Margin Index: To use, bend pages of book backward and follow margin index to pages with black edge markers.

Washington Information Directory

1994-1995

CONGRESSIONAL QUARTERLY INC.

Washington Information Directory 1994-1995

Editor:	Jerry A. Orvedahl
Associate Editor:	Christopher M. Karlsten
Senior Researchers:	Kristen G. Franyo, Amy K. Klein, Barry N. Wolverton
Graphics:	Eloise Fuller
Subject Index:	Patricia R. Ruggiero
Typesetter:	Lisa A. Stanford
Cover:	Design, Dan Royer; photo, © Anthony A. Boccaccio/The Image Bank

The Library of Congress cataloged the first edition of this title as follows:

Washington information directory.   1975/76—
Washington. Congressional Quarterly Inc.

1. Washington, D.C.—Directories. 2. Washington metropolitan area—Directories. 3. United States—Executive departments—Directories.   I. Congressional Quarterly Inc.

F192.3.W33   975.3'0025   75-646321

ISBN 0-87187-798-8
ISSN 0887-8064

Printed in the United States of America

Table of Contents

Chapters

Ready Reference Lists

Boxes and Illustrations

Boxes

Illustrations

Preface

The first sixteen months of President Clinton's administration were a period of exceptional presidential activism. In a reverse of the previous four years, most initiatives originated in the White House rather than the Capitol. The president addressed nearly every explosive issue in the domestic arena, including gay rights, deficit reduction, abortion, free trade, gun control, family leave, and health care. His approval rating among the American public, reflecting the controversial nature of many of the issues, dipped to 36 percent at one point, a record low for a new president.

The president was successful more often than not in getting his initiatives through Congress, but the victories were sometimes bruising. His five-year, $496 billion deficit reduction plan, for example, passed the House in May 1993 by a razor-thin 219-213 vote and passed the Senate 50-49 June 25 on a tie-breaking vote by Vice President Al Gore (the first such tie-breaking vote since 1987). The reconciliation bill then passed on votes of 218-216 in the House and 51-50 in the Senate (another tie-breaking vote). Not a single Republican in either chamber supported the president.

Political alliances were scrambled when in November the president relied heavily on Republican votes to pass the North American Free Trade Agreement. Though opposed by organized labor, by elements of the House Democratic leadership, and by 156 House Democrats, NAFTA passed the House comfortably with the help of 132 Republicans.

The president also succeeded in regulating cable television, amending the Hatch Act to allow federal employees greater latitude in political participation, and passing a simplification of voter registration procedures. But he failed in his attempt to save the superconducting super collider and was forced to compromise on an outright lifting of the ban on gays in the military.

In the spring of 1994 the major domestic issues before the nation were health care reform, which was wending its way through a labyrinth of congressional committees and subcommittees, and a perceived increase in violent crime. Highly publicized crimes created a political climate ripe for an aggressive omnibus crime bill. In one related bill, the House voted 216-214 in favor of a ban on certain military-style assault rifles in a stunning defeat of pro-gun interests. A similar measure had failed by 70 votes only three years earlier.

By spring 1994 Clinton had nearly completed staffing the upper levels of the federal executive branch. By one count, the president had filled all but 16 percent of the 614 most senior positions, and many of those had candidates penciled in. Among the major reorganizations that had already taken place, ACTION and the congressionally chartered Commission on National and Community Service had been merged to form the new Corporation on National and Community Service, and the National Science and Technology Council had been established in the Executive Office of the President. Other reorganizations, including a major overhaul of the Agriculture Dept. and the removal of the Social Security Administration from the Department of Health and Human Services, were working their way through Congress.

The president's extensive legislative agenda competed for national attention with his personal legal difficulties. An investigation was under way into the Clintons' relationship to the failed Whitewater Development Corp., and the president found himself a defendant in a sexual harassment lawsuit filed by Paula Jones, a former employee of the state of Arkansas.

In international affairs, President Clinton's enthusiasm for United Nations peacekeeping missions began to wane after scores of U.S. troops were killed or wounded in Somalia. American troops were hastily withdrawn from that country in March, and the administration became even more reticent to become involved in the continuing civil war in Yugoslavia. Meanwhile, horrific civil wars erupted in Rwanda and Yemen.

These events, both international and domestic, are very often reflected in the pages of this book. The *Washington Information Directory* provides authoritative information on the government and includes the latest information available on twenty-five hundred nonprofit organizations. New sections have been added on Ethics in Government (p. 297) and Peacekeeping and Peace Enforcement (p. 456), and an expanded section on Internal Security and Counterintelligence has been moved to chapter 13 (p. 550). The names and phone numbers of Commerce Dept. desk officers have been added to the embassies appendix (p. 779) and fax numbers have been included for many members of Congress and their district offices (p. 891). Many federal organizations—including the Consumer Product Safety Commission, National Archives and Records Administration, National Science Foundation, National Oceanic and Atmospheric Administration, and Health Resources and Services Administration—either have moved or are in the process of moving to new office space.

As always your comments are important to us and we welcome suggestions for improving the usefulness of this directory. Please direct your comments to the editor.

Jerry A. Orvedahl
Editor

Christopher M. Karlsten
Associate Editor

How to Use This Directory

The *Washington Information Directory* is designed to make your search for information easy and quick.

Each of the eighteen chapters in the directory covers a broad subject area. You will find, for example, chapters on energy, health, science and space, and national security. Within the chapters information is grouped in narrower subject areas. A detailed table of contents can be found at the beginning of each chapter. This subject arrangement allows you to find in one place the departments and agencies of the federal government, congressional committees, and private, nonprofit organizations in the nation's capital that have the information you need.

The directory divides information sources into three categories: (1) agencies, (2) Congress, and (3) nongovernmental organizations. When you look up a subject, you usually will find entries under all three categories. Each entry includes the name, address, and telephone number of the organization; the name and title of the director or the best person to contact for information; and a brief description of the work performed by the organization.

How Information Is Presented

The following section gives a thumbnail explanation of the information available in the directory. Sample entries are given for each of the three categories.

Agencies

The first entry—the National Park Service—is a government agency. Although it is part of the Interior Dept., it is listed in bold type under its commonly known name. Its government parent, the Interior Dept., is shown in parentheses. This approach—common name and bold type—is used for all well-known Washington agencies.

> **National Park Service** (Interior Dept.), Main Interior Bldg. (mailing address: P.O. Box 37127, Washington, DC 20013); 208-4621. Roger G. Kennedy, director. Information, 208-4747.

Press, 208-7394. Fax, 208-7520. Washington, D.C., area activities, 619-7275 (recording).

Administers national parks, monuments, historic sites, and recreation areas. Oversees coordination, planning, and financing of public outdoor recreation programs at all levels of government. Conducts recreation research surveys; administers financial assistance program to states for planning and development of outdoor recreation programs.

Congress

Entries found under the Congress heading are usually Senate or House committees or subcommittees. (Also included under this heading are the Congressional Budget Office, General Accounting Office, Government Printing Office, Library of Congress, and Office of Technology Assessment.) Committee entries include the committee's address, telephone number, chair, and a key staff member. The description gives the committee's jurisdiction or its activities relating to the particular subject. Each section gives both House and Senate committees. Here are entries for House and Senate committees with jurisdiction over the national park system:

House Natural Resources Committee, Subcommittee on National Parks, Forests, and Public Lands, 812 O'Neill Bldg. (300 New Jersey Ave. S.E.) 20515; 226-7736. Bruce F. Vento, D-Minn., chairman; Richard Healy, staff director.

Jurisdiction over legislation on recreation areas, the national park system, the national trails system, and the Bureau of Land Management.

Senate Energy and Natural Resources Committee, Subcommittee on Public Lands, National Parks, and Forests, SD-308 20510; 224-8115. Dale Bumpers, D-Ark., chairman; David Brooks, counsel.

Jurisdiction over legislation on recreation areas, the national park system, the national trails system, and the Bureau of Land Management.

Nongovernmental

Thousands of nonprofit private and special-interest groups have headquarters or branch offices in Washington. Their staffs are often excellent information sources, and they frequently maintain special libraries or information centers. Here is an example of a nongovernmental group with an interest in parks:

Rails-to-Trails Conservancy, 1400 16th St. N.W., #300, 20036; 797-5400. David G. Burwell, president. Fax, 797-5411.

Promotes the conversion of abandoned railroad corridors into hiking and biking trails for public use. Provides public education programs and technical and legal assistance. Publishes trail guides; monitors legislation and regulations.

Reference Aids

Quick Call Numbers

Beginning on p. 2 of the directory is a summary list of information numbers for the executive office of the president, the fourteen federal departments, and the major governmental agencies. You will find in these listings:

• the executive office of the president, including the names and telephone numbers of the president's, vice president's, and first lady's staffs, and contact information for the statutory offices;

• public information and press telephone numbers;

• switchboard and/or locator telephone numbers;

• addresses, names of the people in charge of the agencies or departments, and main offices or bureaus.

Chapter Summaries

On the left-hand page preceding each chapter, you will find a list of key agencies, congressional committees, and policymakers concerned with that chapter's subject area.

Ready Reference Lists

A special section of reference lists, beginning on p. 777, gives information on many different subjects, including congressional offices and committee assignments, foreign embassies, mayors of the nation's major cities, and federal regional offices.

Diplomats. The foreign embassies section (p. 779) gives the names of foreign diplomats in Washington, D.C., and their official addresses and telephone numbers; the names of the U.S. ranking diplomatic officials abroad; and the names and telephone numbers of State Dept. and Commerce Dept. desk officers.

Congressional Offices and Assignments. The 103rd Congress section (p. 891) lists each member's Capitol Hill office address, telephone number, fax number, key professional aide, committee assignments, and district offices. The congressional committees section (p. 975) outlines the jurisdiction and the membership of committees and subcommittees of the 103rd Congress (1993-1995). A list of representatives and senators by state and congressional district begins on p. 885.

Labor Unions. Many nationwide labor unions are included (p. 801) with their addresses, telephone numbers, presidents, and membership numbers. This list is divided between those unions that maintain offices in the Washington, D.C., area and those that do not. A listing for offices within the AFL-CIO's Washington headquarters is at the end of this section.

State and Local Government. To find information on state government, consult the list of state officials (p. 865), which gives the name, address, and telephone number for each governor, lieutenant governor, secretary of state, and attorney general. For local government concerns, see the mayors of major cities (p. 875). This list includes names, telephone numbers, city populations, and forms of city government.

Federal Regional Offices. The regional federal information sources (p. 809) give addresses and telephone numbers for the local offices of federal departments and agencies throughout the country.

Finding Your Way

Indexes

Use the name index (p. 1023) to look up anyone mentioned in the directory. To look up a subject area or a specific organization or agency, use the subject index, which follows the name index. The subject index (p. 1073) is a modified keyword index. Certain frequently used words are considered "throwaway" words and are not indexed when they begin the name of a group. (Some throwaway words are *agency, American, association, bureau, council, department, federal, international, national, society, U.S.,* and *United States.* See p. 1072 for the complete list.) An organization name that begins with one of these words will be indexed under its first main word. For example, the National Aeronautics and Space Administration appears under "Aeronautics and Space Administration, National." Exceptions to this rule occur when one of the throwaway words is a keyword—for example, the American Society of Association Executives. In this case, *American* and *Society* are considered throwaway words, but *Association* is not since it modifies *Executives.*

If you are searching for general information on a particular subject but do not know a specific source, consult the index to find the pages where that topic is covered. For example, if you want general information on the subject of equal employment for women, you can find index entries under both Women and Equal employment opportunity.

Tables of Contents

The summary table of contents (p. *iii*) lists the directory's eighteen chapters. Information boxes and organization charts within the chapters are given on p. *v.* At the beginning of each chapter you will find a detailed table of contents that breaks the chapter into sections organized alphabetically by subject.

Reaching Your Information Source

Writing or Calling

These tips may be helpful when you write or call for information:

(1) Start with a specific question. If necessary, do some homework before you contact a source.

(2) Call the information telephone number first. Often you can get the answer you need without going further. If not, a quick explanation of your query should put you in touch with the person who can answer your question. Rarely will you need to talk to the top administrator.

(3) Call or write your own member of Congress rather than a congressional committee. Your representative has staff people assigned to answer questions from constituents. Contact a committee only if you have a technical question that cannot be answered elsewhere.

(4) Address letters to the director of an office or organization. Your letter will be directed to the person who can answer your question.

(5) Keep in mind the agency or organization, not the name of the director. Personnel changes in Washington are common. When someone retires or moves, that individual's office and telephone number usually remain the same.

Addresses and Area Codes

All addresses and telephone numbers in the *Washington Information Directory* are in Washington, D.C., unless otherwise indicated. Each Washington entry includes the name of the agency or organization, the building or street address, the ZIP code, and the telephone number. The area code for District of Columbia telephone numbers (202) is not included. Here is the beginning of a typical Washington entry:

> **Federal Communications Commission,** 1919 M St.
> N.W. 20554; 632-6600.

To complete the mailing address, you need only to add "Washington, DC."

Maryland and Virginia. The directory lists addresses of information sources in the Maryland and Virginia suburbs of Washington in full. A typical suburban entry would read:

> **Food and Drug Administration** (Health and Human
> Services Dept.), 5600 Fishers Lane, Rockville, MD
> 20857; (301) 443-2410.

Area Codes. Metropolitan Washington area codes are:

202	District of Columbia
301	Maryland
703	Virginia

Capitol Hill

(Dashed lines indicate the city's quadrants, which are noted in the corners of the map)

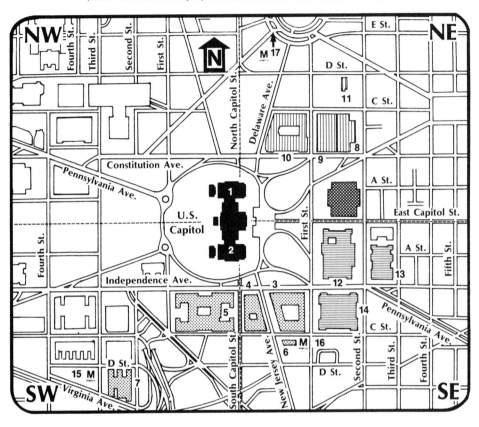

■ U.S. Capitol,
  Washington, D.C. 20510, 20515*

  1 Senate Wing
  2 House Wing

▨ House Office Buildings
  Washington, D.C. 20515

  3 Cannon
  4 Longworth
  5 Rayburn
  6 O'Neill
  7 Ford

▨ Supreme Court
  Washington, D.C. 20543

▥ Senate Office Buildings,
  Washington, D.C. 20510

  8 Hart
  9 Dirksen
  10 Russell
  11 Immigration Building
     (Capitol Police)

▤ Library of Congress,
  Washington, D.C. 20540

  12 Jefferson
  13 Adams
  14 Madison

Ⓜ Subway System

  15 Federal Center SW Station
  16 Capitol South Station
  17 Union Station Station

* Mail sent to the U.S. Capitol should bear the ZIP code of the chamber to which it is addressed.

Building Addresses. Sources located in the headquarters building of a federal executive department are listed as Main State Bldg., Main Interior Bldg., and so forth, plus the ZIP code. Simply add "Washington, DC" to complete the mailing address. If you wish to visit a department, consult the listings for Executive Departments (p. 5) and Federal Agencies (p. 15) to find the street address.

The ZIP code is an essential part of the mailing address, since most departments and agencies have their own ZIP codes. The Defense Dept. has individual ZIP codes for each branch of the armed forces. (The Pentagon, although located in Virginia, has a Washington mailing address.)

Congressional Addresses. The directory abbreviates the names of congressional office buildings. The complete building names and street locations are listed below. To send mail, include the person or committee you are writing, the congressional office building, Washington, DC, and the ZIP code. The ZIP code for Senate buildings is 20510; for House buildings it is 20515.

Capitol

CAP — The letters *H* and *S* before the room number indicate whether the office is on the House or Senate side of the Capitol building.

Senate

SD — Dirksen Senate Office Building on Constitution Ave. between 1st and 2nd Sts. N.E.

SR — Russell Senate Office Building on Constitution Ave. between Delaware Ave. and 1st St. N.E.

SH — Hart Senate Office Building at 2nd St. and Constitution Ave. N.E.

The Senate also has an annex, which houses the Capitol police, in the old Immigration Building at 119 D St. N.E. 20510.

House

CHOB — Cannon House Office Building on Independence Ave. between New Jersey Ave. and 1st St. S.E.

LHOB — Longworth House Office Building on Independence Ave. between S. Capitol St. and New Jersey Ave. S.E.

RHOB — Rayburn House Office Building on Independence Ave. between S. Capitol and 1st Sts. S.W.

The House also has two annexes: the O'Neill Bldg. (formerly House Annex #1) at 300 New Jersey Ave. S.E. and the Ford Bldg. (formerly House Annex #2) at 2nd and D Sts. S.W. Mail to offices in these buildings should include the name of the person addressed; the committee, subcommittee, or office; the name of the building (O'Neill or Ford); and Washington, DC 20515.

Washington
Information Directory

1994-1995

Executive Office . . .

Bill Clinton, president
1600 Pennsylvania Ave. N.W. 20500
Phone: 456-1414
Daily Schedule: 456-2343

Thomas F. "Mack" McLarty III
chief of staff
456-6797

Harold Ickes
deputy chief of staff
456-2533

Philip Lader
deputy chief of staff
456-2533

George Stephanopoulos
senior adviser
456-7105

David R. Gergen
counselor to the president
456-2195

Andrew Friendly
aide to the president
456-2420

Appointments and Scheduling
Nancy Hernreich, deputy assistant
456-6610

Cabinet Affairs
Christine Varney, cabinet secretary
456-6280

Communications
Mark Gearan, director
456-2640

Media Affairs
Jeff Eller, director
456-7150

Press Relations
Dee Dee Myers, press secretary
456-2100

Research
Ann Walker, director
456-7845

Speechwriting
Donald A. Baer, chief speechwriter
456-2777

Counsel to the President
Lloyd N. Cutler
456-2632

Domestic Policy Council
Carol H. Rasco, assistant
456-2216

William A. Galston, deputy assistant
456-2216

Bruce Reed, deputy assistant
456-2216

Ira Magaziner, senior adviser, policy
development
456-6406

Intergovernmental Affairs
Marcia Hale, director
456-7060

Legislative Affairs
Patrick J. Griffin, assistant
456-2230

Susan Brophy, deputy assistant
456-2230

Senate Liaison
Steven Ricchetti, deputy assistant
456-6493

House Liaison
Lorraine Miller, deputy assistant
456-6620

Management and Administration
Vacant, assistant
456-2861

White House Operations
Patsy Thomasson, director
456-7052

National Economic Council
Robert E. Rubin, assistant
456-2174

**National Science and Technology
Council**
John H. Gibbons, chairman
395-5101

. . . of the President

Office of Environmental Policy
Kathleen McGinty, director
456-6224

Political Affairs
Joan Baggett, director
456-1125

Presidential Correspondence
Marsha Scott, director
456-7610

Presidential Personnel
Veronica Biggins, director
456-6676

President's Foreign Intelligence Advisory Board
Les Aspin, chairman
456-2352

    President's Intelligence Oversight Board
    Les Aspin, chairman
    456-2352

Public Liaison
Alexis Herman, director
456-2930

Scheduling and Advance
Ricki Seidman, director
456-7560

Staff Secretary
John D. Podesta, assistant
456-2702

White House Military Office
Vacant, director
456-2150

Office of the Vice President

Albert Gore Jr., vice president
Old Executive Office Bldg., 17th St. and
  Pennsylvania Ave. N.W. 20501
Phone: 456-2326
Chief of Staff: Jack Quinn, 456-6605
Director of Communications:
Lorraine Voles, 456-7034

Office of the First Lady

Hillary Rodham Clinton, first lady
1600 Pennsylvania Ave. N.W. 20500
Phone: 456-6266
Chief of Staff: Margaret A. Williams, 456-
  6266
Press Secretary: Lisa Caputo, 456-2960

Statutory Offices

Council of Economic Advisers
Laura D'Andrea Tyson, chair
395-5084

Council on Environmental Quality
James Baker, acting chair
395-5754

National Drug Control Policy
Lee Brown, director
467-9800

National Security Council
Anthony Lake, assistant
456-2255

Samuel R. Berger, deputy assistant
456-2257

Office of Management and Budget
Leon E. Panetta, director
395-4840

Alice M. Rivlin, deputy director
395-4742

Office of Science and Technology Policy
John H. Gibbons, director
456-7116

Office of U.S. Trade Representative
Mickey Kantor, U.S. trade representative
395-3204

President's Commission on White House Fellowships
Nancy Bekavac, chair
395-4522

Government of the United States

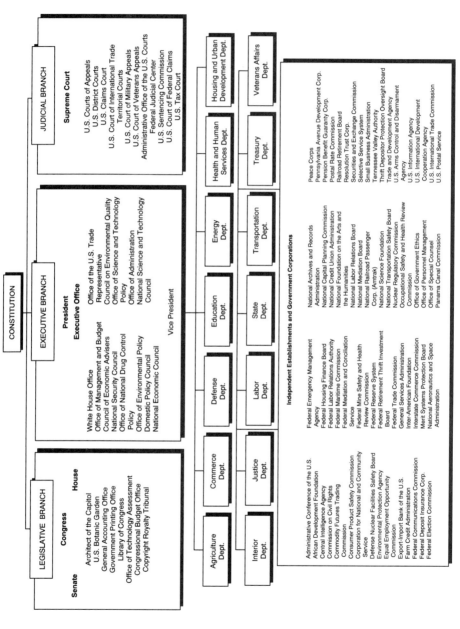

CONSTITUTION

LEGISLATIVE BRANCH

Congress

Senate

House

- Architect of the Capitol
- U.S. Botanic Garden
- General Accounting Office
- Government Printing Office
- Library of Congress
- Office of Technology Assessment
- Congressional Budget Office
- Copyright Royalty Tribunal

EXECUTIVE BRANCH

President

Executive Office

- White House Office
- Office of Management and Budget
- Council of Economic Advisers
- National Security Council
- Office of National Drug Control Policy
- Office of Environmental Policy
- Domestic Policy Council
- National Economic Council
- Office of the U.S. Trade Representative
- Council on Environmental Quality
- Office of Science and Technology Policy
- Office of Administration
- National Science and Technology Council

Vice President

JUDICIAL BRANCH

Supreme Court

- U.S. Courts of Appeals
- U.S. District Courts
- U.S. Claims Court
- U.S. Court of International Trade
- Territorial Courts
- U.S. Court of Military Appeals
- U.S. Court of Veterans Appeals
- Administrative Office of the U.S. Courts
- Federal Judicial Center
- U.S. Sentencing Commission
- U.S. Court of Federal Claims
- U.S. Tax Court

Agriculture Dept.

Commerce Dept.

Defense Dept.

Education Dept.

Energy Dept.

Health and Human Services Dept.

Housing and Urban Development Dept.

Interior Dept.

Justice Dept.

Labor Dept.

State Dept.

Transportation Dept.

Treasury Dept.

Veterans Affairs Dept.

Independent Establishments and Government Corporations

Administrative Conference of the U.S.
African Development Foundation
Central Intelligence Agency
Commission on Civil Rights
Commodity Futures Trading Commission
Consumer Product Safety Commission
Corporation for National and Community Service
Defense Nuclear Facilities Safety Board
Environmental Protection Agency
Equal Employment Opportunity Commission
Export-Import Bank of the U.S.
Farm Credit Administration
Federal Communications Commission
Federal Deposit Insurance Corp.
Federal Election Commission

Federal Emergency Management Agency
Federal Housing Finance Board
Federal Labor Relations Authority
Federal Maritime Commission
Federal Mediation and Conciliation Service
Federal Mine Safety and Health Review Commission
Federal Reserve System
Federal Retirement Thrift Investment Board
Federal Trade Commission
General Services Administration
Inter-American Foundation
Interstate Commerce Commission
Merit Systems Protection Board
National Aeronautics and Space Administration

National Archives and Records Administration
National Capital Planning Commission
National Credit Union Administration
National Foundation on the Arts and the Humanities
National Labor Relations Board
National Mediation Board
National Railroad Passenger Corp. (Amtrak)
National Science Foundation
National Transportation Safety Board
Nuclear Regulatory Commission
Occupational Safety and Health Review Commission
Office of Government Ethics
Office of Personnel Management
Office of Special Counsel
Panama Canal Commission

Peace Corps
Pennsylvania Avenue Development Corp.
Pension Benefit Guaranty Corp.
Postal Rate Commission
Railroad Retirement Board
Resolution Trust Corp.
Securities and Exchange Commission
Selective Service System
Small Business Administration
Tennessee Valley Authority
Thrift Depositor Protection Oversight Board
Trade and Development Agency
U.S. Arms Control and Disarmament Agency
U.S. Information Agency
U.S. International Development Cooperation Agency
U.S. International Trade Commission
U.S. Postal Service

Executive Departments

Agriculture Dept.

14th St. and Independence Ave. S.W. 20250
Locator: 720-8732
Information: 720-2791
Secretary: Mike Espy, 720-3631

Agricultural Marketing Service
14th St. and Independence Ave. S W (mailing
address: P.O. Box 96456, Washington, DC
20090)
Locator: 720-8732
Information: 720-8998
Administrator: Lon Hatamiya, 720-5115

**Agricultural Stabilization and Conserva-
tion Service**
14th St. and Independence Ave. S.W. (mailing
address: P.O. Box 2415, Washington, DC
20013)
Locator: 720-8732
Information: 720-5237
Administrator: Grant Buntrock, 720-3467

**Animal and Plant Health Inspection Ser-
vice**
14th St. and Independence Ave. S.W. (mailing
address: Ag. Box 3041, Washington, DC
20250)
Locator: 720-2791
Information: 720-2511
Administrator: Lonnie J. King, acting, 720-
3861

Commodity Credit Corp.
14th St. and Independence Ave. S.W. (mailing
address: P.O. Box 2415, Washington, DC
20013)
Locator: 720-8732
Information: 720-5237
President: Eugene Moos, 720-3111

Extension Service
14th St. and Independence Ave. S.W. 20250
Locator: 720-8732
Information: 720-3029
Administrator: Leodrey Williams, acting, 720-
3377

Farmers Home Administration
14th St. and Independence Ave. S.W. 20250
Locator: 720-8732
Information: 720-4323
Administrator: Michael Dunn, 720-6903

Federal Grain Inspection Service
14th St. and Independence Ave. S.W. (mailing
address: P.O. Box 96454, Washington, DC
20090)
Locator: 720-8732
Information: 720-5091
Administrator: David R. Shipman, acting, 720-
0219

Food and Nutrition Service
3101 Park Center Dr., Alexandria, VA 22302
Information: (703) 305-2276

Administrator: William Ludwig, (703) 305-2062

Food Safety and Inspection Service
14th St. and Independence Ave. S.W. 20250
Locator: 720-8732
Information: 720-9113
Administrator: H. Russell Cross, 720-7025

Foreign Agricultural Service
14th St. and Independence Ave. S.W. 20250
Locator: 720-8732
Information: 720-7115
Administrator: Richard B. Schroeter, acting, 720-3935

Forest Service
14th St. and Independence Ave. S.W. (mailing address: P.O. Box 96090, Washington, DC 20090)
Locator: 720-8732
Information: 205-1760
Chief: Jack Ward Thomas, 205-1661

Rural Electrification Administration
14th St. and Independence Ave. S.W. 20250
Locator: 720-8732
Information: 720-1260 (press); 720-1255 (public)
Administrator: Wally Byer, 720-9540

Soil Conservation Service
12th St. and Independence Ave. S.W. (mailing address: P.O. Box 2890, Washington, DC 20013)
Locator: 720-8732
Information: 720-4543
Chief: Paul Johnson, 720-4525

Commerce Dept.

Main Commerce Bldg.
14th St. and Constitution Ave. N.W. 20230
Locator: 482-2000
Information: 482-4901 (press); 482-2000 (public)
Secretary: Ronald H. Brown, 482-2112

Bureau of Export Administration
14th St. and Constitution Ave. N.W. 20230
Locator: 482-2000
Information: 482-2721
Under Secretary: William Alan Reinsch, 482-1427

Census Bureau
Suitland and Silver Hill Rds., Suitland, MD (mailing address: Washington, DC 20233)
Locator: (301) 763-7662
Information: (301) 763-4040
Director: Harry A. Scarr, acting, (301) 763-5190

Economic Development Administration
14th St. and Constitution Ave. N.W. 20230
Locator: 482-2000
Information: 482-5112

Assistant Secretary: William W. Ginsberg, 482-5081

International Trade Administration
14th St. and Constitution Ave. N.W. 20230
Locator: 482-2000
Information: 482-3808 (press); 482-2000 (public)
Under Secretary: Jeffrey Garten, 482-2867

Minority Business Development Agency
14th St. and Constitution Ave. N.W. 20230
Locator: 482-2000
Information: 482-1936
Director: Gilbert Colon, acting, 482-5061

National Institute of Standards and Technology
Route I-270 and Quince Orchard Rd., Gaithersburg, MD (mailing address: Bldg. 101, #A1134, Gaithersburg, MD 20899)
Locator: (301) 975-2000
Information: (301) 975-2762
Director: Arati Prabhakar, (301) 975-2300

National Oceanic and Atmospheric Administration
14th St. and Constitution Ave. N.W. 20230
Locator: 482-2000
Information: (301) 443-8910
Administrator: D. James Baker, 482-3436

Patent and Trademark Office
2121 Crystal Park II, #906, Arlington, VA
(mailing address: Washington, DC 20231)
Locator: (703) 308-4455
Information: (703) 305-8341 (press); (703) 308-4357 (public)

Commissioner: Bruce A. Lehman, (703) 305-8600

Technology Administration
14th St. and Constitution Ave. N.W. 20230
Under Secretary: Mary L. Good, 482-1575

U.S. Travel and Tourism Administration
14th St. and Constitution Ave. N.W. 20230
Information: 482-0137
Under Secretary: Greg Farmer, 482-0136

Defense Dept.

The Pentagon, Washington, DC 20301
Switchboard: (703) 545-6700
Information: (703) 695-0192 (defense news); (703) 697-5131 (armed forces news); (703) 697-5737 (public)
Secretary: William Perry, (703) 695-5261

Air Force Dept.
The Pentagon, Washington, DC 20330
Locator: (703) 695-4803
Information: (703) 695-5554
Secretary: Sheila E. Widnall, (703) 697-7376

Army Dept.
The Pentagon, Washington, DC 20310
Information: (703) 697-7550 (press); (703) 695-4462 (public)
Secretary: Togo D. West, Jr., (703) 695-3211

Navy Dept.
The Pentagon, Washington, DC 20350
Locator: (703) 614-9221
Navy Information: (703) 697-5342 (press); (703) 695-0965 (public)
Marine Corps Information: (703) 614-1492 (press and public)
Secretary: John Dalton, (703) 695-3131

Education Dept.

400 Maryland Ave. S.W. 20202
Locator: 708-5366
Information: 401-1576
Secretary: Richard W. Riley, 401-3000

Educational Research and Improvement
555 New Jersey Ave. N.W. 20208
Locator: 708-5366
Information: 401-1576
Assistant Secretary: Sharon Porter Robinson, 219-2050

Elementary and Secondary Education
400 Maryland Ave. S.W. 20202
Locator: 708-5366
Information: 401-1576
Assistant Secretary: Thomas Payzant, 401-0113

Postsecondary Education
7th and D Sts. S.W. 20202
Locator: 708-5366
Information: 401-2311
Assistant Secretary: David Longanecker, 708-5547

Special Education and Rehabilitative Services
330 C St. S.W. (mailing address: 400 Maryland Ave. S.W. 20202)
Locator: 708-5366
Information: 205-8241
Assistant Secretary: Judith Heumann, 205-5465

Vocational and Adult Education
330 C St. S.W. (mailing address: 400 Maryland Ave. S.W. 20202)
Locator: 708-5366
Information: 401-1576
Assistant Secretary: Augusta Kappner, 205-5451

Energy Dept.

1000 Independence Ave. S.W. 20585
Locator: 586-5000
Information: 586-5806 (press); 586-5575 (public)
Secretary: Hazel R. O'Leary, 586-6210

Economic Regulatory Administration
820 1st St. N.E., #810, 20002
Locator: 586-5000
Information: 586-5575
Administrator: Jay F. Thompson, acting, 523-3053

Energy Information Administration
1000 Independence Ave. S.W. 20585
Locator: 586-5000
Information: 586-8800
Administrator: Jay Hakes, 586-4361

Federal Energy Regulatory Commission
825 N. Capitol St. N.E. 20426
Locator: 208-0200
Information: 208-1088 (press); 208-0200 (public)
Chair: Elizabeth Moler, 208-0000

Health and Human Services Dept.

200 Independence Ave. S.W. 20201
Locator: 619-0257
Information: 690-6343 (press); 690-6867 (public)
Secretary: Donna E. Shalala, 690-7000

Administration for Children and Families
901 D St. S.W. (mailing address: 370 L'Enfant Promenade S.W. 20447)
Locator: 619-0257
Information: 401-9215 (press); 401-9200 (public)
Assistant Secretary: Mary Jo Bane, 401-9200

Food and Drug Administration
5600 Fishers Lane, Rockville, MD 20857
Locator: (301) 443-1544
Information: (301) 443-3285 (press); (301) 443-3170 (consumer affairs)

Commissioner: David A. Kessler, (301) 443-2410

Health Care Financing Administration
200 Independence Ave. S.W. 20201
Locator: 619-0257
Information: 690-6113
Administrator: Bruce C. Vladeck, 690-6726

Health Resources and Services Administration
5600 Fishers Lane, Rockville, MD 20857
Locator: 619-0257
Information: (301) 443-3377 (press); (301) 443-2086 (public)
Administrator: William A. Robinson, acting, (301) 443-2216

National Institutes of Health
9000 Rockville Pike, Bethesda, MD 20892

Locator: (301) 496-2351
Information: (301) 496-5787
Director: Harold Varmus, (301) 496-2433

Public Health Service
200 Independence Ave. S.W. 20201
Locator: (301) 443-2403
Information: 690-6867
Assistant Secretary for Health: Philip R. Lee, 690-7694
Surgeon General: Joycelyn Elders, 690-6467

Social Security Administration
6401 Security Blvd., Baltimore, MD 21235
(Washington office: 200 Independence Ave. S.W. 20201)

Locator: (410) 965-8882 in Baltimore
Information: (410) 965-8904 (press); (410) 965-7700 (public) in Baltimore
Commissioner: Shirley S. Chater, 690-6764 in Washington, DC; (410) 965-3120 in Baltimore

Substance Abuse and Mental Health Services Administration
5600 Fishers Lane, Rockville, MD 20857
Locator: 619-0257
Information: (301) 443-8956
Administrator: Elaine M. Johnson, acting, (301) 443-4795

Housing and Urban Development Dept.

HUD Bldg.
451 7th St. S.W. 20410
Locator. 700-1422
Information: 708-0980 (press); 708-0685 (public)
Secretary: Henry G. Cisneros, 708-0417

Community Planning and Development
451 7th St. S.W. 20410
Locator: 708-1422
Information: 708-0980
Assistant Secretary: Andrew Cuomo, 708-2690

Fair Housing and Equal Opportunity
451 7th St. S.W. 20410
Locator: 708-1422
Information: 708-0980
Assistant Secretary: Roberta Achtenberg, 708-4252

Government National Mortgage Assn. (Ginnie Mae)
451 7th St. S.W. 20410
Locator: 708-1422
Information: 708-0685
President: Dwight P. Robinson, 708-0926

Housing—Federal Housing Commissioner
451 7th St. S.W. 20410
Locator: 708-1422
Information: 708-0685
Assistant Secretary: Nicolas P. Retsinas, 708-3600

Policy Development and Research
451 7th St. S.W. 20410
Locator: 708-1422
Information: 708-0685
Assistant Secretary: Michael A. Stegman, 708-1600

Public and Indian Housing
451 7th St. S.W. 20410
Locator: 708-1422
Information: 708-0685
Assistant Secretary: Joseph Shuldiner, designate, 708-0950

Interior Dept.

Main Interior Bldg.
1849 C St. N.W. 20240
Locator: 208-3100
Information: 208-3171
Secretary: Bruce Babbitt, 208-7351

Bureau of Indian Affairs
1849 C St. N.W. 20240
Locator: 208-3100
Information: 219-4150 (press); 208-3711 (public)
Assistant Secretary: Ada E. Deer, 208-7163

Bureau of Land Management
1849 C St. N.W. 20240
Locator: 208-3100
Information: 208-5717
Director: Mike Dombeck, acting, 208-3801

Bureau of Mines
810 7th St. N.W. 20241
Locator: 208-3100
Information: 501-9649
Director: Hermann Enzer, acting, 501-9300

Bureau of Reclamation
1849 C St. N.W. 20240
Locator: 208-3100

Information: 208-4662
Commissioner: Daniel P. Beard, 208-4157

Minerals Management Service
1849 C St. N.W. 20240
Locator: 208-3100
Information: 208-3983
Director: Tom Fry, 208-3500

National Park Service
1849 C St. N.W. (mailing address: P.O. Box 37127, Washington, DC 20013)
Locator: 208-3100
Information: 208-7394 (press); 208-4747 (public)
Director: Roger G. Kennedy, 208-4621

U.S. Fish and Wildlife Service
1849 C St. N.W. 20240
Locator: 208-3100
Information: 208-5634
Director: Mollie H. Beattie, 208-4717

U.S. Geological Survey
12201 Sunrise Valley Dr., Reston, VA 22092
Locator: 208-3100
Information: (703) 648-4460
Director: Gordon P. Eaton, (703) 648-7411

Justice Dept.

Main Justice Bldg.
10th St. and Constitution Ave. N.W. 20530
Locator: 514-2000
Information: 514-2007
Attorney General: Janet Reno, 514-2001

Bureau of Prisons
320 1st St. N.W. 20534
Locator: 307-3135
Information: 307-3198
Director: Kathleen M. Hawk, 307-6300

Antitrust Division
10th St. and Constitution Ave. N.W. 20530
Locator: 514-2000
Assistant Attorney General: Anne K. Bingaman, 514-2401

Civil Division
10th St. and Constitution Ave. N.W. 20530
Locator: 514-2000
Information: 514-2007
Assistant Attorney General: Frank W. Hunger, 514-3301

Civil Rights Division
10th St. and Constitution Ave. N.W. 20530
Locator: 514-2000
Information: 514-2007
Assistant Attorney General: Deval Patrick, 514-2151

Criminal Division
10th St. and Constitution Ave. N.W. 20530
Locator: 514-2000
Assistant Attorney General: Jo Ann Harris, 514-2601

Drug Enforcement Administration
700 Army-Navy Dr., Arlington, VA (mailing address: Washington, DC 20537)
Locator: 307-1000
Information: 307-7977
Administrator: Thomas A. Constantine, 307-8000

Environment and Natural Resources Division
10th St. and Constitution Ave. N.W. 20530
Locator: 514-2000
Information: 616-2765
Assistant Attorney General: Lois J. Schiffer, designate, 514-2701

Federal Bureau of Investigation
10th St. and Pennsylvania Ave. N.W. 20535
Locator: 324-3000
Information: 324-3691
Director: Louis J. Freeh, 324-3444

Foreign Claims Settlement Commission of the United States
600 E St. N.W. 20579
Locator: 616-6988
Chairman: Vacant, 616-6975

Immigration and Naturalization Service
425 Eye St. N.W. 20536
Locator: 514-4316
Information: 514-2648 (press); 514-4316 (public)
Commissioner: Doris Meissner, 514-1900

Office of Justice Programs
633 Indiana Ave. N.W. 20531
Locator: 514-2000
Assistant Attorney General: Laurie Robinson, acting, 307-5933

Tax Division
10th St. and Constitution Ave. N.W. 20530
Locator: 514-2000
Information: 514-2007
Assistant Attorney General: Loretta C. Argrett, 514-2901

U.S. Marshals Service
600 Army-Navy Dr., Arlington, VA 22202
Locator: 514-2000
Information: 307-9065
Director: Eduardo Gonzalez, 307-9001

U.S. Parole Commission
5550 Friendship Blvd., Chevy Chase, MD 20815
Locator: (301) 492-5990
Chairman: Edward F. Reilly, Jr., (301) 492-5990

Labor Dept.

200 Constitution Ave. N.W. 20210
Locator: 219-5000
Information: 219-7316
Secretary: Robert B. Reich, 219-8271

Bureau of Labor Statistics
2 Massachusetts Ave. N.E. 20212

Locator: 606-6400
Information: 606-5902
Commissioner: Katharine G. Abraham, 606-7800

Employment and Training Administration
200 Constitution Ave. N.W. 20210

Locator: 219-5000
Information: 219-6871
Assistant Secretary: Douglas Ross, 219-6050

Employment Standards Administration
200 Constitution Ave. N.W. 20210
Locator: 219-5000
Information: 219-8743
Assistant Secretary: Bernard Anderson, 219-6191

Mine Safety and Health Administration
4015 Wilson Blvd., Arlington, VA 22203
Locator: 219-5000
Information: (703) 235-1452
Assistant Secretary: J. Davitt McAteer, (703) 235-1385

Occupational Safety and Health Administration
200 Constitution Ave. N.W. 20210
Locator: 219-5000
Information: 219-8151
Assistant Secretary: Joseph Dear, 219-7162

Pension and Welfare Benefits Administration
200 Constitution Ave. N.W. 20210
Locator: 219-5000
Information: 219-8921
Assistant Secretary: Olena Berg, 219-8233

State Dept.

Main State Bldg.
2201 C St. N.W. 20520
Locator: 647-3686
Information: 647-2492 (press); 647-4000 (public)
Secretary: Warren Christopher, 647-4910

Bureau of Consular Affairs
2201 C St. N.W. 20520
Locator: 647-3686
Information: 647-1488; 647-0518 (passports); 647-5225 (assistance to U.S. citizens overseas)
Assistant Secretary: Mary Ryan, 647-9576

Bureau of Economic and Business Affairs
2201 C St. N.W. 20520
Locator: 647-3686
Information: 647-1942
Assistant Secretary: Daniel K. Tarullo, 647-7971

Bureau of Intelligence and Research
2201 C St. N.W. 20520
Locator: 647-3686
Information: 647-6575
Assistant Secretary: Toby T. Gati, 647-9177

Bureau of International Organization Affairs
2201 C St. N.W. 20520
Locator: 647-3686
Information: 647-6400
Assistant Secretary: Douglas J. Bennet, 647-9600

Bureau of Oceans and International Environmental and Scientific Affairs
2201 C St. N.W. 20520
Locator: 647-3686
Information: 647-2492 (press); 647-4000 (public)
Assistant Secretary: Elinor G. Constable, 647-1554

Bureau of Politico-Military Affairs
2201 C St. N.W. 20520
Locator: 647-3686
Information: 647-2492 (press); 647-4000 (public)
Assistant Secretary: Robert L. Gallucci, 647-9022

Foreign Service
2201 C St. N.W. 20520
Locator: 647-3686
Director General: Genta Hawkins Holmes, 647-9898

Office of Protocol
2201 C St. N.W. 20520

Locator: 647-3686
Chief: Molly Raiser, 647-4543

Transportation Dept.

400 7th St. S.W. 20590
Locator: 366-4000
Information: 366-4570
Secretary: Federico F. Peña, 366-1111

Federal Aviation Administration
800 Independence Ave. S.W. 20591
Locator: 366-4000
Information: 267-8521 (press); 267-3484 (public)
Administrator: David R. Hinson, 267-3111

Federal Highway Administration
400 7th St. S.W. 20590
Locator: 366-4000
Information: 366-0660
Administrator: Rodney Slater, 366-0650

Federal Railroad Administration
400 7th St. S.W. 20590
Locator: 366-4000
Information: 366-0881
Administrator: Jolene M. Molitoris, 366-0710

Federal Transit Administration
400 7th St. S.W. 20590
Locator: 366-4000
Information: 366-4043
Administrator: Gordon J. Linton, 366-4040

Maritime Administration
400 7th St. S.W. 20590
Locator: 366-4000

Information: 366-5807
Administrator: Vice Adm. Albert J. Herberger, 366-5823

National Highway Traffic Safety Administration
400 7th St. S.W. 20590
Locator: 366-4000
Information: 366-9550
Administrator: Christopher A. Hart, acting, 366-1836

Research and Special Programs Administration
400 7th St. S.W. 20590
Locator: 366-4000
Information: 366-4461
Administrator: Dharmendra K. Sharma, designate, 366-4433

Saint Lawrence Seaway Development Corp.
400 7th St. S.W. 20590
Locator: 366-4000
Information: 366-0091
Administrator: Stanford Parris, 366-0118

U.S. Coast Guard
2100 2nd St. S.W. 20593
Locator: 366-4000
Information: 267-1587
Commandant: Adm. Robert Kramek, designate, 267-2390

Treasury Dept.

Main Treasury Bldg.
15th St. and Pennsylvania Ave. N.W. 20220
Locator: 622-2111
Information: 622-2000

Secretary: Lloyd Bentsen, 622-5300

Bureau of Alcohol, Tobacco, and Firearms
650 Massachusetts Ave. N.W. 20226
Locator: 927-7777

Information: 927-8500
Director: John M. Magaw, 927-8700

Bureau of Engraving and Printing
14th and C Sts. S.W. 20228
Locator: 622-2111
Information: 874-2778
Director: Peter H. Daly, 874-2002

Comptroller of the Currency
250 E St. S.W. 20219
Information: 874-5000
Comptroller: Eugene A. Ludwig, 874-4900

Internal Revenue Service
1111 Constitution Ave. N.W. 20224
Locator: 622-5000
Taxpayer Information: 622-4010 (press); (800) 829-1040 (public)
Commissioner: Margaret Milner Richardson, 622-4115

Office of Thrift Supervision
1700 G St. N.W. 20552

Locator: 906-6000
Information: 906-6677
Director: Jonathan L. Fiechter, acting, 906-6280

U.S. Customs Service
1301 Constitution Ave. N.W. 20229
Locator: 622-2111
Information: 927-1770 (press); 927-6724 (public)
Commissioner: George J. Weise, 927-1000

U.S. Mint
633 3rd St. N.W. 20220
Locator: 622-2111
Information: 874-6450
Director: Philip N. Diehl, designate, 874-6000

U.S. Secret Service
1800 G St. N.W. 20223
Locator: 622-2111
Information: 435-5708
Director: Eljay B. Boward, 435-5700

Veterans Affairs Dept.

801 Eye St. N.W. (mailing address: 810 Vermont Ave. N.W. 20420)
Locator: 233-4010
Information: 535-8165
Secretary: Jesse Brown, 535-8900

Veterans Benefits Administration
801 Eye St. N.W. (mailing address: 810 Vermont Ave. N.W. 20420)
Locator: 233-4010

Information: 872-1151
Chief Benefits Director: Raymond J. Vogel, 535-7920

Veterans Health Administration
801 Eye St. N.W. (mailing address: 810 Vermont Ave. N.W. 20420)
Locator: 233-4010
Chief Medical Director: Dr. John T. Farrar, acting, 535-7010

Federal Agencies

Administrative Conference of the United States
2120 L St. N.W., #500 20037
Information: 254-7065
Chair: Thomasina Rogers, designate, 254-7020

Advisory Council on Historic Preservation
1100 Pennsylvania Ave. N.W. 20004
Executive Director: Robert D. Bush, 606-8503

African Development Foundation
1400 Eye St. N.W. 20005
President: Gregory R. Smith, 673-3916

American Battle Monuments Commission
20 Massachusetts Ave. N.W. 20314
Locator: 272-0533
Information: 272-0533
Secretary: Vacant, 272-0532

Appalachian Regional Commission
1666 Connecticut Ave. N.W., #600 20235
Information: 673-7968
Chair: Jacqueline Phillips, 673-7856

Central Intelligence Agency
Langley, VA (mailing address: Washington, DC 20505)
Locator: (703) 482-1100

Information: (703) 482-7676
Director: R. James Woolsey, (703) 482-1100

Commission of Fine Arts
Judiciary Square, 441 F St. N.W. 20001
Chairman: J. Carter Brown, 504-2200

Commission on Civil Rights
624 9th St. N.W., #700 20425
Locator: 376-8364
Information: 376-8364
Chair: Mary Frances Berry, 376-7700

Commodity Futures Trading Commission
2033 K St. N.W. 20581
Locator: 254-6387
Information: 254-8630
Chair: Mary L. Schapiro, designate, 254-6970

Consumer Product Safety Commission
4330 East-West Highway, Bethesda, MD (mailing address: Washington, DC 20207)
Locator: (301) 504-0100
Information: (301) 504-0580
Chair: Ann Brown, (301) 504-0500

Corporation for National Service
1100 Vermont Ave. N.W. 20525
Information: 606-5000
Chief Executive Officer: Eli J. Segal, 606-5000

Defense Nuclear Facilities Safety Board
625 Indiana Ave. N.W., #700 20004
Chairman: John T. Conway, 208-6400

District of Columbia
441 4th St. N.W., #1100, 20001
Locator: 727-1000
Information: 727-6224
Mayor: Sharon Pratt Kelly, 727-2980

Environmental Protection Agency
401 M St. S.W. 20460
Locator: 260-2090
Information: 260-4355   (press);   260-2080
(public)
Administrator: Carol Browner, 260-4700

Equal Employment Opportunity Commission
1801 L St. N.W., #10006 20507
Locator: 663-4264
Information: 663-4900
Chairman: Gilbert F. Casellas, designate, 663-4001

Export-Import Bank of the United States
811 Vermont Ave. N.W. 20571
Information: 566-8990
President and Chairman: Kenneth D. Brody, 566-8144

Farm Credit Administration
1501 Farm Credit Dr., McLean, VA 22102
Locator: (703) 883-4000
Information: (703) 883-4056
Chairman: Billy Ross Brown, (703) 883-4010

Federal Communications Commission
1919 M St. N.W. 20554
Locator: 632-7106
Information: 632-5050   (press);   632-7000
(public)
Chairman: Reed E. Hundt, 632-6600

Federal Deposit Insurance Corp.
550 17th St. N.W. 20429
Locator: 393-8400
Information: 898-6996
Chair: Ricki R. Tigert, designate, 898-6974

Federal Election Commission
999 E St. N.W. 20463
Locator: 219-3440
Information: 219-4155   (press);   219-3420
(public)
Chairman: Trevor Potter, 219-3440

Federal Emergency Management Agency
500 C St. S.W. 20472
Locator: 646-2500
Information: 646-4600
Director: James Lee Witt, 646-3923

Federal Housing Finance Board
1777 F St. N.W. 20006
Information: 408-2500
Chairman: Vacant, 408-2525

Federal Labor Relations Authority
607 14th St. N.W., #410 20424
Locator: 382-0751
Chair: Jean McKee, 482-6500

Federal Maritime Commission
800 N. Capitol St. N.W. 20573
Locator: 523-5773
Information: 523-5725
Chairman: William D. Hathaway, 523-5911

Federal Mediation and Conciliation Service
2100 K St. N.W. 20427
Locator: 653-5300
Information: 653-5290
Director: John Calhoun Wells, 653-5300

Federal Mine Safety and Health Review Commission
1730 K St. N.W., #600 20006
Information: 653-5633
Chair: Arlene Holen, 653-5648

Federal Reserve System, Board of Governors
20th and C Sts. N.W. 20551
Locator: 452-2266
Information: 452-3204   (press);   452-3215
(public)
Chairman: Alan Greenspan, 452-3201

Federal Retirement Thrift Investment Board
1250 H St. N.W., #400 20005
Executive Director: Francis X. Cavanaugh, 942-1600

Federal Trade Commission
6th St. and Pennsylvania Ave. N.W. 20580
Locator: 326-2000
Information: 326-2180 (press); 326-2222 (public)
Chair: Janet D. Steiger, 326-2100

General Accounting Office
441 G St. N.W. 20548
Locator: 512-3000
Information: 512-4800
Comptroller General: Charles A. Bowsher, 512-5500

General Services Administration
18th and F Sts. N.W. 20405
Locator: 708-5082
Information: 501-0705 (press); 501-5082 (public)
Administrator: Roger Johnson, 501-0800

Government Printing Office
732 N. Capitol St. N.W. 20401
Locator: 512-0000
Information: 512-1991
Publication orders and inquiries: 783-3238
Public Printer: Michael F. DiMario, 512-2034

Inter-American Foundation
901 N. Stuart St., Arlington, VA 22203
Locator: (703) 841-3800
Information: (703) 841-3800
President: Bill K. Perrin, (703) 841-3810

Interstate Commerce Commission
12th St. and Constitution Ave. N.W. 20423
Locator: 927-7119
Information: 927-5340 (press); 927-5350 (public)
Chair: Gail C. McDonald, 927-6020

Legal Services Corp.
750 1st St. N.W. 20002
Locator: 336-8800
Information: 336-8809
President: John P. O'Hara, 336-8800

Marine Mammal Commission
1825 Connecticut Ave. N.W. 20009
Executive Director: John R. Twiss Jr., 606-5504

Merit Systems Protection Board
1120 Vermont Ave. N.W. 20419
Locator: 653-8898
Information: 653-7200
Chairman: Ben Erdreich, 653-7101

National Aeronautics and Space Administration
300 E St. S.W. 20546
Locator: 358-0000
Information: 358-1000
Administrator: Daniel Goldin, 358-1010

National Archives and Records Administration
7th St. and Pennsylvania Ave. N.W. 20408
Locator: 501-5400
Information: 501-5525 (press); 501-5400 (public)
Archivist of the United States: Trudy H. Peterson, acting, 501-5402

National Capital Planning Commission
801 Pennsylvania Ave. N.W. 20576
Executive Director. Reginald W. Griffith, 724-0174

National Commission on Libraries and Information Science
1110 Vermont Ave. N.W., #820, 20005
Chair: Geanne Hurley Simon, 606-9200

National Credit Union Administration
1775 Duke St., Alexandria, VA 22314
Information: (703) 518-6330
Chairman: Norman D'Amours, (703) 518-6300

National Foundation on the Arts and the Humanities

National Endowment for the Arts
1100 Pennsylvania Ave. N.W. 20506
Information: 682-5570 (press); 682-5400 (public)
Chair: Jane Alexander, 682-5414

National Endowment for the Humanities
1100 Pennsylvania Ave. N.W. 20506
Information: 606-8438
Chair: Sheldon Hackney, 606-8310

National Labor Relations Board
1099 14th St. N.W. 20570
Locator: 273-3900
Information: 273-1991
Chairman: William B. Gould IV, 273-1790

National Mediation Board
1301 K St. N.W. 20572
Information: 523-5335
Chair: Kimberly A. Madigan, 523-5920

**National Railroad Passenger Corp.
(Amtrak)**
60 Massachusetts Ave. N.E. 20002
Switchboard: 906-3000
Information: 906-3860 (press); 906-2121 (consumer relations/complaints)
Chairman and President: Thomas M. Downs, 906-3960

National Science Foundation
4201 Wilson Blvd., Arlington VA 22230
Locator: (703) 306-1234
Information: (703) 306-1070
Director: Neal Lane, (703) 306-1000

National Transportation Safety Board
490 L'Enfant Plaza East S.W. 20594
Locator: 382-6600
Information: 382-6600
Chairman: Carl W. Vogt, 382-6502

Nuclear Regulatory Commission
11555 Rockville Pike, Rockville, MD (mailing address: Washington, DC 20555)
Switchboard: (301) 492-7000
Information: (301) 504-2240
Chairman: Ivan Selin, (301) 504-1759

Occupational Safety and Health Review Commission
1120 20th St. N.W. 20036
Information: 606-5398
Chairman: Edwin G. Foulke Jr., 606-5370

Office of Government Ethics
1201 New York Ave. N.W. 20005
Director: Stephen D. Potts, 523-5757

Office of Personnel Management
1900 E St. N.W. 20415
Locator: 606-2118
Information: 606-1800
Director: Jim King, 606-1000

Office of Special Counsel
1730 M St. N.W., #300 20036
Information: 653-7188
Special Counsel: Kathleen Day Koch, 653-7122

Panama Canal Commission
1825 Eye St. N.W., #1050, 20006
Secretary: Michael Rhode Jr., 634-6441

Peace Corps
1990 K St. N.W. 20526
Locator: 606-3886
Information: 606-3010 (press); 606-3387 (public)
Director: Carol Bellamy, 606-3970

Pennsylvania Avenue Development Corp.
1331 Pennsylvania Ave. N.W. 20004
Locator: 724-9091
Information: 724-9073
Chairman, Board of Directors: Richard A. Hauser, 861-1541

Pension Benefit Guaranty Corp.
1200 K St. N.W. 20005
Locator: 778-8800
Information: 326-4000
Executive Director: Martin Slate, 326-4010

Postal Rate Commission
1333 H St. N.W., #300 20268
Information: 789-6800
Chairman: Ed Gleiman, 789-6868

Railroad Retirement Board, Washington Legislative Liaison Office
1310 G St. N.W., #500, 20005
Chairman: Glen L. Bower, Chicago
Liaison Officer: John C. Ficerai, 272-7742

Resolution Trust Corp.
801 17th St. N.W. 20434
Information: 416-6900
Chief Executive Officer: Roger C. Altman, interim, 416-6900

Securities and Exchange Commission
450 5th St. N.W. 20549
Locator: 272-3100
Information: 272-2650
Chairman: Arthur Levitt, 272-2000

Selective Service System
1515 Wilson Blvd., Arlington, VA 22209
Locator: (703) 235-2555
Information: (703) 235-2555
Director: Robert Gambino, (703) 235-2200

Small Business Administration
409 3rd St. S.W. 20416
Locator: 205-6600
Information: 205-7713
Administrator: Erskine Bowles, 205-6605

Smithsonian Institution
1000 Jefferson Dr. S.W. 20560
Locator: 357-1300
Information: 357-2700
Secretary: Robert McCormick Adams, 357-1846

Tennessee Valley Authority
1 Massachusetts Ave. N.W., #300 20001
Chairman: Craven Crowell
Administrative Officer, Washington Office: Jan Evered, 898-2999

U.S. Arms Control and Disarmament Agency
Main State Bldg. (mailing address: 320 21st St. N.W. 20451)
Locator: 647-2034
Information: 647-4800
Director: John D. Holum, 647-9610

U.S. Information Agency
301 4th St. S.W. 20547
Locator: 619-4700
Information: 619-4355
Director: Joseph Duffy, 619-4364

U.S. Institute of Peace
1550 M St. N.W., #700 20005
President: Richard H. Solomon, 457-1700

U.S. International Development Cooperation Agency

Agency for International Development
Main State Bldg.
2201 C St. N.W. 20523
Locator: 663-1449
Information: 647-4200 (press); 647-1850 (public)
Administrator: J. Brian Atwood, 647-9620

Overseas Private Investment Corp.
1100 New York Ave. N.W. 20527
Information: 336-8799
President: Ruth Harkin, 336-0404

U.S. International Trade Commission
500 E St. S.W. 20436
Locator: 205-2000
Information: 205-1819 (press); 205-2000 (public)
Chairman: Don E. Newquist, 205-2781

U.S. Postal Service
475 L'Enfant Plaza S.W. 20260
Locator: 268-2020
Information: 268-2156 (press); 268-2284 (public)
Postmaster General: Marvin T. Runyon, 268-2500

U.S. Trade and Development Agency
1621 N. Kent St., #309, Arlington, VA (mailing address: State Annex 16, Washington, DC 20523)
Director: J. Joseph Grandmaison, (703) 875-4357

Key Agencies:

Commerce Dept.
National Telecommunications and
Information Administration
Main Commerce Bldg.
14th St. and Constitution Ave. N.W. 20230
Information: 482-1551

Federal Communications Commission
1919 M St. N.W. 20554
Information: 632-7000
Press: 632-5050

White House Press Office
The White House
1600 Pennsylvania Ave. N.W. 20500
Information: 456-2100
Press releases: 395-7332

Key Committees:

**House Energy and Commerce
Committee**
2125 RHOB 20515
Phone: 225-2927

**Senate Commerce, Science, and Trans-
portation Committee**
SD-508 20510
Phone: 224-5115

Key Personnel:

Commerce Dept.
Clarence L. Irving Jr., assistant secretary for
communications and information and administrator of the National Telecommunications and Information Administration

Federal Communications Commission
Reed E. Hundt, chairman

The White House
Dee Dee Myers, deputy assistant to the
president and press secretary

1

Communications and the Media

Contents:

Access to the Media

Agencies:

Federal Communications Commission, Political Programming, 2025 M St. N.W., #8202 20554; 632-7586. Milton O. Gross, chief. Information, 632-700. Fax, 653-9659.

Handles complaints and inquiries concerning the equal time rule, which requires equal broadcast opportunities for all legally qualified candidates for the same office. Enforces reasonable access provision of the Communications Act, which obligates all broadcast licensees to afford access to their facilities to candidates for federal office. Enforces identification provision of the Communications Act, which requires sponsorship identification of all paid broadcast announcements.

Congress:

House Energy and Commerce Committee, Subcommittee on Telecommunications and Finance, 316 Ford Bldg. (2nd and D Sts. S.W.) 20515; 226-2424. Edward J. Markey, D-Mass., chairman; David H. Moulton, staff director and chief counsel.

Jurisdiction over legislation related to interstate and foreign communications and the Federal Communications Commission, including the equal time rule.

Senate Commerce, Science, and Transportation Committee, Subcommittee on Communications, SH-227 (mailing address: SD-508, Washington, DC 20510); 224-9340. Daniel K. Inouye, D-Hawaii, chairman; John Windhausen, senior counsel.

Jurisdiction over legislation related to interstate and foreign communications and the Federal Communications Commission, including the equal time rule.

Nongovernmental:

Accuracy in Media, 4455 Connecticut Ave. N.W., #330 20008; 364-4401. Reed Irvine, board chairman. Fax, 364-4098.

Analyzes print and electronic news media for bias, omissions, and errors in news; approaches media with complaints. Maintains speakers bureau.

Center for Media and Public Affairs, 2100 L St. N.W., #300 20037; 223-2942. John Thomas Sheehan, executive director. Fax, 872-4014.

Nonpartisan research and educational organization that studies media coverage of social and political issues and campaigns. Conducts surveys and publishes materials.

Center for Media Education, 1511 K St. N.W., #518 (mailing address: P.O. Box 33039, Washington, DC 20033); 628-2620. Kathryn C. Montgomery, president. Fax, 628-2554.

Educational organization that promotes public interest in media policies and provides nonprofit groups with educational and informational services. Maintains a speakers bureau.

Education and Research Institute, 800 Maryland Ave. N.E. 20002; 546-1710. M. Stanton Evans, chairman. Fax, 546-1638.

Educational organization that conducts seminars and operates the National Journalism Center to train interns in basic skills of media work.

Institute for Public Representation, Georgetown University Law Center, 600 New Jersey Ave. N.W. 20001; 662-9535. Douglas L. Parker, director. Fax, 662-9634.

Public interest law firm that specializes in communications regulatory policy; assists citizens' groups that seek input into local and federal regulation of the electronic media. Interests include freedom of information.

Joint Washington Media Committee, c/o Cohn and Marks, 1333 New Hampshire Ave. N.W. 20036; 452-4837. Richard M. Schmidt Jr., chairman. Fax, 293-4827.

Membership: representatives of media organizations. Consulting group that acts as a clearinghouse and forum for exchange of information on legislative and judicial developments affecting freedom of the press.

Media Access Project, 2000 M St. N.W. 20036; 232-4300. Andrew Jay Schwartzman, executive director. Fax, 223-5302.

Public interest telecommunications law firm that represents the right of the public to receive information from the mass media. Interests include media ownership and the fairness doctrine.

The Media Institute, 1000 Potomac St. N.W., #301 20007; 298-7512. Patrick D. Maines, president. Fax, 337-7092.

Conducts conferences, files court briefs and regulatory comments, and sponsors programs on communications topics. Advocates free-speech rights for individuals, media, and corporate speakers.

Media Research Center, 113 S. West St., 2nd Floor, Alexandria, VA 22314; (703) 683-9733. L. Brent Bozell III, chairman. Fax, (703) 683-9736. Media-watch organization working for balanced news coverage of political issues. Records and analyzes network news programs; analyzes print media; maintains profiles of media executives and library of recordings.

National Assn. of Broadcasters, 1771 N St. N.W. 20036; 429-5300. Edward O. Fritts, president. Press, 429-5480. Library, 429-5490. Membership: radio and television broadcast stations holding an FCC license or construction permit; associate members include producers of equipment and programs. Assists members in areas of management, engineering, and research; interprets laws and regulations governing the broadcast media. Publishes materials about broadcasting industry. Library offers fee-based services by appointment.

National Black Media Coalition, 38 New York Ave. N.E. 20002; 387-8155. Pluria W. Marshall, chair. Fax, 462-4469. Advocates African American involvement in communications at local and national levels. Maintains an equal employment opportunity center. Conducts training classes; negotiates affirmative action plans with large media corporations.

National Captioning Institute, 5203 Leesburg Pike, Falls Church, VA 22041; (703) 998-2400. Philip W. Bravin, president. Fax, (703) 998-2458. Captions television programs for the deaf and hard-of-hearing on behalf of public and commercial television networks, cable TV companies, and home video distributors. Develops, manufactures, and distributes closed-caption decoders for consumer use. Produces and disseminates information about the national closed-captioning service.

Telecommunications Research and Action Center, P.O. Box 12038, Washington, DC 20005; 462-2520. Anna Maria Anthony, editor. Fax, 408-1134. Citizens' interest group that acts as a consumer advocate in telecommunications issues. Works

to promote greater public participation in decisions affecting the media; serves as a clearinghouse for information on media reform and for other public interest groups.

See also Advocacy Institute (p. 274); Democratic National Committee, general counsel (p. 772); Republican National Committee, chief counsel (p. 774)

Freedom of Information Act

Agencies:

Each agency has its own rules and regulations governing public access to its documents; grants for access are determined initially by the agency. Contact the freedom of information officer of the agency involved. For a list of departmental and agency freedom of information officers, see box. (See Freedom of Information Act for explanation, p. 1019.)

Justice Dept., Information and Privacy, Main Justice Bldg., Rm. 7238 20530; 514-3642. Daniel J. Metcalfe and Richard L. Huff, co-directors. Information, 514-2000. Fax, 514-1009. Provides federal agencies with advice and policy guidance on matters related to implementing and interpreting the Freedom of Information Act (FOIA). Litigates selected FOIA and Privacy Act cases; adjudicates administrative appeals from Justice Dept. denials of public requests for access to documents.

Congress:

House Government Operations Committee, Subcommittee on Information, Justice, Transportation, and Agriculture, B349C RHOB 20515; 225-3741. Gary Condit, D-Calif., chairman; Shannon Lahey, acting staff director. Jurisdiction over Freedom of Information Act.

Senate Judiciary Committee, Subcommittee on Technology and the Law, SH-815 20510; 224-3406. Patrick J. Leahy, D-Vt., chairman; Bruce A. Cohen, chief counsel. Jurisdiction over Freedom of Information Act.

Nongovernmental:

American Society of Access Professionals, 7910 Woodmont Ave., #1430, Bethesda, MD 20814; (301) 913-0030. Kathy S. Huggins, executive director. Fax, (301) 913-0001.

Departmental and Agency . . .

Departments

Agriculture
Milt Sloane 720-8164
Commerce
Brenda Dolan 482-4115
Defense
Charlie Y. Talbott .... (703) 697-1180
Air Force
Carolyn Price .... (703) 695-4992
Army
Bill Walker .... (703) 697-6158
Navy
Gwen R. Aitken .... (703) 697-1459
Education
Alexia Roberts 708-9263
Energy
Denise B. Diggin 586-6025
Health and Human Services
Rosario Cirrincione 690-7453
Housing and Urban Development
Anna-Marie Kilmade Gatons 708-3054
Interior
Alexandra Mallus 208-5342
Justice
Patricia D. Harris 514-1938
Labor
Miriam Miller 219-8188
State
Frank M. Machak 647-7740
Transportation
Robert Meeks 366-4542
Treasury
Lana Johnson 622-0930
Veterans Affairs
Michael B. Berger 233-3616

Agencies

Central Intelligence Agency
John H. Wright .... (703) 351-2770
Commission on Civil Rights
Emma Monroig 376-8351
Commodity Futures Trading Commission
Edward Colbert 254-3382
Consumer Product Safety Commission
Todd A. Stevenson .... (301) 504-0785
Corporation for National Service
Kenneth Priebe 606-5000
Environmental Protection Agency
Jeralene B. Green 260-4048
Equal Employment Opportunity Commission
Tom Schlageter 663-4669
Export-Import Bank
Gerald Waid 566-8910
Farm Credit Administration
Ron Erickson .... (703) 883-4056
Federal Communications Commission
Kathy Conley 632-7513
Federal Deposit Insurance Corp.
Lisa Snider 898-3822
Federal Election Commission
Fred S. Eiland 219-4155
Federal Emergency Management Agency
Sandra Jackson 646-3840
Federal Labor Relations Authority
David M. Smith 482-6695
Federal Maritime Commission
Joseph Polkine 523-5725

Membership: federal government employees, attorneys, print and broadcast journalists, and others working with or interested in access-to-information laws. Seeks to improve the administration of the Freedom of Information Act, the Privacy Act, and other access statutes.

Center for National Security Studies, 122 Maryland Ave. N.E. 20002; 675-2327. Kate Martin, director. Fax, 546-1440.

Sponsored by the American Civil Liberties Union (ACLU) Foundation and the Fund for Peace. Specializes in the Freedom of Information Act (FOIA) as it relates to national security matters; produces and distributes litigation handbook and manual on using the FOIA. Sponsors annual conference on FOIA litigation. Library open to the public by appointment.

Freedom of Information Clearinghouse, 2000 P St. N.W. (mailing address: P.O. Box 19367,

...Freedom of Information Contacts

Federal Mine Safety and Health Review Commission
Richard Baker 653-5625

Federal Reserve System
Susan Mitchell 452-3684

Federal Trade Commission
Keith Golden 326-2410

General Services Administration
John Hughes 501-2162

Interstate Commerce Commission
Clyde J. Hart Jr. 927-6317

Legal Services Corp.
JoAnn Gretch 336-8813

Merit Systems Protection Board
Michael Hoxie 653-7200

National Aeronautics and Space Administration
Patricia M. Riep 358-1764

National Archives and Records Administration
Thomas Gedosch .... (301) 713-6730

National Credit Union Administration
Patricia Slye .... (703) 518-6410

National Endowment for the Arts
Marlene Cleaveland 682-5418

National Endowment for the Humanities
David C. Fisher Jr. 606-8322

National Labor Relations Board
John W. Hornbeck 273-3847

National Mediation Board
Judy Semi 523-5996

National Railroad Passenger Corp. (Amtrak)
Medaris Oliveri 906-2728

National Science Foundation
Mary Ellen Schoolmaster 357-9498

National Transportation Safety Board
Michael Levins 382-6700

Nuclear Regulatory Commission
Donnie H. Grimsley ...... (301) 492-8133

Occupational Safety and Health Review Commission
Linda A. Whitsett 606-5398

Office of Personnel Management
Gloria Clark 606-1700

Peace Corps
Tom Peirce................... 606-3261

Pension Benefit Guaranty Corp.
Bill Fitzgerald 778-8839

Resolution Trust Corp.
Maryanne Reinhart 906-5900

Securities and Exchange Commission
GayLa D. Sessoms 942-4320

Selective Service System
Sharon Toon .... (703) 235-2272

Small Business Administration
Beverly Linden 653-6460

U.S. Arms Control and Disarmament Agency
Frederick Smith Jr. 647-3596

U.S. Information Agency
Lola Secora 619-5499

U.S. International Development Cooperation Agency
  Agency for International Development
  James L. Harper 647-1850

U.S. International Trade Commission
Donna R. Koehnke 205-2000

U.S. Postal Service
Betty E. Scherif, acting 268-2924

Washington, DC 20036); 833-3000. Lucinda Sikes, director.

Arm of the Center for Study of Responsive Law, a consumer interest clearinghouse that studies freedom of information policy, among other topics; works with Public Citizen Litigation Group. Collects and disseminates information on federal, state, and foreign freedom of information laws; assists citizens, public interest groups, and the media in seeking information from the govern-

ment; litigates selected cases, generally chosen for their broad effect on case law.

Radio-Television News Directors Assn., 1000 Connecticut Ave. N.W., #615 20036; 659-6510. David Bartlett, president. Fax, 223-4007.

Membership: local and network news directors and other broadcast news professionals. Operates the Freedom of Information Committee, which assists members with news access.

Society of Professional Journalists, First Amendment Center, 1760 Reston Parkway, #407, Reston, VA 22090; (703) 318-1980. Roy Steinfort, director. Fax, (703) 318-0801.

Develops information useful to journalists on freedom of information issues. (Headquarters in Greencastle, Ind.)

See also Institute for Public Representation, Media Access Project, and The Media Institute (p. 22); National Security Archive (p. 549); Reporters Committee for Freedom of the Press (p. 39)

Government Regulation of Communications

General

Agencies:

Federal Communications Commission, 1919 M St. N.W. 20554; 632-6600. Reed E. Hundt, chairman. Information, 632-7000. Press, 632-5050. Library, 632-7100. Fax, 653-5402. Recorded news, 632-0002.

Regulates interstate and foreign communications by radio, television, wire, cable, microwave, and satellite; consults with other government agencies and departments on national and international matters involving wire and radio telecommunications and with state regulatory commissions on telegraph and telephone matters; reviews applications for construction permits and licenses for such services. Library open to the public.

National Telecommunications and Information Administration (Commerce Dept.), Main Commerce Bldg. 20230; 482-1840. Clarence L. Irving Jr., assistant secretary for communications and information and NTIA administrator. Information, 482-1551. Library, 482-3999. Fax, 482-1635.

Develops telecommunications policy for the executive branch; manages federal use of radio spectrum; conducts research on radiowave transmissions and other aspects of telecommunications; serves as information source for federal and state agencies on the efficient use of telecommunications resources; provides noncommercial telecommunications services with grants for construction of facilities.

Congress:

House Appropriations Committee, Subcommittee on Commerce, Justice, State, and Judiciary, H309 CAP 20515; 225-3351. Neal Smith, D-Iowa, chairman; John Osthaus, staff assistant.

Jurisdiction over legislation to appropriate funds for the Federal Communications Commission, the Board for International Broadcasting, the National Telecommunications and Information Administration, and the U.S. Information Agency.

House Energy and Commerce Committee, Subcommittee on Telecommunications and Finance, 316 Ford Bldg. (2nd and D Sts. S.W.) 20515; 226-2424. Edward J. Markey, D-Mass., chairman; David H. Moulton, staff director and chief counsel.

Jurisdiction over legislation related to interstate and foreign communications, including television, cable television, local and long-distance telephone service, radio, wire, microwave, and satellite communications. Jurisdiction over the Federal Communications Commission.

House Government Operations Committee, Subcommittee on Commerce, Consumer, and Monetary Affairs, B377 RHOB 20515; 225-4407. John M. Spratt, Jr., D-S.C., chairman; Theodore Jacobs, staff director. Fax, 225-2441.

Oversees operations of the National Telecommunications and Information Administration.

House Government Operations Committee, Subcommittee on Information, Justice, Transportation, and Agriculture, B349C RHOB 20515; 225-3741. Gary Condit, D-Calif., chairman; Shannon Lahey, acting staff director. Fax, 225-2445.

Oversees operations of the Federal Communications Commission and the Board for International Broadcasting.

House Judiciary Committee, Subcommittee on Economic and Commercial Law, B353 RHOB 20515; 225-2825. Jack Brooks, D-Texas, chairman; Cynthia W. Meadow, chief counsel.

Jurisdiction over legislation related to anticompetitive practices and to monopolies in communications, including cable telecommunication and network practices.

Library of Congress, Copyright Office, 101 Independence Ave. S.E. 20557; 707-8160. Walter D. Sampson, chief, licensing. Information, 707-8150. Fax, 707-0905.

Licenses cable television companies and satellite carriers and collects and distributes royalty payments under the copyright law. Distributes licenses for making and distributing phonorecords and for use of certain noncommercial broadcasting. Administers Section 115 licensing for making and distributing phonorecords.

Senate Appropriations Committee, Subcommittee on Commerce, Justice, State, and Judiciary, S146A CAP 20510; 224-7277. Ernest F. Hollings, D-S.C., chairman; Scott B. Gudes, clerk.

Jurisdiction over legislation to appropriate funds for the Federal Communications Commission, the Board for International Broadcasting, the National Telecommunications and Information Administration, and the U.S. Information Agency.

Senate Commerce, Science, and Transportation Committee, Subcommittee on Communications, SH-227 (mailing address: SD-508, Washington, DC 20510); 224-9340. Daniel K. Inouye, D-Hawaii, chairman; John Windhausen, senior counsel.

Jurisdiction over legislation related to interstate and foreign communications, including television, cable television, local and long-distance telephone service, radio, wire, microwave, and satellite communications. Oversight of the Federal Communications Commission, the National Telecommunications and Information Administration, and the Board for International Broadcasting.

Senate Judiciary Committee, Subcommittee on Antitrust, Monopolies, and Business Rights, SH-308 20510; 224-5701. Howard M. Metzenbaum, D-Ohio, chairman; Gene Kimmelman, chief counsel.

Jurisdiction over all legislation related to anticompetitive practices and to monopolies in communications, including cable telecommunication and network practices.

Nongovernmental:

Computer and Communications Industry Assn., 666 11th St. N.W., #600 20001; 783-0070. Stephanie Biddle, president. Fax, 783-0534.

Membership: manufacturers and suppliers of computer data processing and communications-related products and services. Interests include telecommunications policy, capital formation and tax policy, federal procurement policy, communications and computer industry standards, intellectual property policies, export policy, and antitrust reform.

International Communications Industries Assn., 3150 Spring St., Fairfax, VA 22031; (703) 273-7200. Vacant, executive vice president. Fax, (703) 278-8082.

Membership: video, audiovisual, and microcomputer dealers; manufacturers and producers; and individuals. Interests include unfair competition, small business issues, postal rates, copyright, education, and taxation. Monitors legislation and regulations.

National Assn. of Regulatory Utility Commissioners, 12th St. and Constitution Ave. N.W. (mailing address: P.O. Box 684, Washington, DC 20044-0684); 898-2200. Paul Rodgers, administrative director and general counsel. Press, 898-2205. Fax, 898-2213.

Membership: members of federal, state, municipal, and Canadian regulatory commissions that have jurisdiction over utilities and carriers. Interests include telecommunications regulation.

See also National Assn. of State Utility Consumer Advocates (p. 222)

Enforcement, Judicial, and Legal Actions

Agencies:

Federal Communications Commission, Administrative Law Judges, 2000 L St. N.W. 20554; 632-7680. Joseph Stirmer, chief judge.

Presides over hearings and issues initial decisions in disputes over FCC regulations and applications for licensing.

Federal Communications Commission, Field Operations, 1919 M St. N.W. 20554; 632-6980. Richard M. Smith, chief. Fax, 653-5402. 24-hour watch officer, 632-6975.

Detects violations of radio regulations by monitoring radio transmissions and inspecting stations; investigates complaints of radio frequency interference; furnishes direction-finding aid for ships and aircraft in distress.

Federal Communications Commission, Review Board, 2000 L St. N.W. (mailing address: 1919 M St. N.W., Washington, DC 20554); 632-

Federal Communications Commission

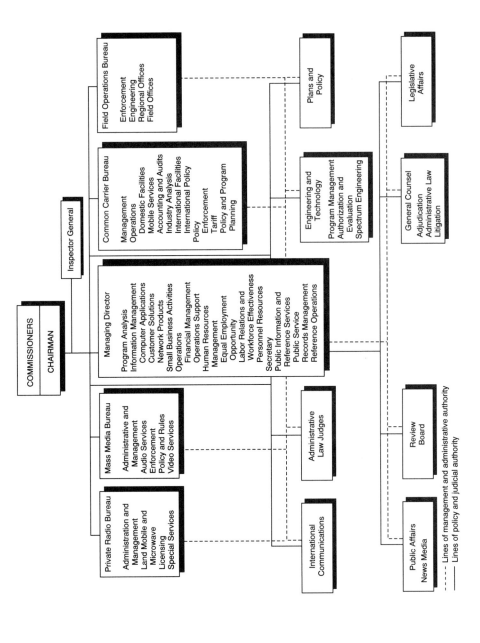

COMMISSIONERS

CHAIRMAN

Inspector General

Private Radio Bureau
Administration and Management
Land Mobile and Microwave
Licensing
Special Services

Mass Media Bureau
Administrative and Management
Audio Services
Enforcement
Policy and Rules
Video Services

Managing Director
Program Analysis
Information Management
Computer Applications
Customer Solutions
Network Products
Small Business Activities
Operations
Financial Management
Operations Support
Human Resources
Management
Equal Employment Opportunity
Labor Relations and Workforce Effectiveness
Personnel Resources
Secretary
Public Information and Reference Services
Public Service
Records Management
Reference Operations

Common Carrier Bureau
Management
Operations
Domestic Facilities
Mobile Services
Accounting and Audits
Industry Analysis
International Facilities
International Policy
Policy
Enforcement
Tariff
Policy and Program Planning

Field Operations Bureau
Enforcement
Engineering
Regional Offices
Field Offices

International Communications

Administrative Law Judges

Public Affairs
News Media

Review Board

General Counsel
Adjudication
Administrative Law
Litigation

Engineering and Technology
Program Management
Authorization and Evaluation
Spectrum Engineering

Plans and Policy

Legislative Affairs

- - - - - Lines of management and administrative authority
————— Lines of policy and judicial authority

7180. Joseph A. Marino, chairman. Fax copies of recent FCC legal actions, 632-0915.

Reviews decisions made by administrative law judges.

Justice Dept., Antitrust Division, 555 4th St. N.W. 20001; 514-5621. Richard L. Rosen, chief, communications and finance. Fax, 514-6381.

Investigates and litigates antitrust cases dealing with communications; participates in agency proceedings and rulemaking concerning communications; monitors and analyzes legislation. Oversees continuing matters concerning the breakup of AT&T.

See also General Counsels box (p. 494)

Congress:

See Government Regulation of Communications, General, Congress (p. 26)

Nongovernmental:

Federal Communications Bar Assn., 1150 Connecticut Ave. N.W., #1050 20036; 833-2684. James Herbert, executive director.

Membership: nonattorneys, law students, and attorneys in communications law who practice before the Federal Communications Commission (FCC), the courts, and state and local regulatory agencies. Cooperates with the FCC and other members of the bar on legal aspects of communications issues.

Regulation of Cable Television

Agencies:

Federal Communications Commission, Cable Television, 1919 M St. N.W. 20554; 416-0903. Ronald Parver, chief. Library, 632-7100.

Processes applications and notifications for licensing of cable television relay service stations (CARS); registers cable television systems; develops, administers, and enforces regulation of cable television and CARS.

Congress:

See Government Regulation of Communications, General, Congress (p. 26)

Nongovernmental:

The Alliance for Community Media, 666 11th St. N.W., #806 20001; 393-2650. T. Andrew

Lewis, executive director. Fax, 393-2653.

Membership: cable television companies, programming managers and producers, independent producers, cable television administrators and regulators, media access centers, and others involved in community communications. Promotes local programming and participation in cable television. Interests include freedom of expression, diversity of information, and developing technologies. Monitors legislation and regulations.

Cable Telecommunications Assn., 3950 Chain Bridge Rd., Fairfax, VA (mailing address: P.O. Box 1005, Fairfax, VA 22030); (703) 691-8875. Stephen Effros, president. Fax, (703) 691-8911.

Membership: independent cable operating companies. Monitors legislation and regulations. Interests include cable rates, telephone company entry into cable television, regulation, and new technologies.

National Cable Television Assn., 1724 Massachusetts Ave. N.W. 20036; 775-3550. Decker Anstrom, president. Information, 775-3629. Fax, 775-3671.

Membership: companies that operate cable television systems and manufacturers and suppliers of hardware and software for the industry. Represents the industry before federal regulatory agencies and Congress and in the courts; provides management and promotional aids and information on legal, legislative, and regulatory matters.

Regulation of International and Satellite Communications

Agencies:

Federal Communications Commission, Common Carrier Bureau, 1919 M St. N.W. 20554; 632-6910. Kathleen B. Levitz, acting chief. Fax, 653-5402.

Develops, recommends, and administers FCC policies involving common carriers that furnish interstate or international communications services for hire. Policy areas include AT&T, Communications Satellite Corp., domestic satellite carriers, cellular radio carriers, and more than 1,400 exchange telephone companies.

Federal Communications Commission, International Communications, 1919 M St. N.W., #658 20554; 632-0935. James Ball, acting director. Fax, 632-0929.

Coordinates the FCC's collection and dissemination of information on communications and telecommunications policy, regulation, and market developments in other countries and the policies and regulations of international organizations. Coordinates the FCC's international policy activities; represents the FCC in international forums.

State Dept., International Communications and Information Policy, Main State Bldg. 20520; 647-5832. Vonya McCann, U.S. coordinator and director. Fax, 647-5957.

Develops and manages international communication information policy for the State Dept. Acts as a liaison for other federal departments and agencies and the private sector in international communications issues. Trade-related telecommunications issues are handled by the Bureau of Economic and Business Affairs.

Congress:

See Government Regulation of Communications, General, Congress (p. 26)

Nongovernmental:

International Assn. of Satellite Users and Suppliers, 45681 Oakbrook Court, #107, Sterling, VA 20166; (703) 759-2094. A. Fred Dassler, executive director. Library, (703) 406-2744. Fax, (703) 759-5094.

Membership: satellite users and suppliers. Provides information on the business application of satellites, new technological developments, and federal regulatory and policy actions. Assists corporations, developing countries, and consortia in efficient satellite usage. Brokers new and reconditioned telecommunications equipment; acts as a liaison between satellite users and suppliers.

International Telecommunications Satellite Organization (INTELSAT), 3400 International Dr. N.W. 20008-3098; 944-6800. Irving Goldstein, director general. Information, 944-7500. Fax, 944-7859.

Membership: more than 120 governments. Owns and operates a global international satellite communications system. Technical offices in California and the United Kingdom provide research and development support.

Satellite Broadcasting and Communications Assn., 225 Reinekers Lane, #600, Alexandria,

VA 22314; (703) 549-6990. Charles Hewitt, president. Fax, (703) 549-7640.

Membership: owners, operators, manufacturers, dealers, and distributors of satellite receiving stations; software and program suppliers; and others working with satellite earth stations and equipment. Promotes private and commercial use of satellite earth stations, particularly for television programming. Monitors legislation and regulations.

Regulation of Private Radio Services

Agencies:

Federal Communications Commission, Private Radio Bureau, 2025 M St. N.W. 20554; 632-6940. Ralph A. Haller, chief. Library, 632-7100. Fax, 634-7651. TDD, 632-6999.

Regulates radio stations engaged in communication for safety, commercial, or personal purposes, including amateur (ham) operators, walkie-talkies, police, fire, ambulance, medical, and ship-to-shore broadcasts. Office in Gettysburg, Pa., handles all licensing applications and concerns: FCC Private Radio Bureau, Licensing Division, 1270 Fairfield Rd., Gettysburg, Pa. 17325; (717) 337-1212.

Congress:

See Government Regulation of Communications, General, Congress (p. 26)

Nongovernmental:

American Mobile Telecommunications Assn., 1150 18th St. N.W., #250 20036; 331-7773. Alan R. Shark, president. Fax, 331-9062.

Membership: mobile telecommunications companies. Represents industry interests before Congress and the Federal Communications Commission (FCC). Serves as an information source on radio frequencies, licensing, and new product and new technology development. Offers research service of FCC records. Monitors legislation and regulations.

Cellular Telecommunications Industry Assn., 1133 21st St. N.W., 3rd Floor 20036; 785-0081. Thomas E. Wheeler, president. Fax, 785-0721.

Membership: system operators, equipment manufacturers, engineering firms, and others engaged in the cellular telephone and mobile communications industry. Promotes interests of members. Monitors legislation and regulations.

Council of Independent Communication Suppliers, 1110 N. Glebe Rd., #500, Arlington, VA 22201; (703) 528-5115. Andrew Daskalakis, chairman. Fax, (703) 524-1074.

Represents independent radio sales and service organizations, communications service providers, and telecommunications consultants and engineers serving the Private Land Mobile Radio Services industry. Informs members of FCC and industry activities and solicits members' views on FCC regulatory proceedings. (Affiliated with Industrial Telecommunications Assn.)

Industrial Telecommunications Assn., 1110 N. Glebe Rd., Arlington, VA 22201; (703) 528-5115. Mark E. Crosby, president. Fax, (703) 524-1074.

FCC-certified frequency advisory committee for the Special Industrial Radio Service and Industrial/Land Transportation pools. Provides frequency coordination, licensing, research, and telecommunications engineering services to Private Land Mobile Radio Services licensees and applicants. Represents telecommunications interests of Special Industrial, Video Production, and Telephone Maintenance Radio Service licensees and informs members of FCC rule changes and industry activities.

National Assn. of Business and Educational Radio, 1501 Duke St., Alexandria, VA 22314; (703) 739-0300. E. B. "Jay" Kitchen Jr., president. Fax, (703) 836-1608.

Membership: individuals; institutions; independent two-way radio dealers, technicians, and service shop owners; and companies holding licenses in the FCC's Business Radio Service. Provides members with information and assistance; supports the expanded availability of private radio facilities and the private land mobile radio spectrum; certifies two-way private land mobile radio technicians. Serves as the FCC-recognized coordinator for frequencies in the Business Radio Service.

Telocator, The Personal Communications Industry Assn., 1019 19th St. N.W., 11th Floor 20036; 467-4770. Thomas A. Stroup, president. Fax, 467-6987.

Membership: FCC-licensed carriers who provide the public with personal communications services, including pagers, conventional radio telephones, and cellular radio telephones. Monitors legislation and regulations; provides members with information, technical assistance, and educational programs. Interests include development of regulatory policies and technological

standards for the industry. Library offers fee-based services by appointment.

Utilities Telecommunications Council, 1140 Connecticut Ave. N.W., #1140 20036; 872-0030. Michael Meehan, executive director. Fax, 872-1331.

Membership: utility companies eligible to hold FCC Power Radio Service licenses. Participates in FCC rulemaking proceedings. Interests include radio spectrum for fixed and mobile communication and technological, legislative, and regulatory developments affecting telecommunications operations of energy utilities.

Regulation of Radio and Television

Agencies:

Federal Communications Commission, Engineering and Technology, 2025 M St. N.W. 20554; 632-7060. Thomas P. Stanley, chief engineer. Library, 632-7100. TDD, 632-6999.

Advises the FCC on technical and spectrum matters and assists in developing U.S. telecommunications policy. Reviews developments in telecommunications and related technologies. Studies characteristics of radio frequency spectrum. Certifies radios and other electronic equipment to meet FCC standards.

Federal Communications Commission, Mass Media Bureau, 1919 M St. N.W. 20554; 632-6460. Roy J. Stewart, chief. Fax, 632-0158.

Licenses, regulates, and develops audio and video services in traditional broadcasting, cable television, and emerging television delivery systems, including high-definition television; processes applications for licensing commercial and noncommercial radio and television broadcast equipment and facilities; handles renewals and changes of ownership; investigates public complaints.

Congress:

See Government Regulation of Communications, General, Congress (p. 26)

Nongovernmental:

Assn. for Maximum Service Television, 1776 Massachusetts Ave. N.W., #310 20036; 861-0344. Margita E. White, president. Fax, 861-0342.

Membership: commercial and educational television stations in the United States. Participates in FCC rulemaking proceedings; specializes in television engineering and other matters concerning the transmission structure of the nation's television system.

Assn. of Independent Television Stations, 1320 19th St. N.W., #300 20036; 887-1970. James B. Hedlund, president. Fax, 887-0950.

Membership: independent television stations. Monitors legislation and regulations affecting the industry. Interests include the must-carry rules, copyright laws, and television advertising and syndication issues.

Electronic Industries Assn., 2001 Pennsylvania Ave. N.W. 20006; 457-4900. Peter F. McCloskey, president. Fax, 457-4985.

Membership: U.S. electronics manufacturers. Interests include competitiveness, common distribution, trade, and government procurement. Monitors legislation and regulations affecting electronics manufacturers. Operates High-Definition Information Center, which collects and disseminates information on electronics, especially high-definition television; represents consumer retailers and manufacturers of home recording equipment under the Home Recording Rights Coalition.

National Assn. of Broadcasters, 1771 N St. N.W. 20036; 429-5300. Edward O. Fritts, president. Press, 429-5480. Library, 429-5490.

Membership: radio and television broadcast stations holding an FCC license or construction permit; associate members include producers of equipment and programs. Interprets laws and regulations governing the broadcast media. Publishes materials about broadcasting industry. Library offers fee-based services by appointment.

Regulation of Telephone and Telegraph

Agencies:

Federal Communications Commission, Common Carrier Bureau, 1919 M St. N.W. 20554; 632-6910. Kathleen B. Levitz, acting chief. Fax, 653-5402.

Develops, recommends, and administers FCC policies involving common carriers that furnish interstate or international communications services for hire. Specific policy areas include AT&T, the Communications Satellite Corp., domestic satellite carriers, cellular radio carriers,

and more than 1,400 exchange telephone companies.

Congress:

See Government Regulation of Communications, General, Congress (p. 26)

Nongovernmental:

Alliance for Public Technology, 901 15th St. N.W. 20005; 408-1403. Barbara O'Connor, chair. Fax, 408-1134.

Membership: public groups and individuals concerned with developing affordable access to information services and telecommunications technology, particularly for the elderly, residential consumers, low-income groups, and people with disabilities.

Competitive Telecommunications Assn., 1140 Connecticut Ave. N.W., #220 20036; 296-6650. James M. Smith, president. Fax, 296-7585.

Membership: providers of long-distance telecommunications services and suppliers to that industry. Analyzes telecommunications issues affecting competitive long-distance carriers; monitors legislation and regulations.

National Telephone Cooperative Assn., 2626 Pennsylvania Ave. N.W. 20037; 298-2300. Michael E. Brunner, executive vice president.

Membership: telephone cooperatives (member-owned telephone companies) in rural areas and small, independent commercial companies serving rural areas. Offers technical assistance and a benefits program to members. Monitors legislation and regulations.

North American Telecommunications Assn., 2000 M St. N.W., #550 20036; 296-9800. Edwin Spievack, president. Fax, 296-4993.

Membership: manufacturers, suppliers, installers, and users of computer and communications systems. Serves as an information source and provides members with a benefits program and legal counsel; conducts training program; monitors legislation and regulations.

Organization for the Protection and Advancement of Small Telephone Companies, 21 Dupont Circle N.W., #700 20036; 659-5990. John N. Rose, executive vice president. Fax, 659-4619.

Membership: local exchange carriers with 50,000 or fewer access lines. Provides members with educational materials and information on regulatory, legislative, and judicial issues in the telecommunications industry. Operates the Foundation for Rural Education and Development.

U.S. Telephone Assn., 900 19th St. N.W. 20005; 326-7300. Roy Neel, president. Fax, 326-7333.
Membership: local telephone companies and manufacturers and suppliers for these companies. Provides members with information on the industry; conducts seminars; participates in FCC regulatory proceedings.

See also Cellular Telecommunications Industry Assn. (p. 30)

Media Accreditation in Washington

Executive Branch

Most federal agencies do not require special press credentials.

Defense Dept., Public Affairs, The Pentagon 20301; (703) 697-9312. Kathleen deLaski, assistant to the secretary of defense. Press, (703) 697-5131. Fax, (703) 693-6853. National Media Pool, (703) 693-1074.
Grants accreditation to Washington-based media organizations to form the National Media Pool. Selected staff of accredited groups are assigned to the media pool on a rotating basis and put on alert for short-notice deployment to the site of military operations.

Foreign Press Center (U.S. Information Agency), 898 National Press Bldg., 529 14th St. N.W. 20045; 724-1640. Phil Brown, director. Fax, 724-0007. Alternate fax, 724-0122. Recorded information, 724-1635.
Provides foreign journalists with access to news sources, including wire services and daily briefings from the White House, State Dept., and Pentagon. Holds live news conferences. Foreign journalists wishing to use the center must present a letter from their organization and a letter from the embassy of the country in which their paper is published.

State Dept., Public Affairs Press Office, Main State Bldg. 20520; 647-2492. Thomas E. Donilon, assistant secretary and department spokesman. Fax, 647-0244.
U.S. journalists seeking accreditation must apply in person with a letter from their editor or publisher and a passport-size photograph. In addition, foreign correspondents need a letter from the embassy of the country in which their organization is based. All journalists must reside in the Washington, D.C., area and must cover the State Dept.'s daily briefing on a regular basis. Applicants should allow three months for security clearance.

White House, Press Office, 1600 Pennsylvania Ave. N.W. 20500; 456-2100. Dee Dee Myers, deputy assistant to the president and press secretary. Press releases, 395-7332. Comments and information, 456-1111.
Journalists seeking permanent accreditation must be accredited by the House or Senate press galleries (this page and p. 35), must be residents of the Washington, D.C., area, and must be full-time employees of a news-gathering organization, expecting to cover the White House on a nearly daily basis. A journalist's editor, publisher, or employer must write to the press office requesting accreditation. Journalists wishing temporary accreditation should have their assignment desk call a day ahead to be cleared for a one-day pass. Press Office also maintains an index of journalists with permanent specialized White House accreditation. Applicants must undergo a Secret Service investigation.

Judicial Branch

Press accreditation is not required by most federal courts, although the policy may vary from court to court.

Supreme Court of the United States, 1 1st St. N.E. 20543; 479-3000. William H. Rehnquist, chief justice; Toni House, public information officer, 479-3211. Library, 479-3177.
Journalists seeking to cover the Court must be accredited by either the White House or the House or Senate press galleries. Contact the public information office to make arrangements.

Legislative Branch

House Periodical Press Gallery, Executive Committee of the Periodical Correspondents' Gallery, H304 CAP 20515; 225-2941. Alexis Simendinger, acting chair (Bureau of National Affairs), 452-4300.

Major Washington Media Contacts

Magazines

Congressional Quarterly Weekly Report
1414 22nd St. N.W. 20037
887-8500

National Journal
1730 M St. N.W. 20036
857-1400

Newsweek
1750 Pennsylvania Ave. N.W. 20006
626-2000

Time
1050 Connecticut Ave. N.W. 20036
861-4000

U.S. News & World Report
2400 N St. N.W. 20037
955-2000

News Services

Associated Press
2021 K St. N.W. 20006
828-6400
City wire, 828-6426

Gannett News Service
1000 Wilson Blvd.
Arlington, VA 22229
(703) 276-5800

Knight-Ridder Newspapers
700 National Press Bldg.
529 14th St. N.W. 20045
383-6000

Newhouse News Service
2000 Pennsylvania Ave. N.W. 20006
383-7800

Reuters
1333 H St. N.W. 20005
898-8300

Scripps-Howard Newspapers
1090 Vermont Ave. N.W. 20005
408-1484

States News Service
1333 F St. N.W. 20004
628-3100

United Press International
1400 Eye St. N.W. 20005
898-8000
City wire, 898-8000

Newspapers, News Bureaus

Baltimore Sun
1627 K St. N.W. 20006
452-8250

Christian Science Monitor
910 16th St. N.W. 20006
785-4400

Los Angeles Times
1875 Eye St. N.W. 20006
293-4650

New York Times
1627 Eye St. N.W. 20006
862-0300

USA Today
1000 Wilson Blvd.
Arlington, VA 22229
(703) 276-3400

Wall Street Journal
1025 Connecticut Ave. N.W. 20036
862-9200

Washington Post
1150 15th St. N.W. 20071
334-6000

Washington Times
3600 New York Ave. N.E. 20002
636-3000

Television/Radio Networks

ABC News
1717 DeSales St. N.W. 20036
887-7777

Cable News Network (CNN)
820 1st St. N.E. 20002
898-7900

CBS News
2020 M St. N.W. 20036
457-4321

C-Span
400 N. Capitol St. N.W. 20001
737-3220

Mutual/NBC Radio Network
1755 S. Jefferson Davis Highway
Arlington, VA 22202
(703) 413-8300

National Public Radio
2025 M St. N.W. 20036
822-2000

NBC News
4001 Nebraska Ave. N.W. 20016
885-4200

Public Broadcasting Service
1320 Braddock Place
Alexandria, VA 22314
(703) 739-5000

Open by application to periodical correspondents whose chief occupation is gathering and reporting news for periodicals not affiliated with lobbying organizations. Accreditation with the House Gallery covers accreditation with the Senate Gallery.

Press Photographers Gallery, Standing Committee of Press Photographers, S317 CAP 20510; 224-6548. John Duricka, chairman (Associated Press), 828-9657. Fax, 224-0280.

Open by application to bona fide news photographers and to heads of photographic bureaus. Accreditation by the standing committee covers both the House and Senate.

Senate Press Gallery, Standing Committee of Correspondents, S316 CAP 20510; 224-0241. Patrick Towell, chairman (Congressional Quarterly), 828-6400.

Open by application to Washington-based reporters who earn more than half their income from news services or from newspapers published at least five times a week. Accreditation with the Senate Gallery covers accreditation with the House Gallery.

Senate Radio and Television Gallery, Executive Committee of the Radio and Television Correspondents' Galleries, S325 CAP 20510; 224-6421. Bill Headline, chairman (C-SPAN), 898-7900. Fax, 224-4882.

Open by application to Washington-based radio and television correspondents and technicians who earn more than half their income from or spend at least half their time in the news gathering profession. Accreditation with the Senate Gallery covers accreditation with the House Gallery.

Police

Metropolitan Police Dept., Police Public Information, 300 Indiana Ave. N.W., #2052 20001; 727-4383. Lt. Beverly Alford, director. Fax, 727-0437. Press passes, 727-3575.

Provides application forms and issues press passes required for crossing police lines within the city of Washington. Passes are issued on a yearly basis; applicants should allow four to six weeks for processing of passes.

Congressional News Media Galleries

The congressional news media galleries serve as liaisons between members of Congress and their staffs and accredited newspaper, magazine, and broadcasting correspondents. The galleries provide accredited correspondents with facilities to cover activities of Congress, and gallery staff members ensure that congressional press releases reach appropriate correspondents. Independent committees of correspondents working through the press galleries are responsible for accreditation of correspondents; *see Media Accreditation in Washington, Legislative Branch, p. 33.*

House Periodical Press Gallery, H304 CAP 20515; 225-2941. David W. Holmes, director.

House Press Gallery, H315 CAP 20515; 225-3945. Thayer Illsley, superintendent.

House Radio and Television Gallery, H321 CAP 20515; 225-5214. Tina Tate, director.

Press Photographers Gallery, S317 CAP 20510; 224-6548. Maurice J. Johnson, superintendent.

Senate Periodical Press Gallery, S320 CAP 20510; 224-0265. Jim Talbert, superintendent.

Senate Press Gallery, S316 CAP 20510; 224-0241. Robert E. Petersen Jr., superintendent.

Senate Radio and Television Gallery, S325 CAP 20510; 224-6421. Larry Janezich, director.

National Park Service (Interior Dept.), National Capital Region, 1100 Ohio Dr. S.W. 20242; 619-7222. Robert G. Stanton, director. Press, 619-7226. Fax, 619-7302. Recorded activities, 619-7275. Permits, 619-7225.

Regional office that administers national parks, monuments, historic sites, and recreation areas in the Washington metropolitan area. Issues special permits required for commercial filming on public park lands. Media representatives covering public events that take place on park lands should notify the Office of Public Affairs and Tourism in advance. A White House or metropolitan police press pass is required in some circumstances.

Professional Interests

General

Agencies:

Federal Communications Commission, Equal Employment Opportunity, 2025 M St. N.W. (mailing address: 1919 M St. N.W., Washington, DC 20554); 632-7069. Glenn Wolfe, chief. Fax, 653-8773.

Responsible for the annual certification of cable television equal employment opportunity compliance. Oversees broadcast employment practices. Publishes annual report on employment trends in cable television and broadcast industries.

Federal Communications Commission, Small Business Activities, 1250 23rd St. N.W. (mailing address: 1919 M St. N.W., Washington, DC 20554); 632-1571. John R. Winston, director. Fax, 632-1580.

Provides technical and legal guidance and assistance to the small, minority, and female business community in the telecommunications industry. Advises the FCC chairman on small, minority, and female business issues. Serves as liaison between federal agencies, state and local governments, and trade associations representing small, minority, and female enterprises concerning FCC policies, procedures, and rule-making activities.

Nongovernmental:

American News Women's Club, 1607 22nd St. N.W. 20008; 332-6770. Diane Smigel, president. Fax, 265-6477.

Membership: writers, reporters, photographers, cartoonists, and professionals in print and broadcast media, government and private industry, publicity, and public relations. Promotes the advancement of women in all media. Sponsors professional receptions and seminars.

Assn. for Suppliers of Printing and Publishing Technologies, 1899 Preston White Dr., Reston, VA 22091-4367; (703) 264-7200. Carol J. Hurlburt, director. Fax, (703) 620-0994.

Trade association representing companies that manufacture and distribute equipment, supplies, systems, software and services for printing and publishing.

Freedom Forum, 1101 Wilson Blvd., Arlington, VA 22209; (703) 528-0800. Charles L. Overby, president. Press, (703) 284-3507. Fax, (703) 522-4692.

Awards grants and operates programs that promote free press, free speech, and freedom of information and that enhance the teaching and practice of journalism.

Interactive Services Assn., 8403 Colesville Rd., #865, Silver Spring, MD 20910; (301) 495-4955. Robert L. Smith Jr., executive director. Fax, (301) 495-4959.

Membership: advertising agencies, cable companies, consulting and research organizations, computer and terminal manufacturers, entrepreneurs, financial institutions, interactive service providers, online and gateway operators, publishers, software vendors, telecommunications companies, service bureaus and packagers, television programmers, and universities and government agencies. Promotes the use of network-based interactive electronic services in homes, offices, and public locations. Library open to the public by appointment.

International Exhibitors Assn., 5501 Backlick Rd., #105, Springfield, VA 22151; (703) 941-3725. Peter J. Mangelli, president. Fax, (703) 941-8275.

Membership: organizations that use exhibits as a marketing medium. Members share information on matters affecting exhibit programs.

National Assn. of Black Journalists, 11600 Sunrise Valley Dr., Reston, VA (mailing address: P.O. Box 4222, Reston, VA 22091-1412); (703) 648-1270. Walterene Swanston, executive director. Fax, (703) 476-6245.

Membership: African American journalists working for radio and television stations, newspapers, and magazines, and others in the field of journalism. Works to increase recognition of the achievements of minority journalists, to expand opportunities for minority students entering the field, and to promote balanced coverage of the African American community by the media. Sponsors scholarships and internship program.

National Assn. of Government Communicators, 669 S. Washington St., Alexandria, VA 22314; (703) 519-3902. Deborah Trocchi, executive director. Fax, (703) 519-7732.

Membership: federal, state, and local government communications employees. Promotes job standards for the government communications profession; monitors administrative and regulatory proposals that affect the field; provides a clearinghouse on government jobs for members.

National Assn. of Hispanic Journalists, 1193 National Press Bldg., 529 14th St. N.W. 20045; 662-7145. Zita Arocha, executive director. Fax, 662-7144.

Membership: professional journalists, educators, students, and corporations interested in encouraging Hispanics to study and enter the field of journalism. Promotes fair representation of Hispanics by the news media. Provides computerized job referral service; compiles and updates national directory of Hispanics in the media; sponsors national high school essay contest, journalism awards, and scholarships.

National Conference of Editorial Writers, 6223 Executive Blvd., Rockville, MD 20852; (301) 984-3015. Cora Everett, executive secretary. Fax, (301) 231-0026.

Membership: editorial writers, editors, syndicated columnists, journalism professors at accredited universities, and commentators on general circulation newspapers and television and radio stations in the United States and Canada. Sponsors critique exchange workshops. Provides critique service upon request.

National Press Foundation, 1282 National Press Bldg., 529 14th St. N.W. 20045; 662-7350. David Yount, president. Fax, 662-1232.

Works to enhance the professional competence of journalists through in-career education and research projects. Sponsors conferences, seminars, fellowships, awards, and writing and research grants, as well as public forums. Supports the National Press Club library. Sponsors training and mentoring of minority youth toward careers in journalism. Incorporates the Washington Journalism Center.

Regional Reporters Assn., 1092 National Press Bldg., 529 14th St. N.W. 20045; 662-7300. Tammy Lytle, president. Fax, 638-1944.

Membership: Washington-based reporters for regional newspapers and radio and television stations. Works to improve regional correspondents' access to all branches of the federal government; encourages professional development; maintains clippings file of stories by regional correspondents; operates computer bulletin board.

Screen Printing Technical Foundation, 10015 Main St., Fairfax, VA 22031-3489; (703) 385-1335. John Crawford, president. Fax, (703) 275-0456.

Provides screen printers, suppliers, and manufacturers with technical guidebooks, training videos, and guidelines for safety programs. Provides member companies with environmental and safety information to prevent accidents.

Society for Technical Communication, 901 N. Stuart St., #904, Arlington, VA 22203-1854; (703) 522-4114. William C. Stolgitis, executive director. Fax, (703) 522-2075.

Membership: writers, publishers, educators, editors, illustrators, and others involved in technical communication in the print and broadcast media. Encourages research and develops training programs for technical communicators; aids educational institutions in devising curricula; awards scholarships.

Telecommunications Industry Assn., 2001 Pennsylvania Ave. N.W., #800 20006-1813; 457-4912. Matthew J. Flanigan, president. Press, 457-4935. Fax, 457-4939. Telex, 710-822-0148 E1Λ WSH.

Membership: telecommunications equipment manufacturers and suppliers. Represents members in telecommunications manufacturing issues; helps to develop standards for telecommunications products; sponsors a job-matching service; cohosts trade shows. (Affiliated with the Electronics Industries Assn.)

Women in Communications, Inc., 3717 Columbia Pike, #310, Arlington, VA 22204; (703) 920-5555. Roni D. Posner, executive director. Fax, (703) 920-5556.

Membership: professionals and students in communications. Maintains job hotline for members and supports women in communications. Works for freedom of expression for all communicators.

Women's Institute for Freedom of the Press, 3306 Ross Pl. N.W. 20008; 966-7783. Martha Leslie Allen, director.

Conducts research and publishes in areas of communications and the media that are of particular interest to women.

World Press Freedom Committee, c/o Newspaper Center, 11600 Sunrise Valley Dr., Reston, VA 22091; (703) 648-1000. Dana R. Bullen, executive director. Fax, (703) 620-4557.

Worldwide organization of print and broadcast groups. Promotes freedom of the press and opposes government censorship. Conducts training programs and assists journalists in central and Eastern Europe and the Third World. Participates in international conferences; maintains equipment clearinghouse.

See also Council on Hemispheric Affairs (p. 465); Washington Center for Politics and Journalism (p. 126)

Broadcasting

Nongovernmental:

American Women in Radio and Television, 1650 Tysons Blvd., #200, McLean, VA 22102; (703) 506-3290. Donna F. Cantor, executive director. Fax, (703) 506-3066.

Membership: professionals in the broadcast industry and full-time students in accredited colleges and universities. Promotes industry cooperation and advancement of women in broadcasting. Maintains foundation for educational and charitable purposes; encourages contacts with foreign women in media and allied fields.

Broadcast Education Assn., 1771 N St. N.W. 20036; 429-5354. Louisa A. Nielsen, executive director. Fax, 429-5406.

Membership: universities, colleges, and faculty members offering specialized training in radio and television broadcasting. Promotes improvement of curriculum and teaching methods. Fosters working relationships among academics, students, and professionals in the industry.

National Academy of Television Arts and Sciences, 9405 Russell Rd., Silver Spring, MD 20910; (301) 587-3993. Dianne Bruno, administrator. Fax, (301) 587-3993.

Membership: professionals in television and related fields and students in communications. Works to upgrade television programming; awards scholarship to a junior, senior, or graduate student in communications. Sponsors annual Emmy Awards. (Headquarters in New York.)

National Assn. of Black-Owned Broadcasters, 1730 M St. N.W. 20036; 463-8970. James L. Winston, executive director. Fax, 429-0657.

Membership: minority owners of radio and television stations and people who work with radio

and television stations. Provides members and the public with information on the broadcast industry and the FCC. Provides members with legal and research facilities. Monitors legislation and regulations.

National Assn. of Broadcasters, 1771 N St. N.W. 20036; 429-5300. Edward O. Fritts, president. Press, 429-5480. Library, 429-5490.

Membership: radio and television broadcast stations holding an FCC license or construction permit; associate members include producers of equipment and programs. Assists members in areas of management, engineering, and research; interprets laws and regulations governing the broadcast media. Publishes materials about broadcasting industry. Library offers fee-based services by appointment.

Public Interest Video Network, 4704 Overbrook Rd., Bethesda, MD 20816; (301) 656-7244. Arlen Slobodow, executive director.

Provides nonprofit, public interest organizations with video production services. Produces and distributes radio and television programming and video news releases to broadcast stations, cable systems, and new television outlets. Serves as consultant on distribution of public affairs programming via satellite to television and radio stations.

Radio-Television News Directors Assn., 1000 Connecticut Ave. N.W., #615 20036; 659-6510. David Bartlett, president. Fax, 223-4007.

Membership: local and network news directors and other broadcast news professionals. Serves as information source for members; provides advice on legislative, political, and judicial problems of electronic journalism.

Press Shield Law

Congress:

House Judiciary Committee, Subcommittee on Intellectual Property and Judicial Administration, 207 CHOB 20515; 225-3926. William J. Hughes, D-N.J., chairman; Hayden W. Gregory, chief counsel.

Jurisdiction over press shield legislation.

Senate Judiciary Committee, Subcommittee on the Constitution, SD-524 20510; 224-5573.

Paul Simon, D-Ill., chairman; Susan D. Kaplan, chief counsel.
Jurisdiction over press shield legislation.

Nongovernmental:

Reporters Committee for Freedom of the Press, 1735 Eye St. N.W. 20006; 466-6312. Jane E. Kirtley, executive director. Fax, 466-6326. Freedom of information hotline, (800) 336-4243.
Membership: reporters, news editors, publishers, and lawyers from the print and broadcast media. Maintains a legal defense and research fund for members of the news media involved in freedom of the press court cases. Library open to the public by appointment.

Student Press Law Center, 1735 Eye St. N.W., #504 20006; 466-5242. Mark Goodman, executive director.
Collects, analyzes, and distributes information on free expression and freedom of information rights of student journalists (print and broadcast) and on violations of those rights in high schools and colleges. Provides free legal assistance to students and faculty advisers experiencing censorship.

See also World Press Freedom Committee (p. 37)

Print Media

Nongovernmental:

American Society of Newspaper Editors, 11600 Sunrise Valley Dr., Reston, VA (mailing address: P.O. Box 4090, Reston, VA 22090-1700); (703) 648-1144. Lee Stinnett, executive director. Fax, (703) 620-4557.
Membership: directing editors of daily newspapers. Campaigns against government secrecy; works to improve the racial mix of newsroom employees; sponsors work/training program for journalists from developing countries; serves as information clearinghouse for newsrooms of daily newspapers.

Assn. of American Publishers, 1718 Connecticut Ave. N.W., #700 20009; 232-3335. Judith Platt, director, communications. Fax, 745-0694.
Membership: publishers of books, journals, tests, and software. Provides members with information on trade matters and market conditions, government policies and pending legisla-

tion, library and educational funding, postal rates, new technology, taxes, copyright, censorship, and libel matters.

Essential Information, 1530 P St. N.W. (mailing address: P.O. Box 19405, Washington, DC 20036); 387-8030. John Richard, director. Fax, 234-5176.
Provides writers and the public with information on public policy matters; awards grants to investigative reporters; sponsors conference on investigative journalism.

Fund for Investigative Journalism, 1755 Massachusetts Ave. N.W., #419 20036; 462-1844. Anne Grant, executive director.
Provides freelance reporters with grants for investigative articles, broadcasts, and books.

International Newspaper Financial Executives, 11600 Sunrise Valley Dr., Reston, VA 22091; (703) 648-1160. Robert J. Kasabian, vice president. Fax, (703) 476-5961.
Membership: controllers and chief financial officers of newspapers. Disseminates information on financial aspects of publishing newspapers. Provides members with information on business office technology, including accounting software and spreadsheet applications.

International Newspaper Marketing Assn., 1801 Robert Fulton Dr., #120, Reston, VA 22091; (703) 476-4662. Earl J. Wilkinson, executive director. Fax, (703) 476-6924.
Membership: newspaper executives. Assists members in improving their newspapers' images. Interests include promotion, marketing, linage, and circulation.

Magazine Publishers of America, 1211 Connecticut Ave. N.W. 20036; 296-7277. George Gross, executive vice president, government affairs. Fax, 296-0343.
Washington office represents members in all aspects of government relations in Washington and state capitals. (Headquarters in New York.)

National Newspaper Assn., 1525 Wilson Blvd., #550, Arlington, VA 22209; (703) 525-7900. Tonda Rush, president. Fax, (703) 525-7901.
Membership: community, weekly, and daily newspapers. Provides members with advisory services; informs members of legislation and regulations that affect their business. An affiliate, the National Newspaper Foundation, con-

ducts management seminars and conferences and awards scholarships to journalism students.

National Newspaper Publishers Assn., 3200 13th St. N.W. 20010; 588-8764. Collis Jones, director of operations. Fax, 588-5029.

Membership: newspapers owned by African Americans serving an African American audience. Assists in improving management and quality of the African American press through workshops and merit awards.

Newsletter Publishers Assn., 1401 Wilson Blvd., #207, Arlington, VA 22209; (703) 527-2333. Frederick D. Goss, executive director. Fax, (703) 841-0629.

Membership: newsletter publishers and specialized information services. Serves as information clearinghouse; acts as liaison between newsletter publishers and the government. Monitors legislation and regulations. Library open to the public.

Newspaper Assn. of America, 11600 Sunrise Valley Dr., Reston, VA 22091-1499; (703) 648-1000. Cathleen Black, president. Press, (703) 648-1117. Library, (703) 648-1090. Fax, (703) 620-4557.

Membership: daily and weekly newspapers and other papers published in the United States, Canada, other parts of the Western Hemisphere, and Europe. Conducts research and disseminates information on newspaper publishing, including labor relations, legal matters, government relations, technical problems and innovations, telecommunications, economic and statistical data, training programs, and public relations. Library open to the public.

Printing Industries of America, 100 Daingerfield Rd., Alexandria, VA 22314; (703) 519-8100. Ray Roper, president. Fax, (703) 548-3227.

Membership: printing firms and businesses that service printing industries. Monitors legislation and regulations. Represents members before Congress and regulatory agencies. Assists members with labor relations, human resources management, and other business management issues. Sponsors graphic arts competition.

Society of National Assn. Publications, 1150 Connecticut Ave. N.W., #1050 20036; 862-9864. Tom Gibson, director. Fax, 833-1308.

Membership: publications owned or controlled by voluntary organizations. Works to develop high publishing standards, including high quality editorial and advertising content in members' publications. Compiles statistics; bestows editorial and graphics awards; monitors postal regulations.

Washington Journalism Center, 1282 National Press Bldg. 529 14th St. N.W. 20045; 662-7351. Bob Meyers, executive director. Fax, 662-1232.

Conducts conferences for journalists on major issues in the news. Sponsors award for environmental writers. (Affiliated with the National Press Foundation.)

Washington Press Club Foundation, 1067 National Press Bldg., 529 14th St. N.W. 20045; 393-0613. Julia D. Hurt, executive director. Fax, 783-0841.

Seeks to advance professionalism in journalism. Awards minority grants and scholarships. Administers an oral history of women in journalism. Sponsors annual Salute to Congress Dinner in late January to welcome Congress back into session. Maintains speakers bureau.

See also The Writer's Center (p. 113)

Public Broadcasting

Agencies:

National Endowment for the Arts (National Foundation on the Arts and the Humanities), Media Arts Program: Film/Radio/Television, 1100 Pennsylvania Ave. N.W. 20506; 682-5452. Brian O'Doherty, director. Fax, 682-5744.

Awards individuals and nonprofit organizations grants for film, video, and radio productions; supports arts programming for public television and radio.

National Endowment for the Humanities (National Foundation on the Arts and the Humanities), Humanities Projects' in Media, 1100 Pennsylvania Ave. N.W., #420 20506; 606-8278. James Dougherty, director.

Awards grants for nonprofit media projects aimed at advancing the humanities.

Congress:

House Appropriations Committee, Subcommittee on Labor, Health and Human Services, and Education, 2358 RHOB 20515; 225-

3508. Neal Smith, D-Iowa, chairman; Mike Stephens, staff assistant.

Jurisdiction over legislation to appropriate funds for the Corporation for Public Broadcasting.

House Energy and Commerce Committee, Subcommittee on Telecommunications and Finance, 316 Ford Bldg. (2nd and D Sts. S.W.) 20515; 226-2424. Edward J. Markey, D-Mass., chairman; David H. Moulton, staff director and chief counsel.

Jurisdiction over legislation related to public broadcasting.

Senate Appropriations Committee, Subcommittee on Labor, Health and Human Services, and Education, SD-186 20510; 224-7283. Tom Harkin, D-Iowa, chairman; Ed Long, clerk.

Jurisdiction over legislation to appropriate funds for the Corporation for Public Broadcasting.

Senate Commerce, Science, and Transportation Committee, Subcommittee on Communications, SH-227 (mailing address: SD-508, Washington, DC 20510); 224-9340. Daniel K. Inouye, D-Hawaii, chairman; John Windhausen, senior counsel.

Jurisdiction over legislation related to public broadcasting.

Nongovernmental:

Assn. of America's Public Television Stations, 1350 Connecticut Ave. N.W., #200 20036; 887-1700. David J. Brugger, president. Fax, 293-2422.

Membership: public television licensees. Provides information on licensees' operating characteristics, financing, and facilities; conducts research; assists licensees in local and regional planning efforts; monitors legislation and regulations affecting public television stations.

Corporation for Public Broadcasting, 901 E St. N.W. 20004; 879-9600. Richard W. Carlson, president. Information, 879-9688. Fax, 783-1019.

Private corporation chartered by Congress under the Public Broadcasting Act of 1967 and funded by the federal government. Supports public broadcasting through grants for public radio and television stations; provides general support for national program production and operation; studies emerging technologies, such as cable and satellite transmission, for possible use by public telecommunications; supports training activities.

National Federation of Community Broadcasters, 666 11th St. N.W. 20001; 393-2355. Lynn Chadwick, president.

Membership: community public radio stations. Works to ensure equitable distribution of federal funds for public broadcasting; represents community broadcasters before the FCC and other government agencies; assists in organizing and expanding community-based broadcast stations; provides public radio system with training and consultation.

National Public Radio, 2025 M St. N.W. 20036; 822-2000. Delano Lewis, president. Information, 822-2300. Fax, 822-2329.

Membership: public radio stations nationwide. Produces and distributes news and public affairs programming, congressional hearings, speeches, cultural and dramatic presentations, and programs for specialized audiences. Provides program distribution service via satellite. Represents member stations before Congress, the FCC, and other regulatory agencies.

Public Broadcasting Service, 1320 Braddock Pl., Alexandria, VA 22314; (703) 739-5000. Ervin Duggan, president. Information, (703) 739-5023. Fax, (703) 739-0775.

Membership: public television stations nationwide. Selects, schedules, promotes, and distributes national programs; provides public television stations with educational, instructional, and cultural programming; also provides news and public affairs, science and nature, fundraising, and children's programming. Assists members with technology development and fund raising.

Key Agencies:

Commerce Dept.
Main Commerce Bldg.
14th St. and Constitution Ave. N.W. 20230
Information: 482-2000

Congressional Budget Office
402 Ford Bldg.
2nd and D Sts. S.W. 20515
Information: 226-2600

Council of Economic Advisers
Old Executive Office Bldg. 20500
Information: 395-5084

Federal Reserve System
20th and C Sts. N.W. 20551
Information: 452-3215

Office of Management and Budget
Old Executive Office Bldg. 20503
Information: 395-3080

Small Business Administration
409 3rd St. S.W. 20416
Information: 205-6740

Treasury Dept.
Main Treasury Bldg.
15th St. and Pennsylvania Ave. N.W. 20220
Information: 622-2000

U.S. Trade Representative
600 17th St. N.W. 20506
Information: 395-3230

Key Committees:

House Banking, Finance, and Urban Affairs Committee
2129 RHOB 20515; 225-4247

House Budget Committee
214 O'Neill Bldg. 20515; 226-7200

House Ways and Means Committee
1102 LHOB 20515; 225-3625

Joint Economic Committee
SD-G01 20510; 224-5171

Joint Taxation Committee
1015 LHOB 20515; 225-3621

Senate Banking, Housing, and Urban Affairs Committee
SD-534 20510; 224-7391

Senate Budget Committee
SD-621 20510; 224-0642

Senate Finance Committee
SD-205 20510; 224-4515

Key Personnel:

Commerce Dept.
Ronald H. Brown, secretary
David J. Barram, deputy secretary
Everett Ehrlich, under secretary for economics and statistics
William Alan Reinsch, under secretary for export administration
Jeffrey Garten, under secretary for international trade administration
Greg Farmer, under secretary for travel and tourism
William W. Ginsberg, assistant secretary for economic development
Charles Meissner, assistant secretary for international economic policy
Raymond E. Vickery Jr., assistant secretary designate for trade development
Bruce A. Lehman, commissioner of patents and trademarks
Lauri Fitz-Pegado, director general designate, U.S. and Foreign Commercial Service

Congressional Budget Office
Robert D. Reischauer, director

Council of Economic Advisers
Laura D'Andrea Tyson, chair

Federal Reserve System
Alan Greenspan, chairman

Office of Management and Budget
Leon E. Panetta, director

Small Business Administration
Erskine Bowles, administrator

Treasury Dept.
Lloyd Bentsen, secretary
Roger C. Altman, deputy secretary
Frank N. Newman, under secretary for domestic finance
Alicia Haydock Munnell, assistant secretary for economic policy
Richard S. Carnell, assistant secretary for financial institutions
Lawrence H. Summers, under secretary for international affairs
Jeffrey Shafer, assistant secretary for international affairs
George Munoz, assistant secretary for management
Leslie Samuels, assistant secretary for tax policy
Gerald Murphy, fiscal assistant secretary
Margaret Milner Richardson, commissioner, Internal Revenue Service

U.S. Trade Representative
Mickey Kantor, U.S. trade representative

2

Economics and Business

Contents:

Business and Economic Policy

General

Agencies:

Census Bureau (Commerce Dept.), Economic Programs, Federal Bldg. 3, Suitland, MD 20233; (301) 763-5274. Charles A. Waite, associate director.

Compiles comprehensive statistics on the level of U.S. economic activity and the characteristics of industrial and business establishments at the national, state, and local levels.

Commerce Dept., Main Commerce Bldg., 14th St. and Constitution Ave. N.W. 20230; 482-2112. Ronald H. Brown, secretary. Information, 482-2000. Press, 482-4901. Library, 482-5511. Fax, 482-5685.

Acts as principal adviser to the president on federal policy affecting industry and commerce; promotes national economic growth and development, competitiveness, international trade, and technological development; provides business and government with economic statistics, research, and analysis; encourages minority business; promotes tourism. Library reference service staff answers questions about commerce and business.

Commerce Dept., Business Analysis, Main Commerce Bldg. 20230; 482-1405. John E. Cremeans, director. Fax, 482-2164.

Develops and maintains macroeconomic models and other analytical tools necessary to analyze a broad range of economic policy issues such as the effects on business of federal legislation, regulations, and programs. Maintains and makes available for public use the Economic Bulletin Board (EBB), the National Trade Data Bank (NTDB), and the National Economic, Social, and Environmental Data Bank.

Commerce Dept., Business Liaison, Main Commerce Bldg. 20230; 482-3942. Melissa Moss, director. Information, 482-1302. Fax, 482-4054. Business assistance, 482-3176.

Serves as the central office for business assistance. Handles requests for information and services as well as complaints and suggestions from businesses; provides businesses with a forum to comment on federal regulations; initiates meetings on policy issues with industry groups, business organizations, trade and small-business

associations, and the corporate community. Business Assistance Office provides information, advice, and guidance on federal policies and programs, selling to government markets, financial assistance programs, and domestic and international business statistics.

Council of Economic Advisers (Executive Office of the President), Old Executive Office Bldg. 20500; 395-5084. Laura D'Andrea Tyson, chair; Thomas P. O'Donnell, chief of staff. Fax, 395-6958.

Advisory body of three members and supporting staff of economists. Monitors and analyzes the economy and advises the president on economic developments, trends, and policies and on the economic implications of other policy initiatives. Prepares the annual *Economic Report of the President* for Congress.

Domestic Policy Council (Executive Office of the President), The White House 20500; 456-2216. Carol H. Rasco, assistant to the president for domestic policy. Fax, 456-2878.

Coordinates the domestic policy-making process to facilitate the implementation of the president's domestic agenda in such areas as business and economics.

Economics and Statistics Administration (Commerce Dept.), Main Commerce Bldg. 20230; 482-3727. Everett Ehrlich, under secretary. Information, 482-2235. Fax, 482-0432.

Advises the secretary on economic policy matters, including consumer and capital spending, inventory status, and the short- and long-term outlook in output and unemployment. Seeks to improve economic productivity and growth. Serves as departmental liaison with the Council of Economic Advisers and other government agencies concerned with economic policy. Supervises and sets policy for the Census Bureau and the Bureau of Economic Analysis.

Federal Reserve System, Board of Governors, 20th and C Sts. N.W. 20551; 452-3201. Alan Greenspan, chairman. Information, 452-3215. Press, 452-3204. Fax, 452-3819.

Sets U.S. monetary policy. Supervises the Federal Reserve System and influences credit conditions through the buying and selling of treasury securities in the open market, by fixing the amount of reserves depository institutions must maintain, and by determining discount rates.

Federal Trade Commission, 6th St. and Pennsylvania Ave. N.W. 20580; 326-2100. Janet D. Steiger, chair. Information, 326-2222. Press, 326-2180. Library, 326-2374. Fax, 326-2050.
Promotes policies designed to maintain strong competitive enterprise within the U.S. economic system. Monitors trade practices and investigates cases involving monopoly, unfair restraints, or deceptive practices. Enforces Truth in Lending and Fair Credit Reporting acts. Library open to the public.

Federal Trade Commission, Economics, 6th St. and Pennsylvania Ave. N.W. 20580; 326-3431. Ronald S. Bond, acting director. Fax, 326-2050.
Provides economic analyses for consumer protection and antitrust investigations, cases, and rulemakings; advises the commission on the effect of government regulations on competition and consumers in various industries; develops special reports on competition, consumer protection, and regulatory issues.

Minority Business Development Agency (Commerce Dept.), Main Commerce Bldg. 20230; 482-5061. Gilbert Colon, acting director. Fax, 482-2693.
Coordinates federal and private programs and resources to promote minority ownership of business. Provides management, technical, and financial assistance through a consortium of minority-business development centers to minority entrepreneurs to start, expand, or manage a business. Develops and monitors national minority business programs. Reports annually on federal agencies' performance in procuring from minority-owned businesses.

National Economic Council (Executive Office of the President), The White House 20500; 456-2174. Robert E. Rubin, assistant to the president for economic policy. Fax, 456-2878.
Comprises cabinet members and other high-ranking executive branch officials. Coordinates domestic and international economic policy-making process to facilitate the implementation of the president's economic agenda.

National Institute of Standards and Technology (Commerce Dept.), National Center for Standards and Certification Information, Route I-270 and Quince Orchard Rd., Bldg. 411, #A163, Gaithersburg, MD 20899; (301) 975-4040. Joanne Overman, supervisor. Fax, (301) 926-1559. Weekly recorded updates: GATT hotline, (301) 975-4041; EC hotline, (301) 921-4164.

Serves as the national repository for information on voluntary industry standards for domestic and foreign products. Provides information on standards, specifications, test methods, codes, and recommended practices.

National Women's Business Council, 409 3rd St. S.W., #5850 20024; 205-3850. Mary Ann Campbell, chair; Amy Millman, executive director. Fax, 205-6825.
Membership: the administrator of the Small Business Administration, secretary of commerce, chairman of the Federal Reserve Board, and six congressionally appointed individuals. Independent, congressionally mandated council established by the Women's Business Ownership Act of 1988. Reviews the status of women-owned businesses nationwide and makes policy recommendations to the president and Congress. Assesses the role of federal, state, and local governments in aiding and promoting women-owned businesses.

Office of Management and Budget (Executive Office of the President), Old Executive Office Bldg. 20503; 395-4840. Leon E. Panetta, director. Information, 395-3080. Fax, 395-3888.
Prepares president's annual budget; works with the Council of Economic Advisers and the Treasury Dept. to develop the federal government's fiscal program; oversees administration of the budget; reviews government regulations; coordinates administration procurement and management policy.

Small Business Administration, 409 3rd St. S.W. 20416; 205-6605. Erskine Bowles, administrator. Information, 205-7713. Press, 205-6740. Library, 205-7033. Fax, 205-7064. TDD, 205-7733. Toll-free information, (800) 827-5722.
Serves as the government's principal advocate of small-business interests through financial, investment, procurement, and management assistance and counseling; evaluates effect of federal programs on and recommends policies for small business.

Technology Administration (Commerce Dept.), Technology Commercialization, Main Commerce Bldg., Rm. 4418 20230; 482-2100. Jon Paugh, director. Press, 482-3037. Library, 482-5511. Fax, 482-0253. Law library, 482-5517.
Encourages industrial research to promote U.S. competitiveness and economic security. Increases private access to federally developed technology by encouraging industry involvement in research conducted at federal labora-

Commerce Dept.

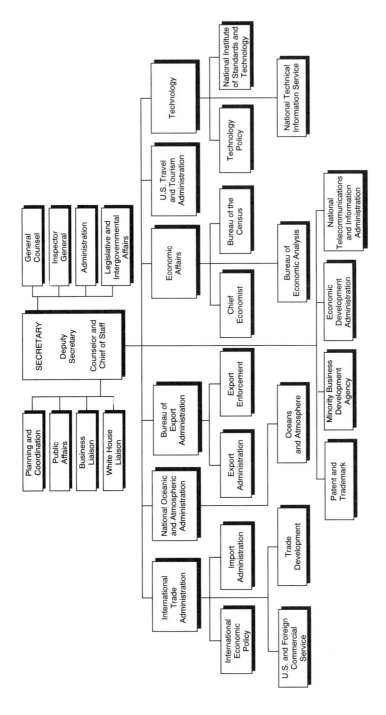

tories; provides state and local agencies and the private sector with information.

Technology Administration (Commerce Dept.), Technology Policy, Main Commerce Bldg., Rm. 4814C 20230; 482-1581. Graham Mitchell, assistant secretary. Fax, 482-4817.
Promotes the removal of barriers to the commercialization of technology; analyzes federal research and development funding; acts as an information clearinghouse.

Treasury Dept., Main Treasury Bldg., 15th St. and Pennsylvania Ave. N.W. 20220; 622-5300. Lloyd Bentsen, secretary. Information, 622-2000. Library, 622-0045. Fax, 622-2599.
Serves as chief financial officer of the government and adviser to the president on economic policy. Formulates and recommends domestic and international financial, economic, tax, and broad fiscal policies; manages the public debt. Library open to the public by appointment.

Treasury Dept., Economic Policy, Main Treasury Bldg. 20220; 622-2200. Alicia Haydock Munnell, assistant secretary. Fax, 622-2633.
Assists and advises the treasury secretary in the formulation and execution of domestic and international economic policies and programs; helps prepare economic forecasts for the federal budget.

Treasury Dept., Financial Management Service, 401 14th St. S.W., #548 20227; 874-7000. Russell D. Morris, commissioner. Fax, 874-6743.
Serves as the government's central financial manager, responsible for cash management and investment of government trust funds, credit administration, and debt collection. Handles central accounting for government fiscal activities; promotes sound financial management practices and increased use of automated payments, collections, accounting, and reporting systems.

Treasury Dept., Treasurer of the United States, Main Treasury Bldg. 20220; 622-0100. Mary Ellen Withrow, treasurer. Fax, 622-2258.
Spokesperson for the treasury secretary in matters dealing with currency, coinage, and savings bonds.

Congress:

Congressional Budget Office, 405 Ford Bldg. (2nd and D Sts. S.W.) 20515; 226-2700. Robert D. Reischauer, director. Information, 226-2600. Fax, 225-7509.
Nonpartisan office that provides the House and Senate with budget-related information and analyses of alternative fiscal policies.

General Accounting Office, 441 G St. N.W. 20548; 512-5500. Charles A. Bowsher, comptroller general. Information, 512-4800. Library, 512-5180. Fax, 512-5507. Documents, 512-6000.
Independent, nonpartisan agency in the legislative branch. Serves as the investigating agency for Congress; carries out legal, accounting, auditing, and claims settlement functions; makes recommendations for more effective government operations; publishes monthly lists of reports available to the public. Library open to the public by appointment.

House Appropriations Committee, H218 CAP 20515; 225-2771. David R. Obey, D-Wis., chairman; Frederick G. Mohrman, staff director.
Jurisdiction over legislation to appropriate funds for all government programs; responsible for rescissions of appropriated funds, transfers of surplus allocations, and new spending under the Congressional Budget Act; maintains data on congressional appropriating process and government spending.

House Appropriations Committee, Subcommittee on Commerce, Justice, State, and Judiciary, H309 CAP 20515; 225-3351. Neal Smith, D-Iowa, chairman; John Osthaus, staff assistant.
Jurisdiction over legislation to appropriate funds for the Commerce Dept., the Securities and Exchange Commission, the Small Business Administration, the Competitiveness Policy Council, the Federal Trade Commission, the International Trade Commission, and the Office of the U.S. Trade Representative.

House Appropriations Committee, Subcommittee on Treasury, Postal Service, and General Government, H164 CAP 20515; 225-5834. Steny H. Hoyer, D-Md., chairman; Bill Smith, staff assistant. Fax, 426-3763.
Jurisdiction over legislation to appropriate funds for the Council of Economic Advisers, Office of Management and Budget, Treasury Dept., and U.S. Tax Court.

House Banking, Finance, and Urban Affairs Committee, Subcommittee on Economic

Treasury Dept.

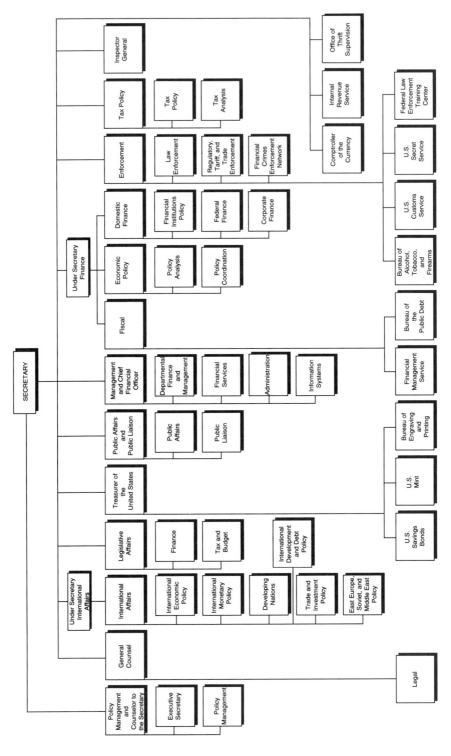

Growth and Credit Formulation, 109 Ford Bldg. (2nd and D Sts. S.W.) 20515; 226-7315. Paul E. Kanjorski, D-Pa., chairman; Robert W. Hall, staff director. Fax, 226-0070.

Jurisdiction over legislation dealing with domestic monetary policy, including the Federal Reserve System (jurisdiction shared with the House Government Operations Committee); financial aid to commerce and industry; the measurement of economic activity; federal loan guarantees; economic development; and economic stabilization measures, including wage and price controls.

House Budget Committee, 214 O'Neill Bldg. (300 New Jersey Ave. S.E.) 20515; 226-7200. Martin Olav Sabo, D-Minn., chairman; Eileen Baumgartner, chief of staff. Fax, 226-7233.

Jurisdiction over congressional budget resolutions, which set levels for federal spending, revenues, deficit, and debt; also jurisdiction over reconciliation bills, which alter existing programs to meet budget goals. Oversight of Congressional Budget Office. Studies budget matters.

House Energy and Commerce Committee, 2125 RHOB 20515; 225-2927. John D. Dingell, D-Mich., chairman; Alan J. Roth, staff director.

Jurisdiction over legislation on interstate and foreign commerce generally, including the Interstate Commerce Commission and the Federal Trade Commission.

House Government Operations Committee, 2157 RHOB 20515; 225-5051. John Conyers Jr., D-Mich., chairman; Julian Epstein, staff director. Fax, 225-4784.

Oversees government budget and accounting issues and the General Accounting Office.

House Government Operations Committee, Subcommittee on Commerce, Consumer, and Monetary Affairs, B377 RHOB 20515; 225-4407. John M. Spratt Jr., D-S.C., chairman; Theodore Jacobs, staff director. Fax, 225-2441.

Oversees operations of the Commerce and Treasury departments, the Federal Reserve System, U.S. Tax Court, and other federal agencies dealing with economic and monetary affairs (jurisdiction shared with House Banking, Finance, and Urban Affairs Committee).

House Ways and Means Committee, 1102 LHOB 20515; 225-3625. Sam M. Gibbons, D-Fla., acting chairman; Janice A. Mays, chief counsel.

Jurisdiction over legislation dealing with the debt ceiling; investment policy; and taxes, including taxation of savings, interest, and dividends. Oversees the Internal Revenue Service; sets excise tax rates for the Bureau of Alcohol, Tobacco, and Firearms.

House Ways and Means Committee, Subcommittee on Select Revenue Measures, 1105 LHOB 20515; 225-9710. Charles B. Rangel, D-N.Y., chairman; Don Longano, staff director.

Jurisdiction over revenue measures referred by the chairman of the House Ways and Means Committee.

Joint Committee on Taxation, 1015 LHOB 20515; 225-3621. Sen. Daniel Patrick Moynihan, D-N.Y., chairman; John Buckley, chief of staff.

Performs staff work for House Ways and Means and Senate Finance committees on domestic and international tax matters in the Internal Revenue Code, the public debt limit, and savings bonds under the Second Liberty Bond Act. Provides those committees with general economic and budgetary analysis. Provides revenue estimates for all tax legislation.

Joint Economic Committee, SD-G01 20510; 224-5171. Rep. David R. Obey, D-Wis., chairman; Richard McGahey, executive director. Fax, 224-0240.

Studies and makes recommendations on economic policy, including fiscal policy; maintains data pertaining to aggregate economic activity; analyzes the president's annual economic report to Congress and communicates findings to the House and Senate.

Senate Appropriations Committee, S128 CAP 20510; 224-4168. Robert C. Byrd, D-W.Va., chairman; James H. English, staff director.

Jurisdiction over legislation to appropriate funds for all government programs; responsible for rescissions of appropriated funds, transfers of surplus allocations, and new spending under the Congressional Budget Act. Maintains data on congressional appropriating process and government spending.

Senate Appropriations Committee, Subcommittee on Commerce, Justice, State, and Judiciary, S146A CAP 20510; 224-7277. Ernest F. Hollings, D-S.C., chairman; Scott B. Gudes, clerk.

Jurisdiction over legislation to appropriate funds for the Commerce Dept., the Securities and Exchange Commission, the Small Business Administration, the Federal Trade Commission, the International Trade Commission, and the Office of the U.S. Trade Representative.

Senate Appropriations Committee, Subcommittee on Treasury, Postal Service, and General Government, SD-190 20510; 224-8271. Dennis DeConcini, D-Ariz., chairman; Patty Lynch, clerk.

Jurisdiction over legislation to appropriate funds for the Executive Office of the President, including the Council of Economic Advisers and the Office of Management and Budget; the Treasury Dept.; and the U.S. Tax Court.

Senate Banking, Housing, and Urban Affairs Committee, SD-534 20510; 224-7391. Donald W. Riegle Jr., D-Mich., chairman; Steven Harris, staff director.

Jurisdiction over legislation dealing with bank regulation, domestic monetary policy, financial aid to commerce and industry, the measurement of economic activity, federal loan guarantees, and economic stabilization measures (including wage and price controls); oversees the Treasury Dept.; oversees the Federal Reserve System (jurisdiction shared with House Government Operations Committee).

Senate Budget Committee, SD-621 20510; 224-0642. Jim Sasser, D-Tenn., chairman; Larry Stein, staff director.

Jurisdiction over congressional budget resolutions, which set levels for federal spending, revenues, deficit, and debt; also jurisdiction over reconciliation bills, which alter existing programs to meet budget goals. Oversight of Congressional Budget Office.

Senate Commerce, Science, and Transportation Committee, SD-508 20510; 224-5115. Ernest F. Hollings, D-S.C., chairman; Kevin Curtin, chief counsel and staff director.

Jurisdiction over interstate and foreign commerce generally, including the Interstate Commerce Commission, the Federal Trade Commission, and many operations of the Commerce Dept.

Senate Finance Committee, SD-205 20510; 224-4515. Daniel Patrick Moynihan, D-N.Y., chairman; Lawrence O'Donnell Jr., staff director.

Jurisdiction over tax legislation; oversees the Internal Revenue Service and the U.S. Tax

Court; sets excise tax rates for the Bureau of Alcohol, Tobacco, and Firearms.

Senate Finance Committee, Subcommittee on Deficits, Debt Management, and Long-Term Economic Growth, SD-205 20510; 224-4515. Bill Bradley, D-N.J., chairman; Michael Dahl, staff contact.

Holds hearings on debt ceiling legislation.

Senate Finance Committee, Subcommittee on Private Retirement Plans and Oversight of the Internal Revenue Service, SD-205 20510; 224-4515. David Pryor, D-Ark., chairman; Steve Glaze, staff contact.

Holds hearings on legislation relating to investment policy and taxation of savings, interest, and dividends.

Senate Finance Committee, Subcommittee on Taxation, SD-205 20510; 224-4515. David L. Boren, D-Okla., chairman; Beth Garrett, staff contact.

Holds hearings on tax legislation.

Senate Governmental Affairs Committee, SD-340 20510; 224-4751. John Glenn, D-Ohio, chairman; Leonard Weiss, staff director. Fax, 224-9682.

Jurisdiction over legislation on government budget and accounting issues other than appropriations; oversight of General Accounting Office operations and of the Office of Management and Budget.

See also Caucus on Deficit Reduction and Economic Growth (p. 760); Congressional Clearinghouse on the Future and Congressional Competitiveness Caucus (p. 756); Congressional Grace Caucus (p. 758); Congressional Leaders United for a Balanced Budget (p. 756)

Nongovernmental:

American Business Conference, 1730 K St. N.W., #1200 20006; 822-9300. Barry Rogstad, president. Fax, 467-4070.

Membership: chief executive officers of midsize, high-growth companies. Seeks a public policy role for growth companies. Studies capital formation, tax policy, regulatory reform, and international trade.

American Chamber of Commerce Executives, 4232 King St., Alexandria, VA 22302; (703) 998-

0072. Paul J. Greeley Jr., president. Fax, (703) 931-5624.

Membership: managers of local, state, and international chambers of commerce. Provides members with educational programs and conferences on topics of interest, including economic development, management systems, and membership drives. Sponsors management councils for members.

American Council for Capital Formation, 1750 K St. N.W., #400 20006; 293-5811. Mark Bloomfield, president. Fax, 785-8165.

Advocates tax and environmental policies conducive to saving, investment, and economic growth. Affiliated with the ACCF Center for Policy Research, which conducts and funds research on capital formation topics.

American Enterprise Institute for Public Policy Research, Economic Policy Studies, 1150 17th St. N.W. 20036; 862-5846. Marvin H. Kosters, director. Fax, 862-7178.

Research and educational organization. Interests include monetary, tax, trade, and regulatory policy and labor and social security issues.

American Society of Assn. Executives, 1575 Eye St. N.W. 20005; 626-2723. R. William Taylor, president. Press, 626-2798. Library, 626-2746. Fax, 371-8825. TDD, 626-2803.

Conducts research and provides educational programs on association management, trends, and developments; maintains a job referral service for executives and students. Library open to the public.

The Brookings Institution, Economic Studies Program, 1775 Massachusetts Ave. N.W. 20036; 797-6121. Henry J. Aaron, director. Information, 797-4029. Fax, 797-6004.

Sponsors economic research and publishes studies on international economics, worldwide economic growth and stability, public finance, urban economics, industrial organization and regulation, labor economics, social policy, and the economics of human resources.

The Business Council, 888 17th St. N.W. 20006; 298-7650. Philip E. Cassidy, executive director. Fax, 785-0296.

Membership: chief executive officers and former officers of major corporations. Serves as a forum for business and government to exchange views and explore public policy as it affects U.S. business interests.

Business-Higher Education Forum, 1 Dupont Circle N.W., #800 20036; 939-9345. Don M. Blandin, director. Fax, 833-4723.

Membership: chief executive officers of major corporations, colleges, and universities. Promotes cooperation between businesses and higher educational institutions. Interests include international economic competitiveness, education and training, research and development, science and technology, and global interdependence.

The Business Roundtable, 1615 L St. N.W., #1100 20036; 872-1260. Samuel L. Maury, executive director. Fax, 466-3509.

Membership: chief executives of the nation's largest corporations. Examines issues of concern to business, including taxation, antitrust law, international trade, employment policy, and the federal budget.

Center for the Study of Public Choice (George Mason University), George's Hall, 4400 University Dr., Fairfax, VA 22030; (703) 993-2330. Robert D. Tollison, director. Fax, (703) 993-2323.

Promotes research in public choice, an interdisciplinary approach to the study of the relationship between economic and political institutions. Interests include constitutional economics, public finance, federalism and local government, econometrics, and trade protection and regulation. Sponsors conferences and seminars. Library open to the public.

Citizens for a Sound Economy, 1250 H St. N.W., #700 20005; 783-3870. Paul Beckner, president. Fax, 783-4687.

Citizens' advocacy group that promotes reduced taxes, free trade, and deregulation. Advocates deficit reduction through spending restraint, competitiveness in financial markets, and increased private involvement in providing public services. Encourages citizens to petition members of Congress. Sponsors the Legal and Regulatory Reform Project, which monitors legislation and regulations and participates in agency rulemaking proceedings.

Committee for a Responsible Federal Budget, 220½ E St. N.E. 20002; 547-4484. Carol Cox Wait, president. Fax, 547-4476.

Educational organization that works to support and improve the congressional budget process. Seeks to increase public awareness of the dangers of federal budget deficits. Offers seminars and symposia; commissions studies and policy analyses.

Committee for Economic Development, 2000 L St. N.W., #700 20036; 296-5860. Van Doorn Ooms, senior vice president and director of research. Fax, 223-0776.
Research organization that makes recommendations on domestic and international economic policy.

Competitive Enterprise Institute, 1001 Connecticut Ave. N.W., #1250 20036; 331-1010. Fred L. Smith Jr., president. Fax, 331-0640.
Advocates free enterprise and limited government. Produces policy analyses on tax, budget, financial services, antitrust, biotechnological, and environmental issues. Monitors legislation and litigates against restrictive regulations through its Free Market Legal Program.

The Conference Board, 1113 M St. N.W. 20005; 371-8126. Meredith Whiting, senior fellow, government affairs.
Membership: senior executives from various industries. Researches science and technology policy, environmental affairs, corporate political activity, management-related issues, the integrated market, and European business activities. Headquarters in New York conducts research and provides economic data on business management, trends, and development.

Council for Social and Economic Studies, 6861 Elm St., #4H, McLean, VA 22101; (703) 442-8010. Roger Pearson, executive director. Fax, (703) 847-9524.
Conducts research and publishes studies on domestic and international economic, social, and political issues.

Council of Better Business Bureaus, 4200 Wilson Blvd., Arlington, VA 22203; (703) 276-0100. James H. McIlhenny, president. Fax, (703) 525-8277.
Mediates disputes between consumers and businesses; promotes ethical business standards; provides voluntary self-regulation of advertising.

Council of State Chambers of Commerce, 122 C St. N.W., #330 20001; 484-8103. J. William McArthur Jr., president. Fax, 737-4806.
Federation of state business organizations. Conducts research on federal spending, state and local taxation, and employee relations and benefits.

Council on Competitiveness, 900 17th St. N.W., #1050 20006; 785-3990. Daniel Burton, president. Fax, 785-3998.
Membership: executives from business, education, and labor. Seeks increased public awareness of economic competition.

Economic Policy Institute, 1730 Rhode Island Ave. N.W., #200 20036; 775-8810. Jeff Faux, president. Fax, 775-0819.
Research and educational organization that publishes analyses on economics, economic development, competitiveness, income distribution, industrial competitiveness, and investment. Conducts public conferences and seminars.

Electronic Industries Assn., 2001 Pennsylvania Ave. N.W., #1000 20006; 457-4914. Gary Shapiro, group vice president, consumer electronics. Fax, 457-4985.
Membership: manufacturers, dealers, installers, and distributors of consumer electronics products. Provides consumer information and data on industry trends; advocates an open market; monitors legislation and regulations.

Ethics Resource Center, 1120 G St. N.W., #200 20005; 737-2258. Gary Edwards, president. Fax, 737-2227.
Educational organization that assists corporations, trade and professional associations, nonprofit groups, academic institutions, schools, and the government in developing and implementing standards of ethical conduct, oversight structures, and ethics training programs.

Foundation for Industrial Modernization, 1331 Pennsylvania Ave. N.W., #1410N 20004-1703; 662-8965. Leo Reddy, president. Fax, 637-3182.
Promotes greater cooperation among industry, government, and academia to revitalize America's infrastructure in order to improve America's global competitiveness, raise its standard of living, raise the skill level of workers, and support environmentally conscious manufacturing. (Affiliated with the National Coalition for Advanced Manufacturing.)

International Mass Retail Assn., 1901 Pennsylvania Ave. N.W., 10th Floor 20006; 861-0774. Robert J. Verdisco, president. Fax, 785-4588.

Membership: discount, specialty, home center, wholesale club, and mass retailers in the United States and abroad. Interests include industry research, trade, and government relations. Monitors legislation and regulations.

Latin American Management Assn., 419 New Jersey Ave. S.E. 20003; 546-3803. Marina Laverdy, acting director. Information on Transportation Dept. lending programs, (800) 522-6623.
Membership: Hispanic manufacturing and technical firms. Promotes Hispanic enterprise, industry, and technology throughout the United States. Seeks to secure public and private contracts for Hispanic firms. Supports public policy beneficial to minority businesses.

Minority Business Enterprise Legal Defense and Education Fund, 220 Eye St. N.E., #240 20002; 543-0040. Anthony W. Robinson, president. Fax, 543-4135.
Acts as an advocate for the minority business community. Represents minority businesses in class action suits; conducts legal research; serves as an information clearinghouse on business and legal trends; monitors legislation and regulations.

National Assn. of Convenience Stores, 1605 King St., Alexandria, VA 22314; (703) 684-3600. Kerley LeBoeuf, president. Fax, (703) 836-4564.
Membership: convenience store retailers and industry suppliers. Advocates industry position on labor, tax, environment, alcohol, and food-related issues; conducts research and training programs; monitors legislation and regulations.

National Assn. of Corporate Directors, 1707 L St. N.W., #560 20036; 775-0509. John M. Nash, president. Fax, 775-4857.
Membership: executives of closely held and public companies, outside and inside directors, and stewards of corporate governance. Serves as a clearinghouse on corporate governance and current board practices. Conducts seminars; runs executive search service; sponsors insurance program for directors and officers.

National Assn. of Manufacturers, 1331 Pennsylvania Ave. N.W., #1500 20004; 637-3000. Jerry Jasinowski, president. Information, 637-3099. Press, 637-3094. Fax, 637-3182.
Represents industry views (mainly of manufacturers) to government on national and international issues. Reviews legislation, administrative rulings, and judicial decisions affecting industry. Sponsors the Human Resources Forum; operates a computer network for members and the public that provides information on legislative and other news; conducts programs on labor relations, occupational safety and health, regulatory and consumer affairs, and other business issues.

National Assn. of State Budget Officers, 400 N. Capitol St. N.W., #299 20001; 624-5382. Brian Roherty, executive director. Fax, 624-7745.
Membership: state budget and financial officers. Sponsors fiscal management training institutes; publishes research reports on budget-related issues. (Affiliate of the National Governors' Assn.)

National Business League, 1511 K St. N.W., #432 20005; 737-4430. Sherman Copelin, president. Fax, 737-4432.
Promotes equal business opportunities for African Americans and other minorities; local chapters provide minority business people with training and technical assistance, including loan procurement and marketing; supports inclusion of courses relevant to minority business in college curricula; maintains data on minority business people. Sponsors the National Student Business League, which promotes professional standards among African American undergraduate business students. Monitors legislation.

National Chamber Litigation Center, 1615 H St. N.W., #230 20062; 463-5337. Stephen Bokat, executive vice president. Fax, 463-5346.
Public policy law firm of the U.S. Chamber of Commerce. Advocates business's positions in court on such issues as employment, environmental, and constitutional law. Provides businesses with legal assistance and representation in legal proceedings before federal courts and agencies.

National Coalition for Advanced Manufacturing (NACFAM), 1331 Pennsylvania Ave. N.W., #1410N 20004-1703; 662-8960. Leo Reddy, president. Fax, 637-3182.
Seeks a public policy environment more supportive of advanced manufacturing and industrial modernization as keys to global economic competitiveness. Advocates greater national focus on industrial base modernization, increased investment in plant and equipment, accelerated development and deployment of advanced manufacturing technology, and reform of technical

education and training. (Affiliated with the Foundation for Industrial Modernization.)

National Commission for Economic Conversion and Disarmament, 1828 Jefferson Pl. N.W. 20036; 728-0815. Gregory A. Bischak, executive director. Fax, 728-0826.

Supports cutbacks in the U.S. military budget and reallocation of funds for civilian economic development. Advocates investment in civilian research and development, transportation, housing, health, education, and the environment.

National Cooperative Business Assn., 1401 New York Ave. N.W., #1100 20005; 638-6222. Russell C. Notar, president. Fax, 638-1374.

Alliance of cooperatives, businesses, and state cooperative associations. Supports development of cooperative businesses; promotes and develops trade among domestic and international cooperatives; monitors legislation and regulations.

National Industrial Council, 1331 Pennsylvania Ave. N.W., #1500N 20004; 637-3053. Barry Buzby, executive director, state associations group; C. Argyll Campbell, executive director, employer associations group, 637-3052. Fax, 637-3182.

Membership: employer associations at the regional, state, and local levels. Works to strengthen U.S. competitive enterprise system. Represents views of industry on business and economic issues; sponsors conferences and seminars. (Department of the National Assn. of Manufacturers.)

National Planning Assn., 1424 16th St. N.W. 20036; 265-7685. Malcolm R. Lovell Jr., president. Fax, 797-5516.

Research organization that conducts studies on domestic and international economic policy issues. Interests include agriculture, human resources, employment, international trade, investment and monetary policy, and U.S. economic competitiveness.

National Retail Federation, 701 Pennsylvania Ave. N.W., #710 20004; 783-7971. Tracy Mullin, president, governmental and public affairs. Fax, 737-2849.

Membership: national and state associations of retailers and major retail corporations. Concerned with federal regulatory activities and legislation that affect retailers, including tax,

employment, trade, and credit issues. Provides information on retailing.

National Venture Capital Assn., 1655 N. Fort Myer Dr., #700, Arlington, VA 22209; (703) 351-5269. Daniel T. Kingsley, executive director. Fax, (703) 351-5268.

Membership: venture capital organizations and individuals and corporate financiers. Promotes understanding of venture capital investment; monitors legislation.

OMB Watch, 1731 Connecticut Ave. N.W. 20009; 234-8494. Gary Bass, executive director. Fax, 234-8584.

Research and advocacy organization that monitors and interprets the policies and activities of the Office of Management and Budget. Sponsors conferences and teaches the governmental decision-making process concerning accountability.

Retail Bakers of America, 14239 Park Center Dr., Laurel, MD 20707; (301) 725-2149. Peter Houstle, executive vice president. Fax, (301) 725-2187.

Membership: single- and multiunit retail bakeries and bakery-delis; donut and other specialty shops; supermarket in-store bakeries and bakery-delis; allied companies that offer equipment, ingredients, supplies, or services to these retailers; and students and teachers of secondary or post-secondary school baking programs. Provides business and training aids. Monitors legislation and regulations.

Security Industry Assn., 1801 K St. N.W., #1203 20006-1301; 466-7420. John Galante, executive director. Fax, 466-0010.

Promotes expansion and professionalism in the security industry. Sponsors trade shows, develops industry standards, supports educational programs and job training, and publishes statistical research. Serves as an information source for the media and the industry.

Ski Industries America, 8377-B Greensboro Dr., McLean, VA 22102; (703) 556-9020. David Ingemie, president. Fax, (703) 821-8276.

Membership: manufacturers and distributors of ski and other outdoor sports equipment, apparel, accessories, and footwear.

Society for Marketing Professional Services, 99 Canal Center Plaza, #250, Alexandria, VA 22314-1588; (703) 549-6117. Patrick E. Winters, executive director. Toll-free, (800) 292-7677. Fax, (703) 549-2498.

Membership: individuals who provide professional services to the building industry. Assists individuals who market design services in the areas of architecture, engineering, planning, interior design, landscape architecture, and construction management. Provides seminars, workshops, and publications for members. Maintains job banks.

U.S. Chamber of Commerce, 1615 H St. N.W. 20062; 463-5300. Richard L. Lesher, president. Information, 659-6000. Press, 463-5682. Fax, 463-5836. Publications, 468-5652.

Federation of businesses and trade and professional associations; state and local chambers of commerce; and American chambers of commerce abroad. Develops and proposes policy on legislative issues important to American business and businessmen; sponsors programs on management, business confidence, small business, consumer affairs, economic policy, minority business, and tax policy; maintains a business forecast and survey center and a trade negotiation information service. Monitors legislation and regulations.

U.S. Chamber of Commerce, Economic Policy, 1615 H St. N.W. 20062; 463-5620. Richard L. Lesher, acting chief economist. Fax, 463-5448.

Represents business community's views on economic policy, including government spending, the federal budget, and tax issues. Forecasts the economy of the United States and other industrialized nations and projects the impact of major policy changes. Studies economic trends and analyzes their effect on the business community.

See also Corporation for Enterprise Development (p. 384); U.S. Business and Industrial Council (p. 70)

National Debt

Agencies:

Federal Financing Bank (Treasury Dept.), Main Treasury ·Bldg. 20220; 622-2470. Charles D. Haworth, secretary; Gary Burner, manager. Fax, 622-0707.

Coordinates federal agency borrowing by purchasing securities issued or guaranteed by fed-eral agencies; funds its operations by borrowing from the treasury.

Treasury Dept., Federal Finance Policy Analysis, Main Treasury Bldg. 20220; 622-1855. Norman Carleton, director.

Analyzes and evaluates economic and financial development, problems and proposals in the areas of treasury financing, public debt management, and related economic matters. Provides analysis and technical assistance on regulatory issues involving government securities and related markets. Monitors and analyzes foreign investment in treasury securities and proposed changes in tax provisions that may affect the market for treasury securities.

Treasury Dept., Financial Institutions, Main Treasury Bldg. 20220; 622-2600. Richard S. Carnell, assistant secretary. Fax, 622-2027.

Advises the under secretary for domestic finance and the treasury secretary on matters of debt management.

Treasury Dept., Government Financing, Main Treasury Bldg. 20220; 622-2460. Charles D. Haworth, director. Fax, 622-0427.

Analyzes federal credit program principles and standards, legislation, and proposals related to government borrowing, lending, and investment. Furnishes actuarial and mathematical analysis required for treasury market financing, the Federal Financing Bank, the U.S. Savings Bonds program, and other government agencies. Manages the Federal Financing Bank.

Treasury Dept., Market Finance, Main Treasury Bldg. 20220; 622-2630. Jill K. Ouseley, director. Fax, 622-0244.

Provides financial and economic data on government financing and public debt management. Coordinates, analyzes, and reviews government borrowing, lending, and investment activities. Monitors the volume of funds raised and supplied in the credit market. Determines interest rates for government loan programs.

Treasury Dept., Public Debt, 999 E St. N.W. 20239; 219-3300. Richard L. Gregg, commissioner. Press, 219-3302. Fax, 219-3391. Investor information, 874-4000. Savings bonds, 447-1775.

Handles public debt securities, treasury notes, and bonds; maintains all records on savings bonds.

Congress:

See *Business and Economic Policy, General, Congress (p. 47)*

Regulation

See also *Business and Economic Policy, General (p. 44); Finance and Investments, Banking (p. 61)*

Agencies:

Office of Management and Budget (Executive Office of the President), Information and Regulatory Affairs, Old Executive Office Bldg., Rm. 350 20500; 395-4852. Sally Katzen, administrator. Fax, 395-3047.

Oversees development of federal regulatory programs. Supervises agency information management activities in accordance with the Paperwork Reduction Act of 1980, as amended; reviews agency analyses of the effect of government regulatory activities on the U.S. economy.

Regulatory Information Service Center (General Services Administration), 750 17th St. N.W., #500 20006; 634-6222. Mark G. Schoenberg, executive director. Information, 634-6220. Fax, 634-6224.

Provides the president, Congress, and the public with information on federal regulatory policies; recommends ways to make regulatory information more accessible to government officials and the public.

Congress:

See *Business and Economic Policy, General, Congress (p. 47)*

Nongovernmental:

U.S. Chamber of Commerce, Legal and Regulatory Affairs, 1615 H St. N.W., #517 20062; 463-5513. Tyler J. Wilson, attorney. Fax, 887-3445.

Advocates business's position on government and regulatory affairs. Monitors legislation and regulations on antitrust and corporate policy, product liability, and business-consumer relations.

Taxes

See also *Business and Tax Law, Tax Violations (p. 499)*

Agencies:

Bureau of Alcohol, Tobacco, and Firearms (Treasury Dept.), Compliance Operations, 650 Massachusetts Ave. N.W. (mailing address: Washington, DC 20226); 927-8710. Arthur Libertucci, associate director. Information, 927-7777.

Enforces and administers revenue laws relating to firearms, alcohol, and tobacco.

Internal Revenue Service (Treasury Dept.), 1111 Constitution Ave. N.W. 20224; 622-4115. Margaret Milner Richardson, commissioner. Toll-free, (800) 829-1040. Press, 622-4010. Fax, 622-6765. TDD, (800) 829-4059.

Administers and enforces internal revenue laws (except those relating to firearms, explosives, alcohol, and tobacco).

Internal Revenue Service (Treasury Dept.), Taxpayer Service, 1111 Constitution Ave. N.W. 20224; 622-4220. Gwen Krauss, director. TDD, (800) 829-4059. Forms and publications, (800) 829-3676. Recorded tax and refund information, (800) 829-4477. Tax information and notice inquiries, (800) 829-1040.

Oversees field offices that provide information and guidance on tax matters, including group assistance in the preparation of returns and assistance to taxpayers who telephone, write, or visit IRS district offices. Arranges tax courses for groups of taxpayers through an IRS taxpayer education coordinator. Provides businesses with a tax kit, which includes tax regulations and forms. Assists foreign-based Americans and foreign nationals who pay U.S. taxes. *(See Regional Federal Information Sources list, p. 836.)*

Justice Dept., Tax Division, Main Justice Bldg. 20530; 514-2901. Loretta C. Argrett, assistant attorney general. Fax, 514-2085.

Acts as counsel for the Internal Revenue Service (IRS) in court litigations between the government and taxpayers (other than those handled by the IRS in the U.S. Tax Court).

Treasury Dept., Main Treasury Bldg. 20220; 622-2986. Cynthia Beerbower, international tax counsel. Fax, 622-0605.

Provides other agencies with technical assistance in international tax matters; negotiates international tax treaties; formulates domestic legislative proposals and reviews tax rules and regulations.

Treasury Dept., Tax Policy, Main Treasury Bldg. 20220; 622-0050. Leslie Samuels, assistant secretary. Fax, 622-0646.

Formulates and implements domestic and international tax policies and programs; conducts analyses of proposed tax legislation and programs; participates in international tax treaty negotiations; responsible for receipts estimates for the annual budget of the United States.

Congress:

See Business and Economic Policy, General, Congress (p. 47)

Judiciary:

U.S. Tax Court, 400 2nd St. N.W. 20217; 606-8700. Lapsley W. Hamblen Jr., chief judge; Charles S. Casazza, clerk of the court, 606-8754.

Tries and adjudicates disputes involving income, estate, and gift taxes and personal holding company surtaxes in cases in which deficiencies have been determined by the Internal Revenue Service.

Nongovernmental:

American Enterprise Institute for Public Policy Research, Fiscal Policy Studies, 1150 17th St. N.W. 20036; 862-5828. John H. Makin, director. Fax, 862-7177.

Research and educational organization that conducts studies on fiscal policy, taxes, and budget issues.

Americans for Tax Reform, 1301 Connecticut Ave. N.W., #401 20036; 785-0266. Peter Roff, executive director. Fax, 785-0261.

Advocates reduction of federal and state taxes; encourages candidates for public office to pledge their opposition to income tax increases through a national pledge campaign.

Business Coalition for Fair Competition, 1101 King St., #200, Alexandria, VA 22314; (703) 739-2782. Art Davis, executive director. Fax, (703) 739-4213.

Membership: trade and professional associations and individual businesses. Concerned with the economic effect of commercial activity by tax-exempt and governmental entities.

Citizens Against Government Waste, 1301 Connecticut Ave. N.W., #400 20036; 467-5300. Thomas A. Schatz, president. Toll-free, (800) 872-3328. Fax, 467-4253.

Nonpartisan organization that seeks to expose waste, mismanagement, and inefficiency in the federal government.

Citizens for a Sound Economy, 1250 H St. N.W., #700 20005; 783-3870. Paul Beckner, president. Fax, 783-4687.

Citizens' advocacy group that promotes reduced taxes, free trade, and deregulation.

Citizens for Tax Justice, 1311 L St. N.W., #400 20005; 626-3780. Robert S. McIntyre, director. Fax, 638-3486.

Coalition that works for progressive taxes at the federal, state, and local levels.

Council of State Chambers of Commerce, 122 C St. N.W., #330 20001; 484-8103. J. William McArthur Jr., president. Fax, 737-4806.

Federation of state business organizations. Conducts research and coordinates members' interests in federal spending and state and local taxation. Represents members and affiliates on corporate state tax issues.

Federation of Tax Administrators, 444 N. Capitol St. N.W. 20001; 624-5890. Harley T. Duncan, executive director. Fax, 624-7888.

Membership: state tax agencies. Provides information upon written request on tax-related issues, including court decisions and legislation. Conducts research and sponsors workshops.

Institute for Research on the Economics of Taxation, 1300 19th St. N.W., #240 20036; 463-1400. Norman B. Ture, president. Fax, 463-6199.

Research organization that analyzes all aspects of taxation. Conducts research on the economic effects of federal tax policies; publishes studies on domestic and international economic policy issues.

Institute of Property Taxation, 888 17th St. N.W., #1150 20006; 452-1213. Billy D. Cook, executive director. Fax, 452-1240.

Membership: corporate property and sales tax personnel and tax professionals who represent business taxpayers. Promotes uniform and equitable property and sales and use taxes; works to minimize the costs of administration and compliance; sponsors conferences, seminars, and symposia. Grants professional designations: Certified Member of the Institute (CMI) for property tax professionals and Certified Sales Member (CSM) for sales tax professionals.

Multistate Tax Commission, 444 N. Capitol St. N.W., #425 20001; 624-8699. Dan R. Bucks, executive director. Library, 624-8819. Fax, 624-8619.
Membership: state governments that have enacted the Multistate Tax Compact. Promotes fair, effective, and efficient state tax systems for interstate and international commerce; works for state tax sovereignty. Encourages uniform state tax laws and regulations for multistate and multinational enterprises. Maintains three regional audit offices that monitor compliance with state tax laws and encourage uniformity in taxpayer treatment. Administers program to identify businesses that do not file tax returns with states.

National Assn. of Manufacturers, Taxation and Fiscal Policy, 1331 Pennsylvania Ave. N.W., #1500N 20004; 637-3072. Monica Lovell, director. Fax, 637-3182.
Represents industry views (mainly of manufacturers) on federal tax and budget policies; conducts conferences; monitors legislation and regulations.

National Taxpayers Union, 713 Maryland Ave. N.E. (mailing address: 325 Pennsylvania Ave. S.E., Washington, DC 20003); 543-1300. David Keating, executive vice president. Fax, 546-2086.
Citizens' interest group that promotes tax and spending reduction at all levels of government. Supports constitutional amendments to balance the federal budget and limit taxes.

The Tax Council, 1801 K St. N.W., #7202 20006; 822-8062. William G. Handfield, executive director. Fax, 466-3918.
Organization of corporations concerned with tax policy and legislation. Interests include tax rate, capital formation, capital gains, foreign source income, and capital cost recovery.

Tax Executives Institute, 1001 Pennsylvania Ave. N.W., #320 20004; 638-5601. Michael J. Murphy, executive director. Fax, 638-5607.

Membership: accountants, lawyers, and other corporate and business employees dealing with tax issues. Sponsors seminars and conferences on federal, state, local, and international tax issues. Develops and monitors tax legislation, regulations, and administrative procedures.

Tax Foundation, 1250 H St. N.W., #750 20005-3908; 783-2760. J. D. Foster, executive director. Fax, 942-7675.
Membership: individuals and businesses interested in federal, state, and local fiscal matters. Conducts research and prepares reports on taxes and government expenditures.

U.S. Conference of Mayors, 1620 Eye St. N.W., 4th Floor 20006; 293-7330. J. Thomas Cochran, executive director. Fax, 293-2352.
Membership: mayors of cities with populations of 30,000 or more. Monitors tax policy and legislation.

Doing Business with the Government

See also Government Housekeeping (p. 300); Labor Standards and Practices (p. 188); Procurement, Acquisition, and Logistics (p. 579); Small Business (p. 90)

Agencies:

Agencies and departments have their own contracting offices to deal with firms, organizations, and individuals seeking to sell goods and services to the government. Government solicitations for bids on goods and services are published in Commerce Business Daily *issued by the Commerce Dept., Publishing Division, 482-0632. For a list of Federal Procurement Officers, see p. 59.*

Committee for Purchase from the Blind and Other Severely Handicapped, 1735 Jefferson Davis Highway, #403, Arlington, VA 22202; (703) 603-7740. Beverly L. Milkman, executive director. Fax, (703) 412-7113.
Presidentially appointed committee that determines which products and services are suitable for federal procurement from qualified nonprofit agencies employing the blind or other severely disabled persons; seeks to increase employment opportunities for these individuals.

Departmental and Agency Procurement Officers

Departments

Agriculture
John Kratzke 720-2582

Commerce
Michael Sade, acting 482-4185

Defense
Eleanor R. Spector .... (703) 695-7145

Education
William Sullivan 708-8264

Energy
Vacant 586-8613

Health and Human Services
Audrey Moten 690-8043

Housing and Urban Development
Roosevelt Jones 708-1290

Interior
Dean Titcomb 208-3433

Justice
James W. Johnston 307-2000

Labor
Daniel P. Murphy.............. 219-4631

State
Robert B. Dickson .... (703) 875-6037

Transportation
Gilbert Trainer 366-4953

Treasury
Robert Welch.................. 622-0520

Veterans Affairs
Gary J. Krump 233-3808

Agencies

Consumer Product Safety Commission
Robert Frost .... (301) 492-6444

Corp. for National Service
Donna Darlington 606-5000

Environmental Protection Agency
Betty L. Bailey................ 260-5020

Export-Import Bank
Daniel A. Garcia, acting 566-8111

Farm Credit Administration
William K. Thompson .... (703) 883-4147

Federal Communications Commission
Sonna L. Stampone 634-6624

Federal Deposit Insurance Corp.
Wayne Greene 942-3233

Federal Maritime Commission
Michael Kilby 523-5900

**Federal Mediation and
Conciliation Service**
Sam Baumgardner 653-5310

Federal Reserve System
James K. Kimmel 452-3296

Federal Trade Commission
Julius Justice 326-2275

General Services Administration
Richard H. Hopf III 501-1043

Interstate Commerce Commission
Tom Yates 927-5370

**National Aeronautics and
Space Administration**
Deidre Lee 358-2090

National Labor Relations Board
Paula M. Roy 273-4210

National Mediation Board
Mary C. Maione-Pricci 523-5950

National Science Foundation
Veronica Bankins 357-7922

Nuclear Regulatory Commission
Ronald T. Thompson ..... (301) 492-4347

Office of Personnel Management
Alfred Chatterton 606-2240

Securities and Exchange Commission
Jean Ryan 272-3900

Small Business Administration
Lucille Brooks 205-6622

**U.S. Arms Control
and Disarmament Agency**
Eugene Johnson 647-8666

U.S. International Trade Commission
Julia Mosley.................. 205-2730

U.S. Postal Service
A. Keith Strange 268-4106

General Services Administration, Acquisition Policy, 18th and F Sts. N.W. 20405; 501-1043. Richard H. Hopf III, associate administrator. Fax, 501-1986.

Develops and implements federal government acquisition policies and procedures; conducts preaward and postaward contract reviews; administers federal acquisition regulations for civilian agencies; suspends and debars contractors for unsatisfactory performance; coordinates and promotes governmentwide career management and training programs for contracting personnel.

General Services Administration, Federal Data Systems, 7th and D Sts. S.W., #5652 20407; 401-1529. Brenda Robinson, director. Fax, 401-1546.

Makes available quarterly information about government procurement contracts over $25,000; collects and disseminates data on the amount of business that companies do with each federal department and agency.

General Services Administration, Small and Disadvantaged Business Utilization, 18th and F Sts. N.W. 20405; 501-1021. Joan Parrott-Fonseca, director. Fax, 208-5938.

Works to increase small-business procurement of government contracts. Provides policy guidance and direction for GSA Business Service Centers, which give advice and assistance to businesses interested in government procurement. *(See Regional Federal Information Sources list, p. 846.)*

Minority Business Development Agency (Commerce Dept.), Main Commerce Bldg. 20230; 482-5061. Gilbert Colon, acting director. Fax, 482-2693.

Assists minority business owners in obtaining federal loans and contract awards; produces an annual report on federal agencies' performance in procuring from minority-owned businesses.

Office of Management and Budget (Executive Office of the President), Federal Procurement Policy, Old Executive Office Bldg., Rm. 352 20503; 395-5802. Allan V. Burman, administrator. Information, 395-3501. Fax, 395-3242.

Coordinates government procurement policies, regulations, procedures, and forms for executive agencies and recipients of federal grants or assistance.

Congress:

General Accounting Office, 441 G St. N.W. 20548; 512-5400. James F. Hinchman, general counsel. Fax, 512-9749.

Independent, nonpartisan agency in the legislative branch. Considers and rules on the proposed or actual award of a government contract upon receipt of a written protest from a bidder.

House Government Operations Committee, 2157 RHOB 20515; 225-5051. John Conyers Jr., D-Mich., chairman; Julian Epstein, staff director. Fax, 225-4784.

Jurisdiction over legislation on the federal procurement system; oversees rules and regulations concerning government procurement.

House Small Business Committee, Subcommittee on Procurement, Taxation, and Tourism, B363 RHOB 20515; 225-9368. James Bilbray, D-Nev., chairman; Felix Martinez, staff director.

Jurisdiction over legislation on programs affecting small business and the federal procurement system; oversees rules and regulations concerning government procurement.

Senate Governmental Affairs Committee, Subcommittee on Oversight of Government Management, SH-442 20510; 224-3682. Carl Levin, D-Mich., chairman; Linda J. Gustitus, staff director.

Jurisdiction over legislation on the federal procurement system; oversees rules and regulations concerning government procurement.

Senate Small Business Committee, Subcommittee on Government Contracting and Paperwork Reduction, SR-428A 20510; 224-5175. Sam Nunn, D-Ga., chairman; Lee Underwood, legislative assistant.

Studies and makes recommendations on legislation concerning government procurement as it affects small business.

Nongovernmental:

Some nongovernmental groups provide members with information about government contracts. Contact representative group for information.

Coalition for Government Procurement, 1990 M St. N.W., #400 20036; 331-0975. Larry Allen, executive director. Fax, 659-5754.

Alliance of business firms that sell to the federal government. Seeks equal opportunities for businesses to sell to the government; monitors practices of the General Services Administration and government procurement legislation and regulations.

Contract Services Assn., 1200 G St. N.W., #750 20005; 347-0600. Gary Engebretson, president. Fax, 347-0608.

Membership: companies that, under contract, provide federal, state, and local governments and other agencies with various technical and support services (particularly in defense, space, transportation, environment, energy, and health care). Analyzes the process by which the government awards contracts to private firms; monitors legislation and regulations.

National Contract Management Assn., 1912 Woodford Rd., Vienna, VA 22182; (703) 448-9231. Jim Goggins, executive vice president. Fax, (703) 448-0939.

Membership: individuals concerned with administering, procuring, negotiating, and managing government contracts and subcontracts. Sponsors Certified Professional Contracts Manager Program and various educational and professional programs.

National Institute of Governmental Purchasing, 11800 Sunrise Valley Dr., Reston, VA 22091; (703) 715-9400. James E. Brinkman, executive vice president. Fax, (703) 715-9897.

Membership: governmental purchasing departments, agencies, and organizations at the federal, state, and local levels in the United States and Canada. Provides public procurement officers with technical assistance and information, training seminars, and professional certification.

Professional Services Council, 8607 Westwood Center Dr., #204, Vienna, VA 22182; (703) 883-2030. Bert M. Concklin, president. Fax, (703) 883-2035.

Membership: associations and firms that provide local, state, federal, and international governments with professional and technical services. Promotes reform of the procurement system; seeks to improve the compilation of data and statistics about the professional and technical services industry.

See also National Industries for the Blind (p. 423)

Finance and Investments

Banking

Agencies:

Comptroller of the Currency (Treasury Dept.), 250 E St. S.W. 20219; 874-4900. Eugene A. Ludwig, comptroller. Information, 874-5000. Fax, 874-4950.

Regulates and examines the operations of national banks; establishes guidelines for bank examinations. Library open to the public.

Comptroller of the Currency (Treasury Dept.), Corporate Activities and Policy Analysis, 250 E St. S.W. 20219; 874-4710. Frank Maguire, senior deputy comptroller. Fax, 874-5352.

Advises the comptroller on policy matters and programs related to bank corporate activities, and is the primary decision maker on national bank corporate applications, including charters, mergers, and acquisitions, conversions, and operating subsidiaries.

Federal Deposit Insurance Corp., Supervision and Resolutions, 550 17th St. N.W. 20429; 898-6849. John W. Stone, executive director. Fax, 898-3772.

Serves as the federal regulator and supervisor of insured state banks that are not members of the Federal Reserve System. Conducts regular examinations and investigations of banks under the jurisdiction of FDIC; advises bank managers on improving policies and practices. Administers the Bank Insurance Fund, which insures deposits in commercial and savings banks, and the Savings Association Insurance Fund, which insures deposits in savings and loan institutions.

Federal Housing Finance Board, 1777 F St. N.W. 20006; 408-2525. Vacant, chairman. Information, 408-2500. Press, 408-2986. Fax, 408-1435.

Oversees the credit and financing operations of the twelve regional banks that comprise the Federal Home Loan Bank system.

Federal Reserve System, Banking Supervision and Regulation, 20th and C Sts. N.W. 20551; 452-2773. Richard Stillenkothen, director. Fax, 452-2770.

Supervises and regulates state banks that are members of the Federal Reserve System; supervises and inspects all bank holding companies;

monitors banking practices; approves bank mergers, consolidations, and other changes in bank structure.

Federal Reserve System, Board of Governors, 20th and C Sts. N.W. 20551; 452-3201. Alan Greenspan, chairman. Information, 452-3215. Press, 452-3204. Fax, 452-3819.

Serves as the central bank and fiscal agent for the government. Examines Federal Reserve banks and state member banks; supervises bank holding companies. Controls wire system transfer operations and supplies currency for depository institutions. *(See Regional Federal Information Sources list, p. 844.)*

Justice Dept., Antitrust Division, 555 4th St. N.W. 20001; 514-5621. Richard L. Rosen, chief, communications and finance. Fax, 514-6381.

Investigates and litigates certain antitrust cases involving financial institutions, including banking, securities, commodity futures, and insurance; participates in agency proceedings and rulemaking in these areas; monitors and analyzes legislation.

National Credit Union Administration, 1775 Duke St., Alexandria, VA 22314-3428; (703) 518-6300. Norman D'Amours, chairman. Information, (703) 518-6330. Fax, (703) 518-6439.

Regulates all federally chartered credit unions; charters new credit unions; supervises and examines federal credit unions and insures their member accounts up to $100,000. Insures state-chartered credit unions that apply and are eligible. Manages the Central Liquidity Facility, which supplies emergency short-term loans to members. Conducts research on economic trends and their effect on credit unions and advises the administration's board on economic and financial policy and regulations.

Office of Management and Budget (Executive Office of the President), Financial Institutions, New Executive Office Bldg. 20503; 395-7241. Alan B. Rhinesmith, chief. Fax, 395-1292.

Monitors the financial condition of deposit insurance funds including the Bank Insurance Fund, the Savings Association Insurance Fund, and the Federal Savings and Loan Insurance Corp. (FSLIC) Resolution Fund. Monitors the Resolution Trust Corp. and the Securities and Exchange Commission. Has limited oversight over the Federal Housing Finance Board and the Federal Home Loan Bank System.

Office of Thrift Supervision (Treasury Dept.), 1700 G St. N.W. 20552; 906-6280. Jonathan L. Fiechter, acting director. Information, 906-6677. Library, 906-6470. Fax, 898-0230.

Charters, regulates, and examines the operations of savings and loan institutions. Library open to the public.

Resolution Trust Corp., 801 17th St. N.W. 20434; 416-6900. Roger C. Altman, interim chief executive officer. Fax, 416-2580. Real estate inventory, (800) 431-0600.

Manages and disposes of failed savings and loan institutions and recovers taxpayers' funds through management and sale of institutions' assets.

Securities and Exchange Commission, Corporation Finance, 450 5th St. N.W. 20549; 272-2800. Linda C. Quinn, director. Fax, 272-2677.

Receives and examines disclosure statements and other information from publicly held companies, including bank holding companies.

Securities and Exchange Commission, Economic Analysis, 450 5th St. N.W. 20549; 272-7102. Susan Woodward, chief economist. Fax, 272-7132.

Provides the commission with economic analyses of proposed rule and policy changes and other information to guide the SEC in influencing capital markets. Evaluates the effect on competition within the securities industry and among competing securities markets; compiles financial statistics on capital formation and the securities industry.

Thrift Depositor Protection Oversight Board, 808 17th St. N.W., 8th Floor 20232; 416-2650. Dietra L. Ford, executive director. Information, 416-2622. Fax, 416-2610.

Membership: the chairmen of the Federal Reserve and the Federal Deposit Insurance Corp. (FDIC); secretary of the treasury; director of the Office of Thrift Supervision; president of the Resolution Trust Corp.; and two independent presidential appointees. Cabinet-level panel that sets policy for the Resolution Trust Corp.

Congress:

House Appropriations Committee, Subcommittee on VA, HUD, and Independent Agencies, H143 CAP 20515; 225-3241. Louis Stokes, D-Ohio, chairman; Paul Thompson, staff assistant.

Jurisdiction over legislation to appropriate funds for the Federal Deposit Insurance Fund and the National Credit Union Administration.

House Banking, Finance, and Urban Affairs Committee, Subcommittee on Financial Institutions Supervision, Regulation, and Deposit Insurance, 212 O'Neill Bldg. (300 New Jersey Ave. S.E.) 20515; 226-3280. Stephen L. Neal, D-N.C., chairman; Peter Kinzler, staff director. Fax, 226-1266.

Jurisdiction over legislation regulating banking and financial institutions.

House Government Operations Committee, Subcommittee on Commerce, Consumer, and Monetary Affairs, B377 RHOB 20515; 225-4407. John M. Spratt Jr., D-S.C., chairman; Theodore Jacobs, staff director. Fax, 225-2441.

Oversees federal bank regulatory agencies, including the Federal Deposit Insurance Corp., National Credit Union Administration, Office of Thrift Supervision, and Resolution Trust Corp.

House Ways and Means Committee, Subcommittee on Oversight, 1135 LHOB 20515; 225-5522. J. J. Pickle, D-Texas, chairman; Beth K. Vance, staff director. Fax, 225-0787.

Oversees government-sponsored enterprises, including the Federal Home Loan Bank System, with regard to the financial risk posed to the federal government.

Senate Appropriations Committee, Subcommittee on VA, HUD, and Independent Agencies, SD-142 20510; 224-7211. Barbara A. Mikulski, D-Md., chair; Kevin F. Kelly, clerk.

Jurisdiction over legislation to appropriate funds for the Federal Deposit Insurance Corp. and the National Credit Union Administration.

Senate Banking, Housing, and Urban Affairs Committee, SD-534 20510; 224-7391. Donald W. Riegle Jr., D-Mich., chairman; Steven Harris, staff director.

Jurisdiction over legislation regulating banking and financial institutions. Oversees federal bank regulatory agencies, including the Federal Deposit Insurance Corp., National Credit Union Administration, Office of Thrift Supervision, and Resolution Trust Corp.; also oversees government-sponsored enterprises, including the Federal Home Loan Bank System.

Nongovernmental:

American Bankers Assn., 1120 Connecticut Ave. N.W. 20036; 663-5000. Donald G. Ogilvie, executive vice president. Information, 663-5221. Library, 663-5040. Fax, 828-4532.

Membership: commercial banks. Operates schools to train banking personnel; conducts conferences; formulates government relations policies for the banking community. Library open to the public by appointment.

American Council of State Savings Supervisors, P.O. Box 34175, Washington, DC 20043; 371-0666. Phylis Bird, executive director.

Membership: state savings and loan supervisors; associate members include state-chartered savings and loan associations and savings institutions. Monitors legislation and regulations on states' rights issues.

American Institute of Certified Public Accountants, 1455 Pennsylvania Ave. N.W., 4th Floor 20004; 434-9203. John E. Hunnicutt, group vice president, government affairs. Fax, 638-4512.

Establishes voluntary professional and ethical regulations for the profession; sponsors conferences and training workshops. Answers technical auditing and accounting questions. (Headquarters in New York.)

American League of Financial Institutions, 900 19th St. N.W., #400 20006; 628-5624. John W. Harshaw, president. Fax, 296-8716.

Membership: minority-controlled federal- and state-chartered savings and loan associations. Provides organizational and managerial advice to members and to other minority groups wishing to form new savings and loan associations; offers on-site technical assistance; monitors legislation and regulations.

Assn. of Financial Services Holding Companies, 888 17th St. N.W., #312 20006; 223-6575. Patrick A. Forte, president. Fax, 331-3836.

Membership: financial services holding companies whose holdings include a federally insured institution. Advocates restructuring of U.S. depository institutions to allow access to capital. Seeks amendment of the Bank Holding Company Act of 1956 to provide all depository institutions access to commercial sources of capital and to allow depository institutions to convert to charters.

Bank Marketing Assn., 1120 Connecticut Ave. N.W. 20036; 663-5268. Michael Riley, managing director. Fax, 828-4540.

Membership: financial institutions and firms that provide products and services to the financial industry. Provides information, educational programs, and services to the financial services industry.

Bankers Assn. for Foreign Trade, 1600 M St. N.W., 7th Floor 20036; 452-0952. Mary Condeelis, executive director. Fax, 452-0959.

Membership: U.S. commercial banks with major international operations; foreign banks with U.S. operations are affiliated as nonvoting members. Monitors activities that affect the operation of foreign and domestic commercial banks.

Bankers' Roundtable, 805 15th St. N.W., #600 20005; 289-4322. Anthony T. Cluff, executive director. Fax, 785-2605.

Membership: bank holding companies registered with the Federal Reserve Board under the Bank Holding Company Act. Conducts research and provides information on banking and financial issues.

Conference of State Bank Supervisors, 1015 18th St. N.W., #1100 20036; 296-2840. James B. Watt, president. Fax, 296-1928.

Membership: state officials responsible for supervision of state-chartered banking institutions. Conducts educational programs and monitors legislation.

Consumer Bankers Assn., 1000 Wilson Blvd., #3012, Arlington, VA 22209; (703) 276-1750. Joe Belew, president. Fax, (703) 528-1290.

Membership: federally insured financial institutions. Provides information on retail banking, including retail banking trends. Operates the Graduate School of Retail Bank Management to train banking personnel; sponsors conferences.

Credit Union National Assn., 805 15th St. N.W. 20005; 682-4200. Charles O. Zuver, senior vice president. Fax, 682-9054.

Confederation of federal and state chartered credit union leagues in every state, the District of Columbia, and Puerto Rico. Monitors legislation and regulations. (Headquarters in Madison, Wis.)

Electronic Funds Transfer Assn., 950 Herndon Parkway, #390, Herndon, VA 22070; (703) 435-

9800. Sean W. Kennedy, president. Fax, (703) 435-7157.

Membership: financial institutions, retailers, system design organizations, equipment manufacturers, and credit card and telecommunications companies. Works for the development of technological and service innovation in electronic funds transfers.

Independent Bankers Assn. of America, 1 Thomas Circle N.W., #950 20005; 659-8111. Kenneth A. Guenther, executive vice president. Toll-free, (800) 422-8439.

Membership: medium-sized and smaller community banks. Interests include farm credit, deregulation, interstate banking, deposit insurance, and financial industry standards.

Mortgage Bankers Assn. of America, 1125 15th St. N.W. 20005; 861-6500. Warren Lasko, executive vice president. Fax, 785-2968.

Membership: institutions involved in real estate finance. Maintains School of Mortgage Banking and sponsors educational seminars; collects statistics on the industry. Library open to the public by appointment.

National Assn. of Federal Credit Unions, 3138 N. 10th St., Arlington, VA 22201; (703) 522-4770. Kenneth L. Robinson, president. Fax, (703) 524-1082.

Membership: federally chartered credit unions. Represents interests of federal credit unions before Congress and regulatory agencies and provides legislative alerts for its members. Sponsors educational meetings focusing on current financial trends, changes in legislation and regulations, and management techniques.

National Assn. of State Credit Union Supervisors, 1901 N. Fort Myer Dr., #201, Arlington, VA 22209; (703) 528-8351. Douglas Duerr, president. Fax, (703) 528-3248.

Membership: state credit union supervisors, state-chartered credit unions, and credit union leagues. Interests include state regulatory systems; conducts educational programs for examiners.

National Automated Clearing House Assn., 607 Herndon Parkway, #200, Herndon, VA 22070; (703) 742-9190. Elliott C. McEtee, president. Fax, (703) 787-0996.

Membership: regional Automated Clearing House (ACH) associations serving financial institutions involved in the ACH payment system.

Establishes rules and standards for the ACH system; works for the development of technological and service innovation in electronic funds transfers; provides information for members.

National Bankers Assn., 1802 T St. N.W. 20009; 588-5432. Samuel Foggie, president. Fax, 588-5443.
Membership: minority-owned banks and minority banking personnel. Monitors legislation and regulations affecting minority banking.

National Society of Public Accountants, 1010 N. Fairfax St., Alexandria, VA 22314; (703) 549-6400. Stanley H. Stearman, executive vice president. Fax, (703) 549-2984.
Seeks to improve the accounting profession and to enhance the status of individual practitioners. Sponsors seminars and correspondence courses on accounting, auditing, business law, and estate planning; monitors legislation and regulations affecting accountants and their small-business clients.

Real Estate Capital Recovery Assn., 1350 Eye St. N.W., #200 20005; 289-8660. David Fensterheim, executive director. Information, 962-9490. Fax, 371-0069.
Membership: companies that help government agencies, banks, savings and loan institutions, and corporations evaluate and manage real estate assets. Acts as liaison between the private sector and government officials responsible for supervising the management and disposition of failed financial institutions.

Savings and Community Bankers of America, 900 19th St. N.W., #400 20006; 857-3100. Paul A. Schosberg, president. Fax, 296-8716.
Membership: insured depository institutions involved in community finance. Provides information and statistics on issues that affect the industry; sponsors conferences with international banks and savings and loan institutions. Monitors economic issues affecting savings institutions; monitors legislation and regulations.

Treasury Management Assn., 7315 Wisconsin Ave. N.W., #1250W, Bethesda, MD 20814; (301) 907-2862. Donald E. Manger, executive director. Fax, (301) 907-2864.
Professional association that provides forum for ideas and perspectives on the treasury management profession and its role in the business environment. Supports treasury professionals through continuing education, professional certification (Certified Cash Manager), publishing and information services, industry standards, and government relations.

Stocks, Bonds, and Securities

See also Business and Economic Policy, National Debt (p. 55)

Agencies:

Federal Reserve System, Board of Governors, 20th and C Sts. N.W. 20551; 452-3201. Alan Greenspan, chairman. Information, 452-3215. Press, 452-3204. Fax, 452-3819.
Regulates amount of credit that may be extended and maintained on certain securities in order to prevent excessive use of credit for purchase or carrying of securities.

Securities and Exchange Commission, 450 5th St. N.W. 20549; 272-2000. Arthur Levitt, chairman. Information, 272-2650. Fax, 272-7050. TDD, 272-7065. Consumer affairs, 272-7440.
Requires public disclosure of financial and other information about companies whose securities are offered for public sale, traded on exchanges, or traded over the counter; issues and enforces regulations to prevent fraud in securities markets and investigates securities frauds and violations; supervises operations of stock exchanges and activities of securities dealers, investment advisers, and investment companies; regulates purchase and sale of securities, properties, and other assets of public utility holding companies and their subsidiaries; participates in bankruptcy proceedings involving publicly held companies; has some jurisdiction over municipal securities trading. Public Reference Section, 272-7450, makes available corporation reports and statements filed with SEC. *(See Regional Federal Information Sources list, p. 862.)*

Securities and Exchange Commission, Economic Analysis, 450 5th St. N.W. 20549; 272-7102. Susan Woodward, chief economist. Fax, 272-7132.
Provides the commission with economic analyses of proposed rule and policy changes and other information to guide the SEC in influencing capital markets. Evaluates the effect of policy and other factors on competition within the securities industry and among competing securities markets; compiles financial statistics on capital formation and the securities industry.

Securities and Exchange Commission, Market Regulation, 450 5th St. N.W. 20549; 272-3000. Brandon Decker, director. Library, 272-2618. Fax, 272-2864.

Oversees and regulates the operations of securities markets, brokers, dealers, and transfer agents. Promotes the establishment of a national system for clearing and settling securities transactions. Works for standards among and oversees self-regulatory organizations, such as national securities exchanges, the National Association of Securities Dealers, and registered clearing agencies. Facilitates the development of a national market system.

Treasury Dept., Financial Institutions Policy, Main Treasury Bldg. 20220; 622-2730. Gordon Eastburn, director. Fax, 622-0256.

Coordinates department efforts on all legislation affecting financial institutions and the government agencies that regulate them. Develops department policy on all matters relating to agencies responsible for supervising financial institutions and financial markets.

Treasury Dept., U.S. Savings Bonds Marketing, 800 K St. N.W. (mailing address: 999 E St. N.W., Washington, DC 20239); 377-7700. Clara R. Apodaca, executive director designate; Fax, 377-7697.

Promotes the sale and retention of U.S. savings bonds through educational and volunteer programs; administers the payroll savings plan for savings bonds.

Congress:

House Energy and Commerce Committee, Subcommittee on Telecommunications and Finance, 316 Ford Bldg. (2nd and D Sts. S.W.) 20515; 226-2424. Edward J. Markey, D-Mass., chairman; David H. Moulton, staff director and chief counsel.

Jurisdiction over stocks and stock exchanges; bonds; over-the-counter markets; and securities legislation, the Securities and Exchange Commission, and the Securities Investor Protection Corp.

House Government Operations Committee, Subcommittee on Commerce, Consumer, and Monetary Affairs, B377 RHOB 20515; 225-4407. John M. Spratt Jr., D-S.C., chairman; Theodore Jacobs, staff director. Fax, 225-2441.

Investigates investment fraud schemes and commodities and securities fraud. Oversees op-

erations of the Securities and Exchange Commission.

Senate Banking, Housing, and Urban Affairs Committee, Subcommittee on Securities, SD-534 20510; 224-9213. Christopher J. Dodd, D-Conn., chairman; Courtney Ward, staff director. Fax, 224-5137.

Jurisdiction over stocks, bonds, stock exchanges, over-the-counter markets, mergers and acquisitions, and securities legislation; the Securities Investor Protection Corp.; and the Securities and Exchange Commission.

Senate Governmental Affairs Committee, Permanent Subcommittee on Investigations, SR-100 20510; 224-3721. Sam Nunn, D-Ga., chairman; Eleanor J. Hill, staff director.

Investigates investment fraud schemes and commodities and securities fraud.

Nongovernmental:

Assn. of Publicly Traded Companies, 1101 Connecticut Ave. N.W., #700 20036; 857-1114. Brian T. Borders, president. Fax, 429-5108.

Membership: companies that issue stock into public capital markets. Promotes fair and efficient capital markets and the ability to manage corporate affairs free from unnecessary government interference. Interests include taxation and accounting rules under the purview of the Financial Accounting Standards Board. Monitors legislation and regulations.

Futures Industry Assn., 2001 Pennsylvania Ave. N.W., #600 20006; 466-5460. John M. Damgard, president. Fax, 296-3184.

Membership: commodity futures brokerage firms and others interested in commodity futures. Serves as a forum for discussion of futures industry; provides market information and statistical data; offers educational programs; works to establish professional and ethical standards for members.

Investment Company Institute, 1401 H St. N.W., 12th Floor 20005; 326-5800. Matthew P. Fink, president. Fax, 326-5806.

Membership: mutual funds and closed-end funds registered under the Investment Company Act of 1940 (including investment advisers to and underwriters of such companies) and the unit investment trust industry. Conducts research and disseminates information on issues affecting mutual funds.

Investment Program Assn., 607 14th St. N.W., #1000 20005; 775-9750. Christopher L. Davis, president. Fax, 331-8446.

Membership: broker/dealer organizations and sponsors, law and accounting firms, financial planners, and partnership consultants. Works to preserve limited partnerships and real estate investment trusts as a form of investment and a source of new capital for the economy. Conducts economic research; monitors legislation and regulations, especially those concerning tax policy.

Investor Responsibility Research Center, 1755 Massachusetts Ave. N.W., #600 20036; 234-7500. Margaret Carroll, executive director. Fax, 332-8570.

Research organization that reports on and analyzes business and public policy issues affecting corporations and investors.

Municipal Securities Rulemaking Board, 1818 N St. N.W., #800 20036; 223-9347. Christopher A. Taylor, executive director. Fax, 872-0347.

Writes rules, subject to approval by the Securities and Exchange Commission, applicable to municipal securities brokers and dealers, in such areas as conduct, industry practices, and professional qualifications. Serves as a self-regulatory agency for the municipal securities industry.

National Assn. of Bond Lawyers, 2000 Pennsylvania Ave. N.W., #9000 20006; 778-2244. Amy K. Dunbar, director, governmental affairs. Fax, 778-2201.

Membership: municipal finance lawyers. Provides members with information on laws relating to the borrowing of money by states and municipalities and to the issuance of state and local government bonds. Monitors legislation and regulations. (Headquarters in Hinsdale, Ill.)

National Assn. of Securities Dealers, 1735 K St. N.W. 20006; 728-8000. Joseph R. Hardiman, president. Fax, 728-8890. Member services, (301) 590-6500. Public disclosure, (800) 289-9999.

Membership: investment brokers and dealers authorized to conduct transactions of the investment banking and securities business under federal and state laws. Serves as the self-regulatory mechanism in the over-the-counter securities market.

National Investor Relations Institute, 2000 L St. N.W., #701 20036; 861-0630. Louis M. Thompson Jr., president. Fax, 861-0633.

Membership: executives engaged in investor relations and financial communications. Provides publications, educational training sessions, and research on investor relations for members; offers conferences and workshops; maintains job placement and referral services for its members.

New York Stock Exchange, 1800 K St. N.W., #1100 20006; 293-5740. Steve Paradise, senior vice president, Washington office. Fax, 331-4158.

Provides limited information on operations of the New York Stock Exchange; Washington office monitors legislation and regulations.

North American Securities Administrators Assn., 1 Massachusetts Ave. N.W., #310 20001-1431; 737-0900. Fowler West, executive director. Fax, 783-3571.

Membership: state, provincial, and territorial securities administrators of the United States, Canada, and Mexico. Serves as the national representative of the state agencies responsible for investor protection. Works to prevent fraud in securities markets and provides a national forum to increase the efficiency and uniformity of state regulation of capital markets. Operates the Central Registration Depository, a nationwide computer link for agent registration and transfers, in conjunction with the National Assn. of Securities Dealers. Monitors legislation and regulations.

Public Securities Assn., 1445 New York Ave. N.W., 8th Floor 20005; 434-8400. Micah S. Green, executive vice president. Fax, 737-4744.

Membership: banks, dealers, and brokers who underwrite, trade, and sell municipal securities, mortgage-backed securities, and government and federal agency securities. Acts as an information and education center for the public securities industry. (Headquarters in New York.)

Securities Industry Assn., 1401 Eye St. N.W., #1000 20005-2225; 296-9410. Marc E. Lackritz, president. Fax, 296-9775.

Membership: investment bankers, securities underwriters, and dealers in stocks and bonds. Represents all segments of the securities industry. (Headquarters in New York.)

Securities Investor Protection Corp., 805 15th St. N.W., #800 20005; 371-8300. James G. Stearns, chairman; Theodore Focht, president and general counsel. Fax, 371-6728.

Private corporation established by Congress to administer the Securities Investor Protection Act. Provides financial protection for customers of member broker-dealers that fail financially.

Tangible Assets and Real Estate

See also Coins and Currency (p. 296)

Agencies:

Bureau of Mines (Interior Dept.), Metals, 810 7th St. N.W. 20241; 501-9450. John M. Lucas, commodities specialist, gold, 501-9417; Robert G. Reese, silver, 501-9413; Roger Loebenstein, platinum group metals, 501-9416; Daniel Edelstein, copper, 501-9416. Fax, 501-3751.

Studies supply and demand of copper and precious metals including gold, silver, platinum group metals, and ferrous metals (iron, iron ore, steel, chromium, and nickel); collects and provides statistical data on production and consumption of precious metals; provides information on gold and silver research, production, and processing methods.

Census Bureau (Commerce Dept.), Industry Division, Suitland and Silver Hill Rds., Suitland, MD (mailing address: Bldg. 4, Rm. 2215, Washington, DC 20233); (301) 763-5938. John P. McNamee, chief, minerals branch. Fax, (301) 763-2632.

Collects, tabulates, and publishes statistics concerning the domestic minerals industry.

Census Bureau (Commerce Dept.), Minerals and Metals, Suitland and Silver Hill Rds., Suitland, MD (mailing address: Washington, DC 20233); (301) 763-5150. Pat Comfer, chief. Fax, (301) 763-7907.

Verifies and publishes monthly import and export statistics collected by bureau district offices on precious metals, petroleum, steel, and other mineral and metal products.

Commodity Futures Trading Commission, 2033 K St. N.W. 20581; 254-6970. Mary L. Schapiro, chair designate. Information, 254-8630. Library, 254-5901. Fax, 254-3061.

Enforces federal statutes relating to commodity futures and options, including gold and silver

futures and options. (A futures contract is an agreement to purchase or sell a commodity for delivery in the future at an agreed price and date. An option is a unilateral contract that gives the buyer the right to buy or sell a specified quantity of a commodity at a specific price within a specified period of time, regardless of the market price of that commodity.) Monitors and regulates gold and silver leverage contracts, which provide for deferred delivery of the commodity and the payment of an agreed portion of the purchase price on margin.

Defense Logistics Agency (Defense Dept.), National Stockpile Center, 1745 Jefferson Davis Highway, #100, Arlington, VA 22202; (703) 607-3235. Crandell McDonald, director. Fax, (703) 607-3215.

Manages the national defense stockpile of strategic and critical materials. Purchases strategic materials including beryllium and newly developed high-tech alloys. Disposes of excess materials including tin, silver, industrial diamond stones, tungsten, and vegetable tannin.

Federal Reserve System, Accounting and Budgets, 20th and C Sts. N.W. 20551; 452-3915. Earl G. Hamilton, assistant director. Fax, 452-6474.

Monitors gold certificate accounts and budgets of Federal Reserve Banks. (Gold certificate accounts are credits issued by the Treasury Dept. against gold held by the Treasury.)

U.S. Mint (Treasury Dept.), 633 3rd St. N.W. 20220; 874-6000. Philip N. Diehl, director designate. Information, 874-6450. Fax, 874-6282.

Produces gold and silver coins for sale to investors.

Congress:

House Banking, Finance, and Urban Affairs Committee, Subcommittee on Consumer Credit and Insurance, 604 O'Neill Bldg. (300 New Jersey Ave. S.E.) 20515; 225-8872. Joseph P. Kennedy II, D-Mass., chairman; Shawn P. Maher, staff director. Fax, 225-7960.

Jurisdiction over legislation to regulate transactions in gold and precious metals.

See also Congressional Copper Caucus (p. 756)

Nongovernmental:

The Gold Institute, 1112 16th St. N.W., #240 20036; 835-0185. John Lutley, president. Fax, 835-0155.

Membership: companies that mine, refine, fabricate, or manufacture gold or gold-containing products; wholesalers of physical gold investment products; banks; and gold bullion dealers. Conducts research on new technological and industrial uses for gold. Compiles statistics by country on mine production of gold and coinage use and on the production, distribution, and use of refined gold.

Industry Council for Tangible Assets, 6728 Old McLean Village Dr., #200, McLean, VA 22101-3906; (703) 847-1740. Eloise Bredder, executive director. Fax, (703) 847-1742.

Membership: bullion, numismatic, philatelic, and gem firms; investment banks; and investment counselors. Monitors legislation concerning regulation of the manufacture, distribution, and sale of tangible assets.

National Assn. of Real Estate Investment Trusts, 1129 20th St. N.W., #305 20036; 785-8717. Mark O. Decker, president. Fax, 785-8723.

Membership: real estate investment trusts and corporations, partnerships, and individuals interested in real estate securities and the industry. Monitors federal and state legislation, federal taxation, securities regulation, standards and ethics, and housing and education; compiles industrywide statistics.

The Silver Institute, 1112 16th St. N.W., #240 20036; 835-0185. John Lutley, executive director. Fax, 835-0155.

Membership: companies that mine, refine, fabricate, or manufacture silver or silver-containing products. Conducts research on new technological and industrial uses for silver. Compiles statistics by country on mine production of silver, coinage use, the production, distribution, and use of refined silver, and the conversion of refined silver into other forms, such as silverware and jewelry.

Silver Users Assn., 1730 M St. N.W., #911 20036; 785-3050. Walter L. Frankland Jr., executive vice president. Fax, 659-5760.

Membership: users of silver, including the photographic industry, silversmiths, and other manufacturers. Conducts research on silver market; monitors government activities in silver; analyzes government statistics on silver consumption and production.

See also American Society of Appraisers and The Appraisal Institute (p. 387)

Industrial Production

General

Agencies:

Census Bureau (Commerce Dept.), Industry Division, Suitland and Silver Hill Rds., Suitland, MD (mailing address: Washington, DC 20233); (301) 763-5850. John P. Govoni, chief. Fax, (301) 763-7582.

Collects, tabulates, and publishes statistics concerning the domestic manufacturing industry.

Economics and Statistics Administration (Commerce Dept.), Main Commerce Bldg. 20230; 482-3727. Everett Ehrlich, under secretary. Information, 482-2235. Fax, 482-0432.

Advises the secretary on economic policy matters, including inventory status and the short- and long-term outlook in output. Seeks to improve economic productivity and growth. Serves as departmental liaison with the Council of Economic Advisers and other government agencies concerned with economic policy. Supervises and sets policy for the Bureau of Economic Analysis.

Congress:

See Business and Economic Policy, General, Congress (p. 47)

Nongovernmental:

American Production and Inventory Control Society, 500 W. Annandale Rd., Falls Church, VA 22046; (703) 237-8344. Donald Ledwig, executive director. Fax, (703) 237-1071.

Membership: purchasing agents and inventory control personnel in manufacturing firms. Disseminates information on production and inventory control, specifically with regard to ensuring an even flow of raw goods into the manufacturing system and of finished goods into the retail system. Conducts certification exams in production and inventory management and integrated resource management.

American Wire Producers Assn., 1101 Connecticut Ave. N.W., #700 20036; 857-1155. Kimberly Korbel, executive director. Fax, 429-5154.

Membership: companies that produce carbon, alloy, and stainless steel wire and wire products in the United States. Interests include imports of rod, wire, and wire products and enforcement of antidumping and countervailing duty laws. Publishes survey of the domestic wire industry. Monitors legislation and regulations affecting the industry.

Flexible Packaging Assn., 1090 Vermont Ave. N.W., #500 20005; 842-3880. Glenn E. Braswell, president. Fax, 842-3841.

Researches packaging trends and technical developments; compiles industry statistics; monitors legislation and regulations.

Industrial Designers Society of America, 1142-E Walker Rd., Great Falls, VA 22066; (703) 759-0100. Robert Schwartz, executive director. Fax, (703) 759-7679.

Membership: designers of products, equipment, instruments, furniture, transportation, packages, exhibits, information services, and related services. Provides the Bureau of Labor Statistics and U.S. Information Agency with industry information. Monitors legislation and regulations.

Industrial Research Institute, 1550 M St. N.W., #1100 20005-1708; 872-6350. Charles F. Larson, executive director. Fax, 872-6356.

Membership: companies that maintain laboratories for industrial research. Seeks to improve the process of industrial research by promoting cooperative efforts among companies, between the academic and research communities, and between industry and the government. Monitors legislation and regulations concerning technology, industry, and national competitiveness.

Institute of Packaging Professionals, 481 Carlisle Dr., Herndon, VA 22070; (703) 318-8970. William C. Pflaum, executive director. Fax, (703) 318-0310.

Represents the interests of packaging professionals. Conducts an annual packaging design competition. Publishes journals and newsletters.

Manufacturers' Alliance for Productivity and Innovation, 1200 18th St. N.W., #400 20036; 331-8430. Kenneth McLennan, president. Fax, 331-7160.

Membership: companies involved in high technology industries, including electronics, telecommunications, precision instruments, computers, the automotive industry, and the aerospace industry. Seeks to increase industrial productivity. Conducts research; organizes discussion councils; monitors legislation and regulations.

National Assn. of Manufacturers, 1331 Pennsylvania Ave. N.W., #1500 20004; 637-3000. Jerry Jasinowski, president. Information, 637-3099. Press, 637-3094. Fax, 637-3182.

Represents industry views (mainly of manufacturers) to government on national and international issues. Reviews legislation, administrative rulings, and judicial decisions affecting industry. Sponsors the Human Resources Forum; operates a computer network for members and the public that provides information on legislative and other news; conducts programs on labor relations, occupational safety and health, regulatory and consumer affairs, and other business issues.

National Assn. of Wholesaler-Distributors, 1725 K St. N.W. 20006; 872-0885. Dirk Van Dongen, president. Fax, 785-0586.

Membership: wholesale distributors and trade associations. Provides members and government policymakers with research, education, and government relations information. Monitors legislation and regulations.

National Tooling and Machining Assn., 9300 Livingston Rd., Ft. Washington, MD 20744; (301) 248-6200. Matthew B. Coffey, president. Fax, (301) 248-7104.

Membership: members of the contract precision metalworking industry, including tool, die, mold, diecasting die, and special machining companies. Assists members in developing and expanding their domestic and foreign markets. Offers training program, insurance, and legal advice; compiles statistical information; monitors legislation and regulations.

U.S. Business and Industrial Council, 220 National Press Bldg., 14th and F Sts. N.W. 20045; 662-8744. Kevin L. Kearns, president. Fax, 662-8754.

National business group that advocates energy independence, reindustrialization, and effective use of natural resources and manufacturing capacity. Current issues include business tax reduction, spending cuts to reduce the deficit, the liability crisis, defense spending, and the trade deficit. Media network distributes op-ed pieces to newspapers and radio stations.

See also Electronic Industries Assn. (p. 32)

Supply Shortages

See also Emergency Preparedness, Industrial Planning and Mobilization (p. 543); Strategic Stockpiles (p. 544)

Agencies:

Bureau of Export Administration (Commerce Dept.), Industrial Resources, Main Commerce Bldg. 20230; 482-4506. John A. Richards, deputy assistant secretary. Fax, 482-5650.

Assists in providing for an adequate supply of strategic and critical materials for defense activities and civilian needs, including military requirements, and other domestic energy supplies; develops plans for industry to meet national emergencies. Studies the effect of imports on national security and recommends actions.

Bureau of Mines (Interior Dept.), Policy Analysis, 810 7th St. N.W. 20241; 501-9729. William L. Miller, chief. Fax, 219-2490.

Provides technical and economic policy analysis of domestic and international regulatory and trade issues concerning mineral production and use. Develops policy options to deal with critical mineral shortages caused by depletion of domestic supplies or disruption of imported supplies. Monitors international political and economic issues that affect the critical strategic position of the United States.

International Trade Administration (Commerce Dept.), Basic Industries, Main Commerce Bldg. 20230; 482-5023. Michael J. Copts, deputy assistant secretary. Fax, 482-5666.

Analyzes and maintains data on metals, minerals, construction, chemicals, rubber, forest products, and energy industries (domestic and international); responds to government and business inquiries about materials shortages in specific industries. Analyzes supply and demand, capacity and production capability, and capital formation requirements.

Insurance

See also Community Planning and Development, Disaster Assistance and Federal Insurance (p. 382); Health Care Financing (p. 348); Housing: Finance, Mortgage Insurance and Guarantees (p. 397); Personnel: Military, Financial Services (p. 571)

Congress:

House Banking, Finance, and Urban Affairs Committee, Subcommittee on Consumer Credit and Insurance, 604 O'Neill Bldg. (300 New Jersey Ave. S.E.) 20515; 225-8872. Joseph P. Kennedy II, D-Mass., chairman; Shawn P. Maher, staff director. Fax, 225-7960.

Jurisdiction over federal flood, crime, fire, and earthquake insurance programs; oversees activities of the insurance industry pertaining to these programs.

House Energy and Commerce Committee, Subcommittee on Commerce, Consumer Protection, and Competitiveness, 151 Ford Bldg. (2nd and D Sts. S.W.) 20515; 226-3160. Cardiss Collins, D-Ill., chairman; David Schooler, staff director.

Jurisdiction over insurance legislation.

Senate Banking, Housing, and Urban Affairs Committee, Subcommittee on Housing and Urban Affairs, SD-535 20510; 224-6348. Paul S. Sarbanes, D-Md., chairman; Paul N. Weech, staff director. Fax, 224-5137.

Jurisdiction over federal flood, crime, and riot insurance programs; oversees insurance industry activities pertaining to these programs.

Senate Judiciary Committee, Subcommittee on Antitrust, Monopolies, and Business Rights, SH-308 20510; 224-5701. Howard M. Metzenbaum, D-Ohio, chairman; Gene Kimmelman, chief counsel.

Jurisdiction over legislation to prevent insurance rate discrimination.

See also Congressional Insurance Caucus (p. 758)

Nongovernmental:

Alliance of American Insurers, 1211 Connecticut Ave. N.W., #400 20036; 822-8811. David M. Farmer, senior vice president, federal affairs.

Membership: property and casualty insurance companies. Provides educational and advisory services for members on insurance issues. (Headquarters in Schaumburg, Ill.)

American Academy of Actuaries, 1720 Eye St. N.W., 7th Floor 20006; 223-8196. James J. Murphy, executive vice president. Fax, 872-1948.

Membership: professional actuaries practicing in the areas of life, health, liability, property, and casualty insurance; pensions; government insurance plans; and general consulting. Provides information on actuarial matters, including insurance and pensions; develops professional standards.

American Council of Life Insurance, 1001 Pennsylvania Ave. N.W. 20004-2599; 624-2000. Richard S. Schweiker, president. Press, 624-2416. Library, 624-2475. Fax, 624-2319. TDD, 624-2090. National Insurance Consumer Helpline, (800) 942-4242.

Membership: life insurance companies authorized to do business in the United States. Conducts research and compiles statistics at state and federal levels. Library on life and health insurance, business, and social sciences open to the public by appointment.

American Insurance Assn., 1130 Connecticut Ave. N.W., #1000 20036; 828-7100. David J. Pratt, senior vice president, federal affairs. Press, 828-7141. Library, 828-7183. Fax, 293-1219.

Membership: companies providing property and casualty insurance. Conducts public relations and educational activities; provides information on issues related to property and casualty insurance. Library open to the public by appointment.

American Society of Pension Actuaries, 4350 N. Fairfax Dr., #820, Arlington, VA 22203-1621; (703) 516-9300. Chester J. Salkind, executive director. Fax, (703) 516-9308.

Membership: professional pension plan actuaries, administrators, consultants, and other benefits professionals. Sponsors educational programs to prepare actuaries and consultants for professional exams; monitors legislation and regulations.

Assn. for Advanced Life Underwriting, 1922 F St. N.W. 20006; 331-6081. David J. Stertzer, executive vice president. Fax, 331-2164.

Membership: specialized underwriters in the fields of estate analysis, business insurance, pension planning, and employee benefit plans. Monitors legislation and regulations on small-business taxes and capital formation.

Assn. of Trial Lawyers of America, 1050 31st St. N.W. 20007; 965-3500. Thomas H. Henderson Jr., executive director. Fax, 625-7312.

Membership: attorneys, judges, law professors, and students. Interests include aspects of legal and legislative activity relating to the adversary system and trial by jury, including property and casualty insurance.

The Council of Insurance Agents and Brokers, 316 Pennsylvania Ave. S.E., #400 20003-1146; 547-6616. Ken A. Crerar, executive vice president. Fax, 546-0597.

Represents commercial property and casualty insurance agencies and brokerage firms.

Independent Insurance Agents of America, 127 S. Peyton St., Alexandria, VA 22314; (703) 683-4422. Jeff Yates, executive vice president. Fax, (703) 683-7556.

Provides educational and advisory services; researches issues pertaining to auto, home, business, life, and health insurance; offers cooperative advertising program to members. Political action committee monitors legislation and regulations.

Insurance Information Institute, 1101 17th St. N.W. 20036; 833-1580. Carolyn Gorman, director, federal affairs. Fax, 223-5779.

Membership: property and casualty insurance companies. Monitors state and federal issues concerning insurance. (Headquarters in New York.)

Mortgage Insurance Companies of America, 727 15th St. N.W. 20005; 393-5566. Suzanne C. Hutchinson, executive vice president. Fax, 393-5557.

Membership: companies that provide default coverage on residential mortgage loans made with down payments of less than 20 percent.

National Assn. of Independent Insurers, 499 S. Capitol St. S.W., #401 20003; 484-2350. Jack Ramirez, senior vice president, government relations. Fax, 484-2356.

Membership: companies providing property and casualty insurance. Monitors legislation and compiles statistics; interests include auto and no-fault insurance and personal lines. (Headquarters in Des Plaines, Ill.)

National Assn. of Insurance Brokers, 1401 New York Ave. N.W., #720 20005; 628-6700. Carl A. Modecki, president. Fax, 628-6707.

Membership: commercial retail insurance brokerages (firms that engage in devising commercial programs for clients). Monitors legislation and regulations that affect insurance brokers, their clients, and the insurance industry.

National Assn. of Insurance Commissioners, 444 N. Capitol St. N.W., #309 20001; 624-7790. Kevin Cronin, Washington counsel. Fax, 624-8579.

Membership: state insurance commissioners, directors, and supervisors. Provides members with information on computer information services, legal and market conduct, and financial services; publishes and distributes research and statistical data on the insurance industry; monitors legislation and regulations. (Headquarters in Kansas City, Mo.)

National Assn. of Life Underwriters, 1922 F St. N.W. 20006; 331-6000. William V. Regan III, executive vice president. Fax, 331-2179.

Federation of affiliated state and local life underwriters. Provides information on life and health insurance and other financial services; sponsors education and training programs.

National Assn. of Professional Insurance Agents, 400 N. Washington St., Alexandria, VA 22314; (703) 836-9340. Donald K. Gardiner, executive vice president. Toll-free, (800) 742-6900. Fax, (703) 836-1279.

Membership: independent insurance agents and brokers. Operates schools to provide agents with basic training; offers seminars and provides educational materials; monitors legislation and regulations.

National Insurance Consumer Organization, 121 N. Payne St., Alexandria, VA (mailing address: P.O. Box 15492, Alexandria, VA 22309); (703) 549-8050. Kathleen O'Reilly, policy director. Fax, (703) 360-9211.

Public interest organization that conducts research and provides consumers with information on buying insurance. Interests include auto, homeowner, renter, life, and health insurance.

Nonprofit Risk Management Center, 1001 Connecticut Ave. N.W., #900 20036; 785-3891. Charles Tremper, executive director.

Assists all groups engaged in charitable service, including nonprofit organizations, government entities, and corporate volunteer programs, to improve the quality of and reduce the cost of their insurance. Provides information on insurance and risk management issues through conferences and publications.

The Product Liability Alliance, 1725 K St. N.W. 20006; 872-0885. James A. Anderson Jr., vice president, government relations. Fax, 785-0586.

Membership: manufacturers, product sellers and their insurers, and trade associations. Promotes enactment of federal product liability tort reform legislation.

Reinsurance Assn. of America, 1301 Pennsylvania Ave. N.W., #900 20004; 638-3690. Franklin W. Nutter, president. Fax, 638-0936.

Membership: companies writing property and casualty reinsurance. Serves as an information clearinghouse.

Intergovernmental Relations: Economic Development

See also Community Planning and Development (p. 378); Military Installations, Base Closings/Economic Impact (p. 560); Rural Development (p. 610); State and Local Government (p. 311)

Agencies:

Appalachian Regional Commission, 1666 Connecticut Ave. N.W., #600 20235; 673-7856. Jacqueline Phillips, federal co chair; Francis Moravitz, executive director, 673-7874. Information, 673-7968. Fax, 673-7934.

Federal-state-local partnership for economic development of the region including Alabama, Georgia, Kentucky, Maryland, Mississippi, New York, North Carolina, Ohio, Pennsylvania, South Carolina, Tennessee, Virginia, and West Virginia. Provides technical and financial assistance and coordinates federal and state efforts for economic development of Appalachia.

Census Bureau (Commerce Dept.), Governments Division, Washington Plaza II, #407, Marlow Heights, MD (mailing address: Washington, DC 20233); (301) 763-7366. Gordon W. Green, chief. Fax, (301) 763-4493.

Compiles the annual *Federal Expenditures by State,* which provides information on federal domestic spending, federal grants programs, and federal aid to states.

Economic Development Administration (Commerce Dept.), Main Commerce Bldg. 20230; 482-5081. William W. Ginsberg, assistant secretary. Information, 482-5112. Fax, 273-4781.

Advises the commerce secretary on domestic economic development. Administers development assistance programs that provide financial and technical aid to economically distressed areas to stimulate economic growth and create jobs. Awards public works and technical assistance grants to public institutions, nonprofit organizations, and native American tribes; assists state and local governments with economic adjustment problems caused by long-term or sudden economic dislocation.

General Services Administration, Federal Domestic Assistance Catalog Staff, 300 7th St. S.W., #101 20405; 708-5126. Robert Brown, director. Fax, 401-8233.

Maintains computerized Federal Assistance Programs Retrieval System, which helps state and local governments to locate programs with the greatest funding potential to meet their developmental needs. Access to database available at designated points in every state. Prepares *Catalog of Federal Domestic Assistance,* which lists all types of assistance, eligibility requirements, application procedure, and suggestions for writing proposals. Copies may be ordered from the Superintendent of Documents, U.S. Government Printing Office, Washington, DC. 20402; 783-3238.

Health and Human Services Dept., Administration for Native Americans, 200 Independence Ave. S.W. 20201; 690-7776. Gary N. Kimble, commissioner designate. Information, 690-7730. Fax, 690-7441.

Awards grants for locally determined social and economic development strategies; promotes native American economic and social self-sufficiency; funds native American and native Hawaiian organizations. Commissioner chairs the Intradepartmental Council on Indian Affairs, which coordinates native American-related programs.

Congress:

General Accounting Office, Intergovernmental Relations Group, 1 Massachusetts Ave. N.W. (mailing address: NGB Income Security, 441 G St. N.W., Washington, DC 20458); 512-7213. George Poindexter, assistant director. Fax, 512-5857.

Independent, nonpartisan agency in the legislative branch. Conducts studies on issues in managing federal assistance programs and fiscal and budgetary conditions of state and local governments; reports findings to Congress.

House Government Operations Committee, Subcommittee on Human Resources and Intergovernmental Relations, B372 RHOB 20515;

225-2548. Edolphus Towns, D-N.Y., chairman; Ron Stroman, staff director. Fax, 225-2382.

Jurisdiction over revenue sharing legislation.

House Public Works and Transportation Committee, Subcommittee on Economic Development, B376 RHOB 20515; 225-6151. Bob Wise, D-W.Va., chairman; Carl J. Lorenz Jr., staff director and counsel.

Jurisdiction over legislation on development of economically depressed areas, including Appalachia, and legislation designed to create jobs; jurisdiction over the Economic Development Administration.

Senate Environment and Public Works Committee, Subcommittee on Water Resources, Transportation, Public Buildings, and Economic Development, SH-415 20510; 224-5031. Daniel Patrick Moynihan, D-N.Y., chairman; Vacant, director.

Jurisdiction over legislation on development of economically depressed areas, including Appalachia, and over legislation designed to create jobs, often with public works and water resource development projects; jurisdiction over the Economic Development Administration.

Senate Finance Committee, SD-205 20510; 224-4515. Daniel Patrick Moynihan, D-N.Y., chairman; Lawrence O'Donnell Jr., staff director.

Jurisdiction over revenue sharing legislation (jurisdiction shared with Senate Governmental Affairs Committee).

Senate Governmental Affairs Committee, Subcommittee on General Services, Federalism, and the District of Columbia, SH-432 20510; 224-4718. Jim Sasser, D-Tenn., chairman; John Wagster, staff director.

Jurisdiction over legislation on revenue sharing (jurisdiction shared with Senate Finance Committee).

See also Congressional Sunbelt Caucus (p. 759); Northeast-Midwest Congressional Coalition and Northeast-Midwest Senate Coalition (p. 760); Western States Senate Coalition (p. 761)

Nongovernmental:

National Assn. of Counties, 440 1st St. N.W., 8th Floor 20001; 393-6226. Larry Naake, executive director. Fax, 393-2630.

Membership: county officials. Conducts research and provides information and technical assistance on issues affecting counties, including economic development programs and federal grants to counties. Monitors legislation and regulations.

National Assn. of Development Organizations, 444 N. Capitol St. N.W., #630 20001; 624-7806. Aliceann Wohlbruck, executive director. Fax, 624-8813.
Membership: organizations interested in regional, local, and rural economic development. Provides information on federal, state, and local development programs and revolving loan funds; sponsors conferences and seminars.

National Assn. of Regional Councils, 1700 K St. N.W., #1300 20006; 457-0710. John W. Epling, executive director. Fax, 296-9352.
Membership: regional councils of local governments. Works with member local governments to encourage areawide economic growth and cooperation between public and private sectors, with emphasis on community development.

National Assn. of State Development Agencies, 750 1st St. N.E., #710 20002-4241; 898-1302. Miles Friedman, executive director. Fax, 898-1312.
Membership: directors of state economic development agencies. Provides economic development consulting service; sponsors conferences and seminars. Interests include financing techniques, job training programs, aid to small business, and state-local coordination strategies.

National Center for Municipal Development, 1620 Eye St. N.W., #300 20006; 429-0160. Mark S. Israel, executive director. Fax, 293-3109.
Affiliated with the National League of Cities and the U.S. Conference of Mayors. Provides municipalities with information in areas such as federal grant programs and allocation formulas.

National Development Council, 3921 Albemarle St. N.W. 20016; 364-9641. Nelson R. Bregon, director. Fax, 364-9648.
Helps low-income communities expand regional economic development. Assists small businesses in finding long-term financing for economic expansion; works to increase employment opportunities. (Headquarters in New York.)

The New England Council, 1455 Pennsylvania Ave. N.W., #1000 (mailing address: 444 North Capitol St. N.W., #418, Washington, DC 20001); 434-8095. Maria Berthoud, director, legislative affairs. Fax, 434-8099.
Provides information on business and economic issues concerning New England; serves as liaison between the New England congressional delegations and business community. (Headquarters in Boston.)

Northeast-Midwest Institute, 218 D St. S.E. 20003; 544-5200. Dick Munson, executive director. Fax, 544-0043.
Public policy research organization that promotes the economic vitality of the northeast and midwest regions. Interests include economic development, human resources, energy, and natural resources.

Sunbelt Institute, 409 3rd St. S.W., #200 20024; 554-0201. Joseph W. Westphal, executive director. Fax, 554-2083.
Bipartisan research organization that examines national policies from a regional perspective. Works with the Congressional Sunbelt Caucus and private and academic sectors. Interests include distribution of federal funding to state and local governments, rural development, and federal procurement funds.

See also Public Technology (p. 314)

International Economics

See also Agriculture: Foreign Programs (p. 605); Foreign Policy and Aid, International Development (p. 451); International Labor Policy and Programs (p. 184)

General

See also Business and Economic Policy, General (p. 44)

Agencies:

Agency for International Development (International Development Cooperation Agency), Policy Analysis and Resources, Main State Bldg., Rm. 3947 20523; 647-8558. George A. Hill, director. Fax, 647-8595.
Provides information and guidance on international economic policy issues that affect the economic growth of developing countries.

Federal Reserve System, International Finance, 20th and C Sts. N.W. 20551; 452-3614. Edwin M. Truman, staff director. Fax, 452-6424.

Provides the Federal Reserve's board of governors with economic analyses of international developments.

International Trade Administration (Commerce Dept.), International Economic Policy, Main Commerce Bldg. 20230; 482-3022. Charles Meissner, assistant secretary. Fax, 482-5444.

Develops and implements trade and investment policies affecting countries, regions, or international organizations to improve U.S. market access abroad. Provides information and analyses of foreign business and economic conditions to the U.S. private sector; monitors consultation and renegotiation of the MTN (Multilateral Trade Negotiations) affecting specific areas; represents the United States in many other trade negotiations including the Uruguay Round of negotiations on the General Agreement on Tariffs and Trade (GATT).

State Dept., Economic and Agricultural Affairs, Main State Bldg. 20520; 647-7575. Joan Edelman Spero, under secretary. Fax, 647-9763.

Advises the secretary on formulation and conduct of foreign economic policies and programs, including international monetary and financial affairs, trade, energy, agriculture, commodities, investments, and international transportation issues. Coordinates economic summit meetings.

State Dept., Economic and Business Affairs, Main State Bldg. 20520; 647-7971. Daniel K. Tarullo, assistant secretary. Fax, 647-5713.

Formulates and implements policies related to U.S. economic relations with foreign countries, including international business practices, trade, finance, investment, development, natural resources, energy, and transportation.

State Dept., International Finance and Development, Main State Bldg. 20520; 647-9496. Alan P. Larson, deputy assistant secretary. Fax, 647-7453.

Formulates and implements policies related to multinational investment and insurance; activities of the World Bank and regional banks in the financial development of various countries; bilateral aid; international monetary reform; international antitrust cases; and international debt, banking, and taxation.

Treasury Dept., International Affairs, Main Treasury Bldg. 20220; 622-0060. Jeffrey Shafer, assistant secretary. Fax, 622-0081.

Coordinates and implements U.S. international economic policy in cooperation with other government agencies. Works to improve the structure and stabilizing operations of the international monetary and investment system; monitors developments in international gold and foreign exchange operations; coordinates policies and programs of development lending institutions; coordinates Treasury Dept. participation in direct and portfolio investment by foreigners in the United States; studies international monetary, economic, and financial issues; analyzes data on international transactions.

Congress:

House Appropriations Committee, Subcommittee on Commerce, Justice, State, and Judiciary, H309 CAP 20515; 225-3351. Neal Smith, D-Iowa, chairman; John Osthaus, staff assistant.

Jurisdiction over legislation to appropriate funds for the Commerce Dept., the Office of the U.S. Trade Representative, and the International Trade Commission.

House Appropriations Committee, Subcommittee on Treasury, Postal Service, and General Government, H164 CAP 20515; 225-5834. Steny H. Hoyer, D-Md., chairman; Bill Smith, staff assistant. Fax, 426-3763.

Jurisdiction over legislation to appropriate funds for the Treasury Dept.

House Banking, Finance, and Urban Affairs Committee, Subcommittee on International Development, Finance, Trade, and Monetary Policy, B304 RHOB 20515; 226-7515. Barney Frank, D-Mass., chairman; Sydney Key, staff director. Fax, 225-3934.

Jurisdiction over international monetary policy, international capital flows, and foreign investment in the United States as they affect domestic monetary policy and the economy; exchange rates; the African Development Bank, Asian Development Bank, Inter-American Development Bank, and World Bank; legislation on international trade, investment, and monetary policy and export expansion matters related to the International Monetary Fund and the Export-Import Bank.

House Energy and Commerce Committee, Subcommittee on Telecommunications and Finance, 316 Ford Bldg. (2nd and D Sts. S.W.) 20515; 226-2424. Edward J. Markey, D-Mass., chairman; David H. Moulton, staff director and chief counsel.

Jurisdiction over legislation on foreign investment in the United States (jurisdiction shared with House Foreign Affairs Committee).

House Foreign Affairs Committee, Subcommittee on Economic Policy, Trade, and the Environment, 702 O'Neill Bldg. (300 New Jersey Ave. S.E.) 20515; 226-7820. Sam Gejdenson, D-Conn., chairman; John Scheibel, staff director. Fax, 225-2029.

Jurisdiction over legislation on foreign investments in the United States (shares jurisdiction with House Energy and Commerce Committee) and foreign trade, including activities of U.S. firms abroad, the Export Administration Act, the International Emergency Economic Powers Act, the Overseas Private Investment Corp., and the revised Trading with the Enemy Act, which authorizes trade restrictions. Oversees the Export-Import Bank of the United States, international financial and monetary institutions, and customs.

House Government Operations Committee, Subcommittee on Commerce, Consumer, and Monetary Affairs, B377 RHOB 20515; 225-4407. John M. Spratt Jr., D-S.C., chairman; Theodore Jacobs, staff director. Fax, 225-2441.

Jurisdiction over operations of the Export-Import Bank, Overseas Private Investment Corp., U.S. International Trade Commission, and the Office of the U.S. Trade Representative.

House Small Business Committee, Subcommittee on Rural Enterprises, Exports, and the Environment, 1F CHOB 20515; 225-8944. Bill Sarpalius, D-Texas, chairman; Christopher Mattson, staff director.

Jurisdiction over legislation on export expansion as it relates to the small-business community.

House Ways and Means Committee, Subcommittee on Oversight, 1135 LHOB 20515; 225-5522. J. J. Pickle, D-Texas, chairman; Beth K. Vance, staff director. Fax, 225-0787.

Oversees the U.S. Customs Service.

House Ways and Means Committee, Subcommittee on Trade, 1136 LHOB 20515; 225-3943. Robert T. Matsui, D-Calif., acting chairman; Bruce Wilson, staff director.

Jurisdiction over legislation on tariffs, trade, and customs and customs administration. Authorizes budgets for the U.S. Customs Service, U.S. International Trade Commission, and the Office of the U.S. Trade Representative.

Joint Economic Committee, SD-G01 20510; 224-5171. Rep. David R. Obey, D-Wis., chairman; Richard McGahey, executive director.

Studies and makes recommendations on international economic policy and programs, trade, and foreign investment policy; monitors economic policy in foreign countries.

Senate Appropriations Committee, Subcommittee on Commerce, Justice, State, and Judiciary, S146A CAP 20510; 224-7277. Ernest F. Hollings, D-S.C., chairman; Scott B. Gudes, clerk.

Jurisdiction over legislation to appropriate funds for the Commerce Dept., the Office of the U.S. Trade Representative, International Trade Commission, and other international economics-related agencies, services, and programs.

Senate Appropriations Committee, Subcommittee on Treasury, Postal Service, and General Government, SD-190 20510; 224-8271. Dennis DeConcini, D-Ariz., chairman; Patty Lynch, clerk.

Jurisdiction over legislation to appropriate funds for the Treasury Dept.

Senate Banking, Housing, and Urban Affairs Committee, Subcommittee on International Finance and Monetary Policy, SD-534 20510; 224-1564. Jim Sasser, D-Tenn., chairman; Charles R. Marr, staff director. Fax, 224-5137.

Jurisdiction over legislation on international monetary and exchange rate policies, foreign investments in the United States, export control, the Export-Import Bank, the International Emergency Economic Powers Act, the Export Administration Act, and the revised Trading with the Enemy Act, which authorizes trade restrictions (some jurisdictions shared with Senate Finance and Foreign Relations committees).

Senate Finance Committee, SD-205 20510; 224-4515. Daniel Patrick Moynihan, D-N.Y., chairman; Lawrence O'Donnell Jr., staff director.

Jurisdiction over legislation on international monetary matters (shares jurisdiction with the

Senate Foreign Relations and Banking, Housing, and Urban Affairs committees).

Senate Finance Committee, Subcommittee on Deficits, Debt Management, and Long-Term Economic Growth, SD-205 20510; 224-4515. Bill Bradley, D-N.J., chairman; Michael Dahl, staff contact.

Holds hearings on tax legislation affecting U.S. firms abroad.

Senate Finance Committee, Subcommittee on International Trade, SD-205 20510; 224-4515. Max Baucus, D-Mont., chairman; Mary Foley, staff contact.

Holds hearings on tariff and trade legislation; oversees the U.S. Customs Service.

Senate Foreign Relations Committee, Subcommittee on International Economic Policy, Trade, Oceans, and Environment, SD-446 20510; 224-4651. Paul S. Sarbanes, D-Md., chairman; Geryld B. Christianson, staff director. Fax, 224-5011.

Jurisdiction over legislation to encourage trade with foreign countries and to protect American business interests abroad. Jurisdiction over legislation affecting multinational corporations; balance of payments; the African Development Bank; the World Bank; the Asian Development Bank; the Inter-American Development Bank; the Overseas Private Investment Corp.; the International Monetary Fund, the Export-Import Bank, and other international monetary organizations; international economic and monetary policy as it relates to U.S. foreign policy (jurisdiction shared with the Senate Finance and Banking, Housing, and Urban Affairs committees).

Senate Small Business Committee, Subcommittee on Export Expansion and Agricultural Development, SR-428A 20510; 224-5175. Harris Wofford, D-Pa., chairman; Daniel Solomon, senior policy analyst, 224-6324.

Jurisdiction over legislation on export expansion as it relates to the small-business community.

See also Export Task Force (p. 759)

International Organizations:

European Community Press and Public Affairs, 2100 M St. N.W. 20037; 862-9500. Andreas A. M. van Agt, ambassador; Peter Doyle, director. Information, 862-9542. Press, 862-9540. Fax, 429-1766.

Information and public affairs office in the United States for the European Union/European Community, which includes the European Economic Community, the European Coal and Steel Community, and the European Atomic Energy Community. Provides commercial policy data on the European Community and provides information and documents on member countries, including economic, development and cooperation, industry, and technology data. Library open to the public by appointment.

International Monetary Fund, 700 19th St. N.W. 20431; 623-7759. Karin Lissakers, U.S. executive director. Fax, 623-4940.

Intergovernmental organization that maintains funds, contributed by and available for use by members, to promote world trade and aid members with temporary balance-of-payments problems.

Organization for Economic Cooperation and Development (OECD), 2001 L St. N.W., #700 20036; 785-6323. Denis Lamb, head, Washington Center. Fax, 785-0350.

Membership: 24 nations including Australia, Canada, Japan, New Zealand, the United States, and Western European nations. Funded by membership contributions. Serves as a forum for members to exchange information and coordinate their economic policies. Washington Center offers OECD publications for sale and maintains reference library that is open to the public. (Headquarters in Paris.)

Nongovernmental:

Atlantic Council of the United States, 1616 H St. N.W. 20006; 347-9353. David C. Acheson, president. Fax, 737-5163.

Conducts studies and makes policy recommendations on international economic issues in the Atlantic and Pacific communities; sponsors conferences and educational exchanges.

The Brookings Institution, Foreign Policy Studies, 1775 Massachusetts Ave. N.W. 20036; 797-6010. John Steinbruner, director. Information, 797-6105. Fax, 797-6003. Publications, 797-6258.

Studies international economic and trade issues as they relate to foreign policy.

Center for International Private Enterprise, 1615 H St. N.W. 20062; 463-5901. Willard Workman, vice president. Fax, 887-3447.

Works to strengthen private voluntary business organizations worldwide and to promote participation in the formation of public policy. Cooperates with local, national, regional, and multilateral institutions promoting private enterprise. (Affiliate of the U.S. Chamber of Commerce.)

Center for National Policy, 1 Massachusetts Ave. N.W., #333 20001; 682-1800. Maureen Steinbruner, president. Fax, 682-1818.

Public policy research and educational organization that serves as a forum for development of national policy alternatives. Publishes studies on major national and international policy issues; sponsors conferences and symposia.

Coalition for Employment through Exports, 1100 Connecticut Ave. N.W., #910 20036; 296-6107. Peggy A. Houlihan, president. Fax, 296-9709.

Alliance of governors and representatives of business and organized labor. Works to ensure adequate lending authority for the Export-Import Bank and other trade finance facilities, as well as to ensure aggressive export financing policies for the United States.

Consumers for World Trade, 2000 L St. N.W., #200 20036; 785-4835. Doreen L. Brown, president. Fax, 416-1734.

Consumer organization that advocates open and competitive trade policies. Represents consumer views in the formulation of foreign trade policy.

Council of the Americas/The Americas Society, 1625 K St. N.W., #1200 20006; 659-1547. Ludlow Flower III, managing director. Fax, 659-0169.

Membership: businesses with interests and investments in Latin America. Seeks to expand the role of private enterprise in the development of Latin America. (Headquarters in New York.)

Economic Strategy Institute, 1100 Connecticut Ave. N.W., #1300 20036; 728-0993. Clyde V. Prestowitz Jr., president. Fax, 728-0998.

Works to increase U.S. economic competitiveness through research on domestic and international economic policies, industrial and technological developments, and global security issues. Testifies before Congress and government agencies.

G7 Council, 1133 Connecticut Ave. N.W., #901 20036; 223-0774. Noelle McGlynn, executive director. Fax, 861-0790.

Membership: international economic policy experts and business leaders, including former G7 officials. Advocates promoting the international economy over national economies. Promotes cooperation and coordination among the G7 countries and other industrial nations.

Institute for International Economics, 11 Dupont Circle N.W., 6th Floor 20036; 328-9000. C. Fred Bergsten, director. Fax, 328-5432.

Conducts studies and makes policy recommendations on international monetary affairs, trade, investment, energy, exchange rates, commodities, and North-South and East-West economic relations.

International Franchise Assn., 1350 New York Ave. N.W., #900 20005; 628-8000. William Cherkasky, president. Fax, 628-0812.

Membership: national and international franchisors. Monitors legislation and regulations; sponsors seminars, workshops, trade shows, and conferences.

International Management and Development Institute, 2600 Virginia Ave. N.W., #1112 20037; 337-1022. Gene E. Bradley, chairman. Fax, 337-6678.

Educational organization that works to improve government-business understanding and international economic cooperation worldwide through policy seminars and research on international economic issues.

National Assn. of Manufacturers, International Economic Affairs, 1331 Pennsylvania Ave. N.W., #1500N 20004; 637-3144. Howard Lewis III, vice president. Fax, 637-3182.

Represents manufacturing business interests on international economic issues, including trade, international investment and financial affairs, and multinational corporations.

National Foreign Trade Council, 1625 K St. N.W., #1090 20006; 887-0278. Frank D. Kittredge, president. Fax, 452-8160.

Membership: U.S. companies engaged in international trade and investment. Advocates open international trading, export expansion, and policies to assist U.S. companies competing in international markets. Provides members with information on international trade topics. Sponsors seminars and conferences.

National Planning Assn., 1424 16th St. N.W. 20036; 265-7685. Malcolm R. Lovell Jr., president. Fax, 797-5516.

Research organization that conducts studies and makes policy recommendations on international economic issues, including international trade, investment, monetary policy, and U.S. economic competitiveness.

Overseas Development Council, 1875 Connecticut Ave. N.W., #1012 20009-5728; 234-8701. John W. Sewell, president. Fax, 745-0067.

Research and educational organization that encourages review of U.S. policy toward developing nations by the business community, educators, policymakers, specialists, the public, and the media. Library open to the public by appointment.

U.S. Chamber of Commerce, International Division, 1615 H St. N.W. 20062; 463-5455. Willard Workman, vice president. Information, 463-5460. Fax, 463-3114.

Provides liaison with network of American chambers of commerce abroad; administers multilateral business councils; responsible for international economic policy development; informs members of developments in international affairs, business economics, and trade; sponsors seminars and conferences.

See also The Delphi International Group (p. 153); Japan Information Access Project (p. 90)

Balance of Payments

Agencies:

Commerce Dept., Balance of Payments, 1441 L St. N.W., BE-58 20230; 606-9545. Christopher L. Bach, chief. Fax, 606-5314.

Compiles, analyzes, and publishes quarterly U.S. balance-of-payments figures.

State Dept., Monetary Affairs, Main State Bldg. 20520; 647-5935. Paul Balabanis, director. Fax, 647-7453.

Formulates balance-of-payments and debt rescheduling policies. Monitors balance-of-payments developments in other countries.

Treasury Dept., International Monetary Affairs, Main Treasury Bldg. 20220; 622-0086. David Klock, senior adviser. Fax, 622-0134.

Analyzes current balance-of-payment statistics and makes short-term projections.

Congress:

See International Economics, General, Congress (p. 76)

Nongovernmental:

See International Economics, General, Nongovernmental (p. 78)

Customs and Tariffs

Agencies:

International Trade Administration (Commerce Dept.), Import Administration, Main Commerce Bldg. 20230; 482-1780. Susan Esserman, assistant secretary designate. Fax, 482-0947.

Enforces antidumping and countervailing duty statutes if foreign goods are subsidized or sold at less than fair market value. Evaluates and processes applications by U.S. international air- and seaport communities seeking to establish limited duty-free zones. Administers the Statutory Import Program, which governs specific tariff schedules and imports and determines whether property left abroad by U.S. agencies may be imported back into the United States.

U.S. Customs Service (Treasury Dept.), 1301 Constitution Ave. N.W. 20229; 927-1000. George J. Weise, commissioner. Press, 927-1770. Library, 927-1350. Fax, 927-1380.

Assesses and collects duties and taxes on imported merchandise; processes persons and baggage entering the United States; collects import and export data for international trade statistics; controls export carriers and goods to prevent fraud and smuggling. Library open to the public.

U.S. Customs Service (Treasury Dept.), Trade Operations, 1301 Constitution Ave. N.W. 20229; 927-0300. Philip Metzger, director. Fax, 927-1096.

Enforces compliance with all commercial import requirements; collects import statistics; assesses and collects countervailing and antidumping duties after determinations have been made by the Commerce Dept. in conjunction with the U.S. International Trade Commission.

U.S. International Trade Commission, 500 E St. S.W. 20436; 205-2781. Don E. Newquist, chairman. Information, 205-2000. Press, 205-1819. Fax, 205-2798.

Advises Congress and the president on tariffs, commercial policy, and foreign trade; investigates effects of tariffs on imports of specific products; assists the Commerce Dept. in determining antidumping and countervailing duties. Library open to the public.

U.S. Trade Representative (Executive Office of the President), 600 17th St. N.W. 20506; 395-3204. Mickey Kantor, U.S. trade representative. Information, 395-3230. Fax, 395-3911.

Serves as principal adviser to the president and primary trade negotiator on international trade policy. Oversees the application of import remedies in cases of unfair trade practices.

See also Transportation: Maritime, Ship and Freight Regulation and Rates (p. 720)

Congress:

See International Economics, General, Congress (p. 76)

Judiciary:

U.S. Court of Appeals for the Federal Circuit, 717 Madison Pl. N.W. 20439; 633-6562. Helen W. Nies, chief judge; Francis X. Gindhart, clerk, 633-6555. Fax, 633-9629.

Reviews decisions of U.S. Court of International Trade (located in New York) on classifications of and duties on imported merchandise; settles legal questions about unfair practices in import trade (such as antidumping cases) found by the U.S. International Trade Commission and on import duties found by the Commerce Dept.

International Investment

See also Foreign Policy and Aid, International Development (p. 451)

Agencies:

Commerce Dept., International Investment, 1441 L St. N.W., #7006 20230; 606-9800. Betty Barker, chief. Fax, 606-5318.

Compiles statistics under the International Investment and Trade in Services Act for an ongoing study of foreign direct investment in

the United States and direct investment abroad by the United States.

International Trade Administration (Commerce Dept.), Trade and Economic Analysis, Main Commerce Bldg. 20230; 482-5145. Jonathan C. Menes, director. Fax, 482-4614.

Analyzes foreign direct investment in the United States. Produces reports and studies including the annual *Foreign Direct Investment in the United States: Transactions.* (Direct foreign investment is defined as foreign ownership of 10 percent or more of a firm's voting stock.)

Investment Policy Advisory Committee (Executive Office of the President), 600 17th St. N.W. 20506; 395-6120. Anne Luzzatto, director, private sector liaison. Fax, 395-7226.

Provides information and policy advice to the U.S. trade representative on direct investment issues relating to international trade, including the operations of multinational enterprise and international investment agreements. Seeks private-sector input on international trade issues; analyzes the effect of international trade policies on industry, labor, and agriculture.

Overseas Private Investment Corp. (OPIC) (International Development Cooperation Agency), 1100 New York Ave. N.W. 20527; 336-8404. Ruth Harkin, president. Information, 336-8799. Fax, 408-9859.

Provides assistance through political risk insurance, direct loans, and loan guarantees to qualified U.S. private investors to support their investments in less developed countries. Offers preinvestment information and counseling. Provides insurance against the risks of inconvertibility of local currency; expropriation; and war, revolution, insurrection, or civil strife.

State Dept., Investment Affairs, Main State Bldg. 20520; 647-1128. Bruce F. Duncomb, director. Fax, 647-0320.

Develops U.S. investment policy. Makes policy recommendations regarding multinational enterprises and the expropriation of and compensation for U.S. property overseas. Negotiates bilateral investment treaties.

Treasury Dept., Foreign Assets Control, 1500 Pennsylvania Ave. N.W., Annex Bldg., 2nd Floor 20220; 622-2510. R. Richard Newcomb, director. Fax, 622-1657.

Has authority under the revised Trading with the Enemy Act, the International Emergency

Economic Powers Act, and the United Nations Participation Act to control financial and commercial dealings with certain countries and their foreign nationals in times of war or emergencies. Regulations involving control of foreign assets and commercial transactions currently apply in varying degrees to Cuba, Haiti, Iran, Iraq, Libya, Montenegro, North Korea, Serbia, Vietnam, and Angola.

Treasury Dept., Foreign Exchange Operations, Main Treasury Bldg. 20220; 622-2650. John Lang, director. Fax, 622-2021.
Monitors foreign exchange market developments and manages the Exchange Stabilization Fund to counter disruptive market conditions and to provide developing countries with bridge loans.

Treasury Dept., International Investment, Main Treasury Bldg. 20220; 622-1860. Donald Crafts, acting director. Fax, 622-0391.
Advises senior department officials on direct foreign investment and transfer of industrial technology.

Congress:

See International Economics, General, Congress (p. 76)

International Organizations:

Inter-American Development Bank, 1300 New York Ave. N.W. 20577; 623-1100. Enrique Iglesias, president; L. Ronald Scheman, U.S. executive director, 623-1030. Information, 623-1000. Press, 623-1371. Library, 623-3210. Fax, 623-3096.
Promotes, through loans and technical assistance, the investment of public and private capital in member nations for economic and social development purposes. Supports and facilitates economic integration of the Latin American region. Library open to the public by appointment.

International Bank for Reconstruction and Development (World Bank), 1818 H St. N.W. 20433; 458-2001. Lewis T. Preston, president; Jan Piercy, U.S. executive director designate, 458-0115. Press, 473-1786. Fax, 676-0578. Bookstore, 473-5545.
International development institution funded by membership subscriptions and borrowings on private capital markets. Encourages the flow of public and private foreign investment into

developing countries through loans and technical assistance. Finances projects on many aspects of foreign economic development, including agriculture, education, health care, public utilities, telecommunications, water supply, and sewerage.

International Bank for Reconstruction and Development (World Bank), Multilateral Investment Guarantee Agency, 1818 H St. N.W. 20433; 473-6138. Akira Iida, executive vice president. Fax, 477-0741.
Seeks to encourage foreign investment in developing countries. Provides guarantees against losses due to currency transfer, expropriation, war, revolution, civil disturbance, and breach of contract. Advises member developing countries on means of improving their attractiveness to foreign investors. Membership open to World Bank member countries and Switzerland.

International Centre for Settlement of Investment Disputes, 701 19th St. N.W. (mailing address: 1818 H St. N.W., Washington, DC 20433); 458-1601. Ibrahim F. I. Shihata, secretary general. Information, 477-1234. Fax, 477-5828.
Affiliate of the World Bank that handles the conciliation and arbitration of investment disputes between contracting states and foreign investors.

International Finance Corp., 1850 Eye St. N.W. (mailing address: 1818 H St. N.W., Washington, DC 20433); 458-2001. Lewis T. Preston, president; William T. Ryrie, executive vice president, 473-0381. Fax, 676-0365.
Promotes private enterprise in developing countries through direct investments in projects that establish new businesses or expand, modify, or diversify existing businesses; provides its own financing or recruits financing from other foreign and local sources. Affiliated with the World Bank.

See also United Nations Development Programme (p. 482)

Nongovernmental:

Assn. of Foreign Investors in U.S. Real Estate, 700 13th St. N.W., #950 20005; 434-4510. James A. Fetgatter, executive director. Fax, 434-4509.
Represents foreign institutions that are interested in the laws, regulations, and economic trends affecting the U.S. real estate market. Informs the public and the government of the

contributions foreign investment makes to the U.S. economy. Examines current issues and organizes seminars for members.

The Bretton Woods Committee, 1990 M St. N.W., #450 20036; 331-1616. James C. Orr, executive director. Fax, 785-9423.

Works to increase public understanding of the World Bank, the original development institutions, and the International Monetary Fund.

Caribbean/Latin American Action, 1818 N St. N.W., #310 20036; 466-7464. Peter B. Johnson, executive director. Fax, 822-0075.

Promotes trade and investment in Caribbean Basin countries; encourages democratic public policy in member countries and works to strengthen private initiatives.

Emergency Committee for American Trade, 1211 Connecticut Ave. N.W., #801 20036; 659-5147. Robert L. McNeill, executive vice chairman. Fax, 659-1347.

Membership. U.S. corporations and banks interested in international trade and investment. Supports open trade and opposes restrictions on U.S. technology exports.

European-American Chamber of Commerce, 801 Pennsylvania Ave. N.W. 20004; 347-9292. Willard M. Berry, president. Fax, 628-5498.

Membership: American companies with operations in Europe and European companies with operations in the U.S. Works for free and fair trade and investment between the United States and the European Community.

Institute of International Finance, 2000 Pennsylvania Ave. N.W., #8500 20006; 857-3600. Charles Dallara, managing director. Fax, 775-1430.

Membership: international commercial banks, multinational corporations, and official lending agencies. Promotes better understanding of international lending transactions by improving the availability and quality of financial information on major country borrowers. Collects and analyzes information to help members evaluate credit risks of public and private borrowers in developing and middle-income countries. Studies and develops alternative solutions to the developing-country debt problem. Examines factors affecting the future of international lending.

National Assn. of Manufacturers, International Economic Affairs, 1331 Pennsylvania Ave. N.W., #1500N 20004; 637-3144. Howard Lewis III, vice president. Fax, 637-3182.

Represents manufacturing business interests on international economic issues, including international investment.

National Assn. of State Development Agencies, 750 1st St. N.E., #710 20002-4241; 898-1302. Miles Friedman, executive director. Fax, 898-1312.

Membership: directors of state economic development agencies. Assists member agencies in encouraging direct capital investment by foreign firms intending to manufacture goods in the United States. Aids in development of export promotion strategies.

R.J. Hudson Consultants, International Political Risk Consultants, P.O. Box 20652, Alexandria, VA 22320-1652; (703) 660-6341. David S. Germroth, executive director.

Assesses the political and economic risks for American businesses and individuals investing abroad.

See also Council of the Americas/The Americas Society (p. 79)

International Trade

See also Agriculture: Foreign Programs (p. 605); Export Controls (p. 545); International Labor Policy and Programs (p. 184)

Agencies:

Advisory Committee for Trade Policy and Negotiations (Executive Office of the President), 600 17th St. N.W. 20506; 395-6120. Anne Luzzatto, director, private sector liaison. Fax, 395-7226.

Serves as chief private sector advisory committee for the president, U.S. trade representative, and Congress on all matters concerning U.S. trade policy. Current activities include the North American Free Trade Agreement and negotiations to strengthen the Uruguay Round of the General Agreement on Tariffs and Trade (GATT).

Bureau of Export Administration (Commerce Dept.), Main Commerce Bldg. 20230; 482-1427. William Alan Reinsch, under secretary. In-

International Trade Associations

The following trade associations have an active interest in international trade.

Association	Contact	Phone
American Apparel Manufacturers Assn.	Carl Priestland	(703) 524-1864
American Cotton Shippers Assn.	Neal Gillen	296-7116
American Electronics Assn.	William K. Krist	682-9110
American Farm Bureau Federation	Paul Drazek	484-3613
American International Automobile Dealers Assn.	Paul Donnellan	(703) 519-7800
American Iron and Steel Institute	Frank Fenton	452-7130
American Textile Manufacturers Institute	Charles V. Bremer	862-0533
Cosmetic, Toiletry, and Fragrance Assn.	E. Edward Kavanaugh	331-1770
Cotton Council International	Vaughn Jordan	745-7805
Electronic Industries Assn.	Mark Rosenker	457-4980
Fiber, Fabric, and Apparel Coalition for Trade	Douglas Bulcao	862-0523
Footwear Industries of America	Fawn Evenson	789-1420
Footwear Retailers of America	Peter Mangione	737-5660
Japan Automobile Manufacturers Assn.	William C. Duncan	296-8537
National Automobile Dealers Assn.	Jake Kelderman	(703) 821-7010
National Cattlemen's Assn.	Alan C. Sobba	347-0228
National Council for U.S.-China Trade	Richard Brecher	429-0340
National Electrical Manufacturers Assn.	Kyle Pitsor	457-8400
National Farmers Union (Farmers Educational and Cooperative Union of America)	Barbara Webb, acting	554-1600
National Grain and Feed Assn.	Todd Kemp	289-0873
National Grain Trade Council	Robert R. Petersen	842-0400
National Retail Federation	Tracy Mullin	783-7971
United Auto Workers	Steven Beckman	828-8500
U.S. Feed Grains Council	Donna F. Dunn	789-0789

formation, 482-2721. Fax, 482-2387. Export licensing information, 482-4811.

Administers Export Administration Act; coordinates export administration programs of federal departments and agencies; maintains control lists and performs export licensing for the purposes of national security, foreign policy, and short supply. Monitors impact of foreign boycotts on the United States; ensures availability of goods and services essential to industrial performance on contracts for national defense. Assesses availability of foreign products and technology to maintain control lists and licensing.

Bureau of Export Administration (Commerce Dept.), Export Enforcement, Main Commerce Bldg. 20230; 482-3618. John Despres, assistant secretary. Fax, 482-4173.

Enforces regulation of exports of U.S. goods and technology for purposes of national security, foreign policy, and short supply. Enforces for-

eign boycotts and compliance with antiboycott provisions of the Export Administration Act.

Export Administration Review Board (Commerce Dept.), Main Commerce Bldg. 20230; 482-5863. Ronald H. Brown, chairman; Richard E. Hull, executive secretary. Fax, 482-3911.

Committee of Cabinet-level secretaries and heads of other government offices. Considers export licensing policies and actions, particularly those concerning national security matters; advises the secretary of commerce on export licensing.

Export-Import Bank of the United States, 811 Vermont Ave. N.W. 20571; 566-8144. Kenneth D. Brody, president and chairman. Information, 566-8990. Fax, 566-7524. TDD, 535-3913. Toll-free hotline, (800) 424-5201; in Washington, D.C., 289-2703.

Independent agency of the U.S. government. Aids in financing exports of U.S. goods and services; offers direct credit to borrowers outside the United States; guarantees export loans made by commercial lenders, working capital guarantees, and export credit insurance; conducts an intermediary loan program. Hotline advises businesses in using U.S. government export programs.

Foreign Trade Zones Board (Commerce Dept.), Main Commerce Bldg. 20230; 482-2862. John J. DaPonte Jr., executive secretary. Fax, 482-0002.

Authorizes public and private corporations to establish foreign trade zones to which foreign and domestic goods can be brought without being subject to customs duties.

International Trade Administration (Commerce Dept.), Main Commerce Bldg. 20230; 482-2867. Jeffrey Garten, under secretary. Press, 482-3808. Library, 482-3611. Fax, 482-5933. Publications, 482-5487.

Serves as the focal point of operational responsibilities in nonagricultural world trade. Participates in formulating international trade policy and implements programs to promote world trade and strengthen the international trade and investment position of the United States. Library open to the public.

International Trade Administration (Commerce Dept.), Basic Industries, Main Commerce Bldg. 20230; 482-5023. Michael J. Copts, deputy assistant secretary. Fax, 482-5666.

Promotes international trade, develops competitive assessments, and assists a diverse group of industries in obtaining overseas projects. Current interests include the North American Free Trade Agreement (NAFTA) and long-term trade with Japan, especially in the automotive industry.

International Trade Administration (Commerce Dept.), Eastern Europe Business Information Center, Main Commerce Bldg. 20230; 482-2645. Susan Blackman, director. Fax, 482-4473. Flash fax, 482-5745.

Provides information on trade and investment in Eastern Europe. Disseminates information on potential trade partners, regulations and incentives, and trade promotion; encourages private enterprise in the region.

International Trade Administration (Commerce Dept.), Export Promotion Services, Main Commerce Bldg. 20230; 482-6220. Janet Barnes, acting manager. Fax, 482-0115.

Promotes and directs programs to expand exports abroad; manages overseas trade missions; conducts trade fair certification programs. Participates in trade fairs and technology seminars to introduce American products abroad. Provides the business community with sales and trade information through an automated system, which allows a direct connection between U.S. and overseas offices.

International Trade Administration (Commerce Dept.), Technology and Aerospace Industries, Main Commerce Bldg. 20230; 482-1872. Ellis R. Mottur, deputy assistant secretary. Fax, 482-0856.

Conducts analyses and competitive assessments of high-tech industries, including aerospace, telecommunications, computer and business equipment, microelectronics, and medical equipment and instrumentation. Develops trade policies for these industries, negotiates market access for U.S. companies, assists in promoting exports through trade missions, shows, and fairs in major overseas markets.

International Trade Administration (Commerce Dept.), Textiles, Apparel, and Consumer Goods Industries, Main Commerce Bldg 20230; 482-3737. Rita D. Hayes, deputy assistant secretary. Fax, 482-2331.

Participates in negotiating bilateral textile and apparel import restraint agreements; responsible for textile, apparel, and consumer goods export expansion programs and reduction of nontariff barriers; provides data on economic conditions in the domestic textile, apparel, and consumer goods markets, including impact of imports.

International Trade Administration (Commerce Dept.), Trade and Economic Analysis, Main Commerce Bldg. 20230; 482-5145. Jonathan C. Menes, director. Fax, 482-4614.

Conducts policy-oriented research and analysis of U.S. international trade and competitive performance; analyzes international economic factors affecting U.S. trade; forecasts and identifies future trade trends and problems. Produces *U.S. Industrial Outlook*, an annual report on U.S. trade performance. Foreign Trade Reference Room open to the public.

International Trade Administration (Commerce Dept.), Trade and Industry Statistics, Main Commerce Bldg. 20230; 482-4211. Bill Sullivan, director. U.S. Foreign Trade Reference Room, 482-2185.

Maintains all U.S. and foreign import and export statistics. U.S. Foreign Trade Reference Room open to the public.

International Trade Administration (Commerce Dept.), Trade Information Center, Main Commerce Bldg. 20230; 482-0543. Tom Cox, director. Toll-free, (800) 872-8723. Fax, 482-4473. TDD, (800) 833-8723.
Counsels U.S. business firms on programs and services provided by the agencies that are members of the Trade Promotion Coordinating Committee to facilitate exports. Agencies include the departments of Agriculture and Commerce, Export-Import Bank, OPIC, and AID. *(See Regional Federal Information Sources list, p. 818.)*

International Trade Administration (Commerce Dept.), U.S. and Foreign Commercial Service, Main Commerce Bldg. 20230; 482-5777. Lauri Fitz-Pegado, director general designate. Fax, 482-5013. TDD, 482-1669.
Acts as liaison with foreign government agencies to monitor and protect U.S. commercial interests abroad. Supports Commerce Dept. overseas trade missions. Provides U.S. firms with information on export markets and overseas business regulations and practices; assists American businesses in resolving trade complaints against foreign companies and governments.

Justice Dept., Antitrust Division, Main Justice Bldg. 20530; 514-2464. Charles S. Stark, chief, foreign commerce. Fax, 514-4508.
Acts as the division's liaison with foreign governments and international organizations including the European Community. Works with the State Dept. to exchange information with foreign governments concerning investigations involving foreign corporations and nationals.

National Institute of Standards and Technology (Commerce Dept.), Standards Code and Information, Route I-270 and Quince Orchard Rd., Gaithersburg, MD 20899; (301) 975-4030. John Donaldson, chief. Fax, (301) 963-2871.
GATT recording, (301) 975-4041. National Center for Standards and Certification Information, (301) 975-4040.
Compiles information on proposed foreign technical regulations. Provides recorded information on selected international trade regulation matters from the GATT (General Agreement on Tariffs and Trade) secretariat in Switzerland. Maintains National Center for Standards and Certification Information to provide U.S. exporters with information on product standards in foreign countries.

President's Export Council (Commerce Dept.), Main Commerce Bldg. 20230; 482-1124. Wendy Haimes Smith, director. Fax, 482-4452.
Advises the president on all aspects of export trade including export controls, promotion, and expansion.

Services Policy Advisory Committee (Executive Office of the President), 600 17th St. N.W. 20506; 395-6120. Anne Luzzatto, director, private sector liaison. Fax, 395-7226.
Advises and makes recommendations to the U.S. trade representative on a wide range of service industry issues in order to remove barriers to international trade. Issues include improving ways to resolve service problems, planning future bilateral and multilateral negotiations, and resolving international investment problems and major domestic problems faced by the service industry.

Small Business Administration, International Trade, 409 3rd St. S.W., #6100 20416; 205-6720. Irene Fisher, director. Library, 205-7033. Fax, 205-7272.
Offers instruction, assistance, and information on exporting through counseling and conferences. Helps businesses gain access to export financing through loan guarantee programs.

State Dept., Economic and Business Affairs, Main State Bldg. 20520; 736-4167. Paul Cleveland, coordinator. Fax, 647-5957.
Serves as primary contact in the State Dept. for U.S. businesses. Coordinates efforts to facilitate U.S. business interests abroad, ensures that U.S. business interests are given sufficient consideration in foreign policy, and provides assistance to firms with problems overseas (such as claims and trade complaints). Works with agencies in the Trade Promotion Coordinating Committee to better integrate assistance to U.S. business overseas.

State Dept., International Trade Controls, Main State Bldg. 20520; 647-1625. Christopher G. Hankin, deputy assistant secretary. Fax, 647-3205.
Develops and implements U.S. economic policy involving international trade matters. Coordinates U.S. participation in multilateral strategic trade control and revisions related to the export of strategically critical high-technology goods.

Cooperates with the Commerce and Defense departments in formulating export control policies and programs.

State Dept., Trade and Commercial Affairs, Main State Bldg., EB/TDC, Rm. 3336 20520; 647-2532. Joanna R. Shelton, deputy assistant secretary. Fax, 647-2302.

Develops and administers policies and programs on international trade, including trade negotiations and agreements, import relief, unfair trade practices, trade relations with developing countries, export development, and export controls (including controls imposed for national security or foreign policy purposes).

Technology Administration (Commerce Dept.), International Technology Policy and Programs, Main Commerce Bldg. 20230; 482-5150. Elliot Maxwell, director. Fax, 482-4826.

Develops and implements policies to enhance the competitiveness of U.S. technology-based industry. Provides information on foreign research and development; coordinates, on behalf of the Commerce Dept., negotiation of international science and technology agreements. Administers the Japan Technology program, which seeks to ensure access for U.S. researchers and industry to Japanese science and technology.

Trade Promotion Coordinating Committee, Main Commerce Bldg., Rm. 3051 20230; 482-5455. Ron Brown, chairman; Ann Lyons, director. Fax, 482-3959.

Coordinates all export promotion and export financing activities of the U.S. government. Comprises representatives from the departments of Commerce, State, Treasury, Defense, Interior, Agriculture, Labor, Transportation, and Energy, OMB, U.S. Trade Representative, Council of Economic Advisers, EPA, Small Business Administration, AID, Export-Import Bank, Overseas Private Investment Corporation, U.S. Trade and Development Agency, and U.S. Information Agency.

Treasury Dept., International Trade, Main Treasury Bldg. 20220; 622-2110. T. Whittier Warthin, director. Fax, 622-1731.

Formulates Treasury Dept. foreign trade policies and coordinates them with other agencies.

Treasury Dept., Trade Finance, Main Treasury Bldg. 20220; 622-1739. William L. McCamey, director. Fax, 622-0967.

Reviews lending policies of the Export-Import Bank, the Commodity Credit Corp., and the Defense Dept.'s foreign military sales program. Serves as U.S. representative to the Export Credits Group, a committee of the Organization for Economic Cooperation and Development, and negotiates international arrangements for export credits.

U.S. International Trade Commission, 500 E St. S.W. 20436; 205-2781. Don E. Newquist, chairman. Information, 205-2000. Press, 205-1819. Fax, 205-2798.

Advises Congress and the president on tariffs, commercial policy, and foreign trade; investigates importation of goods into the United States in terms of their effect on domestic industry and agriculture. Assists Commerce Dept. in determining antidumping and countervailing duties. Library open to the public.

U.S. International Trade Commission, Industries, 500 E St. S.W. 20436; 205-3296. Vern Simpson, director. Fax, 205-3161.

Identifies, analyzes, and develops data on economic and technical matters related to the competitive position of the United States in domestic and world markets in agriculture, mining, and manufacturing.

U.S. Trade and Development Agency, 1621 N. Kent St., #309, Arlington, VA (mailing address: State Annex 16, Rm. 309, Washington, DC 20523); (703) 875-4357. J. Joseph Grandmaison, director. Fax, (703) 875-4009.

Assists U.S. companies exporting to developing and middle income countries. Provides technical assistance and identifies commercial opportunities in these countries.

U.S. Trade Representative (Executive Office of the President), 600 17th St. N.W. 20506; 395-3204. Mickey Kantor, U.S. trade representative. Information, 395-3230. Fax, 395-3911.

Serves as principal adviser to the president and primary trade negotiator on international trade policy. Develops and coordinates U.S. trade policy including commodity and direct investment matters; import remedies; East-West trade policy; U.S. export expansion policy; and the implementation of MTN (Multilateral Trade Negotiations) agreements. Conducts international trade negotiations and represents the United States in General Agreement on Tariffs and Trade (GATT) matters.

Congress:

See *International Economics, General, Congress (p. 76)*

Nongovernmental:

American League for Exports and Security Assistance, 122 C St. N.W., #310 20001; 783-0051. Anna Stout, executive vice president. Fax, 737-4727.

Membership: aerospace and high-technology companies. Provides information on export controls and the preservation of American jobs.

Bankers Assn. for Foreign Trade, 1600 M St. N.W., 7th Floor 20036; 452-0952. Mary Condeelis, executive director. Fax, 452-0959.

Membership: U.S. commercial banks with major international operations; foreign banks with U.S. operations are affiliated as nonvoting members. Monitors activities that affect the operation of foreign and domestic commercial banks.

Emergency Committee for American Trade, 1211 Connecticut Ave. N.W., #801 20036; 659-5147. Robert L. McNeill, executive vice chairman. Fax, 659-1347.

Membership: U.S. corporations and banks interested in international trade and investment. Supports open trade and opposes restrictions on U.S. technology exports.

European-American Chamber of Commerce, 801 Pennsylvania Ave. N.W. 20004; 347-9292. Willard M. Berry, president. Fax, 628-5498.

Membership: American companies with operations in Europe and European companies with operations in the U.S. Works for free and fair trade and investment between the United States and the European Community.

International Network for Women in Enterprise and Trade, 6819 Elm St., #3, McLean, VA (mailing address: P.O. Box 6178, McLean, VA 22106); (703) 893-8541. Christina R. Lane, president. Fax, (703) 241-0090.

Membership: women business owners, executives, and students. Promotes increased participation of women in international commerce. Serves as a forum for the exchange of information on world affairs and business developments.

International Trade Commission Trial Lawyers Assn., 601 13th St. N.W., #500N 20005; 783-5070. Arthur Wineburg, president. Fax, 783-2331.

Disseminates information relating to practice before the International Trade Commission. Monitors and comments on proposed legislation on trade and intellectual property issues.

Japan Productivity Center, 1729 King St., #100, Alexandria, VA 22314; (703) 838-0414. Daisaku Harada, director, U.S. office. Fax, (703) 838-0419.

Promotes education and exchange of information between Japanese and American businesspeople by coordinating overseas meetings and visits for participating countries. (Headquarters in Tokyo.)

U.S.-Arab Chamber of Commerce, 1825 K St. N.W., #1107 20006; 331-8010. Richard Holmes, president. Fax, 331-8297.

Membership: U.S. businesses active in Arab markets. Examines economic policies of U.S. and Arab governments; conducts research on business issues; certifies trade documents and coordinates international trade delegations.

See also American Hellenic Institute (p. 462); Citizens for a Sound Economy (p. 51); National Assn. of Manufacturers (p. 53)

Patents, Copyrights, and Trademarks

Agencies:

Justice Dept., Civil Division, 550 11th St. N.W. 20530; 514-7223. Vito J. DiPietro, director, commercial litigation. Fax, 514-7969.

Represents the United States in patent, copyright, and trademark cases. Includes the defense of patent infringement suits; legal proceedings to establish government priority of invention; defense of administrative acts of the Register of Copyrights; and actions on behalf of the government involving the use of trademarks.

Patent and Trademark Office (Commerce Dept.), 2121 Crystal Park II, #906, Arlington, VA (mailing address: Washington, DC 20231); (703) 305-8600. Bruce A. Lehman, commissioner. Information, (703) 308-4357. Press, (703) 305-8341. Library, (703) 308-0808. Fax, (703) 305-8664.

Grants patents, registers trademarks, and provides patent and trademark information. Scientific library and search file of U.S. and foreign patents available for public use.

State Dept., Intellectual Property and Competition, Main State Bldg., Rm. 2835 20520; 647-1998. Howard Lange, director. Fax, 647-5936.

Handles multilateral and bilateral policy formulation involving patents, copyrights, and trademarks, and international industrial property of U.S. nationals.

U.S. Customs Service (Treasury Dept.), Intellectual Property Rights, 1099 14th St. N.W. (mailing address: 1301 Constitution Ave. N.W., Washington, DC 20229); 482-6960. John Atwood, chief. Fax, 482-6943.

Responsible for Customs recordation of registered trademarks and copyrights. Enforces rules and regulations pertaining to intellectual property rights. Coordinates enforcement of International Trade Commission exclusion orders against unfairly competing goods. Determines admissibility of restricted merchandise and cultural properties. Provides support to and coordinates with international organizations and the Office of the U.S. Trade Representative.

Congress:

House Judiciary Committee, Subcommittee on Intellectual Property and Judicial Administration, 207 CHOB 20515; 225-3926. William J. Hughes, D-N.J., chairman; Hayden W. Gregory, chief counsel.

Jurisdiction over patent, trademark, and copyright legislation, including legislation on home audio and video taping, intellectual property rights, and financial syndication.

House Science, Space, and Technology Committee, Subcommittee on Technology, Environment, and Aviation, B374 RHOB 20515; 225-9662. Tim Valentine, D-N.C., chairman; James H. Turner, staff director.

Jurisdiction over patent and intellectual property policies.

Library of Congress, Copyright Office, 101 Independence Ave. S.E. 20559; 707-8350. Barbara Ringer, acting register of copyrights. Information, 707-3000. Fax, 707-8366.

Provides information on copyright registration procedures and requirements, copyright law, and international copyrights; registers copyright claims and maintains public records of copyright registrations. Copyright record searches

conducted on an hourly fee basis. Files open to public for research during weekday business hours. Does not give legal advice on copyright matters.

Senate Commerce, Science, and Transportation Committee, Subcommittee on Science, Technology, and Space, SH-427 (mailing address: SD-508, Washington, DC 20510); 224-9360. John D. Rockefeller IV, D-W.Va., chairman; Patrick H. Windham, senior professional staff member.

Jurisdiction over patent and intellectual property policies.

Senate Judiciary Committee, Subcommittee on Patents, Copyrights, and Trademarks, SH-327 20510; 224-8178. Dennis DeConcini, D-Ariz., chairman; Karen Robb, chief counsel.

Jurisdiction over patent, trademark, and copyright legislation, including legislation on home audio and video taping, intellectual property rights, and financial syndication.

Judiciary:

U.S. Court of Appeals for the Federal Circuit, 717 Madison Pl. N.W. 20439; 633-6562. Helen W. Nies, chief judge; Francis X. Gindhart, clerk, 633-6555. Fax, 633-9629.

Reviews decisions of U.S. Patent and Trademark Office on applications and interferences regarding patents and trademarks; hears appeals on patent infringement cases from district courts.

Nongovernmental:

American Bar Assn., Intellectual Property Law, 1800 M St. N.W., #200 20036; 331-2617. J. "Jan" Jancin Jr., staff legislative consultant. Fax, 331-2220.

Membership: attorneys practicing intellectual property law, including patent, trademark, copyright, and related unfair competition law. Promotes development and improvement of intellectual property treaties, laws, and regulations and monitors their enforcement; conducts continuing legal education programs.

American Intellectual Property Law Assn., 2001 Jefferson Davis Highway, #203, Arlington, VA 22202; (703) 415-0780. Michael W. Blommer, executive director. Fax, (703) 415-0786.

Membership: lawyers practicing in the field of patents, trademarks, and copyrights (intellectual property law). Holds continuing legal education conferences.

Assn. of American Publishers, 1718 Connecticut Ave. N.W., #700 20009; 232-3335. Carol A. Risher, director, copyrights and new technology. Fax, 745-0694.

Monitors copyright activity in government, Congress, and international forums and institutions; sponsors seminars open to the public for a fee.

Educators Ad Hoc Committee on Copyright Law, c/o National School Boards Assn., 1680 Duke St., Alexandria, VA 22314; (703) 838-6710. August W. Steinhilber, chairman. Fax, (703) 683-7590.

Organization of educators, librarians, and scholars that promotes a broad interpretation of copyright law to permit legitimate scholarly use of published and musical works, videotaped programs, and materials for computer-assisted instruction.

Intellectual Property Owners, 1255 23rd St. N.W., #850 20037; 466-2396. Herbert C. Wamsley, executive director. Fax, 833-3636.

Monitors legislation and conducts educational programs to protect intellectual property and trade secrets through patents, trademarks, and copyrights.

International Copyright Information Center, 1718 Connecticut Ave. N.W., #700 20009; 232-3335. Carol A. Risher, director, copyrights and new technology. Fax, 745-0694.

Serves as a clearinghouse for information on American copyright holders. Aids publishers in developing countries in contacting American publishers for reprint and translation rights.

Japan Information Access Project, 1706 R St. N.W. 20009; 332-5224. Mindy Kotler, director. Fax, 332-6841.

Membership organization that teaches business executives, scientists, engineers, educators, legislators, and journalists how to access, evaluate, and use Japanese-source information in business, science, and technology. Helps American managers integrate Japanese information and U.S. policies toward Japan in their strategic planning. Maintains programs on specific topics, including electronics, financial services, biomedical technologies and pharmaceuticals, and intellectual property.

National Assn. of Manufacturers, Task Force on Intellectual Property, 1331 Pennsylvania Ave. N.W., #1500N 20004-1790; 637-3147. William Morin, director. Fax, 637-3182.

Develops policy and legislation on patents, copyrights, and trademarks.

U.S. Chamber of Commerce, Legal and Regulatory Affairs, 1615 H St. N.W., #517 20062; 463-5513. Tyler J. Wilson, attorney. Fax, 887-3445.

Monitors legislation and regulations on patents, copyrights, and trademarks.

See also Council of Scientific Society Presidents (p. 666); Information Industry Assn. (p. 165); National Assn. of Plant Patent Owners (p. 671); Recording Industry Assn. of America (p. 120)

Small Business

Agencies:

Agency for International Development (AID) (International Development Cooperation Agency), Small and Disadvantaged Business Utilization/Minority Resource Center, 1100 Wilson Blvd., Arlington, VA (mailing address: State Annex 14, Washington, DC 20523); (703) 875-1551. Ivan R. Ashley, director. Fax, (703) 875-1862.

Provides information to U.S. business firms seeking export sales and contracts under AID financing. Devotes special attention to assisting small businesses and minority-owned firms.

Commerce Dept., Business Liaison, Main Commerce Bldg. 20230; 482-3942. Melissa Moss, director. Information, 482-1302. Fax, 482-4054. Business assistance, 482-3176.

Serves as the central office for business assistance. Handles requests for information and services as well as complaints and suggestions from businesses; provides a forum for businesses to comment on federal regulations; initiates meetings on policy issues with industry groups, business organizations, trade and small-business associations, and the corporate community. Business Assistance Office provides information, advice, and guidance on federal policies and programs, selling to government markets, financial assistance programs, and domestic and international business statistics.

Federal Insurance Administration (Federal Emergency Management Agency), 500 C St. S.W. 20472; 646-2781. Vacant, administrator. Fax, 646-3445.

Administers federal crime and flood insurance programs. Makes available to eligible small businesses low-cost flood and crime insurance.

Food and Drug Administration (Health and Human Services Dept.), Small Business, Scientific, and Trade Affairs, 5600 Fishers Lane, Rockville, MD 20857; (301) 443-6776. Mary Ann Danello, director. Fax, (301) 443-5153.

Serves as liaison between the small-business community and the FDA. Assists small businesses in complying with FDA regulatory requirements.

General Services Administration, Small and Disadvantaged Business Utilization, 18th and F Sts. N.W. 20405; 501-1021. Joan Parrott-Fonseca, director. Fax, 208-5938.

Works to increase small-business procurement of government contracts. Provides policy guidance and direction for GSA Business Service Centers, which offer advice and assistance to businesses interested in government procurement. *(See Regional Federal Information Sources list, p. 846.)*

National Science Foundation, Small Business Innovation Research Program, 4201 Wilson Blvd., Arlington, VA 22230; (703) 306-1391. Donald Senich, director. Fax, (703) 306-0337.

Funds research proposals from small science/high-technology firms. Works to increase technological innovation; offers incentives for private organizations to pursue commercial development of NSF-funded research.

National Science Foundation, Small Business Research and Development, 4201 Wilson Blvd., Arlington, VA 22230; (703) 306-1391. Donald Senich, director. Fax, (703) 306-0337.

Serves as liaison between the small-business community and NSF offices awarding grants and contracts. Assists small businesses in obtaining information about NSF programs and grants; makes recommendations on how the NSF can better utilize the capabilities of science- and technology-based small businesses.

Securities and Exchange Commission, Economic Analysis, 450 5th St. N.W. 20549; 272-7102. Susan Woodward, chief economist. Fax, 272-7132.

Provides the commission with economic analyses of proposed rule and policy changes, particularly those that affect small business, and with other information to guide the SEC in influencing capital markets. Evaluates the effect of policy changes and other factors on competition within the securities industry and among competing securities markets.

Small Business Administration, 409 3rd St. S.W. 20416; 205-6605. Erskine Bowles, administrator. Information, 205-7713. Press, 205-6740. Library, 205-7033. Fax, 205-7064. TDD, 205-7733. Toll-free information, (800) 827-5722.

Provides small businesses with financial and management assistance; offers loans to victims of floods, natural disasters, and other catastrophes; licenses, regulates, and guarantees some financing of small-business investment companies; conducts economic and statistical research on small businesses. SBA Answer Desk is an information and referral service. District or regional offices can be contacted for specific loan information. *(See Regional Federal Information Sources list, p. 862.)*

Small Business Administration, Advocacy, 409 3rd St. S.W. 20416; 205-6533. Doris S. Freedman, acting chief counsel. Fax, 205-6561.

Acts as an advocate for small-business viewpoints in regulatory and legislative proceedings. Economic Research Office analyzes the effects of government policies on small business and documents the contributions of small business to the economy.

Small Business Administration, Business Development, 409 3rd St. S.W. 20416; 205-6657. Mary Leslie, associate deputy administrator. Fax, 205-7230.

Conducts programs, through private sector initiatives and business development, to aid women business owners, veterans, the disabled, and owners of small businesses involved in international trade.

Small Business Administration, Business Initiatives, 409 3rd St. S.W. 20416; 205-6665. Monika Edwards Harrison, associate administrator. Fax, 205-7416.

Provides small businesses with instruction and counseling in marketing, accounting, product analysis, production methods, research and development, and management problems.

Small Business Administration, Financial Assistance, 409 3rd St. S.W. 20416; 205-6490. John Cox, assistant administrator. Fax, 205-7519.

Makes available guaranteed, direct, or immediate participation loans to aid in developing small businesses.

Small Business Administration, Minority Small Business and Capital Ownership Development, 409 3rd St. S.W. 20416; 205-6410. Judith Watts, associate administrator. Fax, 205-7549.

Coordinates the services provided by private industry, banks, the SBA, and other government agencies—such as business development and management and technical assistance—to increase the number of small businesses owned by socially and economically disadvantaged Americans.

Congress:

House Government Operations Committee, Subcommittee on Commerce, Consumer, and Monetary Affairs, B377 RHOB 20515; 225-4407. John M. Spratt Jr., D-S.C., chairman; Theodore Jacobs, staff director. Fax, 225-2441.

Reviews regulatory process and effect of specific regulations and paperwork on the small-business community. Oversees operations of the Small Business Administration.

House Small Business Committee, 2361 RHOB 20515; 225-5821. John J. LaFalce, D-N.Y., chairman; Jeanne Roslanowick, staff director. Fax, 225-7209.

Jurisdiction over legislation dealing with the Small Business Administration. Studies and makes recommendations on problems of American small business.

House Small Business Committee, Subcommittee on Minority Enterprise, Finance, and Urban Development, 557 Ford Bldg. (2nd and D Sts. S.W.) 20515; 225-7673. Kweisi Mfume, D-Md., chairman; Bruce Gamble, staff director.

Jurisdiction over legislation on minority business affairs and on development of urban areas.

House Small Business Committee, Subcommittee on Procurement, Taxation, and Tourism, B363 RHOB 20515; 225-9368. James Bilbray, D-Nev., chairman; Felix Martinez, staff director.

Jurisdiction over legislation on programs affecting small business; studies impact of tax policy on small business.

House Small Business Committee, Subcommittee on SBA Legislation and the General Economy, 2361 RHOB 20515; 225-5821. John J. LaFalce, D-N.Y., chairman; Jeanne Roslanowick, staff director.

Jurisdiction over legislation on the Small Business Administration and the economy.

Senate Small Business Committee, SR-428A 20510; 224-5175. Dale Bumpers, D-Ark., chairman; John W. Ball III, staff director.

Jurisdiction over legislation dealing with the Small Business Administration; oversees SBA operations. Studies problems of American small business and on programs involving minority enterprise. Reviews regulatory process and effect of specific regulations and paperwork on the small-business community.

Senate Small Business Committee, Subcommittee on Innovation, Manufacturing, and Technology, SR-428A 20510; 224-5175. Carl Levin, D-Mich., chairman; Alison Pascale, legislative assistant.

Conducts research on issues related to small business manufacturing and technology. Does not report legislation.

Senate Small Business Committee, Subcommittee on Urban and Minority-owned Business Development, SR-428A 20510; 224-5175. John Kerry D-Mass., chairman; Lee Underwood, legislative assistant.

Conducts research on issues related to urban and minority-owned business development. Does not report legislation.

Nongovernmental:

National Assn. of Investment Companies, 1111 14th St. N.W., #700 20005; 289-4336. Jo Ann Price, president. Fax, 289-4329.

Membership: investment companies that provide minority-owned small businesses with venture capital and management guidance. Provides technical assistance; monitors legislation affecting small business.

National Assn. of Small Business Investment Companies, 1199 N. Fairfax Dr., #200, Alexandria, VA 22314; (703) 683-1601. Peter F. McNeish, president. Fax, (703) 683-1605.

Membership: companies licensed by the Small Business Administration to provide small businesses with advisory services, equity financing, and long-term loans.

National Development Council, 3921 Albemarle St. N.W. 20016; 364-9641. Nelson R. Bregon, director. Fax, 364-9648.

Seeks to increase economic development in low-income communities. Assists small businesses in finding long-term financing for expansion; works to increase employment opportunities. (Headquarters in New York.)

National Federation of Independent Business, 600 Maryland Ave. S.W., #700 20024; 554-9000. Jackson Faris, president. Fax, 554-0496.

Membership: independent business and professional people. Monitors public policy issues and legislation affecting small and independent businesses, including taxation, government regulation, labor-management relations, and liability insurance.

National Small Business United, 1155 15th St. N W. 20005; 293-8830. John Paul Galles, executive vice president. Fax, 872-8543.

Membership: manufacturing, wholesale, retail, service, and other small-business firms and regional small-business organizations. Represents the interests of small business before Congress, the administration, and federal agencies. Services to members include a toll-free legislative hotline and group insurance.

Service Corps of Retired Executives Assn., 409 3rd St. S.W., #5900 20024; 205-6762. W. Kenneth Yancey Jr., executive director. Toll-free, (800) 634-0245. Fax, 205-7636.

Independent voluntary organization funded by the Small Business Administration that develops, conducts, and evaluates programs through which retired, semiretired, and active business executives use their knowledge and experience to counsel small businesses.

Small Business Foundation of America, 1155 15th St. N.W., #710 20005; 223-1103. Regina Tracy, executive director. Fax, 872-8543. Toll-free export opportunity hotline, (800) 243-7232; in Washington, D.C., 223-1104.

Sponsors and conducts scientific and economic research on small-business matters. Promotes growth of small businesses. Advocates small-business and entrepreneurial curricula and courses in educational institutions. Assists

small-business organizations and individuals wishing to establish small-business organizations. Serves as an information clearinghouse. Hotline assists small businesses with export-related questions.

Small Business Legislative Council, 1156 15th St. N.W., #510 20005; 639-8500. John Satagaj, president. Fax, 296-5333.

Membership: trade associations that represent small businesses in the manufacturing, wholesale, retail, service, and other sectors. Monitors and proposes legislation and regulations to benefit small businesses.

U.S. Chamber of Commerce, Small Business Center, 1615 H St. N.W. 20062; 463-5503. David Voight, director. Fax, 887-3445.

Seeks to enhance visibility of small business within the national chamber and the U.S. business community. Provides members with information on national small-business programs.

Statistical Data and Projections

Agencies:

Agriculture Dept., Economic Research Service, 1301 New York Ave. N.W. 20005; 219-0300. Kenneth L. Deavers, administrator. Fax, 219-0146.

Analyzes the factors affecting farm production and their relationship to the environment, prices, and income; examines the outlook for various commodities. Studies include rural development and natural resources, agricultural trade and production, government policies, and foreign demand for agricultural products.

Agriculture Dept., National Agricultural Statistics Service, 14th St. and Independence Ave. S.W. 20250; 720-2707. Donald M. Bay, acting administrator. Fax, 720-9013.

Prepares estimates and reports of production, supply, price, and other items relating to the U.S. agricultural economy. Reports include statistics on field crops, fruits and vegetables, cattle, hogs, poultry, and related products.

Bureau of Economic Analysis (Commerce Dept.), 1441 L St. N.W. 20230; 606-9600. Carol Carson, director. Information, 606-9968. Fax, 606-5234.

Compiles, analyzes, and publishes data on measures of aggregate U.S. economic activity, including gross national product; prices by type of expenditure; personal income and outlays; personal savings; corporate profits; leading, coincident, and lagging economic indicators; capital stock; U.S. international transactions; and foreign investment. Provides estimates of personal income and employment by industry for regions, states, metropolitan areas, and counties. Refers specific inquiries to economic specialists in the field.

Bureau of Labor Statistics (Labor Dept.), 2 Massachusetts Ave. N.E. 20212; 606-7800. Katharine G. Abraham, commissioner. Press, 606-5902. Fax, 606-7797.

Provides statistical data on labor economics, including labor force, employment and unemployment, hours of work, wages, employee compensation, prices, living conditions, labor-management relations, productivity, technological developments, occupational safety and health, and structure and growth of the economy. Publishes reports on these statistical trends including the Consumer Price Index, Producer Price Index, and Employment and Earnings.

Census Bureau (Commerce Dept.), Business Division, Suitland and Silver Hill Rds., Suitland, MD (mailing address: Washington, DC 20233); (301) 763-7564. Howard N. Hamilton, chief. Fax, (301) 763-4817.

Provides data of five-year census programs on retail, wholesale, and service industries. Conducts periodic monthly or annual surveys for specific items within these industries.

Census Bureau (Commerce Dept.), Economic Census and Surveys, Suitland and Silver Hill Rds., Suitland, MD (mailing address: Washington, DC 20233-6100); (301) 763-7735. Thomas L. Mesenbourg, chief. Fax, (301) 763-1909.

Provides data and explains proper use of data on county business patterns, classification of industries and commodities, and business statistics. Compiles quarterly reports listing financial data for corporations in certain industrial sectors.

Census Bureau (Commerce Dept.), Foreign Trade, Suitland and Silver Hill Rds., Suitland, MD (mailing address: Washington, DC 20233); (301) 763-5342. C. Harvey Monk, chief. Fax, (301) 763-4171. Trade data inquiries, (301) 763-5140.

Provides data on all aspects of foreign trade in commodities.

Census Bureau (Commerce Dept.), Governments Division, Washington Plaza II, #407, Marlow Heights, MD (mailing address: Washington, DC 20233); (301) 763-7366. Gordon W. Green, chief. Fax, (301) 763-4493.

Provides data and explains proper use of data concerning state and local governments, employment, finance, governmental organization, and taxation.

Census Bureau (Commerce Dept.), Industry Division, Suitland and Silver Hill Rds., Suitland, MD (mailing address: Washington, DC 20233); (301) 763-5850. John P. Govoni, chief. Fax, (301) 763-7582.

Collects and distributes manufacturing and mineral industry data. Reports are organized by commodity, industry, and geographic area.

Council of Economic Advisers (Executive Office of the President), Statistical Office, Old Executive Office Bldg. 20500; 395-5062. Catherine H. Furlong, senior statistician. Fax, 395-5630.

Compiles and reports aggregate economic data, including national income and expenditures, employment, wages, productivity, production and business activity, prices, money stock, credit, finance, government finance, corporate profits and finance, agriculture, and international statistics, including balance of payments and import-export levels by commodity and area. Data published in the *Annual Economic Report* and the monthly *Economic Indicators,* published by the congressional Joint Economic Committee.

Federal Reserve System, International Finance, 20th and C Sts. N.W. 20551; 452-3614. Edwin M. Truman, staff director. Fax, 452-6424.

Compiles and publishes statistical data on international economics in the *Federal Reserve Bulletin;* data include balance of payments, international trade, and exchange rates.

Federal Reserve System, Monetary Affairs, 20th and C Sts. N.W. 20551; 452-3761. Donald L. Kohn, director. Fax, 452-5296.

Analyzes monetary policy and issues related to open market operations, reserve requirements, and discount policy. Reports statistics associated with monetary aggregates; issues related to the government securities market; and economic aspects of other regulatory issues closely related to monetary policy, such as banking, loans, and securities.

Federal Reserve System, Research and Statistics, 20th and C Sts. N.W. 20551; 452-3301. Michael J. Prell, director. Fax, 452-5296. Publications, 452-3245.

Publishes statistical data on business finance, real estate credit, consumer credit, industrial production, construction, and flow of funds.

Internal Revenue Service (Treasury Dept.), Statistics of Income, 500 N. Capitol St. N.W. (mailing address: R:S, 1111 Constitution Ave. N.W., Washington, DC 20224); 874-0700. Fritz Scheuren, director. Fax, 874-0922. Publications, 874-0410.

Provides the public and the Treasury Dept. with statistical information on tax laws. Prepares statistical information for the Commerce Dept. to use in formulating the gross national product (GNP). Publishes *Statistics of Income,* a series available at cost to the public.

International Trade Administration (Commerce Dept.), Basic Industries, Main Commerce Bldg. 20230; 482-5023. Michael J. Copts, deputy assistant secretary. Fax, 482-5666.

Analyzes and maintains data on a wide range of industries including petroleum, coal, gas, biotechnology, metals, agricultural commodities, chemicals and pharmaceuticals, lumber and paper, construction materials, automotive, energy and environmental, and food processing and packaging.

International Trade Administration (Commerce Dept.), Trade and Economic Analysis, Main Commerce Bldg. 20230; 482-5145. Jonathan C. Menes, director. Fax, 482-4614.

Monitors developments in major U.S. industrial sectors. Produces studies, including *U.S. Industrial Outlook,* which reports business planning and marketing data on more than 350 industries and projects economic trends for selected industries.

Office of Management and Budget (Executive Office of the President), Statistical Policy, New Executive Office Bldg., #3228 20503; 395-3093. Katherine K. Wallman, chief. Fax, 395-7245.

Carries out the statistical policy and coordination functions under the Paperwork Reduction Act of 1980; develops long-range plans for improving federal statistical programs; develops policy standards and guidelines for statistical data collection, classification, and publication; evaluates statistical programs and agency performance.

Securities and Exchange Commission, Economic Analysis, 450 5th St. N.W. 20549; 272-7102. Susan Woodward, chief economist. Fax, 272-7132.

Publishes data on trading volume of the stock exchanges; compiles statistics on financial reports of brokerage firms.

Congress:

Congressional Budget Office, 405 Ford Bldg. (2nd and D Sts. S.W.) 20515; 226-2700. Robert D. Reischauer, director. Information, 226-2600. Fax, 225-7509.

Nonpartisan office that provides the House and Senate with budget-related information and analyses of alternative fiscal policies.

House Budget Committee, 214 O'Neill Bldg. (300 New Jersey Ave. S.E.) 20515; 226-7200. Martin Olav Sabo, D-Minn., chairman; Eileen Baumgartner, chief of staff. Fax, 226-7233.

Makes available statistics pertaining to budget proposals put forward by the president and Congress. Oversight of the Congressional Budget Office.

Joint Economic Committee, SD-G01 20510; 224-5171. Rep. David R. Obey, D-Wis., chairman; Richard McGahey, executive director. Fax, 224-0240.

Maintains statistics on nearly all facets of economic activity; provides information to the public or refers individuals to office where information is available; provides statistics on economy pertaining to energy and environment; publishes monthly *Economic Indicators* from data supplied by the Council of Economic Advisers.

Senate Budget Committee, SD-621 20510; 224-0642. Jim Sasser, D-Tenn., chairman; Larry Stein, staff director.

Makes available statistics pertaining to budget proposals put forward by the president and Congress. Oversight of Congressional Budget Office.

International Organizations:

European Community Press and Public Affairs, 2100 M St. N.W. 20037; 862-9500. Andreas A. M. van Agt, ambassador; Peter Doyle, director. Information, 862-9542. Press, 862-9540. Fax, 429-1766.

Provides policy data on the European Community and statistics on member nations. Library open to the public by appointment.

International Bank for Reconstruction and Development (World Bank), 1818 H St. N.W. 20433; 458-2001. Lewis T. Preston, president; Jan Piercy, U.S. executive director designate, 458-0115. Press, 473-1786. Fax, 676-0578. Bookstore, 473-5545.

Collects data on selected economic indicators, world trade, flow of financial resources, and external public debt. Most data and the bank's financial statements are published in the bank's annual report, the *World Debt Tables*, and the *World Development Report*.

International Monetary Fund (IMF), Statistics, 1825 Eye St. N.W. (mailing address: 700 19th St. N.W., Washington, DC 20431); 623-7900. John B. McLenaghan, director. Fax, 623-6460. Publications, 623-7430.

Publishes monthly *International Financial Statistics*, which includes comprehensive financial data for most countries, and *Direction of Trade Statistics*, a quarterly publication, which includes information on the distribution of exports and imports for about 160 countries. Annual statistical publications include the *Balance of Payments Statistics, Direction of Trade Statistics*, the *Government Finance Statistics Yearbook*, and the *International Financial Statistics Yearbook*. Subscriptions available to the public.

Organization for Economic Cooperation and Development (OECD), 2001 L St. N.W., #700 20036; 785-6323. Denis Lamb, head, Washington Center. Fax, 785-0350.

Washington Center maintains library of publications covering a wide range of economic topics, including the *OECD Financial Statistics* and *OECD Economic Surveys*. Offers OECD publications and software for sale. (Headquarters in Paris.)

United Nations Information Centre, 1889 F St. N.W. 20006; 289-8670. Michael Stopford, director. Fax, 289-4267.

Center for reference publications of the United Nations; publications include statistical compilations on international trade and development, national accounts, growth of world industry, and demographic statistics. Library open to the public.

Nongovernmental:

American Statistical Assn., 1429 Duke St., Alexandria, VA 22314; (703) 684-1221. Barbara A. Bailar, executive director. Fax, (703) 684-2037.

Membership: individuals interested in statistics and related quantitative fields. Advises government agencies on statistics and methodology in agency research; promotes development of statistical techniques for use in business, industry, finance, government, agriculture, and science.

Tourism

Agencies:

Immigration and Naturalization Service (Justice Dept.), 425 Eye St. N.W. 20536; 514-1900. Doris Meissner, commissioner. Information, 514-4316. Press, 514-2648. Fax, 514-3296.

Clears aliens and U.S. citizens for entry into the United States. Compiles statistics on tourists.

U.S. Travel and Tourism Administration (Commerce Dept.), Main Commerce Bldg. 20230; 482-0136. Greg Farmer, under secretary. Information, 482-0137. Fax, 482-4279.

Seeks to increase U.S. export earnings by increasing tourism-related trade. Formulates domestic and international trade policy; supports removal of restrictive trade barriers; conducts economic and demographic research; provides medium and small travel companies with technical assistance. Works with states and cities to provide the travel industry and consumers with information on destinations in the United States, including accommodations, transportation, and sightseeing attractions.

U.S. Travel and Tourism Administration (Commerce Dept.), Travel and Tourism Advisory Board, Main Commerce Bldg. 20230; 482-0136. Dana Shelley, director, public affairs. Fax, 482-4279.

Membership: representatives of the U.S. travel industry. Advises the secretary on travel policies; assists in preparing international tourism marketing plans; reviews policies of other federal agencies that affect the travel industry.

Congress:

House Energy and Commerce Committee, Subcommittee on Transportation and Hazardous Materials, 324 Ford Bldg. (2nd and D Sts. S.W.) 20515; 225-9304. Al Swift, D-Wash., chairman; Arthur Endres, staff director and chief counsel.

Jurisdiction over legislation affecting tourism and the U.S. Travel and Tourism Administration.

Senate Commerce, Science, and Transportation Committee, Subcommittee on Foreign Commerce and Tourism, SH-428 (mailing address: SD-508, Washington, DC 20510); 224-9325. John Kerry, D-Mass., chairman; Ivan Schlager, senior counsel.

Jurisdiction over the U.S. Travel and Tourism Administration and over legislation affecting tourism.

See also Congressional Travel and Tourism Caucus (p. 759); Senate Tourism Caucus (p. 761)

Nongovernmental:

American Hotel and Motel Assn., 1201 New York Ave. N.W., #600 20005; 289-3100. Kenneth F. Hine, president. Fax, 289-3199.

Provides operations, technical, educational, marketing, and communications services to members. Monitors legislation and regulations. Library open to the public by appointment.

American Society of Travel Agents, 1101 King St., #200, Alexandria, VA 22314; (703) 739-2782. Earlene Causey, president. Fax, (703) 684-8319.

Membership: representatives of the travel industry. Works to safeguard the traveling public against fraud, misrepresentation, and other unethical practices. Offers training programs for travel agents. Consumer affairs department offers help for anyone with a travel complaint or industry problem.

Hosteling International, 733 15th St. N.W., #840 (mailing address: P.O. Box 37613, Washington, DC 20013); 783-6161. Richard Martyr, executive director. Fax, 783-6171.

Provides opportunities for outdoor recreation and inexpensive travel through hosteling.

Travel and Tourism Government Affairs Council, 1133 21st St. N.W., 8th Floor 20036; 293-5407. Aubrey C. King, executive director. Fax, 293-3155.

Membership: travel and tourism trade organizations. Serves as a forum for the exchange of information on travel and tourism issues. Conducts research, makes policy recommendations, and monitors legislation and regulations. (Affiliate of the Travel Industry Assn. of America.)

Travel Industry Assn. of America, 1133 21st St. N.W., 8th Floor 20036; 293-1433. Edward R. Book, president. Fax, 293-3155.

Membership: business, professional, and trade associations of the travel industry and state and local associations (including official state government tourism offices) promoting tourism to a specific region or site. Encourages travel to and within the United States.

U.S. Travel Data Center, 1133 21st St. N.W., 8th Floor 20036; 293-1040. Suzanne D. Cook, executive director. Fax, 293-3155.

Membership: major components of the travel industry. Conducts research on trends in travel activity, economic effect of travel, effect of government programs on the industry, and travel supply and demand. (Affiliate of the Travel Industry Assn. of America.)

See also Self Help for Hard of Hearing People (p. 424)

Key Agencies:

Education Dept.
400 Maryland Ave. S.W. 20202
Information: 708-5366

National Archives and Records Administration
7th St. and Pennsylvania Ave. N.W. 20408
Information: 501-5400

National Endowment for the Arts
1100 Pennsylvania Ave. N.W. 20506
Information: 682-5400

National Endowment for the Humanities
1100 Pennsylvania Ave. N.W. 20506
Information: 606-8438

Key Committees:

House Education and Labor Committee
2181 RHOB 20515
Phone: 225-4527

Senate Labor and Human Resources Committee
SD-428 20510
Phone: 224-5375

Key Personnel:

Education Dept.
Richard W. Riley, secretary
Madeleine M. Kunin, deputy secretary
Norma Cantu, assistant secretary for civil rights
Sharon Porter Robinson, assistant secretary for educational research and improvement
Thomas Payzant, assistant secretary for elementary and secondary education
Kay L. Casstevens, assistant secretary for legislation and congressional affairs
David Longanecker, assistant secretary for postsecondary education
Judith Heumann, assistant secretary for special education and rehabilitative services
Augusta Kappner, assistant secretary for vocational and adult education
Eugene E. Garcia, director, bilingual education and minority languages affairs

National Archives and Records Administration
Trudy H. Peterson, acting archivist

National Endowment for the Arts
Jane Alexander, chair

National Endowment for the Humanities
Sheldon Hackney, chairman

3

Education
and Culture

Contents:

Culture: Arts and Humanities

General

Agencies:

Bureau of Land Management (Interior Dept.), Cultural Heritage, 1620 L St. N.W., #204 (mailing address: 1849 C St. N.W., #204-LS, Washington, DC 20240); 452-0330. Marilyn Nickels, chief. Fax, 452-7701.

Develops bureau policy on historic preservation, archeological resource protection, consultation with native Americans, curation of artifacts and records, heritage education, and paleontological resource management.

General Services Administration, Living Buildings Program, 18th and F Sts. N.W. 20405; 501-0842. Valerie Matthews, staff contact. Fax, 501-3296.

Arranges the opening of federal buildings for public use for cultural, educational, and recreational activities, including conferences, performing arts functions, and art exhibits.

John F. Kennedy Center for the Performing Arts, 20566; 416-8010. James D. Wolfensohn, chairman; Lawrence J. Wilker, president, 416-8670. Press, 416-8440. Library, 416-8780. Fax, 416-8205. TDD, 416-8728. Performance and ticket information, 467-4600; toll-free, (800) 444-1324.

Independent bureau of the Smithsonian Institution administered by a separate board of trustees. Sponsors educational programs; presents American and international performances in theater, music, dance, and film; sponsors the John F. Kennedy Center Education Program, which produces the annual American College Theater Festival; presents and subsidizes events for young people. Library open to the public.

National Endowment for the Arts (National Foundation on the Arts and the Humanities), 1100 Pennsylvania Ave. N.W. 20506; 682-5414. Jane Alexander, chair. Information, 682-5400. Press, 682-5570. Library, 682-5485. Fax, 682-5612. TDD, 682-5496.

Independent federal grant-making agency. Awards grants to artists and nonprofit arts organizations in design arts, folk arts and crafts, dance, education, literature, museums, music, media arts, opera, theater, and visual arts; awards matching grants to official state arts councils and community arts agencies. Library open to the public by appointment.

National Endowment for the Arts (National Foundation on the Arts and the Humanities), Expansion Arts Program, 1100 Pennsylvania Ave. N.W. 20506; 682-5443. Patrice Powell, acting director. Fax, 682-5002.

Awards matching grants to nonprofit groups for development of community-based arts programs that reflect the culture of minority, inner city, rural, and tribal communities; supports projects that create, present, or teach art.

National Endowment for the Arts (National Foundation on the Arts and the Humanities), Presenting and Commissioning Program, 1100 Pennsylvania Ave. N.W. 20506; 682-5444. Lenwood Sloan, director. Fax, 682-5612.

Awards grants to presenting organizations and artists' communities; funds artists' projects and interdisciplinary art projects.

National Endowment for the Humanities (National Foundation on the Arts and the Humanities), 1100 Pennsylvania Ave. N.W. 20506; 606-8310. Sheldon Hackney, chairman. Information, 606-8438. Fax, 606-8588. TDD, 606-8282.

Independent federal grant-making agency. Awards grants to individuals and institutions for research, scholarship, educational programs, and public programs (including broadcasts, museum exhibitions, lectures, and symposia) in the humanities (defined as study of archeology; history; jurisprudence; language; linguistics; literature; philosophy; the history, criticism, and theory of the arts; and humanistic aspects of the social sciences). Funds preservation of books, newspapers, historical documents, and photographs.

National Endowment for the Humanities (National Foundation on the Arts and the Humanities), Research Programs, 1100 Pennsylvania Ave. N.W. 20506; 606-8200. Guinevere L. Griest, director. Fax, 606-8204.

Awards grants to nonprofit research institutions, groups of scholars, and individuals for advanced research in the humanities. Projects include reference works, translations, editing of historical or literary papers, and cataloging of humanities materials and resources. Conducts publication subsidy program for university and nonprofit presses.

President's Committee on the Arts and the Humanities, 1100 Pennsylvania Ave. N.W., #526 20506; 682-5409. Ellen Lovell, executive director. Fax, 682-5668.

Recommends to the president, the National Endowment for the Arts, and the National Endowment for the Humanities ways to promote private sector support for the arts and humanities; analyzes the effectiveness of federal support for the arts and humanities.

Congress:

House Administration Committee, Subcommittee on Libraries and Memorials, 612 O'Neill Bldg. (300 New Jersey Ave. S.E.) 20515; 226-2307. William L. Clay, D-Mo., chairman; John F. Bass, staff director. Fax, 225-3963.

Jurisdiction over legislation related to the Smithsonian Institution. Oversees operations of the Smithsonian Institution.

House Appropriations Committee, Subcommittee on Interior, 3481 RHOB 20515; 225-3481. Sidney R. Yates, D-Ill., chairman; D. Neal Sigmon, staff assistant.

Jurisdiction over legislation to appropriate funds for government programs for the arts and the humanities, including the operations and programs of the Smithsonian Institution, the National Foundation on the Arts and the Humanities, the Commission of Fine Arts, the Advisory Council on Historic Preservation, and the Institute of Museum Services.

House Education and Labor Committee, Subcommittee on Labor-Management Relations, 320 CHOB 20515; 225-5768. Pat Williams, D-Mont., chairman; Jon Weintraub, staff director.

Jurisdiction over legislation on government programs for the arts and the humanities and for museums and libraries. Oversees operations of the Institute of Museum Services.

House Education and Labor Committee, Subcommittee on Postsecondary Education and Training, 2451 RHOB 20515; 226-3681. William D. Ford, D-Mich., chairman; Omer Waddles, staff director.

Jurisdiction over the National Endowment for the Arts and the National Endowment for the Humanities.

House Government Operations Committee, Subcommittee on Human Resources and Intergovernmental Relations, B372 RHOB 20515; 225-2548. Edolphus Towns, D-N.Y., chairman; Ron Stroman, staff director. Fax, 225-2382.

Oversees operations of the Smithsonian Institution (jurisdiction shared with House Administration Committee) and the National Foundation on the Arts and the Humanities.

Senate Appropriations Committee, Subcommittee on Interior, SD-127 20510; 224-7233. Robert C. Byrd, D-W.Va., chairman; Sue E. Masica, clerk.

Jurisdiction over legislation to appropriate funds for government programs for the arts and the humanities, including the Commission of Fine Arts; the National Foundation on the Arts and the Humanities; and the operations and programs of the Smithsonian Institution, the Institute of Museum Services, and the Advisory Council on Historic Preservation.

Senate Labor and Human Resources Committee, Subcommittee on Education, Arts, and Humanities, SD-648 20510; 224-7666. Claiborne Pell, D-R.I., chairman; David V. Evans, staff director.

Jurisdiction over legislation on government programs for the arts and the humanities, including the National Endowment for the Arts and the National Endowment for the Humanities. Jurisdiction over the Library Services and Construction Act. Oversees operations of the Institute of Museum Services and the National Foundation on the Arts and the Humanities.

Senate Rules and Administration Committee, SR-305 20510; 224-6352. Wendell H. Ford, D-Ky., chairman; James O. King, staff director.

Jurisdiction over legislation related to the Smithsonian Institution. Oversees operations of the Smithsonian Institution.

See also Concerned Senators for the Arts (p. 760); Congressional Arts Caucus (p. 756)

Nongovernmental:

Alliance Française de Washington, 2142 Wyoming Ave. N.W. 20008; 234-7911. Daniel Blondy, executive director. Fax, 234-0125.

Offers courses in French language and literature; presents lectures and films; maintains library of French-language publications for members.

America the Beautiful Fund, 806 15th St. N.W. 20005; 638-1649. Paul Bruce Dowling, executive director.

National service organization that promotes community self-help. Offers advisory services; grants; free seeds for civic and charitable volunteer programs; and national recognition awards to local community groups for activities that promote America's heritage, culture, environment, public parks, and human services.

American Arts Alliance, 1319 F St. N.W., #500 20004; 737-1727. Judith E. Golub, executive director. Fax, 628-1258.

Membership: symphony orchestras; art museums; arts presenters; and theater, dance, and opera companies. Advocates a national public policy for the arts.

American Historical Assn., 400 A St. S.E. 20003; 544-2422. Samuel R. Gammon, executive director. Fax, 544-8307.

Supports public access to government information; publishes original historical research, journal, bibliographies, historical directories, and job placement bulletin. Committee on Women Historians seeks to improve the status of women in the profession; promotes teaching of women's history; collects data and issues biographical directory of women historians.

American Studies Assn., 2101 S. Campus Surge Bldg., University of Maryland, College Park, MD 20742; (301) 405-1364. John F. Stephens, executive director. Fax, (301) 314-9148.

Fosters exchange of ideas about American life; supports and assists programs for teaching American studies abroad and encourages teacher and student exchanges; awards annual prizes for contributions to American studies; provides curriculum resources.

Aspen Institute, 1333 New Hampshire Ave. N.W., #1070 20036; 736-5808. Christopher Makins, vice president. Fax, 986-1913.

Conducts seminars on Western civilization and other traditions and cultures; conducts a variety of studies and workshops on critical contemporary issues. Fields of interest include communications, energy, justice and the law, science and technology, traditional and nontraditional education, international relations, social policies, rural economy, and the environment. (Headquarters in Queenstown, Md.)

Brazilian-American Cultural Institute, 4103 Connecticut Ave. N.W. 20008; 362-8334. José M. Neistein, executive director. Fax, 362-8337.

Conducts courses in Portuguese language and Brazilian literature; sponsors art exhibitions, films, concerts, and other public presentations on Brazilian culture. Library open to the public.

Japan-America Society of Washington, 1020 19th St. N.W., Lower Lobby 20036; 289-8290. Patricia R. Kearns, executive director. Fax, 789-8265.

Conducts programs and produces publications on U.S.-Japan trade, politics, and economic issues; assists Japanese performing artists; offers lectures and films on Japan; operates Japanese-language school; awards annual scholarships to college students studying in the Washington, D.C., metropolitan area; maintains library for members; lends a portable Japanese room to public schools in the Washington, D.C., metropolitan area.

National Assembly of Local Arts Agencies, 927 15th St. N.W., 12th Floor 20005; 371-2830. Robert L. Lynch, president. Fax, 371-0424.

Arts service organization that advocates support for local arts agencies. Provides information on programs, activities, and administration of local arts agencies; on funding sources and guidelines; and on government policies and programs. Monitors legislation and regulations.

National Campaign for Freedom of Expression, 918 F St. N.W., #609 20004; 393-2787. David Mendoza, executive director. Toll-free, (800) 477-6233. Fax, 347-7376.

Membership: artists, artists' organizations, and individuals. Opposes censorship. Promotes political empowerment of artists. Seeks to increase funding for the arts. Monitors legislation and regulations.

National Humanities Alliance, 21 Dupont Circle N.W., #604 20036; 296-4994. John H. Hammer, director. Fax, 872-0884.

Represents scholarly and professional humanities associations; associations of museums, libraries, and historical societies; higher education institutions; state humanities councils; and independent and university-based research centers. Promotes the interests of individuals engaged in research, writing, and teaching.

National League of American PEN Women, 1300 17th St. N.W. 20036; 785-1997. Muriel Freeman, president.

Promotes the development of the creative talents of professional women in the fields of art, letters, and music composition. Conducts and promotes literary, educational, and charitable activities. Offers scholarships, workshops, discussion groups, and professional lectures.

Society for American Archaeology, 900 2nd St. N.E., #12 20002; 789-8200. Ralph Johnson, executive director. Fax, 789-0284.

Promotes greater awareness, understanding, and research of archeology on the American continents; works to preserve and publish results of scientific data and research; serves as information clearinghouse for members.

Washington Project for the Arts, 400 7th St. N.W. 20004; 347-4813. Don Russell, executive director. Fax, 347-8393.

Artist-run organization that provides a forum for contemporary and experimental art in all disciplines. Sponsors exhibitions, performances, visual art, public art and sculpture, and residencies in the United States for national and international artists.

Wolf Trap Foundation for the Performing Arts, 1624 Trap Rd., Vienna, VA 22182; (703) 255-1920. Charles A. Walters Jr., acting president. Information, (703) 255-1900. Fax, (703) 255-1905.

Established by Congress to administer Wolf Trap Farm Park for the Performing Arts. Sponsors performances in theater, music, and dance. Conducts educational programs for children, internships for college students, career-entry programs for young singers, and professional training for teachers and performers. Maintains the grounds and buildings of Wolf Trap Farm Park and provides the Filene Center, an amphitheater, with technical assistance.

See also Institute for the Study of Man (p. 691)

Architecture and Design Arts

See also Community Planning and Development, General (p. 378); Culture: Arts and Humanities, Historic Preservation (p. 109)

Agencies:

Commission of Fine Arts, Judiciary Square, 441 F St. N.W. 20001; 504-2200. J. Carter Brown, chairman; Charles H. Atherton, secretary and administrative officer. Fax, 504-2195.

Advises the president, congressional committees, and government agencies on designs of public buildings, parks, and statuary.

General Services Administration, Art and Historic Preservation Division, 18th and F Sts. N.W. 20405; 501-1256. Dale Lanzone, director. Fax, 219-0104.

Administers the Art and Historic Preservation Program, which sets aside for art projects a percentage of the estimated construction costs for new buildings or renovation costs for existing ones.

National Endowment for the Arts (National Foundation on the Arts and the Humanities), Design Arts Program, 1100 Pennsylvania Ave. N.W. 20506; 682-5437. Alan Brangman, acting director. Fax, 682-5669.

Awards grants for design arts projects in architecture; landscape architecture; urban design and planning; historic preservation; and interior, graphic, industrial, and product design.

Congress:

See Culture: Arts and Humanities, General, Congress (p. 101)

Nongovernmental:

American Institute of Architects, 1735 New York Ave. N.W. 20006; 626-7310. Terrence McDermott, executive vice president. Library, 626-7492. Fax, 626-7426.

Membership: registered American architects. Works to advance the standards of architectural education, training, and practice. Promotes the aesthetic, scientific, and practical efficiency of architecture, urban design, and planning. Offers continuing, career, and professional education programs; sponsors scholarships and an internship program; bestows annual award for design excellence. Houses archival collection, including documents and drawings, of American architects and architecture. Library open to the public. Monitors legislation and regulations.

American Planning Assn., 1776 Massachusetts Ave. N.W. 20036; 872-0611. Michael B. Barker, executive director. Fax, 872-0643.

Membership: professional planners and others interested in urban and rural planning issues. Serves as a clearinghouse for professional planners. Sponsors professional development workshops conducted by the American Institute of Certified Planners. Prepares studies and technical reports; conducts seminars and conferences.

American Society of Interior Designers, 608 Massachusetts Ave. N.E. 20002; 546-3480. John Angle, president. Fax, 546-3240.

Offers certified professional development courses addressing the technical, professional, and business needs of designers; bestows annual scholarships, fellowships, and awards; supports licensing efforts at the state level.

American Society of Landscape Architects, 4401 Connecticut Ave. N.W., #500 20008; 686-2752. David Bohardt, executive vice president. Fax, 686-1001.

Advises government agencies on land-use policy and environmental matters. Accredits university-level programs in landscape architecture; conducts professional education seminars for members.

Associated Landscape Contractors of America, 12200 Sunrise Valley Dr., #150, Reston, VA 22091-3447; (703) 620-6363. Debra H. Atkins, executive director. Fax, (703) 620-6365.

Sponsors regional seminars, technical symposia, and trade shows; conducts research on specialized subjects including landscape maintenance, interior landscaping, reclamation and erosion control, irrigation, design and building, and financial management.

Assn. of Collegiate Schools of Architecture, 1735 New York Ave. N.W. 20006; 785-2324. Richard E. McCommons, executive director. Fax, 626-7421.

Conducts workshops and seminars for architecture school faculty; maintains research council; presents awards for student and faculty excellence in architecture; publishes directory of architecture schools in North America.

Landscape Architecture Foundation, 4401 Connecticut Ave. N.W., #500 20008; 686-0068. David Bohardt, executive vice president. Fax, 686-1001.

Conducts research and provides educational and scientific information on landscape architecture and related fields. Awards scholarships and fellowships in the field of landscape architecture.

The National Architectural Accrediting Board, 1735 New York Ave. N.W. 20006; 783-2007. John Maudlin-Jeronimo, executive director. Fax, 626-7599.

Accredits Bachelor and Master of Architecture degree programs.

National Assn. of Schools of Art and Design, 11250 Roger Bacon Dr., #21, Reston, VA 22090; (703) 437-0700. Samuel Hope, executive director.

Accrediting agency for educational programs in art and design. Provides information on art and design programs at the postsecondary level; offers professional development for executives of art and design programs.

National Council of Architectural Registration Boards, 1735 New York Ave. N.W., #700 20006; 783-6500. Samuel T. Balen, executive vice president. Fax, 783-0290.

Membership: state architectural licensing boards. Develops examination used in U.S. states and territories for licensing architects; certifies architects.

National Landscape Assn., 1250 Eye St. N.W., #500 20005; 789-2900. David L. Peiffer, administrator. Fax, 789-1893.

Serves as an information clearinghouse on the technical aspects of landscape business and design.

See also Dumbarton Oaks and National Building Museum (p. 118)

Broadcasting and Film

See also Public Broadcasting (p. 40)

Agencies:

American Film Institute (John F. Kennedy Center for the Performing Arts), 20566; 828-4000.

Jean Firstenberg, director. Fax, 659-1970. Recorded information, 785-4600.

Awards grants to film makers; preserves films (in Library of Congress archive and other archives); catalogs films; supports research. Shows films of historical and artistic importance. Theater open to the public. Operates the Center for Advanced Film and Television Studies in Los Angeles.

National Archives and Records Administration, Motion Picture, Sound, and Video, 7th St. and Pennsylvania Ave. N.W. 20408; 501-5446. Jack Saunders, chief. Fax, 501-5778.

Selects and preserves audiovisual records produced or acquired by federal agencies; maintains collections from private sector, including newsreels. Research room open to the public.

National Archives and Records Administration, Multimedia and Publications Distribution, 8700 Edgeworth Dr., Capitol Heights, MD 20743; (301) 763-1872. George H. Ziener, director. Information, (301) 763-1896. Fax, (301) 763-6025. Toll-free, (800) 788-6282.

Serves as a clearinghouse for motion pictures, video cassettes, slide sets, audiotapes, interactive video disks, and multimedia kits produced by federal agencies on a wide range of subjects. Sells and rents materials. Provides annual statistical data on audiovisual production, duplication, and distribution by the federal government.

National Endowment for the Arts (National Foundation on the Arts and the Humanities), Media Arts Program: Film/Radio/Television, 1100 Pennsylvania Ave. N.W. 20506; 682-5452. Brian O'Doherty, director. Fax, 682-5744.

Awards individuals and nonprofit organizations grants for film, video, and radio productions; funds film and video exhibitions and workshops; supports the American Film Institute.

National Endowment for the Humanities (National Foundation on the Arts and the Humanities), Humanities Projects in Media, 1100 Pennsylvania Ave. N.W., #420 20506; 606-8278. James Dougherty, director.

Awards grants for nonprofit media projects aimed at advancing knowledge of the humanities.

Congress:

Library of Congress, Motion Picture, Broadcasting, and Recorded Sound, 101 Independence Ave. S.E. 20540-4800; 707-5840. David Francis, chief. Fax, 707-2371. Film and television reading room, 707-8572. Recorded sound reference center, 707-7833.

Collections include archives of representative motion pictures (1942 to present); historic films (1894-1915); early American films (1898-1926); German, Italian, and Japanese features, newsreels, and documentary films (1930-1945); and a selected collection of stills, newspaper reviews, and U.S. government productions. Collection also includes television programs of all types (1948 to present), recordings of radio broadcasts (1924 to present), and sound recordings (1890 to present). American Film Institute film archives are interfiled with the division's collections. Use of collections restricted to scholars and researchers. Reading room open to the public.

Library of Congress, National Film Preservation Board, 101 Independence Ave. S.E. (mailing address: National Film Registry, Library of Congress, Washington, DC 20540); 707-6240. Winston Tabb, administrator. Fax, 707-6269.

Establishes guidelines and receives nominations for the annual selection of twenty-five films of cultural, historical, or aesthetic significance. Selections are entered in the National Film Registry to ensure archival preservation in their original form.

Nongovernmental:

Broadcast Pioneers Library, 1771 N St. N.W. 20036; 223-0088. Catharine Heinz, director.

Maintains library on the history of radio and television. Open to the public by appointment.

Council on International Nontheatrical Events, 1001 Connecticut Ave. N.W., #638 20036; 785-1136. Richard L. Calkins, executive director. Fax, 785-4114.

Selects and enters nontheatrical television documentary films and theatrical short subject films in international film festivals; holds semiannual screening competitions and annual showcase and awards ceremonies.

Motion Picture Assn. of America, 1600 Eye St. N.W. 20006; 293-1966. Jack Valenti, president. Fax, 293-7674.

Membership: motion picture producers and distributors. Advises state and federal governments on copyrights, censorship, cable broadcasting, and other topics; administers volunteer rating system for motion pictures.

Dance

Agencies:

National Endowment for the Arts (National Foundation on the Arts and the Humanities), Dance Program, 1100 Pennsylvania Ave. N.W. 20506; 682-5435. Sali Ann Kriegsman, director. Fax, 682-5790. TDD, 682-5496.

Awards grants to dance services organizations, presenters, companies, and choreographers.

Nongovernmental:

National Assn. of Schools of Dance, 11250 Roger Bacon Dr., #21, Reston, VA 22090; (703) 437-0700. Samuel Hope, executive director.

Accrediting agency for educational programs in dance. Provides information on dance education programs; offers professional development for executives of dance programs.

Education

See also Museum Education Programs box (p. 115)

Agencies:

Education Dept., Arts in Education, 400 Maryland Ave. S.W. 20202; 401-1356. Carolyn N. Andrews, education programs specialist. Fax, 401-2275.

Provides information on arts education programs. Awards grants to the Kennedy Center's arts and education program and to Very Special Arts, a program for the disabled.

John F. Kennedy Center for the Performing Arts, Alliance for Arts Education, 20566; 416-8858. Kathi Levin, director. Fax, 416-8802.

Provides information on exemplary arts education programs; assists education and art agencies with management, public awareness, fund raising, and state planning for arts education.

John F. Kennedy Center for the Performing Arts, Education, 20566; 416-8807. Derek Gordon, associate managing director. Fax, 416-8802. TDD, 416-8822.

Establishes state committees to encourage arts education in schools (Alliance for Arts Education project); presents performances for children at the Kennedy Center (Theatre for Young People); produces annual American College Theater Festival; sponsors the National Symphony Orchestra education program; works in cooperation with the Very Special Arts, a program for the disabled affiliated with the Kennedy Center's education office. Provides teachers and staff of performing arts institutions with opportunities for professional development.

National Endowment for the Arts (National Foundation on the Arts and the Humanities), Arts in Education Program, 1100 Pennsylvania Ave. N.W., #602 20506; 682-5426. Doug Herbert, director. Information, 682-5400. Fax, 682-5613.

Awards grants to state arts agencies for placement of professional practicing artists in educational settings and for other arts education projects.

National Endowment for the Humanities (National Foundation on the Arts and the Humanities), Education Programs, 1100 Pennsylvania Ave. N.W. 20506; 606-8373. James Herbert, executive director. Fax, 606-8243.

Awards grants to improve elementary, secondary, and higher education in the humanities. Projects supported include curricula and materials development and faculty training and development.

National Gallery of Art, Education Resources, 6th St. and Constitution Ave. N.W. 20565; 842-6273. Ruth Perlin, head. Information, 842-6179. Fax, 842-6935. Order desk, 842-6263.

Serves as an educational arm of the gallery; provides audiovisual educational materials to schools, colleges, community groups, libraries, and individuals. Answers written and telephone inquiries about European and American art.

Smithsonian Institution, Elementary and Secondary Education, 900 Jefferson Dr. S.W. 20560; 357-3049. Ann Bay, director. Information, 357-2425. Fax, 357-2116.

Serves as the Smithsonian's central education office. Provides elementary and secondary teachers with programs, publications, audiovisual materials, regional workshops, and summer courses on using museums and primary source materials as teaching tools. Publishes books and other educational materials for children. Offers summer internships to graduating high school seniors.

Nongovernmental:

National Art Education Assn., 1916 Association Dr., Reston, VA 22091-1590; (703) 860-8000. Thomas A. Hatfield, executive director. Fax, (703) 860-2960.

Membership: art teachers (elementary through university) and museum staff. Issues publications on art education theory and practice, research, and current trends; offers placement service for members; provides technical assistance to art educators.

National Assn. of Schools of Art and Design, 11250 Roger Bacon Dr., #21, Reston, VA 22090; (703) 437-0700. Samuel Hope, executive director.

Accrediting agency for educational programs in art and design. Provides information on art and design programs at the postsecondary level; offers professional development for executives of art and design programs.

Young Audiences, 1200 29th St. N.W., Lower Level 20007; 944-2790. Marie C. Barksdale, executive director. Fax, 944-2793.

Sponsors professional musicians, actors, and dancers who present arts education programs in U.S. schools; promotes career opportunities in the performing arts. Seeks to enhance the education of students through exposure to the performing arts. Researches techniques and disseminates information on developing arts education programs.

Folk and Native Arts

Agencies:

Interior Dept., Indian Arts and Crafts Board, Main Interior Bldg. 20240; 208-3773. Geoffrey Stamm, acting general manager. Fax, 208-5196.

Advises artisans and craft guilds; produces a source directory and bibliographies on arts and crafts of native Americans (including Eskimos and Aleuts); maintains museums of native crafts in Montana, South Dakota, and Oklahoma; provides information on native American crafts.

National Endowment for the Arts (National Foundation on the Arts and the Humanities), Folk Arts Program, 1100 Pennsylvania Ave. N.W. 20506; 682-5449. Daniel Sheehy, director. Fax, 682-5699.

Seeks to preserve and enhance multicultural artistic heritage through grants for folk arts projects.

National Museum of American History (Smithsonian Institution), Social and Cultural History, 14th St. and Constitution Ave. N.W. 20560; 357-2735. Rodrif Roth, acting chair. Fax, 357-1853.

Conducts research, develops collections, and cfeates exhibits on political, community, and domestic life, based on collections of folk and popular arts, ethnic and craft objects, textiles, costumes and jewelry, ceramics and glass, graphic arts, musical instruments, photographs, appliances, and machines.

Smithsonian Institution, Folklife Programs and Cultural Studies, 955 L'Enfant Plaza S.W., #2600 20560; 287-3424. Richard Kurin, director. Fax, 287-3699.

Conducts research into traditional U.S. cultures and foreign folklife traditions; produces folkways recordings, films, monographs, and educational programs; presents annual Festival of American Folklife in Washington, D.C.

See also National Endowment for the Humanities (p. 101)

Congress:

Library of Congress, American Folklife Center, 10 1st St. S.E. 20540-8100; 707-6590. Alan Jabbour, director. Fax, 707-2076. TDD, 707-9957. Archive of Folk Culture, 707-5510.

Coordinates national, regional, state and local government, and private folklife activities; contracts with individuals and groups for research and field studies in American folklife and for exhibits and workshops; maintains the National Archive of Folk Culture (an ethnographic collection of American and international folklore, grass-roots oral histories, and ethnomusicology); conducts internships and sponsors fellowships at the archive; sponsors summer concerts of traditional and ethnic music.

Nongovernmental:

American Indian Heritage Foundation, 6051 Arlington Blvd., Falls Church, VA 22044; (703) 237-7500. Princess Pale Moon, president. Fax, (703) 532-1921.

Promotes national and international cultural programs for native Americans. Sponsors the National American Indian Heritage Month; awards higher education grants and scholarships to native Americans; assists tribes in meeting emergency needs.

National Council for the Traditional Arts, 1320 Fenwick Lane, Silver Spring, MD 20910; (301) 565-0654. Joseph T. Wilson, executive director. Fax, (301) 565-0472.

Presents and provides consultation for regional and national folk festivals; offers training programs for park officials on folk culture; conducts ethnocultural surveys; coordinates exhibitions and tours of traditional folk artists with the support of the National Endowment for the Arts. Produces films and videos on traditional arts; sponsors annual national folk festival.

Genealogy

Agencies:

National Archives and Records Administration, Public Programs, 7th St. and Pennsylvania Ave. N.W. 20408; 501-5200. Linda N. Brown, assistant archivist.

Co-sponsors the National Institute of Genealogical Research, a genealogical research class taught annually by National Archives staff and outside professionals; conducts workshops.

National Archives and Records Administration, User Services Branch, 7th St. and Pennsylvania Ave. N.W. 20408; 501-5402. Sharon Fawcett, division chief. Fax, 501-5005. TDD, 501-5404.

Assists individuals interested in researching record holdings of the National Archives, including genealogical records; issues research cards to prospective genealogical, biographical, and other researchers who present photo identification. Still and motion picture research rooms located at 8601 Adelphi Rd., College Park, MD 20740.

Congress:

Library of Congress, Local History and Genealogy Reading Room, 10 1st St. S.E. 20540-5554; 707-5537. Judith Austin, head. Fax, 707-1957.

Provides reference and referral service on topics related to local history, genealogy, and heraldry throughout the United States.

Nongovernmental:

National Genealogical Society, 4527 17th St. North, Arlington, VA 22207; (703) 525-0050. Jean K. Findeis, executive director. Fax, (703) 525-0052.

Encourages study of genealogy and publication of all records that are of genealogical interest.

Maintains a large genealogical library for research. Library open to the public (closed on Tuesday and Thursday; nonmembers charged fee for use).

See also Culture: Arts and Humanities, Historic Preservation, Nongovernmental (p. 110)

Historic Preservation

See also Culture: Arts and Humanities, Washington Area History and Culture (p. 122)

Agencies:

Most federal agencies, such as the General Services Administration, the Defense Dept., and the Agriculture Dept., have historic preservation officers who coordinate agency participation in the federal historic preservation program. Their responsibilities include ensuring that agencies protect historic buildings and other cultural resources that are on or eligible for nomination to the National Register of Historic Places. They also ensure that agency actions do not adversely affect nonfederal property that is on the register or eligible for nomination to it.

Advisory Council on Historic Preservation, 1100 Pennsylvania Ave. N.W. 20004; 606-8503. Robert D. Bush, executive director. Information, 606-8504. Fax, 606-8672.

Advises the president and Congress on historic preservation; reviews and comments on federal projects and programs affecting historic, architectural, archeological, and cultural resources.

National Archives and Records Administration, Advisory Committee on Preservation, 7th St. and Pennsylvania Ave. N.W. 20408; 208-7893. Alan Calmes, executive secretary.

Advises the archivist of the United States on preservation technology and research and on matters related to the continued preservation of records of the National Archives of the United States.

National Archives and Records Administration, Cartographic and Architectural Branch, 8601 Adelphi Rd., College Park, MD 20740-6001; (301) 713-7030. John A. Dwyer, chief. Fax, (301) 713-6516.

Preserves and makes available historical records of federal agencies, including maps, charts, aerial photographs, architectural drawings, patents, and ships' plans. Research room open to the public. Records may be reproduced for a fee.

National Archives and Records Administration, Preservation Policy and Services, 7th St. and Pennsylvania Ave. N.W. 20408; 501-5355. Lewis J. Bellardo, director.

Responsible for conserving textual and nontextual records in the archives. Nontextual records include video sound recordings, motion pictures, still photos, preservation microfilming, and fee reproduction work. Conducts research and testing for materials purchased by and used in the archives.

National Capital Planning Commission, 801 Pennsylvania Ave. N.W. 20576; 724-0174. Reginald W. Griffith, executive director. Fax, 724-0195.

Central planning agency for the federal government in the national capital region, which includes the District of Columbia and suburban Maryland and Virginia. Reviews and approves plans for the preservation of certain historic and environmental features in the national capital region, including the annual federal capital improvement plan.

National Park Service (Interior Dept.), Cultural Resources, 1849 C St. N.W. (mailing address: P.O. Box 37127, Washington, DC 20013); 208-7625. Jerry L. Rogers, associate director. Fax, 208-7520.

Oversees preservation of federal historic sites and administration of buildings programs. Programs include the National Register of Historic Places, National Historic and National Landmark Programs, Historic American Building Survey, Historic American Engineering Record, Archeology and Antiquities Act Program, and Technical Preservation Services. Gives grant and aid assistance and tax benefit information to properties listed in the National Register of Historic Places.

See also National Endowment for the Arts, Design Arts Program (p. 104)

Congress:

Architect of the Capitol, Office of the Curator, HT3 CAP 20515; 225-1222. Barbara A. Wolanin, curator. Fax, 225-3167.

Preserves artwork; maintains collection of drawings, photographs, and manuscripts on and about the Capitol and the House and Senate office buildings. Maintains records of the architect of the Capitol. Library open to the public.

House Banking, Finance, and Urban Affairs Committee, Subcommittee on Housing and Community Development, B303 RHOB 20515; 225-7054. Henry B. Gonzalez, D-Texas, chairman; Nancy Libson, acting staff director. Fax, 225-4680.

Jurisdiction over historic preservation legislation not related to National Park Service properties. Oversees comprehensive planning grants to public bodies that can be used to finance surveys of historic sites and structures.

House Natural Resources Committee, Subcommittee on National Parks, Forests, and Public Lands, 812 O'Neill Bldg. (300 New Jersey Ave. S.E.) 20515; 226-7736. Bruce F. Vento, D-Minn., chairman; Richard Healy, staff director.

Jurisdiction over historic preservation legislation related to National Park Service properties.

Senate Commission on Art, S411 CAP 20510; 224-2955. George J. Mitchell, D-Maine, chairman; James R. Ketchum, curator of the Senate. Fax, 224-8799.

Maintains Senate collection of paintings, sculpture, furniture, and manuscripts; presents exhibits; maintains old Senate and Supreme Court chambers.

Senate Energy and Natural Resources Committee, Subcommittee on Public Lands, National Parks, and Forests, SD-308 20510; 224-8115. Dale Bumpers, D-Ark., chairman; David Brooks, counsel.

Jurisdiction over historic preservation legislation.

Nongovernmental:

American Institute for Conservation of Historic and Artistic Works, 1717 K St. N.W., #301 20006; 452-9545. Sarah Z. Rosenberg, executive director. Fax, 452-9328.

Membership: professional conservators, scientists, students, administrators, cultural institutions, and interested individuals. Promotes the knowledge and practice of the conservation of cultural property; supports research; and disseminates information on conservation.

Children of the American Revolution, 1776 D St. N.W. 20006; 638-3153. Phyllis P. Wathen, administrator.

Membership: descendants, age 22 years and under, of American soldiers or patriots of the American Revolution. Conducts historical, educational, and patriotic activities; preserves places of historical interest.

Council on America's Military Past-U.S.A., P.O. Box 1151, Fort Myer, VA 22211; 479-2258. Col. Herbert M. Hart (USMC, ret.), executive director. Toll-free, (800) 398-4693. Fax, 479-0416.

Membership: historians, archeologists, curators, writers, and others interested in military history and historic preservation. Interests include preservation of historic military establishments and ships.

National Preservation Institute, 401 F St. N.W., #301 20001; 393-0038. James C. Massey, president. Fax, 393-2469.

Provides training and technical assistance in historic preservation and documentation, archeology, architectural photography and history, and computer applications for historic preservation. Awards grants and loans for educational projects concerned with historic preservation.

National Society, Colonial Dames XVII Century, 1300 New Hampshire Ave. N.W. 20036; 293-1700. Sara Pellmann, headquarters secretary; Ann Wellhouse, staff genealogist, 293-1700.

Membership: American women who are lineal descendants of persons who rendered civil or military service and lived in America or one of the British colonies before 1701. Preserves records and shrines; encourages historical research; awards scholarships to undergraduate and graduate students and scholarships in medicine to persons of native American descent.

National Society, Daughters of the American Revolution, 1776 D St. N.W. 20006; 628-1776. Wayne G. Blair, president general. Fax, 879-3252.

Membership: women descended from American Revolutionary War patriots. Conducts historical, educational, and patriotic activities; maintains a genealogical library, American museum, and documentary collection antedating 1830. Library open to the public (nonmembers charged fee for use).

National Society of Colonial Dames of America, 2715 Que St. N.W. 20007; 337-2288. Linda Mattingly, administrator. Fax, 337-0348.

Membership: descendants of colonists in America before 1750. Conducts historical and educational activities; maintains federal house museum.

National Trust for Historic Preservation, 1785 Massachusetts Ave. N.W. 20036; 673-4000. Richard Moe, president. Fax, 673-4038.

Conducts seminars, workshops, and conferences on topics related to preservation, including neighborhood conservation, main street revitalization, rural conservation, and preservation law; offers financial assistance through loan and grant programs; provides advisory services; operates historic house museums, which are open to the public.

Preservation Action, 1350 Connecticut Ave. N.W. 20036; 296-2705. Nellie L. Longsworth, president.

Monitors legislation affecting historic preservation and neighborhood conservation; promotes effective management of historic preservation programs.

Society for Industrial Archeology, c/o NMAH 5014-MRC 629, Washington, DC 20560; (301) 871-9254. Amy Federman, president.

Membership: architects, engineers, historians, students, and collectors. Supports research and preservation of historic American and Canadian industrial, technological, and engineering sites, structures, and equipment; conducts urban tours of industrial sites; offers technical assistance to historians.

U.S. Capitol Historical Society, 200 Maryland Ave. N.E. 20002; 543-8919. Clarence J. Brown, president. Library, 543-0629. Fax, 544-8244.

Membership: members of Congress, individuals, and organizations interested in the preservation of the history and traditions of the U.S. Capitol. Conducts historical research; offers lectures and films; maintains information centers in the Capitol; publishes an annual historical calendar.

See also Commission on Preservation and Access (p. 164)

Holidays and Celebrations

Agencies:

Martin Luther King Jr. Federal Holiday Commission, 451 7th St. S.W., #5182 20410; 708-1005. Gerrie Maccannon, executive officer. Fax, 708-2053.

Established by Congress to encourage appropriate ceremonies and activities for the Martin Luther King Jr. federal holiday observed on the third Monday of January. Assists public and private sectors with holiday planning.

Smithsonian Institution, Folklife Programs and Cultural Studies, 955 L'Enfant Plaza S.W., #2600 20560; 287-3424. Richard Kurin, director. Fax, 287-3699.

Presents annual Festival of American Folklife in Washington, D.C.

Congress:

House Post Office and Civil Service Committee, Subcommittee on Census, Statistics, and Postal Personnel, 515 O'Neill Bldg. (300 New Jersey Ave. S.E.) 20515; 226-7523. Tom Sawyer, D-Ohio, chairman; TerriAnn Lowenthal, staff director.

Jurisdiction over legislation on holidays and celebrations.

Senate Judiciary Committee, SD-224 20510; 224-5225. Joseph R. Biden Jr., D-Del., chairman; Cynthia Hogan, chief counsel.

Jurisdiction over legislation on holidays and celebrations.

Nongovernmental:

National Conference of State Societies, Box 180, LHOB, Washington, DC 20515; 686-6292. Virginia C. Haven, vice president.

Membership: delegates representing the United States, its territories, and the District of Columbia. Principal sponsor of the annual National Cherry Blossom Festival in Washington, D.C.

Language

See also Education: Special Topics, Bilingual (p. 151)

Agencies:

Interagency Language Roundtable, Federal Center for Advancement of Language Learning,

4040 N. Fairfax Dr., #200, Arlington, VA 22203; (703) 312-5057. Craig Miller, chairman. Fax, (703) 528-6746.

Membership: federal departments and agencies involved in language training. Informs members of developments in language training techniques and technology. Promotes exchange of information and materials between government and the academic community. Develops proficiency standards. Holds conferences and workshops on proficiency-based language teaching and testing.

National Endowment for the Humanities, Special Opportunity in Foreign Language Education, 1100 Pennsylvania Ave. N.W., #302 20506; 606-8377. Angela Iovino, assistant director, elementary and secondary education; Elizabeth Welles, program officer, higher education. Fax, 606-8394. Higher education, 606-8340.

Supports foreign language instruction in U.S. schools, colleges, and universities by awarding grant money for teachers, undergraduate language programs, and special projects. Encourages instruction in less commonly taught languages, such as Russian, Japanese, Chinese, and Arabic.

Nongovernmental:

Center for Applied Linguistics, 1118 22nd St. N.W. 20037; 429-9292. Vacant, president. Fax, 659-5641.

Research and technical assistance organization that serves as clearinghouse on application of linguistics to practical language problems; interests include English as a second language, crosscultural training, teacher training and material development, language education, language proficiency test development, bilingual education, sociolinguistics, and psycholinguistics.

Joint National Committee for Language, 300 Eye St. N.E., #211 20002; 546-7855. J. David Edwards, executive director. Fax, 546-7859.

Membership: translators, interpreters, and associations of foreign language teachers (primary through postsecondary level). Supports a national policy on language study and international education. Provides forum and clearinghouse for professional language and international education associations. National Council for Languages and International Studies is political arm.

Linguistic Society of America, 1325 18th St. N.W., #211 20036; 835-1714. Margaret W. Reynolds, executive director.

Membership: individuals and institutions interested in the scientific analysis of language and languages. Holds linguistic institutes and meetings every other year.

National Foreign Language Center (Johns Hopkins University), 1619 Massachusetts Ave. N.W., 4th Floor 20036; 667-8100. David Maxwell, director. Fax, 667-6907.

Nonteaching organization that develops new strategies to strengthen foreign language competence in the United States. Holds conferences to assess adult language skills; develops ways to evaluate different teaching and learning strategies and their cost-effectiveness; researches ways to produce a higher level of retention, understanding, speaking, reading, and writing competence in foreign languages.

U.S. English, 818 Connecticut Ave. N.W., #200 20006; 833-0100. Mauro E. Mujica, chairman of the board. Fax, 833-0108.

Advocates English as the official language of the U.S. government.

See also Teachers of English to Speakers of Other Languages (p. 151)

Literature

Agencies:

National Endowment for the Arts (National Foundation on the Arts and the Humanities), Literature Program, 1100 Pennsylvania Ave. N.W., #722 20506; 682-5451. Gigi Bradford, director. Fax, 682-5729.

Awards grants to writers, poets, and translators of prose and poetry. Administers grants for programs that bring creative writers greater public exposure; awards grants to small presses and literary magazines that publish poetry and fiction.

Congress:

Library of Congress, The Center for the Book, 101 Independence Ave. S.E. 20540-8200; 707-5221. John Y. Cole, director. Fax, 707-9898.

Seeks to broaden public appreciation of books, reading, and libraries; sponsors lectures and conferences on the educational and cultural role of the book, including the history of books and printing, television and the printed word, and the publishing and production of books; cooperates with state centers and with other organizations. Projects and programs are privately funded except for basic administrative support from the Library of Congress.

Library of Congress, Children's Literature Center, 10 1st St. S.E. 20540; 707-5535. Sybille Jagusch, chief. Fax, 707-4632.

Provides reference and information services by telephone, by correspondence, and in person; maintains reference materials on all aspects of the study of children's literature, including critical reviews of current books; sponsors lectures, symposia, and exhibits; publishes annual list of outstanding books for children. Reading room open to the public.

Library of Congress, Poetry and Literature, 10 1st St. S.E. 20540; 707-5394. Rita Dove, poet laureate. Fax, 707-9946.

Advises the library on public literary programs and on the acquisition of literary materials. Arranges for poets to record readings of their work for the library's tape archive. Presents a major work of poetry at an annual program sponsored by the National Endowment for the Arts. The poet laureate is appointed by the Librarian of Congress on the basis of literary distinction.

Nongovernmental:

The Folger Shakespeare Library, 201 E. Capitol St. S.E. 20003; 544-4600. Werner Gundersheimer, director. Information, 544-7077.

Administered by the trustees of Amherst College. Maintains major Shakespearean and Renaissance materials; awards fellowships to scholars for postdoctoral research; presents concerts, poetry and fiction readings, exhibits, and other public events. Offers educational programs for elementary and secondary school students and teachers. Library open to the public by appointment.

The Writer's Center, 4508 Walsh St., Bethesda, MD 20815; (301) 654-8664. Jane Fox, director. Fax, (301) 654-8667.

Membership: writers, editors, graphic artists, and interested individuals. Sponsors workshops in writing and graphic arts, and a reading series of poetry, fiction, and plays. Provides access to word processing, typesetting, and design equipment; maintains a book gallery.

See also Alliance Française de Washington (p. 102); Brazilian-American Cultural Institute (p. 103)

Manuscripts

Agencies:

National Archives and Records Administration, 7th St. and Pennsylvania Ave. N.W. 20408; 501-5402. Trudy H. Peterson, acting archivist of the United States. Information, 501-5400. Press, 501-5525. Recorded information on activities open to the public, 501-5000.

Identifies, preserves, and makes available federal government documents of historic value; administers a network of regional storage centers and archives and operates the presidential library system.

National Archives and Records Administration, Legislative Archives, 7th St. and Pennsylvania Ave. N.W. 20408; 501-5350. Michael Gillette, director. Fax, 219-2176.

Collects and maintains records of congressional committees and legislative files from 1789 to the present. Publishes inventories and guides to these records.

National Archives and Records Administration, National Historical Publications and Records Commission, 7th St. and Pennsylvania Ave. N.W. 20408; 501-5610. Gerald George, executive director. Fax, 501-5601.

Makes plans and recommendations and provides cost estimates for preserving and publishing documentation of U.S. history. Awards grants to government and private cultural institutions that preserve, arrange, edit, and publish documents of historical importance, including the papers of outstanding Americans.

National Archives and Records Administration, Presidential Libraries, 7th St. and Pennsylvania Ave. N.W. 20408; 501-5700. John T. Fawcett, assistant archivist. Fax, 501-5709.

Directs all programs relating to acquisition, preservation, publication, and research use of materials in presidential libraries; conducts oral history projects; publishes finding aids for research sources; provides reference service, including information from and about documentary holdings.

Smithsonian Institution, Archives of American Art, 8th and F Sts. N.W. 20560; 357-2781. Richard J. Wattenmaker, director. Fax, 786-2608.

Collects and preserves manuscript items, such as notebooks, sketchbooks, letters, and journals; photos of works of art; tape-recorded interviews with artists, dealers, and collectors; exhibition catalogs; directories; and biographies and microfilms on the history of visual arts in the United States. Library open to scholars and researchers. Regional centers in Boston, Detroit, New York, and San Marino, Calif., maintain microfilm copies of a selection of the archive collections.

Congress:

Library of Congress, Manuscript Division, 101 Independence Ave. S.E. 20540-4780; 707-5383. James H. Hutson, chief. Fax, 707-6336. Reading Room, 707-5387.

Maintains, describes, and provides reference service on the library's manuscript collections, including the papers of U.S. presidents and other eminent Americans. Manuscript Reading Room primarily serves serious scholars and researchers; historians and reference librarians are available for consultation.

Library of Congress, Rare Book and Special Collections Division, 10 1st St. S.E. 20540; 707-5434. Larry Sullivan, chief. Fax, 707-4142.

Maintains collections of incunabula (books printed before 1501) and other early printed books; early imprints of American history and literature; illustrated books; early Spanish-American, Russian, and Bulgarian imprints; Confederate states imprints; libraries of famous personalities (including Thomas Jefferson, Woodrow Wilson, and Oliver Wendell Holmes); special format collections (miniature books, broadsides, almanacs, and pre-1870 copyright records); special interest collections; and special provenance collections. Reference assistance is provided in the Rare Book and Special Collections Reading Room.

Nongovernmental:

Moorland-Spingarn Research Center (Howard University), 500 Howard Pl. N.W. 20059; 806-7241. Thomas C. Battle, director. Information, 806-7239. Fax, 806-6405.

Collects, preserves, and makes available for study numerous artifacts, books, manuscripts, newspapers, photographs, prints, recordings, and other materials documenting black history and culture in the United States, Africa, Europe, Latin America, and the Caribbean. Maintains extensive collections of black newspapers and magazines; contains the works of African American and African scholars, poets, and nov-

elists; maintains collections on the history of Howard University.

See also George Meany Center for Labor Studies and the George Meany Memorial Archives (p. 198); Historical Society of Washington, D.C. (p. 122)

Museum Programs

Agencies:

Anacostia Museum (Smithsonian Institution), 1901 Fort Pl. S.E. 20020; 287-3306. Steven Newsome, director. Information, 287-3369. Fax, 287-3183. TDD, 357-1729.

Researches, interprets, and documents the history of African Americans, placing special emphasis on the experiences of residents of Georgia, Maryland, North Carolina, South Carolina, Virginia, and the District of Columbia.

Arthur M. Sackler Gallery (Smithsonian Institution), 1050 Independence Ave. S.W. 20560; 357-4880. Milo C. Beach, director. Library, 357-2091. Fax, 357-4911. TDD, 786-2374. Public programs, 357-3200 (recording).

Exhibits Asian and Near Eastern art; features international exhibitions and public programs. Presents films, lectures, and concerts. Library open to the public.

Federal Council on the Arts and the Humanities (National Foundation on the Arts and the Humanities), 1100 Pennsylvania Ave. N.W. 20506; 682-5442. Alice M. Whelihan, indemnity administrator. Fax, 682-5603. TDD, 682-5496.

Membership: administrators of federal agencies sponsoring arts-related activities. Administers the Arts and Artifacts Indemnity Act, which helps museums reduce the costs of commercial insurance for international exhibits.

Freer Gallery of Art (Smithsonian Institution), 12th St. and Jefferson Dr. S.W. 20560; 357-4880. Milo C. Beach, director. Library, 357-2091. Fax, 357-4911. TDD, 786-2374. Public programs, 357-3200 (recording).

Researches and exhibits Asian and Near Eastern art and late 19th and early 20th century American paintings.

Hirshhorn Museum and Sculpture Garden (Smithsonian Institution), 7th St. and Independence Ave. S.W. 20560; 357-3091. James T.

Museum Education Programs

Alexandria Archaeology	(703) 838-4399	National Archives	501-5210
American Assn. of Museums,		National Building Museum	272-2448
Museum Assessment Program	 289-9118	National Gallery of Art	842-6246
Arlington Arts Center	(703) 524-1494	National Museum of Women	
Assn. of Science-Technology		in the Arts	783-5000
Centers	783-7200	Navy Museum	433-4882
B'nai B'rith Klutznick Museum	. . . 857-6583	Octagon Museum	638-3221
C & O Canal	(301) 299-2026	Phillips Collection	387-2151
Capital Children's		Smithsonian Institution	
Museum	543-8600	Central education office	357-3049
Corcoran Gallery of Art	638-3211	Anacostia Museum	287-3369
Daughters of the American		Arthur M. Sackler Gallery	357-4880
Revolution (DAR) Museum	879-3241	Freer Gallery of Art	357-4880
Decatur House (National Trust		Friends of the National Zoo	673-4954
for Historic Preservation)	842-0915	Hirshhorn Museum and	
Dumbarton Oaks	342-3212	Sculpture Garden	357-3235
Federal Reserve Board	452-3686	National Air and Space Museum	786-2106
Folger Shakespeare Library	544-7077	National Museum of African Art	357-4600
Gadsby's Tavern Museum . .	(703) 838-4242	National Museum of American Art	357-3095
Historical Society of		National Museum of American	
Washington, D.C.	785-2068	History	357-3229
J.F.K. Center for the		National Museum of Natural	
Performing Arts - Alliance for		History	357-2747
Arts Education	116 8800	National Portrait Gallery	357-2920
Lyceum	(703) 838-4994	Renwick Gallery	357-2531
Mount Vernon	(703) 780-2000	Textile Museum	483-0981
National Arboretum	475-4815	Woodrow Wilson House	387-4062

Demetrion, director. Information, 357-1618. Library, 357-3222. Fax, 786-2682. TDD, 357-1696.

Preserves and exhibits contemporary American and European paintings and sculpture. Offers films, lectures, concerts, and tours of the collection.

Institute of Museum Services (National Foundation on the Arts and the Humanities), 1100 Pennsylvania Ave. N.W. 20506; 606-8536. Diane Frankle, director. Information, 606-8539. Fax, 357-4911. TDD, 606-8636.

Independent agency established by Congress to assist museums in increasing and improving their services. Awards grants for general operating support, conservation projects, and museum assessment to museums of all disciplines and budget sizes; helps fund museum associations.

National Endowment for the Arts (National Foundation on the Arts and the Humanities), Museum Program, 1100 Pennsylvania Ave.

N.W. 20506; 682-5442. Andrew Oliver Jr., director. Fax, 682-5603. TDD, 682-5496.

Awards grants for installing and cataloging permanent and special collections; traveling exhibits; training museum professionals; conserving and preserving museum collections; and developing arts-related educational programs.

National Endowment for the Humanities (National Foundation on the Arts and the Humanities), Humanities Projects in Museums and Historical Organizations, 1100 Pennsylvania Ave. N.W., #420 20506; 606-8284. Susie Jones, acting director. Fax, 606-8557. TDD, 606-8282.

Awards institutions grants for temporary or long-term exhibitions, publications, audiovisual presentations of exhibitions, and museum-based educational programs emphasizing the humanities. Awards museum professionals development grants for projects that combine humanities education with museum issues.

National Gallery of Art, 6th St. and Constitution Ave. N.W. 20565; 842-6001. Earl A. Powell III, director. Information, 737-4215. Fax, 289-5446.

Autonomous bureau of the Smithsonian Institution administered by a separate board of trustees. Preserves and exhibits European and American paintings, sculpture, and decorative and graphic arts. Offers performances, demonstrations, lectures, symposia, films, tours, and teachers' workshops to enhance exhibitions, the permanent collection, and related topics. Lends art to museums in all fifty states and abroad through the National Lending Service. Publishes monthly calendar of events.

National Museum of African Art (Smithsonian Institution), 950 Independence Ave. S.W. 20560; 357-4858. Sylvia Williams, director. Information, 357-4600. Fax, 357-4879. TDD, 357-4814.

Collects, studies, and exhibits traditional arts of Africa. Temporary exhibits feature objects from the permanent collection and from private and public collections worldwide. Library open to the public by appointment.

National Museum of American Art (Smithsonian Institution), 8th and G Sts. N.W. 20560; 357-3176. Elizabeth Broun, director. Press, 357-2247. Fax, 786-2607. TDD, 786-2414.

Exhibits and interprets American painting, sculpture, photographs, folk art, and graphic art from 18th century to present in permanent collection and temporary exhibition galleries.

National Museum of American History (Smithsonian Institution), 14th St. and Constitution Ave. N.W. 20560; 357-2510. Spencer R. Crew, director. Information, 357-3129. Library, 357-2414. TDD, 357-1563.

Collects and exhibits objects representative of cultural history, applied arts, industry, national and military history, and science and technology. Library open to the public by appointment.

National Museum of Health and Medicine (Defense Dept.), Walter Reed Medical Center, Bldg. 54 South (mailing address: Armed Forces Institute of Pathology, Washington, DC 20306); 576-2348. Dr. Marc Micozzi, director. Fax, 576-2164.

Collects and exhibits medical models, tools, and teaching aids. Maintains permanent exhibits on AIDS, Civil War medicine, and military contributions to medicine and collects specimens illustrating a broad range of pathological conditions. Open to the public. Study collection available by appointment.

National Museum of the American Indian (Smithsonian Institution), 470 L'Enfant Plaza, #7102 20560; 287-2523. W. Richard West Jr., director. Fax, 287-2538.

Established by Congress in 1989 to plan and coordinate development of the National Museum of the American Indian. The museum, scheduled to open in the late 1990s, will collect, preserve, study, and exhibit American Indian languages, literature, history, art, and culture.

National Oceanic and Atmospheric Administration (Commerce Dept.), National Weather Service Science and History Center, 1325 East-West Highway, Silver Spring, MD 20910; (301) 713-0692. Gloria J. Walker, tour coordinator. Fax, (301) 713-0610.

Maintains and exhibits historical collection of the National Weather Service. Displays include meteorological instruments, weather satellites, photographs, and a re-creation of a 19th century weather office.

National Park Service (Interior Dept.), Frederick Douglass National Historic Site, 1411 W St. S.E. 20020; 426-5961. Bill Clark, site manager. Fax, 426-0880.

Museum of the life and work of abolitionist Frederick Douglass and his family. Offers tours of the home and special programs, such as documentary films, videos, and slide presentations; maintains visitor's center and bookstore.

National Portrait Gallery (Smithsonian Institution), 8th and F Sts. N.W. 20560; 357-1915. Alan Fern, director. Information, 357-2390. Library, 357-1886. Fax, 786-2565. TDD, 357-1729.

Exhibits paintings, photographs, sculpture, and prints of individuals who have made significant contributions to the history, development, and culture of the United States. Library open to the public.

Renwick Gallery (Smithsonian Institution), 17th St. and Pennsylvania Ave. N.W. 20560; 357-2531. Michael Monroe, curator-in-charge. Information, 357-2700. Press, 357-2247. Fax, 786-2810. TDD, 357-4522.

Curatorial department of the National Museum of American Art. Exhibits American crafts.

Smithsonian Institution, 1000 Jefferson Dr. S.W. 20560; 357-1846. Robert McCormick Adams, secretary. Information, 357-2700. Library, 357-2139. Fax, 786-2515. TDD, 357-1729. Recorded daily museum highlights, 357-2020.

Conducts research; publishes results of studies, explorations, and investigations; maintains study and reference collections on science, culture, and history; maintains exhibitions in the arts, American history, technology, aeronautics and space explorations, and natural history. Branches of the Smithsonian Institution in Washington, D.C., include the Anacostia Museum, Archives of American Art, Arthur M. Sackler Gallery, Arts and Industries Building, Freer Gallery of Art, Hirshhorn Museum and Sculpture Garden, National Air and Space Museum, National Museum of African Art, National Museum of American Art, National Museum of American History, National Museum of Natural History, National Portrait Gallery, National Zoological Park, and Renwick Gallery. Autonomous bureaus affiliated with the Smithsonian Institution include John F. Kennedy Center for the Performing Arts, National Gallery of Art, and Woodrow Wilson International Center for Scholars. Library open to the public by appointment.

Smithsonian Institution, International Center, 1100 Jefferson Dr. S.W. 20560; 357-4282. Francine C. Berkowitz, coordinator. Fax, 786-2557.

Fosters the development and coordinates the international aspects of Smithsonian activities in research, history, and art. Facilitates international scholarship and encourages international collaboration among individuals and institutions.

Smithsonian Institution, Internship Programs and Services, 900 Jefferson Dr. S.W. 20560; 357-3102. Sarah Landon, coordinator. Fax, 357-3346.

Provides internship placements to undergraduate and graduate students and museum professionals. Emphasizes methods and current practices employed by museum professionals.

Smithsonian Institution, Museum Programs, 900 Jefferson Dr. S.W., #2235 20560; 357-3101. Rex Ellis, director. Fax, 357-3346.

Provides training, services, information, and assistance for the professional enhancement of museum personnel and institutions in the United States and abroad; sponsors museum training workshops; maintains museum reference center; offers career counseling.

Smithsonian Institution, The Smithsonian Associates, 1100 Jefferson Dr. S.W. 20560; 357-2299. Mara Mayor, director. Press, 357-4090. Fax, 786-2536. TDD, 633-9467. National Programs, 357-4800.

National cultural and educational membership organization. Offers adults and young people films and study tours in the arts, humanities, and sciences as well as offers performances, studio arts workshops, and research opportunities.

U.S. Holocaust Memorial Museum, 100 Raoul Wallenberg Pl. S.W. 20024-2150; 488-0400. Sara Bloomfield, executive director. Fax, 488-2690.

Works to preserve documentation about the Holocaust; encourages research; provides educational resources, including conferences and publications. Responsible for the annual Days of Remembrance of the Victims of the Holocaust.

Congress:

Library of Congress, Interpretive Programs, 110 2nd St. S.E. 20540; 707-5223. Irene Burnham, interpretive programs officer. Fax, 707-9063.

Handles exhibits within the Library of Congress; establishes and coordinates traveling exhibits; handles loans of library material.

See also Culture: Arts and Humanities, General, Congress (p. 101)

Nongovernmental:

American Assn. of Museums, 1225 Eye St. N.W., #200 20005; 289-1818. Edward H. Able Jr., executive director. Fax, 289-6578. TDD, 289-8439.

Membership: individuals, museums, and museum professionals. Accredits museums; conducts educational programs for members; promotes international professional exchanges.

Art, Science, and Technology Institute, 2018 R St. N.W. 20009; 667-6322. Laurent Bussaut, executive vice president. Fax, 265-8563.

Research and educational organization. Displays a permanent collection on the art, science, and technology of holography. Conducts research on holographic applications and new forms of expression that combine art, science, and technology.

Art Services International, 700 N. Fairfax St., Alexandria, VA 22314; (703) 548-4554. Lynn K. Berg, director. Fax, (703) 548-3305.

Organizes and circulates fine arts exhibitions to museums worldwide.

Capital Children's Museum, 800 3rd St. N.E. 20002; 543-8600. Ann W. Lewin, president. Information, 675-6874. Fax, 675-4140.

Offers exhibits that involve participation by children. Integrates art, science, the humanities, and technology through "hands-on" learning experiences. (A program of the National Learning Center.)

Corcoran Gallery of Art, 500 17th St. N.W. 20006; 638-3211. David C. Levy, director. Fax, 737-2664.

Exhibits paintings, sculpture, and drawings, primarily American. Collections include European art and works of local Washington artists. The Corcoran School of Art offers a BFA degree and a continuing education program. Library open to the public by appointment.

Dumbarton Oaks, 1703 32nd St. N.W. 20007; 342-3230. Angeliki Laiou, director. Recorded information, 338-8278.

Administered by the trustees of Harvard University. Exhibits Byzantine and pre-Columbian art and artifacts; conducts advanced research and maintains publication programs and library in Byzantine and pre-Columbian studies and in landscape architecture. Gardens open to the public daily (fee charged April through October); library open to qualified scholars by advance application.

National Building Museum, 401 F St. N.W. 20001; 272-2448. Robert W. Duemling, director. Fax, 272-2564.

Celebrates American achievements in building, architecture, urban planning, engineering, and historic preservation through educational programs, exhibitions, tours, lectures, workshops, and publications.

National Museum of Women in the Arts, 1250 New York Ave. N.W. 20005; 783-5000. Rebecca Phillips Abbott, director. Information, 783-7983. Library, 783-7365. Fax, 393-3235. Toll-free, (800) 222-7270.

Acquires, researches, and presents the works of women artists from the Renaissance to the present. Promotes greater representation and awareness of women in the arts. Library open to the public by appointment.

Octagon Museum, 1799 New York Ave. N.W. 20006; 638-3221. Nancy Davis, director. Fax, 626-7420. TDD, 638-1538.

Federal period house open for tours. Presents temporary exhibits on architecture, decorative arts, and Washington history. Sponsors lectures, scholarly research, publications, and educational programs.

The Phillips Collection, 1600 21st St. N.W. 20009; 387-2151. Charles S. Moffett, director. Fax, 387-2436.

Maintains permanent collection of European and American paintings, primarily of the 19th and 20th centuries, and holds special exhibits from the same period. Sponsors lectures, gallery talks, special events, and Sunday concerts (September-May). Library open to researchers and members by appointment.

Textile Museum, 2320 S St. N.W. 20008; 667-0441. Ursula E. McCracken, director. Fax, 483-0994.

Exhibits historic and handmade textiles and carpets. Sponsors symposia, conferences, workshops, lectures, and an annual rug convention. Library open to the public.

Trust for Museum Exhibitions, 1424 16th St. N.W., #502 20036; 745-2566. Ann Van Devanter Townsend, president. Fax, 745-0103.

Provides lending and exhibiting institutions with traveling exhibition services, which include negotiating loans, engaging guest curators, scheduling tours, fund raising, and managing registrarial details and catalog production.

Woodrow Wilson House (National Trust for Historic Preservation), 2340 S St. N.W. 20008; 387-4062. Michael T. Sheehan, director. Fax, 483-1466.

Georgian Revival home that exhibits furnishings and memorabilia from President Woodrow Wilson's political and retirement years.

See also Assn. of Science-Technology Centers (p. 674); National Geographic Society (p. 675)

Music

See also National Endowment for the Humanities (p. 101)

Agencies:

National Endowment for the Arts (National Foundation on the Arts and the Humanities), Music Program, 1100 Pennsylvania Ave. N.W. 20506; 682-5445. Omus Hirshbein, director. Fax, 682-5517. TDD, 682-5496.

Awards grants to music professional training and career development institutions and to music performing, presenting, recording, and service organizations; awards fellowship grants to composers, professional jazz musicians, and solo recitalists.

National Endowment for the Arts (National Foundation on the Arts and the Humanities), Opera-Musical Theater Program, 1100 Pennsylvania Ave. N.W., #703 20506; 682-5447. Tomas Hernandez, director. Fax, 682-5517. TDD, 682-5447.

Awards grants to professional opera and musical theater companies for regional touring; to producers of opera and musical theater works; to composers of new American works; and to organizations that provide services for opera and musical-theater professionals.

National Museum of American History (Smithsonian Institution), Public Programs, 14th St. and Constitution Ave. N.W. 20560; 357-2124. Lonn W. Taylor, assistant director. Fax, 633-9296.

Coordinates and sponsors conferences and tours for school groups and others. Presents concerts that feature jazz by regional artists and ensembles, American popular songs, and American theater music on topics related to the museum's collections and current exhibitions.

National Symphony Orchestra Education Program (John F. Kennedy Center for the Performing Arts), 20566; 416-8800. Carole J. Wysocki, director. Information, 416-8820. Fax, 416-8802.

Presents concerts for students, grades K-12; sponsors fellowship program for talented high school musicians and a young apprentice program for high school students interested in arts management and professional music careers; holds an annual soloist competition open to college and high school pianists, orchestral instrumentalists, and college vocalists; sponsors Youth Orchestra Day for area youth orchestra members selected by their conductors.

Congress:

Library of Congress, Motion Picture, Broadcasting, and Recorded Sound, 101 Independence Ave. S.E. 20540-4800; 707-5840. David Francis, chief. Fax, 707-2371. Recorded sound reference center, 707-7833.

Maintains library's collection of musical and vocal recordings; tapes the library's concert series and other musical events for radio broadcast; produces recordings of music and poetry for sale to the public. Collection also includes sound recordings (1890 to present). Reading room open to the public; listening and viewing by appointment.

Library of Congress, Music Division, 101 Independence Ave. S.E. 20540; 707-5503. James W. Pruett, chief. Fax, 707-0621. Concert information, 707-5502. Performing arts library, 707-6245. Reading room, 707-5507.

Maintains and services, through the Performing Arts Reading Room, the library's collection of music manuscripts, sheet music, books, and instruments. Maintains the performing arts library of the John F. Kennedy Center. Coordinates the library's chamber music concert series; produces, for sale to the public, recordings of concerts sponsored by the division; issues publications relating to the field of music and to division collections.

Nongovernmental:

American Symphony Orchestra League, 777 14th St. N.W., #500 20005; 628-0099. Catherine French, president. Fax, 783-7228.

Service and educational organization dedicated to strengthening symphony and chamber orchestras. Provides artistic, organizational, and financial leadership and service to the music directors, musicians, direct service and governance volunteers, managers, and staff of member orchestras.

Music Educators National Conference, 1806 Robert Fulton Dr., Reston, VA 22091; (703) 860-4000. John J. Mahlmann, executive director. Fax, (703) 860-1531.

Membership: music educators (preschool through university). Publishes books and teaching aids for music educators.

National Assn. for Music Therapy, 8455 Colesville Rd., #930, Silver Spring, MD 20910; (301) 589-3300. Andrea Farbman, executive director. Fax, (301) 589-5175.

Promotes the therapeutic use of music by approving degree programs and clinical training sites for therapists, setting standards for certification of music therapists, and conducting research in the music therapy field.

National Assn. of Schools of Music, 11250 Roger Bacon Dr., #21, Reston, VA 22090; (703) 437-0700. Samuel Hope, executive director.

Accrediting agency for educational programs in music. Provides information on music education programs; offers professional development for executives of music programs.

OPERA America, 777 14th St. N.W., #520 20005; 347-9262. Marc A. Scorca, chief executive officer. Fax, 393-0735.

Membership: professional opera companies in the United States and abroad, producing and presenting organizations, artists, and others affiliated with professional opera. Advises and assists opera companies in daily operations; encourages development of opera and musical theater; produces educational programs; implements programs to increase awareness and appreciation of opera and opera companies.

Recording Industry Assn. of America, 1020 19th St. N.W., #200 20036; 775-0101. Jason S. Berman, president. Fax, 775-7253.

Membership: creators, manufacturers, and marketers of sound recordings. Educates members about new technology in the music industry. Advocates copyright protection and opposes censorship. Works to prevent recording piracy, counterfeiting, bootlegging, and unauthorized record rental and imports. Certifies gold, platinum, and multiplatinum recordings. Publishes statistics on the recording industry.

Washington Area Music Assn., 1690 36th St. N.W. 20007; 338-1134. Mike Schreibman, executive director.

Membership: musicians, concert promoters, lawyers, recording engineers, managers, contractors, and other music industry professionals. Sponsors workshops on industry-related topics. Represents professionals from all musical genres. Serves as a liaison between the Washington-area music community and music communities nationwide. (Affiliated with the Los Ange-

les-based National Academy of Recording Arts and Sciences.)

See also National League of American PEN Women (p. 103); Organization of American States (p. 153)

Theater

Agencies:

Fund for New American Plays (John F. Kennedy Center for the Performing Arts), 20566; 416-8024. Sophy Burnhan, project director. Fax, 416-8026.

Encourages playwrights to write and nonprofit professional theaters to produce new American plays; gives playwrights financial support and provides grants to cover some expenses that exceed standard production costs.

National Endowment for the Arts (National Foundation on the Arts and the Humanities), Theater Program, 1100 Pennsylvania Ave. N.W., #608 20506; 682-5425. Keryl McCord, director. Fax, 682-5512. TDD, 682-5496.

Awards grants to professional theater companies, theater service organizations, and professional theater training institutions. Offers fellowships to playwrights, solo theater artists, stage directors, stage designers, and theater projects involving collaborative work between individual theater artists.

National Park Service, Ford's Theatre National Historic Site, 511 10th St. N.W. 20004; 426-6924. Robert Fudge, site manager. Fax, 347-6269. TDD, 426-1749. Recorded ticket information, 347-4833.

Manages Ford's Theatre, Ford's Theatre Museum, and the Peterson House (house where Lincoln died). Presents interpretive talks, exhibits, and tours. Functions as working stage for theatrical productions.

Smithsonian Institution, Discovery Theater, 900 Jefferson Dr. S.W. 20560; 357-1502. Susan Swarthout, director. Fax, 357-2588. Reservations, 357-1500.

Presents live theatrical performances, including storytelling, dance, music, puppetry, and plays, for young people and their families.

See also John F. Kennedy Center for the Performing Arts (p. 100); National Endowment for the Humanities (p. 101)

Nongovernmental:

National Assn. of Schools of Theatre, 11250 Roger Bacon Dr., #21, Reston, VA 22090; (703) 437-0700. Samuel Hope, executive director.

Accrediting agency for educational programs in theater. Provides information on theater education programs; offers professional development for executives of theater programs.

The Shakespeare Theatre, 450 7th St. N.W. (mailing address: 301 E. Capitol St., S.E., Washington, DC 20003); 547-3230. Jessica L. Andrews, managing director. Fax, 547-0226. TDD, 638-3863. Box office, 393-2700.

Professional resident theater that presents Shakespearean and other classical plays. Offers actor training program for youths, adults, and professional actors. Produces free outdoor summer Shakespeare plays and free Shakespeare plays for schools.

Visual Arts

See also Architecture and Design Arts (p. 104); Broadcasting and Film (p. 105); Museum Programs (p. 114)

Agencies:

National Archives and Records Administration, Still Pictures, 8601 Adelphi Rd., College Park, MD 20740-6001; (301) 713-6660. Elizabeth L. Hill, chief.

Provides the public with copies of still pictures; supplies guides to these materials. Collection includes still pictures from more than 150 federal agencies.

National Endowment for the Arts (National Foundation on the Arts and the Humanities), Visual Arts Program, 1100 Pennsylvania Ave. N.W. 20506; 682-5448. Rosilyn Alter, director. Fax, 682-5721.

Awards grants to individuals and nonprofit organizations for creative works and programs in the visual arts, including painting, sculpture, crafts, video, photography, printmaking, drawing, artists' books, and performance art. Awards matching grants to commissions and artists to present work in public places.

State Dept., Art in Embassies, Main State Bldg. 20520; 647-5723. Vacant, director. Fax, 647-4080.

Exhibits American art in U.S. ambassadorial residences. Acquires art works from the private sector either as loans or as gifts.

See also National Endowment for the Humanities (p. 101)

Congress:

Library of Congress, Prints and Photographs, 101 Independence Ave. S.E. 20540-4840; 707-5836. Stephen E. Ostrow, chief. Fax, 707-6647. Reading Room, 707-6394.

Maintains Library of Congress's collection of pictorial material, not in book format, totaling more than 15 million items. Collection includes artists' prints; historical prints, posters, and drawings; photographs (chiefly documentary); political and social cartoons; and architectural plans, drawings, prints, and photographs. Reference service provided in the Prints and Photographs Reading Room. Reproductions of nonrestricted material available through the Library of Congress's Photoduplication Service; prints and photographs may be borrowed through the Exhibits Office for exhibits by qualified institutions.

Nongovernmental:

Friends of Art and Preservation in Embassies, P.O. Box 19025, Washington, DC 20036; 637-2200. W. Harrison Wellford, board member.

Foundation established to assist the State Dept.'s Office of Foreign Buildings and Art in Embassies programs. Acquires and exhibits American art and preserves high-value furnishings in U.S. embassies and other diplomatic facilities.

National Artists Equity Assn., 1325 G St. N.W., Lower Level (mailing address: P.O. Box 28068, Central Station, Washington, DC 20038); 628-9633. Rodney Reynolds, executive director. Toll-free, (800) 727-6232. Fax, 638-4885.

Membership: professionals in the visual arts, including painters, sculptors, graphic artists, photographers, and potters. Interests include copyrights, health hazards of artists' materials, funding programs of the National Endowment for the Arts, artists' housing and studio space, and legislation and public policy affecting the concerns of visual artists.

National Assn. of Artists' Organizations, 918 F St. N.W., #611 20004; 347-6350. Helen Brunner, executive director. Fax, 347-7376.

Provides technical assistance and sponsors conferences to ensure the continuation and growth of artists' organizations and publications. Monitors legislation and regulations affecting art, artists' organizations, and individual artists.

Washington Area History and Culture

See also Capitol, History (p. 744)

Agencies:

National Park Service (Interior Dept.), National Capital Region, 1100 Ohio Dr. S.W. 20242; 619-7223. Sandra Alley, associate director, public affairs and tourism. Press, 619-7226. Fax, 619-7302. TDD, 619-7222. Recorded information, 619-7275; permits, 619-7225.

Provides visitors with information on Washington-area parks; offers press services for the media and processes special event applications and permits.

Nongovernmental:

D.C. Preservation League, 1511 K St. N.W., #739 20005; 737-1519. Jacqueline V. Prior, executive director. Fax, 737-1823.

Participates in planning, preserving, and developing buildings and sites in Washington, D.C., particularly in the old downtown area. Programs include protection and enhancement of the city's landmarks; educational lectures, tours, and seminars; and technical assistance to neighborhood groups. Monitors legislation and regulations.

Historical Society of Washington, D.C., 1307 New Hampshire Ave. N.W. 20036; 785-2068. John V. Alviti, executive director. Fax, 331-1979.

Maintains research collections on the District of Columbia, including photographs, manuscripts, archives, books, and prints and graphics of Washington (1790 to present); publishes *Washington History* magazine; operates a historic house museum in the Heurich mansion. Museum and library open to the public.

Martin Luther King Memorial Library, Washingtoniana Division, 901 G St. N.W., #307 20001; 727-1213. Roxanna Deane, chief. Fax, 727-1129.

Maintains reference collections of District of Columbia current laws and regulations, history, and culture. Collections include biographies;

travel books; memoirs and diaries; family, church, government, and institutional histories; maps (1612 to present); plat books; city, telephone, and real estate directories (1822 to present); census schedules; newspapers and periodicals (including the *Washington Star* collection); photographs of individuals and buildings; and oral history materials on local neighborhoods, ethnic groups, and businesses.

Supreme Court Historical Society, 111 2nd St. N.E. 20002; 543-0400. David T. Pride, executive director. Fax, 547-7730.

Acquires, preserves, and displays historic items associated with the Court; conducts and publishes scholarly research. Conducts lecture programs; promotes and supports educational and informative activities in the Court.

White House Historical Assn., 740 Jackson Pl. N.W. 20503; 737-8292. Paul D. Houston, executive vice president. Fax, 528-2146.

Publishes books on the White House, including a historical guide, a description of ceremonial events, two volumes of biographical sketches and illustrations of the presidents and first ladies, a book on White House glassware, and a book on White House paintings and sculptures. Net proceeds from book sales go toward the purchase of historic items, such as paintings and furniture, for the White House permanent collection.

See also Octagon Museum (p. 118)

Education

General

See also Science: Education (p. 674)

Agencies:

Education Dept., 400 Maryland Ave. S.W. 20202; 401-3000. Richard W. Riley, secretary. Information, 708-5366. Fax, 401-0596.

Establishes education policy and acts as principal adviser to the president on education matters; administers and coordinates most federal assistance programs on education.

Education Dept., Goals 2000: Educate America, 400 Maryland Ave. S.W. 20202; 401-2000. Mary Anne Schmitt, director. Toll-free, (800) 872-5327. Press, 401-1576. Fax, 401-0689.

Oversees strategy to attain education goals adopted by the president and the governors in 1990, including lower drop-out rate, higher math and science achievement, elimination of illiteracy, and drug-free schools.

Educational Resources Information Center (ERIC) (Education Dept.), 555 New Jersey Ave. N.W. 20208-5720; 219-2088. Robert Stonehill, director. Toll-free, (800) 538-3742. Fax, 219-1817.

Funds and coordinates a national information system comprising sixteen clearinghouses on specific subjects. Documents available in microfiche form at most university libraries. Answers queries and offers referrals to individuals on all facets of education.

See also Domestic Policy Council (p. 300)

Congress:

General Accounting Office, Human Resources, 441 G St. N.W., NGB/ACG 20548; 512-6806. Janet L. Shikles, assistant comptroller general. Fax, 512-5806.

Independent, nonpartisan agency In the legislative branch. Audits, analyzes, and evaluates Education Dept. programs; makes reports available to the public.

House Appropriations Committee, Subcommittee on Labor, Health and Human Services, and Education, 2358 RHOB 20515; 225-3508. Neal Smith, D-Iowa, chairman; Mike Stephens, staff assistant.

Jurisdiction over legislation to appropriate funds for federal education programs (except native American education programs), including adult education, compensatory education, and education for the disadvantaged and disabled.

House Education and Labor Committee, Subcommittee on Elementary, Secondary, and Vocational Education, B-346A RHOB 20515; 225-4368. Dale E. Kildee, D-Mich., chairman; Susan Wilhelm, staff director. Fax, 225-1110.

Jurisdiction over legislation on preschool, elementary, secondary, and vocational education, including community schools and aid to private schools; and legislation barring discrimination in preschool, elementary, secondary, and vocational education.

House Education and Labor Committee, Subcommittee on Select Education and Civil

Rights, 518 O'Neill Bldg. (300 New Jersey Ave. S.E.) 20515; 226-7532. Major R. Owens, D-N.Y., chairman; Maria Cuprill, staff director.

Jurisdiction over legislation on education, including the Office of Educational Research and Improvement; education research; drug and alcohol abuse education; AIDS education and infants with AIDS; environmental education; and education technology. Jurisdiction over legislation on education of people with disabilities, including Gallaudet University and the National Technical Institute for the Deaf. Jurisdiction over the Americans with Disabilities Act.

House Government Operations Committee, Subcommittee on Human Resources and Intergovernmental Relations, B372 RHOB 20515; 225-2548. Edolphus Towns, D-N.Y., chairman; Ron Stroman, staff director. Fax, 225-2382.

Oversees operations of the Education Dept.

Senate Appropriations Committee, Subcommittee on Labor, Health and Human Services, and Education, SD-186 20510; 224-7283. Tom Harkin, D-Iowa, chairman; Ed Long, clerk.

Jurisdiction over legislation to appropriate funds for federal education programs, including adult education, compensatory education, and education for the disadvantaged and disabled.

Senate Labor and Human Resources Committee, Subcommittee on Disability Policy, SH-113 20510; 224-6265. Tom Harkin, D-Iowa, chairman; Robert Silverstein, staff director.

Jurisdiction over legislation on education of people with disabilities, including Gallaudet University and the National Technical Institute for the Deaf; jurisdiction over the Americans with Disabilities Act.

Senate Labor and Human Resources Committee, Subcommittee on Education, Arts, and Humanities, SD-648 20510; 224-7666. Claiborne Pell, D-R.I., chairman; David V. Evans, staff director.

Jurisdiction over legislation on education, including community schools, aid to private schools, the Office of Educational Research and Improvement, education technology, and drug and alcohol abuse education; and legislation barring discrimination in preschool, elementary, secondary, and vocational education. Oversees operations of the Education Dept.

Education Dept.

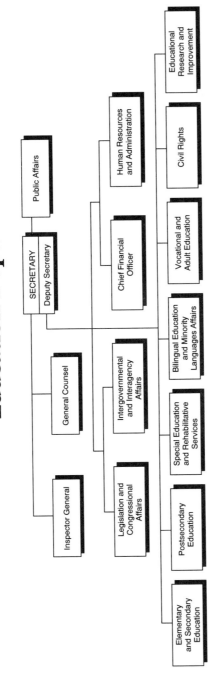

Nongovernmental:

The Carnegie Foundation for the Advancement of Teaching, 1755 Massachusetts Ave. N.W. 20036; 387-7200. Robert Hochstein, assistant to the president. Fax, 462-5567.

Funded by bequest from Andrew Carnegie. Conducts policy studies and issues reports on topics related to education. (Headquarters in Princeton, N.J.)

Center for Law and Education, 1875 Connecticut Ave. N.W., #510 20009-5728; 986-3000. Paul Weckstein, co-director. Fax, 986-6648.

Provides support services on education issues to advocates working on behalf of low-income students and parents. Interests include testing and tracking; bilingual education; discriminatory discipline; special education; special needs for native Americans, migrants, and Hispanics; parent, community, and student participation in education; and vocational and compensatory education. (Headquarters in Cambridge, Mass.)

Charles F. Kettering Foundation, 444 N. Capitol St. N.W., #434 20001; 393-4478. James C. Wilder, director, Washington office. Toll-free, (800) 221-3657. Fax, 393-7644.

Works to improve the domestic policymaking process. Supports international program focusing on unofficial, citizen-to-citizen diplomacy. Encourages greater citizen involvement in formation of public policy. Interests include public education and at-risk youths. (Headquarters in Dayton, Ohio.)

Council for Advancement and Support of Education (CASE), 11 Dupont Circle N.W., #400 20036; 328-5900. Peter McE. Buchanan, president.

Membership: two- and four-year colleges, universities, and independent schools. Offers professional education and training programs to members; advises members on institutional advancement issues, including fund raising, alumni affairs, public relations programs, government relations, and management. Library open to the public by appointment.

Ethics Resource Center, 1120 G St. N.W., #200 20005; 737-2258. Gary Edwards, president. Fax, 737-2227.

Educational organization that produces classroom materials on character education for students in various grade levels. Produces teacher training videos and guides; helps schools evaluate and improve programs in moral education.

Institute for Educational Leadership, 1001 Connecticut Ave. N.W., #310 20036; 822-8405. Michael Usdan, president. Fax, 872-4050.

Works with educators, human services personnel, government officials, and association executives to improve educational opportunities for youths; conducts research on education issues.

National Assn. of State Boards of Education, 1012 Cameron St., Alexandria, VA 22314; (703) 684-4000. Brenda L. Welburn, executive director. Fax, (703) 836-2313.

Membership: members of state boards of education, state board attorneys, and executives to state boards. Provides information, technical and research assistance, and training programs for members. Interests include education governance, finance and policy, teaching, adolescent pregnancy, at-risk youth, vocational and early childhood education, and AIDS and other health education issues.

National Center on Education and the Economy, National Alliance for Restructuring Education, 700 11th St. N.W., #750 20001; 783-3668. Michael Cohen, director. Fax, 783-3672.

Partnership of states, school districts, corporations, foundations, and nonprofit organizations that studies and makes policy recommendations to improve student performance. Interests include organizational change, accountability, and incentives. (Headquarters in Rochester, N.Y.)

National Clearinghouse for Corporate Matching Gifts, 11 Dupont Circle N.W., #400 20036; 328-5900. Cheryl Martin, director. Information, 328-5978. Fax, 387-4973.

Provides companies and educational institutions with information on matching gift programs, in which companies match employee contributions to educational and other nonprofit institutions. Sponsored by the Council for Advancement and Support of Education.

National Learning Center, 800 3rd St. N.E. 20002; 543-8600. Ann W. Lewin, president. Information, 675-6874. Fax, 675-4140.

Designs, implements, and conducts studies in education. Interests include the creation and development of new educational methods, materials, and structures. Maintains the Capital Children's Museum.

National School Public Relations Assn., 1501 Lee Highway, #201, Arlington, VA 22209; (703)

528-5840. Richard D. Bagin, executive director. Fax, (703) 528-7017.

Membership: educators and individuals interested in improving communications in education. Works to improve communication between educators and the public on the needs of schools; provides educators with information on public relations and policy developments.

New American Schools Development Corp., 1000 Wilson Blvd., #2710, Arlington, VA 22209; (703) 908-9500. John Anderson, president. Fax, (703) 908-0622.

Solicits and evaluates school design concepts as part of the Goals 2000 education strategy; funds those shown to improve student performance and offers them for adoption to schools nationwide; provides communities interested in implementing these concepts with financial assistance.

Community Schools

Congress:

See Education, General, Congress (p. 123)

Nongovernmental:

Assn. for Community Based Education, 1805 Florida Ave. N.W. 20009; 462-6333. C. P. Zachariadis, executive director. Fax, 232-8044.

Collects and disseminates information on community-based education programs, free-standing alternative colleges (independent of state or local support), and adult learning centers. Provides technical assistance to develop, expand, and improve community-based education programs.

National Community Education Assn., 3929 Old Lee Highway, Fairfax, VA 22030; (703) 359-8973. Starla Jewell-Kelly, executive director. Fax, (703) 359-0972.

Works for greater recognition of community education programs, services, and personnel. Interests include business-education partnerships to improve schools; life-long learning; school-site child care and latchkey programs; and parental involvement in public education.

Internships

Many government and private agencies, businesses, and educational institutions in Washington conduct internship programs; contact *individual agency or organization for information.*

Nongovernmental:

American Political Science Assn., Congressional Fellowship Program, 1527 New Hampshire Ave. N.W. 20036; 483-2512. Kay Sterling, administrative director. Fax, 483-2657.

Places political scientists, journalists, faculty of medical schools (Robert Wood Johnson Fellowships), and federal agency executives in congressional offices and committees for nine-month fellowships. Individual government agencies nominate federal executive participants.

The Fund for American Studies, 1526 18th St. N.W. 20036; 986-0384. David R. Jones, president.

Educational foundation that sponsors summer institutes on comparative political and economic systems, business and government affairs, and political journalism; grants scholarships to qualified students for these study-internship programs.

National Journalism Center, 800 Maryland Ave. N.E. 20002; 546-1710. M. Stanton Evans, director. Fax, 546-1638.

Sponsors extensive internship program in journalism; offers job placement service. Funded by the Education and Research Institute.

Washington Center, 1101 14th St. N.W., #500 20005; 336-7600. William M. Burke, president. Fax, 336-7609.

Arranges congressional, agency, and public service internships for college students for credit. Fee for internship and housing assistance. Sponsors classes and lectures as part of the internship program. Scholarships and stipends available.

Washington Center for Politics and Journalism, 1901 L St. N.W., #300 (mailing address: P.O. Box 15201, Washington, DC 20003); 296-8455. Terry Michael, executive director. Fax, 775-8169.

Offers internships in political journalism to undergraduate and graduate students. Sixteen-week fall and winter/spring sessions include full-time work in Washington news bureaus and seminars in campaign, governance, and interest group politics for future political reporters.

Youth Policy Institute, 1221 Massachusetts Ave. N.W., #B 20005-5302; 638-2144. David L. Hackett, executive director. Fax, 638-2325.

Seeks to involve youth in public policy decision making. Partly administered and staffed by high school and college students who serve internships of 6 to 12 months; Research Center brings youths to Washington to study public policy proposals; sponsors conferences and workshops. Monitors legislation and government programs dealing with youth. Publishes a resource guide and other materials.

See also Assn. on Third World Affairs (p. 446); Christian College Coalition (this page); Education and Research Institute (p. 22); National Assn. for Equal Opportunity in Higher Education (p. 149)

Private and Parochial Schools

Agencies:

Education Dept., Private Education, 400 Maryland Ave. S.W. 20202; 401-1365. Michelle L. Doyle, director. Fax, 205-3529.

Acts as ombudsman for interests of teachers and students in private schools (elementary and secondary levels); reports to the secretary on matters relating to private education.

Congress:

See Education, General, Congress (p. 123)

Nongovernmental:

Americans United for Separation of Church and State, 8120 Fenton St., Silver Spring, MD 20910; (301) 589-3707. Barry L. Lynn, executive director. Fax, (301) 495-9173.

Citizens' interest group. Opposes federal and state aid to parochial schools; works to ensure religious neutrality in public schools; supports religious free exercise; initiates litigation; monitors legislation and regulations; maintains speakers bureau.

Assn. of Catholic Colleges and Universities, 1 Dupont Circle N.W., #650 20036; 457-0650. Benito M. Lopez Jr., executive director. Fax, 728-0977.

Membership: regionally accredited Catholic colleges and universities and individuals interested in Catholic higher education. Acts as a clearinghouse for information on Catholic institutions of higher education. Affiliated with the National Catholic Educational Assn.

Christian College Coalition, 329 8th St. N.E. 20002; 546-8713. Myron S. Augsburger, president. Fax, 546-8913.

Membership: accredited four-year Christian liberal arts colleges. Offers faculty development conferences on faith and the academic disciplines. Coordinates annual gathering of college administrators. Sponsors internship/seminar programs for students at member colleges. Interests include religious and educational freedom.

Citizens for Educational Freedom, 927 S. Walter Reed Dr., #1, Arlington, VA 22204; (703) 486-8311. Joanne Orlowski, national administrator. Fax, (703) 486-3160.

Citizens' interest group. Advocates federal, state, and local aid to students in nongovernment schools through tax credits and vouchers; supports parental choice in education.

Council for American Private Education, 1726 M St. N.W., #1102 20036-4502; 659-0016. Joyce McCray, executive director. Fax, 659-0018.

Coalition of national private school associations serving private elementary and secondary schools. Acts as a liaison between private education and government, other educational organizations, the media, and the public. Seeks greater access to private schools for all families. Monitors legislation and regulations.

Lutheran Educational Conference of North America, 1001 Connecticut Ave. N.W., #504 20036; 463-6486. Donald A. Stoike, executive director. Fax, 463-6609.

Membership: private Lutheran-related colleges and boards of higher education. Supports federal aid to private higher education.

National Assn. of Independent Schools, 1620 L St. N.W. 20036; 973-9714. Jefferson G. Burnett, director, government relations. Information, 973-9790. Press, 973-9716. Fax, 973-9790.

Membership: independent elementary and secondary schools in the United States and abroad.

National Catholic Educational Assn., 1077 30th St. N.W., #100 20007; 337-6232. Catherine T. McNamee, president. Fax, 333-6706.

Membership: Catholic schools (preschool through college and seminary) and school administrators. Provides consultation services to members for administration, curriculum, continuing education, religious education, campus ministry, boards of education, and union and personnel negotiations; conducts workshops; supports federal aid for private education. Affiliated with the Assn. of Catholic Colleges and Universities.

National Congress of Parents and Teachers, 2000 L St. N.W., #600 20036; 331-1380. Arnold F. Fege, director, governmental relations.

Membership: parent-teacher associations at the preschool, elementary, and secondary levels. Coordinates the National Coalition for Public Education, which opposes tuition tax credits and vouchers for private education. (Headquarters in Chicago.)

National Council of Churches, 110 Maryland Ave. N.E. 20002; 544-2350. James A. Hamilton, director, Washington office.

Membership: Protestant and Orthodox churches. Opposes federal aid to private schools. (Headquarters in New York.)

U.S. Catholic Conference, 3211 4th St. N.E. 20017; 541-3130. Lourdes Sheehan, secretary for education. Press, 541-3200. Fax, 541-3390. TDD, 740-0424.

Represents the Catholic church in the United States in educational matters; advises Catholic schools on federal programs; assists church organizations with religious education.

Professional Interests and Benefits

See also Education: Postsecondary, General (p. 132); Education: Special Groups, Teachers (p. 150)

Nongovernmental:

Academic Collective Bargaining Information Service, University of the District of Columbia, 1321 H St. N.W. 20005; 274-6770. Isadore Goldberg, director. Fax, 727-5598.

Provides employment relations service in the field of higher education. Interests include equal employment opportunity, governance and policy issues, leadership development, unionization, and collective bargaining for faculty and nonfaculty units. Offers seminars, research, evaluation, arbitration, and information services in the field of higher education. Library open to the public.

American Assn. of School Administrators, 1801 N. Moore St., Arlington, VA 22209; (703) 528-0700. Paul D. Houston, executive director. Fax, (703) 528-2146.

Membership: chief school executives, administrators at district or higher level, and teachers of school administration. Promotes opportunities for minorities, women, and the disabled in educational administration and organization.

American Political Science Assn., 1527 New Hampshire Ave. N.W. 20036; 483-2512. Catherine E. Rudder, executive director. Fax, 483-2657.

Membership: political scientists, primarily college and university professors. Works to increase public understanding of politics; provides services to facilitate and enhance research, teaching, and professional development of its members. Acts as liaison with federal agencies, Congress, and the public. Seeks to improve the status of women and minorities in the profession. Offers congressional fellowships, workshops, and awards. Provides information on political science issues.

Assn. of School Business Officials International, 11401 N. Shore Dr., Reston, VA 22090; (703) 478-0405. Donald I. Tharpe, executive director. Fax, (703) 478-0205.

Membership: administrators, directors, and others involved in school business management. Works to educate members on tools, techniques, and procedures of school business management. Researches, analyzes, and disseminates information; conducts workshops.

Council of Chief State School Officers, 1 Massachusetts Ave. N.W., #700 20001-1431; 408-5505. Gordon M. Ambach, executive director. Fax, 408-8072.

Membership: state superintendents and commissioners of education. Works to achieve equal education for all children and to improve ways to measure school performance; provides state education agency personnel and others with leadership, technical assistance, and training. Offers seminars, educational travel, and study programs for members.

International Test and Evaluation Assn., 4400 Fair Lakes Court, Fairfax, VA 22033-3899; (703) 631-6220. R. Alan Plishker, executive director. Fax, (703) 631-6221.

Membership: engineers, scientists, managers, and other industry, government, and academic professionals interested in advancing the field of test and evaluation of products and complex systems. Provides a forum for exchange of information.

National Assn. for Women in Education, 1325 18th St. N.W., #210 20036; 659-9330. Patricia Rueckel, executive director. Fax, 457-0946.

Membership: women in educational administration, teaching, and research, mainly in higher education. Interests include career mobility for women administrators, equitable pensions, and equal educational opportunity and training.

National Assn. of Biology Teachers, 11250 Roger Bacon Dr., #19, Reston, VA 22090; (703) 471-1134. Patricia J. McWethy, executive director.

Provides professional development opportunities through a publications program, in-service workshops, conventions, and national awards programs. Interests include teaching standards, science curriculum, and issues affecting biology education.

National Assn. of School Psychologists, 8455 Colesville Rd., #1000, Silver Spring, MD 20910; (301) 608-0500. Susan Gorin, executive director. Fax, (301) 608-2514.

Advocates for the mental health and educational needs of children; encourages professional growth of members; monitors legislation and regulations.

National Business Education Assn., 1914 Association Dr., Reston, VA 22091; (703) 860-8300. Janet M. Treichel, executive director. Fax, (703) 620-4483.

Membership: business education teachers and others interested in the field. Provides information on business education; offers teaching and testing materials; sponsors conferences; monitors legislation and regulations affecting business education.

National Council for the Social Studies, 3501 Newark St. N.W. 20016; 966-7840. Martharose F. Laffey, executive director. Fax, 966-2061.

Membership: social studies educators, including teachers of history, political science, geography, economics, civics, psychology, sociology, and anthropology. Promotes the teaching of social studies; encourages research; sponsors publications; works with other organizations to advance social studies education.

National Council of State Education Assns., 1201 16th St. N.W., 4th Floor 20036; 822-7745. Larry Diebold, executive director. Fax, 822-7974.

Membership: presidents, vice presidents, executive directors, and secretary-treasurers of state education associations. Holds meetings and training programs for officers and staff of state education associations.

National Council of Teachers of Mathematics, 1906 Association Dr., Reston, VA 22091; (703) 620-9840. James D. Gates, executive director. Fax, (703) 476-2970.

Membership: teachers of mathematics in elementary and secondary schools and two-year colleges; university teacher education faculty; students; and other interested persons. Works for the improvement of classroom instruction at all levels. Serves as forum and information clearinghouse on issues related to mathematics education. Offers educational materials and conferences. Monitors legislation and regulations.

National Science Resources Center, 900 Jefferson Dr. S.W., #1201 20560; 357-4892. Douglas M. Lapp, executive director. Fax, 786-2028.

Sponsored by the Smithsonian Institution and the National Academy of Sciences. Works to improve science and mathematics teaching in elementary schools. Disseminates information; develops curriculum materials; seeks to increase public support for reform of science education.

National Science Teachers Assn., 1840 Wilson Blvd., Arlington, VA 22201-3000; (703) 243-7100. Bill G. Aldridge, executive director. Fax, (703) 243-7177.

Membership: science teachers from elementary through college levels. Seeks to improve science education; provides forum for exchange of information; monitors legislation and regulations. (Affiliated with the American Assn. for the Advancement of Science and the National Aeronautics and Space Administration.)

See also American Federation of Teachers (AFL-CIO) (p. 801); American Historical Assn. and American Studies Assn. (p. 102); National Education Assn. (p. 803)

Research

Agencies:

Education Dept., Center for Education Statistics, 555 New Jersey Ave. N.W. 20208; 219-1828. Emerson J. Elliott, commissioner. Fax, 219-1736. Toll-free information, (800) 424-1616; in Washington, D.C., 219-1652.

Gathers, analyzes, synthesizes, and disseminates qualitative and quantitative data on the characteristics and effectiveness of American education. Helps state and local education agencies improve statistical gathering and processing methods.

Education Dept., Education Information, 555 New Jersey Ave. N.W. 20208; 219-1651. Lewis Walker, chief. Information, 219-1513. Toll-free, (800) 424-1616.

Provides information and answers questions on education statistics and research.

Education Dept., Educational Research and Improvement, 555 New Jersey Ave. N.W. 20208; 219-2050. Sharon Porter Robinson, assistant secretary. Information, 219-1513. Fax, 219-1402. Toll-free education statistics and trends, (800) 424-1616.

Gathers, analyzes, and disseminates information, statistics, and research findings on the conditions and practices of American education. Supports nationally significant model projects, including the National Assessment of Educational Progress (the Nation's Report Card), a survey of the knowledge, skills, understanding, and attitudes of 9, 13, and 17 year olds.

Education Dept., Recognition, 555 New Jersey Ave. N.W. 20208; 219-2134. Jean Narayanan, director. Fax, 219-1407.

Seeks to identify, recognize, and disseminate information about outstanding school programs nationwide that have been effective in or have significantly improved such areas as drug prevention, vocational training, and academics. Operates the National Diffusion Network, the Secretary's School Recognition Program, and the Drug-Free School Recognition Program.

Education Dept., Research, 555 New Jersey Ave. N.W. 20208; 219-2079. Joseph Conaty, acting director. Fax, 219-2030.

Supports fundamental research at every institutional level of education on topics such as the processes of teaching and learning; school organization and improvement; curriculum; and factors that contribute to excellence in education. Administers the Educational Resources Information Center (ERIC), the national information retrieval system on education.

Congress:

See Education, General, Congress (p. 123)

Nongovernmental:

Academy for Educational Development, 1875 Connecticut Ave. N.W. 20009; 884-8000. Stephen F. Moseley, president. Fax, 884-8400.

Conducts, on a contract basis, studies on domestic and international education. Interests include educational finance, management of educational institutions, application of communications technology to health education, agricultural extension, and other development problems, exchange of information, and use of telecommunications for social services. Operates international exchange programs.

American Educational Research Assn., 1230 17th St. N.W. 20036; 223-9485. William J. Russell, executive officer. Fax, 775-1824.

Membership: educational researchers affiliated with universities and colleges, school systems, and federal and state agencies. Publishes original research in education; sponsors publication of reference works in educational research; conducts continuing education programs; studies status of women and minorities in the education field.

Council for Educational Development and Research, 2000 L St. N.W., #601 20036; 223-1593. Dena G. Stoner, executive director. Fax, 785-3859.

Membership: regional educational laboratories and university-based educational research and development organizations; serves as a clearinghouse for information on research conducted by members on various education issues.

Council on Governmental Relations, 1 Dupont Circle N.W., #425 20036; 331-1803. Milton Goldberg, executive director. Fax, 331-8483.

Membership: research universities maintaining federally supported programs. Advises members and makes recommendations to government agencies regarding policies and regulations affecting university research.

Ethics and Public Policy Center, Education and Society Program, 1015 15th St. N.W., #900 20005; 682-1200. George S. Weigel Jr., president. Fax, 408-0632.

Conducts research and holds conferences on the role of formal education in teaching facts, ideas, attitudes, and values.

Madison Center for Educational Affairs, 1155 15th St. N.W., #712 20005; 833-1801. Charles Horner, president. Fax, 775-0851.

Research center that promotes improvements in American education. Monitors and evaluates reform efforts in higher education.

National Institute of Independent Colleges and Universities, 122 C St. N.W. 20001; 347-7520. Frank J. Balz, executive director. Fax, 628-2513.

Conducts research on national attitudes and policies concerning independent higher education; surveys student aid programs and federal tax policies affecting institutional financing; acts as a clearinghouse for state associations. (Affiliated with the National Assn. of Independent Colleges and Universities.)

Rand Corporation, Education and Human Resources Program, 2100 M St. N.W. 20037; 296-5000. Charles R. Roll Jr., director, Washington operations. Fax, 296-7960.

Research organization partially funded by federal agencies. Conducts research on education policy. Sponsors the Center for the Study of the Teaching Profession. (Headquarters in Santa Monica, Calif.)

See also American Federation of Teachers (AFL-CIO) (p. 801); American Institutes for Research (p. 693); Institute for Educational Leadership (p. 125); National Education Assn. (p. 803)

Technology and Media Resources

See also Libraries and Information Science (p. 160)

Congress:

See Education, General, Congress (p. 123)

Nongovernmental:

Assn. for Educational Communications and Technology, 1025 Vermont Ave. N.W., #820 20005; 347-7834. Stanley D. Zenor, executive director. Fax, 347-7839.

Membership: media professionals for government and the military, and schools and school systems (kindergarten through postsecondary). Produces instructional materials and publications on educational technology such as audiovisual teaching and computerized instruction.

Assn. for Information and Image Management, 1100 Wayne Ave., Silver Spring, MD 20910; (301) 587-8202. Susan T. Wolk, executive director. Fax, (301) 587-2711.

Membership: manufacturers and users of image-based information systems. Works to advance the profession of information management; develops standards on such technologies as microfilm and electronic imaging. Library open to the public.

Flexible Packaging Assn., 1090 Vermont Ave. N.W., #500 20005; 842-3880. Glenn E. Braswell, president. Fax, 842-3841.

Conducts packaging programs to teach students practical applications of science and design; coordinates environmental programs on reducing solid waste for schools.

International Communications Industries Assn., 3150 Spring St., Fairfax, VA 22031; (703) 273-7200. Vacant, executive vice president. Fax, (703) 278-8082.

Membership: manufacturers, dealers, and specialists in educational communications products. Provides educators with information on federal funding for audiovisual, video, and computer equipment and materials; monitors trends in educational technology; conducts educational software conference on microcomputers and miniaturization.

Kidsnet, 6856 Eastern Ave. N.W., #208 20012; 291-1400. Karen W. Jaffe, executive director. Fax, 882-7315. America Online, kidsnet@aol.com; CompuServe, 76711,1212.

Computerized clearinghouse that provides information about audio, video, radio, and television programming for preschool through high school. Available by subscription.

See also Academy for Educational Development (p. 130); National Foundation for the Improvement of Education (p. 151)

Education: Postsecondary

General

See also *Education, Professional Interests and Benefits (p. 128); Education: Special Groups, Adult (p. 143); Education: Special Groups, Minorities and Women (p. 146)*

Agencies:

Education Dept., Fund for the Improvement of Postsecondary Education, 7th and D Sts. S.W. 20202-5175; 708-5750. Charles Karelis, director. Fax, 708-6118.

Works to improve postsecondary education by administering grant competitions, including the Comprehensive Program for improvements in postsecondary education; Innovative Projects for Community Service; Drug Prevention Programs in Higher Education; Leadership Projects in Science and the Humanities; Institution-wide Program; National College Student Organizational Network Program; and Higher Education Consortia for Drug Prevention.

Education Dept., Institutional Participation Division, 7th and D Sts. S.W. 20202; 708-4906. Diane M. Sedicum, director. Fax, 205-0782.

Determines the eligibility of postsecondary institutions for participation in funding support programs for faculty development, student financial aid, construction of facilities, and improvements of graduate, continuing, cooperative, and international education.

Education Dept., Postsecondary Education, 7th and D Sts. S.W. 20202; 708-5547. David Longanecker, assistant secretary. Information, 401-2311. Fax, 708-9814.

Administers federal assistance programs for public and private postsecondary institutions; provides financial support for faculty development, construction of facilities, and improvement of graduate, continuing, cooperative, and international education; awards grants and loans for financial assistance to eligible students.

Congress:

House Education and Labor Committee, Subcommittee on Postsecondary Education and Training, 2451 RHOB 20515; 226-3681. William

D. Ford, D-Mich., chairman; Omer Waddles, staff director.

Jurisdiction over legislation on postsecondary education, including community and junior colleges, the Construction Loan Program, financial aid, and legislation barring discrimination in postsecondary education. Jurisdiction over the Women's Educational Equity Act of 1974 as it applies to postsecondary education.

House Ways and Means Committee, Subcommittee on Oversight, 1135 LHOB 20515; 225-5522. J. J. Pickle, D-Texas, chairman; Beth K. Vance, staff director. Fax, 225-0787.

Oversees government-sponsored enterprises, including the Student Loan Marketing Assn. and the College Construction Loan Insurance Assn., with regard to the financial risk posed to the federal government.

Senate Banking, Housing, and Urban Affairs Committee, SD-534 20510; 224-7391. Donald W. Riegle Jr., D-Mich., chairman; Steven Harris, staff director.

Oversees government-sponsored enterprises, including the Student Loan Marketing Assn. and the College Construction Loan Insurance Assn., with regard to the financial risk posed to the federal government.

Senate Labor and Human Resources Committee, Subcommittee on Education, Arts, and Humanities, SD-648 20510; 224-7666. Claiborne Pell, D-R.I., chairman; David V. Evans, staff director.

Jurisdiction over postsecondary education legislation, including community and junior colleges, construction of school facilities, and financial aid, and over legislation barring discrimination in postsecondary education, including the Women's Educational Equity Act of 1974.

Nongovernmental:

Accuracy in Academia, 4455 Connecticut Ave. N.W., #330 20008; 364-3085. Mark Draper, executive director. Fax, 364-4098.

Investigates reports from students of inaccurate information in faculty lectures or in required reading materials that deal with only one side of controversial issues. Approaches faculty members with complaints; publicizes findings in newsletter. Defends rights of professors and students to academic freedom without fear of retaliation. Interests include political discrimination and academic freedom.

Major Washington Colleges and Universities

Agriculture Dept. Graduate School
600 Maryland Ave. S.W. 20024
Switchboard: 447-4419
Director: Philip Hudson, 720-2077

American University
4400 Massachusetts Ave. N.W. 20016
Switchboard: 885-1000
President: Benjamin Ladner
885-2121

Catholic University
620 Michigan Ave. N.E. 20064
Switchboard: 319-5000
President: Patrick Ellis, 319-5100

Columbia Union College
7600 Flower Ave.
Takoma Park, MD 20912
Switchboard: (301) 270-9200
President: Charles Scriven
(301) 891-4128

Gallaudet University
800 Florida Ave. N.E. 20002
Switchboard: 651-5000 (voice and TDD)
President: I. King Jordan
651-5005 (voice and TDD)

George Mason University
4400 University Dr.
Fairfax, VA 22030
Switchboard: (703) 993-1000
President: George W. Johnson
(703) 993-8700

Georgetown University
37th and O Sts. N.W. 20057
Switchboard: 687-0100
President: Leo O'Donovan, 687-4134

George Washington University
2121 Eye St. N.W. 20052
Switchboard: 994-1000
President: Stephen Joel Trachtenberg
994-6500

Howard University
2400 6th St. N.W. 20059
Switchboard: 806-6100
President: Vacant, 806-2500

Marymount University
2807 N. Glebe Rd.
Arlington, VA 22207
Switchboard: (703) 522-5600
President: Eymard Gallagher,
(703) 284-1598

Mount Vernon College
2100 Foxhall Rd. N.W. 20007
Switchboard: 625-0400
President: Lucyann Geiselman, 625-4600

National Defense University
Fort Lesley J. McNair 20319
Switchboard: 475-1145
President: Lt. Gen. Paul G. Cerjan
(USA), 475-1854

National War College
Switchboard: 475-1776
Commandant: Maj. Gen. John C.
Fryer Jr. (USAF), 475-1842

**Industrial College of the
Armed Forces**
Switchboard: 475-1832
Commandant: Rear Adm. Jerome F.
Smith Jr. (USN), 475-1838

**The Paul H. Nitze School of Advanced
International Studies**
(Johns Hopkins University)
1740 Massachusetts Ave. N.W. 20036
Switchboard: 663-5600
Dean: Paul D. Wolfowitz, 663-5624

**Protestant Episcopal Theological
Seminary**
3737 Seminary Rd.
Alexandria, VA 22304
Switchboard: (703) 370-6600
President: Richard Reid, (703) 461-1701

Trinity College
125 Michigan Ave. N.E. 20017
Switchboard: 939-5000
President: Patricia McGuire, 939-5050

University of Maryland
Rt. 1, College Park Campus
College Park, MD 20742
Switchboard: (301) 405-1000
President: William Kirwan
(301) 405-5803

University of the District of Columbia
4200 Connecticut Ave. N.W. 20008
Switchboard: 282-7300
President: Tilden J. LeMelle
282-7550

American Assn. for Higher Education, 1 Dupont Circle N.W., #360 20036; 293-6440. Russell Edgerton, president. Fax, 293-0073.

Membership: college and university educators, students, public officials, and others interested in postsecondary education. Evaluates issues in higher education; interests include statewide and institutional assessment, school-college collaboration, improvement of teaching and learning, and student community service. Conducts studies, conferences, and an annual convention.

American Assn. of Colleges of Pharmacy, 1426 Prince St., Alexandria, VA 22314; (703) 739-2330. Dr. Carl E. Trinca, executive director. Fax, (703) 836-8982.

Represents and advocates for the academic community in the profession of pharmacy. Conducts programs and activities in cooperation with other national health and higher education associations in the Washington, D.C., area.

American Assn. of Collegiate Registrars and Admissions Officers, 1 Dupont Circle N.W., #330 20036; 293-9161. Wayne E. Becraft, executive director. Fax, 872-8857.

Membership: accredited postsecondary institutions represented by staff from recruiting, admissions, registration and records, financial aid, international education, and institutional research. Provides members with guidance, information for professional development, and management assistance; offers national and regional workshops.

American Assn. of Community Colleges, 1 Dupont Circle N.W. 20036; 728-0200. David Pierce, president. Fax, 833-2467.

Membership: two-year community technical and junior colleges, technical institutes, corporate foundations, international associates, and institutional affiliates. Studies include policies for lifelong education, use of mass media in education, humanities in career education, and partnerships among high schools, employers, and members.

American Assn. of State Colleges and Universities, 1 Dupont Circle N.W., #700 20036; 293-7070. James B. Appleberry, president. Fax, 296-5819.

Membership: presidents and chancellors of state colleges and universities. Promotes equity in education; fosters information exchange among members; interests include minority participa-

tion in higher education, student financial aid, international education programs, academic affairs, and teacher education. Monitors legislation and regulations.

American College Testing, 1 Dupont Circle N.W. 20036; 223-2318. Jerry W. Miller, director, Washington office. Fax, 223-0380.

Administers American College Test (ACT) entrance examination for colleges and universities. Provides colleges and universities with testing, counseling, research, and student aid processing services. (Headquarters in Iowa City, Iowa.)

American Conference of Academic Deans, 1818 R St. N.W. 20009; 387-3760. Margaret Williams Curtis, chair. Fax, 265-9532.

Membership: academic deans of two- and four-year accredited liberal arts colleges, private and public. Fosters information exchange among members on college curricular and administrative issues.

American Council on Education, 1 Dupont Circle N.W., #800 20036; 939-9300. Robert H. Atwell, president. Press, 939-9365. Fax, 833-4760.

Membership: colleges, universities, and education associations. Conducts and publishes research; maintains offices dealing with government relations, women in higher education, minority concerns, management of higher education institutions, educational credit (academic credit for nontraditional learning, especially in the armed forces), leadership development, and international education. Library open to the public by appointment.

Assn. for Supervision and Curriculum Development, 1250 N. Pitt St., Alexandria, VA 22314; (703) 549-9110. Gene R. Carter, executive director. Fax, (703) 549-3891.

Membership: teachers, supervisors, directors of instruction, school principals (kindergarten through secondary), university and college faculty, and individuals interested in curriculum development. Sponsors institutes and conferences. Monitors legislation and regulations affecting education.

Assn. of American Colleges and Universities, 1818 R St. N.W. 20009; 387-3760. Paula P. Brownlee, president. Fax, 265-9532.

Membership: public and private colleges, universities, and postsecondary consortia. Works to develop effective academic programs and improve undergraduate curricula and services. Seeks to encourage, enhance, and support the development of broadly based intellectual skills through the study of liberal arts and sciences.

Assn. of American Universities, 1 Dupont Circle N.W. 20036; 466-5030. Cornelius J. Pings, president. Fax, 296-4438.

Membership: public and private universities with emphasis on graduate and professional education and research. Fosters information exchange among presidents of member institutions.

Assn. of Community College Trustees, 1740 N St. N.W. 20036; 775-4667. Ray Taylor, president. Fax, 223-1297.

Provides members of community college governing boards with training in educational programs. Monitors federal education programs.

Assn. of Governing Boards of Universities and Colleges, 1 Dupont Circle N.W. 20036; 296-0400. Richard T Ingram, president. Fax, 223-7053.

Membership: presidents, boards of trustees, regents, commissions, and other groups governing colleges, universities, and institutionally related foundations. Interests include the relationship between the president and board of trustees and other subjects relating to governance. Library open to the public.

Assn. of Jesuit Colleges and Universities, 1 Dupont Circle, N.W., #405 20036; 862-9893. Paul S. Tipton SJ, president. Fax, 862-8523.

Membership: Jesuit colleges and universities. Monitors government regulatory and policy-making activities affecting higher education. Publishes directory of Jesuit colleges, universities, and high schools.

Business-Higher Education Forum, 1 Dupont Circle N.W., #800 20036; 939-9345. Don M. Blandin, director. Fax, 833-4723.

Membership: chief executive officers of major corporations, colleges, and universities. Promotes cooperation between businesses and higher educational institutions. Interests include international economic competitiveness, education and training, research and development, science and technology, and global interdependence.

Career College Assn., 750 1st St. N.E., #900 20002; 336-6700. Stephen J. Blair, president. Fax, 336-6828.

Membership: private postsecondary colleges and career schools in the United States, Western Europe, and the Caribbean. Works to expand the accessibility of postsecondary career education and to improve the quality of education offered by member schools.

College and University Personnel Assn., 1233 20th St. N.W., #301 20036; 429-0311. Richard C. Creal, executive director. Fax, 429-0149.

Membership: college and university human resource administrators. Conducts seminars and workshops; responds to inquiries on human resource administration.

The College Board, 1717 Massachusetts Ave. N.W., #404 20036; 332-7134. Lawrence E. Gladieux, executive director, Washington office. Fax, 462-5558.

Membership: colleges and universities, secondary schools, school systems, and education associations. Contracts with the Educational Testing Service for the administration of college admission tests, and guidance, placement, and financial aid services; for the administration of testing programs that give students credit for advance college-level work in high school; and for the administration of college equivalency exams. Develops guidance and counseling curricula for junior and senior high school students. Conducts research on career development and aspects of counseling and guidance. Library open to the public. (Headquarters in New York.)

Council of Graduate Schools, 1 Dupont Circle N.W., #430 20036; 223-3791. Jules B. LaPidus, president. Fax, 331-7157.

Membership: private and public colleges and universities with significant involvement in graduate education. Produces publications and information about graduate education; provides a forum for member schools to exchange information and ideas.

Council of Independent Colleges, 1 Dupont Circle N.W., #320 20036; 466-7230. Allen P. Splete, president. Fax, 466-7238.

Membership: private four-year liberal arts colleges. Sponsors management development institutes for college presidents and deans; conducts faculty development programs; sponsors national projects on leadership, curriculum development, and related topics. Holds workshops and produces publications.

Educational Testing Service (ETS), 1776 Massachusetts Ave. N.W., #620 20036; 659-0616. George Elford, director, Washington office. Fax, 659-8075.

Administers examinations for admission to educational programs and for graduate and licensing purposes; conducts instructional programs in testing, evaluation, and research in education fields. Washington office handles government and professional relations. Fee for services. (Headquarters in Princeton, N.J.)

National Assn. of College Admission Counselors, 1631 Prince St., Alexandria, VA 22314; (703) 836-2222. Frank E. Burtnett, executive director. Fax, (703) 836-8015.

Membership: high school guidance counselors, independent counselors, college and university admission officers, and financial aid officers. Assists counselors who serve students in the college admission process. Promotes and funds research on admission counseling and on the transition from high school to college. Sponsors national college fairs and continuing education for members.

National Assn. of College and University Attorneys, 1 Dupont Circle N.W., #620 20036; 833-8390. Phillip M. Grier, executive director. Fax, 296-8379.

Provides information on legal developments affecting postsecondary education; advises other education associations on legal issues affecting educational institutions.

National Assn. of College and University Business Officers, 1 Dupont Circle N.W., #500 20036; 861-2500. Caspa L. Harris Jr., president. Fax, 861-2583.

Membership: chief business officers at higher education institutions. Provides members with information on financial management, federal regulations, and other subjects related to the business administration of universities and colleges; conducts workshops on issues such as student aid, institutional budgeting, and accounting.

National Assn. of Independent Colleges and Universities, 122 C St. N.W., #750 20001; 347-7512. David L. Warren, president. Fax, 628-2513.

Membership: independent colleges and universities, and related state associations. Counsels members on federal education programs and tax policy.

National Assn. of State Universities and Land Grant Colleges, 1 Dupont Circle N.W., #710 20036; 778-0818. C. Peter Magrath, president. Fax, 296-6456.

Membership: land grant colleges and state universities. Serves as clearinghouse on issues of public higher education.

National Assn. of Student Personnel Administrators, 1875 Connecticut Ave. N.W., #418 20009-5728; 265-7500. Elizabeth Nuss, executive director. Fax, 797-1157.

Membership: deans, student affairs administrators, faculty, and graduate students. Seeks to develop leadership and improve practices in student affairs administration. Initiates and supports programs and legislation to improve student affairs administration.

National Council of University Research Administrators, 1 Dupont Circle N.W., #220 20036; 466-3894. Natalie Kirkman, executive director. Fax, 223-5573.

Membership: individuals engaged in administering research, training, and educational programs, primarily at colleges and universities. Encourages development of effective policies and procedures in the administration of these programs.

Society for Values in Higher Education, c/o Georgetown University, Washington, DC 20057; 687-3653. M. Kathleen McGrory, executive director. Press, 687-4402. Fax, 687-5094.

Membership: professors in the humanities, social sciences, and sciences. Promotes values-oriented teaching and curricula. Interests include academic ethics; values in administrative decision making; curricula development; ethics in science, technology, and world affairs; and new teaching methods.

U.S. Student Assn., 815 15th St. N.W., #838 20005; 347-8772. Tchiyuka Cornelius, president. Fax, 393-5886.

Represents postsecondary student government associations and state student lobby associations. Interests include civil rights on campus and the financing of higher education. Maintains coalitions on women students of color. Serves as clearinghouse for information on student problems, activities, and government; holds conferences emphasizing student lobbying techniques.

Women's College Coalition, 125 Michigan Ave., N.E. 20017; 234-0443. Jadwiga S. Sebrechts, executive director. Fax, 234-0445.

Membership: public and private, independent and church-related, two- and four-year women's colleges. Interests include the role of women's colleges as model institutions for educating women, gender equity issues, and retention of women in math, science, and engineering. Maintains an information clearinghouse on U.S. undergraduate women's colleges. Conducts research on gender equity issues in education and positive learning environments.

See also American Federation of Teachers (AFL-CIO) (p. 801); Assn. of American Colleges (p. 149); Assn. of Catholic Colleges and Universities and Christian College Coalition (p. 127); National Assn. for Equal Opportunity in Higher Education (p. 149); Servicemembers Opportunity Colleges (p. 554)

College Accreditation

Many college- or university-based and independent postsecondary education programs are accredited by member associations. See specific subject headings and associations within the chapter.

Agencies:

Education Dept., Accrediting Agency Evaluation, 7th and D Sts. S.W., #3036 20202-5244; 708-7417. Karen W. Kershenstein, division director. Fax, 708-9489.

Reviews accrediting agencies and state approval agencies that seek initial or renewed recognition by the secretary of education; provides the National Advisory Committee on Institutional Quality and Integrity with staff support.

Education Dept., National Advisory Committee on Accreditation and Institutional Eligibility, 7th and D Sts. S.W. 2020-5153; 708-5656. Steven Pappas, executive director. Fax, 708-9046.

Develops and recommends to the secretary of education standards for recognizing agencies that accredit academic, vocational, military, and nursing schools.

Nongovernmental:

American Academy for Liberal Education, 1015 18th St. N.W., #204 20036; 452-8611. Susan Wallace, vice president for operations. Fax, 452-8620.

Accredits colleges and universities whose general education program in the liberal arts meets the academy's accreditation requirements. Provides support for institutions that maintain substantial liberal arts programs and which desire to raise requirements to meet AALE standards.

Career College Assn., 750 1st St. N.E., #900 20002; 336-6700. Stephen J. Blair, president. Fax, 336-6828.

Membership: private postsecondary colleges and career schools in the United States, Western Europe, and the Caribbean. Sponsors independent commissions that accredit institutions offering certificates and degrees in many occupational fields in government, business, and industry.

Commission on Recognition of Postsecondary Accreditation, 1 Dupont Circle N.W. 20036; 452-1433. Dorothy Fenwick, director. Fax, 331-9571.

Membership: regional, institutional, and program accrediting organizations. Coordinates and reviews activities of these organizations. Monitors legislation and regulations. Library open to the public.

Construction of Facilities

Agencies:

Education Dept., Higher Education Incentive Programs, 7th and D Sts. S.W. 20202; 260-3245. Alfreda Liebermann, director. Fax, 260-7615.

Provides colleges and universities with loans and grants to construct and refurbish student dormitories and to construct and renovate academic facilities.

See also Architectural and Transportation Barriers Compliance Board (p. 420)

Congress:

See Education: Postsecondary, General, Congress (p. 132)

Nongovernmental:

Assn. of Higher Education Facilities Officers, 1446 Duke St., Alexandria, VA 22314; (703) 684-

1446. Walter A. Schaw, executive vice president. Fax, (703) 549-2772.

Membership: professionals involved in the administration, maintenance, planning, and development of buildings and facilities used by colleges and universities. Interests include maintenance and upkeep of housing facilities. Provides information on campus energy management programs and campus accessibility for people with disabilities.

College Construction Loan Insurance Assn. (Connie Lee), 2445 M St. N.W. 20037; 728-3411. Oliver R. Sockwell, president. Information, 835-0090. Fax, 785-2823. Toll-free, (800) 877-5333.

Congressionally authorized private corporation financed with common stock held by the Student Loan Marketing Assn. (Sallie Mae) and the Education Dept. and with preferred stock held by other investors, including financial and educational institutions. Supports low-cost, long-term financing for higher education academic facilities. Guarantees and reinsures tax-exempt bonds issued by colleges, universities, and teaching hospitals.

Financial Aid to Students

See also Fellowships and Grants (p. 158)

Agencies:

Education Dept., Institutional Participation Division, 7th and D Sts. S.W. 20202; 708-4906. Diane M. Sedicum, director. Fax, 205-0782.

Certifies institutions and schools for participation in student financial aid programs such as the Pell Grant Program, the Perkins Loan Program, the College Work-Study Program, the Supplemental Educational Opportunity Grant Program, the Stafford Student Loan Program (Guaranteed Student Loan)/PLUS Program, and the Supplemental Loans for Students (SLS).

Education Dept., Student Financial Assistance, 7th and D Sts. S.W. (mailing address: 400 Maryland Ave. S.W., Washington, DC 20202); 708-8391. Leo Kornfeld, deputy assistant secretary. Fax, 708-7157. Student Aid Information Center, (800) 433-3243.

Administers federal loan, grant, and work-study programs for postsecondary education to eligible individuals. Administers the Pell Grant Program, the Perkins Loan Program, the Stafford Student Loan Program (Guaranteed Student Loan)/PLUS Program, the College Work-Study Program, the Supplemental Loans for Students (SLS), and the Supplemental Educational Opportunity Grant Program.

Congress:

See Education: Postsecondary, General, Congress (p. 132)

Nongovernmental:

The College Board, 1717 Massachusetts Ave. N.W., #404 20036; 332-7134. Lawrence E. Gladieux, executive director, Washington office. Fax, 462-5558.

Membership: colleges and universities, secondary schools, school systems, and education associations. Researches and analyzes patterns of financing higher education; monitors financial aid and other education legislation. Contracts with the Educational Testing Service to assess a student's financial needs and supplies data to schools where the student applies. Library open to the public. (Headquarters in New York.)

National Assn. of Student Financial Aid Administrators, 1920 L St. N.W., #200 20036-5020; 785-0453. Dallas Martin, president. Fax, 785-1487.

Works to ensure adequate funding for individuals seeking postsecondary education and to ensure proper management and administration of public and private financial aid funds.

National Council of Higher Education Loan Programs, 801 Pennsylvania Ave. S.E., #375 20003; 547-1571. Jean S. Frohlicher, president. Information, 547-7808. Fax, 546-8745.

Membership: agencies and organizations involved in making, servicing, and collecting Guaranteed Student Loans. Works with the Education Dept. to develop forms and procedures for administering the Guaranteed Student Loan Program. Fosters information exchange among members.

Student Loan Marketing Assn. (Sallie Mae), 1050 Thomas Jefferson St. N.W. 20007; 298-2600. Lawrence A. Hough, president. Information, 333-8000.

Government-sponsored private corporation. Provides funds to financial and educational institutions (such as commercial banks, colleges, and universities) that make Stafford Student Loans and other educational loans administered by the Education Dept. available to students. *(See agency sources in this section.)*

See also National Institute of Independent Colleges and Universities (p. 131)

Education: Preschool, Elementary, Secondary

General

See also Education, Private and Parochial Schools (p. 127); Education, Professional Interests and Benefits (p. 128); Education, Research (p. 130); Museum Education Programs box (p. 115)

Agencies:

Education Dept., Bilingual Education and Minority Languages, 330 C St. S.W., #5082 20202; 205-5463. Eugene E. Garcia, director. Fax, 205-8737.

Administers bilingual education programs in elementary and secondary schools to help students of limited English proficiency learn the English language. The program is designed to give students of limited English proficiency better opportunities to achieve academic success and meet grade promotion and graduation requirements.

Education Dept., Drug Planning and Outreach, 400 Maryland Ave. S.W., #1073 20202-6123; 401-3030. William Modzeleski, director. Fax, 401-1069.

Develops policy for the department's drug and violence prevention initiatives for students in elementary and secondary schools and institutions of higher education. Coordinates education efforts in drug and violence prevention with those of other federal departments and agencies.

Education Dept., Elementary and Secondary Education, 400 Maryland Ave. S.W. 20202-6100; 401-0113. Thomas Payzant, assistant secretary. Information, 401-1576. Fax, 401-1112.

Administers federal assistance programs for preschool, elementary, and secondary education (both public and private). Program divisions are Compensatory Education (including Chapter 1 aid for disadvantaged children), School Improvement, Migrant Education, Indian Educa-

tion, Impact Aid, and Drug Planning and Outreach.

Education Dept., Even Start, 400 Maryland Ave. S.W. 20202-6132; 260-0994. Donna Conforti, acting coordinator. Fax, 260-7764.

Develops family-centered education projects to encourage parents to become involved in the education of their children; helps children reach their full potential as learners and offers literacy training to parents.

Education Dept., Follow Through Program, 400 Maryland Ave. S.W. 20202; 401-1692. Robert Alexander, program specialist. Fax, 401-2527.

Assists the overall development of children from low-income families (grades K-3). Augments the educational gains made by children in Head Start and other preschool programs by supplementing basic educational services available in the public school system with services and activities related to physical and mental health, social welfare, and nutrition. Seeks community and parental involvement in the program.

Education Dept., Impact Aid, 400 Maryland Ave. S.W. 20202-6244; 401-3637. Charles E. Hansen, director. Information, 401-0553. Fax, 401-2215.

Provides funds for elementary and secondary educational activities to school districts in federally impacted areas (where federal activities such as military bases enlarge staff and reduce taxable property); provides education funds where school facilities are damaged as a result of a declared major disaster.

Environmental Protection Agency, Pollution Prevention and Toxics, 401 M St. S.W. 20460; 260-3810. Mark A. Greenwood, director. Fax, 260-1764.

Administers the Asbestos Loan and Grant Program by awarding loans and grants to needy public and nonprofit private elementary and secondary schools to eliminate friable asbestos materials that pose a health threat to building occupants.

Health and Human Services Dept., Head Start, 330 C St. S.W. (mailing address: P.O. Box 1182, Washington, DC 20013); 205-8572. Helen Taylor, associate commissioner. Fax, 401-5916.

Awards grants to nonprofit organizations and local governments for operating community Head Start programs (comprehensive development programs for children, ages 3 to 5, of low-income families); manages a limited number of parent and child centers for families with children up to age 3. Conducts research and manages demonstration programs, including those under the Comprehensive Child Care Development Act of 1988; administers the Child Development Associate scholarship program, which trains individuals for careers in child development, often as Head Start teachers.

Smithsonian Institution, Reading Is Fundamental, 600 Maryland Ave. S.W., #600 20024; 287-3371. Ruth Graves, president. Information, 287-3220. Fax, 287-3196.

Conducts programs and workshops to motivate young people to read. Provides young people with books and parents with services to encourage reading at home.

White House Commission on Presidential Scholars (Education Dept.), 400 Maryland Ave. S.W. 20202; 401-1365. JoAnne Livingston, executive director. Fax, 401-1112.

Honorary recognition program that selects high school seniors of outstanding achievement to receive the Presidential Scholars Award. Scholars travel to Washington for national recognition week.

Congress:

House Education and Labor Committee, Subcommittee on Elementary, Secondary, and Vocational Education, B-346A RHOB 20515; 225-4368. Dale E. Kildee, D-Mich., chairman; Susan Wilhelm, staff director. Fax, 225-1110.

Jurisdiction over preschool, elementary, and secondary education legislation, including impact aid legislation, food programs for children in schools, legislation barring discrimination in schools, and the Follow Through Act, which aids children in making the transition from preschool to elementary grades.

Senate Agriculture, Nutrition, and Forestry Committee, Subcommittee on Nutrition and Investigations, SR-328A 20510; 224-2035. Tom Harkin, D-Iowa, chairman; Mark Halverson, legislative assistant.

Jurisdiction over legislation on food programs for children in schools.

Senate Labor and Human Resources Committee, SD-428 20510; 224-5375. Edward M. Kennedy, D-Mass., chairman; Nick Littlefield, chief counsel and staff director.

Jurisdiction over preschool education reauthorization legislation.

Senate Labor and Human Resources Committee, Subcommittee on Education, Arts, and Humanities, SD-648 20510; 224-7666. Claiborne Pell, D-R.I., chairman; David V. Evans, staff director.

Jurisdiction over preschool, elementary, and secondary education legislation, including impact aid legislation; and legislation barring discrimination in schools. Oversight of the Follow Through Act, which aids children in making the transition from preschool to elementary grades.

See also Library of Congress, Children's Literature Center (p. 113)

Nongovernmental:

Assn. for Childhood Education International, 11501 Georgia Ave., #315, Wheaton, MD 20902; (301) 942-2443. Gerald C. Odland, executive director. Toll-free, (800) 423-3563. Fax, (301) 942-3012.

Membership: educators, parents, and professionals who work with children (infancy to adolescence). Works to promote the rights, education, and well-being of children worldwide. Holds annual conference.

Assn. for Supervision and Curriculum Development, 1250 N. Pitt St., Alexandria, VA 22314; (703) 549-9110. Gene R. Carter, executive director. Fax, (703) 549-3891.

Membership: teachers, supervisors, directors of instruction, school principals (kindergarten through secondary), university and college faculty, and individuals interested in curriculum development. Sponsors institutes and conferences. Monitors legislation and regulations affecting education.

Clearinghouse on Educational Choice, 927 S. Walter Reed Dr., Arlington, VA 22204; (703) 486-8311. Robert S. Marlowe, executive director.

Works to educate citizens and policymakers about parental choice in education. Interests include vouchers, tuition tax credits, magnet schools, alternative schools, and the role of parents in the academic achievement of children. Sponsors research, an information clearinghouse, and conferences.

Council for Basic Education, 1319 F St. N.W., #900 20004; 347-4171. A. Graham Down, president. Fax, 347-5047.

Promotes liberal arts education in elementary and secondary schools; seeks to improve liberal arts instruction of teachers and administrators; conducts workshops, seminars, and independent studies for elementary and secondary school teachers; serves as information clearinghouse on education issues.

The Council of the Great City Schools, 1413 K St. N.W. 20005; 393-2427. Mike Casserly, acting director. Fax, 371-1365.

Membership: superintendents and school board members of large urban school districts. Provides research, legislative, and support services for members; interests include elementary and secondary education and school finance.

The Home and School Institute, MegaSkills Education Center, 1500 Massachusetts Ave. N.W. 20005; 466-3633. Dorothy Rich, president.

Works to improve the quality of education for children and parents by integrating the resources of the home, the school, and the community. Develops family training curricula and materials for home use, and training programs and conferences for professionals. Interests include special, bilingual, and career education; and working, single, and teen-age parents.

National Alliance of Business, Center for Excellence in Education, 1201 New York Ave. N.W., #700 20005; 289-2962. Patricia Mitchell, executive director. Fax, 289-1303.

Encourages business leaders, government officials, and educators to work together to restructure the educational system. Provides information on state and local education restructuring initiatives; helps corporations contribute resources to schools; researches entry-level worker skill needs.

National Assessment Governing Board, 800 N. Capitol St. N.W., #825 20002; 357-6938. Roy Truby, executive director. Fax, 357-6945.

Independent board of local, state, and federal officials, educators, and others appointed by the secretary of education and funded under the National Assessment of Educational Progress (NAEP) program. Sets policy for NAEP, a series of tests measuring achievements in U.S. schools since 1969.

National Assn. for the Education of Young Children, 1509 16th St. N.W. 20036-1426; 232-8777. Marilyn M. Smith, executive director. Toll-free, (800) 424-2460. Fax, 328-1846.

Membership: teachers, parents, and directors of early childhood programs. Works to improve the education of and the quality of services to children from birth through age 8. Sponsors professional development opportunities for early childhood educators. Offers an accreditation program and conducts an annual conference; issues publications.

National Assn. of College Admission Counselors, 1631 Prince St., Alexandria, VA 22314; (703) 836-2222. Frank E. Burtnett, executive director. Fax, (703) 836-8015.

Membership: high school guidance counselors, independent counselors, college and university admissions officers, and financial aid officers. Assists counselors who serve students in the college admission process. Promotes and funds research on admission counseling and on the transition from high school to college. Sponsors national college fairs, continuing education for members, and an annual conference.

National Assn. of Elementary School Principals, 1615 Duke St., Alexandria, VA 22314; (703) 684-3345. Samuel G. Sava, executive director. Fax, (703) 548-6021.

Membership: elementary and middle school principals. Conducts workshops for members on federal and state policies and programs and on professional development. Offers assistance in contract negotiations, the image of the principal, and education issues.

National Assn. of Partners in Education, 209 Madison St., #401, Alexandria, VA 22314; (703) 836-4880. Daniel W. Merenda, president. Fax, (703) 836-6941.

Membership: teachers, administrators, volunteers, businesses, community groups, and others seeking to help students achieve academic excellence. Creates and strengthens volunteer and partnership programs. Advocates community involvement in schools.

National Assn. of Secondary School Principals, 1904 Association Dr., Reston, VA 22091; (703) 860-0200. Timothy J. Dyer, executive director. Fax, (703) 476-5432.

Membership: principals and assistant principals of middle and senior high schools, both public and private, and college-level teachers of secondary education. Conducts training programs for members; serves as clearinghouse for information on secondary school administration. Student activities office provides student councils, student activity advisers, and national and junior honor societies with information on national associations.

National Committee for Citizens in Education, 900 2nd St. N.E., #8 20002; 408-0447. Bruce Astrein, executive director. Toll-free, (800) 638-9675. Fax, 408-0452.

Membership: parents, educators, and other interested individuals. Works to improve the quality of public schools by encouraging public involvement. Provides members with training programs, technical assistance, and an information clearinghouse. Monitors legislation and regulations that affect parent and citizen participation in schools.

National Congress of Parents and Teachers, 2000 L St. N.W., #600 20036; 331-1380. Arnold F. Fege, director, governmental relations.

Membership: parent-teacher associations at the preschool, elementary, and secondary levels. Washington office represents members' interests on education, parent involvement, child protection and safety, drug and substance abuse, juvenile justice and missing children, AIDS, the environ.ent, children's television, child care, and nutrition. (Headquarters in Chicago.)

National Head Start Assn., 201 N. Union St., #320, Alexandria, VA 22314; (703) 739-0875. Sarah M. Greene, executive director. Fax, (703) 739-0878.

Membership organization that represents Head Start children, families, and staff. Recommends strategies on issues affecting Head Start programs; provides training and professional development opportunities; monitors legislation and regulations.

National School Boards Assn., 1680 Duke St., Alexandria, VA 22314; (703) 838-6722. Thomas A. Shannon, executive director. Fax, (703) 683-7590.

Federation of state school board associations. Interests include funding of public education, local governance, and quality of education programs. Sponsors seminars, an annual conference, and an information center. Monitors legislation and regulations. Library open to the public by appointment.

National Urban Coalition, 1875 Connecticut Ave. N.W., #400 20009-5728; 986-1460. Ramona H. Edelin, president. Fax, 986-1468.

Membership: business and labor representatives, minority groups, educators, and religious and civic leaders. Operates Say Yes to a Youngster's Future, a community-based education program for low-income students in math, science, and technology; maintains database on urban education programs.

See also Young Audiences (p. 107)

School Lunch Programs

See also Government Financial Assistance Programs, Child Nutrition Programs (p. 407)

Agencies:

Agriculture Dept., Child Nutrition, 3101 Park Center Dr., Alexandria, VA 22302; (703) 305-2590. Alberta Frost, director. Fax, (703) 305-2879.

Administers the transfer of funds to state agencies for the National School Lunch Program; the School Breakfast Program; the Special Milk Program, which helps schools and institutions provide children who do not have access to full meals under other child nutrition programs with fluid milk; the Child and Adult Care Food Program, which provides children in nonresidential child-care centers and family day care homes with year-round meal service; and the Summer Food Service Program, which provides children from low-income families with meals during the summer months.

Agriculture Dept., Food and Nutrition, 3101 Park Center Dr., Alexandria, VA 22302; (703) 305-2062. William Ludwig, administrator. Information, (703) 305-2276. Fax, (703) 305-2908.

Provides state agencies with funds and food for school breakfast and lunch programs (preschool through secondary) at public and nonprofit private schools.

Agriculture Dept., Food Distribution, 3101 Park Center Dr., #503, Alexandria, VA 22302; (703) 305-2680. Vernon Morgan, director. Fax, (703) 305-2420. TDD, (703) 305-2648.

Administers the purchasing and distribution of food to state agencies for child-care centers, public and private schools, public and nonprofit charitable institutions, and summer camps. Coordinates the distribution of special commodities, including surplus cheese and butter. Administers the National Commodity Processing Program, which facilitates distribution, at reduced prices, of processed foods to state agencies.

Agriculture Dept., Nutrition and Technical Services, 3101 Park Center Dr., #607, Alexandria, VA 22302; (703) 305-2585. Joseph E. Shepherd, director. Fax, (703) 305-2549.

Administers the Nutrition Education and Training Program, which provides states with grants for disseminating nutrition information to children and for in-service training of food service and teaching personnel; administers the Child Nutrition Labeling Program, which certifies that foods served in child nutrition programs, particularly school lunch and breakfast programs, meet nutritional requirements; provides information and technical assistance in nutrition and food service management.

National Agricultural Library (Agriculture Dept.), Food and Nutrition Information Center, 10301 Baltimore Blvd., #304, Beltsville, MD 20705; (301) 504-5719. Sandra Facinoli, coordinator. Fax, (301) 504-6409.

Serves as a resource center for school and child nutrition program personnel who need information on food service management and nutrition education. Assists teachers in developing nutrition education programs. Center open to the public.

Congress:

See *Education: Preschool, Elementary, Secondary, General, Congress (p. 140)*

Nongovernmental:

American School Food Service Assn., 1600 Duke St., Alexandria, VA 22314; (703) 739-3900. Barbara Borschow, executive director. Toll-free, (800) 877-8822. Fax, (703) 739-3915.

Membership: state and local food service workers and supervisors, school cafeteria managers, nutrition educators, and others interested in school food programs and child nutrition. Sponsors National School Lunch Week.

Child Nutrition Forum, 1875 Connecticut Ave. N.W., #540 20009-5728; 986-2200. Edward Cooney, coordinator. Fax, 986-2525.

Membership: agriculture, labor, education, and health specialists; school food service officials; and consumer and religious groups. Supports

federal nutrition programs for children; provides information on school nutrition programs; monitors legislation and regulations concerning hunger issues.

Community Nutrition Institute, 2001 S St. N.W., #530 20009; 462-7400. Rodney E. Leonard, executive director. Fax, 462-5241.

Citizens' interest group that provides information on nutrition, food policy issues, and federally funded food programs. Monitors legislation and regulations on nutrition policy.

National Congress of Parents and Teachers, 2000 L St. N.W., #600 20036; 331-1380. Arnold F. Fege, director, governmental relations.

Membership: parent-teacher associations at the preschool, elementary, and secondary levels. Supports school lunch and breakfast programs; active member of the School Lunch Coalition, which supports federally funded nutrition programs for children. (Headquarters in Chicago.)

Education: Special Groups

Adult

See also Education: Special Topics, Vocational (p. 157)

Agencies:

Agriculture Dept., Graduate School, 600 Maryland Ave. S.W. 20024; 720-2077. Philip H. Hudson, director. Information, 447-4419. Fax, 720-3603.

Self-supporting educational institution that is open to the public. Offers continuing education courses for career advancement and personal fulfillment; offers training at agency locations.

Education Dept., Adult Education and Literacy, 330 C St. S.W. (mailing address: 400 Maryland Ave. S.W., Washington, DC 20202-7240); 205-8270. Ronald S. Pugsley, acting director. Fax, 205-8973. Literacy clearinghouse, 205-9996.

Provides state and local education agencies with information on establishing, expanding, improving, and operating adult education and literacy programs. Emphasizes basic and life skills attainment and high school completion. Awards grants to state education agencies for adult education and literacy programs, including grants for education for the homeless and workplace literacy partnerships. Coordinates homeless and adult literacy programs.

Education Dept., Vocational and Adult Education, 330 C St. S.W. (mailing address: 400 Maryland Ave. S.W., Washington, DC 20202-7100); 205-5451. Augusta Kappner, assistant secretary. Fax, 205-8748.

Serves as principal adviser to the secretary on matters related to vocational and adult education. Administers, coordinates, and recommends national policy for improving vocational and adult education programs. Administers grants and contracts for research programs in adult education, dropout prevention, retraining, English literacy, workplace literacy, high technology, and vocational education programs for dislocated workers, migrant farm workers, and the homeless.

See also Bureau of Indian Affairs and Education Dept., Indian Education Programs (p. 147)

Nongovernmental:

American Assn. for Adult and Continuing Education, 1101 Connecticut Ave. N.W., #700 20036; 429-5131. Drew Allbritten, executive director. Fax, 223-4579.

Membership: adult and continuing education professionals. Acts as an information clearinghouse; evaluates adult and continuing education programs; sponsors conferences, seminars, and workshops.

International Assn. for Continuing Education and Training, 1650 Tysons Blvd., #200, McLean, VA 22102; (703) 506-3290. Donna F. Cantor, acting executive director. Fax, (703) 506-3066.

Membership: education and training organizations, and individuals who use the Continuing Education Unit. (The C.E.U. is defined as 10 contact hours of participation in an organized continuing education program that is noncredit.) Develops criteria and guidelines for use of the C.E.U.

National University Continuing Education Assn., 1 Dupont Circle N.W., #615 20036; 659-3130. Kay Kohl, executive director. Fax, 785-0374.

Membership: higher education institutions and nonprofit organizations involved in postsecondary continuing education. Publishes professional materials; prepares statistical analyses;

produces data reports; recognizes accomplishments in the field. Monitors legislation and regulations.

See also American Assn. of Community Colleges (p. 134); Correctional Education Assn. (p. 515); National Community Education Assn. (p. 126)

Gifted and Talented

(also known as exceptional)

Agencies:

Education Dept., Gifted and Talented Education, 555 New Jersey Ave. N.W. 20208; 219-2169. Patricia O'Connell Ross, director. Fax, 219-2106.

Awards grants for developing programs for gifted and talented students, including the limited-English-speaking, economically disadvantaged, and disabled. Oversees the National Research Center, which administers grants for research and analysis of gifted and talented programs. Conducts seminars and produces publications on issues related to gifted and talented programs.

Nongovernmental:

The Council for Exceptional Children, 1920 Association Dr., Reston, VA 22091; (703) 620-3660. George Ayers, executive director. Fax, (703) 264-9494. TDD, (703) 620-3660.

Provides information on gifted and talented education nationwide; maintains clearinghouse of information on the gifted; provides lawmakers with technical assistance; monitors legislation and regulations affecting gifted and talented education. Library open to the public.

Foundation for Exceptional Children, 1920 Association Dr., Reston, VA 22091; (703) 620-1054. Kenneth L. Collins, executive director. Fax, (703) 264-9494.

Membership: individuals interested in meeting the needs of gifted children and children with disabilities. Provides information and assists educators and parents; works to protect the rights of exceptional children; develops education programs and faculty standards. Awards scholarships and grants.

National Assn. for Gifted Children, 1155 15th St. N.W., #1002 20005; 785-4268. Peter D. Rosenstein, executive director.

Membership: teachers, administrators, state coordinators, and parents. Works for programs for intellectually and creatively gifted children in public and private schools.

See also National Assn. of Private Schools for Exceptional Children (p. 146)

Handicapped, Learning Disabled

(also known as exceptional)

See also Health Care and Services for Special Groups, Mentally Retarded (p. 343); Health Care and Services for Special Groups, Physically Disabled (p. 345); Social Services and Rehabilitation Programs, Disabled (p. 420)

Agencies:

Education Dept., Special Education and Rehabilitative Services, 330 C St. S.W. (mailing address: 400 Maryland Ave. S.W., Washington, DC 20202-2500); 205-5465. Judith Heumann, assistant secretary. Fax, 205-9252. TDD, 205-5465. Information clearinghouse, 205-8241.

Administers federal assistance programs for the education and rehabilitation of people with disabilities, as provided for by the Individuals with Disabilities Education Act and the Rehabilitation Act of 1973, as amended, which are administered by the National Institute of Disability and Rehabilitation Research, the Office of Special Education Programs, and the Rehabilitation Services Administration; maintains a national information clearinghouse on people with disabilities.

Education Dept., Special Education Programs, 330 C St. S.W. 20202-2651; 205-5507. Thomas Hehir, director.

Responsible for special education programs and services designed to meet the needs and develop the full potential of children with disabilities. Programs include support for training of teachers and other professional personnel; grants for research; financial aid to help states initiate, expand, and improve their resources; and media services and captioned films for hearing impaired persons.

Gallaudet University, 800 Florida Ave. N.E. 20002; 651-5005. I. King Jordan, president.

Press, 651-5505. Fax, 651-5508. Phone numbers are voice and TDD accessible.

Offers undergraduate and graduate degree programs for the deaf and hearing impaired and graduate training for teachers and other professionals who work with the deaf; conducts research; maintains outreach and regional centers and demonstration doctoral, continuing education, secondary, elementary, and preschool programs (Model Secondary School for the Deaf, Kendall Demonstration Elementary School). Sponsors the International Center on Deafness, the National Information Center on Deafness, and the National Center for the Law and the Deaf.

Smithsonian Institution, Accessibility Program, 900 Jefferson Dr. S.W., #1410 MRC 410 20560; 786-2942. Janice Majewski, coordinator. Fax, 786-2210. TDD, 786-2414.

Coordinates Smithsonian efforts to improve accessibility of its programs and facilities to visitors and staff with disabilities. Serves as a resource for museums and individuals nationwide.

Very Special Arts, 1331 F St. N.W. (mailing address: Education Office, John F. Kennedy Center for the Performing Arts, Washington, DC 20566); 628-2800. Eugene Maillard, chief executive officer. Toll-free, (800) 933-8721. Fax, 737-0725. TDD, 737-0645.

Initiates and supports research and program development providing arts training and demonstration for persons with disabilities. Provides technical assistance and training to Very Special Arts state organizations; acts as an information clearinghouse for arts and persons with disabilities. (Affiliated with the John F. Kennedy Center education office.)

Congress:

Library of Congress, National Library Service for the Blind and Physically Handicapped, 1291 Taylor St. N.W. 20542; 707-5104. Frank Kurt Cylke, director. Toll-free, (800) 424-8567. Fax, 707-0712. Reference, 707-5100.

Administers a national program of free library services for blind and physically disabled persons in cooperation with regional and subregional libraries. Produces and distributes full-length books and magazines in recorded form (disc and cassette) and in Braille. Reference section answers questions relating to blindness and physical disabilities and on library services available to the blind and physically disabled.

Nongovernmental:

American Assn. of University Affiliated Programs for Persons with Developmental Disabilities, 8630 Fenton St., #410, Silver Spring, MD 20910; (301) 588-8252. William E. Jones, executive director. Fax, (301) 588-2842. TDD, (301) 588-3319.

Network of facilities that diagnose and treat the developmentally disabled. Trains graduate students and professionals in the field; helps state and local agencies develop services. Interests include interdisciplinary training and services, early screening to prevent developmental disabilities, and development of equipment and programs to serve persons with disabilities.

American Foundation for the Blind, 1615 M St. N.W., #250 20036; 457-1487. Scott Marshall, associate executive director, governmental relations. Fax, 457-1492.

Research and consulting organization that serves as a clearinghouse for information on blindness and visual impairment. Offers consulting service on educational programs for blind children, adults, and their families. Monitors legislation and regulations prohibiting discrimination on the basis of disability. (Headquarters in New York.)

Assn. for Education and Rehabilitation of the Blind and Visually Impaired, 206 N. Washington St., Alexandria, VA 22314; (703) 548-1884. Kathleen Megivern, executive director.

Membership: professionals and paraprofessionals who work with the blind. Provides information on services for the blind and on employment opportunities for those who work with the blind. Works to improve quality of education and rehabilitation services.

The Council for Exceptional Children, 1920 Association Dr., Reston, VA 22091; (703) 620-3660. George Ayers, executive director. Fax, (703) 264-9494. TDD, (703) 620-3660.

Provides information on the education of exceptional children; maintains clearinghouse of information on people with disabilities, learning disorders, and special education topics; provides lawmakers with technical assistance; monitors legislation and regulations affecting special education. Library open to the public.

Foundation for Exceptional Children, 1920 Association Dr., Reston, VA 22091; (703) 620-1054. Kenneth L. Collins, executive director. Fax, (703) 264-9494.

Membership: individuals interested in meeting the special needs of children with disabilities. Provides information and assists educators and parents; works to protect the rights of exceptional children; develops education programs and faculty standards. Awards scholarships and grants.

National Assn. of Private Schools for Exceptional Children, 1522 K St. N.W., #1032 20005; 408-3338. Sherry L. Kolbe, executive director. Fax, 408-3340.

Promotes greater opportunities for exceptional children; provides legislators and agencies with information and testimony; formulates and disseminates positions and statements on special education issues.

National Assn. of State Directors of Special Education, 1800 Diagonal Rd., #320, Alexandria, VA 22314; (703) 519-3800. Martha J. Fields, executive director. Fax, (703) 519-3808.

Membership: state education agency special education administrators, consultants, and supervisors. Coordinates and provides state education agency personnel with in-service training programs; manages federally sponsored clearinghouse on professions in special education; monitors legislation and research developments in special education.

See also Assn. of Higher Education Facilities Officers (p. 137); The Home and School Institute (p. 141); National Institute for Citizen Education in the Law (p. 522)

Minorities and Women

See also Education: Special Topics, Bilingual (p. 151); Minority and Women's Rights (p. 265)

Agencies:

Administration for Children and Families (Health and Human Services Dept.), Refugee Resettlement, 901 D St. S.W., 6th Floor (mailing address: 370 L'Enfant Promenade S.W., Washington, DC 20447); 401-9246. Lavinia Limon, director. Fax, 401-5487.

Awards grants to states to pay for part of the costs incurred in providing public assistance, health assistance, and educational services to aliens who attained legal status under the Immigration Reform and Control Act of 1986.

Bureau of Indian Affairs (Interior Dept.), Indian Education Programs, Main Interior Bldg. 20240; 208-6123. John W. Tippecconic, director. Fax, 208-3312.

Operates schools for native Americans, including people with disabilities. Provides special assistance to native American pupils in public schools; aids native American college students; sponsors adult education programs.

Commission on Civil Rights, Civil Rights Evaluation, 624 9th St. N.W. 20425; 376-8582. James S. Cunningham, assistant staff director. Library, 376-8110. Fax, 376-8315.

Researches federal policy on education, including desegregation. Library open to the public.

Education Dept., Civil Rights, 330 C St. S.W. 20202; 205-5413. Norma Cantu, assistant secretary. Fax, 205-9862. TDD, 205-8673. Toll-free, (800) 205-8384.

Enforces laws prohibiting use of federal funds for education programs or activities that discriminate on the basis of race, color, sex, national origin, age, or disability; authorized to discontinue funding.

Education Dept., Compensatory Education Programs, 400 Maryland Ave. S.W. 20202-6132; 401-1682. Mary Jean LeTendre, director. Fax, 401-1112.

Administers the Chapter 1 federal assistance program for education of educationally deprived children (preschool through secondary), including native American children, delinquents, and residents in state institutions. Administers the Even Start and Follow Through programs. *(See entries for Even Start and Follow Through, p. 139.)*

Education Dept., Indian Education Programs, 400 Maryland Ave. S.W. 20202; 401-1887. Jon C. Wade, acting director. Fax, 205-2434.

Aids local school districts with programs for native American students; funds schools operated by the Bureau of Indian Affairs and native American-controlled schools and programs, including teacher training programs and curriculum innovations; assists in developing adult education programs; provides fellowships.

Education Dept., Intergovernmental Constituent Services, 400 Maryland Ave. S.W. 20202-3722; 401-3668. James S. Roberts, director. Fax, 401-1971.

Acts as ombudsman for Asian-Pacific, African American, Hispanic, and women's organizations concerned with education issues. Disseminates information on government programs to organizations and educators; reports to the secretary on interests of special populations.

Education Dept., Migrant Education, 400 Maryland Ave. S.W. 20202-6135; 401-0740. Francis Corrigan, director. Fax, 401-1112.

Administers programs that fund education (preschool through postsecondary) for children of migrant workers.

Education Dept., Student Services, 400 Maryland Ave. S.W., #5065 FOB-6 20202-5249; 708-4804. May J. Weaver, branch chief. Fax, 401-6132.

Administers programs for disadvantaged students, including Upward Bound, Talent Search, Student Support Services, the Ronald E. McNair Post-Baccalaureate Achievement Program, and educational opportunity centers; provides special programs personnel with training.

Education Dept., White House Initiative on Historically Black Colleges and Universities, 7th and D Sts. S.W. (mailing address: 400 Maryland Ave. S.W., Washington, DC 20202); 708-8667. Catherine LeBlanc, executive director. Fax, 708-7872.

Supervises and seeks to increase involvement of the private sector in historically black colleges and universities. Works to eliminate barriers to the participation of these colleges and universities in federal and private programs.

Education Dept., Women's Educational Equity Act Program, 400 Maryland Ave. S.W. 20202; 401-1356. Carolyn N. Andrews, program specialist. Fax, 401-2275.

Administers the Women's Educational Equity Act; awards grants and contracts to individuals, higher education institutions, and public and nonprofit private organizations promoting issues related to educational equity for women; maintains liaison with national women's organizations. (Program does not offer financial aid directly to students.)

Interior Dept., Cooperative Activities and Initiatives, Main Interior Bldg. 20240; 208-6403. Ira Hutchison, director. Fax, 208-3620.

Organizes and manages Interior Dept. programs and service assistance activities for historically black colleges and universities, the Hispanic

Association of Colleges and Universities, and Native American Colleges.

Justice Dept., Educational Opportunity, Main Justice Bldg. 20530; 514-4092. Nathaniel Douglas, chief. Fax, 514-8337.

Initiates litigation to ensure equal opportunities in public education; enforces laws dealing with civil rights in public education.

National Advisory Council on Indian Education (Education Dept.), 330 C St. S.W. 20202; 205-8353. Robert K. Chiago, executive director. Fax, 205-8897.

Recommends and reviews educational programs that affect native American children and adults; sponsors conferences and produces publications on native American education issues. Nominates director of native American education programs in Education Dept.

Office of Personnel Management, Affirmative Recruiting and Employment, 1900 E St. N.W., #6332 20415; 606-0800. Donna Beecher, assistant director. Fax, 606-5049. TDD, 606-0023.

Develops and provides guidance to federal agencies on student and needy youth programs, such as work-study and summer employment, as they relate to minorities and women.

Congress:

House Appropriations Committee, Subcommittee on Interior, 3481 RHOB 20515; 225-3481. Sidney R. Yates, D-Ill., chairman; D. Neal Sigmon, staff assistant.

Jurisdiction over legislation to appropriate funds for all native American education activities of the Education Dept. and for the Bureau of Indian Affairs.

House Education and Labor Committee, 2181 RHOB 20515; 225-4527. William D. Ford, D-Mich., chairman; Patricia Rissler, staff director.

Jurisdiction over legislation pertaining to native American education; oversight of native American education programs (jurisdiction shared with the House Natural Resources Committee).

House Education and Labor Committee, Subcommittee on Elementary, Secondary, and Vocational Education, B-346A RHOB 20515; 225-4368. Dale E. Kildee, D-Mich., chairman; Susan Wilhelm, staff director. Fax, 225-1110.

Jurisdiction over legislation barring discrimination in education, including the Women's Educational Equity Act of 1974.

House Education and Labor Committee, Subcommittee on Postsecondary Education and Training, 2451 RHOB 20515; 226-3681. William D. Ford, D-Mich., chairman; Omer Waddles, staff director.

Jurisdiction over legislation barring discrimination in postsecondary education.

Senate Appropriations Committee, Subcommittee on Interior, SD-127 20510; 224-7233. Robert C. Byrd, D-W.Va., chairman; Sue E. Masica, clerk.

Jurisdiction over legislation to appropriate funds for all native American education activities and for the Bureau of Indian Affairs.

Senate Committee on Indian Affairs, SH-838 20510; 224-2251. Daniel K. Inouye, D-Hawaii, chairman; Patricia Zell, staff director. Fax, 224-2309.

Jurisdiction over legislation pertaining to native American education; oversight of native American education programs.

Senate Labor and Human Resources Committee, Subcommittee on Education, Arts, and Humanities, SD-648 20510; 224-7666. Claiborne Pell, D-R.I., chairman; David V. Evans, staff director.

Jurisdiction over legislation barring discrimination in education, including the Women's Educational Equity Act of 1974.

Nongovernmental:

American Assn. of University Women, 1111 16th St. N.W. 20036; 785-7700. Anne L. Bryant, executive director. Library, 785-7763. Fax, 872-1425. TDD, 785-7777.

Membership: graduates of accredited colleges, universities, and recognized foreign institutions. Interests include equity for women in education, the workplace, and the family; and the impact of the federal budget on social programs. Library open to the public by appointment.

Aspira Assn., 1112 16th St. N.W., #340 20036; 835-3600. Hilda Crespo, interim executive director. Fax, 223-1253.

Provides Latino youth with resources necessary for them to remain in school and contribute to their community. Interests include leadership development, parental involvement, and research; monitors legislation and regulations.

Assn. of American Colleges, 1818 R St. N.W. 20009; 387-3760. Joann Stevens, vice president, communications. Fax, 265-9532.
Serves as clearinghouse for information on women professionals in higher education. Interests include women's studies, women's centers, climate issues, and women's leadership and professional development.

East Coast Migrant Head Start Project, 4200 Wilson Blvd., #740, Arlington, VA 22203; (703) 243-7522. Geraldine O'Brien, executive director. Fax, (703) 243-1259.
Establishes Head Start programs for migrant children and offers training and technical assistance to established centers that enroll migrant children.

The Links, 1200 Massachusetts Ave. N.W. 20005; 842-8686. Mary P. Douglass, chief administrative officer. Fax, 842-4020.
Women's service organization that works with the educationally disadvantaged and culturally deprived; focuses on arts, services for youth, and national and international trends and services.

NAACP Legal Defense and Educational Fund, 1275 K St. N.W., #301 20005; 682-1300. Elaine Jones, director. Fax, 682-1312.
Civil rights litigation group that provides legal information about civil rights and advice on educational discrimination against women and minorities; monitors federal enforcement of civil rights laws. Not affiliated with the National Association for the Advancement of Colored People (NAACP). (Headquarters in New York.)

National Alliance of Black School Educators, 2816 Georgia Ave. N.W. 20001; 483-1549. Santee Ruffin, executive director. Fax, 483-8323.
Promotes the education of African American youth and adults; seeks to raise the academic achievement level of all African American students. Sponsors workshops and conferences on major issues in education affecting African American students and educators.

National Assn. for Equal Opportunity in Higher Education, 400 12th St. N.E. 20002; 543-9111. Samuel L. Myers, president. Fax, 543-9113.
Membership: colleges and universities with a predominantly African American enrollment.

Works for increased federal and private support for member institutions and for increased minority representation in private and governmental education agencies; serves as a clearinghouse for information on federal contracts and grants for member institutions; collects, analyzes, and publishes data on member institutions; operates internship program.

National Assn. for the Advancement of Colored People (NAACP), 1025 Vermont Ave. N.W., #1120 20005; 638-2269. Wade J. Henderson, director, Washington bureau. Fax, 638-5936.
Membership: persons interested in civil rights for all minorities. Works for equal opportunity for minorities in all areas, including education; seeks to ensure a quality desegregated education for all through litigation and legislation. (Headquarters in Baltimore.)

National Assn. of Colored Women's Clubs, 5808 16th St. N.W. 20011; 726-2044. Savannah C. Jones, president. Fax, 726-0023.
Seeks to promote education of women and youth; protect and enforce civil rights; raise the standards of the home and family living; promote interracial understanding; and enhance leadership development. Awards scholarships; conducts programs in education, social service, and philanthropy.

National Assn. of State Universities and Land Grant Colleges, Advancement of Public Black Colleges, 1 Dupont Circle N.W., #710 20036; 778-0818. Joyce Payne, director. Fax, 296-6456.
Seeks to heighten awareness and visibility of public African American colleges; promotes institutional advancement. Conducts research and provides information on issues of concern; acts as a liaison with African American public colleges and universities, the federal government, and private associations. Monitors legislation and regulations.

National Council of Educational Opportunity Assns., 1025 Vermont Ave. N.W., #1201 20005; 347-7430. Arnold L. Mitchem, executive director. Fax, 347-0786.
Represents institutions of higher learning, administrators, counselors, teachers, and others committed to advancing equal educational opportunity in colleges and universities. Works to sustain and improve educational opportunity programs such as the federally funded TRIO program, designed to help low-income, first-

generation immigrant, and physically disabled students enroll in and graduate from college.

National Council of La Raza, 810 1st St. N.E., #300 20002; 289-1380. Raul Yzaguirre, president. Fax, 289-8173.

Provides research, policy analysis, and advocacy on educational status and needs of Hispanics; promotes education reform benefiting Hispanics; develops and tests community-based models for helping Hispanic students succeed in school. Interests include counseling, testing, and bilingual, vocational, preschool through postsecondary, and migrant education.

National Educational Service Centers, 777 N. Capitol St. N.E., #305 20002; 408-0060. Richard Roybal, executive director. Fax, 408-0064.

Seeks to increase the number of minorities, especially Hispanics, attending postsecondary schools; supports legislation to increase educational opportunities for Hispanics and other minorities; provides scholarship funds and educational and career counseling. Educational arm of the League of United Latin American Citizens.

National Women's Law Center, 1616 P St. N.W. 20036; 328-5160. Sharon Fischman, communications director. Fax, 328-5137.

Works to expand and protect women's legal rights in education through litigation, advocacy, and public information.

United Negro College Fund, 700 13th St. N.W., #1180 20005; 737-8631. Christa Beverly, director, government affairs. Fax, 737-8651.

Membership: private colleges and universities with historically black enrollment. Raises money for member institutions; monitors legislation and regulations. (Headquarters in New York.)

See also American Assn. of School Administrators (p. 128); American Historical Assn. (p. 102); Center for Law and Education (p. 125); U.S. Student Assn. (p. 136); Women's College Coalition (p. 137)

Teachers

See also Education, Professional Interests and Benefits (p. 128)

Nongovernmental:

American Assn. of Colleges for Teacher Education, 1 Dupont Circle N.W., #610 20036; 293-2450. David G. Imig, executive director. Fax, 457-8095.

Membership: colleges and universities with teacher education programs. Informs members of state and federal policies affecting teacher education and of professional issues such as accreditation, certification, and assessment. Collects and analyzes information on education.

American Assn. of Retired Persons, National Retired Teachers Assn., 601 E St. N.W. 20049; 434-2380. Annette Norsman, director, activities. Fax, 434-6406.

Membership: active and retired teachers and other school personnel (elementary through postsecondary) over age 50. Provides members with information on relevant national issues. Provides state associations of retired school personnel with technical assistance.

Assn. of Teacher Educators, 1900 Association Dr., Reston, VA 22091-1502; (703) 620-3110. Gloria Chernay, executive director. Fax, (703) 620-9530.

Membership: individuals and public and private agencies involved with teacher education. Seeks to improve teacher education at all levels; conducts workshops and conferences; produces and disseminates publications.

International Council on Education for Teaching, 2009 N. 14th St., #609, Arlington, VA 22201; (703) 525-5253. Sandra Klassen, executive director. Fax, (703) 351-9381.

Membership: worldwide network of colleges, universities, educational groups, and individuals interested in improving teacher education. Conducts surveys, research projects, workshops, and seminars. Maintains consulting relationship with the United Nations Educational, Scientific, and Cultural Organization (UNESCO).

National Council for Accreditation of Teacher Education, 2010 Massachusetts Ave. N.W., #200 20036; 466-7496. Arthur E. Wise, president. Fax, 296-6620.

Evaluates and accredits schools, colleges, and academic departments at higher education institutions; publishes list of accredited institutions and standards for accreditation.

National Foundation for the Improvement of Education, 1201 16th St. N.W. 20036; 822-7840. Donna C. Rhodes, executive director. Fax, 822-7779.

Educational and charitable organization created by the National Education Assn. Awards grants to teachers to improve teaching techniques and professional development; administers a dropout prevention grants program; provides teachers with assistance to integrate computer and telecommunications technology into classroom instruction, curriculum management, and administration.

Teachers of English to Speakers of Other Languages, 1600 Cameron St., #300, Alexandria, VA 22314-2751; (703) 836-0774. Susan Bayley, executive director. Fax, (703) 836-7864.

Promotes scholarship and provides information on instruction and research in the teaching of English to speakers of other languages. Offers placement service.

See also American Federation of Teachers (AFL-CIO) (p. 801); Ethics Resource Center (p. 125); National Education Assn. (p. 803); National Science Resources Center (p. 129)

Education: Special Topics

Bilingual

See also Culture: Arts and Humanities, Language (p. 111); Education: Special Groups, Minorities and Women (p. 146)

Agencies:

Education Dept., Bilingual Education and Minority Languages, 330 C St. S.W. (mailing address: 400 Maryland Ave. S.W., Washington, DC 20202-6510); 205-5463. Eugene E. Garcia, director. Fax, 205-8737.

Provides school districts and state education agencies with grants to establish, operate, and improve programs for people with limited English proficiency; promotes development of resources for such programs, including training for parents and education personnel. Administers assistance programs for refugee and immigrant children.

Nongovernmental:

National Assn. for Bilingual Education, 1220 L St. N.W., #605 20005-4018; 898-1829. James J. Lyons, executive director. Fax, 789-2866.

Membership: educators, policy makers, paraprofessionals, publications personnel, students, researchers, and interested individuals. Works to establish professional standards in bilingual education and a national language policy. Conducts annual conference and workshops.

See also Center for Law and Education (p. 125); The Home and School Institute (p. 141); Mexican American Legal Defense and Educational Fund (p. 182); National Council of La Raza (p. 150); Organization of Chinese Americans (p. 272); Teachers of English to Speakers of Other Languages (this page)

Citizenship Education

Nongovernmental:

Close Up Foundation, 44 Canal Center Plaza, Alexandria, VA 22314; (703) 706-3300. Stephen A. Janger, president. Fax, (703) 706-0000.

Sponsors week-long programs on American government for high school students, teachers, older Americans, new Americans, native Americans, Alaskan natives, and Pacific Islanders; offers fellowships for participation in the programs; produces television series for secondary schools; conducts the national Citizen Bee, an academic social studies competition for high school students, and the Civic Achievement Award Program for elementary and junior high school students. Develops specialized programs such as the U.S.-Japan Educational Initiative; summer institutes on energy, environment, and policy choices; and Active Citizenship Today, a program that promotes community service.

Convention II, P.O. Box 1987, Washington, DC 20013; 544-1789. Timothy Leighton, president. Toll-free, (800) 296-5976.

Educational organization that sponsors a model constitutional convention of high school students each February and develops other educational programs in government.

Council for the Advancement of Citizenship, 44 Canal Center Plaza, Alexandria, VA 22314-

1592; (703) 706-3361. Charles M. Tampio, president. Fax, (703) 706-0002.

Consortium of national, state, and local organizations, and interested individuals concerned with promoting responsible citizenship and citizenship education. Sponsors conferences and seminars to increase public awareness of democratic rights and responsibilities; serves as a clearinghouse for information on citizenship education programs; provides local groups with technical assistance.

Horatio Alger Assn., 99 Canal Center Plaza, Alexandria, VA 22314; (703) 684-9444. Terrence J. Giroux, executive director. Fax, (703) 548-3822.

Educates young people about the economic and personal opportunities available in the American free enterprise system. Conducts seminars on careers and public and community service; operates speakers bureau and internship program. Presents the Horatio Alger Youth Award to outstanding high school students. Awards college scholarships.

League of Women Voters Education Fund, 1730 M St. N.W. 20036; 429-1965. Gracia Hillman, executive director. Fax, 429-0854.

Public foundation established by League of Women Voters of the United States. Promotes citizen knowledge of and involvement in representative government; conducts citizen education on current public policy issues; seeks to increase voter registration and turnout; sponsors candidate forums and debates.

National 4-H Council, 7100 Connecticut Ave., Chevy Chase, MD 20815; (301) 961-2820. Richard J. Sauer, president. Fax, (301) 961-2894.

Citizenship education organization that conducts programs for youth and adult groups in Washington. Programs on American government include Wonders of Washington, Citizenship-Washington Focus, and Know America. Citizenship-World Focus deals with international affairs.

Presidential Classroom for Young Americans, 119 Oronoco St., Alexandria, VA 22314; (703) 683-5400. Nila Vehar, executive director. Toll-free, (800) 441-6533. Fax, (703) 548-5728.

Offers civic education programs for high school and college students and adults. Provides week-long series of seminars featuring representatives of each branch of government, the military, the media, private interest groups, and both major

political parties; awards scholarships. Sponsors International Program for high school students.

Washington Workshops Foundation, 3222 N St. N.W. 20007; 965-3434. Sharon E. Sievers, president. Toll-free, (800) 368-5688. Fax, 965-1018.

Educational foundation that provides introductory seminars on American government and politics to junior and senior high school students; advanced congressional seminars to secondary and postsecondary students; and seminars on the business community and on diplomacy and global affairs to secondary and college students.

Home Economics

See also Education: Special Topics, Vocational (p. 157)

Agencies:

Agriculture Dept., Extension Service, 14th St. and Independence Ave. S.W. 20250; 720-3377. Leodrey Williams, acting administrator. Information, 720-3029. Fax, 720-3993.

Oversees county agents and operation of state offices that provide information on home economics, including diet and nutrition, food purchase budgeting, food safety, home gardening, clothing care, and other consumer concerns.

Nongovernmental:

American Home Economics Assn., 1555 King St., Alexandria, VA 22314; (703) 706-4600. Mary Jane Kolar, executive director. Fax, (703) 706-4663.

Membership: professional home economists. Supports consumer and home economics education; develops accrediting standards for undergraduate home economics programs; trains and certifies home economics professionals. Monitors legislation and regulations concerning family and consumer issues.

Future Homemakers of America, 1910 Association Dr., Reston, VA 22091; (703) 476-4900. Alan T. Rains Jr., executive director. Fax, (703) 860-2713.

National student organization that helps young men and women address personal, family, work, and societal issues through vocational home economics.

International Education

See also Overseas Information and Exchange Programs (p. 482)

Agencies:

Japan-United States Friendship Commission, 1120 Vermont Ave. N.W., #925 20005; 275-7712. Eric J. Gangloff, executive director. Fax, 275-7413.

Independent agency established by Congress. Makes grants and administers funds to promote educational and cultural exchanges between Japan and the United States; consults with public and private organizations in both countries.

U.S. Advisory Commission on Public Diplomacy (U.S. Information Agency), 301 4th St. S.W. 20547; 619-4457. Bruce Gregory, staff director. Fax, 619-5489.

Provides bipartisan oversight and assessment of the international information broadcasting, cultural, and educational exchange programs of the U.S. government. Reports to the president, the secretary of state, the USIA director, and Congress.

U.S. Information Agency, Educational and Cultural Affairs, 301 4th St. S.W. 20547; 619-4597. John Loiello, associate director designate. Fax, 619-5068.

Administers Fulbright-Hays scholarship exchange program for U.S. and foreign scholars, university and college faculty, and graduate students; arranges intensive short-term study and observation visits for foreign leaders and professionals who meet and consult with Americans active in their fields; awards grants to private organizations that administer international exchange programs; conducts international exchange programs for youth; distributes American literature and presents American cultural activities (music, art, and drama), news, and editorial material overseas.

U.S. Information Agency, U.S. Speakers Program, 301 4th St. S.W. 20547; 619-4764. C. Anthony Jackson, director. Fax, 619-6520.

Selects experts in various fields to travel abroad to meet with foreign groups and professionals. Covers travel costs and some per diem expenses; provides accident and sickness insurance. Participants share their experiences with colleagues upon returning to the United States.

Congress:

House Foreign Affairs Committee, Subcommittee on International Operations, 2103 RHOB 20515; 225-3424. Howard L. Berman, D-Calif., chairman; Bradley Gordon, staff consultant. Fax, 225-7142.

Jurisdiction over legislation on educational and cultural exchange programs.

Senate Foreign Relations Committee, Subcommittee on Terrorism, Narcotics, and International Operations, SD-446 20510; 224-4651. John Kerry, D-Mass., chairman; Geryld B. Christianson, staff director. Fax, 224-5011.

Jurisdiction over legislation on educational and cultural exchange programs.

See also House/Senate International Education Study Group (p. 757)

International Organizations:

Organization of American States, Inter-American Music Council (Consejo Interamericano de Musica), 1889 F St. N.W. 20006; 458-3158. Efrain Paesky, secretary general. Fax, 458-6198.

Promotes exchange of music and musicians in Western hemisphere; promotes studies and research in musicology and education; interests include ownership of artistic property and copyright problems in the field of music.

Nongovernmental:

Council for International Exchange of Scholars, 3007 Tilden St. N.W., #5M 20008; 686-4000. Jody K. Olsen, executive director. Fax, 362-3442.

Cooperates with the U.S. Information Agency in administering Fulbright grants for university teaching and advanced research abroad. (Affiliated with American Council of Learned Societies, headquartered in New York.)

The Delphi International Group, 1090 Vermont Ave. N.W. 20005; 898-0950. Tonette T. Long, president. Fax, 842-0885.

Assists public and private organizations engaged in international cooperation and business. Works with governments and private counterparts to support foreign professional exchanges. Develops technical training programs and educational curricula for foreign visitors. Provides technical expertise, management support, travel, and business development services.

English-Speaking Union, 15 Dupont Circle, 4th Floor 20036; 234-4602. Diane Nicholson, executive director.

International educational and cultural organization that promotes cultural exchange programs with countries in which English is a major language; offers free English conversational tutoring to non-English-speaking persons; sponsors scholarships for studies in English-speaking countries. (Headquarters in New York.)

Institute of International Education, 1400 K St. N.W. 20005; 898-0600. Barbara P. Gumbiner, senior administrative officer. Fax, 842-1219.

Educational exchange, technical assistance, and training organization that arranges professional programs for international visitors; conducts training courses in energy, environment, journalism, human resource development, educational policy and administration, and business-related fields; provides developing countries with short- and long-term technical assistance in human resource development; arranges professional training and support for staff of human rights organizations; sponsors fellowships and applied internships for midcareer professionals from developing countries; implements contracts and cooperative agreements for organizations, including the U.S. Information Agency, U.S. Agency for International Development, philanthropic foundations, multilateral banks, and other organizations. (Headquarters in New York.)

Meridian International Center, 1630 Crescent Pl. N.W. 20009; 667-6800. Walter L. Cutler, president. Information, 939-5558. Fax, 667-8980.

Conducts international educational and cultural programs; provides foreign visitors and diplomats in the United States with services, including cultural orientation, seminars, and language assistance. Offers world affairs programs and international exhibitions for Americans.

NAFSA: Assn. of International Educators, 1875 Connecticut Ave. N.W., #1000 20009-5728; 462-4811. Naomi F. Collins, director. Fax, 667-3419. E-mail, inbox@nafsa.org. Publications, (800) 836-4994.

Membership: individuals, educational institutions, and others interested in international educational exchange. Provides information on evaluating exchange programs and academic credentials; assists members in complying with federal regulations affecting foreign students and scholars; administers grant programs with an international education focus, including those that benefit foreign and American students, international educators, community development volunteers, and schools with Fulbright programs.

National MultiCultural Institute, 3000 Connecticut Ave. N.W., #438 20008; 483-0700. Elizabeth Salett, president. Fax, 483-5233.

Encourages understanding and communication among people of various backgrounds; seeks to increase awareness of different perspectives and experiences; provides multicultural training, education, and counseling programs for organizations and institutions working with diverse cultural groups.

Town Affiliation Assn. of the U.S., Sister Cities International, 120 S. Payne St., Alexandria, VA 22314; (703) 836-3535. Carol Lynn Greene, executive director. Fax, (703) 836-4815.

Assists U.S. and foreign cities in establishing formal city-to-city affiliations, including exchanges of people, ideas, and materials; acts as program coordinator and information clearinghouse for Sister Cities programs.

World Learning, 1015 15th St. N.W. 20005; 408-5420. Robert Chase, vice president; Karen Wayne, director, au pair/homestay. Fax, 408-5397. School for International Training, (800) 451-4465. Summer Abroad, (800) 345-2929. Incoming Hosts and Volunteers, (800) 327-4678.

Educational organization that develops and administers exchange programs for U.S. and foreign students; offers, through the School for International Training, English- and foreign-language instruction for executives and students. Administers au pair program for American and foreign young people. (Headquarters in Brattleboro, Vt.)

Youth for Understanding, 3501 Newark St. N.W. 20016; 966-6800. William M. Woessner, president. Toll-free, (800) 424-3691. Fax, 895-1104.

Educational organization that administers cross-cultural exchange programs for teenage students. Administers scholarship programs that sponsor student exchanges, including the Congress-Bundestag Scholarship Program.

See also America-Mideast Educational and Training Services (p. 466); Presidential Classroom for Young Americans (p. 152)

Literacy

See also Education: Special Groups, Adult (p. 143)

Agencies:

Education Dept., Adult Education and Literacy, 330 C St. S.W. (mailing address: 400 Maryland Ave. S.W., Washington, DC 20202-7240); 205-8270. Ronald S. Pugsley, acting director. Fax, 205-8973. Literacy clearinghouse, 205-9996.

Provides state and local education agencies with information on establishing, expanding, improving, and operating adult education and literacy programs. Emphasizes basic and life skills attainment and high school completion. Awards grants to state education agencies for adult education and literacy programs, including grants for education for the homeless and workplace literacy partnerships. Coordinates homeless and adult literacy programs.

Education Dept., National Institute for Literacy, 800 Connecticut Ave. N.W., #200 20202; 632-1500. Andy Hartman, director. Fax, 632-1512.

Seeks to eliminate illiteracy in America by the year 2000. Operates a literacy clearinghouse; provides private literacy groups, educational institutions, and federal, state, and local agencies working on illiteracy with assistance; awards grants and fellowships to literacy programs and individuals pursuing careers in the literacy field.

Employment and Training Administration (Labor Dept.), Workplace Literacy, 200 Constitution Ave. N.W. 20210; 219-5677. Guss Morrison, chief. Fax, 219-5455.

Coordinates workplace literacy projects, including technical and basic skills effectiveness training, technology training, adult education studies, and literacy surveys; sponsors, with the Education and Health and Human Services departments, the National Center for Adult Literacy at the University of Pennsylvania.

Smithsonian Institution, Reading Is Fundamental, 600 Maryland Ave. S.W., #600 20024; 287-3371. Ruth Graves, president. Information, 287-3220. Fax, 287-3196.

Conducts programs and workshops to motivate young people to read. Provides young people with books and parents with services to encourage reading at home.

Volunteers in Service to America (VISTA) (Corporation for National Service), Literacy Corps, 1100 Vermont Ave. N.W. 20525; 606-5000. Diana London, acting assistant director. Fax, 606-4921.

Assigns volunteers to local and state education departments and to private, nonprofit organizations that have literacy programs. Other activities include tutor recruitment and training and organization and expansion of local literacy councils.

Congress:

Library of Congress, The Center for the Book, 101 Independence Ave. S.E. 20540-8200; 707-5221. John Y. Cole, director. Fax, 707-9898.

Promotes family and adult literacy; encourages the study of books and stimulates public interest in books, reading, and libraries; sponsors publication of a directory describing national organizations that administer literacy programs. Affiliated state centers sponsor projects and hold events that call attention to the importance of literacy.

Nongovernmental:

AFL-CIO Human Resources Development Institute, 815 16th St. N.W., #405 20006; 638-3912. Patricia Garcia, national coordinator. Fax, 783-6536.

Provides labor unions, employers, education agencies, and community groups with training and technical assistance for workplace education programs focusing on adult literacy, basic skills, and job training.

American Bar Assn., Special Committee on Law and Literacy, 1800 M St. N.W. 20036; 331-2287. Dick Lynch, director. Fax, 331-2220.

Seeks to involve lawyers in literacy programs at the local, state, and national levels; sponsors conferences on literacy and publishes a literacy program manual for state and local bars.

American Library Assn., 110 Maryland Ave. N.E. 20002; 547-4440. Eileen D. Cooke, director, Washington office. Fax, 547-7363.

Educational organization of librarians, trustees, and educators. Washington office supports federal legislation and Library Services and Construction Act funding for literacy projects. (Headquarters in Chicago.)

American Society for Training and Development, 1640 King St., Alexandria, VA (mailing address: P.O. Box 1443, Alexandria, VA 22313); (703) 683-8100. Curtis E. Plott, president. Fax, (703) 683-8103.

Membership: trainers and human resource developers. Publishes information on workplace literacy.

Assn. for Community Based Education, 1805 Florida Ave. N.W. 20009; 462-6333. C. P. Zachariadis, executive director. Fax, 232-8044.

Collects and disseminates information on community-based literacy programs; evaluates effectiveness of programs; conducts training program for literacy practitioners; awards minigrants to existing programs; monitors legislation and regulations.

The Barbara Bush Foundation for Family Literacy, 1002 Wisconsin Ave. N.W. 20007; 338-2006. Benita Somerfield, executive director.

Promotes family literacy programs to break the intergenerational cycle of illiteracy and to establish literacy as a value in American families; awards grants; supports professional development for teachers; encourages recognition of volunteers, educators, students, and effective programs; publishes materials that document effective literacy programs.

General Federation of Women's Clubs, 1734 N St. N.W. 20036-2990; 347-3168. Judith Maggrett, executive director. Fax, 835-0246.

Nondenominational, nonpartisan international organization of women volunteers. Develops literacy projects in response to community needs; sponsors tutoring; provides funding, classroom space, and transportation.

National Alliance of Business, 1201 New York Ave. N.W., #700 20005; 289-2905. Brenda Bell, vice president, program marketing. Fax, 289-1303.

Builds business partnerships with government, labor, and education to improve the quality of the American work force. Provides technical assistance and information on workplace literacy.

National Clearinghouse for ESL Literacy Education, Center for Applied Linguistics, 1118 22nd St. N.W. 20037; 429-9292. Fran Keenan, assistant director. Fax, 659-5641. E-mail, cal@guvax.georgetown.edu.

Provides information and referral service on literacy instruction for adults and out-of-school youth learning English as a second language.

National Governors' Assn., 444 N. Capitol St. N.W. 20001; 624-5346. Lorraine Amico, senior policy analyst. Press, 624-5331. Fax, 624-5313.

Provides state government officials with information and assistance on adult literacy and basic skills services. Seeks to develop a comprehensive and integrated system for meeting the needs of adult learners; conducts research and policy analysis; provides states with technical assistance.

Newspaper Association of America Foundation, 11600 Sunrise Valley Dr., Reston, VA 22091; (703) 648-1051. Betty Sullivan, director, educational programs. Information, (703) 648-1000. Fax, (703) 620-1265.

Sponsors annual literacy conference; publishes a handbook for starting newspaper literacy projects; promotes intergenerational literacy through its Family Focus program; produces a showcase of newspaper literacy projects.

The Southport Institute for Policy Analysis, P.O. Box 25424, Alexandria, VA 22313; 682-4100. Forrest P. Chisman, president. Fax, 682-2121.

Develops policies and programs to improve the basic skills of American workers, especially those working for small- and medium-size employers. Interests include public policy on adult literacy.

United Way of America, 701 N. Fairfax St., Alexandria, VA 22314; (703) 836-7112. Ellen Gilligan, director, education and literacy initiative. Fax, (703) 683-7840.

Produces and distributes literacy information to local United Way chapters; conducts regional forums on literacy for state and local United Way chapters and their communities; provides communities with technical assistance.

See also Correctional Education Assn. (p. 515); Institute for Alternative Futures (p. 666)

Physical Education

Agencies:

Health and Human Services Dept., President's Council on Physical Fitness and Sports, 701 Pennsylvania Ave. N.W., #250 20004; 272-3421. Sandra Perlmutter, executive director. Information, 272-3430. Fax, 504-2064.

Provides schools, state and local governments, recreation agencies, and employers with technical assistance on designing and implementing physical fitness programs; conducts award programs for children and adults and for schools, clubs, and other institutions.

Nongovernmental:

American Alliance for Health, Physical Education, Recreation, and Dance, 1900 Association Dr., Reston, VA 22091; (703) 476-3400. A. Gilson Brown, executive vice president. Fax, (703) 476-9527.

Membership: teachers and others who work with school health, physical education, athletics, recreation, dance, and safety education programs (kindergarten through postsecondary levels). Member associations are American Assn. for Leisure and Recreation, National Assn. for Girls and Women in Sport, Assn. for the Advancement of Health Education, Assn. for Research, Administration, Professional Councils and Societies, National Dance Assn., and National Assn. for Sport and Physical Education.

National Assn. for Girls and Women in Sport, 1900 Association Dr., Reston, VA 22091; (703) 476-3452. Mary Hill, executive director. Fax, (703) 476-9527.

Membership: students, coaches, physical education teachers, athletes, athletic directors, and trainers for girls' and women's sports programs. Seeks to increase sports opportunity for women and girls; provides information on laws relating to equality of sports funds and facilities for women; hosts training sites and rates officials; publishes sports guides; maintains speakers bureau.

Society of State Directors of Health, Physical Education, and Recreation, 9805 Hillridge Dr., Kensington, MD 20895; (301) 949-0709. Simon A. McNeely, executive director. Fax, (301) 949-0709.

Membership: state directors, supervisors, and coordinators for physical and health education and recreation activities in state education departments, and other interested individuals. Seeks to improve school programs on health, physical education, athletics, outdoor education, recreation, and safety.

See also Health, Exercise and Fitness, Nongovernmental (p. 326)
See also National Handicapped Sports Assn. (p. 423); Special Olympics (p. 424)

Vocational

Agencies:

Education Dept., National Discretionary Programs, 330 C St. S.W. (mailing address: 400 Maryland Ave. S.W., Washington, DC 20202-7242); 205-9650. Howard F. Hjelm, director. Fax, 205-8793.

Awards contracts and grants on a competitive basis to state and local education agencies, institutions of higher education, and other organizations for research, demonstration, and training projects in adult and vocational education.

Education Dept., Vocational and Adult Education, 330 C St. S.W. (mailing address: 400 Maryland Ave. S.W., Washington, DC 20202-7100); 205-5451. Augusta Kappner, assistant secretary. Fax, 205-8748.

Serves as principal adviser to the secretary on matters related to vocational and adult education. Administers, coordinates, and recommends national policy for improving vocational and adult education programs. Administers grants and contracts for research programs in vocational education and for vocational education programs for dislocated workers, migrant farm workers, and the homeless.

Education Dept., Vocational Technical Education, 330 C St. S.W. (mailing address: 400 Maryland Ave. S.W., Washington, DC 20202); 205-9441. Winfred I. Warnat, director. Fax, 205-5522.

Provides state and local education agencies with information on establishment, expansion, improvement, and operation of vocational technical education programs. Awards grants to state education agencies for vocational technical education programs.

Congress:

See Education, General, Congress (p. 123)

Nongovernmental:

American Vocational Assn., 1410 King St., Alexandria, VA 22314; (703) 683-3111. Charles H. Buzzell, executive director. Toll-free, (800) 826-9972. Fax, (703) 683-7424.

Membership: teachers, students, supervisors, administrators, and others working or interested in vocational education (middle school through postgraduate). Interests include the impact of high school graduation requirements on vocational education; private sector initiatives; and improving the quality and image of vocational education. Monitors legislation and regulations. Offers conferences, workshops, and an annual convention.

Career College Assn., 750 1st St. N.E., #900 20002; 336-6700. Stephen J. Blair, president. Fax, 336-6828.

Accredits private postsecondary vocational institutions through autonomous commissions affiliated with the association. Acts as an information clearinghouse on trade and technical schools.

International Technology Education Assn., 1914 Association Dr., Reston, VA 22091; (703) 860-2100. Kendall Starkweather, executive director. Fax, (703) 860-0353.

Membership: technology education teachers, supervisors, teacher educators, and individuals studying to be technology education teachers. Technology education includes the curriculum areas of manufacturing, construction, communications, transportation, and energy.

National Assn. of Manufacturers, Employee Relations Committee, 1331 Pennsylvania Ave. N.W. 20004; 637-3129. Peter Lunnie, director. Fax, 637-3182.

Works to enhance the quality of vocational education and to increase support from the business community. Interests include opportunities for dislocated workers, legislation affecting vocational education, and the impact of high technology on the work force.

National Assn. of State Directors of Vocational/Technical Education Consortium, 444 N. Capitol St. N.W., #830 20001; 737-0303. Madeleine B. Hemmings, executive director. Fax, 737-1106.

Membership: state vocational education agency heads, senior staff, and business, labor, and other education officials. Advocates state and national policy to strengthen vocational-technical education to create a foundation of skills for American workers and provide them with opportunities to acquire new and advanced skills.

National Home Study Council, 1601 18th St. N.W. 20009; 234-5100. Michael P. Lambert, executive director. Fax, 332-1386.

Membership: accredited correspondence schools. Accredits home study schools, many of which offer vocational training.

National Institute for Work and Learning, 1875 Connecticut Ave. N.W., 9th Floor 20009; 884-8186. Ivan Charner, vice president. Fax, 884-8422.

Public policy research organization that seeks to improve collaboration between educational and business institutions. Conducts demonstration projects with communities throughout the country on employer-funded tuition aid, youth transition from school to work, and employee education and career development. Conducts research on education and work issues. Library open to the public. (Affiliated with the Academy for Educational Development.)

See also Correctional Education Assn. (p. 515)

Fellowships and Grants

See also Education: Special Topics, International Education (p. 153)

Agencies:

Education Dept., Higher Education Incentive Programs, 7th and D Sts. S.W. 20202; 260-3245. Alfreda Liebermann, director. Fax, 260-7615.

Administers federal fellowship programs, including those offering graduate and professional opportunities.

Harry S. Truman Scholarship Foundation, 712 Jackson Pl. N.W. 20006; 395-4831. Louis H. Blair, executive secretary. Fax, 395-6995.

Memorial to Harry S. Truman established by Congress. Provides students preparing for careers in public service with scholarships. (Candidates are nominated by their respective colleges or universities while in their third year of undergraduate study.)

National Endowment for the Arts (National Foundation on the Arts and the Humanities), 1100 Pennsylvania Ave. N.W. 20506; 682-5414. Jane Alexander, chair. Information, 682-5400. Press, 682-5570. Library, 682-5485. Fax, 682-5612. TDD, 682-5496.

Independent federal grant-making agency. Awards grants to artists and nonprofit arts organizations in design arts, folk arts and crafts, dance, education, literature, museums, music, media arts, opera, theater, and visual arts; awards matching grants to official state arts councils and community arts agencies. Library open to the public by appointment.

National Endowment for the Humanities (National Foundation on the Arts and the Humanities), 1100 Pennsylvania Ave. N.W. 20506; 606-8310. Sheldon Hackney, chairman. Information, 606-8438. Fax, 606-8588. TDD, 606-8282.
Independent federal grant-making agency. Awards grants to individuals and institutions for research, scholarship, educational programs, and public programs (including broadcasts, museum exhibitions, lectures, and symposia) in the humanities (defined as study of archeology; history; jurisprudence; language; linguistics; literature; philosophy; the history, criticism, and theory of the arts; and humanistic aspects of the social sciences). Funds preservation of books, newspapers, historical documents, and photographs.

National Endowment for the Humanities (National Foundation on the Arts and the Humanities), Fellowships and Seminars, 1100 Pennsylvania Ave. N.W. 20506; 606-8458. Marjorie A. Berlincourt, director. Information, 606-8463 Fax, 606-8558. Fellowships information, 606-8466.
Awards postprofessional degree fellowships for advanced research in the humanities. Sponsors summer seminars for school teachers (K-12) and for college teachers.

National Science Foundation, Graduate Education and Research Development, 4201 Wilson Blvd., Arlington, VA 22230; (703) 306-1630. Terence L. Porter, director. Fax, (703) 306-0468. TDD, 357-7492.
Supports activities to strengthen the education of research scientists and engineers; promotes career development; offers pre- and postdoctoral fellowships for study and research; manages the Presidential Faculty Fellows, the National Science Foundation Faculty Awards for Women, the Graduate and Minority Graduate fellowships, and the Visiting Professorships for Women programs.

President's Commission on White House Fellowships, 712 Jackson Pl. N.W. 20503; 395-4522. Brooke Shearer, director. Fax, 395-6179.
Selects White House Fellows through open competition to provide the opportunity for young professionals from all sectors of national life to observe firsthand the processes of the federal government. Beginning each September, fellows work for one year as special assistants to Cabinet members or to principal members of the White House staff. Qualified applicants have demonstrated superior accomplishments early in their careers and have a commitment to community service.

Smithsonian Institution, Fellowships and Grants, 955 L'Enfant Plaza S.W. 20560; 287-3271. Roberta Rubinoff, director. Fax, 287-3691.
Administers fellowships in residence that provide pre- and postdoctoral appointments for study and research at the Smithsonian Institution in history of science and technology, American and cultural history, history of art, anthropology, evolutionary and systematic biology, environmental sciences, astrophysics and astronomy, earth sciences, and tropical biology.

Woodrow Wilson International Center for Scholars, Fellowships, 1000 Jefferson Dr. S.W. 20560; 357-2841. Charles Blitzer, director; Ann C. Sheffield, assistant director for fellowships. Fax, 357-4439.
Awards fellowships to established scholars and professionals from the United States and abroad for humanities and social science research at the center. Publishes guides to scholarly research material in the Washington, D.C., area.

Congress:

House Ways and Means Committee, 1102 LHOB 20515; 225-3625. Sam M. Gibbons, D-Fla., acting chairman; Janice A. Mays, chief counsel.
Jurisdiction over legislation on tax-exempt foundations and charitable trusts.

Senate Finance Committee, SD-205 20510; 224-4515. Daniel Patrick Moynihan, D-N.Y., chairman; Lawrence O'Donnell Jr., staff director.
Jurisdiction over legislation on tax-exempt foundations and charitable trusts.

Nongovernmental:

American Assn. of University Women Educational Foundation, 1111 16th St. N.W. 20036; 728-7603. Tanya Hilton, director. Toll-free, (800) 821-4364. Fax, 872-1425.
Awards fellowships to women who are completing doctoral or postdoctoral research and to fellows in the last year of their professional degree program. Offers fellowships to foreign

women coming to the United States for one year of graduate study. Awards grants to women returning to school for postbaccalaureate education or professional development. Administers the Eleanor Roosevelt Fund, which supports a teacher sabbatical program for women who teach girls math and science in grades K-12. (Affiliate of the American Assn. of University Women.)

American Institute of Architects, American Architectural Foundation, 1735 New York Ave. N.W. 20006; 626-7500. L. William Chapin, president. Library, 626-7492. Fax, 626-7420.

Seeks to advance the quality of American architecture. Works to increase public awareness and understanding, and apply new technology to create more humane environments. Acts as liaison between the profession and the public; awards grants for architecture-oriented projects. Serves as the educational arm of the American Institute of Architects. Also operates the historic Octagon Museum.

American Political Science Assn., Congressional Fellowship Program, 1527 New Hampshire Ave. N.W. 20036; 483-2512. Kay Sterling, administrative director. Fax, 483-2657.

Places political scientists, journalists, faculty of medical schools (Robert Wood Johnson Fellowships), and federal agency executives in congressional offices and committees for nine-month fellowships. Individual government agencies nominate federal executive participants.

Business and Professional Women's Foundation, 2012 Massachusetts Ave. N.W. 20036; 293-1200. Dianne Studes, president. Fax, 861-0298.

Works to improve women's economic status by promoting their employment at all levels in all occupations. Provides mature women seeking training and education with scholarships and loans to increase their job skills. Awards grants for doctoral research on women's economic issues. Library open to the public. (Affiliate of the National Federation of Business and Professional Women's Clubs.)

Congressional Black Caucus Foundation, 1004 Pennsylvania Ave. S.E. 20003; 675-6730. Quintin Lawson, executive director. Fax, 547-3806.

Conducts public policy research on issues of concern to African Americans. Sponsors fellowship programs in which professionals and academic candidates work on congressional committees and subcommittees. Sponsors internship and scholarship programs.

Council for International Exchange of Scholars, 3007 Tilden St. N.W., #5M 20008; 686-4000. Jody K. Olsen, executive director. Fax, 362-3442.

Cooperates with the U.S. Information Agency in administering Fulbright grants for university teaching and advanced research abroad. (Affiliated with American Council of Learned Societies, headquartered in New York.)

Council on Foundations, 1828 L St. N.W., #300 20036; 466-6512. James A. Joseph, president. Fax, 785-3926.

Membership: private, community, operating, and corporate foundations and giving programs. Acts as clearinghouse for information on private philanthropy; sponsors conferences on administering funds.

The Foundation Center, 1001 Connecticut Ave. N.W., #938 20036; 331-1401. Mary Ann de Barbieri, director, Washington office. Fax, 331-1739.

Publishes foundation guides. Serves as clearinghouse on foundations and corporate giving, nonprofit management, fund raising, and grants for individuals. Library open to the public. (Headquarters in New York.)

Women's Research and Education Institute, 1700 18th St. N.W. 20009; 328-7070. Betty Dooley, executive director. Fax, 328-3514.

Provides information and conducts research and policy analysis for members of Congress and other policy makers who support equity for women. Sponsors one-year fellowships for graduate students. Fellows are placed in congressional offices or on committee staffs where they work on policy issues affecting women.

Libraries and Information Science

See also Government Housekeeping, Government Record Keeping (p. 303); Government Printing Office, Regional Depository Libraries (p. 850); Science: Mathematical, Computer, and Physical Sciences, Computer Sciences (p. 686)

Library of Congress

10 1st St. S.E. 20540
James H. Billington, Librarian of Congress, 707-5205.
Switchboard, 707-5000.
Press Inquiries, 707-2905.
Visitor's Information, 707-5458.
General Reference, 707-5522.
Recorded Information, 707-6400.
TDD, 707-6200. Fax, 707-5844.

The Library of Congress is the nation's main book repository. It maintains extensive research collections in every field except clinical medicine and technical agriculture. Collections include books, manuscripts, presidential papers (through Coolidge), films, music, maps, photographs, prints and drawings, recordings of folk songs, speeches, and poetry readings. It provides interlibrary loans, photoduplication services, recordings, concerts, and public programs; publishes catalog cards, bibliographies, and catalogs; provides books on records and tapes, and books in Braille. The Library of Congress also serves as a general reference library for public use for persons above high school age. Admission to its reading rooms is free; users must present photo identification with current address.

The collections of the Library of Congress are housed in three buildings in S.E.: the Thomas Jefferson Bldg. at 10 1st St.; the James Madison Memorial Bldg. at 101 Independence Ave.; and the John Adams Bldg. at 110 2nd St.

Additional information for some of the following divisions is located under specific subject areas in this directory; see index listing of the Library of Congress for page numbers of additional entries.

African and Middle Eastern
Division 707-7937
American Folklife Center 707-6590
American Memory Project 707-6233
Archive of Folk Culture 707-5510
Asian Division 707-5420
Cataloging Distribution Service 707-6171
The Center for the Book 707-5221
Children's Literature Center 707-5535
Computer Catalog Center 707-3370
Concert Office 707-5502
Copyright Office 707-3000
European Division 707-5414
Federal Library and Information
Center Committee 707-4800
Folklife Reading Room 707-5510
Geography and Map Division 707-8530
Hispanic Division 707-5400
Humanities and Social Sciences
Division 707-5530
Interlibrary Loans 707-5444
Interpretative Programs 707-5223
Law Library 707-5065
Law Library Reading Room 707-5079
Local History and Genealogy
Reading Room 707-5537

Machine-Readable Collections
Reading Room 707-5278
Manuscript Division 707-5383
Mary Pickford Theater 707-5677
Microform Reading Room 707-5471
Motion Picture, Broadcasting,
and Recorded Sound
Division 707-5840
Music Division 707-5503
National Library Service for
the Blind and Physically
Handicapped 707-5104
Photoduplication Service 707-5640
Poetry and Literature Center 707-5394
Preservation Office 707-5213
Prints and Photographs
Division 707-5836
Rare Book and Special
Collections Division 707-5434
Science and Technology
Division 707-5664
Serial and Government
Publications Division 707-5647

Departmental and . . .

Departments

Agriculture .... (301) 504-6778
Commerce 482-5511
Defense .... (703) 697-4301
Education 219-1692
Energy 586-9534
Interior 208-5815
Justice 514-3775
Labor 219-6992
State 647-1099
Transportation 366-0746
Treasury 622-0990
Veterans Affairs 233-3085

Agencies

Commission on Civil Rights 376-8110
Commodity Futures Trading
Commission 254-5901
Consumer Product Safety
Commission .... (301) 504-0044
Drug Enforcement
Administration 307-8932

Environmental Protection Agency. . 260-5921
Equal Employment Opportunity
Commission 663-4630
Export-Import Bank of the
United States 566-8897
Farm Credit Administration   (703) 883-4296
Federal Communications
Commission 632-7100
Federal Deposit Insurance Corp.... 898-3631
Federal Election Commission 219-3312
Federal Emergency Management
Agency......................... 646-3771
Federal Labor
Relations Authority 482-6695
Federal Maritime Commission 523-5762
Federal Reserve System 452-3332
Federal Trade Commission 326-2395
General Accounting Office
(Law) 275-2585
(Technical) 275-5180
General Services Administration ... 501-0788
International Bank for Recon-
struction and Development
(World Bank) and International
Monetary Fund 623-7054

Agencies:

Education Dept., Library Programs, 555 New Jersey Ave. N.W. 20208-5571; 219-2293. Ray Fry, director. Fax, 219-1725.

Awards federal grants to support operations of public libraries. Aids research, college, and university libraries with technology applications. Promotes literacy through grants to native American tribes and Hawaiian natives for library services and to state library agencies and local public libraries.

Gallaudet University, Library and Archives, 800 Florida Ave. N.E. 20002; 651-5220. John Day, librarian. Information, 651-5217. Archives, 651-5209; media distribution, 651-5227. All numbers are voice and TDD accessible..

Maintains extensive special collection on deafness, including archival materials relating to deaf cultural history and Gallaudet University.

National Commission on Libraries and Information Science, 1110 Vermont Ave. N.W., #820 20005; 606-9200. Geanne Hurley Simon, chair. Fax, 606-9203.
Advises Congress and the president on national information and library policy issues; works with other agencies, the private sector, libraries, and information networks to improve access to library and information resources for all Americans, including the elderly, disadvantaged, illiterate, and geographically isolated; promotes effective local use of information generated by the federal government.

National Endowment for the Humanities (National Foundation on the Arts and the Humanities), Humanities Projects in Libraries and Archives, 1100 Pennsylvania Ave. N.W. 20506; 606-8271. Thomas C. Phelps, program officer. Fax, 606-8557. TDD, 606-8338.
Awards grants to libraries for projects that enhance public appreciation and understanding of the humanities through books and other

... Agency Libraries

Interstate Commerce
Commission 927-7328
Merit Systems Protection
Board 653-7132
National Aeronautics and
Space Administration 358-0168
National Credit Union
Administration .... (703) 518-6546
National Foundation on the Arts
and the Humanities
   National Endowment for
   the Arts 682-5485
   National Endowment for
   the Humanities 606-8244
National Labor Relations
Board 273-3720
National Library of
Medicine .... (301) 496-6095
National Science Foundation 357-7811
Nuclear Regulatory
Commission .... (301) 492-7748
Occupational Safety and Health
Review Commission 606-5410
Office of Personnel Management .. 606-1381

Office of Thrift Supervision
   (Main Library) 452-3333
   (Law) 906-6470
Peace Corps 606-3307
Postal Rate Commission 789-6877
Public Health Library ...... (301) 443-2673
Securities and Exchange
Commission 272-2618
Small Business Administration
   (Main Library) 205-6644
   (Law) 205-6847
Smithsonian Institution 357-2139
U.S. Arms Control and
Disarmament Agency 647-5969
U.S. International Development
Cooperation Agency
   Agency for International
   Development .... (703) 875-4818
   Overseas Private Investment
   Corporation 336-8565
U.S. International Trade
Commission
   (Main Library) 205-2630
   (Law) 205-3287
U.S. Postal Service 268-2904

---

resources in American library collections. Projects include conferences, exhibitions, essays, and lecture series.

Congress:

House Administration Committee, Subcommittee on Libraries and Memorials, 612 O'Neill Bldg. (300 New Jersey Ave. S.E.) 20515; 226-2307. William L. Clay, D-Mo., chairman; John F. Bass, staff director. Fax, 225-3963.

Oversight of and jurisdiction over legislation on the Library of Congress.

House Appropriations Committee, Subcommittee on Legislative Branch, H302 CAP 20515; 225-5338. Vic Fazio, D-Calif., chairman; Edward E. Lombard, staff professional.

Jurisdiction over legislation to appropriate funds for the Library of Congress, including the Congressional Research Service.

House Education and Labor Committee, Subcommittee on Labor-Management Relations, 320 CHOB 20515; 225-5768. Pat Williams, D-Mont., chairman; Jon Weintraub, staff director.

Jurisdiction over legislation on libraries, including the Library Services and Construction Act.

Joint Committee on the Library, 103 O'Neill Bldg. (300 New Jersey Ave. S.E.) 20515; 226-7633. Rep. Charlie Rose, D-N.C., chairman; Hilary Lieber, staff director.

Studies and makes recommendations on legislation dealing with the Library of Congress.

Library of Congress, 101 Independence Ave. S.E. 20540-1000; 707-5205. James H. Billington, librarian of Congress. Information, 707-2905. Fax, 707-1714.

Main book repository of the United States. *(See box, p. 161.)*

Library of Congress, The Center for the Book, 101 Independence Ave. S.E. 20540-8200; 707-5221. John Y. Cole, director. Fax, 707-9898.

Seeks to broaden public appreciation of books, reading, and libraries; sponsors lectures and conferences on the educational and cultural role of the book, including the history of books and printing, television and the printed word, and the publishing and production of books; cooperates with state centers and with other organizations. Projects and programs are privately funded except for basic administrative support from the Library of Congress.

Library of Congress, Federal Library and Information Center Committee, 701 Pennsylvania Ave. N.W., #725 20004; 707-4800. Mary Berghaus Levering, executive director. Fax, 707-4818.

Membership: one representative from each major federal agency, one representative each from the Library of Congress and the national libraries of medicine and agriculture, and one representative from each of the major Federal Information Centers. Coordinates planning, development, operations, and activities among federal libraries.

Library of Congress, Machine-Readable Collections Reading Room, 10 1st St. S.E., #LJG22 20540; 707-6560. John Kimball, head, automation. Fax, 707-1957.

Acquires, organizes, and services the microcomputer software and CD-ROM collections of the Library of Congress, including full-text encyclopedias and periodical indexes; develops guidelines for acquiring and cataloging machine-readable materials for the Library of Congress. Open to researchers over high school age.

Library of Congress, Preservation, 101 Independence Ave. S.E. 20540; 707-5213. Kenneth E. Harris, director. Fax, 707-3434.

Responsible for preserving book and paper materials in the library's collections.

Senate Appropriations Committee, Subcommittee on Legislative Branch, SD-126 20510; 224-7338. Harry Reid, D-Nev., chairman; Jerry L. Bonham, clerk.

Jurisdiction over legislation to appropriate funds for the Library of Congress, including the Congressional Research Service.

Senate Labor and Human Resources Committee, Subcommittee on Education, Arts, and

Humanities, SD-648 20510; 224-7666. Claiborne Pell, D-R.I., chairman; David V. Evans, staff director.

Jurisdiction over legislation on libraries, including the Library Services and Construction Act.

Senate Rules and Administration Committee, SR-305 20510; 224-6352. Wendell H. Ford, D-Ky., chairman; James O. King, staff director.

Oversight of and jurisdiction over legislation on the Library of Congress.

Nongovernmental:

American Library Assn., 110 Maryland Ave. N.E. 20002; 547-4440. Eileen D. Cooke, director, Washington office. Fax, 547-7363.

Educational organization of librarians, trustees, and educators. Washington office monitors legislation and regulations on libraries and information science. (Headquarters in Chicago.)

American Society for Information Science, 8720 Georgia Ave., #501, Silver Spring, MD 20910; (301) 495-0900. Richard Hill, executive director. Fax, (301) 495-0810. Internet, asis@cni.org.

Membership: librarians, computer scientists, management specialists, behavioral scientists, engineers, and individuals concerned with access to information. Conducts research and educational programs.

Assn. of Research Libraries, 21 Dupont Circle, N.W. 20036; 296-2296. Duane Webster, executive director. Fax, 872-0884.

Membership: major research libraries, primarily university, in the United States and Canada. Interests include development of library resources in all formats, subjects, and languages, development of computer information systems and other bibliographic tools, management of research libraries, preservation of library materials, information policy, and publishing and scholarly communication.

Commission on Preservation and Access, 1400 16th St. N.W., #740 20036-2217; 939-3400. Patricia Battin, president. Fax, 939-3407.

Acts on behalf of the nation's libraries, archives, and universities to develop and encourage collaborative strategies for preserving and making available deteriorating published materials.

Council on Library Resources, 1400 16th St. N.W., #510 20036-2217; 483-7474. W. David Penniman, president. Fax, 483-6410.

Awards grants to libraries and other information-related organizations. Interests include bibliographic services, information science, access to resources, library management, and training for librarians. Does not provide grants for acquisitions or buildings.

Information Industry Assn., 555 New Jersey Ave. N.W., #800 20001; 639-8262. Kenneth B. Allen, president. Fax, 638-4403.

Membership: companies involved in creating, distributing, and using information products, services, and technologies. Interests include government information policy, privacy and information regulation, government procurement rules, intellectual property rights, taxation, and telecommunications. Monitors legislation and regulations.

Special Libraries Assn., 1700 18th St. N.W. 20009-2508; 234-4700. David R. Bender, executive director. Fax, 265-9317.

Membership: libraries serving institutions that use or produce information in specialized areas, including business, engineering, law, the arts and sciences, government, museums, and universities. Sponsors professional development programs and research projects; provides a consultation service; monitors legislation and regulations.

See also Assn. for Information and Image Management (p. 131)

Key Agency:

Labor Dept.
200 Constitution Ave. N.W. 20210
Information: 219-7316

Key Committees:

House Education and Labor Committee
2181 RHOB 20515
Phone: 225-4527

Senate Labor and Human Resources Committee
SD-428 20510
Phone: 224-5375

Key Personnel:

Labor Dept.
Robert B. Reich, secretary

Thomas Glynn, deputy secretary

Joachin F. Otero, deputy under secretary for international labor affairs

Cecilia Bankins, acting assistant secretary for administration and management

Geri Palast, assistant secretary for congressional and intergovernmental affairs

Douglas Ross, assistant secretary for employment and training

Bernard Anderson, assistant secretary for employment standards

J. Davitt McAteer, assistant secretary for mine safety and health

Joseph Dear, assistant secretary for occupational safety and health

Olena Berg, assistant secretary for pension and welfare benefits

Leslie Loble, acting assistant secretary for policy

Anne Lewis, assistant secretary for public affairs

Gen. Preston Taylor Jr., assistant secretary for veterans' employment and training

Katharine G. Abraham, commissioner, Bureau of Labor Statistics

Karen Nussbaum, director, Women's Bureau

4

Employment and Labor

Contents:

Employment and Labor

Agencies:

Labor Dept., 200 Constitution Ave. N.W., #S2018 20210; 219-8271. Robert B. Reich, secretary. Information, 219-7316. Library, 219-6992. Fax, 219-8822. Recorded press releases, 219-6899.

Promotes and develops the welfare of U.S. wage earners; administers federal labor laws; acts as principal adviser to the president on policies relating to wage earners, working conditions, and employment opportunities. Library open to the public.

Labor Dept., Administrative Appeals, 200 Constitution Ave. N.W. 20210; 219-4728. Gresham Smith, acting director. Fax, 219-9315.

Assists the secretary, deputy secretary, and assistant secretary for employment standards in reviewing appeals from decisions of administrative law judges under certain laws and programs. These appeals arise under the Service Contract Act, the Comprehensive Employment and Training Act, the Job Training Partnership Act, the Trade Act, the Surface Transportation Assistance Act, the Energy Reorganization Act, and several environmental laws, unemployment insurance conformity proceedings, and cases brought by the Office of Federal Contract Compliance Programs.

Labor Dept., Administrative Law Judges, 800 K St. N.W. 20001-8002; 633-0341. Nahum Litt, chief administrative law judge; Beverly Queen, docket clerk, 633-0330. Fax, 633-0325.

Preside over formal hearings to determine violations of minimum wage requirements, overtime payments, compensation benefits, employee discrimination, grant performance, alien certification, employee protection, and health and safety regulations set forth under numerous statutes, executive orders, and regulations. With few exceptions, hearings are required to be conducted in accordance with the Administrative Procedure Act.

National Commission for Employment Policy, 1522 K St. N.W., #300 20005; 724-1545. Anthony P. Carnevale, chairman; William Spriggs, associate director. Fax, 724-0019.

Independent agency that advises the president and Congress on national employment and training issues.

Congress:

General Accounting Office, Human Resources, 441 G St. N.W., NGB/ACG 20548; 512-6806. Janet L. Shikles, assistant comptroller general. Fax, 512-5806.

Independent, nonpartisan agency in the legislative branch. Audits, analyzes, and evaluates Labor Dept. programs; makes reports available to the public.

House Appropriations Committee, Subcommittee on Labor, Health and Human Services, and Education, 2358 RHOB 20515; 225-3508. Neal Smith, D-Iowa, chairman; Mike Stephens, staff assistant.

Jurisdiction over legislation to appropriate funds for the Labor Dept., the National Labor Relations Board, National Mediation Board, Federal Mediation and Conciliation Service, and other labor-related agencies.

House Education and Labor Committee, 2181 RHOB 20515; 225-4527. William D. Ford, D-Mich., chairman; Patricia Rissler, staff director.

Jurisdiction over labor and employment legislation.

House Education and Labor Committee, Subcommittee on Postsecondary Education and Training, 2451 RHOB 20515; 226-3681. William D. Ford, D-Mich., chairman; Omer Waddles, staff director.

Jurisdiction over public and full-employment legislation.

Senate Appropriations Committee, Subcommittee on Labor, Health and Human Services, and Education, SD-186 20510; 224-7283. Tom Harkin, D-Iowa, chairman; Ed Long, clerk.

Jurisdiction over legislation to appropriate funds for the Labor Dept., National Labor Relations Board, National Mediation Board, Federal Mediation and Conciliation Service, and other labor-related agencies.

Senate Labor and Human Resources Committee, SD-428 20510; 224-5375. Edward M. Kennedy, D-Mass., chairman; Nick Littlefield, chief counsel and staff director.

Jurisdiction over labor and employment legislation.

Senate Labor and Human Resources Committee, Subcommittee on Employment and Productivity, SD-644 20510; 224-5575. Paul Simon, D-Ill., chairman; Brian Kennedy, staff director.

Jurisdiction over public and full-employment legislation.

Nongovernmental:

See also Labor Unions list (p. 801)

American Enterprise Institute for Public Policy Research, Economic Policy Studies, 1150 17th St. N.W. 20036; 862-5846. Marvin H. Kosters, director. Fax, 862-7178.

Research and educational organization that studies trends in employment, earnings, and income in the United States.

Assn. of Part-Time Professionals, 7700 Leesburg Pike, #216, Falls Church, VA 22043; (703) 734-7975. Maria Laqueur, executive director.

Promotes part-time job opportunities for professional people. Maintains job referral and career counseling services; serves as an information resource center; issues publications on part-time work. Promotes a work environment responsive to individual and family needs.

Center for Social Policy Studies (George Washington University), 1717 K St. N.W., #1200 20006; 833-2530. Sar A. Levitan, director. Fax, 833-2531.

Research organization that focuses on federal social policy, including employment. Reports on productivity, unions, the family and work, poverty and work, work force statistics, the federal work force, government training programs, and other aspects of government employment policy and labor force trends.

Frontlash, 815 16th St. N.W. 20006; 783-3993. Cheryl Graeze, executive director. Toll-free, (800) 833-3250. Fax, 637-3591.

AFL-CIO-funded student organization that initiates college labor clubs. Encourages youth participation in labor-sponsored legislation and in boycott and strike support efforts. Provides educational activities on labor issues; sponsors speakers.

Labor Policy Assn., 1015 15th St. N.W. 20005; 789-8670. Jeffrey C. McGuiness, president. Fax, 789-0064.

Membership: corporate vice presidents in charge of employee relations. Promotes research in employee relations, particularly in federal employment policy and implementation.

National Assn. of Personnel Services, 3133 Mount Vernon Ave., Alexandria, VA 22305; (703) 684-0180. Dianne Callis, president. Fax, (703) 684-0071.

Membership: owners and managers of private personnel services companies, including placement and temporary service firms. Monitors legislation and regulations concerning the private placement industry.

National Assn. of Temporary Services, 119 S. Saint Asaph St., Alexandria, VA 22314; (703) 549-6287. Samuel R. Sacco, executive vice president. Fax, (703) 549-4808.

Membership: companies supplying other companies with workers on a temporary basis. Monitors legislation.

National Council on Employment Policy, 1717 K St. N.W., #1200 20006; 833-2530. Sar A. Levitan, chairman. Fax, 833-2531.

Employment training research organization of labor scholars and practitioners. Researches labor policy issues and labor force statistics.

Society for Human Resource Management, 606 N. Washington St., Alexandria, VA 22314; (703) 548-3440. Michael R. Losey, president. Toll-free, (800) 283-7476. Fax, (703) 836-0367.

Membership: human resource management professionals. Monitors legislation and regulations concerning recruitment, training, and employment practices; occupational safety and health; compensation and benefits; employee and labor relations; and equal employment opportunity. Sponsors seminars and conferences.

Labor Dept.

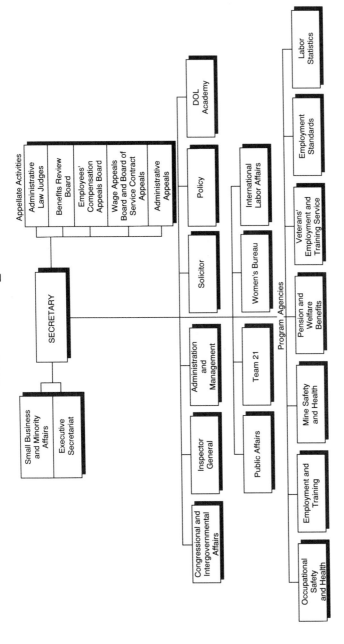

U.S. Chamber of Commerce, Domestic Policy, 1615 H St. N.W. 20062; 463-5500. Lorraine Lavet, director. Press, 463-5682. Fax, 887-3445.

Monitors legislation and regulations affecting the business community, including employee benefits, health care, legal and regulatory affairs, transportation and telecommunications infrastructure, defense conversion, and equal employment opportunity.

Employment and Training

General

See also Civil Service, Hiring, Recruitment, and Training (p. 291); Equal Employment Opportunity, Minorities (p. 182); Equal Employment Opportunity, Women (p. 183); Departmental and Agency Personnel Offices box (p. 288); Military Education and Training (p. 551); Office of Personnel Management, Federal Employment Information Centers (p. 859); Veterans, Readjustment and Job Assistance (p. 439)

Agencies:

Employment and Training Administration (Labor Dept.), 200 Constitution Ave. N.W. 20210; 219-6050. Douglas Ross, assistant secretary. Information, 219-6871. Fax, 219-6827.

Responsible for employment, training, and trade adjustment programs for economically disadvantaged, unemployed, and dislocated workers. Administers and directs policy for the U.S. Employment Service, the Unemployment Insurance Service, and the Office of Work-Based Learning. Administers and directs programs for native American, migrant, young, disabled, and older workers.

Employment and Training Administration (Labor Dept.), Job Training Programs, 200 Constitution Ave. N.W. 20210; 219-6236. Dolores Battle, administrator. Fax, 219-7190.

Administers the Job Training Partnership Act, which provides state and local governments with funds to develop and operate employment and training programs. Oversees the Job Corps (a program for disadvantaged youth) and employment and training programs for native Americans and for disabled, migrant, seasonal, and older workers.

Employment and Training Administration (Labor Dept.), Research and Demonstration, 200 Constitution Ave. N.W. 20210; 219-5677. A. Lafayette Grisby, chief. Fax, 219-5677.

Administers national job training programs and services operating in more than one state and serving persons with disabilities, women, single parents, displaced homemakers, youth, older workers, individuals lacking education credentials or English-language proficiency, public assistance recipients, offenders, and others requiring special assistance.

Employment and Training Administration (Labor Dept.), U.S. Employment Service, 200 Constitution Ave. N.W. 20210; 219-5257. Robert Schaerfl, director. Fax, 219-6643.

Assists states in maintaining a system of local employment-service centers for job seekers and employers.

Employment and Training Administration (Labor Dept.), Work-Based Learning, 200 Constitution Ave. N.W. 20210; 219-6540. James D. Van Erden, administrator. Fax, 219-5428.

Responsible for the Bureau of Apprenticeship and Training and for the Worker Retraining and Adjustment programs (including the Trade Adjustment Assistance Program and the Economic Dislocation and Worker Adjustment Assistance Act); examines training initiatives and technology; and supervises demonstration projects such as school-to-work grants.

National Occupational Information Coordinating Committee, 2100 M St. N.W., #156 20037; 653-5665. Juliette N. Lester, executive director. Fax, 653-2123.

Interagency group that works with the departments of Agriculture, Commerce, Defense, Education, and Labor; provides information on civilian and military occupations, educational institutions, and training programs; develops systems to provide labor market and occupational information for vocational education and employment-related program planners and administrators at the state level; supports state efforts to provide citizens with career information and guidance.

Congress:

House Education and Labor Committee, 2181 RHOB 20515; 225-4527. William D. Ford, D-Mich., chairman; Patricia Rissler, staff director.

Jurisdiction over work incentive programs and education and job training programs for youth and public assistance recipients, including the

Job Opportunities and Basic Skills Training program and the Job Training Partnership Act.

House Education and Labor Committee, Subcommittee on Human Resources, B346C RHOB 20515; 225-1850. Matthew G. Martinez, D-Calif., chairman; Lester Sweeting, staff director and counsel.

Jurisdiction over legislation on employment training programs for elderly workers.

House Education and Labor Committee, Subcommittee on Labor Standards, Occupational Health and Safety, B345A RHOB 20515; 225-1927. Austin J. Murphy, D-Pa., chairman; James Riley, staff director.

Jurisdiction over legislation on minimum wage and wage and hour standards, including the Davis-Bacon Act, the Walsh-Healey Act, and the Fair Labor Standards Act; jurisdiction over mandated benefits, including those for government contractors.

House Education and Labor Committee, Subcommittee on Postsecondary Education and Training, 2451 RHOB 20515; 226-3681. William D. Ford, D-Mich., chairman; Omer Waddles, staff director.

Jurisdiction over employment training legislation, including legislation on apprenticeship programs, on-the-job training, dislocated workers and plant shutdowns, displaced homemakers, and rural workers. Jurisdiction over youth and young adult conservation corps programs.

House Education and Labor Committee, Subcommittee on Select Education and Civil Rights, 518 O'Neill Bldg. (300 New Jersey Ave. S.E.) 20515; 226-7532. Major R. Owens, D-N.Y., chairman; Maria Cuprill, staff director.

Jurisdiction over legislation on vocational rehabilitation and education of people with disabilities.

House Judiciary Committee, Subcommittee on International Law, Immigration, and Refugees, B370B RHOB 20515; 225-5727. Romano L. Mazzoli, D-Ky., chairman; Eugene Pugliese, counsel.

Jurisdiction over legislation on foreign laborers once they are in the United States and on employer sanctions for not complying with the Immigration and Refugee Control Act of 1986.

Senate Finance Committee, Subcommittee on Social Security and Family Policy, SD-205

20510; 224-4515. John B. Breaux, D-La., chairman; Laird D. Burnett, staff contact.

Holds hearings on legislation affecting the Job Opportunities and Basic Skills Training Program.

Senate Judiciary Committee, Subcommittee on Immigration and Refugee Affairs, SD-520 20510; 224-7878. Edward M. Kennedy, D-Mass., chairman; Jeff Blattner, chief counsel.

Jurisdiction over legislation on nonimmigrant foreign laborers once they are in the United States.

Senate Labor and Human Resources Committee, SD-428 20510; 224-5375. Edward M. Kennedy, D-Mass., chairman; Nick Littlefield, chief counsel and staff director.

Jurisdiction over education and job training programs for youth and public assistance recipients, including the Job Training Partnership Act.

Senate Labor and Human Resources Committee, Subcommittee on Aging, SH-615 20510; 224-3239. Barbara A. Mikulski, D-Md., chair; Robyn Lipner, staff director.

Jurisdiction over legislation on employment training programs for elderly workers.

Senate Labor and Human Resources Committee, Subcommittee on Employment and Productivity, SD-644 20510; 224-5575. Paul Simon, D-Ill., chairman; Brian Kennedy, staff director.

Jurisdiction over employment training legislation, including legislation on apprenticeship programs, on-the-job training, and displaced homemakers. Oversight of the Equal Employment Opportunity Commission (jurisdiction shared with the Senate Subcommittee on Labor.)

Senate Labor and Human Resources Committee, Subcommittee on Labor, SH-608 20510; 224-5546. Howard M. Metzenbaum, D-Ohio, chairman; Michele L. Varnhagen, staff director.

Jurisdiction over legislation for workers with disabilities. (Jurisdiction shared with the Subcommittee on Disability Policy.)

Senate Special Committee on Aging, SD-G31 20510; 224-5364. David Pryor, D-Ark., chairman; Theresa M. Forster, staff director.

Studies and makes recommendations on legislation and federal programs affecting older Americans, including the areas of age discrimination, compensation, and unemployment; oversees Older Americans Act programs.

Nongovernmental:

AFL-CIO Human Resources Development Institute, 815 16th St. N.W., #405 20006; 638-3912. Patricia Garcia, national coordinator. Fax, 783-6536.

Provides training and technical assistance to labor unions, employers, education agencies, and community groups for workplace programs focusing on dislocated workers, economically disadvantaged workers, and skill upgrading.

American Labor Education Center, 2000 P St. N.W., #300 20036; 828-5170. Karen Ohmans, director. Fax, 828-5173.

Produces materials and training programs for workers and unions. Interests include occupational health and safety, communication skills, international affairs, and other labor issues.

American Society for Training and Development, 1640 King St., Alexandria, VA (mailing address: P.O. Box 1443, Alexandria, VA 22313); (703) 683-8100. Curtis E. Plott, president. Fax, (703) 683-8103.

Membership: trainers and human resource developers. Promotes workplace training programs and human resource development. Interests include productivity, job training and retraining, participative management, and unemployment. Holds conferences and provides information on technical and skills training.

Employee Relocation Council, 1720 N St. N.W. 20036; 857-0857. H. Cris Collie, executive vice president. Fax, 467-4012.

Membership: corporations that relocate employees and moving, real estate, and relocation management companies. Researches and recommends policies that provide a smooth transition for relocated employees and their families. Holds conferences and issues publications on employee relocation issues.

Interstate Conference of Employment Security Agencies, 444 N. Capitol St. N.W., #142 20001; 628-5588. Emily DeRocco, executive director. Fax, 783-5023.

Membership: state employment security administrators. Informs members of federal legislation on job placement, veterans' affairs, and employment and training programs. Provides labor market information; trains new state administrators and executive staff.

National Alliance of Business, 1201 New York Ave. N.W., #700 20005; 289-2800. William H. Kolberg, president; Joseph Fischer, vice president, job training, 289-2957. Press, 289-2834. Fax, 289-1303.

Assists private industry councils with implementation and operation of the Job Training Partnership Act of 1982, including programs for displaced and economically disadvantaged workers; operates clearinghouse for employment, training, and education programs; conducts seminars and training conferences; provides private industry with consulting services. Promotes work-based learning programs in public schools.

National Assn. of Counties, Training and Employment Program, 440 1st St. N.W., 8th Floor 20001; 393-6226. Neil Bomberg, director. Fax, 393-2630.

Oversees, directs, and offers technical assistance to members participating in federal job training programs; informs members of related legislation. Assists county officials, private industry councils, and service delivery areas in implementing the Job Training Partnership Act of 1982.

National Assn. of Manufacturers, Employee Relations Committee, 1331 Pennsylvania Ave. N.W. 20004; 637-3129. Peter Lunnie, director. Fax, 637-3182.

Interests include opportunities for dislocated workers, striker replacement, vocational education, matters relating to the National Labor Relations Act, and the effect of high technology on the work force.

National Assn. of Private Industry Councils, 1201 New York Ave. N.W., #800 20005; 289-2950. Robert F. A. Knight, president. Fax, 289-1303.

Membership: private industry councils and state job training coordinating councils established under the Job Training Partnership Act of 1982. Interests include job training opportunities for unemployed, economically disadvantaged, and dislocated workers, and youth; and private sector involvement in federal employment and training policy. Provides members with technical assistance; holds conferences and seminars.

National Center on Education and the Economy, National Alliance for Restructuring Education, 700 11th St. N.W., #750 20001; 783-3668. Michael Cohen, director. Fax, 783-3672.

Partnership of states, school districts, corporations, foundations, and nonprofit organizations that studies and makes policy recommendations on work force education and training to enhance America's economic competitiveness. (Headquarters in Rochester, N.Y.)

National Governors' Assn., Center for Policy Research, 444 N. Capitol St. N.W. 20001; 624-5345. Martin Simon, director, training and employment program. Press, 624-5331. Fax, 624-5313.

Provides information and technical assistance to members participating in federal job training programs, including programs authorized under the Job Training Partnership Act of 1982; informs members of related legislation. Provides technical assistance to members participating in employment and training activities concerning work and welfare programs, employment services, adult literacy, dislocated workers, and dropout prevention.

National Institute for Work and Learning, 1875 Connecticut Ave. N.W., 9th Floor 20009; 884-8186. Ivan Charner, vice president. Fax, 884-8422.

Public policy research organization that seeks to improve collaboration between educational and business institutions. Conducts demonstration projects with communities throughout the country on employer-funded tuition aid, youth transition from school to work, employee education, and career development. Conducts research on educational and work issues. Library open to the public. (Affiliated with the Academy for Educational Development.)

Partnership for Training and Employment Careers, 1620 Eye St. N.W. 20006; 887-6120. Cynthia A. Davis, executive director. Fax, 887-8216.

Membership: professionals and policy makers in the employment and training field. Promotes professionalism, information exchange, networking, and professional growth in the work force development field.

The Southport Institute for Policy Analysis, P.O. Box 25424, Alexandria, VA 22313; 682-4100. Forrest P. Chisman, president. Fax, 682-2121.

Works to advance human resource development by addressing issues that affect the quality of the American work force; develops policies and programs to improve the basic skills of American workers, especially those working for small- and medium-size employers; seeks to improve public policy on adult literacy; promotes dialogue on human resource issues between the United States and other countries.

U.S. Chamber of Commerce, Center for Workforce Preparation, 1615 H St. N.W. 20062-2000; 463-5525. Rae Nelson, executive director. Fax, 463-5730.

Works with local chambers on educational reform, human resource, and job training issues.

U.S. Conference of Mayors, 1620 Eye St. N.W., 6th Floor 20006; 293-7330. Joan Crigger, director, employment and training. Fax, 293-2352.

Offers technical assistance to members participating in federal job training programs; monitors related legislation; acts as an information clearinghouse on employment and training programs.

See also Corporation for Enterprise Development (p. 384)

Aliens

Agencies:

Administration for Children and Families (Health and Human Services Dept.), Refugee Resettlement, 901 D St. S.W., 6th Floor (mailing address: 370 L'Enfant Promenade S.W., Washington, DC 20447); 401-9246. Lavinia Limon, director. Fax, 401-5487.

Directs the Refugee Resettlement Program, which reimburses states for financial and medical assistance given to refugees; provides grants for social services, such as employment training and English instruction. Awards funds to private resettlement agencies for the provision of cash assistance to and case management of refugees. Directs the State Legalization Impact Assistance Program, which awards grants to states to pay part of costs for assisting aliens who attained legal status under the Immigration Reform and Control Act of 1986.

Employment and Training Administration (Labor Dept.), Foreign Labor Certification, 200 Constitution Ave. N.W. 20210; 219-5263. Flora

Richardson, chief, foreign labor certifications. Fax, 219-6643.

Sets policies and guidelines for regional offices that certify applications for alien employment in the United States; determines whether U.S. citizens are available for those jobs and whether employment of aliens will adversely affect similarly employed U.S. citizens.

Congress:

See *Employment and Training, General, Congress (p. 171)*

Apprenticeship Programs

Agencies:

Employment and Training Administration (Labor Dept.), Apprenticeship and Training, 200 Constitution Ave. N.W., #N4649 20210; 219-5921. Anthony Swoope, director. Library, 219-6992. Fax, 219-5428.

Promotes establishment of apprenticeship programs in private industry and the public sector. Library open to the public.

Employment and Training Administration (Labor Dept.), Federal Committee on Apprenticeship, 200 Constitution Ave. N.W. 20210; 219-5943. Anthony Swoope, acting executive director. Fax, 219-5428.

Advises the secretary of labor on the role of apprenticeship programs in employment training and on safety standards for those programs; encourages sponsors to include these standards in planning apprenticeship programs.

Congress:

See *Employment and Training, General, Congress (p. 171)*

Nongovernmental:

See *Employment and Training, General, Nongovernmental (p. 173)*

Disabled

See also Social Services and Rehabilitation Programs, Disabled (p. 420)

Agencies:

Committee for Purchase from the Blind and Other Severely Handicapped, 1735 Jefferson Davis Highway, #403, Arlington, VA 22202-3461; (703) 603-7740. Beverly L. Milkman, executive director. Fax, (703) 412-7113.

Presidentially appointed committee that determines which products and services are suitable for federal procurement from qualified nonprofit agencies employing the blind or other severely disabled persons; seeks to increase employment opportunities for these individuals.

Education Dept., Rehabilitation Services Administration, 330 C St. S.W. 20202; 205-5482. Howard Moses, acting commissioner. Fax, 205-9874.

Coordinates and directs federal services for eligible physically and mentally disabled persons, with emphasis on programs that promote employment opportunities. Provides vocational training and job placement services; supports projects with private industry; administers grants for the establishment of supported-employment programs.

Employment Standards Administration (Labor Dept.), Special Employment, 200 Constitution Ave. N.W. 20210; 219-8727. Howard B. Ostmann, chief. Fax, 219-5122.

Administers certification of special lower minimum wage rates for disabled workers with impaired earning capacity in industry, sheltered workshops, hospitals, institutions, and group homes. Provides information on the Family Medical Leave Act.

Equal Employment Opportunity Commission (EEOC), Interagency Committee on Employees with Disabilities, 1801 L St. N.W. 20507; 663-4560. Frank Fritts, acting executive secretary. Fax, 663-7022. TDD, 663-4593.

Established by the Rehabilitation Act of 1973, as amended, and cochaired by the Education Dept. and the EEOC. Works for increased employment of persons with disabilities, affirmative action by the federal government, and an equitable work environment for employees with mental and physical disabilities.

Office of Personnel Management, Affirmative Recruiting and Employment, 1900 E St. N.W., #6332 20415; 606-0800. Donna Beecher, assistant director. Fax, 606-5049. TDD, 606-0023.

Develops policies, programs, and procedures to promote opportunities for qualified workers with disabilities, including veterans, to obtain and advance in federal employment.

President's Committee on Employment of People with Disabilities, 1331 F St. N.W., #300 20004; 376-6200. Richard Douglas, executive director. Fax, 376-6219. TDD, 376-6205.

Promotes training, rehabilitation, and employment opportunities for people with disabilities.

Congress:

See Employment and Training, General, Congress (p. 171)

Nongovernmental:

Dole Foundation for Employment of People with Disabilities, 1819 H St. N.W., #340 20006; 457-0318. Paul G. Hearne, president. Fax, 457-0473.

Awards grants to nonprofit organizations that provide job training and placement programs for people with disabilities. Provides employers, policy makers, and the public with information about employment of people with disabilities.

Mainstream, 3 Bethesda Metro Center, #830, Bethesda, MD 20814; (301) 654-2400. Lawrence C. Pencak, executive director. Fax, (301) 654-2403. TDD, (301) 654-2400.

Seeks to bring persons with disabilities into the work force; directs a demonstration placement program in competitive employment for persons with disabilities; provides publications, videos, and employment services; holds conferences on disability issues. Library open to the public.

See also National Assn. of Rehabilitation Facilities (p. 346)

Dislocated Workers

Agencies:

Employment and Training Administration (Labor Dept.), Worker Retraining and Adjustment Programs, 200 Constitution Ave. N.W. 20210; 219-5577. Robert Colombo, director. Fax, 219-5938.

Responsible for dislocated worker retraining programs.

Congress:

See Employment and Training, General, Congress (p. 171)

Nongovernmental:

National Assn. of Manufacturers, Employee Relations Committee, 1331 Pennsylvania Ave. N.W. 20004; 637-3129. Peter Lunnie, director. Fax, 637-3182.

Interests include opportunities for dislocated workers and vocational education.

National Assn. of Private Industry Councils, 1201 New York Ave. N.W., #800 20005; 289-2950. Robert F. A. Knight, president. Fax, 289-1303.

Membership: private industry councils and state job training coordinating councils established under the Job Training Partnership Act of 1982. Interests include job training opportunities for dislocated workers.

National Governors' Assn., Center for Policy Research, 444 N. Capitol St. N.W. 20001; 624-5335. John Lederer, senior policy analyst. Press, 624-5331. Fax, 624-5313.

Provides information and technical assistance to members participating in federal job training programs, including the Job Training Partnership Act of 1982; informs members of related legislation. Provides technical assistance to members participating in employment and training activities concerning dislocated workers.

Elderly

See also Social Services and Rehabilitation Programs, Elderly (p. 424)

Agencies:

Employment and Training Administration (Labor Dept.), Older Worker Programs, 200 Constitution Ave. N.W. 20210; 219-5904. Charles L. Atkinson, chief. Fax, 219-6338.

Administers the Senior Community Service Employment Program, which provides funds for part-time, community service work-training programs; the programs pay minimum wage and are operated by national sponsoring organizations and state and territorial governments. The program is aimed at economically disadvantaged persons age 55 and over.

Congress:

See Employment and Training, General, Congress (p. 171)

Nongovernmental:

American Assn. of Retired Persons, Senior Community Service Employment Program, 601 E St. N.W. 20049; 434-2020. Glenn L. Northup, director. Fax, 434-6470.

Conducts a federally funded work-experience program for economically disadvantaged older persons; places trainees in community service jobs and helps them reenter the labor force.

National Council of Senior Citizens, Senior AIDES Program, 1331 F St. N.W., 7th Floor 20004; 624-9508. Dorinda Fox, deputy director. Fax, 624-9595.

Operates the Labor Dept.'s Senior Community Service Employment Program, which provides funds for part-time, community service work-training programs and is aimed at low-income individuals age 55 and over.

National Council on the Aging, National Institute on Age, Work, and Retirement, 409 3rd St. S.W. 20024; 479-6981. Joyce Welsh, vice president. Toll-free, (800) 424-9046. Press, 479-6610. Library, 479-6669. Fax, 479-0735. TDD, 479-6674.

Provides business, government, and private organizations concerned with older workers with information, training, and technical assistance. Offers comprehensive retirement and midlife planning programs for the private and public sectors; conducts research on work/retirement behavior and attitudes. Library open to the public.

National Council on the Aging, Senior Community Service Employment Program, 409 3rd St. S.W., 2nd Floor 20024; 479-1200. Donald L. Davis, national project director. Fax, 479-0735.

Works with the Labor Dept. under the authority of the Older Americans Act to provide workers age 55 and over with employment, community service, and training opportunities in their resident communities. Library open to the public.

Migrant and Seasonal Farm Workers

Agencies:

Employment and Training Administration (Labor Dept.), Migrant and Seasonal Farm Worker Programs, 200 Constitution Ave. N.W. 20210; 219-5500. Charles C. Kane, chief. Fax, 219-6338.

Provides funds for programs that help migrant and seasonal farm workers and their families find better jobs in agriculture and other areas. Services include occupational training, education, and job development and placement.

Employment Standards Administration (Labor Dept.), Farm Labor Programs, 200 Constitution Ave. N.W. 20210; 219-7605. Solomon Sugarman, chief. Fax, 219-5122.

Administers and enforces the Migrant and Seasonal Agricultural Worker Protection Act, which protects migrant and seasonal agricultural workers from substandard labor practices by farm labor contractors, agricultural employers, and agricultural associations.

Congress:

See Employment and Training, General, Congress (p. 171)

Nongovernmental:

Migrant Legal Action Program, 2001 S St. N.W. 20009; 462-7744. Roger C. Rosenthal, executive director.

Funded by the Legal Services Corp. Supports and assists local legal services co-funded groups and other organizations and private attorneys with migrant farmworker clients; monitors legislation and regulations; litigates cases dealing with living and working conditions in migrant labor camps.

See also National Council of Agricultural Employers (p. 592)

Public Assistance Recipients

Agencies:

Administration for Children and Families (Health and Human Services Dept.), Family Assistance—Job Opportunities and Basic Skills Training, 901 D St. S.W. (mailing address: 370 L'Enfant Promenade S.W., Washington, DC 20447); 401-9275. Diann Dawson, acting director. Fax, 205-5887.

Provides recipients of Aid to Families with Dependent Children with job assistance, vocational training, and educational aid (including remedial programs, literacy training, and instruction in English as a second language); focuses on women with young children; provides child care options and other support services to make participation possible. Coordinates programs, under the Family Support Act of 1988, with departments of Education and Labor.

Congress:

See *Employment and Training, General, Congress (p. 171)*

Youth

Agencies:

Employment and Training Administration (Labor Dept.), Job Corps, 200 Constitution Ave. N.W. 20210; 219-8550. Peter E. Rell, director. Toll-free, (800) 733-5627. Fax, 219-5183.

Administers with the Interior Dept. a national program of comprehensive job training for disadvantaged youth at residential centers.

Employment Standards Administration (Labor Dept.), Child Labor and Polygraph Standards, 200 Constitution Ave. N.W. 20210; 219-7640. Nila Stovall, chief. Press, 219-8305. Fax, 219-4753. TDD, (800) 326-2577.

Administers and enforces child labor provisions of the Fair Labor Standards Act. Administers the Work Experience and Career Exploration Program aimed at reducing the number of high school dropouts.

Forest Service (Agriculture Dept.), Youth Conservation Corps, 1621 N. Kent St., Arlington, VA (mailing address: P.O. Box 96090, Washington, DC 20090); (703) 235-8861. Ransom Hughes, program manager. Fax, (703) 235-1597.

Administers with the National Park Service and the Fish and Wildlife Service the Youth Conservation Corps, a summer employment and training, public works program for young people ages 15 to 18. The program is conducted in national parks, in national forests, and on national wildlife refuges.

Interior Dept., Cooperative Activities and Initiatives, Main Interior Bldg. 20240; 208-6403. Ira Hutchison, director. Fax, 208-3620.

Oversees and provides professional and technical assistance to the operators of Job Corps centers managed by Interior Dept. bureaus and offices.

Congress:

See *Employment and Training, General, Congress (p. 171)*

Nongovernmental:

Joint Action in Community Service, 5225 Wisconsin Ave. N.W., #404 20015; 537-0996. Harvey Wise, executive director. Fax, 363-0239.

Volunteer organization that works with the Labor Dept.'s Job Corps program for disadvantaged young people ages 16 to 24. Provides follow-up assistance to help them make the transition from training to jobs.

National Alliance of Business, 1201 New York Ave. N.W., #700 20005; 289-2800. William H. Kolberg, president. Press, 289-2834. Fax, 289-1303.

Provides technical assistance in planning and operating youth programs. Encourages businesses to hire disadvantaged young people through targeted jobs tax credit and other programs.

National Assn. of Service and Conservation Corps, 666 11th St. N.W., #500 20001-4542; 737-6272. Kathleen Selz, executive director. Fax, 737-6277.

Membership: individuals and organizations interested in conservation and youth corps programs. Offers technical assistance to those interested in launching programs. Monitors legislation and regulations.

Women in Community Service, 1900 N. Beauregard St., #103, Alexandria, VA 22311; (703) 671-0500. Ruth C. Herman, executive director. Toll-free, (800) 442-9427. Fax, (703) 671-4489.

Membership: Church Women United, National Council of Catholic Women, National Council of Jewish Women, National Council of Negro Women, and American GI Forum Women. Holds contract with Labor Dept. for outreach, support service, and job placement for the Job Corps. Sponsors the Lifeskills Program to assist at-risk women in such areas as job training and money management.

Work, Achievement, Values, and Education (WAVE), 501 School St. S.W., #600 20024; 484-0103. Lawrence C. Brown, president. Fax, 488-7595.

Public service corporation that provides high school dropouts and students at risk, ages 12 to 21, with a program of education and employment services. Provides educational institutions with training and technical assistance.

Equal Employment Opportunity

See also Departmental and Agency Equal Employment Opportunity Contacts box (p. 180); Personnel: Military, Equal Opportunity (p. 569)

General

Agencies:

Commission on Civil Rights, Civil Rights Evaluation, 624 9th St. N.W. 20425; 376-8582. James S. Cunningham, assistant staff director. Library, 376-8110. Fax, 376-8315.

Researches federal policy in areas of equal employment and job discrimination; monitors the economic status of minorities and women, including their employment and earnings. Library open to the public.

Employment Standards Administration (Labor Dept.), Federal Contract Compliance Programs, 200 Constitution Ave. N.W. 20210; 219-9475. Shirley J. Wilcher, deputy assistant secretary. Fax, 219-6195.

Monitors and enforces government contractors' compliance with federal laws and regulations on equal employment opportunities and affirmative action, including employment rights of minorities, women, persons with disabilities, and disabled and Vietnam-era veterans.

Equal Employment Opportunity Commission, 1801 L St. N.W., #10006 20507; 663-4001. Gilbert F. Casellas, chairman designate. Information, 663-4900. Library, 663-4630. Fax, 663-4110. TDD, 663-4141.

Works to end job discrimination by private and government employers based on race, color, religion, sex, national origin, age, or reprisal for protest of employment practices alleged to be unlawful in hiring, promotion, firing, wages, and other terms and conditions of employment. Enforces Title VII of the Civil Rights Act of 1964, as amended, which includes the Pregnancy Discrimination Act; Age Discrimination in Employment Act; Equal Pay Act; and, in the federal sector, disability discrimination laws. Receives charges of discrimination; attempts conciliation or settlement; can bring court ac-

tion to force compliance; has review and appeals responsibility in the federal sector.

Equal Employment Opportunity Commission, Program Operations, 1801 L St. N.W. 20507; 663-4801. James H. Troy, director. Fax, 663-4823.

Provides guidance and technical assistance to employees who suspect discrimination and to employers who are working to comply with equal employment laws.

Justice Dept., Civil Rights, Main Justice Bldg. 20530; 514-3831. James Angus, chief, employment litigation. Library, 514-4098. Fax, 514-1105.

Investigates, negotiates, and litigates allegations of employment discrimination by public schools, universities, state and local governments, and federally funded employers; has enforcement power. Library open to the public by appointment.

Office of Personnel Management, Affirmative Recruiting and Employment, 1900 E St. N.W., #6332 20415; 606-0800. Donna Beecher, assistant director. Fax, 606-5049. TDD, 606-0023.

Responsible for governmentwide recruiting policies and programs; advises and assists federal agency offices in recruiting and promoting minorities, women, students, veterans, and people with disabilities.

Congress:

House Education and Labor Committee, Subcommittee on Postsecondary Education and Training, 2451 RHOB 20515; 226-3681. William D. Ford, D-Mich., chairman; Omer Waddles, staff director.

Jurisdiction over legislation on discrimination based on race, color, religion, sex, age, or national origin in employment where public funds are involved; legislation on public service employment and work force training programs for the unemployed and disadvantaged, including native Americans, youth, and farm laborers. Oversight of federal equal opportunity, age discrimination, and equal pay laws.

House Government Operations Committee, Subcommittee on Employment, Housing, and Aviation, B349A RHOB 20515; 225-6751. Collin C. Peterson, D-Minn., chairman; Wendy Adler, acting staff director.

Departmental and Agency . . .

Departments

Agriculture
David Montoya................ 720-5212

Commerce
Gerald R. Lucas............... 482-0625

Defense
Claiborne Haughton ...... (703) 695-0105

Air Force
Rita Looney .... (703) 695-7381

Army
Luther L. Santiful...... (703) 607-1976

Marines
Howard Mathews....... (703) 614-5650

Navy
Dorothy M. Meletzke ... (703) 695-2248

Education
Vi Sanchez 401-3560

Energy
John J. Pagano................ 586-2218

Health and Human Services
Marcella Haynes 619-0671

Housing and Urban Development
Sandra L. Hobson............. 708-3010

Interior
E. Melodee Stith.............. 208-5693

Justice
Ted McBurrows............... 501-6734

Labor
André C. Whisenton........... 219-6362

State
Evelyn Day................... 647-9294

Transportation
Antonio Califa 366-4648

Treasury
Ronald A. Glaser.............. 622-1160

Veterans Affairs
Gerald K. Hinch 233-2012

Agencies

Commission on Civil Rights
Tino Calabia.................. 376-7533

Commodity Futures Trading Commission
Frank Alston.................. 254-3275

Consumer Product Safety Commission
John W. Barrett Jr. ...... (301) 504-0570

Corporation for National Service
Nancy Voss................... 606-5000

Environmental Protection Agency
Dan J. Rondeau............... 260-4575

Equal Employment Opportunity Commission
Cynthia C. Matthews 663-7081

Export-Import Bank
Pat Steele 377-7800

Farm Credit Administration
Gail Hill................ (703) 883-4144

Federal Communications Commission
Sandra Canery 632-9882

Federal Deposit Insurance Corp.
Mae Culp..................... 942-3102

Federal Election Commission
Kathlene Martin 219-3420

Federal Emergency Management Agency
Adell Betts 646-4122

Oversees operations of the Equal Employment Opportunity Commission and other federal agencies concerned with racial and sexual discrimination in employment.

Senate Governmental Affairs Committee, SD-340 20510; 224-4751. John Glenn, D-Ohio, chairman; Leonard Weiss, staff director. Fax, 224-9682.

Jurisdiction over legislation on discrimination based on race, color, religion, sex, age, or national origin in employment where federal employees are involved.

Senate Labor and Human Resources Committee, SD-428 20510; 224-5375. Edward M. Kennedy, D-Mass., chairman; Nick Littlefield, chief counsel and staff director.
Oversees operation of the Equal Employment Opportunity Commission.

Senate Labor and Human Resources Committee, Subcommittee on Labor, SH-608 20510; 224-5546. Howard M. Metzenbaum, D-Ohio, chairman; Michele L. Varnhagen, staff director.
Jurisdiction over legislation on discrimination based on race, color, religion, sex, age, or national origin in employment except where fed-

...Equal Employment Opportunity Contacts

Federal Labor Relations Authority
James M. Cheskawich.......... 482-6640
Federal Maritime Commission
Mary A. Jackson 523-5806
Federal Mediation and Conciliation Service
Doug Daisey 653-5260
Federal Reserve System
Portia W. Thompson 452-3654
Federal Trade Commission
Barbara B. Wiggs 326-2196
General Services Administration
Grant B. Williams.............. 501-0767
Interstate Commerce Commission
Alexander W. Dobbins.......... 927-7503
Merit Systems Protection Board
Janice E. Fritts 653-6180
National Aeronautics and Space Administration
Yvonne B. Freeman 358-2167
National Credit Union Administration
Lamont R. Gibson....... (703) 518-6325
National Foundation on the Arts and the Humanities
National Endowment for the Arts
Angelia Richardson.......... 682-5454
National Endowment for the Humanities
Margaret Horne.............. 606-8399
National Labor Relations Board
Barbara Gainey 634-1092

National Science Foundation
Ivin L. King 357-9819
National Transportation Safety Board
Craig Keller.................. 382-6707
Nuclear Regulatory Commission
Vandy Miller .... (301) 492-4665
Occupational Safety and Health Review Commission
Larry A. Hoss................. 606-5390
Office of Personnel Management
Teresa A. del Rio 606-2460
Peace Corps
Ronald C. Owens.............. 606-3114
Securities and Exchange Commission
Faith Ruderfer................. 272-2153
Small Business Administration
George H. Robinson 205-6750
Smithsonian Institution
Era Marshall.................. 287-3508
U.S. Arms Control and Disarmament Agency
Robert L. Nealy............... 647-9581
U.S. Information Agency
Delia L. Johnson 619-5157
U.S. International Development Cooperation Agency
Agency for International Development
Jessalyn L. Pendarvis......... 663-1333
U.S. International Trade Commission
William Stutchbery............. 205-3135
U.S. Postal Service
Peter L. Garwood 268-3994

---

eral employees are involved; oversight of federal equal pay laws and of federal agencies concerned with racial and sexual discrimination in employment (jurisdiction shared with the Subcommittee on Employment and Productivity.)

Nongovernmental:

Equal Employment Advisory Council, 1015 15th St. N.W., #1200 20005; 789-8650. Jeffrey A. Norris, president. Fax, 789-2291.
Membership: principal equal employment officers and lawyers. Files amicus curiae (friend of the court) briefs; monitors legislation and regu-

lations; conducts research and provides information on equal employment law and policy.

NAACP Legal Defense and Educational Fund, 1275 K St. N.W., #301 20005; 682-1300. Elaine Jones, director. Fax, 682-1312.
Civil rights litigation group that provides legal information about civil rights legislation and advice on employment discrimination against women and minorities; monitors federal enforcement of equal opportunity rights laws. Not affiliated with the National Association for the Advancement of Colored People (NAACP). (Headquarters in New York.)

National Assn. of Manufacturers, Employee Relations Committee, 1331 Pennsylvania Ave. N.W. 20004; 637-3129. Peter Lunnie, director. Fax, 637-3182.

Monitors Equal Employment Opportunity Commission and Office of Federal Contract Compliance programs. Studies equal employment regulations, human resources, equal rights issues, comparable worth, pregnancy disability, privacy issues, and employment and training.

National Committee on Pay Equity, 1126 16th St. N.W., #411 20036; 331-7343. Susan Bianchi-Sand, executive director. Fax, 331-7406.

Coalition of labor, women's, and civil rights groups. Works to eliminate wage discrimination based on race and sex and to achieve equitable pay for all workers. Acts as an information clearinghouse and provides technical assistance on pay equity matters.

See also American Institutes for Research (p. 693); Lawyers' Committee for Civil Rights Under Law (p. 521); Society for Human Resource Management (p. 169); U.S. Chamber of Commerce, Domestic Policy (p. 187)

Minorities

See also Minority and Women's Rights (p. 265)

Agencies:

Bureau of Indian Affairs (Interior Dept.), Economic Development, Main Interior Bldg., Rm. 2528 20240; 208-2570. Lynn Forcia, chief, job placement and training. Fax, 208-3664.

Develops policies and programs to promote the achievement of economic goals for members of federally recognized tribes who live on or near reservations. Provides job training; assists those who have completed job training programs in finding employment; provides loans and loan guarantees; enhances contracting opportunities for individuals and tribes.

Employment and Training Administration (Labor Dept.), Indian and Native American Programs, 200 Constitution Ave. N.W., #N4641 20210; 219-8502. Charles L. Atkinson, acting chief. Fax, 219-6338.

Administers training and employment-related programs to promote employment opportunity; provides unemployed, underemployed, or economically disadvantaged native Americans and

Alaskan and Hawaiian natives with funds for training, job placement, and support services.

Office of Personnel Management, Affirmative Recruiting and Employment, 1900 E St. N.W., #6332 20415; 606-0870. Federico Perez-Molina, program manager, Hispanic employment. Fax, 606-5049.

Promotes opportunities for Hispanics to compete equally for federal jobs, including high-level positions; acts as technical adviser to managers within each agency.

Congress:

See Equal Employment Opportunity, General, Congress (p. 179)

Nongovernmental:

Coalition of Black Trade Unionists, 1625 L St. N.W. (mailing address: P.O. Box 66268, Washington, DC 20035); 429-1203. Wil Duncan, executive director. Fax, 429-1102.

Monitors legislation affecting African American and other minority trade unionists. Focuses efforts on equal employment opportunity, unemployment, and voter education and registration.

Labor Council for Latin American Advancement, 815 16th St. N.W., #310 20006; 347-4223. Alfredo C. Montoya, executive director. Fax, 347-5095.

Membership: Hispanic trade unionists. Encourages equal employment opportunity, voter registration and education, and participation in the political process.

Mexican American Legal Defense and Educational Fund, 733 15th St. N.W., #920 20005; 628-4074. Mario Moreno, regional counsel, Washington office. Fax, 393-4206.

Provides Mexican-Americans and other Hispanics involved in class-action employment discrimination suits or complaints with legal assistance. Monitors legislation and regulations. (Headquarters in Los Angeles.)

National Assn. for the Advancement of Colored People (NAACP), 1025 Vermont Ave. N.W., #1120 20005; 638-2269. Wade J. Henderson, director, Washington bureau. Fax, 638-5936.

Membership: persons interested in civil rights for all minorities. Advises individuals with employment discrimination complaints. Seeks to eliminate job discrimination and to bring about full employment for all Americans through legislation and litigation. (Headquarters in Baltimore.)

National Council of La Raza, 810 1st St. N.E., #300 20002; 289-1380. Raul Yzaguirre, president. Fax, 289-8173.

Provides research, policy analysis, and advocacy on Hispanic employment status and programs; provides Hispanic community-based groups with technical assistance to help develop effective employment programs with strong educational components. Works to promote understanding of Hispanic employment needs in the private sector. Monitors federal employment legislation and regulations. Interests include women in the workplace, affirmative action, equal opportunity employment, and youth employment.

National Urban League, 1111 14th St. N.W., #600 20005; 898-1604. Robert McAlpine, director, policy and government relations. Fax, 682-0782.

Federation of affiliates concerned with the social welfare of African Americans and other minorities. Testifies before congressional committees and federal agencies on equal employment; studies and evaluates federal enforcement of equal employment laws and regulations. (Headquarters in New York.)

Women

See also Minority and Women's Rights (p. 265)

Agencies:

Labor Dept., Women's Bureau, 200 Constitution Ave. N.W., #S3002 20210; 219-6611. Karen Nussbaum, director. Information, 219-6652. Fax, 219-5529.

Monitors women's employment issues. Promotes employment opportunities for women; sponsors workshops, job fairs, symposia, demonstrations, and pilot projects. Offers technical assistance; conducts research and provides publications on issues that affect working women; represents working women in international forums.

Office of Personnel Management, Federal Women's Program, 1900 E St. N.W. 20415; 606-

0870. Patricia H. Paige, chief, recruiting programs and policy. Fax, 606-5049.

Promotes opportunities for women to obtain and advance in federal employment; coordinates women's programs in federal agencies.

Office of Personnel Management, Women's Executive Leadership Program, 901 N. Stuart St., #308, Arlington, VA (mailing address: P.O. Box 164, Washington, DC 20044); (703) 235-1099. Debra Eddington, manager. Fax, (703) 235-1412.

Trains federally employed women with managerial potential for executive positions in the government. The program is geared toward GS-11 and GS-12 employees.

Congress:

See Equal Employment Opportunity, General, Congress (p. 179)

Nongovernmental:

Federally Employed Women, 1400 Eye St. N.W. 20005; 898-0994. Karen Scott, executive director. Fax, 898-0998.

Membership: women and men who work for the federal government. Works to eliminate sex discrimination in government employment and to increase job opportunities for women; offers training program; monitors legislation and regulations.

Federation of Organizations for Professional Women, 2001 S St. N.W., #500 20009; 328-1415. Viola Young-Horvath, executive director. Fax, 387-1290.

Membership: women's organizations, women's caucuses and committees in professional associations, and people interested in equal educational and employment opportunities for women. Monitors federal programs affecting women; organizes workshops to exchange information; publishes directory of women's organizations nationwide; maintains professional women's legal fund.

Institute for Women's Policy Research, 1400 20th St. N.W., #104 20036; 785-5100. Heidi I. Hartmann, director. Fax, 833-4362.

Public policy research organization that focuses on women's issues, including welfare reform, family and work policies, employment and wages, and discrimination based on gender, race, or ethnicity.

National Council of Career Women, 4200 Wisconsin Ave. N.W., #106-210 20016; 310-4200. Trish Whittaker, president.

Seeks to improve the professional skills of women and increase their employment rate by making them more productive and marketable.

National Federation of Business and Professional Women's Clubs, 2012 Massachusetts Ave. N.W. 20036; 293-1100. Dianne Studes, president. Fax, 861-0298.

Seeks to improve the status of working women through education, legislative action, and local projects. Sponsors Business and Professional Women's Foundation, which awards grants and loans, based on need, to mature women reentering the work force or entering nontraditional fields. Sponsors publication of issues affecting working women. Library open to the public.

National Women's Law Center, 1616 P St. N.W. 20036; 328-5160. Sharon Fischman, communications director. Fax, 328-5137.

Works to expand and protect women's legal rights through litigation, advocacy, and public education.

Wider Opportunities for Women, 1325 G St. N.W., Lower Level 20005; 638-3143. Cynthia Marano, executive director. Fax, 638-4885.

Promotes equal employment opportunities for women through equal access to jobs and training, equal incomes, and an equitable workplace. Conducts nontraditional skills training programs; monitors public policy relating to jobs, affirmative action, vocational education, training opportunities, welfare reform, and pay equity.

Women Work!, 1625 K St. N.W., #300 20006; 467-6346. Jill Miller, executive director. Fax, 467-5366.

Fosters the development of programs and services for former homemakers reentering the job market and provides information about public policy issues that affect displaced homemakers. Refers individuals to local services; monitors legislation.

See also Assn. for Women in Science (p. 666); Business and Professional Women's Foundation (p. 160); Women's Legal Defense Fund (p. 523)

International Labor Policy and Programs

See also International Economics (p. 75)

General

Agencies:

Commerce Dept., Policy Analysis, Main Commerce Bldg., #4858 20230; 482-5703. David A. Peterson, senior policy adviser. Fax, 482-0432.

Responsible with the Labor Dept. and the State Dept. for U.S. government relations with the Geneva-based International Labor Organization (ILO), a tripartite agency of the United Nations that deals with worldwide labor issues.

Labor Dept., Foreign Relations, 200 Constitution Ave. N.W. 20210; 219-7631. John A. Ferch, director. Fax, 219-5613.

Provides foreign governments with technical assistance in labor-related activities on a reimbursable basis. (Funding is provided by the U.S. Agency for International Development, international organizations, and foreign governments.) Participates with the State Dept. in managing the U.S. labor attaché program; conducts the U.S. International Visitors Program. Provides information on foreign labor developments, including foreign labor trends.

Labor Dept., International Labor Affairs, 200 Constitution Ave. N.W., #S2235 20210; 219-6043. Joachin F. Otero, deputy under secretary. Fax, 219-5980.

Assists in developing international economic policy relating to labor; helps represent the United States in multilateral and bilateral trade negotiations.

Labor Dept., International Organizations, 200 Constitution Ave. N.W., #S5311 20210; 219-6241. H. Charles Spring, director. Fax, 219-9074.

Provides administrative support for U.S. participation at the International Labor Organization (ILO) and at the Paris-based Organization for Economic Cooperation and Development (OECD), which studies and reports on world economic issues.

Labor Dept., Labor Advisory Committee for Trade Negotiations and Trade Policy, 200 Constitution Ave. N.W., #C4312 20210; 219-4752. Fernand Lavallee, director. Fax, 219-5381.

Advises the secretary of labor and the U.S. trade representative on trade agreements, trade negotiations, and other matters related to the administration of U.S. trade policy.

Labor Dept., U.S. International Visitors Program, 200 Constitution Ave. N.W., #S5006 20210; 219-7616. John A. Ferch, director. Fax, 219-5613.

Works with the State Dept., the Agency for International Development, and other agencies in arranging visits and training programs for foreign officials interested in U.S. labor and trade unions.

President's Committee on the International Labor Organization (ILO) (Labor Dept.), 200 Constitution Ave. N.W., #S5311 20210; 219-6241. Robert B. Reich, chairman; Joachin F. Otero, committee counselor and U.S. ILO representative, 219-6043. Fax, 219-9074.

Advisory committee of government, employer, and worker representatives, including secretaries of State, Commerce, and Labor, and the president of the AFL-CIO. Reviews developments of the ILO and advises the president, the secretary of labor, and the U.S. representative of the ILO governing body; formulates and coordinates policy on the ILO.

State Dept., Coordinator of International Labor Affairs, Main State Bldg. 20520; 647-3662. Anthony G. Freeman, special assistant to the secretary and coordinator. Fax, 647-0431.

Serves as a liaison between U.S. labor and the State Dept. and as a delegate to the International Labor Organization (ILO); supervises the labor function within the State Dept. and all U.S. embassies abroad.

State Dept., International Organization Affairs, Main State Bldg. 20520; 647-4196. Richard Zorn, deputy director, industrial and communications programs. Fax, 647-8902.

Responsible, with the Labor Dept. and the Commerce Dept., for U.S. government relations with the International Labor Organization (ILO).

International Organizations:

United Nations, International Labor, 1828 L St. N.W., #801 20036; 653-7652. Stephen I. Schlossberg, director. Fax, 653-7687.

Specialized agency of the United Nations. Serves as liaison between the International Labor Organization (ILO), headquartered in Geneva, and U.S. government, employer, and worker groups. Library open to the public by appointment.

Nongovernmental:

American Institute for Free Labor Development, 1015 20th St. N.W., 5th Floor 20036; 659-6300. William C. Doherty, executive director. Fax, 785-1218.

Provides assistance to free and democratic trade unions in Latin America and the Caribbean. Provides trade union leadership courses in collective bargaining, union organization, trade integration, labor-management cooperation, union administration, and political theories. Sponsors social and community development projects, including housing projects, agricultural reforms, and agrarian union projects that focus on production and marketing cooperatives.

Foreign Trade Impact

Agencies:

Economic Development Administration (Commerce Dept.), Trade Adjustment Assistance, Main Commerce Bldg. 20230; 482-3373. Daniel F. Harrington, director. Fax, 482-0466.

Certifies eligibility and provides domestic firms and industries adversely affected by foreign trade with technical assistance under provisions of the Trade Act of 1974.

Employment and Training Administration (Labor Dept.), Trade Adjustment Assistance, 200 Constitution Ave. N.W., #C4318 20210; 219-5555. Marvin M. Fooks, director. Fax, 219-5753.

Assists American workers who are totally or partially unemployed because of increased imports; offers training, job search and relocation assistance, weekly benefits at state unemployment insurance levels, and other reemployment services.

Labor Dept., International Economic Affairs, 200 Constitution Ave. N.W., #S5325 20210; 219-7597. Jorge Perez-Lopez, director. Fax, 219-5071.

Assists in developing U.S. foreign economic policy; examines the effect of foreign trade investment and immigration on income and job opportunities of American workers, domestic production, consumption, and the competitiveness of U.S. products.

U.S. International Trade Commission, 500 E St. S.W. 20436; 205-2781. Don E. Newquist, chairman. Information, 205-2000. Press, 205-1819. Fax, 205-2798.
Investigates the importation of goods into the United States in terms of their effect on domestic industry and agriculture; reports adverse effects to the president and recommends relief. Library open to the public.

Congress:

House Ways and Means Committee, Subcommittee on Trade, 1136 LHOB 20515; 225-3943. Robert T. Matsui, D-Calif., acting chairman; Bruce Wilson, staff director.
Jurisdiction over legislation on foreign trade impact.

Senate Finance Committee, Subcommittee on International Trade, SD-205 20510; 224-4515. Max Baucus, D-Mont., chairman; Mary Foley, staff contact.
Holds hearings on legislation concerning foreign trade impact.

Nongovernmental:

See International Economics, General, Nongovernmental (p. 78); International Economics, International Trade, Nongovernmental (p. 88)

Labor-Management Relations

See also Unions (p. 197)

General

Agencies:

Justice Dept., Organized Crime and Racketeering, 1001 G St. N.W., #300 20530; 514-3666. Gerald A. Toner, assistant chief, labor-management racketeering. Fax, 514-9837.
Reviews and advises on prosecutions of criminal violations involving labor-management relations and internal affairs of labor unions.

Labor Dept., Office of American Workplace, 200 Constitution Ave. N.W. 20210; 219-6045.

Martin Manley, assistant secretary. Fax, 219-4315.
Coordinates the department's labor-management programs and research; conducts conferences and workshops to assist employers and unions in joint efforts to promote innovation and improve productivity in the workplace.

Congress:

House Education and Labor Committee, Subcommittee on Labor-Management Relations, 320 CHOB 20515; 225-5768. Pat Williams, D-Mont., chairman; Jon Weintraub, staff director.
Jurisdiction over legislation on labor-management issues and unfair labor practices and the National Labor Relations Act.

House Government Operations Committee, Subcommittee on Employment, Housing, and Aviation, B349A RHOB 20515; 225-6751. Collin C. Peterson, D-Minn., chairman; Wendy Adler, acting staff director.
Oversight of the Federal Mediation and Conciliation Service, the Labor Dept., and the National Labor Relations Board.

House Government Operations Committee, Subcommittee on Information, Justice, Transportation, and Agriculture, B349C RHOB 20515; 225-3741. Gary Condit, D-Calif., chairman; Shannon Lahey, acting staff director. Fax, 225-2445.
Oversees operations of the National Mediation Board.

House Post Office and Civil Service Committee, Subcommittee on Civil Service, 122 CHOB 20515; 225-4025. Frank McCloskey, D-Ind., chairman; Debbie Kendall, staff director.
Jurisdiction over legislation on federal civil service labor-management issues. Studies the effect of reorganization of agencies on federal employees.

Senate Governmental Affairs Committee, Subcommittee on Federal Services, Post Office, and Civil Service, SH-601 20510; 224-2254. David Pryor, D-Ark., chairman; Kimberly A. Weaver, staff director.
Jurisdiction over legislation on federal civil service labor-management issues, including classification, compensation, and benefits.

Senate Labor and Human Resources Committee, SD-428 20510; 224-5375. Edward M. Kennedy, D-Mass., chairman; Nick Littlefield, chief counsel and staff director.

Oversight of the Labor Dept. and the National Mediation Board.

Senate Labor and Human Resources Committee, Subcommittee on Labor, SH-608 20510; 224-5546. Howard M. Metzenbaum, D-Ohio, chairman; Michele L. Varnhagen, staff director.

Jurisdiction over the National Labor Relations Act and over legislation on labor-management issues and unfair labor practices. Oversight of the Federal Mediation and Conciliation Service and the National Labor Relations Board.

Nongovernmental:

Center on National Labor Policy, 5211 Port Royal Rd., North Springfield, VA 22151; (703) 321-9180. Michael Avakian, general counsel. Fax, (703) 321-7342.

Public interest legal foundation that works to protect employees and employers from alleged excesses of union and government power.

CUE—An Organization for Positive Employee Relations, 1331 Pennsylvania Ave. N.W., #1500N 20004; 637-3043. Bernard H. Trimble, executive director. Fax, 637-3182.

Educational subsidiary of the National Assn. of Manufacturers. Educates management on the benefits of a work environment kept union-free through employee choice or through positive employee-employer relations.

National Assn. of Manufacturers, Industrial Relations, 1331 Pennsylvania Ave. N.W., #1500N 20004; 637-3127. Randolph M. Hale, vice president. Fax, 637-3182.

Conducts research and provides information on corporate industrial relations, including collective bargaining, labor standards, international labor relations, productivity, and other current labor issues; monitors legislation and regulations.

National Right to Work Committee, 8001 Braddock Rd., Springfield, VA 22160; (703) 321-9820. Reed E. Larson, president. Fax, (703) 321-7342.

Citizens' organization opposed to compulsory union membership. Supports right-to-work legislation.

National Right to Work Legal Defense Foundation, 8001 Braddock Rd., Springfield, VA

22160; (703) 321-8510. Rex H. Reed, executive vice president. Fax, (703) 321-9319.

Provides free legal aid for employees in cases of compulsory union membership abuses.

U.S. Chamber of Commerce, Domestic Policy, 1615 H St. N.W. 20062; 463-5500. Lorraine Lavet, director. Press, 463-5682. Fax, 887-3445.

Monitors legislation and regulations affecting labor-management relations.

Disputes/Unfair Labor Practices

Agencies:

Bureau of Labor Statistics (Labor Dept.), Compensation and Working Conditions, 2 Massachusetts Ave. N.E. 20212; 606-6300. George L. Stelluto, associate commissioner. Fax, 606-6310.

Provides data on collective bargaining agreements, wage structures, industrial relations, and work stoppages. Compiles data for *Employment Cost Index,* published quarterly.

Federal Mediation and Conciliation Service, 2100 K St. N.W. 20427; 653-5300. John Calhoun Wells, director. Information, 653-5290. Fax, 653-2002.

Assists labor and management representatives in resolving disputes through collective bargaining, mediation, and voluntary arbitration; awards limited number of small grants toward labor-management cooperation.

Labor Dept., Office of American Workplace, 200 Constitution Ave. N.W. 20210; 219-6045. Martin Manley, assistant secretary. Fax, 219-4315.

Coordinates the department's labor-management programs and research; advises the secretary on issues arising in major contract negotiations.

National Labor Relations Board, 1099 14th St. N.W. 20570; 273-1790. William B. Gould IV, chairman. Information, 273-1991. Library, 273-3720. Fax, 273-4270.

Works to prevent and remedy unfair labor practices by employers and labor unions; conducts elections among employees to determine whether they wish to be represented by a labor union for collective bargaining purposes. Library open to the public.

National Mediation Board, 1301 K St. N.W., #250E 20572; 523-5920. Kimberly A. Madigan, chair. Information, 523-5335. Fax, 523-1494.
Mediates labor disputes in the railroad and airline industries; determines and certifies labor representatives for those industries.

Congress:

See *Labor-Management Relations, General, Congress (p. 186)*

Nongovernmental:

American Arbitration Assn., 1150 Connecticut Ave. N.W. 20036; 296-8510. Garylee Cox, regional vice president. Fax, 872-9574.
Provides dispute resolution services, including arbitration, mediation, minitrials, and elections. (Headquarters in New York.)

See also *Labor Unions list (p. 801)*

Federal and Public Employees

Agencies:

Federal Labor Relations Authority, 607 14th St. N.W., #410 20424-0001; 482-6500. Jean McKee, chairman; Joe Swerdzewski, general counsel, 482-6600. Fax, 482-6635.
Oversees the federal labor-management relations program; administers the law that protects the right of federal government employees to organize, bargain collectively, and participate through labor organizations of their own choosing.

Federal Service Impasses Panel (Federal Labor Relations Authority), 607 14th St. N.W., #220 20424-1000; 482-6670. Edwin D. Brubeck, chairman; Linda A. Lafferty, executive director.
Assists in resolving contract negotiation impasses between federal agencies and labor organizations representing federal employees.

Office of Personnel Management, 1900 E St. N.W. 20415; 606-1700. Lorraine Lewis, general counsel. Fax, 606-0082.
Advises the government on law and legal policy relating to federal labor-management relations; represents the government before the Merit Systems Protection Board.

Office of Personnel Management, Labor Relations and Workforce Performance, 1900 E St.

N.W. 20415; 606-2920. Allan D. Heuerman, assistant director. Fax, 606-2613.
Provides government agencies and unions with information and advice on employee- and labor-management relations. Assists agencies with performance management and incentive awards.

Congress:

See *Labor-Management Relations, General, Congress (p. 186)*

Nongovernmental:

Public Service Research Council, 1761 Business Center Dr., Reston, VA 22090; (703) 438-3966. David Y. Denholm, president. Fax, (703) 438-3935.
Independent, nonpartisan research and educational organization. Opposes collective bargaining, strikes, and binding arbitration in the public sector. Sponsors conferences and seminars. Library open to the public by appointment.

See also *Academic Collective Bargaining Information Service (p. 128); Labor Unions list (p. 801)*

Labor Standards and Practices

See also *Equal Employment Opportunity (p. 179)*

Agencies:

Bureau of Labor Statistics (Labor Dept.), Compensation and Working Conditions, 2 Massachusetts Ave. N.E. 20212; 606-6300. George L. Stelluto, associate commissioner. Fax, 606-6310.
Conducts annual area wage surveys to determine occupational pay information in individual labor markets. Conducts industry wage surveys, which provide wage and employee benefit information; presents data for selected white- and blue-collar jobs.

Employment Standards Administration (Labor Dept.), 200 Constitution Ave. N.W. 20210; 219-6191. Bernard Anderson, assistant secretary. Information, 219-8743. Fax, 219-8457.
Administers and enforces employment laws and regulations. Responsibilities include ensuring compliance among federal contractors, administering benefits claims for federal employees and other workers, and protecting workers' wages and working conditions.

Employment Standards Administration (Labor Dept.), Contract Standards Operations, 200 Constitution Ave. N.W., #S3018 20210; 219-7541. Vacant, director. Fax, 219-5122.

Enforces the Davis-Bacon Act, the Walsh-Healey Public Contracts Act, the Contract Work Hours and Safety Standards Act, the Service Contract Act, and other related government contract labor standards statutes.

Employment Standards Administration (Labor Dept.), Fair Labor Standards Act Enforcement, 200 Constitution Ave. N.W., #S3516 20210; 219-7043. Ethel P. Miller, chief. Fax, 219-5122.

Issues interpretations and rulings of the Fair Labor Standards Act of 1938, as amended (Federal Minimum Wage and Overtime Pay Law).

Employment Standards Administration (Labor Dept.), Federal Contract Compliance Programs, 200 Constitution Ave. N.W. 20210; 219-9475. Shirley J. Wilcher, deputy assistant secretary. Fax, 219-6195.

Monitors and enforces government contractors' compliance with federal laws and regulations on equal employment opportunities and affirmative action, including employment rights of minorities, women, persons with disabilities, and disabled and Vietnam-era veterans.

Employment Standards Administration (Labor Dept.), Policy Planning and Review, 200 Constitution Ave. N.W., #S3506 20210; 219-8412. J. Dean Speer, director, policy and analysis; James W. Gantt, director, planning and review, 219-7474. Fax, 219-5122.

Issues regulations and policy statements on labor standards laws, including the Fair Labor Standards Act, the Davis-Bacon Act, the Service Contract Act, the Migrant and Seasonal Agricultural Workers Protection Act, section H2A of the Immigration Reform and Control Act of 1986, and the Employee Polygraph Protection Act.

Employment Standards Administration (Labor Dept.), Special Employment, 200 Constitution Ave. N.W. 20210; 219-8727. Howard B. Ostmann, chief. Fax, 219-5122.

Authorizes subminimum wages under the Fair Labor Standards Act for certain categories of workers, including full-time students, apprentices, and workers with disabilities. Administers the Fair Labor Standards Act restrictions on working at home in certain industries. Administers special minimum wage provisions appli-

cable in Puerto Rico and American Samoa. Provides information on the Family Medical Leave Act.

Employment Standards Administration (Labor Dept.), Wage and Hour Division, 200 Constitution Ave. N.W., #S3502 20210; 219-8305. Maria Echaveste, administrator. Fax, 219-4753.

Enforces the minimum-wage and overtime provisions of the Fair Labor Standards Act.

Employment Standards Administration (Labor Dept.), Wage Determinations, 200 Constitution Ave. N.W. 20210; 219-7531. Alan L. Moss, director; Vacant, chief, service contract wage determinations, 219-7568; Philip J. Gloss, chief, construction wage determinations, 219-7455. Fax, 219-5771.

Issues prevailing wage determinations under the Service Contract Act of 1965 and under the Davis-Bacon Act and related acts.

Labor Dept., Wage Appeals Board, 200 Constitution Ave. N.W., #N1651 20210; 219-9039. Charles E. Shearer Jr., chairman; Gerald F. Krizan, executive secretary. Fax, 219-6838.

Reviews appeals of wage determinations, final decisions of the Wage and Hour administrator, and decisions of administrative law judges under the Davis-Bacon Act and related acts.

Congress:

House Education and Labor Committee, Subcommittee on Labor Standards, Occupational Health and Safety, B345A RHOB 20515; 225-1927. Austin J. Murphy, D-Pa., chairman; James Riley, staff director.

Jurisdiction over legislation on minimum wage and wage and hour standards, including the Davis-Bacon Act, the Walsh-Healey Act, and the Fair Labor Standards Act; jurisdiction over mandated benefits, including those for government contractors.

House Education and Labor Committee, Subcommittee on Postsecondary Education and Training, 2451 RHOB 20515; 226-3681. William D. Ford, D-Mich., chairman; Omer Waddles, staff director.

Jurisdiction over legislation on job discrimination by government contractors, electronic monitoring, and polygraph testing.

Senate Labor and Human Resources Committee, Subcommittee on Labor, SH-608 20510;

224-5546. Howard M. Metzenbaum, D-Ohio, chairman; Michele L. Varnhagen, staff director. Jurisdiction over legislation on job discrimination by government contractors, minimum wage, wage and hour standards, and mandated benefits, including those for government contractors.

Pensions and Retirement

See also Civil Service, Pay and Employee Benefits (p. 292); Insurance (p. 71); Social Security (p. 409)

Agencies:

Advisory Council on Employee Welfare and Pension Benefit Plans (ERISA Advisory Council) (Labor Dept.), 200 Constitution Ave. N.W., #N5677 20210; 219-8753. William E. Morrow, executive secretary. Information, 219-8776. Fax, 219-6531.

Advises and makes recommendations to the secretary of labor under the Employee Retirement Income Security Act of 1974 (ERISA).

Bureau of Labor Statistics (Labor Dept.), Compensation and Working Conditions, 2 Massachusetts Ave. N.E. 20212; 606-6300. George L. Stelluto, associate commissioner. Fax, 606-6310.

Provides data on pensions and related work benefits.

Federal Retirement Thrift Investment Board, 1250 H St. N.W., #400 20005; 942-1600. Francis X. Cavanaugh, executive director. Fax, 942-1676.

Administers the Thrift Savings Plan, a tax-deferred, defined contribution plan that permits federal employees to save for additional retirement security under a program similar to private 401(k) plans.

Internal Revenue Service (Treasury Dept.), Employee Plans and Exempt Organizations, 1111 Constitution Ave. N.W., #3408 20224; 622-6720. James J. McGovern, assistant commissioner. Fax, 622-6873.

Administers tax aspects of private and self-employed pension plans; determines tax-exempt status; enforces related regulations and minimum standards for funding participation and beneficiary rights under the Employee Retirement Income Security Act of 1974 (ERISA) and the Tax Equity Fiscal Responsibility Act of 1982; provides rules for the uniform interpretation and application of federal tax laws involving tax-exempt organizations and private foundations.

Joint Board for the Enrollment of Actuaries, c/o Treasury Dept. 20220; 376-1421. Leslie S. Shapiro, executive director. Fax, 376-1420.

Joint board, with members from the departments of Labor and Treasury and the Pension Benefit Guaranty Corp., established under the Employee Retirement Income Security Act of 1974 (ERISA). Promulgates regulations for the enrollment of pension actuaries; examines applicants and grants certificates of enrollment; disciplines enrolled actuaries who have engaged in misconduct in the discharge of duties under ERISA.

Justice Dept., Organized Crime and Racketeering, 1001 G St. N.W., #300 20530; 514-3666. Gerald A. Toner, assistant chief, labor-management racketeering. Fax, 514-9837.

Reviews and advises on prosecutions of criminal violations concerning the operation of employee benefit plans in the private sector.

Office of Personnel Management, Retirement Information, 1900 E St. N.W. 20415; 606-0500. Wendy Gross, chief. TDD, 606-0551.

Provides civil servants with information and assistance on federal retirement payments.

Pension and Welfare Benefits Administration (Labor Dept.), 200 Constitution Ave. N.W. 20210; 219-8233. Olena Berg, assistant secretary. Information, 219-8921. Fax, 219-5526.

Administers, regulates, and enforces private employee benefit plan standards established by the Employee Retirement Income Security Act of 1974 (ERISA), with particular emphasis on fiduciary obligations; receives and maintains required reports from employee benefit plan administrators pursuant to ERISA.

Pension Benefit Guaranty Corp., 1200 K St. N.W. 20005-4026; 326-4010. Martin Slate, executive director. Information, 326-4000. Fax, 326-4016. TDD, 326-4179.

Self-financed U.S. government corporation. Insures private-sector, defined-benefit pension plans; guarantees payment of retirement benefits subject to certain limitations established in the Employee Retirement Income Security Act of 1974 (ERISA). Provides insolvent multiemployer pension plans with financial assistance to enable them to pay guaranteed retirement benefits.

See also Railroad Retirement Board (p. 731)

Congress:

General Accounting Office, Human Resources, 441 G St. N.W., NGB/ACG 20548; 512-6806. Janet L. Shikles, assistant comptroller general. Fax, 512-5806.

Independent, nonpartisan agency in the legislative branch. Audits, analyzes, and evaluates federal agency and private sector pension programs; makes reports available to the public.

House Education and Labor Committee, Subcommittee on Labor-Management Relations, 320 CHOB 20515; 225-5768. Pat Williams, D-Mont., chairman; Jon Weintraub, staff director.

Jurisdiction over pension plan, fringe benefit, and retirement income security legislation, including the Employee Retirement Income Security Act of 1974 (ERISA) and the Labor Management Reporting and Disclosure Act.

House Ways and Means Committee, 1102 LHOB 20515; 225-3625. Sam M. Gibbons, D-Fla., acting chairman; Janice A. Mays, chief counsel.

Jurisdiction over legislation related to taxation of pension contributions.

House Ways and Means Committee, Subcommittee on Oversight, 1135 LHOB 20515; 225-5522. J. J. Pickle, D-Texas, chairman; Beth K. Vance, staff director. Fax, 225-0787.

Oversees Pension Benefit Guaranty Corp.

Senate Finance Committee, SD-205 20510; 224-4515. Daniel Patrick Moynihan, D-N.Y., chairman; Lawrence O'Donnell Jr., staff director.

Jurisdiction over legislation related to taxation of pension contributions.

Senate Finance Committee, Subcommittee on Private Retirement Plans and Oversight of the Internal Revenue Service, SD-205 20510; 224-4515. David Pryor, D-Ark., chairman; Steve Glaze, staff contact.

Holds hearings on pension reform legislation; investigates private and self-employed pension plan problems. Oversees Pension Benefit Guaranty Corp.

Senate Governmental Affairs Committee, Permanent Subcommittee on Investigations, SR-100 20510; 224-3721. Sam Nunn, D-Ga., chairman; Eleanor J. Hill, staff director.

Investigates labor racketeering, including pension and health and welfare fund frauds.

Senate Labor and Human Resources Committee, Subcommittee on Labor, SH-608 20510; 224-5546. Howard M. Metzenbaum, D-Ohio, chairman; Michele L. Varnhagen, staff director.

Jurisdiction over pension plan and retirement income security legislation and over the Labor-Management Reporting and Disclosure Act.

Senate Special Committee on Aging, SD-G31 20510; 224-5364. David Pryor, D-Ark., chairman; Theresa M. Forster, staff director.

Studies and makes recommendations on private and self-employed pension plan legislation and mandatory retirement.

Nongovernmental:

American Academy of Actuaries, 1720 Eye St. N.W., 7th Floor 20006; 223-8196. James J. Murphy, executive vice president. Fax, 872-1948.

Membership: professional actuaries practicing in areas of life, health, liability, property, and casualty insurance; pensions; government insurance plans; and general consulting. Provides information on actuarial matters, including insurance and pensions; develops professional standards.

American Assn. of Retired Persons, 601 E St. N.W. 20049; 434-2300. Horace B. Deets, executive director. Fax, 434-2320.

Researches and testifies on private, federal, and other government employee pension legislation and regulations; conducts seminars; provides information on preretirement preparation. Library open to the public.

American Society of Pension Actuaries, 4350 N. Fairfax Dr., #820, Arlington, VA 22203-1621; (703) 516-9300. Chester J. Salkind, executive director. Fax, (703) 516-9308.

Membership: professional pension plan actuaries, administrators, consultants, and other benefits professionals. Sponsors educational programs to prepare actuaries and consultants for professional exams; monitors legislation.

Assn. of Private Pension and Welfare Plans, 1212 New York Ave. N.W. 20005; 289-6700.

James A. Klein, executive director. Fax, 289-4582.

Membership: employers, consultants, banks, and service organizations. Informs members of private pension benefits and compensation.

Center for Economic Organizing, 1522 K St. N.W. 20005; 775-9072. Randy Barber, director. Fax, 775-9074.

Research, consulting, and training organization. Interests include the investment and control of pension funds and the role of unions and the private sector in administering these funds.

Employee Benefit Research Institute, 2121 K St. N.W., #600 20037; 659-0670. Dallas L. Salisbury, president; William S. Custer, research director. Fax, 775-6312.

Researches proposed policy changes on employee benefits. Sponsors studies on retirement income and health, disability, and other benefits.

Employers Council on Flexible Compensation, 927 15th St. N.W., #1000 20005; 659-4300. Kenneth E. Feltman, executive director. Fax, 371-1467.

Represents employers who have or are considering flexible compensation plans. Supports the preservation and expansion of employee choice in savings and pension plans; monitors legislation and regulations.

National Assn. of Manufacturers, Employee Benefits and Compensation Committee, 1331 Pennsylvania Ave. N.W., #1500N 20004; 637-3137. Christopher Bowlin, senior associate director. Fax, 637-3182.

Advises members on development of and changes in the Employee Retirement Income Security Act of 1974 (ERISA), with emphasis on employee benefits, tax policy, and single- and multiemployer pension plans. Studies the Social Security system to ensure that its long-term status remains compatible with private sector retirement plans.

Pension Rights Center, 918 16th St. N.W., #704 20006; 296-3776. Karen W. Ferguson, director. Fax, 833-2472.

Works to preserve and expand pension rights; provides information and technical assistance on pensions.

Retirement Policy Institute, 2158 Florida Ave. N.W. 20008; 483-3140. A. Haeworth Robertson, president.

Researches and educates the public about retirement policy issues. Interests include trends, pension reform, Social Security, and policy alternatives. Monitors legislation and regulations.

Society of Professional Benefit Administrators, 2 Wisconsin Circle, #670, Chevy Chase, MD 20815-7003; (301) 718-7722. Frederick D. Hunt Jr., president. Fax, (301) 718-9440.

Membership: independent third-party administration firms that manage outside claims and benefit plans for client employers. Monitors government compliance requirements. Interests include pensions, health coverage, and the Employee Retirement Income Security Act of 1974 (ERISA).

See also National Council of Senior Citizens and National Council on the Aging (p. 426); United Mine Workers of America Health and Retirement Funds (p. 218)

Safety and Health

General

See also Resources: Coal, Mining Health and Safety (p. 217)

Agencies:

Bureau of Labor Statistics (Labor Dept.), Compensation and Working Conditions, 2 Massachusetts Ave. N.E. 20212; 606-6300. George L. Stelluto, associate commissioner. Fax, 606-6310.

Compiles data on occupational safety and health.

Mine Safety and Health Administration (Labor Dept.), 4015 Wilson Blvd., Arlington, VA 22203; (703) 235-1385. J. Davitt McAteer, assistant secretary. Information, (703) 235-1452.

Administers and enforces the health and safety provisions of the Federal Mine Safety and Health Act of 1977.

National Institute for Occupational Safety and Health (Health and Human Services Dept.), 200 Independence Ave. S.W. 20201; 690-7134. Bryan Hardin, director, Washington office. Toll-free, (800) 356-4674. Fax, 690-7519.

Entity within the Centers for Disease Control and Prevention in Atlanta, Ga. Supports and conducts research on occupational safety and health issues; provides technical assistance and training; develops recommendations for the Labor Dept. Operates an occupational safety and health bibliographic database (mailing address: National Institute for Occupational Safety and Health, Clearinghouse for Occupational Safety and Health Information, 4676 Columbia Parkway, Cincinnati, Ohio 45226).

Occupational Safety and Health Administration (Labor Dept.), 200 Constitution Ave. N.W. 20210; 219-7162. Joseph Dear, assistant secretary. Information, 219-8151. Fax, 219-6064.

Sets and enforces rules and regulations for workplace safety and health. Implements the Occupational Safety and Health Act of 1970. Provides federal agencies and private industries with compliance guidance and assistance.

Occupational Safety and Health Administration (Labor Dept.), Advisory Committee on Construction Safety and Health, 200 Constitution Ave. N.W. 20210; 219-8615. Naomi Mass, chair. Fax, 219-5986.

Advises OSHA on issues concerning workplace safety and health in the construction industry.

Occupational Safety and Health Administration (Labor Dept.), Compliance Programs, 200 Constitution Ave. N.W., #N3468 20210; 219-9308. Roger A. Clark, director. Fax, 219-9187.

Interprets compliance safety standards for agency field personnel and private employees and employers.

Occupational Safety and Health Administration (Labor Dept.), Construction and Engineering, 200 Constitution Ave. N.W., #N3306 20210; 219-8644. Charles Culver, director. Fax, 219-6599.

Provides technical expertise to OSHA's enforcement personnel; initiates studies to determine causes of construction accidents; works with private sector to promote construction safety.

Occupational Safety and Health Administration (Labor Dept.), Federal Advisory Council on Occupational Safety and Health, 200 Constitution Ave. N.W. 20210; 219-9329. Vacant, chairman; John E. Plummer, director, federal agency programs. Fax, 219-9187.

Advises the labor secretary on safety and health initiatives concerning federal employees.

Occupational Safety and Health Administration (Labor Dept.), Federal/State Operations, 200 Constitution Ave. N.W. 20210; 219-7251. Zoltan Bagdy, acting director. Fax, 219-8783.

Makes grants to nonprofit organizations under the New Directions Grant Program to assist in providing education, training, and technical assistance to meet the workplace safety and health needs of employers and employees; administers state enforcement and consultation programs; trains federal and private employees, OSHA and state inspectors, and state consultants.

Occupational Safety and Health Administration (Labor Dept.), Field Programs, 200 Constitution Ave. N.W. 20210; 219-7725. Leo Carey, director. Fax, 219-7986.

Coordinates regional programs, including the field occupational safety and health enforcement program, which provides for workplace inspections, citations of alleged violations of standards and rulemaking, and penalty assessments. Develops policies and procedures used by the field organizations. *(See Regional Federal Information Sources list, p. 831.)*

Occupational Safety and Health Administration (Labor Dept.), Health Standards Programs, 200 Constitution Ave. N.W. 20210; 219-7075. Charles E. Adkins, director. Information, 219-8151. Fax, 219-7125.

Develops new or revised occupational health standards for toxic, hazardous, and carcinogenic substances or other harmful physical agents, such as vibration, noise, and radiation.

Occupational Safety and Health Administration (Labor Dept.), Information and Consumer Affairs, 200 Constitution Ave. N.W. 20210; 219-8148. James F. Foster, director. Fax, 219-5986.

Conducts public hearings on proposed workplace safety and health standards; provides staff assistance and support for the National Advisory Committee for Occupational Safety and Health and the Construction Advisory Committee. Advises the assistant secretary of labor for occupational safety and health on consumer affairs matters.

Occupational Safety and Health Administration (Labor Dept.), National Advisory Committee on Occupational Safety and Health, 200

Constitution Ave. N.W. 20210; 219-8615. J. Thomas Hall, committee management officer. Fax, 219-5986.

Advisory committee of safety and health experts. Advises the secretaries of labor and health and human services on administration of the Occupational Safety and Health Act of 1970.

Occupational Safety and Health Administration (Labor Dept.), Safety Standards, 200 Constitution Ave. N.W. 20210; 219-8061. Thomas J. Shepich, director. Fax, 219-7477.

Develops new or revised occupational safety standards.

Occupational Safety and Health Review Commission, 1120 20th St. N.W., 9th Floor 20036-3419; 606-5370. Edwin G. Foulke Jr., chairman. Information, 606-5398. Fax, 606-5050.

Independent executive branch agency that adjudicates disputes between private employers and the Occupational Safety and Health Administration arising under the Occupational Safety and Health Act of 1970.

Congress:

House Appropriations Committee, Subcommittee on Labor, Health and Human Services, and Education, 2358 RHOB 20515; 225-3508. Neal Smith, D-Iowa, chairman; Mike Stephens, staff assistant.

Jurisdiction over legislation to appropriate funds for the Federal Mine Safety and Health Review Commission and the Occupational Safety and Health Review Commission.

House Education and Labor Committee, Subcommittee on Labor Standards, Occupational Health and Safety, B345A RHOB 20515; 225-1927. Austin J. Murphy, D-Pa., chairman; James Riley, staff director.

Jurisdiction over legislation on workers' compensation and related wage loss; occupational safety and health; mine safety and health; youth camp safety; and migrant and agricultural labor health and safety.

House Small Business Committee, Subcommittee on Rural Enterprises, Exports, and the Environment, 1F CHOB 20515; 225-8944. Bill Sarpalius, D-Texas, chairman; Christopher Mattson, staff director.

Oversees the Occupational Safety and Health Administration as it affects small business.

Senate Appropriations Committee, Subcommittee on Labor, Health and Human Services, and Education, SD-186 20510; 224-7283. Tom Harkin, D-Iowa, chairman; Ed Long, clerk.

Jurisdiction over legislation to appropriate funds for the Federal Mine Safety and Health Review Commission and the Occupational Safety and Health Review Commission.

Senate Labor and Human Resources Committee, Subcommittee on Labor, SH-608 20510; 224-5546. Howard M. Metzenbaum, D-Ohio, chairman; Michele L. Varnhagen, staff director.

Jurisdiction over legislation on occupational safety and health, including workers' compensation and related wage loss, and on migrant and agricultural labor safety and health.

Senate Small Business Committee, SR-428A 20510; 224-5175. Dale Bumpers, D-Ark., chairman; John W. Ball III, staff director.

Jurisdiction over the Occupational Safety and Health Administration as it affects small business.

Nongovernmental:

American Industrial Health Council, 1330 Connecticut Ave. N.W., #300 20036; 659-0060. Ronald A. Lang, president. Fax, 659-1699.

Membership: chemical companies and manufacturers of pharmaceutical, petroleum, aerospace, consumer, and metal products. Monitors regulations affecting methods for assessing health risks in these industries.

American Industrial Hygiene Assn., 2700 Prosperity Ave., #250, Fairfax, VA 22031; (703) 849-8888. O. Gordon Banks, executive director. Fax, (703) 207-3561.

Membership: scientists and engineers who practice industrial hygiene in government, labor, academic institutions, and independent organizations. Promotes the establishment and enforcement of health and safety standards in the workplace and the community; conducts research to identify potential dangers; educates workers about job-related risks; participates in the development of safety regulations.

Industrial Safety Equipment Assn., 1901 N. Moore St., #808, Arlington, VA 22209; (703) 525-1695. Daniel K. Shipp, president. Fax, (703) 528-2148.

Trade organization that drafts industry standards for employee personal safety and protective equipment; encourages development and use of proper equipment to deal with industrial hazards; monitors legislation and regulations.

National Assn. of Manufacturers, Risk Management, 1331 Pennsylvania Ave. N.W., #1500N 20004; 637-3135. Phyllis Eisen, director. Fax, 637-3182.

Conducts research, develops policy, and informs members of product liability reform, toxic injury compensation systems, and occupational safety and health legislation, regulations, and standards.

National Safety Council, 1019 19th St. N.W. 20036; 293-2270. Jane S. Roemer, executive director, public policy. Fax, 293-0032.

Chartered by Congress. Conducts research and provides educational and informational services on occupational safety; encourages the adoption of policies that will reduce accidental deaths and injuries and preventable illnesses; monitors legislation and regulations affecting safety. (Headquarters in Itasca, Ill.)

Public Citizen, Health Research Group, 2000 P St. N.W., #700 20036; 833-3000. Dr. Sidney M. Wolfe, director. Fax, 452-8658.

Citizens' interest group that studies and reports on occupational diseases; monitors the Occupational Safety and Health Administration and participates in OSHA enforcement proceedings.

The Workplace Health and Safety Council, 2300 N St. N.W. 20037; 663-9128. Susan Spangler Nussbaum, executive director. Fax, 663-8007.

Membership: businesses, health and safety managers, general counsels, and academic institutions. Monitors legislation and regulations affecting federal workplace health and safety policies.

See also National Leadership Coalition on AIDS (p. 366)

Workers' Compensation

Agencies:

Bureau of Labor Statistics (Labor Dept.), Safety, Health, and Working Conditions, 2 Massachusetts Ave. N.E. 20212; 606-6304. William M. Eisenberg, assistant commissioner. Fax, 606-6196.

Compiles and publishes statistics on occupational injuries and illnesses.

Employment Standards Administration (Labor Dept.), Workers' Compensation Programs, 200 Constitution Ave. N.W. 20210; 219-7503. Lawrence W. Rogers, director. Fax, 219-4321.

Administers three federal workers' compensation laws: the Federal Employees' Compensation Act; the Longshore and Harbor Workers' Compensation Act and extensions; and Title IV (Black Lung Benefits Act) of the Federal Coal Mine Health and Safety Act.

Labor Dept., Benefits Review Board, 800 K St. N.W. 20001; 633-7501. Nancy S. Dolder, acting chair and chief administrative appeals judge. Fax, 633-0136.

Reviews appeals of workers seeking benefits under the Longshore and Harbor Workers' Compensation·Act and its extensions, including the District of Columbia Workers' Compensation Act, and Title IV (Black Lung Benefits Act) of the Federal Coal Mine Health and Safety Act.

Labor Dept., Employees' Compensation Appeals Board, 300 7th St. S.W. 20210; 401-8600. Michael J. Walsh, chairman. Fax, 401-1821.

Reviews and determines appeals of final determinations of benefits claims made by the Office of Workers' Compensation Programs under the Federal Employees' Compensation Act.

Congress:

See Safety and Health, General, Congress (p. 194)

Nongovernmental:

American Insurance Assn., 1130 Connecticut Ave. N.W., #1000 20036; 828-7100. David J. Pratt, senior vice president, federal affairs. Press, 828-7141. Library, 828-7183. Fax, 293-1219.

Membership: companies providing property and casualty insurance. Offers information on workers' compensation legislation and regulations; conducts educational activities. Library open to the public by appointment.

National Assn. of Manufacturers, Risk Management, 1331 Pennsylvania Ave. N.W., #1500N 20004; 637-3135. Phyllis Eisen, director. Fax, 637-3182.

Conducts research, develops policy, and informs members of workers' compensation law; provides feedback to government agencies.

Statistics and Information

Agencies:

Bureau of Labor Statistics (Labor Dept.), 2 Massachusetts Ave. N.E. 20212; 606-7800. Katharine G. Abraham, commissioner. Information, 606-5888. Press, 606-5902. Fax, 606-7797.

Collects, analyzes, and publishes data and statistics on labor economics, including employment, unemployment, hours of work, wages, employee compensation, prices, consumer expenditures, labor-management relations, productivity, technological developments, occupational safety and health, and structure and growth of the economy. Publishes reports on these statistical trends, including the Consumer Price Index, the Producer Price Index, and Employment and Earnings.

Bureau of Labor Statistics (Labor Dept.), Employment and Unemployment Statistics, 2 Massachusetts Ave. N.E., #4945 20212; 606-6400. Thomas J. Plewes, associate commissioner. Fax, 606-6425.

Monitors employment and unemployment trends on national and local levels; compiles data on worker and industry employment and earnings.

Bureau of Labor Statistics (Labor Dept.), Employment Projections, 2 Massachusetts Ave. N.E. 20212; 606-5700. Ronald E. Kutscher, associate commissioner. Fax, 606-5745.

Develops economic, industrial, and demographic employment projections according to industry and occupation. Provides career guidance material.

Bureau of Labor Statistics (Labor Dept.), Foreign Labor Statistics, 2 Massachusetts Ave. N.E., #2150 20212; 606-5654. Arthur Neef, chief. Fax, 606-5664.

Issues statistical reports on labor force, productivity, employment, prices, and labor costs in foreign countries adjusted to U.S. concepts.

Bureau of Labor Statistics (Labor Dept.), Local Area Unemployment Statistics, 2 Massachusetts Ave. N.E., #4675 20212; 606-6390. Sharon P.

Brown, chief. Information, 606-6392. Fax, 606-6459.

Issues labor force and unemployment statistics for states, metropolitan statistical areas, cities with populations of 25,000 or more, counties, and other areas covered under federal assistance programs.

Bureau of Labor Statistics (Labor Dept.), Monthly Industry Employment Statistics, 2 Massachusetts Ave. N.E., #4860 20212; 606-6528. George Werking, chief. Information, 606-6555. Fax, 606-6644.

Analyzes and publishes national-level employment, hour, and wage statistics based on data submitted by the states; develops statistical information on employment, hours, and wages by industry for the nation, states, and statistical metropolitan areas.

Bureau of Labor Statistics (Labor Dept.), Productivity and Technology, 2 Massachusetts Ave. N.E., #2150 20212; 606-5600. Edwin R. Dean, associate commissioner. Fax, 606-5664.

Develops and analyzes productivity measures for U.S. industries and economy; adjusts productivity measures of foreign countries for comparison with U.S. standards; studies implications of technological changes on employment and occupational distribution.

Census Bureau (Commerce Dept.), Demographic Surveys, Suitland and Silver Hill Rds., Suitland, MD (mailing address: Washington, DC 20233); (301) 763-2776. Sherry L. Courtland, chief. Fax, (301) 763-2703.

Conducts surveys and compiles official monthly employment and unemployment statistics for the Labor Dept.'s Bureau of Labor Statistics.

Employment and Training Administration, Unemployment Insurance Service, 200 Constitution Ave. N.W. 20210; 219-5922. Cynthia L. Ambler, statistician, actuarial services. Fax, 219-8506.

Compiles statistics on state unemployment insurance programs. Studies unemployment issues related to unemployment benefits.

Occupational Safety and Health Administration (Labor Dept.), Statistics, 200 Constitution Ave. N.W., #N3507 20210; 219-6463. Stephen Newell, director. Fax, 219-5161.

Compiles and provides all statistical data for OSHA, such as workplace deaths and company safety records, which are used in setting standards and making policy.

Congress:

House Education and Labor Committee, Subcommittee on Labor-Management Relations, 320 CHOB 20515; 225-5768. Pat Williams, D-Mont., chairman; Jon Weintraub, staff director.

Jurisdiction over legislation on the Bureau of Labor Statistics.

Senate Labor and Human Resources Committee, Subcommittee on Labor, SH-608 20510; 224-5546. Howard M. Metzenbaum, D-Ohio, chairman; Michele L. Varnhagen, staff director.

Jurisdiction over legislation on the Bureau of Labor Statistics.

Unemployment Benefits

Agencies:

Employment and Training Administration (Labor Dept.), Advisory Council on Unemployment Compensation, 200 Constitution Ave. N.W. 20210; 219-4985. Leurie J. Bassi, executive director. Fax, 219-4467.

Membership: employers and employees. Reviews federal/state unemployment compensation programs; advises Congress on the unemployment insurance program.

Employment and Training Administration (Labor Dept.), Trade Adjustment Assistance, 200 Constitution Ave. N.W., #C4318 20210; 219-5555. Marvin M. Fooks, director. Fax, 219-5753.

Assists American workers who are totally or partially unemployed because of increased imports; offers training, job search and relocation assistance, weekly benefits at state unemployment insurance levels, and other reemployment services.

Employment and Training Administration (Labor Dept.), Unemployment Insurance Service, 200 Constitution Ave. N.W. 20210; 219-7831. Mary Ann Wyrsch, director. Fax, 219-8506.

Directs and reviews the state-administered system that provides income support for unemployed workers nationwide; advises state employment security agencies on wage-loss, worker dislocation, and adjustment assistance compensation programs.

Congress:

House Ways and Means Committee, Subcommittee on Human Resources, B317 RHOB 20515; 225-1025. Harold E. Ford, D-Tenn., chairman; Richard Hobbie, staff director. Fax, 225-9480.

Jurisdiction over unemployment benefits legislation.

Senate Finance Committee, Subcommittee on Social Security and Family Policy, SD-205 20510; 224-4515. John B. Breaux, D-La., chairman; Laird D. Burnett, staff contact.

Holds hearings on unemployment benefits legislation.

Nongovernmental:

Interstate Conference of Employment Security Agencies, 444 N. Capitol St. N.W., #142 20001; 628-5588. Emily DeRocco, executive director. Fax, 783-5023.

Membership: state employment security administrators. Informs members of unemployment insurance programs and legislation.

Unions

See also Labor-Management Relations (p. 186); Labor Unions list (p. 801)

Agencies:

Bureau of Labor Statistics (Labor Dept.), Developments in Labor-Management Relations, 2 Massachusetts Ave. N.E., #4175 20212; 606-6274. Alvin Bauman, chief. Fax, 606-6647. Settlements in private sector, 606-6276; work stoppages and union membership, 606-6275.

Compiles data on work stoppages, collective bargaining, settlements, and labor organization membership; maintains public file of major collective bargaining agreements.

Office of the American Workplace (Labor Dept.), Labor-Management Standards, 200 Constitution Ave. N.W., #S2203 20210; 219-6065. Edmundo Gonzalez, deputy assistant secretary. Fax, 219-4315.

Administers and enforces the Labor-Management Reporting and Disclosure Act of 1959 (Landrum-Griffin Act), which guarantees union members certain rights; sets rules for electing union officers, handling union funds, and using trusteeships; requires unions to file annual financial reports with the Labor Dept.

Nongovernmental:

George Meany Center for Labor Studies and the George Meany Memorial Archives, 10000 New Hampshire Ave., Silver Spring, MD 20903; (301) 431-6400. Robert J. Pleasure, executive director. Fax, (301) 434-0371.

Educational institute that offers classes, workshops, and an undergraduate degree program to AFL-CIO-affiliated officers, representatives, and staff. Maintains the AFL-CIO archives and the Institute for the Study of Labor Organizations.

See also Academic Collective Bargaining Information Service (p. 128); American Foreign Service Assn. (p. 468); American Institute for Free Labor Development (p. 185); Coalition of Black Trade Unionists (p. 182).

Key Agencies:

Energy Dept.
1000 Independence Ave. S.W. 20585
Information: 586-5575

Interior Dept.
Main Interior Bldg.
1849 C St. N.W. 20240
Information: 208-3171

Nuclear Regulatory Commission
11555 Rockville Pike
Rockville, MD
(Mailing address: Washington, DC 20555)
Information: (301) 504-2240

Key Committees:

House Energy and Commerce Committee
2125 RHOB 20515
Phone: 225-2927

House Natural Resources Committee
1324 LHOB 20515
Phone: 225-2761

House Science, Space, and Technology Committee
2320 RHOB 20515
Phone: 225-6371

Senate Energy and Natural Resources Committee
SD-304 20510
Phone: 224-4971

Senate Environment and Public Works Committee
SD-456 20510
Phone: 224-6176

Key Personnel:

Energy Dept.

Hazel R. O'Leary, secretary

William H. White, deputy secretary

Charles B. Curtis, under secretary

William J. Taylor III, assistant secretary for congressional and intergovernmental affairs

Christine Ervin, assistant secretary for energy efficiency and renewable energy

Susan Fallows Tierney, assistant secretary for policy, planning, and program evaluation

Tara O'Toole, assistant secretary for environment, safety, and health

Patricia Fry Godley, assistant secretary designate for fossil energy

Jay F. Thompson, acting administrator, Economic Regulatory Administration

Jay Hakes, administrator, Energy Information Administration

Elizabeth Moler, chair, Federal Energy Regulatory Commission

Daniel Dreyfus, director, Civilian Radioactive Waste Management

Martha A. Krebs, director, Office of Energy Research

Interior Dept.

Robert Armstrong, assistant secretary for land and minerals management

Nuclear Regulatory Commission

Ivan Selin, chairman

5

Energy

Contents:

Energy Policy

Agencies:

Agriculture Dept., Energy, 14th St. and Independence Ave. S.W., #438-A 20250-2610; 720-2634. Roger K. Conway, director. Fax, 690-0884.

Advises the secretary on the department's energy-related policies and programs; coordinates energy programs and strategies for the emergency allocation of scarce fuel resources; provides the department with leadership in developing agricultural and rural components of national energy policies.

Bureau of Land Management (Interior Dept.), Energy and Mineral Resources, Main Interior Bldg. 20240; 208-4201. Hillary A. Oden, assistant director. Fax, 208-4800.

Evaluates and classifies onshore oil, natural gas, geothermal resources, and all solid energy and mineral resources, including coal and uranium, on federal lands. Develops and administers regulations for fluid and solid mineral leasing on national lands and on the subsurface of land where fluid and solid mineral rights have been reserved for the federal government.

Bureau of Land Management (Interior Dept.), Minerals Policy Analysis and Economic Evaluation, 1620 L St. N.W., #501 LS (mailing address: Main Interior Bldg., #501 LS, Washington, DC 20240); 452-0380. Sie Ling Chiang, chief. Fax, 452-0399.

Monitors industry trends and developments that affect the bureau's energy and mineral programs. Develops policy and establishes technical standards for mineral economic evaluation and appraisal, including fair-market value determinations.

Energy Dept., 1000 Independence Ave. S.W. 20585; 586-6210. Hazel R. O'Leary, secretary. Information, 586-5575. Press, 586-5806. Fax, 586-4403.

Decides major energy policy issues and acts as principal adviser to the president on energy matters; acts as principal spokesperson for the department.

Energy Dept., 1000 Independence Ave. S.W. 20585; 586-5500. William H. White, deputy secretary. Press, 586-0554. Fax, 586-0148.

Manages departmental programs in energy efficiency and renewable energy, fossil energy, the Energy Information Administration, nuclear energy, civilian radioactive waste management, the power marketing administrations, and the office of the general counsel.

Energy Dept., 1000 Independence Ave. S.W. 20585; 586-6479. Charles B. Curtis, under secretary. Information, 586-4940. Fax, 586-7573.

Manages departmental programs in the areas of national security and defense, environmental safety and health, and waste management (including radioactive and nuclear waste); responsible for all administration and management matters and for regulatory and information programs.

Energy Dept., Economic Impact and Diversity, 1000 Independence Ave. S.W. 20585; 586-8383. Corlis S. Moody, director. Fax, 586-3075.

Researches the effects of federal government energy policies on minority businesses; offers technical and financial assistance to minority businesses, educational institutions, and developmental organizations to encourage their participation in energy research, development, and conservation activities; acts as an information clearinghouse.

Energy Dept., Emergency Management, 1000 Independence Ave. S.W., #GE262 20585; 586-

9892. John J. Nettles Jr., acting director. Fax, 586-3859.

Works to ensure coordinated Energy Dept. responses to energy-related emergencies. Recommends policies to mitigate the effects of energy supply crises on the United States; recommends government responses to energy emergencies.

Energy Dept., Energy Advisory Board, 1000 Independence Ave. S.W., #7B198 20585; 586-7092. Jake W. Stewart, executive director. Fax, 586-3497.

Provides the energy secretary with advice and long-range guidance on the department's research and development, energy, and national defense-related activities.

Energy Dept., Energy Efficiency and Renewable Energy, 1000 Independence Ave. S.W. 20585; 586-9220. Christine Ervin, assistant secretary. Fax, 586-9260.

Develops and manages programs to improve foreign and domestic markets for renewable energy sources including solar, biomass, wind, geothermal, and hydropower and to increase efficiency of energy use among residential, commercial, transportation, utility, and industrial users. Administers financial and technical assistance for state energy programs, weatherization for low-income households, and implementation of energy conservation measures by schools, hospitals, local governments, and public care institutions.

Energy Dept., Energy Research, 1000 Independence Ave. S.W. 20585; 586-5430. Martha A. Krebs, director. Fax, 586-4120.

Advises the secretary on the department's physical science research and energy research and development programs; the use of multipurpose laboratories (except weapons laboratories); and education and training for basic and applied research activities, including fellowships for university researchers. Manages the department's high energy and nuclear physics programs and the fusion energy program. Conducts environmental and health-related research and development programs, including studies of energy-related pollutants and hazardous materials.

Energy Dept., Environment, Safety, and Health, 1000 Independence Ave. S.W. 20585; 586-6151. Tara O'Toole, assistant secretary. Fax, 586-0956.

Ensures that Energy Dept. programs comply with federal policies and standards designed to protect the environment and government property. Oversees health and nonnuclear safety conditions at Energy Dept. facilities.

Energy Dept., Intelligence and National Security, 1000 Independence Ave. S.W. 20585; 586-0645. John G. Keliher, director. Fax, 586-0862.

Provides intelligence community with technical and analytical expertise on foreign nuclear and energy issues. Oversees programs to prevent the spread of weapons of mass destruction, to protect the U.S. nuclear deterrent, and to respond to nuclear and energy emergencies.

Energy Dept., Policy, Planning, and Program Evaluation, 1000 Independence Ave. S.W. 20585; 586-5800. Susan Fallows Tierney, assistant secretary. Fax, 586-0861.

Serves as principal adviser to the secretary, deputy secretary, and under secretary in formulating and evaluating departmental policy. Reviews programs, budgets, regulations, and legislative proposals to ensure consistency with departmental policy.

Energy Information Administration (Energy Dept.), Energy Markets and End Use, 1000 Independence Ave. S.W., #2G-090 20585; 586-1617. W. Calvin Kilgore, director. Fax, 586-9753.

Designs, develops, and maintains statistical and short-term forecasting information systems concerning consumption and other subjects that cut across energy sources. Formulates and administers financial data reporting requirements for major energy companies. Maintains survey on energy supply and use.

Energy Information Administration (Energy Dept.), Integrated Analysis and Forecasting, 1000 Independence Ave. S.W., EI-80, #2F081 20585; 586-2222. Mary J. Hutzler, director. Information, 586-5000. Library, 586-9534. Fax, 586-3045.

Analyzes and forecasts alternative energy futures. Develops, applies, and maintains modeling systems for analyzing the interactions of demand, conversion, and supply for all energy sources and their economic and environmental impacts.

Federal Energy Regulatory Commission (Energy Dept.), 825 N. Capitol St. N.E. 20426; 208-0000. Elizabeth Moler, chair. Information, 208-0200. Press, 208-1088. Fax, 208-0671. Dockets, 208-2020.

Energy Dept.

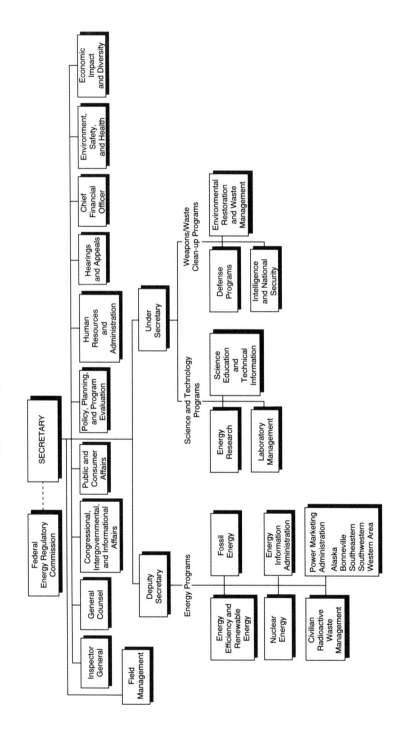

Establishes and enforces: interstate oil pipeline rates, charges, and valuations; and rates and charges for wholesale electric power transmission, sale, and interconnection. Regulates the construction and operation of interstate natural gas facilities and the interstate rates for resale and transportation of natural gas. Under the Natural Gas Wellhead Decontrol Act of 1989, all remaining commission regulation of producer sales prices for natural gas terminated on January 1, 1993. Issues licenses for nonfederal hydroelectric projects and establishes accounting rules and procedures for utilities.

Interior Dept., Land and Minerals Management, Main Interior Bldg. 20240; 208-5676. Robert Armstrong, assistant secretary. Fax, 208-3144.

Directs and supervises the Bureau of Land Management, the Minerals Management Service, and the Office of Surface Mining. Supervises programs associated with land use planning, onshore and offshore minerals, surface mining reclamation and enforcement, and outer continental shelf minerals management.

International Trade Administration (Commerce Dept.), Energy, Environment, and Infrastructure, Main Commerce Bldg. 20230; 482-1466. Joseph J. Yancik, director, energy. Fax, 482-0170.

Conducts research on the effect of federal energy policy on the business community; promotes improved market competitiveness and participation in international trade by the basic energy fuels industries.

National Institute of Standards and Technology (Commerce Dept.), Technology Evaluation and Assessment, Route I-270 and Quince Orchard Rd., Bldg. 411, #A115, Gaithersburg, MD 20899-0001; (301) 975-5500. George Lewett, director. Fax, (301) 975-3839.

Evaluates nonnuclear, energy-related inventions submitted by individuals and small companies and makes recommendations on their development to the Energy Dept.

Office of Management and Budget (Executive Office of the President), Energy and Science, New Executive Office Bldg. 20503; 395-3404. Kathleen Peroff, deputy associate director. Fax, 395-4817.

Advises and assists the president in preparing the budget for energy programs; coordinates OMB energy policy and programs.

Office of Science and Technology Policy (Executive Office of the President), Old Executive Office Bldg., #424 20500; 456-7116. John H. Gibbons, director. Information, 395-7347. Press, 395-6142. Fax, 395-3261.

Provides the president with policy analysis on scientific and technological matters, including energy policy and technology issues; coordinates executive office and federal agency responses to these issues; evaluates the effectiveness of scientific and technological programs.

See also Domestic Policy Council (p. 300)

Congress:

General Accounting Office, Energy and Science Issues, 111 Massachusetts Ave. N.W., #210 20001; 512-6864. Victor S. Rezendes, director. Fax, 512-6880.

Independent, nonpartisan agency in the legislative branch that audits, analyzes, and reports on efficiency and effectiveness of federal energy programs. Addresses governmentwide science issues and the production, regulation, and consumption of all forms of energy.

House Appropriations Committee, Subcommittee on Energy and Water Development, 2362 RHOB 20515; 225-3421. Tom Bevill, D-Ala., chairman; Hunter Spillan, staff assistant.

Jurisdiction over legislation to appropriate funds for the Energy Dept. (except for the Economic Regulatory Administration; Energy Information Administration; strategic petroleum reserve; naval petroleum and oil shale reserves; fossil energy research and development; energy conservation; alternative fuels production; and related matters); the Nuclear Regulatory Commission, the Tennessee Valley Authority, the Federal Energy Regulatory Commission, and the federal power marketing administrations.

House Appropriations Committee, Subcommittee on Interior, 3481 RHOB 20515; 225-3481. Sidney R. Yates, D-Ill., chairman; D. Neal Sigmon, staff assistant.

Jurisdiction over legislation to appropriate funds for the Economic Regulatory Administration; Energy Information Administration; strategic petroleum reserve and naval petroleum and oil shale reserves; clean coal technology; fossil energy research and development; energy conservation; alternate fuels production; and related matters.

House Energy and Commerce Committee, Subcommittee on Energy and Power, 331 Ford Bldg. (2nd and D Sts. S.W.) 20515; 226-2500. Philip R. Sharp, D-Ind., chairman; Shelley N. Fidler, acting staff director.

Jurisdiction over legislation on energy policy, regulation, conservation, exploration, production, distribution, storage, and pricing; commercialization and utilization of new technologies, including liquefied natural gas projects; and measures relating to the Energy Dept., the Federal Energy Regulatory Commission, and the regulatory function of the Economic Regulatory Administration.

House Government Operations Committee, Subcommittee on Environment, Energy, and Natural Resources, B371C RHOB 20515; 225-6427. Mike Synar, D-Okla., chairman; Sandy Harris, staff director. Fax, 225-2392.

Oversight of Energy Dept., Nuclear Regulatory Commission, and Tennessee Valley Authority.

House Natural Resources Committee, Subcommittee on Energy and Mineral Resources, 818 O'Neill Bldg. (300 New Jersey Ave. S.E.) 20515; 225-8331. Richard H. Lehman, D-Calif., chairman; Deborah Lanzone, staff director. Fax, 225-4273.

Jurisdiction over conservation of the U.S. uranium supply, regulation of the nuclear energy industry, disposal of nuclear waste, the U.S. Geological Survey (except water-related programs), mineral land laws, mining, and mineral resources on public lands (jurisdiction over matters involving the Outer Continental Shelf shared with the House Merchant Marine and Fisheries Committee).

House Natural Resources Committee, Subcommittee on Oversight and Investigations, 1328 LHOB 20515; 225-2761. George Miller, D-Calif., chairman; John Lawrence, staff director. Fax, 225-3554.

Jurisdiction over water-related programs of the U.S. Geological Survey, saline water research and development, water resources research programs, and matters related to the Water Resources Planning Act.

House Science, Space, and Technology Committee, 2320 RHOB 20515; 225-6371. George E. Brown Jr., D-Calif., chairman; Robert E. Palmer, chief of staff. Fax, 226-0113.

Jurisdiction over legislation on all nonmilitary energy research and development.

House Small Business Committee, Subcommittee on Regulation, Business Opportunities, and Technology, B363 RHOB 20515; 225-7797. Ron Wyden, D-Ore., chairman; Steve Jenning, staff director.

Studies and makes recommendations on energy allocation and marketing, and energy research and development contracts as they relate to small business.

House Ways and Means Committee, 1102 LHOB 20515; 225-3625. Sam M. Gibbons, D-Fla., acting chairman; Janice A. Mays, chief counsel.

Jurisdiction over legislation on taxes, tariffs, and trade measures relating to energy.

Joint Committee on Taxation, 1015 LHOB 20515; 225-3621. Sen. Daniel Patrick Moynihan, D-N.Y., chairman; John Buckley, chief of staff.

Performs staff work for House Ways and Means and Senate Finance committees on legislation involving internal revenue, including taxation of energy producers, transporters, and consumers. Provides revenue estimates for all tax legislation.

Office of Technology Assessment, Energy and Materials Program, 600 Pennsylvania Ave. S.E. 20003; 228-6260. Emilia Govan, manager. Fax, 228-6336.

Assesses engineering materials, mineral resources, and other energy-related technologies and their consequences.

Senate Appropriations Committee, Subcommittee on Energy and Water Development, SD-132 20510; 224-7260. J. Bennett Johnston, D-La., chairman; W. Proctor Jones, clerk.

Jurisdiction over legislation to appropriate funds for the Energy Dept. (except for the Energy Regulatory Administration; Energy Information Administration; strategic petroleum reserve; fossil energy research, development, and construction; and energy conservation); the Federal Energy Regulatory Commission; the federal power marketing administrations; the Nuclear Regulatory Commission; and the Tennessee Valley Authority.

Senate Appropriations Committee, Subcommittee on Interior, SD-127 20510; 224-7233. Robert C. Byrd, D-W.Va., chairman; Sue E. Masica, clerk.

Jurisdiction over legislation to appropriate funds for the Energy Information Administration; economic regulation; strategic petroleum reserve; energy production, demonstration, and distribution; fossil energy research, development, and construction; energy conservation; civilian (nonnuclear) programs in the Energy Dept.; and related matters.

Senate Energy and Natural Resources Committee, SD-304 20510; 224-4971. J. Bennett Johnston, D-La., chairman; Benjamin Cooper, staff director. Fax, 224-6163.

Jurisdiction over legislation on energy policy, regulation, and conservation; research and development; nonmilitary development of nuclear energy; oil and gas production and distribution (including price); energy-related aspects of deepwater ports; hydroelectric power; coal production and distribution; mining, mineral land laws, and mineral conservation; leasing and the extraction of minerals from the ocean and outer continental shelf lands; and naval petroleum reserves in Alaska. Jurisdiction over legislation on the Federal Energy Regulatory Commission. Oversees the Energy Dept., Tennessee Valley Authority, and the U.S. Geological Survey.

Senate Energy and Natural Resources Committee, Subcommittee on Energy Research and Development, SH-312 20510; 224-7569. Wendell H. Ford, D-Ky., chairman; Vacant, senior professional staff member.

Jurisdiction over legislation on nonmilitary energy research and development, including energy conservation, conservation of U.S. uranium supply, and nuclear fuel cycle policy.

Senate Energy and Natural Resources Committee, Subcommittee on Renewable Energy, Energy Efficiency, and Competitiveness, SH-212 20510; 224-4756. Jeff Bingaman, D-N.M., chairman; Leslie Black Cordess, professional staff member.

Jurisdiction over legislation on regulatory functions of the Economic Regulatory Administration; commercialization and utilization of ̀new technologies; and liquefied natural gas projects.

Senate Finance Committee, Subcommittee on Energy and Agricultural Taxation, SD-205 20510; 224-4515. Tom Daschle, D-S.D., chairman; Ted Sullivan, staff contact.

Holds hearings on legislation concerning taxes, tariffs, and trade measures relating to energy.

Senate Special Committee on Aging, SD-G31 20510; 224-5364. David Pryor, D-Ark., chairman; Theresa M. Forster, staff director.

Studies and makes recommendations on the availability of energy to older people and on the adequacy of federal energy programs for the elderly.

See also Environmental and Energy Study Conference (p. 756); New England Congressional Energy Caucus (p. 760)

Nongovernmental:

Alliance for Acid Rain Control and Energy Policy, 444 N. Capitol St. N.W., #602 20001; 624-5475. Ned Helme, executive director. Fax, 508-3829.

Alliance of governors, corporations, environmentalists, and academicians interested in energy and environmental policy. Advocates creation of a national energy strategy. Monitors legislation and regulations.

American Assn. of Blacks in Energy, 927 15th St. N.W., #200 20005; 371-9530. Kim Hall, general manager.

Encourages participation of African Americans and other minorities in formulating energy policy.

American Bar Assn., Coordinating Group on Energy Law, 1800 M St. N.W. 20036; 331-2651. Penelope S. Ferreira, staff director. Fax, 331-2220.

Evaluates energy developments and their impact on society and the law. Coordinates and assists in energy-related activities and conferences of other American Bar Assn. sections and committees. Conducts continuing education programs on energy law and policy. (Headquarters in Chicago.)

American Boiler Manufacturers Assn., 950 N. Glebe Rd., Arlington, VA 22203; (703) 522-7350. Russell N. Mosher, president. Fax, (703) 522-2665.

Membership: manufacturers of boiler systems and boiler-related products, including fuel-burning systems. Interests include energy and environmental issues.

American Council for an Energy-Efficient Economy, 1001 Connecticut Ave. N.W., #801 20036; 429-8873. Howard Geller, executive director. Fax, 429-2248.

Independent research organization concerned with energy policy, technologies, and conservation. Interests include energy efficiency in buildings and appliances, improved transportation efficiency, industrial efficiency, utility issues, and conservation in developing countries.

Citizen/Labor Energy Coalition, 1120 19th St. N.W., #630 20036; 775-1580. Ira Arlook, president. Fax, 296-4054.

Membership: union, environmental, religious, public interest, senior citizen, and community organizations. Conducts research on energy issues, including energy prices and supply, conservation, alternative energy sources, industry competition, and natural gas. (Headquarters in Chicago.)

Consumer Energy Council of America Research Foundation, 2000 L St. N.W., #802 20036; 659-0404. Ellen Berman, executive director. Fax, 659-0407.

Analyzes economic and social effects of energy policies; develops long-range conservation and load-management strategies for utilities; designs pilot programs for and conducts research on conservation initiatives. Builds consensus among public- and private-sector organizations, state and local groups, businesses, utilities, consumers, environmentalists, government agencies, and others on energy policy issues. Interests include transportation policies, transmission siting and certification, air pollution emissions trading, oil overcharge funds, and appliance rebate programs.

Federal Energy Bar Assn., 1350 Connecticut Ave. N.W. 20036; 223-5625. Lorna Wilson, administrator. Fax, 833-5596.

Friends of the Earth, 218 D St. S.E., 2nd Floor 20003; 544-2600. Jane Perkins, president. Fax, 543-4710.

Citizens' interest group. Interests include nuclear energy and nuclear waste storage and cleanup; synthetic fuels; conservation and renewable energy resources; air and water pollution, including international water projects; and rural energy and agricultural resources. Library open to the public by appointment.

National Assn. of Energy Service Companies, 1440 New York Ave. N.W. 20005; 371-7980. Terry E. Singer, executive director. Fax, 393-5760.

Membership: energy service companies, equipment manufacturers, affiliates of utilities, financial institutions, and governmental and other organizations involved in energy conservation and alternative energy projects. Acts as an energy information clearinghouse; sponsors conferences and seminars; monitors legislation and regulations affecting the industry.

National Constructors Assn., 1730 M St. N.W. 20036; 466-8880. Robert P. McCormick, president.

Membership: designers and builders of oil refineries, chemical plants, steel mills, power plants, and other industrial facilities. Interests include governmental energy policies, regulations, worker safety and health, and labor relations.

National Governors' Assn., Natural Resources Committee, 444 N. Capitol St. N.W., #267 20001; 624-5339. Tom Curtis, staff director. Fax, 624-5313.

Develops governors' recommendations on energy and environmental issues and presents these policies to Congress and federal agencies.

Resources for the Future, 1616 P St. N.W. 20036; 328-5000. Robert Fri, president. Library, 328-5089. Fax, 939-3460.

Research organization that conducts studies on economic and policy aspects of energy, conservation, and development of natural resources, including effects on the environment.

Sierra Club, 408 C St. N.E. 20002; 547-1141. Debbie Sease, legislative director. Fax, 547-6009. Legislative hotline, 675-2394.

Citizens' interest group that promotes protection and responsible use of the Earth's ecosystems and natural resources. Focuses on combating global warming/greenhouse effect through energy conservation, efficient use of renewable energy resources, rapid phase-out of chlorofluorocarbons, and constraints on deforestation. Monitors federal, state, and local legislation relating to natural resources. (Headquarters in San Francisco.)

Southern States Energy Board, P.O. Box 34606, Washington, DC 20043; 667-7303. Carolyn C. Drake, director, Washington office. Fax, 667-7313.

Interstate compact organization that serves as regional representative of 16 southern states and the commonwealths of Puerto Rico and Virgin Islands for energy and environmental issues. (Headquarters in Norcross, Ga.)

SRI International, 1611 N. Kent St., Arlington, VA 22209; (703) 524-2053. Gerald E. Connolly, vice president, Washington office. Fax, (703) 247-8569.

Research organization that conducts policy-related energy studies and scientific research. Projects include surveys of energy supply and demand; analyses of fossil fuel, solar, and nuclear energy; the environmental effects of advanced energy technology; and energy management. (Headquarters in Menlo Park, Calif.)

Union of Concerned Scientists, Energy Policy, 1616 P St. N.W., #310 20036; 332-0900. Alden Meyer, legislative director. Fax, 332-0905.

Independent group of scientists that advocates safe and sustainable national and state energy policies. Conducts research, advocacy, and educational outreach focusing on renewable energy and alternative fuels, transportation policy, carbon reduction strategies, and energy efficiency. (Headquarters in Cambridge, Mass.)

U.S. Chamber of Commerce, Food, Agriculture, Energy, and Natural Resources Policy, 1615 H St. N.W. 20062; 463-5500. Stew Hardy, manager. Fax, 007 3115.

Develops policy on all issues affecting the production, use, and conservation of energy, including transportation, energy taxes, and on- and offshore mining of energy resources.

U.S. Conference of Mayors, Resource Recovery, 1620 Eye St. N.W. 20006; 293-7330. Kevin McCarty, assistant executive director. Fax, 293-2352.

Membership: mayors of cities with populations of 30,000 or more. Works with Congress and the executive branch to promote urban policy on energy and environment issues; analyzes federal legislation, programs, and policies from an urban perspective.

Worldwatch Institute, 1776 Massachusetts Ave. N.W. 20036; 452-1999. Lester R. Brown, president. Fax, 296-7365.

Research organization that focuses on interdisciplinary approach to solving global environmental problems. Interests include energy conservation, renewable resources, solar power, and energy use in developing countries.

See also Resources: Coal (p. 214); Electricity (p. 219); Nuclear Energy (p. 223); Oil and Natural Gas (p. 229); Renewable Energies/ Alternative Fuels, Nongovernmental (p. 237)

See also Federation of American Scientists and National Academy of Sciences (p. 666); The Rand Corporation (p. 691)

Energy Use: Conservation

See also Environment, General (p. 616)

Agencies:

Administration for Children and Families (Health and Human Services Dept.), Community Services, 901 D St. S.W. (mailing address: 370 L'Enfant Promenade S.W., Washington, DC 20447); 401-9333. Donald Sykes, director. Fax, 401-5718.

Administers the Low Income Home Energy Assistance Block Grant Program for heating, cooling, and weatherizing households of low-income persons.

Energy Dept., Building Technologies, 1000 Independence Ave. S.W. 20585; 586-1510. John P. Millhone, deputy assistant secretary. Fax, 586-5954.

Supports private and government efforts to improve the energy efficiency of the nation's buildings and the increased utilization of renewable energy sources. Conducts research and development to make information and energy technologies available.

Energy Dept., Energy Efficiency and Renewable Energy, 1000 Independence Ave. S.W. 20585; 586-9220. Christine Ervin, assistant secretary. Fax, 586-9260.

Works to improve the efficiency of energy use in the commercial, residential, utility, transportation, and industrial sectors. Cooperates with state and local governments and industry partners to improve efficiency of energy use and decrease reliance on energy imports from foreign nations.

Energy Dept., Industrial Technologies, 1000 Independence Ave. S.W. 20585; 586-9232. Alan Streb, deputy assistant secretary. Fax, 586-9234.

Conducts research and disseminates information to increase energy end-use efficiency, promote renewable energy use and industrial applications, and reduce the volume of industrial and municipal waste.

Energy Dept., Technical and Financial Assistance, 1000 Independence Ave. S.W. 20585;

586-9240. Frank M. Stewart, deputy assistant secretary. Fax, 586-5145.

Gives policy guidance for state grant programs on energy conservation. Programs include low-income weatherization assistance, technical assistance for small-energy consumers to conserve and use renewable energy resources, and grants to schools and hospitals to increase energy efficiency. Conducts residential and commercial energy conservation programs. Reviews state plans for use of the funds distributed as restitution under the Petroleum Violation Escrow Fund.

Energy Dept., Transportation Technologies, 1000 Independence Ave. S.W. 20585; 586-8027. Thomas J. Gross, acting deputy assistant secretary. Fax, 586-1637.

Conducts research and development programs to improve transportation energy efficiency. Programs include electric and hybrid vehicles, advanced propulsion systems, advanced materials research, and alternative fuels, including biofuels.

Energy Information Administration (Energy Dept.), Energy End Use and Integrated Statistics, 1000 Independence Ave. S.W. 20585; 586-1112. Lynda T. Carlson, director. Fax, 586-0018.

Maintains data on energy consumption in the residential, commercial, industrial, and transportation sectors. Prepares analyses on energy consumption by sector and fuel type, including the impact of conservation measures. Publishes *Monthly Energy Review* and *State Energy Data Report*.

Housing and Urban Development Dept., Environment and Energy, HUD Bldg., #7240 20410; 708-2894. Richard H. Broun, director. Fax, 708-3363.

Develops policies promoting energy efficiency, conservation, and renewable sources of supply in housing and community development programs, including district heating and cooling systems and wastes-to-energy cogeneration projects.

National Institute of Standards and Technology (Commerce Dept.), Building and Fire Research Laboratory, Route I-270 and Quince Orchard Rd., Bldg. 226, #B306, Gaithersburg, MD 20899; (301) 975-5851. James E. Hill, chief, building environment. Fax, (301) 990-4192.

Develops measurement techniques, test methods, and mathematical models to encourage energy conservation in large buildings. Interests include refrigeration, lighting, infiltration and ventilation, heating and air conditioning, and heat transfer in the building envelope.

See also Federal Aviation Administration, Environment and Energy (p. 617)

Congress:

House Banking, Finance, and Urban Affairs Committee, Subcommittee on Housing and Community Development, B303 RHOB 20515; 225-7054. Henry B. Gonzalez, D-Texas, chairman; Nancy Libson, staff director. Fax, 225-4680.

Jurisdiction over legislation on energy conservation measures in housing (jurisdiction shared with the Energy and Commerce Committee).

House Energy and Commerce Committee, Subcommittee on Energy and Power, 331 Ford Bldg. (2nd and D Sts. S.W.) 20515; 226-2500. Philip R. Sharp, D-Ind., chairman; Shelley N. Fidler, acting staff director.

Jurisdiction over legislation on proposals to label appliances to indicate energy consumption and on emergency fuel allocation.

House Natural Resources Committee, Subcommittee on Energy and Mineral Resources, 818 O'Neill Bldg. (300 New Jersey Ave. S.E.) 20515; 225-8331. Richard H. Lehman, D-Calif., chairman; Deborah Lanzone, staff director. Fax, 225-4273.

Jurisdiction over conservation of the U.S. uranium supply, minerals, petroleum on public lands, and radium.

House Science, Space, and Technology Committee, Subcommittee on Energy, H2390 Ford Bldg. (2nd and D Sts. S.W.) 20515; 225-8056. Marilyn Lloyd, D-Tenn., chair; Francis X. Murray, staff director.

Jurisdiction over legislation on research and development of energy sources and over Energy Dept. basic research programs, including those in energy conservation and utilization; jurisdiction over legislation related to transportation energy conservation programs of the Energy Dept.

Joint Economic Committee, SD-G01 20510; 224-5171. Rep. David R. Obey, D-Wis., chairman; Richard McGahey, executive director. Fax, 224-0240.

Studies and makes recommendations on the conservation and expansion of energy supplies.

Senate Banking, Housing, and Urban Affairs Committee, Subcommittee on Housing and Urban Affairs, SD-535 20510; 224-6348. Paul S. Sarbanes, D-Md., chairman; Paul N. Weech, staff director. Fax, 224-5137.

Jurisdiction over legislation on energy conservation measures in housing.

Senate Energy and Natural Resources Committee, Subcommittee on Energy Research and Development, SH-312 20510; 224-7569. Wendell H. Ford, D-Ky., chairman; Vacant, senior professional staff member.

Jurisdiction over legislation on energy research and development, including energy conservation and conservation of the U.S. uranium supply.

Senate Energy and Natural Resources Committee, Subcommittee on Mineral Resources Development and Production, SD-362 20510; 224-7568. Daniel K. Akaka, D-Hawaii, chairman; Lisa Vehmas, counsel.

Jurisdiction over mineral conservation. Oversees some functions of the Energy Dept.

Senate Energy and Natural Resources Committee, Subcommittee on Renewable Energy, Energy Efficiency, and Competitiveness, SH-212 20510; 224-4756. Jeff Bingaman, D-N.M., chairman; Leslie Black Cordess, professional staff member.

Jurisdiction over energy conservation measures, such as emergency fuel allocation, proposals to label appliances to indicate energy consumption, gasoline rationing, coal conversion, and petroleum on public lands.

Nongovernmental:

Alliance to Save Energy, 1725 K St. N.W., #509 20006; 857-0666. William A. Nitze, president. Fax, 331-9588.

Coalition of government, business, consumer, and labor leaders concerned with increasing the efficiency of energy use. Advocates efficient use of energy; conducts research and demonstration projects and public education programs.

American Council for an Energy-Efficient Economy, 1001 Connecticut Ave. N.W., #801 20036; 429-8873. Howard Geller, executive director. Fax, 429-2248.

Independent research organization concerned with energy policy, technologies, and conservation. Interests include energy efficiency in buildings and appliances, improved transportation efficiency, industrial efficiency, utility issues, and conservation in developing countries.

Energy Conservation Coalition, 6930 Carroll Ave., #600, Takoma Park, MD 20912; (301) 891-1104. Nancy Hirsh, director. Fax, (301) 891-2218.

Coalition of consumer, environmental, scientific, and religious organizations that promotes energy efficiency to reduce carbon dioxide emissions and U.S. dependence on foreign oil and to ensure affordable energy supplies. Conducts research; sponsors workshops; monitors legislation and regulations. (Affiliate of Environmental Action.)

Environmental Defense Fund, 1875 Connecticut Ave. N.W., #1016 20009-5728; 387-3500. Cheryl King, office manager, Washington office. Fax, 234-6049.

Citizens' interest group staffed by lawyers, economists, and scientists. Provides information on energy issues and advocates energy conservation measures. Interests include Antarctica and the Amazon rain forest. Provides utilities and environmental organizations with energy conservation computer models. (Headquarters in New York.)

National Conference of States on Building Codes and Standards, 505 Huntmar Park Dr., #210, Herndon, VA 22070; (703) 437-0100. Robert Brown, acting director, technical services. Fax, (703) 481-3596. TDD, (703) 481-2019.

Membership: delegates appointed by the governors of the states and territories, and individuals and organizations concerned with building standards. Prepares code reports under contract. Works with national and state organizations and governmental agencies to promote the updating and adoption of model energy conservation codes for new and existing buildings. Maintains library of national, state, and local government energy conservation codes. Library open to members.

Many public interest and trade groups have developed energy conservation programs; see also Energy Policy (p. 202); Resources: Coal (p. 214); Electricity (p. 219); Nuclear Energy (p. 223); Oil and Natural Gas (p. 229); Renewable Energies/Alternative Fuels (p. 236)

See also Global Greenhouse Network (p. 621); National Assn. of Regional Councils (p. 313)

International Trade and Cooperation

See also Foreign Policy and Aid, International Development (p. 451)

Agencies:

Agency for International Development (International Development Cooperation Agency), Energy and Infrastructure, 1601 N. Kent St., Arlington, VA (mailing address: Washington, DC 20523); (703) 875-4205. James B. Sullivan, director. Fax, (703) 875-4053.
Assists with the economic growth of developing countries by providing policy, technical, and financial assistance for cost-effective, reliable, and environmentally sound energy programs. Focuses on the Global Warming Initiative, private initiatives, renewable energy, energy efficiency and conservation, technology innovation, and training officials in developing countries.

Energy Dept., Emergency Management, 1000 Independence Ave. S.W., #GE262 20585; 586-9892. John J. Nettles Jr., acting director. Fax, 586-3859.
Monitors international energy situations as they affect domestic market conditions; recommends policies on and government responses to energy emergencies; represents the United States in the International Energy Agency's emergency programs and NATO civil emergency preparedness activities.

Energy Dept., Energy Research, 1000 Independence Ave. S.W. 20585; 586-5430. Martha A. Krebs, director. Fax, 586-4120.
Analyzes international energy and energy technology-related trade. Coordinates development of and establishes policies for research and development agreements among producing and consuming nations; reviews existing international research and development activities; pursues international collaboration in research and in the design, development, and operation of new facilities.

Energy Dept., Policy, Planning, and Program Evaluation, 1000 Independence Ave. S.W. 20585; 586-5800. Susan Fallows Tierney, assistant secretary. Fax, 586-0861.

Advises the secretary on developing and implementing international energy policies consistent with U.S. foreign policy. Evaluates Energy Dept. programs. Represents the department in international discussions on energy matters, including the International Energy Agency of the Organization for Economic Development. Assesses world energy price and supply trends and technological developments; studies effects of international actions on U.S. energy supply.

Energy Information Administration (Energy Dept.), Energy Markets and Contingency Information, 1000 Independence Ave. S.W. 20585; 586-1441. Arthur T. Andersen, director. Fax, 586-9753.
Compiles, interprets, and reports international energy statistics and U.S. energy data for international energy organizations. Analyzes international energy markets; makes projections concerning world prices and trade for energy sources, including oil, natural gas, coal, and electricity; monitors world petroleum market to determine U.S. vulnerability.

Nuclear Regulatory Commission, Exports, Security, and Safety Cooperation, 11555 Rockville Pike, Rockville, MD (mailing address: Washington, DC 20555); (301) 504-2344. Ronald D. Hauber, assistant director. Fax, (301) 504-2395.
Coordinates application review process for exports and imports of nuclear materials, facilities, and components. Makes recommendations on licensing upon completion of review process. Conducts related policy reviews.

State Dept., Global Energy Affairs, Main State Bldg. 20520; 647-2887. Glen Rase, director. Fax, 647-4037.
Coordinates U.S. international energy policy related to commodities, including energy supply, and U.S. participation in the International Energy Agency; monitors cooperative multilateral and bilateral agreements related to energy; coordinates energy-related aspects of U.S. relations with other countries.

State Dept., Nuclear Energy, Main State Bldg. 20520; 647-3310. Richard J. K. Stratford, deputy assistant secretary. Fax, 647-0775.
Coordinates and supervises international nuclear energy policy for the State Dept. Advises the secretary on policy matters relating to nonproliferation and export controls, nuclear technology and safeguards, and nuclear safety. Promotes adherence to the Nuclear Nonproliferation Treaty and other international agreements.

Chairs the Subgroup on Nuclear Export Coordination, the interagency group that reviews nuclear export license applications. Enforces the Atomic Energy Act.

Treasury Dept., International Affairs, Main Treasury Bldg. 20220; 622-2140. David S. Curry, director, Middle East and energy policy. Fax, 622-0037.

Represents the department in the International Energy Agency, World Bank, International Monetary Fund, and other international institutions that address energy matters. Analyzes oil market and provides economic analyses of Arabian peninsular countries.

U.S. International Trade Commission, Energy, Petroleum, Benzenoid, Chemicals, and Rubber and Plastics, 500 E St. S.W. 20436; 205-3368. Edmund Cappuccilli, chief. Fax, 205-3161.

Advisory fact-finding agency on tariffs, commercial policy, and foreign trade matters. Analyzes data on oil, petrochemical, coal, and natural gas products imported by the United States; investigates effects of tariffs on certain imports.

U.S. Trade Representative (Executive Office of the President), 600 17th St. N.W. 20506; 395-3204. Mickey Kantor, U.S. trade representative. Information, 395-3230. Fax, 395-3911.

Serves as principal adviser to the president and primary trade negotiator on international trade policy. Develops and coordinates energy trade matters among government agencies.

Congress:

House Foreign Affairs Committee, 2170 RHOB 20515; 225-5021. Lee H. Hamilton, D-Ind., chairman; Michael H. Van Dusen, chief of staff. Fax, 226-3581.

Jurisdiction over most legislation on U.S. participation in international energy programs and legislation related to the economic aspects of trading nuclear technology and materials with foreign countries.

House Ways and Means Committee, 1102 LHOB 20515; 225-3625. Sam M. Gibbons, D-Fla., acting chairman; Janice A. Mays, chief counsel.

Jurisdiction over legislation on taxes, tariffs, and trade measures relating to energy, such as oil import fees.

Senate Energy and Natural Resources Committee, SD-304 20510; 224-4971. J. Bennett John-

ston, D-La., chairman; Benjamin Cooper, staff director. Fax, 224-6163.

Jurisdiction over legislation relating to U.S. participation in international energy programs (jurisdiction shared with Senate Foreign Relations Committee).

Senate Finance Committee, Subcommittee on Energy and Agricultural Taxation, SD-205 20510; 224-4515. Tom Daschle, D-S.D., chairman; Ted Sullivan, staff contact.

Holds hearings on legislation concerning taxes, tariffs, and trade measures relating to energy, such as oil import fees.

Senate Foreign Relations Committee, SD-446 20510; 224-4651. Claiborne Pell, D-R.I., chairman; Geryld B. Christianson, staff director. Fax, 224-5011.

Jurisdiction over legislation related to the economic aspects of trading nuclear technology and materials.

International Organizations:

European Community Press and Public Affairs, 2100 M St. N.W. 20037; 862-9500. Andreas A. M. van Agt, ambassador; Peter Doyle, director. Information, 862-9542. Press, 862-9540. Fax, 429-1766.

Information and public affairs office in the United States for the European Union/European Community, which includes the European Economic Community, the European Coal and Steel Community, and the European Atomic Energy Community. Provides energy information, statistics, and documents on member countries. Library open to the public by appointment.

International Bank for Reconstruction and Development (World Bank), Industry and Energy, 1776 G St. N.W. (mailing address: 1818 H St. N.W., #G2005, Washington, DC 20433); 473-6826. Richard Stern, director. Fax, 477-0545.

Facilitates investment of capital and makes loans from its own funds for developing the energy resources of less prosperous member countries. Finances lending programs that promote the generation, transmission, and distribution of electric power and the discovery and development of oil and gas in developing countries.

International Energy Agency (Organization for Economic Cooperation and Development), 2001 L St. N.W., #700 20036; 785-6323. Denis Lamb, head, Washington Center. Fax, 785-0350.

Promotes cooperation in energy research and development among developed nations; assists developing countries in negotiations with energy-producing nations; prepares plans for international emergency energy allocation. Publishes statistics and analyses on most aspects of energy. Washington Center maintains reference library open to the public; offers for sale publications of the International Energy Agency. (Headquarters in Paris.)

United Nations Information Centre, 1889 F St. N.W. 20006; 289-8670. Michael Stopford, director. Fax, 289-4267.

Center for reference publications of the United Nations; publications include *World Energy Statistics, Energy Balances and Electricity Profiles,* and other statistical material on energy. Library open to the public.

Nongovernmental:

Atlantic Council of the United States, Energy Policy Committee, 1616 H St. N.W. 20006; 347-9353. Eliane Lomax, assistant director, programs. Fax, 737-5163.

Studies and makes policy recommendations on international energy relationships for all energy sources, including oil, natural gas, coal, synthetic fuels, and nuclear power.

U.S. Energy Assn., 1620 Eye St. N.W., #900 20006; 331-0415. Barry K. Worthington, executive director. Fax, 331-0418.

Membership: energy-related organizations, including professional, trade, and government groups. Participates in the World Energy Council (headquartered in London). Sponsors seminars and conferences on energy resources, policy management, technology, utilization, and conservation.

See also Energy Policy, Nongovernmental (p. 207)

Resources: Coal

General

Agencies:

Bureau of Land Management (Interior Dept.), Solid Minerals, Main Interior Bldg. 20240; 452-0350. Paul Politzer, chief. Fax, 208-4800.

Evaluates and classifies coal resources on federal lands.

Energy Dept., Fuels Programs, 1000 Independence Ave. S.W. 20585; 586-5935. Anthony J. Como, director, coal and electricity. Fax, 586-6050.

Ensures that all new continually operating electric power plants are designed to burn coal or another alternate fuel. Issues orders requiring the conversion of power plants to burn coal. Grants, rescinds, or modifies exemptions from the provisions of the Power Plant and Industrial Fuel Use Act.

Energy Information Administration (Energy Dept.), Coal, Nuclear, Electric, and Alternate Fuels, 1707 H St. N.W. (mailing address: 1000 Independence Ave. S.W., Washington, DC 20585); 254-6234. John Geidl, director. Fax, 254-5765.

Collects data, compiles statistics, and prepares analyses and forecasts on domestic coal supply, including availability, production, costs, processing, transportation, and distribution. Publishes data on the export and import of coal; makes forecasts and provides analyses on coal imports and exports.

Interior Dept., Surface Mining Reclamation and Enforcement, 1951 Constitution Ave. N.W. 20240; 208-4006. Robert Uram, director. Information, 208-2553. Fax, 219-3106.

Administers the Surface Mining Control and Reclamation Act of 1977. Establishes and enforces national standards for the regulation and reclamation of surface coal mining and the surface effects of underground coal mining; oversees state implementation of these standards.

Congress:

General Accounting Office, Energy and Science Issues, 111 Massachusetts Ave. N.W., #201 20001; 512-6866. Gregg A. Fisher, assistant director, energy security and policy. Fax, 512-6880.

Independent, nonpartisan agency in the legislative branch that audits, analyzes, and reports on efficiency and effectiveness of federal energy programs related to coal.

House Education and Labor Committee, Subcommittee on Labor Standards, Occupational Health and Safety, B345A RHOB 20515; 225-1927. Austin J. Murphy, D-Pa., chairman; James Riley, staff director.

Jurisdiction over legislation on coal mining health and safety.

House Energy and Commerce Committee, Subcommittee on Energy and Power, 331 Ford Bldg. (2nd and D Sts. S.W.) 20515; 226-2500. Philip R. Sharp, D-Ind., chairman; Shelley N. Fidler, acting staff director.

Jurisdiction over legislation on coal regulation, utilization, and commercialization.

House Natural Resources Committee, 1324 LHOB 20515; 225-2761. George Miller, D-Calif., chairman; John Lawrence, staff director. Fax, 225-1931.

Jurisdiction over federal legislation affecting coal slurry pipelines. (Jurisdiction shared with House Public Works and Transportation Committee.)

House Natural Resources Committee, Subcommittee on Energy and Mineral Resources, 818 O'Neill Bldg. (300 New Jersey Ave. S.E.) 20515; 225-8331. Richard H. Lehman, D-Calif., chairman; Deborah Lanzone, staff director, Fax, 225-4273.

Jurisdiction over legislation on mining policy and on programs involving mineral and coal leasing.

House Public Works and Transportation Committee, Subcommittee on Surface Transportation, B376 RHOB 20515; 225-9989. Nick J. Rahall II, D-W.Va., chairman; Kenneth House, chief professional staff member.

Jurisdiction over legislation on coal slurry pipelines. (Jurisdiction shared with House Natural Resources Committee.)

House Science, Space, and Technology Committee, Subcommittee on Energy, H2390 Ford Bldg. (2nd and D Sts. S.W.) 20515; 225-8056. Marilyn Lloyd, D-Tenn., chair; Francis X. Murray, staff director.

Jurisdiction over legislation on research and development of fossil fuel energy (including coal and synthetic fuels such as liquefied and gasified coal) and over Energy Dept. basic research programs.

Senate Energy and Natural Resources Committee, SD-304 20510; 224-4971. J. Bennett Johnston, D-La., chairman; Benjamin Cooper, staff director. Fax, 224-6163.

Jurisdiction over legislation on coal slurry pipelines.

Senate Energy and Natural Resources Committee, Subcommittee on Energy Research and Development, SH-312 20510; 224-7569. Wendell H. Ford, D-Ky., chairman; Vacant, senior professional staff member.

Jurisdiction over legislation on fossil fuel research and development (coal and synthetic fuels such as liquefied and gasified coal), clean coal technology, and Energy Dept. research programs.

Senate Energy and Natural Resources Committee, Subcommittee on Mineral Resources Development and Production, SD-362 20510; 224-7568. Daniel K. Akaka, D-Hawaii, chairman; Lisa Vehmas, counsel.

Jurisdiction over legislation on mining policy, including mineral leasing and surface mining.

Senate Labor and Human Resources Committee, Subcommittee on Labor, SH-608 20510; 224-5546. Howard M. Metzenbaum, D-Ohio, chairman; Michèle L. Varnhagen, staff director.

Jurisdiction over legislation on coal mining health and safety.

See also Congressional Mining Caucus (p. 758); Senate Coal Caucus (p. 761)

Nongovernmental:

American Coal Ash Assn., 1913 Eye St. N.W. 20006; 659-2303. Samuel Tyson, executive director. Fax, 223-4984.

Membership: electric utilities that use coal to produce electricity, marketers or brokers of coal ash, coal companies, and suppliers of ash-related equipment. Compiles statistics on coal ash production and utilization. Library open to the public by appointment.

American Coke and Coal Chemicals Institute, 1255 23rd St. N.W. 20037; 452-1140. Mark T. Engle, president. Fax, 833-3636.

Membership: producers of oven coke, metallurgical coal, and chemicals; coke sales agents; tar distillers; and builders of coke ovens and coke oven byproduct plants. Maintains committees on chemicals, coke, manufacturing and environment, safety and health, and traffic.

American Mining Congress, 1920 N St. N.W., #300 20036; 861-2800. John A. Knebel, president. Fax, 861-7535.

Membership: domestic producers of coal, industrial-agricultural minerals, and metals; manufacturers of mining equipment; engineering and consulting firms; and financial institutions. Provides education in practical and scientific mining and metallurgy. Interests include mine leasing programs, mining health and safety, research and development, public lands, coal surface mining, and reclamation. Monitors legislation and regulations.

Assn. of Bituminous Contractors, 1747 Pennsylvania Ave. N.W., #1050 20006; 785-4440. William H. Howe, secretary and general counsel. Fax, 331-8049.

Membership: independent and general contractors that build coal mines. Represents members before the Federal Mine Safety and Health Review Commission and in collective bargaining with the United Mine Workers of America.

Bituminous Coal Operators Assn., 918 16th St. N.W., #303 20006; 783-3195. Joseph P. Brennan, president. Fax, 783-4862.

Membership: firms that mine bituminous coal. Represents members in collective bargaining with the United Mine Workers of America.

National Coal Assn., 1130 17th St. N.W. 20036; 463-2625. Richard L. Lawson, president. Information, 463-2640. Press, 463-2651. Fax, 463-6152.

Membership: coal producers, coal sales and transportation companies, equipment manufacturers, consulting firms, coal resource developers and exporters, coal-burning electric utility companies, and other energy companies. Collects, analyzes, and distributes industry statistics; conducts special studies of competitive fuels, coal markets, production and consumption forecasts, and industry planning. Interests include exports, coal leasing programs, coal transportation, environmental issues, health and safety, national energy policy, slurry pipelines, and research and development, including synthetic fuels.

National Coal Council, 2000 15th St., #500, Arlington, VA 22201; (703) 527-1191. James F. McAvoy, executive director. Fax, (703) 527-1195.

Membership: individuals appointed by the secretary of energy. Represents coal producers, transporters, women and minorities in mining, and manufacturers of coal-producing equipment. Makes recommendations to the secretary on issues involving coal. Library open to the public.

United Mine Workers of America, 900 15th St. N.W. 20005; 842-7200. Richard L. Trumka, president. Fax, 842-7227.

Membership: coal miners. Represents members in collective bargaining with industry. Conducts educational, housing, and health and safety training programs; monitors federal coal mining safety programs.

Exports

See also International Trade and Cooperation (p. 212)

Agencies:

Census Bureau (Commerce Dept.), Foreign Trade, Suitland and Silver Hill Rds., Suitland, MD (mailing address: Washington, DC 20233); (301) 763-5342. C. Harvey Monk, chief. Fax, (301) 763-4171. Trade data inquiries, (301) 763-5140.

Provides information on energy commodities exports, including coal.

Energy Dept., Coal and Technology Exports, 1000 Independence Ave. S.W. 20585; 586-7297. Peter J. Cover, program manager. Fax, 586-1188.

Responsible for coal and technology export promotion activities for the Office of Fossil Energy.

Energy Dept., International Energy Organizations and Policy Development, 1000 Independence Ave. S.W. 20585; 586-6383. Robert Price, director. Fax, 586-6148.

Monitors and evaluates energy policies of foreign nations to determine the effect on international coal trade; works with industry associations and the Commerce Dept. on promoting U.S. coal exports.

Energy Dept., Planning and Environment, 1000 Independence Ave. S.W. 20585; 586-9680. Raymond J. Braitsch, acting director. Fax, 586-1188.

Responsible for energy transportation studies for the Office of Fossil Energy.

Energy Information Administration (Energy Dept.), Coal, Nuclear, Electric, and Alternate Fuels, 1707 H St. N.W. (mailing address: 1000 Independence Ave. S.W., Washington, DC 20585); 254-6234. John Geidl, director. Fax, 254-5765.

Publishes data on the export and import of coal; makes forecasts and provides analyses on coal imports and exports.

International Trade Administration (Commerce Dept.), Energy, Environment, and Infrastructure, Main Commerce Bldg. 20230; 482-1466. Joseph J. Yancik, director, energy. Fax, 482-0170.

Develops and implements programs to promote and expedite the export of coal and other energy fuel resources. Provides coal export counseling services; conducts conferences and workshops.

U.S. International Trade Commission, Energy, Petroleum, Benzenoid, Chemicals, and Rubber and Plastics, 500 E St. S.W. 20436; 205-3368. Edmund Cappuccilli, chief. Fax, 205-3161.

Analyzes data on the quantity and value of domestic and foreign coal and coke traded internationally.

Congress:

See Resources: Coal, General, Congress (p. 214)

Nongovernmental:

Coal Exporters Assn. of the United States, 1130 17th St. N.W. 20036; 463-2639. Moya Phelleps, executive director. Fax, 833-9636.

Membership: exporters of coal and coke. Provides information on coal exports; monitors legislation and regulations affecting the export of coal. (Affiliate of the National Coal Assn.)

See also Resources: Coal, General, Nongovernmental (p. 215)

Mine Leasing

Agencies:

Bureau of Land Management (Interior Dept.), Solid Minerals, Main Interior Bldg. 20240; 452-0350. Paul Politzer, chief. Fax, 208-4800.

Develops and administers federal leasing programs for coal; supervises coal mining operations on federal lands; oversees pre- and postlease operations, including production phases of coal development. Oversees implementation of the Mining Law of 1872 and the Mineral Materials Act of 1955.

Congress:

See Resources: Coal, General, Congress (p. 214)

Nongovernmental:

See Resources: Coal, General, Nongovernmental (p. 215)

Mining Health and Safety

Agencies:

Bureau of Mines (Interior Dept.), Health, Safety, and Mining Technology, 810 7th St. N.W. 20241; 501-9321. Philip G. Meikle, chief. Fax, 501-9957.

Conducts research to improve the health and safety of miners in accordance with the Federal Mine Safety and Health Act of 1977.

Federal Mine Safety and Health Review Commission, 1730 K St. N.W., #600 20006; 653-5648. Arlene Holen, chair. Information, 653-5633. Fax, 653-5030.

Independent agency established by the Federal Mine Safety and Health Act of 1977. Holds fact-finding hearings and issues orders affirming, modifying, or vacating the labor secretary's enforcement actions regarding mine safety and health. Library open to the public.

Labor Dept., Coal Mine Workers' Compensation, 200 Constitution Ave. N.W. 20210; 219-6692. James L. DeMarce, director. Fax, 219-8568.

Administers the department's black lung benefits program. Adjudicates claims, certifies benefit payments, and maintains black lung beneficiary rolls.

Mine Safety and Health Administration (Labor Dept.), 4015 Wilson Blvd., Arlington, VA 22203; (703) 235-1385. J. Davitt McAteer, assistant secretary. Information, (703) 235-1452.

Administers and enforces the health and safety provisions of the Federal Mine Safety and Health Act of 1977. Monitors underground mining and processing operations of minerals, including minerals used in construction materials;

produces educational materials in engineering; and assists with rescue operations following mining accidents.

Congress:

See Resources: Coal, General, Congress (p. 214)

Nongovernmental:

United Mine Workers of America Health and Retirement Funds, 4455 Connecticut Ave. N.W. 20008; 895-3700. Donald Pierce Jr., executive director. Fax, 895-3703.

Labor/management trust fund that provides health and retirement benefits to coal miners. Health benefits are provided to pensioners, their dependents, and, in some cases, their survivors.

See also Resources: Coal, General, Nongovernmental (p. 215)

Pipelines

Agencies:

Energy Dept., Planning and Environment, 1000 Independence Ave. S.W. 20585; 586-9680. Raymond J. Braitsch, acting director. Fax, 586-1188.

Responsible for strategic planning for coal utilization, including transportation and handling.

Congress:

See Resources: Coal, General, Congress (p. 214)

Nongovernmental:

Coal and Slurry Technology Assn., 1156 15th St. N.W., #525 20005; 296-1133. Stuart D. Serkin, executive director. Fax, 223-3504.

Membership: slurry transport and fuel companies and others interested in the slurry fuels industry. Interests include extension of the right of eminent domain to coal slurry pipelines; facilitates the exchange of technical information among members.

See also Resources: Coal, General, Nongovernmental (p. 215)

Prices

Agencies:

Bureau of Labor Statistics (Labor Dept.), Energy, 2 Massachusetts Ave. N.E., #3840 20212; 606-7720. Michael Landess, energy analyst. Fax, 606-7753.

Compiles statistics on coal prices; analyzes price shifts and movement of prices on bituminous and anthracite coal and coke for the Producer Price Index.

Energy Information Administration (Energy Dept.), Coal and Uranium Data Systems, 1707 H St. N.W. (mailing address: 1000 Independence Ave. S.W., Washington, DC 20585); 254-5400. Noel C. Balthasar, chief. Fax, 254-5765.

Collects and publishes statistics on coal prices, production, distribution, consumption, stocks, imports, and exports.

Congress:

See Resources: Coal, General, Congress (p. 214)

Nongovernmental:

See Resources: Coal, General, Nongovernmental (p. 215)

Research and Development

Agencies:

Bureau of Mines (Interior Dept.), Health, Safety, and Mining Technology, 810 7th St. N.W. 20241; 501-9321. Philip G. Meikle, chief. Fax, 501-9957.

Conducts research on mineral extraction to improve the efficiency and lessen the environmental impact of mining.

Energy Dept., Clean Coal Technology, 270 Corporate Center, Germantown, MD (mailing address: FE-22, 270-CC, Washington, DC 20585); (301) 903-9451. C. Lowell Miller, associate deputy assistant secretary. Fax, (301) 903-9438.

Fosters the development and implementation of clean coal technologies in the private sector. Monitors economic and commercial efficiency program and disseminates results. Cofunded by private industry.

Energy Dept., Coal Combustion, Coal Preparation, and Control Systems, 270 Corporate Center, Germantown, MD (mailing address: Washington, DC 20585); (301) 903-0479. Douglas Uthus, director. Fax, (301) 903-2406.

Develops, manages, and conducts analyses for pressurized and atmospheric fluidized-bed combustion; coal-based mixtures combustion; coal combustion retrofit technologies and coal preparation, including sulfur and ash removal; advanced systems that control emissions into the air; and characterization of solid waste produced by advanced coal-based systems that generate electricity for industrial, utility, residential, and commercial applications.

Energy Dept., Coal Conversion, Route 118, Germantown, MD (mailing address: FE-231, Washington, DC 20585); (301) 903-4718. Robert M. Hamilton, acting director. Fax, (301) 903-2406.

Develops, plans, manages, and conducts analyses for Heat Engines Program using coal as the primary base fuel; coal gasification development, including coal conversion into alternative energy forms; and environmental control technologies associated with specific experimental conversion systems. Promotes science and engineering database for gasification systems and develops technologies for direct and indirect liquefaction of coal.

Energy Dept., Fossil Energy, 1000 Independence Ave. S.W. 20585; 586-6660. Patricia Fry Godley, assistant secretary designate. Fax, 586-5146.

Responsible for policy, management, and direction of high-risk, long-term research and development in recovering, converting, and using fossil energy, including coal. Oversees the Clean Coal Program to design and construct environmentally clean coal-burning facilities.

U.S. Geological Survey (Interior Dept.), Coal Geology, 12201 Sunrise Valley Dr., Reston, VA 22092; (703) 648-6401. Robert C. Milici, chief. Fax, (703) 648-6419.

Assesses resources, maintains coal databases, and conducts research on the quality and quantity of the nation's coal resources.

Congress:

See Resources: Coal, General, Congress (p. 214)

Nongovernmental:

See Resources: Coal, General, Nongovernmental (p. 215)

See also Electric Power Research Institute (p. 223)

Resources: Electricity

General

Agencies:

Bureau of Labor Statistics (Labor Dept.), Energy, 2 Massachusetts Ave. N.E., #3840 20212; 606-7720. Michael Landess, energy analyst. Fax, 606-7753.

Compiles and analyzes statistics on electric power price movement and magnitude of price changes in the primary commercial and industrial markets for the Producer Price Index.

Energy Dept., Bonneville Power Administration, 1000 Independence Ave. S.W. 20585; 586-5640. Stephen J. Wright, assistant administrator. Fax, 586-6762.

Coordinates marketing of electric power and energy for the Bonneville Power Administration; serves as liaison between the Bonneville Power Administration and Congress. (Headquarters in Portland, Ore.)

Energy Dept., Fuels Programs, 1000 Independence Ave. S.W. 20585; 586-5935. Anthony J. Como, director, coal and electricity. Fax, 586-6050.

Issues presidential permits required for constructing electric transmission lines that cross the U.S. international border. Authorizes the export of electricity from the United States. Grants, rescinds, or modifies exemptions from the provisions of the Power Plant and Industrial Fuel Use Act.

Energy Dept., Power Marketing Liaison Office, 1000 Independence Ave. S.W., #8G-061 20585; 586-5581. Joel K. Bladow, assistant administrator. Fax, 586-6261.

Serves as a liaison among the Southeastern, Southwestern, Western Area, and Alaska power administrations; other federal agencies; and Congress. Coordinates marketing of electric power from federally owned hydropower projects.

Energy Information Administration (Energy Dept.), Coal, Nuclear, Electric, and Alternate Fuels, 1707 H St. N.W. (mailing address: 1000 Independence Ave. S.W., Washington, DC 20585); 254-6234. John Geidl, director. Fax, 254-5765.

Prepares analyses and forecasts on electric power supplies, including the effects of government policies and regulatory actions on capacity, consumption, finances, and rates. Publishes statistics on electric power industry.

Tennessee Valley Authority, 1 Massachusetts Ave. N.W., #300 20001; 479-4412. Jan Evered, administrative officer, Washington office. Fax, 479-4421.

Coordinates resource conservation, development, and land-use programs in the Tennessee River Valley. Supplies wholesale power to municipal and cooperative electric systems, federal installations, and some industries; interests include nuclear power generation. (Headquarters in Knoxville, Tenn.)

Congress:

General Accounting Office, Energy and Science Issues, 111 Massachusetts Ave. N.W., #201 20001; 512-6864. Michael Blair, assistant director, electricity, conservation, and renewable energy issues. Fax, 512-6880.

Independent, nonpartisan agency in the legislative branch that audits, analyzes, and reports on efficiency and effectiveness of federal energy programs related to electricity.

House Energy and Commerce Committee, Subcommittee on Energy and Power, 331 Ford Bldg. (2nd and D Sts. S.W.) 20515; 226-2500. Philip R. Sharp, D-Ind., chairman; Shelley N. Fidler, acting staff director.

Jurisdiction over legislation on electric utilities regulation, energy plant siting (including nuclear facilities), and proposals to label appliances to indicate energy consumption.

House Natural Resources Committee, Subcommittee on Oversight and Investigations, 1328 LHOB 20515; 225-2761. George Miller, D-Calif., chairman; John Lawrence, staff director. Fax, 225-3554.

Jurisdiction over legislation on the federal power administrations.

House Public Works and Transportation Committee, Subcommittee on Water Resources

and Environment, B370A RHOB 20515; 225-0060. Douglas Applegate, D-Ohio, chairman; Kenneth J. Kopocis, counsel.

Jurisdiction over Tennessee Valley Authority legislation.

House Science, Space, and Technology Committee, Subcommittee on Energy, H2390 Ford Bldg. (2nd and D Sts. S.W.) 20515; 225-8056. Marilyn Lloyd, D-Tenn., chair; Francis X. Murray, staff director.

Jurisdiction over legislation on electric energy research and development.

Senate Energy and Natural Resources Committee, Subcommittee on Energy Research and Development, SH-312 20510; 224-7569. Wendell H. Ford, D-Ky., chairman; Vacant, senior professional staff member.

Jurisdiction over legislation on electric energy research and development.

Senate Energy and Natural Resources Committee, Subcommittee on Water and Power, SD-306 20510; 224-6836. Bill Bradley, D-N.J., chairman; Dana Sebren Cooper, counsel.

Jurisdiction over legislation on the federal power administrations.

Senate Environment and Public Works Committee, Subcommittee on Clean Air and Nuclear Regulation, SH-505 20510; 224-3597. Joseph I. Lieberman, D-Conn., chairman; Joyce Rechtschaffen, counsel.

Jurisdiction over Tennessee Valley Authority legislation.

See also Tennessee Valley Authority Caucus (p. 760)

Nongovernmental:

Electricity Consumers Resource Council, 1333 H St. N.W., 8th Floor 20005; 682-1390. John Anderson, executive director. Fax, 289-6370.

Membership: large industrial users ·of electricity. Promotes development of coordinated federal, state, and local policies concerning electrical supply for industrial users; studies rate structures and their impact on consumers.

The Electrification Council, 701 Pennsylvania Ave. N.W. 20004; 508-5900. Steven Koep, manager. Fax, 508-5335.

Membership: electric industry trade associations and independent manufacturers. Conducts training programs and provides industrial and commercial power consumers with educational materials. Interests include the efficient production, use, and management of energy. Fosters information exchange through the National Electric Industry Trade Ally Partnership.

National Electrical Contractors Assn., 3 Bethesda Metro Center, #1100, Bethesda, MD 20814; (301) 657-3110. John Grau, executive vice president. Fax, (301) 215-4500.

Membership: electrical contractors who build and service electrical wiring, equipment, and appliances. Represents members in collective bargaining with union workers; sponsors research and educational programs.

National Electrical Manufacturers Assn., 2101 L St. N.W. 20037; 457-8400. Malcolm O'Hagan, president. Fax, 457-8411.

Membership: domestic manufacturers of electrical products. Develops and promotes use of electrical standards; compiles and analyzes industry statistics. Interests include efficient energy management, product safety and liability, occupational safety, and the environment. Monitors international trade activities legislation and regulations.

National Independent Energy Producers, 601 13th St. N.W., #320S 20005; 783-2244. Merribel S. Ayres, executive director. Fax, 783-6506.

Membership: companies that generate electricity for sale to utilities and develop cogeneration projects for a variety of users. Membership comprises publicly traded and privately held corporations that represent a broad spectrum of fossil fuel and renewable technologies.

See also Institute of Electrical and Electronics Engineers—United States Activities (p. 677)

Public Utilities

Agencies:

Federal Energy Regulatory Commission (Energy Dept.), Electric Power Regulation, 825 N. Capitol St. N.E. 20426; 208-1200. J. Steven Herod, director. Fax, 208-0180.

Establishes rates and power charges for electric energy transmission, sale, and interconnections. Regulates wholesale electric rates in interstate commerce.

Federal Energy Regulatory Commission (Energy Dept.), Hydropower Licensing, 810 1st St. N.E. 20426; 219-2700. Fred E. Springer, director. Fax, 219-0205.

Issues licenses, permits, and exemptions for hydroelectric power projects. Ensures safety of licensed dams and safeguards the environment.

Rural Electrification Administration (Agriculture Dept.), 14th St. and Independence Ave. S.W. 20250; 720-9540. Wally Byer, administrator. Information, 720-1255. Press, 720-1260. Fax, 720-1725.

Makes loans and loan guarantees to rural electric utilities providing service in rural areas.

Congress:

See Resources: Electricity, General, Congress (p. 220)

Nongovernmental:

American Public Power Assn., 2301 M St. N.W. 20037; 467-2900. Larry Hobart, executive director. Library, 467-2957. Fax, 467-2910.

Membership: local, publicly owned electric utilities nationwide. Represents industry interests before Congress, federal agencies, and the courts; provides educational programs; collects and disseminates information; funds energy research and development projects. Library open to the public by appointment.

Edison Electric Institute, 701 Pennsylvania Ave. N.W. 20004; 508-5000. Thomas R. Kuhn, president. Information, 508-5778.

Membership: investor-owned electric power companies and electric utility holding companies. Interests include electric utility operation and concerns, including conservation and energy management, energy analysis, resources and environment, cogeneration and renewable energy resources, nuclear power, and research. Provides information and statistics relating to electric energy; aids member companies in generating and selling electric energy; and conducts information forums. Library open to the public by appointment.

Electric Generation Assn., 2715 M St. N.W., #150 20007; 965-1134. Margaret A. Welsh, executive director. Fax, 965-1139.

Membership: independent power producers. Works to establish universal standards for reliable and safe interconnection of wholesale electric generation facilities. Supports the implementation of the Energy Policy Act of 1992 and the Clean Air Act. Monitors legislation and regulations.

National Assn. of Regulatory Utility Commissioners, 12th St. and Constitution Ave. N.W. (mailing address: P.O. Box 684, Washington, DC 20044-0684); 898-2200. Paul Rodgers, administrative director and general counsel. Press, 898-2205. Fax, 898-2213.

Membership: members of federal, state, municipal, and Canadian regulatory commissions that have jurisdiction over utilities. Interests include electric utilities.

National Assn. of State Utility Consumer Advocates, 1133 15th St. N.W., #575 20005; 727-3908. Debra Berlyn, executive director. Fax, 727-3911.

Membership: public advocate offices authorized by states to represent ratepayer interests before state and federal utility regulatory commissions. Monitors legislation and regulatory agencies with jurisdiction over electric utilities, telecommunications, and natural gas; conducts conferences and workshops.

National Rural Electric Cooperative Assn., 1800 Massachusetts Ave. N.W. 20036; 857-9524. Bob Bergland, executive vice president. Fax, 857-4150.

Membership: rural electric cooperative systems and public power and utility districts. Provides members with technical assistance; interests include federal power administrations, rates and regulations, research and development, and electricity generated by nuclear power. Library open to the public by appointment.

Research and Development

Agencies:

Energy Dept., Coal Combustion, Coal Preparation, and Control Systems, 270 Corporate Center, Germantown, MD (mailing address: Washington, DC 20585); (301) 903-0479. Douglas Uthus, director. Fax, (301) 903-2406.

Develops, manages, and conducts analyses for pressurized and atmospheric fluidized-bed combustion; coal-based mixtures combustion; coal combustion retrofit technologies and coal preparation, including sulfur and ash removal; advanced systems that control emissions into the air; and characterization of solid waste produced by advanced coal-based systems that generate electricity for industrial, utility, residential, and commercial applications.

Energy Dept., Energy Management, 1000 Independence Ave. S.W. 20585; 586-2826. Marvin E. Gunn Jr., director. Fax, 586-0784.

Responsible for research and development of advanced electric power transmission and distribution technologies and of battery storage systems for use on electric networks. Manages the federal program addressing the potential health effects of electric and magnetic fields. Supports research on the use of hydrogen and on high-temperature superconducting materials and practical devices using such materials.

Energy Dept., Fusion Energy, Route 118, Germantown, MD (mailing address: Washington, DC 20585); (301) 903-4941. N. Anne Davies, associate director. Fax, (301) 903-8584.

Conducts research and development on fusion energy for electric power generation.

National Institute of Standards and Technology (Commerce Dept.), Electricity, Route I-270 and Quince Orchard Rd., Gaithersburg, MD 20899; (301) 975-2400. Oskars Petersons, chief. Fax, (301) 926-3972.

Conducts research to characterize and define performance parameters of electrical/electronic systems, components, and materials; applies research to advance measurement instrumentation and the efficiency of electric power transmission and distribution; develops and maintains national electrical reference standards, primarily for power, energy, and related measurements.

National Institute of Standards and Technology (Commerce Dept.), Electronics and Electrical Engineering Laboratory, Route I-270 and Quince Orchard Rd., Gaithersburg, MD 20899; (301) 975-2220. Judson French, director. Fax, (301) 975-4091.

Provides information on research, development, and applications in the fields of electrical, electronic, quantum electric, and electromagnetic materials engineering. Interests include fundamental physical constants, practical data, measurement methods, theory, standards, technology, and technical services.

Congress:

See Resources: Electricity, General, Congress (p. 220)

Nongovernmental:

Electric Power Research Institute, 2000 L St. N.W., #805 20036; 872-9222. Robert L. Hirsch, vice president. Information, 293-6346. Fax, 293-2697.

Membership: investor- and municipal-owned electric utilities and rural cooperatives. Conducts research and development in power generation and delivery technologies, including fossil fuel, nuclear, and renewable energy sources used by electric utilities. Studies energy management and utilization, including conservation and environmental issues. (Headquarters in Palo Alto, Calif.)

See also Resources: Electricity, General, Nongovernmental (p. 220)

Resources: Nuclear Energy

See also International Trade and Cooperation (p. 212); Nuclear Weapons and Power (p. 563)

General

Agencies:

Bureau of Land Management (Interior Dept.), Energy and Mineral Resources, Main Interior Bldg. 20240; 208-4201. Hillary A. Oden, assistant director. Fax, 208-4800.

Develops and administers federal leasing programs for uranium.

Energy Dept., Nuclear Energy, 1000 Independence Ave. S.W. 20585; 586-6450. Daniel Dreyfus, acting director. Information, 586-9720. Fax, 586-8353.

Administers nuclear fission power generation and fuel technology programs; develops and provides nuclear power sources to meet national civilian and defense requirements. Develops, interprets, and coordinates nuclear safety policy for all Energy Dept. reactors and nuclear facilities.

Energy Information Administration (Energy Dept.), Coal, Nuclear, Electric, and Alternate Fuels, 1707 H St. N.W. (mailing address: 1000 Independence Ave. S.W., Washington, DC 20585); 254-6234. John Geidl, director. Fax, 254-5765.

Prepares analyses and forecasts on the availability, production, prices, processing, transporta-

tion, and distribution of nuclear energy, both domestically and internationally. Collects and publishes data concerning the uranium supply and market.

Nuclear Regulatory Commission, 11555 Rockville Pike, Rockville, MD (mailing address: Washington, DC 20555); (301) 504-1759. Ivan Selin, chairman. Information, (301) 504-2240. Fax, (301) 504-1672.

Regulates commercial uses of nuclear energy; responsibilities include licensing, inspection, and enforcement.

Tennessee Valley Authority, 1 Massachusetts Ave. N.W., #300 20001; 479-4412. Jan Evered, administrative officer, Washington office. Fax, 479-4421.

Coordinates resource conservation, development, and land-use programs in the Tennessee River Valley. Supplies wholesale power to municipal and cooperative electric systems, federal installations, and some industries; interests include nuclear power generation. (Headquarters in Knoxville, Tenn.)

Congress:

General Accounting Office, Energy and Science Issues, 111 Massachusetts Ave. N.W., #201 20001; 512-6864. Victor S. Rezendes, director. Fax, 512-6880.

Independent, nonpartisan agency in the legislative branch that audits, analyzes, and reports on efficiency and effectiveness of federal energy programs related to nuclear energy.

House Energy and Commerce Committee, Subcommittee on Energy and Power, 331 Ford Bldg. (2nd and D Sts. S.W.) 20515; 226-2500. Philip R. Sharp, D-Ind., chairman; Shelley N. Fidler, acting staff director.

Jurisdiction over regulation of commercial nuclear facilities and special oversight functions with respect to all laws, programs, and government activities affecting nonmilitary aspects of nuclear energy. (Jurisdiction shared with House Natural Resources Committee.)

House Natural Resources Committee, Subcommittee on Energy and Mineral Resources, 818 O'Neill Bldg. (300 New Jersey Ave. S.E.) 20515; 225-8331. Richard H. Lehman, D-Calif., chairman; Deborah Lanzone, staff director. Fax, 225-4273.

Jurisdiction over regulation of commercial nuclear facilities; sets liability limits; special oversight functions with respect to all laws, programs, and government activities affecting nonmilitary aspects of nuclear energy, including radiological health and safety, security and safeguards, waste disposal, and licensing and plant siting. (Jurisdiction shared with House Energy and Commerce Committee.)

House Science, Space, and Technology Committee, Subcommittee on Energy, H2390 Ford Bldg. (2nd and D Sts. S.W.) 20515; 225-8056. Marilyn Lloyd, D-Tenn., chair; Francis X. Murray, staff director.

Jurisdiction over legislation and international cooperation on nuclear energy research and development. Oversight responsibilities over safety and operation of Energy Dept. laboratories, including toxic waste cleanup.

Senate Energy and Natural Resources Committee, SD-304 20510; 224-4971. J. Bennett Johnston, D-La., chairman; Benjamin Cooper, staff director. Fax, 224-6163.

Jurisdiction over nonmilitary and nonregulatory aspects of nuclear energy.

Senate Energy and Natural Resources Committee, Subcommittee on Energy Research and Development, SH-312 20510; 224-7569. Wendell H. Ford, D-Ky., chairman; Vacant, senior professional staff member.

Jurisdiction over nuclear energy research and development, including uranium enrichment and nuclear fuel cycle policy.

Senate Environment and Public Works Committee, Subcommittee on Clean Air and Nuclear Regulation, SH-505 20510; 224-3597. Joseph I. Lieberman, D-Conn., chairman; Joyce Rechtschaffen, counsel.

Legislative jurisdiction over nonmilitary environmental regulation and control of nuclear energy, including licensing and plant siting, radiological health and safety, security and safeguards, waste disposal, licensing of certain nuclear exports, and liability insurance for nuclear accidents.

Senate Governmental Affairs Committee, SD-340 20510; 224-4751. John Glenn, D-Ohio, chairman; Leonard Weiss, staff director. Fax, 224-9682.

Jurisdiction over organization and management of nuclear export policy; jurisdiction over legislation on the reform of nuclear licensing procedures and nuclear waste and spent fuel policy, physical security at nuclear installations, and nuclear proliferation.

Nongovernmental:

American Nuclear Energy Council, 410 1st St. S.E., 3rd Floor 20003; 484-2670. Edward M. Davis, president. Fax, 484-7320.

Membership: nuclear energy utilities, manufacturers, engineering contractors, mining companies, and companies interested in the nuclear fuel cycle. Interests include legislation affecting the industry, including nuclear power plant licensing reform and standardization, low- and high-level waste disposal, and the domestic uranium industry.

American Physical Society, 529 14th St. N.W., #1050 20045-2001; 662-8700. Robert L. Park, executive director, public affairs. Fax, 662-8711.

Scientific and educational society of educators, students, scientists, and other interested citizens. Sponsors studies on issues of public concern related to physics, such as reactor safety and energy use. (Headquarters in College Park, Md.)

Americans for Nuclear Energy, 2521 Wilson Blvd., Arlington, VA 22201; (703) 528-4430. Douglas Lee, chairman.

Public interest group that promotes the use of nuclear energy. Monitors federal legislation and regulations affecting nuclear energy.

National Assn. of Regulatory Utility Commissioners, 12th St. and Constitution Ave. N.W. (mailing address: P.O. Box 684, Washington, DC 20044-0684); 898-2200. Paul Rodgers, administrative director and general counsel. Press, 898-2205. Fax, 898-2213.

Membership: members of federal, state, municipal, and Canadian regulatory commissions that have jurisdiction over utilities and carriers. Interests include nuclear energy.

Nuclear Energy Institute, 1776 Eye St. N.W., #400 20006; 293-0770. Phillip Bayne, president. Fax, 785-4019.

Membership: utilities; industries; labor, service, and research organizations; law firms; universities; and government agencies interested in peaceful uses of nuclear energy, including the generation of electricity. Acts as a spokesperson for the nuclear power industry; provides information on licensing and plant siting, research and development, safety and security, and waste disposal.

Nuclear Information and Resource Service, 1424 16th St. N.W., #601 20036; 328-0002. Michael Mariotte, executive director. Fax, 462-2183.

Membership: organizations and individuals concerned about nuclear energy and nuclear waste. Information clearinghouse on nuclear power plants, nuclear waste, and radiation effects. Library open to the public by appointment.

Public Citizen, Critical Mass Energy Project, 215 Pennsylvania Ave. S.E. 20003; 546-4996. Bill McGavern, director. Fax, 547-7392.

Public interest group that promotes energy conservation and renewable energy technologies; opposes nuclear energy. Interests include nuclear plant safety and energy policy issues. Library open to the public by appointment.

Safe Energy Communication Council, 1717 Massachusetts Ave. N.W., #805 20036; 483-8491. Scott Denman, executive director. Fax, 234-9194.

Coalition of national energy, environmental, and public interest media groups that works to increase public awareness of the ability of energy efficiency and renewable energy sources to meet an increasing share of U.S. energy needs and of the economic and environmental liabilities of nuclear power. Provides local, state, and national organizations with technical assistance through media skills training and outreach strategies.

Union of Concerned Scientists, Nuclear Energy, 1616 P St. N.W., #310 20036; 332-0900. Robert Pollard, senior nuclear safety engineer. Fax, 332-0905.

Independent group of scientists concerned with U.S. energy and arms policies, including nuclear policy and nuclear plant safety. (Headquarters in Cambridge, Mass.)

See also Resources: Electricity, General, Nongovernmental (p. 220)
See also National Rural Electric Cooperative Assn. (p. 222)

Licensing and Plant Siting

Agencies:

Federal Emergency Management Agency, Response and Recovery Directorate, 500 C St. S.W. 20472; 646-3692. Richard W. Krimm, associate director. Fax, 646-4060.

Reviews off-site preparedness for commercial nuclear power facilities; evaluates emergency plans before plant licensing and submits findings to the Nuclear Regulatory Commission.

Nuclear Regulatory Commission, Nuclear Material Safety and Safeguards, 11555 Rockville Pike, Rockville, MD (mailing address: Washington, DC 20555); (301) 504-3352. Robert M. Bernero, director. Fax, (301) 504-2197.

Licenses all nuclear facilities and materials except power reactors; directs principal licensing and regulation activities for the management and disposal of nuclear waste.

Nuclear Regulatory Commission, Nuclear Reactor Regulation, 11555 Rockville Pike, Rockville, MD (mailing address: Washington, DC 20555); (301) 504-1270. Thomas Murley, director. Fax, (301) 504-1887.

Licenses nuclear power plants and operators.

Congress:

See Resources: Nuclear Energy, General, Congress (p. 223)

Nongovernmental:

See Resources: Nuclear Energy, General, Nongovernmental (p. 224)

Research and Development

Agencies:

Energy Dept., Advance Light Water Reactors, Routes I-270 and 118, Germantown, MD (mailing address: Washington, DC 20585); (301) 903-5447. David J. McGoff, director. Fax, (301) 903-5588.

Conducts research and development activities for light water reactor programs, nuclear regulation and safety, nuclear reactor economics, and financing for the thermal reactor fuel cycle. Monitors reactors under construction and examines export opportunities for nuclear materials and services.

Energy Dept., Civilian Reactor Development, 19901 Germantown Rd., Germantown, MD (mailing address: NE-42/GTN, Washington, DC 20585); (301) 903-4414. E. C. Brolin, director. Fax, (301) 903-7365.

Conducts advanced liquid metal reactor and high temperature gas reactor research and development; manages the design, construction, and operation of test facilities in support of the advanced reactor program. Oversees the production and sale of isotopes for commercial and medical purposes.

Energy Dept., Fuels Cycle Programs, 19901 Germantown Rd., Germantown, MD (mailing address: Washington, DC 20585); (301) 903-5259. Clinton Bastin, principal coordinator. Fax, (301) 903-3419.

Manages research and development programs for the LMR (liquid metal reactor) fuel cycle, including fuel fabrication development, and reprocessing equipment and systems development for remote operations and maintenance.

Energy Dept., Fusion Energy, Route 118, Germantown, MD (mailing address: Washington, DC 20585); (301) 903-4941. N. Anne Davies, associate director. Fax, (301) 903-8584.

Conducts research and development on fusion energy for electric power generation.

National Institute of Standards and Technology (Commerce Dept.), Physics Laboratory, Route I-270 and Quince Orchard Rd., Gaithersburg, MD 20899; (301) 975-4200. Katharine B. Gebbie, director. Fax, (301) 975-3038.

Provides national standards for radiation measurement methods and technology. Conducts research in measurement science in the fields of electron physics; ionizing radiation dosimetry; neutron physics; and optical, ultraviolet, x-ray, gamma-ray, and infrared radiometry.

Nuclear Regulatory Commission, Nuclear Regulatory Research, 5650 Nicholson Lane, Rockville, MD (mailing address: Washington, DC 20555); (301) 492-3700. Eric Beckjord, director. Fax, (301) 492-3597.

Plans, recommends, and implements nuclear regulatory research, standards development, and resolution of safety issues for nuclear power plants and other facilities regulated by the Nuclear Regulatory Commission; develops and promulgates all technical regulations.

U.S. Geological Survey (Interior Dept.), Energy and Marine Geology, 12201 Sunrise Valley Dr., Reston, VA 22092; (703) 648-6472. Gary Hill, chief. Fax, (703) 648-5464.

Handles exploration research on uranium, thorium, and lithium.

Congress:

See Resources: Nuclear Energy, General, Congress (p. 223)

Nongovernmental:

See Resources: Nuclear Energy, General, Nongovernmental (p. 224)

See also Electric Power Research Institute (p. 223)

Safety, Security, and Waste Disposal

See also Environment, Hazardous Materials (p. 625); Health, Radiation Protection (p. 337); International Trade and Cooperation (p. 212)

Agencies:

Defense Nuclear Facilities Safety Board, 625 Indiana Ave. N.W., #700 20004; 208-6400. John T. Conway, chairman. Fax, 208-6518.

Independent board created by Congress and appointed by the president to provide external oversight of Energy Dept. defense nuclear facilities and make recommendations to the secretary of energy regarding public health and safety.

Energy Dept., Civilian Radioactive Waste Management, 1000 Independence Ave. S.W. 20585; 586-6842. Daniel Dreyfus, director. Fax, 586-2672.

Responsible for developing the waste disposal system for commercial spent nuclear fuels and some military high-level radioactive waste. Sites, licenses, constructs, and operates a permanent repository. Monitors and reports on the adequacy of congressional appropriations for the Nuclear Waste Fund to finance nuclear waste disposal through fees collected from private utility companies that generate electricity.

Energy Dept., Environment, 1000 Independence Ave. S.W. 20585; 586-5680. Ray Berube, deputy assistant secretary. Fax, 586-2268.

Oversees adequacy of decontamination procedures for sites and facilities contaminated by radiation or hazardous and toxic materials.

Energy Dept., Environmental Restoration, 1000 Independence Ave. S.W., #5B050 20585; 586-6331. R. P. Whitfield, associate director. Fax, 586-6523.

Manages Energy Dept. programs that treat and stabilize radioactive waste and that decontaminate and decommission department and some nongovernment facilities and sites; works to develop a reliable national system for low-level waste management and techniques for treatment and immobilization of waste from nuclear power production.

Energy Dept., Health, 20300 Century Blvd., Germantown, MD (mailing address: 1000 Independence Ave. S.W., Washington, DC 20585); (301) 903-7030. Harry Pettengill, deputy assistant secretary. Fax, (301) 903-3445.

Evaluates and establishes standards related to radiation, industrial hygiene, and occupational medicine. Oversees epidemiologic studies.

Energy Dept., Performance Assessment, 19901 Germantown Rd., Germantown, MD (mailing address: Mail Stop 270CC, #5015, Washington, DC 20585); (301) 903-3548. Oliver D. T. Lynch Jr., director. Fax, (301) 903-8403.

Performs nuclear and nonnuclear technical safety appraisals; conducts occupational safety performance assessments; investigates employee complaints.

Energy Dept., Safety and Quality Assurance, 19901 Germantown Rd., Germantown, MD (mailing address: 1000 Independence Ave. S.W., Washington, DC 20585); (301) 903-5532. Joseph E. Fitzgerald Jr., deputy assistant secretary. Fax, (301) 903-3189.

Develops policy and establishes standards to ensure safety and health protection in all department activities; provides oversight of line program management.

Energy Dept., Technology Development, 1000 Independence Ave. S.W. 20585; 586-6382. Clyde Frank, deputy assistant secretary. Fax, 586-6773.

Performs research, development, testing, demonstration, and evaluation for innovative, safe, and cost-effective solutions to the problems of hazardous waste and contamination of soils and groundwater.

Energy Dept., Waste Management, 1000 Independence Ave. S.W., #5B-040 20585; 586-0370. Jill E. Lytle, deputy assistant secretary. Fax, 586-0449.

Provides policy guidance for and oversees waste management operations.

Energy Information Administration (Energy Dept.), Coal, Nuclear, Electric, and Alternate Fuels, 1707 H St. N.W. (mailing address: 1000 Independence Ave. S.W., Washington, DC 20585); 254-6234. John Geidl, director. Fax, 254-5765.

Directs collection of spent fuel data and validation of spent nuclear fuel discharge data for the Civilian Radioactive Waste Management Office.

Environmental Protection Agency, Radiation and Indoor Air, 501 3rd St. N.W. (mailing address: 401 M St. S.W., #6601J, Washington, DC 20460); 233-9320. Margo T. Oge, director. Fax, 233-9651.

Establishes standards to regulate the amount of radiation discharged into the environment from nuclear power plants, uranium mining and milling projects, and other activities that result in radioactive emissions.

Federal Emergency Management Agency, 500 C St. S.W. 20472; 646-3923. James Lee Witt, director. Information, 646-4600. Fax, 646-4562.

Assists state and local governments in preparing for and responding to natural and man-made emergencies, including accidents at nuclear power facilities and accidents involving transportation of radioactive materials; provides planning guidance in the event of such accidents; operates the National Emergency Training Center. Coordinates emergency preparedness and planning for all federal agencies and departments.

National Transportation Safety Board, Hazardous Material and Pipeline Accident, 490 L'Enfant Plaza East S.W. 20594; 382-0670. Larry E. Jackson, acting chief. Fax, 382-6819.

Investigates accidents involved in the transportation of hazardous materials.

Nuclear Regulatory Commission, Advisory Committee on Nuclear Waste Management, 7920 Norfolk Ave., Bethesda, MD (mailing address: Washington, DC 20555); (301) 492-8049. John T. Larkins, executive director. Fax, (301) 492-7617. TDD, (301) 492-8422.

Oversees handling and disposal of high- and low-level nuclear waste, especially the disposal of high-level waste in the Yucca Mountain Repository.

Nuclear Regulatory Commission, Advisory Committee on Reactor Safeguards, 7920 Norfolk Ave., Bethesda, MD (mailing address: Washington, DC 20555); (301) 492-8049. John T. Larkins, executive director. Fax, (301) 492-7617. TDD, (301) 492-8422.

Established by Congress to review and report on safety aspects of proposed and existing nuclear reactor facilities and the adequacy of proposed reactor safety standards; directs the Safety Research Program.

Nuclear Regulatory Commission, Nuclear Material Safety and Safeguards, 11555 Rockville Pike, Rockville, MD (mailing address: Washington, DC 20555); (301) 504-3352. Robert M. Bernero, director. Fax, (301) 504-2197.

Develops and implements safeguards programs; directs licensing and regulation activities for the management and disposal of nuclear waste.

Nuclear Regulatory Commission, Nuclear Reactor Regulation, 11555 Rockville Pike, Rockville, MD (mailing address: Washington, DC 20555); (301) 504-1270. Thomas Murley, director. Fax, (301) 504-1887.

Conducts safety inspections of nuclear reactors. Regulates nuclear materials used or produced at nuclear power plants.

Nuclear Regulatory Commission, Nuclear Regulatory Research, 5650 Nicholson Lane, Rockville, MD (mailing address: Washington, DC 20555); (301) 492-3700. Eric Beckjord, director. Fax, (301) 492-3597.

Plans, recommends, and implements resolution of safety issues for nuclear power plants and other facilities regulated by the Nuclear Regulatory Commission.

Nuclear Waste Technical Review Board, 1100 Wilson Blvd., #910, Arlington, VA 22209; (703) 235-4473. William D. Barnard, executive director. Fax, (703) 235-4495.

Independent board of scientists and engineers appointed by the president to review, evaluate, and report on Energy Dept. development of waste disposal systems and repositories for spent fuel and high-level radioactive waste. Oversees siting, packaging, and transportation of waste, in accordance with the Nuclear Waste Policy Act of 1987.

Transportation Dept., Hazardous Materials Safety, 400 7th St. S.W. 20590; 366-0656. Alan I. Roberts, associate administrator. Fax, 366-5713.

Issues safety regulations and exemptions for the transportation of hazardous materials; works with the International Atomic Energy Agency on standards for international shipments of radioactive materials.

U.S. Geological Survey (Interior Dept.), Earthquakes, Volcanoes, and Engineering, 12201 Sunrise Valley Dr., Reston, VA 22092; (703) 648-6714. Robert L. Wesson, chief. Fax, (703) 648-6717.

Monitors geologic problems relating to land use and environmental developments, including hazards to nuclear reactors; participates, at request of the Nuclear Regulatory Commission, in reviewing safety analysis reports for selected nuclear reactors.

U.S. Geological Survey (Interior Dept.), Regional Geology, 12201 Sunrise Valley Dr., Reston, VA 22092; (703) 648-6960. Mitchell W. Reynolds, chief. Fax, (703) 648-6937.

Studies nuclear test sites and safe disposal of radioactive waste; researches peacetime applications of atomic energy for other government agencies.

Congress:

See Resources: Nuclear Energy, General, Congress (p. 223)

Nongovernmental:

Project on Government Oversight, 2025 Eye St. N.W., #1117 20006; 466-5539. Danielle Bryan, director. Fax, 466-5596.

Works to expose waste, fraud, abuse, and conflicts of interest in federal spending. Examines cleanup efforts at government-owned nuclear facilities to determine cost effectiveness.

See also Resources: Nuclear Energy, General, Nongovernmental (p. 224)

See also League of Women Voters Education Fund, Natural Resources (p. 622)

Resources: Oil and Natural Gas

General

Agencies:

Economic Regulatory Administration (Energy Dept.), 820 1st St. N.E., #810 20002; 523-3053. Jay F. Thompson, acting administrator. Fax, 523-3065.

Manages and directs enforcement of federal statutes and regulations in effect before the decontrol of crude oil and petroleum product prices in January 1981; responsible for the phase-out of economic regulatory actions.

Energy Dept., Fossil Energy, 1000 Independence Ave. S.W. 20585; 586-6660. Patricia Fry Godley, assistant secretary designate. Fax, 586-5146.

Responsible for policy, management, and direction of high-risk, long-term research and development in recovering, converting, and using fossil energy, including petroleum, oil shale, and unconventional sources of natural gas. Handles the strategic petroleum reserve and the naval petroleum and oil shale reserve programs.

Energy Dept., Technical Management, 1000 Independence Ave. S.W. 20585; 586-4415. Paul J. Avila Plaisance, director. Fax, 586-7919.

Directs and manages the development and preparedness for distribution of the strategic petroleum reserve as mandated by the Energy Policy and Conservation Act of 1975.

Energy Information Administration (Energy Dept.), Oil and Gas, 1000 Independence Ave. S.W. 20585; 586-6401. Jimmie L. Petersen, director. Fax, 586-9739.

Collects, interprets, and publishes data on domestic production, use, and distribution of oil and natural gas; analyzes and projects oil and gas reserves, resources, production, capacity, and supply; surveys and monitors alternative fuel needs during emergencies; publishes statistics.

Congress:

General Accounting Office, Energy and Science Issues, 111 Massachusetts Ave. N.W., #201 20001; 512-6864. Gregg A. Fisher, assistant director, energy security and policy. Fax, 512-6880.

Independent, nonpartisan agency in the legislative branch that audits, analyzes, and reports on efficiency and effectiveness of federal energy programs related to oil and natural gas.

House Energy and Commerce Committee, Subcommittee on Energy and Power, 331 Ford Bldg. (2nd and D Sts. S.W.) 20515; 226-2500. Philip R. Sharp, D-Ind., chairman; Shelley N. Fidler, acting staff director.

Jurisdiction over legislation dealing with oil and natural gas, including proposed emergency presidential energy authority (such as rationing), proposals to create civilian petroleum reserves, petroleum and natural gas pricing and pipelines, natural gas imports, regulation of public utilities, energy plant siting, and low head hydro projects.

House Merchant Marine and Fisheries Committee, Subcommittee on Oceanography, Gulf of Mexico, and the Outer Continental Shelf, 575 Ford Bldg. (2nd and D Sts. S.W.) 20515; 226-2460. Solomon P. Ortiz, D-Texas, chairman; Sheila McCready, staff director.

Oversight of and legislative jurisdiction on conservation and development of energy and natural resources in the ocean and the outer continental shelf, including oil and gas. Jurisdiction over legislation on deepwater ports and mineral (Minerals Management Service of the Interior Dept.) and other resources.

House Natural Resources Committee, Subcommittee on Energy and Mineral Resources, 818 O'Neill Bldg. (300 New Jersey Ave. S.E.) 20515; 225-8331. Richard H. Lehman, D-Calif., chairman; Deborah Lanzone, staff director. Fax, 225-4273.

Jurisdiction over legislation on mineral land laws, oil and gas leasing programs, mineral resources on publicly owned land, oil shale development, and Interior Dept. procedures for petroleum leasing.

House Public Works and Transportation Committee, Subcommittee on Surface Transportation, B376 RHOB 20515; 225-9989. Nick J. Rahall II, D-W.Va., chairman; Kenneth House, chief professional.

Jurisdiction over legislation on oil pipeline transportation.

House Science, Space, and Technology Committee, Subcommittee on Energy, H2390 Ford Bldg. (2nd and D Sts. S.W.) 20515; 225-8056.

Marilyn Lloyd, D-Tenn., chair; Francis X. Murray, staff director.

Jurisdiction over legislation on research and development of fossil fuel energy (petroleum, natural gas, oil shale, and tar sand) and over Energy Dept. basic research programs.

Senate Energy and Natural Resources Committee, SD-304 20510; 224-4971. J. Bennett Johnston, D-La., chairman; Benjamin Cooper, staff director. Fax, 224-6163.

Jurisdiction over legislation on strategic petroleum reserves, leasing and development of outer continental shelf lands including territorial affairs, and interstate aspects of production and distribution of natural gas and petroleum, including price regulations.

Senate Energy and Natural Resources Committee, Subcommittee on Energy Research and Development, SH-312 20510; 224-7569. Wendell H. Ford, D-Ky., chairman; Vacant, senior professional staff member.

Jurisdiction over legislation on energy research and development including fossil fuels (petroleum, natural gas, oil shale, and tar sand).

Senate Energy and Natural Resources Committee, Subcommittee on Mineral Resources Development and Production, SD-362 20510; 224-7568. Daniel K. Akaka, D-Hawaii, chairman; Lisa Vehmas, counsel.

Jurisdiction over legislation on production and development of deep seabed mining and deepwater ports (jurisdiction shared with Senate Commerce, Science, and Transportation and Senate Environment and Public Works committees); certain aspects of petroleum, including oil shale and leasing; and all onshore drilling.

Senate Energy and Natural Resources Committee, Subcommittee on Renewable Energy, Energy Efficiency, and Competitiveness, SH-212 20510; 224-4756. Jeff Bingaman, D-N.M., chairman; Leslie Black Cordess, professional staff member.

Jurisdiction over legislation on interstate aspects of production and distribution of natural gas and petroleum, including price, pipeline, and natural gas utilities regulation; jurisdiction over proposed emergency presidential energy authority (such as rationing), and liquefied natural gas. Oversight of the Alaska Natural Gas Transportation System.

Senate Energy and Natural Resources Committee, Subcommittee on Water and Power, SD-306 20510; 224-6836. Bill Bradley, D-N.J., chairman; Dana Sebren Cooper, counsel.

Jurisdiction over legislation on low head hydro projects.

Nongovernmental:

American Gas Assn., 1515 Wilson Blvd., Arlington, VA 22209; (703) 841-8400. Michael Baly III, president. Library, (703) 841-8415. Fax, (703) 841-8406.

Membership: natural gas utilities and pipeline companies. Interests include all technical and operational aspects of the gas industry. Publishes comprehensive statistical record of gas industry; conducts national standard testing for gas appliances; monitors legislation and regulations. Library open to the public by appointment.

American Independent Refiners Assn., 1025 Thomas Jefferson St. N.W., #700E 20007; 625-3840. Valerie Wilbur, representative, government affairs. Fax, 298-7570.

Membership: small and independent petroleum refiners. Interests include allocation, exports, imports, and production guidelines. (Headquarters in Los Angeles.)

American Petroleum Institute, 1220 L St. N.W. 20005; 682-8100. Charles J. DiBona, president. Press, 682-8120. Library, 682-8042. Fax, 682-8029.

Membership: producers, refiners, marketers, and transporters of oil, natural gas, and related products such as gasoline. Provides information on the industry, including data on exports and imports, taxation, transportation, weekly refinery operations (stock levels, output, and input), and drilling activity and costs; conducts research on petroleum and publishes statistical and drilling reports. Library open to the public.

American Public Gas Assn., 11094-D Lee Highway, #102, Fairfax, VA 22030; (703) 352-3890. Robert S. Cave, executive director. Fax, (703) 352-1271.

Membership: municipally owned gas distribution systems. Provides information on federal developments affecting natural gas. Promotes efficiency and works to protect the interests of public gas systems. Sponsors workshops and conferences.

Compressed Gas Assn., 1725 Jefferson Davis Highway, #1004, Arlington, VA 22202-4102; (703) 412-0900. Carl T. Johnson, president. Fax, (703) 412-0128.

Membership: companies that produce and distribute compressed and liquefied gases. Promotes and coordinates technical development and standardization of the industry; monitors legislation and regulations.

Gas Appliance Manufacturers Assn., 1901 N. Moore St., Arlington, VA 22209; (703) 525-9565. C. Reuben Autery, president. Fax, (703) 525-0718.

Membership: manufacturers of gas appliances and equipment for residential and commercial use and related industries. Advocates product improvement and provides market statistics; monitors legislation and regulations.

Gas Research Institute, 1331 Pennsylvania Ave. N.W., #730N 20004; 662-8989. David O. Webb, senior vice president, policy and regulatory affairs Fax, 347-6925.

Membership: interstate and intrastate gas pipelines, natural gas distribution companies, municipal gas distribution systems, and natural gas producers. Manages research related to the natural gas industry. (Headquarters in Chicago.)

Independent Liquid Terminals Assn., 1133 15th St. N.W., #650 20005; 659-2301. John Prokop, president. Fax, 466-4166.

Membership: commercial operators of for-hire bulk liquid terminals and tank storage facilities, including those for crude oil and petroleum. Promotes the safe and efficient handling of various types of liquid commodities. Sponsors workshops and seminars; maintains speakers bureau; publishes directories; monitors legislation and regulations.

Independent Petroleum Assn. of America, 1101 16th St. N.W., 2nd Floor 20036; 857-4722. Denise A. Bode, president. Fax, 857-4799.

Membership: independent oil and gas producers; land and royalty owners; and others with interests in domestic exploration, development, and production of oil and natural gas. Interests include leasing, prices and taxation, foreign trade, environmental restrictions, and improved recovery methods.

Independent Terminal Operators Assn., 1150 Connecticut Ave. N.W., 9th Floor 20036; 828-

4100. William H. Bode, secretary and general counsel. Fax, 828-4130.

Membership: independent operators of petroleum storage facilities. Interests include oil imports; monitors legislation and regulations.

Mid-Continent Oil and Gas Assn., 801 Pennsylvania Ave. N.W., #840 20004; 638-4400. Wayne Gibbens, president. Fax, 638-5967.

Membership: major and independent petroleum companies. Monitors legislation and regulations affecting the petroleum industry.

National Assn. of Regulatory Utility Commissioners, 12th St. and Constitution Ave. N.W. (mailing address: P.O. Box 684, Washington, DC 20044-0684); 898-2200. Paul Rodgers, administrative director and general counsel. Press, 898-2205. Fax, 898-2213.

Membership: members of federal, state, municipal, and Canadian regulatory commissions that have jurisdiction over utilities and carriers. Interests include natural gas.

National Petroleum Council, 1625 K St. N.W. 20006; 393-6100. Marshall W. Nichols, executive director. Fax, 331-8539.

Advisory committee to the secretary of energy on matters relating to the petroleum industry, including oil and natural gas. Publishes reports concerning technical aspects of the oil and gas industries. Library open to the public by appointment.

National Petroleum Refiners Assn., 1899 L St. N.W., #1000 20036; 457-0480. Urvan Sternfels, president. Fax, 457-0486.

Membership: petroleum, petrochemical, and refining companies. Interests include allocation, imports, refining technology, petrochemicals, and environmental regulations.

National Propane Gas Assn., 4301 Fairfax Dr., #340, Arlington, VA 22203; (703) 351-7500. James N. Burroughs, vice president, government relations.

Membership: retail marketers, producers, wholesale distributors, appliance and equipment manufacturers, equipment fabricators, and distributors and transporters of liquefied petroleum gas. Conducts research, safety, and educational programs; provides statistics on the industry. (Headquarters in Lisle, Ill.)

Natural Gas Supply Assn., 1129 20th St. N.W., #300 20036; 331-8900. Nicholas J. Bush, president. Fax, 452-6558.

Membership: major and independent producers of domestic natural gas. Interests include the production, consumption, marketing, and regulation of natural gas; monitors legislation and regulations.

Natural Gas Vehicle Coalition, 1515 Wilson Blvd., #1030, Arlington, VA 22209; (703) 527-3022. Jeffrey Seisler, executive director. Fax, (703) 527-3025.

Membership: natural gas distributors; pipeline, automobile, and engine manufacturers; environmental groups; research and development organizations; and state and local government agencies. Advocates installation of compressed natural gas fuel stations and development of industry standards. Helps market new natural gas products and equipment.

Petroleum Marketers Assn. of America, 1901 N. Fort Myer Dr., #1200, Arlington, VA 22209-1604; (703) 351-8000. Phillip R. Chisholm, executive vice president. Fax, (703) 351-9160.

Membership: state and regional associations representing independent branded and non-branded marketers of petroleum products. Provides information on all aspects of petroleum marketing; monitors legislation and regulations.

Public Citizen, Buyers Up, 2000 P St. N.W., #600 20036; 659-2500. Linda Beaver, national director. Fax, 659-9279.

Administers cooperative purchasing program for consumers of heating oil and heating and cooling services. Monitors energy issues affecting consumers; promotes energy conservation; helps consumers save on energy bills; seeks to increase responsiveness of government and business to consumer needs.

Service Station Dealers of America, 801 N. Fairfax St., #109, Alexandria, VA 22314-1757; (703) 548-4736. Melvin D. Sherbert, president. Fax, (703) 548-0484.

Membership: state associations of gasoline retailers. Interests include environmental issues, retail marketing, oil allocation, imports and exports, prices, and taxation.

Society of Independent Gasoline Marketers of America, 11911 Freedom Dr., #590, Reston,

VA 22090; (703) 709-7000. Kenneth A. Doyle, executive vice president. Fax, (703) 709-7007.

Membership: marketers and wholesalers of brand and nonbrand gasoline. Seeks to ensure adequate supplies of gasoline at competitive prices. Monitors legislation and regulations affecting gasoline supply and price.

See also National Assn. of State Utility Consumer Advocates (p. 222); National Oil Recyclers Assn. (p. 631)

Exports and Imports

See also International Trade and Cooperation (p. 212)

Agencies:

Census Bureau (Commerce Dept.), Foreign Trade, Suitland and Silver Hill Rds., Suitland, MD (mailing address: Washington, DC 20233); (301) 763-5342. C. Harvey Monk, chief. Fax, (301) 763-4171. Trade data inquiries, (301) 763-5140.

Provides information on exports and imports of oil, natural gas, and related products.

Commerce Dept., Balance of Payments, 1441 L St. N.W., BE-58 20230; 606-9545. Christopher L. Bach, chief. Fax, 606-5314.

Provides statistics on U.S. balance of trade, including figures on oil imports.

Energy Dept., Fuels Programs, 1000 Independence Ave. S.W. 20585; 586-9482. Clifford Tomaszewski, director, natural gas. Fax, 586-6050.

Responsible for reviewing and processing natural gas import and export authorizations and for setting natural gas curtailment policy.

Energy Information Administration (Energy Dept.), Petroleum Supply, 1000 Independence Ave. S.W. 20585; 586-6860. Charles C. Heath, director. Fax, 586-5846.

Collects, compiles, interprets, and publishes data on domestic production and distribution of crude oil and refined petroleum products; analyzes and projects availability of petroleum supplies. Publishes statistics on petroleum, including import-export statistics.

U.S. International Trade Commission, Energy, Petroleum, Benzenoid, Chemicals, and Rubber and Plastics, 500 E St. S.W. 20436; 205-3368. Edmund Cappuccilli, chief. Fax, 205-3161.

Provides analytical information on the quantity and value of domestic and foreign petroleum, petrochemicals, and natural gas imported by the United States; investigates effects of tariffs on certain imports.

Congress:

See Resources: Oil and Natural Gas, General, Congress (p. 229)

Nongovernmental:

See Resources: Oil and Natural Gas, General, Nongovernmental (p. 230)

Leasing

Agencies:

Bureau of Land Management (Interior Dept.), Fluid Minerals, Main Interior Bldg. 20240; 452-0340, Erick Kaarlela, chief. Fax, 208-4800.

Develops and administers onshore federal leasing programs for oil and natural gas; evaluates and classifies petroleum resources on onshore federal lands; supervises pre- and postlease operations, including drilling and production phases of oil and natural gas development.

Minerals Management Service (Interior Dept.), Program Development and Coordination, 381 Elden St., Herndon, VA 22070; (703) 787-1178. Thomas A. Readinger, director. Fax, (703) 787-1165.

Administers and updates five-year plans for offshore oil and gas leasing. Provides information on tract selections, guidance on sales procedures, and assistance with postsale guidelines to ensure receipt of fair market value for leases issued on the outer continental shelf.

National Oceanic and Atmospheric Administration (Commerce Dept.), Ocean Resources, Conservation, and Assessment, 1305 East-West Highway, N/ORCA Rm. 10409 SSMC4, Silver Spring, MD 20910; (301) 713-2989. Charles N. Ehler, director. Fax, (301) 713-4389.

Studies and develops policy on oil and gas leasing on the outer continental shelf.

Congress:

See Resources: Oil and Natural Gas, General, Congress (p. 229)

Nongovernmental:

See Resources: Oil and Natural Gas, General, Nongovernmental (p. 230)

Offshore Resources

See also Natural Resources, Outer Continental Shelf (p. 651)

Agencies:

Minerals Management Service (Interior Dept.), Operations and Safety Management, 381 Elden St., Herndon, VA 22070; (703) 787-1570. Henry G. Bartholomew, deputy associate director. Fax, (703) 787-1575.

Administers the Outer Continental Shelf Land Act. Supervises oil and gas operations on outer continental shelf lands; oversees lease operations including exploration, drilling, and production phases of offshore oil and gas development; administers lease provisions for offshore oil and gas.

National Oceanic and Atmospheric Administration (NOAA) (Commerce Dept.), Ecology and Conservation, Main Commerce Bldg., Rm. 6222 20230; 482-5181. Donna Wieting, acting director. Fax, 482-1156.

Makes recommendations to NOAA concerning environmental and ecological problems. Assesses the accuracy and coordinates the implementation of environmental impact statements for all federal projects, including offshore oil and natural gas facilities.

U.S. Geological Survey (Interior Dept.), Energy and Marine Geology, 12201 Sunrise Valley Dr., Reston, VA 22092; (703) 648-6472. Gary Hill, chief. Fax, (703) 648-5464.

Handles resource assessment and research activities for oil and natural gas, both onshore and offshore.

Congress:

See Resources: Oil and Natural Gas, General, Congress (p. 229)

Nongovernmental:

National Ocean Industries Assn., 1120 G St. N.W., #900 20005; 347-6900. Robert B. Stewart, president. Fax, 347-8650.

Membership: manufacturers, producers, suppliers and support and service companies involved in marine, offshore, and ocean work. Interests include offshore oil and gas supply and production.

See also Resources: Oil and Natural Gas, General, Nongovernmental (p. 230)

Oil Shale and Tar Sands

Agencies:

Energy Dept., Naval Petroleum and Oil Shale Reserves, 1000 Independence Ave. S.W. 20585; 586-4685. Capt. Kenneth W. Meeks (USN), deputy assistant secretary. Fax, 586-4446.

Develops, conserves, operates, and maintains oil shale reserves for producing oil, natural gas, and other petroleum products.

Congress:

See Resources: Oil and Natural Gas, General, Congress (p. 229)

Nongovernmental:

See Resources: Oil and Natural Gas, General, Nongovernmental (p. 230)

Pipelines

Agencies:

Federal Energy Regulatory Commission (Energy Dept.), Pipeline and Producer Regulation, 825 N. Capitol St. N.E. 20426; 208-0700. Kevin P. Madden, director. Fax, 208-0193.

Establishes and enforces maximum rates and charges for oil and natural gas pipelines; establishes oil pipeline operating rules; issues certificates for and regulates construction, sale, and acquisition of natural gas pipeline facilities. Ensures compliance with the Natural Gas Policy Act, the Natural Gas Act, and other statutes.

National Transportation Safety Board, Hazardous Material and Pipeline Accident; 490 L'Enfant Plaza East S.W. 20594; 382-0670. Larry E. Jackson, acting chief. Fax, 382-6819.

Investigates natural gas and petroleum pipeline accidents.

Transportation Dept., Hazardous Materials Safety, 400 7th St. S.W. 20590; 366-0656. Alan I. Roberts, associate administrator. Fax, 366-5713.

Designates substances as hazardous materials and regulates their transportation in interstate commerce; coordinates international standards regulations.

Transportation Dept., Pipeline Safety, 400 7th St. S.W., #2335 20590; 366-4595. George Tenley, associate administrator. Fax, 366-4566.

Issues and enforces federal regulations for oil, natural gas, and petroleum products pipeline safety.

Congress:

See Resources: Oil and Natural Gas, General, Congress (p. 229)

Nongovernmental:

Assn. of Oil Pipe Lines, 1725 K St. N.W. 20006; 331-8228. Patrick H. Corcoran, executive director. Fax, 822-1964.

Membership: oil pipeline companies. Compiles statistics; monitors legislation and regulations.

Interstate Natural Gas Assn. of America, 555 13th St. N.W., #300W 20004; 626-3200. Jerald V. Halvorsen, president. Fax, 626-3239.

Membership: U.S. interstate and Canadian interprovincial natural gas pipeline companies. Commissions studies and provides information on the natural gas pipeline industry.

See also Resources: Oil and Natural Gas, General, Nongovernmental (p. 230)

Prices

Agencies:

Bureau of Labor Statistics (Labor Dept.), Energy, 2 Massachusetts Ave. N.E., #3840 20212; 606-7720. Michael Landess, energy analyst. Fax, 606-7753.

Compiles statistics on oil and gas prices; analyzes price shifts and movement of prices on natural gas, liquid petroleum gas, refined petroleum products, and crude oil for the Producer Price Index.

Economic Regulatory Administration (Energy Dept.), Enforcement Litigation, 820 1st St. N.E., #810 20002; 523-3011. Milton C. Lorenz, chief counsel. Fax, 523-3042.

Administers and enforces pricing and allocation regulations in effect prior to the decontrol of crude oil and petroleum product prices in January 1981.

Energy Information Administration (Energy Dept.), Petroleum Marketing, 1000 Independence Ave. S.W. 20585; 586-5214. John S. Cook, director. Information, 586-8800.

Interprets and publishes data on domestic prices of all petroleum products and crude oil; analyzes petroleum industry.

Energy Information Administration (Energy Dept.), Reserves and Natural Gas, 1000 Independence Ave. S.W. 20585; 586-6090. Diane Lique, director. Fax, 586-1076.

Interprets and publishes monthly and annual data on the estimated wellhead and market value of natural gas.

Federal Energy Regulatory Commission (Energy Dept.), Pipeline and Producer Regulation, 825 N. Capitol St. N.E. 20426; 208-0700. Kevin P. Madden, director. Fax, 208-0193.

Establishes and enforces rates and charges for oil and natural gas pipelines. Ensures compliance with the Natural Gas Policy Act, the Natural Gas Act, and other statutes.

Congress:

See Resources: Oil and Natural Gas, General, Congress (p. 229)

Nongovernmental:

See Resources: Oil and Natural Gas, General, Nongovernmental (p. 230)

Research and Development

Agencies:

Energy Dept., Fossil Energy, 1000 Independence Ave. S.W. 20585; 586-6660. Patricia Fry Godley, assistant secretary designate. Fax, 586-5146.

Responsible for policy, management, and direction of high-risk, long-term research and development in recovering, converting, and using fossil energy, including petroleum, oil shale, and unconventional sources of natural gas.

Energy Dept., Oil and Gas Exploration and Production, 1000 Independence Ave. S.W. 20585; 586-5600. Donald A. Juckett, director. Fax, 586-6221.

Responsible for programs in unconventional oil and gas recovery; studies ways to improve efficiency of oil recovery in depleted reservoirs; coordinates and evaluates research and development among government, universities, and industrial research organizations.

Congress:

See Resources: Oil and Natural Gas, General, Congress (p. 229)

Nongovernmental:

See Resources: Oil and Natural Gas, General, Nongovernmental (p. 230)

Taxation

Agencies:

Internal Revenue Service (Treasury Dept.), Pass Through and Special Industries, Branch 8, 1111 Constitution Ave. N.W., #5314 20224; 622-3130. Jeffrey M. Nelson, chief. Fax, 622-4524.

Administers excise tax programs, including taxes on diesel, gasoline, and special fuels. Advises district offices, internal IRS offices, and general inquirers on tax policy, rules, and regulations.

Treasury Dept., Tax Analysis, Main Treasury Bldg. 20220; 622-1782. Geraldine Gerardi, director, business taxation. Fax, 622-1772.

Develops and provides economic analysis of business taxation policy relating to energy matters, including tax incentives for alternative energy usage and development, gasoline and automobile efficiency taxes, and tax incentives designed to encourage industrial conversion from oil to coal in industrial facilities.

Congress:

See Resources: Oil and Natural Gas, General, Congress (p. 229)

Nongovernmental:

American Petroleum Institute, Taxation Dept., 1220 L St. N.W. 20005; 682-8465. Andy Yood, director. Library, 682-8046. Fax, 682-8049.

Provides information on petroleum taxation. Library open to the public in the afternoon.

See also Resources: Oil and Natural Gas, General, Nongovernmental (p. 230)

Resources: Renewable Energies/Alternative Fuels

See also Natural Resources, General (p. 634)

General

Agencies:

Energy Dept., Alternative Fuels, EE33/MS6B-025 FORS, 1000 Independence Ave. S.W. 20585; 586-9118. Jerry Allsup, director. Fax, 586-8134.

Conducts research on and develops technology for alternative fuels (including alcohol and natural gas fuels) for use in transportation vehicles and construction equipment with gasoline, diesel, and advanced engine designs.

Energy Dept., Utility Technologies, 1000 Independence Ave. S.W. 20585; 586-9275. Robert L. San Martin, deputy assistant secretary. Fax, 586-1640.

Conducts research, development, and deployment activities to facilitate use of renewable energy resources, including solar, wind, photovoltaic, biomass, geothermal, and hydropower.

Energy Dept., Waste Material Management, 1000 Independence Ave. S.W. 20585; #EE222 586-6750. Kurt Sissons, director. Fax, 586-3237.

Conducts research on municipal waste conversion for use as an energy source.

Energy Information Administration (Energy Dept.), Coal, Nuclear, Electric, and Alternate Fuels, 1707 H St. N.W. (mailing address: 1000 Independence Ave. S.W., Washington, DC 20585); 254-6234. John Geidl, director. Fax, 254-5765.

Prepares analyses on the availability, production, costs, processing, transportation, and distribution of uranium and alternative energy supplies, including biomass, solar, wind, waste, wood, and alcohol.

Congress:

General Accounting Office, Energy and Science Issues, 111 Massachusetts Ave. N.W., #201 20001; 512-6866. Gregg A. Fisher, assistant director, energy security and policy. Fax, 512-6880.

Independent, nonpartisan agency in the legislative branch that audits, analyzes, and reports on efficiency and effectiveness of federal energy programs related to renewable energies.

House Banking, Finance, and Urban Affairs Committee, Subcommittee on Housing and Community Development, B303 RHOB 20515; 225-7054. Henry B. Gonzalez, D-Texas, chairman; Nancy Libson, staff director. Fax, 225-4680.

Jurisdiction over legislation on energy conservation measures in housing, including the Solar Bank.

House Energy and Commerce Committee, Subcommittee on Energy and Power, 331 Ford Bldg. (2nd and D Sts. S.W.) 20515; 226-2500. Philip R. Sharp, D-Ind., chairman; Shelley N. Fidler, acting staff director.

Jurisdiction over legislation on regulation, commercialization, and utilization of hydroelectric power, synthetic and alcohol fuels, and renewable energy resources, including wind, solar, and ocean thermal energy.

House Merchant Marine and Fisheries Committee, Subcommittee on Oceanography, Gulf of Mexico, and the Outer Continental Shelf, 575 Ford Bldg. (2nd and D Sts. S.W.) 20515; 226-2460. Solomon P. Ortiz, D-Texas, chairman; Sheila McCready, staff director.

Jurisdiction over legislation concerning the development and conservation of energy and natural resources found in the ocean and the outer continental shelf.

House Natural Resources Committee, Subcommittee on Energy and Mineral Resources, 818 O'Neill Bldg. (300 New Jersey Ave. S.E.) 20515; 225-8331. Richard H. Lehman, D-Calif., chairman; Deborah Lanzone, staff director. Fax, 225-4273.

Jurisdiction over legislation affecting the use of geothermal resources.

House Natural Resources Committee, Subcommittee on Oversight and Investigations, 1328 LHOB 20515; 225-2761. George Miller, D-Calif., chairman; John Lawrence, staff director. Fax, 225-3554.

Jurisdiction over legislation on irrigation and reclamation projects and electrical power marketing administrations.

House Science, Space, and Technology Committee, Subcommittee on Energy, H2390 Ford Bldg. (2nd and D Sts. S.W.) 20515; 225-8056. Marilyn Lloyd, D-Tenn., chair; Francis X. Murray, staff director.

Jurisdiction over Energy Dept. basic research programs, including legislation on research and development of solar, wind, geothermal, and fossil fuel energy (including synthetic fuels such as liquefied and gasified coal), and other nonfossil and nonnuclear energy sources.

Senate Banking, Housing, and Urban Affairs Committee, Subcommittee on Housing and Urban Affairs, SD-535 20510; 224-6348. Paul S. Sarbanes, D-Md., chairman; Paul N. Weech, staff director. Fax, 224-5137.

Jurisdiction over legislation on energy conservation measures in housing, including the Solar Bank.

Senate Commerce, Science, and Transportation Committee, Subcommittee on National Ocean Policy Study, SH-425 (mailing address: SD-508, Washington, DC 20510); 224-4912. Ernest F. Hollings, D-S.C., chairman; Penny Dalton, staff member.

Studies ocean resources development and conservation. (Subcommittee does not report legislation.)

Senate Energy and Natural Resources Committee, Subcommittee on Energy Research and Development, SH-312 20510; 224-7569. Wendell H. Ford, D-Ky., chairman; Vacant, senior professional staff member.

Jurisdiction over legislation on synfuels research and development, including the U.S. Synthetic Fuels Corp.; and over Energy Dept. basic research programs, including research and development of solar, wind, geothermal, and fossil fuel energy (including synthetic fuels such as liquefied and gasified coal), and other advanced energy systems.

Senate Energy and Natural Resources Committee, Subcommittee on Mineral Resources Development and Production, SD-362 20510; 224-7568. Daniel K. Akaka, D-Hawaii, chairman; Lisa Vehmas, counsel.

Jurisdiction over legislation on energy and nonfuel mineral resources.

Senate Energy and Natural Resources Committee, Subcommittee on Renewable Energy, Energy Efficiency, and Competitiveness, SH-212

20510; 224-4756. Jeff Bingaman, D-N.M., chairman; Leslie Black Cordess, professional staff member.

Jurisdiction over legislation on commercialization of new energy technologies, including wind, solar, ocean thermal conversion, and alcohol fuels.

Senate Energy and Natural Resources Committee, Subcommittee on Water and Power, SD-306 20510; 224-6836. Bill Bradley, D-N.J., chairman; Dana Sebren Cooper, counsel.

Jurisdiction over legislation on hydroelectric power, irrigation and reclamation projects, power marketing administrations, and the impact of energy developments on water resources.

Nongovernmental:

Conservation and Renewable Energy Inquiry and Referral Service, P.O. Box 8900, Silver Spring, MD 20907. Sue Ellen Hersh, director. Toll-free, (800) 523-2929.

Provides information on renewable energy and energy conservation; makes referrals to other organizations for technical information on renewable energy resources.

Council on Alternate Fuels, 1110 N. Glebe Rd., #610, Arlington, VA 22201; (703) 276-6655. Michael Koleda, president. Fax, (703) 276-7662.

Membership: companies interested in technologies for converting solid, liquid, and gaseous fossil fuels and biomass into other forms. Interests include coal gasification, combined cycle power generation, and liquid transportation fuels from coal, natural gas, and biomass.

Hearth Products Assn., 1101 Connecticut Ave. N.W., #700 20036; 857-1181. Carter E. Keithley, president. Fax, 223-4579.

Membership: all sectors of the hearth products industry. Sponsors the Hearth Education Foundation, which provides industry training programs on the safe and efficient use of alternative fuels and appliances.

National Independent Energy Producers, 601 13th St. N.W., #320S 20005; 783-2244. Merribel S. Ayres, executive director. Fax, 783-6506.

Membership: companies that generate electricity for sale to utilities and develop cogeneration projects for a variety of users. Membership comprises publicly traded and privately held corporations that represent a broad spectrum of fossil fuel-fired and renewable technologies.

See also Energy Policy, Nongovernmental (p. 207)

See also Edison Electric Institute (p. 221); Electric Power Research Institute (p. 223); Public Citizen, Critical Mass Energy Project (p. 225); World Resources Institute (p. 639)

Alcohol Fuels

Agencies:

Bureau of Alcohol, Tobacco, and Firearms (Treasury Dept.), Distilled Spirits and Tobacco, 650 Massachusetts Ave. N.W. 20226; 927-8210. Robert Mosley, chief. Fax, 927-8602.

Develops guidelines for regional offices responsible for issuing permits for producing gasohol and other ethyl alcohol fuels, whose uses include heating and operating machinery.

Farmers Home Administration (Agriculture Dept.), Business and Industry, 14th St. and Independence Ave. S.W., #6321 20250; 690-4100. Dwight A. Carmon, director. Fax, 690-3803.

Makes loan guarantees to rural businesses, including those seeking to develop alcohol fuels production facilities.

Congress:

See Resources: Renewable Energies/Alternative Fuels, General, Congress (p. 236)

See also Congressional Alcohol Fuels Caucus (p. 755)

Nongovernmental:

American Agriculture Movement, 100 Maryland Ave. N.E. 20002; 544-5750. Ray Chancey, director. Fax, 547-9155. Recorded hotline, 544-6024.

Membership: family farmers and ranchers concerned with government agriculture policy. Interests include alcohol fuel production and use.

American Methanol Institute, 800 Connecticut Ave. N.W., #620 20006; 467-5050. Raymond A. Lewis, president. Fax, 331-9055.

Membership: methanol producers and related industries. Encourages use of methanol fuels and development of chemical-derivative markets. Monitors legislation and regulations.

Renewable Fuels Assn., 1 Massachusetts Ave. N.W. 20001-1431; 289-3835. Eric Vaughn, president.

Membership: companies and state governments involved in developing the domestic ethanol industry. Distributes publications on ethanol performance.

See also Resources: Renewable Energies/Alternative Fuels, General, Nongovernmental (p. 237)

Geothermal Energy

Agencies:

Bureau of Land Management (Interior Dept.), Fluid Minerals, Main Interior Bldg. 20240; 452-0340. Erick Kaarlela, chief. Fax, 208-4800.

Develops and administers federal leasing programs for geothermal energy; evaluates and classifies geothermal resources on federal lands; supervises pre- and postlease operations, including drilling and production phases of geothermal development.

Energy Dept., Geothermal Technology, 1000 Independence Ave. S.W., EE-122, #5H065 20585; 586-5340. John E. Mock, director. Fax, 586-5124.

Responsible for long-range research and technology development of geothermal energy resources.

U.S. Geological Survey (Interior Dept.), Earthquakes, Volcanoes, and Engineering, 12201 Sunrise Valley Dr., Mail Stop 905, Reston, VA 22092; (703) 648-6709. James R. Riehle, deputy, volcano and geothermal research. Fax, (703) 648-6717.

Provides staff support to the U.S. Geological Survey through programs in geothermal research and volcano hazards.

Congress:

See Resources: Renewable Energies/Alternative Fuels, General, Congress (p. 236)

Nongovernmental:

See Resources: Renewable Energies/Alternative Fuels, General, Nongovernmental (p. 237)

Solar, Ocean, and Wind Energy

Agencies:

Energy Dept., Solar Energy Conversion, 1000 Independence Ave. S.W., #EE-13 20585; 586-1720. Robert H. Annan, director. Fax, 586-5127.
Conducts research and development on solar electric power generation to encourage private development of photovoltaic, solar thermal, and biomass power technologies. Collaborates in the commercialization of solar technologies.

Energy Dept., Wind/Hydro/Ocean, 1000 Independence Ave. S.W. 20585; 586-8086. Ronald R. Loose, director. Fax, 586-5124.
Researches and develops small and large wind energy conversion systems and ocean thermal energy conversion systems (primarily to supply electric power). Works to resolve environmental issues that constrain development.

National Oceanic and Atmospheric Administration (Commerce Dept.), Ocean Minerals and Fnergy, 1305 East-West Highway, N/ORM1, Silver Spring, MD 20910, (301) 713-3159, M. Karl Jugel, acting chief. Fax, (301) 713-4009.
Responsible for scientific research on regulatory, developmental, and environmental aspects of deep seabed mining and ocean thermal energy conversion projects.

Congress:

See Resources: Renewable Energies/Alternative Fuels, General, Congress (p. 236)

Nongovernmental:

American Wind Energy Assn., 777 N. Capitol St. N.E., #805 20002; 408-8988. Randall S. Swisher, executive director. Fax, 408-8536.
Membership: manufacturers, developers, operators, and distributors of wind machines; utility companies; and individuals interested in wind energy. Advocates the use of wind energy as an alternative energy source; makes industry data available to the public and to federal and state legislators. Promotes export of wind energy technology.

National Ocean Industries Assn., 1120 G St. N.W., #900 20005; 347-6900. Robert B. Stewart, president. Fax, 347-8650.
Membership: manufacturers, producers, suppliers, and support and service companies involved in marine, offshore, and ocean work. Interests include ocean thermal energy and new energy sources.

Passive Solar Industries Council, 1511 K St. N.W., #600 20005; 628-7400. Helen English, executive director. Fax, 393-5043.
Membership: building industry associations, corporations, small businesses, and independent professionals. Provides information on the passive solar industry and related legislation, regulations, and programs. Publishes guidelines on passive solar design.

Solar Energy Industries Assn., 777 N. Capitol St. N.E., #805 20002; 408-0660. Scott Sklar, director. Fax, 408-8536.
Membership: industries and individuals with interests in the production and use of solar energy. Interests include photovoltaic, solar thermal power, solar hot water, and solar space heating and cooling technologies. Monitors legislation and regulations.

Solartherm, 1315 Apple Ave., Silver Spring, MD 20910; (301) 587-8686. Carl Schleicher, president.
Membership: scientists and scientific organizations. Conducts research and market development activities for low-cost solar energy systems and for alternative energy systems, including high-temperature solar, solid waste, ocean, and wind energy systems.

See also Resources: Renewable Energies/ Alternative Fuels, General, Nongovernmental (p. 237)

Statistics

Agencies:

Bureau of Labor Statistics (Labor Dept.), Energy, 2 Massachusetts Ave. N.E., #3840 20212; 606-7720. Michael Landess, energy analyst. Fax, 606-7753.
Compiles and analyzes statistics for the Producer Price Index on prices, price shifts, and movement of prices for natural gas and petroleum, coal, and electric power.

Energy Information Administration (Energy Dept.), 1000 Independence Ave. S.W. 20585; 586-4361. Jay Hakes, administrator. Fax, 586-0329.

Collects, processes, and publishes data on all energy reserves, financial status of energy-producing companies, production, demand, consumption, and other areas; provides long- and short-term analyses of energy trends and data.

Energy Information Administration (EIA) (Energy Dept.), National Energy Information Center, 1000 Independence Ave. S.W., EI-231 20585; 586-8800. Nancy Nicoletti, chief. Fax, 586-0727.

Catalogs and distributes energy data; acts as a clearinghouse for statistical information on energy; makes referrals for technical information. Reading room of EIA publications open to the public.

Congress:

See Energy Policy, Congress (p. 205)

International Organizations:

European Community Press and Public Affairs, 2100 M St. N.W. 20037; 862-9500. Andreas A. M. van Agt, ambassador; Peter Doyle, director. Information, 862-9542. Press, 862-9540. Fax, 429-1766.

Provides energy statistics on member countries. Library open to the public by appointment.

United Nations Information Centre, 1889 F St. N.W. 20006; 289-8670. Michael Stopford, director. Fax, 289-4267.

Center for reference publications of the United Nations; publications include *World Energy Statistics, Energy Balances and Electricity Profiles,* and other statistical materials on energy. Library open to the public.

Nongovernmental:

American Gas Assn., Statistics, 1515 Wilson Blvd., Arlington, VA 22209; (703) 841-8490. Ellen J. Hahn, director. Fax, (703) 841-8697.

Issues statistics on gas industry, including supply and reserves. Library open to the public by appointment.

American Petroleum Institute, Finance, Accounting, and Statistics, 1220 L St. N.W. 20005; 682-8495. Edward H. Murphy, director. Information, 682-8513. Library, 682-8042. Fax, 962-4730.

Provides statistics on petroleum industry, including data on exports and imports, weekly refinery operations (stock levels, output, and input), drilling activity and costs, taxation, and transportation. Publishes monthly supply-and-demand table for crude oil and weekly statistical bulletin. Library open to the public.

Edison Electric Institute, Statistics, 701 Pennsylvania Ave. N.W. 20004; 508-5583. Thomas R. Daugherty, director. Fax, 508-5380.

Provides statistics on electric utility operations, including the *Statistical Yearbook of the Electric Utility Industry,* which contains data on the capacity, generation, sales, and finances of the electric utility industry.

National Coal Assn., Policy Analysis, 1130 17th St. N.W., 5th Floor 20036; 463-2654. Constance D. Holmes, senior vice president. Fax, 833-9636.

Collects, analyzes, and distributes industry statistics on production, transportation, and consumption of coal.

See also Resources: Coal (p. 214); Electricity (p. 219); Nuclear Energy (p. 223); Oil and Natural Gas (p. 229); Renewable Energies/ Alternative Fuels, Nongovernmental (p. 237).

Key Agencies:

Bureau of Indian Affairs
Interior Dept.
Main Interior Bldg.
18th and C Sts. N.W. 20240
Information: 208-3711

Commission on Civil Rights
624 9th St. N.W. 20425
Information: 376-8364

Consumer Product Safety Commission
4330 East-West Highway, Bethesda, MD
(Mailing address: Washington, DC 20207)
Information: (301) 504-0580

Executive Office
Office for Public Liaison
Old Executive Office Bldg. 20500
Information: 456-2930

Health and Human Services Dept.
Office for Civil Rights
330 Independence Ave. S.W. 20201
Information: 619-0585

Justice Dept.
Civil Rights Division
Main Justice Bldg.
10th St. and Constitution Ave. N.W. 20530
Information: 514-2007

Key Committees:

House Agriculture Committee
1301 LHOB 20515
Phone: 225-2171

House Appropriations Committee
H218 CAP 20515
Phone: 225-2771

House Government Operations Committee
2157 RHOB 20515
Phone: 225-5051

Senate Agriculture, Nutrition, and Forestry Committee
SR-328A 20510
Phone: 224-2035

Senate Appropriations Committee
S128 CAP 20510
Phone: 224-4168

Senate Labor and Human Resources Committee
SD-428 20510
Phone: 224-5375

Key Personnel:

Commission on Civil Rights
Mary Frances Berry, chair

Consumer Product Safety Commission
Ann Brown, chair

Executive Office
Alexis Herman, assistant to the president and director, public liaison

Health and Human Services Dept.
Dennis Hayashi, director, civil rights

Interior Dept.
Ada E. Deer, assistant secretary, Indian affairs

Justice Dept.
Deval Patrick, assistant attorney general, civil rights

6

Advocacy
and Public Service

Contents:

Consumer Affairs

See also Federal and Private Toll-Free Numbers for Emergency and Consumer Use (box, p. 248)

General

Agencies:

Bureau of Labor Statistics (Labor Dept.), Prices and Living Conditions, 2 Massachusetts Ave. N.E. 20212; 606-6960. Kenneth V. Dalton, associate commissioner. Fax, 606-7080.

Collects, processes, analyzes, and disseminates data relating to prices and consumer expenditures; maintains the Consumer Price Index.

Consumer Affairs Council, 1620 L St. N.W., #700 20036; 634-4319. Polly Baca, director; Howard Seltzer, executive secretary. Fax, 634-4135. Main phone is voice and TDD accessible.

Composed of consumer representatives from federal agencies. Reviews consumer policy and provides leadership in improving the management, coordination, and effectiveness of federal agency consumer programs.

Consumer Product Safety Commission, 4330 East-West Highway, Bethesda, MD (mailing address: Washington, DC 20207); (301) 504-0500. Ann Brown, chair. Information, (301) 504-0580. Library, (301) 504-0544. Fax, (301) 504-0124. Product safety hotline, (800) 638-2772. TDD, (800) 638-8270.

Establishes and enforces product safety standards; collects data; studies the causes and prevention of product-related injuries; identifies hazardous products and recalls them from the marketplace. Library open to the public.

Federal Trade Commission, Consumer and Competition Advocacy, 6th St. and Pennsylvania Ave. N.W. 20580; 326-3344. Michael O. Wise, acting director. Fax, 326-3050.

Promotes the interests of consumers by encouraging market competition. Conducts research and advises government agencies and bodies on consumer and competition issues.

General Services Administration, Consumer Information Center, 18th and F Sts. N.W. 20405; 501-1794. Teresa N. Nasif, director. Fax, 501-4281.

Publishes quarterly consumer information catalog that lists free and low-cost federal publications. Copies may be obtained from the Consumer Information Centers, Pueblo, Colo. 81009. Copies also available at Federal Information Centers. *(See Regional Federal Information Sources list, p. 847.)*

U.S. Office of Consumer Affairs (Health and Human Services Dept.), 1620 L St. N.W., #700 20036; 634-9610. Polly Baca, director. Press, 634-4310. Fax, 634-4135. Consumer inquiries, 634-4310.

Coordinates federal consumer programs and serves as a resource center for government agencies; advises state and local governments on administration of consumer programs; assists agencies and businesses in developing consumer complaint mechanisms. Publishes *Consumer's Resource Handbook* and *Consumer News.*

Agency and department consumer contacts:

Agriculture Dept., Consumer Adviser, 14th St. and Independence Ave. S.W. 20250; 720-3975. Bill Wasserman, director. Fax, 690-3100.

Commerce Dept., Consumer Affairs, Main Commerce Bldg., Rm. 5718 20230; 482-5001. Lajuan Johnson, director. Fax, 482-6007.

Commission on Civil Rights, Public Affairs, 624 9th St. N.W. 20425; 376-8312. Charles Rivera, director. Fax, 376-8315. TDD, 376-8116.

Consumer Product Safety Commission, Information and Public Affairs, 4330 East-West Highway, Bethesda, MD (mailing address: Washington, DC 20207); (301) 504-0580. Kathleen Begala, director, public affairs. Fax, (301) 504-0862. Product safety hotline, (800) 638-2772; TDD, (800) 638-8270.

Defense Dept., Personnel Support and Policy Services, The Pentagon 20301-4000; (703) 697-9283. Lt. Col. J. A. Mangual, assistant director. Fax, (703) 697-2519.

Education Dept., Intergovernmental and Interagency Affairs, 400 Maryland Ave. S.W 20202; 401-0404. Ronn Hunt, program specialist. Press, 401-1304. Fax, 401-1971.

Energy Dept., Consumer and Public Liaison 1000 Independence Ave. S.W., PA-2 20585 586-5373. Betty Nolan, director. Fax, 586-0539

Environmental Protection Agency, Public Information Center, 401 M St. S.W., #3404 20460; 260-7751. Alison Cook, director. Fax, 260-6257.

Federal Communications Commission, Public Service, 1919 M St. N.W. 20554; 632-7000. Martha Contee, chief. Fax, 632-0942.

Federal Deposit Insurance Corp., Consumer Affairs, 550 17th St. N.W. 20429; 898-6777. Janice M. Smith, director. Information, 898-3773. Fax, 898-3522. TDD, (800) 898-6726. Toll-free, (800) 934-3342.

Federal Maritime Commission, Informal Inquiries and Complaints, 800 N. Capitol St. N.W. 20573; 523-5807. Joseph Farrell, director. Fax, 523-0014.

Federal Reserve System, Consumer and Community Affairs, 20th and C Sts. N.W. 20551; 452-2631. Griffith L. Garwood, director. Fax, 728-5850. Complaints, 452-3693.

Federal Trade Commission, Consumer Protection, 6th St. and Pennsylvania Ave. N.W. 20580; 326-3238. Christian S. White, acting director. Fax, 326-2050.

Food and Drug Administration (Health and Human Services Dept.), Consumer Affairs, 5600 Fishers Lane, Rockville, MD 20857; (301) 443-5006. Alexander Grant, associate commissioner. Fax, (301) 443-9767. Consumer inquiries, (301) 443-3170.

General Services Administration, Consumer Information Center, 18th and F Sts. N.W. 20405; 501-1794. Teresa N. Nasif, director. Fax, 501-4281.

Health and Human Services Dept., Consumer Affairs, 1620 L St. N.W. 20036; 634-4319. Gina Ley Steiner, consumer contact. Fax, 634-4135. Main phone is voice and TDD accessible.

Interior Dept., Communications, Main Interior Bldg. 20240; 208-6416. Kevin Sweeney, director. Fax, 208-5048.

Interstate Commerce Commission, Compliance and Consumer Assistance, 12th St. and Constitution Ave. N.W. 20423; 927-5500. Bernard Gaillard, director. Fax, 927-5529. TDD, 927-5721.

Justice Dept., Civil Division, 550 11th St. N.W. (mailing address: P.O. Box 386, Washington, DC 20044); 514-6786. Eugene M. Thirolf, director, consumer litigation. Fax, 514-8742.

Labor Dept., 200 Constitution Ave. N.W. 20210; 219-6060. Al Cruz, coordinator, consumer affairs. Fax, 219-8699.

Merit Systems Protection Board, 1120 Vermont Ave. N.W., #900 20419; 653-7126. Michael W. Crum, deputy executive director. TDD, 653-8896.

National Institute of Standards and Technology (Commerce Dept.), Route I-270 and Quince Orchard Rd., Gaithersburg, MD (mailing address: Administrative Bldg., A-47, Gaithersburg, MD 20899); (301) 975-3058. Peggy Saunders, head, publications and program inquiries. Fax, (301) 975-2128. Reference Desk, (301) 975-3052.

Nuclear Regulatory Commission, Public Affairs, 11555 Rockville Pike, Rockville, MD (mailing address: Washington, DC 20555); (301) 504-2240. Elizabeth A. Haydon, coordinator, consumer affairs. Fax, (301) 504-3716.

Postal Rate Commission, Consumer Advocate, 1333 H St. N.W. 20268; 789-6830. Stephen A. Gold, director. Fax, 789-6861.

Securities and Exchange Commission, Filings, Information, and Consumer Services, 450 5th St. N.W. 20549; 272-7440. Wilson Butler, director. Fax, 272-7050.

Small Business Administration, 409 3rd St. S.W. 20416; 205-6931. Mary Ann Fresco, consumer affairs officer. Fax, 205-7416.

State Dept., Economic and Business Affairs, Main State Bldg. 20520; 736-4167. Paul Cleveland, coordinator. Fax, 647-5957.

Transportation Dept., Consumer Affairs, 400 7th St. S.W., #10405 20590; 366-2220. Hoyte Decker, assistant director. Fax, 366-7907.

Treasury Dept., Public Affairs and Public Liaison, Main Treasury Bldg. 20220; 622-2920. Joan Logue-Kinder, assistant secretary designate. Fax, 622-2808.

U.S. Coast Guard (Transportation Dept.), Navigation, Safety, and Waterway Services, 2100 2nd St. S.W. (mailing address: Commandant G-NAB-5, U.S. Coast Guard, Washington, DC 20593); 267-0972. Richard P. Bergen, chief, consumer affairs. Fax, 267-4285. Coast Guard hotline, (800) 368-5647.

U.S. Postal Service, Consumer Affairs, 475 L'Enfant Plaza S.W. 20260; 268-2284. Ann McK. Robinson, consumer advocate. Fax, 268-2304. TDD, 268-2310.

Veterans Affairs Dept., Consumer Affairs, 810 Vermont Ave. N.W. 20420; 535-8962. Rosa Maria Fontanez, director. Fax, 535-8963.

Congress:

House Agriculture Committee, Subcommittee on Department Operations and Nutrition, 1301A LHOB 20515; 225-1496. Charles W. Stenholm, D-Texas, chairman; Stan Ray, staff director.
Jurisdiction over legislation on nutrition issues, research, pesticides, food safety, food stamps, and consumer programs generally.

House Agriculture Committee, Subcommittee on Environment, Credit, and Rural Development, 1430 LHOB 20515; 225-0301. Tim Johnson, D-S.D., chairman; Anne Simmons, staff director.
Jurisdiction over legislation on agriculture credit, including the Farm Credit Administration.

House Agriculture Committee, Subcommittee on Foreign Agriculture and Hunger, 1336 LHOB 20515; 225-1867. Timothy J. Penny, D-Minn., chairman; Jane Shey, staff director.
Jurisdiction over hunger issues generally.

House Agriculture Committee, Subcommittee on Livestock, 1336 LHOB 20515; 225-1867. Harold L. Volkmer, D-Mo., chairman; Tim DeCoster, staff director.
Jurisdiction over legislation concerning inspection of aquacultural species (seafood), dairy products, meats, poultry, and livestock.

House Appropriations Committee, Subcommittee on Agriculture, Rural Development, FDA, and Related Agencies, 2362 RHOB 20515; 225-2638. Richard J. Durbin, D-Ill.,

chairman; Robert B. Foster, staff assistant. Fax, 225-3598.
Jurisdiction over legislation to appropriate funds for the Food and Drug Administration, Food Safety and Inspection Service, and Human Nutrition Information Service.

House Appropriations Committee, Subcommittee on Commerce, Justice, State, and Judiciary, H309 CAP 20515; 225-3351. Neal Smith, D-Iowa, chairman; John Osthaus, staff assistant.
Jurisdiction over legislation to appropriate funds for the Federal Trade Commission.

House Appropriations Committee, Subcommittee on VA, HUD, and Independent Agencies, H143 CAP 20515; 225-3241. Louis Stokes, D-Ohio, chairman; Paul Thompson, staff assistant.
Jurisdiction over legislation to appropriate funds for the Consumer Information Center of the General Services Administration, the Consumer Product Safety Commission, and the U.S. Office of Consumer Affairs of the Health and Human Services Dept.

House Banking, Finance, and Urban Affairs Committee, Subcommittee on Consumer Credit and Insurance, 604 O'Neill Bldg. (300 New Jersey Ave. S.E.) 20515; 225-8872. Joseph P. Kennedy II, D-Mass., chairman; Shawn P. Maher, staff director. Fax, 225-7960.
Jurisdiction over legislation on consumer protection, including fair lending and regulatory issues.

House Energy and Commerce Committee, Subcommittee on Commerce, Consumer Protection, and Competitiveness, 151 Ford Bldg. (2nd and D Sts. S.W.) 20515; 226-3160. Cardiss Collins, D-Ill., chairman; David Schooler, staff director.
Jurisdiction over product liability and consumer protection legislation, the Consumer Product Safety Commission, and interstate and foreign commerce, including general trade matters within the jurisdiction of the full committee.

House Energy and Commerce Committee, Subcommittee on Health and the Environment, 2415 RHOB 20515; 225-4952. Henry A. Waxman, D-Calif., chairman; Karen Nelson, staff director.
Jurisdiction over legislation on vaccines; labeling and packaging, including tobacco products

and alcoholic beverages; and the use of vitamins. Oversight of the Food and Drug Administration.

House Energy and Commerce Committee, Subcommittee on Transportation and Hazardous Materials, 324 Ford Bldg. (2nd and D Sts. S.W.) 20515; 225-9304. Al Swift, D-Wash., chairman; Arthur Endres, staff director and chief counsel.

Jurisdiction over legislation affecting the regulation of commercial practices and the Federal Trade Commission.

House Government Operations Committee, Subcommittee on Commerce, Consumer, and Monetary Affairs, B377 RHOB 20515; 225-4407. John M, Spratt Jr., D-S.C., chairman; Theodore Jacobs, staff director. Fax, 225-2441.

Oversight of the Federal Trade Commission, Consumer Product Safety Commission, and Bureau of Alcohol, Tobacco, and Firearms.

House Government Operations Committee, Subcommittee on Human Resources and Intergovernmental Relations, B372 RHOB 20515; 225-2548. Edolphus Towns, D-N.Y., chairman; Ron Stroman, staff director. Fax, 225-2382.

Oversees government food and consumer services, including the Food and Nutrition Service and the Food Safety and Inspection Service.

House Science, Space, and Technology Committee, Subcommittee on Science, 2319 RHOB 20515; 225-8844. Rick Boucher, D-Va., chairman; Grace L. Ostenso, staff director.

Jurisdiction over legislation related to the U.S. Fire Administration and Building and Fire Research Laboratory of the National Institute of Standards and Technology; oversight of federal fire prevention and the Earthquake Hazards Reduction Act. Jurisdiction over research and development involving government nutritional programs.

Senate Agriculture, Nutrition, and Forestry Committee, Subcommittee on Agricultural Credit, SR-328A 20510; 224-2035. Kent Conrad, D-N.D., chairman; Kevin Price, legislative assistant.

Jurisdiction over legislation on agricultural credit, including the Farm Credit Administration, the Farm Credit System, and the Farmers Home Administration.

Senate Agriculture, Nutrition, and Forestry Committee, Subcommittee on Agricultural Research, Conservation, Forestry, and General Legislation, SR-328A 20510; 224-2035. Tom Daschle, D-S.D., chairman; Tom Buis, legislative assistant.

Jurisdiction over legislation on inspection and certification of meat, flowers, fruits, vegetables, and livestock.

Senate Agriculture, Nutrition, and Forestry Committee, Subcommittee on Nutrition and Investigations, SR-328A 20510; 224-2035. Tom Harkin, D-Iowa, chairman; Mark Halverson, legislative assistant.

Jurisdiction over legislation on food, nutrition, and hunger.

Senate Appropriations Committee, Subcommittee on Agriculture, Rural Development, and Related Agencies, SD-140 20510; 224-7240. Dale Bumpers, D-Ark., chairman; Rocky L. Kuhn, clerk.

Jurisdiction over legislation to appropriate funds for the Food and Drug Administration; the Food Safety and Inspection Service and the Human Nutrition Information Service (of the Agriculture Dept.); and other consumer-related services and programs.

Senate Appropriations Committee, Subcommittee on Commerce, Justice, State, and Judiciary, S146A CAP 20510; 224-7277. Ernest F. Hollings, D-S.C., chairman; Scott B. Gudes, clerk.

Jurisdiction over legislation to appropriate funds for the Federal Trade Commission.

Senate Appropriations Committee, Subcommittee on VA, HUD, and Independent Agencies, SD-142 20510; 224-7211. Barbara A. Mikulski, D-Md., chair; Kevin F. Kelly, clerk.

Jurisdiction over legislation to appropriate funds for the Consumer Information Center of the General Services Administration, the Consumer Product Safety Commission, and the U.S. Office of Consumer Affairs.

Senate Banking, Housing, and Urban Affairs Committee, SD-534 20510; 224-7391. Donald W. Riegle Jr., D-Mich., chairman; Steven Harris, staff director.

Jurisdiction over legislation on consumer protection, including the Community Reinvestment

Federal and Private Toll-Free Numbers...

Departments

Agriculture
Meat and poultry safety inquiries .... (800) 535-4555; 720-3333 in Washington, D.C.

Commerce
Export counseling .... (800) 872-8723; (410) 962-3560 in Maryland and Washington, D.C.

Defense
Army espionage hotline .... (800) 225-5779

Education
Student financial aid info. .... (800) 433-3243

Energy
Renewable energy conservation info. ...... (800) 523-2929

Health and Human Services
AIDS info. .... (800) 342-2437; 332-2437 in Washington, D.C. Spanish speaking, (800) 344-7432; 328-0697 in Washington, D.C.; TDD, (800) 243-7889
Cancer info. .... (800) 422-6237
Civil rights info. .... (800) 368-1019; 863-0100 in Washington, D.C.
General health info. .... (800) 336-4797
Medicare hotline .... (800) 638-6833
National Runaway Switchboard .... (800) 621-4000
Social Security benefits info. .... (800) 772-1213

Housing and Urban Development
Housing discrimination hotline .... (800) 669-9777; TDD, (800) 927-9275

Justice
Juvenile justice info. .... (800) 638-8736; (301) 251-5500 in Maryland
Racial, religious, and sexual preference
disputes hotline .... (800) 347-4283

Transportation
Airline safety hotline .... (800) 322-7873; 267-8592 in Washington, D.C.
Auto safety hotline .... (800) 424-9393; 366-0123 in Washington, D.C.
Hazardous material, chemical, and oil spills (800) 424-8802 [a]; 426-2675 in Washington, D.C.

Treasury
Drug smuggling reports .... (800) 232-5378
Explosive materials discovery,
theft, loss reports .... (800) 800-3855; 927-7777 in Washington, D.C.
Tax form requests .... (800) 829-3676
Tax refund info. .... (800) 829-4477
Taxpayer assistance .... (800) 829-1040; (410) 962-2590 in Baltimore, Md.

Agencies

Consumer Product Safety Commission
Product safety info. .... (800) 638-2772

Environmental Protection Agency
Safe drinking water hotline .... (800) 426-4791
Hazardous waste and cleanup info. .... (800) 424-9346; (703) 412-9810 in Washington, D.C., area
Pesticides and related medical info. ...... (800) 858-7378

Export-Import Bank
Export finance hotline .... (800) 424-5201; 566-8860 in Washington, D.C.

... for Emergency and Consumer Use

Federal Deposit Insurance Corp.
Banking complaints and inquiries .... (800) 934-3342; 898-3536 in Washington, D.C.

Federal Election Commission
Political fundraising laws info. .... (800) 424-9530; 219-3420 in Washington, D.C.

Federal Emergency Management Agency
Crime insurance service .... (800) 638-8780; (301) 251-1660 in Washington, D.C., area
Emergency management and training info. (800) 638-1821[b]; (301) 447-1032 in Maryland
Flood insurance service .... (800) 638-6620

National Archives and Records Administration
Audiovisual material sales and info. ...... (800) 788-6282; (301) 763-1896 in Maryland

Nuclear Regulatory Commission
Nuclear power info. .... (800) 368-5642[b,c,d]; (301) 492-7000 in Maryland

Office of Special Counsel
Prohibited personnel practices info. .... (800) 872-9855; 653-7188 in Washington, D.C.

Small Business Administration
Small business assistance .... (800) 827-5722; 606-4000 in Washington, D.C.

Veterans Benefits Administration
Debt management hotline .... (800) 027-0648
Insurance hotline .... (800) 669-8477
Radiation hotline .... (800) 827-0365

Private Organizations

Agent Orange Veterans Payment Program .... (800) 225-4712

GED Hotline on Adult Education .... (800) 626-9433

International Service Agencies
Overseas charities info. .... (800) 638-8079; (301) 881-2468 in Maryland

National Center for Missing and Exploited Children .... (800) 843-5678

National Insurance Consumer Helpline . (800) 942-4242

National Literacy Hotline .... (800) 228-8813

National Organ Procurement and Transplantation Network .... (800) 243-6667

National Organization for Victim Assistance .... (800) 879-6682; 232-6682 in Washington, D.C.

---

[a] May not be called from Washington, D.C.

[b] May not be called from Puerto Rico and the Virgin Islands

[c] May not be called from Hawaii

[d] May not be called from Alaska

Act and the Fair Credit Reporting Act, and regulatory oversight issues.

Senate Commerce, Science, and Transportation Committee, SD-508 20510; 224-5115. Ernest F. Hollings, D-S.C., chairman; Kevin Curtin, chief counsel and staff director.

Jurisdiction over regulation of consumer products and services, including testing related to toxic substances. Jurisdiction over legislation related to the U.S. Fire Administration and the Building and Fire Research Laboratory of the National Institute of Standards and Technology; oversight of federal fire prevention and the Earthquake Hazards Reduction Act.

Senate Commerce, Science, and Transportation Committee, Subcommittee on the Consumer, SH-227 (mailing address: SD-508, Washington, DC 20510); 224-0415. Richard H. Bryan, D-Nev., chairman; Moses Boyd, senior counsel.

Jurisdiction over legislation on the Federal Trade Commission, the Consumer Product Safety Commission, the National Traffic Safety Administration, and the U.S. Fire Administration. Jurisdiction over product safety and liability; flammable products; insurance; and labeling and packaging legislation, including advertising and packaging of tobacco products and alcoholic beverages.

Senate Labor and Human Resources Committee, SD-428 20510; 224-5375. Edward M. Kennedy, D-Mass., chairman; Nick Littlefield, chief counsel and staff director.

Jurisdiction over legislation on vaccines, drug labeling and packaging, inspection and certification of fish and processed food, and the use of vitamins.

Nongovernmental:

Automotive Consumer Action Program, 8400 Westpark Dr., McLean, VA 22102; (703) 821-7144. Deborah M. Hopkins, manager, consumer affairs. Fax, (703) 821-7075.

Third-party mediation program that promotes national standards and procedures in resolving auto dealer/manufacturer and consumer disputes.

Center for Auto Safety, 2001 S St. N.W. 20009; 328-7700. Clarence M. Ditlow III, executive director.

Public interest organization that receives written consumer complaints against auto manufac-

turers; monitors federal agencies responsible for regulating and enforcing auto and highway safety rules.

Center for Study of Responsive Law, 1530 P St. N.W. (mailing address: P.O. Box 19367, Washington, DC 20036); 387-8030. John Richard, administrator.

Consumer interest clearinghouse that conducts research and holds conferences on public interest law. Interests include white-collar crime, the environment, occupational health and safety, the postal system, banking deregulation, insurance, freedom of information policy, and broadcasting.

Citizen Action, 1120 19th St. N.W., #630 20036; 775-1580. Ira Arlook, president. Fax, 296-4054.

Coalition of statewide citizens' groups working for state and national legislative reform. Interests include health care, insurance reform, global warming, energy policy, and toxics right-to-know. Monitors legislation and regulations.

Commission for the Advancement of Public Interest Organizations, P.O. Box 53424, Washington, DC 20009; 462-0505. Samuel Epstein, staff contact.

Seeks to enlarge the constituency and capabilities of public interest movements. Acts as clearinghouse for public interest groups, for citizens seeking help on community problems, and for government agencies seeking to increase citizen participation in their programs.

Consumer Federation of America, 1424 16th St. N.W., #604 20036; 387-6121. Stephen Brobeck, executive director.

Federation of national, regional, state, and local proconsumer organizations. Promotes consumer interests in banking, credit, and insurance; telecommunications; housing; food, drugs, and medical care; safety; energy and natural resources development; and indoor air quality.

Consumers Union of the United States, 1666 Connecticut Ave. N.W., #310 20009-1039; 462-6262. Mark Silbergeld, director, Washington office. Fax, 265-9548.

Consumer advocacy group that represents consumer interests before Congress and regulatory agencies and litigates consumer affairs cases involving the government. Publishes *Consumer Reports* magazine. (Headquarters in Yonkers, N.Y.)

Council of Better Business Bureaus, Alternative Dispute Resolution, 4200 Wilson Blvd., #800, Arlington, VA 22203; (703) 247-9361. Robert E. Gibson, senior vice president. Fax, (703) 276-0634.

Administers mediation and arbitration programs through Better Business Bureaus nationwide to assist in resolving disputes between businesses and consumers. Assists with unresolved disputes between car owners and automobile manufacturers. Maintains pools of certified arbitrators nationwide. Provides mediation training.

National Assn. of Consumer Agency Administrators, 1010 Vermont Ave. N.W., #514 20005; 347-7395. Susan Grant, executive director. Fax, 347-2563.

Membership: state and local government consumer affairs professionals. Seeks to enhance consumer services available to the public. Acts as a clearinghouse for consumer information and legislation. Serves as liaison with federal agencies and Congress. Offers training programs, seminars, and conferences.

National Consumers League, 815 15th St. N.W., #928N 20005; 639-8140. Linda F. Golodner, president. Fax, 737-2164. TDD, 737-5084.

Citizens' interest group that engages in research and educational activities related to consumer issues. Interests include health care; child labor; food, drug, and product safety; environment; telecommunications; and financial services.

National Insurance Consumer Organization, 121 N. Payne St., Alexandria, VA (mailing address: P.O. Box 15492, Alexandria, VA 22309); (703) 549-8050. Kathleen O'Reilly, policy director. Fax, (703) 360-9211.

Public interest organization that conducts research and provides consumers with information on buying insurance. Interests include auto, homeowner, renter, life, and health insurance.

Public Citizen, 2000 P St. N.W. 20036; 833-3000. Joan Claybrook, president.

Public interest consumer advocacy organization comprising the following projects: Buyers Up, Congress Watch, Critical Mass Energy Project, Health Research Group, and Litigation Group.

Trial Lawyers for Public Justice, 1625 Massachusetts Ave. N.W., #100 20036; 797-8600.

Arthur Bryant, executive director. Fax, 232-7203.

Membership: consumer activists, trial lawyers, and public interest lawyers. Litigates to influence corporate and government decisions about products or activities adversely affecting health or safety. Interests include toxic torts, environmental protection, civil rights and civil liberties, workers' safety, consumer protection, and the preservation of the civil justice system.

U.S. Chamber of Commerce, Legal and Regulatory Affairs, 1615 H St. N.W., #517 20062; 463-5513. Tyler J. Wilson, attorney. Fax, 887-3445.

Monitors legislation and regulations regarding business and consumer issues, including legislation and policies affecting the Federal Trade Commission, the Consumer Product Safety Commission, and other agencies.

U.S. Public Interest Research Group (USPIRG), 215 Pennsylvania Ave. S.E. 20003; 546-9707. Gene Karpinski, executive director. Fax, 546-2461.

Conducts research and advocacy on consumer and environmental issues, including telephone rates, banking practices, insurance, campaign finance reform, product safety, toxic and solid waste, safe drinking water, and energy; monitors private and governmental actions affecting consumers; supports efforts to challenge consumer fraud and illegal business practices. Serves as national office for state groups.

See also Administration of Justice, General, Nongovernmental, for public interest law groups (p. 493)

Advertising

Agencies:

Bureau of Alcohol, Tobacco, and Firearms (Treasury Dept.), Compliance Operations, 650 Massachusetts Ave. N.W. (mailing address: Washington, DC 20226); 927-8710. Arthur Libertucci, associate director. Information, 927-7777.

Regulates the advertising of alcoholic beverages and the labeling and size of alcoholic beverage containers; authorized to refer violations to Justice Dept. for criminal prosecution.

Comptroller of the Currency (Treasury Dept.), Law Dept., 250 E St. S.W. 20219; 874-5200.

William P. Bowden Jr., chief counsel. Library, 874-4720. Fax, 874-5374.

Enforces regulations concerning advertising by nationally chartered banks; may issue cease-and-desist orders.

Federal Highway Administration (Transportation Dept.), Right of Way, 400 7th St. S.W. 20590; 366-0342. Barbara K. Orski, director. Fax, 366-3713.

Administers laws concerning outdoor advertising and junkyards along interstate and federally aided primary highways.

Federal Reserve System, Consumer and Community Affairs, 20th and C Sts. N.W. 20551; 452-2631. Griffith L. Garwood, director. Fax, 728-5850. Complaints, 452-3693.

Receives consumer complaints concerning advertising by state-chartered banks that are members of the Federal Reserve System and refers them to district banks.

Federal Trade Commission, Advertising Practices, 6th St. and Pennsylvania Ave. N.W. 20580; 326-3090. C. Lee Peeler, associate director. Fax, 326-3259.

Monitors advertising claims of products for validity; investigates allegations of deceptive advertising practices; handles complaints from consumers, public interest groups, businesses, and Congress regarding the truthfulness and fairness of advertising practices. Enforces statutes and rules preventing misrepresentations in print and broadcast advertising.

Food and Drug Administration (Health and Human Services Dept.), Drug Marketing, Advertising, and Communications, 5600 Fishers Lane, HFD-240, Rockville, MD 20857; (301) 594-6824. Janet L. Rose, acting director. Fax, (301) 594-6771.

Monitors prescription drug advertising and labeling; investigates complaints; conducts market research on health care communications and drug issues.

Office of Thrift Supervision (Treasury Dept.), Consumer Programs, 1700 G St. N.W. 20552; 906-6238. Gilda Morse, manager. Fax, 906-7494. Consumer complaints, (800) 842-6929.

Investigates consumer complaints of false and deceptive advertising by federally insured savings and loan associations.

Congress:

See Consumer Affairs, General, Congress (p. 246)

Nongovernmental:

American Advertising Federation, 1101 Vermont Ave. N.W., #500 20005; 898-0089. Wallace Snyder, president. Fax, 898-0159.

Membership: advertising companies (ad agencies, advertisers, media, and services), clubs, associations, and college chapters. A founder of the National Advertising Review Board, a self-regulatory body. Sponsors annual awards for outstanding advertising.

American Assn. of Advertising Agencies, 1899 L St. N.W. 20036; 331-7345. John Kamp, senior vice president, Washington office. Fax, 857-3675.

Cosponsors the National Advertising Review Board (a self-regulatory body), the Advertising Council, and the Media/Advertising Partnership for a Drug Free America; monitors legislation and regulations. (Headquarters in New York.)

Assn. of National Advertisers, 1725 K St. N.W. 20006; 785-1525. Daniel L. Jaffe, executive vice president. Fax, 659-3711.

Cosponsors the National Advertising Review Board, a self-regulatory body; monitors legislation and regulations. (Headquarters in New York.)

Center for the Study of Commercialism, 1875 Connecticut Ave. N.W., #300 20009-5728; 332-9110. Michael Jacobson, co-founder. Fax, 265-4954.

Studies and opposes the adverse effects of advertising and commercialism on American culture.

Council of Better Business Bureaus, Advertising Review, 4200 Wilson Blvd., #800, Arlington, VA 22203; (703) 276-0100. Cassie Redmond, director, public affairs. Fax, (703) 525-8277.

Membership: businesses and better business bureaus in the United States and Canada. Promotes ethical business practices and issues industry guidelines on advertising. Conducts programs that promote truth in advertising.

Direct Marketing Assn., 1101 17th St. N.W., #705 20036; 347-1222. Lorna Christie, vice president, ethics and consumer affairs. Fax, 785-2231.

Membership: telemarketers; users, creators, and producers of direct mail; and suppliers to the industry. Conducts research and promotes knowledge and use of direct response marketing. Handles consumer complaints about telephone and mail-order purchases. Operates a mail preference service, which removes consumer names from unwanted mailing lists, and a telephone preference service, which helps consumers handle unsolicited telephone sales calls. (Headquarters in New York.)

Outdoor Advertising Assn. of America, 1850 M St. N.W., #1040 20036; 833-5566. Nancy Fletcher, president. Fax, 833-1522.

Membership: outdoor advertising companies, operators, suppliers, and affiliates. Serves as a clearinghouse for public service advertising campaigns; monitors legislation and regulations.

State Advertising Coalition, 1899 L St. N.W., #700 20036; 296-6395. Maureen Riehl, executive director. Fax, 296 6396.

Coalition of the American Advertising Federation, the American Assn. of Advertising Agencies, and the Assn. of National Advertisers. Monitors state and local legislation and regulation of advertising and public relations.

Alcohol

See also Health, Substance Abuse (p. 338); Transportation: Motor Vehicle, Safety (p. 727)

Agencies:

Bureau of Alcohol, Tobacco, and Firearms (Treasury Dept.), Compliance Operations, 650 Massachusetts Ave. N.W. (mailing address: Washington, DC 20226); 927-8710. Arthur Libertucci, associate director. Information, 927-7777.

Regulates labeling of and enforces taxation of alcoholic beverages.

Congress:

See Consumer Affairs, General, Congress (p. 246)

Nongovernmental:

Beer Institute, 1225 Eye St. N.W., #825 20005; 737-2337. Ray McGrath, president. Fax, 737-7004.

Membership: domestic and international brewers and suppliers to the domestic brewing industry. Monitors legislation and regulations.

Center for Science in the Public Interest, 1875 Connecticut Ave. N.W., #300 20009-5728; 332-9110. Michael Jacobson, executive director. Fax, 265-4954.

Concerned with policy on alcohol, particularly with the marketing, labeling, and taxation of alcoholic beverages.

Distilled Spirits Council of the United States, 1250 Eye St. N.W., #900 20005; 628-3544. F. A. Meister, president. Fax, 682-8888.

Membership: manufacturers and marketers of liquor sold in the United States. Provides consumer information on alcohol-related issues and topics. Monitors legislation and regulations.

Licensed Beverage Information Council, 1225 Eye St. N.W., #500 20005; 682-4776. Monita W. Fontaine, executive director. Fax, 682-4707.

Membership: alcoholic beverage industry associations. Conducts multimedia programs in conjunction with government agencies for health care professionals and the public on alcoholism, drinking and pregnancy, teenage alcohol abuse, and drunk driving. Sponsors educational programs on alcohol-related issues.

National Alcoholic Beverage Control Assn., 4216 King St. West, Alexandria, VA 22302; (703) 578-4200. James M. Sgueo, executive director. Fax, (703) 820-3551.

Membership: distilleries, trade associations, and state agencies that control the purchase, distribution, and sale of alcoholic beverages. Monitors legislation and regulations.

National Assn. of Beverage Retailers, 5101 River Rd., #108, Bethesda, MD 20816; (301) 656-1494. John B. Burcham Jr., executive director. Fax, (301) 656-7539.

Membership: state associations of on- and off-premise licensees. Monitors legislation and regulations affecting the alcoholic beverage industry.

National Assn. of State Alcohol and Drug Abuse Directors, 444 N. Capitol St. N.W., #642

20001; 783-6868. William Butynski, executive director. Fax, 783-2704.
Provides information on treatment and prevention of alcohol abuse.

National Beer Wholesalers Assn., 1100 S. Washington St., Alexandria, VA 22314-4494; (703) 683-4300. Ronald A. Sarasin, president. Fax, (703) 683-8965.
Sponsors programs on preventing alcohol abuse; monitors legislation and regulations for family-owned and family-operated beer distributors.

National Licensed Beverage Assn., 4214 King St. West, Alexandria, VA 22302-1507; (703) 671-7575. Debra A. Leach, executive director. Fax, (703) 845-0310.
Membership: bars, taverns, restaurants, cocktail lounges, stores, and hotels that sell alcoholic beverages. Sponsors program that trains bartenders, waiters, and waitresses to deal with alcohol abusers.

Wine and Spirits Wholesalers of America, 1023 15th St. N.W., #400 20005; 371-9792. Douglas W. Metz, managing director. Fax, 789-2405.
Membership: wholesale distributors of domestic and imported wine and distilled spirits. Provides information on drinking awareness.

See also National Wine Coalition and Wine Institute (p. 599)

Consumer Education

Most department and agency consumer offices sponsor consumer education programs and provide informational materials and publications. See list of agency and department consumer contacts beginning on p. 244.

Agencies:

Agriculture Dept., Food Safety and Inspection Service, 14th St. and Independence Ave. S.W. 20250; 690-0351. Marjorie Davidson, director, public awareness. Information, 720-9113. Fax, 720-9063. Toll-free hotline, (800) 535-4555; in Washington, D.C., 720-3333.
Sponsors food safety educational programs to inform the public about measures to prevent foodborne illnesses; sponsors lectures, publications, public service advertising campaigns, exhibits, and audiovisual presentations. Toll-free hotline answers food safety questions.

Agriculture Dept., Science and Education, 14th St. and Independence Ave. S.W. 20250; 720-5923. R. D. Plowman, acting assistant secretary. Fax, 690-2842.
Coordinates agricultural research, extension, and teaching programs in the food and agricultural sciences, including human nutrition, home economics, consumer services, agricultural economics, environmental quality, natural and renewable resources, forestry and range management, animal and plant production and protection, aquaculture, and the processing, distribution, marketing, and utilization of food and agricultural products.

Consumer Product Safety Commission (CPSC), Information and Public Affairs, 4330 East-West Highway, Bethesda, MD (mailing address: Washington, DC 20207); (301) 504-0580. Kathleen Begala, director, public affairs. Fax, (301) 504-0862. Product safety hotline, (800) 638-2772; TDD, (800) 638-8270.
Provides information concerning consumer product safety; works with local and state governments, school systems, and private groups to develop product safety information and education programs. Toll-free hotline accepts consumer complaints on hazardous products and injuries associated with a product and offers recorded information on product recalls and CPSC safety recommendations.

Federal Trade Commission (FTC), Consumer and Business Education, 6th St. and Pennsylvania Ave. N.W. 20580; 326-3268. Irene M. Vawter, assistant director. Fax, 326-2050. TDD, 326-2502.
Develops educational material about FTC activities for consumers and businesses.

Food and Drug Administration (FDA) (Health and Human Services Dept.), Consumer Affairs, 5600 Fishers Lane, Rockville, MD 20857; (301) 443-5006. Alexander Grant, associate commissioner. Fax, (301) 443-9767. Consumer inquiries, (301) 443-3170.
Responds to inquiries on issues related to the FDA. Conducts consumer health education programs for specific groups, including women, the elderly, and the educationally and economically disadvantaged. Serves as liaison with national health and consumer organizations.

Health and Human Services Dept., Consumer Affairs, 1620 L St. N.W. 20036; 634-4319. Howard Seltzer, director, policy. Fax, 634-4135. Main phone is voice and TDD accessible.

Works with federal agencies, educational organizations, and the private sector to develop consumer education programs.

Congress:

See Consumer Affairs, General, Congress (p. 246)

Nongovernmental:

American Home Economics Assn., 1555 King St., Alexandria, VA 22314; (703) 706-4600. Mary Jane Kolar, executive director. Fax, (703) 706-4663.

Membership: professional home economists. Monitors legislation and regulations concerning family and consumer issues. Supports consumer and homemaking education.

See also Consumer Affairs, General, Nongovernmental (p. 250)

Credit Practices

See also Housing: Finance (p. 395)

Agencies:

Comptroller of the Currency (Treasury Dept.), Compliance Management, 250 E St. S.W. 20219; 874-5216. Stephen Cross, deputy comptroller. Fax, 874-5221.

Develops policy for enforcing consumer laws and regulations that affect national banks, including the Truth-in-Lending, Community Reinvestment, and Equal Credit Opportunity acts.

Comptroller of the Currency (Treasury Dept.), Economic Analysis and Public Affairs, 250 E St. S.W. 20219; 874-4910. Konrad S. Alt, senior deputy comptroller.

Oversees the agency's economic research and analysis program and provides policy advice on issues relating to community development. Advises the comptroller on relations with the media, the banking industry, Congress, and consumer and community development groups.

Comptroller of the Currency (Treasury Dept.), Law Dept., 250 E St. S.W. 20219; 874-5200. William P. Bowden Jr., chief counsel. Library, 874-4720. Fax, 874-5374.

Enforces and oversees compliance by nationally chartered banks with laws prohibiting discrimi-

nation in credit transactions on the basis of sex or marital status.

Federal Deposit Insurance Corp., Consumer Affairs, 550 17th St. N.W. 20429; 898-6777. Janice M. Smith, director. Information, 898-3773. Fax, 898-3522. TDD, (800) 898-6726. Toll-free, (800) 934-3342.

Coordinates and monitors complaints filed by consumers against federally insured state banks that are not members of the Federal Reserve System; handles complaints concerning truth-in-lending and other fair credit provisions, including charges of discrimination on the basis of sex or marital status; responds to general banking inquiries; answers questions on deposit insurance coverage.

Federal Deposit Insurance Corp., Supervision and Resolutions, 550 17th St. N.W. 20429; 898-6849. John W. Stone, executive director. Fax, 898-3772.

Examines and supervises federally insured state banks that are not members of the Federal Reserve System for violations of truth-in-lending and other fair credit provisions.

Federal Reserve System, Consumer and Community Affairs, 20th and C Sts. N.W. 20551; 452-2631. Griffith L. Garwood, director. Fax, 728-5850. Complaints, 452-3693.

Receives consumer complaints concerning truth-in-lending, fair credit billing, equal credit opportunity, electronic fund transfer, home mortgage disclosure, and consumer leasing acts; receives complaints about unregulated practices; refers complaints to district banks. The Federal Reserve monitors enforcement of fair lending laws with regard to state-chartered banks that are members of the Federal Reserve System.

Federal Trade Commission, Credit Practices, 601 Pennsylvania Ave. N.W. 20580; 326-3224. David Medine, associate director. Fax, 326-3259. TDD, 326-2502.

Enforces truth-in-lending and fair credit billing provisions for creditors not handled by other agencies, such as retail stores and small loan companies; enforces the Fair Credit Reporting Act, which protects consumers from unfair credit ratings and practices; enforces the Fair Debt Collection Practices Act, Electronic Funds Transfer Act, Equal Credit Opportunity Act, Consumer Leasing Act, Holder in Due Course Rule, and Credit Practices Rule.

Justice Dept., Civil Division, 550 11th St. N.W. (mailing address: P.O. Box 386, Washington, DC 20044); 514-6786. Eugene M. Thirolf, director, consumer litigation. Fax, 514-8742.

Files suits to enforce the Truth-in-Lending Act and other federal statutes protecting consumers, generally upon referral by client agencies.

National Credit Union Administration, Examination and Insurance, 1775 Duke St., Alexandria, VA 22314-3428; (703) 518-6360. D. Michael Riley, director. Fax, (703) 518-6569. Toll-free investment hotline, (800) 755-5999.

Oversees and enforces compliance by federally chartered credit unions with the Truth-in-Lending Act, the Equal Credit Opportunity Act, and other federal statutes protecting consumers.

Office of Thrift Supervision (Treasury Dept.), Consumer Programs, 1700 G St. N.W. 20552; 906-6238. Gilda Morse, manager. Fax, 906-7494. Consumer complaints, (800) 842-6929.

Receives and processes complaints filed against savings and loan institutions, including charges of discrimination against minorities and women.

Small Business Administration, Civil Rights Compliance, 409 3rd St. S.W. 20416; 205-6751. J. Arnold Feldman, chief. Fax, 205-7064. TDD, 205-7150.

Reviews complaints against the Small Business Administration by recipients of its assistance in cases of alleged discrimination in credit transactions; monitors recipients for civil rights compliance.

Congress:

See Consumer Affairs, General, Congress (p. 246)

Nongovernmental:

American Bankers Assn., Communications, 1120 Connecticut Ave. N.W. 20036; 663-7501. Virginia Dean, executive director. Library, 663-5040. Fax, 296-9258.

Provides information on credit, truth-in-lending laws, other fair credit provisions, and financial management issues. Library open to the public by appointment.

American Financial Services Assn., 919 18th St. N.W. 20006; 296-5544. Lana R. Batts, president. Fax, 223-0321.

Membership: consumer installment credit industry including consumer finance, sales finance, and industrial banking companies. Conducts research, provides consumer finance education, and monitors legislation and regulations.

Bankcard Holders of America, 6862 Elm St., #300, McLean, VA 22101; (703) 917-9805. Elgie Holstein, director.

Consumer advocacy and educational organization that educates its members and the public about credit and consumer credit rights. Maintains speakers bureau and toll-free consumer credit dispute hotline for members; provides credit and financial referral service, credit card protection information, and lists of banks offering no annual fee, low interest rate, and secured credit cards. Publishes materials on consumer credit. Testifies before Congress and state legislatures on consumer credit issues.

National Foundation for Consumer Credit, 8611 2nd Ave., #100, Silver Spring, MD 20910; (301) 589-5600. Durant Abernethy, president. Toll-free, (800) 388-2227. Fax, (301) 495-5623.

Membership: financial institutions, labor unions, religious groups, finance companies, retail stores, social service organizations, and academics. Establishes nationwide credit counseling centers to educate families about proper budgeting and to assist families with financial difficulties.

National Retail Federation, 701 Pennsylvania Ave. N.W., #710 20004; 783-7971. Michael Altier, vice president. Fax, 737-2849.

Membership: national and state associations of retailers and major retail corporations. Provides information on credit, truth-in-lending laws, and other fair credit practices.

See also Consumer Affairs, General, Nongovernmental (p. 250)

Fire Prevention and Control

See also Consumer Affairs, Flammable Products (p. 257)

Agencies:

Federal Emergency Management Agency, National Fire Academy, 16825 S. Seton Ave., Emmitsburg, MD 21727; (301) 447-1117. James

F. Coyle, acting superintendent. Fax, (301) 447-1178.

Trains fire officials and related professionals in fire prevention and management, current firefighting technologies, and the administration of fire prevention organizations.

Forest Service (Agriculture Dept.), Fire and Aviation Management, 201 14th St. S.W. (mailing address: P.O. Box 96090, Washington, DC 20090); 205-1483. Mary Jo Lavin, acting director. Fax, 205-1272.

Responsible for aviation and fire management programs, including fire control planning and prevention, suppression of fires, and the use of prescribed fires. Provides state foresters with financial and technical assistance for fire protection in forests and on rural lands.

National Institute of Standards and Technology (Commerce Dept.), Building and Fire Research Laboratory, Route I-270 and Quince Orchard Rd., Gaithersburg, MD 20899; (301) 975-5900. Richard N. Wright, director. Library, (301) 975-6859. Fax, (301) 975-4032.

Conducts basic and applied research on fire and fire resistance of construction materials; develops testing methods, standards, design concepts, and technologies for fire protection and prevention.

National Institute of Standards and Technology (Commerce Dept.), Fire Safety Engineering, Route I-270 and Quince Orchard Rd., Gaithersburg, MD 20899; (301) 975-6863. Andrew J. Fowell, chief. Fax, (301) 975-4052.

Conducts research on fire safety. Develops models to measure the behavior and mitigate the impact of large-scale fires. Operates the Fire Research Information Service and a large-scale fire test facility.

Occupational Safety and Health Administration (Labor Dept.), Safety Standards, 200 Constitution Ave. N.W. 20210; 219-8061. Thomas J. Shepich, director. Fax, 219-7477.

Administers regulations for fire safety standards; sponsors programs for maritime, fire protection, construction, mechanical, and electrical industries.

U.S. Fire Administration (Federal Emergency Management Agency), 16825 S. Seton Ave., Emmitsburg, MD 21727; (301) 447-1018. Edward M. Wall, deputy administrator. Information, 646-2442. Fax, (301) 447-1270.

Conducts research and collects, analyzes, and disseminates data on combustion, fire prevention, firefighter safety, and the management of fire prevention organizations; studies and develops arson prevention programs and fire prevention codes; maintains the National Fire Data System.

Congress:

See *Consumer Affairs, General, Congress (p. 246)*

See also *Congressional Fire Services Caucus (p. 748)*

Nongovernmental:

International Assn. of Fire Chiefs, 4025 Fair Ridge Dr., Fairfax, VA 22033-2868; (703) 273-0911. Garry L. Briese, executive director. Fax, (703) 273-9363.

Membership: firefighting chiefs and managers. Conducts research on fire control through grants from the departments of Commerce, Labor, and Transportation; testifies before congressional committees; monitors legislation and regulations affecting fire safety codes.

National Fire Protection Assn., 1110 N. Glebe Rd., #560, Arlington, VA 22201; (703) 516-4346. Anthony R. O'Neill, vice president, government affairs. Fax, (703) 516-4350.

Membership: individuals and organizations interested in fire protection. Develops and updates fire protection codes and standards; sponsors technical assistance programs; collects fire data statistics. Monitors legislation and regulations. (Headquarters in Quincy, Mass.)

Flammable Products

See also *Consumer Affairs, Fire Prevention and Control (p. 256); Consumer Affairs, Product Safety/Testing (p. 264)*

Agencies:

Consumer Product Safety Commission, Hazard Identification and Reduction, 4330 East-West Highway, Bethesda, MD (mailing address: Washington, DC 20207); (301) 504-0554. Bert G. Simson, assistant executive director. Fax, (301) 504-0024.

Proposes, evaluates, and develops standards and test procedures for safety and fire resistance in accordance with the Flammable Fabrics Act and the Federal Hazardous Substances Act. Reports injuries resulting from use of products.

National Institute of Standards and Technology (Commerce Dept.), Fire Science, Route I-270 and Quince Orchard Rd., Gaithersburg, MD 20899; (301) 975-6864. Richard G. Gann, chief. Fax, (301) 975-4052.
Conducts research on fire and metrology. Studies smoke components of flames, the burning of polymeric materials, and fire detection and suppression systems.

Congress:

See Consumer Affairs, General, Congress (p. 246)

Nongovernmental:

American Apparel Manufacturers Assn., 2500 Wilson Blvd., #301, Arlington, VA 22201; (703) 524-1864. G. Stewart Boswell, president. Fax, (703) 522-6741.
Membership: manufacturers of apparel and allied needle-trade products. Interests include product flammability.

American Fiber Manufacturers Assn., 1150 17th St. N.W., #310 20036; 296-6508. Paul T. O'Day, president. Fax, 296-3052.
Membership: American companies that produce manufactured fiber. Interests include flammable-materials research and environmental, safety, and trade issues.

American Textile Manufacturers Institute, 1801 K St. N.W., #900 20006-1301; 862-0500. Carlos F. J. Moore, executive vice president. Fax, 862-0570.
Membership: textile spinning, weaving, knitting, and finishing industries; and sheet, towel, and carpeting manufacturers. Sponsors programs to educate the public about flammable fabrics.

National Cotton Council of America, 1521 New Hampshire Ave. N.W. 20036; 745-7805. John Maguire, vice president, Washington office. Fax, 483-4040.
Membership: all segments of the U.S. cotton industry. Sponsors programs to educate the public about flammable fabrics. (Headquarters in Memphis.)

See also Consumer Affairs, General, Nongovernmental (p. 250)

Food and Nutrition

See also Commodities (p. 593); Government Financial Assistance Programs, Child Nutrition Programs (p. 407); Government Financial Assistance Programs, Food Stamps (p. 408)

Agencies:

Agriculture Dept., Agricultural Research Service, 14th St. and Independence Ave. S.W. 20250; 720-3656. R. D. Plowman, administrator. Fax, 720-5427.
Conducts studies on agricultural problems of domestic and international concern through nationwide network of research centers. Studies include research on human nutrition; livestock production and protection; crop production, protection, and processing; postharvest technology; and food distribution and market value.

Agriculture Dept., Extension Service, 14th St. and Independence Ave. S.W. 20250; 720-3377. Leodrey Williams, acting administrator. Information, 720-3029. Fax, 720-3993.
Oversees county agents and operation of state offices that provide information on nutrition, diet, food purchase budgeting, food safety, home gardening, and other consumer concerns.

Agriculture Dept., Food and Consumer Services, 14th St. and Independence Ave. S.W. 20250; 720-7711. Ellen Haas, assistant secretary. Fax, 690-3100.
Directs the Food and Nutrition Service and the Human Nutrition Information Service, which include all Agriculture Dept. domestic food assistance programs. Oversees office of the consumer adviser for agricultural products.

Agriculture Dept., Food Safety and Inspection Service, 14th St. and Independence Ave. S.W. 20250; 720-7025. H. Russell Cross, administrator. Information, 720-9113. Fax, 690-4437. Consumer inquiries, (800) 535-4555; in Washington, D.C., 720-3333.
Inspects and provides safe handling and labeling guidelines for meat and poultry products.

Agriculture Dept., Human Nutrition Information Service, 6505 Belcrest Rd., #360, Hyattsville, MD 20782; (301) 436-7725. Janice G. Lilja, acting administrator. Fax, (301) 436-7626.
Conducts household food consumption surveys; conducts research on nutrition education and on methods for assessing food intake; maintains the

National Nutrient Data Bank, a computerized file of the nutrient composition of 4,500 food items; develops dietary guidelines and provides nutrition information.

Animal and Plant Health Inspection Service (Agriculture Dept.), 14th St. and Independence Ave. S.W. (mailing address: Ag. Box 3041, Washington, DC 20250); 720-3861. Lonnie J. King, acting administrator. Information, 720-2511. Fax, 720-3054.

Administers animal disease control programs in cooperation with states; inspects imported animals, flowers, and plants; licenses the manufacture and marketing of veterinary biologics to ensure purity and effectiveness.

Food and Drug Administration (Health and Human Services Dept.), Center for Food Safety and Applied Nutrition, 200 C St. S.W. 20204; 205-4850. Fred R. Shank, director. Fax, 205-5025.

Develops standards of composition and quality of foods (except meat and poultry but including fish), develops safety regulations for food and color additives for foods, cosmetics, and drugs; monitors pesticide residues in foods; conducts food safety and nutrition research; develops analytical methods for measuring food additives, nutrients, pesticides, and chemical and microbiological contaminants; recommends action to Justice Dept.

National Agricultural Library (Agriculture Dept.), Food and Nutrition Information Center, 10301 Baltimore Blvd., #304, Beltsville, MD 20705; (301) 504-5719. Sandra Facinoli, coordinator. Fax, (301) 504-6409.

Serves individuals and agencies seeking information or educational materials on food and human nutrition; lends books and audiovisual materials for educational purposes; maintains a software demonstration center; provides reference services; develops resource lists of health and nutrition publications. Center open to the public.

National Institute of Diabetes and Digestive and Kidney Diseases (National Institutes of Health, Health and Human Services Dept.), Nutritional Sciences, 5333 Westbard Ave., Bethesda, MD 20892; (301) 594-7573. Dr. Van S. Hubbard, director. Information, (301) 496-3583. Fax, (301) 594-7504.

Supports research on nutritional requirements, dietary fiber, obesity, eating disorders, energy regulation, clinical nutrition, trace minerals, and basic nutrient functions.

National Oceanic and Atmospheric Administration (Commerce Dept.), Trade and Industry Services, 1335 East-West Highway, Silver Spring, MD 20910; (301) 713-2355. Richard Cano, chief, inspection services. Fax, (301) 713-1081.

Administers voluntary inspection program for fish products and fish processing plants; certifies fish for wholesomeness, safety, and condition; grades for quality.

See also Agricultural Marketing Service (p. 588)

Congress:

See Consumer Affairs, General, Congress (p. 246)

Nongovernmental:

American Board of Nutrition, 9650 Rockville Pike, Bethesda, MD 20814; (301) 530-7110. David Schnakenberg, executive officer. Fax, (301) 571-1892.

Establishes standards for specialists in the field of human and clinical nutrition; certifies those who meet its qualifications.

American Frozen Food Institute, 1764 Old Meadow Lane, #350, McLean, VA 22102; (703) 821-0770. Steven C. Anderson, president. Fax, (703) 821-1350.

Membership: frozen food packers, distributors, and suppliers. Provides production statistics.

American Institute of Nutrition, 9650 Rockville Pike, Bethesda, MD 20814; (301) 530-7050. Richard G. Allison, executive officer. Fax, (301) 571-1892.

Membership: nutrition scientists. Conducts research in nutrition and related fields and promotes the exchange of information among members; promotes nutrition education; offers awards for nutrition research.

American Meat Institute, 1700 N. Moore St., #1600, Arlington, VA (mailing address: P.O. Box 3556, Washington, DC 20007); (703) 841-2400. J. Patrick Boyle, president. Fax, (703) 527-0938.

Membership: national and international meat and poultry packers and processors. Provides information on consumer issues such as food additives, meat and poultry pricing, and nutrition.

The American Society for Clinical Nutrition, 9650 Rockville Pike, Bethesda, MD 20814-3998; (301) 530-7110. David Schnakenberg, executive officer. Fax, (301) 571-1892.

Membership: clinical nutritionists. Supports research on the role of human nutrition in health and disease; encourages undergraduate and graduate nutrition education. (Affiliated with American Institute of Nutrition.)

American Society for Parenteral and Enteral Nutrition, 8630 Fenton St., #412, Silver Spring, MD 20910; (301) 587-6315. Barney Sellers, executive director. Fax, (301) 587-2365.

Membership: health care professionals who provide patients with nutritional support during hospitalization and rehabilitation at home. Develops nutrition guidelines; provides educational materials; conducts annual meetings.

Beyond Beef, 1130 17th St. N.W., #300 20036; 775-1132. Jeremy Rifkin, president. Fax, 775-0074.

Works to reduce beef consumption by fifty percent by the year 2000, to replace beef in the diet with organically raised grains, fruits, and vegetables, and to promote humanely and organically raised cattle. Opposes genetically engineered food.

Center for Science in the Public Interest, 1875 Connecticut Ave. N.W., #300 20009-5728; 332-9110. Michael Jacobson, executive director. Fax, 265-4954.

Conducts research on food and nutrition. Interests include eating habits, food safety regulations, food additives, organically produced foods, alcoholic beverages, and links between diet and disease.

Community Nutrition Institute, 2001 S St. N.W., #530 20009; 462-4700. Rodney E. Leonard, executive director. Fax, 462-5241.

Citizens' interest group that provides information on nutrition and food policy issues. Monitors legislation and regulations affecting food safety and nutrition.

Council for Responsible Nutrition, 1300 19th St. N.W., #310 20036; 872-1488. J. B. Cordaro, president. Fax, 872-9594.

Membership: manufacturers, distributors, and suppliers of nutritional supplements and products. Provides information on the nutritional supplement industry; monitors Food and Drug Administration, Federal Trade Commission, and Consumer Product Safety Commission regulations.

Farm Animal Reform Movement, P.O. Box 30654, Bethesda, MD 20824; (301) 530-1737. Alex Hershaft, president. Fax, (301) 530-5747.

Works to end use of animals for food. Interests include consumer health, agricultural resources, and environmental quality. Monitors legislation and regulations. Conducts national educational campaigns, including the Great American Meatout.

Food and Drug Law Institute, 1000 Vermont Ave. N.W. 20005; 371-1420. John Villforth, president. Fax, 371-0649.

Membership: providers of products and services to the food, drug, medical device, and cosmetics industries, including major food and drug companies and lawyers. Arranges conferences on technological and legal developments in the industry; sponsors law courses, fellowships, and legal writing. Library open to the public.

Food Marketing Institute, 800 Connecticut Ave. N.W., #500 20006; 452-8444. Timothy Hammonds, president. Library, 429-8295. Fax, 429-4549.

International organization of food retailers and wholesalers. Conducts programs in research, education, industry relations, and public affairs. Library open to the public by appointment.

Food Research and Action Center, 1875 Connecticut Ave. N.W., #540 20009-5728; 986-2200. Robert Fersh, executive director. Fax, 986-2525.

Public interest advocacy, research, and legal center that works to end hunger and poverty in the United States. Offers legal assistance, organizational aid, training, and information to groups seeking to improve or expand federal food programs, including food stamps, child nutrition, and WIC (women, infants, and children) programs; monitors legislation and regulations; conducts studies relating to hunger and poverty; coordinates network of antihunger organizations.

Grocery Manufacturers of America, 1010 Wisconsin Ave. N.W., #900 20007; 337-9400. C. Manly Molpus, president. Fax, 337-4508.

Membership: manufacturers of products sold through the retail grocery trade. Monitors legislation and regulations.

International Bottled Water Assn., 113 N. Henry St., Alexandria, VA 22314-2973; (703) 683-5213. Sylvia E. Swanson, executive vice president.

Serves as a clearinghouse for industry-related consumer, regulatory, and technical information. Monitors state and federal legislation and regulations.

International Life Sciences Institute North America, 1126 16th St. N.W., #300 20036; 659-0074. Florence E. Boyce, administrator. Fax, 659-3859.

Acts as liaison among scientists from international government agencies, concerned industries, research institutes, and universities regarding the safety of foods and chemical ingredients. Conducts research on caffeine, food coloring, oral health, human nutrition, and other food issues. Promotes international cooperation among scientists.

National Food Processors Assn., 1401 New York Ave. N.W., #400 20005; 639-5939. John R. Cady, president. Fax, 637-8068.

Membership: canned and frozen food processing companies and suppliers. Conducts research for improving safety and quality of food processing; maintains updated series of legal requirements concerning contents and characteristics of canned foods; provides members with statistical and economic information and legal assistance.

National Restaurant Assn., 1200 17th St. N.W. 20036; 331-5900. William P. Fisher, executive vice president. Fax, 331-2429.

Membership: restaurants, cafeterias, clubs, contract feeders, caterers, institutional food services, and other members of the food industry. Supports food service education and research; monitors legislation and regulations.

National Soft Drink Assn., 1101 16th St. N.W. 20036; 463-6732. William L. Ball III, president. Fax, 463-8172.

Membership: companies engaged in producing or distributing soft drinks. Acts as industry liaison with government and the public.

Physicians Committee for Responsible Medicine, 5100 Wisconsin Ave. N.W. (mailing address: P.O. Box 6322, Washington, DC 20015); 686-2210. Dr. Neal D. Barnard, president. Fax, 686-2216.

Membership: health professionals, medical students, and other individuals. Provides individuals and institutions with nutrition information and low-fat, cholesterol-free recipes; promotes preventive medicine.

Public Citizen, Health Research Group, 2000 P St. N.W., #700 20036; 833-3000. Dr. Sidney M. Wolfe, director. Fax, 452-8658.

Citizens' interest group that studies and reports on unsafe foods; monitors and petitions the Food and Drug Administration.

Public Voice for Food and Health Policy, 1001 Connecticut Ave. N.W., #522 20036; 659-5930. Mark Epstein, executive director. Fax, 659-3683.

Research, education, and advocacy organization that promotes the consumer interest in food and health policy issues. Monitors legislation and regulations affecting food safety, agriculture, health, nutrition, and the environment.

Snack Food Assn., 1711 King St., #1, Alexandria, VA 22314; (703) 836-4500. James W. Shufelt, president. Toll-free, (800) 628-1334. Fax, (703) 836-8262.

Membership: snack food manufacturers and suppliers. Promotes industry sales; compiles statistics; conducts research and surveys; assists members with training and education; monitors legislation and regulations; provides consumers with industry information.

Worldwatch Institute, 1776 Massachusetts Ave. N.W. 20036; 452-1999. Lester R. Brown, president. Fax, 296-7365.

Research organization whose interests include environmental origins of world health trends, world population growth, and malnutrition.

See also Agriculture, General, Nongovernmental (p. 589)

See also American Institute for Cancer Research (p. 369); Consumer Federation of America (p. 250)

Labeling and Packaging

See also Consumer Affairs, Alcohol (p. 253); Consumer Affairs, Tobacco (p. 265); Health, Medical Devices (p. 328); Health, Pharmaceuticals (p. 331)

Agencies:

Agriculture Dept., Food Safety and Inspection Service, 14th St. and Independence Ave. S.W. 20250; 720-7025. H. Russell Cross, administrator. Information, 720-9113. Fax, 690-4437. Consumer inquiries, (800) 535-4555; in Washington, D.C., 720-3333.
Provides labeling guidelines for meat and poultry products.

Consumer Product Safety Commission, Hazard Identification and Reduction, 4330 East-West Highway, Bethesda, MD (mailing address: Washington, DC 20207); (301) 504-0554. Bert G. Simson, assistant executive director. Fax, (301) 504-0024.
Establishes labeling and packaging regulations. Develops standards in accordance with the Poison Prevention Packaging Act, the Federal Hazardous Substances Act, and the Consumer Products Safety Act.

Federal Trade Commission, Consumer Protection, 601 Pennsylvania Ave. N.W., 4th Floor 20580; 326-2996. Dean C. Graybill, associate director, enforcement. Fax, 326-3259.
Enforces labeling acts for textile, wool, and fur fiber products and for energy appliances; enforces packaging and labeling acts requiring identification of the manufacturer and listing of correct weight and other identifying information for most products, excluding food, drugs, and cosmetics.

Food and Drug Administration (Health and Human Services Dept.), Center for Food Safety and Applied Nutrition, 200 C St. S.W. 20204; 205-4850. Fred R. Shank, director. Fax, 205-5025.
Develops and enforces labeling regulations for foods (except meat and poultry but including fish) and cosmetics; develops and enforces standards on form and fill of packaging for foods and cosmetics; develops and enforces safety regulations for food and cosmetic packaging materials; recommends action to Justice Dept.

National Institute of Standards and Technology (Commerce Dept.), Standards Services, Route I-270 and Quince Orchard Rd., Gaithersburg, MD 20899; (301) 975-4005. Carroll S. Brickenkamp, chief, weights and measures. Information, (301) 975-4004. Fax, (301) 926-0647.
Promotes uniform standards among the states for packaging and labeling products and for measuring devices, including scales and commercial measurement instruments; advises manufacturers on labeling and packaging laws and on measuring device standards.

Congress:

See Consumer Affairs, General, Congress (p. 246)

Nongovernmental:

Flexible Packaging Assn., 1090 Vermont Ave. N.W., #500 20005; 842-3880. Glenn E. Braswell, president. Fax, 842-3841.
Membership: companies that supply or manufacture flexible packaging.

Packaging Machinery Manufacturers Institution, 1343 L St. N.W. 20005; 347-3838. Chuck Yuska, president. Fax, 628-2471.
Membership: manufacturers of packaging and packaging-related converting machinery. Provides industry information and statistics; offers educational programs to members.

See also Consumer Affairs, General, Nongovernmental (p. 250)

Privacy

Agencies:

Federal Communications Commission, Common Carrier Bureau, 2025 M St. N.W., #6008 20554; 634-1860. James Keegan, chief, domestic facilities. Fax, 634-6625.
Establishes federal policy governing interstate caller identification services.

Federal Trade Commission, Credit Practices, 601 Pennsylvania Ave. N.W. 20580; 326-3238. Christian S. White, acting director, consumer protection. Fax, 326-2050.
Enforces the Fair Credit Reporting Act, which requires credit bureaus to furnish correct and complete information to businesses evaluating credit, insurance, or job applications.

Office of Management and Budget (Executive Office of the President), Information Policy, 725 17th St. N.W. 20503; 395-3785. Robert N. Veeder, senior policy analyst. Fax, 395-7285.
Oversees implementation of the Privacy Act of 1974. Issues guidelines and regulations.

U.S. Office of Consumer Affairs (Health and Human Services Dept.), Consumer, Industry, and International Relations, 1620 L St. N.W. 20036; 634-4329. Polly Baca, director. Fax, 634-4135.
Works to protect consumer privacy in the areas of telecommunications, direct marketing, credit and banking, and insurance and medical records.

Congress:

House Judiciary Committee, Subcommittee on Civil and Constitutional Rights, 806 O'Neill Bldg. (300 New Jersey Ave. S.E.) 20515; 226-7680. Don Edwards, D-Calif., chairman; Catherine A. LeRoy, chief counsel.
Jurisdiction over legislation on the release of personal information by government agencies.

Senate Judiciary Committee, Subcommittee on the Constitution, SD-524 20510; 224-5573. Paul Simon, D-Ill., chairman; Susan D. Kaplan, chief counsel.
Jurisdiction over legislation on the release of personal information by government agencies.

Nongovernmental:

American Civil Liberties Union, Privacy and Technology, 122 Maryland Ave. N.E. 20002; 544-1681. Laura Murphy Lee, director, Washington office. Fax, 546-0738.
Studies the ways in which technology affects privacy. Interests include the Privacy Act of 1974, telecommunications, video and library lists, credit and medical records, criminal justice systems, drug testing, DNA database security, and patient confidentiality. (Headquarters in New York.)

American Society for Industrial Security, 1655 N. Fort Myer Dr., #1200, Arlington, VA 22209; (703) 522-5800. E. J. Criscuoli, executive vice president. Fax, (703) 243-4954.
Membership: security professionals. Interests include all aspects of security, with emphases on counterterrorism, computer security, privacy issues, government security, and the availability of job-related information for employers determining an employee's suitability for employment.

Assn. of Direct Response Fundraising Counsel, 1319 F St. N.W., #300 20004; 347-0929. Robert S. Tigner, general counsel. Fax, 347-9606.
Membership: businesses in the direct response fund-raising industry. Establishes standards of ethical practice in such areas as ownership of direct mail donor lists and mandatory disclosures by fund-raising counsel. Educates nonprofit organizations and the public on direct mail fund raising.

Communications Workers of America, 501 3rd St. N.W. 20001; 434-1100. Morton Bahr, president. Fax, 434-1201.
Membership: telecommunications workers. Opposes electronic monitoring of productivity, eavesdropping by employers, and misuse of drug and polygraph tests.

Computer Professionals for Social Responsibility, 666 Pennsylvania Ave. S.E., #303 20003; 544-9240. Marc Rotenberg, director, Washington office. Fax, 547-5482. Electronic mail, rotenberg@washofc.cpsr.org.
Membership: computer professionals. Conducts research, conferences, and litigation on the social effects of computer and communications technology. The Computing and Civil Liberties Project investigates privacy, information access, and civil liberties issues. (Headquarters in Palo Alto, Calif.)

Consumers Union of the United States, 1666 Connecticut Ave. N.W., #310 20009; 462-6262. Mark Silbergeld, director, Washington office. Fax, 265-9548.
Consumer advocacy group active in protecting the privacy of consumers. Interests include credit report accuracy. (Headquarters in Yonkers, N.Y.)

Direct Marketing Assn., 1101 17th St. N.W., #705 20036; 347-1222. Richard Barton, senior vice president, government affairs. Fax, 785-2231.
Membership: telemarketers; users, creators, and producers of direct mail; and suppliers to the industry. Evaluates direct marketing methods that make use of personal consumer information. Offers free service whereby consumers may remove their names from national mailing and

telephone marketing lists. (Headquarters in New York.)

National Assn. of State Utility Consumer Advocates, 1133 15th St. N.W., #575 20005; 727-3908. Debra Berlyn, executive director. Fax, 727-3911.

Membership: public advocate offices authorized by states to represent ratepayer interests before state and federal utility regulatory commissions. Supports privacy protection for telephone customers.

National Consumers League, 815 15th St. N.W., #928N 20005; 639-8140. Linda F. Golodner, president. Fax, 737-2164. TDD, 737-5084.

Citizens' interest group concerned with privacy rights of consumers. Interests include credit and financial records, medical records, direct marketing, telecommunications, and workplace privacy.

U.S. Public Interest Research Group (USPIRG), 215 Pennsylvania Ave. S.E. 20003; 546-9707. Edmund Mierzwinski, consumer advocate. Fax, 546-2461.

Coordinates grass-roots efforts to advance consumer protection laws. Works for the protection of privacy rights, particularly in the area of fair credit reporting.

See also Information Industry Assn. (p. 165)

Product Safety/Testing

Agencies:

Consumer Product Safety Commission, 4330 East-West Highway, Bethesda, MD (mailing address: Washington, DC 20207); (301) 504-0500. Ann Brown, chair. Information, (301) 504-0580. Library, (301) 504-0544. Fax, (301) 504-0124. Product safety hotline, (800) 638-2772. TDD, (800) 638-8270.

Establishes and enforces product safety standards; collects data; studies causes and prevention of product-related injuries; identifies hazardous products and recalls them from the marketplace. Library open to the public.

Consumer Product Safety Commission, Compliance and Enforcement, 4330 East-West Highway, Bethesda, MD (mailing address: Washington, DC 20207); (301) 504-0621. David

Schmeltzer, assistant executive director. Fax, (301) 504-0359.

Identifies and acts on any defective consumer product already in distribution; conducts surveillance and enforcement programs to ensure industry compliance with existing safety standards; conducts enforcement litigation. Participates in developing standards to ensure that the final result is enforceable; monitors recall of defective products and issues warnings to consumers when appropriate.

Consumer Product Safety Commission, Engineering Sciences, 4330 East-West Highway, Bethesda, MD (mailing address: Washington, DC 20207); (301) 504-0504. James Bradley, acting associate executive director. Fax, (301) 504-0124.

Develops and evaluates consumer product safety standards, test methods, performance criteria, design specifications, and quality standards; conducts and evaluates engineering tests. Collects scientific and technical data to determine potential hazards of consumer products.

Consumer Product Safety Commission, Epidemiology, 4330 East-West Highway, Bethesda, MD (mailing address: Washington, DC 20207); (301) 504-0440. Robert D. Verhalen, associate executive director. Fax, (301) 504-0234.

Collects data on consumer product-related hazards and potential hazards; determines the frequency, severity, and distribution of various types of injuries and investigates their causes; assesses the effects of product safety standards and programs on consumer injuries; conducts epidemiological studies and research in the field of consumer product-related injuries.

National Injury Information Clearinghouse (Consumer Product Safety Commission), 4330 East-West Highway, Bethesda, MD (mailing address: Washington, DC 20207); (301) 504-0424. Joel I. Friedman, director. Fax, (301) 504-0124.

Analyzes types and frequency of injuries resulting from consumer and recreational products. Collects injury information from consumer complaints, investigations, coroners' reports, death certificates, newspaper clippings, and statistically selected hospital emergency rooms nationwide.

Congress:

See Consumer Affairs, General, Congress (p. 246)

Nongovernmental:

American Academy of Pediatrics, 601 13th St. N.W., #400N 20005; 347-8600. Elizabeth J. Noyes, director, government liaison. Toll-free, (800) 336-5475. Fax, 393-6137.

Promotes legislation and regulations concerning child health and safety. Committee on Injury and Poison Prevention drafts policy statements and publishes information on toy safety, poisons, and other issues that affect children. (Headquarters in Elk Grove Village, Ill.)

Cosmetic Ingredient Review, 1101 17th St. N.W. 20036; 331-0651. F. Allen Andersen, director. Fax, 331-1969.

Voluntary self-regulatory program funded by the Cosmetic, Toiletry, and Fragrance Assn. Reviews and evaluates the data used by the cosmetics industry to assess the safety of cosmetic ingredients.

See also Consumer Affairs, General, Nongovernmental (p. 250)

Tobacco

See also Commodities, Tobacco and Peanuts (p. 601)

Agencies:

Bureau of Alcohol, Tobacco, and Firearms (Treasury Dept.), Compliance Operations, 650 Massachusetts Ave. N.W. (mailing address: Washington, DC 20226); 927-8710. Arthur Libertucci, associate director. Information, 927-7777.

Enforces and administers revenue laws relating to tobacco.

Centers for Disease Control and Prevention (Health and Human Services Dept.), Smoking and Health/Liaison, 330 C St. S.W. 20201; 205-8500. Karen M. Deasy, director, liaison office. Fax, 205-8313.

Produces and issues the surgeon general's annual report on smoking and health; conducts public information and education programs on smoking and health. Conducts epidemiological studies, surveys, and analyses on tobacco use. Serves as liaison between governmental and nongovernmental organizations that work on tobacco initiatives. (Headquarters in Atlanta.)

Federal Trade Commission, Advertising Practices, 601 Pennsylvania Ave. N.W., 4th Floor 20580; 326-3150. Judith Wilkenfeld, assistant director. Fax, 326-3259.

Regulates advertising of tobacco products under the Federal Cigarette Labeling and Advertising Act and the Comprehensive Smokeless Tobacco Health Education Act. Regulates labeling and advertising of tobacco products; administers health warnings on packages; monitors and tests claims on tobacco products for validity. Works with the Justice Dept. in enforcing the ban on tobacco advertising in the broadcast media; investigates deceptive claims and violations of laws and may refer violations to the Justice Dept. for criminal prosecution.

Congress:

See Consumer Affairs, General, Congress (p. 246)

See also Congressional Task Force on Tobacco and Health (p. 759)

Nongovernmental:

Action on Smoking and Health, 2013 H St. N.W. 20006; 659-4310. John F. Banzhaf III, executive director. Toll-free, (800) 427-4228.

Educational and legal organization that works to ensure protection of nonsmokers from cigarette smoking; provides information about smoking hazards and nonsmokers' rights.

Coalition on Smoking OR Health, 1150 Connecticut Ave. N.W., #820 20036; 452-1184. Joy Epstein, administrator, federal issues. Fax, 452-1417.

Coalition of the American Lung Assn., the American Cancer Society, and the American Heart Assn. Works to bring the health hazards of smoking and tobacco to the attention of federal, state, and local legislators and agencies.

Minority and Women's Rights

See also Constitutional Law and Civil Liberties (p. 500); Education: Special Groups, Minorities and Women (p. 146); Equal Employment Opportunity (p. 179); Health Care and Services for Special Groups, Minorities and Economically Disadvantaged Groups (p. 344)

Check the index and specific subject area for minority and women's groups not listed in this section.

General

Agencies:

Commission on Civil Rights, 624 9th St. N.W., #700 20425; 376-7700. Mary Frances Berry, chair. Information, 376-8364. Library, 376-8110. Fax, 376-7672. TDD, 376-8116. Complaints, (800) 552-6843; in Washington, D.C., 376-8582. Assesses federal laws and policies of government agencies and studies legal developments to determine the nature and extent of denial of equal protection under the law on the basis of race, color, religion, sex, national origin, age, or disability in many areas, including employment, voting rights, education, administration of justice, and housing. Reports and makes recommendations to the president and Congress; serves as national clearinghouse for civil rights information. Conducts studies relating to discrimination against certain groups, including women, African Americans, Hispanics, Asians, and Pacific Island Americans. Library open to the public.

Executive Office of the President, Public Liaison, Old Executive Office Bldg. 20500; 456-2930. Alexis Herman, assistant to the president and director. Press, 456-2100. Fax, 456-6218. Serves as liaison between the administration and the public on issues of domestic and international concern, including women's and minority issues and the elderly.

Health and Human Services Dept., Civil Rights, 330 Independence Ave. S.W. 20201; 619-0403. Dennis Hayashi, director. Information, 619-0585. Fax, 619-3818. TDD, (800) 537-7697. Toll-free hotline, (800) 368-1019; in Washington, D.C., 863-0100. Administers and enforces laws prohibiting discrimination on the basis of race, color, sex, national origin, religion, age, or disability in programs receiving federal funds from the department; authorized to discontinue funding.

Justice Dept., Civil Rights, Main Justice Bldg. 20530; 514-2151. Deval Patrick, assistant attorney general. Information, 514-2007. Library, 514-4098. Fax, 514-0293. TDD, 472-1953. Enforces federal civil rights laws prohibiting discrimination on the basis of race, color, religion, sex, disability, age, or national origin in voting, education, employment, credit, housing, public accommodations and facilities, and federally assisted programs.

Justice Dept., Community Relations Service, 5550 Friendship Blvd., Chevy Chase, MD 20815; (301) 492-5929. Geoffrey Weiss, acting director. Press, (301) 492-5969. Fax, (301) 492-5984. Toll-free hotline, (800) 347-4283.

Provides conciliation, mediation, and technical advisory services; assists local governments, law enforcement agencies, and communities dealing with racial or ethnic tensions of a potentially violent or economically disruptive nature. Operates a toll-free hotline for reporting incidences of discrimination based on race, gender, sexual orientation, national origin, or religious preference.

Congress:

House Government Operations Committee, Subcommittee on Employment, Housing, and Aviation, B349A RHOB 20515; 225-6751. Collin C. Peterson, D-Minn., chairman; Wendy Adler, acting staff director.

Oversees operations of the Equal Employment Opportunity Commission.

House Government Operations Committee, Subcommittee on Information, Justice, Transportation, and Agriculture, B349C RHOB 20515; 225-3741. Gary Condit, D-Calif., chairman; Shannon Lahey, acting staff director. Fax, 225-2445.

Oversees operations of the Commission on Civil Rights.

House Judiciary Committee, Subcommittee on Civil and Constitutional Rights, 806 O'Neill Bldg. (300 New Jersey Ave. S.E.) 20515; 226-7680. Don Edwards, D-Calif., chairman; Catherine A. LeRoy, chief counsel.

Jurisdiction over civil and constitutional rights legislation.

Senate Judiciary Committee, Subcommittee on the Constitution, SD-524 20510; 224-5573. Paul Simon, D-Ill., chairman; Susan D. Kaplan, chief counsel.

Jurisdiction over civil and constitutional rights legislation; oversees operations of the Commission on Civil Rights.

Senate Labor and Human Resources Committee, SD-428 20510; 224-5375. Edward M. Kennedy, D-Mass., chairman; Nick Littlefield, chief counsel and staff director.

Oversees operations of the Equal Employment Opportunity Commission.

African Americans

Agencies:

See *Minority and Women's Rights, General, agencies (p. 266)*

Congress:

See *Minority and Women's Rights, General, Congress (p. 266)*

See also *Congressional Black Caucus (p. 758)*

Nongovernmental:

Blacks in Government, 1820 11th St. N.W. 20001; 667-3280. Marion A. Bowden, president. Fax, 667-3705.

Advocacy organization for public employees. Promotes equal opportunity and career advancement for African American government employees; provides career development information; seeks to eliminate racism in the federal work force; sponsors programs, business meetings, and social gatherings; represents interests of African American government workers to Congress and the executive branch; promotes voter education and registration.

Congressional Black Caucus Foundation, 1004 Pennsylvania Ave. S.E. 20003; 675-6730. Quintin Lawson, executive director. Fax, 547-3806.

Conducts research and programs on public policy issues of concern to African Americans. Sponsors fellowship programs in which professionals and academic candidates work on congressional committees and subcommittees. Holds issue forums and leadership seminars. Provides elected officials, organizations, and researchers with statistical, demographic, public policy, and political information. Sponsors internship and scholarship programs.

Joint Center for Political and Economic Studies, 1090 Vermont Ave. N.W., #1100 20005; 789-3500. Eddie N. Williams, president. Library, 789-5519. Fax, 789-6390.

Researches and analyzes issues of concern to African Americans, focusing on economic and social policy issues and African American political participation. Publishes an annual profile of African American elected officials in federal, state, and local government; holds forums on public policy issues. Library open to the public by appointment.

Lincoln Institute for Research and Education, 1001 Connecticut Ave. N.W., #1135 20036; 223-5112. J. A. Parker, president.

Public policy research group that studies issues of interest to middle-class African Americans, including business, economics, employment, education, national defense, health, and culture. Sponsors seminars.

National Assn. for the Advancement of Colored People (NAACP), 1025 Vermont Ave. N.W., #1120 20005; 638-2269. Wade J. Henderson, director, Washington bureau. Fax, 638-5936.

Membership: persons interested in civil rights for all minorities. Works for the political, educational, social, and economic equality and empowerment of minorities through legal, legislative, and direct action and educational programs. (Headquarters in Baltimore.)

National Assn. of Colored Women's Clubs, 5808 16th St. N.W. 20011; 726-2044. Savannah C. Jones, president. Fax, 726-0023.

Conducts programs in education, social service, and philanthropy. Works to protect and enforce civil rights; raise the standards of the home and family living; promote interracial understanding; and enhance leadership development. Awards scholarships.

National Black Caucus of Local Elected Officials, c/o National League of Cities, 1301 Pennsylvania Ave. N.W., #600 20004; 626-3120. Jeff Fletcher, director, public affairs. Fax, 626-3043.

Membership: elected officials at the local level and other interested individuals. Concerned with issues affecting African Americans, including housing, economics, the family, and human rights.

National Black Caucus of State Legislators, 444 N. Capitol St. N.W., #622 20001; 624-5457. Charles Bremer, executive director. Fax, 508-3826.

Membership: African American state legislators. Promotes effective leadership among African American state legislators; serves as an information network and clearinghouse for members.

National Center for Neighborhood Enterprise, 1367 Connecticut Ave. N.W., 2nd Floor 20036; 331-1103. Robert L. Woodson Sr., chairman. Fax, 296-1541.

Seeks new approaches to the problems confronting the African American community. Interests include economic development, the encouragement of entrepreneurship, housing, family development, and educational opportunity.

National Council of Negro Women, 1667 K St. N.W., #700 20006; 659-0006. Dorothy I. Height, president. Fax, 785-8733.

Coalition of domestic and international organizations and individuals interested in issues that affect African American women. Encourages the development of African American women; sponsors programs on family health care, career development, child care, juvenile offenders, housing discrimination against women, teenage pregnancy, and literacy improvement among female heads of households; promotes social and economic well-being of African American women through its Development Projects training program.

National Urban League, 1111 14th St. N.W., #600 20005; 898-1604. Robert McAlpine, director, policy and government relations. Fax, 682-0782.

Federation of affiliates concerned with the social welfare of African Americans and other minorities. Seeks elimination of racial segregation and discrimination; monitors legislation, policies, and regulations to determine impact on minorities; interests include employment, health, welfare, education, housing, and community development. (Headquarters in New York.)

Project 21, 300 Eye St. N.E., #3 20002; 543-1286. Ron Nehring, director. Fax, 543-4779.

Emphasizes spirit of entrepreneurship, sense of family, and traditional values among African Americans. (Initiative of the National Center for Public Policy Research.)

See also Minority Business Enterprise Legal Defense and Education Fund (p. 53)

Hispanics

Agencies:

See Minority and Women's Rights, General, agencies (p. 266)

Congress:

See Minority and Women's Rights, General, Congress (p. 266)

See also Congressional Hispanic Caucus (p. 758)

Nongovernmental:

Congressional Hispanic Caucus Institute, 504 C St. N.E. 20002; 543-1771. Rita Elizondo, executive director. Fax, 546-2143. Toll-free college scholarship information, (800) 392-3532.

Addresses issues of concern to Hispanic Americans and fosters awareness of the contributions of Hispanics to American society. Develops programs to familiarize Hispanic students with policy-related careers and to encourage their professional growth and development. Acts as an information clearinghouse on educational opportunities.

League of United Latin American Citizens, 777 N. Capitol St. N.E., #305 20002; 408-0060. Richard Roybal, executive director, national educational service centers. Fax, 408-0064.

Seeks full social, political, economic, and educational rights for Hispanics in the United States. Programs include housing projects for the poor, employment and training for youth and women, and political advocacy on issues affecting Hispanics. (Headquarters in Las Vegas.)

Mexican American Legal Defense and Educational Fund, 733 15th St. N.W., #920 20005; 628-4074. Mario Moreno, regional counsel, Washington office. Fax, 393-4206.

Gives legal assistance to Mexican-Americans and other Hispanics in such areas as equal employment, voting rights, bilingual education, and immigration; awards scholarship funds to Hispanic law students. Monitors legislation and regulations. (Headquarters in Los Angeles.)

National Conference of Catholic Bishops/ United States Catholic Conference, Secretariat for Hispanic Affairs, 3211 4th St. N.E., 4th Floor 20017; 541-3152. Ronaldo Cruz, director. Fax, 541-3322.

Acts as an information clearinghouse on communications and pastoral and liturgical activities; serves as liaison for other churches, institutions, and government and private agencies concerned with Hispanics; provides information on legislation; acts as advocate for Hispanics within the National Conference of Catholic Bishops.

National Conference of Puerto Rican Women, 5 Thomas Circle N.W. 20005; 387-4716. Edna Banchs Laverdi, president.

Promotes participation of Puerto Rican and other Hispanic women in the economic, social, and political aspects of life in the United States.

National Council of La Raza, 810 1st St. N.E., #300 20002; 289-1380. Raul Yzaguirre, president. Fax, 289-8173.

Offers technical assistance to Hispanic community organizations; operates policy analysis center with interests in education, employment and training, immigration, language issues, civil rights, and housing and community development. Special projects focus on the Hispanic elderly, teenage pregnancy, health, and AIDS. Monitors legislation and regulations.

National Puerto Rican Coalition, 1700 K St. N.W., #500 20006; 223-3915. Louis Nunez, president. Fax, 429-2223.

Membership: Puerto Rican organizations and individuals. Analyzes and advocates for public policy that benefits Puerto Ricans; offers training and technical assistance to Puerto Rican organizations and individuals, develops national communication network for Puerto Rican community-based organizations and individuals.

See also Aspira Assn. (p. 148); National Coalition of Hispanic Health and Human Services Organizations (p. 345)

Lesbians and Gays

Agencies:

See Minority and Women's Rights, General, agencies (p. 266)

Congress:

See Minority and Women's Rights, General, Congress (p. 266)

Nongovernmental:

Gay and Lesbian Activists Alliance, 1734 14th St. N.W. 20009; 667-5139. Jeff Coudriet, president.

Political action and educational organization that supports lesbian and gay rights legislation. Rates political leaders based on their support of lesbian and gay rights legislation.

Human Rights Campaign Fund, 1012 14th St. N.W., 6th Floor 20005; 628-4160. Tim McFeeley, executive director. Fax, 347-5323.

Promotes legislation affirming the rights of lesbians and gays. Interests include civil rights; funding for AIDS research; and discrimination in housing, immigration, and the military.

Mattachine Society of Washington, 5020 Cathedral Ave. N.W., Washington, DC 20016; 363-3881. Franklin E. Kameny, president.

Acts as a clearinghouse on homosexual rights; works to eliminate discrimination against homosexuals in the issuance of security clearances, the armed services, the civil service, and other fields; provides legal counsel and advisory services; maintains speakers bureau. Gay Information and Assistance program provides referrals and information on issues related to homosexuality.

National Gay and Lesbian Task Force Policy Institute, 1734 14th St. N.W. 20009-4309; 332-6483. Torie Osborn, executive director. Fax, 332-0207. TDD, 332-6219.

Educates the media and the public on issues affecting the lesbian and gay community. Interests include health issues, civil rights, antigay violence, sodomy law reform, gays in the military and on campus, and recognition of gay and lesbian families. Monitors legislation.

National Organization for Women (NOW), 1000 16th St. N.W., #700 20036; 331-0066. Patricia Ireland, president. Fax, 785-8576. TDD, 331-9002.

Membership: women and men interested in feminist civil rights. Works to end discrimination against lesbians and gays. Promotes the development and enforcement of legislation prohibiting discrimination on the basis of sexual orientation.

Native Americans

Agencies:

Bureau of Indian Affairs (Interior Dept.), Main Interior Bldg. 20240; 208-7163. Ada E. Deer, assistant secretary. Information, 208-3711. Press, 219-4150. Fax, 208-6334.

Works with federally recognized Indian tribal governments and Alaska native communities in a government-to-government relationship. Encourages and supports tribal efforts to govern themselves and to provide needed programs and services on the reservations. Manages land held in trust for Indian tribes and individuals. Funds educational benefits, road construction and maintenance, social services, police protection, economic development efforts, and special assistance to develop governmental and administrative skills.

Health and Human Services Dept., Administration for Native Americans, 200 Independence Ave. S.W. 20201; 690-7776. Gary N. Kimble, commissioner designate. Information, 690-7730. Fax, 690-7441.

Awards grants for locally determined social and economic development strategies; promotes native American economic and social self-sufficiency; funds tribes and native American and native Hawaiian organizations. Commissioner serves as chairman of the Intradepartmental Council on Indian Affairs, which coordinates native American-related programs.

See also Minority and Women's Rights, General, agencies (p. 266)

Congress:

House Natural Resources Committee, Subcommittee on Native American Affairs, 1522 LHOB 20515; 226-7393. Bill Richardson, D-N.M., chairman; Tadd Johnson, staff director. Fax, 226-0522.

Jurisdiction over native American legislation, including land management and trust responsibilities, education, health, special services, loan programs, and claims against the United States.

Senate Committee on Indian Affairs, SH-838 20510; 224-2251. Daniel K. Inouye, D-Hawaii, chairman; Patricia Zell, staff director. Fax, 224-2309.

Jurisdiction over legislation on native Americans; oversight of all programs that affect native Americans.

Judiciary:

U.S. Court of Federal Claims, 717 Madison Pl. N.W. 20005; 219-9668. Loren A. Smith, chief judge; David A. Lampen, clerk, 219-9657. Fax, 219-9649.

Deals with native American tribal claims against the government that are founded upon the Constitution, congressional acts, government regulations, and contracts. Examples include claims for land, water, and mineral rights and for the accounting of funds held for native Americans under various treaties.

Nongovernmental:

National Congress of American Indians, 900 Pennsylvania Ave. S.E. 20003; 546-9404. Rachel Joseph, acting executive director. Fax, 546-3741.

Membership: native American and Alaska native governments and individuals. Provides information and serves as general advocate for tribes. Monitors legislative and regulatory activities affecting native American affairs.

Navajo Nation, 1101 17th St. N.W., #250 20036; 775-0393. Michael Begaye, director, Washington office. Fax, 775-8075.

Monitors legislative and regulatory activities affecting the Navajo people; serves as a clearinghouse that provides information on the Navajo Nation. (Headquarters in Window Rock, Ariz.)

See also Americans for the Restitution and Righting of Old Wrongs (p. 521); Friends Committee on National Legislation (p. 278); Native American Rights Fund (p. 522)

Women

Agencies:

See Minority and Women's Rights, General, agencies (p. 266)

Congress:

See Minority and Women's Rights, General, Congress (p. 266)

See also Congressional Caucus for Women's Issues (p. 756)

Nongovernmental:

B'nai B'rith Women, 1828 L St. N.W., #250 20036; 857-1300. Elaine Kotell Binder, executive director. Fax, 857-1380.

Jewish women's organization. Interests include emotional health of children and youth; family issues such as choice, domestic violence, and long-term health care; civil and constitutional rights; community services; anti-Semitism; and Jews in the former Soviet Union.

Center for Women Policy Studies, 2000 P St. N.W. 20036; 872-1770. Leslie R. Wolfe, president. Fax, 296-8962.

Policy and advocacy organization concerned with women's issues, including educational and employment equity for women, women and AIDS, violence against women, economic opportunity for low-income women, women's health, and reproductive laws.

Church Women United, 110 Maryland Ave. N.E. 20002; 544-8747. Nancy S. Chupp, legislative director. Fax, 543-1297.

Christian women's organization. Interests include defense policy, employment, family stability, health, human rights, justice, world peace, and hunger and poverty issues, especially as they affect women and children.

Leadership America, 700 N. Fairfax St., #610, Alexandria, VA 22314; (703) 549-1102. Kae G. Dakin, executive director. Fax, (703) 836-9205.

Educational program designed to increase women's influence in the national decision-making process. Conducts seminars on public policy issues for women in leadership positions. Affiliate of the Foundation for Women's Resources, headquartered in Austin, Texas.

National Organization for Women (NOW), 1000 16th St. N.W., #700 20036; 331-0066. Patricia Ireland, president. Fax, 785-8576. TDD, 331-9002.

Membership: women and men interested in feminist civil rights. Uses traditional and non-traditional forms of political activism, including nonviolent civil disobedience, to improve the status of all women regardless of age, income, sexual orientation, or race.

National Women's Law Center, 1616 P St. N.W. 20036; 328-5160. Sharon Fischman, communications director. Fax, 328-5137.

Works to expand and protect women's legal rights through litigation, advocacy, and public information. Interests include reproductive rights, health, education, employment, women in prison, income security, and family support.

Older Women's League, 666 11th St. N.W., #700 20001; 783-6686. Joan Kuriansky, executive director. Fax, 638-2356.

Grass-roots organization concerned with the social and economic problems of middle-aged and older women. Interests include health care, Social Security, pension rights, housing, employ-ment, women as care givers, effects of budget cuts, and issues relating to death and dying.

Pension Rights Center, Women's Pension Project, 918 16th St. N.W., #704 20006; 296-3776. M. Cindy Hounsell, coordinating attorney. Fax, 833-2472.

Provides information on women's pension issues; conducts workshops and seminars; monitors legislation and regulations.

Quota International, 1420 21st St. N.W. 20036; 331-9694. Kathleen Thomas, executive director. Fax, 331-4395.

Membership: executives and professionals. Sponsors community and internationally based programs for women and children. Interests include hearing- and speech-impaired individuals, child drug abuse, battered wives, nutrition, immunization programs for children, and day-care services.

The Woman Activist Fund, 2310 Barbour Rd., Falls Church, VA 22043; (703) 573-8716. Flora Crater, president.

Advocacy group that conducts research on individuals and groups in elective and appointive office, especially those who make decisions affecting women and minorities. Publishes annual ratings of these officials.

Women's Action for New Directions, 110 Maryland Ave. N.E., #205 20002; 543-8505. Sima Osdoby, director of policy and program. Fax, 675-6469.

Monitors legislation affecting women. (Headquarters in Arlington, Mass.)

Women's Research and Education Institute, 1700 18th St. N.W. 20009; 328-7070. Betty Dooley, executive director. Fax, 328-3514.

Provides data, research, and policy analyses on women's issues. Sponsors fellowships in congressional offices; promotes public education through conferences, symposia, and briefings; serves as an information clearinghouse; publishes periodic report on the status of women in the United States. Interests include health care, housing, women and tax policy, military women, alternative work options, employment, older women, and home-based work.

See also Fund for the Feminist Majority (p. 769)

Other Minority Groups

Agencies:

See *Minority and Women's Rights, General,* agencies (p. 266)

Congress:

See *Minority and Women's Rights, General, Congress* (p. 266)

Nongovernmental:

American-Arab Anti-Discrimination Committee, 4201 Connecticut Ave. N.W., #500 20008; 244-2990. Albert Mokhiber, president. Fax, 244-3196.

Nonsectarian organization that seeks to protect the rights of Americans of Arab descent. Works to combat discrimination against Arab Americans in employment, education, and political life and to prevent stereotyping of Arabs in the media.

Anti-Defamation League of B'nai B'rith, 1100 Connecticut Ave. N.W., #1020 20036; 452-8320. Jess N. Hordes, director, Washington office. Fax, 296-2371.

Jewish organization interested in civil rights and liberties. Seeks to combat anti-Semitism and other forms of bigotry. Interests include discrimination in employment, housing, voting, and education; U.S. foreign policy in the Middle East; and the treatment of Jews worldwide. Monitors legislation and regulations affecting Jewish interests and the civil rights of all Americans. (Headquarters in New York.)

Japanese American Citizens League, 1001 Connecticut Ave. N.W., #704 20036; 223-1240. Karen K. Narasaki, Washington representative. Fax, 296-8082.

Monitors legislative and regulatory activities affecting the rights of Japanese Americans. Supports civil rights of all Americans, with a focus on Asian and Pacific Americans. (Headquarters in San Francisco.)

Organization of Chinese American Women, 1300 N St. N.W. 20005; 638-0330. Pauline W. Tsui, executive director. Fax, 638-2196.

Seeks to overcome racial and sexual discrimination and to ensure equal education and employment opportunities in professional and nonprofessional fields; provides members with

leadership, skills, and employment training; assists newly arrived immigrants.

Organization of Chinese Americans, 1001 Connecticut Ave. N.W., #707 20036; 223-5500. Daphne Kwok, executive director. Fax, 296-0540.

Advocacy group seeking equal opportunities for Chinese Americans. Interests include cultural heritage, education, voter registration, hate crimes, immigration, and civil rights issues; opposes adoption of English as official U.S. language.

Organization of Pan-Asian American Women, P.O. Box 39128, Washington, DC 20016; 659-9370. Emily Woo, president. Fax, 682-9109.

Membership: Asian-Pacific American women. Focuses on public policy issues concerning Asian-Pacific women. Interests include the global status of women, civil rights, immigration and refugee issues, affirmative action, economic development, educational equity, health, and domestic violence; places special emphasis on leadership and professional development and coalition building.

Philanthropy, Public Service, and Voluntarism

Agencies:

Corporation for National Service, 1100 Vermont Ave. N.W. 20525; 606-5000. Eli J. Segal, chief executive officer. Fax, 606-4928. TDD, 606-5256. Volunteer recruiting information, (800) 424-8867; in Washington, D.C., 606-5000.

Independent corporation that administers federally sponsored domestic volunteer programs that provide disadvantaged citizens with services. Engages Americans of all ages and backgrounds in community-based service. Addresses U.S. education, human, public safety, and environmental needs. Works to foster civic responsibility and provide educational opportunity for those who make a substantial commitment to service. Programs include Foster Grandparent Program, Retired and Senior Volunteer Program, Senior Companion Program, and Volunteers in Service to America (VISTA).

Corporation for National Service, Program Demonstration and Development, 1100 Vermont Ave. N.W., #8200 20525; 606-5000. Hank

Oltmann, acting director. Fax, 606-4921. TDD, 606-5256.

Administers the Drug Alliance Program, which supports public and private drug education and drug prevention efforts.

Corporation for National Service, Retired and Senior Volunteer Program, Foster Grandparent Program, and Senior Companion Program, 1100 Vermont Ave. N.W. 20525; 606-4855. Thomas E. Endres, acting assistant director, older Americans volunteer programs. Information, 606-5108. Fax, 606-4921.

Oversees regional offices and provides them with financial assistance for programs administered by community agencies, including the Retired and Senior Volunteer Program, which encourages older citizens to use their talents and experience in community service; the Foster Grandparent Program, which gives low-income persons age 60 and over opportunities to work with exceptional children and children with special needs; and the Senior Companion Program, which recruits low-income persons age 60 and over to help other adults, especially seniors with special needs.

Corporation for National Service, University Year for VISTA, 1100 Vermont Ave. N.W. 20525; 606-5000. Diana London, acting assistant director. Fax, 606-4921.

Provides grants to public and private nonprofit organizations that encourage postsecondary students to volunteer in community activities that address poverty-related problems.

Internal Revenue Service (Treasury Dept.), Employee Plans and Exempt Organizations, 1111 Constitution Ave. N.W., #3408 20224; 622-6720. James J. McGovern, assistant commissioner. Fax, 622-6873.

Provides rules for the uniform interpretation and application of federal tax laws affecting tax-exempt organizations and private foundations.

Peace Corps, 1990 K St. N.W. 20526; 606-3970. Carol Bellamy, director. Information, 606-3387. Press, 606-3010. Library, 606-3307. Fax, 606-3110. Toll-free, (800) 424-8580.

Promotes world peace and mutual understanding between the United States and developing nations. Administers volunteer programs in developing nations to provide educational, health, energy and conservation, housing, food production, and economic development assistance.

Volunteers in Service to America (VISTA) (Corporation for National Service), 1100 Vermont Ave. N.W. 20525; 606-5000. Diana London, acting assistant director. Fax, 606-4921.

Assigns full-time volunteers to public and private nonprofit organizations to alleviate poverty in local communities. Volunteers receive stipends.

Congress:

General Accounting Office, Human Resources, 441 G St. N.W., NGB/ACG 20548; 512-6806. Janet L. Shikles, assistant comptroller general. Fax, 512-5806.

Independent, nonpartisan agency in the legislative branch. Audits, analyzes, and evaluates Corporation for National Service programs; makes reports available to the public.

House Appropriations Committee, Subcommittee on Labor, Health and Human Services, and Education, 2358 RHOB 20515; 225-3508. Neal Smith, D-Iowa, chairman; Mike Stephens, staff assistant.

Appropriates funds for Corporation for National Service programs.

House Government Operations Committee, Subcommittee on Employment, Housing, and Aviation, B349A RHOB 20515; 225-6751. Collin C. Peterson, D-Minn., chairman; Wendy Adler, acting staff director.

Oversight of the Corporation for National Service.

House Ways and Means Committee, 1102 LHOB 20515; 225-3625. Sam M. Gibbons, D-Fla., acting chairman; Janice A. Mays, chief counsel.

Jurisdiction over legislation on tax-exempt foundations and charitable trusts.

Senate Appropriations Committee, Subcommittee on Labor, Health and Human Services, and Education, SD-186 20510; 224-7283. Tom Harkin, D-Iowa, chairman; Ed Long, clerk.

Appropriates funds for Corporation for National Service programs.

Senate Finance Committee, SD-205 20510; 224-4515. Daniel Patrick Moynihan, D-N.Y., chairman; Lawrence O'Donnell Jr., staff director.

Jurisdiction over legislation on tax-exempt foundations and charitable trusts.

Senate Labor and Human Resources Committee, SD-428 20510; 224-5375. Edward M. Kennedy, D-Mass., chairman; Nick Littlefield, chief counsel and staff director.

Oversight of the Corporation for National Service and domestic activities of the Red Cross.

Nongovernmental:

Accountants for the Public Interest, 1012 14th St. N.W., #906 20005; 347-1668. Mildred E. MacVicar, executive director. Fax, 347-1663.

Membership: accountants who provide volunteer services to nonprofit organizations, small businesses, and individuals unable to afford professional accounting services.

Advocacy Institute, 1730 Rhode Island Ave. N.W., #600 20036; 659-8475. Michael Pertschuk and David Cohen, co-directors. Fax, 659-8484.

Public interest organization that offers counseling and training in advocacy skills and strategies to nonprofit groups interested in such issues as civil and human rights, public health, arms control, and environmental and consumer affairs. Aids groups in making better use of resources, such as access to the media and coalition building.

Assn. of Junior Leagues International, 1319 F St. N.W., #604 20004; 393-3364. Christine Benero, director, Washington office. Fax, 393-4517.

Educational and charitable women's organization that promotes voluntarism and works for community improvement through leadership of trained volunteers. Interests include children, women, domestic violence, aging, education, and child health issues. (Headquarters in New York.)

Council of Better Business Bureaus, Philanthropic Advisory Service, 4200 Wilson Blvd., #800, Arlington, VA 22203; (703) 276-0100. Bennett M. Weiner, vice president. Fax, (703) 525-8277.

Serves as a donor information service on charities that solicit nationally or have national or international program services; issues reports on the operations of national charitable organizations; provides charities with counseling and educational materials on compliance with the standards for charitable solicitations.

Council on Foundations, 1828 L St. N.W., #300 20036; 466-6512. James A. Joseph, president. Fax, 785-3926.

Membership: Independent community, family, public and company-sponsored foundations, corporate giving programs, and foundations in other countries. Promotes responsible and effective philanthropy through educational programs, publications, government relations, and promulgation of a set of principles and practices for effective grantmaking.

Ecumenical Resource Consultants, 1843 Kalorama Rd. N.W. 20009; 328-9517. Ronald J. Meshanko, president. Fax, 328-9527.

Consultation group that aids nonprofit organizations in writing grant proposals and locating government, foundation, or corporate funding sources for social services projects. Proposals are in the areas of aging, child care, drug abuse, education, rehabilitation, health, housing, nutrition, refugees, economic development, community organizing, media, women's issues, and youth employment.

The Foundation Center, 1001 Connecticut Ave. N.W., #938 20036; 331-1401. Mary Ann de Barbieri, director, Washington office. Fax, 331-1739.

Publishes foundation guides. Serves as a clearinghouse on foundations and corporate giving, nonprofit management, fund raising, and grants for individuals. Library open to the public. (Headquarters in New York.)

The Funding Center, 209 Madison St., #200, Alexandria, VA 22314; (703) 683-0000. Barry Nickelsberg, executive director. Fax, (703) 683-3834.

Counsels nonprofit organizations in fund raising and related services; identifies public and private sources of funding; conducts workshops.

General Federation of Women's Clubs, 1734 N St. N.W. 20036-2990; 347-3168. Judith Maggrett, executive director. Fax, 835-0246.

Nondenominational, nonpartisan international organization of women volunteers. Interests include conservation, education, home life, international and public affairs, and the arts.

Gifts in Kind America, 700 N. Fairfax St., #300, Alexandria, VA 22314; (703) 836-2121. Susan Corrigan, president. Fax, (703) 549-1481.

Created by United Way of America to encourage donation of newly manufactured products by corporations. Works with companies to develop in-kind programs, coordinates the distribution of gifts to nonprofit agencies, collects tax documentation from recipients, and conducts communitywide public relations activities to encourage product giving.

Independent Sector, 1828 L St. N.W., #1200 20036; 223-8100. Sara E. Melendez, president. Fax, 457-0609.

Membership: corporations, foundations, and national voluntary, charitable, and philanthropic organizations. Encourages volunteering, giving, and not-for-profit initiatives by the private sector for public causes.

Institute for Justice, 1001 Pennsylvania Ave. N.W., #200S 20004-2505; 457-4240. Chip Mellor, president. Fax, 457-8574.

Sponsors seminars to train law students, grassroots activists, and practicing lawyers in applying advocacy strategies in public interest litigation. Seeks to protect from arbitrary government interference free speech, private property rights, parental school choice, and economic liberty. Litigates cases.

National Assembly of National Voluntary Health and Social Welfare Organizations, 1319 F St. N.W., #601 20004; 347-2080. Gordon A. Raley, executive director. Fax, 393-4517.

Membership: national voluntary health and human service organizations. Provides collective leadership in the areas of health and human service. Provides members' professional staff and volunteers with a forum to share information. Supports public policies, programs, and resources that advance the effectiveness of health and human service organizations and their service delivery.

National Center for Nonprofit Boards, 2000 L St. N.W., #510 20036; 452-6262. Nancy R. Axelrod, executive director. Fax, 452-6299.

Works to improve the effectiveness of nonprofit organizations by strengthening their boards of directors. Operates an information clearinghouse; publishes materials on governing nonprofit organizations; assists organizations in conducting training programs, workshops, and

conferences for board members and chief executives.

National Committee for Responsive Philanthropy, 2001 S St. N.W., #620 20009; 387-9177. Robert O. Bothwell, executive director. Fax, 332-5084.

Directs philanthropic giving to benefit the socially, economically, and politically disenfranchised. Advocates for groups that represent the poor, minorities, and women. Conducts research; organizes local coalitions; monitors legislation and regulations.

National Service Secretariat, 5140 Sherier Pl. N.W. 20016; 244-5828. Donald J. Eberly, executive director.

Promotes and supports national volunteer service. Acts as a clearinghouse for information on public service. Sponsors the Coalition for National Service. Monitors legislation.

National Society of Fund Raising Executives, 1101 King St., #700, Alexandria, VA 22314; (703) 684-0410. Patricia F. Lewis, president. Fax, (703) 684-0540.

Membership: individuals who serve as fund-raising executives for nonprofit institutions or as members of counseling firms engaged in fund-raising management. Promotes ethical standards; offers workshops; certifies members; monitors legislation and regulations. NSFRE Foundation promotes philanthropy and voluntarism. Library open to the public by appointment.

The Points of Light Foundation, 1737 H St. N.W. 20006; 223-9186. Richard Schubert, president. Fax, 223-9256.

Motivates leaders to mobilize their members for volunteer community service aimed at solving social problems. Offers technical assistance, training, and information services to nonprofit organizations, public agencies, corporations, and others interested in volunteering.

Progressive Policy Institute, 518 C St. N.E. 20002; 547-0001. Will Marshall, president. Fax, 544-5014.

Encourages civic participation in solving U.S. problems through voluntary national service, community-based institutions, and public-private partnerships.

Support Center of Washington, 2001 O St. N.W. 20036; 833-0300. Sherburne Laughlin, executive director. Fax, 857-0077.
Works to increase the effectiveness and efficiency of nonprofit organizations by providing financial management, accounting, and fundraising assistance. Other services include legal and tax information, marketing and resource development, and training programs.

United Way of America, 701 N. Fairfax St., Alexandria, VA 22314; (703) 836-7100. Elaine L. Chao, president. Fax, (703) 683-7840.
Service association for independent local United Way organizations in the United States. Services include staff training; fund-raising, planning, and communications assistance; resource management; and national public service advertising.

Youth Service America, 1101 15th St. N.W., #200 20005; 296-2992. Roger Landrum, president. Fax, 296-4030.
Advocates youth service at national, state, and local levels. Promotes opportunities for young people to be engaged in community service. Provides service and conservation corps and school- and university-based programs with technical assistance; acts as a clearinghouse on youth service.

See also Alliance of Nonprofit Mailers (p. 308); America the Beautiful Fund (p. 102); Commission for the Advancement of Public Interest Organizations (p. 250); International Voluntary Services (p. 454); Service Corps of Retired Executives Assn. (p. 93); Volunteers in Overseas Cooperative Assistance (p. 455)

Religion and Ethics

See also Constitutional Law and Civil Liberties, Religion (p. 504); Education, Private and Parochial Schools (p. 127)

Nongovernmental:

The Alban Institute, 4550 Montgomery Ave., #433N, Bethesda, MD 20814; (301) 718-4407. Leslie L. Buhler, acting president. Toll-free, (800) 486-1318.
Nondenominational research, consulting, and educational organization that provides church and synagogue congregations with support and services. Interests include planning and growth, conflict resolution, leadership and staff training, spiritual development, and mission and stewardship. Conducts continuing education programs.

American Baptist Churches U.S.A., 110 Maryland Ave. N.E. 20002; 544-3400. Robert W. Tiller, director, governmental relations. Fax, 544-0277.
Serves as liaison between U.S. Baptist churches and government organizations. Interests include immigration, foreign and military policy, human services, employment, the environment, and civil rights. (Headquarters in Valley Forge, Pa.)

American Ethical Union, Washington Ethical Action, 6214 Crathie Lane, Bethesda, MD 20816; (301) 229-3759. Herbert Blinder, director, Washington office.
Federation of ethical culture societies in the United States. Interests include human rights, ethics, world peace, health, welfare, education, and civil liberties. Monitors legislation and regulations. (Headquarters in New York.)

American Friends Service Committee, 1822 R St. N.W. 20009; 483-3341. James Matlack, director, Washington office. Fax, 232-3197.
Independent organization affiliated with the Religious Society of Friends (Quakers) in America. Sponsors domestic and international service, development, justice, and peace programs. Interests include peace education; the arms race and disarmament; social and economic justice; gay and lesbian rights, racism, sexism, and civil rights; refugees and immigration policy; crisis response and relief efforts; and international development efforts, especially in Central America, the Middle East, and southern Africa. (Headquarters in Philadelphia.)

American Jewish Committee, 1156 15th St. N.W., #1201 20005; 785-4200. Jason F. Isaacson, director, government and international affairs. Fax, 785-4115.
Human relations agency devoted to protecting civil and religious rights for all people. Interests include church-state issues, research on human behavior, Israel and the Middle East, Jews in the former Soviet Union, immigration, social discrimination, civil and women's rights, employment, education, housing, and international cooperation for peace and human rights. (Headquarters in New York.)

American Jewish Congress, 2027 Massachusetts Ave. N.W. 20036; 332-4001. Mark J. Pelavin, Washington representative. Fax, 387-3434.

Jewish community relations and civil liberties organization. Seeks to combat anti-Semitism and other forms of bigotry in employment, education, housing, and voting. Areas of activity include church-state relations; government involvement in education; public school prayer; constitutional, minority, women's, and human rights; world Jewry; U.S. foreign policy in the Middle East; Arab investment in the United States; and the Arab boycott of Israel. Monitors legislation. (Headquarters in New York.)

Americans United for Separation of Church and State, 8120 Fenton St., Silver Spring, MD 20910; (301) 589-3707. Barry L. Lynn, executive director. Fax, (301) 495-9173.

Citizens' interest group. Opposes federal and state aid to parochial schools; works to ensure religious neutrality in public schools; supports religious free exercise; initiates litigation; monitors legislation and regulations; maintains speakers bureau.

Baptist Joint Committee on Public Affairs, 200 Maryland Ave. N.E. 20002; 544-4226. James M. Dunn, executive director. Fax, 544-2094.

Membership: national Baptist conventions and conferences. Conducts research and operates an information service. Interests include religious liberty, separation of church and state, First Amendment issues, and government regulation of religious institutions.

Baptist World Alliance, 6733 Curran St., McLean, VA 22101; (703) 790-8980. Denton Lotz, general secretary. Fax, (703) 893-5160.

International Baptist organization. Conducts religious teaching and works to create a better understanding among nations. Organizes development efforts and disaster relief in less developed nations. Interests include human rights and religious liberty.

B'nai B'rith International, 1640 Rhode Island Ave. N.W. 20036; 857-6500. Sidney M. Clearfield, executive vice president. Fax, 296-0638.

Provides information and coordinates political action on public policy issues important to the international Jewish community. The B'nai B'rith Youth Organization offers educational and leadership training programs for teenagers

and counseling and career guidance services. Other interests include community volunteer programs, senior citizen housing, and the security and development of Israel. Sponsors the B'nai B'rith Hillel Foundations, which offer educational, religious, recreational, and social programs for Jewish college and university students. Operates the B'nai B'rith Klutznick National Jewish Museum. Affiliated with the Anti-Defamation League and B'nai B'rith Women.

Catholic Charities USA, 1731 King St., #200, Alexandria, VA 22314; (703) 549-1390. Fred Kammer SJ, president. Fax, (703) 549-1656.

Member agencies and institutions provide persons of all backgrounds with social services, including adoption, education, counseling, food, and housing services. National office promotes public policies that address human needs and social injustice. Provides members with advocacy and professional support, including technical assistance, training, and resource development; disseminates publications.

Catholic Information Center, 741 15th St. N.W. 20005; 783-2062. Michael Curtin, director.

Provides information on Roman Catholicism and the Catholic church. Offers free counseling services. Library open to the public.

Christian Life Commission of the Southern Baptist Convention, 400 N. Capitol St. N.W., #594 20001; 638-3223. James A. Smith, director, government relations. Fax, 347-3658.

Public policy office of the Southern Baptist Convention. Educates churches and members about moral/political issues in U.S. government. Interests include abortion, pornography, religious liberty, First Amendment, drugs and alcohol, hunger, and race relations. (Headquarters in Nashville.)

Christian Science Committee on Publication, 910 16th St. N.W. 20006; 857-0427. Philip G. Davis, federal representative. Fax, 331-0587.

Public service organization that provides information on the religious convictions and practices of Christian Scientists; monitors legislation and regulations; maintains a speakers bureau. (Headquarters in Boston.)

Church of the Brethren, 110 Maryland Ave. N.E. 20002; 546-3202. Timothy A. McElwee, director, Washington office. Fax, 544-5852.

Organizes and coordinates political activities on social policy issues of concern to the church. Interests include the arms race and military spending, civil rights and liberties, health care, conditions for the poor, refugees and immigrants, world hunger, conditions in the Middle East and Central America, and religious freedom. Sponsors seminars. (Headquarters in Elgin, Ill.)

Episcopal Church, 110 Maryland Ave. N.E., #309 20002; 547-7300. Betty A. Coats and Robert J. Brooks, co-directors, Washington office. Fax, 547-4457.

Informs Congress, the executive branch, and governmental agencies about the actions and resolutions of the Episcopal church. Monitors legislation and regulations. (Headquarters in New York.)

Episcopal Peace Fellowship, 1317 G St. N.W. (mailing address: P.O. Box 28156, Washington, DC 20038); 783-3380. Mary H. Miller, executive secretary.

Organizes Episcopalians committed to the biblical concept of peace. Supports conscientious objectors who resist military service and who refuse to pay taxes that support the military; seeks to end the death penalty. Maintains network of local chapters; serves as a clearinghouse for peace education materials.

Ethics and Public Policy Center, Religion and Society Program, 1015 15th St. N.W., #900 20005; 682-1200. George S. Weigel Jr., president. Fax, 408-0632.

Research organization that analyzes the public policy positions of organized religions.

Evangelical Lutheran Church in America, 122 C St. N.W., #125 20001; 783-7507. Kay Dowhower, director, governmental affairs. Toll-free, (800) 959-1988. Fax, 783-7502.

Monitors legislation and regulations on public policy issues of interest to the Lutheran church. (Headquarters in Chicago.)

Friends Committee on National Legislation, 245 2nd St. N.E. 20002-5795; 547-6000. Joe Volk, executive secretary. Fax, 547-6019. Recorded information, 547-4343.

Conducts research on economic justice, world disarmament, international cooperation, and human rights. Advocates on behalf of native Americans in such areas as treaty rights, self-determination, and U.S. trust responsibilities.

Conducts research and education activities through the FCNL Education Fund. Monitors legislation and regulations. Affiliated with the Religious Society of Friends (Quakers).

The General Board of Church and Society of the United Methodist Church, 100 Maryland Ave. N.E. 20002; 488-5600. Thom White Wolf Fassett, general secretary. Fax, 488-5619.

Conducts research on social, political, and economic issues. Interests include social welfare, the environment, civil liberties, criminal justice, and foreign policy; assists member churches.

General Conference of Seventh-day Adventists, 12501 Old Columbia Pike, Silver Spring, MD 20904; (301) 680-6000. Robert S. Folkenberg, president. Fax, (301) 680-6090.

World headquarters of the Seventh-day Adventist church. Interests include education, health care, humanitarian relief, and development. Supplies educational tools for the blind and the hearing-impaired. Operates schools worldwide. Organizes community, service-oriented youth groups.

Institute on Religion and Democracy, 1331 H St. N.W., #900 20005; 393-3200. Diane L. Knippers, president. Fax, 638-4948.

Interdenominational bipartisan organization that supports democratic and constitutional forms of government consistent with the values of Christianity. Serves as a resource center to promote Christian perspectives on U.S. foreign policy questions. Interests include international conflicts, religious liberties, and the growth of democratic forms of government worldwide.

Interfaith Impact for Justice and Peace, 110 Maryland Ave. N.E. 20002; 543-2800. Jim Bell, executive director. Fax, 547-8107. Legislative update recording, (800) 424-7290.

Coalition of national religious organizations. Develops information and recommendations on U.S. policy concerning health and human services, international development and economics, food and agriculture, and the environment.

International Religious Liberty Assn., 12501 Old Columbia Pike, Silver Spring, MD 20904; (301) 680-6680. Bert B. Beach, secretary general. Fax, (301) 680-6695.

Seeks to preserve and expand religious liberty and freedom of conscience; advocates separation of church and state; sponsors international and domestic meetings and congresses.

Jesuit Conference, Social Ministries, 1424 16th St. N.W., #300 20036-2286; 462-7008. Peter Klink SJ, director. Fax, 462-7009.

Information and advocacy organization of Jesuits and laypersons concerned with peace and social justice issues in the United States. Interests include peace and disarmament, economic justice, and issues affecting minorities, especially native Americans, Hispanics, and African Americans.

Leadership Conference of Women Religious, 8808 Cameron St., Silver Spring, MD 20910-4113; (301) 588-4955. Margaret Cafferty, executive director. Fax, (301) 587-4575.

Membership: Roman Catholic women religious who are the principal administrators of their congregations in the United States. Offers programs and support to members. Conducts research; serves as an information clearinghouse.

Maryknoll Fathers and Brothers (Catholic Foreign Mission Society of America), 4834 16th St. N.W. 20011; 726-4252. Joseph L. Thaler, regional director.

Conducts religious teaching and other mission work for the poor in Africa, Asia, and Latin America. (Headquarters in Ossining, N.Y.)

Mennonite Central Committee, 110 Maryland Ave. N.E. 20002; 544-6564. Kenneth Martens Friesen, acting director, Washington office. Fax, 544-2820.

Christian organization engaged in service and development projects. Monitors legislation and regulations affecting issues of interest to Mennonite churches. Interests include human rights in developing countries, military spending, the environment, world hunger, poverty, and civil and religious liberties. (Headquarters in Akron, Pa.)

National Assn. of Evangelicals, 1023 15th St. N.W., #500 20005; 789-1011. Robert P. Dugan Jr., director, public affairs. Fax, 842-0392.

Represents Christian evangelical denominations. Interests include religious liberty, economic policy, church-state relations, foreign policy, and immigration and refugee policy. Monitors legislation and regulations. (Headquarters in Wheaton, Ill.)

National Catholic Conference for Interracial Justice, 3033 4th St. N.E. 20017; 529-6480. Jerome Ernst, executive director. Fax, 526-1262.

Promotes the Roman Catholic church's teachings on racial justice and multicultural and multiracial understanding.

National Conference of Catholic Bishops/ United States Catholic Conference, 3211 4th St. N.E. 20017; 541-3000. Robert N. Lynch, general secretary. Press, 541-3200. Fax, 541-3322.

Serves as a forum for bishops to exchange ideas, debate concerns of the church, and draft responses to religious and social issues. Provides information on doctrine and policies of the Roman Catholic church; develops religious education and training programs; formulates policy positions on social issues, including the economy, employment, federal budget priorities, voting rights, energy, health, housing, rural affairs, international military and political matters, human rights, the arms race, global economics, and immigration and refugee policy.

National Conference on Soviet Jewry, 1640 Rhode Island Ave. N.W., #501 20036; 898-2500. Mark B. Levin, executive director. Fax, 898-0296.

Promotes religious and personal freedom for Jews wishing to leave the former Soviet Union in accordance with international law and for those choosing to remain. Provides them with legal advice and technical assistance. Organizes conferences, rallies, vigils, commemorations, and letter-writing campaigns; monitors legislation.

National Council of Catholic Women, 1275 K St. N.W., #975 20005; 682-0334. Annette Kane, executive director. Fax, 682-0338.

Federation of Roman Catholic women's organizations. Provides a forum for Catholic women to research and discuss issues affecting the church and society; monitors legislation and regulations. Interests include employment, family life, abortion, care for the elderly, day care, world hunger, global water supplies, genetic engineering research, pornography legislation, and substance abuse. Special programs include volunteer respite care, leadership training for women, and drug and alcohol abuse education.

National Council of Churches, 110 Maryland Ave. N.E. 20002; 544-2350. James A. Hamilton, director, Washington office.

Membership: Protestant and Orthodox churches. Interests include racial and social equality; social welfare, economic justice, and peace issues; church-state relations; prayer in public schools;

and federal aid to private schools. (Headquarters in New York.)

National Council of Jewish Women, 1101 15th St. N.W. 20005; 296-2588. Sammie Moshenberg, director, Washington office. Fax, 331-7792.

Jewish women's education, community service, and advocacy organization. Interests include economic equity for women; reproductive, civil, and constitutional rights; juvenile justice; child care; education and welfare programs; Israel; aging issues; and work and family issues. (Headquarters in New York.)

NETWORK, 806 Rhode Island Ave. N.E. 20018; 526-4070. Kathy Thornton, national coordinator. Fax, 832-4635.

Catholic organization that coordinates political activity on public policy issues. Interests include arms control, military spending, human rights, and economic justice for women and children.

Presbyterian Church (U.S.A.), 110 Maryland Ave. N.E., #104 20002; 543-1126. Elenora Giddings Ivory, director, Washington office. Fax, 543-7755.

Provides information on the views of the general assembly of the Presbyterian church on public policy issues; monitors legislation affecting issues of concern. Interests include arms control, budget priorities, foreign policy, civil rights, religious liberty, church-state relations, economic justice, and public policy issues affecting women. (Headquarters in Louisville, Ky.)

Progressive National Baptist Convention, 601 50th St. N.E. 20019; 396-0558. Tyrone S. Pitts, general secretary. Fax, 398-4998.

Baptist denomination that supports missionaries, implements education programs, and advocates for civil and human rights.

Union of American Hebrew Congregations, Religious Action Center of Reform Judaism, 2027 Massachusetts Ave. N.W. 20036; 387-2800. David Saperstein, director, Washington office. Fax, 667-9070.

Religious and educational organization concerned with social justice and religious liberty. Mobilizes the American Jewish community and serves as its advocate on issues concerning Jews around the world, including economic justice, civil rights, and international peace. (Headquarters in New York.)

Unitarian Universalist Assn. of Congregations in North America, 100 Maryland Ave. N.E. 20002; 547-0254. Robert Z. Alpern, director. Fax, 544-2854.

Monitors public policy and legislation. Interests include civil and religious liberties; arms limitation and disarmament; Middle East policy; the federal budget; human rights; and public policy affecting women, including reproductive rights policy. (Headquarters in Boston.)

United Church of Christ, 110 Maryland Ave. N.E., #207 20002; 543-1517. Jay Lintner, director, Washington office. Fax, 543-5994.

Studies public policy issues and promotes church policy on these issues; organizes political activity to implement church views. Interests include health care, international peace, economic justice, and civil rights. (Headquarters in Cleveland.)

Women's Alliance for Theology, Ethics, and Ritual, 8035 13th St., Silver Spring, MD 20910; (301) 589-2509. Diann Neu and Mary Hunt, co-directors. Fax, (301) 589-3150.

Feminist theological organization that focuses on issues concerning women and religion. Interests include social issues; work skills for women with disabilities; human rights in Argentina, Chile, and Uruguay; and liturgies, rituals, counseling, and research.

See also Center of Concern (p. 447); Ethics Resource Center (p. 52); Society for Values in Higher Education (p. 136)

Key Agencies:

Census Bureau
Suitland and Silver Hill Rds.
Suitland, MD
(Mailing address: Washington, DC 20233)
Information: (301) 763-4040

General Services Administration
18th and F Sts. N.W. 20405
Information: 708-5082

Government Printing Office
732 N. Capitol St. N.W. 20401
Information: 512-0000

Merit Systems Protection Board
1120 Vermont Ave. N.W. 20419
Information: 653-7200

National Archives and Records Administration
7th St. and Pennsylvania Ave. N.W. 20408
Information: 501-5400

Office of Government Ethics
1201 New York Ave. N.W., #500 20005
Information: 523-5757

Office of Personnel Management
1900 E St. N.W. 20415
Information: 606-1800

Office of Special Counsel
1730 M St. N.W., #300 20036-4505
Information: 653-7188

U.S. Postal Service
475 L'Enfant Plaza S.W. 20260
Information: 268-2284

Key Committees:

House Government Operations Committee
2157 RHOB 20515
Phone: 225-5051

House Post Office and Civil Service Committee
309 CHOB 20515
Phone: 225-4054

Senate Governmental Affairs Committee
SD-340 20510
Phone: 224-4751

Key Personnel:

Census Bureau
Harry A. Scarr, acting director

General Services Administration
Roger Johnson, administrator

Government Printing Office
Michael F. DiMario, public printer

Merit Systems Protection Board
Ben Erdreich, chairman

National Archives and Records Administration
Trudy H. Peterson, acting archivist of the United States

Office of Government Ethics
Stephen D. Potts, director

Office of Personnel Management
Jim King, director

Office of Special Counsel
Kathleen Day Koch, special counsel

U.S. Postal Service
Marvin T. Runyon, postmaster general

7

Government Personnel and Services

Contents:

Census: Population Data

The Census Bureau publishes a pamphlet, "Telephone Contacts for Data Users," that lists key Census Bureau personnel and their fields of specialty. Copies may be obtained from the Census Bureau, Data User Services Division, User Training Branch, Washington, D.C. 20233; (301) 763-1510. For a specific inquiry about computer data, call (301) 763-4100.

Agencies:

Census Bureau (Commerce Dept.), Suitland and Silver Hill Rds., Suitland, MD (mailing address: Washington, DC 20233); (301) 763-5190. Harry A. Scarr, acting director. Information, (301) 763-4040. Library, (301) 763-5042. Fax, (301) 763-5013. TDD, (301) 763-2811.

Conducts surveys and censuses (including the decennial census of population and housing); collects and analyzes demographic, social, economic, housing, agricultural, and foreign trade data and data on governments; publishes statistics for use by Congress, business, state and local governments, planners, and the public. Library open to the public.

Census Bureau (Commerce Dept.), Decennial Management, Suitland and Silver Hill Rds., Suitland, MD (mailing address: Washington, DC 20233); (301) 763-5180. Charles D. Jones, acting chief. Fax, (301) 763-4422.

Provides data from the 1990 decennial census (including general plans and procedures), economic, demographic, and population statistics, and information on trends.

Census Bureau (Commerce Dept.), Demographic Surveys, Suitland and Silver Hill Rds., Suitland, MD (mailing address: Washington, DC 20233); (301) 763-2776. Sherry L. Courtland, chief. Fax, (301) 763-2703.

Provides and explains proper use of data on consumer spending, crime, employment and unemployment, income, and housing. Conducts surveys on various subjects, including population, prisoners, health, and travel.

Census Bureau (Commerce Dept.), Housing and Household Economic Statistics, 3737 Branch Ave., Hillcrest Heights, MD (mailing address: Washington, DC 20233); (301) 763-8550. Daniel H. Weinberg, chief. Fax, (301) 763-8412.

Develops statistical programs for the decennial census and for other surveys on housing, income, poverty, and the labor force. Collects and explains the proper use of economic, social, and demographic data. Responsible for the technical planning, analysis, and publication of data from current surveys, including the decennial census, the American Housing Survey, Current Population Survey, and Survey of Income and Program Participation.

Census Bureau (Commerce Dept.), Population, Suitland and Silver Hill Rds., Suitland, MD (mailing address: Washington, DC 20233); (301) 763-7646. Arthur J. Norton, chief. Fax, (301) 763-4144.

Prepares population estimates and projections for national, state, and local areas and congressional districts. Provides data on demographic and social statistics in the following areas: families and households, marital status and living arrangements, farm population, migration and mobility, population distribution, ancestry, fertility, child care, race and ethnicity, language patterns, school enrollment, educational attainment, and voting.

Congress:

House Appropriations Committee, Subcommittee on Commerce, Justice, State, and Judiciary, H309 CAP 20515; 225-3351. Neal Smith, D-Iowa, chairman; John Osthaus, staff assistant.

Jurisdiction over legislation to appropriate funds for the Commerce Dept., including the Census Bureau.

House Post Office and Civil Service Committee, Subcommittee on Census, Statistics, and Postal Personnel, 515 O'Neill Bldg. (300 New Jersey Ave. S.E.) 20515; 226-7523. Tom Sawyer, D-Ohio, chairman; TerriAnn Lowenthal, staff director.

Jurisdiction over census legislation and statistics collection, demography, and population issues; oversight of the Census Bureau.

Senate Appropriations Committee, Subcommittee on Commerce, Justice, State, and Judiciary, S146A CAP 20510; 224-7277. Ernest F. Hollings, D-S.C., chairman; Scott B. Gudes, clerk.

Jurisdiction over legislation to appropriate funds for the Commerce Dept., including the Census Bureau.

Senate Governmental Affairs Committee, Subcommittee on Regulation and Government Information, SH-605 20510; 224-9000. Joseph I. Lieberman, D-Conn., chairman; John Nakahata, staff director.

Jurisdiction over census legislation and statistics collection, demography, and population issues; oversight of the Census Bureau.

Nongovernmental:

Population Assn. of America, 1722 N St. N.W. 20036; 429-0891. Ina Young, executive administrator. Fax, 785-0146.

Membership: university, government, and industry researchers in demography. Holds annual technical sessions to present papers on population issues and statistics.

Population Reference Bureau, 1875 Connecticut Ave. N.W., #520 20009-5728; 483-1100. Peter J. Donaldson, president. Fax, 328-3937.

Educational organization engaged in information dissemination, training, and policy analysis on population trends and issues. Interests include international development and family planning programs, the environment, and U.S. social and economic policy. Library open to the public.

Civil Service

General

See also Ethics in Government (p. 297); Government Housekeeping, General (p. 300)

Agencies:

General Services Administration, Information Security Oversight, 750 17th St. N.W. 20006; 634-6150. Steven Garfinkel, director. Fax, 634-6131.

Oversees the security classification system throughout the executive branch; reports to the president on implementation of the security classification system. Develops and disseminates security education materials. Oversees the Classified Information Nondisclosure Agreement, which bars federal employees from disclosing classified and sensitive government information.

Office of Personnel Management (OPM), 1900 E St. N.W. 20415; 606-1000. Jim King, director. Information, 606-1800. Library, 606-1381. Fax, 606-2573. TDD, 606-2118. Locator, 606-2400; job information, 606-2701.

Administers civil service rules and regulations; sets policy for personnel management, labor-management relations, work force effectiveness, and employment within the executive branch; manages federal personnel activities, including recruitment, pay comparability, and benefit programs. Library open to the public.

Office of Personnel Management, Compensation Policy, 1900 E St. N.W. 20415; 606-2880. Barbara L. Fiss, assistant director. Fax, 606-4264.

Responsible for policy development and administration of compensation systems for almost two million federal civilian white-collar and blue-collar employees.

Office of Personnel Management, Human Resources Development, 1900 E St. N.W. 20415-0001; 606-1575. Carol J. Okins, director.

Offers leadership training services and sets governmentwide policy on human resources development. Oversees the Senior Executive Service Program, Executive Management Development Centers, and Federal Executive Institute.

Office of Personnel Management, International Affairs, 1900 E St. N.W. 20415; 606-0961. Carmen Lomellin, director. Fax, 606-4787.

Coordinates briefings on the U.S. civil service and OPM for foreign visitors from civil services and public administration departments worldwide. Acts as OPM's official representative in any international forum. Interacts with other agencies and organizations concerning international activities.

Office of Personnel Management, Personnel Systems and Oversight, 1900 E St. N.W. 20415-0001; 606-2800. Jean M. Barber, associate director.

Works to improve personnel management within agencies by developing and implementing policy on white- and blue-collar pay systems,

Office of Personnel Management

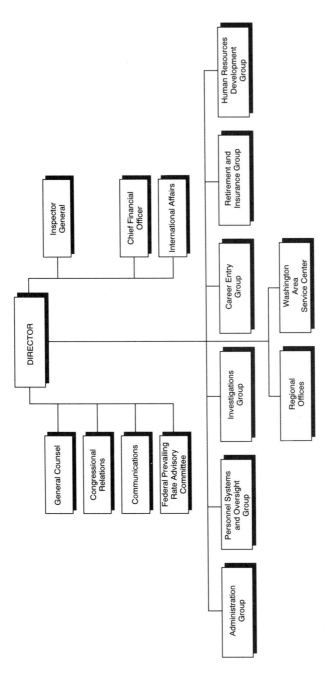

- DIRECTOR

- Inspector General
- Chief Financial Officer
- International Affairs

- General Counsel
- Congressional Relations
- Communications
- Federal Prevailing Rate Advisory Committee

- Administration Group
- Personnel Systems and Oversight Group
- Investigations Group
  - Regional Offices
- Career Entry Group
  - Washington Area Service Center
- Retirement and Insurance Group
- Human Resources Development Group

incentive awards, labor-management relations, employee benefits, and information systems. Assesses agencies' effectiveness in managing personnel. Evaluates agencies' compliance with personnel laws and regulations.

Office of Personnel Management, Statistical Analysis and Services, 1900 E St. N.W. 20415; 606-2850. John E. Curnow, chief. Fax, 606-1719.

Produces information for the Office of Personnel Management, Congress, and the public on statistical aspects of the federal civilian work force, including trends in composition, grade levels, minority employment, sizes of agencies, and salaries.

Congress:

House Appropriations Committee, Subcommittee on Treasury, Postal Service, and General Government, H164 CAP 20515; 225-5834. Steny H. Hoyer, D-Md., chairman; Bill Smith, staff assistant. Fax, 426-3763.

Jurisdiction over legislation to appropriate funds for the Office of Personnel Management and the Merit Systems Protection Board.

House Education and Labor Committee, Subcommittee on Labor Standards, Occupational Health and Safety, B345A RHOB 20515; 225-1927. Austin J. Murphy, D-Pa., chairman; James Riley, staff director.

Jurisdiction over legislation on federal employees' compensation.

House Government Operations Committee, Subcommittee on Employment, Housing, and Aviation, B349A RHOB 20515; 225-6751. Collin C. Peterson, D-Minn., chairman; Wendy Adler, acting staff director.

Oversight of the Office of Personnel Management and the Merit Systems Protection Board.

House Post Office and Civil Service Committee, Subcommittee on Civil Service, 122 CHOB 20515; 225-4025. Frank McCloskey, D-Ind., chairman; Debbie Kendall, staff director.

Jurisdiction over legislation on civil service labor-management issues, hiring and recruiting, rights of privacy, and code of ethics; and legislation related to the Hatch Act, which deals with the political activity of civil service employees. Oversight of the Senior Executive Service and intergovernmental personnel programs. Studies the effects of reorganization of agencies on federal employees.

House Post Office and Civil Service Committee, Subcommittee on Compensation and Employee Benefits, 209 CHOB 20515; 226-7546. Eleanor Holmes Norton, D-D.C., chair; Cedric Hendricks, staff director.

Jurisdiction over legislation on civil service employee pay allowances, dual compensation, job classifications, benefits, leave, and retirement.

Senate Appropriations Committee, Subcommittee on Treasury, Postal Service, and General Government, SD-190 20510; 224-8271. Dennis DeConcini, D-Ariz., chairman; Patty Lynch, clerk.

Jurisdiction over legislation to appropriate funds for the Office of Personnel Management and the Merit Systems Protection Board.

Senate Governmental Affairs Committee, Subcommittee on Federal Services, Post Office, and Civil Service, SH-601 20510; 224-2254. David Pryor, D-Ark., chairman; Kimberly A. Weaver, staff director.

Jurisdiction over legislation on civil service labor-management issues; hiring, recruiting, and job classifications; compensation, including pay allowances and benefits; code of ethics; rights of privacy; intergovernmental personnel programs; effects of reorganization; leave and retirement; and legislation related to the Hatch Act, which deals with the political activity of civil service employees. Oversight of the Senior Executive Service, the Office of Personnel Management, and the Merit Systems Protection Board.

See also Federal Government Service Task Force (p. 756)

Nongovernmental:

See also Labor Unions list (p. 801)

American Council of the Blind Government Employees, 1155 15th St. N.W. 20005; 467-5081. Mitch Pomerantz, president. Toll-free, (800) 424-8666. Fax, 467-5085.

Membership: federal, state, and local government employees and retirees who are blind or visually impaired and other interested persons. Seeks to improve government employment opportunities for visually disabled persons. Offers technical assistance. (Affiliated with American Council of the Blind.)

Departments

Agriculture .... 720-5625, recording

Commerce 482-5138

Defense (civilian) .... (703) 697-9205
Air Force (civilian) .... (703) 695-4389
Army (civilian) .... (703) 693-7911
Navy (civilian) .... (703) 697-6181
Defense Intelligence Agency (703) 284-1321
Defense Logistics Agency . (703) 274-7087
(703) 274-7372, vacancies recording
Defense Mapping Agency . (301) 227-1980

Education 401-0553
401-0559, vacancies

Energy .... 586-4333, job hotline

Health and Human Services ... 619-2123
Food and Drug
Administration .... (301) 443-1970
Health Resources and Services
Administration .... (301) 443-6707
(301) 443-1230, vacancies recording
Public Health Service and
National Institutes
of Health ..... (301) 496-2403, recording
Social Security
Administration .... (410) 965-4506
Substance Abuse and Mental Health
Services Administration .. (301) 443-5407
(301) 443-2282, vacancies recording

Housing and Urban
Development 708-0408
708-3203, vacancies recording

Departmental and Agency . . .

Interior 208-5701
Justice 514-6810
514-6877, vacancies recording

Labor 219-6646

State 647-7252
647-7284, civil service employment
(703) 875-7490, vacancies recording

Transportation 366-9392

Treasury .... 622-1029, vacancies recording

Veterans Affairs 233-2459

Agencies

Administrative Office of
the U.S. Courts 273-2760
vacancies recording

Agency for International
Development 663-2368
overseas, clerical, and secretarial;
663-1512, professional

Commodity Futures Trading
Commission 254-3275

Consumer Product Safety
Commission .... (301) 504-0100

Corporation for National
Service 606-5263

Environmental Protection
Agency ...... 260-5055, vacancies recording

Equal Employment Opportunity
Commission 663-4337

Blacks in Government, 1820 11th St. N.W. 20001; 667-3280. Marion A. Bowden, president. Fax, 667-3705.

Advocacy organization for public employees. Promotes equal opportunity and career advancement for African American government employees; provides career development information; seeks to eliminate racism in the federal work force; sponsors programs, business meetings, and social gatherings; represents interests of African American government workers to Congress and the executive branch; promotes voter education and registration.

Council for Excellence in Government, 1620 L St. N.W., #850 20036; 728-0418. Patricia G. McGinnis, president.

Membership: business and professional leaders with previous executive-level government experience. Works to broaden understanding of public service and management in the government; conducts outreach activities that encourage public and media discussion of public service and management; serves as a forum for business and government executives to discuss and develop new ideas for public service and management.

... Personnel Offices

Export-Import Bank 566-8834

Farm Credit
Administration .. (703) 883-4139, recording

Federal Communications
Commission 632-7104
632-0101, vacancies recording

Federal Deposit Insurance
Corp. 393-8400

Federal Election Commission ... 219-4290

Federal Emergency Management
Agency 646-4040

Federal Labor Relations
Authority 382-0748

Federal Mediation and
Conciliation Service 653-5260

Federal Reserve Board 452-3880

Federal Trade Commission 326-2020
vacancies recording

General Accounting Office 275-5067
recording

General Services
Administration 501-0398

Government Printing Office 512-1200

Interstate Commerce
Commission 927-7288

Merit Systems Protection
Board 653-5916

National Aeronautics and
Space Administration 358-1560

National Archives and Records
Administration .... (301) 713-6760

National Credit Union
Administration .... (703) 518-6510

National Endowment for
the Arts 682-5405

National Endowment for
the Humanities 606-8415

National Labor Relations
Board 273-3980

National Mediation Board 523-5950

National Science
Foundation .... (703) 306-1182

National Transportation
Safety Board 382-6717

Nuclear Regulatory
Commission .... (301) 492-8234

Office of Personnel
Management .... 606-2424, recording

Securities and Exchange
Commission 272-2550

Small Business Administration   205-6780

Smithsonian Institution 287-3100
287-3102, vacancies recording

U.S. Arms Control and
Disarmament Agency 647-2034

U.S. Information Agency 619-4617
619-4539, vacancies recording

U.S. International Trade
Commission 205-2651

U.S. Postal Service 268-3646

Federal Managers Assn., 1641 Prince St., Alexandria, VA 22314; (703) 683-8700. Bruce Moyer, executive director. Fax, (703) 683-8707.
Seeks to improve the effectiveness of federal supervisors and managers and the operations of the federal government.

Federally Employed Women, 1400 Eye St. N.W. 20005; 898-0994. Karen Scott, executive director. Fax, 898-0998.
Membership: women and men who work for the federal government. Works to eliminate sex discrimination in government employment and to increase job opportunities for women; offers

training programs; monitors legislation and regulations.

Professional Managers Assn., P.O. Box 895, Ben Franklin Station, Washington, DC 20044; 927-3990. Helene Benson, president. Fax, 927-4979.
Membership: midlevel career federal managers. Conducts research on management practices in the federal government; works to improve the working atmosphere, pay and benefits, and public image of government employees; provides educational materials.

Public Employees Roundtable, 1201 Constitution Ave. N.W., #1220 (mailing address: P.O. Box 14270, Ben Franklin Station, Washington, DC 20044-4270); 927-5000. Joan B. Keston, executive director. Fax, 927-5001.

Membership: professional and managerial associations representing a wide range of public employees at all levels. Sponsors conferences, celebrations, and publicity events to educate the public about the contributions of public employees. Sponsors annual scholarship program for college students pursuing a public service career.

Senior Executives Assn., P.O. Box 7610, Ben Franklin Station, Washington, DC 20044; 927-7000. Carol A. Bonosaro, president.

Professional association representing Senior Executive Service members and other federal career executives. Sponsors professional education. Interests include management improvement, compensation and benefits, and public recognition of career executives' activities. Monitors legislation and regulations.

Dismissals and Disputes

Agencies:

Merit Systems Protection Board, 1120 Vermont Ave. N.W. 20419; 653-7101. Ben Erdreich, chairman. Information, 653-7200. Library, 653-7200. Fax, 653-2261. TDD, 653-8896.

Independent quasi-judicial agency that handles hearings and appeals involving federal employees; protects the integrity of federal merit systems and ensures adequate protection for employees against abuses by agency management. Library open to the public.

Merit Systems Protection Board, Appeals Counsel, 1120 Vermont Ave. N.W. 20419; 653-8888. Stephen E. Alpern, director. Fax, 653-2260.

Analyzes and processes petitions for review of appeals decisions from the regional offices; prepares opinions and orders for board consideration; analyzes and processes cases that are reopened and prepares proposed dispositions.

Merit Systems Protection Board, Policy and Evaluations, 1120 Vermont Ave. N.W. 20419; 653-7208. Evangeline W. Swift, director. Fax, 653-7211.

Conducts studies on the civil service and other executive branch merit systems; reports to the president and Congress on whether federal employees are adequately protected against political abuses and prohibited personnel practices. Conducts annual oversight review of the Office of Personnel Management.

Merit Systems Protection Board, Washington Regional Office, 5203 Leesburg Pike, #1109, Falls Church, VA 22041; (703) 756-6250. P. J. Winzer, director. Fax, (703) 756-7112.

Hears and decides appeals of adverse personnel actions (such as removals, suspensions for more than 14 days, and reductions in grade or pay), retirement, and performance-related actions for federal civilian employees who work in the Washington area or in overseas areas not covered by other board regional offices. Federal civilian employees who work outside Washington, D.C., should contact the Merit Systems Protection Board regional office in their area. *(See Regional Federal Information Sources list, p. 853.)*

Office of Personnel Management, 1900 E St. N.W. 20415; 606-1700. Lorraine Lewis, general counsel. Fax, 606-0082.

Represents the federal government before the Merit Systems Protection Board, other administrative tribunals, and the courts.

Office of Special Counsel, 1730 M St. N.W., #300 20036-4505; 653-7122. Kathleen Day Koch, special counsel. Information, 653-7188. Fax, 653-5151. Issues relating to the Hatch Act, (800) 854-2824.

Investigates allegations of prohibited personnel practices, including reprisals against whistle-blowers (federal employees who disclose waste, fraud, inefficiency, and wrongdoing by supervisors of federal departments and agencies). Initiates necessary corrective or disciplinary action. Enforces the Hatch Act.

Congress:

See Civil Service, General, Congress (p. 287)

Judiciary:

U.S. Court of Appeals for the Federal Circuit, 717 Madison Pl. N.W. 20439; 633-6562. Helen W. Nies, chief judge; Francis X. Gindhart, clerk, 633-6555. Fax, 633-9629.

Reviews decisions of the Merit Systems Protection Board.

Nongovernmental:

See Civil Service, General, Nongovernmental (p. 287)

Hiring, Recruitment, and Training

Agencies:

The Federal Job Information/Testing Center in Washington, D.C. (606-2700), provides the public with information on applications for civil service jobs. Persons outside Washington, D.C., should contact the regional federal job office in their area. (See Regional Federal Information Sources list, p. 859.) For a list of federal personnel offices in Washington, D.C., see p. 288.

Office of Personnel Management, Academic and Special Projects, 1900 E St. N.W., #1416 20415; 606-3283. Anna Briatico, chief. Fax, 606-1768.

Visits college campuses to inform soon-to-be graduates about opportunities in the federal work force. (See also Office of Personnel Management, Federal Employment Information Centers, p. 859.)

Office of Personnel Management, Affirmative Recruiting and Employment, 1900 E St. N.W., #6332 20415; 606-0800. Donna Beecher, assistant director. Fax, 606-5049. TDD, 606-0023.

Develops policies, programs, and procedures for governmentwide recruiting and academic relations programs, including diversity employment efforts related to women, minorities, students, persons with disabilities, and veterans.

Office of Personnel Management, Career Entry, 1900 E St. N.W. 20415; 606-0800. Leonard R. Klein, associate director. Fax, 606-1540.

Develops civil service tests for most federal jobs through GS-15; develops qualification standards and governmentwide staffing policies; administers special programs to find jobs for displaced federal employees, minorities, veterans, women, youth, and persons with disabilities; administers the Administrative Law Judges program, federal recruitment efforts, and special personnel programs.

Office of Personnel Management, Classification, 1900 E St. N.W. 20415; 606-2950. Ray Moran, acting assistant director. Fax, 606-4891.

Develops job classification standards for agencies within the federal government.

Office of Personnel Management, Employee Development Policy and Programs, 901 N. Stuart St., #1310, Arlington, VA 20415; (703) 235-1006. Don Mizaur, acting assistant director. Fax, (703) 235-1492.

Responsible for governmentwide training policy of the civilian work force. Oversees the Government Affairs Institute, the National Independent Study Center in Denver, and a network of contractors who provide agencies with training design and organization development services.

Office of Personnel Management, Executive and Management Development, 901 N. Stuart St., #305B, Arlington, VA 20415; (703) 235-1111. Kirke Harper, acting assistant director. Fax, (703) 235-1414.

Administers training programs for government executives. Programs include the Federal Executive Institute, European Training Program, Management Development Centers, and five other long-term development programs: the Presidential Management Intern Program, the Women's Executive Leadership Program, the Executive Potential Program, the Senior Executive Service Candidate Development Program, and the LEGIS Fellows Program.

Office of Personnel Management, Executive and Management Policy, 1900 E St. N.W. 20415; 606-1610. Judith M. Jaffe, assistant director. Fax, 606-2126.

Responsible for training and curriculum development programs for government executives and supervisors. Administers executive personnel systems, including those for the Senior Executive Service (SES) and personnel in supergrade positions not in SES.

Office of Personnel Management, Federal Investigations, 600 E St. N.W., #200 (mailing address: P.O. Box 886, Washington, DC 20044-0886); 376-3800. Peter Garcia, assistant director. Fax, 376-3840.

Initiates and conducts investigations of new federal employees; determines whether applicants and appointees are suitable for positions other than those involving national security.

Office of Personnel Management, Job Information Center, 1900 E St. N.W. 20415; 606-2700. Joe Ruiz, chief.

Responds to questions concerning entry into the federal work force; posts job vacancies and informs applicants of qualification requirements and application procedures; provides pamphlets on federal employment. *(See also Office of Personnel Management, Federal Employment Information Centers, p. 859.)*

Office of Personnel Management, Personnel Mobility Program, 901 N. Stuart St., Arlington, VA (mailing address: P.O. Box 164, Washington, DC 20044); (703) 235-1113. Ardrey Harris, chief. Fax, (703) 235-1412.

Oversees temporary personnel exchanges among federal agencies, state and local governments, institutions of higher education, and other organizations.

See also Office of Personnel Management, Presidential Management Intern Program (p. 309)

Congress:

See Civil Service, General, Congress (p. 287)

Nongovernmental:

See Civil Service, General, Nongovernmental (p. 287)

Labor-Management Relations

See also Civil Service, Dismissals and Disputes (p. 290); Civil Service, Pay and Employee Benefits (this page); Labor-Management Relations, General (p. 186)

Agencies:

Federal Labor Relations Authority, 607 14th St. N.W., #410 20424-0001; 482-6500. Jean McKee, chairman; Joe Swerdzewski, general counsel, 482-6600. Fax, 482-6635.

Oversees the federal labor-management relations program; administers the law that protects the right of federal employees to organize, bargain collectively, and participate through labor organizations of their own choosing.

Federal Service Impasses Panel (Federal Labor Relations Authority), 607 14th St. N.W., #220 20424-1000; 482-6670. Edwin D. Brubeck, chairman; Linda A. Lafferty, executive director.

Assists in resolving contract negotiation impasses between federal agencies and labor organizations representing federal employees.

Office of Personnel Management, 1900 E St. N.W. 20415; 606-1700. Lorraine Lewis, general counsel. Fax, 606-0082.

Advises the government on law and legal policy relating to federal labor-management relations; represents the government before the Merit Systems Protection Board.

Office of Personnel Management, Labor Relations and Workforce Performance, 1900 E St. N.W. 20415; 606-2920. Allan D. Heuerman, assistant director. Fax, 606-2613.

Provides government agencies and unions with information and advice on employee- and labor-management relations. Assists agencies with performance management and incentive awards.

Office of Personnel Management, National Partnership Council, 1900 E St. N.W. 20415-0001; 606-1035. Pat Stewart and Doug Walker, executive secretariat, 606-1479. Fax, 606-2264.

Membership: officials of executive departments, government agencies, and federal workers' unions. Advises the president on labor-management relations in the executive branch. Proposes legislation consistent with the National Performance Review's recommendations on flexible hiring and on reforming the General Schedule classification system.

Congress:

See Civil Service, General, Congress (p. 287)

Nongovernmental:

See Labor Unions list (p. 801)

See also American Foreign Service Assn. (p. 468)

Pay and Employee Benefits

Agencies:

Bureau of Labor Statistics (Labor Dept.), Occupational Pay and Employee Benefit Levels, 2 Massachusetts Ave. N.E. 20212; 606-6225. Jordan N. Pfuntner, chief. Fax, 606-7856.

Conducts occupational pay surveys on area and national industries.

General Schedule (GS) for Federal Civilian White-Collar Employees

Salaries for federal white-collar civil service employees vary from agency to agency but most agencies follow this blueprint when developing their respective pay systems. In January 1994, most general schedule employees began receiving locality pay as a salary supplement. Intended to reduce the discrepancy between federal and nonfederal rates of pay in designated geographical areas, locality pay is calculated as a percentage of salary. Percentages used to calculate locality pay, by area of employment, are: Atlanta, 3.86; Boston, 5.47; Chicago, 5.34; Cincinnati, 4.22; Cleveland, 3.34; Dallas, 4.21; Dayton, 3.77; Denver, 4.54; Detroit, 4.84; Houston, 6.52; Huntsville, 4.10; Indianapolis, 3.68; Kansas City, 3.30; Los Angeles (including Santa Barbara Co. and Edwards A.F.B.), 5.69; Memphis, 3.09; New York, 5.77; Norfolk, 3.28; Oklahoma City, 3.34; Philadelphia, 4.96; Sacramento, 3.69; St. Louis, 3.09; Salt Lake City, 3.09; San Antonio, 3.09; San Diego, 3.88; San Francisco, 6.18; Seattle, 3.92; Washington, D.C. (including St. Mary's Co., Md.), 4.23; and rest of the United States (not including Alaska, Hawaii, or U.S. territories or possessions), 3.09.

GS Grade	Step 1	2	3	4	5	6	7	8	9	10
1	$11,903	$12,300	$12,695	$13,090	$13,487	$13,720	$14,109	$14,503	$14,521	$14,891
2	13,382	13,701	14,145	14,521	14,683	15,115	15,547	15,979	16,411	16,843
3	14,603	15,090	15,577	16,064	16,551	17,038	17,525	18,012	18,499	18,986
4	16,393	16,939	17,485	18,031	18,577	19,123	19,669	20,215	20,761	21,307
5	18,340	18,951	19,562	20,173	20,784	21,395	22,006	22,617	23,228	23,839
6	20,443	21,124	21,805	22,486	23,167	23,848	24,529	25,210	25,891	26,572
7	22,717	23,474	24,231	24,988	25,745	26,502	27,259	28,016	28,773	29,530
8	25,159	25,998	26,837	27,676	28,515	29,354	30,193	31,032	31,871	32,710
9	27,789	28,715	29,641	30,567	31,493	32,419	33,345	34,271	35,197	36,123
10	30,603	31,623	32,643	33,663	34,683	35,703	36,723	37,743	38,763	39,783
11	33,623	34,744	35,865	36,986	38,107	39,228	40,349	41,470	42,591	43,712
12	40,298	41,641	42,984	44,327	45,670	47,013	48,356	49,699	51,042	52,385
13	47,920	49,517	51,114	52,711	54,308	55,905	57,502	59,099	60,696	62,293
14	56,627	58,515	60,403	62,291	64,179	66,067	67,955	69,843	71,731	73,619
15	66,609	68,829	71,049	73,269	75,489	77,709	79,929	82,149	84,369	86,589

Source: Office of Personnel Management.

Federal Pay Comparability Act of 1990

The Federal Pay Comparability Act of 1990 (PL 101-509) further defines procedures for adjusting federal pay rates established by the Federal Pay Comparability Act of 1970 (PL 91-656). Under pay reform revisions enacted to close the gap between federal and private-sector salaries, federal workers receive raises equal to the average annual salary increases in the private sector. Employees are guaranteed salary increases of up to 5 percent annually, based on the Bureau of Labor Statistics' Employment Cost Index, which tracks changes in private local labor markets. Beginning in 1994, federal workers in high-cost cities will qualify for locality-based pay boosts.

The president appoints members of the Federal Salary Council, which makes recommendations for pay adjustments. The recommendations are reviewed by the "pay agent" of the president. (The pay agent is selected by the president and consists of the secretary of labor and the directors of the Office of Management and Budget and the Office of Personnel Management.) Under the 1990 law the president can opt not to increase salaries only in the event of war or negative growth of the gross national product for two consecutive quarters. After 1995 the president will have broader discretion to alter the agreement.

Also included in the act is a Pay-for-Performance Labor-Management Committee, which increases the linkage between accomplishment and compensation. It replaces the GS-16 to GS-18 pay levels with a single pay band within which agencies may establish pay rates.

General Services Administration, Workplace Initiatives, 18th and F Sts. N.W., #6119 20405; 501-3464. Faith Wohl, director. Fax, 208-7578.

Administers employee child care programs, including the Telecommuting program, which allows employees to work from their homes, and the Working Family Community Service program. Maintains list of child care contacts in GSA regional centers. *(See Regional Federal Information Sources list, p. 846.)*

Labor Dept., Federal Employeés' Compensation, 200 Constitution Ave. N.W. 20210; 219-7552. Thomas Markey, director. Fax, 219-7260.

Administers the Federal Employees Compensation Act, which provides workers' compensation for federal employees and others.

Office of Personnel Management, Employee Health Services, 1900 E St. N.W. 20415; 606-1740. Ron Patterson, chief. Fax, 606-2613.

Sets policy and guides federal agencies in establishing and maintaining alcohol and drug abuse programs as well as fitness programs.

Office of Personnel Management, Federal Prevailing Rate Advisory Committee, 1900 E St. N.W. 20415; 606-1500. Anthony F. Ingrassia, chairman. Fax, 606-5104.

Advises OPM on pay systems for federal blue-collar workers.

Office of Personnel Management, Insurance Programs, 1900 E St. N.W. 20415; 606-0770. Lucretia F. Myers, assistant director. Fax, 606-0751.

Administers group life insurance for federal employees and retirees; negotiates rates and benefits with health insurance carriers; settles disputed claims.

Office of Personnel Management, Performance Management and Incentive Awards, 1900 E St. N.W. 20415; 606-2720. Doris A. Hausser, chief. Fax, 606-2395. Incentive Awards, 606-2828.

Performance Management division sets policy and implements the performance appraisal and pay-for-performance system for all federal employees. Consults with agencies to help them develop their own systems; reviews and approves agencies' plans before implementation. Sets policy for performance appraisal and awards for federal employees. Incentive Awards division provides agencies with technical assistance and guidance on the Federal Incentive Awards Program and other awards programs that recognize achievements of federal workers.

Office of Personnel Management, Retirement and Insurance Policy, 1900 E St. N.W. 20415; 606-0788. Reginald M. Jones Jr., assistant director. Fax, 606-1108.

Develops and interprets federal policy and regulations on retirement and insurance benefits.

Office of Personnel Management, Retirement Information, 1900 E St. N.W. 20415; 606-0500. Wendy Gross, chief. TDD, 606-0551.

Responds to telephone inquiries on retirement law and health and life insurance; handles reports of annuitants' deaths; conducts interviews on individual cases; makes appropriate referrals.

Office of Personnel Management, Retirement Programs, 1900 E St. N.W. 20415; 606-0300. Frank Titus, assistant director. Fax, 606-1998.

Administers the civil service and federal employees' retirement systems; responsible for monthly annuity payments and other benefits; organizes and maintains retirement records; distributes information on retirement and on insurance programs for annuitants.

Office of Personnel Management, Salary Systems, 1900 E St. N.W., #6H31 20415; 606-2838. Ruth M. O'Donnell, chief. Fax, 606-4264.

Responsible for the annual pay adjustment review process and, beginning January 1994, local adjustment allowances (locality pay) for federal white-collar workers. Works jointly with the Office of Management and Budget and the Labor Dept. to aid the director of OPM in the role of "pay agent" for the president. Report available to the public after presidential consideration. *(See General Schedule (GS) for Federal Civilian White-Collar Employees, p. 293.)*

Office of Personnel Management, Special Compensation, 1900 E St. N.W. 20415; 606-1413. Bryce Baker, chief. Fax, 606-1349.

Authorizes pay incentives for staffing and makes allowances for uniforms, employee relocation, hazardous duty, and commutes to remote workplaces.

Office of Personnel Management, Wage Systems, 1900 E St. N.W. 20415; 606-2848. Barbara K. Fudge, chief. Fax, 606-1349.

Administers the federal wage system that establishes pay scales for federal blue-collar employees. Responds to inquiries on federal blue-collar pay rates and pay administration matters.

Congress:

See Civil Service, General, Congress (p. 287)

Nongovernmental:

National Assn. of Retired Federal Employees, 1533 New Hampshire Ave. N.W. 20036; 234-

0832. Charles W. Carter, president. Toll-free, (800) 456-8410. Fax, 797-9697.

Works to preserve the integrity of the civil service retirement system. Provides members with information about benefits for retired federal employees and for survivors of deceased federal employees. Monitors legislation and regulations.

National Committee on Public Employee Pension Systems, 1221 Connecticut Ave. N.W. 20036; 293-3960. Hastings Keith and Ralph Wood, co-chairmen. Fax, 293-7614.

Seeks reform of pension policies for public employees, particularly at the federal level. Goals include placing caps on cost of living adjustments for pension plans and redefining early retirement and disability to bring them in line with private sector standards.

Political Activity and the Hatch Act

Enacted in 1939 and revised in 1993, the Hatch Act limits the political activities of most federal employees and most District of Columbia government employees. Its provisions do not extend to employees of the executive office of the president, to individuals who are appointed by the president and confirmed by the Senate, or to members of the armed forces, whose conduct is governed by separate Defense Dept. rules. The Hatch Act prohibits federal employees from participating in political activity while on duty, including wearing a campaign button. While off duty, most federal employees may hold office in a political party, participate in campaigns and rallies, publicly endorse candidates, and raise political funds from within their agency's political action committee. However, they may not run for partisan elective offices or solicit contributions from the public. Stricter provisions on off-duty political activity apply to employees in certain sensitive agencies, including the Federal Election Commission, Federal Bureau of Investigation, Secret Service, the intelligence agencies, the Criminal Division of the Justice Dept., and others.

Agencies:

Office of Special Counsel, 1730 M St. N.W., #300 20036-4505; 653-9001. Michael G. Lawrence, director, congressional affairs. Fax, 653-5161.

Interprets federal laws, including the Hatch Act, concerning political activities allowed by certain federal employees; investigates allegations of Hatch Act violations and conducts prosecutions.

Congress:

See *Civil Service, General, Congress (p. 287)*

Nongovernmental:

American Civil Liberties Union, Fund of the National Capital Area, 1400 20th St. N.W. 20036; 457-0800. Pearl Hoffman, coordinator, litigation screening committee. Fax, 452-1868.

Civil liberties organization that advises and represents in court proceedings selected civil service employees charged with illegal political activity. Supports broader opportunities for political participation by federal employees. Maintains public education programs.

Coins and Currency

Agencies:

Bureau of Engraving and Printing (Treasury Dept.), 14th and C Sts. S.W. 20228; 874-2002. Peter H. Daly, director. Information, 874-2778. Fax, 874-3879.

Designs, engraves, and prints currency, bonds, notes, bills, certificates, and Federal Reserve notes; revenue, customs, postage, and savings stamps; and other security documents for the federal government. Provides information on history, design, and engraving of currency; offers public tours; maintains reading room where materials are brought for special research (for appointment, write to the Public and External Affairs office).

Bureau of Engraving and Printing (Treasury Dept.), Currency Standards, 14th and C Sts. S.W. (mailing address: P.O. Box 37048, Washington, DC 20013); 874-3425. Paul R. Frey, chief. Information, 874-2361. Mutilation redemption, 874-2532. Unfit currency and destruction of currency, 874-2771. Claims, 874-2397.

Redeems U.S. currency that has been mutilated; develops regulations and procedures for the destruction of unfit U.S. currency.

Federal Reserve System, Board of Governors, 20th and C Sts. N.W. 20551; 452-3201. Alan Greenspan, chairman. Information, 452-3215. Press, 452-3204. Fax, 452-3819.

Influences the availability of money as part of its responsibility for monetary policy; maintains reading room for inspection of records that are available to the public.

National Museum of American History (Smithsonian Institution), National Numismatic Collection, 14th St. and Constitution Ave. N.W. 20560; 357-1798. Elvira Clain-Stefanelli, executive director. Fax, 357-1853.

Develops and maintains collections of ancient, medieval, modern, U.S., and world coins; U.S. and world currencies; tokens; medals; orders and decorations; and primitive media of exchange. Conducts research and responds to public inquiries.

Treasury Dept., Main Treasury Bldg. 20220; 622-5300. Lloyd Bentsen, secretary. Information, 622-2000. Library, 622-0045. Fax, 622-2599.

Oversees the manufacture of U.S. coins and currency; submits to Congress final reports on the minting of coins or any changes in currency. Library open to the public by appointment.

Treasury Dept., Financial Management Service, 401 14th St. S.W., #548 20227; 874-7000. Russell D. Morris, commissioner. Fax, 874-6743.

Prepares and publishes for the president, Congress, and the public monthly, quarterly, and annual statements of government financial transactions, including reports on U.S. currency and coin in circulation.

Treasury Dept., Treasurer of the United States, Main Treasury Bldg. 20220; 622-0100. Mary Ellen Withrow, treasurer. Fax, 622-2258.

Signs currency; promotes selling and holding of U.S. savings bonds. Oversees operation of the U.S. Mint and the Bureau of Engraving and Printing.

U.S. Mint (Treasury Dept.), 633 3rd St. N.W. 20220; 874-6000. Philip N. Diehl, director designate. Information, 874-6450. Fax, 874-6282.

Manufactures and distributes all domestic coins; safeguards government's holdings of precious metals; manufactures and sells commemorative coins and medals of historic interest. Maintains an exhibit and sales area at Union Station in Washington, D.C.

Congress:

House Appropriations Committee, Subcommittee on Treasury, Postal Service, and General Government, H164 CAP 20515; 225-5834. Steny H. Hoyer, D-Md., chairman; Bill Smith, staff assistant. Fax, 426-3763.

Jurisdiction over legislation to appropriate funds for the Treasury Dept., including the U.S. Mint and the Bureau of Engraving and Printing.

House Banking, Finance, and Urban Affairs Committee, Subcommittee on Consumer Credit and Insurance, 604 O'Neill Bldg. (300 New Jersey Ave. S.E.) 20515; 225-8872. Joseph P. Kennedy II, D-Mass., chairman; Shawn P. Maher, staff director. Fax, 225-7960.

Jurisdiction over legislation on coins and currency, medals, proof and mint sets, and other special coins. Oversight of the U.S. Mint and the Bureau of Engraving and Printing.

House Ways and Means Committee, 1102 LHOB 20515; 225-3625. Sam M. Gibbons, D-Fla., acting chairman; Janice A. Mays, chief counsel.

Oversight of the Treasury Dept. (except the U.S. Mint and the Bureau of Engraving and Printing).

Senate Appropriations Committee, Subcommittee on Treasury, Postal Service, and General Government, SD-190 20510; 224-8271. Dennis DeConcini, D-Ariz., chairman; Patty Lynch, clerk.

Jurisdiction over legislation to appropriate funds for the Treasury Dept., including the U.S. Mint and the Bureau of Engraving and Printing.

Senate Banking, Housing, and Urban Affairs Committee, SD-534 20510; 224-7391. Donald W. Riegle Jr., D-Mich., chairman; Steven Harris, staff director.

Jurisdiction over legislation on coins and currency, medals, proof and mint sets, and other special coins. Oversight of the U.S. Mint and the Bureau of Engraving and Printing.

Senate Finance Committee, SD-205 20510; 224-4515. Daniel Patrick Moynihan, D-N.Y., chairman; Lawrence O'Donnell Jr., staff director.

Oversight of the Treasury Dept.

Ethics in Government

See also Political Activity and the Hatch Act (p. 295)

Agencies:

Office of Government Ethics, 1201 New York Ave. N.W., #500 20005-3917; 523-5757. Stephen D. Potts, director. Fax, 523-6325.

Administers executive branch policies relating to financial disclosure, employee conduct, and conflict-of-interest laws.

Office of Special Counsel, 1730 M St. N.W., #300 20036-4505; 653-7122. Kathleen Day Koch, special counsel. Information, 653-7188. Fax, 653-5151. Issues relating to the Hatch Act, (800) 854-2824.

Investigates allegations of prohibited personnel practices and prosecutes individuals who violate civil service regulations. Receives and refers federal employee disclosures of waste, fraud, inefficiency, and mismanagement. Enforces the Hatch Act.

President's Council on Integrity and Efficiency (Executive Office of the President), New Executive Office Bldg. 20503; 395-6911. Bill Colbin, chairman. Fax, 395-3047.

Membership: inspectors general of the major federal departments and agencies. Established by the president to coordinate the inspectors general program. Works to eliminate fraud, waste, and mismanagement in federal programs.

See also Departmental and Agency Inspectors General box (p. 298)

Congress:

House Appropriations Committee, Subcommittee on Treasury, Postal Service, and General Government, H164 CAP 20515; 225-5834. Steny H. Hoyer, D-Md., chairman; Bill Smith, staff assistant. Fax, 426-3763.

Jurisdiction over legislation to appropriate funds for the Office of Government Ethics.

House Government Operations Committee, 2157 RHOB 20515; 225-5051. John Conyers Jr., D-Mich., chairman; Julian Epstein, staff director. Fax, 225-4784.

Oversight of the Office of Government Ethics.

Departmental and Agency . . .

Departmental and agency inspectors general are responsible for identifying and reporting program fraud and abuse, criminal activity, and unethical conduct in the federal government. In the legislative branch the General Accounting Office also has fraud and abuse hotlines: (800) 424-5454; 272-5557 in Washington, D.C.

Departments

Agriculture
Charles R. Gillum, acting 720-8001
Fraud and abuse hotline . . (800) 424-9121
690-1622 in Washington, D.C.

Commerce
Frank DeGeorge. 482-4661
Fraud and abuse hotline . . (800) 424-5197
482-2495 in Washington, D.C.

Defense
Vacant . . . . (703) 695-4249
Fraud and abuse hotline . . (800) 424-9098
(703) 693-5080 in the Washington, D.C., area

Education
James B. Thomas Jr. 205-5439
Fraud and abuse hotline . . (800) 647-8733
755-2770 in Washington, D.C.

Energy
John C. Layton 586-4393

Fraud and abuse hotline . . (800) 541-1625
586-4073 in Washington, D.C.

Health and Human Services
June Gibbs Brown. 619-3148
Fraud and abuse hotline . . (800) 368-5779

Housing and Urban Development
Susan Gaffney 708-0430
Fraud and abuse hotline . . (800) 347-3735
708-4200 in Washington, D.C.

Interior
Joyce Fleischman, acting 208-5745
Fraud and abuse hotline . . (800) 424-5081
(703) 235-9399 in the Washington, D.C., area

Justice
Michael R. Bromwich, designate 514-3435
Fraud and abuse hotline . . (800) 869-4499

Labor
Charles C. Masten. 219-7296
Fraud and abuse hotline . . (800) 347-3756
219-5227 in Washington, D.C.

State
Sherman M. Funk. 647-9450
Fraud and abuse hotline 647-3320

Transportation
A. Mary Schiavo 366-1959
Fraud and abuse hotline . . (800) 424-9071
366-1461 in Washington, D.C.

House Post Office and Civil Service Committee, Subcommittee on Civil Service, 122 CHOB 20515; 225-4025. Frank McCloskey, D-Ind., chairman; Debbie Kendall, staff director.
Jurisdiction over legislation on civil service issues, including issues of ethical conduct, and over the code of ethics.

Senate Appropriations Committee, Subcommittee on Treasury, Postal Service, and General Government, SD-190 20510; 224-8271. Dennis DeConcini, D-Ariz., chairman; Patty Lynch, clerk.
Jurisdiction over legislation to appropriate funds for the Office of Government Ethics.

Senate Governmental Affairs Committee, Subcommittee on Federal Services, Post Office,

and Civil Service, SH-601 20510; 224-2254. David Pryor, D-Ark., chairman; Kimberly A. Weaver, staff director.
Jurisdiction over legislation on civil service issues, including issues of ethical conduct, and over the code of ethics. Oversight of the Office of Government Ethics.

Nongovernmental:

Center for Public Integrity, 1634 Eye St., #902 20006; 783-3900. Charles Lewis, executive director. Fax, 783-3906.

Educational foundation supported by corporations, labor unions, foundations, and individuals. Produces and distributes comprehensive reports that examine in detail ethics-related issues.

... Inspectors General

Treasury
Valerie Lau, designate 622-1090
Fraud and abuse hotline .. (800) 359-3898
Veterans Affairs
Stephen A. Trodden 233-2636
Fraud and abuse hotline .. (800) 488-8244
233-5394 in Washington, D.C.

Agencies

Agency for International Development
Jeffrey Rush Jr., designate 647-7844
Fraud and abuse hotline .. (703) 875-4999
Central Intelligence Agency
Frederick P. Hitz......... (703) 874-2553
Environmental Protection Agency
John C. Martin 260-3137
Fraud and abuse hotline .. (800) 424-4000
260-4977 in Washington, D.C.
Federal Deposit Insurance Corporation
James Renick 942-3619
Fraud and abuse hotline .. (800) 904-9042
Federal Emergency Management Agency
Russell F. Miller 646-3910
Fraud and abuse hotline .. (800) 323-8603
General Services Administration
William Barton............... 501-0450
Fraud and abuse hotline .. (800) 424-5210
501-1780 in Washington, D.C.

Merit Systems Protection Board
T. Paul Riegert 653-2514
Fraud and abuse hotline 653-7054
National Aeronautics and Space Administration
Bill D. Colvin................ 358-1274
Fraud and abuse hotline .. (800) 424-9183
358-1220 in Washington, D.C.
National Science Foundation
Linda Sundro................ 357-9457
Nuclear Regulatory Commission
David C. Williams........ (301) 492-9093
Fraud and abuse hotline .. (800) 233-3497
Office of Personnel Management
Patrick E. McFarland.......... 606-1200
Fraud and abuse hotline 606-2423
Resolution Trust Corporation
John J. Adair .... (703) 908-7800
Fraud and abuse hotline .. (800) 833-3310
Small Business Administration
James F. Hoobler 205-6580
Fraud and abuse hotline 970-6766
U.S. Information Agency
Marian C. Bennett 401-7931
Fraud and abuse hotline 401-7202
U.S. Postal Service
Kenneth J. Hunter 268-4267
Fraud and abuse hotline .. (800) 654-8896
484-5480 in Washington, D.C.

Fund for Constitutional Government, 121 Constitution Ave. N.E. 20002; 546-3799. Anne B. Zill, president. Fax, 543-3156.

Seeks to expose and correct corruption in the federal government and private sector through research and public education.

Government Accountability Project, 810 1st St. N.E., #630 20002; 408-0034. Louis Clark, executive director. Fax, 408-9855.

Membership: federal employees, union members, professionals, and interested citizens. Provides legal and strategic counsel to public and private employees who seek to expose corporate and government actions that are illegal, wasteful, or repressive; aids such employees in personnel action taken against them; assists grass-

roots organizations investigating corporate wrongdoing, government inaction, or corruption.

Project on Government Oversight, 2025 Eye St. N.W., #1117 20006; 466-5539. Danielle Bryan, director. Fax, 466-5596.

Public interest organization that works to expose waste, fraud, abuse, and conflicts of interest in all aspects of federal spending.

Executive Reorganization

Agencies:

Office of Management and Budget (Executive Office of the President), Personnel and General Services/Administration and Coordination,

New Executive Office Bldg. 20503; 395-6112. William R. Feezle, senior management associate. Fax, 395-5175.

Plans the president's government reorganization initiatives and implements reorganization plans approved by Congress.

Congress:

House Government Operations Committee, Subcommittee on Legislation and National Security, B373 RHOB 20515; 225-5147. John Conyers Jr., D-Mich., chairman; James C. Turner, staff director. Fax, 225-2373.

Jurisdiction over executive and legislative reorganization legislation.

House Post Office and Civil Service Committee, Subcommittee on Civil Service, 122 CHOB 20515; 225-4025. Frank McCloskey, D-Ind., chairman; Debbie Kendall, staff director.

Studies the effect of reorganization of agencies on federal employees.

Senate Governmental Affairs Committee, SD-340 20510; 224-4751. John Glenn, D-Ohio, chairman; Leonard Weiss, staff director. Fax, 224-9682.

Jurisdiction over executive and legislative reorganization legislation.

Senate Governmental Affairs Committee, Subcommittee on Federal Services, Post Office, and Civil Service, SH-601 20510; 224-2254. David Pryor, D-Ark., chairman; Kimberly A. Weaver, staff director.

Studies the effect of reorganization of agencies on federal employees.

Government Housekeeping

General

See also Civil Service, General (p. 285)

Agencies:

Domestic Policy Council (Executive Office of the President), The White House 20500; 456-2216. Carol H. Rasco, assistant to the president for domestic policy. Fax, 456-2878.

Comprises cabinet officials and staff members. Coordinates the domestic policy-making process

to facilitate the implementation of the president's domestic agenda in such areas as agriculture, education, energy, environment, health, housing, labor, and veterans affairs.

Federal Bureau of Investigation (Justice Dept.), Personnel, 9th St. and Pennsylvania Ave. N.W. 20535; 324-3514. Manuel J. Gonzalez, assistant director. Fax, 324-1091.

Performs background investigations of presidential appointees.

General Services Administration (GSA), 18th and F Sts. N.W. 20405; 501-0800. Roger Johnson, administrator. Information, 708-5082. Press, 501-0705. Library, 501-0788. TDD, 708-9300.

Establishes policies for managing federal government property, including construction and operation of buildings and procurement and distribution of supplies and equipment; manages transportation, telecommunications, and automated data processing for federal agencies. Manages disposal of surplus federal property.

General Services Administration, Acquisition Policy, 18th and F Sts. N.W. 20405; 501-1043. Richard H. Hopf III, associate administrator. Fax, 501-1986.

Develops and implements federal government acquisition policies and procedures; conducts preaward and postaward contract reviews; administers federal acquisition regulations for civilian agencies; suspends and debars contractors for unsatisfactory performance; coordinates and promotes governmentwide career management and training programs for contracting personnel.

General Services Administration, Board of Contract Appeals, 18th and F Sts. N.W. 20405; 501-0585. Stephen M. Daniels, chairman. Fax, 501-4425.

Resolves disputes arising out of contracts with the General Services Administration, the Treasury Dept., the Education Dept., the Commerce Dept., and other independent agencies.

General Services Administration, Federal Information Centers, 18th and F Sts. N.W. 20405; 501-1939. Warren Snaider, contract technical representative. Fax, 501-1680. TDD, (800) 326-2996. Information, P.O. Box 600, Cumberland, MD 21502; (301) 722-9098.

Contracts the Federal Information Centers, which respond to inquiries about federal programs and services. The centers give information or locate particular agencies or persons best suited to help with specific concerns. *(See Regional Federal Information Sources list, p. 847.)*

General Services Administration, Federal Property Resources Service, 18th and F Sts. N.W. 20405; 501-0210. John V. Neale Jr., acting commissioner. Fax, 219-2072.

Manages and disposes of federal real estate.

General Services Administration, National Capital Region, 7th and D Sts. S.W. 20407; 708-9100. Thurman M. Davis, regional administrator. Fax, 708-9966.

Provides federal agencies with space, supplies, telecommunications, transportation, data processing, and construction services; has equal status with regional offices. *(See Regional Federal Information Sources list, p. 846.)*

Office of Management and Budget (Executive Office of the President), Federal Procurement Policy, Old Executive Office Bldg., Rm. 352 20503; 395-5802. Allan V. Burman, administrator. Information, 395-3501. Fax, 395-3242.

Coordinates government procurement policies, regulations, procedures, and forms for executive agencies and recipients of federal grants or assistance.

Office of Management and Budget (Executive Office of the President), Treasury and Postal, New Executive Office Bldg. 20503; 395-6156. Margaret Young, chief. Fax, 395-6825.

Examines, evaluates, and suggests improvements for agencies and programs within the Treasury Dept. (including the Internal Revenue Service and the Customs Dept.), the U.S. Postal Service, the District of Columbia government, and the Executive Office of the President.

See also General Services Administration, Business Service Centers in Regional Federal Information Sources list (p. 846)

Congress:

House Appropriations Committee, Subcommittee on Treasury, Postal Service, and General Government, H164 CAP 20515; 225-5834. Steny H. Hoyer, D-Md., chairman; Bill Smith, staff assistant. Fax, 426-3763.

Jurisdiction over legislation to appropriate funds for the Office of Management and Budget, the General Services Administration (except the Consumer Information Center), the National Archives and Records Administration, and the Executive Office of the President.

House Government Operations Committee, 2157 RHOB 20515; 225-5051. John Conyers Jr., D-Mich., chairman; Julian Epstein, staff director. Fax, 225-4784.

Jurisdiction over legislation on all procurement practices. Also examines the efficiency of government operations, including federal regulations and program management.

House Government Operations Committee, Subcommittee on Information, Justice, Transportation, and Agriculture, B349C RHOB 20515; 225-3741. Gary Condit, D-Calif., chairman; Shannon Lahey, acting staff director. Fax, 225-2445.

Jurisdiction over legislation concerning the National Archives and Records Administration.

House Government Operations Committee, Subcommittee on Legislation and National Security, B373 RHOB 20515; 225-5147. John Conyers Jr., D-Mich., chairman; James C. Turner, staff director. Fax, 225-2373.

Jurisdiction over legislation concerning reduction of paperwork and improvement of federal information management; oversight responsibilities for operations of the White House, the Executive Office of the President, and the Office of Management and Budget. Jurisdiction over legislation for the General Services Administration.

Senate Appropriations Committee, Subcommittee on Treasury, Postal Service, and General Government, SD-190 20510; 224-8271. Dennis DeConcini, D-Ariz., chairman; Patty Lynch, clerk.

Jurisdiction over legislation to appropriate funds for the General Services Administration (except the Consumer Information Center), National Archives and Records Administration, and Executive Office of the President.

Senate Governmental Affairs Committee, Subcommittee on General Services, Federalism, and the District of Columbia, SH-432 20510; 224-4718. Jim Sasser, D-Tenn., chairman; John Wagster, staff director.

Jurisdiction over legislation for the General Services Administration.

Senate Governmental Affairs Committee, Subcommittee on Oversight of Government Management, SH-442 20510; 224-3682. Carl Levin, D-Mich., chairman; Linda J. Gustitus, staff director.

Jurisdiction over the Ethics and Government Act of 1978 and over legislation on all procurement practices. Examines the efficiency of government operations, including federal regulations and program management.

Senate Governmental Affairs Committee, Subcommittee on Regulation and Government Information, SH-605 20510; 224-9000. Joseph I. Lieberman, D-Conn., chairman; John Nakahata, staff director.

Jurisdiction over legislation for the National Archives and Records Administration; government procurement and legislation to reduce the volume of federal paperwork; and the improvement of federal information management; oversight responsibilities for operations of the White House and the Office of Management and Budget.

Data Processing and Telecommunications

See also Science: Mathematical, Computer, and Physical Sciences, Computer Sciences (p. 686)

Agencies:

General Services Administration, Information Resources Management Service, 18th and F Sts. N.W. 20405; 501-1000. Joe M. Thompson, commissioner. Fax, 501-0022. TDD, 501-2860.

Purchases and leases automatic data processing (ADP) and telecommunications equipment and services for the federal government; advises agencies and administers governmentwide implementation of ADP and telecommunications systems; operates federal networks for telecommunications and data communications, including the Federal Telecommunications Services. Plans and directs programs for improving federal records and information management.

Federal Buildings

Agencies:

General Services Administration, Physical Security and Law Enforcement, 18th and F Sts. N.W. 20405; 501-0887. Garrett J. DeYulia, assistant commissioner. Fax, 501-1998.

Oversees security and law enforcement programs for federal buildings, employees, and visitors to federal buildings.

General Services Administration, Public Buildings Service, 18th and F Sts. N.W. 20405; 501-1100. Kenneth Kimbrough, commissioner. Fax, 219-2310.

Administers the construction, maintenance, and operation of buildings owned or leased by the federal government.

General Services Administration, Safety and Environmental Management, 18th and F Sts. N.W. 20405; 501-1464. Henry J. Singer, director. Fax, 501-3257.

Oversees safety programs for federal buildings, employees, and visitors to federal buildings.

Congress:

See Government Housekeeping, General, Congress (p. 301)

Government Publications

See also Access to Congressional Information (p. 736); Government Printing Office, Regional Depository Libraries in Regional Federal Information Sources list (p. 850)

Agencies:

National Archives and Records Administration, Federal Register, 800 N. Capitol St. N.W., #700 (mailing address: Office of the Federal Register, National Archives and Records Administration, Washington, DC 20408); 523-3187. Martha L. Girard, director. Fax, 523-6866. TDD, 523-5229.

Compiles and publishes the *Federal Register* of rules, regulations, and notices from government agencies; publishes *Code of Federal Regulations, United States Government Manual, Weekly Compilation of Presidential Documents, Public Papers of the President, United States Statutes at Large,* and slip laws.

National Technical Information Service (Commerce Dept.), 5285 Port Royal Rd., Springfield, VA 22161; (703) 487-4636. Donald R. Johnson, director. Fax, (703) 487-4098. Sales center, (703) 487-4650; rush orders, (800) 336-4700.

Distribution center that sells government-funded research and development reports and other technical analyses prepared by federal agencies, their contractors, or grantees. Publishes biweekly abstract journal, *Government Reports Announcements*, and index; publishes weekly abstract newsletter. Offers microfiche and computerized bibliographic search services. Online database available through commercial vendors and in machine-readable form through lease agreement.

Congress:

General Accounting Office (GAO), Document Handling and Information Services Facility, 700 4th St. N.W. (mailing address: P.O. Box 6015, Gaithersburg, MD 20877); 512-4448. Keith Bonney, staff contact. Fax, (301) 258-4066. Publications and orders, 512-6000.

Provides GAO publications and information about GAO publications on request.

Government Printing Office (GPO), 732 N. Capitol St. N.W. 20401; 512-2034. Michael F. DiMario, public printer. Fax, 512-1347. Congressional documents orders and inquiries, 512-2471; general government publications orders and inquiries, 783-3238; complaints, 512-2302.

Prints, distributes, and sells selected publications of the U.S. Congress, government agencies, and executive departments. Makes available, for a fee, the *Monthly Catalog of U.S. Government Publications*, a comprehensive listing of all publications issued by the various departments and agencies each month. Popular government publications may also be purchased at GPO bookstores in larger cities. *(See Regional Federal Information Sources list, p. 849.)*

House Administration Committee, H326 CAP 20515; 225-2061. Charlie Rose, D-N.C., chairman; Robert E. Shea, staff director. Fax, 225-4345.

Jurisdiction over the printing, cost of printing, binding, and distribution of congressional publications; jurisdiction (in conjunction with the Senate Rules and Administration Committee and the Joint Committee on Printing) over the Government Printing Office, executive papers, and depository libraries.

Joint Committee on Printing, SH-818 20510; 224-5241. Sen. Wendell H. Ford, D-Ky., chairman; John Chambers, staff director. Fax, 224-1176.

Oversees public printing, binding, and distribution of government publications; executive papers and depository libraries; and activities of the Government Printing Office (in conjunction with the House Administration and Senate Rules and Administration committees).

Library of Congress, Serial and Government Publications, 101 Independence Ave. S.E. 20540; 707-5647. Karen Renninger, chief. Fax, 707-6128.

Operates Newspaper and Periodical Reading Room; maintains library's collection of current domestic and foreign newspapers, current periodicals, and serially issued publications of federal, state, and foreign governments; has maintained full government publication depository since 1979. Responds to written or telephone requests for information on government publications.

Senate Rules and Administration Committee, SR-305 20510; 224-6352. Wendell H. Ford, D-Ky., chairman; James O. King, staff director.

Jurisdiction over the printing, cost of printing, binding, and distribution of congressional publications; jurisdiction (in conjunction with the House Administration Committee and the Joint Committee on Printing) over the Government Printing Office, executive papers, and depository libraries.

Government Record Keeping

Agencies:

General Services Administration, Acquisition Reviews, 18th and F Sts. N.W. 20405; 501-1126. Kenneth Touloumes, director. Fax, 501-2856.

Provides procurement authorization for federal agencies in areas of information resources management.

General Services Administration, Management Reviews, 18th and F Sts. N.W. 20405; 501-1332. Susan Robson Tobin, director. Fax, 219-0987.

Reviews agencies' information resources management and procurement of information technology.

National Archives and Records Administration, 7th St. and Pennsylvania Ave. N.W. 20408; 501-5402. Trudy H. Peterson, acting archivist of the United States. Information, 501-5400. Press, 501-5525. Recorded information on activities open to the public, 501-5000.

Identifies, preserves, and makes available federal government documents of historic value; administers a network of regional storage centers and archives; operates the presidential library system; publishes legislative, regulatory, and other widely used documents.

National Archives and Records Administration, Electronic Records, 8601 Adelphi Rd., College Park, MD 20740-6001; (301) 713-6630. Kenneth S. Thibodeau, director. Fax, (301) 713-7275. Reference service, 501-5579.

Preserves, maintains, and makes available electronic records of the U.S. government in all subject areas. Provides researchers with magnetic tape copies of records on a cost-recovery basis. Distributes lists of holdings.

National Archives and Records Administration, Federal Records Centers, 8601 Adelphi Rd., College Park, MD 20740-6001; (301) 713-7200. David F. Peterson, assistant archivist. Fax, (301) 713-7205.

Stores federal records and assists agencies in microfilming records, protecting vital operating records, improving filing and classification systems, and developing disposition schedules.

National Archives and Records Administration, Federal Register, 800 N. Capitol St. N.W., #700 (mailing address: Office of the Federal Register, National Archives and Records Administration, Washington, DC 20408); 523-4534. Martha L. Girard, director. Fax, 523-6866. TDD, 523-5229.

Compiles and publishes the *Federal Register* of rules, regulations, and notices from government agencies; publishes *Code of Federal Regulations, United States Government Manual, Weekly Compilation of Presidential Documents, Public Papers of the President, United States Statutes at Large,* and slip laws.

National Archives and Records Administration, Legislative Archives, 7th St. and Pennsylvania Ave. N.W. 20408; 501-5350. Michael Gillette, director. Fax, 219-2176.

Collects and maintains records of congressional committees and legislative files from 1789 to the present. Publishes inventories and guides to these records.

National Archives and Records Administration, Multimedia and Publications Distribution, 8700 Edgeworth Dr., Capitol Heights, MD 20743; (301) 763-1872. George H. Ziener, director. Information, (301) 763-1896. Fax, (301) 763-6025. Toll-free, (800) 788-6282.

Rents and sells government-produced films, slides, filmstrips, audiotapes, interactive video disks, videotapes, and multimedia kits on a wide range of subjects. Publishes catalogs of audiovisual materials produced by the U.S. government and an annual overview of federal audiovisual activity.

National Archives and Records Administration, National Archives, 7th St. and Pennsylvania Ave. N.W. 20408; 501-5300. Trudy H. Peterson, assistant archivist. Fax, 219-1543.

Receives and preserves federal agency records that warrant permanent preservation by the government; makes them available for federal and public use.

National Archives and Records Administration, Presidential Documents and Legislative Division, 800 N. Capitol St. N.W., #700 (mailing address: Office of the Federal Register, National Archives and Records Administration, Washington, DC 20408); 523-5230. Frances D. McDonald, director. Fax, 523-6866. TDD, 523-5229. Public Laws Update Service (PLUS), 523-6641.

Assigns public law numbers to enacted legislation, executive orders, and proclamations; responds to inquiries on public law numbers; assists inquirers in finding presidential signing or veto messages in the *Weekly Compilation of Presidential Documents* and the *Public Papers of the Presidents* series; compiles slip laws and annual *United States Statutes at Large;* compiles indexes for finding statutory provisions; operates PLUS, which provides information by telephone on new legislation. Publications are available from the U.S. Government Printing Office, Washington, D.C. 20402; 783-3238.

National Archives and Records Administration, Public Programs, 7th St. and Pennsylvania Ave. N.W. 20408; 501-5200. Linda N. Brown, assistant archivist.

Plans and directs activities to acquaint the public with materials of the National Archives; conducts tours, workshops, and classes; stages exhibits; produces books and pamphlets; issues teaching packets using historic documents.

National Archives and Records Administration, Records Administration, 8601 Adelphi Rd., College Park, MD 20740; (301) 713-7100. James W. Moore, assistant archivist. Fax, (301) 713-6850.

Administers programs that establish standards, guidelines, and procedures for agency records administration, including developing documentation standards, administering vital records, and maintaining and preserving records. Manages training programs; monitors certain records not contained in National Archives depositories.

National Archives and Records Administration, Records Declassification, 7th St. and Pennsylvania Ave. N.W. 20408; 501-5345. Jeanne Schauble, director. Fax, 219-1543.

Directs the review and declassification of records and security-classified materials in the National Archives in accordance with Executive Order 12356 and the Freedom of Information Act; assists other federal archival agencies in declassifying security-classified documents in their holdings.

National Archives and Records Administration, Textual Projects, 7th St. and Pennsylvania Ave. N.W. 20408; 501-5460. Geraldine N. Phillips, director. Fax, 299-1543.

Prepares inventories, microfilm publications, and guides to civil and military records in the archives. Prepares descriptions of holdings. Acquires and appraises new records.

National Archives and Records Administration, Textual Reference, 7th St. and Pennsylvania Ave. N.W. 20408; 501-5380. R. Michael McReynolds, director. Fax, 501-5005.

Provides reference service for unpublished civil and military federal government records. Maintains central catalog of all library materials. Compiles comprehensive bibliographies of materials related to archival administration and records management. Permits research in American history, archival science, and records management. Maintains collections of the papers of the Continental Congress (1774-1789), U.S. State Dept. diplomatic correspondence (1789-1963), and general records of the U.S. government.

Congress:

See Government Housekeeping, General, Congress (p. 301)

Supplies and Transportation

Agencies:

General Services Administration, Federal Supply Service, 1941 Jefferson Davis Highway, Arlington, VA 22202; (703) 305-6667. Roger D. Daniero, commissioner. Fax, (703) 305-5500.

Responsible for providing federal agencies with common-use goods and nonpersonal services and for procurement and supply, transportation and travel management, and disposal of surplus personal property.

General Services Administration, Transportation and Property Management, 1941 Jefferson Davis Highway, #815, Arlington, VA 22202; (703) 305-7660. Allan W. Beres, assistant commissioner. Fax, (703) 305-6905.

Manages governmentwide programs and activities relating to the use of excess personal property (except Automated Data Processing [ADP] equipment); provides transportation, travel, aircraft, mail, relocation, and vehicle fleet services. Produces *Federal Travel Regulations* and *Federal Travel Directory*.

Congress:

See Government Housekeeping, General, Congress (p. 301)

Postal Service

General

Agencies:

U.S. Postal Service, 475 L'Enfant Plaza S.W. 20260; 268-2500. Marvin T. Runyon, postmaster general. Information, 268-2284. Press, 268-2156. Library, 268-2904. Fax, 268-4860. Locator, 268-2000.

Offers postal service throughout the country as an independent establishment of the executive branch. Library open to the public.

U.S. Postal Service, Inspection Service, 475 L'Enfant Plaza S.W. 20260; 268-4267. Kenneth J.

Hunter, chief postal inspector. Fax, 268-4563. Fraud and abuse hotline, (800) 654-8896.

Investigates criminal violations of postal laws, such as theft of mail or posted valuables, assaults on postal employees, organized crime in postal-related matters, and prohibited mailings. Conducts internal audits; investigates postal activities to detect problems in mail flow operations and to determine effectiveness of procedures; monitors compliance of individual post offices with postal regulations; functions as the inspector general for the postal service.

Congress:

House Appropriations Committee, Subcommittee on Treasury, Postal Service, and General Government, H164 CAP 20515; 225-5834. Steny H. Hoyer, D-Md., chairman; Bill Smith, staff assistant. Fax, 426-3763.

Jurisdiction over legislation to appropriate funds for the U.S. Postal Service and the Postal Rate Commission.

House Government Operations Committee, Subcommittee on Information, Justice, Transportation, and Agriculture, B349C RHOB 20515; 225-3741. Gary Condit, D-Calif., chairman; Shannon Lahey, acting staff director. Fax, 225-2445.

Oversight of the U.S. Postal Service and the Postal Rate Commission.

House Post Office and Civil Service Committee, 309 CHOB 20515; 225-4054. William L. Clay, D-Mo., chairman; Gail E. Weiss, staff director.

Jurisdiction over postal service legislation.

House Post Office and Civil Service Committee, Subcommittee on Postal Operations and Services, 406 CHOB 20515; 225-9124. Barbara-Rose Collins, D-Mich., chair; Meredith Copper, staff director.

Jurisdiction over postal service legislation, including legislation on postal service consumer protection, labor relations, automation of postal facilities, postal fraud, mail rates and classifications, postal finances and expenditures (except those relating to matters within the jurisdiction of the Subcommittee on Census, Statistics, and Postal Personnel), philately, mail transportation, and military mail. Analyzes the impact on federal jobs of the use of mail consultants and contractors by government agencies.

Senate Appropriations Committee, Subcommittee on Treasury, Postal Service, and General Government, SD-190 20510; 224-8271. Dennis DeConcini, D-Ariz., chairman; Patty Lynch, clerk.

Jurisdiction over legislation to appropriate funds for the U.S. Postal Service and the Postal Rate Commission.

Senate Governmental Affairs Committee, Permanent Subcommittee on Investigations, SR-100 20510; 224-3721. Sam Nunn, D-Ga., chairman; Eleanor J. Hill, staff director.

Investigates postal fraud.

Senate Governmental Affairs Committee, Subcommittee on Federal Services, Post Office, and Civil Service, SH-601 20510; 224-2254. David Pryor, D-Ark., chairman; Kimberly A. Weaver, staff director.

Jurisdiction over postal service legislation, including legislation on postal service consumer protection, labor relations, automation of postal facilities, postal fraud, mail rates, and classifications for the postal service and philately; postal finances and expenditures; and mail transportation and military mail. Oversight of the U.S. Postal Service and the Postal Rate Commission. Analyzes the impact on federal jobs of the use of mail consultants and contractors by government agencies.

Consumer Complaints and Services

Agencies:

U.S. Postal Service, Consumer Affairs, 475 L'Enfant Plaza S.W. 20260; 268-2284. Ann McK. Robinson, consumer advocate. Fax, 268-2304. TDD, 268-2310.

Handles consumer complaints; oversees investigations into consumer problems; intercedes in local areas when problems are not adequately resolved; provides information on specific products and services; represents consumers' viewpoint before postal management bodies; initiates projects to improve postal service.

U.S. Postal Service, Consumer Protection, 475 L'Enfant Plaza S.W. 20260; 268-3081. Jennifer Angelo, chief counsel. Fax, 268-4997.

Initiates civil administrative proceedings to stop mail delivery that solicits money by lottery or misrepresentation; enforces statutes designed to prevent receipt of unwanted sexual material.

U.S. Postal Service, Enforcement, 475 L'Enfant Plaza S.W. 20260; 268-3076. George C. Davis, chief counsel. Fax, 268-4997.

Reviews and processes cases falling under the Program Fraud Civil Remedies Act of 1986.

U.S. Postal Service, Sales and Account Management, 475 L'Enfant Plaza S.W. 20260; 268-2222. John R. Wargo, manager. Fax, 268-5193.

Analyzes, develops, and markets postal products and services, primarily to commercial customers; oversees regional marketing and communications; acts as liaison with major customer groups such as Mailers' Technical Advisory Committee; manages the National and Regional Postal Forums. *(See Regional Federal Information Sources list, p. 863.)*

U.S. Postal Service, Stamp Acquisition and Distribution, 475 L'Enfant Plaza S.W., #4474E 20260-6810; 268-6854. Michael Spates, manager. Fax, 268-6631.

Designs, manufactures, and distributes postage stamps and postal stationery; develops inventory controls; directs domestic and international mail order services and philatelic marketing programs.

Congress:

See Postal Service, General, Congress (p. 306)

Employee and Labor Relations

Agencies:

U.S. Postal Service, Diversity Development, 475 L'Enfant Plaza S.W. 20260; 268-6566. Veronica Collazo, vice president. Fax, 268-6573.

Responsible for policy and planning with regard to affirmative action hiring and supplier/vendor selection.

U.S. Postal Service, Employee Relations, 475 L'Enfant Plaza S.W. 20260; 268-3783. Suzanne J. Henry, vice president. Fax, 268-3074.

Drafts and implements employment policies and practices, safety and health guidelines, training and development programs, and compensation guidelines.

U.S. Postal Service, Labor Relations, 475 L'Enfant Plaza S.W. 20260; 268-3816. Joseph J. Mahon Jr., vice president. Fax, 268-3074.

Handles collective bargaining and contract administration for the U.S. Postal Service and

processes complaints regarding equal employment opportunity.

U.S. Postal Service, Postal Career Executive Service, 475 L'Enfant Plaza S.W. 20260; 268-4255. Janet Qualters, human resources analyst. Fax, 268-6195.

Matches needs of U.S. Postal Service with career goals and job preferences of its executive employees.

Congress:

See Postal Service, General, Congress (p. 306)

Nongovernmental:

See also Labor Unions list (p. 801)

National Assn. of Postal Supervisors, 490 L'Enfant Plaza S.W., #3200 20024-2120; 484-6070. Vincent Palladino, president. Fax, 488-7288.

Membership: present and former postal supervisors. Cooperates with other postal management associations, unions, and the U.S. Postal Service to improve the efficiency of the postal service; promotes favorable working conditions and broader career opportunities for all postal employees; provides members with information on current functions and legislative issues of the postal service.

National Assn. of Postmasters of the United States, 8 Herbert St., Alexandria, VA 22305; (703) 683-9027. Kenneth Vlietstra, executive director. Fax, (703) 683-6820.

Membership: present and former postmasters of the United States. Promotes quality mail service and favorable relations between the postal service and the public; works with other postal groups and levels of management in the interest of postal matters and the welfare of its members.

National Star Route Mail Contractors Assn., 324 E. Capitol St. N.E. 20003-3897; 543-1661. John V. Maraney, executive director. Fax, 543-8863.

Membership: contractors for highway mail transport and selected rural route deliverers. Acts as liaison between contractors and the U.S. Postal Service and the Labor Dept. concerning contracts, wages, and other issues. Monitors legislation and regulations.

Mail Rates and Classification

Agencies:

Postal Rate Commission, 1333 H St. N.W., #300 20268; 789-6868. Ed Gleiman, chairman; Stephen Sharfman, legal adviser, 789-6820. Information, 789-6800. Fax, 789-6861.

Submits recommendations to the governors of the U.S. Postal Service concerning proposed changes in postage rates, fees, and mail classifications; issues advisory opinions on proposed changes in postal services; studies and submits recommendations on public complaints concerning postal rates and nationwide service. Reviews appeals of post office closings.

U.S. Postal Service, Business Mail Acceptance, 475 L'Enfant Plaza S.W. 20260; 268-5174. Anita Bizzotto, manager. Fax, 268-4404.

Implements policies on and answers customer inquiries about domestic and international mail classification matters.

U.S. Postal Service, Mailing Standards, 475 L'Enfant Plaza S.W. 20260; 268-3359. Gail Sonnenberg, vice president. Fax, 268-6507.

Issues policy statements on domestic and international mail classification matters. Ensures the accuracy of policies developed by the Postal Rate Commission with respect to domestic mail classification schedules.

U.S. Postal Service, Marketing and Sales, 475 L'Enfant Plaza S.W. 20260; 268-2650. John Alepa, pricing manager. Fax, 554-2581.

Sets prices for postal service product lines using competitive pricing methods.

Congress:

See Postal Service, General, Congress (p. 306)

Nongovernmental:

Advertising Mail Marketing Assn., 1333 F St. N.W., #710 20004-1108; 347-0055. Gene A. Del Polito, executive director. Fax, 347-0789. Recorded postal information, (202) 347-0799; bulletin board service, (202) 347-5128.

Membership: companies and organizations interested in third-class mail. Provides members with information about postal policy, postal rates, and legislation regarding postal regulations.

Alliance of Nonprofit Mailers, 2001 S St. N.W. 20009-1125; 462-5132. Neal Denton, executive director. Press, 462-5156. Fax, 462-0423.

Works to maintain reasonable mail rates for nonprofit organizations. Represents member organizations before Congress, the U.S. Postal Service, the Postal Rate Commission, and the courts on nonprofit postal rate and mail classification issues.

Direct Marketing Assn., 1101 17th St. N.W., #705 20036; 347-1222. Richard Barton, senior vice president, government affairs. Fax, 785-2231.

Membership: telemarketers; users, creators, and producers of direct mail; and suppliers to the industry. Serves as liaison between members and the U.S. Postal Service. Monitors federal legislation and regulations concerning postal rates. (Headquarters in New York.)

Mail Advertising Service Assn. International, 1421 Prince St., Alexandria, VA 22314; (703) 836-9200. David A. Weaver, president. Fax, (703) 548-8204.

Membership: U.S. and foreign letter and printing shops that engage in direct mail advertising. Serves as a clearinghouse for members on improving methods of using the mails for advertising.

National Federation of Nonprofits, 815 15th St. N.W., #822 20005; 628-4380. Lee M. Cassidy, executive director. Fax, 628-4383.

Membership: educational, cultural, fraternal, religious, and scientific organizations that mail nonprofit second-, third-, or fourth-class mail. Serves as liaison between members and the U.S. Postal Service; represents nonprofit members' interests on the Mailers' Technical Advisory Committee. Monitors legislation and regulations.

Parcel Shippers Assn., 1211 Connecticut Ave. N.W., #610 20036; 296-3690. David A. Bunn, executive vice president. Fax, 296-0343.

Voluntary organization of business firms concerned with the shipment of small parcels. Works to improve parcel post rates and service; represents members before the Postal Rate Commission in matters regarding parcel post rates; monitors legislation and regulations.

Stamps/Postal History

Agencies:

National Museum of American History (Smithsonian Institution), National Postal Museum, 2 Massachusetts Ave. N.E. 20212; 633-9360. James H. Bruns, director. Fax, 633-9393.

Exhibits postal history and philately collections; provides information on world postal history and philately.

U.S. Postal Service, Stamp Acquisition and Distribution, 475 L'Enfant Plaza S.W., #4474E 20260-6810; 268-6854. Michael Spates, manager. Fax, 268-6631.

Designs, manufactures, and distributes postage stamps and postal stationery; directs philatelic marketing programs.

U.S. Postal Service, Stamp Management, 475 L'Enfant Plaza S.W. 20260; 268-2312. James Tolbert, manager. Fax, 268-6631.

Manages the stamp selection function; develops the basic stamp pre-production design; manages relationship with philatelic community; provides support to the philately product management group.

Congress:

See *Postal Service, General, Congress (p. 306)*

Nongovernmental:

Samuel Gompers Stamp Club, P.O. Box 1233, Springfield, VA 22151; (703) 451-7008. Edwin M. Schmidt, secretary-treasurer.

Membership: active and retired trade union members and other philatelists with an interest in labor topics. Promotes the creation and collection of trade union stamps and trade union philatelist memorabilia.

Public Administration

Agencies:

Administrative Conference of the United States, 2120 L St. N.W., #500 20037; 254-7020. Thomasina Rogers, chair designate. Fax, 254-3077.

Independent agency whose members are agency heads and department officials, private lawyers, university faculty, and other experts in law and government. Studies and recommends improvements in federal administration and legal procedures. Library open to the public.

Office of Personnel Management, Presidential Management Intern Program, 901 N. Stuart St., #308, Arlington, VA 22203; (703) 235-1106. Rita Rutsohn, director. Fax, (703) 235-1411.

Seeks to attract to federal service individuals with high management potential and advanced academic degrees in areas applicable to managing and developing federal programs and policies. After presidential management interns have served two years in a federal agency or department, they are eligible for conversion to career civil service appointment.

President's Commission on White House Fellowships, 712 Jackson Pl. N.W. 20503; 395-4522. Brooke Shearer, director. Fax, 395-6179.

Provides young professionals from all sectors of national life with the opportunity to observe firsthand the processes of the federal government. Beginning each September, fellows work for one year as special assistants to Cabinet members or to principal members of the White House staff. Qualified applicants have demonstrated superior accomplishments early in their careers and have a commitment to community service.

President's Council on Management Improvement, New Executive Office Bldg. 20503; 395-6190. Phil Lader, chairman. Information, 395-5090. Fax, 395-6835.

Responsible for implementing the management improvement initiatives of the administration. Develops and oversees improved government-wide management and administrative systems; formulates long-range plans to promote these systems; works to resolve interagency management problems and to implement reforms.

Congress:

House Government Operations Committee, 2157 RHOB 20515; 225-5051. John Conyers Jr., D-Mich., chairman; Julian Epstein, staff director. Fax, 225-4784.

Jurisdiction over legislation on all procurement practices. Also examines the efficiency of government operations, including federal regulations and program management.

House Government Operations Committee, Subcommittee on Information, Justice, Transportation, and Agriculture, B349C RHOB

20515; 225-3741. Gary Condit, D-Calif., chairman; Shannon Lahey, acting staff director. Fax, 225-2445.

Oversees operations of the Administrative Conference of the United States.

House Standards of Official Conduct Committee, HT-2 CAP 20515; 225-7103. Jim McDermott, D-Wash., chairman; Bernard Raimo Jr., chief counsel. Fax, 225-7392.

Jurisdiction over the Ethics in Government Act of 1978.

Senate Governmental Affairs Committee, Subcommittee on Oversight of Government Management, SH-442 20510; 224-3682. Carl Levin, D-Mich., chairman; Linda J. Gustitus, staff director.

Jurisdiction over the Ethics in Government Act of 1978 and over legislation on all procurement practices. Examines the efficiency of government operations, including federal regulations and program management.

Senate Judiciary Committee, Subcommittee on Courts and Administrative Practice, SH-223 20510; 224-4022. Howell Heflin, D-Ala., chairman; Jim Whiddon, chief counsel.

Oversees operations of the Administrative Conference of the United States; jurisdiction over administrative practices and procedures.

Nongovernmental:

American Society for Public Administration, 1120 G St. N.W., #700 20005; 393-7878. John P. Thomas, executive director. Fax, 638-4952.

Membership: government administrators, public officials, educators, researchers, and others interested in public administration. Presents awards to distinguished professionals in the field; sponsors workshops and conferences; disseminates information about public administration. Promotes high ethical standards for public service.

Assn. of Government Accountants, 2200 Mount Vernon Ave., Alexandria, VA 22301; (703) 684-6931. Lee Woods, executive director. Fax, (703) 548-9367.

Membership: individuals engaged in government accounting, auditing, budgeting, and information systems.

Federally Employed Women, 1400 .Eye St. N.W. 20005; 898-0994. Karen Scott, executive director. Fax, 898-0998.

Membership: women and men who work for the federal government. Works to eliminate sex discrimination in government employment and to increase job opportunities for women; offers training programs; monitors legislation and regulations.

International City and County Management Assn., 777 N. Capitol St. N.E. 20002; 962-3610. William H. Hansell Jr., executive director. Fax, 962-3500.

Membership: city and county managers, council of government directors, and municipal administrators. Sponsors a training institute that offers correspondence courses in municipal administration; maintains an information service on local government management practices. Library open to the public by appointment.

International Personnel Management Assn., 1617 Duke St., Alexandria, VA 22314; (703) 549-7100. Donald K. Tichenor, executive director. Fax, (703) 684-0948.

Membership: personnel professionals from federal, state, and local governments. Provides information on training procedures, management techniques, and legislative developments on the federal, state, and local levels.

National Academy of Public Administration, 1120 G St. N.W., #850 20005; 347-3190. R. Scott Fosler, president. Fax, 393-0993.

Membership: scholars and administrators in public management. Offers assistance to federal, state, and local government agencies, public officials, foreign governments, foundations, and corporations on problems related to public administration.

National Assn. of Schools of Public Affairs and Administration, 1120 G St. N.W., #730 20005; 628-8965. Alfred M. Zuck, executive director. Fax, 626-4978.

Membership: universities and government agencies interested in the advancement of education, research, and training in public management. Serves as a clearinghouse for information on public administration and public affairs programs in colleges and universities. Accredits masters degree programs.

National Women's Political Caucus, 1275 K St. N.W., #750 20005; 898-1100. Mary Beth Lambert, political director. Fax, 898-0458.

Seeks to increase the number of women in policy-making positions in federal, state, and local government. Identifies, recruits, trains, and supports women candidates for public office. Monitors agencies and provides names of qualified women for high- and midlevel appointments.

Women in Government Relations, Inc., 1029 Vermont Ave. N.W., #510 20005; 347-5432. Janet Allen, executive director. Fax, 347-5434.

Membership: professionals in business, trade associations, and government whose jobs involve governmental relations at the federal, state, or local level. Serves as a forum for exchange of information among its members.

State and Local Government

See also Governors, Lieutenant Governors, Secretaries of State, and Attorneys General list (p. 865); Intergovernmental Relations: Economic Development (p. 73); Mayors of Major Cities list (p. 875)

Agencies:

Advisory Commission on Intergovernmental Relations, 800 K St. N.W., #450 20001; 653-5540. John Kincaid, executive director. Fax, 653-5429.

Bipartisan commission composed of members from the executive and legislative branches of federal, state, and local governments as well as members from the general public who are appointed by the president. Studies structure and function of governments and the financial relationships of the different levels; makes recommendations to state, local, and federal officials.

Census Bureau (Commerce Dept.), Governments Division, Washington Plaza II, #407, Marlow Heights, MD (mailing address: Washington, DC 20233); (301) 763-7366. Gordon W. Green, chief. Fax, (301) 763-4493.

Compiles annual *Federal Expenditures by State* (available to the public), which provides information on overall federal grants-in-aid expenditures to state and local governments; collects data on finances, employment, and structure of the public sector; and serves as national clearinghouse on state and local audit reports.

Computer data obtainable from Data User Services, (301) 763-4100.

Executive Office of the President, Intergovernmental Affairs, White House 20500; 456-7060. Marcia Hale, director. Fax, 456-6220.

Serves as liaison with state and local governments; provides information on administration programs and policies.

General Services Administration, Federal Domestic Assistance Catalog Staff, 300 7th St. S.W., #101 20405; 708-5126. Robert Brown, director. Fax, 401-8233.

Operates computerized Federal Assistance Programs Retrieval System, which helps state and local governments to locate federal assistance or federal aid programs with the greatest funding potential to meet their developmental needs. Access to database available at designated points in every state. Prepares *Catalog of Federal Domestic Assistance* (published annually in June and updated in December), which lists all types of federal aid and explains types of assistance, eligibility requirements, application process, and suggestions for writing proposals. Copies may be ordered from the Superintendent of Documents, U.S. Government Printing Office, Washington, D.C. 20402; 783-3238.

Housing and Urban Development Dept., Policy Development and Research, HUD Bldg. 20410; 708-1600. Michael A. Stegman, assistant secretary. Fax, 619-8000.

Assesses urban economic development and the fiscal capacity of state and local governments.

Office of Management and Budget (Executive Office of the President), Federal Financial Management, New Executive Office Bldg. 20503; 395-4534. Vacant, controller. Fax, 395-4915.

Facilitates exchange of information on financial management standards, techniques, and processes among officers of state and local governments.

Congress:

General Accounting Office, Human Resources, 441 G St. N.W., NGB/ACG 20548; 512-6806. Janet L. Shikles, assistant comptroller general. Fax, 512-5806.

Independent, nonpartisan agency in the legislative branch. Responsible for intergovernmental relations activities. Reviews the effects of federal grants and regulations on state and local governments; works to reduce intergovernmental conflicts and costs; seeks to improve the allocation and targeting of federal funds to state and local governments through changes in federal funding formulas.

House Government Operations Committee, Subcommittee on Human Resources and Intergovernmental Relations, B372 RHOB 20515; 225-2548. Edolphus Towns, D-N.Y., chairman; Ron Stroman, staff director. Fax, 225-2382.

Jurisdiction over legislation dealing with the interrelationship among federal, state, and local governments, including revenue sharing legislation.

Senate Finance Committee, SD-205 20510; 224-4515. Daniel Patrick Moynihan, D-N.Y., chairman; Lawrence O'Donnell Jr., staff director.

Jurisdiction over legislation dealing with the interrelationship among federal, state, and local governments, including revenue sharing legislation (jurisdiction shared with Senate Governmental Affairs Committee).

Senate Governmental Affairs Committee, Subcommittee on General Services, Federalism, and the District of Columbia, SH-432 20510; 224-4718. Jim Sasser, D-Tenn., chairman; John Wagster, staff director.

Jurisdiction over legislation dealing with the interrelationship between federal, state, and local governments, including revenue sharing legislation (jurisdiction shared with Senate Finance Committee).

Nongovernmental:

Academy for State and Local Government, 444 N. Capitol St. N.W., #345 20001; 434-4850. Enid F. Beaumont, director. Fax, 434-4851.

Offers technical assistance, training, and research to the Council of State Governments, International City/County Management Assn., National Assn. of Counties, National Conference of State Legislatures, National Governors' Assn., National League of Cities, and U.S. Conference of Mayors. Promotes cooperation among federal, state, and local governments; the private sector; and researchers. Interests include tax policy, finance, and state and local relations. Works to improve state and local litigation in the Supreme Court. Promotes the exchange of information from overseas with state and local officials.

American Legislative Exchange Council, 214 Massachusetts Ave. N.E., #240 20002; 547-4646. Samuel A. Brunelli, executive director. Fax, 547-8142.

Educational and research organization for state legislators. Conducts research and provides information and model state legislation on public policy issues. Supports the development of state policies to limit government, expand free markets, promote economic growth, and preserve individual liberty.

Center for Policy Alternatives, 1875 Connecticut Ave. N.W., #710 20009-5728; 387-6030. Linda Tarr-Whelan, president. Fax, 986-2539.

Clearinghouse and research center that assists state and local officials in developing policy initiatives. Interests include state and local economic development and tax reform, toxic chemicals and environmental problems, governmental reform, health policy, voter registration, and women's rights issues; provides technical assistance.

Coalition of Northeastern Governors, Policy Research Center, 400 N. Capitol St. N.W., #382 20001; 624-8450. Anne D. Stubbs, executive director. Fax, 624-8463.

Membership: governors of nine northeastern states (Conn., Maine, Mass., N.H., N.J., N.Y., Pa., R.I., Vt.). Addresses common issues of concern such as energy, economic development, employment, transportation, and the environment; serves as an information clearinghouse and liaison among member states and with the federal government.

Council of Governors Policy Advisors, 400 N. Capitol St., #390 20001; 624-5386. Alice Tetelman, executive director. Fax, 624-7846.

Membership: chiefs of staff, policy directors, agency heads, and other top policy advisers. Provides a forum to share ideas on policy development and to debate issues; conducts policy research; provides members with management training and technical assistance. Interests include state policies for economic development, human investment, capital planning and budgeting, agricultural and rural development, and telecommunications. Affiliated with National Governors Association. Formerly known as the Council of State Planning Agencies.

Council of State Governments, 444 N. Capitol St. N.W. 20001; 624-5460. Abe Frank, director, Washington office. Fax, 624-5452.

Membership: governing bodies of states, commonwealths, and territories. Monitors legislation and executive policy. Promotes interstate, federal-state, and state-local cooperation; interests include education, transportation, human services, housing, natural resources, and economic development. Provides services to affiliates and associated organizations, including the National Assn. of State Treasurers, National Assn. of Secretaries of State, National Assn. of Government Labor Officials, and other state administrative organizations in specific fields. (Headquarters in Lexington, Ky.)

Government Finance Officers Assn., 1750 K St. N.W., #650 20006; 429-2750. Catherine L. Spain, director, federal liaison center. Fax, 429-2755.

Membership: state and local government finance managers. Offers training and publications in public financial management. Conducts research in public fiscal management, design and financing of government programs, and formulation and analysis of government fiscal policy. (Headquarters in Chicago.)

Municipal Treasurers' Assn. of the United States and Canada, 1229 19th St. N.W. 20036; 833-1017. Stacey Crane, executive director. Fax, 833-0375.

Provides continuing education and certification programs. Monitors legislation and regulations.

National Assn. of Bond Lawyers, 2000 Pennsylvania Ave. N.W., #9000 20006; 778-2244. Amy K. Dunbar, director, governmental affairs. Fax, 778-2201.

Membership: municipal finance lawyers. Provides members with information on laws relating to the borrowing of money by states and municipalities and to the issuance of state and local government bonds. Monitors legislation and regulations. (Headquarters in Hinsdale, Ill.)

National Assn. of Counties, 440 1st St. N.W., 8th Floor 20001; 393-6226. Larry Naake, executive director. Fax, 393-2630.

Membership: county officials. Conducts research, provides information, and offers technical assistance on issues affecting counties. Monitors legislation and regulations.

National Assn. of Regional Councils, 1700 K St. N.W., #1300 20006; 457-0710. John W. Epling, executive director. Fax, 296-9352.

Membership: regional councils of local governments. Works to improve local governments' ability to deal with common public needs, address regional issues, and reduce public expense. Interests include housing, urban planning, transportation, the environment, energy conservation, economic development, and aging.

National Assn. of State Budget Officers, 400 N. Capitol St. N.W., #299 20001; 624-5382. Brian Roherty, executive director. Fax, 624-7745.

Membership: state budget and financial officers. Sponsors training institutes on fiscal management; publishes research reports on state budget-related issues. (Affiliate of the National Governors' Assn.)

National Assn. of Towns and Townships, 1522 K St. N.W., #600 20005-1202; 737-5200. Jeffrey H. Schiff, executive director. Fax, 289-7996.

Provides local government officials from small jurisdictions with technical assistance, educational services, and public policy support; conducts research and coordinates training for local government officials nationwide.

National Conference of State Legislatures, 444 N. Capitol St. N.W., #515 20001; 624-5400. Carl Tubbesing, director, Washington office. Fax, 737-1069.

Coordinates and represents state legislatures at the federal level; conducts research and publishes reports in areas of interest to state legislatures; conducts an information exchange program on intergovernmental relations; sponsors seminars for state legislators and their staffs. Maintains audiovisual library; monitors legislation and regulations. (Headquarters in Denver.)

National Conference of State Societies, Box 180, LHOB, Washington, DC 20515; 686-6292. Virginia C. Haven, vice president.

Membership: delegates representing the United States, its territories, and the District of Columbia. Sponsors educational, cultural, and civic programs. Principal sponsor of the annual National Cherry Blossom Festival in Washington, D.C.

National Governors' Assn., 444 N. Capitol St. N.W., #267 20001; 624-5300. Raymond C. Scheppach, executive director. Press, 624-5330. Fax, 624-5313.

Membership: governors of states, commonwealths, and territories. Provides members with policy and technical assistance. Makes policy recommendations to Congress and the president in community and economic development; education; international trade and foreign relations; energy and the environment; human resources; agriculture; transportation, commerce, and technology; communications; and criminal justice and public protection.

National Institute of Municipal Law Officers, 1000 Connecticut Ave. N.W., #902 20036; 466-5424. Benjamin L. Brown, general counsel. Fax, 785-0152.

Organization of cities and municipalities that are represented through their chief legal officers. Acts as a research service for members in all areas of municipal law; participates in litigation of municipal and constitutional law issues.

National League of Cities, 1301 Pennsylvania Ave. N.W. 20004; 626-3000. Donald Borut, executive director. Information, 626-3120. Press, 626-3158. Fax, 626-3043.

Membership: cities and state municipal leagues. Provides city leaders with training, technical assistance, and publications; investigates needs of local governments in implementing federal programs that affect cities.

Public Risk Management Assn., 1117 N. 19th St., #900, Arlington, VA 22209; (703) 528-7701. Dennis Kirschbaum, executive director. Fax, (703) 528-7966.

Membership: state and local government risk management practitioners, including benefits and insurance managers. Develops and teaches cost-effective management techniques for handling public liability issues.

Public Technology, 1301 Pennsylvania Ave. N.W. 20004; 626-2400. Costis Toregas, president. Fax, 626-2498.

Cooperative research, development, and technology-transfer organization of cities and counties in North America. Assists local governments in increasing efficiency, reducing costs, improving services, and developing public enterprise programs to help local officials create revenues and serve citizens.

U.S. Conference of Mayors, 1620 Eye St. N.W., 4th Floor 20006; 293-7330. J. Thomas Cochran, executive director. Fax, 293-2352.

Membership: mayors of cities with populations of 30,000 or more. Promotes city-federal cooperation; publishes reports and conducts meetings on federal programs, policies, and initiatives that affect urban interests. Serves as a clearinghouse for information on urban problems.

See also Coastal States Organization (p. 651); Multistate Tax Commission (p. 58); National Assn. of State Development Agencies and National Center for Municipal Development (p. 75)

Key Agencies:

Health and Human Services Dept.
200 Independence Ave. S.W. 20201
Information: 690-6867

Key Committees:

House Energy and Commerce Committee
2125 RHOB 20515
Phone: 225-2927

House Government Operations Committee
2157 RHOB 20515
Phone: 225-5051

House Ways and Means Committee
1102 LHOB 20515
Phone: 225-3625

Senate Finance Committee
SD-205 20510
Phone: 224-4515

Senate Labor and Human Resources Committee
SD-428 20510
Phone: 224-5375

Key Personnel:

Health and Human Services Dept.

Donna E. Shalala, secretary

Walter D. Broadnax, deputy secretary

Mary Jo Bane, assistant secretary for children and families

Dr. Philip R. Lee, assistant secretary for health

Avis LaVelle, assistant secretary for public affairs

Dr. David A. Kessler, commissioner, Food and Drug Administration

Bruce C. Vladeck, administrator, Health Care Financing Administration

William A. Robinson, acting administrator, Health Resources and Services Administration

Harold Varmus, director, National Institutes of Health

Elaine M. Johnson, acting administrator, Substance Abuse and Mental Health Services Administration

Dr. Joycelyn Elders, surgeon general

8

Health

Contents:

Health

See also Consumer Affairs, Food and Nutrition (p. 258)

General

Agencies:

Agency for Health Care Policy and Research (Health and Human Services Dept.), 2101 E. Jefferson St., #600, Rockville, MD 20852; (301) 594-6662. J. Jarrett Clinton, administrator. Fax, (301) 594-2168.
Works to enhance the quality, appropriateness, and effectiveness of health care services and to improve access to services. Promotes improvements in clinical practices and in organizing, financing, and delivering health care services. Conducts and supports research, demonstration projects, evaluations, and training; disseminates information on a wide range of activities.

Centers for Disease Control and Prevention (Health and Human Services Dept.), 5600 Fishers Lane, Parklawn Bldg., #1834, Rockville, MD 20857; (301) 443-2610. Dr. Gary R. Noble, associate director, Washington office. Fax, (301) 443-8182. (Also located at 200 Independence Ave. S.W. 20201; 690-8598).
Surveys national disease trends and epidemics and environmental health problems; administers block grants to states for preventive health services; promotes national health education program; administers foreign quarantine program and occupational safety and health programs; assists state and local health departments and programs with control of sexually transmitted diseases, treatment of tuberculosis, childhood immunization, and health promotion regarding chronic diseases and injury. (Headquarters in Atlanta: 1600 Clifton Rd. N.E. 30333. Public inquiries, (404) 639-3534.)

Disease Prevention and Health Promotion (Health and Human Services Dept.), National Health Information Center, 11426-28 Rockville Pike, Rockville, MD (mailing address: P.O. Box 1133, Washington, DC 20013-1133); (301) 565-4167. Lisa Swanberg, project director. Toll-free, (800) 336-4797.
Provides referrals on health topics and resources.

Food and Drug Administration (Health and Human Services Dept.), 5600 Fishers Lane, Rockville, MD 20857; (301) 443-2410. Dr. David A. Kessler, commissioner. Information, (301) 443-3170. Press, (301) 443-3285. Fax, (301) 443-3100.
Conducts research and develops standards on the composition, quality, and safety of drugs, cosmetics, medical devices, radiation-emitting products, foods, food additives, and infant formulas; develops labeling and packaging standards; conducts inspections of manufacturers; issues orders to companies to recall and/or cease

selling or producing hazardous products; enforces rulings and recommends action to Justice Dept. when necessary. Library open to the public.

Food and Drug Administration (Health and Human Services Dept.), Regulatory Affairs, 5600 Fishers Lane, #1490, Rockville, MD 20857; (301) 443-1594. Ronald G. Chesemore, associate commissioner. Fax, (301) 443-6591.

Directs and coordinates the FDA's compliance activities; manages field offices; advises FDA commissioner on regulatory policies.

Health and Human Services Dept., 200 Independence Ave. S.W. 20201; 690-7694. Dr. Philip R. Lee, assistant secretary for health. Information, 690-6867. Fax, 690-6274.

Directs activities of the Public Health Service. Serves as the secretary's principal adviser on health concerns; exercises specialized responsibilities in various health areas, including population affairs and international health.

Health and Human Services Dept., Disease Prevention and Health Promotion, 330 C St. S.W. 20201; 205-8611. Dr. J. Michael McGinnis, deputy assistant secretary for health and assistant surgeon general. Toll-free, (800) 336-4797. Fax, 205-9478.

Develops national policies and programs for disease prevention and health promotion; coordinates activities of the Public Health Service and agencies involved in health promotion; assists the private sector and agencies with health promotion activities.

Health and Human Services Dept., National Center for Health Statistics, 6525 Belcrest Rd., #1140, Hyattsville, MD 20782; (301) 436-7016. Dr. Manning Feinleib, director. Information, (301) 436-8500. Fax, (301) 436-5202.

Compiles, analyzes, and disseminates national health statistics on population health characteristics, health facilities and human resources, health costs and expenditures, and health hazards.

Health and Human Services Dept., National Committee on Vital and Health Statistics, 6525 Belcrest Rd., #1100, Hyattsville, MD 20782; (301) 436-7050. Gail F. Fisher, executive secretary. Fax, (301) 436-4233.

Advises the secretary on health problem statistics; works with agencies and committees of

other nations on health problems of mutual concern.

Health and Human Services Dept., Planning and Evaluation, 200 Independence Ave. S.W. 20201; 690-7858. David T. Ellwood, assistant secretary. Fax, 690-7383.

Provides policy advice and makes recommendations to the secretary on the full range of department planning, including Medicare, Medicaid, health care services, human resources, health care facilities development and financing, biomedical research, and health care planning.

Health Resources and Services Administration (Health and Human Services Dept.), 5600 Fishers Lane, #1405, Rockville, MD 20857; (301) 443-2216. William A. Robinson, acting administrator. Information, (301) 443-2086. Press, (301) 443-3377. Fax, (301) 443-2605.

Administers federal health services programs related to access, quality, equity, and cost of health care. Supports state and community efforts to deliver care to underserved areas and groups with special health needs.

Health Resources and Services Administration (Health and Human Services Dept.), Organ Transplantation, 5600 Fishers Lane, #11A22, Rockville, MD 20857; (301) 443-7577. Judith Braslow, director. Fax, (301) 594-6095.

Implements provisions of the National Organ Transplant Act. Provides information on federal, state, and private programs involved in organ transplantation; supports a national computerized network for organ procurement and matching; maintains information on transplant recipients; awards grants to organ procurement organizations.

National Institute for Occupational Safety and Health (Health and Human Services Dept.), 200 Independence Ave. S.W. 20201; 690-7134. Bryan Hardin, director, Washington office. Toll-free, (800) 356-4674. Fax, 690-7519.

Entity within the Centers for Disease Control and Prevention in Atlanta, Ga. Supports and conducts research on occupational safety and health issues; provides technical assistance and training; develops recommendations for the Labor Dept. Operates an occupational safety and health bibliographic database (mailing address: National Institute for Occupational Safety and Health, Clearinghouse for Occupational Safety and Health Information, 4676 Columbia Parkway, Cincinnati, Ohio 45226).

Health and Human Services Dept.

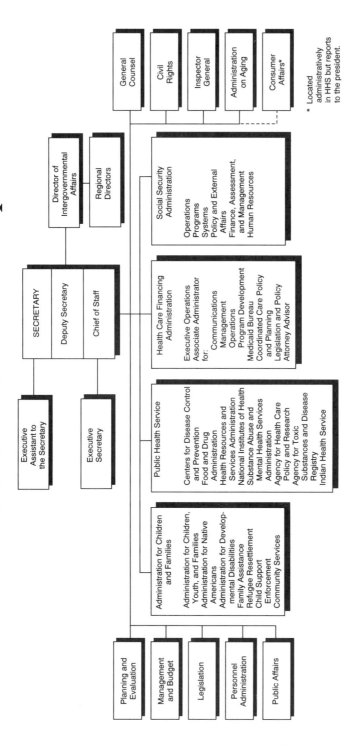

SECRETARY
Deputy Secretary
Chief of Staff

Executive Assistant to the Secretary

Executive Secretary

Director of Intergovernmental Affairs

Regional Directors

General Counsel

Civil Rights

Inspector General

Administration on Aging

Consumer Affairs*

* Located administratively in HHS but reports to the president.

Planning and Evaluation

Management and Budget

Legislation

Personnel Administration

Public Affairs

Administration for Children and Families

Administration for Children, Youth, and Families
Administration for Native Americans
Administration for Developmental Disabilities
Family Assistance
Refugee Resettlement
Child Support Enforcement
Community Services

Public Health Service

Centers for Disease Control and Prevention
Food and Drug Administration
Health Resources and Services Administration
National Institutes of Health
Substance Abuse and Mental Health Services Administration
Agency for Health Care Policy and Research
Agency for Toxic Substances and Disease Registry
Indian Health Service

Health Care Financing Administration

Executive Operations
Associate Administrator for:
  Communications
  Management
  Operations
  Program Development
Medicaid Bureau
Coordinated Care Policy and Planning
Legislation and Policy
Attorney Advisor

Social Security Administration

Operations
Programs
Systems
Policy and External Affairs
Finance, Assessment, and Management
Human Resources

National Institutes of Health (Health and Human Services Dept.), 9000 Rockville Pike, Bldg. 1, #126, Bethesda, MD 20892; (301) 496-2433. Harold Varmus, director. Press, (301) 496-5787. Fax, (301) 496-8276.

Supports and conducts biomedical research into the causes and prevention of diseases and furnishes information to health professionals and the public. Comprises 16 research institutes *(see Health Research section in this chapter)* and 8 components (the National Library of Medicine, the Warren Grant Magnuson Clinical Center, the National Center for Nursing Research, the National Center for Research Resources, the John E. Fogarty International Center, the National Center for Human Genome Research, the Division of Research Grants, and the Division of Computer Research and Technology). All institutes are located in Bethesda or Rockville, Md., except the National Institute of Environmental Health Sciences at Research Triangle Park, N.C. 27709 (P.O. Box 12233).

National Library of Medicine (Health and Human Services Dept.), 8600 Rockville Pike, Bethesda, MD 20894; (301) 496-6221. Dr. Donald A. B. Lindberg, director. Fax, (301) 496-4450.

Offers medical library services and computer-based reference service to the public, health professionals, libraries in medical schools and hospitals, and research institutions; operates a toxicology information service for the scientific community, industry, and federal agencies; assists medical libraries through the Regional Medical Library Network and research in medical library science. Assists nonprofit scientific biomedical publications and assists in the improvement of basic library resources.

Public Health Service (Health and Human Services Dept.), 200 Independence Ave. S.W. 20201; 690-7694. Dr. Philip R. Lee, assistant secretary for health. Information, 690-6867. Fax, 690-6274.

Promotes the protection and advancement of physical and mental health; establishes national health policy; maintains cooperative international health-related agreements and programs; administers programs to develop health resources and improve delivery of health services; works to prevent and control communicable diseases; conducts and supports research in medicine and related sciences; and provides scientific information. Protects against impure or unsafe foods, drugs, and cosmetics; develops education for the health professions.

Public Health Service (Health and Human Services Dept.), 200 Independence Ave. S.W. 20201; 690-6467. Joycelyn Elders, surgeon general. Fax, (301) 443-3574.

Advises the public on health issues such as smoking, AIDS, immunization, diet, nutrition, disease prevention, and general health issues. Oversees activities of all members of the Public Health Service Commission Corps.

Substance Abuse and Mental Health Services Administration (Health and Human Services Dept.), 5600 Fishers Lane, #12-105, Rockville, MD 20857; (301) 443-4795. Elaine M. Johnson, acting administrator. Information, (301) 443-8956. Fax, (301) 443-0284.

Coordinates activities of the Center for Substance Abuse Treatment, Center for Mental Health Services, and Center for Substance Abuse Prevention, which sponsors the National Clearinghouse for Alcohol and Drug Information.

See also Domestic Policy Council (p. 300)

Congress:

General Accounting Office, Human Resources, 1 Massachusetts Ave. N.W. (mailing address: NGB/Health Care Delivery Issues, 441 G St. N.W., Washington, DC 20548); 512-7101. David Baine, director, health care delivery issues. Fax, 512-6114.

Independent, nonpartisan agency in the legislative branch. Audits all federal government health programs, including those administered by the departments of Defense, Health and Human Services, and Veterans Affairs.

House Appropriations Committee, Subcommittee on Agriculture, Rural Development, FDA, and Related Agencies, 2362 RHOB 20515; 225-2638. Richard J. Durbin, D-Ill., chairman; Robert B. Foster, staff assistant. Fax, 225-3598.

Jurisdiction over legislation to appropriate funds for the Food and Drug Administration, Food Safety and Inspection Service, and Human Nutrition Information Service.

House Appropriations Committee, Subcommittee on Labor, Health and Human Services, and Education, 2358 RHOB 20515; 225-3508. Neal Smith, D-Iowa, chairman; Mike Stephens, staff assistant.

Jurisdiction over legislation to appropriate funds for health agencies in the Health and

Human Services Dept. (excluding the Food and Drug Administration and native American health and health facilities construction activities); the National Commission on Acquired Immune Deficiency Syndrome; and the National Council on Disability.

House Energy and Commerce Committee, Subcommittee on Health and the Environment, 2415 RHOB 20515; 225-4952. Henry A. Waxman, D-Calif., chairman; Karen Nelson, staff director.

Jurisdiction over most health legislation, including Medicaid, national health insurance proposals, public health and quarantine, alcohol abuse, drug abuse (including medical and psychological rehabilitation programs for drug abusers), dental health, medical devices, long-term and nursing home care, orphan drugs, preventive health and emergency medical care, family planning, population research, mental health, and prenatal, maternal, and child health care. Oversight of the Food and Drug Administration.

House Government Operations Committee, Subcommittee on Human Resources and Intergovernmental Relations, B372 RHOB 20515; 225-2548. Edolphus Towns, D-N.Y., chairman; Ron Stroman, staff director. Fax, 225-2382.

Oversees operations of the Health and Human Services Dept.

House Natural Resources Committee, Subcommittee on Energy and Mineral Resources, 818 O'Neill Bldg. (300 New Jersey Ave. S.E.) 20515; 225-8331. Richard H. Lehman, D-Calif., chairman; Deborah Lanzone, staff director. Fax, 225-4273.

Jurisdiction over nonmilitary environmental regulation and control of nuclear energy, including radiological health.

House Ways and Means Committee, Subcommittee on Health, 1114 LHOB 20515; 225-7785. Pete Stark, D-Calif., chairman; David Abernethy, staff director.

Jurisdiction over legislation dealing with health care research and delivery programs supported by tax revenues, including Medicare, and proposals to establish a national health insurance system (jurisdiction shared with the House Energy and Commerce Committee).

Senate Appropriations Committee, Subcommittee on Agriculture, Rural Development, and Related Agencies, SD-140 20510; 224-7240. Dale Bumpers, D-Ark., chairman; Rocky L. Kuhn, clerk.

Jurisdiction over legislation to appropriate funds for the Food and Drug Administration; Food Safety and Inspection Service and the Human Nutrition Information Service (of the Agriculture Dept.); and other health-related services and programs.

Senate Appropriations Committee, Subcommittee on Labor, Health and Human Services, and Education, SD-186 20510; 224-7283. Tom Harkin, D-Iowa, chairman; Ed Long, clerk.

Jurisdiction over legislation to appropriate funds for health agencies in the Health and Human Services Dept. (excluding the Food and Drug Administration and native American health programs).

Senate Environment and Public Works Committee, Subcommittee on Clean Air and Nuclear Regulation, SH-505 20510; 224-3597. Joseph I. Lieberman, D-Conn., chairman; Joyce Rechtschaffen, counsel.

Jurisdiction over nonmilitary environmental regulation and control of nuclear energy, including radiological health.

Senate Finance Committee, SD-205 20510; 224-4515. Daniel Patrick Moynihan, D-N.Y., chairman; Lawrence O'Donnell Jr., staff director.

Jurisdiction over health programs supported by tax revenues, including Medicaid and Medicare.

Senate Judiciary Committee, SD-224 20510; 224-5225. Joseph R. Biden Jr., D-Del., chairman; Cynthia Hogan, chief counsel.

Jurisdiction over legislation on drug abuse, which includes regulatory aspects of federal drug abuse programs and criminal justice system rehabilitation programs for juvenile drug abusers.

Senate Labor and Human Resources Committee, SD-428 20510; 224-5375. Edward M. Kennedy, D-Mass., chairman; Nick Littlefield, chief counsel and staff director.

Jurisdiction over most health legislation, including insurance, dental health, emergency medical care, mental health, medical devices, public health and quarantine, family planning, population research, prenatal, and some maternal and child health care legislation, including the dangers of lead-based paint and sudden infant death syndrome; jurisdiction over legislation on radiation hazards of consumer products and machines used in industry. Oversees operations of the Health and Human Services Dept.

Senate Labor and Human Resources Committee, Subcommittee on Children, Families, Drugs, and Alcoholism, SH-639 20510; 224-5630. Christopher J. Dodd, D-Conn., chairman; Sarah Flanagan, staff director.

Jurisdiction over alcohol and drug abuse legislation, including federal grants for alcohol and drug abuse treatment programs and research, and medical and psychological rehabilitation programs for alcohol and drug abusers.

See also Congressional Task Force on Tobacco and Health (p. 759); Rural Health Care Coalition (p. 760); Senate Rural Health Caucus (p. 761)

International Organizations:

International Bank for Reconstruction and Development (World Bank), Population, Health, and Nutrition, 1750 Pennsylvania Ave. N.W., #S11-141 (mailing address: 1818 H St. N.W., Washington, DC 20433); 458-2381. Janet de Merode, director. Fax, 522-3235.

Provides developing member countries with loans to help improve citizens' primary health care and nutrition and to help slow population growth through family planning.

Pan American Health Organization, 525 23rd St. N.W. 20037; 861-3200. Dr. Carlyle Guerra de Macedo, director. Information, 861-3458. Library, 861-3305. Fax, 223-5971.

Regional office for the Americas of the World Health Organization, headquartered in Geneva, Switzerland. Works to extend health services to underserved populations of its member countries and to control or eradicate communicable diseases; promotes cooperation among governments to solve public health problems. Library open to the public by appointment.

World Federation of Public Health Assns., 1015 15th St. N.W. 20005; 789-5696. Diane Kuntz, executive secretary. Fax, 789-5681.

International health organization composed of national public health associations whose membership includes health professionals and laypersons interested in improving community health. Sponsors triennial international congress.

Nongovernmental:

American Assn. for World Health, 1129 20th St. N.W., #400 20036; 466-5883. Richard L. Wittenberg, president. Fax, 466-5896.

Works to inform Americans about world health problems and increase American support for organizations dealing with these problems. Distributes educational materials; sponsors World Health Day, World No-Tobacco Day, and World AIDS Day. Association board serves as the U.S. Committee for the World Health Organization and the Pan American Health Organization.

American College of Preventive Medicine, 1015 15th St. N.W., #403 20005; 789-0003. Hazel K. Keimowitz, executive director. Fax, 289-8274.

Membership: physicians in general preventive medicine, public health, occupational medicine, and aerospace medicine. Provides educational opportunities; advocates public policies consistent with scientific principles of the discipline; supports the investigation and analysis of issues relevant to the field.

American Industrial Health Council, 1330 Connecticut Ave. N.W., #300 20036; 659-0060. Ronald A. Lang, president. Fax, 659-1699.

Coalition of industrial firms and trade associations concerned about potential health effects associated with industrial and commercial activities. Advocates using scientific information to evaluate and assess health risks; promotes the development and use of scientifically valid risk assessment data by regulatory agencies. Provides information on health hazards of toxic substances, genetic testing, and causes of cancer and birth defects.

American Medical Informatics Assn., 4915 St. Elmo Ave., #302, Bethesda, MD 20814; (301) 657-1291. Gail Mutnik, executive director. Fax, (301) 657-1296.

Provides information on medical systems and use of computers in the health care field. Promotes use of computers and information systems in patient care; conducts and promotes research on medical technology; encourages development of universal standards, terminology, and coding systems.

American Osteopathic Healthcare Assn., 5301 Wisconsin Ave. N.W., #630 20015; 686-1700. David Kushner, president. Fax, 686-7615.

Conducts educational programs on management techniques for executives of member hospitals; monitors legislation and regulations.

American Public Health Assn., 1015 15th St. N.W., #300 20005; 789-5600. Dr. Fernando Trevino, executive director. Fax, 789-5661.

Membership: health care professionals, educators, environmentalists, social workers, industrial hygienists, and individuals. Interests include all aspects of health care and education. Establishes standards for scientific procedures in public health; conducts research on the causes and origin of communicable diseases. Produces data on the number of women and minority workers in public health and on their health status.

Assn. for the Advancement of Health Education, 1900 Association Dr., Reston, VA 22091; (703) 476-3437. Becky J. Smith, executive director. Fax, (703) 476-6638.

Membership: health educators and allied health professionals in community and volunteer health agencies, educational institutions, and businesses. Develops health education programs; monitors legislation.

Assn. of Teachers of Preventive Medicine, 1015 15th St. N.W., #405 20005; 682-1698. Kay B. Doggett, executive director. Fax, 842-1980.

Membership: medical educators, practitioners, administrators, students, and health care agencies. Works to advance education in preventive medicine; interests include public health, clinical prevention, and aerospace and occupational medicine. Promotes collaborative research and programs; fosters information exchange.

Health Education Foundation, 2600 Virginia Ave. N.W., #502 20037; 338-3501. Dr. Morris Chafetz, president. Fax, 342-8728.

Seeks to develop health information programs; operates information reference service.

Institute for Women's Policy Research, 1400 20th St. N.W., #104 20036; 785-5100. Heidi I. Hartmann, director. Fax, 833-4362.

Public policy research organization that focuses on women's issues, including health care and comprehensive family and medical leave programs.

International Patient Education Council, 15881 Crabbs Branch Way, Rockville, MD (mailing address: P.O. Box 1438, Rockville, MD

20849); (301) 948-1863. Maryanne Biddison, executive director.

Membership: physicians, registered nurses, hospitals, health maintenance organizations, and other health-related groups. Develops patient education programs and provides health care professionals with information.

Managed Health Care Assn., 1225 Eye St. N.W., #300 20005; 371-8232. Carol Cronin, executive director. Fax, 842-0621.

Organization of private-sector employers that promotes the expansion and improvement of managed health care. Provides health care management professionals with education and training. Supports innovation in the design and operation of managed care programs. Provides a forum for information exchange among employers, managed care organizations, and health care providers. Serves as a technical resource on managed health care systems.

National Chronic Pain Outreach Assn., 7979 Old Georgetown Rd., #100, Bethesda, MD 20814-2429; (301) 652-4948. Laura S. Hitchcock, executive director. Fax, (301) 907-0745.

Works to improve the lives of people with chronic pain. Serves as a clearinghouse for information on pain management; educates the public and health care professionals; helps develop support groups by providing publications and tapes.

National Council for International Health, 1701 K St. N.W., #600 20006; 833-5900. Eliot T. Putnam Jr., president. Fax, 833-0075.

Seeks to strengthen U.S. participation in international health activities, especially in developing countries. Serves as an information clearinghouse for the international health community. Promotes cooperation among private and public organizations involved in international health activities. Provides policy analysis and public education. Holds the International Health Conference. Sponsors career services program and international health seminars.

National Health Council, 1730 M St. N.W., #500 20036; 785-3913. Joseph C. Isaacs, president. Fax, 785-5923.

Membership: voluntary health agencies, associations, and business, insurance, and government groups interested in health. Conducts research on health and health-related issues; serves as an information clearinghouse on health careers; monitors legislation and regulations.

National Health Lawyers Assn., 1120 Connecticut Ave. N.W., #950 20036; 833-1100. Marylou King, vice president. Fax, 833-1105.

Membership: corporate, institutional, and government lawyers interested in the health field; law students; and health professionals. Serves as an information clearinghouse on health law; sponsors health law educational programs and seminars.

National Health Policy Forum, 2021 K St. N.W., #800 20006; 872-1390. Judith Miller Jones, director. Fax, 785-0114.

Nonpartisan policy analysis and research organization that provides federal agencies and congressional staff with information on financing and delivery of health care services. Affiliated with George Washington University.

National Hospice Organization, 1901 N. Moore St., #901, Arlington, VA 22209; (703) 243-5900. John J. Mahoney, president. Fax, (703) 525-5762. Toll-free information and referral helpline, (800) 658-8898.

Membership: institutions and individuals providing hospice care and other interested organizations and individuals. Promotes supportive care for the terminally ill and their families; sets hospice program standards; provides information on hospices; monitors legislation and regulations.

National Women's Health Network, 1325 G St. N.W. 20005; 347-1140. Beverly Baker, executive director. Fax, 347-1168.

Acts as an information clearinghouse on women's health issues; monitors federal health policies and legislation. Interests include older women's health issues, contraception, breast cancer, abortion, unsafe drugs, and AIDS.

Public Citizen, Health Research Group, 2000 P St. N.W., #700 20036; 833-3000. Dr. Sidney M. Wolfe, director. Fax, 452-8658.

Citizens' interest group that conducts policy-oriented research on health care issues. Interests include hospital quality and costs, doctors' fees, physician discipline and malpractice, state administration of Medicare programs, workplace safety and health, unnecessary surgery, comprehensive health planning, dangerous drugs, carcinogens, medical devices, and overuse of medical and dental X-rays. Favors a single-payer (Canadian-style), comprehensive health program.

Rand Corporation, Health Sciences Program, 2100 M St. N.W. 20037; 296-5000. Charles R. Roll Jr., director, Washington operations. Fax, 296-7960.

Research organization that assesses alternative reimbursement schemes for health care. Interests include the role and changing character of academic medicine, medical human resources and technology, and care of the elderly. (Headquarters in Santa Monica, Calif.)

U.S. Conference of Local Health Officers, 1620 Eye St. N.W., 4th Floor 20006; 293-7330. J. Thomas Cochran, executive director. Fax, 293-2352.

Membership: city, county, and district health officers. Provides members with information on national, state, and local health developments; submits health policy proposals to the federal government; monitors legislation and regulations affecting local health departments.

Dental

See also Health Research, Dental (p. 369)

Agencies:

Health Resources and Services Administration (Health and Human Services Dept.), Associated, Dental, and Public Health Professions, 5600 Fishers Lane, #8-101, Rockville, MD 20857; (301) 443-6853. Dr. Neil Sampson, director. Fax, (301) 443-1164.

Funds and conducts research on dental employment, education, and delivery systems. Areas of study include geographic distribution of dentists, general practice vs. specialization, women and minorities in dentistry, curriculum development, and dental health care delivery.

Congress:

See Health, General, Congress (p. 321)

Nongovernmental:

American Assn. of Dental Schools, 1625 Massachusetts Ave. N.W., #502 20036; 667-9433. Dr. Preston A. Littleton Jr., executive director. Fax, 667-0642.

Membership: individuals interested in dental education; undergraduate and graduate schools of dentistry; and allied dental education programs in the United States, Canada, and Puerto Rico. Provides information on dental teaching and research and on admission requirements of

U.S. and Canadian dental schools; publishes a directory of dental educators.

American College of Dentists, 839 Quince Orchard Blvd., #J, Gaithersburg, MD 20878; (301) 977-3223. Dr. Sherry Keramidas, executive director. Fax, (301) 977-3330.

Honorary society of dentists. Fellows are elected based on their contributions to education, research, dentistry, and community and civic organizations. Interests include ethics, professionalism, and dentistry in the health-care system.

American Dental Assn., 1111 14th St. N.W. 20005; 898-2400. Leonard P. Wheat, director, government relations. Fax, 898-2437.

Conducts research; provides dental education materials; compiles statistics on dentistry and dental care. Monitors legislation and regulations. (Headquarters in Chicago.)

American Dental Trade Assn., 4222 King St. West, Alexandria, VA 22302-1597; (703) 379-7755. Nikolaj M. Petrovic, president. Fax, (703) 931-9429.

Membership: dental laboratories and distributors and manufacturers of dental equipment and supplies. Collects and disseminates statistical and management information; conducts studies, programs, and projects of interest to the industry; acts as liaison with government agencies.

National Assn. of Dental Laboratories, 555 E. Braddock Rd., Alexandria, VA 22314; (703) 683-5263. Robert W. Stanley, executive director. Fax, (703) 549-4788.

Membership: dental laboratories, industry manufacturers and suppliers, and schools of dental technology. Interests include certification, improving education in dental technology, and content of alloys used in dentistry; monitors state and federal legislation.

National Dental Assn., 5506 Connecticut Ave. N.W., #24 20015; 244-7555. Robert S. Johns, executive director. Fax, 244-5992.

Promotes the interests of African American and other minority dentists through educational programs and federal legislation and programs.

See also Health, General, Nongovernmental (p. 323)

Exercise and Fitness

Agencies:

Health and Human Services Dept., President's Council on Physical Fitness and Sports, 701 Pennsylvania Ave. N.W., #250 20004; 272-3421. Sandra Perlmutter, executive director. Information, 272-3430. Fax, 504-2064.

Provides schools, state and local governments, recreation agencies, and employers with technical assistance on designing and implementing physical fitness programs; conducts award programs for children and adults and for schools, clubs, and other institutions.

Nongovernmental:

American Running and Fitness Assn., 4405 East-West Highway, #405, Bethesda, MD 20814; (301) 913-9517. Susan Kalish, executive director. Toll-free, (800) 776-2732. Fax, (301) 913-9520.

Membership: athletes, sports medicine professionals, health clubs, businesses, and individuals. Promotes proper nutrition and regular exercise. Provides members with medical advice and referrals, fitness information, and assistance in developing fitness programs.

Road Runners Club of America, 1150 S. Washington St., #250, Alexandria, VA 22314; (703) 836-0558. Henley Gibble, executive director. Fax, (703) 836-4430.

Develops and promotes road races and fitness programs, including the Children's Running Development Program. Issues guidelines on road races. Interests include safety, wheelchair participation, and baby joggers/strollers in races; facilitates communication between clubs. Supports running for people with disabilities.

See also Education: Special Topics, Physical Education, Nongovernmental (p. 157)

See also American Hiking Society (p. 652); National Handicapped Sports Assn. (p. 423); Special Olympics (p. 424)

Family Planning and Population

See also Census: Population Data (p. 284); Constitutional Law and Civil Liberties, Abortion and Reproductive Issues (p. 503)

Agencies:

Agency for International Development (International Development Cooperation Agency), Population, 1601 N. Kent St., Arlington, VA (mailing address: G/RND/POP, #811, Washington, DC 20523); (703) 875-4402. Elizabeth S. Maguire, acting director. Fax, (703) 875-4413.
Awards grants to foreign governments and private educational and interest groups for research, employment training, programs, and materials (especially contraceptives) for family planning abroad.

Census Bureau (Commerce Dept.), Fertility Statistics, Suitland and Silver Hill Rds., Suitland, MD (mailing address: Washington, DC 20233); (301) 763-5303. Martin O'Connell, chief. Fax, (301) 763-3862.
Provides data and statistics on fertility. Conducts census and survey research on the number of children, birth expectations, and current child spacing patterns of women in the United States, especially working mothers. Conducts studies on child care.

Family Life Information Exchange (Health and Human Services Dept.), P.O. Box 37299, Washington, DC 20013-7299; (301) 585-6636. Jenrose Weldon, director.
Federally contracted program that collects and disseminates information on family planning and related topics, including adoption and adolescent abstinence.

National Institute of Child Health and Human Development (National Institutes of Health, Health and Human Services Dept.), Center for Population Research, 6100 Executive Blvd., Rockville, MD 20852; (301) 496-1101. Dr. Florence P. Haseltine, director. Fax, (301) 496-0962.
Supports biomedical research on reproductive processes influencing human fertility and infertility; develops methods for regulating fertility; evaluates the safety and effectiveness of contraceptive methods; conducts research on the reproductive motivation of individuals and the causes and consequences of population change.

Public Health Service (Health and Human Services Dept.), Population Affairs, 4330 East-West Highway, #115, Bethesda, MD 20814; (301) 594-4000. Gerald Bennett, acting director. Fax, (301) 492-3017.
Responsible for planning, monitoring, and evaluating population research, voluntary family planning, and adolescent family life programs.

Congress:

See Health, General, Congress (p. 321)

International Organizations:

International Bank for Reconstruction and Development (World Bank), Population, Health, and Nutrition, 1750 Pennsylvania Ave. N.W., #S11-141 (mailing address: 1818 H St. N.W., Washington, DC 20433); 458-2381. Janet de Merode, director. Fax, 522-3235.
Provides member countries with loans and technical advice for family planning projects designed to slow population growth. (Works in conjunction with regional World Bank offices.)

Nongovernmental:

Alan Guttmacher Institute, 1120 Connecticut Ave. N.W., #960 20036; 296-4012. Cory L. Richards, vice president for public policy. Fax, 223-5756.
Conducts research, policy analysis, and public education in the areas of reproductive health, fertility regulation, population, and related areas of health and social policy. (Headquarters in New York.)

Center for Population Options, 1025 Vermont Ave. N.W., #210 20005; 347-5700. Marge Clark, executive director. Fax, 347-2263.
Seeks to reduce the incidence of unintended teenage pregnancy and AIDS through public education, training and technical assistance, research, and media programs.

Center for Population Research (Georgetown University), 1437 37th St. N.W. 20057; 687-6807. Beth J. Soldo, director.
Research, consulting, and education center involved in international and domestic population issues, including child nutrition and health, fertility, and the aging process.

International Federation for Family Life Promotion, 2009 N. 14th St., #512, Arlington, VA 22201-2514; (703) 516-0388. Claude A. Lanctot, executive director. Fax, (703) 516-0390.
Organization of individuals and groups worldwide interested in natural family planning. Works with federal and private agencies and international organizations to promote natural family planning research, education, and services; conducts training programs for natural family planning instructors.

National Abortion Federation, 1436 U St. N.W., #103 20009; 667-5881. Sylvia Stengle, executive director. Toll-free, (800) 772-9100. Fax, 667-5890.

Federation of facilities providing abortion services. Offers information on medical, legal, and social aspects of abortion; sets quality standards for abortion care. Conducts training workshops and seminars; monitors legislation and regulations.

National Family Planning and Reproductive Health Assn., 122 C St. N.W., #380 20001; 628-3535. Judith DeSarno, president. Fax, 737-2690. Recording, 563-7742.

Membership: health professionals and others interested in family planning and reproductive health. Operates a network for information, referral, research, policy analysis, and training designed to improve and expand the delivery of family planning services and reproductive health care.

Planned Parenthood Federation of America, 1120 Connecticut Ave. N.W., #461 20036; 785-3351. William W. Hamilton Jr., director, Washington office. Fax, 293-4349.

Educational, research, and medical services organization. Washington office conducts research and monitors legislation on fertility-related health topics, including abortion, reproductive health, contraception, family planning, and international population control. (Headquarters in New York accredits affiliated local centers, which offer medical services, birth control, and family planning information.)

Population Action International, 1120 19th St. N.W., #550 20036; 659-1833. Dr. J. Joseph Speidel, president. Fax, 293-1795.

Promotes population stabilization through public education and universal access to voluntary family planning. Library open to the public by appointment.

Population-Environment Balance, 1325 G St. N.W., #1003 20005; 879-3000. Mark W. Nowak, executive director. Fax, 879-3019.

Grass-roots organization that advocates U.S. population stabilization to safeguard the environment.

Population Institute, 107 2nd St. N.E. 20002; 544-3300. Werner Fornos, president. Fax, 544-0068.

Encourages leaders of developing nations to balance population growth through resource management; works with leaders of industrial nations to help achieve a balance between population and natural resources.

Population Reference Bureau, 1875 Connecticut Ave. N.W., #520 20009-5728; 483-1100. Peter J. Donaldson, president. Fax, 328-3937.

Educational organization engaged in information dissemination, training, and policy analysis on population trends and issues. Interests include family planning and international development programs, the environment, and U.S. social and economic policy. Library open to the public.

World Population Society, 1333 H St. N.W., #106 20005; 898-1303. Frank H. Oram, executive director.

Membership: professionals in population activities and others concerned with population matters. Encourages multidisciplinary approaches to population problems; promotes technical cooperation in programs to reduce population growth among developing nations; organizes international conferences.

Zero Population Growth, 1400 16th St. N.W., #320 20036; 332-2200. Susan Weber, executive director. Fax, 332-2302.

Membership: persons interested in sustainable world populations. Promotes the expansion of domestic and international family planning programs; supports a voluntary population stabilization policy and women's access to abortion services; works to protect the earth's resources and environment.

See also Health, General, Nongovernmental (p. 323)

See also Program for Appropriate Technology in Health (p. 455)

Medical Devices

See also Consumer Affairs, Labeling and Packaging (p. 262)

Agencies:

Food and Drug Administration (Health and Human Services Dept.), Center for Devices and Radiological Health, 1390 Piccard Dr., Rockville, MD 20850; (301) 443-4690. Dr. D. Bruce Burlington, director. Fax, (301) 594-1320.

Evaluates safety, efficacy, and labeling of medical devices; classifies medical devices; develops FDA surveillance and compliance programs; establishes performance standards; assists in legal actions concerning medical devices; provides small manufacturers of medical devices with technical and other nonfinancial assistance; plans, collects, and coordinates research and testing activities and data; conducts training and educational programs. Library open to the public.

Food and Drug Administration (Health and Human Services Dept.), Small Manufacturers Assistance, 1901 Chapman Ave., Rockville, MD (mailing address: 5600 Fishers Lane, Rockville, MD 20857); (301) 443-6597. John Stigi, director. Toll-free, (800) 638-2041. Fax, (301) 443-8818.

Serves as liaison between small-business manufacturers of medical devices and the FDA. Assists manufacturers in complying with FDA regulatory requirements; sponsors seminars.

Congress:

See Health, General, Congress (p. 321)

Nongovernmental:

Health Industry Distributors Assn., 225 Reinekers Lane, #650, Alexandria, VA 22314-2875; (703) 549-4432. Wayne Kay, president. Fax, (703) 549-6495.

Membership: medical products distributors and home health care providers. Administers educational programs and conducts training seminars; monitors legislation and regulations.

Health Industry Manufacturers Assn., 1200 G St. N.W., #400 20005; 783-8700. Alan H. Magazine, president. Fax, 783-8750.

Membership: manufacturers of medical devices, diagnostic products, and health care information systems. Interests include safe and effective medical devices. Conducts educational seminars and monitors legislation and regulations.

National Assn. for Medical Equipment Services, 625 Slaters Lane, #200, Alexandria, VA 22314; (703) 836-6263. Corrine Parver, president. Fax, (703) 836-6730.

Membership: home medical equipment suppliers, manufacturers, and state associations. Promotes legislative and regulatory policy that improves access to quality home medical equipment.

See also American Orthotic and Prosthetic Assn. and Hearing Industries Assn. (p. 346); Public Citizen, Health Research Group (p. 325)

Mental Health

Agencies:

National Institute of Mental Health (National Institutes of Health, Health and Human Services Dept.), 5600 Fishers Lane, #17-99, Rockville, MD 20857; (301) 443-3673. Dr. Frederick K. Goodwin, director. Information, (301) 443-4513. Press, (301) 443-3600. Fax, (301) 443-2578.

Conducts research on the cause, diagnosis, treatment, and prevention of mental disorders; assists states and communities with mental health programs; provides information on mental health problems and programs.

National Institute of Mental Health (National Institutes of Health, Health and Human Services Dept.), Clinical and Treatment Research, 5600 Fishers Lane, #18C-26, Rockville, MD 20857; (301) 443-3683. Jane H. Steinberg, acting director. Fax, (301) 443-6000.

Sponsors and directs research, research training, and resource development in psychopathology, classification, assessment, etiology, genetics, clinical course, outcome, and treatment of mental disorders. Focuses on schizophrenic disorders, affective and anxiety disorders, and mental disorders of children and adolescents, the elderly, minorities, and other special populations. Coordinates the NIMH Medications Development Program.

National Institute of Mental Health (National Institutes of Health, Health and Human Services Dept.), Depression, Awareness, Recognition, and Treatment, 5600 Fishers Lane, #10-85, Rockville, MD 20857; (301) 443-4140. Isabel Davidoff, director. Fax, (301) 443-4045.

Educates the public and health professionals about depression and its treatment; develops workplace educational programs for managers, employees, and health program directors; produces and disseminates materials.

National Institute of Mental Health (National Institutes of Health, Health and Human Services Dept.), Prevention Research, 5600 Fishers Lane, #10-85, Rockville, MD 20857; (301) 443-4283. Eve Moscicki, chief. Information, (301) 443-4513. Fax, (301) 443-4045.

Provides funds for research and research training in the prevention of mental disorders and behavioral dysfunctions, including the promotion of mental health; focuses on preventive intervention strategies.

National Institute of Mental Health (National Institutes of Health, Health and Human Services Dept.), Special Populations, 5600 Fishers Lane, #17C-14, Rockville, MD 20857; (301) 443-2847. Delores Parron, associate director. Fax, (301) 443-1328.

Sets research policy on women and racial and ethnic minorities. Administers the minority institutions programs, which support research on and research training for minorities in the mental health field.

National Institute of Mental Health (National Institutes of Health, Health and Human Services Dept.), Violence and Traumatic Stress, 5600 Fishers Lane, Parklawn Bldg., #10C-24, Rockville, MD 20857; (301) 443-3728. Susan D. Solomon, chief. Fax, (301) 443-1726.

Supports research on mental health consequences of traumatic events, including disasters, combat, terrorism, and interpersonal violence. Conducts and funds programs to reduce trauma. Studies perpetrators of violence and the relationship between mental health issues and the law.

Substance Abuse and Mental Health Services Administration (Health and Human Services Dept.), Center for Mental Health Services, 5600 Fishers Lane, #15-105, Rockville, MD 20857; (301) 443-0001. Dr. Bernard S. Arons, director. Information, (301) 443-2792. Fax, (301) 443-1563.

Develops outreach programs for the mentally ill and their families; assists people with AIDS or HIV, victims of violence and physical or sexual abuse, the elderly, and refugees; assists state and local governments and the private sector in expanding mental health services, including rehabilitative services.

Congress:

See Health, General, Congress (p. 321)

Nongovernmental:

American Bar Assn., Commission on Mental and Physical Disability Law, 1800 M St. N.W., #200 20036; 331-2240. John Parry, director. Fax, 331-2220.

Serves as a clearinghouse for information on mental and physical disability law and offers computerized legal research services.

American Counseling Assn., 5999 Stevenson Ave., Alexandria, VA 22304; (703) 823-9800. Patricia Schwallie-Giddis, acting executive director. Toll-free, (800) 347-6647. Fax, (703) 823-0252. TDD, (703) 370-1943.

Membership: professional counselors and counselor educators. Provides members with leadership training, continuing education programs, and advocacy services; develops professional and ethical standards for the counseling profession; accredits counselor education programs; monitors legislation and regulations. Library open to the public.

American Mental Health Counselors Assn., 5999 Stevenson Ave., Alexandria, VA 22304; (703) 823-9800. Mary Lyn Pike, executive director. Fax, (703) 751-1696.

Membership: professional counselors and graduate students in the mental health field. Sponsors leadership training and continuing education programs for members; serves as a liaison between counselors and clients; monitors legislation and regulations. (Affiliated with the American Counseling Assn.)

American Psychiatric Assn., 1400 K St. N.W. 20005; 682-6083. Dr. Melvin Sabshin, medical director. Information, 682-6000. Press, 682-6220. Library, 682-6080. Fax, 682-6114.

Membership: psychiatrists. Promotes availability of high-quality psychiatric care; provides the public with information; assists state and local agencies; conducts educational programs for professionals and students in the field. Library open to the public by appointment.

American Psychological Assn., 750 1st St. N.E. 20002-4242; 336-5500. Raymond D. Fowler, executive vice president. Library, 336-5640. Fax, 336-6069. TDD, 336-6123.

Membership: professional psychologists and educators. Supports research, training, and professional services; works toward improving the qualifications, training programs, and competence of psychologists; monitors federal legislation on mental health issues.

Anxiety Disorders Assn. of America, 6000 Executive Blvd., #513, Rockville, MD 20852; (301) 231-9350. Joel Klaverkamp, executive director. Fax, (301) 231-7392.

Membership: people with phobias and anxiety disorders, their support persons, and mental health professionals. Provides self-help groups with technical and networking support; encourages research and treatment for anxiety disorders.

Assn. of Black Psychologists, 821 Kennedy St. N.W. (mailing address: P.O. Box 55999, Washington, DC 20040); 722-0808. Anna M. Jackson, president. Fax, 722-5941.

Membership: African American psychologists and psychology students. Develops policies to foster mental health in the African American community.

Mental Health Law Project, 1101 15th St. N.W., #1212 20005; 467-5730. Leonard S. Rubenstein, director. Fax, 223-0409.

Public interest law firm. Conducts test case litigation to defend rights of persons with mental disabilities. Provides legal support for legal services offices, protection and advocacy agencies, and private attorneys.

National Alliance for the Mentally Ill, 2101 Wilson Blvd., #302, Arlington, VA 22201; (703) 524-7600. Laurie M. Flynn, executive director. Fax, (703) 524-9094. Helpline, (800) 950-6264.

Membership: mentally ill individuals and their families and friends. Works to eradicate mental illness and improve the lives of those affected by brain diseases; sponsors public education and research; monitors legislation and regulations.

National Assn. of Private Psychiatric Hospitals, 1319 F St. N.W. 20004; 393-6700. Robert L. Trachtenberg, executive director. Fax, 783-6041.

Membership: private psychiatric hospitals that care for psychiatrically ill children, adolescents, adults, and persons suffering from substance abuse and addiction. Interests include cost containment and cost effectiveness of quality psychiatric care. Promotes research for new treatments, continuing education for psychiatrists and administrators, and preventive programs. Maintains standards for quality of care. Provides statistical information.

National Assn. of State Mental Health Program Directors, 66 Canal Center Plaza, #302, Alexandria, VA 22314-1591; (703) 739-9333. Robert W. Glover, executive director. Fax, (703) 548-9517.

Membership: officials in charge of state mental health agencies. Compiles data on state mental health programs.

National Community Mental Healthcare Council, 12300 Twinbrook Parkway, Rockville, MD 20852; (301) 984-6200. Charles G. Ray, chief executive officer.

Membership: community mental health agencies and state community mental health associations. Conducts research on community mental health activities; provides information, technical assistance, and referrals; monitors legislation and regulations affecting community mental health facilities.

National Mental Health Assn., 1021 Prince St., Alexandria, VA 22314-2971; (703) 684-7722. John A. Smith, acting president. Toll-free, (800) 969-6642. Fax, (703) 684-5968.

Citizens' interest group. Encourages research on mental illness; helps to establish community mental health centers; visits hospitals and other mental health facilities to ensure quality care; participates in litigation supporting patients' rights; produces educational materials including films. Serves as clearinghouse for mental health issues.

See also Prenatal, Maternal, and Child Health Care, Nongovernmental (p. 335)

See also Institute for Alternative Futures (p. 666); National Assn. of School Psychologists (p. 129)

Pharmaceuticals

See also Consumer Affairs, Labeling and Packaging (p. 262); Health, Substance Abuse (p. 338)

Agencies:

Food and Drug Administration (Health and Human Services Dept.), Center for Drug Evaluation and Research, 5600 Fishers Lane, Parklawn Bldg., #13B-45, Rockville, MD 20857; (301) 443-2894. Gerald Meyer, acting director. Information, (301) 594-1012. Press, (301) 443-3285. Fax, (301) 443-2763.

Reviews and approves generic drugs.

Food and Drug Administration (Health and Human Services Dept.), Generic Drugs, 7500 Standish Pl., Rockville, MD 20857; (301) 594-0340. Douglas L. Sporn, acting director. Fax, (301) 594-0183.

Oversees generic drug review process to ensure the safety and effectiveness of approved drugs.

Food and Drug Administration (Health and Human Services Dept.), Health Affairs, 5600 Fishers Lane, Parklawn Bldg., #1536, Rockville, MD 20857; (301) 443-6143. Dr. Stuart Nightingale, associate commissioner. Fax, (301) 443-1309.

Serves as liaison between FDA and health professionals for medical and scientific information and policy issues; coordinates agency's international activities on importing and exporting pharmaceuticals. Interests include food and drug patents.

Public Health Service (Health and Human Services Dept.), National Vaccine Program, 200 Independence Ave. S.W., #730E 20201; 401-8141. Anthony Robbins, director designate. Fax, 690-5761.

Coordinates public and private efforts in vaccine research, development, testing, licensing, production, and use.

Public Health Service (Health and Human Services Dept.), Orphan Products Board, 5600 Fishers Lane, #8-73, Rockville, MD 20857; (301) 443-4718. Dr. Richard J. Bertin, executive secretary. Information, (301) 443-4903. Fax, (301) 443-4915.

Promotes the development of drugs, devices, and alternative medical food therapies for rare diseases or conditions. Coordinates activities on the development of orphan drugs among federal agencies, manufacturers, and organizations representing patients.

Congress:

See Health, General, Congress (p. 321)

Nongovernmental:

American Assn. of Colleges of Pharmacy, 1426 Prince St., Alexandria, VA 22314; (703) 739-2330. Dr. Carl E. Trinca, executive director. Fax, (703) 836-8982.

Represents and advocates for pharmacists in the academic community. Conducts programs and activities in cooperation with other national health and higher education associations.

American Managed Care Pharmacy Assn., 2300 9th St. South, #210, Arlington, VA 22204; (703) 920-8480. Delbert D. Konnor, executive vice president. Fax, (703) 920-8491.

Membership: companies providing home-delivered pharmaceutical services. Monitors standards for drug delivery and legislation and regulations on health care costs and home-delivery pharmaceuticals.

American Pharmaceutical Assn., 2215 Constitution Ave. N.W. 20037; 628-4410. Dr. John A. Gans, executive vice president. Toll-free, (800) 237-2742. Library, 429-7524. Fax, 783-2351.

Membership: practicing pharmacists, pharmaceutical scientists, and pharmacy students. Promotes professional education and training; publishes scientific journals and handbook on nonprescription drugs. Library open to the public by appointment.

American Society for Pharmacology and Experimental Therapeutics, 9650 Rockville Pike, Bethesda, MD 20814-3995; (301) 530-7060. Kay Croker, executive officer. Fax, (301) 530-7061.

Membership: researchers and teachers involved in basic and clinical pharmacology in the United States and Canada.

American Society of Hospital Pharmacists, 7272 Wisconsin Ave., Bethesda, MD 20814; (301) 657-3000. Joseph A. Oddis, executive vice president. Fax, (301) 657-1615.

Membership: pharmacists who practice in organized health care settings such as hospitals, health maintenance organizations, and long-term care facilities. Provides publishing and educational programs designed to help members improve pharmaceutical services; accredits pharmacy residency and pharmacy technician training programs; monitors legislation and regulations.

Animal Health Institute, 501 Wythe St., Alexandria, VA (mailing address: P.O. Box 1417-D50, Alexandria, VA 22313); (703) 684-0011. Richard H. Ekfelt, president. Fax, (703) 684-0125.

Membership: manufacturers of drugs and other products (including vaccines, pesticides, and vitamins) for pets and food-producing animals. Monitors legislation and regulations.

Drug Policy Foundation, 4455 Connecticut Ave. N.W., #B500 20008; 537-5005. Arnold S. Trebach, president. Fax, 537-3007.

Assists in litigation to change federal laws to legalize prescriptions for heroin and marijuana in treatment of cancer and other serious diseases. Monitors legislation and regulations.

Food and Drug Law Institute, 1000 Vermont Ave. N.W. 20005; 371-1420. John Villforth, president. Fax, 371-0649.

Membership: providers of products and services to the food, drug, medical device, and cosmetics industries, including major food and drug companies and lawyers. Arranges conferences on technological and legal developments in the industry; sponsors law courses, fellowships, and legal writing. Library open to the public.

National Assn. of Chain Drug Stores, 413 N. Lee St., Alexandria, VA (mailing address: P.O. Box 1417-D49, Alexandria, VA 22313); (703) 549-3001. Ronald L. Ziegler, president. Fax, (703) 836-4869.

Membership: chain drug retailers; associate members include manufacturers, suppliers, publishers, and advertising agencies. Provides information on the pharmacy profession, community pharmacy practice, and retail prescription drug economics.

National Assn. of Retail Druggists, 205 Daingerfield Rd., Alexandria, VA 22314; (703) 683-8200. Charles M. West, executive vice president. Fax, (703) 683-3619.

Membership: independent drug store owners and pharmacists working in retail drugstores. Interests include drug regulation and national health insurance. Provides consumer information on such issues as prescription drugs, poison control, and mail order drug fraud.

National Council on Patient Information and Education, 666 11th St. N.W., #810 20001; 347-6711. Robert M. Bachman, executive director. Fax, 638-0773.

Membership: organizations of health care professionals, pharmaceutical manufacturers, federal agencies, voluntary health organizations, and consumer groups. Works to increase information available to patients about prescription medicines; conducts educational programs; distributes public service announcements for television and radio.

National Pharmaceutical Council, 1894 Preston White Dr., Reston, VA 22091; (703) 620-6390. Mark R. Knowles, president. Fax, (703) 476-0904.

Membership: pharmaceutical manufacturers that research and produce trade-name prescription medication and other pharmaceutical products. Provides information on the quality and cost-effectiveness of pharmaceutical products and the economics of drug programs.

National Wholesale Druggists' Assn., 1821 Michael Faraday Dr., #400, Reston, VA 22090-5348; (703) 787-0000. Ronald J. Streck, president. Fax, (703) 787-6930.

Membership: full-service drug wholesalers. Works to improve relations among supplier and customer industries; serves as a forum on major industry issues; researches and disseminates information on management practices for drug wholesalers; monitors legislation and regulations.

Nonprescription Drug Manufacturers Assn., 1150 Connecticut Ave. N.W. 20036; 429-9260. James D. Cope, president.

Membership: manufacturers and distributors of nonprescription medicines; associate members include suppliers, advertising agencies, and research and testing laboratories. Promotes the role of self-medication in health care. Monitors legislation and regulations. Library open to the public by appointment.

Parenteral Drug Assn., 7500 Old Georgetown Rd., #620, Bethesda, MD 20814; (301) 986-0293. Edmund M. Fry, executive vice president. Fax, (301) 986-0296.

Educates pharmaceutical professionals on parenteral and sterile-product technologies. Promotes pharmaceutical research. Serves as a liaison with pharmaceutical manufacturers, suppliers, users, academics, and government regulatory officials.

Pharmaceutical Manufacturers Assn., 1100 15th St. N.W., #900 20005; 835-3400. Gerald J. Mossinghoff, president. Fax, 835-3414.

Membership: companies that discover, develop, and manufacture prescription drugs. Provides consumer information on drug abuse, the safe and effective use of prescription medicines, and developments in important areas, including AIDS. Provides pharmaceutical industry statistics.

U.S. Pharmacopeial Convention, 12601 Twinbrook Parkway, Rockville, MD 20852; (301) 881-0666. Jerome A. Halperin, executive director. Fax, (301) 816-8299.

Establishes and revises standards for drug strength, quality, purity, packaging, labeling, and storage. Publishes drug use information, official drug quality standards, patient education materials, and consumer drug references.

See also Health Professionals, Nongovernmental (p. 355)

See also Institute for Alternative Futures (p. 666)

Prenatal, Maternal, and Child Health Care

See also Government Financial Assistance Programs, Child Nutrition Programs (p. 407); Social Services and Rehabilitation Programs, Children, Youth, and Families (p. 415); Day Care (p. 419)

Agencies:

Centers for Disease Control and Prevention (Health and Human Services Dept.), 5600 Fishers Lane, Parklawn Bldg., #1834, Rockville, MD 20857; (301) 443-2610. Dr. Gary R. Noble, associate director, Washington office. Fax, (301) 443-8182. (Also located at 200 Independence Ave. S.W. 20201; 690-8598).

Surveys national disease trends and incidences; conducts research and assists state and local health agencies that receive grants for the control of childhood diseases preventable by immunization. (Headquarters in Atlanta: 1600 Clifton Rd. N.E. 30333. Public inquiries, (404) 639-3534.)

Health and Human Services Dept., Adolescent Pregnancy Programs, 4340 East-West Highway, #1115, Bethesda, MD 20814; (301) 594-4004. Patrick J. Sheeran, acting director. Fax, (301) 492-2017.

Coordinates the Adolescent Family Life Program, which funds community health care and pregnancy prevention programs. Administers a program that provides pregnant adolescents and children of teenage parents with health care services and a program that focuses on sexual abstinence. Funds research programs to investigate adolescent sexual behavior, adoption, and early childbearing.

Health Care Financing Administration (Health and Human Services Dept.), Medicaid, 6325 Security Blvd., Baltimore, MD 21207; (410) 966-3230. Sally Richardson, director. Fax, (410) 966-0255.

Develops health care policies and programs for needy children under Medicaid; works with the Public Health Service and other related agencies to coordinate the department's child health resources.

Health Resources and Services Administration (Health and Human Services Dept.), Maternal and Child Health, 5600 Fishers Lane, #18-05, Rockville, MD 20857; (301) 443-2170. Dr. Audrey H. Nora, director. Fax, (301) 443-1797.

Administers block grants to states for mothers and children and for children with special health needs; awards funding for research training, genetic disease testing, counseling and information dissemination, hemophilia diagnostic and treatment centers, and demonstration projects to improve the health of mothers and children. Interests also include pediatric AIDS health care and emergency medical services for children.

Health Resources and Services Administration (Health and Human Services Dept.), National Maternal and Child Health Clearinghouse, 8201 Greensboro Dr., #600, McLean, VA 22102; (703) 821-8955. Linda Cramer, project director. Fax, (703) 821-2098.

Disseminates information on various aspects of maternal and child health and genetics.

Health Resources and Services Administration (Health and Human Services Dept.), National Vaccine Injury Compensation Program, 200 Independence Ave. S.W., #730E 20201; 401-8141. Chester Robinson, acting director. Toll-free hotline, (800) 338-2382.

Provides no-fault compensation to individuals injured by certain childhood vaccines (diphtheria and tetanus toxoids and pertussis vaccine; measles, mumps, and rubella vaccine; and oral polio and inactivated polio vaccine).

National Institute of Child Health and Human Development (National Institutes of Health, Health and Human Services Dept.), 9000 Rockville Pike, Bethesda, MD 20892; (301) 496-3454. Dr. Duane F. Alexander, director. Information, (301) 496-5133. Fax, (301) 402-1104.

Conducts research and research training on biological and behavioral human development. Interests include reproduction and population studies, perinatal biology and infant mortality, congenital defects, nutrition, human learning and behavior, and mental retardation.

National Institute of Child Health and Human Development (National Institutes of Health, Health and Human Services Dept.), Center for Research for Mothers and Children, 6100 Executive Blvd., Rockville, MD (mailing address: 9000 Rockville Pike, Bethesda, MD 20892); (301) 496-5097. Dr. Sumner J. Yaffe, director. Fax, (301) 402-2085.

Supports biomedical and behavioral science research and training for maternal and child health care. Areas of study include fetal development, maternal-infant health problems, HIV-related diseases in childbearing women, roles of nutrients and hormones in child growth, developmental disabilities, and behavioral development.

National Sudden Infant Death Syndrome Resource Center (Health and Human Services Dept.), 8201 Greensboro Dr., McLean, VA 22102; (703) 821-8955. Olivia Cowdrill, director. Fax, (703) 821-2098.

Provides information about sudden infant death syndrome (SIDS), apnea, and related issues; makes referrals to local SIDS programs and parent support groups. Publishes educational information about SIDS.

Congress:

See Health, General, Congress (p. 321)

Nongovernmental:

Alan Guttmacher Institute, 1120 Connecticut Ave. N.W., #460 20036; 296-4012. Cory L. Richards, vice president for public policy. Fax, 223-5756.

Conducts research, policy analysis, and public education in reproductive health issues, including maternal and child health. (Headquarters in New York.)

Alliance to End Childhood Lead Poisoning, 227 Massachusetts Ave. N.E., #200 20002; 543-1147. Don Ryan, executive director. Fax, 543-4466.

Works to increase awareness of childhood lead poisoning and to develop and implement prevention programs.

American Academy of Child and Adolescent Psychiatry, 3615 Wisconsin Ave. N.W. 20016;

966-7300. Virginia Q. Anthony, executive director. Fax, 966-2891.

Membership: child and adolescent psychiatrists. Sponsors annual meeting and review for medical board examinations; provides information on child abuse, youth suicide, and drug abuse; monitors legislation concerning mentally ill children.

American Academy of Pediatrics, 601 13th St. N.W., #400N 20005; 347-8600. Elizabeth J. Noyes, director, government liaison. Toll-free, (800) 336-5475. Fax, 393-6137.

Helps set standards for delivery of health care to children; participates in accrediting pediatric education programs; supports continuing education; advocates for maternal and child health legislation and regulations. Interests include nutrition, pediatric AIDS, primary care, research, injury control, substance abuse, and access to immunizations. (Headquarters in Elk Grove Village, Ill.)

American Assn. of Children's Residential Centers, 1021 Prince St., Alexandria, VA 22314-2971; (703) 838-7522. Claudia Waller, executive director. Fax, (703) 684-5968.

Membership: mental health residential agencies and individuals interested in clinical practice in residential care for emotionally disturbed children. Represents interests of emotionally disturbed children and their families before the federal government; conducts educational conferences and provides information on residential treatment.

American College of Nurse-Midwives, 818 Connecticut Ave. N.W., #900 20006; 728-9866. Ronald E. Nitzsche, chief operating officer. Information, 728-9860. Press, 728-9875. Fax, 728-9897.

Membership: certified nurse-midwives who preside at deliveries. Interests include preventive health care for women.

American College of Obstetricians and Gynecologists, 409 12th St. S.W. 20024; 638-5577. Dr. Ralph Hale, executive director. Press, 484-3321. Fax, 484-5107.

Membership: medical specialists in obstetrics and gynecology. Monitors legislation and regulations on maternal and child health care.

American Society for Psychoprophylaxis in Obstetrics, 1101 Connecticut Ave. N.W., #700

20036; 857-1128. Linda Harmon, executive director. Toll-free, (800) 368-4404. Fax, 857-1128.

Membership: supporters of the Lamaze method of childbirth, including parents, physicians, childbirth educators, and other health professionals. Trains and certifies Lamaze educators. Provides referral service for parents seeking Lamaze classes.

Assn. for the Care of Children's Health, 7910 Woodmont Ave., #300, Bethesda, MD 20814; (301) 654-6549. William Sciarillo, executive director. Fax, (301) 986-4553.

International multidisciplinary organization of nurses, child life specialists, physicians, social workers, psychologists, parents, and others. Provides information concerning children's emotional health in hospitals and other health care settings; serves as an educational resource for psychosocial child health issues.

Children's Defense Fund, 25 E St. N.W. 20001; 628-8787. Marian Wright Edelman, president. Fax, 662-3510.

Advocacy group concerned with programs for children and youth. Assesses adequacy of the Early and Periodic Screening, Diagnosis, and Treatment Program for Medicaid-eligible children. Promotes adequate prenatal care for adolescent and lower-income women; works to prevent adolescent pregnancy.

Cystic Fibrosis Foundation, 6931 Arlington Rd., Bethesda, MD 20814; (301) 951-4422. Robert Beall, president. Toll-free, (800) 344-4823. Fax, (301) 951-6378.

Conducts research on cystic fibrosis, an inherited genetic disease affecting the respiratory and digestive systems. Provides funding for care centers and information on the disease.

Human Growth Foundation, 7777 Leesburg Pike, #202S, Falls Church, VA 22043; (703) 883-1773. Fran Price, executive director. Toll-free, (800) 451-6434. Fax, (703) 883-1776.

Promotes research into growth and growth disorders; provides those affected by growth disorders and their families with education and support; encourages exchange of information with the medical profession. Sponsors Human Growth Month and national conferences; awards research grants.

International Federation for Family Life Promotion, 2009 N. 14th St., #512, Arlington, VA 22201-2514; (703) 516-0388. Claude A. Lanctot, executive director. Fax, (703) 516-0390.

Promotes breast feeding, primary health care, family life education, and natural family planning.

March of Dimes Birth Defects Foundation, 1901 L St. N.W., #260 20036; 659-1800. Kay Johnson, director, policy and government affairs. Fax, 296-2964.

Works to prevent birth defects, low birthweight, and infant mortality. Awards grants for research and provides funds for treatment of birth defects; monitors legislation and regulations. Medical services grantees provide prenatal counseling. (Headquarters in White Plains, N.Y.)

National Assn. of Children's Hospitals and Related Institutions, 401 Wythe St., Alexandria, VA 22314; (703) 684-1355. Lawrence A. McAndrews, president. Fax, (703) 684-1589.

Advocates and promotes education and research on child health care related to children's hospitals; compiles statistics and provides information on the number, length, and quality of pediatric hospitalizations.

National Center for Education in Maternal and Child Health, 2000 15th St. North, #701, Arlington, VA 22201; (703) 524-7802. Dr. Rochelle Mayer, director. Fax, (703) 524-9335.

Collects and disseminates information about maternal and child health to health professionals and the general public. Carries out special projects for the U.S. Maternal and Child Health Bureau. Library open to the public by appointment. (Affiliated with Georgetown University.)

National Consortium for Child Mental Health Services, 3615 Wisconsin Ave. N.W. 20016; 966-7300. Virginia Q. Anthony, executive director. Fax, 966-2891.

Membership: organizations interested in developing mental health services for children. Fosters information exchange; advises local, state, and federal agencies that develop children's mental health services. (Affiliated with American Academy of Child and Adolescent Psychiatry.)

National Organization on Adolescent Pregnancy, Parenting, and Prevention, 4421-A East-West Highway, Bethesda, MD 20814; (301) 913-0378. Kathleen Sheeran, executive director. Fax, (301) 913-0380.

Membership: health and social work professionals, community and state leaders, and individuals. Promotes services to prevent and resolve problems associated with adolescent sexuality, pregnancy, and parenting. Helps to develop stable and supportive family relationships through program support and evaluation; monitors legislation and regulations.

National Organization on Fetal Alcohol Syndrome, 1815 H St. N.W., #750 20006; 785-4585. Patti Munter, executive director. Toll-free, (800) 666-6327. Fax, 466-6456.

Works to eradicate alcohol-related birth defects through public education, conferences, medical school curriculum, and partnerships with federal programs interested in fetal alcohol syndrome.

Nurture/Center to Prevent Childhood Malnutrition, 4948 St. Elmo Ave., #208, Bethesda, MD 20814; (301) 907-8601. Sandra Huffman, president. Fax, (301) 907-8603.

Works to improve child nutrition worldwide through policy analysis and evaluation of community-based self-help nutrition projects in the United States, Peru, and Ghana. (Affiliated with the Dept. of International Health, Johns Hopkins University.)

Zero to Three/National Center for Clinical Infant Programs, 2000 14th St. North, #380, Arlington, VA 22201; (703) 528-4300. Eleanor Stokes Szanton, executive director. Fax, (703) 528-6848. TDD, (703) 528-0419.

Works to improve infant health, mental health, and development. Sponsors training programs for professionals; offers fellowships. Provides private and government organizations with information on infant development issues.

See also Health, General, Nongovernmental (p. 323)

See also Program for Appropriate Technology in Health (p. 455)

Radiation Protection

See also Resources: Nuclear Energy (p. 223)

Agencies:

Armed Forces Radiobiology Research Institute, National Naval Medical Center, 8901 Wisconsin Ave., Bethesda, MD 20889; (301) 295-

1210. Capt. Robert L. Bumgarner (USN), director. Fax, (301) 295-4967.

Serves as the principal ionizing radiation radiobiology research laboratory under the jurisdiction of the Defense Nuclear Agency. Library open to the public.

Environmental Protection Agency, Radiation and Indoor Air, 501 3rd St. N.W. (mailing address: 401 M St. S.W., #6601J, Washington, DC 20460); 233-9320. Margo T. Oge, director. Fax, 233-9651.

Establishes standards to regulate the amount of radiation discharged into the environment from nuclear power plants, uranium mining and milling projects, and other activities that result in radioactive emissions. Works to reduce naturally occurring radon gas in buildings through studies, training programs, and state grants.

Food and Drug Administration (Health and Human Services Dept.), Center for Devices and Radiological Health, 1390 Piccard Dr., Rockville, MD 20850; (301) 443-4690. Dr. D. Bruce Burlington, director. Fax, (301) 594-1320.

Develops and administers national programs to control unnecessary exposure to radiation. Establishes standards for the emission of ionizing and nonionizing radiation from consumer and medical products. Provides physicians and consumers with guidelines on radiation-emitting products. Conducts factory inspections of microwave ovens, video display terminals, and other products; develops procedures for compliance with agency regulations. Conducts research on the health effects of radiation exposure and on the measurement and control of radiation emission. Conducts training and educational programs. Library open to the public.

See also Defense Nuclear Agency, Environment and Modeling (p. 437)

Congress:

See Health, General, Congress (p. 321)

Nongovernmental:

Friends of the Earth, Nuclear Project, 218 D St. S.E., 2nd Floor 20003; 547-5882. David Albright, president.

Advocates research and public access to information on the health and environmental hazards of civilian and military technology. Library open to the public by appointment.

National Council on Radiation Protection and Measurements, 7910 Woodmont Ave., #800, Bethesda, MD 20814; (301) 657-2652. W. R. Ney, executive director. Toll-free, (800) 229-2652. Fax, (301) 907-8768.

Corporation chartered by Congress that collects and analyzes information and provides recommendations on radiation protection and measurement. Studies radiation emissions from household items and from office and medical equipment.

See also American College of Radiology (p. 357); Public Citizen, Health Research Group (p. 325)

Substance Abuse

See also Consumer Affairs, Alcohol (p. 253); Consumer Affairs, Tobacco (p. 265); Criminal Law, Drug Abuse (p. 510)

Agencies:

Corporation for National Service, Drug Alliance Program, 1100 Vermont Ave. N.W. 20525; 606-4857. Calvin T. Dawson, director. Fax, 606-4921.

Supports volunteer parent groups and youth groups that work to create a drug-free environment; works to generate parental involvement in drug abuse prevention and education and to create coalitions to address drug abuse prevention; sponsors conferences, workshops, and seminars on drug use and youth; awards grants; trains volunteers; promotes public and private sector involvement in drug awareness.

Education Dept., Drug-Free Schools in Communities, 400 Maryland Ave. S.W. 20202; 401-1599. Allen King, director. Information, 401-2310. Fax, 401-1112.

Provides local school systems, state educational agencies, and institutions of higher education with leadership, training, educational materials, and technical assistance to develop programs that prevent drug and alcohol abuse.

Education Dept., Drug Planning and Outreach, 400 Maryland Ave. S.W., #1073 20202-6123; 401-3030. William Modzeleski, director. Fax, 401-1069.

Develops policy for the department's drug and violence prevention initiatives for students in elementary and secondary schools and institutions of higher education. Coordinates education efforts in drug and violence prevention with those of other federal departments and agencies.

Executive Office of the President, National Drug Control Policy, Old Executive Office Bldg. 20500; 467-9800. Lee Brown, director. Information, 467-9890. Fax, 467-9899.

Establishes policies and oversees the implementation of a national drug control strategy; recommends changes to reduce demand for and supply of illegal drugs; advises the National Security Council on drug control policy.

Food and Drug Administration (Health and Human Services Dept.), Health Affairs, 5600 Fishers Lane, Parklawn Bldg., #1536, Rockville, MD 20857; (301) 443-6143. Dr. Stuart Nightingale, associate commissioner. Fax, (301) 443-1309.

Coordinates interagency reviews of international control of abusive drugs.

Health Resources and Services Administration (Health and Human Services Dept.), Special Populations, 4350 East-West Highway, West Towers Bldg., 9th Floor, Bethesda, MD 20814; (301) 594-4420. Joan Holloway, director. Fax, (301) 594-4989.

Funds a program that links primary care and substance abuse treatment.

National Clearinghouse for Alcohol and Drug Information (Health and Human Services Dept.), Center for Substance Abuse Prevention, 11426-28 Rockville Pike, #200, Rockville, MD (mailing address: P.O. Box 2345, Rockville, MD 20852); (301) 468-2600. Dr. David W. Rowden, director. Toll-free, (800) 729-6686. Fax, (301) 468-6433. TDD, (301) 230-2867.

Provides information and publications on alcohol and drugs.

National Institute on Alcohol Abuse and Alcoholism (National Institutes of Health, Health and Human Services Dept.), 6000 Executive Blvd., #400, Rockville, MD 20892-7003; (301) 443-3885. Dr. Enoch Gordis, director. Information, (301) 443-3860. Fax, (301) 443-7043.

Supports basic and applied research on preventing and treating alcoholism and alcohol-related problems; conducts research and disseminates findings on alcohol abuse and alcoholism.

National Institute on Drug Abuse (National Institutes of Health, Health and Human Services Dept.), 5600 Fishers Lane, #10-05, Rockville, MD 20857; (301) 443-6480. Alan I. Leshner, director. Information, (301) 443-1124. Press, (301) 443-6245. Fax, (301) 443-9127. Toll-free, (800) 843-4971.

Conducts and sponsors research on the prevention, effects, and treatment of drug abuse. Operates toll-free hotline for employers trying to eradicate drug abuse in the workplace.

Office of Personnel Management, Employee Health Services, 1900 E St. N.W. 20415; 606-1740. Ron Patterson, chief. Fax, 606-2613.

Sets policy and guides federal agencies in establishing and maintaining alcohol and drug abuse programs.

Substance Abuse and Mental Health Services Administration (Health and Human Services Dept.), Center for Substance Abuse Prevention, 5515 Security Lane, Rockville, MD (mailing address: 5600 Fishers Lane, Rockville, MD 20857); (301) 443-0365. Elaine Johnson, director. Fax, (301) 443-5447.

Promotes strategies to prevent alcohol and drug abuse; provides information about substance abuse.

Substance Abuse and Mental Health Services Administration (Health and Human Services Dept.), Center for Substance Abuse Treatment, 5600 Fishers Lane, Rockwall 2, #1075, Rockville, MD 20857; (301) 443-2467. Dr. Lisa W. Scheckel, acting director. Information, (301) 443-5052. Fax, (301) 443-9363.

Develops and supports policies and programs that improve and expand treatment services for alcoholics and drug addicts. Administers grants that support private and public addiction prevention and treatment services. Conducts research on and evaluates alcohol treatment programs and other drug treatment programs and delivery systems.

Congress:

See *Health, General, Congress (p. 321)*

Nongovernmental:

American Council for Drug Education, 204 Monroe St., #110, Rockville, MD 20850; (301) 294-0600. William F. Current, executive director. Toll-free, (800) 488-3784. Fax, (301) 294-0603.

Works to prevent drug abuse through public education. Produces and distributes educational material; opposes legalizing psychoactive drugs.

American Society of Addiction Medicine, 5225 Wisconsin Ave. N.W. 20015; 244-8948. James F. Callahan, executive vice president. Fax, 537-7252.

Membership: physicians and medical students. Supports the study and provision of effective treatment and care for people with alcohol and drug dependencies; educates physicians; administers certification program in addiction medicine. Monitors legislation and regulations.

Employee Assistance Professionals Assn., 2101 Wilson Blvd., #500, Arlington, VA 22201; (703) 522-6272. Michael L. Benjamin, chief operating officer. Fax, (703) 522-4585.

Represents professionals in the workplace who assist employees and their family members with personal and behavioral problems, including health, marital, family, financial, alcohol, drug, legal, emotional, stress, or other personal problems that adversely affect employee job performance and productivity.

International Commission for the Prevention of Alcoholism, 12501 Old Columbia Pike, Silver Spring, MD 20904; (301) 680-6719. Thomas R. Neslund, executive director. Fax, (301) 680-6090.

Membership: health officials, physicians, educators, clergy, and judges. Promotes prevention of alcohol and drug dependencies; provides information about medical effects of alcohol and drugs; sponsors conferences.

National Assn. of Alcoholism and Drug Abuse Counselors, 3717 Columbia Pike, #300, Arlington, VA 22204; (703) 920-4644. Linda P. Kaplan, executive director. Toll-free, (800) 548-0497. Fax, (703) 920-4672.

Provides information on drug dependency treatment, research, and resources. Works with private groups and federal agencies concerned with treating and preventing alcoholism and drug abuse; certifies addiction counselors; provides members with liability and health insurance; holds workshops and conferences for treatment professionals.

National Assn. of State Alcohol and Drug Abuse Directors, 444 N. Capitol St. N.W., #642 20001; 783-6868. William Butynski, executive director. Fax, 783-2704.

Membership: state alcohol and drug abuse agencies. Provides information on alcohol and other drug abuse treatment and prevention services and resources; contracts with federal and state agencies to design and conduct research on alcohol and drug abuse programs.

National Council on Alcoholism and Drug Dependence, 1511 K St. N.W., #926 20005; 737-8122. Sarah Kayson, director, public policy. Fax, 628-4731.

Membership: local affiliates and individuals interested in alcoholism, other drug dependencies, and their related problems. Monitors legislation and regulations. Affiliates offer information and referral services. (Headquarters in New York.)

See also National Organization on Fetal Alcohol Syndrome (p. 337)

Health Care and Services for Special Groups

General

Agencies:

Administration for Children and Families (Health and Human Services Dept.), 901 D St. S.W. (mailing address: 370 L'Enfant Promenade S.W., Washington, DC 20447); 401-9200. Mary Jo Bane, assistant secretary. Information, 401-9215. Fax, 401-5770.

Administers and funds programs for the elderly; native Americans; children, youth, and families; and those with developmental disabilities. Responsible for Social Services Block Grants to the states. Provides agencies with technical assistance; coordinates Head Start program, National Runaway Switchboard operations, and programs for abused children and the elderly.

Health Resources and Services Administration (Health and Human Services Dept.), Health Resources Development, 5600 Fishers Lane, Parklawn Bldg., #705, Rockville, MD 20857; (301) 443-1993. Dr. Stephen Bowen, director. Fax, (301) 443-9645.

Administers programs that provide communities with grants for the delivery of health care services to persons infected with the human immunodeficiency virus (HIV); supports health facilities for uncompensated care, construction

grants, and loans; provides grants to organ procurement transplantation programs; plans, directs, coordinates, and monitors activities relating to emergency medical services and trauma system planning and implementation.

Health Resources and Services Administration (Health and Human Services Dept.), Special Populations, 4350 East-West Highway, West Towers Bldg., 9th Floor, Bethesda, MD 20814; (301) 594-4420. Joan Holloway, director. Fax, (301) 594-4989.

Awards grants to community-based organizations to provide primary health care services to special populations, including HIV-infected persons, women considered to be at risk, homeless individuals, substance abusers, elderly people, and native Hawaiian and Pacific Basin residents.

Congress:

House Education and Labor Committee, Subcommittee on Human Resources, B346C RHOB 20515; 225-1850. Matthew G. Martinez, D-Calif., chairman; Lester Sweeting, staff director and counsel.

Jurisdiction over legislation on general programs for the elderly, including health and nutrition programs.

House Education and Labor Committee, Subcommittee on Labor Standards, Occupational Health and Safety, B345A RHOB 20515; 225-1927. Austin J. Murphy, D-Pa., chairman; James Riley, staff director.

Jurisdiction over workers' health and safety legislation, including legislation on migrant and farm labor matters.

House Energy and Commerce Committee, Subcommittee on Health and the Environment, 2415 RHOB 20515; 225-4952. Henry A. Waxman, D-Calif., chairman; Karen Nelson, staff director.

Jurisdiction over legislation on the mentally retarded, migrant health care, people with disabilities, long-term and nursing home programs, health care for the poor (including Medicaid and national health insurance proposals), and medical research on aging. (Jurisdiction over native American health care shared with House Natural Resources Committee.)

House Natural Resources Committee, Subcommittee on Native American Affairs, 1522 LHOB 20515; 226-7393. Bill Richardson, D-

N.M., chairman; Tadd Johnson, staff director. Fax, 226-0522.

Jurisdiction over legislation pertaining to native American health care and special services; oversight of native American health care programs. (Jurisdiction shared with House Energy and Commerce Committee.)

House Science, Space, and Technology Committee, Subcommittee on Science, 2319 RHOB 20515; 225-8844. Rick Boucher, D-Va., chairman; Grace L. Ostenso, staff director.

Jurisdiction over research and development involving programs for people with disabilities.

House Ways and Means Committee, Subcommittee on Health, 1114 LHOB 20515; 225-7785. Pete Stark, D-Calif., chairman; David Abernethy, staff director.

Jurisdiction over proposals for national health insurance (jurisdiction shared with the House Energy and Commerce Committee), Medicare, and other health matters.

Senate Committee on Indian Affairs, SH-838 20510; 224-2251. Daniel K. Inouye, D-Hawaii, chairman; Patricia Zell, staff director. Fax, 224-2309.

Jurisdiction over legislation pertaining to native American health care; oversight of native American health care programs.

Senate Finance Committee, Subcommittee on Health for Families and the Uninsured, SD-205 20510; 224-4515. Donald W. Riegle Jr., D-Mich., chairman; Debbie Chang, staff contact.

Holds hearings on health legislation for low-income individuals, including Medicaid and national health insurance proposals.

Senate Finance Committee, Subcommittee on Medicare and Long-Term Care, SD-205 20510; 224-4515. John D. Rockefeller IV, D-W.Va., chairman; Ellen Doneski, staff contact.

Holds hearings on Medicare and Medicaid provisions dealing with long-term care.

Senate Labor and Human Resources Committee, SD-428 20510; 224-5375. Edward M. Kennedy, D-Mass., chairman; Nick Littlefield, chief counsel and staff director.

Jurisdiction over legislation on migrant health care, health care for the poor and elderly (excluding Medicaid and Medicare), government-

run health care facilities, and medical research on aging.

Senate Labor and Human Resources Committee, Subcommittee on Disability Policy, SH-113 20510; 224-6265. Tom Harkin, D-Iowa, chairman; Robert Silverstein, staff director.

Jurisdiction over legislation concerning people with disabilities and developmental disabilities.

Senate Special Committee on Aging, SD-G31 20510; 224-5364. David Pryor, D-Ark., chairman; Theresa M. Forster, staff director.

Studies and makes recommendations on the overall health problems of the elderly, including quality and cost of long-term care, and on access to and quality of health care for minority elderly; oversight of federally funded programs for the elderly, including Medicare, Medicaid, and programs concerning day-to-day care.

Elderly

See also Health Care Financing, Medicaid and Medicare (p. 350); Social Services and Rehabilitation Programs, Elderly (p. 424)

Agencies:

Health Care Financing Administration (Health and Human Services Dept.), Long-Term Care Services, 6325 Security Blvd., Baltimore, MD 21207; (410) 966-6807. Helene Fredeking, director. Fax, (410) 966-6730.

Monitors compliance of nursing homes and long-term care facilities with government standards. Coordinates survey certification to determine which nursing homes qualify to participate in Medicaid and Medicare programs; criteria evaluated include quality of care and environmental conditions. Administers the nursing home resident assessment system to determine health care needs and lifestyle preferences of residents at the time of admission.

National Institute on Aging (National Institutes of Health, Health and Human Services Dept.), 9000 Rockville Pike, Bldg. 31, #5C35, Bethesda, MD 20892-3100; (301) 496-9265. Dr. Richard J. Hodes, director. Information, (301) 496-1752. Fax, (301) 496-2525.

Conducts and funds research and disseminates information on the biological, medical, behavioral, and social aspects of aging and the common problems of the elderly.

Congress:

See Health Care and Services for Special Groups, General, Congress (p. 340)

Nongovernmental:

Alliance for Aging Research, 2021 K St. N.W., #305 20006; 293-2856. Daniel Perry, executive director. Fax, 785-8574.

Membership: senior corporate and foundation executives, science leaders, and congressional representatives. Promotes scientific research on aging and the problems of the elderly.

Alzheimer's Assn., 1319 F St. N.W., #710 20004-1106; 393-7737. Stephen R. McConnell, senior vice president, public policy. Toll-free, (800) 272-3900. Fax, 393-2109.

Offers family support services and educates the public about Alzheimer's disease, a neurological disorder mainly affecting the brain tissue in older adults. Promotes research and long-term care protection. Monitors legislation and regulations. (Headquarters in Chicago.)

American Assn. of Homes for the Aging, 901 E St. N.W., #500 20004; 783-2242. Michael F. Rodgers, senior vice president. Fax, 783-2255.

Membership: nonprofit homes, housing, and health-related facilities for the elderly sponsored by religious, fraternal, labor, private, and governmental organizations. Conducts research on long-term care for the elderly; sponsors institutes and workshops on accreditation, financing, and institutional life; monitors legislation and regulations.

American Assn. of Retired Persons, Health Care Campaign, 601 E St. N.W. 20049; 434-3828. Barbara Herzog, director. Fax, 434-6477.

Advocates improvements in Medicare and Medicaid and equal access to health care for all individuals; offers consumer information and health education material. Provides members with group health insurance and mail-order pharmacy services.

American Health Care Assn., 1201 L St. N.W. 20005; 842-4444. Paul R. Willging, executive vice president. Information, 898-2839. Press, 898-2855. Library, 898-2839. Fax, 842-3860. Publication orders, (800) 321-0343.

Membership: owners and administrators of private proprietary and nonprofit nursing homes, long-term care homes, and residential care facilities. Sponsors and provides educational programs and materials. Library open to the public by appointment.

The Gerontological Society of America, 1275 K St. N.W., #350 20005; 842-1275. Paul A. Kerschner, executive director. Fax, 842-1150.

Scientific organization of researchers, educators, and professionals in the field of aging. Promotes the scientific study of aging and the application of these studies to public policy.

National Assn. for Home Care, 519 C St. N.E. 20002; 547-7424. Val Halamandaris, president. Fax, 547-3540.

Membership: home care professionals and paraprofessionals. Advocates the rights of the elderly, infirm, and terminally ill to remain independent in their own homes as long as possible. Monitors legislation and regulations involving home care and hospice.

National Citizens' Coalition for Nursing Home Reform, 1224 M St. N.W., #301 20005-5183; 393-2018. Elma L. Holder, executive director. Information, 393-2018. Fax, 393-4122.

Seeks to improve the long-term care system and quality of life for residents in nursing homes and other facilities for the elderly. Promotes citizen participation in all aspects of nursing homes; acts as clearinghouse for nursing home advocacy. Coordinates the Campaign for Quality Care, concerned with implementing the Nursing Home Reform Law of 1987.

National Council of Senior Citizens, 1331 F St. N.W. 20004; 347-8800. Lawrence T. Smedley, executive director. Information, 624-9549. Press, 624-9540. Library, 624-9366. Fax, 624-9595.

Federation of senior citizen clubs, associations, councils, and other groups. Supports expansion of Medicare, protection of the Social Security system, improved health programs, national health care, and reduced cost of drugs. Nursing Home Information Service provides information on nursing home standards and regulations.

National Council on the Aging, 409 3rd St. S.W. 20024; 479-1200. Daniel Thursz, president. Library, 479-6669. Fax, 479-0735. TDD, 479-6674.

Membership: individuals, voluntary agencies and associations, businesses, and labor unions serving or concerned with the elderly. Acts as an information clearinghouse on aging; operates institutes on adult day care, community-based long-term care, health promotion, rural aging, and financial issues for the elderly; provides fellowships for medical students. Library open to the public.

National Hispanic Council on Aging, 2713 Ontario Rd. N.W. 20009; 265-1288. Marta Sotomayor, president. Fax, 745-2522.

Membership: senior citizens, health care workers, professionals in the field of aging, and others in the United States and Puerto Rico who are interested in topics related to Hispanics and aging. Provides research training, consulting, and technical assistance; sponsors seminars, workshops, and management internships.

National Osteoporosis Foundation, 1150 17th St. N.W., #500 20036; 223-2226. Sandra C. Raymond, executive director. Toll-free, (800) 223-9994. Fax, 223-2237.

Seeks to reduce osteoporosis through educational programs, research, and patient advocacy.

Mentally Retarded

See also Health, Mental Health (p. 329); Social Services and Rehabilitation Programs, Disabled (p. 420)

Agencies:

Education Dept., Rehabilitation Services Administration, 330 C St. S.W. 20202; 205-5482. Howard Moses, acting commissioner. Fax, 205-9874.

Allocates funds to state agencies and nonprofit organizations for programs serving eligible physically and mentally disabled persons; services provided by these funds include medical and psychological treatment as well as establishment of supported-employment and independent-living programs.

Health Care Financing Administration (Health and Human Services Dept.), Long-Term Care Services, 6325 Security Blvd., Baltimore, MD 21207; (410) 966-6807. Helene Fredeking, director. Fax, (410) 966-6730.

Monitors compliance of psychiatric hospitals and long-term and intermediate care facilities with government standards; coordinates health care programs for the mentally retarded.

President's Committee on Mental Retardation (Health and Human Services Dept.), 330 Independence Ave. S.W. 20201; 619-0634. Gary H. Blumenthal, executive director. Information, 619-3463. Fax, 205-9519.

Compiles information, conducts studies, and promotes research on mental retardation; advises the president and the secretary of health and human services; acts as a liaison among federal, state, local, and private organizations concerned with mental retardation.

Congress:

See Health Care and Services for Special Groups, General, Congress (p. 340)

Nongovernmental:

American Assn. on Mental Retardation, 444 N. Capitol St. N.W., #846 20001; 387-1968. M. Doreen Croser, executive director. Toll-free, (800) 424-3688. Fax, 387-2193.

Membership: physicians, educators, administrators, social workers, psychologists, psychiatrists, students, and others interested in mental retardation and related developmental disabilities. Provides information on legal rights, services, and facilities for people with mental retardation.

The Arc, 1522 K St. N.W., #516 20005; 785-3388. Paul Marchand, director, governmental affairs. Fax, 467-4179.

Membership: individuals interested in assisting people with mental retardation. Provides information on government programs and legislation concerning mental retardation; oversees and encourages support for local groups that provide direct services for people with mental retardation. (Headquarters in Arlington, Texas.)

National Assn. of State Directors of Developmental Disability Services, 113 Oronoco St., Alexandria, VA 22314; (703) 683-4202. Robert M. Gettings, executive director. Fax, (703) 684-1395.

Membership: chief administrators of state mental retardation programs. Coordinates exchange of information on mental retardation programs among the states; provides information on state programs.

National Children's Center, 6200 2nd St. N.W. 20011; 722-2300. Shearer Bailey, acting executive director. Fax, 722-2383.

Provides educational, social, and clinical services to infants, children, and adults with mental retardation and other developmental disabilities. Services provided through a 24-hour intensive treatment program, group homes and independent living programs, educational services, adult treatment programs, and early intervention programs for infants with disabilities or infants at high risk.

See also American Assn. of University Affiliated Programs for Persons with Developmental Disabilities (p. 146)

Migrants

See also Employment and Training, Migrant and Seasonal Farm Workers (p. 177)

Agencies:

Health Resources and Services Administration (Health and Human Services Dept.), Primary Health Care, 4350 East-West Highway, 7th Floor, Bethesda, MD 20814; (301) 594-4303. Antonio Duran, director, migrant health. Fax, (301) 594-4997.
Awards grants to state and local organizations to administer migrant health projects; administers national migrant health advisory council.

Congress:

See Health Care and Services for Special Groups, General, Congress (p. 340)

Nongovernmental:

East Coast Migrant Health Project, 1234 Massachusetts Ave. N.W., #623 20005; 347-7377. Jennifer Schmidt, executive director. Fax, 347-6385.
Sponsored by the National Migrant Worker Council and funded by the Health and Human Services Dept. Assigns health professionals and allied health care personnel to health facilities along the East Coast; assists migrants in addressing health and social needs; and familiarizes providers with migrants' special health care needs.

Migrant Legal Action Program, 2001 S St. N.W. 20009; 462-7744. Roger C. Rosenthal, executive director.
Funded by the Legal Services Corp. Assists local legal services groups and private attorneys representing farm workers. Monitors legislation,

regulations, and enforcement activities of the Environmental Protection Agency and the Occupational Safety and Health Administration in the area of pesticide use as it affects the health of migrant farm workers. Litigates cases concerning living and working conditions in migrant labor camps.

See also National Assn. of Community Health Centers (p. 345)

Minorities and Economically Disadvantaged Groups

See also Health Care Financing, Medicaid and Medicare (p. 350)
For information about sickle cell disease, see Health Research, Genetics (p. 371)

Agencies:

Health Resources and Services Administration (Health and Human Services Dept.), National Health Service Corps, 4350 East-West Highway, 8th Floor, Bethesda, MD (mailing address: Rockville, MD 20857); (301) 594-4130. Dr. Donald L. Weaver, director. Fax, (301) 594-4076.
Supplies communities experiencing a shortage of health care personnel with doctors and other medical professionals.

Health Resources and Services Administration (Health and Human Services Dept.), Primary Care Services, 4350 East-West Highway, Bethesda, MD 20814; (301) 594-4300. Richard C. Bohrer, director. Fax, (301) 594-4983.
Awards grants to public and nonprofit migrant, community, and health care centers to provide direct health care services in areas that are medically underserved.

National Institutes of Health (Health and Human Services Dept.), Research on Minority Health, 9000 Rockville Pike, Bldg. 1, #260, Bethesda, MD 20892; (301) 402-1366. Dr. John Ruffin, associate director. Fax, (301) 402-2517.
Coordinates the development of NIH policies and objectives related to minority health research and research training programs. Encourages minorities to work in the biomedical research field.

Public Health Service (Health and Human Services Dept.), Indian Health Service, 5600 Fishers Lane, #6-05, Rockville, MD 20857; (301)

443-1083. Dr. Michael H. Trujillo, director. Information, (301) 443-3593. Fax, (301) 443-4794.

Operates hospitals and health centers that provide native Americans and Alaska natives with preventive and remedial health care. Provides or improves sanitation and water supply systems in native American communities.

Public Health Service (Health and Human Services Dept.), Minority Health, 5515 Security Lane, #1100, Rockville, MD 20852; (301) 443-5084. Claudia Baquet, deputy assistant secretary. Information, (301) 587-1938. Fax, (301) 443-8280.

Oversees the implementation of the secretary's Task Force on Black and Minority Health and legislative mandates; develops programs to meet the health care needs of minorities; awards grants to coalitions of minority community organizations and to minority AIDS education and prevention projects.

Congress:

See Health Care and Services for Special Groups, General, Congress (p. 340)

Nongovernmental:

Americans for the Restitution and Righting of Old Wrongs (ARROW), 1000 Connecticut Ave. N.W. 20036; 296-0685. E. Thomas Colosimo, executive director.

Provides native American tribal leaders with health services management and training programs; recruits physicians and nurses to volunteer their services on reservation hospitals. Works to prevent child, drug, and alcohol abuse.

National Assn. of Community Health Centers, 1330 New Hampshire Ave. N.W., #122 20036; 659-8008. Thomas Van Coverden, executive director. Fax, 659-8519.

Membership: community health centers, migrant and homeless health programs, and other community health care programs. Provides the medically underserved with health services; seeks to ensure the continued development of community health care programs through policy analysis, research, technical assistance, publications, education, and training.

National Coalition of Hispanic Health and Human Services Organizations, 1501 16th St. N.W. 20036; 387-5000. Jane L. Delgado, president. Fax, 797-4353.

Assists agencies and groups serving the Hispanic community in general health care and in targeting health and psychosocial problems; provides information, technical assistance, health care provider training, and policy analysis; coordinates and supports research. Interests include mental health, chronic diseases, substance abuse, maternal and child health, youth issues, juvenile delinquency, and access to care.

National Health Law Program, 1815 H St. N.W., #705 20006; 887-5310. Stan Dorm, managing attorney, Washington office. Fax, 785-6792.

Organization of lawyers representing the economically disadvantaged, minorities, and the elderly in issues concerning federal, state, and local health care programs. Offers technical assistance and training for health law specialists. (Headquarters in Los Angeles.)

See also Health, General, Nongovernmental (p. 323)

See also Georgetown University Center for Health Policy Studies (p. 353)

Physically Disabled

See also Education: Special Groups, Handicapped, Learning Disabled (p. 145); Social Services and Rehabilitation Programs, Disabled (p. 420)

Agencies:

Education Dept., Clearinghouse on Disability Information, 330 C St. S.W. 20202-2524; 205-8241. Susan Murray, director. Fax, 205-9252. Main phone is voice and TDD accessible.

Provides information on federal legislation and programs and national organizations concerning individuals with disabilities.

Education Dept., Rehabilitation Services Administration, 330 C St. S.W. 20202; 205-5482. Howard Moses, acting commissioner. Fax, 205-9874.

Allocates funds to state agencies and nonprofit organizations for programs serving eligible physically and mentally disabled persons; services provided by these funds include medical and psychological treatment as well as establishment of supported-employment and independent-living programs.

National Institute of Child Health and Human Development (National Institutes of Health, Health and Human Services Dept.), National Center for Medical Rehabilitation Research, 6100 Executive Blvd., #2A-03, Rockville, MD (mailing address: 9000 Rockville Pike, Bldg. 6100E, #2A-03, Bethesda, MD 20892); (301) 402-2242. Dr. Marcus Fuhrer, director. Fax, (301) 402-0832.

Conducts and supports research to develop improved technologies, techniques, and prosthetic and orthotic devices; promotes medical rehabilitation training.

National Institute on Deafness and Other Communication Disorders (National Institutes of Health, Health and Human Services Dept.), 9000 Rockville Pike, Bldg. 31, #3602, Bethesda, MD 20892; (301) 402-0900. Dr. James B. Snow Jr., director. Information, (301) 496-7243. Fax, (301) 402-1590. TDD, (301) 496-6596.

Conducts and supports research and research training and disseminates information on hearing disorders and other communication processes, including diseases that affect hearing, balance, smell, taste, voice, speech, and language.

Congress:

See Health Care and Services for Special Groups, General, Congress (p. 340)

See also Library of Congress, National Library Service for the Blind and Physically Handicapped (p. 145)

Nongovernmental:

Alexander Graham Bell Assn. for the Deaf, 3417 Volta Pl. N.W. 20007; 337-5220. Donna M. Dickman, executive director.

Provides hearing-impaired children with information and special education programs; works to improve employment opportunities for deaf persons; acts as a support group for parents of deaf persons.

American Council of the Blind, 1155 15th St. N.W., #720 20005; 467-5081. Oral O. Miller, national representative. Fax, 467-5085. Toll-free, 3:00-5:30 p.m. E.S.T., (800) 424-8666..

Membership organization serving blind and visually impaired individuals. Interests include Social Security, telecommunications, rehabilitation services, transportation, education, and architectural access. Provides blind individuals with information and referral services, including legal referrals; advises state organizations and agencies serving the blind; sponsors scholarships for the blind and visually impaired.

American Orthotic and Prosthetic Assn., 1650 King St., #500, Alexandria, VA 22314; (703) 836-7116. Ian R. Horen, executive director. Fax, (703) 836-0838.

Membership: companies that manufacture or supply artificial limbs and braces. Provides information on the profession.

American Physical Therapy Assn., 1111 N. Fairfax St., Alexandria, VA 22314-1488; (703) 684-2782. Francis Mallon, acting executive vice president. Toll-free, (800) 999-2782. Fax, (703) 684-7343.

Membership: active and retired accredited physical therapists, assistants, and students. Establishes professional standards and accredits physical therapy programs; seeks to improve physical therapy education, practice, and research. Library open to the public by appointment.

Better Hearing Institute, 5021-B Backlick Rd., Annandale, VA (mailing address: P.O. Box 1840, Washington, DC 20013); (703) 642-0580. Joseph J. Rizzo, executive director. Toll-free, (800) 327-9355. Fax, (703) 750-9302. Main phone is voice and TDD accessible.

Educational service that provides the hearing-impaired with consumer information and other assistance.

Hearing Industries Assn., 515 King St., #320, Alexandria, VA 22314; (703) 684-5744. Carole M. Rogin, president. Fax, (703) 684-6048.

Membership: hearing aid manufacturers and companies that supply hearing aid components. Provides information on hearing loss and hearing aids.

National Assn. of Rehabilitation Facilities, 1910 Association Dr., #200, Reston, VA 22091; (703) 648-9300. Robert E. Schwartz, executive director. Toll-free, (800) 368-3513. Fax, (703) 648-0346.

Promotes improved rehabilitation facilities; sponsors workshops, seminars, and on-the-job training contracts.

National Assn. of the Deaf, 814 Thayer Ave., Silver Spring, MD 20910; (301) 587-1788. Nancy J. Bloch, executive director. Fax, (301) 587-1791. TDD, (301) 587-1789.

Membership: deaf and hard-of-hearing individuals; hearing, speech, and language professionals; parents; state associations; and others concerned with the problems of the deaf. Interests include rehabilitation, education, employment, and discrimination; serves as an information clearinghouse on deafness; coordinates activities of state associates; publishes deafness-related materials; monitors legislation and regulations.

National Easter Seal Society, 1350 New York Ave. N.W., #915 20005; 347-3066. Joseph D. Romer, senior vice president, public affairs. Fax, 737-7914. TDD, 347-7385.

Federation of state and local groups with programs that help people with disabilities achieve independence. Washington office monitors legislation and regulations. Affiliates assist individuals with a broad range of disabilities, including muscular dystrophy, cerebral palsy, stroke, speech and hearing loss, blindness, amputation, and learning disabilities. Services include physical, occupational, vocational, and speech therapy; speech, hearing, physical, and vocational evaluation; psychological testing and counseling; personal and family counseling; and special education programs. (Headquarters in Chicago.)

National Head Injury Foundation, 1776 Massachusetts Ave. N.W., #100 20036; 296-6443. George Zitnay, president. Toll-free, (800) 444-6443. Fax, 296-8850. Family helpline, (800) 444-6443.

Works to improve the quality of life for persons with traumatic brain injuries and for their families. Promotes the prevention of head injuries through public awareness and education programs. Offers state-level support services for individuals and their families; monitors legislation and regulations.

National Information Center on Deafness, 800 Florida Ave. N.E. 20002; 651-5051. Loraine DiPietro, director. Fax, 651-5054. TDD, 651-5052.

Provides information on topics dealing with hearing loss and deafness. (Affiliated with Gallaudet University.)

National Rehabilitation Assn., 633 S. Washington St., Alexandria, VA 22314; (703) 836-0850. Ann Tourigny, executive director. Fax, (703) 836-0848. TDD, (703) 836-0849.

Membership: administrators, counselors, therapists, disability examiners, vocational evaluators, instructors, job placement specialists, disability managers in the corporate sector, and others interested in rehabilitation of people with physical and mental disabilities. Sponsors conferences and workshops; monitors legislation and regulations.

Prevention of Blindness Society, 1775 Church St. N.W. 20036; 234-1010. Arnold Simonse, executive director. Fax, 234-1020.

Conducts preschool and elementary school screening program and glaucoma testing; provides information and referral service on eye health care; assists low-income persons in obtaining eye care and provides eyeglasses for a nominal fee to persons experiencing financial stress.

Registry of Interpreters for the Deaf, 8719 Colesville Rd., #310, Silver Spring, MD 20910; (301) 608-0050. Janet L. Bailey, president. Fax, (301) 608-0508.

Trains and certifies interpreters; maintains registry of certified interpreters; establishes certification standards. Sponsors training workshops and conferences.

Spina Bifida Assn. of America, 4590 MacArthur Blvd. N.W., #250 20007-4226; 944-3285. Lawrence Pencak, executive director. Toll-free, (800) 621-3141. Fax, 944-3295.

Membership: individuals with spina bifida, their supporters, and concerned professionals. Offers educational programs and support services; acts as a clearinghouse, provides referral services, and conducts seminars; monitors legislation and regulations.

Telecommunications for the Deaf, 8719 Colesville Rd., #300, Silver Spring, MD 20910; (301) 589-3786. Alfred Sonnenstrahl, executive director. Fax, (301) 589-3797. TDD, (301) 589-3006.

Membership: individuals, organizations, and businesses using telecommunications for the deaf (TDD) equipment. Provides information on TDD equipment. Interests include closed captioning for television, emergency access (911), TDD relay services, visual alerting systems, and TDD/computer conversion. Publishes an international TDD telephone directory.

Telephone Pioneers of America, Aids for the Handicapped Program, 1710 H St. N.W., 5th

Floor 20006; 392-6248. Marsha Siccarelli, administrator. Fax, 467-0525.

Encourages the development of electronic inventions that aid people with mental, visual, hearing, motion, and speech disabilities. Interests include phone devices for the deaf, sports activities for the blind, and teaching devices for autistic children. (Headquarters in Denver, Colo.)

See also American Council of the Blind Government Employees (p. 287); American Speech-Language-Hearing Assn. (p. 358); National Captioning Institute (p. 23)

Health Care Financing

See also Health Planning and Facilities (p. 351); Insurance (p. 71)

General

Agencies:

Health Care Financing Administration (Health and Human Services Dept.), Prepaid Health Care, Operations and Oversight, 330 Independence Ave. S.W. 20201; 619-1063. Elizabeth Handley, acting director. Fax, 619-2011.

Sets national policies for federally qualified health maintenance organizations (HMOs) and competitive medical plans; monitors HMO compliance with federal regulations. Administers and promotes prepaid health plan participation in Medicare programs.

Congress:

Congressional Budget Office, Health and Human Resources, 418A Ford Bldg. (2nd and D Sts. S.W.) 20515; 226-2669. Nancy M. Gordon, assistant director. Fax, 225-3149.

Studies major health issues, especially alternative federal health care policies; conducts research on health issues such as Medicare, Medicaid, health maintenance organizations, and health coverage for the uninsured.

Congressional Budget Office, Human Resources Cost Estimates Unit, 431 Ford Bldg. (2nd and D Sts. S.W.) 20515; 226-2820. Charles Seagrave, chief. Fax, 226-2963.

Studies major health insurance budget issues, especially Medicaid and Medicare. Provides cost estimates for congressional proposals in the area

of human resources, including proposals on health and Social Security.

House Energy and Commerce Committee, Subcommittee on Health and the Environment, 2415 RHOB 20515; 225-4952. Henry A. Waxman, D-Calif., chairman; Karen Nelson, staff director.

Jurisdiction over national health insurance proposals (jurisdiction shared with the House Ways and Means Committee) and legislation on malpractice insurance, Medicaid, and health maintenance organizations.

House Ways and Means Committee, Subcommittee on Health, 1114 LHOB 20515; 225-7785. Pete Stark, D-Calif., chairman; David Abernethy, staff director.

Jurisdiction over national health insurance proposals (jurisdiction shared with the House Energy and Commerce Committee) and legislation on health insurance supported by tax revenues, including Medicare.

Senate Finance Committee, Subcommittee on Health for Families and the Uninsured, SD-205 20510; 224-4515. Donald W. Riegle Jr., D-Mich., chairman; Debbie Chang, staff contact.

Holds hearings on national health insurance proposals (jurisdiction shared with the Senate Labor and Human Resources Committee) and on legislation on health insurance and Medicaid for low-income individuals.

Senate Labor and Human Resources Committee, SD-428 20510; 224-5375. Edward M. Kennedy, D-Mass., chairman; Nick Littlefield, chief counsel and staff director.

Jurisdiction over national health insurance proposals (jurisdiction shared with the Senate Finance Committee) and legislation on malpractice insurance and health maintenance organizations.

See also Congressional Insurance Caucus (p. 758)

Nongovernmental:

American Managed Care and Review Assn., 1227 25th St. N.W., #610 20037; 728-0506. Charles W. Stellar, president. Fax, 728-0609.

Represents health care provider organizations and other managed health care plans. Monitors legislation and regulations concerning health insurance and other issues of interest to managed health care plans; conducts training sessions on improving health care delivery in managed care practice settings; supports use of peer review and cost controls by member groups; provides managed care organizations with legal and consulting services.

American Medical Assn., 1101 Vermont Ave. N.W. 20005; 789-7400. Lee Stillwell, president, government affairs. Fax, 789-7485.

Membership: physicians, house staff, residents, and medical students. Monitors legislation and regulations on health matters and malpractice insurance. Provides information on health care. (Headquarters in Chicago.)

The Brookings Institution, Economic Studies Program, 1775 Massachusetts Ave. N.W. 20036; 797-6266. Joshua M. Wiener, senior fellow, health issues. Fax, 797-2965.

Studies federal health care issues and health programs, including Medicare, Medicaid, and long-term care.

Council for Affordable Health Insurance, 112 S. West St., Alexandria, VA 22314, (703) 036-6200. Greg Scandlen, executive director. Fax, (703) 836-6550.

Membership: small and mid-size insurance companies that favor free-market health care financing reform. Promotes reform measures, including establishment of medical savings accounts, tax equity, limited rating bands (rates that vary with age, physical condition, or geography), universal access, medical price disclosure prior to treatment, and caps on malpractice awards. Serves as a liaison with businesses, provider organizations, and public interest groups. Monitors legislation and regulations.

Employers Council on Flexible Compensation, 927 15th St. N.W., #1000 20005; 659-4300. Kenneth E. Feltman, executive director. Fax, 371-1467.

Represents employers who have or are considering flexible compensation plans. Supports the preservation and expansion of employee choice in health insurance coverage; monitors legislation and regulations.

Group Health Assn. of America, 1129 20th St. N.W., #600 20036; 778-3200. Karen Ignagni, president. Fax, 331-7487.

Membership: health maintenance organizations. Provides legal counsel and conducts educational programs. Monitors legislation and regulations. Library open to the public by appointment.

Health Insurance Assn. of America, 1025 Connecticut Ave. N.W. 20036; 223-7780. Willis D. Gradison Jr., president. Fax, 223-7889.

Membership: health insurance companies that write and sell health insurance policies. Promotes effective management of health care expenditures; provides statistical information on health insurance issues; monitors legislation and regulations.

Health Security Action Council, 1757 N St. N.W. 20036; 223-9685. Denise E. Holmes, director. Fax, 293-3457.

Membership: individuals; representatives of labor, education, and the elderly; and consumer organizations supporting national health insurance and other health plans. Conducts surveys on the effects of federal legislation on state and local health programs; provides educational and informational materials.

National Academy of Social Insurance, 1776 Massachusetts Ave. N.W., #615 20036; 452-8097. Pamela J. Larson, executive director. Fax, 452-8111.

Promotes research and education on Social Security, health care financing, and related public and private programs; assesses social insurance programs and their relationship to other programs; supports research and leadership development. Acts as a clearinghouse for social insurance information.

National Assn. of Health Underwriters, 1000 Connecticut Ave. N.W., #810 20036; 223-5533. Michael Lane, executive vice president. Fax, 785-2274.

Studies issues affecting the health insurance industry; certifies health underwriters; conducts advanced health insurance underwriting and research seminars at universities; maintains a speakers bureau.

National Assn. of Manufacturers, Employee Benefits, 1331 Pennsylvania Ave. N.W. 20004; 637-3124. Sharon Canner, director, industrial relations.

Interests include health care, employee benefits, cost containment, mandated benefits, Medicare, and other federal programs that affect employers.

National Health Care Anti-Fraud Assn., 1255 23rd St. N.W., #850 20037; 659-5955. William J. Mahon, executive director. Fax, 833-3636.

Membership: health insurance companies and regulatory and law enforcement agencies. Members work to identify, investigate, and prosecute individuals defrauding health care reimbursement systems.

Society of Professional Benefit Administrators, 2 Wisconsin Circle, #670, Chevy Chase, MD 20815-7003; (301) 718-7722. Frederick D. Hunt Jr., president. Fax, (301) 718-9440.

Membership: independent third-party administration firms that manage employee benefit plans for client employers. Interests include health care and insurance legislation and regulations, revision of Medicare programs, and health care cost containment. Monitors industry trends, government compliance requirements, and developments in health care financing.

See also Health, General, Nongovernmental (p. 323)

See also Employee Benefit Research Institute (p. 353); Healthcare Financial Management Assn. (p. 360); Healthcare Leadership Council (p. 353)

Medicaid and Medicare

Agencies:

Health Care Financing Administration (Health and Human Services Dept.), 200 Independence Ave. S.W. 20201; 690-6726. Bruce C. Vladeck, administrator. Information, 690-6113. Fax, 690-6262.

Administers Medicare (a health insurance program for persons with disabilities or age 65 or older, who are eligible to participate) and Medicaid (a health insurance program for persons judged unable to pay for health services).

Health Care Financing Administration (Health and Human Services Dept.), Data Management and Strategy, 7008 Security Blvd., #126, Baltimore, MD (mailing address: 6325 Security Blvd., Baltimore, MD 21207); (410) 597-5110. Regina McPhillips, director. Fax, (410) 597-5123.

Serves as primary federal statistical office for disseminating economic data on Medicare.

Health Care Financing Administration (Health and Human Services Dept.), Health Standards and Quality, 6325 Security Blvd., Baltimore, MD 21207; (410) 966-6841. Barbara J. Gagel, director. Fax, (410) 966-6730.

Develops, establishes, and enforces standards that regulate the quality of care hospitals and other health care facilities provide under Medicare and Medicaid programs. Oversees operations of survey and peer review organizations that enforce health care standards, primarily for institutional care. Monitors providers' and suppliers' compliance with standards.

Health Care Financing Administration (Health and Human Services Dept.), Medicaid, 6325 Security Blvd., Baltimore, MD 21207; (410) 966-3230. Sally Richardson, director. Fax, (410) 966-0255.

Administers and monitors Medicaid programs to ensure program quality and financial integrity; promotes beneficiary awareness and access to services.

Health Care Financing Administration (Health and Human Services Dept.), Policy Development, 6325 Security Blvd., Baltimore, MD 21207; (410) 966-5674. Thomas Ault, director; Robert Wren, director, Medicare coverage and eligibility policy, (410) 966-5661. Fax, (410) 966-0594.

Issues regulations and guidelines for administration of the Medicare program.

Health Care Financing Administration (Health and Human Services Dept.), Program Operations, 6325 Security Blvd., Baltimore, MD 21207; (410) 965-8050. Carol J. Walton, director. Fax, (410) 966-5882.

Manages the contractual framework for the Medicare program; establishes and enforces performance standards for contractors who process and pay Medicare claims.

Health Care Financing Administration (Health and Human Services Dept.), Survey and Certification, 6325 Security Blvd., Baltimore, MD 21207; (410) 966-6823. Wayne Smith, chief, acute care services. Fax, (410) 966-6730.

Certifies facilities that participate in federal Medicare and Medicaid programs. Determines whether facilities meet federal health and safety standards required for participation in such programs.

Congress:

See Health Care Financing, General, Congress (p. 348)

Nongovernmental:

Federation of American Health Systems, 1111 19th St. N.W. 20036; 833-3090. Michael D. Bromberg, executive director. Fax, 861-0063.

Membership: investor-owned, for-profit hospitals and health care systems. Studies Medicaid and Medicare reforms. Maintains speakers bureau; compiles statistics on investor-owned hospitals. Monitors legislation and regulations.

See also Health, General, Nongovernmental (p. 323)

See also American Assn. of Retired Persons, Health Care Campaign (p. 342); National Committee to Preserve Social Security and Medicare (p. 410)

Health Planning and Facilities

See also Health, General (p. 318); Health Care Financing (p. 348)

Agencies:

Health and Human Services Dept., National Clearinghouse for Primary Care Information, 8201 Greensboro Dr., #600, McLean, VA 22102; (703) 821-8955. Judy A. Cramer, project director. Fax, (703) 506-0384.

Supports the planning, development, and delivery of ambulatory health care to urban and rural areas in need of medical personnel and services; gives information to health care providers, administrators, and other interested persons.

Health and Human Services Dept., Planning and Evaluation, 200 Independence Ave. S.W. 20201; 690-7858. David T. Ellwood, assistant secretary. Fax, 690-7383.

Coordinates health policy and evaluation activities for the department; researches and analyzes health financing programs, health promotion and illness prevention programs, the adequacy and efficiency of health resources and services programs, health care planning, and health care facilities development and financing.

Health Care Financing Administration (Health and Human Services Dept.), Research and Demonstrations, 6325 Security Blvd., Baltimore, MD 21207-5187; (410) 966-6507. George Schieber, director. Fax, (410) 966-6511.

Conducts studies and demonstrations of alternative payment methods for health care providers; works to improve efficiency of health care delivery and financing. Researches issues pertaining to access and measurement of quality and effectiveness of care under Medicare and Medicaid.

Health Care Financing Administration (Health and Human Services Dept.), Survey and Certification, 6325 Security Blvd., Baltimore, MD 21207-5187; (410) 966-6763. Anthony Tirone, director. Fax, (410) 966-6730.

Enforces health care and safety standards for hospitals, nursing homes, and other long-term care facilities; clinical and other laboratories; clinics; and other health care facilities.

Health Resources and Services Administration (Health and Human Services Dept.), Health Resources Development, 5600 Fishers Lane, Parklawn Bldg., #705, Rockville, MD 20857; (301) 443-1993. Dr. Stephen Bowen, director. Fax, (301) 443-9645.

Reviews applications for hospital mortgage insurance; monitors repayment of insured mortgages and direct and guaranteed loans; publishes guidelines for constructing and equipping health facilities; directs efforts to improve their operational effectiveness and efficiency. Plans, directs, coordinates, and monitors activities relating to emergency medical services and trauma system planning and implementation.

Health Resources and Services Administration (Health and Human Services Dept.), Rural Health Policy, 5600 Fishers Lane, #905, Rockville, MD 20857; (301) 443-0835. Jeffrey Human, director. Fax, (301) 443-2803.

Works with federal agencies, states, and the private sector to develop solutions to health care problems in rural communities. Studies the effects of Medicare and Medicaid programs on rural access to health care. Collects and analyzes data concerning the problems of rural health care providers and populations. Provides the National Advisory Committee on Rural Health with staff support.

Congress:

House Energy and Commerce Committee, Subcommittee on Health and the Environment,

2415 RHOB 20515; 225-4952. Henry A. Waxman, D-Calif., chairman; Karen Nelson, staff director.

Jurisdiction over legislation on health planning, health facilities construction, and government-run health care facilities, including Public Health Service hospitals.

House Ways and Means Committee, Subcommittee on Oversight, 1135 LHOB 20515; 225-5522. J. J. Pickle, D-Texas, chairman; Beth K. Vance, staff director. Fax, 225-0787.

Oversees government-sponsored enterprises, including the College Construction Loan Insurance Assn., with regard to the financial risks posed to the federal government.

Office of Technology Assessment, Health Program, 600 Pennsylvania Ave. S.E. (mailing address: Washington, DC 20510-8025); 228-6590. Sean Tunis, program manager. Fax, 228-6603.

Acts on requests from House and Senate committees for research studies on general health care issues, including health care technologies and the cost and quality of child, adolescent, and elderly health care.

Senate Banking, Housing, and Urban Affairs Committee, SD-534 20510; 224-7391. Donald W. Riegle Jr., D-Mich., chairman; Steven Harris, staff director.

Oversees government-sponsored enterprises, including the College Construction Loan Insurance Assn., with regard to the financial risk posed to the federal government.

Senate Labor and Human Resources Committee, SD-428 20510; 224-5375. Edward M. Kennedy, D-Mass., chairman; Nick Littlefield, chief counsel and staff director.

Jurisdiction over legislation on health planning, health facilities construction, and government-run health care facilities, including Public Health Service hospitals.

Nongovernmental:

American College of Health Care Administrators, 325 S. Patrick St., Alexandria, VA 22314; (703) 549-5822. Richard L. Thorpe, executive vice president. Fax, (703) 739-7901.

Membership: administrators of long-term health care organizations and facilities, including home health care programs, hospices, daycare centers for the elderly, nursing and hospital facilities, retirement communities, and mental health care centers. Conducts research on statistical characteristics of nursing home and other medical administrators; conducts seminars; offers education courses; provides certification for administrators. Library open to the public by appointment.

American Hospital Assn., 50 F St. N.W. 20001; 638-1100. Richard J. Davidson, president. Fax, 626-2345.

Membership: hospitals, other inpatient care facilities, outpatient centers, Blue Cross plans, areawide planning agencies, regional medical programs, hospital schools of nursing, and individuals. Conducts research and education projects in such areas as provision of comprehensive care, hospital economics, hospital facilities and design, and community relations; monitors legislation and regulations; participates with other health care associations in establishing hospital care standards.

Assn. for Healthcare Philanthropy, 313 Park Ave., #400, Falls Church, VA 22046; (703) 532-6243. William C. McGinly, president. Fax, (703) 532-7170.

Membership: hospital and health care executives who manage fund-raising activities.

Assn. of Academic Health Centers, 1400 16th St. N.W., #410 20036; 265-9600. Dr. Roger J. Bulger, president. Fax, 265-7514.

Membership: academic health centers (composed of a medical school, a teaching hospital, and at least one other health professional school or program). Participates in studies and public debates on health professionals' training and education, patient care, and biomedical research.

Assn. of State and Territorial Health Officials, 415 2nd St. N.E., #200 20002; 546-5400. George K. Degnon, executive vice president.

Membership: executive officers of state and territorial health departments. Serves as legislative review agency and information source for members.

Assn. of University Programs in Health Administration, 1911 N. Fort Myer Dr., #503, Arlington, VA 22209; (703) 524-5500. Henry A. Fernandez, president. Fax, (703) 525-4791.

Membership: colleges and universities with programs in health administration. Offers consultation services to health administration programs;

maintains task forces on undergraduate education, ethics, epidemiology, AIDS, health law, health facilities, long-term care, international development, institutional research, information management, quality improvement, and technology assessment.

College Construction Loan Insurance Assn. (Connie Lee), 2445 M St. N.W. 20037; 728-3411. Oliver R. Sockwell, president. Information, 835-0090. Fax, 785-2823. Toll-free, (800) 877-5333.

Congressionally authorized private corporation financed with common stock held by the Student Loan Marketing Assn. (Sallie Mae) and the Education Dept. and with preferred stock held by other investors, including financial and educational institutions. Insures and reinsures bonds and loans for teaching hospitals.

Employee Benefit Research Institute, 2121 K St. N.W., #600 20037; 659-0670. Dallas L. Salisbury, president; William S. Custer, research director. Fax, 775-6312.

Conducts research on health insurance coverage, health care utilization, and health care cost containment; studies health care delivery and financing alternatives, including long-term care, flexible benefits, and retiree health financing options.

Federation of American Health Systems, 1111 19th St. N.W. 20036; 833-3090. Michael D. Bromberg, executive director. Fax, 861-0063.

Membership: investor-owned, for-profit hospitals and health care systems. Interests include health reform, cost containment, and Medicare and Medicaid reforms. Maintains speakers bureau; compiles statistics on investor-owned hospitals. Monitors legislation and regulations.

Forum for Healthcare Planning, 2111 Wilson Blvd., #850, Arlington, VA 22201; (703) 516-6192. J. Michael McGehee, executive director. Fax, (703) 516-9242.

Membership: hospital administrators, health care consultants, architects, planners, educators, researchers, and government and community leaders. Provides educational programs on public policy and health care planning issues.

Foundation for Hospice and Homecare, 519 C St. N.E. 20002; 547-6586. Bill J. Halamandaris, chief executive officer. Fax, 546-8968.

Promotes high-quality hospice, home care, and other community services for those with chronic health problems or life-threatening illness. Conducts research and provides information on related issues. Works to educate the public concerning health and social policy matters. Monitors legislation and regulations. Oversees the National HomeCaring Council, which provides training, education, accreditation, and certification in the field.

Georgetown University Center for Health Policy Studies, 2233 Wisconsin Ave. N.W., #525 20007; 342-0107. Jack Hadley, co-director. Fax, 625-6685.

Research branch of Georgetown University School of Medicine. Studies long-term and indigent health care policy and funding.

Healthcare Leadership Council, 1500 K St. N.W., #360 20005; 347-5731. Pamela G. Bailey, president. Fax, 347-5836.

Membership: health care leaders who examine major health issues, including access and affordability. Works to implement new public policies.

Intergovernmental Health Policy Project, 2021 K St. N.W., #800 20006; 872-1445. Richard Merritt, director. Fax, 785-0114.

Researches state health laws and programs. Provides health policymakers, administrators, and others with information on state health programs and policies.

National Assn. of Counties, 440 1st St. N.W., 8th Floor 20001; 393-6226. Thomas L. Joseph, associate legislative director, health. Fax, 393-2630.

Promotes federal understanding of county government's role in providing, funding, and overseeing health care services at the local level. Interests include indigent health care, Medicaid and Medicare, prevention of and services for HIV infection and AIDS, long-term care, mental health, maternal and child health, and traditional public health programs conducted by local health departments.

National Assn. of Public Hospitals, 1212 New York Ave. N.W., #800 20005; 408-0223. Larry S. Gage, president. Fax, 408-0235.

Membership: city and county public hospitals, state universities, and hospital districts and authorities. Works to improve and expand health care in hospitals; interests include Medicaid patients and vulnerable populations, including AIDS patients, the homeless, the mentally ill, and non-English-speaking patients. Monitors legislation and regulations. Holds annual regional meetings.

National Governors' Assn., Committee on Human Resources, 444 N. Capitol St. N.W. 20001; 624-5340. Margaret Siegel, director. Information, 624-5300. Fax, 624-5313.

Monitors health issues, including malpractice, state health care cost containment, Medicaid, and health care block grants. Develops and manages health care policy projects focusing on access to and financing of health and long-term care and services, particularly for the poor.

Rand Corporation, 2100 M St. N.W. 20037; 296-5000. Charles R. Roll Jr., director, Washington operations. Fax, 296-7960.

Conducts research on health issues, studies health economics, and publishes results. (Headquarters in Santa Monica, Calif.)

U.S. Conference of Local Health Officers, 1620 Eye St. N.W., 4th Floor 20006; 293-7330. J. Thomas Cochran, executive director. Fax, 293-2352.

Membership: city, county, and district health officers. Provides members with information on national, state, and local health developments; submits health policy proposals to the federal government; monitors legislation and regulations affecting local health departments.

Washington Business Group on Health, 777 N. Capitol St. N.E., #800 20002; 408-9320. Mary Jane England, president. Fax, 408-9332. TDD, 408-9333.

Membership: large corporations with an interest in health. Monitors health care legislation and regulations of interest to large corporations. Interests include reimbursement policies, Medicare, retiree medical cost, hospital cost containment, health planning, and corporate health education.

See also Health, General, Nongovernmental (p. 323)

See also American Health Care Assn. (p. 342); Institute of Medicine (p. 364)

Health Professionals

Agencies:

Health and Human Services Dept., Commissioned Personnel, 5600 Fishers Lane, #4A15, Rockville, MD 20857; (301) 443-3067. Rear Adm. Suzanne Dahlman (CC), director. Fax, (301) 443-6730.

Administers the Public Health Service Commissioned Corps, which helps health professionals become commissioned officers with the same benefits offered in the other uniformed services.

Health Care Financing Administration (Health and Human Services Dept.), Health Standards and Quality, 6325 Security Blvd., Baltimore, MD 21207; (410) 966-6851. Michael McMullan, director, peer review. Fax, (410) 966-6730.

Oversees professional review and other medical review programs; establishes guidelines; prepares issue papers relating to legal aspects of professional review and quality assurance.

Health Resources and Services Administration (Health and Human Services Dept.), Health Education Assistance Loan Branch, 5600 Fishers Lane, Rockville, MD 20857; (301) 443-1540. Stephen J. Boehlert, chief. Fax, (301) 594-6911.

Administers federal program of insured loans to graduate students in medicine, osteopathy, dentistry, veterinary medicine, optometry, podiatry, public health, pharmacy, clinical psychology, chiropractics, and health administration under the Health Professions Education Assistance Act of 1976.

Health Resources and Services Administration (Health and Human Services Dept.), Health Professions, 5600 Fishers Lane, #805, Rockville, MD 20857; (301) 443-5794. Fitzhugh Mullan, director; Clay E. Simpson Jr., director, disadvantaged assistance, (301) 443-2100. Fax, (301) 443-2111.

Supports education of health professionals, nurse training, and targeting of resources to areas of national priority, including disease prevention, health promotion, bedside nursing, and care of the elderly. Administers regional centers that provide training for faculty and practitioners in geriatric health care and in the treatment of patients with HIV-related disorders or AIDS.

Health Resources and Services Administration (Health and Human Services Dept.), Health Services Scholarships, 4350 East-West Highway, 10th Floor, Rockville, MD 20857; (301) 594-4410. Norris S. Lewis, director. Fax, (301) 594-4985. Toll-free applications and information hotlines, (800) 638-0824 and (800) 221-9393.

Administers service-obligated scholarship and loan repayment programs that support students in medical and health professional schools.

Health Resources and Services Administration (Health and Human Services Dept.), National Practitioners Data Bank, 5600 Fishers Lane, Parklawn Bldg., #8-67, Rockville, MD 20857; (301) 443-2300. Thomas C. Croft, director, quality assurance. Toll-free, (800) 767-6732. Fax, (301) 443-6725.

Provides information on reports of malpractice payments, adverse state licensure, clinical privileges, and society membership actions (only to eligible state licensing boards, hospitals, and other health care entities) about physicians, dentists, and other licensed health care practitioners.

National Institutes of Health (Health and Human Services Dept.), Minority Biomedical Research Support Program, 5333 Westbard Ave., Bethesda, MD 20892; (301) 594-7949. Dr. Ciriaco Q. Gonzales, director. Fax, (301) 594-7732.

Awards grants to eligible minority universities and colleges to support biomedical research by minority students and faculty; funds development of research facilities.

See also Health Resources and Services Administration, National Health Service Corps (p. 344)

Congress:

House Energy and Commerce Committee, Subcommittee on Health and the Environment, 2415 RHOB 20515; 225-4952. Henry A. Waxman, D-Calif., chairman; Karen Nelson, staff director.

Jurisdiction over legislation on the education, training, and distribution of health professionals.

House Ways and Means Committee, Subcommittee on Health, 1114 LHOB 20515; 225-7785. Pete Stark, D-Calif., chairman; David Abernethy, staff director.

Jurisdiction over Professional Standards Review Organizations legislation.

Senate Labor and Human Resources Committee, SD-428 20510; 224-5375. Edward M. Kennedy, D-Mass., chairman; Nick Littlefield, chief counsel and staff director.

Jurisdiction over legislation on the education, training, and distribution of health professionals and over Professional Standards Review Organizations legislation.

Nongovernmental:

American Academy of Family Physicians, 2021 Massachusetts Ave. N.W. 20036; 232-9033. Rosemarie Sweeney, vice president. Fax, 232-9044.

Membership: family physicians, residents, and medical students. Monitors legislation and regulations; sponsors continuing medical education programs; promotes family practice residency programs. (Headquarters in Kansas City, Mo.)

American Academy of Otolaryngology-Head and Neck Surgery, Inc., 1 Prince St., Alexandria, VA 22314; (703) 836-4444. Dr. Jerome C. Goldstein, executive vice president. Press, (703) 519-1560. Fax, (703) 683-5100. TDD, (703) 519-1585.

Coordinates research in ear, nose, and throat disorders and head and neck surgery; provides continuing education; monitors legislation and regulations. Related interests include allergies, plastic and reconstructive surgery, and medical problems resulting from the use of tobacco.

American Academy of Physician Assistants, 950 N. Washington St., Alexandria, VA 22314; (703) 836-2272. Stephen C. Crane, executive vice president. Fax, (703) 684-1924.

Membership: physician assistants. Sponsors continuing medical education programs for re-certification of physician assistants; offers malpractice insurance; and monitors legislation and regulations. Interests include federal support for physician assistants' education programs; health issues related to underserved populations, Medicare coverage of physician assistants' services, and state laws regulating practice. Maintains speakers bureau.

American Assn. for Clinical Chemistry, Inc., 2101 L St. N.W., #202 20037; 857-0717. Richard G. Flaherty, executive vice president. Fax, 887-5093.

Membership: chemists, physicians, and other scientists specializing in clinical chemistry. Provides educational and professional development services; presents awards for outstanding achievement; monitors legislation and regulations.

American Assn. of Colleges of Nursing, 1 Dupont Circle N.W., #530 20036; 463-6930. Geraldine Bednash, executive director. Fax, 785-8320.

Promotes quality baccalaureate and graduate nursing education; works to secure federal support of nursing education, nursing research, and student financial assistance; operates databank providing information on enrollments, graduations, salaries, and other conditions in nursing higher education.

American Assn. of Colleges of Osteopathic Medicine, 6110 Executive Blvd., #405, Rockville, MD 20852; (301) 468-0990. Sherry R. Arnstein, executive director.

Works with federal policy makers on health policy issues; administers a centralized admission program for osteopathic medical colleges; assesses faculty needs; supports increase in the number of minority and economically disadvantaged students in osteopathic colleges; maintains an information database.

American Assn. of Colleges of Pharmacy, 1426 Prince St., Alexandria, VA 22314; (703) 739-2330. Dr. Carl E. Trinca, executive director. Fax, (703) 836-8982.

Membership: teachers and administrators representing colleges of pharmacy accredited by the American Council on Pharmaceutical Education. Sponsors educational programs; conducts research; provides career information; helps administer the Pharmacy College Admissions Test.

American Assn. of Colleges of Podiatric Medicine, 1350 Piccard Dr., #322, Rockville, MD 20850; (301) 990-7400. Anthony J. McNevin, president. Toll-free, (800) 922-9266. Fax, (301) 990-2807.

Membership: schools of podiatric medicine and affiliate teaching hospitals in the United States. Serves as an information clearinghouse on podiatric medical education; conducts research and policy analysis; administers centralized admissions program to colleges of podiatric medicine and to graduate residency programs; advises on establishing new colleges of podiatric medicine.

American Assn. of Dental Schools, 1625 Massachusetts Ave. N.W., #502 20036; 667-9433. Dr. Preston A. Littleton Jr., executive director. Fax, 667-0642.

Membership: individuals interested in dental education; undergraduate and graduate schools of dentistry; hospital dental education programs; and allied dental education programs in the United States, Canada, and Puerto Rico. Provides information on dental teaching and research and on admission requirements of U.S. and Canadian dental schools; publishes a directory of dental educators.

American Assn. of Healthcare Consultants, 11208 Waples Mill Rd., #109, Fairfax, VA 22030; (703) 691-2242. Vaughan A. Smith, president. Fax, (703) 691-2247.

Membership organization that develops credentials and standards for consulting services in all aspects of health planning and management; supports continuing education and training of health care professionals. Enforces code of professional ethics. (Affiliate of the American College of Health Care Executives.)

American Board of Opticianry, 10341 Democracy Lane, Fairfax, VA 22030; (703) 691-8356. Nancy Roylance, executive director. Fax, (703) 691-3929.

Establishes standards for opticians who dispense eyeglasses. Administers professional exams and awards certification; maintains registry of certified eyeglass dispensers. Adopts and enforces continuing education requirements; assists state licensing boards; approves educational offerings for recertification requirements.

American Chiropractic Assn., 1701 Clarendon Blvd., Arlington, VA 22209; (703) 276-8800. J. Ray Morgan, executive vice president. Fax, (703) 243-2593.

Promotes professional growth and recognition for chiropractors. Interests include health care coverage, sports injuries, physical fitness, internal disorders, and orthopedics. Supports foundation for chiropractic education and research. Monitors legislation and regulations.

American College of Cardiology, 9111 Old Georgetown Rd., Bethesda, MD 20814; (301) 897-2691. F. Lynn May, executive vice president. Fax, (301) 897-9745.

Membership: physicians, surgeons, and scientists specializing in cardiovascular health care;

sponsors programs in continuing medical education. Library open to the public.

American College of Emergency Physicians, 900 17th St. N.W., #1250 20006; 728-0610. Vacant, director, government affairs. Fax, 728-0617.

Monitors legislation affecting emergency medicine and practitioners. Interests include Medicare and Medicaid legislation and regulations, graduate medical education, indigent care, prehospital care, drunk driving, public health, and tax policy. (Headquarters in Dallas.)

American College of Nuclear Physicians, 1200 19th St. N.W., #300 20036; 857-1135. Carol A. Lively, executive director. Fax, 223-4579.

Fosters professional standards among nuclear physicians; works to ensure the proper and safe practice of nuclear medicine at a reasonable cost; seeks to advance and improve the science of nuclear medicine.

American College of Osteopathic Surgeons, 123 N. Henry St., Alexandria, VA 22314; (703) 684-0416. Guy D. Beaumont, executive director. Fax, (703) 684-3280.

Membership: surgeons in disciplines of orthopedics, neurosurgery, thoracic surgery, cardiovascular surgery, urology, plastic surgery, and general surgery. Offers members continuing education programs.

American College of Physicians, 700 13th St. N.W., #250 20005; 393-1650. Howard B. Shapiro, director, public policy. Fax, 783-1347.

Membership: internists, nonsurgical specialists, and physicians-in-training. Supports research and continuing education and issues recommendations on and evaluations of health problems. Monitors legislation and regulations relating to health policy. (Headquarters in Philadelphia.)

American College of Radiology, 1891 Preston White Dr., Reston, VA 22091; (703) 648-8900. John J. Curry, executive director. Fax, (703) 648-9176.

Membership: certified radiologists in the United States and Canada. Develops programs in radiation protection, technologist training, practice standards, and health care insurance; maintains a placement service for radiologists.

American College of Surgeons, 1640 Wisconsin Ave. N.W. 20007; 337-2701. Cynthia A. Brown, manager, Washington office. Fax, 337-4271.

Monitors legislation and regulations concerning surgery; conducts continuing education programs and sponsors scholarships for graduate medical education. Interests include hospital cancer programs, emergency treatment, and hospital accreditation. (Headquarters in Chicago.)

American Group Practice Assn., 1422 Duke St., Alexandria, VA 22314; (703) 838-0033. Donald W. Fisher, executive vice president. Fax, (703) 548-1890.

Membership: medical and dental group practices. Compiles statistics on group practice; sponsors a foundation for research and education programs.

American Medical Assn., 1101 Vermont Ave. N.W. 20005; 789-7400. Lee Stillwell, president, government affairs. Fax, 789-7485.

Membership: physicians, house staff, residents, and medical students. Provides information on the medical profession and health care; cooperates in setting standards for medical schools and hospital intern and residency training programs; offers physician placement service and counseling on management practices; provides continuing medical education. Monitors legislation and regulations. (Headquarters in Chicago.)

American Medical Peer Review Assn., 810 1st St. N.E., #410 20002; 371-5610. Andrew Webber, executive vice president. Fax, 371-8954.

Seeks to improve physicians' ability to assess the quality of medical care services; assists in developing methods to monitor the appropriateness of medical care; monitors legislation.

American Medical Women's Assn., 801 N. Fairfax St., #400, Alexandria, VA 22314; (703) 838-0500. Eileen McGrath, executive director. Fax, (703) 549-3864.

Membership: Female physicians, interns, residents, and medical students. Promotes continuing education; evaluates manufacturers' research on products for women's health; provides student educational loans; monitors legislation and regulations that affect women's health.

American Nurses Assn., 600 Maryland Ave. S.W., #100W 20024-2571; 554-4444. Shirley A. Girouard, executive director. Fax, 554-2262.

Membership: registered nurses. Sponsors the American Nurses Foundation. Monitors legislation and regulations.

American Occupational Therapy Assn., 1383 Piccard Dr., Rockville, MD 20849-1725; (301) 948-9626. Jeanette Bair, executive director. Toll-free, (800) 366-9799. Fax, (301) 948-5512. TDD, (800) 377-8555.

Membership: registered occupational therapists, certified occupational therapy assistants, and students. Associate members include businesses and organizations supportive of occupational therapy. Accredits colleges and universities and certifies therapists.

American Optometric Assn., 1505 Prince St., Alexandria, VA 22314; (703) 739-9200. Jeffrey G. Mays, director, Washington office. Fax, (703) 739-9497.

Membership: optometrists and optometry students. Monitors legislation and regulations and acts as liaison with international optometric groups and government optometrists; conducts continuing education programs for optometrists and provides information on eye care. (Headquarters in St. Louis, Mo.)

American Osteopathic Assn., 300 5th St. N.E. 20002; 544-5060. Elizabeth W. Beckwith, director, Washington office. Fax, 544-3525.

Membership: osteopathic physicians. Promotes general health and education; accredits osteopathic educational institutions; monitors legislation and regulations. (Headquarters in Chicago.)

American Podiatric Medical Assn., 9312 Old Georgetown Rd., Bethesda, MD 20814; (301) 571-9200. Frank J. Malouff, executive director. Fax, (301) 530-2752.

Membership: podiatrists. Accredits colleges of podiatric medicine and podiatric residency programs. Interests include the status of podiatrists in the military, federally supported financial assistance for podiatric students, and national health care initiatives.

American Society for Clinical Laboratory Science, 7910 Woodmont Ave., #1301, Bethesda, MD 20814-3015; (301) 657-2768. Lynn Podell Robinson, executive director. Fax, (301) 657-2909.

Membership: laboratory technologists. Monitors legislation and regulations concerning the clinical laboratory industry; conducts continuing education programs for medical technologists and laboratory workers.

American Society of Clinical Pathologists, 1001 Pennsylvania Ave. N.W., #725 20004-2508; 347-4450. Robin E. Stombler, director, Washington office. Fax, 347-4453.

Membership: pathologists, residents, and other physicians; clinical scientists; registered certified medical technologists; and technicians. Monitors legislation and regulations; promotes continuing education, educational standards, and research in pathology. (Headquarters in Chicago.)

American Society of Consultant Pharmacists, 1321 Duke St., Alexandria, VA 22314-3563; (703) 739-1300. R. Tim Webster, executive director. Fax, (703) 739-1321.

Membership: dispensing and clinical pharmacists who provide services to long-term care facilities. Monitors legislation and federal regulations on pharmacy issues and long-term care. Makes grants and conducts research in the science and practice of consultant pharmacy.

American Society of Internal Medicine, 2011 Pennsylvania Ave. N.W., #800 20006; 835-2746. Dr. Alan R. Nelson, executive vice president. Fax, 835-0443.

Federation of societies representing internists nationwide. Concerned with the social, economic, and political factors affecting the delivery of medical care.

American Speech-Language-Hearing Assn., 10801 Rockville Pike, Rockville, MD 20852; (301) 897-5700. Frederick T. Spahr, executive director. Fax, (301) 571-0457. TDD, (301) 897-0157. Toll-free hotline (except Alaska, Hawaii, and Maryland), (800) 638-8255 (voice and TDD accessible).

Membership: specialists in speech-language pathology and audiology. Sponsors professional education programs; acts as accrediting agent for graduate college programs and for public clinical education programs in speech-language pathology and audiology. Advocates the rights of the communicatively disabled; provides information on speech, hearing, and language problems. Provides referrals to speech-language pathologists and audiologists through toll-free hotline.

American Veterinary Medical Assn., 1101 Vermont Ave. N.W., #710 20005; 789-0007. Robert R. Jorgensen, executive director. Fax, 842-4360.

Monitors legislation and regulations affecting veterinary medicine. (Headquarters in Schaumburg, Ill.)

Assn. for Hospital Medical Education, 1101 Connecticut Ave. N.W., #700 20036; 857-1196. Michael S. Hamm, executive director. Fax, 223-4579.

Membership: physicians and others engaged in graduate and continuing medical education at community teaching hospitals. Conducts graduate and continuing education programs.

Assn. of American Medical Colleges, 2450 N St. N.W. 20037; 828-0400. Dr. Robert G. Petersdorf, president. Fax, 828-1125.

Membership: U.S. schools of medicine, councils of deans, teaching hospitals, academic societies, and medical students. Administers Medical College Admissions Test.

Assn. of American Veterinary Medical Colleges, 1101 Vermont Ave. N.W., #710 20005-3521; 371-9195. Lester M. Crawford, executive director. Fax, 842-4360.

Membership: U.S. and Canadian schools and colleges of veterinary medicine and veterinary science departments in agricultural colleges. Produces veterinary reports; sponsors continuing education programs.

Assn. of Schools and Colleges of Optometry, 6110 Executive Blvd., #690, Rockville, MD 20852; (301) 231-5944. Martin A. Wall, executive director. Fax, (301) 770-1828.

Membership: optometry schools and colleges; monitors legislation and regulations affecting optometric education. Provides information about the Optometry College Admissions Test to students.

Assn. of Schools of Allied Health Professions, 1730 M St. N.W., #500 20036; 293-4848. Thomas Elwood, executive director. Fax, 293-4852.

Membership: two- and four-year colleges and academic health science centers with allied health professional training programs; administrators, educators, and practitioners; and professional societies. Serves as information resource; works with the Health and Human Services Dept. to conduct surveys of allied health education programs; monitors legislation and regulations. Interests include health promotion and disease prevention, ethics in health care, and the participation of women and persons with disabilities in allied health.

Assn. of Schools of Public Health, 1015 15th St. N.W., #404 20005; 842-4668. Michael K. Gemmell, executive director. Fax, 289-8274.

Membership: accredited graduate schools of public health. Promotes improved education and training of professional public health personnel. Library open to the public.

College of American Pathologists, 1350 Eye St. N.W., #590 20005-3305; 371-6617. Jayne A. Hart, vice president. Fax, 371-0028.

Membership: physicians who are board certified in clinical and/or anatomic pathology. Accredits laboratories and provides them with proficiency testing programs. (Headquarters in Northfield, Ill.)

Contact Lens Society of America, 11735 Bowman Green Dr., Reston, VA 22090; (703) 437-5100. Tina M. Schott, executive director. Fax, (703) 437-0727.

Membership: contact lens professionals. Conducts courses and continuing education seminars for contact lens fitters and technicians.

Council on Education for Public Health, 1015 15th St. N.W. 20005; 789-1050. Patricia P. Evans, executive director. Fax, 289-8274.

Accredits schools of public health and graduate programs in community health education and community health preventive medicine. Works to strengthen public health programs through consultation, research, and other services.

Eye Bank Assn. of America, 1001 Connecticut Ave. N.W., #601 20036; 775-4999. Patricia Aiken-O'Neill, president. Fax, 429-6036.

Membership: U.S. and Canadian eye banks. Sets and enforces medical standards for eye banking; seeks to increase donations to eye, tissue, and organ banks; conducts training and certification programs for eye bank technicians; compiles statistics.

Foundation for Chiropractic Education and Research, 1701 Clarendon Blvd., Arlington, VA 22209; (703) 276-7445. Stephen R. Seater, executive director. Fax, (703) 276-8178.

Funds research to demonstrate the efficacy of chiropractic. Awards research grants, fellowships, and research residencies.

Healthcare Financial Management Assn., 1050 17th St. N.W., #700 20036; 296-2920. Wendy W. Herr, group executive. Toll-free, (800) 252-4362. Fax, 223-9771.

Membership: health care financial management specialists. Offers educational programs; provides information on financial management of health care. Library open to the public. (Headquarters in Westchester, Ill.)

International Chiropractors Assn., 1110 N. Glebe Rd., Arlington, VA 22201; (703) 528-5000. Ronald Hendrickson, executive vice president. Fax, (703) 528-5023.

Membership: chiropractors, students, educators, and laypersons. Seeks to increase public awareness of chiropractic. Supports research on health issues; administers scholarship program; monitors legislation and regulations.

International Council of Societies of Pathology, 7001 Georgia St., Chevy Chase, MD 20815; 576-2961. Dr. F. K. Mostofi, secretary-treasurer. Fax, 576-3056.

Seeks to develop and maintain international cooperative research and education programs in pathology. Assists the World Health Organization and other international organizations in the delivery of medical care.

National Assn. of County Health Officials, 440 1st St. N.W., #500 20001; 783-5550. Nancy Rawding, executive director. Fax, 783-1583.

Represents local health departments. Promotes partnership among local, state, and federal health agencies. Works to improve the capacity of local health departments to assess local health needs, develop public health policies, and ensure delivery of community services. Provides the forum to develop the technical competence, managerial capacity, and leadership potential of local public health officials. Affiliated with the National Assn. of Counties.

National Assn. of Healthcare Access Management, 1200 19th St. N.W., #300 20036; 857-1125. Carol A. Lively, executive director. Fax, 223-4579.

Promotes professional growth and recognition of health care patient access managers; provides instructional videotapes; sponsors educational programs.

National Center for Homeopathy, 801 N. Fairfax St., Alexandria, VA 22314; (703) 548-7790. Sharon Stevenson, associate executive director. Fax, (703) 548-7792.

Educational organization for professionals, groups, associations, and individuals interested in homeopathy and homeotherapeutics. Funds scientific research; sponsors educational programs for laypersons and health care professionals. Library open to the public.

National Certification Agency for Medical Laboratory Personnel, 7910 Woodmont Ave., #1301, Bethesda, MD 20814; (301) 654-1622. Andrea Guevara, executive director. Fax, (301) 657-2909.

Independent certification organization that develops and conducts examinations for clinical laboratory scientists and technicians; certifies qualified applicants.

National Medical Assn., 1012 10th St. N.W. 20001; 347-1895. Rosemary A. Davis, executive vice president. Fax, 842-3293.

Membership: minority physicians. Supports increased participation of minorities in the health professions, especially medicine.

National Organization for Competency Assurance, 1101 Connecticut Ave. N.W., #700 20036; 857-1165. Michael S. Hamm, executive director. Fax, 223-4579.

Membership: certifying agencies and other groups that issue credentials to health professionals. Promotes public understanding of competency assurance certification programs for health professions and occupations; monitors regulations; oversees commission that establishes certification program standards.

Vision Council of America, 1800 N. Kent St., #904, Arlington, VA 22209; (703) 243-1508. Susan Burton, executive director. Fax, (703) 243-1537.

Sponsors trade shows and public relations programs for the ophthalmic industry. Educates the public on developments in the optical industry.

See also Health, General, Nongovernmental (p. 323)

See also American Academy of Ophthalmology (p. 370); American College of Obstetricians and Gynecologists (p. 335); American Hospital Assn. (p. 352); Health Volunteers Overseas (p. 453)

Health Research

General

Agencies:

Armed Forces Radiobiology Research Institute, National Naval Medical Center, 8901 Wisconsin Ave., Bethesda, MD 20889; (301) 295-1210. Capt. Robert L. Bumgarner (USN), director. Fax, (301) 295-4967.

Serves as the principal ionizing radiation radiobiology research laboratory under the jurisdiction of the Defense Nuclear Agency. Library open to the public.

Energy Dept., Energy Management, 1000 Independence Ave. S.W. 20585; 586-2826. Marvin E. Gunn Jr., director. Fax, 586-0784.

Manages the federal program that addresses the potential health effects of electric and magnetic fields.

National Institutes of Health (Health and Human Services Dept.), 9000 Rockville Pike, Bldg. 1, #126, Bethesda, MD 20892; (301) 496-2433. Harold Varmus, director. Press, (301) 496-5787. Fax, (301) 496-8276.

Supports and conducts biomedical research on the causes and .prevention of diseases; furnishes health professionals and the public with information.

National Institutes of Health (Health and Human Services Dept.), Computer Research and Technology, 9000 Rockville Pike, Bldg. 12A, #3033, Bethesda, MD 20892; (301) 496-5703. Dr. David Rodbard, director. Information, (301) 496-6203. Fax, (301) 402-1754.

Responsible for incorporating computers into biomedical research and administrative procedures of NIH. Serves as the primary scientific and technological resource for NIH in the areas of high performance computing, database applications, mathematics, statistics, laboratory automation, engineering, and computer science and technology.

National Institutes of Health (Health and Human Services Dept.), John E. Fogarty International Center, 9000 Rockville Pike, Bldg. 31, #B2C02, Bethesda, MD 20892; (301) 496-1415. Philip E. Schambra, director. Fax, (301) 402-2173.

Coordinates international epidemiologic research on chronic and infectious diseases. Disseminates information on biomedical research in the United States and abroad; studies international health issues. Directs Fogarty International Center/World Health Organization programs in biomedical research and training.

National Institutes of Health (Health and Human Services Dept.), National Center for Research Resources, 9000 Rockville Pike, Bldg. 12A, #4007, Bethesda, MD 20892; (301) 496-5793. Dr. Judith L. Vaitukaitis, director. Fax, (301) 402-0006.

Discovers, develops, and provides biomedical researchers with access to critical research technologies and resources, including sophisticated instrumentation, models of human disease, and clinical research environments.

National Institutes of Health (Health and Human Services Dept.), National Institute of Nursing Research, 9000 Rockville Pike, Bldg. 31, #5B03, Bethesda, MD 20892; (301) 496-8230. Ada Sue Hinshaw, director. Information, (301) 496-0207. Fax, (301) 480-4969.

Provides grants and awards for nursing research and research training. Programs include research in health promotion and disease prevention, acute and chronic illness, and delivery of nursing care.

National Institutes of Health (Health and Human Services Dept.), Protection from Research Risks, 9000 Rockville Pike, Bldg. 31, #5B-63, Bethesda, MD 20892; (301) 496-7005. Gary B. Ellis, director. Fax, (301) 402-2071. Human subjects, (301) 496-8101. Animal welfare, (301) 496-7163.

Monitors the use of humans and animals in research to ensure that programs and procedures comply with Public Health Service and Health and Human Services Dept. regulations; conducts and develops educational programs for the protection of human subjects and the humane care and use of laboratory animals; helps other organizations address ethical issues in medicine and research.

National Institutes of Health (Health and Human Services Dept.), Research Grants, 5333 Westbard Ave., #449, Bethesda, MD 20892; (301) 594-7248. Jerome G. Green, director. Fax, (301) 594-7384.

Conducts scientific merit review of research grant and fellowship applications submitted to NIH. Assists in formulating grant and award

National Institutes of Health

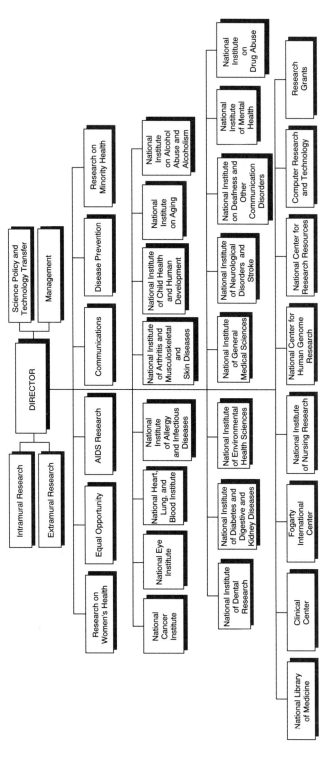

policies. Compiles, stores, and analyzes information on operating grant programs. Disseminates information on obtaining research grants.

National Institutes of Health (Health and Human Services Dept.), Research on Minority Health, 9000 Rockville Pike, Bldg. 1, #260, Bethesda, MD 20892; (301) 402-1366. Dr. John Ruffin, associate director. Fax, (301) 402-2517.

Coordinates the development of NIH policies and objectives related to minority health research and research training programs. Encourages minorities to work in the biomedical research field.

National Institutes of Health (Health and Human Services Dept.), Research on Women's Health, 9000 Rockville Pike, Bldg. 1, #201, Bethesda, MD 20892; (301) 402-1770. Dr. Vivian W. Pinn, director. Fax, (301) 402-1798.

Establishes NIH goals and policies for research related to women's health; supports expansion of research on diseases and conditions that affect women; monitors appropriate numerical participation of women in clinical research.

The Warren Grant Magnuson Clinical Center (National Institutes of Health, Health and Human Services Dept.), 9000 Rockville Pike, Bethesda, MD 20892; (301) 496-4114. John Gallin, director. Information, (301) 496-2563. Fax, (301) 402-0244.

Serves as a clinical research center for the National Institutes of Health.

Congress:

House Agriculture Committee, Subcommittee on Department Operations and Nutrition, 1301A LHOB 20515; 225-1496. Charles W. Stenholm, D-Texas, chairman; Stan Ray, staff director.

Jurisdiction over legislation on animals used for experimentation.

House Energy and Commerce Committee, Subcommittee on Health and the Environment, 2415 RHOB 20515; 225-4952. Henry A. Waxman, D-Calif., chairman; Karen Nelson, staff director.

Jurisdiction over legislation on health research, the treatment of cancer, AIDS, medical research on human subjects, and developmental disabilities (including epilepsy, cerebral palsy, autism, and mental retardation).

House Science, Space, and Technology Committee, Subcommittee on Science, 2319 RHOB 20515; 225-8844. Rick Boucher, D-Va., chairman; Grace L. Ostenso, staff director.

Jurisdiction over legislation on research and development involving health, nutrition, and medical programs.

Office of Technology Assessment, Biological Applications Program, 600 Pennsylvania Ave. S.E., #354 20003; 228-6670. Michael Gough, manager. Fax, 228-6293.

Conducts studies for Congress on applications of biological research, such as in neurology, on forensic uses of DNA technology, and on the biotechnology industry.

Senate Labor and Human Resources Committee, SD-428 20510; 224-5375. Edward M. Kennedy, D-Mass., chairman; Nick Littlefield, chief counsel and staff director.

Jurisdiction over legislation on health research, animals used for experimentation, the treatment of cancer and AIDS, medical research on human subjects (including recombinant DNA), and research and development activities involving biomedical programs and biotechnology.

Senate Labor and Human Resources Committee, Subcommittee on Disability Policy, SH-113 20510; 224-6265. Tom Harkin, D-Iowa, chairman; Robert Silverstein, staff director.

Jurisdiction over legislation on disabilities and developmental disabilities, including epilepsy, cerebral palsy, autism, and mental retardation.

Nongovernmental:

American Physiological Society, 9650 Rockville Pike, Bethesda, MD 20814-3991; (301) 530-7105. Alice W. Hellerstein, public affairs officer. Fax, (301) 571-8305.

Researches how the body and its organ systems function. Fosters scientific research, education, and the dissemination of scientific knowledge. Offers research awards and fellowships, programs to promote science education, and fellowships to encourage minority participation in physiological research. Works to establish standards for the humane care and use of laboratory animals.

Howard Hughes Medical Institute, 4000 Jones Bridge Rd., Chevy Chase, MD 20815-6789; (301) 215-8500. Dr. Purnell W. Choppin, president. Fax, (301) 215-8558.

Conducts biomedical research programs in major academic medical centers and universities. Areas of research include cell biology and regulation, genetics, immunology, neuroscience, and structural biology. Maintains a grants program in science education, including graduate, undergraduate, and precollege levels.

Institute of Medicine, 2101 Constitution Ave. N.W. 20418; 334-3300. Dr. Kenneth I. Shine, president. Information, 334-2352. Library, 334-2125. Fax, 334-1694.

Independent research organization chartered by the National Academy of Sciences. Conducts studies of policy issues related to health and medicine and issues position statements. National Academy of Sciences library open to the public by appointment.

Johns Hopkins University Applied Physics Laboratory, Johns Hopkins Rd., Laurel, MD 20723-6099; (301) 953-5000. Dr. G. L. Smith, director. Fax, (301) 953-1093. TDD, (301) 953-5666.

Research and development organization that, with affiliated medical centers, conducts research on the application of high-level technology and instrumentation to medical problems.

Research!America, 1522 King St., Alexandria, VA 22314; (703) 739-2577. Mary Woolley, president. Toll-free, (800) 366-2873. Fax, (703) 739-2372.

Membership: academic and professional societies, voluntary health organizations, corporations, and individuals interested in promoting medical research. Provides information on the benefits of medical research and seeks to increase funding for research.

SRI International, 1611 N. Kent St., Arlington, VA 22209; (703) 524-2053. Gerald E. Connolly, vice president, Washington office. Fax, (703) 247-8569.

Research and consulting organization. Conducts studies on biotechnology, genetic engineering, drug metabolism, cancer, toxicology, disease control systems, and other areas of basic and applied research. (Headquarters in Menlo Park, Calif.)

Undersea and Hyperbaric Medical Society, 10531 Metropolitan Ave., Kensington, MD 20895; (301) 942-2980. Leon J. Greenbaum Jr., executive director. Fax, (301) 942-7804.

Works to advance undersea and hyperbaric medicine and its supporting sciences. Studies the effect of greater than normal atmospheric pressure on the human body. Serves as a forum for information exchange on scientific issues.

See also Health, General, Nongovernmental (p. 323)

See also American Institutes for Research (p. 693)

AIDS (Acquired Immune Deficiency Syndrome)

See also Health Research, Blood (p. 367)

Agencies:

Centers for Disease Control and Prevention (Health and Human Services Dept.), 5600 Fishers Lane, Parklawn Bldg., #1834, Rockville, MD 20857; (301) 443-2610. Dr. Gary R. Noble, associate director, Washington office. Fax, (301) 443-8182. (Also located at 200 Independence Ave. S.W. 20201; 690-8598).

Conducts research to prevent and control AIDS; promotes public awareness through guidelines for health care workers, educational packets for schools, and monthly reports on incidences of AIDS. (Headquarters in Atlanta: 1600 Clifton Rd. N.E. 30333. Public inquiries, (404) 639-3534.)

Food and Drug Administration (FDA) (Health and Human Services Dept.), Center for Biologics Evaluation and Research, 8800 Rockville Pike, Bethesda, MD (mailing address: 1401 Rockville Pike, #200 North, Rockville, MD 20852); (301) 496-3556. Kathryn C. Zoon, director. Press, (301) 443-3285. Fax, (301) 402-0763.

Develops testing standards for vaccines, blood supply, and blood products and derivatives to prevent transmission of the human immunodeficiency virus (HIV); regulates biological therapeutics; serves as the focus for AIDS activities within the FDA.

Food and Drug Administration (Health and Human Services Dept.), Center for Drug Evaluation and Research, 5600 Fishers Lane, Parklawn Bldg., #13B-45, Rockville, MD 20857; (301) 443-2894. Gerald Meyer, acting director. Information, (301) 594-1012. Press, (301) 443-3285. Fax, (301) 443-2763.

Approves new drugs for AIDS and AIDS-related diseases. Reviews and approves applications to investigate and market new drugs.

Health Resources and Services Administration (Health and Human Services Dept.), AIDS Program, 5600 Fishers Lane, Rockville, MD 20857; (301) 443-4588. Dr. Stephen Bowen, associate administrator. Information, (301) 443-3377. Fax, (301) 443-1551.

Administers grants to support health care programs for AIDS patients, including those that reimburse low-income patients for drug expenses. Provides patients with AIDS and HIV-related disorders with ambulatory and community-based care. Conducts AIDS/HIV education and training activities for health professionals.

National Institute of Allergy and Infectious Diseases (National Institutes of Health, Health and Human Services Dept.), AIDS, 6003 Executive Blvd., Solar Bldg., #2A18, Rockville, MD 20852; (301) 496-8000. Dr. John Killen, director. Information, (301) 496-5717. Fax, (301) 402-1505. Toll-free hotline, (800) 342-2437.

Primary institute at NIH for AIDS research. Conducts a network of AIDS clinical trials and preclinical drug development research. Supports epidemiological studies and research into AIDS vaccines. Studies the pathogenesis of HIV infection.

Public Health Service (Health and Human Services Dept.), Minority Health, 5515 Security Lane, #1100, Rockville, MD 20852; (301) 443-5084. Claudia Baquet, deputy assistant secretary. Information, (301) 587-1938. Fax, (301) 443-8280.

Awards grants to minority AIDS education and prevention projects to administer health promotion, education, and disease prevention programs.

Public Health Service (Health and Human Services Dept.), National AIDS Policy, 200 Independence Ave. S.W. 20201; 690-5471. Arthur Lawrence, acting director. Information, 690-6867. Fax, 690-7054.

Coordinates national AIDS policy, sets priorities, recommends funding, and helps implement all Public Health Service HIV programs. Monitors progress of prevention and control programs; serves as a liaison with governmental and private organizations.

Walter Reed Army Institute of Research, Retrovirology, 13 Taft Court, Rockville, MD 20850; (301) 295-6414. Col. Donald S. Burke, director. Fax, (301) 295-6422.

Conducts and funds AIDS research for the Army retrovirus program; oversees AIDS testing for Defense Dept. personnel.

The Warren Grant Magnuson Clinical Center (National Institutes of Health, Health and Human Services Dept.), Transfusion Medicine, 9000 Rockville Pike, Bldg. 10, #1C711, Bethesda, MD 20892; (301) 496-9702. Dr. Harvey Klein, chief. Information, (301) 496-4506. Fax, (301) 402-1360.

Supplies blood and blood components for patient care and research. Research topics include AIDS.

See also National Museum of Health and Medicine (p. 116)

Congress:

See Health Research, General, Congress (p. 363)

Nongovernmental:

AIDS Action Council, 1875 Connecticut Ave. N.W., #700 20009; 986-1300. Daniel T. Bross, executive director. Fax, 986-1345.

Promotes and monitors legislation on AIDS research and education and on related public policy issues.

American Red Cross, National Headquarters, 17th and D Sts. N.W., 2nd Floor 20006; 737-8300. Elizabeth H. Dole, president. Fax, 783-3432.

Humanitarian relief and health education organization chartered by Congress. Conducts public education campaigns on AIDS.

Human Rights Campaign Fund, 1012 14th St. N.W., 6th Floor 20005; 628-4160. Tim McFeeley, executive director. Fax, 347-5323.

Promotes legislation to fund AIDS research.

Mattachine Society of Washington, 5020 Cathedral Ave. N.W., Washington, DC 20016; 363-3881. Franklin E. Kameny, president.

Provides referrals and information on AIDS.

National Assn. of People with AIDS, 1413 K St. N.W. 20005; 898-0414. William J. Freeman, executive director. Fax, 898-0435.

Membership: people with AIDS or HIV disease. Provides persons affected by AIDS or HIV disease with information and social service referrals; contributes to educational campaigns about AIDS.

National Leadership Coalition on AIDS, 1730 M St. N.W., #905 20036; 429-0930. B. J. Stiles, president. Fax, 872-1977.

Works with businesses to create AIDS health policies, guidelines, and education programs. Provides information and a business support network.

National Minority AIDS Council, 300 Eye St. N.E., #400 20002; 544-1076. Paul A. Kawata, executive director. Fax, 544-0378.

Works to encourage leadership within minority communities responding to the HIV/AIDS epidemic; provides community-based AIDS programs with technical assistance. Monitors legislation and regulations. Disseminates information on AIDS, especially information on the impact of the disease on minority communities.

Pediatric AIDS Coalition, 601 13th St. N.W., #400N 20005; 347-8600. Damian Thorman, chair. Toll-free, (800) 336-5475. Fax, 393-6137.

Coalition of child health and advocacy groups. Works to ensure that the needs of children with AIDS are addressed in AIDS legislation. Promotes pediatric AIDS prevention, education, research, and treatment programs. Monitors legislation and regulations.

See also National Assn. of Public Hospitals (p. 353); National Foundation for Infectious Diseases (p. 373)

Animal Experimentation

Agencies:

Animal and Plant Health Inspection Service (Agriculture Dept.), Regulatory Enforcement and Animal Care, 6505 Belcrest Rd., Hyattsville, MD 20782; (301) 436-8323. Dr. Dale F. Schwindaman, deputy administrator. Fax, (301) 436-8341.

Administers laws that regulate the handling, breeding, and care of animals used in research.

National Institutes of Health (Health and Human Services Dept.), Protection from Research Risks, 9000 Rockville Pike, Bldg. 31, #5B-63, Bethesda, MD 20892; (301) 496-7005. Gary B.

Ellis, director. Fax, (301) 402-2071. Animal welfare, (301) 496-7163.

Monitors the use of animals in research to ensure that programs and procedures comply with Public Health Service and Health and Human Services Dept. regulations; conducts and develops educational programs and materials; evaluates the effectiveness of HHS policies and programs for the humane care and use of laboratory animals; helps other organizations address ethical issues in medicine and research.

Congress:

See Health Research, General, Congress (p. 363)

See also Congressional Animal Welfare Caucus (p. 757); Congressional Friends of Animals (p. 758)

Nongovernmental:

American Humane Assn., 322 Massachusetts Ave. N.E. 20002; 543-7780. Adele Douglass, Washington representative. Fax, 546-3266.

Membership: societies, government agencies, and individuals concerned with child protection laws. Monitors legislation and regulations to ensure the proper use of laboratory animals; assists local societies in establishing shelters and investigating cruelty cases; maintains training programs for humane society personnel; and assists in public school education programs. (Headquarters in Denver, Colo.)

Animal Welfare Institute, P.O. Box 3650, Washington, DC 20007; 337-2332. Christine Stevens, president. Fax, 338-9478.

Educational group that opposes cruel treatment of animals used in research.

Humane Society of the United States, 2100 L St. N.W. 20037; 452-1100. John A. Hoyt, chief executive. Information, 778-6114. Fax, 778-6132.

Citizens' interest group that seeks to reduce suffering of animals used in medical research and testing. Promotes the use of nonanimal alternatives, elimination of unnecessary testing, and refinement of procedures to minimize pain. Interests include legislation regulating the use of live animals in research and testing.

National Assn. for Biomedical Research, 818 Connecticut Ave. N.W., #303 20006; 857-0540. Frankie L. Trull, president. Fax, 659-1902.

Membership: scientific and medical professional societies, academic institutions, and research-oriented corporations. Supports the humane use of animals in medical research, education, and product safety testing.

National Research Council, Institute of Laboratory Animal Resources, 2101 Constitution Ave. N.W. 20418; 334-2590. Dr. Thomas L. Wolfle, director. Fax, 334-1687.

Maintains an information center and answers inquiries concerning animal models for use in biomedical research, location of unique animal colonies, and availability of animals and genetic stocks from colonies and breeders. Develops guidelines on topics related to animal care and use in research, testing, and education; conducts conferences. (The National Research Council is the operating arm of the National Academy of Sciences and the National Academy of Engineering.)

People for the Ethical Treatment of Animals, 4928 Wyaconda Rd., Rockville, MD (mailing address: P.O. Box 42516, Washington, DC 20015); (301) 770-7444. Alex Pacheco, president. Information, (301) 770-8980. Fax, (301) 770-8969.

Educational and activist group supporting animal rights. Provides information on topics including laboratory research animals, factory farming, cosmetics, and vegetarianism. Monitors legislation; conducts workshops.

Physicians Committee for Responsible Medicine, 5100 Wisconsin Ave. N.W. (mailing address: P.O. Box 6322, Washington, DC 20015); 686-2210. Dr. Neal D. Barnard, president. Fax, 686-2216.

Membership: health professionals, medical students, and other individuals. Investigates alternatives to animal use in medical research experimentation, product testing, and education.

Society for Animal Protective Legislation, P.O. Box 3719, Washington, DC 20007; 337-2334. Christine Stevens, secretary. Fax, 338-9478.

Citizens' interest group that supports legislation to ensure the proper treatment of laboratory animals.

Arthritis

Agencies:

National Arthritis and Musculoskeletal and Skin Diseases Information Clearinghouse (National Institute of Arthritis and Musculoskeletal and Skin Diseases, National Institutes of Health, Health and Human Services Dept.), 9000 Rockville Pike, Bethesda, MD 20892; (301) 495-4484. Laura Hanley, information specialist. Fax, (301) 587-4352.

Provides physicians and the public with educational materials and federal community demonstration projects related to rheumatic, musculoskeletal, and skin diseases.

National Institute of Arthritis and Musculoskeletal and Skin Diseases (National Institutes of Health, Health and Human Services Dept.), 9000 Rockville Pike, Bldg. 31, #4032, Bethesda, MD 20892; (301) 496-4353. Dr. Lawrence E. Shulman, director. Information, (301) 496-8188. Fax, (301) 480-6069.

Conducts and funds research on arthritis and other rheumatic and bone diseases and musculoskeletal disorders. Funds national arthritis centers.

Blood

See also Health Care and Services for Special Groups, Minorities and Economically Disadvantaged Groups (p. 344); Health Research, Genetics (p. 371); Health Research, Heart and Stroke (p. 372)

Agencies:

National Heart, Lung, and Blood Institute (National Institutes of Health, Health and Human Services Dept.), Blood Diseases and Resources, 7550 Wisconsin Ave., #516, Bethesda, MD 20892; (301) 496-4868. Dr. Clarice Reid, acting director. Information, (301) 496-4236. Fax, (301) 402-3202.

Administers and conducts research and training programs to improve the diagnosis, prevention, and treatment of blood diseases and related disorders. Works to ensure the efficient and safe use and adequate supply of high-quality blood and blood products. Directs a program of research, education, and service delivery support for the Bone Marrow Transplantation Branch.

National Heart, Lung, and Blood Institute (National Institutes of Health, Health and Human Services Dept.), Bone Marrow Transplantation, 7550 Wisconsin Ave., #5C04, Bethesda, MD 20892; (301) 496-8387. Clarice Reid, acting director. Fax, (301) 402-1622.

Promotes expansion of the National Marrow Donor Registry. Supports the development and testing of methods for identifying and motivating marrow donors who are unrelated to recipients; matching unrelated-donors with potential recipients; and collecting, preserving and distributing unrelated-donor marrow.

National Heart, Lung, and Blood Institute (National Institutes of Health, Health and Human Services Dept.), Education Programs Information Center, P.O. Box 30105, Bethesda, MD 20824-0105; (301) 251-1222. Paula Books, manager. Press, (301) 496-4236. Fax, (301) 251-1223.

Acquires, maintains, and disseminates information on cholesterol, high blood pressure, and blood resources. Provides reference and referral services. Library open to the public.

National Institute of Diabetes and Digestive and Kidney Diseases (National Institutes of Health, Health and Human Services Dept.), Hematology, 5333 Westbard Ave., Westwood Bldg., #3A05, Bethesda, MD 20892; (301) 594-7541. David G. Badman, director. Information, (301) 496-3583. Fax, (301) 594-7501.

Supports basic research on and clinical studies of the states of blood cell formation, mobilization, and release. Interests include anemia associated with chronic diseases, iron and white blood cell metabolism, and genetic control of hemoglobin.

The Warren Grant Magnuson Clinical Center (National Institutes of Health, Health and Human Services Dept.), Transfusion Medicine, 9000 Rockville Pike, Bldg. 10, #1C711, Bethesda, MD 20892; (301) 496-9702. Dr. Harvey Klein, chief. Information, (301) 496-4506. Fax, (301) 402-1360.

Supplies blood and blood components for research and patient care. Provides training programs and conducts research in the preparation and transfusion of blood and blood products. Research topics include hepatitis, automated cell separation, immunohematology, and AIDS transmittal through transfusions.

Nongovernmental:

American Assn. of Blood Banks, 8101 Glenbrook Rd., Bethesda, MD 20814-2749; (301) 907-6977. Joel Solomon, executive officer. Fax, (301) 907-6895.

Membership: physicians, nurses, technologists, and administrators in the blood banking field. Inspects and accredits blood bank and transfusion services; sponsors certification exam for blood bank personnel; sponsors, with the College of American Pathologists, hepatitis and AIDS testing programs.

American Red Cross, National Headquarters, 17th and D Sts. N.W., 2nd Floor 20006; 737-8300. Elizabeth H. Dole, president. Fax, 783-3432.

Humanitarian relief and health education organization chartered by Congress. Collects blood and maintains blood centers; conducts research in various areas, including the production of interferon; operates a rare-donor registry, including a joint sickle cell anemia program with the NAACP; operates transfusion alternative program. Conducts training programs in nursing and first aid; trains volunteers for work in local chapters, hospitals, and community health centers. Administers national bone marrow registry.

Cancer

Agencies:

National Cancer Institute (National Institutes of Health, Health and Human Services Dept.), 9000 Rockville Pike, Bethesda, MD 20892; (301) 496-5615. Dr. Samuel Broder, director. Information, (301) 496-5583. Fax, (301) 402-0338. Cancer Information Services toll-free hotline, (800) 422-6237.

Conducts and funds research on the causes, diagnosis, treatment, prevention, control, and biology of cancer and the rehabilitation of cancer patients; administers the National Cancer Program; coordinates international research activities. Sponsors regional and national cancer information services.

National Cancer Institute (National Institutes of Health, Health and Human Services Dept.), Cancer Prevention and Control, 9000 Rockville Pike, Bldg. 31, #10A52, Bethesda, MD 20892; (301) 496-6616. Dr. Peter Greenwald, director. Fax, (301) 496-9931.

Funds projects for innovative and effective approaches to preventing and controlling cancer.

Coordinates support for establishing multidisciplinary cancer care and clinical research activities in community hospitals. Supports cancer research training, clinical and continuing education, and career development.

National Cancer Institute (National Institutes of Health, Health and Human Services Dept.), Organ Systems Coordinating Branch, 9000 Rockville Pike, Bethesda, MD 20892; (301) 496-8528. Andrew Chiarodo, chief. Fax, (301) 402-0181.

Encourages the study of cancers in solid tumors. Encourages multidisciplinary research linking laboratory and clinical medicine.

President's Cancer Panel, c/o National Cancer Institute, 9000 Rockville Pike, Bethesda, MD 20892; (301) 496-1148. Dr Maureen O. Wilson, executive secretary. Fax, (301) 402-1508.

Presidentially appointed committee that monitors and evaluates the National Cancer Program; reports to the president and Congress.

Congress:

See Health Research, General, Congress (p. 363)

Nongovernmental:

American Cancer Society, 316 Pennsylvania Ave. S.E., #200 20003; 546-4011. Kerrie Wilson, vice president, public affairs. Fax, 546-1682.

Supports medical research, education for health care professionals, and public information programs on cancer. Monitors legislation. (Headquarters in Atlanta.)

American Institute for Cancer Research, 1759 R St. N.W. 20009; 328-7744. Marilyn Gentry, executive director. Toll-free, (800) 843-8114. Fax, 328-7226.

Funds cancer research in areas of diet and nutrition; sponsors education programs. Library open to the public by appointment.

American Society of Clinical Oncology, 750 17th St. N.W., #1100 20006; 778-2396. Stacey Beckhardt, director, government relations. Fax, 778-2330.

Membership: physicians and scientists specializing in cancer prevention, treatment, education, and research. Promotes exchange of information in clinical research and patient care relating to all stages of cancer. (Headquarters in Chicago.)

Assn. of Community Cancer Centers, 11600 Nebel St., #201, Rockville, MD 20852; (301) 984-9496. Lee E. Mortenson, executive director. Fax, (301) 770-1949.

Membership: individuals from community hospitals involved in multidisciplinary cancer programs, including research, management, and patient care. Promotes the National Cancer Program.

Candlelighters Childhood Cancer Foundation, 7910 Woodmont Ave., #460, Bethesda, MD 20814; (301) 657-8401. James R. Kitterman, executive director. Toll-free, (800) 366-2223. Fax, (301) 718-2686.

Membership: families of children with cancer, survivors of childhood cancer, and health and education professionals. Serves as an information and educational network; sponsors self-help groups for parents of children and adolescents with cancer; operates Ombudsman Program for employment and insurance problems; monitors legislation and regulations. Library open to the public by appointment.

Leukemia Society of America, 2900 Eisenhower Ave., #419, Alexandria, VA 22314; (703) 960-1100. David M. Timko, executive director. Fax, (703) 960-0920.

Seeks to expand knowledge of leukemia and allied diseases. Conducts leukemia research; provides research scholarships and fellowships; maintains speakers bureau. Local chapters provide leukemia patients with financial assistance, counseling, and referrals. (Headquarters in New York.)

See also Health, General, Nongovernmental (p. 323)

See also Drug Policy Foundation (p. 332); National Hospice Organization (p. 325)

Dental

See also Health, Dental (p. 325)

Agencies:

National Institute of Dental Research (National Institutes of Health, Health and Human Services Dept.), 9000 Rockville Pike, Bldg. 31, #2C39, Bethesda, MD 20892; (301) 496-3571. Dr. Harald Loe, director. Information, (301) 496-4261. Fax, (301) 402-2185.

Conducts and funds research on the causes, prevention, and treatment of oral diseases and conditions.

Nongovernmental:

International Assn. for Dental Research, 1111 14th St. N.W. 20005; 898-1050. John J. Clarkson, executive director. Fax, 789-1033.

Membership: professionals engaged in dental research. Conducts annual convention, conferences, and symposia.

Diabetes, Digestive Diseases

Agencies:

National Diabetes Information Clearinghouse (National Institute of Diabetes and Digestive and Kidney Diseases, National Institutes of Health, Health and Human Services Dept.), 9000 Rockville Pike, Rockville, MD (mailing address: Box NDIC, Bethesda, MD 20892); (301) 654-3327. Beatrice Jakubowski, information specialist. Fax, (301) 496-2830.

Provides health professionals and the public with information on the symptoms, causes, treatments, and general nature of diabetes.

National Digestive Diseases Information Clearinghouse (National Institute of Diabetes and Digestive and Kidney Diseases, National Institutes of Health, Health and Human Services Dept.), 9000 Rockville Pike, Bethesda, MD (mailing address: Box NDDIC, Bethesda, MD 20892); (301) 654-3810. Frances Heilig, information specialist. Fax, (301) 496-2830.

Provides health professionals and the public with information on the symptoms, causes, treatments, and general nature of digestive ailments.

National Institute of Diabetes and Digestive and Kidney Diseases (National Institutes of Health, Health and Human Services Dept.), Diabetes, Endocrinology, and Metabolic Diseases, 9000 Rockville Pike, Bldg. 31, #9A16, Bethesda, MD 20892; (301) 496-7348. Dr. Richard Eastman, director. Fax, (301) 496-2830.

Awards grants and contracts to support basic and clinical research of diabetes mellitus and its complications.

National Institute of Diabetes and Digestive and Kidney Diseases (National Institutes of Health, Health and Human Services Dept.),

Digestive Diseases and Nutrition, 9000 Rockville Pike, Bldg. 31, #9A23, Bethesda, MD 20892; (301) 496-1333. Dr. Jay H. Hoofnagle, director. Fax, (301) 496-2830.

Awards grants and contracts to support basic and clinical research on digestive diseases.

Nongovernmental:

American Diabetes Assn., 1660 Duke St., Alexandria, VA 22314; (703) 549-1500. John H. Graham IV, chief executive officer. Toll-free, (800) 232-3472. Fax, (703) 836-7439.

Conducts and funds research on diabetes. Provides local affiliates with education, information, and referral services.

Juvenile Diabetes Foundation, 1850 K St. N.W., #450 20006; 778-8069. Michael Romansky, Washington counsel. Toll-free, (800) 223-1138. Fax, 778-8087.

Conducts research, education, and public awareness programs aimed at improving the lives of diabetics and finding a cure for diabetes. Monitors legislation and regulations. (Headquarters in New York.)

Eye

Agencies:

National Eye Institute (National Institutes of Health, Health and Human Services Dept.), 9000 Rockville Pike, Bldg. 31A, #6803, Bethesda, MD 20892; (301) 496-2234. Dr. Carl Kupfer, director. Information, (301) 496-5248. Fax, (301) 496-9970.

Conducts and funds research on the eye and visual disorders.

Nongovernmental:

American Academy of Ophthalmology, 1101 Vermont Ave. N.W., #700 20005; 737-6662. Cynthia Root Moran, director. Fax, 737-7061.

Membership: eye physicians and surgeons. Provides information on eye diseases. Monitors legislation and regulations. (Headquarters in San Francisco.)

Assn. for Research in Vision and Ophthalmology, 9650 Rockville Pike, Bethesda, MD 20814-3998; (301) 571-1844. Joanne Angle, executive director. Fax, (301) 571-8311.

Promotes eye and vision research; issues awards for significant research and administers research grant program.

International Eye Foundation, 7801 Norfolk Ave., Bethesda, MD 20814; (301) 986-1830. Victoria M. Sheffield, executive director. Fax, (301) 986-1876.

Operates eye health care and blindness prevention programs in developing countries. Sends volunteer surgeons and public health specialists to provide care; trains paramedical and public health personnel in developing countries in various aspects of public eye health care. Implements programs to control vitamin A deficiency and onchocerciasis (river blindness). Provides technology transfer and ophthalmic equipment and medicines.

Genetics

Agencies:

Health Resources and Services Administration (Health and Human Services Dept.), Genetic Services, 5600 Fishers Lane, #18A18, Rockville, MD 20857; (301) 443-1080. Dr. Jane Lin-Fu, chief. Fax, (301) 443-4842.

Awards funds, including demonstration grants, to develop or enhance regional and state genetic screening, diagnostic, counseling, and follow-up programs; screens newborns for sickle cell disease; enrolls those affected in a comprehensive care program. Provides comprehensive care for individuals and families with Cooley's anemia. Offers educational programs.

National Heart, Lung, and Blood Institute (National Institutes of Health, Health and Human Services Dept.), Sickle Cell Disease, 7550 Wisconsin Ave., #508, Bethesda, MD 20892; (301) 496-6931. Dr. Clarice D. Reid, chief. Fax, (301) 402-4843.

Supports research into the diagnosis and treatment of sickle cell anemia and continuing education programs for professionals and the public.

National Institute of Allergy and Infectious Diseases (National Institutes of Health, Health and Human Services Dept.), Genetics and Transplantation, 6003 Executive Blvd., Rockville, MD (mailing address: 9000 Rockville Pike, Solar Bldg., #4A14, Bethesda, MD 20892); (301) 496-5598. Dr. Stephen M. Rose, chief. Information, (301) 496-5717. Fax, (301) 402-2571.

Studies the molecular genetics of the immune system; conducts basic and clinical research on the link between genetics of the immune system and the success of transplantation.

National Institute of Diabetes and Digestive and Kidney Diseases (National Institutes of Health, Health and Human Services Dept.), Hematology, 5333 Westbard Ave., Westwood Bldg., #3A05, Bethesda, MD 20892; (301) 594-7541. David G. Badman, director. Information, (301) 496-3583. Fax, (301) 594-7501.

Supports basic and clinical studies of the states of blood cell formation, mobilization, and release. Interests include genetic control of hemoglobin.

National Institute of General Medical Sciences (National Institutes of Health, Health and Human Services Dept.), Genetics, 5333 Westbard Ave., #910, Bethesda, MD 20892; (301) 594-7773. Dr. Judith H. Greenberg, director. Information, (301) 496-7301. Fax, (301) 594-7724.

Supports research and research training in genetics.

National Institutes of Health (Health and Human Services Dept.), Human Genome Research, 9000 Rockville Pike, Bldg. 38A, #605, Bethesda, MD 20892; (301) 496-0844. Dr. Francis S. Collins, director. Information, (301) 402-0911. Fax, (301) 402-0837.

Plans, coordinates, and reviews progress of human genome research to map all genes in human DNA, as well as those of model organisms. Works to improve techniques for cloning, storing, and handling DNA and to enhance data processing and analysis; promotes exchange of information on new mapping data.

National Institutes of Health (Health and Human Services Dept.), Recombinant DNA Activities, 9000 Rockville Pike, Bldg. 31, #4B11, Bethesda, MD 20892; (301) 496-9838. Dr. Nelson A. Wivel, director. Fax, (301) 496-9839.

Coordinates NIH policy and procedure regarding recombinant DNA research and biotechnology; implements NIH guidelines and reviews research proposals requiring NIH approval.

Congress:

See Health Research, General, Congress (p. 363)

Nongovernmental:

Genetics Society of America, 9650 Rockville Pike, Bethesda, MD 20814; (301) 571-1825. Elaine Strass, executive director. Fax, (301) 530-7079.

Encourages professional cooperation among persons working in genetics and related sciences; holds annual convention.

Howard University, Center for Sickle Cell Disease, 2121 Georgia Ave. N.W. 20059; 806-7930. Dr. Oswaldo Castro, director. Fax, 806-4517.

Screens and tests for sickle cell disease; conducts research; promotes public education and community involvement; provides counseling and patient care.

Kennedy Institute of Ethics, Georgetown University, 1437 37th St. N.W. 20057; 687-8099. Dr. Robert M. Veatch, director. Fax, 687-6770. Library, (800) 633-3849; in Washington, D.C., 687-3885.

Sponsors research on medical ethical issues, including legal and ethical definitions of death, allocation of scarce health resources, and recombinant DNA and human gene therapy; supplies National Library of Medicine (National Institutes of Health) with online database on bioethics; publishes annual bibliography. Library open to the public.

March of Dimes Birth Defects Foundation, 1901 L St. N.W., #260 20036; 659-1800. Kay Johnson, director, policy and government affairs. Fax, 296-2964.

Works to prevent and treat birth defects. Monitors legislation and regulations; awards grants for research and provides funds for treatment of birth defects. (Headquarters in White Plains, N.Y.)

National Center for Education in Maternal and Child Health, 2000 15th St. North, #701, Arlington, VA 22201; (703) 524-7802. Dr. Rochelle Mayer, director. Fax, (703) 524-9335.

Produces directories and bibliographies on human genetics and genetic disorders; provides referral services. Library open to the public by appointment. (Affiliated with Georgetown University.)

See also Howard Hughes Medical Institute (p. 363); Biotechnology Industry Organization (p. 669); National Research Council, Institute

of Laboratory Animal Resources (p. 367); SRI International (p. 364)

Heart and Stroke

Agencies:

National Heart, Lung, and Blood Institute (National Institutes of Health, Health and Human Services Dept.), Education Programs Information Center, P.O. Box 30105, Bethesda, MD 20824-0105; (301) 251-1222. Paula Books, manager. Press, (301) 496-4236. Fax, (301) 251-1223.

Acquires, maintains, and disseminates information on cholesterol, high blood pressure, smoking, blood resources, and asthma to the public and health professionals. Provides reference and referral services. Library open to the public.

National Heart, Lung, and Blood Institute (National Institutes of Health, Health and Human Services Dept.), Heart and Vascular Diseases, 7550 Wisconsin Ave., Bethesda, MD 20892; (301) 496-2553. Dr. Michael Horan, director. Fax, (301) 402-3508.

Conducts and funds research on the prevention, causes, and treatment of heart and vascular diseases.

National Institute of Neurological Disorders and Stroke (National Institutes of Health, Health and Human Services Dept.), 9000 Rockville Pike, Bldg. 31, #8A52, Bethesda, MD 20892; (301) 496-9746. Dr. Patricia A. Grady, acting director. Information, (301) 496-5751. Fax, (301) 496-0296.

Conducts and funds stroke research.

Nongovernmental:

American Heart Assn., 1150 Connecticut Ave. N.W., #810 20036; 822-9380. Scott Ballin, vice president. Fax, 822-8993.

Membership: physicians, scientists, and other interested individuals. Monitors legislation and regulations concerning heart disease and stroke research and treatment; supports heart disease and stroke research and community service programs that provide information about heart disease and stroke. (Headquarters in Dallas.)

Citizens for Public Action on Blood Pressure and Cholesterol, 7200 Wisconsin Ave., #1002, Bethesda, MD 20814; (301) 907-7790. Gerald J. Wilson, executive director. Fax, (301) 907-7792.

Works to ensure public health resources for cholesterol and blood pressure education, screening, and treatment; prepares patient and professional educational materials and programs; monitors legislation and regulations on heart disease research, programs, and services.

Infectious Diseases, Allergies

Agencies:

National Institute of Allergy and Infectious Diseases (National Institutes of Health, Health and Human Services Dept.), 9000 Rockville Pike, Bethesda, MD 20892; (301) 496-2263. Dr. Anthony S. Fauci, director. Information, (301) 496-5717. Fax, (301) 496-4409.

Conducts research on infectious diseases and allergies, and other immunological disorders.

Navy Dept. (Defense Dept.), Naval Medical Research Institute, 8901 Wisconsin Ave., Bethesda, MD 20889-5607; (301) 295-0021. Capt. Robert G. Walter, commanding officer. Fax, (301) 295-2720.

Performs basic and applied biomedical research in areas of military importance, including infectious diseases, hyperbaric medicine, wound repair enhancement, environmental stress, and immunobiology. Provides support to field laboratories and naval hospitals.

Nongovernmental:

Asthma and Allergy Foundation of America, 1125 15th St. N.W., #502 20005; 466-7643. Mary Worstell, executive director. Toll-free, (800) 727-8462. Fax, 466-8940.

Provides information on asthma and allergies; maintains specialists referral service and speakers bureau; conducts self-management program for asthmatic children and their parents; awards research grants; provides teachers and school and occupational nurses with in-service training.

National Foundation for Infectious Diseases, 4733 Bethesda Ave., #750, Bethesda, MD 20814; (301) 656-0003. Dr. Richard J. Duma, executive director. Fax, (301) 907-0878.

Raises and disburses funds to support research on infectious diseases; educates the public and health professionals about infectious diseases; conducts an annual adult immunization awareness campaign; sponsors forum on AIDS, hepatitis, and other infectious diseases.

Kidney Disease

Agencies:

Health Care Financing Administration (Health and Human Services Dept.), Coverage and Eligibility Policy, 6325 Security Blvd., Baltimore, MD 21207; (410) 966-4635. Jackie L. Sheridan, chief, alternative delivery organizations. Fax, (410) 966-0169.

Administers coverage policy for Medicare persons with chronic kidney failure. Coordinates coverage under new treatment methods.

National Institute of Allergy and Infectious Diseases (National Institutes of Health, Health and Human Services Dept.), Genetics and Transplantation, 6003 Executive Blvd., Rockville, MD (mailing address: 9000 Rockville Pike, Solar Bldg., #4A14, Bethesda, MD 20892); (301) 496-5598. Dr. Stephen M. Rose, chief. Information, (301) 496-5717. Fax, (301) 402-2571.

Provides funds for studies of transplantation immunobiology, including kidney transplants.

National Institute of Diabetes and Digestive and Kidney Diseases (National Institutes of Health, Health and Human Services Dept.), Kidney, Urologic, and Hematological Diseases, 5333 Westbard Ave., #3A04, Bethesda, MD 20892; (301) 594-7584. Dr. Gladys H. Hirschman, director, chronic renal disease. Information, (301) 496-3583. Fax, (301) 594-7501.

Funds research on the prevention and treatment of renal disorders. Conducts research and reviews grant proposals concerning maintenance therapy for persons with chronic renal disease.

National Kidney and Urologic Diseases Information Clearinghouse (National Institute of Diabetes and Digestive and Kidney Diseases, National Institutes of Health, Health and Human Services Dept.), 9000 Rockville Pike, Bethesda, MD (mailing address: Box NKUDIC, Bethesda, MD 20892); (301) 654-4415. Cathy House, information specialist. Fax, (301) 496-2830.

Supplies health care providers and the public with information on the symptoms, causes, and treatments of kidney and urologic diseases.

Nongovernmental:

American Kidney Fund, 6110 Executive Blvd., #1010, Rockville, MD 20852; (301) 881-3052. Frank Soldovere, executive director. Toll-free, (800) 638-8299. Fax, (301) 881-0898.

Voluntary health organization that gives financial assistance to kidney disease victims. Disseminates public education materials; sponsors research grants for professionals; promotes organ donation for transplantation.

National Kidney Foundation, 725 15th St. N.W., #800 20005; 628-7171. Charles L. Plante, Washington representative. Fax, 628-5264.

Supports funding for kidney dialysis and other forms of treatment for kidney disease; provides information on detection and screening of kidney diseases. (Headquarters in New York.)

Lung

Agencies:

National Heart, Lung, and Blood Institute (National Institutes of Health, Health and Human Services Dept.), Education Programs Information Center, P.O. Box 30105, Bethesda, MD 20824-0105; (301) 251-1222. Paula Books, manager. Press, (301) 496-4236. Fax, (301) 251-1223.

Acquires, maintains, and disseminates information on smoking and asthma. Provides reference and referral services. Library open to the public.

National Heart, Lung, and Blood Institute (National Institutes of Health, Health and Human Services Dept.), Lung Diseases, 5333 Westbard Ave., Bethesda, MD 20892; (301) 594-7430. Suzanne Hurd, director. Information, (301) 251-1223. Press, (301) 496-4236. Fax, (301) 594-7487.

Directs research and training programs in lung diseases including research on causes, treatments, prevention, and health education.

Nongovernmental:

American Lung Assn., 1726 M St. N.W., #902 20036; 785-3355. Fran Du Melle, director, Washington office. Fax, 452-1805.

Fights lung disease through research, educational programs, and public awareness campaigns. Interests include antismoking campaigns, lung-related research, air pollution, school health education, and all lung diseases, including tuberculosis and occupational lung diseases. (Headquarters in New York.)

Cystic Fibrosis Foundation, 6931 Arlington Rd., Bethesda, MD 20814; (301) 951-4422. Robert Beall, president. Toll-free, (800) 344-4823. Fax, (301) 951-6378.

Conducts research on cystic fibrosis, an inherited genetic disease affecting the respiratory and digestive systems. Provides funding for care centers and information on the disease.

Metabolic Diseases

See also Health Research, Diabetes, Digestive Diseases (p. 370)

Agencies:

National Institute of Diabetes and Digestive and Kidney Diseases (National Institutes of Health, Health and Human Services Dept.), Diabetes, Endocrinology, and Metabolic Diseases, 9000 Rockville Pike, Bldg. 31, #9A16, Bethesda, MD 20892; (301) 496-7348. Dr. Richard Eastman, director. Fax, (301) 496-2830.

Provides grants and contracts to support diabetes and disease research.

Nongovernmental:

See Cystic Fibrosis Foundation, this page

Neurological and Muscular Disorders

Agencies:

National Institute of Neurological Disorders and Stroke (National Institutes of Health, Health and Human Services Dept.), 9000 Rockville Pike, Bldg. 31, #8A52, Bethesda, MD 20892; (301) 496-9746. Dr. Patricia A. Grady, acting director. Information, (301) 496-5751. Fax, (301) 496-0296.

Conducts research on neurological diseases.

Congress:

See Health Research, General, Congress (p. 363)

Nongovernmental:

Alzheimer's Assn., 1319 F St. N.W., #710 20004-1106; 393-7737. Stephen R. McConnell, senior vice president, public policy. Toll-free, (800) 272-3900. Fax, 393-2109.

Offers family support services and educates the public about Alzheimer's disease, a neurological disorder mainly affecting the brain tissue in older adults. Promotes research and long-term care protection. (Headquarters in Chicago.)

Epilepsy Foundation of America, 4351 Garden City Dr., Landover, MD 20785; (301) 459-3700. William McLin, executive vice president. Toll-free, (800) 332-1000. Library, (800) 332-4050. Fax, (301) 577-2684.

Promotes research and treatment of epilepsy; disseminates information and educational materials. Affiliates provide people with epilepsy with direct services and make referrals when necessary. Makes grants for epilepsy research. Library open to the public by appointment.

Foundation for the Advancement of Chiropractic Tenets and Science, 1110 N. Glebe Rd., Arlington, VA 22201; (703) 528-5000. Ronald Hendrickson, executive vice president. Fax, (703) 528-5023.

Offers financial aid for education and research programs in colleges and independent institutions; studies chiropractic services in the United States. (Affiliate of the International Chiropractors Assn.)

National Coalition for Research in Neurological Disorders, 1250 24th St. N.W. 20037; 293-5453. Lawrence S. Hoffheimer, executive director. Fax, 466-2888.

Coalition of voluntary agencies, physicians, and scientists. Works to increase federal funding for neurological disorder research; conducts educational programs.

National Foundation for Brain Research, 1250 24th St. N.W., #300 20037; 293-5453. Lawrence S. Hoffheimer, executive director. Fax, 466-2888.

Membership: professional societies, voluntary organizations, and businesses that support research into neurological and addictive brain disorders, including Alzheimer's disease, obsessive-compulsive behavior, dyslexia, drug addiction and alcoholism, stroke, Tay-Sachs disease, and depression. Sponsors programs that heighten public and professional awareness of brain disorders. Serves as a liaison with government agencies, medical and scientific societies, volunteer health organizations, and industry.

National Multiple Sclerosis Society, 2021 K St. N.W. 20006; 296-5363. Diane Afes, acting executive director, Washington office. Fax, 296-3425.

Seeks to advance medical knowledge of multiple sclerosis, a disease of the central nervous system. Patient services include individual and family counseling, exercise programs, equipment loans, medical and social service referrals, transportation assistance, back-to-work training programs, and in-service training seminars. (Headquarters in New York.)

United Cerebral Palsy Assns., 1522 K St. N.W., #1112 20005; 842-1266. John D. Kemp, executive director. Toll-free, (800) 872-5827. Fax, 842-3519. Main phone is voice and TDD accessible.

National network of state and local affiliates that assists individuals with cerebral palsy and other severe physical disabilities and their families. Provides parent education, early intervention, and employment services; family support and respite programs; and vocational training. Promotes research on cerebral palsy; supports the use of assistive technology and community-based living arrangements for persons with cerebral palsy and other severe physical disabilities.

See also National Easter Seal Society (p. 347)

Skin

Agencies:

National Institute of Arthritis and Musculoskeletal and Skin Diseases (National Institutes of Health, Health and Human Services Dept.), 9000 Rockville Pike, Bldg. 31, #4C32, Bethesda, MD 20892; (301) 496-4353. Dr. Lawrence E. Shulman, director. Information, (301) 496-8188. Fax, (301) 480-6069.

Supports research on the treatment of skin diseases, including psoriasis, eczema, and acne.

Nongovernmental:

American Academy of Facial Plastic and Reconstructive Surgery, 1110 Vermont Ave. N.W., #220 20005; 842-4500. Stephen C. Duffy, executive vice president. Fax, 371-1514. Toll-free information and physician referral, (800) 332-3223.

Promotes research and study in the field. Helps train residents in facial plastic and reconstructive surgery; offers continuing medical education. Sponsors scientific and medical meetings, international symposia, fellowship training program, seminars, and workshops. Provides videotapes on facial plastic and reconstructive surgery.

See also American Academy of Otolaryngology-Head and Neck Surgery, Inc. (p. 355)

Key Agencies:

Federal Emergency Management Agency
500 C St. S.W. 20472
Information: 646-4600

Housing and Urban Development Dept.
HUD Bldg.
451 7th St. S.W. 20410
Information: 708-0685

Key Committees:

House Banking, Finance, and Urban Affairs Committee
2129 RHOB 20515
Phone: 225-4247

Senate Banking, Housing, and Urban Affairs Committee
SD-534 20510
Phone: 224-7391

Key Personnel:

Federal Emergency Management Agency
James Lee Witt, director

Richard W. Krimm, associate director, Response and Recovery Directorate

Vacant, administrator, Federal Insurance Administration

Housing and Urban Development Dept.
Henry G. Cisneros, secretary

Terrence R. Duvernay, deputy secretary

Marilynn A. Davis, assistant secretary for administration

Andrew Cuomo, assistant secretary for community planning and development

William J. Gilmartin, assistant secretary for congressional and intergovernmental relations

Roberta Achtenberg, assistant secretary for fair housing and equal opportunity

Nicolas P. Retsinas, assistant secretary for housing—Federal Housing commissioner

Michael A. Stegman, assistant secretary for policy development and research

Joseph Shuldiner, assistant secretary for public and Indian housing

Dwight P. Robinson, president, Government National Mortgage Assn.

9

Housing
and Urban Affairs

Contents:

Community Planning and Development

See also Intergovernmental Relations: Economic Development (p. 73)

General

Agencies:

Administration for Children and Families (Health and Human Services Dept.), Community Services, 901 D St. S.W. (mailing address: 370 L'Enfant Promenade S.W., Washington, DC 20447); 401-9333. Donald Sykes, director. Fax, 401-5718.

Administers the Community Services Block Grant and Discretionary Grant programs.

Housing and Urban Development Dept., Block Grant Assistance, HUD Bldg., Rm. 7286 20410; 708-3587. Don I. Patch, director. Information, 708-1112. Press, 708-0685. Fax, 708-3363.

Develops regulations and procedures for the community development block grant program and the Section 108 Loan Guarantee Program. Manages close-out functions of the Urban Renewal Program.

Housing and Urban Development Dept., Community Planning and Development, HUD Bldg., Rm. 7100 20410; 708-2690. Andrew Cuomo, assistant secretary. Information, 708-0980. Fax, 708-3336.

Provides cities and states with community and economic development and housing assistance, including community development block grants, urban development action grants, and rental rehabilitation grant programs. Encourages public-private partnerships in urban development and private sector initiatives. Oversees enterprise zone development program.

Housing and Urban Development Dept., Field Coordination, HUD Bldg. 20410; 708-2565. Frank L. Davis, director. Fax, 708-3363.

Acts as liaison and coordinates all activities between the Office of Community Planning and Development and regional and field offices; evaluates the performance of regional and field offices. *(See Regional Federal Information Sources list, p. 824.)*

Housing and Urban Development Dept., HUD USER, P.O. Box 6091, Rockville, MD 20850; (301) 251-5154. Tony Cain, director. Toll-free, (800) 245-2691. Fax, (301) 251-5747.

Research information service and clearinghouse for HUD research reports. Provides information on past and current HUD research; maintains HUD USER ON-LINE, a bibliographic database accessible to the public. Performs custom search requests for a nominal fee; blueprints available upon request.

Housing and Urban Development Dept., Interstate Land Sales Registration, HUD Bldg., Rm. 9160 20410; 708-0502. Bruce J. Weichmann, director. Fax, 708-0299.

Administers the Interstate Land Sales Full Disclosure Act, which requires land developers who sell undeveloped land through interstate commerce or the mails to disclose required information about the land to the purchaser prior to signing a sales contract and to file information with the federal government.

Housing and Urban Development Dept., Policy Coordination, HUD Bldg., Rm. 7208 20410; 708-1283. Joseph F. Smith, director. Fax, 708-3363.

Conducts policy analyses and evaluations of community planning and development programs, including rehabilitation loans and community development block grant, urban development action grant, rental rehabilitation grant, and urban homesteading programs.

Housing and Urban Development Dept., Policy Development and Research, HUD Bldg. 20410; 708-1600. Michael A. Stegman, assistant secretary. Fax, 619-8000.

Evaluates community development programs.

Housing and Urban Development Dept., Program Evaluation, HUD Bldg., Rm. 8136 20410; 708-0574. Kevin Neary, director. Fax, 619-8360.

Conducts research, program evaluations, and demonstrations for all HUD housing, community development, and fair housing and equal opportunity programs.

Housing and Urban Development Dept., State and Small Cities, HUD Bldg., Rm. 7184 20410; 708-1322. Richard J. Kennedy, director. Fax, 708-1744.

Provides states with grants for distribution to small cities not entitled to community development block grants. Tribes and insular areas also are eligible for the grants. Funds support community development programs in low- and moderate-income communities and communities with urgent needs.

Housing and Urban Development Dept., Technical Assistance, HUD Bldg., Rm. 7148 20410; 708-2090. Syl C. Angel, director. Fax, 708-3363.

Develops program policies and designs and implements technical assistance plans for state and local governments for use in community planning and development programs. Administers community development work-study programs and community development grants for historically black colleges and universities; the Neighborhood Development Demonstration Program, which provides grants to create jobs, expand businesses, develop housing, or deliver necessary housing; and the New Communities Program.

National Capital Planning Commission, 801 Pennsylvania Ave. N.W. 20576; 724-0174. Reginald W. Griffith, executive director. Fax, 724-0195.

Central planning agency for the federal government in the national capital region, which includes the District of Columbia and suburban Maryland and Virginia. Reviews and approves plans for the physical growth and development of the national capital area, using environmental, historic, and land-use criteria.

Congress:

House Banking, Finance, and Urban Affairs Committee, Subcommittee on Consumer Credit and Insurance, 604 O'Neill Bldg. (300 New Jersey Ave. S.E.) 20515; 225-8872. Joseph P. Kennedy II, D-Mass., chairman; Shawn P. Maher, staff director. Fax, 225-7960.

Jurisdiction over federal insurance, including flood insurance.

House Banking, Finance, and Urban Affairs Committee, Subcommittee on Economic Growth and Credit Formulation, 109 Ford Bldg. (2nd and D Sts. S.W.) 20515; 226-7315. Paul E. Kanjorski, D-Pa., chairman; Robert W. Hall, staff director. Fax, 226-0070.

Jurisdiction over Urban Development Action Grants and enterprise zones.

House Banking, Finance, and Urban Affairs Committee, Subcommittee on Housing and Community Development, B303 RHOB 20515; 225-7054. Henry B. Gonzalez, D-Texas, chairman; Nancy Libson, staff director. Fax, 225-4680.

Jurisdiction over all community development legislation; urban planning, design, and research; urban redevelopment and relocation; and community development training and fellowships.

House Public Works and Transportation Committee, Subcommittee on Water Resources and Environment, B370A RHOB 20515; 225-0060. Douglas Applegate, D-Ohio, chairman; Kenneth J. Kopocis, counsel.

Jurisdiction over disaster relief legislation; oversight of U.S. disaster relief programs.

Senate Banking, Housing, and Urban Affairs Committee, Subcommittee on Housing and Urban Affairs, SD-535 20510; 224-6348. Paul S. Sarbanes, D-Md., chairman; Paul N. Weech, staff director. Fax, 224-5137.

Jurisdiction over community development legislation (including Urban Development Action Grants and enterprise zones); federal insurance (including flood insurance); urban planning, design, and research; and urban redevelopment and relocation.

Senate Environment and Public Works Committee, Subcommittee on Water Resources, Transportation, Public Buildings, and Economic Development, SH-415 20510; 224-5031. Daniel Patrick Moynihan, D-N.Y., chairman; Vacant, director.

Jurisdiction over disaster relief legislation; oversight of U.S. disaster relief programs. Oversight of the public buildings service of the General Services Administration.

Nongovernmental

American Institute of Architects, 1735 New York Ave. N.W. 20006; 626-7310. Terrence McDermott, executive vice president. Library, 626-7492. Fax, 626-7426.

Membership: registered American architects. Works to advance the standards of architectural education, training, and practice. Promotes the aesthetic, scientific, and practical efficiency of architecture, urban design, and planning. Offers continuing, career, and professional education programs; sponsors scholarships and an internship program; bestows annual award for design excellence. Houses archival collection, including documents and drawings, of American architects and architecture. Library open to the public. Monitors legislation and regulations.

American Planning Assn., 1776 Massachusetts Ave. N.W. 20036; 872-0611. Michael B. Barker, executive director. Fax, 872-0643.

Membership: professional planners and others interested in urban and rural planning issues. Sponsors professional development workshops conducted by the American Institute of Certified Planners. Prepares studies and technical reports; conducts seminars and conferences.

American Resort Development Assn., 1220 L St. N.W., #510 20005; 371-6700. Thomas Franks, president. Fax, 289-8544.

Membership: developers, builders, financiers, marketing companies, and others involved in resort, recreational, and community development. Serves as an information clearinghouse; monitors federal and state legislation affecting land, timeshare, and community development industries.

Center for Community Change, 1000 Wisconsin Ave. N.W. 20007; 342-0519. Pablo Eisenberg, executive director. Fax, 342-1132.

Provides community-based organizations serving minorities and the economically disadvantaged with technical assistance. Areas of assistance include community development block grants, housing, economic and resource development, rural development projects, and program planning.

Community Information Exchange, 1029 Vermont Ave. N.W., #710 20005; 628-2981. Kathleen M. Desmond, president. Fax, 783-1485.

Serves community-based nonprofit organizations and other subscribers with interests in revitalizing low-income communities. Provides technical information on community development, case examples, inventory of funding sources, referrals to experts, subject files, publications, and sample documents. Available by online computer access or staff-assisted searches.

Council of State Community Development Agencies, 444 N. Capitol St. N.W., #224 20001; 393-6435. John M. Sidor, executive director. Fax, 393-3107.

Membership: directors and staff of state community development agencies. Promotes common interests among the states, including community and economic development, housing, infrastructure, and state and local planning.

The Housing and Development Law Institute, 1614 20th St. N.W. 20009; 265-8102. William F. Maher, executive director. Fax, 332-6652.

Assists public agencies that administer assisted housing and community development programs in addressing common legal concerns and problems; conducts seminars on legal issues and practices in the housing and community development field. (Affiliated with the National Assn. of Housing and Redevelopment Officials.)

Institute for Local Self-Reliance, 2425 18th St. N.W. 20009; 232-4108. Neil Seldman, president. Fax, 332-0463.

Conducts research and provides technical assistance on environmentally sound economic development for government, small businesses, and community organizations.

International Institute of Site Planning, 715 G St. S.E. 20003; 546-2322. Beatriz de W. Coffin, director. Fax, 546-2722.

Directs research and provides information on site planning development and design of sites and buildings; conducts study/travel programs.

Local Initiatives Support Corp., 1825 K St. N.W., #909 20006; 296-4580. Michael Tierney, program director. Fax, 835-8931.

Provides community development corporations with financial and technical assistance to build affordable housing and revitalize distressed neighborhoods. (Headquarters in New York.)

NAIOP, Assn. for Commercial Real Estate, 2201 Cooperative Way, 3rd Floor, Herndon, VA 22071; (703) 904-7100. Thomas J. Bisacquino, executive vice president. Fax, (703) 904-7942.

Membership: developers, planners, designers, builders, financiers, and managers of industrial and office properties. Monitors legislation and regulations on capital gains, real estate taxes, impact fees, growth management, environmental issues, and hazardous waste liability.

National Assn. of Counties, 440 1st St. N.W., 8th Floor 20001; 942-4204. Haron N. Battle, associate legislative director, community and economic development. Information, 393-6226. Fax, 393-2620.

Membership: county governments. Monitors legislation and regulations affecting housing and community and economic development. Conducts research and provides information on community development block grants, assisted low-income housing, urban development action grants, and other housing and economic development programs. Analyzes the effects of census data on housing.

National Assn. of Housing and Redevelopment Officials, 1320 18th St. N.W. 20036; 429-2960. Richard Y. Nelson Jr., executive director. Fax, 429-9684.

Membership: housing, community, and urban development practitioners and organizations, and state and local government agencies and personnel. Works with federal government agencies to improve community development and housing programs; conducts training programs.

National Assn. of Neighborhoods, 1651 Fuller St. N.W. 20009; 332-7766. Deborah Crain, executive director. Fax, 332-2314.

Federation of neighborhood groups that provides technical assistance to local governments, neighborhood groups, and businesses. Seeks to increase influence of local groups on decisions affecting neighborhoods; sponsors training workshops promoting neighborhood awareness.

National Assn. of Regional Councils, 1700 K St. N.W., #1300 20006; 457-0710. John W. Epling, executive director. Fax, 296-9352.

Membership: regional councils of local governments. Develops policy proposals on issues with regional impact, including housing and community development.

National Center for Neighborhood Enterprise, 1367 Connecticut Ave. N.W., 2nd Floor 20036; 331-1103. Robert L. Woodson Sr., chairman. Fax, 296-1541.

Public policy research and demonstration organization. Interests include economic development, education, family preservation, and crime prevention. Attempts to identify model neighborhood-based economic and social development projects. Gives technical assistance to enterprises undertaking neighborhood development.

National Community Development Assn., 522 21st St. N.W., #120 20006; 293-7587. John A. Sasso, executive secretary. Fax, 887-5546.

Membership: local governments that administer federally supported community and economic development, housing, and human service programs.

National Congress for Community Economic Development, 1875 Connecticut Ave. N.W., #524 20009-5728; 234-5009. Stephen Glaude, president. Fax, 234-4510.

Membership: organizations engaged in revitalizing economically distressed communities. Services include advocacy, fund raising and technical assistance, information and referrals, conferences, and training. Library open to the public.

National Council of La Raza, 810 1st St. N.E., #300 20002; 289-1380. Raul Yzaguirre, president. Fax, 289-8173.

Helps Hispanic community-based groups obtain funds, develop and build low-income housing and community facilities, and develop and finance community economic development projects; conducts research and provides policy analysis on the housing status and needs of Hispanics; monitors legislation on fair housing and government funding for low-income housing.

National Housing Conference, 815 15th St. N.W., #601 20005; 393-5772. Robert J. Reid, executive director. Fax, 393-5656.

Membership: state and local housing officials, community development specialists, builders, bankers, lawyers, civic leaders, tenants, architects and planners, labor and religious groups, and national housing and housing-related organizations. Mobilizes public support for community development and affordable housing programs; conducts educational sessions.

National League of Cities, 1301 Pennsylvania Ave. N.W. 20004; 626-3000. Donald Borut, executive director. Information, 626-3120. Press, 626-3158. Fax, 626-3043.

Membership: cities and state municipal leagues. Aids city leaders in developing programs; investigates needs of local governments in implementing federal community development programs.

National Neighborhood Coalition, 810 1st St. N.E., #300 20002; 289-1551. Bud Kanitz, executive director. Fax, 289-8173.

Membership: national and regional organizations that have neighborhood-based affiliates, provide technical assistance to neighborhood groups, or conduct research on issues affecting neighborhoods. Monitors national programs and policies that affect inner-city neighborhoods; conducts monthly information forums.

National Realty Committee, 1420 New York Ave. N.W., #1100 20005; 639-8400. Steven A. Wechsler, president. Fax, 639-8442.

Membership: real estate owners, advisers, builders, investors, lenders, and managers. Serves as forum for public policy issues including taxes, the environment, capital, credit, and investments.

Partners for Livable Places, 1429 21st St. N.W. 20036; 887-5990. Robert H. McNulty, president. Fax, 466-4845.

Promotes working partnerships among public, private, and governmental sectors to improve the quality of life and economic development at local and regional levels. Conducts conferences and workshops; maintains library and referral clearinghouse. (International headquarters in Indianapolis.)

U.S. Conference of Mayors, 1620 Eye St. N.W., 4th Floor 20006; 293-7330. J. Thomas Cochran, executive director. Fax, 293-2352.

Membership: mayors of cities with populations of 30,000 or more. Promotes city-federal cooperation; publishes reports and conducts meetings on federal programs, policies, and initiatives that affect urban interests. Serves as a clearinghouse for information on urban problems.

The Urban Institute, Center for Public Finance and Housing, 2100 M St. N.W. 20037; 857-8585. G. Thomas Kingsley, director. Fax, 452-1840.

Research organization that deals with urban problems. Researches and evaluates use of community development block grant funds and neighborhood rehabilitation programs. Conducts economic research on the infrastructure of urban areas.

Urban Land Institute, 625 Indiana Ave. N.W., #400 20004-2930; 624-7000. Richard Rosan, executive vice president. Toll-free, (800) 321-5011. Fax, 624-7140.

Membership: land developers, planners, state and federal agencies, financial institutions, home builders, consultants, and realtors. Provides information on land-use planning, development, and management; sends teams to communities to examine land-use and development

problems; monitors trends in new community development. Library open to the public by appointment for a fee.

Disaster Assistance and Federal Insurance

Agencies:

Army Dept. (Defense Dept.), Corps of Engineers, Readiness Branch, 20 Massachusetts Ave. N.W., #6218 20314; 272-0251. Edward J. Hecker, chief. Information, 272-0010. Fax, 504-4150.

Assists in repairing and restoring damaged flood control structures and federally authorized hurricane and shore protection projects damaged by wind or water; provides emergency assistance during floods or coastal storms. Gives technical assistance and participates in debris removal and cleanup operations at request of the Federal Emergency Management Agency.

Federal Emergency Management Agency, Response and Recovery Directorate, 500 C St. S.W. 20472; 646-3692. Richard W. Krimm, associate director. Fax, 646-4060.

Administers the president's disaster relief program, including disaster research, preparedness, temporary housing, funding for repair of damaged public facilities, debris removal, and hazard mitigation; provides financial and technical assistance in the event of natural or technological disasters including earthquakes; assists in developing civil emergency planning. Coordinates other federal agency disaster assistance activities.

Federal Insurance Administration (Federal Emergency Management Agency), 500 C St. S.W. 20472; 646-2781. Vacant, administrator. Fax, 646-3445.

Administers federal crime and flood insurance programs, including the National Flood Insurance Program. Makes available to eligible homeowners low-cost flood and crime insurance. Flood insurance information: 731-5300, Washington, D.C., local area; (800) 638-6620, toll-free, nationwide nonclaims business; (800) 638-6831, Alaska and Hawaii; (800) 492-6605, Maryland. Crime insurance information: 251-1660, Washington, D.C., local area; (800) 638-8780, nationwide.

Small Business Administration, Disaster Assistance, 409 3rd St. S.W., #8100 20416; 205-6734.

Bernard Kulik, assistant administrator. Fax, 205-7728.

Provides victims of physical disasters with disaster and economic injury loans for homes, businesses, and personal property. Lends to individual homeowners, business concerns of all sizes, and nonprofit institutions to repair or replace damaged structures and furnishings, business machinery, equipment, and inventory.

Transportation Dept., Emergency Transportation, 400 7th St. S.W., #8404 20590; 366-5270. Lloyd E. Milburn, director. Fax, 366-3769.

Develops, coordinates, and reviews transportation emergency preparedness programs for use in emergencies affecting national defense and in emergencies caused by natural disasters and crisis situations.

Congress:

See *Community Planning and Development, General, Congress (p. 379)*

Nongovernmental:

American Red Cross, Disaster Services, 615 N. Saint Asaph St., Alexandria, VA 22314; (703) 838-7653. Donald W. Jones, vice president. Information, (703) 838-7617. Fax, (703) 838-7661.

Chartered by Congress to administer disaster relief. Provides disaster victims with food, clothing, shelter, first aid, and medical care; promotes disaster preparedness and prevention.

Salvation Army Disaster Service, 503 E St. N.W. 20001; 783-9085. James Allen, emergency disaster services coordinator.

Provides disaster victims and rescuers with emergency support, including food, clothing, and counseling services.

Urban Redevelopment and Relocation

Agencies:

Housing and Urban Development Dept., Affordable Housing, HUD Bldg. 20410; 708-2685. Vacant, director. Fax, 708-1744. TDD, 708-1112.

Administers the Section 312 Rehabilitation Loan Program, which makes low-interest loans for property rehabilitation to low- and moderate-income homeowners and to investor owners of multifamily and commercial properties. Coordinates with cities to convey publicly owned,

abandoned property to low-income families in exchange for their commitment to repair, occupy, and maintain property.

Housing and Urban Development Dept., Block Grant Assistance, HUD Bldg., Rm. 7286 20410; 708-3587. Don I. Patch, director. Information, 708-1112. Press, 708-0685. Fax, 708-3363.

Manages close-out functions of the Urban Renewal Program.

Housing and Urban Development Dept., Economic Development, HUD Bldg., Rm. 7136 20410; 708-2290. Roy O. Priest, director. Fax, 708-7543.

Manages economic development programs including Urban Development Action Grants and enterprise zone initiatives. Encourages private-public partnerships for development through neighborhood development corporations. Coordinates conferences and workshops on economic development and affordable housing programs.

Housing and Urban Development Dept., Enterprise Zone Development, HUD Bldg., Rm. 7136 20410; 708-2035. Michael McMahon, director. Fax, 708-7543.

Provides information about federal enterprise zones in economically distressed urban and rural areas.

Housing and Urban Development Dept., Homeownership and Opportunity for People Everywhere (HOPE 3), HUD Bldg., Rm. 7158 20410; 708-0324. John D. Garrity, director. Fax, 708-1744.

Provides low-income families and individuals with opportunities to buy homes. Provides eligible home buyers with federal assistance to purchase homes or to rehabilitate single-family properties. Awards grants to nonprofit or public agencies in cooperation with nonprofit agencies to acquire or rehabilitate single-family properties for sale and occupancy by eligible families at affordable prices.

Housing and Urban Development Dept., Relocation and Real Estate, HUD Bldg., Rm. 7156 20410; 708-0336. Harold J. Huecker, director. Fax, 708-1744.

Administers the Uniform Relocation Assistance and Land Acquisition Policies Act of 1970, as amended, and other laws requiring that relocation assistance be given to persons displaced by federally assisted housing and community development programs.

Congress:

See Community Planning and Development, General, Congress (p. 379)

Nongovernmental:

Corporation for Enterprise Development, 777 N. Capitol St. N.E., #801 20002; 408-9788. Brian Dabson, president. Fax, 408-9793.

Research and consulting organization that promotes economic self-sufficiency among low-income people through enterprise development, including microbusinesses to generate self-employment for the unemployed. Provides state and local governments and community organizations with technical assistance and policy analysis.

International Downtown Assn., 915 15th St. N.W., #600 20005; 783-4963. Richard H. Bradley, president. Fax, 347-2161.

Membership: organizations, corporations, public agencies, and individuals interested in the development and management of city downtown areas. Supports cooperative efforts between the public and private sectors to revitalize downtowns and adjacent neighborhoods; provides members with information, technical assistance, and advice; administers the Downtown Development Foundation.

National Assn. for the Advancement of Colored People (NAACP), 1025 Vermont Ave. N.W., #1120 20005; 638-2269. Wade J. Henderson, director, Washington bureau. Fax, 638-5936.

Membership: persons interested in civil rights for all minorities. Works to eliminate discrimination in housing and urban affairs. Interests include programs for urban redevelopment, urban homesteading, and low-income housing. Supports programs that make affordable rental housing available to minorities and that maintain African American ownership of urban and rural land. (Headquarters in Baltimore.)

National Assn. of Home Builders, 1201 15th St. N.W. 20005; 822-0200. Kent W. Colton, executive vice president. Fax, 822-0374.

Membership: contractors, builders, architects, engineers, mortgage lenders, and others interested in home building and commercial real estate construction. Offers educational programs and information on urban revitalization and housing rehabilitation. Library open to the public.

National Center for Urban Ethnic Affairs, P.O. Box 20, Cardinal Station, Washington, DC 20064; 319-5128. John A. Kromkowski, president. Information, 232-3600. Fax, 319-6289.

Educational and research organization that preserves and revitalizes urban neighborhoods through community organization and development; provides technical support and encourages interethnic and interracial cooperation, particularly between recent and older immigrants.

National Council for Urban Economic Development, 1730 K St. N.W., #915 20006; 223-4735. Jeffrey Finkle, executive director. Fax, 223-4745.

Membership: public economic development directors, chamber of commerce staff, utility executives, academicians, and others who design and implement development programs. Provides information to its members on job creation, attraction, and retention.

National Housing and Rehabilitation Assn., 1726 18th St. N.W. 20009; 328-9171. Peter H. Bell, executive director. Fax, 265-4435.

Membership: development firms and organizations and city, state, and local agencies concerned with multifamily and commercial development. Monitors government policies affecting multifamily development and rehabilitation. Presents project case studies and new financing mechanisms.

National Urban Coalition, 1875 Connecticut Ave. N.W., #400 20009-5728; 986-1460. Ramona H. Edelin, president. Fax, 986-1468.

Membership: business and labor representatives, minority groups, educators, and religious and civic leaders. Maintains task force on urban housing and urban health. Works with affiliates to broker funds for housing, community, and economic development projects and for innovative urban education programs.

Neighborhood Reinvestment Corp., 1325 G St. N.W., #800 20005; 376-2400. George Knight, executive director. Fax, 376-2600.

Chartered by Congress to assist localities in developing and operating local neighborhood-based programs designed to reverse decline in urban residential neighborhoods. Programs include Neighborhood Housing Services, Mutual Housing Association, Neighborhood Preservation Projects, and the Apartment Improvement Program.

See also National Assn. of Housing and Redevelopment Officials and National League of Cities (p. 381); The Urban Institute (p. 382)

Housing

General

Agencies:

General Services Administration, Federal Domestic Assistance Catalog Staff, 300 7th St. S.W., #101 20405; 708-5126. Robert Brown, director. Fax, 401-8233.

Maintains computerized system to aid state and local governments in locating federal assistance programs with the greatest funding potential to meet their developmental needs. Access to database available at designated points in every state.

Housing and Urban Development Dept., HUD Bldg., 451 7th St. S.W. 20410; 708-0417. Henry G. Cisneros, secretary. Information, 708-0685. Press, 708-0980. Library, 708-3180. Fax, 708-0299.

Responsible for federal programs concerned with housing needs, fair housing opportunity, and improving and developing the nation's urban and rural communities. Administers mortgage insurance, rent subsidy, preservation, rehabilitation, and antidiscrimination in housing programs. Advises the president on federal policy and makes legislative recommendations on housing and community development issues.

Housing and Urban Development Dept., Environment and Energy, HUD Bldg., Rm. 7240 20410; 708-2894. Richard H. Broun, director. Fax, 708-3363.

Issues policies and sets standards for environmental and land-use planning and for environmental management practices. Develops policies promoting energy efficiency, conservation, and renewable sources of supply in housing and community development programs, including district heating and cooling systems and wastes-to-energy cogeneration projects.

Housing and Urban Development Dept., Housing—Federal Housing Commissioner, HUD Bldg., Rm. 9100 20410; 708-3600. Nicolas P. Retsinas, assistant secretary. Fax, 708-2580.

Administers housing programs including the production, financing, and management of housing; directs preservation and rehabilitation of the housing stock; manages regulatory programs.

Housing and Urban Development Dept., HUD USER, P.O. Box 6091, Rockville, MD 20850; (301) 251-5154. Tony Cain, director. Toll-free, (800) 245-2691. Fax, (301) 251-5747.

Research information service and clearinghouse for HUD research reports. Provides information on past and current HUD research; maintains HUD USER ON-LINE, a bibliographic database accessible to the public. Performs custom search requests for a nominal fee; blueprints available upon request.

Housing and Urban Development Dept., Library and Information Services, HUD Bldg., Rm. 8141 20410; 708-1420. Audrey McKenzie, information specialist. Fax, 708-1485. Reference, 708-2370.

Provides information and referrals and distributes publications about HUD programs on a walk-in, write-in, or phone-in basis. Written or walk-in requests for HUD handbooks and other publications are handled by HUD field offices. *(See Regional Federal Information Sources list, p. 824.)*

Housing and Urban Development Dept., Policy Development and Research, HUD Bldg. 20410; 708-1600. Michael A. Stegman, assistant secretary. Fax, 619-8000.

Studies ways to improve the effectiveness and equity of HUD programs; analyzes housing and urban issues, including national housing goals, the operation of housing financial markets, the management of housing assistance programs, and statistics on federal and housing insurance programs; conducts the American Housing Survey; develops policy recommendations to improve federal housing programs. Works to increase the affordability of rehabilitated and newly constructed housing through technological and regulatory improvements.

Office of Management and Budget, Housing, New Executive Office Bldg., Rm. 9226 20503; 395-4610. F. Stevens Redburn, chief. Fax, 395-1307.

Housing and Urban Development Dept.

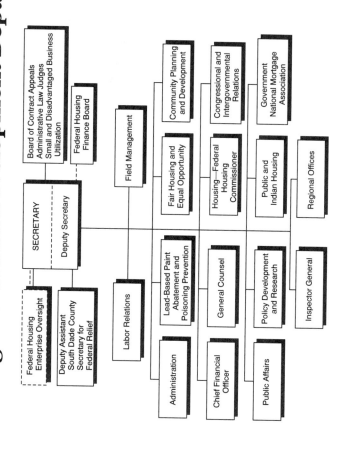

Assists and advises the OMB director in budget preparation, reorganizations, and evaluations of Housing and Urban Development Dept. housing programs.

Congress:

House Appropriations Committee, Subcommittee on VA, HUD, and Independent Agencies, H143 CAP 20515; 225-3241. Louis Stokes, D-Ohio, chairman; Paul Thompson, staff assistant.

Jurisdiction over legislation to appropriate funds for all programs of the Housing and Urban Development Dept., the Federal Emergency Management Agency, the National Credit Union Administration, the Neighborhood Reinvestment Corporation, and the National Institute of Building Sciences.

House Banking, Finance, and Urban Affairs Committee, Subcommittee on Housing and Community Development, B303 RHOB 20515; 225-7054. Henry B. Gonzalez, D-Texas, chairman; Nancy Libson, staff director. Fax, 225-4680.

Jurisdiction over all housing legislation, including construction standards and materials, condominiums and cooperatives, home ownership aid, manufactured homes, single and multifamily housing, and rural housing; oversees the Farmers Home Administration and other housing-related services and programs.

House Government Operations Committee, Subcommittee on Employment, Housing, and Aviation, B349A RHOB 20515; 225-6751. Collin C. Peterson, D-Minn., chairman; Wendy Adler, acting staff director.

Oversight of the Housing and Urban Development Dept.

Senate Appropriations Committee, Subcommittee on VA, HUD, and Independent Agencies, SD-142 20510; 224-7211. Barbara A. Mikulski, D-Md., chair; Kevin F. Kelly, clerk.

Jurisdiction over legislation to appropriate funds for all programs of the Housing and Urban Development Dept., the Federal Emergency Management Agency, the National Credit Union Administration, the Neighborhood Reinvestment Corporation, and the National Institute of Building Sciences.

Senate Banking, Housing, and Urban Affairs Committee, Subcommittee on Housing and Urban Affairs, SD-535 20510; 224-6348. Paul S. Sarbanes, D-Md., chairman; Paul N. Weech, staff director. Fax, 224-5137.

Jurisdiction over legislation concerning housing issues, including rural housing, construction standards and materials, condominiums and cooperatives, home ownership aid, manufactured homes, and single and multifamily housing. Oversees the Housing and Urban Development Dept. and the Farmers Home Administration.

Nongovernmental:

American Society of Appraisers, 535 Herndon Parkway, #150, Herndon, VA (mailing address: P.O. Box 17265, Washington, DC 20041); (703) 478-2228. A. W. Carson, executive director. Toll-free, (800) 272-8258. Fax, (703) 742-8471.

Membership: accredited appraisers of real property, including land, houses, and commercial buildings; businesses; machinery and equipment; yachts; aircraft; public utilities; personal property, including antiques, fine art, residential contents, gems, and jewelry. Affiliate members include students and professionals interested in appraising. Provides technical information; accredits appraisers; provides consumer information program.

American Society of Civil Engineers, 1015 15th St. N.W., #600 20005-2605; 789-2200. Ed Pfrang, executive director. Fax, 822-6583.

Develops and produces consensus standards for construction documents and building codes. Maintains the Civil Engineering Research Foundation, which focuses national attention and resources on the research needs of the civil engineering profession.

The Appraisal Foundation, 1029 Vermont Ave. N.W., #900 20005; 347-7722. David S. Bunton, executive vice president. Fax, 347-7727.

Seeks to ensure that appraisers are qualified to offer their services by promoting uniform professional standards and establishing licensing and certification requirements.

The Appraisal Institute, 2600 Virginia Ave. N.W., #300 20037; 296-4447. Donald E. Kelly, vice president, Washington office. Fax, 296-9464.

Provides Congress, regulatory agencies, and the executive branch with information on appraisal matters. (Headquarters in Chicago.)

National Assn. of Counties, 440 1st St. N.W., 8th Floor 20001; 942-4204. Haron N. Battle, associate legislative director, community and economic development. Information, 393-6226. Fax, 393-2620.

Membership: county governments. Monitors legislation and regulations affecting housing. Conducts research and provides information on housing.

National Assn. of Home Builders, 1201 15th St. N.W. 20005; 822-0200. Kent W. Colton, executive vice president. Fax, 822-0374.

Membership: contractors, builders, architects, engineers, mortgage lenders, and others interested in home building and commercial real estate construction. Offers educational programs and information on housing policy and mortgage finance in the United States. Library open to the public.

National Assn. of Real Estate Brokers, 1629 K St. N.W., #306 20006; 785-4477. H. Bernie Jackson, vice president. Fax, 785-1244.

Membership: minority real estate brokers, appraisers, contractors, property managers, and salespersons. Works to prevent discrimination in housing policies and practices; conducts regional seminars on federal policy, legislation, and regulations; advises members on procedures for procuring federal contracts.

National Assn. of Realtors, 777 14th St. N.W. 20005; 383-1264. Stephen Driesler, senior vice president, government and political relations. Fax, 383-1134.

Sets standards of ethics for the real estate business; promotes education, research, and exchange of information. Monitors legislation and regulations. (Headquarters in Chicago.)

National Home Buyers and Home Owners Assn., 1050 17th St. N.W. 20036; 659-6500. Benny L. Kass, general counsel. Fax, 293-2608.

Promotes consumer interests in housing, including condominiums; publishes a homebuyer's checklist in English and Spanish.

The Urban Institute, Center for Public Finance and Housing, 2100 M St. N.W. 20037; 857-8585. G. Thomas Kingsley, director. Fax, 452-1840.

Research organization that deals with urban problems. Researches federal, state, and local programs and policies; housing needs and markets; discrimination and segregation; and other housing policy problems, including housing allowances and public housing programs.

Construction Standards and Materials

Agencies:

Environmental Protection Agency, Radiation and Indoor Air, 501 3rd St. N.W. (mailing address: 401 M St. S.W., #6601J, Washington, DC 20460); 233-9320. Margo T. Oge, director. Fax, 233-9651.

Establishes standards for radon measurement; administers national and state radon surveys; develops model building codes for state and local governments; provides states and building contractors with technical assistance and training on radon detection and mitigation; collects data and provides the public with information. Administers carpeting program and other programs related to indoor air quality control. Coordinates federal and private efforts to address pollution problems in buildings.

Federal Housing Administration (Housing and Urban Development Dept.), Manufactured Housing and Construction Standards, L'Enfant Plaza, 490 East #3214 (mailing address: HUD Bldg., #B133, Washington, DC 20410); 755-7430. G. Robert Fuller, director. Fax, 755-7445.

Establishes and maintains standards for selection of new materials and methods of construction; evaluates technical suitability of products and materials; develops uniform, preemptive, and mandatory national standards for manufactured housing; enforces standards through design review and quality control inspection of factories; administers a national consumer protection program.

Housing and Urban Development Dept., Affordable Housing Research and Technology, HUD Bldg., Rm. 8132 20410; 708-4370. David Engel, acting director. Fax, 619-8360.

Develops and implements research programs addressing regulatory barriers to housing, such as zoning, land development, and building zones. Implements building technology research programs on environmental hazards in housing, such as radon. Reviews and assesses changes in building codes and standards. Conducts demonstrations on innovative building construction techniques.

International Trade Administration (Commerce Dept.), Basic Industries, Main Commerce Bldg. 20230; 482-5023. Michael J. Copts, deputy assistant secretary. Fax, 482-5666.

Analyzes and maintains data on the capital goods, international construction, engineering, and architecture industries. Monitors production costs, prices, financial and labor conditions, technological changes, distribution, markets, trade patterns, and other aspects of these industries. Promotes international trade, develops competitive assessments, and assists engineering and construction companies in obtaining overseas construction projects.

National Institute of Standards and Technology (Commerce Dept.), Building and Fire Research Laboratory, Route I-270 and Quince Orchard Rd., Gaithersburg, MD 20899; (301) 975-5900. Richard N. Wright, director. Library, (301) 975-6859. Fax, (301) 975-4032.

Performs analytical, laboratory, and field research in the area of building technology and its applications for building usefulness, safety, and economy; produces performance criteria and evaluation, test, and measurement methods for building owners, occupants, designers, manufacturers, builders, and federal, state, and local regulatory authorities.

Congress:

See Housing, General, Congress (p. 387)

Nongovernmental:

Air Conditioning and Refrigeration Institute, 4301 N. Fairfax Dr., #425, Arlington, VA 22203; (703) 524-8800. Philip A. Squair, legislative regulatory representative. Fax, (703) 528-3816.

Represents manufacturers of central air conditioning and commercial refrigeration equipment. Develops product performance rating standards and administers programs to verify manufacturers' certified ratings.

American Forest and Paper Assn., 1111 19th St. N.W. 20036; 463-2700. Bob Glowinski, vice president, American Wood Council. Fax, 463-2785.

Membership: manufacturers of wood and specialty products and related associations. Interests include tax, housing, environmental, international trade, natural resources, and land-use issues that affect the wood products industry.

American Portland Cement Alliance, 1212 New York Ave. N.W., #520 20005; 408-9494. Richard C. Creighton, president. Fax, 408-9392.

Membership: producers of portland cement. Monitors legislation and regulations of interest to the U.S. cement industry.

American Subcontractors Assn., 1004 Duke St., Alexandria, VA 22314-3588; (703) 684-3450. Chris S. Stinebert, executive vice president. Fax, (703) 836-3482.

Membership: construction subcontractors, specialty contractors, and their suppliers. Addresses business, contract, and payment issues affecting all subcontractors. Interests include procurement laws, payment practices, and lien laws. Monitors legislation and regulations.

Asphalt Roofing Manufacturers Assn., 6000 Executive Blvd., #201, Rockville, MD 20852-3803; (301) 231-9050. Richard D. Snyder, executive vice president. Fax, (301) 881-6572.

Membership: manufacturers of bitumen-based roofing products. Assists in developing local building codes and standards for asphalt roofing products. Provides technical information; supports research; monitors legislation and regulations.

Associated Builders and Contractors, 1700 N. 17th St., Rosslyn, VA 22209; (703) 812-2000. Daniel J. Bennet, executive vice president. Fax, (703) 812-8202.

Membership: construction contractors engaged primarily in nonresidential construction, subcontractors, and suppliers. Sponsors apprenticeship and training programs. Provides labor relations information; compiles statistics. Monitors legislation and regulations.

Associated General Contractors of America, 1957 E St. N.W. 20006-5194; 393-2040. Hubert Beatty, executive vice president. Fax, 347-4004.

Membership: general contractors engaged primarily in nonresidential construction; subcontractors; suppliers; accounting, insurance and bonding, and law firms. Conducts training programs, conferences, seminars, and market development activities for members. Produces position papers on construction issues. Monitors legislation and regulations.

Assn. of the Wall and Ceiling Industries, 307 East Annandale, #200, Alexandria, VA 22314; (703) 534-8300. Gary McKenzie, co-executive director. Fax, (703) 534-8307.

Membership: contractors and suppliers working in the wall and ceiling industries. Sponsors conferences and seminars. Monitors legislation and regulations. Library open to the public.

Brick Institute of America, 11490 Commerce Park Dr., Reston, VA 22091-1525; (703) 620-

0010. Nelson J. Cooney, president. Fax, (703) 620-3928.

Membership: manufacturers of clay brick. Provides technical expertise and assistance; promotes bricklaying vocational education programs; maintains collection of technical publications on brick masonry construction; monitors legislation and regulations.

Building Owners and Managers Assn. International, 1201 New York Ave. N.W., #300 20005; 408-2662. Mark W. Hurwitz, executive vice president. Fax, 371-0181.

Membership: office building owners and managers. Reviews changes in model codes and building standards; conducts seminars and workshops on building operation and maintenance issues; sponsors educational and training programs; monitors legislation and regulations.

Building Systems Councils of the National Assn. of Home Builders, 1201 15th St. N.W. 20005; 822-0576. Barbara K. Martin, executive director. Fax, 861-2141.

Membership: manufacturers and suppliers of home building products and services. Represents all segments of the industry, including consumers. Assists in developing National Assn. of Home Builders policies regarding building codes, legislation, and government regulations affecting manufacturers of model code complying, factory-built housing; sponsors educational programs; conducts plant tours of member operations.

Construction Management Assn. of America, 7918 Jones Branch Dr., McLean, VA 22102; (703) 356-2622. Karl F. Borgstrom, executive director. Fax, (703) 356-6388.

Promotes the development of construction management as a profession through publications, education, a certification program, and an information network. Serves as an advocate for construction management in the legislative, executive, and judicial branches of government.

Construction Specifications Institute, 601 Madison St., Alexandria, VA 22314; (703) 684-0300. Joseph A. Gascoigne, executive director. Fax, (703) 684-0465.

Membership: architects, engineers, contractors, and others in the construction industry. Promotes construction technology; maintains speakers bureau; publishes reference materials to help individuals prepare construction documents; sponsors certification programs for construction specifiers and manufacturing representatives.

Council of American Building Officials, 5203 Leesburg Pike, Falls Church, VA 22041; (703) 931-4533. Richard P. Kuchnicki, chief executive officer. Fax, (703) 379-1546.

Seeks to ensure consistency among model codes; encourages uniformity in administration of building regulations; maintains a one- and two-family dwelling code, a model energy code, and manufactured home construction and safety standards; provides review board for the American National Standards Institute disabled accessibility standard; oversees building certification program.

Gypsum Assn., 810 1st St. N.E., #510 20002; 289-5440. Jerry A. Walker, executive director. Fax, 289-3707.

Membership: manufacturers of gypsum wallboard and plaster. Assists members, code officials, builders, designers, and others with technical problems and building code questions; publishes Fire Resistance Design Manual referenced by major building codes; conducts safety programs for member companies; monitors legislation and regulations.

Kitchen Cabinet Manufacturers Assn., 1899 Preston White Dr., Reston, VA 22091-4326; (703) 264-1690. C. Richard Titus, executive vice president. Fax, (703) 620-6530.

Represents cabinet manufacturers and suppliers to the industry. Provides government relations, management statistics, marketing information, and plant tours and administers cabinet testing and certification programs.

Mechanical Contractors Assn. of America, 1385 Piccard Dr., Rockville, MD 20850; (301) 869-5800. James R. Noble, executive vice president. Fax, (301) 990-9690.

Membership: mechanical contractors and members of related professions. Seeks to improve building standards and codes. Provides information, publications, and training programs; conducts seminars and annual convention; monitors legislation and regulations.

NAHB Research Center, 400 Prince George's Blvd., Upper Marlboro, MD 20772; (301) 249-4000. Liza K. Bowles, president. Fax, (301) 249-0305.

Conducts contract research and product labeling and certification for industry, government, and trade associations related to home building and light commercial industrial building. Research includes energy conservation, new technologies, public health issues, affordable housing, special needs housing for the elderly and persons with disabilities, building codes and standards, land development, and environmental issues. (Affiliated with the National Assn. of Home Builders.)

NAHB Research Center, Radon Research and Indoor Air Quality, 400 Prince George's Blvd., Upper Marlboro, MD 20772; (301) 249-4000. Bob Dewey, manager. Fax, (301) 249-0305.

Serves as information clearinghouse on radon and new home construction; develops site evaluation and radon prevention techniques; monitors development of indoor air quality related codes and standards; measures indoor radon levels and other indoor pollutants. Conducts educational programs; provides home builders and state and local governments with training and technical assistance. Conducts infiltration measurements. (Affiliated with the National Assn. of Home Builders.)

National Assn. of Brick Distributors, 1600 Spring Hill Rd., #305, Vienna, VA 22182; (703) 749-6223. Kenneth S. Dash, president. Fax, (703) 749-6227.

Membership: brick and clay product distributors and manufacturers. Serves as sales and marketing arm of the brick industry; holds annual convention and trade exhibit; conducts educational seminars.

National Assn. of Home Builders, 1201 15th St. N.W. 20005; 822-0200. Kent W. Colton, executive vice president. Fax, 822-0374.

Membership: contractors, builders, architects, engineers, mortgage lenders, and others interested in home building and commercial real estate construction. Participates in updating and developing building codes and standards; offers technical information. Library open to the public.

National Assn. of Minority Contractors, 1333 F St. N.W., #500 20004; 347-8259. Samuel A. Carradine Jr., executive director. Fax, 628-1876.

Membership: minority businesses and related firms, associations, and individuals serving those businesses in the construction industry. Advises members on commercial and government business; develops resources for technical

assistance and training; provides bid information on government contracts.

National Assn. of Plumbing-Heating-Cooling Contractors, 180 S. Washington St., Falls Church, VA (mailing address: P.O. Box 6808, Falls Church, VA 22040); (703) 237-8100. Allen Inlow, chief executive officer. Toll-free, (800) 533-7694. Fax, (703) 237-7442.

Provides education, training, and research for plumbing, heating, and cooling contractors and their employees. Offers career information, internships, and scholarship programs for business and engineering students to encourage careers in the mechanical/electrical contracting field.

National Assn. of the Remodeling Industry, 4301 N. Fairfax Dr., #310, Arlington, VA 22203; (703) 276-7600. William C. Carmichael, executive vice president. Fax, (703) 243-3465.

Membership: remodeling contractors, manufacturers, wholesalers, distributors, lenders, and utilities. Sponsors educational programs on construction products and techniques; provides information on industry statistics and small-business practices; monitors legislation and regulations; publishes consumer information.

National Conference of States on Building Codes and Standards, 505 Huntmar Park Dr., #210, Herndon, VA 22070; (703) 437-0100. Robert Wible, executive director. Library, (703) 481-2023. Fax, (703) 481-3596.

Membership: delegates appointed by governors of the 50 states and territories and individuals and organizations concerned with building standards. Works with HUD to ensure that manufactured housing conforms to HUD standards and codes; seeks to streamline building codes administration in order to reduce housing costs; assists states in improving their building codes, standards, and regulations; promotes local, state, and interstate cooperation; encourages uniform comprehensive building codes and standards. Library open to the public by appointment.

National Institute of Building Sciences, 1201 L St. N.W. 20005; 289-7800. David A. Harris, president. Fax, 289-1092.

Public-private partnership authorized by Congress to improve the regulation of building construction, facilitate the safe introduction of innovative building technology, and disseminate performance criteria and other technical information.

Roof Coatings Manufacturers Assn., 6000 Executive Blvd., #201, Rockville, MD 20852-3803; (301) 230-2501. Richard D. Snyder, executive director. Fax, (301) 881-6572.

Represents the manufacturers of cold-applied protective roof coatings, cements, and systems, and the suppliers of products, equipment, and services to and for the roof coating manufacturing industry.

Safe Buildings Alliance, 655 15th St. N.W. 20005; 879-5120. John F. Welch, president. Fax, 638-2103.

Membership: former producers of building materials containing asbestos. Interests include issues related to asbestos in buildings, including the development of uniform federal and state standards for asbestos identification and abatement, nonremoval alternatives to asbestos in buildings, and the regulation of inspectors and abatement contractors. Provides information; maintains speakers bureau.

See also Asbestos Information Assn./North America (p. 624); National Lumber and Building Material Dealers Assn. (p. 643)

Manufactured Housing

Agencies:

Federal Housing Administration (Housing and Urban Development Dept.), Manufactured Housing and Construction Standards, 490 L'Enfant Plaza East, #3214 (mailing address: HUD Bldg., Rm. B133, Washington, DC 20410); 755-7430. G. Robert Fuller, director. Fax, 755-7445.

Establishes, maintains, and enforces manufactured home safety and construction standards.

Federal Housing Administration (Housing and Urban Development Dept.), Title I Insurance, 490 L'Enfant Plaza East, #3214 (mailing address: HUD Bldg., Rm. B133, Washington, DC 20410); 755-7400. Robert J. Coyle, director. Fax, 708-0299.

Administers programs for insuring approved lending institutions against loss on manufactured home and property improvement loans.

Housing and Urban Development Dept., Affordable Housing Research and Technology, HUD Bldg., Rm. 8132 20410; 708-4370. David Engel, acting director. Fax, 619-8360.

Formulates policy and conducts research on energy issues in housing. Develops energy standards for manufactured housing.

Congress:

See Housing, General, Congress (p. 387)

Nongovernmental:

Center for Auto Safety, 2001 S St. N.W. 20009; 328-7700. Clarence M. Ditlow III, executive director.

Monitors Federal Trade Commission warranty regulations and HUD implementation of federal safety and construction standards for manufactured mobile homes.

Council of American Building Officials, 5203 Leesburg Pike, Falls Church, VA 22041; (703) 931-4533. Richard P. Kuchnicki, chief executive officer. Fax, (703) 379-1546.

Seeks to ensure consistency among model codes; maintains manufactured home construction and safety standards established by the council; oversees building certification program.

Manufactured Housing Institute, 1745 Jefferson Davis Highway, #511, Arlington, VA 22202; (703) 413-6620. Jerry C. Connors, president. Fax, (703) 413-6621.

Represents park owners, financial lenders, and builders, suppliers, and retailers of manufactured homes. Provides information on manufactured home construction standards, finance, site development, property management, and marketing.

See also Building Systems Councils of the National Assn. of Home Builders (p. 390); National Assn. of Home Builders and National Conference of States on Building Codes and Standards (p. 391)

Multifamily Housing: Cooperatives, Condominiums, and Rentals

Agencies:

Federal Housing Administration (Housing and Urban Development Dept.), Administrative Support, HUD Bldg., Rm. 9128 20410; 708-0820. Theodore A. Ford, director. Fax, 708-3716.

Develops policies and procedures for procurement contracting related to the rehabilitation, repair, rental, maintenance, management, demolition, and sale of acquired multifamily and single-family properties and properties under the federal surplus land program. Provides housing program offices with reconditioning and contracting services.

Federal Housing Administration (Housing and Urban Development Dept.), Insured Multifamily Housing Development, HUD Bldg., Rm. 6134 20410; 708-3000. Linda D. Cheatham, director. Fax, 708-3104.

Establishes procedures for the development of housing under the multifamily mortgage insurance programs. Administers the mortgage insurance programs for rental, cooperative, and condominium housing.

Federal Housing Administration (Housing and Urban Development Dept.), Insured Single Family Housing, HUD Bldg., Rm. 9266 20410; 708-3046. John J. Coonts, director. Fax, 708-2582.

Offers a mortgage insurance program for new and existing single-family dwellings (one to four units), including certain cooperatives and condominiums.

Federal Housing Administration (Housing and Urban Development Dept.), Multifamily Housing Management, HUD Bldg., Rm. 6160 20410; 708-3730. Albert Sullivan, director. Fax, 401-3270.

Services mortgages developed under HUD's multifamily mortgage insurance programs, including the Community Disposal Program; reviews management of multifamily housing projects and administers project-based subsidy programs; advises state housing agencies that administer multifamily projects.

Federal Housing Administration (Housing and Urban Development Dept.), Multifamily Housing Programs, HUD Bldg., Rm. 6106 20410; 708-2495. Helen Dunlap, deputy assistant secretary. Fax, 708-2583.

Determines risk and administers programs associated with government-insured mortgage programs, architectural procedures, and land development programs for multifamily housing. Administers some housing assistance programs for low-income persons.

Congress:

See Housing, General, Congress (p. 387)

Nongovernmental:

Community Associations Institute, 1630 Duke St., Alexandria, VA 22314; (703) 548-8600. Barbara Byrd-Lawler, executive vice president. Fax, (703) 684-1581.

Membership: builders, lenders, owners, managers, realtors, insurance companies, public officials, and others associated with condominium or homeowner associations. Provides members with information on creating, financing, and maintaining common facilities and services in condominiums and other planned developments.

Cooperative Housing Foundation, 1010 Wayne Ave., #240, Silver Spring, MD 20910; (301) 587-4700. Michael Doyle, president. Fax, (301) 587-2626.

Works under contract with the Agency for International Development, United Nations, and World Bank to establish local cooperative housing organizations in the United States and to strengthen local government housing departments abroad. Develops and strengthens nonprofit technical service organizations; conducts training workshops; assists tenant groups in converting units into cooperatives; conducts research.

National Apartment Assn., 1111 14th St. N.W., #900 20005; 842-4050. Charles Richard Covert Jr., executive vice president. Fax, 842-4056.

Membership: state and local associations of owners, managers, investors, developers, and builders of apartment houses or other rental properties; conducts educational and professional certification programs; monitors legislation and regulations.

National Assn. of Home Builders, 1201 15th St. N.W. 20005; 822-0200. Kent W. Colton, executive vice president. Fax, 822-0374.

Membership: contractors, builders, architects, engineers, mortgage lenders, and others interested in home building and commercial real estate construction. Offers a Registered Apartment Managers certification program; provides educational programs and information on apartment construction and management, condominiums and cooperatives, multifamily rehabilitation, and low-income and federally assisted housing. Library open to the public.

National Assn. of Housing and Redevelopment Officials, 1320 18th St. N.W. 20036; 429-

2960. Richard Y. Nelson Jr., executive director. Fax, 429-9684.

Membership: housing, community, and urban development practitioners and organizations, and state and local government agencies and personnel. Conducts studies and provides training and certification in the operation and management of rental housing; develops performance standards for low-income rental housing operations.

National Assn. of Housing Cooperatives, 1614 King St., Alexandria, VA 22314; (703) 549-5201. Herbert J. Levy, executive director. Fax, (703) 549-5204.

Membership: housing cooperative members. Promotes housing cooperatives, particularly for low- and moderate-income families; sets standards; provides technical assistance in all phases of cooperative housing; sponsors educational programs and on-site training; monitors legislation; maintains an information clearinghouse on housing cooperatives.

National Center for Housing Management, 1275 K St. N.W., #700 20005; 872-1717. Roger G. Stevens Jr., president. Fax, 789-1179.

Private corporation created by executive order to meet housing management and training needs. Conducts research, demonstrations, and educational and training programs in all types of multifamily housing management. Develops and implements certification systems for housing management programs.

National Cooperative Business Assn., 1401 New York Ave. N.W., #1100 20005; 638-6222. Russell C. Notar, president. Fax, 638-1374.

Alliance of cooperatives, businesses, and state cooperative associations. Provides information about starting and managing cooperatives; monitors legislation and regulations.

National Housing and Rehabilitation Assn., 1726 18th St. N.W. 20009; 328-9171. Peter H. Bell, executive director. Fax, 265-4435.

Membership: development firms and organizations and city, state, and local agencies concerned with multifamily and commercial development. Monitors government policies affecting multifamily development and rehabilitation. Presents project case studies and new financing mechanisms.

National Multi Housing Council, 1850 M St. N.W., #540 20036; 659-3381. Jonathan L. Kempner, president. Fax, 775-0112.

Membership: owners, financiers, managers, and developers of multifamily housing. Advocates policies and programs at the federal, state, and local levels to increase the supply and quality of multifamily units in the United States; serves as a clearinghouse on rent control, condominium conversion, taxes, fair housing, housing for seniors, and environmental issues.

Property Management Assn., 8811 Colesville Rd., #G106, Silver Spring, MD 20910; (301) 587-6543. John P. Bachner, executive vice president. Fax, (301) 589-2017.

Membership: property managers and firms that offer products and services needed in the property management field. Conducts seminars and promotes information exchange on property management practices.

See also Housing, General, Nongovernmental (p. 387)

Single Family Housing

Agencies:

Federal Housing Administration (Housing and Urban Development Dept.), Insured Single Family Housing, HUD Bldg., Rm. 9266 20410; 708-3046. John J. Coonts, director. Fax, 708-2582.

Develops, administers, and services all HUD-insured mortgages on single-family dwellings (one to four units). Guides lenders in originating, servicing, and handling claims of HUD-insured mortgages; guides and assists approved mortgages with HUD requirements; makes policy and provides guidance for HUD field and regional offices on underwriting mortgages, servicing, and disposing of single family properties; establishes acceptable financial risks for the operation of government-insured home mortgage programs.

Federal Housing Administration (Housing and Urban Development Dept.), Single Family Housing, HUD Bldg., Rm. 9282 20410; 708-3175. Vacant, deputy assistant secretary. Fax, 708-2582.

Determines risk and administers programs associated with government-insured mortgage programs, architectural procedures, land development programs for single family housing, and interstate land sales. Administers requirements to obtain and maintain federal government approval of mortgages.

Congress:

See Housing, General, Congress (p. 387)

Nongovernmental:

Home Owners Warranty Corp., 1110 N. Glebe Rd., Arlington, VA 22201; (703) 516-4100. H. Kenneth Seeber, president. Fax, (703) 516-4056.
Administers the Home Owners Warranty Program, which provides for a ten-year insured warranty on new homes through builders registered with the Home Owners Warranty Corp., and the Remodeler Protection Program, which provides coverage for up to ten years.

See also Housing, General, Nongovernmental (p. 387)

Statistics

Agencies:

Census Bureau (Commerce Dept.), Construction Statistics, 3737 Branch Ave., Hillcrest Heights, MD (mailing address: Washington, DC 20233); (301) 763-7163. W. Joel Richardson, chief. Fax, (301) 763-8318.
Publishes statistics on new housing construction, including housing starts, sales, and completions; housing authorized by building permits; price index of single-family homes sold; and characteristics of new housing.

Census Bureau (Commerce Dept.), Housing and Household Economic Statistics, 3737 Branch Ave., Hillcrest Heights, MD (mailing address: Washington, DC 20233); (301) 763-8550. Daniel H. Weinberg, chief. Fax, (301) 763-8412.
Publishes decennial census of housing and the American Housing Survey, which describe housing inventory characteristics. Also publishes a quarterly survey on housing vacancy and a survey of market absorption.

Office of Thrift Supervision (OTS) (Treasury Dept.), Supervisory Systems, 1700 G St. N.W. 20552; 906-6720. Patrick Berbakos, deputy assistant director. Fax, 906-6660.
Provides housing and mortgage statistics, including terms and rates of conventional home mortgages, and asset and liability information for thrift institutions insured by the Savings Association Insurance Fund.

Housing: Finance

General

See also Housing, General (p. 385)

Agencies:

Housing and Urban Development Dept., Economic Affairs, HUD Bldg., Rm. 8204 20410; 708-3080. Frederick J. Eggers, deputy assistant secretary. Fax, 619-8000.
Directs research in public finance and urban economic development; assembles data on housing markets; conducts annual housing surveys; analyzes financial instruments used in housing.

Housing and Urban Development Dept., Housing—Federal Housing Commissioner, HUD Bldg., Rm. 9100 20410; 708-3600. Nicolas P. Retsinas, assistant secretary. Fax, 708-2580.
Administers all Federal Housing Administration (FHA) mortgage insurance programs; approves and monitors all lending institutions that conduct business with HUD.

Congress:

House Banking, Finance, and Urban Affairs Committee, Subcommittee on Financial Institutions Supervision, Regulation, and Deposit Insurance, 212 O'Neill Bldg. (300 New Jersey Ave. S.E.) 20515; 226-3280. Stephen L. Neal, D-N.C., chairman; Peter Kinzler, staff director. Fax, 226-1266.
Jurisdiction over legislation on federal financial regulatory agencies and authorized activities of federally chartered and federally supervised financial institutions.

House Banking, Finance, and Urban Affairs Committee, Subcommittee on Housing and Community Development, B303 RHOB 20515; 225-7054. Henry B. Gonzalez, D-Texas, chairman; Nancy Libson, staff director. Fax, 225-4680.
Jurisdiction over mortgage banking legislation, including mortgage insurance, secondary mortgage markets, and mortgage credit (except programs administered by the Veterans Administration).

House Ways and Means Committee, Subcommittee on Oversight, 1135 LHOB 20515; 225-5522. J. J. Pickle, D-Texas, chairman; Beth K. Vance, staff director. Fax, 225-0787.

Oversees government-sponsored enterprises, including the Federal Home Loan Mortgage Corp. and the Federal National Mortgage Assn., with regard to the financial risk posed to the federal government.

Senate Banking, Housing, and Urban Affairs Committee, SD-534 20510; 224-7391. Donald W. Riegle Jr., D-Mich., chairman; Steven Harris, staff director.

Jurisdiction over legislation on federal financial regulatory agencies and authorized activities of federally chartered and federally supervised financial institutions. Oversees government sponsored enterprises, including the Federal Home Loan Mortgage Corp. and the Federal National Mortgage Assn.

Senate Banking, Housing, and Urban Affairs Committee, Subcommittee on Housing and Urban Affairs, SD-535 20510; 224-6348. Paul S. Sarbanes, D-Md., chairman; Paul N. Weech, staff director. Fax, 224-5137.

Jurisdiction over mortgage banking legislation, including mortgage insurance and secondary mortgage markets.

Nongovernmental:

American Land Title Assn., 1828 L St. N.W., #705 20036; 296-3671. James R. Maher, executive vice president. Fax, 223-5843.

Membership: land title insurance underwriting companies, abstracters, and title insurance agents. Searches, reviews, and insures land titles to protect real estate investors, including home buyers and mortgage lenders; provides industry information; monitors legislation and regulations.

Assn. of Local Housing Finance Agencies, 1101 Connecticut Ave. N.W., #700 20036; 857-1197. John C. Murphy, executive director. Fax, 223-4579.

Membership: professionals of city and county government that finance affordable housing. Provides professional development programs in new housing finance and other areas; monitors legislation and regulations.

National Council of State Housing Agencies, 444 N. Capitol St. N.W., #438 20001; 624-7710.

John McEvoy, executive director. Fax, 624-5899.

Membership: state housing finance agencies. Promotes greater opportunities for lower-income people to rent or buy affordable housing.

Mortgage Banking

Agencies:

Federal Housing Finance Board, 1777 F St. N.W. 20006; 408-2525. Vacant, chairman. Information, 408-2500. Press, 408-2986. Fax, 408-1435. Public reading room, 408-2969.

Regulates and supervises the credit and financing operations of the twelve Federal Home Loan Banks, which provide a flexible credit reserve for member institutions engaged in home mortgage lending. Member institutions of the Federal Home Loan Banks include savings and loans, savings banks, commercial banks, credit unions, insurance companies, and other financial intermediaries.

Office of Thrift Supervision (OTS) (Treasury Dept.), 1700 G St. N.W. 20552; 906-6280. Jonathan L. Fiechter, acting director. Information, 906-6677. Library, 906-6470. Fax, 898-0230. Mortgage rates recording, 906-6988. Toll-free recording, (800) 424-5405.

Charters, regulates, and examines the operations of savings and loan institutions. Library open to the public.

Congress:

See Housing: Finance, General, Congress (p. 395)

Nongovernmental:

American Council of State Savings Supervisors, P.O. Box 34175, Washington, DC 20043; 371-0666. Phylis Bird, executive director.

Membership: state savings and loan supervisors; associate members include state-chartered savings and loan associations and savings institutions. Monitors legislation and regulations on states' rights issues.

American League of Financial Institutions, 900 19th St. N.W., #400 20006; 628-5624. John W. Harshaw, president. Fax, 296-8716.

Membership: minority-controlled federal- and state-chartered savings and loan associations. Provides members and other minority groups with organizational and managerial advice; offers on-site technical assistance to resolve problems in operations. Encourages financing of low- and moderate-income housing and promotes community reinvestment activities. Monitors legislation and regulations.

Savings and Community Bankers of America, 900 19th St. N.W., #400 20006; 857-3100. Paul A. Schosberg, president. Fax, 296-8716.

Membership: insured depository institutions involved in community finance. Provides information on issues that affect the industry. Monitors economic issues affecting savings institutions; publishes homebuyers survey; monitors legislation and regulations.

The Urban Institute, Center for Public Finance and Housing, 2100 M St. N.W. 20037; 857-8585. G. Thomas Kingsley, director. Fax, 452-1840.

Research organization that deals with urban problems. Evaluates federal insurance and tax policies as they affect housing; conducts research for state governments on improvements to state tax policy; studies alternative mortgage instruments and secondary markets.

See also Mortgage Bankers Assn. of America (p. 398); National Urban Coalition (p. 384)

Mortgage Insurance and Guarantees

Agencies:

Federal Housing Administration (Housing and Urban Development Dept.), Insured Multifamily Housing Development, HUD Bldg., Rm. 6134 20410; 708-3000. Linda D. Cheatham, director. Fax, 708-3104.

Establishes procedures for the development of housing under the multifamily mortgage insurance programs. Administers the mortgage insurance programs for rental, cooperative, and condominium housing.

Federal Housing Administration (Housing and Urban Development Dept.), Insured Single Family Housing, HUD Bldg., Rm. 9266 20410; 708-3046. John J. Coonts, director. Fax, 708-2582.

Establishes acceptable financial risks for the operation of government-insured mortgage programs for single-family properties (one to four units); monitors and oversees HUD-approved local counseling agencies for Federal Housing Administration programs.

Federal Housing Administration (Housing and Urban Development Dept.), Title I Insurance, 490 L'Enfant Plaza East S.W., #3214 (mailing address: HUD Bldg., Rm. B133, Washington, DC 20410); 755-7400. Robert J. Coyle, director. Fax, 708-0299.

Administers programs for insuring approved lending institutions against loss on manufactured home and property improvement loans.

Congress:

See Housing: Finance, General, Congress (p. 395)

Nongovernmental:

Mortgage Insurance Companies of America, 727 15th St. N.W. 20005; 393-5566. Suzanne C. Hutchinson, executive vice president. Fax, 393-5557.

Membership: companies that provide default coverage on residential, high-ratio mortgage loans. Insures lenders against loss from default on low down payment home mortgages and provides coverage that acts as a credit enhancement on mortgage securities.

Secondary Mortgage Market

Agencies:

Government National Mortgage Assn. (Ginnie Mae) (Housing and Urban Development Dept.), HUD Bldg., Rm. 6100 20410; 708-0926. Dwight P. Robinson, president. Fax, 708-0490.

Supports government housing objectives by establishing secondary markets for residential mortgages. Serves as a vehicle for channeling funds from the securities markets into the mortgage market through mortgage-backed securities programs and helps to increase the supply of credit available for housing. Guarantees privately issued securities backed by Federal Housing Administration, Veterans Affairs Dept., and Farmers Home Administration mortgages.

Congress:

See Housing: Finance, General, Congress (p. 395)

Nongovernmental:

Federal Agricultural Mortgage Corp. (Farmer Mac), 919 18th St. N.W., #200 20006; 872-7700. Thomas R. Clark, vice president.

Private corporation chartered by Congress to provide a secondary mortgage market for farm and rural housing loans. Guarantees principal and interest repayment on securities backed by farm and rural housing loans.

Federal Home Loan Mortgage Corp. (Freddie Mac), 8200 Jones Branch Rd., McLean, VA 22102; (703) 903-3000. Leland C. Brendsel, chairman. Information, (703) 759-8160. Fax, (703) 903-3495.

Chartered by Congress to increase the flow of funds for residential mortgages by buying conventional mortgages and selling mortgage securities to major investors.

Federal National Mortgage Assn. (Fannie Mae), 3900 Wisconsin Ave. N.W. 20016; 752-7000. James A. Johnson, chairman. Information, 752-7124. Press, 752-5962. Library, 752-7750. Fax, 752-6014.

Congressionally chartered, shareholder-owned corporation. Makes mortgage funds available by buying conventional and government-insured mortgages in the secondary mortgage market; raises its capital through sale of short- and long-term obligations, mortgages, and stock; issues and guarantees mortgage-backed securities.

Mortgage Bankers Assn. of America, 1125 15th St. N.W. 20005; 861-6500. Warren Lasko, executive vice president. Fax, 785-2968.

Membership: institutions involved in real estate finance. Maintains School of Mortgage Banking; collects statistics on the industry. Conducts seminars and workshops in specialized areas of mortgage finance. Monitors legislation and regulations affecting mortgage finance. Library open to the public by appointment.

Housing: Special Concerns

See also Social Services and Rehabilitation Programs, Homeless (p. 426); Veterans, Housing Loans (p. 439)

General

Agencies:

Farmers Home Administration (Agriculture Dept.), 14th St. and Independence Ave. S.W. 20250; 720-6903. Michael Dunn, administrator. Information, 720-4323. Fax, 690-0311.

Offers financial assistance to apartment dwellers, homeowners, and farmers in rural areas.

Farmers Home Administration (Agriculture Dept.), Equal Opportunity, 14th St. and Independence Ave. S.W. 20250; 245-5528. Walter Y. Fredericks, acting director. Fax, 245-5499.

Enforces compliance with laws prohibiting discrimination in credit transactions on the basis of sex, marital status, race, color, religion, age, or handicap. Ensures equal opportunity in granting Farmers Home Administration housing, farm ownership, and operating loans, and a variety of community and business program loans.

Housing and Urban Development Dept., Homeownership and Opportunity for People Everywhere (HOPE 3), HUD Bldg., Rm. 7158 20410; 708-0324. John D. Garrity, director. Fax, 708-1744.

Provides low-income families and individuals with opportunities to buy homes. Provides eligible home buyers with federal assistance to purchase homes or to rehabilitate single-family properties. Awards grants to nonprofit or public agencies in cooperation with nonprofit agencies to acquire or rehabilitate single-family properties for sale and occupancy by eligible families at affordable prices.

Justice Dept., Civil Rights, Main Justice Bldg. 20530; 514-2151. Deval Patrick, assistant attorney general. Information, 514-2007. Library, 514-4098. Fax, 514-0293. TDD, 472-1953.

Enforces federal civil rights laws prohibiting discrimination on the basis of race, color, religion, sex, disability, age, or national origin in housing, public accommodations and facilities, and credit and federally assisted programs.

Congress:

House Banking, Finance, and Urban Affairs Committee, Subcommittee on Housing and Community Development, B303 RHOB 20515; 225-7054. Henry B. Gonzalez, D-Texas, chairman; Nancy Libson, staff director. Fax, 225-4680.

Jurisdiction over all housing legislation, including housing allowances, housing for the elderly and people with disabilities, public housing, and subsidized housing.

House Judiciary Committee, Subcommittee on Civil and Constitutional Rights, 806 O'Neill Bldg. (300 New Jersey Ave. S.E.) 20515; 226-

7680. Don Edwards, D-Calif., chairman; Catherine A. LeRoy, chief counsel.

Jurisdiction over fair housing legislation pertaining to discrimination against minorities.

Senate Banking, Housing, and Urban Affairs Committee, Subcommittee on Housing and Urban Affairs, SD-535 20510; 224-6348. Paul S. Sarbanes, D-Md., chairman; Paul N. Weech, staff director. Fax, 224-5137.

Jurisdiction over all housing legislation, including housing allowances, housing for the elderly and people with disabilities, public housing, and subsidized housing.

Senate Judiciary Committee, Subcommittee on the Constitution, SD-524 20510; 224-5573. Paul Simon, D-Ill., chairman; Susan D. Kaplan, chief counsel.

Jurisdiction over fair housing legislation, including legislation pertaining to discrimination against minorities. (Jurisdiction shared with the Labor and Human Resources Committee.)

Senate Special Committee on Aging, SD-G31 20510; 224-5364. David Pryor, D-Ark., chairman; Theresa M. Forster, staff director.

Studies and makes recommendations on housing access for the elderly.

Nongovernmental:

National Foundation for Affordable Housing Solutions, 11200 Rockville Pike, Rockville, MD 20852; (301) 468-3100. Martin C. Schwartzberg, president. Fax, (301) 231-0369.

Works to maintain the existing stock of affordable housing; encourages development of new affordable housing through public/private partnerships; designs and tests model programs for linking social services to housing.

National Housing Conference, 815 15th St. N.W., #601 20005; 393-5772. Robert J. Reid, executive director. Fax, 393-5656.

Membership: state and local housing officials, community development specialists, builders, bankers, lawyers, civic leaders, tenants, architects and planners, labor and religious groups, and national housing and housing-related organizations. Mobilizes public support for community development and affordable housing programs; conducts educational sessions.

National Low Income Housing Coalition, 1012 14th St. N.W., #1200 20005; 662-1530. Cushing N. Dolbeare, acting president. Fax, 393-1973.

Membership: individuals and organizations interested in low-income housing. Works for decent, affordable housing and freedom of housing choice for low-income citizens. Provides information and technical assistance through the Low Income Housing Information Service. Monitors legislation.

National Rural Housing Coalition, 601 Pennsylvania Ave. N.W., #850 20004; 393-5229. Robert A. Rapoza, legislative director. Fax, 393-3034.

Advocates improved housing for low-income rural families; works to increase public awareness of rural housing problems; monitors legislation.

National Trust for Historic Preservation, 1785 Massachusetts Ave. N.W. 20036; 673-4000. Richard Moe, president. Fax, 673-4038.

Conducts seminars, workshops, and conferences on topics related to preservation, including neighborhood conservation, main street revitalization, rural conservation, and preservation law; offers financial assistance through loan and grant programs; provides advisory services; operates historic house museums, which are open to the public.

See also Local Initiatives Support Corp. (p. 380)

Elderly and Disabled

Agencies:

Farmers Home Administration (Agriculture Dept.), Housing Programs, 14th St. and Independence Ave. S.W. 20250; 720-5177. Ronnie O. Tharrington, assistant administrator. Fax, 690-3025.

Makes loans in rural communities (population under 20,000) to borrowers, including the elderly and people with disabilities, below a certain income level, for buying, building, or improving single-family houses. Administers the Rural Rental Housing Program, which provides loans for building rental units in rural communities and grab bars and doorways that accommodate wheelchairs. Administers Rural Housing Preservation Grants, which provide communities with funds for rehabilitating single-family housing owned or occupied by low-income persons or families. Offers Congregate Housing

Program, in conjunction with the Administration on Aging, which gives housing assistance and social services to the handicapped and the elderly.

Federal Housing Administration (Housing and Urban Development Dept.), Elderly and Assisted Housing, HUD Bldg., Rm. 6130 20410; 708-2730. Margaret Milner, director. Fax, 708-2583.

Administers rental assistance, moderate rehabilitation, and housing programs for the elderly and people with disabilities. Provides grants for housing for the elderly and people with disabilities under Section 202 of the Housing Act of 1959.

Housing and Urban Development Dept., Fair Housing and Equal Opportunity, HUD Bldg., Rm. 5100 20410; 708-4252. Roberta Achtenberg, assistant secretary. Information, 708-0980. Fax, 708-4483. Housing discrimination hotline, (800) 669-9777; in Washington, D.C., 708-3500.

Monitors compliance with legislation requiring equal opportunities in housing for people with disabilities. Monitors compliance with construction codes to accommodate people with disabilities in multifamily dwellings. Hotline answers inquiries about housing discrimination.

Congress:

See Housing: Special Concerns, General, Congress (p. 398)

Nongovernmental:

American Assn. of Homes for the Aging, 901 E St. N.W., #500 20004-2037; 783-2242. Michael Rodgers, senior vice president, policy and governmental affairs. Fax, 783-2255.

Membership: nonprofit nursing homes, housing, and health-related facilities for the elderly. Provides research and technical assistance on housing and long-term care for the elderly; conducts certification program for retirement housing professionals. Operates a capital formation program to procure financing for new housing facilities for the elderly; monitors legislation and regulations.

American Assn. of Retired Persons, 601 E St. N.W. 20049; 434-6030. Katrinka Smith Sloan, manager, consumer affairs. Fax, 434-6466.

Membership association concerned with problems of preretired and retired persons, including

housing. Offers consultation and information services to organizations and consumers interested in housing for older persons. Supports affordable and appropriate housing for older Americans, including shared housing, continuing care, and home equity conversion. Library open to the public.

Assisted Living Facilities Assn. of America, 9401 Lee Highway, #402, Fairfax, VA 22031; (703) 691-8100. Carol F. Fisk, executive director. Fax, (703) 691-8106.

Promotes the development of standards and increased awareness for the assisted living industry. Provides members with information on policy, funding access, and quality of care. Interests include funding alternatives to make assisted living available to all who need it. Monitors legislation and regulations.

B'nai B'rith International, Senior Citizens Housing Committee, 1640 Rhode Island Ave. N.W. 20036; 857-6581. Mark D. Olshan, director. Fax, 857-0980.

Works with local groups to sponsor federally assisted housing for independent low-income senior citizens and the handicapped, regardless of race or religion.

Council of American Building Officials, 5203 Leesburg Pike, Falls Church, VA 22041; (703) 931-4533. Richard P. Kuchnicki, chief executive officer. Fax, (703) 379-1546.

Provides review board for the American National Standards Institute handicapped accessibility standards, which ensure that buildings are accessible to people with physical disabilities.

National Council on the Aging, 409 3rd St. S.W. 20024; 479-1200. Daniel Thursz, president. Library, 479-6669. Fax, 479-0735. TDD, 479-6674.

Membership: individuals, voluntary agencies and associations, businesses, and labor unions serving or concerned with the elderly. Acts as an information clearinghouse on aging; sponsors institutes for the elderly on housing and independent living, rural housing and health needs, and financial issues; provides the elderly with information, technical assistance, and training programs on housing operations and services. Library open to the public.

See also National Multi Housing Council (p. 394)

Minorities

Agencies:

Bureau of Indian Affairs (Interior Dept.), Housing Assistance, 1849 C St. N.W. (mailing address: Main Interior Bldg., Mail Stop 2525, Washington, DC 20240); 208-3671. A. Ronald Thurman, chief. Fax, 208-3086.

Administers one-time grant program that assists federally recognized tribes in renovating and improving existing housing and in constructing new housing; advises tribes about assistance available through other programs.

Housing and Urban Development Dept., Fair Housing and Equal Opportunity, HUD Bldg., Rm. 5100 20410; 708-4252. Roberta Achtenberg, assistant secretary. Information, 708-0980. Fax, 708-4483. Housing discrimination hotline, (800) 669-9777; in Washington, D.C., 708-3500.

Monitors compliance with legislation requiring equal opportunities in housing for minorities, people with disabilities, and families with children. Monitors compliance with construction codes to accommodate people with disabilities in multifamily dwellings. Hotline answers inquiries about housing discrimination.

Housing and Urban Development Dept., Funded Programs, HUD Bldg., Rm. 5234 20410; 708-0455. Marcella Brown, director. Fax, 708-2755.

Awards grants to public and private organizations and to state and local agencies. Funded projects work to educate the public about fair housing rights; programs are designed to prevent or eliminate discriminatory housing practices.

Housing and Urban Development Dept., Native American Programs, HUD Bldg., Rm. 4140 20410; 708-1015. Dom Nessi, director. Fax, 401-5351.

Works through tribal and state housing authorities to assess housing needs; directs native Americans to HUD programs; provides native American housing authorities with financial and technical assistance for developing low-income projects in native American areas.

Housing and Urban Development Dept., State and Small Cities, HUD Bldg., Rm. 7184 20410; 708-1322. Richard J. Kennedy, director. Fax, 708-1744.

Provides states with grants for distribution to small cities not entitled to community development block grants; tribes and insular areas also are eligible for the grants.

Office of Thrift Supervision (Treasury Dept.), Consumer Programs, 1700 G St. N.W. 20552; 906-6238. Gilda Morse, manager. Fax, 906-7494. Consumer complaints, (800) 842-6929.

Handles complaints of discrimination against minorities and women by savings and loan associations; gives technical assistance to minority-owned or minority-controlled savings and loan institutions.

Congress:

See *Housing: Special Concerns, General, Congress (p. 398)*

Nongovernmental:

Center for Community Change, 1000 Wisconsin Ave. N.W. 20007; 342-0519. Pablo Eisenberg, executive director. Fax, 342-1132.

Provides community-based organizations serving minorities and the economically disadvantaged with technical assistance. Areas of assistance include community development block grants, housing, economic and resource development, rural development projects, and program planning.

NAACP Legal Defense and Educational Fund, 1275 K St. N.W., #301 20005; 682-1300. Elaine Jones, director. Fax, 682-1312.

Civil rights litigation group that provides legal information on civil rights and advice on housing discrimination against women and minorities; monitors federal enforcement of civil rights laws. Not affiliated with the National Association for the Advancement of Colored People (NAACP). (Headquarters in New York.)

National American Indian Housing Council, 900 2nd St. N.E., #220 20002; 789-1754. Ruth A. Jaure, executive director. Fax, 789-1758.

Membership: native American housing authorities. Clearinghouse for information on native American housing issues; works for safe and sanitary dwellings for native American and Alaska native communities; monitors HUD policies and housing legislation; provides members with training and technical assistance in managing housing assistance programs.

National Assn. for the Advancement of Colored People (NAACP), 1025 Vermont Ave. N.W., #1120 20005; 638-2269. Wade J. Henderson, director, Washington bureau. Fax, 638-5936.

Membership: persons interested in civil rights for all minorities. Works to eliminate discrimination in housing and urban affairs. (Headquarters in Baltimore.)

National Assn. of Real Estate Brokers, 1629 K St. N.W., #306 20006; 785-4477. H. Bernie Jackson, vice president. Fax, 785-1244.

Membership: minority real estate brokers, appraisers, contractors, property managers, and salespersons. Works to prevent discrimination in housing policies and practices; conducts regional seminars on federal policy, legislation, and regulations; advises members on procedures for procuring federal contracts.

National Urban League, 1111 14th St. N.W., #600 20005; 898-1604. Robert McAlpine, director, policy and government relations. Fax, 682-0782.

Federation of affiliates concerned with the social welfare of African Americans and other minorities. Conducts research studies and demonstration projects on housing and urban affairs. (Headquarters in New York.)

See also National Council of La Raza (p. 381)

Public and Subsidized Housing

See also Social Services and Rehabilitation Programs, Homeless (p. 426); Social Services and Rehabilitation Programs, Low-Income Groups and Public Assistance Recipients (p. 428)

Agencies:

Federal Housing Administration (Housing and Urban Development Dept.), Moderate Rehabilitation, HUD Bldg., Rm. 4226 20410; 708-7424. Gary Bowen, director. Fax, 401-6867.

Provides rental subsidies to lower-income families living in housing that was formerly substandard but has been upgraded through the program.

Federal Housing Administration (Housing and Urban Development Dept.), Rental Assistance, HUD Bldg., Rm. 4226 20410; 708-2841. Madeline Hastings, director. Fax, 401-6867.

Administers certificate and housing voucher programs authorized by Section 8 of the Housing Act of 1937, as amended.

Housing and Urban Development Dept., Assisted Housing, HUD Bldg., Rm. 4204 20410; 708-1380. Maryann Russ, director. Fax, 401-3963.

Establishes policies and procedures for low-income public housing programs, including security, special needs for the elderly and people with disabilities, standards for rental and occupancy, and financial management.

Housing and Urban Development Dept., Construction, Rehabilitation, and Maintenance, HUD Bldg., Rm. 4138 20410; 708-1800. Janice Rattley, director. Fax, 401-5351.

Establishes development policies and procedures for low-income housing programs, including criteria for site approval and construction standards; establishes policies for utilities and maintenance engineering; oversees administration of the Comprehensive Improvement Assistance Program for modernizing existing public housing.

Housing and Urban Development Dept., Entitlement Communities, HUD Bldg., Rm. 7282 20410; 708-1577. James R. Broughman, director. Fax, 708-3363.

Provides entitled cities and counties with block grants to provide housing and economic opportunity for low- and moderate-income people.

Congress:

See Housing: Special Concerns, General, Congress (p. 398)

Nongovernmental:

Affordable Housing Consortium, 11200 Rockville Pike, 4th Floor, Rockville, MD 20852; (301) 468-3100. Martin Schwartzberg, president. Fax, (301) 231-0369.

Facilitates the transfer of rental housing properties from private ownership to community-based nonprofits and public entities for long-term use by low-income tenants. Ensures the long-term viability of the properties and the enhanced self-sufficiency of their residents.

Housing Assistance Council, 1025 Vermont Ave. N.W., #606 20005; 842-8600. Moises Loza, executive director. Toll-free, (800) 989-4422 Fax, 347-3441.

Operates in rural areas and in cities of fewer than 25,000 citizens. Advises low-income and minority groups seeking federal assistance for improving rural housing and community facilities; studies and makes recommendations for state and local housing policies; makes low-interest loans for housing programs for low-income and minority groups living in rural areas, including native Americans and farm workers.

National Assn. of Home Builders, 1201 15th St. N.W. 20005; 822-0200. Kent W. Colton, executive vice president. Fax, 822-0374.
Membership: contractors, builders, architects, engineers, mortgage lenders, and others interested in home building and commercial real estate construction. Offers educational programs and information on low-income federally assisted housing. Library open to the public.

National Leased Housing Assn., 2300 M St. N.W., #260 20037; 785-8888. Denise Muha, executive director. Fax, 785-2008.

Membership: public and private organizations and individuals who follow developments in multifamily, government-assisted housing programs. Monitors legislation and federal regulations and conducts training seminars.

The Urban Institute, Center for Public Finance and Housing, 2100 M St. N.W. 20037; 857-8585. G. Thomas Kingsley, director. Fax, 452-1840.

Research organization that studies and proposes solutions to urban problems. Researches housing policy problems, including housing management, public housing programs, and rent control.

See also nongovernmental sections of Community Planning and Development, General (p. 379); Community Planning and Development, Urban Redevelopment and Relocation (p. 384); Housing, Multifamily Housing: Cooperatives, Condominiums, and Rentals (p. 393)

Key Agencies:

Agriculture Dept.
Food and Nutrition Service
3101 Park Center Dr.
Alexandria, VA 22302
Information: (703) 305-2276

Health and Human Services Dept.
200 Independence Ave. S.W. 20201
Information: 690-6867

Social Security Administration (Health and Human Services Dept.)
6401 Security Blvd., Baltimore, MD 21235
(Washington office: 200 Independence Ave. S.W. 20201)
Information: (410) 965-7700, Baltimore

Veterans Affairs Dept.
801 Eye St. N.W. (mailing address: 810 Vermont Ave. N.W. 20420)
Information: 535-8165

Key Committees:

House Education and Labor Committee
2181 RHOB 20515
Phone: 225-4527

House Veterans' Affairs Committee
335 CHOB 20515
Phone: 225-3527

House Ways and Means Committee
1102 LHOB 20515
Phone: 225-3625

Senate Finance Committee
SD-205 20510
Phone: 224-4515

Senate Labor and Human Resources Committee
SD-428 20510
Phone: 224-5375

Senate Special Committee on Aging
SD-G31 20510
Phone: 224-5364

Senate Veterans' Affairs Committee
SR-414 20510
Phone: 224-9126

Key Personnel:

Agriculture Dept.
Ellen Haas, assistant secretary for food and consumer services

Health and Human Services Dept.
Donna E. Shalala, secretary
Mary Jo Bane, assistant secretary for children and families
Shirley S. Chater, commissioner, Social Security Administration

Labor Dept.
Gen. Preston Taylor Jr., assistant secretary for veterans' employment and training

Veterans Affairs Dept.
Jesse Brown, secretary
Hershel W. Gober, deputy secretary
David Burge, acting assistant secretary for policy and planning
Raymond J. Vogel, under secretary for benefits
Dr. John T. Farrar, acting under secretary for health, Veterans Health Administration
Jerry Bowen, director, national cemetery system

10

Social Services and Veterans' Programs

Contents:

Government Financial Assistance Programs

General

Agencies:

Health and Human Services Dept., 200 Independence Ave. S.W., #61SF 20201; 690-7000. Donna E. Shalala, secretary. Fax, 690-7203.
Acts as principal adviser to the president on health, welfare, and income security plans, policies, and programs of the federal government. Encompasses the Social Security Administration, Health Care Financing Administration, Administration for Children and Families, the Public Health Service, and the Centers for Disease Control and Prevention.

Congress:

General Accounting Office, Human Resources, 441 G St. N.W., NGB/ACG 20548; 512-6806. Janet L. Shikles, assistant comptroller general. Fax, 512-5806.
Independent, nonpartisan agency in the legislative branch. Audits, analyzes, and evaluates Health and Human Services Dept. programs; makes reports available to the public.

House Agriculture Committee, Subcommittee on Department Operations and Nutrition, 1301A LHOB 20515; 225-1496. Charles W. Stenholm, D-Texas, chairman; Stan Ray, staff director.
Jurisdiction over food stamp legislation.

House Appropriations Committee, Subcommittee on Labor, Health and Human Services, and Education, 2358 RHOB 20515; 225-3508. Neal Smith, D-Iowa, chairman; Mike Stephens, staff assistant.
Jurisdiction over legislation to appropriate funds for all Health and Human Services Dept. programs, except the Food and Drug Administration and native American health programs.

House Education and Labor Committee, Subcommittee on Elementary, Secondary, and Vocational Education, B-346A RHOB 20515; 225-

4368. Dale E. Kildee, D-Mich., chairman; Susan Wilhelm, staff director. Fax, 225-1110.
Jurisdiction over legislation on the National School Lunch Program, the School Breakfast Program, the Summer Food Program for Children, the Special Milk Program for Children, and the Special Supplemental Food Program for Women, Infants, and Children (WIC).

House Ways and Means Committee, Subcommittee on Human Resources, B317 RHOB 20515; 225-1025. Harold E. Ford, D-Tenn., chairman; Richard Hobbie, staff director. Fax, 225-9480.
Jurisdiction over legislation on Aid to Families with Dependent Children, child support enforcement, child welfare, child care, foster care, adoption assistance, supplemental security income, unemployment compensation and insurance, low-income energy assistance, eligibility of welfare recipients for food stamps, and welfare programs.

Senate Agriculture, Nutrition, and Forestry Committee, SR-328A 20510; 224-2035. Patrick J. Leahy, D-Vt., chairman; Charles Riemenschneider, chief of staff.
Jurisdiction over legislation on low-income energy assistance programs.

Senate Agriculture, Nutrition, and Forestry Committee, Subcommittee on Nutrition and Investigations, SR-328A 20510; 224-2035. Tom Harkin, D-Iowa, chairman; Mark Halverson, legislative assistant.
Jurisdiction over legislation on commodity donations, the Food Stamp Program, the National School Lunch Program, the School Breakfast Program, the Summer Food Program for Children, the Special Milk Program for Children, the Special Supplemental Food Program for Women, Infants, and Children (WIC), and nutritional programs for the elderly.

Senate Appropriations Committee, Subcommittee on Labor, Health and Human Services, and Education, SD-186 20510; 224-7283. Tom Harkin, D-Iowa, chairman; Ed Long, clerk.
Jurisdiction over legislation to appropriate funds for all Health and Human Services Dept.

programs, except the Food and Drug Administration and native American health programs.

Senate Finance Committee, Subcommittee on Social Security and Family Policy, SD-205 20510; 224-4515. John B. Breaux, D-La., chairman; Laird D. Burnett, staff contact.

Holds hearings on legislation concerning Aid to Families with Dependent Children, child support enforcement, child welfare, child care, foster care, adoption assistance, supplemental security income, unemployment compensation and insurance, and welfare programs.

Senate Labor and Human Resources Committee, Subcommittee on Children, Families, Drugs, and Alcoholism, SH-639 20510; 224-5630. Christopher J. Dodd, D-Conn., chairman; Sarah Flanagan, staff director.

Jurisdiction over eligibility of welfare recipients for food stamps.

Aid to Families with Dependent Children

Agencies·

Administration for Children and Families (Health and Human Services Dept.), Family Assistance, 901 D St. S.W. (mailing address: 370 L'Enfant Promenade S.W., Washington, DC 20447); 401-9275. Diann Dawson, acting director. Fax, 205-5887.

Administers federal matching grants to states for the income maintenance payments made under the Aid to Families with Dependent Children (AFDC) program. Administers federal matching grants to states for payments made to families under the Emergency Assistance Program. Prepares studies and compiles statistics on AFDC programs.

Congress:

See *Government Financial Assistance Programs, General, Congress (p. 406)*

Child Nutrition Programs

See also Consumer Affairs, Food and Nutrition (p. 258)

Agencies:

Agriculture Dept., Child Nutrition, 3101 Park Center Dr., Alexandria, VA 22302; (703) 305-

2590. Alberta Frost, director. Fax, (703) 305-2879.

Administers the transfer of funds to state agencies for the National School Lunch Program; the School Breakfast Program; the Special Milk Program, which helps schools and institutions provide children who do not have access to full meals under other child nutrition programs with fluid milk; the Child and Adult Care Food Program, which provides children in nonresidential child-care centers and family day care homes with year-round meal service; and the Summer Food Service Program, which provides children from low-income families with meals during the summer months.

Agriculture Dept., Food and Nutrition, 3101 Park Center Dr., Alexandria, VA 22302; (703) 305-2062. William Ludwig, administrator. Information, (703) 305-2276. Fax, (703) 305-2908.

Administers all Agriculture Dept. domestic food assistance programs, including the distribution of funds and food for school breakfast and lunch programs (preschool through secondary) to public and nonprofit private schools; the food stamp program; and a special supplemental food program for women, infants, and children (WIC).

Agriculture Dept., Food Distribution, 3101 Park Center Dr., #503, Alexandria, VA 22302; (703) 305-2680. Vernon Morgan, director. Fax, (703) 305-2420. TDD, (703) 305-2648.

Administers the purchasing and distribution of food to state agencies for child care centers, public and private schools, public and nonprofit charitable institutions, and summer camps. Coordinates the distribution of special commodities, including surplus cheese and butter. Administers the National Commodity Processing Program, which facilitates distribution, at reduced prices, of processed foods to state agencies.

Agriculture Dept., Nutrition and Technical Services, 3101 Park Center Dr., #607, Alexandria, VA 22302; (703) 305-2585. Joseph E. Shepherd, director. Fax, (703) 305-2549.

Administers the Nutrition Education and Training Program, which provides states with grants for disseminating nutrition information to children and for in-service training of food service and teaching personnel; administers the Child Nutrition Labeling Program, which certifies that foods served in child nutrition programs, particularly school lunch and breakfast programs, meet nutritional requirements.

Agriculture Dept., Supplemental Food Programs, 3101 Park Center Dr., Alexandria, VA 22302; (703) 305-2746. Stanley C. Garnett, director. Fax, (703) 305-2420.

Provides health departments and agencies with federal funding for food supplements and administrative expenses to make food, nutrition education, and health services available to infants, young children, and pregnant, nursing, and postpartum women.

Congress:

See Government Financial Assistance Programs, General, Congress (p. 406)

Nongovernmental:

Child Nutrition Forum, 1875 Connecticut Ave. N.W., #540 20009-5728; 986-2200. Edward Cooney, coordinator. Fax, 986-2525.

Membership: agriculture, labor, education, and health specialists; school food service officials; and consumer and religious groups. Supports federal nutrition programs for children; provides information on school nutrition programs; monitors legislation and regulations concerning hunger issues.

National Congress of Parents and Teachers, 2000 L St. N.W., #600 20036; 331-1380. Arnold F. Fege, director, governmental relations.

Membership: parent-teacher associations at the preschool, elementary, and secondary levels. Supports school lunch and breakfast programs; active member of the School Lunch Coalition, which supports federally funded nutrition programs for children. (Headquarters in Chicago.)

Nurture/Center to Prevent Childhood Malnutrition, 4948 St. Elmo Ave., #208, Bethesda, MD 20814; (301) 907-8601. Sandra Huffman, president. Fax, (301) 907-8603.

Works to improve child nutrition worldwide through policy analysis and evaluation of community-based self-help nutrition projects in the United States, Peru, and Ghana. (Affiliated with the Dept. of International Health, Johns Hopkins University.)

Food Stamps

See also Social Services and Rehabilitation Programs, Low-Income Groups and Public Assistance Recipients (p. 428)

Agencies:

Agriculture Dept., Food Stamp Program, 3101 Park Center Dr., Alexandria, VA 22302; (703) 305-2026. Bonny O'Neil, acting deputy administrator. Information, (703) 305-2276. Fax, (703) 305-2454. TDD, (703) 305-2349.

Administers, through state welfare agencies, the Food Stamp Program, which provides needy persons with food coupons to increase food purchasing power. Provides matching funds to cover half the cost of coupon issuance.

Congress:

See Government Financial Assistance Programs, General, Congress (p. 406)

Nongovernmental:

See Interfaith Impact for Justice and Peace (p. 278)

Refugees and Repatriated Americans

See also Foreign Policy and Aid, Disaster Relief and Refugees (p. 449); Immigration and Naturalization (p. 468)

Agencies:

Administration for Children and Families (Health and Human Services Dept.), Refugee Resettlement, 901 D St. S.W., 6th Floor (mailing address: 370 L'Enfant Promenade S.W., Washington, DC 20447); 401-9246. Lavinia Limon, director. Fax, 401-5487.

Directs a domestic resettlement program for refugees; reimburses states for costs incurred in giving refugees monetary and medical assistance; awards funds to private resettlement agencies for providing refugees with monetary assistance and case management; provides states and nonprofit agencies with grants for social services such as English and employment training.

Administration for Children and Families (Health and Human Services Dept.), Repatriate Program, 901 D St. S.W. 20447; 401-9246. Lavinia Limon, director. Information, 401-9324.

Administers and operates a repatriation program available to State Dept.-certified U.S. citizens returning from foreign countries because of destitution, illness, or emergencies. Reimburses state and local governments for transportation from port of entry; food, shelter, and clothing; and medical care, including hospitalization.

State Dept., Refugee Programs, Main State Bldg. 20520-5824; 647-7360. Phyllis E. Oakley, acting director. Information, 663-1026. Fax, 647-8162.

Develops and implements programs and policies on international refugee matters, including repatriation and resettlement programs; funds and monitors overseas relief, assistance, and repatriation programs; manages refugee admission to the United States.

Congress:

House Judiciary Committee, Subcommittee on International Law, Immigration, and Refugees, B370B RHOB 20515; 225-5727. Romano L. Mazzoli, D-Ky., chairman; Eugene Pugliese, counsel.

Jurisdiction over legislation concerning refugees and repatriated Americans; oversight of private immigration relief bills.

Senate Judiciary Committee, Subcommittee on Immigration and Refugee Affairs, SD-520 20510; 224-7878. Edward M. Kennedy, D-Mass., chairman; Jeff Blattner, chief counsel.

Jurisdiction over legislation concerning refugees and repatriated Americans; oversight of private immigration relief bills.

Nongovernmental:

Center for Intercultural Education and Development, 3520 Prospect St. N.W. (mailing address: P.O. Box 2298, Georgetown University, Washington, DC 20057); 298-0200. Julio Giulietti SJ, director. Fax, 338-0608.

Promotes the development of a comprehensive and humane refugee policy through public information and educational programs, lectures, immigration and migration policy research, and on-location training sessions in refugee camps and resettlement homes. Assists refugees in adjusting to life in the United States.

Southeast Asia Resource Action Center, 1628 16th St. N.W. 20009; 667-4690. Le Xuan Khoa, president. Fax, 667-6449.

Assists Southeast Asians in the United States with resettlement. Advocates for refugee rights. Interests include education, citizenship development, Indochinese self-help organizations, and economic development.

U.S. Catholic Conference, Migration and Refugee Services, 3211 4th St. N.E. 20017; 541-3220. Richard Ryscavage, executive director. Press, 541-3315. Fax, 541-3399.

Provides refugees and immigrants with resettlement services and legal counseling; operates training programs for volunteers and professionals; develops and implements USCC policy on migration, immigration, and refugee issues.

Social Security

General

For Health and Human Services Dept. Organization Chart, see p. 320.

See also Pensions and Retirement (p. 190)

Agencies:

Health and Human Services Dept., Income Assistance Policy, 200 Independence Ave. S.W. 20201; 690-7148. Canta Pian, director. Fax, 690-6562.

Advises the secretary on policy related to Social Security and welfare programs.

Social Security Administration (Health and Human Services Dept.), Hearings and Appeals, 5107 Leesburg Pike, Falls Church, VA 22041; (703) 305-0200. Daniel L. Skoler, associate commissioner. Fax, (703) 305-0208.

Administers a nationwide system of administrative law judges who conduct hearings and decide appealed cases concerning benefits provisions. Reviews decisions for appeals council action, if necessary, and renders the secretary's final decision. Reviews benefits cases on health insurance, disability, retirement and survivors' benefits, and supplemental security income.

Social Security Administration (Health and Human Services Dept.), Operations, 6401 Security Blvd., Baltimore, MD 21235; (410) 965-3143. Janice L. Warden, deputy commissioner. Toll-free, (800) 772-1213. Fax, (410) 965-1344. TDD, (410) 965-4404.

Issues Social Security numbers, maintains earnings and beneficiary records, authorizes claims, certifies benefits, and makes postadjudicative changes in beneficiary records for retirement, survivors', and disability insurance and black lung claims. Maintains toll-free number for workers who want information on future Social Security benefits.

Social Security Administration (Health and Human Services Dept.), Research and Statistics, 6401 Security Blvd., Baltimore, MD 21235; (410) 965-2841. Peter M. Wheeler, associate commissioner. Fax, (410) 965-3308. Publications, (202) 282-7136.

Compiles statistics on beneficiaries; conducts research on the economic status of beneficiaries and the relationship between Social Security and the economy; analyzes the effects of Social Security legislation; disseminates results of research and statistical programs through publications.

Congress:

General Accounting Office, Human Resources, 441 G St. N.W., NGB/ACG 20548; 512-6806. Janet L. Shikles, assistant comptroller general. Fax, 512-5806.

Independent, nonpartisan agency in the legislative branch that audits, analyzes, and evaluates Health and Human Services Dept. programs, including Social Security, Medicare, and Medicaid; makes reports available to the public.

House Appropriations Committee, Subcommittee on Labor, Health and Human Services, and Education, 2358 RHOB 20515; 225-3508. Neal Smith, D-Iowa, chairman; Mike Stephens, staff assistant.

Jurisdiction over legislation to appropriate funds for all Health and Human Services Dept. programs, except the Food and Drug Administration and native American health programs.

House Ways and Means Committee, Subcommittee on Human Resources, B317 RHOB 20515; 225-1025. Harold E. Ford, D-Tenn., chairman; Richard Hobbie, staff director. Fax, 225-9480.

Jurisdiction over legislation on supplemental security income for the elderly, blind, and disabled.

House Ways and Means Committee, Subcommittee on Social Security, B316 RHOB 20515; 225-9263. Andrew Jacobs Jr., D-Ind., chairman; Sandra Casber Wise, staff director. Fax, 225-9480.

Jurisdiction over Social Security disability and retirement and survivors' legislation.

Senate Appropriations Committee, Subcommittee on Labor, Health and Human Services, and Education, SD-186 20510; 224-7283. Tom Harkin, D-Iowa, chairman; Ed Long, clerk.

Jurisdiction over legislation to appropriate funds for all Health and Human Services Dept. programs, except the Food and Drug Administration and native American health programs.

Senate Finance Committee, Subcommittee on Social Security and Family Policy, SD-205 20510; 224-4515. John B. Breaux, D-La., chairman; Laird D. Burnett, staff contact.

Holds hearings on supplemental security income for the elderly, blind, and disabled; Social Security disability; and retirement and survivors' legislation.

Senate Special Committee on Aging, SD-G31 20510; 224-5364. David Pryor, D-Ark., chairman; Theresa M. Forster, staff director.

Studies and makes recommendations on Social Security and other retirement benefits for the elderly.

See also Congressional Social Security Caucus (p. 759)

Nongovernmental:

National Academy of Social Insurance, 1776 Massachusetts Ave. N.W., #615 20036; 452-8097. Pamela J. Larson, executive director. Fax, 452-8111.

Promotes research and education on Social Security, health care financing, and related public and private programs; assesses social insurance programs and their relationship to other programs; supports research and leadership development. Acts as a clearinghouse for social insurance information.

National Committee to Preserve Social Security and Medicare, 2000 K St. N.W., #800 20006; 822-9459. Martha McSteen, president. Fax, 822-9612.

Educational and advocacy organization that focuses on Social Security and Medicare programs and on related income security and health issues. Interests include retirement income protection, health care reform, and the quality of life of seniors. Monitors legislation and regulations.

Save Our Security Coalition and Education Fund, 1331 F St. N.W., 5th Floor 20004; 624-

9557. Roberta Feinstein Havel, executive director. Fax, 624-9595.

Coalition of aging, disability, and labor groups concerned with Social Security programs and health care. Serves as an information clearinghouse on Social Security, Medicare, and other health and social insurance issues. Conducts research, works as an advocate, and makes recommendations to strengthen the Social Security program.

Disability

Agencies:

Social Security Administration (Health and Human Services Dept.), Disability, 6401 Security Blvd., Baltimore, MD 21235; (410) 965-3424. Hilton W. Friend, acting associate commissioner. Information, (410) 965-7700. Fax, (410) 965-6503.

Provides direction for administration of the disability insurance program, which is paid out of the Social Security Trust Fund.

Social Security Administration (Health and Human Services Dept.), Disability and International Operations, 1500 Woodlawn Dr., Baltimore, MD (mailing address: 7200 Security West Tower, Baltimore, MD 21241); (410) 966-7000. Joseph R. Muffolett, director. Toll-free, (800) 772-1213. Fax, (410) 966-2329.

Reviews and authorizes claims for benefits under the disability insurance program and all claims for beneficiaries living abroad; certifies benefits payments; maintains beneficiary rolls.

Congress:

See *Social Security, General, Congress (p. 410)*

Elderly Needy, Blind, and Disabled: Supplemental Security Income

Agencies:

Employment Standards Administration (Labor Dept.), Coal Mine Workers' Compensation, 200 Constitution Ave. N.W. 20210; 219-6692. James L. DeMarce, director. Fax, 219-8568.

Provides direction for administration of the black lung benefits program. Adjudicates claims filed on or after July 1, 1973; certifies these benefit payments and maintains black lung beneficiary rolls. *(For claims filed before July 1,*

1973, contact Social Security Administration, Disability, below.)

Social Security Administration (Health and Human Services Dept.), Disability, 6401 Security Blvd., Baltimore, MD 21235; (410) 965-3424. Hilton W. Friend, acting associate commissioner. Information, (410) 965-7700. Fax, (410) 965-6503.

Administers disability and blindness provisions of the Supplemental Security Income (SSI) program. Responsible for claims filed under black lung benefits program before July 1, 1973.

Social Security Administration (Health and Human Services Dept.), Supplemental Security Income, 6401 Security Blvd., Baltimore, MD 21235; (410) 965-0300. Linda Davis Randle, acting associate commissioner. Fax, (410) 966-0980.

Provides direction and technical guidance for administration of the Supplemental Security Income (SSI) program for the elderly, blind, and disabled. Provides guidance on administration of state supplementary benefits programs; monitors state compliance with mandatory minimum federal supplements.

Congress:

See *Social Security, General, Congress (p. 410)*

Retirement and Survivors' Benefits

Agencies:

Social Security Administration (Health and Human Services Dept.), Operations, 6401 Security Blvd., Baltimore, MD 21235; (410) 965-3143. Janice L. Warden, deputy commissioner. Toll-free, (800) 772-1213. Fax, (410) 965-1344. TDD, (410) 965-4404.

Issues Social Security numbers, maintains earnings and beneficiary records, authorizes claims, certifies benefits, and makes postadjudicative changes in beneficiary records for retirement, survivors', and disability insurance claims. Maintains toll-free number for workers who want information on future Social Security benefits.

Social Security Administration (Health and Human Services Dept.), Retirement and Survivors Insurance, 6401 Security Blvd., Baltimore, MD 21235; (410) 965-2302. Sandy Crank, associate commissioner. Fax, (410) 965-8582.

Develops policies and procedures for administering the retirement and survivors' insurance programs.

Congress:

See Social Security, General, Congress (p. 410)

Social Services and Rehabilitation Programs

General

See also Philanthropy, Public Service, and Voluntarism (p. 272); Religion and Ethics (p. 276)

For Health and Human Services Dept. Organization Chart, see p. 320.

Agencies:

Administration for Children and Families (Health and Human Services Dept.), 901 D St. S.W. (mailing address: 370 L'Enfant Promenade S.W., Washington, DC 20447); 401-9200. Mary Jo Bane, assistant secretary. Information, 401-9215. Fax, 401-5770.

Administers and funds programs for the elderly; native Americans; children, youth, and families; and those with developmental disabilities. Responsible for Social Services Block Grants to the states; coordinates Health and Human Services Dept. policy and regulations on child protection, day care, foster care, adoption services, child abuse and neglect, home management, and special services for people with disabilities. Administers Head Start program and funds the National Runaway Switchboard, (800) 621-4000.

Bureau of Indian Affairs (Interior Dept.), Social Services, 1951 Constitution Ave. N.W. (mailing address: 1849 C St. N.W., Mail Stop 310-SIB, Washington, DC 20240); 208-2721. David Hickman, chief. Fax, 208-2648.

Gives assistance, in accordance with state payment standards, to native Americans who do not qualify for other forms of direct aid. Provides family and individual counseling and child welfare services. Administers the Indian Child Welfare Act grants to native American tribes and organizations to establish and operate native American child protection services.

Corporation for National Service, 1100 Vermont Ave. N.W. 20525; 606-5000. Eli J. Segal, chief executive officer. Fax, 606-4854. TDD,

606-5256. Volunteer recruiting information, (800) 424-8867; in Washington, D.C., 606-5000.

Independent corporation that administers federally sponsored domestic volunteer programs that provide disadvantaged citizens with services, including Volunteers in Service to America (VISTA), Retired Senior and Volunteer Program, Foster Grandparent Program, Senior Companion Program, and University Year for VISTA.

Health and Human Services Dept., Administration for Native Americans, 200 Independence Ave. S.W. 20201; 690-7776. Gary N. Kimble, commissioner designate. Information, 690-7730. Fax, 690-7441.

Awards grants for locally determined social and economic development strategies; promotes native American economic and social self-sufficiency; funds tribes and native American and native Hawaiian organizations. Commissioner serves as chairman of the Intradepartmental Council on Indian Affairs, which coordinates native American-related programs.

Health and Human Services Dept., Aging, Disability, and Long-Term Care Policy, 200 Independence Ave. S.W. 20201; 690-6443. Robyn Stone, deputy assistant secretary. Fax, 401-7733.

Coordinates policy and evaluation procedures for social services programs to ensure efficient use of resources. Conducts research and analyses of programs, including long-term care services for the elderly; social services programs for families; and programs for people with disabilities.

See also Domestic Policy Council (p. 300)

Congress:

General Accounting Office, Human Resources, 441 G St. N.W., NGB/ACG 20548; 512-6806. Janet L. Shikles, assistant comptroller general. Fax, 512-5806.

Independent, nonpartisan agency in the legislative branch that audits, analyzes, and evaluates Health and Human Services Dept. and Corporation for National Service programs; makes reports available to the public.

House Agriculture Committee, 1301 LHOB 20515; 225-2171. E. "Kika" de la Garza, D-Texas, chairman; Dianne Powell, staff director. Fax, 225-8510.

Jurisdiction over legislation on commodity donations, food stamps, and food programs for women, children, and the elderly.

House Appropriations Committee, Subcommittee on Labor, Health and Human Services, and Education, 2358 RHOB 20515; 225-3508. Neal Smith, D-Iowa, chairman; Mike Stephens, staff assistant.

Jurisdiction over legislation to appropriate funds for the Health and Human Services Dept. (except the Food and Drug Administration and native American health programs), Corporation for National Service programs, and the National Council on Disability.

House Appropriations Committee, Subcommittee on Transportation, 2358 RHOB 20515; 225-2141. Bob Carr, D-Mich., chairman; Del Davis, staff assistant.

Jurisdiction over legislation to appropriate funds for the Architectural and Transportation Barriers Compliance Board.

House Appropriations Committee, Subcommittee on VA, HUD, and Independent Agencies, H143 CAP 20515; 225-3241. Louis Stokes, D-Ohio, chairman; Paul Thompson, staff assistant.

Jurisdiction over legislation to appropriate funds for the Interagency Council on the Homeless.

House Education and Labor Committee, Subcommittee on Human Resources, B346C RHOB 20515; 225-1850. Matthew G. Martinez, D-Calif., chairman; Lester Sweeting, staff director and counsel.

Jurisdiction over legislation on Community Services Block Grant Program, Head Start, native Americans programs, antipoverty programs, applications of the Older Americans Act (including volunteer older Americans programs under the Corporation for National Service) and related legislation, runaway youth, child and youth development, Child Care Development Block Grant, and child-family services.

House Education and Labor Committee, Subcommittee on Select Education and Civil Rights, 518 O'Neill Bldg. (300 New Jersey Ave. S.E.) 20515; 226-7532. Major R. Owens, D-N.Y., chairman; Maria Cuprill, staff director.

Jurisdiction over legislation on child abuse and domestic violence, child adoption, education of children with disabilities, vocational rehabilitation for people with disabilities and developmental disabilities, day care, and domestic volunteer programs.

House Energy and Commerce Committee, Subcommittee on Health and the Environment, 2415 RHOB 20515; 225-4952. Henry A. Waxman, D-Calif., chairman; Karen Nelson, staff director.

Jurisdiction over developmental disability legislation.

House Ways and Means Committee, Subcommittee on Human Resources, B317 RHOB 20515; 225-1025. Harold E. Ford, D-Tenn., chairman; Richard Hobbie, staff director. Fax, 225-9480.

Jurisdiction over legislation dealing with the Aid to Families with Dependent Children program and social services for the elderly, blind, and disabled.

Senate Agriculture, Nutrition, and Forestry Committee, Subcommittee on Nutrition and Investigations, SR-328A 20510; 224-2035. Tom Harkin, D-Iowa, chairman; Mark Halvorson, legislative assistant.

Jurisdiction over legislation on commodity donations, food stamps, and food programs for women, children, and the elderly.

Senate Appropriations Committee, Subcommittee on Labor, Health and Human Services, and Education, SD-186 20510; 224-7283. Tom Harkin, D-Iowa, chairman; Ed Long, clerk.

Jurisdiction over legislation to appropriate funds for the Health and Human Services Dept. (except the Food and Drug Administration and native American health programs), Corporation for National Service programs, and the National Council on Disability.

Senate Appropriations Committee, Subcommittee on Transportation, SD-156 20510; 224-7281. Frank R. Lautenberg, D-N.J., chairman; Patrick J. McCann, clerk.

Jurisdiction over legislation to appropriate funds for the Architectural and Transportation Barriers Compliance Board.

Senate Appropriations Committee, Subcommittee on VA, HUD, and Independent Agencies, SD-142 20510; 224-7211. Barbara A. Mikulski, D-Md., chair; Kevin F. Kelly, clerk.

Jurisdiction over legislation to appropriate funds for the Interagency Council on the Homeless.

Senate Finance Committee, Subcommittee on Social Security and Family Policy, SD-205 20510; 224-4515. John B. Breaux, D-La., chairman; Laird D. Burnett, staff contact.

Holds hearings on legislation concerning the Aid to Families with Dependent Children program and social services for the elderly, blind, and disabled.

Senate Labor and Human Resources Committee, Subcommittee on Aging, SH-615 20510; 224-3239. Barbara A. Mikulski, D-Md., chairman; Robyn Lipner, staff director.

Jurisdiction over applications of the Older Americans Act and related legislation.

Senate Labor and Human Resources Committee, Subcommittee on Children, Families, Drugs, and Alcoholism, SH-639 20510; 224-5630. Christopher J. Dodd, D-Conn., chairman; Sarah Flanagan, staff director.

Jurisdiction over legislation on day care, child abuse and domestic violence, Corporation for National Service programs, low-income energy assistance, adoption reform, Community Services Block Grant Program, Head Start, native Americans programs, antipoverty programs, youth, child and youth development, Child Care Development Block Grant, and child-family services.

Senate Labor and Human Resources Committee, Subcommittee on Disability Policy, SH-113 20510; 224-6265. Tom Harkin, D-Iowa, chairman; Robert Silverstein, staff director.

Jurisdiction over legislation on developmental disabilities and on vocational rehabilitation for people with disabilities and developmental disabilities.

Senate Special Committee on Aging, SD-G31 20510; 224-5364. David Pryor, D-Ark., chairman; Theresa M. Forster, staff director.

Oversight of all matters affecting older Americans. Studies and reviews public and private policies and programs that affect the elderly, including retirement income and maintenance, housing, health, welfare, employment, education, recreation, and participation in family and community life; provides other Senate committees with information. Cannot report legislation.

Nongovernmental:

Americans for the Restitution and Righting of Old Wrongs (ARROW), 1000 Connecticut Ave. N.W. 20036; 296-0685. E. Thomas Colosimo, executive director.

Gives direct aid, including supplemental scholarships, clothing, and food, to needy native American students. Works to prevent drug, alcohol, and child abuse.

Catholic Charities USA, 1731 King St., #200, Alexandria, VA 22314; (703) 549-1390. Fred Kammer SJ, president. Fax, (703) 549-1656.

Member agencies and institutions provide persons of all backgrounds with social services, including adoption, education, counseling, food, and housing services. National office promotes public policies that address human needs and social injustice. Provides members with advocacy and professional support, including technical assistance, training, and resource development; disseminates publications.

Center for the Study of Social Policy, 1250 Eye St. N.W. 20005; 371-1565. Tom Joe, director. Fax, 371-1472.

Conducts research on government financing and delivery of social services programs, especially those related to children and families. Research focuses on long-term care for the elderly, health care reform, social welfare, the working poor, and people with disabilities. Offers technical assistance to states implementing reform in child and family services.

City Cares of America, 1737 H St. N.W. 20006; 887-0500. Alan K. Chambers, executive director. Fax, 887-6844.

Promotes community service among young professionals by replicating the Cares community-service model nationwide. Works to enhance the management and service capabilities of existing Cares organizations, enabling them to meet more effectively the needs of their communities.

Council on Social Work Education, 1600 Duke St., Alexandria, VA 22314; (703) 683-8080. Donald W. Beless, executive director. Fax, (703) 683-8099.

Promotes quality education in social work. Accredits social work programs.

National Assn. of Social Workers, 750 1st St. N.E. 20002; 408-8600. Sheldon Goldstein, executive director. Fax, 336-8310.

Membership: graduates of accredited social work education programs and students in accredited programs. Promotes the interests of social workers and their clients; promotes professional standards; certifies members of the Academy of Certified Social Workers; conducts research; acts as an information clearinghouse.

Salvation Army, 615 Slaters Lane, Alexandria, VA (mailing address: P.O. Box 269, Alexandria, VA 22313); (703) 684-5500. Kenneth Hodder, commissioner. Fax, (703) 684-3478.
International religious social welfare organization that provides social services, including counseling, youth and senior citizens' services, emergency help, foster care, settlement and day care, tutoring for the retarded, programs for people with disabilities, prison work, summer camps, community centers, employment services, rehabilitation programs for alcoholics, missing persons bureaus, and residences for the homeless.

Social Legislation Information Service, 440 1st St. N.W. 20001; 638-2952. Marjorie Kopp, editor. Fax, 638-4004.
Membership: individuals, libraries, and national, state, and local agencies interested in social welfare. Reports on federal legislation and activities of federal agencies relating to children, the elderly, and people with disabilities; delinquents; health, education, and welfare; and housing, employment, and other social welfare issues. (Division of the Child Welfare League of America.)

U.S. Conference of City Human Services Officials, 1620 Eye St. N.W., 4th Floor 20006; 293-7330. Laura DeKoven Waxman, deputy executive director. Fax, 293-2352.
Promotes improved social services for specific urban groups through meetings, technical assistance, and training programs for members; fosters information exchange among federal, state, and local governments, human services experts, and other groups concerned with human services issues. (Affiliate of the U.S. Conference of Mayors.)

The Urban Institute, 2100 M St. N.W. 20037; 833-7200. William Gorham, president. Information, 857-8702. Library, 857-8688. Fax, 223-3043.
Nonpartisan, public policy research and education organization. Interests include states' use of federal funds; delivery of social services to specific groups, including children of mothers in the

Aid to Families with Dependent Children program; retirement policy, income, and community-based services for the elderly; job placement and training programs for welfare recipients; health care cost containment and access; food stamps; child nutrition; the homeless; housing; immigration; and tax policy. Library open to the public by appointment.

See also Center for Social Policy Studies (p. 169); National Assn. of Colored Women's Clubs (p. 267)

Children, Youth, and Families

See also Government Financial Assistance Programs, Aid to Families with Dependent Children and Child Nutrition Programs (p. 407)

Agencies:

Administration for Children and Families (Health and Human Services Dept.), 901 D St. S.W. (mailing address: 370 L'Enfant Promenade S.W., Washington, DC 20447); 401-9200. Mary Jo Bane, assistant secretary. Information, 401-9215. Fax, 401-5770.
Plans, manages, and coordinates national assistance programs that promote stability, economic security, responsibility, and self-support for families; supervises programs and use of funds to provide the most needy with aid and to increase alternatives to public assistance. Programs include Aid to Families with Dependent Children, Child Support Enforcement, Low-Income Home Energy Assistance, Community Services Block Grant, and Refugee and Entrant Assistance.

Administration for Children and Families (Health and Human Services Dept.), Child Support Enforcement, 901 D St. S.W. (mailing address: 370 L'Enfant Promenade S.W., Washington, DC 20447); 401-9370. Lawrence Love, acting director. Information, 401-9373.
Helps states develop, manage, and operate child support programs. Maintains the Federal Parent Locator Service, which provides state and local child support agencies with information for locating absent parents. State enforcement agencies locate absent parents, establish paternity, establish and enforce support orders, and collect child support payments.

Administration for Children, Youth, and Families (Health and Human Services Dept.), Children's Bureau, 330 C St. S.W. (mailing address:

P.O. Box 1182, Washington, DC 20013); 690-0618. Carol W. Williams, associate commissioner. Fax, 690-6721.

Administers grants to agencies and institutes of higher learning for research projects and for training personnel in the child welfare field. Administers formula grants to strengthen child welfare services provided by state and local public welfare agencies. Provides states with technical assistance in group and foster care, adoption, and family services. Administers the Child Care and Development Block Grant.

Administration for Children, Youth, and Families (Health and Human Services Dept.), Family and Youth Services, 330 C St. S.W. (mailing address: P.O. Box 1182, Washington, DC 20013); 205-8102. Terry Lewis, acting associate commissioner. Fax, 205-8221.

Administers federal discretionary grant programs for projects serving runaway and homeless youth and for projects that deter youth involvement in gangs. Provides youth service agencies with training and technical assistance. Monitors federal policies, programs, and legislation. Supports research on gangs, runaways, and homeless youth.

Administration for Children, Youth, and Families (Health and Human Services Dept.), National Center on Child Abuse and Neglect, 330 C St. S.W. (mailing address: P.O. Box 1182, Washington, DC 20013); 205-8586. David W. Lloyd, director. Information, (703) 385-7565. Fax, 205-8221.

Maintains clearinghouse of programs for preventing and treating child abuse and neglect; makes grants to agencies and states for identification and treatment programs.

Agriculture Dept., Extension Service, 4-H Youth Program, 14th St. and Independence Ave. S.W. 20250; 720-5853. Alma C. Hobbs, deputy administrator. Fax, 720-9366.

Administers education programs with state land-grant universities and county governments for rural and urban youth ages 5 to 19. Projects provide youth with experience in the fields of science and technological literacy, environment, natural resources, health, leadership, citizenship, service, and personal development.

Corporation for National Service, Drug Alliance Program, 1100 Vermont Ave. N.W. 20525; 606-4857. Calvin T. Dawson, director. Fax, 606-4921.

Supports volunteer parent groups and youth groups that work to create a drug-free environment; works to generate parental involvement in drug abuse prevention and education and to create coalitions to address drug abuse prevention; sponsors conferences, workshops, and seminars on drug use and youth; awards grants to nonprofit volunteer groups working against drug abuse; awards grants for creating new parent-volunteer groups; trains volunteers; promotes involvement of the public and private sectors in drug awareness.

See also Bureau of Indian Affairs (p. 412)

Congress:

See Social Services and Rehabilitation Programs, General, Congress (p. 412)

See also Congressional Coalition on Adoption (p. 756)

Nongovernmental:

Adoptees in Search, P.O. Box 41016, Bethesda, MD 20824; (301) 656-8555. Joanne W. Small, executive director. Fax, (301) 652-2106.

Membership: adult adoptees, adoptive parents, and birth parents. Provides adult adoptees seeking information about their roots with professional consultation, guidance, and support services. Promotes awareness of adoption practice and laws that affect adopted adults. Advocates legislative change of the sealed record policy.

Adoption Service Information Agency, 7720 Alaska Ave. N.W. 20012; 726-7193. Theodore Kim, president. Fax, 722-4928.

Provides information on international, primarily Korean, adoption; sponsors seminars and workshops for adoptive and prospective adoptive parents.

American Assn. for Marriage and Family Therapy, 1100 17th St. N.W. 20036; 452-0109. Michael Bowers, executive director. Fax, 223-2329.

Membership: professional marriage and family therapists. Promotes professional standards in marriage and family therapy through training programs; provides the public with educational material and referral service for marriage and family therapy.

American Bar Assn., Center on Children and the Law, 1800 M St. N.W. 20036; 331-2250. Howard Davidson, director. Fax, 331-2225.

Works to increase lawyer representation of children; sponsors speakers and conferences; monitors legislation and provides information. Interests include child sexual abuse and exploitation, missing and runaway children, parental kidnapping, child support, foster care, and adoption of children with special needs.

American Enterprise Institute for Public Policy Research, Social and Individual Responsibility Project, 1150 17th St. N.W. 20036; 862-5904. Douglas J. Besharov, director. Fax, 862-7178.

Research and education organization that conducts studies on social welfare policies, including family and welfare policies. Interests include children, child abuse and neglect, divorce, family breakdown, poverty, and welfare programs.

American Family Society, 5013 Russett Rd., Rockville, MD 20853; (301) 460-4455. K. Wayne Scott, president. Fax, (301) 460-6422.

Provides families and organizations with self-help resource materials. Sponsors the Great American Family Program; promotes National Family Week.

American Humane Assn., 322 Massachusetts Ave. N.E. 20002; 543-7780. Adele Douglass, Washington representative. Fax, 546-3266.

Membership: societies, individuals, and government agencies concerned with child protection laws. Prepares model state legislation on child abuse and its prevention; publishes surveys on child abuse and state abuse laws. (Headquarters in Denver.)

American Youth Work Center, 1751 N St. N.W. 20036; 785-0764. William Treanor, executive director. Fax, 728-0657.

International citizens' interest group concerned with juvenile justice and community-based youth services, including runaway shelters, hotlines, crisis intervention centers, drug programs, alternative education, and job training and placement. Provides youth programs with technical assistance; works with agencies and individuals dealing with young people; serves as clearinghouse and resource center; sponsors training sessions, conferences, and a college internship program.

Boy Scouts of America, 9190 Wisconsin Ave., Bethesda, MD 20814; (301) 530-9360. Ron L. Carroll, scout executive. Fax, (301) 564-3648.

Educational services organization for boys ages 7 to 17. Promotes citizen participation and physical fitness. The Explorers Program, which includes young men and women ages 14 to 20, provides vocational opportunities. (Headquarters in Irving, Texas.)

Boys and Girls Clubs of America, 611 Rockville Pike, Rockville, MD 20852; (301) 251-6676. Robbie Callaway, assistant national director. Fax, (301) 294-3052.

Educational service organization for boys and girls, most from disadvantaged circumstances. Works to prevent juvenile delinquency; promotes youth employment, health and fitness, leadership, and citizenship. Interests include child care, child safety and protection, drug and alcohol abuse prevention, runaway and homeless youth, youth employment, child nutrition, tax reform and charitable contributions, and other issues that affect disadvantaged youth. (Headquarters in Atlanta.)

Center for the Support of Children, 5315 Nebraska Ave. N.W. 20015; 363-5923. Laurene T. McKillop, executive director. Fax, 363-7999.

Assists state and local decision makers and service providers in creating and implementing policy for children and families; seeks to strengthen relationships among policy makers, service providers and recipients, and funding sources; provides training, technical assistance, and strategic planning; focuses on child support, paternity, child welfare, child care, and other family responsibility issues that affect adolescents, young families, and child support service professionals.

Child Welfare League of America, 440 1st St. N.W., #310 20001-2085; 638-2952. David Liederman, executive director. Fax, 638-4004.

Membership: public and private child welfare agencies and individuals. Develops standards for the field; provides information on adoption, foster care, group home services, child protection, residential care for children and youth, services to pregnant adolescents and young parents, and other child welfare issues.

Children's Defense Fund, 25 E St. N.W. 20001; 628-8787. Marian Wright Edelman, president. Fax, 662-3510.

Advocacy group concerned with programs and policies for children and youth, particularly poor and minority children. Interests include health care, education, child care, job training and employment, and family support; works to ensure educational and job opportunities for youth.

The Children's Foundation, 725 15th St. N.W. 20005; 347-3300. Kay Hollestelle, executive director.

Advocacy group for children and those who care for them. Works to improve available child care; promotes enforcement of child support; offers information, technical assistance, and professional support to child care providers.

Christian Children's Fund, 1717 Massachusetts Ave. N.W., #601 20036; 462-2161. Arthur Simon, director, Washington liaison office. Fax, 462-0601.

Works to ensure the survival, protection, and development of children in over forty countries. Promotes the improvement in quality of life of children within the context of family, community, and culture. Helps children in unstable situations brought on by war, natural disasters, and other high-risk circumstances.

Family Service America, Inc., 1319 F St. N.W., #204 20004; 347-1124. Ronald H. Field, senior vice president, public policy. Fax, 393-4517. Toll-free information and referrals, (800) 221-2681.

Membership: family service agencies in the United States and abroad. Provides families with support services and counseling. Promotes affordable and accessible family-centered health and mental health care, affordable and safe housing, education and job training, and fiscal and workplace policies that strengthen family viability. Monitors legislation. (Headquarters in Milwaukee.)

Girl Scouts of the U.S.A., 1025 Connecticut Ave. N.W., #309 20036; 659-3780. Carmen Delgado Votaw, director, government relations. Fax, 331-8065.

Educational service organization for girls ages 5 to 17. Promotes personal development through social action, leadership, and other projects. Interests include career education, youth camp safety, child sexual exploitation, child health care, runaways, and juvenile justice. (Headquarters in New York.)

Mothers at Home, 8310-A Old Courthouse Rd., Vienna, VA 22182; (703) 827-5903. Cathy Myers, co-director. Toll-free, (800) 783-4666. Press, (703) 534-7858. Fax, (703) 790-8587.

Provides information and support for mothers who stay home, or who would like to stay home, to rear their children. Monitors legislation and regulations.

National Black Child Development Institute, 1023 15th St. N.W., #600 20005; 387-1281. Evelyn K. Moore, executive director. Fax, 234-1738.

Advocacy group for African American children, youth, and families. Interests include child care, foster care, adoption, health, and education. Provides information on government policies that affect African American children, youth, and families.

National Center for Missing and Exploited Children, 2101 Wilson Blvd., #550, Arlington, VA 22201; (703) 235-3900. Ernest Allen, president. Fax, (703) 235-4067. TDD, (800) 826-7653. Toll-free hotline, (800) 843-5678.

Private organization funded primarily by the Justice Dept. Assists parents and citizens' groups in locating and safely returning missing children; offers technical assistance to law enforcement agencies; coordinates public and private missing children programs; maintains database that coordinates information on missing children.

National Child Support Enforcement Assn., 400 N. Capitol St. N.W., #372 20001; 624-8180. Eleanor Landstreet, executive director. Fax, 624-8828.

Promotes enforcement of child support obligations and educates professionals on child support issues; fosters exchange of ideas among child support professionals; monitors legislation and regulations.

National Collaboration for Youth, 1319 F St. N.W. 20004; 347-2080. Gordon A. Raley, executive director. Fax, 393-4517.

Membership: national youth-serving organizations. Works to improve members' youth development programs through information exchange and other support. Raises public awareness of youth issues. Monitors legislation and regulations.

National Council for Adoption, 1930 17th St. N.W. 20009; 328-1200. William L. Pierce, president. Fax, 332-0935.

Organization of individuals, agencies, and corporations interested in adoption. Supports adoption through legal, ethical agencies; advocates the right to confidentiality in adoption. Conducts research and holds conferences; provides information; supports pregnancy counseling, maternity services, and counseling for infertile couples.

National 4-H Council, 7100 Connecticut Ave., Chevy Chase, MD 20815; (301) 961-2820. Richard J. Sauer, president. Fax, (301) 961-2894.

Educational organization incorporated to expand and strengthen the 4-H program (for young people ages 9 to 19) of the Agriculture Dept.'s Cooperative Extension Service and state land-grant universities. Programs include citizenship and leadership training and international exchanges.

National Network of Runaway and Youth Services, 1319 F St. N.W., #401 20004; 783-7949. Della M. Hughes, executive director. Fax, 783-7955. AIDS hotline for youth-serving agencies, (800) 878-2437.

Membership: providers of services related to runaway and homeless youth. Monitors legislation and regulations that affect youth rights; offers technical assistance to new and existing youth projects; operates Safe Choices Project, which provides youth with AIDS prevention education.

National Urban League, 1111 14th St. N.W., #600 20005; 898-1604. Robert McAlpine, director, policy and government relations. Fax, 682-0782.

Federation of affiliates concerned with the social welfare of African Americans and other minorities. Conducts research. Youth Development division provides local leagues with technical assistance for youth programs and seeks training opportunities for youth within Urban League programs. (Headquarters in New York.)

Orphan Foundation of America, 1500 Massachusetts Ave. N.W., #448 20005; 861-0762. Eileen McCaffrey, executive director. Toll-free, (800) 950-4673. Fax, 223-9079.

Advocates for orphaned, abandoned, and homeless teenagers. Provides research, information, scholarships, emergency cash grants, volunteer programs, guidance, and support. Interests include the rights of orphaned children, adoption, transition from youth foster care to young adult independence, and breaking the welfare cycle. Resource center provides training and educational materials.

See also Catholic Charities U.S.A. (p. 414); National Center for Prosecution of Child Abuse (p. 509); National Organization on Adolescent Pregnancy, Parenting, and Prevention (p. 336); Salvation Army (p. 415)

Day Care

Agencies:

General Services Administration, Workplace Initiatives, 18th and F Sts. N.W., #6119 20405; 501-3464. Faith Wohl, director. Fax, 208-7578.

Administers employee child care programs, including the Telecommuting program, which allows employees to work from their homes, and the Working Family Community Service program. Maintains list of child care contacts in GSA regional centers. *(See Regional Federal Information Sources list, p. 846.)*

See also Administration for Children and Families (p. 412)

Congress:

See Social Services and Rehabilitation Programs, General, Congress (p. 412)

Nongovernmental:

Child Welfare League of America, 440 1st St. N.W., #310 20001-2085; 638-2952. David Liederman, executive director. Fax, 638-4004.

Membership: public and private welfare agencies and individuals. Develops standards for the profession and provides information on day care in centers and homes.

Children's Defense Fund, 25 E St. N.W. 20001; 628-8787. Helen Blank, senior child care associate. Fax, 662-3520.

Advocacy group concerned with federal and state programs for children and youth; provides parents and child-care advocates with information on child-care policy.

The Children's Foundation, 725 15th St. N.W. 20005; 347-3300. Kay Hollestelle, executive director.

Advocacy group for children and those who care for them. Works to improve available child care; offers information, technical assistance, and professional support to child care providers.

Council for Early Childhood Professional Recognition, Child Development Associate National Credentialing Program, 1341 G St. N.W., #400 20005-3105; 265-9090. Carol Phillips, executive director. Toll-free, (800) 424-4310. Fax, 265-9161.

Promotes and establishes standards for quality child care through an accrediting program. Awards credentials to family day care, preschool, home visitor, and infant-toddler caregivers.

National Assn. for the Education of Young Children, 1509 16th St. N.W. 20036-1426; 232-8777. Marilyn M. Smith, executive director. Toll-free, (800) 424-2460. Fax, 328-1846.

Membership: early childhood professionals and parents. Works to improve the quality of early childhood care and education. Administers national accreditation system for early childhood programs. Maintains information service.

See also Catholic Charities U.S.A. (p. 414); National Community Education Assn. (p. 126); Salvation Army (p. 415)

Disabled

See also Education: Special Groups, Handicapped, Learning Disabled (p. 145); Health Care and Services for Special Groups, Mentally Retarded (p. 343); Health Care and Services for Special Groups, Physically Disabled (p. 345); Social Security, Elderly Needy, Blind, and Disabled: Supplemental Security Income (p. 411)

Agencies:

Administration for Children and Families (Health and Human Services Dept.), Administration on Developmental Disabilities, 200 Independence Ave. S.W. 20201; 690-6590. Bob Williams, commissioner. Fax, 690-6904.

Establishes state protection and advocacy systems for people with developmental disabilities, including persons with mental retardation, cerebral palsy, epilepsy, and autism; awards discretionary grants to university-affiliated programs and to programs of national significance. Administers formula grants to states for individuals who incurred developmental disabilities before the age of 22.

Architectural and Transportation Barriers Compliance Board, 1331 F St. N.W., #1000 20004; 272-5434. Lawrence W. Roffee, executive director. Fax, 272-5447. Toll-free technical assistance, (800) 872-2253.

Enforces standards requiring that certain federally funded buildings and facilities be accessible to persons with disabilities; provides technical assistance and information on designing these facilities; sets guidelines for the Americans with Disabilities Act.

Education Dept., Clearinghouse on Disability Information, 330 C St. S.W. 20202-2524; 205-8241. Susan Murray, director. Fax, 205-9252. Main phone is voice and TDD accessible.

Provides information on federal legislation and programs and national organizations concerning individuals with disabilities.

Education Dept., National Institute on Disability and Rehabilitation Research, 330 C St. S.W. (mailing address: 400 Maryland Ave. S.W., Washington, DC 20202); 205-8134. Katherine D. Seelman, director. Fax, 205-8997. TDD, 205-9136.

Assists research programs in rehabilitating people with disabilities; provides information on developments in the field; awards grants and contracts for scientific, technical, and methodological research; coordinates federal research programs on rehabilitation; offers fellowships to individuals conducting research in the field.

Education Dept., Rehabilitation Services Administration, 330 C St. S.W. 20202; 205-5482. Howard Moses, acting commissioner. Fax, 205-9874.

Coordinates and directs major federal programs for eligible physically and mentally disabled persons. Administers distribution of grants for training and employment programs and for establishing supported-employment and independent-living programs. Provides vocational training and job placement.

President's Committee on Employment of People with Disabilities, 1331 F St. N.W., #300 20004; 376-6200. Richard Douglas, executive director. Fax, 376-6219. TDD, 376-6205.

Seeks to eliminate physical and psychological barriers to people with disabilities through education and information programs; promotes education, training, rehabilitation, and employment opportunities for people with disabilities.

President's Committee on Mental Retardation (Health and Human Services Dept.), 330 Independence Ave. S.W. 20201; 619-0634. Gary H. Blumenthal, executive director. Information, 619-3463. Fax, 205-9519.

Compiles information, conducts studies, and promotes research on mental retardation; advises the president and the secretary of health and human services; acts as a liaison among federal, state, local, and private organizations concerned with mental retardation.

Social Security Administration (Health and Human Services Dept.), Disability, 6401 Security Blvd., Baltimore, MD 21235; (410) 965-3424. Hilton W. Friend, acting associate commissioner. Information, (410) 965-7700. Fax, (410) 965-6503.

Administers and regulates the disability insurance program and disability provisions of the Supplemental Security Income (SSI) program.

See also Administration for Children and Families (p. 412)

Congress:

See Social Services and Rehabilitation Programs, General, Congress (p. 412)

Nongovernmental:

Affiliated Leadership League of and for the Blind of America, 1101 17th St. N.W., #803 20036; 833-0092. Robert K. Humphreys, administrator and counsel. Fax, 833-0086.

Membership: service and educational organizations and public and private agencies serving the blind and visually impaired. Advocates rights of blind consumers. Promotes accreditation for organizations serving the blind; acts as an information clearinghouse; monitors legislation and regulations.

American Assn. on Mental Retardation, 444 N. Capitol St. N.W., #846 20001; 387-1968. M. Doreen Croser, executive director. Toll-free, (800) 424-3688. Fax, 387-2193.

Membership: physicians, educators, administrators, social workers, psychologists, psychiatrists, students, and others interested in mental retardation and related developmental disabilities. Provides information on legal rights, services, and facilities for people with mental retardation.

American Council of the Blind, 1155 15th St. N.W., #720 20005; 467-5081. Oral O. Miller, national representative. Fax, 467-5085. Toll-free, 3:00–5:30 p.m. E.S.T., (800) 424-8666.

Membership organization serving blind and visually impaired individuals. Interests include Social Security, telecommunications, rehabilitation services, transportation, education, and architectural access. Provides blind individuals

with information and referral services, including legal referrals; advises state organizations and agencies serving the blind; sponsors scholarships for the blind and visually impaired.

American Foundation for Autistic Children, 4917 Dorset Ave., Chevy Chase, MD 20815; (301) 656-9213. Mooza V. P. Grant, president.

Works with children and parents of autistic and self-injurious children. Conducts research and provides information on autism; works with education and health institutions. Interests include developing residential facilities for older children.

American Foundation for the Blind, 1615 M St. N.W., #250 20036; 457-1487. Scott Marshall, associate executive director, governmental relations. Fax, 457-1492.

Voluntary research and consulting organization that serves as a clearinghouse for information on blindness. Offers consulting service on programs for blind children, adults, and their families; consultation focuses on aging, civil rights, education, employment, health, rehabilitation, social welfare services, and technology. (Headquarters in New York.)

American Network of Community Options and Resources, 4200 Evergreen Lane, #315, Annandale, VA 22003; (703) 642-6614. Joni Fritz, executive director.

Monitors and supports legislation and federal regulations that promote quality care and services for people with disabilities; advises and works with regulatory and consumer agencies that serve people with developmental disabilities; provides information and sponsors seminars and workshops for members; publishes directory that lists member agencies offering residential services in 48 states and the District of Columbia.

American Occupational Therapy Assn., 1383 Piccard Dr., Rockville, MD 20849-1725; (301) 948-9626. Jeanette Bair, executive director. Toll-free, (800) 366-9799. Fax, (301) 948-5512. TDD, (800) 377-8555.

Membership: registered occupational therapists, certified occupational therapy assistants, and students. Associate members include businesses and organizations supportive of occupational therapy. Accredits colleges and universities and certifies therapists.

American Physical Therapy Assn., 1111 N. Fairfax St., Alexandria, VA 22314-1488; (703) 684-2782. Francis Mallon, acting executive vice president. Toll-free, (800) 999-2782. Fax, (703) 684-7343.

Membership: active and retired accredited physical therapists, assistants, and students. Establishes professional standards and accredits physical therapy programs; seeks to improve physical therapy education, practice, and research. Library open to the public by appointment.

American Rehabilitation Counseling Assn., 5999 Stevenson Ave., Alexandria, VA 22304; (703) 823-9800. Patricia Schwallie-Giddis, acting executive director. Toll-free, (800) 347-6647. Fax, (703) 823-0252. TDD, (703) 370-1943.

Membership: rehabilitation counselors, counselor educators and graduate students in the mental health field, and other interested persons. Establishes counseling and research standards; encourages establishment of rehabilitation facilities; conducts leadership training and continuing education programs; serves as a liaison between counselors and clients; monitors legislation and regulations. Library open to the public. (Affiliated with the American Counseling Assn.)

American Society for Deaf Children, 814 Thayer Ave., Silver Spring, MD 20910; (800) 942-2732. Jeff Cohen, president. Toll-free, (800) 942-2732 (voice- and TDD-accessible).

Provides families of deaf and hard-of-hearing children with referral services, parent-to-parent support, and information on deafness. (Headquarters in Sulpher, Okla.)

The Arc, 1522 K St. N.W., #516 20005; 785-3388. Paul Marchand, director, governmental affairs. Fax, 467-4179.

Membership: individuals interested in assisting people with mental retardation. Gathers and provides information on government programs and legislation concerning mental retardation; oversees and encourages support for local groups that provide direct services for people with mental retardation. (Headquarters in Arlington, Texas.)

Assn. for Education and Rehabilitation of the Blind and Visually Impaired, 206 N. Washington St., Alexandria, VA 22314; (703) 548-1884. Kathleen Megivern, executive director.

Membership: professionals and paraprofessionals who work with the blind. Provides information on services for the blind and on employment opportunities for those who work with the blind. Works to improve quality of education and rehabilitation services.

The Assn. for Persons with Severe Handicaps, 206 W. Glenndale Ave., Alexandria, VA 22301; (703) 683-5586. Celane M. McWhorter, director, government relations. Fax, (703) 683-3643. Main phone is voice and TDD accessible.

International organization that promotes dignity, education, and independence for persons with severe disabilities. Monitors legislation and regulations. (Headquarters in Seattle.)

Autism Society of America, 7910 Woodmont Ave., #650, Bethesda, MD 20814; (301) 657-0881. Veronica Zysk, office manager. Fax, (301) 657-0869.

Monitors legislation and regulations affecting support, education, training, research, and other services for autistic persons. Offers referral service and information to the public.

Best Buddies of America, 1350 New York Ave. N.W. 20005; 347-7265. Gustav Chiarello, field director, eastern region.

Volunteer organization that pairs college students in one-to-one friendships with persons who are mentally retarded.

Council of State Administrators of Vocational Rehabilitation, P.O. Box 3776, Washington, DC 20007; 638-4634. Joseph H. Owens, executive director.

Membership: chief administrative officers of public rehabilitation agencies that prepare persons with mental and physical disabilities for competitive employment. Provides a forum to study and act on matters affecting the rehabilitation of persons with disabilities.

Epilepsy Foundation of America, 4351 Garden City Dr., Landover, MD 20785; (301) 459-3700. William McLin, executive vice president. Toll-free, (800) 332-1000. Library, (800) 332-4050. Fax, (301) 577-2684.

Promotes research and treatment of epilepsy; makes research grants; disseminates information and educational materials. Affiliates provide people with epilepsy with direct services and make referrals when necessary. Library open to the public by appointment.

Girl Scouts of the U.S.A., 1025 Connecticut Ave. N.W., #309 20036; 659-3780. Carmen Delgado Votaw, director, government relations. Fax, 331-8065.

Educational service organization for girls ages 5 to 17. Promotes personal development through social action, leadership, and programs such as Girl Scouting for Handicapped Girls. (Headquarters in New York.)

Goodwill Industries International, Inc., 9200 Wisconsin Ave., Bethesda, MD 20814; (301) 530-6500. David M. Cooney, president. Fax, (301) 530-1516. TDD, (301) 530-0836.

Membership: autonomous agencies that provide disabled and disadvantaged individuals with Goodwill Industries services, which include vocational rehabilitation evaluation, training, employment, and placement services.

National Assn. of Protection and Advocacy Systems, 900 2nd St. N.E., #211 20002; 408-9514. Curtis Decker, executive director. Fax, 408-9520. TDD, 408-9521.

Membership: agencies working for the rights of the mentally ill or developmentally disabled and clients of the vocational rehabilitation system. Monitors legislation and regulations; provides state agencies with training and technical assistance; maintains an electronic mail network.

National Assn. of State Directors of Developmental Disability Services, 113 Oronoco St., Alexandria, VA 22314; (703) 683-4202. Robert M. Gettings, executive director. Fax, (703) 684-1395.

Membership: chief administrators of state mental retardation programs. Coordinates exchange of information on mental retardation programs among the states; provides information on state programs.

National Assn. of the Deaf, 814 Thayer Ave., Silver Spring, MD 20910; (301) 587-1788. Nancy J. Bloch, executive director. Fax, (301) 587-1791. TDD, (301) 587-1789.

Membership: deaf and hard-of-hearing individuals; hearing, speech, and language professionals; state associations; parents; and others concerned with the problems of the deaf. Interests include rehabilitation, education, employment, and discrimination. Serves as an information clearinghouse on deafness; coordinates activities of state associates; publishes deafness-related materials; monitors legislation and regulations.

National Easter Seal Society, 1350 New York Ave. N.W., #915 20005; 347-3066. Joseph D. Romer, senior vice president, public affairs. Fax, 737-7914. TDD, 347-7385.

Federation of state and local groups with programs that help people with disabilities achieve independence. Washington office monitors legislation and regulations. Affiliates assist individuals with a broad range of disabilities, including muscular dystrophy, cerebral palsy, stroke, speech and hearing loss, blindness, amputation, and learning disabilities. Services include physical, occupational, vocational, and speech therapy; speech, hearing, physical, and vocational evaluation; psychological testing and counseling; personal and family counseling; supported employment; special education programs; social clubs and day and residential camps; and transportation, referral, and follow-up programs. (Headquarters in Chicago.)

National Handicapped Sports Assn., 451 Hungerford Dr., #100, Rockville, MD 20850; (301) 217-0960. Kirk M. Bauer, executive director. Fax, (301) 217-0968. TDD, (301) 217-0963.

Conducts sports and recreation activities and physical fitness programs for people with disabilities and their families and friends; produces videotaped exercise programs for people with physical disabilities; conducts workshops and competitions.

National Industries for the Blind, 1901 N. Beauregard St., Alexandria, VA 22311; (703) 998-0770. Patricia Beattie, director, legislative affairs. Fax, (703) 998-8268.

Works to develop and improve opportunities for evaluating, training, employing, and advancing people who are blind and multidisabled blind. Assists associated agencies for the blind in manufacturing quality products and services for procurement by the federal government. (Headquarters in Wayne, N.J.)

National Information Center for Children and Youth with Disabilities, P.O. Box 1492, Washington, DC 20013; 884-8200. Suzanne Ripley, director. Toll-free, (800) 695-0285. Fax, 416-0312.

Federally funded clearinghouse that provides free information to parents, educators, caregivers, advocates, and others who help children and youth with disabilities become active participants in school, work, and the community. Offers personal responses to specific questions, referrals to other organizations, prepared information packets, and technical assistance to families and professional groups.

National Multiple Sclerosis Society, 2021 K St. N.W. 20006; 296-5363. Diane Afes, acting executive director, Washington office. Fax, 296-3425.

Seeks to advance medical knowledge of multiple sclerosis, a disease of the central nervous system. Patient services include individual and family counseling, exercise programs, equipment loans, medical and social service referrals, transportation assistance, back-to-work training programs, and in-service training seminars for nurses, homemakers, and physical and occupational therapists. (Headquarters in New York.)

National Organization on Disability, 910 16th St. N.W., #600 20006; 293-5960. Alan A. Reich, president. Toll-free, (800) 248-2253. Fax, 293-7999. TDD, 293-5968.

Administers the Community Partnership Program, a network of communities that works to remove barriers and address educational, employment, social, and transportation needs of people with disabilities. Provides members with information and technical assistance; sponsors annual community awards competition; makes referrals; monitors legislation and regulations.

National Rehabilitation Assn., 633 S. Washington St., Alexandria, VA 22314; (703) 836-0850. Ann Tourigny, executive director. Fax, (703) 836-0848. TDD, (703) 836-0849.

Membership: administrators, counselors, therapists, disability examiners, vocational evaluators, instructors, job placement specialists, disability managers in the corporate sector, and others interested in rehabilitation of people with physical and mental disabilities. Sponsors conferences and workshops; monitors legislation and regulations.

RESNA, 1101 Connecticut Ave. N.W., #700 20036; 857-1199. James R. Geletka, executive director. Fax, 223-4579.

Membership: engineers, health professionals, persons with disabilities, and others concerned with rehabilitation engineering technology. Promotes and supports developments in rehabilitation engineering; acts as an information clearinghouse.

Self Help for Hard of Hearing People, 7910 Woodmont Ave., #1200, Bethesda, MD 20814;

(301) 657-2248. Donna Sorkin, executive director. Fax, (301) 913-9413. TDD, (301) 657-2249.

Promotes understanding of the nature, causes, and remedies of hearing loss. Provides hearing-impaired people with support and information. Seeks to educate the public about hearing loss and the problems of hearing-impaired people. Provides travelers with information on assistive listening devices in museums, theaters, and places of worship.

Special Olympics, 1350 New York Ave. N.W., #500 20005; 628-3630. Vacant, president. Fax, 737-1937.

Offers individuals with mental retardation opportunities for year-round sports training; sponsors athletic competition in 22 individual and team sports.

United Cerebral Palsy Assns., 1522 K St. N.W., #1112 20005; 842-1266. John D. Kemp, executive director. Toll-free, (800) 872-5827. Fax, 842-3519. Main phone is voice and TDD accessible.

National network of state and local affiliates that assists individuals with cerebral palsy and other severe physical disabilities and their families. Provides parent education, early intervention, and employment services; family support and respite programs; and vocational training. Promotes research on cerebral palsy; supports the use of assistive technology and community-based living arrangements for persons with cerebral palsy and other severe physical disabilities.

See also American Blind Lawyers Assn. (p. 520); Assn. of Higher Education Facilities Officers (p. 137); Catholic Charities USA (p. 414); National Assn. for Music Therapy (p. 120); National Institute for Citizen Education in the Law (p. 522); Road Runners Club of America (p. 326); Salvation Army (p. 415)

Elderly

See also Pensions and Retirement (p. 190); Social Security, Elderly Needy, Blind, and Disabled: Supplemental Security Income (p. 411)

Agencies:

Corporation for National Service, Retired and Senior Volunteer Program, Foster Grandparent Program, and Senior Companion Program, 1100 Vermont Ave. N.W. 20525; 606-4855. Thomas E. Endres, acting assistant director, older Americans volunteer programs. Information, 606-5108. Fax, 606-4921.

Oversees regional offices and provides them with financial assistance for programs administered by community agencies, including the Retired and Senior Volunteer Program, which encourages older citizens to use their talents and experience in community service; the Foster Grandparent Program, which gives low-income persons age 60 and over opportunities to work with exceptional children and children with special needs; and the Senior Companion Program, which recruits low-income persons age 60 and over to help other adults, especially seniors with special needs.

Health and Human Services Dept., Administration on Aging, 330 Independence Ave. S.W. 20201; 619-0556. Fernando M. Torres-Gil, assistant secretary. Information, 619-0641. Fax, 619-3759.

Acts as advocate for the elderly; serves as the principal agency for implementing programs under the Older Americans Act. Develops programs to promote the economic welfare and personal independence of older people; provides advice and assistance to promote the development of state-administered, community-based social services for older people; supports curriculum development and training in gerontology.

Health and Human Services Dept., Federal Council on the Aging, 330 Independence Ave. S.W. 20201; 619-2451. Brian T. Lutz, executive director. Fax, 619-3759.

Independent advisory council appointed jointly by Congress and the president and authorized under the Older Americans Act to review, evaluate, and make recommendations on federal policies that affect the elderly. Conducts conferences and workshops; disseminates information.

See also Administration for Children and Families (p. 412)

Congress:

See Social Services and Rehabilitation Programs, General, Congress (p. 412)

Nongovernmental:

American Assn. of Homes for the Aging, 901 E St. N.W., #500 20004; 783-2242. Michael F. Rodgers, senior vice president. Fax, 783-2255.

Membership: nonprofit homes, housing, and health-related facilities for the elderly sponsored by religious, fraternal, labor, private, and governmental organizations. Provides members with technical assistance; conducts research on long-term care for the elderly; conducts educational programs for licensing and accrediting members; monitors legislation and regulations.

American Assn. of Retired Persons, 601 E St. N.W. 20049; 434-2300. Horace B. Deets, executive director. Fax, 434-2320.

Conducts educational and counseling programs in areas concerning the elderly such as widowed persons service, health promotion, housing, and consumer protection. Library open to the public.

Families USA, 1334 G St. N.W. 20005; 737-6340. Ron Pollack, executive director. Fax, 347-2417.

Organization of American families whose interests include health and long-term care, income security, Social Security, Medicare, and Medicaid. Engages in research and public education activities. Monitors legislation and regulations affecting the elderly.

Gray Panthers Project Fund, 2025 Pennsylvania Ave. N.W., #821 20006; 466-3132. Dixie Horning, director. Fax, 466-3133.

Educational and advocacy organization that promotes national health care and economic and social justice for people of all ages, including the elderly.

International Federation on Aging, 601 E St. N.W. 20049; 434-2430. Nigel Martin, secretary general. Fax, 434-6458.

International federation of organizations that serves the elderly. Serves as an advocate for the elderly and promotes international exchange of policy and program information.

National Alliance of Senior Citizens, 1700 18th St. N.W., #401 20009; 986-0117. Peter J. Luciano, chief executive officer.

Membership: persons age 45 and older. Interests include Social Security, health care, Medicare, pensions, and crime against older Americans.

National Assn. of Area Agencies on Aging, 1112 16th St. N.W., #100 20036; 296-8130. Richard Browdie, executive director. Fax, 296-8134.

Works to establish an effective national policy on aging; provides local agencies with training and technical assistance; disseminates information to these agencies and the public; monitors legislation and regulations.

National Assn. of State Units on Aging, 1225 Eye St. N.W., #725 20005; 898-2578. Daniel A. Quirk, executive director.

Membership: state and territorial governmental units that deal with the elderly. Provides members with information, technical assistance, and professional training; monitors legislation and regulations.

National Caucus and Center on Black Aged, 1424 K St. N.W. 20005; 637-8400. Samuel J. Simmons, president. Fax, 347-0895.

Concerned with issues that affect elderly African Americans. Sponsors employment and housing programs for the elderly and education and training for professionals in the gerontology field; monitors legislation and regulations.

National Council of Senior Citizens, 1331 F St. N.W. 20004; 347-8800. Lawrence T. Smedley, executive director. Information, 624-9549. Press, 624-9540. Library, 624-9366. Fax, 624-9595.

Federation of senior citizen clubs, associations, councils, and other groups. Seeks to nationalize health care services and to strengthen benefits to the elderly, including improved Social Security payments, increased employment, and education and health programs. Offers prescription drug program, Medicare supplement, and group travel.

National Council on the Aging, 409 3rd St. S.W. 20024; 479-1200. Daniel Thursz, president. Library, 479-6669. Fax, 479-0735. TDD, 479-6674.

Membership: individuals, voluntary agencies and associations, businesses, and labor unions serving or concerned with the elderly. Acts as an information clearinghouse on aging. Conducts research; offers information, training, and technical assistance to those working with the elderly; sponsors institutes on older worker employment services and senior centers; sponsors programs on literacy, retirement, family caregivers, and women. Library open to the public.

National Hispanic Council on Aging, 2713 Ontario Rd. N.W. 20009; 265-1288. Marta Sotomayor, president. Fax, 745-2522.

Membership: senior citizens, health care workers, professionals in the field of aging, and others in the United States and Puerto Rico who are interested in topics related to Hispanics and aging. Provides research training, consulting, and technical assistance; sponsors seminars, workshops, and management internships.

See also Catholic Charities U.S.A. (p. 414); National Senior Citizens Law Center (p. 522); Salvation Army (p. 415)

Homeless

Agencies:

Education Dept., Adult Education and Literacy, 330 C St. S.W. (mailing address: 400 Maryland Ave. S.W., Washington, DC 20202-7240); 205-8270. Ronald S. Pugsley, acting director. Fax, 205-8973. Literacy clearinghouse, 205-9996.

Awards discretionary grants to state education agencies to establish, expand, improve, and operate adult education programs for the homeless. Provides state and local agencies and community-based organizations with technical assistance to establish education programs for homeless adults.

Education Dept., Education for Homeless Children and Youth, 400 Maryland Ave. S.W. 20202; 401-0728. Francine Vinson, coordinator. Fax, 401-1112.

Provides formula grants to education agencies in the states, the District of Columbia, Puerto Rico, the Virgin Islands, American Somoa, and the Northern Mariana Islands to educate homeless children and youth and to establish an office of coordinator of education for homeless children and youth in each jurisdiction.

Federal Emergency Management Agency, Disaster Assistance, 500 C St. S.W. 20472; 646-3652. Fran McCarthy, program specialist. Fax, 646-2723.

Coordinates the Emergency Food and Shelter Program under the McKinney Act. Gives supplemental assistance to programs that provide the homeless with shelter, food, and support services.

Housing and Urban Development Dept., Community Planning and Development, HUD

Bldg., Rm. 7100 20410; 708-2690. Andrew Cuomo, assistant secretary. Fax, 708-3336.

Gives supplemental assistance to facilities that aid the homeless; awards grants for innovative programs that address the needs of homeless families with children.

Housing and Urban Development Dept., Special Needs Assistance Programs, HUD Bldg., Rm. 7262 20410; 708-4300. Barbara Richards, acting director. Fax, 708-3617.

Advises and represents the secretary on homelessness matters; promotes cooperation among federal agencies on homelessness issues; coordinates assistance programs for the homeless under the McKinney Act. Trains HUD field staff in administering homelessness programs. Distributes funds to eligible nonprofit organizations, cities, counties, tribes, and territories for shelter plus care, transitional housing, and permanent housing for the disabled homeless. Programs provide for acquisition and rehabilitation of buildings, prevention of homelessness, counseling, and medical care. Administers the Federal Surplus Property Program and spearheads the initiative to lease HUD hold homes to the homeless.

National Institute on Alcohol Abuse and Alcoholism (National Institutes of Health, Health and Human Services Dept.), Homeless Demonstration and Evaluation, 6000 Executive Blvd., Rockville, MD 20892-7003; (301) 443-0786. Robert Huebner, acting chief. Fax, (301) 443-9334.

Provides funds and assistance to establish community-based research demonstration projects for substance abuse treatment of homeless individuals; evaluates project effectiveness.

Congress:

See Social Services and Rehabilitation Programs, General, Congress (p. 412)

Nongovernmental:

American Institute of Architects, Search for Shelter, 1735 New York Ave. N.W. 20006; 626-7468. Charles Buki, director. Fax, 626-7421.

Helps architects and community groups form partnerships that address local issues affecting the homeless and near-homeless, special-needs populations, and people living in substandard conditions. Conducts public awareness workshops. Supports architectural planning for transitional and permanent housing and administers programs that produce new or renovated units.

Housing Assistance Council, 1025 Vermont Ave. N.W., #606 20005; 842-8600. Moises Loza, executive director. Toll-free, (800) 989-4422. Fax, 347-3441.

Provides low-income housing development groups in rural areas with seed money loans and technical assistance; assesses rural housing needs responses; makes recommendations for federal and state involvement; publishes technical guides and reports on rural housing issues.

National Alliance to End Homelessness, 1518 K St. N.W. 20005; 638-1526. Thomas L. Kenyon, president. Fax, 638-4664.

Seeks to form a public-private partnership to abate problems of the homeless; promotes policies and programs that reduce the homeless population; awards grants to nonprofit organizations concerned with housing issues.

National Coalition for the Homeless, 1612 K St. N.W., #1004 20006; 265-2371. Fred Karnas, executive director. Fax, 775-1316. Recorded hotline, 775-1372.

Works to ensure housing for all people; conducts research and provides information on homelessness, job creation, counseling, and family and child care; monitors legislation and regulations; litigates on behalf of homeless people.

National Law Center on Homelessness and Poverty, 918 F St. N.W., #412 20004; 638-2535. Maria Foscarinis, director. Fax, 628-2737.

Legal advocacy group that monitors legislation affecting the homeless. Works to protect and expand the rights of the homeless through impact litigation, and conducts research on homelessness issues. Acts as a clearinghouse for legal information and technical assistance.

Salvation Army, 615 Slaters Lane, Alexandria, VA (mailing address: P.O. Box 269, Alexandria, VA 22313); (703) 684-5500. Kenneth Hodder, commissioner. Fax, (703) 684-3478.

International religious social welfare organization that provides the homeless with residences and social services, including counseling, emergency help, and employment services.

Share Our Strength, 1511 K St. N.W., #940 20005; 393-2925. Bill Shore, executive director. Toll-free, (800) 969-4767. Fax, 347-5868.

Network of restaurateurs, writers, and artists who fight hunger by raising funds and by heightening public awareness of hunger. Awards grants to domestic and international hunger relief organizations; encourages the restaurant industry to donate food surplus to homeless shelters and soup kitchens; educates the public on hunger matters.

U.S. Conference of Mayors, Task Force on Hunger and Homelessness, 1620 Eye St. N.W., 4th Floor 20006; 293-7330. Laura DeKoven Waxman, assistant executive director. Fax, 293-2352.

Tracks trends in hunger, homelessness, and community programs that address homelessness and hunger in U.S. cities; issues reports; monitors legislation and regulations.

See also National Assn. of Community Health Centers (p. 345); National Assn. of Public Hospitals (p. 353); National Network of Runaway and Youth Services (p. 419)

Low-Income Groups and Public Assistance Recipients

See also Government Financial Assistance Programs, General (p. 406); Housing: Special Concerns, Public and Subsidized Housing (p. 402); Legal Services and Education (p. 520)

Agencies:

Administration for Children and Families (Health and Human Services Dept.), 901 D St. S.W. (mailing address: 370 L'Enfant Promenade S.W., Washington, DC 20447); 401-9200. Mary Jo Bane, assistant secretary. Information, 401-9215. Fax, 401-5770.

Administers programs for low-income families and individuals. Responsible for Social Service Block Grants to the states; coordinates HHS policy and regulations on day care, foster care, adoption services, child abuse and neglect, home management, Head Start, special services for the disabled and aging, and grants to native Americans.

Administration for Children and Families (Health and Human Services Dept.), Community Services, 901 D St. S.W. (mailing address: 370 L'Enfant Promenade S.W., Washington, DC 20447); 401-9333. Donald Sykes, director. Fax, 401-5718.

Administers the Community Services Block Grant and Discretionary Grant programs and the Low Income Home Energy Assistance Block Grant Program for heating, cooling, and weatherizing low-income households.

Administration for Children and Families (Health and Human Services Dept.), Family Assistance—Job Opportunities and Basic Skills Training, 901 D St. S.W. (mailing address: 370 L'Enfant Promenade S.W., Washington, DC 20447); 401-9275. Diann Dawson, acting director. Fax, 205-5887.

Provides recipients of Aid to Families with Dependent Children with job search assistance, vocational training, and educational aid (including remedial programs, literacy training, and instruction in English as a second language); focuses on women with young children; provides child care options and other support services to make participation possible. Coordinates programs, under the Family Support Act of 1988, with departments of Education and Labor.

Agriculture Dept., Food Distribution, 3101 Park Center Dr., #503, Alexandria, VA 22302; (703) 305-2680. Vernon Morgan, director. Fax, (703) 305-2420. TDD, (703) 305-2648.

Administers the Emergency Food Assistance Program, under which butter, cheese, milk, rice, and other surplus commodities are distributed to the needy. Administers the National Commodity Processing Program, which facilitates distribution, at reduced prices, of processed foods to state agencies, including charitable institutions, child-care food programs, nutrition programs for the elderly, state correctional institutions, and summer food service programs.

Education Dept., Follow Through Program, 400 Maryland Ave. S.W. 20202-2527; 401-1692. Robert Alexander, program specialist. Fax, 401-2527.

Assists the overall development of children from low-income families (grades K-3). Supplements basic educational services available in the public school system with services and activities related to physical and mental health, social welfare, and nutrition. Seeks community and parental involvement in the program.

Health and Human Services Dept., Head Start, 330 C St. S.W. (mailing address: P.O. Box 1182, Washington, DC 20013); 205-8572. Helen Taylor, associate commissioner. Fax, 401-5916.

Awards grants to nonprofit organizations and local governments for operating community Head Start programs (comprehensive development programs for children, ages 3 to 5, of low-income families); manages a limited number of parent and child centers for families with children up to age 3. Conducts research and manages demonstration programs, including those under the Comprehensive Child Care Development Act of 1988; administers the Child Development Associate scholarship program, which trains individuals for careers in child development, often as Head Start teachers.

Volunteers in Service to America (VISTA) (Corporation for National Service), 1100 Vermont Ave. N.W. 20525; 606-5000. Diana London, acting assistant director. Fax, 606-4921.

Assigns full-time volunteers to public and private nonprofit organizations to alleviate poverty in local communities. Volunteers receive stipends.

Congress:

See *Social Services and Rehabilitation Programs, General, Congress (p. 412)*

Nongovernmental:

Accountants for the Public Interest, 1012 14th St. N.W., #906 20005; 347-1668. Mildred E. MacVicar, executive director. Fax, 347-1663.

Membership: accountants who provide volunteer services to nonprofit organizations, small businesses, and individuals unable to afford professional accounting services.

American Public Welfare Assn., 810 1st St. N.E., #500 20002-4267; 682-0100. A. Sidney Johnson III, executive director. Fax, 289-6555.

Membership: state and local human services agencies and individuals working or interested in public welfare. Develops national social policy positions; promotes professional development for members.

Center for Community Change, 1000 Wisconsin Ave. N.W. 20007; 342-0519. Pablo Eisenberg, executive director. Fax, 342-1132.

Provides community-based organizations serving minorities and the economically disadvantaged with technical assistance. Areas of assistance include community development block grants, housing, economic and resource development, rural development projects, and program planning.

Center for Law and Social Policy, 1616 P St. N.W., #150 20036; 328-5140. Alan W. Houseman, director. Fax, 328-5195.

Public interest law firm that represents low-income citizens in cases involving family policy issues, including child support, child care, education, employment and training, minimum wage laws, health care, and public benefits. Represents local legal services programs before the Legal Services Corp., Congress, and the courts.

Center on Budget and Policy Priorities, 777 N. Capitol St. N.E. 20002; 408-1080. Robert Greenstein, director. Fax, 408-1056.

Research group that analyzes federal, state, and local government policies affecting low- and moderate-income Americans.

Coalition on Human Needs, 1000 Wisconsin Ave. N.W. 20007; 342-0726. Jennifer A. Vasiloff, executive director. Fax, 342-1132.

Coalition of religious, civil rights, labor, service, and policy groups. Works to provide low-income individuals with education, job training, health care, food, and shelter; monitors and reports on legislation and regulations that affect the poor; helps local groups organize to protect human service programs in their communities.

Food Research and Action Center, 1875 Connecticut Ave. N.W., #540 20009-5728; 986-2200. Robert Fersh, executive director. Fax, 986-2525.

Public interest advocacy, research, and legal center that works to end hunger and poverty in the United States; offers legal assistance, organizational aid, training, and information to groups seeking to improve or expand federal food programs, including food stamp, child nutrition, and WIC (women, infants, and children) programs; monitors legislation and regulations; conducts studies relating to hunger and poverty; coordinates network of antihunger organizations.

National Assn. for the Advancement of Colored People (NAACP), 1025 Vermont Ave. N.W., #1120 20005; 638-2269. Wade J. Henderson, director, Washington bureau. Fax, 638-5936.

Membership: persons interested in civil rights for all minorities. Interests include welfare reform and related social welfare matters. Administers programs that create employment and affordable housing opportunities and that improve health care. Monitors legislation and regulations. (Headquarters in Baltimore.)

National Assn. of Community Action Agencies, 1875 Connecticut Ave. N.W., #416 20009; 265-7546. Edward L. Block, executive director. Fax, 265-8850.

Provides community action agencies with information, training, and technical assistance; advocates, at all levels of government, for low-income people.

National Assn. of Housing Cooperatives, 1614 King St., Alexandria, VA 22314; (703) 549-5201. Herbert J. Levy, executive director. Fax, (703) 549-5204.

Membership: housing cooperative members. Promotes housing cooperatives, particularly for low- and moderate-income families; monitors legislation.

National Community Action Foundation, 2100 M St. N.W. 20037; 775-0223. David Bradley, executive director. Fax, 775-0225.

Organization for community action agencies concerned with issues that affect the poor. Provides information on Community Services Block Grant, low-income energy assistance, employment and training, weatherization for low-income housing, nutrition, and the Head Start program.

National Urban Coalition, 1875 Connecticut Ave. N.W., #400 20009-5728; 986-1460. Ramona H. Edelin, president. Fax, 986-1468.

Membership: business and labor representatives, minority groups, educators, and religious and civic leaders. Operates Say Yes to a Youngster's Future, a community-based education program for low-income students in math, science, and technology; maintains database on urban education programs and task force on urban housing and urban health.

National Urban League, 1111 14th St. N.W., #600 20005; 898-1604. Robert McAlpine, director, policy and government relations. Fax, 682-0782.

Federation of affiliates concerned with the social welfare of African Americans and other minorities. Conducts research. Social Welfare

Division disseminates welfare rights information to local leagues. (Headquarters in New York.)

Poverty and Race Research Action Council, 1711 Connecticut Ave. N.W., #207 20009-5728; 387-9887. Chester Hartman, executive director. Fax, 387-0764.

Provides nonprofit organizations with funding for research on race and poverty. Promotes advocacy work.

See also Catholic Charities USA (p. 414); Corporation for Enterprise Development (p. 384): National Head Start Assn. (p. 142); Salvation Army (p. 415)

Veterans

See also Personnel: Military, Retirement (p. 578)

General

Agencies:

Air Force Dept. (Defense Dept.), Force Support and Personnel, The Pentagon 20330; (703) 614-4752. Ruby B. DeMesme, acting deputy assistant secretary. Fax, (703) 693-4244.

Civilian office that monitors and reviews Air Force veterans' personnel policies.

Army Dept. (Defense Dept.), Army Career and Alumni Program, 2461 Eisenhower Ave., Alexandria, VA 22331; (703) 325-3591. P. V. Botelho, chief. Toll-free, (800) 445-2049. Fax, (703) 325-8092.

Military office that provides Army military personnel with information concerning transaction benefits.

Navy Dept. (Defense Dept.), Manpower, The Pentagon 20350; (703) 695-4350. Vacant, deputy assistant secretary. Fax, (703) 614-3889.

Civilian office that directs and reviews Navy and Marine Corps veterans' policies.

Veterans Affairs Dept., 801 Eye St. N.W. (mailing address: 810 Vermont Ave. N.W., Washington, DC 20420); 535-8900. Jesse Brown, secretary. Information, 535-8165. Fax, 535-8667.

Administers programs benefiting veterans, including disability compensation, pensions, education, home loans, insurance, vocational rehabilitation, medical care at veterans' hospitals and outpatient facilities, and burial benefits.

Veterans Affairs Dept., National Veteran Analysis and Statistics, 810 Vermont Ave. N.W. 20420; 233-6852. Conrad R. Hoffman, director. Fax, 233-2633.

Serves as the single, departmentwide repository, clearinghouse, and publication source for veterans' demographic and statistical information.

Veterans Affairs Dept., Policy and Planning, 810 Vermont Ave. N.W. 20420; 273-5033. David Burge, acting assistant secretary. Fax, 273-5993.

Develops policy and provides policy makers with analytical reports on improving services to veterans and their families.

Congress:

General Accounting Office, Human Resources, 441 G St. N.W., NGB/ACG 20548; 512-6806. Janet L. Shikles, assistant comptroller general. Fax, 512-5806

Independent, nonpartisan agency in the legislative branch that audits, analyzes, and evaluates Veterans Affairs Dept. programs; makes reports available to the public.

House Appropriations Committee, Subcommittee on VA, HUD, and Independent Agencies, H143 CAP 20515; 225-3241. Louis Stokes, D-Ohio, chairman; Paul Thompson, staff assistant.

Jurisdiction over legislation to appropriate funds for the Veterans Affairs Dept., the Board of Veterans Appeals, the U.S. Court of Veterans Appeals, and other veterans' programs.

House Government Operations Committee, Subcommittee on Human Resources and Intergovernmental Relations, B372 RHOB 20515; 225-2548. Edolphus Towns, D-N.Y., chairman; Ron Stroman, staff director. Fax, 225-2382.

Oversight jurisdiction of the Veterans Affairs Dept. (shares oversight jurisdiction with the House Veterans' Affairs Committee).

House Veterans' Affairs Committee, 335 CHOB 20515; 225-3527. G. V. "Sonny" Montgomery, D-Miss., chairman; Mack G. Fleming, counsel and staff director. Fax, 225-5486.

Oversight and legislative jurisdiction of the Veterans Affairs Dept. (shares oversight jurisdiction with the House Government Operations Committee).

House Veterans' Affairs Committee, Subcommittee on Compensation, Pension, and Insurance, 335 CHOB 20515; 225-3569. Jim Slattery, D-Kan., chairman; John Brizzi, staff director and chief counsel.

Jurisdiction over legislation on veterans' pensions and life insurance and on service-connected disability payments to veterans, survivors, and dependents.

House Veterans' Affairs Committee, Subcommittee on Education, Training, and Employment, 337A CHOB 20515; 225-9166. G. V. "Sonny" Montgomery, D-Miss., chairman; Jill T. Cochran, staff director.

Jurisdiction over legislation on education, training, vocational rehabilitation, employment, and readjustment to civilian life for veterans and disabled veterans. Jurisdiction over legislation on educational assistance for survivors of deceased veterans.

House Veterans' Affairs Committee, Subcommittee on Hospitals and Health Care, 338 CHOB 20515; 225-9154. J. Roy Rowland, D-Ga., chairman; Ralph Ibson, chief counsel.

Jurisdiction over legislation on hospitals, medical programs, outpatient programs, state veterans' homes, and construction of medical facilities.

House Veterans' Affairs Committee, Subcommittee on Housing and Memorial Affairs, 337 CHOB 20515; 225-9164. George E. Sangmeister, D-Ill., chairman; Gloria Royce, staff director.

Jurisdiction over legislation on cemeteries and burial benefits for veterans, housing loans, and special housing loans for paraplegics.

Senate Appropriations Committee, Subcommittee on VA, HUD, and Independent Agencies, SD-142 20510; 224-7211. Barbara A. Mikulski, D-Md., chair; Kevin F. Kelly, clerk.

Jurisdiction over legislation to appropriate funds for the Veterans Affairs Dept., the Board of Veterans Appeals, the U.S. Court of Veterans Appeals, and other veterans' programs.

Senate Banking, Housing, and Urban Affairs Committee, Subcommittee on Housing and

Veterans Affairs Dept.

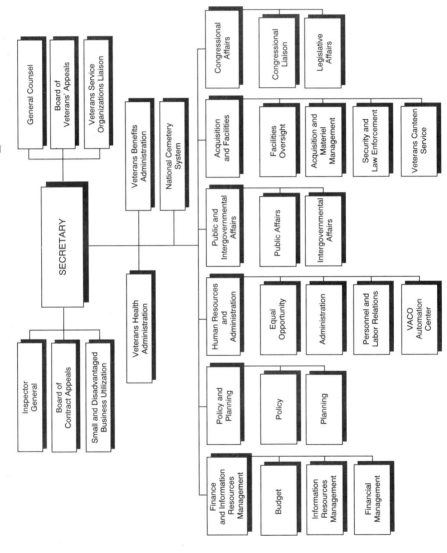

Urban Affairs, SD-535 20510; 224-6348. Paul S. Sarbanes, D-Md., chairman; Paul N. Weech, staff director. Fax, 224-5137.

Jurisdiction over legislation on veterans' housing loan programs (jurisdiction shared with the Veterans' Affairs Committee).

Senate Veterans' Affairs Committee, SR-414 20510; 224-9126. John D. Rockefeller IV, D-W.Va., chairman; Jim Gottlieb, staff director. Fax, 224-9575.

Jurisdiction over veterans' legislation, including pensions; service-connected disability payments to veterans, survivors, and dependents; education and training; vocational rehabilitation for veterans with disabilities; veterans' life insurance, hospitals, medical programs, and outpatient programs; construction of medical facilities; readjustment to civilian life; housing loans and special housing loans for paraplegics; employment; cemetery and burial benefits; state veterans' homes; and educational assistance for survivors of deceased veterans. Oversight of and legislative jurisdiction over the Veterans Affairs Dept.

See also Vietnam Era Veterans in Congress (p. 757)

Nongovernmental:

American Veterans Committee, 6309 Bannockburn Dr., Bethesda, MD 20817; (301) 320-6490. June A. Willenz, executive director. Information, (301) 229-5671. Fax, (301) 320-6490.

Membership: veterans of the World Wars and the Korean, Vietnam, and Persian Gulf wars. Promotes the philosophy, "citizens first, veterans second"; works for international cooperation and peace. (Affiliated with World Veterans Federation, headquartered in Paris.)

National Assn. for Uniformed Services, 5535 Hempstead Way, Springfield, VA 22151; (703) 750-1342. Maj. Gen. James C. Pennington (USA, ret.), president. Fax, (703) 354-4380.

Membership: active, reserve, and retired officers and enlisted personnel of all uniformed services, their spouses, widows, and widowers. Supports legislation that benefits military personnel and veterans.

Vietnam Veterans of America, 1224 M St. N.W. 20005; 628-2700. Paul S. Egan, executive director. Fax, 628-5880.

Membership organization that provides information on legislation that affects Vietnam era veterans and their families. Engages in legislative and judicial advocacy in areas relevant to Vietnam era veterans.

See also Friends of the Vietnam Veterans Memorial (p. 559); Naval Reserve Assn. (p. 578); Public Law Education Institute (p. 584)

Appeals of VA Decisions

Agencies:

Veterans Affairs Dept., Board of Veterans Appeals, 810 Vermont Ave. N.W. 20420; 233-3001. Charles L. Cragin, chairman. Information, 233-3336. Press, 233-3275. Library, 233-4046. Fax, 233-4787.

Final appellate body within the department; reviews claims for veterans' benefits on appeal from agencies of original jurisdiction. Decisions of the board are subject to review by the U.S. Court of Veterans' Appeals.

Judiciary:

U.S. Court of Appeals for the Federal Circuit, 717 Madison Pl. N.W. 20439; 633-6562. Helen W. Nies, chief judge; Francis X. Gindhart, clerk; 633-6555. Fax, 633-9629.

Reviews decisions concerning the Veteran's Judicial Review Provisions.

U.S. Court of Veterans Appeals, 1625 Indiana Ave. N.W. 20004; 501-5970. Frank Q. Nebeker, chief judge. Fax, 501-5849.

Independent court that reviews decisions of the VA's Board of Veterans Appeals concerning benefits. Deals mainly with disability benefits claims.

Nongovernmental:

American Legion National Organization, Claims Service, 1608 K St. N.W. 20006; 861-2762. John Hanson, director. Fax, 833-4452.

Membership: honorably discharged wartime veterans of World War I, World War II, the Korean War, the Vietnam War, or conflicts in Lebanon, Grenada, Panama, and the Persian Gulf. Assists veterans with appeals before the Veterans Affairs Dept. for benefits claims.

Veterans of Foreign Wars of the United States, Appeals, 200 Maryland Ave. N.E. 20002; 543-

2239. George Estry, chief appeals consultant. Fax, 543-6719.

Assists veterans and their dependents and survivors with appeals before the Veterans Affairs Dept. for benefits claims. Assists with cases in the U.S. Court of Veterans Appeals.

Vietnam Veterans of America Legal Services Program, 2001 S St. N.W., #610 20009; 265-8305. David Addlestone, national service representative; John Kahler, service representative liaison. Fax, 328-0063.

Assists Vietnam veterans with appeals before the Veterans Affairs Dept. for benefits claims.

See also veterans' service organizations in Veterans, Benefits, Compensation, Insurance, and Pensions, Nongovernmental (this page)

Benefits, Compensation, Insurance, and Pensions

Agencies:

Veterans Affairs Dept., Compensation and Pension Service, 810 Vermont Ave. N.W. 20420; 233-2264. J. Gary Hickman, director. Fax, 233-4811.

Administers disability payments.

Veterans Affairs Dept., Veterans Assistance Service, 810 Vermont Ave. N.W. 20420; 233-2567. David A. Brigham, director. Fax, 233-4810.

Provides information on and assistance with benefits legislated by Congress for veterans of active military, naval, or air service (including the Public Health Service, the National Oceanic and Atmospheric Administration, and the World War II Merchant Marines).

Veterans Benefits Administration (Veterans Affairs Dept.), 801 Eye St. N.W. (mailing address: 810 Vermont Ave. N.W., Washington, DC 20420); 535-7920. Raymond J. Vogel, under secretary. Information, 872-1151. Fax, 535-8026. Toll-free insurance hotline, (800) 669-8477.

Administers nonmedical benefits programs for veterans and their dependents and survivors. Benefits include veterans' compensation and pensions, survivors' benefits, education and rehabilitation assistance, home loan benefits, insurance coverage, and burials. (Directs benefits delivery nationwide through regional offices and veterans' insurance offices in Philadelphia and St. Paul.)

See also Veterans, General, Agencies (p. 430)

Congress:

See Veterans, General, Congress (p. 431)

Nongovernmental:

Most of the following private veterans' service organizations are either chartered by Congress or recognized by the Veterans Affairs Dept. (VA) to assist veterans in the preparation, presentation, and prosecution of claims for benefits under laws administered by the VA. Congressionally chartered groups must conform to certain federal regulations of incorporation and must submit annual reports to Congress; groups recognized by the VA do not. Both kinds of groups must assist all veterans, not just their members.

American Legion National Organization, 1608 K St. N.W. 20006; 861-2711. John F. Sommer Jr., executive director. Fax, 861-2786.

Membership: honorably discharged wartime veterans of World War I, World War II, the Korean War, the Vietnam War, or conflicts in Lebanon, Grenada, Panama, and the Persian Gulf. Chartered by Congress to assist veterans with claims for benefits.

American Red Cross, Military and Social Services, 18th and D Sts. N.W. 20006; 639-3148. Sue A. Richter, vice president. Fax, 737-2616.

Assists veterans and their dependents with claims for benefits on a limited basis.

American Veterans of World War II, Korea, and Vietnam (Amvets), 4647 Forbes Blvd., Lanham, MD 20706-4380; (301) 459-9600. James J. Kenney, executive director. Fax, (301) 459-7924.

Congressionally chartered veterans organization. Assists veterans with claims for benefits. Monitors legislation, regulations, and public policy issues related to veterans, national defense, and foreign relations. Sponsors programs for youth and hospitalized veterans.

Army and Air Force Mutual Aid Assn., 468 Sheridan Ave., Fort Myer, VA 22211-5002; (703) 522-3060. Bradley J. Snyder, president. Toll-free, (800) 336-4538. Fax, (703) 875-0076.

Private service organization recognized by the Veterans Affairs Dept. to assist veterans with claims for benefits.

Blinded Veterans Assn., 477 H St. N.W. 20001; 371-8880. John Williams, director, administration. Toll-free, (800) 669-7079. Fax, 371-8258.
Chartered by Congress to assist veterans with claims for benefits. Seeks out blinded veterans to make them aware of benefits and services available to them.

Catholic War Veterans U.S.A., 441 N. Lee St., Alexandria, VA 22314; (703) 549-3622. William Gill, executive director. Fax, (703) 684-5196.
Recognized by the Veterans Affairs Dept. to assist veterans with claims for benefits. Conducts community service programs for children; offers scholarships; supports benefits for Vietnam veterans commensurate with those received by World War II veterans.

Disabled American Veterans, 807 Maine Ave. S.W. 20024; 554-3501. Arthur H. Wilson, executive director. Fax, 554-3581.
Chartered by Congress to assist veterans with claims for benefits. Assists families of veterans with disabilities.

Fleet Reserve Assn., 125 N. West St., Alexandria, VA 22314; (703) 683-1400 Norman E. Pearson, national executive secretary. Fax, (703) 549-6610.
Membership: active duty, reserve, and retired Navy, Marine Corps, and Coast Guard personnel. Recognized by the Veterans Affairs Dept. to assist veterans and widows of veterans with benefit claims.

Jewish War Veterans of U.S.A., 1811 R St. N.W. 20009; 265-6280. Col. Herb Rosenbleeth (USA, ret.), national executive director. Fax, 234-5662.
Recognized by the Veterans Affairs Dept. to assist veterans with claims for benefits. Offers programs in community relations and services, foreign affairs, national defense, and veterans' affairs; monitors legislation and regulations that affect veterans.

Marine Corps League, 8626 Lee Highway, Fairfax, VA (mailing address: P.O. Box 3070, Merrifield, VA 22116); (703) 207-9588. William "Brooks" Corley Jr., executive director. Fax, (703) 207-0047.

Membership: active duty, retired, and reserve Marine Corps groups. Chartered by Congress to assist veterans with claims for benefits. Operates a volunteer service program in VA hospitals.

Military Order of the Purple Heart of the U.S.A., 5413-B Backlick Rd., Springfield, VA 22151; (703) 642-5360. Michael B. Prothero, adjutant general. Fax, (703) 642-2054.
Membership: veterans awarded the Purple Heart for combat wounds. Chartered by Congress to assist veterans with claims for benefits. Conducts service and welfare work on behalf of disabled and needy veterans and their families.

Non-Commissioned Officers Assn., 225 N. Washington St., Alexandria, VA 22314; (703) 549-0311. Charles R. Jackson, president. Fax, (703) 549-0245.
Congressionally chartered and accredited by the Veterans Affairs Dept. to assist veterans and widows of veterans with claims for benefits. Provides legislative assistance. (Headquarters in San Antonio, Tex.)

Paralyzed Veterans of America, 801 18th St. N.W. 20006; 872-1300. Gordon H. Mansfield, executive director. Fax, 785-4452. TDD, 416-7622.
Congressionally chartered organization that assists veterans with claims for benefits. Distributes information on special education for paralyzed veterans; supports and raises funds for medical research.

United Spanish War Veterans, 810 Vermont Ave. N.W. (mailing address: P.O. Box 1915, Washington, DC 20013); 347-1898. Beulah M. Cope, adjutant general.
Chartered by Congress to assist Spanish-American War veterans and their spouses and children with pensions and benefits.

Veterans of Foreign Wars of the United States, National Veterans Service, 200 Maryland Ave. N.E. 20002; 543-2239. Frederico Juarbe Jr., director. Fax, 543-6719.
Chartered by Congress to assist veterans with claims for benefits.

Veterans of World War I of the U.S.A., P.O. Box 8027, Alexandria, VA 22306; (703) 780-5660. Muriel Sue Parkhurst, executive director.
Fraternal organization of veterans of wartime service in World War I. Chartered by Congress

to assist veterans with claims for benefits. Maintains representatives in VA hospitals.

See also Personnel: Military, Financial Services, Nongovernmental (p. 572); Veterans, General, Nongovernmental (p. 433)

Burial Benefits

Agencies:

Veterans Affairs Dept., Compensation and Pension Service, 810 Vermont Ave. N.W. 20420; 233-2264. J. Gary Hickman, director. Fax, 233-4811.

Handles claims for burial and plot allowances by veterans' survivors.

Veterans Affairs Dept., National Cemetery System, 801 Eye St. N.W. (mailing address: 810 Vermont Ave. N.W., Washington, DC 20420); 535-7810. Jerry Bowen, director. Fax, 535-8293.

Administers VA national cemeteries; furnishes markers and headstones for deceased veterans; administers state grants to establish, expand, and improve veterans' cemeteries.

Congress:

See Veterans, General, Congress (p. 431)

Nongovernmental:

See veterans' service organizations in Veterans, Benefits, Compensation, Insurance, and Pensions (p. 434)

Business Assistance

Agencies:

Farmers Home Administration (Agriculture Dept.), Farmer Programs, 14th St. and Independence Ave. S.W. 20250; 720-4671. Lou Anne Kling, acting assistant administrator. Fax, 690-3573.

Gives preference to honorably discharged veterans in processing applications for FHA farm loans.

Small Business Administration, Veterans Affairs, 409 3rd St. S.W. 20416; 205-6773. Leon Bechet, director. Fax, 205-7064.

Coordinates programs to give special consideration to veterans in loan, counseling, procurement, and training programs and in transition training sessions.

Correction of Military Records

See also Military Grievances, Discipline, and Appeals, Correction of Military Records (p. 554); Review Boards (p. 557)

Agencies:

Defense Dept., Legal Policy, The Pentagon, #4C 763 20301-4000; (703) 697-3387. Capt. Jerry Kirkpatrick (USN), director. Fax, (703) 693-6708.

Coordinates policy for armed services boards charged with correcting military records and reviewing discharges.

Nongovernmental:

American Legion National Organization, Review and Correction Boards Unit, 1608 K St. N.W. 20006; 861-2764. Carol Rutherford, supervisor. Information, 861-2700. Fax, 861-2728.

Membership: honorably discharged wartime veterans of World War I, World War II, the Korean War, and the Vietnam War. Represents before the Defense Dept. veterans seeking to upgrade less-than-honorable discharges and to correct alleged errors in military records.

Disabled American Veterans, 807 Maine Ave. S.W. 20024; 554-3501. Arthur H. Wilson, executive director. Fax, 554-3581.

Chartered by Congress to assist veterans with claims for benefits. Represents before the Defense Dept. veterans seeking to correct alleged errors in military records.

Marine Corps League, 8626 Lee Highway, Fairfax, VA (mailing address: P.O. Box 3070, Merrifield, VA 22116); (703) 207-9588. William "Brooks" Corley Jr., executive director. Fax, (703) 207-0047.

Membership: active duty, retired, and reserve Marine Corps groups. Represents before the Defense Dept. veterans seeking to upgrade less-than-honorable discharges.

National Veterans Legal Services Project, 2001 S St. N.W., #610 20009; 265-8305. David Addlestone and Barton Stichman, co-directors. Fax, 328-0063.

Represents veterans before the Defense Dept., Veterans Affairs Dept., Court of Veterans Appeals, and other courts for benefits, records correction, and military discharge upgrade claims.

Veterans of Foreign Wars of the United States, Military Claims, 200 Maryland Ave. N.E. 20002; 543-2239. Robert Gardner, chief.

Represents before the Defense Dept. veterans seeking to upgrade less-than-honorable discharges.

See also veterans' service organizations in Veterans, Benefits, Compensation, Insurance, and Pensions (p. 434)

Education and Vocational Rehabilitation

Agencies:

Education Dept., Veterans Educational Outreach Program, 7th and D Sts. S.W., #3113 (mailing address: 400 Maryland Ave. S.W., Washington, DC 20202-5170); 708-7861. Ronald D. Amon, program manager. Fax, 708-8141.

Provides postsecondary institutions with funds, based on their eligible veterans' enrollment. Institutions receiving funds must maintain a veterans' affairs office and provide veterans with outreach, recruitment, counseling, and special education programs. Emphasis is on helping disabled and educationally disadvantaged veterans.

Veterans Affairs Dept., Education Service, 810 Vermont Ave. N.W. 20420; 233-5154. Celia Dollarhide, director. Fax, 233-8319.

Administers VA's education program, including financial support for veterans' education and for spouses and dependent children of disabled and deceased disabled veterans; provides eligible veterans and dependents with educational assistance under the G.I. Bill and Veterans Educational Assistance Program.

Veterans Affairs Dept., Vocational Rehabilitation Service, 810 Vermont Ave. N.W. 20420; 233-3935. Dennis R. Wyant, director. Fax, 233-8319.

Administers VA's vocational rehabilitation and counseling program, which provides service-disabled veterans with services and assistance; helps veterans to become employable and to obtain and maintain suitable employment.

Congress:

See Veterans, General, Congress (p. 431)

Nongovernmental:

Interstate Conference of Employment Security Agencies, 444 N. Capitol St. N.W., #142 20001; 628-5588. Emily DeRocco, executive director. Fax, 783-5023.

Membership: state employment security administrators. Monitors legislation and regulations that affect veterans' employment and training programs involving state employment security agencies.

See also veterans' service organizations in Veterans, Benefits, Compensation, Insurance, and Pensions (p. 434)

Health Care and Hospitals

Agencies:

Defense Nuclear Agency (Defense Dept.), Environment and Modeling, 6801 Telegraph Rd., Alexandria, VA 22310; (703) 325-7744. Dr. David Auton, chief. Information, (703) 285-5610. Fax, (703) 325-2951. Toll-free, (800) 462-3683.

Reviews personnel participation in atmospheric nuclear tests; provides veterans who participated in these tests with information.

Health and Human Services Dept., Veterans Affairs and Military Liaison, 200 Independence Ave. S.W. 20201; 690-6156. Peter E. M. Beach, director. Fax, 690-5672.

Advises the secretary on health issues that affect veterans and soon-to-be-discharged military personnel. Works to identify the health-related needs of and facilitate the delivery of services to veterans and their families.

Veterans Affairs Dept., Academic Affairs, 801 Eye St. N.W. (mailing address: 810 Vermont Ave. N.W., Washington, DC 20420); 535-7091. Elizabeth M. Short, associate chief medical director. Fax, 535-7522.

Administers education and training programs for personnel in VA hospitals and field facilities in all allied health fields.

Veterans Affairs Dept., Clinical Programs, 801 Eye St. N.W. (mailing address: 810 Vermont Ave. N.W., Washington, DC 20420); 535-7393.

Dr. David H. Law, acting associate deputy chief medical director. Fax, 535-7593.

Manages clinical programs of the VA medical care system.

Veterans Affairs Dept., Dentistry, 801 Eye St. N.W. (mailing address: 810 Vermont Ave. N.W., Washington, DC 20420); 535-7079. Dr. Chester P. Paczkowski, assistant chief medical director.

Administers VA oral health care programs; coordinates oral research, education, and training of VA oral health personnel and outpatient dental care in private practice.

Veterans Affairs Dept., Geriatrics and Extended Care, 801 Eye St. N.W. (mailing address: 810 Vermont Ave. N.W., Washington, DC 20420); 535-7165. Dr. Thomas T. Yoshikawa, assistant chief medical director. Fax, 535-7006.

Administers research, educational, and clinical health care programs in geriatrics, including VA and community nursing homes, personal care homes, VA domiciliaries, state veterans' homes, and hospital-based home care.

Veterans Affairs Dept., Mental Health and Behavioral Sciences Service, 801 Eye St. N.W. (mailing address: 810 Vermont Ave. N.W., Washington, DC 20420); 535-7304. Dr. Paul Errera, director. Fax, 535-7581.

Develops posttraumatic and inpatient psychiatry programs for the homeless and for drug and alcohol abusers.

Veterans Affairs Dept., Research and Development, 801 Eye St. N.W. (mailing address: 810 Vermont Ave. N.W., Washington, DC 20420); 535-7160. Dr. Dennis B. Smith, associate chief medical director. Fax, 535-7159.

Formulates and implements policy for the research and development program of the Veterans Health Administration; advises the chief medical director on research-related matters; represents the VA in interactions with external organizations in matters related to biomedical and health services research.

Veterans Affairs Dept., Strategic Planning and Policy, 801 Eye St. N.W. (mailing address: 810 Vermont Ave. N.W., Washington, DC 20420); 535-7052. James M. Gregg, director.

Coordinates and develops departmental planning to distribute funds to VA field facilities.

Veterans Affairs Dept., Voluntary Service, 801 Eye St. N.W. (mailing address: 810 Vermont Ave. N.W., Washington, DC 20420); 535-7405. Jim W. Delgado, director. Fax, 535-7761.

Supervises volunteer programs in VA medical centers.

Veterans Health Administration (Veterans Affairs Dept.), 801 Eye St. N.W. (mailing address: 810 Vermont Ave. N.W., Washington, DC 20420); 535-7010. Dr. John T. Farrar, acting under secretary for health. Fax, 535-7630.

Recommends policy and administers medical and hospital services for eligible veterans. Publishes guidelines on treatment of veterans exposed to Agent Orange.

Congress:

See Veterans, General, Congress (p. 431)

Nongovernmental:

American Gold Star Mothers, 2128 LeRoy Pl. N.W. 20008; 265-0991. Jeanne K. Penfold, president.

Membership: mothers who have lost sons or daughters in military service (World War I to the present). Members serve as volunteers in VA hospitals.

American War Mothers, 2615 Woodley Pl. N.W. 20008; 462-2791. Beverly G. Marvel, president.

Membership: mothers and stepmothers of military personnel from all branches of service. Members serve as volunteers in VA hospitals.

National Assn. of Veterans Administration Physicians and Dentists, 1620 Eye St. N.W. #220 20006-4005; 363-3838. Samuel Spagnolo, president. Fax, 223-8323.

Seeks to improve the quality of care and conditions at VA hospitals. Monitors legislation and regulations on veterans' health care.

Paralyzed Veterans of America, 801 18th St. N.W. 20006; 872-1300. Gordon H. Mansfield, executive director. Fax, 785-4452. TDD, 416-7622.

Congressionally chartered veterans' service organization. Consults with the Veterans Affairs Dept. on the establishment and operation of spinal cord injury treatment centers.

See also Marine Corps League and Veterans of World War I of the U.S.A. (p. 435)

Housing Loans

Agencies:

Veterans Affairs Dept., Loan Guaranty Service, 810 Vermont Ave. N.W. 20420; 233-2332. R. Keith Pedigo, director. Fax, 233-8478.

Guarantees private institutional financing of home loans for veterans; provides disabled veterans with direct loans and grants for specially adapted housing.

Congress:

See Veterans, General, Congress (p. 431)

Nongovernmental:

See veterans' service organizations in Veterans, Benefits, Compensation, Insurance, and Pensions (p. 434)

Readjustment and Job Assistance

Agencies:

Labor Dept., Veterans' Employment and Training, 200 Constitution Ave. N.W. 20210; 219-9116. Gen. Preston Taylor Jr. (USA, ret.), assistant secretary. Fax, 219-4773.

Monitors state employment offices to see that preference is given to veterans seeking jobs; advises the secretary on veterans' affairs.

Labor Dept., Veterans' Employment, Re-employment, and Training, 200 Constitution Ave. N.W., #S-1316 20210; 219-9110. Hary Puente-Duany, director. Fax, 219-7341.

Investigates veterans' complaints of job or benefits loss because of active or reserve duty military service.

Office of Personnel Management, Affirmative Recruiting and Employment, 1900 E St. N.W., #6332 20415; 606-0800. Donna Beecher, assistant director. Fax, 606-5049. TDD, 606-0023.

Responsible for governmentwide recruiting policies and programs. Assists federal agencies in recruiting and promoting minorities, women, students, veterans, and people with disabilities.

Veterans Affairs Dept., Advisory Committee on the Readjustment of Vietnam Veterans, 801 Eye St. N.W. (mailing address: 810 Vermont Ave. N.W., Washington, DC 20420); 535-7504. David W. Gorman, chairman. Fax, 535-7398.

Studies Vietnam veteran readjustment issues such as medical service, compensation, and pension for posttraumatic stress disorder; examines Vet Center operations and Vietnam veteran employment issues.

Veterans Affairs Dept., Readjustment Counseling, 801 Eye St. N.W. (mailing address: 810 Vermont Ave. N.W., Washington, DC 20420); 535-7554. Dr. Arthur S. Blank Jr., director.

Responsible for community-based centers for veterans nationwide. Provides counseling services for war-related psychological problems.

Congress:

See Veterans, General, Congress (p. 431)

Nongovernmental:

Blinded Veterans Assn., 477 H St. N.W. 20001; 371-8880. John Williams, director, administration. Toll-free, (800) 669-7079. Fax, 371-8258.

Provides blind and disabled veterans with vocational rehabilitation and employment services.

Disabled American Veterans, Employment, 807 Maine Ave. S.W. 20024; 554-3501. Ronald W. Drach, national employment director. Fax, 554-3581.

Recommends veterans' employment policy to federal agencies; monitors legislation and regulations on veterans' employment.

Non-Commissioned Officers Assn., 225 N. Washington St., Alexandria, VA 22314; (703) 549-0311. Charles R. Jackson, president.

Congressionally chartered fraternal organization of active and retired enlisted military personnel. Sponsors job fairs to assist members in finding employment. (Headquarters in San Antonio.)

Paralyzed Veterans of America, 801 18th St. N.W. 20006; 872-1300. Gordon H. Mansfield, executive director. Fax, 785-4452. TDD, 416-7622.

Congressionally chartered organization that assists veterans with claims for benefits. Promotes access to educational and public facilities and to public transportation for people with disabilities; seeks modification of workplaces.

See also veterans' service organizations in Veterans, Benefits, Compensation, Insurance, and Pensions (p. 434)

Key Agencies:

Immigration and Naturalization Service
425 Eye St. N.W. 20536
Information: 514-4316

State Dept.
Main State Bldg.
2201 C St. N.W. 20520
Information: 647-4000

**U.S. International Development
Cooperation Agency**
Main State Bldg.
320 21st St. N.W. 20523
Information: 647-1850

Key Committees:

House Foreign Affairs Committee
2170 RHOB 20515
Phone: 225-5021

Senate Foreign Relations Committee
SD-446 20510
Phone: 224-4651

Key Personnel:

Immigration and Naturalization Service
Doris Meissner, commissioner

Interior Department
Leslie Turner, assistant secretary for territorial and international affairs

State Department
Warren Christopher, secretary
Molly Raiser, chief of protocol
Strobe Talbott, deputy secretary
Joan Edelman Spero, under secretary for economic and agricultural affairs
Lynn E. Davis, under secretary for international security affairs
Peter Tarnoff, under secretary for political affairs

Samuel W. Lewis, director, Policy Planning Staff
George E. Moose, assistant secretary for African affairs
Winston Lord, assistant secretary for East Asian and Pacific affairs
Stephen A. Oxman, assistant secretary for European and Canadian affairs
Alexander Watson, assistant secretary for Inter-American affairs
Robert Pelletreau, assistant secretary for Near Eastern affairs
Robin L. Raphel, assistant secretary for South Asian affairs
Mary Ryan, assistant secretary for consular affairs
Anthony C. E. Quainton, assistant secretary for diplomatic security
Daniel K. Tarullo, assistant secretary for economic and business affairs
John Shattuck, assistant secretary for human rights and humanitarian affairs
Toby T. Gati, assistant secretary for intelligence and research
Robert Gelbard, assistant secretary for international narcotics matters
Douglas J. Bennet, assistant secretary for international organization affairs
Elinor G. Constable, assistant secretary for oceans and international environmental and scientific affairs
Robert L. Gallucci, assistant secretary for politico-military affairs
Thomas E. Donilon, assistant secretary for public affairs and department spokesman
Genta Hawkins Holmes, director general, Foreign Service

**U.S. International Development
Cooperation Agency**
J. Brian Atwood, administrator
J. Brian Atwood, administrator, Agency for International Development

11

International Affairs

Contents:

Foreign Policy and Aid

See also International Economics (p. 75)

General

Agencies:

Defense Dept., Regional Security Affairs, The Pentagon, Rm. 4E838 20301; (703) 695-4351. Charles W. Freeman Jr., assistant secretary. Fax, (703) 697-7230.

Advises the secretary of defense and recommends policies on regional security issues (except those involving countries of the former Soviet Union).

National Security Council (Executive Office of the President), The White House 20500; 456-2255. Anthony Lake, assistant to the president for national security affairs. Press, 456-2947. Fax, 456-2883.

Advises the president on matters relating to national security; collects information on foreign policy and defense issues; coordinates the national security, defense, and intelligence functions of departments such as State and Defense.

Office of Science and Technology Policy (Executive Office of the President), National Security and International Affairs, Old Executive Office Bldg., Rm. 494 20500; 456-2894. Jane Wales, associate director. Information, 395-6142. Fax, 395-1571.

Supports and advises the president on national security policy, international science matters, and other science policy areas. Coordinates international science and technology issues at the interagency level.

President's Foreign Intelligence Advisory Board (Executive Office of the President), Old Executive Office Bldg. 20503; 456-2352. Les Aspin, chairman; Eugene Yeates, executive director. Fax, 395-3403.

Members appointed by the president. Assesses the quality, quantity, and adequacy of foreign intelligence collection and of counterintelligence activities by all government agencies; advises the president on matters concerning intelligence and national security.

State Dept., Main State Bldg., 2201 C St. N.W. 20520; 647-4910. Warren Christopher, secretary. Information, 647-4000. Press, 647-2492. Fax, 647-0464.

Directs and coordinates U.S. foreign relations and interdepartmental activities of the U.S. government overseas.

State Dept., Consular Affairs, Main State Bldg., Rm. 6811 20520-4818; 647-9576. Mary Ryan, assistant secretary. Information, 647-1488. Fax, 647-0341. Passport services, 647-0518. Assistance to U.S. citizens overseas, 647-5225.

Issues passports to U.S. citizens and visas to immigrants and nonimmigrants seeking to enter the United States. Provides protection, assistance, and documentation for American citizens abroad.

State Dept., Counselor's Office, Main State Bldg., Rm. 7250 20520; 647-6240. Timothy E. Wirth, counselor. Fax, 647-0753.

Advises the secretary of state on international issues.

State Dept., Foreign Missions, Main State Bldg., Rm. 2238 20520-7207; 647-3416. Eric James Boswell, director. Fax, 647-1919.

Regulates the benefits, privileges, and immunities granted to foreign missions and their personnel in the United States on the basis of the treatment accorded U.S. missions abroad and considerations of national security, public safety, and welfare.

State Dept., Intelligence and Research, Main State Bldg., Rm. 6533 20520-6510; 647-9177. Toby T. Gati, assistant secretary. Fax, 647-4296.

Coordinates foreign-policy-related research, analysis, and intelligence programs for the State Dept. and other federal agencies.

State Dept., Policy Planning Staff, Main State Bldg., Rm. 7311 20520; 647-2372. Samuel W. Lewis, director. Fax, 647-4147.

Advises the secretary and other State Dept. officials on foreign policy matters.

State Dept., Political Affairs, Main State Bldg., Rm. 7240 20520; 647-2471. Peter Tarnoff, under secretary. Fax, 647-4780.

Assists in the formulation and conduct of foreign policy and in the overall direction of the department; coordinates interdepartmental activities of the U.S. government abroad.

State Dept., Protocol, Main State Bldg., Rm. 1235 20520; 647-4543. Molly Raiser, chief. Press, 647-1685. Fax, 647-1560.

Serves as principal adviser to the president, vice president, secretary of state, and other high-ranking government officials on matters of diplomatic procedure governed by law or international customs and practice.

Congress:

General Accounting Office, National Security and International Affairs, 441 G St. N.W. 20548; 512-2800. Frank C. Conahan, assistant comptroller general. Fax, 512-7686.

Independent, nonpartisan agency in the legislative branch. Audits, analyzes, and evaluates international programs; makes unclassified reports available to the public.

House Appropriations Committee, Subcommittee on Commerce, Justice, State, and Judiciary, H309 CAP 20515; 225-3351. Neal Smith, D-Iowa, chairman; John Osthaus, staff assistant.

Jurisdiction over legislation to appropriate funds for the State Dept. (except migration and refugee assistance), the U.S. Arms Control and Disarmament Agency, the Foreign Claims Settlement Commission, the U.S. Information Agency, the Commission on Security and Co-operation in Europe, and the Japan-United States Friendship Commission.

House Appropriations Committee, Subcommittee on Foreign Operations, Export Financing, and Related Programs, H307 CAP 20515; 225-2041. David R. Obey, D-Wis., chairman; Terry R. Peel, staff assistant. Fax, 226-7922.

Jurisdiction over legislation to appropriate funds for foreign operations, including migration, refugee, economic, and military assistance programs of the State Dept.; the Export-Import Bank; the International Bank for Reconstruction and Development (World Bank); the Inter-American Development Bank; the International Monetary Fund; the International Development Cooperation Agency, including the Agency for International Development; the Peace Corps; and related international organizations.

House Foreign Affairs Committee, 2170 RHOB 20515; 225-5021. Lee H. Hamilton, D-Ind., chairman; Michael H. Van Dusen, chief of staff. Fax, 226-3581.

Jurisdiction over foreign affairs legislation, including economic and military assistance programs.

House Foreign Affairs Committee, Subcommittee on Africa, 709 O'Neill Bldg. (300 New Jersey Ave. S.E.) 20515; 226-7807. Harry A. Johnston, D-Fla., chairman; Clifford Kupchan, staff director. Fax, 225-2029.

Jurisdiction over foreign affairs legislation dealing with Africa. Concurrent jurisdiction over matters assigned to the functional House Foreign Affairs subcommittees insofar as they affect the region.

House Foreign Affairs Committee, Subcommittee on Asia and the Pacific, 707 O'Neill Bldg. (300 New Jersey Ave. S.E.) 20515; 226-7801. Gary L. Ackerman, D-N.Y., chairman; Russell J. Wilson, staff director. Fax, 225-2029.

Jurisdiction over foreign affairs legislation dealing with East Asia and the Pacific, the Near East, and South Asia, from Afghanistan to the Far East. Concurrent jurisdiction over matters assigned to the functional House Foreign Affairs subcommittees insofar as they affect the region.

House Foreign Affairs Committee, Subcommittee on Europe and the Middle East, B359 RHOB 20515; 225-3345. Lee H. Hamilton, D-Ind., chairman; Katherine Wilkens, staff director.

Jurisdiction over foreign affairs legislation dealing with Europe, Greenland, the Middle East (including Iran, Iraq, Egypt, Israel, Lebanon, Syria, Jordan, Saudi Arabia, Gulf states, and Turkey), and the former Soviet Union. Concurrent jurisdiction over matters assigned to the functional House Foreign Affairs subcommittees insofar as they affect the region.

House Foreign Affairs Committee, Subcommittee on International Operations, 2103 RHOB 20515; 225-3424. Howard L. Berman, D-Calif., chairman; Bradley Gordon, staff consultant. Fax, 225-7142.

Jurisdiction over legislation on and operations of the State Dept., U.S. foreign embassies, and the United States Information Agency. Jurisdiction over authorization of budget for the Agency for International Development and the Arms Control and Disarmament Agency, and for U.S. contributions to the United Nations and other international organizations.

State Dept.

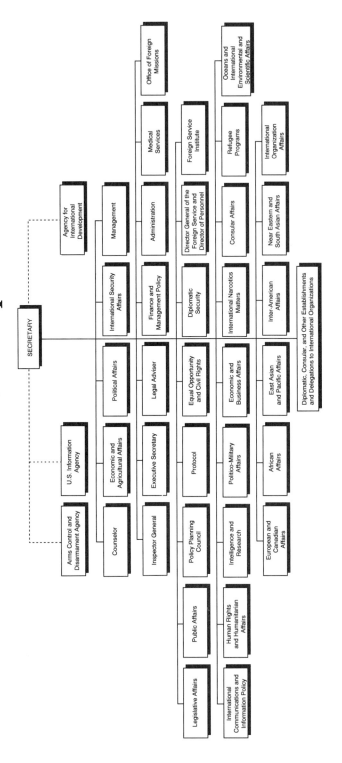

SECRETARY

Arms Control and Disarmament Agency

U.S. Information Agency

Agency for International Development

Counselor

Economic and Agricultural Affairs

Political Affairs

International Security Affairs

Management

Inspector General

Executive Secretary

Legal Adviser

Finance and Management Policy

Administration

Medical Services

Policy Planning Council

Protocol

Equal Opportunity and Civil Rights

Diplomatic Security

Director General of the Foreign Service and Director of Personnel

Foreign Service Institute

Intelligence and Research

Politico-Military Affairs

Economic and Business Affairs

International Narcotics Matters

Consular Affairs

Refugee Programs

Oceans and International Environmental and Scientific Affairs

European and Canadian Affairs

African Affairs

East Asian and Pacific Affairs

Inter-American Affairs

Near Eastern and South Asian Affairs

International Organization Affairs

Legislative Affairs

Public Affairs

International Communications and Information Policy

Human Rights and Humanitarian Affairs

Office of Foreign Missions

Diplomatic, Consular, and Other Establishments and Delegations to International Organizations

House Foreign Affairs Committee, Subcommittee on International Security, International Organizations, and Human Rights, B358 RHOB 20515; 226-7825. Tom Lantos, D-Calif., chairman; Bob King, staff director. Fax, 226-3581.

Oversight of State and Defense department operations regarding arms transfers, export licenses, sales, administration of security assistance, and foreign military training and advisory programs.

House Foreign Affairs Committee, Subcommittee on Western Hemisphere Affairs, 705 O'Neill Bldg. (300 New Jersey Ave. S.E.) 20515; 226-7812. Robert G. Torricelli, D-N.J., chairman; Rob Henken, staff director. Fax, 225-2029.

Jurisdiction over foreign affairs legislation dealing with Canada, Latin America, the Caribbean, and Mexico. Concurrent jurisdiction over matters assigned to the functional House Foreign Affairs subcommittees insofar as they affect the region.

House Government Operations Committee, Subcommittee on Legislation and National Security, B373 RHOB 20515; 225-5147. John Conyers Jr., D-Mich., chairman; James C. Turner, staff director. Fax, 225-2373.

Oversees operations of the State Dept., the Peace Corps, the U.S. International Development Cooperation Agency, and other agencies concerned with foreign affairs.

House Merchant Marine and Fisheries Committee, Subcommittee on Coast Guard and Navigation, 541 Ford Bldg. (2nd and D Sts. S.W.) 20515; 226-3587. W. J. "Billy" Tauzin, D-La., chairman; Elizabeth Megginson, staff director.

Jurisdiction over legislation on the Panama Canal; international arrangements to prevent collisions at sea; and enforcement of laws and treaties on marine pollution control and abatement.

Library of Congress, African and Middle Eastern Division, 110 2nd St. S.E. 20540; 707-7937. Beverly Gray, chief. Fax, 707-1724.

Maintains collections of African, Near Eastern, and Hebraic material. Prepares bibliographies and special studies relating to Africa and the Middle East. Reference service and reading rooms available to the public.

Library of Congress, Asian Division, 110 2nd St. S.E. 20540; 707-5420. Hisao Matsumopo, acting chief. Fax, 707-1724.

Maintains collections of Chinese, Korean, Japanese, Southeast Asian, and South Asian material covering all subjects except law, technical agriculture, and clinical medicine. Reference service is provided in the Asian Reading Room.

Library of Congress, European Division, 10 1st St. S.E. 20540; 707-5414. Michael Haltzel, chief. Fax, 707-8482. Reading room, 707-4515.

Provides reference service on the library's European collections (except collections on Spain, Portugal, and the British Isles). Prepares bibliographies and special studies relating to European countries, including the former Soviet Union. Maintains current unbound Slavic language periodicals and newspapers, which are available in the European Reading Room.

Library of Congress, Hispanic Division, 10 1st St. S.E. 20540; 707-5400. Georgette Dorn, chief. Fax, 707-2005. Reference staff and reading room, 707-5397.

Reading room staff (in the Hispanic Division Room) orients researchers and scholars in the area of Iberian and Latin American studies. Primary and secondary source materials are available in the library's general collections for the study of all periods, from pre-Columbian to the present. All major subject areas are represented with emphasis on history, literature, and the social sciences; the "Archive of Hispanic Literature on Tape" is available in the reading room.

Senate Appropriations Committee, Subcommittee on Commerce, Justice, State, and Judiciary, S146A CAP 20510; 224-7277. Ernest F. Hollings, D-S.C., chairman; Scott B. Gudes, clerk.

Jurisdiction over legislation to appropriate funds for the State Dept. (except counterterrorism, migration and refugee assistance, and international narcotics control), the U.S. Arms Control and Disarmament Agency, the Foreign Claims Settlement Commission, the U.S. Information Agency, and other foreign policy and aid-related services and programs.

Senate Appropriations Committee, Subcommittee on Foreign Operations, SD-136 20510; 224-7209. Patrick J. Leahy, D-Vt., chairman; Eric D. Newsom, clerk.

Jurisdiction over legislation to appropriate funds for foreign operations, including migration, refugee, development, economic, and military assistance programs of the State Dept.

Senate Commerce, Science, and Transportation Committee, SD-508 20510; 224-5115. Ernest F. Hollings, D-S.C., chairman; Kevin Curtin, chief counsel and staff director.

Jurisdiction over legislation on interoceanic canals, including the Panama Canal (jurisdiction shared with Senate Armed Services Committee).

Senate Foreign Relations Committee, SD-446 20510; 224-4651. Claiborne Pell, D-R.I., chairman; Geryld B. Christianson, staff director. Fax, 224-5011.

Jurisdiction over legislation on foreign affairs, including economic and military assistance programs. Oversight responsibilities for operations of the State Dept., the Foreign Service, U.S. participation in the United Nations, the U.S. International Development Cooperation Agency, and other agencies concerned with foreign affairs.

Senate Foreign Relations Committee, Subcommittee on African Affairs, SD-446 20510; 224-4651. Paul Simon, D-Ill., chairman; Geryld B. Christianson, staff director. Fax, 224-5011.

Jurisdiction over foreign affairs legislation dealing with Africa, with the exception of countries bordering on the Mediterranean Sea from Egypt to Morocco.

Senate Foreign Relations Committee, Subcommittee on East Asian and Pacific Affairs, SD-446 20510; 224-4651. Charles S. Robb, D-Va., chairman; Geryld B. Christianson, staff director. Fax, 224-5011.

Jurisdiction over foreign affairs legislation dealing with East Asia and the Pacific, including the mainland of Asia from China and Korea to Burma, Hong Kong, Japan, the Philippines, Malaysia, Indonesia, Australia and New Zealand, Oceania, and the South Pacific islands.

Senate Foreign Relations Committee, Subcommittee on European Affairs, SD-446 20510; 224-4651. Joseph R. Biden Jr., D-Del., chairman; Geryld B. Christianson, staff director. Fax, 224-5011.

Jurisdiction over foreign affairs legislation dealing with Europe (including Greece and Turkey), the United Kingdom, Greenland, Iceland, the former Soviet Union, and the North Polar region.

Senate Foreign Relations Committee, Subcommittee on Near Eastern and South Asian Affairs, SD-446 20510; 224-4651. Daniel Patrick Moynihan, D-N.Y., chairman; Geryld B. Christianson, staff director. Fax, 224-5011.

Jurisdiction over foreign affairs legislation dealing with the Near East and South Asia, including the Arab states and Israel, Bhutan, Bangladesh, India, Pakistan, Afghanistan, Nepal, Sri Lanka, and across North Africa from Egypt to Morocco.

Senate Foreign Relations Committee, Subcommittee on Western Hemisphere and Peace Corps Affairs, SD-446 20510; 224-4651. Christopher J. Dodd, D-Conn., chairman; Geryld B. Christianson, staff director. Fax, 224-5011.

Jurisdiction over foreign affairs legislation dealing with Canada, Latin America, the Caribbean, and Mexico; oversight of all matters of the Peace Corps and the U.S. delegation to the Organization of American States.

Nongovernmental:

ACCESS, 1511 K St. N.W., #643 20005; 783-6050. Mary E. Lord, executive director. Fax, 783-4767.

Nonadvocacy organization that serves as information clearinghouse on international security, peace, and world affairs. Works to expand the public debate on international issues by providing referral to a variety of viewpoints. Maintains database of resources and speakers bureau.

American Enterprise Institute for Public Policy Research, Foreign and Defense Policy Studies, 1150 17th St. N.W. 20036; 862-5814. Jeane Kirkpatrick, director. Press, 862-5829. Fax, 862-7178.

Research and educational organization that conducts conferences, seminars, and debates and sponsors research on international affairs.

Assn. on Third World Affairs, 1629 K St. N.W., #802 20006; 331-8455. Lorna Hahn, executive director. Fax, 775-7465.

Membership: individuals and groups interested in developing nations. Promotes research projects; arranges lectures and conferences; sponsors student interns.

Assn. to Unite the Democracies, 1506 Pennsylvania Ave. S.E. 20003; 544-5150. Charles Patrick, president. Toll-free, (800) 288-6483. Fax, 544-3742.

Educational organization that promotes and conducts research on unity among the industrial democracies, including the United States, Japan, Western European countries, and new and emerging democracies in the former Soviet bloc.

Atlantic Council of the United States, 1616 H St. N.W. 20006; 347-9353. David C. Acheson, president. Fax, 737-5163.

Conducts studies and makes policy recommendations on American foreign security and international economic policies in the Atlantic and Pacific communities.

The Brookings Institution, Foreign Policy Studies, 1775 Massachusetts Ave. N.W. 20036; 797-6010. John Steinbruner, director. Information, 797-6105. Fax, 797-6003. Publications, 797-6258.

Conducts studies on foreign policy, national security, regional affairs, and international energy and economic policies.

Carnegie Endowment for International Peace, 2400 N St. N.W. 20037; 862-7997. Morton I. Abramowitz, president. Fax, 862-2610.

Conducts research on international affairs and American foreign policy. Program activities cover a broad range of military, political, and economic issues; sponsors panel discussions.

Center for Democracy, 1101 15th St. N.W., #505 20005; 429-9141. Allen Weinstein, president. Fax, 293-1768.

Nonpartisan organization that works to promote the democratic process and strengthen democratic institutions in the United States and worldwide. Monitors elections and provides democratizing governments with technical and informational assistance.

Center for Strategic and International Studies, 1800 K St. N.W. 20006; 887-0200. David M. Abshire, president. Information, 775-3176. Fax, 775-3199. Publications: 775-3119.

Independent bipartisan research institute that studies international and domestic policy issues. Interests include science and technology, international business and economics, political-military affairs, arms control, international communications, fiscal policy, and health care reform.

Center of Concern, 3700 13th St. N.E. 20017; 635-2757. James Hug, executive director. Fax, 832-9494.

Independent, interdisciplinary organization that conducts social analysis, theological reflection, policy advocacy, and public education on issues of international justice and peace.

The Citizens Network for Foreign Affairs, 1634 Eye St. N.W., #702 20006; 639-8889. John H. Costello, president. Fax, 639-8648.

Bipartisan public education and public policy organization that works to inform the American public about U.S. international economic interests. Advocates a more collaborative partnership between the public and private sectors to promote global economic growth.

Council for American Security, 1700 K St. N.W., #650 20006; 296-3711. Stephen Edelen, president. Fax, 296-3786.

Foreign policy research and educational organization interested in defense and foreign policy issues pertaining to the Americas, Europe, and the former Soviet Union. Conducts research; offers congressional testimony.

Council on Foreign Relations, 2400 N St. N.W. 20037; 862-7780. Alton Frye, senior vice president and national director.

Promotes understanding of U.S. foreign policy and international affairs. Awards research grants through its International Affairs Fellowship Program. (Headquarters in New York.)

Eisenhower World Affairs Institute, 918 16th St. N.W., #501 20006; 223-6710. Jane L. Kratovil, executive director. Fax, 452-1837.

Conducts educational and leadership development programs to strengthen democratic institutions in the United States and abroad. Supports scholarship and public affairs dialogues.

Friends Committee on National Legislation, 245 2nd St. N.E. 20002-5795; 547-6000. Joe Volk, executive secretary. Fax, 547-6019. Recorded information, 547-4343.

Seeks to broaden public interest in and affect legislation on the Middle East and Central American peace processes, developing countries, and the work of the United Nations. Affiliated with the Religious Society of Friends (Quakers).

German Marshall Fund of the United States, 11 Dupont Circle N.W. 20036; 745-3950. Frank E. Loy, president. Fax, 265-1662.

U.S. foundation funded by the Federal Republic of Germany as a memorial to the Marshall Plan. Seeks to strengthen U.S.-European relations; explores changing U.S.-European economic roles; supports reform in central and Eastern Europe; builds environmental partnerships; promotes contacts between individuals with similar responsibilities in different countries; awards grants; offers fellowships.

Institute for Policy Studies, 1601 Connecticut Ave. N.W. 20009; 234-9382. Michael Shuman, director. Fax, 387-7915.

Research and educational organization. Interests include foreign policy, the U.S. military-industrial complex, international development, human rights, and national security.

International Center, 731 8th St. S.E. 20003; 547-3800. Lindsay Mattison, executive director. Fax, 546-4784.

Research organization concerned with U.S. relations with Africa, Asia, Latin America, and the former Soviet Union. Seeks to inform the government and the public of the effect of American policies abroad. Assists local groups worldwide in establishing agro-forestry projects through the New Forests Project. Sponsors internships.

International Freedom Foundation, 200 G St. N.E. 20002; 546-5788. Jeffrey L. Pandin, executive director. Fax, 546-5488.

Promotes individual liberty, free-market principles, and the building of democratic institutions through research, analysis, and public education.

International Republican Institute, 1212 New York Ave. N.W., 9th Floor 20005; 408-9450. Bruce McColm, president. Fax, 408-9462.

Created under the National Endowment for Democracy Act. Fosters democratic self-rule through closer ties and cooperative programs with political parties and other nongovernmental institutions overseas.

National Democratic Institute for International Affairs, 1717 Massachusetts Ave. N.W., #503 20036; 328-3136. Kenneth Wollack, president. Fax, 939-3166.

Conducts nonpartisan international programs to help maintain and strengthen democratic institutions worldwide. Focuses on party building, governance, and electoral systems.

National Endowment for Democracy, 1101 15th St. N.W. 20005; 293-9072. Carl Gershman, president. Fax, 223-6042.

Grant-making organization that receives funding from Congress. Awards grants to private organizations involved in democratic development abroad, including the areas of democratic political processes; pluralism; and education, culture, and communications.

National Security Archive, 1755 Massachusetts Ave. N.W., #500 20036; 797-0882. Thomas Blanton, executive director. Fax, 387-6315.

Research institute and library that provides information on U.S. foreign policy and national security affairs. Maintains collection of declassified and unclassified national security documents. Archive open to the public by appointment.

Overseas Development Council, 1875 Connecticut Ave. N.W., #1012 20009-5728; 234-8701. John W. Sewell, president. Fax, 745-0067.

Research and educational organization that encourages review of U.S. policy toward developing nations by the business community, educators, policy makers, specialists, the public, and the media. Library open to the public by appointment.

The Paul H. Nitze School of Advanced International Studies, 1740 Massachusetts Ave. N.W. 20036; 663-5624. Paul Wolfowitz, dean. Information, 663-5600. Press, 663-5644. Fax, 663-5621.

Offers graduate programs in international relations and public policy. Sponsors the Johns Hopkins Foreign Policy Institute, an educational and research organization that addresses current world problems; the Center of Canadian Studies; the Center of Brazilian Studies; the E. O. Reischauer Center for East Asian Studies; and the Hopkins-Nanjing Center for Chinese and American Studies. Operates branch in Bologna, Italy.

R.J. Hudson Consultants, International Political Risk Consultants, P.O. Box 20652, Alexandria, VA 22320-1652; (703) 660-6341. David S. Germroth, executive director.

Addresses issues that affect U.S. foreign policy. Assesses the political and economic risks for American businesses and individuals investing abroad.

Union of Concerned Scientists, Foreign Policy, 1616 P St. N.W., #310 20036; 332-0900. Jonathan Dean, senior arms control adviser. Fax, 332-0905.

Membership: scientists and others who advocate peaceful conflict resolution through international cooperation. Works to increase funding and effectiveness of peacekeeping operations, to improve methods of detecting crises, and to encourage post-conflict peacebuilding. (Headquarters in Cambridge, Mass.)

U.S. Catholic Conference, International Justice and Peace, 3211 4th St. N.E. 20017; 541-3199. Drew Christiansen, director. Fax, 541-3339.

Works with the U.S. State Dept., foreign government offices, and international organizations on issues of peace, justice, and human rights.

U.S. Global Strategy Council, 1800 K St. N.W., #1102 20006; 466-6029. Ray S. Cline, chairman. Fax, 331-0109.

Advocates development of long-term, global policies to promote national security, economic well-being, and international stability. Interests include economic, political, social, and military changes in Asia, the Pacific basin, the Caribbean, and Latin America; reform in South Africa; international terrorism; and international economic competition.

World Federalist Assn., 418 7th St. S.E. 20003; 546-3950. Tim Barner, executive director. Toll-free, (800) 546-3761. Fax, 546-3749.

Sponsors projects and conducts research related to international affairs; seeks to broaden public support for world order organizations and a restructured United Nations.

Disaster Relief and Refugees

See also Government Financial Assistance Programs, Refugees and Repatriated Americans (p. 408); Immigration and Naturalization (p. 468)

Agencies:

Agency for International Development (International Development Cooperation Agency), U.S. Foreign Disaster Assistance, Main State Bldg., Rm. 1262A 20523; 647-8924. Nan Vorton, director. Information, 647-5916. Fax, 647-5269.

Administers federal disaster relief and preparedness assistance to foreign countries. Aids displaced persons in disaster situations and helps other countries manage natural and manmade disasters.

Defense Dept., Democracy and Peacekeeping, The Pentagon 20301-2900; (703) 695-2310. Edward L. Warner III, assistant secretary, strategy, requirements, and resources.

Develops policy and plans for department provision of humanitarian assistance, refugee affairs, and U.S. international information programs.

State Dept., Refugee Programs, Main State Bldg. 20520-5824; 647-7360. Phyllis E. Oakley, acting director. Information, 663-1026. Fax, 647-8162.

Develops and implements policies and programs on international refugee matters, including repatriation and resettlement programs; funds and monitors overseas relief, assistance, and repatriation programs; manages refugee admission to the United States.

Congress:

House Foreign Affairs Committee, 2170 RHOB 20515; 225-5021. Lee H. Hamilton, D-Ind., chairman; Michael H. Van Dusen, chief of staff. Fax, 226-3581.

Jurisdiction over international disaster assistance legislation, including the Foreign Assistance Act.

House Judiciary Committee, Subcommittee on International Law, Immigration, and Refugees, B370B RHOB 20515; 225-5727. Romano L. Mazzoli, D-Ky., chairman; Eugene Pugliese, counsel.

Jurisdiction over refugee and immigration legislation.

Senate Foreign Relations Committee, SD-446 20510; 224-4651. Claiborne Pell, D-R.I., chairman; Geryld B. Christianson, staff director. Fax, 224-5011.

Jurisdiction over international disaster assistance legislation.

Senate Judiciary Committee, Subcommittee on Immigration and Refugee Affairs, SD-520 20510; 224-7878. Edward M. Kennedy, D-Mass., chairman; Jeff Blattner, chief counsel.

Jurisdiction over legislation on refugees, immigration, and naturalization. Oversight of private immigration relief bills.

International Organizations:

International Organization for Migration, 1750 K St. N.W., #1110 20006; 862-1826. Hans-Petter Boc, chief of mission. Fax, 862-1879.

Nonpartisan organization that plans and operates refugee resettlement, national migration, and emergency relief programs at the request of its member governments. Recruits skilled professionals for developing countries. (Headquarters in Geneva.)

United Nations High Commissioner for Refugees, 1718 Connecticut Ave. N.W. 20009; 387-8546. Rene van Rooyen, Washington representative. Fax, 387-9038.

Works with governments and voluntary organizations to protect and assist refugees worldwide. Promotes long-term alternatives to refugee camps, including voluntary repatriation, local integration, and resettlement overseas. (Headquarters in Geneva.)

See also Pan American Development Foundation (p. 454)

Nongovernmental:

American Red Cross, National Headquarters, 17th and D Sts. N.W., 2nd Floor 20006; 737-8300. Elizabeth H. Dole, president. Fax, 783-3432.

Service organization chartered by Congress to provide domestic and international disaster relief and to act as a medium of communication between the U.S. armed forces and their families in time of war. Coordinates the distribution of supplies, funds, and technical assistance for relief in major foreign disasters through the International Federation of Red Cross and Red Crescent Societies and the International Committee of the Red Cross, both headquartered in Geneva.

Center for Intercultural Education and Development, 3520 Prospect St. N.W. (mailing address: P.O. Box 2298, Georgetown University, Washington, DC 20057); 298-0200. Julio Giulietti SJ, director. Fax, 338-0608.

Promotes the development of a comprehensive and humane refugee policy through public information and educational programs, lectures, immigration and migration policy research, and on-location training sessions in refugee camps and resettlement homes. Assists refugees in adjusting to life in the United States.

Central American Refugee Center, 3112 Mt. Pleasant St. N.W. 20010; 328-9799. Saul Solorzano, executive director. Fax, 328-0023.

Human rights organization that seeks recognition of refugees' rights, including the right not to be deported. Provides legal representation for refugees seeking asylum; encourages church congregations to assist refugees in applying for political asylum. Interests include community education, documentation of human rights abuses, and social services.

Church World Service, 110 Maryland Ave. N.E. 20002; 543-6336. Carol Capps, director, development policy. Fax, 546-6232.

International relief, refugee, and development agency of the National Council of Churches. Provides food and medical assistance in drought- and famine-stricken areas; disaster relief services in the United States; and development assistance in developing countries. Monitors legislation and regulations. (Headquarters in New York.)

International Rescue Committee, 1825 Connecticut Ave. N.W., #314 20009; 667-7714. Ray Evans, director, Washington office. Fax, 232-7376.

Provides worldwide emergency aid, resettlement services, and educational support for refugees; recruits volunteers. (Headquarters in New York.)

Jesuit Refugee Service/USA, 1424 16th St. N.W. 20036; 462-5200. Robert W. McChesney SJ, national coordinator. Fax, 328-9212.

U.S. Jesuit organization that aids refugees in Africa, Southeast Asia, Central America, and Mexico. Provides information on refugee problems; places individual Jesuits, sisters, and lay people in refugee work abroad. Monitors refugee- and immigration-related legislation. (International headquarters in Rome.)

Lutheran World Relief, 110 Maryland Ave. N.E. 20002; 543-6336. Carol Capps, director, development policy. Fax, 546-6232.

Provides food to drought- and famine-stricken areas; relief services to refugees and victims of natural disasters; and development assistance to promote reforestation, long-term medical care, improved food supplies, increased availability of water, and other needs. Monitors legislation and regulations. (Headquarters in New York.)

Refugee Policy Group, 1424 16th St. N.W. 20036; 387-3015. Dennis Gallagher, executive director. Fax, 667-5034.

Conducts policy analyses and research on domestic and international refugee issues; sponsors symposia. Library open to the public by appointment.

Refugee Voices, 3041 4th St. N.E. 20017-1102; 832-0020. Frank Moan, director. Toll-free, (800) 688-7338. Fax, 832-5616.

Advocates on behalf of refugees; produces radio programs to educate Americans about the plight of refugees; coordinates information network; monitors legislation and regulations.

U.S. Committee for Refugees, 1717 Massachusetts Ave. N.W., #701 20036; 347-3507. Roger P. Winter, director. Fax, 347-3418.

Public information and educational organization that monitors the world refugee situation and informs the public about refugee issues. Interests include human rights abuses and health care. Publishes position papers and an annual survey. (Headquarters in New York.)

World Vision, Relief and Development, 220 Eye St. N.E., #270 20002; 547-3743. Thomas R. Getman, director, government relations. Fax, 547-4834.

Provides children and families around the world with aid, including emergency disaster relief; helps impoverished communities become self-sustaining through agriculture, health care, community organization, food programming, nutritional training, income generation and credit, and other development projects. (Headquarters in Monrovia, Calif.)

See also Foreign Policy and Aid, International Development, Nongovernmental (p. 452)

International Development

See also Agriculture: Foreign Programs, Foreign Assistance and World Food Shortage (p. 606); International Economics, International Investment (p. 81); International Trade and Cooperation (p. 212)

Agencies:

Agency for International Development (International Development Cooperation Agency), Main State Bldg., Rm. 5942 20523; 647-9620. J.

Brian Atwood, administrator. Information, 647-1850. Press, 647-4200. Fax, 647-0148.

Provides developing countries and the nations of central and Eastern Europe with economic assistance and disaster relief. Assists with transnational problems. Promotes free markets and economic growth, sound environmental policies, and natural resource management. Maintains economic, social, and demographic data for the developing countries of Africa, Central and South America, Asia, and the Near East.

Agency for International Development (International Development Cooperation Agency), Asia and Near East Bureau, Main State Bldg., Rm. 6212 20523; 647-8298. Margaret Carpenter, assistant administrator. Fax, 647-6901.

Oversees U.S. foreign assistance programs in South and East Asia and the Near East.

Agency for International Development (International Development Cooperation Agency), Global Programs, Field Support and Research, Main State Bldg., Rm. 4942 20523; 647-1827. Sally Shelton-Colby, assistant administrator designate. Fax, 647-3028.

Administers grants to research and educational institutions for development of foreign assistance programs, particularly in the areas of agricultural and rural development, energy, health, nutrition, population and family planning, forestry, and natural resources.

Agency for International Development (International Development Cooperation Agency), Humanitarian Response, Main State Bldg., Rm. 5314A 20523-0059; 647-0220. M. Douglas Stafford, assistant administrator. Fax, 647-0218.

Manages U.S. foreign disaster assistance, U.S. government food aid programs, grants to private voluntary and cooperative development organizations, and American sponsored schools and hospitals around the world. Manages U.S. government relief efforts in Somalia.

Agency for International Development (International Development Cooperation Agency), International Training, 1621 N. Kent St., Arlington, VA (mailing address: Main State Bldg., Washington, DC 20523-1601); (703) 875-4200. Dennis Diamond, director. Fax, (703) 875-4346.

Administers the AID Participant Training Program, which provides students and midcareer professionals from developing countries with academic and technical training, and the Entrepreneur International Initiative, a short-term training/trade program that matches developing country entrepreneurs with American counterparts to familiarize them with American goods, services, and technology. Participants train in U.S. universities, businesses, labor organizations, state and local governments, and community organizations.

Agency for International Development (International Development Cooperation Agency), Policy Analysis and Resources, Main State Bldg., Rm. 3947 20523; 647-8558. George A. Hill, director. Fax, 647-8595.

Provides information and guidance on international economic policy issues that affect developing countries.

Foreign Agricultural Service (Agriculture Dept.), 14th St. and Independence Ave. S.W. 20250; 720-5173. Christopher E. Goldthwait, general sales manager. Information, 720-7115. Fax, 690-1595.

Administers the U.S. foreign food aid program with the Agency for International Development. Responsible for Title I of the Food for Peace program, the Food for Progress program, and the Section 416(b) program, which provides developing countries with surplus commodities.

Inter-American Foundation, 901 N. Stuart St., Arlington, VA 22203; (703) 841-3810. Bill K. Perrin, president. Information, (703) 841-3800. Fax, (703) 841-0973.

Supports small-scale Latin American and Caribbean social development efforts through grassroots development programs, grants, and fellowships.

Peace Corps, 1990 K St. N.W. 20526; 606-3970. Carol Bellamy, director. Information, 606-3387. Press, 606-3010. Library, 606-3307. Fax, 606-3110. Toll-free, (800) 424-8580.

Promotes world peace and mutual understanding between the United States and developing nations. Administers volunteer programs in developing nations to provide educational, health, energy and conservation, housing, food production, and economic development assistance.

State Dept., Development Finance, Main State Bldg., Rm. 2529 20520; 647-9426. Louis Warren, director. Fax, 647-0320.

Provides liaison between the International Bank for Reconstruction and Development (World Bank), regional development banks, and the

U.S. Export-Import Bank to facilitate U.S. assistance to developing nations. Helps to formulate State Dept. and U.S. government positions on multilateral lending.

Treasury Dept., Multilateral Development Banks, Main Treasury Bldg., Rm. 5400 20220; 622-1231. Matthew P. Hennesey, director. Information, 622-2960. Fax, 622-1228.

Provides support for U.S. participation in multilateral development banks: the World Bank Group, the Inter-American Development Bank, the African Development Bank/Fund, the Asian Development Bank, and the European Bank for Reconstruction and Development.

U.S. International Development Cooperation Agency, Main State Bldg., 320 21st St. N.W. 20523; 647-8578. J. Brian Atwood, administrator. Information, 647-1850. Press, 647-4274. Fax, 647-1770.

Independent agency that includes the Agency for International Development (AID) and the Overseas Private Investment Corporation (OPIC). Formulates U.S. international policies affecting developing nations; coordinates U.S.-supported bilateral and multilateral development assistance activities; responsible for the development aspects of U.S. participation in international organizations, including United Nations development programs; shares with the Treasury Dept. responsibility for U.S. participation in multilateral development banks such as the World Bank; shares with the Agriculture Dept. responsibility for the Food for Peace program.

Congress:

See Foreign Policy and Aid, General, Congress (p. 443)

Nongovernmental:

Adventist Development and Relief Agency International, 12501 Old Columbia Pike, Silver Spring, MD 20904; (301) 680-6380. Ralph S. Watts Jr., president. Toll-free, (800) 424-2372. Press, (301) 680-6340. Fax, (301) 680-6370.

Worldwide agency of the Seventh-day Adventist church. Works to alleviate poverty in developing countries and responds to disasters. Sponsors activities that improve health, foster economic and social well-being, and build self-reliance.

Alliance for Communities in Action, P.O. Box 30154, Bethesda, MD 20814; (301) 229-7707.

Richard Schopfer, executive director. Fax, (301) 229-0457.

Collaborates with local and international development organizations to promote self-help projects for small Latin American communities and small-business projects for skilled workers. Provides funding, technical assistance, and supplies for health, housing, food production, and water projects. Promotes microenterprise development projects.

American Council for Voluntary InterAction, 1717 Massachusetts Ave. N.W., #801 20036; 667-8227. Carolyn M. Long, vice president. Fax, 667-8236.

Provides a forum for exchange of information among private U.S. voluntary agencies on development assistance issues, including food aid and other relief services, migration, and refugee affairs. Monitors legislation and regulations.

American Near East Refugee Aid, 1522 K St. N.W., #202 20005; 347-2558. Peter Gubser, president. Fax, 682-1637.

Assists Palestinian and Lebanese grass-roots organizations in providing their communities with health and welfare services, employment, and educational opportunities. Provides relief in response to civilian emergencies. (Field offices in Jerusalem and Gaza.)

Assn. for the Advancement of Policy, Research, and Development in the Third World, P.O. Box 70257, Washington, DC 20024; 723-7010. Mekki Mtewa, executive director. Fax, 723-7010.

Serves as a forum for the exchange of scientific and technological information to aid developing countries; conducts research; sponsors workshops, seminars, and an annual conference on international development. Affiliated with the International Development Foundation.

The Bretton Woods Committee, 1990 M St. N.W., #450 20036; 331-1616. James C. Orr, executive director. Fax, 785-9423.

Works to increase public understanding of the World Bank, the regional development institutions, and the International Monetary Fund.

CARE, 2025 Eye St. N.W. 20006; 223-2277. Charles L. Sykes, vice president, Washington liaison office. Fax, 296-8695.

Assists the developing world's poor through emergency aid and community self-help programs that focus on farming assistance, reforestation, health, and job creation. (Headquarters in Atlanta, Ga.)

Christian Children's Fund, 1717 Massachusetts Ave. N.W., #601 20036; 462-2161. Arthur Simon, director, Washington liaison office. Fax, 462-0601.

Nonsectarian humanitarian organization that promotes improved child welfare standards and services worldwide by supporting long-term sustainable development. Provides children in unstable situations brought on by war, natural disaster, and other circumstances with material aid, counseling, medical care, and other services. Provides aid to children of all backgrounds.

Citizens Democracy Corps, 1735 Eye St. N.W., #720 20006; 872-0933. Carol Stremlau, acting executive director. Fax, 872-0923.

Provides small- and medium-sized businesses with voluntary assistance programs and publishes a compendium of U.S. nonprofit organizations working in the newly independent states and in central and eastern Europe.

Cooperative Housing Foundation, 1010 Wayne Ave., #240, Silver Spring, MD 20910; (301) 587-4700. Michael Doyle, president. Fax, (301) 587-2626.

Works under contract with the Agency for International Development, United Nations, and World Bank to establish local cooperative housing organizations in the United States and to strengthen local government housing departments abroad.

The Development Group for Alternative Policies, 927 15th St. N.W., 4th Floor 20005; 898-1566. Douglas Hellinger, managing director. Fax, 898-1612.

Works with grass-roots organizations in developing countries to promote changes in international economic policies that do not benefit the poor.

Health Volunteers Overseas, Washington Station, P.O. Box 65157, Washington, DC 20035; 296-0928. Nancy Kelly, executive director. Fax, 296-8018.

Operates training programs in developing countries for health professionals who wish to teach low-cost medical care delivery practices.

Holy Childhood Assn., 1720 Massachusetts Ave. N.W. 20036; 775-8637. Francis Wright, national director. Fax, 429-2987.

Religious education and relief organization that provides educational materials to teach American children about underprivileged children in foreign countries. Provides financial aid for programs and facilities that benefit underprivileged children abroad under age 14.

Institute for International Research, Clearinghouse on Development Communication, 1815 N. Fort Myer Dr., Arlington, VA 22209; (703) 527-5546. Valerie Lamont, director. Fax, (703) 527-4661.

International documentation clearinghouse that reports on the applications of communications for developing countries. Library open to development professionals.

International Center for Research on Women, 1717 Massachusetts Ave. N.W., #302 20036; 797-0007. Mayra Buvinic, president. Fax, 797-0020.

Research and educational organization that seeks to increase women's economic participation in developing countries. Conducts policy research, provides technical services, and educates the public on women's contributions to societies.

International Development Foundation, P.O. Box 70257, Washington, DC 20024; 723-7010. Mekki Mtewa, chairman. Fax, 723-7010.

Collaborates with multinational corporations and government agencies to identify, evaluate, and fund development projects. Promotes cooperation among intergovernmental organizations in developing nations. Sponsors international leadership seminars and workshops for industry, government, and community leaders and internships for young professionals from abroad.

International Service Agencies, 6000 Executive Blvd., #608, Rockville, MD 20852; (301) 881-2468. Renee Acosta, executive director. Toll-free, (800) 638-8079. Fax, (301) 881-2524.

Fund-raising federation of private international aid organizations. Promotes long-term self-help projects in developing countries in the areas of health, agriculture, education and job training, construction, and emergency disaster assistance.

International Voluntary Services, 1424 16th St. N.W., #6031 20036; 387-5533. Don Luce, president. Fax, 387-4234.

Provides developing countries with volunteers in the areas of health, agriculture, small business, and community and rural development. Library open to the public.

National Peace Corps Assn., 2119 S St. N.W. 20008; 462-5938. Charles F. Dambach, president. Fax, 462-5873.

Membership: former Peace Corps volunteers, staff, and interested individuals. Promotes a global perspective in the United States; seeks to educate the public about the developing world; supports Peace Corps programs; maintains network of returned volunteers.

New TransCentury Foundation, 1901 N. Fort Myer Dr., #1017, Arlington, VA 22209; (703) 351-5500. Lisa Wiggins, president. Fax, (703) 351-5510.

International development research and consulting organization. Provides developing countries with technical assistance; assists individuals seeking work in international development. Interests include agriculture, health, labor and migration, refugee resettlement, credit entrepreneurship (loans to entrepreneurs to start businesses), and assistance to private voluntary and nongovernmental organizations.

Pan American Development Foundation, 1889 F St. N.W., #850 20006; 458-3969. Peter Reitz, executive director. Fax, 458-6316.

Works with the public and private sectors to improve the quality of life throughout the Caribbean and Latin America. Associated with the Organization of American States (OAS).

Partners for Livable Places, 1429 21st St. N.W. 20036; 887-5990. Robert H. McNulty, president. Fax, 466-4845.

Provides technical assistance, support services, and information to assist communities in creating better living environments. Works in the Caribbean area, South America, and Europe on public/private partnerships and resource development to improve living environments. Conducts conferences and workshops; maintains library and referral clearinghouse. (International headquarters in Indianapolis.)

Partners of the Americas, 1424 K St. N.W. 20005; 628-3300. William S. Reese, president. Fax, 628-3306.

Membership: individuals in the United States, Latin America, and the Caribbean. Sponsors technical assistance projects and exchanges between the United States, Latin America, and the Caribbean; supports self-help projects in agriculture, public health, and education.

Pax World Service, 1111 16th St. N.W., #120 20036; 293-7290. Charolett Rhoads, president. Fax, 293-7023.

Promotes international understanding and development by providing financial support for selected programs and projects. Focuses on meeting basic human needs through small-scale, community-based initiatives.

Planning Assistance, 1832 Jefferson Pl. N.W. 20036; 466-3290. Robert Learmonth, executive director. Fax, 466-3293.

Provides managerial assistance to governmental and nongovernmental organizations seeking to create, expand, or improve their social and economic development programs. Focuses on development in Africa, Asia, and Latin America.

Program for Appropriate Technology in Health, 1990 M St. N.W., #700 20036; 822-0033. Carol Corso, director, communication. Fax, 457-1466.

Seeks to improve the safety and availability of health products and technologies worldwide, particularly in developing countries. Interests include reproductive health, immunization, maternal-child health, AIDS, and nutrition. (Headquarters in Seattle.)

Salvation Army World Service Office, 927 15th St. N.W., 4th Floor 20005; (703) 684-5528. Dean B. Seiler, executive director. Fax, (703) 684-5536.

Works in Latin America, the Caribbean, Africa, Asia, and the South Pacific to provide technical and financial assistance in support of local Salvation Army programs of health service, employment skills training, community development, disaster relief and assistance, and local leadership training.

Town Affiliation Assn. of the U.S., Sister Cities International, 120 S. Payne St., Alexandria, VA 22314; (703) 836-3535. Carol Lynn Greene, executive director. Fax, (703) 836-4815.

Encourages and helps U.S. communities to link with counterparts in other nations and exchange people, ideas, and cultures on a long-term, continuing basis; serves as an information clearinghouse; administers technical assistance in developing nations; sponsors youth programs and scholarships.

Volunteers in Overseas Cooperative Assistance, 50 F St. N.W., #1075 20001; 383-4961. Donald D. Cohen, president. Fax, 783-7204.

Recruits professionals for voluntary, short-term technical assistance to cooperatives, environmental groups, and agricultural enterprises, upon request, in developing countries and emerging democracies.

Volunteers in Technical Assistance, 1600 Wilson Blvd., #500, Arlington, VA (mailing address: P.O. Box 12438, Arlington, VA 22209); (703) 276-1800. Henry R. Norman, president. Fax, (703) 243-1865.

Provides individuals and groups in developing countries with information and technical resources aimed at fostering self-sufficiency. Assistance includes needs assessment and program development support; consulting services; information systems and training; communications; and management of long-term field projects.

World Mercy Fund, 121 S. Saint Asaph St., Alexandria, VA 22314; (703) 548-4646. Patrick Leonard, president. Fax, (703) 548-6963.

Provides the developing world with medical, educational, agricultural, and other forms of aid.

See also Nurture/Center to Prevent Childhood Malnutrition (p. 337)

Military Assistance

Agencies:

Defense Dept., Defense Security Assistance Agency, The Pentagon, Rm. 4E841 20301-2800; (703) 695-3291. Lt. Gen. Thomas G. Rhame (USA), director. Information, (703) 695-5931. Press, (703) 697-5131. Fax, (703) 695-0081.

Develops budgetary proposals and Defense Dept. policies on arms transfers. Selects and manages U.S. personnel in security assistance assignments overseas; manages weapons systems sales; maintains special defense acquisition funds and priority defense items information systems that study and track U.S. arms transfers. Administers foreign military sales programs.

State Dept., Defense Relations and Security Assistance, Main State Bldg., Rm. 7424 20520; 647-7972. Barbara Tobias, director. Fax, 647-9779.

Formulates the security systems budget; aids in administering security assistance programs, such as military grants and credit sales.

State Dept., International Security Affairs, Main State Bldg., Rm. 7208 20520-7512; 647-1049. Lynn E. Davis, under secretary. Fax, 736-4397.

Works with the secretary of state to develop policy on foreign security assistance programs and technology transfer.

U.S. Arms Control and Disarmament Agency, Weapons and Technology Control, Main State Bldg., Rm. 4734 20451; 647-3496. Joseph P. Smaldone, chief. Fax, 736-4833.

Evaluates arms control implications of proposed conventional arms transfers and exports of technology with possible military applications. Participates in policy development on weapons proliferation issues, particularly those concerning missiles and chemical weapons. Seeks to advance regional and global conventional arms control proposals.

Congress:

See Foreign Policy and Aid, General, Congress (p. 443)

Peacekeeping and Peace Enforcement

See also Defense Policy, General (p. 528); Foreign Policy and Aid, General (p. 442)

Agencies:

Commission on Security and Cooperation in Europe (Helsinki Commission), 234 Ford Bldg. (2nd and D Sts. S.W.) 20515; 225-1901. Sen. Dennis DeConcini, D-Ariz., chairman; Samuel G. Wise, staff director. Fax, 226-4199.

Independent agency created by Congress. Membership includes individuals from the executive and legislative branches. Studies and evaluates international peacekeeping and peace enforcement operations, particularly as they relate to the Helsinki Accords.

Defense Dept., Democracy and Peacekeeping, The Pentagon 20301-2900; (703) 695-2310. Edward L. Warner III, assistant secretary, strategy, requirements, and resources.

Develops policy and plans for the defense of human rights worldwide and for U.S. participation in international peacekeeping and peace enforcement activities. Develops policy related to creating, identifying, training, exercising, and committing military forces for peacekeeping and peace enforcement activities.

National Security Council (Executive Office of the President), The White House 20500; 456-2255. Anthony Lake, assistant to the president for national security affairs. Press, 456-2947. Fax, 456-2883.

Advises the president on foreign policy and defense issues, including participation and proposed participation of U.S. armed forces in international peacekeeping operations.

State Dept., International Organization Affairs, Main State Bldg., Rm. 6323 20520-6319; 647-9600. Douglas J. Bennet, assistant secretary. Information, 647-6400. Fax, 647-6510.

Coordinates and develops policy guidelines for U.S. participation in the United Nations and in other international organizations and conferences.

State Dept., Policy Planning Staff, Main State Bldg., Rm. 7311 20520; 647-2372. Samuel W. Lewis, director. Fax, 647-4147.

Advises the secretary and other State Dept. officials on foreign policy matters, including international peacekeeping and peace enforcement operations.

State Dept., United Nations Political Affairs, Main State Bldg., Rm. 6334 20520-6319; 647-2392. Joseph C. Snyder III, director. Fax, 647-0039.

Deals with United Nations political and institutional matters and international security affairs.

U.S. Institute of Peace, 1550 M St. N.W., #700 20005; 457-1700. Richard H. Solomon, president. Fax, 429-6063.

Independent organization created and funded by Congress to promote the peaceful resolution of international conflict through negotiation and mediation. Provides federal agencies and individuals with training, research programs, and information; awards grants to institutions and individuals; and provides fellowships to scholars from the United States and abroad. Library open to the public by appointment.

Congress:

General Accounting Office, National Security and International Affairs, 441 G St. N.W. 20548; 512-2800. Frank C. Conahan, assistant comptroller general. Fax, 512-7686.

Independent, nonpartisan agency in the legislative branch. Audits, analyzes, and evaluates international programs, including U.S. participation in international peacekeeping and peace enforcement operations; makes unclassified reports available to the public.

Nongovernmental:

American Peace Society, 1319 18th St. N.W. 20036; 296-6261. Evron M. Kirkpatrick, president. Fax, 296-5149.

Conducts research and publishes journals dealing with international problems.

National Peace Foundation, 1835 K St. N.W., #610 20006; 223 1770. Stephen P. Strickland, president. Toll-free, (800) 237-3223. Fax, 223-1718.

Supports conflict resolution education and the U.S. Institute of Peace. Holds conferences and provides information on peace education and managing and resolving conflict.

United Nations Assn. of the USA, 1010 Vermont Ave. N.W. 20005; 347-5004. Steven A. Dimoff, executive director, Washington office. Fax, 628-5945.

Research and educational organization focusing on international institutions, multilateral diplomacy, U.S. foreign policy, and international economics. Coordinates Model United Nations program for high school and university students. Monitors legislation and regulations. (Headquarters in New York.)

Regional Affairs: Africa

See also Foreign Embassies, U.S. Ambassadors, and Country Desk Officers list (p. 779)

Agencies:

African Development Foundation, 1400 Eye St. N.W. 20005; 673-3916. Gregory R. Smith, president. Fax, 673-3810.

Established by Congress to work with and fund organizations and individuals involved in development projects at the local level in Africa. Gives preference to projects involving extensive participation by local Africans.

Agency for International Development (International Development Cooperation Agency), Africa Bureau, Main State Bldg., Rm. 6936 20523; 647-9232. John F. Hicks, assistant administrator. Fax, 647-7621.

Advises AID administrator on U.S. policy toward developing countries in Sub-Saharan Africa.

State Dept., Bureau of African Affairs, Main State Bldg., Rm. 6234A 20520; 647-2530. George E. Moose, assistant secretary. Press, 647-7373. Fax, 647-6301.

Advises the secretary on U.S. policy toward Sub-Saharan Africa. Directors, assigned to specific countries within the bureau, aid the assistant secretary.

State Dept., Central African Affairs (Burundi, Cameroon, Central African Republic, Chad, Congo, Equatorial Guinea, Gabon, Rwanda, Sao Tome and Principe, and Zaire), Main State Bldg., Rm. 4246 20520; 647-2080. Arlene Render, director. Fax, 647-1726.

State Dept., East African Affairs (Indian Ocean Territory, Comoros, Djibouti, Eritrea, Ethiopia, Kenya, Madagascar, Mauritius, Seychelles, Somalia, Sudan, Tanzania, and Uganda), Main State Bldg., Rm. 5240 20520; 647-9742. David Shinn, director. Fax, 647-0810.

State Dept., Southern African Affairs (Angola, Botswana, Lesotho, Malawi, Mozambique, Namibia, South Africa, Swaziland, Zambia, and Zimbabwe), Main State Bldg., Rm. 4238 20520; 647-9836. April Glaspie, director. Fax, 647-5007.

State Dept., West African Affairs (Benin, Burkina Faso, Cape Verde, Côte d'Ivoire, The Gambia, Ghana, Guinea, Guinea-Bissau, Liberia, Mali, Mauritania, Niger, Nigeria, Senegal, Sierra Leone, Togo, and Western Sahara), Main State Bldg., Rm. 4250 20520; 647-3406. Vacant, director. Fax, 647-4855.

U.S. Information Agency, African Affairs, 301 4th St. S.W. 20547; 619-4894. Robert LaGamma, director. Fax, 619-5925.

Administers USIA programs throughout Sub-Saharan Africa in support of U.S. policies. Manages U.S. information service offices in individual African countries that conduct cultural and educational exchange programs through lectures, radio broadcasts, films, and television. Advises the president, Congress, and federal agencies on U.S. policies toward African nations.

See also State Dept., Bureau of Near Eastern Affairs (p. 465); State Dept., Bureau of South Asian Affairs, and U.S. Information Agency, North Africa, Near East, and South Asian Affairs (p. 466)

Congress:

See Foreign Policy and Aid, General, Congress (p. 443)

International Organizations:

International Bank for Reconstruction and Development (World Bank), Africa, 1818 H St. N.W. 20433; 473-4000. Edward V. K. Jaycox, vice president. Information, 473-4619. Fax, 473-7917.

Encourages public and private foreign investment in the countries of Sub-Saharan Africa through loans, loan guarantees, and technical assistance. Finances economic development projects in agriculture, environmental protection, education, public utilities, telecommunications, water supply, sewerage, public health, and other areas.

International Bank for Reconstruction and Development (World Bank), Middle East and North Africa, 600 19th St. N.W. (mailing address: 1818 H St. N.W., Washington, DC 20433); 473-5250. Caio Koch-Weser, vice president. Fax, 477-0810.

Encourages public and private foreign investment in the countries of North Africa through loans, loan guarantees, and technical assistance. Finances economic development projects in agriculture, environmental protection, education, public utilities, telecommunications, water supply, sewerage, public health, and other areas.

Nongovernmental:

African-American Institute, 1625 Massachusetts Ave. N.W., #210 20036; 667-5636. Jerry L. Drew, director, Washington office. Fax, 265-6332.

Arranges U.S. itineraries for African visitors sponsored by the U.S. Information Agency (USIA). Sponsors policy studies program to educate Congress on African issues. Promotes trade and investment in Africa. (Headquarters in New York.)

African National Congress, 707 8th St. S.E., #200 (mailing address: P.O. Box 15575, Washington, DC 20003); 543-9433. Lindiwe Mabuza, chief representative. Fax, 543-9435.

Liberation movement organization that seeks to dismantle the apartheid system in South Africa and build a democratic, nonracist, nonsexist society. Monitors legislation and negotiations on issues pertaining to apartheid and development. Maintains speakers bureau.

Africare, 440 R St. N.W. 20001; 462-3614. C. Payne Lucas, president. Fax, 387-1034.

Seeks to improve the quality of life in rural Africa through development of water resources, increased food production, and delivery of health services. Resource center open to the public by appointment.

American African Affairs Assn., 1001 Connecticut Ave. N.W., #1135 20036; 223-5110. J. A. Parker, co-chairman.

Educational organization that provides information on African states. Interests include world communism and the role of the United States in development.

TransAfrica, 1744 R St. N.W. 20009-2410; 797-2301. Randall Robinson, executive director. Fax, 797-2382.

Focuses on U.S. foreign policy toward African nations, the Caribbean, and peoples of African descent. Provides members with information on foreign policy issues. Operates the Free South Africa Movement, which coordinates legislative and research activities opposing apartheid.

Washington Office on Africa, 110 Maryland Ave. N.E. 20002; 546-7961. Imani Countess, executive director. Fax, 546-1545.

Monitors legislation and executive actions concerning southern Africa; issues action alerts. Library open to the public by appointment.

Regional Affairs: East Asia and the Pacific

See also Foreign Embassies, U.S. Ambassadors, and Country Desk Officers list (p. 779)

Agencies:

Agency for International Development (International Development Cooperation Agency), Asia and Near East Bureau, Main State Bldg., Rm. 6212 20523; 647-8298. Margaret Carpenter, assistant administrator. Fax, 647-6901.

Advises AID administrator on U.S. economic development policy in Asia, the Pacific, and the Near East.

Japan-United States Friendship Commission, 1120 Vermont Ave. N.W., #925 20005; 275-7712. Eric J. Gangloff, executive director. Fax, 275-7413.

Independent agency established by Congress that makes grants and administers funds and programs promoting educational and cultural exchanges between Japan and the United States; consults with public and private organizations in both countries.

State Dept., Bureau of East Asian and Pacific Affairs, Main State Bldg. 20520-6310; 647-9596. Winston Lord, assistant secretary. Press, 647-2530. Fax, 647-7350

Advises the secretary on U.S. policy toward East Asian and Pacific countries. Directors, assigned to specific countries within the bureau, aid the assistant secretary.

State Dept., Australia and New Zealand Affairs, Main State Bldg., Rm. 4209 20520; 647-9690. Mike P. Owens, director. Fax, 647-4402.

State Dept., Chinese and Mongolian Affairs, Main State Bldg., Rm. 4318 20520; 647-6300. Donald Keyser, director. Fax, 647-6820.

State Dept., Japanese Affairs, Main State Bldg., Rm. 4206 20520; 647-2913. Stephen Ecton, director. Fax, 647-4402.

State Dept., Korean Affairs, Main State Bldg., Rm. 5313 20520; 647-7717. David E. Brown, director. Fax, 647-7388.

State Dept., Pacific Island Affairs, Main State Bldg., Rm. 5317 20520; 647-0108. Lynne Lambert, director. Fax, 647-0118.

State Dept., Philippines, Indonesia, Malaysia, Brunei, and Singapore Affairs, Main State Bldg., Rm. 6206 20520; 647-3276. W. Scott Butcher, director. Fax, 647-0996.

State Dept., Taiwan Coordination Staff, Main State Bldg., Rm. 4312 20520; 647-7711. Joseph Borich, director. Fax, 647-6820.

State Dept., Thailand and Burma Affairs, Main State Bldg., Rm. 4312 20520; 647-7108. John D. Finney, director. Fax, 647-6820.

State Dept., Vietnam, Laos, and Cambodia Affairs, Main State Bldg., Rm. 5210 20520; 647-3132. James Hall, director. Fax, 647-3069.

U.S. Information Agency, East Asia and Pacific Affairs, 301 4th St. S.W. 20547; 619-4829. Jodie Lewinsohn, director. Fax, 619-6684.

Administers USIA programs throughout the East Asian and Pacific region in support of U.S. policies. Conducts informational, educational, and cultural exchange programs. Advises the president, Congress, and federal agencies on U.S. policy toward nations in East Asia and the Pacific.

Congress:

See Foreign Policy and Aid, General, Congress (p. 443)

International Organizations:

International Bank for Reconstruction and Development (World Bank), East Asia and Pacific, 701 19th St. N.W. (mailing address: 1818 H St. N.W., Rm. E-10-0-33, Washington, DC 20433); 458-1384. Gautam S. Kaji, vice president. Fax, 477-0169.

Encourages public and private investment in the countries of East Asia and the Pacific through loans, loan guarantees, and technical assistance. Finances economic development projects in agriculture, environmental protection, education, public utilities, telecommunications, water supply, sewerage, public health, and other areas.

Nongovernmental:

American Institute in Taiwan, 1700 N. Moore St., #1700, Arlington, VA 22209; (703) 525-8474. Natale H. Bellocchi, managing director. Fax, (703) 841-1385.

Chartered by Congress to coordinate commercial, cultural, and other activities between the people of the United States and Taiwan. Represents U.S. interests and maintains offices in Taiwan.

The Asia Foundation, 2301 E St. N.W. 20037; 223-5268. Vance Hyndman, Washington director. Fax, 785-4582.

Provides Asian countries and the Pacific islands with grants and technical assistance to strengthen legislatures, legal and judicial systems, market economies, the media, and nongovernmental organizations. (Headquarters in San Francisco.)

Asia Resource Center, 538 7th St. S.E. (mailing address: P.O. Box 15275, Washington, DC 20003); 547-1114. Roger Rumpf, director. Fax, 543-2364.

Educational organization that provides information on developments in the Asian Pacific region, including information on peace and justice issues.

The Asia Society, 1785 Massachusetts Ave. N.W. 20036; 387-6500. Judith Sloan, director, Washington office. Fax, 387-6945.

Membership: individuals interested in Asia and the Pacific. Sponsors seminars and lectures on political, economic, and cultural issues. (Headquarters in New York.)

Coordination Council for North American Affairs, 4201 Wisconsin Ave. N.W. 20016; 895-1800. Mou-Shih Ding, representative.

Represents political, economic, and cultural interests of the government of the Republic of China (Taiwan) in the United States; handles former embassy functions.

Heritage Foundation, Asian Studies Center, 214 Massachusetts Ave. N.E. 20002; 546-4400. Seth Cropsey, director. Fax, 675-1779.

Conducts research and provides information on U.S. policies in Asia and the Pacific. Interests include economic and trade issues and political, economic, and military policies toward Taiwan, mainland China, Australia, and New Zealand. Hosts speakers and visiting foreign policy delegations; sponsors conferences.

Japan-America Society of Washington, 1020 19th St. N.W., Lower Lobby 20036; 289-8290. Patricia R. Kearns, executive director. Fax, 789-8265.

Conducts programs and produces publications on U.S.-Japan trade, politics, and economic issues; assists Japanese performing artists; offers lectures and films on Japan; operates Japanese-language school; awards annual scholarships to college students studying in the Washington,

D.C., metropolitan area; maintains library for members; lends a portable Japanese room to public schools in the Washington, D.C., metropolitan area.

Japan Economic Institute of America, 1000 Connecticut Ave. N.W. 20036; 296-5633. Arthur J. Alexander, president. Fax, 296-8333.

Research organization supported by Japan's Ministry of Foreign Affairs. Publishes current information on the Japanese economy and U.S.-Japan economic relations. Library open to the public.

Japan Information Access Project, 1706 R St. N.W. 20009; 332-5224. Mindy Kotler, director. Fax, 332-6841.

Membership organization that teaches business executives, scientists, engineers, educators, legislators, and journalists how to access, evaluate, and use Japanese-source information in business, science, and technology. Helps American managers integrate Japanese information and U.S. policies toward Japan in their strategic planning. Maintains programs on specific topics, including electronics, financial services, biomedical technologies and pharmaceuticals, and intellectual property.

U.S.-Asia Institute, 232 E. Capitol St. N.E. 20003; 544-3181. Joji Konoshima, president. Fax, 543-1748.

Organization of individuals interested in Asia. Encourages communication among political and business leaders in the United States and Asia. Interests include foreign policy, international trade, Asian and American cultures, education, and employment. Conducts research and sponsors conferences and workshops in cooperation with the State Dept. to promote greater understanding between the United States and Asian nations. Conducts programs that take congressional staff members to Singapore, Indonesia, Malaysia, and China.

See also Assn. on Third World Affairs (p. 446); Church Coalition for Human Rights in the Philippines and Human Rights Watch (p. 477); Institute for European, Russian, and Eurasian Studies (p. 463)

Regional Affairs: Europe and Canada

See also Foreign Policy and Aid, Regional Affairs: Independent States and Commonwealth (p. 462)

See also Foreign Embassies, U.S. Ambassadors, and Country Desk Officers list (p. 779)

Agencies:

Agency for International Development (International Development Cooperation Agency), Europe and the New Independent States Bureau, Main State Bldg., Rm. 6724 20523; 647-9119. Thomas Dine, assistant administrator. Fax, 647-9973.

Advises AID administrator on U.S. economic development policy in Europe and the new independent states.

State Dept., Bureau of European and Canadian Affairs, Main State Bldg., Rm. 6228 20520; 647-9626. Stephen A. Oxman, assistant secretary. Information, 647-6925. Fax, 647-0967.

Advises the secretary on U.S. policy toward European countries and Canada. Directors, assigned to specific countries within the bureau, aid the assistant secretary.

State Dept., Canadian Affairs, Main State Bldg., Rm. 5227 20520; 647-2170. James Hooper, director. Fax, 647-4088.

State Dept., Central European Affairs (Austria, Germany, Liechtenstein, and Switzerland), Main State Bldg., Rm. 4228 20520; 647-1484. J. D. Bindenagel, director. Fax, 647-5117.

State Dept., Eastern European Affairs (Albania, Bulgaria, Czech Republic, Estonia, Hungary, Latvia, Lithuania, Poland, Romania, Slovak Republic, and the former Yugoslavia: Bosnia-Herzegovina, Croatia, and Serbia), Main State Bldg., Rm. 5220 20520; 647-4136. Terry R. Snell, director. Fax, 647-0555.

State Dept., European Community and Regional Affairs, Main State Bldg., Rm. 6519 20520; 647-3932. Shaun Donnelly, director. Fax, 647-9959.

Handles all matters (emphasizing those that are trade-related) concerning the European Community, the Council of Europe, and the Organization for Economic Cooperation and Development. Monitors East-West trade, export controls, and economic activities for the North Atlantic Treaty Organization and the Conference on Security and Cooperation in Europe.

State Dept., European Security and Political Affairs, Main State Bldg., Rm. 6227 20520; 647-1626. James B. Cunningham, director. Fax, 647-0967.

Coordinates and advises, with the Defense Dept. and other agencies, the U.S. mission to the North Atlantic Treaty Organization and the U.S. delegation to the Conference on Security and Cooperation in Europe regarding political, military, and arms control matters.

State Dept., Northern European Affairs (Belgium, Bermuda, Denmark, Finland, Iceland, Ireland, Luxembourg, the Netherlands, Norway, Sweden, and the United Kingdom), Main State Bldg., Rm. 4513 20520; 647-5687. John Tefft, director. Fax, 647-3463.

State Dept., Southern European Affairs (Cyprus, Greece, and Turkey), Main State Bldg., Rm. 5509 20520; 647-6112. Marshall P. Adair, director. Fax, 647-5087.

State Dept., Western European Affairs (France, Italy, Malta, Portugal, San Marino, Spain, and the Vatican), Main State Bldg., Rm. 5226 20520; 647-3072. Eileen Heaphy, director. Fax, 647-3459.

U.S. Information Agency, European Affairs, 301 4th St. S.W. 20547; 619-4563. Vacant, director. Fax, 619-6821.

Administers USIA programs in Canada and Europe in support of U.S. policies. Manages U.S. information service offices in individual countries that conduct cultural and educational exchange programs through lectures, radio broadcasts, films, and television. Advises the president, Congress, and federal agencies on U.S. policies toward Europe and Canada.

Congress:

See Foreign Policy and Aid, General, Congress (p. 443)

See also Ad Hoc Congressional Committee or Irish Affairs (p. 755); Friends of Ireland (p. 757)

International Organizations:

European Community Press and Public Affairs, 2100 M St. N.W. 20037; 862-9500. Andreas A. M. van Agt, ambassador; Peter Doyle, director. Information, 862-9542. Press, 862-9540. Fax, 429-1766.

Information and public affairs office in the United States for the European Union/European Community, which includes the European Economic Community, the European Coal and Steel Community, and the European Atomic Energy Community. Provides social policy data on the European Community and provides statistics and documents on member countries, including those related to energy, economics, development and cooperation, commerce, agriculture, industry, and technology. Library open to the public by appointment.

International Bank for Reconstruction and Development (World Bank), Eastern Europe and Central Asia, 600 19th St. N.W. (mailing address: 1818 H St. N.W., Washington, DC 20433); 473-6860. Wilfried P. Thalwitz, vice president. Fax, 477-1942.

Encourages public and private foreign investment in the countries of Eastern and southern Europe through loans, loan guarantees, and technical assistance. Finances economic development projects in agriculture, environmental protection, education, public utilities, telecommunications, water supply, sewerage, public health, and other areas.

Nongovernmental:

American Hellenic Institute, 1730 K St. N.W., #1005 20006; 785-8430. Eugene Rossides, chairman. Fax, 785-5178.

Works to strengthen trade and commerce between Greece and Cyprus and the United States and within the American Hellenic community.

Irish American Unity Conference, 837 National Press Bldg., 529 14th St. N.W. 20036; 662-8830. Robert Linnon, president. Fax, 662-8831.

Encourages nonviolent means of resolving conflict in Northern Ireland. Conducts symposia and provides information on Northern Ireland; monitors legislation and regulations.

Joint Baltic American National Committee, 400 Hurley Ave., Rockville, MD (mailing address: P.O. Box 4578, Rockville, MD 20850); (301) 340-1954. Mati Koiva, chairman. Fax, (301) 309-1406.

Represents Estonian, Latvian, and Lithuanian organizations in the United States; acts as a representative on issues affecting the Baltic states.

National Italian American Foundation, 666 11th St. N.W., #800 20001; 638-0220. Alfred M. Rotondaro, executive director. Fax, 638-0002.

Membership: U.S. citizens of Italian ancestry. Promotes recognition of Italian-American contributions to American society. Funds cultural events, educational symposia, antidefamation programs, and scholarships. Represents the interests of Italian Americans before Congress. Serves as an umbrella organization for local Italian-American clubs throughout the United States.

See also Human Rights Watch (p. 477); Institute for European, Russian, and Eurasian Studies (p. 463); Irish National Caucus (p. 478)

Regional Affairs: Independent States and Commonwealth

See also Foreign Embassies, U.S. Ambassadors, and Country Desk Officers list (p. 779)

Agencies:

State Dept., Independent States and Commonwealth Affairs, Main State Bldg., Rm. 4223 20520; 647-6729. Larry C. Napper, director. Fax, 647-3506.

Handles relations with the former Soviet Union except for the Baltic states; assists other agencies in dealings with the former Soviet Union.

U.S. Information Agency, European Affairs, 301 4th St. S.W. 20547; 619-4563. Leonard J. Baldyga, director. Fax, 619-6821.

Administers USIA programs in Canada and Europe, including the former Soviet Union, in support of U.S. policies. Manages U.S. information service offices in individual countries that conduct cultural and educational exchange programs through lectures, radio broadcasts, films, and television. Advises the president, Congress, and federal agencies on U.S. policies toward the former Soviet Union and Eastern Europe.

Congress:

See Foreign Policy and Aid, General, Congress (p. 443)

See also Congressional Coalition for Soviet Jews (p. 756); U.S.-Former Soviet Union Energy Caucus (p. 760)

International Organizations:

International Bank for Reconstruction and Development (World Bank), Eastern Europe and Central Asia, 600 19th St. N.W. (mailing address: 1818 H St. N.W., Washington, DC 20433); 473-6860. Wilfried P. Thalwitz, vice president. Fax, 477-1942.

Encourages public and private foreign investment in central Asia, including the countries of the former Soviet Union, through loans, loan guarantees, and technical assistance. Finances economic development projects in agriculture, environmental protection, education, public utilities, telecommunications, water supply, sewerage, public health, and other areas.

Nongovernmental:

Committee on American-Russian Relations, 201 Massachusetts Ave. N.E. 20002; 546-3960. Alfred Friendly Jr., president. Fax, 546-5947.

Membership: individuals and organizations interested in U.S.-Russian relations. Seeks to strengthen public understanding of political and economic developments in Russia and of diplomatic and arms control initiatives. Supports democratic institutions and the development of a free-market economy in Russia.

Free Congress Research and Education Foundation, 717 2nd St. N.E. 20002; 546-3004. Paul M. Weyrich, president. Fax, 543-8425.

Public policy research and education foundation. Through the Krieble Institute, provides citizens of the former Soviet bloc with training in democratic processes and free enterprise.

Institute for European, Russian, and Eurasian Studies (George Washington University), 2130 H St. N.W., #601 20052; 994-6340. James R. Millar, director. Fax, 994-5436.

Studies and researches European, Russian, and Eurasian affairs. Sino-Soviet Information Center open to the public.

National Conference on Soviet Jewry, 1640 Rhode Island Ave. N.W., #501 20036; 898-2500. Mark B. Levin, executive director. Fax, 898-0296.

Membership: national Jewish organizations. Coordinates efforts by members to aid Jews in the former Soviet Union, including Jewish families attempting to emigrate.

Ukrainian National Information Service, 214 Massachusetts Ave. N.E., #225 20002; 547-0018. Tamara Gallo, director. Fax, 543-5502.

Information bureau of the Ukrainian Congress Committee of America in New York. Provides information and monitors U.S. policy on Ukraine and the Ukrainian community in the United States and abroad. (Headquarters in New York.)

See also Human Rights Watch (p. 477)

Regional Affairs: Latin America

See also Foreign Embassies, U.S. Ambassadors, and Country Desk Officers list (p. 779)

Agencies:

Agency for International Development (International Development Cooperation Agency), Latin America and the Caribbean Bureau, Main State Bldg., Rm. 4529A 20523; 647-9108. Mark L. Schneider, assistant administrator. Fax, 647-9671.

Advises AID administrator on U.S. policy toward developing Latin American and Caribbean countries. Designs and implements assistance programs for developing nations.

Panama Canal Commission, 1825 Eye St. N.W., #1050 20006; 634-6441. Michael Rhode Jr., secretary. Fax, 634-6439.

Independent federal agency that manages, operates, and maintains the Panama Canal and its complementary works, installations, and equipment; provides for the orderly transit of vessels through the canal.

State Dept., Bureau of Inter-American Affairs, Main State Bldg., Rm. 6263 20520-6258; 647-5780. Alexander Watson, assistant secretary. Information, 647-4726. Fax, 647-0791.

Advises the secretary on U.S. policy toward Latin American and Caribbean countries. Directors, assigned to specific countries within the bureau, aid the assistant secretary.

State Dept., Andean Affairs (Bolivia, Colombia, Ecuador, Peru, and Venezuela), Main State Bldg., Rm. 5906 20520-6258; 647-1715. Ford Cooper, director. Fax, 647-2628.

State Dept., Brazilian Affairs, Main State Bldg., Rm. 4908 20520-6258; 647-6541. David Miller, director. Fax, 736-7481.

State Dept., Caribbean Affairs, Main State Bldg., Rm. 3248 20520-6258; 647-3210. John Leonard, director. Fax, 647-4477.
Includes the British Associated States, Aruba, Bahamas, Barbados, Caicos Islands, Cayman Islands, Dominica, Dominican Republic, French Guiana, Grenada, Guadeloupe, Guyana, Haiti, Jamaica, Martinique, Netherlands Antilles, Suriname, Trinidad and Tobago, and Turks Islands.

State Dept., Central American Affairs (Belize, Costa Rica, El Salvador, Guatemala, Honduras, and Nicaragua), Main State Bldg., Rm. 4915 20520-6258; 647-4010. John R. Hamilton, director. Fax, 647-2597.

State Dept., Cuban Affairs, Main State Bldg., Rm. 3250 20520-6258; 647-9272. Dennis Hays, director. Fax, 736-4476.

State Dept., Mexican Affairs, Main State Bldg., Rm. 4258 20520-6258; 647-9894. Robert C. Felder, director. Fax, 647-5752.

State Dept., Panamanian Affairs, Main State Bldg., Rm. 4909 20520-6258; 647-4982. John R. Dawson, director. Fax, 647-2901.

State Dept., Southern Cone Affairs (Argentina, Chile, Paraguay, and Uruguay), Main State Bldg., Rm. 5911 20520-6258; 647-2407. Donald Planty, director. Fax, 736-4475.

State Dept., U.S. Mission to the Organization of American States, Main State Bldg., Rm. 6494 20520-6258; 647-9376. Hattie Babbitt, U.S. permanent representative. Press, 647-9378. Fax, 736-4758.
Formulates U.S. policy and represents U.S. interests at the Organization of American States (OAS).

U.S. Information Agency, American Republics, 301 4th St. S.W. 20547; 619-4860. Donald R. Hamilton, director. Fax, 619-5172.
Administers USIA programs throughout Central and South America and the Caribbean in support of U.S. policies. Manages U.S. information service offices in individual countries that conduct cultural and educational exchange programs through lectures, radio broadcasts, films,

and television. Advises the president, Congress, and federal agencies on U.S. policies toward Latin America.

Congress:

See Foreign Policy and Aid, General, Congress (p. 443)

See also U.S. Interparliamentary Group—Mexico (p. 757)

International Organizations:

International Bank for Reconstruction and Development (World Bank), Latin America and the Caribbean, 1850 Eye St. N.W. (mailing address: 1818 H St. N.W., Washington, DC 20433); 473-9001. S. Shahid Husain, vice president. Fax, 676-9271.

Encourages public and private foreign investment in the countries of Latin America and the Caribbean through loans, loan guarantees, and technical assistance. Finances economic development projects in agriculture, environmental protection, education, public utilities, telecommunications, water supply, sewerage, public health, and other areas.

Organization of American States (OAS), 17th St. and Constitution Ave. N.W. 20006; 458-3000. João Clemente Baena Soares, secretary general. Information, 458-3760. Library, 458-6037. Fax, 458-3967.

Membership: the United States, Canada, and all independent Latin American and Caribbean countries. Funded by quotas paid by member states and by contributions to special multilateral funds. Works to promote democracy, eliminate poverty, and resolve disputes among member nations. Provides member states with technical and advisory services in cultural, educational, scientific, social, and economic areas. Library open to the public.

Nongovernmental:

Center for International Policy, 1755 Massachusetts Ave. N.W., #324 20036; 232-3317. William Goodfellow, director. Fax, 232-3440.

Research and educational organization concerned with the Central American peace process. Studies peace agreements; publishes pictorial reports designed to popularize the peace accord.

Council of the Americas/The Americas Society, 1625 K St. N.W., #1200 20006; 659-1547. Ludlow Flower III, managing director. Fax, 659-0169.

Membership: businesses with interests and investments in Latin America. Seeks to expand the role of private enterprise in the development of Latin America. (Headquarters in New York.)

Council on Hemispheric Affairs, 724 9th St. N.W., #401 20001; 393-3322. Laurence R. Birns, director. Fax, 393-3423.

Seeks to expand interest in inter-American relations and increase press coverage of Latin America and Canada. Monitors U.S., Latin American, and Canadian relations, with emphasis on human rights, trade, growth of democratic institutions, freedom of the press, and hemispheric economic and political developments; provides educational materials and analyzes issues. Issues annual survey on human rights and freedom of the press.

The Cuban American National Foundation, 1000 Thomas Jefferson St. N.W., #505 20007; 265-2822. Thomas Cox, regional director. Fax, 338-0308.

Conducts research and provides information on Cuba; supports the establishment of a democratic government in Cuba. Library open to the public by appointment.

Inter-American Dialogue, 1211 Connecticut Ave. N.W., #510 20036; 265-5350. Peter Hakim, president. Fax, 265-5425.

Serves as a forum for communication and exchange among leaders of the Americas. Provides analyses and policy recommendations on issues of hemispheric concern. Interests include economic integration, the Latin American debt crisis, and the strengthening of democracy in Latin America. Sponsors conferences and seminars.

Network in Solidarity with the People of Guatemala, 1500 Massachusetts Ave. N.W., #241 20005; 223-6474. Michael Willis, coordinator. Fax, 223-8221.

Membership: organizations interested in promoting social justice and human rights in Central America. Opposes U.S. intervention in Central America; seeks to inform the public about human rights and U.S. policy in Guatemala.

Religious Task Force on Central America, 1747 Connecticut Ave. N.W. 20009; 387-7652.

Lee Miller and Margaret Swedish, coordinators.

Network of religious-based organizations and individuals concerned about Central America. Opposes U.S. military aid and intervention in Central America; provides information and promotes human rights and social justice in the region.

Washington Office on Latin America, 110 Maryland Ave. N.E., #404 20002; 544-8045. George Vickers, director. Fax, 546-5288.

Acts as a liaison between government policymakers and groups and individuals concerned with human rights and U.S. policy in Latin America. Serves as an information resource center; monitors legislation.

See also Assn. on Third World Affairs (p. 446); Central American Refugee Center (p. 450); Human Rights Watch (p. 477); Pan American Development Foundation and Partners of the Americas (p. 454)

Regional Affairs: Near East and South Asia

See also Foreign Embassies, U.S. Ambassadors, and Country Desk Officers list (p. 779)

Agencies:

Agency for International Development (International Development Cooperation Agency), Asia and Near East Bureau, Main State Bldg., Rm. 6212 20523; 647-8298. Margaret Carpenter, assistant administrator. Fax, 647-6901.

Advises AID administrator on U.S. economic development policy in Asia and the Near East.

State Dept., Bureau of Near Eastern Affairs, Main State Bldg., Rm. 6242 20520-6243; 647-7209. Robert Pelletreau, assistant secretary. Information, 647-5150. Fax, 736-4462.

State Dept., Bureau of South Asian Affairs, Main State Bldg., Rm. 6254 20520-6243; 736-4325. Robin L. Raphel, assistant secretary. Information, 736-4255. Fax, 736-4333.

State Dept., Arabian Peninsula Affairs (Bahrain, Kuwait, Oman, Qatar, Republic of Yemen, Saudi Arabia, and United Arab Emirates), Main State Bldg., Rm. 4224 20520-6243; 647-6184. Margaret M. Dean, director. Fax, 736-4459.

State Dept., Bhutan, India, Maldives, Nepal, and Sri Lanka Affairs, Main State Bldg., Rm. 5251 20520-6243; 647-2141. Ronald Lorton, director. Fax, 736-4463.

State Dept., Egyptian Affairs, Main State Bldg., Rm. 6251A 20520-6243; 647-2365. Richard H. Jones, director. Fax, 736-4460.

State Dept., Israel and Arab-Israeli Affairs, Main State Bldg., Rm. 6247 20520-6243; 647-3672. Thomas J. Miller, director. Fax, 736-4461.

State Dept., Lebanon, Jordan, Palestine, and Syria Affairs, Main State Bldg., Rm. 6250 20520-6243; 647-2670. Pete Martinez, director. Fax, 647-0989.

State Dept., North African Affairs (Algeria, Libya, Morocco, and Tunisia), Main State Bldg., Rm. 5250 20520; 647-4679. Stephen Buck, director. Fax, 736-4458.

State Dept., Northern Gulf Affairs (Iran and Iraq), Main State Bldg., Rm. 4515 20520; 647-5692. Vacant, director. Fax, 736-4464.

State Dept., Pakistan, Afghanistan, and Bangladesh Affairs, Main State Bldg., Rm. 5247 20520-6243; 647-7593. John C. Holzman, director. Fax, 647-3001.

U.S. Information Agency, North Africa, Near East, and South Asian Affairs, 301 4th St. S.W. 20547; 619-4520. Kent Obee, director. Fax, 619-5605.

Administers USIA programs throughout North Africa, the Near East, and South Asia in support of U.S. policies. Manages U.S. information services offices in individual countries that conduct cultural and educational exchange programs through lectures, radio broadcasts, films, and television. Advises the president, Congress, and federal agencies on U.S. policies toward North Africa, the Near East, and South Asia.

Congress:

See *Foreign Policy and Aid, General, Congress* (p. 443)

See also *Congressional Caucus for Syrian Jewry* (p. 758)

International Organizations:

International Bank for Reconstruction and Development (World Bank), Middle East and North Africa, 600 19th St. N.W. (mailing address: 1818 H St. N.W., Washington, DC 20433); 473-5250. Caio Koch-Weser, vice president. Fax, 477-0810.

Encourages public and private foreign investment in the countries of the Middle East through loans, loan guarantees, and technical assistance. Finances economic development projects in agriculture, education, public utilities, telecommunications, water supply, sewerage, and other areas.

International Bank for Reconstruction and Development (World Bank), South Asia, 701 19th St. N.W. (mailing address: 1818 H St. N.W., Washington, DC 20433); 458-1430. D. Joseph Wood, vice president. Fax, 477-6050.

Encourages public and private foreign investment in the countries of South Asia through loans, loan guarantees, and technical assistance. Finances economic development projects in agriculture, environmental protection, education, public utilities, telecommunications, water supply, sewerage, public health, and other areas.

Nongovernmental:

America-Mideast Educational and Training Services, 1100 17th St. N.W. 20036; 785-0022. Robert S. Dillon, president. Fax, 822-6563.

Promotes understanding and cooperation between Americans and the people of the Arab world through education, information, and development programs. Produces educational material to help improve teaching about the Arab world in American schools and colleges.

American Israel Public Affairs Committee, 440 1st St. N.W., #600 20001; 639-5200. Howard Kohr, executive director. Fax, 347-4889.

Works to maintain and improve relations between the United States and Israel.

American Jewish Congress, 2027 Massachusetts Ave. N.W. 20036; 332-4001. Mark J. Pelavin, Washington representative. Fax, 387-3434.

National Jewish organization that advocates the maintenance and improvement of U.S.-Israeli relations through legislation, public education, and joint economic ventures. Interests include the Arab boycott of Israel and foreign investment in the United States. (Headquarters in New York.)

The Asia Foundation, 2301 E St. N.W. 20037; 223-5268. Vance Hyndman, Washington director. Fax, 785-4582.

Provides grants and technical assistance in Asia and the Pacific islands to strengthen legislatures, legal and judicial systems, market economies, the media, and nongovernmental organizations. (Headquarters in San Francisco.)

Foundation for Middle East Peace, 555 13th St. N.W. 20004; 637-6558. Merle Thorpe Jr., president. Fax, 637-5910.

Educational organization that seeks to promote understanding and resolution of the Israeli-Palestinian conflict. Makes grants to both Arab and Jewish organizations and public policy research centers working toward peaceful resolution of the conflict; provides media with information.

The Institute for Palestine Studies, Georgetown Station, P.O. Box 25301, Washington, DC 20007; 342-3990. Philip Mattar, executive director.

Scholarly research institute that specializes in the history and development of the Palestine problem, the Arab-Israeli conflict, and their peaceful resolution. (Headquarters in Beirut, Lebanon.)

League of Arab States, 1100 17th St. N.W., #602 20036; 265-3210. Abdulah Spreh, ambassador. Fax, 331-1525.

Intergovernmental organization of Arab states. Seeks to improve Arab-American relations and provide greater understanding of Arab culture and involvement in world affairs. Maintains the Arab Information Center. (Headquarters in Cairo.)

Middle East Institute, 1761 N St. N.W. 20036-2882; 785-1141. Robert V. Keeley, president. Library, 785-0183. Fax, 331-8861. Language Dept., 785-2710.

Membership: individuals interested in the Middle East. Seeks to broaden knowledge of the Middle East through research, conferences and seminars, language classes, lectures, and exhibits. Library open to the public.

Middle East Research and Information Project, 1500 Massachusetts Ave. N.W., #119

20005; 223-3677. Peggy Hutchison, publisher. Press, 223-3657. Fax, 223-3604.

Works to educate the public about the contemporary Middle East. Focuses on U.S. policy in the region and issues of human rights and social justice.

National Assn. of Arab-Americans, 1212 New York Ave. N.W., #300 20005-3987; 842-1840. Khalil Jahshan, executive director. Fax, 842-1614.

Organization of Americans of Arab descent or heritage. Acts as a representative on political issues for its membership; sponsors Mid-East Policy and Research Center.

National Council on U.S.-Arab Relations, 1735 Eye St. N.W., #515 20006; 293-0801. John Duke Anthony, president. Fax, 293-0903.

Assists educational and cultural organizations working to improve mutual understanding between the United States and the Arab world. Serves as a clearinghouse on Arab issues and maintains speakers bureau.

United Palestinian Appeal, 2100 M St. N.W., #409 20037; 659-5007. Munir Nasser, director. Fax, 296-0224.

Charitable organization partially funded by American corporations doing business in the Middle East. Provides funds for community development projects, hospitals, schools, and orphanages and for programs helping people with disabilities, the elderly, and the homeless; seeks to improve the quality of life for Palestinians in the Middle East, especially those in occupied territories.

Washington Institute for Near East Policy, 1828 L St. N.W., #1050 20036; 452-0650. Robert Satloff, director. Fax, 223-5364.

Research and educational organization that seeks to improve the effectiveness of American policy in the Near East by promoting debate among policymakers, journalists, and scholars.

See also American Near East Refugee Aid (p. 453); The Asia Society (p. 460); Assn. on Third World Affairs (p. 446); Human Rights Watch (p. 477); U.S.-Asia Institute (p. 460)

Foreign Service

For information on the annual foreign service exam, contact the State Dept., Recruitment Division, P.O. Box 9317, Arlington, VA 22209; (703) 875-7247.

Agencies:

State Dept., Career Development and Assignments, Main State Bldg., Rm. 2328 (mailing address: PER/CDA, Washington, DC 20520-2810); 647-1692. Jennifer Ward, director. Fax, 647-0277.
Coordinates programs related to the professional development of American members of the foreign service, including career development and assignment counseling programs; training; and presidential appointments and resignations.

State Dept., Family Liaison, Main State Bldg., Rm. 1212A (mailing address: Washington, DC 20520-7512); 647-1076. Kendall Montgomery, director. Fax, 647-1670.
Provides support for U.S. foreign affairs personnel and their families in Washington and abroad. Maintains liaison offices that give support services to the U.S. foreign affairs community overseas. Services include dependent employment assistance and continuing education programs; educational assistance for families with children; and information on adoption and separation, regulations, allowance, and finances. Assists families in emergencies.

State Dept., Foreign Service, Main State Bldg., Rm. 6218 20520; 647-9898. Genta Hawkins Holmes, director general. Fax, 647-5080.
Administers the foreign service.

State Dept., National Foreign Affairs Training Center, 4000 Arlington Blvd., Arlington, VA 22204; (703) 302-6703. Lawrence Taylor, director. Fax, (703) 302-7461. Registrar, (703) 875-7143.
Provides training for U.S. government personnel involved in foreign affairs agencies, including employees of the State Dept., the Agency for International Development, the U.S. Information Agency, the Defense Dept., and other agencies.

Congress:

House Foreign Affairs Committee, Subcommittee on International Operations, 2103 RHOB 20515; 225-3424. Howard L. Berman, D-Calif., chairman; Bradley Gordon, staff consultant. Fax, 225-7142.
Jurisdiction over foreign service legislation.

Senate Foreign Relations Committee, Subcommittee on Terrorism, Narcotics, and International Operations, SD-446 20510; 224-4651. John Kerry, D-Mass., chairman; Geryld B. Christianson, staff director. Fax, 224-5011.
Jurisdiction over foreign service legislation.

Nongovernmental:

American Foreign Service Assn., 2101 E St. N.W. 20037; 338-4045. Susan Reardon, executive director. Fax, 338-6820.
Membership: active and retired foreign service employees of the State Dept., Agency for International Development (AID), Foreign Commercial Service, Foreign Agricultural Service, and the U.S. Information Agency. Offers scholarship program; maintains club for members; represents State, AID, and USIA foreign service personnel in labor-management negotiations. Interests include business-government collaboration, U.S. economic competitiveness, international trade, and labor unions.

Public Members Assn. of the Foreign Service, 9200 Briary Lane, Fairfax, VA 22031; (703) 978-3023. E. D. Frankhouser, president.
Educational association of individuals who have served as public members of foreign service inspection teams or of State Dept. or other agency selection boards and advisory committees. Explains foreign policy and foreign service aims to the public; conducts seminars.

Immigration and Naturalization

See also Foreign Policy and Aid, Disaster Relief and Refugees (p. 449); International Law and Agreements, Boundaries (p. 474)

Agencies:

Administration for Children and Families (Health and Human Services Dept.), Refugee Resettlement, 901 D St. S.W., 6th Floor (mailing address: 370 L'Enfant Promenade S.W., Washington, DC 20447); 401-9246. Lavinia Limon, director. Fax, 401-5487.

Directs the Refugee Resettlement Program, which reimburses states for financial and medical assistance given to refugees; awards funds to private resettlement agencies for the provision of cash assistance to and case management of refugees; provides grants for social services, such as employment training and English instruction. Directs the State Legalization Impact Assistance Program, which awards grants to states to pay part of costs of providing certain types of assistance to aliens who attained legal status under the Immigration Reform and Control Act of 1986.

Commission on Immigration Reform, 1825 Connecticut Ave. N.W., #511 20009; 673-5348. Barbara Jordan, chair. Fax, 673-5354.

Evaluates the impact of recent reforms in immigration policy and recommends further policy changes.

Immigration and Naturalization Service (Justice Dept.), 425 Eye St. N.W. 20536; 514-1900. Doris Meissner, commissioner. Information, 514-4316. Press, 514-2648. Fax, 514-3296.

Administers and enforces immigration and naturalization laws relating to the admission, exclusion, deportation, and naturalization of aliens; responsible for preventing illegal entry into the United States; investigates, apprehends, and deports illegal aliens; oversees Border Patrol enforcement activities. Field offices provide aliens with information on application for asylum and U.S. citizenship. *(See Regional Federal Information Sources list, p. 830.)*

Justice Dept., Main Justice Bldg. 20530; 514-2001. Janet Reno, attorney general. Information, 514-2000. Fax, 514-0468.

Administers and enforces immigration and naturalization laws. Justice Dept. encompasses the Immigration and Naturalization Service, the Board of Immigration Appeals, and the Foreign Claims Settlement Commission of the United States.

Justice Dept., Civil Division, Main Justice Bldg. 20530; 514-3301. Frank W. Hunger, assistant attorney general; Robert L. Bombaugh, immigration litigation director, 501-7030. Information, 514-2007. Fax, 514-8071.

Handles most civil litigation arising under immigration and nationality laws.

Justice Dept., Community Relations Service, 5550 Friendship Blvd., Chevy Chase, MD

20815; (301) 492-5929. Geoffrey Weiss, acting director. Press, (301) 492-5969. Fax, (301) 492-5984. Toll-free hotline, (800) 347-4283.

Responsible for the Cuban/Haitian Entrant Program, which seeks to resettle these entrants in the United States and provides humanitarian assistance. Administers a similar program for Central Americans entering the United States through Mexico. Provides unaccompanied minors with language training and physical protection.

Justice Dept., Executive Office for Immigration Review, 5107 Leesburg Pike, Falls Church, VA 22041; (703) 305-0470. David L. Milhollan, director.

Quasi-judicial body separate from the Immigration and Naturalization Service. Interprets immigration laws; conducts hearings and hears appeals on immigration issues.

Justice Dept., Special Investigations, 1001 G St. N.W., #1000 20530; 616-2492. Neal M. Sher, director. Fax, 616-2491.

Identifies Nazi war criminals who illegally entered the United States after World War II. Handles legal action to ensure denaturalization and/or deportation.

Labor Dept., International Economic Affairs, 200 Constitution Ave. N.W., #S5325 20210; 219-7597. Jorge Perez-Lopez, director. Fax, 219-5071.

Assists in developing U.S. immigration policy.

State Dept., Visa Services, 2401 E St. N.W. 20522-0113; 663-1155. Diane Dillard, deputy assistant secretary. Information, 663-1291. Fax, 663-1247.

Supervises the visa issuance system, which is administered by officers of U.S. consulates abroad.

Congress:

House Judiciary Committee, Subcommittee on International Law, Immigration, and Refugees, B370B RHOB 20515; 225-5727. Romano L. Mazzoli, D-Ky., chairman; Eugene Pugliese, counsel.

Jurisdiction over immigration and naturalization legislation.

Senate Judiciary Committee, Subcommittee on Immigration and Refugee Affairs, SD-520

20510; 224-7878. Edward M. Kennedy, D-Mass., chairman; Jeff Blattner, chief counsel.

Jurisdiction over legislation on refugees, immigration, and naturalization. Oversight of the Immigration and Naturalization Service, the U.S. Board of Immigration Appeals, international migration and refugee laws and policies, and private immigration relief bills.

Nongovernmental:

American Council for Nationalities Service, 1717 Massachusetts Ave. N.W. 20036; 347-3507. Roger P. Winter, executive director. Fax, 347-3418.

Helps immigrants and refugees adjust to American society; assists in resettling recently arrived immigrants and refugees; offers information, counseling services, and temporary living accommodations through its member agencies nationwide; issues publications on immigration law, refugees, and refugee resettlement. Operates U.S. Committee for Refugees, which collects and disseminates information on refugee issues in the United States and abroad. Monitors legislation and regulations.

American Immigration Lawyers Assn., 1400 Eye St. N.W., #1200 20005; 371-9377. Warren R. Leiden, executive director. Fax, 371-9449.

Bar association for attorneys interested in immigration law. Provides information and continuing education programs on immigration law and policy; offers workshops and conferences; monitors legislation and regulations.

Center for Intercultural Education and Development, 3520 Prospect St. N.W. (mailing address: P.O. Box 2298, Georgetown University, Washington, DC 20057); 298-0200. Julio Giulietti SJ, director. Fax, 338-0608.

Promotes the development of a comprehensive and humane refugee policy through public information and educational programs, lectures, immigration and migration policy research, and on-location training sessions in refugee camps and resettlement homes. Assists refugees in adjusting to life in the United States.

Federation for American Immigration Reform, 1666 Connecticut Ave. N.W., #400 20009; 328-7004. Daniel Stein, executive director. Fax, 387-3447.

Organization of individuals interested in immigration reform. Monitors immigration laws and policies.

Lutheran Immigration and Refugee Service, 122 C St. N.W., #300 20001-2172; 783-7509. John Fredriksson, Washington representative.

Provides refugees in the United States with resettlement assistance, follow-up services, and immigration counseling. Funds local projects that provide social and legal services to all refugees, including undocumented persons. (Headquarters in New York.)

National Council of La Raza, 810 1st St. N.E., #300 20002; 289-1380. Raul Yzaguirre, president. Fax, 289-8173.

Provides research, policy analysis, and advocacy relating to immigration policy and programs. Monitors federal legislation on immigration, legalization, employer sanctions, employment discrimination resulting from federal immigration laws, and eligibility of immigrants for federal benefit programs. Assists community-based groups involved in immigration and education services and educates employers about immigration laws.

U.S. Catholic Conference, Migration and Refugee Services, 3211 4th St. N.E. 20017; 541-3220. Richard Ryscavage, executive director. Press, 541-3315. Fax, 541-3399.

Provides refugees and immigrants with resettlement services and legal counseling; operates training programs for volunteers and professionals; develops and implements USCC policy on migration, immigration, and refugee issues.

See also Institute for Public Representation (p. 521); National Center for Urban Ethnic Affairs (p. 384)

International Law and Agreements

General

Agencies:

Commission on Security and Cooperation in Europe (Helsinki Commission), 234 Ford Bldg. (2nd and D Sts. S.W.) 20515; 225-1901. Sen. Dennis DeConcini, D-Ariz., chairman; Samuel G. Wise, staff director. Fax, 226-4199.

Independent agency created by Congress. Membership includes individuals from the executive and legislative branches. Monitors and encourages compliance with the Helsinki Accords, a series of agreements with provisions on security, economic, environmental, human rights, and humanitarian issues; conducts hearings; serves as an information clearinghouse for issues in Eastern and Western Europe, Canada, and the United States relating to the Helsinki Accords.

INTERPOL (Justice Dept.), 600 E St. N.W. (mailing address: Washington, DC 20530); 272-8383. Shelley G. Altenstadter, chief. Fax, 272-5941.

U.S. national central bureau for INTERPOL; interacts in international investigations on behalf of U.S. police; coordinates the exchange of investigative information dealing with common law crimes, including drug trafficking, counterfeiting, missing persons, and terrorism; assists with extradition processes. Coordinates law enforcement requests for investigative assistance in the United States and abroad. Serves as liaison between foreign and U.S. law enforcement agencies at federal, state, and local levels. (Headquarters in Lyons, France.)

Justice Dept., Foreign Agents Registration Unit, 1400 New York Ave. N.W. 20530; 514-1216. Joseph E. Clarkson, chief. Fax, 514-2836.

Receives and maintains the registrations of agents representing foreign countries, companies, organizations, and individuals. Compiles annual report on foreign agent registrations. Foreign agent registration files are open for public inspection.

Securities and Exchange Commission, International Affairs, 450 5th St. N.W. 20549; 272-2306. Michael D. Mann, director. Fax, 504-2282.

Serves as liaison with enforcement and diplomatic officials abroad; seeks to enhance international cooperation in enforcement activities for the securities market; obtains evidence from abroad relating to investigations and litigation. Develops agreements with foreign countries to assist commission enforcement and regulatory efforts.

State Dept., Diplomatic Security, Main State Bldg., Rm. 6316 20520; 647-6290. Anthony C. E. Quainton, assistant secretary. Fax, 647-0953.

Provides a secure environment for conducting American diplomacy and promoting American interests abroad and in the United States.

State Dept., International Claims and Investment Disputes, 2100 K St. N.W. 20037; 632-7810. Ronald J. Bettauer, assistant legal adviser. Fax, 632-5283.

Handles claims by foreign governments and their nationals against the U.S. government, as well as claims against the State Dept. for negligence under the Federal Tort Claims Act. Administers the Iranian claims program and negotiates agreements with other foreign governments on claims settlements.

State Dept., Law Enforcement and Intelligence Affairs, Main State Bldg., Rm. 5419A 20520; 647-7324. Robert K. Harris, assistant legal adviser. Fax, 647-4802.

Negotiates extradition treaties, legal assistance treaties in criminal matters, and other agreements relating to international criminal matters.

State Dept., Legal Adviser, Main State Bldg., Rm. 6423 20520; 647-9598. Conrad Harper, legal adviser. Information, 647-6575. Fax, 647-1037.

Provides the department with legal advice on international problems; participates in international negotiations; represents the U.S. government in international litigation and in international conferences related to legal issues.

State Dept., Politico-Military Affairs, Main State Bldg., Rm. 7325A 20520; 647-9022. Robert L. Gallucci, assistant secretary. Fax, 647-1346.

Negotiates U.S. military base and operating rights overseas; acts as liaison between the Defense Dept. and State Dept.; controls military travel to sensitive or restricted areas abroad; arranges diplomatic clearance for overflights and ship visits.

State Dept., Treaty Affairs, Main State Bldg., Rm. 5420 20520; 647-1345. Robert E. Dalton, assistant legal adviser. Fax, 736-7541.

Provides legal advice on treaties and other international agreements, including constitutional questions, drafting, negotiation, and interpretation of treaties; maintains records of treaties and executive agreements.

Technology Administration (Commerce Dept.), International Technology Policy and Programs, Main Commerce Bldg. 20230; 482-5150. Elliot Maxwell, director. Fax, 482-4826.

Provides information on foreign research and development; coordinates, on behalf of the Commerce Dept., negotiation of international science and technology agreements.

Transportation Dept., International Aviation, 400 7th St. S.W. 20590; 366-2423. Paul L. Gretch, director. Fax, 366-3694.

Responsible for international aviation regulation and negotiations, including fares, tariffs, and foreign licenses; represents the United States at international aviation meetings.

Congress:

House Foreign Affairs Committee, 2170 RHOB 20515; 225-5021. Lee H. Hamilton, D-Ind., chairman; Michael H. Van Dusen, chief of staff. Fax, 226-3581.

Jurisdiction over legislation on international law enforcement, boundaries, and narcotics control; executive agreements; regional security agreements; counterterrorism policy; protection of Americans abroad, including the Foreign Airports Security Act; and the United Nations.

House Foreign Affairs Committee, Subcommittee on International Operations, 2103 RHOB 20515; 225-3424. Howard L. Berman, D-Calif., chairman; Bradley Gordon, staff consultant. Fax, 225-7142.

Jurisdiction over legislation dealing with embassy security.

House Foreign Affairs Committee, Subcommittee on International Security, International Organizations, and Human Rights, B358 RHOB 20515; 226-7825. Tom Lantos, D-Calif., chairman; Bob King, staff director. Fax, 226-3581.

Jurisdiction over legislation on international terrorism, including the Anti-Terrorism Assistance Program; international human rights, including implementation of the Universal Declaration of Human Rights; and international law enforcement issues, including narcotics control programs.

House Judiciary Committee, 2138 RHOB 20515; 225-3951. Jack Brooks, D-Texas, chairman; Jon Yarowsky, general counsel.

Jurisdiction over legislation on exchange of prisoners between the United States and Canada and the United States and Mexico.

House Judiciary Committee, Subcommittee on Civil and Constitutional Rights, 806 O'Neill Bldg. (300 New Jersey Ave. S.E.) 20515; 226-7680. Don Edwards, D-Calif., chairman; Catherine A. LeRoy, chief counsel.

Jurisdiction over legislation on control of international terrorism (shared with House Foreign Affairs Committee).

Senate Foreign Relations Committee, SD-446 20510; 224-4651. Claiborne Pell, D-R.I., chairman; Geryld B. Christianson, staff director. Fax, 224-5011.

Jurisdiction over legislation on human rights, international boundaries, regional security agreements, executive agreements, international narcotics control, embassy security, and international counterterrorism policy, including the Anti-Terrorism Assistance Program (jurisdiction shared with Senate Judiciary Committee); jurisdiction over legislation on exchange of prisoners between the United States and Canada and the United States and Mexico.

Senate Foreign Relations Committee, Subcommittee on Terrorism, Narcotics, and International Operations, SD-446 20510; 224-4651. John Kerry, D-Mass., chairman; Geryld B. Christianson, staff director. Fax, 224-5011.

Jurisdiction over legislation dealing with international terrorism; protection of Americans abroad, including the Foreign Airports Security Act; the international flow of illegal drugs; and the United Nations.

Senate Governmental Affairs Committee, Permanent Subcommittee on Investigations, SR-100 20510; 224-3721. Sam Nunn, D-Ga., chairman; Eleanor J. Hill, staff director.

Investigates international narcotics trafficking.

Senate Judiciary Committee, SD-224 20510; 224-5225. Joseph R. Biden Jr., D-Del., chairman; Cynthia Hogan, chief counsel.

Jurisdiction over legislation relating to the control of international terrorism (jurisdiction shared with the Senate Foreign Relations Committee).

Nongovernmental:

American Arbitration Assn., 1150 Connecticut Ave. N.W. 20036; 296-8510. Garylee Cox, regional vice president. Fax, 872-9574.

Provides dispute resolution services and information on international arbitration; administers certain international arbitration systems. (Headquarters in New York.)

American Bar Assn., International Legal Exchange Program, 1700 Pennsylvania Ave. N.W., #620 20006; 393-7122. Edison W. Dick, executive director. Fax, 347-9015.

Organizes the exchange of lawyers between the United States and other countries and arranges short-term placements for foreign lawyers with law firms nationwide.

American Bar Assn., Standing Committee on World Order Under Law, 1800 M St. N.W. 20036; 331-2651. Penelope S. Ferreira, director. Fax, 331-2220.

Examines legal issues relating to international peace and security, human rights, peaceful resolution of international conflicts, and the United Nations; develops model treaties; makes policy recommendations. (Headquarters in Chicago.)

American Society of International Law, 2223 Massachusetts Ave. N.W. 20008; 939-6000. Charlotte Ku, executive director. Fax, 797-7133.

Membership: lawyers, political scientists, economists, government officials, and students. Conducts research and study programs on international law; sponsors the International Law Students Assn. Library open to the public.

Inter-American Bar Assn., 815 15th St. N.W., #921 20005; 393-1217. José A. Toro, secretary general. Fax, 393-1241.

Membership: lawyers and bar associations in the Western Hemisphere with associate members in Europe and Asia. Works to promote uniformity of national and international laws; holds conferences; makes recommendations to national governments and organizations. Library open to the public.

Inter-American Bar Foundation, 1819 H St. N.W., #320A 20006; 293-1455. Donald K. Duvall, president. Fax, 828-0157.

Sponsors inter-American workshops and training programs for lawyers; offers scholarships and fellowships; conducts research; translates legal works of general interest throughout the hemisphere; maintains a digest of legal developments; conducts Administration of Justice program in Latin America.

World Jurists' Assn. of the World Peace Through Law Center, 1000 Connecticut Ave. N.W., #202 20036; 466-5428. Raul Goco, president. Fax, 452-8540.

Membership: lawyers, law professors, judges, law students, and nonlegal professionals worldwide. Promotes world peace through adherence to international law; conducts research; holds biennial world conferences.

Americans Abroad

Agencies:

Foreign Claims Settlement Commission of the United States (Justice Dept.), 600 E St. N.W. 20579; 616-6975. Vacant, chairman; Judith H. Lock, administrative officer, 208-7728. Fax, 616-6993.

Processes claims by U.S. nationals against foreign governments for property losses sustained.

State Dept., Citizens Consular Services, Main State Bldg., Rm. 4817 20520-4818; 647-3666. Carmen A. DiPlacido, director. Fax, 647-2835. Recorded information, 647-3444.

Deals with nonemergency matters concerning U.S. citizens abroad, including legal documents, reports of birth and death, matters of child custody, U.S. properties overseas, provisional conservatorship of estates of U.S. citizens who die abroad, absentee ballots, federal benefits, citizenship and passport activities, and seaman and shipping problems.

State Dept., Citizens Emergency Center, Main State Bldg., Rm. 4800 20520-4010; 647-5226. Maura Harty, director. Fax, 647-6201. Recorded consular information sheets, 647-5225.

Assists with emergency matters concerning U.S. citizens abroad, including missing persons, deaths, financial assistance to stranded persons, and U.S. nationals arrested abroad.

State Dept., International Claims and Investment Disputes, 2100 K St. N.W. 20037; 632-7810. Ronald J. Bettauer, assistant legal adviser. Fax, 632-5283.

Handles claims by U.S. government and citizens against foreign governments; handles claims by owners of U.S. flag vessels for reimbursements of fines, fees, licenses, and other direct payments for illegal seizures by foreign governments in international waters under the Fishermen's Protective Act.

State Dept., Passport Services, Main State Bldg., Rm. 6811 20520; 647-5366. Barry J. Kefauver, deputy assistant secretary. Information, 647-1488. Fax, 647-0341. Passport information, 647-0518.

Administers passport laws and issues passports. (Most branches of the U.S. Postal Service and most U.S. district and state courts are authorized to accept applications and payment for passports and to administer the required oath to

U.S. citizens. Completed applications are sent from the post office or court to the nearest State Dept. regional passport office for processing.) Maintains a variety of records received from the Overseas Citizens Services, including consular certificates of witness to marriage and reports of birth and death. *(See Regional Federal Information Sources list, p. 832.)*

Congress:

House Foreign Affairs Committee, 2170 RHOB 20515; 225-5021. Lee H. Hamilton, D-Ind., chairman; Michael H. Van Dusen, chief of staff. Fax, 226-3581.
Jurisdiction over legislation on protection of Americans abroad, including the Foreign Airports Security Act.

House Select Committee on Intelligence, H405 CAP 20515; 225-4121. Dan Glickman, D-Kan., chairman; Michael Sheehy, chief counsel. Fax, 225-1991.
Oversight of directives and procedures governing intelligence activities affecting the rights of Americans abroad.

Senate Foreign Relations Committee, SD-446 20510; 224-4651. Claiborne Pell, D-R.I., chairman; Geryld B. Christianson, staff director. Fax, 224-5011.
Jurisdiction over legislation on protection of Americans abroad.

Senate Select Committee on Intelligence, SH-211 20510; 224-1700. Dennis DeConcini, D-Ariz., chairman; Norm Bradley, staff director.
Oversight of directives and procedures governing intelligence activities affecting the rights of Americans abroad.

Boundaries

Agencies:

International Boundary Commission, United States and Canada, U.S. Section, 1250 23rd St. N.W., #405 20037; 736-9100. Vacant, commissioner. Fax, 736-9107.
Defines and maintains the demarcation of the international boundary line between the United States and Canada.

International Joint Commission, United States and Canada, U.S. Section, 1250 23rd St. N.W.,

#100 20440; 736-9000. David LaRoche, secretary. Fax, 736-9015.
Handles disputes concerning the use of boundary waters; negotiates questions dealing with the rights, obligations, and interests of the United States and Canada along the border; establishes procedures for the adjustment and settlement of questions.

Saint Lawrence Seaway Development Corp. (Transportation Dept.), 400 7th St. S.W. 20590; 366-0118. Stanford Parris, administrator. Information, 366-0091. Fax, 366-7147.
Operates and maintains the Saint Lawrence Seaway within U.S. territorial limits; conducts development programs and coordinates activities with its Canadian counterpart.

State Dept., Mexican Affairs, Main State Bldg., Rm. 4258 20520-6258; 647-9894. Stephen Gibson, U.S. coordinator, U.S.—Mexico border affairs. Fax, 647-5752.
Acts as liaison between the State Dept. and the U.S. section of the International Boundary and Water Commission, United States and Mexico (based in El Paso, Texas), in international boundary and water matters as defined by U.S.-Mexican treaties and agreements.

Congress:

See International Law and Agreements, General, Congress (p. 472)

See also Congressional Border Caucus (p. 758)

Counterterrorism

Agencies:

Defense Dept., Special Operations and Low Intensity Conflict, The Pentagon, Rm. 2E258 20301; (703) 693-2895. H. Allen Holmes, assistant secretary. Fax, (703) 693-6335.
Serves as special staff assistant and civilian adviser to the defense secretary on matters related to special operations and international terrorism.

Federal Bureau of Investigation (Justice Dept.), Counterterrorism, 10th St. and Pennsylvania Ave. N.W. 20535; 324-4664. David M. Tubbs, chief. Press, 324-3691. Fax, 324-4658.
Federal law enforcement agency with primary jurisdiction over the U.S. government's counterterrorism activities. Responsible for preventing,

interdicting, and investigating the criminal activities of domestic and international terrorist groups and individuals in the United States.

INTERPOL (Justice Dept.), 600 E St. N.W. (mailing address: Washington, DC 20530); 272-8383. Shelley G. Altenstadter, chief. Fax, 272-5941.

U.S. national central bureau for INTERPOL; interacts in international investigations of terrorism on behalf of U.S. police. Sponsors forums enabling foreign governments to discuss counterterrorism policy. Serves as liaison between foreign and U.S. law enforcement agencies. (Headquarters in Lyons, France.)

Justice Dept., Terrorism and Violent Crime, 10th St. and Pennsylvania Ave. N.W., #2513 20530; 514-0849. James S. Reynolds, chief. Fax, 514-8714.

Investigates and prosecutes incidents of international terrorism involving U.S. interests, domestic violent crime, firearms, and explosives violations. Provides legal advice on federal statutes relating to murder, assault, kidnapping, threats, robbery, weapons and explosives control, malicious destruction of property, and aircraft and sea piracy.

State Dept., Counterterrorism, Main State Bldg., Rm. 2507 20520; 647-9892. Barbara K. Bodine, acting coordinator. Information, 647-7633. Fax, 647-0221.

Implements U.S. counterterrorism policy and coordinates activities with foreign governments; responds to terrorist acts; works to promote a stronger counterterrorism stance worldwide.

State Dept., Diplomatic Security, Main State Bldg., Rm. 6316 20520; 647-6290. Anthony C. E. Quainton, assistant secretary. Fax, 647-0953.

Conducts Anti-Terrorism Assistance Program, which provides training to foreign governments fighting terrorism.

Transportation Dept., Intelligence and Security, 400 7th St. S.W. 20590; 366-6535. Rear Adm. Paul E. Busick (USCG), director. Fax, 366-7261.

Advises the secretary on transportation intelligence and security policy. Acts as liaison with the intelligence community, federal agencies, corporations, and interest groups; administers counterterrorism strategic planning processes.

Congress:

See International Law and Agreements, General, Congress (p. 472)

Nongovernmental:

American Society for Industrial Security, 1655 N. Fort Myer Dr., #1200, Arlington, VA 22209; (703) 522-5800. E. J. Criscuoli, executive vice president. Fax, (703) 243-4954.

Membership: security administrators charged with protecting the assets and personnel of private and public organizations. Sponsors seminars and workshops on counterterrorism.

See also United States Global Strategy Council (p. 449)

Extradition

Agencies:

Justice Dept., Enforcement Operations, 1001 G St. N.W. 20530; 514-3684. Gerald Shur, senior associate director. Fax, 514-5143.

Implements prisoner transfer treaties with foreign countries.

Justice Dept., International Affairs, 1400 New York Ave. N.W. (mailing address: P.O. Box 27330, Washington, DC 20038); 514-0000. George W. Proctor, director. Fax, 514-0080.

Performs investigations necessary for extradition of fugitives from the United States and other nations. Handles requests for legal assistance including documentary evidence from the United States and other nations.

State Dept., Law Enforcement and Intelligence Affairs, Main State Bldg., Rm. 5419A 20520; 647-7324. Robert K. Harris, assistant legal adviser. Fax, 647-4802.

Negotiates and approves extradition of fugitives between other nations and the United States.

Congress:

See International Law and Agreements, General, Congress (p. 472)

Nongovernmental:

Center for National Security Studies, 122 Maryland Ave. N.E. 20002; 675-2327. Kate Martin, director. Fax, 546-1440.

Sponsored by the American Civil Liberties Union Foundation and the Fund for Peace. Monitors and conducts research on extradition, intelligence, national security, and civil liberties. Library open to the public by appointment.

Fishing/Law of the Sea

Agencies:

National Oceanic and Atmospheric Administration (Commerce Dept.), National Marine Fisheries Service, 1335 East-West Highway, Silver Spring, MD 20910; (301) 713-2239. Rolland A. Schmitten, assistant administrator. Information, (301) 713-2370. Fax, (301) 713-2258.

Administers marine fishing regulations, including offshore fishing rights and international agreements.

State Dept., Oceans, Main State Bldg., Rm. 7831 20520; 647-2396. David A. Colson, deputy assistant secretary. Fax, 647-0217.

Coordinates U.S. negotiations concerning international fishing and oceans issues. Handles both foreign fleets fishing in U.S. waters and U.S. fleets fishing in foreign waters or the open seas.

Congress:

House Foreign Affairs Committee, Subcommittee on Economic Policy, Trade, and the Environment, 702 O'Neill Bldg. (300 New Jersey Ave. S.E.) 20515; 226-7820. Sam Gejdenson, D-Conn., chairman; John Scheibel, staff director. Fax, 225-2029.

Oversees and has jurisdiction over legislation concerning international fishing laws and Law of the Sea (jurisdiction shared with House Merchant Marine and Fisheries Committee).

House Merchant Marine and Fisheries Committee, Subcommittee on Fisheries Management, 534 Ford Bldg. (2nd and D Sts. S.W.) 20515; 226-3514. Thomas J. Manton, D-N.Y., chairman; Jim Mathews, staff director.

Jurisdiction over legislation concerning international fishing laws (jurisdiction shared with House Foreign Affairs Committee).

House Merchant Marine and Fisheries Committee, Subcommittee on Oceanography, Gulf of Mexico, and the Outer Continental Shelf, 575 Ford Bldg. (2nd and D Sts. S.W.) 20515; 226-2460. Solomon P. Ortiz, D-Texas, chairman; Sheila McCready, staff director.

Jurisdiction over legislation concerning Law of the Sea. (Jurisdiction over international aspects shared with House Foreign Affairs Committee.)

Senate Commerce, Science, and Transportation Committee, SD-508 20510; 224-5115. Ernest F. Hollings, D-S.C., chairman; Kevin Curtin, chief counsel and staff director.

Jurisdiction over legislation concerning international fishing laws and Law of the Sea (jurisdiction shared with the Senate Foreign Relations Committee).

Senate Commerce, Science, and Transportation Committee, Subcommittee on National Ocean Policy Study, SH-425 (mailing address: SD-508, Washington, DC 20510); 224-4912. Ernest F. Hollings, D-S.C., chairman; Penny Dalton, staff member.

Studies issues concerning international fishing laws and Law of the Sea (jurisdiction shared with Senate Foreign Relations Committee). (Subcommittee does not report legislation.)

Senate Foreign Relations Committee, Subcommittee on International Economic Policy, Trade, Oceans, and Environment, SD-446 20510; 224-4651. Paul S. Sarbanes, D-Md., chairman; Geryld B. Christianson, staff director. Fax, 224-5011.

Oversight of Law of the Sea matters.

Nongovernmental:

Council on Ocean Law, 1600 H St. N.W., 2nd Floor 20006; 347-3766. Charles Higginson, executive director. Fax, 842-0030.

Promotes American interests in international ocean law; provides educational materials.

U.S. Tuna Foundation, 1101 17th St. N.W., #609 20036; 857-0610. David G. Burney, executive director. Fax, 331-9686.

Membership: tuna processors, vessel owners, and fishermen's unions. Provides information and research on the tuna industry; offers advice on fisheries to the U.S. delegation to the United Nations Law of the Sea Conference.

Human Rights

Agencies:

Commission on Security and Cooperation in Europe (Helsinki Commission), 234 Ford Bldg. (2nd and D Sts. S.W.) 20515; 225-1901. Sen.

Dennis DeConcini, D-Ariz., chairman; Samuel G. Wise, staff director. Fax, 226-4199.

Independent agency created by Congress. Membership includes individuals from the executive and legislative branches. Monitors and encourages compliance with the human rights provisions of the Helsinki Accords; conducts hearings; serves as an information clearinghouse for human rights issues in Eastern and Western Europe, Canada, and the United States relating to the Helsinki Accords.

State Dept., Human Rights and Humanitarian Affairs, Main State Bldg., Rm. 7802 20520; 647-2126. John Shattuck, assistant secretary. Fax, 647-9519.

Implements U.S. policies relating to human rights; prepares annual review of human rights worldwide; provides the Immigration and Naturalization Service with advisory opinions regarding asylum petitions.

Congress:

See International Law and Agreements, General, Congress (p. 472)

See also Congressional Friends of Human Rights Monitors (p. 756)

Nongovernmental:

American Council for the Advancement of Human Rights, 1875 Connecticut Ave. N.W., #1140 20009-5728; 588-5300. Robert B. Fitzpatrick, president. Fax, 588-5023.

Research organization that seeks ratification by the U.S. Senate of existing international human rights treaties, especially those that the United States has signed. Treaties of interest include American Convention on Human Rights and the International Covenant on Civil and Political Rights.

Amnesty International USA, 304 Pennsylvania Ave. S.E. 20003; 544-0200. James O'Dea, director, Washington office. Fax, 546-7142.

International organization that works for the release of men and women imprisoned anywhere in the world for their beliefs, political affiliation, color, ethnic origin, sex, language, or religion, provided they have neither used nor advocated violence. Opposes torture and the death penalty; urges fair trials for all political prisoners. Library open to the public. (U.S. headquarters in New York.)

Church Coalition for Human Rights in the Philippines, 110 Maryland Ave. N.E. 20002; 543-1094. Kathryn J. Johnson, executive director. Fax, 546-0090.

Coalition of churches and church-related organizations concerned with human rights, political prisoners, and military aid to the Philippines. Provides information and sponsors educational forums on human rights violations in the Philippines.

Guatemala Human Rights Commission/USA, 3321 12th St. N.E. 20017; 529-6599. Alice Zachmann, coordinator. Fax, 526-4611.

Provides information and collects and makes available reports on human rights violations in Guatemala; publishes a bimonthly report of documented cases of specific abuses and a quarterly bulletin of human rights news and analysis. Takes on special projects to further sensitize the public and the international community to human rights abuses in Guatemala.

Human Rights Watch, 1522 K St. N.W., #910 20005; 371-6592. Holly Burkhalter, Washington director. Fax, 371-0124.

International, nonpartisan human rights organization that monitors human rights violations worldwide. Coordinates five committees—Africa Watch, Americas Watch, Asia Watch, Helsinki Watch, and Middle East Watch. Coordinates thematic projects on women's rights, arms sales, and prisons. Sponsors fact-finding missions to various countries; publicizes violations and encourages international protests; maintains file on human rights violations. (Headquarters in New York.)

International Assn. of Official Human Rights Agencies, 444 N. Capitol St. N.W., #634 20001; 624-5410. R. Edison Elkins, executive director. Fax, 624-8185.

Works with government and human rights agencies to identify needs common to civil rights enforcement. Offers management training for human rights executives and civil rights workshops for criminal justice agencies; develops training programs in investigative techniques, settlement and conciliation, and legal theory. Serves as an information clearinghouse on human rights laws and enforcement.

International Human Rights Law Group, 1601 Connecticut Ave. N.W., #700 20009; 232-8500. Reed Brody, executive director. Fax, 232-6731.

Public interest law center concerned with promoting and protecting international human rights. Conducts educational programs and conferences; provides information and legal assistance regarding human rights violations; monitors the electoral and judicial process in several countries.

Irish National Caucus, 413 E. Capitol St. S.E. 20003; 544-0568. Sean McManus, president. Fax, 543-2491.
Educational organization concerned with protecting human rights in Northern Ireland. Supports efforts to unify Ireland by peaceful means. Seeks to end discrimination in Northern Ireland through implementation of the McBride principles, initiated in 1984.

See also Central American Refugee Center (p. 450); Council on Hemispheric Affairs (p. 465); Institute for Policy Studies (p. 448); Network in Solidarity with the People of Guatemala and Religious Task Force on Central America (p. 465); U.S. Catholic Conference (p. 449); Washington Office on Latin America (p. 465)

Narcotics

See also Criminal Law, Drug Abuse (p. 510)

Agencies:

Defense Dept., Counter-Narcotics Operations, The Pentagon, Rm. 2B913 20301; (703) 695-1476. Capt. William G. Bozin, chief.
Responsible for countering the importation of narcotics into the United States.

Defense Dept., Democracy and Peacekeeping, The Pentagon 20301-2900; (703) 695-2310. Edward L. Warner III, assistant secretary, strategy, requirements, and resources.
Coordinates and monitors Defense Dept. support of civilian drug law enforcement agencies and interagency efforts to detect and monitor the maritime and aerial transit of illegal drugs into the United States. Represents the secretary of defense on drug control matters outside the department.

Drug Enforcement Administration (Justice Dept.), 700 Army-Navy Dr., Arlington, VA (mailing address: Washington, DC 20537); 307-8000. Thomas A. Constantine, administrator. Information, 307-7977. Fax, 307-7335.

Assists foreign narcotics agents; cooperates with the State Dept., embassies, the Agency for International Development, and international organizations to strengthen narcotics law enforcement and to reduce supply and demand in developing countries; trains and advises narcotics enforcement officers in developing nations.

State Dept., International Narcotics Matters, Main State Bldg., Rm. 7333 20520-7310; 647-8464. Robert Gailbard, assistant secretary. Fax, 647-8269.
Coordinates international drug control activities, including policy development, diplomatic initiatives, bilateral and multilateral assistance for crop control, interdiction and related enforcement activities in producer and transit nations, development assistance, technical assistance for demand reduction, and training for foreign personnel in narcotics enforcement and related procedures.

U.S. Coast Guard (Transportation Dept.), Operational Law Enforcement, 2100 2nd St. S.W. 20593; 267-1155. Capt. J. F. Carmichael, chief. Fax, 267-4082.
Enforces or assists in the enforcement of federal laws and treaties and other international agreements to which the United States is party, on, over, and under the high seas and waters subject to the jurisdiction of the United States; conducts investigations into suspected violations of such laws and international agreements, including drug smuggling and trafficking.

Congress:

See International Law and Agreements, General, Congress (p. 472)

See also Senate Caucus on International Narcotics Control (p. 761)

Regional Security Agreements

Agencies:

Defense Dept., African Affairs, The Pentagon, Rm. 4B746 20301; (703) 697-2864. James L. Woods, deputy assistant secretary. Fax, (703) 695-4620.
Advises the assistant secretary for international security affairs on matters dealing with Sub-Saharan Africa.

Defense Dept., East Asia and Pacific Affairs, The Pentagon, Rm. 4C839 20301; (703) 695-

4175. Kent Wiedemann, deputy assistant secretary. Fax, (703) 695-8222.

Advises the assistant secretary for international security affairs on matters dealing with East Asia and the Pacific.

Defense Dept., European and NATO Policy, The Pentagon, Rm. 4D800 20301; (703) 697-7207. Joseph Kruzel, deputy assistant secretary. Fax, (703) 695-6506.

Advises the assistant secretary for international security policy on matters dealing with Europe and NATO (North Atlantic Treaty Organization).

Defense Dept., Inter-American Affairs, The Pentagon, Rm. 4C800 20301; (703) 697-5884. Mari-Luci Jaramillo, deputy assistant secretary. Fax, (703) 695-8404.

Advises the assistant secretary for international security affairs on inter-American matters; aids in the development of U.S. policy toward Latin America.

Defense Dept., Near Eastern and South Asian Affairs, The Pentagon, Rm. 4D765 20301; (703) 695-5223. Molly Williamson, deputy assistant secretary. Fax, (703) 693-6795.

Advises the assistant secretary for international security affairs on matters dealing with the Near East and South Asia.

Defense Dept., Regional Security Affairs, The Pentagon, Rm. 4E838 20301; (703) 695-4351. Chas. W. Freeman Jr., assistant secretary. Fax, (703) 697-7239.

Advises the secretary of defense and recommends policies on regional security issues (except those involving countries of the former Soviet Union).

Permanent Joint Board on Defense/United States and Canada, 1111 Jefferson Davis Highway, Arlington, VA 22202; (703) 604-0487. Vacant, chairman; Lt. Col. Jerre D. Fallis (USAF), military secretary. Fax, (703) 604-0486.

Comprises representatives from the State Dept. and Defense Dept.; chairman appointed by the president. Conducts studies relating to sea, land, and air defense problems. (Canadian counterpart located in Ottawa.)

State Dept., European Security and Political Affairs, Main State Bldg., Rm. 6227 20520; 647-1626. James B. Cunningham, director. Fax, 647-0967.

Coordinates and advises, with the Defense Dept. and other agencies, the U.S. mission to the North Atlantic Treaty Organization and the U.S. delegation to the Conference on Security and Cooperation in Europe regarding political, military, and arms control matters.

State Dept., Politico-Military Affairs, Main State Bldg., Rm. 7325A 20520; 647-9022. Robert L. Gallucci, assistant secretary. Fax, 647-1346.

Responsible for security affairs policy and operations for the non-European area.

State Dept., United Nations Political Affairs, Main State Bldg., Rm. 6334 20520-6319; 647-2392. Joseph C. Snyder III, director. Fax, 647-0039.

Deals with United Nations political and institutional matters and international security affairs.

Congress:

See International Law and Agreements, General, Congress (p. 472)

International Organizations:

Inter-American Defense Board, 2600 16th St. N.W. 20441; 939-6600. Maj. Gen. James R. Harding (USA), chairman. Fax, 939-6620.

Membership: military officers from 20 countries of the Western Hemisphere. Plans and prepares for the collective self-defense of the American continents. Develops procedures for standardizing military organization and operations; operates the Inter-American Defense College.

Joint Mexican-United States Defense Commission, U.S. Section, 1111 Jefferson Davis Highway, Arlington, VA 22202; (703) 604-0483. Maj. Gen. John C. Ellerson (USA), chairman.

Comprises military delegates of the two countries. Studies problems concerning the common defense of the United States and Mexico.

See also Organization of American States (p. 464)

International Organizations and Conferences

Agencies:

Environmental Protection Agency, International Activities, 401 M St. S.W. 20460; 260-4870. Alan Hecht, acting assistant administrator. Fax, 260-9653.

Coordinates the agency's work on international environmental issues and programs, including management of bilateral agreements and participation in multilateral organizations and negotiations.

State Dept., Agricultural Trade Policy and Programs, Main State Bldg., Rm. 3526 20520; 647-3090. Thomas L. Robinson, director. Fax, 647-1894.

Develops U.S. food and agricultural policies involving trade, aid, producer/consumer relations, and food security. Proposes and implements State Dept. foreign policy goals on agricultural issues, including trade, aid, and export credits. Represents the department in agricultural commodity organizations and forums such as the General Agreement on Tariffs and Trade (GATT).

State Dept., International Conferences, Main State Bldg., Rm. 1517 20520-6319; 647-6875. Frank R. Provyn, managing director. Fax, 647-1301.

Coordinates U.S. participation in international conferences.

State Dept., International Organization Affairs, Main State Bldg., Rm. 6323 20520-6319; 647-9600. Douglas J. Bennet, assistant secretary. Information, 647-6400. Fax, 647-6510.

Coordinates and develops policy guidelines for U.S. participation in the United Nations and in other international organizations and conferences.

Congress:

House Foreign Affairs Committee, Subcommittee on International Security, International Organizations, and Human Rights, B358 RHOB 20515; 226-7825. Tom Lantos, D-Calif., chairman; Bob King, staff director. Fax, 226-3581.

Jurisdiction over legislation on the United Nations and other international organizations.

House Government Operations Committee, 2157 RHOB 20515; 225-5051. John Conyers Jr., D-Mich., chairman; Julian Epstein, staff director. Fax, 225-4784.

Oversight jurisdiction of relationship of the United States to international organizations, including the United Nations.

Library of Congress, Serial and Government Publications, 101 Independence Ave. S.E. 20540; 707-5647. Karen Renninger, chief. Information, 707-5690. Fax, 707-6128.

Collects and maintains information on governmental and nongovernmental organizations that are internationally based, financed, and sponsored. Responds to written or telephone requests to provide information on the history, structure, operation, and activities of these organizations. Some book material available for interlibrary loan through the Library of Congress Loan Division.

Senate Foreign Relations Committee, Subcommittee on Terrorism, Narcotics, and International Operations, SD-446 20510; 224-4651. John Kerry, D-Mass., chairman; Geryld B. Christianson, staff director. Fax, 224-5011.

Jurisdiction over legislation on the United Nations and other international organizations and conferences.

International Organizations:

European Community Press and Public Affairs, 2100 M St. N.W. 20037; 862-9500. Andreas A. M. van Agt, ambassador; Peter Doyle, director. Information, 862-9542. Press, 862-9540. Fax, 429-1766.

Information and public affairs office in the United States for the European Union/European Community, which includes the European Economic Community, the European Coal and Steel Community, and the European Atomic Energy Community. Member countries are Belgium, Denmark, France, Germany, Great Britain, Greece, Ireland, Italy, Luxembourg, the Netherlands, Portugal, and Spain. Provides social policy data on the European Community and provides statistics and documents on member countries, including those related to energy, economics, development and cooperation, commerce, agriculture, industry, and technology. Library open to the public by appointment.

Food and Agriculture Organization of the United Nations, Liaison Office for North

America, 1001 22nd St. N.W., #300 20437; 653-2400. Vacant, director. Library, 653-2402. Fax, 653-5760.

Serves as the main forum of the international community on world food, agriculture, fisheries, and forestry problems; provides developing nations with technical assistance to improve and increase agricultural productivity. Library open to the public by appointment. (International headquarters in Rome.)

Inter-American Development Bank, 1300 New York Ave. N.W. 20577; 623-1100. Enrique Iglesias, president; L. Ronald Scheman, U.S. executive director, 623-1030. Information, 623-1000. Press, 623-1371. Library, 623-3210. Fax, 623-3096.

Promotes, through loans and technical assistance, the investment of public and private capital in member countries for social and economic development purposes. Facilitates economic integration of the Latin American region. Library open to the public by appointment.

International Bank for Reconstruction and Development (World Bank), 1818 H St. N.W. 20433; 458-2001. Lewis T. Preston, president; Jan Piercy, U.S. executive director designate, 458-0115. Press, 473-1786. Fax, 676-0578. Bookstore, 473-5545.

International development institution funded by membership subscriptions and borrowings on private capital markets. Encourages the flow of public and private foreign investment into developing countries through loans and technical assistance. Finances foreign economic development projects in agriculture, environmental protection, education, public utilities, telecommunications, water supply, sewerage, public health, and other areas.

International Centre for Settlement of Investment Disputes, 701 19th St. N.W. (mailing address: 1818 H St. N.W., Washington, DC 20433); 458-1601. Ibrahim F. I. Shihata, secretary general. Information, 477-1234. Fax, 477-5828.

World Bank affiliate that handles the conciliation and arbitration of investment disputes between contracting states and foreign investors.

International Development Assn., 1818 H St. N.W. 20433; 458-2001. Lewis T. Preston, president. Press, 473-1786. Fax, 676-0578.

Affiliate of the World Bank funded by membership contributions and transfers of funds from the World Bank. Extends interest-free credits to poorest member countries for high-priority development projects.

International Finance Corp., 1850 Eye St. N.W. (mailing address: 1818 H St. N.W., Washington, DC 20433); 458-2001. Lewis T. Preston, president; William S. Ryrie, executive vice president, 473-0381. Fax, 676-0365.

Promotes private enterprise in developing countries through direct investments in projects that establish new businesses or expand, modify, or diversify existing businesses; provides its own financing or recruits financing from other sources. Affiliated with the World Bank.

International Monetary Fund (IMF), 700 19th St. N.W. 20431; 623-7759. Karin Lissakers, U.S. executive director. Fax, 623-4940.

Intergovernmental organization that maintains funds, contributed and available for use by members, to promote world trade and aid members with temporary balance-of-payments problems.

International Organization for Migration, 1730 K St. N.W., #1110 20006; 862-1826. Hans-Petter Boe, chief of mission. Fax, 862-1879.

Nonpartisan organization that plans and operates refugee resettlement, national migration, and humanitarian assistance programs at the request of its member governments. Recruits skilled professionals for developing countries. (Headquarters in Geneva.)

Organization for Economic Cooperation and Development (OECD), 2001 L St. N.W., #700 20036; 785-6323. Denis Lamb, head, Washington Center. Fax, 785-0350.

Membership: 24 nations including Australia, Canada, Japan, New Zealand, the United States, and Western European nations. Serves as a forum for members to exchange information and attempt to coordinate their economic policies. Washington Center maintains reference library open to the public. (Headquarters in Paris.)

Organization of American States (OAS), 17th St. and Constitution Ave. N.W. 20006; 458-3000. João Clemente Baena Soares, secretary general. Information, 458-3760. Library, 458-6037. Fax, 458-3967.

Membership: the United States, Canada, and all independent Latin American and Caribbean countries. Funded by quotas paid by member states and by contributions to special multilateral funds. Works to promote democracy, eliminate poverty, and resolve disputes among member nations. Provides member states with technical and advisory services in cultural, educational, scientific, social, and economic areas. Library open to the public.

Pan American Health Organization, 525 23rd St. N.W. 20037; 861-3200. Dr. Carlyle Guerra de Macedo, director. Information, 861-3458. Library, 861-3305. Fax, 223-5971.
Regional office for the Americas of the World Health Organization, headquartered in Geneva, Switzerland. Works to extend health services to underserved populations in member countries and to control or eradicate communicable diseases; promotes cooperation among governments to solve public health problems. Library open to the public by appointment.

United Nations Development Programme, 1889 F St. N.W. 20006; 289-8674. David Scotton, director, Washington office. Fax, 842-2998.
Funded by voluntary contributions from member nations and by nonmember recipient nations. Administers and coordinates technical assistance programs provided through the United Nations system. Seeks to increase economic and social development in developing nations. (Headquarters in New York.)

United Nations Economic Commission for Latin America and the Caribbean, 1735 Eye St. N.W., #809 20006; 955-5613. Isaac Cohen, director. Fax, 296-0826.
Membership: Latin American and some industrially developed Western nations. Seeks to strengthen economic relations between countries both within and outside Latin America through research and analysis of socioeconomic problems, training programs, and advisory services to member governments. (Headquarters in Santiago, Chile.)

United Nations Information Centre, 1889 F St. N.W. 20006; 289-8670. Michael Stopford, director. Fax, 289-4267.
Center for reference publications of the United Nations; library, open to the public, includes all official U.N. records and publications.

Nongovernmental:

United Nations Assn. of the USA, 1010 Vermont Ave. N.W. 20005; 347-5004. Steven A.

Dimoff, executive director, Washington office. Fax, 628-5945.
Research and educational organization focusing on international institutions, multilateral diplomacy, U.S. foreign policy, and international economics. Coordinates Model United Nations program for high school and university students. Monitors legislation and regulations. (Headquarters in New York.)

U.S. Committee for the United Nations Children's Fund (UNICEF), 110 Maryland Ave. N.E., #304 20002; 547-7946. Martin F. Rendon, director, congressional relations. Information, 547-0204. Fax, 543-8144.
Serves as information reference service on UNICEF; maintains film library and files of some documents relating to UNICEF. Interests include international humanitarian assistance, U.S. voluntarism, child survival, and international health. (Headquarters in New York.)

United Way International, 901 N. Pitt St., 1st Floor, Alexandria, VA 22314; (703) 519-0092. Russy D. Sumariwalla, president. Fax, (703) 519-0097.
Membership: independent United Way organizations in other countries. Provides United Way fund-raising campaigns with technical assistance; trains volunteers and professionals; operates an information exchange for affiliated organizations.

See also Atlantic Council of the United States (p. 447)

Overseas Information and Exchange Programs

See also Education: Special Topics, International Education (p. 153); Science: International Programs (p. 681)

Agencies:

Board for International Broadcasting, 1201 Connecticut Ave. N.W. 20036; 254-8040. Daniel A. Mica, chairman. Fax, 254-3929.
Established by Congress to oversee the operations of Radio Free Europe/Radio Liberty and to assess the quality and effectiveness of broadcasts with regard to U.S. foreign policy objectives; reports annually to the president and to Congress.

U.S. Advisory Commission on Public Diplomacy (U.S. Information Agency), 301 4th St. S.W. 20547; 619-4457. Bruce Gregory, staff director. Fax, 619-5489.

Provides bipartisan oversight and assessment of the international information broadcasting, cultural, and educational exchange programs of the U.S. government. Reports to the president, the secretary of state, the USIA director, and Congress.

U.S. Information Agency (USIA), 301 4th St. S.W. 20547; 619-4364. Joseph Duffy, director. Information, 619-4355. Fax, 619-6988.

Independent agency responsible for international information, education, and exchange programs designed to promote understanding of American society and culture and U.S. foreign policy. Oversees more than 200 posts in 130 foreign countries.

Voice of America (U.S. Information Agency), 330 Independence Ave. S.W. 20547; 619-3375. Geoffrey Cowan, director designate. Information, 619-2538. Fax, 619-0085. Locator, 619-4700.

Official radio broadcast service of the U.S. Information Agency. Offers overseas broadcasts of news, editorials, and features dealing with developments in American foreign and domestic affairs. Operates African, East Asian and Pacific, European, American Republics, North African, Near East and South Asian affairs offices, as well as the World English program.

Congress:

House Foreign Affairs Committee, Subcommittee on International Operations, 2103 RHOB 20515; 225-3424. Howard L. Berman, D-Calif., chairman; Bradley Gordon, staff consultant. Fax, 225-7142.

Jurisdiction over legislation on educational and cultural exchange programs.

Senate Foreign Relations Committee, Subcommittee on Terrorism, Narcotics, and International Operations, SD-446 20510; 224-4651. John Kerry, D-Mass., chairman; Geryld B. Christianson, staff director. Fax, 224-5011.

Jurisdiction over legislation on educational and cultural exchange programs.

Nongovernmental:

American Council of Teachers of Russian, 1776 Massachusetts Ave. N.W., #700 20036; 833-7522. Lisa Choate, assistant director. Fax, 833-7523.

Conducts educational exchanges with the countries of the former Soviet Union and Eastern Europe. Assists the countries of the former Soviet Union in implementing education reforms.

The American Council of Young Political Leaders, 1000 Connecticut Ave. N.W., #800 20036; 857-0999. Gerry Cobb, executive director. Fax, 857-0027.

Bipartisan political education organization that promotes understanding of foreign policy between state and local leaders and their counterparts abroad. Sponsors conferences and political study tours for U.S. and foreign political leaders between the ages of 25 and 41.

Business-Higher Education Forum, 1 Dupont Circle N.W., #800 20036; 939-9345. Don M. Blandin, director. Fax, 833-4723.

Membership: chief executive officers of major corporations, colleges, and universities. Promotes the development of industry-university alliances around the world. Provides countries in central and Eastern Europe with technical assistance in enterprise development, management training, market economics, education, and infrastructure development.

Foreign Services Research Institute, 2718 Unicorn Lane N.W. (mailing address: P.O. Box 6317, Washington, DC 20015); 362-1588. John E. Whiteford Boyle, president.

Provides information on American culture to embassies, foreign business firms, and foreign educational establishments. Advises on placement of foreign students; maintains library on U.S. and foreign educational and cultural data. Represents the International Academy of Independent Scholars, which aids retired scholars in research, library access, and travel.

Foreign Student Service Council, 2337 18th St. N.W. 20009; 232-4979. Michael Novelli, director. Fax, 667-9305.

Organizes seminar programs, partially sponsored by the U.S. Information Agency, for foreign students studying in American universities; offers hospitality through volunteer host families; and administers a housing referral service that arranges living accommodations in Washington-area homes. Maintains speakers bureau.

International Copyright Information Center, 1718 Connecticut Ave. N.W., #700 20009; 232-

3335. Carol A. Risher, director, copyrights and new technology. Fax, 745-0694.

Aids publishers in developing countries in contacting American publishers for reprint and translation rights.

Japan-America Society of Washington, 1020 19th St. N.W., Lower Lobby 20036; 289-8290. Patricia R. Kearns, executive director. Fax, 789-8265.

Conducts programs and produces publications on U.S.-Japan trade, politics, and economic issues; assists Japanese performing artists; offers lectures and films on Japan; operates Japanese-language school; awards annual scholarships to college students studying in the Washington, D.C., metropolitan area; maintains library for members; lends a portable Japanese room to public schools in the Washington, D.C., metropolitan area.

Japan Information Access Project, 1706 R St. N.W. 20009; 332-5224. Mindy Kotler, director. Fax, 332-6841.

Membership organization that teaches business executives, scientists, engineers, educators, legislators, and journalists how to access, evaluate, and use Japanese-source information in business, science, and technology. Helps American managers integrate Japanese information and U.S. policies toward Japan in their strategic planning. Maintains programs on specific topics, including electronics, financial services, biomedical technologies and pharmaceuticals, and intellectual property.

Legacy International, 128 N. Fayette St., Alexandria, VA 22314; (703) 549-3630. Ira Kaufman, executive director. Fax, (703) 549-0262.

Promotes cross-cultural understanding of global issues through training and education programs and youth exchanges in the United States, central Europe, the Middle East, and Central Asia. Interests include environmentally sound development, conflict resolution, and leadership training.

NAFSA: Assn. of International Educators, 1875 Connecticut Ave. N.W., #1000 20009-5728; 462-4811. Naomi F. Collins, director. Fax, 667-3419. E-mail, inbox@nafsa.org. Publications, (800) 836-4994.

Membership: individuals, educational institutions, and others interested in international educational exchange. Provides information on evaluating exchange programs and academic credentials; assists members in complying with federal regulations affecting foreign students and scholars; administers grant programs with an international education focus.

Radio Free Europe/Radio Liberty, 1201 Connecticut Ave. N.W. 20036; 457-6914. Jane Lester, corporate secretary. Information, 457-6900. Press, 457-6950. Library, 457-6907. Fax, 457-6992.

Independent radio broadcast service funded by federal grants. Radio Free Europe broadcasts programs to Bulgaria, Czech Republic, Estonia, Hungary, Latvia, Lithuania, Poland, Romania, and Slovakia; programming includes entertainment, news, and specials on political developments in Eastern Europe. Radio Liberty broadcasts to the former Soviet Union. Broadcasts to Afghanistan through Radio Free Afghanistan. Library open to the public by appointment. (Headquarters in Munich.)

World Learning, 1015 15th St. N.W. 20005; 408-5420. Robert Chase, vice president; Karen Wayne, director, au pair/homestay. Fax, 408-5397. School for International Training, (800) 451-4465. Summer Abroad, (800) 345-2929. Incoming Hosts and Volunteers, (800) 327-4678.

Training organization that manages development assistance and training grants and contracts for the United Nations, U.S. government agencies, and others. Provides U.N. visitors and other guests with language training and housing searches. Other projects include subgrants to and training for local nongovernmental organizations (particularly in management, project implementation, health, and environmental issues) and selected refugee training services. Administers au pair program for American and foreign young people. (Headquarters in Brattleboro, Vt.)

See also Academy for Educational Development (p. 130); Eisenhower World Affairs Institute (p. 447)

Territories, Trust Territories, and Freely Associated States

Territories

Agencies:

Interior Dept., Territorial and International Affairs, Main Interior Bldg., Rm. 4328 20240;

208-3075. Leslie Turner, assistant secretary. Fax, 208-3390.

Promotes economic, social, and political development of the territories of Guam, American Samoa, the Virgin Islands, and the Commonwealth of the Northern Mariana Islands.

Congress:

American Samoa's Delegate to Congress, 109 CHOB 20515; 225-8577. Eni F. H. Faleomavaega, D-American Samoa, delegate. Fax, 225-8757.

Represents American Samoa in Congress.

Guam's Delegate to Congress, 507 CHOB 20515; 225-1188. Robert A. Underwood, D-Guam, delegate. Fax, 226-0341.

Represents Guam in Congress.

House Appropriations Committee, Subcommittee on Interior, 3481 RHOB 20515; 225-3481. Sidney R. Yates, D-Ill., chairman; D. Neal Sigmon, staff assistant.

Jurisdiction over legislation to appropriate funds for territorial affairs.

House Natural Resources Committee, Subcommittee on Insular and International Affairs, 1626 LHOB 20515; 225-9297. Ron de Lugo, D-Virgin Island, chairman; Jeffrey L. Farrow, staff director. Fax, 225-5255.

Jurisdiction over legislation on U.S. territorial possessions. Oversight and investigative authority over activities, policies, and programs for Guam, American Samoa, Puerto Rico, and the Virgin Islands.

Puerto Rican Resident Commissioner, 1517 LHOB 20515; 225-2615. Carlos A. Romero-Barceló, NPP-Puerto Rico, resident commissioner. Fax, 225-2154.

Represents the Commonwealth of Puerto Rico in Congress.

Senate Appropriations Committee, Subcommittee on Interior, SD-127 20510; 224-7233. Robert C. Byrd, D-W.Va., chairman; Sue E. Masica, clerk.

Jurisdiction over legislation to appropriate funds for territorial affairs.

Senate Energy and Natural Resources Committee, SD-304 20510; 224-4971. J. Bennett Johnston, D-La., chairman; Benjamin Cooper, staff director. Fax, 224-6163.

Jurisdiction over legislation on U.S. territorial possessions. Oversight and investigative authority over activities, policies, and programs for Guam, American Samoa, Puerto Rico, and the Virgin Islands.

Virgin Islands Delegate to Congress, 2427 RHOB 20515; 225-1790. Ron de Lugo, D-Virgin Islands, delegate. Fax, 225-9392.

Represents the Virgin Islands in Congress.

Nongovernmental:

Puerto Rico Federal Affairs Administration, 1100 17th St. N.W., #800 20036; 778-0710. Wanda Rubianes, director. Information, 778-0732. Press, 778-0731. Fax, 778-0733.

Represents the governor and the government of the Commonwealth of Puerto Rico before Congress and the executive branch; conducts research; monitors legislation and regulations; serves as official press information center for the Commonwealth of Puerto Rico.

U.S. Virgin Islands Division of Tourism, 900 17th St. N.W. 20006; 293-3707. Flora Boynes-Spencer, regional manager. Fax, 785-2542.

Provides information about the U.S. Virgin Islands and promotes tourism there. (Headquarters in St. Thomas.)

Trust Territories and Freely Associated States

Agencies:

Interior Dept., Territorial and International Affairs, Main Interior Bldg., Rm. 4328 20240; 208-3075. Leslie Turner, assistant secretary. Fax, 208-3390.

Promotes economic, social, and political development of the Trust Territory of the Pacific Islands (Republic of Palau). Supervises federal programs for the freely associated states (Federated States of Micronesia and the Republic of the Marshall Islands).

State Dept., Pacific Island Affairs, Main State Bldg., Rm. 5317 20520; 647-0108. Lynne Lambert, director. Fax, 647-0118.

Conducts U.S. relations with the freely associated states. Develops procedures for the transition of the remaining Trust Territory of the Pacific Islands (Republic of Palau) to a freely associated state. Works to gain international recognition for the freely associated states.

Congress:

House Appropriations Committee, Subcommittee on Interior, 3481 RHOB 20515; 225-3481. Sidney R. Yates, D-Ill., chairman; D. Neal Sigmon, staff assistant.

Jurisdiction over legislation to appropriate funds for territorial affairs.

House Natural Resources Committee, Subcommittee on Insular and International Affairs, 1626 LHOB 20515; 225-9297. Ron de Lugo, D-Virgin Islands, chairman; Jeffrey L. Farrow, staff director. Fax, 225-5255.

Jurisdiction, oversight, and investigative authority over activities, policies, and programs for the Trust Territory of the Pacific Islands (Republic of Palau) and the freely associated states (Federated States of Micronesia and the Republic of the Marshall Islands).

Senate Appropriations Committee, Subcommittee on Interior, SD-127 20510; 224-7233. Robert C. Byrd, D-W.Va., chairman; Sue E. Masica, clerk.

Jurisdiction over legislation to appropriate funds for territorial and international affairs.

Senate Energy and Natural Resources Committee, SD-304 20510; 224-4971. J. Bennett Johnston, D-La., chairman; Benjamin Cooper, staff director. Fax, 224-6163.

Jurisdiction, oversight, and investigative authority over activities, policies, and programs for the Trust Territory of the Pacific Islands (Republic of Palau) and the freely associated states (Federated States of Micronesia and the Republic of the Marshall Islands).

Nongovernmental:

Republic of Palau, 444 N. Capitol St. N.W., #619 20001; 624-7793. Charles Uong, administrative officer. Fax, 624-7795.

Represents the government and people of the Trust Territory of Palau before Congress, the federal government, and other organizations; provides Palauan officials and students coming to the United States with administrative and technical assistance; acts as a source of general information on Palau.

Key Agency:

Justice Dept.
Main Justice Bldg.
10th St. and Constitution Ave. N.W. 20530
Information: 514-2000

Key Committees:

House Judiciary Committee
2138 RHOB 20515
Phone: 225-3951

Senate Judiciary Committee
SD-224 20510
Phone: 224-5225

Key Judiciary:

Administrative Office of the U.S. Courts
1 Columbus Circle N.E. 20544
Information: 273-1120

Supreme Court of the United States
1 1st St. N.E. 20543
Information: 479-3211

Key Personnel:

Administrative Office of the U.S. Courts
L. Ralph Mecham, director

Justice Dept.
Janet Reno, attorney general
Jamie S. Gorelick, deputy attorney general
William C. Bryson, acting associate attorney
general

Anne K. Bingaman, assistant attorney general, antitrust division
Frank W. Hunger, assistant attorney general, civil division
Deval Patrick, assistant attorney general, civil rights division
Jo Ann Harris, assistant attorney general, criminal division
Lois J. Schiffer, assistant attorney general designate, environment and natural resources
Laurie Robinson, acting assistant attorney general, justice programs
Walter Dellinger, assistant attorney general, legal counsel
Sheila Foster Anthony, assistant attorney general, legislative affairs
Loretta C. Argrett, assistant attorney general, tax division
Kathleen M. Hawk, director, Bureau of Prisons
Thomas A. Constantine, administrator, Drug Enforcement Administration
Louis J. Freeh, director, Federal Bureau of Investigation
Carl Stern, director, public affairs
Drew S. Days III, solicitor general
Eduardo Gonzalez, director, U.S. Marshals Service

Supreme Court
William H. Rehnquist, chief justice
(Associate justices listed in order of their appointment)
Harry A. Blackmun
John Paul Stevens
Sandra Day O'Connor
Antonin Scalia
Anthony M. Kennedy
David H. Souter
Clarence Thomas
Ruth Bader Ginsburg

12

Law
and Justice

Contents:

Administration of Justice

General

Agencies:

Justice Dept., Main Justice Bldg., 10th St. and Constitution Ave. N.W. 20530; 514-2001. Janet Reno, attorney general. Information, 514-2000. Fax, 514-0468.

Investigates and prosecutes violations of federal laws; represents the government in federal cases and interprets laws under which other departments act. Supervises federal corrections system; administers immigration and naturalization laws. Justice Dept. organization includes divisions on antitrust, civil law, civil rights, criminal law, environment and natural resources, and tax, as well as the Federal Bureau of Investigation, Bureau of Prisons, Office of Legal Counsel, Office of Policy Development, Office of Professional Responsibility, U.S. Parole Commission, Immigration and Naturalization Service, Board of Immigration Appeals, Executive Office for Immigration Review, Drug Enforcement Administration, Foreign Claims Settlement Commission of the United States, Office of Justice Programs, U.S. Marshals Service, and U.S. Trustees.

Justice Dept., Main Justice Bldg. 20530; 514-2201. Drew S. Days III, solicitor general. Fax, 514-9769. Information on pending cases, 514-2217.

Represents the federal government before the Supreme Court of the United States.

Justice Dept., Executive Office for U.S. Attorneys, Main Justice Bldg. 20530; 514-2121. Anthony Moscato, director. Information, 514-1020. Fax, 514-0323.

Provides the offices of U.S. attorneys with technical assistance and supervision in areas of legal counsel, personnel, and training. Publishes the *U.S. Attorneys' Manual.* Administers the Attorney General's Advocacy Institute, which conducts workshops and seminars to develop the litigation skills of the department's attorneys in criminal and civil trials. Develops and implements Justice Dept. procedures and policy for collecting criminal fines.

Justice Dept., Justice Programs, 633 Indiana Ave. N.W. 20531; 307-5933. Laurie Robinson, acting assistant attorney general. Fax, 514-7805.

Sets program policy, provides staff support, and coordinates administration for the National Institute of Justice, which conducts research on criminal justice; the Bureau of Justice Statistics, which gathers and evaluates national crime data; the Office for Victims of Crime, which funds state victim compensation and assistance programs; the Office of Juvenile Justice and Delinquency Prevention, which administers federal juvenile delinquency programs; and the Bureau of Justice Assistance, which provides funds for anticrime programs.

Justice Dept., Policy Development, Main Justice Bldg. 20530; 514-4601. Eleanor Dean Acheson, assistant attorney general. Fax, 514-2424.

Studies, develops, and coordinates Justice Dept. policy. Drafts and reviews legislative proposals. Oversees implementation of the Freedom of Information and Privacy acts.

Justice Dept., Professional Responsibility, Main Justice Bldg. 20530; 514-3365. Michael E. Shaheen Jr., counsel. Fax, 514-4371.

Receives and reviews allegations of misconduct by Justice Dept. employees; refers cases that warrant further review to appropriate investigative agency or unit; makes recommendations to the attorney general for action on certain misconduct cases.

State Justice Institute, 1650 King St., #600, Alexandria, VA 22314; (703) 684-6100. David I. Tevelin, executive director. Fax, (703) 684-7618.

Quasi-governmental corporation established by Congress. Awards grants to state courts and to state agencies working to improve judicial administration in the state courts. Interests include judicial education, court technology, victim assistance, and federal-state relations.

Congress:

General Accounting Office, General Government, 820 1st St. N.E., #200 20002; 512-8777. Henry R. Wray, director. Fax, 512-8692. Documents, 512-6241.

Independent, nonpartisan agency in the legislative branch. Audits, analyzes, and evaluates federal administration of justice programs and activities; makes some reports available to the public.

House Appropriations Committee, Subcommittee on Commerce, Justice, State, and Judiciary, H309 CAP 20515; 225-3351. Neal Smith, D-Iowa, chairman; John Osthaus, staff assistant.

Jurisdiction over legislation to appropriate funds for the Justice Dept., the federal judiciary, the Legal Services Corp., the State Justice Institute, juvenile justice and delinquency prevention, district courts, and other judicial-related services and programs.

House Government Operations Committee, Subcommittee on Information, Justice, Transportation, and Agriculture, B349C RHOB 20515; 225-3741. Gary Condit, D-Calif., chairman; Shannon Lahey, acting staff director. Fax, 225-2445.

Oversees operations of the Justice Dept., the federal judiciary (except the U.S. Tax Court), the Legal Services Corp., and the State Justice Institute.

House Judiciary Committee, 2138 RHOB 20515; 225-3951. Jack Brooks, D-Texas, chairman; Jon Yarowsky, general counsel.

Jurisdiction over legislation on judicial proceedings, constitutional amendments, civil liberties, ethics in government, federal judiciary, federal corrections system, interstate compacts, patents, copyrights and trademarks, bankruptcy, mutiny, espionage and counterfeiting, immigration and naturalization, revision and codification of the statutes of the United States, internal security, local courts in the territories and possessions, protection of trade and commerce against unlawful restraints and monopolies, legislation relating to claims against the United States, and state and territorial boundary lines.

Senate Appropriations Committee, Subcommittee on Commerce, Justice, State, and Judiciary, S146A CAP 20510; 224-7277. Ernest F. Hollings, D-S.C., chairman; Scott B. Gudes, clerk.

Jurisdiction over legislation to appropriate funds for the Justice Dept., the federal judiciary, the Legal Services Corp., the State Justice Institute, juvenile justice and delinquency prevention, district courts, and other judicial-related services and programs.

Senate Judiciary Committee, SD-224 20510; 224-5225. Joseph R. Biden Jr., D-Del., chairman; Cynthia Hogan, chief counsel.

Jurisdiction over legislation on judicial proceedings, constitutional amendments, civil liberties, ethics in government, federal judiciary, federal corrections system, interstate compacts, government information, patents, copyrights and trademarks, bankruptcy, mutiny, espionage and counterfeiting, immigration and naturalization, revision and codification of the statutes of the United States, internal security, local courts in the territories and possessions, protection of trade and commerce against unlawful restraints and monopolies, legislation relating to claims against the United States, and state and territorial boundary lines. Oversees operations of the Justice Dept., the federal judiciary (except the U.S. Tax Court), the Legal Services Corp., and the State Justice Institute.

Judiciary:

Administrative Office of the U.S. Courts, 1 Columbus Circle N.E. 20544; 273-3000. L. Ralph Mecham, director. Information, 273-1120. Library, 273-1888. Fax, 273-3011.

Supervises all administrative matters of the federal court system, except the Supreme Court. Examines dockets of the courts; prepares statistical data and reports on the business of the courts. Provides the Judicial Conference of the United States with staff assistance; drafts legislative proposals relating to the federal court system. Supervises offices of federal magistrates and federal public defenders.

Federal Judicial Center, 1 Columbus Circle N.E. 20002; 273-4160. William W. Schwarzer, director. Fax, 273-4019.

Conducts research on the operations of the federal court system; develops and conducts continuing education and training programs for judges and judicial personnel; and makes recommendations to improve the administration of the courts.

Judicial Conference of the United States, 1 Columbus Circle N.E. 20544; 273-3000. William H. Rehnquist, chief justice of the United States,

Justice Dept.

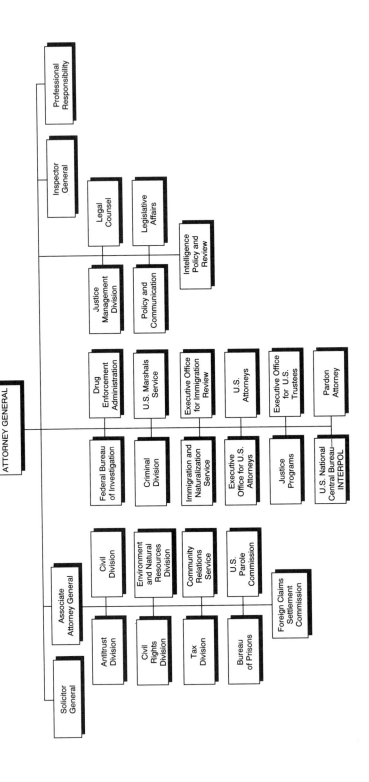

ATTORNEY GENERAL

Professional Responsibility

Inspector General

Legal Counsel

Legislative Affairs

Justice Management Division

Policy and Communication

Intelligence Policy and Review

Drug Enforcement Administration

U.S. Marshals Service

Executive Office for Immigration Review

U.S. Attorneys

Executive Office for U.S. Trustees

Pardon Attorney

Federal Bureau of Investigation

Criminal Division

Immigration and Naturalization Service

Executive Office for U.S. Attorneys

Justice Programs

U.S. National Central Bureau— INTERPOL

Solicitor General

Associate Attorney General

Civil Division

Environment and Natural Resources Division

Community Relations Service

U.S. Parole Commission

Foreign Claims Settlement Commission

Antitrust Division

Civil Rights Division

Tax Division

Bureau of Prisons

chairman; L. Ralph Mecham, secretary. Information, 273-1140. Fax, 273-1145.

Serves as the policymaking and governing body for the administration of the federal judicial system; advises Congress on the creation of new federal judgeships.

Supreme Court of the United States, 1 1st St. N.E. 20543; 479-3000. William H. Rehnquist, chief justice; William R. Suter, clerk, 479-3011. Library, 479-3173. Supreme Court opinions and information, 479-3211.

Highest appellate court in the federal judicial system. Interprets the U.S. Constitution, federal legislation, and treaties. Provides information on new cases filed, the status of pending cases, and admissions to the Supreme Court Bar. Library open to Supreme Court bar members only. *(For complete list of justices, see p. 488.)*

Nongovernmental:

Alliance for Justice, 1601 Connecticut Ave. N.W., #601 20009; 332-3224. Nan Aron, executive director. Fax, 265-2150.

Membership: public interest lawyers and advocacy, environmental, civil rights, and consumer organizations. Promotes reform of the legal system to ensure access to the courts; monitors selection of federal judges; works to preserve the rights of nonprofit organizations to advocate on behalf of their constituents.

American Alliance for Rights and Responsibilities, 1725 K St. N.W., #1112 20006; 785-7844. Roger Conner, executive director. Fax, 785-4370.

Advocates balance between individual rights and responsibility. Supports individuals and groups working to improve civic responsibility, mutual obligation, and voluntary restraint; conducts research and litigates cases to promote individual responsibility.

American Bar Assn., Washington Office, 1800 M St. N.W. 20036; 331-2215. Robert D. Evans, director. Information, 331-2208. Press, 331-2293. Library, 331-2207. Fax, 331-2220. TDD, 331-3884.

Comprises the Public Service Division, the Government and Public Sector Division, International Law and Practice Section, Criminal Justice Section, Taxation Section, Individual Rights and Responsibilities Section, Dispute Resolution Section, and others. Acts as a clearinghouse for the association's legislative activities and communicates the status of important

bills and regulations to state and local bar associations and to all sections concerned with major governmental activities that affect the legal profession. (Headquarters in Chicago.)

American Tort Reform Assn., 1212 New York Ave. N.W., #515 20005; 682-1163. Martin F. Connor, president. Fax, 682-1022.

Membership: businesses, associations, trade groups, professional societies, and individuals interested in reforming the civil justice system in the United States. Develops model state legislation and position papers on tort reform. Works with state coalitions in support of tort reform legislation.

Assn. of Trial Lawyers of America, 1050 31st St. N.W. 20007; 965-3500, Thomas H. Henderson Jr., executive director. Fax, 625-7312.

Membership: attorneys, judges, law professors, and students. Works to strengthen the civil justice system and the right to trial by jury. Interests include victims' rights, property and casualty insurance, revisions of federal rules of evidence, criminal code, jurisdictions of courts, juries, and consumer law.

Center for Study of Responsive Law, 1530 P St. N.W. (mailing address: P.O. Box 19367, Washington, DC 20036); 387-8030. John Richard, administrator.

Consumer interest clearinghouse. Conducts research and holds conferences on public interest law. Interests include white-collar crime, the environment, occupational health and safety, the postal system, banking deregulation, insurance, freedom of information policy, and broadcast issues.

Federal Bar Assn., 1815 H St. N.W., #408 20006; 638-0252. John G. Blanche III, executive staff director. Library, 638-1956. Fax, 775-0295.

Membership: attorneys employed by the federal government or practicing before federal courts or agencies. Conducts research and offers programs in a variety of legal fields, including antitrust law, civil rights and liberties, narcotic and dangerous drugs, legal education (primarily continuing education), and legal services.

Help Abolish Legal Tyranny—An Organization of Americans for Legal Reform (HALT-ALR), 1319 F St. N.W. 20004; 347-9600. William Fry, executive director. Fax, 347-9606.

Departmental and Agency . . .

Departments

Agriculture
James Gilliland 720-3351

Commerce
Carol C. Darr, acting 482-4772

Defense
Stephen W. Preston, acting (703) 695-3341

Air Force
Gilbert Casellas .... (703) 697-0941

Army
William T. Coleman III,
designate .... (703) 697-9235

Navy
Steven Honigman ...... (703) 614-1994

Education
Judith A. Winston............. 401-2600

Energy
Robert R. Nordhaus 586-5281

Health and Human Services
Harriet S. Rabb.............. 690-7741

Housing and Urban Development
Nelson A. Diaz................ 708-2244

Interior
John Leshy.................. 208-4423

Justice
Walter Dellinger.............. 514-2041

Labor
Thomas S. Williamson Jr....... 219-7675

State
Conrad Harper............... 647-9598

Transportation
Stephen H. Kaplan........... 366-4702

Treasury
Jean Hanson................. 622-0287

Veterans Affairs
Mary Lou Keener 535-8111

Agencies

**Administrative Conference of the
United States**
Gary J. Edles 254-7020

**Advisory Council on Historic
Preservation**
John M. Fowler 606-8503

Central Intelligence Agency
Elizabeth R. Rindskopf ... (703) 482-1951

Commission on Civil Rights
Vacant 376-8351

Commodity Futures Trading Commission
Patrick G. Nicolette, acting..... 254-9880

Consumer Product Safety Commission
Eric Rubel.............. (301) 504-0980

Corporation for National Service
Terry Russell 606-5000

Environmental Protection Agency
Gene C. Nelson 260-8040

**Equal Employment Opportunity
Commission**
Vacant 663-4705

Export-Import Bank of the United States
Carol F. Lee 566-8334

Farm Credit Administration
Jean Noonan............ (703) 883-4020

Federal Communications Commission
William Kennard.............. 632-7020

Federal Deposit Insurance Corp.
Douglas H. Jones, acting 898-3680

Federal Election Commission
Lawrence M. Noble........... 219-3690

Federal Emergency Management Agency
John P. Carey................ 646-4105

Federal Energy Regulatory Commission
Susan Tomasky 208-1000

Federal Labor Relations Authority
Joseph Swerdzewski 482-6600

Federal Maritime Commission
Robert D. Bourgoin........... 523-5740

Public interest organization concerned with legal reform. Conducts research on alternative dispute resolution programs for delivery of legal services, including arbitration, legal clinics, and mediation services; provides educational and self-help manuals on use of the legal system. Operates The Law Store, a legal document preparation service created to research, test, and promote innovative techniques for improving access to legal services for the average citizen.

Lawyers for Civil Justice, 2100 M St. N.W., #305 20006; 429-0045. Barry Bauman, executive director. Fax, 429-6982.

... General Counsels

Federal Mediation and Conciliation Service
Eileen B. Hoffman 653-5305

Federal Reserve System
J. Virgil Mattingly Jr. 452-3430

Federal Trade Commission
Jay C. Shaffer, acting 326-2480

General Services Administration
Emily C. Hewitt. 501-2200

International Bank for Reconstruction and Development (World Bank)
Ibrahim F. I. Shihata 458-1601

Interstate Commerce Commission
Henri F. Rush, acting 927-7312

Merit Systems Protection Board
Llewellyn M. Fischer 653-7168

National Aeronautics and Space Administration
Edward A. Frankle 358-2450

National Credit Union Administration
Robert M. Fenner . . . . (703) 518-6540

National Foundation on the Arts and the Humanities

National Endowment for the Arts
Karen Christenson. 682-5418

National Endowment for the Humanities
Michael S. Shapiro 606-8322

National Labor Relations Board
Daniel Silverman, acting 273-3700

National Mediation Board
Ronald M. Etters. 523-5944

National Railroad Passenger Corp. (Amtrak)
Stephen C. Rogers. 906-3995

National Science Foundation
Lawrence Rudolph, acting 357-9435

National Transportation Safety Board
Daniel D. Campbell. 382-6540

Nuclear Regulatory Commission
William C. Parler. . . . . (301) 504-1743

Occupational Safety and Health Review Commission
Earl R. Ohman Jr.. 606-5410

Office of Personnel Management
Lorraine Lewis 606-1700

Peace Corps
Brian Sexton. 606-3114

Pension Benefit Guaranty Corp.
Carol Connor Flowe 778-8820

Postal Rate Commission
Stephen Sharfman, acting 789-6820

Securities and Exchange Commission
Simon Lorne. 272-3171

Small Business Administration
John T. Spotila 205-6642

Smithsonian Institution
Peter G. Powers. 357-2583

U.S. Arms Control and Disarmament Agency
Mary Elizabeth Hoinkes, acting. 647-3582

U.S. Information Agency
Leslie R. Jin, designate 619-4979

U.S. International Development Cooperation Agency

Agency for International Development
Wandra G. Mitchell 647-8548

Overseas Private Investment Corporation
Charles D. Toy. 336-8410

U.S. International Trade Commission
Lyn M. Schlitt 205-3061

U.S. Postal Service
Mary S. Elcano 268-2950

Membership: defense trial lawyers and corporate and insurance attorneys. Informs members of developments in the civil justice field. Interests include tort reform, litigation cost containment, and tort and product liability; monitors legislation and regulations affecting the civil justice system.

National Assn. for the Advancement of Colored People (NAACP), 1025 Vermont Ave. N.W., #1120 20005; 638-2269. Wade J. Henderson, director, Washington bureau. Fax, 638-5936.
Membership: persons interested in civil rights for all minorities. Seeks, through litigation, to

end discrimination in all areas, including discriminatory practices in the administration of justice. Studies and recommends policy on court administration and jury selection. Maintains branch offices in many state and federal prisons. (Headquarters in Baltimore.)

National Bar Assn., 1225 11th St. N.W. 20001; 842-3900. John Crump, executive director. Fax, 289-6170.

Membership: primarily minority attorneys, legal professionals, judges, and law students. Interests include legal education and improvement of the judicial process. Sponsors legal education seminars in all states that require continuing legal education for lawyers.

National Center for State Courts, 1110 N. Glebe Rd., #1090, Arlington, VA 22201; (703) 841-0200. Thomas A. Henderson, Washington liaison. Fax, (703) 841-0206.

Works to improve state court systems through research, technical assistance, and training programs. Monitors legislation affecting court systems; interests include judicial immunity and state-federal jurisdiction. Serves as secretariat for several state court organizations, including the Conference of Chief Justices, Conference of State Court Administrators, and American Judges Assn. (Headquarters in Williamsburg, Va.)

National Legal Center for the Public Interest, 1000 16th St. N.W., #301 20036; 296-1683. Ernest B. Hueter, president. Fax, 293-2118.

Public interest law center and information clearinghouse. Studies judicial issues and the impact of the legal system on the private sector; sponsors seminars; does not litigate cases.

Rand Corporation, 2100 M St. N.W. 20037; 296-5000. Charles R. Roll Jr., director, Washington operations. Fax, 296-7960.

Analyzes current problems of the American civil and criminal justice systems and evaluates recent and pending changes and reforms. Researches criminal behavior and patterns and the effectiveness of current policies for preventing and deterring criminal activity. (Headquarters in Santa Monica, Calif.)

Trial Lawyers for Public Justice, 1625 Massachusetts Ave. N.W., #100 20036; 797-8600. Arthur Bryant, executive director. Fax, 232-7203.

Membership organization that litigates cases involving toxic torts, environmental protection, civil rights and liberties, consumer safety, workers' rights, and the preservation of the civil justice system. Serves as an information clearinghouse.

U.S. Chamber of Commerce, Legal and Regulatory Affairs, 1615 H St. N.W., #517 20062; 463-5513. Tyler J. Wilson, attorney. Fax, 887-3445.

Federation of individuals, firms, corporations, trade and professional associations, and local, state, and regional chambers of commerce. Monitors legislation and regulations in administrative law, antitrust policy, civil justice reform, and product liability reform.

Washington Legal Foundation, 2009 Massachusetts Ave. N.W. 20036; 588-0302. Daniel J. Popeo, general counsel. Fax, 588-0386.

Public interest law and policy center. Interests include constitutional law, government regulation, media law, and criminal justice; litigates on behalf of small businesses, members of Congress, and victims of violent crimes who bring civil suits against their attackers.

World Jurists' Assn. of the World Peace Through Law Center, 1000 Connecticut Ave. N.W., #202 20036; 466-5428. Raul Goco, president. Fax, 452-8540.

Membership: lawyers, law professors, judges, law students, and nonlegal professionals worldwide. Conducts research and prepares reports on issues related to international and comparative law; holds biennial world conferences. (Affiliated with World Assn. of Judges, World Assn. of Law Professors, and World Assn. of Lawyers.)

See also The Product Liability Alliance (p. 73)

Judicial Appointments

Agencies:

Justice Dept., Main Justice Bldg. 20530; 514-2001. Janet Reno, attorney general. Information, 514-2000. Fax, 514-0468.

Investigates and processes prospective candidates for presidential appointment (subject to Senate confirmation) to the federal judiciary.

Congress:

House Judiciary Committee, Subcommittee on Economic and Commercial Law, B353 RHOB 20515; 225-2825. Jack Brooks, D-Texas, chairman; Cynthia W. Meadow, chief counsel.

Jurisdiction over legislation on federal judicial appointments, which includes legislation to create new federal judgeships; conducts hearings on presidential appointees to federal judgeships.

Senate Judiciary Committee, SD-224 20510; 224-5225. Joseph R. Biden Jr., D-Del., chairman; Cynthia Hogan, chief counsel.

Jurisdiction over legislation on federal judicial appointments, which includes legislation to create new federal judgeships; conducts hearings on presidential appointees to federal judgeships.

Judiciary:

Administrative Office of the U.S. Courts, 1 Columbus Circle N.E. 20544; 273-3000. L. Ralph Mecham, director. Information, 273-1120. Library, 273-1888. Fax, 273-3011.

Supervises all administrative matters of the federal court system, except the Supreme Court. Transmits to Congress the recommendations of the Judicial Conference of the United States concerning creation of federal judgeships and other legislative proposals.

Judicial Conference of the United States, 1 Columbus Circle N.E. 20544; 273-3000. William H. Rehnquist, chief justice of the United States, chairman; L. Ralph Mecham, secretary. Information, 273-1140. Fax, 273-1145.

Policymaking and governing body of the federal judicial system. Advises Congress on the creation of federal judgeships.

Nongovernmental:

Alliance for Justice, Judicial Selection Project, 1601 Connecticut Ave. N.W., #601 20009; 332-3224. George Kassouf, director. Fax, 265-2150.

Monitors candidates for vacancies in the federal judiciary; independently reviews nominees' records; maintains statistics on the judiciary.

Business and Tax Law

Antitrust

Agencies:

Comptroller of the Currency (Treasury Dept.), 250 E St. S.W. 20219; 874-4900. Eugene A. Ludwig, comptroller. Information, 874-5000. Fax, 874-4950.

Regulates and examines operations of national banks; establishes guidelines for bank examinations; handles mergers of national banks with regard to antitrust law. Library open to the public.

Federal Communications Commission, Common Carrier Bureau, 1919 M St. N.W. 20554; 632-6910. Kathleen B. Levitz, acting chief. Fax, 653-5402.

Regulates mergers and consolidations involving common carriers that furnish interstate or international communications services.

Federal Deposit Insurance Corp., Supervision and Resolutions, 550 17th St. N.W. 20429; 898-6849. John W. Stone, executive director. Fax, 898-3772.

Studies and analyzes applications for mergers, consolidations, acquisitions, and assumption transactions between insured banks.

Federal Energy Regulatory Commission (Energy Dept.), 825 N. Capitol St. N.E. 20426; 208-0000. Elizabeth Moler, chair. Information, 208-0200. Press, 208-1088. Fax, 208-0671. Dockets, 208-2020.

Regulates mergers, consolidations, and acquisitions of electric utilities; regulates the acquisition of interstate natural gas pipeline facilities.

Federal Maritime Commission, 800 N. Capitol St. N.W., 10th Floor 20573; 523-5911. William D. Hathaway, chairman. Information, 523-5725. Library, 523-5762. Fax, 523-4224.

Regulates foreign and domestic ocean shipping of the United States; reviews agreements (on rates, schedules, and other matters) filed by common carriers for compliance with antitrust laws and grants antitrust immunity. Library open to the public.

Federal Reserve System, Banking Supervision and Regulation, 20th and C Sts. N.W. 20551;

452-2773. Richard Stillenkothen, director. Fax, 452-2770.

Approves bank mergers, consolidations, and other alterations in bank structure.

Federal Trade Commission, Competition, 6th St. and Pennsylvania Ave. N.W. 20580; 326-2556. Mary Lou Steptoe, acting director. Fax, 326-2050. TDD, 326-2502.

Enforces antitrust laws and investigates possible violations; seeks voluntary compliance and pursues civil judicial remedies; reviews premerger filings; coordinates activities with Antitrust Division of the Justice Dept.

Interstate Commerce Commission, 12th St. and Constitution Ave. N.W. 20423; 927-6020. Gail C. McDonald, chairman. Information, 927-5350. Press, 927-5340. Library, 927-7328. Fax, 927-1472.

Regulates the licensing, rates, and finances of interstate rail, bus, truck, and water carriers; reviews and approves applications for mergers, sales, consolidations, and acquisitions of carriers. Library open to the public.

Justice Dept., Antitrust Division, Main Justice Bldg., Rm. 3109 20530; 514-2401. Anne K. Bingaman, assistant attorney general. Fax, 616-2645.

Enforces antitrust laws to prevent monopolies and unlawful restraint of trade; has civil and criminal jurisdiction; coordinates activities with Bureau of Competition of the Federal Trade Commission.

Justice Dept., Antitrust Division, 555 4th St. N.W. 20001; 514-5621. Richard L. Rosen, chief, communications and finance. Fax, 514-6381.

Investigates and litigates certain antitrust cases involving either communications industries or financial institutions, including banking, securities, commodity futures, and insurance firms; participates in agency proceedings and rulemaking in these areas.

Justice Dept., Antitrust Division, Main Justice Bldg. 20530; 514-2481. Janie Ingalls, chief, legal procedures. Fax, 514-3763.

Maintains files and handles requests for information on federal civil and criminal antitrust cases; provides the president and Congress with copies of statutory reports prepared by the division on a variety of competition-related issues; issues opinion letters on whether certain business activity violates antitrust laws.

Justice Dept., Antitrust Division, 555 4th St. N.W. 20001; 307-0467. Gail Kursh, chief, professions and intellectual property. Fax, 514-1517.

Litigates certain antitrust cases involving health care and professional services, professional associations, sports and labor groups, and the motion picture, publishing, newspaper, and pharmaceutical industries. Handles certain violations of antitrust laws that involve patents, copyrights, and trademarks.

Justice Dept., Antitrust Division, 555 4th St. N.W. 20001; 307-6349. Roger Phones, chief, transportation, energy, and agriculture. Fax, 307-2784.

Enforces antitrust laws in the airline, railroad, motor carrier, barge line, ocean carrier, and energy industries; litigates antitrust cases pertaining to agriculture and related commodities.

Congress:

House Banking, Finance, and Urban Affairs Committee, Subcommittee on Financial Institutions Supervision, Regulation, and Deposit Insurance, 212 O'Neill Bldg. (300 New Jersey Ave. S.E.) 20515; 226-3280. Stephen L. Neal, D-N.C., chairman; Peter Kinzler, staff director. Fax, 226-1266.

Jurisdiction over legislation on mergers and acquisitions as they affect the economy.

House Judiciary Committee, Subcommittee on Economic and Commercial Law, B353 RHOB 20515; 225-2825. Jack Brooks, D-Texas, chairman; Cynthia W. Meadow, chief counsel.

Jurisdiction over legislation affecting anticompetitive and monopolistic practices and over Justice Dept. antitrust enforcement policies. Oversight of the Sherman Act and the Clayton Act.

House Small Business Committee, Subcommittee on Regulation, Business Opportunities, and Technology, B363 RHOB 20515; 225-7797. Ron Wyden, D-Ore., chairman; Steve Jenning, staff director.

Jurisdiction over legislation on all antitrust matters relating to small business; investigates anticompetitive and monopolistic practices.

Senate Judiciary Committee, Subcommittee on Antitrust, Monopolies, and Business Rights,

SH-308 20510; 224-5701. Howard M. Metzenbaum, D-Ohio, chairman; Gene Kimmelman, chief counsel.

Jurisdiction over legislation affecting anticompetitive and monopolistic practices and over Justice Dept. antitrust enforcement polices. Oversight of the Sherman Act and the Clayton Act.

Senate Small Business Committee, Subcommittee on Competitiveness, Capital Formation, and Economic Opportunity, SR-428A 20510; 224-5175. Joseph I. Lieberman, D-Conn., chairman; Ken Glueck, legislative assistant.

Investigates antitrust matters relating to small business; investigates anticompetitive and monopolistic practices.

Nongovernmental:

American Corporate Counsel Assn., 1225 Connecticut Ave. N.W. 20036; 296-4522. Frederick J. Krebs, executive director. Fax, 331-7454.

Membership: practicing attorneys in corporate law departments. Provides information on corporate law issues, including securities, health and safety, the environment, intellectual property, litigation, international legal affairs, pro bono work, and labor benefits. Monitors legislation and regulations, with primary focus on issues affecting in-house attorneys' ability to practice law.

The Business Roundtable, 1615 L St. N.W., #1100 20036-5610; 872-1260. Samuel L. Maury, executive director. Fax, 466-3509.

Membership: chief executives of the nation's largest corporations. Examines issues of concern to business, including antitrust law.

See also American Bar Assn., Center for Study of Responsive Law, and Federal Bar Assn. (p. 493); Federal Communications Bar Assn. (p. 29); National Chamber Litigation Center (p. 53); U.S. Chamber of Commerce, Economic Policy (p. 55)

Bankruptcy

Agencies:

Justice Dept., Executive Office for U.S. Trustees, 901 E St. N.W., #700 20530; 307-1391. John E. Logan, director. Fax, 307-0672.

Handles the administration and oversight of bankruptcy and liquidation cases filed under the Bankruptcy Reform Act. Provides individual U.S. trustee offices with administrative and management support.

Justice Dept., Policy Development, Main Justice Bldg. 20530; 514-4601. Eleanor Dean Acheson, assistant attorney general. Fax, 514-2424.

Studies and develops policy for improvement of the criminal and civil justice systems, including bankruptcy reform policy.

Congress:

House Judiciary Committee, Subcommittee on Economic and Commercial Law, B353 RHOB 20515; 225-2825. Jack Brooks, D-Texas, chairman; Cynthia W. Meadow, chief counsel.

Jurisdiction over bankruptcy legislation.

Senate Judiciary Committee, Subcommittee on Courts and Administrative Practice, SH-223 20510; 224-4022. Howell Heflin, D-Ala., chairman; Jim Whiddon, chief counsel.

Jurisdiction over bankruptcy legislation.

Judiciary:

Administrative Office of the U.S. Courts, Bankruptcy Division, 1 Columbus Circle N.E. 20544; 273-1900. Francis F. Szczebak, chief. Fax, 273-1917.

Provides administrative assistance and support in the operation of the U.S. Bankruptcy Court.

Nongovernmental:

American Bankruptcy Institute, 510 C St. N.E. 20002; 543-1234. Harry D. Dixon Jr., chairman. Fax, 543-2762.

Membership: lawyers; federal and state legislators; and representatives of accounting and financial services firms, lending institutions, credit organizations, and consumer groups. Provides information and educational services on insolvency, reorganization, and bankruptcy issues; sponsors conferences, seminars, and workshops.

Tax Violations

See also Business and Economic Policy, Taxes (p. 56)

Agencies:

Internal Revenue Service (Treasury Dept.), Field Service, 1111 Constitution Ave. N.W. 20224; 622-7800. Daniel J. Wiles, assistant chief counsel. Fax, 622-6889.

Oversees field office litigation of civil cases that involve underpayment of taxes when the taxpayer chooses to challenge the determinations of the Internal Revenue Service (IRS) in the U.S. Tax Court, or when the taxpayer chooses to pay the amount in question and sue the IRS for a refund. Reviews briefs and defense letters prepared by field offices for tax cases; prepares tax litigation advice memoranda; formulates litigation strategy. Makes recommendations concerning appeal and certiorari. Litigates insurance and declaratory judgment cases in the U.S. Tax Court.

Justice Dept., Tax Division, Main Justice Bldg. 20530; 514-2901. Loretta C. Argrett, assistant attorney general. Fax, 514-2085.

Authorizes prosecution of most criminal cases involving tax violations investigated and developed by the Internal Revenue Service (IRS); represents IRS in civil litigation except in U.S. Tax Court proceedings; represents other agencies, including the departments of Defense and Interior, in cases with state or local tax authorities.

Congress:

House Ways and Means Committee, 1102 LHOB 20515; 225-3625. Sam M. Gibbons, D-Fla., acting chairman; Janice A. Mays, chief counsel.

Jurisdiction over legislation concerning changes in enforcement of tax laws.

Senate Finance Committee, Subcommittee on Private Retirement Plans and Oversight of the Internal Revenue Service, SD-205 20510; 224-4515. David Pryor, D-Ark., chairman; Steve Glaze, staff contact.

Holds hearings on legislation concerning changes in enforcement of tax laws.

Judiciary:

U.S. Tax Court, 400 2nd St. N.W. 20217; 606-8700. Lapsley W. Hamblen Jr., chief judge; Charles S. Casazza, clerk of the court, 606-8754.

Tries and adjudicates disputes involving income, estate, and gift taxes and personal holding company surtaxes in cases in which deficiencies

have been determined by the Internal Revenue Service.

Nongovernmental:

American Bar Assn., Taxation Section, 1800 M St. N.W. 20036; 331-2230. Christine Brunswick, director. Fax, 331-2698.

Studies and recommends policies on taxation; provides information on tax issues; sponsors continuing legal education programs; monitors tax laws and legislation.

Constitutional Law and Civil Liberties

General

Agencies:

Commission on Civil Rights, 624 9th St. N.W., #700 20425; 376-7700. Mary Frances Berry, chairman. Information, 376-8364. Library, 376-8110. Fax, 376-7672. TDD, 376-8116. Complaints, (800) 552-6843; in Washington, D.C., 376-8582.

Assesses federal laws and policies of government agencies and reviews legal developments to determine the nature and extent of denial of equal protection on the basis of race, color, religion, sex, national origin, age, or disability; investigates complaints of denials of voting rights. Library open to the public.

Education Dept., Civil Rights, 330 C St. S.W. 20202; 205-5413. Norma Cantu, assistant secretary. Fax, 205-9862. TDD, 205-8673. Toll-free, (800) 205-8384.

Enforces laws prohibiting use of federal funds for education programs or activities that discriminate on the basis of race, color, sex, national origin, age, or disability; authorized to discontinue funding.

Health and Human Services Dept., Civil Rights, 330 Independence Ave. S.W. 20201; 619-0403. Dennis Hayashi, director. Information, 619-0585. Fax, 619-3818. TDD, (800) 537-7697. Toll-free hotline, (800) 368-1019; in Washington, D.C., 863-0100.

Administers and enforces laws prohibiting discrimination on the basis of sex, race, color, religion, national origin, age, or disability in health care and social services programs funded by the department; authorized to discontinue funding.

Justice Dept., Civil Rights, Main Justice Bldg. 20530; 514-2151. Deval Patrick, assistant attorney general. Information, 514-2007. Library, 514-4098. Fax, 514-0293. TDD, 472-1953.
Enforces federal civil rights laws prohibiting discrimination on the basis of race, color, religion, sex, disability, age, or national origin in voting, education, employment, credit, housing, public accommodations and facilities, and federally assisted programs.

Justice Dept., Legal Counsel, Main Justice Bldg. 20530; 514-2041. Walter Dellinger, assistant attorney general. Fax, 514-0539.
Advises the attorney general, the president, and executive agencies on questions regarding constitutional law.

Justice Dept., Redress Administration, 200 Constitution Ave. N.W., #1519 20001; 219-4396. Paul Suddes, administrator. Toll-free, (800) 219-6900. Fax, 219-9314. TDD, 219-4710.
Locates, identifies, and administers redress payments to Japanese-Americans interned in the United States during World War II.

Labor Dept., Civil Rights, 200 Constitution Ave. N.W. 20210; 219-8927. Annabelle Lockhart, director. Fax, 219-5658.
Resolves complaints of discrimination on the basis of race, color, religion, sex, national origin, age, or disability in programs funded by the department.

Congress:

House Government Operations Committee, Subcommittee on Information, Justice, Transportation, and Agriculture, B349C RHOB 20515; 225-3741. Gary Condit, D-Calif., chairman; Shannon Lahey, acting staff director. Fax, 225-2445.
Oversees operations of the Commission on Civil Rights.

House Judiciary Committee, 2138 RHOB 20515; 225-3951. Jack Brooks, D-Texas, chairman; Jon Yarowsky, general counsel.
Jurisdiction over legislation on proposed amendments to the Constitution; subcommittee jurisdiction determined by subject of proposed amendment.

House Judiciary Committee, Subcommittee on Civil and Constitutional Rights, 806 O'Neill Bldg. (300 New Jersey Ave. S.E.) 20515; 226-7680. Don Edwards, D-Calif., chairman; Catherine A. LeRoy, chief counsel.
Jurisdiction over legislation dealing with civil rights enforcement, the Voting Rights Act and affirmative action, civil liberties (including First Amendment rights and computer-related issues), and constitutional issues involving criminal law, habeas corpus, the death penalty, and the exclusionary rule.

House Judiciary Committee, Subcommittee on Intellectual Property and Judicial Administration, 207 CHOB 20515; 225-3926. William J. Hughes, D-N.J., chairman; Hayden W. Gregory, chief counsel.
Jurisdiction over legislation on court administration and management and over rules of civil judicial procedure.

Senate Judiciary Committee, Subcommittee on the Constitution, SD-524 20510; 224-5573. Paul Simon, D-Ill., chairman; Susan D. Kaplan, chief counsel.
Jurisdiction over legislation on proposed amendments to the Constitution, civil rights enforcement, the Voting Rights Act and affirmative action, civil liberties (including the First Amendment, excluding computers), constitutional issues involving criminal law, habeas corpus, the death penalty, and the exclusionary rule; oversees operations of the Commission on Civil Rights.

Senate Judiciary Committee, Subcommittee on Courts and Administrative Practice, SH-223 20510; 224-4022. Howell Heflin, D-Ala., chairman; Jim Whiddon, chief counsel.
Jurisdiction over legislation on court administration and management and over rules of civil judicial procedure.

Judiciary:

Supreme Court of the United States, 1 1st St. N.E. 20543; 479-3000. William H. Rehnquist, chief justice; William K. Suter, clerk, 479-3011. Library, 479-3037. Supreme Court opinions and information, 479-3211.
Highest appellate court in the federal judicial system. Interprets the U.S. Constitution, federal legislation, and treaties. Provides information on new cases filed, the status of pending cases, and admissions to the Supreme Court Bar. *(For complete list of justices, see p. 488.)*

Nongovernmental:

American Civil Liberties Union (ACLU), 122 Maryland Ave. N.E. 20002; 544-1681. Laura Murphy Lee, director, Washington office. Fax, 546-0738.

Initiates test court cases and advocates legislation to guarantee constitutional rights and civil liberties. Focuses on First Amendment rights, minority and women's rights, gay and lesbian rights, and privacy; supports legalized abortion, opposes government-sponsored school prayer and legislative restrictions on television content. Washington office monitors legislative and regulatory activities and public policy. Library open to the public by appointment. (Headquarters in New York maintains docket of cases.)

Center for Individual Rights, 1300 19th St., #260 20036; 833-8400. Michael S. Greve, executive director. Fax, 833-8410.

Public interest law firm that supports reform of the civil justice system on the basis of private rights and individual responsibility. Interests include economic regulation, freedom of speech, and libel law.

Citizens' Commission on Civil Rights, 2000 M St. N.W., #400 20036; 659-5565. Corrine M. Yu, director and counsel. Fax, 223-5302.

Bipartisan commission of former federal officials. Monitors compliance of federal agencies and judicial bodies with civil rights laws; conducts social science research and provides technical and legal assistance to other civil rights and public interest groups; interests include low- and moderate-income housing, voting rights, employment, school desegregation, and education of the disadvantaged.

Ethics and Public Policy Center, Law and Society Program, 1015 15th St. N.W., #900 20005; 682-1200. George S. Weigel Jr., president. Fax, 408-0632.

Examines current issues of jurisprudence, especially those relating to constitutional interpretation.

Institute for Justice, 1001 Pennsylvania Ave. N.W., #200S 20004-2505; 457-4240. Chip Mellor, president. Fax, 457-8574.

Sponsors seminars to train law students, grassroots activists, and practicing lawyers in applying advocacy strategies in public interest litigation. Seeks to protect from arbitrary government interference free speech, private property rights,

parental school choice, and economic liberty. Litigates cases.

The Jefferson Foundation, 1529 18th St. N.W. 20036; 234-3688. Mary Kennedy, executive director. Fax, 483-6018.

Studies historical trends in American government. Conducts research and provides information on proposed constitutional reforms designed to improve the structure and functioning of the government. Sponsors Jefferson Meetings on the Constitution to stimulate public discussion of constitutional issues.

Landmark Legal Foundation Center for Civil Rights, 1 Farragut Square South, 6th Floor 20006; 393-3360. Peter Huchinson, director. Fax, 393-3345.

Public interest organization that seeks to advance civil rights by supporting the elimination of racial quotas and other laws that treat minorities as special cases; seeks to advance economic liberty as a fundamental civil right. (Headquarters in Kansas City, Mo.)

Leadership Conference on Civil Rights, 1629 K St. N.W., #1010 20006; 466-3311. Ralph G. Neas, executive director. Fax, 466-3435.

Coalition of national organizations representing minorities, women, labor, senior citizens, people with disabilities, and religious groups. Works for enactment and enforcement of civil rights and social welfare legislation; acts as clearinghouse for information on civil rights legislation and regulations.

Legal Affairs Council, 3554 Chain Bridge Rd., #301, Fairfax, VA 22030; (703) 591-7767. Richard A. Delgaudio, president. Fax, (703) 222-1293.

Provides conservative activists with financial and legal assistance for court challenges of alleged violations of human and civil rights, especially First Amendment rights.

NAACP Legal Defense and Educational Fund, 1275 K St. N.W., #301 20005; 682-1300. Elaine Jones, director. Fax, 682-1312.

Civil rights litigation group that provides legal information on civil rights issues, including employment, housing, and educational discrimination; monitors federal enforcement of civil rights laws. Not affiliated with the National Assn. for the Advancement of Colored People (NAACP). (Headquarters in New York.)

National Assn. for the Advancement of Colored People (NAACP), 1025 Vermont Ave. N.W., #1120 20005; 638-2269. Wade J. Henderson, director, Washington bureau. Fax, 638-5936.

Membership: persons interested in civil rights for all minorities. Works for the political, educational, social, and economic equality of minorities through legal, legislative, and direct action, and educational programs. (Headquarters in Baltimore.)

National Committee Against Repressive Legislation, 3321 12th St. N.E., 3rd Floor 20017-4008; 529-4225. Kit Gage, Washington representative.

Educational organization that seeks to protect First Amendment rights of free speech and association. Interests include privacy, protection of due process rights, government secrecy and surveillance, and control of federal intelligence agencies; sponsors educational programs; organizes grass-roots political activities; maintains speakers bureau. (Headquarters in Los Angeles.)

National Organization for Women (NOW), 1000 16th St. N.W., #700 20036; 331-0066. Patricia Ireland, president. Fax, 785-8576. TDD, 331-9002.

Membership: women and men interested in civil rights for women. Works to end discrimination based on gender, to preserve abortion rights, and to pass an equal rights amendment to the Constitution.

See also Lawyers' Committee for Civil Rights Under Law (p. 521)

Abortion and Reproductive Issues

See also Health, Family Planning and Population (p. 326)

Congress:

House Judiciary Committee, Subcommittee on Civil and Constitutional Rights, 806 O'Neill Bldg. (300 New Jersey Ave. S.E.) 20515; 226-7680. Don Edwards, D-Calif., chairman; Catherine A. LeRoy, chief counsel.

Jurisdiction over proposed abortion amendments to the Constitution.

Senate Judiciary Committee, Subcommittee on the Constitution, SD-524 20510; 224-5573.

Paul Simon, D-Ill., chairman; Susan D. Kaplan, chief counsel.

Jurisdiction over proposed abortion amendments to the Constitution.

See also Congressional Pro-Life Caucus (p. 758)

Nongovernmental:

Ad Hoc Committee in Defense of Life, 1187 National Press Bldg., 529 14th St. N.W. 20045; 347-8686. Robert McFadden, Washington bureau chief.

Nonpartisan group that supports legislation and an amendment to the Constitution prohibiting abortion. (Headquarters in New York.)

Catholics for a Free Choice, 1436 U St. N.W. 20009; 986-6093. Frances Kissling, president. Fax, 332-7995.

International educational organization that supports the right to legal reproductive health care, especially to family planning and abortion. Works to reduce the incidence of abortion and to increase women's choices in childbearing and child-rearing through advocacy of social and economic programs for women, families, and children.

Human Life International, 7845 Airpark Rd., #E, Gaithersburg, MD 20879; (301) 670-7884. Paul Marx, president. Fax, (301) 869-7363.

Educational organization that opposes abortion, sterilization, infanticide, euthanasia, and contraception.

March for Life, P.O. Box 90300, Washington, DC 20090; 543-3377. Nellie J. Gray, president. Fax, 543-8202.

Membership: individuals and organizations that support government action prohibiting abortion. Monitors legislation and regulations. Sponsors annual march in Washington each January 22.

National Abortion Rights Action League (NARAL), 1156 15th St. N.W., 7th Floor 20005; 973-3000. Kate Michelman, president. Press, 973-3032. Fax, 973-3097.

Membership: persons favoring legalized abortion. Promotes grass-roots support of political candidates in favor of legalized abortion.

National Coalition Against Surrogacy, 1130 17th St. N.W., #630 20036; 466-2823. Andrew Kimbrell, policy director. Fax, 429-9602.

Works to protect the rights of surrogate mothers and to bar surrogacy contracts in the United States.

National Committee for a Human Life Amendment, 1511 K St. N.W., #335 20005; 393-0703. Michael A. Taylor, executive director.

Supports legislation and a constitutional amendment prohibiting abortion.

National Conference of Catholic Bishops/ United States Catholic Conference, Committee for Pro-Life Activities, 3211 4th St. N.E. 20017; 541-3070. Gail Quinn, executive director. Fax, 541-3054.

Provides information on the position of the Roman Catholic Church on abortion; monitors legislation on abortion and related issues; provides alternatives to abortion through Catholic charities.

National Right to Life Committee, 419 7th St. N.W. 20004; 626-8800. David N. O'Steen, executive director. Fax, 737-9189.

Association of 50 state right-to-life organizations. Opposes abortion, infanticide, and euthanasia; supports legislation prohibiting abortion except when the life of the mother is endangered. Monitors legislation and regulations. Operates an information clearinghouse and speakers bureau.

National Women's Health Network, 1325 G St. N.W. 20005; 347-1140. Beverly Baker, executive director. Fax, 347-1168.

Advocacy organization interested in women's health. Seeks to preserve legalized abortion; monitors legislation and regulations; testifies before Congress.

National Women's Political Caucus, 1275 K St. N.W. 20005; 898-1100. Jody Newman, executive director. Fax, 898-0458.

Advocacy group that seeks greater involvement of women in politics. Provides information on constitutional amendments related to abortion; supports legalized abortion.

Religious Coalition for Reproductive Choice, 1025 Vermont Ave. N.W., #1130 20005; 628-7700. Ann Thompson Cook, executive director. Fax, 628-7716.

Coalition of religious groups favoring legalized abortion. Opposes constitutional amendments and federal and state legislation restricting access to abortion services.

Voters for Choice, 2604 Connecticut Ave. N.W., 2nd Floor 20008-1521; 588-5200. Julie Burton, executive director. Fax, 588-0600.

Independent, nonpartisan political committee that supports candidates favoring legalized abortion. Provides candidates at all levels of government with campaign strategy information; opposes constitutional amendments and legislation restricting abortion.

See also American Civil Liberties Union (p. 502); National Council of Catholic Women (p. 279); National Organization for Women (p. 503)

Religion

See also Education, Private and Parochial Schools (p. 127); Religion and Ethics (p. 276)

Congress:

House Judiciary Committee, Subcommittee on Civil and Constitutional Rights, 806 O'Neill Bldg. (300 New Jersey Ave. S.E.) 20515; 226-7680. Don Edwards, D-Calif., chairman; Catherine A. LeRoy, chief counsel.

Jurisdiction over proposed constitutional amendments, including the First Amendment right to religious freedom.

Senate Judiciary Committee, Subcommittee on the Constitution, SD-524 20510; 224-5573. Paul Simon, D-Ill., chairman; Susan D. Kaplan, chief counsel.

Jurisdiction over proposed constitutional amendments; oversight of the First Amendment right to religious freedom.

Nongovernmental:

American Jewish Congress, 2027 Massachusetts Ave. N.W. 20036; 332-4001. Mark J. Pelavin, Washington representative. Fax, 387-3434.

Advocacy organization that seeks to uphold civil and constitutional rights. Litigates cases involving prayer in public schools, tuition tax credits, equal access, and religious symbols on public property. (Headquarters in New York.)

Americans for Religious Liberty, P.O. Box 6656, Silver Spring, MD 20916; (301) 598-2447. Edd Doerr, executive director.

Educational organization concerned with issues involving the separation of church and state. Opposes government-sponsored school prayer and tax support for religious institutions; supports religious neutrality in public education; defends abortion rights. Provides legal services in litigation cases. Maintains speakers bureau.

Americans United for Separation of Church and State, 8120 Fenton St., Silver Spring, MD 20910; (301) 589-3707. Barry L. Lynn, executive director. Fax, (301) 495-9173.

Citizens' interest group that opposes government-sponsored prayer in public schools and tax aid for parochial schools.

Council on Religious Freedom, 4545 42nd St. N.W., #201 20016; 363-8098. Lee Boothby, vice president.

Seeks to preserve principles of religious liberty through litigation and educational programs. Opposes prayer in public schools.

International Religious Liberty Assn., 12501 Old Columbia Pike, Silver Spring, MD 20904; (301) 680-6680. Bert B. Beach, secretary general. Fax, (301) 680-6695.

Seeks to preserve and expand religious liberty and freedom of conscience; advocates separation of church and state; sponsors international and domestic meetings and congresses.

National Assn. of Evangelicals, 1023 15th St. N.W., #500 20005; 789-1011. Robert P. Dugan Jr., director, public affairs. Fax, 842-0392.

Membership: evangelical churches, organizations (including schools), and individuals. Supports religious freedom. Monitors legislation and regulations. (Headquarters in Wheaton, Ill.)

National Council of Churches, 110 Maryland Ave. N.E. 20002; 544-2350. James A. Hamilton, director, Washington office.

Membership: Protestant-Anglican and Orthodox churches. Opposes government-sponsored prayer in public schools. Provides information on the school prayer issue. (Headquarters in New York.)

See also American Civil Liberties Union (p. 502)

Separation of Powers

Congress:

House Government Operations Committee, Subcommittee on Legislation and National Security, B373 RHOB 20515; 225-5147. John Conyers Jr., D-Mich., chairman; James C. Turner, staff director. Fax, 225-2373.

Jurisdiction over legislation on some aspects of executive privilege and separation of powers (jurisdiction over separation of powers shared with House Judiciary Committee).

House Judiciary Committee, 2138 RHOB 20515; 225-3951. Jack Brooks, D-Texas, chairman; Jon Yarowsky, general counsel.

Jurisdiction over legislation dealing with separation of powers and presidential succession (jurisdiction over separation of powers shared with House Government Operations Committee).

Senate Judiciary Committee, Subcommittee on the Constitution, SD-524 20510; 224-5573. Paul Simon, D-Ill., chairman; Susan D. Kaplan, chief counsel.

Jurisdiction over legislation on separation of powers, presidential succession, and some aspects of executive privilege.

Criminal Law

General

Agencies:

Federal Bureau of Investigation (Justice Dept.), 10th St. and Pennsylvania Ave. N.W. 20535; 324-3444. Louis J. Freeh, director. Information, 324-3691. Fax, 324-4705.

Investigates all violations of federal criminal laws except those assigned specifically to other federal agencies. Exceptions include alcohol, counterfeiting, tobacco, and customs violations (departments of Treasury and Commerce); postal violations (U.S. Postal Service); and illegal entry of aliens (Justice Dept.'s Immigration and Naturalization Service). Services provided to other law enforcement agencies include fingerprint identification, laboratory services, police training, and the National Crime Information Center (communications network among FBI, state, and local police agencies).

INTERPOL (Justice Dept.), 600 E St. N.W. (mailing address: Washington, DC 20530); 272-8383. Shelley G. Altenstadter, chief. Fax, 272-5941.
U.S. national central bureau for INTERPOL; participates in international investigations on behalf of U.S. police; coordinates the exchange of investigative information on crimes, including drug trafficking, counterfeiting, missing persons, and terrorism. Coordinates law enforcement requests for investigative assistance in the United States and abroad. Assists with extradition processes. Serves as liaison between foreign and U.S. law enforcement agencies at federal, state, and local levels. (Headquarters in Lyons, France.)

Justice Dept., Criminal Division, Main Justice Bldg. 20530; 514-2601. Jo Ann Harris, assistant attorney general. Fax, 514-9412.
Enforces all federal criminal laws except those specifically assigned to the antitrust, civil rights, environment and natural resources, and tax divisions of the Justice Dept. Supervises and directs U.S. attorneys in the field on criminal matters and litigation; supervises international extradition proceedings. Coordinates federal enforcement efforts against white-collar crime, fraud, and child pornography; handles civil actions under customs, liquor, narcotics, gambling, and firearms laws; coordinates enforcement activities against organized crime. Directs the National Asset Forfeiture Program for seizing the proceeds of criminal activity. Investigates and prosecutes criminal offenses involving public integrity and subversive activities, including treason, espionage, and sedition; Nazi war crimes; and related criminal offenses. Handles all civil cases relating to internal security and counsels federal departments and agencies regarding internal security matters. Drafts responses on proposed and pending criminal law legislation.

Justice Dept., Enforcement Operations, 1001 G St. N.W. 20530; 514-3684. Gerald Shur, senior associate director. Fax, 514-5143.
Coordinates federal witness security and victim compensation programs; selects individuals to enter the programs.

Justice Dept., Victims of Crime, 633 Indiana Ave. N.W. 20531; 307-5983. Carolyn Hightower, acting director. Fax, 514-6383.
Provides funds to state victim compensation and assistance programs, including counseling for victims of rape, child abuse, and spouse abuse; supports victim assistance programs for native Americans. Operations are financed by the crime victims fund, which is financed by federal criminal fines, penalties, and bond forfeitures. Provides information on victim and witness services.

National Institute of Justice (Justice Dept.), 633 Indiana Ave. N.W. 20531; 307-2942. Jeremy Travis, director designate. Fax, 307-6394.
Conducts research on all aspects of criminal justice, including crime prevention, enforcement, adjudication, and corrections; evaluates criminal justice programs; develops model programs using new techniques. Maintains the National Criminal Justice Reference Service, which provides information on criminal justice research, including information on AIDS issues for law enforcement officials: toll-free, (800) 851-3420; in Maryland, (301) 251-5500.

Congress:

House Education and Labor Committee, Subcommittee on Human Resources, B346C RHOB 20515; 225-1850. Matthew G. Martinez, D-Calif., chairman; Lester Sweeting, staff director and counsel.
Jurisdiction over legislation on juvenile justice and related issues, including the role of children in the courts (jurisdiction shared with House Judiciary Committee). Oversight of the Juvenile Justice and Delinquency Prevention Act, the Runaway and Homeless Youth Act, and juvenile justice programs administered by the Office of Justice Programs.

House Energy and Commerce Committee, Subcommittee on Health and the Environment, 2415 RHOB 20515; 225-4952. Henry A. Waxman, D-Calif., chairman; Karen Nelson, staff director.
Jurisdiction over legislation on drug abuse and rehabilitation of drug abusers, including narcotics addicts who have had contact (arrest or conviction) with the federal criminal justice system.

House Government Operations Committee, Subcommittee on Commerce, Consumer, and Monetary Affairs, B377 RHOB 20515; 225-4407. John M. Spratt Jr., D-S.C., chairman; Theodore Jacobs, staff director. Fax, 225-2441.
Oversight of Bureau of Alcohol, Tobacco, and Firearms.

House Judiciary Committee, 2138 RHOB 20515; 225-3951. Jack Brooks, D-Texas, chairman; Jon Yarowsky, general counsel.

Jurisdiction over internal security legislation.

House Judiciary Committee, Subcommittee on Civil and Constitutional Rights, 806 O'Neill Bldg. (300 New Jersey Ave. S.E.) 20515; 226-7680. Don Edwards, D-Calif., chairman; Catherine A. LeRoy, chief counsel.

Jurisdiction over legislation on control of domestic terrorism; oversight of the intelligence operations of the Federal Bureau of Investigation (jurisdiction shared with House Select Committee on Intelligence).

House Judiciary Committee, Subcommittee on Crime and Criminal Justice, 362 Ford Bldg. (2nd and D Sts. S.W.) 20515; 226-2406. Charles E. Schumer, D-N.Y., chairman; David Yassky, counsel.

Responsible for all aspects of criminal law and procedure and revision of the U.S. criminal code. Jurisdiction over legislation on speedy trials and pretrial procedures; grand juries; juvenile justice and related issues (jurisdiction shared with House Education and Labor Committee); organized crime; gun control; some aspects of narcotics abuse, including control, enforcement, criminal penalties, regulation of trade, and import-export control; sentences, parole, and pardons; the U.S. Parole Commission; and capital punishment. Investigates federal arson prevention and control activities.

House Judiciary Committee, Subcommittee on Intellectual Property and Judicial Administration, 207 CHOB 20515; 225-3926. William J. Hughes, D-N.J., chairman; Hayden W. Gregory, chief counsel.

Jurisdiction over legislation on federal corrections institutions (including prisoner health care), judicial ethics, federal trial juries, and organized crime, including the Racketeer Influenced and Corrupt Organizations Act (RICO).

House Post Office and Civil Service Committee, Subcommittee on Postal Operations and Services, 406 CHOB 20515; 225-9124. Barbara-Rose Collins, D-Mich., chairman; Meredith Cooper, staff director.

Jurisdiction over legislation on postal fraud.

House Select Committee on Intelligence, H405 CAP 20515; 225-4121. Dan Glickman, D-Kan., chairman; Michael Sheehy, chief counsel. Fax, 225-1991.

Jurisdiction over legislation on control of domestic terrorism; oversight of the intelligence operations of the Federal Bureau of Investigation (jurisdiction shared with House Judiciary Committee).

Senate Foreign Relations Committee, Subcommittee on Terrorism, Narcotics, and International Operations, SD-446 20515; 224-4651. John Kerry, D-Mass., chairman; Geryld B. Christianson, staff director. Fax, 224-5011.

Jurisdiction over legislation dealing with the international flow of illegal drugs.

Senate Governmental Affairs Committee, SD-340 20510; 224-4751. John Glenn, D-Ohio, chairman; Leonard Weiss, staff director. Fax, 224-9682.

Oversight of Bureau of Alcohol, Tobacco, and Firearms.

Senate Governmental Affairs Committee, Permanent Subcommittee on Investigations, SR-100 20510; 224-3721. Sam Nunn, D-Ga., chairman; Eleanor J. Hill, staff director.

Investigates organized criminal activity, national and international narcotics trafficking, postal fraud, prison crime, child pornography, government contracts fraud, insurance fraud, entitlement fraud, fraud involving the use of computers, and securities theft and fraud. Investigates federal arson prevention and control activities.

Senate Judiciary Committee, SD-224 20510; 224-5225. Joseph R. Biden Jr., D-Del., chairman; Cynthia Hogan, chief counsel.

Responsible for all aspects of criminal law and procedure and revision of the U.S. criminal code. Jurisdiction over legislation on internal security, speedy trials and pretrial procedures, grand juries, federal trial juries, federal corrections institutions (including prisoner health care), sentences, parole, pardons, the U.S. Parole Commission, and capital punishment. Jurisdiction over legislation dealing with organized crime, including the Racketeer Influenced and Corrupt Organizations Act (RICO); judicial ethics; gun control; control of domestic terrorism; some aspects of narcotics abuse, including control, enforcement, criminal penalties, regulation of trade, and import-export control.

Senate Judiciary Committee, Subcommittee on Juvenile Justice, SH-305 20510; 224-4933. Herb Kohl, D-Wis., chairman; Jon Leibowitz, chief counsel.

Jurisdiction over legislation on juvenile justice and related issues, including the role of children in the courts. Oversight of the Juvenile Justice and Delinquency Prevention Act, the Runaway and Homeless Youth Act, and juvenile justice programs administered by the Office of Justice Programs.

Senate Labor and Human Resources Committee, Subcommittee on Children, Families, Drugs, and Alcoholism, SH-639 20510; 224-5630. Christopher J. Dodd, D-Conn., chairman; Sarah Flanagan, staff director.

Jurisdiction over legislation on drug abuse and rehabilitation of drug abusers, including narcotics addicts who have had contact (arrest or conviction) with the federal criminal justice system.

Senate Select Committee on Intelligence, SH-211 20510; 224-1700. Dennis DeConcini, D-Ariz., chairman; Norm Bradley, staff director.

Oversight of the intelligence operations of the Federal Bureau of Investigation.

Nongovernmental:

American Bar Assn., Criminal Justice, 1800 M St. N.W. 20036; 331-2260. Thomas C. Smith, director. Fax, 331-2220.

Responsible for all matters pertaining to criminal law and procedure for the association. Studies and makes recommendations on all facets of the criminal and juvenile justice system, including sentencing, juries, pretrial procedures, grand juries, white-collar crime, and the Racketeer Influenced and Corrupt Organizations Act (RICO). (Headquarters in Chicago.)

Institute of Criminal Law and Procedure, Georgetown University Law Center, 600 New Jersey Ave. N.W. 20001; 662-9070. Samuel Dash, director. Fax, 662-9444.

Contract research organization affiliated with Georgetown University Law Center. Conducts research on the criminal justice system, including plea bargaining and police-prosecutor relations.

National Assn. of Attorneys General, 444 N. Capitol St. N.W., #339 20001; 434-8053. Christine Milliken, executive director. Information, 434-8000.

Membership: attorneys general of the states, territories, and commonwealths. Fosters interstate cooperation on legal and law enforcement issues, conducts policy research and analysis, and facilitates communication between members and all levels of government. *(For list of attorneys general, see State Officials, p. 865.)*

National Assn. of Crime Victim Compensation Boards, P.O. Box 16003, Alexandria, VA 22302-8003; (703) 370-2996. Dan Eddy, executive director. Fax, (703) 370-2996.

Provides state compensation agencies with training and technical assistance. Provides public information on victim compensation.

National Assn. of Criminal Defense Lawyers, 1627 K St. N.W. 20006; 872-8688. R. Keith Stroup, executive director. Fax, 331-8269.

Membership: criminal defense attorneys. Provides members with continuing legal education programs, a brief bank, an ethics hotline, and specialized assistance in areas such as DNA and Section 8300 cash reporting requirements. Offers free legal assistance to members who are harassed, charged with contempt, or receive a bar grievance for providing ethical but aggressive representation. Monitors legislation and regulations. Interests include eliminating mandatory minimum sentencing, opposing the death penalty, and minimizing the effect on civil liberties of the war on drugs.

National Crime Prevention Council, 1700 K St. N.W. 20006; 466-6272. John A. Calhoun, executive director. Fax, 296-1356.

Educates public on crime prevention through media campaigns, supporting materials, and training workshops; sponsors McGruff public service campaign; maintains database on crime prevention programs; runs demonstration programs in schools.

National District Attorneys' Assn., 99 Canal Center Plaza, #510, Alexandria, VA 22314; (703) 549-9222. Newman Flanagan, executive director. Fax, (703) 836-3195.

Sponsors conferences and workshops on criminal justice; provides information on district attorneys, criminal justice, the courts, child abuse, environmental crime, and national traffic laws.

National Organization for Victim Assistance, 1757 Park Rd. N.W. 20010; 232-6682. Marlene A. Young, executive director. Fax, 462-2255. Toll-free information hotline, (800) 879-6682; (202) 232-6682 in Washington, D.C., area.

Membership: persons involved with victim and witness assistance programs, criminal justice professionals, researchers, crime victims, and others interested in victims' rights. Monitors legislation; provides victims and victim support programs with technical assistance, referrals, and program support; provides information on victims' rights.

National Victim Center, 2111 Wilson Blvd., #300, Arlington, VA 22201; (703) 276-2880. Robert S. Ross Jr., executive director. Fax, (703) 276-2889.

Works with victims' groups and criminal justice agencies to protect the rights of crime victims through state and federal statutes and policies. Promotes greater responsiveness to crime victims through training and education; provides research and technical assistance in the development of victim-related legislation.

See also Assn. of Trial Lawyers of America and Federal Bar Assn. (p. 493)

Child Abuse, Domestic Violence, and Sexual Assault

Agencies:

Administration for Children, Youth, and Families (Health and Human Services Dept.), Family and Youth Services, 330 C St. S.W. (mailing address: P.O. Box 1182, Washington, DC 20013); 205-8102. Terry Lewis, acting associate commissioner. Fax, 205-8221.

Administers federal discretionary grant programs for projects serving runaway and homeless youth and for projects that deter youth involvement in gangs. Provides youth service agencies with training and technical assistance. Monitors federal policies, programs, and legislation. Supports research on gangs, runaways, and homeless youth.

Justice Dept., Child Exploitation and Obscenity Section, 1001 G St. N.W., #310 20530; 514-5780. George C. Burgasser, acting chief. Fax, 514-1793.

Enforces federal obscenity and child pornography laws; prosecutes cases involving violations of these laws. Maintains collection of briefs, pleadings, and other material for use by federal, state, and local prosecutors.

National Institute of Justice (Justice Dept.), 633 Indiana Ave. N.W. 20531; 307-2942. Jeremy Travis, director designate. Fax, 307-6394.

Conducts research on all aspects of criminal justice, including AIDS issues for law enforcement officials. Studies on rape and domestic violence available from the National Criminal Justice Reference Service: toll-free, (800) 851-3420; in Maryland, (301) 251-5500.

National Institute of Mental Health (National Institutes of Health, Health and Human Services Dept.), Violence and Traumatic Stress, 5600 Fishers Lane, Parklawn Bldg., #10C-24, Rockville, MD 20857; (301) 443-3728. Susan D. Solomon, chief. Fax, (301) 443-1726.

Supports research on the causes of rape and sexual assault, mental health consequences of interpersonal violence and abuse, treatment of victims and offenders, and effectiveness of programs designed to reduce trauma. Studies the relationship between mental health issues and the law.

Congress:

See Criminal Law, General, Congress (p. 506)

Nongovernmental:

American Bar Assn., Center on Children and the Law, 1800 M St. N.W. 20036; 331-2250. Howard Davidson, director. Fax, 331-2225.

Provides child welfare community with training and technical assistance. Interests include child abuse and neglect, adoption, foster care, and medical neglect.

National Center for Prosecution of Child Abuse, 99 Canal Center Plaza, #510, Alexandria, VA 22314; (703) 739-0321. Patricia Toth, director. Fax, (703) 549-6259.

Provides prosecutors involved in child abuse cases with training and information. Monitors legislation concerning child abuse.

See also Social Services and Rehabilitation Programs, Children, Youth, and Families, Nongovernmental (p. 416)

See also Center for Women Policy Studies (p. 271)

Drug Abuse

See also Health, Substance Abuse (p. 338); International Law and Agreements, Narcotics (p. 478)

Agencies:

Defense Dept., Drug Enforcement Policy and Support, The Pentagon 20310-1510; (703) 695-7996. Brian E. Sheridan, deputy assistant secretary. Fax, (703) 693-7588.

Advises the secretary on Defense Dept. policies and programs in support of federal counter-narcotics operations and the implementation of the president's National Drug Control Strategy.

Drug Enforcement Administration (Justice Dept.), 700 Army-Navy Dr., Arlington, VA (mailing address: Washington, DC 20537); 307-8000. Thomas A. Constantine, administrator. Information, 307-7977. Fax, 307-7335.

Enforces federal laws and statutes relating to narcotics and other dangerous drugs, including addictive drugs, depressants, stimulants, and hallucinogens; manages the National Narcotics Intelligence System in cooperation with federal, state, and local officials; investigates violations and regulates legal trade in narcotics and dangerous drugs. Provides school and community officials with drug abuse policy guidelines. Provides the public with information on drugs and drug abuse.

Executive Office of the President, National Drug Control Policy, Old Executive Office Bldg. 20500; 467-9800. Lee Brown, director. Information, 467-9890. Fax, 467-9899.

Establishes policies and oversees the implementation of a national drug control strategy; recommends changes to reduce demand for and supply of illegal drugs; advises the National Security Council on drug control policy.

Federal Bureau of Investigation (Justice Dept.), 10th St. and Pennsylvania Ave. N.W. 20535; 324-3444. Louis J. Freeh, director. Information, 324-3691. Fax, 324-4705.

Shares responsibility with the Drug Enforcement Administration for investigating violations of federal criminal drug laws; investigates organized crime involvement with illegal narcotics trafficking.

Food and Drug Administration (Health and Human Services Dept.), Center for Drug Evaluation and Research, 5600 Fishers Lane, Parklawn Bldg., #13B-45, Rockville, MD 20857; (301) 443-2894. Gerald Meyer, acting director. Information, (301) 594-1012. Press, (301) 443-3285. Fax, (301) 443-2763.

Makes recommendations to the Justice Dept.'s Drug Enforcement Administration on narcotics and dangerous drugs to be controlled.

Interior Dept., Enforcement and Security Management, Main Interior Bldg. 20240; 208-4108. John J. Gannon, director. Fax, 208-5048.

Administers drug and law enforcement programs for the Interior Dept., including programs in national parks, ranges, and fish and wildlife refuges. Cooperates with local law enforcement agencies, state park rangers, and other drug enforcement agencies.

Justice Dept., Justice Assistance, 633 Indiana Ave. N.W. 20531; 514-6278. Nancy Gist, director. Fax, 514-5956.

Awards grants and provides eligible state and local governments with training and technical assistance to enforce laws relating to narcotics and other dangerous drugs.

Justice Dept., Narcotic and Dangerous Drugs, 1400 New York Ave. N.W. 20530; 514-0917. Geoffery R. Greiveldinger, acting chief. Fax, 514-6112.

Investigates and prosecutes participants in criminal syndicates involved in the large-scale importation, manufacture, shipment, or distribution of illegal narcotics and other dangerous drugs. Trains agents and prosecutors in the techniques of major drug litigation.

U.S. Coast Guard (Transportation Dept.), Operational Law Enforcement, 2100 2nd St. S.W. 20593; 267-1155. Capt. J. F. Carmichael, chief. Fax, 267-4082.

Combats smuggling of narcotics and other dangerous drugs into the United States via the Atlantic and Pacific oceans and the Gulf of Mexico; works with U.S. Customs Service on drug law enforcement.

U.S. Customs Service (Treasury Dept.), 1301 Constitution Ave. N.W. 20229; 927-1600. John E. Hensley, assistant commissioner, enforcement. Information, 566-5286. Fax, 633-7645.

Interdicts and seizes contraband, including narcotics and other dangerous drugs smuggled into the United States. To report information on drug smuggling, call (800) 232-5378. Library open to the public.

Congress:

See Criminal Law, General, Congress (p. 506)

Nongovernmental:

Drug Policy Foundation, 4455 Connecticut Ave. N.W., #B500 20008; 537-5005. Arnold S. Trebach, president. Fax, 537-3007.
Supports reform of current drug control policy. Advocates medical treatment to control drug abuse. Opposes random drug testing and litigates cases that deal with drug testing in the workplace.

National Assn. of Chiefs of Police, 1000 Connecticut Ave. N.W., #9 20036; 293-9088. Dennis Martin, president.
Conducts research and provides organizations interested in reducing drug demand with information, programs, and training. Administers Going Straight, a campaign that works to create drug free schools.

National Assn. of State Alcohol and Drug Abuse Directors, 444 N. Capitol St. N.W., #642 20001; 783-6868. William Butynski, executive director. Fax, 783-2704.
Provides information on drug abuse treatment and prevention; contracts with federal and state agencies for design of programs to fight drug abuse.

National Organization for the Reform of Marijuana Laws (NORML), 1001 Connecticut Ave. N.W., #1010 (mailing address: P.O. Box 53356, Washington, DC 20077-3788); 483-5500. Richard Cowan, director. Fax, 483-0057.
Citizens' interest and educational organization. Researches social, economic, and legal effects of marijuana use and laws governing drug testing; acts as clearinghouse on marijuana laws; supports the decriminalization of marijuana for medical and personal use.

Rand Corporation, Drug Policy Research Center, 2100 M St. N.W. 20037; 296-5000. Barbara Williams, senior adviser. Fax, 296-7960.
Studies and analyzes the nation's drug problems and policies. Provides policy makers with information. (Headquarters in Santa Monica, Calif.)

See also American Prosecutors Research Institute, National Drug Prosecution Center (p. 523)

Gun Control

Agencies:

Bureau of Alcohol, Tobacco, and Firearms (Treasury Dept.), Law Enforcement, 650 Massachusetts Ave. N.W. 20226; 927-7970. Charles R. Thomson, acting associate director. Fax, 927-7756.
Enforces and administers laws to eliminate illegal possession and use of firearms. Investigates criminal violations and regulates legal trade. To report thefts, losses, or discoveries of explosive materials, call (800) 800-3855.

Congress:

See Criminal Law, General, Congress (p. 506)

Nongovernmental:

Citizens Committee for the Right to Keep and Bear Arms, 600 Pennsylvania Ave. S.E., #205 20003; 543-3363. John M. Snyder, director, publications and public affairs.
Concerned with rights of gun owners. Maintains National Advisory Council, comprising members of Congress, which provides advice on issues concerning the right to keep and bear arms. (Headquarters in Bellevue, Wash.)

Coalition to Stop Gun Violence, 100 Maryland Ave. N.E. 20002; 544-7190. Michael K. Beard, president. Fax, 544-7213.
Membership: organizations and individuals seeking to ban handguns. Provides national, state, and local groups operating handgun education programs with materials; engages in research and field work to support legislation to ban or control handguns.

Educational Fund to End Handgun Violence, 110 Maryland Ave. N.E. 20002; 544-7227. Joshua Horwitz, executive director.
Works to reduce handgun violence through education; assists schools and organizations in establishing antiviolence programs; maintains a firearms litigation clearinghouse.

Gun Owners of America, 8001 Forbes Pl., #102, Springfield, VA 22151; (703) 321-8585. Lawrence D. Pratt, executive director. Fax, (703) 321-8408.

Seeks to preserve the right to bear arms and to protect the rights of law-abiding gun owners. Monitors legislation and regulations, provides information, and provides gun owners with legal assistance in suits against the federal government.

Handgun Control, 1225 Eye St. N.W., #1100 20005; 898-0792. Richard M. Aborn, president. Fax, 371-9615.

Public interest organization that works for handgun control legislation and serves as an information clearinghouse.

National Rifle Assn. of America, 11250 Waples Mill Rd., Fairfax, VA 22030; (703) 267-1000. Wayne La Pierre, executive vice president. Fax, (703) 267-3976.

Membership: target shooters, hunters, gun collectors, gunsmiths, police officers, and others interested in firearms. Promotes shooting sports and recreational shooting and safety; studies and makes recommendations on firearms laws. Opposes gun control legislation.

Juvenile Justice

See also Social Services and Rehabilitation Programs, Children, Youth, and Families (p. 415)

Agencies:

Education Dept., Compensatory Education Programs, 400 Maryland Ave. S.W. 20202-6132; 401-1682. Mary Jean LeTendre, director. Fax, 401-1112.

Funds state and local institutions responsible for providing neglected or delinquent children with free public education.

Executive Office of the President, Coordinating Council on Juvenile Justice and Delinquency Prevention, 633 Indiana Ave. N.W. 20531; 307-5911. Janet Reno, chairman; Bonnie Halford, staff director, 616-3553. Fax, 514-6382.

Membership: the attorney general; secretaries of education, health and human services, housing and urban development, and labor; and directors of federal agencies concerned with juvenile justice and delinquency prevention programs. Coordinates federal juvenile delinquency activities and programs involved with missing and exploited children. Makes policy recommendations to Congress and the president.

Justice Dept., Juvenile Justice and Delinquency Prevention, 633 Indiana Ave. N.W. 20531; 307-5911. John J. Wilson, acting administrator. Fax, 514-6382. Technical information, 307-0751. Juvenile Justice Clearinghouse, (800) 638-8736.

Administers most federal programs related to prevention and treatment of juvenile delinquency, missing and exploited children, and research and evaluation of juvenile justice system; coordinates youth programs of the departments of Agriculture, Education, Housing and Urban Development, Interior, and Labor, and of the Substance Abuse and Mental Health Services Administration, including the Center for Studies of Crime and Delinquency. Operates the Juvenile Justice Clearinghouse.

National Institute of Mental Health (National Institutes of Health, Health and Human Services Dept.), Violence and Traumatic Stress, 5600 Fishers Lane, Parklawn Bldg., #10C-24, Rockville, MD 20857; (301) 443-3728. Susan D. Solomon, chief. Fax, (301) 443-1726.

Supports research on crime and juvenile delinquency; funds studies in several mental health-related areas, including community-based prevention and treatment, violent behavior, and delinquent and criminal behavior. Studies the relationship between mental health issues and the law.

Congress:

See Criminal Law, General, Congress (p. 506)

Nongovernmental:

National Institute for Citizen Education in the Law, D.C. Street Law Diversion Program, 711 G St. S.E. 20003; 546-6644. Jeffrey Chinn, director. Fax, 546-6649.

Provides first-offender youths with alternatives to adjudication or probation by placing them in a street law education program, which teaches them about legal rights and responsibilities. Offers information and technical assistance for establishing and operating similar diversion projects.

National Office for Social Responsibility, 222 S. Washington St., Alexandria, VA 22314; (703) 549-5305. Robert J. Gemignani, president. Fax, (703) 836-7269.

Provides training and technical assistance for public-private partnerships in employment training, education, and criminal and juvenile justice.

Organized Crime

Agencies:

Justice Dept., Narcotic and Dangerous Drugs, 1400 New York Ave. N.W. 20530; 514-0917. Geoffery R. Greiveldinger, acting chief. Fax, 514-6112.

Investigates and prosecutes participants in criminal syndicates involved in the large-scale importation, manufacture, shipment, or distribution of illegal narcotics and other dangerous drugs. Trains agents and prosecutors in the techniques of major drug litigation.

Justice Dept., Organized Crime and Racketeering, 1001 G St. N.W. 20530; 514-3594. Paul E. Coffey, chief. Fax, 514-6301.

Enforces federal criminal laws when subjects under investigation are alleged racketeers or part of syndicated criminal operations; coordinates efforts of federal, state, and local law enforcement agencies against organized crime in cases of infiltration of legitimate businesses and labor unions, public corruption, labor-management racketeering, and violence that disrupts the criminal justice process.

Congress:

See Criminal Law, General, Congress (p. 506)

Other Violations

See also Campaigning, Campaign Conduct and Election Administration (p. 739)

Agencies:

Bureau of Alcohol, Tobacco, and Firearms (Treasury Dept.), Law Enforcement, 650 Massachusetts Ave. N.W. 20226; 927-7970. Charles R. Thomson, acting associate director. Fax, 927-7756.

Enforces and administers laws relating to alcohol, tobacco, firearms, arson, explosives, and destructive devices; investigates criminal violations and regulates legal trade. To report thefts, losses, or discoveries of explosive materials, call (800) 800-3855.

Justice Dept., Fraud, 1400 New York Ave. N.W. 20530; 514-0640. Gerald E. McDowell, chief. Fax, 514-6118.

Administers federal enforcement activities relating to crimes against consumers, computer and credit card fraud, and white-collar crime, which includes fraud in government programs, security and commodity exchanges, and banking practices.

Justice Dept., Money Laundering, 1400 New York Ave. N.W. 20530; 514-1758. Theodore S. Greenberg, chief. Fax, 616-1344.

Investigates and prosecutes money-laundering offenses involving illegal transfer of funds within the United States and from the United States to other countries. Oversees and coordinates legislative policy proposals.

Justice Dept., Terrorism and Violent Crime, 10th St. and Pennsylvania Ave. N.W., #2513 20530; 514-0849. James S. Reynolds, chief. Fax, 514-8714.

Investigates and prosecutes incidents of international terrorism involving U.S. interests, domestic violent crime, firearms, and explosives violations. Provides legal advice on federal statutes relating to murder, assault, kidnapping, threats, robbery, weapons and explosives control, malicious destruction of property, and aircraft and sea piracy.

U.S. Customs Service (Treasury Dept.), 1301 Constitution Ave. N.W. 20229; 927-1600. John E. Hensley, assistant commissioner, enforcement. Information, 566-5286. Fax, 633-7645.

Combats smuggling and the unreported transportation of funds in excess of $10,000; enforces statutes relating to the processing and regulation of people, carriers, cargo, and mail into and out of the United States. Investigates counterfeiting, child pornography, and commercial fraud cases. Library open to the public.

U.S. Postal Service, Inspection Service, 475 L'Enfant Plaza S.W. 20260; 268-4267. Kenneth J. Hunter, chief postal inspector. Fax, 268-4563. Fraud and abuse hotline, (800) 654-8896.

Protects mail, postal funds, and property from violations of postal laws, such as mail fraud or distribution of obscene materials.

U.S. Secret Service (Treasury Dept.), 1800 G St. N.W. 20223; 435-5700. Eljay B. Boward, director. Information, 435-5708. Fax, 435-5246.

Enforces and administers counterfeiting and forgery laws. Investigates electronic fund transfer, credit card, and other types of access fraud, and threats against the president, vice president, and foreign heads of state visiting the United States.

Congress:

See Criminal Law, General, Congress (p. 506)

Sentencing and Corrections

Agencies:

Bureau of Prisons (Justice Dept.), 320 1st St. N.W. 20534; 307-6300. Kathleen M. Hawk, director. Information, 307-3198. Fax, 514-6878. Inmate locator service, 307-3126.

Supervises operations of federal correctional institutions and community treatment facilities, and commitment and management of federal inmates; oversees contracts with local institutions for confinement and support of federal prisoners. Regional offices are responsible for administration; central office in Washington coordinates operations and issues standards and policy guidelines. Central office includes Industries, Education, and Vocational Training— Unicor, which provides prison-manufactured goods and services for sale to federal agencies; and the National Institute of Corrections, an information center on state and local corrections programs. *(See Regional Federal Information Sources list, p. 827.)*

Bureau of Prisons (Justice Dept.), Health Services, 320 1st St. N.W. 20534; 307-3055. Dr. Kenneth P. Moritsugu, medical director. Fax, 307-0826.

Administers health care and treatment programs for prisoners in federal institutions.

Bureau of Prisons (Justice Dept.), Industries, Education, and Vocational Training—UNICOR, 320 1st St. N.W. 20534; 508-8400. Steve Schwalb, chief operating officer. Fax, 638-0720.

Administers program whereby inmates in federal prisons produce goods and services that are sold to the federal government.

Bureau of Prisons (Justice Dept.), National Institute of Corrections, 500 1st St. N.W. 20534; 307-3106. Larry Solomon, acting director. Fax, 307-3361. TDD, 307-3156.

Awards grants and offers technical assistance and training for upgrading state and local corrections systems through staff development, research, and evaluation of correctional operations and programs. Acts as a clearinghouse on correctional information.

Justice Dept., 500 1st St. N.W. 20530; 616-6070. Margaret C. Love, pardon attorney. Fax, 616-6069.

Receives and reviews petitions to the president for all forms of executive clemency, including pardons and sentence reductions; initiates investigations and prepares the deputy attorney general's recommendations to the president on petitions.

Justice Dept., Justice Assistance, 633 Indiana Ave. N.W. 20531; 514-6278. Nancy Gist, director. Fax, 514-5956.

Provides states and communities with funds and technical assistance for corrections demonstration projects.

National Institute of Justice (Justice Dept.), 633 Indiana Ave. N.W. 20531; 307-2942. Jeremy Travis, director designate. Fax, 307-6394.

Conducts research on all aspects of criminal justice, including crime prevention, enforcement, adjudication, and corrections. Maintains the National Criminal Justice Reference Service, which provides information on corrections research: toll-free, (800) 851-3420; in Maryland, (301) 251-5500.

U.S. Parole Commission (Justice Dept.), 5550 Friendship Blvd., #420, Chevy Chase, MD 20815; (301) 492-5990. Edward F. Reilly Jr., chairman. Fax, (301) 492-6694. Chairman's fax, (301) 492-5307.

Makes release decisions for all federal prisoners serving sentences of more than one year; has jurisdiction over paroled federal prisoners and over other prisoners on mandatory release under the "good time" statutes. U.S. probation officers supervise parolees and mandatory releases. *(See Regional Federal Information Sources list, p. 830.)*

U.S. Sentencing Commission, 1 Columbus Circle N.E., #2-500 South Lobby 20002; 273-4500. William W. Wilkins Jr., chairman. Fax, 273-4529.

Researches and drafts sentencing guidelines and policy for all federal courts to coincide with the abolition of the use of parole in the federal corrections system.

Congress:

See *Criminal Law, General, Congress (p. 506)*

Judiciary:

Administrative Office of the U.S. Courts, 1 Columbus Circle N.E. 20544; 273-3000. L. Ralph Mecham, director. Information, 273-1120. Library, 273-1888. Fax, 273-3011.

Supervises all administrative matters of the federal court system, except the Supreme Court; collects statistical data on business of the courts.

Administrative Office of the U.S. Courts, Probation and Pretrial Services, 1 Columbus Circle N.E. 20745; 273-1600. Donald L. Chamlee, chief. Fax, 273-1603.

Supervises federal probation and pretrial services officers, subject to primary control by the respective district courts in which they serve. Responsible for general oversight of field offices; tests new probation programs such as probation teams and deferred prosecution.

Nongovernmental:

American Bar Assn., Criminal Justice, 1800 M St. N.W. 20036; 331-2260. Thomas C. Smith, director. Fax, 331-2220.

Studies and makes recommendations on all aspects of the correctional system, including overcrowding in prisons and the privatization of prisons and correctional institutions. (Headquarters in Chicago.)

American Civil Liberties Union Foundation, National Prison Project, 1875 Connecticut Ave. N.W. 20009-5728; 234-4830. Alvin J. Bronstein, executive director. Fax, 234-4890.

Litigates on behalf of prisoners through class action suits. Seeks to improve prison conditions and the penal system; serves as resource center for prisoners' rights; operates an AIDS education project.

American Correctional Assn., 8025 Laurel Lakes Court, Laurel, MD 20707-5075; (301) 206-5098. James A. Gondles Jr., executive director. Toll-free, (800) 222-5646. Fax, (301) 206-5061.

Membership: corrections administrators and staff in juvenile and adult institutions, community corrections facilities, and jails; affiliates include state and regional corrections associations in the United States and Canada. Conducts and publishes research; provides state and local governments with technical assistance. Interests include correctional standards and accreditation programs. Library open to the public.

Amnesty International USA, 304 Pennsylvania Ave. S.E. 20003; 544-0200. James O'Dea, director, Washington office. Fax, 546-7142.

International organization that opposes retention or reinstitution of the death penalty; advocates humane treatment of all prisoners. (U.S. headquarters in New York.)

Correctional Education Assn., 8025 Laurel Lakes Court, Laurel, MD 20707; (301) 490-1440. Stephen J. Steurer, executive director. Fax, (301) 206-5061.

Membership: educators and administrators who work with students in correctional settings. Provides members with information and technical assistance to improve quality of educational programs and services offered in correctional settings. Interests include postsecondary and vocational education, special education, jail education, and libraries and literacy.

Families Against Mandatory Minimums, 1001 Pennsylvania Ave. N.W., #200 South 20004; 457-5790. Julie Stewart, president. Fax, 457-8564.

Seeks to repeal statutory mandatory minimum prison sentences. Works to increase public awareness of inequity of mandatory minimum sentences.

NAACP Legal Defense and Educational Fund, 1275 K St. N.W., #301 20005; 682-1300. Elaine Jones, director. Fax, 682-1312.

Civil rights litigation group that supports abolition of capital punishment; assists attorneys representing prisoners on death row; focuses public attention on race discrimination in the application of the death penalty. Not affiliated with the National Assn. for the Advancement of Colored People (NAACP). (Headquarters in New York.)

National Center on Institutions and Alternatives, 635 Slaters Lane, G100, Alexandria, VA 22314; (703) 684-0373. Jerome G. Miller, president. Fax, (703) 684-6037.

Seeks to reduce incarceration as primary form of punishment imposed by criminal justice system;

advocates use of extended community service, work-release, and halfway house programs; provides defense attorneys and courts with specific recommendations for sentencing and parole.

Prison Fellowship Ministries, 1856 Old Reston Ave., Reston, VA (mailing address: P.O. Box 17500, Washington, DC 20041); (703) 478-0100. Thomas C. Pratt, president. Fax, (703) 478-0452.

Religious organization that ministers to prisoners and ex-prisoners, victims, and the families involved. Offers counseling, seminars, and postrelease support for readjustment; works to increase the fairness and effectiveness of the criminal justice system.

The Sentencing Project, 918 F St. N.W., #501 20004; 628-0871. Malcolm Young, executive director. Fax, 628-1091.

Develops and promotes sentencing programs that reduce reliance on incarceration; provides technical assistance to sentencing programs; publishes research and information on criminal justice reform.

See also Episcopal Peace Fellowship (p. 278); National Legal Aid and Defender Assn. (p. 522); National Sheriffs' Assn. (p. 519)

Law and Government

Claims Against the Government

Agencies:

Agency sources involved in specific issues such as native American claims, foreign claims, or veterans' benefits may be found in the appropriate chapter. See index.

Justice Dept., Civil Division, Main Justice Bldg. 20530; 514-3301. Frank W. Hunger, assistant attorney general. Information, 514-2007. Fax, 514-8071.

Represents the United States in the U.S. Court of Federal Claims, except in cases involving taxes, lands, patents, or native American claims.

Justice Dept., Environment and Natural Resources, Main Justice Bldg. 20530; 514-2701. Lois J. Schiffer, assistant attorney general designate. Fax, 514-0557.

Represents the United States in the U.S. Court of Federal Claims in cases arising from acquisition of property or related matters.

Justice Dept., Tax Division, Main Justice Bldg. 20530; 514-2901. Loretta C. Argrett, assistant attorney general. Fax, 514-2085.

Represents the United States in court cases and related litigation involving refund claims arising under internal revenue laws.

State Dept., International Claims and Investment Disputes, 2100 K St. N.W. 20037; 632-7810. Ronald J. Bettauer, assistant legal adviser. Fax, 632-5283.

Handles claims by U.S. government and citizens against foreign governments; claims by foreign governments and their nationals against the U.S. government; claims against the State Dept. for negligence (in the United States or abroad) under the Federal Tort Claims Act; and claims by owners of U.S. flag vessels for reimbursement of fines, fees, licenses, and other direct payments for illegal seizures by foreign governments in international waters under the Fishermen's Protective Act. Negotiates agreements with foreign governments on claims settlements.

Congress:

General Accounting Office, General Government, 441 G St. N.W. 20548; 512-3102. Sharon S. Green, director, claims group. Fax, 512-2507. Documents, 512-6241.

Independent, nonpartisan agency in the legislative branch. Settles general claims and demands by or against the United States; jurisdiction in claims settlement concurrent with U.S. district courts and U.S. Court of Federal Claims. Provides the Justice Dept. with technical support and assistance in its prosecution or defense of suits to which the United States is party.

House Judiciary Committee, Subcommittee on Administrative Law and Governmental Relations, B351A RHOB 20515; 225-5741. John Bryant, D-Texas, chairman; Paul J. Drolet, chief counsel.

Jurisdiction over legislation related to claims against the United States.

Senate Judiciary Committee, SD-224 20510; 224-5225. Joseph R. Biden Jr., D-Del., chairman; Cynthia Hogan, chief counsel.

Jurisdiction over legislation related to claims against the United States.

Judiciary:

U.S. Court of Federal Claims, 717 Madison Pl. N.W. 20005; 219-9668. Loren A. Smith, chief judge; David A. Lampen, clerk, 219-9657. Fax, 219-9649.

Renders judgment on any nontort claims for monetary damages against the United States founded upon the Constitution, statutes, government regulations, and government contracts. Examples include compensation for taking of property, claims arising under construction and supply contracts, certain patent cases, and cases involving the refund of federal taxes. Hears cases involving native American claims.

Interstate Compacts

Congress:

House Judiciary Committee, Subcommittee on Administrative Law and Governmental Relations, B351A RHOB 20515; 225-5741. John Bryant, D-Texas, chairman; Paul J. Drolet, chief counsel.

Jurisdiction over all interstate compacts dealing with such matters as hazardous waste transportation, water rights, and boundaries. (Congressional approval of interstate compacts is required by the Constitution.)

Senate Judiciary Committee, Subcommittee on Antitrust, Monopolies, and Business Rights, SH-308 20510; 224-5701. Howard M. Metzenbaum, D-Ohio, chairman; Gene Kimmelman, chief counsel.

Jurisdiction over interstate compacts dealing with such matters as hazardous waste transportation, water rights, and boundaries. (Congressional approval of interstate compacts is required by the Constitution.)

Law Enforcement

See also Criminal Law (p. 505)

General

Agencies:

Federal Bureau of Investigation (Justice Dept.), National Law Institute, 1900 Half St. S.W. 20535; 252-7466. Pamela A. McCullough, Washington representative. Fax, 252-7351.

Conducts educational programs for officials trained in law who advise federal, state, and local law enforcement agencies; topics include First Amendment rights, hiring policies, and recent developments in constitutional law. (Headquarters in Quantico, Va.)

Federal Law Enforcement Training Center (Treasury Dept.), 650 Massachusetts Ave. N.W., #3100 20026; 927-8940. John C. Dooher, associate director. Fax, 927-8782.

Trains federal law enforcement personnel from seventy-one agencies, excluding the Federal Bureau of Investigation and the Drug Enforcement Administration. (Headquarters in Glynco, Ga.)

Justice Dept., Community Relations Service, 5550 Friendship Blvd., Chevy Chase, MD 20815; (301) 492-5929. Geoffrey Weiss, acting director. Press, (301) 492-5969. Fax, (301) 492-5984. Toll-free hotline, (800) 347-4283.

Assists local governments, law enforcement agencies, and communities responding to potentially violent racial/ethnic tension; provides conflict resolution services for violent or economically disruptive racial/ethnic confrontations. Operates a toll-free hotline for reporting incidences of discrimination based on race, gender, sexual orientation, national origin, or religious preference.

Justice Dept., Justice Assistance, 633 Indiana Ave. N.W. 20531; 514-6278. Nancy Gist, director. Fax, 514-5956.

Provides funds to eligible state and local governments and to nonprofit organizations for criminal justice programs, primarily those that combat drug trafficking and other drug-related crime.

National Institute of Standards and Technology (Commerce Dept.), Law Enforcement Standards Laboratory, Route I-270 and Quince Orchard Rd., Gaithersburg, MD (mailing address: Bldg. 225, #A323, Gaithersburg, MD 20899); (301) 975-2757. Daniel Frank, acting director. Fax, (301) 948-0978.

Answers inquiries and makes referrals concerning methods of testing and development of law enforcement equipment; maintains information on equipment standards and current research; prepares reports and formulates standards for the National Institute of Justice and the National Highway Traffic Safety Administration.

Treasury Dept., Financial Crimes Enforcement Network, 2070 Chain Bridge Rd., Vienna, VA 22182; (703) 905-3591. Julius McGruder, acting director. Fax, (703) 905-3690.

Administers information network to aid federal, state, local, and foreign law enforcement agencies in the detection, investigation, and prosecution of money-laundering operations and other financial crimes.

U.S. Marshals Service (Justice Dept.), 600 Army-Navy Dr., Arlington, VA 22202; 307-9001. Eduardo Gonzalez, director. Information, 307-9065. Fax, (703) 557-9783.

Provides the federal judiciary system and the attorney general with support services, primarily in fugitive apprehension, court and witness security, prisoner custody and transportation, prisoner support, maintenance and disposal of seized and forfeited property, and special operations. Administers the Federal Witness Protection program.

Congress:

House Judiciary Committee, Subcommittee on Civil and Constitutional Rights, 806 O'Neill Bldg. (300 New Jersey Ave. S.E.) 20515; 226-7680. Don Edwards, D-Calif., chairman; Catherine A. LeRoy, chief counsel.

Jurisdiction over legislation dealing with the use, collection, evaluation, and release of criminal justice data. Oversight of legislation on information policy, electronic privacy, computer security, and trade and licensing.

House Judiciary Committee, Subcommittee on Crime and Criminal Justice, 362 Ford Bldg. (2nd and D Sts. S.W.) 20515; 226-2406. Charles E. Schumer, D-N.Y., chairman; David Yassky, counsel.

Jurisdiction over legislation related to Office of Justice Programs, which includes the Bureau of Justice Assistance, Bureau of Justice Statistics, National Institute of Justice, Office of Juvenile Justice and Delinquency Prevention, and the Office for Victims of Crime.

Office of Technology Assessment, Biological Applications Program, 600 Pennsylvania Ave. S.E., #354 20003; 228-6670. Michael Gough, manager. Fax, 228-6293.

Conducts studies for Congress on applications of biological research, including forensic use of DNA technology.

Senate Judiciary Committee, SD-224 20510; 224-5225. Joseph R. Biden Jr., D-Del., chairman; Cynthia Hogan, chief counsel.

Jurisdiction over legislation related to Office of Justice Programs, which includes the Bureau of Justice Assistance, Bureau of Justice Statistics, National Institute of Justice, Office of Juvenile Justice and Delinquency Prevention, and the Office for Victims of Crime.

Senate Judiciary Committee, Subcommittee on Technology and the Law, SH-815 20510; 224-3406. Patrick J. Leahy, D-Vt., chairman; Bruce A. Cohen, chief counsel.

Jurisdiction over legislation dealing with the use, collection, evaluation, and release of criminal justice data. Oversight of legislation on information policy, electronic privacy, computer security, and trade and licensing.

Nongovernmental:

American Federation of Police, 1000 Connecticut Ave. N.W., #9 20036; 293-9088. Gerald S. Arenberg, director, Washington office.

Membership: governmental and private law enforcement officers. Provides members with insurance benefits and training programs.

International Assn. of Chiefs of Police, 515 N. Washington St., Alexandria, VA 22314-2357; (703) 836-6767. Daniel N. Rosenblatt, executive director.

Membership: foreign and U.S. police executives and administrators. Consults and conducts research on all aspects of police activity; conducts training programs and develops educational aids; conducts public education programs.

Law Enforcement Alliance of America, 7700 Leesburg Pike, #421, Falls Church, VA 22043; (703) 847-2677. Jim Fotis, executive director. Fax, (703) 556-6485.

Membership: law enforcement professionals, citizens, and victims of crime. Advocacy group on law and order issues.

National Assn. of Chiefs of Police, 1000 Connecticut Ave. N.W., #9 20036; 293-9088. Dennis Martin, president.

Membership: U.S. chiefs of police and supervisory command rank officers. Conducts educational and in-service training programs; conducts research.

National Criminal Justice Assn., 444 N. Capitol St. N.W., #618 20001; 347-4900. Gwen A. Holden, executive vice president. Fax, 508-3859.
Membership: criminal justice organizations and professionals. Provides members and interested individuals with technical assistance and information.

National Law Enforcement Council, 888 16th St. N.W., #600 20006; 835-8020. Donald Baldwin, executive director. Fax, 331-4291.
Membership: national law enforcement organizations. Fosters information exchange and explores the effects of public policy on law enforcement.

National Organization of Black Law Enforcement Executives, 4609 Pine Crest Office Park Dr., 2nd Floor, Alexandria, VA 22312; (703) 658-1529. Joseph Wright, executive director. Fax, (703) 658-9479.
Membership: minority police chiefs and senior law enforcement executives. Works to increase community involvement in the criminal justice system and to enhance the role of minorities in law enforcement. Provides urban police departments with assistance in police operations, community relations, and devising strategies to combat urban and hate crimes.

National Sheriffs' Assn., 1450 Duke St., Alexandria, VA 22314; (703) 836-7827. Charles "Bud" Meeks, executive director. Fax, (703) 683-6541.
Membership: sheriffs and other municipal, state, and federal law enforcement officers. Conducts research and training programs for members in law enforcement, court procedures, and corrections.

Police Executive Research Forum, 2300 M St. N.W., #910 20037; 466-7820. Chuck Wexler, executive director. Fax, 466-7826.
Membership: law enforcement executives from moderate to large police departments. Conducts research on law enforcement issues and methods of disseminating criminal justice and law enforcement information.

Police Foundation, 1001 22nd St. N.W. 20037; 833-1460. Hubert Williams, president. Fax, 659-9149.
Research and education foundation that conducts studies to improve police procedures; provides technical assistance for innovative law enforcement strategies, including community-oriented policing.

Crime Data and Research

Agencies:

Federal Bureau of Investigation (Justice Dept.), Criminal Justice Information Services, 10th St. and Pennsylvania Ave. N.W. 20535; 324-8901. Steven L. Pomerantz, assistant director. Fax, 324-8906.
Computerized information system on wanted criminals, persons named in arrest warrants, runaways, and stolen property (including cars). Information available to federal, state, and local law enforcement authorities only. Provides telecommunications support for the Interstate Identification Index File, which lists databases for criminal histories and records throughout the country and is maintained by the FBI Identification Division.

Federal Bureau of Investigation (Justice Dept.), Uniform Crime Reporting, 7th and D Sts. N.W. 20535; 324-2614. J. Harper Wilson, chief. Information, 324-5015. Fax, 324-6495.
Compiles data in eight major crime categories: arson, forcible rape, robbery, aggravated assault, larceny-theft, motor vehicle theft, burglary, and murder. Publishes *Crime in the United States* annually.

Justice Dept., Justice Statistics, 633 Indiana Ave. N.W. 20531; 307-0765. Jan Chaiken, director designate. Fax, 307-5846.
Collects, evaluates, publishes, and provides statistics on criminal justice. Data available from the National Criminal Justice Reference Service, P.O. Box 6000, Rockville, Md. 20857; toll-free, (800) 732-3277; in Maryland, (301) 251-5500.

National Institute of Justice (Justice Dept.), 633 Indiana Ave. N.W. 20531; 307-2942. Jeremy Travis, director designate. Fax, 307-6394.
Conducts research on all aspects of criminal justice, including crime prevention, enforcement, adjudication, and corrections; evaluates criminal justice programs; develops model programs using new techniques. Maintains the National Criminal Justice Reference Service, which provides information on criminal justice research, including information on AIDS issues for law enforcement officials: toll-free, (800) 851-3420; in Maryland, (301) 251-5500.

Congress:

See *Law Enforcement, General, Congress* (p. 518)

Judiciary:

Administrative Office of the U.S. Courts, Statistics, 1 Columbus Circle N.E. 20544; 273-2240. Steven R. Schlesinger, chief. Fax, 273-2247.
Compiles information and statistics from civil, criminal, appeals, and bankruptcy cases. Publishes statistical reports on court management; juror utilization; federal offenders; equal access to justice; the Financial Privacy Act; caseloads of federal, public, and community defenders; and types of cases adjudicated.

Nongovernmental:

Center for Criminal Justice Studies, 309 Massachusetts Ave. N.E. 20002; 547-8191. Elizabeth Langston, executive director. Fax, 547-8190.
Conducts research, seminars, and conferences on criminal justice and law enforcement. Serves as a clearinghouse for research and information on criminal justice and law enforcement.

Justice Research and Statistics Assn., 444 N. Capitol St. N.W., #445 20001-1512; 624-8560. Joan C. Weiss, executive director. Fax, 624-5269.
Provides information on the collection, analysis, dissemination, and use of data concerning crime and criminal justice at the state level; serves as liaison between the Justice Dept. Bureau of Justice Statistics and the states; develops standards for states on the collection, analysis, and use of statistics.

See also *Institute of Criminal Law and Procedure (p. 508); International Assn. of Chiefs of Police (p. 518)*

Legal Services and Education

General

Agencies:

Legal Services Corp., 750 1st St. N.W., 10th Floor 20002; 336-8800. John P. O'Hara, president. Library, 336-8804. Fax, 336-8959.
Independent federal corporation established by Congress. Awards grants to local agencies that provide the poor with legal services. Library open to the public.

Congress:

House Government Operations Committee, Subcommittee on Information, Justice, Transportation, and Agriculture, B349C RHOB 20515; 225-3741. Gary Condit, D-Calif., chairman; Shannon Lahey, acting staff director. Fax, 225-2445.
Oversees operations of the Legal Services Corp.

House Judiciary Committee, Subcommittee on Administrative Law and Governmental Relations, B351A RHOB 20515; 225-5741. John Bryant, D-Texas, chairman; Paul J. Drolet, chief counsel.
Jurisdiction over legislation on the Legal Services Corp.

Senate Labor and Human Resources Committee, SD-428 20510; 224-5375. Edward M. Kennedy, D-Mass., chairman; Nick Littlefield, chief counsel and staff director.
Legislative and oversight jurisdiction over operations of the Legal Services Corp.

Senate Special Committee on Aging, SD-G31 20510; 224-5364. David Pryor, D-Ark., chairman; Theresa M. Forster, staff director.
Conducts studies and makes recommendations on provision of adequate legal services to the elderly.

Nongovernmental:

American Bar Assn., Dispute Resolution, 1800 M St. N.W. 20036; 331-2661. Larry Ray, director. Fax, 331-2220.
Acts as a clearinghouse on dispute resolution; supports methods for resolving disputes other than litigation; provides technical assistance.

American Blind Lawyers Assn., 1155 15th St. N.W. 20005; 467-5081. Dave Adams, president. Fax, 467-5085.
Membership: blind lawyers and law students. Provides members with legal information; acts as an information clearinghouse on legal materials available in Braille, in large print, and on tape. (Affiliated with American Council of the Blind.)

American Inns of Court Foundation, 127 S. Peyton St., #201, Alexandria, VA 22314; (703)

684-3590. Don Stumbaugh, executive director. Fax, (703) 684-3607.

Promotes professionalism, ethics, civility, and legal skills of judges, lawyers, academicians, and law students in order to improve the quality and efficiency of the justice system.

Americans for the Restitution and Righting of Old Wrongs (ARROW), 1000 Connecticut Ave. N.W. 20036; 296-0685. E. Thomas Colosimo, executive director.

Helps train nonlawyer native American court clerks, administrators, law enforcement officers, and social workers to improve the tribal system of law, order, and justice; publishes training materials for tribal court officers. Provides program and financial management support for training of native American court officers.

Center for Dispute Settlement, 1666 Connecticut Ave. N.W. 20009; 265-9572. Linda R. Singer, executive director. Fax, 328-9162.

Designs, implements, and evaluates alternative and nonjudicial methods of dispute resolution; mediates disputes; provides training in dispute resolution

Center for Law and Education, 1875 Connecticut Ave. N.W., #510 20009-5728; 986-3000. Paul Weckstein, co-director. Fax, 986-6648.

Assists local legal services programs in matters concerning education, civil rights, and provision of legal services to low-income persons; litigates some cases for low-income individuals. (Headquarters in Cambridge, Mass.)

Center for Law and Social Policy, 1616 P St. N.W., #150 20036; 328-5140. Alan W. Houseman, director. Fax, 328-5195.

Public interest law firm that represents low-income citizens in cases involving family policy issues, including child support, child care, education, employment and training, minimum wage laws, health care, and public benefits. Represents local legal services programs before the Legal Services Corp., Congress, and the courts.

Consumers Union of the United States, 1666 Connecticut Ave. N.W., #310 20009-1039; 462-6262. Mark Silbergeld, director, Washington office. Fax, 265-9548.

Represents consumer interests before Congress and regulatory agencies; litigates consumer affairs cases involving government agencies. (Headquarters in Yonkers, N.Y.)

Help Abolish Legal Tyranny—An Organization of Americans for Legal Reform (HALT-ALR), 1319 F St. N.W. 20004; 347-9600. William Fry, executive director. Fax, 347-9606.

Public interest organization concerned with legal reform. Conducts research on alternative dispute resolution programs for delivery of legal services, including arbitration, legal clinics, and mediation services; provides educational and self-help manuals on the use of the legal system. Operates The Law Store, a legal document preparation service created to research, test, and promote innovative techniques for improving access to legal services for the average citizen.

Institute for Justice, 1001 Pennsylvania Ave. N.W., #200S 20004-2505; 457-4240. Chip Mellor, president. Fax, 457-8574.

Sponsors seminars to train law students, grassroots activists, and practicing lawyers in applying advocacy strategies in public interest litigation. Seeks to protect from arbitrary government interference free speech, private property rights, parental school choice, and economic liberty. Litigates cases.

Institute for Public Representation, Georgetown University Law Center, 600 New Jersey Ave. N.W. 20001; 662-9535. Douglas L. Parker, director. Fax, 662-9634.

Public interest law firm funded by Georgetown University Law Center. Studies federal administrative law and federal court litigation. Interests include consumer protection, civil rights, women's issues, court reform, immigration and refugee policy, communications law, freedom of information, environmental protection, and corporate responsibility.

International Trade Commission Trial Lawyers Assn., 601 13th St. N.W., #500N 20005; 783-5070. Arthur Wineburg, president. Fax, 783-2331.

Disseminates information relating to practice before the International Trade Commission. Monitors and comments on proposed legislation on trade and intellectual property issues.

Lawyers' Committee for Civil Rights Under Law, 1450 G St. N.W., #450 20005; 662-8600. Barbara Arnwine, executive director. Fax, 783-0857.

Provides minority groups and the poor with legal assistance in such areas as voting rights, employment discrimination, education, environment, and equal access to government services and benefits.

Mexican American Legal Defense and Educational Fund, 733 15th St. N.W., #920 20005; 628-4074. Mario Moreno, regional counsel, Washington office. Fax, 393-4206.

Provides Mexican-Americans and other Hispanics with legal assistance in such areas as equal employment, voting rights, bilingual education, and immigration; awards scholarships to Hispanic law students; monitors legislation and regulations. (Headquarters in Los Angeles.)

Migrant Legal Action Program, 2001 S St. N.W. 20009; 462-7744. Roger C. Rosenthal, executive director.

Funded by the Legal Services Corp. Provides support and assistance to local legal services cofunded groups and other organizations and private attorneys with migrant farmworker clients; monitors legislation and federal regulations.

National Court Reporters Assn., 8224 Old Courthouse Rd., Vienna, VA 22182; (703) 556-6272. Brian E. Cartier, executive director. Fax, (703) 556-6291. TDD, (703) 556-6289.

Membership organization that certifies and offers continuing education for court reporters. Acts as a clearinghouse on technology and information for and about court reporters.

National Health Law Program, 1815 H St. N.W., #705 20006; 887-5310. Stan Dorm, managing attorney, Washington office. Fax, 785-6792.

Organization of lawyers representing the economically disadvantaged, minorities, and the elderly in issues concerning federal, state, and local health care programs. Offers technical assistance and training for health law specialists. (Headquarters in Los Angeles.)

National Institute for Citizen Education in the Law, 711 G St. S.E. 20003-2861; 546-6644. Jason Newman and Edward O'Brien, co-directors. Fax, 546-6649. TDD, 546-7591.

Educational organization that promotes public understanding of the law and the legal system, particularly through citizen participation. Provides information, curriculum materials, training, and technical assistance to public and private school systems at elementary and secondary levels, law schools, departments of corrections, local juvenile justice systems, bar associations, community groups, and state and local governments interested in establishing law-related education programs, including mediation. Administers programs for students with disabilities.

National Institute for Dispute Resolution, 1901 L St. N.W., #600 20036; 466-4764. Margery F. Baker, president. Fax, 466-4769.

Promotes the development of fair, effective, and efficient conflict resolution processes; fosters the use of such processes and programs in new arenas locally, nationally, and internationally; stimulates innovative approaches to the resolution of future conflict. Provides information and technical assistance regarding the use of dispute resolution processes.

National Legal Aid and Defender Assn., 1625 K St. N.W., #800 20006; 452-0620. Clinton Lyons, executive director. Fax, 872-1031.

Membership: local organizations and individuals providing indigent clients, including prisoners, with legal aid and defender services. Serves as a clearinghouse for member organizations; publishes directory of legal aid and defender programs.

National Resource Center for Consumers of Legal Services, 1444 Eye St. N.W., 8th Floor 20005; 842-3503. Thomas Chiancone, assistant director. Fax, 842-4354.

Promotes the development of prepaid and group legal services plans; gives technical assistance to lawyers, benefits counselors, labor unions, cooperatives, and other consumer groups establishing such plans; maintains information clearinghouse of existing plans, educational materials, and research studies of legal services.

National Senior Citizens Law Center, 1815 H St. N.W. 20006; 887-5280. Burton D. Fretz, executive director. Fax, 785-6792.

Organization funded by the Legal Services Corp. Litigates on behalf of legal services programs and elderly poor clients and client groups. Represents clients before Congress and federal departments and agencies. Interests include Social Security and Supplemental Security Income, Medicare, Medicaid, nursing home residents' rights, home health care, public and private pensions, and protective services.

Native American Rights Fund, 1712 N St. N.W. 20036; 785-4166. Richard Dauphinais, directing attorney, Washington office. Fax, 822-0068.

Provides native Americans and Alaskan natives with legal assistance in land claims, water rights, hunting, and other areas. (Headquarters in Boulder.)

Public Citizen Litigation Group, 2000 P St. N.W. 20036; 833-3000. David Vladeck, director.

Conducts litigation for Public Citizen, a citizens' interest group, in the areas of consumer rights, employee rights, health and safety, government and corporate accountability, and separation of powers; represents other individuals and citizens' groups with similar interests.

Women's Legal Defense Fund, 1875 Connecticut Ave. N.W., #710 20009-5728; 986-2600. Judith Lichtman, president. Fax, 986-2539.

Advocacy organization that advances legal rights of women, primarily in the areas of employment and family law; provides technical expertise; litigates selected cases.

See also American Civil Liberties Union (p. 502); National Law Center on Homelessness and Poverty (p. 427); National Women's Law Center (p. 271); Public Law Education Institute (p. 584); Trial Lawyers for Public Justice (p. 251)

Professional Education

Agencies:

Justice Dept., Legal Education and Continuing Professional Growth, 601 D St. N.W. 20530; 501-7467. Donna Bucella, director. Fax, 208-7235.

Designs and implements continuing legal education programs for attorneys in all federal departments and agencies. Attorney General's Advocacy Institute trains Justice Dept. lawyers, including those who work for U.S. Attorney offices nationwide. Legal Education Institute provides attorneys in other agencies with advocacy training.

Nongovernmental:

American Prosecutors Research Institute, National Drug Prosecution Center, 99 Canal Center Plaza, #510, Alexandria, VA 22314; (703) 549-6790. Jennifer Panagopoulos, chief administrator. Fax, (703) 836-3195.

Trains prosecutors to investigate and prosecute drug cases; develops legislation to revise drug laws. Established by a grant from the Justice Dept.

Assn. of American Law Schools, 1201 Connecticut Ave. N.W., #800 20036; 296-8851. Carl C. Monk, executive director. Fax, 296-8869.

Membership: schools of law, subject to approval by association. Represents member organizations before federal government and private agencies; evaluates member institutions; conducts workshops on the teaching of law; assists law schools with faculty recruitment; publishes faculty placement bulletin and annual directory of law teachers.

Council on Legal Education Opportunity, 1800 M St. N.W., #160 South 20036; 785-4840. Irshad Abdal-Haqq, executive director. Fax, 223-5633.

Helps economically and educationally disadvantaged students attend law schools; conducts summer programs to prepare students for law school.

National Consumer Law Center, 1875 Connecticut Ave. N.W., #510 20009-5728; 986-6060. Margot Saunders, managing attorney. Fax, 986-6648.

Provides lawyers funded by the Legal Services Corp. with research and assistance; provides lawyers with training in consumer and energy law. (Headquarters in Boston.)

See also Federal Bar Assn. (p. 493); Mexican American Legal Defense and Educational Fund (p. 522); National Bar Assn. (p. 496); National Institute for Citizen Education in the Law (p. 522)

Research and Information

Congress:

Library of Congress, Law Library, 101 Independence Ave. S.E. 20540; 707-5065. M. Kathleen Price, law librarian. Fax, 707-1820. Reading room, 707-5080.

Maintains collections of foreign, international, and comparative law organized jurisdictionally by country; covers all legal systems—common law, civil law, Roman law, canon law, religious law, and ancient and medieval law. Services include a public reading room; a microtext facility with microfilm readers, reader-printers, microfiche readers, an opaque card reader, and coin-operated copying machines; and five foreign law/rare book reading areas. Staff of legal specialists does not provide advice on legal matters.

Judiciary:

Administrative Office of the U.S. Courts, 1 Columbus Circle N.E. 20544; 273-3000. L. Ralph Mecham, director. Information, 273-1120. Library, 273-1888. Fax, 273-3011.

Supervises all administrative matters of the federal court system, except the Supreme Court; prepares statistics and reports on the business of the courts, including reports on juror utilization, caseloads of federal, public, and community defenders, and types of cases adjudicated.

Supreme Court of the United States, Library, 1 1st N.E. 20543; 479-3037. Shelley L. Dowling, librarian.

Maintains collection of Supreme Court documents dating from the mid-1800s. Records, briefs, and documents available for public use.

See also Federal Judicial Center (p. 491)

Nongovernmental:

National Consumer Law Center, 1875 Connecticut Ave. N.W., #510 20009-5728; 986-6060. Margot Saunders, managing attorney. Fax, 986-6648.

Provides lawyers funded by the Legal Services Corp. with research and assistance; researches problems of low-income consumers and develops alternative solutions. (Headquarters in Boston.)

National District Attorneys' Assn., American Prosecutors Research Institute, 99 Canal Center Plaza, #510, Alexandria, VA 22314; (703) 549-4253. Jennifer Panagopoulos, deputy director. Fax, (703) 836-3195.

Conducts research, provides prosecutors and others interested in criminal law with information, and analyzes policies related to improvements in criminal prosecution.

See also American Bar Assn. and Federal Bar Assn. (p. 493); HALT-ALR (p. 493); National Resource Center for Consumers of Legal Services (p. 522)

Key Agencies:

Defense Dept.
The Pentagon 20301
Information: (703) 697-5737

**U.S. Arms Control and Disarmament
Agency**
Main State Bldg.
2201 C St. N.W.
(Mailing address: 320 21st St. N.W. 20451)
Information: 647-4800

Key Committees:

House Armed Services Committee
2120 RHOB 20515
Phone: 225-4151

Senate Armed Services Committee
SR-228 20510
Phone: 224-3871

Key Personnel:

Defense Dept.
William Perry, secretary
John M. Deutch, deputy secretary
Paul Kaminski, under secretary designate
for acquisition and technology
Edwin Dorn, under secretary for personnel
and readiness
Frank G. Wisner, under secretary for policy
Lt. Gen. Emmett Paige Jr., assistant secre-
tary for command, control, communica-
tions, and intelligence
Joshua Gotbaum, assistant secretary for
economic security

Dr. Stephen Joseph, assistant secretary for
health affairs

Sandra Stuart, assistant secretary for legislative affairs

Ashton B. Carter, assistant secretary for
nuclear security and counter-proliferation

Charles W. Freeman Jr., assistant secretary
for regional security affairs

Deborah Lee, assistant secretary for reserve
affairs

H. Allen Holmes, assistant secretary for
special operations and low intensity
conflict

Edward L. Warner III, assistant secretary
for strategy, requirements, and resources

Anita K. Jones, director, research and
engineering

Sheila E. Widnall, secretary of the Air Force

Togo D. West Jr., secretary of the Army

John Dalton, secretary of the Navy

Gen. John M. Shalikashvili (USA), chairman,
Joint Chiefs of Staff

Gen. Merrill A. McPeak, chief of staff, Air
Force

Gen. Gordon Sullivan, chief of staff, Army

Gen. Carl E. Mundy Jr., commandant of the
Marine Corps

Adm. Jeremy Michael Boorda, chief of naval operations

Lt. Gen. James R. Clapper Jr. (USAF),
director, Defense Intelligence Agency

**U.S. Arms Control and Disarmament
Agency**
John D. Holum, director

13

National Security

Contents:

Defense Policy

See also International Law and Agreements, Regional Security Agreements (p. 478)

General

Agencies:

Air Force Dept. (Defense Dept.), The Pentagon 20330-1670; (703) 697-7376. Sheila E. Widnall, secretary. Information: Operations, (703) 695-5554; Readiness and Support, (703) 695-0640; Strategic and Space, (703) 695-5766; Tactical and Airlift, (703) 695-9664.
Civilian office that develops and reviews Air Force national security policies in conjunction with the chief of staff of the Air Force and the secretary of defense.

Air Force Dept. (Defense Dept.), The Pentagon 20330-1670; (703) 697-9225. Gen. Merrill A. McPeak, chief of staff. Fax, (703) 693-9297.

Military office that develops and directs Air Force national security policies in conjunction with the secretary of the Air Force and the secretary of defense.

Army Dept. (Defense Dept.), The Pentagon 20310-0101; (703) 695-3211. Togo D. West Jr., secretary. Press, (703) 697-7550. Fax, (703) 697-8036.

Civilian office that develops and reviews Army national security policies in conjunction with the chief of staff of the Army and the secretary of defense.

Army Dept. (Defense Dept.), The Pentagon 20310-0200; (703) 695-2077. Gen. Gordon Sullivan, chief of staff. Information, (703) 614-0741. Press, (703) 697-7589. Fax, (703) 695-9439.

Military office that develops and administers Army national security policies in conjunction with the secretary of the Army and the secretary of defense.

Defense Dept., The Pentagon 20301-1000; (703) 695-5261. William Perry, secretary. Information, (703) 697-5737. Press, (703) 695-0192 (defense news); (703) 697-5131 (armed forces news); (703) 695-3324 (tours).

Civilian office that develops national security policies and has overall responsibility for administering national defense; responds to public and congressional inquiries about national defense matters.

Defense Dept., Environmental Security, 400 Army-Navy Dr., Arlington VA 20301; (703) 695-6639. Sherri Wasserman Goodman, deputy under secretary.

Integrates environmental, safety, and occupational health considerations into U.S. defense and economic policies. Works to ensure responsible performance in defense operations, to maintain quality installations, to reduce the costs of complying with environmental laws, and to clean up past contamination.

Defense Dept., Joint Chiefs of Staff, The Pentagon 20318; (703) 697-9121. Gen. John M. Shalikashvili (USA), chairman; Vice Adm. Richard Macke (USN), joint staff director, (703) 614-5221. Information, (703) 697-4272. Fax, (703) 697-8758.

Joint military staff office that assists the president, the National Security Council, and the secretary of defense in developing national security policy and in coordinating operations of the individual armed services.

Defense Dept., Policy, The Pentagon 20301-2000; (703) 697-7200. Frank G. Wisner, under secretary.

Civilian office responsible for policy matters relating to international security issues and political military affairs. Oversees such areas as arms control, foreign military sales, intelligence collection and analysis, and NATO and regional security affairs.

Defense Dept., Special Operations and Low Intensity Conflict, The Pentagon, Rm. 2E258 20301; (703) 693-2895. H. Allen Holmes, assistant secretary. Fax, (703) 693-6335.

Serves as special staff assistant and civilian adviser to the defense secretary on matters related to special operations and low intensity conflict. Responsible for the Army's Green Berets, the Navy Seals, and other special operation forces.

Defense Dept., Strategy, Requirements, and Resources, The Pentagon 20301; (703) 697-7728. Edward L. Warner III, assistant secretary.

Develops and coordinates national security strategy and defense strategy and advises on the resources, forces, and contingency plans necessary to implement those strategies. Ensures the integration of defense strategy into the department's resource allocation, force structure development, weapons system acquisition, and budgetary processes. Evaluates the capability of forces to accomplish defense strategy.

Marine Corps (Defense Dept.), Navy Annex, Arlington, VA (mailing address: Headquarters, U.S. Marine Corps, Washington, DC 20380); (703) 614-2500. Gen. Carl E. Mundy Jr., commandant. Information, (703) 614-8010. Press, (703) 614-1492. Fax, (703) 697-7246.

Military office that develops and directs Marine Corps national security policies in conjunction with the secretary of defense and the secretary of the Navy.

Navy Dept. (Defense Dept.), The Pentagon 20350-1000; (703) 695-3131. John Dalton, secretary. Information, (703) 695-0965. Press, (703) 697-5342. Fax, (703) 614-3477.

Civilian office that develops and reviews Navy and Marine Corps national security policies in conjunction with the chief of naval operations, the commandant of the Marine Corps, and the secretary of defense.

Navy Dept. (Defense Dept.), NO9B30, #3, 521-Pentagon 20350-2000; (703) 695-6007. Adm. Jeremy Michael Boorda, chief of naval operations. Information, (703) 695-0965. Press, (703) 697-5342. Fax, (703) 697-6290.

Military office that develops Navy national security policies in conjunction with the secretary of defense and the secretary of the Navy and in cooperation with the commandant of the Marine Corps.

State Dept., Politico-Military Affairs, Main State Bldg., Rm. 7325A 20520; 647-9022. Robert L. Gallucci, assistant secretary. Fax, 647-1346.

Responsible for security affairs policy; acts as a liaison between the Defense Dept. and the State Dept.

U.S. Coast Guard (Transportation Dept.), Strategic Planning, 2100 2nd St. S.W. 20593-0001;

Defense Dept.

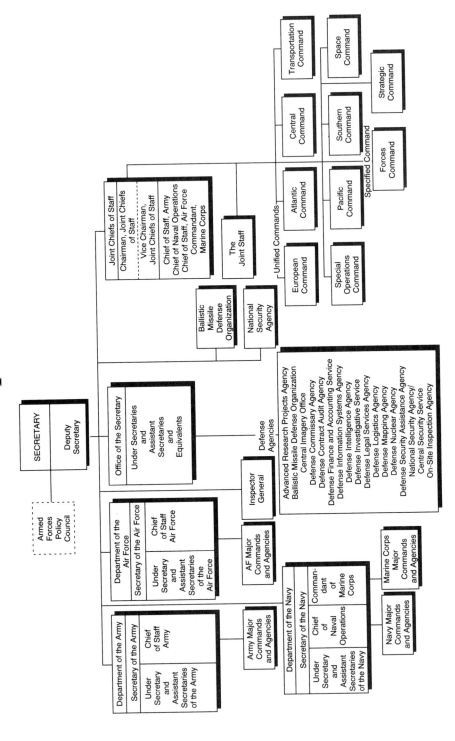

267-2690. Capt. James T. Doherty, chief. Fax, 267-6813.

Makes five-to-fifteen-year projections on trends in politics, economics, sociology, technology, and society, and how those trends will affect the Coast Guard.

U.S. Institute of Peace, 1550 M St. N.W., #700 20005; 457-1700. Richard H. Solomon, president. Fax, 429-6063.

Independent organization created and funded by Congress to promote the peaceful resolution of international conflict through negotiation and mediation. Provides federal agencies and individuals with training, research programs, and information. Awards grants to institutions and individuals and provides fellowships to scholars from the United States and abroad. Library open to the public by appointment.

Congress:

House Appropriations Committee, Subcommittee on Defense, H144 CAP 20515; 225-2847. John P. Murtha, D-Pa., chairman; Donald E. Richbourg, senior staff assistant Fax, 225-7850.

Jurisdiction over legislation to appropriate funds for the Defense Dept. (excluding military construction, civil defense, and military assistance to foreign countries), the Central Intelligence Agency, and the intelligence community.

House Appropriations Committee, Subcommittee on Treasury, Postal Service, and General Government, H164 CAP 20515; 225-5834. Steny H. Hoyer, D-Md., chairman; Bill Smith, staff assistant. Fax, 426-3763.

Jurisdiction over legislation to appropriate funds for the Executive Office of the President, including the National Security Council.

House Armed Services Committee, 2120 RHOB 20515; 225-4151. Ronald V. Dellums, D-Calif., chairman; Marilyn A. Elrod, staff director.

Jurisdiction over defense legislation. Oversight of the Defense Dept., including the Army, Navy, and Air Force departments.

Senate Appropriations Committee, Subcommittee on Defense, SD-119 20510; 224-7255. Daniel K. Inouye, D-Hawaii, chairman; Richard L. Collins, clerk.

Jurisdiction over legislation to appropriate funds for the Defense Dept. (excluding military

construction, family housing, civil defense, nuclear materials, and military assistance to foreign countries), the Central Intelligence Agency, and the intelligence community.

Senate Armed Services Committee, SR-228 20510; 224-3871. Sam Nunn, D-Ga., chairman; Arnold Punaro, staff director.

Jurisdiction over defense legislation. Oversight of the Defense Dept., including the Army, Navy, and Air Force departments.

Senate Armed Services Committee, Subcommittee on Coalition Defense and Reinforcing Forces, SR-228 20510; 224-3871. Carl Levin, D-Mich., chairman; John Hamre, professional staff member.

Jurisdiction over legislation concerning NATO and East Asia defenses, cooperation with allies, defense modeling and simulation, equipment requirements and programs for reserve forces, and to the extent not covered by the full committee, issues of peacekeeping and peace enforcement.

Senate Armed Services Committee, Subcommittee on Regional Defense and Contingency Forces, SR-228 20510; 224-3871. Edward M. Kennedy, D-Mass., chairman; Creighton Greene, professional staff member.

Jurisdiction over legislation concerning Southwest Asia defenses and defense-related programs of the U.S. Coast Guard. Oversees policy aspects of security assistance programs and the Defense Security Assistance Agency; oversees the Military Sealift Command, Military Traffic Management Command, and budget accounts for research, development, and procurement of airlift and sealift capability.

See also Army Caucus (p. 757); Congressional Military Reform Caucus (p. 756)

Nongovernmental

Air Force Assn., 1501 Lee Highway, Arlington, VA 22209; (703) 247-5800. Gen. Monroe W. Hatch Jr. (USAF, ret.), executive director. Press, (703) 247-5850. Fax, (703) 247-5853.

Membership: civilians and active, reserve, retired, and cadet personnel of the Air Force. Informs members and the public of developments in the aerospace field; monitors legislation and Defense Dept. policies. Library on aviation history open to the public by appointment.

Air Force Dept.

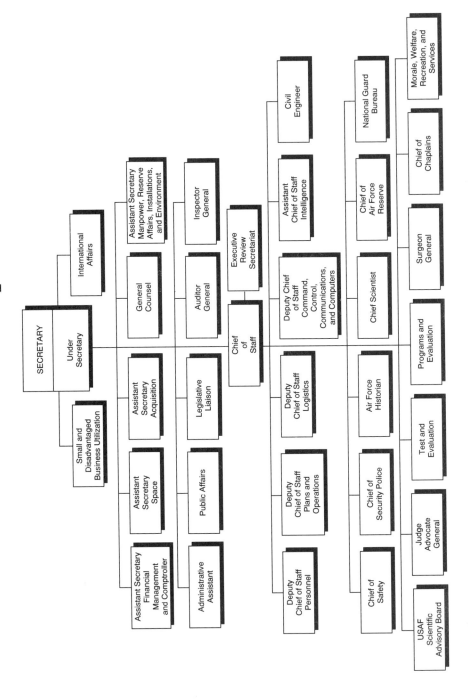

American Conservative Union, 38 Ivy St. S.E. 20003; 546-6555. Jeff Hollingsworth, executive director. Fax, 546-7370.

Legislative interest organization concerned with national defense policy, legislation related to nuclear weapons, U.S. strategic position vis-à-vis the former Soviet Union, missile defense programs, and U.S. strategic alliance commitments.

American Defense Institute, 1055 N. Fairfax St., 2nd Floor, Alexandria, VA 22314; (703) 519-7000. Capt. Eugene B. McDaniel (USN, ret.), president. Fax, (703) 519-8627.

Nonpartisan organization that advocates a strong national defense. Acts as an information clearinghouse on issues related to national security. Seeks to educate young Americans on matters of defense and foreign policy.

American Enterprise Institute for Public Policy Research, Foreign and Defense Policy Studies, 1150 17th St. N.W. 20036; 862-5814. Jeane Kirkpatrick, director. Press, 862-5829. Fax, 862-7178.

Research and educational organization that conducts conferences, seminars, and debates and sponsors research on national security, defense policy, and arms control.

American Security Council, 1155 15th St. N.W., #1101 20005-2706; 296-9500. Gregg Hilton, executive director. Fax, 296-9547.

Bipartisan, prodefense organization that advocates continuation of the strategic modernization program and stable funding for the space program, new technologies, and conventional forces. Monitors legislation and conducts educational activities. (Headquarters in Ballston, Va.)

Assn. of National Security Alumni, 2001 S St. N.W., #740 20009; 483-9325. David Mac-Michael, director, Washington office. Fax, 328-9702.

Research organization established by former members of the U.S. national security apparatus who oppose covert activity as a means of implementing U.S. foreign and domestic policies.

Assn. of the United States Army, 2425 Wilson Blvd., Arlington, VA 22201; (703) 841-4300. Gen. Jack Merritt (USA, ret.), president. Fax, (703) 525-9039.

Membership: civilians and active and retired members of the armed forces. Conducts symposia on defense issues and researches topics that affect the military.

Atlantic Council of the United States, 1616 H St. N.W. 20006; 347-9353. David C. Acheson, president. Fax, 737-5163.

Conducts studies and makes policy recommendations on American foreign security and international economic policies in the Atlantic and Pacific communities; sponsors conferences and educational exchanges.

The Brookings Institution, Foreign Policy Studies, 1775 Massachusetts Ave. N.W. 20036; 797-6010. John Steinbruner, director. Information, 797-6105. Fax, 797-6003. Publications, 797-6258.

Research and educational organization that focuses on major national security topics, including U.S. armed forces, weapons decisions, employment policies, and the security aspects of U.S. foreign relations.

Business Executives for National Security, 1615 L St. N.W., #330 20036, 296-2125. Robert W Gaskin, vice president. Fax, 296-2490.

Monitors legislation on national security issues from a business perspective; holds conferences, congressional forums, and other meetings on national security issues; works with other organizations on defense policy issues.

Center for Defense Information, 1500 Massachusetts Ave. N.W. 20005; 862-0700. Rear Adm. Eugene J. Carroll (USN, ret.), director. Fax, 862-0708.

Educational organization that advocates a strong defense while opposing excessive expenditures for weapons and policies that increase the risk of war. Interests include the defense budget, weapons systems, and troop levels. Provides Congress, the Pentagon, State Dept., media, and public with appraisals of military matters. Library open to the public.

Center for Naval Analyses, 4401 Ford Ave., Alexandria, VA 22302; (703) 824-2000. Robert J. Murray, president. Fax, (703) 824-2942.

Conducts research on weapons acquisitions, tactical problems, and naval operations.

Center for Security Policy, 1250 24th St. N.W., #300 20037; 466-0515. Frank J. Gaffney Jr., director. Fax, 466-0518.

Army Dept.

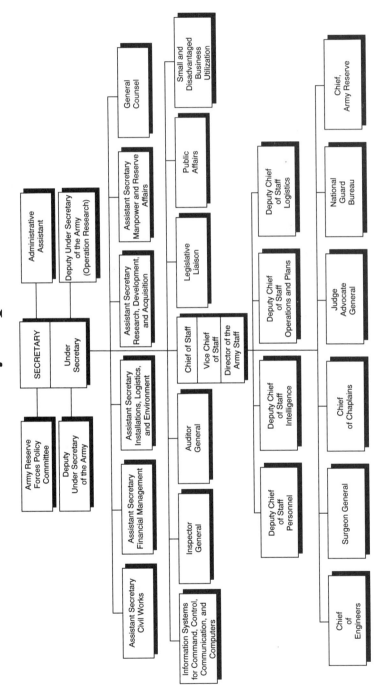

Educational institution concerned with U.S. defense and foreign policy. Interests include relations between the United States and the former Soviet Union, arms control compliance and verification policy, and technology transfer policy.

The Conservative Caucus, 450 Maple Ave. East, Vienna, VA 22180; (703) 938-9626. Howard Phillips, chairman.

Legislative interest organization that promotes grass-roots activity on national defense and foreign policy.

Defense Orientation Conference Assn., 9271 Old Keene Mill Rd., #200, Burke, VA 22015; (703) 451-1200. John W. Ohlsen, executive vice president.

Membership: citizens interested in national defense. Promotes continuing education of members on national security issues through tours of defense installations in the United States and abroad.

Ethics and Public Policy Center, Foreign Policy Program, 1015 15th St N.W., #900 20005; 682-1200. George S. Weigel Jr., president. Fax, 408-0632.

Conducts research and holds conferences on foreign policy, including role of the U.S. military abroad.

Henry L. Stimson Center, 21 Dupont Circle N.W., 5th Floor 20036; 223-5956. Michael Krepon, president. Fax, 785-9034. TDD, 296-3241.

Research and educational organization that studies arms control and international security, focusing on policy, technology, and politics.

Hudson Institute, 1015 18th St. N.W., #200 20036; 223-7774. Lt. Gen. William E. Odom (USA, ret.), director, national security studies. Fax, 223-8537.

Public policy research organization that conducts studies on U.S. overseas bases, U.S.-NATO relations, and missile defense programs. Focuses on long-range implications for U.S. national security. (Headquarters in Indianapolis.)

International Security Council, 2000 L St. N.W., #506 20036; 828-0802. Joseph Churba, president. Fax, 429-2563.

Educational organization that sponsors lectures and seminars on a wide variety of topics related to international security. Emphasizes the need for a strong U.S. defense and firm commitments between the United States and its allies.

Military Order of the World Wars, 435 N. Lee St., Alexandria, VA 22314; (703) 683-4911. Lt. Gen. H. R. Temple Jr. (USA, ret.), chief of staff. Fax, (703) 683-4501.

Membership: retired and active duty commissioned warrant officers and flight officers. Supports a strong national defense; supports patriotic education in schools; presents awards to outstanding Reserve Officers Training Corps (ROTC) cadets.

National Campaign for a Peace Tax Fund, 2121 Decatur Pl. N.W. 20008; 483-3751. Marian Franz, executive director. Fax, 986-0667.

Membership: individuals opposed to military spending. Supports legislation permitting taxpayers who are conscientiously opposed to military expenditures to have the military portion of their income tax money placed in a separate, nonmilitary fund.

Navy League of the United States, 2300 Wilson Blvd., Arlington, VA 22201; (703) 528-1775. Rear Adm. John Dalrymple (USN, ret.), executive director. Fax, (703) 528-2333.

Membership: retired and reserve military personnel and civilians interested in the U.S. Navy, Marine Corps, Coast Guard, and Merchant Marine. Distributes literature, provides speakers, and conducts seminars to promote interests of the sea services; monitors legislation.

Rand Corporation, 2100 M St. N.W. 20037; 296-5000. Charles R. Roll Jr., director, Washington operations. Fax, 296-7960.

Conducts research on national security issues, including political/military affairs of the former Soviet Union and U.S. strategic policy. (Headquarters in Santa Monica, Calif.)

U.S. Defense Committee, 3238 Wynford Dr., Fairfax, VA 22031; (703) 280-4226. Henry L. Walther, president.

Membership: individuals advocating a strong foreign policy and national defense. Opposes nuclear freeze proposals; supports missile defense programs; conducts research on U.S. policy in Central America; supports reductions in U.S. funding for the United Nations.

See also ACCESS (p. 446); Defense Budget Project (p. 540); George C. Marshall Institute (p. 666)

Navy Dept.

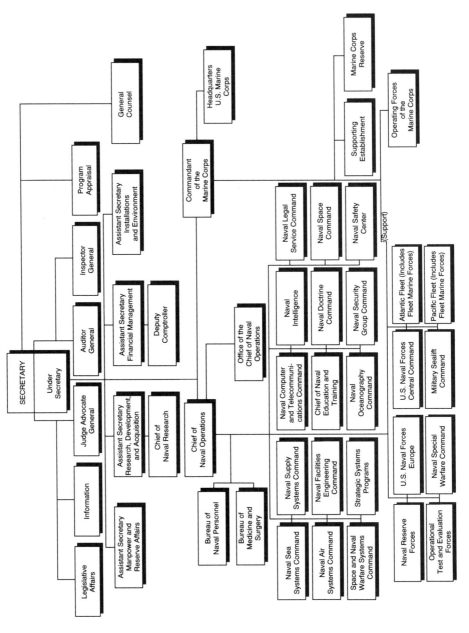

Arms Control and Disarmament

See also Defense Policy, General (p. 528); Export Controls (p. 545)

Agencies:

Defense Dept., Counter-Proliferation Policy, The Pentagon, Rm. 1E443 20301-2600; (703) 697-6963. Mitchel B. Wallerstein, deputy assistant secretary. Fax, (703) 693-7812.

Develops department policy concerning established arms control forums such as the Conference on Security and Cooperation in Europe (Helsinki commission).

Defense Dept., Nuclear Security and Counter-Proliferation, The Pentagon 20301-2600; (703) 695-0942. Ashton B. Carter, assistant secretary. Fax, (703) 693-9146.

Advises the secretary on reducing and countering nuclear, biological, chemical, and missile threats to the United States and its forces and allies; arms control negotiations, implementation, and verification policy; denuclearization, threat reduction, and nuclear safety, security, and dismantlement in the states of the former Soviet Union; and technology transfer.

Defense Dept., On-Site Inspection Agency, 300 W. Service Rd., Dulles International Airport, Chantilly, VA (mailing address: P.O. Box 17498, Washington, DC 20041-0498); (703) 742-4449. Brig. Gen. Gregory G. Govan (USA), director. Information, (703) 742-4326. Fax, (703) 742-4343.

Implements all activities associated with the inspection process of the Intermediate-range Nuclear Forces (INF) Treaty. Recruits, trains, and manages U.S. teams inspecting treaty-related facilities in Europe and the former Soviet Union; escorts inspectors from the former Soviet Union visiting U.S. facilities; plans inspection activities for proposed agreements, including Conventional Forces in Europe, Chemical Weapons, Strategic Arms Reductions Talks (START), and Nuclear Testing Talks. Provides support to U.N. Special Commission on Iraq.

State Dept., Strategic and Theater Policy, Main State Bldg., Rm. 7418 20520; 647-7775. Richard D. Sokolsky, director. Fax, 647-1346.

Develops policies related to nuclear and conventional arms control, strategic defenses, nuclear testing, and assistance to the former Soviet Union aimed toward eliminating weapons of mass destruction.

U.S. Arms Control and Disarmament Agency, Main State Bldg., 2201 C St. N.W. (mailing address: 320 21st St. N.W., Washington, DC 20451); 647-9610. John D. Holum, director. Information, 647-4800. Fax, 647-4920.

Advises the president and the secretary of state on arms control policy. Conducts and coordinates research for arms control policy formulation. Prepares for and manages U.S. participation in arms control negotiations; develops verification procedures for arms control agreements; disseminates information to the public.

Congress:

House Armed Services Committee, 2120 RHOB 20515; 225-4151. Ronald V. Dellums, D-Calif., chairman; Marilyn A. Elrod, staff director.

Oversight of international arms control and disarmament matters.

House Foreign Affairs Committee, Subcommittee on International Security, International Organizations, and Human Rights, B358 RHOB 20515; 226-7825. Tom Lantos, D-Calif., chairman; Bob King, staff director. Fax, 226-3581.

Jurisdiction over arms control, disarmament, and nuclear nonproliferation legislation. Oversight of the U.S. Arms Control and Disarmament Agency and State and Defense department activities involving arms transfers and arms sales.

Senate Armed Services Committee, Subcommittee on Nuclear Deterrence, Arms Control, and Defense Intelligence, SR-228 20510; 224-3871. Jim Exon, D-Neb., chairman; Bill E. Hoehn Jr., professional staff member.

Oversight of arms control and disarmament matters.

Senate Foreign Relations Committee, SD-446 20510; 224-4651. Claiborne Pell, D-R.I., chairman; Geryld B. Christianson, staff director. Fax, 224-5011.

Jurisdiction over arms control, disarmament, and nuclear nonproliferation legislation. (Jurisdiction shared with Senate Armed Services Committee.)

See also Arms Control and Foreign Policy Caucus (p. 755)

Nongovernmental:

Arms Control Assn., 1726 M St. N.W., #201 20036; 463-8270. Spurgeon M. Keeny Jr., executive director. Fax, 463-8273.

Nonpartisan organization interested in arms control. Seeks to broaden public interest in arms control, disarmament, and national security policy.

Center for Defense Information, 1500 Massachusetts Ave. N.W. 20005; 862-0700. Rear Adm. Eugene J. Carroll (USN, ret.), director. Fax, 862-0708.

Educational organization that advocates a strong defense while opposing excessive expenditure for weapons and policies that increase the risk of war. Interests include the defense budget, weapons systems, and troop levels. Library open to the public.

Chemical and Biological Arms Control Institute, 2111 Eisenhower Ave., #301, Alexandria, VA 22314; (703) 739-1033. Michael Moodie, president. Fax, (703) 739-1525.

Promotes arms control, nonproliferation, and the elimination of chemical, biological, and other weapons of mass destruction through research, analysis, technical support, and education.

Committee on American-Russian Relations, 201 Massachusetts Ave. N.E. 20002; 546-3960. Alfred Friendly Jr., president. Fax, 546-5947.

Membership: individuals and organizations interested in U.S.-Russian relations. Seeks to strengthen public understanding of political and economic developments in Russia and of diplomatic and arms control initiatives. Supports democratic institutions and the development of a free-market economy in Russia.

Council for a Livable World, 110 Maryland Ave. N.E. 20002; 543-4100. John Isaacs, president. Fax, 543-6297. Arms control hotline, 543-0006.

Citizens' interest group that supports arms control, reduced military spending, peace enforcement, peacekeeping, and tight restrictions on international arms sales.

Federation of American Scientists, 307 Massachusetts Ave. N.E. 20002; 546-3300. Jeremy J. Stone, president. Fax, 675-1010.

Conducts studies and monitors legislation on U.S. nuclear arms policy; advocates an end to the arms race; provides the public with information on arms control and related issues. Interests include the Strategic Defense Initiative (SDI) and arms control compliance.

Friends Committee on National Legislation, 245 2nd St. N.E. 20002-5795; 547-6000. Joe Volk, executive secretary. Fax, 547-6019. Recorded information, 547-4343.

Supports world disarmament; international cooperation; domestic, economic, peace, and social justice issues; and improvement in relations between the United States and the former Soviet Union. Opposes conscription. Affiliated with the Religious Society of Friends (Quakers).

Friends of the Earth, 218 D St. S.E., 2nd Floor 20003; 544-2600. Jane Perkins, president. Fax, 543-4710.

Citizens' interest group that advocates a freeze on the production and testing of nuclear weapons and transfer of federal funds from production to cleanup efforts. Advises other organizations on political strategy and organizational techniques. Monitors military compliance with environmental law. Library open to the public by appointment.

High Frontier, 2800 Shirlington Rd., Arlington, VA 22206; (703) 671-4111. Lt. Gen. Daniel O. Graham (USA, ret.), director. Fax, (703) 931-6432.

Educational organization that provides information on missile defense programs and proliferation. Advocates development of a single-stage-to-orbit space vehicle. Operates speakers bureau. Monitors defense legislation.

Institute for Science and International Security, 236 Massachusetts Ave. N.E., #500 20002; 547-5909. Tom Zamara Collina, director.

Conducts research and analysis on nuclear weapons production and nonproliferation issues.

Lawyers Alliance for World Security, 1601 Connecticut Ave. N.W., #600 20009; 745-2450. John Parachini, executive director. Fax, 667-0444.

Public education organization that seeks to broaden interest in and understanding of arms control and disarmament with regard to nuclear, conventional, chemical, and biological weapons. Sponsors educational programs for government officials, including legislators from the Commonwealth of Independent States. (Affiliated with the Committee for National Security.)

National Commission for Economic Conversion and Disarmament, 1828 Jefferson Pl. N.W. 20036; 728-0815. Gregory A. Bischak, executive director. Fax, 728-0826.

Supports cutbacks in the U.S. military budget and reallocation of funds for civilian economic development. Advocates investment in civilian research and development, transportation, housing, health, education, and the environment.

National Peace Foundation, 1835 K St. N.W., #610 20006; 223-1770. Stephen P. Strickland, president. Toll-free, (800) 237-3223. Fax, 223-1718.

Supports conflict resolution education and the U.S. Institute of Peace. Holds conferences and provides information on peace education and managing and resolving conflict.

Nuclear Control Institute, 1000 Connecticut Ave. N.W., #804 20036; 822-8444. Paul Leventhal, president. Fax, 452-0892.

Promotes nuclear nonproliferation; works to prevent the use of nuclear explosive materials (plutonium and highly enriched uranium) as reactor fuels; advocates terminating the export of nuclear technologies and facilities that could be used in the manufacture of nuclear weaponry; works to reverse the growth of the nuclear arsenals of nuclear weapon states; studies and recommends measures to prevent nuclear terrorism.

Peace Action, 1819 H St. N.W., #640 20006; 862-9740. Monica Green, executive director. Fax, 862-9762.

Grass-roots organization that works to halt the nuclear arms race and supports a negotiated comprehensive test ban treaty. Seeks a reduction in the military budget and a transfer of those funds to nonmilitary programs. Works for an end to the international arms trade.

Peace Links, 747 8th St. S.E., 2nd Floor 20003; 544-0805. Carol Williams, director. Fax, 544-0809.

Seeks to educate Americans about alternatives to war as a means of resolving conflicts; promotes improved relations between people from the former Soviet Union and Americans through an exchange program and a letter-writing program; provides educational information, primarily to women's groups, concerning the arms race and national security issues.

Physicians for Social Responsibility, 1101 14th St. N.W., #700 20005; 898-0150. Julia A. Moore, executive director. Fax, 898-0172.

Membership: doctors, dentists, and other individuals concerned about the threat of nuclear war. Conducts public education programs, monitors policy decisions on arms control, and serves as a liaison with other concerned groups.

Union of Concerned Scientists, Nonproliferation, 1616 P St. N.W., #310 20036; 332-0900. Ken Luongo, Washington representative, arms control and international security policy. Fax, 332-0905.

Independent group of scientists that works to prevent proliferation of nuclear weapons and production capabilities. Focuses on the Nuclear Nonproliferation Treaty, the production of weapons-grade fissile materials, and export controls. (Headquarters in Cambridge, Mass.)

Women Strike for Peace, 110 Maryland Ave. N.E., #302 20002; 543-2660. Edith Villastrigo, national legislative coordinator. Fax, 546-0090.

Promotes opposition to nuclear weapons, nuclear power plants, and U.S. intervention in developing countries. Supports nuclear disarmament with international controls. Provides the public with information on foreign policy, the arms race, and prevention of nuclear war.

Women's Action for New Directions, 110 Maryland Ave. N.E., #205 20002; 543-8505. Sima Osdoby, director of policy and program. Fax, 675-6469.

Seeks to redirect federal spending priorities from military spending toward domestic needs; works to develop citizen expertise through education and political involvement; provides educational programs and material about nuclear and conventional weapons; monitors defense legislation, budget policy legislation, and legislation affecting women. (Headquarters in Arlington, Mass.)

See also American Conservative Union and Center for Security Policy (p. 533); Henry L. Stimson Center and Hudson Institute (p. 535)

Budget Management

Agencies:

Defense Contract Audit Agency (Defense Dept.), Cameron Station, Alexandria, VA

22304-6178; (703) 274-6785. William H. Reed, director. Fax, (703) 617-7450.

Performs all contract audits for the Defense Dept. Provides Defense Dept. personnel responsible for procurement and contract administration with accounting and financial advisory services regarding the negotiation, administration, and settlement of contracts and subcontracts.

Defense Dept., Comptroller, The Pentagon, Rm. 3E822 20301-1100; (703) 695-3237. John J. Hamre, comptroller. Fax, (703) 614-2378.

Supervises and reviews the preparation and implementation of the defense budget. Advises the secretary of defense on fiscal matters. Collects and distributes information on the department's management of resources.

Office of Management and Budget (Executive Office of the President), National Security, New Executive Office Bldg. 20503; 395-3884. Donald E. Gessaman, deputy associate director. Fax, 395-3307.

Supervises preparation of the Defense Dept.'s portion of the federal budget.

Congress:

General Accounting Office, National Security and International Affairs, 441 G St. N.W. 20548; 512-2800. Frank C. Conahan, assistant comptroller general. Fax, 512-7686.

Independent, nonpartisan agency in the legislative branch. Audits, analyzes, and evaluates defense spending programs; makes unclassified reports available to the public.

See also Defense Policy, General, Congress (p. 531)

Nongovernmental:

Defense Budget Project, 777 N. Capitol St. N.E., #710 20002; 408-1517. Andrew Krepinevich, director. Fax, 408-1526.

Conducts detailed analyses of defense spending; makes results available to members of Congress, the executive branch, the media, academics, and other organizations.

Emergency Preparedness

General

Agencies:

Energy Dept., Emergency Management, 1000 Independence Ave. S.W., Rm. GE262 20585; 586-9892. John J. Nettles Jr., acting director. Fax, 586-3859.

Assists federal agencies, state and local governments, and industry in preparing for and responding to energy emergencies.

Federal Emergency Management Agency, 500 C St. S.W. 20472; 646-3923. James Lee Witt, director. Information, 646-4600. Fax, 646-4562.

Assists state and local governments in preparing for and responding to natural, man-made, and national security-related emergencies. Develops plans and policies for hazard mitigation, preparedness planning, emergency response, and recovery. Coordinates emergency preparedness and planning for all federal agencies and departments.

Federal Emergency Management Agency, Emergency Information Coordination Center, 500 C St. S.W., #M27 20472; 646-2999. Laura Lorenz, manager. Fax, 646-2600. Operations, 646-2400.

Serves as a central point of contact for federal agencies and members of Congress for coordinating national response to disasters and emergencies.

Public Health Service (Health and Human Services Dept.), Emergency Preparedness, 7600 Fishers Lane, #4-81, Rockville, MD 20857; (301) 443-1167. Frank Young, director. Fax, (301) 443-5146.

Works with the Federal Emergency Management Agency and other federal agencies and departments to develop plans and maintain operational readiness for responding to requests for assistance during major disasters; develops and coordinates medical equipment and training plans for major disasters; maintains logistical plans and communication networks with federal, state, and local emergency preparedness organizations.

Congress:

House Appropriations Committee, Subcommittee on VA, HUD, and Independent Agencies, H143 CAP 20515; 225-3241. Louis Stokes, D-Ohio, chairman; Paul Thompson, staff assistant.

Jurisdiction over legislation to appropriate funds for the Federal Emergency Management Agency.

House Armed Services Committee, 2120 RHOB 20515; 225-4151. Ronald V. Dellums, D-Calif., chairman; Marilyn A. Elrod, staff director.

Jurisdiction over legislation for emergency communications and industrial planning and mobilization.

House Armed Services Committee, Subcommittee on Oversight and Investigations, 2540 RHOB 20515; 225-2086. Norman Sisisky, D-Va., chairman; Warren Nelson, professional staff member. Fax, 226-0105.

Jurisdiction over civil defense legislation.

House Armed Services Committee, Subcommittee on Readiness, 2339 RHOB 20515; 225-9644. Earl Hutto, D-Fla., chairman; Steve Rossetti, professional staff member. Fax, 225-4032.

Jurisdiction over legislation concerning emergency mobilization of merchant fleets (jurisdiction shared with House Merchant Marine and Fisheries Committee) and national defense stockpiles, including military, civilian, and industrial requirements.

House Merchant Marine and Fisheries Committee, Subcommittee on Merchant Marine, 543 Ford Bldg. (2nd and D Sts. S.W.) 20515; 226-3533. William O. Lipinski, D-Ill., chairman; Keith Lesnick, staff director.

Jurisdiction over legislation concerning emergency mobilization of merchant fleets (jurisdiction shared with House Armed Services Committee).

Senate Appropriations Committee, Subcommittee on VA, HUD, and Independent Agencies, SD-142 20510; 224-7211. Barbara A. Mikulski, D-Md., chair; Kevin F. Kelly, clerk.

Jurisdiction over legislation to appropriate funds for the Federal Emergency Management Agency.

Senate Armed Services Committee, Subcommittee on Defense Technology, Acquisition, and Industrial Base, SR-228 20510; 224-3871. Jeff Bingaman, D-N.M., chairman; John W. Douglass, professional staff member.

Jurisdiction over legislation concerning national defense stockpiles, including military, civilian, and industrial requirements.

Senate Armed Services Committee, Subcommittee on Military Readiness and Defense Infrastructure, SR-228 20510; 224-3871. John Glenn, D-Ohio, chairman; David S. Lyles, professional staff member.

Jurisdiction over emergency preparedness legislation, including civil defense, emergency mobilization of merchant fleets, emergency communications, and industrial planning and mobilization.

Civil Defense—Community Programs

Agencies:

Civil Air Patrol, National Capital Wing, Bolling Air Force Base 20332; 404-7776. Col. Gene Hartman, wing commander. Fax, 767-5695.

Official auxiliary of the U.S. Air Force. Conducts search-and-rescue missions for the Air Force; participates in emergency airlift and disaster relief missions. (Headquarters at Maxwell Air Force Base, Ala.)

Federal Emergency Management Agency, Emergency Management Institute, 16825 S. Seton Ave., Emmitsburg, MD 21727; (301) 447-1286. John W. McKay, superintendent. Fax, (301) 447-1497.

Provides federal, state, and local government personnel and private organizations engaged in emergency management with technical, professional, and vocational training. Educational programs include hazard mitigation, emergency preparedness, and disaster response.

Federal Emergency Management Agency, National Preparedness Directorate, 500 C St. S.W. 20472; 646-2967. Vacant, associate director. Fax, 646-3155.

Develops and coordinates policies and capabilities that ensure continuity of essential executive branch functions during national emergencies. Specific programs include: continuity of government, mobilization preparedness, national information systems, disaster support, situation assessment, and facilities management.

Federal Emergency Management Agency, Response and Recovery Directorate, 500 C St. S.W. 20472; 646-3692. Richard W. Krimm, associate director. Fax, 646-4060.
Provides state and local governments with funding and technical assistance to develop plans for national security emergencies.

Congress:

See Emergency Preparedness, General, Congress (p. 541)

Nongovernmental:

American Red Cross, Disaster Services, 615 N. Saint Asaph St., Alexandria, VA 22314; (703) 838-7653. Donald W. Jones, vice president. Information, (703) 838-7617. Fax, (703) 838-7661.
Provides local civil defense programs with supporting services. Gives emergency welfare assistance to disaster victims, communities, and local governments during and after a national disaster.

International Assn. of Chiefs of Police, Advisory Committee for Patrol and Tactical Operations, 515 N. Washington St., Alexandria, VA 22314-2357; (703) 836-6767. Jerry Needle, staff liaison. Fax, (703) 836-4543.
Membership: foreign and U.S. police executives and administrators. Maintains liaison with civil defense and emergency service agencies; prepares guidelines for police cooperation with emergency and disaster relief agencies during emergencies.

Coast Guard and Merchant Marine

Agencies:

Maritime Administration (Transportation Dept.), National Security Plans, 400 7th St. S.W. 20590; 366-5900. Thomas M. P. Christensen, director. Fax, 488-0941.
Plans for the transition of merchant shipping from peacetime to wartime operations under the direction of the National Shipping Authority. (The National Shipping Authority is a stand-by organization that is activated upon the declaration of a war or other national emergency.)

Maritime Administration (Transportation Dept.), Ship Operations, 400 7th St. S.W. 20590; 366-1875. Michael Delpercio Jr., director. Fax, 366-3954.

Maintains the National Defense Reserve Fleet, a fleet of older vessels traded in by U.S. flag operators that are called into operation during emergencies; manages and administers the Ready Reserve Force, a fleet of ships available for operation within five to ten days, to meet the nation's sea-lift readiness requirements.

U.S. Coast Guard (Transportation Dept.), Defense Operations, 2100 2nd St. S.W. 20593; 267-2039. Capt. Donald R. Grosse, chief. Fax, 267-4278.
Ensures that the Coast Guard can mobilize effectively during national emergencies, including those resulting from enemy military attack. (The Coast Guard is part of the Transportation Dept. during peacetime; in certain emergency circumstances, including war, some of its functions become components of the Navy and come under the jurisdiction of the Defense Dept.)

Congress:

See Emergency Preparedness, General, Congress (p. 541)

Nongovernmental:

See Transportation: Maritime, General, Nongovernmental (p. 716)

Emergency Communications

Agencies:

Air Force Dept. (Defense Dept.), Command, Control, Communications, and Computers, The Pentagon 20330-1250; (703) 695-6324. Lt. Gen. Carl G. O'Berry, deputy chief of staff. Fax, (703) 614-0156.
Responsible for policy, planning, programming, and evaluating performance of the Air Force's C-4 system.

Air Force Dept. (Defense Dept.), Communications, Computers, and Support Systems, The Pentagon 20330-1060; (703) 697-3624. Lloyd Mosemann, deputy assistant secretary. Fax, (703) 697-8313.
Responsible for Air Force communications and support systems.

Army Dept. (Defense Dept.), Information Systems for Command, Control, Communications, and Computers, The Pentagon 20310-0107; (703) 695-4366. Lt. Gen. Peter A. Kind, director. Fax, (703) 695-3091.

Oversees policy and budget for the Army's information systems and programs.

Defense Dept., Command, Control, and Communications, The Pentagon, Rm. 3E194 20301; (703) 695-2396. Deborah Castleman, deputy assistant secretary.

Civilian office with policy oversight for all C-3 matters.

Defense Dept., Command, Control, Communications, and Computer Systems, The Pentagon 20318-6000; (703) 695-6478. Lt. Gen. Albert J. Edmonds, director. Fax, (703) 614-2945.

Military office that sets policy throughout the Defense Dept. for C-4 matters.

Defense Dept., White House Communications Agency, Washington Navy Yard—Anacostia, Bldg. 399 20374; 757-5530. Col. Thomas J. Hawes, commander. Fax, 757-5529.

Responsible for presidential communications.

Federal Communications Commission, Emergency Broadcast System, 1919 M St. N.W. 20554; 632-3906. Helena Mitchell, chief. Fax, 632-1148.

Develops rules and regulations for the Emergency Broadcast System, which issues radio reports during local, state, and national emergencies, including war, natural disasters, or major accidents involving hazardous materials. Assists officials of state and local Emergency Broadcast Systems.

Federal Communications Commission, Program Analysis, 1919 M St. N.W. 20554; 632-0923. H. Walker Feaster, associate managing director. Fax, 632-1588.

Plans for operation of common carrier, broadcast, and private radio services of all types during a national emergency; develops priorities for public use of private line service communications during an emergency.

National Communications System (Defense Dept.), 701 S. Courthouse Rd., Arlington, VA 22204; (703) 692-0018. Lt. Gen. Alonzo E. Short Jr. (USA), manager. Information, (703) 692-9270. Fax, (703) 746-7138.

Ensures that the federal government has the necessary communications facilities to permit its continued operation during a national emergency, including war; provides the Federal Emergency Management Agency with communications support as it directs the nation's recovery from a major disaster.

Navy Dept. (Defense Dept.), Naval Computer and Telecommunications Command, 4401 Massachusetts Ave. N.W. 20394-5460; 282-0550. Capt. Thomas A. Stark, commander. Fax, 282-0357.

Provides, operates, and maintains all Navy onshore communications resources; nontactical information resources for command, control, and administration of the the Navy; and Defense Communication System.

President's National Security Telecommunications Advisory Committee, c/o National Communications System, 701 S. Courthouse Rd., Arlington, VA 22204-2198; (703) 692-9274. Lt. Col. Michael S. Cleary, director. Fax, (703) 746-5240.

Advises the president on specific measures to improve national security telecommunications.

Congress:

See *Emergency Preparedness, General, Congress (p. 541)*

Industrial Planning and Mobilization

Agencies:

Bureau of Export Administration (Commerce Dept.), Industrial Resources, Main Commerce Bldg. 20230; 482-4506. John A. Richards, deputy assistant secretary. Fax, 482-5650.

Administers the Defense Production Act and provides industry with information on the allocation of resources falling under the jurisdiction of the act; conducts studies on industrial mobilization for the federal government.

Defense Dept., Dual Use Technology and International Programs, The Pentagon, Rm. 3E1082 20301; (703) 697-4172. Kenneth S. Flamm, principal deputy assistant secretary. Fax, (703) 693-2026.

Advises the under secretary of defense for acquisition on dual use technology; cooperative research and development, production, procurement, and follow-on support programs with foreign nations; technology transfer; and the technology and industrial base generally.

Defense Dept., Economic Security, The Pentagon, Rm. 3E808 20301-3310; (703) 695-7178. Joshua Gotbaum, assistant secretary. Fax, (703) 614-9284.

Sets policy for economic conversion of military resources, base realignments and closings, dual use technology, international programs and use of the industrial base, and community relations.

Defense Logistics Agency (Defense Dept.), Materiel Management, Cameron Station, Alexandria, VA 22304; (703) 274-6101. Maj. Gen. Ray E. McCoy (USA), deputy director. Fax, (703) 617-0577.

Oversees operations of Emergency Supply Operations Centers that acquire, maintain, and distribute items used in first-line weapons systems.

Congress:

See Emergency Preparedness, General, Congress (p. 541)

Nongovernmental:

American Defense Preparedness Assn., 2101 Wilson Blvd., Arlington, VA 22201; (703) 522-1820. Lt. Gen. Lawrence F. Skibbie (USA, ret.), president. Fax, (703) 522-1885.

Membership: U.S. citizens and businesses interested in national security. Also open to individuals and businesses in nations with defense agreements with the United States. Provides information and expertise on defense preparedness issues; works to increase public awareness of national defense preparedness through education programs; serves as a forum for dialogue between the defense industry and the government.

National Defense Transportation Assn., 50 S. Pickett St., #220, Alexandria, VA 22304; (703) 751-5011. Lt. Gen. Edward Honor (USA, ret.), president. Fax, (703) 823-8761.

Membership: transportation service and manufacturing companies. Maintains liaison with the Defense Dept., Transportation Dept., and Federal Emergency Management Agency to prepare emergency transportation plans.

National Security Industrial Assn., 1025 Connecticut Ave. N.W., #300 20036; 775-1440. Adm. James R. Hogg (USN, ret.), president. Fax, 775-1309.

Membership: industrial, research, legal, and educational organizations interested in national security. Promotes communication between government and industry; conducts symposia, conferences, and visits to military installations for its members.

Shipbuilders Council of America, 4301 N. Fairfax Dr., #330, Arlington, VA 22203; (703) 276-1700. John J. Stocker, president. Fax, (703) 276-1707.

Membership: shipbuilders and allied industries and associations. Promotes the maintenance of a privately owned reserve fleet for times of national emergency. Serves as a liaison between the government and the shipbuilding and ship repairing industries.

Strategic Stockpiles

Agencies:

Defense Dept., Defense National Stockpile Center, Crystal Square 4, #100, 1745 Jefferson Davis Highway, Arlington, VA 22202; (703) 607-3218. Richard J. Connelly, administrator. Fax, (703) 607-3215.

Stockpiles strategic and critical materials for use in wartime or national emergencies.

Defense Dept., Materiel and Resource Management Policy, The Pentagon 20301; (703) 697-9238. Jeffrey A. Jones, director. Fax, (703) 697-3428.

Civilian office that develops energy policy for the Defense Dept. Works with the Energy Dept. to develop policy for strategic petroleum reserves, petroleum logistics, facilities energies, and naval petroleum and oil shale reserves. Promotes conservation and efficiency of energy resources.

Defense Dept., Production Base, The Pentagon 20301; (703) 695-0123. Kenneth R. Foster, deputy director. Fax, (703) 693-7038.

Develops and oversees strategic and critical materials policies including oversight of the National Defense Stockpile.

Energy Dept., Naval Petroleum and Oil Shale Reserves, 1000 Independence Ave. S.W., #3H076 20585; 586-4685. Capt. Kenneth W. Meeks (USN), deputy assistant secretary. Fax, 586-4446.

Develops, conserves, operates, and maintains naval petroleum and oil shale reserves for producing oil, natural gas, and other petroleum products as authorized by the Naval Petroleum Reserves Production Act of 1976.

Energy Dept., Technical Management, 1000 Independence Ave. S.W. 20585; 586-4415. Paul J. Avila Plaisance, director. Fax, 586-7919.

Directs and manages the development and preparedness for distribution of the strategic petroleum reserve as mandated by the Energy Policy and Conservation Act of 1975.

National Institute of Standards and Technology (Commerce Dept.), Materials Science and Engineering Laboratory, Route I-270 and Quince Orchard Rd., Gaithersburg, MD (mailing address: Bldg. 223, #B309, Gaithersburg, MD 20899); (301) 975-5658. Lyle H. Schwartz, director. Fax, (301) 926-8349.

Advises the secretary and Congress on strategic resources issues. Conducts studies; coordinates development of departmental positions on federal policies and programs; develops and maintains consultation program with business interests; prepares reports on critical and strategic materials for members of the Council for Mutual Economic Assistance.

Congress:

See Emergency Preparedness, General, Congress (p. 541)

Export Controls

Agencies:

Bureau of Export Administration (Commerce Dept.), Main Commerce Bldg. 20230; 482-1427. William Alan Reinsch, under secretary. Information, 482-2721. Fax, 482-2387. Export licensing information, 482-4811.

Administers Export Administration Act; maintains control lists and performs export licensing for the purposes of national security, foreign policy, and prevention of short supply.

Bureau of Export Administration (Commerce Dept.), Export Enforcement, Main Commerce Bldg. 20230; 482-3618. John Despres, assistant secretary. Fax, 482-4173.

Enforces regulation of exports of U.S. goods and technology for purposes of national security, foreign policy, and prevention of short supply. Enforces foreign boycotts and compliance with antiboycott provisions of the Export Administration Act.

Defense Dept., Defense Technology Security Administration, The Pentagon 20301; (703) 604-5215. Peter M. Sullivan, acting deputy under secretary. Fax, (703) 604-4779.

Analyzes export control factors affecting national security; develops and implements Defense Dept. policies for trade security and for the transfer and control of advanced military technology.

Energy Dept., Nonproliferation Policy, 1000 Independence Ave. S.W., #GA017 (mailing address: 1540.3, Washington, DC 20585); 586-6175. Edward Fei, acting director. Fax, 586-6789.

Develops policies concerning nuclear material and equipment exports, nuclear material transfers and retransfers, and regional nonproliferation.

Export Administration Review Board (Commerce Dept.), Main Commerce Bldg. 20230; 482-5863. Ronald H. Brown, chairman; Richard E. Hull, executive secretary. Fax, 482-3911.

Committee of Cabinet-level secretaries and heads of other government offices. Considers export licensing policies and actions, especially those concerning national security and other major policy matters; advises the secretary of commerce on export licensing.

National Security Council (Executive Office of the President), The White House 20506; 395-3331. Michael Punk, director, international economic affairs, 395-3622; Robert Bell, director, defense policy/arms control, 395-3330. Information, 395-2947.

Advises, in conjunction with the National Economic Council, the president on national security issues, including export controls on dual-use commodities and technologies.

Nuclear Regulatory Commission, Exports, Security, and Safety Cooperation, 11555 Rockville Pike, Rockville, MD (mailing address: Washington, DC 20555); (301) 504-2344. Ronald D. Hauber, assistant director. Fax, (301) 504-2395.

Coordinates application review process for exports and imports of nuclear materials, facilities, and components; makes recommendations on licensing upon completion of review; conducts related policy reviews.

President's Export Council (Commerce Dept.), Subcommittee on Export Administration, Main Commerce Bldg., Rm. 1608 (mailing address:

Rm. 3886C, Washington, DC 20230); 482-2583. Betty A. Ferrell, coordinator. Fax, 482-5270.

Advises the president and secretary of commerce on matters related to the Export Administration Act of 1979, which deals with controlling trade for reasons of national security, foreign policy, and short supply. Seeks ways to minimize the negative effect of export controls while protecting U.S. national security and foreign policy interests.

State Dept., Defense Trade Controls, 1701 N. Fort Myer Dr., Arlington, VA (mailing address: State Dept. Annex 6, Washington, DC 20522); (703) 875-6650. William B. Robinson, director. Fax, (703) 875-6647.

Administers government control over the commercial export of defense articles, services, and related technical data and other authorizations related to the permanent export and temporary import of such items.

State Dept., International Trade Controls, Main State Bldg. 20520; 647-1625. Christopher G. Hankin, deputy assistant secretary. Fax, 647-3205.

Coordinates U.S. participation in multilateral strategic trade control and revisions related to the export of strategically critical high-technology goods. Cooperates with the Commerce and Defense departments in formulating export control policies and programs.

State Dept., Nuclear Energy, Main State Bldg. 20520; 647-3310. Richard J. K. Stratford, deputy assistant secretary. Fax, 647-0775.

Carries out the department's nuclear control responsibilities as mandated under the Nuclear Non-Proliferation Act of 1978; reviews and makes recommendations to the executive branch on requests to the Nuclear Regulatory Commission for licensing.

Treasury Dept., Foreign Assets Control, 1500 Pennsylvania Ave. N.W., Annex Bldg., 2nd Floor 20220; 622-2510. R. Richard Newcomb, director. Fax, 622-1657.

Has authority under the revised Trading with the Enemy Act, the International Emergency Economic Powers Act, and the United Nations Participation Act to control financial and commercial dealings with certain countries and their foreign nationals in times of war or emergencies. Regulations involving foreign assets control and commercial transactions currently apply in varying degrees to Cuba, Haiti, Iran, Iraq, Libya, Montenegro, North Korea, Serbia, Vietnam, and Angola.

U.S. Arms Control and Disarmament Agency, Nonproliferation and Regional Arms Control, Main State Bldg., Rm. 4936 20451; 647-3466. Norman Wuls, acting assistant director. Information, 647-8677. Fax, 647-6721. Publications, 647-4800.

Advises the president and the secretary of state on exports of conventional, nuclear, chemical, and biological weapons and missiles that deliver them.

Congress:

House Armed Services Committee, Subcommittee on Military Acquisitions, 2343 RHOB 20515; 225-6703. Ronald V. Dellums, D-Calif., chairman; Doug Necessary, professional staff member. Fax, 226-0105.

Jurisdiction over legislation on foreign military sales and the proliferation of weapons technology.

House Foreign Affairs Committee, Subcommittee on Economic Policy, Trade, and the Environment, 702 O'Neill Bldg. (300 New Jersey Ave. S.E.) 20515; 226-7820. Sam Gejdenson, D-Conn., chairman; John Scheibel, staff director. Fax, 225-2029.

Jurisdiction over foreign trade legislation and legislation related to export control, including the Export Administration Act and the revised Trading with the Enemy Act, which authorize trade restrictions, and the International Emergency Economic Powers Act.

House Foreign Affairs Committee, Subcommittee on International Security, International Organizations, and Human Rights, B358 RHOB 20515; 226-7825. Tom Lantos, D-Calif., chairman; Bob King, staff director. Fax, 226-3581.

Oversight of State and Defense department operations regarding arms transfers, export licenses, and sales.

House Science, Space, and Technology Committee, Subcommittee on Technology, Environment, and Aviation, B374 RHOB 20515; 225-9662. Tim Valentine, D-N.C., chairman; James H. Turner, staff director.

Jurisdiction over legislation on transfers of technology between the United States and foreign countries.

Senate Armed Services Committee, Subcommittee on Nuclear Deterrence, Arms Control, and Defense Intelligence, SR-228 20510; 224-3871. Jim Exon, D-Neb., chairman; Bill E. Hoehn Jr., professional staff member.

Jurisdiction over legislation on foreign military sales and the proliferation of weapons technology.

Senate Banking, Housing, and Urban Affairs Committee, Subcommittee on International Finance and Monetary Policy, SD-534 20510; 224-1564. Jim Sasser, D-Tenn., chairman; Charles R. Marr, staff director. Fax, 224-5137.

Jurisdiction over foreign trade legislation and legislation related to export control, including the Export Administration Act and the revised Trading with the Enemy Act, which authorize trade restrictions, and the International Emergency Economic Powers Act.

Senate Foreign Relations Committee, SD-446 20510; 224-4651. Claiborne Pell, D-R.I., chairman; Geryld B. Christianson, staff director. Fax, 224-5011.

Oversight of State and Defense department operations regarding arms transfers, export licenses, and sales.

Senate Governmental Affairs Committee, Permanent Subcommittee on Investigations, SR-100 20510; 224-3721. Sam Nunn, D-Ga., chairman; Eleanor J. Hill, staff director.

Investigates transfers of technology between the United States and foreign countries.

Nongovernmental:

American League for Exports and Security Assistance, 122 C St. N.W., #310 20001; 783-0051. Anna Stout, executive vice president. Fax, 737-4727.

Membership: aerospace and defense companies. Provides information on export controls and the preservation of American jobs.

Emergency Committee for American Trade, 1211 Connecticut Ave. N.W., #801 20036; 659-5147. Robert L. McNeill, executive vice chairman. Fax, 659-1347.

Membership: U.S. corporations and banks interested in international trade and investment. Supports open trade and opposes restrictions on U.S. technology exports.

Nuclear Control Institute, 1000 Connecticut Ave. N.W., #804 20036; 822-8444. Paul Leventhal, president. Fax, 452-0892.

Promotes nuclear nonproliferation; works to prevent the use of nuclear explosive materials (plutonium and highly enriched uranium) as reactor fuels; advocates terminating the export of nuclear technologies and facilities that could be used in the manufacture of nuclear weaponry; works to reverse the growth of the nuclear arsenals of nuclear weapon states; studies and recommends measures to prevent nuclear terrorism.

Intelligence

Agencies:

Air Force Dept. (Defense Dept.), Intelligence, The Pentagon 20330; (703) 695-5613. Maj. Gen. Ervin Rokke, assistant chief of staff. Fax, (703) 697-4903.

Military office that directs Air Force intelligence activities and coordinates activities with other intelligence agencies.

Army Dept. (Defense Dept.), Intelligence, The Pentagon 20310; (703) 695-3033. Lt. Gen. Ira Owens, deputy chief of staff. Fax, (703) 697-8849.

Military office that directs Army intelligence activities and coordinates activities with other intelligence agencies.

Central Intelligence Agency, Langley, VA (mailing address: Washington, DC 20505); (703) 482-1100. R. James Woolsey, director. Information, (703) 482-7676.

Coordinates the intelligence functions of government agencies as they relate to national security and advises the National Security Council on those functions; gathers and evaluates intelligence relating to national security and distributes the information to government agencies in the national security field.

Defense Dept., Command, Control, Communications, and Intelligence, The Pentagon 20301-6000; (703) 695-0348. Lt. Gen. Emmett Paige Jr., assistant secretary. Fax, (703) 614-8060.

Civilian office that advises and makes recommendations to the secretary of defense on the management of all Defense Dept. intelligence and communications programs, resources, and activities.

Defense Dept., Intelligence Oversight, The Pentagon 20301-7200; (703) 697-1346. Charles A. Hawkins Jr., assistant to the secretary. Fax, (703) 614-1629.

Responsible for the independent oversight of all Defense Dept. intelligence and counterintelligence activities; reviews intelligence operations and investigates and reports on possible violations of federal law or regulations.

Defense Intelligence Agency (Defense Dept.), The Pentagon 20340; (703) 695-7353. Lt. Gen. James R. Clapper Jr. (USAF), director. Information, (703) 695-0071. Fax, (703) 695-7336.

Collects and evaluates military-related intelligence information to satisfy the requirements of the secretary of defense, Joint Chiefs of Staff, selected components of the Defense Dept., and other authorized agencies. Monitors and reviews the operations of and develops guidelines for Defense Dept. intelligence functions.

Energy Dept., Intelligence, 1000 Independence Ave. S.W. 20585; 586-2610. James L. Ford, director. Fax, 586-0751.

Gathers and maintains information as it relates to national security, including military applications of nuclear energy.

Justice Dept., Intelligence Policy and Review, Main Justice Bldg., Rm. 6325 20530; 514-5600. Allen Kornblum, acting counsel. Fax, 514-7858.

Provides the attorney general with legal advice and recommendations on national security matters. Reviews executive orders, directives, and procedures relating to the intelligence community; approves certain intelligence-gathering activities. Provides interpretations and applications of the Constitution, statutes, regulations, and directives relating to U.S. national security activities. Represents the United States before the Foreign Intelligence Surveillance Court.

Marine Corps (Defense Dept.), Intelligence, Navy Annex, Arlington, VA (mailing address: Headquarters, U.S. Marine Corps, Washington, DC 20380); (703) 614-2443. Maj. Gen. Paul K. Van Riper, director. Fax, (703) 614-5888.

Military office that directs Marine Corps intelligence activities and coordinates activities with other intelligence agencies.

National Security Agency (Defense Dept.), 9800 Savage Rd., Fort Meade, MD 20755-6000; (301) 688-6311. Vice Adm. John M. McConnell (USN), director. Information, (301) 688-6524.

Maintains and operates the Defense Dept.'s Computer Security Center; collects national security intelligence through technical means; ensures communications and computer security within the government.

National Security Council (Executive Office of the President), The White House 20500; 456-2255. Anthony Lake, assistant to the president for national security affairs. Press, 456-2947. Fax, 456-2883.

Advises the president on national security matters; collects information on foreign policy and defense issues; coordinates the national security, defense, and intelligence functions of departments such as State and Defense.

Navy Dept. (Defense Dept.), Naval Intelligence, The Pentagon 20350-2000; (703) 695-0124. Rear Adm. Edward D. Sheafer Jr., director. Press, (703) 697-3671. Fax, (703) 614-0230.

Military office that directs Navy intelligence activities and coordinates activities with other intelligence agencies.

President's Foreign Intelligence Advisory Board (Executive Office of the President), Old Executive Office Bldg. 20503; 456-2352. Les Aspin, chairman; Eugene Yeates, executive director. Fax, 395-3403.

Members appointed by the president. Advises the president and makes recommendations to government intelligence agencies on the improvement of U.S. intelligence-gathering efforts. Assesses the quality, quantity, and propriety of intelligence collection and analysis and of counterintelligence activities. Advises the president on matters concerning national security.

State Dept., Intelligence and Research, Main State Bldg., Rm. 6533 20520-6510; 647-9177. Toby T. Gati, assistant secretary. Fax, 647-4296.

Coordinates foreign-policy-related research, analysis, and intelligence programs for the State Dept. and other federal agencies.

U.S. Coast Guard (Transportation Dept.), Intelligence, 2100 2nd St. S.W. 20593-0001; 267-2126. Capt. James A. Smith, chief. Fax, 267-6954.

Manages all Coast Guard intelligence activities and programs.

Congress:

House Armed Services Committee, Subcommittee on Military Acquisitions, 2343 RHOB 20515; 225-6703. Ronald V. Dellums, D-Calif., chairman; Doug Necessary, professional staff member. Fax, 226-0105.

Jurisdiction over military intelligence activities affecting national security.

House Foreign Affairs Committee, Subcommittee on International Security, International Organizations, and Human Rights, B358 RHOB 20515; 226-7825. Tom Lantos, D-Calif., chairman; Bob King, staff director. Fax, 226-3581.

Oversight of foreign intelligence activities.

House Government Operations Committee, Subcommittee on Legislation and National Security, B373 RHOB 20515; 225-5147. John Conyers Jr., D-Mich., chairman; James C. Turner, staff director. Fax, 225-2373.

Oversight responsibilities for the operations of agencies related to national security, including the Defense Dept., Central Intelligence Agency, National Security Agency, and Defense Intelligence Agency.

House Select Committee on Intelligence, H405 CAP 20515; 225-4121. Dan Glickman, D-Kan., chairman; Michael Sheehy, chief counsel. Fax, 225-1991.

Studies, makes recommendations, and proposes legislation on intelligence agencies' activities and policies, including the attorney general's implementation of guidelines for Federal Bureau of Investigation intelligence activities and the conduct of electronic surveillance for foreign intelligence purposes; oversees the Central Intelligence Agency, National Security Agency, Defense Intelligence Agency, and other intelligence activities of the U.S. government to ensure conformity with the U.S. Constitution and laws; authorizes budgets for the intelligence community.

Senate Armed Services Committee, Subcommittee on Nuclear Deterrence, Arms Control, and Defense Intelligence, SR-228 20510; 224-3871. Jim Exon, D-Neb., chairman; Bill E. Hoehn Jr., professional staff member.

Jurisdiction over military intelligence activities affecting national security.

Senate Foreign Relations Committee, SD-446 20510; 224-4651. Claiborne Pell, D-R.I., chairman; Geryld B. Christianson, staff director. Fax, 224-5011.

Oversight of foreign intelligence activities.

Senate Governmental Affairs Committee, SD-340 20510; 224-4751. John Glenn, D-Ohio, chairman; Leonard Weiss, staff director. Fax, 224-9682.

Oversees operations of the National Security Council.

Senate Select Committee on Intelligence, SH-211 20510; 224-1700. Dennis DeConcini, D-Ariz., chairman; Norm Bradley, staff director.

Studies, makes recommendations, and proposes legislation on intelligence agencies' activities and policies; oversees the Central Intelligence Agency, National Security Agency, Defense Intelligence Agency, the intelligence activities of the Federal Bureau of Investigation, and other intelligence operations of the U.S. government to ensure conformity with the U.S. Constitution and laws; authorizes appropriations for the intelligence community.

Nongovernmental:

Assn. of Former Intelligence Officers, 6723 Whittier Ave., #303A, McLean, VA 22101; (703) 790-0320. David D. Whipple, executive director. Fax, (703) 790-0264.

Membership: former military and civilian intelligence officers. Encourages public support for intelligence agencies; supports increased intelligence education in colleges and universities.

Center for National Security Studies, 122 Maryland Ave. N.E. 20002; 675-2327. Kate Martin, director. Fax, 546-1440.

Sponsored by the Fund for Peace and the American Civil Liberties Union Foundation. Monitors and conducts research on civil liberties and intelligence and national security, including activities of the Central Intelligence Agency and the Federal Bureau of Investigation. Library open to the public by appointment.

National Security Archive, 1755 Massachusetts Ave. N.W., #500 20036; 797-0882. Thomas Blanton, executive director. Fax, 387-6315.

Research institute and library that provides information on U.S. foreign policy and national security affairs. Maintains collection of declassified and unclassified national security documents. Archive open to the public by appointment.

Internal Security and Counterintelligence

See also Emergency Preparedness, Emergency Communications (p. 542); Export Controls (p. 545); Intelligence (p. 547)

Agencies:

Air Force Dept. (Defense Dept.), Criminal Investigation and Counterintelligence, The Pentagon, Rm. 4E1081 20330-1140; (703) 697-1955. Col. Gerald Lane, director. Fax, (703) 697-4293.

Develops and implements policy with regard to investigations of hostile intelligence, terrorism, and other crimes as they relate to Air Force security.

Army Dept. (Defense Dept.), Counterintelligence and Security Countermeasures, The Pentagon, Rm. 2D489 20310-1001; (703) 697-3934. Col. Nick Chiccarello, director.

Responsible for the security and effectiveness of the Army's electronic warfare systems. Develops new ways to interfere with enemy electronic warfare systems.

Defense Dept., Counterintelligence and Security Countermeasures, The Pentagon 20301-6000; (703) 695-6609. John Elliff, director.

Responsible for security and effectiveness of the military's electronic warfare systems. Develops new ways to interfere with enemy electronic warfare systems.

Defense Dept., Defense Investigative Service, 1340 Braddock Pl., Alexandria, VA 22314-1651; (703) 325-5308. John F. Donnelly, director. Fax, (703) 325-6545.

Administers four programs to protect classified government information and resources: Personnel Security Investigations; Defense Industrial Security; Arms, Ammunition, and Explosives Security; and Key Asset Protection.

Defense Dept., Defense Investigative Service, 1340 Braddock Pl., Alexandria, VA 22314-1651; (703) 325-5277. Gregory A. Gwash, deputy director, industrial security.

Ensures that U.S. industry, while performing on government contracts or engaging in research and development, properly safeguards the classified information in its possession.

Federal Bureau of Investigation (Justice Dept.), National Security, 10th St. and Pennsylvania Ave. N.W. 20535; 324-4880. Robert M. Bryant, assistant director. Information, 324-4444. Fax, 324-4705.

Investigates violations of federal law relating to sabotage, espionage, counterespionage, treason, insurrection and rebellion, seditious conspiracy, advocation of the overthrow of the government, and other matters affecting national internal security. Conducts counterespionage activities against hostile intelligence services and their agents in the United States.

General Services Administration, Information Security Oversight, 750 17th St. N.W. 20006; 634-6150. Steven Garfinkel, director. Fax, 634-6131.

Administers governmentwide national security classification program under which information is classified, declassified, and safeguarded for national security purposes.

Justice Dept., Internal Security, 1400 New York Ave. N.W. 20530; 514-1187. John L. Martin, chief. Fax, 514-2836.

Enforces federal statutes relating to internal security, including treason, espionage, sedition, sabotage, and the export of military and strategic commodities and technology; supervises the registration requirements of Foreign Agents Registration Act.

National Security Agency (Defense Dept.), 9800 Savage Rd., Fort Meade, MD 20755-6000; (301) 688-6311. Vice Adm. John M. McConnell (USN), director. Information, (301) 688-6524.

Maintains and operates the Defense Dept.'s Computer Security Center; ensures communications and computer security within the government.

Navy Dept. (Defense Dept.), Naval Criminal Investigative Service, Washington Navy Yard S.E. 20388; 433-8800. Roy D. Nedrow, director. Fax, 433-9619.

Handles investigative responsibilities for naval counterintelligence and security; processes security clearances for the Navy.

State Dept., Countermeasures and Information Security, 2121 Virginia Ave. N.W. 20522-1003; 663-0538. William D. Clarke, deputy assistant secretary. Fax, 663-0653.
Safeguards all electronic information and systems in the State Dept., both domestic and abroad. Also responsible for Physical Security Program for State Dept. officials and for the Diplomatic Courier Service.

State Dept., Diplomatic Security Service, 2121 Virginia Ave. N.W. 20522-1003; 663-0473. Mark E. Mulvey, director. Fax, 663-0831.
Oversees the safety and security of all U.S. government employees at U.S. embassies and consulates abroad. Responsible for the safety of the Secretary of State and all foreign dignitaries. Conducts background investigations of potential government employees, investigates passport and visa fraud, and warns government employees of any counterintelligence dangers they might encounter.

State Dept., Foreign Missions, Main State Bldg., Rm. 2238 20520-7207; 647-3416. Eric James Boswell, director. Fax, 647-1919.
Authorized to control the numbers, locations, and travel privileges of foreign diplomats and diplomatic staff in the United States.

Congress:

See Intelligence, Congress (p. 549)

Military Education and Training

Agencies:

Air Force Dept. (Defense Dept.), Air Force Academy Group, The Pentagon 20330-1040; (703) 695-4005. Scott Mills, chief. Information, (703) 697-2919. Fax, (703) 695-7999.
Military office that receives congressional nominations for the Air Force Academy; counsels congressional offices on candidate selection.

Air Force Dept. (Defense Dept.), Force Support and Personnel, The Pentagon 20330; (703) 614-4752. Ruby B. DeMesme, acting deputy assistant secretary. Fax, (703) 693-4244.
Civilian office that monitors and reviews education policies of the U.S. Air Force Academy at Colorado Springs and officer candidates' training and Reserve Officers Training Corps (ROTC) programs for the Air Force. Advises the

secretary of the Air Force on education matters, including graduate education, voluntary education programs, and flight, specialized, and recruit training.

Air Force Dept. (Defense Dept.), Personnel Programs, The Pentagon 20330-1040; (703) 695-6770. Maj. Gen. Michael D. McGinty, director. Fax, (703) 697-0903.
Supervises operations and policies of all professional military education, including continuing education programs. Oversees operations and policies of Air Force service schools, including technical training for newly enlisted Air Force personnel.

Army Dept. (Defense Dept.), Education, 2461 Eisenhower Ave., Alexandria, VA 22331-0472; (703) 325-3538. Col. Roy Edwards, chief. Fax, (703) 325-9811.
Military office that manages the operations and policies of voluntary education programs for Army personnel. Administers the tuition assistance program.

Army Dept. (Defense Dept.), Military Personnel Management, The Pentagon 20310; (703) 695-2497. Maj. Gen. F. E. Vollrath, director. Fax, (703) 693-5980.
Military office that supervises operations and policies of the U.S. Military Academy and officer candidates' training and Reserve Officers Training Corps (ROTC) programs. Advises the chief of staff of the Army on academy and education matters.

Army Dept. (Defense Dept.), Training, Education, and Community Support, The Pentagon 20310; (703) 697-0919. Lt. Col. William E. Marshall, assistant deputy. Fax, (703) 614-5975.
Coordinates all education and training programs for active and reserve members of the Army. Monitors and reviews morale, welfare, recreation, and family support issues.

Army Dept. (Defense Dept.), Training Operations, The Pentagon 20310; (703) 697-1406. Col. Scott C. Marcy, chief. Fax, (703) 697-0936.
Military office that runs civilian and military training readiness programs; monitors and reviews operations and policies of Army service schools and advises the chief of staff of the Army on education matters; administers certain service schools and serves as an information source for others.

Army Dept. (Defense Dept.), West Point Liaison, 200 Stovall St., Alexandria, VA 22332; (703) 325-7414. Jorja L. Graves, chief. Fax, (703) 325-6073.

Military office that receives congressional nominations for West Point; counsels congressional offices on candidate selection.

Civil Air Patrol, National Capital Wing, Bolling Air Force Base 20332; 404-7776. Col. Gene Hartman, wing commander. Fax, 767-5695.

Official auxiliary of the U.S. Air Force. Sponsors a cadet training and education program for junior and senior high school age students. Cadets who have earned the Civil Air Patrol's Mitchell Award are eligible to enter the Air Force at an advanced pay grade. Conducts an aerospace education program for adults. (Headquarters at Maxwell Air Force Base, Ala.)

Defense Dept., Accession Policy, The Pentagon 20301; (703) 695-5525. Wayne S. Sellman, director. Fax, (703) 614-9272.

Reviews and develops education policies of the service academies, service schools, graduate and voluntary education programs, education programs for active duty personnel, tuition assistance programs, and officer candidates' training and Reserve Officers Training Corps (ROTC) programs for the Defense Dept. Advises the secretary of defense on education matters.

Defense Dept., Readiness and Training, The Pentagon, Rm. 3B930 20301-4000; (703) 695-2618. Michael Parmentier, director. Fax, (703) 693-7382.

Develops, reviews, and analyzes legislation, policies, plans, programs, resource levels, and budgets for the training of military personnel and military units.

Defense Systems Management College (Defense Dept.), 9820 Belvoir Rd., #G38, Fort Belvoir, VA 22060-5565; (703) 805-3360. Brig. Gen. Claude M. Bolton Jr. (USA), commandant. Fax, (703) 805-2639. Registrar, (703) 805-2227.

Academic institution that offers courses to military and civilian personnel who specialize in acquisition and procurement. Conducts research to support and improve management of defense systems acquisition programs.

Education Dept., National Advisory Committee on Accreditation and Institutional Eligibility, 7th and D Sts. S.W. 20202-5153; 708-5656.

Steven Pappas, executive director. Fax, 708-9046.

Makes recommendations to the secretary of education on degree-granting authority of military institutions.

Industrial College of the Armed Forces (Defense Dept.), Fort Lesley J. McNair, 4th and P Sts. S.W. 20319; 475-1832. Rear Adm. Jerome F. Smith Jr. (USN), commandant, 475-1838. Fax, 475-0717.

Division of National Defense University. Offers professional level courses for senior military officers and senior civilian government officials. Academic program focuses on management of national resources, mobilization, and industrial preparedness.

Marine Corps (Defense Dept.), Training and Education, U.S. Marine Corps, Code MCCDC, Quantico, VA 22134; (703) 640-3730. Brig. Gen. Carl W. Fulford, director. Fax, (703) 640-3724.

Military office that develops and implements training and education programs for regular and reserve personnel and units.

National Defense University (Defense Dept.), Fort Lesley J. McNair, 4th and P Sts. S.W. 20319; 287-9400. Lt. Gen. Paul G. Cerjan (USA), president. Fax, 287-9410.

Nondegree, professional university sponsored by the Joint Chiefs of Staff to prepare senior military officers and government employees for increasingly responsible roles within the government. Offers resident programs, correspondence courses, and research fellowships.

National War College (Defense Dept.), Fort Lesley J. McNair, 4th and P Sts. S.W. 20319-6000; 475-1842. Maj. Gen. John C. Fryer Jr. (USAF), commandant. Information, 475-1776. Fax, 475-1745.

Division of National Defense University. Offers professional level courses for senior military officers and senior civilian government officials. Academic program focuses on the formulation and implementation of national security policy and military strategy.

Navy Dept. (Defense Dept.), Manpower, The Pentagon 20350; (703) 695-4350. Vacant, deputy assistant secretary. Fax, (703) 614-3889.

Civilian office that reviews policies of the U.S. Naval Académy, Navy and Marine Corps service schools, and officer candidates' training and

Reserve Officer Training Corps (ROTC) programs. Advises the secretary of the Navy on education matters, including voluntary education programs.

Navy Dept. (Defense Dept.), Naval Training, The Pentagon 20350; (703) 697-4071. Vice Adm. Robert K. U. Kihune, director. Fax, (703) 693-6480.

Develops and implements naval training policies. Oversees Navy service college and graduate school programs. Administers training programs for Naval Reserve Officer Training Corps, Naval Junior ROTC, and officer and enlisted personnel.

Uniformed Services University of the Health Sciences (Defense Dept.), 4301 Jones Bridge Rd., Bethesda, MD 20814; (301) 295-3013. Dr. James A. Zimble, president. Information, (301) 295-3030. Fax, (301) 295-3542.

Fully accredited four-year medical school under the auspices of the Defense Dept. Prepares individuals for careers as medical officers in the uniformed services of the Army, Navy, Air Force, and the U.S. Public Health Service. Maintains graduate program that awards doctorates in basic sciences and medical zoology; awards master's degrees in public health and tropical medicine.

U.S. Coast Guard (Transportation Dept.), Officer Recruiting, 2100 2nd St. S.W. 20593; 267-1729. Lt. Cmdr. Sergio Cerda, chief. Fax, 267-4277.

Military office that monitors operations and policies of the U.S. Coast Guard Academy at New London, Conn., direct commissioned officer programs, and officer candidates' training programs for the Coast Guard.

U.S. Coast Guard (Transportation Dept.), Personnel and Training, 2100 2nd St. S.W. 20593-0001; 267-0905. Rear Adm. William C. Donnell, chief. Fax, 267-4205.

Responsible for hiring, recruiting, and training all military and nonmilitary Coast Guard personnel.

U.S. Naval Academy (Navy Dept.), Annapolis, MD 21402; (410) 267-2202. Rear Adm. Thomas C. Lynch, superintendent; Capt. A. Coward IV, director, candidate guidance, (410) 267-4361. Fax, (410) 267-2303. Visitor's information, (410) 263-6933.

Provides undergraduate education for young men and women who have been nominated by members of their state's congressional delegation. Graduates are commissioned as either an ensign in the U.S. Navy or a second lieutenant in the U.S. Marine Corps. (Toll-free from Washington, D.C., metropolitan area: superintendent, (301) 261-2273; candidate guidance, (301) 261-2714.)

Congress:

House Armed Services Committee, Subcommittee on Military Forces and Personnel, 2343 RHOB 20515; 225-7560. Ike Skelton, D-Mo., chairman; Michael R. Higgins, professional staff member. Fax, 226-0105.

Jurisdiction over legislation on precommissioning programs and on military service academies and schools.

Senate Armed Services Committee, Subcommittee on Force Requirements and Personnel, SR-228 20510; 224-3871. Richard C. Shelby, D-Ala., chairman; Frederick F. Y. Pang, professional staff member.

Jurisdiction over legislation on precommissioning programs and on military service academies and schools.

Nongovernmental:

Assn. of Military Colleges and Schools of the U.S., 9115 McNair Dr., Alexandria, VA 22309; (703) 360-1678. Lt. Gen. Willard W. Scott (USA, ret.), executive director.

Membership: nonfederal military colleges, academies, junior colleges, and secondary schools. Monitors legislation and Defense Dept. policies, with emphasis on the Reserve Officers Training Corps (ROTC) and aid to private education.

The George and Carol Olmsted Foundation, 1515 N. Courthouse Rd., Arlington, VA 22201; (703) 527-9070. Barbara S. Schimpff, executive vice president.

Administers grants for military academies and scholarship programs for selected officers of the armed forces.

Military Order of the World Wars, 435 N. Lee St., Alexandria, VA 22314; (703) 683-4911. Lt. Gen. H. R. Temple Jr. (USA, ret.), chief of staff. Fax, (703) 683-4501.

Membership: retired and active duty commissioned warrant officers and flight officers.

Presents awards to outstanding Reserve Officers Training Corps (ROTC) cadets.

Navy League of the United States, 2300 Wilson Blvd., Arlington, VA 22201; (703) 528-1775. Rear Adm. John Dalrymple (USN, ret.), executive director. Fax, (703) 528-2333.

Sponsors Naval Sea Cadet Corps and Navy League Sea Cadet Corps for young people ages 11 through 18 years. Graduates are eligible to enter the Navy at advanced pay grades.

Servicemembers Opportunity Colleges, 1 Dupont Circle N.W. 20036; 667-0079. Steve F. Kime, director. Toll-free, (800) 368-5622. Fax, 667-0622.

Partnership of higher education associations, educational institutions, the Defense Dept., and the military services. Offers credit courses and degree programs to military personnel and their families stationed in the United States and around the world.

See also Air Force Historical Foundation (p. 558); Naval Reserve Assn. (p. 578)

Military Grievances, Discipline, and Appeals

General

Congress:

House Armed Services Committee, Subcommittee on Military Forces and Personnel, 2343 RHOB 20515; 225-7560. Ike Skelton, D-Mo., chairman; Michael R. Higgins, professional staff member. Fax, 226-0105.

Jurisdiction over legislation on military personnel matters, including courts martial and appeals and military grievance procedures.

Senate Armed Services Committee, Subcommittee on Force Requirements and Personnel, SR-228 20510; 224-3871. Richard C. Shelby, D-Ala., chairman; Frederick F. Y. Pang, professional staff member.

Jurisdiction over legislation on military personnel matters, including courts martial and appeals and military grievance procedures.

Correction of Military Records

See also Review Boards (p. 557); Veterans, Correction of Military Records (p. 436)

Agencies:

Air Force Dept. (Defense Dept.), Board for the Correction of Military Records, 1535 Command Dr., EE Wing, 3rd Floor, Andrews AFB, MD 20331-7002; (301) 981-5726. C. Bruce Braswell, executive director. Fax, (301) 981-9207.

Civilian board that reviews appeals for corrections to Air Force personnel records and makes recommendations to the secretary of the Air Force.

Army Dept. (Defense Dept.), Board for the Correction of Military Records, 1941 Jefferson Davis Highway, 2nd Floor, Arlington, VA 22202; (703) 607-1611. David R. Kinneer, executive secretary. Fax, (703) 607-2036.

Civilian board that reviews appeals for corrections to Army personnel records and makes recommendations to the secretary of the Army.

Defense Dept., Legal Policy, The Pentagon, Rm. 4C763 20301-4000; (703) 697-3387. Capt. Jerry Kirkpatrick (USN), director. Fax, (703) 693-6708.

Coordinates policy for armed services boards charged with correcting military records.

Navy Dept. (Defense Dept.), Board for Correction of Naval Records, Navy Annex, Arlington, VA (mailing address: Washington, DC 20370); (703) 614-1402. W. Dean Pfeiffer, executive director. Fax, (703) 614-9857.

Civilian board that reviews appeals for corrections to Navy and Marine Corps personnel records and makes recommendations to the secretary of the Navy.

U.S. Coast Guard (Transportation Dept.), Board for Correction of Military Records, 400 7th St. S.W. 20590; 366-9335. Robert H. Joost, chairman. Fax, 366-7152.

Civilian board that reviews appeals for corrections to Coast Guard personnel records and makes recommendations to the general counsel of the Transportation Dept.

Congress:

See *Military Grievances, Discipline, and Appeals, General, Congress (p. 554)*

Courts Martial/Appeals/ Clemency/Parole

Agencies:

Air Force Dept. (Defense Dept.), Air Force Personnel Council, 1535 Command Dr., EE Wing, Andrews AFB, MD 20331-7002; (301) 981-5739. Brig. Gen. Elwood P. Hinman III, director. Fax, (301) 981-9282.

Military office that administers review boards, including the Clemency and Parole Board, which in turn reviews cases of military prisoners and makes recommendations to the secretary of the Air Force.

Air Force Dept. (Defense Dept.), Judge Advocate General, The Pentagon 20330; (703) 614-5732. Maj. Gen. Nolan Sklute, judge advocate general. Fax, (703) 614-8894.

Military office that prosecutes and defends Air Force personnel during military legal proceedings.

Army Dept. (Defense Dept.), Army Clemency and Parole Board, Crystal Mall 4, 1941 Jefferson Davis Highway, Arlington, VA 22202; (703) 607-1504. James E. Vick, chairman. Fax, (703) 607-2036.

Civilian and military board that reviews cases of military prisoners and makes recommendations to the secretary of the Army; reviews suspension of less-than-honorable discharges and restoration of prisoners to active duty or parole.

Army Dept. (Defense Dept.), Judge Advocate General, The Pentagon 20310; (703) 697-5151. Maj. Gen. Michael J. Nardotti Jr., judge advocate general. Fax, (703) 697-4337.

Military office that prosecutes and defends Army personnel during military legal proceedings. Serves as an administrative office for military appeals court, which hears legal proceedings involving Army personnel.

Defense Dept., U.S. Court of Military Appeals, 450 E St. N.W. 20442; 272-1448. Thomas F. Granahan, clerk of the court. Fax, 504-4672.

Serves as the appellate court for cases involving dishonorable or bad conduct discharges, confinement of a year or more, and the death penalty, and for cases certified to the court by the judge advocate general of an armed service. Less serious cases are reviewed by the individual armed services. Library open to the public.

Navy Dept. (Defense Dept.), Judge Advocate General, 200 Stovall St., Alexandria, VA 22332; (703) 614-7420. Rear Adm. Harold E. Grant, judge advocate general. Fax, (703) 697-4610.

Military office that administers legal proceedings involving Navy and Marine personnel.

Navy Dept. (Defense Dept.), Naval Clemency and Parole Board, 801 N. Randolph St., Arlington, VA 22203; (703) 696-4170. Col. Bernard F. Lubby, executive secretary. Fax, (703) 696-6671.

Military board that reviews cases of Navy and Marine Corps prisoners and makes recommendations to the secretary of the Navy.

Congress:

See *Military Grievances, Discipline, and Appeals, General, Congress (p. 554)*

Nongovernmental·

Judge Advocates Assn., 1815 H St. N.W. 20006; 628-0979. Michael E. Campiglia, director. Fax, 775-0295.

Membership: active duty, reserve, and retired military lawyers; civilian lawyers practicing in the military law field; and members of the Court of Military Appeals. Informs members of developments and proposed changes in military law.

Public Law Education Institute, 1601 Connecticut Ave. N.W. 20009; 232-1400. Thomas Alder, president.

Conducts research and serves as an information clearinghouse on military law, the draft, selective service, veterans' affairs, and tort law related to military affairs.

Deserters

See also *Review Boards (p. 557)*

Agencies:

Air Force Dept. (Defense Dept.), Enlisted Promotion, Evaluation, and Retention Policy, The Pentagon 20330-1040; (703) 697-1661. Chief Master Sgt. Jimmy Tanner, head. Fax, (703) 227-0903.

Military office that develops Air Force policies and responds to inquiries relating to enlisted promotion, evaluation, and retention policy issues.

Army Dept. (Defense Dept.), Military Personnel, Management, and Equal Opportunity Policy, The Pentagon 20310-0111; (703) 697-2631. Robert M. Emmerichs, deputy assistant secretary. Fax, (703) 614-5975.

Civilian office that recommends, monitors, and reviews Army policies relating to deserters.

Army Dept. (Defense Dept.), Military Police Support Agency, 4401 Ford Ave., #225, Alexandria, VA 22302; (703) 756-1880. Jeff Porter, action officer. Fax, (703) 756-1081.

Military office that develops Army policies and responds to inquiries relating to deserters.

Defense Dept., Legal Policy, The Pentagon, Rm. 4C763 20301-4000; (703) 697-3387. Capt. Jerry Kirkpatrick (USN), director. Fax, (703) 693-6708.

Coordinates and reviews Defense Dept. policies and programs relating to deserters.

Marine Corps (Defense Dept.), Corrections, Headquarters, U.S. Marine Corps, Code MHC, Arlington, VA 22214; (703) 696-1064. Chief Warrant Off. 3 James A. Hart, head. Fax, (703) 696-2080.

Military office that develops Marine Corps policies and responds to inquiries relating to deserters. Oversees Marine Corps brigs (correctional facilities).

Navy Dept. (Defense Dept.), Deserter Branch, Navy Annex, Arlington, VA (mailing address: Washington, DC 20370); (703) 614-2551. Cmdr. A. B. Stakem, head. Fax, (703) 614-4009.

Military office that develops Navy policies and responds to inquiries relating to deserters.

Navy Dept. (Defense Dept.), Manpower, The Pentagon 20350-1000; (703) 695-4350. Vacant, deputy assistant secretary. Fax, (703) 614-3889.

Civilian office that develops and reviews Navy and Marine Corps policies relating to deserters.

Congress:

See Military Grievances, Discipline, and Appeals, General, Congress (p. 554)

Grievances

Agencies:

Air Force Dept. (Defense Dept.), Air Force Review Boards, 1535 Command Dr., E Wing, #K307, Andrews AFB, MD 20331-7002; (301) 981-3137. Joe G. Lineberger, deputy. Fax, (301) 981-3136.

Civilian office that responds to complaints from Air Force military personnel and assists in seeking corrective action.

Air Force Dept. (Defense Dept.), Inquiries Support Office, The Pentagon 20330-1140; (703) 614-6321. Lt. Col. Ted Neeves, chief. Fax, (703) 614-6461.

Military office that handles complaints and requests for assistance from civilians and Air Force and other military personnel.

Army Dept. (Defense Dept.), Assistance, The Pentagon 20310-1700; (703) 695-1581. Col. Thomas Mulrine, chief. Fax, (703) 693-0155.

Military office that handles complaints and requests for assistance from Army military personnel and their spouses.

Army Dept. (Defense Dept.), Military Personnel, Management, and Equal Opportunity Policy, The Pentagon 20310-0111; (703) 697-2631. Robert M. Emmerichs, deputy assistant secretary. Fax, (703) 614-5975.

Civilian office that receives complaints from Army military personnel and assists in seeking corrective action.

Defense Dept., Military Equal Opportunity, The Pentagon 20301; (703) 697-6381. Col. Hubert Bridges (USA), director. Fax, (703) 697-6553.

Receives civil rights complaints from military personnel and assists in seeking corrective action.

Marine Corps (Defense Dept.), Inspection, Navy Annex, Arlington, VA (mailing address: Headquarters, U.S. Marine Corps, Code IG, Washington, DC 20380); (703) 614-1698. Maj. Gen. R. L. Phillips, inspector general. Fax, (703) 697-6690.

Military office that receives complaints from Marine Corps personnel and assists in seeking corrective action.

Navy Dept. (Defense Dept.), Management Support, Navy Annex, Arlington, VA (mailing address: Washington, DC 20370); (703) 614-2820. Capt. Stephen R. Cleal, director. Fax, (703) 693-6905.

Military office that handles complaints and requests for assistance from Navy military personnel and members of Congress.

Navy Dept. (Defense Dept.), Manpower and Reserve Affairs, The Pentagon 20350; (703) 697-2179. Frederick F. Y. Pang, assistant secretary. Fax, (703) 614-3889.

Civilian office that receives complaints from Navy and Marine Corps military personnel and assists in seeking corrective action.

Congress:

See *Military Grievances, Discipline, and Appeals, General, Congress (p. 554)*

Review Boards

See also *Veterans, Correction of Military Records (p. 436)*

Agencies:

Air Force Dept. (Defense Dept.), Air Force Personnel Council, 1535 Command Dr., EE Wing, Andrews AFB, MD 20331-7002; (301) 981-5739. Brig. Gen. Elwood P. Hinman III, director. Fax, (301) 981-9282.

Military office that administers boards that review appeal cases. Administers the Air Force Board of Review, Disability Review Board, Clemency and Parole Board, Discharge Review Board, Decorations Board, Personnel Board, and the Physical Disability Appeal Board.

Army Dept. (Defense Dept.), Army Council of Review Boards, 1941 Jefferson Davis Highway, Arlington, VA 22202; (703) 607-1607. Col. Roger A. Wright, director. Fax, (703) 607-2036.

Military office that administers boards that review appeal cases. Administers the Ad Hoc Review Board, Army Grade Determination Board, Disability Rating Review Board, Discharge Review Board, Elimination Review Board, Security Review Board, and Physical Disability Appeal Board.

Defense Dept., Legal Policy, The Pentagon, Rm. 4C763 20301-4000; (703) 697-3387. Capt. Jerry Kirkpatrick (USN), director. Fax, (703) 693-6708.

Coordinates policy for the discharge review boards of the armed services.

Navy Dept. (Defense Dept.), Naval Council of Personnel Boards, 801 N. Randolph St., Arlington, VA 22203; (703) 696-4355. Capt. F. I. Grant (USN), director. Fax, (703) 696-4556.

Military office that administers boards that review appeal cases for the Navy and the Marine Corps. Composed of the Regional Physical Evaluation Boards, the Naval Discharge Review Board, and the Naval Clemency and Parole Board.

Military History

Agencies:

Air Force Dept. (Defense Dept.), Air Force History, Bolling Air Force Base 20332; 767-5764. Richard P. Hallion, chief. Library, 767-0412. Fax, 767-5527.

Publishes historical studies, monographs, and reference works; directs worldwide Air Force History Program and provides guidance to the Air Force Historical Research Agency at Maxwell Air Force Base in Alabama; supports Air Force Air Staff agencies and responds to inquiries from the public and the U.S. government. Library open to the public.

Army Dept. (Defense Dept.), Center of Military History, 1099 14th St. N.W. 20005-3402; 504-5400. Brig. Gen. Harold W. Nelson, chief. Information, 504-5421. Library, 504-5416. Fax, 504-5390.

Publishes the official history of the Army. Provides information on Army history; coordinates Army museum system and art program. Works with Army school system to ensure that history is included in curriculum. Sponsors professional appointments, fellowships, and awards.

Defense Dept., Historical Office, The Pentagon 20301-1950; (703) 697-4216. Alfred Goldberg, historian.

Collects, compiles, and publishes documents and data on the history of the office of the secretary of defense and the Defense Dept.; coordinates historical activities of the Defense Dept. and prepares special studies at the request of the secretary.

Defense Dept., Joint History Office, The Pentagon 20318-9999; (703) 697-3088. Brig. Gen. David A. Armstrong (USA, ret.), director. Fax, (703) 697-0909.

Provides historical support services, including historical research, and writes the official history of the Joint Chiefs of Staff.

Marine Corps (Defense Dept.), Historical Center, Washington Navy Yard S.E. 20374; 433-2273. Brig. Gen. Edwin H. Simmons (USMC, ret.), director. Information, 433-3534. Library, 433-4253. Fax, 433-7265. Reference, 433-3483.

Maintains official Marine Corps archives; writes official histories of the corps for government agencies and the public; answers inquiries about Marine Corps history; maintains museum; conducts prearranged tours of the historical center and museum. Library open to the public.

National Archives and Records Administration, Textual Reference, 7th St. and Pennsylvania Ave. N.W. 20408; 501-5380. R. Michael McReynolds, director. Fax, 501-5005.

Contains Army records from the Revolutionary War to the war in Vietnam, Navy records from the Revolutionary War to the Korean War, and Air Force records from 1947 to 1954. Handles records captured from enemy powers at the end of World War II and a small collection of records captured from the Vietnamese. Conducts research in response to specific inquiries; makes records available for reproduction or examination in research room.

National Museum of American History (Smithsonian Institution), Armed Forces History, 14th St. and Constitution Ave. N.W. 20560; 357-1883. James S. Hutchins, curator/supervisor. Fax, 357-1853.

Maintains collections relating to the history of the U.S. armed forces and the American flag; includes manuscripts, documents, correspondence, uniforms, ordnance material of European and American origin, and other personal memorabilia of armed forces personnel of all ranks.

National Museum of Health and Medicine (Defense Dept.), Walter Reed Medical Center, Bldg. 54 South (mailing address: Armed Forces Institute of Pathology, Washington, DC 20306); 576-2348. Dr. Marc Micozzi, director. Fax, 576-2164.

Maintains exhibits related to pathology and the history of medicine, particularly the history of

military medicine. Open to the public. Study collection available by appointment.

Navy Dept. (Defense Dept.), Naval Historical Center, Washington Navy Yard S.E. (mailing address: 901 M St. S.E. Bldg. 57 WNY, Washington, DC 20374-5060); 433-2210. Dean C. Allard, director. Library, 433-4131. Fax, 433-3593. Museum, 433-4882; Art Gallery, 433-3815; Archives, 433-3171.

Produces publications on naval history. Maintains historical files on Navy ships, operations, shore installations, and aviation. Collects Navy art, artifacts, and photographs. Library and archives open to the public.

U.S. Coast Guard (Transportation Dept.), Historian, 2100 2nd St. S.W. 20593-0001; 267-2596. Robert Browning, historian. Fax, 267-4307.

Collects and maintains Coast Guard historical materials, including service artifacts, documents, photographs, and books. Also publishes books and pamphlets, including the *Commandant's Bulletin*.

Nongovernmental:

Aerospace Education Foundation, 1501 Lee Highway, Arlington, VA 22209; (703) 247-5839. Phil Lacombe, director. Fax, (703) 247-5853.

Promotes knowledge and appreciation of U.S. military and civilian aerospace development and history. Sponsors educational symposia and scholarships for Reserve Officers Training Corps (ROTC) graduates. (Affiliated with the Air Force Assn.)

Air Force Historical Foundation, 1535 Command Dr., Stop 44 #A-122, Andrews AFB, MD 20331; (301) 736-1959. Col. Louis H. Cummings (USAF, ret.), executive director. Fax, (301) 981-3574.

Membership: individuals interested in the history of the U.S. Air Force and U.S. air power. Awards scholarships to Air Force Reserve Officers' Training Corps graduates for master's and doctoral level training in fields related to Air Force needs. Bestows grants and awards on Air Force Academy and Air War College students and to other active duty personnel. Funds research and publishes books on aviation and Air Force history.

The Battle of Normandy Foundation, 1730 Rhode Island Ave. N.W., #612 20036; 728-0672. Anthony C. Stout, president. Fax, 728-0619.

Executive agent to 50th Anniversary Commission: D-Day, the Battle of Normandy and Liberation of Europe, which is planning national and international commemoration of 50th anniversary of World War II. Supports the Battle of Normandy Museum in Caen, France. Administers the Normandy Scholar Program, which sends American university students to Europe to study World War II.

Council on America's Military Past-U.S.A., P.O. Box 1151, Fort Myer, VA 22211; 479-2258. Col. Herbert M. Hart (USMC, ret.), executive director. Toll-free, (800) 398-4693. Fax, 479-0416.

Membership: historians, archeologists, curators, writers, and others interested in military history and historic preservation. Interests include preservation of historic military establishments and ships.

Friends of the Vietnam Veterans Memorial, 2030 Clarendon Blvd., #412, Arlington, VA 22201; (703) 525-1107. Ira Hamburg, executive director. Fax, (703) 525-1109.

Seeks to remind Americans of the significance of the Vietnam War. Assists visitors at the memorial by providing information and escorts; mails name rubbings free of charge to families and friends of individuals whose names are inscribed on the memorial; acts as an information clearinghouse; provides locator service to connect families and friends of those who died in Vietnam.

Naval Historical Foundation, Washington Navy Yard S.E. 20374; 433-2005. Adm. James L. Holloway III (USN, ret.), president. Fax, 889-3565.

Collects private documents and artifacts relating to naval history; maintains collection on deposit with the Library of Congress for public reference.

U.S. Navy Memorial Foundation, 701 Pennsylvania Ave. N.W., #123 20004; 737-2300. Rear Adm. James E. Miller (USN, ret.), president. Toll-free, (800) 821-8892. Fax, 737-2308.

Educational foundation authorized by Congress. Focuses on American naval history; built and supports the Navy memorial to honor those who serve or have served in the Navy or Coast Guard.

Women in Military Service for America Memorial Foundation, 5510 Columbia Pike, #302,

Arlington, VA (mailing address: Dept. 560, Washington, DC 20042-0560); (703) 533-1155. Brig. Gen. Wilma L. Vaught (USAF, ret.), president. Toll-free, (800) 222-2294. Fax, (703) 931-4208.

Authorized by Congress to create, support, and build on federal land in Washington, D.C., and its environs, a national memorial to honor women who serve or have served in the U.S. armed forces.

See also Air Force Assn. (p. 531)

Military Installations

General

Agencies:

Defense Dept., Environmental Security, 400 Army-Navy Dr., Arlington VA 20301; (703) 695-6639. Sherri Wasserman Goodman, deputy under secretary.

Integrates environmental, safety, and occupational health considerations into U.S. defense and economic policies. Works to ensure responsible performance in defense operations, to maintain quality installations, to reduce the costs of complying with environmental laws, and to clean up past contamination.

Defense Dept., Regional Security Affairs, The Pentagon, Rm. 4E838 20301; (703) 695-4351. Charles W. Freeman Jr., assistant secretary. Fax, (703) 697-7230.

Negotiates and monitors defense cooperation agreements, including base rights, access and prepositioning, exchange programs, and status of forces agreements with foreign governments in assigned geographic areas of responsibility.

Congress:

House Armed Services Committee, Subcommittee on Military Installations and Facilities, 2120 RHOB 20515; 225-7120. Dave McCurdy, D-Okla., chairman; Alma B. Moore, professional staff member. Fax, 225-9077.

Jurisdiction over legislation on military base operations and closings, military construction, military housing, and military real estate leasing and buying.

Senate Armed Services Committee, Subcommittee on Military Readiness and Defense

Infrastructure, SR-228 20510; 224-3871. John Glenn, D-Ohio, chairman; David S. Lyles, professional staff member.

Jurisdiction over legislation on military base operations and closings, military construction, military housing, and military real estate leasing and buying.

Base Closings/Economic Impact

Agencies:

Air Force Dept. (Defense Dept.), Base Realignment and Transition, The Pentagon 20330; (703) 695-6766. Col. Wayne Mayfield, chief. Fax, (703) 693-9707.

Military office that plans for the closing of Air Force bases.

Air Force Dept. (Defense Dept.), Bases and Units, The Pentagon 20330; (703) 614-2122. Col. James C. Moore, chief. Fax, (703) 697-1685.

Manages Air Force bases and units worldwide.

Air Force Dept. (Defense Dept.), Installations, The Pentagon 20330-1660; (703) 695-3592. James F. Boatright, deputy assistant secretary. Fax, (703) 693-7568.

Civilian office that plans and reviews the closing of Air Force bases.

Army Dept. (Defense Dept.), Employment and Classification, The Pentagon 20310-0300; (703) 695-4011. James Alward, acting chief. Fax, (703) 695-8411.

Military office responsible for employment policies to assist civilian personnel in cases of Defense Dept. program changes, including base closings.

Army Dept. (Defense Dept.), Installations and Housing, The Pentagon 20310-0110; (703) 697-8161. Paul W. Johnson, deputy assistant secretary. Fax, (703) 614-7394.

Civilian office that manages all Army installations and reviews the closing of Army facilities.

Defense Base Closure and Realignment Commission, 1700 N. Moore St., #1425, Arlington, VA 22209; (703) 696-0504. Jim Courter, chairman. Fax, (703) 696-0550.

Independent commission appointed by the president to study and recommend closure or realignment of military installations. Reviews list of installations provided by the secretary of

defense. Recommendation criteria include current and future mission requirements; cost and personnel implications; availability and condition of land, facilities, and air space; and local economic impact and effect on community infrastructure.

Defense Dept., Civilian Adjustment and Reemployment, 2461 Eisenhower Ave., #164, Alexandria, VA 22314; (703) 325-2050. Douglas R. Earich, director. Fax, (703) 325-2056.

Seeks to find jobs for personnel laid off due to program changes and base closings. Helps manage program changes and base closings.

Defense Dept., Economic Adjustment, 400 Army-Navy Dr., #200, Arlington, VA 22202-2884; (703) 697-9155. Paul J. Dempsey, director. Fax, (703) 697-3021.

Civilian office that helps community officials develop strategies and coordinated plans to alleviate the economic effect of major defense program changes, including base closings, reductions in force, and contract cutbacks. Assists communities where defense activities are being expanded. Serves as the staff for the Economic Adjustment Committee, an interagency group that coordinates federal defense economic adjustment activities.

Marine Corps (Defense Dept.), Land Use and Military Construction, 3033 Wilson Blvd., Arlington, VA 22209; (703) 696-0865. Col. Robert Watkins, head. Fax, (703) 696-1020.

Military office that reviews studies on base closings.

Navy Dept. (Defense Dept.), Installations and Facilities, Crystal Plaza 5, 2211 Jefferson Davis Highway, Arlington, VA 22244; (703) 602-2686. Vacant, deputy assistant secretary. Fax, (703) 602-2145.

Civilian office that assists in planning for the economic and personnel adjustments that accompany program changes at Navy facilities, including base closings.

Navy Dept. (Defense Dept.), Shore Activities, The Pentagon 20350-2000; (703) 695-2420. Rear Adm. Patrick W. Drennon, director. Fax, (703) 614-7298.

Military office that plans for program changes at Navy facilities and assists in planning for the economic and personnel adjustments that accompany such changes, including base closings.

Congress:

See *Military Installations, General, Congress* (p. 559)

See *also* *Congressional Fairness Network* (p. 758)

Commissaries, PXs, and Service Clubs

Agencies:

Air Force Dept. (Defense Dept.), Defense Commissary Liaison Office, The Pentagon 20330-1000; (703) 695-3265. Dan Sclater, legislative liaison. Fax, (703) 695-3650.
Military office that serves as a liaison for defense commissary services.

Air Force Dept. (Defense Dept.), Force Support and Personnel, The Pentagon 20330; (703) 614-4752. Ruby B. DeMesme, acting deputy assistant secretary. Fax, (703) 693-4244.
Civilian office that monitors and reviews policies for Air Force commissaries, PXs, and service clubs and reviews their operations.

Army Dept. (Defense Dept.), Military Personnel, Management, and Equal Opportunity Policy, The Pentagon 20310-0111; (703) 697-2631. Robert M. Emmerichs, deputy assistant secretary. Fax, (703) 614-5975.
Civilian office that monitors policies for Army commissaries, PXs, and service clubs and reviews their operations.

Army Dept. (Defense Dept.), Troop Support, The Pentagon 20310-0500; (703) 695-2711. Col. William L. Hand, chief. Fax, (703) 614-4031.
Military office that monitors operations and policies of clothing, equipment, food, field, and Army commissary services.

Defense Dept., Army and Air Force Exchange, The Pentagon 20330; (703) 695-2958. T. Don Clay, chief, Washington office. Fax, (703) 614-8594.
Coordinates Army and Air Force PX matters with other Defense Dept. offices. (Headquarters in Dallas.)

Defense Dept., Personnel Support Policy and Services, The Pentagon 20301; (703) 697-9283. Col. (select) Lester K. C. Chang (USAF), acting director. Fax, (703) 697-2519.

Directs the operations and policies of armed forces commissaries, PXs, and service clubs.

Navy Dept. (Defense Dept.), Manpower and Reserve Affairs, The Pentagon 20350; (703) 697-2179. Frederick F. Y. Pang, assistant secretary. Fax, (703) 614-3889.
Civilian office that develops policies for Navy and Marine Corps commissaries, exchanges, and service clubs and reviews their operations.

Navy Dept. (Defense Dept.), Navy Club, 1111 Jefferson Davis Highway, Arlington, VA 22202; (703) 602-5096. Capt. Lawrence M. Kelly, head. Fax, (703) 746-6471.
Military office that provides technical guidance for Navy clubs.

Navy Dept. (Defense Dept.), Navy Exchange Program, Crystal Mall 3, 1931 Jefferson Davis Highway, Arlington, VA 22202; (703) 607-0072. Capt. R. J. Blood, director. Fax, (703) 607-1167.
Military office that serves as a liaison between Navy Supply Command and Navy Exchange Service Command, which includes commissaries and PXs. (Support Services located in Virginia Beach, Va.)

Congress:

House Armed Services Committee, Subcommittee on Readiness, 2339 RHOB 20515; 225-9644. Earl Hutto, D-Fla., chairman; Steve Rossetti, professional staff member. Fax, 225-4032.
Jurisdiction over legislation on military commissaries, PXs, and service clubs.

Senate Armed Services Committee, SR-228 20510; 224-3871. Sam Nunn, D-Ga., chairman; Arnold Punaro, staff director.
Jurisdiction over legislation on military commissaries, PXs, and service clubs.

Nongovernmental:

American Logistics Assn., 1133 15th St. N.W., #640 20005; 466-2520. Richard D. Murray, president. Fax, 296-4419.
Membership: suppliers and employees of military commissaries, PXs, and service clubs. Acts as liaison between the Defense Dept. and service contractors; monitors legislation and testifies on issues of interest to members.

International Military Community Executives Assn., 1800 Diagonal Rd., #285, Alexandria, VA 22314; (703) 548-0093. Paul Reece, executive director. Fax, (703) 548-0095.

Provides members with education and training seminars on government affairs, public relations, hospitality and recreation management, and communication. Operates certification program.

Construction, Housing, and Real Estate

Agencies:

Air Force Dept. (Defense Dept.), Housing and Civil Engineering, The Pentagon 20330-1260; (703) 695-0236. Col. Dwight E. Clark, director. Fax, (703) 697-3266.

Military office that plans and directs construction of Air Force housing on military installations in the United States and overseas.

Air Force Dept. (Defense Dept.), Installations, The Pentagon 20330-1660; (703) 695-3592. James F. Boatright, deputy assistant secretary. Fax, (703) 693-7568.

Civilian office that plans and reviews construction policies and programs of Air Force military facilities (including the Military Construction Program), housing programs, and real estate buying, selling, and leasing in the United States.

Air Force Dept. (Defense Dept.), Military Construction, The Pentagon 20330; (703) 697-7799. Col. Karsten Rothenberg, director. Fax, (703) 695-8175.

Military office that plans and directs construction of Air Force facilities (except housing) in the United States and overseas.

Air Force Dept. (Defense Dept.), Real Estate Agency, 172 Luke Ave., #104, AFREA/MI, Bolling Air Force Base 20332-5113; 767-4275. Anthony R. Jonkers, director. Fax, 767-4384.

Acquires, manages, and disposes of land for the Air Force worldwide. Maintains a complete land and facilities inventory.

Army Dept. (Defense Dept.), Army Housing, DAIM-FDH, Fort Belvoir, VA 22060-5518; (703) 355-2401. Dean Stefanides, director. Fax, (703) 355-3481.

Military office that plans and directs the construction and maintenance of Army family housing.

Army Dept. (Defense Dept.), Corps of Engineers, 20 Massachusetts Ave. N.W. 20314-1000; 272-0001. Lt. Gen. Arthur E. Williams (USACE), chief of engineers. Information, 272-0011. Fax, 272-1683.

Military office that establishes policy and directs civil works and military construction projects of the Army Corps of Engineers; directs the Army's real estate leasing and buying for military installations and civil works projects.

Army Dept. (Defense Dept.), Installations and Housing, The Pentagon 20310-0110; (703) 697-8161. Paul W. Johnson, deputy assistant secretary. Fax, (703) 614-7394.

Civilian office that reviews construction of Army military facilities, housing programs, and the buying and leasing of real estate in the United States and overseas.

Defense Dept., Conservation and Installations, 400 Army-Navy Dr., #206, Arlington, VA 22202-2884; (703) 604-5763. Russ Milnes, director. Fax, (703) 604-5934.

Civilian office that oversees Defense Dept. housing programs at military installations. Works to improve the quality of housing services at military installations.

Defense Dept., Conservation Installation, 400 Army-Navy Dr., #206, Arlington, VA 22204-2884; (703) 695-7820. Russel E. Milnes, assistant deputy under secretary. Fax, (703) 697-7548.

Civilian office that develops Defense Dept. policy for acquisition, management, and disposal of military real property. Ensures responsiveness of military physical plant to the changing needs of the military; provides service members and their dependents with military housing; monitors Defense Dept. experiment with decentralized management of military commands.

Marine Corps (Defense Dept.), Facilities, 3033 Wilson Blvd., Arlington, VA (mailing address: Headquarters, U.S. Marine Corps, Code LFF, 2 Navy Annex, Washington, DC 20380-1775); (703) 696-0864. Col. Hank Rudge, head. Fax, (703) 696-0849.

Military office that develops and implements Marine Corps policy for family housing and maintenance of real property.

Marine Corps (Defense Dept.), Land Use and Military Construction, 3033 Wilson Blvd., Arlington, VA 22209; (703) 696-0865. Col. Robert Watkins, head. Fax, (703) 696-1020.

Military office responsible for military construction and the acquisition, management, and disposal of Marine Corps real property.

Navy Dept. (Defense Dept.), Installations and Facilities, Crystal Plaza 5, 2211 Jefferson Davis Highway, Arlington, VA 22244; (703) 602-2686. Vacant, deputy assistant secretary. Fax, (703) 602-2145.

Civilian office that monitors and reviews construction of Navy military facilities and housing and the buying and leasing of real estate in the United States and overseas.

Navy Dept. (Defense Dept.), Real Estate, 200 Stovall St., Alexandria, VA 22332; (703) 325-0437. A. J. Roth, director. Fax, (703) 325-2839.

Military office that directs the Navy's real estate leasing and buying for military installations.

Navy Dept. (Defense Dept.), Shore Activities, The Pentagon 20350-2000; (703) 695-2420. Rear Adm. Patrick W. Drennon, director. Fax, (703) 614-7298.

Military office that oversees the development of construction programs for Navy military facilities in the United States and abroad; directs construction of Navy housing at military installations.

U.S. Coast Guard (Transportation Dept.), Housing Programs, 2100 2nd St. S.W. 20593-0001; 267-6263. Herbert Levin, chief. Fax, 267-4862.

Provides temporary housing for active personnel and their families.

Congress:

House Appropriations Committee, Subcommittee on Military Construction, B300 RHOB 20515; 225-3047. W. G. "Bill" Hefner, D-N.C., chairman; William A. Marinelli, staff assistant.

Jurisdiction over legislation to appropriate funds for military construction, including family housing and NATO infrastructure.

Senate Appropriations Committee, Subcommittee on Military Construction, SD-131 20510; 224-7276. Jim Sasser, D-Tenn., chairman; Michael Walker, clerk.

Jurisdiction over legislation to appropriate funds for military construction, including family housing and NATO infrastructure.

See also Military Installations, General, Congress (p. 559)

Nuclear Weapons and Power

Agencies:

Defense Dept., Atomic Energy, The Pentagon 20301-3050; (703) 697-5161. Harold Palmer Smith, assistant secretary. Fax, (703) 695-0476.

Civilian office responsible for the safety, security, and survivability of nuclear and chemical weapons and for the modernization and upgrading of the nuclear and chemical weapons stockpile. Coordinates nuclear weapons policy with the Energy Dept.

Defense Dept., Nuclear Security and Counter-Proliferation, The Pentagon 20301-2600; (703) 695-0942. Ashton B. Carter, assistant secretary. Fax, (703) 693-9146.

Advises the secretary on policy and strategy for nuclear offensive and defensive forces, including the structure, requirements, and posture of strategic forces, strategic reserve forces, theater nuclear forces, warning systems, and space systems and their employment; surety, reliability, safety, and security of nuclear forces; and strategic and theater missile defense.

Defense Dept., Research and Engineering, The Pentagon 20301-3030; (703) 697-5776. Anita K. Jones, director. Fax, (703) 693-7167.

Civilian office that directs Defense Dept. strategic nuclear weapons research and development programs and coordinates the research and development programs of the individual armed services.

Defense Nuclear Agency (Defense Dept.), 6801 Telegraph Rd., Alexandria, VA 22310; (703) 325-7004. Maj. Gen. Kenneth L. Hagemann (USAF), director. Information, (703) 325-7095. Fax, (703) 325-2960.

Military office responsible for nuclear weapons research testing in the Defense Dept.; coordinates Defense Dept. nuclear weapons activities with civilian nuclear research agencies; manages nuclear weapons stockpile; coordinates inspections of nuclear weapons storage sites; publishes technical documents on nuclear weaponry.

Defense Nuclear Agency (Defense Dept.), Environment and Modeling, 6801 Telegraph Rd., Alexandria, VA 22310; (703) 325-7744. Dr.

David Auton, chief. Information, (703) 285-5610. Fax, (703) 325-2951. Toll-free, (800) 462-3683.

Reviews personnel participation in atmospheric nuclear tests. Provides military personnel who participated in these tests with information.

Energy Dept., Defense Programs, 1000 Independence Ave. S.W., #4A019 20585; 586-2177. Victor H. Reis, assistant secretary. Fax, 586-1567.

Responsible for nuclear weapons research, development, testing, and production; performs laser fusion research and development; provides the assistant secretary for international affairs and the director of arms control and nonproliferation with support in the area of nonproliferation controls.

Energy Dept., Nonproliferation Policy, 1000 Independence Ave. S.W., #GA017 (mailing address: 1540.3, Washington, DC 20585); 586-6175. Edward Fei, acting director. Fax, 586-6789.

Develops and implements policies concerning nuclear materials and equipment; participates in international negotiations involving nuclear policy; supports activities of the International Atomic Energy Agency; develops policies concerning nuclear reprocessing requests.

Energy Dept., Nuclear Energy, 1000 Independence Ave. S.W. 20585; 586-6450. Daniel Dreyfus, acting director. Information, 586-9720. Fax, 586-8353.

Develops and provides nuclear power sources to meet defense requirements for space and terrestrial applications; designs and develops naval nuclear propulsion plants and reactor cores.

National Security Council (Executive Office of the President), Defense Policy/Arms Control, The White House 20506; 395-3330. Robert Bell, director.

Advises the assistant to the president for national security affairs on matters concerning nuclear weapons policy.

Navy Dept. (Defense Dept.), Naval Sea Systems Command, National Center 2, Arlington, VA (mailing address: Washington, DC 20362-5101); (703) 602-3887. Adm. Bruce DeMars, director, naval nuclear propulsion. Fax, (703) 603-1906.

Responsible for naval nuclear propulsion.

State Dept., Nuclear Energy, Main State Bldg. 20520; 647-3310. Richard J. K. Stratford, deputy assistant secretary. Fax, 647-0775.

Coordinates U.S. government activities that support safeguards against proliferation of nuclear weapons.

Congress:

House Appropriations Committee, Subcommittee on Energy and Water Development, 2362 RHOB 20515; 225-3421. Tom Bevill, D-Ala., chairman; Hunter Spillan, staff assistant.

Jurisdiction over legislation to appropriate funds for atomic energy defense activities within the Energy Dept.; Defense Nuclear Facilities Safety Board; Nuclear Regulatory Commission; Nuclear Waste Technical Review Board; Nuclear Safety Oversight Commission; and Office of Nuclear Waste Negotiator.

House Armed Services Committee, Subcommittee on Military Acquisitions, 2343 RHOB 20515; 225-6703. Ronald V. Dellums, D-Calif., chairman; Doug Necessary, professional staff member. Fax, 226-0105.

Jurisdiction over military applications of nuclear energy.

House Energy and Commerce Committee, Subcommittee on Energy and Power, 331 Ford Bldg. (2nd and D Sts. S.W.) 20515; 226-2500. Philip R. Sharp, D-Ind., chairman; Shelley N. Fidler, acting staff director.

Jurisdiction over legislation on siting of nuclear facilities.

House Foreign Affairs Committee, Subcommittee on Economic Policy, Trade, and the Environment, 702 O'Neill Bldg. (300 New Jersey Ave. S.E.) 20515; 226-7820. Sam Gejdenson, D-Conn., chairman; John Scheibel, staff director. Fax, 225-2029.

Jurisdiction over legislation on commercial and economic aspects of nuclear technology and materials.

House Natural Resources Committee, Subcommittee on Energy and Mineral Resources, 818 O'Neill Bldg. (300 New Jersey Ave. S.E.) 20515; 225-8331. Richard H. Lehman, D-Calif., chairman; Deborah Lanzone, staff director. Fax, 225-4273.

Jurisdiction over commercial nuclear facilities, including setting liability limits.

Senate Appropriations Committee, Subcommittee on Energy and Water Development, SD-132 20510; 224-7260. J. Bennett Johnston, D-La., chairman; W. Proctor Jones, clerk.

Jurisdiction over legislation to appropriate funds for the Nuclear Regulatory Commission, Nuclear Safety Oversight Commission, Nuclear Waste Technical Review Board, Office of Nuclear Waste Negotiator, Defense Nuclear Facilities Safety Board, and atomic energy defense activities within the Energy Dept.

Senate Armed Services Committee, SR-228 20510; 224-3871. Sam Nunn, D-Ga., chairman; Arnold Punaro, staff director.

Jurisdiction over national security aspects of nuclear energy.

Senate Energy and Natural Resources Committee, Subcommittee on Energy Research and Development, SH-312 20510; 224-7569. Wendell H. Ford, D-Ky., chairman; Vacant, senior professional staff member.

Jurisdiction over commercial nuclear facilities, including setting liability limits; nuclear fuel cycle policy, including uranium resources; nuclear facilities siting; and breeder reactor development.

Nongovernmental:

See Defense Policy, Arms Control and Disarmament, Nongovernmental (p. 538)

Personnel: Civilian

Agencies:

Air Force Dept. (Defense Dept.), Civilian Personnel, The Pentagon 20330; (703) 695-2141. J. R. Graham, director. Fax, (703) 695-6049.

Implements and evaluates Air Force civilian personnel policies; serves as the principal adviser to the secretary of the Air Force on civilian personnel matters.

Air Force Dept. (Defense Dept.), Civilian Policy, The Pentagon 20330-1040; (703) 695-7381. John L. Schrader, chief. Fax, (703) 695-6049.

Civilian office that monitors and reviews Air Force equal employment opportunity programs and policies.

Army Dept. (Defense Dept.), Civilian Personnel, The Pentagon 20310-0300; (703) 695-4237.

Carol Ashby Smith, director. Fax, (703) 695-8411.

Develops and reviews Army civilian personnel policies and advises the secretary of the Army on civilian personnel matters.

Army Dept. (Defense Dept.), Equal Employment Opportunity, Crystal Mall 4, #919, 1941 Jefferson Davis Highway, Arlington, VA 22202; (703) 607-1978. Luther L. Santiful, director. Fax, (703) 607-2042.

Civilian office that administers equal employment opportunity programs and policies for civilian employees of the Army.

Defense Dept., Personnel and Readiness, The Pentagon 20301-4000; (703) 695-5254. Edwin Dorn, under secretary. Fax, (703) 693-0170.

Civilian office that coordinates civilian personnel policies of the Defense Dept. and reviews civilian personnel policies of the individual services. Handles equal opportunity policies.

Marine Corps (Defense Dept.), Civilian Personnel, Navy Annex, #4336, Arlington, VA (mailing address: Headquarters, U.S. Marine Corps, Code MPC-30, Washington, DC 20380); (703) 614-5624. Frank T. Catenaccio, head; Howard Mathews, deputy equal employment opportunities officer, (703) 614-5650. Fax, (703) 614-8506.

Develops and implements personnel and equal employment opportunity programs for civilian employees of the Marine Corps.

Navy Dept. (Defense Dept.), Civilian Personnel Management, 800 N. Quincy St., Arlington, VA 22203; (703) 696-4546. Roberta K. Peters, director. Fax, (703) 696-5338.

Develops and reviews Navy civilian personnel policies and advises the secretary of the Navy on civilian personnel matters.

Navy Dept. (Defense Dept.), Civilian Personnel Policy/Equal Employment Opportunity, The Pentagon 20350; (703) 695-2248. Dorothy M. Meletzke, deputy assistant secretary. Fax, (703) 614-3889.

Civilian office that develops and reviews Navy and Marine Corps civilian personnel and equal opportunity programs and policies.

U.S. Coast Guard (Transportation Dept.), Civilian Equal Opportunity, 2100 2nd St. S.W. 20593-0001; 267-0040. Marcia H. Coates, chief. Fax, 267-4282.

Administers the Affirmative Employment Program relating to civilian Coast Guard positions; processes complaints.

Congress:

House Armed Services Committee, Subcommittee on Military Forces and Personnel, 2343 RHOB 20515; 225-7560. Ike Skelton, D-Mo., chairman; Michael R. Higgins, professional staff member. Fax, 226-0105.

Jurisdiction over legislation on civilian personnel strength and programs in the military.

Senate Armed Services Committee, Subcommittee on Force Requirements and Personnel, SR-228 20510; 224-3871. Richard C. Shelby, D-Ala., chairman; Frederick F. Y. Pang, professional staff member.

Jurisdiction over legislation on civilian personnel strength and programs in the military.

Personnel: Military

General

Agencies:

Air Force Dept. (Defense Dept.), Force Support and Personnel, The Pentagon 20330; (703) 614-4752. Ruby B. DeMesme, acting deputy assistant secretary. Fax, (703) 693-4244.

Civilian office that coordinates military personnel policies of the Air Force Dept.

Air Force Dept. (Defense Dept.), Personnel, The Pentagon 20330-1040; (703) 697-6088. Lt. Gen. Billy J. Boles, deputy chief of staff. Fax, (703) 614-5436. Toll-free casualty assistance, (800) 433-0048.

Military office that coordinates military personnel policies of the Air Force Dept.

Army Dept. (Defense Dept.), Personnel, The Pentagon 20310; (703) 695-6003. Lt. Gen. Thomas P. Carney, deputy chief of staff. Fax, (703) 693-6607.

Military office that coordinates military and civilian personnel policies of the Army Dept.

Army Dept. (Defense Dept.), U.S. Army Service Center for the Armed Forces, The Pentagon 20310; (703) 695-5643. Col. Donald C. Cook Jr., commander. Fax, 693-3730.

Assists Defense Dept. personnel (military, civilian, retirees, and dependents) with travel requests, movement of household goods, and processing of passports; provides support for the Armed Forces Hostess Assn. and for the chaplain's office. Operates the Pentagon library and motorpool and the Pentagon Officers' Athletic Center.

Defense Dept., Military Manpower and Personnel Policy, The Pentagon 20301-4000; (703) 697-4166. Lt. Gen. Robert M. Alexander (USAF), deputy assistant secretary. Fax, (703) 614-7046.

Military office that coordinates military personnel policies of the Defense Dept. and reviews military personnel policies of the individual services.

Defense Dept., Personnel and Readiness, The Pentagon 20301-4000; (703) 695-5254. Edwin Dorn, under secretary. Fax, (703) 693-0171.

Civilian office responsible for personnel and manpower policies of the Defense Dept.; focal point for all readiness issues.

Navy Dept. (Defense Dept.), Manpower, The Pentagon 20350; (703) 695-4350. Vacant, deputy assistant secretary. Fax, (703) 614-3889.

Civilian office that coordinates military personnel policies of the Navy and the Marine Corps.

Navy Dept. (Defense Dept.), Military Personnel Policy and Career Progression, Navy Annex, Arlington, VA (mailing address: Washington, DC 20370); (703) 614-5571. Rear Adm. L. F. Gunn, assistant chief. Fax, (703) 614-1189.

Military office that coordinates military personnel policies of the Navy Dept.

U.S. Coast Guard (Transportation Dept.), Personnel and Training, 2100 2nd St. S.W. 20593-0001; 267-0905. Rear Adm. William C. Donnell, chief. Fax, 267-4205.

Responsible for hiring, recruiting, and training all military and nonmilitary Coast Guard personnel.

Congress:

House Armed Services Committee, Subcommittee on Military Forces and Personnel, 2343 RHOB 20515; 225-7560. Ike Skelton, D-Mo., chairman; Michael R. Higgins, professional staff member. Fax, 226-0105.

Jurisdiction over legislation on military personnel, including drug and alcohol abuse, equal opportunity, banking and insurance, family services, medical care and benefits, pay and compensation, recruitment, military reserve strength, and retirement benefits.

Senate Armed Services Committee, Subcommittee on Force Requirements and Personnel, SR-228 20510; 224-3871. Richard C. Shelby, D-Ala., chairman; Frederick F. Y. Pang, professional staff member.

Jurisdiction over legislation on military personnel, including drug and alcohol abuse, equal opportunity, banking and insurance, family services, medical care and benefits, Americans missing in action (MIAs), education of overseas dependents, pay and compensation, recruitment, military reserve strength, and retirement benefits.

Nongovernmental:

Air Force Sergeants Assn., 5211 Auth Rd., Suitland, MD 20746; (301) 899-3500. James D. Staton, executive director. Fax, (301) 899-8136.

Membership: active duty, reserve, and retired enlisted personnel of all grades and members of the National Guard. Monitors defense policies and legislation on issues such as the proposed phasing out of federal subsidies for medical and retirement benefits, and commissaries.

American Veterans of World War II, Korea, and Vietnam (Amvets), 4647 Forbes Blvd., Lanham, MD 20706-4380; (301) 459-9600. James J. Kenney, executive director. Fax, (301) 459-7924.

Membership: veterans of World War II, Korea, and Vietnam. Helps members obtain benefits; participates in community programs; operates a volunteer service that donates time to hospitalized veterans. Monitors legislation and regulations.

Army Distaff Foundation, 6200 Oregon Ave. N.W. 20015; 541-0105. Maj. Gen. Calvert P. Benedict (USA, ret.), executive director. Toll-free, (800) 541-4255. Fax, 364-2856.

Supports recreation facilities and transportation services for residents of the Knollwood residential facility, a continuing-care retirement community for Army widows and widowers, retired career Army officers, and relatives of career Army officers.

EXPOSE, Ex-partners of Servicemen (Women) for Equality, P.O. Box 11191, Alexandria, VA 22312; (703) 941-5844. Mary Wurzel, president. Fax, (703) 212-6951.

Membership: former spouses of military personnel, both officers and enlisted, and other interested parties. Seeks federal laws to restore to ex-spouses benefits lost through divorce, including retirement pay; survivors' benefits; and medical, commissary, and exchange benefits. Provides information concerning related federal laws and regulations. Serves as an information clearinghouse.

National Assn. for Uniformed Services, 5535 Hempstead Way, Springfield, VA 22151; (703) 750-1342. Maj. Gen. James C. Pennington (USA, ret.), president. Fax, (703) 354-4380.

Membership: active, reserve, and retired officers and enlisted personnel of all uniformed services, their spouses, widows, and widowers. Supports legislation that benefits military personnel and veterans.

National Assn. of Military Widows, 4023 N. 25th Rd., Arlington, VA 22207; (703) 527-4565. Jean Arthurs, president.

Provides military widows with referral information on survivor benefit programs; helps locate widows eligible for benefits; monitors legislation. Interests include health and education.

National Conference on Ministry to the Armed Forces, 4141 N. Henderson Rd., Arlington, VA 22203; (703) 276-7905. Clifford T. Weathers, coordinator. Fax, (703) 276-7906.

Offers support to the Armed Forces Chaplains Board and the chief of chaplains of each service; disseminates information on matters affecting service personnel welfare.

National Interreligious Service Board for Conscientious Objectors, 1612 K St. N.W., #1400 20006; 293-3220. L. William Yolton, executive director. Fax, 293-3218.

Seeks to defend and extend the rights of conscientious objectors. Provides information and advocacy about the military draft and national service. Offers counseling and information to military personnel seeking discharge or transfer to noncombatant positions within the military.

Society of Military Widows, 5535 Hempstead Way, Springfield, VA 22151; (703) 750-1342. Margaret Tilton, president. Fax, (703) 354-4380.

Serves the interests of widows of servicemen who died while in active military service. Monitors legislation concerning military widows' benefits; provides support programs and information.

United Service Organizations (USO), 601 Indiana Ave. N.W. 20004; 783-8121. Chapman B. Cox, president, World USO. Fax, 638-4716.
Voluntary civilian organization chartered by Congress. Provides military personnel and their families in the United States and overseas with social, educational, and recreational programs.

U.S. Army Warrant Officers Assn., 462 Herndon Parkway, #207, Herndon, VA 22070; (703) 742-7727. Don Hess, executive vice president. Fax, (703) 742-7728.
Membership: active duty, reserve, and retired Army warrant officers. Monitors and makes recommendations to Defense Dept., Army Dept., and Congress on policies and programs affecting Army warrant officers.

Cemeteries and Burials

See also Veterans, Burial Benefits (p. 436)

Agencies:

American Battle Monuments Commission (Executive Office of the President), 20 Massachusetts Ave. N.W. 20314; 272-0532. Vacant, secretary. Information, 272-0533. Fax, 272-1375.
Maintains military cemeteries and memorials on foreign soil and certain memorials in the United States; provides next of kin with grave site and related information.

Army Dept. (Defense Dept.), Arlington National Cemetery, Arlington, VA 22211; (703) 695-3175. John C. Metzler Jr., superintendent. Fax, (703) 697-4967.
Arranges and provides eligibility information for burials at Arlington National Cemetery.

Army Dept. (Defense Dept.), Ceremonies and Special Events, Fort Lesley J. McNair, 4th and P Sts. S.W. 20319; 475-1399. Thomas L. Groppel, director. Fax, 475-2695.
Responsible for ceremonies at the Tomb of the Unknown Soldier in Arlington National Cemetery; arranges for military ceremonies at civilian cemeteries in the military district of Washington and surrounding area.

Congress:

House Appropriations Committee, Subcommittee on VA, HUD, and Independent Agencies, H143 CAP 20515; 225-3241. Louis Stokes, D-Ohio, chairman; Paul Thompson, staff assistant.
Jurisdiction over legislation to appropriate funds for the American Battle Monuments Commission and for cemeterial expenses for the Army Dept., including Arlington National Cemetery.

House Veterans' Affairs Committee, Subcommittee on Housing and Memorial Affairs, 337 CHOB 20515; 225-9164. George E. Sangmeister, D-Ill., chairman; Gloria Royce, staff director.
Jurisdiction over legislation on national cemeteries, including Arlington National Cemetery.

Senate Appropriations Committee, Subcommittee on VA, HUD, and Independent Agencies, SD-142 20510; 224-7211. Barbara A. Mikulski, D-Md., chair; Kevin F. Kelly, clerk.
Jurisdiction over legislation to appropriate funds for the American Battle Monuments Commission and for cemeterial expenses for the Army Dept., including Arlington National Cemetery.

Senate Veterans' Affairs Committee, SR-414 20510; 224-9126. John D. Rockefeller IV, D-W.Va., chairman; Jim Gottlieb, staff director. Fax, 224-9575.
Jurisdiction over legislation on national cemeteries, including Arlington National Cemetery.

Drug and Alcohol Abuse

Agencies:

Air Force Dept. (Defense Dept.), Social Actions, The Pentagon 20330; (703) 614-8488. Maj. Cheryl L. Daly, chief. Fax, (703) 695-4083.
Military office that monitors and reviews Air Force drug and alcohol abuse programs.

Army Dept. (Defense Dept.), Military Personnel, Management, and Equal Opportunity Policy, The Pentagon 20310-0111; (703) 697-2631. Robert M. Emmerichs, deputy assistant secretary. Fax, (703) 614-5975.
Civilian office that monitors and reviews Army drug and alcohol abuse programs and makes recommendations to the secretary of the Army.

Army Dept. (Defense Dept.), Personnel Readiness, The Pentagon 20310; (703) 697-2449. Lt. Col. Jeanette Harris, chief. Fax, (703) 697-2407.

Military office that develops Army policies for combating alcohol and drug abuse by military and civilian personnel; monitors and evaluates individual programs of the major Army commands.

Army Dept. (Defense Dept.), Surgeon General/Personnel Readiness, 5109 Leesburg Pike, Falls Church, VA 22041; (703) 756-8005. Lt. Col. Terry Schultz, chief. Fax, (703) 756-8002.

Military office that develops Army medical programs related to drug and alcohol abuse and health promotion policy.

Defense Dept., Professional Affairs and Quality Assurance, The Pentagon 20301; (703) 695-6800. Dr. John Mazzuchi, acting deputy assistant secretary. Fax, (703) 614-3537.

Reviews and directs drug and alcohol abuse identification, education, prevention, treatment, and rehabilitation programs within the Defense Dept.

Marine Corps (Defense Dept.), Alcohol, Drug, and Health Affairs, U.S. Marine Corps, Code MHH, Washington, DC 20380-1775; (703) 696-1174. James H. McHugh, head. Fax, (703) 696-1186.

Military office that directs Marine Corps drug and alcohol abuse policies and programs.

Navy Dept. (Defense Dept.), Drug and Alcohol Program, Navy Annex, Arlington, VA (mailing address: Washington, DC 20370-5630); (703) 614-8008. Capt. W. R. Towcimak, director. Fax, (703) 697-4466.

Military office that develops and administers Navy drug and alcohol abuse programs.

Navy Dept. (Defense Dept.), Manpower, The Pentagon 20350; (703) 695-4350. Vacant, deputy assistant secretary. Fax, (703) 614-3889.

Civilian office that develops and reviews Navy and Marine Corps drug and alcohol abuse programs.

Congress:

See Personnel: Military, General, Congress (p. 566)

Emergency Leave

Nongovernmental:

American Red Cross, Emergency Communications, 431 18th St. N.W. 20006; 639-3462. William Martin, manager. Fax, 347-4486.

Contacts military personnel in family emergencies; provides military personnel with verification of family situations for emergency leave applications.

See also Air Force Aid Society (p. 571)

Equal Opportunity

Agencies:

Air Force Dept. (Defense Dept.), Social Actions, The Pentagon 20330; (703) 614-8488. Maj. Cheryl L. Daly, chief. Fax, (703) 695-4083.

Military office that develops and administers Air Force equal opportunity programs and policies.

Army Dept. (Defense Dept.), Equal Opportunity Programs, The Pentagon 20310; (703) 697-8721. Maj. Kevin Clement, chief. Fax, (703) 697-2407.

Military office that develops and administers equal opportunity programs and policies for the Army.

Army Dept. (Defense Dept.), Military Personnel, Management, and Equal Opportunity Policy, The Pentagon 20310-0111; (703) 697-2631. Robert M. Emmerichs, deputy assistant secretary. Fax, (703) 614-5975.

Civilian office that develops military equal opportunity programs and policies for the Army.

Defense Dept., Defense Advisory Committee on Women in the Services, The Pentagon, Rm. 3D769 20301-4000; (703) 697-2122. Col. Vickie Longenecker (USA), director. Fax, (703) 697-8256.

Advises the secretary of defense and provides the public with information on matters relating to women in the military, especially recruitment and retention.

Defense Dept., Equal Opportunity Policy, The Pentagon, Rm. 3A272 20301-4000; (703) 695-0105. Claiborne Haughton, director. Fax, (703) 697-1553.

Develops military equal opportunity policy and civilian equal employment opportunity policy for the Defense Dept.

Defense Dept., Military Equal Opportunity, The Pentagon 20301; (703) 697-6381. Col. Hubert Bridges (USA), director. Fax, (703) 697-1553.

Receives civil rights complaints from military personnel and assists in seeking corrective action.

Marine Corps (Defense Dept.), Equal Opportunity, Headquarters, U.S. Marine Corps, Code MHE, Washington, DC 20380; (703) 696-1145. Lt. Col. Oke Johnson, head. Fax, (703) 696-2039.

Military office that develops and administers Marine Corps equal opportunity programs.

Navy Dept. (Defense Dept.), Equal Opportunity, Navy Annex, Arlington, VA (mailing address: Washington, DC 20370); (703) 614-2007. Cmdr. R. D. Watts, director. Fax, (703) 693-6891.

Military office that develops and administers Navy equal opportunity programs and policies.

U.S. Coast Guard (Transportation Dept.), Military Equal Opportunity, 2100 2nd St. S.W. 20593-0001; 267-0036. Cmdr. J. J. Seeley, chief. Fax, 267-4282.

Administers equal opportunity regulations with respect to promotion and advancement of Coast Guard military personnel.

Congress:

See *Personnel: Military, General, Congress* (p. 566)

Nongovernmental:

See *Human Rights Campaign Fund* (p. 269)

Family Services

Agencies:

Air Force Dept. (Defense Dept.), Family Matters, The Pentagon 20330; (703) 697-4720. Col. Robert B. Brady, chief. Fax, (703) 695-4083.

Military office that monitors and reviews policy relating to services provided to Air Force families and civilian employees with family concerns.

Army Dept. (Defense Dept.), Armed Forces Hostess Assn., The Pentagon 20310-6604; (703) 697-3180. Patsy Rutledge, president.

Volunteer office staffed by wives of military personnel of all services. Serves as an information clearinghouse for military and civilian Defense Dept. families; maintains information on military bases in the United States and abroad; issues information handbook for families in the Washington area.

Army Dept. (Defense Dept.), Community and Family Support Center, 2461 Eisenhower Ave., Alexandria, VA 22331-0500; (703) 325-9008. Brig. Gen. John G. Meyer Jr., commanding general. Fax, (703) 325-6315.

Military office that directs operations of Army recreation, community service, child development, and youth activity centers. Handles dependent education in conjunction with the Defense Dept.

Defense Dept., Family Policy and Support, The Pentagon 20301-4000; (703) 697-7191. Gail H. McGinn, director. Fax, (703) 695-1977.

Coordinates policies of the individual services relating to the families of military personnel.

Marine Corps (Defense Dept.), Family Programs, 3033 Wilson Blvd., Arlington, VA (mailing address: Headquarters, U.S. Marine Corps, Code MHF, Washington, DC 20380-1775); (703) 696-2046. Judy Hampton, head. Fax, (703) 696-1143.

Sponsors family service centers located on major Marine Corps installations. Oversees the administration of policies affecting the quality of life of Marine Corps military families. Administers education and relocation assistance programs. Offers child development services.

Navy Dept. (Defense Dept.), Force Support and Families, The Pentagon 20350; (703) 614-3553. Von Harrison, deputy assistant secretary. Fax, (703) 614-3889.

Civilian office that oversees the administration of all policies affecting the quality of life of families of Navy military personnel.

Navy Dept. (Defense Dept.), Naval Personnel, Navy Annex, Arlington, VA (mailing address: Washington, DC 20370-6600); (703) 697-6411. Capt. M. S. Debien, director. Fax, (703) 697-6464.

Oversees Navy family service centers; provides naval personnel and families being sent overseas with information and support; addresses problems of abuse and sexual assault within families; helps Navy spouses find employment; facilitates communication between Navy families and Navy officials. Assists in relocating Navy families during transition from military to civilian life.

U.S. Coast Guard (Transportation Dept.), Family Support Programs, 2100 2nd St. S.W. 20593-0001; 267-6726. Cmdr. B. E. Leek, chief. Fax, 267-4862.
Offers broad array of human services to individuals in the Coast Guard and their families, including child care, elderly care, educational services, domestic violence counseling, and health care.

Congress:

See Personnel: Military, General, Congress (p. 566)

Nongovernmental:

Air Force Aid Society, 1745 Jefferson Davis Highway, Arlington, VA 22202; (703) 607-3072. Gen. John A. Shaud (USAF, ret.), director. Fax, (703) 607-3022.
Membership: Air Force active duty, reserve, and retired military personnel and their dependents. Provides active duty and retired Air Force military personnel with personal emergency loans for basic needs, travel, or dependents' health expenses; assists families of active, deceased, or retired Air Force personnel with postsecondary education, loans, and grants.

American Red Cross, Emergency Communications, 431 18th St. N.W. 20006; 639-3462. William Martin, manager. Fax, 347-4486.
Contacts military personnel in family emergencies; provides military personnel with verification of family situations for emergency leave applications.

National Military Family Assn., 6000 Stevenson Ave., Alexandria, VA 22304; (703) 823-6632. Michele Webb, president. Fax, (703) 751-4857.
Membership: active duty and retired military, National Guard, and reserve personnel of all U.S. uniformed services, their families, and interested individuals. Works to improve the quality of life for military families.

Navy-Marine Corps Relief Society, 801 N. Randolph St., Arlington, VA 22203-1978; (703)

696-4904. Vice Adm. Jimmy Pappas (USN, ret.), president. Fax, (703) 696-0144.
Assists Navy and Marine Corps personnel and their families in times of need. Disburses interest-free loans and grants. Provides educational loans, visiting nurse services, thrift shops, food lockers, budget counseling, and volunteer training.

See also No Greater Love (p. 574)

See also Personnel: Military, General, Nongovernmental (p. 567)

Financial Services

Agencies:

Air Force Dept. (Defense Dept.), Financial Management, The Pentagon 20330; (703) 697-1974. Robert F. Hale, assistant secretary and comptroller.
Advises the secretary of the Air Force on policies relating to financial services for military and civilian personnel.

Army Dept. (Defense Dept.), Casualty Operations, 2461 Eisenhower Ave., Alexandria, VA 22331-0481; (703) 325-8627. Lt. Col. Michael Stinello, head. Fax, (703) 325-0134.
Verifies beneficiaries of deceased Army personnel for benefits distribution.

Defense Dept., Accounting Policy, The Pentagon 20301; (703) 697-0536. Nelson E. Toye, director. Fax, (703) 697-4608.
Develops policy for banks and credit unions on military installations for all service branches.

Marine Corps (Defense Dept.), Casualty Section, 3033 Wilson Blvd., Arlington, VA (mailing address: Commandant of the Marine Corps, Code MHP-10, Washington, DC 20380); (703) 696-2069. Maj. D. J. Greco, head. Fax, (703) 696-2072.
Confirms beneficiaries of deceased Marine Corps personnel for benefits distribution.

Navy Dept. (Defense Dept.), Casualty Assistance, Navy Annex, Arlington, VA (mailing address: Commander, Bureau of Naval Personnel, PERS663, Washington, DC 20370-6630); (703) 614-2926. Tim Trant, head. Fax, (703) 614-3345.
Confirms beneficiaries of deceased Navy personnel for benefits distribution.

Congress:

House Banking, Finance, and Urban Affairs Committee, Subcommittee on Financial Institutions Supervision, Regulation, and Deposit Insurance, 212 O'Neill Bldg. (300 New Jersey Ave. S.E.) 20515; 226-3280. Stephen L. Neal, D-N.C., chairman; Peter Kinzler, staff director. Fax, 226-1266.

Jurisdiction over legislation regulating banking and credit unions on military bases (jurisdiction shared with Subcommittee on General Oversight, Investigations, and the Resolution of Failed Financial Institutions).

House Banking, Finance, and Urban Affairs Committee, Subcommittee on General Oversight, Investigations, and the Resolution of Failed Financial Institutions, 139 RHOB 20515; 225-2828. Floyd H. Flake, D-N.Y., chairman; Gloria Bryant, staff director. Fax, 225-7145.

Oversight of banking and credit unions on military bases (shared with Subcommittee on Financial Institutions Supervision, Regulation, and Deposit Insurance).

Senate Banking, Housing, and Urban Affairs Committee, SD-534 20510; 224-7391. Donald W. Riegle Jr., D-Mich., chairman; Steven Harris, staff director.

Oversees and has jurisdiction over legislation on banking and credit unions on military bases.

See also Personnel: Military, General, Congress (p. 566)

Nongovernmental:

Armed Forces Benefit Assn., 909 N. Washington St., Alexandria, VA 22314; (703) 549-4455. Lt. Gen. C. C. Blanton (USAF, ret.), president. Fax, (703) 548-6497.

Membership: active and retired personnel of the uniformed services, federal civilian employees, and dependents. Offers low-cost insurance and financial and banking services worldwide.

Army and Air Force Mutual Aid Assn., 468 Sheridan Ave., Fort Myer, VA 22211-5002; (703) 522-3060. Bradley J. Snyder, president. Toll-free, (800) 336-4538. Fax, (703) 875-0076.

Private service organization that offers member and family assistance services to active duty Army and Air Force officers, retired officers who became members before their retirement, and retired officers under age 60.

Defense Credit Union Council, 805 15th St. N.W., #300 20005; 682-5993. James W. Rowe, president. Fax, 682-9054.

Trade association of credit unions serving the Defense Dept.'s military and civilian personnel. Works with the National Credit Union Administration to solve problems concerning the operation of credit unions for the military community; maintains liaison with the Defense Dept.

Medical Benefits

Agencies:

Air Force Dept. (Defense Dept.), Force Support and Personnel, The Pentagon 20330; (703) 614-4752. Ruby B. DeMesme, acting deputy assistant secretary. Fax, (703) 693-4244.

Civilian office that reviews and monitors medical benefits programs for Air Force military personnel.

Air Force Dept. (Defense Dept.), Managed Care, Bolling Air Force Base 20332; 767-5066. Col. Robert E. Shields, chief. Fax, 404-7366.

Military office that develops and administers medical benefits and entitlement programs for Air Force military personnel.

Army Dept. (Defense Dept.), Military Personnel, Management, and Equal Opportunity Policy, The Pentagon 20310-0111; (703) 697-2631. Robert M. Emmerichs, deputy assistant secretary. Fax, (703) 614-5975.

Civilian office that reviews and monitors medical benefits programs for Army military personnel and makes recommendations to the secretary of the Army.

Army Dept. (Defense Dept.), Personnel Readiness, The Pentagon 20310; (703) 697-2449. Lt. Col. Jeanette Harris, chief. Fax, (703) 697-2407.

Military office that develops Army policies on HIV-positive Army personnel, suicide prevention, and general health promotion.

Army Dept. (Defense Dept.), Professional Services, 5111 Leesburg Pike, Falls Church, VA 22041-3258; (703) 756-0113. Brig. Gen. Russ Zajtchak, director. Fax, (703) 756-0121.

Military office that administers medical benefits programs for Army military personnel; answers inquiries regarding eligibility and formulates clinical policy.

Defense Dept., Health Affairs, The Pentagon 20301-1200; (703) 697-2111. Dr. Stephen Joseph, assistant secretary. Fax, (703) 614-3537.

Civilian office that administers the medical benefits programs for active duty and retired military personnel and dependents in the Defense Dept.; develops policies relating to medical programs.

Navy Dept. (Defense Dept.), Health Affairs, The Pentagon 20350; (703) 614-0855. Cmdr. Chris Music, director. Fax, (703) 693-4959.

Civilian office that reviews medical programs for Navy and Marine Corps military personnel and develops and reviews policies relating to these programs.

Navy Dept. (Defense Dept.), Patient Administration, 23rd and E Sts. N.W. 20372; 653-1081. Cmdr. Ernie Ghent, director. Fax, 653-0899.

Military office that develops and administers medical benefits programs for Navy and Marine Corps military personnel.

U.S. Coast Guard (Transportation Dept.), Health and Safety, 2100 2nd St. S.W. 20593-0001; 267-1098. Rear Adm. Alan M. Steinman, chief. Fax, 267-4346.

Oversees all health and safety aspects of the Coast Guard, including the operation of medical and dental clinics, sick bays on ships, and mess halls and galleys. Investigates Coast Guard accidents, such as the grounding of ships and downing of aircraft.

See also Uniformed Services University of the Health Sciences (p. 553)

Congress:

See Personnel: Military, General, Congress (p. 566)

Nongovernmental:

Assn. of Military Surgeons of the United States, 9320 Old Georgetown Rd., Bethesda, MD 20814; (301) 897-8800. Lt. Gen. Max B. Bralliar (USAF, ret.), executive director. Fax, (301) 530-5446.

Membership: health professionals, including nurses, dentists, pharmacists, and physicians, who work or have worked for the U.S. Public Health Service, the VA, or the Army, Navy, or Air Force, and students. Works to improve all phases of federal health services.

Commissioned Officers Assn. of the U.S. Public Health Service, 1400 Eye St. N.W., #725 20005; 289-6400. William J. Lucca Jr., executive director. Fax, 682-0487.

Membership: commissioned officers of the U.S. Public Health Service. Supports expansion of federal health care facilities, including military facilities.

See also Veterans, Health Care and Hospitals, Nongovernmental (p. 438)

Military Bands

Agencies:

Army Dept. (Defense Dept.), Ceremonies and Special Events, Fort Lesley J. McNair, 4th and P Sts. S.W. 20319-5050; 475-1281. Maj. Robert Boggs, coordinator.

Coordinates and schedules public ceremonies and special events, including appearances of all armed forces bands and honor guards.

Defense Dept., Community Relations, The Pentagon 20301-1400; (703) 697-7385. Col. Peter Fisher (USA), public affairs officer, (703) 695-2113. Fax, (703) 697-2577.

Provides armed forces bands with policy guidance for related public events.

Congress:

See Personnel: Military, General, Congress (p. 566)

Missing in Action and Prisoners of War

Agencies:

Air Force Dept. (Defense Dept.), Personnel, The Pentagon 20330-1040; (703) 697-6088. Lt. Gen. Billy J. Boles, deputy chief of staff. Fax, (703) 614-5436. Toll-free casualty assistance, (800) 433-0048.

Military office that responds to inquiries about missing in action (MIA) personnel for the Air Force; refers inquiries to the Military Personnel Center at Randolph Air Force Base in San Antonio, Texas.

Army Dept. (Defense Dept.), Casualty and Memorial Affairs Operations, 2461 Eisenhower Ave., Alexandria, VA 22331; (703) 325-5305. Lt. Col. Mack M. Brooks, chief, POWs and MIAs. Fax, (703) 325-1808.

Military office that responds to inquiries about missing in action (MIA) personnel for the Army and distributes information about Army MIAs to the next of kin.

Defense Dept., POW/MIA Affairs, The Pentagon 20301-2400; (703) 284-1295. James W. Wold (USAF, ret.), deputy assistant secretary designate. Fax, (703) 908-0924.

Civilian office responsible for policy matters relating to prisoners of war and missing in action issues. Represents the Defense Dept. before Congress, the media, veterans organizations, and POW/MIA families.

Defense Dept., Public Communication, The Pentagon, Rm. 2B777 20301-1400; (703) 697-5737. Harold Heilsnis, director. Fax, (703) 695-1149.

Responds to public inquiries on Defense Dept. personnel, including those listed as missing in action.

Marine Corps (Defense Dept.), Casualty Section, 3033 Wilson Blvd., Arlington, VA (mailing address: Headquarters, U.S. Marine Corps, Code MHP-10, Washington, DC 20380-1775); (703) 696-2069. A. Hammers, assistant head. Fax, (703) 696-2072.

Military office that responds to inquiries about missing in action (MIA) personnel for the Marine Corps and distributes information about Marine Corps MIAs to the next of kin.

Navy Dept. (Defense Dept.), Naval Personnel, Navy Annex, Arlington, VA (mailing address: Washington, DC 20370-6600); (703) 697-6411. Capt. M. S. Debien, director. Fax, (703) 697-6464.

Military office that responds to inquiries about missing in action (MIA) personnel for the Navy and distributes information about Navy MIAs.

State Dept., Vietnam, Laos, and Cambodia Affairs, Main State Bldg., Rm. 5210 20520; 647-3132. James Gagnon, deputy director. Fax, 647-3069.

Handles issues related to Americans missing in action in Indochina; serves as liaison with Congress, international organizations, and foreign governments on developments in these countries.

Congress:

House Armed Services Committee, Subcommittee on Oversight and Investigations, 2540 RHOB 20515; 225-2086. Norman Sisisky, D-Va., chairman; Warren Nelson, professional staff member. Fax, 226-0105.

Jurisdiction over legislation on Americans missing in action (MIAs).

Senate Armed Services Committee, Subcommittee on Force Requirements and Personnel, SR-228 20510; 224-3871. Richard C. Shelby, D-Ala., chairman; Frederick F. Y. Pang, professional staff member.

Jurisdiction over legislation on Americans missing in action (MIAs).

Nongovernmental:

National League of Families of American Prisoners and Missing in Southeast Asia, 1001 Connecticut Ave. N.W., #919 20036; 223-6846. Ann Mills Griffiths, executive director. Fax, 785-9410. Recording, 659-0133.

Membership: family members of MIAs and POWs and returned POWs of the Vietnam War. Works for the release of all prisoners of war, an accounting of the missing, and repatriation of the remains of those who have died serving their country in Southeast Asia. Works to raise public awareness of these issues; maintains regional and state coordinators; sponsors an annual recognition day.

No Greater Love, 1750 New York Ave. N.W. 20006; 783-4665. Carmella LaSpada, chief executive officer. Fax, 783-1168.

Provides programs of remembrance, friendship, and care for families of Americans killed in war or by acts of terrorism.

See also American Veterans of World War II, Korea, and Vietnam (p. 567)

Overseas Dependents' Education

Agencies:

Defense Dept., Dependents Education, 4040 N. Fairfax Dr., Arlington, VA 22203-1635; (703) 696-4247. John L. Stremple, director. Fax, (703) 696-8918.

Civilian office that maintains school system for dependents of all military personnel and eligible civilians overseas; advises the secretary of defense on overseas education matters; supervises selection of teachers in schools for military dependents.

Congress:

House Armed Services Committee, Subcommittee on Readiness, 2339 RHOB 20515; 225-9644. Earl Hutto, D-Fla., chairman; Steve Rossetti, professional staff member. Fax, 225-4032.
Jurisdiction over legislation concerning overseas military dependents' education programs.

House Education and Labor Committee, Subcommittee on Elementary, Secondary, and Vocational Education, B-346A RHOB 20515; 225-4368. Dale E. Kildee, D-Mich., chairman; Susan Wilhelm, staff director. Fax, 225-1110.
Jurisdiction over legislation concerning overseas and domestic military dependents' education programs (jurisdiction shared with House Armed Services Committee).

Senate Armed Services Committee, Subcommittee on Force Requirements and Personnel, SR-228 20510; 224-3871. Richard C. Shelby, D-Ala., chairman; Frederick F. Y. Pang, professional staff member.
Jurisdiction over legislation concerning military dependents' education programs.

See also Personnel: Military, General, Congress (p. 566)

Pay and Compensation

Agencies:

Air Force Dept. (Defense Dept.), Force Support and Personnel, The Pentagon 20330; (703) 614-4752. Ruby B. DeMesme, acting deputy assistant secretary. Fax, (703) 693-4244.
Civilian office that monitors and reviews Air Force military pay and compensation policies.

Air Force Dept. (Defense Dept.), Military Compensation, The Pentagon 20330; (703) 695-1111. Col. Susan Fischer, chief. Fax, (703) 697-8453.
Military office that develops and administers Air Force military personnel pay and compensation policies.

Army Dept. (Defense Dept.), Military Compensation and Entitlements, The Pentagon 20310; (703) 695-2491. Lt. Col. Edgar Stanton, chief. Fax, (703) 693-1832.

Military office that develops and administers Army military personnel pay and compensation policies.

Army Dept. (Defense Dept.), Military Personnel, Management, and Equal Opportunity Policy, The Pentagon 20310-0111; (703) 697-2631. Robert M. Emmerichs, deputy assistant secretary. Fax, (703) 614-5975.

Civilian office that monitors and reviews Army pay and compensation policy and makes recommendations to the secretary of the Army.

Defense Dept., Compensation, The Pentagon 20301; (703) 695-3176. Capt. David C. Lundahl (USN), director. Fax, (703) 697-8725.

Coordinates military pay and compensation policies with the individual service branches and advises the secretary of defense on compensation policy.

Marine Corps (Defense Dept.), Policy, Navy Annex, Arlington, VA (mailing address: Headquarters, U.S. Marine Corps, Washington, DC 20380), (703) 614-3440. Maj. S. L. Walsh, compensation/incentive officer. Fax, (703) 614-2649.

Military office that develops and administers Marine Corps personnel pay and compensation policies.

Navy Dept. (Defense Dept.), Manpower, The Pentagon 20350; (703) 695-4350. Vacant, deputy assistant secretary. Fax, (703) 614-3889.

Civilian office that develops and reviews Navy and Marine Corps pay and compensation policies.

Navy Dept. (Defense Dept.), Military Compensation Policy, Navy Annex, Arlington, VA (mailing address: Washington, DC 20350); (703) 614-5633. Capt. E. F. Uricoli, head. Fax, (703) 695-3311.

Military office that develops and administers Navy military personnel pay and compensation policies.

Congress:

See Personnel: Military, General, Congress (p. 566)

Recruitment

Agencies:

Air Force Dept. (Defense Dept.), Accession Policy, The Pentagon 20330; (703) 697-8917. Lt. Col. Doc Holaday, chief. Fax, (703) 614-1436.
Military office that coordinates Air Force recruiting activities with the recruitment service at Randolph Air Force Base in San Antonio, Texas.

Air Force Dept. (Defense Dept.), Force Support and Personnel, The Pentagon 20330; (703) 614-4752. Ruby B. DeMesme, acting deputy assistant secretary. Fax, (703) 693-4244.
Civilian office that monitors and reviews Air Force recruitment policies and programs.

Army Dept. (Defense Dept.), Enlisted Accessions, The Pentagon 20310; (703) 697-6744. Col. Richard Durden, chief. Fax, (703) 695-0183.
Military office that develops policies and administers Army recruitment programs.

Army Dept. (Defense Dept.), Personnel Procurement and Manpower Systems, The Pentagon 20310; (703) 697-8201. Col. Jeanne Hamilton, assistant deputy. Fax, (703) 614-5975.
Civilian office that monitors and reviews Army recruitment policies and programs and makes recommendations to the secretary of the Army.

Defense Dept., Accession Policy, The Pentagon 20301; (703) 695-5525. Wayne S. Sellman, director. Fax, (703) 614-9272.
Civilian office that develops Defense Dept. recruiting programs and policies, including advertising, market research, and enlistment standards. Coordinates with the individual services on recruitment of military personnel.

Defense Dept., Defense Advisory Committee on Women in the Services, The Pentagon, Rm. 3D769 20301-4000; (703) 697-2122. Col. Vickie Longenecker (USA), director. Fax, (703) 697-8256.
Advises the secretary of defense on recruiting and retaining women in the armed services.

Marine Corps (Defense Dept.), Personnel Procurement, Navy Annex, Arlington, VA (mailing address: Commandant, U.S. Marine Corps, Code MR, Headquarters, 2 Navy Annex, Washington, DC 20380-1775); (703) 614-2508. Maj.

Gen. James R. Davis, director. Fax, (703) 614-8428.
Military office that administers and develops policies for Marine Corps officer and enlisted recruitment programs.

Navy Dept. (Defense Dept.), Military Personnel Policy and Career Progression, Navy Annex, Arlington, VA (mailing address: Washington, DC 20370); (703) 614-5571. Rear Adm. L. F. Gunn, assistant chief. Fax, (703) 614-1189.
Military office that develops policies and plans for Navy recruitment programs.

Navy Dept. (Defense Dept.), Navy Recruiting Command, 801 N. Randolph St., Arlington, VA 22203; (703) 696-4181. Adm. Marsha J. Evans, commander. Fax, (703) 696-8957.
Military office that administers Navy recruitment programs.

Navy Dept. (Defense Dept.), Recruiting, The Pentagon 20350; (703) 697-2427. Lt. Col. Peter Karonis (USMC), special assistant. Fax, (703) 693-4957.
Civilian office that develops and reviews Navy and Marine Corps recruitment policies and programs.

Congress:

See *Personnel: Military, General, Congress* (p. 566)

Reserves

See also *Military Education and Training* (p. 551)

Agencies:

Air Force Dept. (Defense Dept.), Air Force Reserve, The Pentagon 20330-1150; (703) 695-9225. Maj. Gen. John J. Closner, chief. Information, (703) 697-1761. Fax, (703) 614-4026.
Military office that coordinates and directs Air Force Reserve matters (excluding the Air National Guard).

Air Force Dept. (Defense Dept.), Air National Guard, The Pentagon 20310-2500; (703) 693-4750. Maj. Gen. Donald W. Shepperd, director. Information, (703) 695-0421. Fax, (703) 697-2943.

Military office that coordinates and directs Air National Guard matters.

Air Force Dept. (Defense Dept.), Reserve Affairs, The Pentagon 20330-1660; (703) 697-6375. Maury Ison, acting deputy assistant secretary. Fax, (703) 695-2701.

Civilian office that reviews and monitors Air Force Reserve, Air National Guard, and Civil Air Patrol policies.

Army Dept. (Defense Dept.), Army National Guard, The Pentagon 20310-2500; (703) 697-5559. Maj. Gen. John R. D'Araujo Jr., director. Information, (703) 695-0421. Fax, (703) 697-8060.

Military office that coordinates and directs Army National Guard matters.

Army Dept. (Defense Dept.), Army Reserve, The Pentagon 20310-2400; (703) 697-1784. Maj. Gen. Roger W. Sandler, chief. Information, (703) 696-3961. Fax, (703) 697-1891.

Military office that coordinates and directs Army Reserve matters (excluding the Army National Guard).

Army Dept. (Defense Dept.), Manpower and Reserve Affairs, The Pentagon 20310-0111; (703) 697-9253. William D. Clark, acting assistant secretary. Fax, (703) 614-5975.

Civilian office that reviews Army Reserve policies.

Defense Dept., Reserve Affairs, The Pentagon 20301-1500; (703) 695-0063. Deborah Lee, assistant secretary. Fax, (703) 693-5371.

Civilian office that develops Defense Dept. reserve policies; coordinates and reviews reserve programs.

Marine Corps (Defense Dept.), Reserve Affairs, Navy Annex, Arlington, VA (mailing address: Headquarters, U.S. Marine Corps, Washington, DC 20380); (703) 614-1161. Brig. Gen. Steven Berkheiser, assistant deputy chief of staff. Fax, (703) 614-3099.

Military office that coordinates and directs Marine Corps Reserve matters.

Navy Dept. (Defense Dept.), Naval Reserve, The Pentagon 20350-2000; (703) 695-5353. Rear Adm. Thomas F. Hall, director. Information, (703) 695-5588. Fax, (703) 695-3357.

Military office that coordinates and directs Naval Reserve matters.

Navy Dept. (Defense Dept.), Reserve Affairs, The Pentagon 20350-1000; (703) 614-5410. Wade R. Sanders, deputy assistant secretary. Fax, (703) 614-3889. Marine Corps Reserve Affairs, (703) 697-9326.

Civilian office that reviews Navy and Marine Corps Reserve policies.

U.S. Coast Guard (Transportation Dept.), Readiness and Reserve, 2100 2nd St. S.W. 20593-0001; 267-2350. Rear Adm. Gregory A. Penington, chief. Fax, 267-4553.

Oversees and ensures Coast Guard readiness to perform its peacetime mission and its wartime role. Responsible for training all reserve forces.

Congress:

See Personnel: Military, General, Congress (p. 566)

Nongovernmental:

Adjutants General Assn. of the United States, 1 Massachusetts Ave. N.W. 20001 1121; 789-0031. Maj. Gen. John L. Matthews, adjutant general of Utah, president; Capt. Victor Dubina, public relations director. Fax, 682-9358.

Organization of the adjutants general of the National Guard. Holds conferences to coordinate National Guard activities with the Defense Dept.

Assn. of Civilian Technicians, 12510-B Lake Ridge Dr., Lake Ridge, VA 22192; (703) 690-1330. John T. Hunter, president. Fax, (703) 494-0961.

Membership: federal civil service employees of the National Guard. Represents members before federal agencies and Congress.

Enlisted Assn. of the National Guard of the United States, 1219 Prince St., Alexandria, VA 22314; (703) 519-3846. Master Sgt. Michael P. Cline (ret.), executive director. Toll-free, (800) 234-3264. Fax, (703) 519-3849.

Membership: active and retired enlisted members and veterans of the National Guard. Promotes a strong national defense and National Guard. Sponsors scholarships, conducts seminars, and provides information concerning members and their families.

Marine Corps Reserve Officers Assn., 201 N. Washington St., #206, Alexandria, VA 22314; (703) 548-7607. Col. Laurence R. Gaboury (USMC, ret.), executive director. Fax, (703) 519-8779.

Membership: active duty and retired Marine Corps Reserve officers. Promotes the interests of the Marine Corps and the Marine Corps Reserve; conducts annual military conference.

National Guard Assn. of the United States, 1 Massachusetts Ave. N.W. 20001-1431; 789-0031. Maj. Gen. Robert F. Ensslin Jr. (USNG, ret.), executive director. Fax, 682-9358.

Membership: active duty and retired officers of the National Guard. Works to promote a strong national defense and to maintain a strong, ready National Guard.

Naval Reserve Assn., 1619 King St., Alexandria, VA 22314; (703) 548-5800. Rear Adm. James E. Forrest (USN, ret.), executive director. Fax, (703) 683-3647.

Membership: active duty, inactive, and retired Navy and Naval Reserve officers. Supports and promotes U.S. military and naval policies, particularly the interests of the Navy and Naval Reserve. Offers education programs for naval reservists and potential naval commissioned officers. Provides the public with information on national security issues. Assists members with Naval Reserve careers, military retirement, and veterans' benefits.

Reserve Officers Assn. of the United States, 1 Constitution Ave. N.E. 20002; 479-2200. Maj. Gen. Evan Hultman (USAR, ret.), executive director. Fax, 479-0416.

Membership: active and inactive commissioned officers of all uniformed services. Supports continuation of a reserve force to enhance national security.

See also veterans' service organizations in Veterans, General, Nongovernmental (p. 433)

Retirement

See also Veterans (p. 430)

Agencies:

Air Force Dept. (Defense Dept.), Force Support and Personnel, The Pentagon 20330; (703) 614-4752. Ruby B. DeMesme, acting deputy assistant secretary. Fax, (703) 693-4244.

Civilian office that monitors and reviews Air Force military retirement programs.

Air Force Dept. (Defense Dept.), Retirements and Separations, The Pentagon 20330-1040; (703) 697-9012. Major Rich Cervetti, head. Fax, (703) 227-0903.

Military office that coordinates Air Force separation and retirement matters with the Military Personnel Center at Randolph Air Force Base, San Antonio, Texas.

Army Dept. (Defense Dept.), Military Personnel, Management, and Equal Opportunity Policy, The Pentagon 20310-0111; (703) 697-2631. Robert M. Emmerichs, deputy assistant secretary. Fax, (703) 614-5975.

Civilian office that monitors and reviews Army military retirement programs and makes recommendations to the secretary of the Army.

Army Dept. (Defense Dept.), Retirement Services, 2461 Eisenhower Ave., Alexandria, VA 22331; (703) 325-9158. Lt. Col. Gary F. Smith (ret.), chief. Toll-free, (800) 336-4909. Fax, (703) 325-6327.

Military office that administers retirement programs for Army military personnel.

Defense Dept., Compensation, The Pentagon 20301; (703) 695-3176. Capt. David C. Lundahl (USN), director. Fax, (703) 697-8725.

Develops retirement policies and reviews administration of retirement programs for all Defense Dept. military personnel.

Marine Corps (Defense Dept.), Retired Activities, Navy Annex, Arlington, VA (mailing address: Headquarters, U.S. Marine Corps, Code MMSR-6, Washington, DC 20380); (703) 614-1901. Carolyn Dawson, head. Fax, (703) 614-4400.

Military office that administers retirement programs and benefits for Marine Corps retirees.

Marine Corps (Defense Dept.), Separation and Retirement, Navy Annex, Arlington, VA (mailing address: Headquarters, U.S. Marine Corps, Code MMSR, Washington, DC 20380); (703) 614-1735. James P. Rathbun, head. Fax, (703) 614-4400.

Military office that processes Marine Corps military personnel retirements but does not administer benefits.

Navy Dept. (Defense Dept.), Manpower, The Pentagon 20350; (703) 695-4350. Vacant, deputy assistant secretary. Fax, (703) 614-3889.

Civilian office that directs and reviews Navy and Marine Corps military retirement programs.

Navy Dept. (Defense Dept.), Retired Activities, Navy Annex, Arlington, VA (mailing address: Washington, DC 20370); (703) 614-3197. June Herrin, head. Fax, (703) 693-6471.

Military office that administers retirement programs and benefits for Navy military personnel.

Navy Dept. (Defense Dept.), Retirements Branch, Navy Annex, Arlington, VA (mailing address: Washington, DC 20370); (703) 614-2690. Cmdr. Tom E. Lisowski, head. Fax, (703) 614-9482.

Military office that processes Navy military personnel retirements but does not administer benefits.

U.S. Soldiers' and Airmen's Home, 3700 N. Capitol St. N.W. 20317; 722-3228. Maj. Gen. Donald C. Hilbert (USA, ret.), director. Information, 722-3386. Fax, 722-9087.

Gives domiciliary and medical care to retired regular enlisted personnel of the Army and Air Force or career service personnel unable to earn a livelihood.

Congress:

See Personnel: Military, General, Congress (p. 566)

Nongovernmental:

Retired Enlisted Assn., 909 N. Washington St., #300, Alexandria, VA 22314; (703) 684-1981. John M. Adams, executive director, government affairs. Fax, (703) 548-4876.

Membership: enlisted personnel who have retired for length of service or medical reasons from the active, reserve, or guard components of the armed forces. Runs scholarship, legislative, and veterans service programs. (Headquarters in Aurora, Colo.)

Retired Officers Assn., 201 N. Washington St., Alexandria, VA 22314; (703) 549-2311. Vice Adm. Thomas J. Kilcline (USN, ret.), president. Fax, (703) 838-8173.

Membership: officers and former officers of the uniformed services. Assists members, their dependents, and survivors with service status and retirement problems; provides employment assistance. Monitors legislation affecting veterans affairs, health, and military compensation issues.

Procurement, Acquisition, and Logistics

See also Nuclear Weapons and Power (p. 563); Research and Development (p. 582)

Agencies:

Air Force Dept. (Defense Dept.), Acquisition, The Pentagon 20330-1060; (703) 697-6361. Vacant, assistant secretary. Fax, (703) 693-6400.

Civilian office that directs and reviews Air Force procurement policies and programs.

Air Force Dept. (Defense Dept.), Contracting, The Pentagon 20330 1060; (703) 695-6332. Brig. Gen. Robert W. Drewes, deputy assistant secretary. Fax, (703) 693-2947.

Develops, implements, and enforces contracting policies on Air Force acquisitions worldwide, including research and development services, weapons systems, logistics services, and operational contracts.

Air Force Dept. (Defense Dept.), Fighter, C², and Weapons Programs, The Pentagon 20330-1060; (703) 695-2147. Brig. Gen. John W. Hawley, director. Fax, (703) 697-5653.

Military office that directs Air Force acquisition and development programs within the tactical arena.

Army Dept. (Defense Dept.), Procurement, The Pentagon 20310-0103; (703) 695-1862. George E. Dausman, deputy assistant secretary. Fax, (703) 614-9505.

Directs and reviews Army procurement policies and programs.

Defense Contract Audit Agency (Defense Dept.), Cameron Station, Alexandria, VA 22304-6178; (703) 274-6785. William H. Reed, director. Fax, (703) 617-7450.

Performs all contract audits for the Defense Dept. Provides Defense Dept. personnel responsible for procurement and contract administration with accounting and financial advisory services.

Defense Dept., Acquisition and Technology, The Pentagon 20301-3015; (703) 695-2381. Paul Kaminski, under secretary designate. Information, (703) 695-4893. Fax, (703) 693-2576.

Formulates and directs policy relating to the department's purchasing system. Oversees all defense procurement and acquisition programs.

Defense Dept., Armed Services Board of Contract Appeals, 5109 Leesburg Pike, Falls Church, VA 22041; (703) 756-8501. Paul Williams, chairman. Fax, (703) 756-8535.

Adjudicates disputes arising under Defense Dept. contracts.

Defense Dept., Defense Acquisition Regulation Council, The Pentagon 20301; (703) 697-7267. Nancy Ladd, director. Fax, (703) 697-9845.

Develops procurement regulations for the Defense Dept.

Defense Dept., Logistics, The Pentagon 20301-3500; (703) 697-1368. Jeffrey A. Jones, assistant deputy under secretary. Fax, (703) 693-0555.

Formulates and implements department policies and programs regarding spare parts management. Oversees acquisition of spare parts.

Defense Dept., Operational Test and Evaluation, The Pentagon 20301-1700; (703) 697-3654. Philip E. Coyle, III, director designate. Fax, (703) 693-5248.

Ensures that major acquisitions, including weapons systems, are operationally effective and suitable prior to full-scale investment. Provides the secretary of defense and Congress with independent assessment of these programs.

Defense Logistics Agency (Defense Dept.), Cameron Station, Alexandria, VA 22304-6100; (703) 274-6111. Vice Adm. Edward M. Straw (USN), director. Information, (703) 274-6135. Fax, (703) 274-4965.

Administers defense contracts; acquires, stores, and distributes food, clothing, medical, and other supplies used by the military services and other federal agencies; administers programs related to logistical support for the military

services; and assists military services with developing, acquiring, and using technical information and defense materiel and disposing of materiel no longer needed.

Defense Systems Management College (Defense Dept.), 9820 Belvoir Rd., #G38, Fort Belvoir, VA 22060-5565; (703) 805-3360. Brig. Gen. Claude M. Bolton Jr. (USA), commandant. Fax, (703) 805-2639. Registrar, (703) 805-2227.

Offers courses to military and civilian personnel who specialize in acquisition and procurement. Conducts research to improve management of defense systems acquisitions programs.

Marine Corps (Defense Dept.), Contract Division, 3033 Wilson Blvd., Arlington, VA 22201; (703) 696-1013. Philip E. Zanfagna Jr., director. Fax, (703) 696-1016.

Military office that directs Marine Corps procurement programs.

Navy Dept. (Defense Dept.), Acquisition Policy, Integrity, and Accountability, Crystal Plaza 5, #578, 2211 Jefferson Davis Highway, Arlington, VA 22244-5104; (703) 602-2338. Rear Adm. Eugene Harshbarger, deputy. Fax, (703) 602-4643.

Civilian office that directs and reviews Navy acquisition and procurement policy.

Navy Dept. (Defense Dept.), Logistics, The Pentagon 20350-2000; (703) 695-2154. Vice Adm. Stephen F. Loftus, deputy chief. Fax, (703) 695-0605.

Military office that directs policy for Navy procurement and acquisition programs.

Navy Dept. (Defense Dept.), Military Sealift Command, Washington Navy Yard 20398-5100; 433-0001. Vice Adm. Michael P. Kalleres, commander. Information, 433-0330. Fax, 433-6638.

Transports Defense Dept. and other U.S. government cargo by sea; operates ships that maintain supplies for the armed forces and scientific agencies.

U.S. Coast Guard (Transportation Dept.), Acquisition, 2100 2nd St. S.W. 20593-0001; 267-2007. Rear Adm. G. F. Woolever, chief. Fax, 267-4279.

Administers all procurement made through the Acquisition Contract Support division.

U.S. Coast Guard (Transportation Dept.), Logistics Management, 2100 2nd St. S.W. 20593-

0001; 267-1407. Capt. Robert Kirk Jones, chief. Fax, 267-4516.

Sets policy and procedures for the procurement, distribution, maintenance, and replacement of materiel and personnel.

U.S. Department of Justice—Defense Procurement Fraud Unit, 1400 New York Ave. N.W., #3100 (mailing address: P.O. Box 28188, Central Station, Washington, DC 20038); 514-0819. Barbara Corprew, deputy chief. Fax, 514-0152.

Interdepartmental unit that investigates fraud in defense contracting.

Congress:

General Accounting Office, National Security and International Affairs, 441 G St. N.W. 20548; 512-2800. Frank C. Conahan, assistant comptroller general. Fax, 512-7686.

Independent, nonpartisan agency in the legislative branch. Audits, analyzes, and evaluates Defense Dept. acquisition programs; makes unclassified reports available to the public.

House Armed Services Committee, Subcommittee on Military Acquisitions, 2343 RHOB 20515; 225-6703. Ronald V. Dellums, D-Calif., chairman; Doug Necessary, professional staff member. Fax, 226-0105.

Jurisdiction over legislation on military procurement (excluding construction) and military contract services.

House Armed Services Committee, Subcommittee on Readiness, 2339 RHOB 20515; 225-9644. Earl Hutto, D-Fla., chairman; Steve Rossetti, professional staff member. Fax, 225-4032.

Jurisdiction over legislation on naval petroleum reserves and leasing of capital equipment.

House Government Operations Committee, Subcommittee on Legislation and National Security, B373 RHOB 20515; 225-5147. John Conyers Jr., D-Mich., chairman; James C. Turner, staff director. Fax, 225-2373.

Oversight of defense procurement.

Senate Armed Services Committee, SR-228 20510; 224-3871. Sam Nunn, D-Ga., chairman; Arnold Punaro, staff director.

Jurisdiction over legislation on military procurement (excluding construction), naval petroleum reserves, and military contract services.

Nongovernmental:

Contract Services Assn., 1200 G St. N.W., #750 20005; 347-0600. Gary Engebretson, president. Fax, 347-0608.

Membership: companies that, under contract, provide federal, state, and local governments and other agencies with various technical and support services (interests include defense and space). Analyzes the process by which the government awards contracts to private firms; monitors legislation and regulations.

Council of Defense and Space Industry Assns., 1250 Eye St. N.W., #1100 20005; 371-8414. Ruth W. Franklin, administrative officer. Fax, 371-8470.

Makes recommendations on federal procurement policies. Interests include estimating and accounting systems, contract clauses, defective pricing data, industrial security, management systems control, patents and technical data, property acquisition and control, and contract cost principles.

Electronic Industries Assn., Government Division, 2001 Pennsylvania Ave. N.W. 20006-1813; 457-4940. Dan C. Heinemeier, vice president. Fax, 457-4910.

Membership: companies engaged in the research, development, integration, or manufacture of electronic equipment or services for defense and other government applications. Monitors federal policy and practices in acquiring electronic products and services; represents the electronics industry's views on acquisition regulations in the Defense Dept. and other federal agencies; serves as the focal point through which the Defense Dept. communicates with the electronics industry on procurement policy and other matters affecting the business-government relationship.

National Security Industrial Assn., 1025 Connecticut Ave. N.W., #300 20036; 775-1440. Adm. James R. Hogg (USN, ret.), president. Fax, 775-1309.

Membership: industrial, research, legal, and educational organizations interested in national security. Interests include federal procurement regulations and defense policies that affect contractors.

See also Doing Business with the Government, Nongovernmental (p. 60)

See also Center for Naval Analyses (p. 533)

Research and Development

See also Nuclear Weapons and Power (p. 563); Procurement, Acquisition, and Logistics (p. 579)

Agencies:

Air Force Dept. (Defense Dept.), Acquisition, The Pentagon 20330-1060; (703) 697-6361. Vacant, assistant secretary. Fax, (703) 693-6400.

Civilian office that directs and reviews Air Force research, development, and acquisition of weapons systems.

Army Dept. (Defense Dept.), Research, Development, and Acquisition, The Pentagon 20310; (703) 695-6153. George E. Dausman, acting assistant secretary. Fax, (703) 697-4003.

Civilian office that directs and reviews Army research and development of weapons systems and missiles.

Defense Dept., Ballistic Missile Defense Organization, The Pentagon 20301-7100; (703) 695-7060. Lt. Gen. Malcolm R. O'Neil (USA), director. Information, (703) 695-8743. Fax, (703) 693-1693.

Manages and directs the ballistic missile defense acquisition and research and development programs. Seeks to deploy improved theater missile defense systems and to develop options for effective national missile defenses while increasing the contribution of defensive systems to U.S. and allied security.

Defense Dept., Defense Advanced Research Projects Agency, 3701 N. Fairfax Dr., Arlington, VA 22203; (703) 696-2400. Gary L. Denman, director. Fax, (703) 696-2209.

Seeks to ensure U.S. technological superiority by determining which proposals for future projects related to national security deserve further research.

Defense Dept., Defense Research and Engineering, The Pentagon, Rm. 3E1045 20301; (703) 695-0598. John Bachkosky, deputy director. Fax, (703) 614-6829.

Civilian office responsible for policy, guidance, and oversight of the Defense Dept.'s Science and Technology Program. Serves as focal point for in-house laboratories, university research, and other scientific matters.

Defense Dept., Research and Engineering, The Pentagon 20301-3030; (703) 697-5776. Anita K. Jones, director. Fax, (703) 693-7167.

Principal technical adviser to the under secretary of defense for acquisition and technology on space-related matters. Oversees maintenance of U.S. technology base and works to select the best technology programs to achieve and preserve a qualitative lead in deployed systems.

Defense Technical Information Center (Defense Dept.), Cameron Station, Alexandria, VA 22304-6145; (703) 274-6800. Kurt N. Molholm, administrator. Information, (703) 274-7633. Fax, (703) 617-7718. Registration, (703) 274-6871.

Acts as a central repository for the Defense Dept.'s collection of current and completed research and development efforts in all fields of science and technology. Disseminates research and development information to contractors, grantees, and registered organizations working on government research and development projects, particularly for the Defense Dept. Users must register with the center.

Marine Corps (Defense Dept.), Systems Command, Quantico, VA 22134-5010; (703) 640-2411. Maj. Gen. J. A. Brabham Jr., commander. Fax, (703) 640-3792.

Military office that directs Marine Corps research, development, and acquisition.

Naval Research Laboratory, Research, 4555 Overlook Ave. S.W. 20375-5000; 767-3301. Timothy Coffey, director. Information, 767-2541. Fax, 404-8110.

Conducts scientific research and develops advanced technology for the Navy. Areas of research include radar systems, radiation technology, tactical electronic warfare, and weapons guidance systems.

Navy Dept. (Defense Dept.), Research, Development, and Acquisition, The Pentagon 20350; (703) 695-6315. Nora Slatkin, assistant secretary. Fax, (703) 697-0172.

Civilian office that directs and reviews Navy and Marine Corps research and development of weapons systems.

Navy Dept. (Defense Dept.), Test Evaluation and Technology Requirements, The Pentagon 20350-2000; (703) 697-5533. Rear Adm. W. P. Houley, director. Fax, (703) 697-8368.

Military office that directs Navy test and evaluation and development of weapons systems.

Office of Science and Technology Policy (Executive Office of the President), National Security and International Affairs, Old Executive Office Bldg., Rm. 494 20500; 456-2894. Jane Wales, associate director. Information, 395-6142. Fax, 395-1571.

Supports and advises the president on national security policy, international science matters, and other science policy areas. Coordinates international science and technology issues at the interagency level.

President's National Security Telecommunications Advisory Committee, c/o National Communications System, 701 S. Courthouse Rd., Arlington, VA 22204-2198; (703) 692-9274. Lt. Col. Michael S. Cleary, director. Fax, (703) 746-5240.

Advises the president on specific measures to improve national security telecommunications.

State Dept., Intelligence and Research, Main State Bldg., Rm. 6533 20520-6510; 647-9177. Toby T. Gati, assistant secretary. Fax, 647-4296.

Coordinates foreign-policy-related research, analysis, and intelligence programs for the State Dept. and other federal agencies.

U.S. Coast Guard (Transportation Dept.), Engineering Logistics and Development, 2100 2nd St. S.W. 20593-0001; 267-1844. Rear Adm. Peter A. Bunch, chief. Fax, 267-4245.

Develops and maintains engineering standards for the building of ships and other Coast Guard craft.

Congress:

House Armed Services Committee, Subcommittee on Research and Technology, 2120B RHOB 20515; 225-6527. Patricia Schroeder, D-Colo., chair; Doug Roach, staff contact, Air Force; William Andahazy, staff contact, Army; Jean Reed, staff contact, Navy. Fax, 225-6890.

Jurisdiction over legislation on military research and development, reinvestment, and conversion.

Senate Armed Services Committee, SR-228 20510; 224-3871. Sam Nunn, D-Ga., chairman; Arnold Punaro, staff director.

Jurisdiction over military research and development legislation.

Nongovernmental:

American Society of Naval Engineers, 1452 Duke St., Alexandria, VA 22314; (703) 836-6727. Capt. Charles J. Smith (USN, ret.), executive director. Fax, (703) 836-7491.

Membership: civilian, active duty, and retired naval engineers. Provides forum for an exchange of information between industry and government involving all phases of naval engineering.

ANSER (Analytic Services), 1215 Jefferson Davis Highway, #800, Arlington, VA 22202; (703) 416-2000. John M. Fabian, president. Fax, (703) 416-3050.

Systems analysis organization funded by government contracts. Conducts weapon systems analysis.

Armed Forces Communications and Electronics Assn., 4400 Fair Lakes Court, Fairfax, VA 22033; (703) 631-6100. Adm. James B. Busey IV (USN, ret.), president. Fax, (703) 631-4693.

Membership: industrial organizations, scientists, and military and government personnel in the fields of communications, electronics, and electrical engineering. Consults with the Defense Dept. and other federal agencies on design and maintenance of command, control, communications, computer, and intelligence systems; holds shows displaying latest communications products.

Institute for Defense Analyses, 1801 N. Beauregard St., Alexandria, VA 22311; (703) 845-2300. Gen. Larry D. Welch (USAF, ret.), president. Fax, (703) 845-2588.

Federally funded research and development center that focuses on national security and defense. Conducts research, systems evaluation, and policy analysis for Defense Dept. and other agencies.

Johns Hopkins University Applied Physics Laboratory, Johns Hopkins Rd., Laurel, MD 20723-6099; (301) 953-5000. Dr. G. L. Smith, director. Fax, (301) 953-1093. TDD, (301) 953-5666.

Research and development organization that primarily conducts research for the Navy on guided missiles and weapons systems; develops research satellites for the Navy and the National Aeronautics and Space Administration.

Logistics Management Institute, 6400 Goldsboro Rd., Bethesda, MD 20817-5886; (301) 320-2000. Gen. William G. T. Tuttle Jr. (USA, ret.), president. Library, (301) 320-7249. Fax, (301) 320-5617.

Conducts research on military and nonmilitary logistics, including transportation, supply and maintenance, force management, weapons support, acquisition, health systems, international programs, energy and environment, mathematical modeling, installations, operations, and information systems. Library open to the public by appointment.

Society of American Military Engineers, 607 Prince St., Alexandria, VA 22314; (703) 549-3800. Vice Adm. A. B. Beran (USCG, ret.), executive director. Fax, (703) 684-0231.

Membership: military and civilian engineers and architects. Conducts research on subjects related to military engineering.

SRI International, 1611 N. Kent St., Arlington, VA 22209; (703) 524-2053. Gerald E. Connolly, vice president, Washington office. Fax, (703) 247-8569.

Research organization supported by government and private contracts. Conducts research on military technology, including lasers and computers. Other interests include strategic planning and armed forces interdisciplinary research. (Headquarters in Menlo Park, Calif.)

See also Center for Defense Information (p. 533)

Selective Service

Agencies:

Justice Dept., General Litigation and Legal Advice, 1001 G St. N.W., #200 20530; 514-1026. Roger B. Cubbage, deputy chief. Fax, 514-6113.

Investigates and prosecutes cases involving violation of federal selective service laws.

Selective Service System, 1515 Wilson Blvd., Arlington, VA 22209-2425; (703) 235-2200. Robert Gambino, director. Information, (703) 235-2555. Fax, (703) 235-2212.

Supplies the armed forces with military manpower when authorized; registers male citizens of the United States ages 18 to 25.

Congress:

House Appropriations Committee, Subcommittee on VA, HUD, and Independent Agencies, H143 CAP 20515; 225-3241. Louis Stokes, D-Ohio, chairman; Paul Thompson, staff assistant.

Jurisdiction over legislation to appropriate funds for the Selective Service System.

House Armed Services Committee, Subcommittee on Military Forces and Personnel, 2343 RHOB 20515; 225-7560. Ike Skelton, D-Mo., chairman; Michael R. Higgins, professional staff member. Fax, 226-0105.

Jurisdiction over selective service legislation.

House Government Operations Committee, Subcommittee on Legislation and National Security, B373 RHOB 20515; 225-5147. John Conyers Jr., D-Mich., chairman; James C. Turner, staff director. Fax, 225-2373.

Oversees operations of the Selective Service System.

Senate Appropriations Committee, Subcommittee on VA, HUD, and Independent Agencies, SD-142 20510; 224-7211. Barbara A. Mikulski, D-Md., chair; Kevin F. Kelly, clerk.

Jurisdiction over legislation to appropriate funds for the Selective Service System.

Senate Armed Services Committee, Subcommittee on Force Requirements and Personnel, SR-228 20510; 224-3871. Richard C. Shelby, D-Ala., chairman; Frederick F. Y. Pang, professional staff member.

Oversees operations of the Selective Service System.

Nongovernmental:

National Interreligious Service Board for Conscientious Objectors, 1612 K St. N.W., #1400 20006; 293-3220. L. William Yolton, executive director. Fax, 293-3218.

Monitors legislation concerning defense personnel and conscientious objection. Provides information and counseling on military service and conscientious objection.

Public Law Education Institute, 1601 Connecticut Ave. N.W. 20009; 232-1400. Thomas Alder, president.

Conducts research and serves as an information clearinghouse on military law, the draft, selective service, veterans' affairs, and tort law related to military affairs.

Key Agency:

Agriculture Dept.
14th St. and Independence Ave. S.W.
20250
Information: 720-2791

Key Committees:

House Agriculture Committee
1301 LHOB 20515
Phone: 225-2171

Senate Agriculture, Nutrition, and Forestry Committee
SR-328A 20510
Phone: 224-2035

Key Personnel:

Agriculture Dept.

Mike Espy, secretary

Richard Rominger, deputy secretary

Eugene Moos, under secretary for international affairs and commodity programs

Bob Nash, under secretary for small community and rural development

Keith J. Collins, acting assistant secretary for economics

Ellen Haas, assistant secretary for food and consumer services

Patricia Jensen, acting assistant secretary for marketing and inspection services

James Lyons, assistant secretary for natural resources and environment

R.D. Plowman, acting assistant secretary for science and education

14

Agriculture

Contents:

Agriculture

General

Agencies:

Agricultural Marketing Service (Agriculture Dept.), 14th St. and Independence Ave. S.W. (mailing address: P.O. Box 96456, Washington, DC 20090-6456); 720-5115. Lon Hatamiya, administrator. Information, 720-8998. Fax, 720-8477.

Administers marketing, standardization, grading, inspection, and regulatory programs; maintains a market news service to inform producers of market price changes; conducts agricultural marketing research and development programs; studies agricultural transportation issues.

Agricultural Stabilization and Conservation Service (Agriculture Dept.), 14th St. and Independence Ave. S.W. (mailing address: P.O. Box 2415, Washington, DC 20013); 720-3467. Grant Buntrock, administrator. Information, 720-5237. Fax, 720-9105.

Oversees farm commodity programs that provide crop loans and purchases. Administers price support programs that provide crop payments when market prices fall below specified levels; conducts programs to help obtain adequate farm and commercial storage and drying equipment for farm products; directs conservation and environmental cost sharing projects and programs to assist farmers during natural disasters and other emergencies.

Agricultural Stabilization and Conservation Service (Agriculture Dept.), Natural Resources Analysis, 14th St. and Independence Ave. S.W. (mailing address: P.O. Box 2415, Washington, DC 20013); 720-9685. Thomas L. Browning, director. Fax, 720-8261.

Studies economic issues relating to conservation and land-use programs and availability of storage for agricultural products. Oversees the service's regulatory activities.

Agriculture Dept., 14th St. and Independence Ave. S.W. 20250; 720-3631. Mike Espy, secretary. Information, 720-2791. Library, 720-3434. Fax, 720-2166. Recorded news, 488-8358.

Serves as principal adviser to the president on agricultural policy; works to increase and maintain farm income and to develop markets abroad for U.S. agricultural products.

Agriculture Dept., Board of Contract Appeals, 14th St. and Independence Ave. S.W. 20250-0600; 720-7023. Edward Houry, chairman. Fax, 720-3059.

Considers appeals of decisions made by contracting officers involving agencies within the Agriculture Dept., including decisions on contracts for construction, property, and services.

Agriculture Dept., Economic Analysis Staff, 14th St. and Independence Ave. S.W. 20250-0100; 720-5955. Keith J. Collins, director. Fax, 690-4915.

Prepares economic and statistical analyses used to plan and evaluate short- and intermediate-range agricultural policy. Evaluates Agriculture Dept. policy and proposals and legislation for their impact on the agricultural economy.

Agriculture Dept., Economics, 14th St. and Independence Ave. S.W. 20250; 720-4164. Keith J. Collins, acting assistant secretary. Fax, 690-4915.

Administers the department's economic agencies, including the National Agricultural Statistics Service, Economic Research Service, World Agricultural Outlook Board, Office of Energy, Economics Management Staff, and Economic Analysis Staff.

Agriculture Dept., Food and Consumer Services, 14th St. and Independence Ave. S.W. 20250; 720-7711. Ellen Haas, assistant secretary. Fax, 690-3100.

Directs the Food and Nutrition Service and the Human Nutrition Information Service, which include all Agriculture Dept. domestic food assistance programs. Oversees office of the consumer adviser for agricultural products.

See also Domestic Policy Council (p. 300)

Congress:

General Accounting Office, Food and Agriculture Issues, 441 G St. N.W. 20548; 512-5138. John W. Harman, director. Fax, 512-8774.

Independent, nonpartisan agency in the legislative branch that audits the Agriculture Dept. and analyzes and reports on its handling of food and agriculture issues.

House Agriculture Committee, 1301 LHOB 20515; 225-2171. E. "Kika" de la Garza, D-Texas, chairman; Dianne Powell, staff director. Fax, 225-8510.

Jurisdiction over legislation on agriculture, agricultural economics and research, agricultural extension services and experiment stations, agricultural engineering, animal industry and diseases, forestry industries, pests and pesticides, rural issues and family farms, and nutrition; oversees Agriculture Dept. operations.

House Appropriations Committee, Subcommittee on Agriculture, Rural Development, FDA, and Related Agencies, 2362 RHOB 20515; 225-2638. Richard J. Durbin, D-Ill., chairman; Robert B. Foster, staff assistant. Fax, 225-3598.

Jurisdiction over legislation to appropriate funds for the Agriculture Dept. (except the Forest Service), the Farm Credit Administration, the Commodity Futures Trading Commission, and other agriculture-related services and programs.

House Government Operations Committee, Subcommittee on Information, Justice, Transportation, and Agriculture, B349C RHOB 20515; 225-3741. Gary Condit, D-Calif., chairman; Shannon Lahey, acting staff director. Fax, 225-2445.

Oversees operations of the Agriculture Dept. (except Food and Consumer Services, Food Safety and Inspection Service, and the Forest Service).

House Ways and Means Committee, Subcommittee on Oversight, 1135 LHOB 20515; 225-5522. J. J. Pickle, D-Texas, chairman; Beth K. Vance, staff director. Fax, 225-0787.

Oversees government-sponsored enterprises, including the Farm Credit Banks and the Federal Agricultural Mortgage Corp., with regard to the financial risk they pose to the federal government.

Senate Agriculture, Nutrition, and Forestry Committee, SR-328A 20510; 224-2035. Patrick J. Leahy, D-Vt., chairman; Charles Riemenschneider, chief of staff.

Jurisdiction over legislation on agriculture, agricultural economics and research, agricultural extension services and experiment stations, agricultural engineering, animal industry and diseases, forestry, pests and pesticides, rural issues, nutrition, and family farms; oversees Agriculture Dept. operations.

Senate Appropriations Committee, Subcommittee on Agriculture, Rural Development, and Related Agencies, SD-140 20510; 224-7240. Dale Bumpers, D-Ark., chairman; Rocky L. Kuhn, clerk.

Jurisdiction over legislation to appropriate funds for the Agriculture Dept. (except the Forest Service), the Farm Credit Administration, the Commodity Futures Trading Commission, and other agriculture-related services and programs.

Senate Banking, Housing, and Urban Affairs Committee, SD-534 20510; 224-7391. Donald W. Riegle Jr., D-Mich., chairman; Steven Harris, staff director.

Oversees government-sponsored enterprises, including the Farm Credit Banks and the Federal Agricultural Mortgage Corp., with regard to the financial risk they pose to the federal government.

Senate Banking, Housing, and Urban Affairs Committee, Subcommittee on Economic Stabilization and Rural Development, SD-534 20510; 224-7391. Richard C. Shelby, D-Ala., chairman; Christin Givhan, staff director.

Jurisdiction over legislation on economic stabilization and growth, including regulatory relief issues, barriers to development in rural areas, price controls, and asset disposition policies.

See also Northeast Agricultural Caucus (p. 760)

Nongovernmental:

Agribusiness Council, 2550 M St. N.W., #275 20037; 296-4563. Nicholas E. Hollis, president. Fax, 887-9178.

Works to strengthen U.S. competitiveness in overseas agricultural markets. Promotes cooperation between private industry and government to improve international agricultural trade and development. Sponsors trade missions to developing countries. (U.S. affiliate of Agri-Energy Roundtable.)

Agriculture Council of America, 927 15th St. N.W., #800 20005; 682-9200. W. Patrick Nichols, president. Fax, 289-6648.

Membership: farmers and ranchers, farm commodity organizations, and agribusiness firms. Promotes good relations between the agriculture industry and consumers through FoodWatch, a public education program that addresses food

Agriculture Dept.

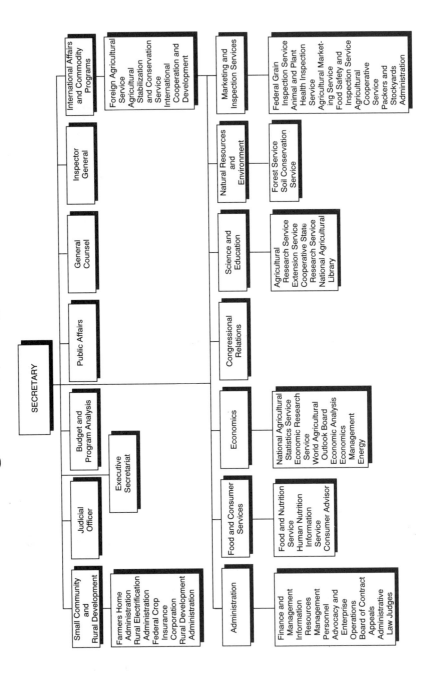

safety concerns; sponsors programs to improve the image of farmers and the agriculture industry.

Agri-Energy Roundtable, 2550 M St. N.W., #275 20037; 887-0528. Nicholas E. Hollis, executive director. Fax, 887-9178.

Membership: companies, international organizations, and affiliated agro-industry associations in emerging countries. International clearinghouse that encourages cooperation in energy and agricultural development between industrialized and developing nations.

American Agriculture Movement, 100 Maryland Ave. N.E. 20002; 544-5750. Ray Chancey, director. Fax, 547-9155. Recorded hotline, 544-6024.

Membership: family farmers and ranchers concerned with government agriculture policy. Supports parity pricing for all agricultural products; works to improve economic status of U.S. farmers.

American Farm Bureau Federation, 600 Maryland Ave. S.W., #800 20024; 484-3600. Richard W. Newpher, executive director, Washington office. Fax, 484-3604.

Federation of state farm bureaus in 50 states and Puerto Rico. Promotes agricultural research. Interests include commodity programs, domestic production, marketing, education, research, financial assistance to the farmer, foreign assistance programs, rural development, the world food shortage, and inspection and certification of food. (Headquarters in Park Ridge, Ill.)

American Farmland Trust, 1920 N St. N.W., #400 20036; 659-5170. Ralph Grossi, president. Fax, 659-8339.

Works with farmers to promote farming practices that lead to a healthy environment. Interests include preservation of farmlands from urban development, establishment of safeguards against soil erosion, and agricultural resource conservation policy development at all government levels. Initiates local preservation efforts and assists individuals and organizations engaged in safeguarding agricultural properties.

Federal Agricultural Mortgage Corp. (Farmer Mac), 919 18th St. N.W., #200 20006; 872-7700. Thomas R. Clark, vice president.

Private corporation chartered by Congress to provide a secondary mortgage market for farm and rural housing loans. Guarantees principal and interest repayment on securities backed by farm and rural housing loans.

Henry A. Wallace Institute for Alternative Agriculture, 9200 Edmonston Rd., #117, Greenbelt, MD 20770-1551; (301) 441-8777. I. Garth Youngberg, executive director.

Supports the adoption of low-cost, resource-conserving, and environmentally sound farming methods. Provides scientific information and sponsors research and education programs on alternative agricultural methods. Monitors legislation and regulations.

International Assn. of Refrigerated Warehouses, 7315 Wisconsin Ave., #1200N, Bethesda, MD 20814; (301) 652-5674. J. William Hudson, president. Fax, (301) 652-7269.

Membership: owners and operators of public refrigerated warehouses. Interests include labor, transportation, taxes, environment, safety, regulatory compliance, and food distribution. Monitors legislation and regulations.

International Food Information Council, 1100 Connecticut Ave. N.W., #430 20036; 296-6540. Vacant, president. Fax, 296-6547.

Membership: food and beverage companies and manufacturers of food ingredients. Provides the media, health professionals, and consumers with scientific information about food and food ingredients.

National-American Wholesale Grocers Assn., 201 Park Washington Court, Falls Church, VA 22046; (703) 532-9400. John R. Block, president. Fax, (703) 538-4673.

Trade association of grocery wholesale distribution companies that supply and service independent grocers throughout the United States and Canada. Provides members with research, technical, educational, and government service programs.

National Assn. of State Departments of Agriculture, 1156 15th St. N.W., #1020 20005; 296-9680. Richard W. Kirchhoff, executive vice president. Fax, 296-9686.

Membership: state agriculture commissioners. Serves as liaison between federal agencies and state governments to coordinate agricultural policies and laws.

National Center for Food and Agricultural Policy, 1616 P St. N.W. 20036; 328-5074. Dale E. Hathaway, director. Fax, 939-3460.

Research and educational organization concerned with international food and agricultural issues. Examines public policy concerning agriculture, food safety and quality, natural resources, and the environment. Library open to the public.

National Council of Agricultural Employers, 1735 Eye St. N.W., #704 20006; 728-0300. Sharon M. Hughes, executive vice president. Fax, 728-0303.

Membership: employers of agricultural labor. Encourages establishment and maintenance of conditions conducive to an adequate supply of domestic and foreign farm labor.

National Farmers Union (Farmers Educational and Cooperative Union of America), 600 Maryland Ave. S.W., #202W 20024; 554-1600. Larry Mitchell, director, government relations. Fax, 554-1654.

Membership: family farmers belonging to state affiliates. Interests include commodity programs, domestic production, marketing, education, research, energy and natural resources, financial assistance to farmers, Social Security for farmers, foreign programs, rural development, the world food shortage, and inspection and certification of food. Sponsors Green Thumb, a community service employment and training project. (Headquarters in Denver.)

National Food Brokers Assn., 1010 Massachusetts Ave. N.W. 20001; 789-2844. Robert C. Schwarze, president. Fax, 842-0839.

Membership: individuals and firms that sell food and nonfood products wholesale for a commission or a brokerage fee in the United States and other countries. Works to eliminate unfair business practices; supports competition among large and small businesses. Sponsors seminars; conducts conferences and sales training programs; provides group insurance plans. Monitors legislation and regulations. Library open to the public by appointment.

National Food Processors Assn., 1401 New York Ave. N.W., #400 20005; 639-5939. John R. Cady, president. Fax, 637-8068.

Membership: food processing companies and suppliers. Promotes agricultural interests of the food processing industry; maintains information

clearinghouse on environmental and crop protection; conducts pesticide residue analysis of products; serves as liaison between members and the government; monitors legislation and regulations.

National Grange, 1616 H St. N.W. 20006; 628-3507. Robert E. Barrow, master. Fax, 347-1091.

Membership: farmers and others involved in agricultural production and rural community service activities. Coordinates community service programs with state grange organizations.

Union of Concerned Scientists, Agriculture and Biotechnology, 1616 P St. N.W., #310 20036; 332-0900. Margaret Mellon, director. Fax, 332-0905.

Independent group of scientists that advocates policies to encourage low-input sustainable agricultural practices and to reduce the environmental and health effects caused by conventional agricultural practices and high chemical inputs.

U.S. Chamber of Commerce, Food, Agriculture, Energy, and Natural Resources Policy, 1615 H St. N.W. 20062; 463-5500. Stew Hardy, manager. Fax, 887-3445.

Develops policy on issues affecting production, transportation, and sale of agricultural products. Interests include food safety, pesticides, nutrition labeling, seafood inspection, backhauling, and international trade.

See also Consumer Affairs, Food and Nutrition, Nongovernmental (p. 259)

Farm Supplies

Agencies:

Agricultural Marketing Service (Agriculture Dept.), Seed Regulatory and Testing, Bldg. 506, BARC East, Soil Conservation Rd., Beltsville, MD 20705; (301) 504-9237. Jim Triplitt, chief. Fax, (301) 504-5454.

Administers interstate programs prohibiting false advertising and labeling of seeds. Regulates interstate shipment of seeds. Tests seeds for a fee under the Agricultural Marketing Act.

Tennessee Valley Authority, 1 Massachusetts Ave. N.W., #300 20001; 479-4412. Jan Evered, administrative officer, Washington office. Fax, 479-4421.

Coordinates resource conservation, development, and land-use programs in the Tennessee River Valley. Conducts fertilizer research through its National Fertilizer Development Center. (Headquarters in Knoxville, Tenn.)

Congress:

See Agriculture, General, Congress (p. 588)

Nongovernmental:

American Seed Trade Assn., 601 13th St. N.W., #570S 20005; 638-3128. David R. Lambert, executive vice president. Fax, 638-3171.

Membership: producers and merchandisers of seeds. Conducts seminars on research developments in corn, sorghum, soybean, garden seeds, and other farm seeds; promotes overseas seed market development.

The Fertilizer Institute, 501 2nd St. N.E. 20002; 675-8250. Gary D. Myers, president. Fax, 544-8123.

Membership: manufacturers, dealers, and distributors of fertilizer. Provides statistical data and other information concerning the effects of fertilizer and its relationship to world food production, food supply, and the environment.

Irrigation Assn., 1911 N. Fort Myer Dr., Arlington, VA 22209; (703) 524-1200. Charles S. Putnam, executive director. Fax, (703) 524-9544.

Membership: manufacturers, distributors, contractors, and government and university researchers in the field of irrigation. Provides technical information on the use of agricultural irrigation; sponsors courses on irrigation education.

See also American Assn. of Nurserymen (p. 670); National Agricultural Aviation Assn. (p. 709); National Assn. of Plant Patent Owners (p. 671)

Commodities

General

Agencies:

Agricultural Stabilization and Conservation Service (Agriculture Dept.), 14th St. and Independence Ave. S.W. (mailing address: P.O. Box 2415, Washington, DC 20013); 720-3467. Grant

Buntrock, administrator. Information, 720-5237. Fax, 720-9105.

Administers farm commodity programs providing crop loans and purchases; provides crop payments when market prices fall below specified levels; sets acreage allotments and marketing quotas.

Agriculture Dept., Marketing and Inspection Services, 14th St. and Independence Ave. S.W. (mailing address: Ag. Box 0109, Washington, DC 20250-0109); 720-4256. Patricia Jensen, acting assistant secretary. Fax, 720-5775.

Administers inspection and grading services and regulatory programs for agricultural commodities through the Agricultural Marketing Service, Agricultural Cooperative Service, Animal and Plant Health Inspection Service, Federal Grain Inspection Service, Food Safety and Inspection Service, and Packers and Stockyards Administration.

Agriculture Dept., National Plant Germplasm System, #331, Bldg. 5, BARC West, Beltsville, MD 20705; (301) 504-5311. Vacant, director. Fax, (301) 504-6231.

Network of organizations and individuals interested in preserving the genetic diversity of crop plants, including cotton, wheat and other grains, fruits and vegetables, rice, sugar, tobacco, and peanuts. Collects, preserves, evaluates, and catalogs germplasm and distributes it for specific purposes.

Animal and Plant Health Inspection Service (Agriculture Dept.), 14th St. and Independence Ave. S.W. (mailing address: Ag. Box 3041, Washington, DC 20250); 720-3861. Lonnie J. King, acting administrator. Information, 720-2511. Fax, 720-3054.

Administers quarantine regulations governing imports of agricultural commodities into the United States; certifies that U.S. exports are free of pests and disease.

Commodity Credit Corp. (Agriculture Dept.), 14th St. and Independence Ave. S.W. (mailing address: P.O. Box 2415, Washington, DC 20013); 720-3111. Eugene Moos, president. Information, 720-5237.

Finances commodity stabilization programs, domestic and export surplus commodity disposal, foreign assistance, storage activities, and related programs.

Commodity Futures Trading Commission, 2033 K St. N.W. 20581; 254-6970. Mary L. Schapiro, chair designate. Information, 254-8630. Library, 254-5901. Fax, 254-3061.

Administers the Commodity Exchange Act, which regulates all commodity futures and options to prevent fraudulent trade practices. (A futures contract is an agreement to purchase or sell a commodity for delivery in the future at an agreed price and date. An option is a unilateral contract that gives the buyer the right to buy or sell a specified quantity of a commodity at a specific price within a specified period of time, regardless of the market price of that commodity.)

Congress:

House Agriculture Committee, Subcommittee on Department Operations and Nutrition, 1301A LHOB 20515; 225-1496. Charles W. Stenholm, D-Texas, chairman; Stan Ray, staff director.

Jurisdiction over legislation on emergency commodity distribution.

House Agriculture Committee, Subcommittee on Environment, Credit, and Rural Development, 1430 LHOB 20515; 225-0301. Tim Johnson, D-S.D., chairman; Anne Simmons, staff director.

Jurisdiction over legislation on the Commodity Futures Trading Commission and the Commodity Exchange Act.

House Agriculture Committee, Subcommittee on Foreign Agriculture and Hunger, 1336 LHOB 20515; 225-1867. Timothy J. Penny, D-Minn., chairman; Jane Shey, staff director.

Jurisdiction over legislation on international commodity agreements and foreign agricultural trade of commodities (jurisdiction shared with House Foreign Affairs Committee).

House Agriculture Committee, Subcommittee on General Farm Commodities, 1430 LHOB 20515; 225-0301. Bill Sarpalius, D-Texas, chairman; Anne Simmons, staff director.

Jurisdiction over legislation on feed grains, wheat, and oilseeds, including tung nuts, flaxseed, soybeans, dry edible beans, cotton, cottonseed, and rice.

House Agriculture Committee, Subcommittee on Livestock, 1336 LHOB 20515; 225-1867. Harold L. Volkmer, D-Mo., chairman; Tim DeCoster, staff director.

Jurisdiction over legislation on dairy commodity programs and wool.

House Agriculture Committee, Subcommittee on Specialty Crops and Natural Resources, 105 CHOB 20515; 225-8906. Charlie Rose, D-N.C., chairman; Keith Pitts, staff director.

Jurisdiction over legislation on tobacco, peanuts, and sugar and on the inspection and certification of flowers, fruits, and vegetables.

House Foreign Affairs Committee, Subcommittee on Economic Policy, Trade, and the Environment, 702 O'Neill Bldg. (300 New Jersey Ave. S.E.) 20515; 226-7820. Sam Gejdenson, D-Conn., chairman; John Scheibel, staff director. Fax, 225-2029.

Jurisdiction over legislation on international commodity agreements and foreign agricultural trade of commodities (jurisdiction shared with House Agriculture Committee).

Senate Agriculture, Nutrition, and Forestry Committee, SR-328A 20510; 224-2035. Patrick J. Leahy, D-Vt., chairman; Charles Riemenschneider, chief of staff.

Jurisdiction over the Commodity Futures Trading Commission and the Commodity Exchange Act.

Senate Agriculture, Nutrition, and Forestry Committee, Subcommittee on Agricultural Production and Stabilization of Prices, SR-328A 20510; 224-2035. David Pryor, D-Ark., chairman; Bobby Franklin, legislative assistant.

Jurisdiction over legislation on agricultural commodities, including feed grains; wheat; oilseeds, including tung nuts, flaxseed, soybeans, dry edible beans, cotton, cottonseed, and rice; dairy products; wool; tobacco; peanuts; and sugar (jurisdiction over legislation on sugar imports shared with Senate Finance Committee).

Senate Agriculture, Nutrition, and Forestry Committee, Subcommittee on Agricultural Research, Conservation, Forestry, and General Legislation, SR-328A 20510; 224-2035. Tom Daschle, D-S.D., chairman; Tom Buis, legislative assistant.

Jurisdiction over legislation on the inspection and certification of flowers, fruits, and vegetables.

Senate Agriculture, Nutrition, and Forestry Committee, Subcommittee on Domestic and Foreign Marketing and Product Promotion, SR-328A 20510; 224-2035. David L. Boren, D-Okla., chairman; Brian Ellis, legislative assistant.

Oversight of international commodity agreements and export controls on agricultural commodities.

Senate Agriculture, Nutrition, and Forestry Committee, Subcommittee on Nutrition and Investigations, SR-328A 20510; 224-2035. Tom Harkin, D-Iowa, chairman; Mark Halverson, legislative assistant.

Jurisdiction over legislation on commodity donations and emergency commodity distribution.

Senate Finance Committee, SD-205 20510; 224-4515. Daniel Patrick Moynihan, D-N.Y., chairman; Lawrence O'Donnell Jr., staff director.

Jurisdiction over some legislation on sugar, including sugar imports (jurisdiction shared with Senate Agriculture, Nutrition, and Forestry Committee).

See also Congressional Soybean Caucus (p. 756); Congressional Textile Caucus (p. 759); Senate Textile Steering Committee (p. 761)

Nongovernmental:

See Agriculture, General, Nongovernmental (p. 589)

Cotton

Agencies:

Agricultural Marketing Service (Agriculture Dept.), Cotton, 14th St. and Independence Ave. S.W. (mailing address: P.O. Box 96456, Washington, DC 20090); 720-3193. Jesse F. Moore, director. Fax, 690-1718.

Administers cotton marketing programs; sets cotton grading standards and conducts quality inspections based on those standards. Maintains market news service to inform producers of daily price changes.

Agricultural Stabilization and Conservation Service (Agriculture Dept.), Cotton, Grain, and Rice Price Support, 14th St. and Independence Ave. S.W. (mailing address: P.O. Box 2415,

Washington, DC 20013); 720-7641. Tom VonGarlem, acting director. Fax, 690-3307.

Develops cotton price support and loan programs through the payment-in-kind program, loans and diversion payments to farmers, direct purchases of commodities from farmers, and payments to support "target prices" fixed by law for upland cotton.

Agricultural Stabilization and Conservation Service (Agriculture Dept.), Fibers and Rice Analysis, 14th St. and Independence Ave. S.W. (mailing address: P.O. Box 2415, Washington, DC 20013); 720-7954. Wayne Bjorlie, director. Fax, 690-1346.

Develops production adjustment and price support programs to balance supply and demand for certain commodities, including cotton.

Congress:

See Commodities, General, Congress (p. 594)

International Organizations:

International Cotton Advisory Committee, 1629 K St. N.W., #702 20006; 463-6660. Lawrence H. Shaw, executive director. Fax, 463-6950.

Membership: cotton producing and consuming countries. Provides information on cotton production, trade, consumption, stocks, and prices.

Nongovernmental:

Cotton Council International, 1521 New Hampshire Ave. N.W. 20036; 745-7805. Allen Terhaar, executive director. Fax, 483-4040.

Division of National Cotton Council of America. Promotes U.S. raw cotton exports.

Cotton Warehouse Assn. of America, 1150 Connecticut Ave. N.W., #507 20036; 331-4337. Donald L. Wallace Jr., executive vice president. Fax, 331-4330.

Membership: cotton compress and warehouse workers. Serves as a liaison between members and government agencies; monitors legislation and regulations.

National Cotton Council of America, 1521 New Hampshire Ave. N.W. 20036; 745-7805. John Maguire, vice president, Washington office. Fax, 483-4040.

Membership: all segments of the U.S. cotton industry. Provides statistics and information on such topics as cotton history and processing. (Headquarters in Memphis.)

Dairy Products

Agencies:

Agricultural Marketing Service (Agriculture Dept.), Dairy, 14th St. and Independence Ave. S.W. (mailing address: P.O. Box 96456, Washington, DC 20090-6456); 720-4392. Willard H. Blanchard, director. Fax, 720-4844.

Administers dairy product marketing and promotion programs; grades dairy products; maintains market news service on daily price changes; sets minimum price that farmers receive for milk (not responsible for setting retail prices for milk purchased by consumers).

Agricultural Stabilization and Conservation Service (Agriculture Dept.), Dairy, 14th St. and Independence Ave. S.W. (mailing address: P.O. Box 2415, Washington, DC 20013); 720-3385. Indulis Kancitis, director. Fax, 690-0767.

Administers dairy stabilization and price support programs, including purchases and dispositions of dairy products acquired under price supports.

Agricultural Stabilization and Conservation Service (Agriculture Dept.), Dairy Analysis, 14th St. and Independence Ave. S.W. (mailing address: P.O. Box 2415, Washington, DC 20013); 720-6733. Charles Shaw, director. Fax, 690-1346.

Develops production adjustment and price support programs to balance supply and demand for dairy products.

Congress:

See Commodities, General, Congress (p. 594)

Nongovernmental:

American Butter Institute, 888 16th St. N.W. 20006; 296-4250. Jerome J. Kosak, executive director. Fax, 659-1496.

Membership: butter manufacturers, packagers, and distributors. Interests include dairy price supports and programs, packaging and labeling, and imports. Monitors legislation and regulations.

Dairy and Food Industries Supply Assn., 6245 Executive Blvd., Rockville, MD 20852; (301)

984-1444. John M. Martin, president. Fax, (301) 881-7832.

Membership: equipment manufacturers, suppliers, and servicers for the food and dairy processing industry. Participates in the sanitary standards program for dairy and food processing; sponsors biennial Food and Dairy Expo and food engineering scholarships.

International Ice Cream Assn., 888 16th St. N.W. 20006; 296-4250. E. Linwood Tipton, president. Fax, 331-7820.

Membership: manufacturers and distributors of ice cream and other frozen desserts. Conducts market research; monitors legislation and regulations.

Milk Industry Foundation, 888 16th St. N.W. 20006; 296-4250. E. Linwood Tipton, president. Fax, 331-7820.

Membership: processors of fluid milk and fluidmilk products. Conducts market research; monitors legislation and regulations.

National Cheese Institute, 888 16th St. N.W. 20006; 296-4250. E. Linwood Tipton, executive director. Fax, 331-7820.

Membership: cheese manufacturers, packagers, processors, and distributors. Interests include dairy price supports and programs, packaging and labeling, and imports. Monitors legislation and regulations.

National Dairy Promotion and Research Board, 2111 Wilson Blvd., #600, Arlington, VA 22201; (703) 528-4800. Cynthia Carson, chief executive officer. Fax, (703) 524-9558.

Independent board appointed by the secretary of agriculture. Promotes dairy products; collects, allocates, and evaluates the use of checkoff funds (assessments on the marketing of milk) received from producers of dairy products. Conducts product, market, and nutrition research; reports findings to the industry and to the public. Agriculture Dept. reports annually to Congress on the board's programs.

National Independent Dairy-Foods Assn., 321 D St. N.E. 20002; 543-3838. Robert L. Redding Jr., executive vice president. Fax, 543-4575.

Membership: independent dairy product processors. Interests include developing a more flexible parity-price formula.

National Milk Producers Federation, 1840 Wilson Blvd., 4th Floor, Arlington, VA 22201; (703

243-6111. James C. Barr, chief executive officer. Fax, (703) 841-9328.

Membership: dairy farmer cooperatives. Provides information on development and modification of sanitary regulations, product standards, and marketing procedures for dairy products.

Eggs

Agencies:

Agricultural Marketing Service (Agriculture Dept.), Poultry, 14th St. and Independence Ave. S.W. (mailing address: P.O. Box 96456, Washington, DC 20090-6456); 720-4476. D. Michael Holbrook, director. Fax, 690-3165.

Supervises egg industry's research and promotion program. Sets grading standards and inspects eggs and egg products for wholesomeness.

Congress:

See Commodities, General, Congress (p. 594)

Nongovernmental:

Egg Nutrition Center, 2301 M St. N.W., #405 20037; 833-8850. Cathy McCharen, director. Fax, 463-0102.

Provides information on egg nutrition and related health issues. Disseminates information on cholesterol and heart disease.

United Egg Producers, 1 Massachusetts Ave. N.W., #800 20001-1431; 842-2345. Christine Nelson, director, government relations. Fax, 682-0775.

Membership: regional egg marketing cooperatives. Monitors legislation and regulations. (Headquarters in Atlanta, Ga.)

Feed Grains and Wheat

Agencies:

Agricultural Marketing Service (Agriculture Dept.), Livestock and Seed, 14th St. and Independence Ave. S.W. (mailing address: P.O. Box 96456, Washington, DC 20090-6456); 720-5705. Barry L. Carpenter, director. Fax, 720-3499.

Administers grain marketing program; maintains market news service to inform producers of grain market situation and daily price changes.

Agricultural Stabilization and Conservation Service (Agriculture Dept.), Cotton, Grain, and Rice Price Support, 14th St. and Independence Ave. S.W. (mailing address: P.O. Box 2415, Washington, DC 20013); 720-7641. Tom VonGarlem, acting director. Fax, 690-3307.

Develops wheat and feed grain price support and loan programs through the payment-in-kind program, loans and diversion payments to farmers, direct purchases of commodities from farmers, and payments to support "target prices" fixed by law for wheat and feed grains.

Agricultural Stabilization and Conservation Service (Agriculture Dept.), Grains Analysis, 14th St. and Independence Ave. S.W. (mailing address: P.O. Box 2415, Washington, DC 20013); 720-4417. Phil Sronce, director. Fax, 690-1346.

Develops production adjustment and price support programs to balance supply and demand for certain commodities, including wheat, rye, and other grains.

Federal Grain Inspection Service (Agriculture Dept.), 14th St. and Independence Ave. S.W. (mailing address: P.O. Box 96454, Washington, DC 20090); 720-0219. David R. Shipman, acting administrator. Information, 720-5091. Fax, 205-9237.

Administers inspection and weighing program for grain and processed commodities; conducts quality inspections based on established standards.

Congress:

See Commodities, General, Congress (p. 594)

Nongovernmental:

American Corn Millers Federation, 600 Maryland Ave. S.W., #305W 20024; 554-1614. Betsy Faga, president. Fax, 554-1616.

Trade association representing the dry corn milling industry. Sponsors research programs for milled white corn products.

American Feed Industry Assn., 1501 Wilson Blvd., Arlington, VA 22209; (703) 524-0810. David A. Bossman, president. Fax, (703) 524-1921.

Membership: feed manufacturers and their suppliers. Conducts seminars on feed grain production, marketing, advertising, and quality control.

Corn Refiners Assn., 1701 Pennsylvania Ave. N.W. 20006; 331-1634. Terry L. Claassen, president. Fax, 331-2054.

Promotes research on technical aspects of corn refining and product development; awards research grants to colleges and universities. Monitors legislation and regulations.

Millers National Federation, 600 Maryland Ave. S.W., #305W 20024; 484-2200. Roy Henwood, president. Fax, 488-7416.

Membership: companies owning wheat and rye flour mills. Seeks to inform the public, the industry, and government about issues affecting the domestic flour milling industry. Monitors legislation and regulations.

National Assn. of Wheat Growers, 415 2nd St. N.E. 20002; 547-7800. Carl Schwensen, executive vice president. Fax, 546-2638.

Federation of state wheat grower associations. Sponsors annual seminar on legislative issues.

National Corn Growers Assn., 201 Massachusetts Ave. N.E., #C4 20002; 546-7611. Keith Heard, executive vice president. Fax, 544-5142.

Promotes the use, marketing, and efficient production of corn; conducts research and educational activities; monitors legislation and regulations. (Headquarters in St. Louis.)

National Grain and Feed Assn., 1201 New York Ave. N.W., #830 20005; 289-0873. Kendell Keith, president. Fax, 289-5388.

Membership: all segments of the grain and feed industry. Arbitration panel resolves disputes over trade and commercial regulations.

National Grain Trade Council, 1300 L St. N.W., #925 20005; 842-0400. Robert R. Petersen, president.

Federation of grain exchanges and national associations of grain processors, handlers, merchandisers, distributors, exporters, and warehouse workers.

North American Export Grain Assn., 1300 L St. N.W., #900 20005; 682-4030. Steven A. McCoy, president. Fax, 682-4033.

Membership: grain exporting firms and others interested in the grain export industry. Provides information on grain export allowances, rates, distribution, and current market trends; sponsors seminars. Monitors legislation and regulations.

Terminal Elevator Grain Merchants' Assn., 1300 L St. N.W., #925 20005; 842-0400. Robert R. Petersen, secretary.

Membership: companies owning terminal elevators. Monitors legislation and regulations concerning grain inspection programs, transportation of grain, and general farm policy.

U.S. Feed Grains Council, 1400 K St. N.W., #1200 20005; 789-0789. Kenneth Hobbie, president. Fax, 898-0522.

Membership: feed grain producers and exporters; railroads; banks; and chemical, machinery, malting, and seed companies interested in feed grain exports. Promotes development of U.S. feed grain markets overseas.

U.S. Wheat Associates, 1620 Eye St. N.W., #801 20006; 463-0999. Winston Wilson, president. Fax, 785-1052.

Membership: wheat farmers. Develops export markets for the U.S. wheat industry; provides information on wheat production and marketing.

Fruits and Vegetables

Agencies:

Agricultural Marketing Service (Agriculture Dept.), Fruit and Vegetable, 14th St. and Independence Ave. S.W. (mailing address: P.O. Box 96456, Washington, DC 20090-6456); 720-4722. Charles R. Brader, director. Fax, 720-0016.

Administers fruit and vegetable marketing service and regulatory programs, including marketing orders and research and promotional programs for fruits, vegetables, and specialty crops; sets grading standards for fresh and processed fruits and vegetables; conducts quality inspections based on those standards; maintains market news service to inform producers of daily price changes.

Agriculture Dept., Economic Research Service, 1301 New York Ave. N.W. 20005; 219-0883. Fred Hoff, chief, specialty agriculture. Fax, 219-0042.

Conducts market research; studies and forecasts domestic supply-and-demand trends for fruits and vegetables.

Congress:

See Commodities, General, Congress (p. 594)

See also Congressional Corn Caucus (p. 758)

Nongovernmental:

International Apple Institute, 6707 Old Dominion Dr., #320, McLean, VA (mailing address: P.O. Box 1137, McLean, VA 22101-1137); (703) 442-8850. Ellen Terpstra, president. Fax, (703) 790-0845.

Represents commercial apple growers in thirty states plus processors, distributors, exporters, importers, and retailers of apples. Compiles statistics, promotes research and marketing for the industry, and provides information about apples and nutrition to educators. Monitors legislation and regulations.

International Banana Assn., 1929 39th St. N.W. 20006; 223-1183. Robert M. Moore, president. Fax, 223-1194.

Works to improve global distribution and increased consumption of bananas; collects and disseminates information about the banana industry; serves as a liaison between the U.S. government and banana-producing countries on issues of concern to the industry.

National Wine Coalition, 1730 Rhode Island Ave. N.W., #402 20036; 785-9510. Gordon W. Murchie, executive director. Fax, 785-9402.

Membership: members of the winemaking industry and wine consumers. Seeks to educate the public about the social and cultural role of wine. Conducts research; monitors legislation and regulations.

United Fresh Fruit and Vegetable Assn., 727 N. Washington St., Alexandria, VA 22314; (703) 836-3410. Thomas Stenzel, president. Fax, (703) 836-7745.

Membership: growers, shippers, wholesalers, retailers, food service operators, importers, and exporters involved in producing and marketing fresh fruits and vegetables. Represents the industry before the government and the public sector. Library open to the public by appointment.

Wine Institute, 601 13th St. N.W., #580 South 20005; 408-0870. Robert P. Koch, vice president, federal government relations. Fax, 371-0061.

Membership: California wine and brandy producers. Monitors legislation and regulations. (Headquarters in San Francisco.)

Oilseeds and Rice

Agencies:

Agricultural Marketing Service (Agriculture Dept.), Livestock and Seed, 14th St. and Independence Ave. S.W. (mailing address: P.O. Box 96456, Washington, DC 20090-6456); 720-5705. Barry L. Carpenter, director. Fax, 720-3499.

Administers rice marketing program; maintains market news service to inform producers of rice market situation and daily price changes.

Agricultural Stabilization and Conservation Service (Agriculture Dept.), Cotton, Grain, and Rice Price Support, 14th St. and Independence Ave. S.W. (mailing address: P.O. Box 2415, Washington, DC 20013); 720-7641. Tom VonGarlem, acting director. Fax, 690-3307.

Develops rice and oilseeds price support and loan programs through the payment-in-kind program, loans and diversion payments to farmers, direct purchases of commodities from farmers, and payments to support "target prices" fixed by law for rice and oilseeds.

Agricultural Stabilization and Conservation Service (Agriculture Dept.), Fibers and Rice Analysis, 14th St. and Independence Ave. S.W. (mailing address: P.O. Box 2415, Washington, DC 20013); 720-7954. Wayne Bjorlie, director. Fax, 690-1346.

Develops production adjustment and price support programs to balance supply and demand for certain commodities, including rice.

Agricultural Stabilization and Conservation Service (Agriculture Dept.), Oilseeds Analysis, 14th St. and Independence Ave. S.W. (mailing address: P.O. Box 2415, Washington, DC 20013); 720-4146. Brad Karmen, director. Fax, 720-8261.

Develops production adjustment and price support programs to balance supply and demand for oilseeds.

Federal Grain Inspection Service (Agriculture Dept.), 14th St. and Independence Ave. S.W. (mailing address: P.O. Box 96454, Washington, DC 20090); 720-0219. David R. Shipman, acting administrator. Information, 720-5091. Fax, 205-9237.

Administers inspection and weighing program for soybeans, rice, sunflower seeds, and other processed commodities; conducts quality inspections based on established standards.

Congress:

See Commodities, General, Congress (p. 594)

Nongovernmental:

American Soybean Assn., 1000 Connecticut Ave. N.W., #1106 20036; 371-5511. John Gordley, Washington representative. Fax, 331-7036.

Membership: soybean farmers. Promotes expanded world markets and research for the benefit of soybean growers. (Headquarters in St. Louis.)

National Institute of Oilseed Products, 412 1st St. S.E. 20003; 484-2773. Rick Meyers, Washington representative. Fax, 484-0770.

Membership: companies and individuals involved in manufacturing and trading oilseed products. Provides statistics on oilseed product imports and exports. (Headquarters in Monterey, Calif.)

National Oilseed Processors Assn., 1255 23rd St. N.W., #850 20037; 452-8040. Sheldon J. Hauck, president. Fax, 835-0400.

Provides information on soybean crops, products, and commodity programs and on the soybean processing industry.

Rice Millers' Assn., 4301 N. Fairfax Dr., #305, Arlington, VA 22203; (703) 351-8161. David R. Graves, president. Fax, (703) 351-8162.

Membership: rice milling and related firms. Provides U.S. and foreign rice trade and industry information; assists in establishing quality standards for rice production and milling. Monitors legislation and regulations.

Soy Protein Council, 1255 23rd St. N.W., #850 20037; 467-6610. Sheldon J. Hauck, executive vice president. Fax, 833-3636.

Membership: firms that process and sell vegetable proteins or food products containing vegetable proteins. Provides information on the nutritional properties of vegetable proteins.

Sugar

Agencies:

Agricultural Stabilization and Conservation Service (Agriculture Dept.), Sweeteners Analysis, 14th St. and Independence Ave. S.W. (mailing address: P.O. Box 2415, Washington, DC

20013); 720-3391. Robert Barry, director. Fax, 720-8261.

Develops production adjustment and price support programs to balance supply and demand for certain commodities, including sugar and honey.

Agriculture Dept., Economic Research Service, 1301 New York Ave. N.W. 20005; 219-0883. Fred Hoff, chief, specialty agriculture. Fax, 219-0042.

Conducts market research; studies and forecasts domestic supply-and-demand trends for sugar and other sweeteners.

Congress:

See Commodities, General, Congress (p. 594)

See also Senate Sweetener Caucus (p. 761)

Nongovernmental:

American Sugar Beet Growers Assn., 1156 15th St. N.W., #1101 20005; 833-2398. Luther Markwart, executive vice president.

Membership: sugar beet growers associations. Monitors legislation and regulations; serves as liaison between member associations and government agencies, including the departments of Agriculture and Commerce and the Office of the U.S. Trade Representative.

Chocolate Manufacturers Assn./American Cocoa Research Institute, 7900 Westpark Dr., #A320, McLean, VA 22102; (703) 790-5011. Lawrence T. Graham, president. Fax, (703) 790-5752.

Membership: U.S. chocolate manufacturers and distributors. Sponsors educational programs; offers grants for cocoa research.

Hawaiian Sugar Planters' Assn., 1156 15th St. N.W., #1103 20005; 331-7448. John C. Roney, vice president.

Membership: Hawaiian sugar cane producers and processors. Conducts agricultural research; monitors legislation and regulations. (Headquarters in Aiea, Hawaii.)

National Confectioners Assn., 7900 Westpark Dr., #A320, McLean, VA 22102; (703) 790-5750. Lawrence T. Graham, president. Fax, (703) 790-5752.

Membership: confectionery manufacturers and suppliers. Provides information on confectionery consumption and nutrition; sponsors educational programs and research on candy technology; monitors legislation and regulations.

The Sugar Assn., 1101 15th St. N.W., #600 20005; 785-1122. Charles D. Shamel, president. Fax, 785-5019.

Membership: sugar processors, growers, refiners, and planters. Provides nutritional information on sugar. Library open to the public by appointment.

U.S. Beet Sugar Assn., 1156 15th St. N.W. 20005; 296-4820. Van R. Olsen, president. Fax, 331-2065.

Membership: beet sugar processors. Provides information on sugar processing. Library open to the public by appointment.

U.S. Cane Sugar Refiners' Assn., 1730 Rhode Island Ave. N.W. 20036; 331-1458. Nicholas Kominus, president.

Membership: independent sugar cane refiners. Monitors legislation and regulations.

Tobacco and Peanuts

See also Consumer Affairs, Tobacco (p. 265)

Agencies:

Agricultural Marketing Service (Agriculture Dept.), Tobacco, 300 12th St. S.W. (mailing address: P.O. Box 96456, Washington, DC 20090-6456); 205-0567. Larry J. Hopkins, director. Fax, 205-0099.

Administers tobacco marketing programs; sets tobacco standards and conducts quality inspections based on those standards, including tests for prohibited pesticides in imported flue-cured and burley tobacco; maintains market news service to inform producers of daily price changes.

Agricultural Stabilization and Conservation Service (Agriculture Dept.), Tobacco and Peanuts Analysis, 14th St. and Independence Ave. S.W. (mailing address: P.O. Box 2415, Washington, DC 20013); 720-8839. Robert H. Miller, director. Fax, 720-8261.

Develops production adjustment and price support programs to balance supply and demand for tobacco and peanuts.

Agriculture Dept., Economic Research Service, 1301 New York Ave. N.W. 20005; 219-0883. Fred Hoff, chief, specialty agriculture. Fax, 219-0042.

Conducts market research; studies and forecasts domestic supply-and-demand trends for tobacco.

Congress:

See Commodities, General, Congress (p. 594)

Nongovernmental:

Burley and Dark Leaf Tobacco Assn., 1100 17th St. N.W., #505 20036; 296-6820. Mark Eaton, vice president and managing director. Fax, 467-6349.

Membership: growers of burley and dark leaf tobacco. Promotes tobacco sales.

Cigar Assn. of America, 1100 17th St. N.W., #504 20036; 223-8204. Norman F. Sharp, president. Fax, 833-0379.

Membership: growers and suppliers of cigar leaf tobacco and manufacturers, packagers, importers, and distributors of cigars. Monitors legislation and regulations.

National Peanut Council, 1500 King St., #301, Alexandria, VA 22314; (703) 838-9500. Kim Cutchins, president. Fax, (703) 838-9089.

Membership: peanut growers, shellers, brokers, and manufacturers, as well as allied companies. Provides information on economic and nutritional value of peanuts; coordinates research; promotes U.S. peanut exports, domestic production, and market development.

Smokeless Tobacco Council, 1627 K St. N.W., #700 20006; 452-1252. Jeffery L. Schlagenhauf, president. Fax, 452-0118.

Members: smokeless tobacco manufacturers. Monitors legislation and regulations.

Tobacco Associates, 1725 K St. N.W. 20006; 828-9144. Kirk Wayne, president. Fax, 828-9149.

Membership: producers of flue-cured tobacco. Promotes exports of flue-cured tobacco; provides information to encourage overseas market development.

The Tobacco Institute, 1875 Eye St. N.W., #800 20006; 457-4800. Samuel D. Chilcote Jr., president. Fax, 457-9350.

Membership: manufacturers of tobacco products. Provides information on the economics and history of the tobacco industry.

Education and Research

See also Consumer Affairs, Food and Nutrition (p. 258)

Agencies:

Agriculture Dept., Agricultural Cooperative Service, 14th St. and Independence Ave. S.W. (mailing address: P.O. Box 96576, Washington, DC 20090); 720-7558. Randall E. Torgerson, administrator. Information, 720-2556. Fax, 720-4641.

Conducts economic research and provides technical assistance to help farmers market their products and purchase supplies; helps people living in rural areas to obtain business services through cooperatives.

Agriculture Dept., Agricultural Research Service, 14th St. and Independence Ave. S.W. 20250; 720-3656. R. D. Plowman, administrator. Fax, 720-5427.

Conducts research on crops, livestock, poultry, soil and water conservation, agricultural engineering, and control of insects and other pests; develops new uses for farm commodities.

Agriculture Dept., Cooperative State Research Service, 14th St. and Independence Ave. S.W. 20250; 720-4423. John Patrick Jordan, administrator. Fax, 720-8987.

Administers grant program for research at agricultural experimental stations, land-grant colleges, and eligible schools of forestry; helps state experiment stations, land-grant colleges, and other agencies in the Agriculture Dept. to plan and coordinate research programs.

Agriculture Dept., Economic Research Service, 1301 New York Ave. N.W. 20005; 219-0300. Kenneth L. Deavers, administrator. Fax, 219-0146.

Analyzes factors affecting farm production and their relationship to the environment, prices and income, and the outlook for various commodities, including aquaculture and industrial crops. Studies include rural development and natural resources, agricultural trade and production, government policies, and foreign demand for agricultural products.

Agriculture Dept., Extension Service, 14th St. and Independence Ave. S.W. 20250; 720-3377. Leodrey Williams, acting administrator. Information, 720-3029. Fax, 720-3993.

Conducts educational programs to assist farmers, processors, and others in efficient production and marketing of agricultural products. Conducts educational programs on sustainable agriculture. Serves as national headquarters for the 4-H youth programs and coordinates activities with state and local clubs.

Agriculture Dept., Grants and Program Systems, 901 D St. S.W. 20250; 401-1761. William D. Carlson, associate administrator. Fax, 401-1804.

Administers grants to colleges, universities, small businesses, and other organizations to promote research in food, agriculture, and related areas. Maintains administrative responsibility for programs in aquaculture, critical materials (domestic rubber), small-farm resource development, and higher education.

Agriculture Dept., Higher Education, 14th St. and Independence Ave. S.W. 20250; 720-7854. K. Jane Coulter, deputy administrator. Fax, 690-4082.

Provides national leadership and coordination on issues relating to higher education; assists colleges and universities in developing and maintaining education programs in the food and agricultural sciences. Seeks to ensure that colleges and universities produce the requisite number of graduates to satisfy the nation's need for individuals trained in the field.

Agriculture Dept., National Agricultural Statistics Service, 14th St. and Independence Ave. S.W. 20250; 720-2707. Donald M. Bay, acting administrator. Fax, 720-9013. Weekly weather and crop information, bulletin subscriptions, 720-4021.

Prepares estimates and reports on production, supply, prices, and other items relating to the U.S. agricultural economy. Reports include statistics on field crops, fruits and vegetables, cattle, hogs, poultry, and related products.

Agriculture Dept., Science and Education, 14th St. and Independence Ave. S.W. 20250; 720-5923. R. D. Plowman, acting assistant secretary. Fax, 690-2842.

Coordinates agricultural research, extension, and teaching programs in the food and agricultural sciences, including human nutrition, home economics, consumer services, agricultural economics, environmental quality, natural and renewable resources, forestry and range management, animal and plant production and protection, aquaculture, and the processing, distribution, marketing, and utilization of food and agricultural products.

Agriculture Dept., Special Emphasis Outreach Program, 14th St. and Independence Ave. S.W. 20250; 720-7314. David Montoya, director. Fax, 690-2345.

Works with state governments to foster participation by minority individuals and institutions in food and agricultural research, teaching programs, and related areas. Assists the USDA in developing and improving opportunities in agricultural enterprises for minority individuals and institutions.

Census Bureau (Commerce Dept.), Agriculture, 3737 Branch Ave., Hillcrest Heights, MD (mailing address: Washington, DC 20233); (301) 763-8555. Vacant, chief. Toll-free, (800) 523-3215. Library, (301) 763-8241. Fax, (301) 763-8315.

Conducts a quinquennial agricultural census that provides data on crops, livestock, operator characteristics, land use, farm production expenditures, machinery and equipment, and irrigation for counties, states, regions, and the nation.

National Science and Technology Council (Executive Office of the President), 744 Jackson Pl. N.W. 20506; 395-5101. John H. Gibbons, chairman. Fax, 395-5076.

Coordinates research and development activities and programs that involve more than one federal agency. Concerns include food, agriculture, and forestry research.

Congress:

House Agriculture Committee, Subcommittee on Department Operations and Nutrition, 1301A LHOB 20515; 225-1496. Charles W. Stenholm, D-Texas, chairman; Stan Ray, staff director.

Jurisdiction over legislation on agricultural education and over legislation on agricultural research (jurisdiction shared with House Science, Space, and Technology Committee).

House Science, Space, and Technology Committee, Subcommittee on Science, 2319 RHOB 20515; 225-8844. Rick Boucher, D-Va., chairman; Grace L. Ostenso, staff director.

Jurisdiction over legislation concerning agricultural research and development.

Senate Agriculture, Nutrition, and Forestry Committee, Subcommittee on Agricultural Research, Conservation, Forestry, and General Legislation, SR-328A 20510; 224-2035. Tom Daschle, D-S.D., chairman; Tom Buis, legislative assistant.

Jurisdiction over legislation on agricultural education and research.

Nongovernmental:

Academy for Educational Development, 1255 23rd St. N.W., #400 20037; 862-1900. William Smith, executive vice president, social development. Fax, 862-1947.

Conducts, on a contract basis, studies of international agricultural development; encourages exchange of agricultural information between researchers and farmers.

Agricultural Research Institute, 9650 Rockville Pike, Bethesda, MD 20814; (301) 530-7122. Stan Cath, executive director. Fax, (301) 530-7007.

Membership: corporations, trade organizations, professional societies, universities, experiment stations, and government agencies involved in research. Identifies critical agricultural needs and problems; sponsors conferences and workshops.

Future Farmers of America, 5632 Mount Vernon Memorial Highway, Alexandria, VA (mailing address: P.O. Box 15160, Alexandria, VA 22309); (703) 360-3600. Larry C. Case, national adviser. Fax, (703) 360-5524.

Membership: local chapters of high school students enrolled in agricultural education and agribusiness programs. Coordinates leadership training and other activities with local chapters across the United States.

International Fund for Agricultural Research, 1611 N. Kent St., #600, Arlington, VA 22209; (703) 276-1611. Richard L. Sawyer, president. Fax, (703) 522-8077.

Supports international agricultural research efforts to combat poverty, hunger, malnutrition, and environmental degradation in developing countries. Encourages international cooperation between public and private research institutions.

National Council of Farmer Cooperatives, 50 F St. N.W., #900 20001; 626-8700. Wayne A. Boutwell, president. Fax, 626-8722.

Educational organization of farmer cooperatives. Conducts educational programs and encourages research on agricultural cooperatives; provides statistics and analyzes trends; presents awards for research papers.

National 4-H Council, 7100 Connecticut Ave., Chevy Chase, MD 20815; (301) 961-2820. Richard J. Sauer, president. Fax, (301) 961-2894.

Educational organization incorporated to strengthen and complement the 4-H program (for young people ages 9 to 19) of the Agriculture Dept.'s Cooperative Extension Service and state land-grant universities. Programs include citizenship and leadership training and international exchanges.

See also Agriculture, General, Nongovernmental (p. 589)

Financial Assistance to the Farmer

Agencies:

Agricultural Stabilization and Conservation Service (Agriculture Dept.), 14th St. and Independence Ave. S.W. (mailing address: P.O. Box 2415, Washington, DC 20013); 720-3467. Grant Buntrock, administrator. Information, 720-5237. Fax, 720-9105.

Administers farm commodity programs providing crop loans and purchases; provides crop payments when market prices fall below specified levels; sets acreage allotments and marketing quotas; assists farmers in areas affected by natural disasters.

Commodity Credit Corp. (Agriculture Dept.), 14th St. and Independence Ave. S.W. (mailing address: P.O. Box 2415, Washington, DC 20013); 720-3111. Eugene Moos, president. Information, 720-3467.

Administers and finances the commodity stabilization program through loans, purchases, and supplemental payments; sells through domestic and export markets commodities acquired by the government under this program; administers some aspects of foreign food aid through the Food for Peace program; provides storage facilities.

Farm Credit Administration, 1501 Farm Credit Dr., McLean, VA 22102-5090; (703) 883-4000. Billy Ross Brown, chairman. Information, (703) 883-4056. Fax, (703) 734-5784. TDD, (703) 883-4444.

Examines and regulates the cooperative Farm Credit System, which comprises federal land bank associations, production credit associations, federal land credit associations, agriculture credit associations, farm credit banks, and banks for cooperatives. Oversees credit programs and related services for harvesters of aquatic products, farmers, ranchers, producers, and their associations.

Farm Credit Administration, Examination, 1501 Farm Credit Dr., McLean, VA 22102-5090; (703) 883-4160. David C. Baer, chief examiner. Fax, (703) 893-2978.

Enforces and oversees compliance with the Farm Credit Act. Monitors cooperatively owned member banks' and associations' compliance with laws prohibiting discrimination in credit transactions on the basis of sex or marital status.

Farmers Home Administration (Agriculture Dept.), 14th St. and Independence Ave. S.W. 20250; 720-6903. Michael Dunn, administrator. Information, 720-4323. Fax, 690-0311.

Rural development credit agency that provides farmers with loans for farm land purchases, soil conservation, and operating costs. Administers emergency disaster loans and rural housing loans; offers technical assistance in farm operation.

Farmers Home Administration (Agriculture Dept.), Equal Opportunity, 14th St. and Independence Ave. S.W. 20250; 245-5528. Walter Y. Fredericks, acting director. Fax, 245-5499.

Enforces compliance with the Equal Credit Opportunity Act, which prohibits discrimination on the basis of sex, marital status, race, color, religion, disability, or age, in public assistance for rural housing and farm loan programs.

Federal Crop Insurance Corp. (Agriculture Dept.), 2101 L St. N.W. 20036; 254-8460. Kenneth D. Ackerman, manager. Information, 254-8399. Fax, 254-8379.

Provides farmers with insurance against crops lost because of bad weather, insects, disease, and other natural causes.

Congress:

House Agriculture Committee, 1301 L!HOB 20515; 225-2171. E. "Kika" de la Garza, D-Texas, chairman; Dianne Powell, staff director. Fax, 225-8510.
Jurisdiction over legislation on price supports.

House Agriculture Committee, Subcommittee on Environment, Credit, and Rural Development, 1430 LHOB 20515; 225-0301. Tim Johnson, D-S.D., chairman; Anne Simmons, staff director.
Jurisdiction over legislation on agricultural credit, loans, natural disaster assistance, production adjustment programs, and insurance, including crop insurance.

Senate Agriculture, Nutrition, and Forestry Committee, Subcommittee on Agricultural Credit, SR-328A 20510; 224-2035. Kent Conrad, D-N.D., chairman; Kevin Price, legislative assistant.
Jurisdiction over legislation on agricultural credit, loans, and natural disaster assistance.

Senate Agriculture, Nutrition, and Forestry Committee, Subcommittee on Agricultural Production and Stabilization of Prices, SR-328A 20510; 224-2035. David Pryor, D-Ark., chairman; Bobby Franklin, legislative assistant.
Jurisdiction over legislation on price supports, production adjustment programs, and insurance, including crop insurance.

Nongovernmental:

See Agriculture, General, Nongovernmental (p. 589)

Foreign Programs

Commercial Programs

Agencies:

Foreign Agricultural Service (Agriculture Dept.), 14th St. and Independence Ave. S.W. 20250; 720-3935. Richard B. Schroeter, acting administrator. Information, 720-7115. Fax, 690-2159.
Promotes exports of U.S. commodities and assists with trade negotiations; coordinates activities of U.S. representatives in foreign countries who report on crop and market conditions; sponsors trade fairs in foreign countries to promote export of U.S. agricultural products; analyzes world demand and production of various commodities; monitors sales by private exporters.

State Dept., Agricultural Trade Policy and Programs, Main State Bldg., Rm. 3526 20520; 647-3090. Thomas L. Robinson, director. Fax, 647-1894.
Participates in formulating the department's agricultural trade policy concerning the export trade in temperate agricultural products such as grain, oilseeds, and dairy products, and imports of meat. Handles questions pertaining to international negotiations on all agricultural products covered under the General Agreement on Tariffs and Trade (GATT) and offered by commodity organizations, including coffee, tea, bananas, cocoa, sugar, cotton, and hard fibers.

State Dept., Textiles, Main State Bldg., Rm. 3336 20520; 647-3569. John Lyle, director. Fax, 647-2302.
Negotiates bilateral textile trade agreements with foreign governments concerning cotton, wool, and synthetic textile and apparel products.

U.S. Agricultural Export Development Council, 1225 Eye St. N.W., #500 20005; 682-4734. Helen Miller, executive coordinator. Fax, 682-4707.
Membership: producer and agribusiness organizations. Works with the Foreign Agricultural Service on projects to create, expand, and maintain agricultural markets abroad. Sponsors seminars and workshops.

Congress:

House Agriculture Committee, Subcommittee on Foreign Agriculture and Hunger, 1336 LHOB 20515; 225-1867. Timothy J. Penny, D-Minn., chairman; Jane Shey, staff director.
Jurisdiction over legislation on international commodity agreements, foreign agricultural trade of commodities, and foreign market development (jurisdiction shared with House Foreign Affairs Committee).

House Foreign Affairs Committee, Subcommittee on Economic Policy, Trade, and the Environment, 702 O'Neill Bldg. (300 New Jersey Ave. S.E.) 20515; 226-7820. Sam Gejdenson, D-Conn., chairman; John Scheibel, staff director. Fax, 225-2029.

Jurisdiction over legislation on international commodity agreements, foreign agricultural trade of commodities and foreign market development (oversight shared with House Agriculture Committee), and export controls on agricultural commodities.

House Small Business Committee, Subcommittee on Rural Enterprises, Exports, and the Environment, 1F CHOB 20515; 225-8944. Bill Sarpalius, D-Texas, chairman; Christopher Mattson, staff director.

Jurisdiction over legislation on export expansion and agricultural development as it relates to the small-business community.

Senate Agriculture, Nutrition, and Forestry Committee, Subcommittee on Domestic and Foreign Marketing and Product Promotion, SR-328A 20510; 224-2035. David L. Boren, D-Okla., chairman; Brian Ellis, legislative assistant.

Jurisdiction over legislation on international commodity agreements, foreign agricultural trade of commodities, foreign market development, and export controls on agricultural commodities.

Senate Finance Committee, SD-205 20510; 224-4515. Daniel Patrick Moynihan, D-N.Y., chairman; Lawrence O'Donnell Jr., staff director.

Jurisdiction over some sugar legislation, including sugar imports (jurisdiction shared with Senate Agriculture, Nutrition, and Forestry Committee).

Senate Small Business Committee, Subcommittee on Export Expansion and Agricultural Development, SR-428A 20510; 224-5175. Harris Wofford, D-Pa., chairman; Daniel Solomon, senior policy analyst, 224-6324.

Jurisdiction over legislation on export expansion and agricultural development as it relates to the small-business community.

Nongovernmental:

See Agriculture, General, Nongovernmental (p. 589)

Foreign Assistance and World Food Shortage

Agencies:

Agency for International Development (International Development Cooperation Agency), Main State Bldg., Rm. 5942 20523; 647-9620. J. Brian Atwood, administrator. Information, 647-1850. Press, 647-4200. Fax, 647-0148.

Provides developing countries and the nations of central and Eastern Europe with economic and humanitarian assistance; offers technical assistance to increase agricultural production. Jointly administers the Food for Peace program with the Agriculture Dept.'s Foreign Agricultural Service.

Agriculture Dept., International Cooperation and Development, 14th St. and Independence Ave. S.W. (mailing address: Washington, DC 20250); 690-0776. Lynette Wagner, acting administrator. Information, 690-1801. Fax, 720-6103.

Coordinates and conducts the department's international cooperation and development programs in agriculture and related fields. Programs include technical assistance and training, scientific and technical cooperation, administration of collaborative research, representation of USDA and U.S. government interests in international organization affairs, and facilitation of private sector involvement in country and regional agricultural development. Programs are conducted cooperatively with other USDA and U.S. government agencies, universities, and the private sector.

Agriculture Dept., World Agricultural Outlook Board, 12th St. and Independence Ave. S.W. 20250; 720-6030. James R. Donald, chairman. Fax, 690-1805.

Serves as the central information source for the department's world agricultural economic intelligence effort. Oversees Agriculture Dept.'s global agricultural economic outlook and forecasting work.

Foreign Agricultural Service (Agriculture Dept.), 14th St. and Independence Ave. S.W. 20250; 720-5173. Christopher E. Goldthwait, general sales manager. Information, 720-7115. Fax, 690-1595.

Administers Commodity Credit Corporation commercial export programs, including export credit guarantee and export enhancement programs. Administers, with the Agency for International Development, U.S. foreign food aid programs, including Title I of the Food for Peace program, the Food for Progress program, and the Section 416(b) program, which provides developing countries with surplus commodities. Represents the United States in developing export markets.

State Dept., Agricultural Trade Policy and Programs, Main State Bldg., Rm. 3526 20520; 647-3090. Thomas L. Robinson, director. Fax, 647-1894.

Makes recommendations on international food policy issues such as the effects of U.S. food aid on foreign policy; studies and drafts proposals on the U.S. role in Food for Peace and World Food programs.

Congress:

House Agriculture Committee, Subcommittee on Foreign Agriculture and Hunger, 1336 LHOB 20515; 225-1867. Timothy J. Penny, D-Minn., chairman; Jane Shey, staff director.

Jurisdiction over international commodity donations and over legislation on U.S. domestic food production for foreign assistance programs under Public Law 480, including the Food for Peace program and the Foreign Agricultural Service. (The House Foreign Affairs Committee has jurisdiction over legislation on overseas food distribution.)

House Foreign Affairs Committee, 2170 RHOB 20515; 225-5021. Lee H. Hamilton, D-Ind., chairman; Michael H. Van Dusen, chief of staff. Fax, 226-3581.

Jurisdiction over legislation on overseas food distribution for foreign assistance programs under Public Law 480, including the Food for Peace program and the Foreign Agricultural Service. (The House Agriculture Committee has jurisdiction over legislation on domestic food production for Public Law 480 programs.)

Senate Agriculture, Nutrition, and Forestry Committee, Subcommittee on Domestic and Foreign Marketing and Product Promotion, SR-328A 20510; 224-2035. David L. Boren, D-Okla., chairman; Brian Ellis, legislative assistant.

Jurisdiction over legislation on food production and distribution for foreign assistance programs under Public Law 480, including the Food for Peace program and the Foreign Agricultural Service.

Senate Agriculture, Nutrition, and Forestry Committee, Subcommittee on Nutrition and Investigations, SR-328A 20510; 224-2035. Tom Harkin, D-Iowa, chairman; Mark Halverson, legislative assistant.

Jurisdiction over legislation on commodity donations, food, nutrition, and hunger in the United States and in foreign countries.

International Organizations:

Food and Agriculture Organization of the United Nations, Liaison Office for North America, 1001 22nd St. N.W., #300 20437; 653-2400. Vacant, director. Library, 653-2402. Fax, 653-5760.

Serves as the main forum of the international community on world food, agriculture, fisheries, and forestry problems; provides developing nations with technical assistance to improve and increase food and agricultural production. Library open to the public by appointment. (International headquarters in Rome.)

Nongovernmental:

Agricultural Cooperative Development International, 50 F St. N.W., #900 20001; 638-4661. Ron Gollehon, president. Fax, 626-0726.

Membership: farm supply, processing, and marketing cooperatives; farm credit banks; national farmer organizations; and insurance cooperatives. Provides cooperatives with training and technical, management, and marketing assistance; supports farm credit systems, agribusiness, and government agencies in developing countries. Contracts with the Agency for International Development to start farm cooperatives in other countries. Affiliated with the National Council of Farmer Cooperatives.

American Red Cross, National Headquarters, 17th and D Sts. N.W., 2nd Floor 20006; 737-8300. Elizabeth H. Dole, president. Fax, 783-3432.

Humanitarian relief and health education organization chartered by Congress. Provides food and supplies to assist in major disaster and refugee situations worldwide.

Bread for the World, 1100 Wayne Ave., #1000, Silver Spring, MD 20910; (301) 608-2400. David Beckmann, president. Fax, (301) 608-2401.

Christian citizens' movement that works to eradicate world hunger. Organizes and coordinates political action on issues and public policy affecting the causes of hunger. Interests include domestic food assistance programs, international famine, and hunger relief.

CARE, 2025 Eye St. N.W. 20006; 223-2277. Charles L. Sykes, vice president, Washington liaison office. Fax, 296-8695.

Assists the developing world's poor through emergency aid and community self-help programs that focus on farming assistance, reforestation, health, and job creation. (Headquarters in Atlanta, Ga.)

Interfaith Impact for Justice and Peace, 110 Maryland Ave. N.E. 20002; 543-2800. Jim Bell, executive director. Fax, 547-8107. Legislative update recording, (800) 424-7290.

Coalition of religious organizations. Develops recommendations on U.S. food and agricultural policies; provides information on food stamps, development assistance, food aid, U.S. farm policy, and international economic issues.

International Food Policy Research Institute, 1200 17th St. N.W. 20036; 862-5600. Per Pinstrup-Andersen, director. Library, 862-5614. Fax, 467-4439.

Research organization that analyzes the world food situation and suggests ways of making food more available in developing countries. Provides various governments with information on national and international food policy. Sponsors conferences and seminars; publishes research reports. Library open to the public by appointment.

RESULTS, 236 Massachusetts Ave. N.E., #300 20002; 543-9340. Sam Harris, director. Fax, 546-3228.

Works to end world hunger; encourages grassroots and legislative support of programs and proposals dealing with hunger and hunger-related issues; monitors legislation and regulations.

U.S. National Committee for World Food Day, 1001 22nd St. N.W. 20437; 653-2404. Patricia Young, national coordinator. Fax, 653-5760.

Consortium of farm, religious, nutrition, education, consumer, relief, and development organizations. Coordinates widespread community participation in World Food Day. Distributes materials about food and hunger issues and encourages long-term action.

Winrock International Institute for Agricultural Development, 1611 N. Kent St., Arlington, VA 22209; (703) 525-9430. Richard Cobb, vice president. Fax, (703) 525-1744.

Seeks to increase the output of crops and livestock and to raise rural incomes in developing nations. Interests include agricultural planning, strengthening research systems, training personnel, and implementing production programs. (Headquarters in Morrilton, Ark.)

World Mercy Fund, 121 S. Saint Asaph St., Alexandria, VA 22314; (703) 548-4646. Patrick Leonard, president. Fax, (703) 548-6963.

Provides the developing world with medical, educational, agricultural, and other forms of technical assistance and training.

See also Agriculture, General, Nongovernmental (p. 589); Foreign Policy and Aid, International Development, Nongovernmental (p. 452)

See also The Fertilizer Institute (p. 593); International Fund for Agricultural Research (p. 603); National Cooperative Business Assn. (p. 612)

Livestock and Poultry

Agencies:

Agricultural Marketing Service (Agriculture Dept.), Livestock and Seed, 14th St. and Independence Ave. S.W. (mailing address: P.O. Box 96456, Washington, DC 20090-6456); 720-5705. Barry L. Carpenter, director. Fax, 720-3499.

Administers meat marketing program; maintains market news service to inform producers of meat market situation and daily price changes; develops, establishes, and revises U.S. standards for classes and grades of livestock and meat; grades, examines, and certifies meat and meat products.

Agricultural Marketing Service (Agriculture Dept.), Poultry, 14th St. and Independence Ave. S.W. (mailing address: P.O. Box 96456, Washington, DC 20090-6456); 720-4476. D. Michael Holbrook, director. Fax, 690-3165.

Sets poultry grading standards and conducts quality inspections based on those standards.

Agriculture Dept., Food Safety and Inspection Service, 14th St. and Independence Ave. S.W.

20250; 720-7025. H. Russell Cross, administrator. Information, 720-9113. Fax, 690-4437. Consumer inquiries, (800) 535-4555; in Washington, D.C., 720-3333.

Inspects and provides safe handling and labeling guidelines for meat and poultry products.

Agriculture Dept., Livestock and Meat Standardization, 14th St. and Independence Ave. S.W. (mailing address: P.O. Box 96456, Washington, DC 20090); 720-4486. Herbert Abraham, chief. Fax, 720-1112.

Sets meat grading standards. Writes and maintains meat purchase specifications.

Agriculture Dept., Packers and Stockyards Administration, 14th St. and Independence Ave. S.W. 20250; 720-7051. Calvin W. Watkins, acting administrator. Information, 720-9528. Fax, 690-2173.

Maintains competition in the marketing of livestock, poultry, and meat by prohibiting deceptive and monopolistic marketing practices; tests market scales and conducts check weighings for accuracy.

Agriculture Dept., Program Review and Resource Management, 14th St. and Independence Ave. S.W. (mailing address: P.O. Box 96456, Washington, DC 20090); 720-1930. Gary Benton, chief. Fax, 720-3499.

Conducts quality inspections based on meat grading standards set by the Agriculture Dept.'s Livestock and Meat Standardization office.

Congress:

House Agriculture Committee, Subcommittee on Livestock, 1336 LHOB 20515; 225-1867. Harold L. Volkmer, D-Mo., chairman; Tim DeCoster, staff director.

Jurisdiction over legislation on inspection and certification of meat, livestock, and poultry and over animal welfare.

Senate Agriculture, Nutrition, and Forestry Committee, Subcommittee on Agricultural Research, Conservation, Forestry, and General Legislation, SR-328A 20510; 224-2035. Tom Daschle, D-S.D., chairman; Tom Buis, legislative assistant.

Jurisdiction over legislation on inspection and certification of meat, livestock, and poultry and over animal welfare.

Nongovernmental:

American Meat Institute, 1700 N. Moore St., #1600, Arlington, VA (mailing address: P.O. Box 3556, Washington, DC 20007); (703) 841-2400. J. Patrick Boyle, president. Fax, (703) 527-0938.

Membership: national and international meat and poultry packers and processors. Provides statistics on meat and poultry production and consumption, livestock, and feed grains. Funds meat research projects and consumer education programs; sponsors conferences and correspondence courses on meat production and processing; monitors legislation and regulations.

American Sheep Industry Assn., 412 1st St. S.E., #1 Lower Level 20003; 484-2778. Larry Meyers, Washington representative. Fax, 484-0770.

Membership: sheep, wool, and mohair producers. Interests include sheep breeds, lamb and wool marketing, and wool research. Monitors legislation and regulations. (Headquarters in Denver.)

Animal Health Institute, 501 Wythe St., Alexandria, VA (mailing address: P.O. Box 1417-D50, Alexandria, VA 22313); (703) 684-0011. Richard H. Ekfelt, president. Fax, (703) 684-0125.

Membership: manufacturers of drugs and other products (including vaccines, pesticides, and vitamins) for pets and food-producing animals. Monitors legislation and regulations.

Beyond Beef, 1130 17th St. N.W., #300 20036; 775-1132. Jeremy Rifkin, president. Fax, 775-0074.

Works to reduce beef consumption by fifty percent by the year 2000, to replace beef in the diet with organically raised grains, fruits, and vegetables, and to reform the cattle production system and promote humanely and organically raised beef. Opposes genetically engineered food.

Farm Animal Reform Movement, P.O. Box 30654, Bethesda, MD 20824; (301) 530-1737. Alex Hershaft, president. Fax, (301) 530-5747.

Works to end use of animals for food. Interests include consumer health, agricultural resources, and environmental quality. Conducts national educational campaigns, including the Great American Meatout. Monitors legislation and regulations.

National Assn. of Meat Purveyors, 1920 Association Dr., #400, Reston, VA 22091; (703) 758-1900. Deven L. Scott, executive vice president. Fax, (703) 758-8001.

Membership: meat, poultry, fish, and game companies specializing in the food service industry. Interests include quality standards and standard procedures for meat, poultry, fish, and game handling; conducts seminars.

National Broiler Council, 1155 15th St. N.W. 20005; 296-2622. George B. Watts, president. Fax, 293-4005.

Membership: producers and processors of broiler chickens. Provides information on production, marketing, and consumption of broiler chickens.

National Cattlemen's Assn., 1301 Pennsylvania Ave. N.W., #300 20004; 347-0228. Thomas Cook, vice president, government affairs. Fax, 638-0607.

Membership: individual cattlemen, state cattlemen's groups, and breed associations. Provides information on beef research, agricultural labor, beef grading, foreign trade, taxes, marketing, cattle economics, branding, animal health, and environmental management. (Headquarters in Englewood, Colo.)

National Meat Canners Assn., 1700 N. Moore St., Arlington, VA (mailing address: P.O. Box 3556, Washington, DC 20007); (703) 841-2400. Jerome Breiter, executive secretary. Fax, (703) 841-9656.

Membership: canners of prepared meats and meat food products. Provides information on the canned meat industry.

National Pork Board, 501 School St. S.W., #400 20024; 554-3601. Jim Smith, director, market relations. Fax, 554-3602.

Independent board appointed by the secretary of agriculture. Promotes pork product consumption; collects, allocates, and evaluates the use of checkoff funds (assessments on the sale of pork) received from pork producers. Uses funds for pork product promotion, research, and consumer education programs. Provides pork producers with information. (Headquarters in Des Moines, Iowa.)

National Pork Producers Council, 501 School St. S.W., #400 20024; 554-3600. Richard Pasco, vice president, government affairs. Fax, 554-3602.

Membership: pork producers and independent pork producer organizations. Interests include pork production, nutrition, the environment, trade, and federal regulations. Monitors legislation and regulations. (Headquarters in Des Moines, Iowa.)

National Turkey Federation, 11319 Sunset Hills Rd., Reston, VA 22090; (703) 435-7206. Stuart E. Proctor Jr., president. Fax, (703) 481-0837.

Membership: turkey growers, hatcheries, breeders, and processors. Promotes turkey consumption; monitors legislation and regulations.

U.S. Hide, Skin, and Leather Assn., 1700 N. Moore St., #1600, Arlington, VA 22209; (703) 841-5485. Jerome J. Breiter, president. Fax, (703) 841-9656.

Membership: meatpackers, brokers, dealers, processors, and exporters of hides and skins. Maintains liaison with allied trade associations and participates in programs on export statistics, hide price reporting, and freight rates; conducts seminars and consumer information programs. (Division of American Meat Institute.)

See also Public Lands Council (p. 645)

Rural Development

Agencies:

Agricultural Stabilization and Conservation Service (Agriculture Dept.), Conservation and Environmental Protection, 14th St. and Independence Ave. S.W. (mailing address: P.O. Box 2415, Washington, DC 20013); 720-6221. James McMullen, director. Fax, 720-4619.

Makes direct cash payments to farmers as a cost-sharing method for agricultural conservation and pollution abatement projects in rural areas.

Agriculture Dept., Agricultural Cooperative Service, 14th St. and Independence Ave. S.W. (mailing address: P.O. Box 96576, Washington, DC 20090); 720-7558. Randall E. Torgerson, administrator. Information, 720-2556. Fax, 720-4641.

Provides cooperative enterprises that process and market farm products and other cooperatively owned, rural-based industries with technical and research assistance. Helps to develop new cooperatives.

Agriculture Dept., Extension Service, 14th St. and Independence Ave. S.W. 20250; 720-3377. Leodrey Williams, acting administrator. Information, 720-3029. Fax, 720-3993.

Conducts workshops on management of farmer cooperatives and educational programs on sustainable agriculture. Provides small farmers with management and marketing programs; offers training and assistance to rural communities and local officials.

Agriculture Dept., Small Community and Rural Development, 14th St. and Independence Ave. S.W. 20250; 720-4581. Bob Nash, under secretary. Fax, 720-2080.

Acts as chief adviser to the secretary on agricultural credit and related matters; coordinates rural development policies and programs throughout the federal government; supervises the Farmers Home Administration, Rural Electrification Administration, and Federal Crop Insurance Corp.

Agriculture Dept., Small Scale Agriculture, 901 D St. S.W. (mailing address: USDA-CSRS, Aerospace Bldg., Washington, DC 20250); 401-1805. Howard W. "Bud" Kerr Jr., director. Fax, 401-1804.

Provides department programs and initiatives dealing with small farms with leadership and guidance; works with federal, state, and local farming authorities and private industry to ensure that program priorities are met and publicized.

Farmers Home Administration (Agriculture Dept.), Farmer Programs, 14th St. and Independence Ave. S.W. 20250; 720-4671. Lou Anne Kling, acting assistant administrator. Fax, 690-3573.

Supports rural development through farm program loans, including real estate, farm production, and emergency loans.

Farmers Home Administration (Agriculture Dept.), Housing Programs, 14th St. and Independence Ave. S.W. 20250; 720-5177. Ronnie O. Tharrington, assistant administrator. Fax, 690-3025.

Supports rural development through single-family housing loans, rent supplement programs, and rural rental housing programs.

Farmers Home Administration (Agriculture Dept.), Program Operations, 14th St. and Independence Ave. S.W. 20250-0700; 720-2564.

Wayne Fawbush, deputy administrator. Fax, 720-8445.

Lender of last resort for farm credit. Supports rural development through loan and grant programs for rural rental and farm labor housing, business and industry loans, and community programs, including water and waste disposal systems.

Housing and Urban Development Dept., State and Small Cities, HUD Bldg., Rm. 7184 20410; 708-1322. Richard J. Kennedy, director. Fax, 708-1744.

Administers grants to states for statewide planning and assistance to cities and counties with fewer than 50,000 persons.

Rural Development Administration (Agriculture Dept.), 14th St. and Independence Ave. S.W. 20250; 690-4730. Wilbur T. Peer, acting administrator. Fax, 690-4737.

Promotes rural economic development by financing community facilities and assisting community businesses.

Rural Electrification Administration (Agriculture Dept.), 14th St. and Independence Ave. S.W. 20250; 720-9540. Wally Byer, administrator. Information, 720-1255. Press, 720-1260. Fax, 720-1725.

Makes loans and loan guarantees to rural electric and telephone utilities providing service in rural areas. Administers the Rural Telephone Bank, which provides supplemental financing from nonfederal sources for telephone systems. Also makes loans that promote economic development and creation of jobs in rural areas.

Congress:

House Agriculture Committee, Subcommittee on Environment, Credit, and Rural Development, 1430 LHOB 20515; 225-0301. Tim Johnson, D-S.D., chairman; Anne Simmons, staff director.

Jurisdiction over legislation on family farming and rural development, including rural electrification and telephone development; oversight of Rural Electrification Administration.

House Small Business Committee, Subcommittee on Rural Enterprises, Exports, and the Environment, 1F CHOB 20515; 225-8944. Bill Sarpalius, D-Texas, chairman; Christopher Mattson, staff director.

Jurisdiction over rural economy and family farming legislation as it relates to the small-business community.

Senate Agriculture, Nutrition, and Forestry Committee, Subcommittee on Rural Development and Rural Electrification, SR-328A 20510; 224-2035. Howell Heflin, D-Ala., chairman; Chuck Penry, legislative assistant.

Jurisdiction over legislation on family farming and rural development, including rural electrification and telephone development; oversight of Rural Electrification Administration.

Senate Banking, Housing, and Urban Affairs Committee, Subcommittee on Economic Stabilization and Rural Development, SD-534 20510; 224-7391. Richard C. Shelby, D-Ala., chairman; Christin Givhan, staff director.

Jurisdiction over legislation on economic stabilization and growth, including regulatory relief issues and barriers to development in rural areas.

Senate Small Business Committee, Subcommittee on Rural Economy and Family Farming, SR-428A 20510; 224-5175. Paul Wellstone, D-Minn., chairman; Brian Ahlberg, legislative assistant.

Jurisdiction over rural economy and family farming legislation as it relates to the small-business community.

See also Congressional Rural Caucus (p. 758); Rural Health Care Coalition (p. 760); Senate Rural Health Caucus (p. 761)

Nongovernmental:

Farm Credit Council, 50 F St. N.W. 20001; 626-8710. William R. Weber, president.

Membership: cooperative farm lending institutions, district farm credit councils, and a central bank for cooperatives. Monitors legislation and regulations concerning cooperative farm lenders and their ability to provide credit and related services.

Federal Agricultural Mortgage Corp. (Farmer Mac), 919 18th St. N.W., #200 20006; 872-7700. Thomas R. Clark, vice president.

Private corporation chartered by Congress to provide a secondary mortgage market for farm and rural housing loans. Guarantees principal and interest repayment on securities backed by farm and rural housing loans.

National Cooperative Business Assn., 1401 New York Ave. N.W., #1100 20005; 638-6222. Russell C. Notar, president. Fax, 638-1374.

Alliance of cooperatives, businesses, and state cooperative associations. Provides information about starting and managing agricultural cooperatives in the United States and in developing nations; monitors legislation and regulations.

National Council of Farmer Cooperatives, 50 F St. N.W., #900 20001; 626-8700. Wayne A. Boutwell, president. Fax, 626-8722.

Educational organization of farmer cooperatives. Encourages research on agricultural cooperatives; provides statistics and analyzes trends. Monitors legislation and regulations on agricultural trade, transportation, energy, and tax issues.

National Rural Electric Cooperative Assn., 1800 Massachusetts Ave. N.W. 20036; 857-9524. Bob Bergland, executive vice president. Fax, 857-4150.

Membership: rural electric cooperative systems and public power and utility districts. Provides members with technical assistance. Library on rural electrification, water resources, and energy open to the public by appointment.

National Telephone Cooperative Assn., 2626 Pennsylvania Ave. N.W. 20037; 298-2300. Michael E. Brunner, executive vice president. Fax, 298-2320.

Membership: telephone cooperatives (member-owned telephone companies) in rural areas and small, independent commercial companies serving rural areas. Offers technical assistance and a benefits program to members. Monitors legislation and regulations.

Rural Coalition, P.O. Box 5199, Arlington, VA 22205-0299; (703) 534-1845. Lorette Picciano-Hanson, executive director.

Alliance of organizations that develop public policies benefiting rural communities. Studies agriculture and rural development issues, including health, jobs and the environment, education, minority farmers, farmworkers, native Americans, protection of natural resources, and rural investment. Provides rural groups with technical assistance.

Key Agencies:

Environmental Protection Agency
401 M St. S.W. 20460
Information: 260-2080

Interior Dept.
Main Interior Bldg.
1849 C St. N.W. 20240
Information: 208-3171

National Oceanic and Atmospheric
Administration
14th St. and Constitution Ave. N.W. 20230
Information: 482-2000

Key Committees:

House Merchant Marine and
Fisheries Committee
1334 LHOB 20515
Phone: 225-4047

House Natural Resources Committee
1324 LHOB 20515
Phone: 225-2761

Senate Energy and Natural
Resources Committee
SD-304 20510
Phone: 224-4971

Senate Environment and
Public Works Committee
SD-456 20510
Phone: 224-6176

Key Personnel:

Environmental Protection Agency

Carol Browner, administrator

Interior Dept.

Bruce Babbitt, secretary
Vacant, deputy secretary
George T. Frampton Jr., assistant secretary for fish, wildlife, and parks
Robert Armstrong, assistant secretary for land and minerals management
Elizabeth Ann Rieke, assistant secretary for water and science
Mike Dombeck, acting director, Bureau of Land Management
Hermann Enzer, acting director, Bureau of Mines
Daniel P. Beard, commissioner, Bureau of Reclamation
Roger G. Kennedy, director, National Park Service
Mollie H. Beattie, director, U.S. Fish and Wildlife Service
Gordon P. Eaton, director, U.S. Geological Survey

National Oceanic and Atmospheric
Administration

D. James Baker, administrator

15

Environment
and Natural Resources

Contents:

Environment

General

See also Energy chapter (p. 201); Natural Resources, General (p. 634); Science: Environmental and Earth Sciences (p. 677)

Agencies:

Agriculture Dept., Natural Resources and Environment, 14th St. and Independence Ave. S.W. 20250; 720-7173. James Lyons, assistant secretary. Fax, 720-4732.

Formulates and promulgates policy relating to environmental activities and natural resources; administers forest, conservation, and natural resource aspects of the National Environmental Policy Act.

Council on Environmental Quality (Executive Office of the President), 722 Jackson Pl. N.W. 20503; 395-5754. Ray Clark, acting chair. Fax, 395-3744.

Advises the president on environmental issues and prepares annual report on environmental quality for Congress; develops regulations for implementation of environmental impact statement law; provides information on environmental affairs. (The council is to be abolished and succeeded by the new White House Office on Environmental Policy.)

Energy Dept., Environment, Safety, and Health, 1000 Independence Ave. S.W. 20585; 586-6151. Tara O'Toole, assistant secretary. Fax, 586-0956.

Ensures that Energy Dept. programs comply with federal policies and standards designed to protect the environment and government property. Approves all environmental impact statements prepared by the department. Oversees health and nonnuclear safety conditions at Energy Dept. facilities.

Environmental Protection Agency, 401 M St. S.W. 20460; 260-4700. Carol Browner, administrator. Information, 260-2080. Press, 260-4355.

Administers federal environmental policies, research, and regulations; provides information on environmental subjects, including water pollution, pollution prevention, hazardous and solid waste disposal, air and noise pollution, pesticides and toxic substances, and radiation.

Environmental Protection Agency, Enforcement, 401 M St. S.W. 20460; 260-4134. Steve Herman, assistant administrator. Fax, 260-0500.

Principal adviser to the administrator on enforcement of standards for air, water, toxic substances and pesticides, hazardous and solid waste management, radiation, and emergency preparedness programs. Investigates criminal and civil violations of environmental standards; oversees federal facilities' environmental compliance and site cleanup; serves as EPA's liaison office for federal agency compliance with the National Environmental Policy Act; manages environmental review of other agencies' projects and activities and coordinates EPA native American environmental programs.

Environmental Protection Agency, Health and Environmental Assessment, 401 M St. S.W. 20460; 260-7315. William H. Farland, director. Fax, 260-0393.

Evaluates animal and human health data to define environmental health hazards and estimate risk to humans.

Environmental Protection Agency, National Workforce Development Staff, 401 M St. S.W. 20460; 260-2574. Patricia Powers, director. Fax, 260-0211.

Awards grants to selected institutions for the development of environmental education programs, curricula, and materials. Operates an environmental employment program for persons age 55 and over.

Environmental Protection Agency, Policy, Planning, and Evaluation, 401 M St. S.W. 20460; 260-4332. David Gardiner, assistant administrator. Fax, 260-0275.

Coordinates agency planning, policy development, and standard-setting activities.

Environmental Protection Agency, Research and Development, 401 M St. S.W. 20460; 260-7676. Robert J. Huggett, assistant administrator designate. Fax, 260-9761.

Develops scientific data and methods to support EPA standards and regulations; conducts exposure and risk assessments; researches applied and long-term technologies to reduce risks from pollution.

Environmental Protection Agency, Science Advisory Board, 401 M St. S.W. 20460; 260-4126. Donald G. Barnes, staff director. Fax, 260-9232. Internet, barnes.don@epamail.epagov.

Coordinates nongovernment scientists and engineers who advise the administrator on scientific and technical aspects of environmental problems and issues. Evaluates EPA research projects, the technical basis of regulations and standards, and policy statements.

Environmental Protection Agency, Wetlands Protection, 499 S. Capitol St. S.W., #727 (mailing address: 401 M St. S.W., #4502-F, Washington, DC 20460); 260-7791. John W. Meagher, director. Fax, 260-2356.

Manages dredge-and-fill program under section 404 of the Clean Water Act. Coordinates federal policies affecting wetlands. Promotes public awareness of wetland preservation and management. Encourages the development of stronger wetland programs at the state level.

Federal Aviation Administration (Transportation Dept.), Environment and Energy, 800 Independence Ave. S.W. 20591; 267-3576. Louise E. Maillett, director. Fax, 267-5594.

Responsible for environmental affairs for aviation, including implementation and administration of aviation-related environmental acts. Administers and monitors the agency's hazardous materials program.

Housing and Urban Development Dept., Environment and Energy, HUD Bldg., Rm. 7240 20410; 708-2894. Richard H. Broun, director. Fax, 708-3363.

Issues policies and sets standards for environmental and land-use planning and environmental management practices. Oversees HUD implementation of requirements on environment, historic preservation, archeology, flood plain management, coastal zone management, sole source aquifers, farmland protection, endangered species, airport clear zones, explosive hazards, radon, and noise.

Justice Dept., Environment and Natural Resources, 601 Pennsylvania Ave. N.W. (mailing address: P.O. Box 23985, Washington, DC 20026-3985); 272-9877. Chuck DeMonaco, acting chief, environmental crimes. Fax, 272-9881.

Conducts criminal enforcement actions on behalf of the United States for all environmental protection statutes, including air, water, pesticides, hazardous wastes, wetland matters investigated by the Environmental Protection Agency, and other criminal environmental enforcement.

Justice Dept., Environment and Natural Resources, Main Justice Bldg. (mailing address: P.O. Box 23986, Washington, DC 20026-3986); 514-2219. Letitia J. Grishaw, chief, environmental defense. Fax, 514-2584.

Conducts litigation on air, water, noise, pesticides, solid waste, toxic substances, Superfund, and wetlands in cooperation with the Environmental Protection Agency; represents the EPA in suits involving judicial review of EPA actions; represents the U.S. Army Corps of Engineers in cases involving dredge-and-fill activity in navigable waters and adjacent wetlands; represents the Coast Guard in oil and hazardous spill cases; defends all federal agencies in environmental litigation.

Justice Dept., Environment and Natural Resources, Main Justice Bldg. (mailing address: P.O. Box 7611, Ben Franklin Station, Washington, DC 20044); 514-4291. John C. Cruden, chief, environmental enforcement. Fax, 514-8058.

Conducts civil enforcement actions on behalf of the United States for all environmental protection statutes, including air, water, pesticides, hazardous waste, wetland matters investigated by the Environmental Protection Agency, and other civil environmental enforcement.

National Oceanic and Atmospheric Administration (Commerce Dept.), National Environmental Satellite, Data, and Information Service, 4401 Suitland Rd., #2069, Suitland, MD (mailing address: Federal Bldg. 4, #2069, Washington, DC 20233); (301) 763-7190. Robert S. Winokur, assistant administrator. Information, (301) 763-2560. Fax, (301) 763-4011.

Provides satellite observations of the environment by operating polar orbiting and geostationary satellites; develops satellite techniques; increases the utilization of satellite data in environmental services.

National Science and Technology Council (Executive Office of the President), 744 Jackson Pl. N.W. 20506; 395-5101. John H. Gibbons, chairman. Fax, 395-5076.

Coordinates research and development activities and programs that involve more than one federal agency. Activities concern earth sciences, materials, and radiation policy.

State Dept., Oceans and International Environmental and Scientific Affairs, Main State Bldg., Rm. 7831 20520-7818; 647-1554. Elinor G. Constable, assistant secretary. Fax, 647-0217.

Environmental Protection Agency

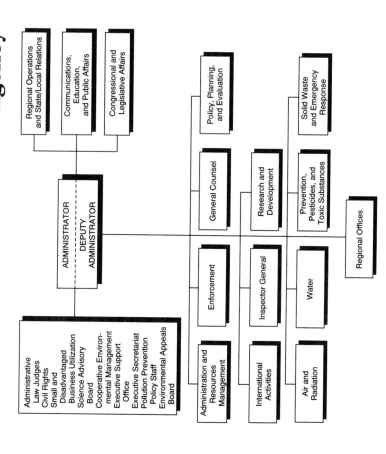

ADMINISTRATOR

DEPUTY ADMINISTRATOR

Regional Operations and State/Local Relations

Communications, Education, and Public Affairs

Congressional and Legislative Affairs

Administrative Law Judges
Civil Rights
Small and Disadvantaged Business Utilization
Science Advisory Board
Cooperative Environmental Management
Executive Support Office
Executive Secretariat
Pollution Prevention Policy Staff
Environmental Appeals Board

Administration and Resources Management

Enforcement

Policy, Planning, and Evaluation

General Counsel

International Activities

Inspector General

Research and Development

Air and Radiation

Water

Prevention, Pesticides, and Toxic Substances

Solid Waste and Emergency Response

Regional Offices

Concerned with foreign policy as it affects natural resources and the environment, human health, the global climate, energy production, and oceans and fisheries.

Transportation Dept., Environmental Division, 400 7th St. S.W., #9217 20590; 366-4366. Eugene L. Lehr, chief. Fax, 366-7618.

Develops environmental policy and makes recommendations to the secretary; monitors Transportation Dept. implementation of environmental legislation; reviews and comments on the environmental impact statements of major transportation projects; serves as liaison with other federal agencies and state and local governments on environmental matters related to transportation.

See also Domestic Policy Council (p. 300)

Congress:

General Accounting Office, Environmental Programs, 441 G St. N.W. 20548; 512-6111. Richard L. Hembra, director. Fax, 512-8774.

Independent, nonpartisan agency in the legislative branch. Audits, analyzes, and evaluates programs of the Environmental Protection Agency; makes reports available to the public.

House Appropriations Committee, Subcommittee on VA, HUD, and Independent Agencies, H143 CAP 20515; 225-3241. Louis Stokes, D-Ohio, chairman; Paul Thompson, staff assistant.

Jurisdiction over legislation to appropriate funds for the Environmental Protection Agency, Office of Environmental Policy, Council on Environmental Quality, National Science Foundation, and other environment-related services and programs.

House Energy and Commerce Committee, Subcommittee on Health and the Environment, 2415 RHOB 20515; 225-4952. Henry A. Waxman, D-Calif., chairman; Karen Nelson, staff director.

Jurisdiction over legislation concerning environmental affairs, including global warming.

House Energy and Commerce Committee, Subcommittee on Transportation and Hazardous Materials, 324 Ford Bldg. (2nd and D Sts. S.W.) 20515; 225-9304. Al Swift, D-Wash., chairman; Arthur Endres, staff director and chief counsel.

Jurisdiction over legislation on solid waste disposal, pollution, toxic substances, noise pollution control, and hazardous materials (except EPA research and development programs). Jurisdiction over the Comprehensive Environmental Response, Compensation, and Liability Act (the Superfund), the Resource Conservation and Recovery Act, and the Toxic Substances Control Act (jurisdiction shared with House Science, Space, and Technology Committee).

House Government Operations Committee, Subcommittee on Environment, Energy, and Natural Resources, B371C RHOB 20515; 225-6427. Mike Synar, D-Okla., chairman; Sandy Harris, staff director. Fax, 225-2392.

Oversight of the Environmental Protection Agency, the Office of Environmental Policy, the Nuclear Regulatory Commission, the U.S. Fish and Wildlife Service, and the Council on Environmental Quality.

House Science, Space, and Technology Committee, Subcommittee on Energy, H2390 Ford Bldg. (2nd and D Sts. S.W.) 20515; 225-8056. Marilyn Lloyd, D-Tenn., chair; Francis X. Murray, staff director.

Jurisdiction over legislation on Energy Dept. environmental science activities.

House Science, Space, and Technology Committee, Subcommittee on Technology, Environment, and Aviation, B374 RHOB 20515; 225-9662. Tim Valentine, D-N.C., chairman; James H. Turner, staff director.

Jurisdiction over legislation on Environmental Protection Agency research and development programs concerning air, water, noise, and solid waste pollution. Jurisdiction over research and development programs of the National Environmental Policy Act, the Comprehensive Environmental Response, Compensation, and Liability Act (the Superfund), the Resource Conservation and Recovery Act, and the Toxic Substances Control Act (jurisdiction shared with House Energy and Commerce Committee).

House Small Business Committee, Subcommittee on Rural Enterprises, Exports, and the Environment, 1F CHOB 20515; 225-8944. Bill Sarpalius, D-Texas, chairman; Christopher Mattson, staff director.

Studies and makes recommendations on environmental and pollution issues as they relate to small business.

Senate Appropriations Committee, Subcommittee on VA, HUD, and Independent Agencies, SD-142 20510; 224-7211. Barbara A. Mikulski, D-Md., chair; Kevin F. Kelly, clerk.

Jurisdiction over legislation to appropriate funds for the Environmental Protection Agency, Office of Environmental Policy, Council on Environmental Quality, National Science Foundation, and other environment-related services and programs.

Senate Commerce, Science, and Transportation Committee, Subcommittee on National Ocean Policy Study, SH-425 (mailing address: SD-508, Washington, DC 20510); 224-4912. Ernest F. Hollings, D-S.C., chairman; Penny Dalton, staff member.

Studies issues related to the National Environmental Satellite Service. (Subcommittee does not report legislation.)

Senate Environment and Public Works Committee, SD-456 20510; 224-6176. Max Baucus, D-Mont., chairman; Peter L. Scher, staff director.

Jurisdiction over most legislation relating to environmental affairs, including global warming and Environmental Protection Agency research and development programs concerning air, water, noise, solid waste, hazardous materials, and toxic substances; jurisdiction over legislation relating to the National Environmental Policy Act, the Comprehensive Environmental Response, Compensation, and Liability Act (the Superfund), the Resource Conservation and Recovery Act, and the Toxic Substances Control Act. Oversight of the Environmental Protection Agency, the Office of Environmental Policy, the Nuclear Regulatory Commission, the U.S. Fish and Wildlife Service, the Council on Environmental Quality, and the National Science Foundation.

Senate Small Business Committee, SR-428A 20510; 224-5175. Dale Bumpers, D-Ark., chairman; John W. Ball III, staff director.

Studies and makes recommendations on environmental and pollution issues as they relate to small businesses.

See also Environmental and Energy Study Conference (p. 756)

Nongovernmental:

American Academy of Environmental Engineers, 130 Holiday Court, #100, Annapolis, MD 21401; (410) 266-3311. William C. Anderson, executive director. Fax, (410) 266-7653. Direct dial from Washington, D.C.: (301) 261-8958.

Membership: state-licensed environmental engineers who have passed examinations in environmental engineering specialties, including general environment, air pollution control, solid waste management, hazardous waste management, industrial hygiene, radiation protection, water supply, and wastewater.

American Bar Assn., Standing Committee on Environmental Law, 1800 M St. N.W., #2005 20036; 331-2276. Elissa Lichtenstein, director. Fax, 331-2220.

Studies and sponsors domestic and international projects in environmental law and policy; coordinates environmental law activities throughout the ABA. (Headquarters in Chicago.)

Americans for the Environment, 1400 16th St. N.W. 20036; 797-6665. Roy Morgan, president. Fax, 797-6646.

Seeks to protect natural resources by influencing public policy. Encourages citizen involvement in the electoral process; offers training, education, and information in environmental fields and in political campaign management.

Citizens for the Environment, 1250 H St. N.W., #700 20005-3908; 783-3870. Paul Beckner, executive director. Fax, 783-4687.

Education and research organization that seeks market-oriented solutions to environmental problems. Develops initiatives to balance environmental and economic considerations; supports private efforts to manage wildlife habitats. (Affiliated with Citizens for a Sound Economy Foundation.)

Concern, 1794 Columbia Rd. N.W., 20009; 328-8160. Susan Boyd, executive director. Fax, 387-3378.

Environmental education organization interested in issues such as global warming, energy, sustainable agriculture, pesticides, water resources, and waste reduction.

Co-op America, 1850 M St. N.W., #700 20036; 872-5307. Alisa Gravitz, executive director. Toll-free, (800) 424-2667. Fax, 331-8166.

Network of consumers interested in environmental protection through recycling and other practices. Publishes a directory of environmentally responsible businesses and provides members with a catalog of products from those businesses, a financial planning guide for investment, and boycott information.

Edison Electric Institute, 701 Pennsylvania Ave. N.W. 20004; 508-5000. Thomas R. Kuhn, president. Information, 508-5778.

Membership: investor-owned electric power companies and electric utility holding companies. Interests include electric utility operation and concerns, including conservation and energy management, energy analysis, resources and environment, cogeneration and renewable energy resources, nuclear power, and research. Library open to the public by appointment.

Environmental Action, 6930 Carroll Ave., #600, Takoma Park, MD 20912; (301) 891-1100. Margaret Morgan-Hubbard, director. Fax, (301) 891-2218.

Citizens' interest group. Monitors legislation and regulations on environmental issues; conducts research and educational programs; provides information on public utilities, toxic substances, solid and hazardous waste, alternative energy, and energy conservation.

Environmental and Energy Study Institute, 122 C St. N.W., #700 20001; 628-1400. Robert O'Blake, chairman; Ken Murphy, executive director. Fax, 628-1825.

Nonpartisan policy education and analysis group established in cooperation with the congressional Environmental and Energy Study Conference to foster informed debate on environmental and energy issues. Interests include policies for sustainable development.

Environmental Defense Fund, 1875 Connecticut Ave. N.W., #1016 20009-5728; 387-3500. Cheryl King, office manager, Washington office. Fax, 234-6049.

Citizens' interest group staffed by lawyers, economists, and scientists. Takes legal action on environmental issues; provides information on pollution prevention, environmental health, energy conservation, toxic substances, acid rain, the Amazon rain forest, drinking water safety and enforcement, and litigation of water pollution standards. (Headquarters in New York.)

Environmental Law Institute, 1616 P St. N.W., 2nd Floor 20036; 328-5150. J. William Futrell,

president. Press, 939-3815. Library, 939-3814. Fax, 328-5002.

Research and education organization partially funded by government agencies. Conducts research on federal and state environmental law; publishes materials on environmental issues; sponsors education and training courses. Library open to the public by appointment.

Environmental Safety, 1700 N. Moore St., #1920, Arlington, VA 22209; (703) 527-8300. William Drayton, president. Fax, (703) 527-8383.

Monitors the effectiveness of laws relating to the containment, disposal, and transportation of toxic wastes; informs the public of its findings. Works with states to test and improve ways to implement environmental protection laws at the state level.

Friends of the Earth, 218 D St. S.E., 2nd Floor 20003; 544-2600. Jane Perkins, president. Fax, 543-4710.

Citizens' interest group concerned with environmental and energy-related issues, including protection of farmland, food resources, and public health; synthetic fuels; clean air, water, and groundwater; energy conservation; nuclear energy, waste, storage, and weapons; radiation and health; agricultural, ocean, and coastal resources; international water projects; transportation of hazardous wastes; global warming; and toxic substances and pesticides. Library open to the public by appointment.

Global Greenhouse Network, 1130 17th St. N.W., #630 20036; 466-2823. Jeremy Rifkin, president. Fax, 429-9602.

Coalition of public interest groups and legislators concerned with global warming. Focuses on the reduction of fossil fuel use, energy conservation, improved agricultural practices, and reforestation.

Izaak Walton League of America, 1401 Wilson Blvd., Level B, Arlington, VA 22209; (703) 528-1818. Maitland Sharpe, executive director. Fax, (703) 528-1836.

Grass-roots organization that promotes conservation of natural resources and the environment. Interests include air and water pollution and wildlife habitat protection. Provides information on acid rain and stream cleanup efforts at the local level.

League of Women Voters Education Fund, Natural Resources, 1730 M St. N.W. 20036; 429-1965. Elizabeth Kraft, director. Fax, 429-0854.

Education foundation affiliated with the League of Women Voters. Promotes citizen understanding of nuclear and solid waste issues; holds regional workshops to educate community leaders on these issues.

National Assn. of Conservation Districts, 509 Capitol Court N.E. 20002; 547-6223. Ernest C. Shea, executive vice president. Fax, 547-6450.

Membership: conservation districts (local subdivisions of state governments). Interests include erosion and sediment control, control of pollution from diffuse sources, and rural development.

National Assn. of Environmental Professionals, 5165 MacArthur Blvd. N.W. 20016; 966-1500. Susan Eisenberg, executive director. Fax, 966-1977.

Membership: environmental administrators, educators, and individuals in government, industry, and academia who are interested in national environmental policy and issues.

National Audubon Society, 666 Pennsylvania Ave. S.E., #200 20003; 547-9009. Elizabeth Raisbeck, senior vice president for regional and government affairs. Fax, 547-9022.

Citizens' interest group that promotes environmental preservation. Provides information on water resources, public lands, rangelands, forests, parks, national wildlife refuge system, wildlife and marine conservation.

National Environmental Development Assn., 1440 New York Ave. N.W. 20005; 638-1230. Terry Yosic, executive vice president. Fax, 639-8685.

Membership: corporations, labor unions, organizations, and individuals. Provides information on balancing environmental and economic needs. Manages projects concerning clean air, clean water, resource conservation and recovery, indoor air quality, and risk assessment.

National Wildlife Federation, 1400 16th St. N.W. 20036; 797-6800. Jay D. Hair, president. Fax, 797-6646.

Provides information on the environment, including air, water, and solid waste pollution and toxic substances; takes legal action on environmental issues. Laurel Ridge Conservation Education Center in Vienna, Va., provides educational materials and outdoor programs.

Natural Resources Defense Council, 1350 New York Ave. N.W. 20005; 783-7800. Thomas Cochran, office manager. Fax, 783-5917.

Environmental organization staffed by lawyers and scientists who undertake litigation and research. Interests include toxic substances and air, water, and ozone pollution. (Headquarters in New York.)

Population-Environment Balance, 1325 G St. N.W., #1003 20005; 879-3000. Mark W. Nowak, executive director. Fax, 879-3019.

Grass-roots organization that advocates U.S. population stabilization to safeguard the environment.

Renew America, 1400 16th St. N.W. 20036; 232-2252. Kenneth Brown, executive director. Fax, 232-2617.

Advances solutions to environmental problems by encouraging the replication of successful community-based initiatives.

Resources for the Future, 1616 P St. N.W. 20036; 328-5000. Robert Fri, president. Fax, 939-3460.

Engages in research and education on environmental issues, including multiple use of public lands, costs and benefits of pollution control, endangered species, hazardous waste policy, environmental risk management, and climate resources. Library open to the public by appointment.

Sierra Club, 408 C St. N.E. 20002; 547-1141. Debbie Sease, legislative director. Fax, 547-6009. Legislative hotline, 675-2394.

Citizens' interest group that promotes protection of natural resources. Interests include the Clean Air Act; the Arctic National Wildlife Refuge; protection of national forests, parks, and wilderness; toxins; global warming; and international development lending reform. Monitors legislation and regulations. (Headquarters in San Francisco.)

Union of Concerned Scientists, Environment, 1616 P St. N.W., #310 20036; 332-0900. Alden Meyer, legislative director. Fax, 332-0905.

Membership: scientists and others who advocate a comprehensive approach to resolving global environmental and resource concerns. Global Resources Campaign addresses interrelationships among environmental degradation, resource depletion, population growth, poverty, and development issues through independent technical research and public education. (Headquarters in Cambridge, Mass.)

U.S. Chamber of Commerce, Environment Policy, 1615 H St. N.W. 20062-2000; 463-5533. Mary E. Bernhard, manager. Fax, 887-3445.

Monitors operations of federal departments and agencies responsible for environmental programs and policies. Analyzes and evaluates legislation and regulations that affect the environment.

U.S. Public Interest Research Group (USPIRG), 215 Pennsylvania Ave. S.E. 20003; 546-9707. Gene Karpinski, executive director. Fax, 546-2461.

Coordinates grass-roots efforts to advance environmental and consumer protection laws; conducts research on environmental issues, including toxic and solid waste, air and water pollution, pesticides, endangered species, forest and wildlife preservation, alternative energy sources, and energy conservation; compiles reports and disseminates information on such issues; drafts and monitors environmental laws; testifies on behalf of proposed environmental legislation.

World Wildlife Fund, 1250 24th St. N.W. 20037; 293-4800. Kathryn S. Fuller, president. Fax, 293-9345.

Conducts research and publishes reports on environmental and conservation issues, including pollution reduction, forestry management, coastal and international land use, rural resource conservation, park management, sustainable development, and dispute resolution.

Worldwatch Institute, 1776 Massachusetts Ave. N.W. 20036; 452-1999. Lester R. Brown, president. Fax, 296-7365.

Research organization that focuses on interdisciplinary approach to solving global environmental problems. Interests include natural resources and human needs, environmental threats to food production, and quality of life.

See also America the Beautiful Fund (p. 102); National Governors' Assn. (p. 313); The Nature Conservancy (p. 638); World Resources

Institute (p. 630); Zero Population Growth (p. 328)

Air Pollution

Agencies:

Environmental Protection Agency, Air and Radiation, 401 M St. S.W., West Towers, MC 6101 20460; 260-7400. Mary D. Nichols, assistant administrator. Fax, 260-5155.

Administers air quality standards and planning programs of the Clean Air Act Amendments of 1990. Supervises the Office of Air Quality Planning and Standards in Durham, N.C., which develops air quality standards and provides information on air pollution control issues, including industrial air pollution. Administers the Air Pollution Technical Information Center in Research Triangle Park, N.C., which collects and provides technical literature on air pollution.

Environmental Protection Agency, Atmospheric Programs, 401 M St. S.W. 20460; 233-9140. Paul Stolpman, director. Fax, 233-9586.

Responsible for acid rain and stratospheric ozone programs; examines strategies for mitigating climate and atmospheric change.

Environmental Protection Agency, Mobile Sources, 401 M St. S.W. 20460; 260-7645. Richard D. Wilson, director. Fax, 260-3730.

Enforces Clean Air Act provisions for mobile sources, including motor vehicle air pollution control programs. Ann Arbor, Mich., office enforces aircraft emission standards.

Environmental Protection Agency, Radiation and Indoor Air, 501 3rd St. N.W. (mailing address: 401 M St. S.W., #6601J, Washington, DC 20460); 233-9320. Margo T. Oge, director. Fax, 233-9651.

Establishes standards for measuring radon; administers national and state radon surveys; conducts soil gas studies; provides states with technical assistance and training on radon detection and mitigation; collects data on radon mitigation and provides technical and public information. Administers environmental tobacco smoke, carpeting, and other indoor air quality control programs; coordinates federal and private efforts to address pollution problems in buildings.

Environmental Protection Agency, Stationary Source Compliance, 2800 Crystal Dr., Arlington, VA (mailing address: 401 M St. S.W., #6306W, Washington, DC 20460); (703) 308-8600. John B. Rasnic, director. Fax, (703) 308-8739.

Administers Clean Air Act provisions for stationary sources, including steel, petroleum, coal-fired boilers and furnaces, electric utilities, natural gas, sources of volatile organic compounds, and other industrial air pollution standards. Maintains data on the compliance status of various sources.

Federal Aviation Administration (Transportation Dept.), Environment and Energy, 800 Independence Ave. S.W. 20591; 267-3576. Louise E. Maillett, director. Fax, 267-5594.

Enforces government standards for aircraft emissions; conducts research on ozone depletion and high-altitude aircraft.

National Acid Precipitation Assessment Program (Executive Office of the President), 722 Jackson Pl. N.W. 20503; 296-1002. Derek Winstanley, director. Fax, 296-1009.

Interagency program created by Congress to coordinate federally funded research on causes, effects, and control of acid rain and air pollution.

U.S. Geological Survey (Interior Dept.), Energy and Marine Geology, 12201 Sunrise Valley Dr., Reston, VA 22092; (703) 648-6472. Gary Hill, chief. Fax, (703) 648-5464.

Conducts research to determine radon levels present in certain geographic areas and to measure the likelihood of radon occurrence.

Congress:

House Energy and Commerce Committee, Subcommittee on Health and the Environment, 2415 RHOB 20515; 225-4952. Henry A. Waxman, D-Calif., chairman; Karen Nelson, staff director.

Jurisdiction over legislation on indoor and outdoor air pollution, including the Clean Air Act.

Senate Environment and Public Works Committee, Subcommittee on Clean Air and Nuclear Regulation, SH-505 20510; 224-3597. Joseph I. Lieberman, D-Conn., chairman; Joyce Rechtschaffen, counsel.

Jurisdiction over legislation on indoor and outdoor air pollution, including the Clean Air Act.

Nongovernmental:

Alliance for Acid Rain Control and Energy Policy, 444 N. Capitol St. N.W., #602 20001; 624-5475. Ned Helme, executive director. Fax, 508-3829.

Alliance of governors, corporations, environmentalists, and academicians interested in environmental and energy policy, including acid rain. Monitors legislation and regulations.

Alliance for Responsible CFC Policy, 2111 Wilson Blvd., #850, Arlington, VA 22201; (703) 243-0344. Kevin Fay, director. Fax, (703) 243-2874.

Coalition of users and producers of chlorofluorocarbons (CFCs). Seeks further study of the ozone depletion theory.

Asbestos Information Assn./North America, 1745 Jefferson Davis Highway, #406, Arlington, VA 22202; (703) 412-1150. B. J. Pigg, president. Fax, (703) 412-1152.

Membership: firms that manufacture, sell, and use products containing asbestos fiber and those that mine, mill, and sell asbestos. Provides information on asbestos and health and on industry efforts to eliminate problems associated with asbestos dust; serves as liaison between the industry and federal and state governments.

Assn. of Local Air Pollution Control Officials, 444 N. Capitol St. N.W., #307 20001; 624-7864. S. William Becker, executive director. Fax, 624-7863.

Membership: local representatives of air pollution control programs nationwide that are responsible for implementing provisions of the Clean Air Act. Disseminates policy and technical information; analyzes air pollution issues; monitors legislation and regulations; conducts seminars, workshops, and conferences.

Center for Auto Safety, 2001 S St. N.W. 20009; 328-7700. Clarence M. Ditlow III, executive director.

Public interest organization that conducts research on air pollution caused by auto emissions; monitors fuel economy regulations.

Center for Clean Air Policy, 444 N. Capitol St. N.W., #602 20001; 624-7709. Ned Helme, executive director. Fax, 508-3829.

Membership: governors, corporations, environmentalists, and academicians. Analyzes economic and environmental effects of air pollution and related environmental problems. Serves as a liaison among government, corporate, community, and environmental groups.

Climate Institute, 324 4th St. N.E. 20002; 547-0104. John C. Topping Jr., president. Fax, 547-0111.

Educates the public and policy makers on climate change caused by pollutants (greenhouse effect, or global warming) and on the depletion of the ozone layer. Develops strategies on mitigating climate change in eight other countries.

Environmental Defense Fund, 1875 Connecticut Ave. N.W., #1016 20009-5728; 387-3500. Cheryl King, office manager, Washington office. Fax, 234-6049.

Citizens' interest group staffed by lawyers, economists, and scientists. Conducts research and provides information on pollution prevention, environmental health, and protection of the Amazon rain forest and the ozone layer. (Headquarters in New York.)

Environmental Industry Council, 529 14th St. N.W., #655 20045; 737-3018. John Adams, executive director. Fax, 466-8500.

Membership: manufacturers of pollution control equipment and systems and trade associations involved in pollution control. Monitors legislation and regulations affecting the industry.

Manufacturers of Emission Controls Assn., 1707 L St. N.W., #570 20036; 296-4797. Bruce I. Bertelsen, executive director. Fax, 331-1388.

Membership: manufacturers of motor vehicle and stationary source emission control equipment. Provides information on emission technology and industry capabilities.

State and Territorial Air Pollution Program Administrators, 444 N. Capitol St. N.W., #307 20001; 624-7864. S. William Becker, executive director. Fax, 624-7863.

Membership: state and territorial air quality officials responsible for implementing programs established under the Clean Air Act. Disseminates policy and technical information and analyzes air quality issues; monitors legislation and regulations; conducts seminars, workshops, and conferences.

See also Environment, General, Nongovernmental (p. 620)

See also American Council for an Energy-Efficient Economy (p. 211)

Hazardous Materials

See also Environment, Water Pollution (p. 632)

Agencies:

Agency for Toxic Substances and Disease Registry (Health and Human Services Dept.), 200 Independence Ave. S.W., #719B 20201; 690-7536. Andrea A. Wargo, associate administrator. Fax, 690-6985.

Works with federal, state, and local agencies to minimize or eliminate adverse effects of exposure to toxic substances at spill and waste disposal sites; maintains a registry of persons exposed to hazardous substances and of diseases and illnesses resulting from exposure to hazardous or toxic substances; maintains inventory of hazardous substances; maintains registry of sites closed or restricted because of contamination by hazardous material. (Headquarters in Atlanta.)

Agriculture Dept., National Agricultural Pesticide Impact Assessment Program, 14th St. and Independence Ave. S.W. 20250-0114; 720-4751. Nancy N. Ragsdale, director. Information, 720-4751. Fax, 720-1767.

Coordinates the pesticide assessment program under the Insecticide, Fungicide, and Rodenticide Act; maintains liaison with the Environmental Protection Agency on pesticide issues.

Defense Dept., Environmental Security, 400 Army-Navy Dr., Arlington, VA 20301; (703) 695-6639. Sherri Wasserman Goodman, deputy under secretary.

Integrates environmental, safety, and occupational health considerations into U.S. defense and economic policies. Works to ensure responsible performance in defense operations, to maintain quality installations, to reduce the costs of complying with environmental laws, and to clean up past contamination.

Environmental Protection Agency, Chemical Control, 401 M St. S.W. 20460; 260-3945. Charlie M. Aver, director. Fax, 260-8168.

Selects and implements control measures for new and existing chemicals that present a risk to human health and the environment. Oversees and manages regulatory evaluation and decision-making processes. Evaluates alternative remedial control measures under the Toxic Substances Control Act and makes recommendations concerning the existence of unreasonable risk from exposure to chemicals. Develops generic and chemical-specific rules for new chemicals.

Environmental Protection Agency, Chemical Emergency Preparedness and Prevention, 401 M St. S.W., South East 393 20460; 260-8600. Jim Makris, director. Fax, 260-7906. Toll-free hotline, (800) 535-0202; in Washington, D.C., area, (703) 486-3310.

Develops and administers chemical emergency preparedness and prevention programs; reviews effectiveness of programs; prepares community right-to-know regulations. Provides guidance materials, technical assistance, and training. Implements the preparedness and community right-to-know provisions of the Superfund Amendments and Reauthorization Act of 1986.

Environmental Protection Agency, Enforcement, 401 M St. S.W. 20460; 260-4134. Steve Herman, assistant administrator. Fax, 260-0500.

Enforces laws that protect public health and the environment from hazardous materials, pesticides, and toxic substances.

Environmental Protection Agency, Pesticide Programs, 1921 Jefferson Davis Highway, Arlington, VA (mailing address: 401 M St. S.W., Washington, DC 20460); (703) 305-7090. Douglas D. Campt, director. Toll-free, (800) 858-7378. Fax, (703) 305-6244.

Evaluates data to determine the risks and benefits of pesticides; sets standards for safe use of pesticides, including those for use on foods. Develops rules that govern labeling and literature accompanying pesticide products.

Environmental Protection Agency, Pollution Prevention and Toxics, 401 M St. S.W. 20460; 260-3810. Mark A. Greenwood, director. Fax, 260-1764.

Assesses the health and environmental hazards of existing chemical substances and mixtures; collects information on chemical use, exposure, and effects; maintains inventory of existing chemical substances; reviews new chemicals and regulates the manufacture, distribution, use, and disposal of harmful chemicals.

Environmental Protection Agency, Prevention, Pesticides, and Toxic Substances, 401 M St. S.W., MC 7101 20460; 260-2902. Lynn R. Goldman, assistant administrator. Fax, 260-1847. Toxic substances control, 554-1404.

Studies and makes recommendations for regulating chemical substances under the Toxic Substances Control Act; compiles list of chemical substances subject to the act; registers, controls, and regulates use of pesticides and toxic substances.

Environmental Protection Agency, Solid Waste and Emergency Response, 401 M St. S.W., #5101 20460; 260-4610. Elliott P. Laws, assistant administrator. Fax, 260-3527. Superfund/Resource conservation and recovery hotline, (800) 424-9346; from Washington, D.C., (703) 920-9810. TDD, (800) 553-7672; from Washington, D.C., (703) 486-3323.

Administers and enforces the Superfund Act; manages the handling, cleanup, and disposal of hazardous wastes.

Justice Dept., Environment and Natural Resources, Main Justice Bldg. (mailing address: P.O. Box 7611, Ben Franklin Station, Washington, DC 20044); 514-4291. John C. Cruden, chief, environmental enforcement. Fax, 514-8058.

Represents the United States in civil cases under environmental laws that involve the handling, storage, treatment, transportation, and disposal of hazardous waste. Recovers federal money spent to clean up hazardous waste sites or sues defendants to clean up sites under Superfund.

National Response Center (Transportation Dept.), 2100 2nd St. S.W. 20593; 267-2675. Cmdr. David W. Beach, chief. Fax, 479-7165. Toll-free hotline, (800) 424-8802.

Maintains 24-hour hotline for reporting pollution and oil or hazardous materials accidents. Notifies appropriate federal officials to reduce the effects of accidents.

National Transportation Safety Board, Hazardous Material and Pipeline Accident, 490 L'Enfant Plaza East S.W. 20594; 382-0670. Larry E. Jackson, acting chief. Fax, 382-6819.

Investigates natural gas and liquid pipeline accidents and other accidents involving the transportation of hazardous materials.

State Dept., Environmental Protection, Main State Bldg., Rm. 4325 20520; 647-9266. Day Mount, director. Fax, 647-5947.

Advances U.S. interests internationally on atmospheric and marine pollution, chemicals and toxic substances, and ocean wastes and their transportation. Interests include hazardous wastes and acid rain.

Transportation Dept., Hazardous Materials Safety, 400 7th St. S.W. 20590; 366-0656. Alan I. Roberts, associate administrator. Fax, 366-5713.

Issues safety regulations and exemptions for the transportation of hazardous materials.

Transportation Dept., Pipeline Safety, 400 7th St. S.W., #2335 20590; 366-4595. George Tenley, associate administrator. Fax, 366-4566.

Issues and enforces federal regulations for hazardous liquids pipeline safety.

Transportation Dept., Research and Special Programs Administration, 400 7th St. S.W. 20590; 366-4433. Dharmendra K. Sharma, administrator designate. Fax, 366-7431.

Coordinates department's research and development programs to improve safety of systems, including hazardous materials shipments and pipeline safety, and to ensure effectiveness, efficiency, and viability of transportation systems.

Congress:

House Agriculture Committee, Subcommittee on Department Operations and Nutrition, 1301A LHOB 20515; 225-1496. Charles W. Stenholm, D-Texas, chairman; Stan Ray, staff director.

Jurisdiction over legislation on pesticides.

House Energy and Commerce Committee, Subcommittee on Transportation and Hazardous Materials, 324 Ford Bldg. (2nd and D Sts. S.W.) 20515; 225-9304. Al Swift, D-Wash., chairman; Arthur Endres, staff director and chief counsel.

Jurisdiction over legislation on pollution; toxic substances, including the Toxic Substances Control Act; hazardous substances, including the Comprehensive Environmental Response, Compensation, and Liability Act (the Superfund); and other hazardous materials programs (jurisdiction shared with House Science, Space, and Technology and House Public Works and Transportation committees).

House Public Works and Transportation Committee, Subcommittee on Water Resources and Environment, B370A RHOB 20515; 225-0060. Douglas Applegate, D-Ohio, chairman; Kenneth J. Kopocis, counsel.

Shares jurisdiction over legislation on the Comprehensive Environmental Response, Compensation, and Liability Act (the Superfund) with House Energy and Commerce and House Science, Space, and Technology committees.

House Science, Space, and Technology Committee, Subcommittee on Technology, Environment, and Aviation, B374 RHOB 20515; 225-9662. Tim Valentine, D-N.C., chairman; James H. Turner, staff director.

Jurisdiction over legislation and environmental research and development on pollution; toxic substances, including the Toxic Substances Control Act; and the Comprehensive Environmental Response, Compensation, and Liability Act (the Superfund) (jurisdiction shared with House Energy and Commerce and House Public Works and Transportation committees).

Senate Environment and Public Works Committee, Subcommittee on Superfund, Recycling, and Solid Waste Management, SH-505 20510; 224-3597. Frank R. Lautenberg, D-N.J., chairman; Leonard Shen, counsel.

Jurisdiction over legislation for hazardous substances, including the Comprehensive Environmental Response, Compensation, and Liability Act (the Superfund).

Senate Environment and Public Works Committee, Subcommittee on Toxic Substances, Research, and Development, SH-505 20510; 224-3597. Harry Reid, D-Nev., chairman; Jerry Reynoldson, director.

Jurisdiction over legislation on pollution; environmental research and development; pesticides; and toxic substances, including the Toxic Substances Control Act. Oversight of the Comprehensive Environmental Response, Compensation, and Liability Act (the Superfund) and of hazardous materials programs.

Nongovernmental:

Chemical Specialties Manufacturers Assn., 1913 Eye St. N.W. 20006; 872-8110. Ralph Engel, president. Fax, 872-8114.

Membership: manufacturers, marketers, packagers, and suppliers in the chemical specialties industry. Specialties include cleaning compounds and detergents, insecticides, disinfectants, automotive and industrial products, polishes and floor finishes, and aerosol products. Monitors scientific developments; conducts surveys and research; provides chemical safety information and consumer education programs; sponsors National Poison Prevention Week and Aerosol Education Bureau; monitors legislation and regulations.

The Chlorine Institute, Inc., 2001 L St. N.W., #506 20036; 775-2790. Robert G. Smerko, president. Fax, 223-7225.

Safety, health, and environmental protection center of the chlor-alkali (chlorine, caustic soda, caustic potash, and hydrogen chloride) industry. Interests include employee health and safety, resource conservation and pollution abatement, control of chlorine emergencies, product specifications, and public and community relations. Sponsors and coordinates research; publishes technical pamphlets and drawings.

Citizens Clearinghouse for Hazardous Wastes, 119 Rowell Court, Falls Church, VA (mailing address: P.O. Box 6806, Falls Church, VA 22040); (703) 237-2249. Lois Gibbs, executive director.

Provides citizens' groups, individuals, and municipalities with support and information on solid and hazardous waste. Sponsors workshops, speakers bureau, leadership development conference, and convention on waste disposal technology. Operates a toxicity data bank on environmental and health effects of common chemical compounds; maintains a registry of technical experts to assist in solid and hazardous waste problems; gathers information on polluting corporations.

Clean Sites, 1199 N. Fairfax St., Alexandria, VA 22314; (703) 683-8522. Edwin H. Clark II, president. Information, (703) 739-1283. Fax, (703) 548-8773.

Works to accelerate hazardous waste cleanup. Helps involved parties and governments reach legal settlements, divide cleanup costs among responsible parties, and manage cleanup activities. Provides financial services in collecting and disbursing cleanup funds. Conducts research on waste cleanup.

Greenpeace, 1436 U St. N.W. 20009; 462-1177. Barbara Dudley, executive director. Fax, 462-4507.

Seeks to protect the environment through research, education, and grass-roots organizing. Works to prevent careless disposal and incineration of hazardous waste; encourages the development of methods to reduce production of hazardous waste. Monitors legislation and regulations.

Hazardous Materials Advisory Council, 1110 Vermont Ave. N.W., #250 20005; 728-1460. Jonathan Collom, president. Fax, 728-1459.

Membership: shippers, carriers, container manufacturers, and emergency response and spill cleanup companies. Promotes safety in the domestic and international transportation of hazardous materials. Provides information and educational services; sponsors conferences, workshops, and seminars. Advocates uniform hazardous materials regulations.

Hazardous Waste Treatment Council, 915 15th St. N.W., 5th Floor 20005; 783-0870. Richard Fortuna, executive director. Fax, 737-2038.

Membership: waste treatment and disposal companies. Interests include hazardous waste neutralization, recycling, and destruction processes and the use of permanent remedies in the cleanup of problem sites; works to restrict burning of hazardous waste and burying of untreated waste in landfills. Provides the public with information.

Household Products Recycling and Disposal Council, 1201 Connecticut Ave. N.W., #300D 20036; 659-5535. Betsy Garside, administrator. Fax, 835-8879.

Information service that makes referrals and disseminates information on the proper disposal of household chemical waste. (Affiliated with the Chemical Specialties Manufacturers Assn.)

National Agricultural Chemicals Assn., 1156 15th St. N.W., #400 20005; 296-1585. Jay J. Vroom, president. Fax, 463-0474.

Membership: pesticide manufacturers. Provides information on pesticide safety, development, and use. Monitors legislation and regulations.

National Coalition Against the Misuse of Pesticides, 701 E St. S.E., #200 20003; 543-5450. Jay Feldman, executive director.

Coalition of family farmers, farmworkers, consumers, home gardeners, physicians, lawyers, and others concerned about pesticide hazards and safety. Issues information to increase public awareness of environmental, public health, and economic problems caused by pesticide abuse; promotes alternatives to pesticide use, such as the integrated pest management program.

National Pest Control Assn., 8100 Oak St., Dunn Loring, VA 22027; (703) 573-8330. Harvey S. Gold, executive vice president. Fax, (703) 573-4116.

Membership: pest control operators. Monitors federal regulations that affect pesticide use; provides members with technical information.

Rachel Carson Council, 8940 Jones Mill Rd., Chevy Chase, MD 20815; (301) 652-1877. Diana Post, executive director.

Disseminates information on the toxicity of chemical contaminants and pesticides and their effects on human health and the environment. Library open to the public by appointment.

See also Environment, General, Nongovernmental (p. 620)

See also Chemical Manufacturers Assn. (p. 685); League of Women Voters Education Fund, Natural Resources (p. 622)

International Affairs

Agencies:

Environmental Protection Agency, International Activities, 401 M St. S.W. 20460; 260-4870. Alan Hecht, acting assistant administrator. Fax, 260-9653.

Coordinates the agency's work on international environmental issues and programs, including management of bilateral agreements and participation in multilateral organizations and negotiations.

International Joint Commission, United States and Canada, U.S. Section, 1250 23rd St. N.W., #100 20440; 736-9000. Joel Fisher, environmental adviser. Fax, 736-9015.

Deals with disputes between the United States and Canada on transboundary water and air resources. Investigates issues upon request of the governments of the United States and Canada. Reviews applications for water resource projects.

State Dept., Environmental Protection, Main State Bldg., Rm. 4325 20520; 647-9266. Day Mount, director. Fax, 647-5947.

Advances U.S. interests internationally on atmospheric and marine pollution, chemicals and toxic substances, and ocean wastes and their transportation. Interests include hazardous wastes and acid rain.

Congress:

House Foreign Affairs Committee, Subcommittee on Economic Policy, Trade, and the Environment, 702 O'Neill Bldg. (300 New Jersey Ave. S.E.) 20515; 226-7820. Sam Gejdenson, D-Conn., chairman; John Scheibel, staff director. Fax, 225-2029.

Jurisdiction over legislation on international environmental agreements and policy (jurisdiction shared with Subcommittee on International Security, International Organizations, and Human Rights).

Senate Foreign Relations Committee, Subcommittee on International Economic Policy, Trade, Oceans, and Environment, SD-446 20510; 224-4651. Paul S. Sarbanes, D-Md., chairman; Geryld B. Christianson, staff director. Fax, 224-5011.

Jurisdiction over legislation on international environmental agreements and policy, including international marine affairs in the Antarctic and Arctic areas.

Nongovernmental:

American Committee for International Conservation, c/o Center for Marine Conservation, 1725 DeSales St. N.W., #500 20036; 429-5609. Roger E. McManus, president. Fax, 872-0619.

Committee of national conservation organizations. Supports the International Union for Conservation of Nature and Natural Resources and monitors U.S. conservation activities overseas. Interested in development of a world conservation strategy and preservation of critical habitats.

Canada-United States Environmental Council, c/o Defenders of Wildlife, 1101 14th St. N.W. 20005; 682-9400. James G. Deane, co-chairman. Fax, 682-1334.

Membership: environmental and conservation groups. Interests include acid rain, Great Lakes pollution, and protection of arctic wildlife habitats. Promotes cooperation between the United States and Canada on environmental concerns.

Greenpeace, 1436 U St. N.W. 20009; 462-1177. Barbara Dudley, executive director. Fax, 462-4507.

Seeks to protect the environment through research, education, and grass-roots organizing. Interests include chemical and nuclear waste dumping, solid and hazardous waste disposal, and protection of marine mammals and endangered species. Supports the establishment of Antarctica as a world park, free of industry, military presence, and nuclear power and weaponry. Monitors legislation and regulations.

Volunteers in Overseas Cooperative Assistance, 50 F St. N.W., #1075 20001; 383-4961. Donald D. Cohen, president. Fax, 783-7204.

Recruits professionals for voluntary, short-term technical assistance to cooperatives, environmental groups, and agricultural enterprises, upon request, in developing countries and emerging democracies.

World Resources Institute, Center for International Development and Environment, 1709 New York Ave. N.W., #700 20006; 638-6300. Thomas H. Fox, director. Fax, 638-0036.

International organization that conducts research on environmental problems and studies the interrelationships of natural resources, economic growth, and human needs. Interests include forestry and land use, renewable energy, fisheries, and sustainable agriculture. Assesses environmental policies of aid agencies.

See also Environment, General, Nongovernmental (p. 620); Natural Resources, General, Nongovernmental (p. 637)

Recycling and Solid Waste Management

Agencies:

Environmental Protection Agency, Solid Waste and Emergency Response, 401 M St. S.W., #5101 20460; 260-4610. Elliott P. Laws, assistant administrator. Fax, 260-3527. Superfund/Resource conservation and recovery hotline, (800) 424-9346; from Washington, D.C., (703) 920-9810. TDD, (800) 553-7672; from Washington, D.C., (703) 486-3323.

Administers and enforces the Resource Conservation and Recovery Act.

Congress:

House Energy and Commerce Committee, Subcommittee on Transportation and Hazardous Materials, 324 Ford Bldg. (2nd and D Sts. S.W.) 20515; 225-9304. Al Swift, D-Wash., chairman; Arthur Endres, staff director and chief counsel.

Jurisdiction over legislation on solid waste disposal, including the Resource Conservation and Recovery Act. (Jurisdiction shared with House Science, Space, and Technology and House Public Works and Transportation committees.)

House Science, Space, and Technology Committee, Subcommittee on Technology, Environment, and Aviation, B374 RHOB 20515; 225-9662. Tim Valentine, D-N.C., chairman; James H. Turner, staff director.

Jurisdiction over legislation and research and development on solid waste disposal, including the Resource Conservation and Recovery Act. (Jurisdiction shared with House Energy and Commerce and House Public Works and Transportation committees.)

Senate Environment and Public Works Committee, Subcommittee on Superfund, Recycling, and Solid Waste Management, SH-505 20510; 224-3597. Frank R. Lautenberg, D-N.J., chairman; Leonard Shen, counsel.

Jurisdiction over research and development and legislation on solid waste disposal, including the Resource Conservation and Recovery Act.

Nongovernmental:

Aluminum Recycling Assn., 1000 16th St. N.W. 20036; 785-0951. Richard M. Cooperman, executive director. Fax, 785-0210.

Membership: producers of recycled aluminum specification ingot. Provides information and conducts research on aluminum recycling from aluminum-based scrap, excluding cans. Interests include aluminum recycling production technology.

American Plastics Council, 1275 K St. N.W., #400 20005; 371-5319. Donald B. Shea, group vice president. Fax, 371-5679.

Seeks to increase plastics recycling; conducts research on disposal of plastic products; sponsors research on waste-handling methods, incineration, and degradation; supports programs that test alternative waste management technologies. Monitors legislation and regulations.

(Affiliated with the Society of the Plastics Industry.)

Assn. of Foam Packaging Recyclers, 1025 Connecticut Ave. N.W., #515 20036; 822-6424. R. Jerry Johnson, executive director. Toll-free, (800) 944-8448. Fax, 331-0538.

Membership: companies that recycle foam packaging material. Coordinates national network of collection centers for postconsumer foam packaging products; helps to establish new collection centers. (Affiliated with the Polystyrene Packaging Council.)

Assn. of State and Territorial Solid Waste Management Officials, 444 N. Capitol St. N.W. 20001; 624-5828. Thomas Kennedy, executive director. Fax, 624-7875.

Membership: state and territorial solid waste management officials. Works with the Environmental Protection Agency to develop policy on solid and hazardous waste.

Council on Packaging in the Environment, 1001 Connecticut Ave. N.W., #401 20036; 331-0099. Edward J. Stana, president. Fax, 466-5447.

Coalition of consumer product companies, manufacturers, recyclers, retailers, and trade associations that provides information about packaging—its uses, societal benefits, and environmental effects—and addresses the effects and management of packaging in municipal solid waste systems.

Flexible Packaging Assn., 1090 Vermont Ave. N.W., #500 20005; 842-3880. Glenn E. Braswell, president. Fax, 842-3841.

Coordinates environmental programs on reducing solid waste for schools and the public.

Foodservice and Packaging Institute, 1901 N. Moore St., #1111, Arlington, VA 22209; (703) 527-7505. Joseph W. Bow, president. Fax, (703) 527-7512.

Membership: manufacturers, suppliers, and distributors of disposable products used in food service, packaging, and consumer products. Promotes the use of disposables for commercial and home use; sponsors research on recycling and composting technology; monitors environmental legislation.

Glass Packaging Institute, 1627 K St. N.W., #800 20006; 887-4850. Joseph Cattaneo, executive vice president. Fax, 785-5377.

Membership: manufacturers of glass containers and their suppliers. Promotes industry policies to protect the environment, conserve natural resources, and reduce energy consumption; conducts research; monitors legislation affecting the industry. Interests include glass recycling.

Institute for Local Self-Reliance, 2425 18th St. N.W. 20009; 232-4108. Neil Seldman, president. Fax, 332-0463.

Conducts research and provides technical assistance on environmentally sound economic development for government, small businesses, and community organizations. Advocates the development of a materials policy at local, state, and regional levels to reduce per capita consumption of raw materials and to shift from dependence on fossil fuels to reliance on renewable resources.

Institute of Scrap Recycling Industries, Inc., 1325 G St. N.W., #1000 20005; 466-4050. Herschel Cutler, executive director. Fax, 775-9109.

Represents processors, brokers, and consumers of scrap paper, glass, plastic, textiles, rubber, and ferrous and nonferrous metals.

National Assn. of Chemical Recyclers, 1200 G St. N.W., 8th Floor 20005; 434-8740. Brenda D. Pulley, executive director. Fax, 434-8741.

Membership: commercial chemical recyclers and others interested in the industry. Promotes the recovery and reuse of spent solvent as an alternative to waste disposal. Seeks to educate members on the safest and most efficient methods of recycling. Sponsors seminars and conferences. Monitors legislation and regulations.

National Oil Recyclers Assn., 1101 Pennsylvania Ave. N.W., #800 20004; 628-4900. Christopher Harris, general counsel. Fax, 628-4912.

Promotes oil recycling and appropriate use of used oil as industrial fuel; concerned with protecting public health and the environment. Provides information on oil recycling, including collection programs for do-it-yourself oil changers. Monitors legislation and regulations.

National Recycling Coalition, 1101 30th St. N.W., #305 20007; 625-6406. Marsha L. Rhea, executive director. Fax, 625-6409.

Membership: public officials; community recycling groups; local, state, and national agencies; environmentalists; waste haulers; solid waste disposal consultants; and private recycling companies. Encourages recycling to preserve resources. Offers programs such as the Recycling Advisory Council and the Buy Recycled Business Alliance.

National Solid Wastes Management Assn., 1730 Rhode Island Ave. N.W., #1000 20036; 659-4613. Eugene J. Wingerter, executive director. Fax, 775-5917.

Membership: organizations engaged in refuse collection, processing, and disposal, including resource recovery. Provides information on solid and hazardous waste management, resource recovery, and waste equipment; sponsors workshops.

Polystyrene Packaging Council, 1025 Connecticut Ave. N.W., #515 20036; 822-6424. R. Jerry Johnson, executive director. Fax, 331-0538.

Membership: manufacturers and suppliers of polystyrene foam products. Promotes effective use and recycling of polystyrene; studies and reports on solid waste disposal issues, including waste-to-energy incineration and use of landfills. Monitors legislation and regulations.

Shippers of Recycled Textiles, 7910 Woodmont Ave., #1212, Bethesda, MD 20814; (301) 656-1077. Bernard D. Brill, executive vice president. Fax, (301) 656-1079.

Membership: organizations and individuals involved in shipping and distributing recycled textiles and other textile products. Publishes statistics on the amount of waste material recycled. (Affiliated with the International Association of Wiping Cloth Manufacturers.)

Solid Waste Assn. of North America, 1100 Wayne Ave., #700, Silver Spring, MD (mailing address: P.O. Box 7219, Silver Spring, MD 20907); (301) 585-2898. H. Lanier Hickman Jr., executive director. Toll-free, (800) 456-4723. Fax, (301) 589-7068. Toll-free clearinghouse, (800) 677-9424.

Membership: government officials who manage municipal solid waste programs. Interests include waste reduction, collection, recycling, and disposal. Monitors legislation and regulations; conducts training and certification programs. Operates solid waste information clearinghouse partially funded by the EPA.

U.S. Conference of Mayors, Municipal Waste Management Assn., 1620 Fye St. N.W., 3rd

Floor 20006; 293-7330. David Gatton, managing director. Fax, 293-2352.

Organization of local governments and private companies involved in planning and developing solid waste management programs, including waste-to-energy and recycling. Assists communities with financing, environmental assessments, and associated policy implementation.

See also Automotive Recyclers Assn. (p. 726)

Water Pollution

Agencies:

Environmental Protection Agency, Ground and Drinking Water, 401 M St. S.W., #4601 20460; 260-5508. James R. Elder, director. Fax, 260-4383. Toll-free hotline, (800) 426-4791.

Develops standards for the quality of drinking water supply systems; regulates underground injection of waste and protection of groundwater wellhead areas under the Safe Drinking Water Act; provides information on public water supply systems.

Environmental Protection Agency, Municipal Support, 401 M St. S.W., #4204 20460; 260-5859. Michael J. Quigley, director. Fax, 260-1827.

Directs programs to assist in the design and construction of municipal sewage systems; develops programs to ensure efficient operation and maintenance of municipal wastewater treatment facilities; implements programs for prevention of water pollution.

Environmental Protection Agency, Science and Technology, 401 M St. S.W., #4301 20460; 260-5400. Tudor T. Davies, director. Fax, 260-5394.

Develops and coordinates water pollution control programs for the Environmental Protection Agency; monitors water quality nationwide and maintains a data collection system; assists state and regional agencies in establishing water quality standards and planning local water resources management; develops guidelines for industrial wastewater discharge.

Environmental Protection Agency, Waste Water, Enforcement, and Compliance, 401 M St. S.W., #4201 20460; 260-5850. Michael B. Cook, director. Fax, 260-1040.

Oversees the issuance of and compliance with water permits. Responsible for the Pretreatment Program regulating industrial discharges to local sewage treatment.

National Drinking Water Advisory Council, 401 M St. S.W., #4601 20460; 260-2285. Charlene Shaw, contact. Fax, 260-4383.

Advises the EPA administrator on activities, functions, and policies relating to implementation of the Safe Drinking Water Act.

National Oceanic and Atmospheric Administration (Commerce Dept.), Ocean Resources, Conservation, and Assessment, 1305 East-West Highway, N/ORCA #10409 SSMC4, Silver Spring, MD 20910; (301) 713-2989. Charles N. Ehler, director. Fax, (301) 713-4389.

Provides information on damage to marine ecosystems caused by pollution. Provides information on spill trajectory projections and chemical hazard analyses. Researches trends of toxic contamination on U.S. coastal regions.

U.S. Coast Guard (Transportation Dept.), Marine Environmental Protection, 2100 2nd St. S.W. 20593; 267-0518. Capt. M. J. Donoghue, chief. Fax, 267-4085.

Oversees cleanup operations after spills of oil and other hazardous substances in U.S. waters, on the outer continental shelf, and in international waters. Reviews coastal zone management and enforces international standards for pollution prevention and response.

U.S. Coast Guard (Transportation Dept.), National Pollution Funds, 4200 Wilson Blvd., #1000, Arlington, VA 22203; (703) 235-4700. Daniel F. Sheehan, director. Fax, (703) 235-4840.

Certifies the financial responsibility of vessels and companies involved in oil exploration and transportation in U.S. waters and on the outer continental shelf; manages the Oil Spill Liability Trust Fund under the Oil Pollution Act of 1990.

Congress:

House Energy and Commerce Committee, Subcommittee on Health and the Environment, 2415 RHOB 20515; 225-4952. Henry A. Waxman, D-Calif., chairman; Karen Nelson, staff director.

Jurisdiction over legislation on drinking water purity, including the Safe Drinking Water Act.

House Merchant Marine and Fisheries Committee, Subcommittee on Coast Guard and Navigation, 541 Ford Bldg. (2nd and D Sts. S.W.) 20515; 226-3587. W. J. "Billy" Tauzin, D-La., chairman; Elizabeth Megginson, staff director.

Jurisdiction over legislation on oil spills and financial responsibility requirements and on marine pollution control and abatement.

House Merchant Marine and Fisheries Committee, Subcommittee on Environment and Natural Resources, 545 Ford Bldg. (2nd and D Sts. S.W.) 20515; 226-3547. Gerry E. Studds, D-Mass., chairman; Daniel M. Ashe, staff director.

Jurisdiction over legislation concerning coastal marine pollution and elements of the Clean Water Act and the National Environmental Policy Act.

House Merchant Marine and Fisheries Committee, Subcommittee on Oceanography, Gulf of Mexico, and the Outer Continental Shelf, 575 Ford Bldg. (2nd and D Sts. S.W.) 20515; 226-2460. Solomon P. Ortiz, D-Texas, chairman; Sheila McCready, staff director.

Jurisdiction over legislation on ocean dumping, including the Ocean Dumping Act (jurisdiction shared with House Public Works and Transportation Committee).

House Public Works and Transportation Committee, Subcommittee on Water Resources and Environment, B370A RHOB 20515; 225-0060. Douglas Applegate, D-Ohio, chairman; Kenneth J. Kopocis, counsel.

Jurisdiction over most legislation on oil spills and financial responsibility requirements and on water pollution, including the Clean Water Act.

House Science, Space, and Technology Committee, Subcommittee on Space, 2320 RHOB 20515; 225-7858. Ralph M. Hall, D-Texas, chairman; William S. Smith, staff director.

Jurisdiction over legislation on ocean dumping and ocean pollution research and development. (Jurisdiction shared with the House Merchant Marine and Fisheries Committee.)

Senate Environment and Public Works Committee, Subcommittee on Clean Water, Fisheries, and Wildlife, SH-505 20510; 224-3597. Bob Graham, D-Fla., chairman; Bill Leary, counsel.

Jurisdiction over legislation on ocean dumping, ocean pollution research and development, drinking water purity, water pollution, oil spills and financial responsibility requirements, and marine pollution control and abatement; jurisdiction over the Clean Water Act, National Environmental Policy Act, Safe Drinking Water Act, and Ocean Dumping Act.

See also Chesapeake Bay Congressional Caucus (p. 755)

Nongovernmental:

Clean Water Action, 1320 18th St. N.W., 3rd Floor 20036; 457-1286. David R. Zwick, president. Fax, 457-0287.

Citizens' organization interested in clean, safe, and affordable water. Works to influence public policy through education, technical assistance, monitoring of legislation and regulations, and grass-roots organizing. Interests include toxins and pollution, drinking water, water conservation, sewage treatment, pesticides, mass burn incineration, bay and estuary protection, and consumer water issues.

League of Women Voters Education Fund, Natural Resources, 1730 M St. N.W. 20036; 429-1965. Elizabeth Kraft, director. Fax, 429-0854.

Education foundation affiliated with the League of Women Voters. Conducts a national project concerning community drinking water systems and groundwater. Sponsors research and develops educational materials on water issues; helps local leagues manage demonstration programs.

Water Environment Federation, 601 Wythe St., Alexandria, VA 22314; (703) 684-2400. Quincalee Brown, executive director. Fax, (703) 684-2492.

Membership: civil and environmental engineers, wastewater treatment plant operators, scientists, and others concerned with water quality. Works to preserve and improve water quality worldwide. Provides the public with technical information and educational materials.

See also Environment, General, Nongovernmental (p. 620)

Natural Resources

General

See also Energy chapter (p. 201); Environment, General (p. 616)

Agencies:

Agriculture Dept., Natural Resources and Environment, 14th St. and Independence Ave. S.W. 20250; 720-7173. James Lyons, assistant secretary. Fax, 720-4732.

Responsible for the department's resource management programs. Administers, through the Forest Service, national forests and grasslands and their resources, including timber, water, forage, fish, and wildlife. Manages a national soil and water conservation program and a soil classification survey through the Soil Conservation Service. Compiles data on soil, water, and related natural resources and monitors resource use trends for conservation and development purposes.

Bureau of Land Management (Interior Dept.), Land and Renewable Resources, Main Interior Bldg. 20240; 208-4896. Michael J. Penfold, assistant director. Fax, 208-5010.

Develops and implements natural resource programs for renewable resources use and protection, including management of forested land, rangeland, wild horses and burros, wildlife habitats, endangered species, soil and water quality, rights of way, recreation, and cultural programs.

Interior Dept., Main Interior Bldg., 1849 C St. N.W. 20240; 208-7351. Bruce Babbitt, secretary. Information, 208-3171. Library, 208-5821. Fax, 208-5048.

Principal U.S. conservation agency. Manages most federal land; responsible for conservation and development of mineral and water resources; responsible for conservation, development, and use of fish and wildlife resources; operates recreation programs for federal parks, refuges, and public lands; preserves and administers the nation's scenic and historic areas; reclaims arid lands in the West through irrigation; administers native American lands and relationships with tribal governments.

Interior Dept., Program Analysis, Main Interior Bldg. 20240; 208-5978. Brooks Yeager, director. Fax, 208-4867.

Analyzes how policies affect the department; makes recommendations and develops policy options for resolving natural resource problems.

Justice Dept., Environment and Natural Resources, Main Justice Bldg. 20530; 514-2701. Lois J. Schiffer, assistant attorney general designate. Fax, 514-0557.

Handles civil suits involving the federal government in all areas of natural resources; handles some criminal suits involving pollution control.

National Oceanic and Atmospheric Administration (Commerce Dept.), 14th St. and Constitution Ave. N.W. 20230; 482-3436. D. James Baker, administrator. Information, 482-2000. Fax, 408-9674.

Conducts research in marine and atmospheric sciences; issues weather forecasts and warnings vital to public safety and the national economy; surveys resources of the sea; analyzes economic aspects of fisheries operations; develops and implements policies on international fisheries; provides states with grants to conserve coastal zone areas; protects marine mammals; maintains a national environmental center with data from satellite observations and other sources including meteorological, oceanic, geodetic, and seismological data centers; provides colleges and universities with grants for research, education, and marine advisory services; prepares and provides nautical and aeronautical charts and maps.

National Science and Technology Council (Executive Office of the President), 744 Jackson Pl. N.W. 20506; 395-5101. John H. Gibbons, chairman. Fax, 395-5076.

Coordinates research and development activities and programs that involve more than one federal agency. Activities concern earth sciences, materials, and forestry research.

Office of Science and Technology Policy (Executive Office of the President), Old Executive Office Bldg., Rm. 424 20500; 456-7116. John H. Gibbons, director. Information, 395-7347. Press, 395-6142. Fax, 395-3261.

Provides the president with policy analysis and assistance on issues related to natural resources.

State Dept., Ecology, Health, and Conservation, Main State Bldg. 20520; 647-2418. Robert Pringle, director, ecology, health, and conservation. Fax, 647-5947.

Represents the United States in international affairs relating to natural resources. Interests include wildlife, tropical forests, and biological diversity.

State Dept., Oceans and International Environmental and Scientific Affairs, Main State Bldg., Rm. 7831 20520-7818; 647-1554. Elinor G. Constable, assistant secretary. Fax, 647-0217.

Concerned with foreign policy as it affects natural resources and the environment, human health, the global climate, energy production, and oceans and fisheries.

Tennessee Valley Authority, 1 Massachusetts Ave. N.W., #300 20001; 479-4412. Jan Evered, administrative officer, Washington office. Fax, 479-4421.

Coordinates resource conservation, development, and land-use programs in the Tennessee River Valley. Activities include forestry and wildlife development. (Headquarters in Knoxville, Tenn.)

Congress:

General Accounting Office, Natural Resources Management, 441 G St. N.W. 20548; 512-7756. James Duffus III, director. Fax, 512-8774.

Independent, nonpartisan agency in the legislative branch that audits, analyzes, and reports on efficiency and effectiveness of Interior Dept. programs concerned with managing natural resources.

House Appropriations Committee, Subcommittee on Commerce, Justice, State, and Judiciary, H309 CAP 20515; 225-3351. Neal Smith, D-Iowa, chairman; John Osthaus, staff assistant.

Jurisdiction over legislation to appropriate funds for the Marine Mammal Commission and the Commerce Dept., including the National Oceanic and Atmospheric Administration.

House Appropriations Committee, Subcommittee on Energy and Water Development, 2362 RHOB 20515; 225-3421. Tom Bevill, D-Ala., chairman; Hunter Spillan, staff assistant.

Jurisdiction over legislation to appropriate funds for the Bureau of Reclamation in the Interior Dept., the federal power marketing administrations in the Energy Dept., the civil programs of the Army Corps of Engineers, the Tennessee Valley Authority, and related agencies.

House Appropriations Committee, Subcommittee on Interior, 3481 RHOB 20515; 225-3481. Sidney R. Yates, D-Ill., chairman; D. Neal Sigmon, staff assistant.

Jurisdiction over legislation to appropriate funds for the Interior Dept. (except the Bureau of Reclamation), the Forest Service in the Agriculture Dept., and the Bureau of Mines; for

Interior Dept.

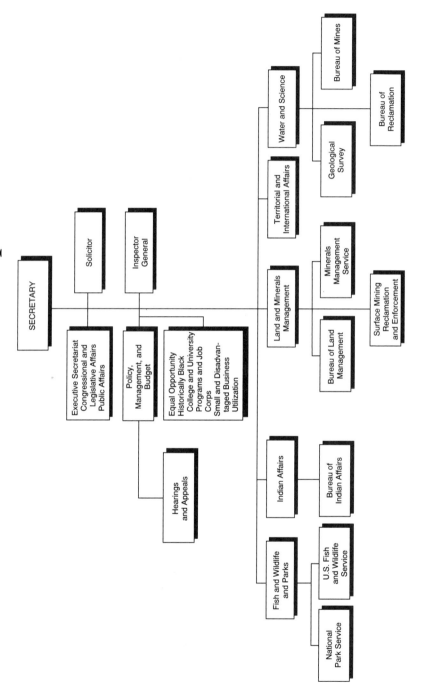

clean coal technology, fossil energy, and naval petroleum and oil shale reserves, and for other natural resources-related services and programs.

House Government Operations Committee, Subcommittee on Environment, Energy, and Natural Resources, B371C RHOB 20515; 225-6427. Mike Synar, D-Okla., chairman; Sandy Harris, staff director. Fax, 225-2392.

Oversight of the Interior Dept. and of the Agriculture Dept.'s Forest Service.

House Merchant Marine and Fisheries Committee, Subcommittee on Environment and Natural Resources, 545 Ford Bldg. (2nd and D Sts. S.W.) 20515; 226-3547. Gerry E. Studds, D-Mass., chairman; Daniel M. Ashe, staff director.

Jurisdiction over legislation on many natural resource issues, including conservation.

House Natural Resources Committee, 1324 LHOB 20515; 225-2761. George Miller, D-Calif., chairman; John Lawrence, staff director. Fax, 225-1931.

Jurisdiction over legislation on natural resource issues, including water control.

House Science, Space, and Technology Committee, Subcommittee on Technology, Environment, and Aviation, B374 RHOB 20515; 225-9662. Tim Valentine, D-N.C., chairman; James H. Turner, staff director.

Jurisdiction over research and development legislation related to natural resources.

Senate Agriculture, Nutrition, and Forestry Committee, Subcommittee on Agricultural Research, Conservation, Forestry, and General Legislation, SR-328A 20510; 224-2035. Tom Daschle, D-S.D., chairman; Tom Buis, legislative assistant.

Jurisdiction over legislation on many natural resources issues, including conservation, forestry, and water control; oversight of the Interior Dept. and of the Agriculture Dept.'s Forest Service.

Senate Appropriations Committee, Subcommittee on Commerce, Justice, State, and Judiciary, S146A CAP 20510; 224-7277. Ernest F. Hollings, D-S.C., chairman; Scott B. Gudes, clerk.

Jurisdiction over legislation to appropriate funds for the Marine Mammal Commission and the Commerce Dept., including the National Oceanic and Atmospheric Administration.

Senate Appropriations Committee, Subcommittee on Energy and Water Development, SD-132 20510; 224-7260. J. Bennett Johnston, D-La., chairman; W. Proctor Jones, clerk.

Jurisdiction over legislation to appropriate funds for the Bureau of Reclamation in the Interior Dept., the federal power marketing administrations in the Energy Dept., the civil programs of the Army Corps of Engineers, the Tennessee Valley Authority, and related agencies.

Senate Appropriations Committee, Subcommittee on Interior, SD-127 20510; 224-7233. Robert C. Byrd, D-W.Va., chairman; Sue E. Masica, clerk.

Jurisdiction over legislation to appropriate funds for the Interior Dept, the Forest Service in the Agriculture Dept., and the Bureau of Mines; for clean coal technology, fossil energy, and naval petroleum and oil shale reserves; and for other natural resources-related services and programs.

Senate Energy and Natural Resources Committee, SD-304 20510; 224-4971. J. Bennett Johnston, D-La., chairman; Benjamin Cooper, staff director. Fax, 224-6163.

Jurisdiction over legislation on many aspects of natural resources, including research and development.

See also Tennessee Valley Authority Caucus (p. 760)

Nongovernmental:

American Committee for International Conservation, c/o Center for Marine Conservation, 1725 DeSales St. N.W., #500 20036; 429-5609. Roger E. McManus, president. Fax, 872-0619.

Committee of national conservation organizations. Supports the International Union for Conservation of Nature and Natural Resources and monitors U.S. conservation activities overseas. Interested in developing a world conservation strategy and preserving critical habitats.

Conservation International, 1015 18th St. N.W., #1000 20036; 429-5660. Russell Mittermeier, president. Fax, 887-5188.

Works to conserve tropical rain forests through economic development; promotes exchange of debt relief for conservation programs that involve local people and organizations. Provides private groups and governments with information and technical advice on conservation efforts; supports conservation data gathering in Latin America and the Caribbean.

Friends of the Earth, 218 D St. S.E., 2nd Floor 20003; 544-2600. Jane Perkins, president. Fax, 543-4710.

Citizens' interest group that promotes preservation of natural resources, particularly water resources, energy, and coastal and marine environments. Library open to the public by appointment.

Izaak Walton League of America, 1401 Wilson Blvd., Level B, Arlington, VA 22209; (703) 528-1818. Maitland Sharpe, executive director. Fax, (703) 528-1836.

Grass-roots organization that promotes conservation of natural resources and the environment.

National Assn. of Conservation Districts, 509 Capitol Court N.E. 20002; 547-6223. Ernest C. Shea, executive vice president. Fax, 547-6450.

Membership: conservation districts (local subdivisions of state governments). Develops national policies on the conservation and development of water, land, forests, and other natural resources. Interests include erosion and sediment control, control of pollution from diffuse sources, and rural development.

National Audubon Society, 666 Pennsylvania Ave. S.E., #200 20003; 547-9009. Elizabeth Raisbeck, senior vice president for regional and government affairs. Fax, 547-9022.

Citizens' interest group that promotes environmental preservation. Provides information on water resources, public lands, rangelands, forests, parks, wildlife and marine conservation, and the national wildlife refuge system. (Headquarters in New York.)

National Wildlife Federation, 1400 16th St. N.W. 20036; 797-6800. Jay D. Hair, president. Fax, 797-6646.

Promotes conservation of natural resources; provides information on wildlife, fish, water, the outer continental shelf, oceans, land, rangelands, forests, air, solid waste management, parks and recreation, and toxic materials; takes legal action on environmental issues. Laurel Ridge Conservation Education Center in Vienna, Va., conducts outdoor programs.

Natural Resources Defense Council, 1350 New York Ave. N.W. 20005; 783-7800. Thomas Cochran, office manager. Fax, 783-5917.

Environmental organization staffed by lawyers and scientists who undertake litigation and research. Interests include air, water, land use, forests, toxic materials, natural resources management and conservation, preservation of endangered plant species, and ozone pollution. (Headquarters in New York.)

The Nature Conservancy, 1815 N. Lynn St., Arlington, VA 22209; (703) 841-5300. John C. Sawhill, president. Fax, (703) 841-1283.

Acquires land to protect endangered species; provides information and maintains international system of natural sanctuaries; operates the Heritage Program, a cooperative effort with state governments to identify and inventory threatened and endangered plants and animals.

Renewable Natural Resources Foundation, 5430 Grosvenor Lane, Bethesda, MD 20814; (301) 493-9101. Robert D. Day, executive director. Fax, (301) 493-6148.

Consortium of professional, scientific, and education organizations working to advance scientific and public education in renewable natural resources. Encourages the application of sound scientific practices to resource management and conservation. Fosters interdisciplinary cooperation among its member organizations.

Resources for the Future, 1616 P St. N.W. 20036; 328-5000. Robert Fri, president. Library, 328-5089. Fax, 939-3460.

Engages in research and education on natural resource issues, including forestry, multiple use of public lands, costs and benefits of pollution control, energy and national security, environmental risk management, and climate resources. Library open to the public by appointment.

Sierra Club, 408 C St. N.E. 20002; 547-1141. Debbie Sease, legislative director. Fax, 547-6009. Legislative hotline, 675-2394.

Citizens' interest group that promotes protection of natural resources. Interests include the Arctic National Wildlife Refuge and protection of national forests, parks, and wilderness. Monitors legislation and regulations. (Headquarters in San Francisco.)

U.S. Chamber of Commerce, Food, Agriculture, Energy, and Natural Resources Policy,

1615 H St. N.W. 20062; 463-5500. Stew Hardy, manager. Fax, 887-3445.

Develops policy on all issues affecting the production, use, and conservation of natural resources. Interests include management, development, use, and protection of natural resources such as fuel and nonfuel minerals, timber, water, public lands, on- and offshore energy, wetlands, and endangered species.

The Wilderness Society, 900 17th St. N.W. 20006; 833-2300. John Roush, president. Fax, 429-3958.

Promotes preservation of wilderness and the responsible management of all federal lands, including national parks and forests, wilderness areas, wildlife refuges, and land administered by the Interior Dept.'s Bureau of Land Management.

Wildlife Management Institute, 1101 14th St. N.W., #801 20005; 371-1808. Rollin D. Sparrowe, president. Fax, 408-5059.

Research and consulting organization that provides technical services and information about natural resources. Interests include forests, rangelands, and land, water, and wildlife resources.

World Resources Institute, 1709 New York Ave. N.W. 20006; 638-6300. Jonathan Lash, president. Press, 662-3484. Library, 662-2504. Fax, 638-0036.

Conducts and supports research on global resource policy. Holds briefings, seminars, and conferences. Library open to the public by appointment.

World Wildlife Fund, 1250 24th St. N.W. 20037; 293-4800. Kathryn S. Fuller, president. Fax, 293-9345.

Supports and conducts scientific research and conservation projects to promote biological diversity and to save endangered species and their habitats, including tropical forests in Latin America, Asia, and Africa. Awards grants and provides local conservation groups with technical assistance that supports habitat protection. Analyzes environmental policy on wetlands conservation, pollution, and use of public lands.

See also The Rand Corporation (p. 691)

Fish Resources

See also International Law and Agreements, Fishing/Law of the Sea (p. 476)

Agencies:

Atlantic States Marine Fisheries Commission, 1776 Massachusetts Ave. N.W., #600 20036; 452-8700. John H. Dunnigan, executive director. Fax, 452-9110.

Interstate compact commission of marine fisheries representatives from 15 states along the Atlantic seaboard. Assists states in developing joint fisheries programs; works with other fisheries organizations and the federal government on environmental, natural resource, and conservation issues.

Interior Dept., Fish, Wildlife, and Parks, Main Interior Bldg. 20240; 208-4416. George T. Frampton Jr., assistant secretary. Fax, 208-4684.

Responsible for programs associated with the development, conservation, and use of fish, wildlife, recreational, historical, and national park system resources. Coordinates marine environmental quality and biological resources programs with other federal agencies.

Justice Dept., Environment and Natural Resources, 601 Pennsylvania Ave. N.W. (mailing address: P.O. Box 7369, Ben Franklin Station, Washington, DC 20044-7369); 272-4421. James C. Kilbourne, chief, wildlife and marine resources. Fax, 724-6941.

Supervises suits involving the protection of marine mammals and birds and regulation of fisheries subject to U.S. jurisdiction, including areas within the outer continental shelf.

National Oceanic and Atmospheric Administration (Commerce Dept.), National Marine Fisheries Service, 1335 East-West Highway, Silver Spring, MD 20910; (301) 713-2239. Rolland A. Schmitten, assistant administrator. Information, (301) 713-2370. Fax, (301) 713-2258.

Administers marine fishing regulations, including offshore fishing rights and international agreements; conducts marine resources research; studies use and management of these resources; administers the Magnuson Fishery Conservation and Management Act; manages and protects marine resources, especially endangered species, within exclusive economic zones.

U.S. Fish and Wildlife Service (Interior Dept.), Main Interior Bldg. 20240; 208-4717. Mollie H. Beattie, director. Information, 208-5634. Fax, 208-6965.

Meets federal mandates concerning inland sport fisheries and fishery research activities and improves fish resources through responsible management of fish habitats; provides conservation education and information programs on fish.

U.S. Fish and Wildlife Service (Interior Dept.), Fish and Wildlife Ecological Services, Main Interior Bldg., Rm. 3024 20240; 208-4646. Michael J. Spear, assistant director. Fax, 208-6916.

Monitors federal policy on fish and wildlife. Reviews all federal and federally licensed projects to determine environmental effect on fish and wildlife; administers grant-in-aid money to states for fish and wildlife programs; responsible for maintaining the endangered species list and for protecting and restoring species to healthy numbers.

U.S. Fish and Wildlife Service (Interior Dept.), Fisheries, Main Interior Bldg., Rm. 3245 20240; 208-6394. Gary B. Edwards, assistant director. Fax, 208-4674.

Develops, manages, and protects interstate and international fisheries, including fisheries of the Great Lakes, fisheries on federal lands, endangered species of fish, and anadromous species. Administers the National Fish Hatchery System.

U.S. Fish and Wildlife Service (Interior Dept.), National Biological Survey, Main Interior Bldg. 20240; 208-3733. F. Eugene Hester, deputy director.

Performs research in support of biological resource management. Monitors the status of and trends in the nation's biotic resources. Conducts research on fish diseases, nutrition, and culture techniques; studies ecology of the Great Lakes and the effects of pesticides and herbicides on fish.

Congress:

House Merchant Marine and Fisheries Committee, Subcommittee on Fisheries Management, 534 Ford Bldg. (2nd and D Sts. S.W.) 20515; 226-3514. Thomas J. Manton, D-N.Y., chairman; Jim Mathews, staff director.

Jurisdiction over legislation on fish and fish hatcheries, the Magnuson Fishery Conservation and Management Act, fisheries research, aquaculture, and seafood safety.

Senate Commerce, Science, and Transportation Committee, Subcommittee on National Ocean Policy Study, SH-425 (mailing address: SD-508, Washington, DC 20510); 224-4912. Ernest F. Hollings, D-S.C., chairman; Penny Dalton, staff member.

Studies all aspects of fish and fish hatcheries, including the Magnuson Fishery Conservation and Management Act, fisheries research, aquaculture, and seafood safety. (Subcommittee does not report legislation.)

Nongovernmental:

American Fisheries Society, 5410 Grosvenor Lane, #110, Bethesda, MD 20814; (301) 897-8616. Paul Brouha, executive director. Fax, (301) 897-8096.

Membership: biologists and other scientists interested in fisheries. Promotes the fisheries profession, the advancement of fisheries science, and conservation of renewable aquatic resources. Monitors legislation and regulations.

International Assn. of Fish and Wildlife Agencies, 444 N. Capitol St. N.W., #544 20001; 624-7890. R. Max Peterson, executive vice president. Fax, 624-7891.

Membership: federal, state, and provincial fish and wildlife management agencies in the United States, Canada, and Mexico. Encourages balanced fish and wildlife resource management.

National Fisheries Education and Research Foundation, 1525 Wilson Blvd., #500, Arlington, VA 22209; (703) 524-9216. Adrienne Paradis, executive director. Fax, (703) 524-4619.

Research and educational organization that conducts technical research and sponsors consumer education projects on fish and seafood products.

National Fisheries Institute, 1525 Wilson Blvd., #500, Arlington, VA 22209; (703) 524-8880. Lee J. Weddig, executive vice president. Fax, (703) 524-4619.

Membership: vessel owners and distributors, processors, wholesalers, importers, traders, and brokers of fish and shellfish. Monitors legislation and regulations on fisheries.

National Food Processors Assn., 1401 New York Ave. N.W., #400 20005; 639-5939. John R. Cady, president. Fax, 637-8068.

Membership: food processing companies and suppliers. Serves as industry liaison between seafood processors and the federal government.

Sport Fishing Institute, 1010 Massachusetts Ave. N.W., #320 20001; 898-0770. Gilbert C. Radonski, president. Fax, 371-2085.
Membership: outdoor recreation industries, associations, and manufacturers of sport fishing equipment.

Trout Unlimited, 1500 Wilson Blvd., Arlington, VA 22209; (703) 522-0200. Charles Gauvin, president. Fax, (703) 284-9400.
Membership: individuals interested in the protection and enhancement of cold-water fish and their habitat. Sponsors research projects with federal and state fisheries agencies; maintains programs for water quality surveillance and cleanup of streams and lakes.

U.S. Tuna Foundation, 1101 17th St. N.W., #609 20036; 857-0610. David G. Burney, executive director. Fax, 331-9686.
Membership: tuna processors, vessel owners, and fishermen's unions. Interests include fishing legislation and government relations.

See also Natural Resources, General, Nongovernmental (p. 637)

Forest and Rangeland Resources

Agencies:

Forest Service (Agriculture Dept.), 14th St. and Independence Ave. S.W. (mailing address: P.O. Box 96090, Washington, DC 20090); 205-1661. Jack Ward Thomas, chief. Information, 205-1760. Fax, 205-1765.
Manages national forests and grasslands for outdoor recreation and sustained yield of renewable natural resources, including timber, water, forage, fish, and wildlife. Cooperates with state and private foresters; conducts forestry research.

Forest Service (Agriculture Dept.), National Forest System, 14th St. and Independence Ave. S.W. (mailing address: P.O. Box 96090, Washington, DC 20090); 205-1523. Jim Overbay, deputy. Fax, 205-1858.
Manages 191 million acres of forests and rangelands. Products and services from these lands include timber, water, forage, wildlife, minerals, and recreation.

Forest Service (Agriculture Dept.), Research, 14th St. and Independence Ave. S.W. (mailing address: P.O. Box 96090, Washington, DC 20090); 205-1665. Jerry A. Sesco, deputy chief. Fax, 205-1530.
Conducts biological, physical, and economic research related to forestry, including studies on harvesting methods, acid deposition, international forestry, the effects of global climate changes on forests, and forest products. Provides information on the establishment, improvement, and growth of trees, grasses, and other forest vegetation. Works to protect forest resources from fire, insects, diseases, and animal pests. Examines the effect of forest use activities on water quality, soil erosion, and sediment production. Conducts continuous forest survey and analyzes outlook for future supply and demand.

Forest Service (Agriculture Dept.), State and Private Forestry, 14th St. and Independence Ave. S.W. (mailing address: P.O. Box 96090, Washington, DC 20090); 205-1657. Joan Comanor, acting deputy chief. Fax, 205-1174.
Assists state and private forest owners with the protection and management of 574 million acres of forest and associated watershed lands. Assistance includes fire control, protecting forests from insects and diseases, land-use planning, developing multiple-use management, and improving practices in harvesting, processing, and marketing of forest products.

Forest Service (Agriculture Dept.), Youth Conservation Corps, 1621 N. Kent St., Arlington, VA (mailing address: P.O. Box 96090, Washington, DC 20090); (703) 235-8861. Ransom Hughes, program manager. Fax, (703) 235-1597.
Administers, with the National Park Service and the Fish and Wildlife Service, the Youth Conservation Corps, a summer employment and training, public works program for youths ages 15 to 18. The program is conducted in national parks, in national forests, and on national wildlife refuges.

Congress:

House Agriculture Committee, Subcommittee on Specialty Crops and Natural Resources, 105 CHOB 20515; 225-8906. Charlie Rose, D-N.C., chairman; Keith Pitts, staff director.
Jurisdiction over legislation on forestry in general and forest reserves acquired from state, local, or private sources.

House Natural Resources Committee, Subcommittee on National Parks, Forests, and Public Lands, 812 O'Neill Bldg. (300 New Jersey Ave. S.E.) 20515; 226-7736. Bruce F. Vento, D-Minn., chairman; Richard Healy, staff director.

Jurisdiction over legislation on forest reserves and public lands (except in Alaska), the national park system, the national forest system, the national wilderness preservation system, the wild and scenic rivers system, national recreation areas, the national trails system, the establishment of wildlife refuges on public lands, and the Bureau of Land Management.

House Natural Resources Committee, Subcommittee on Oversight and Investigations, 1328 LHOB 20515; 225-2761. George Miller, D-Calif., chairman; John Lawrence, staff director. Fax, 225-3554.

Jurisdiction over legislation on forest reserves and public lands in Alaska.

Senate Agriculture, Nutrition, and Forestry Committee, Subcommittee on Agricultural Research, Conservation, Forestry, and General Legislation, SR-328A 20510; 224-2035. Tom Daschle, D-S.D., chairman; Tom Buis, legislative assistant.

Jurisdiction over legislation on forestry in general and forest reserves acquired from state, local, or private sources.

Senate Energy and Natural Resources Committee, Subcommittee on Public Lands, National Parks, and Forests, SD-308 20510; 224-8115. Dale Bumpers, D-Ark., chairman; David Brooks, counsel.

Jurisdiction over legislation on forest reserves, public lands, the national park system, the national forest system, the national wilderness preservation system, the wild and scenic rivers system, national recreation areas, the national trails system, the establishment of wildlife refuges on public lands, and the Bureau of Land Management.

See also Forestry 2000 Task Force (p. 759)

Nongovernmental:

American Forest & Paper Assn., 1111 19th St. N.W. 20036; 463-2700. Jo Cooper, vice president, environment and regulatory affairs. Fax, 463-2785.

Membership: manufacturers of wood and specialty products and related associations. Interests include tax, housing, environmental, international trade, natural resources, and land-use issues that affect the wood products industry.

American Forest Council, 1111 19th St. N.W., #800 20036; 463-2455. Laurence Wiseman, president. Fax, 463-2785.

Membership: wood and paper companies. Provides information on forest resources and industrial policies concerning forest management and land use; commissions public opinion research on resource and environmental issues.

American Forests, 1516 P St. N.W. 20005; 667-3300. R. Neil Sampson, executive vice president. Fax, 667-7751.

Citizens' interest group that promotes protection and responsible management of forests and natural resources. Provides information on conservation, public land policy, urban forestry, and timber management. Runs an international tree planting campaign to help mitigate global warming.

American Hardwood Export Council, 1111 19th St. N.W., #800 20036; 463-2720. Elizabeth Ward, executive director. Fax, 463-2785.

Trade association of companies and associations that export hardwood products. Aids members in developing and expanding export capabilities in new and existing markets.

American Pulpwood Assn., 1025 Vermont Ave. N.W., #1020 20005; 347-2900. Richard Lewis, president. Fax, 783-2685.

Membership: logging contractors, pulpwood dealers, and pulpwood consumers. Administers programs to improve the productivity, safety, and efficiency of pulpwood harvesting and transport; provides information on new equipment, tools, and methods; works to ensure continued access to the timberland base; monitors legislation and regulations.

American Wood Preservers Institute, 1945 Old Gallows Rd., #150, Vienna, VA 22182; (703) 893-4005. Victor E. Lindenheim, president. Fax, (703) 893-8492.

Membership: wood preservers, including manufacturers, formulators of wood preserving chemicals, and wood treating companies. Monitors legislation and regulations that affect the industry. Acts as a liaison between the industry and federal agencies, including the Environmental

Protection Agency. Sponsors annual environmental seminar and legislative conference.

International Society of Tropical Foresters, 5400 Grosvenor Lane, Bethesda, MD 20814; (301) 897-8720. Warren T. Doolittle, president. Fax, (301) 897-3690.

Concerned with managing and protecting tropical forests. Distributes information and facilitates communication on tropical forestry issues.

National Lumber and Building Material Dealers Assn., 40 Ivy St. S.E. 20003; 547-2230. Gary W. Donnelly, executive vice president. Fax, 547-7640.

Membership: federated associations of retailers in the lumber and building material industries. Monitors legislation and regulations that affect the lumber industry.

Save America's Forests, 4 Library Court S.E. 20003; 544-9219. Carl Ross and Mark Winstein, co-directors.

Coalition of environmental and public interest groups, businesses, and individuals. Advocates recycling and comprehensive nationwide laws to prevent deforestation and to protect forest ecosystems.

Society of American Foresters, 5400 Grosvenor Lane, Bethesda, MD 20814; (301) 897-8720. William H. Banzhaf, executive vice president. Fax, (301) 897-3690.

Association of forestry professionals. Provides technical information on forestry; accredits forestry programs in universities and colleges.

See also Natural Resources, General, Nongovernmental (p. 637)

See also International Center (p. 448)

Land Resources

Agencies:

Bureau of Land Management (Interior Dept.), Main Interior Bldg., Rm. 5660 20240; 208-3801. Mike Dombeck, acting director. Information, 208-5717. Fax, 208-5242.

Manages public lands and federally owned mineral resources, including oil, gas, and coal. Resources managed and leased include wildlife habitats, timber, minerals, open space, wilderness areas, forage, and recreational resources.

Surveys federal lands and maintains public land records. Encourages multipurpose land use.

Bureau of Mines (Interior Dept.), Research, 810 7th St. N.W. 20241; 501-9290. David R. Forshey, associate director. Fax, 501-9957.

Conducts research on conservation methods for all aspects of mining; develops new procedures for mining technology; studies health and safety in mining; conducts studies and programs on mine land reclamation and restoration.

Bureau of Reclamation (Interior Dept.), Technical Liaison, Main Interior Bldg. 20240; 208-4054. Robert Ledzian, chief. Fax, 208-4021.

Responsible for acquisition, administration, management, and disposal of lands in 17 western states associated with bureau water resource development projects.

Interior Dept., Board of Land Appeals, 4015 Wilson Blvd., Arlington, VA 22203; (703) 235-3750. James L. Byrnes, chief administrative judge. Fax, (703) 235-9014.

Adjunct office of the interior secretary that decides appeals from decisions rendered by the Bureau of Land Management, the Minerals Management Service, the Office of Surface Mining, and the Bureau of Indian Affairs concerning the use and disposition of public lands; issues final decisions concerning the Surface Mining Control and Reclamation Act of 1977.

Interior Dept., Land and Minerals Management, Main Interior Bldg. 20240; 208-5676. Robert Armstrong, assistant secretary. Fax, 208-3144.

Directs and supervises the Bureau of Land Management, the Minerals Management Service, and the Office of Surface Mining. Supervises programs associated with land use planning, onshore and offshore minerals, surface mining reclamation and enforcement, and outer continental shelf minerals management.

Interior Dept., North American Wetlands Conservation Council, 4401 N. Fairfax Dr., Arlington, VA 22203; (703) 358-1784. Robert G. Streeter, coordinator. Fax, (703) 358-2282.

Membership: government and private-sector conservation experts. Works to protect, restore, and manage wetlands and other habitats for migratory birds and other animals and to maintain migratory bird and waterfowl populations.

Interior Dept., Surface Mining Reclamation and Enforcement, 1951 Constitution Ave. N.W. 20240; 208-4006. Robert Uram, director. Information, 208-2553. Fax, 219-3106.

Regulates surface mining of coal and surface effects of underground coal mining. Responsible for reclamation of abandoned coal mine lands.

Soil Conservation Service (Agriculture Dept.), 12th St. and Independence Ave. S.W. (mailing address: P.O. Box 2890, Washington, DC 20013); 720-4525. Paul Johnson, chief. Information, 720-4543. Fax, 720-7690.

Responsible for soil and water conservation programs, including watershed protection, flood prevention, river basin surveys, and resource conservation and development. Provides landowners, operators, state and local units of government, and community groups with technical assistance in carrying out local soil and water conservation programs. Inventories and monitors soil, water, and related resource data and resource use trends. Provides information about soil surveys, farmlands, and other natural resources.

Tennessee Valley Authority, 1 Massachusetts Ave. N.W., #300 20001; 479-4412. Jan Evered, administrative officer, Washington office. Fax, 479-4421.

Coordinates resource conservation, development, and land-use programs in the Tennessee River Valley. Provides information on land usage in the region. (Headquarters in Knoxville, Tenn.)

Congress:

House Agriculture Committee, Subcommittee on Environment, Credit, and Rural Development, 1430 LHOB 20515; 225-0301. Tim Johnson, D-S.D., chairman; Anne Simmons, staff director.

Jurisdiction over legislation on irrigation, soil conservation, and small-scale stream channelization, watershed, and flood control programs.

House Natural Resources Committee, Subcommittee on Energy and Mineral Resources, 818 O'Neill Bldg. (300 New Jersey Ave. S.E.) 20515; 225-8331. Richard H. Lehman, D-Calif., chairman; Deborah Lanzone, staff director. Fax, 225-4273.

Jurisdiction over legislation on land use planning, including surface mining.

House Natural Resources Committee, Subcommittee on National Parks, Forests, and Public Lands, 812 O'Neill Bldg. (300 New Jersey Ave. S.E.) 20515; 226-7736. Bruce F. Vento, D-Minn., chairman; Richard Healy, staff director.

Jurisdiction over legislation on public lands (except in Alaska), the land and water conservation fund, and the Bureau of Land Management.

Senate Agriculture, Nutrition, and Forestry Committee, Subcommittee on Agricultural Research, Conservation, Forestry, and General Legislation, SR-328A 20510; 224-2035. Tom Daschle, D-S.D., chairman; Tom Buis, legislative assistant.

Jurisdiction over legislation on irrigation, soil conservation, and stream channelization, watershed, and flood control programs involving structures of less than 4,000 acre-feet in storage capacity.

Senate Energy and Natural Resources Committee, Subcommittee on Mineral Resources Development and Production, SD-362 20510; 224-7568. Daniel K. Akaka, D-Hawaii, chairman; Lisa Vehmas, counsel.

Jurisdiction over legislation on land use planning, including surface mining; coal production, distribution, and utilization; and coal severance tax.

Senate Energy and Natural Resources Committee, Subcommittee on Public Lands, National Parks, and Forests, SD-308 20510; 224-8115. Dale Bumpers, D-Ark., chairman; David Brooks, counsel.

Jurisdiction over legislation on public lands, the land and water conservation fund, the Bureau of Land Management, and the Alaska National Interest Lands Conservation Act.

Nongovernmental:

American Geological Institute, 4220 King St., Alexandria, VA 22302; (703) 379-2480. Marcus E. Milling, executive director. Fax, (703) 379-7563.

Membership: earth science societies and associations. Maintains computerized database of the world's geoscience literature (available to the public for a fee).

American Land Rights Assn., 233 Pennsylvania Ave. S.E., #301 20003; 544-6156. Myron Ebell, Washington representative. Fax, 544-6774.

Membership: individuals who own homes, property, or other equity interests within federal- or state-managed areas. Monitors national land acquisition policies and legislation. Interests include private lands under the management of the federal government. (Headquarters in Battle Ground, Wash.)

American Resort Development Assn., 1220 L St. N.W., #510 20005; 371-6700. Thomas Franks, president. Fax, 289-8544.

Membership: developers, builders, financiers, marketing companies, and others involved in resort, recreational, and community development. Serves as an information clearinghouse; monitors federal and state legislation affecting land, timeshare, and community development industries.

ASFE/The Assn. of Professional Firms Practicing in the Geosciences, 8811 Colesville Rd., #G106, Silver Spring, MD 20910; (301) 565-2733. John P. Bachner, executive vice president. Fax, (301) 589-2017.

Membership: consulting geotechnical and geoenvironmental engineering firms. Conducts seminars and a peer review program on quality control policies and procedures in geotechnical engineering.

Land Trust Alliance, 1319 F St. N.W., #501 20004-1106; 638-4725. Jean Hocker, president. Fax, 638-4730.

Membership: organizations and individuals who work to conserve land resources. Serves as a forum for the exchange of information; conducts research and public education programs; monitors legislation and regulations.

National Assn. of Conservation Districts, 509 Capitol Court N.E. 20002; 547-6223. Ernest C. Shea, executive vice president. Fax, 547-6450.

Membership: conservation districts (local subdivisions of state governments). Develops conservation and development policies on land, forests, and other natural resources. Interests include erosion and sediment control; forestry, flood plain, and range management; and rural development.

National Wetlands Technical Council, c/o Environmental Law Institute, 1616 P St. N.W. 20036; 939-3848. Moira McDonald, staff contact.

Membership: technical experts in wetland science. Fosters information exchange with policy makers on issues that affect wetlands.

Public Lands Council, 1301 Pennsylvania Ave. N.W. 20004; 347-5355. William G. Myers III, executive director. Fax, 737-4086.

Membership: cattle and sheep ranchers who hold permits and leases to graze livestock on public lands.

Scenic America, 21 Dupont Circle N.W. 20036; 833-4300. Sally Oldham, president. Fax, 833-4304.

Membership: national, state, and local groups concerned with land-use control, growth management, and landscape protection. Works to enhance the scenic quality of America's communities and countryside. Provides information and technical assistance on scenic byways, tree preservation, economics of aesthetic regulation, billboard and sign control, scenic areas preservation, and growth management.

See also Natural Resources, General, Nongovernmental (p. 637)

See also National Cattlemen's Assn. (p. 610)

Metal Resources

Agencies:

Bureau of Mines (Interior Dept.), Environmental Technology, 810 7th St. N.W. 20241; 501-9271. William B. Schmidt, chief. Fax, 501-9957.

Develops technology for treating hazardous and nonhazardous waste materials, cleaning contaminated water, and mitigating other environmental effects associated with past mining and metal industry operations. Provides other federal agencies with technical assistance in conducting environmental research.

Bureau of Mines (Interior Dept.), Health, Safety, and Mining Technology, 810 7th St. N.W. 20241; 501-9321. Philip G. Meikle, chief. Fax, 501-9957.

Conducts research on conservation methods in mining; develops new procedures for mining technology; studies health and safety issues in mining.

Bureau of Mines (Interior Dept.), Information and Analysis, 810 7th St. N.W. 20241; 501-9450.

Donald G. Rogich, chief, mineral commodities. Fax, 219-9876.

Collects and publishes worldwide commercial and technological information related to metals and industrial minerals. Provides information on metals research, production, and processing methods.

Bureau of Mines (Interior Dept.), Minerals and Materials Science, 810 7th St. N.W. 20241; 501-9274. Robert S. Kaplan, chief. Fax, 501-9957.

Conducts minerals and materials research, including the development of processes for extracting and recovering low-grade ores; supervises the development of materials for engineering and mining.

Congress:

House Natural Resources Committee, Subcommittee on Energy and Mineral Resources, 818 O'Neill Bldg. (300 New Jersey Ave. S.E.) 20515; 225-8331. Richard H. Lehman, D-Calif., chairman; Deborah Lanzone, staff director. Fax, 225-4273.

Jurisdiction over legislation on metallic and nonmetallic minerals.

Senate Energy and Natural Resources Committee, Subcommittee on Mineral Resources Development and Production, SD-362 20510; 224-7568. Daniel K. Akaka, D-Hawaii, chairman; Lisa Vehmas, counsel.

Jurisdiction over legislation on metallic minerals.

See also Congressional Copper Caucus (p. 756); Congressional Mining Caucus (p. 758); Congressional Steel Caucus (p. 759); Senate Steel Caucus (p. 761)

Nongovernmental:

Aluminum Assn., 900 19th St. N.W., #300 20006; 862-5100. David N. Parker, president. Library, 862-5117. Fax, 862-5164.

Represents the aluminum industry. Develops voluntary standards and technical data; compiles statistics concerning the industry. Library open to the public by appointment.

American Iron and Steel Institute, 1101 17th St. N.W., 13th Floor 20036; 452-7100. Andrew G. Sharkey III, president. Fax, 463-6573.

Represents the iron and steel industry. Publishes statistics on iron and steel production;

monitors legislation and regulations; promotes the use of steel; conducts research.

American Mining Congress, 1920 N St. N.W., #300 20036; 861-2800. John A. Knebel, president. Fax, 861-7535.

Membership: domestic producers of coal and industrial-agricultural minerals and metals; manufacturers of mining equipment; engineering and consulting firms; and financial institutions. Interests include mine leasing programs, mine health and safety, research and development, public lands, and minerals availability. Monitors legislation and regulations.

American Zinc Assn., 1112 16th St. N.W., #240 20036; 835-0164. George F. Vary, executive director. Fax, 835-0155.

Provides information on zinc; monitors legislation and regulations.

Sheet Metal and Air Conditioning Contractors National Assn., 4201 Lafayette Center Dr., Chantilly, VA 22021; (703) 803-2980. John W. Sroka, executive vice president. Fax, (703) 803-3732.

Membership: sheet metal and air conditioning contractors. Provides information on standards and installation and fabrication methods. Operates the National Environmental Balancing Bureau with the Mechanical Contractors Assn. of America.

Mineral Resources

See also Emergency Preparedness, Strategic Stockpiles (p. 544); Natural Resources, Outer Continental Shelf (p. 651)

Agencies:

Bureau of Land Management (Interior Dept.), Energy and Mineral Resources, Main Interior Bldg. 20240; 208-4201. Hillary A. Oden, assistant director. Fax, 208-4800.

Evaluates and classifies onshore oil, natural gas, geothermal resources, and all solid energy and mineral resources, including coal and uranium on federal lands. Develops and administers regulations for fluid and solid mineral leasing on national lands and on the subsurface of land where fluid and solid mineral rights have been reserved for the federal government.

Bureau of Land Management (Interior Dept.), Minerals Policy Analysis and Economic Evaluation, 1620 L St. N.W., #501 LS (mailing address: Main Interior Bldg., #501 LS, Washington, DC 20240); 452-0380. Sie Ling Chiang, chief. Fax, 452-0399.

Develops mineral management and environmental policies by analyzing the impact of proposed or existing policies on the markets for mineral and energy resources. Establishes standards, policies, and guidelines for mineral economic evaluation for lease, exchange, conveyance, or other dispositions.

Bureau of Mines (Interior Dept.), 810 7th St. N.W. 20241; 501-9300. Hermann Enzer, acting director. Information, 501-9649. Fax, 501-9960.

Researches and develops technologies for extracting, processing, using, and recycling mineral resources. Collects, compiles, analyzes, and publishes statistical and economic information on all phases of nonfuel mineral resource development, including exploration, production, shipping, demand, stocks, prices, imports, and exports.

Bureau of Mines (Interior Dept.), Policy Analysis, 810 7th St. N.W. 20241; 501-9729. William L. Miller, chief. Fax, 219-2490.

Provides technical and economic policy analysis on domestic and international regulatory and trade issues concerning mineral production and use. Develops policy options to deal with critical mineral shortages caused by depletion of domestic supplies or disruption of imported supplies. Analyzes key environmental issues that affect and are affected by the minerals industries.

Federal Emergency Management Agency, Resources Preparedness and Capabilities, 500 C St. S.W. 20472; 646-3544. Thomas R. McQuillan, acting director. Fax, 646-3397.

Supports the enhancement and availability of a mineral resources base to respond to national emergencies; administers the Defense Production Act; promotes inter- and intra-agency development of mineral resource mobilization plans and policies.

Interior Dept., Board of Land Appeals, 4015 Wilson Blvd., Arlington, VA 22203; (703) 235-3750. James L. Byrnes, chief administrative judge. Fax, (703) 235-9014.

Adjunct office of the interior secretary that decides appeals from decisions rendered by the Bureau of Land Management, the Minerals Management Service, the Office of Surface Mining, and the Bureau of Indian Affairs concerning the use and disposition of public minerals; issues final decisions concerning the Surface Mining Reclamation Control Act of 1977.

Interior Dept., Land and Minerals Management, Main Interior Bldg. 20240; 208-5676. Robert Armstrong, assistant secretary. Fax, 208-3144.

Directs and supervises the Bureau of Land Management, the Minerals Management Service, and the Office of Surface Mining. Supervises programs associated with land-use planning, onshore and offshore minerals, surface mining reclamation and enforcement, and outer continental shelf minerals management.

Interior Dept., Water and Science, Main Interior Bldg. 20240; 208-3186. Elizabeth Ann Rieke, assistant secretary. Fax, 371-2815.

Administers departmental water, scientific, and research activities. Directs and supervises the Bureau of Mines, the Bureau of Reclamation, and the U.S. Geological Survey.

International Trade Administration (Commerce Dept.), Trade and Industry Statistics, Main Commerce Bldg. 20230; 482-4211. Bill Sullivan, director. U.S. Foreign Trade Reference Room, 482-2185.

Maintains U.S. and foreign import and export statistics on strategic minerals. U.S. Foreign Trade Reference Room open to the public.

Minerals Management Service (Interior Dept.), Operations and Safety Management, 381 Elden St., Herndon, VA 22070; (703) 787-1570. Henry G. Bartholomew, deputy associate director. Fax, (703) 787-1575.

Oversees postlease operations, including exploration, drilling, and production phases of oil and gas development. Ensures compliance with environmental statutes and regulations.

Minerals Management Service (Interior Dept.), Resources and Environmental Management, 381 Elden St., Herndon, VA 22070; (703) 787-1500. James W. Workman, deputy associate director. Fax, (703) 787-1209.

Oversees prelease operations; administers offshore oil and gas leasing.

Minerals Management Service (Interior Dept.), Royalty Management Program, Main Interior

Bldg. 20240; 208-3512. R. Dale Fazio, chief. Fax, 208-3982.

Collects royalties on minerals produced on federal and native American lands. (Accounting center in Denver.)

State Dept., International Commodities, Main State Bldg. 20520; 647-2744. Wesley S. Scholz, director. Fax, 647-8758.

Handles foreign policy aspects of minerals, international commodity arrangements, and national defense stockpile policy, including deep seabed mining and Antarctic mineral development.

U.S. Geological Survey (Interior Dept.), Mineral Resources, 12201 Sunrise Valley Dr., Reston, VA 22092; (703) 648-6100. Willis H. White, chief. Fax, (703) 648-6057.

Coordinates mineral resource activities for the Geological Survey, including geochemical and geophysical instrumentation and research.

Congress:

House Natural Resources Committee, Subcommittee on Energy and Mineral Resources, 818 O'Neill Bldg. (300 New Jersey Ave. S.E.) 20515; 225-8331. Richard H. Lehman, D-Calif., chairman; Deborah Lanzone, staff director. Fax, 225-4273.

Jurisdiction over mineral supply and leasing legislation; oversight and legislative jurisdiction over the Bureau of Mines, onshore functions of the Minerals Management Service, mineral aspects of the Office of Surface Mining, mineral leasing of the Bureau of Land Management, and offshore hardrock mineral development programs.

House Natural Resources Committee, Subcommittee on Oversight and Investigations, 1328 LHOB 20515; 225-2761. George Miller, D-Calif., chairman; John Lawrence, staff director. Fax, 225-3554.

Oversight and legislative jurisdiction over outer continental shelf aspects of the Minerals Management Service.

Senate Energy and Natural Resources Committee, Subcommittee on Mineral Resources Development and Production, SD-362 20510; 224-7568. Daniel K. Akaka, D-Hawaii, chairman; Lisa Vehmas, counsel.

Jurisdiction over mineral supply and leasing legislation; oversight and legislative jurisdiction

over the Bureau of Mines, Office of Surface Mining, the Minerals Management Service, and offshore hardrock mineral development programs.

Senate Energy and Natural Resources Committee, Subcommittee on Public Lands, National Parks, and Forests, SD-308 20510; 224-8115. Dale Bumpers, D-Ark., chairman; David Brooks, counsel.

Jurisdiction over legislation on the Bureau of Land Management.

Nongovernmental:

American Mining Congress, 1920 N St. N.W., #300 20036; 861-2800. John A. Knebel, president. Fax, 861-7535.

Membership: domestic producers of coal and industrial-agricultural minerals and metals; manufacturers of mining equipment; engineering and consulting firms; and financial institutions. Interests include mine leasing programs, mine health and safety, research and development, public lands, and minerals availability. Monitors legislation and regulations.

Glass Packaging Institute, 1627 K St. N.W., #800 20006; 887-4850. Joseph Cattaneo, executive vice president. Fax, 785-5377.

Membership: manufacturers of glass containers and their suppliers. Administers the Nickel Solution Trust with interests in recycling, legislation and government regulations, and research affecting glass packaging. Promotes conservation of natural resources in the industry.

Mineralogical Society of America, 1130 17th St. N.W., #330 20036; 775-4344. Susan L. Meyers, office manager. Fax, 775-0018.

Membership: mineralogists, petrologists, crystallographers, geochemists, educators, students, and others interested in mineralogy. Conducts research; sponsors educational programs; promotes industrial application of mineral studies.

Salt Institute, 700 N. Fairfax St., Alexandria, VA 22314; (703) 549-4648. Richard L. Hanneman, president. Fax, (703) 548-2194.

Membership: North American salt companies and overseas companies that produce dry salt for use in food, animal feed, highway deicing, water softening, and chemicals. Monitors legislation and regulations. Sponsors education and training projects with the Bureau of Mines and the Food and Drug Administration.

See also Natural Resources, General, Nongovernmental (p. 637)

Native American Trust Resources Management

Agencies:

Bureau of Indian Affairs (Interior Dept.), Trust Responsibilities, Main Interior Bldg. 20240; 208-5831. Patrick A. Hayes, director. Fax, 219-1255.

Assists in developing and managing bureau programs involving native American trust resources (agriculture, minerals, forestry, wildlife, water, transportation, irrigation, environmental protection, and real property management).

Interior Dept., Office of the Solicitor, Main Interior Bldg. 20240; 208-3401. Michael Anderson, associate solicitor, Indian affairs. Fax, 219-1791.

Advises the Bureau of Indian Affairs and the secretary of interior on all legal matters, including its trust responsibilities toward native Americans and their natural resources.

Justice Dept., Environment and Natural Resources, 601 Pennsylvania Ave. N.W. (mailing address: P.O. Box 663, Ben Franklin Station, Washington, DC 20044); 272-6414. Edward J. Passarelli, leader, claims and Indian team. Fax, 272-6815.

Represents the United States in suits, including trust violations, brought by individual native Americans and native American tribes against the government.

Justice Dept., Environment and Natural Resources, 601 Pennsylvania Ave. N.W. 20004; 272-4111. Hank J. Meshorer, chief, Indian resources. Fax, 272-4471.

Represents the United States as trustee for native Americans in court actions involving protection of native American land and resources.

Minerals Management Service (Interior Dept.), Royalty Management Program, Main Interior Bldg. 20240; 208-3512. R. Dale Fazio, chief. Fax, 208-3982.

Collects royalties on minerals produced on federal and native American lands. (Accounting center in Denver.)

Congress:

House Natural Resources Committee, Subcommittee on Native American Affairs, 1522 LHOB 20515; 226-7393. Bill Richardson, D-N.M., chairman; Tadd Johnson, staff director. Fax, 226-0522.

Jurisdiction over native American legislation, including land management and trust responsibilities and claims against the United States.

Senate Committee on Indian Affairs, SH-838 20510; 224-2251. Daniel K. Inouye, D-Hawaii, chairman; Patricia Zell, staff director. Fax, 224-2309.

Jurisdiction over native American legislation, including land management and trust responsibilities and claims against the United States.

Nongovernmental:

See Minority and Women's Rights, Native Americans (p. 269)

See also Rural Coalition (p. 612)

Ocean Resources

See also International Law and Agreements, Fishing/Law of the Sea (p. 476); Science: Environmental and Earth Sciences, Oceanography (p. 680)

Agencies:

National Oceanic and Atmospheric Administration (Commerce Dept.), National Environmental Satellite, Data, and Information Service, 4401 Suitland Rd., #2069, Suitland, MD (mailing address: Federal Bldg. 4, #2069, Washington, DC 20233); (301) 763-7190. Robert S. Winokur, assistant administrator. Information, (301) 763-2560. Fax, (301) 763-4011.

Disseminates worldwide environmental data through a system of meteorological, oceanographic, geophysical, and solar-terrestrial data centers.

National Oceanic and Atmospheric Administration (Commerce Dept.), National Sea Grant College Program, 1335 East-West Highway, Silver Spring, MD 20910; (301) 713-2448. David B. Duane, director. Fax, (301) 713-0799.

Provides institutions with grants for marine research, education, and advisory services; provides marine environmental information.

National Oceanic and Atmospheric Administration (Commerce Dept.), Ocean and Coastal Resource Management, 1305 East-West Highway, NXI, SSMC4 #13634, Silver Spring, MD 20910; (301) 713-3155. Jeff Benoit, director. Fax, (301) 713-4269.

Administers the Coastal Zone Management Act, the National Estuarine Research Reserve System, the National Marine Sanctuary Program, the Deep Seabed Hard Mineral Resources Act, and the Ocean Thermal Energy Conversion Act to carry out NOAA's goals for preservation, conservation, and restoration of the ocean and coastal environment.

National Oceanic and Atmospheric Administration (Commerce Dept.), Ocean Minerals and Energy, 1305 East-West Highway, N/ORM1, Silver Spring, MD 20910; (301) 713-3159. M. Karl Jugel, acting chief. Fax, (301) 713-4009.

Responsible for scientific research on regulatory, developmental, and environmental aspects of deep seabed mining and ocean thermal energy conversion projects.

National Oceanic and Atmospheric Administration (Commerce Dept.), Ocean Resources, Conservation, and Assessment, 1305 East-West Highway, N/ORCA #10409 SSMC4, Silver Spring, MD 20910; (301) 713-2989. Charles N. Ehler, director. Fax, (301) 713-4389.

Conducts national studies and develops policies on ocean management and use along the U.S. coastline and the exclusive economic zone.

National Oceanic and Atmospheric Administration (Commerce Dept.), Officer Corps, 11400 Rockville Pike, Rockville, MD 20852; (301) 443-2383. Rear Adm. Sigmund R. Petersen, director. Recruiting, (301) 443-8984.

Uniformed service of the Commerce Dept. that operates and manages NOAA's fleet of hydrographic, oceanographic, and fisheries research ships and aircraft. Supports NOAA's scientific programs.

National Oceanic and Atmospheric Administration (Commerce Dept.), Sanctuaries and Reserves, 1305 East-West Highway, 12th Floor, Silver Spring, MD 20910; (301) 713-3125. Francesca Cava, chief. Fax, (301) 713-0404.

Administers the National Marine Sanctuary program, which seeks to protect and restore the ecology and recreational resources of ocean waters. Administers the National Estuarine Research Reserve System, which helps to acquire,

develop, and operate estuarine areas as natural field laboratories for research and education.

Congress:

House Merchant Marine and Fisheries Committee, Subcommittee on Environment and Natural Resources, 545 Ford Bldg. (2nd and D Sts. S.W.) 20515; 226-3547. Gerry E. Studds, D-Mass., chairman; Daniel M. Ashe, staff director.

Jurisdiction over legislation concerning research on ocean life and the National Environmental Policy Act as it applies to ocean resources.

House Merchant Marine and Fisheries Committee, Subcommittee on Oceanography, Gulf of Mexico, and the Outer Continental Shelf, 575 Ford Bldg. (2nd and D Sts. S.W.) 20515; 226-2460. Solomon P. Ortiz, D-Texas, chairman; Sheila McCready, staff director.

Jurisdiction over legislation concerning deep seabed mining, ocean environment and charting, coastal zone management, Law of the Sea, Sea Grant programs and extension services, and commerce and transportation aspects of outer continental shelf lands.

Senate Commerce, Science, and Transportation Committee, SD-508 20510; 224-5115. Ernest F. Hollings, D-S.C., chairman; Kevin Curtin, chief counsel and staff director.

Jurisdiction over legislation concerning research on ocean life, the National Environmental Policy Act as it applies to ocean resources, deep seabed mining, ocean environment and charting, coastal zone management, Law of the Sea, Sea Grant programs and extension services, and commerce and transportation aspects of outer continental shelf lands.

Senate Commerce, Science, and Transportation Committee, Subcommittee on National Ocean Policy Study, SH-425 (mailing address: SD-508, Washington, DC 20510); 224-4912. Ernest F. Hollings, D-S.C., chairman; Penny Dalton, staff member.

Studies all aspects of ocean policy including marine science funding and the outer continental shelf. Studies issues involving marine research, coastal zone management, ocean environment, and the Law of the Sea. Studies deep seabed mining, ocean charting, and the National Environmental Policy Act as it applies to ocean resources. (Subcommittee does not report legislation.)

Nongovernmental:

Coastal States Organization, 444 N. Capitol St. N.W., #322 20001; 508-3860. David C. Slade, executive director. Fax, 508-3843.

Nonpartisan organization that represents governors of U.S. coastal states, territories, and commonwealths on management of coastal, Great Lakes, and marine resources. Interests include ocean dumping, coastal pollution, wetlands preservation and restoration, national oceans policy, and the outer continental shelf. Gathers and analyzes data to assess state coastal needs; sponsors and participates in conferences and workshops.

Marine Technology Society, 1828 L St. N.W., #906 20036; 775-5966. Martin J. Finerty Jr., general manager. Fax, 429-9417.

Membership: scientists, engineers, technologists, and others interested in marine science and technology. Provides information on marine science, technology, and education.

National Ocean Industries Assn., 1120 G St. N.W., #900 20005; 347-6900. Robert B. Stewart, president. Fax, 347-8650.

Membership: manufacturers, producers, suppliers, and support and service companies involved in marine, offshore, and ocean work. Interests include offshore oil and gas supply and production, deep-sea mining, ocean thermal energy, and new energy sources.

Outer Continental Shelf

Agencies:

Minerals Management Service (Interior Dept.), Offshore Minerals Management, Main Interior Bldg. 20240; 208-3530. Thomas M. Gernhofer, associate director. Fax, 208-6048.

Administers the Outer Continental Shelf Lands Act. Evaluates, classifies, and supervises oil, gas, and other mineral reserves and operations on outer continental shelf lands; manages the submerged lands of the outer continental shelf.

U.S. Geological Survey (Interior Dept.), Energy and Marine Geology, 12201 Sunrise Valley Dr., Reston, VA 22092; (703) 648-6472. Gary Hill, chief. Fax, (703) 648-5464.

Handles resource assessment, exploration research, and marine geologic and environmental studies on the U.S. outer continental shelf.

Congress:

House Merchant Marine and Fisheries Committee, Subcommittee on Oceanography, Gulf of Mexico, and the Outer Continental Shelf, 575 Ford Bldg. (2nd and D Sts. S.W.) 20515; 226-2460. Solomon P. Ortiz, D-Texas, chairman; Sheila McCready, staff director.

Jurisdiction over legislation on ocean environment and coastal zone matters, including leasing and development of the outer continental shelf under the Outer Continental Shelf Lands Act.

Senate Commerce, Science, and Transportation Committee, Subcommittee on National Ocean Policy Study, SH-425 (mailing address: SD-508, Washington, DC 20510); 224-4912. Ernest F. Hollings, D-S.C., chairman; Penny Dalton, staff member.

Studies outer continental shelf matters related to coastal zone management, marine research, and ocean environment. (Subcommittee does not report legislation.)

Senate Energy and Natural Resources Committee, SD-304 20510; 224-4971. J. Bennett Johnston, D-La., chairman; Benjamin Cooper, staff director. Fax, 224-6163.

Jurisdiction over legislation on ocean environment and coastal zone matters, including leasing and development of the outer continental shelf under the Outer Continental Shelf Lands Act; and on the environmental impact of offshore drilling on the outer continental shelf (jurisdiction shared with Senate Commerce, Science, and Transportation and Senate Environment and Public Works committees).

Senate Environment and Public Works Committee, Subcommittee on Clean Water, Fisheries, and Wildlife, SH-505 20510; 224-3597. Bob Graham, D-Fla., chairman; Bill Leary, counsel.

Jurisdiction over legislation on the environmental impact of offshore drilling on the outer continental shelf. (Jurisdiction shared with Senate Commerce, Science, and Transportation and Senate Energy and Natural Resources committees.)

Nongovernmental:

See Natural Resources, Ocean Resources, Nongovernmental (this page)

Parks and Recreation

Agencies:

Bureau of Land Management (Interior Dept.), Recreation and Wilderness Resources, 1620 L St. N.W. (mailing address: 204LS, 1849 C St. N.W., Washington, DC 20240); 452-7790. Frank Snell, chief. Fax, 452-7709.
Identifies and manages recreational and wilderness resources on public lands.

Bureau of Reclamation (Interior Dept.), Technical Liaison, Main Interior Bldg. 20240; 208-4054. Robert Ledzian, chief. Fax, 208-4021.
Responsible for acquisition, administration, management, and disposal of lands in 17 western states associated with bureau water resource development projects. Provides overall policy guidance for land use, including agreements with public agencies for outdoor recreation, fish and wildlife enhancement, and land use authorizations such as leases, licenses, permits, and rights of way.

Forest Service (Agriculture Dept.), Recreation Management, 14th St. and Independence Ave. S.W. (mailing address: P.O. Box 96090, Washington, DC 20090); 205-1706. Lyle Laverty, director. Fax, 205-1145.
Develops policy and sets guidelines on administering national forests for recreational purposes.

Interior Dept., Fish, Wildlife, and Parks, Main Interior Bldg. 20240; 208-4416. George T. Frampton Jr., assistant secretary. Fax, 208-4684.
Responsible for programs associated with the development, conservation, and use of fish, wildlife, recreational, historical, and national park system resources. Coordinates marine environmental quality and biological resources programs with other federal agencies.

Interior Dept., National Park System Advisory Board, Main Interior Bldg. (mailing address: P.O. Box 37127, Washington, DC 20013); 208-4030. Dave Jervis, assistant chief, policy. Fax, 208-4260.
Advises the secretary on matters relating to the national park system; makes recommendations on the historical significance of national trails and landmarks.

National Park Service (Interior Dept.), Main Interior Bldg. (mailing address: P.O. Box 37127, Washington, DC 20013); 208-4621. Roger G.

Kennedy, director. Information, 208-4747. Press, 208-7394. Fax, 208-7520. Washington, D.C., area activities, 619-7275 (recording).
Administers national parks, monuments, historic sites, and recreation areas. Oversees coordination, planning, and financing of public outdoor recreation programs at all levels of government. Conducts recreation research surveys; administers financial assistance program to states for planning and development of outdoor recreation programs.

Congress:

House Natural Resources Committee, Subcommittee on National Parks, Forests, and Public Lands, 812 O'Neill Bldg. (300 New Jersey Ave. S.E.) 20515; 226-7736. Bruce F. Vento, D-Minn., chairman; Richard Healy, staff director.
Jurisdiction over legislation on recreation areas, the national park system, the national trails system, and the Bureau of Land Management.

Senate Energy and Natural Resources Committee, Subcommittee on Public Lands, National Parks, and Forests, SD-308 20510; 224-8115. Dale Bumpers, D-Ark., chairman; David Brooks, counsel.
Jurisdiction over legislation on recreation areas, the national park system, the national trails system, and the Bureau of Land Management.

Nongovernmental:

American Hiking Society, 243 Church St., Vienna, VA (mailing address: P.O. Box 20160, Washington, DC 20041); (703) 255-9304. Bruce Ward, president. Fax, (703) 255-9308.
Membership: individuals and clubs interested in preserving America's trail system and protecting the interests of hikers and other trail users. Sponsors research on trail construction and a trail maintenance summer program. Provides information on outdoor volunteer opportunities on public lands.

American Recreation Coalition, 1331 Pennsylvania Ave. N.W., #726 20004; 662-7420. Derrick A. Crandall, president. Fax, 662-7424.
Membership: organized recreationalists, national and regional corporations offering recreational products and services, and recreation industry trade associations. Works to increase public and private sector activity in public recreation, land and water management, and energy policy. Provides information on innovative recreational planning.

National Park Foundation, 1101 17th St. N.W. 20036; 785-4500. Alan A. Rubin, president. Fax, 785-3539.

Chartered by Congress and chaired by the interior secretary. Encourages private-sector support of the national park system; provides grants and sponsors educational and cultural activities.

National Parks and Conservation Assn., 1776 Massachusetts Ave. N.W., #200 20036; 223-6722. Paul C. Pritchard, president. Toll-free, (800) 628-7275. Fax, 659-0650.

Citizens' interest group that seeks to protect national parks and other park system areas.

National Recreation and Park Assn., 2775 S. Quincy St., Arlington, VA 22206; (703) 820-4940. Dean Tice, executive director. Fax, (703) 671-6772. TDD, (703) 578-5559.

Membership: park and recreation professionals and citizens interested in parks and recreation. Provides technical assistance for park and recreational programs.

Rails-to-Trails Conservancy, 1400 16th St. N.W., #300 20036; 797-5400. David G. Burwell, president. Fax, 797-5411.

Promotes the conversion of abandoned railroad corridors into hiking and biking trails for public use. Provides public education programs and technical and legal assistance. Publishes trail guides; monitors legislation and regulations.

Student Conservation Assn., 1800 N. Kent St., #1260, Arlington, VA 22209; (703) 524-2441. Marta Kelly, national director. Fax, (703) 524-2451.

Educational organization that provides youth and adults with opportunities for training and work experience in natural resource management and conservation. Volunteers serve in national parks, forests, wildlife refuges, and other public lands. (Headquarters in Charlestown, N.H.)

World Wildlife Fund, 1250 24th St. N.W. 20037; 293-4800. Kathryn S. Fuller, president. Fax, 293-9345.

International conservation organization that provides funds and technical assistance for establishing and maintaining parks.

See also Natural Resources, General, Nongovernmental (p. 637)

Water Resources

See also Environment, Water Pollution (p. 632)

Agencies:

Army Dept. (Defense Dept.), Corps of Engineers, 20 Massachusetts Ave. N.W. 20314-1000; 272-0001. Lt. Gen. Arthur E. Williams (USACE), chief of engineers. Information, 272-0011. Fax, 272-1683.

Provides local governments with disaster relief, flood control, navigation, and hydroelectric power services.

Bureau of Reclamation (Interior Dept.), Main Interior Bldg. 20240; 208-4157. Daniel P. Beard, commissioner. Information, 208-4662. Fax, 208-3484.

Administers federal programs for water and power resource development and management in 17 western states; oversees municipal and industrial water supply, hydroelectric power generation, irrigation, flood control, water quality improvement, river regulation, fish and wildlife enhancement, and outdoor recreation.

Delaware River Basin Commission, 1010 Massachusetts Ave. N.W., #100 20001; 343-5761. Irene B. Brooks, U.S. commissioner. Fax, 343-1013.

Federal-interstate commission. Oversees projects to develop the Delaware River Basin that include regulation and development of ground and surface water supplies for municipal, industrial, and agricultural uses; development of hydropower; abatement of stream pollution; flood damage reduction; and protection of fish and wildlife.

Interstate Commission on the Potomac River Basin, 6110 Executive Blvd., #300, Rockville, MD 20852; (301) 984-1908. Herbert M. Sachs, executive director. Fax, (301) 984-5841.

Interstate compact commission established by Congress to control and reduce water pollution and to restore and protect living resources in the Potomac River and its tributaries. Monitors water quality; seeks innovative methods to solve water supply and land resource problems. Provides information and educational materials on the Potomac River basin.

Office of Management and Budget (Executive Office of the President), Water Resources, New

Executive Office Bldg. 20503; 395-4590. Bruce D. Long, chief. Fax, 395-4652.

Reviews all plans and budgets related to federal or federally assisted water and related land resource projects.

Smithsonian Environmental Research Center (Smithsonian Institution), Contees Wharf Rd., Edgewater, MD (mailing address: P.O. Box 28, Edgewater, MD 21037); (410) 798-4424. David L. Correll, director. Fax, (301) 261-7954.

Studies the interaction of the Rhode River with its watershed, the effect of humans on the system, and the long-term effects of water quality on the plant and animal population.

Susquehanna River Basin Commission, 1010 Massachusetts Ave. N.W., #100 20001; 343-4091. John R. McCarty, U.S. commissioner. Fax, 343-1013.

Federal-interstate compact commission that manages water and water-related resources to develop the Susquehanna River basin. Regulates and develops ground and surface water supplies for municipal, industrial, and agricultural uses; works to reduce stream pollution and flood damage, and to protect fish and wildlife.

Tennessee Valley Authority, 1 Massachusetts Ave. N.W., #300 20001; 479-4412. Jan Evered, administrative officer, Washington office. Fax, 479-4421.

Coordinates resource conservation, development, and land-use programs in the Tennessee River Valley. Operates the river control system; projects include flood control, navigation development, and multiple-use reservoirs. (Headquarters in Knoxville, Tenn.)

U.S. Geological Survey (Interior Dept.), National Water Information Center, 12201 Sunrise Valley Dr., Reston, VA 22092. James F. Daniel, assistant chief hydrologist, scientific information management. Toll-free, (800) 426-9000.

Referral service for governmental and private water resources organizations. Assists in identifying, locating, and acquiring data on water resources. Information available through cooperating organizations and 76 assistance centers.

U.S. Geological Survey (Interior Dept.), Water Resources, 12201 Sunrise Valley Dr., Reston, VA 22092; (703) 648-5215. Philip Cohen, chief hydrologist. Fax, (703) 648-5295.

Administers the Water Resources Research Act of 1990. Assesses the quantity and quality of surface and groundwater resources; collects, analyzes, and disseminates data on water use and the effect of human activity and natural phenomena on hydrologic systems. Provides federal agencies, state and local governments, international organizations, and foreign governments with scientific and technical assistance.

Congress:

House Agriculture Committee, Subcommittee on Environment, Credit, and Rural Development, 1430 LHOB 20515; 225-0301. Tim Johnson, D-S.D., chairman; Anne Simmons, staff director.

Jurisdiction over legislation on small watershed programs, including stream channelization.

House Energy and Commerce Committee, Subcommittee on Energy and Power, 331 Ford Bldg. (2nd and D Sts. S.W.) 20515; 226-2500. Philip R. Sharp, D-Ind., chairman; Shelley N. Fidler, acting staff director.

Jurisdiction over legislation on hydroelectric power and ocean thermal energy resource commercialization, utilization, and conversion.

House Natural Resources Committee, Subcommittee on National Parks, Forests, and Public Lands, 812 O'Neill Bldg. (300 New Jersey Ave. S.E.) 20515; 226-7736. Bruce F. Vento, D-Minn., chairman; Richard Healy, staff director.

Jurisdiction over legislation on water rights, including federally reserved water rights on public lands.

House Natural Resources Committee, Subcommittee on Oversight and Investigations, 1328 LHOB 20515; 225-2761. George Miller, D-Calif., chairman; John Lawrence, staff director. Fax, 225-3554.

Jurisdiction over legislation on irrigation and reclamation projects, compacts relating to use and apportionment of interstate water resources, and power marketing administrations.

House Public Works and Transportation Committee, Subcommittee on Water Resources and Environment, B370A RHOB 20515; 225-0060. Douglas Applegate, D-Ohio, chairman; Kenneth J. Kopocis, counsel.

Jurisdiction over legislation on water resources; watershed and flood control programs; U.S. Army Corps of Engineers water resources projects; wetlands protection; navigation and river basin programs; small watershed programs of the Soil Conservation Service; groundwater programs; and construction, operation, and maintenance of harbors.

House Science, Space, and Technology Committee, Subcommittee on Technology, Environment, and Aviation, B374 RHOB 20515; 225-9662. Tim Valentine, D-N.C., chairman; James H. Turner, staff director.
Jurisdiction over water resources research legislation.

Senate Agriculture, Nutrition, and Forestry Committee, Subcommittee on Agricultural Research, Conservation, Forestry, and General Legislation, SR-328A 20510; 224-2035. Tom Daschle, D-S.D., chairman; Tom Buis, legislative assistant.
Jurisdiction over legislation on small watershed programs, including stream channelization, and on flood control programs that involve structures of less than 4,000 acre-feet in storage capacity.

Senate Energy and Natural Resources Committee, Subcommittee on Renewable Energy, Energy Efficiency, and Competitiveness, SH-212 20510; 224-4756. Jeff Bingaman, D-N.M., chairman; Leslie Black Cordess, professional staff member.
Jurisdiction over legislation on ocean thermal energy resource commercialization, utilization, and conversion.

Senate Energy and Natural Resources Committee, Subcommittee on Water and Power, SD-306 20510; 224-6836. Bill Bradley, D-N.J., chairman; Dana Sebren Cooper, counsel.
Jurisdiction over legislation on hydroelectric power; irrigation and reclamation projects; water rights, including federally reserved water rights on public lands; compacts relating to use and apportionment of interstate water resources; and power marketing administrations.

Senate Environment and Public Works Committee, Subcommittee on Clean Water, Fisheries, and Wildlife, SH-505 20510; 224-3597. Bob Graham, D-Fla., chairman; Bill Leary, counsel.
Jurisdiction over legislation on wetlands protection and groundwater programs.

Senate Environment and Public Works Committee, Subcommittee on Water Resources,

Transportation, Public Buildings, and Economic Development, SH-415 20510; 224-5031. Daniel Patrick Moynihan, D-N.Y., chairman; Vacant, director.
Jurisdiction over water resources and water resources research legislation; watershed and flood control programs; U.S. Army Corps of Engineers water resources projects; navigation and river basin programs; small watershed programs of the Soil Conservation Service; and construction, operation, and maintenance of harbors.

See also Tennessee Valley Authority Caucus (p. 760)

Nongovernmental:

American Rivers, 801 Pennsylvania Ave. S.E., #400 20003; 547-6900. Kevin J. Coyle, president. Fax, 543-6142.
Works to preserve the nation's river system and to control river development and dam and canal construction.

American Water Resources Assn., 5410 Grosvenor Lane, #220, Bethesda, MD 20814; (301) 493-8600. Kenneth D. Reid, executive vice president. Fax, (301) 493-5844.
Collects and provides information on all aspects of water resources. Interests include research and education on planning, managing, and developing water resources.

American Water Works Assn., 1401 New York Ave. N.W. 20005; 628-8303. John H. Sullivan, deputy executive director, Washington office. Fax, 628-2846.
Membership: municipal water utilities, manufacturers of equipment for water industries, water treatment companies, and individuals. Provides information on drinking water treatment; publishes voluntary standards for the water industry. (Headquarters in Denver.)

Environmental Defense Fund, 1875 Connecticut Ave. N.W., #1016 20009-5728; 387-3500. Cheryl King, office manager, Washington office. Fax, 234-6049.
Citizens' interest group staffed by lawyers, economists, and scientists. Takes legal action on environmental issues; provides information on pollution prevention, environmental health, water resources, and water marketing. (Headquarters in New York.)

Izaak Walton League of America, 1401 Wilson Blvd., Level B, Arlington, VA 22209; (703) 528-1818. Maitland Sharpe, executive director. Fax, (703) 528-1836.
Grass-roots organization that promotes conservation of natural resources and the environment. Coordinates a citizen action program to monitor and improve the condition of local streams.

National Assn. of Conservation Districts, 509 Capitol Court N.E. 20002; 547-6223. Ernest C. Shea, executive vice president. Fax, 547-6450.
Membership: conservation districts (local subdivisions of state governments). Develops national policies on the conservation and development of water resources.

National Assn. of Flood and Stormwater Management Agencies, 1225 Eye St. N.W., #300 20005; 682-3761. Susan Gilson, executive director. Fax, 842-0621.
Membership: state, county, and local governments concerned with management of water resources. Monitors legislation and regulations.

National Assn. of Regulatory Utility Commissioners, 12th St. and Constitution Ave. N.W. (mailing address: P.O. Box 684, Washington, DC 20044-0684); 898-2200. Paul Rodgers, administrative director and general counsel. Press, 898-2205. Fax, 898-2213.
Membership: members of federal, state, municipal, and Canadian regulatory commissions that have jurisdiction over utilities. Interests include water.

National Assn. of Water Companies, 1725 K St. N.W., #1212 20006; 833-8383. James B. Groff, executive director. Fax, 331-7442.
Membership: privately owned, regulated water companies. Provides members with information on legislative and regulatory issues and other subjects.

National Rural Community Assistance Program, 602 S. King St., #402, Leesburg, VA 22075; (703) 771-8636. Kathleen Stanley, executive director. Fax, (703) 771-8753.
Federally funded organization that conducts program to improve water delivery and disposal of waste water for rural residents, particularly low-income families.

National Utility Contractors Assn., 4301 N. Fairfax Dr., #360, Arlington, VA 22203-1627;

(703) 358-9300. William G. Harley, executive director.
Membership: contractors who perform water, sewer, and other underground utility construction. Sponsors conferences; conducts surveys; compiles statistics; monitors public works legislation and regulations.

National Water Resources Assn., 3800 N. Fairfax Dr., #4, Arlington, VA 22203; (703) 524-1544. Thomas F. Donnelly, executive vice president. Fax, (703) 524-1548.
Membership: conservation and irrigation districts, municipalities, and others interested in water resources. Works for the development and maintenance of water resource projects in the western reclamation states. Represents interests of members before Congress and regulatory agencies.

Water Resources Congress, 8133 Leesburg Pike, #760, Vienna, VA 22182; (703) 525-4881. Kathleen A. Phelps, executive director. Fax, (703) 556-4449.
Membership: individuals, port authorities, barge and towing companies, private and public utilities, corporations, and others interested in development of water resources. Provides information about water resource management.

See also Natural Resources, General, Nongovernmental (p. 637)

Wildlife and Marine Mammals

Agencies:

Forest Service (Agriculture Dept.), Wildlife and Fisheries, 14th St. and Independence Ave. S.W. (mailing address: P.O. Box 96090, Washington, DC 20250); 205-1205. Robert D. Nelson, director. Fax, 205-1599.
Provides national policy direction and management for fish, endangered species, and wildlife programs on lands managed by the Forest Service.

Interior Dept., Fish, Wildlife, and Parks, Main Interior Bldg. 20240; 208-4416. George T. Frampton Jr., assistant secretary. Fax, 208-4684.
Responsible for programs associated with the development, conservation, and use of fish, wildlife, recreational, historical, and national park system resources. Coordinates marine environmental quality and biological resources programs with other federal agencies.

Interior Dept., North American Wetlands Conservation Council, 4401 N. Fairfax Dr., Arlington, VA 22203; (703) 358-1784. Robert G. Streeter, coordinator. Fax, (703) 358-2282.

Membership: government and private-sector conservation experts. Works to protect, restore, and manage wetlands and other habitats for migratory birds and other animals and to maintain migratory bird and waterfowl populations.

Justice Dept., Environment and Natural Resources, 601 Pennsylvania Ave. N.W. (mailing address: P.O. Box 7369, Ben Franklin Station, Washington, DC 20044-7369); 272-4421. James C. Kilbourne, chief, wildlife and marine resources. Fax, 724-6941.

Responsible for criminal enforcement and civil litigation under federal fish and wildlife conservation statutes, including protection of wildlife, fish, and plant resources within U.S. jurisdiction; monitors interstate and foreign commerce of these resources.

Marine Mammal Commission, 1825 Connecticut Ave. N.W. 20009; 606-5504. John R. Twiss Jr., executive director. Fax, 606-5510.

Established by Congress to ensure protection and conservation of marine mammals; conducts research and makes recommendations on federal programs that affect marine mammals.

National Oceanic and Atmospheric Administration (Commerce Dept.), Protected Resources, 1335 East-West Highway, Silver Spring, MD 20910; (301) 713-2332. William W. Fox Jr., director. Fax, (301) 713-0376.

Provides advice and guidance on the conservation and protection of marine mammals and endangered species and on the conservation, restoration, and enhancement of their habitats. Develops national guidelines and policies for relevant research programs; prepares and reviews management and recovery plans and environmental impact analyses.

U.S. Fish and Wildlife Service (Interior Dept.), Main Interior Bldg. 20240; 208-4717. Mollie H. Beattie, director. Information, 208-5634. Fax, 208-6965.

Maintains and improves wildlife resources through responsible management of migratory birds and endangered wildlife; control of population imbalances; habitat preservation; administration of the National Wildlife Refuge Sys-

tem; enforcement of federal wildlife laws; and research, including bird banding, harvest and survival rate studies, breeding, migrating and wintering surveys, and disease studies.

U.S. Fish and Wildlife Service (Interior Dept.), Fish and Wildlife Ecological Services, Main Interior Bldg., Rm. 3024 20240; 208-6846. Michael J. Spear, assistant director. Fax, 208-6916.

Monitors federal policy on fish and wildlife. Reviews all federal and federally licensed projects to determine environmental effect on fish and wildlife; administers grant-in-aid money to states for fish and wildlife programs; responsible for maintaining the endangered species list and for protecting and restoring species to healthy numbers.

U.S. Fish and Wildlife Service (Interior Dept.), Migratory Bird Conservation Commission, 4401 N. Fairfax Dr., Arlington, VA 22203; (703) 358-1713. Geoffrey L. Haskett, secretary. Fax, (703) 358-2223.

Established by the Migratory Bird Conservation Act of 1929. Decides which areas to purchase for use as migratory bird refuges.

U.S. Fish and Wildlife Service (Interior Dept.), National Biological Survey, Main Interior Bldg. 20240; 208-3733. F. Eugene Hester, deputy director.

Performs research in support of biological resource management. Monitors the status of and trends in the nation's biotic resources. Conducts research on fish and wildlife, including the effect of disease and environmental contaminants on wildlife populations. Studies endangered species to assess their status and population trends and to restore the species to viable population levels.

U.S. Fish and Wildlife Service (Interior Dept.), North American Waterfowl and Wetlands, 4401 N. Fairfax Dr., Arlington, VA 22203; (703) 358-1784. Robert G. Streeter, executive director. Fax, (703) 358-2282.

Coordinates U.S. activities with Canada to protect waterfowl habitats, restore waterfowl populations, and set research priorities under the North American Waterfowl Management Plan.

U.S. Fish and Wildlife Service (Interior Dept.), Refuges and Wildlife, Main Interior Bldg. 20240; 208-5333. David L. Olsen, assistant director. Fax, 208-3082.

Determines policy for the management of wildlife, including migratory birds; administers hunting regulations and establishes hunting seasons for migratory birds; marks and bands waterfowl; manages the National Wildlife Refuge System; enforces federal wildlife regulations for hunting and importing wildlife; manages land acquisition for wildlife refuges; and oversees the federal duck stamp program, which generates revenue for wetlands acquisition.

Congress:

House Government Operations Committee, Subcommittee on Environment, Energy, and Natural Resources, B371C RHOB 20515; 225-6427. Mike Synar, D-Okla., chairman; Sandy Harris, staff director. Fax, 225-2392.

Oversight of the U.S. Fish and Wildlife Service.

House Merchant Marine and Fisheries Committee, Subcommittee on Environment and Natural Resources, 545 Ford Bldg. (2nd and D Sts. S.W.) 20515; 226-3547. Gerry E. Studds, D-Mass., chairman; Daniel M. Ashe, staff director.

Jurisdiction over legislation on fisheries and wildlife, habitat preservation and research programs, endangered species and marine mammal protection, wildlife refuges, estuarine protection, wetlands conservation, and biological diversity. General oversight of the U.S. Fish and Wildlife Service, the Office of Environmental Policy, and the Marine Mammal Commission.

Senate Environment and Public Works Committee, Subcommittee on Clean Water, Fisheries, and Wildlife, SH-505 20510; 224-3597. Bob Graham, D-Fla., chairman; Bill Leary, counsel.

Jurisdiction over legislation on fisheries and wildlife, habitat preservation and research programs, endangered species and marine mammal protection, wildlife refuges, estuarine protection, wetlands conservation, and biological diversity; oversight of the U.S. Fish and Wildlife Service, the Office of Environmental Policy, and the Marine Mammal Commission.

Nongovernmental:

American Horse Protection Assn., 1000 29th St. N.W., #T100 20007; 965-0500. Robin C. Lohnes, executive director. Fax, 965-9621.

Membership: individuals, corporations, and foundations interested in protecting wild and domestic horses.

Animal Welfare Institute, P.O. Box 3650, Washington, DC 20007; 337-2332. Christine Stevens, president. Fax, 338-9478.

Educational group that opposes steel jaw animal traps and supports the protection of marine mammals. Interests include preservation of endangered species, reform of cruel methods of raising food animals, and humane treatment of laboratory animals.

Center for Marine Conservation, 1725 DeSales St. N.W., #500 20036; 429-5609. Roger E. McManus, president. Fax, 872-0619.

Conducts research, policy analysis, and educational and public information programs to protect marine wildlife and habitats and coastal resources. Interests include conservation of species, fisheries, and habitats.

Defenders of Wildlife, 1101 14th St. N.W., #1400 20005; 682-9400. Rodger O. Schlickeisen, president. Fax, 682-1331.

Advocacy group that provides information on endangered species, wildlife refuges, and biodiversity issues.

Ducks Unlimited, 1155 Connecticut Ave. N.W., #800 20036; 452-8824. Scott Sutherland, director, federal relations. Fax, 467-4750.

Works to restore populations of North American waterfowl and to preserve wetland habitats in Canada, the United States, and Mexico. Monitors legislation and regulations. (Headquarters in Memphis, Tenn.)

Greenpeace, 1436 U St. N.W. 20009; 462-1177. Barbara Dudley, executive director. Fax, 462-4507.

Seeks to protect the environment through research, education, and grass-roots organizing. Works to stop commercial slaughter of whales, seals, and dolphins; to preserve marine habitats; and to establish Antarctica as a world park, free of industry, military presence, and nuclear power and weaponry. Monitors legislation and regulations.

Humane Society of the United States, 2100 L St. N.W. 20037; 452-1100. John A. Hoyt, chief executive. Information, 778-6114. Fax, 778-6132.

Works for the humane treatment and protection of animals. Interests include protecting endangered wildlife and marine mammals and their habitats and ending inhumane or cruel conditions in zoos.

International Assn. of Fish and Wildlife Agencies, 444 N. Capitol St. N.W., #544 20001; 624-7890. R. Max Peterson, executive vice president. Fax, 624-7891.

Membership: federal, state, and provincial fish and wildlife management agencies in the United States, Canada, and Mexico. Encourages balanced fish and wildlife resource management.

National Fish and Wildlife Foundation, 1120 Connecticut Ave. N.W., #900 20036; 857-0166. Amos S. Eno, executive director. Fax, 857-0162.

Forges partnerships between the public and private sectors in support of conservation activities that identify the root causes of environmental problems.

National Institute for Urban Wildlife, 10921 Trotting Ridge Way, Columbia, MD 21044; (301) 596-3311. Gomer E. Jones, president.

Scientific and educational organization interested in the conservation of wildlife and wildlife habitats in urban areas. Works with developers and environmentalists to integrate wildlife into development programs; provides guidelines on urban planning issues, including urban recreational fishing, highway-wildlife relationships, natural resource management for military installations, and vegetation in urban open spaces.

National Wildlife Federation, 1400 16th St. N.W. 20036; 797-6800. Jay D. Hair, president. Fax, 797-6646.

Educational organization that promotes preservation of natural resources; provides information on wildlife.

The Nature Conservancy, 1815 N. Lynn St., Arlington, VA 22209; (703) 841-5300. John C. Sawhill, president. Fax, (703) 841-1283.

Acquires land to protect endangered species; provides information and maintains international system of natural sanctuaries; operates the Heritage Program, a cooperative effort with state governments to identify and inventory threatened and endangered plants and animals.

Society for Animal Protective Legislation, P.O. Box 3719, Washington, DC 20007; 337-2334. Christine Stevens, secretary. Fax, 338-9478.

Citizens' interest group that supports legislation to protect animals.

Wildlife Habitat Enhancement Council, 1010 Wayne Ave., #920, Silver Spring, MD 20910; (301) 588-8994. Joyce M. Kelly, president. Fax, (301) 588-4629.

Membership: corporations, conservation groups, and individuals. Supports use of underdeveloped private lands for the benefit of wildlife, fish, and plant life. Provides technical assistance and educational programs; fosters information sharing among members.

Wildlife Legislative Fund of America/Wildlife Conservation Fund of America, 1000 Connecticut Ave. N.W., #1202 20036; 446-4407. David P. Dexter, director, federal affairs. Fax, 466-8727.

Seeks to protect the right of sportsmen to hunt, fish, and trap; promotes scientific wildlife management practices. Provides educational, research, and legal services. (Headquarters in Columbus, Ohio.)

Wildlife Management Institute, 1101 14th St. N.W., #801 20005; 371-1808. Rollin D. Sparrowe, president. Fax, 408-5059.

Research and consulting organization that provides information on natural resources, particularly on wildlife management. Interests include threatened and endangered species, nongame and hunted wildlife, waterfowl, large land mammals, and predators.

The Wildlife Society, 5410 Grosvenor Lane, Bethesda, MD 20814; (301) 897-9770. Harry E. Hodgdon, executive director. Fax, (301) 530-2471.

Membership: wildlife biologists and resource management specialists. Provides information on management techniques; sponsors conferences; maintains list of job opportunities for members.

World Wildlife Fund, 1250 24th St. N.W. 20037; 293-4800. Kathryn S. Fuller, president. Fax, 293-9345.

International conservation organization that supports and conducts scientific research and conservation projects to promote biological diversity and to save endangered species and their habitats. Awards grants for habitat protection.

See also National Audubon Society (p. 622)

Key Agencies:

Commerce Dept.
Main Commerce Bldg.
14th St. and Constitution Ave. N.W. 20230
Information: 482-2000

National Aeronautics and Space Administration
300 E St. S.W.
(Mailing address: NASA Headquarters, Mail Code A, Washington, DC 20546)
Information: 358-1000

National Science Foundation
4201 Wilson Blvd., Arlington, VA 22230
Information: (703) 306-1070

Office of Science and Technology Policy
Old Executive Office Bldg. 20500
Information: 395-7347

Key Committees:

House Science, Space, and Technology Committee
2320 RHOB 20515
Phone: 225-6371

Senate Commerce, Science, and Transportation Committee
SD-508 20510
Phone: 224-5115

Key Personnel:

Commerce Dept.
Mary L. Good, under secretary, Technology Administration
Graham Mitchell, assistant secretary for technology policy
Arati Prabhakar, director, National Institute of Standards and Technology

National Aeronautics and Space Administration
Daniel Goldin, administrator

National Science Foundation
Neal Lane, director

Office of Science and Technology Policy
John H. Gibbons, director

Science
and Space

Contents:

Science

Agencies:

Energy Dept., Energy Research, 1000 Independence Ave. S.W. 20585; 586-5430. Martha A. Krebs, director. Fax, 586-4120.

Advises the secretary on the department's physical science research and energy research and development programs; the well-being and management of the nonweapons multipurpose laboratories; and education and training activities required for basic and applied research activities, including fellowships for university researchers. Manages the department's high energy physics, nuclear physics, fusion energy, basic energy sciences, and applied mathematical and computing sciences programs. Manages environmental and health-related research and development programs, including studies of energy-related pollutants and hazardous materials. Provides and operates the large-scale facilities required for research in the physical and life sciences.

National Aeronautics and Space Administration, Space Science Data Operations, Goddard Space Flight Center, Code 630, Greenbelt, MD 20771; (301) 286-7354. James L. Green, chief. Information, (301) 286-6695. Fax, (301) 286-4952.

Develops and operates systems for processing, archiving, and disseminating space physics and astrophysics data.

National Museum of American History (Smithsonian Institution), Dibner Library of the History of Science and Technology, 14th St. and Constitution Ave. N.W. 20560; 357-1568. Ellen Wells, head, special collections. Fax, 633-9102.

Collection includes major holdings in the history of science and technology dating from the fifteenth to the twentieth centuries. Extensive collections in natural history, archaeology, almanacs, physical and mathematical sciences, and scientific instrumentation. Open to the public by appointment.

National Museum of American History (Smithsonian Institution), Library, 14th St. and Constitution Ave. N.W. 20560; 357-2414. Rhoda Ratner, chief librarian. Fax, 357-4256.

Collection includes materials on the history of science and technology, with concentrations in engineering, transportation, and applied science. Maintains collection of trade catalogs and materials about expositions and world fairs. Open to the public by appointment.

National Museum of Natural History (Smithsonian Institution), 10th St. and Constitution Ave. N.W. 20560; 357-2664. Frank H. Talbot, director. Information, 786-2950. Fax, 357-4779.

Conducts research and maintains exhibitions and collections relating to the natural sciences. Collections are organized into seven research and curatorial departments: anthropology, botany, entomology, invertebrate zoology, mineral sciences, paleobiology, and vertebrate zoology.

National Science and Technology Council (Executive Office of the President), 744 Jackson Pl. N.W. 20506; 395-5101. John H. Gibbons, chairman. Fax, 395-5076.

Coordinates research and development activities and programs that involve more than one federal agency. Activities concern biotechnology; earth sciences; human subjects; international science; engineering and technology; life sciences; food, agriculture, and forestry; and research, computing, materials, and radiation policy coordination.

National Science Board (National Science Foundation), 4201 Wilson Blvd., Arlington, VA 22230; (703) 306-2000. James J. Duderstadt, chairman; Marta Cehelsky, executive officer. Information, (703) 306-1070. Fax, (703) 306-0181.

Formulates policy for the National Science Foundation; advises the president on national science policy.

National Science Foundation, 4201 Wilson Blvd., Arlington, VA 22230; (703) 306-1000. Neal Lane, director. Information, (703) 306-1070. Fax, (703) 306-0109.

Sponsors scientific and engineering research; develops and helps implement science and engineering education programs; fosters dissemination of scientific information; promotes international cooperation within the scientific community; and assists with national science policy planning.

National Science Foundation, Planning and Assessment, 4201 Wilson Blvd., #1285, Arlington, VA 22230; (703) 306-1090. Charles N. Brownstein, director. Fax, (703) 306-0109.

Assesses NSF programs and nationwide science research and education initiatives. Analyzes science funding and personnel data to predict the usefulness of proposed initiatives in advancing science education and research.

Office of Management and Budget (OMB) (Executive Office of the President), Energy and Science, New Executive Office Bldg. 20503; 395-3404. Kathleen Peroff, deputy associate director. Fax, 395-4817.

Assists and advises the OMB director in budget preparation; analyzes and evaluates programs in space and science, including the activities of the National Science Foundation and the National Aeronautics and Space Administration; coordinates OMB science, energy, and space policies and programs.

Office of Science and Technology Policy (Executive Office of the President), Old Executive Office Bldg., Rm. 424 20500; 456-7116. John H. Gibbons, director. Information, 395-7347. Press, 395-6142. Fax, 395-3261.

Serves as the president's principal adviser on science and technology policy. Assists with review of research and development budgets of federal agencies, including the departments of Energy, Commerce, and Health and Human Services; the National Science Foundation; and the National Aeronautics and Space Administration. Works with the Office of Management and Budget, other executive offices, Congress, and federal agencies to develop research programs consistent with the president's science and technology goals. Administers the Federal Coordinating Council for Science, Engineering, and Technology.

Smithsonian Institution, Central Reference and Loan Services, 10th St. and Constitution Ave. N.W., Natural History Bldg., #27 20560; 357-2139. Martin Smith, chief librarian. Fax, 786-2443. TDD, 357-2328.

Maintains collection of general reference, biographical, and interdisciplinary materials; serves as an information resource on institution libraries, a number of which have collections in scientific subjects, including horticulture, botany, science and technology, and anthropology.

Technology Administration (Commerce Dept.), Main Commerce Bldg. 20230; 482-1575. Mary L. Good, under secretary. Fax, 482-4498.

Seeks to enhance U.S. competitiveness by encouraging the development of new technologies and the conversion of technological knowledge into products and services. Oversees the National Institute of Standards and Technology and the National Technical Information Service.

Congress:

General Accounting Office, Resources, Community, and Economic Development, 441 G St. N.W., #1842 20548; 512-3200. Keith Fultz, assistant comptroller general. Fax, 512-8774.

Independent, nonpartisan agency in the legislative branch. Reviews and analyzes issues involving federal science, technology, and public policy; audits and oversees the National Science Foundation and the Office of Science and Technology Policy; serves as liaison with the National Academy of Sciences and the National Academy of Engineering; audits and evaluates the performance of the Commerce Dept. (including the National Oceanic and Atmospheric Administration and the National Institute of Standards and Technology); makes reports available to the public.

House Administration Committee, Subcommittee on Libraries and Memorials, 612 O'Neill Bldg. (300 New Jersey Ave. S.E.) 20515; 226-2307. William L. Clay, D-Mo., chairman; John F. Bass, staff director. Fax, 225-3963.

Oversight of and jurisdiction over legislation on the Smithsonian Institution.

House Appropriations Committee, Subcommittee on Commerce, Justice, State, and Judiciary, H309 CAP 20515; 225-3351. Neal Smith, D-Iowa, chairman; John Osthaus, staff assistant.

Jurisdiction over legislation to appropriate funds for the Commerce Dept., including the National Oceanic and Atmospheric Administration, the National Institute of Standards and Technology, and the National Technical Information Service.

House Appropriations Committee, Subcommittee on Interior, 3481 RHOB 20515; 225-3481. Sidney R. Yates, D-Ill., chairman; D. Neal Sigmon, staff assistant.

Jurisdiction over legislation to appropriate funds for the Smithsonian Institution and the U.S. Geological Survey.

House Appropriations Committee, Subcommittee on VA, HUD, and Independent Agencies, H143 CAP 20515; 225-3241. Louis Stokes, D-Ohio, chairman; Paul Thompson, staff assistant.

Jurisdiction over legislation to appropriate funds for the National Science Foundation and the Office of Science and Technology Policy.

House Government Operations Committee, Subcommittee on Human Resources and Intergovernmental Relations, B372 RHOB 20515; 225-2548. Edolphus Towns, D-N.Y., chairman; Ron Stroman, staff director. Fax, 225-2382.

Oversees operations of the National Science Foundation.

House Judiciary Committee, Subcommittee on Intellectual Property and Judicial Administration, 207 CHOB 20515; 225-3926. William J. Hughes, D-N.J., chairman; Hayden W. Gregory, chief counsel.

Jurisdiction over legislation concerning electronic privacy and computer security.

House Merchant Marine and Fisheries Committee, Subcommittee on Oceanography, Gulf of Mexico, and the Outer Continental Shelf, 575 Ford Bldg. (2nd and D Sts. S.W.) 20515; 226-2460. Solomon P. Ortiz, D-Texas, chairman; Sheila McCready, staff director.

Jurisdiction over legislation on the National Oceanic and Atmospheric Administration.

House Natural Resources Committee, Subcommittee on Energy and Mineral Resources, 818 O'Neill Bldg. (300 New Jersey Ave. S.E.) 20515; 225-8331. Richard H. Lehman, D-Calif., chairman; Deborah Lanzone, staff director. Fax, 225-4273.

Jurisdiction over U.S. Geological Survey legislation, except water-related programs.

House Natural Resources Committee, Subcommittee on Oversight and Investigations, 1328 LHOB 20515; 225-2761. George Miller, D-Calif., chairman; John Lawrence, staff director. Fax, 225-3554.

Jurisdiction over water-related programs of the U.S. Geological Survey.

House Science, Space, and Technology Committee, 2320 RHOB 20515; 225-6371. George E. Brown Jr., D-Calif., chairman; Robert E. Palmer, chief of staff. Fax, 226-0113.

Jurisdiction over legislation on scientific research and development; science scholarships, programs, policy, resources, employment, and exploration; and technology.

House Science, Space, and Technology Committee, Subcommittee on Science, 2319 RHOB 20515; 225-8844. Rick Boucher, D-Va., chairman; Grace L. Ostenso, staff director.

Jurisdiction over legislation on the National Science Foundation, the Office of Science and Technology Policy, and the Office of Technology Assessment; science research and development programs; math, science, and engineering education; international scientific cooperation; and nuclear research and development projects.

House Science, Space, and Technology Committee, Subcommittee on Technology, Environment, and Aviation, B374 RHOB 20515; 225-9662. Tim Valentine, D-N.C., chairman; James H. Turner, staff director.

Jurisdiction over technology policy (including technology transfer), cooperative research and development, patent and intellectual property policy, biotechnology, and recombinant DNA research. Legislative jurisdiction over the National Institute of Standards and Technology, the Technology Administration, the National Technical Information Service, and the Office of Technology Assessment.

Library of Congress, Science and Technology, 10 1st St. S.E. 20540; 707-5664. John F. Price, acting chief. Fax, 707-1925. Science reading room, 707-5639. Technical reports, 707-5655.

Offers reference service by telephone, by correspondence, and in person. Maintains a collection of more than three million technical reports.

Office of Technology Assessment, 600 Pennsylvania Ave. S.E. (mailing address: U.S. Congress, Washington, DC 20510); 224-3695. Roger Herdman, director; Sen. Edward M. Kennedy, D-Mass., chairman; Rep. Don Sundquist, R-Tenn., vice chairman, Technology Assessment

Board. Information, 224-9241. Press, 228-6204. Fax, 228-6218. Publications, 224-8996.

Provides Congress with information and analyses on the political, physical, economic, and social effects of technological applications.

Senate Appropriations Committee, Subcommittee on Commerce, Justice, State, and Judiciary, S146A CAP 20510; 224-7277. Ernest F. Hollings, D-S.C., chairman; Scott B. Gudes, clerk.

Jurisdiction over legislation to appropriate funds for the Commerce Dept., including the National Oceanic and Atmospheric Administration, National Institute of Standards and Technology, and the National Technical Information Service.

Senate Appropriations Committee, Subcommittee on Interior, SD-127 20510; 224-7233. Robert C. Byrd, D-W.Va., chairman; Sue E. Masica, clerk.

Jurisdiction over legislation to appropriate funds for the Smithsonian Institution and the U.S. Geological Survey.

Senate Appropriations Committee, Subcommittee on VA, HUD, and Independent Agencies, SD-142 20510; 224-7211. Barbara A. Mikulski, D-Md., chair; Kevin F. Kelly, clerk

Jurisdiction over legislation to appropriate funds for the National Science Foundation, the Office of Science and Technology Policy, and the National Institute of Building Science.

Senate Commerce, Science, and Transportation Committee, SD-508 20510; 224-5115. Ernest F. Hollings, D-S.C., chairman; Kevin Curtin, chief counsel and staff director.

Jurisdiction over legislation on the Commerce Dept. and its scientific activities, including the National Oceanic and Atmospheric Administration and all ocean-related matters, and science aspects of the Office of Science and Technology Policy.

Senate Commerce, Science, and Transportation Committee, Subcommittee on Science, Technology, and Space, SH-427 (mailing address: SD-508, Washington, DC 20510); 224-9360. John D. Rockefeller IV, D-W.Va., chairman; Patrick H. Windham, senior professional staff member.

Oversight of the National Institute of Standards and Technology and other departments and

agencies with an emphasis on science. Jurisdiction over scientific research and development; science fellowships, scholarships, grants, programs, policy, resources, employment, and exploration; and technology. Jurisdiction over international scientific cooperation, technology transfer, and cooperative research and development (including global change and the space station); resolutions of joint cooperation with foreign governments on science and technology; and international intellectual property rights.

Senate Energy and Natural Resources Committee, Subcommittee on Mineral Resources Development and Production, SD-362 20510; 224-7568. Daniel K. Akaka, D-Hawaii, chairman; Lisa Vehmas, counsel.

Jurisdiction over legislation on the U.S. Geological Survey.

Senate Judiciary Committee, Subcommittee on Technology and the Law, SH-815 20510; 224-3406. Patrick J. Leahy, D-Vt., chairman; Bruce A. Cohen, chief counsel.

Jurisdiction over legislation concerning electronic privacy, computer security, and technology.

Senate Labor and Human Resources Committee, Subcommittee on Education, Arts, and Humanities, SD-648 20510; 224-7666. Claiborne Pell, D-R.I., chairman; David V. Evans, staff director.

Oversees and has jurisdiction over legislation on the National Science Foundation.

Senate Rules and Administration Committee, SR-305 20510; 224-6352. Wendell H. Ford, D-Ky., chairman; James O. King, staff director.

Jurisdiction over legislation concerning the Smithsonian Institution and the Botanic Garden.

See also Congressional Biotechnology Caucus (p. 756); Technology Assessment Board (p. 757)

Nongovernmental:

American Assn. for Laboratory Accreditation, 656 Quince Orchard Rd., #620, Gaithersburg, MD 20878; (301) 670-1377. John W. Locke, president. Fax, (301) 869-1495.

Accredits and monitors laboratories that test construction materials and perform biological, chemical, electrical, geotechnical, environmental, mechanical, metals and metal fasteners, metrological, asbestos, radon, and thermal testing. Certifies laboratory reference materials.

American Assn. for the Advancement of Science, 1333 H St. N.W. 20005; 326-6640. Richard S. Nicholson, executive officer. Information, 326-6400. Fax, 371-9526.

Membership: scientists, affiliated scientific organizations, and individuals interested in science. Fosters scientific education; monitors and seeks to influence public policy and public understanding of science and technology; encourages scientific literacy among minorities and women. Sponsors national and international symposia, workshops, and meetings; publishes *Science* magazine.

American Assn. for the Advancement of Science, Scientific Freedom, Responsibility and Law Program, 1333 H St. N.W., #1002 20005; 326-6793. Mark S. Frankel, director. Press, 326-6440. Library, 326-6610. Fax, 289-4950. TDD, 326-6630.

Focuses on professional ethics and law in science and engineering and on the social implications of science and technology. Collaborates with other professional groups on these activities.

American Council of Independent Laboratories, 1629 K St. N.W. 20006; 887-5872. Joseph F. O'Neil, executive director. Fax, 887-0021. Laboratory Referral Service, 887-5873.

Membership: independent commercial laboratories. Promotes professional and ethical business practices in providing analysis, testing, and research in engineering, microbiology, analytical chemistry, life sciences, and environmental geosciences.

Assn. for Women in Science, 1522 K St. N.W. 20005; 408-0742. Catherine Didion, executive director. Fax, 408-8321.

Promotes equal opportunity for women in scientific professions; provides career and funding information.

Council of Scientific Society Presidents, 1155 16th St. N.W. 20036; 872-4452. Martin Apple, executive director. Fax, 872-4079.

Membership: presidents, presidents-elect, and immediate past presidents of scientific societies. Supports science and science education. Serves as a forum for discussion of current scientific

issues, including merit review of federally supported science projects, minority participation in scientific careers, intellectual property rights, ethics in science, and national science policy.

Federation of American Scientists, 307 Massachusetts Ave. N.E. 20002; 546-3300. Jeremy J. Stone, president. Fax, 675-1010.

Conducts studies and monitors legislation on issues and problems related to science and technology, especially U.S. nuclear arms policy, energy, arms transfer, and civil aerospace issues.

George C. Marshall Institute, 1730 M St. N.W., #502 20036; 296-9655. Jeffrey Salmon, executive director. Fax, 296-9714.

Analyzes the technical and scientific aspects of public policy issues; produces publications on global warming, space, national security, and technology policy.

Government-University-Industry Research Roundtable, 2101 Constitution Ave. N.W. 20418; 334-3486. Don I. Phillips, executive director. Fax, 334-1505.

Forum sponsored by the National Academy of Sciences, National Academy of Engineering, and Institute of Medicine. Provides scientists, engineers, and members of government, academia, and industry with an opportunity to discuss ways of improving the infrastructure for science and technology research.

Institute for Alternative Futures, 108 N. Alfred St., Alexandria, VA 22314; (703) 684-5880. Clem Bezold, executive director. Fax, (703) 684-0640.

Research and educational organization that explores the implications of trends and emerging issues through seminars and publications. Works with state and local governments, Congress, and associations. Interests include pharmaceutical research and development, mental health, telecommunications, artificial intelligence, and literacy.

National Academy of Sciences, 2101 Constitution Ave. N.W. 20418; 334-2000. Bruce Alberts, president. Information, 334-2138. Library, 334-2125. Fax, 334-1684. Publications, (800) 624-6242; in Washington, D.C., 334-3313.

Congressionally chartered independent organization of scholars in scientific, engineering, and medical research that advises the federal government on questions of science and technology. Interests include all branches of science and technology. Library open to the public by appointment. (The National Research Council is the operating arm of the National Academy of Sciences, the National Academy of Engineering, and the Institute of Medicine.)

National Geographic Society, Committee for Research and Exploration, 1145 17th St. N.W. 20036-4688; 857-7439. Steven Stettes, secretary.

Sponsors basic research grants in the sciences, including anthropology, archaeology, astronomy, biology, botany, ecology, physical and human geography, geology, oceanography, paleontology, and zoology.

Scientific Apparatus Makers Assn., 225 Reinikers Lane, #625, Alexandria, VA 22314; (703) 836-1360. Cynthia A. Esher, president. Fax, (703) 836-6644.

Membership: manufacturers and distributors of high technology scientific and industrial instruments, laboratory apparatus, and process controls. Works to increase worldwide demand for products.

See also Art, Science, and Technology Institute (p. 117)

Science: Biology and Life Sciences

Biology

Agencies:

Armed Forces Radiobiology Research Institute, National Naval Medical Center, 8901 Wisconsin Ave., Bethesda, MD 20889; (301) 295-1210. Capt. Robert L. Bumgarner (USN), director. Fax, (301) 295-4967.

Serves as the principal ionizing radiation radiobiology research laboratory under the jurisdiction of the Defense Nuclear Agency. Library open to the public.

National Aeronautics and Space Administration (NASA), Life Sciences, 2 Independence Square S.W. 20546; 358-2530. Joan Vernikos, director. Fax, 358-4168.

Conducts space medicine and life sciences research for NASA.

National Museum of Natural History (Smithsonian Institution), Library, 10th St. and Constitution Ave. N.W., #51 20560; 357-1496. Ann Juneau, chief librarian. Fax, 357-1896.

Maintains reference collections covering systematic biology and taxonomy, invertebrate biology and vertebrate zoology, paleobiology, botany, general geology and mineral sciences, oceanography, entomology, ecology, evolution, limnology, anthropology, and ethnology; permits on-site use of the collections. Open to the public by appointment; makes interlibrary loans.

National Oceanic and Atmospheric Administration (Commerce Dept.), National Marine Fisheries Service, 1335 East-West Highway, Silver Spring, MD 20910; (301) 713-2239. Rolland A. Schmitten, assistant administrator. Information, (301) 713-2370. Fax, (301) 713-2258.

Conducts research and collects data on marine ecology and biology; collects, analyzes, and provides information through the Marine Resources Monitoring, Assessment, and Prediction Program. Administers the Magnuson Fishery Conservation and Management Act and marine mammals and endangered species protection programs. Works with the Army Corps of Engineers on research into habitat restoration and conservation.

National Science Foundation, Biological Sciences, 4201 Wilson Blvd., #605, Arlington, VA 22230; (703) 306-1400. Mary E. Clutter, assistant director. Information, (703) 306-1234. Fax, (703) 306-0343.

Provides grants for research in the cellular and molecular biosciences, environmental biology, integrative biology and neuroscience, and biological instrumentation and resources.

Navy Dept. (Defense Dept.), Naval Medical Research Institute, 8901 Wisconsin Ave., Bethesda, MD 20889-5607; (301) 295-0021. Capt. Robert G. Walter, commanding officer. Fax, (301) 295-2720.

Performs basic and applied biomedical research in areas of military importance, including infectious diseases, hyperbaric medicine, wound repair enhancement, environmental stress, and immunobiology. Provides support to field laboratories and naval hospitals.

Office of Science and Technology Policy (Executive Office of the President), Science, Old Executive Office Bldg. 20500; 395-5130. M. R. C. Greenwood, associate director. Fax, 395-5164.

Analyzes policies and advises the president on life science issues; coordinates executive office and federal agency actions related to these issues. Evaluates the effectiveness of life science programs.

Smithsonian Environmental Research Center (Smithsonian Institution), P.O. Box 28, Contees Wharf Rd., Edgewater, MD 21037; (410) 798-4424. David L. Correll, director. Fax, (301) 261-7954.

Performs laboratory and field research that measures physical, chemical, and biological interactions to determine the mechanisms of environmental responses to humans' use of air, land, and water. Evaluates properties of the environment that affect the functions of living organisms. Maintains research laboratories, public education program, facilities for controlled environments, and estuarine and terrestrial lands.

Congress:

See Science, Congress (p. 663)

Nongovernmental:

American Institute of Biological Sciences, 730 11th St. N.W. 20001-4521; 628-1500. Clifford J. Gabriel, executive director. Toll-free, (800) 992-2427. Fax, 628-1509.

Membership: biologists, students, biological associations, industrial research laboratories, and others interested in biology. Promotes interdisciplinary cooperation among members engaged in biological research and education; conducts educational programs for members; sponsors Congressional Science Fellowship; administers projects supported by government grants; monitors legislation and regulations.

American Society for Biochemistry and Molecular Biology, 9650 Rockville Pike, Bethesda, MD 20814; (301) 530-7145. Charles C. Hancock, executive officer. Fax, (301) 571-1824.

Professional society of biological chemists; membership by election. Monitors legislation and regulations.

The American Society for Cell Biology, 9650 Rockville Pike, Bethesda, MD 20814-3992; (301) 530-7153. Elizabeth Marincola, executive director. Fax, (301) 530-7139. CompuServe, 71031,306; Internet, 71031.306@compuserve.com.

Membership: scientists who have education or research experience in cell biology or an allied

field. Organizes courses, workshops, and symposia on advances in cell biology. Monitors legislation and regulation.

American Society for Microbiology, 1325 Massachusetts Ave. N.W. 20005; 942-9265. Michael I. Goldberg, executive director. Fax, 942-9333.

Membership: microbiologists. Encourages education, training, scientific investigation, and application of research results in microbiology and related subjects.

American Type Culture Collection, 12301 Parklawn Dr., Rockville, MD 20852; (301) 881-2600. Raymond H. Cypess, director. Fax, (301) 770-2587.

Independent organization devoted to preserving cultures of microorganisms, viruses, and plant and animal cell lines; distributes them for study among scientists. Conducts workshops and training courses on using these materials.

The Biometric Society, 1429 Duke St., #401, Alexandria, VA 22314; (703) 836-8311.

Membership: biologists, mathematicians, statisticians, and individuals interested in the applications of biometry. Promotes advancement of quantitative biological science through the development of theories and the application of mathematical and statistical techniques. (Biometry is the branch of biology that examines data statistically and by quantitative analysis.)

Biophysical Society, 9650 Rockville Pike, Bethesda, MD 20814; (301) 530-7114. Emily M. Gray, executive director. Fax, (301) 530-7133.

Membership: scientists, professors, and researchers engaged in biophysics or related fields. Encourages development and dissemination of knowledge in biophysics.

Carnegie Institution of Washington, 1530 P St. N.W. 20005; 387-6400. Maxine F. Singer, president. Fax, 387-8092.

Conducts research in the physical and biological sciences at the following centers: the observatories of the Carnegie Institution with headquarters in Pasadena, Calif.; Geophysical Laboratory and Dept. of Terrestrial Magnetism in Washington, D.C.; Dept. of Plant Biology in Stanford, Calif.; and Dept. of Embryology in Baltimore, Md. Refers specific inquiries to appropriate department. Library open to the public by appointment.

Federation of American Societies for Experimental Biology, 9650 Rockville Pike, Bethesda, MD 20814; (301) 530-7090. Michael J. Jackson, executive director. Information, (301) 530-7075. Fax, (301) 530-7049.

Federation of nine scientific and educational groups: American Physiological Society, American Society for Biochemistry and Molecular Biology, American Society for Pharmacology and Experimental Therapeutics, American Assn. of Pathologists, American Institute of Nutrition, American Assn. of Immunologists, American Society for Cell Biology, Biophysical Society, and American Assn. of Anatomists. Serves as support group for member societies.

See also American Assn. for the Advancement of Science (p. 666); Howard Hughes Medical Institute (p. 363)

Biotechnology

See also Agriculture: Education and Research (p. 602); Health Research, Genetics (p. 371)

Agencies:

Agriculture Dept., Grants and Program Systems, 901 D St. S.W. 20250; 401-1761. William D. Carlson, associate administrator. Fax, 401-1804.

Administers competitive research grants for biotechnology in the agricultural field. Oversees research in biotechnology.

Environmental Protection Agency, Prevention, Pesticides, and Toxic Substances, 401 M St. S.W. 20460; 260-6900. Elizabeth Milewski, special assistant, biotechnology. Fax, 260-0949.

Conducts reviews of bacterial byproducts of biotechnology and selected industrial chemicals produced by biotechnology.

National Institute of Standards and Technology (Commerce Dept.), Chemical Science and Technology Laboratory, Route I-270 and Quince Orchard Rd., Gaithersburg, MD 20899; (301) 975-3145. Hratch G. Semerjian, director. Fax, (301) 975-3845.

Conducts basic and applied research in biotechnology.

National Institutes of Health (Health and Human Services Dept.), Recombinant DNA Activities, 9000 Rockville Pike, Bldg. 31, Rm. 4B11, Bethesda, MD 20892; (301) 496-9838. Dr. Nelson A. Wivel, director. Fax, (301) 496-9839.

Reviews special requests submitted to NIH involving recombinant DNA technology and implements policies regarding this research. Assists in and develops NIH biotechnology policy.

National Library of Medicine (Health and Human Services Dept.), National Center for Biotechnology Information, 8600 Rockville Pike, Bethesda, MD 20894; (301) 496-2475. Dr. David J. Lipman, director. Fax, (301) 480-9241.

Creates automated systems for storing and analyzing knowledge of molecular biology and genetics. Develops new information technologies to aid in understanding the molecular processes that control human health and disease. Conducts basic research in computational molecular biology.

National Science Foundation, Biological Sciences, 4201 Wilson Blvd., #605, Arlington, VA 22230; (703) 306-1400. Mary E. Clutter, assistant director. Information, (703) 306-1234. Fax, (703) 306-0343.

Provides grants for research in the cellular and molecular biosciences, environmental biology, integrative biology and neuroscience, and biological instrumentation and resources.

Office of Science and Technology Policy (Executive Office of the President), Biotechnology Research Subcommittee of the Committee of Life Sciences and Health, N.I.S.T. Bldg. 222, #A345, Gaithersburg, MD 20899; (301) 975-2627. Dr. Lura Powell, chair. Fax, (301) 330-3447.

Serves as a forum for addressing biotechnology research issues, sharing information, identifying gaps in scientific knowledge, and developing consensus among concerned federal agencies. Facilitates continuing cooperation among federal agencies on topical issues.

Congress:

See Science, Congress (p. 663)

Nongovernmental:

Biotechnology Industry Organization, 1625 K St. N.W., #1100 20006; 857-0244. Carl Feldbaum, president. Fax, 857-0237.

Membership: industrial companies engaged in biotechnology. Monitors government activities at all levels; promotes educational activities; conducts workshops.

Foundation on Economic Trends, 1130 17th St. N.W., #630 20036; 466-2823. Jeremy Rifkin, president. Fax, 429-9602.

Examines the environmental, economic, and social consequences of genetic engineering. Pursues public policy initiatives.

Friends of the Earth, 1025 Vermont Ave. N.W., #300 20005; 783-7400. Jack Doyle, senior analyst, technology and corporate policy. Fax, 783-0444.

Monitors legislation and regulations on issues related to seed industry consolidation and patenting laws and on business developments in agricultural biotechnology and their effect on farming, food production, genetic resources, and the environment.

Kennedy Institute of Ethics, Georgetown University, 1437 37th St. N.W. 20057; 687-8099. Dr. Robert M. Veatch, director. Fax, 687-6770. Library, (800) 633-3849; in Washington, D.C., 687-3885.

Sponsors research on medical ethics. Interests include legal and ethical definitions of death, allocation of scarce health resources, and recombinant DNA and human gene therapy. Supplies National Library of Medicine (National Institutes of Health) with online database on bioethics; publishes annual bibliography. Library open to the public.

Botany and Horticulture

Agencies:

National Arboretum (Agriculture Dept.), 3501 New York Ave. N.E. 20002; 475-4829. Thomas S. Elias, director. Library, 475-4828. Fax, 475-5252.

Maintains public display of plants on 444 acres; provides information and makes referrals concerning cultivated plants (exclusive of field crops and fruits); conducts plant breeding and research; maintains herbarium. Library open to the public on Tuesdays and Thursdays.

National Museum of Natural History (Smithsonian Institution), Botany, 10th St. and Constitution Ave. N.W. 20560; 357-2534. Warren L. Wagner, chairman. Fax, 786-2563.

Conducts botanical research; furnishes information on the identification, distribution, and local names of flowering plants; studies threatened and endangered plant species.

National Museum of Natural History (Smithsonian Institution), Botany Library, 10th St. and Constitution Ave. N.W. 20560; 357-2715. Ruth F. Schallert, librarian. Fax, 357-1896.

Collections include taxonomic botany, plant morphology, general botany, history of botany, grasses, and algae. Permits on-site use of collections (appointment preferred); makes interlibrary loans.

Smithsonian Institution, Horticulture Library, Arts and Industries Bldg., 900 Jefferson Dr. S.W. 20560; 357-1544. Susan Gurney, chief librarian. Fax, 786-2026.

Collection includes books, periodicals, trade catalogs, and videotapes on horticulture, garden history, and landscape design. Specializes in American gardens and gardening of the late nineteenth and early twentieth centuries. Open to the public by appointment.

Congress:

U.S. Botanic Garden, 1st St. and Maryland Ave. S.W. 20024; 225-8333. Jeffrey P. Cooper-Smith, executive director. Fax, 225-1561. Flower and plant information, 225-7099 (recording).

Collects, cultivates, and grows various plants for public display and study; conservatory open to the public; identifies botanic specimens and furnishes information on proper growing methods. Conducts horticultural classes and tours. Sponsors four seasonal flower shows annually.

See also Science, Congress (p. 663)

Nongovernmental:

American Assn. of Nurserymen, 1250 Eye St. N.W., #500 20005; 789-2900. Robert J. Dolibois, executive vice president. Fax, 789-1893.

Membership: wholesale growers, garden center retailers, landscape firms, and suppliers to the horticultural community. Monitors legislation and regulations on agricultural, environmental, and small-business issues; conducts educational seminars on business management for members. (Affiliated with the National Assn. of Plant Patent Owners.)

American Horticultural Society, 7931 E. Boulevard Dr., Alexandria, VA 22308; (703) 768-5700. H. Marc Cathey, president. Toll-free, (800) 777-7931. Fax, (703) 765-6032.

Promotes the expansion of horticulture in the United States through educational programs for amateur and professional horticulturists. Acts as a horticultural clearinghouse; maintains the Gardener's Information Service.

American Society for Horticultural Science, 113 S. West St., #400, Alexandria, VA 22314-2824; (703) 836-4606. Christine A. Radiske, executive director. Fax, (703) 836-2024.

Membership: educators, government workers, firms, associations, and individuals interested in horticultural science. Promotes and encourages interest in scientific research and education in horticulture.

American Society of Plant Physiologists, 15501 Monona Dr., Rockville, MD 20855; (301) 251-0560. Kenneth M. Beam, executive director. Fax, (301) 279-2996.

Membership: plant physiologists, plant biochemists, and molecular biologists. Publishes journals; provides placement service for members.

National Assn. of Plant Patent Owners, 1250 Eye St. N.W., #500 20005; 789-2900. Craig Regelbrugge, administrator. Fax, 789-1893.

Membership: owners of patents on newly propagated horticultural plants. Informs members of plant patents issued, provisions of patent laws, and changes in practice. Promotes the development, protection, production, and distribution of new varieties of horticultural plants. Works with international organizations of plant breeders on matters of common interest. (Affiliated with the American Assn. of Nurserymen.)

Society of American Florists, 1601 Duke St., Alexandria, VA 22314; (703) 836-8700. Drew Gruenburg, senior vice president. Fax, (703) 836-8705.

Membership: growers, wholesalers, and retailers in the floriculture and ornamental horticulture industries. Interests include labor, pesticides, the environment, international trade, and toxicity of plants. Mediates industry problems.

See also National Geographic Society (p. 667)

Zoology

Agencies:

National Museum of Natural History (Smithsonian Institution), Entomology, 10th St. and

Constitution Ave. N.W. 20560; 357-2078. Jonathan A. Coddington, chairman. Library, 357-2354. Fax, 786-2894.

Conducts research in entomology. Maintains the national collection of insects; lends insect specimens to specialists for research and classification. Library open to the public by appointment.

National Museum of Natural History (Smithsonian Institution), Invertebrate Zoology, 10th St. and Constitution Ave. N.W. 20560; 357-2030. Brian Kensley, chairman. Fax, 357-3043.

Conducts research on the identity, morphology, histology, life history, distribution, classification, and ecology of marine, terrestrial, and fresh water invertebrate animals (except insects); maintains the national collection of invertebrate animals; aids exhibit and educational programs; conducts pre- and postdoctoral fellowship programs; provides facilities for visiting scientists in the profession.

National Museum of Natural History (Smithsonian Institution), Vertebrate Zoology, 10th St. and Constitution Ave. N.W. 20560; 357-2740. G. David Johnson, chairman. Fax, 357-4779.

Conducts research on the systematics, ecology, and behavior of mammals, birds, reptiles, amphibians, and fish; maintains the national collection of specimens.

National Zoological Park (Smithsonian Institution), 3001 Connecticut Ave. N.W. 20008; 673-4721. Michael H. Robinson, director. Information, 673-4821. Library, 673-4771. Fax, 673-4607. TDD, 673-4823. Recorded information, 673-4800.

Maintains a public zoo for exhibiting animals. Conducts research on animal behavior, ecology, nutrition, reproductive physiology, pathology, and veterinary medicine; operates an annex near Front Royal, Va., for the long-term propagation and study of endangered species. Houses a unit of the Smithsonian Institution library with volumes in zoology, biology, ecology, animal behavior, and veterinary medicine; makes interlibrary loans. Library open to qualified researchers by appointment.

Congress:

See Science, Congress (p. 663)

Nongovernmental:

American Assn. of Zoological Parks and Aquariums, 7970-D Old Georgetown Rd., Bethesda, MD 20814-2493; (301) 907-7777. Kris Vehrs, director, government affairs. Fax, (301) 907-2980.

Membership: interested individuals and professionally run zoos and aquariums in North America. Administers professional accreditation program; participates in conservation, education, and research activities. (Headquarters in Wheeling, W.Va.)

Entomological Society of America, 9301 Annapolis Rd., Lanham, MD 20706; (301) 731-4535. W. Darryl Hansen, executive director. Fax, (301) 731-4538.

Scientific research organization that promotes the science of entomology and the interests of professionals in the field. Advises on crop protection, food chain, and individual and urban health matters dealing with insect pests.

See also National Geographic Society (p. 667)

Science: Data and Statistics

Agencies:

National Aeronautics and Space Administration, National Space Science Data Center, Goddard Space Flight Center, Greenbelt Rd., Greenbelt, MD (mailing address: Code 633, Greenbelt, MD 20771); (301) 286-7355. Joseph H. King, head. Fax, (301) 286-1771.

Develops and operates information and data systems; maintains digital data and film archives and an online data catalog system. (Mail data requests c/o National Space Science Data Center, Code 633.4/Request Coordination Office, (301) 286-6695.)

National Aeronautics and Space Administration, Space Science Data Operations, Goddard Space Flight Center, Code 630, Greenbelt, MD 20771; (301) 286-7354. James L. Green, chief. Information, (301) 286-6695. Fax, (301) 286-4952.

Develops and operates systems for processing, archiving, and disseminating space physics and astrophysics data.

National Institute of Standards and Technology (Commerce Dept.), Information Services, Route I-270 and Quince Orchard Rd., Gaithersburg, MD 20899; (301) 975-2786. Paul Vassallo, director. Fax, (301) 869-8071. Publications, (301) 975-3058. Reference desk, (301) 975-3052.

Conducts publications program for the institute and maintains a research information center, which includes material on engineering, chemistry, physics, mathematics, and the materials and computer sciences.

National Institute of Standards and Technology (Commerce Dept.), Measurement Services, Route I-270 and Quince Orchard Rd., Gaithersburg, MD (mailing address: B354 Physics Bldg., Gaithersburg, MD 20899); (301) 975-3602. Stanley D. Rasberry, director. Fax, (301) 948-3825.

Disseminates physical, chemical, and engineering measurement standards and provides services to ensure accurate and compatible measurements, specifications, and codes on a national and international scale.

National Institute of Standards and Technology (Commerce Dept.), Standard Reference Data, Route I-270 and Quince Orchard Rd., Gaithersburg, MD (mailing address: A323 Physics Bldg., Gaithersburg, MD 20899); (301) 975-2200. Malcolm W. Chase, chief. Fax, (301) 926-0416. Information and publications, (301) 975-2208.

Collects and disseminates critically evaluated physical, chemical, and materials properties data in the physical sciences and engineering for use by industry, government, and academic laboratories. Develops databases in a variety of formats, including disk, CD-ROM, and magnetic tape.

National Institute of Standards and Technology (Commerce Dept.), Statistical Engineering, Route I-270 and Quince Orchard Rd., Gaithersburg, MD 20899; (301) 975-2839. Robert Lundegard, chief. Fax, (301) 990-4127.

Promotes within industry and government the use of effective statistical techniques for planning analysis of experiments in the physical sciences; interprets experiments and data collection programs.

National Oceanic and Atmospheric Administration (NOAA) (Commerce Dept.), Library and Information Services, 1315 East-West Highway, 2nd Floor, Silver Spring, MD 20910; (301) 713-2607. Carol Watts, director. Fax, (301) 713-4598. Reference service, (301) 713-2660.

Collection includes reports, journals, monographs, and microforms on atmospheric and oceanic science. Maintains bibliographic database of other NOAA libraries, an online service, and reference materials on CD-ROM. Makes interlibrary loans; open to the public.

National Oceanic and Atmospheric Administration (Commerce Dept.), National Environmental Satellite, Data, and Information Service, 4401 Suitland Rd., #2069, Suitland, MD (mailing address: Federal Bldg. 4, #2069, Washington, DC 20233); (301) 763-7190. Robert S. Winokur, assistant administrator. Information, (301) 763-2560. Fax, (301) 763-4011.

Acquires and disseminates global environmental (marine, atmospheric, solid earth, and solar-terrestrial) data. Operates the following data facilities: National Climatic Data Center, Asheville, N.C.; National Geophysical Data Center, Boulder, Colo.; National Oceanographic Data Center, Washington, D.C. Maintains comprehensive data and information referral service.

National Oceanic and Atmospheric Administration (Commerce Dept.), National Oceanographic Data Center, 1825 Connecticut Ave. N.W. 20235; 606-4594. Bruce C. Douglas, director. Fax, 606-4586. Information and requests, 606-4549.

Offers a wide range of oceanographic data on magnetic tape, disk, and hard copy; provides research scientists with data processing services; prepares statistical summaries and graphical data products. (Additional fee charged for requests requiring more than minimal work.)

National Science Foundation, Science Resources Studies, 4201 Wilson Blvd., #965, Arlington, VA 22230; (703) 306-1780. Kenneth Brown, director. Fax, (703) 306-0510.

Projects national scientific and technical resources and requirements.

National Technical Information Service (Commerce Dept.), 5285 Port Royal Rd., Springfield, VA 22161; (703) 487-4636. Donald R. Johnson, director. Fax, (703) 487-4098. Sales center, (703) 487-4650; rush orders, (800) 336-4700.

Distribution center that sells to the public foreign and U.S. government-funded research and development reports and other technical analyses prepared by federal agencies, their contractors, or grantees. Offers microfiche and computerized bibliographic search services. Online database available through commercial vendors

and in machine-readable form through lease agreement.

U.S. Geological Survey (Interior Dept.), National Mapping Division, 12201 Sunrise Valley Dr., Reston, VA 22092; (703) 648-5748. Allen H. Watkins, chief. Fax, (703) 648-5792. Information and data services, (703) 648-5780.

Provides government agencies and the public with geographic and cartographic information, maps, and technical assistance; conducts research; develops and maintains a digital geographic/cartographic database and assists users in applying spatial data.

Congress:

General Accounting Office (GAO), Document Handling and Information Services Facility, 700 4th St. N.W. (mailing address: P.O. Box 6015, Gaithersburg, MD 20877); 512-4448. Keith Bonney, staff contact. Fax, (301) 258-4066. Publications and orders, 512-6000.

Provides GAO technical publications and information about GAO publications on request

Library of Congress, Science and Technology, 10 1st St. S.E. 20540; 707-5664. John F. Price, acting chief. Fax, 707-1925. Science reading room, 707-5639. Technical reports, 707-5655.

Offers reference service by telephone, by correspondence, and in person. Maintains a collection of more than three million technical reports.

See also Science, Congress (p. 663)

Nongovernmental:

American Statistical Assn., 1429 Duke St., Alexandria, VA 22314; (703) 684-1221. Barbara A. Bailar, executive director. Fax, (703) 684-2037.

Membership: individuals interested in statistics and related quantitative fields. Advises government agencies on statistics and methodology in agency research; promotes development of statistical techniques for use in business, industry, finance, government, agriculture, and science.

Commission on Professionals in Science and Technology, 1500 Massachusetts Ave. N.W. 20005; 223-6995. Betty M. Vetter, executive director.

Membership: scientific societies, corporations, and individuals. Analyzes and publishes data on scientific and engineering human resources in the United States.

Science: Education

Agencies:

Education Dept., Formula Grants, 400 Maryland Ave. S.W. 20202; 401-0841. Doris Crudup, chief, mathematics and science. Fax, 401-2275.

Implements the state entitlement section of the Dwight D. Eisenhower Mathematics and Science Program, which funds programs for improving teacher education in mathematics and science, and programs for improving instruction for the underrepresented and underserved, including women, minorities, people with disabilities, individuals with limited English proficiency, and migrants.

Education Dept., Higher Education, 7th and D Sts. S.W. 20202-5251; 708-4662. Argelia Velez-Rodriguez, senior officer, minority science and engineering improvement. Fax, 708-8141.

Funds programs to improve science and engineering education in predominantly minority colleges and universities; promotes increased participation by minority students and faculty in science and engineering fields; encourages minority schools and universities to apply for grants that will generate precollege student interest in science.

National Oceanic and Atmospheric Administration (Commerce Dept.), National Sea Grant College Program, 1335 East-West Highway, Silver Spring, MD 20910; (301) 713-2448. David B. Duane, director. Fax, (301) 713-0799.

Provides grants, primarily to colleges and universities, for marine resource development; sponsors undergraduate and graduate education and the training of technicians at the college level.

National Science Foundation, Education and Human Resources, 4201 Wilson Blvd., #805, Arlington, VA 22230; (703) 306-1600. Luther S. Williams, assistant director. Fax, (703) 306-0399.

Develops and supports programs to strengthen science and math education. Provides fellowships and grants for graduate research and teacher education, instructional materials, and studies on the quality of existing science and math programs.

National Science Foundation, Science Resources Studies, 4201 Wilson Blvd., #965, Arlington, VA 22230; (703) 306-1780. Kenneth Brown, director. Fax, (703) 306-0510.

Develops and analyzes national statistics and models on training, use, and characteristics of scientists, engineers, and technicians.

Congress:

See *Science, Congress (p. 663)*

Nongovernmental:

American Assn. for the Advancement of Science, Education and Human Resources Programs, 1333 H St. N.W., #1126 20005; 326-6670. Shirley M. Malcom, head. Fax, 371-9849.

Membership: scientists, scientific organizations, and others interested in science and technology education. Works to increase and provide information on the status of women, minorities, and people with disabilities in the sciences and engineering; focuses on expanding science education opportunities for women, minorities, and people with disabilities.

American Assn. of Physics Teachers, 1 Physics Ellipse, College Park, MD 20740; (301) 209-3300. Bernard V. Khoury, executive officer. Fax, (301) 209-0845.

Membership: physics teachers and others interested in physics education. Seeks to advance the institutional and cultural role of physics education. Sponsors seminars and conferences; provides educational information and materials. (Affiliated with the American Institute of Physics.)

American Society for Engineering Education, 1818 N St. N.W., #600 20036; 331-3500. Frank L. Huband, executive director. Press, 331-3537. Fax, 265-8504.

Membership: engineering faculty and administrators, professional engineers, government agencies, and engineering colleges, corporations, and professional societies. Conducts research, conferences, and workshops on engineering education. Monitors legislation and regulations.

Assn. of Science-Technology Centers, 1025 Vermont Ave. N.W., #500 20005; 783-7200. Ellen Griffee, director, government relations. Fax, 783-7207.

Membership: science centers and science museums. Works to further public understanding and appreciation of science and technology. Provides traveling exhibition service, produces publications, and holds conferences. Serves as an information clearinghouse.

Commission on Professionals in Science and Technology, 1500 Massachusetts Ave. N.W. 20005; 223-6995. Betty M. Vetter, executive director.

Membership: scientific societies, corporations, and individuals. Analyzes and publishes data on scientific and engineering human resources in the United States. Interests include employment of minorities and women, salary ranges, and supply and demand of scientists and engineers.

Mathematical Assn. of America, 1529 18th St. N.W. 20036; 387-5200. Marcia P. Sward, executive director. Toll-free, (800) 331-1622. Fax, 265-2384.

Membership: mathematics professors and individuals with a professional interest in mathematics. Seeks to improve the teaching of collegiate mathematics. Conducts curriculum research and development.

National Assn. of Biology Teachers, 11250 Roger Bacon Dr., #19, Reston, VA 22090; (703) 471-1134. Patricia J. McWethy, executive director.

Membership: biology teachers and others interested in biology education at the elementary, secondary, and collegiate levels. Provides professional development opportunities through its publication program, summer workshops, conventions, and national award programs. Interests include teaching standards, science curriculum, and issues affecting biology education.

National Council of Teachers of Mathematics, 1906 Association Dr., Reston, VA 22091; (703) 620-9840. James D. Gates, executive director. Fax, (703) 476-2970.

Membership: teachers of mathematics in elementary and secondary schools and two-year colleges, university teacher education faculty and students, and other interested persons. Works to improve classroom instruction at all levels. Serves as forum and information clearinghouse on issues related to mathematics education. Offers educational materials and conferences. Monitors legislation and regulations.

National Geographic Society, 17th and M Sts. N.W. 20036; 857-7000. Gilbert M. Grosvenor,

president. Press, 857-7027. Fax, 775-6141. TDD, 857-7198.

Educational and scientific organization. Publishes *National Geographic, Research and Exploration, National Geographic Traveler,* and *World* magazines; produces maps, books, and films; maintains an exhibit hall; offers film-lecture series; produces television specials. Library open to the public.

National Science Resources Center, 900 Jefferson Dr. S.W., #1201 20560; 357-4892. Douglas M. Lapp, executive director. Fax, 786-2028.

Sponsored by the Smithsonian Institution and the National Academy of Sciences. Works to improve science teaching in elementary schools. Disseminates information; develops curriculum materials; seeks to increase public support for reform of science education.

National Science Teachers Assn., 1840 Wilson Blvd., Arlington, VA 22201-3000; (703) 243-7100. Bill G. Aldridge, executive director. Fax, (703) 243-7177.

Membership: science teachers from elementary through college levels. Seeks to improve science education; provides forum for exchange of information; monitors legislation and regulations. (Affiliated with the American Assn. for the Advancement of Science and the National Aeronautics and Space Administration.)

National Technical Assn., 206 N. Washington St., #202, Alexandria, VA (mailing address: P.O. Box 7045, Washington, DC 20032); 829-6100. Mildred Fitzgerald-Johnson, executive director. Fax, (703) 684-3952.

Membership: predominantly minority architects, mathematicians, engineers, scientists, others in associated careers, and students entering technical areas. Works to increase minority participation in technical fields; conducts student technical symposia and national scientific and technical awareness program.

Science Service, Inc., 1719 N St. N.W. 20036; 785-2255. Alfred S. McLaren, president. Fax, 785-1243.

Corporation organized to increase public understanding of science and to distribute scientific information. Publishes *Science News* and *Directory of Science Training Programs for High Ability Precollege Students.* Administers the Westinghouse Science Talent Search and the International Science and Engineering Fair.

World Future Society, 7910 Woodmont Ave., #450, Bethesda, MD 20814; (301) 656-8274. Edward Cornish, president.
Scientific and educational organization interested in future social and technological developments. Publishes books and magazines.

Science: Engineering

Agencies:

National Institute of Standards and Technology (Commerce Dept.), Electronics and Electrical Engineering Laboratory, Route I-270 and Quince Orchard Rd., Gaithersburg, MD 20899; (301) 975-2220. Judson French, director. Fax, (301) 975-4091.
Provides focus for research, development, and applications in the fields of electrical, electronic, quantum electric, and electromagnetic materials engineering. Interests include fundamental physical constants, practical data, measurement methods, theory, standards, technology, and technical services.

National Institute of Standards and Technology (Commerce Dept.), Manufacturing Engineering Laboratory, Route I-270 and Quince Orchard Rd., Bldg. 220, Rm. B322, Gaithersburg, MD 20899; (301) 975-3400. Michael J. Wozny, director. Fax, (301) 948-5668.
Collects technical data, develops standards in production engineering, and publishes findings; produces the technical base for proposed standards and technology for industrial and mechanical engineering; provides instrument design, fabrication, and repair.

National Science Foundation, Engineering, 4201 Wilson Blvd., #505, Arlington, VA 22230; (703) 306-1300. Joseph Bordogna, assistant director. Fax, (703) 306-0289.
Supports fundamental research and education in engineering through grants and special equipment awards. Programs are designed to enhance international competitiveness and to improve the quality of engineering in the United States. Oversees the following divisions: Electrical and Communications Systems, Chemical and Thermal Systems, Engineering Education Centers, Mechanical and Structural Systems, Design and Manufacturing Systems, Biological and Critical Systems, and Industrial Innovation Interface.

Office of Science and Technology Policy (Executive Office of the President), Science, Old

Executive Office Bldg. 20500; 395-5130. M. R. C. Greenwood, associate director. Fax, 395-5164.
Analyzes policies and advises the president on physical science and engineering issues; coordinates executive office and federal agency actions related to these issues. Evaluates the effectiveness of physical science and engineering programs.

See also National Institute of Standards and Technology, Information Services (p. 672)

Congress:

See Science, Congress (p. 663)

Nongovernmental:

ACEC Research and Management Foundation, 1015 15th St. N.W. 20005; 347-7474. Thomas E. Kern, executive director. Fax, 898-0068.
Conducts research and educational activities to improve engineering practices and professional cooperation. Awards scholarships to undergraduate engineering students.

American Assn. of Engineering Societies, 1111 19th St. N.W., #608 20036; 296-2237. Mitchell Bradley, executive director. Fax, 296-1151.
Addresses crosscutting technology policy concerns that affect the public interest. Represents the U.S. engineering community as delegate to the World Federation of Engineering Organizations and the Pan American Union of Engineering Associations. Surveys engineering salaries, degrees, and enrollments.

American Consulting Engineers Council, 1015 15th St. N.W., #802 20005; 347-7474. James L. MacFarlane, president. Fax, 898-0068.
Membership: practicing consulting engineering firms and state, local, and regional consulting engineers councils. Monitors legislation and regulations; serves as an information clearinghouse for member companies in such areas as legislation, legal cases, marketing, management, professional liability, business practices, and insurance.

American Society of Mechanical Engineers, 1828 L St. N.W., #906 20036; 785-3756. Philip W. Hamilton, director, public affairs. Fax, 429-9417.
Serves as a clearinghouse for sharing of information among federal, state, and local governments

and the engineering profession. Monitors legislation and regulations. (Headquarters in New York.)

Institute of Electrical and Electronics Engineers—United States Activities, 1828 L St. N.W., #1202 20036; 785-0017. W. Thomas Suttle, staff director, professional activities. Fax, 785-0835.

U.S. arm of an international technological and professional organization concerned with all areas of electrotechnology policy, including aerospace, computers, communications, biomedicine, electric power, and consumer electronics. (Headquarters in New York.)

International Society for Hybrid Microelectronics, 1850 Centennial Park Dr., #105, Reston, VA 22091; (703) 758-1060. Richard Breck, executive director. Toll-free, (800) 232-4746. Fax, (703) 758-1066.

Membership: persons involved in the microelectronics industry. Integrates disciplines of science and engineering; fosters exchange of information among complementary technologies, including ceramics, thin and thick films, surface mount, semiconductor packaging, discrete semiconductor devices, monolithic circuits, and multichip modules; disseminates technical knowledge.

International Test and Evaluation Assn., 4400 Fair Lakes Court, Fairfax, VA 22033-3899; (703) 631-6220. R. Alan Pliskker, executive director. Fax, (703) 631-6221.

Membership: engineers, scientists, managers, and other industry, government, and academic professionals interested in advancing the field of test and evaluation of products and complex systems. Provides a forum for information exchange.

National Academy of Engineering, 2101 Constitution Ave. N.W. 20418; 334-3200. Robert Mayer White, president. Information, 334-2138. Library, 334-2125. Fax, 334-1597. Publications, (800) 624-6242; in Washington, D.C., 334-3313.

Independent society whose members are elected in recognition of important contributions to the field of engineering and technology. Shares responsibility with the National Academy of Sciences for examining questions of science and technology at the request of the federal government. Library open to the public by appointment. (Affiliated with the National Academy of Sciences.)

National Institute for Engineering Ethics, 1420 King St., Alexandria, VA 22314; (703) 684-2845. Arthur E. Schwartz, general counsel. Fax, (703) 836-4875.

Promotes the study and application of ethics in engineering. Provides students and practicing engineers with case studies and videotaped training programs. (Affiliated with the National Society of Professional Engineers.)

National Society of Professional Engineers, 1420 King St., Alexandria, VA 22314; (703) 684-2800. Donald G. Weinert, executive director. Information, (703) 684-2882. Fax, (703) 836-4875.

Membership: graduate engineers from technical disciplines of engineering. Holds engineering seminars; operates an information center. Participates in MathCounts, a national math competition for junior high school students. Sponsors National Engineers Week. (Affiliated with the National Institute for Engineering Ethics.)

See also American Society for Engineering Education (p. 674)

Science: Environmental and Earth Sciences

See also Environment (p. 616)

Atmospheric Sciences

Agencies:

National Oceanic and Atmospheric Administration (Commerce Dept.), National Weather Service Science and History Center, 1325 East-West Highway, Silver Spring, MD 20910; (301) 713-0692. Gloria J. Walker, tour coordinator. Fax, (301) 713-0610.

Maintains and exhibits historical collection of the National Weather Service. Displays include meteorological instruments, weather satellites, photographs, and a re-creation of a 19th century weather office.

National Science Foundation, Atmospheric Sciences, 4201 Wilson Blvd., #775, Arlington, VA 22230; (703) 306-1520. Richard Greenfield, director. Fax, (703) 306-0377.

Supports research on the earth's atmosphere and the sun's effect on it, including studies of the physics, chemistry, and dynamics of the earth's upper and lower atmospheres; climate processes and variations; and the natural global cycles of gases and particles in the earth's atmosphere.

National Weather Service (National Oceanic and Atmospheric Administration, Commerce Dept.), 1325 East-West Highway, Silver Spring, MD 20910; (301) 713-0689. E. W. Friday, director. Information, (301) 713-0622. Fax, (301) 713-0610.

Issues warnings of hurricanes, severe storms, and floods; provides weather forecasts and services for the general public and for aviation, agricultural, and marine interests. National Weather Service forecast office, (703) 260-0107; weather forecast for Washington, D.C., and vicinity, (703) 260-0307; marine forecast, (703) 260-0505; recreational forecast, (703) 260-0705; climate data, (703) 260-0707; river stages, (703) 260-0305; long-range forecast for anywhere in the United States, (301) 763-8155; pilot weather, (800) 992-7433.

National Weather Service (National Oceanic and Atmospheric Administration, Commerce Dept.), National Meteorological Center, 5200 Auth Rd., Camp Springs, MD (mailing address: Washington, DC 20233); (301) 763-8016. Ronald D. McPherson, director. Fax, (301) 763-8434.

The National Meteorological Center and the National Environmental Satellite, Data, and Information Service are part of the World Weather Watch Programme developed by the United Nations' World Meteorological Organization. Collects data and exchanges it with other nations; provides other national weather service offices, private meteorologists, and government agencies with forecast products.

Congress:

See *Science, Congress (p. 663)*

Nongovernmental:

See *American Assn. for the Advancement of Science (p. 666); National Geographic Society (p. 667)*

Geology and Earth Sciences

Agencies:

National Aeronautics and Space Administration, Mission to Planet Earth, 300 E St. S.W. (mailing address: NASA Headquarters, Mail

Code Y, Washington, DC 20546); 358-1700. Charles Kennel, associate administrator. Information, 358-1547. Fax, 358-3092.

Conducts programs dealing with the earth as observed from space; conducts upper atmospheric and terrestrial studies and meteorological and ocean research.

National Museum of Natural History (Smithsonian Institution), Mineral Sciences, 10th St. and Constitution Ave. N.W., MRC-119 20560; 357-1412. Jeffrey E. Post, chairman. Fax, 357-2476.

Conducts research on meteorites, mineralogy, petrology, volcanology, and geochemistry. Maintains the Global Volcanism Network, which reports worldwide volcanic and meteoric events and seismic activity.

National Museum of Natural History (Smithsonian Institution), Naturalist Center, 10th St. and Constitution Ave. N.W. 20560; 357-2804. Richard H. Efthim, manager. Fax, 786-2778.

Maintains natural history research and reference library with books and 30,000 objects, including minerals, rocks, plants, animals, shells and corals, insects, invertebrates, micro- and macrofossil materials, and microbiological and anthropological materials. Facilities include study equipment such as microscopes, dissecting instruments, and plant presses; teacher reference center; and audiovisual library. Library open to the public. Reservations required for groups of six or more.

National Museum of Natural History (Smithsonian Institution), Paleobiology, 10th St. and Constitution Ave. N.W. 20560; 357-2162. William DiMichele, chairman. Fax, 786-2832.

Conducts research on invertebrate paleontology, paleobotany, sedimentology, and vertebrate paleontology; provides information on paleontology. Maintains national collection of fossil organisms and sediment samples.

National Oceanic and Atmospheric Administration (Commerce Dept.), Library and Information Services, 1315 East-West Highway, 2nd Floor, Silver Spring, MD 20910; (301) 713-2607. Carol Watts, director. Fax, (301) 713-4598. Reference service, (301) 713-2660.

Collection includes books and periodicals on earth sciences. Maintains bibliographic database of other NOAA libraries, an online service, and reference materials on CD-ROM. Makes interlibrary loans; open to the public.

National Science Foundation, Earth Sciences, 4201 Wilson Blvd., #785, Arlington, VA 22230; (703) 306-1550. James F. Hays, director. Fax, (703) 306-0382.

Provides grants for research in geology, geophysics, geochemistry, and related fields, including tectonics, hydrologic sciences, and continental dynamics.

National Science Foundation, Polar Programs, 4201 Wilson Blvd., #755, Arlington, VA 22230; (703) 306-1030. Neal Sullivan, director; Guy G. Guthridge, manager, polar information, (703) 306-1031. Fax, (703) 306-0139.

Funds and manages U.S. activity in Antarctica; provides grants for arctic programs in polar biology and medicine, earth sciences, atmospheric sciences, meteorology, ocean sciences, and glaciology. The Polar Information Program serves as a clearinghouse for polar data and makes referrals on specific questions.

U.S. Arctic Research Commission, 4350 N. Fairfax Dr., #630, Arlington, VA 22203; (703) 525-0111. Philip L. Johnson, executive director. Fax, (703) 525-0114.

Presidential advisory commission that develops policy for arctic research; assists the interagency Arctic Research Policy Committee in implementing a national plan of arctic research; recommends improvements in logistics, data management, and dissemination of arctic information.

U.S. Geological Survey (Interior Dept.), Earthquakes, Volcanoes, and Engineering, 12201 Sunrise Valley Dr., Reston, VA 22092; (703) 648-6714. Robert L. Wesson, chief. Fax, (703) 648-6717.

Manages geologic, geophysical, and engineering investigations, including assessments of hazards from earthquakes, volcanoes, and landslides; conducts research on the mechanisms and occurrences of earthquakes and volcanoes and their relationship to the behavior of the crust and upper mantle; develops methods for predicting the time, place, and magnitude of earthquakes; conducts research on igneous and geothermal systems; conducts engineering and geologic studies on landslides and ground failures.

U.S. Geological Survey (Interior Dept.), Geologic Division, 12201 Sunrise Valley Dr., Reston, VA 22092; (703) 648-6600. Benjamin A. Morgan, chief geologist. Fax, (703) 648-6683.

Conducts field and laboratory research programs on the geology of the United States. Interests include environmental geology; earthquakes, volcanoes, and landslides; mineral and energy resources; geochemistry and geophysics; and marine and coastal geology.

U.S. Geological Survey (Interior Dept.), Information and Data Services, 12201 Sunrise Valley Dr., Reston, VA (mailing address: 508 National Center, Reston, VA 22092); (703) 648-5780. Gary W. North, assistant chief. Fax, (703) 648-5939.

Produces maps, bulletins, professional papers, and brochures; sells survey maps and atlases, aerial and space images, and digital spatial data over the counter and through authorized dealers.

U.S. Geological Survey (Interior Dept.), Library, 12201 Sunrise Valley Dr., Reston, VA 22092; (703) 648-4305. Edward H. Liszewski, acting chief librarian. Fax, (703) 648-6373.

Maintains collection of books, periodicals, serials, maps, and technical reports on geology, mineral and water resources, mineralogy, physics, paleontology, petrology, chemistry, and soil and environmental sciences. Open to the public; makes interlibrary loans.

U.S. Geological Survey (Interior Dept.), Regional Geology, 12201 Sunrise Valley Dr., Reston, VA 22092; (703) 648-6960. Mitchell W. Reynolds, chief. Fax, (703) 648-6937.

Manages geological investigations and analyses to determine the geologic framework of the United States and to provide basic geological data for assessing land as a resource. Activities include geologic mapping, developing and applying geochronologic methods of age determination, including paleontologic and isotopic geologies, and lunar and planetary investigations.

Congress:

See Science, Congress (p. 663)

Nongovernmental:

American Geological Institute, 4220 King St., Alexandria, VA 22302; (703) 379-2480. Marcus E. Milling, executive director. Fax, (703) 379-7563.

Membership: earth science societies and associations. Maintains a computerized database with information on geology, engineering and environmental geology, oceanography, and other geological fields. (Service available to the public for a fee.)

American Geophysical Union, 2000 Florida Ave. N.W. 20009; 462-6903. A. F. Spilhaus Jr., executive director. Fax, 328-0566.

Membership: scientists and technologists in the field of geophysics. Maintains extensive publications program.

See also American Assn. for the Advancement of Science (p. 666); National Geographic Society (p. 667)

Oceanography

See also Natural Resources, Ocean Resources (p. 649)

Agencies:

National Museum of Natural History (Smithsonian Institution), Botany, 4210 Silver Hill Rd., Suitland, MD (mailing address: Smithsonian Institution, Washington, DC 20560); (301) 238-3548. Ernani Menez, curator, marine plants. Fax, (301) 238-3361.

Processes, sorts, and distributes to scientists specimens of marine plants; engages in taxonomic sorting, community analysis, and specimen and sample data management; assists national and international agencies with environmental analysis programs.

National Museum of Natural History (Smithsonian Institution), Invertebrate Zoology, 10th St. and Constitution Ave. N.W., MRC 163 20560; 357-4673. Rafael Lemaitre, curator, crustaceans. Fax, 357-3043.

Conducts research and answers scientific inquiries on the Smithsonian's marine invertebrate collections; engages in taxonomic sorting, community analysis, and specimen and sample data management.

National Museum of Natural History (Smithsonian Institution), Library, 10th St. and Constitution Ave. N.W., #51 20560; 357-1496. Ann Juneau, chief librarian. Fax, 357-1896.

Maintains collections covering oceanography; permits on-site use of the collections. Open to the public by appointment; makes interlibrary loans.

National Museum of Natural History (Smithsonian Institution), Vertebrate Zoology, 4210 Silver Hill Rd., Suitland, MD (mailing address: Smithsonian Institution, Washington, DC 20560); (301) 238-3798. Leslie Knapp, curator, fishes.

Processes, sorts, and distributes to scientists specimens of marine vertebrates; engages in taxonomic sorting, community analysis, and specimen and sample data management.

National Oceanic and Atmospheric Administration (Commerce Dept.), Library and Information Services, 1315 East-West Highway, 2nd Floor, Silver Spring, MD 20910; (301) 713-2607. Carol Watts, director. Fax, (301) 713-4598. Reference service, (301) 713-2660.

Collection includes reports, journals, monographs, data catalogs, directories, and microforms on marine science and physical oceanography. Maintains bibliographic database of other NOAA libraries, an online service, and reference materials on CD-ROM. Makes interlibrary loans; open to the public.

National Oceanic and Atmospheric Administration (Commerce Dept.), National Ocean Service, 1305 East-West Highway SSMC Bldg. 4, Silver Spring, MD 20910; (301) 713-3074. Stan Wilson, assistant administrator. Fax, (301) 713-4269.

Manages charting and geodetic services, oceanography and marine services, coastal resource coordination, and marine survey operations.

National Oceanic and Atmospheric Administration (Commerce Dept.), National Oceanographic Data Center, 1825 Connecticut Ave. N.W. 20235; 606-4594. Bruce C. Douglas, director. Fax, 606-4586. Information and requests, 606-4549.

Offers a wide range of oceanographic data on magnetic tape, disk, and hard copy; provides research scientists with data processing services; prepares statistical summaries and graphical data products. (Additional fee charged for requests requiring more than minimal work.)

National Oceanic and Atmospheric Administration (Commerce Dept.), Officer Corps, 11400 Rockville Pike, Rockville, MD 20852; (301) 443-2383. Rear Adm. Sigmund R. Petersen, director. Recruiting, (301) 443-8984.

Uniformed service of the Commerce Dept. that operates and manages NOAA's fleet of hydrographic, oceanographic, and fisheries research ships and aircraft. Supports NOAA's scientific programs.

National Science Foundation, Ocean Sciences Research, 4201 Wilson Blvd., #725, Arlington, VA 22230; (703) 306-1582. Michael Reeve, head. Fax, (703) 306-0390.

Awards grants to academic institutions and private corporations for research in all areas of the marine sciences, including biological, chemical, and physical oceanography, marine geology, and marine geophysics.

National Science Foundation, Oceanographic Centers and Facilities, 4201 Wilson Blvd., #725, Arlington, VA 22230; (703) 306-1576. Donald F. Heinrichs, head. Fax, (703) 306-0390.

Awards grants and contracts for acquiring, upgrading, and operating oceanographic research facilities that lend themselves to shared usage. Facilities supported include ships, submersibles, and shipboard and shorebased data logging and processing equipment. Supports development of new drilling techniques and systems.

U.S. Geological Survey (Interior Dept.), Energy and Marine Geology, 12201 Sunrise Valley Dr., Reston, VA 22092; (703) 648-6472. Gary Hill, chief. Fax, (703) 648-5464.

Surveys the continental margins and the ocean floor to provide information on the mineral resources potential of submerged lands.

Congress:

House Merchant Marine and Fisheries Committee, Subcommittee on Oceanography, Gulf of Mexico, and the Outer Continental Shelf, 575 Ford Bldg. (2nd and D Sts. S.W.) 20515; 226-2460. Solomon P. Ortiz, D-Texas, chairman; Sheila McCready, staff director.

Jurisdiction over legislation on most oceanographic matters, including deep seabed mining, ocean charting, and the National Oceanic and Atmospheric Administration.

Senate Commerce, Science, and Transportation Committee, SD-508 20510; 224-5115. Ernest F. Hollings, D-S.C., chairman; Kevin Curtin, chief counsel and staff director.

Jurisdiction over legislation on most oceanographic matters, including deep seabed mining (jurisdiction shared with the Senate Energy and Natural Resources Committee), ocean charting, and the National Oceanic and Atmospheric Administration.

Senate Commerce, Science, and Transportation Committee, Subcommittee on National Ocean Policy Study, SH-425 (mailing address: SD-508, Washington, DC 20510); 224-4912. Ernest F. Hollings, D-S.C., chairman; Penny Dalton, staff member.

Studies national ocean policy and programs. (Subcommittee does not report legislation.)

Senate Energy and Natural Resources Committee, Subcommittee on Mineral Resources Development and Production, SD-362 20510; 224-7568. Daniel K. Akaka, D-Hawaii, chairman; Lisa Vehmas, counsel.

Jurisdiction over legislation on deep seabed mining (jurisdiction shared with the Senate Commerce, Science, and Transportation Committee).

Nongovernmental:

Marine Technology Society, 1828 L St. N.W., #906 20036; 775-5966. Martin J. Finerty Jr., general manager. Fax, 429-9417.

Membership: scientists, engineers, technologists, and others interested in marine science and technology. Provides information on marine science, technology, and education.

National Ocean Industries Assn., 1120 G St. N.W., #900 20005; 347-6900. Robert B. Stewart, president. Fax, 347-8650.

Membership: manufacturers, producers, suppliers, and support and service companies involved in marine, offshore, and ocean work. Interests include offshore oil and gas supply and production, deep-sea mining, ocean thermal energy, and new energy sources.

See also National Geographic Society (p. 667)

Science: International Programs

Agencies:

National Institute of Standards and Technology (Commerce Dept.), International and Academic Affairs, I-270 and Quince Orchard Rd., Administration Bldg., Rm. A505, Gaithersburg, MD 20899; (301) 975-3072. George A. Sinnott, director. Fax, (301) 975-3530.

Represents the institute in international functions; coordinates programs with foreign institutions; assists scientists from foreign countries who visit the institute for consultation. Administers a postdoctoral research associates program.

National Oceanic and Atmospheric Administration (Commerce Dept.), National Environmental Satellite, Data, and Information Service, 4401 Suitland Rd., #2069, Suitland, MD (mailing address: Federal Bldg. 4, #2069, Washington, DC 20233); (301) 763-7190. Robert S. Winokur, assistant administrator. Information, (301) 763-2560. Fax, (301) 763-4011.

The National Environmental Satellite, Data, and Information Services and the National Meteorological Center are part of the World Weather Watch Programme developed by the United Nations' World Meteorological Organization. Manages U.S. civil earth-observing satellite systems and atmospheric, oceanographic, geophysical, and solar data centers. Provides the public, businesses, and government agencies with environmental data and information products and services.

National Science Foundation, International Programs, 4201 Wilson Blvd., #935, Arlington, VA 22230; (703) 306-1710. Marcel Bardon, director. Fax, (703) 306-0476.

Coordinates and manages the foundation's international scientific activities and cooperative research and exchange programs; provides planning support for U.S. participation in international scientific organizations. Collects, analyzes, and distributes information on foreign scientific research and development.

National Weather Service (National Oceanic and Atmospheric Administration, Commerce Dept.), National Meteorological Center, 5200 Auth Rd., Camp Springs, MD (mailing address: Washington, DC 20233); (301) 763-8016. Ronald D. McPherson, director. Fax, (301) 763-8434.

The National Meteorological Center and the National Environmental Satellite, Data, and Information Service are part of the World Weather Watch Programme developed by the United Nations' World Meteorological Organization. Collects data and exchanges it with other nations; provides other national weather service offices, private meteorologists, and government agencies with forecast products.

Office of Science and Technology Policy (Executive Office of the President), National Security and International Affairs, Old Executive Office Bldg., Rm. 494 20500; 456-2894. Jane Wales, associate director. Fax, 395-1571.

Advises the president on international science and technology matters as they affect national security; coordinates international science and technology initiatives at the interagency level.

Smithsonian Institution, International Relations, 1100 Jefferson Dr. S.W. 20560; 357-4282. Francine C. Berkowitz, director. Fax, 786-2557.

Fosters the development and coordinates the international aspects of Smithsonian scientific activities; facilitates basic research in the natural sciences and encourages international collaboration among individuals and institutions.

State Dept., Oceans and International Environmental and Scientific Affairs, Main State Bldg., Rm. 7831 20520-7818; 647-1554. Elinor G. Constable, assistant secretary. Information, 647-6575. Press, 647-2492. Fax, 647-0217.

Formulates and implements policies and proposals for U.S. international scientific, technological, environmental, oceanic and marine, arctic and antarctic, and space programs; coordinates international science and technology policy with other federal agencies.

State Dept., Scientific Programs, Main State Bldg. 20520; 647-2752. Raymond E. Wanner, deputy director. Fax, 647-8902.

Oversees U.S. participation in international scientific and technical organizations, including the International Atomic Energy Agency, the United Nations Environment Programme, and the World Meteorological Organization. Works to ensure that United Nations agencies follow United Nations Conference on Environment and Development recommendations on sustainable growth.

See also Education: Special Topics, International Education (p. 153); Overseas Information and Exchange Programs (p. 482)

Congress:

See Science, Congress (p. 663)

Nongovernmental:

American Assn. for the Advancement of Science, International Programs, 1333 H St. N.W. 20005; 326-6650. Richard Getzinger, director. Fax, 289-4958.

Administers programs concerned with international science and engineering; works to further understanding of global problems with scientific and technological components; provides policy makers at national and international levels with information from the scientific community.

Japan Information Access Project, 1706 R St. N.W. 20009; 332-5224. Mindy Kotler, director. Fax, 332-6841.

Membership organization that teaches business executives, scientists, engineers, educators, legislators, and journalists how to access, evaluate, and use Japanese-source information in business, science, and technology. Helps American managers integrate Japanese information and U.S. policies toward Japan in their strategic planning. Maintains programs on specific topics, including electronics, financial services, biomedical technologies and pharmaceuticals, and intellectual property.

Science: Mathematical, Computer, and Physical Sciences

General

Agencies:

National Institute of Standards and Technology (Commerce Dept.), Route I-270 and Quince Orchard Rd., Gaithersburg, MD (mailing address: Bldg. 101, #A1134, Gaithersburg, MD 20899); (301) 975-2300, Arati Prabhakar, director. Information (301) 975-2762. Fax, (301) 869-8972.

Nonregulatory agency that serves as national reference and measurement laboratory for the physical and engineering sciences. Works with industry, government agencies, and academia; conducts research in electronics, manufacturing, physics, chemistry, radiation, materials science, applied mathematics, computer science and technology, and engineering sciences.

National Institute of Standards and Technology (Commerce Dept.), Computing and Applied Mathematics Laboratory, Route I-270 and Quince Orchard Rd., Gaithersburg, MD 20899; (301) 975-2732. Joan R. Rosenblatt, director. Fax, (301) 963-9137.

Offers support in mathematical and computer sciences to all institute programs and federal agencies; provides consultations, methods, and research supporting the institute's scientific and engineering projects. Manages and operates NIST central computing facilities.

National Oceanic and Atmospheric Administration (Commerce Dept.), Library and Information Services, 1315 East-West Highway, 2nd Floor, Silver Spring, MD 20910; (301) 713-2607. Carol Watts, director. Fax, (301) 713-4598. Reference service, (301) 713-2660.

Collection includes books and journals on mathematics, computer science, satellite technology, and atmospheric physics; supports the National Environmental Satellite Data and Information Service of NOAA. Maintains bibliographic database of other NOAA libraries, an online service, and reference materials on CD-ROM. Makes interlibrary loans; open to the public.

Office of Science and Technology Policy (Executive Office of the President), Technology, Old Executive Office Bldg. 20500; 395-6175. Lionel S. Johns, associate director. Fax, 395-4155.

Analyzes policies and advises the president on physical sciences and computational science and technology issues; coordinates executive office and federal agency actions related to these issues.

Congress:

See Science, Congress (p. 663)

Nongovernmental:

Carnegie Institution of Washington, 1530 P St. N.W. 20005; 387-6400. Maxine F. Singer, president. Fax, 387-8092.

Conducts research in the physical and biological sciences at the following centers: the observatories of the Carnegie Institution with headquarters in Pasadena, Calif.; Geophysical Laboratory and Dept. of Terrestrial Magnetism in Washington, D.C.; Dept. of Plant Biology in Stanford, Calif.; and Dept. of Embryology in Baltimore, Md. Refers specific inquiries to appropriate department. Library open to the public by appointment.

See also American Assn. for the Advancement of Science (p. 666)

Astronomy

Agencies:

National Aeronautics and Space Administration, Space Science, 300 E St. S.W. (mailing address: NASA Headquarters, Mail Code S, Washington, DC 20546); 358-1409. Wesley T.

Huntress Jr., associate administrator. Information, 358-1547. Fax, 358-3092.

Administers programs that study the composition, energy, mass, position, size, and properties of celestial bodies within the universe, as observed from Earth. Administers NASA's rocket programs.

National Science Foundation, Astronomical Sciences, 4201 Wilson Blvd., #4510, Arlington, VA 22230; (703) 306-1820. Hugh M. Van Horn, director. Fax, (703) 306-0525.

Provides grants for ground-based astronomy and astronomical research on planetary astronomy, stellar astronomy and astrophysics, galactic astronomy, extragalactic astronomy and cosmology, and advanced technologies and instrumentation. Maintains astronomical facilities.

U.S. Naval Observatory (Defense Dept.), 3450 Massachusetts Ave. N.W. 20392-5420; 653-1538. Richard E. Blumberg, superintendent. Information, 653-1541. Fax, 653-1497. Tours, 653-1507.

Determines the precise positions and motions of celestial bodies. Operates the U.S. master clock. Provides the U.S. Navy and Defense Dept. with astronomical and timing data for navigation, precise positioning, and command, control, and communications.

Congress:

See Science, Congress (p. 663); Space, General, Congress (p. 695)

Nongovernmental:

American Astronomical Society, 2000 Florida Ave. N.W., #400 20009; 328-2010. Peter B. Boyce, executive officer. Press, (301) 286-8607. Fax, 234-2560. Internet, aas@blackhole.aas.org.

Membership: astronomers and other professionals interested in the advancement of astronomy in the United States, Canada, and Mexico. Holds scientific meetings; awards research grants.

Assn. of Universities for Research in Astronomy, 1625 Massachusetts Ave. N.W., #701 20036; 483-2101. Goetz Oertel, president. Fax, 483-2106.

Consortium of universities. Manages three ground-based observatories and the international Gemini Project for the National Science-

Foundation and manages the Space Telescope Science Institute for the National Aeronautics and Space Administration.

Chemistry

Agencies:

National Institute of Standards and Technology (Commerce Dept.), Chemical Science and Technology Laboratory, Route I-270 and Quince Orchard Rd., Gaithersburg, MD 20899; (301) 975-3145. Hratch G. Semerjian, director. Fax, (301) 975-3845.

Develops uniform chemical measurement methods; provides federal agencies and industry with advisory and research services in the areas of analytical chemistry, biotechnology, chemical engineering, and physical chemistry; conducts interdisciplinary research efforts with other NIST laboratories.

National Institute of Standards and Technology (Commerce Dept.), Materials Science and Engineering Laboratory, Route I-270 and Quince Orchard Rd., Gaithersburg, MD (mailing address: Bldg. 223, #B309, Gaithersburg, MD 20899); (301) 975-5658. Lyle H. Schwartz, director. Fax, (301) 926-8349.

Provides measurements, data, standards, reference materials, concepts, and technical information fundamental to the processing, microstructure, properties, and performance of materials; addresses the scientific basis for new advanced materials; operates a research nuclear reactor for advanced materials characterization measurements; operates four materials data centers.

National Science Foundation, Chemistry, 4201 Wilson Blvd., #1055, Arlington, VA 22230; (703) 306-1840. John B. Hunt, acting director. Fax, (703) 306-0534. Toll-free fax, (800) 338-3128.

Awards grants to research programs in organic and macromolecular chemistry, physical chemistry, analytical and surface chemistry, and inorganic, bioinorganic, and organometallic chemistry; provides funds for instruments needed in chemistry research; coordinates interdisciplinary research.

National Science Foundation, Materials Research, 4201 Wilson Blvd., #1065, Arlington, VA 22230; (703) 306-1810. John H. Hopps Jr., director. Fax, (703) 306-0515.

Provides grants for research in condensed matter physics; solid state chemistry and polymers;

metals, ceramics, and electronic materials; and materials theory. Provides major instrumentation for these activities. Supports multidisciplinary research in these areas through materials research laboratories and groups.

See also National Institute of Standards and Technology, Information Services (p. 672)

Congress:

See Science, Congress (p. 663)

Nongovernmental:

American Assn. for Clinical Chemistry, Inc., 2101 L St. N.W., #202 20037; 857-0717. Richard G. Flaherty, executive vice president. Fax, 887-5093.

Membership: chemists, physicians, and other scientists specializing in clinical chemistry. Provides educational and professional development services; presents awards for outstanding achievement; monitors legislation and regulations.

American Chemical Society, 1120 Vermont Ave. N.W. 20005; 872-4600. John K. Crum, executive director. Fax, 872-4615.

Scientific and educational society of professional chemists and chemical engineers. Maintains educational programs, including those that evaluate college chemistry departments and high school chemistry curricula. Administers grants and fellowships for basic research; presents achievement awards. Library open to the public.

American Chemical Society, Petroleum Research Fund, 1155 16th St. N.W. 20036; 872-4481. Joseph E. Rogers Jr., administrator. Fax, 872-6319.

Makes grants to nonprofit institutions for advanced scientific education and fundamental research related to the petroleum industry (chemistry, geology, engineering).

American Institute of Chemists, 7315 Wisconsin Ave., #502E, Bethesda, MD 20814; (301) 652-2447. Macey Elliott, executive director. Fax, (301) 657-3549.

Professional society of chemists and chemical engineers. Sponsors a national certification program; monitors legislation and regulations; sponsors scientific exchanges to the People's Republic of China, the former Soviet Union, and other countries. Publishes annual professional

directory. AIC Foundation sponsors the Student Award Program.

AOAC International, 2200 Wilson Blvd., #400, Arlington, VA 22201; (703) 522-3032. Ronald R. Christensen, executive director. Fax, (703) 522-5468.

International association of analytical science professionals, companies, government agencies, nongovernmental organizations, and institutions. Supports the development, testing, validation, and publication of reliable chemical and biological methods of analyzing foods, drugs, feed, fertilizers, pesticides, water, forensic materials, and other substances affecting public health and safety and the environment.

Chemical Manufacturers Assn., 2501 M St. N.W. 20037; 887-1100. Frederick L. Webber, president. Fax, 887-1237.

Membership: manufacturers of basic industrial chemicals. Provides members with technical research, communications services, and legal affairs counseling. Monitors legislation and regulations; interests include environmental safety and health, transportation, energy, and international trade.

Society of the Plastics Industry, 1275 K St. N.W., #400 20005; 371-5200. Larry Thomas, president. Fax, 371-1022.

Promotes the plastics industry. Monitors legislation and regulations.

Synthetic Organic Chemical Manufacturers Assn., 1330 Connecticut Ave. N.W., #300 20036; 659-0060. Graydon R. Powers, president. Fax, 659-1699.

Membership: companies that manufacture, distribute, and market organic chemicals, and providers of custom chemical services. Monitors legislation and regulations. Interests include international trade, environmental and occupational safety, and health issues; conducts workshops and seminars. Promotes commercial opportunities for members.

See also American Industrial Health Council (p. 323); Chemical Specialties Manufacturers Assn. (p. 627)

Computer Sciences

Agencies:

National Institute of Standards and Technology (Commerce Dept.), Computer Systems Laboratory, Route I-270 and Quince Orchard Rd., Gaithersburg, MD 20899; (301) 975-2822. James H. Burrows, director. Fax, (301) 948-1784.
Advises federal agencies on automatic data processing management and use of information technology; helps federal agencies maintain up-to-date computer technology support systems, emphasizing computer security techniques; recommends federal information processing standards; conducts research in computer science and technology.

National Science Foundation, Computer and Computation Research, 4201 Wilson Blvd., #1145, Arlington, VA 22230; (703) 306-1910. Bruce Barnes, acting director. Fax, (703) 306-0557.
Awards grants for research in computer science and engineering, including programs in computer and computation theory; numeric, symbolic, and geometric computation; computer systems; and software engineering.

National Science Foundation, Information, Robotics, and Intelligence Systems, 4201 Wilson Blvd., #1115, Arlington, VA 22230; (703) 306-1930. Y. T. Chien, director. Fax, (703) 306-0599.
Supports research on designing, developing, managing, and using information systems, including database and expert systems, knowledge models and cognitive systems, machine intelligence and robotics, information technology and organizations, and interactive systems.

See also National Institute of Standards and Technology, Information Services (p. 672)

Congress:

See Science, Congress (p. 663)

Nongovernmental:

Computer and Business Equipment Manufacturers Assn., 1250 Eye St. N.W. 20005; 737-8888. Rhett Dawson, president. Press, 626-5725. Fax, 638-4922.
Membership: manufacturers and assemblers of information processing, business, and communications products and supplies. Studies domestic and international issues affecting the high-technology industry. Interests include international trade, taxation, proprietary rights, telecommunications, standards, and government procurement. Provides industry marketing statistics.

Computer and Communications Industry Assn., 666 11th St. N.W., #600 20001; 783-0070. Stephanie Biddle, president. Fax, 783-0534.
Membership: manufacturers and suppliers of computer data processing and communications-related products and services. Interests include telecommunications policy, capital formation and tax policy, federal procurement policy, communications and computer industry standards, intellectual property policies, export policy, and antitrust reform.

Computer Dealers and Lessors Assn., 1212 Potomac St. N.W. 20007; 333-0102. Greg Carroll, president. Fax, 333-0180.
Membership: companies that buy, sell, and lease new and used computers and other high-technology equipment. Acts as liaison with equipment manufacturers; enforces industry code of ethics; conducts industry surveys; monitors legislation and regulations.

Computer Law Assn., 3028 Javier Rd., #500E, Fairfax, VA 22031-4622; (703) 560-7747. Barbara Fieser, executive director. Fax, (703) 207-7028.
Membership: lawyers, law students, and nonattorneys concerned with the legal aspects of computers and computer communications. Sponsors programs and provides information on such issues as software protection, contracting, communications, international distribution, financing, taxes, copyrights, patents, and electronic data interchange.

Information Technology Assn. of America, 1616 N. Fort Myer Dr., Arlington, VA 22209; (703) 284-5340. Luanne James, president. Fax, (703) 525-2279.
Membership: organizations in the computer software and services industry. Monitors legislation and regulations; conducts research; holds seminars and workshops on education and small-business interests, government relations, competitive practices, communications, software, trade, and government procurement.

Institute of Electrical and Electronics Engineers—United States Activities, 1828 L St.

N.W., #1202 20036; 785-0017. W. Thomas Suttle, staff director, professional activities. Fax, 785-0835.

U.S. arm of an international technological and professional organization. Interests include promoting career and technology policy interests of members. (Headquarters in New York.)

International Assn. of Knowledge Engineers, 973D Russel Ave., Gaithersburg, MD 20879; (301) 948-5390. Julie Walker, executive director. Fax, (301) 926-4243. Toll-free bulletin board, (800) 833-6464.

Membership: corporations, institutions, and practitioners of knowledge engineering (the design of reasoning machines and computer systems to receive, organize, and maintain human knowledge). Promotes the development of technology, disseminates information among members, and establishes standards in the field. Certifies members; maintains job bank.

International Council for Computer Communication, P.O. Box 9745, Washington, DC 20016; (703) 836-7787. John D. McKendree, treasurer.

Membership: elected representatives from computer communication and medical, legal, and policy disciplines. Promotes scientific research in and development of computer communication; encourages evaluation of applications of computer communication for educational, scientific, medical, economic, legal, cultural, and other peaceful purposes; sponsors international conferences, seminars, and workshops. (Affiliated with the International Federation for Information Processing in Geneva, Switzerland.)

National Computer Graphics Assn., 2722 Merrilee Dr., #200, Fairfax, VA 22031; (703) 698-9600. Jim Schuping, president. Fax, (703) 560-2752.

Membership: individuals and corporations interested in developing, promoting, and improving computer graphics applications in business, industry, government, academia, science, and the arts. Provides a forum for computer graphics managers, users, and vendors; serves as a clearinghouse for information about computer graphics; sponsors national and regional conferences and expositions.

Software Publishers Assn., 1730 M St. N.W., #700 20036; 452-1600. Kenneth A. Wasch, executive director. Fax, 223-8756.

Membership: publishers of microcomputer software. Conducts investigations and litigation to protect members' copyrights; monitors legislation and regulations; collects pertinent data, including monthly sales information; offers contracts reference and credit information exchange services; sponsors conferences and seminars.

World Computer Graphics Assn., 5201 Leesburg Pike, #201, Falls Church, VA 22041; (703) 578-0301. Caby C. Smith, president. Fax, (703) 578-3386.

Membership: associations and organizations interested or engaged in computer graphics. Promotes formation of international computer graphics associations; works to increase awareness of computer graphics for industry, government, and personal and home use; sponsors international conferences and expositions.

See also American Institutes for Research (p. 693); American Medical Informatics Assn. (p. 323); Computer Professionals for Social Responsibility (p. 263); Institute for Alternative Futures (p. 666)

Mathematics

Agencies:

National Institute of Standards and Technology (Commerce Dept.), Computing and Applied Mathematics Laboratory, Route I-270 and Quince Orchard Rd., Gaithersburg, MD 20899; (301) 975-2732. Joan R. Rosenblatt, director. Fax, (301) 963-9137.

Develops improved mathematical and statistical models and computational methods; consults on their use. Manages and operates NIST central computing facilities.

National Science Foundation, Mathematical Sciences, 4201 Wilson Blvd., #1025, Arlington, VA 22230; (703) 306-1870. Frederic Y. M. Wan, director. Fax, (703) 306-0555.

Provides grants for research in the mathematical sciences in the following areas: classical and modern analysis, geometric analysis, topology and foundations, algebra and number theory, applied and computational mathematics, and statistics and probability. Maintains special projects program, which supports scientific computing equipment for mathematics research and several research institutes. Sponsors conferences, workshops, and postdoctoral research fellowships.

See also National Institute of Standards and Technology, Information Services (p. 672)

Congress:

See Science, Congress (p. 663)

Nongovernmental:

American Statistical Assn., 1429 Duke St., Alexandria, VA 22314; (703) 684-1221. Barbara A. Bailar, executive director. Fax, (703) 684-2037.
Membership: individuals interested in statistics and related quantitative fields. Advises government agencies on statistics and methodology in agency research; promotes development of statistical techniques for use in business, industry, finance, government, agriculture, and science.

Conference Board of the Mathematical Sciences, 1529 18th St. N.W. 20036; 293-1170. Ronald C. Rosier, administrative officer. Fax, 265-2384.
Membership: presidents of fifteen mathematical sciences professional societies. Serves as a forum for discussion of issues of concern to the mathematical sciences community.

Mathematical Assn. of America, 1529 18th St. N.W. 20036; 387-5200. Marcia P. Sward, executive director. Toll-free, (800) 331-1622. Fax, 265-2384.
Membership: mathematics professors and individuals with a professional interest in mathematics. Seeks to improve the teaching of collegiate mathematics. Conducts curriculum research and development.

Physics

Agencies:

Energy Dept., High Energy and Nuclear Physics, 19901 Germantown Rd., Germantown, MD (mailing address: Washington, DC 20585); (301) 903-3713. Wilmot N. Hess, associate director. Fax, (301) 903-3833.
Provides grants and facilities for research in high energy and nuclear physics. Constructs, operates, and maintains particle accelerators used in high energy and nuclear physics research.

National Institute of Standards and Technology (Commerce Dept.), Materials Science and Engineering Laboratory, Route I-270 and Quince Orchard Rd., Gaithersburg, MD (mailing address: Bldg. 223, #B309, Gaithersburg, MD 20899); (301) 975-5658. Lyle H. Schwartz, director. Fax, (301) 926-8349.
Provides measurements, data, standards, reference materials, concepts, and technical information fundamental to the processing, microstructure, properties, and performance of materials; addresses the scientific basis for new advanced materials; operates a research nuclear reactor for advanced materials characterization measurements; operates four materials data centers.

National Institute of Standards and Technology (Commerce Dept.), Physics Laboratory, Route I-270 and Quince Orchard Rd., Gaithersburg, MD 20899; (301) 975-4200. Katharine B. Gebbie, director. Fax, (301) 975-3038.
Conducts research to improve measurement capability and quantitative understanding of basic physical processes that underlie measurement science; investigates structure and dynamics of atoms and molecules; provides national standards for time and frequency and for measurement of radiation; develops radiometric and wavelength standards; analyzes national measurement needs.

National Science Foundation, Materials Research, 4201 Wilson Blvd., #1065, Arlington, VA 22230; (703) 306-1810. John H. Hopps Jr., director. Fax, (703) 306-0515.
Provides grants for research in condensed matter physics; solid state chemistry and polymers; metals, ceramics, and electronic materials; and materials theory. Provides major instrumentation for these activities. Supports multidisciplinary research in these areas through materials research laboratories and groups. Supports national user facilities in the areas of synchrotron radiation, high magnetic fields, neutron scattering, and high-resolution electron microscopy.

National Science Foundation, Physics, 4201 Wilson Blvd., #935, Arlington, VA 22230; (703) 306-1710. Marcel Bardon, director. Fax, (703) 306-0476.
Awards grants for research programs in atomic, molecular, and optical physics; elementary particle physics; and nuclear, theoretical, and gravitational physics.

See also National Institute of Standards and Technology, Information Services (p. 672)

Congress:

See Science, Congress (p. 663)

Nongovernmental:

American Physical Society, 529 14th St. N.W., #1050 20045-2001; 662-8700. Robert L. Park, executive director, public affairs. Fax, 662-8711.

Scientific and educational society of educators, students, citizens, and scientists, including industrial scientists. Sponsors studies on issues of public concern related to physics, such as reactor safety and energy use. Informs members of national and international developments. (Headquarters in College Park, Md.)

See also Health, Radiation Protection (p. 337)

Weights and Measures/Metric System

Agencies:

National Institute of Standards and Technology (Commerce Dept.), Measurement Services, Route I-270 and Quince Orchard Rd., Gaithersburg, MD (mailing address: B354 Physics Bldg., Gaithersburg, MD 20899); (301) 975-3602. Stanley D. Rasberry, director. Fax, (301) 948-3825.

Disseminates physical, chemical, and engineering measurement standards and provides services to ensure accurate and compatible measurements, specifications, and codes on a national and international scale.

National Institute of Standards and Technology (Commerce Dept.), Metric Program, Route I-270 and Quince Orchard Rd., Gaithersburg, MD 20899; (301) 975-3690. Gary Carver, chief. Fax, (301) 948-1416.

Coordinates federal metric conversion transition to ensure consistency; provides the public with technical and general information about the metric system; assists state and local governments, businesses, and educators with metric conversion activities.

National Institute of Standards and Technology (Commerce Dept.), National Conference on Weights and Measures, P.O. Box 4025, Gaithersburg, MD 20885; (301) 975-4005. Carroll S. Brickenkamp, executive secretary. Information, (301) 975-4004. Fax, (301) 926-0647.

Membership: state and local officials who deal with weights and measures, industry and business representatives, individuals, and associations. Serves as a national forum on issues related to weights and measures administration; develops consensus on uniform laws and regulations, specifications, and tolerances for weighing and measuring devices.

National Institute of Standards and Technology (Commerce Dept.), Weights and Measures, Route I-270 and Quince Orchard Rd., Gaithersburg, MD 20899; (301) 975-4005. Carroll S. Brickenkamp, chief. Information, (301) 975-4004. Fax, (301) 926-0647.

Promotes uniformity in weights and measures law and enforcement. Provides weights and measures agencies with training and technical assistance; assists state and local agencies in adapting their weights and measures to meet national standards; conducts research; sets uniform standards and regulations; sponsors the National Conference on Weights and Measures.

Congress:

House Science, Space, and Technology Committee, Subcommittee on Technology, Environment, and Aviation, B374 RHOB 20515; 225-9662. Tim Valentine, D-N.C., chairman; James H. Turner, staff director.

Jurisdiction over legislation on weights and measurement systems; monitors the National Institute of Standards and Technology.

Senate Commerce, Science, and Transportation Committee, Subcommittee on Science, Technology, and Space, SH-427 (mailing address: SD-508, Washington, DC 20510); 224-9360. John D. Rockefeller IV, D-W.Va., chairman; Patrick H. Windham, senior professional staff member.

Jurisdiction over legislation on weights and measurement systems; monitors the National Institute of Standards and Technology.

Nongovernmental:

American National Metric Council, 4330 East-West Highway, #1117, Bethesda, MD 20814; (301) 718-6508. John Deam, president. Fax, (301) 656-0989.

Membership: companies, libraries, organizations, and individuals. Coordinates voluntary transition to the metric system in the United States and assists with industry transition;

serves as information source on U.S. metric planning and use.

Science: Research Applications

Agencies:

Defense Technical Information Center (Defense Dept.), Cameron Station, Alexandria, VA 22304-6145; (703) 274-6800. Kurt N. Molholm, administrator. Information, (703) 274-7633. Fax, (703) 617-7718. Registration, (703) 274-6871.

Acts as a central repository for the Defense Dept.'s collection of current and completed research and development efforts in all fields of science and technology. Disseminates research and development information to contractors, grantees, and registered organizations working on government research and development projects, particularly for the Defense Dept. Users must register with the center.

National Aeronautics and Space Administration, Space Science, 300 E St. S.W. (mailing address: NASA Headquarters, Mail Code S, Washington, DC 20546); 358-1409. Wesley T. Huntress Jr., associate administrator. Information, 358-1547. Fax, 358-3092.

Provides information on technology developed during NASA's activities that have practical applications in other fields; maintains a data bank. (Accepts written requests for specific technical information.)

National Institute of Standards and Technology (Commerce Dept.), Route I-270 and Quince Orchard Rd., Gaithersburg, MD (mailing address: Bldg. 101, #A1134, Gaithersburg, MD 20899); (301) 975-2300. Arati Prabhakar, director. Information, (301) 975-2762. Fax, (301) 869-8972.

Nonregulatory agency that serves as national reference and measurement laboratory for the physical and engineering sciences. Works with industry, government agencies, and academia; conducts research in electronics, manufacturing, physics, chemistry, radiation, materials science, applied mathematics, computer science and technology, and engineering sciences.

National Science Foundation, Human Resource Development, 4201 Wilson Blvd., #815, Arlington, VA 22230; (703) 306-1640. Roosevelt Calbert, director. Fax, (703) 306-0423.

Supports and encourages participation in scientific and engineering research by women, minorities, and people with disabilities. Awards grants and scholarships.

Technology Administration (Commerce Dept.), Main Commerce Bldg. 20230; 482-1575. Mary L. Good, under secretary. Fax, 482-4498.

Seeks to enhance U.S. competitiveness by encouraging the development of new technologies and the conversion of technological knowledge into products and services. Oversees the National Institute of Standards and Technology and the National Technical Information Service.

Technology Administration (Commerce Dept.), Technology Policy, Main Commerce Bldg. 20230; 482-1581. Graham Mitchell, assistant secretary. Fax, 482-4817.

Promotes the removal of barriers to the commercialization of technology; analyzes federal research and development funding; acts as an information clearinghouse.

Congress:

Office of Technology Assessment (OTA), 600 Pennsylvania Ave. S.E. (mailing address: U.S. Congress, Washington, DC 20510); 224-3695. Roger Herdman, director; Sen. Edward M. Kennedy, D-Mass., chairman; Rep. Don Sundquist, R-Tenn., vice chairman, Technology Assessment Board. Information, 224-9241. Press, 228-6204. Fax, 228-6218. Publications, 224-8996.

Provides congressional committees with assessments of the impact of technologies and with analyses of policy alternatives.

See also Science, Congress (p. 663)

See also Technology Assessment Board (p. 757)

Nongovernmental:

National Center for Advanced Technologies, 1250 Eye St. N.W., #1100 20005; 371-8571. J. Clifford Schoep, president. Information, 371-8451. Fax, 371-8470.

Encourages U.S. competition in the world market by uniting government, industry, and university efforts to develop advanced technologies. (Affiliated with the Aerospace Industries Assn. of America.)

Public Technology, 1301 Pennsylvania Ave. N.W. 20004; 626-2400. Costis Toregas, president. Fax, 626-2498.

Cooperative research, development, and technology-transfer organization of cities and counties in North America. Applies available technological innovations and develops other methods to improve public services.

The Rand Corporation, 2100 M St. N.W., #800 20037; 296-5000. David Chu, director, Washington operations. Fax, 296-7960.

Research organization. Interests include energy, emerging technologies and critical systems, space and transportation, technology policies, international cooperative research, water resources, ocean and atmospheric sciences, and other technologies in defense and nondefense areas. (Headquarters in Santa Monica, Calif.)

SRI International, 1611 N. Kent St., Arlington, VA 22209; (703) 524-2053. Gerald E. Connolly, vice president, Washington office. Fax, (703) 247-8569.

Research and consulting organization that conducts basic and applied research for government, industry, and business. Interests include engineering and physical and life sciences. (Headquarters in Menlo Park, Calif.)

See also Industrial Research Institute (p. 70)

Science: Social Sciences

Anthropology

Agencies:

National Museum of Natural History (Smithsonian Institution), Anthropology, 10th St. and Constitution Ave. N.W. 20560; 357-2363. Dennis J. Stanford, chairman. Information, 357-1592. Fax, 357-2208.

Conducts research on paleo-Indian archaeology and prehistory, New World origins, and paleoecology. Maintains anthropological and human studies film archives. Museum maintains public exhibitions of human cultures.

National Museum of Natural History (Smithsonian Institution), Library, 10th St. and Constitution Ave. N.W., #51 20560; 357-1496. Ann Juneau, chief librarian. Fax, 357-1896.

Maintains reference collections covering anthropology and ethnology; permits on-site use of the collections. Open to the public by appointment; makes interlibrary loans.

Congress:

See Science, Congress (p. 663)

Nongovernmental:

American Anthropological Assn., 4350 N. Fairfax Dr., #640, Arlington, VA 22203; (703) 528-1902. John M. Cornman, executive director. Fax, (703) 528-3546.

Membership: anthropologists, educators, students, and others interested in anthropological studies. Publishes research studies of member organizations, sponsors workshops, and disseminates to members information concerning developments in anthropology.

Institute for the Study of Man, 6861 Elm St., #4H, McLean, VA 22101; (703) 442-8010. Roger Pearson, executive director. Fax, (703) 847-9524.

Publishes academic journals, books, and monographs in areas related to anthropology, psychology, genetics, archaeology, linguistics, and cultural history.

See also American Assn. for the Advancement of Science (p. 666); National Geographic Society (p. 667)

Geography and Mapping

Agencies:

Census Bureau (Commerce Dept.), Geography, 5001 Silver Hill Rd., Suitland, MD (mailing address: Washington, DC 20233); (301) 763-5636. Robert W. Marx, chief. Fax, (301) 763-4749.

Provides maps for use in conducting censuses and surveys and for showing their results geographically; determines names and current boundaries of legal geographic units; defines names and boundaries of selected statistical areas; develops geographic code schemes; maintains computer files of area measurements, geographic boundaries, and map features with address ranges.

Defense Mapping Agency (Defense Dept.), 8613 Lee Highway, Fairfax, VA 22031; (703) 285-9290. Maj. Gen. Raymund E. O'Mara (USAF), director. Fax, (703) 285-9325.

Provides all elements of the Defense Dept., including operational forces worldwide, with maps, charts, and digital data.

National Archives and Records Administration, Cartographic and Architectural Branch, 8601 Adelphi Rd., College Park, MD 20740-6001; (301) 713-7030. John A. Dwyer, chief. Fax, (301) 713-6516.

Makes information available on federal government cartographic records, architectural drawings, and aerial mapping films; prepares descriptive guides and inventories of records. Library open to the public. Records may be reproduced for a fee.

National Oceanic and Atmospheric Administration (Commerce Dept.), National Geodetic Survey, 1305 East-West Highway SSMC Bldg. 3, Silver Spring, MD 20910; (301) 713-3222. Capt. Melvyn C. Grunthal, chief. Information, (301) 443-8631. Fax, (301) 443-8701.

Supplies the framework for surveying, mapping, and construction projects throughout the United States; develops and maintains a national geodetic reference system, which serves as a common reference for latitude, longitude, height, scale, orientation, and gravity measurements.

State Dept., Office of the Geographer, Main State Bldg. 20520; 647-2021. William B. Wood, director. Fax, 647-4296.

Advises the State Dept. and other federal agencies on geographic and cartographic matters. Furnishes technical and analytical research and advice in the field of geography.

U.S. Board on Geographic Names, 12201 Sunrise Valley Dr., Reston, VA (mailing address: National Center 523, Reston, VA 22092); (703) 648-4544. Roger L. Payne, executive secretary, Domestic Names Committee; Randall Flynn, executive secretary, Foreign Names Committee, (703) 285-9518. Fax, (703) 648-5542.

Interagency organization established by Congress to standardize geographic names. Board members are representatives from the departments of Agriculture, Commerce, Defense, Interior, and State; the Central Intelligence Agency; the Government Printing Office; the Library of Congress; and the Postal Service.

U.S. Geological Survey (Interior Dept.), Earth Science Information Center, 12201 Sunrise Valley Dr., Reston, VA (mailing address: National Center 507, Reston, VA 22092); (703) 648-5935. John Shanton, chief. Information, (703) 648-6045. Fax, (703) 648-5548. Toll-free, (800) 872-6277.

Collects, organizes, and distributes cartographic, geographic, hydrologic, and other earth science information; offers maps, reports, and other publications, digital cartographic data, aerial photographs, and space imagery and manned spacecraft photographs for sale. Acts as clearinghouse on cartographic and geographic data covering the United States.

U.S. Geological Survey (Interior Dept.), Information and Data Services, 12201 Sunrise Valley Dr., Reston, VA (mailing address: National Center 508, Reston, VA 22092); (703) 648-5780. Gary W. North, assistant chief. Fax, (703) 648-5939.

Produces maps, bulletins, professional papers, and brochures; sells survey maps and atlases, aerial and space images, and digital spatial data over the counter and through authorized dealers.

U.S. Geological Survey (Interior Dept.), National Mapping Division, 12201 Sunrise Valley Dr., Reston, VA 22092; (703) 648-5748. Allen H. Watkins, chief. Fax, (703) 648-5792. Information and data services, (703) 648-5780.

Provides government agencies and the public with geographic and cartographic information, maps, and technical assistance; conducts research; collects, compiles, and analyzes information about features of the earth's surface; develops and maintains a digital geographic/cartographic database and assists users in applying spatial data; coordinates federal mapping activities; encourages the development of surveying and mapping techniques.

Congress:

Library of Congress, Geography and Map Division, 101 Independence Ave. S.E. 20540; 707-8530. Ralph Ehrenberg, chief. Fax, 707-8531. Reference, 707-6277.

Maintains cartographic collection of maps, atlases, globes, and reference books. Reference service provided; reading room open to the public. Interlibrary loans available through the library's loan division; photocopies, when not limited by copyright or other restriction, available through the library's photoduplication service.

See also Science, Congress (p. 663)

Nongovernmental:

American Congress on Surveying and Mapping, 5410 Grosvenor Lane, #100, Bethesda, MD 20814-2160; (301) 493-0200. John Lisack Jr., executive director. Fax, (301) 493-8245.

Membership: professionals in surveying, cartography, geodesy, and geographic/land information systems. Sponsors workshops and seminars for surveyors and mapping scientists; participates in accreditation of college and university surveying and related degree programs; grants fellowships; develops and administers certification programs for hydrographers and technician surveyors; monitors legislation and regulations.

American Society for Photogrammetry and Remote Sensing, 5410 Grosvenor Lane, #210, Bethesda, MD 20814-2160; (301) 493-0290. William D. French, executive director. Fax, (301) 493-0208.

Promotes use of photogrammetry, remote sensing, and geographic information systems (computerized mapping systems used in urban, regional, and environmental planning) for earth resource evaluation and preparation of maps; publishes scientific and technical manuals.

Assn. of American Geographers, 1710 16th St. N.W. 20009; 234-1450. Ronald F. Abler, executive director. Fax, 234 2144.

Membership: educators, students, business executives, government employees, and scientists in the field of geography. Seeks to advance professional studies in geography and encourages the application of geographic research in education, government, and business.

National Geographic Society, Cartographic Division, 1145 17th St. N.W. 20036; 775-7861. John F. Shupe, chief cartographer, 857-7772. Library, 775-6175. Map orders, (800) 638-4077; in Washington, D.C., 971-1200.

Educational and scientific organization. Supports and conducts research on cartography, mapping, and geography. Produces and sells to the public political, physical, and thematic maps, atlases, and globes.

See also American Assn. for the Advancement of Science (p. 666)

Sociology and Behavioral Science

Agencies:

National Science Foundation, Social, Behavioral, and Economic Sciences, 4201 Wilson Blvd., #905, Arlington, VA 22230; (703) 306-1700. Cora B. Marrett, assistant director. Fax, (703) 306-0495.

Awards grants for research in behavioral and cognitive sciences, social and economic sciences, science resources studies, and international programs. Provides support for science and technology centers and for workshops, symposia, and conferences.

Congress:

See Science, Congress (p. 663)

Nongovernmental:

American Institutes for Research, 3333 K St. N.W. 20007; 342-5000. David A. Goslin, president. Fax, 342-5033.

Conducts research and analysis in the behavioral and social sciences, including education research, health research, and data analysis to assess fairness and equity in the workplace; assists in designing and writing documents; assesses usability of software, systems, and other products; studies human-machine interface.

American Psychological Assn., 750 1st St. N.E. 20002-4242; 336-5500. Raymond D. Fowler, executive vice president. Library, 336-5640. Fax, 336-6069. TDD, 336-6123.

Membership: professional psychologists and educators. Supports research, training, and professional services; works toward improving the qualifications, competence, and training programs of psychologists.

American Sociological Assn., 1722 N St. N.W. 20036; 833-3410. Felice Levine, executive officer. Fax, 785-0146. TDD, 872-0486.

Membership: sociologists, social scientists, and others interested in research, teaching, and application of sociology. Sponsors professional development program, teaching resources center, and education programs; offers fellowships for minorities.

Consortium of Social Science Assns., 1522 K St. N.W., #836 20005; 842-3525. Howard J. Silver, executive director. Fax, 842-2788.

Consortium of associations in the fields of anthropology, economics, history, political science, psychology, sociology, statistics, geography, linguistics, law, and social science. Advocates support for research and monitors federal funding in the social and behavioral sciences; conducts seminars.

Human Resources Research Organization, 66 Canal Center Plaza, #400, Alexandria, VA 22314; (703) 549-3611. William C. Osborn, president.

Research and development organization in the field of industrial psychology. Studies, designs, develops, and evaluates personnel systems, chiefly in the workplace. Interests include personnel selection, promotion, career progression, performance appraisal, training, and program evaluation.

See also American Assn. for the Advancement of Science (p. 666)

Space

General

Agencies:

Commerce Dept., Air and Space Commercialization, Main Commerce Bldg., Rm. 5027 20230; 482-6125. Keith Calhoun-Senghor, director. Fax, 482-5173.

Promotes private investment in space activities; seeks to remove legal, policy, and institutional impediments to space commerce; represents private sector interests at the federal level; coordinates commercial space policy for the Commerce Dept.

National Aeronautics and Space Administration (NASA), 300 E St. S.W. (mailing address: NASA Headquarters, Mail Code A, Washington, DC 20546); 358-1010. Daniel Goldin, administrator. Information, 358-1000. Fax, 358-2810.

Conducts research on problems of flight within and outside the earth's atmosphere; develops, constructs, tests, and operates experimental aeronautical and space vehicles; conducts activities for manned and unmanned exploration of space; maintains information center.

National Aeronautics and Space Administration, Advanced Concepts and Technology, 300 E St. S.W. (mailing address: NASA Headquarters, Mail Code C, Washington, DC 20546); 358-0701. Greg Reck, acting associate administrator. Fax, 358-3878.

Manages research and technology for civil space initiatives; promotes commercialization of space; conducts cost analyses of proposed initiatives.

National Aeronautics and Space Administration, Aeronautics, 300 E. St. S.W. (mailing address: NASA Headquarters, Mail Code R, Washington, DC 20546); 358-2693. Wesley L. Harris, associate administrator. Fax, 358-4066.

Conducts basic and applied research in aerodynamics, materials, structures, avionics, propulsion, human factors, and safety; manages the following NASA research centers: Ames (Mountain View, Calif.); Dryden (Edwards, Calif.); Langley (Hampton, Va.); and Lewis (Cleveland, Ohio).

National Aeronautics and Space Administration, Exploration, 300 E St. S.W. (mailing address: NASA Headquarters, Mail Code X, Washington, DC 20546); 358-1879. Michael D. Griffin, associate administrator. Fax, 358-4336.

Contributes to scientific and technical knowledge of the moon and Mars; develops strategies necessary for successful missions to the moon and Mars; works with other government agencies, including the Defense and Energy departments, to develop technologies for future missions.

National Aeronautics and Space Administration, International Relations, 300 E St. S.W. (mailing address: NASA Headquarters, Mail Code IR, Washington, DC 20546); 358-0900. Peter G. Smith, director. Information, 358-1639. Fax, 358-3029.

Acts as liaison with space agencies of foreign countries; negotiates and implements international agreements for cooperation in space; works with other U.S. government agencies on international issues regarding space and aeronautics.

National Aeronautics and Space Administration, NASA Advisory Council, 300 E St. S.W. (mailing address: NASA Headquarters, Mail Code IC, Washington, DC 20546); 358-0791. Sylvia K. Kraemer, executive secretary. Fax, 358-2983.

Advises the administrator on NASA's aeronautics and space plans and programs. The council comprises the following advisory committees: Aeronautics, Technology and Commercialization, Life and Microgravity Sciences and Applications, Space Science, History, Space Station, Minority Business Resource, and Earth Systems Science and Applications.

National Aeronautics and Space Administration, Safety and Mission Quality, 300 E St. S.W. (mailing address: NASA Headquarters, Mail Code Q, Washington, DC 20546); 358-2406. Col. Frederick D. Gregory (USAF), associate administrator. Fax, 358-2699.

Evaluates the safety and reliability of NASA systems and programs. Alerts officials to technical execution and physical readiness of NASA projects.

National Aeronautics and Space Administration, Space Communications, 300 E St. S.W. (mailing address: NASA Headquarters, Mail Code O, Washington, DC 20546); 358-2020. Charles T. Force, associate administrator. Fax, 358-3530.

Plans, develops, and operates worldwide tracking, data acquisition, data processing, and communications systems, facilities, and services essential to the agency's space flight missions, including the Space Tracking Data Network at Goddard Space Flight Center in Greenbelt, Md., and the Deep Space Network operated by the Jet Propulsion Laboratory in Pasadena, Calif. Gives support to planetary spacecraft, earth-orbiting satellites, shuttle missions, sounding rockets, balloons, and aeronautical test vehicles.

National Aeronautics and Space Administration, Space Flight, 300 E St. S.W. (mailing address: NASA Headquarters, Mail Code M, Washington, DC 20546); 358-2015. Maj. Gen. Jeremiah W. Pearson (USMC, ret.), associate administrator. Fax, 358-2838.

Responsible for space transportation systems operations. Manages the Johnson Space Center, Kennedy Space Center, Marshall Space Flight Center, and Stennis Space Center. Administers the development, testing, and production phases of the space shuttle. Manages the shuttle space lab program and the space station.

National Air and Space Museum (Smithsonian Institution), 6th St. and Independence Ave. S.W. 20560; 357-1745. Martin Harwit, director. Press, 357-1552. Library, 357-3133. TDD, 357-1505. Education office, 786-2106. Daily space and earth phenomena report, 357-2000 (recording). Tours, 357-1400.

Collects, preserves, and exhibits astronautical objects and equipment of historical interest, including manned spacecraft and communications and weather satellites. Library open to the public by appointment.

Office of Science and Technology Policy (Executive Office of the President), Technology, Old Executive Office Bldg. 20500; 395-6175. Lionel S. Johns, associate director. Fax, 395-4155.

Analyzes policies and advises the president on space science issues; coordinates executive office and federal agency actions related to these issues.

Transportation Dept., Commercial Space Transportation, 400 7th St. S.W. 20590; 366-2937. Frank C. Weaver, director. Fax, 366-7256.

Promotes and facilitates the operation of commercial expendable space launch vehicles by the private sector; licenses and regulates these activities.

See also Civil Air Patrol (p. 706)

Congress:

General Accounting Office, National Security and International Affairs, 441 G St. N.W. 20548; 512-2800. Frank C. Conahan, assistant comptroller general. Fax, 512-7686.

Independent, nonpartisan agency in the legislative branch. Audits, analyzes, and evaluates the performance of the National Aeronautics and Space Administration. Makes unclassified reports available to the public.

House Appropriations Committee, Subcommittee on VA, HUD, and Independent Agencies, H143 CAP 20515; 225-3241. Louis Stokes, D-Ohio, chairman; Paul Thompson, staff assistant.

Jurisdiction over legislation to appropriate funds for the National Aeronautics and Space Administration.

House Government Operations Committee, Subcommittee on Commerce, Consumer, and Monetary Affairs, B377 RHOB 20515; 225-4407. John M. Spratt Jr., D-S.C., chairman; Theodore Jacobs, staff director. Fax, 225-2441.

Oversees operations of the National Oceanic and Atmospheric Administration.

National Aeronautics and Space Administration

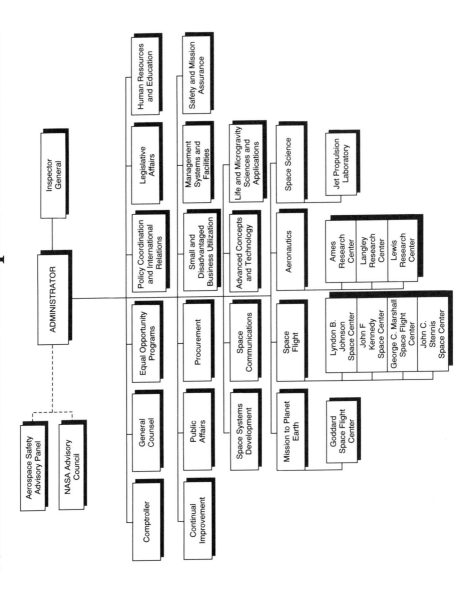

House Government Operations Committee, Subcommittee on Legislation and National Security, B373 RHOB 20515; 225-5147. John Conyers Jr., D-Mich., chairman; James C. Turner, staff director. Fax, 225-2373.

Oversees operations of the National Aeronautics and Space Administration.

House Science, Space, and Technology Committee, Subcommittee on Space, 2320 RHOB 20515; 225-7858. Ralph M. Hall, D-Texas, chairman; William S. Smith, staff director.

Jurisdiction over legislation on space programs, national research and development in space exploration, space commercialization, earth-observing systems, the Office of Science, Technology, and Space Policy, the National Aeronautics and Space Administration, and the satellite and atmospheric systems of the National Oceanic and Atmospheric Administration, including the National Environmental Satellite, Data, and Information Service.

Senate Appropriations Committee, Subcommittee on VA, HUD, and Independent Agencies, SD-142 20510; 224-7211. Barbara A. Mikulski, D-Md., chair; Kevin F. Kelly, clerk.

Jurisdiction over legislation to appropriate funds for the National Aeronautics and Space Administration and the Office of Science, Technology, and Space Policy.

Senate Commerce, Science, and Transportation Committee, Subcommittee on National Ocean Policy Study, SH-425 (mailing address: SD-508, Washington, DC 20510); 224-4912. Ernest F. Hollings, D-S.C., chairman; Penny Dalton, staff member.

Studies issues relating to the National Environmental Satellite, Data, and Information Service and the satellite and atmospheric systems of the National Oceanic and Atmospheric Administration. (Subcommittee does not report legislation.)

Senate Commerce, Science, and Transportation Committee, Subcommittee on Science, Technology, and Space, SH-427 (mailing address: SD-508, Washington, DC 20510); 224-9360. John D. Rockefeller IV, D-W.Va., chairman; Patrick H. Windham, senior professional staff member.

Jurisdiction over legislation on nonmilitary space programs, national research and development in space exploration, space commercialization, and earth-observing systems. Oversight and legislative jurisdiction over the National Aeronautics and Space Administration and the Office of Science, Technology, and Space Policy.

See also Congressional Space Caucus (p. 759)

Nongovernmental:

Aerospace Education Foundation, 1501 Lee Highway, Arlington, VA 22209; (703) 247-5839. Phil Lacombe, director. Fax, (703) 247-5853.

Promotes knowledge and appreciation of U.S. military and civilian aerospace development and history. Sponsors educational symposia and scholarships for Reserve Officers Training Corps (ROTC) graduates. (Affiliated with the Air Force Assn.)

Aerospace Industries Assn. of America, 1250 Eye St. N.W., #1100 20005; 371-8400. Don Fuqua, president. Information, 371-8552. Press, 371-8544. Library, 371-8565. Fax, 371-8573.

Represents U.S. manufacturers of commercial, military, and business aircraft; helicopters; aircraft engines; missiles; spacecraft; and related components and equipment. Library open to the public by appointment.

American Astronautical Society, 6352 Rolling Mill Pl., #102, Springfield, VA 22152; (703) 866-0020. Carolyn Brown, executive director. Fax, (703) 866-3526.

Scientific and technological society of researchers, scientists, astronauts, and other professionals in the field of astronautics and spaceflight engineering. Organizes national and local meetings and symposia.

American Institute of Aeronautics and Astronautics, 901 D St. S.W. (mailing address: 370 L'Enfant Promenade S.W., Washington, DC 20024); 646-7400. Cort Durocher, executive director. Information, 646-7432. Fax, 646-7508.

Membership: engineers, scientists, and students in the fields of aeronautics and astronautics. Holds workshops on aerospace technical issues for congressional subcommittees. Offers computerized database through its Technical Information Service in New York.

Institute for Security and Cooperation in Outer Space, 3400 International Dr. N.W., #2K-500 20008; 537-0831. Connie Van Praet, director. Fax, 966-7393.

Educates the public on the benefits of international cooperation in a weapons-free space environment. Conducts policy research on international civil and military space initiatives. (Associated with the New York-based United Nations Department of Public Information.)

National Research Council, Aeronautics and Space Engineering Board, 2001 Wisconsin Ave. N.W. (mailing address: 2101 Constitution Ave. N.W., #HA292, Washington, DC 20418); 334-2855. JoAnn Clayton, director. Information, 334-2855. Press, 334-2138. Library, 334-2125. Fax, 334-2620. Publications, 334-2855.

Membership: aeronautics and space experts. Advises government agencies on aeronautics and space engineering research, technology, and experiments. Library open to the public by appointment. (The National Research Council is the operating arm of the National Academy of Sciences and the National Academy of Engineering.)

National Research Council, Space Studies Board, 2001 Wisconsin Ave. N.W. (mailing address: 2101 Constitution Ave. N.W., #HA584, Washington, DC 20418); 334-3477. Marc S. Allen, director. Information, 334-2855. Press, 334-2138. Library, 334-2125. Fax, 334-3701. Publications, 334-3313.

Advises NASA and other federal agencies on space science and applications programs; provides research assessments and long-term research strategies. Interests include astronomy, lunar and planetary exploration, solar and space physics, earth science, space biology and medicine, and microgravity materials research. Library open to the public by appointment.

National Space Society, 922 Pennsylvania Ave. S.E. 20003; 543-1900. Lori Garver, executive director. Fax, 546-4189.

Membership: individuals interested in space programs and applications of space technology. Provides information on NASA and commercial space activities; promotes public education on space exploration and development.

Resources for the Future, 1616 P St. N.W. 20036; 328-5000. Robert Fri, president. Fax, 939-3460.

Examines the economic aspects of U.S. space policy, including policy on the space shuttle, unmanned rockets, communications satellites, and the space station. Focuses on the role of private business versus that of government.

Space Policy Institute (George Washington University), 2130 H St. N.W. 20052; 994-7292. John M. Logsdon, director. Fax, 994-1639.

Conducts research on space policy issues; organizes seminars, symposia, and conferences. Focuses on civilian space activities, including competitive and cooperative interactions on space between the United States and other countries.

Spacecause, 922 Pennsylvania Ave. S.E. 20003; 543-1900. Mark M. Hopkins, president. Fax, 546-4189.

Coalition of the public, academia, and business that supports a stronger government policy priority on civilian space activities; monitors legislation and regulations.

Young Astronaut Council, 1308 19th St. N.W. 20036; 682-1984. T. Wendell Butler, president. Fax, 775-1773.

Promotes improved math and science skills through aerospace activities for children ages 3 to 16. Encourages children to pursue careers in aerospace fields.

See also George C. Marshall Institute (p. 666); National Aviation Club (p. 710)

Research and Technology

Agencies:

National Aeronautics and Space Administration, Advanced Concepts and Technology, 300 E St. S.W. (mailing address: NASA Headquarters, Mail Code C, Washington, DC 20546); 358-0701. Greg Reck, acting associate administrator. Fax, 358-3878.

Conducts advanced space research and technology activities at all NASA centers. Manages research and technology for the civil space initiative and for space exploration.

National Aeronautics and Space Administration, Exploration, 300 E St. S.W. (mailing address: NASA Headquarters, Mail Code X, Washington, DC 20546); 358-1879. Michael D. Griffin, associate administrator. Fax, 358-4336.

Contributes to scientific and technical knowledge of the moon and Mars; develops strategies necessary for successful missions to the moon and Mars; works with other government agencies, including the Defense and Energy departments, to develop technologies for future missions.

National Aeronautics and Space Administration, International Space Station, 300 E St. S.W. (mailing address: NASA Headquarters, Mail Code D, Washington, DC 20546); 358-4424. Wil C. Trafton, director. Information, 358-1778. Fax, 358-2949.

Responsible for developing a permanently manned orbiting space station to serve as a research facility for scientific, technological, and commercial activities.

National Aeronautics and Space Administration, National Space Science Data Center, Goddard Space Flight Center, Greenbelt Rd., Greenbelt, MD (mailing address: Code 633, Greenbelt, MD 20771); (301) 286-7355. Joseph H. King, head. Fax, (301) 286-1771.

Acquires, catalogs, and distributes NASA mission data to the international space science community, including research organizations, universities, and other interested organizations worldwide. Provides software tools and network access to promote collaborative data analysis. (Mail data requests c/o National Space Science Data Center, Code 633.4/Request Coordination Office, (301) 286-6695.)

National Aeronautics and Space Administration, Space Science, 300 E St. S.W. (mailing address: NASA Headquarters, Mail Code S, Washington, DC 20546); 358-1409. Wesley T. Huntress Jr., associate administrator. Information, 358-1547. Fax, 358-3092.

Makes information available on technological developments that have resulted from NASA programs. (Accepts written requests for specific technical information.)

National Aeronautics and Space Administration, Space Systems Development, 300 E St. S.W. (mailing address: NASA Headquarters, Mail Code D, Washington, DC 20546); 358-4600. Arnold D. Aldrich, associate administrator. Information, 358-1776. Fax, 358-2920.

Supervises large propulsion systems, including the national launch system and its main engine, and other flight systems. Responsible for planning the Advanced Transportation Systems Program.

Congress:

See *Space, General, Congress (p. 695)*

Space Sciences

Agencies:

National Aeronautics and Space Administration, Goddard Space Flight Center, Greenbelt, MD 20771; (301) 286-5121. John M. Klineberg, director. Information, (301) 286-8955. Fax, (301) 286-1714.

Conducts space and earth science research; performs advanced planning for space missions; develops and manages spacecraft and scientific instrumentation; functions as the control center for earth orbital satellites; operates the NASA tracking and data relay satellite system.

National Aeronautics and Space Administration, Life and Microgravity Sciences and Applications, 300 E St. S.W. (mailing address: NASA Headquarters, Mail Code U, Washington, DC 20546); 358-0122. Harry Holloway, associate administrator. Information, 358-1547. Fax, 358-4174.

Conducts all in-orbit exploration of space. Areas of research include life sciences, materials, and microgravity effects in space.

Office of Science and Technology Policy (Executive Office of the President), Technology, Old Executive Office Bldg. 20500; 395-6175. Lionel S. Johns, associate director. Fax, 395-4155.

Advises the president on space science issues; coordinates executive office and federal agency actions related to these issues.

Congress:

See *Space, General, Congress (p. 695)*

Nongovernmental:

National Research Council, Space Studies Board, 2001 Wisconsin Ave. N.W. (mailing address: 2101 Constitution Ave. N.W., #HA584, Washington, DC 20418); 334-3477. Marc S. Allen, director. Information, 334-2855. Press, 334-2138. Library, 334-2125. Fax, 334-3701. Publications, 334-3313.

Advises NASA and other federal agencies on space science and applications programs; provides research assessments and long-term research strategies. Interests include astronomy, lunar and planetary exploration, solar and space physics, earth science, space biology and medicine, and microgravity materials research. Library open to the public by appointment. (The National Research Council is the operating arm of the National Academy of Sciences and the National Academy of Engineering.)

Key Agencies:

Interstate Commerce Commission
12th St. and Constitution Ave. N.W. 20423
Information: 927-5350

National Transportation Safety Board
490 L'Enfant Plaza East S.W. 20594
Information: 382-6600

Transportation Dept.
400 7th St. S.W. 20590
Information: 366-4570

Key Committees:

House Public Works and Transportation Committee
2165 RHOB 20515
Phone: 225-4472

Senate Commerce, Science, and Transportation Committee
SD-508 20510
Phone: 224-5115

Key Personnel:

Interstate Commerce Commission
Gail C. McDonald, chair

National Transportation Safety Board
Carl W. Vogt, chairman

Transportation Dept.
Federico F. Peña, secretary

Morton Downey, deputy secretary

Raymond G. Romero, assistant secretary designate for aviation and international affairs

Frank Kruesi, assistant secretary for transportation policy

David R. Hinson, administrator, Federal Aviation Administration

Rodney Slater, administrator, Federal Highway Administration

Jolene M. Molitoris, administrator, Federal Railroad Administration

Gordon J. Linton, administrator, Federal Transit Administration

Vice Adm. Albert J. Herberger, administrator, Maritime Administration

Christopher A. Hart, acting administrator, National Highway Traffic Safety Administration

Dharmendra K. Sharma, administrator designate, Research and Special Programs Administration

Stanford Parris, administrator, Saint Lawrence Seaway Development Corp.

Adm. Robert Kramek, commandant designate, U.S. Coast Guard

17

Transportation

Contents:

Transportation

See also Energy Use: Conservation (p. 209)

General

Agencies:

Census Bureau (Commerce Dept.), Business Division, Suitland and Silver Hill Rds., Suitland, MD (mailing address: Washington, DC 20233); (301) 763-2735. William G. Bostic Jr., chief, transportation branch. Fax, (301) 763-2928.

Provides data and explains proper use of data for the bureau's Truck Inventory and Use Survey and Nationwide Truck Activity and Commodity Survey; conducts research programs.

Interstate Commerce Commission, 12th St. and Constitution Ave. N.W. 20423; 927-6020. Gail C. McDonald, chair. Information, 927-5350. Press, 927-5340. Library, 927-7328. Fax, 927-1472.

Regulates interstate surface transportation for foreign and U.S. vehicles in the United States, including railroads, trucking companies, bus lines, freight forwarders of household goods, water carriers, coal slurry pipelines, and transportation brokers. Operates consumer protection programs; consumer complaints should be directed to the nearest regional office. Library open to the public. *(See Regional Federal Information Sources list, p. 852)*

Interstate Commerce Commission, Compliance and Consumer Assistance, 12th St. and Constitution Ave. N.W. 20423; 927-5500. Bernard Gaillard, director. Fax, 927-5529. TDD, 927-5721.

Oversees compliance with and enforcement of economic laws and regulations concerning interstate surface carriers, including household goods movers, buses, trucks, trains, and inland and coastal waterway transportation.

Interstate Commerce Commission, Proceedings, 12th St. and Constitution Ave. N.W. 20423; 927-7513. David M. Konschnik, director. Fax, 927-6419. TDD, 927-5721.

Regulates licensing, rates, service standards, and financial transactions for inland waterways, interstate trucking, passenger carriage, pipelines, and railroads; provides information and assistance; handles complaints and rulemaking proceedings; recommends legislative changes to the commission.

Interstate Commerce Commission, Public Assistance, 12th St. and Constitution Ave. N.W. 20423; 927-7597. Dan King, acting director. Fax, 927-5158. TDD, 927-5721.

Assists small-business owners and transportation firms in filing protests on rates and filing for new operating authority or extensions for motor, rail, and inland water carriers. Provides information on how to obtain service where there is none.

National Transportation Safety Board, 490 L'Enfant Plaza East S.W. 20594; 382-6502. Carl W. Vogt, chairman. Information, 382-6600. Fax, 382-6609.

Promotes transportation safety through independent investigations of accidents and other safety problems. Makes recommendations for safety improvement.

National Transportation Safety Board, Research and Engineering, 490 L'Enfant Plaza East S.W. 20594; 382-6560. Bernard S. Loeb, director. Fax, 382-6008.

Evaluates effectiveness of federal, state, and local safety programs. Identifies transportation safety issues not addressed by government or industry. Conducts studies on specific safety problems.

Office of Management and Budget (Executive Office of the President), Transportation, New Executive Office Bldg. 20503; 395-5704. Roger Adkins, chief. Fax, 395-4797.

Assists and advises the OMB director on budget preparation, proposed legislation, and evaluations of Transportation Dept. programs, policies, and activities.

Transportation Dept., 400 7th St. S.W. 20590; 366-1111. Federico F. Peña, secretary. Information, 366-4570. Fax, 366-7202.

Deals with most areas of transportation. Comprises the Coast Guard, Federal Aviation Administration, Federal Highway Administration, Federal Railroad Administration, Maritime Administration, National Highway Traffic Safety Administration, Research and Special Programs Administration, Federal Transit Administration, and Saint Lawrence Seaway Development Corp.

Transportation Dept., Aviation and International Affairs, 400 7th St. S.W. 20590; 366-4551. Raymond G. Romero, assistant secretary designate. Fax, 366-7127.

Formulates domestic aviation policy. Formulates international aviation, maritime, and across-the-border railroad and trucking policy. Assesses the performance of the nation's aviation network in meeting public needs. Conducts research on the social and economic conditions of the aviation industry; analyzes the effect of government policies on the aviation industry.

Transportation Dept., Consumer Affairs, 400 7th St. S.W., #10405 20590; 366-2220. Hoyte Decker, assistant director. Fax, 366-7907.

Refers consumer complaints to appropriate departmental offices; advises the secretary on consumer issues; coordinates citizen participation activities and promotes joint projects with consumer interest groups; serves as ombudsman for consumer protection affairs; publishes educational materials.

Transportation Dept., Environmental Division, 400 7th St. S.W., #9217 20590; 366-4366. Eugene L. Lehr, chief. Fax, 366-7618.

Develops environmental policy and makes recommendations to the secretary; monitors Transportation Dept. implementation of environmental legislation; reviews and comments on environmental impact statements for major transportation projects; acts as liaison with other federal agencies and state and local governments on environmental matters related to transportation.

Transportation Dept., Intelligence and Security, 400 7th St. S.W. 20590; 366-6535. Rear Adm. Paul E. Busick (USCG), director. Fax, 366-7261.

Advises the secretary on transportation intelligence and security policy. Acts as liaison with the intelligence community, federal agencies, corporations, and interest groups; administers counterterrorism strategic planning processes.

Transportation Dept., Research and Special Programs Administration, 400 7th St. S.W. 20590; 366-4433. Dharmendra K. Sharma, administrator designate. Fax, 366-7431.

Coordinates department's research and development programs to improve safety of systems, including hazardous materials shipments and pipeline safety, and to ensure effectiveness, efficiency, and viability of transportation systems; responsible for economic matters that concern the airline industry, including fares and tariffs; oversees Transportation Systems Center in Cambridge, Mass., and Transportation Safety Institute in Oklahoma City, Okla.

Transportation Dept., Transportation Policy, 400 7th St. S.W. 20590; 366-4544. Frank Kruesi, assistant secretary. Fax, 366-7127.

Oversees policy development for all domestic transportation except aviation. Assesses the performance of the domestic transportation network; analyzes the effect of government policies on domestic transportation industries.

Transportation Dept., Transportation Regulatory Affairs, 400 7th St. S.W. 20590; 366 4220. Frank C. Weaver, director. Fax, 366-7618.

Conducts economic and regulatory policy research, primarily on intercity transportation systems, and recommends policy to the secretary; reviews environmental and safety regulatory issues. Prepares material for filings before various regulatory agencies and boards. Promotes deregulation of transportation industries.

U.S. Customs Service (Treasury Dept.), Inspection and Control, 1301 Constitution Ave. N.W. 20229; 927-0500. Charles W. Winwood, assistant commissioner. Fax, 927-1442.

Enforces statutes relating to the processing and regulation of people, baggage, cargo, and mail in and out of the United States; assesses and collects customs duties, excise taxes, fees, and penalties due on imported merchandise; administers certain navigation laws.

Congress:

General Accounting Office, Transportation, 901 D St. S.W., #802 20024; 401-6001. Allen Li, associate director. Fax, 401-6025.

Independent, nonpartisan agency in the legislative branch. Audits, analyzes, and evaluates performance of the Transportation Dept.; makes reports available to the public.

Transportation Dept.

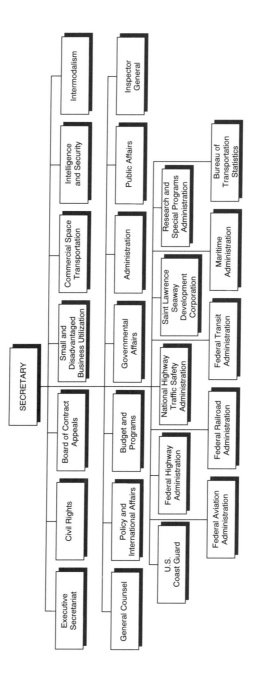

House Appropriations Committee, Subcommittee on Commerce, Justice, State, and Judiciary, H309 CAP 20515; 225-3351. Neal Smith, D-Iowa, chairman; John Osthaus, staff assistant.

Jurisdiction over legislation to appropriate funds for the Maritime Administration and Federal Maritime Commission.

House Appropriations Committee, Subcommittee on Transportation, 2358 RHOB 20515; 225-2141. Bob Carr, D-Mich., chairman; Del Davis, staff assistant.

Jurisdiction over legislation to appropriate funds for the Transportation Dept. (except the Maritime Administration) and related agencies, including the National Transportation Safety Board and the Interstate Commerce Commission.

House Government Operations Committee, Subcommittee on Information, Justice, Transportation, and Agriculture, B349C RHOB 20515; 225-3741. Gary Condit, D-Calif., chairman; Shannon Lahey, acting staff director. Fax, 225-2445.

Oversees operations of the Transportation Dept. and the National Transportation Safety Board.

House Public Works and Transportation Committee, 2165 RHOB 20515; 225-4472. Norman Y. Mineta, D-Calif., chairman; Paul Schoellhamer, chief of staff.

Jurisdiction over legislation on transportation, except railroads.

Senate Appropriations Committee, Subcommittee on Commerce, Justice, State, and Judiciary, S146A CAP 20510; 224-7277. Ernest F. Hollings, D-S.C., chairman; Scott B. Gudes, clerk.

Jurisdiction over legislation to appropriate funds for the Maritime Administration and the Federal Maritime Commission.

Senate Appropriations Committee, Subcommittee on Transportation, SD-156 20510; 224-7281. Frank R. Lautenberg, D-N.J., chairman; Patrick J. McCann, clerk.

Jurisdiction over legislation to appropriate funds for the Transportation Dept. (except the Maritime Administration) and related agencies, including the National Transportation Safety Board and the Interstate Commerce Commission.

Senate Commerce, Science, and Transportation Committee, SD-508 20510; 224-5115. Ernest F. Hollings, D-S.C., chairman; Kevin Curtin, chief counsel and staff director.

Jurisdiction over legislation on transportation; oversight of the Transportation Dept. and the National Transportation Safety Board.

Senate Special Committee on Aging, SD-G31 20510; 224-5364. David Pryor, D-Ark., chairman; Theresa M. Forster, staff director.

Studies and makes recommendations on the availability of transportation for the elderly.

Nongovernmental:

American Public Works Assn., 1301 Pennsylvania Ave. N.W., #501 20004; 393-2792. Charles Bryley, director, Washington office. Fax, 737-9153.

Membership: engineers, architects, and others who maintain and manage public works facilities and services. Conducts research and promotes exchange of information on transportation-related issues. (Headquarters in Kansas City.)

Assn. of Transportation Practitioners, 19564 Club House Rd., Gaithersburg, MD 20879-3002; (301) 670-6733. E. Dale Jones, executive director. Fax, (301) 670-6735.

Provides members with continuing educational development in transportation law and practice. Interests include railroad, motor, energy, pipeline, antitrust, labor, safety, and environmental matters.

Bicycle Federation of America, 1506 21st St. N.W., #200 20036; 463-6622. William C. Wilkinson III, executive director. Fax, 463-6625.

Promotes bicycle use; conducts research, planning, and training projects; develops safety education and public information materials. Works to increase public awareness of the benefits and opportunities of bicycling. Manages the Bicycle Institute of America and the Pedestrian Federation of America.

Community Transportation Assn. of America, 1440 New York Ave. N.W., #440 20005; 628-1480. David Raphael, executive director. Toll-free, (800) 527-8279. Fax, 737-9197.

Concerned with rural, small-city, and specialized transportation.

The Institute of Navigation, 1800 Diagonal Rd., #480, Alexandria, VA 22314-2840; (703) 683-7101. David Scull, executive director. Fax, (703) 683-7105.

Membership: individuals and organizations interested in navigation. Encourages research in navigation and establishment of uniform practices in navigation operations and education; conducts symposia on air, space, marine, and land navigation.

Institute of Transportation Engineers, 525 School St. S.W., #410 20024; 554-8050. Thomas W. Brahms, executive director. Fax, 863-5486.

Membership: international professional transportation engineers. Conducts research, seminars, and training sessions; provides professional and scientific information on transportation standards and recommended practices.

The National Industrial Transportation League, 1700 N. Moore St., Arlington, VA 22209; (703) 524-5011. Edward M. Emmett, president. Fax, (703) 524-5017.

Membership: air, water, and surface shippers and receivers, including industries, corporations, chambers of commerce, and trade associations. Monitors legislation and regulations.

National Research Council, Transportation Research Board, 2001 Wisconsin Ave. N.W. (mailing address: 2101 Constitution Ave. N.W., Washington, DC 20418); 334-2936. Thomas B. Deen, executive director. Information, 334-2933. Library, 334-2989. Fax, 334-2527. Publications, 334-3213. Toll-free, (800) 424-9818.

Promotes research in transportation systems planning and administration and in the design, construction, maintenance, and operation of transportation facilities. Provides information to state and national highway and transportation departments; operates research information services; conducts special studies, conferences, and workshops; publishes technical reports. Library open to the public by appointment. (The National Research Council is the operating arm of the National Academy of Sciences and the National Academy of Engineering.)

Rebuild America Coalition, c/o American Public Works Assn., 1301 Pennsylvania Ave. N.W., #501 20004; 393-2792. Carol Everett, executive director. Fax, 737-9153.

Coalition of public and private organizations concerned with maintaining the infrastructure of the United States. Advocates government encouragement of innovative technology, financing, and public-private partnerships to build and rebuild public facilities.

Union of Concerned Scientists, Transportation, 1616 P St. N.W., #310 20036; 332-0900. Alden Meyer, legislative director. Fax, 332-0905.

Independent group of scientists concerned with market-based strategies to reduce the environmental, economic, and public health effects of the U.S. transportation system.

See also National Assn. of Regional Councils (p. 313)

Transportation: Air

General

See also Environment, Air Pollution (p. 623)

Agencies:

Civil Air Patrol, National Capital Wing, Bolling Air Force Base 20332; 404-7776. Col. Gene Hartman, wing commander. Fax, 767-5695.

Official civilian auxiliary of the U.S. Air Force. Primary function is to conduct search-and-rescue missions for the Air Force. Maintains an aerospace education program for adults and a cadet program for junior and senior high school students. (Headquarters at Maxwell Air Force Base, Ala.)

Federal Aviation Administration (Transportation Dept.), 800 Independence Ave. S.W. 20591; 267-3111. David R. Hinson, administrator. Press, 267-3883. Fax, 267-5047.

Regulates air commerce to improve aviation safety; promotes development of a national system of airports; develops and operates a common system of air traffic control and air navigation for both civilian and military aircraft; prepares the annual National Aviation System Plan.

Federal Aviation Administration (Transportation Dept.), Aviation Education, 400 7th St. S.W., #PL 100, AHT 100 20590; 366-7500. Phillip S. Woodruff, director. Fax, 366-3786.

Provides schools and colleges with educational materials; sponsors aviation education activities for the public and the education community.

Federal Aviation Administration (Transportation Dept.), Aviation Policy, Plans, and Management Analysis, 800 Independence Ave. S.W. 20591; 267-3274. John M. Rodgers, director. Fax, 267-3324.

Responsible for economic and regulatory policy and analysis, aviation activity forecasts, and strategic planning within the FAA.

Federal Aviation Administration (Transportation Dept.), Chief Scientist, 800 Independence Ave. S.W. 20591; 267-9451. Robert E. Machol, chief scientist. Fax, 267-5117.

Responsible for long-range technical program requirements. Makes independent assessment of readiness of systems FAA intends to purchase. Coordinates efforts with those of other government agencies and the private sector. Advises the administrator, the associate administrator for system engineering and development, and the executive director for development on technical and scientific matters. Conducts workshops and symposia.

Federal Aviation Administration (Transportation Dept.), International Aviation, 800 Independence Ave. S.W. 20591; 267-3213. Joan W. Bauerlein, director. Fax, 267-5306.

Coordinates all activities of the FAA that involve foreign relations; acts as liaison with the State Dept. and other agencies concerning international aviation; provides other countries with technical assistance on civil aviation problems; formulates international civil aviation policy.

Federal Aviation Administration (Transportation Dept.), Statistics and Forecast, 800 Independence Ave. S.W., #935, APO-110 20591; 267-3357. Robert L. Bowles, manager. Fax, 267-3324.

Maintains statistics relating to civil aircraft, air personnel and airports, age and type of pilots and air personnel, passenger data, activity counts at FAA air traffic control facilities, and related information.

Federal Aviation Administration (Transportation Dept.), System Engineering and Development, 1250 Maryland Ave. S.W. (mailing address: 800 Independence Ave. S.W., Washington, DC 20591); 287-8535. Martin T. Pozesky, associate administrator. Fax, 287-8500.

Advises and assists in developing advanced technologies to meet National Airspace System Development requirements.

Federal Aviation Administration (Transportation Dept.), Training and Higher Education, 400 7th St. S.W., AHT-30, Plaza Level 100 20590; 366-7503. Joseph P. Kisicki, director; Larry Lackey, manager, airway science grants, 366-6641. Fax, 366-3786.

Administers science curriculum program that promotes aviation education in colleges and universities by developing and certifying school curricula. Provides airway science grants for the construction of facilities and equipment used in airway science education programs.

Justice Dept., Civil Division, 1425 New York Ave. N.W., #10100 (mailing address: P.O. Box 14271, Washington, DC 20044-4271); 616-4000. Gary W. Allen, director, torts branch, aviation/admiralty litigation. Information, 616-2777. Fax, 616-4002.

Represents the federal government in civil suits arising from aviation incidents and accidents.

National Air and Space Museum (Smithsonian Institution), 6th St. and Independence Ave. S.W. 20560; 357-1745. Martin Harwit, director. Press, 357-1552. Library, 357-3133. TDD, 357-1505. Education office, 786-2106. Tours, 357-1400.

Maintains exhibits and collections on aeronautics, pioneers of flight, and early aircraft through modern air technology. Library open to the public by appointment.

National Mediation Board, 1301 K St. N.W., #250E 20572; 523-5920. Kimberly A. Madigan, chair. Information, 523-5335. Fax, 523-1494.

Mediates labor disputes in the airline industry; determines and certifies labor representatives for the industry.

Transportation Dept., Aviation and Surface Transportation Audits, 400 7th St. S.W. 20590; 366-1437. Alexis M. Stefani, director. Fax, 366-3530.

Provides auditing services for the Essential Air Service Program, which guarantees federally subsidized air service to small communities, and other airline economic programs. Audits internal departmental programs.

Transportation Dept., Consumer Affairs, 400 7th St. S.W., #10405 20590; 366-2220. Hoyte Decker, assistant director. Fax, 366-7907.

Addresses complaints about airline service and consumer-protection matters. Conducts investigations, provides assistance, and reviews regulations affecting air carriers.

Congress:

General Accounting Office, Transportation, 901 D St. S.W., #802 20024; 401-6001. Allen Li, associate director. Fax, 401-6025.

Independent, nonpartisan agency in the legislative branch. Audits, analyzes, and evaluates performance of the Transportation Dept., including the Federal Aviation Administration; makes reports available to the public.

House Appropriations Committee, Subcommittee on Transportation, 2358 RHOB 20515; 225-2141. Bob Carr, D-Mich., chairman; Del Davis, staff assistant.

Jurisdiction over legislation to appropriate funds for the Federal Aviation Administration.

House Public Works and Transportation Committee, Subcommittee on Aviation, 2251 RHOB 20515; 225-9161. James L. Oberstar, D-Minn., chairman; David A. Heymsfeld, chief counsel.

Jurisdiction over legislation on civil aviation, including airport funding, airline deregulation, safety issues, and the Federal Aviation Administration (except research and development). Jurisdiction over aviation noise pollution legislation.

House Science, Space, and Technology Committee, Subcommittee on Technology, Environment, and Aviation, B374 RHOB 20515; 225-9662. Tim Valentine, D-N.C., chairman; James H. Turner, staff director.

Jurisdiction over legislation on civil aviation research and development, including the National Aeronautics and Space Administration (authorization relating to aeronautics) and the Federal Aviation Administration.

Senate Appropriations Committee, Subcommittee on Transportation, SD-156 20510; 224-7281. Frank R. Lautenberg, D-N.J., chairman; Patrick J. McCann, clerk.

Jurisdiction over legislation to appropriate funds for the Federal Aviation Administration.

Senate Commerce, Science, and Transportation Committee, SD-508 20510; 224-5115. Ernest F. Hollings, D-S.C., chairman; Kevin Curtin, chief counsel and staff director.

Jurisdiction over legislation on the National Aeronautics and Space Administration, including nonmilitary aeronautical research and development.

Senate Commerce, Science, and Transportation Committee, Subcommittee on Aviation, SH-428 (mailing address: SD-508, Washington, DC 20510); 224-9350. Wendell H. Ford, D-Ky., chairman; Carol J. Carmody, professional staff member.

Jurisdiction over legislation on civil aviation, including airport funding, airline deregulation, safety issues, research and development, the National Transportation Safety Board, and the Federal Aviation Administration. Jurisdiction over aviation noise pollution legislation.

See also Congressional Aviation Forum (p. 757)

Nongovernmental:

Aeronautical Repair Station Assn., 121 N. Henry St., Alexandria, VA 22314-2903; (703) 739-9543. Farah MacLeod, executive director. Fax, (703) 739-9488.

Membership: Federal Aviation Administration-certified repair stations; associate members are suppliers and distributors of components and parts. Monitors legislation and regulations; works to improve relations between repair stations and manufacturers. Interests include reducing costs and problems associated with product liability and establishing uniformity in the application, interpretation, and enforcement of FAA regulations.

Aerospace Industries Assn. of America, 1250 Eye St. N.W., #1100 20005; 371-8400. Don Fuqua, president. Information, 371-8552. Press, 371-8544. Library, 371-8565. Fax, 371-8573.

Represents U.S. manufacturers of commercial, military, and business aircraft; helicopters; aircraft engines; missiles; spacecraft; and related components and equipment. Library open to the public by appointment.

AIR Conference (Airline Industrial Relations Conference), 1920 N St. N.W., #250 20036; 861-7550. Robert J. DeLucia, vice president. Fax, 861-7557.

Membership: domestic and international scheduled air carriers. Monitors developments and collects data on trends in airline labor relations.

Air Freight Assn., 1710 Rhode Island Ave. N.W., 2nd Floor 20036; 293-1030. Stephen A. Alterman, executive vice president. Fax, 293-4377.

Membership: cargo airlines and other firms authorized by the Transportation Dept. to engage in domestic and international air freight forwarding.

Air Transport Assn. of America, 1301 Pennsylvania Ave. N.W. 20004; 626-4000. James E. Landry, president. Fax, 626-4166.

Membership: U.S. scheduled air carriers. Promotes aviation safety and the facilitation of air transportation for passengers and cargo. Monitors legislation and regulations.

Aircraft Owners and Pilots Assn., 500 E St. S.W., #920 20024; 479-4050. Thomas B. Chapman, vice president. Fax, 484-1312.

Membership: owners and pilots of general aviation aircraft. Washington office monitors legislation and regulations. Headquarters office provides members with maps, trip planning, speakers bureau, and other services; issues airport directory and handbook for pilots; sponsors the Air Safety Foundation. (Headquarters in Frederick, Md.)

American Helicopter Society, 217 N. Washington St., Alexandria, VA 22314; (703) 684-6777. Morris E. Flater, executive director. Fax, (703) 739-9279.

Membership: individuals and organizations interested in vertical flight. Acts as an information clearinghouse for technical data on helicopter design improvement, aerodynamics, and safety. Operates the Vertical Flight Foundation, which grants scholarships to students interested in helicopter technology.

American Institute of Aeronautics and Astronautics, 901 D St. S.W. (mailing address: 370 L'Enfant Promenade S.W., Washington, DC 20024); 646-7400. Cort Durocher, executive director. Information, 646-7432. Fax, 646-7508.

Membership: engineers, scientists, and students in the fields of aeronautics and astronautics. Holds workshops on aerospace technical issues for congressional subcommittees. Offers computerized database through its Technical Information Service in New York.

Aviation Consumer Action Project, 2000 P St. N.W. (mailing address: P.O. Box 19029, Washington, DC 20036); 638-4000. Geraldine Frankoski, director.

Consumer advocacy organization that represents interests of airline passengers before the Federal Aviation Administration on safety issues and before the Transportation Dept. on economic and regulatory issues; testifies before Congress. (Affiliated with Public Citizen.)

General Aviation Manufacturers Assn., 1400 K St. N.W., #801 20005; 393-1500. Edward W. Stimpson, president. Fax, 842-4063.

Membership: U.S. manufacturers of business, commuter, and personal aircraft and manufacturers of engines, avionics, and equipment. Monitors legislation and regulations; sponsors safety and public information programs.

Helicopter Assn. International, 1635 Prince St., Alexandria, VA 22314; (703) 683-4646. Frank L. Jensen Jr., president. Fax, (703) 683-4745.

Membership: owners, manufacturers, and operators of helicopters, and affiliated companies in the civil helicopter industry. Provides information on use and operation of helicopters; offers business management and aviation safety courses; sponsors annual industry exposition; monitors legislation and regulations.

National Aeronautic Assn., 1815 N. Fort Myer Dr., #700, Arlington, VA 22209; (703) 527-0226. Walter D. Miller, executive director. Fax, (703) 527-0229.

Membership: persons interested in development of general and sporting aviation. Supervises sporting aviation competitions; oversees and approves official aircraft, aeronautics, and astronautics records in the United States. Interests include aeromodeling, aerobatics, helicopters, ultralights, home-built aircraft, parachuting, soaring, hang gliding, and ballooning.

National Agricultural Aviation Assn., 1005 E St. S.E. 20003; 546-5722. James Boillot, executive director. Fax, 546-5726.

Membership: qualified agricultural pilots; operating companies that seed, fertilize, and spray land by air; and allied industries. Compiles statistics on agricultural aviation.

National Air Carrier Assn., 1730 M St. N.W., #806 20036; 833-8200. Edward J. Driscoll, president. Fax, 659-9479.

Membership: air carriers certified for charter and scheduled operations. Monitors legislation and regulations.

National Air Transportation Assn., 4226 King St., Alexandria, VA 22302; (703) 845-9000. Alden Lange, acting executive director. Fax, (703) 845-8176.

Membership: aviation sales and service companies and on-demand air transport companies. Manages education foundation; compiles statistics; provides business assistance programs; monitors legislation and regulations.

National Aviation Club, P.O. Box 2717, Arlington, VA 22202; (703) 960-0014. Eugene P. Deatrick, executive vice president. Fax, (703) 960-0015.

Membership: individuals and corporations interested in aviation and aerospace. Sponsors speakers and seminars on aviation and aerospace issues; presents awards for achievements in aviation.

National Business Aircraft Assn., 1200 18th St. N.W., #200 20036; 783-9000. John W. Olcott, president. Fax, 331-8364.

Membership: companies owning and operating aircraft for business use, suppliers, and maintenance and air fleet service companies. Monitors legislation and regulations; conducts seminars and workshops in business aviation management. Sponsors annual civilian aviation exposition.

Regional Airline Assn., 1200 19th St. N.W., #300 20036-2401; 857-1170. Walter S. Coleman, president. Fax, 429-5113.

Membership: regional airlines that operate aircraft with 60 or fewer seats and that provide scheduled cargo, mail, and passenger service. Issues annual report on the industry.

RTCA Inc., 1140 Connecticut Ave. N.W., #1020 20036; 833-9339. David S. Watrous, president. Fax, 833-9434.

Membership: federal agencies, aviation organizations, and commercial firms interested in aeronautical systems. Develops and publishes standards for aviation, including minimum operational performance standards for specific equipment; conducts research, makes recommendations, and issues reports on the field of aviation electronics and telecommunications.

See also Transportation Communications International Union (AFL-CIO) (p. 804)

Airports

Agencies:

Bureau of Land Management (Interior Dept.), Lands, 1620 L St. N.W., #1000 (mailing address: Main Interior Bldg., Rm. 1849, Washington, DC 20240); 452-7780. Ray Brady, acting chief. Fax, 452-7708.

Operates the Airport Lease Program, which leases public lands for use as public airports.

Federal Aviation Administration (Transportation Dept.), Airports, 800 Independence Ave. S.W. 20591; 267-9471. Cynthia Rich, assistant administrator. Fax, 267-5301.

Makes grants for development and improvement of publicly operated and owned airports and some privately owned airports; certifies airports; oversees construction and accessibility standards for people with disabilities. Questions about local airports are usually referred to a local FAA field office. *(See Regional Federal Information Sources list, p. 832.)*

Congress:

See Transportation: Air, General, Congress (p. 708)

Nongovernmental:

Airports Council International, 1220 19th St. N.W., #200 20036; 293-8500. George P. Howard, president. Fax, 331-1362.

Membership: authorities, boards, commissions, and municipal departments operating public airports. Serves as liaison with government agencies and other aviation organizations; works to improve passenger and freight facilitation; acts as clearinghouse on engineering and operational aspects of airport development; monitors legislation and regulations.

American Assn. of Airport Executives, 4212 King St., Alexandria, VA 22302; (703) 824-0500. Charles M. Barclay, president. Fax, (703) 820-1395.

Membership: airport managers, superintendents, consultants, authorities and commissions, government officials, and others interested in the construction, management, and operation of airports. Conducts examination for and awards the professional designation of Accredited Airport Executive.

See also Aircraft Owners and Pilots Assn. (p. 709)

Regulation and Assistance

Agencies:

Federal Aviation Administration (Transportation Dept.), Environment and Energy, 800 Independence Ave. S.W. 20591; 267-3576. Louise E. Maillett, director. Fax, 267-5594.

Responsible for environmental affairs and energy conservation for aviation, including implementation and administration of various aviation-related environmental acts.

Transportation Dept., Airline Statistics, 400 7th St. S.W. 20590; 366-9059. James W. Mitchell, director. Fax, 366-3383.

Develops, interprets, and enforces accounting and reporting regulations for the aviation industry; issues air carrier reporting instructions, waivers, and due-date extensions.

Transportation Dept., Aviation Analysis, 400 7th St. S.W. 20590; 366-1030. John V. Coleman, director. Fax, 366-7638.

Analyzes essential air service needs of communities; directs subsidy policy and programs; guarantees air service to small communities; conducts research for the department on airline mergers, international route awards, and employee protection programs; administers the air carrier fitness provisions of the Federal Aviation Act; registers domestic and foreign air carriers; enforces charter regulations for tour operators.

Transportation Dept., Aviation and International Affairs, 400 7th St. S.W. 20590; 366-4551. Raymond G. Romero, assistant secretary designate. Fax, 366-7127.

Responsible for economic matters concerning the airline industry, including airline licensing, international aviation concerns, and antitrust functions.

Congress:

See Transportation: Air, General, Congress (p. 708)

Nongovernmental:

National Assn. of State Aviation Officials, 8401 Colesville Rd., #505, Silver Spring, MD 20910; (301) 588-0587. Edward Scott, executive vice president. Fax, (301) 588-1288.

Membership: state aeronautics agencies that deal with aviation issues, including regulation. Seeks uniform aviation laws; manages an aviation research and education foundation.

Research and Development

Agencies:

Federal Aviation Administration (Transportation Dept.), Airway Facilities, 800 Independence Ave. S.W. 20591; 267-8181. Joachin Archilla, acting associate administrator. Fax, 267-5015.

Conducts research and development programs aimed at providing procedures, facilities, and devices needed for a safe and efficient system of air navigation and air traffic control.

Federal Aviation Administration (Transportation Dept.), National Airspace System Development, 800 Independence Ave. S.W. 20591; 267-3555. John E. Turner, associate administrator. Fax, 267-3552.

Advises and assists in developing concepts for applying new technologies to meet long-range national airspace system requirements and for system acquisition, engineering, and management activities.

National Aeronautics and Space Administration (NASA), Aeronautics, 300 E St. S.W. (mailing address: NASA Headquarters, Mail Code R, Washington, DC 20546); 358-2693. Wesley L. Harris, associate administrator. Fax, 358-4066.

Administers the NASA aeronautics program; conducts basic and applied research in aerodynamics, materials, structures, avionics, propulsion, human factors, and safety; manages the following NASA research centers: Ames (Mountain View, Calif.); Dryden (Edwards, Calif.); Langley (Hampton, Va.); and Lewis (Cleveland, Ohio).

Congress:

See Transportation: Air, General, Congress (p. 708)

Nongovernmental:

Aerospace Education Foundation, 1501 Lee Highway, Arlington, VA 22209; (703) 247-5839. Phil Lacombe, director. Fax, (703) 247-5853.
Promotes knowledge and appreciation of U.S. civilian and military aerospace development and history. (Affiliated with the Air Force Assn.)

Safety and Security

Agencies:

Federal Aviation Administration (Transportation Dept.), Accident Investigation, 800 Independence Ave. S.W. 20591; 267-9612. David F. Thomas, director. Fax, 267-5043.
Investigates aviation accidents and incidents to detect unsafe conditions and trends in the national airspace system and to coordinate corrective action.

Federal Aviation Administration (Transportation Dept.), Air Traffic, 800 Independence Ave. S.W. 20591; 267-3666. William H. Pollard, associate administrator. Fax, 267-5456.
Operates the national air traffic control system; employs air traffic controllers at airport towers, en route air traffic control centers, and flight service stations; maintains the National Flight Data Center.

Federal Aviation Administration (Transportation Dept.), Aircraft Certification Service, 800 Independence Ave. S.W. 20591; 267-8235. Thomas E. McSweeny, director. Fax, 267-5364.
Certifies all aircraft for airworthiness; approves designs and specifications for new aircraft, aircraft engines, propellers, and appliances; supervises aircraft manufacturing and testing.

Federal Aviation Administration (Transportation Dept.), Aviation Medicine, 800 Independence Ave. S.W. 20591; 267-3535. Dr. Jon L. Jordan, federal air surgeon. Fax, 267-5399.
Responsible for the medical activities and policies of the FAA; designates, through regional offices, aviation medical examiners who conduct periodic medical examinations of all air personnel; maintains a Civil Aeromedical Institute in Oklahoma City.

Federal Aviation Administration (Transportation Dept.), Aviation Safety, 800 Independence Ave. S.W. 20591; 267-9613. Charles Huettner, acting associate administrator. Fax, 267-5496.
Responsible for safety promotion and for the quality and integrity of safety-data studies and analyses.

Federal Aviation Administration (Transportation Dept.), Civil Aviation Security, 800 Independence Ave. S.W. 20591; 267-9863. Cathal L. Flynn, assistant administrator. Fax, 267-8496.
Responsible for domestic and foreign air carrier and airport security, including FAA antihijacking, antitheft, and sabotage prevention programs; formulates regulations for airport security, antihijacking controls, air cargo security, and hazardous materials; enforces regulations; inspects airports for compliance.

Federal Aviation Administration (Transportation Dept.), Flight Standards, 800 Independence Ave. S.W. 20591; 267-8237. Thomas C. Accardi, director. Fax, 267-5230.
Responsible for examination and certification (except medical) of air personnel and air agencies; evaluates and develops standards for flight procedures and air operations; certifies repair stations; supervises maintenance operations of airlines and general aviation aircraft.

Federal Bureau of Investigation (Justice Dept.), Criminal Investigative Division, 10th St. and Pennsylvania Ave. N.W. 20535; 324-4260. Larry Potts, assistant director. Fax, 324-2175.
Investigates cases of aircraft hijacking, destruction of aircraft, and air piracy. Works with FAA to ensure security of national air carrier systems against terrorist and nonterrorist threats.

Federal Communications Commission, Field Operations, 1919 M St. N.W. 20554; 632-6980. Richard M. Smith, chief. Fax, 653-5402. 24-hour watch officer, 632-6975.
Provides technical services to aid the Federal Aviation Administration in locating aircraft in distress.

Justice Dept., General Litigation and Legal Advice, 1001 G St. N.W. 20530; 514-1028. Mary C. Spearing, chief. Fax, 514-6113.
Maintains supervisory responsibility over all federal criminal statutes not otherwise assigned, including enforcement of federal air piracy and related laws.

National Oceanic and Atmospheric Administration (Commerce Dept.), Coast and Geodetic Survey, 1305 East-West Highway SSMC, Bldg. 3, Silver Spring, MD 20910; (301) 713-3163. Rear

Adm. J. Austin Yeager, director. Fax, (301) 443-8701.

Directs programs and conducts research to support fundamental scientific and engineering activities and resource development for safe navigation of national airspace. Maintains the National Geodetic Reference System.

National Transportation Safety Board, Aviation Safety, 490 L'Enfant Plaza East S.W. 20594; 382-6610. Timothy P. Forté, director. Fax, 382-6879.

Responsible for management, policies, and programs in aviation safety and for aviation accident investigations. Manages programs on special investigations, safety issues, and safety objectives. Acts as U.S. representative in international investigations.

Congress:

See *Transportation: Air, General, Congress* (p. 708)

Nongovernmental:

Aerospace Medical Assn., 320 S. Henry St., Alexandria, VA 22314; (703) 739-2240. Dr. Russell B. Rayman, executive director. Fax, (703) 739-9652.

Membership: physicians, flight surgeons, aviation medical examiners, flight nurses, scientists, technicians, and specialists in clinical, operational, and research fields of aerospace medicine. Promotes programs to improve aerospace medicine and maintain safety in aviation by examining and monitoring the health of aviation personnel; participates in aircraft investigation and cockpit design.

Air Traffic Control Assn., 2300 Clarendon Blvd., #711, Arlington, VA 22201; (703) 522-5717. Gabriel A. Hartl, president. Fax, (703) 527-7251.

Membership: air traffic controllers, flight service station specialists, pilots, aviation engineers and manufacturers, and others interested in air traffic control systems. Compiles information and data concerning air traffic control; provides information to members, Congress, and federal agencies; acts as liaison between members and Congress.

Flight Safety Foundation, 2200 Wilson Blvd., #500, Arlington, VA 22201; (703) 522-8300. John H. Enders, vice chairman. Fax, (703) 525-6047.

Membership: aerospace manufacturers, domestic and foreign airlines, energy and insurance companies, educational institutions, and organizations and corporations interested in flight safety. Sponsors seminars and conducts studies on air safety for governments and industries. Administers award programs that recognize achievements in air safety.

International Society of Air Safety Investigators, Technology Trading Park, 5 Export Dr., Sterling, VA 20164-4421; (703) 430-9668. Robin Critzer, office manager. Fax, (703) 450-1745.

Membership: specialists who investigate and seek to define the causes of aircraft accidents. Encourages improvement of air safety and investigative procedures.

See also *Transportation: Air, General, Nongovernmental (p. 708)*

See also *National Safety Council (p. 729)*

Transportation: Maritime

General

Agencies:

Army Dept. (Defense Dept.), Corps of Engineers, 20 Massachusetts Ave. N.W. (mailing address: Washington, DC 20314); 272-0099. Brig. Gen. Stanley G. Genega, director, civil works. Fax, 272-8992.

Coordinates field offices that oversee projects concerning harbors, dams, levees, waterways, locks, reservoirs, and other constructions designed to facilitate transportation and flood control.

Federal Maritime Commission, 800 N. Capitol St. N.W., 10th Floor 20573; 523-5911. William D. Hathaway, chairman. Information, 523-5725. Library, 523-5762. Fax, 523-4224.

Regulates foreign and domestic ocean shipping of the United States; enforces maritime shipping laws and regulations regarding rates and charges, freight forwarding, passengers, and port authorities. Library open to the public.

Justice Dept., Civil Division, 1425 New York Ave. N.W., #10100 (mailing address: P.O. Box 14271, Washington, DC 20044-4271); 616-4000. Gary W. Allen, director, torts branch, aviation/admiralty litigation. Information, 616-2777. Fax, 616-4002.

Represents the federal government in civil suits concerning the maritime industry, including ships, shipping, and merchant marine personnel. Handles civil cases arising from admiralty incidents and accidents.

Maritime Administration (Transportation Dept.), 400 7th St. S.W. 20590; 366-5823. Vice Adm. Albert J. Herberger, administrator. Information, 366-5807. Fax, 366-3890.

Conducts research on shipbuilding and operations; administers subsidy programs; provides financing guarantees and a tax-deferred fund for shipbuilding; operates the U.S. Merchant Marine Academy in Kings Point, N.Y.

Maritime Administration (Transportation Dept.), Policy and International Affairs, 400 7th St. S.W. 20590; 366-5772. Reginald A. Bourdon, associate administrator. Fax, 366-3746.

Conducts studies and makes policy recommendations to the administrator. Compiles data gathered by foreign maritime representatives on the operating and construction costs of ships; implements bilateral maritime agreements; participates in international maritime policy-making.

Maritime Administration (Transportation Dept.), Shipbuilding and Ship Operations, 400 7th St. S.W. 20590; 366-5737. Harlan T. Haller, associate administrator. Fax, 366-3954.

Works with private industry to develop standardized ship designs and improved shipbuilding techniques and materials. Responsible for maintenance and readiness of National Defense Reserve Fleet and Ready Reserve Fleet.

Maritime Administration (Transportation Dept.), Technology Assessment, 400 7th St. S.W. 20590; 366-1925. Paul Mentz, director. Fax, 366-3889.

Conducts technology assessment activities related to the development and use of water transportation systems for commercial and national security purposes. Makes recommendations concerning future trends in such areas as trade, emerging technologies, fuels, and materials.

Navy Dept. (Defense Dept.), Military Sealift Command, Washington Navy Yard 20398-5100; 433-0001. Vice Adm. Michael P. Kalleres, commander. Information, 433-0330. Fax, 433-6638.

Transports Defense Dept. and other U.S. government cargo by sea; operates ships that maintain supplies for the armed forces and scientific agencies; transports fuels for the Energy Dept.

Congress:

House Appropriations Committee, Subcommittee on Commerce, Justice, State, and Judiciary, H309 CAP 20515; 225-3351. Neal Smith, D-Iowa, chairman; John Osthaus, staff assistant.

Jurisdiction over legislation to appropriate funds for the Maritime Administration and Federal Maritime Commission.

House Appropriations Committee, Subcommittee on Energy and Water Development, 2362 RHOB 20515; 225-3421. Tom Bevill, D-Ala., chairman; Hunter Spillan, staff assistant.

Jurisdiction over legislation to appropriate funds for the civil programs of the U.S. Army Corps of Engineers.

House Appropriations Committee, Subcommittee on Transportation, 2358 RHOB 20515; 225-2141. Bob Carr, D-Mich., chairman; Del Davis, staff assistant.

Jurisdiction over legislation to appropriate funds for the U.S. Coast Guard, Interstate Commerce Commission, Saint Lawrence Seaway Development Corp., and Panama Canal Commission.

House Government Operations Committee, Subcommittee on Information, Justice, Transportation, and Agriculture, B349C RHOB 20515; 225-3741. Gary Condit, D-Calif., chairman; Shannon Lahey, acting staff director. Fax, 225-2445.

Oversees operations of the Federal Maritime Commission.

House Merchant Marine and Fisheries Committee, Subcommittee on Coast Guard and Navigation, 541 Ford Bldg. (2nd and D Sts. S.W.) 20515; 226-3587. W. J. "Billy" Tauzin, D-La., chairman; Elizabeth Megginson, staff director.

Jurisdiction over legislation on the U.S. Coast Guard, maritime safety, and marine pollution control and abatement.

House Merchant Marine and Fisheries Committee, Subcommittee on Merchant Marine, 543 Ford Bldg. (2nd and D Sts. S.W.) 20515; 226-

3533. William O. Lipinski, D-Ill., chairman; Keith Lesnick, staff director.

Jurisdiction over legislation on most merchant marine matters, including government subsidies and assistance; merchant marine personnel programs; port regulation, safety, and security; and ship and freight regulation and rates.

House Public Works and Transportation Committee, Subcommittee on Water Resources and Environment, B370A RHOB 20515; 225-0060. Douglas Applegate, D-Ohio, chairman; Kenneth J. Kopocis, counsel.

Jurisdiction over legislation on deepwater ports and Saint Lawrence Seaway rates and regulations and over legislation authorizing construction, operation, and maintenance of inland waterways and the Maritime Administration.

House Science, Space, and Technology Committee, Subcommittee on Technology, Environment, and Aviation, B374 RHOB 20515; 225-9662. Tim Valentine, D-N.C., chairman; James H. Turner, staff director.

Oversight of research and development activities of the U.S. Coast Guard and the Maritime Administration.

Senate Appropriations Committee, Subcommittee on Commerce, Justice, State, and Judiciary, S146A CAP 20510; 224-7277. Ernest F. Hollings, D-S.C., chairman; Scott B. Gudes, clerk.

Jurisdiction over legislation to appropriate funds for the Maritime Administration and the Federal Maritime Commission.

Senate Appropriations Committee, Subcommittee on Energy and Water Development, SD-132 20510; 224-7260. J. Bennett Johnston, D-La., chairman; W. Proctor Jones, clerk.

Jurisdiction over legislation to appropriate funds for the civil functions of the U.S. Army Corps of Engineers.

Senate Appropriations Committee, Subcommittee on Transportation, SD-156 20510; 224-7281. Frank R. Lautenberg, D-N.J., chairman; Patrick J. McCann, clerk.

Jurisdiction over legislation to appropriate funds for the U.S. Coast Guard, Interstate Commerce Commission, Saint Lawrence Seaway Development Corp., and Panama Canal Commission.

Senate Commerce, Science, and Transportation Committee, SD-508 20510; 224-5115. Ernest F. Hollings, D-S.C., chairman; Kevin Curtin, chief counsel and staff director.

Oversight of and legislative jurisdiction over the U.S. Coast Guard, the Maritime Administration, maritime safety, and ports, including security and regulation; oversight of the Federal Maritime Commission. Jurisdiction over marine pollution control and abatement.

Senate Commerce, Science, and Transportation Committee, Subcommittee on Merchant Marine, SH-425 (mailing address: SD-508, Washington, DC 20510); 224-4914. John B. Breaux, D-La., chairman; Harold J. Creel Jr., senior counsel.

Jurisdiction over legislation on Saint Lawrence Seaway and merchant marine matters, including ship and freight regulation and rates, merchant marine personnel programs, and government subsidies and assistance to foreign and U.S. vessels.

Senate Commerce, Science, and Transportation Committee, Subcommittee on National Ocean Policy Study, SH-425 (mailing address: SD-508, Washington, DC 20510); 224-4912. Ernest F. Hollings, D-S.C., chairman; Penny Dalton, staff member.

Studies issues involving deepwater ports (jurisdiction shared with Senate Energy and Natural Resources and Senate Environment and Public Works committees). Studies legislation on the U.S. Coast Guard. (Subcommittee does not report legislation.)

Senate Energy and Natural Resources Committee, Subcommittee on Mineral Resources Development and Production, SD-362 20510; 224-7568. Daniel K. Akaka, D-Hawaii, chairman; Lisa Vehmas, counsel.

Jurisdiction over legislation on deepwater ports (jurisdiction shared with Senate Commerce, Science, and Transportation and Senate Environment and Public Works committees).

Senate Environment and Public Works Committee, Subcommittee on Water Resources, Transportation, Public Buildings, and Economic Development, SH-415 20510; 224-5031. Daniel Patrick Moynihan, D-N.Y., chairman; Vacant, director.

Jurisdiction over legislation authorizing construction, operation, and maintenance of inland waterways and harbors (jurisdiction on deepwater ports beyond three-mile limit shared with Senate Energy and Natural Resources and Senate Commerce, Science, and Transportation committees).

Nongovernmental:

AFL-CIO Maritime Committee, 1150 17th St. N.W., #700 20036; 835-0404. Talmage E. Simpkins, executive director. Fax, 872-0912.

Membership: AFL-CIO maritime unions. Provides information on the maritime industry and unions. Monitors legislation and regulations. Interests include seamen's service contracts and pension plans, maritime safety, U.S. merchant marine, and the rights of Panama Canal residents.

American Institute of Merchant Shipping, 1000 16th St. N.W. 20036; 775-4399. Ernest J. Corrado, president. Fax, 659-3795.

Membership: U.S.-flag tankers, dry bulk carriers, containerships, and other oceangoing vessels engaged in domestic and international trade. Provides information on international maritime matters, maritime safety, and regulatory and legislative issues.

American Maritime Congress, 1300 Eye St. N.W., #250W 20005-3314; 842-4900. Gloria Cataneo Rudman, executive director. Fax, 842-3492.

Organization of U.S.-flag carriers engaged in oceanborne transportation. Conducts research and provides information on the U.S.-flag merchant marine.

The American Waterways Operators, 1600 Wilson Blvd., #1000, Arlington, VA 22209; (703) 841-9300. Thomas Allegretti, president. Fax, (703) 841-0389.

Membership: commercial shipyard owners and operators of barges, tugboats, and towboats on navigable coastal and inland waterways. Monitors legislation and regulations; acts as liaison with Congress, the U.S. Coast Guard, the Army Corps of Engineers, and the Maritime Administration.

Boat Owners Assn. of the United States, 880 S. Pickett St., Alexandria, VA 22304; (703) 461-2864. Michael Sciulla, vice president, government affairs. Fax, (703) 461-2845.

Membership: owners of recreational boats. Represents boat-owner interests before the federal government; offers consumer protection and other services to members.

Maritime Institute for Research and Industrial Development, 1133 15th St. N.W. 20005; 463-6505. C. James Patti, president. Fax, 223-9093.

Membership: U.S.-flag ship operators. Promotes the development of the U.S. Merchant Marine. Interests include bilateral shipping agreements, the use of private commercial merchant vessels by the Defense Dept., and enforcement of cargo preference laws for U.S.-flag ships.

National Assn. of Waterfront Employers, 2011 Pennsylvania Ave. N.W., #301 20006; 296-2810. Thomas D. Wilcox, executive director. Fax, 331-7479.

Membership: private stevedore and marine terminal companies, their subsidiaries, and other waterfront-related employers. Legislative interests include trade, antitrust, insurance, and user-fee issues. Monitors legislation and regulations.

National Marine Manufacturers Assn., 3050 K St. N.W., #145 20007; 944-4980. Mary M. Mann, director, federal government relations. Fax, 944-4988.

Membership: recreational marine equipment manufacturers. Promotes boating safety and the development of boating facilities. Monitors legislation and regulations; serves as liaison with Congress and regulatory agencies. (Headquarters in Chicago.)

National Waterways Conference, 1130 17th St. N.W. 20036; 296-4415. Harry N. Cook, president. Fax, 835-3861.

Membership: petroleum, coal, chemical, electric power, building materials, iron and steel, and grain companies; port authorities; water carriers; and other waterways interests. Conducts research on the economics of water transportation; sponsors educational programs on waterways; monitors legislation and regulations.

Shipbuilders Council of America, 4301 N. Fairfax Dr., #330, Arlington, VA 22203; (703) 276-1700. John J. Stocker, president. Fax, (703) 276-1707.

Membership: shipbuilders and allied industries and associations. Works to ensure a stable shipbuilding and ship repairing industry in the United States. Promotes the maintenance of a privately owned reserve fleet for times of national emergency. Monitors legislation and regulations; sponsors lectures; conducts discussions to promote industry consensus and cooperation.

Transportation Institute, 5201 Auth Way, Camp Springs, MD 20746; (301) 423-3335. James L. Henry, president. Fax, (301) 423-0634.

Membership: U.S.-flag maritime shipping companies. Conducts research on freight regulation and rates, government subsidies and assistance, domestic and international maritime matters, maritime safety, ports, Saint Lawrence Seaway, shipbuilding, and regulation of shipping.

See also Labor Unions list (p. 801)

Coast Guard

Agencies:

U.S. Coast Guard (Transportation Dept.), 2100 2nd St. S.W. 20593; 267-2390. Adm. Robert Kramek, commandant designate. Information, 267-1587. Fax, 267-4158.

Carries out search-and-rescue missions in and around navigable waters and on the high seas; enforces federal laws on the high seas and navigable waters of the United States and its possessions; conducts marine environmental protection programs; administers boating safety programs; inspects and regulates construction, safety, and equipment of merchant marine vessels; establishes and maintains a system of navigation aids; maintains a state of military readiness to assist the Navy in time of war or when directed by the president.

Congress:

See Transportation: Maritime, General, Congress (p. 714)

Government Subsidies and Assistance

Agencies:

Maritime Administration (Transportation Dept.), Maritime Aids, 400 7th St. S.W. 20590; 366-0364. Richard E. Bowman, associate administrator. Fax, 366-7901.

Administers maritime aid programs, including the Construction Reserve Fund, Operating Differential Subsidy, Financing Guarantee, and Marine Insurance programs.

Maritime Administration (Transportation Dept.), Maritime Subsidy Board, 400 7th St. S.W. 20590; 366-5746. James E. Saari, secretary. Fax, 366-9206.

Administers subsidy contracts for the construction and operation of U.S.-flag ships engaged in foreign trade.

Maritime Administration (Transportation Dept.), Ship Financing, 400 7th St. S.W. 20590; 366-5744. Mitchell D. Lax, director. Fax, 366-7901.

Provides ship financing guarantees and administers the Capital Construction Fund Program.

Maritime Administration (Transportation Dept.), Ship Operating Assistance, 400 7th St. S.W. 20590; 366-2323. James E. Caponiti, director. Fax, 366-7901.

Calculates rates for commercial American steamship lines to enable them to compete with foreign shipping lines that operate at lower cost. Conducts financial analysis of commercial shipping and calculates guideline rates for carriage of preference cargos.

Maritime Administration (Transportation Dept.), Trade Analysis and Insurance, 400 7th St. S.W. 20590; 366-2400. Edmond J. Fitzgerald, director. Fax, 366-7901.

Recommends subsidies for ship construction and operation to the Maritime Subsidy Board.

Congress:

See Transportation: Maritime, General, Congress (p. 714)

Nongovernmental:

See Transportation Institute (this page)

Maritime Safety

See also Transportation, General (p. 702)

Agencies:

Federal Communications Commission, Field Operations, 1919 M St. N.W. 20554; 632-6980. Richard M. Smith, chief. Fax, 653-5402. 24-hour watch officer, 632-6975.

Provides technical services to the U.S. Coast Guard for locating ships in distress.

National Oceanic and Atmospheric Administration (Commerce Dept.), Coast and Geodetic Survey, 1305 East-West Highway SSMC, Bldg. 3, Silver Spring, MD 20910; (301) 713-3163. Rear Adm. J. Austin Yeager, director. Fax, (301) 443-8701.

Directs programs and conducts research to support fundamental scientific and engineering activities and resource development for safe navigation of the nation's waterways and territorial seas. Maintains the National Geodetic Reference System.

National Response Center (Transportation Dept.), 2100 2nd St. S.W. 20593; 267-2675. Cmdr. David W. Beach, chief. Fax, 479-7165. Toll-free hotline, (800) 424-8802.

Maintains 24-hour hotline for reporting pollution and oil or hazardous materials accidents. Notifies appropriate federal officials to reduce the effects of accidents.

National Transportation Safety Board, Marine, 490 L'Enfant Plaza East S.W. 20594; 382-6860. Marjorie Murtagh, chief. Fax, 382-0692.

Investigates selected marine transportation accidents, including major marine accidents that involve U.S. Coast Guard operations or functions. Determines the facts upon which the board establishes probable cause; makes recommendations on matters pertaining to marine transportation safety and accident prevention.

Occupational Safety and Health Administration (Labor Dept.), Construction and Maritime Compliance Assistance, 200 Constitution Ave. N.W. 20210; 219-8136. Roy F. Gurnham, director. Fax, 219-9187.

Interprets construction and maritime compliance safety standards for agency field personnel and private employees and employers.

U.S. Coast Guard (Transportation Dept.), Auxiliary Boating and Consumer Division, 2100 2nd St. S.W. 20593; 267-1077. Capt. C. B. Doherty, chief. Fax, 267-4423.

Establishes and enforces safety standards for recreational boats and associated equipment; coordinates public education and information programs.

U.S. Coast Guard (Transportation Dept.), Marine Investigation, 2100 2nd St. S.W. 20593; 267-1430. Capt. Larry H. Gibson, chief. Fax, 267-1416.

Investigates accidents involving commercial vessels that result in loss of life, serious injury, or substantial damage.

U.S. Coast Guard (Transportation Dept.), Marine Safety Center, 400 7th St. S.W. 20590; 366-6480. Capt. T. H. Walsh, commanding officer. Fax, 366-3877.

Reviews and approves commercial vessel plans and specifications to ensure technical compliance with federal safety and pollution abatement standards.

U.S. Coast Guard (Transportation Dept.), Marine Safety, Security, and Environmental Protection, 2100 2nd St. S.W. 20593; 267-2200. Rear Adm. Arthur E. Henn, chief. Fax, 267-4839.

Establishes and enforces regulations for port safety and security; environmental protection; vessel safety, inspection, design, documentation, and investigation; licensing of merchant vessel personnel; and shipment of hazardous materials. Sets policy for three Coast Guard programs: Port Environmental Safety, Waterway Management, and Environmental Response.

U.S. Coast Guard (Transportation Dept.), Marine Technical and Hazardous Materials, 2100 2nd St. S.W. 20593; 267-2967. Capt. G. D. Marsh, chief. Fax, 267-4816.

Ensures that commercial vessels and deepwater ports are designed and operate in accordance with federal safety and pollution abatement standards. Determines which chemicals may be safely transported by water. Monitors and conducts research and development projects on the safety of commercial vessels and hazardous materials.

U.S. Coast Guard (Transportation Dept.), Merchant Vessel Inspection and Documentation, 2100 2nd St. S.W. 20593; 267-2978. Capt. George M. Williams, chief. Fax, 267-1069.

Inspects and certifies merchant vessels.

U.S. Coast Guard (Transportation Dept.), Navigation, Safety, and Waterway Services, 2100 2nd St. S.W. (mailing address: Commandant G-N, Washington, DC 20593); 267-2267. Rear Adm. W. J. Ecker, chief. Fax, 267-4674.

Administers Long Range and Short Range Aids to Navigation programs; regulates the construction, maintenance, and operation of bridges across U.S. navigable waters. Conducts search and-rescue and polar and domestic ice-breaking operations. Establishes and enforces safety standards, including operator requirements and national construction standards for boats. Regulates waterways under U.S. jurisdiction.

Congress:

See Transportation: Maritime, General, Congress (p. 714)

Nongovernmental:

National Council of Fishing Vessel Safety and Insurance, 1525 Wilson Blvd., #500, Arlington, VA 22209; (703) 524-9218. Adrienne Paradis, executive secretary. Fax, (703) 524-4619.

Membership: vessel owner associations, insurance companies, adjusters, maritime attorneys, naval architects, and safety professionals. Coordinates national program to reduce loss of life and vessels and to reduce insurance costs for the fishing industry.

National Safe Boating Council, 2100 2nd St. S.W. (mailing address: c/o Commandant G-NAB-3, U.S. Coast Guard, Washington, DC 20593); 267-1060. Hunt Anderson, U.S. Coast Guard representative. Fax, 267-4423.

Membership: national organizations that promote recreational boating safety. Conducts annual seminar; works with the U.S. Coast Guard to sponsor activities during National Safe Boating Week.

Radio Technical Commission for Maritime Services, 655 15th St. N.W., #300 20005; 639-4006. William T. Adams, president. Fax, 347-8540.

Membership: government agencies and private organizations. Conducts research, makes recommendations, and issues reports on maritime telecommunications standards.

U.S. Coast Guard Auxiliary, 2100 2nd St. S.W. 20593-0001; 267-0982. Capt. A. A. Sarra, chief director. Fax, 267-4409.

Volunteer, nonmilitary organization created by Congress to assist the Coast Guard in promoting water safety. Offers public education programs; administers the Courtesy Marine Examination Program, a safety equipment check provided free to the public; works with the Coast Guard and state boating officials to maintain marine safety.

See also AFL-CIO Maritime Committee and American Institute of Merchant Shipping (p. 716); Transportation Institute (p. 717)

Merchant Marine Personnel

Agencies:

Maritime Administration (Transportation Dept.), Maritime Labor and Training, 400 7th St. S.W. 20590; 366-5755. Bruce J. Carlton, acting director. Fax, 366-3889.

Supports the training of merchant marine officers at the U.S. Merchant Marine Academy in Kings Point, N.Y., and at maritime academies in California, Maine, Massachusetts, Michigan, New York, and Texas. Monitors maritime industry labor practices and policies; promotes consonant labor relations.

U.S. Coast Guard (Transportation Dept.), Marine Investigation, 2100 2nd St. S.W. 20593; 267-1430. Capt. Larry H. Gibson, chief, Fax, 267-1416.

Handles disciplinary proceedings for merchant marine personnel. Compiles and analyzes records of marine casualties.

U.S. Coast Guard (Transportation Dept.), Merchant Vessel Personnel, 2100 2nd St. S.W. 20593; 267-0214. Capt. John McGowan, chief. Fax, 267-4570.

Supervises licensing of merchant marine personnel and the issuance of certificates to seamen in establishing minimal crewing requirements for merchant vessels. Oversees pilotage and regulates rates for pilotage on the Great Lakes.

Congress:

See Transportation: Maritime, General, Congress (p. 714)

Nongovernmental:

See International Longshoremen's and Warehousemen's Union and International Longshoremen's Assn. (p. 803); Seafarers International Union of North America (p. 804); Transportation Institute (p. 717)

Ports

Agencies:

Federal Maritime Commission, Agreements and Information Management, 800 N. Capitol St. N.W. 20573; 523-5793. Geneal Anderson, chief. Fax, 523-3782.

Analyzes agreements between terminal operators and shipping companies for docking facilities. Monitors terminal tariffs for compliance with rules.

Maritime Administration (Transportation Dept.), Marketing, 400 7th St. S.W. 20590; 366-4721. Nan Harllee, associate administrator. Fax, 366-5522.

Responsible for direction and administration of international and domestic market promotion, port and intermodal transportation development, port readiness for national defense, and research and development.

U.S. Coast Guard (Transportation Dept.), Port Safety and Security, 2100 2nd St. S.W. 20593; 267-0489. Capt. A. J. Sabol, chief. Fax, 267-0506.

Enforces rules and regulations governing the safety and security of ports and anchorages and the movement of vessels in U.S. waters. Supervises cargo transfer operations, storage, and stowage; conducts harbor patrols and waterfront facility inspections; establishes security zones and monitors vessel movement.

Congress:

See *Transportation: Maritime, General, Congress (p. 714)*

Nongovernmental:

American Assn. of Port Authorities, 1010 Duke St., Alexandria, VA 22314; (703) 684-5700. Erik Stromberg, president. Fax, (703) 684-6321.

Membership: port authorities in the Western Hemisphere. Provides technical and economic information on port finance, construction, operation, and security.

See also *Transportation Institute (p. 717)*

Saint Lawrence Seaway

Agencies:

Saint Lawrence Seaway Development Corp. (Transportation Dept.), 400 7th St. S.W. 20590; 366-0118. Stanford Parris, administrator. Information, 366-0091. Fax, 366-7147.

Operates and maintains the Saint Lawrence Seaway within U.S. territorial limits; conducts development programs and coordinates activities with its Canadian counterpart.

Congress:

See *Transportation: Maritime, General, Congress (p. 714)*

Nongovernmental:

See *Transportation Institute (p. 717)*

Ship and Freight Regulation and Rates

See also *International Economics, Customs and Tariffs (p. 80)*

Agencies:

Federal Maritime Commission, Tariffs, Certification, and Licensing, 800 N. Capitol St. N.W., 9th Floor 20573; 523-5796. Bryant L. VanBrakle, director. Fax, 523-5830.

Regulates the rates charged for shipping in domestic commerce and monitors the rates in foreign commerce; licenses and enforces regulations concerning ocean freight forwarders; issues certificates of financial responsibility to ensure that carriers refund fares and meet their liability in case of death, injury, or nonperformance.

Interstate Commerce Commission, Proceedings, 12th St. and Constitution Ave. N.W. 20423; 927-7513. David M. Konschnik, director. Fax, 927-6419. TDD, 927-5721.

Regulates licensing, rates, and financial matters for carriers that use the inland waterways.

Interstate Commerce Commission, Public Assistance, 12th St. and Constitution Ave. N.W. 20423; 927-7597. Dan King, acting director. Fax, 927-5158. TDD, 927-5721.

Assists small-business owners and transportation firms in filing protests on rates and filing for new operating authority or extensions. Provides information on obtaining service.

Congress:

See Transportation: Maritime, General, Congress (p. 714)

Nongovernmental:

See American Institute of Merchant Shipping (p. 716); Transportation Institute (p. 717)

Transportation: Motor Vehicle

General

See also Environment, Air Pollution (p. 623); Insurance (p. 71)

Agencies:

Federal Highway Administration (Transportation Dept.), 400 7th St. S.W. 20590; 366-0650. Rodney Slater, administrator. Information, 366-0660. Fax, 366-3244.
Administers federal-aid highway programs with money from the Highway Trust Fund; works to improve highway and motor vehicle safety; coordinates research and development programs on highway and traffic safety, construction, costs, and environmental impact of highway transportation; administers regional and territorial highway building programs and the highway beautification program.

Congress:

General Accounting Office, Transportation, 901 D St. S.W., #802 20024; 401-6001. Allen Li, associate director. Fax, 401-6025.
Independent, nonpartisan agency in the legislative branch. Audits, analyzes, and evaluates performance of the Transportation Dept., including highway and mass transit issues.

House Appropriations Committee, Subcommittee on Transportation, 2358 RHOB 20515; 225-2141. Bob Carr, D-Mich., chairman; Del Davis, staff assistant.
Jurisdiction over legislation to appropriate funds for the Transportation Dept., including the Federal Highway Administration and the National Highway Traffic Safety Administration.

House Energy and Commerce Committee, Subcommittee on Transportation and Hazardous Materials, 324 Ford Bldg. (2nd and D Sts. S.W.) 20515; 225-9304. Al Swift, D-Wash., chairman; Arthur Endres, staff director and chief counsel.
Jurisdiction over motor vehicle safety legislation and the National Highway Traffic Safety Administration.

House Government Operations Committee, Subcommittee on Information, Justice, Transportation, and Agriculture, B349C RHOB 20515; 225-3741. Gary Condit, D-Calif., chairman; Shannon Lahey, acting staff director. Fax, 225-2445.
Oversees operations of the Interstate Commerce Commission.

House Public Works and Transportation Committee, Subcommittee on Surface Transportation, B376 RHOB 20515; 225-9989. Nick J. Rahall II, D-W.Va., chairman; Kenneth House, chief professional.
Jurisdiction over legislation on regulation of commercial vehicles and interstate surface transportation, including the Federal Highway Administration, National Highway Traffic Safety Administration, Federal Aid to Highways, and highway trust fund programs and activities.

House Science, Space, and Technology Committee, Subcommittee on Technology, Environment, and Aviation, B374 RHOB 20515; 225-9662. Tim Valentine, D-N.C., chairman; James H. Turner, staff director.
Special oversight of surface transportation research and development programs of executive branch departments and agencies.

Senate Appropriations Committee, Subcommittee on Transportation, SD-156 20510; 224-7281. Frank R. Lautenberg, D-N.J., chairman; Patrick J. McCann, clerk.
Jurisdiction over legislation to appropriate funds for the Transportation Dept., including the Federal Highway Administration and National Highway Traffic Safety Administration.

Senate Commerce, Science, and Transportation Committee, SD-508 20510; 224-5115. Ernest F. Hollings, D-S.C., chairman; Kevin Curtin, chief counsel and staff director.
Jurisdiction over motor vehicle safety legislation; oversight of the Interstate Commerce Commission.

Senate Commerce, Science, and Transportation Committee, Subcommittee on Surface Transportation, SH-428 (mailing address: SD-508, Washington, DC 20510); 224-9350. Jim Exon, D-Neb., chairman; Vacant, senior professional staff member.

Jurisdiction over legislation on regulation of commercial motor carriers and interstate buses. Oversight of surface transportation research and development, including Federal Highway Administration activities (except federal highway construction).

Senate Environment and Public Works Committee, Subcommittee on Water Resources, Transportation, Public Buildings, and Economic Development, SH-415 20510; 224-5031. Daniel Patrick Moynihan, D-N.Y., chairman; Vacant, director.

Jurisdiction over legislation on the Federal Highway Administration, National Highway Traffic Safety Administration, highway trust fund programs, and federal aid to highways.

See also Congressional Automotive Caucus (p. 757); Congressional Truck Caucus (p. 759)

Nongovernmental:

American Automobile Assn., 1440 New York Ave. N.W., #200 20005; 942-2050. Richard F. Hebert, managing director. Fax, 783-4798.

Membership: state and local automobile associations. Provides members with travel services. Interests include all aspects of highway transportation, travel and tourism, safety, drunk driving, economics, federal aid, and legislation that affects motorists. (Headquarters in Heathrow, Fla.)

American Bus Assn., 1100 New York Ave. N.W., #1050 20005; 842-1645. George T. Snyder Jr., executive vice president. Fax, 842-0850.

Membership: intercity privately owned bus companies, state associations, travel/tourism businesses, bus manufacturers, and those interested in the bus industry. Monitors legislation and regulations.

American Trucking Assns., 2200 Mill Rd., Alexandria, VA 22314; (703) 838-1700. Thomas J. Donohue, president. Toll-free, (800) 282-5463. Press, (703) 838-1873. Library, (703) 838-1880. Fax, (703) 684-5720.

Membership: state trucking associations, individual trucking and motor carrier organizations,

and related supply companies. Maintains departments on industrial relations, law, management systems, research, safety, traffic, state laws, taxation, communications, legislation, economics, and engineering. Library open to the public by appointment.

Highway Loss Data Institute, 1005 N. Glebe Rd., Arlington, VA 22201; (703) 247-1600. Brian O'Neill, president. Fax, (703) 247-1678.

Research organization that gathers, processes, and publishes data on the ways in which insurance losses vary among different kinds of vehicles. (Affiliated with Insurance Institute for Highway Safety.)

Motorcycle Industry Council, 1235 Jefferson Davis Highway, #600, Arlington, VA 22202; (703) 416-0444. Melvin R. Stahl, senior vice president.

Membership: manufacturers and distributors of motorcycles, mopeds and related parts, accessories, and equipment. Monitors legislation and regulations. (Headquarters in Irvine, Calif.)

National Institute for Automotive Service Excellence, 13505 Dulles Technology Dr., Herndon, VA 22071; (703) 713-3800. Ronald H. Weiner, president. Fax, (703) 713-0727.

Administers program for testing and certifying automotive technicians; researches methods to improve technician training.

National Parking Assn., 1112 16th St. N.W. 20036; 296-4336. Barbara O'Dell, president. Fax, 331-8523.

Membership: parking garage owners, operators, and consultants. Offers information and research services; monitors legislation and regulations; sponsors seminars and educational programs on garage design and equipment.

National Private Truck Council, 66 Canal Center Plaza, #600, Alexandria, VA 22314; (703) 683-1300. Gene S. Bergoffen, executive vice president. Fax, (703) 683-1217.

Membership: manufacturers, producers, distributors, and retail establishments that operate fleets of vehicles incidental to their nontransportation businesses. Interests include truck safety, maintenance, and economics. Supports economic deregulation of the trucking industry and uniformity in state taxation of the industry. Private Management Fleet Institute conducts continuing education, truck research, and certification programs.

NATSO, Inc., 1199 N. Fairfax St., Alexandria, VA (mailing address: P.O. Box 1285, Alexandria, VA 22313); (703) 549-2100. W. Dewey Clower, president. Fax, (703) 684-4525.

Membership: travel plaza and truck stop operators and suppliers to the truck stop industry. Provides credit information and educational training programs; monitors legislation and regulations. Operates the American Truck Stop Foundation, which promotes highway safety.

Trucking Management, 2233 Wisconsin Ave. N.W., #412 20007; 965-7660. Arthur H. Bunte Jr., president. Fax, 965-7663.

Represents trucking employers. Negotiates and administers labor contracts with the Teamsters Union.

See also Labor Unions list (p. 801); Resources: Oil and Natural Gas, General, Nongovernmental (p. 230)

Highways

Agencies:

Federal Highway Administration (Transportation Dept.), National Highway Institute, 6300 Georgetown Pike, McLean, VA 22101; (703) 285-2770. George M. Shrieves, director. Fax, (703) 285-2791.

Develops and administers, in cooperation with state highway departments, training programs for agency, state, and local highway department employees.

Federal Highway Administration (Transportation Dept.), Policy, 400 7th St. S.W. 20590; 366-0585. Gloria J. Jeff, associate administrator. Fax, 366-9626.

Develops policy and administers the Federal Highway Administration's international programs. Conducts policy studies and legislation analyses; makes recommendations; compiles and reviews highway-related data. Represents the administration at international conferences; administers foreign assistance programs.

Federal Highway Administration (Transportation Dept.), Program Development, 400 7th St. S.W. 20590; 366-0371. Anthony R. Kane, associate administrator. Fax, 366-3713.

Provides guidance and oversight for planning, design, construction, and maintenance operations relating to federal aid, direct federal construction, environmental analysis and planning, right-of-way issues, and other highway programs; establishes design guidelines and specifications for highways built with federal funds.

Federal Highway Administration (Transportation Dept.), Research and Development, 6300 Georgetown Pike, McLean, VA 22101; (703) 285-2051. John A. Clements, associate administrator. Fax, (703) 285-2379.

Conducts highway research and development programs; studies safety, location, design, construction, operation, and maintenance of highways; cooperates with state and local highway departments in utilizing results of its research.

Federal Highway Administration (Transportation Dept.), Right of Way, 400 7th St. S.W. 20590; 366-0342. Barbara K. Orski, director. Fax, 366-3713.

Funds and oversees acquisition of land by states for federally assisted highways; provides financial assistance to relocate people and businesses forced to move by highway construction; cooperates in administering program for the use of air rights in connection with federally aided highways; administers Highway Beautification Act to control billboards and junkyards along interstate and federally aided primary highways.

Congress:

See Transportation: Motor Vehicle, General, Congress (p. 721)

Nongovernmental:

American Assn. of State Highway and Transportation Officials, 444 N. Capitol St. N.W. 20001; 624-5800. Francis B. Francois, executive director. Fax, 624-5806.

Membership: the Federal Highway Administration and transportation departments of the states, District of Columbia, Guam, and Puerto Rico. Maintains committees on transportation planning, finance, maintenance, safety, and construction.

American Road and Transportation Builders Assn., 501 School St. S.W. 20024; 488-2722. T. Peter Ruane, president. Fax, 488-3631.

Membership: highway and transportation contractors; federal, state, and local engineers and officials; construction equipment manufacturers and distributors; and others interested in the transportation construction industry. Serves as liaison with government; provides information on highway engineering and construction developments.

Intelligent Vehicle Highway Society of America, 400 Virginia Ave. S.W., #800 20024-2730; 484-4847. Jim Constantino, executive director. Fax, 484-3483.

Advocates application of electronic, computer, and communications technology to make motor vehicle use more efficient. Coordinates research and development of intelligent vehicle and highway systems by government, academia, and industry.

International Bridge, Tunnel, and Turnpike Assn., 2120 L St. N.W., #305 20037; 659-4620. Neil D. Schuster, executive director. Fax, 659-0500.

Membership: public and private operators of toll facilities and associated industries. Conducts research; compiles statistics.

International Road Federation, 525 School St. S.W. 20024; 554-2106. Richard B. Robertson, director general. Fax, 479-0828.

Membership: road associations and automobile construction and related industries. Administers fellowship program that allows foreign engineering students to study at U.S. graduate schools. Maintains interest in roads and highways worldwide.

The Road Information Program, 1200 18th St. N.W., #314 20036; 466-6706. William M. Wilkins, executive director. Fax, 785-4722.

Organization of transportation specialists; conducts research on economic and technical transportation issues; promotes consumer awareness of the condition of the national road and bridge system.

Manufacturing

Nongovernmental:

American Automobile Manufacturers Assn., 1401 H St. N.W., #900 20005; 326-5500. Andrew Card, president. Fax, 326-5567.

Membership: domestic manufacturers of passenger and commercial cars, trucks, and buses

for highway use. Comprises federal liaison, motor truck, and economic and international affairs departments. (Headquarters in Detroit, Mich.)

Assn. of International Automobile Manufacturers, 1001 N. 19th St., #1200, Arlington, VA 22209; (703) 525-7788. Philip A. Hutchinson, president. Fax, (703) 525-8817.

Membership: importers of cars and automotive equipment. Serves as an information clearinghouse on import regulations at the state and federal levels.

Japan Automobile Manufacturers Assn., 1050 17th St. N.W., #410 20036; 296-8537. William C. Duncan, general director, Washington office. Fax, 872-1212.

Membership: Japanese motor vehicle manufacturers. Interests include energy, market, trade, and environmental issues. (Headquarters in Tokyo.)

Recreation Vehicle Industry Assn., 1896 Preston White Dr., Reston, VA (mailing address: P.O. Box 2999, Reston, VA 22090); (703) 620-6003. David J. Humphreys, president. Fax, (703) 620-5071.

Membership: manufacturers of recreation vehicles and their suppliers. Monitors legislation and regulations; compiles shipment statistics and other technical data; provides consumers and the media with information on the industry. Assists members' compliance with American National Standards Institute requirements for recreation vehicles and park trailers.

Truck Trailer Manufacturers Assn., 1020 Princess St., Alexandria, VA 22314; (703) 549-3010. Richard P. Bowling, president.

Membership: truck trailer manufacturing and supply companies. Serves as liaison between its members and government agencies; works to improve safety standards and industry efficiency.

Moving and Freight

Agencies:

Interstate Commerce Commission, 12th St and Constitution Ave. N.W. 20423; 927-6020 Gail C. McDonald, chair. Information, 927 5350. Press, 927-5340. Library, 927-7328. Fax 927-1472.

Grants operating rights to trucking companies, bus lines, and freight forwarders of household goods; regulates carrier rates; reviews and approves applications for mergers, consolidations, and issuance of railroad securities; operates consumer protection programs that alert the public to regulations governing movement of household goods. Consumer complaints should be directed to nearest regional office. Library open to the public. *(See Regional Federal Information Sources list, p. 809.)*

Congress:

See *Transportation: Motor Vehicle, General, Congress (p. 721)*

Nongovernmental:

American Movers Conference, 1611 Duke St., Alexandria, VA 22314; (703) 683-7410. Joseph M. Harrison, president. Fax, (703) 638-7527.

Membership: local, intrastate, interstate, and international movers of household and other goods. Represents members' views before the Interstate Commerce Commission and other government agencies. (Affiliated with American Trucking Assns.)

Household Goods Carriers' Bureau, 1611 Duke St., Alexandria, VA 22314; (703) 683-7410. Joseph M. Harrison, president. Fax, (703) 683-7527.

Membership: movers certified by the Interstate Commerce Commission to move household goods in interstate commerce. Maintains a committee on rates and tariffs.

Interstate Truckload Carriers Conference, 2200 Mill Rd., Alexandria, VA 22314; (703) 838-1950. J. Terry Turner, executive director. Fax, (703) 836-6610.

Represents intercity common and contract trucking companies before Congress, federal agencies, courts, and the media.

National Assn. of Chemical Distributors (NACD), 1101 17th St. N.W., #1200 20036; 296-9200. Joseph Cook, executive vice president. Fax, 296-0023.

Membership: firms that purchase, inventory, and transport chemical raw materials for distribution to industry. Monitors legislation and regulations. Provides members with information on such topics as training, safe handling and transport of chemicals, liability insurance, and

environmental issues. Manages the NACD Educational Foundation.

National Institute of Certified Moving Consultants, 11150 Main St., #402, Fairfax, VA 22030; (703) 934-9111. Gary F. Petty, president. Fax, (703) 934-9712.

Membership: sales and marketing personnel in the moving industry. Provides certification and training programs.

National Motor Freight Traffic Assn., 2200 Mill Rd., 4th Floor, Alexandria, VA 22314; (703) 838-1810. Martin E. Foley, executive director. Fax, (703) 683-1094.

Membership: motor carriers of general goods in interstate and intrastate commerce. Publishes *National Motor Freight Classification*, an index used by common carriers to determine freight rates.

National Moving and Storage Technical Foundation, 11150 Main St., #402, Fairfax, VA 22030; (703) 934-9111. Gary F. Petty, executive director. Fax, (703) 934-9712.

Sponsors educational programs and provides financial support for research on the moving and storage industry.

See also *American Trucking Assns. (p. 722)*

Parts and Components

Nongovernmental:

American Retreaders Assn., 1707 Pepper Tree Court, Bowie, MD 20716; (301) 577-5040. Roy Littlefield, director, government affairs. Fax, (301) 306-0523.

Membership: manufacturers, distributors, and retailers of retreaded tires. Monitors legislation and regulations; interests include environmental and small-business issues and quality control in the industry. Promotes government procurement of retreaded tires. (Headquarters in Louisville, Ky.)

Automotive Parts and Accessories Assn., 4600 East-West Highway, 3rd Floor, Bethesda, MD 20814; (301) 654-6664. Lawrence S. Hecker, president. Fax, (301) 654-3299.

Membership: domestic and international manufacturers, manufacturers' representatives, retailers, and distributors in the automotive aftermarket industry, which involves service of a vehicle after it leaves the dealership. Offers educational programs, conducts research, and provides members with technical and international trade services; acts as liaison with government; sponsors annual marketing conference and trade shows.

Automotive Parts Rebuilders Assn., 4401 Fair Lakes Court, #210, Fairfax, VA 22033; (703) 968-2772. William C. Gager, president. Fax, (703) 968-2878.
Membership: rebuilders of automotive parts. Conducts educational programs on transmission, brake, clutch, water pump, air conditioning, electrical parts, heavy duty brake, and carburetor rebuilding.

Automotive Recyclers Assn., 3975 Fair Ridge Dr., #T20N, Fairfax, VA 22033-2906; (703) 385-1001. William P. Steinkuller, executive vice president. Fax, (703) 385-1494.
Membership: retail and wholesale firms selling recycled auto and truck parts. Works to increase the efficiency of businesses in the automotive recycling industry. Cooperates with public and private agencies to encourage further automotive recycling efforts.

Electronic Industries Assn., 2001 Pennsylvania Ave. N.W., #1000 20006; 457-4914. Gary Shapiro, group vice president, consumer electronics. Fax, 457-4985.
Membership: manufacturers, dealers, installers, and distributors of consumer electronics products. Provides consumer information and data on industry trends; advocates an open market; monitors legislation and regulations.

National Tire Dealers and Retreaders Assn., 1250 Eye St. N.W., #400 20005; 789-2300. Philip P. Friedlander Jr., executive vice president. Fax, 682-3999.
Membership: independent tire dealers and retreaders. Monitors federal and state legislation and regulations; holds seminars; conducts market research studies.

Regulation

Agencies:

Federal Highway Administration (Transportation Dept.), Motor Carrier Standards, 400 7th St. S.W. 20590; 366-1790. James E. Scapellato, director. Fax, 366-7298.
Regulates motor vehicle size and weight on federally aided highways; conducts studies on

issues relating to motor carrier transportation; promotes uniformity in state and federal motor carrier laws and regulations.

Interstate Commerce Commission, 12th St. and Constitution Ave. N.W. 20423; 927-6020. Gail C. McDonald, chair. Information, 927-5350. Press, 927-5340. Library, 927-7328. Fax, 927-1472.
Grants operating rights to trucking companies, bus lines, and freight forwarders of household goods; regulates carrier rates; reviews and approves applications for mergers, consolidations, and issuance of railroad securities; operates consumer protection programs that alert the public to regulations governing movement of household goods. Library open to the public.

Interstate Commerce Commission, Compliance and Consumer Assistance, 12th St. and Constitution Ave. N.W. 20423; 927-5500. Bernard Gaillard, director. Fax, 927-5529. TDD, 927-5721.
Handles consumer problems and complaints involving interstate moving companies, buses, trains, and small shipments.

Interstate Commerce Commission, Economics, 12th St. and Constitution Ave. N.W. 20423; 927-7684. Milon Yager, director. Fax, 927-6225. TDD, 927-5721.
Monitors bus and trucking regulatory reform; develops and maintains various economic, mathematical, and statistical tools; acts as liaison with government agencies, industries, and organizations on major transportation issues.

Congress:

See Transportation: Motor Vehicle, General, Congress (p. 721)

Nongovernmental:

National Assn. of Regulatory Utility Commissioners, 12th St. and Constitution Ave. N.W. (mailing address: P.O. Box 684, Washington, DC 20044-0684); 898-2200. Paul Rodgers, administrative director and general counsel. Press, 898-2205. Fax, 898-2213.
Membership: members of federal, state, municipal, and Canadian regulatory commissions that have jurisdiction over motor and common carriers. Interests include motor carriers.

See also Transportation: Motor Vehicle, General, Nongovernmental (p. 722)

See also American Assn. of Motor Vehicle Administrators (p. 728)

Safety

See also Consumer Affairs, Alcohol (p. 253)

Agencies:

Federal Highway Administration (Transportation Dept.), Highway Safety, 400 7th St. S.W. 20590; 366-2171. R. Clarke Bennett, director. Fax, 366-2249.

Develops roadway safety standards, including standards for traffic control systems and devices. Administers program to make safety improvements to highways.

Federal Highway Administration (Transportation Dept.), Motor Carrier Field Operations, 400 7th St. S.W. 20590; 366-2952. Michael F. Trentacoste, director. Fax, 366-7908.

Plans and directs the federal and state Motor Carrier Safety Assistance programs to improve commercial vehicle safety on U.S. highways. Assigns safety fitness ratings based on motor carrier safety data.

Federal Highway Administration (Transportation Dept.), Motor Carrier Standards, 400 7th St. S.W. 20590; 366-1790. James E. Scapellato, director. Fax, 366-7298.

Interprets and disseminates national safety regulations regarding commercial drivers' qualifications, maximum hours of service, accident reporting, and transportation of hazardous materials. Sets minimum levels of financial responsibility for trucks and buses. Responsible for Commercial Driver's License Information Program.

Federal Highway Administration (Transportation Dept.), Traffic Management and Intelligent Vehicle Highway Systems, 400 7th St. S.W. 20590; 366-0372. Susan B. Lauffer, acting director. Fax, 366-2249.

Studies safety of highway systems, including traffic plans and highway communication systems.

National Highway Traffic Safety Administration (Transportation Dept.), 400 7th St. S.W. 20590; 366-1836. Christopher A. Hart, acting administrator. Information, 366-9550. Fax, 366-2106. Toll-free 24-hour hotline, (800) 424-9393; in Washington D.C., 366-0123.

Implements motor vehicle safety programs; issues federal motor vehicle safety standards; conducts testing programs to determine compliance with these standards; funds local and state motor vehicle and driver safety programs; conducts research on motor vehicle development, equipment, and auto and traffic safety. The Auto Safety Hotline handles consumer problems and complaints involving safety-related defects.

National Highway Traffic Safety Administration (Transportation Dept.), Motor Vehicle Safety Research Advisory Committee, 400 7th St. S.W. 20590; 366-1537. George L. Parker, chairman. Fax, 366-5930.

Serves as an independent source of ideas for motor vehicle safety research; provides the National Highway Traffic Safety Administration with information and recommendations.

National Highway Traffic Safety Administration (Transportation Dept.), National Driver Register, 400 7th St. S.W. 20590; 366-4800. Robert McGee, chief; Willetta Wilson, committee management coordinator. Fax, 366-2746.

Maintains and operates the National Driver Register, a program in which states exchange information on motor vehicle driving records to ensure that drivers with suspended licenses in one state cannot obtain licenses in any other state.

National Transportation Safety Board, Highway, 490 L'Enfant Plaza East S.W. 20594; 382-6850. Claude H. Harris, chief. Fax, 382-6715.

In cooperation with states, investigates selected highway transportation accidents to compile the facts upon which the board determines probable cause; works to prevent similar recurrences; makes recommendations on matters pertaining to highway safety and accident prevention.

Congress:

See Transportation: Motor Vehicle, General, Congress (p. 721)

Nongovernmental:

Advocates for Highway and Auto Safety, 777 N. Capitol St. N.E., #410 20002; 408-1711. Judith Lee Stone, president. Fax, 408-1699.

Coalition of insurers, citizens' groups, and safety organizations. Works to reduce deaths, injuries, and economic costs associated with motor vehicle crashes and fraud and theft involving motor vehicles. Interests include safety belts and child safety seats, air bags, drunk and drugged driving abuse, motorcycle helmets, vehicle crashworthiness, and speed limits. Monitors legislation and regulations.

American Assn. of Motor Vehicle Administrators, 4200 Wilson Blvd., #1100, Arlington, VA 22203; (703) 522-4200. John Strandquist, executive director. Fax, (703) 522-1553.

Membership: officials responsible for administering and enforcing motor vehicle and traffic laws in the United States and Canada. Promotes uniform laws and regulations for vehicle registration, drivers' licenses, and motor carrier services; provides administrative evaluation services for safety equipment.

American Bus Assn., 1100 New York Ave. N.W., #1050 20005; 842-1645. George T. Snyder Jr., executive vice president. Fax, 842-0850.

Membership: intercity privately owned bus companies, state associations, travel/tourism businesses, bus manufacturers, and those interested in the bus industry. Monitors legislation and regulations; maintains committee on safety standards.

American Trucking Assns., Safety, 2200 Mill Rd., Alexandria, VA 22314; (703) 838-1847. Stephen Campbell, vice president. Fax, (703) 683-1934.

Membership: state trucking associations, individual trucking and motor carrier organizations, and related supply companies. Provides information on safety for the trucking industry. Develops safety training programs for motor carriers and drivers.

Automotive Safety Foundation, 1776 Massachusetts Ave. N.W. 20036; 857-1200. Lester P. Lamm, president. Fax, 857-1220.

Conducts highway safety programs to reduce automobile-related accidents and deaths. (Affiliated with Highway Users Federation for Safety and Mobility.)

Center for Auto Safety, 2001 S St. N.W. 20009; 328-7700. Clarence M. Ditlow III, executive director.

Public interest group. Receives consumer complaints against auto manufacturers; monitors

government agencies that enforce auto safety and fuel economy rules.

Commercial Vehicle Safety Alliance, 5430 Grosvenor Lane, #130, Bethesda, MD 20814; (301) 564-1623. William R. Fiste, executive director. Fax, (301) 564-0588.

Membership: U.S., Canadian, and Mexican officials responsible for administering and enforcing commercial motor carrier safety laws. Works to increase on-highway inspections, prevent duplication of inspections, improve the safety of equipment operated on highways, and improve compliance with hazardous materials transportation regulations.

Commission of Accredited Truck Driving Schools, 2011 Pennsylvania Ave. N.W., #500 20006; 467-6473. Carol Kataldo, executive director. Fax, 457-9121.

Membership: accredited truck driving training schools. Works with government and the industry on safety issues and promotes sound educational and ethical standards among truck driving schools; supports research on truck driver education and safety.

Highway Users Federation for Safety and Mobility, 1776 Massachusetts Ave. N.W. 20036; 857-1200. Lester P. Lamm, president. Fax, 857-1220.

Membership: companies and associations representing major industry and highway user groups. Monitors legislation and regulations. Acts as an information clearinghouse. (Affiliated with the Automotive Safety Foundation.)

Institute of Transportation Engineers, 525 School St. S.W., #410 20024; 554-8050. Thomas W. Brahms, executive director. Fax, 863-5486.

Membership: international professional transportation engineers. Interests include safe and efficient surface transportation; provides professional and scientific information on transportation standards and recommended practices.

Insurance Institute for Highway Safety, 1005 N. Glebe Rd., Arlington, VA 22201; (703) 247-1500. Brian O'Neill, president. Fax, (703) 247-1678.

Membership: property and casualty insurance associations and individual insurance companies. Conducts research and provides data on highway safety; seeks ways to reduce losses from vehicle crashes. (Affiliated with Highway Loss Data Institute.)

National Assn. of Governors' Highway Safety Representatives, 750 1st St. N.E., #720 20002; 789-0942. Barbara L. Harsha, executive director. Fax, 789-0946.

Membership: state officials who manage highway safety programs. Maintains information clearinghouse on state highway safety programs; interprets technical data concerning highway safety. Represents the states in policy debates on national highway safety issues.

National Commission Against Drunk Driving, 1900 L St. N.W., #705 20036; 452-6004. Terrance Schiavone, president. Fax, 223-7012.

Works to increase public awareness of the problem of drunk and impaired drivers, especially repeat offenders. Administers work site traffic safety programs for corporate managers. Monitors the implementation of recommendations made by the Presidential Commission Against Drunk Driving.

National Safety Council, 1019 19th St. N.W. 20036; 293-2270. Jane S. Roemer, executive director, public policy. Fax, 293-0032.

Chartered by Congress. Conducts research and provides educational and informational services on motor vehicle accident prevention; encourages the adoption of policies that will reduce accidental deaths and injuries; monitors legislation and regulations affecting safety rules. (Headquarters in Itasca, Ill.)

National School Transportation Assn., 6213 Old Keene Mill Court, Springfield, VA (mailing address: P.O. Box 2639, Springfield, VA 22152); (703) 644-0700. Karen Finkel, executive director. Fax, (703) 644-9385.

Membership: private owners who operate school buses on contract, bus manufacturers, and allied companies. Primary area of interest and research is school bus safety.

School Bus Manufacturers Institute, 7508 Ben Avon Rd., Bethesda, MD 20817; (301) 229-8441. Berkley C. Sweet, executive vice president.

Membership: major manufacturers of conventional school buses. Represents manufacturers before Congress and government agencies, primarily on issues of engineering and safety.

Tire Industry Safety Council, 1400 K St. N.W., #900 20005; 783-1022. Eric Bolton, director. Fax, 783-3512.

Membership: American tire manufacturers. Provides consumers with information on tire care and safety.

United Bus Owners of America, 1300 L St. N.W., #1050 20005; 484-5623. Wayne J. Smith, executive director. Fax, 898-0484.

Provides information, offers technical assistance, conducts research, and monitors legislation. Interests include insurance, safety programs, and credit.

See also Licensed Beverage Information Council (p. 253); NATSO, Inc. (p. 722)

Sales and Leasing

Nongovernmental:

American Automotive Leasing Assn., 1001 Connecticut Ave. N.W. 20036; 223-2600. Mary T. Tavenner, executive director. Fax, 331-1899.

Membership: automobile and truck commercial leasing companies. Monitors legislation and regulations.

American Car Rental Assn., 927 15th St. N.W., #1000 20005; 789-2240. Jan M. Armstrong, executive vice president. Fax, 371-1467.

Membership: companies involved in the short-term renting of automobiles. Acts as liaison with legislative bodies and regulatory agencies. Maintains information clearinghouse and membership directory.

National Automobile Dealers Assn., 8400 Westpark Dr., McLean, VA 22102; (703) 821-7000. Frank E. McCarthy, executive vice president. Fax, (703) 821-7075.

Membership: domestic and imported franchised new car and truck dealers. Publishes the *National Automobile Dealers Used Car Guide* (Blue Book).

Recreation Vehicle Dealers Assn. of North America, 3930 University Dr., Fairfax, VA 22030; (703) 591-7130. Robert J. Strawn Jr., president. Toll-free, (800) 336-0355. Fax, (703) 591-0734.

Serves as liaison between the recreation vehicle industry and government; interests include government regulation of safety, trade, warranty, and franchising; provides members with educational services; works to improve service standards for consumers.

Truck Renting and Leasing Assn., 2011 Pennsylvania Ave. N.W., 5th Floor 20006; 775-4859. J. Michael Payne, chief executive officer. Fax, 457-9121.

Membership: truck renting and leasing companies and system suppliers to the industry. Acts as liaison with legislative bodies and regulatory agencies. Interests include federal motor carrier safety issues, highway funding, operating taxes and registration fees at the state level, and uniformity of state taxes.

Transportation: Railroad

General

Agencies:

Federal Railroad Administration (Transportation Dept.), 400 7th St. S.W. 20590; 366-0710. Jolene M. Molitoris, administrator. Information, 366-0881. Fax, 366-7009.

Develops national rail policies; enforces rail safety laws; administers financial assistance programs available to states and the rail industry; conducts research and development on improved rail safety.

Federal Railroad Administration (Transportation Dept.), Railroad Development, 400 7th St. S.W. 20590; 366-9660. James T. McQueen, associate administrator. Fax, 366-0646.

Administers federal assistance programs for national, regional, and local rail services, including freight service assistance, service continuation, and passenger service. Conducts research and development on new rail technologies.

National Railroad Passenger Corp. (Amtrak), 60 Massachusetts Ave. N.E. 20002; 906-3960. Thomas M. Downs, chairman and president. Press, 906-3860. Fax, 906-3865. Consumer relations/complaints, 906-2121; travel and ticket information, (800) 872-7245.

Quasi-public corporation created by the Rail Passenger Service Act of 1970 to improve and develop intercity passenger rail service.

National Transportation Safety Board, Railroad, 490 L'Enfant Plaza East S.W. 20594; 382-6843. Robert Lauby, chief. Fax, 382-6884.

Investigates passenger train accidents, including rapid rail transit and rail commuter systems, and freight rail accidents with substantial damage to determine probable cause; investigates all

employee and passenger fatalities; makes recommendations on rail transportation safety and accident prevention.

Congress:

House Appropriations Committee, Subcommittee on Transportation, 2358 RHOB 20515; 225-2141. Bob Carr, D-Mich., chairman; Del Davis, staff assistant.

Jurisdiction over legislation to appropriate funds for the Federal Railroad Administration, National Railroad Passenger Corp. (Amtrak), and Interstate Commerce Commission.

House Energy and Commerce Committee, Subcommittee on Transportation and Hazardous Materials, 324 Ford Bldg. (2nd and D Sts. S.W.) 20515; 225-9304. Al Swift, D-Wash., chairman; Arthur Endres, staff director and chief counsel.

Jurisdiction over railroad legislation, including railroad labor and retirement.

House Government Operations Committee, Subcommittee on Information, Justice, Transportation, and Agriculture, B349C RHOB 20515; 225-3741. Gary Condit, D-Calif., chairman; Shannon Lahey, acting staff director. Fax, 225-2445.

Oversees operations of the Federal Railroad Administration, Interstate Commerce Commission, and National Railroad Passenger Corp. (Amtrak).

Senate Appropriations Committee, Subcommittee on Transportation, SD-156 20510; 224-7281. Frank R. Lautenberg, D-N.J., chairman; Patrick J. McCann, clerk.

Jurisdiction over legislation to appropriate funds for the Federal Railroad Administration, National Railroad Passenger Corp. (Amtrak), and Interstate Commerce Commission.

Senate Commerce, Science, and Transportation Committee, Subcommittee on Surface Transportation, SH-428 (mailing address: SD-508, Washington, DC 20510); 224-9350. Jim Exon, D-Neb., chairman; Vacant, senior professional staff member.

Jurisdiction over railroad legislation (except railroad labor and retirement); oversees the Federal Railroad Administration, Interstate Commerce Commission, and National Railroad Passenger Corp. (Amtrak).

Senate Labor and Human Resources Committee, Subcommittee on Labor, SH-608 20510; 224-5546. Howard M. Metzenbaum, D-Ohio, chairman; Michele L. Varnhagen, staff director.

Jurisdiction over legislation on railroad labor and retirement.

See also Senate Rail Caucus (p. 761)

Nongovernmental:

American Short Line Railroad Assn., 1120 G St. N.W., #520 20005; 628-4500. William E. Loftus, president. Fax, 628-6430.

Membership: independently owned short line railroad systems. Assists members with technical and legal questions; compiles information on laws, regulations, and other matters affecting the industry.

Assn. of American Railroads, 50 F St. N.W. 20001; 639-2100. Edwin L. Harper, president. Information, 639-2550. Press, 639-2555. Fax, 639-2868.

Provides information on freight railroad operations, safety and maintenance, economics and finance, management, and law and legislation; conducts research; issues statistical reports. Library open to the public by appointment.

National Assn. of Railroad Passengers, 900 2nd St. N.E., #308 20002; 408-8362. Ross Capon, executive director. Fax, 408-8287.

Consumer organization. Works to expand and improve U.S. intercity and commuter rail passenger service, increase federal funds for mass transit, ensure fair treatment for rail freight transportation, and address environmental concerns pertaining to mass transit. Opposes subsidies for intercity trucking; works with Amtrak on scheduling, new services, fares, and advertising.

Railway Progress Institute, 700 N. Fairfax St., #601, Alexandria, VA 22314; (703) 836-2332. Robert A. Matthews, president. Fax, (703) 548-0058.

Membership: railroad and rail rapid transit suppliers. Conducts research on safety and new technology; monitors legislation.

Railroad Employees

Agencies:

National Mediation Board, 1301 K St. N.W., #250E 20572; 523-5920. Kimberly A. Madigan, chair. Information, 523-5335. Fax, 523-1494.

Mediates labor disputes in the railroad industry; determines and certifies labor representatives in the industry.

Railroad Retirement Board, Washington Legislative Liaison, 1310 G St. N.W., #500 20005; 272-7742. John C. Ficerai, liaison officer. Fax, 272-7728.

Assists congressional offices with inquiries on retirement, spouse, survivor, and unemployment benefits for railroad employees and retirees. (Headquarters in Chicago.)

Congress:

See Transportation: Railroad, General, Congress (p. 730)

Nongovernmental:

National Railway Labor Conference, 1901 L St. N.W., #500 20036; 862-7200. Charles I. Hopkins Jr., chairman. Fax, 862-7230.

Assists member railroad lines with labor matters; negotiates with railroad labor representatives.

Railway Labor Executives' Assn., 400 N. Capitol St. N.W. 20001; 737-1541. R. J. Irvin, executive secretary-treasurer. Fax, 783-3107.

Membership: executives of railroad labor organizations. Confers on legislative matters, including pensions and retirement.

Regulation and Assistance

Agencies:

Federal Railroad Administration (Transportation Dept.), Policy, 400 7th St. S.W. 20590; 366-0173. Sally Hill Cooper, associate administrator. Fax, 366-7688.

Manages new and revised policies, plans, and projects related to railroad economics, finance, system planning, and operations. Conducts studies, analyses, tests, and demonstrations. Makes recommendations to the transportation secretary on issues before regulatory agencies.

Federal Railroad Administration (Transportation Dept.), Safety, 400 7th St. S.W. 20590; 366-0895. Grady C. Cothen Jr., associate administrator. Fax, 366-7136.

Administers and enforces federal laws and regulations that promote railroad safety, including track maintenance, inspection and equipment standards, operating practices, and transportation of explosives and other hazardous materials. Conducts inspections and reports on railroad equipment facilities and accidents.

Interstate Commerce Commission, Compliance and Consumer Assistance, 12th St. and Constitution Ave. N.W. 20423; 927-5500. Bernard Gaillard, director. Fax, 927-5529. TDD, 927-5721.

Oversees U.S. rail operations with respect to equipment utilization, rate violations, freight car distribution, and other matters.

Interstate Commerce Commission, Economics, 12th St. and Constitution Ave. N.W. 20423; 927-7684. Milon Yager, director. Fax, 927-6225. TDD, 927-5721.

Evaluates rail merger and consolidation proposals; issues economic and environmental analyses of railway system proposals; monitors effects of rail regulatory legislation.

Interstate Commerce Commission, Railroad Service Board, 12th St. and Constitution Ave. N.W. 20423; 927-5500. Bernard Gaillard, chairman. Fax, 927-5529. TDD, 927-5721.

Issues temporary emergency orders pertaining to the operation of rail carriers, including orders for rerouting because of carrier disability.

Congress:

See *Transportation: Railroad, General, Congress (p. 730)*

Nongovernmental:

National Assn. of Regulatory Utility Commissioners, 12th St. and Constitution Ave. N.W. (mailing address: P.O. Box 684, Washington, DC 20044-0684); 898-2200. Paul Rodgers, administrative director and general counsel. Press, 898-2205. Fax, 898-2213.

Membership: members of federal, state, municipal, and Canadian regulatory commissions that have jurisdiction over motor and common carriers. Interests include railroads.

Transportation: Urban Mass Transit

Agencies:

Federal Transit Administration (Transportation Dept.), 400 7th St. S.W. 20590; 366-4040. Gordon J. Linton, administrator. Information, 366-4043. Fax, 366-3472.

Responsible for developing improved mass transportation facilities, equipment, techniques, and methods; assists state and local governments in financing mass transportation systems.

Federal Transit Administration (Transportation Dept.), Budget and Policy, 400 7th St. S.W. 20590; 366-4050. Vacant, associate administrator. Fax, 366-7116.

Develops budgets, programs, legislative proposals, and policies for the federal transit program; evaluates program proposals and their potential impact on local communities; coordinates private sector initiatives of the agency.

Federal Transit Administration (Transportation Dept.), Grants Management, 400 7th St. S.W. 20590; 366-4020. Robert H. McManus, associate administrator. Fax, 366-7951.

Administers capital planning and operating assistance grants and loan activities; monitors transit projects in such areas as environmental impact, special provisions for the elderly and people with disabilities, efficiency, and investment.

Federal Transit Administration (Transportation Dept.), Technical Assistance and Safety, 400 7th St. S.W. 20590; 366-4052. Lawrence L. Schulman, associate administrator. Fax, 366-3765.

Provides industry, transit properties, and state and local governments with contracts, cooperative agreements, and grants for testing, developing, and demonstrating methods of improved mass transportation service and technology. Supports drug control efforts in transit systems.

National Transportation Safety Board, Railroad, 490 L'Enfant Plaza East S.W. 20594; 382-6843. Robert Lauby, chief. Fax, 382-6884.

Investigates passenger train accidents, including rapid rail transit and rail commuter systems, and freight rail accidents with substantial damage to determine probable cause; investigates all employee and passenger fatalities; makes recommendations on rail transportation safety and accident prevention.

Congress:

General Accounting Office, Transportation, 901 D St. S.W., #802 20024; 401-6001. Allen Li, associate director. Fax, 401-6025.

Independent, nonpartisan agency in the legislative branch. Audits, analyzes, and evaluates performance of the Transportation Dept., including highway and mass transit issues; makes reports available to the public.

House Appropriations Committee, Subcommittee on Transportation, 2358 RHOB 20515; 225-2141. Bob Carr, D-Mich., chairman; Del Davis, staff assistant.

Jurisdiction over legislation to appropriate funds for the Federal Transit Administration and intercity mass transit systems, including the Washington Metropolitan Area Transit Authority.

House Public Works and Transportation Committee, Subcommittee on Surface Transportation, B376 RHOB 20515; 225-9989. Nick J. Rahall II, D-W.Va., chairman; Kenneth House, chief professional.

Jurisdiction over legislation on urban mass transportation and intercity mass transit systems.

Senate Appropriations Committee, Subcommittee on Transportation, SD-156 20510; 224-7281. Frank R. Lautenberg, D-N.J., chairman; Patrick J. McCann, clerk.

Jurisdiction over legislation to appropriate funds for the Federal Transit Administration, urban mass transportation, and intercity mass transit systems.

Senate Banking, Housing, and Urban Affairs Committee, Subcommittee on Housing and Urban Affairs, SD-535 20510; 224-6348. Paul S. Sarbanes, D-Md., chairman; Paul N. Weech, staff director. Fax, 224-5137.

Jurisdiction over legislation on urban mass transportation and intercity mass transit systems.

Nongovernmental:

American Public Transit Assn., 1201 New York Ave. N.W. 20005; 898-4000. Jack R. Gilstrap, executive vice president. Information, 898-4089. Fax, 898-4049.

Membership: rapid rail and motor bus systems and manufacturers, suppliers, and consulting firms. Compiles data on the industry; promotes research; monitors legislation and regulations.

Assn. for Commuter Transportation, 1518 K St. N.W., #503 20005; 393-3497. Kenneth Sufka, executive director.

Membership: corporations, public agencies, transit authorities, transport management associations, van-pool management companies, and individuals. Monitors legislation and regulations; serves as a clearinghouse for ride-sharing information and materials; maintains speaker referral service. Interests include tax equity for commuters and employer transportation requirements of the Clean Air Act amendments.

National Research Council, Transportation Research Board, 2001 Wisconsin Ave. N,W (mailing address: 2101 Constitution Ave. N.W., Washington, DC 20418); 334-3250. Suzanne D. Crowther, manager, urban mass transportation research information service. Information, 334-3262. Fax, 334-3495.

Provides information on research projects and publications covering such topics as public transportation technology and management, elderly and disabled passenger needs, and rural transport systems. Fee for services. (The National Research Council is the operating arm of the National Academy of Sciences, the National Academy of Engineering, and the Institute of Medicine.)

United Bus Owners of America, 1300 L St. N.W., #1050 20005; 484-5623. Wayne J. Smith, executive director. Fax, 898-0484.

Provides information, offers technical assistance, conducts research, and monitors legislation. Interests include insurance, safety programs, and credit.

See also American Bus Assn. (p. 728)

The offices of all members of Congress and all congressional committees and subcommittees can be reached by calling 224-3121.

Key Agency:

Federal Election Commission
999 E St. N.W. 20463
Information: 219-3420
Toll-free: (800) 424-9530

Key Committees:

House Administration Committee
H326 CAP 20515
Phone: 225-2061

House Standards of Official Conduct Committee
HT-2 CAP 20515
Phone: 225-7103

Senate Rules and Administration Committee
SR-305 20510
Phone: 224-6352

Senate Select Committee on Ethics
SH-220 20510
Phone: 224-2981

Key Personnel:

Federal Election Commission
Trevor Potter, chairman

House

Thomas S. Foley, D-Wash., Speaker of the House
Richard A. Gephardt, D-Mo., majority leader
David E. Bonior, D-Mich., majority whip
Robert H. Michel, R-Ill., minority leader
Newt Gingrich, R-Ga., minority whip
Steny H. Hoyer, D-Md., chairman, House Democratic Caucus
Dick Armey, R-Texas, chairman, House Republican Conference

Senate

Robert C. Byrd, D-W.Va., president pro tempore
George J. Mitchell, D-Maine, majority leader
Wendell H. Ford, D-Ky., majority whip
Bob Dole, R-Kan., Republican leader
Alan K. Simpson, R-Wyo., assistant Republican leader
David Pryor, D-Ark., secretary, Senate Democratic Conference
Thad Cochran, R-Miss., chairman, Senate Republican Conference

Political Party Committees:

Democratic National Committee
430 S. Capitol St. S.E. 20003
Phone: 863-8000
David Wilhelm, chairman

Republican National Committee
310 1st St. S.E. 20003
Phone: 863-8500
Haley Barbour, chairman

18

Congress
and Politics

Contents:

Access to Congressional Information

Bills, Documents, Hearings, and Reports

See also Regional Depository Libraries list (p. 850)

Agencies:

National Archives and Records Administration, Presidential Documents and Legislative Division, 800 N. Capitol St. N.W., #700 (mailing address: Office of the Federal Register, National Archives and Records Administration, Washington, DC 20408); 523-5230. Frances D. McDonald, director. Fax, 523-6866. TDD, 523-5229. Public Laws Update Service (PLUS), 523-6641.

Assigns public law numbers to enacted legislation, executive orders, and proclamations; responds to inquiries on public law numbers; assists inquirers in finding presidential signing or veto messages in the *Weekly Compilation of Presidential Documents* and the *Public Papers of the Presidents* series; compiles slip laws and annual *United States Statutes at Large;* compiles indexes for finding statutory provisions. Operates Public Laws Update Service (PLUS), which provides information by telephone on new legislation. Publications available from the U.S. Government Printing Office, Washington, D.C. 20402; 783-3238.

House and Senate:

Government Printing Office, Documents, 732 N. Capitol St. N.W. (mailing address: Superintendent of Documents, Government Printing Office, Washington, DC 20401); 512-0571. Wayne P. Kelley, superintendent. Fax, 512-2233. Congressional order desk, 512-2470. Publications, 783-3238.

Prints, distributes, and sells congressional hearings, documents, prints, public laws, reports, and House calendars.

House:

House Document Room, B-18 Ford Bldg. (2nd and D Sts. S.W.) 20515; 225-3456. Gerard Walsh, manager. Fax, 226-4362.

Maintains and distributes House bills, reports, public laws, and documents to members' offices, committee staffs, and the general public. Telephone requests are accepted.

Senate:

Senate Document Room, SH-B04 20510; 224-7860. Jeanie Bowles, superintendent.

Maintains and distributes Senate bills, reports, public laws, and documents. (To obtain material send a self-addressed mailing label with request. Telephone requests are not accepted.)

Senate Executive Clerk, S138 CAP 20510; 224-4341. Gerald A. Hackett, executive clerk.

Maintains and distributes copies of treaties submitted to the Senate for ratification; provides information on submitted treaties and nominations. (Shares distribution responsibility with Senate Document Room, 224-7860.)

Congressional Record

The Congressional Record, *published daily when Congress is in session, is a printed account of proceedings on the floor of the House and Senate. A Daily Digest section with page references summarizes the day's action, both on the floor and in committees, and lists committee meetings scheduled for the following day. An index is published monthly and at the close of sessions of Congress. The law stipulates that the* Record *shall be a verbatim report of proceedings and that members of Congress may revise their remarks before they are published. Material inserted but not spoken on the floor is indicated as such in the text of the* Record. *The* Congressional Record Scanner *abstracts each day's* Congressional Record. *It is published daily by Congressional Quarterly, 1414 22nd St. N.W. 20037; 887-6279.*

To purchase copies:

Government Printing Office Main Bookstore, Congressional Order Desk, 710 N. Capitol St. N.W. (mailing address: Superintendent of Documents, Government Printing Office, Washington, DC 20402); 512-2470. Fax, 512-2250.

U.S. Capitol Historical Society, Information Center, East-Front Lobby, CAP 20515; 224-0038.

To read copies:

Library of Congress, Law Library Reading Room, 101 Independence Ave. S.E. 20540; 707-5079. Kathleen M. Price, head, law library. Fax, 707-3585.

Copies of the *Congressional Record* are available for reading. Terminals in the reading room provide access to a computer system containing bill digests from the 93rd Congress to date.

Martin Luther King Memorial Library, 901 G St. N.W., #400 20001; 727-1101. Hardy R. Franklin, director. Information, 727-0321. Fax, 727-1129.

Maintains collection of *Congressional Record* paperback volumes (1980 to date), bound volumes (1939-1976), microfilm (1827-1964), and microfiche (1977-1985).

See also Regional Depository Libraries list (p. 850)

To subscribe:

Government Printing Office Main Bookstore, Congressional Order Desk, 710 N. Capitol St. N.W. (mailing address: Superintendent of Documents, Government Printing Office, Washington, DC 20402); 512-2470. Fax, 512-2250.

Legislative Jurisdiction over Printing

House and Senate:

Joint Committee on Printing, SH-818 20510; 224-5241. Sen. Wendell H. Ford, D-Ky., chairman; John Chambers, staff director. Fax, 224-1176.

Controls arrangement and style of the *Congressional Record;* determines which congressional prints, documents, and reports are inserted; oversight of public printing, binding, and distribution of government publications; oversees activities of the Government Printing Office (in conjunction with the House Administration and Senate Rules and Administration committees).

House:

House Administration Committee, H326 CAP 20515; 225-2061. Charlie Rose, D-N.C., chairman; Robert E. Shea, staff director. Fax, 225-4345.

Jurisdiction over congressional printing, binding, and distribution; cost of printing; and printing of and corrections to the *Congressional Record*. Jurisdiction (in conjunction with the Joint Committee on Printing and the Senate Rules and Administration Committee) over the Government Printing Office, executive papers, and depository libraries.

Senate:

Senate Rules and Administration Committee, SR-305 20510; 224-6352. Wendell H. Ford, D-Ky., chairman; James O. King, staff director.
Jurisdiction (in conjunction with the House Administration Committee and the Joint Committee on Printing) over the Government Printing Office and legislation on printing of and corrections to the *Congressional Record*.

Scheduled Committee Meetings

House and Senate:

Congressional Record (Daily Digest). Lists the following day's congressional committee meetings and hearings as well as persons testifying. Provides summary of the day's committee action.

Information can also be obtained from individual committee offices. See 103rd Congress section (p. 975)

Nongovernmental:

Associated Press, 2021 K St. N.W., #600 20006; 828-6400. John Wolman, bureau chief. Fax, 828-6422. Daybook editor, 828-6468.
Publishes daybook that lists congressional committee meetings and hearings and their location and subject matter. No fee for listing events in daybook. (Headquarters in N.Y.)

The Congressional Monitor, 1414 22nd St. N.W. 20037; 887-6279. Fax, 728-1863.
Lists daily committee meetings and hearings, complete witness list, floor proceedings, and future scheduled committee meetings and hearings. Fee for services.

Legi-Slate, 777 N. Capitol St. N.E., #900 20002; 898-2300. Toll-free, (800) 877-6999. Fax, 842-4748.
Provides online congressional hearing and markup schedules, including time and location,

meeting agendas, and full witness listings. Fee for services. Affiliated with the Washington Post Company.

United Press International, 1400 Eye St. N.W. 20005; 898-8000. Fax, 789-2362.
Wire service that lists congressional committee meetings and hearings, location, and subject matter. Fee for services.

Washington Alert, 1414 22nd St. N.W. 20037; 887-8511. Fax, 728-1863.
Provides online congressional hearing and markup schedules, including time and location, meeting agendas, and full witness listings. Fee for services. Affiliated with Congressional Quarterly Inc.

Washington Post, 1150 15th St. N.W. 20071; 334-7410. Information, 334-6000.
Lists congressional committee meetings and hearings, locations, and subject matter. Fee for services.

Scheduled Floor Proceedings

House:

Congressional Record (see p. 737)

Clerk of the House of Representatives, Records and Registration, 1036 LHOB 20515; 225-1300. Patricia Bias, director.
Provides videotapes of House floor proceedings. Fee for services.

House Democratic Cloakroom, H222 CAP 20515; 225-7330. Barry K. Sullivan, manager.
Recorded messages: House floor action, 225-7400; legislative program, 225-1600.

House Republican Cloakroom, H223 CAP 20515; 225-7350. Timothy J. Harroun, manager.
Recorded messages: House floor action, 225-7430; legislative program, 225-2020.

Senate:

Congressional Record (see p. 737)

Senate Democratic Cloakroom, S225 CAP 20510; 224-4691. Recorded message: Senate floor action, 224-8541.

Senate Republican Cloakroom, S226 CAP 20510; 224-6191. Recorded message: Senate floor action, 224-8601.

Nongovernmental:

See The Congressional Monitor *(p. 738)*

Status of Legislation

House and Senate:

Calendars of the U.S. House of Representatives and History of Legislation, Senate Document Room, SH-B04 20510; 224-7860. Jeanie Bowles, superintendent.

Issued weekly when the House is in session. Provides capsule legislative history of all measures reported by House and Senate committees; provides additional reference material. Subject index included in each Monday edition or in the edition published on the first day the House is in session. (Also available from the House Document Room, B 10 Ford Bldg., 2nd and D Sts. S.W. 20515; 225-3456, and from the Superintendent of Documents, Government Printing Office, Washington, DC 20402; 512-2470.)

Legislative Information Service, 696 Ford Bldg. (2nd and D Sts. S.W.) 20515; 225-1772. Deborah Turner, chief.

Records, stores, and provides legislative status information on all bills and resolutions pending in Congress. Provides information through LEGIS, a computer-based service, on all legislation introduced since the 93rd Congress.

Library of Congress, Computer Catalog Center, 10 1st St. S.E. 20540; 707-3370. Judy Austin, acting team leader, history and political science, 707-4473. Fax, 707-1957.

Makes available a computer system containing information on all legislation introduced since the 93rd Congress (1973), arranged by member's name, subject, committee, and bill or resolution number. Terminals available for use by the public.

Campaigning

Campaign Conduct and Election Administration

See also Access to the Media (p. 22); Civil Service, Political Activity and the Hatch Act (p. 295); Pay and Perquisites, Standards of Conduct (p. 763)

Agencies:

Federal Election Commission (FEC), National Clearinghouse on Election Administration, 999 E St. N.W. 20463; 219-3670. Penelope Bonsall, director. Toll-free, (800) 424-9530. Fax, 219-8500.

Conducts studies on voter registration, voting procedures, and election administration; serves as an information clearinghouse on election administration; provides information on National Voter Registration Act of 1993; produces research publications, which are available through the Government Printing Office.

Justice Dept., Election Crimes, 1400 New York Ave. N.W. (mailing address: P.O. Box 27518, Washington, DC 20038); 514-1421. Craig Donsanto, director. Fax, 514-3003.

Supervises enforcement of federal criminal laws related to elections. Oversees investigation of deprivation of voting rights; intimidation and coercion of voters; denial or promise of federal employment or other benefits; illegal political contributions, expenditures, and solicitations; and all other election violations referred to the division.

Congress:

House Administration Committee, H326 CAP 20515; 225-2061. Charlie Rose, D-N.C., chairman; Robert E. Shea, staff director. Fax, 225-4345.

Jurisdiction over legislation and other matters related to all federal elections including the election of the president, vice president, and members of the House; corrupt practices; contested House elections; and voter registration.

House Administration Committee, Subcommittee on Elections, 717 O'Neill Bldg. (300 New Jersey Ave. S.E.) 20515; 226-7616. Al Swift, D-Wash., chairman; Herbert S. Stone, staff director. Fax, 225-4466.

Jurisdiction over legislation related to election law changes, voter registration, overseas voters, and broadcast of early projections. Oversees operations of the Federal Election Commission.

House Appropriations Committee, Subcommittee on Treasury, Postal Service, and General Government, H164 CAP 20515; 225-5834. Steny H. Hoyer, D-Md., chairman; Bill Smith, staff assistant. Fax, 426-3763.

Jurisdiction over legislation to appropriate funds for the Federal Election Commission.

House Commission on Congressional Mailing Standards, 176A Ford Bldg. (2nd and D Sts. S.W.) 20515; 225-0436. William L. Clay, D-Mo., chairman; Julie Tagen, staff director. Fax, 226-0245.

Receives complaints, conducts investigations, and issues decisions on disputes arising from the alleged abuse of franked mail by House members during congressional election campaigns.

House District of Columbia Committee, 1309 LHOB 20515; 225-4457. Pete Stark, D-Calif., chairman; Broderick D. Johnson, staff director. Fax, 225-2099.

Oversight of election laws in the District of Columbia.

House Judiciary Committee, Subcommittee on Economic and Commercial Law, B353 RHOB 20515; 225-2825. Jack Brooks, D-Texas, chairman; Cynthia W. Meadow, chief counsel.

Jurisdiction over proposed constitutional amendments related to the electoral college, campaign reform, and presidential succession.

Senate Appropriations Committee, Subcommittee on Treasury, Postal Service, and General Government, SD-190 20515; 224-8271. Dennis DeConcini, D-Ariz., chairman; Patty Lynch, clerk.

Jurisdiction over legislation to appropriate funds for the Federal Election Commission.

Senate Governmental Affairs Committee, Subcommittee on Federal Services, Post Office, and Civil Service, SH-601 20510; 224-2254. David Pryor, D-Ark., chairman; Kimberly A. Weaver, staff director.

Jurisdiction over legislation on voter registration by mail.

Senate Governmental Affairs Committee, Subcommittee on General Services, Federalism, and the District of Columbia, SH-432 20510; 224-4718. Jim Sasser, D-Tenn., chairman; John Wagster, staff director.

Oversight of election laws in the District of Columbia.

Senate Judiciary Committee, Subcommittee on the Constitution, SD-524 20510; 224-5573. Paul Simon, D-Ill., chairman; Susan D. Kaplan, chief counsel.

Jurisdiction over proposed constitutional amendments related to the electoral college, campaign reform, and presidential succession.

Senate Rules and Administration Committee, SR-305 20510; 224-6352. Wendell H. Ford, D-Ky., chairman; James O. King, staff member.

Jurisdiction over legislation and other matters related to all federal elections including the election of the president, vice president, members of the Senate, and presidential succession; corrupt practices; political action committees; election law changes; and broadcast of early election projections. Oversees voter registration by mail and operations of the Federal Election Commission.

Nongovernmental:

American Assn. of Political Consultants, 900 2nd St. N.E., #110 20002; 371-9585. Thomas N. Edmonds, president. Fax, 371-9597.

Membership: political consultants, media specialists, campaign managers, corporate public affairs officers, pollsters, public officials, academicians, fund raisers, lobbyists, and congressional staffers. Focuses on ethics of the profession; provides members with opportunities to meet industry leaders and learn new techniques and emerging technologies.

American Bar Assn., Standing Committee on Election Law, 1800 M St. N.W. 20036; 331-2652. Richard P. Mandelbaum, director. Fax, 331-2220.

Studies ways to improve the federal election process.

Campaign Finance

Agencies:

Federal Election Commission (FEC), 999 E St. N.W. 20463; 219-3440. Trevor Potter, chairman;

John C. Surina, staff director. Information, 219-3420. Press, 219-4155. Library, 219-3312. Fax, 219-3880. Toll-free information, (800) 424-9530.

Formulates, administers, and enforces policy with respect to the Federal Election Campaign Act of 1971 as amended, including campaign disclosure requirements, contribution and expenditure limitations, and public financing of presidential nominating conventions and campaigns. Receives campaign finance reports; makes rules and regulations; conducts audits and investigations. Serves as an election information clearinghouse. Copies of campaign finance reports available for inspection. Library open to the public.

Federal Election Commission, Public Records, 999 E St. N.W. 20463; 219-4140. Kent Cooper, assistant staff director. Toll-free, (800) 424-9530. Fax, 219-3880.

Makes available for public inspection and copying the detailed campaign finance reports on contributions and expenditures filed by candidates for federal office, their supporting political committees, and individuals and committees making expenditures on behalf of a candidate. Maintains copies of all reports and statements filed since 1972.

Justice Dept., Election Crimes, 1400 New York Ave. N.W. (mailing address: P.O. Box 27518, Washington, DC 20038); 514-1421. Craig Donsanto, director. Fax, 514-3003.

Supervises enforcement of federal criminal laws related to illegal political contributions, expenditures, and solicitations.

Congress:

Clerk of the House of Representatives, Records and Registration, 1036 LHOB 20515; 225-1300. Patricia Bias, director.

Receives reports of campaign receipts and expenditures of House candidates and committees. Open for public inspection.

House Administration Committee, H326 CAP 20515; 225-2061. Charlie Rose, D-N.C., chairman; Robert E. Shea, staff director. Fax, 225-4345.

Jurisdiction over campaign finance legislation, including the Federal Election Campaign Act.

House Ways and Means Committee, 1102 LHOB 20515; 225-3625. Sam M. Gibbons, D-Fla., acting chairman; Janice A. Mays, chief counsel. Jurisdiction over legislation on taxes and credits for public financing of federal elections.

Secretary of the Senate, Public Records, SH-232 20510; 224-0329. Elizabeth Williams, chief, campaign financing and Federal Election Commission liaison. Fax, 224-1851.

Receives reports of campaign receipts and expenditures of Senate candidates and committees. Open for public inspection.

Senate Finance Committee, SD-205 20510; 224-4515. Daniel Patrick Moynihan, D-N.Y., chairman; Lawrence O'Donnell Jr., staff director. Jurisdiction over legislation on taxes and credits for public financing of federal elections.

Senate Rules and Administration Committee, SR-305 20510; 224-6352. Wendell H. Ford, D-Ky., chairman; James O. King, staff director. Jurisdiction over campaign finance legislation.

Nongovernmental:

Center for Responsive Politics, 1320 19th St. N.W. 20036; 857-0044. Ellen Miller, executive director. Fax, 857-7809.

Conducts research on Congress and related issues, with particular interest in campaign finance and congressional operations.

Common Cause, Campaign Finance Monitoring Project, 2030 M St. N.W. 20036; 833-1200. Reuben Silvers, research associate.

Citizens' interest group. Records and analyzes campaign contributions to congressional candidates and campaign committees, particularly those from political action committees, and soft money contributions to national political parties.

National Library on Money & Politics, 1320 19th St. N.W. 20036; 857-0318. Ellen S. Miller, executive director. Fax, 857-7809.

Conducts research and analysis of political money and provides the media and others with direct assistance on the subject. A project of the Center for Responsive Politics.

See also Common Cause, State Issues Development (p. 742)

Election Demographics and Statistics

Congress:

Clerk of the House of Representatives, H105 CAP 20515; 225-7000. Donnald K. Anderson, clerk.

Publishes biennial compilation of statistics on congressional and presidential elections. Available from the clerk's office.

Senate Rules and Administration Committee, SR-305 20510; 224-6352. Wendell H. Ford, D-Ky., chairman; James O. King, staff director.

Distributes *Senate Election Law Guidebook*, a compilation of Senate campaign information, including federal and state laws governing election to the U.S. Senate. Available from the Senate Document Room.

Nongovernmental:

Elections Research Center, 5508 Greystone St., Chevy Chase, MD 20815; (301) 654-3540. Richard M. Scammon, director.

Compiles *America Votes*, a biennial handbook containing statistics of presidential, congressional, and gubernatorial elections by state, district, and county. Contracts election research projects.

See also Committee for the Study of the American Electorate (p. 768)

Reapportionment and Redistricting

Agencies:

Census Bureau (Commerce Dept.), Data User Services, 8903 Presidential Parkway, Upper Marlboro, MD (mailing address: Washington, DC 20233); (301) 763-4100. Marshall L. Turner Jr., chief. Fax, (301) 763-4794.

Disseminates census data on counties, municipalities, and other small areas to state legislatures for use in redrawing congressional district boundaries.

Census Bureau (Commerce Dept.), Population, Suitland and Silver Hill Rds., Suitland, MD (mailing address: Washington, DC 20233); (301) 763-7646. Arthur J. Norton, chief. Fax, (301) 763-4144.

Computes every ten years the population figures that determine the number of representatives

each state may have in the House of Representatives.

Congress:

Clerk of the House of Representatives, H105 CAP 20515; 225-7000. Donnald K. Anderson, clerk.

Receives population figures compiled by the Census Bureau that form the basis for reapportionment of the House; informs state governors of new apportionment figures.

House Judiciary Committee, 2138 RHOB 20515; 225-3951. Jack Brooks, D-Texas, chairman; Jon Yarowsky, general counsel.

Jurisdiction over reapportionment legislation.

Senate Judiciary Committee, SD-224 20510; 224-5225. Joseph R. Biden Jr., D-Del., chairman; Cynthia Hogan, chief counsel.

Jurisdiction over reapportionment legislation.

Nongovernmental:

Common Cause, State Issues Development, 2030 M St. N.W. 20036; 833-1200. Anna Pegler Gordon, research associate for state issues. Fax, 659-3716.

Citizens' interest group. Seeks to alter procedures governing redistricting by the establishment of independent redistricting commissions.

Capitol

Capitol switchboard: 224-3121.

See also 103rd Congress section for each member's office (p. 891)

Buildings, Grounds, and Security

House and Senate:

Architect of the Capitol, SB15 CAP 20515; 228-1793. George M. White, architect. Fax, 228-1893.

Maintains the Capitol and its grounds, the House and Senate office buildings, the Capitol power plant, the Robert A. Taft Memorial, and the buildings and grounds of the Supreme Court and the Library of Congress; operates the Botanic Garden and Senate restaurants. Acquires property and plans and constructs buildings for Congress, the Supreme Court, and the Library of Congress. Assists in deciding which artwork, historical objects, and exhibits are to be accepted for display in the Capitol. Flag office flies American flags over the Capitol at legislators' request.

Capitol Police, 119 D St. N.E. 20510; 224-9806. Gary L. Abrecht, chief. Fax, 224-4505.

Responsible for security for the Capitol, House and Senate office buildings, and Botanic Garden; approves demonstration permits.

Joint Committee on the Library, 103 O'Neill Bldg. (300 New Jersey Ave. S.E.) 20515; 226-7633. Rep. Charlie Rose, D-N.C., chairman; Hilary Lieber, staff director.

Oversees the placing of all works of art in the Capitol (in conjunction with the House Administration and Senate Rules and Administration committees); oversees development and maintenance of the Botanic Garden and the Library of Congress (in conjunction with the House Public Works and Transportation and Senate Rules and Administration committees).

U.S. Botanic Garden, 1st St. and Maryland Ave. S.W. 20024; 225-8333. Jeffrey P. Cooper-Smith, executive director. Fax, 225-1561. Flower and plant information, 225-7099 (recording).

Collects, cultivates, and grows various plants for public display and study. Sponsors four seasonal flower shows annually.

House:

House Administration Committee, H326 CAP 20515; 225-2061. Charlie Rose, D-N.C., chairman; Robert E. Shea, staff director. Fax, 225-4345.

Responsible for all matters related to security of the House office buildings and the House wing of the Capitol; jurisdiction over operations of the Botanic Garden, Library of Congress, Smithsonian Institution, and Capitol art collection (in conjunction with the Joint Committee on the Library and the Senate Rules and Administration Committee).

House Appropriations Committee, Subcommittee on Legislative Branch, H302 CAP 20515; 225-5338. Vic Fazio, D-Calif., chairman; Edward E. Lombard, staff assistant.

Jurisdiction over legislation to appropriate funds for the House of Representatives and the Senate, the Architect of the Capitol, the Library of Congress, and House offices.

House Office Building Commission, H226 CAP 20515; 225-4500. Thomas S. Foley, D-Wash., chairman; Nathan A. Marceca, staff contact. Fax, 225-3738.

Studies and approves all matters related to construction and alterations of House office buildings. Assigns office space to House committees.

House Public Works and Transportation Committee, Subcommittee on Public Buildings and Grounds, B376 RHOB 20515; 225-9961. James A. Traficant Jr., D-Ohio, chairman; Susan F. Brita, staff director.

Jurisdiction over legislation relating to the Capitol and House office buildings, including naming of buildings and facilities. Oversees planning, construction, renovation, maintenance, and care of the grounds and buildings of the Capitol, House, Library of Congress, and Botanic Garden (in conjunction with the Joint Committee on the Library). Participates with other House committees in the oversight of security.

Superintendent of the House Office Buildings, B341 RHOB 20515; 225-4141. Robert R. Miley, superintendent. Fax, 225-3003.

Oversees construction, maintenance, and operation of House office buildings; assigns office space to House members under rules of procedure established by the Speaker's office and the House Office Building Commission.

Senate:

Senate Appropriations Committee, Subcommittee on Legislative Branch, SD-126 20510; 224-7338. Harry Reid, D-Nev., chairman; Jerry L. Bonham, clerk.

Jurisdiction over legislation to appropriate funds for the Senate, the Architect of the Capitol, the Botanic Garden, the Library of Congress, and Senate offices.

Senate Commission on Art, S411 CAP 20510; 224-2955. George J. Mitchell, D-Maine, chairman; James R. Ketchum, curator of the Senate. Fax, 224-8799.

Accepts artwork and historical objects for display in Senate office buildings and the Senate wing of the Capitol. Maintains and exhibits Senate collections (paintings, sculpture, furniture, and manuscripts); oversees and maintains old Senate and Supreme Court chambers.

Senate Rules and Administration Committee, SR-305 20510; 224-6352. Wendell H. Ford, D-Ky., chairman; James O. King, staff director.

Responsible for all matters related to the Senate office buildings, including oversight of alterations, and the Senate wing of the Capitol; jurisdiction over authorization of funds for constructing and acquiring additional office space; oversees the maintenance and care of the grounds and buildings of the Botanic Garden and the Library of Congress and the placement of all works of art in the Capitol (in conjunction with the House Administration Committee and the Joint Committee on the Library). Assigns office space to Senate members and committees.

Superintendent of the Senate Office Buildings, SD-G45 20510; 224-3141. Larry R. Stoffel, superintendent. Fax, 224-0652.

Oversees maintenance of Senate office buildings.

Events and Demonstrations

House and Senate:

Capitol Police, Special Events, 119 D St. N.E. 20510; 224-8891. John E. Daniels, deputy chief, protective services; John Krug, special events contact. Fax, 228-2429.

Handles administrative and protective aspects of all special events held on the Capitol grounds. Accepts applications and submits requests for approval to the police board for demonstration permits and visiting musical performances. Coordinates all VIP arrivals.

House:

Office of the Speaker, Speaker's Rooms, H209 CAP 20515; 225-2204. Kathleen Miller, legislative assistant. Fax, 225-9483.

Approves events permits and visiting band performances on the House side of the Capitol. To arrange for visiting band performances and events, contact your representative.

Senate:

Sergeant at Arms of the Senate, S321 CAP 20510; 224-2341. Robert L. Benoit, sergeant at

arms; Robert Bean, deputy sergeant at arms. Fax, 224-7690.

Approves visiting band performances on the Senate steps. To arrange for visiting band performances, contact your senator.

Galleries

See also Media Accreditation in Washington, Legislative Branch (p. 33)

House:

The House public gallery is open daily from 9:00 a.m. to 4:30 p.m. (Hours are extended when chamber is in session.) Free gallery passes are available from any congressional office.

Doorkeeper of the House of Representatives, H154 CAP 20515; 225-3505. James T. Molloy, doorkeeper; James L. Jenkins, chief gallery doorman. Fax, 225-9475.

Enforces rules and regulations of the House public gallery.

Senate:

The Senate public gallery is open daily from 9:00 a.m. to 4:30 p.m. (Hours are extended when chamber is in session.) Free gallery passes are available from any congressional office.

Sergeant at Arms of the Senate, S321 CAP 20510; 224-2341. Robert L. Benoit, sergeant at arms; Robert Bean, deputy sergeant at arms. Fax, 224-7690.

Enforces rules and regulations of the Senate public gallery.

History

House and Senate:

Architect of the Capitol, Office of the Curator, HT3 CAP 20515; 225-1222. Barbara A. Wolanin, curator. Fax, 225-3167.

Preserves artwork; maintains collection of drawings, photographs, and manuscripts on and about the Capitol and the House and Senate office buildings. Maintains records of the architect of the Capitol. Library open to the public.

House:

Office of the Historian, 385 Ford Bldg. (2nd and D Sts. S.W.) 20515; 225-1153. Raymond W. Smock, historian. Fax, 225-6178.

Conducts historical research. Advises members on the disposition of their records and papers; maintains information on manuscript collections of former members; maintains biographical files on former members. Recent publications include *Biographical Directory of the United States Congress, 1774-1989: Bicentennial Edition; Guide to Research Collections of Former Members of the United States House of Representatives, 1789-1987: Bicentennial Edition; Black Americans in Congress, 1870-1989;* and *Women in Congress, 1917-1989.*

Senate:

Office of Conservation and Preservation, S410 CAP 20510; 224-4550. Carl Fritter, acting director. Fax, 224-6592.

Develops and coordinates programs related to the conservation and preservation of Senate records and materials for the Secretary of the Senate.

Senate Historical Office, SH-201 20510; 224-6900. Richard Baker, historian. Fax, 224-5329.

Serves as an information clearinghouse on Senate history, traditions, and members. Collects, organizes, and distributes to the public previously unpublished Senate documents; collects and preserves photographs and pictures related to Senate history; conducts an oral history program; advises senators and Senate committees on the disposition of their noncurrent papers and records. Produces publications on the history of the Senate.

Nongovernmental:

U.S. Capitol Historical Society, 200 Maryland Ave. N.E. 20002; 543-8919. Clarence J. Brown, president. Library, 543-0629. Fax, 544-8244.

Membership: members of Congress, individuals, and organizations interested in the preservation of the history and traditions of the U.S. Capitol. Conducts historical research; offers lectures and films; maintains information centers in the Capitol; produces a historical calendar annually.

Tours

House and Senate:

Sergeant at Arms of the Senate, Capitol Guide Service, Rotunda CAP 20510; 225-6827. Frances Rademaekers, chief of guide service.

Offers the general public free guided tours of the interior of the U.S. Capitol, 9:00 a.m. to 3:45 p.m. daily.

Congress at Work

Members are selected to serve in each of the following offices, committees, or organizations by party organizations in each chamber.

See 103rd Congress section for congressional offices and committee membership (p. 891)

Leadership

Presiding Officer of the House:

Speaker of the House of Representatives, Speaker's Office, H204 CAP 20515; 225-5604. Thomas S. Foley, D-Wash., Speaker; Heather S. Foley, chief of staff. Speaker's Rooms, H209 CAP 20515; 225-2204.

Presides over the House while in session; preserves decorum and order; announces vote results; recognizes members for debate and introduction of bills, amendments, and motions; refers bills and resolutions to committees; decides points of order; appoints House members to conference committees; votes at his own discretion.

House Democrats:

House Democratic Caucus, 718 O'Neill Bldg. (300 New Jersey Ave. S.E.) 20515; 226-3210. Steny H. Hoyer, D-Md., chairman; Melissa Schulman, executive director. Fax, 225-0282.

Membership: House Democrats. Selects Democratic leadership; formulates party rules and floor strategy; considers caucus members' recommendations on major issues; votes on the Democratic Steering and Policy Committee's recommendations for House committee chairmen and Democratic committee assignments.

House Democratic Steering and Policy Committee, H226 CAP 20515; 225-8550. Thomas S.

U.S. House of Representatives

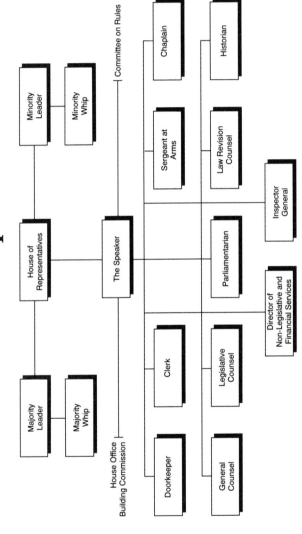

Foley, D-Wash., chairman; George Kundanis, executive director. Fax, 225-3738.

Studies and makes recommendations to the Democratic leadership on party policy and priorities; makes Democratic committee assignments and nominates committee chairmen subject to approval by the House Democratic Caucus and entire House of Representatives.

Majority Leader of the House of Representatives, H148 CAP 20515; 225-0100. Richard A. Gephardt, D-Mo., majority leader; Craig Hanna, executive floor assistant. Fax, 225-7414.

Serves as chief strategist and floor spokesman for the majority party in the House.

Majority Whip of the House of Representatives, H107 CAP 20515; 225-3130. David E. Bonior, D-Mich., majority whip; Sarah Dufendach, administrative assistant.

Serves as assistant majority leader in the House; helps marshal majority forces in support of party strategy.

House Republicans:

House Republican Committee on Committees, H230 CAP 20515; 225-0600. Robert H. Michel, R-Ill., chairman; Sue Bell, staff contact.

Makes Republican committee assignments.

House Republican Conference, 1618 LHOB 20515; 225-5107. Dick Armey, R-Texas, chairman; Kerry Knott, executive director. Fax, 225-0809.

Membership: House Republicans. Selects Republican leadership; formulates party rules and floor strategy, and considers party positions on major legislation; votes on Republican Committee on Committees' recommendations for the ranking member of each House committee; publishes legislative digest analyzing pending legislation.

House Republican Policy Committee, 1616 LHOB 20515; 225-6168. Henry J. Hyde, R-Ill., chairman; Tom Smeeton, executive director.

Studies legislation and makes recommendations on House Republican policies and positions on proposed legislation.

House Republican Research Committee, 1622 LHOB 20515; 225-0871. Duncan Hunter, R-Calif., chairman; John Sacharanski, executive director. Fax, 225-7675.

Provides information and research on public policy issues for Republican House members.

Minority Leader of the House of Representatives, H230 CAP 20515; 225-0600. Robert H. Michel, R-Ill., minority leader; William Pitts, floor assistant.

Serves as chief strategist and floor spokesman for the minority party in the House.

Minority Whip of the House of Representatives, 1620 LHOB 20515; 225-0197. Newt Gingrich, R-Ga., minority whip; Dan Meyer, chief of staff. Fax, 225-5646.

Serves as assistant minority leader in the House; helps marshal minority forces in support of party strategy.

Presiding Officer of the Senate:

Vice President of the United States, President of the Senate, U.S. Capitol, S212 CAP 20510; 224-8391. Albert Gore Jr., vice president; Thurgood Marshall Jr., assistant to the vice president for legislative affairs. Senate office· SD-202 20510; 224 2424. Executive office: White House 20500; 456-2326.

Presides over the Senate while in session; preserves decorum and order; announces vote results; recognizes members for debate and introduction of bills, amendments, and motions; decides points of order; votes only in the case of a tie. (President pro tempore of the Senate presides in the absence of the vice president.)

President Pro Tempore of the Senate, S128 CAP 20510; 224-2848. Robert C. Byrd, D-W.Va., president pro tempore; Barbara Vidineiks, chief of staff.

Presides over the Senate in the absence of the vice president.

Senate Democrats:

Majority Leader of the Senate, S221 CAP 20510; 224-5556. George J. Mitchell, D-Maine, majority leader; John Hilley, chief of staff. Press, 224-2939.

Serves as chief strategist and floor spokesman for the Democratic party in the Senate.

Majority Whip of the Senate, S148 CAP 20510; 224-2158. Wendell H. Ford, D-Ky., majority whip; Missy Smith, executive assistant.

U.S. Senate

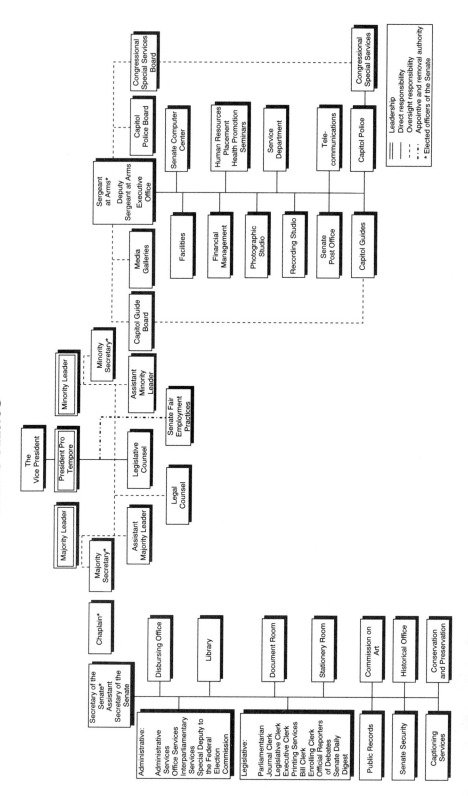

Serves as assistant majority leader in the Senate; helps marshal majority forces in support of party strategy.

Senate Democratic Conference, S309 CAP 20510; 224-3735. George J. Mitchell, D-Maine, chairman; David Pryor, D-Ark., secretary; C. Abbott Saffold, secretary for the majority.

Membership: Democratic senators. Selects Democratic leadership; formulates party rules and floor strategy and considers party positions on major legislation; votes on Democratic Steering Committee's recommendations for Senate committee chairs and Democratic committee assignments.

Senate Democratic Policy Committee, SH-619 20510; 224-3232. George J. Mitchell, D-Maine, chairman; Greg Billings, staff director.

Studies and makes recommendations to the Democratic leadership on legislation for consideration by the Senate.

Senate Democratic Steering Committee, S309 CAP 20510; 224-3735. Daniel K. Inouye, D-Hawaii, chairman; C. Abbott Saffold, secretary for the majority.

Makes Democratic committee assignments and selects committee chairmen, subject to approval by the Senate Democratic Conference.

Senate Republicans:

Assistant Republican Leader of the Senate, S229 CAP 20510; 224-2708. Alan K. Simpson, R-Wyo., assistant Republican leader; Michael Tongour, chief counsel. Fax, 224-3913.

Serves as assistant minority leader in the Senate; helps marshal minority forces in support of party strategy.

Republican Leader of the Senate, S230 CAP 20510; 224-3135. Bob Dole, R-Kan., Republican leader; Sheila Burke, chief of staff.

Serves as chief strategist and floor spokesman for the minority party in the Senate.

Senate Republican Committee on Committees, SD-183 20510; 224-2644. Conrad Burns, R-Mont., chairman; Jack Ramirez, staff contact.

Makes Republican committee assignments subject to approval by the Senate Republican Conference. (The committee convenes once every two years at the beginning of each new Congress.)

Senate Republican Conference, SH-405 20510; 224-2764. Thad Cochran, R-Miss., chairman; Will Feltus, staff director.

Membership: Republican senators. Serves as caucus and central coordinating body of the party. Organizes and elects Senate Republican leadership; votes on Republican committee assignments. Staff provides various support and media services for Republican members.

Senate Republican Policy Committee, SR-347 20510; 224-2946. Don Nickles, R-Okla., chairman; Kelly D. Johnston, staff director.

Studies and makes recommendations to the minority leader on the priorities and scheduling of legislation on the Senate floor; prepares policy papers and develops Republican policy initiatives.

Officers

House:

Chaplain of the House of Representatives, HB25 CAP 20515; 225-2509. James David Ford, chaplain.

Opens each day's House session with a prayer and offers other religious services to House members, their families, and staffs. (Prayer sometimes offered by visiting chaplain.)

Clerk of the House of Representatives, H105 CAP 20515; 225-7000. Donnald K. Anderson, clerk.

Chief administrative and budgetary officer of the House. Responsible for direction of duties of House employees; receives lobby registrations and reports of campaign expenditures and receipts of House candidates; disburses funds appropriated for House expenditures; responsible for other activities necessary for the continuing operation of the House.

Doorkeeper of the House of Representatives, H154 CAP 20515; 225-3505. James T. Molloy, doorkeeper; William P. Sims, chief doorman. Fax, 225-9475.

Supervises House document room, publications distribution service, the House cloakrooms, and telephone services; announces at the House door all messages from the president and the Senate; announces visitors; oversees House doormen and pages; maintains order in the House galleries and in adjacent rooms and corridors; supervises operation of Office of Photography.

General Counsel of the House of Representatives, H112 CAP 20515; 225-9700. Thomas Spulak, general counsel. Fax, 226-1360.

Advises House members and committees on legal matters.

Legislative Counsel of the House of Representatives, 136 CHOB 20515; 225-6060. David E. Meade, legislative counsel. Fax, 225-3437.

Assists House members and committees in drafting legislation.

Minority Doorkeeper of the House of Representatives, H228 CAP 20515; 225-0600. William Pitts, minority doorkeeper. Fax, 225-7733.

Assists the minority leadership and members.

Minority Postmaster of the House of Representatives, HB13 CAP 20515; 225-4768. Jay Pierson, minority postmaster.

Assists the minority leadership and members on legislative matters.

Minority Sergeant at Arms of the House of Representatives, HB13B CAP 20515; 225-2139. Vacant, minority sergeant at arms. Fax, 225-1488.

Assists the minority leadership and members on leadership matters.

Sergeant at Arms of the House of Representatives, H124 CAP 20515; 225-2456. Werner W. Brandt, sergeant at arms. Fax, 225-3233.

Maintains order on the House floor; executes orders from the Speaker of the House; oversees the accounts of pay and mileage of members, delegates, the resident commissioner from Puerto Rico, and staff; maintains all retirement, life insurance, and health benefit records of House members. Sits on the Capitol Police Board and Capitol Guide Board; oversees Capitol security (with Senate Sergeant at Arms) and protocol.

Senate:

Chaplain of the Senate, SH-204A 20510; 224-2510. Richard C. Halverson, chaplain. Fax, 224-9686.

Opens each day's Senate session with a prayer and offers other religious services to Senate members, their families, and staffs. (Prayer sometimes offered by visiting chaplain.)

Legal Counsel of the Senate, SH-642 20510; 224-4435. Michael Davidson, legal counsel. Fax, 224-3391.

Advises Senate members and committees on legal matters.

Legislative Counsel of the Senate, SD-668 20510; 224-6461. Francis L. Burk Jr., legislative counsel. Fax, 224-0567.

Assists Senate members and committees in drafting legislation.

Majority Secretary of the Senate, S309 CAP 20510; 224-3735. C. Abbott Saffold, majority secretary; Martin Paone, assistant secretary.

Assists the majority leader and the majority party in the Senate.

Minority Secretary of the Senate, S337 CAP 20510; 224-3835. Howard O. Greene Jr., minority secretary; John L. Doney, assistant secretary. Fax, 224-2860.

Assists the minority leader and minority party in the Senate.

Secretary of the Senate, S208 CAP 20510; 224-2115. Martha S. Pope, secretary; Michelle Haynes, administrative assistant. Fax, 224-1664.

Chief administrative officer of the Senate. Responsible for direction of duties of Senate employees and administration of oaths; receives lobby registrations and reports of campaign expenditures and receipts of Senate candidates; responsible for other Senate activities.

Sergeant at Arms of the Senate, S321 CAP 20510; 224-2341. Robert L. Benoit, sergeant at arms; Robert Bean, deputy sergeant at arms. Fax, 224-7690.

Oversees the Senate wing of the Capitol; doormen; Senate pages; and telecommunication, photographic, supply, and janitorial services. Maintains order on the Senate floor and galleries; oversees Capitol security (with House Sergeant at Arms); sits on the Capitol Police Board and Capitol Guide Board.

Operations/Reorganization

House:

House Rules Committee, H312 CAP 20515; 225-9486. Joe Moakley, D-Mass., chairman; George C. Crawford, staff director. Fax, 225-5373.

Sets rules for floor debate on legislation reported by regular standing committees; grants emergency waivers, under the House rules and the Congressional Budget Act of 1974, of required reporting dates for bills and resolutions authorizing new budget authority; has jurisdiction over resolutions creating committees; has legislative authority to recommend changes in the rules of the House; has jurisdiction over recesses and final adjournments of Congress.

Senate:

Senate Rules and Administration Committee, SR-305 20510; 224-6352. Wendell H. Ford, D-Ky., chairman; James O. King, staff director.

Jurisdiction over all matters related to the rules governing the conduct of business in the Senate, including floor, committee, and gallery procedures. Also studies and makes recommendations on computer and other technical services in the Senate; oversees operation of the computer information system for the Senate.

Parliamentary Questions

House and Senate:

See U.S. Group—Interparliamentary Union (p. 757)

House:

Parliamentarian of the House of Representatives, H209 CAP 20515; 225-7373. William H. Brown, parliamentarian.

Advises presiding officers on parliamentary procedures and committee jurisdiction over legislation; prepares and maintains a compilation of the precedents of the House.

Senate:

Parliamentarian of the Senate, S132 CAP 20510; 224-6128. Alan S. Frumin, parliamentarian.

Advises presiding officers on parliamentary procedures and committee jurisdiction over legislation; prepares and maintains a compilation of the precedents of the Senate.

Congressional Support Groups

Legislative Assistance

House and Senate:

Congressional Budget Office, 405 Ford Bldg. (2nd and D Sts. S.W.) 20515; 226-2700. Robert D. Reischauer, director. Information, 226-2600. Fax, 225-7509.

Nonpartisan office that provides the House and Senate with budget-related information and analyses of alternative fiscal policies.

General Accounting Office, 441 G St. N.W. 20548; 512-5500. Charles A. Bowsher, comptroller general. Information, 512-4800. Library, 512-5180. Fax, 512-5507. Documents, 512-6000.

Independent, nonpartisan agency in the legislative branch. Serves as the investigating agency for Congress; carries out legal, accounting, auditing, and claims settlement functions; makes recommendations for more effective government operations; publishes monthly lists of reports available to the public. Library open to the public by appointment.

Law Revision Counsel, 304 Ford Bldg. (2nd and D Sts. S.W.) 20515; 226-2411. Edward F. Willett Jr., law revision counsel. Fax, 225-0010.

Develops and updates an official classification of U.S. laws.

Office of Technology Assessment (OTA), 600 Pennsylvania Ave. S.E. (mailing address: U.S. Congress, Washington, DC 20510); 224-3695. Roger Herdman, director; Sen. Edward M. Kennedy, D-Mass., chairman; Rep. Don Sundquist, R-Tenn., vice chairman, Technology Assessment Board. Information, 224-9241. Press, 228-6204. Fax, 228-6218. Publications, 224-8996.

Provides Congress with information and analyses on the political, physical, economic, and social effects of technological applications.

House:

Legislative Counsel of the House of Representatives, 136 CHOB 20515; 225-6060. David E. Meade, legislative counsel. Fax, 225-3437.

Assists House members and committees in drafting legislation.

Departmental and Agency . . .

Departments

Agriculture
Fred Slaybach 720-7907

Commerce
Loretta Dunn 482-3663

Defense
Sandra Stuart .... (703) 697-6210

Air Force
Maj. Gen. Paul E.
Stein .... (703) 697-8153

Army
Maj. Gen. Jerry C. Harrison (703) 697-6767

Navy
Rear Adm. Robert
Natter .... (703) 697-7146

Education
Kay Caffstevens 401-0020

Energy
William Taylor 586-5450

Health and Human Services
Kimberly Parker 690-6786

Housing and Urban Development
John Biechman 708-0380

Interior
Melanie Beller 208-7693

Justice
Sheila Anthony 514-3752

Labor
Geri D. Palast 219-4692

State
Wendy Sherman 647-4204

Transportation
Regina Sullivan 366-9714

Treasury
Michael Levy 622-1900

Veterans Affairs
Edward Scott 273-5615

Agencies

Commission on Civil Rights
Mary Mathews 376-8317

Commodity Futures Trading Commission
Mac Smith 254-6372

Consumer Product Safety Commission
Robert J. Wager .... (301) 504-0515

Corporation for National Service
Gene Sofer 606-5000

Environmental Protection Agency
Robert Hickmott 260-5200

Equal Employment Opportunity Commission
Philip B. Calkins, acting 663-4900

Export-Import Bank of the United States
Ira Fishman 566-8967

Farm Credit Administration
Christine Quinn, acting .... (703) 883-4056

Federal Communications Commission
Judith L. Harris 632-6405

Federal Deposit Insurance Corp.
Alice C. Goodman 898-8730

Federal Election Commission
Christina VanBrakle 219-4136

Federal Emergency Management Agency
Martha S. Braddock 646-4500

Federal Labor Relations Authority
Francisco J. Martinez-Alvarez.... 482-6500

Federal Maritime Commission
David Miles 523-5740

Federal Mediation and Conciliation Service
Theodore Chaskelson 653-5270

... Congressional Liaisons

Federal Reserve System
Donald J. Winn 452-3456

Federal Trade Commission
Dorian Hall 326-2195

**General Services
Administration**
Bill Ratchford 501-0563

**Interstate Commerce
Commission**
Dixie E. Horton 927-6050

Legal Services Corporation
Florene Yarbrough, acting 336-8800

**Merit Systems Protection
Board**
Martha Ann Richardson 653-7175

**National Aeronautics and
Space Administration**
Mary D. Kerwin, acting 358-1942

**National Credit Union
Administration**
Robert Loftus .... (703) 518-6300

**National Foundation on
the Arts and the Humanities**
**National Endowment for
the Arts**
Richard Woodruff 682-5434

**National Endowment for the
Humanities**
Ann S. Young 606-8328

**National Labor Relations
Board**
John C. Truesdale 273-1991

National Mediation Board
Ronald M. Etters 523-5944

National Science Foundation
Joel Widder .... (703) 306-1070

**National Transportation
Safety Board**
Charlotte Casey 382-6757

**Nuclear Regulatory
Commission**
Dennis K. Rathbun .... (301) 504-1776

**Occupational Safety and Health
Review Commission**
Linda A. Whitsett 606-5398

**Office of Personnel
Management**
James N. Woodruff 606-1424

Office of Special Counsel
Michael G. Lawrence 653-9001

**Pension Benefit Guaranty
Corporation**
Martin Slate 326-4010

Postal Rate Commission
Charles L. Clapp 789-6840

**Securities and Exchange
Commission**
Kathryn Fulton 272-2500

Selective Service System
Lewis C. Brodsky .... (703) 235-2053

Small Business Administration
Kris Swedin 205-6700

Smithsonian Institution
Mark Rodgers 357-2962

Tennessee Valley Authority
Jan Evered 898-2999

**U.S. Arms Control and
Disarmament Agency**
Ivo Spalatin 647-3612

U.S. Information Agency
Douglas Wilson 619-6828

**U.S. International Development
Cooperation Agency**
**Agency for International
Development**
Jill Buckley 647-8264

**U.S. International Trade
Commission**
Charles Hansen 205-3151

U.S. Postal Service
Robert Harris 268-2506

Senate:

Legislative Counsel of the Senate, SD-668 20510; 224-6461. Francis L. Burk Jr., legislative counsel. Fax, 224-0567.

Assists Senate members and committees in drafting legislation.

Liaison Offices

House and Senate:

Office of Personnel Management, Congressional Liaison, B332 RHOB 20515; 225-4955. Charlene Luskey, chief. Fax, 632-0832.

Provides House and Senate members with information on federal civil service matters, especially those pertaining to federal employment, retirement, and health benefits programs.

House:

Air Force Liaison, B322 RHOB 20515; 225-6656. Col. Vince Evans, chief. Fax, 475-0680.

Provides House members with services and information on all matters related to the U.S. Air Force.

Army Liaison, B325 RHOB 20515; 225-3853. Col. Jay McNulty, chief. Fax, 475-1561.

Provides House members with services and information on all matters related to the U.S. Army.

Navy-Marine Corps Liaison, B324 RHOB 20515; 225-7124. Capt. Kraig M. Kennedy, director; Lt. Col. John Sattler, Marine Corps director.

Provides House members with services and information on all matters related to the U.S. Navy and the U.S. Marine Corps.

U.S. Coast Guard Liaison, B320 RHOB 20515; 225-4775. Cmdr. Woody Lee, chief. Fax, 426-6081.

Provides House members with services and information on all matters related to the U.S. Coast Guard.

Veterans Affairs Dept. Congressional Liaison Service, B328 RHOB 20515; 225-2280. Philip Mayo, chief. Fax, 453-5225.

Provides House members with services and information on all matters related to veterans' benefits and services.

White House Legislative Affairs, White House 20500; 456-2230. Patrick Griffin, assistant to the president for legislative affairs; Lorraine Miller, deputy assistant (House), 456-6620.

Serves as a liaison between the president and the House of Representatives.

Senate:

Air Force Liaison, SR-182 20510; 224-2481. Col. Robert Behler, chief. Fax, 475-0854.

Provides senators with services and information on all matters related to the U.S. Air Force.

Army Liaison, SR-183 20510; 224-2881. Col. Frank Hurd, chief. Fax, 475-9051.

Provides senators with services and information on all matters related to the U.S. Army.

Navy-Marine Corps Liaison, SR-182 20510; 224-4681. Capt. Cutler Dawson, Navy director; Col. Terry Paul, Marine Corps director. Fax, 475-0890.

Provides senators with services and information on all matters related to the U.S. Navy and the U.S. Marine Corps.

U.S. Coast Guard Liaison, SR-183 20510; 224-2913. Cmdr. John Jaskot, chief. Fax, 755-1695.

Provides senators with services and information on all matters related to the U.S. Coast Guard.

Veterans Affairs Dept. Congressional Liaison, SH-321 20510; 224-5351. Edwin L. Arnold, chief. Fax, 453-5218.

Provides senators with services and information on all matters related to veterans' benefits and services.

White House Legislative Affairs, White House 20500; 456-2230. Patrick Griffin, assistant to the president for legislative affairs; Steven J. Ricchetti, deputy assistant (Senate), 456-7054.

Serves as a liaison between the president and the Senate.

Libraries

House and Senate:

Joint Committee on the Library, 103 O'Neill Bldg. (300 New Jersey Ave. S.E.) 20515; 226-7633. Rep. Charlie Rose, D-N.C., chairman; Hilary Lieber, staff director.

Studies and makes recommendations on proposals concerning the management and expansion of the Library of Congress.

Library of Congress, Congressional Research Service, 101 Independence Ave. S.E. 20540; 707-5775. Daniel P. Mulhollan, director. Information, 707-5700. Fax, 707-2615. (Services not available to public.)

Provides members of Congress and committees with general reference assistance; prepares upon request background reports, analytical studies, reading lists, bibliographies, and pros and cons of policy issues; conducts public issue seminars and workshops for committees, members, and staffs; makes available the services of subject specialists. (Divisions: American Law, 707-6006; Congressional Reference, 707-5741; Economics, 707-7800; Education and Public Welfare, 707-6228; Environmental and Natural Resources Policy, 707-7232; Foreign Affairs and National Defense, 707-5064; Government, 707-7852; Library Services, 707-5804; Science Policy Research, 707-7040.)

Library of Congress, Law Library, 101 Independence Ave. S.E. 20540; 707-5065. M. Kathleen Price, law librarian. Fax, 707-1820. Reading room, 707-5080.

Maintains collections of foreign, international, and comparative law organized jurisdictionally by country; covers all legal systems, including common law, civil law, Roman law, canon law, religious law, and ancient and medieval law. Reading room open to the public.

For Library of Congress divisions, see Library of Congress box (p. 161)

House:

House Administration Committee, H326 CAP 20515; 225-2061. Charlie Rose, D-N.C., chairman; Robert E. Shea, staff director. Fax, 225-4345.

Jurisdiction over legislation on the House library; manages, in conjunction with the Joint Library and the Senate Rules and Administration committees, policies and programs of the Library of Congress.

Library of the House, B18 CHOB 20515; 225-0462. E. Raymond Lewis, librarian.

Serves as the statutory and official depository of House reports, hearings, prints, and documents for the Clerk of the House.

Senate:

Library of the Senate, S332 CAP 20510; 224-7106. Roger K. Haley, librarian.

Maintains special collection for Senate private use of primary source legislative materials, including reports, hearings, prints, documents, and debate proceedings. (Not open to the public.)

Senate Rules and Administration Committee, SR-305 20510; 224-6352. Wendell H. Ford, D-Ky., chairman; James O. King, staff director.

Manages, in conjunction with the House Administration and the Joint Library committees, policies and programs of the Library of Congress.

Organizations of Members

House and Senate:

Ad Hoc Congressional Committee on Irish Affairs, 203 CHOB 20515; 225-3965. Rep. Hamilton Fish Jr., R-N.Y., Rep. Benjamin A. Gilman, R-N.Y., and Rep. Thomas J. Manton, D-N.Y., co-chairmen; Elaine Simek, staff contact.

Advisory Commission on Intergovernmental Relations, 800 K St. N.W. 20575; 653-5536. William F. Winter, chairman; Joan Casey, staff contact.

Arms Control and Foreign Policy Caucus, 501 Ford Bldg. (2nd and D Sts. S.W.) 20515; 226-3440. Sen. James M. Jeffords, R-Vt., chair; Edith Wilkie, executive director.

California Democratic Congressional Delegation, 503 O'Neill Bldg. (300 New Jersey Ave. S.E.) 20515; 226-2313. Rep. Don Edwards, D-Calif., chairman; Pamela Barry, staff contact.

Commission on Security and Cooperation in Europe, 234 Ford Bldg. (2nd and D Sts. S.W.) 20515; 225-1901. Sen. Dennis DeConcini, D-Ariz., and Rep. Steny H. Hoyer, D-Md., co-chairmen; Samuel G. Wise, staff director. Fax, 226-4199.

Congressional Alcohol Fuels Caucus, 2463 RHOB 20515; 225-5271. Rep. Richard J. Durbin, D-Ill., and Rep. Jim Leach, R-Iowa, co-chairmen; Tom Faletti, staff contact.

Congressional Arts Caucus, 345 Ford Bldg. (2nd and D Sts. S.W.) 20515; 226-2456. Rep. Louise M. Slaughter, D-N.Y., chair; Rhoda Glickman, executive director. Fax, 225-9470.

Congressional Biotechnology Caucus, 2241 RHOB 20515; 225-2815. Sen. Frank R. Lautenberg, D-N.J., Sen. Hank Brown, R-Colo., Rep. Calvin Dooley, D-Calif., and Rep. Thomas J. Bliley Jr., R-Va., co-chairmen; James Derderian, staff contact.

Congressional Caucus for Women's Issues, 2471 RHOB 20515; 225-6740. Rep. Patricia Schroeder, D-Colo., and Rep. Olympia J. Snowe, R-Maine, co-chairs; Lesley Primmer, executive director. Fax, 225-2593.

Congressional Caucus on Advanced Materials, B374 RHOB 20515; 225-9662. Sen. John McCain, R-Ariz., and Rep. Tim Valentine, D-N.C., co-chairmen; Sherri Stone, staff contact.

Congressional Coalition for Soviet Jews, 1640 Rhode Island Ave. N.W., #501 20036; 898-2500. Richard Wexler, chairman; Mark B. Levin, staff contact. Fax, 898-0822.

Congressional Coalition on Adoption, SH-302 20510; 224-2752. Rep. Thomas J. Bliley Jr., R-Va., Rep. James L. Oberstar, D-Minn., Sen. Paul Simon, D-Ill., and Sen. Larry E. Craig, R-Idaho, co-chairmen; Brooke Roberts, staff contact.

Congressional Competitiveness Caucus, SH-511 20510; 224-2651. Sen. Max Baucus, D-Mont., Sen. Charles E. Grassley, R-Iowa, Rep. Marcy Kaptur, D-Ohio, and Rep. Jim Kolbe, R-Ariz., co-chairs; Ed Gresser, staff contact.

Congressional Copper Caucus, 405 CHOB 20515; 225-2542. Rep. Jim Kolbe, R-Ariz., and Sen. Pete V. Domenici, R-N.M., co-chairmen; Steve Bloch, staff contact.

Congressional Fire Services Caucus, 1705 LHOB 20515; 225-4131. Rep. Steny H. Hoyer, D-Md., chairman; Bill Castelli, staff contact.

Congressional Friends of Human Rights Monitors, 2264 RHOB 20515; 225-6465. Rep. Tony P. Hall, D-Ohio, chairman; Rick Carne, staff contact.

Congressional International AIDS Task Force, 1707 LHOB 20515; 225-3106. Rep. Jim

McDermott, D-Wash., chairman; Rita Patel, staff contact.

Congressional Leaders United for a Balanced Budget, 442 CHOB 20515; 225-2211. Rep. James M. Inhofe, R-Okla., and Rep. Charles W. Stenholm, D-Texas, co-chairmen; Laurie Rains, staff contact.

Congressional Military Reform Caucus, SH-104 20510; 224-2441. Sen. William V. Roth Jr., R-Del., chairman; Mark Forman, staff contact.

Congressional Olympic Caucus, SR-380 20510; 224-5852. Sen. Bill Bradley, D-N.J., and Sen. Ben Nighthorse Campbell, D-Colo., co-chairmen; Eva Burkley, staff contact.

Congressional Populist Caucus, 2335 RHOB 20515; 225-5905. Rep. Lane Evans, D-Ill., and Sen. Tom Harkin, D-Iowa, co-chairmen; Tom O'Donald, staff contact. Fax, 225-5396.
Organization of members of the House and Senate that focuses on issues of economic equity and justice for all Americans.

Congressional Senior Citizen Intern Program, SD-G31 20510; 224-5364. Rep. William J. Hughes, D-N.J., Rep. Ralph Regula, R-Ohio, Sen. Nancy Landon Kassebaum, R-Kan., and Sen. David Pryor, D-Ark., co-chairs; Michael Langan, staff contact. Fax, 224-9926.

Congressional Soybean Caucus, 2463 RHOB 20515; 225-5271. Rep. Doug Bereuter, R-Neb., Sen. Christopher S. Bond, R-Mo., Rep. Richard J. Durbin, D-Ill., Sen. Charles E. Grassley, R-Iowa, Sen. Howell Heflin, D-Ala., Rep. Jim Leach, R-Iowa, Rep. Timothy J. Penny, D-Minn., and Sen. Paul Simon, D-Ill., co-chairmen; Pat Souders, staff contact. Fax, 225-0170.

Congressional Sportsman's Caucus, 1727 LHOB 20515; 225-4565. Rep. Bill Brewster, D-Okla., Sen. Conrad Burns, R-Mont., and Rep. Don Young, R-Alaska, co-chairmen; Colin Chapman, staff contact.

Environmental and Energy Study Conference, 515 Ford Bldg. (2nd and D Sts. S.W.) 20515; 226-3300. Sen. John McCain, R-Ariz., and Rep. Jan Meyers, R-Kan., co-chairs; Linda Cartwright staff contact. Fax, 226-3302.

Federal Government Service Task Force, 30 Ford Bldg. (2nd and D Sts. S.W.) 20515; 226-

2494. Rep. Steny H. Hoyer, D-Md., Rep. Vic Fazio, D-Calif., Rep. Norm Dicks, D-Wash., Rep. James P. Moran Jr., D-Va., and Sen. Paul S. Sarbanes, D-Md., co-chairmen; Nicholas Nolan, executive director. Fax, 225-9265.

Friends of Ireland, 306 CHOB 20515; 225-4636. Rep. Frank McCloskey, D-Ind., chairman; Paul Weber, staff contact.

House/Senate International Education Study Group, SR-444 20510; 224-2823. Sen. Christopher J. Dodd, D-Conn., chairman; Suzanne Day, staff contact.

Long Island Congressional Caucus, 2445 RHOB 20515; 225-2601. Rep. Gary L. Ackerman, D-N.Y., chairman; Jedd Moskowitz, staff contact.

New York State Congressional Delegation, 2252 RHOB 20515; 225-4365. Rep. Charles B. Rangel, D-N.Y., chairman; Frank Jasmine, staff contact. Fax, 225-0816.

Pennsylvania Congressional Delegation, 2423 RHOB 20515; 225-1145. Rep. John P. Murtha, D-Pa., dean; Colette Dawn Marchesini, director. Fax, 225-5709.

Porkbusters Coalition, 2342 RHOB 20515; 225-3515. Rep. Harris W. Fawell, R-Ill., and Rep. Timothy J. Penny, D-Minn., co-chairmen; Kristin Wolgemuth, staff contact. Fax, 225-9420.

Technology Assessment Board, SR-315 20510; 224-4543. Sen. Edward M. Kennedy, D-Mass., chairman; Ron Weich, staff contact.
Oversees the Office of Technology Assessment.

U.S. Assn. of Former Members of Congress, 1755 Massachusetts Ave. N.W., #422 20036; 332-3532. James W. Symington, president. Fax, 543-7145.

U.S. Group—Interparliamentary Union, SH-231B 20510; 224-3047. Sen. Barbara Boxer, D-Calif., chair; Jan Paulk, staff contact.
Membership: elected parliamentarians throughout the world. All members of Congress are members of the union.

U.S. Group of the North Atlantic Assembly, SH-231B 20510; 224-3047. Sen. Howell Heflin, D-Ala., chairman; Jan Paulk, staff contact.

U.S. Interparliamentary Group—Canada, SH-231B 20510; 224-3047. Sen. Howard M. Metzenbaum, D-Ohio, chairman; Jan Paulk, staff contact.

U.S. Interparliamentary Group—Mexico, SH-231B 20510; 224-3047. Sen. Christopher J. Dodd, D-Conn., chairman; Jan Paulk, staff contact.

Vietnam Era Veterans in Congress, 2335 RHOB 20515; 225-5905. Sen. Tom Daschle, D-S.D., Rep. Lane Evans, D-Ill., Sen. John Kerry, D-Mass., and Rep. H. Martin Lancaster, D-N.C., co-chairmen; Jeff Lande, staff contact. Fax, 225-5396.

House:

Albanian Issues Caucus, 1434 LHOB 20515; 225-2464. Eliot L. Engel, D-N.Y., and Susan Molinari, R-N.Y., co-chairs; Jason Steinbaum, staff contact.

Army Caucus, 236 CHOB 20515; 225-2831. Greg Laughlin, D-Texas, and John M. McHugh, R-N.Y., co-chairmen; Bob Grasso, staff contact.

Chesapeake Bay Congressional Caucus, 1810 LHOB 20515; 225-4016. Benjamin L. Cardin, D-Md., chairman; Chris Lynch, staff contact.

Congressional Animal Welfare Caucus, 1020 LHOB 20515; 225-6205. John A. Boehner, R-Ohio, and Charles W. Stenholm, D-Texas, co-chairmen; John Fish, staff contact.

Congressional Automotive Caucus, 2239 RHOB 20515; 225-3611. Dale E. Kildee, D-Mich., and Bud Shuster, R-Pa., co-chairmen; Larry Rosenthal, staff contact.

Congressional Aviation Forum, 2371 RHOB 20515; 225-6216. Dan Glickman, D-Kan., and James V. Hansen, R-Utah, co-chairmen; Sherry Ruffing, staff contact.

Congressional Bearing Caucus, 343 CHOB 20515; 225-4476. Nancy L. Johnson, R-Conn., and John M. Spratt Jr., D-S.C., co-chairs; Ron Lefrancois, staff contact. Fax, 225-4488.

Congressional Beef Caucus, 108 CHOB 20515; 225-6730. Calvin Dooley, D-Calif., and Bob Smith, R-Ore., co-chairmen; Pete Thompson, staff contact.

Congressional Biomedical Research Caucus, 2410 RHOB 20515; 225-4315. Sonny Callahan, R-Ala., George W. Gekas, R-Pa., Bill Richardson, D-N.M., and J. Roy Rowland, D-Ga., co-chairmen; Sheilah Borne, staff contact.

Congressional Black Caucus, H2-344 Ford Bldg. (2nd and D Sts. S.W.) 20515; 226-7790. Kweisi Mfume, D-Md., chairman; Amelia Parker, executive director.

Congressional Black Caucus Task Force on Haiti, 2305 RHOB 20515; 225-6231. Major R. Owens, D-N.Y., chairman; Jackie Ellis, staff contact.

Congressional Boating Caucus, 2207 RHOB 20515; 225-2106. David E. Bonior, D-Mich., chairman; Eric Pfuehler, staff contact. Fax, 226-1169.

Congressional Border Caucus, 440 CHOB 20515; 225-4831. Ronald D. Coleman, D-Texas, chairman; Scott Sutherland, staff contact. Fax, 225-4825.

Membership: House members with districts adjacent to the U.S.-Mexican border.

Congressional Caucus for Syrian Jewry, 2412 RHOB 20515; 225-6616. Benjamin A. Gilman, R-N.Y., and Charles E. Schumer, D-N.Y., co-chairmen; John Wolfe, staff contact.

Congressional Coalition on Population and Development, 2465 RHOB 20515; 225-5911. Anthony C. Beilenson, D-Calif., and Constance A. Morella, R-Md., co-chairs; Jim Pickup, staff contact.

Congressional Corn Caucus, 418 CHOB 20515; 225-5476. Fred Grandy, R-Iowa, and Timothy J. Penny, D-Minn., co-chairmen; Linda Throsner, staff contact.

Congressional Fairness Network, 1221 LHOB 20515; 225-3261. Glen Browder, D-Ala., chairman; Vickie Plunkett, staff contact.

Members whose districts may be affected by military base closings.

Congressional Footwear Caucus, 235 CHOB 20515; 225-8273. Joe Moakley, D-Mass., chairman; John Weinfurter, staff contact. Fax, 225-3984.

Congressional Friends of Animals, 2182 RHOB 20515; 225-3531. Tom Lantos, D-Calif., and Charlie Rose, D-N.C., co-chairmen; Rebecca Davis, staff contact.

Congressional Grace Caucus, 206 CHOB 20515; 225-5611. C. Christopher Cox, R-Calif., and Frank Pallone Jr., D-N.J., co-chairmen; Joe Duggan, staff contact. Fax, 225-9177.

Bipartisan coalition that seeks to focus attention on the cost-cutting recommendations made by the Grace commission (President's Private Sector Survey on Cost Control) and other commissions.

Congressional Hispanic Caucus, H2-244 Ford Bldg. (2nd and D Sts. S.W.) 20515; 226-3430. José E. Serrano, D-N.Y., chairman; Rick Lopez, staff contact. Fax, 225-7569.

Congressional Human Rights Caucus, H2-590 Ford Bldg. (2nd and D Sts. S.W.) 20515; 226-4040. John Porter, R-Ill., and Tom Lantos, D-Calif., co-chairmen; Alex Arriaga and Heidi Gaasch, co-directors.

Congressional Insurance Caucus, 2411 RHOB 20515; 225-2276. Dan Burton, R-Ind., chairman; Jeffrey Schaffner, staff contact. Fax, 225-0016.

Congressional Mining Caucus, 2202 RHOB 20515; 225-6155. Bill Emerson, R-Mo., Austin J. Murphy, D-Pa., and Barbara F. Vucanovich, R-Nev., co-chairs; Carter Cornick, staff contact. Fax, 225-2319.

Congressional Pro-Life Caucus, 2353 RHOB 20515; 225-7669. Christopher H. Smith, R-N.J., chairman; Maggie Wynne, staff contact. Fax, 225-3502.

Congressional Rural Caucus, 175B Ford Bldg. (2nd and D Sts. S.W.) 20515; 225-8242. Jill L. Long, D-Ind., chair; Brad Captain, staff contact.

Congressional Social Security Caucus, 2407 RHOB 20515; 225-5961. C. W. Bill Young, R-Fla., chairman; Harry Glenn, staff contact.

Congressional Space Caucus, 2350 RHOB 20515; 225-4261. Herbert H. Bateman, R-Va., and Norman Y. Mineta, D-Calif., co-chairmen; Melinda Dobson, staff contact. Fax, 225-4382.

Congressional Steel Caucus, 2423 RHOB 20515; 225-2065. John P. Murtha, D-Pa., chairman; Judy Grundy, staff contact.

Congressional Sunbelt Caucus, H2-561 Ford Bldg. (2nd and D Sts. S.W.) 20515; 226-2374. Dave McCurdy, D-Okla., and E. Clay Shaw Jr., R-Fla., co-chairmen; Joseph W. Westphal, executive director. Fax, 226-2375.

Congressional Task Force on Tobacco and Health, 2463 RHOB 20515; 225-5271. Richard J. Durbin, D-Ill., and James V. Hansen, R-Utah, co-chairmen; Tom Faletti, staff contact.

Congressional Task Force to End the Arab Boycott, 2412 RHOB 20515; 225-6616. Ileana Ros-Lehtinen, R-Fla., and Charles E. Schumer, D-N.Y., co-chairs; John Wolfe, staff contact.

Congressional Textile Caucus, 1536 LHOB 20515; 225-5501. John M. Spratt Jr., D-S.C., chairman; Tom Kahn, staff contact.

Congressional Travel and Tourism Caucus, 246 Ford Bldg. (2nd and D Sts. S.W.) 20515; 225-3935. James L. Oberstar, D-Minn., chairman; Halle Czechowski, staff contact.

Congressional Truck Caucus, 2188 RHOB 20515; 225-2431. James L. Oberstar, D-Minn., and Bud Shuster, R-Pa., co-chairmen; Ann Eppard, staff contact.

Congressional Urban Caucus, 341 CHOB 20515; 225-4731. John Lewis, D-Ga., and Christopher Shays, R-Conn., co-chairmen; Deidra Ball, staff contact.

Conservative Democratic Forum, 1211 LHOB 20515; 225-6605. Charles W. Stenholm, D-Texas, coordinator; Rebecca Tice, staff contact. Fax, 225-2234.

Conservative Opportunity Society, 1020 LHOB 20515; 225-6205. John A. Boehner, R-Ohio, chairman; Christy Carson, staff contact. Fax, 25-0704.

Defense Conversion Committee of the Speaker's Working Group on Policy Development, 2416 RHOB 20515; 225-2076. Ronald V. Dellums, D-Calif., and Sam Gejdenson, D-Conn., co-chairmen; Gail Bysiewicz, staff contact.

Democratic Study Group, 1422 LHOB 20515; 225-5858. Mike Synar, D-Okla., chairman; Scott Lilly, executive director. Fax, 225-4022.

Represents views of mainstream Democrats. Primary source of legislative research for House Democrats.

Export Task Force, 1111 LHOB 20515; 225-4811. Nancy L. Johnson, R-Conn., and Ron Wyden, D-Ore., co-chairs; Mark Ucellis, staff contact.

Forestry 2000 Task Force, 2418 RHOB 20515; 225-4931. Sonny Callahan, R-Ala., J. Roy Rowland, D-Ga., Bob Smith, R-Ore., and Ron Wyden, D-Ore., co-chairmen; Beth Ann Midkiff, staff contact.

House Commission on Congressional Mailing Standards, 176A Ford Bldg. (2nd and D Sts. S.W.) 20515; 225-0436. William L. Clay, D-Mo., chairman; Julie Tagen, staff contact. Fax, 226-0245.

House Democratic Freshman Leadership, 319 CHOB 20515; 225-3315. James E. Clyburn, D-S.C., president; Debra Derr, staff contact.

House Great Lakes Task Force, 530 Ford Bldg. (2nd and D Sts. S.W.) 20515; 226-3920. Amo Houghton, R-N.Y., William O. Lipinski, D-Ill., James L. Oberstar, D-Minn., and Fred Upton, R-Mich., co-chairmen; Marc Gaden, coordinator.

House Republican Freshman Class Leadership, 307 CHOB 20515; 225-1956. Howard P. "Buck" McKeon, R-Calif., president; Bob Cochran, staff contact.

House Task Force on Angola, 2442 RHOB 20515; 225-4422. Jeff Crank, staff contact. Fax, 225-1942.

House Task Force on U.S.-Mexico Economic Relations, 405 CHOB 20515; 225-2542. Jim Kolbe, R-Ariz., chairman; Sean Mulvaney, staff contact.

House Wednesday Group, H2-386 Ford Bldg. (2nd and D Sts. S.W.) 20515; 226-3236. Jim Kolbe, R-Ariz., chairman; Katharine Mottley, staff contact. Fax, 225-3637.

Membership: House Republicans who meet Wednesday evenings to discuss mutual problems, issues, and legislation.

House Working Group on Mental Illness and Health Issues, 218 CHOB 20515; 225-5711. Mike Kopetski, D-Ore., Ronald K. Machtley, R-R.I., Ted Strickland, D-Ohio, and Bob Wise, D-W.Va., co-chairmen; Scott Barstow, staff contact.

Long Island Sound Congressional Caucus, 1034 LHOB 20515; 225-5541. Christopher Shays, R-Conn., chairman; Allison Klinton, staff contact.

Lower Mississippi Delta Congressional Caucus, 2454 RHOB 20515; 225-4404. Blanche Lambert, D-Ark., chair; Bill Emerson, R-Mo., vice chair; Julie Pickett, staff contact.

New England Congressional Energy Caucus, 326 CHOB 20515; 225-4911. Ronald K. Machtley, R-R.I., and Edward J. Markey, D-Mass., co-chairmen; John Deasy, staff contact. Fax, 225-4417.

'92 Group, 1714 LHOB 20515; 225-5406. Lauren Cotter, staff contact. Fax, 225-1081.

Group of House members committed to expanding the legislative influence of Republican members and to becoming the majority House party.

Northeast Agricultural Caucus, 1127 LHOB 20515; 225-3665. Sherwood Boehlert, R-N.Y., and Louise M. Slaughter, D-N.Y., co-chairs; Heming Nelson, staff contact.

Northeast-Midwest Congressional Coalition, H2-530 Ford Bldg. (2nd and D Sts. S.W.) 20515; 226-3920. Dean A. Gallo, R-N.J., and Marcy Kaptur, D-Ohio, co-chairs; Merrill Wagner, staff contact.

Notch Coalition, 438 CHOB 20515; 225-4765. Fred Grandy, R-Iowa, and H. James Saxton, R-N.J., co-chairmen; Kristen Naney, staff contact.

Republican Study Committee, 433 CHOB 20515; 225-0587. Dan Burton, R-Ind., chairman; Ed Buckham, staff contact. Fax, 225-8705.

Membership: conservative House Republicans.

Republican Task Force on American Air Power, c/o House Republican Research Committee, 1622 LHOB 20515; 225-0871. Randy "Duke" Cunningham, R-Calif., and Sam Johnson, R-Texas, co-chairmen; Kevin Fitzpatrick, staff contact.

Rural Health Care Coalition, 1211 LHOB 20515; 225-6605. Pat Roberts, R-Kan., and Charles W. Stenholm, D-Texas, co-chairmen; Colleen Kepner, staff contact. Fax, 225-2234.

Special Task Force on the Development of Parliamentary Institutions in Eastern Europe, 2459 RHOB 20515; 225-3605. Martin Frost, D-Texas, chairman; Kristi Walseth, staff contact.

Task Force on Reform, 414 CHOB 20515; 225-3011. Eric D. Fingerhut, D-Ohio, and Karen Shepherd, D-Utah, co-chairs; Mike Burke, staff contact.

Tennessee Valley Authority Caucus, 1230 LHOB 20515; 225-4311. Bob Clement, D-Tenn., chairman; Jay Hansen, staff contact. Fax, 226-1035.

U.S.-Former Soviet Union Energy Caucus, 236 CHOB 20515; 225-2831. Greg Laughlin, D-Texas, and Curt Weldon, R-Pa., co-chairmen; Frank Lisane, staff contact.

Senate:

Caucus on Deficit Reduction and Economic Growth, SH-724 20510; 224-2043. Kent Conrad, D-N.D., chairman; Mary Naylor, staff contact.

Commission on Ethics, SR-364 20510; 224-6244. Richard H. Bryan, D-Nev., chairman; Jean Marie Neal, staff contact.

Concerned Senators for the Arts, SR-14C 20510; 224-2315. Howard M. Metzenbaum, D-Ohio, and Claiborne Pell, D-R.I., co-chairmen Cheryl Birdsall, staff contact.

Northeast-Midwest Senate Coalition, SH-51 20510; 224-0606. James M. Jeffords, R-Vt., an

Daniel Patrick Moynihan, D-N.Y., co-chairmen; Gray Maxwell, staff contact.

Senate Arms Control Observer Group, SH-637 20510; 224-2162. Robert C. Byrd, D-W.Va., Richard G. Lugar, R-Ind., Sam Nunn, D-Ga., Claiborne Pell, D-R.I., and Ted Stevens, R-Alaska, co-chairmen; Monica Chavez, staff contact.

Senate Caucus on International Narcotics Control, SD-224 20510; 224-5225. Joseph R. Biden Jr., D-Del., and Alfonse M. D'Amato, R-N.Y., co-chairmen; Chris Putala, staff contact.

Senate Coal Caucus, SR-173A 20510; 224-4343. Wendell H. Ford, D-Ky., chairman; Sandi Markland, staff contact.

Senate Footwear Caucus, SH-322 20510; 224-2523. William S. Cohen, R-Maine, and George J. Mitchell, D-Maine, co-chairmen; Eben Adams, staff contact.

Senate Grace Caucus, SH-330 20510; 224-5653. Herb Kohl, D-Wis., and Hank Brown, R-Colo., co-chairmen; Kate Sparks, staff contact.
Bipartisan coalition that seeks to focus attention on the cost-cutting recommendations made by the Grace commission (President's Private Sector Survey on Cost Control).

Senate Great Lakes Task Force, SH-503 20510; 224-3353. Dave Durenberger, R-Minn., and John Glenn, D-Ohio, co-chairmen; Mike Gordon, staff contact.

Senate National Guard Caucus, SR-293 20510; 224-5721. Christopher S. Bond, R-Mo., and Wendell H. Ford, D-Ky., co-chairmen; Brent Franzel, staff contact.

Senate Rail Caucus, SR-154 20510; 224-3244. Max Baucus, D-Mont., and Dave Durenberger, R-Minn., co-chairmen; Sue Pihlstrom, staff contact.

Senate Rural Health Caucus, SH-511 20510; 224-3254. Tom Harkin, D-Iowa, and Bob Dole, R-Kan., co-chairmen; Anne Ford, staff contact.

Senate Steel Caucus, SH-109 20510; 224-6472. John D. Rockefeller IV, D-W.Va., and Arlen Specter, R-Pa., co-chairmen; Ken Levinson, acting staff contact.

Senate Steering Committee, SR-237 20510; 224-5597. Malcolm Wallop, R-Wyo., chairman; Jade C. West, staff director.
Membership: conservative Senate members.

Senate Sweetener Caucus, SH-516 20510; 224-4623. John B. Breaux, D-La., and Larry E. Craig, R-Idaho, co-chairmen; John Broussard, staff contact.

Senate Textile Steering Committee, SR-125 20510; 224-6121. Ernest F. Hollings, D-S.C., chairman; Ivan Schlager, staff contact.

Senate Tourism Caucus, SD-183 20510; 224-2644. Conrad Burns, R-Mont., and Ernest F. Hollings, D-S.C., co-chairmen; Pat Joyce, staff contact.

Western States Senate Coalition, 444 N. Capitol St. N.W., #414 20001; 224-3004. Dennis DeConcini, D-Ariz., Orrin G. Hatch, R-Utah, Harry Reid, D-Nev., and Ted Stevens, R-Alaska, co-chairmen; Dick Cocozza, staff contact. Fax, 224-2354.

Pay and Perquisites

Foreign Travel

House:

Clerk of the House of Representatives, Records and Registration, 1036 LHOB 20515; 225-1300. Patricia Bias, director.
Receives and maintains reports from committee chairmen on foreign travel by House members and staff. Open for public inspection.

Senate:

Secretary of the Senate, Public Records, SH-232 20510; 224-0758. Shirley Tucker, staff contact. Fax, 224-1851.
Receives and maintains reports from committee chairmen on foreign travel by Senate members and staff. Open for public inspection.

Franking Privilege

Franking is the privilege of sending official mail postage free; legislative personnel authorized to use the frank are the vice president of the United States, members of Congress, resident commissioners, and certain officials of the Senate and House.

House:

House Commission on Congressional Mailing Standards, 176A Ford Bldg. (2nd and D Sts. S.W.) 20515; 225-0436. William L. Clay, D-Mo., chairman; Julie Tagen, staff director. Fax, 226-0245.

Oversight of the use of franked mail by House members.

House Post Office and Civil Service Committee, 309 CHOB 20515; 225-4054. William L. Clay, D-Mo., chairman; Gail E. Weiss, staff director.

Jurisdiction over the use of the franking privilege.

Nonlegislative and Financial Services, Postal Operations of the House of Representatives, B225 LHOB 20515; 225-3856. Michael J. Shinay, director. Fax, 225-6530.

Supervises the postal facilities in the Capitol and the House office buildings.

Senate:

Senate Rules and Administration Committee, SR-305 20510; 224-6352. Wendell H. Ford, D-Ky., chairman; James O. King, staff director.

Jurisdiction over the use of the franking privilege.

Senate Select Committee on Ethics, SH-220 20510; 224-2981. Richard H. Bryan, D-Nev., chairman; Victor M. Baird, staff director. Fax, 224-7416.

Oversight of the use of franked mail by Senate members; takes action on misuse of the frank.

Nongovernmental:

National Taxpayers Union, 713 Maryland Ave. N.E. (mailing address: 325 Pennsylvania Ave. S.E., Washington, DC 20003); 543-1300. David Keating, executive vice president. Fax, 546-2086.

Citizens' interest group that publishes reports on congressional franking.

Medical Treatment

House and Senate:

Attending Physician, H166 CAP 20515; 225-5421. Dr. Robert C. J. Krasner, attending physician; Robert F. Moran, administrative assistant.

Provides members with first-aid, emergency care, and medical consultation; provides House and Senate employees and tourists with first-aid and emergency care.

Salaries and Expenses

House:

Clerk of the House of Representatives, H105 CAP 20515; 225-7000. Donnald K. Anderson, clerk.

Prepares and submits quarterly reports covering the receipts and expenditures of the House for three months, including disbursements by each committee and each member's office and staff. Reports available from the House Document Room, 225-3456.

House Administration Committee, Subcommittee on Accounts, 611 O'Neill Bldg. (300 New Jersey Ave. S.E.) 20515; 226-7540. Martin Frost, D-Texas, chairman; Robert Mansker, staff director. Fax, 225-3195.

Responsible for all matters related to the House's internal operational budget, including members' allowances and expenses, remuneration of House employees, and such unforeseen expenditures as special investigations.

House Post Office and Civil Service Committee, 309 CHOB 20515; 225-4054. William L. Clay, D-Mo., chairman; Gail E. Weiss, staff director.

Jurisdiction over proposed changes in the salary of members of Congress.

Senate:

Secretary of the Senate, S208 CAP 20510; 224-2115. Martha S. Pope, secretary; Michelle Haynes, administrative assistant. Fax, 224-1664.

Prepares and submits semiannual reports covering the receipts and expenditures of the Senate for six months, including data on each committee and each member's office and staff. Reports available from the Government Printing Office, 275-3030.

Senate Governmental Affairs Committee, SD-340 20510; 224-4751. John Glenn, D-Ohio, chairman; Leonard Weiss, staff director. Fax, 224-9682.

Jurisdiction over proposed changes in the salary of members of Congress.

Senate Rules and Administration Committee, SR-305 20510; 224-6352. Wendell H. Ford, D-Ky., chairman; James O. King, staff director.

Responsible for all matters related to the Senate's internal operational budget, including members' allowances and expenses, remuneration of Senate employees, and such unforeseen expenditures as special investigations. Oversees budgets of the Secretary of the Senate, the Sergeant at Arms, and the Architect of the Capitol.

Nongovernmental:

National Taxpayers Union, 713 Maryland Ave. N.E. (mailing address: 325 Pennsylvania Ave. S.E., Washington, DC 20003); 543-1300. David Keating, executive vice president. Fax, 546-2086.

Citizens' interest group that publishes reports on congressional pensions.

Standards of Conduct

Agencies:

Justice Dept., Public Integrity, 1400 New York Ave. N.W. 20005; 514-1431. Lee J. Radek, chief. Fax, 514-3003.

Conducts investigations of wrongdoing in selected cases that involve alleged corruption of public office or violations of election law by public officials, including members of Congress.

House:

Clerk of the House of Representatives, Records and Registration, 1036 LHOB 20515; 225-1300. Patricia Bias, director.

Receives and maintains the financial disclosure records of House members, officers, employees, candidates, and certain legislative organizations. Open for public inspection.

House Standards of Official Conduct Committee, HT-2 CAP 20515; 225-7103. Jim McDermott, D-Wash., chairman; Bernard Raimo Jr., chief counsel. Fax, 225-7392.

Enforces the House Code of Official Conduct (rules governing the behavior of House members and employees); has full legislative jurisdiction over all matters under that code; reviews members' financial disclosures.

Senate:

Secretary of the Senate, Public Records, SH-232 20510; 224-0322. Susan Casteel, staff contact, ethics. Fax, 224-1851.

Receives and maintains the financial disclosure records of Senate members, officers, employees, candidates, and legislative organizations. Open for public inspection.

Senate Select Committee on Ethics, SH-220 20510; 224-2981. Richard H. Bryan, D-Nev., chairman; Victor M. Baird, staff director. Fax, 224-7416.

Receives complaints and investigates allegations of improper conduct; administers the code of official conduct; recommends disciplinary action; makes recommendations to the Senate on additional laws, rules, and regulations that may be necessary; investigates allegations of unauthorized disclosure of classified information and documents by members, officers, and employees of the Senate.

Televised Coverage, Recordings, and Photographs

House:

Clerk of the House of Representatives, House Recording Studio, B310 RHOB 20515; 225-3941. William C. Moody, director.

Assists House members in making film and tape recordings. Provides daily gavel-to-gavel television coverage of House floor proceedings.

Office of Photography, B302 RHOB 20515; 225-2840. Keith Jewell, director.

Provides House members with photographic assistance.

Senate:

Sergeant at Arms of the Senate, Senate Photographic Studio, SD-10 20510; 224-3669. Steve Benza, director. Fax, 228-5774.

Provides Senate members with photographic assistance.

Sergeant at Arms of the Senate, Senate Recording Studio, ST71 CAP 20510; 224-4977. James R. Grahne, director. Fax, 224-8701.

Assists Senate members in making radio and video tape recordings and live satellite broadcasts; televises Senate floor proceedings for broadcast by C-SPAN (Cable-Satellite Public Affairs Network).

Political Advocacy

Lobby and Foreign Agents Registrations

Agencies:

Justice Dept., Foreign Agents Registration Unit, 1400 New York Ave. N.W. 20530; 514-1216. Joseph E. Clarkson, chief. Fax, 514-2836.

Receives and maintains the registration of agents representing foreign countries, companies, organizations, and individuals. Compiles annual report on foreign agent registrations. Foreign agent registration files are open for public inspection.

House:

Clerk of the House of Representatives, Records and Registration, 1036 LHOB 20515; 225-1300. Patricia Bias, director.

Receives and maintains lobby registrations and quarterly financial reports of lobbyists. Administers the statutes of the Federal Regulation of Lobbying Act of 1946 and counsels lobbyists. Receives and maintains agency filings made under the requirements of Section 319 of the Department of the Interior and Related Agencies Appropriations Act for fiscal 1990 (known as the Byrd amendment). Maintains a list of House legislative service organizations (caucuses). Open for public inspection.

House Judiciary Committee, Subcommittee on Administrative Law and Governmental Relations, B351A RHOB 20515; 225-5741. John Bryant, D-Texas, chairman; Paul J. Drolet, chief counsel.

Jurisdiction over legislation on the regulation of lobbying and disclosure requirements for registered lobbyists.

Senate:

Secretary of the Senate, Public Records, SH-232 20510; 224-0758. Shirley Tucker, staff contact. Fax, 224-1851.

Receives and maintains lobby registrations and quarterly financial reports of lobbyists. Open for public inspection.

Senate Governmental Affairs Committee, Subcommittee on Oversight of Government Management, SH-442 20510; 224-3682. Carl Levin, D-Mich., chairman; Linda J. Gustitus, staff director.

Jurisdiction over legislation on regulation of lobbying and disclosure requirements for registered lobbyists.

Nongovernmental:

American League of Lobbyists, P.O. Box 30005, Alexandria, VA 22310; (703) 960-3011. Patti Jo Baber, executive director. Fax, (703) 960-4070.

Membership: lobbyists and government relations and public affairs professionals. Works to improve the skills, ethics, and public image of lobbyists. Monitors lobby legislation; conducts educational programs on public issues, lobbying techniques, and other topics of interest to membership.

Political Action Committees

Nongovernmental:

The following are among the top twenty Washington-based political action committees (PACs) in each of three categories: (1) Labor, (2) Nonconnected, and (3) Trade, Membership, and Health. This list is based on disbursements reported to the Federal Election Commission (FEC) under the Federal Election Campaign Act of 1971, as amended. The FEC does not require phone numbers; in some cases phone numbers are not available.

Labor:

Active Ballot Club (United Food and Commercial Workers International Union, AFL-CIO), 1775 K St. N.W. 20006; 223-3111. Jerry Menapace, treasurer. Fax, 466-1562.

AFL-CIO Committee on Political Education/ Political Contributions Committee, 815 16th St. N.W. 20006; 637-5101. Thomas R. Donahue, treasurer.

Air Line Pilots Assn. PAC, 1625 Massachusetts Ave. N.W., 8th Floor 20036; 797-4039. Duane E. Woerth, treasurer. Fax, 797-4052.

American Federation of State, County, and Municipal Employees—PEOPLE, Qualified, 1625 L St. N.W. 20036; 429-1000. William Lucy, treasurer.

American Federation of Teachers Committee on Political Education, 555 New Jersey Ave. N.W. 20001; 879-4436. Edward J. McElroy, treasurer.

Carpenters' Legislative Improvement Committee (United Brotherhood of Carpenters and Joiners of America, AFL-CIO), 101 Constitution Ave. N.W. 20001; 546-6206. James S. Bledsoe, treasurer.

Committee on Letter Carriers Political Education (National Assn. of Letter Carriers), 100 Indiana Ave. N.W. 20001; 393-4695. Florence Johnson, treasurer.

CWA-COPE Political Contributions Committee (Communications Workers of America, AFL-CIO), 501 3rd St. N.W., #1000 20001; 434-1410. Barbara J. Easterling, treasurer. Fax, 434-1481.

Democratic Republican Independent Voter Education Committee (International Brotherhood of Teamsters, Chauffeurs, Warehousemen, and Helpers of America), 25 Louisiana Ave. N.W. 20001; 624-8741. Wallace D. Clements, treasurer.

District No. 1-MEBA/NMU (AFL-CIO) Political Action Fund, 1125 15th St. N.W., #501 20005; 872-0902. Michael D. Derby, treasurer.

International Brotherhood of Electrical Workers Committee on Political Education, 1125 15th St. N.W., #1202 20005; 728-6020. Jack F. Moore, treasurer.

Ironworkers Political Action League, 1750 New York Ave. N.W., #400 20006; 383-4800. James E. Cole, treasurer.

Laborers' Political League of Laborers' International Union of North America, 905 16th St. N.W. 20006; 737-8320. James J. Norwood, treasurer.

Machinists Non-Partisan Political League (International Assn. of Machinists and Aerospace Workers, AFL-CIO), 9000 Machinists Pl., Upper Marlboro, MD 20772; (301) 967-4500. Donald E. Wharton, treasurer. Fax, (301) 967-4588.

National Education Assn. PAC, 1201 16th St. N.W. 20036; 822-7300. Ken Melley, treasurer.

Political Fund Committee of the American Postal Workers Union, AFL-CIO, 1300 L St. N.W. 20005; 842-4210. Douglas C. Holbrook, treasurer.

Seafarers Political Activity Donation (Seafarers International Union of North America), 5201 Auth Way, Camp Springs, MD 20746; (301) 899-0675. John Fay, treasurer.

Service Employees International Union Committee on Political Education Political Campaign Committee, 1313 L St. N.W. 20005; 898-3361. Richard W. Cordtz, treasurer.

Sheet Metal Workers International Assn. Political Action League, 1750 New York Ave. N.W. 20006; 662-0887. Lawrence J. Cassidy, treasurer.

United Assn. Political Education Committee, 901 Massachusetts Ave. N.W. 20001; 628-5823. Marion A. Lee, treasurer.

Nonconnected:

Americans for Free International Trade PAC Inc., 2011 Pennsylvania Ave. N.W., 5th Floor 20006; 659-8545. Wayne Williams, treasurer.

Campaign America, 900 2nd St. N.E., #118 20002; 408-5105. Judith F. Taggart, treasurer.

Conservative Campaign Fund, 8321 Old Courthouse Rd., #215, Vienna, VA 22182. Peter T. Flaherty, treasurer.

Council for a Livable World, 110 Maryland Ave. N.E. 20002; 543-4100. Philip Schrag, treasurer. Fax, 543-6297.

Supports congressional candidates who advocate arms control.

Effective Government Committee, 607 14th St. N.W., #800 20005; 347-6112. David Jones, treasurer.

Emily's List, 1112 16th St. N.W., #750 20036; 887-1957. Ellen R. Malcolm, treasurer.

English Language PAC, P.O. Box 9558, Washington, DC 20016. Jan C. Zall, treasurer.

Ernst & Young PAC, 1200 19th St. N.W., #400 20036; 327-6000. James G. Maguire, treasurer.

GOPAC Inc., 440 1st St. N.W., #400 20001; 484-2282. Lisa B. Nelson, treasurer.

The House Leadership Fund, P.O. Box 39236, Washington, DC 20016. Jan Clark, treasurer.

Independent Action Inc., 1511 K St. N.W., #619 20005; 628-4321. Mark Ingram, treasurer. Democratic PAC supporting mostly challengers. Interests include civil rights, prochoice, health care, educational funding, and environmental legislation.

National Abortion Rights Action League PAC, 1156 15th St. N.W., 7th Floor 20005; 973-3000. Evan J. Goldman, treasurer. Supports candidates who are fully prochoice.

National Committee for an Effective Congress, 507 Capitol Court N.E. 20002; 547-1151. James E. Byron, treasurer. Supports liberal or progressive candidates in marginal races.

National PAC, 600 Pennsylvania Ave. S.E., #207 20003; 879-7710. Marvin Josephson, treasurer. Supports candidates who advocate close U.S.-Israeli relations.

National Right to Life PAC, 419 7th St. N.W., #500 20004; 626-8800. Amarie Natividad, treasurer.

Republicans for Choice, 1315 Duke St., Alexandria, VA 22314; (703) 960-9882. Roseann Garber, treasurer.

Ruff-PAC, 666 Pennsylvania Ave. S.E., #402 20003; 546-0023. Tammy J. Lyles, treasurer. Supports candidates who support a free market economy and a strong national defense.

United Conservatives of America, 768 Walker Rd., #290, Great Falls, VA 22066. Robert G. Mills, treasurer.

Voters for Choice/Friends of Family Planning, 2604 Connecticut Ave. N.W. 20008; 588-5200. Linda Tarr-Whelan, treasurer.

Women's Pro-Israel National PAC, 2020 Pennsylvania Ave. N.W., #275 20006. Joyce Ullman, treasurer.

Trade, Membership, and Health:

Action Committee for Rural Electrification, 1800 Massachusetts Ave. N.W. 20036; 857-9535. Patrick E. Gioffre, treasurer.

American Bankers Assn. PAC, 1120 Connecticut Ave. N.W., #851 20036; 663-5113. Gary W. Fields, treasurer.

American Chiropractic Assn. PAC, 1701 Clarendon Blvd., Arlington, VA 22209; (703) 276-8800. Richard E. Thompson, treasurer.

American Dental PAC, 1111 14th St. N.W., 11th Floor 20005; 898-2424. Dr. Lewis Earle, treasurer.

American Medical Assn. PAC, 1101 Vermont Ave. N.W. 20005; 789-7400. Kevin Walker, treasurer.

American Optometric Assn. PAC, 1505 Prince St., #300, Alexandria, VA 22314. Ernest Schlabach, treasurer.

Assn. of Trial Lawyers of America PAC, 1050 31st St. N.W. 20007; 965-3500. Joan C. Pollitt, treasurer.

Build PAC of the National Assn. of Home Builders, 15th and M Sts. N.W. 20005; 822-0470. Phillip L. Blair, treasurer.

Dealers Election Action Committee of the National Automobile Dealers Assn., 8400 Westpark Dr., McLean, VA 22102; (703) 821-7111. Leonard Fichtner, treasurer.

Independent Insurance Agents of America Inc. PAC, 412 1st St. S.E., #300 20003; 863-7000. Paul A. Equale, treasurer.

National Assn. of Broadcasters Television and Radio PAC, 1771 N St. N.W. 20036; 429-5319. James C. May, treasurer.

National Assn. of Life Underwriters PAC, 1922 F St. N.W. 20006; 331-6000. Paul M. Smith Sr., treasurer.

National Assn. of Retired Federal Employees PAC, 1533 New Hampshire Ave. N.W. 20036; 234-0832. Benny Lewis Parker, treasurer.

National Assn. of Social Workers Political Action for Candidate Election, 750 1st St. N.E. 20002; 408-8600. Maurice Boisvert, treasurer.

National Beer Wholesalers' Assn. PAC, 1100 S. Washington St., Alexandria, VA 22314; (703) 683-4300. Ronald A. Sarasin, treasurer.

National Cable Television Assn.'s PAC, 1724 Massachusetts Ave. N.W. 20036; 775-3650. William C. Oldaker, treasurer.

National Committee to Preserve Social Security and Medicare PAC, 2000 K St. N.W., 8th Floor 20006; 822-9459. Jeff Galginaitis, treasurer.

NRA Political Victory Fund, 11250 Waples Mill Rd., Fairfax, VA 22030; (703) 267-1000. Maryrose Jennison, treasurer.

Veterans of Foreign Wars PAC, 200 Maryland Ave. N.E., #506 20002; 544-5868. J. Douglas Forrest, treasurer.

Women's Campaign Fund Inc., 120 Maryland Ave. N.E. 20002; 544-4484. Ann Kinney, treasurer.

Political Interest Groups

See also Religion and Ethics, Nongovernmental (p. 276)

Nongovernmental:

AARP/Vote, 601 E St. N.W. 20049; 434-3741. James T. Butler, director. Fax, 434-3745.
Nonpartisan voter education program of the American Association of Retired Persons. Maintains nationwide volunteer network that raises issues of concern to older persons in political campaigns.

American Conservative Union, 38 Ivy St. S.E. 20003; 546-6555. Jeff Hollingsworth, executive director. Fax, 546-7370.
Legislative interest organization that focuses on defense, foreign policy, economics, and legal issues.

American Freedom Coalition, 7777 Leesburg Pike, #314N, Falls Church, VA 22043; (703) 790-8700. Robert G. Grant, president. Fax, (703) 790-8711.
Legislative interest organization that supports traditional values. Concerns include religious freedom, family, political reform, civil rights, education, economic freedom, and national defense.

Americans for Democratic Action, 1625 K St. N.W., #1150 20006; 785-5980. Rep. John Lewis, D-Ga., president; Amy Isaacs, director. Fax, 785-5969.
Legislative interest organization that seeks to strengthen civil, constitutional, women's, family, workers', and human rights.

Arab American Institute, 918 16th St. N.W. 20006; 429-9210. James Zogby, director. Fax, 429-9214.
Advocacy group concerned with political issues affecting Arab Americans. Seeks to involve the Arab-American community in party politics and the electoral process.

The Campaign for New Priorities, 424 C St. N.E., Lower Level 20002; 544-8222. Robert L. Borosage, acting director. Fax, 544-8226.
Coordinates efforts of citizens and organizations to increase federal domestic-program funding by reducing military spending. Works to increase spending on education, job retraining, the environment and infrastructure, and civilian research and development.

Cato Institute, 1000 Massachusetts Ave. N.W. 20001; 842-0200. Edward H. Crane III, president. Fax, 842-3490.
Public policy research organization that advocates limited government and individual liberty. Interests include privatization and deregulation, low and simple taxes, and reduced government spending. Encourages voluntary solutions to social and economic problems.

Center for National Policy, 1 Massachusetts Ave. N.W., #333 20001; 682-1800. Maureen Steinbruner, president. Fax, 682-1818.

Ratings of Members

The following organizations either publish voting records on selected issues or annually rate members of Congress; organizations marked with an asterisk (*) rate members biennially.

See also Labor Unions list (p. 801)

American Conservative Union, 38 Ivy St. S.E. 20003; 546-6555.

***American Farm Bureau Federation,** 600 Maryland Ave. S.W., #800 20024; 484-3600.

American Federation of Labor-Congress of Industrial Organizations, 815 16th St. N.W. 20006; 637-5000.

***American Security Council,** 1155 15th St. N.W., #1101 20005-2706; 296-9500.

Americans for Democratic Action, 1625 K St. N.W., #210 20006; 785-5980.

***Common Cause,** 2030 M St. N.W. 20036; 833-1200.

Competitive Enterprise Institute, 1001 Connecticut Ave. N.W., #1250 20036; 331-1010.

Consumer Federation of America, 1424 16th St. N.W., #604 20036; 387-6121.

Environmental Voter, 1707 L St. N.W., #550 20036; 785-8683.

Gay and Lesbian Activists Alliance, 2 Massachusetts Ave. N.E. (mailing address: P.O. Box 75265, Washington, D.C. 20013); 667-5139.

Leadership Conference on Civil Rights, 1629 K St. N.W., #1010 20006; 466-3311.

***Liberty Lobby,** 300 Independence Ave. S.E. 20003; 546-5611.

National Abortion Rights Action League—Political Action Committee (NARAL—PAC), 1156 15th St. N.W., 7th Floor 20005; 973-3000.

***National Assn. for the Advancement of Colored People (NAACP),** 1025 Vermont Ave. N.W., #1120 20005; 638-2269.

National Assn. of Social Workers— PACE (Political Action for Candidate Election), 750 1st St. N.E. 20002; 408-8600.

National Council of Senior Citizens, 1331 F St. N.W. 20004; 347-8800.

National Federation of Independent Business, 600 Maryland Ave. S.W., #700 20024; 554-9000.

National Gay and Lesbian Task Force Policy Institute, 1734 14th St. N.W. 20009; 332-6483.

National Taxpayers Union, 713 Maryland Ave. N.E. (mailing address: 325 Pennsylvania Ave. S.E. 20003); 543-1300.

National Women's Political Caucus, 1275 K St. N.W., #750 20005; 898-1100.

Public Citizen, Congress Watch, 215 Pennsylvania Ave. S.E., 3rd Floor 20003; 546-4996.

U.S. Chamber of Commerce Legislative and Public Affairs, 1615 H St. N.W. 20062; 463-5604.

U.S. Student Assn., 815 15th St. N.W., #838 20005; 347-8772.

The Woman Activist Fund, 2310 Barbour Rd., Falls Church, VA 22043; (703) 573-8716.

Public policy research and educational organization that serves as a forum for development of national policy alternatives. Studies issues of national and international concern including problems of governance.

Citizens Against Government Waste, 1301 Connecticut Ave. N.W., #400 20036; 467-5300. Thomas A. Schatz, president. Toll-free, (800) 872-3328. Fax, 467-4253.

Nonpartisan organization that seeks to expose waste, mismanagement, and inefficiency in the federal government.

Committee for the Study of the American Electorate, 421 New Jersey Ave. S.E. 20003; 546-3221. Curtis Gans, director.
Nonpartisan research group that studies issues involving low and declining American voter participation.

Common Cause, 2030 M St. N.W. 20036; 833-1200. Fred Wertheimer, president. Fax, 659-3716.
Citizens' legislative interest group that works for institutional reform in federal and state government. Advocates partial public financing of congressional election campaigns, ethics in government, nuclear arms control, oversight of

defense spending, tax reform, and a reduction of political action committee influence in Congress.

Concerned Women for America, 370 L'Enfant Promenade S.W., #800 20024; 488-7000. Jim Woodall, vice president. Fax, 488-0806.

Educational and legal defense foundation that seeks to protect the rights of the family and preserve Judeo-Christian values. Monitors legislation affecting family and religious issues.

Congressional Economic Leadership Institute, 201 Massachusetts Ave. N.E., #C8 20002; 546-5007. Bob Vastine, president. Fax, 546-7037.

Nonpartisan research group that serves as a forum for the discussion of economic issues between Congress and the private sector.

The Conservative Caucus, 450 Maple Ave. East, Vienna, VA 22180; (703) 938-9626. Howard Phillips, chairman.

Legislative interest organization that promotes grass-roots activity on issues such as national defense and economic and tax policy. The Conservative Caucus Research, Analysis, and Education Foundation studies public issues including Central American affairs, defense policy, and federal funding of political advocacy groups.

Family Research Council, 700 13th St. N.W., #500 20005; 393-2100. Gary L. Bauer, president. Fax, 393-2134.

Legislative interest organization that analyzes issues affecting the family and seeks to ensure that the interests of the family are considered in the formulation of public policy.

Foundation for Public Affairs, 1019 19th St. N.W., #200 20036; 872-1750. Leslie Swift-Rosenzweig, executive director. Fax, 835-8343.

Public policy research and educational foundation that serves as an information clearinghouse on interest groups and corporate public affairs programs. Monitors the activities of public policy groups and advises on methods of operation, staff, budget size, and other administrative topics. Provides commentary on groups' effectiveness and political orientation. (Affiliated with the Public Affairs Council.)

Free Congress Research and Education Foundation, 717 2nd St. N.E. 20002; 546-3004. Paul M. Weyrich, president. Fax, 543-8425.

Research and education foundation that promotes traditional values, conservative governance, and institutional reform. Studies judicial/political issues, electoral process, and public policy. Trains citizens to participate in a democracy. Operates a 24-hour satellite television network.

Fund for the Feminist Majority, 1600 Wilson Blvd., #801, Arlington, VA 22209; (703) 522-2214. Eleanor Smeal, president. Fax, (703) 522-2219.

Legislative interest group that seeks to increase the number of feminists running for public office; promotes a national feminist agenda.

Gay and Lesbian Activists Alliance, 1734 14th St. N.W. 20009; 667-5139. Jeff Coudriet, president.

Political action and education organization that supports lesbian and gay rights legislation. Rates political leaders based on their support of lesbian and gay rights legislation.

Heritage Foundation, 214 Massachusetts Ave. N.E. 20002; 546-4400. Edwin J. Feulner Jr., president. Fax, 546-8328.

Public policy research organization that conducts research and analysis and sponsors lectures, debates, and policy forums advocating individual freedom, limited government, the free market system, and a strong national defense.

The Jefferson Foundation, 1529 18th St. N.W. 20036; 234-3688. Mary Kennedy, executive director. Fax, 483-6018.

Research and educational organization that studies constitutional reforms proposed by Congress that seek to improve the function and structure of government; works to increase public knowledge of government structural reforms through citizen participation in Jefferson Meetings on the Constitution.

Joint Center for Political and Economic Studies, 1090 Vermont Ave. N.W., #1100 20005; 789-3500. Eddie N. Williams, president. Library, 789-5519. Fax, 789-6390.

Research and educational organization that analyzes issues of concern to African Americans, focusing on economic and social policy issues and African American political participation; publishes an annual profile of African American elected officials in federal, state, and local government. Library open to the public by appointment.

Labor Council for Latin American Advancement, 815 16th St. N.W., #310 20006; 347-4223. Alfredo C. Montoya, executive director. Fax, 347-5095.

Membership: Hispanic trade unionists. Conducts nonpartisan voter registration and education programs and encourages increased participation by Hispanic workers in the political process.

Lead or Leave, 1100 Connecticut Ave. N.W., #1300 20036; 857-0808. Jeremy Hartman, executive assistant. Fax, 457-1453.

Nonpartisan organization that encourages younger Americans to get involved in politics. Seeks to form a consensus on economic issues facing young people, in particular the federal budget deficit, and works at the local level to promote the desire for deficit reduction and fiscal responsibility.

League of Women Voters of the United States, 1730 M St. N.W. 20036; 429-1965. Gracia Hillman, executive director. Fax, 429-0854.

Membership: women and men interested in nonpartisan political action and study. Works to increase participation in government; provides information on voter registration and balloting. Interests include social policy, natural resources, international relations, and representative government.

Liberty Lobby, 300 Independence Ave. S.E. 20003; 546-5611. Vince Ryan, chairman, board of policy.

Legislative interest organization that opposes a balanced budget amendment, busing, gun control, hate crimes legislation, the Genocide Convention, foreign aid, and U.S. involvement in the United Nations. Supports states' rights, reduced government spending and lower taxes, protective immigration laws, and repeal of the Sixteenth, Seventeenth, and Twenty-Fifth amendments.

National Assn. of Latino Elected and Appointed Officials, 514 C St. N.E. 20002-5810; 546-2536. Karen Escalante, national director; Kelly Wagner, administrator. Fax, 546-4121. Toll-free hotline, (800) 446-2536.

Research and advocacy group that provides civic affairs information and assistance on legislation affecting Hispanics. Encourages Hispanic participation in local, state, and national politics. Interests include the health and social, economic, and educational welfare of Hispanics.

National Black Caucus of Local Elected Officials, c/o National League of Cities, 1301 Pennsylvania Ave. N.W., #600 20004; 626-3120. Jeff Fletcher, director, public affairs. Fax, 626-3043.

Membership: elected officials at the local level and other interested individuals. Concerned with issues affecting African Americans, including housing, economics, the family, and human rights.

National Black Caucus of State Legislators, 444 N. Capitol St. N.W., #622 20001; 624-5457. Charles Bremer, executive director. Fax, 508-3826.

Membership: African American state legislators. Promotes effective leadership among African American state legislators; serves as an information network and clearinghouse for members.

National Forum Foundation, 511 C St. N.E. 20002; 543-3515. James S. Denton, president. Fax, 547-4101.

Nonpartisan organization that promotes political and economic freedom in the United States and abroad. Provides support to the emerging democracies of Europe and Eurasia through long- and short-term training programs and direct assistance. Emphasizes programs that encourage the development of democratic governance and free-market economies.

National Jewish Coalition, 415 2nd St. N.E. 20002; 547-7701. Matt Brooks, executive director.

Legislative interest group that works to build support among Republican party decision makers on issues of concern to the Jewish community; studies domestic and foreign policy issues affecting the Jewish community; supports a strong relationship between the United States and Israel.

National Jewish Democratic Council, 711 2nd St. N.E., #100 20002; 544-7636. Steve Gutow, executive director. Fax, 544-7645.

Encourages Jewish involvement in the Democratic party and its political campaigns. Monitors and analyzes domestic and foreign policy issues that concern the American Jewish community.

National Organization for Women (NOW), 1000 16th St. N.W., #700 20036; 331-0066. Patricia Ireland, president. Fax, 785-8576. TDD, 331-9002.

Advocacy organization that works for women's civil rights. Acts through demonstrations, court cases, and legislative efforts to improve the status of all women. Interests include increasing the number of women in elected and appointed office, improving women's economic status and health coverage, ending violence against women, preserving abortion rights, and abolishing discrimination based on gender, race, age, and sexual orientation.

National Rainbow Coalition, 1700 K St. N.W., #800 20006; 728-1180. Jesse L. Jackson, president. Fax, 728-1192.

Independent political organization concerned with U.S. domestic and foreign policy. Interests include D.C. statehood, civil rights, defense policy, agriculture, poverty, the economy, energy, and the environment.

National Taxpayers Union, 713 Maryland Ave. N.E. (mailing address: 325 Pennsylvania Ave. S.E., Washington, DC 20003); 543-1300. David Keating, executive vice president. Fax, 546-2086.

Citizens' interest group that promotes tax and spending reduction at all levels of government. Supports constitutional amendments to balance the federal budget and limit taxes.

National Woman's Party, 144 Constitution Ave. N.E. 20002; 546-1210. Helen Arnold, president. Fax, 543-2365.

Membership: women seeking equality under the law. Supports the Equal Rights Amendment and other legislation to eliminate discrimination against women.

National Women's Political Caucus, 1275 K St. N.W. 20005; 898-1100. Jody Newman, executive director. Fax, 898-0458.

Advocacy group that seeks greater involvement of women in politics; supports women for elective and appointive political office; serves as an information clearinghouse on women in politics, particularly during election campaigns; publishes directory of women holding federal and state offices.

People for the American Way, 2000 M St. N.W., #400 20036; 467-4999. Arthur J. Kropp, president. Fax, 293-2672.

Nonpartisan organization that promotes protection of First Amendment rights through a national grass-roots network of members and volunteers. Conducts public education programs on constitutional issues. Provides radio, television, and newspaper advertisements; maintains speakers bureau. Library open to the public by appointment.

Progressive Policy Institute, 518 C St. N.E. 20002; 547-0001. Will Marshall, president. Fax, 544-5014.

Public policy research and educational organization that supports individual opportunity, equal justice under law, and popular government. Center for Civic Enterprise promotes civic participation in solving national problems through voluntary national service.

Project Vote, 1511 K St. N.W., #326 20005; 638-9016. Sanford Newman, executive director. Fax, 383-5905.

Civic organization that registers low-income and minority individuals and educates them on the power of the vote.

Public Advocate, 6001 Leesburg Pike, Falls Church, VA 22041; (703) 845-1808. Eugene Delgaudio, executive director.

Educational grass-roots organization that promotes a limited role for federal government.

Public Affairs Council, 1019 19th St. N.W., #200 20036; 872-1790. Raymond L. Hoewing, president.

Membership: corporate public affairs executives. Informs and counsels members on public affairs programs. Sponsors conferences on election issues, government relations, and political trends. Sponsors the Foundation for Public Affairs.

Public Citizen, Congress Watch, 215 Pennsylvania Ave. S.E., 3rd Floor 20003; 546-4996. Pamela Gilbert, director. Fax, 547-7392.

Citizens' interest group. Interests include consumer protection, financial services, public health and safety, government reform, energy, and the environment.

Term Limits Legal Institute, 900 2nd St. N.E., #200A 20002; 371-0450. Cleta Detherage Mitchell, director. Fax, 371-0210.

Handles lawsuits defending the constitutionality of congressional term limits; provides counseling and education on term limits legislation.

20/20 Vision, 1828 Jefferson Pl. N.W. 20036; 833-2020. Robin Caiola, legislative director. Toll-free, (800) 669-1782. Fax, 833-5307.

Advocacy group that encourages members to spend twenty minutes each month in communicating their opinions to policymakers. Targets legislative issues in particular districts and provides information on current issues. Interests include reducing military spending and protecting the environment.

U.S. Chamber of Commerce, Membership Grassroots Operations, 1615 H St. N.W. 20062; 463-5604. Donald J. Kroes, vice president. Fax, 463-5836.

Federation that works to enact probusiness legislation; tracks election law legislation; coordinates the chamber's candidate endorsement program and its grass-roots lobbying activities.

U.S. Term Limits, 1511 K St. N.W., #540 20005; 393-6440. Paul Jacob, executive director. Fax, 393-6434.

Works through states to encourage congressional term limit legislation; favors a constitutional amendment to mandate congressional term limits.

The Urban Institute, 2100 M St. N.W. 20037; 833-7200. William Gorham, president. Information, 857-8702. Library, 857-8688. Fax, 223-3043.

Public policy research and education organization. Investigates U.S. social and economic problems; encourages discussion on solving society's problems, improving and implementing government decisions, and increasing citizens' awareness of public choices. Library open to the public by appointment.

The Woman Activist Fund, 2310 Barbour Rd., Falls Church, VA 22043; (703) 573-8716. Flora Crater, president.

Advocacy group that conducts research on individuals and groups in elective and appointive office, especially those who make decisions affecting women and minorities. Publishes annual ratings of these officials.

See also Coalition of Black Trade Unionists (p. 182); Voters for Choice (p. 504)

Political Party Organizations

Democratic

Democratic Congressional Campaign Committee, 430 S. Capitol St. S.E. 20003; 863-1500. Rep. Vic Fazio, D-Calif., chairman; Genie Norris, executive director. Fax, 485-3512.

Provides Democratic House candidates with financial and other campaign services.

Democratic Governors' Assn., 430 S. Capitol St. S.E. 20003; 479-5153. Gov. Evan Bayh, D-Ind., chairman; Katherine Whelan, executive director. Fax, 479-5156.

Serves as a liaison between governors' offices and Democratic party organizations; assists Democratic gubernatorial candidates.

Democratic Leadership Council, 518 C St. N.E. 20002; 546-0007. Sen. John B. Breaux, D-La., chairman; Alvin From, president. Fax, 544-5002.

Organization of Democratic members of Congress, governors, state and local officials, and concerned citizens. Builds consensus within the Democratic party on public policy issues, including economic growth, national security, national service, and expansion of opportunity for all Americans.

Democratic National Committee, 430 S. Capitol St. S.E. 20003; 863-8000. David Wilhelm, chairman. Press, 479-5118. Fax, 863-8028.

Formulates and promotes Democratic party policies and positions; assists Democratic candidates for state and national office; organizes national political activities; works with state and local officials and organizations.

Democratic National Committee, 430 S. Capitol St. S.E. 20003; 863-8000. Joe Sandler, general counsel.

Responsible for legal affairs of the DNC, including equal time and fairness cases before the Federal Communications Commission. Advises the DNC and state parties on redistricting and campaign finance law compliance.

Democratic National Committee, Assn. of State Democratic Chairs, 430 S. Capitol St. S.E. 20003; 479-5120. Ann Fishman, executive director. Fax, 479-5123.

Acts as a liaison between state parties and the DNC; works to strengthen state parties for national, state, and local elections; conducts fund-raising activities.

Democratic National Committee, Communications, 430 S. Capitol St. S.E. 20003; 863-8020. Jim Whitney, director. Fax, 488-5081.

Assists federal, state, and local Democratic candidates and officials in delivering a coordinated message on current issues; works to improve and expand relations with the press and to increase the visibility of Democratic officials and the Democratic party.

Democratic National Committee, Finance, 430 S. Capitol St. S.E. 20003; 863-8111. Laura Hartigan, director. Fax, 863-7109.

Responsible for developing the Democratic party's financial base. Coordinates fund-raising efforts for and gives financial support to Democratic candidates in national, state, and local campaigns.

Democratic National Committee, Political Division, 430 S. Capitol St. S.E. 20003; 863-7128. Donald Sweitzer, director. Fax, 863-7188.

Responsible for electoral activities at the federal, state, and local levels, sponsors workshops to recruit Democratic candidates and to provide instruction in campaign techniques; conducts party constituency outreach programs; coordinates voter registration.

Democratic National Committee, Research, 430 S. Capitol St. S.E. 20003; 479-5130. Eric Berman, director. Fax, 488-5056.

Provides Democratic elected officials, candidates, state party organizations, and the general public with information on Democratic party policy and programs.

Democratic Senatorial Campaign Committee, 430 S. Capitol St. S.E. 20003; 224-2447. Sen. Bob Graham, D-Fla., chairman; Don Foley, executive director. Fax, 485-3120.

Provides Democratic senatorial candidates with financial, research, and consulting services.

Women's National Democratic Club, Committee on Public Policy, 1526 New Hampshire Ave. N.W. 20036; 232-7363. Mary Nenno, president. Fax, 986-2791.

Studies issues and presents views to congressional committees, the Democratic Party Platform Committee, Democratic leadership groups, elected officials, and other interested groups.

Republican

College Republican National Committee, 440 1st St. N.W., #303 20001; 662-1330. George Fondren, executive director. Fax, 393-0898.

Membership: Republican college students. Promotes grass-roots support for the Republican party and provides campaign assistance.

National Federation of Republican Women, 124 N. Alfred St., Alexandria, VA 22314; (703) 548-9688. Charlotte Mousel, president. Fax, (703) 548-9836.

Political education and volunteer arm of the Republican party. Organizes volunteers for support of Republican candidates for national, state, and local offices; encourages candidacy of Republican women; sponsors campaign management schools. Recruits Republican women candidates for office.

National Republican Congressional Committee, 320 1st St. S.E. 20003; 479-7000. Rep. Bill Paxon, R-N.Y., chairman; Maria Cino, executive director. Fax, 863-0693.

Provides Republican House candidates with campaign assistance, including financial, public relations, media, and direct mail services.

National Republican Senatorial Committee, 425 2nd St. N.E. 20002; 675-6000. Sen. Phil Gramm, R-Texas, chairman; William D. Harris, executive director. Fax, 675-6058.

Provides Republican senatorial candidates with financial and public relations services.

Republican Governors Assn., 310 1st St. S.E. 20003; 863-8587. Gov. John R. McKernan Jr., R-Maine, chairman; Chris Henick, executive director. Fax, 863-8659.

Serves as a liaison between governors' offices and Republican party organizations; assists Republican candidates for governor.

Republican National Committee (RNC), 310 1st St. S.E. 20003; 863-8500. Haley Barbour, chairman. Information, 863-8790. Press, 863-8550. Fax, 863-8820.

Develops and promotes Republican party policies and positions; assists Republican candidates for state and national office; organizes national political activities; works with state and local officials and organizations.

Republican National Committee, 310 1st St. S.E. 20003; 863-8638. Michael A. Hess, chief counsel. Fax, 863-8654.

Responsible for legal affairs of the RNC, including equal time and fairness cases before the Federal Communications Commission. Advises the RNC and state parties on redistricting and campaign finance law compliance.

Republican National Committee, Communications, 310 1st St. S.E. 20003; 863-8614. Chuck Greener, director. Fax, 863-8773.

Assists federal, state, and local Republican candidates and officials in delivering a coordinated message on current issues; works to improve and expand relations with the press and to increase the visibility of Republican officials and the Republican message.

Republican National Committee, Finance, 310 1st St. S.E. 20003; 863-8720. Albert Mitchler, executive director. Fax, 863-8634.

Responsible for developing the Republican party's financial base. Coordinates fund-raising efforts for and gives financial support to Republican candidates in national, state, and local campaigns.

Republican National Committee, National Hispanic Assembly, 440 1st St. N.W., #414 20001; 662-1355. Alfred Villalovos, chairman. Fax, 662-1408.

Encourages Hispanics to join the Republican party; offers advisory services to Hispanic Republican candidates at state and local levels; provides Republican officeholders and party organizations with information on issues and demographics.

Republican National Committee, Political Operations, 310 1st St. S.E. 20003; 863-8600. Robin Carle, director. Fax, 863-8657.

Responsible for electoral activities at the federal, state, and local levels; sponsors workshops to recruit Republican candidates and provide instruction in campaign techniques; operates party constituency outreach programs; coordinates voter registration.

Ripon Society, 227 Massachusetts Ave. N.E., #210 20002; 546-1292. Jean Hayes, executive director. Fax, 547-6560.

Membership: moderate and progressive Republicans. Works for the adoption of moderate and progressive positions and policies within the Republican party.

Staff Support

Congressional Employees

House:

House Administration Committee, H326 CAP 20515; 225-2061. Charlie Rose, D-N.C., chairman; Robert E. Shea, staff director. Fax, 225-4345.

Jurisdiction over employment of persons by the House. Handles issues of compensation, retirement, and other benefits for members, officers, and employees. Oversight of the House contingent fund, office equipment, and police, parking, restaurant, and other related services.

House Placement Office, 219 Ford Bldg. (2nd and D Sts. S.W.) 20515; 226-6731. John McDermott, chief.

Provides members, committees, and administrative offices of the House of Representatives with placement and referral services.

Senate:

Senate Placement Office, SH-142B 20510; 224-9167. Carol Collett, manager.

Provides members, committees, and administrative offices of the Senate with placement and referral services.

Senate Rules and Administration Committee, SR-305 20510; 224-6352. Wendell H. Ford, D-Ky., chairman; James O. King, staff director.

Jurisdiction over Senate contingent fund, which provides salaries for professional committee staff members and general funds for personal Senate staffs.

Nongovernmental:

Congressional Management Foundation, 513 Capitol Court N.E., #100 20002; 546-0100. Rick Shapiro, executive director. Fax, 547-0936.

Nonpartisan organization that provides members of Congress and their staffs with management information and services through seminars, consultation, research, and publications.

Pages

Pages are patronage appointees in the 11th grade who run errands and act as messengers for members of Congress.

House:

Doorkeeper of the House of Representatives, H154 CAP 20515; 225-3505. James T. Molloy, doorkeeper; Karen Soltys, office manager. Fax, 225-9475.

Responsible for day-to-day activities of pages.

House of Representatives Page Board, 2239 RHOB 20515; 225-3611. Dale E. Kildee, D-Mich., chairman; Christopher Mansour, co-ordinator. Fax, 225-6393.

Oversees and enforces rules and regulations concerning the House page program.

House of Representatives Page School, LJ-A5, Library of Congress 20540-9996; 225-9000. Robert F. Knautz, principal. Fax, 225-9001.

Provides pages of the House with junior year high school education.

Senate:

Senate Page School, Library of Congress, 10 1st St. S.E., #310 20540; 224-3926. Kathryn Weeden, principal. Fax, 224-1838.

Provides education for pages of the Senate.

Sergeant at Arms of the Senate, S321 CAP 20510; 224-2341. Robert L. Benoit, sergeant at arms; Robert Bean, deputy sergeant at arms. Fax, 224-7690.

Oversees and enforces rules and regulations concerning Senate pages after they have been appointed.

Staff Organizations

House and Senate:

Capitol Hill Women's Political Caucus, P.O. Box 599, LHOB, Washington, DC 20515; 986-0994. Heidi Yeager and Renee Rogers, co-chairs.

Membership: women and men from congressional offices, public interest groups, federal agencies, law firms, and lobbying organizations. Promotes legislation that supports equal employment policy, reproductive choice, child care, and other issues of concern to women; seeks to encourage participation, election, and appointment of women in the political and governing process; serves as an information clearinghouse for female members of Congress and the public. Affiliated with the National Women's Political Caucus.

Congressional Staff Club, 810 O'Neill Bldg. (300 New Jersey Ave. S.E.) 20515; 226-3250. James Guyton, president.

Organization of House and Senate staff members. Meets to discuss mutual concerns and promote better relationships among congressional offices.

Federal Bar Assn., 1815 H St. N.W., #408 20006; 638-0252. John G. Blanche III, executive staff director. Library, 638-1956. Fax, 775-0295.

Organization of bar members who are present or former staff members of the House, Senate, Library of Congress, Supreme Court, General Accounting Office, or Government Printing Office; or attorneys in legislative practice.

Republican Women of Capitol Hill, 208 CHOB 20515; 224-5647. Jenny Sandahl, president.

Membership: present and former Republican female staff members who have worked for senators or members of Congress, the Congressional Campaign Committee, the Senatorial Campaign Committee, or the RNC. Promotes communication among congressional staffs.

House:

Administrative Assistants Assn. of the U.S. House of Representatives, c/o 223 CHOB 20515; 225-5341. Dave Nathan, president.

Professional and social organization of House chiefs of staff. Meets to discuss mutual concerns and exchange information. Sponsors orientation program for new chiefs of staff. Meets with administrative, congressional, and international personnel for off-the-record briefings.

House Legislative Assistants Assn., c/o 223 CHOB 20515; 225-5341. Mark Brownell, president.

Nonpartisan professional organization of legislative assistants, legislative directors, legal counsels, and committee staff. Meets to discuss mutual concerns, exchange information, and hear guest speakers; holds seminars on issues pending on the House floor.

Senate:

Senate Press Secretaries Assn., c/o SD-229 20510; 224-4843. Lynnette Moten, president.

Bipartisan organization of present and former senatorial press secretaries and assistant press secretaries. Meets to discuss mutual concerns and to hear guest speakers.

Ready
Reference Lists

The lists in this section are a convenient source of names, addresses, and telephone numbers for foreign diplomats in this country; U.S. ambassadors; labor unions; regional offices of federal government departments and agencies; state officials, such as governors and lieutenant governors; and mayors of major cities. The alphabetical organization of the lists makes them easy to use, giving you information right at your finger tips.

A section on the 103rd Congress contains lists of senators and representatives by state, as well as alphabetically by last name, and includes complete contact information for each member of Congress. In this section you also will find complete lists of all House, Senate, and joint committees and subcommittees, including the partisan committees in both houses of Congress.

Contents:

Corresponding with a Foreign Service Post

Business correspondence to a foreign service post should be addressed to a section or position rather than to an officer by name in case that officer has transferred to another post. Do not combine any of the following address forms, since this can cause delays in delivery; in some cases the letter may be returned to you.

Posts with APO/FPO addresses:
use domestic postage
name of section
name of post
PSC or unit number, box number
APO + two-letter code (AA, AE, or AP)
+ ZIP Code

**Posts without APO/FPO addresses
(via diplomatic pouch)**
use domestic postage
name of post
Department of State
Washington, DC 20521 + 4-digit postal code
(see below)

When sending mail via diplomatic pouch (see address form above), add the 4-digit code of the destination post to the 20521 ZIP Code. Following are 4-digit codes for U.S. embassies abroad.

Abidjan 2010	Colombo 6100	London 8400	Quito 3420
Abu Dhabi 6010	Conakry 2110	Lusaka 2310	Rabat 9400
Accra 2020	Copenhagen 5280	Luxembourg 5380	Rangoon 4250
Addis Ababa 2030	Cotonou 2120	Madrid 8500	Reykjavik 5640
Algiers 6030	Dakar 2130	Majuro 4380	Riga 4520
Almaty 7030	Damascus 6110	Malabo 2320	Riyadh 6300
Amman 6050	Dar Es Salaam 2140	Managua 3240	Rome 9500
Ankara 7000	Dhaka 6120	Manama 6210	St. George's 3180
Antananarivo 2040	Djibouti 2150	Manila 8600	St. John's 3010
Asunción 3020	Doha 6130	Maputo 2330	San Jose 3440
Athens 7100	Dublin 5290	Maseru 2340	San Salvador 3450
Baku 7050	Florence 5670	Mbabane 2350	Sanaa 6330
Bamako 2050	Freetown 2160	Mexico City 8700	Santiago 3460
Bandar Seri	Gaborone 2170	Minsk 7010	Santo Domingo 3470
Begawan 4020	Georgetown 3170	Mogadishu 2360	Sarajevo 7130
Bangkok 7200	Guatemala City 3190	Monrovia 8800	Seoul 9600
Bangui 2060	The Hague 5770	Montevideo 3360	Singapore 4280
Banjul 2070	Harare 2180	Moscow 5430	Sofia 5740
Barcelona 5400	Havana 3200	Muscat 6220	Stockholm 5750
Beijing 7300	Helsinki 5310	Nairobi 8900	Suva 4290
Beirut 6070	Islamabad 8100	Nassau 3370	Tallinn 4530
Belgrade 5070	Jakarta 8200	N'Djamena 2410	Tashkent 7110
Belize City 3050	Kampala 2190	New Delhi 9000	Tbilisi 7060
Bern 5110	Kathmandu 6190	Niamey 2420	Tegucigalpa 3480
Bishkek 7040	Khartoum 2200	Nicosia 5450	Tel Aviv 9700
Bissau 2080	Kiev 5850	Nouakchott 2430	Tirane 9510
Bogota 3030	Kigali 2210	Oslo 5460	Tokyo 9800
Bonn 7400	Kingston 3210	Ottawa 5480	Tunis 6360
Brasilia 7500	Kinshasa 2220	Ouagadougou 2440	Ulaanbaatar 4410
Bratislava 5840	Kolonia 4120	Panama City 9100	Valletta 5800
Brazzaville 2090	Kuala Lumpur 4210	Paramaribo 3390	Vatican City 5660
Bridgetown 3120	Kuwait City 6200	Paris 9200	Victoria 2510
Brussels 7600	Lagos 8300	Phnom Penh 4540	Vienna 9900
Bucharest 5260	La Paz 3220	Port-au-Prince 3400	Vientiane 4350
Budapest 5270	Libreville 2270	Port Louis 2450	Warsaw 5010
Buenos Aires 3130	Lilongwe 2280	Port Moresby 4240	Wellington 4360
Bujumbura 2100	Lima 3230	Port-of-Spain 3410	Windhoek 2540
Cairo 7700	Lisbon 5320	Prague 5630	Yaounde 2520
Canberra 7800	Ljubljana 7140	Praia 2460	Yerevan 7020
Caracas 3140	Lome 2300	Pretoria 9300	Zagreb 5080
			Zurich 5130

Foreign Embassies, U.S. Ambassadors, and Country Desk Officers

In the list that follows, the surnames of all foreign diplomats are shown in capital letters. The listing also includes U.S. ambassadors or ranking diplomatic officials abroad and gives the names and telephone numbers of the U.S. State Dept. and U.S. Commerce Dept. desk officers assigned to follow political, cultural, and economic developments in each country.

Afghanistan
Chargé d'Affaires ad interim: Abdul RAHIM.
Chancery: 2341 Wyoming Ave. N.W. 20008; 234-3770; fax, 328-3516.

Embassy in Kabul temporarily closed.

State Dept. Desk Officer: John Hoover, 647-9552.

Commerce Dept. Desk Officer: Timothy Gilman, 482-2954.

Albania
Ambassador: Roland BIMO.
Chancery (temp.): 1511 K St. N.W., #1010 20005; 223-4942; fax, 628-7342.

U.S. Ambassador Designate in Tirane: Joseph Edward Lake.

State Dept. Desk Officer: John Benton, 647-3187.

Commerce Dept. Desk Officer: Lynn Fabrizio, 482-0360.

Algeria
Ambassador: Nourredine Yazid ZERHOUNI.
Chancery: 2118 Kalorama Rd. N.W. 20008; 265-2800.

U.S. Ambassador Designate in Algiers: Ronald E. Neumann.

State Dept. Desk Officer: Steven Kashkett, 647-4680.

Commerce Dept. Desk Officer: Christopher Cerone, 482-1860.

Andorra
Relations with Andorra are maintained by the U.S. Consulate in Barcelona, Spain. Carolee Heileman, U.S. consul general.

State Dept. Desk Officer: Sherwood McGinnis, 647-1412.

Angola
U.S. Ambassador in Luanda: Edmund T. DeJarnette Jr.
State Dept. Desk Officer: Dennis Hankins, 647-8434.
Commerce Dept. Desk Officer: Finn Holm-Olsen, 482-4228.

Antigua and Barbuda
Ambassador: Patrick Albert LEWIS.
Chancery: 3400 International Dr. N.W., #4M 20008; 362-5211; fax, 362-5225.

U.S. Chargé d'Affaires in St. John's: Bryant J. Salter.

State Dept. Desk Officer: Andrew Siegel, 647-2130.

Commerce Dept. Desk Officer: Michelle Brooks, 482-2527.

Argentina
Ambassador: Raul Enrique GRANILLO OCAMPO.
Chancery: 1600 New Hampshire Ave. N.W. 20009; 939-6400.

U.S. Ambassador in Buenos Aires: James R. Cheek.

State Dept. Desk Officer: Donald Cooke, 647-2401.

Commerce Dept. Desk Officer: Randy Mye, 482-1548.

Armenia
Ambassador: Rouben Robert SHUGARIAN.
Chancery: 1660 L St. N.W., #210 20036; 628-5766.

U.S. Ambassador in Yerevan: Harry J. Gilmore.

State Dept. Desk Officer: Kirk Bennett, 647-8671.

Australia
Ambassador: Donald Eric RUSSELL.
Chancery: 1601 Massachusetts Ave. N.W. 20036; 797-3000; fax, 797-3168.

U.S. Ambassador in Canberra: Edward Perkins.

State Dept. Desk Officer: Louis McCall, 647-9691.

Commerce Dept. Desk Officer: Gary Bouck, 482-2471.

Austria
Ambassador: Helmut TUERK.
Chancery: 3524 International Court N.W. 20008-3035; 895-6700; fax, 895-6750.

U.S. Ambassador in Vienna: Swanee G. Hunt.

State Dept. Desk Officer: Deborah Kavin, 647-2005.

Commerce Dept. Desk Officer: Philip Combs, 482-2920.

Azerbaijan
Ambassador: Hafiz Mir Jalal Oglu PASHAYEV.
Chancery (temp.): 927 15th St. N.W., #700 20005; 842-0001; fax, 842-0004.

U.S. Ambassador Designate in Baku: Richard Dale Kauzlarich.

State Dept. Desk Officer: Kirk Bennett, 647-8671.

Bahamas
Ambassador: Timothy Baswell DONALDSON.
Chancery: 2220 Massachusetts Ave. N.W. 20008; 319-2660; fax, 319-2668.

U.S. Ambassador Designate in Nassau: Sidney Williams.

State Dept. Desk Officer: Stephen Pattison, 647-2621.

Commerce Dept. Desk Officer: Mark Siegelman, 482-5680.

Bahrain
Ambassador: Muhammed Abdul GHAFFAR.
Chancery: 3502 International Dr. N.W. 20008; 342-0741.

U.S. Ambassador Designate in Manama: David M. Ransom.

State Dept. Desk Officer: David Young, 647-6572.

Commerce Dept. Desk Officer: Claude Clement, 482-1860.

Bangladesh
Ambassador: Humayun KABIR.
Chancery: 2201 Wisconsin Ave. N.W. 20007; 342-8372.

U.S. Ambassador Designate in Dhaka: David Merrill.

State Dept. Desk Officer: Paul Wohlers, 647-9552.

Commerce Dept. Desk Officer: John Simmons, 482-1860.

Barbados
Ambassador: Rudi Valentine WEBSTER.
Chancery: 2144 Wyoming Ave. N.W. 20008; 939-9200.

U.S. Ambassador Designate in Bridgetown: Jeanette Hyde.

State Dept. Desk Officer: Andrew Siegel, 647-2130.

Commerce Dept. Desk Officer: Michelle Brooks, 482-2527.

Belarus
Ambassador: Serguei Nikolaevich MARTYNOV.
Chancery: 1619 New Hampshire Ave. N.W. 20009; 986-1604; fax, 986-1805.

U.S. Ambassador in Minsk: David H. Swartz.

State Dept. Desk Officer: Michael Snowden, 647-8671.

Belgium
Ambassador: Juan CASSIERS.
Chancery: 3330 Garfield St. N.W. 20008; 333-6900; fax, 333-3079.

U.S. Ambassador in Brussels: Alan J. Blinken.

State Dept. Desk Officer: Elisabeth Brocking, 647-6664.

Commerce Dept. Desk Officer: Simon Bensimon, 482-5401.

Belize

Ambassador: Dean R. LINDO.
Chancery: 2535 Massachusetts Ave. N.W. 20008; 332-9636; fax, 332-6888.

U.S. Ambassador in Belize City: Eugene L. Scassa.

State Dept. Desk Officer: John Connerley, 647-3381.

Commerce Dept. Desk Officer: Michelle Brooks, 482-2527.

Benin

Ambassador: Candide Pierre AHOUAN-SOU.
Chancery: 2737 Cathedral Ave. N.W. 20008; 232-6656; fax, 265-1996.

U.S. Ambassador in Cotonou: Ruth A. Davis.

State Dept. Desk Officer: Ann Syrett, 647-2637.

Commerce Dept. Desk Officer: Debra Henke, 482-5149.

Bhutan

State Dept. Desk Officer: Andrew Young, 647-1450.
Commerce Dept. Desk Officer: Timothy Gilman, 482-2954.

Bolivia

Chargé d'Affaires ad interim: Luis Fernando GONZALEZ-QUINTANILLA.
Chancery: 3014 Massachusetts Ave. N.W. 20008; 483-4410; fax, 328-3712.

U.S. Ambassador in La Paz: Charles R. Bowers.

State Dept. Desk Officer: Randolph Marcus, 647-3076.

Commerce Dept. Desk Officer: Rebecca Hunt, 482-2521.

Bosnia-Herzegovina

U.S. Chargé d'Affaires: Victor Jackovich (resident in Vienna, Austria).
State Dept. Desk Officer: Susan Bremner, 647-4138.

Botswana

Ambassador: Botsweletse Kingsley SEBELE.
Chancery: 3400 International Dr. N.W., #7M 20008; 244-4990; fax, 244-4164.

U.S. Ambassador in Gaborone: Howard F. Jeter.

State Dept. Desk Officer: Robert Jackson, 647-8252.

Commerce Dept. Desk Officer: Finn Holm-Olsen, 482-2521.

Brazil

Ambassador: Rubens RICUPERO.
Chancery: 3006 Massachusetts Ave. N.W. 20008; 745-2700; fax, 745-2827.

U.S. Ambassador in Brasilia: Melvyn Levitsky.

State Dept. Desk Officer: David Miller, 647-6541.

Commerce Dept. Desk Officer: Horace Jennings, 482-3872.

Brunei

Chargé d'Affaires ad interim: Janeh SUKAIMI.
Chancery: 2600 Virginia Ave. N.W., #300 20037; 342-0159; 342-0158.

U.S. Ambassador in Bandar Seri Begawan: Theresa A. Tull.

State Dept. Desk Officer: Nan Nida, 647-3278.

Commerce Dept. Desk Officer: Raphael Cung, 482-3647.

Bulgaria

Ambassador: Ognian Raytchev PISHEV.
Chancery: 1621 22nd St. N.W. 20008; 387-7969; fax, 234-7973.

U.S. Ambassador in Sofia: William D. Montgomery.

State Dept. Desk Officer: Andrew Chritton, 647-3187.

Commerce Dept. Desk Officer: Lynn Fabrizio, 482-4915.

Burkina Faso

Ambassador: Gaetan R. OUEDRAOGO.
Chancery: 2340 Massachusetts Ave. N.W. 20008; 332-5577.

U.S. Ambassador in Ouagadougou: Donald J. McConnell.

State Dept. Desk Officer: Geeta Pasi, 647-2865.

Commerce Dept. Desk Officer: Philip Michelini, 482-4388.

Burma
Ambassador: U THAUNG.
Chancery: 2300 S St. N.W. 20008; 332-9044.

U.S. Ambassador in Rangoon: Vacant.

State Dept. Desk Officer: Karl E. Wycoff, 647-7108.

Commerce Dept. Desk Officer: Jean Kelly, 482-3877.

Burundi
Ambassador: Julien KAVAKURE.
Chancery: 2233 Wisconsin Ave. N.W., #212 20007; 342-2574.

U.S. Ambassador in Bujumbura: Robert Krueger.

State Dept. Desk Officer: Kevin Aiston, 647-3139.

Commerce Dept. Desk Officer: Philip Michelini, 482-4388.

Cambodia
Permanent Mission of Cambodia to the United Nations, 820 2nd Ave., New York, NY 10017; (212) 697-2009. Thiounn PRASITH, permanent representative.

U.S. Ambassador in Phnom Penh: Charles H. Twining.

State Dept. Desk Officer: Daniel Shields, 647-3133.

Commerce Dept. Desk Officer: Hong-Phong B Pho, 482-3877.

Cameroon
Chargé d'Affaires ad interim: Pierre NDZENGUE.
Chancery: 2349 Massachusetts Ave. N.W. 20008; 265-8790.

U.S. Ambassador in Yaounde: Harriet W. Isom.

State Dept. Desk Officer: Steven Honley, 647-1707.

Commerce Dept. Desk Officer: Debra Henke, 482-5149.

Canada
Ambassador: Raymond CHRETIEN.
Chancery: 501 Pennsylvania Ave. N.W. 20001; 682-1740; fax, 682-7726.

U.S. Ambassador in Ottawa: James Johnston Blanchard.

State Dept. Desk Officer: James Hooper, 647-2170.

Commerce Dept. Desk Officer: Jonathan Doh, 482-3101.

Cape Verde, Republic of
Ambassador: Carlos Alberto Santos SILVA.
Chancery: 3415 Massachusetts Ave. N.W. 20007; 965-6820; fax, 965-1207.

U.S. Ambassador in Praia: Joseph M. Segars.

State Dept. Desk Officer: Herb Thomas, 647-3391.

Commerce Dept. Desk Officer: Philip Michelini, 482-4388.

Central African Republic
Ambassador: Jean-Pierre SOHAHONG-KOMBET.
Chancery: 1618 22nd St. N.W. 20008; 483-7800; fax, 332-9893.

U.S. Ambassador in Bangui: Robert E. Gribbin III.

State Dept. Desk Officer: Mary Grandfield, 647-3139.

Commerce Dept. Desk Officer: Philip Michelini, 482-4388.

Chad
Ambassador: Laoumaye Mekonyo KOUMBAIRIA.
Chancery: 2002 R St. N.W. 20009; 462-4009; fax, 265-1937.

U.S. Ambassador in N'Djamena: Laurence E. Pope II.

State Dept. Desk Officer: Mary Grandfield, 647-1704.

Commerce Dept. Desk Officer: Philip Michelini, 482-4388.

Chile
Ambassador: Patricio SILVA.
Chancery: 1732 Massachusetts Ave. N.W. 20036; 785-1746; fax, 887-5579.

U.S. Ambassador Designate in Santiago: Gabriel Guerra-Mondragon.

State Dept. Desk Officer: Alexander Featherstone, 647-2401.

Commerce Dept. Desk Officer: Roger Turner, 482-1495.

China, People's Republic of
Ambassador: LI Daoyu.
Chancery: 2300 Connecticut Ave. N.W. 20008; 328-2500.

U.S. Ambassador in Beijing: J. Stapleton Roy.

State Dept. Desk Officer: Don Keyser, 647-6300.

Commerce Dept. Desk Officer: Cheryl McQueen, 482-3932.

China (Taiwan) (See **Taiwan**)

Colombia
Ambassador: Gabriel SILVA.
Chancery: 2118 Leroy Place N.W. 20008; 387-8338; fax, 232-8643.

U.S. Ambassador in Bogota: Myles Robert Rene Frechette.

State Dept. Desk Officer: Anne Wells, 647-3023.

Commerce Dept. Desk Officer: Paul Moore, 482-1659.

Comoros
Ambassador Amini Ali MOUMIN.
Chancery (temp.): Permanent Mission of the Comoros to the United Nations, 336 E. 45th St., 2nd Floor, New York, NY 10017; (212) 972-8010; fax, (212) 983-4712.

Embassy in Moroni closed September 1993.

State Dept. Desk Officer: Oliver Griffith, 647-5684.

Commerce Dept. Desk Officer: Chandra Watkins, 482-4564.

Congo, Republic of the
Appointed Ambassador: Pierre Damien BOUSSOUKOU-BOUMBA.
Chancery: 4891 Colorado Ave. N.W. 20011; 726-0825; fax, 726-1860.

U.S. Ambassador in Brazzaville: William C. Ramsay.

State Dept. Desk Officer: Lori Magnusson, 647-3139.

Commerce Dept. Desk Officer: Debra Henke, 482-5149.

Costa Rica
Ambassador: Gonzalo J. FACIO.
Chancery: 2114 S St. N.W. 20008; 234-2945; fax, 265-4795.

U.S. Chargé d'Affaires in San Jose: Joseph Becelia.

State Dept. Desk Officer: Eric Farnsworth, 647-4980.

Commerce Dept. Desk Officer: Mark Siegelman, 482-5680.

Côte d'Ivoire
Ambassador: Charles GOMIS.
Chancery: 2424 Massachusetts Ave. N.W. 20008; 797-0300.

U.S. Ambassador in Abidjan: Hume A. Horan.

State Dept. Desk Officer: Ann Syrett, 647-2637.

Commerce Dept. Desk Officer: Philip Michelini, 482-4388.

Croatia
Ambassador: Peter A. SARCEVIC.
Chancery (temp.): 236 Massachusetts Ave. N.E. 20002; 543-5580.

U.S. Ambassador in Zagreb: Peter W. Galbraith.

State Dept. Desk Officer: Michael Hammer, 647-4138.

Cuba
Chancery: Cuba's interests in the United States are represented by Switzerland. The Cuban Interests Section is located at 2630 and 2639 16th St. N.W. 20009; 797-8518. Alfonso FRAGA PEREZ, counselor.

U.S. interests in Cuba are represented through the Swiss Embassy. Joseph G. Sullivan, U.S. principal officer in Havana.

State Dept. Desk Officer: Dennis Hays, 647-9272.

Cyprus
Ambassador: Andreas J. JACOVIDES.
Chancery: 2211 R St. N.W. 20008; 462-5772.

U.S. Ambassador Designate in Nicosia: Richard Boucher.

State Dept. Desk Officer: Joseph Merante, 647-6113.

Commerce Dept. Desk Officer: Ann Corro, 482-3945.

The Czech Republic
Ambassador: Michael ZANTOVSKY.
Chancery: 3900 Spring of Freedom St. N.W. 20008; 363-6315; fax, 966-8540.

U.S. Ambassador in Prague: Adrian A. Basora.

State Dept. Desk Officer: Tom Gibbon, 647-3187.

Commerce Dept. Desk Officer: Mark Mowrey, 482-4915.

Denmark
Ambassador: Peter P. DYVIG.
Chancery: 3200 Whitehaven St. N.W. 20008; 234-4300; fax, 328-1470.
U.S. Ambassador in Copenhagen: Richard B. Stone.
State Dept. Desk Officer: Richard Norland, 647-5669.
Commerce Dept. Desk Officer: Maryanne Kendall, 482-3254.

Djibouti, Republic of
Ambassador: Roble OLHAYE.
Chancery: 1156 15th St. N.W., #515 20005; 331-0270; fax, 331-0302.
U.S. Ambassador Designate in Djibouti: Martin L. Cheshes.
State Dept. Desk Officer: Ted Andrews, 647-7369.
Commerce Dept. Desk Officer: Chandra Watkins, 482-4564.

Dominica
Ambassador: Edward I. WATTY (resident in Dominica).
U.S. Ambassador Designate: Jeanette Hyde (resident in Bridgetown, Barbados).
State Dept. Desk Officer: Andrew Siegel, 647-2130.
Commerce Dept. Desk Officer: Michelle Brooks, 482-2527.

Dominican Republic
Ambassador: Jose del Carmen ARIZA.
Chancery: 1715 22nd St. N.W. 20008; 332-6280; fax, 265-8057.
U.S. Ambassador in Santo Domingo: Donna Jean Hrinak.
State Dept. Desk Officer: David Summers, 647-2620.
Commerce Dept. Desk Officer: Mark Siegelman, 482-5680.

Ecuador
Ambassador: Edgar TERAN-TERAN.
Chancery: 2535 15th St. N.W. 20009; 234-7200.
U.S. Ambassador in Quito: Peter Romero.

State Dept. Desk Officer: Edward Ramotowski, 647-3338.

Commerce Dept. Desk Officer: Paul Moore, 482-1659.

Egypt
Ambassador: Ahmed Maher El SAYED.
Chancery: 3522 International Court N.W. 20008; 895-5400; fax, 895-5497.
U.S. Ambassador in Cairo: Edward S. Walker Jr.
State Dept. Desk Officer: Richard H. Jones, 647-2365.
Commerce Dept. Desk Officer: Corey Wright, 482-1860.

El Salvador
Ambassador: Ana Christina SOL.
Chancery: 2308 California St. N.W. 20008; 265-9671.
U.S. Ambassador in San Salvador: Alan H. Flanigan.
State Dept. Desk Officers: Lari Martinez and Glenn Griffin, 647-3681.
Commerce Dept. Desk Officer: Helen Lee, 482-2528.

Equatorial Guinea
Ambassador: Damaso Obiang NDONG.
Chancery (temp.): 57 Magnolia Ave., Mount Vernon, NY 10553; (914) 738-9584; fax, (914) 667-6838.
U.S. Ambassador in Malabo: John E. Bennett.
State Dept. Desk Officer: Steven Honley, 647-3139.
Commerce Dept. Desk Officer: Philip Michelini, 482-4388.

Eritrea
Ambassador: Hagos GHEBREHIWET.
Chancery: 910 17th St. N.W., #400 20006; 429-1991; fax, 429-9004.
U.S. Ambassador in Asmara: Robert G. Houdek.
State Dept. Desk Officer: George Colvin, 647-6485.
Commerce Dept. Desk Officer: Chandra Watkins, 482-4564.

Estonia
Ambassador: Toomas Hendrik ILVES.
Chancery: 1030 15th St. N.W., #1000 20005, 789-0320; fax, 789-0471.

U.S. Ambassador in Tallinn: Robert C. Frasure.

State Dept. Desk Officer: Walter Andrusyszyn, 647-3188.

Ethiopia
Ambassador: Berhane GEBRE-CHRISTOS.
Chancery: 2134 Kalorama Rd. N.W. 20008; 234-2281; fax, 328-7950.

U.S. Ambassador in Addis Ababa: Irvin Hicks.

State Dept. Desk Officer: George Colvin, 647-8852.

Commerce Dept. Desk Officer: Chandra Watkins, 482-4564.

Fiji
Ambassador: Pita Kewa NACUVA.
Chancery: 2233 Wisconsin Ave. N.W., #240 20007; 337-8320; fax, 337-1996.

U.S. Ambassador in Suva: Vacant.

State Dept. Desk Officer: Edward Michael, 647-3546.

Finland
Ambassador: Jukka VALTASAARI.
Chancery: 3216 New Mexico Ave. N.W. 20016; 363-2430; fax, 363-8233.

U.S. Ambassador Designate in Helsinki: Derek Shearer.

State Dept. Desk Officer: Carolyn Johnson, 647-6071.

Commerce Dept. Desk Officer: Maryanne Kendall, 482-3254.

France
Ambassador: Jacques ANDREANI.
Chancery: 4101 Reservoir Rd. N.W. 20007; 944-6000.

U.S. Ambassador in Paris: Pamela C. Harriman.

State Dept. Desk Officer: Anne Carson, 647-2633.

Commerce Dept. Desk Officer: Elena Mikalis, 482-6008.

Gabon
Ambassador: Paul BOUNDOUKOU-LATHA.
Chancery: 2233 Wisconsin Ave. N.W., #200 20007; 797-1000.

U.S. Ambassador in Libreville: Joseph C. Wilson IV.

State Dept. Desk Officer: Lori Magnusson, 647-1707.

Commerce Dept. Desk Officer: Debra Henke, 482-5149.

Gambia, The
Ambassador: Ousman A. SALLAH.
Chancery: 1155 15th St. N.W., #1000 20005; 785-1399; fax, 785-1430.

U.S. Ambassador in Banjul: Andrew J. Winter.

State Dept. Desk Officer: Ray McGrath, 647-4567.

Commerce Dept. Desk Officer: Philip Michelini, 482-4388.

Georgia
Ambassador: Peter CHKHEIDZE.

Chancery: 1511 K St. N.W., #424 20005; 393-6060.

U.S. Ambassador in Tbilisi: Kent N. Brown.

State Dept. Desk Officer: Steve Carrig, 647-8671.

Germany, Federal Republic of
Ambassador: Immo STABREIT.
Chancery: 4645 Reservoir Rd. N.W. 20007; 298-4000; fax, 298-4249.

U.S. Ambassador in Bonn: Richard C. Holbrooke.

State Dept. Desk Officer: Craig Thielmann, 647-2005.

Commerce Dept. Desk Officer: John Larsen, 482-2435.

Ghana
Ambassador: Joseph L. S. ABBEY.
Chancery: 3512 International Dr. N.W. 20008; 686-4520; fax, 686-4527.

U.S. Ambassador in Accra: Kenneth L. Brown.

State Dept. Desk Officer: Herb Thomas, 647-3391.

Commerce Dept. Desk Officer: Debra Henke, 482-5149.

Greece
Ambassador: Loucas TSILAS.
Chancery: 2221 Massachusetts Ave. N.W. 20008; 939-5800; fax, 939-5824.

U.S. Ambassador in Athens: Thomas M. T. Niles.

State Dept. Desk Officer: William Schofield, 647-6113.

Commerce Dept. Desk Officer: Ann Corro, 482-3945.

Grenada
Ambassador: Denneth MODESTE.
Chancery: 1701 New Hampshire Ave. N.W. 20009; 265-2561.

U.S. Chargé d'Affaires in St. George's: Ollie P. Anderson Jr.

State Dept. Desk Officer: Andrew Siegel, 647-2130.

Commerce Dept. Desk Officer: Michelle Brooks, 482-2527.

Guatemala
Ambassador: Edmond MULET.
Chancery: 2220 R St. N.W. 20008; 745-4952; fax, 745-1908.

U.S. Ambassador in Guatemala City: Marilyn McAfee.

State Dept. Desk Officer: Charles Herrington, 647-1145.

Commerce Dept. Desk Officer: Helen Lee, 482-2528.

Guinea
Ambassador: Elhadj Boubacar BARRY.
Chancery: 2112 Leroy Place N.W. 20008; 483-9420; fax, 483-8688.

U.S. Ambassador in Conakry: Joseph A. Saloom III.

State Dept. Desk Officer: Gayleagha Brown, 647-2865.

Commerce Dept. Desk Officer: Philip Michelini, 482-4388.

Guinea-Bissau
Ambassador: Alfredo Lopes CABRAL.
Chancery: 918 16th St. N.W., Mezzanine Suite 20006; 872-4222; fax, 872-4226.

U.S. Ambassador in Bissau: Roger A. McGuire.

State Dept. Desk Officer: Herb Thomas, 647-3391.

Commerce Dept. Desk Officer: Philip Michelini, 482-4388.

Guyana
Ambassador: Odeen ISHMAEL.
Chancery: 2490 Tracy Place N.W. 20008; 265-6900.

U.S. Ambassador in Georgetown: George F. Jones.

State Dept. Desk Officer: Daniel Kiang, 647-2130.

Commerce Dept. Desk Officer: Michelle Brooks, 482-2527.

Haiti
Ambassador: Jean CASIMIR.
Chancery: 2311 Massachusetts Ave. N.W. 20008; 332-4090; fax, 745-7215.

U.S. Ambassador in Port-au-Prince: William Lacy Swing.

State Dept. Desk Officer: Ellen Engels, 647-4195.

Commerce Dept. Desk Officer: Mark Siegelman: 482-5680.

The Holy See
The Most Reverend Agostino CACCIA-VILLAN, apostolic pro-nuncio.
Office: 3339 Massachusetts Ave. N.W. 20008; 333-7121.

U.S. Ambassador in Vatican City: Raymond Flynn.

State Dept. Desk Officer: Edwin Nolan, 647-2453.

Honduras
Ambassador: Rene Arturo BENDANA-VALENZUELA.
Chancery: 3007 Tilden St. N.W. 20008; 966-7702; fax, 966-9751.

U.S. Ambassador in Tegucigalpa: William T. Pryce.

State Dept. Desk Officer: Kathleen Hennessey, 647-4980.

Commerce Dept. Desk Officer: Helen Lee, 482-2528.

Hungary
Ambassador: Pal TAR.
Chancery: 3910 Shoemaker St. N.W. 20008; 362-6730; fax, 966-8135.

U.S. Ambassador Designate in Budapest: Donald M. Blinken.

State Dept. Desk Officer: Jeff Levine, 647-3298.

Commerce Dept. Desk Officer: Brian Toohey, 482-4915.

Iceland
Ambassador: Einar BENEDIKTSSON.
Chancery: 2022 Connecticut Ave. N.W.
20008; 265-6653; fax, 265-6656.
Kendall, 482-3254.

U.S. Ambassador in Reykjavik: Parker W. Borg.

State Dept. Desk Officer: Elisabeth Brocking, 647-6664.

Commerce Dept. Desk Officer: Maryanne Kendall, 482-3254.

India
Ambassador: Siddhartha S. RAY.
Chancery: 2107 Massachusetts Ave. N.W.
20008; 939-7000.

U.S. Ambassador Designate in New Delhi: Frank G. Wisner.

State Dept. Desk Officer: Steve Blake, 647-2141.

Commerce Dept. Desk Officer: John Crown, 482-2954.

Indonesia
Ambassador: Arifin Mohamad SIREGAR.
Chancery: 2020 Massachusetts Ave. N.W.
20036; 775-5200; fax, 775-5365.

U.S. Ambassador in Jakarta: Robert L. Barry.

State Dept. Desk Officer: Karen Brown, 647-3277.

Commerce Dept. Desk Officer: Karen Goddin, 482-3877.

Iran
Chancery: Iran's interests in the United States are represented by Pakistan.
An Iranian Interests Section is located at 2209 Wisconsin Ave. N.W. 20007; 965-4990.

U.S. interests in Iran are represented through the Swiss Embassy in Tehran.

State Dept. Desk Officer: Christopher Henzel, 647-6111.

Commerce Dept. Desk Officer: Paul Thanos, 482-1860.

Iraq
Chancery: Iraq's interests in the United States are represented by Algeria.
An Iraqi Interests Section is located at 1801 P St. N.W. 20036; 483-7500; fax, 462-5066.
Embassy in Baghdad temporarily closed.

State Dept. Desk Officers: Stephen Kimmel and Angela Dickey, 647-5692.

Commerce Dept. Desk Officer: Paul Thanos, 482-1860.

Ireland
Ambassador: Dermot A. GALLAGHER.
Chancery: 2234 Massachusetts Ave. N.W.
20008; 462-3939.

U.S. Ambassador in Dublin: Jean Kennedy Smith.

State Dept. Desk Officer: David Schafer, 647-5669.

Commerce Dept. Desk Officer: Boyce Fitzpatrick, 482-2177.

Israel
Ambassador: Itamar RABINOVICH.
Chancery: 3514 International Dr. N.W.
20008; 364-5500; fax, 364-5610.

U.S. Ambassador Designate in Tel Aviv: Edward Djerejian.

State Dept. Desk Officer: Thomas Miller, 647-3672.

Commerce Dept. Desk Officer: Paul Thanos, 482-1860.

Italy
Ambassador: Boris BIANCHERI.
Chancery: 1601 Fuller St. N.W. 20009; 328-5500.

U.S. Ambassador in Rome: Reginald Bartholomew.

State Dept. Desk Officer: Alexander Karagiannis, 647-2453.

Commerce Dept. Desk Officer: Boyce Fitzpatrick, 482-2177.

Jamaica
Ambassador: Richard Leighton BERNAL.
Chancery: 1850 K St. N.W., #355 20006; 452-0660; fax, 452-0081.

U.S. Ambassador in Kingston: Vacant.

State Dept. Desk Officer: Stephen Pattison, 647-2621.

Commerce Dept. Desk Officer: Mark Siegelman, 482-5680.

Japan
Ambassador: Takakazu KURIYAMA.
Chancery: 2520 Massachusetts Ave. N.W.
20008; 939-6700; fax, 328-2187.
482-2425.

U.S. Ambassador in Tokyo: Walter F. Mondale.

State Dept. Desk Officer: Steve Ecton, 647-3152.

Commerce Dept. Desk Officer: Ed Leslie, 482-2425.

Jordan
Ambassador: Fayez A. TARAWNEH.
Chancery: 3504 International Dr. N.W. 20008; 966-2664; fax, 966-3110.

U.S. Ambassador Designate in Amman: Wesley W. Egan Jr.

State Dept. Desk Officer: Roberta Newell, 647-1022.

Commerce Dept. Desk Officer: Paul Thanos, 482-1860.

Kampuchea (See **Cambodia**)

Kazakhstan
Ambassador: Alim SH. DJAMBOURCHINE.
Chancery (temp.): 3421 Massachusetts Ave. N.W. 20008; 333-4504; fax, 333-4509.

U.S. Ambassador in Almaty: William H. Courtney.

State Dept. Desk Officer: Jason Hyland, 647-8956.

Kenya
Ambassador: Denis D. AFANDE.
Chancery: 2249 R St. N.W. 20008; 387-6101.

U.S. Ambassador in Nairobi: Aurelia Brazeal.

State Dept. Desk Officer: Chris Wilson, 647-5684.

Commerce Dept. Desk Officer: Chandra Watkins, 482-4564.

Kiribati
U.S. Ambassador: Michael W. Marine (resident in Suva, Fiji).

State Dept. Desk Officer: Edward Michael, 647-3546.

Korea, Democratic People's Republic (North)
Permanent Mission of North Korea to the United Nations, 225 E. 86th St., New York, NY 10028; (212) 722-3536. Pak GIL YON, ambassador.

State Dept. Desk Officer: David Brown, 647-7717.

Korea, Republic of (South)
Ambassador: Seung-Soo HAN.
Chancery: 2450 Massachusetts Ave. N.W. 20008; 939-5600.

U.S. Ambassador in Seoul: James T. Laney.

State Dept. Desk Officer: David Brown, 647-7717.

Commerce Dept. Desk Officer: Jeffrey Donius, 482-4390.

Kuwait
Ambassador: Mohammed Sabah Al-Salim AL-SABAH.
Chancery: 2940 Tilden St. N.W. 20008; 966-0702; fax, 966-0517.

U.S. Ambassador in Kuwait City: Ryan Clark Crocker.

State Dept. Desk Officer: Ethan Goldrich, 647-6562.

Commerce Dept. Desk Officer: Corey Wright, 482-5506.

Kyrgyzstan
Ambassador: Roza OTUNBAYEVA.
Chancery (temp.): 1511 K St. N.W., #705 20005; 347-3732; fax, 347-3718.

U.S. Ambassador in Bishkek: Edward Hurwitz.

State Dept. Desk Officer: Jason Hyland, 647-8956.

Laos
Ambassador: Hiem PHOMMACHANH.
Chancery: 2222 S St. N.W. 20008; 332-6416; fax, 332-4923.

U.S. Ambassador in Vientiane: Victor L. Tomseth.

State Dept. Desk Officer: Cheryl Sim, 647-3133.

Commerce Dept. Desk Officer: Hong-Phong B Pho, 482-3877.

Latvia
Ambassador: Ojars Eriks KALNINS.
Chancery: 4325 17th St. N.W. 20011; 726-8213.

U.S. Ambassador in Riga: Ints M. Silins.

State Dept. Desk Officer: Walter Andrusyszyn, 647-3188.

U.S. State Department Contacts
for Nonsovereign Regions

The U.S. State Department assigns desk officers to monitor affairs in the following nonsovereign territories, islands, and regions.

Territory, Island, or Region	Desk Officer	Phone
Anguilla	Andrew Siegel	647-2130
Aruba	Sandra Stevens	647-2621
Bermuda	Barbara Stephenson	647-8027
British Indian Ocean Territory	Oliver Griffith	647-5684
British Virgin Islands	Stephen Pattison	647-2621
Cayman Islands	Stephen Pattison	647-2621
Cook Island	Edward Michael	647-3546
Diego Garcia	Oliver Griffith	647-5864
Freely Associated States	Lynne Lambert	647-0108
French Antilles (French Guiana)	Nancy Jackson	647-2130
French Polynesia	Edward Michael	647-3546
Guadeloupe	Nancy Jackson	647-2130
Hong Kong	Diane Kelly	647-6796
Macao	Diane Kelly	047-C70C
Martinique	Nancy Jackson	647-2620
Montserrat	Andrew Siegel	647-2130
Netherlands Antilles	Sandra Stevens	647-2621
New Caledonia	Edward Michael	647-3546
Niue	Edward Michael	647-3546
Northern Ireland	David Schafer	647-5669
Palau	Lynne Lambert	647-0108
Palestine	Traci Dougherty	647-1096
Puerto Rico	David Summers	647-2620
Scotland	Barbara Stephenson	647-8027
Tahiti	Edward Michael	647-3546
Tokelau	Edward Michael	647-3546
Turks and Caicos	Stephen Pattison	647-2621
U.S. Virgin Islands	David Summers	647-2620
Wallis and Futuna	Edward Michael	647-3546
Western Sahara	Gayleagha Brown	647-2865

Lebanon

Ambassador: Simon Massoud KARAM.
Chancery: 2560 28th St. N.W. 20008; 939-6300; fax, 939-6324.

U.S. Ambassador in Beirut: Mark G. Hambley.

State Dept. Desk Officer: Juan Alsace, 647-1030.

Commerce Dept. Desk Officer: Thomas Sams, 482-1860.

Lesotho

Ambassador: Teboho E. KITLELI
Chancery: 2511 Massachusetts Ave. N.W. 20008; 797-5533; fax, 234-6815.

U.S. Ambassador in Maseru: Vacant.

State Dept. Desk Officer: Robert Jackson, 647-8252.

Commerce Dept. Desk Officer: Finn Holm-Olsen, 482-4228.

Liberia
Chargé d'Affaires ad interim: Konah K. BLACKETT.
Chancery: 5201 16th St. N.W. 20011; 723-0437.
U.S. Ambassador in Monrovia: Vacant.
State Dept. Desk Officer: William Jackson, 647-3395.
Commerce Dept. Desk Officer: Philip Michelini, 482-4388.

Libya
State Dept. Desk Officer: David Setter, 647-4674.
Commerce Dept. Desk Officer: Claude Clement, 482-1860.

Liechtenstein
Chancery: Liechtenstein's interests in the United States are represented by Switzerland, 2900 Cathedral Ave. N.W. 20008; 745-7900; fax, 387-2564.
U.S. interests in Liechtenstein are represented by the U.S. Consulate in Zurich, Switzerland. Sheldon I. Krebs, U.S. consul general.
State Dept. Desk Officer: Deborah Kavin, 647-2005.

Lithuania
Ambassador: Stasys LOZORAITIS.
Chancery: 2622 16th St. N.W. 20009; 234-5860; fax, 328-0466.
U.S. Ambassador in Vilnius: Darryl N. Johnson.
State Dept. Desk Officer: Walter Andrusyszyn, 647-3188.

Luxembourg
Ambassador: Alphonse BERNS.
Chancery: 2200 Massachusetts Ave. N.W. 20008; 265-4171; fax, 328-8270.
U.S. Ambassador in Luxembourg: Edward M. Rowell.
State Dept. Desk Officer: Garold Larson, 647-6664.

Commerce Dept. Desk Officer: Simon Bensimon, 482-5401.

Macedonia, Former Yugoslav Republic of
State Dept. Desk Officer: Monique Quesada, 647-4138.

Madagascar
Ambassador: Pierrot J. RAJAONARIVELO.
Chancery: 2374 Massachusetts Ave. N.W. 20008; 265-5525.
U.S. Ambassador in Antananarivo: Dennis P. Barrett.
State Dept. Desk Officer: Oliver Griffith, 647-5684.
Commerce Dept. Desk Officer: Chandra Watkins, 482-4564.

Malawi
Ambassador: Robert B. MBAYA.
Chancery: 2408 Massachusetts Ave. N.W. 20008; 797-1007.
U.S. Ambassador in Lilongwe: Peter R. Chaveas.
State Dept. Desk Officer: Philip Egger, 647-8433.
Commerce Dept. Desk Officer: Finn Holm-Olsen, 482-4228.

Malaysia
Ambassador: Dato ABDUL MAJID.
Chancery: 2401 Massachusetts Ave. N.W. 20008; 328-2700; fax, 483-7661.
U.S. Ambassador in Kuala Lumpur: John S. Wolf.
State Dept. Desk Officer: John Heffern, 647-3278.
Commerce Dept. Desk Officer: Raphael Cung, 482-3647.

Maldives, Republic of
Permanent Mission of the Republic of the Maldives to the United Nations, 2 United Nations Plaza, New York, NY 10017; (212) 599-6195. Ambassador: Ahmad RASHEED.
U.S. Ambassador: Steven R. Mann (resident in Colombo, Sri Lanka).
State Dept. Desk Officer: Alison Krupnick, 647-2351.
Commerce Dept. Desk Officer: John Simmons, 482-2954.

Mali
Ambassador: Siragatou Ibrahim CISSE.
Chancery: 2130 R St. N.W. 20008; 332-2249.
U.S. Ambassador in Bamako: William H. Dameron III.
State Dept. Desk Officer: Getta Pasi, 647-2865.
Commerce Dept. Desk Officer: Philip Michelini, 482-4388.

Malta
Ambassador: Albert BORG OLIVIER DE PUGET.
Chancery: 2017 Connecticut Ave. N.W. 20008; 462-3611; fax, 387-5470.
U.S. Ambassador Designate in Valletta: Joseph R. Paolino Jr.
State Dept. Desk Officer: Edwin Nolan, 647-2453.
Commerce Dept. Desk Officer: Robert McLaughlin, 482-3748.

Marshall Islands
Ambassador: Wilfred I. KENDALL.
Chancery: 2433 Massachusetts Ave. N.W. 20008; 234-5414; fax, 232-3236.
U.S. Ambassador in Majuro: David C. Fields.
State Dept. Desk Officer: Hollis Summers, 647-0108.

Mauritania
Ambassador: Mohamed Fall AININA.
Chancery: 2129 Leroy Place N.W. 20008; 232-5700.
U.S. Ambassador Designate in Nouakchott: Dorothy Myers Sampas.
State Dept. Desk Officer: Gayleagha Brown, 647-2865.
Commerce Dept. Desk Officer: Philip Michelini, 482-4388.

Mauritius
Ambassador: Anund Priyay NEEWOOR.
Chancery: 4301 Connecticut Ave. N.W., #441 20008; 244-1491; fax, 966-0983.
U.S. Ambassador in Port Louis: Leslie Alexander.
State Dept. Desk Officer: Oliver Griffith, 647-5684.
Commerce Dept. Desk Officer: Chandra Watkins, 482-4564.

Mexico
Ambassador: Jorge MONTANO.
Chancery: 1911 Pennsylvania Ave. N.W. 20006; 728-1600.
U.S. Ambassador in Mexico City: James R. Jones.
State Dept. Desk Officer: Robert Felder, 647-9894.
Commerce Dept. Desk Officer: Rebecca Banister, 482-0300.

Micronesia
Ambassador: Jesse B. MAREHALAU.
Chancery: 1725 N St. N.W. 20036; 223-4383; fax, 223-4391.
U.S. Ambassador Designate in Kolonia: March Fong Eu.
State Dept. Desk Officer: Hollis Summers, 647-0108.

Moldova
U.S. Ambassador in Chisinau: Mary C. Pendleton.
State Dept. Desk Officer: Steve Carrig, 647-0071.

Monaco
Monaco's foreign affairs interests are represented by France.
Monacoan Consul: Francis W. CRESCI, 845 3rd Ave., New York, NY 10022; (212) 759-5227.
Relations with Monaco are maintained by the U.S. Embassy in Paris, France. Pamela C. Harriman, U.S. Ambassador.
State Dept. Desk Officer: Anne Carson, 647-2633.

Mongolia
Ambassador: Luvsandorj DAWAGIV.
Chancery: 2833 M St. N.W. 20007; 333-7117; fax, 298-9227.
U.S. Ambassador in Ulaanbaatar: Donald C. Johnson.
State Dept. Desk Officer: Aubrey A. Carlson, 647-9141.
Commerce Dept. Desk Officer: Sheila Baker, 482-3932.

Morocco
Ambassador: Mohamed BENAISSA.
Chancery: 1601 21st St. N.W. 20009; 462-7979; fax, 265-0161.

U.S. Ambassador Designate in Rabat: Marc Charles Ginsburg.

State Dept. Desk Officer: Edward Vazquez, 647-4675.

Commerce Dept. Desk Officer: Claude Clement, 482-1860.

Mozambique
Ambassador: Hipolito Pereira Zozimo PATRICIO.

Chancery: 1990 M St. N.W., #570 20036; 293-7146; fax, 835-0245.

U.S. Ambassador in Maputo: Dennis Coleman Jett.

State Dept. Desk Officer: Chris Richey, 647-8252.

Commerce Dept. Desk Officer: Finn Holm-Olsen, 482-4228.

Namibia
Ambassador: Tuliameni KALOMOH.

Chancery: 1605 New Hampshire Ave. N.W. 20009; 986-0540; fax, 986-0443.

U.S. Ambassador in Windhoek: Marshall F. McCallie.

State Dept. Desk Officer: Alan Yu, 647-9429.

Commerce Dept. Desk Officer: Finn Holm-Olsen, 482-4228.

Nauru
U.S. Ambassador: Edward Perkins (resident in Canberra, Australia).

State Dept. Desk Officer: Edward Michael, 647-3546.

Nepal
Ambassador: Yog Prasad UPADHYAY.

Chancery: 2131 Leroy Place N.W. 20008; 667-4550.

U.S. Ambassador Designate in Kathmandu: Sandra L. Vogelgesang.

State Dept. Desk Officer: Denise Valois, 647-2351.

Commerce Dept. Desk Officer: Timothy Gilman, 482-2954.

Netherlands
Ambassador: Adriaan Pieter Roetert JACOBOVITS DE SZEGED.

Chancery: 4200 Linnean Ave. N.W. 20008; 244-5300; fax, 362-3430.

U.S. Ambassador in The Hague: Vacant.

State Dept. Desk Officer: Garold Larson, 647-6664.

Commerce Dept. Desk Officer: Simon Bensimon, 482-5401.

New Zealand
Ambassador: Denis Bazeley Gordon MC-LEAN.

Chancery: 37 Observatory Circle N.W. 20008; 328-4800.

U.S. Ambassador Designate in Wellington: Josiah Beeman.

State Dept. Desk Officer: Gus Recinos, 647-9691.

Commerce Dept. Desk Officer: Gary Bouck, 482-2471.

Nicaragua
Ambassador: Roberto Genaro MAYORGA-CORTES.

Chancery: 1627 New Hampshire Ave. N.W. 20009; 939-6570.

U.S. Ambassador in Managua: John F. Maisto.

State Dept. Desk Officer: Carl Schonander, 647-2205.

Commerce Dept. Desk Officer: Jay Dowling, 482-1648.

Niger
Ambassador: Adamou SEYDOU.

Chancery: 2204 R St. N.W. 20008; 483-4224.

U.S. Ambassador in Niamey: John S. Davison.

State Dept. Desk Officer: Getta Pasi, 647-2865.

Commerce Dept. Desk Officer: Philip Michelini, 482-4388.

Nigeria
Ambassador: Zubair Mahmud KAZAURE.

Chancery: 1333 16th St. N.W. 20036; 986-8400.

U.S. Ambassador in Lagos: Walter C Carrington.

State Dept. Desk Officer: Timothy An drews, 647-4567.

Commerce Dept. Desk Officer: Debr Henke, 482-5149.

Norway
Ambassador: Kjeld VIBE.
Chancery: 2720 34th St. N.W. 20008; 333-6000; fax, 337-0870.

U.S. Ambassador in Oslo: Thomas Loftus.

State Dept. Desk Officer: Richard Norlan, 647-5669.

Commerce Dept. Desk Officer: James Devlin, 482-4414.

Oman
Chargé d'Affaires ad interim: Riyadh MACKI.
Chancery: 2535 Belmont Rd. N.W. 20008; 387-1980; fax, 745-4933.

U.S. Ambassador in Muscat: David J. Dunford.

State Dept. Desk Officer: David Young, 647-6558.

Commerce Dept. Desk Officer: Paul Thanos, 482-1860.

Pakistan
Ambassador: Maleeha LODHI.
Chancery: 2315 Massachusetts Ave. N.W. 20008; 939-6200; fax, 387-0484.

U.S. Ambassador in Islamabad: John C. Monjo.

State Dept. Desk Officer: Francisco Gonzalez, 647-9823.

Commerce Dept. Desk Officer: Timothy Gilman, 482-2954.

Panama
Ambassador: Jaime FORD Boyd.
Chancery: 2862 McGill Terrace N.W. 20008; 483-1407.

U.S. Ambassador designate in Panama City: Robert A. Pastor.

State Dept. Desk Officer: Georgia T. Wright, 647-4986.

Commerce Dept. Desk Officer: Helen Lee, 482-2528.

Papua New Guinea
Ambassador: Margaret TAYLOR.
Chancery: 1615 New Hampshire Ave. N.W., 3rd Floor 20009; 745-3680; fax, 745-3679.

U.S. Ambassador in Port Moresby: Richard W. Teare.

State Dept. Desk Officer: Edward Michael, 647-3546.

Paraguay
Ambassador: Juan Esteban AGUIRRE.
Chancery: 2400 Massachusetts Ave. N.W. 20008; 483-6960; fax, 234-4508.

U.S. Ambassador in Asunción: Vacant.

State Dept. Desk Officer: Sandy Campbell, 647-2296.

Commerce Dept. Desk Officer: Randy Mye, 482-1548.

Peru
Ambassador: Ricardo V. LUNA.
Chancery: 1700 Massachusetts Ave. N.W. 20036; 833-9860; fax, 659-8124.

U.S. Ambassador in Lima: Alvin Adams Jr.

State Dept. Desk Officer: Bruce Williamson, 647-3360.

Commerce Dept. Desk Officer: Rebecca Hunt, 482-2521.

Philippines
Ambassador: Raul Ch. RABE.
Chancery: 1600 Massachusetts Ave. N.W. 20036; 467-9300; fax, 328-7614.

U.S. Ambassador in Manila: John C. Negroponte.

State Dept. Desk Officer: W. Scott Butcher, 647-1222.

Commerce Dept. Desk Officer: George Paine, 482-3877.

Poland
Chargé d'Affaires ad interim: Maciej KOZLOWSKI.
Chancery: 2640 16th St. N.W. 20009; 234-3800; fax, 328-6271.

U.S. Ambassador Designate in Warsaw: Nicholas Rey.

State Dept. Desk Officer: John Boris, 647-4138.

Commerce Dept. Desk Officer: Mark Mowrey, 482-4915.

Portugal
Ambassador: Francisco Jose Laco Treichler KNOPFLI.
Chancery: 2125 Kalorama Rd. N.W. 20008; 328-8610; fax, 462-3726.

U.S. Ambassador designate in Lisbon: Elizabeth Bagley.

State Dept. Desk Officer: Mark Davison, 647-1412.

Commerce Dept. Desk Officer: Mary Beth Double, 482-4508.

Qatar
Ambassador: Sheikh Abdulrahman bin Saud AL-THANI.
Chancery: 600 New Hampshire Ave. N.W., #1180 20037; 338-0111.
U.S. Ambassador in Doha: Kenton W. Keith.
State Dept. Desk Officer: Daniel Goodspeed, 647-6572.
Commerce Dept. Desk Officer: Paul Thanos, 482-1860.

Romania
Ambassador: Aurel-Dragos MUNTEANU.
Chancery: 1607 23rd St. N.W. 20008; 332-4846; fax, 232-4748.
U.S. Ambassador in Bucharest: John R. Davis, Jr.
State Dept. Desk Officer: Brady Kiesling, 647-3187.
Commerce Dept. Desk Officer: Lynn Fabrizio, 482-4915.

Russia
Ambassador: Vladimir Petrovich LUKIN.
Chancery: 1125 16th St. N.W. 20036; 628-7551.
U.S. Ambassador in Moscow: Thomas R. Pickering.
State Dept. Desk Officer: Larry C. Napper, 647-9806.
Commerce Dept. Desk Officer: Lynn Fabrizio, 482-0988.

Rwanda
Ambassador: Aloys UWIMANA.
Chancery: 1714 New Hampshire Ave. N.W. 20009; 232-2882; fax, 232-4544.
U.S. embassy in Kigali closed temporarily.
State Dept. Desk Officer: Kevin Aiston, 647-3139.
Commerce Dept. Desk Officer: Philip Michelini, 482-4388.

St. Kitts and Nevis
Chargé d'Affaires ad interim: Aubrey Eric HART.

Chancery: 2100 M St. N.W., #608 20037; 833-3550; fax, 833-3553.
U.S. Chargé d'Affaires: Bryant J. Salter (resident in St. Johns, Antigua).
State Dept. Desk Officer: Andrew Siegel, 647-2130.
Commerce Dept. Desk Officer: Michelle Brooks, 482-2527.

Saint Lucia
Ambassador: Joseph Edsel EDMUNDS.
Chancery: 2100 M St. N.W., #309 20037; 463-7378; fax, 887-5746.
U.S. Ambassador Designate: Jeanette Hyde (resident in Bridgetown, Barbados).
State Dept. Desk Officer: Andrew Siegel, 647-2130.
Commerce Dept. Desk Officer: Michelle Brooks, 482-2527.

Saint Vincent and the Grenadines
Ambassador: Kingsley C. A. LAYNE.
Chancery: 1717 Massachusetts Ave. N.W., #102 20036; 462-7806; fax, 462-7807.
U.S. Ambassador Designate: Jeanette Hyde (resident in Bridgetown, Barbados).
State Dept. Desk Officer: Andrew Siegel, 647-2130.
Commerce Dept. Desk Officer: Michelle Brooks, 482-2527.

Samoa (See **Western Samoa**)

San Marino
Consul General: Baron Enrico di PORTINOVA.
Consulate: 1899 L St. N.W. 20036; 223-3517.
Diplomatic relations with San Marino are maintained by the U.S. Consulate in Florence, Italy. Sue H. Patterson, U.S. consul general.
State Dept. Desk Officer: Edwin Nolan, 647-2453.

Sao Tome and Principe
Chargé d'affaires: Domingos FERREIRA.
Chancery (temp.): Permanent Mission of Sao Tome and Principe to the United Nations, 801 2nd Ave., New York, NY 10017 (212) 697-4211.
U.S. Ambassador to Sao Tome and Principe Joseph C. Wilson IV (resident in Libreville Gabon).

State Dept. Desk Officer: Lori Magnusson, 647-1707.

Commerce Dept. Desk Officer: Philip Michelini, 482-4388.

Saudi Arabia
Ambassador: Prince Bandar BIN SULTAN.
Chancery: 601 New Hampshire Ave. N.W. 20037; 342-3800.

U.S. Ambassador designate in Riyadh: Raymond Edwin Mabus Jr.

State Dept. Desk Officer: Les Hickman, 647-7550.

Commerce Dept. Desk Officer: Christopher Cerone, 482-1860.

Senegal
Appointed Ambassador: Mamadou Mansour SECK.
Chancery: 2112 Wyoming Ave. N.W. 20008; 234-0540.

U.S. Ambassador in Dakar: Mark Johnson.

State Dept. Desk Officer: Gayleagha Brown, 647-2865.

Serbia-Montenegro
Chargé d'Affaires ad interim: Rudolf PERINE.
Chancery: 2410 California St. N.W. 20008; 462-6566.

U.S. Ambassador in Belgrade: Vacant.

State Dept. Desk Officer: Stuart Jones, 647-4138.

Seychelles
Ambassador: Marc Michael MARENGO.
Chancery (temp.): Permanent Mission of Seychelles to the United Nations, 820 2nd Ave., #900F New York, NY 10017; (212) 687-9766; fax, (212) 922-9177.

U.S. Ambassador designate in Victoria: Carl B. Stokes.

State Dept. Desk Officer: Oliver Griffith, 647-8852.

Commerce Dept. Desk Officer: Chandra Watkins, 482-4564.

Sierra Leone
Ambassador: Thomas Kahota KARGBO.
Chancery: 1701 19th St. N.W. 20009; 939-9261.

U.S. Ambassador in Freetown: Lauralee M. Peters.

State Dept. Desk Officer: Ray McGrath, 647-4567.

Commerce Dept. Desk Officer: Philip Michelini, 482-4388.

Singapore
Ambassador: S. R. NATHAN.
Chancery: 3501 International Place N.W. 20008; 537-3100; fax, 537-0876.

U.S. Ambassador Designate in Singapore: Timothy A. Chorba.

State Dept. Desk Officer: Nan Nida, 647-3278.

Commerce Dept. Desk Officer: Raphael Cung, 482-3647.

The Slovak Republic
Chargé d'Affaires ad interim: Peter BURIAN.
Chancery (temp.): 2201 Wisconsin Ave. N.W., #380 20007; 965-5161; fax, 965-5166.

U.S. Ambassador Designate in Bratislava: Theodore E. Russell.

State Dept. Desk Officer: Tom Gibbon, 647-3187.

Commerce Dept. Desk Officer: Mark Mowrey, 482-4915.

Slovenia
Ambassador: Ernest PETRIC.
Chancery (temp.): 1300 19th St. N.W., #410 20036; 667-5363.

U.S. Ambassador in Ljubljana: E. Allan Wendt.

State Dept. Desk Officer: Marc Norman, 647-4138.

Solomon Islands
Ambassador: Francis BUGOTU.
Chancery (temp.): Permanent Mission of the Solomon Islands to the United Nations, 820 2nd Ave., New York, NY 10017; (212) 599-6193.

Embassy in Honiara closed July 1993.

State Dept. Desk Officer: Edward Michael, 647-3546.

Somalia
Somali embassy ceased operations May 8, 1991.

U.S. embassy in Mogadishu is unstaffed.

State Dept. Desk Officer: Ted Andrews, 647-7369.

Commerce Dept. Desk Officer: Chandra Watkins, 482-4564.

South Africa
Ambassador: Harry Heinz SCHWARZ.
Chancery: 3051 Massachusetts Ave. N.W. 20008; 232-4400.
U.S. Ambassador in Pretoria: Princeton N. Lyman.
State Dept. Desk Officer: Susan Keogh-Fisher, 647-8432.
Commerce Dept. Desk Officer: Emily Solomon, 482-5148.

Spain
Ambassador: Jaime de OJEDA.
Chancery: 2700 15th St. N.W. 20009; 265-0190.
U.S. Ambassador in Madrid: Richard Gardner.
State Dept. Desk Officer: Sherwood McGinnis, 647-1412.
Commerce Dept. Desk Officer: Mary Beth Double, 482-4508.

Sri Lanka
Ambassador: Ananda W. P. GURUGE.
Chancery: 2148 Wyoming Ave. N.W. 20008; 483-4025; fax, 232-7181.
U.S. Ambassador in Colombo: Teresita C. Schaffer.
State Dept. Desk Officer: Alison Krupnick, 647-2351.
Commerce Dept. Desk Officer: John Simmons, 482-2954.

Sudan
Ambassador: Ahmed SULIMAN.
Chancery: 2210 Massachusetts Ave. N.W. 20008; 338-8565; fax, 667-2406.
U.S. Ambassador in Khartoum: Donald K. Petterson.
State Dept. Desk Officer: Joe Fishbein, 647-8852.
Commerce Dept. Desk Officer: Chandra Watkins, 482-4564.

Suriname
Ambassador: Willem A. UDENHOUT.
Chancery: 4301 Connecticut Ave. N.W., #108 20008; 244-7488; fax, 244-5878.
U.S. Ambassador in Paramaribo: John P. Leonard.

State Dept. Desk Officer: Sandra Stevens, 647-2620.
Commerce Dept. Desk Officer: Michelle Brooks, 482-2527.

Swaziland
Ambassador: Absalom Vusani MAMBA.
Chancery: 3400 International Dr. N.W. 20008; 362-6683; fax, 244-8059.
U.S. Ambassador in Mbabane: Stephen H. Rogers.
State Dept. Desk Officer: Robert Jackson, 647-8252.
Commerce Dept. Desk Officer: Finn Holm-Olsen, 482-4228.

Sweden
Ambassador: Carl Henrik SIHVER LILJE-GREN.
Chancery: 600 New Hampshire Ave. N.W., #1200 20037; 944-5600; fax, 342-1319.
U.S. Ambassador Designate in Stockholm: Thomas L. Siebert.
State Dept. Desk Officer: Carolyn Johnson, 647-6071.
Commerce Dept. Desk Officer: James Devlin, 482-4414.

Switzerland
Ambassador: Carlo JAGMETTI.
Chancery: 2900 Cathedral Ave. N.W. 20008; 745-7900; fax, 387-2564.
U.S. Ambassador in Bern: M. Larry Lawrence.
State Dept. Desk Officer: Deborah Kavin, 647-2005.
Commerce Dept. Desk Officer: Philip Combs, 482-2920.

Syria
Ambassador: Walid AL-MOUALEM.
Chancery: 2215 Wyoming Ave. N.W. 20008; 232-6313; fax, 234-9548.
U.S. Ambassador in Damascus: Christopher W. S. Ross.
State Dept. Desk Officer: Liane Dorsey, 647-1131.
Commerce Dept. Desk Officer: Corey Wright, 482-5506.

Taiwan
Representation maintained by the Coordination Council for North American Af-

fairs, 4201 Wisconsin Ave. N.W. 20016; 895-1800.

The United States maintains unofficial relations with Taiwan through the American Institute in Taiwan. Washington office: 1700 N. Moore St., Arlington, VA 22209-1996; (703) 525-8474; Natale H. Bellocchi, managing director.

State Dept. Desk Officer (Coordination Staff): Joseph Borich, 647-7711.

Commerce Dept. Desk Officer: Robert Chu, 482-4390.

Tajikistan

U.S. Ambassador in Dushanbe: Stanley T. Escudero.

State Dept. Desk Officer: Lowry Taylor, 647-8956.

Tanzania

Ambassador: Charles Musama NYIRABU. Chancery: 2139 R St. N.W. 20008; 939-6125; fax, 797-7408.

U.S. Ambassador Designate in Dar Es Salaam: Brady Anderson.

State Dept. Desk Officer: Oliver Griffith, 647-5684.

Commerce Dept. Desk Officer: Finn Holm-Olsen, 482-4228.

Thailand

Ambassador: M. L. Birabhongse KASEMSRI. Chancery: 2300 Kalorama Rd. N.W. 20008; 483-7200; fax, 234-4498.

U.S. Ambassador in Bangkok: David F. Lambertson.

State Dept. Desk Officer: Karl E. Wycoff, 647-7108.

Commerce Dept. Desk Officer: Jean Kelly, 482-3877.

Togo

Ambassador: Edem Frederic HEGBE. Chancery: 2208 Massachusetts Ave. N.W. 20008; 234-4212; fax, 232-3190.

U.S. Ambassador in Lomé: Johnny Young.

State Dept. Desk Officer: Ann Syrett, 647-2637.

Commerce Dept. Desk Officer: Debra Henke, 482-5149.

Tonga

Ambassador: Sione KITE (resident in London).

U.S. Ambassador: Vacant (resident in Suva, Fiji).

State Dept. Desk Officer: Edward Michael, 647-3546.

Trinidad and Tobago

Ambassador: Corinne Averille MCKNIGHT. Chancery: 1708 Massachusetts Ave. N.W. 20036; 467-6490; fax, 785-3130.

U.S. Ambassador designate in Port-of-Spain: Brian J. Donnelly.

State Dept. Desk Officer: Daniel Kiang, 647-2130.

Commerce Dept. Desk Officer: Michelle Brooks, 482-2527.

Tunisia

Ambassador: Ismail KHELIL. Chancery: 1515 Massachusetts Ave. N.W. 20005; 862-1850.

U.S. Ambassador designate in Tunis: Mary Ann Casey.

State Dept. Desk Officer: Sue Saarnio, 647-3614.

Commerce Dept. Desk Officer: Corey Wright, 482-1860.

Turkey

Ambassador: Nuzhet KANDEMIR. Chancery: 1714 Massachusetts Ave. N.W. 20036; 659-8200.

U.S. Ambassador Designate in Ankara: Richard C. Barkley.

State Dept. Desk Officer: John Hamilton, 647-6114.

Commerce Dept. Desk Officer: Ann Corro, 482-3945.

Turkmenistan

U.S. Ambassador in Ashgabat: Joseph S. Hulings III.

State Dept. Desk Officer: Lowry Taylor, 647-8956.

Tuvalu

U.S. Ambassador: Vacant (resident in Suva, Fiji).

State Dept. Desk Officer: Edward Michael, 647-3546.

Uganda
Ambassador: Stephen Kapimpina KATENTA-APULI.
Chancery: 5909 16th St. N.W. 20011; 726-7100; fax, 726-1727.
U.S. Ambassador designate in Kampala: E. Michael Southwick.
State Dept. Desk Officer: Chris Wilson, 647-5684.
Commerce Dept. Desk Officer: Chandra Watkins, 482-4564.

Ukraine
Ambassador: Oleh H. BILORUS.
Chancery: 3350 M St. N.W. 20007; 333-0606; fax, 333-0817.
U.S. Ambassador in Kiev: William Miller.
State Dept. Desk Officer: Edward Salazar, 647-8671.
Commerce Dept. Desk Officer: Chris Lucyk, 482-2018.

United Arab Emirates
Ambassador: Mohammad bin Hussein AL-SHAALI.
Chancery: 3000 K St. N.W., #600 20007; 338-6500.
U.S. Ambassador in Abu Dhabi: William A. Rugh.
State Dept. Desk Officer: Daniel Goodspeed, 647-6558.
Commerce Dept. Desk Officer: Christopher Cerone, 482-1860.

United Kingdom
Ambassador: Robin RENWICK.
Chancery: 3100 Massachusetts Ave. N.W. 20008; 462-1340; fax, 898-4255.
U.S. Ambassador Designate in London: William J. Crowe Jr.
State Dept. Desk Officers: Kathleen Stephens, 647-8027; David Schafer (Northern Ireland), 647-5669.
Commerce Dept. Desk Officer: Robert McLaughlin, 482-3748.

Uruguay
Ambassador: Eduardo MACGILLYCUDDY.
Chancery: 1910 I St. N.W. 20006; 331-1313.

U.S. Ambassador in Montevideo: Thomas J. Dodd.
State Dept. Desk Officer: Sandy Campbell, 647-2296.
Commerce Dept. Desk Officer: Roger Turner, 482-1495.

Uzbekistan
Ambassador: Mukhamed Bobir MALIKOV.
Chancery: 1511 K St. N.W., #619 20005; 638-4266; fax, 638-4268.
U.S. Ambassador in Tashkent: Henry L. Clarke.
State Dept. Desk Officer: Deidi Delahanty, 647-8956.

Vanuatu
U.S. Ambassador: Richard W. Teare (resident in Port Moresby, Papua New Guinea).
State Dept. Desk Officer: Edward Michael, 647-3546.

Venezuela
Ambassador: Simon Alberto CONSALVI.
Chancery: 1099 30th St. N.W. 20007; 342-2214.
U.S. Ambassador in Caracas: Jeffrey Davidow.
State Dept. Desk Officer: Perry Ball, 647-3338.
Commerce Dept. Desk Officer: Laura Zeiger-Hartfield, 482-3748.

Vietnam
Permanent Mission of the Socialist Republic of Vietnam to the United Nations, 20 Waterside Plaza, New York, NY 10010; (212) 679-3779. Le Van Bang, permanent representative.
State Dept. Desk Officer: Andrew Rothman, 647-3132.

Western Samoa
Ambassador: Tuiloma Neroni SLADE.
Chancery: 820 Second Ave., #800 New York, NY 10017; (212) 599-6196; fax, (212) 599-0797.
U.S. Ambassador Designate: Josiah Beeman (resident in Wellington, New Zealand).
State Dept. Desk Officer: Edward Michael, 647-3546.

Yemen, Republic of
Ambassador: Mohsin A. ALAINI.
Chancery: 2600 Virginia Ave. N.W., #705 20037; 965-4760; fax, 337-2017.

U.S. Ambassador in Sanaa: Arthur H. Hughes.

State Dept. Desk Officer: Steve Zate, 647-6572.

Commerce Dept. Desk Officer: Paul Thanos, 482-1860.

Yugoslavia (See **Serbia-Montenegro**)

Zaire
Ambassador: TATANENE Manata.
Chancery: 1800 New Hampshire Ave. N.W. 20009; 234-7690.

U.S. Ambassador in Kinshasa: Vacant.

State Dept. Desk Officer: Terrence McCulley, 647-2080.

Commerce Dept. Desk Officer: Philip Michelini, 482-4388.

Zambia
Ambassador: Dunstan Weston KAMANA.
Chancery: 2419 Massachusetts Ave. N.W. 20008; 265-9717.

U.S. Ambassador in Lusaka: Gordon L. Streeb.

State Dept. Desk Officer: Philip Egger, 647-8433.

Commerce Dept. Desk Officer: Finn Holm-Olsen, 482-4228.

Zimbabwe
Ambassador: Amos Bernard Muvengwa MIDZI.
Chancery: 1608 New Hampshire Ave. N.W. 20009; 332-7100; fax, 483-9326.

U.S. Ambassador in Harare: E. Gibson Lanpher.

State Dept. Desk Officer: Robert Jackson, 647-9429.

Commerce Dept. Desk Officer: Finn Holm-Olsen, 482-4228.

Labor Unions

These lists were compiled from material supplied by the Bureau of National Affairs' *Directory of U.S. Labor Organizations* and information gathered by Congressional Quarterly in April 1994. Only organizations with a membership of 25,000 or more are included in this appendix. Asterisks (*) indicate unions that are affiliated with the AFL-CIO.

The following unions are either headquartered or have representative offices in the Washington, D.C., area.

*Amalgamated Clothing and Textile Workers Union
815 16th St. N.W. 20006
Phone: 628-0214
Membership: 237,000
President: Jack Sheinkman
Headquarters: 15 Union Square, New York, NY 10003; (212) 242-0700

*Amalgamated Transit Union
5025 Wisconsin Ave. N.W. 20016
Phone: 537-1645
Membership: 165,000
President: James La Sala

American Assn. of University Professors
1012 14th St. N.W., #500 20005
Phone: 737-5900
Membership: 40,000
President: Linda Pratt

*American Federation of Government Employees
80 F St. N.W. 20001
Phone: 737-8700
Membership: 200,000
President: John Sturdivant

*American Federation of State, County and Municipal Employees
1625 L St. N.W. 20036
Phone: 429-1000
Membership: 1,300,000
President: Gerald W. McEntee

*American Federation of Teachers
555 New Jersey Ave. N.W. 20001
Phone: 879-4400
Membership: 780,000
President: Albert Shanker

American Federation of Television and Radio Artists
5480 Wisconsin Ave., Chevy Chase, MD 20815
Phone: (301) 657-2560
Membership: 77,000
President: John Badila
Headquarters: 260 Madison Ave., New York, NY 10016; (212) 532-0800

*American Nurses' Assn.
600 Maryland Ave. S.W. 20024
Phone: 554-4444
Membership: 206,000
President: Lucille A. Joel

*American Postal Workers Union
1300 L St. N.W. 20005
Phone: 842-4200
Membership: 228,000
President: Moe Biller

*Assn. of Flight Attendants
1625 Massachusetts Ave. N.W. 20036
Phone: 328-5400
Membership: 31,000
President: Susan Bianchi-Sand

*Bakery, Confectionery, and Tobacco Workers' International Union
10401 Connecticut Ave., Kensington, MD 20895
Phone: (301) 933-8600
Membership: 135,000
President: Frank Hurt

*Brotherhood of Maintenance of Way Employees
400 N. Capitol St. N.W. 20001
Phone: 638-2135
Membership: 55,000
President: Mac A. Fleming
Headquarters: 26555 Evergreen Rd., Southfield, MI 48076; (313) 948-1010

*Communications Workers of America
501 3rd St. N.W. 20001
Phone: 434-1100
Membership: 650,000
President: Morton Bahr

Federation of Nurses and Health Professionals
555 New Jersey Ave. N.W. 20001
Phone: 879-4491
Membership: 50,000
President: Albert Shanker

*Graphic Communications International Union
1900 L St. N.W. 20036
Phone: 462-1400
Membership: 113,000
President: James J. Norton

*Hotel Employees and Restaurant Employees International Union
1219 28th St. N.W. 20007
Phone: 393-4373
Membership: 269,000
President: Edward T. Hanley

*International Air Line Pilots Assn.
1625 Massachusetts Ave. N.W. 20036
Phone: 797-4010
Membership: 31,000
President: J. Randolph Babbit

*International Assn. of Bridge, Structural and Ornamental Iron Workers
1750 New York Ave. N.W. 20006
Phone: 383-4800
Membership: 140,000
President: Jake West

*International Assn. of Fire Fighters
1750 New York Ave. N.W. 20006
Phone: 737-8484
Membership: 151,000
President: Alfred K. Whitehead

*International Assn. of Machinists and Aerospace Workers
9000 Machinists Pl., Upper Marlboro, MD 20772
Phone: (301) 967-4500
Membership: 500,000
President: George J. Kourpias

*International Brotherhood of Boilermakers, Iron Ship Builders, Blacksmiths, Forgers and Helpers
2722 Merrilee Dr., Fairfax, VA 22031
Phone: (703) 560-1493
Membership: 79,000
President: Charles W. Jones
Headquarters: 753 State Ave., Kansas City, KS 66101; (913) 371-2640

*International Brotherhood of Electrical Workers
1125 15th St. N.W. 20005
Phone: 833-7000
Membership: 730,000
President: John J. Barry

*International Brotherhood of Painters and Allied Trades of the United States and Canada
1750 New York Ave. N.W. 20006
Phone: 637-0700
Membership: 143,000
President: A. L. Monroe

*International Brotherhood of Teamsters, Chauffeurs, Warehousemen and Helpers of America
25 Louisiana Ave. N.W. 20001
Phone: 624-6800
Membership: 1,500,000
President: Ronald Carey

*International Chemical Workers Union
1126 16th St. N.W. 20036
Phone: 659-3747
Membership: 40,000
President: Frank D. Martino
Headquarters: 1655 W. Market St., Akron, OH 44313; (216) 867-2444

*International Ladies' Garment Workers' Union
815 16th St. N.W. 20006
Phone: 347-7417
Membership: 175,000
President: Jay Mazur
Headquarters: 1710 Broadway, New York, NY 10019; (212) 265-7000

*International Longshoremen's and Warehousemen's Union
1133 15th St. N.W. 20005
Phone: 463-6265
Membership: 50,000
President: Dave A. Arian
Headquarters: 1188 Franklin St., San Francisco, CA 94109; (415) 775-0533

*International Longshoremen's Assn.
815 16th St. N.W. 20006
Phone: 628-4546
Membership: 60,000
President: John Bowers
Headquarters: 17 Battery Place, New York, NY 10004; (212) 425-1200

*International Union, United Automobile, Aerospace and Agricultural Implement Workers of America (UAW)
1757 N St. N.W. 20036
Phone: 828-8500
Membership: 900,000
President: Owen F. Bieber
Headquarters: 8000 E. Jefferson Ave., Detroit, MI 48214; (313) 926-5000

*International Union of Bricklayers and Allied Craftsmen
815 15th St. N.W. 20005
Phone: 783-3788
Membership: 84,000
President: John T. Joyce

*International Union of Electronic, Electrical, Salaried, Machine and Furniture Workers
1126 16th St. N.W. 20036
Phone: 296-1201
Membership: 150,000
President: William H. Bywater

*International Union of Operating Engineers
1125 17th St. N.W. 20036
Phone: 429-9100
Membership: 375,000
President: Frank Hanley

*International Union of Police Assns.
1016 Duke St., Alexandria, VA 22314
Phone: (703) 549-7473
Membership: 25,000
President: Robert B. Kliesmet

*Laborers' International Union of North America
905 16th St. N.W. 20006
Phone: 737-8320
Membership: 500,000
President: Arthur A. Coia

*National Assn. of Letter Carriers
100 Indiana Ave. N.W. 20001
Phone: 393-4695
Membership: 312,000
President: Vincent R. Sombrotto

National Education Assn.
1201 16th St. N.W. 20036
Phone: 833-4000
Membership: 2,000,000
President: Keith Geiger

*National Federation of Federal Employees
1016 16th St. N.W. 20036
Phone: 862-4400
Membership: 45,000
President: Sheila Velazco

*National Marine Engineers' Beneficial Assn.
125 15th St. N.W., #501 20005
Phone: 466-7060
Membership: 53,000
President: Louis Parise

National Rural Letter Carriers' Assn.
1448 Duke St., Alexandria, VA 22314
Phone: (703) 684-5545
Membership: 80,600
President: William R. Brown Jr.

National Treasury Employees Union
901 E St. N.W. 20004
Phone: 783-4444
Membership: 150,000
President: Robert M. Tobias

*The Newspaper Guild
8611 2nd Ave., Silver Spring, MD 20910
Phone: (301) 585-2990
Membership: 31,777
President: Charles Dale

*Office and Professional Employees International Union
815 16th St. N.W. 20006
Phone: 393-4464
Membership: 135,000
President: Michael Goodwin
Headquarters: 256 W. 14th St., New York, NY 10011; (212) 675-3210

*Oil, Chemical and Atomic Workers International Union
2722 Merrilee Dr., Fairfax, VA 22031
Phone: (703) 876-9300
Membership: 110,000
President: Robert E. Wages
Headquarters: P.O. Box 2812, Denver, CO 80201; (303) 987-2229

*Operative Plasterers' and Cement Masons' International Assn. of the United States and Canada
1125 17th St. N.W. 20036
Phone: 393-6569
Membership: 39,000
President: Dominic Martell

Screen Actors Guild
5480 Wisconsin Ave., Chevy Chase, MD 20815
Phone: (301) 657-2560
Membership: 78,000
President: John Badila
Headquarters: 7065 Hollywood Blvd., Hollywood, CA 90028; (213) 465-4600

*Seafarers International Union of North America
5201 Auth Way, Camp Springs, MD 20746
Phone: (301) 899-0675
Membership: 85,000
President: Michael Sacco

*Service Employees' International Union
1313 L St. N.W. 20005
Phone: 898-3200
Membership: 1,000,000
President: John J. Sweeney

*Sheet Metal Workers' International Assn.
1750 New York Ave. N.W. 20006
Phone: 783-5880
Membership: 126,000
President: Arthur Moore

*Transportation Communications International Union
815 16th St. N.W. 20006
Phone: 783-3660

Membership: 130,000
President: Robert A. Scardelletti
Headquarters: 3 Research Place, Rockville, MD 20850; (301) 948-4910

*United Assn. of Journeymen and Apprentices of the Plumbing and Pipe Fitting Industry of the United States and Canada
901 Massachusetts Ave. N.W. 20001
Phone: 628-5823
Membership: 220,000
President: Marvin J. Boede

*United Brotherhood of Carpenters and Joiners of America
101 Constitution Ave. N.W. 20001
Phone: 546-6206
Membership: 550,000
President: Sigurd Lucassen

United Electrical, Radio and Machine Workers of America
1800 Diagonal Rd., Alexandria, VA 22314
Phone: (703) 684-3123
Membership: 60,000
President: John H. Hovis Jr.
Headquarters: 535 Smithfield St., Pittsburgh, PA 15222; (412) 471-8919

*United Food and Commercial Workers International Union
1775 K St. N.W. 20006
Phone: 223-3111
Membership: 1,300,000
President: Douglas H. Dority

United Mine Workers of America
900 15th St. N.W. 20005
Phone: 842-7200
Membership: 186,000
President: Richard L. Trumka

*United Steelworkers of America
815 16th St. N.W. 20006
Phone: 638-6929
Membership: 459,000
President: George F. Becker
Headquarters: 5 Gateway Center, Pittsburgh, PA 15222; (412) 562-3400

*United Transportation Union
400 N. Capitol St. N.W. 20001
Phone: 347-0900
Membership: 145,000
President: G. Thomas DuBose
Headquarters: 14600 Detroit Ave., Cleveland, OH 44107-4250; (216) 228-9400

*United Union of Roofers, Waterproofers, and Allied Workers
1125 17th St. N.W. 20036
Phone: 638-3228
Membership: 25,000
President: Earl J. Kruse

*Utility Workers Union of America
815 16th St. N.W. 20006
Phone: 347-8105
Membership: 55,000
President: Marshall M. Hicks

The following unions are headquartered outside the Washington, D.C., area and do not have representative offices there.

Actors' Equity Assn.
165 W. 46th St., New York, NY 10036
Phone: (212) 869-8530
Membership: 29,000
President: Ron Silver

*American Federation of Grain Millers
4949 Olson Memorial Highway, Minneapolis, MN 55422
Phone: (612) 545-0211
Membership: 28,000
President: Larry R. Jackson

*American Federation of Musicians of the United States and Canada
1501 Broadway, #600, New York, NY 10036
Phone: (212) 869-1330
Membership: 180,000
President: Mark Tully Massagli

*Associated Actors and Artistes of America
165 W. 46th St., New York, NY 10036
Phone: (212) 869-0358
Membership: 99,000
President: Theodore Bikel

California School Employees Assn.
2045 Lundy Ave. (mailing address: P.O. Box 640), San Jose, CA 95106
Phone: (408) 263-8000
Membership: 108,000
President: Steve Araujo

*Glass, Molders, Pottery, Plastics and Allied Workers International Union
608 E. Baltimore Pike (mailing address: P.O. Box 607), Media, PA 19063

Phone: (215) 565-5051
Membership: 86,400
President: James E. Hatfield

*International Alliance of Theatrical Stage Employees and Moving Picture Machine Operators of the United States and Canada
1515 Broadway, New York, NY 10036
Phone: (212) 730-1770
Membership: 50,000
President: Alfred W. DiTolla

*International Brotherhood of Firemen and Oilers
1100 Circle 75 Parkway, #350, Atlanta, GA 30339
Phone: (404) 933-9104
Membership: 25,000
President: Jimmy L. Walker

*International Union, Aluminum, Brick, and Glass Workers
3362 Hollenberg Dr., Bridgeton, MO 63044
Phone: (314) 739-6142
Membership: 42,000
President: Ernie J. LaBaff

*International Woodworkers of America
25 Cornell Ave., Gladstone, OR 97027
Phone: (503) 656-1475
Membership: 25,000
President: Wilson J. Hubbell

National Union of Hospital and Health Care Employees
505 8th Ave., New York, NY 10018
Phone: (212) 239-3590
Membership: 40,000
President: Henry Nicholas

*Retail, Wholesale and Department Store Union
30 E. 29th St., New York, NY 10016
Phone: (212) 684-5300
Membership: 130,000
President: Lenore Miller

State Employees Assn. of North Carolina
P.O. Drawer 27727, Raleigh, NC 27611
Phone: (919) 833-6436
Membership: 58,000
President: Chuck Hunt

*Transport Workers Union of America
80 West End Ave., New York, NY 10023
Phone: (212) 873-6000
Membership: 96,000
President: Sonny Hall

*United Paperworkers International Union
P.O. Box 1475, Nashville, TN 37202
Phone: (615) 834-8590
Membership: 202,000
President: Wayne E. Glenn

*United Rubber, Cork, Linoleum and Plastic Workers of America
570 White Pond Dr., Akron, OH 44320
Phone: (216) 869-0320
Membership: 100,000
President: Kenneth Coss

AFL-CIO
(American Federation of Labor-
Congress of Industrial Organizations)

815 16th St. N.W. 20006
Phone: 637-5000
Lane Kirkland, president

The AFL-CIO is a voluntary federation of national and international labor unions in the United States; each union is autonomous and conducts its own contract negotiations. The federation represents members before Congress and other branches of government. The economic research department examines issues affecting American workers. Library open to the public.

Departments:

Civil Rights
Richard Womack, director; 637-5270

Committee on Political Education
John Perkins, director; 637-5101

Community Services
Joe Velasquez, director; 637-5189

Economic Research
Rudolph A. Oswald, director; 637-5160

Education
Dorothy Shields, director; 637-5141

Employee Benefits
Karen Ignagni, director; 637-5204

Information
Rex Hardesty, director; 637-5010

International Affairs
Charles Gray, director; 637-5050

Legal Dept.
Laurence S. Gold, general counsel; 637-5390

Legislation
Robert McGlotten, director; 637-5075

Occupational Safety and Health
Peg Seminario, director; 637-5366

Organization and Field Services
Joseph J. Shantz, director; 637-5280

Trade and Industrial Departments:

Building and Construction Trades
Robert A. Georgine, president; 347-1461

Food and Allied Service Trades
Robert F. Harbrant, president; 737-7200

Industrial Union
Howard D. Samuel, president; 842-7800

Maritime Trades
Michael Sacco, president; 628-6300

Metal Trades
Paul J. Burnsky, president; 347-7255

Professional Employees
Jack Golodner, president; 638-0320

Public Employees
Al Bilik, president; 393-2820

Transportation Trades
Walter J. Shea, president; 628-9262

Union Label and Service Trades
James E. Hatfield, president; 628-2131

State and Territory Abbreviations

Please refer to the following U.S. Postal Service abbreviations for the states and territories when using the list of Regional Federal Information Sources.

AK	Alaska	MS	Mississippi
AL	Alabama	MT	Montana
AR	Arkansas	NC	North Carolina
AS	American Samoa	ND	North Dakota
AZ	Arizona	NE	Nebraska
CA	California	NH	New Hampshire
CM	Northern Mariana Islands	NJ	New Jersey
CO	Colorado	NM	New Mexico
CT	Connecticut	NV	Nevada
CZ	Canal Zone	NY	New York
DC	District of Columbia	OH	Ohio
DE	Delaware	OK	Oklahoma
FL	Florida	OR	Oregon
GA	Georgia	PA	Pennsylvania
GU	Guam	PR	Puerto Rico
HI	Hawaii	RI	Rhode Island
IA	Iowa	SC	South Carolina
ID	Idaho	SD	South Dakota
IL	Illinois	TN	Tennessee
IN	Indiana	TT	Trust Territory
KS	Kansas	TX	Texas
KY	Kentucky	UT	Utah
LA	Louisiana	VA	Virginia
MA	Massachusetts	VI	Virgin Islands
MD	Maryland	VT	Vermont
ME	Maine	WA	Washington
MI	Michigan	WI	Wisconsin
MN	Minnesota	WV	West Virginia
MO	Missouri	WY	Wyoming

Regional Federal Information Sources

Departments

Agriculture Dept.—Animal and Plant Health Inspection Service (Animal Damage Control Program)

Area Served	Telephone	Address
AK, AZ, CA, CO, HI, ID, KS, MT, ND, NE, NM, NV, OK, OR, SD, TX, UT, WA, WY	(303) 969-6560	12345 W. Alameda Parkway, #204, Lakewood, CO 80228
AL, AR, CT, DC, DE, FL, GA, IA, IL, IN, KY, LA, MA, MD, ME, MI, MN, MO, MS, NC, NH, NJ, NY, OH, PA, RI, SC, TN, VA, VT, WI, WV	(615) 781-5418	7000 Executive Center Dr., #370, Brentwood, TN 37027

Agriculture Dept.—Animal and Plant Health Inspection Service (Plant Protection and Quarantine Programs)

Area Served	Telephone	Address
AK, AZ, CA, CO, GU, HI, ID, MT, ND, NV, OR, SD, UT, WA, WY	(916) 551-3220	9580 Micron Ave., #I, Sacramento, CA 95827
AL, FL, GA, KY, MS, NC, PR, SC, TN, VI	(601) 863-1813	3505 25th Ave., Bldg. 1 North, Gulfport, MS 39501
AR, IA, KS, LA, MO, NE, NM, OK, TX	(210) 504-4150	3505 Boca Chica Blvd., #360, Brownsville, TX 78521-4065
CT, DC, DE, IL, IN, MA, MD, ME, MI, MN, NH, NJ, NY, OH, PA, RI, VA, VT, WI, WV	(609) 235-9120	505 S. Lenola Rd., 2nd Floor, Moorestown, NJ 08057-1549

Agriculture Dept.—Animal and Plant Health Inspection Service (Regulatory Enforcement and Animal Care)

Area Served	Telephone	Address
AK, AZ, CA, CO, HI, ID, MT, NM, NV, OR, UT, WA, WY	(916) 551-1561	9580 Micron Ave., #J, Sacramento, CA 95827-2623

AL, FL, GA, KY, MS, NC, PR, SC, TN	(813) 225-7690	501 East Polk St., #820, Tampa FL 33602
AR, KS, LA, MO, OK, TX	(817) 885-6901	501 Felix St., Bldg. #11 (mailing address: P.O. Box 6258), Ft. Worth, TX 76115
CT, DC, DE, MA, MD, ME, MI, NH, NJ, NY, OH, PA, RI, VA, VT, WV	(410) 962-7463	2568-A Riva Rd., #302, Annapolis, MD 21401-7400
IA, IL, IN, MN, ND, NE, SD, WI	(612) 370-2255	100 N. 6th St., #625, Minneapolis, MN 55403

Agriculture Dept.—Animal and Plant Health Inspection Service (Veterinary Services)

Area Served	Telephone	Address
AK, AZ, CA, CO, HI, ID, MT, NM, NV, OR, UT, WA, WY	(303) 784-6201	384 Inverness Dr. South, #150 (mailing address: P.O. Box 3857), Englewood, CO 80112
AL, FL, GA, KY, MS, NC, PR, SC, TN, VI	(813) 228-2952	501 E. Polk St., #880, Tampa, FL 33602-3954
AR, IA, KS, LA, MO, ND, NE, OK, SD, TX	(817) 885-7850	100 W. Pioneer Parkway, #100, Arlington, TX 76010
CT, DC, DE, IL, IN, MA, MD, ME, MI, MN, NH, NJ, NY, OH, PA, RI, VA, VT, WV, WI	(518) 370-5026	Bldg. 12, GSA Depot, Scotia, NY 12302

Agriculture Dept.—Extension Service

Area Served	Telephone	Address
AK	(907) 474-7246	University of Alaska, 103 AHRB, Fairbanks, AK 99775-5200
AL	(205) 844-4444	Auburn University, 109 Duncan Hall, Auburn, AL 36849-5612
	(205) 851-5783	Alabama A & M University, P.O. Box 967, Normal, AL 35762
	(205) 727-8798	Tuskegee University, 101 Moton Hall, Tuskegee, AL 36088
AR	(501) 686-2565	University of Arkansas, P.O. Box 391, Little Rock, AR 72203
	(501) 543-8131	University of Arkansas, 1200 N. University Dr. (mailing address: Box 4005), Pine Bluff, AR 71601
AS		Mapusaga Campus, P.O. Box 2609, Pago Pago, AS 96799
AZ	(602) 621-7209	College of Agriculture, University of Arizona, 301 Forbes Bldg., Tucson, AZ 85721
CA	(510) 987-0060	University of California, Agriculture and Natural Resources, 300 Lakeside Dr., 6th Floor, Oakland, CA 94612-3560

CM	(670) 234-9022	Northern Marianas College, P.O. Box 1250, Saipan, CM 96950
CO	(303) 491-6281	Colorado State University, 1 Administration Bldg., Fort Collins, CO 80523
CT	(203) 486-2917	College of Agriculture & Natural Resources, University of Connecticut, 1376 Storrs Rd. (mailing address: Box U-66), Storrs, CT 06269-4066
DC	(202) 576-6993	University of the District of Columbia, 901 Newton St. N.E., Washington, DC 20017
DE	(302) 831-2504	University of Delaware, 131 Townsend Hall, S. College Ave., Newark, DE 19717-1303
	(302) 739-4929	Delaware State University, Dover, DE 19901
FL	(904) 392-1761	University of Florida, 1038 McCarty Hall, Gainesville, FL 32611
	(904) 599-3546	Florida A & M University, 215 Perry-Paige Bldg., Tallahassee, FL 32307
GA	(706) 542-3824	University of Georgia, 111 Conner Hall, Athens, GA 30602-7504
	(912) 825-6296	Ft. Valley State College, Box 4061, Ft. Valley, GA 31030-3298
GU	(671) 734-2562	University of Guam, UOG Station, Mangilao, GU 96913
HI	(808) 956-8234	University of Hawaii, 3050 Maile Way, Gilmore 202, Honolulu, HI 96822
IA	(515) 294-6192	Iowa State University, 315 Beardshear, Ames, IA 50011
ID	(208) 885-6639	University of Idaho, Agricultural Science Bldg., Moscow, ID 83843
IL	(217) 333-2660	University of Illinois, 122 Mumford Hall, 1301 W. Gregory Dr., Urbana, IL 61801
IN	(317) 494-8489	Purdue University, 104 Agricultural Administration Bldg., West Lafayette, IN 47907
KS	(913) 532-7137	Kansas State University, 123 Umberger Hall, Manhattan, KS 66506-3401
KY	(606) 257-4772	University of Kentucky, Agricultural Science Bldg., Lexington, KY 40546-0091
	(502) 227-6310	Kentucky State University, Atwood Research Facility, Frankfort, KY 40601
LA	(504) 388-6083	Louisiana State University, Knapp Hall, Baton Rouge, LA 70803-1900
	(504) 771-2242	Southern University and A & M College, Baton Rouge, LA 70813
MA	(413) 545-2766	University of Massachusetts, 117 Stockbridge Hall, Amherst, MA 01003
MD	(301) 445-8076	University of Maryland, 3300 Metzerott Rd., Adelphi, MD 20783
	(301) 651-2229	University of Maryland, Eastern Shore, Princess Anne, MD 21853

ME	(207) 581-3186	University of Maine, 102 Libby Hall, Orono, ME 04469
MI	(517) 355-2308	Michigan State University, 106 Ag Hall, East Lansing, MI 48824
MN	(612) 624-2703	University of Minnesota, 240 Coffey Hall, 1420 Eckles Ave., St. Paul, MN 55108
MO	(314) 882-7754	University of Missouri, 309 University Hall, Columbia, MO 65211
	(314) 681-5521	Lincoln University, P.O. Box 69, Jefferson City, MO 65102-0029
MS	(601) 325-3036	Mississippi State University, 201 Bost Ext. Center (mailing address: Box 5446), Mississippi State, MS 39762
	(601) 877-6118	Alcorn State University, P.O. Box 114, Lorman, MS 39096
MT	(406) 994-4371	Montana State University, 212 Montana Hall, Bozeman, MT 59717
NC	(919) 515-2811	North Carolina State University, Box 7602, Raleigh, NC 27695-7602
	(919) 334-7691	North Carolina A & T State University, Box 21928, Greensboro, NC 27420-1928
ND	(701) 237-8944	North Dakota State University, NDSU Ext. Service, 311 Morrill Hall, Fargo, ND 58105
NE	(402) 472-2966	University of Nebraska, 214 Ag. Hall, Lincoln, NE 68583-0703
NH	(603) 862-1520	University of New Hampshire, 103 Taylor Hall, Durham, NH 03824
NJ	(908) 932-9306	The State University of Rutgers, Box 231, Cook College, New Brunswick, NJ 08903
NM	(505) 646-3016	New Mexico State University, Box 3AE, Las Cruces, NM 88003
NV	(702) 784-6611	University of Nevada, Mail Stop 222, Reno, NV 89557-0004
NY	(607) 255-2237	Cornell University, 276 Roberts Hall, Ithaca, NY 14853-5901
OH	(614) 292-4067	Ohio State University, 2120 Fyffe Rd., Columbus, OH 43210
OK	(405) 744-5398	Oklahoma State University, 139 Agricultural Hall, Stillwater, OK 74078-0500
	(405) 466-3833	Langston University, Ag Research Bldg., Box 730, Langston, OK 73050
OR	(503) 737-2713	Oregon State University, Corvallis, OR 97331
PA	(814) 865-2541	Penn State University, 201 Agriculture Administration Bldg., University Park, PA 16802
PR	(809) 832-4040	University of Puerto Rico, College Station, Mayaguez, PR 00708
RI	(401) 792-2474	University of Rhode Island, 113 Woodward Hall, Kingston, RI 02881
SC	(803) 656-3382	Clemson University, 103 Barre Hall, Clemson, SC 29634

	(803) 531-6819	South Carolina State College, 300 College St. N.E. (mailing address: Box 1765), Orangeburg, SC 29117
SD	(605) 688-4792	South Dakota State University, Ag Hall 154 (mailing address: P.O. Box 2207D), Brookings, SD 57007-9988
TN	(615) 974-7114	University of Tennessee, Box 1071, Knoxville, TN 37901-1071
	(615) 320-3419	Tennessee State University, 3500 John E. Merritt Blvd., Nashville, TN 37209-1561
TT	(691) 320-2728	College of Micronesia, AES/CES, P.O. Box 1179, Kolonia, Pohnpei 96941
TX	(409) 845-7967	Texas A & M University, 106 System Administration Bldg., College Station, TX 77843
	(409) 857-2023	Prairie View A & M University, P.O. Box 3059, Prairie View, TX 77446-3059
UT	(801) 750-2200	Utah State University, Ag. Science Bldg., Logan, UT 84322-4800
VA	(703) 231-9892	Virginia Tech, College of Ag and Life Sciences, 101 Hutcheson Hall, Blacksburg, VA 24061-0402
	(804) 524-5961	Virginia State University, P.O. Box 9081, Petersburg, VA 23803
VI	(809) 778-0246	University of the Virgin Islands, Box 10,000, Kingshill, St. Croix, VI 00850
VT	(802) 656-2980	University of Vermont, 601 Main St., Burlington, VT 05401-3439
WA	(509) 335-2933	Washington State University, 411 Hulbert Hall, Pullman, WA 99164-6230
WI	(608) 262-3786	University of Wisconsin, 432 N. Lake St., 527 Ext. Bldg., Madison, WI 53706
WV	(304) 293-8187	West Virginia University, 305 Stewart Hall (mailing address: P.O. Box 6031), Morgantown, WV 26506
WY	(307) 766-5124	University of Wyoming, P.O. Box 3354, College of Agriculture, Laramie, WY 82071

Agriculture Dept.—Farmers Home Administration

Area Served	Telephone	Address
AK	(907) 745-2176	634 S. Bailey, #103, Palmer, AK 99645
AL	(205) 279-3400	4121 Carmichael Rd., #601, Montgomery, AL 36106-3683
AR	(501) 324-6281	700 W. Capitol (mailing address: P.O. Box 2778), Little Rock, AR 72203
AZ	(602) 280-8700	Phoenix, AZ 85012
CA	(916) 668-2000	194 W. Main St., #F, Woodland, CA 95695
CO	(303) 236-2801	655 Parfet St., #E-100, Denver, CO 80215
CT, MA, RI	(413) 253-4300	451 West St., Amherst, MA 01002

DC, DE, MD	(302) 697-4300	4611 S. Dupont Highway (mailing address: P.O. Box 400), Camden, DE 19934-9998
FL	(904) 338-3400	4440 N.W. 25th Pl. (mailing address: P.O. Box 147010), Gainesville, FL 32614-7010
GA	(706) 546-2173	355 E. Hancock Ave., Athens, GA 30610
HI	(808) 933-3000	154 Waianuenue Ave., Hilo, HI 96720
IA	(515) 284-4663	210 Walnut St., Des Moines, IA 50309
ID	(208) 334-1301	3232 Elder St., Boise, ID 83705
IL	(217) 398-5235	1817 S. Neil St., #103, Champaign, IL 61820
IN	(317) 290-3100	5975 Lakeside Blvd., Indianapolis, IN 46278
KS	(913) 271-2700	1201 S.W. Summit Executive Dr. (mailing address: P.O. Box 4653), Topeka, KS 66604
KY	(606) 224-7300	771 Corporate Dr., #200, Lexington, KY 40503
LA	(318) 473-7920	3727 Government St., Alexandria, LA 71302
ME	(207) 990-9160	444 Stillwater Ave., #2 (mailing address: P.O. Box 405), Bangor, ME 04402-0405
MI	(517) 337-6635	3001 Coolidge Rd., #200, East Lansing, MI 48823
MN	(612) 290-3842	375 Jackson St., St. Paul, MN 55101
MO	(314) 876-0976	601 Business Loop 70 West, #235, Columbia, MO 65203
MS	(601) 965-4316	100 W. Capitol St., #831, Jackson, MS 39269
MT	(406) 585-2580	900 Technology Blvd., Unit 1, #B, Bozeman, MT 59715
NC	(919) 790-2731	4405 Bland Rd., #260, Raleigh, NC 27609
ND	(701) 250-4781	220 E. Rosser, #208 (mailing address: P.O. Box 1737), Bismarck, ND 58502
NE	(402) 437-5551	100 Centennial Mall North, #308, Lincoln, NE 68508
NH, VI, VT	(802) 828-6001	89 Main St., Montpelier, VT 05602
NJ	(609) 265-3600	1016 Woodlane Rd., #22, Mt. Holly, NJ 08060
NM	(505) 766-2462	517 Gold Ave. S.W., #3414, Albuquerque, NM 87102
NV	(702) 887-1222	1179 Fairview Dr., #C, Carson City, NV 89701
NY	(315) 423-5290	James M. Hanley Federal Bldg., #871 (mailing address: P.O. Box 7318), Syracuse, NY 13261-7318
OH	(614) 469-5606	200 N. High St., Columbus, OH 43215
OK	(405) 624-4250	USDA Agricultural Center Bldg., Stillwater, OK 74074
OR	(503) 326-2731	1220 S.W. 3rd Ave., #1590, Portland, OR 97204
PA	(717) 782-4476	1 Credit Union Place, #330, Harrisburg, PA 17110-2996
PR	(809) 766-5095	159 Carlos E. Chardon St., #501, Hato Rey, PR 00918-5481
SC	(803) 765-5163	1835 Assembly St., Columbia, SC 29201

SD	(605) 353-1430	200 4th St. S.W., Huron, SD 57350
TN	(615) 783-1308	3322 W. End Ave., #300, Nashville, TN 37203-1071
TX	(817) 774-1301	101 S. Main, #102, Temple, TX 76501
UT	(801) 524-4063	125 S. State St., #5438, Salt Lake City, UT 84138
VA	(804) 287-1550	1606 Santa Rosa Rd., #238, Richmond, VA 23229
WA	(509) 664-0240	Federal Bldg., #319 (mailing address: P.O. Box 2427), Wenatchee, WA 98807
WI	(715) 345-7625	4949 Kirschling Court, Stevens Point, WI 54481
WV	(304) 291-4791	75 High St. (mailing address: P.O. Box 678), Morgantown, WV 26505
WY	(307) 261-5271	Federal Bldg., #1005, 100 East B (mailing address: P.O. Box 820), Casper, WY 82602

Agriculture Dept.—Federal Crop Insurance Corporation

Area Served	Telephone	Address
AL, FL, GA, SC	(912) 242-3044	401 N. Patterson St., #M-113, Valdosta, GA 31601
AR, KY, LA, MS, TN	(601) 965-4771	100 W. Capitol, #318, Jackson, MS 39269
AZ, CA, NV, UT	(916) 551-2153	1303 J St., #450, Sacramento, CA 95814
CO, KS, MO, NE	(913) 266-0248	3401 S.W. Van Buren, Topeka, KS 66603
CT, DE, MA, MD, ME, NC, NH, NJ, NY, PA, RI, VA, VT, WV	(919) 790-2749	4407 Bland Rd., #160, Raleigh, NC 27609
IA, MN, WI	(612) 290-3304	30 E. 7th St., #2190, St. Paul, MN 55101
ID, OR, WA	(509) 353-2147	N. 112 University Blvd., #204, Spokane, WA 99206-5275
IL, IN, MI, OH	(217) 492-4186	2305 W. Monroe St., Springfield, IL 62704
MT, ND, SD, WY	(406) 657-6447	2110 Overland Ave., #106, Billings, MT 59102-6440
NM, OK, TX	(405) 231-5057	205 N.W. 63rd St., #170, Oklahoma City, OK 73116

Agriculture Dept.—Food and Nutrition Service

Area Served	Telephone	Address
AK, AS, AZ, CA, GU, HI, ID, NV, OR, TT, WA	(415) 705-1350	550 Kearny St., #400, San Francisco, CA 94108-2518
AL, FL, GA, KY, MS, NC, SC, TN	(404) 730-2588	77 Forsyth St. S.W., #107, Atlanta, GA 30303-3427
AR, LA, NM, OK, TX	(214) 767-0256	1100 Commerce St., #5A15, Dallas, TX 75242-1005
CO, IA, KS, MO, MT, ND, NE, SD, UT, WY	(303) 844-0312	1244 Speer Blvd., #903, Denver, CO 80204-3585

CT, MA, ME, NH, NY, RI, VT	(617) 565-6395	10 Causeway St., #501, Boston, MA 02222-1068
DC, DE, MD, NJ, PA, PR, VA, VI, WV	(609) 259-5091	300 Corporate Blvd., Robbinsville, NJ 08691-1598
IL, IN, MI, MN, OH, WI	(312) 353-1044	77 W. Jackson Blvd., 20th Floor, Chicago, IL 60604-3507

Agriculture Dept.—Food Safety and Inspection Service

Area Served	Telephone	Address
AK, AS, AZ, CA, CM, CO, GU, HI, ID, MT, ND, NV, OR, SD, UT, WA, WY	(510) 273-7402	620 Central Ave., Bldg. 2C, Alameda, CA 94501
AL, FL, GA, KY, MS, NC, PR, SC, TN, VA, VI, WV	(404) 347-3911	1718 Peachtree St. N.W., #299 South, Atlanta, GA 30309
AR, KS, LA, MO, NE, NM, OK, TX	(214) 767-9116	1100 Commerce St., #5F41, Dallas, TX 75242
CT, DC, DE, MA, MD, ME, NH, NJ, NY, PA, RI, VA, VT	(215) 597-4217	701 Market St., 2-B South, Philadelphia, PA 19106-1516
IA, IL, IN, MI, MN, OH, WI	(515) 284-6300	11338 Aurora Ave., Des Moines, IA 50322

Agriculture Dept.—Forest Service

Area Served	Telephone	Address
AK	(907) 586-8863	709 W. 9th St. (mailing address: P.O. Box 21628), Juneau, AK 99802
AL, AR, FL, GA, KY, LA, MS, NC, OK, PR, SC, TN, TX, VA, VI	(404) 347-2384	1720 Peachtree Rd. N.W., Atlanta, GA 30367
AZ, NM	(505) 842-3292	517 Gold Ave. S.W., Albuquerque, NM 87102
CA, HI	(415) 705-2874	630 Sansome St., San Francisco, CA 94111
CO, KS, NE, SD (except northwestern), WY (eastern)	(303) 275-5350	740 Simms St. (mailing address: P.O. Box 25127), Lakewood, CO 80401
CT, DE, IA, IL, IN, MA, MD, ME, MI, MN, MO, NH, NJ, NY, OH, PA, RI, VT, WI, WV	(414) 297-3693	310 W. Wisconsin Ave., #500, Milwaukee, WI 53203
ID (northern), MT, ND, SD (northwestern), WY (northwestern)	(406) 329-3511	200 E. Broadway St. (mailing address: P.O. Box 7669), Missoula, MT 59807
ID (southern), NV, UT, WY (western)	(801) 625-5352	324 25th St., Ogden, UT 84401
OR, WA	(503) 326-2971	333 S.W. 1st Ave. (mailing address: P.O. Box 3623), Portland, OR 97208

Commerce Dept.—Census Bureau

Area Served	Telephone	Address
AK, HI, ID, MT, NV, OR, WA	(206) 728-5390	101 Stewart St., #500, Seattle, WA 98101-1098
AL, FL, GA	(404) 730-3832	101 Marietta St. N.W., #3200, Atlanta, GA 30303-2700
AR, IA, KS, MN, MO, OK	(913) 757-3728	400 State Ave., #600, Kansas City, KS 66101-2410
AZ, CO, ND, NE, NM, SD, UT, WY	(303) 969-6750	6900 W. Jefferson Ave. (mailing address: P.O. Box 272020), Denver, CO 80227-9020
CA	(818) 904-6393	15350 Sherman Way, #300, Van Nuys, CA 91406-4224
CT, MA, ME, NH, NY (except New York City), RI, VT	(617) 424-0500	2 Copley Place, #301 (mailing address: P.O. Box 9108), Boston, MA 02117-9108
DC, KY, NC, SC, TN, VA	(704) 344-6142	901 Center Park Dr., #106, Charlotte, NC 28217-2935
DE, MD, NJ, PA	(215) 597-4920	105 S. 7th St., Philadelphia, PA 19106-3395
IL, IN, WI	(312) 353-6251	175 W. Jackson Blvd., #557, Chicago, IL 60604 2689
LA, MS, TX	(214) 767-7500	6303 Harry Hines Blvd., #210, Dallas, TX 75235-5269
MI, OH, WV	(313) 259-1158	1395 Brewery Park Blvd. (mailing address: P.O. Box 33405), Detroit, MI 48232-5405
NY (city), PR, VI	(212) 264-3860	26 Federal Plaza, #37-130, New York, NY 10278-0044

Commerce Dept.—Economic Development Administration

Area Served	Telephone	Address
AK, AS, AZ, CA, CM, GU, HI, ID, NV, OR, WA, Marshall Islands, Micronesia	(206) 553-0596	915 2nd Ave., #1856, Seattle, WA 98174
AL, FL, GA, KY, MS, NC, SC, TN	(404) 730-3002	401 W. Peachtree St. N.W., #1820, Atlanta, GA 30308-3510
AR, LA, NM, OK, TX	(512) 482-5461	611 E. 6th St., #201, Austin, TX 78701
CO, IA, KS, MO, MT, ND, NE, SD, UT, WY	(303) 844-4714	1244 Speer Blvd., #670, Denver, CO 80204
CT, DC, DE, MA, MD, ME, NH, NJ, NY, PA, PR, RI, VA, VI, VT, WV	(215) 597-4603	105 S. 7th St., 1st Floor, Philadelphia, PA 19106
IL, IN, MI, MN, OH, WI	(312) 353-7706	111 N. Canal St., #855, Chicago, IL 60606-7204

Commerce Dept.—International Trade Administration

Area Served	Telephone	Address
AK	(907) 271-6237	4201 Tudor Centre Dr., #319, Anchorage, AK 99508
AL	(205) 731-1331	2015 2nd Ave. North, #302, Birmingham, AL 35203
AR	(501) 324-5794	425 W. Capitol Ave., #700, Little Rock, AR 72201
AZ	(602) 640-2513	2901 N. Central Ave., #970, Phoenix, AZ 85012
CA	(310) 575-7104	11000 Wilshire Blvd., #9200, Los Angeles, CA 90024
	(714) 660-1688	3300 Irvine Ave., #305, Newport Beach, CA 92660
	(619) 557-5395	6363 Greenwich Dr., #230, San Diego, CA 92122
	(415) 705-2300	250 Montgomery St., 14th Floor, San Francisco, CA 94104
	(408) 291-7625	5201 Great American Parkway, #333, Santa Clara, CA 95054
CO, WY	(303) 844-6622	1625 Broadway, #680, Denver, CO 80202
CT	(203) 240-3530	450 Main St., #610B, Hartford, CT 06103
DC	(301) 975-3904	c/o National Institute of Standards and Technology, Bldg. 411, #A102, Gaithersburg, MD 20899
DE	(215) 962-4980	660 American Ave., #201, King of Prussia, PA 19406
FL	(305) 536-5267	51 S.W. 1st Ave., #224, Miami, FL 33130
	(813) 461-0011	128 N. Osceola Ave., Clearwater, FL 34615
	(407) 648-6235	200 E. Robinson St., #695, Orlando, FL 32801
	(904) 488-6469	107 W. Gaines St., #366G, Tallahassee, FL 32399-2000
GA	(404) 452-9101	4360 Chamblee-Dunwoody Rd., #310, Atlanta, GA 30341
	(912) 652-4204	120 Barnard St., #A-107, Savannah, GA 31401
HI	(808) 541-1782	300 Ala Moana Blvd., #4106 (mailing address P.O. Box 50026), Honolulu, HI 96850
IA	(515) 284-4222	210 Walnut St., #817, Des Moines, IA 5030?
ID, MT	(208) 334-3857	700 W. State St., 2nd Floor, Boise ID 83720
IL	(312) 353-4450	55 E. Monroe St., #2440, Chicago, IL 60603
	(312) 353-4332	c/o Illinois Institute of Technology, 201 ? Loop Rd., Wheaton, IL 60187
	(815) 987-4347	515 N. Court St. (mailing address: P.O. Bo? 1747), Rockford, IL 61110-0247
IN	(317) 582-2300	11405 N. Pennsylvania St., #106, Carmel, I? 46302
KS	(316) 269-6160	151 N. Volutsia, Wichita, KS 67214-4695

KY	(502) 582-5066	520 S. 4th St., 3rd Floor, Louisville, KY 40202
LA	(504) 589-6546	501 Magazine St., #1043, New Orleans, LA 70130
MA, VT	(617) 565-8563	164 Northern Ave., #307, Boston, MA 02210
MD	(410) 962-3560	40 S. Gay St., #413, Baltimore, MD 21202
	(301) 975-3904	c/o National Institute of Standards and Technology, Bldg. 411, #A102, Gaithersburg, MD 20899
ME	(207) 622-8249	187 State St., Augusta ME 04333
MI	(313) 226-3650	477 Michigan Ave., #1140, Detroit, MI 48226
	(616) 456-2411	300 Monroe N.W., #409, Grand Rapids, MI 49503
MN, ND	(612) 348-1638	110 S. 4th St., #108, Minneapolis, MN 55401
MO	(314) 425-3302	8182 Maryland Ave., #303, St. Louis, MO 63105
	(816) 426-3141	601 E. 12th St., #635, Kansas City, MO 64106
MS	(601) 965-4388	201 W. Capital St., #310, Jackson, MS 39201-2005
NC	(919) 333-5345	400 W. Market St., #400, Greensboro, NC 27401
NE, SD	(402) 221-3664	11133 O St., Omaha, NE 68137
NH	(603) 334-6074	601 Spaulding Turnpike, #29, Portsmouth, NH 03801
NJ	(609) 989-2100	3131 Princeton Pike Bldg. #6, #100, Trenton, NJ 08648
NM	(505) 827-0350	c/o New Mexico Dept. of Economic Development, 1100 St. Francis Dr., Santa Fe, NM 87503
NV	(702) 784-5203	1755 E. Plumb Lane, #152, Reno, NV 89502
NY	(716) 846-4191	111 W. Huron St., #1312, Buffalo, NY 14202
	(716) 263-6480	111 E. Ave., #220, Rochester, NY 14604
	(212) 264-0634	26 Federal Plaza, #3718, New York, NY 10278
OH	(513) 684-2944	550 Main St., #9504, Cincinnati, OH 45202
	(216) 522-4750	600 Superior Ave., #700, Cleveland, OH 44114
OK	(405) 231-5302	6601 Broadway Extension, Oklahoma City, OK 73116
	(918) 581-7650	440 S. Houston St., Tulsa, OK 74127
OR	(503) 326-3001	121 S.W. Salmon, #242, Portland, OR 97204
PA	(215) 962-4980	660 American Ave., #201, King of Prussia, PA 19406
	(412) 644-2850	1000 Liberty Ave., #2002, Pittsburgh, PA 15222
PR	(809) 766-5555	Federal Bldg., Chardon Ave., #G-55, Hato Rey, PR 00918
RI	(401) 528-5104	7 Jackson Walkway, Providence, RI 02903
SC	(803) 765-5345	1835 Assembly St., #172, Columbia, SC 29201

	(803) 727-4051	c/o Trident Technical College, 66 Columbus St. (mailing address: P.O. Box 118067, CE-P), Charleston, SC 29423
TN	(615) 736-5161	404 James Robertson Parkway, #114, Nashville, TN 37219-1505
	(901) 544-4137	22 N. Front St., #200, Memphis, TN 38103
	(615) 545-4637	301 E. Church Ave., Knoxville, TN 37915
TX	(214) 767-0542	2050 N. Stemmons Freeway, #170 (mailing address: P.O. Box 58130), Dallas, TX 75258
	(512) 482-5939	410 E. 5th St., #414-A (mailing address: P.O. Box 12728), Austin, TX 78711
	(713) 229-2578	500 Dallas, #1160, Houston, TX 77002
UT	(801) 524-5116	324 S. State St., #105, Salt Lake City, UT 84111
VA	(804) 771-2246	704 E. Franklin St., #550, Richmond, VA 23219
WA	(206) 553-5615	3131 Elliott Ave., #290, Seattle, WA 98121
	(509) 735-2751	320 N. Johnson St., #350, Kennewick, WA 99336
WI	(414) 297-3473	517 E. Wisconsin Ave., #596, Milwaukee, WI 53202
WV	(304) 347-5123	405 Capitol St., #807, Charleston, WV 25301

Commerce Dept.—Minority Business Development Agency

Area Served	Telephone	Address
AK, AS, AZ, CA, HI, ID, NV, OR, WA	(415) 744-3001	221 Main St., #1280, San Francisco, CA 94105
AL, FL, GA, KY, MS, NC, SC, TN	(404) 730-3300	401 W. Peachtree St. N.W., #1930, Atlanta, GA 30308
AR, CO, LA, MT, ND, NM, OK, SD, TX, UT, WY	(214) 767-8001	1100 Commerce St., #7B23, Dallas, TX 75242
CT, DC, DE, MA, MD, ME, NH, NJ, NY, PA, PR, RI, VA, VI, VT, WV	(212) 264-3262	26 Federal Plaza, #3720, New York, NY 10278
IA, IL, IN, KS, MI, MN, MO, NE, OH, WI	(312) 353-0182	55 E. Monroe St., #1440, Chicago, IL 60603

Commerce Dept.—National Oceanic and Atmospheric Administration

Area Served	Telephone	Address
AK, AZ, CA, HI, ID, MT, NV, OR, UT, WA	(206) 526-6046	7600 Sand Point Way N.E., BIN C-15700, Seattle, WA 98115
AL, AR, FL, GA, IA, IL, IN, KY, LA, MN, MO, MS, OH, TN, WI	(816) 426-7621	601 E. 12th St., #1836, Kansas City, MO 6410●
CO, KS, ND, NE, NM, OK, SD, TX, WY	(303) 497-6286	325 Broadway, Boulder, CO 80303

| CT, DE, MA, MD (except Washington, D.C., area), ME, NC, NH, NJ, NY, PA, PR, RI, SC, VA (except Sterling), VI, VT, WV | (804) 441-6864 | 253 Monticello Ave., Norfolk, VA 23510 |
| DC, MD (Washington, D.C., area), VA (Sterling) | (202) 482-6090 | 14th St. and Constitution Ave. N.W., Washington, D.C. 20230 |

Education Dept.

Area Served	Telephone	Address
AK, ID, OR, WA	(206) 553-0460	915 2nd Ave., #3362, Seattle, WA 98174-1099
AL, FL, GA, KY, MS, NC, SC, TN	(404) 331-2502	101 Marietta Tower Bldg. (mailing address: P.O. Box 1777), Atlanta, GA 30301
AR, LA, NM, OK, TX	(214) 767-3626	1200 Main Tower Bldg., #2125, Dallas, TX 75202
AS, AZ, CA, CM, GU, HI, NV, TT	(415) 556-4920	50 United Nations Plaza, #205, San Francisco, CA 94102
CO, MT, ND, SD, UT, WY	(303) 844-3544	1244 Speer Blvd., #310, Denver, CO 80204-3582
CT, MA, ME, NH, RI, VT	(617) 223-9317	John W. McCormack Post Office and Courthouse, #540, Boston, MA 02109-4557
DC, DE, MD, PA, VA, WV	(215) 596-1001	3535 Market St., #R-16350, Philadelphia, PA 19104
IA, KS, MO, NE	(816) 891-7972	10220 N. Executive Hills Blvd., 9th Floor, Kansas City, MO 64153-1367
IL, IN, MI, MN, OH, WI	(312) 353-5215	401 S. State St., #700A, Chicago, IL 60605-1225
NJ, NY, PR, VI	(212) 264-7005	26 Federal Plaza, #36-120, New York, NY 10278-0195

Energy Dept.—Federal Energy Regulatory Commission

Area Served	Telephone	Address
AK, ID, MT, OR, WA, WY	(503) 326-5840	1120 S.W. 5th Ave., #1340, Portland, OR 97204
AL, AR, FL, GA, LA, MS, NC, OK, PR, SC, TN, TX, VA	(404) 452-2360	3125 Presidential Parkway, #300, Atlanta, GA 30340
AZ, CA, CO, HI, NM, NV, UT	(415) 744-3075	901 Market St., #350, San Francisco, CA 94103
CT, DC, DE, MA, MD, ME, NH, NJ, NY, PA, RI, VT, WV	(212) 631-8110	19 W. 34th St., #400, New York, NY 10001
IA, IL, IN, KS, KY, MI, MN, MO, ND, NE, OH, SD, WI	(312) 353-6173	230 S. Dearborn St., #3130, Chicago, IL 60604

Energy Dept.—Field Offices

The Energy Dept.'s Operations Offices do not serve specific states. Instead, the Operations Offices manage government-owned, contractor-operated energy research and development facilities. Contact the Operations Office nearest you for referral to the proper oversight office.

Telephone	Address
(510) 637-1774	1301 Clay St., Oakland, CA 94612-5208
(303) 275-4778	1617 Cole Blvd., Golden, CO 80401
(208) 526-0111	785 DOE Pl., Idaho Falls, ID 83401
(708) 252-2001	9800 S. Cass Ave., Argonne, IL 60439
(505) 845-4154	P.O. Box 5400, Albuquerque, NM 87185-5400
(702) 295-1212	P.O. Box 98518, Las Vegas, NV 89193-8518
(513) 738-6319	7400 Willey Rd., Cincinnati, OH 45030
(803) 725-6211	P.O. Box A, Aiken, SC 29801
(615) 576-5454	P.O. Box 2001, Oak Ridge, TN 37831
(509) 376-7411	P.O. Box 550, Richland, WA 99352

Health and Human Services Dept.

Area Served	Telephone	Address
AK, ID, OR, WA	(206) 553-0420	2201 6th Ave., Mail Stop RX-0, Seattle, WA 98121
AL, FL, GA, KY, MS, NC, SC, TN	(404) 331-2442	101 Marietta Tower, Atlanta, GA 30323
AR, LA, NM, OK, TX	(214) 767-3301	1200 Main Tower Bldg., Dallas, TX 75202
AS, AZ, CA, GU, HI, NV	(415) 556-6746	50 United Nations Plaza, #431, San Francisco, CA 94102
CO, MT, ND, SD, UT, WY	(303) 844-4545	1961 Stout St., #10006, Denver, CO 80294
CT, MA, ME, NH, RI, VT	(617) 565-1500	John F. Kennedy Federal Bldg., #2411, Boston, MA 02203
DC, DE, MD, PA, VA, WV	(215) 596-6492	3535 Market St. (mailing address: P.O. Box 13716), Philadelphia, PA 19101
IA, KS, MO, NE	(816) 426-2821	601 E. 12th St., Kansas City, MO 64106
IL, IN, MI, MN, OH, WI	(312) 353-5160	105 W. Adams, 23rd Floor, Chicago, IL 60603
NJ, NY, PR, VI	(212) 264-4600	26 Federal Plaza, New York, NY 10278

Health and Human Services Dept.—Administration for Children and Families

Area Served	Telephone	Address
AK, ID, OR, WA	(206) 553-2775	2201 6th Ave., Seattle, WA 98121
AL, FL, GA, KY, MS, NC, SC, TN	(404) 331-5733	101 Marietta Tower, #821, Atlanta, GA 30323
AR, LA, NM, OK, TX	(214) 767-9648	1200 Main Tower Bldg., Dallas, TX 75202
AZ, CA, HI, NV	(415) 556-7800	50 United Nations Plaza, MS-450, San Francisco, CA 94102

CO, MT, ND, SD, UT, WY	(303) 844-2622	1961 Stout St., #1185, Denver, CO 80294-3538
CT, MA, ME, NH, RI, VT	(617) 565-1020	John F. Kennedy Federal Bldg., #2000, Boston, MA 02203
DC, DE, MD, PA, VA, WV	(215) 596-0362	3535 Market St. (mailing address: P.O. Box 13716), Philadelphia, PA 19104
IA, KS, MO, NE	(816) 426-3981	601 E. 12th St., #384, Kansas City, MO 64106
IL, IN, MI, MN, OH, WI	(312) 353-4237	105 W. Adams St., 20th Floor, Chicago, IL 60606
NJ, NY, PR, VI	(212) 264-2890	26 Federal Plaza, #4048, New York, NY 10278

Health and Human Services Dept.—Food and Drug Administration

Area Served	Telephone	Address
AK, AZ, CA, HI, ID, MT, NV, OR, WA	(415) 556-0439	50 United Nations Plaza, #568, San Francisco, CA 94102
AL, FL, GA, LA, MS, NC, PR, SC, TN	(404) 347-4266	60 8th St. N.E., Atlanta, GA 30309
AR, CO, IA, KS, MO, NE, NM, OK, TX, UT, WY	(214) 655-8100	7920 Elmbrook Dr., #102, Dallas, TX 75247-4982
CT, MA, ME, NH, NY, RI, VT	(718) 965-5416	830 3rd Ave., Brooklyn, NY 11232
DC, DE, KY, MD, NJ, OH, PA, VA, WV	(215) 597-8058	2nd and Chestnut Sts., Philadelphia, PA 19106
IL, IN, MI, MN, ND, SD, WI	(312) 353-1047	20 N. Michigan Ave., #550, Chicago, IL 60606

Health and Human Services Dept.—Public Health Service

Area Served	Telephone	Address
AK, ID, OR, WA	(206) 442-0430	2201 6th Ave., Seattle, WA 98121
AL, FL, GA, KY, MS, NC, SC, TN	(404) 331-2316	101 Marietta Tower Bldg., Atlanta, GA 30323
AR, LA, NM, OK, TX	(214) 767-3879	1200 Main Tower Bldg., Dallas, TX 75202
AS, AZ, CA, GU, HI, NV, TT	(415) 556-5810	50 United Nations Plaza, San Francisco, CA 94102
CO, MT, ND, SD, UT, WY	(303) 844-6163	1961 Stout St., Denver, CO 80294
CT, MA, ME, NH, RI, VT	(617) 565-1426	John F. Kennedy Federal Bldg., Boston, MA 02203
DC, DE, MD, PA, VA, WV	(215) 596-6637	3535 Market St. (mailing address: P.O. Box 13716), Philadelphia, PA 19101
IA, KS, MO, NE	(816) 426-3291	601 E. 12th St., Kansas City, MO 64106
IL, IN, MI, MN, OH, WI	(312) 353-1385	105 W. Adams St., Chicago, IL 60603
NJ, NY, PR, VI	(212) 264-2561	26 Federal Plaza, New York, NY 10278

Health and Human Services Dept.—Social Security Administration

Area Served	Telephone	Address
AK, ID, OR, WA	(206) 615-2100	2201 6th Ave., Mail Stop RX50, Seattle, WA 98121
AL, FL, GA, KY, MS, NC, SC, TN	(404) 331-2475	101 Marietta Tower Bldg., #1904, Atlanta, GA 30323
AR, LA, NM, OK, TX	(214) 767-4210	1200 Main Tower Bldg., #1440, Dallas, TX 75202
AS, AZ, CA, CM, GU, HI, NV	(415) 744-4676	75 Hawthorne St., 7th Floor, San Francisco, CA 94105
CO, MT, ND, SD, UT, WY	(303) 844-2388	1961 Stout St., #1185, Denver, CO 80294
CT, MA, ME, NH, RI, VT	(617) 565-2870	John F. Kennedy Federal Bldg., #1100, Boston, MA 02203
DC, DE, MD, PA, VA, WV	(215) 597-5157	300 Spring Garden St. (mailing address: P.O. Box 8788), Philadelphia, PA 19101
IA, KS, MO, NE	(816) 426-6548	601 E. 12th St., #436, Kansas City, MO 64106
IL, IN, MI, MN, OH, WI	(312) 353-8277	600 W. Madison St., Chicago, IL 60661
NJ, NY, PR, VI	(212) 264-3915	26 Federal Plaza, #40-102, New York, NY 10278

Housing and Urban Development Dept.

Area Served	Telephone	Address
AK, ID, OR, WA	(206) 220-5101	909 1st Ave., #200, Seattle, WA 98104-1000
AL, FL, GA, KY, MS, NC, PR, SC, TN, VI	(404) 331-5136	75 Spring St. S.W., Atlanta, GA 30303-3388
AR, LA, NM, OK, TX	(817) 885-5401	1600 Throckmorton (mailing address: P.O. Box 2905), Fort Worth, TX 76113-2905
AS, AZ, CA, GU, HI, NV	(415) 556-4752	450 Golden Gate Ave. (mailing address: P.O. Box 36003), San Francisco, CA 94102-3448
CO, MT, ND, SD, UT, WY	(303) 844-4513	1405 Curtis St., Denver, CO 80202-2349
CT, MA, ME, NH, RI, VT	(617) 565-5234	10 Causeway St., #375, Boston, MA 02222-1092
DC, DE, MD, PA, VA, WV	(215) 597-2560	105 S. 7th St., Philadelphia, PA 19106-3392
IA, KS, MO, NE	(913) 236-2162	400 State Ave., #200, Kansas City, KS 66101-2406
IL, IN, MI, MN, OH, WI	(312) 353-5680	77 W. Jackson Blvd., Chicago, IL 60604-3507
NJ, NY	(212) 264-6500	26 Federal Plaza, New York, NY 10278-0068

Interior Dept.—Bureau of Indian Affairs

Area Served	Telephone	Address
AK (except Metlakatla)	(907) 586-7177	P.O. Box 3-8000, Juneau, AK 99802-1219
AK (Metlakatla), ID, MT, OR, WA	(503) 231-6702	911 11th Ave. N.E., Portland, OR 97232-416◄

AL, CT, FL, LA, MA, ME, MS, NC, NY, RI	(703) 235-2571	1951 Constitution Ave. N.W., Mail Stop 260, Washington, DC 20245
AZ, CA, NV, UT (except Navajo Reservations)	(602) 379-6600	1 N. 1st St. (mailing address: P.O. Box 10), Phoenix, AZ 85001-0010
AZ, NM, UT (Navajo Reservations)	(602) 871-5151	P.O. Box M, Window Rock, AZ 86515-0714
CA	(916) 978-4691	2800 Cottage Way, Sacramento, CA 95825-1884
CO, NM, TX	(505) 766-3170	615 1st St. N.W. (mailing address: Box 26567), Albuquerque, NM 87125-6567
IA, MI, MN, WI	(612) 373-1000	15 S. 5th St., 10th Floor, Minneapolis, MN 55401-1020
KS, OK (western), TX	(405) 247-6673	WCD Office Complex, Box 368, Anadarko, OK 73005-0368
MO, OK (eastern)	(918) 687-2296	5th and W. Okmulgee, Muskogee, OK 74401-4898
MT, WY	(406) 657-6315	316 N. 26th St., Billings, MT 58101-1397
ND, NE, SD	(605) 226-7343	115 4th Ave. S.E., Aberdeen, SD 57401-4382

Interior Dept.—Bureau of Land Management

Area Served	Telephone	Address
AK	(907) 271-5555	222 W. 7th Ave., #13, Anchorage, AK 99513-7599
AL, AR, CT, DC, DE, FL, GA, IA, IL, IN, KY, LA, MA, MD, ME, MI, MN, MO, MS, NC, NH, NJ, NY, OH, PA, RI, SC, TN, VA, VT, WI, WV	(703) 440-1713	7450 Boston Blvd., Springfield, VA 22153
AZ	(602) 650-0504	3707 N. 7th St. (mailing address: P.O. Box 16563), Phoenix, AZ 85011
CA	(916) 978-4746	2800 Cottage Way, E-2841, Sacramento, CA 95825
CO	(303) 239-3667	2850 Youngfield St., Lakewood, CO 80215-7076
ID	(208) 384-3014	3380 Americana Terrace, Boise, ID 83706
KS, NM, OK, TX	(505) 438-7514	1474 Rodeo Rd. (mailing address: P.O. Box 27115), Santa Fe, NM 87502-0115
MT, ND, SD	(406) 255-2913	222 N. 32nd St. (mailing address: P.O. Box 36800), Billings, MT 59107
NE, WY	(307) 775-6011	2515 Warren Ave. (mailing address: P.O. Box 1828), Cheyenne, WY 82003
NV	(702) 785-6586	850 Harvard Way (mailing address: P.O. Box 12000), Reno, NV 89520-0006
OR, WA	(503) 280-7027	1300 N.E. 44th Ave. (mailing address: P.O. Box 2965), Portland, OR 97208
UT	(801) 539-4021	324 S. State St. (mailing address: P.O. Box 45155), Salt Lake City, UT 84145-0155

Interior Dept.—National Park Service

Area Served	Telephone	Address
AK	(907) 257-2696	2525 Gambell St., Anchorage, AK 99503
AL, FL, GA, KY, MS, NC, PR, SC, TN, VI	(404) 331-4998	75 Spring St. S.W., Atlanta, GA 30303
AR, AZ (northeast), LA, NM, OK, TX	(505) 988-6012	P.O. Box 728, Santa Fe, NM 87501
AZ (except northeast), CA, HI, NV	(415) 744-3929	600 Harrison St., #600, San Francisco, CA 94107
CO, MT, ND, SD, UT, WY	(303) 969-2503	P.O. Box 25287, Denver, CO 80225
CT, MA, ME, NH, NJ, NY, RI, VT	(617) 223-5199	15 State St., Boston, MA 02109
DC, and metropolitan area parks in MD, VA, and WV	(202) 619-7222	1100 Ohio Dr. S.W., Washington, DC 20242
DE, PA, most of MD, VA, and WV	(215) 597-3679	143 S. 3rd St., Philadelphia, PA 19106
IA, IL, IN, KS, MI, MN, MO, NE, OH, WI	(402) 221-3448	1709 Jackson St., Omaha, NE 68102
ID, OR, WA	(206) 220-4013	909 1st Ave., Seattle, WA 98104

Interior Dept.—U.S. Fish and Wildlife Service

Area Served	Telephone	Address
AK	(907) 786-3542	1011 E. Tudor Rd., Anchorage, AK 99503
AL, AR, FL, GA, KY, LA, MS, NC, PR, SC, TN, VI	(404) 679-7289	1875 Century Blvd., Atlanta, GA 30345
AZ, NM, OK, TX	(505) 766-2321	500 Gold Ave. S.W., Albuquerque, NM 87103
CA, HI, ID, NV, OR, WA	(503) 231-2122	911 N.E. 11th Ave., Portland, OR 97232-4181
CO, KS, MT, ND, NE, SD, UT, WY	(303) 236-7904	134 Union Blvd., Lakewood, CO 80228
CT, DE, MA, MD, ME, NH, NJ, NY, PA, RI, VA, VT, WV	(617) 965-5100	300 Westgate Center Dr., Hadley, MA 01035
DC	(202) 208-5634	1849 C St. N.W., Washington, DC 20240
IA, IL, IN, MI, MN, MO, OH, WI	(612) 725-3500	Whipple Federal Bldg., Fort Snelling, Twin Cities, MN 55111

Interior Dept.—U.S. Geological Survey

Area Served	Telephone	Address
AK, AZ, CA, HI, ID, NV, OR, WA	(415) 329-4309	345 Middlefield Rd., Menlo Park, CA 94025
AL, AR, CT, DC, DE, FL, GA, IL, IN, KY, LA, MA, MD, ME, MI, MS, NC, NH, NJ, NY, OH, PA, PR, RI, SC, TN, VA, VI, VT, WI, WV	(703) 648-6045	12201 Sunrise Valley Dr., Reston, VA 22092

| CO, IA, KS, MN, MO, MT, ND, NE, NM, OK, SD, TX, UT, WY | (303) 236-5829 | Denver Federal Center, Box 25046, Denver, CO 80225 |

Justice Dept.—Bureau of Prisons

Area Served	Telephone	Address
AK, AZ, CA, HI, ID, MT, NV, OR, UT, WA, WY	(510) 803-4700	7950 Dublin Blvd., 3rd Floor, Dublin, CA 94568
AL, FL, GA, MS, PR, VI	(404) 624-5202	523 McDonough Blvd. S.E., Atlanta, GA 30315
AR, LA, NM, OK, TN, TX	(214) 767-9700	4211 Cedar Springs Rd., Dallas, TX 75219
CO, IA, IL, KS, MN, MO, ND, NE, SD, WI	(913) 621-3939	4th and State Ave., 8th Floor, Kansas City, KS 66101-2492
CT, MA, ME, NH, NJ, NY, PA, RI, VT	(215) 597-6317	2nd and Chestnut Sts., 7th Floor, Philadelphia, PA 19106
DC, DE, IN, KY, MD, MI, NC, OH, SC, VA, WV	(301) 317-3100	10010 Junction Dr., #100N, Annapolis Junction, MD 20701

Justice Dept.—Drug Enforcement Administration

Area Served	Telephone	Address
AK, ID, OR, WA	(206) 553-5443	220 W. Mercer St., Seattle, WA 98119
AL, AR, LA, MS	(504) 840-1100	3838 N. Causeway Blvd., #1800, Metairie, LA 70002
AZ	(602) 640-5700	3010 N. 2nd St., #301, Phoenix, AZ 85012
CA (northern)	(415) 556-6771	450 Golden Gate Ave. (mailing address: P.O. Box 36035), San Francisco, CA 94102
CA (southern)	(619) 585-4200	402 W. 35th St., National City, CA 91950
CA (southern), GU, HI, NV	(310) 894-2650	225 E. Temple St., 20th Floor, Los Angeles, CA 90012
CO, MT, NM, UT, WY	(303) 784-6300	115 Inverness Dr. East, Denver, CO 80112
CT, MA, ME, NH, RI, VT	(617) 557-2100	50 Staniford St., #200, Boston, MA 02114
DC, MD, VA, WV	(202) 401-7834	400 6th St. S.W., Washington, DC 20024
DE, PA	(215) 597-9530	600 Arch St., Philadelphia, PA 19106
FL, PR, VI	(305) 590-4870	8400 N.W. 53rd St., Miami, FL 33166
GA, NC, SC, TN	(404) 331-4401	75 Spring St. S.W., Atlanta, GA 30303
IA, KS, MO, NE, SD	(314) 425-3241	7911 Forsyth Blvd., St. Louis, MO 63105
IL, IN, MN, ND, WI	(312) 353-7875	219 S. Dearborn St., Chicago, IL 60604
KY, MI, OH	(313) 226-7290	231 W. Lafayette, Detroit, MI 48226
NJ	(201) 645-6060	970 Broad St., Newark, NJ 07102
NY	(212) 337-3900	99 10th Ave., New York, NY 10011
OK, TX (northern)	(214) 767-7151	1880 Regal Row, Dallas, TX 75235
TX (southern)	(700) 527-9000	333 W. Loop North, Houston, TX 77024

Justice Dept.—Federal Bureau of Investigation

Area Served	Telephone	Address
AK	(907) 276-4441	222 W. 7th Ave., #241, Anchorage, AK 99513-7598
AL	(205) 252-7705	2121 Federal Bldg., #1400, Birmingham, AL 35203
	(205) 438-3674	1 St. Louis St., Mobile, AL 36602
AR	(501) 221-9100	10825 Financial Centre Parkway, #200, Little Rock, AR 72211
AZ	(602) 279-5511	201 E. Indianola, #400, Phoenix, AZ 85102
CA	(213) 477-6565	11000 Wilshire Blvd., Los Angeles, CA 90024
	(916) 481-9110	2800 Cottage Way, Sacramento, CA 95825
	(619) 231-1122	880 Front St., #6S-31, San Diego, CA 92188
	(415) 553-7400	450 Golden Gate Ave., San Francisco, CA 94102
CO, WY	(303) 629-7171	Federal Office Bldg., #1823, Denver, CO 80202
CT	(203) 777-6311	150 Court St., New Haven, CT 06510
DC (metro area)	(202) 324-3000	1900 Half St. S.W., Washington, DC 20535
DE, MD	(301) 265-8080	7142 Ambassador Rd., Baltimore, MD 21244
FL	(904) 721-1211	7820 Arlington Expressway, #200, Jacksonville, FL 32211
	(305) 944-9101	16320 N.W. 2nd Ave., North Miami Beach, FL 33169
	(813) 228-7661	500 Zack St., #610, Tampa, FL 33602
GA	(404) 521-3900	2635 Century Parkway N.E., #400, Atlanta, GA 30345
HI	(808) 521-1411	300 Ala Moana Blvd., #4307, Honolulu, HI 96850
IA, NE	(402) 493-8688	1075 Burt St., Omaha, NE 68114
ID, MT, UT	(801) 579-1400	257 E. 200 South St., #1200, Salt Lake City, UT 84011
IL	(312) 431-1333	219 S. Dearborn St., #905, Chicago, IL 60604
	(217) 522-9675	400 W. Monroe St., #400, Springfield, IL 62704
IN	(317) 639-3301	575 N. Pennsylvania St., #679, Indianapolis, IN 46204
KS, MO	(816) 221-6100	U.S. Courthouse, #300, Kansas City, MO 64106
KY	(502) 583-3941	600 Martin Luther King Pl., #500, Louisville, KY 40202
LA	(504) 522-4671	1250 Poydras St., #2200, New Orleans, LA 70113
MA, ME, NH, RI	(617) 742-5533	One Center Plaza, #600, Boston, MA 02108
MI	(313) 965-2323	477 Michigan Ave., Detroit, MI 48226

MN, ND, SD	(612) 376-3200	111 Washington Ave. South, #1100, Minneapolis, MN 55401
MO	(314) 241-5357	1520 Market St., #2704, St. Louis, MO 63103
MS	(601) 948-5000	100 W. Capitol St., #1553, Jackson, MS 39269
NC	(704) 529-1030	6010 Kenley Lane, Charlotte, NC 28217
NJ (except Gloucester, Salem, and Camden counties)	(201) 622-5613	Gateway One, Market St., Newark, NJ 07102
NJ (Gloucester, Salem, and Camden counties), PA (eastern)	(215) 629-0800	600 Arch St., Philadelphia, PA 19106
NM	(505) 224-2000	415 Silver S.W., #300, Albuquerque, NM 87102
NV	(702) 385-1281	700 E. Charleston Blvd., Las Vegas, NV 89104
NY, VT	(518) 465-7551	445 Broadway, 5th Floor, Albany, NY 12201-1219
	(716) 856-7800	111 W. Huron St., #1400, Buffalo, NY 14202
	(212) 335-2700	26 Federal Plaza, New York, NY 10278
OH	(513) 421-4310	550 Main St., #9023, Cincinnati, OH 45202
	(216) 522-1400	1240 E. 9th St., #3005, Cleveland, OH 44199
OK	(405) 842-7471	50 Penn Pl., #1600, Oklahoma City, OK 73118
OR	(503) 224-4181	1500 S.W. 1st Ave., Portland, OR 97201
PA (western), WV	(412) 471-2000	700 Grant St., #300, Pittsburgh, PA 15219
PR	(809) 498-5284	U.S. Courthouse and Federal Office Bldg., #526, Hato Rey, San Juan, PR 00918
SC	(803) 254-3011	1835 Assembly St., #1357, Columbia, SC 29201
TN	(615) 544-0751	710 Locust St., 6th Floor, Knoxville, TN 37901
	(901) 525-7373	167 N. Main St., #841, Memphis, TN 38103
TX	(214) 720-2200	1801 N. Lamar, #300, Dallas, TX 75202
	(915) 533-7451	700 E. San Antonio Ave., #C-600, El Paso, TX 79901
	(713) 868-2266	2500 East T. C. Jester, #200, Houston, TX 77008
	(512) 225-6741	615 E. Houston St., #200, San Antonio, TX 78205
VA	(804) 623-3111	200 Granby St., #839, Norfolk, VA 23510
	(804) 261-1044	111 Greencourt Rd., Richmond, VA 23228
WA	(206) 622-0460	915 2nd Ave., #710, Seattle, WA 98174
WI	(414) 276-4684	330 E. Kilbourn Ave., #600, Milwaukee, WI 53202-6627

Justice Dept.—Immigration and Naturalization Service

Area Served	Telephone	Address
AK, CO, IA, ID, IL, IN, KS, MI, MN, MO, MT, ND, NE, OH, OR, SD, UT, WA, WI, WY	(612) 725-3850	Bishop Henry Whipple Federal Bldg., #480, Fort Snelling, Twin Cities, MN 55111
AL, AR, FL, GA, KY, LA, MS, NC, NM, OK, SC, TN, TX	(214) 767-7011	7701 N. Stemmons Freeway, Dallas, TX 75247
AZ, CA, GU, HI, NV	(714) 643-4236	24000 Avila Rd. (mailing address: P.O. Box 30080), Laguna Niguel, CA 92677
CT, DE, MA, MD, ME, NH, NJ, NY, PA, PR, RI, VA, VI, VT, WV	(802) 660-5000	70 Kimball Ave., South Burlington, VT 05403

Justice Dept.—U.S. Parole Commission

Area Served	Telephone	Address
AK, CO, IA, ID, IL, IN, KS, KY, MI, MN, MO, MT, ND, NE, NV, OH, OK, OR, SD, UT, WA, WI, WY	(816) 891-7770	10920 Ambassador Dr., #220, Kansas City, MO 64153
AL, CT, CZ, DC, DE, FL, GA, MA, MD, ME, NC, NH, NJ, NY, PA, PR, RI, SC, VA, VI, VT, WV	(301) 492-5821	5550 Friendship Blvd., #420, Chevy Chase, MD 20815-7286
AR, AS, AZ, CA, GU, HI, LA, MS, NM, TN, TX	(214) 767-0024	525 Griffin St., #820, Dallas, TX 75202-5097

Labor Dept.

Area Served	Telephone	Address
AK, ID, OR, WA	(206) 553-7620	1111 3rd Ave., #805, Seattle, WA 98101
AL, FL, GA, KY, MS, NC, SC, TN	(404) 347-4495	1371 Peachtree St. N.E., #317, Atlanta, GA 30367
AR, LA, NM, OK, TX	(214) 767-4776	525 Griffin St., #734, Dallas, TX 75202
AZ, CA, GU, HI, NV	(415) 744-6673	71 Stevenson St., #1035, San Francisco, CA 94105
CO, MT, ND, SD, UT, WY	(303) 844-4235	1961 Stout St., #1468, Denver, CO 80294
CT, MA, ME, NH, RI, VT	(617) 565-2075	1 Congress St., 11th Floor, Boston, MA 02114
DC, DE, MD, PA, VA, WV	(215) 596-1139	3535 Market St., #14120, Philadelphia, PA 19104
IA, KS, MO, NE	(816) 426-5481	911 Walnut St., #2509, Kansas City, MO 64106
IL, IN, MI, MN, OH, WI	(312) 353-6976	230 S. Dearborn St., #3192, Chicago, IL 60604
NJ, NY, PR, VI	(212) 337-2319	201 Varick St., #605, New York, NY 10014

Labor Dept.—Bureau of Labor Statistics

Area Served	Telephone	Address
AK, AS, AZ, CA, GU, HI, ID, NV, OR, WA	(415) 744-7166	71 Stevenson St. (mailing address: P.O. Box 193766), San Francisco, CA 94119
AL, FL, GA, KY, MS, NC, SC, TN	(404) 347-2161	1371 Peachtree St. N.E., Atlanta, GA 30367
AR, LA, NM, OK, TX	(214) 767-6953	525 Griffin St., Dallas, TX 75202
CO, IA, KS, MO, MT, ND, NE, SD, UT, WY	(816) 426-2378	911 Walnut St., Kansas City, MO 64106
CT, MA, ME, NH, RI, VT	(617) 565-2331	1 Congress St., Boston, MA 02114
DC, DE, MD, PA, VA, WV	(215) 596-1151	3535 Market St., Philadelphia, PA 19101
IL, IN, MI, MN, OH, WI	(312) 353-7226	230 S. Dearborn St., Chicago, IL 60604
NJ, NY, PR, VI	(212) 337-2500	201 Varick St., #808, New York, NY 10014

Labor Dept.—Employment and Training Administration

Area Served	Telephone	Address
AK, ID, OR, WA	(206) 553-7700	909 1st Ave., Seattle, WA 98174
AL, FL, GA, KY, MS, NC, SC, TN	(404) 347-4411	1371 Peachtree St. N.E., Atlanta, GA 30367
AR, LA, NM, OK, TX	(214) 767-8263	525 Griffin Square Bldg., Dallas, TX 75202
AZ, CA, HI, NV	(415) 744-6650	71 Stevenson St., San Francisco, CA 94102
CO, MT, ND, SD, UT, WY	(303) 844-4477	1961 Stout St., Denver, CO 80294
CT, MA, ME, NH, RI, VT	(617) 565-3630	John F. Kennedy Federal Bldg., Boston, MA 02203
DC, DE, MD, PA, VA, WV	(215) 596-6336	P.O. Box 8796, Philadelphia, PA 19101
IA, KS, MO, NE	(816) 426-3796	911 Walnut St., Kansas City, MO 64106
IL, IN, MI, MN, OH, WI	(312) 353-0313	230 S. Dearborn St., Chicago, IL 60604
NJ, NY, PR, VI	(212) 337-2139	201 Varick St., New York, NY 10014

Labor Dept.—Occupational Safety and Health Administration

Area Served	Telephone	Address
AK, ID, OR, WA	(206) 553-5930	1111 3rd Ave., #715, Seattle, WA 98101-3212
AL, FL, GA, KY, MS, NC, SC, TN	(404) 347-3573	1375 Peachtree St. N.E., #587, Atlanta, GA 30367
AR, LA, NM, OK, TX	(214) 767-4731	525 Griffin St., #602, Dallas, TX 75202
AS, AZ, CA, GU, HI, NV, TT	(415) 744-6670	71 Stevenson St., #415, San Francisco, CA 94105
CO, MT, ND, SD, UT, WY	(303) 844-3061	1961 Stout St., Denver, CO 80294
CT, MA, ME, NH, RI, VT	(617) 565-7164	133 Portland St., 1st Floor, Boston, MA 02114
DC, DE, MD, PA, VA, WV	(215) 596-1201	3535 Market St., #2100, Philadelphia, PA 19104

IA, KS, MO, NE	(816) 426-5861	911 Walnut St., #406, Kansas City, MO 64106
IL, IN, MI, MN, OH, WI	(312) 353-2220	230 S. Dearborn St., #3244, Chicago, IL 60604
NJ, NY, PR, VI	(212) 337-2378	201 Varick St., #670, New York, NY 10014

State Dept.—Passport Offices

Area Served	Telephone	Address
AK, CO, ID, MN, MT, ND, NE, OR, SD, WA, WY	(206) 220-7787	915 2nd Ave., #992, Seattle, WA 98174-1091
AL, AR, KS, KY, LA, MO, MS, OH, OK, TN	(504) 589-2335	701 Loyola Ave., #T-12005, New Orleans, LA 70113-1931
AS, CM, GU, HI, TT; Wake, Midway, and Pacific islands	(808) 541-1918	300 Ala Moana Blvd., #C-106, Honolulu, HI 96850-0001
AZ, NM, TX	(713) 653-3158	1919 Smith St., #1100, Houston, TX 77002-8049
CA (northern), NV (except Clark County), UT	(415) 744-4008	525 Market St., #200, San Francisco, CA 94105-2773
CA (southern), NV (Clark County)	(310) 575-7080	11000 Wilshire Blvd., #13100, Los Angeles, CA 90024-3615
CT (walk-in applications only)	(203) 325-1803	Broad and Atlantic Sts., 1 Landmark Square, Stamford, CT 06901-2767
DC, MD, NC, VA, WV	(202) 326-6021	1425 K St. N.W., Washington, DC 20522-1705
DE, NJ, PA	(215) 597-8027	600 Arch St., #4426, Philadelphia, PA 19106-1685
FL, GA, PR, SC, VI	(305) 536-7691	51 S.W. 1st Ave., 3rd Level, Miami, FL 33130-1680
IA, IL, IN, MI, WI	(312) 353-7164	230 S. Dearborn St., #380, Chicago, IL 60604-1564
MA, ME, NH, RI, VT	(617) 565-7190	10 Causeway St., #247, Boston, MA 02222-1094
NY	(212) 399-5930	630 5th Ave., #270, New York, NY 10111
walk-in applications only	(212) 206-7020	201 Varick St., #1108, New York, NY 10014

Transportation Dept.—Federal Aviation Administration

Area Served	Telephone	Address
AK	(907) 271-5296	222 W. 7th Ave., #14, Anchorage, AK 99513
AL, FL, GA, KY, MS, NC, PR, SC, TN, VI	(404) 305-5100	1701 Columbia Ave., College Park, GA 30337
AR, LA, NM, OK, TX	(817) 222-5800	2601 Meacham Blvd., Fort Worth, TX 76137
AZ, CA, NV	(310) 297-1431	15000 Aviation Blvd., Hawthorne, CA (mailing address: P.O. Box 92007, Worldway Postal Center, Los Angeles, CA 90009)
CO, ID, MT, OR, UT, WA, WY	(206) 227-2004	1601 Lind Ave. S.W., Renton, WA 98055-4056
CT, MA, ME, NH, RI, VT	(617) 238-7372	12 New England Executive Park, Burlington, MA 01803

DC, DE, MD, NJ, NY, PA, VA, WV	(718) 553-2680	JFK International Airport (Fitzgerald Federal Bldg.), Jamaica, NY 11430
IA, KS, MO, NE	(816) 426-5449	601 E. 12th St., #1501, Kansas City, MO 64106
IL, IN, MI, MN, ND, OH, SD, WI	(708) 294-7067	2300 E. Devon Ave., Des Plaines, IL 60018

Transportation Dept.—Federal Highway Administration

Area Served	Telephone	Address
AK, ID, OR, WA	(503) 326-2064	222 S.W. Columbia St., #600, Portland, OR 97201
AL, FL, GA, KY, MS, NC, SC, TN	(404) 347-4078	1720 Peachtree Rd. N.W., #200, Atlanta, GA 30367
AR, LA, NM, OK, TX	(817) 334-3232	819 Taylor St., #8A00 (mailing address: P.O. Box 902003), Fort Worth, TX 76102
AZ, CA, HI, NV	(415) 744-2639	211 Main St., #1100, San Francisco, CA 94105
CO, MT, ND, SD, UT, WY	(303) 969-6722	555 Zang St., #400, Lakewood, CO 80228
CT, MA, ME, NH, NJ, NY, PR, RI, VT	(518) 472-6476	Clinton Ave. and N. Pearl St., #719, Albany, NY 12207
DC, DE, MD, PA, VA, WV	(410) 962-0093	10 S. Howard St., #4000, Baltimore, MD 21201
IA, KS, MO, NE	(816) 926-7490	6301 Rockhill Rd. (mailing address: P.O. Box 419715), Kansas City, MO 64131
IL, IN, MI, MN, OH, WI	(708) 206-3186	18209 Dixie Highway, Homewood, IL 60430-2294

Transportation Dept.—Federal Railroad Administration

Area Served	Telephone	Address
AK, ID, MT, ND, OR, SD, WA, WY	(206) 696-7536	703 Broadway, #650, Vancouver, WA 98660
AL, FL, GA, KY, MS, NC, SC, TN	(404) 347-2751	1720 Peachtree Rd. N.W., #440, Atlanta, GA 30309
AR, LA, NM, OK, TX	(817) 334-3601	8701 Bedford-Euless Rd., #425, Hurst, TX 76053
AZ, CA, HI, NV, UT	(916) 551-1260	650 Capitol Mall, #707, Sacramento, CA 95814
CO, IA, KS, MO, NE	(816) 426-2497	911 Walnut St., #1807, Kansas City, MO 64106-2095
CT, MA, ME, NH, NJ, NY, RI, VT	(617) 494-2321	55 Broadway, #1077, Cambridge, MA 02142
DE, MD, OH, PA, VA, WV	(215) 521-8200	Scott Plaza Two, #550, Philadelphia, PA 19113
IL, IN, MI, MN, WI	(312) 353-6203	111 N. Canal St., #655, Chicago, IL 60606

Transportation Dept.—Federal Transit Administration

Area Served	Telephone	Address
AK, ID, OR, WA	(206) 220-7954	915 2nd Ave., #3142, Seattle, WA 98174

AL, FL, GA, KY, MS, NC, PR, SC, TN	(404) 347-3948	1720 Peachtree Rd. N.W., #400, Atlanta, GA 30309
AR, LA, NM, OK, TX	(817) 860-9663	524 E. Lamar Blvd., #175, Arlington, TX 76011
AS, CA, GU, HI	(415) 744-3133	211 Main St., #1160, San Francisco, CA 94105
AZ, CO, MT, ND, NV, SD, UT, WY	(303) 844-3242	216 16th St., #650, Denver, CO 80202-5120
CT, MA, ME, NH, RI, VT	(617) 494-2055	55 Broadway, Cambridge, MA 02142
DC, DE, MD, PA, VA, WV	(215) 656-6900	1760 Market St., #500, Philadelphia, PA 19103
IA, KS, MO, NE	(816) 523-0204	6301 Rockhill Rd., #303, Kansas City, MO 64131
IL, IN, MI, MN, OH, WI	(312) 353-2789	55 E. Monroe St., #1415, Chicago, IL 60603
NJ, NY, VI	(212) 264-8162	26 Federal Plaza, #2940, New York, NY 10278

Transportation Dept.—Maritime Administration

Area Served	Telephone	Address
AK, AZ, CA, CO, HI, ID, MT, ND, NM, NV, OR, SD, UT, WA, WY	(415) 744-2580	211 Main St., San Francisco, CA 94105
AL, AR, FL (western), IA, KS, KY, LA, MO, MS, NE, OK, TN, TX	(504) 589-6556	365 Canal St., New Orleans, LA 70130
CT, DE, MA, MD, ME, NH, NJ, NY (downstate), PA (eastern), PR, RI, VT	(212) 264-1300	26 Federal Plaza, #3737, New York, NY 10278
FL (eastern), GA, NC, SC, VA, WV	(804) 441-6393	7737 Hampton Blvd., Norfolk, VA 23505
IL, IN, MI, MN, NY (upstate), OH, PA (western), WI	(708) 298-4535	2300 E. Devon Ave., #366, Des Plaines, IL 60018

Transportation Dept.—National Highway Traffic Safety Administration

Area Served	Telephone	Address
AK, ID, OR, WA	(206) 220-7640	915 2nd Ave., #3140, Seattle, WA 98174
AL, FL, GA, KY, MS, NC, SC, TN	(404) 347-4537	1720 Peachtree Rd. N.W., #501, Atlanta, GA 30309
AR, LA, NM, OK, TX	(817) 334-4300	819 Taylor St., Fort Worth, TX 76102-6177
AS, AZ, CA, GU, HI, NV	(415) 744-3089	211 Main St., #1000, San Francisco, CA 94105
CO, MT, ND, SD, UT, WY	(303) 969-6917	555 Zang St., 4th Floor, Denver, CO 80228
CT, MA, ME, NH, RI, VT	(617) 494-3427	Transportation System Center, Kendall Square, Code 903, Cambridge, MA 02142
DC, DE, MD, PA, VA, WV	(410) 768-7111	7526 Connelley Dr., #L, Hanover, MD 21076
IA, KS, MO, NE	(816) 822-7233	P.O. Box 412515, Kansas City, MO 64141
IL, IN, MI, MN, OH, WI	(708) 206-3300	18209 Dixie Highway, #A, Homewood, IL 60430
NJ, NY, PR, VI	(914) 682-6162	222 Mamaroneck Ave., #204, White Plains, NY 10605

Treasury Dept.—Bureau of Alcohol, Tobacco, and Firearms; Compliance Operations

Area Served	Telephone	Address
AK, AZ, CA, HI, ID, MT, NV, OR, UT, WA	(415) 744-7013	221 Main St., 11th Floor, San Francisco, CA 94105
AL, FL, GA, MS, NC, PR, SC, TN, VA	(404) 679-5010	2600 Century Parkway N.E., #300, Atlanta, GA 30345
AR, CO, IA, KS, LA, MO, NE, NM, OK, TX, WY	(214) 767-2280	1114 Commerce St., 7th Floor, Dallas, TX 75242
CT, DC, DE, MA, MD, ME, NH, NJ, NY, PA, RI, VT	(212) 264-2328	6 World Trade Center, #620, New York, NY 10048
IL, IN, KY, MI, MN, ND, OH, SD, WV, WI	(312) 353-1967	300 S. Riverside Plaza, #310, Chicago, IL 60606-6616

Treasury Dept.—Bureau of Alcohol, Tobacco, and Firearms; Law Enforcement

Area Served	Telephone	Address
AK, HI, ID, MT, OR, WA, WY	(206) 220-6440	915 2nd Ave., #806, Seattle, WA 98174
AL, MS	(205) 731-1205	2121 8th Ave. North, #725, Birmingham, AL 35203
AR, LA	(504) 589-2048	10001 Lake Forest Blvd., #309, New Orleans, LA 70127
AZ (except southwestern), NM	(602) 640-2840	3003 N. Central Ave., #1010, Phoenix, AZ 85012
AZ (southwestern), CA (southern)	(213) 894-4812	350 S. Figueroa St., #800, Los Angeles, CA 90071
CA (northern), CO, NV, UT	(415) 744-7001	221 Main St., #1250, San Francisco, CA 94105
CT, MA, ME, NH, RI, VT	(617) 565-7042	10 Causeway St., #701, Boston, MA 02222-1081
DC, VA	(202) 219-7751	607 14th St. N.W., #620, Washington, D.C. 20005
DE, MD	(410) 962-0897	103 S. Gay St., 2nd Floor, Baltimore, MD 21202
FL	(305) 597-4800	8420 N.W. 52nd St., #120, Miami, FL 33166
GA	(404) 331-6526	101 Marietta St. N.W., #406, Atlanta, GA 30303
IA, KS, NE	(816) 426-7188	811 Grand Ave., #106, Kansas City, MO 64106
IL (northern), IN (northern)	(312) 353-6935	300 S. Riverside Plaza, #350 South, Chicago, IL 60606
IL (southern), MO	(314) 425-5560	100 S. 4th St., #550, St. Louis, MO 63102
IN (southern), KY, WV (western)	(502) 582-5211	510 W. Broadway, #807, Louisville, KY 40202

MI	(313) 393-6000	1155 Brewery Park Blvd., #300, Detroit, MI 48207-2602
MN, ND, SD, WI	(612) 290-3092	30 E. 7th St., #1870, St. Paul, MN 55101
NC, SC	(704) 344-6125	4530 Park Rd., #400, Charlotte, NC 28209
NJ (northern), NY, PR	(212) 264-4658	90 Church St., #1016, New York, NY 10007
NJ (southern), PA, WV (eastern)	(215) 597-7266	2nd and Chestnut Sts., #504, Philadelphia, PA 19106
OH	(216) 522-7210	7251 Engle Rd., #301, Middleburg Hts., OH 44130
OK, TX (northern)	(214) 767-2250	1200 Main Tower Bldg., #2250, Dallas, TX 75250
TN	(615) 781-5364	215 Centerview Dr., #215, Brentwood, TN 37027
TX (southern)	(713) 449-2073	15355 Vantage Parkway West, #210, Houston, TX 77032

Treasury Dept.—Comptroller of the Currency

Area Served	Telephone	Address
AK, AZ, CA, CO, GU, HI, ID, MT, NV, OR, UT, WA, WY	(415) 545-5900	50 Fremont St., #3900, San Francisco, CA 94105-2292
AL, FL, GA, MS, NC, SC, TN, VA, WV	(404) 659-8855	245 Peachtree Center Ave. N.E., #600, Atlanta, GA 30303-1223
AR, LA, NM, OK, TX	(214) 720-0656	500 N. Ackard St., Dallas, TX 75201-3342
CT, DC, DE, MA, MD, ME, NH, NJ, NY, PA, PR, RI, VI, VT	(212) 819-9860	1114 Avenue of the Americas, #3900, New York, NY 10036-7703
IA, KS, MN, MO, ND, NE, SD	(816) 556-1800	2345 Grand Ave., #700, Kansas City, MO 64108-2683
IL, IN, KY, MI, OH, WI	(312) 663-8000	440 S. LaSalle St., #2700, Chicago, IL 60605-1073

Treasury Dept.—Internal Revenue Service

Area Served	Telephone	Address
AK, CA, HI, ID, NV, OR, WA	(415) 556-3009	1650 Mission St., #316, San Francisco, CA 94103
AL, AR, FL, GA, LA, MS, NC, SC, TN	(404) 331-4337	401 W. Peachtree St., #201, Atlanta, GA 30365
AZ, CO, KS, NM, OK, TX, UT, WY	(214) 308-1681	4050 Alpha Rd., MS-6400, Dallas, TX 75244
CT, MA, ME, NH, NY, RI, VT	(212) 264-0693	P.O. Box 269, Church St. Station, New York, NY 10007
DC, DE, MD, NJ, PA, VA	(215) 597-2080	841 Chestnut St., 2nd Floor, Philadelphia, PA 19107
IA, IL, MN, MO, MT, ND, NE, SD, WI	(312) 886-0333	300 S. Riverside Plaza, Chicago, IL 60606
IN, KY, MI, OH, WV	(513) 684-2841	P.O. Box 1699, Cincinnati, OH 45201

Treasury Dept.—Office of Thrift Supervision

Area Served	Telephone	Address
AK, AZ, CA, HI, ID, MT, NV, OR, UT, WA, WY	(415) 616-1500	1 Montgomery St., #400 (mailing address: P.O. Box 7165), San Francisco, CA 94120
AL, DC, FL, GA, MD, NC, PR, SC, VI	(404) 888-0771	1475 Peachtree St. N.E. (mailing address: P.O. Box 105217), Atlanta, GA 30348-5217
AR, CO, IA, KS, LA, MN, MO, MS, ND, NE, NM, OK, SD, TX	(214) 281-2000	122 W. John Carpenter Freeway, #600, Irving, TX (mailing address: P.O. Box 619027, Dallas/Ft. Worth, TX 75261-9027)
CT, DE, MA, ME, NH, NJ, NY, PA, VT, WV	(201) 413-1000	10 Exchange Place Centre, 18th Floor, Jersey City, NJ 07302
IL, IN, KY, MI, OH, TN, WI	(312) 540-5900	111 E. Wacker Dr., #800, Chicago, IL 60601-4360

Treasury Dept.—U.S. Customs Service

Area Served	Telephone	Address
AK, CA, HI, ID (southern), NV, OR, WA	(310) 980-3100	1 World Trade Center, #705, Long Beach, CA 90831-0700
AL, AR, LA, MS, TN	(504) 589-6324	423 Canal St., #337, New Orleans, LA 70130
AZ, NM, OK, TX	(713) 953-6843	5850 San Felipe St., Houston, TX 77057
CO, IA, ID (northern), IL, IN, KS, KY, MI, MN, MO, MT, ND, NE, OH, SD, UT, WI, WY	(312) 353-4733	610 Canal St., Chicago, IL 60607
CT, MA, MD, ME, NH, NJ (southern), NY (western), PA, RI, VT	(617) 565-6210	10 Causeway St., #801, Boston, MA 02222-1056
FL, GA, NC, PR, SC, VA, VI, WV	(305) 536-5952	909 S.E. 1st Ave., Miami, FL 33131
NJ (northern), NY (eastern)	(212) 466-4444	6 World Trade Center, New York, NY 10048

Veterans Affairs Dept.—Benefits

Area Served	Telephone*	Address
AK	(907) 257-4700	2925 DeBarr Rd., Anchorage, AK 99508-2989
AL	(205) 262-7781	474 S. Court St., Montgomery, AL 36104
AR	(501) 370-3800	P.O. Box 1280, North Little Rock, AR 72115
AZ	(602) 263-5411	3225 N. Central Ave., Phoenix, AZ 85012
CA	(310) 479-4011	11000 Wilshire Blvd., Los Angeles, CA 90024
	(619) 297-8220	2022 Camino Del Rio North, San Diego, CA 92108
	(415) 495-8900	211 Main St., San Francisco, CA 94105
CO	(303) 980-1300	44 Union Blvd. (mailing address: P.O. Box 25126), Denver, CO 80225

*Telephone numbers are for local callers only. Others may dial (800) 827-1000.

CT	(203) 278-3230	450 Main St., Hartford, CT 06103
DC, and metropolitan MD and VA	(202) 872-1151	941 N. Capitol St. N.E., Washington, DC 20421
DE	(302) 998-0191	1601 Kirkwood Highway, Wilmington, DE 19805
FL	(813) 898-2121	144 1st Ave. South, St. Petersburg, FL 33701
GA	(404) 881-1776	730 Peachtree St. N.E., Atlanta, GA 30365
HI	(808) 541-1000	300 Ala Moana Blvd. (mailing address: P.O. Box 50188), Honolulu, HI 96850
IA	(515) 284-0219	210 Walnut St., Des Moines, IA 50309
ID	(208) 334-1010	550 W. Fort St. (mailing address: Box 044), Boise, ID 83724
IL	(312) 663-5510	536 S. Clark St. (mailing address: P.O. Box 8136), Chicago, IL 60680
IN	(317) 226-5566	575 N. Pennsylvania St., Indianapolis, IN 46204
KS	(316) 682-2301	5500 E. Kellogg, Wichita, KS 67218
KY	(502) 584-2231	545 S. 3rd St., Louisville, KY 40202
LA	(504) 589-7191	701 Loyola Ave., New Orleans, LA 70113
MA	(617) 227-4600	JFK Federal Bldg., Boston, MA 02203
MD	(410) 685-5454	31 Hopkins Plaza, Baltimore, MD 21201
ME	(207) 623-8000	Rt. 17 East, Togus, ME 04330
MI	(313) 964-5110	477 Michigan Ave., Detroit, MI 48226
MN	(612) 726-1454	Federal Bldg., Fort Snelling, St. Paul, MN 55111
MO	(314) 342-1171	1520 Market St., St. Louis, MO 63103
MS	(601) 965-4873	100 W. Capitol St., Jackson, MS 39269
MT	(700) 447-7975	Fort Harrison, MT 59636
NC	(919) 748-1800	251 N. Main St., Winston-Salem, NC 27155
ND	(701) 293-3656	655 1st Ave. North, Fargo, ND 58102
NE	(402) 437-5001	5631 S. 48th St., Lincoln, NE 68516
NH	(603) 666-7785	275 Chestnut St., Manchester, NH 03101
NJ	(201) 645-2150	20 Washington Pl., Newark, NJ 07102
NM	(505) 766-3361	500 Gold Ave. S.W., Albuquerque, NM 87102
NV	(702) 329-9244	1201 Terminal Way, Reno, NV 89520
NY	(716) 846-5191	111 W. Huron St., Buffalo, NY 14202
	(212) 620-6901	252 7th Ave., New York, NY 10001
OH	(216) 621-5050	1240 E. 9th St., Cleveland, OH 44199
OK	(918) 687-2500	125 S. Main St., Muskogee, OK 74401
OR	(503) 221-2431	1220 S.W. 3rd Ave., Portland, OR 97204
PA	(215) 438-5225	5000 Wissahickon Ave. (mailing address: P.O. Box 8079), Philadelphia, PA 19101
	(412) 281-4233	1000 Liberty Ave., Pittsburgh, PA 15222
PR	(809) 766-5141	U.S. Courthouse and Federal Bldg., Carlos E. Chardon St. (mailing address: GPO Box 4867), Hato Rey, San Juan, PR 00936

RI	(401) 273-4910	380 Westminster Mall, Providence, RI 02903
SC	(803) 765-5861	1801 Assembly St., Columbia, SC 29201
SD	(605) 336-3496	2501 W. 22nd St. (mailing address: P.O. Box 5046), Sioux Falls, SD 57117
TN	(615) 736-5251	110 9th Ave. South, Nashville, TN 37203
TX	(713) 664-4664	2515 Murworth Dr., Houston, TX 77054
	(817) 772-3060	1400 N. Valley Mills Dr., Waco, TX 76799
UT	(801) 524-5960	125 S. State St. (mailing address: P.O. Box 11500), Salt Lake City, UT 84147
VA	(703) 982-6440	210 Franklin Rd. S.W., Roanoke, VA 24011
VT	(802) 296-5177	N. Hartland Rd., White River Junction, VT 05001
WA	(206) 624-7200	915 2nd Ave., Seattle, WA 98174
WI	(414) 383-8680	5000 W. National Ave., Milwaukee, WI 53295
WV	(304) 529-5720	640 4th Ave., Huntington, WV 25701
WY	(307) 778-7396	2360 E. Pershing Blvd., Cheyenne, WY 82001

Veterans Affairs Dept.—Public Affairs

Area Served	Telephone	Address
AK, CA, HI, ID, NV, OR, WA, Philippines	(310) 824-4497	Wilshire and Sawtelle Blvds., #214 (mailing address: P.O. Box 84041), Los Angeles, CA 90073
AL, FL, GA, MS, NC, PR, SC, TN	(404) 347-3236	730 Peachtree St. N.E., #710, Atlanta, GA 30365
AR, AZ, LA, NM, OK, TX	(214) 767-9270	4500 S. Lancaster Rd., #124, Dallas, TX 75216
CO, IA, KS, MN, MO, MT, ND, NE, SD, UT, WY	(303) 980-2995	44 Union Blvd., #630 (mailing address: P.O. Box 25126), Denver, CO 80225
CT, MA, ME, NH, NY, RI, VT	(212) 620-6525	252 7th Ave., #400T, New York, NY 10001
DC, DE, MD, NJ, PA, VA, WV	(202) 535-8074	801 Eye St. N.W., #1003 (mailing address: VA Central Office), Washington, DC 20420
IL, IN, KY, MI, OH, WI	(312) 353-4076	536 S. Clark St., #668 (mailing address: P.O. Box 8136), Chicago, IL 60680

Agencies

Commission on Civil Rights

Area Served	Telephone	Address
AK, AZ, CA, HI, ID, NM, NV, OR, TX, WA	(213) 894-3437	3660 Wilshire Blvd., #810, Los Angeles, CA 90010
AL, AR, IA, KS, LA, MO, MS, NE, OK	(816) 426-5253	911 Walnut St., #3103, Kansas City, MO 64106
CO, MT, ND, SD, UT, WY	(303) 866-1040	1700 Broadway, #710, Denver, CO 80290
CT, DC, DE, MA, MD, ME, NH, NJ, NY, PA, RI, VA, VT, WV	(202) 376-7533	624 9th St. N.W., #500, Washington, DC 20425

| FL, GA, KY, NC, SC, TN | (404) 730-2476 | 101 Marietta St., #2821, Atlanta, GA 30303 |
| IL, IN, MI, MN, OH, WI | (312) 353-8311 | 55 W. Monroe St., #410, Chicago, IL 60603 |

Commodity Futures Trading Commission

Area Served	Telephone	Address
AK, AZ, CA, HI, ID, MT, NV, OR, UT, WA, WY	(310) 575-6783	10900 Wilshire Blvd., #400, Los Angeles, CA 90024
AL, CT, DE, FL, GA, KY, MA, MD, ME, MS, NC, NH, NJ, NY, PA, RI, SC, TN, VA, VT, WV	(212) 466-2061	1 World Trade Center, #3747, New York, NY 10048
AR, CO, IA, KS, LA, MN, MO, ND, NE, NM, OK, SD, TX	(816) 931-7600	4900 Main St., #721, Kansas City, MO 64112
IL, IN, MI, OH, WI	(312) 353-5990	300 S. Riverside Plaza, #1600 North, Chicago, IL 60606

Consumer Product Safety Commission

Area Served	Telephone	Address
AK, AR, AS, AZ, CA, CO, GU, HI, ID, LA, MT, NM, NV, OK, OR, TX, UT, WA, WY	(415) 744-2966	600 Harrison St., #245, San Francisco, CA 94107-1370
AL, GA, IA, IL, IN, KS, KY, MI, MN, MO, MS, ND, NE, OH, SD, TN, WI	(312) 353-8260	230 S. Dearborn St., #2944, Chicago, IL 60604-1601
CT, DC, DE, FL, MA, MD, ME, NC, NH, NJ, NY, PA, PR, RI, SC, VA, VI, VT, WV	(212) 466-1612	6 World Trade Center, Vesey St., #350, New York, NY 10048-0950

Corporation for National Service

Area Served	Telephone	Address
AK, ID, OR, WA	(206) 553-7739	915 2nd Ave., #3190, Seattle, WA 98174-1103
AL, FL, GA, MS, NC, SC, TN	(404) 331-2860	101 Marietta St. N.W., #1003, Atlanta, GA 30323-2301
AR, KS, LA, MO, NM, OK, TX	(214) 767-9494	1100 Commerce St., #6B11, Dallas, TX 75242-0696
AS, AZ, CA, GU, HI, NV	(415) 744-3013	211 Main St., #530, San Francisco, CA 94105-1914
CO, MT, ND, NE, SD, UT, WY	(303) 844-2671	1405 Curtis St., #2930, Denver, CO 80202-2349
CT, MA, ME, NH, RI, VT	(617) 565-7000	10 Causeway St., #473, Boston, MA 02222-1039
DC, DE, KY, MD, OH, PA, VA, WV	(215) 597-9972	801 Arch St., #103, Philadelphia, PA 19107

IA, IL, IN, MI, MN, WI	(312) 353-5107	77 W. Jackson Blvd., #442, Chicago, IL 60604-2702
NJ, NY, PR, VI	(212) 466-3481	6 World Trade Center Bldg., #758, New York, NY 10048-0206

Environmental Protection Agency

Area Served	Telephone	Address
AK, ID, OR, WA	(206) 553-4973	1200 6th Ave., Seattle, WA 98101
AL, FL, GA, KY, MS, NC, SC, TN	(404) 347-3004	345 Courtland St. N.E., Atlanta, GA 30365
AR, LA, NM, OK, TX	(214) 655-2200	1445 Ross Ave., Dallas, TX 75202
AS, AZ, CA, GU, HI, NV	(415) 744-1020	75 Hawthorne St., San Francisco, CA 94105
CO, MT, ND, SD, UT, WY	(303) 293-1692	999 18th St., Denver, CO 80202
CT, MA, ME, NH, RI, VT	(617) 565-3424	John F. Kennedy Federal Bldg., Boston, MA 02203
DC, DE, MD, PA, VA, WV	(215) 597-9825	841 Chestnut St., Philadelphia, PA 19107
IA, KS, MO, NE	(913) 551-7003	726 Minnesota Ave., Kansas City, KS 66101
IL, IN, MI, MN, OH, WI	(312) 353-2072	77 W. Jackson Blvd., Chicago, IL 60604
NJ, NY, PR, VI	(212) 264-2515	26 Federal Plaza, New York, NY 10278

Equal Employment Opportunity Commission

Area Served	Telephone	Address
AK, ID, OR, WA	(206) 553-0968	2815 2nd Ave., #500, Seattle, WA 98121
AL, MS	(205) 731-0082	1900 3rd Ave. North, #101, Birmingham, AL 35203
AR, TN	(901) 722-2617	1407 Union Ave., #621, Memphis, TN 38104
AS, CA (northern), CM, GU, HI, TT	(415) 744-6500	901 Market St., #500, San Francisco, CA 94103
AZ, NM	(602) 640-5000	4520 N. Central Ave., #300, Phoenix, AZ 85012-1848
CA (southern), NV	(213) 894-1000	255 E. Tempe, 4th Floor, Los Angeles, CA 90012
CO, MT, ND, NE, SD, WY, UT	(303) 866-1300	1845 Sherman St., 2nd Floor, Denver, CO 80203
CT, MA, ME, NH, NY, PR, RI, VI, VT	(212) 748-8500	7 World Trade Center, 18th Floor, New York, NY 10048
CZ, FL	(305) 536-4491	1 N.E. 1st St., 6th Floor, Miami, FL 33132-2491
DC, MD, VA	(202) 275-7377	1400 L St. N.W., #200, Washington, DC 20005
DE, NJ, PA, WV	(215) 656-7000	1421 Cherry St., 10th Floor, Philadelphia, PA 19102
GA	(404) 331-6531	75 Piedmont Ave. N.E., #1100, Atlanta, GA 30335
IA, MN, WI	(414) 297-1111	310 W. Wisconsin Ave., #800, Milwaukee, WI 53203-2292
IL	(312) 353-2713	500 W. Madison St., #2800, Chicago, IL 60661

IN, KY	(317) 226-7212	101 W. Ohio St., #1900, Indianapolis, IN 46204-4203
KS, MO	(314) 425-6585	625 N. Euclid St., 5th Floor, St. Louis, MO 63108
LA	(504) 589-2329	701 Loyola Ave., #600, New Orleans, LA 70113-9936
MI	(313) 226-7636	477 Michigan Ave., #1540, Detroit, MI 48226-9704
NC, SC	(704) 567-7100	5500 Central Ave., Charlotte, NC 28212-2708
OH	(216) 522-2001	1660 W. 2nd St., #850, Cleveland, OH 44113-1454
OK, TX (northern)	(214) 655-3355	207 S. Houston St., 3rd Floor, Dallas, TX 75202-4726
TX (central)	(713) 653-3377	1919 Smith St., 7th Floor, Houston, TX 77002
TX (southern)	(210) 229-4810	5410 Fredericksburg Rd., #200, San Antonio, TX 78229-9934

Federal Communications Commission

Area Served	Telephone	Address
AK, HI, ID, MT, OR, WA	(206) 821-9037	11410 N.E. 122nd Way, Kirkland, WA 98034-6927
AL, FL, GA, NC, PR, SC, TN, VA, VI	(404) 279-4621	3575 Koger Blvd., Duluth, GA 30136-4958
AR, CO, IA, KS, LA, MO, MS, ND, NE, NM, OK, SD, TX, WY	(816) 353-9035	8800 E. 63rd St., Kansas City, MO 64133-4895
AZ, CA, NV, UT	(510) 732-9046	3777 Depot Rd., Hayward, CA 94545-2756
CT, DC, DE, MA, MD, ME, NH, NJ, NY, PA, RI, VT, WV	(617) 770-4023	1 Batterymarch Park, Quincy, MA 02169-7495
IL, IN, KY, MI, MN, OH, WI	(708) 298-5405	1550 Northwest Highway, Park Ridge, IL 60068-1460

Federal Deposit Insurance Corp.

Area Served	Telephone	Address
AK, AZ, CA, GU, HI, ID, MT, NV, OR, UT, WA, WY	(415) 546-0160	25 Ecker St., #2300, San Francisco, CA 94105
AL, FL, GA, NC, SC, VA, WV	(404) 525-0308	245 Peachtree Center Ave. N.E., #1200, Atlanta, GA 30303
AR, KY, LA, MS, TN	(901) 685-1603	5100 Poplar Ave., #1900, Memphis, TN 38137
CO, NM, OK, TX	(214) 220-3342	1910 Pacific Ave., #1900, Dallas, TX 75201
CT, MA, ME, NH, RI, VT	(617) 320-1600	200 Lowder Brook Dr., Westwood, MA 02090
DC, DE, MD, NJ, NY, PA, PR, VI	(212) 704-1200	452 5th Ave., 19th Floor, New York, NY 10018
IA, KS, MN, MO, ND, NE, SD	(816) 234-8000	2345 Grand Ave., #1500, Kansas City, MO 64108
IL, IN, MI, OH, WI	(312) 207-0210	30 S. Wacker Dr., #3100, Chicago, IL 60606

Federal Emergency Management Agency

Area Served	Telephone	Address
AK, ID, OR, WA	(206) 487-4604	130 228th St. S.W., Bothell, WA 98021-9796
AL, FL, GA, KY, MS, NC, SC, TN	(404) 853-4200	1371 Peachtree St. N.E., Atlanta, GA 30309-3108
AR, LA, NM, OK, TX	(817) 898-5104	800 N. Loop 288, Denton, TX 76201-3698
AS, AZ, CA, CM, GU, HI, NV, TT	(415) 923-7100	Bldg. 105, Presidio of San Francisco, San Francisco, CA 94129-1250
CO, MT, ND, SD, UT, WY	(303) 235-4811	Denver Federal Center, Denver, CO 80225-0267
CT, MA, ME, NH, RI, VT	(617) 223-9540	442 John W. McCormack Post Office and Courthouse, Boston, MA 02109-4595
DC, DE, MD, PA, VA, WV	(215) 931-5500	105 S. 7th St., Philadelphia, PA 19106
IA, KS, MO, NE	(816) 283-7060	911 Walnut St., #200, Kansas City, MO 64106
IL, IN, MI, MN, OH, WI	(312) 408-5501	175 W. Jackson Blvd., 4th Floor, Chicago, IL 60604
NJ, NY, PR, VI	(212) 225-7209	26 Federal Plaza, #1337, New York, NY 10278

Federal Labor Relations Authority

Area Served	Telephone	Address
AK, AZ, CA, HI, ID, NV, OR, WA	(415) 744-4000	901 Market St., #220, San Francisco, CA 94103
AL, FL, GA, KY, MS, NC, SC, TN	(404) 347-2324	1371 Peachtree St. N.E., #122, Atlanta, GA 30309-3102
AR, CZ, LA, NM, OK, TX	(214) 767-4996	525 Griffin St., #926, LB 107, Dallas, TX 75202
CO, IA, KS, MO, MT, ND, NE, SD, UT, WY	(303) 844-5224	1244 Speer Blvd., #100, Denver, CO 80204
CT, DE, MA, ME, NH, NJ, NY, PA, PR, RI, VI, VT	(617) 424-5730	99 Summer St., #1500, Boston, MA 02110-1200
DC, MD, VA, WV	(202) 653-8500	1255 22nd St. N.W., #400, Washington, DC 20037
IL, IN, MI, MN, OH, WI	(312) 353-6306	55 W. Monroe, #1150, Chicago, IL 60603

Federal Maritime Commission

Area Served	Telephone	Address
AK, CA (northern), ID, MT, OR, TT, WA, WY	(415) 744-7016	525 Market St., #3510, San Francisco, CA 94105
AL, AR, GA, IA, IL, IN, KY, LA, MI, MN, MO, MS, NC, OH, SC, TN, WI	(504) 589-6662	365 Canal St., #2260, New Orleans, LA 70130
AZ, CA (southern), HI, NV, UT	(310) 980-3423	11 Golden Shore, #270, Long Beach, CA 90802
CO, KS, ND, NE, NM, OK, SD, TX	(713) 229-2841	14950 Heathrow Forest Parkway, #110, Houston, TX 77032-3842

CT, DE, MA, MD, ME, NH, NJ, NY, PA, RI, VA, VT, WV	(212) 264-1425	6 World Trade Center, #614, New York, NY 10048-0949
DC	(202) 523-5860	800 N. Capitol St., #928, Washington, DC 20573
FL	(305) 655-3184	18441 N.W. 2nd Ave., #302, Miami, FL 33169
PR, VI	(809) 766-5581	150 Carlos Chardon Ave., #762, Hato Rey, PR 00918-1735

Federal Mediation and Conciliation Service

Area Served	Telephone	Address
AK, CA (northern), CO, ID, MT, NV (except southeastern), OR, UT, WA, WY	(206) 553-3800	2001 6th Ave., #310, Seattle, WA 98121
AL, AR, FL, GA, LA, MS, SC (southern and western), TN, VA (southwestern)	(404) 347-2473	1720 Peachtree St. N.W., #318, Atlanta, GA 30309
AS, AZ, CA (southern), CM, GU, HI, NM, NV (southeastern), TT, TX	(213) 965-3814	225 W. Broadway, #610, Glendale, CA 91204
CT, MA, ME, NH, NJ (northern), NY (downstate), PR, RI, VI, VT	(212) 399-5038	1633 Broadway, 2nd Floor, New York, NY 10019
DC, DE, KY (northeastern), MD, NC, NJ (southern), NY (upstate), OH (southeastern), PA, SC (northern and eastern), VA (except southwestern), WV	(215) 597-7690	600 Arch St., #3456, Philadelphia, PA 19106
IA, MN, ND, NE, SD, WI (western)	(612) 370-3300	1300 Godward St., #3950, Minneapolis, MN 55413
IL (northern), IN (northern), MI (northern), WI (eastern)	(708) 887-4750	908 N. Elm St., #203, Hinsdale, IL 60521
IL (southern), IN (southern), KS, KY (except northeastern), MO, OK	(314) 576-3293	12140 Woodcrest Executive Dr., #325, St. Louis, MO 63141
MI (southern), OH (except southeastern)	(216) 522-4800	6161 Oak Tree Blvd., #100, Independence, OH 44131

Federal Reserve Districts

Area Served	Telephone	Address
AK, AZ, CA, HI, ID, NV, OR, UT, WA	(415) 974-2000	101 Market St. (mailing address: P.O. Box 7702), San Francisco, CA 94120
AL, FL, GA, LA (southern), MS (southern), TN (central and southern)	(404) 521-8500	104 Marietta St. N.W. (mailing address: P.O. Box 1731), Atlanta, GA 30303-2713

AR, IL (southern), IN (southern), KY (western), MO (central and eastern), MS (northern), TN (western)	(314) 444-8444	411 Locust St. (mailing address: P.O. Box 442), St. Louis, MO 63166
CO, KS, MO (western), NE, NM (northern), OK, WY	(816) 881-2000	925 Grand Ave., Kansas City, MO 64198-0001
CT, MA, ME, NH, RI, VT	(617) 973-3000	600 Atlantic Ave. (mailing address: P.O. Box 2076), Boston, MA 02106-2076
DC, MD, NC, SC, VA, WV (southern)	(804) 697-8000	701 E Byrd St. (mailing address: P.O. Box 27622), Richmond, VA 23261
DE, NJ (southern), PA (central and eastern)	(215) 574-6000	10 Independence Mall (mailing address: P.O. Box 66), Philadelphia, PA 19105
IA, IL (northern), IN (central and northern), MI (except Upper Peninsula), WI (except northwestern)	(312) 322-5322	230 S. LaSalle St. (mailing address: P.O. Box 834), Chicago, IL 60690-0834
KY (eastern), OH, PA (western), WV (northern)	(216) 579-2000	1455 E. 6th St. (mailing address: P.O. Box 6387), Cleveland, OH 44101-1387
LA (northern), NM (southern), TX	(214) 922-6000	2200 N. Pearl St. (Station K), Dallas, TX 75201
MI (Upper Peninsula), MN, MT, ND, SD, WI (northwestern)	(612) 340-2345	250 Marquette Ave., Minneapolis, MN 55401-0291
NJ (central, northern), NY	(212) 720-5000	33 Liberty St., New York, NY 10045

Federal Trade Commission

Area Served	Telephone	Address
AK, ID, OR, WA	(206) 220-6350	915 2nd Ave., Seattle, WA 98174
AL, FL, GA, MS, NC, SC, TN, VA	(404) 347-4837	1718 Peachtree St. N.W., Atlanta, GA 30367
AR, LA, NM, OK, TX	(214) 767-5503	100 N. Central Expressway, Dallas, TX 75201
AZ, CA (southern)	(310) 575-7890	11000 Wilshire Blvd., Los Angeles, CA 90024
CA (northern), HI, NV	(415) 744-7920	901 Market St., San Francisco, CA 94103
CO, KS, MT, ND, NE, SD, UT, WY	(303) 844-2271	1405 Curtis St., Denver, CO 80202-2393
CT, MA, ME, NH, RI, VT	(617) 565-7240	10 Causeway St., Boston, MA 02222-1073
DC, DE, MD, MI, OH, PA, WV	(216) 522-4210	668 Euclid Ave., Cleveland, OH 44114
IA, IL, IN, KY, MN, MO, WI	(312) 353-8516	55 E. Monroe St., Chicago, IL 60603
NJ, NY	(212) 264-1207	150 William St., New York, NY 10038

General Accounting Office

Area Served	Telephone	Address
AK, ID, OR, WA	(206) 287-4800	915 2nd Ave., Seattle, WA 98174
AL, FL, GA, SC, TN	(404) 679-1900	2635 Century Parkway, Atlanta, GA 30345

AR, LA, MS, TX	(214) 855-2600	1445 Ross Ave., Dallas, TX 75202
AZ, CA (southern)	(213) 346-8000	350 S. Figueroa St., Los Angeles, CA 90071
CA (northern), NV	(415) 904-2000	301 Howard St., San Francisco, CA 94105
CO, MT, ND, NM, SD, UT, WY	(303) 572-7306	1224 Speer Blvd., Denver, CO 80204
CT, MA, ME, NH, RI, VT	(617) 565-7500	10 Causeway St., Boston, MA 02222
DE, MD, NJ (southern), PA	(215) 574-4000	841 Chestnut St., Philadelphia, PA 19107
IA, KS, MO, NE, OK	(913) 384-7400	5799 Broadmoor, Mission, KS 66202
IL, MN, WI	(312) 220-7600	200 W. Adams St., Chicago, IL 60606
IN, KY, OH (southern), WV	(513) 684-7120	600 Vine St., Cincinnati, OH 45202
MI, OH (northern)	(313) 256-8000	477 Michigan Ave., Detroit, MI 48226
NC, VA	(804) 552-8100	5029 Corporate Woods Dr., Virginia Beach, VA 23426
NJ (northern), NY, PR, VI	(212) 264-0730	7 World Trade Center, 25th Floor, New York, NY 10048

General Services Administration

Area Served	Telephone	Address
AK, ID, OR, WA	(206) 931-7000	GSA Center, Auburn, WA 98001
AL, FL, GA, KY, MS, NC, SC, TN	(404) 331-3200	401 W. Peachtree St., Atlanta, GA 30365-2550
AR, LA, NM, OK, TX	(817) 334-2321	819 Taylor St., Fort Worth, TX 76102
AZ, CA, HI, NV	(415) 744-5001	525 Market St., San Francisco, CA 94105
CO, MT, ND, SD, UT, WY	(303) 236-7329	Denver Federal Center, Bldg. 41, Denver, CO 80225-0006
CT, MA, ME, NH, RI, VT	(617) 565-5860	10 Causeway St., Boston, MA 02222
DC, MD (Montgomery and Prince George's counties), VA (northern)	(202) 708-9100	7th and D Sts. S.W., Washington, DC 20407
DE, MD (except Montgomery and Prince George's counties), PA, VA (southern), WV	(215) 597-1237	100 Penn Square East, Philadelphia, PA 19107
IA, KS, MO, NE	(816) 926-7201	1500 E. Bannister Rd., Kansas City, MO 64131
IL, IN, MI, MN, OH, WI	(312) 353-5395	230 S. Dearborn St., Chicago, IL 60604
NJ, NY, PR, VI	(212) 264-2600	26 Federal Plaza, New York, NY 10278

General Services Administration—Business Service Centers

General Services Administration (GSA) Business Service Centers furnish advice and assistance to business persons interested in contracting with GSA and other federal agencies and departments; emphasis is placed on helping small and disadvantaged business.

Area Served	Telephone	Address
AK, ID, OR, WA	(206) 931-7956	400 15th St. S.W., Auburn, WA 98001
AL, FL, GA, KY, MS, NC, SC, TN	(404) 331-5103	401 W. Peachtree St., #2900, Atlanta, GA 30365-2550

AR, LA, NM, OK, TX	(817) 334-3284	819 Taylor St., Fort Worth, TX 76102
AZ, CA (southern), NV (Clark County)	(213) 894-3210	300 N. Los Angeles St., Los Angeles, CA 90012-2000
CA (northern), HI, NV (except Clark County)	(415) 744-5050	525 Market St., San Francisco, CA 94105
CO, MT, ND, SD, UT, WY	(303) 236-7408	B41 Denver Federal Center, #145, Denver, CO 80225-0006
CT, MA, ME, NH, RI, VT	(617) 565-8100	10 Causeway St., #290, Boston, MA 02222
DC, and metropolitan MD and VA	(202) 708-5804	7th and D Sts. S.W., Washington, DC 20407
DE, MD, PA, VA, WV	(215) 656-5525	100 Penn Square East, Philadelphia, PA 19107
IA, KS, MO, NE	(816) 926-7203	1500 E. Bannister Rd., Kansas City, MO 64131
IL, IN, MI, MN, OH, WI	(312) 353-5383	230 S. Dearborn St., Chicago, IL 60604
NJ, NY, PR, VI	(212) 264-1234	26 Federal Plaza, New York, NY 10278

General Services Administration—Federal Information Centers

Federal Information Centers are clearinghouses for information about the federal government. Persons interested in the operations, services, and programs of the federal government may contact a center for answers to their questions or for help in locating the office which has the information they seek. Those persons who do not live in one of the metropolitan areas listed below may call the FIC at (301) 722-9098, or they may write to Federal Information Center, P.O. Box 600, Cumberland, Md. 21502. TDD users may reach the FIC by dialing (800) 326-2996, toll free.

State	Telephone	Metropolitan Area Served
AK	(800) 729-8003	Anchorage
AL	(800) 366-2998	Birmingham Mobile
AR	(800) 366-2998	Little Rock
AZ	(800) 359-3997	Phoenix
CA	(800) 726-4995	Los Angeles San Diego San Francisco Santa Ana
	(916) 973-1695	Sacramento
CO	(800) 359-3997	Colorado Springs Denver Pueblo
CT	(800) 347-1997	Hartford New Haven
FL	(800) 347-1997	Fort Lauderdale Jacksonville Miami Orlando St. Petersburg Tampa West Palm Beach

GA	(800) 347-1997	Atlanta
HI	(800) 733-5996	Honolulu
IA	(800) 735-8004	All points in Iowa
IL	(800) 366-2998	Chicago
IN	(800) 366-2998	Gary
	(800) 347-1997	Indianapolis
KS	(800) 735-8004	All points in Kansas
KY	(800) 347-1997	Louisville
LA	(800) 366-2998	New Orleans
MA	(800) 347-1997	Boston
MD	(800) 347-1997	Baltimore
MI	(800) 347-1997	Detroit Grand Rapids
MN	(800) 366-2998	Minneapolis
MO	(800) 366-2998	St. Louis
	(800) 735-8004	Other points in Missouri
NC	(800) 347-1997	Charlotte
NE	(800) 366-2998	Omaha
	(800) 735-8004	Other points in Nebraska
NJ	(800) 347-1997	Newark Trenton
NM	(800) 359-3997	Albuquerque
NY	(800) 347-1997	Albany Buffalo New York Rochester Syracuse
OH	(800) 347-1997	Akron Cincinnati Cleveland Columbus Dayton Toledo
OK	(800) 366-2998	Oklahoma City, Tulsa
OR	(800) 726-4995	Portland
PA	(800) 347-1997	Philadelphia Pittsburgh
RI	(800) 347-1997	Providence
TN	(800) 347-1997	Chattanooga
	(800) 366-2998	Memphis Nashville

TX	(800) 366-2998	Austin Dallas Fort Worth Houston San Antonio
UT	(800) 359-3997	Salt Lake City
VA	(800) 347-1997	Norfolk Richmond Roanoke
WA	(800) 726-4995	Seattle Tacoma
WI	(800) 366-2998	Milwaukee

Government Printing Office—Bookstores

Government Printing Office (GPO) bookstores carry a limited stock of government publications. Titles not found in a bookstore can be ordered from GPO in Washington, D.C., by calling (202) 783-3238. Allow 4-5 days to receive an order at a GPO bookstore, and 4-6 weeks to have it mailed direct. Book order numbers can be obtained from your nearest bookstore when ordering books from GPO in Washington, D.C.

City	Telephone	Address
Atlanta, GA	(404) 347-1900	999 Peachtree St. N.E. 30309
Birmingham, AL	(205) 731-1056	2021 3rd Ave. North 35203
Boston, MA	(617) 720-4180	10 Causeway St. 02222
Chicago, IL	(312) 353-5133	401 S. State St. 60605
Cleveland, OH	(216) 522-4922	1240 E. 9th St. 44199
Columbus, OH	(614) 469-6956	200 N. High St. 43215
Dallas, TX	(214) 767-0076	1100 Commerce St. 75242
Denver, CO	(303) 844-3964	1961 Stout St. 80294
Detroit, MI	(313) 226-7816	477 Michigan Ave. 48226
Houston, TX	(713) 228-1187	801 Travis St. 77002
Jacksonville, FL	(904) 353-0569	100 W. Bay St. 32202
Kansas City, MO	(816) 767-2256	5600 E. Bannister Rd. 64137
Los Angeles, CA	(213) 239-9844	505 S. Flower St. 90071
Milwaukee, WI	(414) 297-1304	310 W. Wisconsin Ave. 53203
New York, NY	(212) 264-3825	26 Federal Plaza 10278
Philadelphia, PA	(215) 636-1900	100 N. 17th St. 19103
Pittsburgh, PA	(412) 644-2721	1000 Liberty Ave. 15222
Portland, OR	(503) 221-6217	1305 S.W. 1st Ave. 97201
Pueblo, CO	(719) 544-3142	201 W. 8th St. 81003
San Francisco, CA	(415) 252-5334	450 Golden Gate Ave. 94102
Seattle, WA	(206) 553-4270	915 2nd Ave. 98174
Washington, DC	(202) 512-0132	710 N. Capitol St. N.W. 20401
	(202) 653-5075	1510 H St. N.W. 20005

Government Printing Office—Regional Depository Libraries

Regional depository libraries are designated to receive and retain one copy of all federal government documents which must be made available for public inspection. Selective depository libraries, which are not listed here, offer only certain types of documents chosen by the library. For a list of all depository libraries, write to the Government Printing Office, 710 N. Capitol St. N.W., Washington, D.C. 20402.

Area Served	Telephone	Address
AK, WA	(206) 753-4027	Washington State Library, MS AJ-11, Olympia, WA 98504
AL	(205) 244-3650	Auburn University at Montgomery, Library, Government Information, 7300 University Dr., Montgomery, AL 36117-3596
	(205) 348-6046	University of Alabama Libraries, Box 870266, Tuscaloosa, AL 35487-0266
AR	(501) 682-2326	Arkansas State Library, Documents Service, 1 Capitol Mall, Little Rock, AR 72201
AS, CM, GU, HI	(808) 956-8230	University of Hawaii, Hamilton Library, Government Documents, Maps, and Microforms, 2550 The Mall, Honolulu, HI 96822
AZ	(602) 542-4444	Arizona Dept. of Library, Archives and Public Records, State Capitol Bldg., 3rd Floor, Phoenix, AZ 85007
CA	(916) 653-0085	California State Library, Government Publications Section, P.O. Box 942837, Sacramento, CA 94237-0001
CO	(303) 492-8834	University of Colorado at Boulder, Government Publications Library, Campus Box 184, Boulder, CO 80309-0184
	(303) 640-8876	Denver Public Library, Government Publications Dept., 1357 Broadway, Denver, CO 80203
CT, RI	(203) 566-4971	Connecticut State Library, 231 Capitol Ave., Hartford, CT 06106
DC, DE, MD	(301) 405-9165	University of Maryland, McKeldin Library, Documents/Maps Room, College Park, MD 20742
FL, PR, VI	(904) 392-0367	University of Florida Libraries, Documents Dept., #241, Library West, Gainesville, FL 32611
GA	(706) 542-8949	University of Georgia Libraries, Government Documents Dept., Athens, GA 30602
IA	(319) 335-5925	University of Iowa Libraries, Government Publications Dept., Iowa City, IA 52242
ID	(208) 885-6344	University of Idaho Libraries, Documents Section, Moscow, ID 83844
IL	(217) 782-4887	Illinois State Library, Federal Documents, 300 S. 2nd St., Springfield, IL 62701-1796
IN	(317) 232-3686	Indiana State Library, Serials and Documents 140 N. Senate Ave., Indianapolis, IN 46204

KS	(913) 864-4660	University of Kansas, 6001 Malott Hall, Government Documents and Maps, Lawrence, KS 66045-2800
KY	(606) 257-8400	University of Kentucky Libraries, Government Publications/Maps, Lexington, KY 40506-0039
LA	(504) 388-2570	Louisiana State University, Middletown Library, Business Administration and Government Documents, Baton Rouge, LA 70803
	(318) 257-4962	Louisiana Technical University, Prescott Memorial Library, Documents Dept., Ruston, LA 71272-0046
MA	(617) 536-5400	Boston Public Library, Government Documents, 666 Boylston St., Boston, MA 02117
ME, NH, VT	(207) 581-1681	University of Maine, Raymond Folger Library, Government Documents, Orono, ME 04469
MI	(313) 833-1025	Detroit Public Library, 5201 Woodward Ave., Detroit, MI 48202-4093
	(517) 373-1307	Library of Michigan, Government Documents Service, 717 W. Allegan St. (mailing address: P.O. Box 30007), Lansing, MI 48909
MN, SD	(612) 626-7520	University of Minnesota, 409 Wilson Library, Government Publications, 309 S. 19th St., Minneapolis, MN 55455
MO	(314) 882-6733	University of Missouri at Columbia, Ellis Library, Government Documents, Columbia, MO 65201
MS	(601) 232-5857	University of Mississippi, Williams Library, Documents Dept., University, MS 38677
MT	(406) 243-6700	University of Montana, Maureen and Mike Mansfield Library, Documents Dept., Missoula, MT 59812
NC	(919) 962-1151	University of North Carolina at Chapel Hill, Davis Library, CB #3912, BA/SS Department-Documents, Chapel Hill, NC 27599
ND	(701) 237-8863	North Dakota State University Library, Documents Office, P.O. Box 5599, Fargo, ND 58105
	(701) 777-3316	University of North Dakota, Chester Fritz Library, Documents Dept., Grand Forks, ND 58202
NE	(402) 472-2562	University of Nebraska at Lincoln, Love Library, Federal Documents Dept., Lincoln, NE 68588-4010
NJ	(201) 733-7812	Newark Public Library, U.S. Documents Division, 5 Washington St., Newark, NJ 07101-0630
NM	(505) 277-5441	University of New Mexico, General Library, Government Publications and Maps Dept., Albuquerque, NM 87131
	(505) 827-3852	New Mexico State Library, Documents Dept., 325 Don Gaspar Ave., Santa Fe, NM 87503

NV	(702) 784-6579	University of Nevada Library, Government Publications Dept., Reno, NV 89557-0044
NY	(518) 474-3940	New York State Library, Legislative and Governmental Service, Cultural Education Center, Empire State Plaza, Albany, NY 12230
OH	(614) 644-1971	State Library of Ohio, Documents Section, 65 S. Front St., Columbus, OH 43266-0334
OK	(405) 521-2502	Oklahoma Dept. of Libraries, Government Documents Division, 200 N.E. 18th St., Oklahoma City, OK 73105
	(405) 744-6546	Oklahoma State University Library, Documents Dept., Stillwater, OK 74078
OR	(503) 725-4123	Portland State University, Millar Library, Documents Dept., P.O. Box 1151, Portland, OR 97207
PA	(717) 787-3752	State Library of Pennsylvania, Government Publications, Box 1601, Harrisburg, PA 17105
SC	(803) 656-5174	Clemson University, Cooper Library, Documents Dept., Box 343001, Clemson, SC 29634
	(803) 777-4841	University of South Carolina, Thomas Cooper Library, Documents/Microform Dept., Sumter and Green St., Columbia, SC 29208
TN	(901) 678-2206	Memphis State University Library, Government Documents Dept., Memphis, TN 38152
TX	(512) 463-5455	Texas State Library, Documents Dept. (mailing address: Box 12927, Capitol Station), Austin, TX 78711
	(806) 742-2236	Texas Technical University Library, Documents Reference Dept., Lubbock, TX 79409
UT, WY	(801) 750-1000	Utah State University, Merrill Library, UMC-30, Government Documents Dept., Logan, UT 84322
VA	(804) 924-3133	University of Virginia, Alderman Library, Government Documents Dept., Charlottesville, VA 22903-2498
WI	(608) 264-6525	State Historical Society of Wisconsin Library, Government Publications, 816 State St., Madison, WI 53706
	(414) 278-2167	Milwaukee Public Library, Documents Dept., 814 W. Wisconsin Ave., Milwaukee, WI 53233
WV	(304) 293-3051	West Virginia University Library, Government Documents Section, Morgantown, WV 26506-6069

Interstate Commerce Commission

Area Served	Telephone	Address
AK, AZ, CA, CO, HI, ID, MT, NM, NV, OR, UT, WA, WY	(415) 744-6520	211 Main St., #500, San Francisco, CA 94105

AL, CT, DC, DE, FL, GA, KY, MA, MD, ME, MS, NC, NH, NJ, NY, OH, PA, RI, SC, TN, VA, VT, WV	(215) 596-4040	3535 Market St., #16400, Philadelphia, PA 19104
AR, IA, IL, IN, KS, LA, MI, MN, MO, ND, NE, OK, SD, TX, WI	(312) 353-6204	55 W. Monroe, #550, Chicago, IL 60603

Legal Services Corporation

Area Served	Telephone	Address
AK, CA, GU, HI, NV, OR, TT, WA	(415) 273-6415	1330 Broadway, #1444, Oakland, CA 94612
AL, AR, AZ, CO, CT, DC, DE, FL, GA, IA, ID, IL, IN, KS, KY, LA, MA, MD, ME, MI, MN, MO, MS, MT, NC, ND, NE, NH, NJ, NM, NY, OH, OK, PA, PR, RI, SC, SD, TN, TX, UT, VA, VI, VT, WI, WV, WY, all native American programs and components, regardless of geographic location	(202) 336-8800	750 1st St. N.E., Washington, DC 20002

Merit Systems Protection Board

Area Served	Telephone	Address
AK, HI, ID, OR, WA, all Pacific overseas areas, including AS, CM, GU, and TT	(206) 220-7975	915 2nd Ave., #1840, Seattle, WA 98174-1056
AL, FL, GA, MS, NC, SC	(404) 730-2751	401 W. Peachtree St. N.W., 10th Floor, Atlanta, GA 30308-3519
AR, LA, OK, TX	(214) 767-0555	1100 Commerce St., #6F20, Dallas, TX 75242-9979
AZ, CO, KS, MT, ND, NE, NM, NV, SD, UT, WY	(303) 231-5200	730 Simms St., #301 (mailing address: P.O. Box 25025), Denver, CO 80225-0025
CA	(415) 744-3081	525 Market St., #2800, San Francisco, CA 94105-2736
CT, MA, ME, NH, RI, VT	(617) 424-5700	99 Summer St., #1810, Boston, MA 02110-1200
DC, MD, VA (Washington metro area), all overseas areas not otherwise covered	(703) 756-6250	5203 Leesburg Pike, #1109, Falls Church, VA 22041-3473
DE, NJ (southern), PA, VA (except Washington metro area), WV	(215) 597-9960	2nd and Chestnut Sts., #501, Philadelphia, PA 19106-2987
IA, IL (southern), KY, MO, TN	(314) 425-4295	911 Washington Ave., #410, St. Louis, MO 63101-1203
IL (northern), IN, MI, MN, OH, WI	(312) 353-2923	230 S. Dearborn St., 31st Floor, Chicago, IL 60604-1669

| NJ (northern), NY, PR, VI | (212) 264-9372 | 26 Federal Plaza, #3137A, New York, NY 10278-0022 |

National Archives and Records Administration

Area Served	Telephone	Address
AK	(907) 271-2441	654 W. 3rd Ave., Anchorage, AK 99501
AL, FL, GA, KY, MS, NC, SC, TN	(404) 763-7477	1557 St. Joseph Ave., East Point, GA 30344
AR, LA, NM, OK, TX	(817) 334-5525	501 W. Felix St. (mailing address: P.O. Box 6216), Fort Worth, TX 76115
AS, CA (except southern), CM, GU, HI, NV (except Clark County), TT	(415) 876-9018	1000 Commodore Dr., San Bruno, CA 94066
AZ, CA (southern), NV (Clark County)	(714) 643-4241	24000 Avila Rd. (mailing address: P.O. Box 6719), Laguna Niguel, CA 92607-6719
CO, MT, ND, SD, UT, WY	(303) 236-0817	Denver Federal Center, P.O. Box 25307, Denver, CO 80225
CT, MA, ME, NH, RI, VT	(617) 647-8100	380 Trapelo Rd., Waltham, MA 02154
DE, MD, PA, VA, WV	(215) 597-3000	9th and Market Sts., Philadelphia, PA 19107
IA, KS, MO, NE	(816) 926-6272	2312 E. Bannister Rd., Kansas City, MO 64131
ID, OR, WA	(206) 526-6347	6125 Sand Point Way N.E., Seattle, WA 98115
IL, IN, MI, MN, OH, WI	(312) 353-0162	7358 S. Pulaski Rd., Chicago, IL 60629
NJ, NY, PR, VI	(212) 337-1300	201 Varick St., New York, NY 10014

National Credit Union Administration

Area Served	Telephone	Address
AK, AS, CA, GU, HI, ID, MT, NV, OR, WA	(510) 825-6125	2300 Clayton Rd., #1350, Concord, CA 94520
AL, AR, FL, GA, KY, LA, MS, NC, SC, TN	(404) 396-4042	7000 Central Parkway, #1600, Atlanta, GA 30328
AZ, CO, IA, KS, MN, ND, NE, NM, OK, SD, TX, UT, WY	(512) 482-4500	4807 Spicewood Springs Rd., #5200, Austin, TX 78759-8490
CT, MA, ME, NH, NY, PR, RI, VI, VT	(518) 464-4180	9 Washington Square, Washington Ave. Extension, Albany, NY 12205
DC, DE, MD, NJ, PA, VA, WV	(703) 838-0401	1775 Duke St., #4206, Alexandria, VA 22314-3437
IL, IN, MI, MO, OH, WI	(708) 245-1000	4225 Naperville Rd., #125, Lisle, IL 60532

National Endowment for the Humanities

Area Served	Telephone	Address
AK	(907) 272-5341	430 W. 7th Ave., #1, Anchorage, AK 99501
AL	(205) 930-0540	2217 10th Ct. South, Birmingham, AL 35205

AR	(501) 221-0091	10816 Executive Center Dr., #310, Little Rock, AR 72211-4383
AS	(684) 633-4255	Dept. of Education, P.O. Box 1935, Pago Pago, AS 96799
AZ	(602) 257-0335	1242 N. Central Ave., Phoenix, AZ 85004
CA	(415) 391-1474	312 Sutter St., #601, San Francisco, CA 94108
CM	(670) 235-4785	Caller Box AAA 3394, Saipan, MP 96950
CO	(303) 573-7733	1623 Blake St., #200, Denver, CO 80202
CT	(203) 347-6888	41 Lawn Ave., Wesleyan Station, Middletown, CT 06459
DC	(202) 347-1732	1331 H St. N.W., #902, Washington, DC 20005
DE	(302) 633-2400	1812 Newport Gap Pike, Wilmington, DE 19808
FL	(813) 272-3473	1514-1/2 E. 8th Ave., Tampa, FL 33605-3473
GA	(404) 523-6220	50 Hurt Plaza S.E., #440, Atlanta, GA 30303-2936
GU	(671) 472-4507	123 Archbishop Flores St., #C, Agana, GU 96910
HI	(808) 732-5402	3599 Waialae Ave., #23, Honolulu, HI 96816
IA	(319) 335-4153	University of Iowa, Oakdale Campus N210 OH, Iowa City, IA 52242
ID	(208) 345-5346	217 W. State St., Boise, ID 03702
IL	(312) 939-5212	618 S. Michigan Ave., Chicago, IL 60605
IN	(317) 638-1500	1500 N. Delaware St., Indianapolis, IN 46202
KS	(913) 357-0359	112 S.W. 6th Ave., #210, Topeka, KS 66603
KY	(606) 257-5932	University of Kentucky, 417 Clifton Ave., Lexington, KY 40508-3406
LA	(504) 523-4352	1001 Howard Ave., #3110, New Orleans, LA 70113
MA	(413) 536-1385	1 Woodbridge St., South Hadley, MA 01075
MD	(410) 625-4830	601 N. Howard St., Baltimore, MD 21201
ME	(207) 773-5051	371 Cumberland Ave. (mailing address: P.O. Box 7202), Portland, ME 04112
MI	(517) 372-7770	119 Pere Marquette Dr., #3B, Lansing, MI 48912-1231
MN	(612) 224-5739	26 E. Exchange St., Lower Level South, St. Paul, MN 55101
MO	(314) 621-7705	911 Washington Ave., #215, St. Louis, MO 63101-1208
MS	(601) 982-6752	3825 Ridgewood Rd., #311, Jackson, MS 39211
MT	(406) 243-6022	P.O. Box 8036, Hellgate Station, Missoula, MT 59807
NC	(919) 334-5325	425 Spring Garden St., Greensboro, NC 27401
ND	(701) 255-3360	2900 Broadwave, #3 (mailing address: P.O. Box 2191), Bismarck, ND 58502

NE	(402) 474-2131	215 Centennial Mall South, #225, Lincoln, NE 68508
NH	(603) 224-4071	19 Pillsbury St. (mailing address: P.O. Box 2228), Concord, NH 03302-2228
NJ	(908) 932-7726	390 George St., #602, New Brunswick, NJ 08901-2019
NM	(505) 277-3705	209 Onate Hall, University of New Mexico, Albuquerque, NM 87131
NV	(702) 784-6587	1101 N. Virginia St., Reno, NV 89507
NY	(212) 233-1131	198 Broadway, 10th Floor, New York, NY 10038
OH	(614) 461-7802	695 Bryden Rd. (mailing address: P.O. Box 06354), Columbus, OH 43206-0354
OK	(405) 235-0280	428 W. California, #270, Oklahoma City, OK 73102
OR	(503) 241-0543	812 S.W. Washington, #225, Portland, OR 97205
PA	(215) 925-1005	320 Walnut St., #305, Philadelphia, PA 19106
PR	(809) 721-2087	Box S-4307, Old San Juan, PR 00904
RI	(401) 273-2250	60 Ship St., Providence, RI 02903
SC	(803) 771-8864	1200 Catawba, Columbia, SC 29250
SD	(605) 688-6113	Box 7050, University Station, Brookings, SD 57007
TN	(615) 320-7001	1003 18th Ave. South, Nashville, TN 37212
TX	(512) 440-1991	3809 S. 2nd St., Austin, TX 78704
UT	(801) 531-7868	350 S. 400 East, #110, Salt Lake City, UT 84111
VA	(804) 924-3296	145 Ednam Dr., Charlottesville, VA 22903-4629
VI	(809) 776-4044	GERS Bldg., 3rd Floor, Kronprindsens Gade (mailing address: P.O. Box 1829), St. Thomas, VI 00803
VT	(802) 888-3183	Main St. (mailing address: P.O. Box 58), Hyde Park, VT 05655
WA	(206) 682-1770	615 2nd Ave., #300, Seattle, WA 98104
WI	(608) 263-7970	716 Langdon St., Madison, WI 53706
WV	(304) 346-8500	723 Kanawha Blvd. East, #800, Charleston, WV 25301
WY	(307) 766-3142	P.O. Box 3643, University Station, Laramie, WY 82071-3643

National Labor Relations Board

Many area offices are responsible for serving parts of states; therefore, some states appear on this list more than once. For assistance, call or write to the nearest office.

Area Served	Telephone	Address
AK, ID, MT, OR, WA	(206) 220-6300	915 2nd Ave., Seattle, WA 98174
AL, FL, LA, MS	(504) 589-6361	1515 Poydras St., New Orleans, LA 70112

AL, GA, TN	(404) 331-2896	101 Marietta St. N.W., Atlanta, GA 30323
AR, KY, MS, TN	(901) 722-2725	1407 Union Ave., Memphis, TN 38104-3627
AZ, NM, NV, TX	(602) 379-3361	234 N. Central Ave., Phoenix, AZ 85004
CA	(213) 894-5200	811 Wilshire Blvd., Los Angeles, CA 90017
CA	(310) 575-7352	11000 Wilshire Blvd., Los Angeles, CA 90024
CA, HI	(415) 744-6810	901 Market St., San Francisco, CA 94103
CA, NV	(510) 637-3300	1301 Clay St., #300N, Oakland, CA 94612-5211
CO, ID, MT, NE, UT, WY	(303) 844-3551	600 17th St., Denver, CO 80202
CT	(203) 240-3522	1 Commercial Plaza, Hartford, CT 06103
DC, DE, MD, PA, VA, WV	(410) 962-2822	111 Market Place, Baltimore, MD 21202
DE, NJ, PA	(215) 597-7601	615 Chestnut St., Philadelphia, PA 19106
FL, GA	(813) 228-2641	201 E. Kennedy Blvd., Tampa, FL 33602-5824
IA, IL	(309) 671-7080	300 Hamilton Blvd., Peoria, IL 61602
IA, MN, ND, SD, WI	(612) 348-1757	110 S. 4th St., Minneapolis, MN 55401
IL, IN	(312) 353-7570	200 W. Adams St., Chicago, IL 60606
IL, MO	(314) 425-4167	611N 10th St., St. Louis, MO 63101
IN	(317) 226-7430	575 N. Pennsylvania St., Indianapolis, IN 46204
KS, MO, NE, OK	(913) 236-2777	5799 Broadmoor, Mission, KS 66202
KY, OH, WV	(513) 684-3686	550 Main St., Cincinnati, OH 45202
MA, ME, NH, RI, VT	(617) 565-6700	10 Causeway St., Boston, MA 02222
MI	(313) 226-3200	477 Michigan Ave., Detroit, MI 48226
MI, WI	(414) 297-3861	310 W. Wisconsin Ave., Milwaukee, WI 53203
NC, SC, TN, WV	(919) 631-5201	251 N. Main St., Winston-Salem, NC 27101
NJ	(201) 645-2100	970 Broad St., Newark, NJ 07102
NY	(212) 264-0300	26 Federal Plaza, New York, NY 10278
	(718) 330-7713	1 MetroTech Center, Jay St. and Myrtle Ave., Brooklyn, NY 11201-4201
	(716) 846-4931	111 W. Huron St., Buffalo, NY 14202
OH	(216) 522-3715	1240 E. 9th St., Cleveland, OH 44199
OK, TX	(817) 334-2921	819 Taylor St., Fort Worth, TX 76102
PA, WV	(412) 644-2977	1000 Liberty Ave., Pittsburgh, PA 15222
PR, VI	(809) 766-5347	150 Carlos E. Chardon Ave., Hato Rey, PR 00918

The following divisions of regional responsibilities among NTSB offices are those for the board's aviation, highway, and railroad safety oversight. For information on NTSB oversight of marine and pipeline activities, please call (202) 382-6600.

National Transportation Safety Board—Aviation Oversight

Area Served	Telephone	Address
AK, ID, MT, OR, UT, WA, WY	(206) 764-3782	19518 Pacific Highway South, #201, Seattle, WA 98188
AL, FL, GA, MS, NC, PR, SC, TN, VI	(305) 597-4610	8405 N.W. 53rd St., #B-103, Miami, FL 33166

AR, CO, LA, NM, OK, TX	(817) 885-6800	1200 Copeland Rd., #300, Arlington, TX 76011
AZ, CA, HI, NV	(310) 297-1041	1515 W. 109th St., #555, Gardena, CA 90248
CT, DC, DE, KY, MA, MD, ME, NH, NJ, NY, OH, PA, RI, VA, VT, WV	(201) 334-6420	2001 Route 46, #203, Parsippany, NJ 07054
IA, IL, IN, KS, MI, MN, MO, ND, NE, SD, WI	(708) 377-8177	31 W. 775 North Ave., West Chicago, IL 60185

National Transportation Safety Board—Highway Oversight

Area Served	Telephone	Address
AL, FL, GA, KY, MS, NC, SC, TN, VA, WV	(404) 347-7385	1720 Peachtree St. N.W., Atlanta, GA 30309
AR, IA, IL, IN, KS, LA, MN, MO, ND, NE, NM, OK, SD, TX, WI	(817) 885-6800	1200 Copeland Rd., #300, Arlington, TX 76011
AZ, CA, CO, ID, MT, NV, OR, UT, WA, WY	(310) 297-1041	1515 W. 190th St., #555, Gardena, CA 90248
CT, DC, DE, MA, MD, ME, MI, NH, NJ, NY, OH, PA, RI, VT	(201) 334-6615	2001 Rt. 46, #203, Parsippany, NJ 07054

National Transportation Safety Board—Railroad Oversight

Area Served	Telephone	Address
AL, AR, IA, IL, IN, KS, KY, LA, MI, MN, MO, MS, ND, NE, OK, SD, TN, TX, WI	(708) 377-8177	31 W. 775 North Ave., West Chicago, IL 60185
AZ, CA, CO, ID, MT, NM, NV, OR, UT, WA, WY	(310) 297-1041	1515 W. 190th St., #555, Gardena, CA 90248
CT, DC, DE, FL, GA, MA, MD, ME, NC, NH, NJ, NY, OH, PA, RI, SC, VA, VT, WV	(201) 334-6645	2001 Rt. 46, #203, Parsippany, NJ 07054

Nuclear Regulatory Commission

Area Served	Telephone	Address
AK, AR, AZ, CA, CO, HI, ID, KS, LA, MT, ND, NE, NM, NV, OK, OR, SD, TX, UT, WA, WY	(817) 860-8100	611 Ryan Plaza Dr., #400, Arlington, TX 76011-8064
AL, FL, GA, KY, MS, NC, PR, SC, TN, VA, VI, WV	(404) 331-4503	101 Marietta St. N.W., #2900, Atlanta, GA 30323
CT, DC, DE, MA, MD, ME, NH, NJ, NY, PA, RI, VT	(215) 337-5000	475 Allendale Rd., King of Prussia, PA 19406-1415
IA, IL, IN, MI, MN, MO, OH, WI	(708) 829-9500	801 Warrenville Rd., Lisle, IL 60532-4351

Office of Personnel Management

Area Served	Telephone	Address
AK, AS, CA, GU, HI, ID, NV, OR, WA	(415) 744-7237	211 Main St., 7th Floor, San Francisco, CA 94105
AL, FL, GA, MS, NC, SC, TN, VA	(404) 331-3459	75 Spring St. S.W., Atlanta, GA 30303
AR, AZ, CO, LA, MT, NM, OK, TX, UT, WY	(214) 767-8227	1100 Commerce St., Dallas, TX 75242
CT, DE, MA, MD, ME, NH, NJ, NY, PA, PR, RI, VI, VT	(215) 597-4543	600 Arch St., Philadelphia, PA 19106
DC	(202) 606-1000	1900 E St. N.W., #5A09, Washington, DC 20415
IA, IL, IN, KS, KY, MI, MN, MO, ND, NE, OH, SD, WI, WV	(312) 353-2901	239 S. Dearborn St., Chicago, IL 60604

Office of Personnel Management—Federal Employment Information Centers

The offices listed below provide general information on federal employment, explain how to apply for specific jobs, supply application materials, and conduct written examinations. For a list of the federal personnel offices located in Washington, D.C., see p. 288.

Area Served	Telephone	Address
AK	(907) 271-5821	222 W. 7th Ave., #22, Anchorage, AK 99513-7572
AL, MS, TN	(205) 837-0894	520 Wynn Dr. N.W., Huntsville, AL 35816-3426
AR, OK	(405) 231-4948	(Mailing address: 8610 Broadway, #305, San Antonio, TX 78217)
AZ	(602) 640-4800	3225 N. Central Ave., #1415, Phoenix, AZ 85012
CA	(619) 557-6165	880 Front St., #4218, San Diego, CA 92101-8821
	(415) 744-5627	211 Main St. (mailing address: P.O. Box 7405), San Francisco, CA 94120
CA, NV (Clark, Lincoln, and Nye counties)	(818) 575-6510	9650 Flair Dr., #100A, El Monte, CA 91731
CA, NV (except Clark, Lincoln, and Nye counties)	(916) 551-1464	1029 J St., #202, Sacramento, CA 95814
CO, MT, UT, WY	(303) 969-7050	12345 W. Alameda Parkway, Lakewood, CO (mailing address: P.O. Box 25167, Denver, CO 80225)
	(303) 969-7052	(In Montana and Wyoming)
	(303) 969-7053	(In Utah)
CT, MA, ME, NH, RI, VT	(617) 565-5900	10 Causeway St., Boston, MA 02222
DC	(202) 606-2700	1900 E St. N.W., #1416, Washington, DC 20415

DE	(215) 597-7440	600 Arch St., Philadelphia, PA 19106
FL	(305) 536-6738	51 S.W. 1st Ave., #1222, Miami, FL 33130
	(407) 648-6148	3444 McCrory Pl., #125, Orlando, FL 32803-3701
GA	(404) 331-4315	75 Spring St. S.W., #940A, Atlanta, GA 30303
HI	(808) 541-2791	300 Ala Moana Blvd., #5316, Honolulu, HI 96850
IA (except Scott County)	(816) 426-7757	(Mailing address: 601 E. 12th St., #134, Kansas City, MO 64106)
IA (Scott County)	(312) 353-6192	(Mailing address: 175 W. Jackson Blvd., #530, Chicago, IL 60604)
ID, WA	(206) 220-6400	915 2nd Ave., #110, Seattle, WA 98174
IL (except Madison and St. Clair counties)	(312) 353-6192	175 W. Jackson Blvd., #530, Chicago, IL 60604
IL (Madison and St. Clair counties)	(314) 539-2285	(Mailing address: 400 Old Post Office Bldg., 815 Olive St., St. Louis, MO 63101)
IN	walk-in service only	575 N. Pennsylvania St., Indianapolis, IN
IN (Clark, Dearborn, and Floyd counties)	(513) 225-2720	(Mailing address: 200 W. 2nd St., #506, Dayton, OH 45402)
IN (except Clark, Dearborn, and Floyd counties)	(313) 226-6950	(Mailing address: 477 Michigan Ave., #565, Detroit, MI 48226)
KS	walk-in service only	120 S. Market St., #101, Wichita, KS
	(816) 426-7820	(Mailing address: 601 E. 12th St., #134, Kansas City, MO 64106)
KY (except Henderson County), OH (southern)	(513) 225-2720	200 W. 2nd St., #506, Dayton, OH 45402
KY (Henderson County), MI, OH (northern)	(313) 226-6950	477 Michigan Ave., #565, Detroit, MI 48226
LA	(504) 589-2764	1515 Poydras St., #608, New Orleans, LA 70112
MD	(410) 962-3822	300 W. Pratt St., Baltimore, MD 21201
MN, ND, SD, WI (except Dane, Grant, Green, Iowa, Jefferson, Kenosha, Lafayette, Milwaukee, Racine, Rock, Walworth, and Waukesha counties)	(612) 725-3430	1 Federal Dr., #501, Ft. Snelling, Twin Cities, MN 55111
MO (eastern)	(314) 539-2285	400 Old Post Office Bldg., 815 Olive St., St. Louis, MO 63101
MO (western)	(816) 426-5702	601 E. 12th St., #134, Kansas City, MO 64106
NC, SC	(919) 790-2822	4407 Bland Rd., #202, Raleigh, NC 27609
NE	(816) 426-7819	(Mailing address: 601 E. 12th St., #134, Kansas City, MO 64106)
NJ	walk-in service only	970 Broad St., 2nd Floor, Newark, NJ
	(215) 597-7440	(Mailing address: 600 Arch St., Philadelphia, PA 19106)

NM	(505) 766-2906	505 Marquette Ave., #910, Albuquerque, NM 87102
NY	(212) 264-0422	26 Federal Plaza, 2nd Floor, #120, New York, NY 10278
	(315) 423-5660	100 S. Clinton St. (mailing address: P.O. Box 7257), Syracuse, NY 13260
OR	(503) 326-3141	1220 S.W. 3rd Ave., #376, Portland, OR 97204
PA	(717) 782-4494	Federal Bldg., #168 (mailing address: P.O. Box 761), Harrisburg, PA 17108
	(215) 597-7440	600 Arch St., Philadelphia, PA 19106
	walk-in service only	1000 Liberty Ave., #119, Pittsburgh, PA (mailing address: 600 Arch St., Philadelphia, PA 19106)
PR	(809) 766-5242	150 Carlos Chardon Ave., #340, Hato Rey, PR 00918-1710
TN	walk-in service only	200 Jefferson Ave., #1312, Memphis, TN (mailing address: 520 Wynn Dr. N.W., Huntsville, AL 35816-3426)
TX	(512) 884-8113	(For Corpus Christi area)
	(214) 767-8035	1100 Commerce St., #6B10, Dallas, TX 75242
	(512) 412-0722	(For Harlingen area)
	(713) 759-0455	(For Houston area)
	(210) 805-2423	8610 Broadway, #305, San Antonio, TX 78217
VA	(804) 441-3355	200 Granby St., #220, Norfolk, VA 23510-1886
	walk-in service only	5145 E. Virginia Beach Blvd., Norfolk, VA
VI	(809) 774-8790	(Mailing address: 150 Carlos Chardon Ave., #340, Hato Rey, PR 00918-1710)
WI (Dane, Grant, Green, Iowa, Jefferson, Kenosha, Lafayette, Milwaukee, Racine, Rock, Walworth, and Waukesha counties)	(312) 353-6189	(Mailing address: 175 W. Jackson Blvd., #530, Chicago, IL 60604)
WV	(513) 225-2866	(Mailing address: 200 W. 2nd St., #506, Dayton, OH 45402)

Railroad Retirement Board

Main Office: 844 N. Rush St., Chicago, IL 60611; (312) 751-4500

Area Served	Telephone	Address
AK, AZ, CA, CO, HI, ID, MT, NM, NV, OR, TX (southwestern), UT, WA, WY	(510) 637-2977	1301 Clay St., #390N, Oakland, CA 94612-5202
AL, AR, FL, GA, KY, LA, MS, NC, SC, TN, TX (northeastern), VA, WV	(404) 331-2691	101 Marietta St., Atlanta, GA 30323

CT, DC, DE, MA, MD, ME, NH, NJ, NY, PA (eastern), RI, VT	(215) 656-6948	1421 Cherry St., Philadelphia, PA 19102
DC, Legislative Liaison Office	(202) 653-9540	2000 L St. N.W., Washington, DC 20036
IA, IL (southern), KS, MI (northern), MN, MO, ND, NE, OK, SD, TX (central, southern, and northern), WI	(816) 426-3278	601 E. 12th St., Kansas City, MO 64106
IL (northern and central), IN, MI (southern), OH, PA (western)	(216) 522-4043	1240 E. 9th St., Cleveland, OH 44199

Resolution Trust Corporation

Area Served	Telephone	Address
AK, AR, IA, ID, IL, IN, KS, KY, MI, MN, MO, MT, ND, NE, OH, OK, OR, SD, WA, WI, WY	(816) 531-2212	4900 Main St., #200, Kansas City, MO 64112
AL, DC, DE, FL, GA, MD, NC, SC, TN, VA, WV	(404) 881-4840	100 Colony Square, #2100, Atlanta, GA 30361
AZ, CO, HI, NM, NV, UT	(303) 556-6500	1515 Arapahoe St., Tower 3, #800, Denver, CO 80202
CA	(714) 852-7700	4000 MacArthur Blvd., 10th Floor, Newport Beach, CA 92660-2516
CT, MA, ME, NH, NJ, NY, PA, VT	(215) 650-8500	1000 Adams Ave., Norristown, PA 19403
LA, MS, TX	(214) 443-2300	3500 Maple Ave., Dallas, TX 75214

Securities and Exchange Commission

Area Served	Telephone	Address
AK, AZ, CA, GU, HI, ID, MT, NV, OR, WA	(213) 965-3998	5670 Wilshire Blvd., 11th Floor, Los Angeles, CA 90036-3648
AL, FL, GA, LA, MS, NC, PR, SC, TN, VI	(305) 536-5765	1401 Brickell Ave., #200, Miami, FL 33131
AR, CO, KS, ND, NE, NM, OK, SD, TX, UT, WY	(303) 391-6800	1801 California St., #4800, Denver, CO 80202-2648
CT, DC, DE, MA, ME, MD, NH, NJ, NY, PA, RI, VA, VT, WV	(212) 748-8000	7 World Trade Center, #1300, New York, NY 10048
IA, IL, IN, KY, MI, MN, MO, OH, WI	(312) 353-7390	500 W. Madison St., #1400, Chicago, IL 60661-2511

Small Business Administration

Area Served	Telephone	Address
AK, ID, OR, WA	(206) 553-5676	2615 4th Ave., #440, Seattle, WA 98121

AL, FL, GA, KY, MS, NC, SC, TN	(404) 347-4999	1375 Peachtree St. N.E., 5th Floor, Atlanta, GA 30367-8102
AR, LA, NM, OK, TX	(214) 767-7611	8625 King George Dr., Bldg. C, Dallas, TX 75235-3391
AZ, CA, GU, HI, NV	(415) 744-6402	71 Stevenson St., 20th Floor, San Francisco, CA 94105-2939
CO, MT, ND, SD, UT, WY	(303) 294-7021	999 18th St., #701, Denver, CO 80202
CT, MA, ME, NH, RI, VT	(617) 451-2030	155 Federal St., 9th Floor, Boston, MA 02110
DC, DE, MD, PA, VA, WV	(215) 962-3700	475 Allendale Rd., #201, King of Prussia, PA 19406
IA, KS, MO, NE	(816) 426-3605	911 Walnut St., 13th Floor, Kansas City, MO 64106
IL, IN, MI, MN, OH, WI	(312) 353-0357	300 S. Riverside Plaza, #1975S, Chicago, IL 60606-6607
NJ, NY, PR, VI	(212) 264-1450	26 Federal Plaza, New York, NY 10278

U.S. Postal Service

Area Served	Telephone	Address
AK, AZ, CA, HI, ID, MT, NM, NV, OR, TT, TX (ZIP codes 797-799 and 885), UT, WA, Pacific Possessions	(415) 742-4922	850 Cherry Ave., San Bruno, CA 94099-0100
AL, AR, FL, GA, LA, MS, OK, TN, TX (except ZIP codes 797-799 and 885)	(901) 722-7333	1407 Union Ave., Memphis, TN 38166-0100
CO, IA, IL, IN (except ZIP codes 420, 423, 424, 470, 476, 477), KS, MI, MN, MO, ND, NE, SD, WI, WY	(312) 765-5000	433 W. Van Buren St., Chicago, IL 60699-0100
CT, MA, ME, NH, NJ (ZIP codes 070-079, 085-089), NY, PR, RI, VI, VT	(203) 285-7001	6 Griffin Rd. North, Windsor, CT 06006-0100
DC, DE, IN (ZIP codes 420, 423, 424, 470, 476, 477), KY, MD, NC, NJ (ZIP codes 080-084), OH, PA, SC, VA, WV	(215) 931-5001	P.O. Box 8601, Philadelphia, PA 19197-0100

Governors, Lieutenant Governors, Secretaries of State, and Attorneys General

This list was compiled from material supplied by the Council of State Governments, the National Assn. of Attorneys General, the National Assn. of Secretaries of State, the National Governors' Assn., and information gathered by Congressional Quarterly. Also included are the Washington representatives of states that maintain offices in the nation's capital.

Political affiliations are indicated as follows: Democrat (D), Independent (I), Republican (R), and New Progressive Party (NPP).

Alabama
Gov. Jim Folsom (D)
State Capitol, Montgomery 36130
Press: Barbara Thomas (205) 242-7150

Vacant, lieutenant governor
725 State Capitol, Montgomery 36130
(205) 242-7900; fax, (205) 242-4666

Secy. of State Jim Bennett (D)
State House, 600 Dexter Ave., Montgomery 36130
(205) 242-7205; fax, (205) 242-4993

Atty. Gen. Jimmy Evans (D)
State House, 11 S. Union St., Montgomery 36130
(205) 242-7300

In Washington, D.C.:
Ronn Flippo, Washington Representative
State of Alabama
R. G. Flippo and Associates
701 Pennsylvania Ave. N.W., #800 20004
508-4397

Alaska
Gov. Walter J. Hickel (I)
State Capitol, P.O. Box 110001, Juneau 99811-0001
Press: John Manly (907) 465-3500

Lt. Gov. John B. Coghill (I)
State Capitol, P.O. Box 110015, Juneau 99811-0015
(907) 465-3520; fax, (907) 463-5364

(No office of Secretary of State)

Atty. Gen. Charles E. Cole (D)
State Capitol, P.O. Box 110300, Juneau 99811-0300
(907) 465-3600

In Washington, D.C.:
John W. Katz, director
Washington Office of the Governor
State of Alaska
444 N. Capitol St. N.W., #336 20001
624-5858

American Samoa
Gov. A. P. Lutali (D)
Office of the Governor, Pago Pago 96799
Press: Aleki Sene (011 684) 633-1121

Lt. Gov. Tauese P. Sunia (D)
Office of the Lieutenant Governor, Pago Pago 96799
(011 684) 633-4116; fax, (011 684) 633-2269

(No office of Secretary of State)

Atty. Gen. Malaetasi Togafau (D)
P.O. Box 7, Pago Pago 96799
(011 684) 633-4163

In Washington, D.C.:
Marc Sisk, Washington Representative
Washington Office of the Governor
2828 Pennsylvania Ave. N.W., #203 20007
338-8088

Arizona
Gov. Fife Symington (R)
Executive Office, Phoenix 85007
Press: Doug Cole (602) 542-1342

(No office of Lieutenant Governor)

Secy. of State Richard Mahoney (D)
700 State Capitol, West Wing, 1700 W. Washington, Phoenix 85007-2808
(602) 542-0681; fax, (602) 542-1575

Atty. Gen. Grant Woods (R)
1275 W. Washington St., Phoenix 85007-2926
(602) 542-4266

Arkansas
Gov. Jim Guy Tucker (D)
State Capitol, Room 250, Little Rock 72201
Press: Max Parker (501) 682-2345

Lt. Gov. Mike Huckabee (R)
270 State Capitol, Little Rock 72201
(501) 682-2144; fax, (501) 682-2894

Secy. of State Bill McCuen (D)
256 State Capitol, Little Rock 72201
(501) 682-1010; fax, (501) 682-1284

Atty. Gen. Winston Bryant (D)
Tower Bldg., 323 Center St., Little Rock 72201-
2610
(501) 682-2007

California
Gov. Pete Wilson (R)
State Capitol, 1st Floor, Sacramento 95814
Press: Dan Schnur (916) 445-4571

Lt. Gov. Leo T. McCarthy (D)
5777 W. Century Blvd., #1650, Los Angeles 90045-
5631
(310) 412-6118; fax, (916) 323-4998

Secy. of State March Fong Eu (D)
1230 J St., Sacramento 95814
(916) 445-6371; fax, (916) 324-4573

Atty. Gen. Daniel E. Lungren (R)
1515 K St., #511, Sacramento 95814
(916) 324-5437

In Washington, D.C.:
David Wetmore, acting director
Washington Office of the Governor
State of California
444 N. Capitol St. N.W., #134 20001
624-5270

Colorado
Gov. Roy Romer (D)
State Capitol, Room 127, Denver 80203-1792
Press: Cindy Parmenter (303) 866-4572

Lt. Gov. C. Michael Callihan (D)
130 State Capitol, Denver 80203-1792
(303) 866-2087; fax, (303) 866-5469

Secy. of State Natalie Meyer (R)
1560 Broadway, #200, Denver 80202
(303) 894-2200; fax, (303) 894-2242

Atty. Gen. Gale A. Norton (R)
1525 Sherman St., Denver 80203
(303) 866-3052

Connecticut
Gov. Lowell P. Weicker Jr. (I)
State Capitol, 201 State Capitol Ave., Hartford
06106
Press: Avice Meehan (203) 566-4840

Lt. Gov. Eunice Groark (I)
304 State Capitol, Hartford 06106
(203) 566-2614; fax, (203) 566-4792

Secy. of State Pauline Kezer (R)
104 State Capitol, Hartford 06106
(203) 566-2739; fax, (203) 566-6318

Atty. Gen. Richard Blumenthal (D)
55 Elm St., Hartford 06141
(203) 566-2026

In Washington, D.C.:
Jan Kaplan, director
Washington Office of the Governor
State of Connecticut
444 N. Capitol St. N.W., #317 20001
347-4535

Delaware
Gov. Tom Carper (D)
820 N. French St., Wilmington 19801
Press: Sheri L. Woodruff (302) 577-3210

Lt. Gov. Ruth Ann Minner (D)
Tatnall Bldg., 3rd Floor, Dover 19901
(302) 739-4151; fax, (302) 577-3019

Secy. of State William T. Quillen (R)
Townsend Bldg., P.O. Box 898, Dover 19903
(302) 739-4111; fax, (302) 739-3811

Atty. Gen. Charles M. Oberly III (D)
820 N. French St., Wilmington 19801
(302) 577-3838

In Washington, D.C.:
Liz Ryan, director
Washington Office
State of Delaware
400 N. Capitol St. N.W., #230 20001
624-7724

Florida
Gov. Lawton Chiles (D)
206 Capitol, Tallahassee 32399
Press: Jo Miglino (904) 488-5394

Lt. Gov. Buddy MacKay (D)
PL05 State Capitol, Tallahassee 32399-0001
(904) 488-4711; fax, (904) 922-2894

Secy. of State Jim Smith (R)
2 Capitol, Plaza Level, Tallahassee 32399
(904) 922-0234; fax, (904) 487-2214

Atty. Gen. Robert A. Butterworth (D)
PL01 State Capitol, Tallahassee 32399-1050
(904) 487-1963

In Washington, D.C.:
Debby Kilmer, director
Washington Office
State of Florida
444 N. Capitol St. N.W., #349 20001
624-5885

Georgia
Gov. Zell Miller (D)
State Capitol, Room 100, Atlanta 30334
Press: Chuck Reece (404) 651-7774

Lt. Gov. Pierre Howard (D)
240 State Capitol, Atlanta 30334
(404) 656-5030; fax, (404) 656-6739

Secy. of State Max Cleland (D)
214 State Capitol, Atlanta 30334
(404) 656-2881; fax, (404) 656-0513

Atty. Gen. Michael J. Bowers (D)
40 Capitol Square S.W., Atlanta 30334-1300
(404) 656-4585

Guam
Gov. Joseph Ada (R)
Executive Chambers, P.O. Box 2950, Agana 96910
Press: Mark Forbes (011 671) 472-8931

Lt. Gov. Frank F. Blas (R)
Executive Chambers, P.O. Box 2950, Agana 96910
(011 671) 472-8931; fax, (011 671) 477-4826

(No office of Secretary of State)

Atty. Gen. Elizabeth Barrett-Anderson
120 W. O'Brien Dr., Agana 96910
(011 671) 475-3324

Hawaii
Gov. John Waihee (D)
State Capitol, Honolulu 96813
Press: Carolyn Tanaka (808) 586-0029

Lt. Gov. Benjamin J. Cayetano (D)
State Capitol, P.O. Box 3226, Honolulu 96801
(808) 586-0255; fax, (808) 586-0231

(No office of Secretary of State)

Atty. Gen. Robert A. Marks (D)
425 Queen St., Honolulu 96813
(808) 586-1282

In Washington, D.C.:
Philip Shimer, Washington representative
State of Hawaii
444 N. Capitol St. N.W., #706 20001
508-3830

Idaho
Gov. Cecil D. Andrus (D)
State Capitol, Boise 83720
Press: Scott Peyron (208) 334-2249

Lt. Gov. C. L. "Butch" Otter (R)
225 State House, Boise 83720
(208) 334-2200; fax, (208) 334-3259

Secy. of State Pete T. Cenarrusa (R)
203 State Capitol, Boise 83720
(208) 334-2300; fax, (208) 334-2282

Atty. Gen. Larry EchoHawk (D)
State House, Room 207, Boise 83720-1000
(208) 334-2400

Illinois
Gov. Jim Edgar (R)
State Capitol, Springfield 62706
Press: Mike Lawrence (217) 782-7355

Lt. Gov. Bob Kustra (R)
214 State Capitol, Springfield 62706
(217) 782-7884; fax, (217) 524-6262

Secy. of State George H. Ryan Sr. (R)
213 State Capitol, Springfield 62706
(217) 782-2201; fax, (217) 785-0358

Atty. Gen. Roland W. Burris (D)
100 W. Randolph St., Chicago 60601
(312) 814-2503

In Washington, D.C.:
Terri Moreland, director
Washington Office
State of Illinois
444 N. Capitol St. N.W., #240 20001
624-7760

Indiana
Gov. Evan Bayh (D)
206 State House, Indianapolis 46204
Press: Fred Nation (317) 232-4578

Lt. Gov. Frank L. O'Bannon (D)
333 State Capitol, Indianapolis 46204
(317) 232-4545; fax, (317) 232-4788

Secy. of State Joseph H. Hogsett (D)
201 State House, Indianapolis 46204
(317) 232-6531; fax, (317) 233-3283

Atty. Gen. Pamela Fanning Carter (D)
219 State House, Indianapolis 46204
(317) 232-6201

In Washington, D.C.:
Jeff Viohl, director
Washington Office
State of Indiana
1001 G St. N.W., #400 East 20001
628-3343

Iowa

Gov. Terry E. Branstad (R)
State Capitol, Des Moines 50319
Press: Dick Vohs (515) 281-3150

Lt. Gov. Joy Corning (R)
9 State Capitol, Des Moines 50319
(515) 281-3421; fax, (515) 281-6611

Secy. of State Elaine Baxter (D)
State House, Des Moines 50319
(515) 281-5204; fax, (515) 242-5952

Atty. Gen. Bonnie J. Campbell (D)
Hoover State Office Bldg., Des Moines 50319
(515) 281-3053

In Washington, D.C.:
Phil Smith, director
Washington Office
State of Iowa
444 N. Capitol St. N.W., #359S 20001
624-5442

Kansas

Gov. Joan Finney (D)
State Capitol, 2nd Floor, Topeka 66612-1590
Press: Martha Walker (913) 296-2714

Lt. Gov. James Francisco (D)
State Capitol, 2nd Floor, Topeka 66612-1504
(913) 296-2213; fax, (913) 296-5669

Secy. of State Bill Graves (R)
State Capitol, 2nd Floor, Topeka 66612
(913) 296-4575; fax, (913) 296-4570

Atty. Gen. Robert T. Stephan (R)
Judicial Bldg., Topeka 66612-1597
(913) 296-2215

Kentucky

Gov. Brereton C. Jones (D)
State Capitol, 700 Capitol Ave., Frankfort 40601
Press: Bill Griffin (502) 564-2611

Lt. Gov. Paul E. Patton (D)
142 State Capitol, Frankfort 40601
(502) 564-7562; fax, (502) 564-5959

Secy. of State Bob Babbage (D)
150 State Capitol, Frankfort 40601-3493
(502) 564-3490; fax, (502) 564-5687

Atty. Gen. Chris Gorman (D)
116 State Capitol, Frankfort 40601
(502) 564-7600

In Washington, D.C.:
Pat Miller, director
Washington Office of the Governor
Commonwealth of Kentucky
400 N. Capitol St. N.W., #351S 20001
624-7741

Louisiana

Gov. Edwin W. Edwards (D)
P.O. Box 94004, Baton Rouge 70804-9004
Press: Kim Hunter (504) 342-9037

Lt. Gov. Melinda Schwegmann (D)
Pentagon Court Barracks, P.O. Box 44243, Baton Rouge 70804
(504) 342-7009; fax, (504) 342-1949

Secy. of State W. Fox McKeithen (R)
P.O. Box 94125, Baton Rouge 70804
(504) 342-4479; fax, (504) 342-5577

Atty. Gen. Richard P. Ieyoub (D)
Dept. of Justice, P.O. Box 94095, Baton Rouge 70804-4095
(504) 342-7013

Maine

Gov. John R. McKernan Jr. (R)
State House, Station 1, Augusta 04333
Press: Cory G. Tilley (207) 287-2531

(No office of Lieutenant Governor)

President of the Senate
Dennis Dutremble (D)
State House, Station 3, Augusta 04333
(207) 289-1500; fax, (207) 289-1308

Secy. of State Bill Diamond (D)
Nash Bldg., Station 148, Augusta 04333-0148
(207) 626-8400; fax, (207) 287-8598

Atty. Gen. Michael E. Carpenter (D)
State House, Augusta 04330
(207) 626-8800

Maryland

Gov. William Donald Schaefer (D)
State House, 100 State Circle, Room 204, Annapolis 21401
Press: Page Boinest (410) 974-2316

Lt. Gov. Melvin A. Steinberg (D)
State House, Annapolis 21401
(410) 974-2804; fax, (410) 974-5252

Secy. of State Tyras S. Athey (D)
State House, Annapolis 21401
(410) 974-5521; fax, (410) 974-5190

Atty. Gen. J. Joseph Curran Jr. (D)
200 St. Paul Place, Baltimore 21202
(410) 576-6300

In Washington, D.C.:
Kenneth Mannella, director
Governor's Washington Office
State of Maryland
444 N. Capitol St. N.W., #311 20001
638-2215

Massachusetts
Gov. William F. Weld (R)
State House, Room 265, Boston 02133
Press: Ray Howell (617) 727-2759

Lt. Gov. Argeo Paul Cellucci (R)
360 State House, Executive Office, Boston 02133
(617) 727-3600; fax, (617) 727-9731

Secy. of the Commonwealth
Michael J. Connolly (D)
337 State House, Boston 02133
(617) 727-9180; fax, (617) 742-4722

Atty. Gen. Scott Harshbarger (D)
1 Ashburton Pl., Boston 02108-1698
(617) 727-2200

In Washington, D.C.:
Jordan St. John, director
Office of Federal-State Relations
Commonwealth of Massachusetts
444 N. Capitol St. N.W., #217 20001
624-7713

Michigan
Gov. John Engler (R)
P.O. Box 30013, Lansing 48909
Press: John Truscott (517) 335-6397

Lt. Gov. Connie Binsfeld (R)
5215 Capitol Bldg., P.O. Box 30026, Lansing 48909
(517) 373-6800; fax, (517) 335-6763

Secy. of State Richard H. Austin (D)
Treasury Bldg., 430 W. Allegan St., 1st Floor, Lansing 48918
(517) 373-2510; fax, (517) 373-0727

Atty. Gen. Frank J. Kelley (D)
P.O. Box 30212, Lansing 48909-0212
(517) 373-1110

In Washington, D.C.:
LeAnne Redick, director
Washington Office
State of Michigan
444 N. Capitol St. N.W., #411 20001
624-5840

Minnesota
Gov. Arne H. Carlson (R)
130 State Capitol, St. Paul 55155
Press: Cyndy Brucato (612) 296-0017

Lt. Gov. Joanell Dyrstad (R)
130 State Capitol, St. Paul 55155
(612) 296-0078; fax, (612) 296-2089

Secy. of State Joan Growe (D)
180 State Office Bldg., 100 Constitution Ave., St. Paul 55155-1299
(612) 296-2079; fax, (612) 297-5844

Atty. Gen. Hubert H. Humphrey III (D)
102 State Capitol, St. Paul 55155
(612) 296-6196

In Washington, D.C.:
Kathee McCright, director
Washington Office
State of Minnesota
400 N. Capitol St. N.W., #365S 20001
624-5308

Mississippi
Gov. Kirk Fordice (R)
P.O. Box 139, Jackson 39205
Press: Johnna Plummer (601) 359-3111

Lt. Gov. Eddie Briggs (R)
315 New Capitol, P.O. Box 1018, Jackson 39215-1018
(601) 359-3200; fax, (601) 359-3935

Secy. of State Dick Molpus (D)
401 Mississippi St. (mailing address: P.O. Box 136), Jackson 39205-0136
(601) 359-1350; fax, (601) 354-6243

Atty. Gen. Mike Moore (D)
Dept. of Justice, P.O. Box 220, Jackson 39205-0220
(601) 359-3692

In Washington, D.C.:
Linda V. Barnett, director
State of Mississippi
444 N. Capitol St. N.W., #367 20001
434-4870

Missouri
Gov. Mel Carnahan (D)
State Capitol, P.O. Box 720, Jefferson City 65102
Press: Chris Sifford (314) 751-4108

Lt. Gov. Roger B. Wilson (D)
121A State Capitol, Jefferson City 65101
(314) 751-4727; fax, (314) 751-9422

Secy. of State Judith Moriarty (D)
208 State Capitol, P.O. Box 778, Jefferson City 65102
(314) 751-3318; fax, (314) 751-2490

Atty. Gen. Jeremiah W. "Jay" Nixon (D)
P.O. Box 899, Jefferson City 65102
(314) 751-3321

In Washington, D.C.:
Jill Friedman, director
Washington Office
State of Missouri
400 N. Capitol St. N.W., #376 20001
624-7720

Montana
Gov. Marc Racicot (R)
State Capitol, Helena 59620
Press: Amy Townsend (406) 444-5523

Lt. Gov. Dennis Rehberg (R)
207 Capitol Station, Helena 59620
(406) 444-5551; fax, (406) 444-5529

Secy. of State Mike Cooney (D)
225 State Capitol, Helena 59620
(406) 444-2034; fax, (406) 444-3976

Atty. Gen. Joseph P. Mazurek (D)
Justice Bldg., 215 N. Sanders, Helena 59620-1401
(406) 444-2026

Nebraska
Gov. E. Benjamin Nelson (D)
State Capitol, Lincoln 68509
Press: Karen Kilgarin (402) 471-2244

Lt. Gov. Kim Robak (D)
2315 State Capitol, P.O. Box 94863, Lincoln 68509-4863
(402) 471-2256; fax, (402) 471-6031

Secy. of State Allen J. Beermann (R)
2300 State Capitol, P.O. Box 94608, Lincoln 68509-4608
(402) 471-2554; fax, (402) 471-3666

Atty. Gen. Don Stenberg (R)
State Capitol, P.O. Box 98920, Lincoln 68509
(402) 471-2682

Nevada
Gov. Bob Miller (D)
State Capitol, Carson City 89710
Press: Michael Campbell (702) 687-5670

Lt. Gov. Sue Wagner (R)
Capitol Complex, Carson City 89710
(702) 687-3037; fax, (702) 687-3420

Secy. of State Cheryl A. Lau (R)
Capitol Complex, Carson City 89710
(702) 687-5203; fax, (702) 687-3471

Atty. Gen. Frankie Sue Del Papa (D)
Heroes Memorial Bldg., 198 S. Carson,
Carson City 89710
(702) 687-4170

In Washington, D.C.:
R. Leo Penne, director
Washington Office
State of Nevada
444 N. Capitol St. N.W., #209 20001
624-5405

New Hampshire
Gov. Stephen Merrill (R)
State House, Concord 03301
Press: Jim Rivers (603) 271-2121

(No office of Lieutenant Governor)

President of the Senate
Ralph D. Hough (R)
302 State House, Concord 03301
(603) 271-2111; fax, (603) 271-2105

Secy. of State William Gardner (D)
204 State House, Concord 03301
(603) 271-3242; fax, (603) 271-6316

Atty. Gen. Jeffrey R. Howard (R)
State House Annex, 25 Capitol St., Concord
03301-6397
(603) 271-3658

New Jersey
Gov. Christine Todd Whitman (R)
State House, CN-001, Trenton 08625
Press: Carl Golden (609) 292-8956

(No office of Lieutenant Governor)

President of the Senate
Donald T. DiFrancesco (R)
259 State House Annex, CN-099, Trenton 08625
(609) 292-5199; fax, (609) 599-3458

Secy. of State Daniel J. Dalton (D)
CN-300, Trenton 08625
(609) 984-1900; fax, (609) 292-7665

Atty. Gen. Robert J. Del Tufo (D)
Richard J. Hughes Justice Complex, 25 Market St.,
CN-080, Trenton 08625
(609) 292-4925

In Washington, D.C.:
Lyle Dennis, director
Washington Office of the Governor
State of New Jersey
444 N. Capitol St. N.W., #201 20001
638-0631

New Mexico
Gov. Bruce King (D)
State Capitol, Santa Fe 87503
Press: John A. McKean (505) 827-3035

Lt. Gov. Casey Luna (D)
State Capitol, Santa Fe 87503
(505) 827-3050; fax, (505) 989-8318

Secy. of State Stephanie Gonzales (D)
420 State Capitol, Santa Fe 87503
(505) 827-3600; fax, (505) 827-3634

Atty. Gen. Tom Udall (D)
P.O. Drawer 1508, Santa Fe 87504-1508
(505) 827-6000

New York
Gov. Mario M. Cuomo (D)
Executive Chamber, State Capitol, Albany 12224
Press: Anne W. Crowley (518) 474-8418

Lt. Gov. Stan Lundine (D)
326 State Capitol, Albany 12224
(518) 474-4623; fax, (518) 473-2444

Secy. of State Gail S. Shaffer (D)
162 Washington Ave., Albany 12231
(518) 474-0050; fax, (518) 474-4765

Atty. Gen. Robert Abrams (D)
120 Broadway, New York 10271
(212) 416-8519

In Washington, D.C.:
Sandra W. Cuneo, director
New York State Office of Federal Affairs
444 N. Capitol St. N.W., #301 20001
434-7100

North Carolina
Gov. James B. Hunt Jr. (D)
State Capitol, Raleigh 27603
Press: Rachel Perry (919) 733-5612

Lt. Gov. Dennis A. Wicker (D)
State Capitol, 116 W. Jones St., Raleigh 27603-8006
(919) 733-7350; fax, (919) 733-6595

Secy. of State Rufus L. Edmisten (D)
300 N. Salisbury St., Raleigh 27603-5909
(919) 733-5140; fax, (919) 733-5172

Atty. Gen. Michael F. Easley (D)
Dept. of Justice, P.O. Box 629, Raleigh 27602-0629
(919) 733-3377

In Washington, D.C.:
Debra Bryant, director
Washington Office
State of North Carolina
444 N. Capitol St. N.W., #332 20001
624-5830

North Dakota
Gov. Edward T. Schafer (R)
State Capitol, 600 E. Boulevard Ave., Bismarck 58505
Press: Jody VonRueden (701) 224-2200

Lt. Gov. Rosemarie Myrdal (R)
State Capitol, Bismarck 58505
(701) 224-2202; fax, (701) 224-2205

Secy. of State Alvin Jaeger (R)
State Capitol, 1st Floor, 600 E. Boulevard Ave.,
Bismarck 58505-0500
(701) 224-3670; fax, (701) 224-2992

Atty. Gen. Heidi Heitkamp (D)
State Capitol, 600 E. Boulevard Ave., Bismarck
58505-0040
(701) 224-2210

Northern Mariana Islands
Gov. Frolian C. Tenorio (D)
Capitol Hill, Saipan, M.P. 96950
·Press: Bruce Lloyd (011 670) 322-5094

Lt. Gov. Jesus Borja (D)
Capitol Hill, Saipan, M.P. 96950
(011 670) 322-5091; fax, (011 670) 322-5096

Acting Atty. Gen. Richard Weil
Capitol Hill, Saipan, M.P. 96950
(011 670) 322-4311

In Washington, D.C.:
Juan N. Babauta, resident representative
Commonwealth of the
Northern Mariana Islands
2121 R St. N.W. 20008
673-5869

Ohio
Gov. George V. Voinovich (R)
77 S. High St., 30th Floor, Columbus 43266-0601
Press: John Meyer (614) 644-0957

Lt. Gov. Mike DeWine (R)
State Office Tower II, 77 S. High St., 30th Floor,
Columbus 43215
(614) 466-3396; fax, (614) 644-0575

Secy. of State Bob Taft (R)
30 E. Broad St., 14th Floor, Columbus 43266-0418
(614) 466-2655; fax, (614) 644-0649

Atty. Gen. Lee Fisher (D)
State Office Tower, 30 E. Broad St., Columbus
43266-0410
(614) 466-3376

In Washington, D.C.:
Ted Hollingsworth, director
Washington Office
State of Ohio
444 N. Capitol St. N.W., #546 20001
624-5844

Oklahoma
Gov. David Walters (D)
State Capitol, Oklahoma City 73105
Press: Randy Splaingard (405) 523-4251

Lt. Gov. Jack Mildren (D)
211 State Capitol, Oklahoma City 73105
(405) 521-2161; fax, (405) 525-2702

Secy. of State John Kennedy (D)
101 State Capitol, Oklahoma City 73105
(405) 521-3911; fax, (405) 521-3771

Atty. Gen. Susan B. Loving (D)
112 State Capitol, 2300 N. Lincoln Blvd.,
Oklahoma City 73105
(405) 521-3921

Oregon
Gov. Barbara Roberts (D)
State Capitol, Salem 97310
Press: Gwenn Baldwin (503) 378-6575

(No office of Lieutenant Governor)

Secy. of State Phil Keisling (D)
136 State Capitol, Salem 97310
(503) 378-4139; fax, (503) 373-7414

Atty. Gen. Theodore R. Kulongoski (D)
100 Justice Bldg., Salem 97310
(503) 378-6002

In Washington, D.C.:
Robert Schule, Washington representative
Governor of Oregon
The Wexler Group
1317 F St. N.W. 20004
638-2121

Pennsylvania
Gov. Robert P. Casey (D)
Main Capitol Bldg., Room 308, Harrisburg 17120
Press: Vincent P. Carocci (717) 783-1116

Lt. Gov. Mark S. Singel (D)
200 Main Capitol, Harrisburg 17120-0002
(717) 787-3300; fax, (717) 783-0150

Secy. of the Commonwealth Brenda K. Mitchell
(D)
302 N. Capitol Bldg., Harrisburg 17120
(717) 787-7630; fax, (717) 787-1734

Atty. Gen. Ernest D. Preate Jr. (R)
Strawberry Square, Harrisburg 17120
(717) 787-3391

In Washington, D.C.:
Philip F. Jehle, director
Washington Office of the Governor
Commonwealth of Pennsylvania
444 N. Capitol St. N.W., #700 20001
624-7828

Puerto Rico
Gov. Pedro Rosselló (NPP)
La Fortaleza, San Juan 00901
Press: George McDougall (809) 721-7000

(No office of Lieutenant Governor)

Secy. of State Baltasar Corrada Del Rio (NPP)
State Capitol, P.O. Box 3271, San Juan 00902-3271
(809) 723-4343; fax, (809) 725-7302

Acting Atty. Gen. Pedro R. Pierluisi
Dept. of Justice, P.O. Box 192, San Juan 00902
(809) 721-7700

In Washington, D.C.:
Wanda Rubianes, director
Puerto Rico Federal Affairs Administration
1100 17th St. N.W. 20036
778-0710

Rhode Island
Gov. Bruce Sundlun (D)
State House, Room 124, Providence 02903
Press: Barbara Cottam (401) 277-2080

Lt. Gov. Robert A. Weygand (D)
317 State House, Providence 02903
(401) 277-2371; fax, (401) 277-2012

Secy. of State Barbara Leonard (R)
217 State House, Providence 02903
(401) 277-2357; fax, (401) 277-1356

Atty. Gen. Jeffrey B. Pine (R)
72 Pine St., Providence 02903
(401) 274-4400

South Carolina
Gov. Carroll A. Campbell Jr. (R)
P.O. Box 11369, Columbia 29211
Press: Tucker A. Eskew (803) 734-9840

Lt. Gov. Nick A. Theodore (D)
State House, P.O. Box 142, Columbia 29202
(803) 734-2080; fax, (803) 734-2082

Secy. of State Jim Miles (R)
Wade Hampton Bldg., P.O. Box 11350, Columbia
29211
(803) 734-2170; fax, (803) 734-2164

Atty. Gen. T. Travis Medlock (D)
Robert C. Dennis Office Bldg., P.O. Box
11549, Columbia 29211
(803) 734-3970

In Washington, D.C.:
Nikki McNamee, director
Washington Office of the Governor
State of South Carolina
444 N. Capitol St. N.W., #203 20001
624-7784

South Dakota
Gov. Walter D. Miller (R)
500 E. Capitol, Pierre 57501
Press: Janelle Toman (605) 773-3212

Lt. Gov. Steve T. Kirby (R)
500 E. Capitol, Pierre 57501
(605) 773-3212; fax, (605) 773-4711

Secy. of State Joyce Hazeltine (R)
500 E. Capitol, Pierre 57501
(605) 773-3537; fax, (605) 773-6580

Atty. Gen. Mark Barnett (R)
500 E. Capitol, Pierre 57501-5070
(605) 773-3215

Tennessee
Gov. Ned Ray McWherter (D)
State Capitol, Room G-9, Nashville 37243-0001
Press: Ken Renner (615) 741-3763

Lt. Gov. John S. Wilder (D)
1 Legislative Plaza, Nashville 37219
(615) 741-2368; fax, (615) 741-9349

Secy. of State Riley Darnell (D)
State Capitol, 1st Floor, Nashville 37243-0305
(615) 741-2819; fax, (615) 741-5962

Atty. Gen. Charles W. Burson (D)
450 James Robertson Parkway, Nashville 37243-0495
(615) 741-3491

Texas
Gov. Ann W. Richards (D)
P.O. Box 12428, Austin 78711
Press: Bill Cryer (512) 463-1826

Lt. Gov. Bob Bullock (D)
P.O. Box 12068, Austin 78711
(512) 463-0001; fax, (512) 463-0039

Secy. of State John Hannah Jr. (D)
P.O. Box 12697, Austin 78711
(512) 463-5701; fax, (512) 475-2761

Atty. Gen. Dan Morales (D)
P.O. Box 12548, Capitol Station, Austin 78711-2548
(512) 463-2191

In Washington, D.C.:
Jane Hickie, director
Office of State-Federal Relations
State of Texas
122 C St. N.W., #200 20001
638-3927

Utah
Gov. Mike Leavitt (R)
210 State Capitol, Salt Lake City 84114
Press: Vicki Varela (801) 538-1000

Lt. Gov. Olene S. Walker (R)
203 State Capitol, Salt Lake City 84114
(801) 538-1040; fax, (801) 538-1557

(No office of Secretary of State)

Atty. Gen. Jan Graham (D)
State Office Bldg., Salt Lake City 84114
(801) 538-1326

In Washington, D.C.:
Joanne Snow Neumann, director
Washington Office
State of Utah
444 N. Capitol St. N.W., #370 20001
624-7704

Vermont
Gov. Howard Dean (D)
109 State St., Montpelier 05609
Press: Glen Gershaneck (802) 828-3333

Lt. Gov. Barbara Snelling (R)
State House, Montpelier 05633
(802) 828-2226; fax, (802) 828-3198

Secy. of State Don Hooper (D)
109 State St., Montpelier 05609-1101
(802) 828-2148; fax, (802) 828-2496

Atty. Gen. Jeffrey L. Amestoy (R)
109 State St., Montpelier 05609-1001
(802) 828-3171

Virgin Islands
Gov. Alexander A. Farrelly (D)
Government House, Charlotte Amalie,
St. Thomas 00802
Press: James A. O'Bryan Jr. (809) 774-0294

Lt. Gov. Derek Hodge (D)
18 Kongens Gade, St. Thomas 00802
(809) 774-2991; fax, (809) 773-0330

(No office of Secretary of State)

Atty. Gen. Rosalie Ballentine
Dept. of Justice, G.E.R.S. Complex, #48B-50C
Kronprinsdens Gade, St. Thomas 00802
(809) 774-5666

In Washington, D.C.:
Carlyle Corbin, Washington representative
Office of the Governor of the Virgin Islands
900 17th St. N.W. 20006
293-3707

Virginia
Gov. George F. Allen (R)
State Capitol, Richmond 23219
Press: Ken Stroupe (804) 786-2211

Lt. Gov. Donald S. Beyer Jr. (D)
Supreme Court Bldg., 101 N. 8th St., Richmond 23219
(804) 786-2078; fax, (804) 786-7514

Secy. of the Commonwealth Betsy Davis Beamer (R)
Capitol Square, P.O. Box 2454, Richmond 23201
(804) 786-2441; fax, (804) 371-0017

Atty. Gen. Stephen Rosenthal (D)
101 N. 8th St., 5th Floor, Richmond 23219
(804) 786-2071

In Washington, D.C.:
Dian Copelin, director
Virginia Liaison Office
444 N. Capitol St. N.W., #214 20001
783-1769

Washington
Gov. Mike Lowry (D)
Legislative Bldg., Olympia 98504
Press: Anne Fennessy (206) 753-6780

Lt. Gov. Joel Pritchard (R)
304 Legislative Bldg., P.O. Box 40400, Olympia 98504-0400
(206) 786-7700; fax, (206) 786-7520

Secy. of State Ralph Munro (R)
Legislative Bldg., 2nd Floor (mailing address: P.O.
Box 40220), Olympia 98504-0220
(206) 753-7121; fax, (206) 586-5629

Atty. Gen. Christine O. Gregoire (D)
Bldg. 3, 905 Plum St. (mailing address: P.O. Box
40100), Olympia 98504-0100
(206) 753-6200

West Virginia
Gov. Gaston Caperton (D)
State Capitol, Room W-156, Charleston 25305
Press: Carolyn Curry (304) 558-6345

(No office of Lieutenant Governor)

President of the Senate
Keith Burdette (D)
229 Main Unit, Capitol Complex, Charleston
25305
(304) 357-7801; fax, (304) 357-7829

Secy. of State Ken Hechler (D)
Bldg. 1, 1900 Kanawha Blvd. East, #157K, Charleston 25305
(304) 558-6000; fax, (304) 558-0900

Atty. Gen. Darrell V. McGraw Jr. (D)
State Capitol, Charleston 25305
(304) 558-2021

Wisconsin
Gov. Tommy G. Thompson (R)
State Capitol, P.O. Box 7863, Madison 53707
Press: Stephanie Smith (608) 266-6925

Lt. Gov. Scott McCallum (R)
22 E. State Capitol, Madison 53702
(608) 266-3516; fax, (608) 267-3571

Secy. of State Douglas La Follette (D)
30 W. Mifflin St., 9th and 10th Floors, Madison
53703
(608) 266-8888; fax, (608) 267-6813

Atty. Gen. James E. Doyle (D)
114 East, State Capitol, P.O. Box 7857, Madison
53707-7857
(608) 266-1221

In Washington, D.C.:
Mary Sheehy, director
Washington Office
State of Wisconsin
444 N. Capitol St. N.W., #613 20001
624-5870

Wyoming
Gov. Mike Sullivan (D)
State Capitol, Cheyenne 82002
Press: Dennis E. Curran (307) 777-7434

(No office of Lieutenant Governor)

Secy. of State Kathy Karpan (D)
State Capitol, Cheyenne 82002-0020
(307) 777-5333; fax, (307) 777-6217

Atty. Gen. Joseph B. Meyer (R)
State Capitol, Cheyenne 82002
(307) 777-7841

Mayors of Major Cities

Listed below are mayors of cities with a population of 75,000 or more. The list is organized alphabetically by state. It gives the population of each city, the month and year that the mayor's term expires, and the local area code and municipal telephone number. The list also gives the form of government for each city: council-elected executive (CE), council-manager (CM), commission (CO), or mayor-council (MC).

Some cities have representatives in Washington with offices located at 1620 Eye St. N.W. 20006; 429-0160. The Washington office for New York City is at 555 New Jersey Ave. N.W. 20001; 393-3903; and the office for Los Angeles is at 1301 Pennsylvania Ave. N.W. 20004; 347-0915.

This list was compiled from information gathered by Congressional Quarterly; *The Municipal Year Book,* published by the International City Management Assn.; and material from the United States Conference of Mayors.

City/State	Population (in thousands)	Mayor	Term Expires	Form of Govt.	Telephone Number
Alabama					
Birmingham	266	Richard Arrington Jr.	10/95	MC	205-254-2277
Huntsville	160	Steve Hettinger	10/96	MC	205-532-7304
Mobile	196	Michael C. Dow	10/97	CO	205-434-7395
Montgomery	187	Emory Folmar	11/95	MC	205-241-2000
Tuscaloosa	78	Alvin DuPont	10/97	CO	205-349-2010
Alaska					
Anchorage	226	Tom Fink	7/94	MC	907-343-4409
Arizona					
Chandler	91	Jay Tivshraeny	3/96	CM	602-786-2200
Glendale	152	Elaine Scruggs	4/96	CM	602-435-4250
Mesa	288	Willie Wong	6/94	CM	602-644-2388
Phoenix	983	Paul Johnson	12/95	CM	602-262-7111
Scottsdale	130	Herbert R. Drinkwater	4/96	CM	602-994-2433
Tempe	142	Harry E. Mitchell	7/94	CM	602-350-8225
Tucson	405	George Miller	12/95	CM	602-791-4201
Arkansas					
Little Rock	176	Jim Dailey	12/94	CM	501-371-4510
California					
Alameda	76	E.W. Withrow, Jr.	4/95	CM	510-748-4545
Alhambra	82	Boyd Condie	2/95	CM	818-570-5007
Anaheim	266	Tom Daly	11/94	CM	714-254-5100
Bakersfield	175	Bob Price	12/96	CM	805-326-3770

City/State	Population (in thousands)	Mayor	Term Expires	Form of Govt.	Telephone Number
Berkeley	103	Loni Hancock	12/94	CM	510-644-6484
Burbank	94	Bill Wiggins	5/95	CM	818-953-9708
Carson	84	Michael I. Mitoma	4/96	CM	310-830-7600
Chula Vista	135	Tim Nader	11/94	CM	619-691-5044
Compton	90	Omar Bradley	6/95	CM	310-605-5591
Concord	111	Mark DeSaulnier	11/94	CM	510-671-3158
Corona	76	William Miller	12/94	CM	714-736-2201
Costa Mesa	96	Sandy Genis	12/94	CM	714-754-5327
Daly City	92	Madolyn L. Agrimonti	11/94	CM	415-991-8000
Downey	91	Robert S. Brazelton	6/94	CM	310-869-7331
El Cajon	89	Joan Shoemaker	7/94	CM	619-441-1776
El Monte	106	Patricia Wallach	4/96	CM	818-580-2001
Escondido	109	Jerry Harmon	7/94	CM	619-741-4610
Fairfield	77	Chuck Hammond	12/97	CM	707-428-7395
Fontana	88	William Kragness	11/94	CM	714-350-7600
Fremont	173	William Ball	11/94	CM	510-494-4811
Fresno	354	Jim Patterson	3/97	CM	209-498-1561
Fullerton	114	A. B. Catlin	12/94	CM	714-738-6311
Garden Grove	143	Frank Kessler	12/94	CM	714-741-5040
Glendale	180	Larry Zarian	4/97	CM	818-548-4000
Hayward	111	Roberta Cooper	4/98	CM	510-293-5342
Huntington Beach	182	Grace Winchell	12/94	CM	714-536-5511
Inglewood	110	Edward Vincent	1/95	CM	310-412-5300
Irvine	110	Mike Ward	11/94	CM	714-724-6000
Lancaster	97	Frank Roberts	4/95	CM	805-723-6019
Long Beach	429	Ernie Kell	6/94	CM	310-590-6309
Los Angeles	3,485	Richard Riordan	6/97	MC	213-485-3311
Modesto	165	Richard A. Lang	11/95	CM	209-577-5230
Moreno Valley	119	Bonnie Flickinger	12/94	CM	714-243-3008
Norwalk	94	Mike Mendez	4/95	CM	310-929-2677
Oakland	372	Elihu Mason Harris	1/95	CM	510-238-3141
Oceanside	128	Dick Lyon	12/96	CM	619-966-4401
Ontario	133	James L. Fatland	11/94	CM	714-986-1151
Orange	111	Gene Beyer	11/94	CM	714-744-5500
Oxnard	142	Manuel M. Lopez	11/94	CM	805-385-7430
Pasadena	132	Rick Cole	5/95	CM	818-405-4311
Pomona	132	Eddie Cortez	4/95	CM	714-620-2051
Rancho Cucamonga	101	Dennis L. Stout	12/94	CM	714-989-1851
Richmond	87	Rosemary Corbin	11/97	CM	510-620-6503
Riverside	227	Ron Loveridge	12/97	CM	909-782-5551
Sacramento	369	Joseph Serna Jr.	6/96	CM	916-264-5407
Salinas	109	Allen Styles	6/95	CM	408-758-7203
San Bernardino	164	Tom Minor	6/97	MC	714-384-5133
San Buenaventura	93	Tom Buford	12/95	CM	805-654-7827
San Diego	1,111	Susan Golding	12/96	CM	619-236-6330
San Francisco	724	Frank Jordan	1/96	MC	415-554-6141
San Jose	782	Susan Hammer	1/95	CM	408-277-4237
San Mateo	85	Jerry Hill	12/94	CM	415-377-3423
Santa Ana	294	Dan Young	11/94	CM	714-647-6910
Santa Barbara	86	Hal Conklin	12/97	CM	805-963-0611
Santa Clara	94	Everett N. Souza	11/94	CM	408-984-3250
Santa Clarita	111	George Pederson	12/94	CM	805-259-2481
Santa Fe Springs	156	Al Sharp	3/97	CM	310-868-051
Santa Monica	87	Judy Abdo	11/94	CM	310-458-820
Santa Rosa	113	Bill Knight	12/94	CM	707-524-536

City/State	Population *(in thousands)*	Mayor	Term Expires	Form of Govt.	Telephone Number
Simi Valley	100	Gregory Stratton	11/94	CM	805-583-6701
South Gate	86	Albert Robles	4/95	CM	213-563-9500
Stockton	211	Joan Darrah	12/96	CM	209-944-8244
Sunnyvale	117	Frances Rowe	11/95	CM	408-730-7473
Thousand Oaks	104	Elois Zeanah	12/94	CM	805-497-8611
Torrance	133	Dee Hardison	3/98	CM	310-328-5310
Vallejo	109	Anthony Intintoli Jr.	12/95	CM	707-648-4377
Visalia	76	Basil A. Perch	11/95	CM	209-738-3313
West Covina	96	Brad McFadden	4/95	CM	818-814-8401
Westminster	78	Charles V. Smith	11/94	CM	714-898-3311
Whittier	78	Michael Sullens	4/96	CM	310-945-8225
Colorado					
Arvada	89	Robert Erie	11/95	CM	303-421-2550
Aurora	222	Paul E. Tauer	11/95	CM	303-695-7015
Boulder	83	Leslie L. Durgin	11/95	CM	303-441-3002
Colorado Springs	281	Robert M. Isaac	4/95	CM	719-578-6600
Denver	468	Wellington E. Webb	7/95	MC	303-640-2721
Fort Collins	88	Ann Azari	4/95	CM	303-221-6505
Lakewood	126	Linda Morton	11/95	CM	303-987-7040
Pueblo	99	Joyce Lawrence	12/94	CM	719-584-0800
Westminster	75	Nancy Heil	11/95	CM	303-430-2400
Connecticut					
Bridgeport	142	Joseph P. Ganim	12/95	MC	203-576-7201
Hartford	140	Mike Peters	12/95	CM	203-543-8500
New Haven	130	John DeStefano	12/95	MC	203-787-8200
Norwalk	77	Frank J. Esposito	11/95	MC	203-854-7701
Stamford	108	Stanley Esposito	12/94	MC	203-977-4152
Waterbury	109	Edward D. Bergin	12/95	MC	203-574-6712
District of Columbia					
Washington, D.C.	607	Sharon Pratt Kelly	1/95	MC	202-727-6319
Florida					
Cape Coral	75	Roger G. Butler	11/96	MC	813-574-0436
Clearwater	99	Rita Garvey	4/96	CM	813-462-6700
Coral Springs	79	John Sommerer	3/96	CM	305-344-1000
Fort Lauderdale	149	Jim Naugle	3/97	CM	305-761-5003
Gainesville	85	James S. Painter	5/94	CM	904-334-2006
Hialeah	188	Julio J. Martinez	11/97	MC	305-883-5802
Hollywood	122	Mara Giulianti	3/96	CM	305-921-3321
Jacksonville	635	Edward Austin	7/95	MC	904-630-1776
Miami	359	Steve Clark	11/97	CM	305-250-5300
Miami Beach	93	Seymour Gelber	11/95	CM	305-673-7030
Orlando	165	Glenda Hood	10/96	MC	407-246-2221
St. Petersburg	239	David Fischer	3/97	CM	813-893-7117
Tallahassee	125	Penny Shaw Herman	2/95	CM	904-599-8181
Tampa	280	Sandra W. Freedman	3/95	MC	813-223-8251
Georgia					
Albany	78	Paul Keenan	1/96	CM	912-431-3244
Atlanta	394	Bill Campbell	12/97	MC	404-330-6100
Columbus	179	Frank Martin	1/95	CM	404-571-4700
Macon	107	Tommy Olmstead	12/95	MC	912-751-7170
Savannah	138	Susan Weiner	12/95	CM	912-651-6444

City/State	Population (in thousands)	Mayor	Term Expires	Form of Govt.	Telephone Number
Hawaii					
Honolulu	365	Frank F. Fasi	1/97	MC	808-523-4141
Maui County	97	Linda Crocket Lingle	12/94	CE	808-243-7855
Idaho					
Boise	126	Brent Coles	12/97	MC	208-384-4422
Illinois					
Arlington Heights	75	Arlene J. Mulder	4/97	CM	708-253-2340
Aurora	100	David L. Pierce	4/97	MC	708-892-8811
Chicago	2,784	Richard M. Daley	4/95	MC	312-744-3300
Decatur	84	Erik K. Brechnitz	5/95	CM	217-424-2804
Elgin	77	George Van De Voorde	4/95	CM	708-931-5595
Joliet	77	Arthur Schultz	5/95	CM	815-740-2495
Naperville	85	Samuel T. Macrane	5/95	CM	708-420-6111
Peoria	114	James A. Maloof	5/97	CM	309-672-8519
Rockford	139	Charles E. Box	4/97	MC	815-987-5590
Springfield	105	Ossie Langfelder	4/95	CO	217-789-2200
Indiana					
Evansville	126	Frank F. McDonald II	12/95	MC	812-426-5581
Fort Wayne	184	Paul Helmke	1/96	MC	219-427-1111
Gary	117	Thomas V. Barnes	1/96	MC	219-881-1302
Hammond	84	Duane W. Dedelow Jr.	1/96	MC	219-853-6301
Indianapolis	731	Stephen Goldsmith	12/95	MC	317-327-3600
South Bend	106	Joseph Kernan	12/95	MC	219-284-9261
Iowa					
Cedar Rapids	109	Larry Serbousek	12/95	MC	319-398-5051
Davenport	95	Pat Gibbs	12/95	MC	319-326-7701
Des Moines	193	John P. Dorrian	12/95	CM	515-237-1645
Sioux City	81	Robert Scott	12/94	CM	712-279-6102
Kansas					
Kansas City	150	Joe Steineger	4/95	CM	913-573-5010
Overland Park	112	Ed Eilert	4/97	CM	913-381-5252
Topeka	120	Harry Felker	4/97	CO	913-295-3940
Wichita	304	Elma Broadfoot	4/95	CM	316-268-4331
Kentucky					
Lexington	225	Pam Miller	12/98	MC	606-258-3000
Louisville	269	Jerry Abramson	12/97	MC	502-625-3061
Louisiana					
Baton Rouge	220	Tom Edward McHugh	12/96	MC	504-389-3000
Lafayette	94	Kenneth F. Bowen	6/96	MC	318-261-8300
New Orleans	497	Mark Morial	5/98	MC	504-586-4000
Shreveport	199	Hazel Beard	11/94	MC	318-226-6250
Maryland					
Baltimore	736	Kurt Schmoke	12/95	MC	410-396-3835
Massachusetts					
Boston	574	Thomas Menino	1/98	MC	617-635-4001
Brockton	93	Winthrop H. Farwell Jr.	1/96	MC	508-580-7120
Cambridge	96	Kenneth Reeves	12/95	CM	617-349-4320

City/State	Population (in thousands)	Mayor	Term Expires	Form of Govt.	Telephone Number
Fall River	93	John R. Mitchell	1/96	MC	508-324-2000
Lowell	103	Richard Howe	1/96	CM	508-970-4040
Lynn	81	Patrick J. McManus	12/95	MC	617-598-4000
New Bedford	100	Rosemary Tierney	1/96	MC	508-979-1400
Newton	83	Theodore D. Mann	12/97	MC	617-552-7100
Quincy	85	James A. Sheets	1/96	MC	617-376-1990
Somerville	76	Michael E. Capuano	1/96	MC	617-625-6600
Springfield	157	Robert T. Markel	1/96	MC	413-787-6100
Worcester	170	Raymond V. Mariano	1/96	CM	508-799-1153
Michigan					
Ann Arbor	110	Ingrid B. Sheldon	11/94	CM	313-994-2766
Dearborn	89	Michael Guido	1/98	MC	313-943-2300
Detroit	1,028	Dennis Archer	12/97	MC	313-224-6340
Farmington Hills	75	Nancy Bates	12/94	CM	313-473-9504
Flint	141	Woodrow Stanley	11/95	MC	313-766-7346
Grand Rapids	189	John H. Logie	1/96	CM	616-456-3166
Kalamazoo	80	Edward Annen	11/95	CM	616-337-8792
Lansing	127	David Hollister	12/97	MC	517-483-4141
Livonia	101	Robert D. Bennett	1/96	MC	313-421-2000
Southfield	76	Donald F. Fracassi	12/97	CM	313-354-9600
Sterling Heights	118	Richard J. Notte	11/95	CM	313-977-6123
Warren	145	Ronald L. Bonkowski	11/95	MC	313-574-4520
Westland	85	Robert J. Thomas	12/97	MC	313-467-3185
Minnesota					
Bloomington	86	Neil Peterson	12/95	CM	612-881-5811
Duluth	85	Gary Doty	1/96	MC	218-723-3295
Minneapolis	368	Sharon Sayles Belton	12/97	MC	612-673-2100
St. Paul	272	Norm Coleman	12/97	MC	612-266-8510
Mississippi					
Jackson	197	Kane Ditto	7/97	CO	601-960-1084
Missouri					
Independence	112	Ron Stewart	4/98	CM	816-325-7026
Kansas City	435	Emanuel Cleaver II	4/95	CM	816-274-2595
St. Louis	397	Freeman R. Bosley Jr.	4/97	MC	314-622-3201
Springfield	144	N. L. McCartney	4/95	CM	417-864-1651
Montana					
Billings	81	Richard L. Larsen	12/95	CM	406-657-8296
Nebraska					
Lincoln	192	Mike Johanns	5/95	MC	402-471-7511
Omaha	336	P. J. Morgan	6/97	MC	402-444-5000
Nevada					
Las Vegas	258	Jan Laverty Jones	6/95	CM	702-229-6241
Reno	134	Peter J. Sferrazza	6/95	CM	702-334-2001
New Hampshire					
Manchester	100	Ray Wieczorek	1/96	MC	603-624-6500
Nashua	80	Rob Wagner	1/96	MC	603-594-3341
New Jersey					
Camden	87	Arnold W. Webster	12/96	MC	609-757-7200
Dover Twp.	75	Joseph H. Vicari	12/94	MC	908-341-1000

City/State	Population (in thousands)	Mayor	Term Expires	Form of Govt.	Telephone Number
Elizabeth	110	J. Christian Bollwage	12/96	MC	908-820-4170
Hamilton Twp.	83	John K. Rafferty	12/95	MC	609-890-3502
Jersey City	229	Bret Schundler	5/97	MC	201-547-5200
Newark	275	Sharpe James	7/94	MC	201-733-6400
Paterson	141	William J. Pascrell Jr.	7/94	MC	201-881-3300
Trenton	89	Douglas H. Palmer	7/94	MC	609-989-3030
Woodbridge	90	James E. McGreevey	1/96	MC	908-634-4500
New Mexico					
Albuquerque	385	Martin Chavez	11/97	MC	505-768-3000
New York					
Albany	101	Gerald D. Jennings	12/97	MC	518-434-5100
Buffalo	328	Anthony Masiello	12/97	MC	716-851-4841
New York City	7,323	Rudolph Giuliani	12/97	MC	212-788-3000
Rochester	232	Bill Johnson	12/97	MC	716-428-7045
Syracuse	164	Roy Bernardi	12/96	MC	315-448-8005
Yonkers	188	Terence Zaleski	12/95	CM	914-377-6000
North Carolina					
Charlotte	396	Richard Vinroot	12/95	CM	704-336-2244
Durham	137	Sylvia S. Kerckhoff	12/95	CM	919-560-4333
Fayetteville	76	Fred Hanna	12/94	CM	919-433-1992
Greensboro	184	Carolyn Allen	12/97	CM	919-373-2000
Raleigh	208	Tom Fetzer	12/95	CM	919-890-3050
Winston-Salem	143	Martha S. Wood	12/97	CM	919-727-2058
Ohio					
Akron	223	Donald L. Plusquellic	1/96	MC	216-375-2345
Canton	84	Richard Watkins	1/96	MC	216-489-3283
Cincinnati	364	Roxanne Qualls	11/95	CM	513-352-3250
Cleveland	506	Michael R. White	12/97	MC	216-664-2220
Columbus	633	Greg Lashutka	12/95	MC	614-645-7671
Dayton	182	Michael R. Turner	1/98	CM	513-443-3636
Parma	88	Michael Ries	1/96	MC	216-885-8000
Toledo	333	Carty Finkbeiner	1/98	CM	419-245-1001
Youngstown	96	Patrick J. Ungaro	12/97	MC	216-742-8701
Oklahoma					
Lawton	81	John T. Marley	2/95	CM	405-357-6100
Norman	80	William Nation	4/95	CM	405-366-5406
Oklahoma City	445	Ronald Norick	4/98	CM	405-297-2424
Tulsa	374	M. Susan Savage	2/98	CO	918-596-7777
Oregon					
Eugene	113	Ruth Bascom	1/98	CM	503-687-501C
Portland	437	Vera Katz	12/96	CO	503-823-412C
Salem	108	R. G. Andersen-Wyckoff	12/94	CM	503-588-625!
Pennsylvania					
Allentown	105	William Heydt	12/97	MC	215-437-754
Erie	109	Joyce Savocchio	12/97	MC	814-870-120
Philadelphia	1,586	Edward Rendell	1/96	MC	215-686-218
Pittsburgh	370	Tom Murphy	12/97	MC	412-255-262
Reading	78	Warren H. Haggerty Jr.	12/95	CO	215-655-600
Scranton	82	James Conners	12/97	MC	717-348-410

City/State	Population (in thousands)	Mayor	Term Expires	Form of Govt.	Telephone Number
Puerto Rico					
Arecibo	93	Angel M. Roman Velez	12/96	MC	809-879-2299
Bayamon	214	Ramon L. Rivera	12/96	MC	809-787-8836
Caguas	133	Angel O. Berrios Diaz	12/96	MC	809-743-3400
Carolina	178	Jose E. Aponte	12/96	MC	809-757-2705
Guaynabo	81	Alejandro Cruz	12/96	MC	809-720-2388
Mayaguez	100	Jose Guillermo Rodriguez	12/96	MC	809-834-8586
Ponce	188	Rafael Cordero	12/96	MC	809-840-4141
San Juan	438	Hector Luis Acevedo	12/96	MC	809-721-0100
Toa Baja	89	Victor M. Soto	12/96	MC	809-794-1135
Rhode Island					
Cranston	76	Michael A. Traficante	12/94	MC	401-461-5380
Providence	161	Vincent A. Cianci Jr.	12/94	MC	401-421-7740
Warwick	85	Lincoln Chafee	12/94	MC	401-738-2000
South Carolina					
Charleston	80	Joseph P. Riley Jr.	1/96	MC	803-577-4727
Columbia	98	Robert D. Coble	6/94	CM	803-733-8221
South Dakota					
Sioux Falls	101	Jack White	6/96	CO	605-339-7094
Tennessee					
Chattanooga	152	Gene Roberts	4/97	CO	615-757-5152
Clarksville	75	Donald W. Trotter	1/95	MC	615-645-7444
Knoxville	165	Victor Ashe	12/95	MC	615-521-2040
Memphis	610	Willie W. Herenton	12/95	MC	901-576-6000
Nashville	488	Philip N. Bredesen	9/95	MC	615-862-6000
Texas					
Abilene	107	Gary McCaleb	5/96	CM	915-676-6205
Amarillo	158	Kel Seliger	5/95	CM	806-378-3000
Arlington	262	Richard Greene	5/95	CM	817-275-3271
Austin	466	Bruce Todd	6/94	CM	512-499-2250
Beaumont	114	David W. Moore	5/96	CM	409-880-3716
Brownsville	99	Pat Ahumada	11/95	CM	512-548-6000
Carrollton	82	Gary W. Blanscet	5/96	CM	214-466-3001
Corpus Christi	257	Mary Rhodes	4/95	CM	512-880-3100
Dallas	1,007	Steve Bartlett	5/95	CM	214-670-4054
El Paso	515	Larry Francis	6/95	MC	915-541-4145
Fort Worth	448	Kay Granger	5/95	CM	817-871-6117
Garland	181	James B. Ratliff	5/96	CM	214-205-2400
Grand Prairie	100	Charles V. England	5/96	CM	214-660-8024
Houston	1,631	Bob Lanier	12/97	MC	713-247-2200
Irving	155	Bobby Joe Raper	5/95	CM	214-721-2410
Laredo	123	Saul N. Ramirez Jr.	10/94	CM	210-791-7300
Lubbock	186	David R. Langston	5/96	CM	806-762-6411
McAllen	84	Othal E. Brand Sr.	5/97	CM	210-682-6181
Mesquite	101	Cathye Ray	5/95	CM	214-288-7711
Midland	89	J. D. Faircloth	6/94	CM	915-685-7204
Odessa	90	Lorraine Perryman	5/96	CM	915-337-7381
Pasadena	119	Johnny Isbell	6/97	MC	713-477-1511
Plano	129	James N. Muns	5/96	CM	214-578-7107
Richardson	75	Gary Slagel	5/95	CM	214-238-4100
San Angelo	84	Dick Funk	5/95	CM	915-657-4241

City/State	Population (in thousands)	Mayor	Term Expires	Form of Govt.	Telephone Number
San Antonio	936	Nelson W. Wolff	5/95	CM	210-299-7060
Tyler	75	Smith P. Reynolds Jr.	5/96	CM	903-531-1250
Waco	104	Robert Sheehy Jr.	5/96	CM	817-750-5750
Wichita Falls	96	Michael Lam	5/96	CM	817-761-7404
Utah					
Provo	87	George O. Stewart	12/97	MC	801-379-6524
Salt Lake City	160	Deedee Corradini	12/95	CO	801-535-7704
Sandy City	75	Thomas M. Dolan	1/98	MC	801-568-7100
West Valley	87	Brent Anderson	12/94	MC	801-966-3600
Virginia					
Alexandria	111	Patricia Ticer	6/94	CM	703-838-4930
Chesapeake	152	William E. Ward	6/96	CM	804-547-6462
Hampton	134	James L. Eason	6/96	CM	804-727-6315
Newport News	170	Barry E. Duval	7/94	CM	804-247-8403
Norfolk	261	Mason C. Andrews	7/94	CM	804-441-2679
Portsmouth	104	Gloria O. Webb	6/96	CM	804-393-8746
Richmond	203	Walter T. Kenney	7/94	CM	804-780-7977
Roanoke	96	David A. Bowers	6/96	CM	703-981-2444
Virginia Beach	393	Meyera E. Oberndorf	6/96	CM	804-427-4581
Washington					
Bellevue	87	Don Davidson	12/95	CM	206-455-7810
Seattle	516	Norman Rice	12/97	MC	206-684-4000
Spokane	177	Jack Geraughty	12/97	CM	509-625-6250
Tacoma	177	Jack Hyde	12/97	CM	206-591-5100
Wisconsin					
Green Bay	96	Samuel Halloin	7/95	MC	414-448-3005
Kenosha	80	John Antaramian	4/96	MC	414-656-8100
Madison	191	Paul Soglin	4/95	MC	608-266-4611
Milwaukee	628	John O. Norquist	4/96	MC	414-278-2200
Racine	84	N. Owen Davies	4/95	MC	414-636-9111

Pronunciation Guide for Congress

The following is an informal pronunciation guide for some of the most-often-mispronounced names of members of Congress:

SENATE

Alfonse M. D'Amato, R-N.Y. — da-MAH-toe
Dennis DeConcini, D-Ariz. — dee-con-SEE-nee
Pete V. Domenici, R-N.M. — da-MEN-ih-chee
D. M. "Lauch" Faircloth, R-N.C. — LOCK
Dianne Feinstein, D-Calif. — FINE-stine
Daniel K. Inouye, D-Hawaii — in-NO-ay

HOUSE

Jim Bacchus, D-Fla. — BACK-us
Spencer Bachus, R-Ala. — BACK-us
Scotty Baesler, D-Ky. — BAA-sler
James A. Barcia, D-Mich. — BAR-sha
Xavier Becerra, D-Calif. — HAH-vee-air beh-SEH-ra
Anthony C. Beilenson, D-Calif. — BEE-lin-son
Doug Bereuter, R-Neb. — BEE-right-er
Michael Bilirakis, R-Fla. — bil-li-RACK-us
John A. Boehner, R-Ohio — BAY-ner
Henry Bonilla, R-Texas — bo-NEE-uh
David E. Bonior, D-Mich. — BON-yer
Rick Boucher, D-Va. — BOUGH-cher
Steve Buyer, R-Ind. — BOO-yer
Charles T. Canady, R-Fla. — CAN-uh-dee
Michael D. Crapo, R-Idaho — CRAY-poe
Peter A. DeFazio, D-Ore. — da-FAH-zee-o
Peter Deutsch, D-Fla. — DOYCH
Lincoln Diaz-Balart, R-Fla. — DEE-az BAA-lart
Eni F. H. Faleomavaega, D-Am. Samoa — EN-ee FOL-ee-oh-mav-ah-ENG-uh
Harris W. Fawell, R-Ill. — FAY-well
Vic Fazio, D-Calif. — FAY-zee-o
Thomas M. Foglietta, D-Pa. — fo-lee-ET-uh
Elton Gallegly, R-Calif. — GAL-uh-glee
Sam Gejdenson, D-Conn. — GAY-den-son
Robert W. Goodlatte, R-Va. — GOOD-lat
Luis V. Gutierrez, D-Ill. — loo-EES goo-tee-AIR-ez

George J. Hochbrueckner, D-N.Y. — HOCK-brewk-ner
Peter Hoekstra, R-Mich. — HOKE-struh
Amo Houghton, R-N.Y. — HO-tun
James M. Inhofe, R-Okla. — IN-hoff
John R. Kasich, R-Ohio — KAY-sick
Gerald D. Kleczka, D-Wis. — KLETCH-kuh
Scott L. Klug, R-Wis. — KLOOG
Jim Kolbe, R-Ariz. — COLE-bee
Mike Kopetski, D-Ore. — ka-PET-skee
Greg Laughlin, D-Texas — LAWF-lin
Rick A. Lazio, R-N.Y. — LAZZ-ee-o
Richard H. Lehman, D-Calif. — LEE-mun
Nita M. Lowey, D-N.Y. — LOW-e
Ronald K. Machtley, R-R.I. — MAKE-lee
Donald Manzullo, R-Ill. — man-ZOO-low
Marjorie Margolies-Mezvinsky, D-Pa. — mar-GO-lees mez-VIN-skee
Kweisi Mfume, D-Md. — kwy-EE-say mm-FU-may
David Minge, D-Minn. — MIN-gee
David R. Obey, D-Wis. — O-bee
Frank Pallone Jr., D-N.J. — pa-LOAN
Ed Pastor, D-Ariz.— pas-TORE
Nancy Pelosi, D-Calif. — pa-LOH-see
Tom Petri, R-Wis. — PEE-try
Glenn Poshard, D-Ill. — pa-SHARD
Arthur Ravenel Jr., R-S.C. — RAV-nel
Ralph Regula, R-Ohio — REG-you-luh
Dana Rohrabacher, R-Calif. — ROAR-ah-BAH-ker
Ileana Ros-Lehtinen, R-Fla. — il-ee-AH-na ross-LAY-tin-nen
Marge Roukema, R-N.J. — ROCK-ah-muh
Bill Sarpalius, D-Texas — sar-PAUL-us
José E. Serrano, D-N.Y. — ho-ZAY sa-RAH-no (rolled 'R')
Bart Stupak, D-Mich. — STEW-pack
W. J. "Billy" Tauzin, D-La. — TOE-zan
Frank Tejeda, D-Texas — tuh-HAY-duh
Robert G. Torricelli, D-N.J. — tor-uh-SELL-ee
Jolene Unsoeld, D-Wash. — UN-sold
Nydia M. Velázquez, D-N.Y. — NID-ee-uh veh-LASS-kez
Barbara F. Vucanovich, R-Nev. — voo-CAN-oh-vitch
Bill Zeliff, R-N.H. — ZELL-iff

103rd Congress
State Delegations to the 103rd Congress

The list below gives the names of senators and representatives of each state delegation for the 103rd Congress. The senators are listed by seniority and the representatives by district. As of June 17, 1994, there were 56 Democrats and 44 Republicans in the Senate and 256 Democrats, 178 Republicans, and 1 independent in the House of Representatives.

Alabama
Sen. Howell Heflin (D)
Sen. Richard C. Shelby (D)
1. Sonny Callahan (R)
2. Terry Everett (R)
3. Glen Browder (D)
4. Tom Bevill (D)
5. Bud Cramer (D)
6. Spencer Bachus (R)
7. Earl F. Hilliard (D)

Alaska
Sen. Ted Stevens (R)
Sen. Frank H. Murkowski (R)
AL Don Young (R)

Arizona
Sen. Dennis DeConcini (D)
Sen. John McCain (R)
1. Sam Coppersmith (D)
2. Ed Pastor (D)
3. Bob Stump (R)
4. Jon Kyl (R)
5. Jim Kolbe (R)
6. Karan English (D)

Arkansas
Sen. Dale Bumpers (D)
Sen. David Pryor (D)
1. Blanche Lambert (D)
2. Ray Thornton (D)
3. Tim Hutchinson (R)
4. Jay Dickey (R)

California
Sen. Barbara Boxer (D)
Sen. Dianne Feinstein (D)

1. Dan Hamburg (D)
2. Wally Herger (R)
3. Vic Fazio (D)
4. John T. Doolittle (R)
5. Robert T. Matsui (D)
6. Lynn Woolsey (D)
7. George Miller (D)
8. Nancy Pelosi (D)
9. Ronald V. Dellums (D)
10. Bill Baker (R)
11. Richard W. Pombo (R)
12. Tom Lantos (D)
13. Pete Stark (D)
14. Anna G. Eshoo (D)
15. Norman Y. Mineta (D)
16. Don Edwards (D)
17. Sam Farr (D)
18. Gary Condit (D)
19. Richard H. Lehman (D)
20. Calvin Dooley (D)
21. Bill Thomas (R)
22. Michael Huffington (R)
23. Elton Gallegly (R)
24. Anthony C. Beilenson (D)
25. Howard "Buck" McKeon (R)
26. Howard L. Berman (D)
27. Carlos J. Moorhead (R)
28. David Dreier (R)
29. Henry A. Waxman (D)
30. Xavier Becerra (D)
31. Matthew G. Martinez (D)
32. Julian C. Dixon (D)
33. Lucille Roybal-Allard (D)
34. Esteban E. Torres (D)
35. Maxine Waters (D)
36. Jane Harman (D)
37. Walter R. Tucker (D)
38. Steve Horn (R)

39. Ed Royce (R)
40. Jerry Lewis (R)
41. Jay C. Kim (R)
42. George E. Brown Jr. (D)
43. Ken Calvert (R)
44. Al McCandless (R)
45. Dana Rohrabacher (R)
46. Robert K. Dornan (R)
47. C. Christopher Cox (R)
48. Ron Packard (R)
49. Lynn Schenk (D)
50. Bob Filner (D)
51. Randy "Duke" Cunningham (R)
52. Duncan Hunter (R)

Colorado
Sen. Hank Brown (R)
Sen. Ben Nighthorse Campbell (D)
1. Patricia Schroeder (D)
2. David E. Skaggs (D)
3. Scott McInnis (R)
4. Wayne Allard (R)
5. Joel Hefley (R)
6. Dan Schaefer (R)

Connecticut
Sen. Christopher J. Dodd (D)
Sen. Joseph I. Lieberman (D)
1. Barbara B. Kennelly (D)
2. Sam Gejdenson (D)
3. Rosa DeLauro (D)
4. Christopher Shays (R)
5. Gary Franks (R)
6. Nancy L. Johnson (R)

Delaware
Sen. William V. Roth Jr. (R)
Sen. Joseph R. Biden Jr. (D)
AL Michael N. Castle (R)

Florida
Sen. Bob Graham (D)
Sen. Connie Mack (R)
1. Earl Hutto (D)
2. Pete Peterson (D)
3. Corrine Brown (D)
4. Tillie Fowler (R)
5. Karen L. Thurman (D)
6. Cliff Stearns (R)
7. John L. Mica (R)
8. Bill McCollum (R)
9. Michael Bilirakis (R)
10. C.W. Bill Young (R)
11. Sam M. Gibbons (D)
12. Charles T. Canady (R)
13. Dan Miller (R)
14. Porter J. Goss (R)
15. Jim Bacchus (D)
16. Tom Lewis (R)
17. Carrie Meek (D)
18. Ileana Ros-Lehtinen (R)
19. Harry A. Johnston (D)
20. Peter Deutsch (D)
21. Lincoln Diaz-Balart (R)
22. E. Clay Shaw Jr. (R)
23. Alcee L. Hastings (D)

Georgia
Sen. Sam Nunn (D)
Sen. Paul Coverdell (R)
1. Jack Kingston (R)
2. Sanford Bishop (D)
3. Mac Collins (R)
4. John Linder (R)
5. John Lewis (D)
6. Newt Gingrich (R)
7. George "Buddy" Darden (D)
8. J. Roy Rowland (D)
9. Nathan Deal (D)
10. Don Johnson (D)
11. Cynthia McKinney (D)

Hawaii
Sen. Daniel K. Inouye (D)
Sen. Daniel K. Akaka (D)
1. Neil Abercrombie (D)
2. Patsy T. Mink (D)

Idaho
Sen. Larry E. Craig (R)
Sen. Dirk Kempthorne (R)

1. Larry LaRocco (D)
2. Michael D. Crapo (R)

Illinois
Sen. Paul Simon (D)
Sen. Carol Moseley-Braun (D)
1. Bobby L. Rush (D)
2. Mel Reynolds (D)
3. William O. Lipinski (D)
4. Luis V. Gutierrez (D)
5. Dan Rostenkowski (D)
6. Henry J. Hyde (R)
7. Cardiss Collins (D)
8. Philip M. Crane (R)
9. Sidney R. Yates (D)
10. John Porter (R)
11. George E. Sangmeister (D)
12. Jerry F. Costello (D)
13. Harris W. Fawell (R)
14. Dennis Hastert (R)
15. Thomas W. Ewing (R)
16. Donald Manzullo (R)
17. Lane Evans (D)
18. Robert H. Michel (R)
19. Glenn Poshard (D)
20. Richard J. Durbin (D)

Indiana
Sen. Richard G. Lugar (R)
Sen. Daniel R. Coats (R)
1. Peter J. Visclosky (D)
2. Philip R. Sharp (D)
3. Tim Roemer (D)
4. Jill L. Long (D)
5. Steve Buyer (R)
6. Dan Burton (R)
7. John T. Myers (R)
8. Frank McCloskey (D)
9. Lee H. Hamilton (D)
10. Andrew Jacobs Jr. (D)

Iowa
Sen. Charles E. Grassley (R)
Sen. Tom Harkin (D)
1. Jim Leach (R)
2. Jim Nussle (R)
3. Jim Ross Lightfoot (R)
4. Neal Smith (D)
5. Fred Grandy (R)

Kansas
Sen. Bob Dole (R)
Sen. Nancy Landon Kassebaum (R)

1. Pat Roberts (R)
2. Jim Slattery (D)
3. Jan Meyers (R)
4. Dan Glickman (D)

Kentucky
Sen. Wendell H. Ford (D)
Sen. Mitch McConnell (R)
1. Tom Barlow (D)
2. Ron Lewis (R)
3. Romano L. Mazzoli (D)
4. Jim Bunning (R)
5. Harold Rogers (R)
6. Scotty Baesler (D)

Louisiana
Sen. J. Bennett Johnston (D)
Sen. John B. Breaux (D)
1. Robert L. Livingston (R)
2. William J. Jefferson (D)
3. W.J. "Billy" Tauzin (D)
4. Cleo Fields (D)
5. Jim McCrery (R)
6. Richard H. Baker (R)
7. Jimmy Hayes (D)

Maine
Sen. William S. Cohen (R)
Sen. George J. Mitchell (D)
1. Thomas H. Andrews (D)
2. Olympia J. Snowe (R)

Maryland
Sen. Paul S. Sarbanes (D)
Sen. Barbara A. Mikulski (D)
1. Wayne T. Gilchrest (R)
2. Helen Delich Bentley (R)
3. Benjamin L. Cardin (D)
4. Albert R. Wynn (D)
5. Steny H. Hoyer (D)
6. Roscoe G. Bartlett (R)
7. Kweisi Mfume (D)
8. Constance A. Morella (R)

Massachusetts
Sen. Edward M. Kennedy (D)
Sen. John Kerry (D)
1. John W. Olver (D)
2. Richard E. Neal (D)
3. Peter I. Blute (R)
4. Barney Frank (D)
5. Martin T. Meehan (D)
6. Peter G. Torkildsen (R)
7. Edward J. Markey (D)

8. Joseph P. Kennedy II (D)
9. Joe Moakley (D)
10. Gerry E. Studds (D)

Michigan
Sen. Donald W. Riegle Jr. (D)
Sen. Carl Levin (D)
1. Bart Stupak (D)
2. Peter Hoekstra (R)
3. Vernon J. Ehlers (R)
4. Dave Camp (R)
5. James A. Barcia (D)
6. Fred Upton (R)
7. Nick Smith (R)
8. Bob Carr (D)
9. Dale E. Kildee (D)
10. David E. Bonior (D)
11. Joe Knollenberg (R)
12. Sander M. Levin (D)
13. William D. Ford (D)
14. John Conyers Jr. (D)
15. Barbara-Rose Collins (D)
16. John D. Dingell (D)

Minnesota
Sen. Dave Durenberger (R)
Sen. Paul Wellstone (D)
1. Timothy J. Penny (D)
2. David Minge (D)
3. Jim Ramstad (R)
4. Bruce F. Vento (D)
5. Martin Olav Sabo (D)
6. Rod Grams (R)
7. Collin C. Peterson (D)
8. James L. Oberstar (D)

Mississippi
Sen. Thad Cochran (R)
Sen. Trent Lott (R)
1. Jamie L. Whitten (D)
2. Bennie Thompson (D)
3. G. V. "Sonny" Montgomery (D)
4. Mike Parker (D)
5. Gene Taylor (D)

Missouri
Sen. John C. Danforth (R)
Sen. Christopher S. Bond (R)
1. William L. Clay (D)
2. James M. Talent (R)
3. Richard A. Gephardt (D)
4. Ike Skelton (D)
5. Alan Wheat (D)
6. Pat Danner (D)

7. Mel Hancock (R)
8. Bill Emerson (R)
9. Harold L. Volkmer (D)

Montana
Sen. Max Baucus (D)
Sen. Conrad Burns (R)
AL Pat Williams (D)

Nebraska
Sen. Jim Exon (D)
Sen. Bob Kerrey (D)
1. Doug Bereuter (R)
2. Peter Hoagland (D)
3. Bill Barrett (R)

Nevada
Sen. Harry Reid (D)
Sen. Richard H. Bryan (D)
1. James Bilbray (D)
2. Barbara F. Vucanovich (R)

New Hampshire
Sen. Robert C. Smith (R)
Sen. Judd Gregg (R)
1. Bill Zeliff (R)
2. Dick Swett (D)

New Jersey
Sen. Bill Bradley (D)
Sen. Frank R. Lautenberg (D)
1. Robert E. Andrews (D)
2. William J. Hughes (D)
3. H. James Saxton (R)
4. Christopher H. Smith (R)
5. Marge Roukema (R)
6. Frank Pallone Jr. (D)
7. Bob Franks (R)
8. Herbert C. Klein (D)
9. Robert G. Torricelli (D)
10. Donald M. Payne (D)
11. Dean A. Gallo (R)
12. Dick Zimmer (R)
13. Robert Menendez (D)

New Mexico
Sen. Pete V. Domenici (R)
Sen. Jeff Bingaman (D)
1. Steven H. Schiff (R)
2. Joe Skeen (R)
3. Bill Richardson (D)

New York
Sen. Daniel Patrick Moynihan (D)
Sen. Alfonse M. D'Amato (R)

1. George J. Hochbrueckner (D)
2. Rick A. Lazio (R)
3. Peter T. King (R)
4. David A. Levy (R)
5. Gary L. Ackerman (D)
6. Floyd H. Flake (D)
7. Thomas J. Manton (D)
8. Jerrold Nadler (D)
9. Charles E. Schumer (D)
10. Edolphus Towns (D)
11. Major R. Owens (D)
12. Nydia M. Velázquez (D)
13. Susan Molinari (R)
14. Carolyn B. Maloney (D)
15. Charles B. Rangel (D)
16. Jose E. Serrano (D)
17. Eliot L. Engel (D)
18. Nita M. Lowey (D)
19. Hamilton Fish Jr. (R)
20. Benjamin A. Gilman (R)
21. Michael R. McNulty (D)
22. Gerald B.H. Solomon (R)
23. Sherwood Boehlert (R)
24. John M. McHugh (R)
25. James T. Walsh (R)
26. Maurice D. Hinchey (D)
27. Bill Paxon (R)
28. Louise M. Slaughter (D)
29. John J. LaFalce (D)
30. Jack Quinn (R)
31. Amo Houghton (R)

North Carolina
Sen. Jesse Helms (R)
Sen. Lauch Faircloth (R)
1. Eva Clayton (D)
2. Tim Valentine (D)
3. H. Martin Lancaster (D)
4. David Price (D)
5. Stephen L. Neal (D)
6. Howard Coble (R)
7. Charlie Rose (D)
8. W.G. "Bill" Hefner (D)
9. Alex McMillan (R)
10. Cass Ballenger (R)
11. Charles H. Taylor (R)
12. Melvin Watt (D)

North Dakota
Sen. Byron Dorgan (D)
Sen. Kent Conrad (D)
AL Earl Pomeroy (D)

Ohio
Sen. John Glenn (D)
Sen. Howard M. Metzenbaum (D)

1. David Mann (D)
2. Rob Portman (R)
3. Tony P. Hall (D)
4. Michael G. Oxley (R)
5. Paul E. Gillmor (R)
6. Ted Strickland (D)
7. David L. Hobson (R)
8. John A. Boehner (R)
9. Marcy Kaptur (D)
10. Martin R. Hoke (R)
11. Louis Stokes (D)
12. John R. Kasich (R)
13. Sherrod Brown (D)
14. Tom Sawyer (D)
15. Deborah Pryce (R)
16. Ralph Regula (R)
17. James A. Traficant Jr. (D)
18. Douglas Applegate (D)
19. Eric D. Fingerhut (D)

Oklahoma
Sen. David L. Boren (D)
Sen. Don Nickles (R)
1. James M. Inhofe (R)
2. Mike Synar (D)
3. Bill Brewster (D)
4. Dave McCurdy (D)
5. Ernest Jim Istook (R)
6. Frank Lucas (R)

Oregon
Sen. Mark O. Hatfield (R)
Sen. Bob Packwood (R)
1. Elizabeth Furse (D)
2. Bob Smith (R)
3. Ron Wyden (D)
4. Peter A. DeFazio (D)
5. Mike Kopetski (D)

Pennsylvania
Sen. Arlen Specter (R)
Sen. Harris Wofford (D)
1. Thomas M. Foglietta (D)
2. Lucien E. Blackwell (D)
3. Robert A. Borski (D)
4. Ron Klink (D)
5. William F. Clinger (R)
6. Tim Holden (D)
7. Curt Weldon (R)
8. Jim Greenwood (R)
9. Bud Shuster (R)
10. Joseph M. McDade (R)
11. Paul E. Kanjorski (D)
12. John P. Murtha (D)
13. Marjorie Margolies-
    Mezvinsky (D)

14. William J. Coyne (D)
15. Paul McHale (D)
16. Robert S. Walker (R)
17. George W. Gekas (R)
18. Rick Santorum (R)
19. Bill Goodling (R)
20. Austin J. Murphy (D)
21. Tom Ridge (R)

Rhode Island
Sen. Claiborne Pell (D)
Sen. John H. Chafee (R)
1. Ronald K. Machtley (R)
2. Jack Reed (D)

South Carolina
Sen. Strom Thurmond (R)
Sen. Ernest F. Hollings (D)
1. Arthur Ravenel Jr. (R)
2. Floyd D. Spence (R)
3. Butler Derrick (D)
4. Bob Inglis (R)
5. John M. Spratt Jr. (D)
6. James E. Clyburn (D)

South Dakota
Sen. Larry Pressler (R)
Sen. Tom Daschle (D)
AL Tim Johnson (D)

Tennessee
Sen. Jim Sasser (D)
Sen. Harlan Mathews (D)
1. James H. Quillen (R)
2. John J. "Jimmy" Duncan
   Jr. (R)
3. Marilyn Lloyd (D)
4. Jim Cooper (D)
5. Bob Clement (D)
6. Bart Gordon (D)
7. Don Sundquist (R)
8. John Tanner (D)
9. Harold E. Ford (D)

Texas
Sen. Phil Gramm (R)
Sen. Kay Bailey Hutchison
   (R)
1. Jim Chapman (D)
2. Charles Wilson (D)
3. Sam Johnson (R)
4. Ralph M. Hall (D)
5. John Bryant (D)
6. Joe L. Barton (R)
7. Bill Archer (R)

8. Jack Fields (R)
9. Jack Brooks (D)
10. J.J. Pickle (D)
11. Chet Edwards (D)
12. Pete Geren (D)
13. Bill Sarpalius (D)
14. Greg Laughlin (D)
15. E. "Kika" de la Garza (D)
16. Ronald D. Coleman (D)
17. Charles W. Stenholm (D)
18. Craig Washington (D)
19. Larry Combest (R)
20. Henry B. Gonzalez (D)
21. Lamar Smith (R)
22. Tom DeLay (R)
23. Henry Bonilla (R)
24. Martin Frost (D)
25. Michael A. Andrews (D)
26. Dick Armey (R)
27. Solomon P. Ortiz (D)
28. Frank Tejeda (D)
29. Gene Green (D)
30. Eddie Bernice Johnson
    (D)

Utah
Sen. Orrin G. Hatch (R)
Sen. Robert F. Bennett (R)
1. James V. Hansen (R)
2. Karen Shepherd (D)
3. Bill Orton (D)

Vermont
Sen. Patrick J. Leahy (D)
Sen. James M. Jeffords (R)
AL Bernard Sanders (I)

Virginia
Sen. John W. Warner (R)
Sen. Charles S. Robb (D)
1. Herbert H. Bateman (R)
2. Owen B. Pickett (D)
3. Robert C. Scott (D)
4. Norman Sisisky (D)
5. Lewis F. Payne Jr. (D)
6. Robert W. Goodlatte (R)
7. Thomas J. Bliley Jr. (R)
8. James P. Moran Jr. (D)
9. Rick Boucher (D)
10. Frank R. Wolf (R)
11. Leslie L. Byrne (D)

Washington
Sen. Slade Gorton (R)
Sen. Patty Murray (D)
1. Maria Cantwell (D)

2. Al Swift (D)
3. Jolene Unsoeld (D)
4. Jay Inslee (D)
5. Thomas S. Foley (D)
6. Norm Dicks (D)
7. Jim McDermott (D)
8. Jennifer Dunn (R)
9. Mike Kreidler (D)

West Virginia
Sen. Robert C. Byrd (D)
Sen. John D. Rockefeller IV (D)

1. Alan B. Mollohan (D)
2. Bob Wise (D)
3. Nick J. Rahall II (D)

Wisconsin
Sen. Herb Kohl (D)
Sen. Russell D. Feingold (D)
1. Peter Barca (D)
2. Scott L. Klug (R)
3. Steve Gunderson (R)
4. Gerald D. Kleczka (D)

5. Thomas M. Barrett (D)
6. Tom Petri (R)
7. David R. Obey (D)
8. Toby Roth (R)
9. F. James Sensenbrenner Jr. (R)

Wyoming
Sen. Malcolm Wallop (R)
Sen. Alan K. Simpson (R)
AL Craig Thomas (R)

Representatives' Offices, Committee Assignments

The list below gives, in alphabetical order, the names of House members and their party, state, and district affiliation, followed by the addresses and telephone numbers for their Washington offices. Address abbreviations used are as follows: CHOB (Cannon House Office Bldg., on Independence Ave. between New Jersey Ave. and 1st St. S.E.), LHOB (Longworth House Office Bldg., on Independence Ave. between S. Capitol St. and New Jersey Ave. S.E.), RHOB (Rayburn House Office Bldg., on Independence Ave. between S. Capitol and 1st Sts. S.E.), O'Neill Bldg. (formerly House Annex #1, at 300 New Jersey Ave. S.E.), and Ford Bldg. (formerly House Annex #2, at 2nd and D Sts. S.W.). The area code for Washington is 202. The list also gives the name of a top administrative aide for each member of the House.

The address, telephone number, and director for the House members' district offices are listed. Each representative's committee assignments, except for partisan committees, are given as the final entry. For representatives' partisan committee assignments, see p. 997.

As of June 17, 1994, there were 256 Democrats, 178 Republicans, and 1 independent in the House of Representatives. The information for this list was gathered by Congressional Quarterly from House offices in Washington, D.C.

Abercrombie, Neil, D-Hawaii (1)
CAPITOL HILL OFFICE:
  1440 LHOB 20515; 225-2726
    Admin. Assistant   Patrick McCain

DISTRICT OFFICE:
  300 Ala Moana Blvd., #4104, Honolulu 96850;
(808) 541-2570; District Director: Steve Beaudry.

COMMITTEE ASSIGNMENTS:
  Armed Services
  Natural Resources

Ackerman, Gary L., D-N.Y. (5)
CAPITOL HILL OFFICE:
  2445 RHOB 20515; 225-2601
  Fax: 225-1589
    Admin. Assistant   Jedd Moskowitz

DISTRICT OFFICES:
  218-14 Northern Blvd., Bayside 11361; (718)
423-2154; Office Director: Arthur Flug.
  229 Main St., Huntington 11743; (516) 423-
2154; Office Director: Anne McShane.

COMMITTEE ASSIGNMENTS:
  Foreign Affairs
  Merchant Marine and Fisheries
  Post Office and Civil Service

Allard, Wayne, R-Colo. (4)
CAPITOL HILL OFFICE:
  422 CHOB 20515; 225-4676
    Admin. Assistant   Roy Palmer

DISTRICT OFFICES:
  315 W. Oak, #307, Fort Collins 80521; (303)
493-9132; District Director: Mike Bennett.
  822 7th St., #350, Greeley 80631; (303) 351-
7582; Office Manager: Sean Conway.
  19 W. 4th St., La Junta 81050; (719) 384-7370;
Office Manager: Doris Morgan.
  212 E. Kiowa, Fort Morgan 80701; (303) 867-
8909; Office Manager: Lewis Frank.
  705 S. Division, Sterling 80751; (303) 522-1788;
Office Manager: Lewis Frank.

COMMITTEE ASSIGNMENTS:
  Agriculture
  Budget
  Natural Resources

Andrews, Michael A., D-Texas (25)
CAPITOL HILL OFFICE:
303 CHOB 20515; 225-7508
Fax: 225-2045
Chief of Staff   Ann M. Rowan

DISTRICT OFFICES:
1001 E. Southmore, #810, Pasadena 77502;
(713) 473-4334; District Director: Joseph Giam-
fortone.
515 Rusk St., #12102, Houston 77002; (713)
229-2244; District Administrator: Joseph Giam-
fortone.

COMMITTEE ASSIGNMENTS:
Budget
Joint Economic
Ways and Means

Andrews, Robert E., D-N.J. (1)
CAPITOL HILL OFFICE:
1005 LHOB 20515; 225-6501
Fax: 225-6583
Admin. Assistant   Ted Long

DISTRICT OFFICES:
16 Somerdale Square, Somerdale 08083; (609)
627-9000; Chief of Staff: Lynn C. Kmiec.
63 N. Broad St., Woodbury 08096; (609) 848-
3900; District Representative: Leanne Hasbrouk.

COMMITTEE ASSIGNMENTS:
Education and Labor
Foreign Affairs

Andrews, Thomas H., D-Maine (1)
CAPITOL HILL OFFICE:
1530 LHOB 20515; 225-6116
Fax: 225-9065
Admin. Assistant   Craig S. Brown

DISTRICT OFFICE:
136 Commercial St., Portland 04101; (207) 772-
8240; Office Manager: Kim Monaghan.

COMMITTEE ASSIGNMENTS:
Armed Services
Merchant Marine and Fisheries
Small Business

Applegate, Douglas, D-Ohio (18)
CAPITOL HILL OFFICE:
2183 RHOB 20515; 225-6265
Fax: 225-3087
Admin. Assistant   Jim Hart

DISTRICT OFFICES:
Ohio Valley Towers, Steubenville 43952; (614)
283-3716; Office Director: Julie Ellen.
46060 National Rd. West, St. Clairsville 43950;

(614) 695-4600; Office Director: Susan Conaway.
225 Underwood St., Zanesville 43701; (614)
452-7023; Office Director: Mary Funk.
1330 4th St. N.W., New Philadelphia 44663;
(216) 343-9112; Office Director: Nancy Leggett.

COMMITTEE ASSIGNMENTS:
Public Works and Transportation
Veterans' Affairs

Archer, Bill, R-Texas (7)
CAPITOL HILL OFFICE:
1236 LHOB 20515; 225-2571
Fax: 225-4381
Admin. Assistant   Don Carlson

DISTRICT OFFICE:
1003 Wirt Rd., #311, Houston 77055; (713)
467-7493; District Director: Anne U. Clutterbuck.

COMMITTEE ASSIGNMENTS:
Joint Taxation
Ways and Means (Ranking)

Armey, Dick, R-Texas (26)
CAPITOL HILL OFFICE:
301 CHOB 20515; 225-7772
Admin. Assistant   Brian F. Gunderson

DISTRICT OFFICE:
9901 Valley Ranch Parkway East, #3050, Irving
75063; (214) 556-2500; Office Director: Jean
Campbell.

COMMITTEE ASSIGNMENTS:
Education and Labor
Joint Economic

Bacchus, Jim, D-Fla. (15)
CAPITOL HILL OFFICE:
432 CHOB 20515; 225-3671
Admin. Assistant   Linda Hennessee

DISTRICT OFFICE:
900 Dixon Blvd., Coco 32922; (407) 632-1776;
Office Manager: Donna McGinnis.

COMMITTEE ASSIGNMENTS:
Banking, Finance, and Urban Affairs
Science, Space, and Technology

Bachus, Spencer, R-Ala. (6)
CAPITOL HILL OFFICE:
216 CHOB 20515; 225-4921
Fax: 225-2082
Admin. Assistant   Jennifer Oldham

DISTRICT OFFICES:
1900 International Park Dr., #107, Birmingham
.

35243; (205) 969-2296; District Director: Donna Williams.

3500 McFarland Blvd., P.O. Drawer 569, Northport 35476; (205) 333-9894; Congressional Aide: Margaret Pyle.

COMMITTEE ASSIGNMENTS:
Banking, Finance, and Urban Affairs
Veterans' Affairs

Baesler, Scotty, D-Ky. (6)
CAPITOL HILL OFFICE:
508 CHOB 20515; 225-4706
Fax: 225-2122
Admin. Assistant   Chuck Atkins

DISTRICT OFFICE:
444 E. Main St., #103, Lexington 40507; (606) 253-1124.

COMMITTEE ASSIGNMENTS:
Agriculture
Education and Labor
Veterans' Affairs

Baker, Bill, R-Calif. (10)
CAPITOL HILL OFFICE:
1724 LHOB 20515; 225-1880
Fax: 225-2150
Admin. Assistant   John Walker

DISTRICT OFFICE:
1801 N. California Blvd., #103, Walnut Creek 94596; (510) 932-8899; District Manager: Ann Jordan.

COMMITTEE ASSIGNMENTS:
Public Works and Transportation
Science, Space, and Technology

Baker, Richard H., R-La. (6)
CAPITOL HILL OFFICE:
434 CHOB 20515; 225-3901
Fax: 225-7313
Admin. Assistant   Christy Casteel

DISTRICT OFFICES:
5757 Corporate Blvd., #104, Baton Rouge 70808; (504) 929-7711; Office Director: Christy Casteel.
3406 Rosalino St., Alexandria 71301; (318) 445-5504; District Director: Cathy Brown.
100 E. Texas St., Leesville 71446; (318) 238-5443; Office Director: Vacant.

COMMITTEE ASSIGNMENTS:
Banking, Finance, and Urban Affairs
Natural Resources
Small Business

Ballenger, Cass, R-N.C. (10)
CAPITOL HILL OFFICE:
2238 RHOB 20515; 225-2576
Fax: 225-0316
Admin. Assistant   Patrick Murphy

DISTRICT OFFICES:
P.O. Box 1830, Hickory 28603; (704) 327-6100; Office Director: Tommy Luckadoo.
P.O. Box 1881, Clemmons 27012; (919) 766-9455; District Representative: Marsha Sucharski.

COMMITTEE ASSIGNMENTS:
District of Columbia
Education and Labor
Foreign Affairs

Barca, Peter W., D-Wis. (1)
CAPITOL HILL OFFICE:
1719 LHOB 20515; 225-3031
Chief of Staff   Diane Evans

DISTRICT OFFICES:
20 S. Main St., #20, Janesville 53545; (608) 752-9074; District Director: Kathy Soderbloom.
411 6th St., Racine 53403; (414) 632-4446; District Director: John Dickert.

COMMITTEE ASSIGNMENTS:
Public Works and Transportation
Science, Space, and Technology

Barcia, James A., D-Mich. (5)
CAPITOL HILL OFFICE:
1717 LHOB 20515; 225-8171
Admin. Assistant   Roger Szemraj

DISTRICT OFFICES:
301 E. Gennessee Rd., #502, Saginaw 48607; (517) 754-6075; District Director: Jim Lewis.
3741 E. Wilder Rd., Bay City 48706; (517) 667-0003; District Representative: Debbie Zarazua.
5409 Pierson Rd., Flushing 48433; (313) 732-7501; District Representative: Mark Salogar.

COMMITTEE ASSIGNMENTS:
Public Works and Transportation
Science, Space, and Technology

Barlow, Tom, D-Ky. (1)
CAPITOL HILL OFFICE:
1533 LHOB 20515; 225-3115
Fax: 225-3115
Admin. Assistant   Bobby Miller

DISTRICT OFFICE:
1 Executive Blvd., #LL1, Paducah 42001; (502) 444-7216; District Director: Bob Buchanan.

COMMITTEE ASSIGNMENTS:
Agriculture
Merchant Marine and Fisheries
Natural Resources

Barrett, Bill, R-Neb. (3)
CAPITOL HILL OFFICE:
1213 LHOB 20515; 225-6435
Fax: 225-0207
Admin. Assistant   Jeri Finke

DISTRICT OFFICES:
312 W. 3rd St., Grand Island 68801; (308) 381-5555; Office Director: D. Vogel.
1502 2nd Ave., Scottsbluff 69361; (308) 632-3333; Office Director: Greg Stull.

COMMITTEE ASSIGNMENTS:
Agriculture
Education and Labor
House Administration
Joint Library

Barrett, Thomas M., D-Wis. (5)
CAPITOL HILL OFFICE:
313 CHOB 20515; 225-3571
Admin. Assistant   Janet Piraino

DISTRICT OFFICE:
135 W. Wells St., #618, Milwaukee 53203; (414) 297-1331; District Director: Anne DeLeo.

COMMITTEE ASSIGNMENTS:
Banking, Finance, and Urban Affairs
Government Operations
Natural Resources

Bartlett, Roscoe G., R-Md. (6)
CAPITOL HILL OFFICE:
312 CHOB 20515; 225-2721
Fax: 225-2193
Admin. Assistant   Joe Karpinski

DISTRICT OFFICES:
4317 Buckeystown Pike, Frederick 21701; (301) 694-3030; District Assistant: Rita Downs.
100 W. Franklin St., Hagerstown 21740; (301) 797-6043; District Assistant: Rita Downs.
15 E. Main St., #110, Westminster 21157; (410) 857-1115; District Assistant: Nancy Stocksdale.
50 Broadway St., Frostburg 21532; (301) 689-0034; District Assistant: Myra Kidd.

COMMITTEE ASSIGNMENTS:
Armed Services
Science, Space, and Technology

Barton, Joe L., R-Texas (6)
CAPITOL HILL OFFICE:
1514 LHOB 20515; 225-2002
Fax: 225-3052
Admin. Assistant   Cathy Gillespie

DISTRICT OFFICES:
303 W. Knox St., #101, Ennis 75119; (817) 543-1000; Office Director: Linda Gillespie.
3509 Hulen St., #110, Fort Worth 76107; (817) 543-1000; District Representative: Christi Townsend.
2019 E. Lamar Blvd., #100, Arlington 76006; (817) 543-1000; District Manager: Harold Samuels.

COMMITTEE ASSIGNMENTS:
Energy and Commerce
Science, Space, and Technology

Bateman, Herbert H., R-Va. (1)
CAPITOL HILL OFFICE:
2350 RHOB 20515; 225-4261
Fax: 225-4382
Admin. Assistant   Dan Scandling

DISTRICT OFFICES:
739 Thimble Shoals Blvd., Newport News 23606; (804) 873-1132; Fax: (804) 599-0424; Staff Director: Dee Benton.
4712 Southpoint Parkway, Fredericksburg 22407; (703) 898-2975; Fax: (703) 898-3280; Office Director: John Goolrick.
P.O. Box 447, Accomac 23301; (804) 787-7836; Fax: (804) 787-9540; Office Director: Suzanne Beasley.

COMMITTEE ASSIGNMENTS:
Armed Services
Merchant Marine and Fisheries

Becerra, Xavier, D-Calif. (30)
CAPITOL HILL OFFICE:
1710 LHOB 20515; 225-6235
Fax: 225-2202
Admin. Assistant   Elsa Marquez

DISTRICT OFFICE:
2435 Colorado Blvd., #200, Los Angeles 90041; (213) 550-8962; Fax: (213) 550-1440; Admin. Assistant: Henry Lozano.

COMMITTEE ASSIGNMENTS:
Education and Labor
Judiciary
Science, Space, and Technology

Beilenson, Anthony C., D-Calif. (24)
CAPITOL HILL OFFICE:
2465 RHOB 20515; 225-5911
Admin. Assistant   Jan Faulstich

DISTRICT OFFICES:
21031 Ventura Blvd., #1010, Woodland Hills 91364; (818) 999-1990; Office Manager: Virginia Hatfield.
200 North Westlake Blvd., #211, Thousand Oaks 91362; (805) 496-4333; Office Manager: Diane Kinzer Brown.

COMMITTEE ASSIGNMENTS:
Budget
Rules

Bentley, Helen Delich, R-Md. (2)
CAPITOL HILL OFFICE:
1610 LHOB 20515; 225-3061
Fax: 225-4251
Admin. Assistant   Pat Wait

DISTRICT OFFICE:
200 E. Joppa Rd., #400, Towson 21286; (410) 337-7222; Fax: (410) 337-0021; Office Manager: Sandy Dawson.

COMMITTEE ASSIGNMENTS:
Appropriations
Merchant Marine and Fisheries

Bereuter, Doug, R-Neb. (1)
CAPITOL HILL OFFICE:
2348 RHOB 20515; 225-4806
Admin. Assistant   Susan Olson

DISTRICT OFFICES:
1045 K St., Lincoln 68508; (402) 438-1598; District Office Manager: Jim Barr.
502 N. Broad St., Freemont 68025; (402) 727-0888; District Office Manager: Dave Heineman.

COMMITTEE ASSIGNMENTS:
Banking, Finance, and Urban Affairs
Foreign Affairs
Select Intelligence

Berman, Howard L., D-Calif. (26)
CAPITOL HILL OFFICE:
2201 RHOB 20515; 225-4695
Chief of Staff   Gene Smith

DISTRICT OFFICE:
10200 Sepulveda Blvd., #130, Mission Hills 91345; (818) 891-0543; Office Director: Rose Castaneda.

COMMITTEE ASSIGNMENTS:
Budget
Foreign Affairs
Judiciary

Bevill, Tom, D-Ala. (4)
CAPITOL HILL OFFICE:
2302 RHOB 20515; 225-4876
Admin. Assistant   Don Smith

DISTRICT OFFICES:
1710 Alabama Ave., #247, Jasper 35501; (205) 221-2310; Office Director: Missie Hudson.
107 Federal Bldg., Gadsden 35901; (205) 546-0201; Office Director: Mary Cochran.
102-104 Federal Bldg., Cullman 35055; (205) 734-6043; Office Director: Evelyn Stevens.

COMMITTEE ASSIGNMENT:
Appropriations

Bilbray, James, D-Nev. (1)
CAPITOL HILL OFFICE:
2431 RHOB 20515; 225-5965
Fax: 225-8808
Admin. Assistant   Michael H. Talisnik

DISTRICT OFFICES:
1785 E. Sahara Ave., #445, Las Vegas 89104; (702) 792-2424; Office Director: Renee Diamond.
40 Water St., Henderson 89015; (702) 565-4788; District Representative: Sally Rigg.

COMMITTEE ASSIGNMENTS:
Armed Services
Select Intelligence
Small Business

Bilirakis, Michael, R-Fla. (9)
CAPITOL HILL OFFICE:
2240 RHOB 20515; 225-5755
Admin. Assistant   Robert Meyers

DISTRICT OFFICES:
1100 Cleveland St., #1600, Clearwater 34615; (813) 441-3721; District Admin.: Pat Faber.
4111 Land O' Lakes Blvd., #306, Land O' Lakes 34639; (813) 996-7441; Caseworker: Shirley Miaoulis.

COMMITTEE ASSIGNMENTS:
Energy and Commerce
Veterans' Affairs

Bishop, Sanford D., Jr., D-Ga. (2)
CAPITOL HILL OFFICE:
1632 LHOB 20515; 225-3631
Chief of Staff   Fred S. Humphries

DISTRICT OFFICES:
17 10th St., Columbus 31901; (706) 323-6894; Field Representative: Ted Jones.
682 Cherry St., #1113, Macon 31201; (912) 741-2221; Fax: (912) 741-2144; Field Representative: Alfred Ellis.

401 N. Patterson St., Valdosta 31601; (912) 247-9705; Fax: (912) 241-1035; District Director: Charles Stripling.

225 Pine Ave., Albany 31701; (912) 439-8067; Fax: (912) 436-2099; Field Representative: Steve Belk.

101 S. Main St., Dawson 31742; (912) 995-3991; Fax: (912) 995-4894.

COMMITTEE ASSIGNMENTS:
Agriculture
Post Office and Civil Service
Veterans' Affairs

Blackwell, Lucien E., D-Pa. (2)
CAPITOL HILL OFFICE:
410 CHOB 20515; 225-4001
Fax: 225-7362
Chief of Staff   Corliss Clemonts-James

DISTRICT OFFICE:
3901 Market St., Philadelphia 19104; (215) 347-2543; Fax: (215) 387-2477; District Manager: Maurice Floyd.

COMMITTEE ASSIGNMENTS:
Budget
Public Works and Transportation

Bliley, Thomas J., Jr., R-Va. (7)
CAPITOL HILL OFFICE:
2241 RHOB 20515; 225-2815
Admin. Assistant   Linda Pedigo

DISTRICT OFFICES:
4914 Fitzhugh Ave., #101, Richmond 23230; (804) 771-2809; District Representative: Karen Marcus.

763 Madison Rd., #207, Culpeper 22701; (703) 825-8960; District Representative: Anita Essalih.

COMMITTEE ASSIGNMENTS:
District of Columbia (Ranking)
Energy and Commerce

Blute, Peter I., R-Mass. (3)
CAPITOL HILL OFFICE:
1029 LHOB 20515; 225-6101
Staff Director   Matt Trant

DISTRICT OFFICES:
1079 Mechanics Tower, Worcester 01608; (508) 752-6789; Fax: (508) 752-9888; District Manager: Mary Jane McKenna.

7 N. Main St., #200, Attleboro 02703; (508) 223-3100; Fax: (508) 223-3323; District Manager: Mary Jane McKenna.

1039 S. Main St., Fall River 02724; (508) 675-3400; Fax: (508) 675-7755; District Manager: Mary Jane McKenna.

COMMITTEE ASSIGNMENTS:
Public Works and Transportation
Science, Space, and Technology

Boehlert, Sherwood, R-N.Y. (23)
CAPITOL HILL OFFICE:
1127 LHOB 20515; 225-3665
Fax: 225-1891
Admin. Assistant   Dan Costello

DISTRICT OFFICE:
10 Broad St., #200, Utica 13501; (315) 793-8146; Office Director: Randy Wilcox.

COMMITTEE ASSIGNMENTS:
Post Office and Civil Service
Public Works and Transportation
Science, Space, and Technology

Boehner, John A., R-Ohio (8)
CAPITOL HILL OFFICE:
1020 LHOB 20515; 225-6205
Chief of Staff   Barry Jackson

DISTRICT OFFICES:
5617 Liberty-Fairfield Rd., Hamilton 45011; (513) 894-6003; Deputy Chief of Staff: Mick Kriegen.

12 S. Plum St., Troy 45373; (513) 339-1524; Field Representative: Chuck Mohler.

COMMITTEE ASSIGNMENTS:
Agriculture
Education and Labor
House Administration

Bonilla, Henry, R-Texas (23)
CAPITOL HILL OFFICE:
1529 LHOB 20515; 225-4511
Fax: 225-2237
Chief of Staff   Steve Ruhlen

DISTRICT OFFICES:
11120 Wurzbach, #300, San Antonio 78230; (210) 697-9055; District Manager: Phil Ricks.

1300 Matamoros St., #113B, Laredo 78040; (210) 726-4682; Fax: (210) 726-4684; Constituent Liaison: Patricia V. Zuniga.

111 E. Broadway, #101, Del Rio 78840; (210) 774-6547; Fax: (210) 774-5693; Constituent Liaison: Ida Nino.

4400 N. Big Spring, #211, Midland 79705; (915) 686-8833; Fax: (915) 686-8819; Constituent Liaison: Melissa Columbus.

COMMITTEE ASSIGNMENT:
Appropriations

Bonior, David E., D-Mich. (10)
CAPITOL HILL OFFICE:
2207 RHOB 20515; 225-2106
Admin. Assistant Sarah Dufendach

DISTRICT OFFICES:
59 N. Walnut, #305, Mt. Clemens 48043; (313) 469-3232; Office Director: Ed Bruley.
526 Water St., Port Huron 48060; (313) 987-8889; Constituent Service Representative: Timothy Morse.

COMMITTEE ASSIGNMENT:
Rules

Borski, Robert A., D-Pa. (3)
CAPITOL HILL OFFICE:
2161 RHOB 20515; 225-8251
Fax: 225-4628
Admin. Assistant Alan Slomowitz

DISTRICT OFFICES:
7141 Frankford Ave., Philadelphia 19135; (215) 335-3355; Fax: (215) 333-4508; Office Director: Jack Dempsey.
2630 Memphis St., Philadelphia 19125; (215) 426-4616; Fax: (215) 426-7741; District Representative: Sis Dolan.

COMMITTEE ASSIGNMENTS:
Foreign Affairs
Public Works and Transportation
Standards of Official Conduct

Boucher, Rick, D-Va. (9)
CAPITOL HILL OFFICE:
2245 RHOB 20515; 225-3861
Fax: 225-0442
Chief of Staff Roger Goodman

DISTRICT OFFICES:
188 E. Main St., Abingdon 24210; (703) 628-1145; Fax: (703) 628-2203; District Administrator: Rebecca Coleman.
311 Shawnee Ave. East, Big Stone Gap 24219; (703) 523-1412; Fax: (703) 523-1412; District Administrator: Rebecca Coleman.
112 N. Washington Ave., P.O. Box 1268, Pulaski 24301; (703) 980-4310; Fax: (703) 980-0529; District Administrator: Rebecca Coleman.

COMMITTEE ASSIGNMENTS:
Energy and Commerce
Judiciary
Science, Space, and Technology

Brewster, Bill, D-Okla. (3)
CAPITOL HILL OFFICE:
1727 LHOB 20515; 225-4565

Fax: 225-9029
Chief of Staff Patrick Raffaniello

DISTRICT OFFICES:
131 E. 12th, Ada 74820; (405) 436-1980; Office Manager: James Ross.
123 W. 7th Ave., #206, Stillwater 74074; (405) 743-1400; Office Manager: Robert Felts.
118 Carl Albert Federal Bldg., McAlester 74501; (918) 423-5951; Office Manager: Sue Bollinger.
101 W. Main St., Ardmore 73401; (405) 226-6300.

COMMITTEE ASSIGNMENT:
Ways and Means

Brooks, Jack, D-Texas (9)
CAPITOL HILL OFFICE:
2449 RHOB 20515; 225-6565
Fax: 225-1584
Admin. Assistant Sharon Matts

DISTRICT OFFICES:
201 Federal Bldg., Beaumont 77701; (409) 839-2508; Fax: (409) 832-0738; Office Manager: Dianna Coffey.
601 25th St., #217, Galveston 77550; (409) 766-3608; Fax: (409) 763-4133; Office Manager: Dorethea Lewis.

COMMITTEE ASSIGNMENT:
Judiciary (Chairman)

Browder, Glen, D-Ala. (3)
CAPITOL HILL OFFICE:
1221 LHOB 20515; 225-3261
Fax: 225-9020
Admin. Assistant Bob McNeil

DISTRICT OFFICES:
Federal Bldg., Anniston 36202; (205) 236-5655; Fax: (205) 237-9203; Office Director: Ray Minter.
Federal Bldg., Opelika 36801; (205) 745-6222; Fax: (205) 742-0109; Office Director: Alice Lloyd.
115 E. Northside, Tuskegee 36803; (205) 727-6490; Office Director: Lifus Johnson.

COMMITTEE ASSIGNMENTS:
Armed Services
Budget

Brown, Corrine, D-Fla. (3)
CAPITOL HILL OFFICE:
1037 LHOB 20515; 225-0123
Fax: 225-2256
Admin. Assistant Ronnie Simmons

DISTRICT OFFICES:
815 S. Main St., #275, Jacksonville 32207; (904)

398-8567; Fax: (904) 398-8812; Area Director: Shelanda Shaw.

75 Ivanhoe Blvd., Orlando 32802; (904) 872-0656; Fax: (904) 872-5763; Area Director: Reginald B. McGill.

401 S.E. 1st Ave., #316, Gainesville 32601; (904) 375-6003; Fax: (904) 375-6008; Congressional Aide: Jean Haley.

250 N. Beach St., #80-1, Daytona Beach 32114; (904) 254-4622; Fax: (904) 254-4659; Congressional Aide: Naomi Cooper.

COMMITTEE ASSIGNMENTS:
Government Operations
Public Works and Transportation
Veterans' Affairs

Brown, George E., Jr., D-Calif. (42)
CAPITOL HILL OFFICE:
2300 RHOB 20515; 225-6161
Fax: 225-8671
Admin. Assistant   Bill Goold

DISTRICT OFFICE:
657 La Cadena Dr., Colton 92324; (909) 825-2472; District Admin.: Wilmer Carter.

COMMITTEE ASSIGNMENTS:
Agriculture
Science, Space, and Technology (Chairman)

Brown, Sherrod, D-Ohio (13)
CAPITOL HILL OFFICE:
1407 LHOB 20515; 225-3401
Chief of Staff   Rhod Shaw

DISTRICT OFFICES:
1936 Cooper Foster Park Rd., Lorain 44053; (216) 282-5100; District Director: Deanna Hill.

15561 W. High St., Middlefield 44062; (216) 632-5913; District Manager: Joyce Edelinsky.

5201 Abbe Rd., Elyria 44035; (216) 934-5100; District Manager: Deanne Hill.

COMMITTEE ASSIGNMENTS:
Energy and Commerce
Foreign Affairs
Post Office and Civil Service

Bryant, John, D-Texas (5)
CAPITOL HILL OFFICE:
205 CHOB 20515; 225-2231
Fax: 225-0327
Admin. Assistant   Randy White

DISTRICT OFFICE:
8035 East R. L. Thornton Freeway, #518, Dallas 75228; (214) 767-6554; Office Director: Norma Minnis.

COMMITTEE ASSIGNMENTS:
Budget
Energy and Commerce
Judiciary

Bunning, Jim, R-Ky. (4)
CAPITOL HILL OFFICE:
2437 RHOB 20515; 225-3465
Fax: 225-0003
Admin. Assistant   David A. York

DISTRICT OFFICES:
1717 Dixie Highway, #160, Fort Wright 41011; (606) 341-2602; District Director: Debbie McKinney.

704 W. Jefferson St., #219, Lagrange 40031; (502) 222-2188; Office Manager: Oteka Brab.

1405 Greenup Ave., #236, Ashland 41101; (606) 325-9898; Office Manager: Darlynn Barber.

COMMITTEE ASSIGNMENTS:
Budget
Standards of Official Conduct
Ways and Means

Burton, Dan, R-Ind. (6)
CAPITOL HILL OFFICE:
2411 RHOB 20515; 225-2276
Fax: 225-0016
Admin. Assistant   Kevin Binger

DISTRICT OFFICES:
8900 Keystone at the Crossing, #1050, Indianapolis 46240; (317) 848-0201; District Manager: Jim Atterholt.

435 E. Main St., #J-3, Greenwood 46142; (317) 882-3640; Office Director: Mary Frederick.

COMMITTEE ASSIGNMENTS:
Foreign Affairs
Post Office and Civil Service
Veterans' Affairs

Buyer, Steve, R-Ind. (5)
CAPITOL HILL OFFICE:
1419 LHOB 20515; 225-5037
Admin. Assistant   Kelly Craven

DISTRICT OFFICE:
120 E. Mulberry St., #106, Kokomo 46901; (317) 454-7551; District Director: Linda Ameen.

COMMITTEE ASSIGNMENTS:
Armed Services
Veterans' Affairs

Byrne, Leslie L., D-Va. (11)
CAPITOL HILL OFFICE:
1609 LHOB 20515; 225-1492
Admin. Assistant   Maggi Luca

DISTRICT OFFICE:
7620 Little River Turnpike, #203, Annandale 22003; (703) 750-1992; District Manager: Jan Reeves.

COMMITTEE ASSIGNMENTS:
Post Office and Civil Service
Public Works and Transportation

Callahan, Sonny, R-Ala. (1)
CAPITOL HILL OFFICE:
2418 RHOB 20515; 225-4931
Admin. Assistant   Jo Bonner

DISTRICT OFFICE:
2970 Cottage Hill Rd., #126, Mobile 36606; (205) 690-2811; District Representative: Taylor Ellis.

COMMITTEE ASSIGNMENT:
Appropriations

Calvert, Ken, R-Calif. (43)
CAPITOL HILL OFFICE:
1523 LHOB 20515; 225-1986
Admin. Assistant   Ed Slevin

DISTRICT OFFICE:
3400 Central Ave., #200, Riverside 92506; (909) 784-4300; Fax: (909) 784-5255; District Manager: Sue Miller.

COMMITTEE ASSIGNMENTS:
Natural Resources
Science, Space, and Technology

Camp, Dave, R-Mich. (4)
CAPITOL HILL OFFICE:
137 CHOB 20515; 225-3561
Fax: 225-9679
Admin. Assistant   John Guzik

DISTRICT OFFICES:
135 Ashman, Midland 48640; (517) 631-2552; District Director: Scott Haines.
308 W. Main St., Owosso 48867; (517) 723-6759; Constituent Representative: Sandy Harvey.
3508 W. Houghton Lake Dr., #1, Houghton Lake 48629; (517) 366-4922; Constituent Representative: Tarin Boven.

COMMITTEE ASSIGNMENT:
Ways and Means

Canady, Charles T., R-Fla. (12)
CAPITOL HILL OFFICE:
1107 LHOB 20515; 225-1252
Admin. Assistant   Clark Reid

DISTRICT OFFICE:
124 S. Tennessee Ave., #125, Lakeland 33801; (813) 688-2651; District Manager: Sue Loftin.

COMMITTEE ASSIGNMENTS:
Agriculture
Judiciary

Cantwell, Maria, D-Wash. (1)
CAPITOL HILL OFFICE:
1520 LHOB 20515; 225-6311
Fax: 225-2286
Admin. Assistant   Lisa Piccione

DISTRICT OFFICES:
21905 64th Ave. West, #101, Mountlake Terrace 98043; (206) 640-0233; Fax: (206) 776-7168; District Director: Mike Deller.
P.O. Box 185, Poulsbo 98370; (206) 697-3112; District Director: Mike Deller.

COMMITTEE ASSIGNMENTS:
Foreign Affairs
Merchant Marine and Fisheries
Public Works and Transportation

Cardin, Benjamin L., D-Md. (3)
CAPITOL HILL OFFICE:
227 CHOB 20515; 225-4016
Admin. Assistant   David Koshgarian

DISTRICT OFFICES:
540 E. Belvedere Ave., #201, Baltimore 21212; (301) 433-8886; Office Director: Bailey Fine.
412 S. Highland Ave., Baltimore 21224; (301) 563-9177; Staff Assistant: Peter Hammen.
8336 Belair Rd., Baltimore 21236; (410) 529-4152; Staff Assistant: Anne Irby.

COMMITTEE ASSIGNMENTS:
House Administration
Standards of Official Conduct
Ways and Means

Carr, Bob, D-Mich. (8)
CAPITOL HILL OFFICE:
2347 RHOB 20515; 225-4872
Fax: 225-1260
Chief of Staff   Howard Edelson

DISTRICT OFFICES:
2848 E. Grand River Ave., #1, East Lansing 48823; (517) 351-7203; Office Director: Vacant.
3487 S. Linden Rd., Suite D, Flint 48507; (313) 230-0873; District Director: Eddie McDonald.
10049 E. Grand River, #300A, Brighton 48116; (810) 220-1002; Fax: (810) 220-1020; Office Director: Vacant.

COMMITTEE ASSIGNMENT:
Appropriations

Castle, Michael N., R-Del. (AL)
CAPITOL HILL OFFICE:
1205 LHOB 20515; 225-4165
Fax: 225-2291
Admin. Assistant   Michael Ratchford

DISTRICT OFFICES:
201 N. Walnut St., #107, Wilmington 19801;
(302) 428-1902; District Director: Jeff Dayton.
Freer Federal Bldg., #2005, Dover 19901; (302)
736-1666; Fax: (302) 736-6580; Constituent Aide:
Carrie Townsend.

COMMITTEE ASSIGNMENTS:
Banking, Finance, and Urban Affairs
Education and Labor
Merchant Marine and Fisheries

Chapman, Jim, D-Texas (1)
CAPITOL HILL OFFICE:
2417 RHOB 20515; 225-3035
Admin. Assistant   Billy Moore

DISTRICT OFFICES:
P.O. Box 538, Sulphur Springs 75482; (903) 885-
8682; District Admin.: Bill Brannon.
100 E. Houston St., Marshall 75671; (903) 938-
8386; District Admin.: Leonard Rockwell.

COMMITTEE ASSIGNMENT:
Appropriations

Clay, William L., D-Mo. (1)
CAPITOL HILL OFFICE:
2306 RHOB 20515; 225-2406
Chief of Staff   Harriet Pritchett

DISTRICT OFFICES:
6197 Delmar Blvd., St. Louis 63112; (314) 725-
5770; District Director: Pearlie I. Evans.
Central City Shopping Center, #49, St. Louis
63136; (314) 388-0321; District Coordinator: Virginia
Cook.

COMMITTEE ASSIGNMENTS:
Education and Labor
House Administration
Post Office and Civil Service (Chairman)

Clayton, Eva, D-N.C. (1)
CAPITOL HILL OFFICE:
222 CHOB 20515; 225-3101
Fax: 225-3354
Admin. Assistant   Lenwood Long

DISTRICT OFFICES:
134 N. Main St., Warrenton 27589; (919) 257-
4800; Fax: (919) 257-2088; District Manager: Charles
Worth.
400 W. 5th St., Greenville 27838; (919) 758-8800;

Fax: (919) 758-1021; District Manager: Charles
Worth.

COMMITTEE ASSIGNMENTS:
Agriculture
Small Business

Clement, Bob, D-Tenn. (5)
CAPITOL HILL OFFICE:
1230 LHOB 20515; 225-4311
Fax: 226-1035
Admin. Assistant   David A. Flanders

DISTRICT OFFICES:
552 U.S. Courthouse, Nashville 37203; (615) 736-
5295; Chief of Staff: Dottie Moore.
101 5th Ave. East, #201, Springfield 37172; (615)
384-6600; Office Manager: Nancy Hall.
2701 Jefferson St., #103, Nashville 37208; (615)
320-1363; Admin. Assistant: Gail Stafford.

COMMITTEE ASSIGNMENTS:
Public Works and Transportation
Veterans' Affairs

Clinger, William F., R-Pa. (5)
CAPITOL HILL OFFICE:
2160 RHOB 20515; 225-5121
Fax: 225-4681
Staff Director   Jim Clarke

DISTRICT OFFICES:
315 S. Allen St., #116, State College 16801; (814)
238-1776; Office Manager: Rebecca Mills.
605 Integra Bank Bldg., Warren 16365; (814)
726-3910; District Admin.: Rick Peltz.

COMMITTEE ASSIGNMENTS:
Government Operations (Ranking)
Public Works and Transportation

Clyburn, James E., D-S.C. (6)
CAPITOL HILL OFFICE:
319 CHOB 20515; 225-3315
Admin. Assistant   Vacant

DISTRICT OFFICES:
1703 Gervais St., Columbia 29201; (803) 799-
1100; District Director: Robert Nance.
181 E. Evans St., Florence 29502; (803) 662-1212;
Area Director: Charlene Lowery.
4900 LaCrosse Rd., North Charleston 29419;
(803) 747-9660; Fax: (803) 744-2715; Area Director:
Davis Marshall.

COMMITTEE ASSIGNMENTS:
Public Works and Transportation
Veterans' Affairs

Coble, Howard, R-N.C. (6)
CAPITOL HILL OFFICE:
403 CHOB 20515; 225-3065
Fax: 225-8611
Admin. Assistant   Edward McDonald

DISTRICT OFFICES:
324 West Market St., #247, Greensboro 27401; (910) 333-5005; Fax: (910) 333-5048; Office Manager: Chris Beaman.
510 Ferndale Blvd., High Point 27262; (910) 886-5106; Fax: (910) 886-8740; District Representative: Carolyn McGahey.
124 W. Elm St., P.O. Box 814, Graham 27253; (910) 229-0159; Fax: (910) 228-7974; District Representative: Janine Osborne.
1404 Piedmont Dr., P.O. Box 1813, Lexington 27293; (704) 246-8230; Fax: (704) 246-4275; District Representative: Connie Leonard.
241 Sunset Ave., #101, Asheboro 27203; (910) 626-3060; Fax: (910) 626-4533; District Representative: Nancy Ellis.

COMMITTEE ASSIGNMENTS:
Judiciary
Merchant Marine and Fisheries

Coleman, Ronald D., D-Texas (16)
CAPITOL HILL OFFICE:
440 CHOB 20515; 225-4831
Chief of Staff   Paul Rogers

DISTRICT OFFICE:
700 E. San Antonio St., #723, El Paso 79901; (915) 534-6200; District Director: Luis Mata.

COMMITTEE ASSIGNMENTS:
Appropriations
Select Intelligence

Collins, Barbara-Rose, D-Mich. (15)
CAPITOL HILL OFFICE:
1108 LHOB 20515; 225-2261
Fax: 225-6645
Chief of Staff   Miniard Culpepper

DISTRICT OFFICE:
1155 Brewery Park, #353, Detroit 48207; (313) 567-2233; Fax: (313) 567-6029; District Director: Fred Dwihal.

COMMITTEE ASSIGNMENTS:
Government Operations
Post Office and Civil Service
Public Works and Transportation

Collins, Cardiss, D-Ill. (7)
CAPITOL HILL OFFICE:
2308 RHOB 20515; 225-5006
Admin. Assistant   Bud Myers

DISTRICT OFFICES:
230 S. Dearborn St., #3880, Chicago 60604; (312) 353-5754; Fax: (312) 353-2682; District Admin.: Jim Garrett.
328 W. Lake St., Oak Park 60302; (708) 383-1400; Fax: (708) 383-9417; Executive District Admin.: Bob Kettlewell.

COMMITTEE ASSIGNMENTS:
Energy and Commerce
Government Operations

Collins, Mac, R-Ga. (3)
CAPITOL HILL OFFICE:
1118 LHOB 20515; 225-5901
Fax: 225-2515
Admin. Assistant   Jay Morgan

DISTRICT OFFICES:
173 N. Main St., Jonesboro 30236; (404) 603-3395; District Director: Ronny Chance.
5704 Beallwood Connector, #200, Columbus 31904; (706) 327-7228; District Director: Shirley Gillespie.

COMMITTEE ASSIGNMENTS:
Public Works and Transportation
Small Business

Combest, Larry, R-Texas (19)
CAPITOL HILL OFFICE:
1511 LHOB 20515; 225-4005
Fax: 225-9615
Admin. Assistant   Rob Lehman

DISTRICT OFFICES:
1205 Texas Ave., #613, Lubbock 79401; (806) 763-1611; Office Manager: Mary Whistler.
3800 E. 42nd St., #205, Odessa 79762; (915) 362-2631; Office Manager: Jenny Welch.
5809 S. Western, #205, Amarillo 79110; (806) 353-3945; Office Manager: Margo Burgess.
511 W. Ohio, #114, Midland 79701; (915) 687-0926.

COMMITTEE ASSIGNMENTS:
Agriculture
Select Intelligence (Ranking)
Small Business

Condit, Gary A., D-Calif. (18)
CAPITOL HILL OFFICE:
1123 LHOB 20515; 225-6131
Fax: 225-0819
Chief of Staff   Mike Lynch

DISTRICT OFFICES:
415 W. 18th St., Merced 95340; (209) 383-4455; Fax: (209) 726-1065; District Representative: Mary Stefani.
920 16th St., Suite C, Modesto 95354; (209) 527-

1914; Fax: (209) 527-5748; District Representative: Vacant.

COMMITTEE ASSIGNMENTS:
Agriculture
Government Operations

Conyers, John, Jr., D-Mich. (14)
CAPITOL HILL OFFICE:
2426 RHOB 20515; 225-5126
Fax: 225-0072
Office Manager   Carla Brooks

DISTRICT OFFICE:
231 W. Lafayette, #669, Detroit 48226; (313) 961-5670; Fax: (313) 226-2085; Acting Office Director: Michelle White.

COMMITTEE ASSIGNMENTS:
Government Operations (Chairman)
Judiciary
Small Business

Cooper, Jim, D-Tenn. (4)
CAPITOL HILL OFFICE:
125 CHOB 20515; 225-6831
Fax: 225-4520
Chief of Staff   Greg Hinote

DISTRICT OFFICES:
210 E. Depot St., P.O. Box 725, Shelbyville 37160; (615) 684-1114; District Coordinator: Walter Wood.
City Hall, 7 S. High St., Winchester 37398; (615) 967-4150; Office Director: Judy Wofford.
208 E. 1st North St., #1, Morristown 37816; (615) 587-9000; Office Director: Joyce Hopson.
311 S. Main St., Crossville 38555; (615) 484-1864; Office Director: Mickey Eldridge.

COMMITTEE ASSIGNMENTS:
Budget
Energy and Commerce

Coppersmith, Sam, D-Ariz. (1)
CAPITOL HILL OFFICE:
1607 LHOB 20515; 225-2635
Chief of Staff   Andy Gordon

DISTRICT OFFICE:
404 S. Mill Ave., #C-201, Tempe 85281; (602) 921-5500; District Director: Susan Goldsmith.

COMMITTEE ASSIGNMENTS:
Public Works and Transportation
Science, Space, and Technology

Costello, Jerry F., D-Ill. (12)
CAPITOL HILL OFFICE:
119 CHOB 20515; 225-5661
Fax: 225-0285
Admin. Assistant   Brian Lott

DISTRICT OFFICE:
327 W. Main St., Belleville 62220; (618) 233-8026; Fax: (618) 233-8765; Personal Assistant: Amy Huggins.

COMMITTEE ASSIGNMENTS:
Budget
Public Works and Transportation

Cox, C. Christopher, R-Calif. (47)
CAPITOL HILL OFFICE:
206 CHOB 20515; 225-5611
Fax: 225-9177
Chief of Staff   Jan Fujiwara

DISTRICT OFFICE:
4000 MacArthur Blvd., East Tower, #430, Newport Beach 92660; (714) 756-2244; District Representative: Greg Haskin.

COMMITTEE ASSIGNMENTS:
Budget
Government Operations
Joint Economic

Coyne, William J., D-Pa. (14)
CAPITOL HILL OFFICE:
2455 RHOB 20515; 225-2301
Admin. Assistant   Coleman J. Conroy

DISTRICT OFFICE:
1000 Liberty Ave., #2009, Pittsburgh 15222; (412) 644-2870; Office Director: James P. Rooney.

COMMITTEE ASSIGNMENTS:
Budget
Ways and Means

Cramer, Robert E. "Bud," D-Ala. (5)
CAPITOL HILL OFFICE:
1318 LHOB 20515; 225-4801
Fax: 225-4392
Admin. Assistant   Mike Adcock

DISTRICT OFFICES:
403 Franklin St., Huntsville 35801; (205) 551-0190; District Coordinator: Douglas Grise.
737-E Avalon Ave., Muscle Shoals 35661; (205) 381-3450; Case Worker: Ethel McDonald.
Morgan County Courthouse, P.O. Box 668, Decatur 35602; (205) 355-9400; Caseworker: Peggy Allen.

COMMITTEE ASSIGNMENTS:
Public Works and Transportation
Science, Space, and Technology
Select Intelligence

Crane, Philip M., R-Ill. (8)
CAPITOL HILL OFFICE:
233 CHOB 20515; 225-3711
Fax: 225-7830
Chief of Staff   Robert C. Coleman

DISTRICT OFFICES:
1450 S. New Wilke Rd., #101, Arlington Heights 60005; (708) 394-0790; Office Director: Jack McKenney.
300 N. Milwaukee Ave., Suite C, Lake Villa 60046; (708) 265-9000; Office Director: Carole Toft.

COMMITTEE ASSIGNMENTS:
Joint Taxation
Ways and Means

Crapo, Michael D., R-Idaho (2)
CAPITOL HILL OFFICE:
437 CHOB 20515; 225-5531
Fax: 225-8216
Chief of Staff   John Hoehne

DISTRICT OFFICES:
304 N. 8th St., Boise 83702; (208) 334-1953; Office Manager: Janet Jeffries.
250 S. 4th, #220, Pocatello 83201; (208) 236-6734; Field Representative: Dawn Hatch.
488 Blue Lakes Blvd., #105, Twin Falls 83301; (208) 734-7219; Field Representative: Dawn Hatch.

COMMITTEE ASSIGNMENT:
Energy and Commerce

Cunningham, Randy "Duke," R-Calif. (51)
CAPITOL HILL OFFICE:
117 CHOB 20515; 225-5452
Fax: 225-2558
Admin. Assistant   Frank Collins

DISTRICT OFFICE:
613 West Valley Parkway, #320, Escondido 92025; (619) 737-8438; Fax: (619) 737-9132; District Director: Kathy Stafford-Taulbee.

COMMITTEE ASSIGNMENTS:
Armed Services
Education and Labor
Merchant Marine and Fisheries

Danner, Pat, D-Mo. (6)
CAPITOL HILL OFFICE:
1217 LHOB 20515; 225-7041
Fax: 225-8221
Admin. Assistant   Doug Gray

DISTRICT OFFICES:
5754 N. Broadway, Bldg. 3, #2, Kansas City 64118; (816) 455-2256; Fax: (816) 455-2153; District Admin.: Lou Carson.
201 S. 8th St., #330, St. Joseph 64501; (816) 233-9818; Fax: (816) 233-9848; District Admin.: Rosie Haertling.

COMMITTEE ASSIGNMENTS:
Public Works and Transportation
Small Business

Darden, George "Buddy," D-Ga. (7)
CAPITOL HILL OFFICE:
2303 RHOB 20515; 225-2931
Admin. Assistant   Robert Gaylor

DISTRICT OFFICES:
376 Powder Springs St., #100, Marietta 30064; (404) 422-4480; Fax: (404) 331-3404; Office Manager: Jane Cook.
301 Federal Bldg., Rome 30161; (706) 291-7777; Fax: (706) 291-5636; District Aide: Cecil Burk.
200 Ridley Ave., LaGrange 30240; (706) 882-4578; Fax: (706) 882-4662; Office Manager: Hilda Railey.
315 Bradley St., Carrollton 30117; (404) 832-0553; Fax: (404) 832-0728; Office Manager: Bill Hamrick.

COMMITTEE ASSIGNMENTS:
Appropriations
Standards of Official Conduct

Deal, Nathan, D-Ga. (9)
CAPITOL HILL OFFICE:
1406 LHOB 20515; 225-5211
Fax: 225-8272
Chief of Staff   David Cook

DISTRICT OFFICES:
311 Green St., #302, Gainesville 30501; (404) 535-2592; Fax: (404) 535-2765; District Coordinator: Don Parks.
415 E. Walnut Ave., #108, Dalton 30721; (706) 226-5320; Fax: (706) 278-0840; Staff Assistant: Vivian Campbell.
109 N. Main St., Lafayette 30728; (706) 638-7042; Fax: (706) 638-7049; Staff Assistant: Gwen Clark.

COMMITTEE ASSIGNMENTS:
Natural Resources
Public Works and Transportation
Science, Space, and Technology

DeFazio, Peter A., D-Ore. (4)
CAPITOL HILL OFFICE:
1233 LHOB 20515; 225-6416
Admin. Assistant   Penny Dodge

DISTRICT OFFICES:
211 E. 7th Ave., Eugene 97401; (503) 465-6732;
Office Director: Betsy Boyd.
215 S. 2nd St., Coos Bay 97420; (503) 269-2609;
Office Director: Jana Doer.
P.O. Box 126, Roseburg 97470; (503) 440-3523;
Office Director: Chris Conroy.

COMMITTEE ASSIGNMENTS:
Natural Resources
Public Works and Transportation

de la Garza, E. "Kika," D-Texas (15)
CAPITOL HILL OFFICE:
1401 LHOB 20515; 225-2531
Admin. Assistant   Bernice McGuire

DISTRICT OFFICES:
La Posada Village, 1418 Beech, McAllen 78501;
(210) 682-5545; Staff Assistant: Vacant.
401 E. 2nd St., Alice 78332; (512) 664-2215; Staff
Assistant: Vacant.

COMMITTEE ASSIGNMENT:
Agriculture (Chairman)

DeLauro, Rosa, D-Conn. (3)
CAPITOL HILL OFFICE:
327 CHOB 20515; 225-3661
Fax: 225-4890
Admin. Assistant   Paul Frick

DISTRICT OFFICE:
265 Church St., New Haven 06510; (203) 562-
3718; District Director: Marlene Woodmam.

COMMITTEE ASSIGNMENT:
Appropriations

DeLay, Tom, R-Texas (22)
CAPITOL HILL OFFICE:
407 CHOB 20515; 225-5951
Fax: 225-5241
Admin. Assistant   Ken Carroll

DISTRICT OFFICE:
12603 Southwest Freeway, #285, Stafford
77477; (713) 240-3700; Office Director: Janice
Reynolds.

COMMITTEE ASSIGNMENT:
Appropriations

Dellums, Ronald V., D-Calif. (9)
CAPITOL HILL OFFICE:
2108 RHOB 20515; 225-2661
Admin. Assistant   Carlottia Scott

DISTRICT OFFICE:
1301 Clay St., #1000-N, Oakland 94612; (510)
763-0370; Fax: (510) 273-7023; District Director: Lee
Halterman.

COMMITTEE ASSIGNMENTS:
Armed Services (Chairman)
District of Columbia

de Lugo, Ron, D-Virgin Islands (AL)
CAPITOL HILL OFFICE:
2427 RHOB 20515; 225-1790
Admin. Assistant   Sheila Ross

DISTRICT OFFICES:
3013 Golden Rock, #313, St. Croix 00820; (809)
778-5900; District Supervisor: Sam Bough.
256 Federal Bldg., St. Thomas 00801; (809) 774-
4408; District Supervisor: Sam Bough.

COMMITTEE ASSIGNMENTS:
Education and Labor
Natural Resources
Public Works and Transportation

Derrick, Butler, D-S.C. (3)
CAPITOL HILL OFFICE:
221 CHOB 20515; 225-5301
Admin. Assistant   Lynne J. Richardson

DISTRICT OFFICES:
315 S. McDuffie St., P.O. Box 4126, Anderson
29622; (803) 224-7401; District Manager: Wayne
Adams.
120 Main St., #129, Greenwood 29646; (803)
223-8251; Office Manager: Elestine Norman.
211 York St. N.E., #5, Aiken 29801; (803) 649-
5571; Office Manager: Martha Rowland.

COMMITTEE ASSIGNMENTS:
House Administration
Rules

Deutsch, Peter, D-Fla. (20)
CAPITOL HILL OFFICE:
425 CHOB 20515; 225-7931
Admin. Assistant   Jim Smith

DISTRICT OFFICES:
10100 Pines Blvd., Pembroke Pines 33025; (305)
437-3936; District Director: Perle Siegel.
1010 Kennedy Dr., #310, Key West 33040; (305)
294-5815; Office Director: Deborah Robertson.

COMMITTEE ASSIGNMENTS:
  Banking, Finance, and Urban Affairs
  Foreign Affairs
  Merchant Marine and Fisheries

Diaz-Balart, Lincoln, R-Fla. (21)
CAPITOL HILL OFFICE:
  509 CHOB 20515; 225-4211
  Fax: 225-8576
    Chief of Staff   Steve Vermillion

DISTRICT OFFICE:
  8525 N.W. 53rd Terrace, Miami 33166; (305)
470-8555; District Director: Ana Carbonell.

COMMITTEE ASSIGNMENTS:
  Foreign Affairs
  Merchant Marine and Fisheries

Dickey, Jay, R-Ark. (4)
CAPITOL HILL OFFICE:
  1338 LHOB 20515; 225-3772
  Fax: 225-1314
    Admin. Assistant   Vacant

DISTRICT OFFICES:
  100 E. 8th Ave., #2521, Pine Bluff 71601; (501)
536-3376; Fax: (501) 536-4050, District Manager:
Richard Bearden.
  101 Reserve, #201, Hot Springs 71913; (501)
623-5800; Fax: (501) 623-5363; Caseworker: Susan
Carter.
  101 S. Jackson, #201, El Dorado 71730; (501)
862-0236; Fax: (501) 862-0890; District Manager:
Vacant.

COMMITTEE ASSIGNMENTS:
  Agriculture
  Natural Resources
  Small Business

Dicks, Norm, D-Wash. (6)
CAPITOL HILL OFFICE:
  2467 RHOB 20515; 225-5916
  Fax: 226-1176
    Office Manager   Donna Taylor

DISTRICT OFFICES:
  1717 Pacific Ave., #2244, Tacoma 98402; (206)
593-6536; Fax: (206) 593-6551; Office Director: Tim
Zenk.
  500 Pacific Ave., #301, Bremerton 98310; (206)
479-4011; Fax: (206) 553-7445; Office Director: Cheri
Williams.

COMMITTEE ASSIGNMENTS:
  Appropriations
  Select Intelligence

Dingell, John D., D-Mich. (16)
CAPITOL HILL OFFICE:
  2328 RHOB 20515; 225-4071
    Admin. Assistant   Marda Robillard

DISTRICT OFFICES:
  5465 Schaefer Rd., Dearborn 48126; (313) 846-
1276; District Coordinator: Constance Shorter.
  214 E. Elm Ave., #105, Monroe 48161; (313) 243-
1849; District Representative: Donna Hoffer.

COMMITTEE ASSIGNMENT:
  Energy and Commerce (Chairman)

Dixon, Julian C., D-Calif. (32)
CAPITOL HILL OFFICE:
  2400 RHOB 20515; 225-7084
    Admin. Assistant   Andrea Tracy Holmes

DISTRICT OFFICE:
  5100 W. Goldleaf Circle, #208, Los Angeles
90056; (213) 678-5424; Admin. Assistant: Patricia
Miller.

COMMITTEE ASSIGNMENTS:
  Appropriations
  Select Intelligence

Dooley, Cal, D-Calif. (20)
CAPITOL HILL OFFICE:
  1227 LHOB 20515; 225-3341
    Chief of Staff   Lisa Quigley

DISTRICT OFFICE:
  224 W. Lacey Blvd., Hanford 93230; (800) 464-
4294; District Director: Chris Sundstrom.

COMMITTEE ASSIGNMENTS:
  Agriculture
  Banking, Finance, and Urban Affairs
  Natural Resources

Doolittle, John T., R-Calif. (4)
CAPITOL HILL OFFICE:
  1524 LHOB 20515; 225-2511
    Admin. Assistant   David Lopez

DISTRICT OFFICE:
  2130 Professional Dr., #190, Roseville 95661;
(916) 786-5560; District Office Coordinator: Richard
Robinson.

COMMITTEE ASSIGNMENTS:
  Agriculture
  Natural Resources

Dornan, Robert K., R-Calif. (46)
CAPITOL HILL OFFICE:
2402 RHOB 20515; 225-2965
Admin. Assistant   Joe Eule

DISTRICT OFFICE:
300 Plaza Alicante, #360, Garden Grove 92640;
(714) 971-9292; District Admin.: Patricia Fanelli.

COMMITTEE ASSIGNMENTS:
Armed Services
Select Intelligence

Dreier, David, R-Calif. (28)
CAPITOL HILL OFFICE:
411 CHOB 20515; 225-2305
Staff Director   Brad Smith

DISTRICT OFFICE:
112 N. 2nd Ave., Covina 91723; (818) 339-9078;
District Representative: Mark Harmsen.

COMMITTEE ASSIGNMENT:
Rules

Duncan, John J. "Jimmy," Jr., R-Tenn. (2)
CAPITOL HILL OFFICE:
115 CHOB 20515; 225-5435
Fax: 225-6440
Admin. Assistant   Judy Whitbred

DISTRICT OFFICES:
501 W. Main St., #318, Knoxville 37902; (615)
523-3772; Office Director: Mildred McRae.
McMinn County Courthouse, Athens 37303;
(615) 745-4671; Office Director: Linda Higdon.
419 1st American Bank Bldg., Maryville 37801;
(615) 984-5464; Office Director: Sara Sayles.

COMMITTEE ASSIGNMENTS:
Natural Resources
Public Works and Transportation

Dunn, Jennifer, R-Wash. (8)
CAPITOL HILL OFFICE:
1641 LHOB 20515; 225-7761
Admin. Assistant   Phil Bond

DISTRICT OFFICE:
50 116th Ave. S.E., #201, Bellevue 98004; (206)
450-0161; District Manager: Phil Watkins.

COMMITTEE ASSIGNMENTS:
House Administration
Public Works and Transportation
Science, Space, and Technology

Durbin, Richard J., D-Ill. (20)
CAPITOL HILL OFFICE:
2463 RHOB 20515; 225-5271
Fax: 225-0170
Admin. Assistant   Ed Greelegs

DISTRICT OFFICES:
525 S. 8th St., P.O. Box 790, Springfield 62703;
(217) 492-4062; Office Director: Mike Daley.
221 E. Broadway, Centralia 62801; (618) 532-
4887; Office Director: Lucy Murphy.
400 St. Louis St., #2, Edwardsville 62025.

COMMITTEE ASSIGNMENT:
Appropriations

Edwards, Chet, D-Texas (11)
CAPITOL HILL OFFICE:
328 CHOB 20515; 225-6105
Chief of Staff   Vacant

DISTRICT OFFICE:
700 S. University Parks Dr., #710, Waco 76706;
(817) 752-9600; Fax: (817) 752-7769; District Director:
Jim Haddox.

COMMITTEE ASSIGNMENTS:
Armed Services
Veterans' Affairs

Edwards, Don, D-Calif. (16)
CAPITOL HILL OFFICE:
2307 RHOB 20515; 225-3072
Admin. Assistant   Roberta Haeberle

DISTRICT OFFICE:
1042 W. Hedding St., #100, San Jose 95126;
(408) 345-1711; District Coordinator: Terry Poche.

COMMITTEE ASSIGNMENTS:
Foreign Affairs
Judiciary
Veterans' Affairs

Ehlers, Vernon J., R-Mich. (3)
CAPITOL HILL OFFICE:
1526 LHOB 20515; 225-3831
Chief of Staff   Mary Lobisco

DISTRICT OFFICE:
166 Federal Bldg., Grand Rapids 49503; (616)
451-8383.

COMMITTEE ASSIGNMENTS:
Public Works and Transportation
Science, Space, and Technology

Emerson, Bill, R-Mo. (8)
CAPITOL HILL OFFICE:
2454 RHOB 20515; 225-4404
Chief of Staff   Lloyd Smith

DISTRICT OFFICES:
339 Broadway, Cape Girardeau 63701; (314) 335-0101.
612 Pine, #101, Rolla 65401; (314) 364-2455; Office Director: Iris Bernhardt.

COMMITTEE ASSIGNMENTS:
Agriculture
Public Works and Transportation

Engel, Eliot L., D-N.Y. (17)
CAPITOL HILL OFFICE:
1433 LHOB 20515; 225-2464
Admin. Assistant   John Calvelli

DISTRICT OFFICES:
3655 Johnson Ave., Bronx 10463; (718) 796-9700; Chief of Staff: Arnold Linhardt.
177 Dreiser Loop, #3, Bronx 10475; (718) 320-2314; Chief of Staff: Arnold Linhardt.
655 E. 233rd St., Bronx 10466; (718) 652-0400; Chief of Staff: Jennifer Story.
87 Nepperhan Ave., #213, Yonkers 10701; (914) 423-0700; Chief of Staff: Shirley Saunders.
29 W. 4th St., Mount Vernon 10550; (914) 699-4100; Chief of Staff: Linda Lynch.

COMMITTEE ASSIGNMENTS:
Education and Labor
Foreign Affairs

English, Karan, D-Ariz. (6)
CAPITOL HILL OFFICE:
1024 LHOB 20515; 225-2190
Admin. Assistant   Shannon Davis

DISTRICT OFFICES:
117 E. Aspen Ave., Flagstaff 86001; (602) 774-1314; Fax: (602) 774-2411; District Director: Ed Delaney.
1818 E. Southern Ave., #3B, Mesa 85204; (602) 497-1156; Executive Assistant: Sarah Luna.

COMMITTEE ASSIGNMENTS:
Education and Labor
Natural Resources

Eshoo, Anna G., D-Calif. (14)
CAPITOL HILL OFFICE:
1505 LHOB 20515; 225-8104
Fax: 225-8890
Chief of Staff   John Flaherty

DISTRICT OFFICE:
698 Emerson St., Palo Alto 94301; (415) 323-2984; District Director: Bruce Ives.

COMMITTEE ASSIGNMENTS:
Merchant Marine and Fisheries
Science, Space, and Technology

Evans, Lane, D-Ill. (17)
CAPITOL HILL OFFICE:
2335 RHOB 20515; 225-5905
Admin. Assistant   Dennis J. King

DISTRICT OFFICES:
1535 47th Ave., #5, Moline 61265; (309) 793-5760; District Representative: Philip Hare.
1640 N. Henderson St., Galesburg 61401; (309) 342-4411; Office Manager: Joyce Bean.
City Hall, Monmouth 61462; (309) 734-9304; District Representative: Philip Hare.
121 Scotland, Maclan Plaza, Macomb 61455; (309) 837-5263; Office Manager: Joyce Bean.

COMMITTEE ASSIGNMENTS:
Armed Services
Natural Resources
Veterans' Affairs

Everett, Terry, R-Ala. (2)
CAPITOL HILL OFFICE:
208 CHOB 20515; 225-2901
Admin. Assistant   Clay Swanzy

DISTRICT OFFICES:
116 S. Main, #211, Enterprise 36330; (205) 393-2996; Office Director: Judy Jenkins.
3001 Zelda Rd., Montgomery 36106; (205) 277-9113; Field Director: Steve Pelham.
100 W. Troy St., Dothan 36303; (205) 794-9680; Office Director: Marcus Paramore.
City Hall Bldg., Main St., Opp 36467; (205) 493-9253; Office Director: Frances Spurlin.

COMMITTEE ASSIGNMENTS:
Agriculture
Armed Services
Veterans' Affairs

Ewing, Thomas W., R-Ill. (15)
CAPITOL HILL OFFICE:
1317 LHOB 20515; 225-2371
Chief of Staff   Mike Stokke

DISTRICT OFFICES:
2401 E. Washington St., #101, Bloomington 61704; (309) 662-9371; District Caseworker: Karen McCall.
210 W. Water St., Pontiac 61764; (815) 844-7660; Deputy Chief of Staff: Aaron Quick.
102 E. Main St., Busey Plaza, #307, Urbana 61801; (217) 328-0165; District Press Secretary: Terry Greene.

70 Meadowview Center, #200, Kankakee 60901; (815) 937-0875; District Caseworker: Dorla Meents.
4 N. Vermilion St., #503, Danville 61832; (217) 431-8230; Caseworker: Vacant.

COMMITTEE ASSIGNMENTS:
Agriculture
Public Works and Transportation

Faleomavaega, Eni F. H., D-Am. Samoa (AL)
CAPITOL HILL OFFICE:
109 CHOB 20515; 225-8577
Legislative Director   Martin R. Yerick

DISTRICT OFFICE:
P.O. Drawer X, Pago Pago 96799; (684) 633-1372; District Manager: Oreta Togafau.

COMMITTEE ASSIGNMENTS:
Education and Labor
Foreign Affairs
Natural Resources

Farr, Sam, D-Calif. (17)
CAPITOL HILL OFFICE:
1216 LHOB 20515; 225-2861
Admin. Assistant   Rochelle Dornatt

DISTRICT OFFICES:
380 Alvarado St., Monterey 93940; (408) 649-3555; Chief of Staff: Donna Blitzer.
701 Ocean St., #318, Santa Cruz 95060; (408) 429-1976; Office Director: Sally Johnson.
100 W. Alisal, Salinas 93901; (408) 424-2229; Office Director: Juan Uranga.

COMMITTEE ASSIGNMENTS:
Agriculture
Armed Services
Natural Resources

Fawell, Harris W., R-Ill. (13)
CAPITOL HILL OFFICE:
2342 RHOB 20515; 225-3515
Chief of Staff   Alan Mertz

DISTRICT OFFICE:
115 W. 55th St., #100, Clarendon Hills 60514; (708) 655-2052; District Director: Barbara Graham.

COMMITTEE ASSIGNMENTS:
Education and Labor
Science, Space, and Technology

Fazio, Vic, D-Calif. (3)
CAPITOL HILL OFFICE:
2113 RHOB 20515; 225-5716

Fax: 225-3350
Chief of Staff   Monica Maples

DISTRICT OFFICE:
722B Main St., Woodland 95695; (916) 666-5521; District Director: Richard Harris.

COMMITTEE ASSIGNMENT:
Appropriations

Fields, Cleo, D-La. (4)
CAPITOL HILL OFFICE:
513 CHOB 20515; 225-8490
Chief of Staff   Robert Moore

DISTRICT OFFICES:
700 N. 10th St., #210, Baton Rouge 70802; (504) 343-9772; Fax: (504) 343-9693; District Director: Johnny Anderson.
610 Texas St., #201, Shreveport 71101; (318) 221-9924; Fax: (318) 424-7605; Office Director: Lynn Braggs.
301 N. Main St., 2nd Floor, Opelousas 70570; (318) 942-9691; Office Director: Charles Cravins.
211 N. 3rd St., #102, Monroe 71201; (318) 322-8887; Fax: (318) 322-0454; Office Director: King Dawson.

COMMITTEE ASSIGNMENTS:
Banking, Finance, and Urban Affairs
Small Business

Fields, Jack, R-Texas (8)
CAPITOL HILL OFFICE:
2228 RHOB 20515; 225-4901
Admin. Assistant   Robert E.H. Ferguson

DISTRICT OFFICES:
9810 FM1960 Bypass West, #165, Deerbrook Plaza, Humble 77338; (713) 540-8000; District Representative: Jim Finley.
300 W. Davis, #507, Conroe 77301; (409) 756-8044; District Representative: Jim Finley.
111 E. University Dr., #216, College Station 77840; (409) 846-6068; District Representative: Jim Finley.

COMMITTEE ASSIGNMENTS:
Energy and Commerce
Merchant Marine and Fisheries (Ranking)

Filner, Bob, D-Calif. (50)
CAPITOL HILL OFFICE:
504 CHOB 20515; 225-8045
Fax: 225-9073
Chief of Staff   David Ginsborg

DISTRICT OFFICE:
333 F St., Suite A, Chula Vista 91910; (619) 422-5963; Fax: (619) 422-7290; District Director: Vincent Hall.

COMMITTEE ASSIGNMENTS:
Public Works and Transportation
Veterans' Affairs

Fingerhut, Eric D., D-Ohio (19)
CAPITOL HILL OFFICE:
431 CHOB 20515; 225-5731
Chief of Staff David Fleshler

DISTRICT OFFICE:
2550 Som Center Rd., #385, Willoughby Hills 44094; (216) 943-1919; District Manager: Robert Triozzi.

COMMITTEE ASSIGNMENTS:
Banking, Finance, and Urban Affairs
Foreign Affairs
Science, Space, and Technology

Fish, Hamilton, Jr., R-N.Y. (19)
CAPITOL HILL OFFICE:
2354 RHOB 20515; 225-5441
Admin. Assistant Nicholas Hayes

DISTRICT OFFICES:
1440 Route 9, Wappingers Falls 12590; (914) 297-5711; Office Director: Helen Fuimarello.
1 Vink Dr., Carmel 10512; (914) 225-5200; Office Director: Dolly Pederson
2 Church St., Ossining 10562; (914) 762-7561; District Admin.: Janice Traber.

COMMITTEE ASSIGNMENT:
Judiciary (Ranking)

Flake, Floyd H., D-N.Y. (6)
CAPITOL HILL OFFICE:
1035 LHOB 20515; 225-3461
Chief of Staff Edwin Reed

DISTRICT OFFICE:
196-06 Linden Blvd., St. Albans 11412; (718) 949-5600; Fax: (718) 949-5972; District Manager: Samuel Moon.

COMMITTEE ASSIGNMENTS:
Banking, Finance, and Urban Affairs
Government Operations
Small Business

oglietta, Thomas M., D-Pa. (1)
CAPITOL HILL OFFICE:
341 CHOB 20515; 225-4731
Admin. Assistant Anthony Green

DISTRICT OFFICES:
6th and Arch Sts., William J. Green Bldg., Philadelphia 19106; (215) 925-6840; Office Policy Director: Maria Walker.

4835 N. Broad St., Philadelphia 19141; (215) 324-9410; Office Manager: Shirley Gregory.
1806 S. Broad St., Philadelphia 19145; (215) 463-8702; Policy Director: Maria Walker.
511-13 Welsh St., Chester 19013; (215) 874-7094; Staff Director: Vacant.

COMMITTEE ASSIGNMENT:
Appropriations

Foley, Thomas S., D-Wash. (5)
CAPITOL HILL OFFICE:
1201 LHOB 20515; 225-2006
Fax: 225-1642
Admin. Assistant Susan Bell Moos
H-204 The Capitol 20515; 225-5604
(Speaker's office)

DISTRICT OFFICES:
W. 601 1st Ave., Spokane 99204; (509) 353-2155; District Assistant: Janet Gilpatrick.
12929 E. Sprague, Spokane 99216; (509) 926-4434; Legis. Assistant: Jeanne Zappone.
28 W. Main, Walla Walla 99362; (509) 522-6372; District Assistant: Patricia Gregg.

COMMITTEE ASSIGNMENT:
Joint Inaugural Ceremonies

Ford, Harold E., D-Tenn. (9)
CAPITOL HILL OFFICE:
2211 RHOB 20515; 225-3265
Fax: 225-9215
Admin. Assistant Terri Winston

DISTRICT OFFICE:
167 N. Main St., #369, Memphis 38103; (901) 544-4131; Office Admin.: Mildred Horn.

COMMITTEE ASSIGNMENT:
Ways and Means

Ford, William D., D-Mich. (13)
CAPITOL HILL OFFICE:
2107 RHOB 20515; 225-6261
Admin. Assistant David Geiss

DISTRICT OFFICES:
Federal Bldg., Wayne 48184; (313) 722-1411; Office Manager: Robin Marshall.
31 S. Huron, Ypsilanti 48197; (313) 482-6636; Office Director: Dee Dogan.
106 E. Washington, Ann Arbor 48104; (313) 741-4210; Office Manager: Ellen Offen.

COMMITTEE ASSIGNMENT:
Education and Labor (Chairman)

Fowler, Tillie, R-Fla. (4)
CAPITOL HILL OFFICE:
413 CHOB 20515; 225-2501
Chief of Staff   David Gilliland

DISTRICT OFFICES:
4452 Hendricks Ave., Jacksonville 32207; (904) 739-6600; Fax: (904) 367-0066; District Manager: Susie Wiles.
533 N. Nova Rd., Ormand Beach 32174; (904) 672-0754; Fax: (904) 673-8964; District Representative: Georgia Flynn.

COMMITTEE ASSIGNMENTS:
Armed Services
Merchant Marine and Fisheries

Frank, Barney, D-Mass. (4)
CAPITOL HILL OFFICE:
2404 RHOB 20515; 225-5931
Admin. Assistant   Peter Kovar

DISTRICT OFFICES:
29 Crafts St., Newton 02158; (617) 332-3920; District Director: Dorothy M. Reichard.
222 Milliken Place, Fall River 02722; (508) 674-3551; Office Manager: Amelia Wright.
558 Pleasant St., New Bedford 02740; (508) 999-6462; Office Manager: Elsie Souza.
89 Main St., Bridgewater 02324; (508) 697-9403; Office Manager: Garth Patterson.

COMMITTEE ASSIGNMENTS:
Banking, Finance, and Urban Affairs
Budget
Judiciary

Franks, Bob, R-N.J. (7)
CAPITOL HILL OFFICE:
429 CHOB 20515; 225-5361
Admin. Assistant   Gregg Edwards

DISTRICT OFFICES:
2333 Morris Ave., #B17, Union 07083; (908) 686-5576; District Director: Janet Thompson.
73 Main St., #4, Woodbridge 07095; (908) 602-0075; Office Manager: Vacant.
1 Railroad Ave., Franklin 08873; (908) 873-0811; Office Manager: Vacant.

COMMITTEE ASSIGNMENTS:
Budget
Public Works and Transportation

Franks, Gary A., R-Conn. (5)
CAPITOL HILL OFFICE:
435 CHOB 20515; 225-3822
Chief of Staff   Rick Genua

DISTRICT OFFICES:
135 Grand St., #210, Waterbury 06702; (203)

573-1418; Chief of Staff: Rick Genua.
30 Main St., Danbury 06810; (203) 790-1263; Chief of Staff: Rick Genua.

COMMITTEE ASSIGNMENT:
Energy and Commerce

Frost, Martin, D-Texas (24)
CAPITOL HILL OFFICE:
2459 RHOB 20515; 225-3605
Admin. Assistant   Matt Angle

DISTRICT OFFICES:
3020 S.E. Loop 820, Fort Worth 76140; (817) 293-9231; District Director: Cinda Crawford.
400 S. Zang Blvd., Dallas 75208; (214) 767-2816; Office Manager: Judy Scheberle.
318 W. Main St., #102, Arlington 76010; (817) 795-3291; Office Manager: Mike Spears.
100 N. Main St., #534, Corsicana 75110; (903) 874-0760; Fax: (903) 874-0468; Staff Assistant: Penny Jones.

COMMITTEE ASSIGNMENTS:
House Administration
Joint Library
Rules

Furse, Elizabeth, D-Ore. (1)
CAPITOL HILL OFFICE:
316 CHOB 20515; 225-0855
Admin. Assistant   Jennie Kugel

DISTRICT OFFICE:
2701 N.W. Vaughn St., #860, Portland 97210; (503) 326-2901; District Manager: Phyllis Oster.

COMMITTEE ASSIGNMENTS:
Armed Services
Banking, Finance, and Urban Affairs
Merchant Marine and Fisheries

Gallegly, Elton, R-Calif. (23)
CAPITOL HILL OFFICE:
2441 RHOB 20515; 225-5811
Admin. Assistant   Paul Bateman

DISTRICT OFFICE:
300 Esplanade Dr., #1800, Oxnard 93030; (80⁵ 485-2300; Office Manager: Paula Sheil.

COMMITTEE ASSIGNMENTS:
Foreign Affairs
Judiciary
Natural Resources

Gallo, Dean A., R-N.J. (11)
CAPITOL HILL OFFICE:
2447 RHOB 20515; 225-5034
Chief of Staff   Donna Mullins

DISTRICT OFFICES:
101 Gibraltar Dr., #2-D, Parsippany-Troy Hills Township, Morris Plains 07950; (201) 984-0711; Office Manager: Carol Ricker.
22 N. Sussex St., Dover 07801; (201) 328-7413; District Representative: Pam Thievon.
3 Fairfield Ave., West Caldwell 07006; (201) 228-9262; Office Director: Joan Hamilton.

COMMITTEE ASSIGNMENT:
Appropriations

Gejdenson, Sam, D-Conn. (2)
CAPITOL HILL OFFICE:
2416 RHOB 20515; 225-2076
Admin. Assistant   Robert Baskin

DISTRICT OFFICES:
74 W. Main St., P.O. Box 2000, Norwich 06360; (203) 886-0139; Office Director: Naomi Otterness.
94 Court St., Middletown 06457; (203) 346-1123; Congressional Aide: Patty Shea.

COMMITTEE ASSIGNMENTS:
Foreign Affairs
House Administration
Joint Printing
Natural Resources

Gekas, George W., R-Pa. (17)
CAPITOL HILL OFFICE:
2410 RHOB 20515; 225-4315
Admin. Assistant   Allan Cagnoli

DISTRICT OFFICES:
3605 Vartan Way, 2nd Floor, Harrisburg 17110; (717) 232-5123; District Secretary: Arlene Eckels.
400 S. 8th St., #108B, Lebanon 17042; (717) 273-1451; Office Director: Reg Nylan.
222 S. Market St., #102-A, Elizabethtown 17022; (717) 367-6669; Office Director: Michelle Splane.

COMMITTEE ASSIGNMENTS:
Judiciary
Select Intelligence

Gephardt, Richard A., D-Mo. (3)
CAPITOL HILL OFFICE:
1432 LHOB 20515; 225-2671
Fax: 225-7452
Admin. Assistant   Rodney Sippel
H-148 The Capitol 20515; 225-0100
(Majority Leader's office)

DISTRICT OFFICE:
11140 S. Towne Square, St. Louis 63123; (314) 94-3400; Fax: (314) 845-7088; Office Director: Mary enick.

COMMITTEE ASSIGNMENTS:
Budget
Joint Inaugural Ceremonies

Geren, Pete, D-Texas (12)
CAPITOL HILL OFFICE:
1730 LHOB 20515; 225-5071
Fax: 225-2786
Admin. Assistant   Laura Redding

DISTRICT OFFICE:
1600 W. Seventh St., #740, Ft. Worth 76102; (817) 338-0909; Fax: (817) 335-5852; District Director: Bill Souder.

COMMITTEE ASSIGNMENTS:
Armed Services
Public Works and Transportation
Science, Space, and Technology

Gibbons, Sam M., D-Fla. (11)
CAPITOL HILL OFFICE:
2204 RHOB 20515; 225-3376
Chief of Staff   Barbara Toffling

DISTRICT OFFICE:
2002 N. Lois Ave., #260, Tampa 33607; (813) 870-2101; Office Director: Greg Wonders.

COMMITTEE ASSIGNMENTS:
Joint Taxation
Ways and Means (Acting Chairman)

Gilchrest, Wayne T., R-Md. (1)
CAPITOL HILL OFFICE:
412 CHOB 20515; 225-5311
Admin. Assistant   Tony Caligiuri

DISTRICT OFFICES:
335 High St., Chestertown 21620; (410) 778-9407.
1 Plaza East, Salisbury 21801; (410) 749-3184.
101 Crain Hwy. N.W., #509, Glen Burnie 21061; (410) 760-3372.

COMMITTEE ASSIGNMENTS:
Merchant Marine and Fisheries
Public Works and Transportation

Gillmor, Paul E., R-Ohio (5)
CAPITOL HILL OFFICE:
1203 LHOB 20515; 225-6405
Admin. Assistant   Mark Wellman

DISTRICT OFFICES:
120 Jefferson St., 2nd Floor, Port Clinton 43452; (419) 734-1999; Senior District Representative: Tom Brown.
1655 N. Clinton St., Defiance 43512; (419) 782-

1996; Office Manager: Barb Barker.
  148 E. South Boundary, Perrysburg 43551; (419) 872-2500; District Representative: Tim Brown.
  County Administration Bldg., Norwalk 44857; (419) 668-0206; Office Manager: Vacant.

COMMITTEE ASSIGNMENT:
  Energy and Commerce

Gilman, Benjamin A., R-N.Y. (20)
CAPITOL HILL OFFICE:
  2185 RHOB 20515; 225-3776
  Admin. Assistant   Nancy L. Colandrea

DISTRICT OFFICES:
  44 East Ave., P.O. Box 358, Middletown 10940; (914) 343-6666; Office Manager: Molly Aumick.
  377 Route 59, Monsey 10952; (914) 357-9000; District Assistant: Carmel Wilson.
  32 Main St., Hastings-on-Hudson 10706; (914) 478-5550; District Assistant: Valerie Jennings.

COMMITTEE ASSIGNMENTS:
  Foreign Affairs (Ranking)
  Post Office and Civil Service

Gingrich, Newt, R-Ga. (6)
CAPITOL HILL OFFICE:
  2428 RHOB 20515; 225-4501
  Admin. Assistant   Annette E. Thompson

DISTRICT OFFICE:
  3823 Roswell Rd., #200, Marietta 30062; (404) 565-6398; Office Director: Jeff Wansley.

COMMITTEE ASSIGNMENTS:
  House Administration
  Joint Printing

Glickman, Dan, D-Kan. (4)
CAPITOL HILL OFFICE:
  2371 RHOB 20515; 225-6216
  Admin. Assistant   Marc A. Pearl

DISTRICT OFFICES:
  401 N. Market, Wichita 67202; (316) 262-8396; District Director: Melissa Gregory.
  325 N. Penn, Independence 67301; (316) 331-8056; District Aide: John Lechliter.

COMMITTEE ASSIGNMENTS:
  Agriculture
  Judiciary
  Science, Space, and Technology
  Select Intelligence (Chairman)

Gonzalez, Henry B., D-Texas (20)
CAPITOL HILL OFFICE:
  2413 RHOB 20515; 225-3236
  Legislative Director   Jennifer Sada

DISTRICT OFFICE:
  727 E. Durango Blvd., #B124, San Antonio 78206; (512) 229-6195; Legis. Director: Jennifer Cell Sada.

COMMITTEE ASSIGNMENT:
  Banking, Finance, and Urban Affairs (Chairman)

Goodlatte, Robert W., R-Va. (6)
CAPITOL HILL OFFICE:
  214 CHOB 20515; 225-5431
  Admin. Assistant   Tim Phillips

DISTRICT OFFICES:
  10 Franklin Rd. S.E., #540, Roanoke 24011; (703) 857-2672; District Director: Steve Landes.
  114 N. Central Ave., Staunton 24401; (703) 885-3861; District Representative: Pete Larkin.
  2 S. Main St., Harrisonburg 22801; (703) 432-2391; District Representative: Phoebe Orebaugh.
  916 Main St., #300, Lynchburg 24505; (804) 845-8306; District Representative: Clarkie Jester.

COMMITTEE ASSIGNMENTS:
  Agriculture
  Judiciary

Goodling, Bill, R-Pa. (19)
CAPITOL HILL OFFICE:
  2263 RHOB 20515; 225-5836
  Fax: 226-1000
  Admin. Assistant   Pete Tartline

DISTRICT OFFICES:
  200 S. George St., York 17405; (717) 843-8887; District Coordinator: Nancy Newcomer.
  212 N. Hanover St., Carlisle 17013; (717) 243-5432; Office Director: Charles Walters.
  140 Baltimore St., #210, Gettysburg 17325; (717) 334-3430; Office Director: Georgiana Wetmore.
  2020 Yale Ave., Camp Hill 17011; (717) 763-1988; Staff Assistant: Dot Forrey.
  44 Frederick St., Hanover 17331; (717) 632-7855; Office Director: Georgiana Wetmore.

COMMITTEE ASSIGNMENTS:
  Education and Labor (Ranking)
  Foreign Affairs

Gordon, Bart, D-Tenn. (6)
CAPITOL HILL OFFICE:
  103 CHOB 20515; 225-4231
  Admin. Assistant   Steve Rogers

DISTRICT OFFICES:
  106 S. Maple St., Murfreesboro 37130; (615) 896-1986; Fax: (615) 896-8218; District Director Kent Syler.
  17 S. Jefferson St., Cookeville 38501; (615) 528-5907; District Representative: Billy G. Smith.

COMMITTEE ASSIGNMENTS:
  Budget
  Rules

Goss, Porter J., R-Fla. (14)

CAPITOL HILL OFFICE:
  330 CHOB 20515; 225-2536
  Fax: 225-6820
    Chief of Staff   Sheryl Wooley

DISTRICT OFFICES:
  2000 Main St., #303, Fort Meyers 33901; (813) 332-4677; Fax: (813) 332-1743; District Scheduler: Linda Uhler.
  3301 Tamiami Trail E., Bldg. F, #212, Naples 33962; (813) 774-8060; Fax: (813) 774-7262; Community Outreach Coordinator: Kelleen Jackson.

COMMITTEE ASSIGNMENTS:
  Rules
  Standards of Official Conduct

Grams, Rod, R-Minn. (6)

CAPITOL HILL OFFICE:
  1713 LHOB 20515; 225-2271
    Admin. Assistant   Chris Crikstrup

DISTRICT OFFICE:
  2013 2nd Ave. North, #30, Anoka 55303; (612) 427-5921; District Office Manager: Barb Sykora.

COMMITTEE ASSIGNMENTS:
  Banking, Finance, and Urban Affairs
  Science, Space, and Technology

Grandy, Fred, R-Iowa (5)

CAPITOL HILL OFFICE:
  418 CHOB 20515; 225-5476
    Acting Admin. Assistant   Nancy Sheppard

DISTRICT OFFICES:
  4501 Southern Hills Dr., #21, Sioux City 51106; (712) 276-5800; District Director: Lori Grosbeck.
  822 Central Ave., #102, Fort Dodge 50501; (515) 573-2738; District Representative: Ryan Ludvigson.
  14 W. 5th St., Spencer 51301; (712) 262-6480; Staff Assistant: Lois Clark.

COMMITTEE ASSIGNMENTS:
  Standards of Official Conduct (Ranking)
  Ways and Means

Green, Gene, D-Texas (29)

CAPITOL HILL OFFICE:
  1004 LHOB 20515; 225-1688
    Admin. Assistant   Moses Mercado

DISTRICT OFFICES:
  5502 Lawndale, Houston 77023; (713) 923-9961;

District Manager: Rhonda Jackson.
  420 W. 19th St., Houston 77008; Office Manager: Vacant.

COMMITTEE ASSIGNMENTS:
  Education and Labor
  Government Operations
  Merchant Marine and Fisheries

Greenwood, James C., R-Pa. (8)

CAPITOL HILL OFFICE:
  515 CHOB 20515; 225-4276
    Admin. Assistant   Judy Borger

DISTRICT OFFICES:
  69 E. Oakland Ave., Doylestown 18901; (215) 348-7511; Administrative Assistant: Pete Krauss.
  1 Oxford Valley, #800, Langhorne 19047; (215) 752-7711; Executive Assistant: Pete Johnson.

COMMITTEE ASSIGNMENT:
  Energy and Commerce

Gunderson, Steve, R-Wis. (3)

CAPITOL HILL OFFICE:
  2235 RHOB 20515; 225-5506
    Admin. Assistant   Kris Deininger

DISTRICT OFFICE:
  622 E. State Highway 54, P.O. Box 247, Black River Falls 54615; (715) 284-7431; Fax: (715) 284-5503; District Director: Marlene Hanson.

COMMITTEE ASSIGNMENTS:
  Agriculture
  Education and Labor

Gutierrez, Luis V., D-Ill. (4)

CAPITOL HILL OFFICE:
  1208 LHOB 20515; 225-8203
  Fax: 225-7810
    Admin. Assistant   Doug Scofield

DISTRICT OFFICE:
  318 N. Elston Ave., Chicago 60618; (312) 509-0999; Fax: (312) 509-0152; Site Director: Steve Shavers.

COMMITTEE ASSIGNMENTS:
  Banking, Finance, and Urban Affairs
  Foreign Affairs
  Veterans' Affairs

Hall, Ralph M., D-Texas (4)

CAPITOL HILL OFFICE:
  2236 RHOB 20515; 225-6673
    Admin. Assistant   James D. Cole

DISTRICT OFFICES:
104 N. San Jacinto St., Rockwall 75087; (214) 771-9118; Office Director: Diane Milliken.
211 Federal Bldg., Tyler 75702; (903) 597-3729; Office Director: Martha Glover.
119 Federal Bldg., Sherman 75090; (903) 892-1112; Office Director: Mike Allen.
Cooke County Courthouse, Gainesville 76240; (817) 668-6370; Fax: (817) 668-6478; Office Director: Marsha Shasteen.

COMMITTEE ASSIGNMENTS:
Energy and Commerce
Science, Space, and Technology

Hall, Tony P., D-Ohio (3)
CAPITOL HILL OFFICE:
2264 RHOB 20515; 225-6465
Chief of Staff   Rick Carne

DISTRICT OFFICE:
200 W. 2nd St., #501, Dayton 45402; (513) 225-2843; District Director: William Monita.

COMMITTEE ASSIGNMENT:
Rules

Hamburg, Dan, D-Calif. (1)
CAPITOL HILL OFFICE:
114 CHOB 20515; 225-3311
Fax: 225-7710
Admin. Assistant   Meg Ryan-O'Donnell

DISTRICT OFFICES:
910 A Waugh Lane, Ukiah 95482; (707) 462-1716; Staff Assistant: Dave Nelson.
229 Eye St., #12, Crescent City 95531; (707) 465-0112; Staff Assistant: Cinda Caine-Cornell.
710 E St., Eureka 95501; (707) 441-4949; Staff Assistant: Claire Courtney.
1040 Main St., #103, Napa 94559; (707) 254-8508; Staff Assistant: Arlene Corsello.
817 Missouri St., #3, Fairfield 94533; (707) 426-0287; Staff Assistant: Martin Netis.

COMMITTEE ASSIGNMENTS:
Merchant Marine and Fisheries
Public Works and Transportation

Hamilton, Lee H., D-Ind. (9)
CAPITOL HILL OFFICE:
2187 RHOB 20515; 225-5315
Chief of Staff   Jonathan Friedman

DISTRICT OFFICE:
1201 E. 10th St., #107, Jeffersonville 47130; (812) 288-3999; Fax: (812) 288-3877; Admin. Assistant: Wayne Vance.

COMMITTEE ASSIGNMENTS:
Foreign Affairs (Chairman)
Joint Economic

Hancock, Mel, R-Mo. (7)
CAPITOL HILL OFFICE:
129 CHOB 20515; 225-6536
Admin. Assistant   Duncan Haggart

DISTRICT OFFICES:
2840 E. Chestnut Expressway, Springfield 65802; (417) 862-4317; Office Manager: Barbara Dixon.
302 Federal Bldg., Joplin 64801; (417) 781-1041; Office Manager: Bea White.

COMMITTEE ASSIGNMENT:
Ways and Means

Hansen, James V., R-Utah (1)
CAPITOL HILL OFFICE:
2466 RHOB 20515; 225-0453
Admin. Assistant   Nancee W. Blockinger

DISTRICT OFFICES:
324 25th St., #1017, Ogden 84401; (801) 393-8362.
435 E. Tabernacle, #301, St. George 84770; (801) 628-1017; Office Director: Vacant.

COMMITTEE ASSIGNMENTS:
Armed Services
Natural Resources
Select Intelligence

Harman, Jane, D-Calif. (36)
CAPITOL HILL OFFICE:
325 CHOB 20515; 225-8220
Fax: 226-0684
Admin. Assistant   Vacant

DISTRICT OFFICE:
5200 W. Century Blvd., #960, Los Angeles 90045; (310) 348-8220; District Manager: Judy Sitzer.

COMMITTEE ASSIGNMENTS:
Armed Services
Science, Space, and Technology

Hastert, Dennis, R-Ill. (14)
CAPITOL HILL OFFICE:
2453 RHOB 20515; 225-2976
Fax: 225-0697
Chief of Staff   Scott B. Palmer

DISTRICT OFFICES:
27 N. River St., Batavia 60510; (708) 406-1114; Fax: (708) 406-1808; Office Manager: Lisa Post.

1007 Main St., Mendota 61342; (815) 538-3322; Fax: (815) 538-3324; Office Manager: Bonnie Walsh.

COMMITTEE ASSIGNMENTS:
Energy and Commerce
Government Operations

Hastings, Alcee L., D-Fla. (23)
CAPITOL HILL OFFICE:
1039 LHOB 20515; 225-1313
Fax: 226-0690
Admin. Assistant Vacant

DISTRICT OFFICES:
2701 W. Oakland Park Blvd., Fort Lauderdale 33311; (305) 733-2800; Fax: (305) 735-9444; District Representative: Arthur Kennedy.
5725 Corporate Way, #208, West Palm Beach 33407; (407) 684-0565; Fax: (407) 684-3613; Representative: Mikel Jones.

COMMITTEE ASSIGNMENTS:
Foreign Affairs
Merchant Marine and Fisheries
Post Office and Civil Service

Hayes, Jimmy, D-La. (7)
CAPITOL HILL OFFICE:
2432 RHOB 20515; 225-2031
Fax: 225-1175
Chief of Staff John Doyle

DISTRICT OFFICES:
109 E. Vermillion, Lafayette 70501; (318) 233-4773; District Director: Louis Perrett.
901 Lake Shore Dr., #402, Lake Charles 70601; (318) 433-1613; Office Director: Cheryl Senegal.

COMMITTEE ASSIGNMENTS:
Government Operations
Public Works and Transportation
Science, Space, and Technology

Hefley, Joel, R-Colo. (5)
CAPITOL HILL OFFICE:
2442 RHOB 20515; 225-4422
Executive Assistant Anna Osborne

DISTRICT OFFICES:
104 S. Cascade Ave., #105, Colorado Springs 80903; (719) 520-0055; Office Director: Connie Solomon.
9605 Maroon Circle, #220, Englewood 80112; (303) 792-3923; Staff Assistant: Angela D'Aurio.

COMMITTEE ASSIGNMENTS:
Armed Services
Natural Resources
Small Business

Hefner, W. G. "Bill," D-N.C. (8)
CAPITOL HILL OFFICE:
2470 RHOB 20515; 225-3715
Admin. Assistant Bill McEwen

DISTRICT OFFICES:
101 Union St. South, P.O. Box 385, Concord 28026; (704) 786-1612; Office Manager: Virginia Jochems.
507 W. Innes St., P.O. Box 4220, Salisbury 28144; (704) 636-0635; District Office Manager: Sharon Banner-Sheelor.
230 E. Franklin, P.O. Box 1503, Rockingham 28379; (919) 997-2070; Office Director: David Perry.

COMMITTEE ASSIGNMENT:
Appropriations

Herger, Wally, R-Calif. (2)
CAPITOL HILL OFFICE:
2433 RHOB 20515; 225-3076
Fax: 225-3245
Admin. Assistant John P. Magill

DISTRICT OFFICES:
55 Independence Circle, #104, Chico 95926; (916) 893-8363; Office Director: Fran Peace.
410 Hemsted Dr., #115, Redding 96002; (916) 223-5898; Field Representative: Shannon Phillips.

COMMITTEE ASSIGNMENTS:
Budget
Ways and Means

Hilliard, Earl F., D-Ala. (7)
CAPITOL HILL OFFICE:
1007 LHOB 20515; 225-2665
Fax: 226-0772
Admin. Assistant Tunstall Wilson

DISTRICT OFFICES:
P.O. Box 2627, Tuscaloosa 35403; (205) 752-3578; Office Director: Kay Presley.
15 Lee St., #301, Montgomery 36104; (205) 262-4724; Office Director: Robert Lange.
Federal Bldg., Selma 36701; (205) 872-2684; Office Director: Betty Calloway.
1800 5th Ave. North, #305, Birmingham 35203; (205) 328-2841; Office Director: Elvira Willoughby.

COMMITTEE ASSIGNMENTS:
Agriculture
Small Business

Hinchey, Maurice D., D-N.Y. (26)
CAPITOL HILL OFFICE:
1313 LHOB 20515; 225-6335
Fax: 226-0774
Admin. Assistant Eleanor Nash-Brown

DISTRICT OFFICES:
291 Wall St., Kingston 12401; (914) 331-4466; Fax: (914) 331-7456; Office Manager: Hazel Spano.
100A Federal Bldg., Binghampton 13901; (607) 773-2768; Fax: (607) 773-1789; Office Manager: Kay Coudriet.
Carriage House, Terrace Hill, Ithaca 14850; (607) 273-1388; Fax: (607) 273-8847; Office Manager: Marsha Mosher.

COMMITTEE ASSIGNMENTS:
Banking, Finance, and Urban Affairs
Natural Resources

Hoagland, Peter, D-Neb. (2)
CAPITOL HILL OFFICE:
1113 LHOB 20515; 225-4155
Fax: 225-4684
Admin. Assistant   Kathleen Ambrose

DISTRICT OFFICE:
8424 Zorinsky Federal Bldg., Omaha 68102; (402) 344-8701; Fax: (402) 344-8706; Office Director: Paul Landow.

COMMITTEE ASSIGNMENT:
Ways and Means

Hobson, David L., R-Ohio (7)
CAPITOL HILL OFFICE:
1507 LHOB 20515; 225-4324
Chief of Staff   Mary Beth Carozza

DISTRICT OFFICES:
150 N. Limestone St., Springfield 45501; (513) 325-0474; District Director: Eileen Austria.
212 S. Broad St., Lancaster 43130; (614) 654-5149; District Director: Eileen Austria.

COMMITTEE ASSIGNMENTS:
Appropriations
Budget
Standards of Official Conduct

Hochbrueckner, George J., D-N.Y. (1)
CAPITOL HILL OFFICE:
229 CHOB 20515; 225-3826
Fax: 225-0776
Admin. Assistant   Tom Downs

DISTRICT OFFICES:
3771 Nesconset Highway, #213, Centereach 11720; (516) 689-6767; Fax: (516) 751-6112; District Director: Ellen Joyce.
437 E. Main St., Riverhead 11901; (516) 727-2152; Office Director: Ellen Joyce.

COMMITTEE ASSIGNMENTS:
Armed Services
Merchant Marine and Fisheries

Hoekstra, Peter, R-Mich. (2)
CAPITOL HILL OFFICE:
1319 LHOB 20515; 225-4401
Fax: 226-0779
Executive Assistant   Cindy Harrington

DISTRICT OFFICES:
42 W. 10th St., Holland 49423; (616) 395-0030; Fax: (616) 395-0271; District Manager: Jim Johnson.
900 3rd St., #203, Muskegon 49440; (616) 722-8386; Fax: (616) 722-0176; Office Manager: Jerry Kooiman.
120 W. Harris St., Cadillac 49601; (616) 775-0050; Fax: (616) 775-0298; Office Manager: Jill Brown.

COMMITTEE ASSIGNMENTS:
Education and Labor
Public Works and Transportation

Hoke, Martin R., R-Ohio (10)
CAPITOL HILL OFFICE:
212 CHOB 20515; 225-5871
Fax: 226-0994
Admin. Assistant   Ed Cassidy

DISTRICT OFFICE:
21270 Lorain Rd., Fairview Park 44126; (216) 356-2010.

COMMITTEE ASSIGNMENTS:
Budget
Science, Space, and Technology

Holden, Tim, D-Pa. (6)
CAPITOL HILL OFFICE:
1421 LHOB 20515; 225-5546
Fax: 226-0996
Admin. Assistant   Tom Gajewski

DISTRICT OFFICES:
633 Court St., 1st Floor, Reading 19601; (215) 371-9931; Fax: (215) 371-9939; Staff Director: Tim Smith.
101 N. Centre St., #303, Pottsville 17901; (717) 622-4212; Fax: (717) 628-2561; Office Manager: Connie Caldonetti.
Northumberland County Courthouse, Market Square, Sunbury 17801; (717) 988-1902; Office Manager: Connie Caldonetti.

COMMITTEE ASSIGNMENTS:
Agriculture
Armed Services

Horn, Steve, R-Calif. (38)
CAPITOL HILL OFFICE:
1023 LHOB 20515; 225-6676
Fax: 226-1012
Chief of Staff   Jim Dykstra

DISTRICT OFFICE:
4010 Watson Plaza Dr., #160, Lakewood 90712; (310) 425-1336; Fax: (310) 425-4591; District Manager: Connie Sziebl.

COMMITTEE ASSIGNMENTS:
Government Operations
Public Works and Transportation

Houghton, Amo, R-N.Y. (31)
CAPITOL HILL OFFICE:
1110 LHOB 20515; 225-3161
Fax: 225-5574
Admin. Assistant   Brian Fitzpatrick

DISTRICT OFFICES:
32 Dennison Parkway West, Corning 14830; (607) 937-3333; Fax: (607) 937-6047; Office Director: Jackie O'Neill.
122 Federal Bldg., Prendergast and 3rd Sts., Jamestown 14701; (716) 484-0252; Fax: (716) 484-8178; Office Director: Mickey Brown.
Westgate Plaza, W. State St., Olean 14760; (716) 372-2127; Fax: (716) 373-4750; Office Manager: Nancy Clark.

COMMITTEE ASSIGNMENT:
Ways and Means

Hoyer, Steny H., D-Md. (5)
CAPITOL HILL OFFICE:
1705 LHOB 20515; 225-4131
Chief of Staff   William Black

DISTRICT OFFICES:
4201 Northview Dr., #403, Bowie 20716; (301) 464-6440; District Director: John Bohanon.
21A Industrial Park Dr., #101, Waldorf 20602; (301) 843-1577; District Director: John Bohanon.

COMMITTEE ASSIGNMENTS:
Appropriations
House Administration

Huffington, Michael, R-Calif. (22)
CAPITOL HILL OFFICE:
113 CHOB 20515; 225-3601
Fax: 226-1015
Admin. Assistant   Fleming Saunders

DISTRICT OFFICES:
1819 State St., Suite D, Santa Barbara 93101; (805) 682-6600; District Director: David Gray.
1060 Palm St., Suite A, San Luis Obispo 93401; (805) 542-0426; Fax: (805) 542-0364; District Assistant: Brian Nestande.
910 E. Stowell Rd., Santa Maria 93454; (805) 349-9357; Office Manager: Anna Nickerson.

COMMITTEE ASSIGNMENTS:
Banking, Finance, and Urban Affairs
Small Business

Hughes, William J., D-N.J. (2)
CAPITOL HILL OFFICE:
241 CHOB 20515; 225-6572
Fax: 225-8530
Admin. Assistant   Mark Brown

DISTRICT OFFICES:
222 New Rd., #5, Linwood 08221; (609) 927-9063; Fax: (609) 927-9329; Staff Assistant: Jessie Simmons.
151 N. Broadway, P.O. Box 248, Pennsville 08070; (609) 678-3333; Fax: (609) 678-9020; Staff Assistant: Bernice Willadsen.

COMMITTEE ASSIGNMENTS:
Judiciary
Merchant Marine and Fisheries

Hunter, Duncan, R-Calif. (52)
CAPITOL HILL OFFICE:
133 CHOB 20515; 225-5672
Fax: 225-0235
Admin. Assistant   Victoria J. Middleton

DISTRICT OFFICES:
366 S. Pierce St., El Cajon 92020; (619) 579-3001; Fax: (619) 579-2251; District Admin.: Wendell Cutting.
1101 Airport Rd., Suite G, Imperial 92251; (619) 353-5420; Fax: (619) 353-3003; Office Director: Carole Starr.

COMMITTEE ASSIGNMENT:
Armed Services

Hutchinson, Tim, R-Ark. (3)
CAPITOL HILL OFFICE:
1541 LHOB 20515; 225-4301
Chief of Staff   Ray Reid

DISTRICT OFFICES:
422 Federal Bldg., Fayetteville 72701; (501) 442-5258; District Assistant: Todd Deatherage.
P.O. Box 579, Harrison 72601; (501) 741-6900; District Assistant: Karen Hopper.
P.O. Box 1624, Fort Smith 72902; (501) 782-7787; Senior District Assistant: Archie Lantz.

COMMITTEE ASSIGNMENTS:
Public Works and Transportation
Veterans' Affairs

Hutto, Earl, D-Fla. (1)
CAPITOL HILL OFFICE:
2435 RHOB 20515; 225-4136

Fax: 225-5785
Admin. Assistant   Gary P. Pulliam

DISTRICT OFFICES:
P.O. Box 17689, Pensacola 32522; (904) 478-1123; Fax: (904) 478-8071; District Admin.: Ben Collins.
Courthouse Annex, Shalimar 32579; (904) 651-3111; Fax: (904) 651-8928; District Representative: Larry Williamson.
P.O. Box 459, Panama City 32402; (904) 872-8813; Fax: (904) 872-8326; District Representative: Earl J. Hadaway.

COMMITTEE ASSIGNMENTS:
Armed Services
Merchant Marine and Fisheries

Hyde, Henry J., R-Ill. (6)
CAPITOL HILL OFFICE:
2110 RHOB 20515; 225-4561
Fax: 226-1240
Chief of Staff   Judy Wolverton

DISTRICT OFFICE:
50 E. Oak St., #200, Addison 60101; (708) 832-5950; Office Manager: Alice Horstman.

COMMITTEE ASSIGNMENTS:
Foreign Affairs
Judiciary

Inglis, Bob, R-S.C. (4)
CAPITOL HILL OFFICE:
1237 LHOB 20515; 225-6030
Fax: 226-1177
Admin. Assistant   Jeff Fedorchak

DISTRICT OFFICES:
300 E. Washington St., #101, Greenville 29601; (803) 232-1141; Fax: (803) 233-2160; District Admin.: Max Metcalf.
201 Magnolia St., #108, Spartanburg 29301; (803) 582-6422; Fax: (803) 573-9478; Constituent Services Manager: Ray Wynn.
405 W. Main St., Union 29379; (803) 427-2205; Fax: (803) 429-8879; Constituent Liaison: Toni Greer.

COMMITTEE ASSIGNMENTS:
Budget
Judiciary

Inhofe, James M., R-Okla. (1)
CAPITOL HILL OFFICE:
442 CHOB 20515; 225-2211
Fax: 225-9187
Chief of Staff   D. Stephen Edwards

DISTRICT OFFICE:
1924 S. Utica, #530, Tulsa 74104; (918) 581-7111; Fax: (918) 581-7770.

COMMITTEE ASSIGNMENTS:
Armed Services
Merchant Marine and Fisheries
Public Works and Transportation

Inslee, Jay, D-Wash. (4)
CAPITOL HILL OFFICE:
1431 LHOB 20515; 225-5816
Fax: 226-1137
Chief of Staff   Lisa Garza

DISTRICT OFFICES:
701 N. 1st St., Suite B, Yakima 98901; (509) 452-3243; Fax: (509) 452-3438.
3311 W. Clearwater, #105, Kennewick 99336; (509) 783-0310; Fax: (509) 735-9573.
112 N. Mission St., Wenatchee 98801; (509) 662-4294; Fax: (509) 662-4295; District Caseworker: Stephanie Gilliland.

COMMITTEE ASSIGNMENTS:
Agriculture
Science, Space, and Technology

Istook, Ernest Jim, Jr., R-Okla. (5)
CAPITOL HILL OFFICE:
1116 LHOB 20515; 225-2132
Admin. Assistant   Brian Lopina

DISTRICT OFFICES:
5400 N. Grand Blvd., #505, Oklahoma City 73112; (405) 942-3636; District Director: Dwight Dissler.
5th and Grand, Ponca City 74601; (405) 762-6778; Northern Region Field Representative: Mike Wilt.
1st Court Place, #205, Bartlesville 74003; (918) 336-5546; Northern Region Field Representative: Mike Wilt.

COMMITTEE ASSIGNMENT:
Appropriations

Jacobs, Andrew, Jr., D-Ind. (10)
CAPITOL HILL OFFICE:
2313 RHOB 20515; 225-4011
Admin. Assistant   David Wildes

DISTRICT OFFICE:
46 E. Ohio St., #441A, Indianapolis 46204; (317) 226-7331; Office Manager: Loretta Raikes.

COMMITTEE ASSIGNMENT:
Ways and Means

Jefferson, William J., D-La. (2)
CAPITOL HILL OFFICE:
428 CHOB 20515; 225-6636
Chief of Staff Lionel Collins

DISTRICT OFFICE:
501 Magazine St., New Orleans 70130; (504) 589-2274; Office Director: Stephanie Edwards.

COMMITTEE ASSIGNMENTS:
District of Columbia
Ways and Means

Johnson, Don, D-Ga. (10)
CAPITOL HILL OFFICE:
226 CHOB 20515; 225-4101
Fax: 226-1466
Admin. Assistant Beverly Bell

DISTRICT OFFICES:
220 College Ave., #400, Athens 30601; (706) 353-6444; Fax: (706) 353-9669; District Coordinator: Jane Kidd.
2050 Walton Way, #212, Augusta 30904; (706) 736-3373; Fax: (706) 736-3696; Office Manager: Roberta Dush.
1108 Hunter St., Newton County Courthouse, Covington 30209; (706) 787-8667; Staff Assistant: Cathy Dobbs.

COMMITTEE ASSIGNMENTS:
Armed Services
Science, Space, and Technology

Johnson, Eddie Bernice, D-Texas (30)
CAPITOL HILL OFFICE:
1721 LHOB 20515; 225-8885
Fax: 226-1477
Admin. Assistant Bobby Johnson

DISTRICT OFFICE:
2515 McKinney Ave., #1565, Dallas 75201; (214) 922-8885; District Manager: Chris Reed-Brown.

COMMITTEE ASSIGNMENTS:
Public Works and Transportation
Science, Space, and Technology

Johnson, Nancy L., R-Conn. (6)
CAPITOL HILL OFFICE:
343 CHOB 20515; 225-4476
Fax: 225-4488
Admin. Assistant Eric Thompson

DISTRICT OFFICE:
480 Myrtle St., #200, New Britain 06053; (203) 223-8412; District Director: John Barrasso.

COMMITTEE ASSIGNMENTS:
Standards of Official Conduct
Ways and Means

Johnson, Sam, R-Texas (3)
CAPITOL HILL OFFICE:
1030 LHOB 20515; 225-4201
Fax: 225-1485
Admin. Assistant Shannon Smith

DISTRICT OFFICES:
9400 N. Central Expressway, #610, Dallas 75231; (214) 739-0182; Fax: (214) 739-2183; District Director: Mary Lynn Murrell.
1912 Ave. K, #204, Plano 75074; (214) 423-2017; District Director: Mary Lynn Murrell.

COMMITTEE ASSIGNMENTS:
Banking, Finance, and Urban Affairs
Science, Space, and Technology
Small Business

Johnson, Tim, D-S.D. (AL)
CAPITOL HILL OFFICE:
2438 RHOB 20515; 225-2801
Fax: 225-2427
Admin. Assistant Drey Samuelson

DISTRICT OFFICES:
515 South Dakota Ave., Sioux Falls 57102; (605) 332-8896; Fax: (605) 332-2824; Office Director: Sharon Bertram.
809 South St., #104, Rapid City 57701; (605) 341-3990; Fax: (605) 341-2207; Office Director: Darrell Shoemaker.
20 6th Ave. S.W., Suite C, Aberdeen 57401; (605) 226-3440; Fax: (605) 226-2439; Office Director: Sharon Stroschein.

COMMITTEE ASSIGNMENTS:
Agriculture
Natural Resources

Johnston, Harry A., D-Fla. (19)
CAPITOL HILL OFFICE:
204 CHOB 20515; 225-3001
Fax: 225-8791
Chief of Staff Suzanne M. Stoll

DISTRICT OFFICES:
1501 Corporate Dr., #250, Boynton Beach 33426; (407) 732-4000; Fax: (407) 736-2455; District Assistant: Diane Kohl Birnbaum.
5790 Margate Blvd., Margate 33063; (305) 972-6454; District Assistant: Diane Kohl Birnbaum.

COMMITTEE ASSIGNMENTS:
Budget
Foreign Affairs

Kanjorski, Paul E., D-Pa. (11)
CAPITOL HILL OFFICE:
2429 RHOB 20515; 225-6511
Fax: 225-9024
Admin. Assistant   Karen Feather

DISTRICT OFFICES:
10 E. South St., Wilkes-Barre 18701; (717) 825-2200; Appts. Secretary: Ellen Donlavage.
9th and Spruce Sts., Kulpmont 17834; (717) 373-1541; Staff Assistant: Henry Sgro.

COMMITTEE ASSIGNMENTS:
Banking, Finance, and Urban Affairs
Post Office and Civil Service

Kaptur, Marcy, D-Ohio (9)
CAPITOL HILL OFFICE:
2104 RHOB 20515; 225-4146
Fax: 225-7711
Chief of Staff   Fariborz S. Fatemi

DISTRICT OFFICE:
234 Summit St., #719, Toledo 43604; (419) 259-7500; District Manager: Steve Katich.

COMMITTEE ASSIGNMENT:
Appropriations

Kasich, John R., R-Ohio (12)
CAPITOL HILL OFFICE:
1131 LHOB 20515; 225-5355
Chief of Staff   Don Thibaut

DISTRICT OFFICE:
200 N. High St., #500, Columbus 43215; (614) 469-7318; Office Manager: Sally Testa.

COMMITTEE ASSIGNMENTS:
Armed Services
Budget (Ranking)

Kennedy, Joseph P., II, D-Mass. (8)
CAPITOL HILL OFFICE:
1210 LHOB 20515; 225-5111
Admin. Assistant   Michael Powell

DISTRICT OFFICES:
529 Main St., #605, Charlestown 02129; (617) 242-0200; Office Director: Brian O'Connor.
801A Tremont St., Roxbury 02118; (617) 445-1281; Office Director: Jim Spencer.

COMMITTEE ASSIGNMENTS:
Banking, Finance, and Urban Affairs
Veterans' Affairs

Kennelly, Barbara B., D-Conn. (1)
CAPITOL HILL OFFICE:

201 CHOB 20515; 225-2265
Fax: 225-1031
Admin. Assistant   Ross Brown

DISTRICT OFFICE:
1 Corporate Center, Hartford 06103; (203) 278-8888; Fax: (203) 278-2111; District Director: Robert Croce.

COMMITTEE ASSIGNMENTS:
Budget
House Administration
Ways and Means

Kildee, Dale E., D-Mich. (9)
CAPITOL HILL OFFICE:
2239 RHOB 20515; 225-3611
Fax: 225-6393
Admin. Assistant   Christopher Mansour

DISTRICT OFFICES:
1829 N. Perry St., Pontiac 48340; (810) 373-9337; Fax: (810) 373-6955; District Director: Gary Sullenger.
316 W. Water St., Flint 48503; (810) 239-1437; Fax: (810) 239-1439; District Director: Gary Sullenger.

COMMITTEE ASSIGNMENTS:
Budget
Education and Labor
House Administration

Kim, Jay C., R-Calif. (41)
CAPITOL HILL OFFICE:
502 CHOB 20515; 225-3201
Fax: 226-1485
Admin. Assistant   Sandra Garner

DISTRICT OFFICES:
1131 W. 6th St., #160A, Ontario 91762; (909) 988-1055; Fax: (909) 988-5723; Chief of Staff: Sandra Garner.
18200 Yorba Linda Blvd., #203A, Yorba Linda 92686; (714) 572-8574; Fax: (714) 572-8577; Constituent Liaison: Phyllis Schneider.

COMMITTEE ASSIGNMENTS:
Public Works and Transportation
Small Business

King, Peter T., R-N.Y. (3)
CAPITOL HILL OFFICE:
118 CHOB 20515; 225-7896
Fax: 226-2279
Admin. Assistant   Jon Hymes

DISTRICT OFFICE:
1003 Park Blvd., Massapequa 11762; (516) 541-4225; Fax: (516) 541-6602; District Manager: Randy Yunker.

COMMITTEE ASSIGNMENTS:
Banking, Finance, and Urban Affairs
Merchant Marine and Fisheries
Veterans' Affairs

Kingston, Jack, R-Ga. (1)
CAPITOL HILL OFFICE:
1229 LHOB 20515; 225-5831
Fax: 226-2269
Admin. Assistant   Paul Powell

DISTRICT OFFICES:
6605 Abercorn St., #102, Savannah 31405; (912) 352-0101; Fax: (912) 352-0105; District Director: Peggy Lee Mowers.
Statesboro Federal Bldg., #220, Statesboro 30458; (912) 489-8797; Fax: (912) 764-8549; Office Manager: Floy Thackston.
805 Gloucester St., #304, Brunswick 31520; (912) 265-9010; Fax: (912) 265-9013; Office Manager: Becki Bernier.
208 Tebeau St., Waycross 31501; (912) 287-1180; Fax: (912) 287-1182; Office Manager: Malcolm Vass.

COMMITTEE ASSIGNMENTS:
Agriculture
Merchant Marine and Fisheries

Kleczka, Gerald D., D-Wis. (4)
CAPITOL HILL OFFICE:
2301 RHOB 20515; 225-4572
Fax: 225-8135
Admin. Assistant   Jennifer McKenzie

DISTRICT OFFICES:
5032 W. Forest Home Ave., Milwaukee 53219; (414) 297-1140; Fax: (414) 327-6151; Chief of Staff: Kathy Hein.
414 W. Moreland Blvd., #105, Waukesha 53188; (414) 549-6360; Fax: (414) 549-6723; Constituent Liaison: Laurie Grabow.

COMMITTEE ASSIGNMENTS:
House Administration
Joint Printing
Ways and Means

Klein, Herb, D-N.J. (8)
CAPITOL HILL OFFICE:
1728 LHOB 20515; 225-5751
Fax: 226-2273
Admin. Assistant   William J. Pascrell

DISTRICT OFFICE:
Robert A. Roe Federal Bldg., 200 Federal Plaza,

#500, Paterson 07505; (201) 523-5152; Fax: (201) 523-0637; District Manager: Peter Rendina, Jr.

COMMITTEE ASSIGNMENTS:
Banking, Finance, and Urban Affairs
Science, Space, and Technology

Klink, Ron, D-Pa. (4)
CAPITOL HILL OFFICE:
1130 LHOB 20515; 225-2565
Fax: 226-2274
Admin. Assistant   Brent Ayer

DISTRICT OFFICES:
11279 Center Highway, North Huntingdon 15642; (412) 864-8681; Fax: (412) 864-8691; District Manager: Joe Brimmeier.
250 Insurance St., #305, Beaver 15009; (412) 728-3005; Fax: (412) 728-3095; Caseworker: Brian Hayden.
2700 D Rochester Rd., Mars 16046; (412) 772-6080; Fax: (412) 772-6099; Caseworker: Dick Picio.
134 N. Mercer St., New Castle 16101; (412) 654-9036; Fax: (412) 654-9076; Caseworker: Jim Comianos.

COMMITTEE ASSIGNMENTS:
Banking, Finance, and Urban Affairs
Education and Labor
Small Business

Klug, Scott L., R-Wis. (2)
CAPITOL HILL OFFICE:
1224 LHOB 20515; 225-2906
Fax: 225-6942
Admin. Assistant   Brandon Scholz

DISTRICT OFFICE:
16 N. Carroll St., #600, Madison 53703; (608) 257-9200; Office Director: Judy Lowell.

COMMITTEE ASSIGNMENT:
Energy and Commerce

Knollenberg, Joe, R-Mich. (11)
CAPITOL HILL OFFICE:
1218 LHOB 20515; 225-5802
Fax: 226-2356
Admin. Assistant   Paul Welday

DISTRICT OFFICES:
30833 Northwestern Hwy., #214, Farmington Hills 48334; (810) 851-1366; Field Representative: Pat Wierzbicki.
15439 Middlebelt, Livonia 48154; (313) 425-7557; Field Representative: Denise Radtke.

COMMITTEE ASSIGNMENTS:
Banking, Finance, and Urban Affairs
Small Business

Kolbe, Jim, R-Ariz. (5)
CAPITOL HILL OFFICE:
405 CHOB 20515; 225-2542
Fax: 225-0378
Chief of Staff   Laurie Fenton

DISTRICT OFFICES:
1661 N. Swan Rd., #112, Tucson 85712; (602) 881-3588; Fax: (602) 322-9490; District Manager: Patricia Klein.
77 Calle Portal, #B160, Sierra Vista 85635; (602) 459-3115; Fax: (602) 459-5419; District Aide: Billie Fabijan.

COMMITTEE ASSIGNMENTS:
Appropriations
Budget

Kopetski, Mike, D-Ore. (5)
CAPITOL HILL OFFICE:
218 CHOB 20515; 225-5711
Fax: 225-9477
Admin. Assistant   Phil Rotondi

DISTRICT OFFICES:
530 Center St. N.E., #340, Salem 97301; (503) 588-9100; Fax: (503) 588-0963; Office Director: Lisa Howard.
615 High St., Oregon City 97045; (503) 650-1273; Office Director: Vacant.

COMMITTEE ASSIGNMENT:
Ways and Means

Kreidler, Mike, D-Wash. (9)
CAPITOL HILL OFFICE:
1535 LHOB 20515; 225-8901
Fax: 226-2361
Admin. Assistant   Bob Crane

DISTRICT OFFICES:
312 4th St. S.E., Puyallup 98372; (206) 840-5688; District Manager: Evan Simpson.
31919 1st Ave., South #140, Federal Way 98003; (206) 946-0553; District Manager: Evan Simpson.

COMMITTEE ASSIGNMENTS:
Energy and Commerce
Veterans' Affairs

Kyl, Jon, R-Ariz. (4)
CAPITOL HILL OFFICE:
2440 RHOB 20515; 225-3361
Fax: 225-1143
Chief of Staff   Ted Maness

DISTRICT OFFICE:
4250 Camelback Rd., #140K, Phoenix 85018; (602) 840-1891; Fax: (602) 840-4848.

COMMITTEE ASSIGNMENTS:
Armed Services
Government Operations
Standards of Official Conduct

LaFalce, John J., D-N.Y. (29)
CAPITOL HILL OFFICE:
2310 RHOB 20515; 225-3231
Fax: 225-8693
Admin. Assistant   Ronald Maselka

DISTRICT OFFICES:
Federal Bldg., Buffalo 14202; (716) 846-4056; District Representative: Peter Hadrovic.
Main Post Office Bldg., Niagara Falls 14302; (716) 284-9976; Staff Assistant: Rebekah Muscoreil.
409 S. Union St., Rochester 14559; (716) 352-4777; Staff Assistant: Hannelore Heyen.

COMMITTEE ASSIGNMENTS:
Banking, Finance, and Urban Affairs
Small Business (Chairman)

Lambert, Blanche, D-Ark. (1)
CAPITOL HILL OFFICE:
1204 LHOB 20515; 225-4076
Fax: 225-4654
Admin. Assistant   Russ Orban

DISTRICT OFFICE:
615 S. Main St., #211, Jonesboro 72401; (501) 972-4600; Fax: (501) 972-4605; District Office Manager: Earline Norwood.

COMMITTEE ASSIGNMENTS:
Agriculture
Energy and Commerce
Merchant Marine and Fisheries

Lancaster, H. Martin, D-N.C. (3)
CAPITOL HILL OFFICE:
2436 RHOB 20515; 225-3415
Fax: 225-0666
Admin. Assistant   Edmund B. Welch

DISTRICT OFFICE:
134 N. John St., #108, Goldsboro 27530; (919) 736-1844; Fax: (919) 734-4731; Admin. Assistant: David Warren Hepler.

COMMITTEE ASSIGNMENTS:
Armed Services
Merchant Marine and Fisheries
Small Business

Lantos, Tom, D-Calif. (12)
CAPITOL HILL OFFICE:
2182 RHOB 20515; 225-3531
Admin. Assistant   Robert R. King

DISTRICT OFFICE:
400 El Camino Real, #820, San Mateo 94402; (415) 342-0300; Office Director: Evelyn Szelenyi.

COMMITTEE ASSIGNMENTS:
Foreign Affairs
Government Operations

LaRocco, Larry, D-Idaho (1)
CAPITOL HILL OFFICE:
1117 LHOB 20515; 225-6611
Fax: 226-1213
Chief of Staff   Garry Wenske

DISTRICT OFFICES:
304 N. 8th St., Boise 83702; (208) 343-4211; Fax: (208) 343-4791; District Representative: Tom Knappenberger.
408 Sherman Ave., Coeur d'Alene 83814; (208) 667-2110; Fax: (208) 765-0111; Staff Assistant: Jeff Bell.
621 Main St., Lewiston 83501; (208) 746-6694; Fax: (208) 746-5344; Staff Assistant: Debi Fitzgerald.
109 S. Kimball Ave., Caldwell 83605; (208) 459-2362; Fax: (208) 459-7529; Staff Assistant: Julie McCoy.

COMMITTEE ASSIGNMENTS:
Banking, Finance, and Urban Affairs
Natural Resources

Laughlin, Greg, D-Texas (14)
CAPITOL HILL OFFICE:
236 CHOB 20515; 225-2831
Admin. Assistant   Bob Grasso

DISTRICT OFFICES:
312 S. Main St., Victoria 77901; (512) 576-1231; Deputy District Director: Emmett Alvarez.
Hays County Courthouse, 102 M LBJ, Annex 3, San Marcos 78666; (512) 396-1400; Deputy District Director: Linda Collinsworth.
111 N. 10th St., West Columbia 77486; (409) 345-1414; Deputy District Director: Dawn Jensen.

COMMITTEE ASSIGNMENTS:
Merchant Marine and Fisheries
Post Office and Civil Service
Public Works and Transportation
Select Intelligence

Lazio, Rick A., R-N.Y. (2)
CAPITOL HILL OFFICE:
314 CHOB 20515; 225-3335
Fax: 225-4669
Admin. Assistant   Vacant

DISTRICT OFFICE:
126 W. Main St., Babylon 11702; (516) 893-9010; Fax: (516) 893-9017; District Manager: Barbara Vogl.

COMMITTEE ASSIGNMENTS:
Banking, Finance, and Urban Affairs
Budget

Leach, Jim, R-Iowa (1)
CAPITOL HILL OFFICE:
2186 RHOB 20515; 225-6576
Fax: 226-1278
Admin. Assistant   Bill Tate

DISTRICT OFFICES:
209 W. 4th St., Davenport 52801; (319) 326-1841; Fax: (319) 326-5464; District Admin. Assistant: Linda Weeks.
308 Tenth St. S.E., Cedar Rapids 52403; (319) 363-4773; Fax: (319) 363-5008; Staff Assistant: Tom Cope.
102 S. Clinton St., #505, Iowa City 52240; (319) 351-0789; Fax: (319) 351-5789; Staff Assistant: Ginny Burris.

COMMITTEE ASSIGNMENTS:
Banking, Finance, and Urban Affairs (Ranking)
Foreign Affairs

Lehman, Richard H., D-Calif. (19)
CAPITOL HILL OFFICE:
1226 LHOB 20515; 225-4540
Admin. Assistant   Janice Morris

DISTRICT OFFICE:
2377 W. Shaw Ave., #105, Fresno 93711; (209) 248-0800; Fax: (209) 248-0619; District Representative: David Brodie.

COMMITTEE ASSIGNMENTS:
Energy and Commerce
Natural Resources

Levin, Sander M., D-Mich. (12)
CAPITOL HILL OFFICE:
106 CHOB 20515; 225-4961
Fax: 226-1033
Admin. Assistant   Rikki Baum

DISTRICT OFFICE:
2107 E. 14 Mile Rd., Sterling Heights 48310; (810) 268-4444; Fax: (810) 268-0918; Office Manager: Bonnie Hart.

COMMITTEE ASSIGNMENT:
Ways and Means

Levy, David A., R-N.Y. (4)
CAPITOL HILL OFFICE:
116 CHOB 20515; 225-5516
Fax: 225-4672
Admin. Assistant   John Falardeau

DISTRICT OFFICE:
203 Rockaway Ave., Valley Stream 11580; (516) 872-9550; Fax: (516) 872-2959; District Manager: Robert Barra.

COMMITTEE ASSIGNMENTS:
Foreign Affairs
Public Works and Transportation

Lewis, Jerry, R-Calif. (40)
CAPITOL HILL OFFICE:
2312 RHOB 20515; 225-5861
Fax: 225-6498
Admin. Assistant   Arlene Willis

DISTRICT OFFICE:
1150 Brookside Ave., #J-5, Redlands 92374; (714) 862-6030; Fax: (714) 335-9155; District Representative: Marilyn Glick.

COMMITTEE ASSIGNMENTS:
Appropriations
Select Intelligence

Lewis, John, D-Ga. (5)
CAPITOL HILL OFFICE:
329 CHOB 20515; 225-3801
Fax: 225-0351
Admin. Assistant   Linda Earley Chastang

DISTRICT OFFICE:
100 Peachtree St., #1920, Atlanta 30303; (404) 659-0116; Fax: (404) 331-0947; Chief of Staff: James Waller.

COMMITTEE ASSIGNMENTS:
District of Columbia
Ways and Means

Lewis, Tom, R-Fla. (16)
CAPITOL HILL OFFICE:
2351 RHOB 20515; 225-5792
Fax: 225-1860
Admin. Assistant   Karen Hogan

DISTRICT OFFICES:
4440 PGA Blvd., #406, Palm Beach Gardens 33410; (407) 627-6192; Fax: (407) 626-4749; District Manager: Ed Chase.
7601 S. U.S. Highway 1, #200, Port St. Lucie 34952; (407) 283-7989; Fax: (407) 871-0651; District Manager: Ann Decker.

COMMITTEE ASSIGNMENTS:
Agriculture
Science, Space, and Technology

Lightfoot, Jim Ross, R-Iowa (3)
CAPITOL HILL OFFICE:

2444 RHOB 20515; 225-3806
Fax: 225-6973
Admin. Assistant   Frank Purcell

DISTRICT OFFICES:
501 W. Lowell, Shenandoah 51601; (712) 246-1984; District Admin.: Eleanor Sligar.
220 W. Salem Ave., Indianola 50125; (515) 961-0591; Caseworker: Janice Goode.
413 Kellogg, Ames 50010; (515) 232-1288; District Representative: Dorothy Smith.
347 E. 2nd St., Ottumwa 52501; (515) 683-3551; District Representative: Jill Hrdlicka.
311 N. 3rd St., Burlington 52601; (319) 753-6415; District Representative: Violet Love.

COMMITTEE ASSIGNMENT:
Appropriations

Linder, John, R-Ga. (4)
CAPITOL HILL OFFICE:
1605 LHOB 20515; 225-4272
Fax: 225-4696
Admin. Assist.   Bob Varga

DISTRICT OFFICE:
3003 Chamblee-Tucker Rd., #140, Atlanta 30341; (404) 936-9400; Executive Director: Barbara Sedowski.

COMMITTEE ASSIGNMENTS:
Banking, Finance, and Urban Affairs
Science, Space, and Technology
Veterans' Affairs

Lipinski, William O., D-Ill. (3)
CAPITOL HILL OFFICE:
1501 LHOB 20515; 225-5701
Fax: 225-1012
Admin. Assistant   George Edwards

DISTRICT OFFICE:
5832 S. Archer Ave., Chicago 60638; (312) 886-0481; Special Assistant: Vacant.

COMMITTEE ASSIGNMENTS:
Merchant Marine and Fisheries
Public Works and Transportation

Livingston, Robert L., R-La. (1)
CAPITOL HILL OFFICE:
2368 RHOB 20515; 225-3015
Fax: 225-0739
Admin. Assistant   J. Allen Martin

DISTRICT OFFICE:
111 Veterans Blvd., #700, Metairie 70005; (504) 589-2753; Fax: (504) 589-2607; District Director: Rick LeGendre.

COMMITTEE ASSIGNMENTS:
Appropriations
House Administration

Lloyd, Marilyn, D-Tenn. (3)
CAPITOL HILL OFFICE:
2406 RHOB 20515; 225-3271
Fax: 225-6974
Admin. Assistant   Sue Sloan Carlton

DISTRICT OFFICES:
253 Jay Solomon Federal Office Bldg., Chattanooga 37401; (615) 267-9108; Fax: (615) 267-4719; Admin. Assistant: Anita Ebersole.
1211 Federal Bldg., Oak Ridge 37830; (615) 576-1977; Fax: (615) 576-3221; Admin. Assistant: Martha Wallus.

COMMITTEE ASSIGNMENTS:
Armed Services
Science, Space, and Technology

Long, Jill L., D-Ind. (4)
CAPITOL HILL OFFICE:
1513 LHOB 20515; 225-4436
Fax: 225-8810
Admin. Assistant   Inga Smulkstys

DISTRICT OFFICES:
1300 S. Harrison St., #3105, Fort Wayne 46802; (219) 424-3041; District Director: Mary Schmidt.
105 E. Mitchell, Kendallville 46755; (219) 347-5471; District Director: Mary Schmidt.
1190 U.S. 27 North, Berne 46711; (219) 589-8699; District Director: Mary Schmidt.

COMMITTEE ASSIGNMENTS:
Agriculture
Veterans' Affairs

Lowey, Nita M., D-N.Y. (18)
CAPITOL HILL OFFICE:
1424 LHOB 20515; 225-6506
Fax: 225-0546
Admin. Assistant   Scott Fleming

DISTRICT OFFICES:
222 Mamaroneck Ave., #310, White Plains 10605; (914) 428-1707; Fax: (914) 328-1505; District Director: Deborah Bohren.
97-45 Queens Blvd., #505, Rego Park 11374; (718) 897-3602; Fax: (718) 897-3804; Office Manager: Mary Colletta.

COMMITTEE ASSIGNMENT:
Appropriations

Machtley, Ronald K., R-R.I. (1)
CAPITOL HILL OFFICE:

326 CHOB 20515; 225-4911
Fax: 225-4417
Admin. Assistant   Jenny Rademacher

DISTRICT OFFICES:
268 Pawtucket Ave., East Providence 02916; (401) 434-3568; District Director: Marc Palazzo.
127 Social St., #172, Woonsocket 02895; (401) 762-4052; Congressional Assistant: Rita Bouthiller.
320 Thames St., #267, Newport 02840; (401) 848-7920; Congressional Assistant: Marilyn Borsare.

COMMITTEE ASSIGNMENTS:
Armed Services
Small Business

Maloney, Carolyn B., D-N.Y. (14)
CAPITOL HILL OFFICE:
1504 LHOB 20515; 225-7944
Fax: 225-4709
Admin. Assistant   Jeremy Rabinovitz

DISTRICT OFFICES:
28-11 Astoria Blvd., Long Island City 11102; (718) 932-1804; District Representative: Dominic Fucile.
950 3rd Ave., 19th Floor, New York 10022; (212) 832-6531; Fax: (212) 832-7576; Chief of Staff: John Wade.
619 Lorimer St., Brooklyn 11211; (718) 349-1260; District Representative: Mary Odomirok.

COMMITTEE ASSIGNMENTS:
Banking, Finance, and Urban Affairs
Government Operations

Mann, David, D-Ohio (1)
CAPITOL HILL OFFICE:
503 CHOB 20515; 225-2216
Admin. Assistant   Hannah Margetich

DISTRICT OFFICE:
1014 Vine St., #2210, Cincinnati 45202; (513) 684-2723; Chief of Operations: Timothy Riker.

COMMITTEE ASSIGNMENTS:
Armed Services
Judiciary

Manton, Thomas J., D-N.Y. (7)
CAPITOL HILL OFFICE:
203 CHOB 20515; 225-3965
Admin. Assistant   Steven Vest

DISTRICT OFFICES:
46-12 Queens Blvd., Sunnyside 11104; (718) 706-1400; District Director: Bill Driscoll.
21-14 Williamsbridge Rd., Bronx 10461; (718) 931-1400; Office Manager: Fran Mahoney.

COMMITTEE ASSIGNMENTS:
Energy and Commerce
House Administration
Merchant Marine and Fisheries

Manzullo, Donald, R-Ill. (16)
CAPITOL HILL OFFICE:
506 CHOB 20515; 225-5676
Fax: 225-5284
Admin. Assistant   James Thacker

DISTRICT OFFICES:
3929 Broadway, #1, Rockford 61108; (815) 394-1231; Director: Pam Bunting.
181 N. Virginia Ave., Crystal Lake 60014; (815) 356-9800; Caseworker: Laurie Saathoff.

COMMITTEE ASSIGNMENTS:
Foreign Affairs
Small Business

Margolies-Mezvinsky, Marjorie, D-Pa. (13)
CAPITOL HILL OFFICE:
1516 LHOB 20515; 225-6111
Admin. Assistant   Vacant

DISTRICT OFFICES:
1 Presidential Blvd., #200, Bala Cynwyd 19004; (610) 667-3666; Fax: (610) 667-3223; Chief of Staff: Linda August.
12 E. Butler Ave., #111, Ambler 19002; (215) 542-7666; Chief of Staff: Linda August.
Routes 73 and 113, P.O. Box 639, Skippack 19474; (610) 287-5666; Chief of Staff: Linda August.

COMMITTEE ASSIGNMENTS:
Energy and Commerce
Government Operations
Small Business

Markey, Edward J., D-Mass. (7)
CAPITOL HILL OFFICE:
2133 RHOB 20515; 225-2836
Admin. Assistant   Dan Rabinovitz

DISTRICT OFFICE:
15 High St., Medford 02155; (617) 396-2900; Office Manager: Carol Lederman.

COMMITTEE ASSIGNMENTS:
Energy and Commerce
Natural Resources

Martinez, Matthew G., D-Calif. (31)
CAPITOL HILL OFFICE:
2231 RHOB 20515; 225-5464
Fax: 225-5467
Admin. Assistant   Maxine Grant

DISTRICT OFFICE:
320 S. Garfield Ave., #214, Alhambra 91801; (818) 458-4524; Fax: (818) 458-7457; Chief of Staff: Maxine Grant.

COMMITTEE ASSIGNMENTS:
Education and Labor
Foreign Affairs

Matsui, Robert T., D-Calif. (5)
CAPITOL HILL OFFICE:
2311 RHOB 20515; 225-7163
Fax: 225-0566
Admin. Assistant   Tom Keaney

DISTRICT OFFICE:
650 Capitol Mall, Sacramento 95814; (916) 551-2846; Fax: (916) 444-6117; Office Director: Collette Johnson-Schulke.

COMMITTEE ASSIGNMENT:
Ways and Means

Mazzoli, Romano L., D-Ky. (3)
CAPITOL HILL OFFICE:
2246 RHOB 20515; 225-5401
Fax: 225-5249
Staff Director   Jane Kirby

DISTRICT OFFICE:
600 Dr. Martin Luther King Jr. Place, #216, Louisville 40202; (502) 582-5129; Chief of Staff: Charles Mattingly.

COMMITTEE ASSIGNMENTS:
Judiciary
Small Business

McCandless, Al, R-Calif. (44)
CAPITOL HILL OFFICE:
2422 RHOB 20515; 225-5330
Fax: 226-1040
Chief of Staff   Signy Ellerton Cale

DISTRICT OFFICES:
73-710 Fred Waring Dr., #112, Palm Desert 92260; (619) 340-2900; District Director: Pat Cross.
22690 Cactus Ave., #155, Moreno Valley 92553; (909) 656-1444; Field Representative: Jann Foley.

COMMITTEE ASSIGNMENTS:
Banking, Finance, and Urban Affairs
Government Operations

McCloskey, Frank, D-Ind. (8)
CAPITOL HILL OFFICE:
306 CHOB 20515; 225-4636
Fax: 225-4688
Chief of Staff   Melinda Plaisier

DISTRICT OFFICES:
101 N.W. Martin Luther King Jr. Blvd., #124, Evansville 47708; (812) 465-6484; Area Director: Carolyn Johnson-Millender.
120 W. 7th St., #208, Bloomington 47401; (812) 334-1111; Area Director: Julio Alonso.

COMMITTEE ASSIGNMENTS:
Armed Services
Foreign Affairs
Post Office and Civil Service

McCollum, Bill, R-Fla. (8)

CAPITOL HILL OFFICE:
2266 RHOB 20515; 225-2176
Fax: 225-0999
Chief of Staff   Vaughn S. Forrest

DISTRICT OFFICE:
605 E. Robinson St., #650, Orlando 32801; (407) 872-1962; District Representative: John Ariale.

COMMITTEE ASSIGNMENTS:
Banking, Finance, and Urban Affairs
Judiciary

McCrery, Jim, R-La. (5)

CAPITOL HILL OFFICE:
225 CHOB 20515; 225-2777
Fax: 225-8039
Admin. Assistant   Richard Hunt

DISTRICT OFFICES:
6425 Youree Dr., Shreveport 71105; (318) 226-5080; District Manager: Vacant.
2400 Forsythe St., 2nd Floor, Monroe 71201; (318) 388-6105; Eastern District Manager: Lee Fletcher.

COMMITTEE ASSIGNMENT:
Ways and Means

McCurdy, Dave, D-Okla. (4)

CAPITOL HILL OFFICE:
2344 RHOB 20515; 225-6165
Fax: 225-9746
Admin. Assistant   Steve Patterson

DISTRICT OFFICES:
330 W. Gray, #110, Norman 73070; (405) 329-6500; Fax: (405) 329-2543; Office Director: Vaughn Clark.
103 Federal Bldg., Lawton 73501; (405) 357-2131; Fax: (405) 357-7789; Field Representative: Sue Dinges.

COMMITTEE ASSIGNMENTS:
Armed Services
Science, Space, and Technology

McDade, Joseph M., R-Pa. (10)

CAPITOL HILL OFFICE:
2370 RHOB 20515; 225-3731
Fax: 225-9594
Admin. Assistant   Deborah Weatherly

DISTRICT OFFICES:
538 Spruce St., #514, Scranton 18503; (717) 346-3834; Office Director: Michael Russen.
240 W. 3rd St., #230, Williamsport 17701; (717) 327-8161; Office Director: Ruth Calistri.

COMMITTEE ASSIGNMENT:
Appropriations (Ranking)

McDermott, Jim, D-Wash. (7)

CAPITOL HILL OFFICE:
1707 LHOB 20515; 225-3106
Admin. Assistant   Charles M. Williams

DISTRICT OFFICE:
1809 7th Ave., #1212, Seattle 98101; (206) 553-7170; District Admin.: Nancy James.

COMMITTEE ASSIGNMENTS:
District of Columbia
Standards of Official Conduct (Chairman)
Ways and Means

McHale, Paul, D-Pa. (15)

CAPITOL HILL OFFICE:
511 CHOB 20515; 225-6411
Fax: 225-5320
Admin. Assistant   Herb Giobbi

DISTRICT OFFICES:
26 E. 3rd St., Bethlehem 18015; (610) 866-0916; District Manager: Vacant.
1 Center Square, #203, Allentown 18101; (610) 439-8861; Senior Staff Assistant: John Gormley.
168 Main St., Pennsburg 18073; (215) 541-0614; Senior Staff Assistant: Judy Edwards.
1603 Lehigh St., Easton 18042; (610) 258-8383; Senior Staff Assistant: Cynthia Duelley.

COMMITTEE ASSIGNMENTS:
Armed Services
Science, Space, and Technology

McHugh, John M., R-N.Y. (24)

CAPITOL HILL OFFICE:
416 CHOB 20515; 225-4611
Chief of Staff   Cary Brick

DISTRICT OFFICES:
200 Washington St., #404A, Watertown 13601; (315) 782-3150.
104 Federal Bldg., Plattsburgh 12901; (518) 563-1406.
104 W. Utica St., Oswego 13126; (315) 342-5664.

COMMITTEE ASSIGNMENTS:
Armed Services
Government Operations

McInnis, Scott, R-Colo. (3)
CAPITOL HILL OFFICE:
512 CHOB 20515; 225-4761
Admin. Assistant   Stephannie Finley

DISTRICT OFFICES:
134 W. B St., Pueblo 81003; (719) 543-8200; District Director: Steve Arveschoug.
327 N. 7th St., Grand Junction 81501; (303) 245-7107; District Director: Steve Arveschoug.
1060 Main Ave., #107, Durango 81301; (303) 259-2754; District Director: Steve Arveschoug.
526 Pine St., #112, Glenwood Springs 81601; (303) 928-0637; District Director: Steve Arveschoug.

COMMITTEE ASSIGNMENTS:
Natural Resources
Small Business

McKeon, Howard P. "Buck," R-Calif. (25)
CAPITOL HILL OFFICE:
307 CHOB 20515; 225-1956
Fax: 226-0683
Chief of Staff   Bob Cochran

DISTRICT OFFICES:
23929 W. Valencia Blvd., #410, Santa Clarita 91355; (805) 254-2111; Fax: (805) 254-2380; District Director: Armando Azarloza.
1008 West Ave. N-4, Suite D, Palmdale 93551; (805) 948-7833; Fax: (805) 948-0398; Field Representative: Kelly Hand.
17134 Devonshire Ave., #201, Northridge 91325; (818) 885-1032; Field Representative: Vacant.

COMMITTEE ASSIGNMENTS:
Education and Labor
Public Works and Transportation

McKinney, Cynthia A., D-Ga. (11)
CAPITOL HILL OFFICE:
124 CHOB 20515; 225-1605
Fax: 226-0691
Chief of Staff   Andrea Young

DISTRICT OFFICES:
1 S. DeKalb Center, #9, 2853 Candler Rd., Decatur 30034; (404) 244-9902; Fax: (404) 244-9570; District Director: Pat Scott.
120 Barnard St., #305, Savannah 31401; (912) 652-4118; District Representative: Theresa White.
505 Courthouse Lane, #100, Augusta 30901; District Representative: Lola S. Russell.

COMMITTEE ASSIGNMENTS:
Agriculture
Foreign Affairs

McMillan, Alex, R-N.C. (9)
CAPITOL HILL OFFICE:
401 CHOB 20515; 225-1976
Chief of Staff   Frank Hill

DISTRICT OFFICES:
401 W. Trade St., #214, Charlotte 28202; (704) 372-1976; Congressional Liaison: Barbara Johnson-Waters.
224 S. New Hope Rd., Suite H, Gastonia 28054; (704) 861-1976; Congressional Liaison: Barbara Johnson-Waters.

COMMITTEE ASSIGNMENTS:
Budget
Energy and Commerce

McNulty, Michael R., D-N.Y. (21)
CAPITOL HILL OFFICE:
217 CHOB 20515; 225-5076
Chief of Staff   Lana Helfrich

DISTRICT OFFICES:
827 Leo W. O'Brien Federal Bldg., Albany 12207; (518) 465-0700; Fax: (518) 427-5107; Admin. Assistant: Charlie Diamond.
U.S. Post Office, Schenectady 12305; (518) 374-4547; Office Manager: Bob Carr.
9 Market St., Amsterdam 12010; (518) 843-3400; Office Manager: Elaine DeVito.
33 2nd St., Troy 12180; (518) 271-0822; Office Manager: Domenica Millington.

COMMITTEE ASSIGNMENT:
Ways and Means

Meehan, Martin T., D-Mass. (5)
CAPITOL HILL OFFICE:
1223 LHOB 20515; 225-3411
Fax: 226-0771
Admin. Assistant   Steve Joncas

DISTRICT OFFICES:
11 Kearney Square, Lowell 01852; (508) 459-0101; Fax: (508) 459-1907; District Director: Steve Joncas.
11 Lawrence St., #806, Lawrence 01840; (508) 681-6200; Fax: (508) 682-6070; Office Director: Bob LaRochelle.
255 Main St., #102, Marlborough 01752; (508) 460-9292; Fax: (508) 460-6869; Office Director: Mary Ann Prescal-Ricca.

COMMITTEE ASSIGNMENTS:
Armed Services
Small Business

Meek, Carrie P., D-Fla. (17)
CAPITOL HILL OFFICE:
404 CHOB 20515; 225-4506

Fax: 226-0777
Chief of Staff   Peggy Demon

DISTRICT OFFICE:
25 W. Flagler St., #1015, Miami 33130; (305) 381-9541; Fax: (305) 381-8376; District Director: Guy Forchion.

COMMITTEE ASSIGNMENT:
Appropriations

Menendez, Robert, D-N.J. (13)
CAPITOL HILL OFFICE:
1531 LHOB 20515; 225-7919
Fax: 226-0792
Admin. Assistant   Michael Hutton

DISTRICT OFFICES:
654 Ave. C, Bayonne 07002; (201) 823-2900; District Coordinator: Jose Alvarez.
911 Bergen Ave., Jersey City 07306; (201) 222-2828; Fax: (201) 222-0188; District Coordinator: Jose Alvarez.
275 Hobart St., Perth Amboy 08861; (908) 324-6212; Fax: (908) 324-7470; District Coordinator: Jose Alvarez.

COMMITTEE ASSIGNMENTS:
Foreign Affairs
Public Works and Transportation

Meyers, Jan, R-Kan. (3)
CAPITOL HILL OFFICE:
2338 RHOB 20515; 225-2865
Admin. Assistant   Kirk Walder

DISTRICT OFFICES:
204 Federal Bldg., Kansas City 66101; (913) 621-0832; Admin. Assistant: Michael Murray.
7133 W. 95th St., #217, Overland Park 66212; (913) 383-2013; Staff Assistant: Lori Phillips.
708 W. 9th St., Lawrence 66044; (913) 842-9313; Fax: (913) 842-9276; Staff Assistant: Ann Wiklund.

COMMITTEE ASSIGNMENTS:
Foreign Affairs
Small Business (Ranking)

Mfume, Kweisi, D-Md. (7)
CAPITOL HILL OFFICE:
2419 RHOB 20515; 225-4741
Fax: 225-3178
Chief of Staff   Tammy Hawley

DISTRICT OFFICES:
3000 Druid Park Dr., Baltimore 21215; (410) 367-1900; Fax: (410) 367-5331; Office Manager: Lenora Briscoe.
2203 N. Charles St., Baltimore 21218; (410) 235-2700; Office Manager: Lenora Briscoe.
1825 Woodlawn Dr., #106, Baltimore 21207;

(410) 298-5997; Fax: (410) 962-7983; Director of District Operations: Ruth Simms.

COMMITTEE ASSIGNMENTS:
Banking, Finance, and Urban Affairs
Joint Economic
Small Business
Standards of Official Conduct

Mica, John L., R-Fla. (7)
CAPITOL HILL OFFICE:
427 CHOB 20515; 225-4035
Fax: 226-0821
Admin. Assistant   Russell Roberts

DISTRICT OFFICES:
237 Fernwood Blvd., #105, Fern Park 32730; (407) 339-8080; Fax: (407) 339-8595; District Representative: Dick Harkey.
840 Deltona Blvd., Suite G, Deltona 32725; (407) 860-1499; Fax: (407) 860-5730.
1396 Dunlawton Ave., #2B, Port Orange 32127; (904) 756-9798; Fax: (904) 756-9903; District Representative: John Booker.

COMMITTEE ASSIGNMENTS:
Government Operations
Public Works and Transportation

Michel, Robert H., R-Ill. (18)
CAPITOL HILL OFFICE:
2112 RHOB 20515; 225-6201
Chief of Staff   Ray Lahood
H-230 The Capitol 20515; 225-0600
(Minority Leader's office)

DISTRICT OFFICES:
100 N.E. Monroe, #107, Peoria 61602; (309) 671-7027; Chief of Staff: Ray Lahood.
236 W. State St., Jacksonville 62650; (217) 245-1431; Office Director: Craig Findley.

COMMITTEE ASSIGNMENT:
Joint Inaugural Ceremonies

Miller, Dan, R-Fla. (13)
CAPITOL HILL OFFICE:
510 CHOB 20515; 225-5015
Fax: 226-0828
Chief of Staff   Kathy Wood

DISTRICT OFFICES:
1751 Mound St., #A-2, Sarasota 34236; (813) 951-6643; Fax: (813) 951-2972; District Director: Ralph Devitto.
2424 Manatee Ave., #104, Bradenton 34205; (813) 747-9081; Fax: (813) 749-5310; District Representative: Sandy Groseclose.

COMMITTEE ASSIGNMENTS:
Budget
Education and Labor

Miller, George, D-Calif. (7)
CAPITOL HILL OFFICE:
2205 RHOB 20515; 225-2095
Admin. Assistant   Daniel Weiss

DISTRICT OFFICES:
367 Civic Dr., #14, Pleasant Hill 94523; (510)
602-1880; Office Director: Mary Lansing.
3220 Blume Dr., #281, Richmond 94806; (510)
262-6500; Staff Assistant: Hank Royal.

COMMITTEE ASSIGNMENTS:
Education and Labor
Natural Resources (Chairman)

Mineta, Norman Y., D-Calif. (15)
CAPITOL HILL OFFICE:
2221 RHOB 20515; 225-2631
Chief of Staff   David Castagnetti

DISTRICT OFFICE:
1245 S. Winchester Blvd., #310, San Jose 95128;
(408) 984-6045; Fax: (408) 984-5409.

COMMITTEE ASSIGNMENT:
Public Works and Transportation (Chairman)

Minge, David, D-Minn. (2)
CAPITOL HILL OFFICE:
1508 LHOB 20515; 225-2331
Fax: 226-0836
Admin. Assistant   Rick Jauert

DISTRICT OFFICES:
542 1st St. South, Montevideo 56265; (612) 269-
9311; District Director: Norma Brick-Samuelson.
938 4th Ave., P.O. Box 367, Windom 56101;
(507) 831-0115; Deputy District Director: Vacant.
108 E. 3rd St., Chaska 55318; (612) 448-6567;
Deputy District Director: Vacant.

COMMITTEE ASSIGNMENTS:
Agriculture
Science, Space, and Technology

Mink, Patsy T., D-Hawaii (2)
CAPITOL HILL OFFICE:
2135 RHOB 20515; 225-4906
Fax: 225-4987
Legislative Director   Laura Efurd

DISTRICT OFFICE:
300 Ala Moana, #5104, Honolulu 96813; (808)
541-1986; Fax: (808) 538-0233; Office Director: Colleen Saiki.

COMMITTEE ASSIGNMENTS:
Budget
Education and Labor
Natural Resources

Moakley, Joe, D-Mass. (9)
CAPITOL HILL OFFICE:
235 CHOB 20515; 225-8273
Chief of Staff   John Weinfurter

DISTRICT OFFICES:
World Trade Center, #220, Boston 02110; (617)
565-2920; Office Director: Roger Kineavy.
4 Court St., Taunton 02780; (508) 824-6676; Office Director: Karen Pacheco.
166 Main St., Brockton 02401; (508) 586-5555;
Office Director: Joe Moynihan.

COMMITTEE ASSIGNMENT:
Rules (Chairman)

Molinari, Susan, R-N.Y. (13)
CAPITOL HILL OFFICE:
123 CHOB 20515; 225-3371
Fax: 226-1272
Chief of Staff   Paul Lobo

DISTRICT OFFICES:
14 New Dorp Lane, Staten Island 10306; (718)
987-8400; Fax: (718) 987-8938; District Manager: Barbara Palumbo.
9818 4th Ave., Brooklyn 11209; (718) 630-5277;
Fax: (718) 630-5388; Constituent Representative: Eileen Long.

COMMITTEE ASSIGNMENTS:
Education and Labor
Public Works and Transportation

Mollohan, Alan B., D-W.Va. (1)
CAPITOL HILL OFFICE:
2242 RHOB 20515; 225-4172
Admin. Assistant   Mary McGovern

DISTRICT OFFICES:
209 Post Office Bldg., Clarksburg 26301; (304)
623-4422; Area Representative: Ann Marie Merandi.
Federal Bldg., #213, Morgantown 26505; (304)
292-3019; Area Representative: Lotta Neer.
1117 Federal Bldg., Parkersburg 26101; (304)
428-0493; Area Representative: Allenetta Kaufman.
316 Federal Bldg., Wheeling 26003; (304) 232-
5390; Area Representative: Cathy Abraham.

COMMITTEE ASSIGNMENTS:
Appropriations
Budget

Montgomery, G. V. "Sonny," D-Miss. (3)
CAPITOL HILL OFFICE:
2184 RHOB 20515; 225-5031
Fax: 225-3375
Admin. Assistant   Andre Clemandot

DISTRICT OFFICES:
P.O. Box 5618, Meridian 39301; (601) 693-6681;
Office Director: Jeanette Noe.
110D Airport Rd., Pearl 39208; (601) 932-2401;
Office Director: Dan Kimbrough.
2080 Airport Rd., Columbus 39701; (601) 327-
2766; Office Director: Clara Peterson.

COMMITTEE ASSIGNMENTS:
Armed Services
Veterans' Affairs (Chairman)

Moorhead, Carlos J., R-Calif. (27)
CAPITOL HILL OFFICE:
2346 RHOB 20515; 225-4176
Admin. Assistant   Maxine Dean

DISTRICT OFFICES:
301 E. Colorado Blvd., #618, Pasadena 91101;
(818) 792-6168; Fax: (818) 792-6528; District Representative: Peter Musurlian.
420 N. Brand Blvd., #304, Glendale 91203; (818)
247-8445; Fax: (818) 247-4908; Staff Assistant: Marilyn McKay.

COMMITTEE ASSIGNMENTS:
Energy and Commerce (Ranking)
Judiciary

Moran, James P., Jr., D-Va. (8)
CAPITOL HILL OFFICE:
430 CHOB 20515; 225-4376
Admin. Assistant   Mame Reiley

DISTRICT OFFICE:
5115 Franconia Rd., Alexandria 22310; (703) 971-
4700; Fax: (703) 922-9436; Office Director: Susan
Warner.

COMMITTEE ASSIGNMENT:
Appropriations

Morella, Constance A., R-Md. (8)
CAPITOL HILL OFFICE:
223 CHOB 20515; 225-5341
Fax: 225-1389
Admin. Assistant   David A. Nathan

DISTRICT OFFICE:
51 Monroe St., #507, Rockville 20850; (301)
424-3501; Fax: (301) 424-5992; Office Director: Mary
Brown.

COMMITTEE ASSIGNMENTS:
Post Office and Civil Service
Science, Space, and Technology

Murphy, Austin J., D-Pa. (20)
CAPITOL HILL OFFICE:
2210 RHOB 20515; 225-4665
Fax: 225-4772
Admin. Assistant   Frederick P. McLuckie

DISTRICT OFFICES:
306 Fallowfield Ave., Charleroi 15022; (412) 489-
4217; Office Manager: Ken Laird.
96 N. Main St., Washington 15301; (412) 228-
2777; Staff Assistant: David Mark.
RD#3, Box 352-BB, Uniontown 15401; (412)
438-1490; Office Manager: Jacque Joseph.
8 S. 4th St., Youngwood 15697; (412) 925-1370;
Office Manager: Paulette Bieneck.
93 High St., #306, Waynesburg 15370; (412) 627-
7611; Office Manager: Dave Coder.

COMMITTEE ASSIGNMENTS:
Education and Labor
Natural Resources

Murtha, John P., D-Pa. (12)
CAPITOL HILL OFFICE:
2423 RHOB 20515; 225-2065
Executive Assistant   William Allen

DISTRICT OFFICE:
P.O. Box 780, Johnstown 15907; (814) 535-2642;
Fax: (814) 539-6229; District Admin. Assistant: John
Hugya.

COMMITTEE ASSIGNMENT:
Appropriations

Myers, John T., R-Ind. (7)
CAPITOL HILL OFFICE:
2372 RHOB 20515; 225-5805
Admin. Assistant   Sallie Davis

DISTRICT OFFICES:
107 Federal Bldg., Terre Haute 47808; (812) 238-
1619; District Director: Lynn Nicoson.
107 Halleck Bldg., Lafayette 47901; (317) 423-
1661; Secretary: Jane Long.

COMMITTEE ASSIGNMENTS:
Appropriations
Post Office and Civil Service (Ranking)

Nadler, Jerrold, D-N.Y. (8)
CAPITOL HILL OFFICE:
424 CHOB 20515; 225-5635
Fax: 225-6923
Admin. Assistant   Amy Green

DISTRICT OFFICE:
1841 Broadway, #800, New York 10023; (212) 489-3530; Fax: (212) 977-3546; Chief of Staff: Neil Goldstein.

COMMITTEE ASSIGNMENTS:
Judiciary
Public Works and Transportation

Neal, Richard E. , D-Mass. (2)
CAPITOL HILL OFFICE:
131 CHOB 20515; 225-5601
Fax: 225-8112
Admin. Assistant   Morgan Broman

DISTRICT OFFICES:
1550 Main St., Springfield 01103; (413) 785-0325; Fax: (413) 747-0604; Office Director: James Leydon.
4 Congress St., Milford 01757; (508) 634-8198; Office Director: Virginia Purcell.

COMMITTEE ASSIGNMENT:
Ways and Means

Neal, Stephen L. , D-N.C. (5)
CAPITOL HILL OFFICE:
2469 RHOB 20515; 225-2071
Fax: 225-4060
Admin. Assistant   Robert Wrigley

DISTRICT OFFICE:
2000 W. 1st St., #508, Winston-Salem 27104; (910) 631-5125; Fax: (910) 725-4493; Office Director: Jim Phillips.

COMMITTEE ASSIGNMENTS:
Banking, Finance, and Urban Affairs
Government Operations

Norton, Eleanor Holmes, D-D.C. (AL)
CAPITOL HILL OFFICE:
1415 LHOB 20515; 225-8050
Fax: 225-3002
Admin. Assistant   Donna Brazile

DISTRICT OFFICES:
815 15th St. N.W., Washington, D.C., #100, 20005; (202) 783-5065; Fax: (202) 783-5211; District Director: Renee Redwood.
1150 Chicago Ave. S.E., Washington, D.C., 20020; (202) 678-8900; Fax: (202) 678-8844; District Director: Renee Redwood.

COMMITTEE ASSIGNMENTS:
District of Columbia
Post Office and Civil Service
Public Works and Transportation

Nussle, Jim, R-Iowa (2)
CAPITOL HILL OFFICE:
308 CHOB 20515; 225-2911
Fax: 225-9129
Admin. Assistant   Steve Greiner

DISTRICT OFFICES:
3356 Kimball Ave., Waterloo 50702; (319) 235-1109; District Director: Scott Krebsbach.
2300 John F. Kennedy Rd., Dubuque 52002; (319) 557-7740; District Director: Scott Krebsbach.
223 W. Main St., Manchester 52057; (319) 927-5141; District Director: Scott Krebsbach.
1825 4th St. S.W., Mason City 50401; (515) 423-0303; District Director: Scott Krebsbach.

COMMITTEE ASSIGNMENTS:
Agriculture
Banking, Finance, and Urban Affairs

Oberstar, James L. , D-Minn. (8)
CAPITOL HILL OFFICE:
2366 RHOB 20515; 225-6211
Admin. Assistant   William G. Richard

DISTRICT OFFICES:
231 Federal Bldg., Duluth 55802; (218) 727-7474; Office Director: Jackie Morris.
316 Lake St., Chisholm 55719; (218) 254-5761; Staff Assistant: DeAnn Stish.
501 Laurel St., Brainard 56401; (218) 828-4400; Staff Assistant: Ken Hasskamp.
13065 Orono Parkway, Elk River 55330; (612) 241-0188; Staff Assistant: Ken Hasskamp.

COMMITTEE ASSIGNMENTS:
Foreign Affairs
Public Works and Transportation

Obey, David R. , D-Wis. (7)
CAPITOL HILL OFFICE:
2462 RHOB 20515; 225-3365
Staff Director   Joseph R. Crapa

DISTRICT OFFICE:
317 1st St., Wausau 54401; (715) 842-5606; Staff Director: Jerry Madison.

COMMITTEE ASSIGNMENTS:
Appropriations
Joint Economic (Chairman)

Olver, John W. , D-Mass. (1)
CAPITOL HILL OFFICE:
1323 LHOB 20515; 225-5335
Fax: 226-1224
Admin. Assistant   Jonathan D. Klein

DISTRICT OFFICES:
78 Center St., Pittsfield 01201; (413) 442-0946; District Representative: Cindy Lynch.
187 High St., Holyoke 01040; (413) 532-7010; District Director: Patricia Lewis Sackrey.
881 Main St., #223, Fitchburg 01420; (508) 342-8722; District Director: Polli Moryl-Kreidler.

COMMITTEE ASSIGNMENT:
Appropriations

Ortiz, Solomon P., D-Texas (27)
CAPITOL HILL OFFICE:
2136 RHOB 20515; 225-7742
Admin. Assistant   Florencio Rendon

DISTRICT OFFICES:
3649 Leopard St., #510, Corpus Christi 78408; (512) 883-5868; Fax: (512) 884-9201; Office Director: Joe Galindo.
3505 Boca Chica Blvd., #200, Brownsville 78521; (210) 541-1242; Fax: (210) 544-6915; Office Director: Melissa Van Holsbeke.

COMMITTEE ASSIGNMENTS:
Armed Services
Merchant Marine and Fisheries

Orton, Bill, D-Utah (3)
CAPITOL HILL OFFICE:
1122 LHOB 20515; 225-7751
Staff Director   George Krumbhaar

DISTRICT OFFICE:
51 S. University Ave., #317, Provo 84601; (801) 379-2500; Staff Director: Niles Ellwood.

COMMITTEE ASSIGNMENTS:
Banking, Finance, and Urban Affairs
Budget

Owens, Major R., D-N.Y. (11)
CAPITOL HILL OFFICE:
2305 RHOB 20515; 225-6231
Admin. Assistant   Jacqueline Ellis

DISTRICT OFFICE:
289 Utica Ave., Brooklyn 11213; (718) 773-3100; Fax: (718) 735-7143; District Director: Dan Simonette.

COMMITTEE ASSIGNMENTS:
Education and Labor
Government Operations

Oxley, Michael G., R-Ohio (4)
CAPITOL HILL OFFICE:
2233 RHOB 20515; 225-2676
Chief of Staff   Jim Conzelman

DISTRICT OFFICES:
3121 W. Elm Plaza, Lima 45805; (419) 999-6455; District Representative: Kelly Kirk.
100 E. Main Cross, Findlay 45840; (419) 423-3210; District Representative: Bonnie Dunbar.
24 W. 3rd St., #314, Mansfield 44902; (419) 522-5757; District Representative: Phil Holloway.

COMMITTEE ASSIGNMENT:
Energy and Commerce

Packard, Ron, R-Calif. (48)
CAPITOL HILL OFFICE:
2162 RHOB 20515; 225-3906
Fax: 225-0134
Chief of Staff   David C. Coggin

DISTRICT OFFICES:
221 E. Vista Way, #205, Vista 92084; (619) 631-1364; Fax: (619) 631-1367; District Representative: Don Polese.
629 Camino de Los Mares, #204, San Clemente 92673; (714) 496-2343; Fax: (714) 496-2988; District Director: Mike Eggers.

COMMITTEE ASSIGNMENT:
Appropriations

Pallone, Frank, Jr., D-N.J. (6)
CAPITOL HILL OFFICE:
420 CHOB 20515; 225-4671
Admin. Assistant   Russell McGurk

DISTRICT OFFICES:
540 Broadway, #118, Long Branch 07740; (908) 571-1140; Fax: (908) 870-3890; Office Director: Michael Beson.
67-69 Church St., Kilmer Square, New Brunswick 08901; (908) 249-8892; Fax: (908) 249-1335; Office Director: Jim McCann.
IEI Airport Plaza, #18, Highway 36, Hazlet 07730; (908) 264-9104; Fax: (908) 739-4668; Office Director: Gen Hawley.

COMMITTEE ASSIGNMENTS:
Energy and Commerce
Merchant Marine and Fisheries

Parker, Mike, D-Miss. (4)
CAPITOL HILL OFFICE:
1410 LHOB 20515; 225-5865
Fax: 225-5886
Admin. Assistant   Arthur D. Rhodes

DISTRICT OFFICES:
245 E. Capitol St., #222, Jackson 39201; (601) 965-4085; Fax: (601) 965-4695; Office Manager: Ed Cole.

230 S. Whitworth St., Brookhaven 39601; (601) 835-0706; Staff Assistant: Christi Thueman.

Chancery Court Annex, Columbia 39429; (601) 731-1622; Community Development Liaison: Rick Hux.

521 Main St., Natchez 39120; (601) 446-7250; Staff Assistant: Martha Salters.

176 W. Court Ave., Mendenhall 39114; (601) 847-0873; Community Development Liaison: Malone Bryant.

728 1/2 Sawmill Rd., Laurel 39440; (601) 425-4999; Staff Assistant: Donna Gibbes.

COMMITTEE ASSIGNMENTS:
Budget
Public Works and Transportation

Pastor, Ed, D-Ariz. (2)
CAPITOL HILL OFFICE:
408 CHOB 20515; 225-4065
Fax: 225-1655
Admin. Assistant   Gene Fisher

DISTRICT OFFICES:
332 E. McDowell, #10, Phoenix 85004; (602) 256-0551; Fax: (602) 257-9103; District Director: Ron Piceno.

2432 E. Broadway, Tucson 85719; (602) 624-9986; Fax: (602) 624-3872; Southern Arizona District Director: Linda Leatherman.

281 W. 24th St., #117, Yuma 85364; (602) 329-9151; Fax: (602) 329-6684; Staff Assistant: Charlene Fernandez.

COMMITTEE ASSIGNMENT:
Appropriations

Paxon, Bill, R-N.Y. (27)
CAPITOL HILL OFFICE:
1314 LHOB 20515; 225-5265
Fax: 225-5910
Admin. Assistant   Michael Hook

DISTRICT OFFICES:
5500 Main St., Williamsville 14221; (716) 634-2324; Fax: (716) 631-7610; Chief of Staff: Matt Koch.

10 E. Main St., Victor 14564; (716) 742-1600; Fax: (716) 742-1976; Office Director: Mark Aesch.

COMMITTEE ASSIGNMENT:
Energy and Commerce

Payne, Donald M., D-N.J. (10)
CAPITOL HILL OFFICE:
417 CHOB 20515; 225-3436
Fax: 225-4160
Admin. Assistant   Maxine James

DISTRICT OFFICE:
970 Broad St., #1435-B, Newark 07102; (201) 645-3213; District Representative: Richard Thigpen.

COMMITTEE ASSIGNMENTS:
Education and Labor
Foreign Affairs
Government Operations

Payne, L. F., Jr., D-Va. (5)
CAPITOL HILL OFFICE:
1119 LHOB 20515; 225-4711
Fax: 226-1147
Admin. Assistant   Vacant

DISTRICT OFFICES:
700 Main St., #301, Danville 24541; (804) 792-1280; Fax: (804) 797-5942; Casework Supervisor: Jennifer Moorefield.

103 S. Main St., Farmville 23901; (804) 392-8331; Fax: (804) 392-6448; Office Manager: Margaret Watkins.

103 E. Water St., #302, Charlottesville 22902; (804) 295-6372; Fax: (804) 295-6059; District Manager: Greg Kelly.

COMMITTEE ASSIGNMENT:
Ways and Means

Pelosi, Nancy, D-Calif. (8)
CAPITOL HILL OFFICE:
240 CHOB 20515; 225-4965
Fax: 225-8259
Admin. Assistant   Judith Lemons

DISTRICT OFFICE:
450 Golden Gate Ave., San Francisco 94102; (415) 556-4862; Fax: (415) 861-1670; District Representative: Michael Yaki.

COMMITTEE ASSIGNMENTS:
Appropriations
Select Intelligence
Standards of Official Conduct

Penny, Timothy J., D-Minn. (1)
CAPITOL HILL OFFICE:
436 CHOB 20515; 225-2472
Fax: 225-0051
Acting Admin. Assistant   Jane Shey

DISTRICT OFFICE:
108 West Park Square, P.O. Box 368, Owatonna 55060; (507) 455-9151; District Director: Jim Hagerty.

COMMITTEE ASSIGNMENTS:
Agriculture
Veterans' Affairs

Peterson, Collin C., D-Minn. (7)
CAPITOL HILL OFFICE:
1133 LHOB 20515; 225-2165
Press Secretary   Rebecca Donovan

DISTRICT OFFICES:
714 Lake Ave., Detroit Lakes 56501; (218) 847-5056; District Director: Vacant.
3333 W. Division, #210, St. Cloud 56301; (612) 259-0559; District Director: Vacant.
2603 Wheat Dr., Red Lake Falls 56750; (218) 253-4356; District Director: Vacant.

COMMITTEE ASSIGNMENTS:
Agriculture
Government Operations

Peterson, Pete, D-Fla. (2)
CAPITOL HILL OFFICE:
426 CHOB 20515; 225-5235
Chief of Staff   Suzanne Farmer

DISTRICT OFFICES:
930 Thomasville Rd., #101, Tallahassee 32303; (904) 561-3979; Fax: (904) 691-2902; District Manager: Tom Pitcock.
30 W. Government St., Panama City 32401; (904) 785-0812; Fax: (904) 763-3764; District Representative: Ken Davis.

COMMITTEE ASSIGNMENT:
Appropriations

Petri, Tom, R-Wis. (6)
CAPITOL HILL OFFICE:
2262 RHOB 20515; 225-2476
Admin. Assistant   Joseph Flader

DISTRICT OFFICES:
P.O. Box 1816, Fond du Lac 54936; (414) 922-1180; District Director: Sue Kerkman.
115 Washington Ave., Oshkosh 54901; (414) 231-6333; District Representative: Frank Frassetto.

COMMITTEE ASSIGNMENTS:
Education and Labor
Post Office and Civil Service
Public Works and Transportation

Pickett, Owen B., D-Va. (2)
CAPITOL HILL OFFICE:
2430 RHOB 20515; 225-4215
Fax: 225-4218
Admin. Assistant   Jeanne Evans

DISTRICT OFFICES:
112 E. Little Creek Rd., Norfolk 23505; (804) 583-5892; Constituent Service Manager: Julia Jacobs Hopkins.
2710 Virginia Beach Blvd., Virginia Beach 23452; (804) 486-3710; Constituent Service Manager: Arleen Haushalter.

COMMITTEE ASSIGNMENTS:
Armed Services
Merchant Marine and Fisheries

Pickle, J. J., D-Texas (10)
CAPITOL HILL OFFICE:
242 CHOB 20515; 225-4865
Fax: 225-2477
Admin. Assistant   Barbara Pate

DISTRICT OFFICE:
763 Federal Bldg., Austin 78701; (512) 482-5921; District Admin.: Paul Hilgers.

COMMITTEE ASSIGNMENTS:
Joint Taxation
Ways and Means

Pombo, Richard W., R-Calif. (11)
CAPITOL HILL OFFICE:
1519 LHOB 20515; 225-1947
Fax: 226-0861
Chief of Staff   Matt Miller

DISTRICT OFFICES:
2321 W. March Lane, #205, Stockton 95207; (209) 951-3091; District Director: Steve Ding.
10398 Rockingham Dr., #2, Sacramento 95827; (916) 368-1048; District Director: Vacant.

COMMITTEE ASSIGNMENTS:
Agriculture
Merchant Marine and Fisheries
Natural Resources

Pomeroy, Earl, D-N.D. (AL)
CAPITOL HILL OFFICE:
318 CHOB 20515; 225-2611
Admin. Assistant   Karen Frederickson

DISTRICT OFFICES:
657 2nd Ave., #266, Fargo 58102; (701) 235-9760; Fax: (701) 235-9767; Eastern Field Representative: Joan Carlson.
220 E. Rosser Ave., #376, Bismarck 58501; (701) 224-0355; Fax: (701) 224-0431; State Director: Gail Skaley.

COMMITTEE ASSIGNMENTS:
Agriculture
Budget

Porter, John Edward, R-Ill. (10)
CAPITOL HILL OFFICE:
1026 LHOB 20515; 225-4835
Fax: 225-0157
Admin. Assistant   Robert C. Gustafson

DISTRICT OFFICES:
102 Wilmot Rd., #200, Deerfield 60015; (708) 940-0202; Fax: (708) 940-7143; Executive Assistant: Ginny Hotaling.
18 N. County St., #601A, Waukegan 60085; (708) 662-0101; Office Director: Dee Jay Davis.

1650 Arlington Heights Rd., #204, Arlington Heights 60004; (708) 392-0303; Office Director: Bonnie Nelson.

COMMITTEE ASSIGNMENT:
Appropriations

Portman, Rob, R-Ohio (2)
CAPITOL HILL OFFICE:
238 CHOB 20515; 225-3164
Admin. Assistant   John Bridgland

DISTRICT OFFICE:
8044 Montgomery Rd., #540, Cincinnati 45236; (513) 791-0381; Fax: (513) 791-1696; District Manager: Annette Wishard.

COMMITTEE ASSIGNMENTS:
Government Operations
Small Business

Poshard, Glenn, D-Ill. (19)
CAPITOL HILL OFFICE:
107 CHOB 20515; 225-5201
Admin. Assistant   David Stricklin

DISTRICT OFFICES:
New Route 13W, Marion 62959; (618) 993-8532; Staff Assistant: Lisa Champlin.
201 E. Nolen St., West Frankfort 62896; (618) 937-6402; Staff Assistant: Jim Kirkpatrick.
363 S. Main St., Decatur 62521; (217) 362-9011; Staff Assistant: Louise Nolan.
600 Airport Rd., Mattoon 61938; (217) 234-7032; Staff Assistant: Paul Black.
801 W. 9th St., P.O. Box 818, Mt. Carmel 62863; (618) 262-7723; Staff Assistant: Shirley Stevenson.
444 S. Willow St., Effingham 62401; (217) 342-7220; Staff Assistant: Sam Medernach.

COMMITTEE ASSIGNMENTS:
Public Works and Transportation
Small Business

Price, David, D-N.C. (4)
CAPITOL HILL OFFICE:
2458 RHOB 20515; 225-1784
Fax: 225-6314
Admin. Assistant   Paul H. Feldman

DISTRICT OFFICES:
225 Hillsborough St., #330, Raleigh 27603; (919) 856-4611; Office Director: Joan Ewing.
1777 Chapel Hill-Durham Blvd., #202, Chapel Hill 27514; (919) 967-8500; Office Director: Gay Eddy.

COMMITTEE ASSIGNMENTS:
Appropriations
Budget

Pryce, Deborah, R-Ohio (15)
CAPITOL HILL OFFICE:
128 CHOB 20515; 225-2015
Fax: 226-0986
Admin. Assistant   Tom Wolfe

DISTRICT OFFICE:
200 N. High St., #400, Columbus 43215; (614) 469-5614; Fax: (614) 469-6937; District Representative: Marcee McCreary.

COMMITTEE ASSIGNMENTS:
Banking, Finance, and Urban Affairs
Government Operations

Quillen, James H., R-Tenn. (1)
CAPITOL HILL OFFICE:
102 CHOB 20515; 225-6356
Fax: 225-7812
Chief of Staff   Frances Light Currie

DISTRICT OFFICE:
157 Post Office Bldg., Kingsport 37662; (615) 247-8161; Office Manager: Betty Vaughn.

COMMITTEE ASSIGNMENT:
Rules

Quinn, Jack, R-N.Y. (30)
CAPITOL HILL OFFICE:
331 CHOB 20515; 225-3306
Fax: 225-0347
Admin. Assistant   MaryLou Palmer

DISTRICT OFFICE:
403 Main St., #510, Buffalo 14203; (716) 845-5257.

COMMITTEE ASSIGNMENTS:
Public Works and Transportation
Veterans' Affairs

Rahall, Nick J., II, D-W.Va. (3)
CAPITOL HILL OFFICE:
2269 RHOB 20515; 225-3452
Admin. Assistant   Kent Keyser

DISTRICT OFFICES:
110 1/2 Main St., Beckley 25801; (304) 252-5000; Office Director: Dick Nevi.
601 Federal St., #1005, Bluefield 24701; (304) 325-6222; Office Director: Debbie Stevens.
815 5th Ave., Huntington 25701; (304) 522-6425; Office Director: J. Randolph Cheetham.
R.K. Bldg., Logan 25601; (304) 752-4934; Office Director: Debrina Workman.
101 N. Court St., Lewisburg 24901; (304) 647-3228; Office Director: Wade Griffith.

COMMITTEE ASSIGNMENTS:
Natural Resources
Public Works and Transportation

Ramstad, Jim, R-Minn. (3)
CAPITOL HILL OFFICE:
322 CHOB 20515; 225-2871
Fax: 225-6351
Admin. Assistant   Maybeth Christensen

DISTRICT OFFICE:
8120 Penn Ave., Bloomington 55431; (612) 881-4600; Fax: (612) 881-1943; District Manager: Erik Paulsen.

COMMITTEE ASSIGNMENTS:
Joint Economic
Judiciary
Small Business

Rangel, Charles B., D-N.Y. (15)
CAPITOL HILL OFFICE:
2252 RHOB 20515; 225-4365
Admin. Assistant   Frank Jasmine

DISTRICT OFFICES:
163 W. 125th St., New York 10027; (212) 663-3900; Fax: (212) 663-4277; Office Director: Vivian Jones.
601 W. 181st St., New York 10033; (212) 927-5333; Fax: (212) 795-2334; Office Director: Vacant.
2110 1st Ave., New York 10029; (212) 348-9630; Fax: (212) 423-0489; Office Director: Miriam Falcon-Lopez.

COMMITTEE ASSIGNMENT:
Ways and Means

Ravenel, Arthur, Jr., R-S.C. (1)
CAPITOL HILL OFFICE:
231 CHOB 20515; 225-3176
Admin. Assistant   Sharon Chellis

DISTRICT OFFICES:
334 Meeting St., #640, Charleston 29403; (803) 727-4175.
206 Laurel St., Conway 29526; (803) 248-2660; District Assistant: Barbara Browning.
829 E. Front St., Georgetown 29440; (803) 527-6868; District Assistant: Elma Harrelson.

COMMITTEE ASSIGNMENTS:
Armed Services
Merchant Marine and Fisheries

Reed, Jack, D-R.I. (2)
CAPITOL HILL OFFICE:
1510 LHOB 20515; 225-2735
Admin. Assistant   J. B. Poersch

DISTRICT OFFICE:
100 Midway Place, #5, Cranston 02920; (401) 943-3100; Office Director: Ray Simone.

COMMITTEE ASSIGNMENTS:
Education and Labor
Judiciary
Merchant Marine and Fisheries
Select Intelligence

Regula, Ralph, R-Ohio (16)
CAPITOL HILL OFFICE:
2309 RHOB 20515; 225-3876
Fax: 225-3059
Press Secretary   Connie Jones

DISTRICT OFFICE:
4150 Belden Village St. N.W., Canton 44718; (216) 489-4414; Fax: (216) 489-4448; Office Manager: Jeanette Griffin.

COMMITTEE ASSIGNMENT:
Appropriations

Reynolds, Mel, D-Ill. (2)
CAPITOL HILL OFFICE:
514 CHOB 20515; 225-0773
Admin. Assistant   Charles Kelly

DISTRICT OFFICES:
525 E. 103rd St., Chicago 60628; (312) 568-7900; District Administrator: Damon Rockett.
17926 S. Halstead, #1 West, Homewood 60430; (708) 957-9955; District Administrator: Damon Rockett.

COMMITTEE ASSIGNMENT:
Ways and Means

Richardson, Bill, D-N.M. (3)
CAPITOL HILL OFFICE:
2349 RHOB 20515; 225-6190
Admin. Assistant   Isabelle Watkins

DISTRICT OFFICES:
411 Paseo de Peralta, Santa Fe 87501; (505) 988-7230; Office Director: Sam Taylor.
Gallup City Hall, 2nd and Aztec Sts., Gallup 87301; (505) 722-6522; Office Director: Rose Custer.
602 Mitchell St., Clovis 88101; (505) 769-3380; Office Director: Becky Geer.
San Miguel County Courthouse, P.O. Box 1805, Las Vegas 87701; (505) 425-7270.

COMMITTEE ASSIGNMENTS:
Energy and Commerce
Natural Resources
Select Intelligence

Ridge, Tom, R-Pa. (21)
CAPITOL HILL OFFICE:
1714 LHOB 20515; 225-5406
Fax: 225-1081
Admin. Assistant Mark Campbell

DISTRICT OFFICES:
108 Federal Bldg., Erie 16501; (814) 456-2038;
Office Director: Ann DiTullio.
305 Chestnut St., Meadville 16335; (814) 724-
8414; Office Director: Jody Bruckner.
91 E. State St., Sharon 16146; (412) 981-8440;
Office Director: Carol Weber.
327 N. Main St., Butler 16001; (412) 285-7005;
Office Manager: Joan Janisak.

COMMITTEE ASSIGNMENTS:
Banking, Finance, and Urban Affairs
Post Office and Civil Service
Veterans' Affairs

Roberts, Pat, R-Kan. (1)
CAPITOL HILL OFFICE:
1126 LHOB 20515; 225-2715
Admin. Assistant Leroy Towns

DISTRICT OFFICES:
P.O. Box 550, Dodge City 67801; (316) 227-2244;
Office Director: Phyllis Ross.
P.O. Box 1334, Salina 67402; (913) 825-5409; Of-
fice Director: Betty Duwe.
P.O. Box 128, Norton 67654; (913) 877-2454;
Office Director: Karen Reedy.
335 N. Washington, #180, Hutchinson 67501;
(316) 665-6138.

COMMITTEE ASSIGNMENTS:
Agriculture (Ranking)
House Administration
Joint Library
Joint Printing (Ranking)

Roemer, Tim, D-Ind. (3)
CAPITOL HILL OFFICE:
415 CHOB 20515; 225-3915
Admin. Assistant Bernie Toon

DISTRICT OFFICE:
217 N. Main, South Bend 46601; (219) 288-3301;
Office Manager: Julie Vuckovich.

COMMITTEE ASSIGNMENTS:
Education and Labor
Science, Space, and Technology

Rogers, Harold, R-Ky. (5)
CAPITOL HILL OFFICE:
2468 RHOB 20515; 225-4601
Fax: 225-0940
Admin. Assistant Kevin Fromer

DISTRICT OFFICES:
203 E. Mt. Vernon, Somerset 42501; (606) 679-
8346; Fax: (606) 678-4856; District Admin.: Robert
Mitchell.
601 Main St., Hazard 41701; (606) 439-0794;
Field Representative: Dudley Crouch.
806 Hambley Blvd., Pikeville 41501; (606) 432-
4388; Office Manager: Sandy Runyon.

COMMITTEE ASSIGNMENT:
Appropriations

Rohrabacher, Dana, R-Calif. (45)
CAPITOL HILL OFFICE:
1027 LHOB 20515; 225-2415
Fax: 225-0145
Chief of Staff Gary L. Curran

DISTRICT OFFICE:
16162 Beach Blvd., #304, Huntington Beach
92647; (714) 847-2433; Fax: (714) 847-5153; District
Director: Kathleen Hollingsworth.

COMMITTEE ASSIGNMENTS:
District of Columbia
Foreign Affairs
Science, Space, and Technology

Romero-Barcelo, Carlos, D-P.R. (AL)
CAPITOL HILL OFFICE:
1517 LHOB 20515; 225-2615
Fax: 225-2154
Admin. Assistant Pedro Rivera-Casiano

DISTRICT OFFICE:
P.O. Box 4751, San Juan 00902; (809) 723-6333;
Fax: (809) 729-6824; District Manager: Domingo
Garcia.

COMMITTEE ASSIGNMENTS:
Education and Labor
Natural Resources

Rose, Charlie, D-N.C. (7)
CAPITOL HILL OFFICE:
2230 RHOB 20515; 225-2731
Fax: 225-0345
Admin. Assistant Andrea Turner-Scott

DISTRICT OFFICES:
208 Post Office Bldg., Wilmington 28401; (910)
343-4959; Fax: (910) 763-7790; Staff Assistant: Judy
Bentley.
218 Federal Bldg., Fayetteville 28301; (910) 323-
0260; Fax: (910) 323-0069; District Coordinator: Judith Kirchman.

COMMITTEE ASSIGNMENTS:
Agriculture
House Administration (Chairman)
Joint Library (Chairman)
Joint Printing

Ros-Lehtinen, Ileana, R-Fla. (18)
CAPITOL HILL OFFICE:
127 CHOB 20515; 225-3931
Fax: 225-5620
Admin. Assistant   Mauricio Tamargo

DISTRICT OFFICE:
5757 Blue Lagoon Dr., #240, Miami 33126; (305) 262-1800; District Director: Debra Musgrove.

COMMITTEE ASSIGNMENTS:
Foreign Affairs
Government Operations

Rostenkowski, Dan, D-Ill. (5)
CAPITOL HILL OFFICE:
2111 RHOB 20515; 225-4061
Fax: 225-4064
Admin. Assistant   Virginia Fletcher

DISTRICT OFFICES:
818 W. Fullerton, Chicago 60614; (312) 276-6000; Office Director: Nancy A. Panzke.
4849 N. Milwaukee, #101, Chicago 60630; (312) 481-0111; Office Director: Carol Giffey.

COMMITTEE ASSIGNMENTS:
Joint Taxation
Ways and Means

Roth, Toby, R-Wis. (8)
CAPITOL HILL OFFICE:
2234 RHOB 20515; 225-5665
Fax: 225-0087
Admin. Assistant   Joe Western

DISTRICT OFFICES:
2101 S. Oneida St., Green Bay 54304; (414) 494-2800; Fax: (414) 494-2916; Office Director: Ann Boltz.
1120 Pierce Ave., Marinette 54143; (715) 735-5704; Field Representative: Robert Michaelis.
126 N. Oneida St., Appleton 54911; (414) 739-4167; Fax: (414) 739-9721; Office Director: John Fink.

COMMITTEE ASSIGNMENTS:
Banking, Finance, and Urban Affairs
Foreign Affairs

Roukema, Marge, R-N.J. (5)
CAPITOL HILL OFFICE:
2244 RHOB 20515; 225-4465
Admin. Assistant   Steve Wilson

DISTRICT OFFICES:
1200 E. Ridgewood Ave., Ridgewood 07450; (201) 447-3900; Fax: (201) 447-3749; District Administrator: Frank Covelli.
1500 Route 517, Hackettstown 07840; (908) 850-4747; Fax: (908) 850-3406; Staff Assistant: Carol Dougherty.

COMMITTEE ASSIGNMENTS:
Banking, Finance, and Urban Affairs
Education and Labor

Rowland, J. Roy, D-Ga. (8)
CAPITOL HILL OFFICE:
2134 RHOB 20515; 225-6531
Admin. Assistant   Barbara Schlein

DISTRICT OFFICES:
P.O. Box 6258, Macon 31208; (912) 474-0150; District Coordinator: Bill Stembridge.
P.O. Box 2047, Dublin 31040; (912) 275-0024; Office Manager: Vickie Willis.
1810 N. Ashley St., #5, Valdosta 31602; (912) 333-0118; District Representative: Jimmy Brooks.
200 Carl Vinson Parkway, Warner Robins 31088; (912) 328-6404; District Representative: Bill Stembridge.
2410 Westgate Blvd., #109, Albany 31707; (912) 889-9040; Office Manager: Vacant.
101 S. Peterson Ave., Douglas 31533; (912) 384-6275; Office Manager: Vacant.
225 Tift Ave., Tifton 31794; (912) 388-0400; Office Manager: Vacant.

COMMITTEE ASSIGNMENTS:
Energy and Commerce
Veterans' Affairs

Roybal-Allard, Lucille, D-Calif. (33)
CAPITOL HILL OFFICE:
324 CHOB 20515; 225-1766
Chief of Staff   Henry Contreras

DISTRICT OFFICE:
255 E. Temple St., #1860, Los Angeles 90012; (213) 628-9230; Fax: (213) 628-8578; District Director: Yolanda Chavez.

COMMITTEE ASSIGNMENTS:
Banking, Finance, and Urban Affairs
Small Business

Royce, Ed, R-Calif. (39)
CAPITOL HILL OFFICE:
1404 LHOB 20515; 225-4111
Admin. Assistant   Joan Bates Korich

DISTRICT OFFICE:
305 N. Harbor Blvd., #300, Fullerton 92632; (714) 992-8081 and (310) 604-6019; Fax: (714) 992-1668; Admin. Assistant: Marcia Gilchrist.

COMMITTEE ASSIGNMENTS:
Foreign Affairs
Science, Space, and Technology

Rush, Bobby L., D-Ill. (1)
CAPITOL HILL OFFICE:
1725 LHOB 20515; 225-4372
Fax: 226-0333
Admin. Assistant   Maurice Daniel

DISTRICT OFFICES:
655 E. 79th St., Chicago 60619; (312) 224-6500; Fax: (312) 224-9624; District Administrator: Thomas Gray.
9730 S. Western Ave., #237, Evergreen Park 60642; (708) 422-4055; Fax: (708) 422-5199; Office Director: Thomas Gray.

COMMITTEE ASSIGNMENTS:
Banking, Finance, and Urban Affairs
Government Operations
Science, Space, and Technology

Sabo, Martin Olav, D-Minn. (5)
CAPITOL HILL OFFICE:
2336 RHOB 20515; 225-4755
Admin. Assistant   Michael Erlandson

DISTRICT OFFICE:
110 S. 4th St., #462, Minneapolis 55401; (612) 348-1649; Office Director: Kathleen Anderson.

COMMITTEE ASSIGNMENTS:
Appropriations
Budget (Chairman)

Sanders, Bernard, I-Vt. (AL)
CAPITOL HILL OFFICE:
213 CHOB 20515; 225-4115
Fax: 225-6790
Admin. Assistant   Jane O'Meara-Sanders

DISTRICT OFFICE:
1 Church St., 2nd Floor, Burlington 05401; (802) 862-0697; Fax: (802) 860-6370; District Office Director: Jane O'Meara-Sanders.

COMMITTEE ASSIGNMENTS:
Banking, Finance, and Urban Affairs
Government Operations

Sangmeister, George E., D-Ill. (11)
CAPITOL HILL OFFICE:
1032 LHOB 20515; 225-3635
Admin. Assistant   Emma Bechler

DISTRICT OFFICES:
101 N. Joliet St., Joliet 60431; (815) 740-2028.
102 W. Madison St., Ottawa 61350; (815) 433-0085; Office Manager: Tom Walsh.
213 Gold Coast Lane, Calumet City 60409; (708) 862-2590; Office Manager: Vacant.

COMMITTEE ASSIGNMENTS:
Judiciary
Public Works and Transportation
Veterans' Affairs

Santorum, Rick, R-Pa. (18)
CAPITOL HILL OFFICE:
1222 LHOB 20515; 225-2135
Fax: 225-7747
Admin. Assistant   Mark Rodgers

DISTRICT OFFICES:
606 Weyman Rd., Pittsburgh 15236; (412) 882-3205; Admin. Assistant: Mark Rodgers.
541 5th Ave., McKeesport 15132; (412) 664-4049.

COMMITTEE ASSIGNMENT:
Ways and Means

Sarpalius, Bill, D-Texas (13)
CAPITOL HILL OFFICE:
126 CHOB 20515; 225-3706
Fax: 225-6142
Chief of Staff   Phil C. Duncan

DISTRICT OFFICES:
801 S. Fillmore, #400, Amarillo 79101; (806) 371-8844; Fax: (806) 371-0651; Congressional Aide: Rosa Bragg.
208 Federal Bldg., 1000 Lamar, Wichita Falls 76301; (817) 767-0541; District Director: Aaron Alejandro.
1104 N. Locust St., Denton 76201; (817) 898-1564; Community Representative: Lisa Hunsacker.
1112 Texas Ave., Lubbock 79401; (806) 763-8608; Fax: (806) 763-8439; Community Representative: Maggie Trejo.

COMMITTEE ASSIGNMENTS:
Agriculture
Small Business

Sawyer, Tom, D-Ohio (14)
CAPITOL HILL OFFICE:
1414 LHOB 20515; 225-5231
Admin. Assistant   TerriAnn Lowenthal

DISTRICT OFFICE:
411 Wolf Ledges Parkway, #105, Akron 44311; (216) 375-5710; Office Director: Judi Shapiro.

COMMITTEE ASSIGNMENTS:
Education and Labor
Foreign Affairs
Post Office and Civil Service
Standards of Official Conduct

Saxton, H. James, R-N.J. (3)
CAPITOL HILL OFFICE:
438 CHOB 20515; 225-4765
Fax: 225-0778
Admin. Assistant   Bill Jarrell

DISTRICT OFFICES:
100 High St., 2nd Floor, Mt. Holly 08060; (609) 261-5800; District Representative: Sandy Condit.
7 Hadley Ave., Toms River 08753; (908) 914-2020; Staff Assistant: Pat Brogan.
1 Maine Ave., Cherry Hill 08002; (609) 428-0520; Staff Assistant: Dee Denton.

COMMITTEE ASSIGNMENTS:
Armed Services
District of Columbia
Joint Economic
Merchant Marine and Fisheries

Schaefer, Dan, R-Colo. (6)
CAPITOL HILL OFFICE:
2448 RHOB 20515; 225-7882
Chief of Staff   Holly Propst

DISTRICT OFFICE:
3615 S. Huron St., #101, Englewood 80110; (303) 762-8890; District Director: Andree Krause.

COMMITTEE ASSIGNMENT:
Energy and Commerce

Schenk, Lynn, D-Calif. (49)
CAPITOL HILL OFFICE:
315 CHOB 20515; 225-2040
Fax: 225-2042
Admin. Assistant   Fran Callanan

DISTRICT OFFICES:
3900 5th Ave., #200, San Diego 92103; (619) 291-1430; Fax: (619) 291-8956; District Director: Laurie Black.
825 Imperial Beach Blvd., Imperial Beach 91932; (619) 291-1430; Fax: (619) 291-8956; District Director: Laurie Black.

COMMITTEE ASSIGNMENTS:
Energy and Commerce
Merchant Marine and Fisheries

Schiff, Steven H., R-N.M. (1)
CAPITOL HILL OFFICE:
1009 LHOB 20515; 225-6316
Fax: 225-4975
Admin. Assistant   Peter Rintye

DISTRICT OFFICE:
625 Silver Ave. S.W., #140, Albuquerque 87102; (505) 766-2538; Fax: (505) 766-1674; District Director: Mary Martinek.

COMMITTEE ASSIGNMENTS:
Government Operations
Judiciary
Science, Space, and Technology
Standards of Official Conduct

Schroeder, Patricia, D-Colo. (1)
CAPITOL HILL OFFICE:
2208 RHOB 20515; 225-4431
Admin. Assistant   Dan Buck

DISTRICT OFFICE:
1600 Emerson St., Denver 80218; (303) 866-1230; Office Director: Kip Cheroutes.

COMMITTEE ASSIGNMENTS:
Armed Services
Judiciary
Post Office and Civil Service

Schumer, Charles E., D-N.Y. (9)
CAPITOL HILL OFFICE:
2412 RHOB 20515; 225-6616
Fax: 225-4183
Chief of Staff   Marcus Kunian

DISTRICT OFFICES:
1628 Kings Highway, Brooklyn 11229; (718) 965-5400; District Admin.: Florence Stachel.
7315 Yellowstone Blvd., Forest Hills 11375; (718) 268-8200; District Admin.: Florence Stachel.
90-16 Rockaway Beach Blvd., Rockaway 11693; (718) 945-9200; District Admin.: Florence Stachel.

COMMITTEE ASSIGNMENTS:
Banking, Finance, and Urban Affairs
Foreign Affairs
Judiciary

Scott, Robert C., D-Va. (3)
CAPITOL HILL OFFICE:
501 CHOB 20515; 225-8351
Special Assistant   Joni Ivey

DISTRICT OFFICES:
2600 Washington Ave., #1010, Newport News 23607; (804) 380-1000; Fax: (804) 928-6694; Office Manager: Gisele Russell.
501 N. 2nd St., #401, Richmond 23219; (804)

644-4845; Fax: (804) 648-6026; Legislative Assistant: Deitra Trent.

COMMITTEE ASSIGNMENTS:
Education and Labor
Judiciary
Science, Space, and Technology

Sensenbrenner, F. James, Jr., R-Wis. (9)
CAPITOL HILL OFFICE:
2332 RHOB 20515; 225-5101
Admin. Assistant   Todd Schultz

DISTRICT OFFICE:
120 Bishops Way, Brookfield 53005; (414) 784-1111; Office Director: Tom Schreibel.

COMMITTEE ASSIGNMENTS:
Judiciary
Science, Space, and Technology

Serrano, Jose E., D-N.Y. (16)
CAPITOL HILL OFFICE:
336 CHOB 20515; 225-4361
Fax: 225-6001
Chief of Staff   Ellyn M. Toscano

DISTRICT OFFICE:
890 Grand Concourse, Bronx 10451; (718) 538-5400; Fax: (718) 860-6306; Office Director: Cheryl Simmons.

COMMITTEE ASSIGNMENT:
Appropriations

Sharp, Philip R., D-Ind. (2)
CAPITOL HILL OFFICE:
2217 RHOB 20515; 225-3021
Fax: 225-8140
Admin. Assistant   Ron Gyure

DISTRICT OFFICES:
2900 W. Jackson, #101, Muncie 47304; (317) 747-5566.
Main Post Office Bldg., Richmond 47374; (317) 966-6125; Caseworker: Sally Cook.
331 Franklin St., Suite A, Columbus 47201; (812) 372-3637; Staff Assistant: Carol Sewell.

COMMITTEE ASSIGNMENTS:
Energy and Commerce
Natural Resources

Shaw, E. Clay, Jr., R-Fla. (22)
CAPITOL HILL OFFICE:
2267 RHOB 20515; 225-3026
Fax: 225-8398
Admin. Assistant   Lee Johnson

DISTRICT OFFICES:
1512 E. Broward Blvd., #101, Ft. Lauderdale 33301; (305) 522-1800; Fax: (305) 768-0511; Office Director: Dorothy Stuart.
222 Lakeview Ave., #162, West Palm Beach 33401; (407) 832-3007; Office Manager: Vacant.

COMMITTEE ASSIGNMENT:
Ways and Means

Shays, Christopher, R-Conn. (4)
CAPITOL HILL OFFICE:
1034 LHOB 20515; 225-5541
Fax: 225-9629
Admin. Assistant   Betsy Wright Hawkings

DISTRICT OFFICES:
10 Middle St., Bridgeport 06604; (203) 579-5870; Office Director: Dick Slawsky.
888 Washington Blvd., Stamford 06901; (203) 357-8277; Office Director: Vacant.
125 East Ave., Norwalk 06851; (203) 866-6469; Office Director: Vacant.

COMMITTEE ASSIGNMENTS:
Budget
Government Operations

Shepherd, Karen, D-Utah (2)
CAPITOL HILL OFFICE:
414 CHOB 20515; 225-3011
Fax: 226-0354
Admin. Assistant   Mike Burke

DISTRICT OFFICE:
125 S. State St., #2311, Salt Lake City 84138; (801) 524-4394; Fax: (801) 524-4394; District Manager: Robyn Matheson.

COMMITTEE ASSIGNMENTS:
Natural Resources
Public Works and Transportation

Shuster, Bud, R-Pa. (9)
CAPITOL HILL OFFICE:
2188 RHOB 20515; 225-2431
Fax: 225-2486
Chief of Staff   Ann Eppard

DISTRICT OFFICES:
R.D. 2, Box 711, Altoona 16601; (814) 946-1653 Office Director: Judy Giansanti.
179 E. Queen St., Chambersburg 17201; (717) 264-8308; Office Director: Mike Joyce.

Sisisky, Norman, D-Va. (4)
CAPITOL HILL OFFICE:
2352 RHOB 20515; 225-6365
Fax: 226-1170
Admin. Assistant   Jan Faircloth

DISTRICT OFFICES:
309 County St., 1 Bristol Square, #204, Portsmouth 23704; (804) 393-2068; Office Director: Vacant.
43 Rives Rd., Petersburg 23805; (804) 732-2544; Office Director: Rick Franklin.
425H S. Main St., Emporia 23847; (804) 634-5575; Office Director: Rick Franklin.

COMMITTEE ASSIGNMENTS:
Armed Services
Small Business

Skaggs, David E., D-Colo. (2)
CAPITOL HILL OFFICE:
1124 LHOB 20515; 225-2161
Chief of Staff   Stephen Saunders

DISTRICT OFFICE:
9101 Harlan, #130, Westminster 00030, (303) 650-7886; District Director: Sue Damour.

COMMITTEE ASSIGNMENTS:
Appropriations
Select Intelligence

Skeen, Joe, R-N.M. (2)
CAPITOL HILL OFFICE:
2367 RHOB 20515; 225-2365
Chief of Staff   Suzanne Eisold

DISTRICT OFFICES:
1065-B S. Main, Suite A, Las Cruces 88005; (505) 527-1771; District Representative: Dorothy Thomas.
257 Federal Bldg., Roswell 88201; (505) 622-0055; District Representative: Alice Eppers.

COMMITTEE ASSIGNMENT:
Appropriations

Skelton, Ike, D-Mo. (4)
CAPITOL HILL OFFICE:
2227 RHOB 20515; 225-2876
Admin. Assistant   Jack Pollard

DISTRICT OFFICES:
319 S. Lamine St., Sedalia 65301; (816) 826-2675; Office Director: Berna Dean Nierman.
1616 Industrial Dr., Jefferson City 65109; (314) 35-3499; Office Director: Ann Kutscher.

219 N. Adams St., Lebanon 65536; (417) 532-7964; Office Director: Shirley Clark.
514-B N. Seven Highway, Blue Springs 64014; (816) 228-4242; Office Director: Bob Hagedorn.

COMMITTEE ASSIGNMENTS:
Armed Services
Small Business

Slattery, Jim, D-Kan. (2)
CAPITOL HILL OFFICE:
2243 RHOB 20515; 225-6601
Admin. Assistant   Howard Bauleke

DISTRICT OFFICES:
700 S.W. Jackson, #803, Topeka 66603; (913) 233-2503; District Director: Phil Kirk.
1001 N. Broadway, Suite C, P.O. Box 1306, Pittsburg 66752; (316) 231-6040; S.E. Kan. Director: Paula Gilchrist.

COMMITTEE ASSIGNMENTS:
Energy and Commerce
Veterans' Affairs

Slaughter, Louise M., D-N.Y. (28)
CAPITOL HILL OFFICE:
2421 RHOB 20515; 225-3615
Fax: 225-7822
Admin. Assistant   Tom Bantle

DISTRICT OFFICE:
100 State St., #3120, Rochester 14614; (716) 232-4850; District Representative: Mike Keane.

COMMITTEE ASSIGNMENTS:
Budget
Rules

Smith, Bob, R-Ore. (2)
CAPITOL HILL OFFICE:
108 CHOB 20515; 225-6730
Chief of Staff   Paul Unger

DISTRICT OFFICE:
259 Barnett Rd., Suite E, Medford 97501; (503) 776-4646; Office Director: Leigh Johnson.

COMMITTEE ASSIGNMENTS:
Agriculture
Natural Resources

Smith, Christopher H., R-N.J. (4)
CAPITOL HILL OFFICE:
2353 RHOB 20515; 225-3765
Fax: 225-7768
Admin. Assistant   Martin Dannenfelser

COMMITTEE ASSIGNMENT:
Public Works and Transportation (Ranking)

DISTRICT OFFICES:
1720 Greenwood Ave., Trenton 08609; (609) 890-2800; Fax: (609) 890-0172; Office Director: Joyce Golden.
427 High St., #1, Burlington City 08016; (609) 386-5534; Fax: (609) 386-6878; Office Director: Pidge Carroll.
38-A Whiting Shopping Center, Whiting 08759; (908) 350-2300; Fax: (908) 350-6260; Office Director: Loretta Charbonneau.

COMMITTEE ASSIGNMENTS:
Foreign Affairs
Veterans' Affairs

Smith, Lamar, R-Texas (21)
CAPITOL HILL OFFICE:
2443 RHOB 20515; 225-4236
Admin. Assistant   John Lampmann

DISTRICT OFFICES:
1100 N.E. Loop 410, #640, San Antonio 78209; (210) 821-5024; District Director: O'Lene Stone.
201 W. Wall St., #104, Midland 79701; (915) 687-5232; Office Director: Ann Bradford.
33 E. Twohig, #302, San Angelo 76903; (915) 653-3971; Office Director: Jo Anne Powell.
1006 Junction Highway, Kerrville 78028; (512) 895-1414; Office Director: Kathy Temple.
221 E. Main, #318, Round Rock 78664; (512) 218-4221; Office Director: Jodell Brooks.

COMMITTEE ASSIGNMENTS:
Budget
Judiciary

Smith, Neal, D-Iowa (4)
CAPITOL HILL OFFICE:
2373 RHOB 20515; 225-4426
Admin. Assistant   Tom Dawson

DISTRICT OFFICES:
544 Insurance Exchange Bldg., Des Moines 50309; (515) 284-4634; Office Director: Kay Bolton.
40 Pearl St., Council Bluffs 51503; (712) 323-5976; Office Director: Jane Bell.

COMMITTEE ASSIGNMENTS:
Appropriations
Small Business

Smith, Nick, R-Mich. (7)
CAPITOL HILL OFFICE:
1708 LHOB 20515; 225-6276
Fax: 225-6281
Chief of Staff   Jon Gauthier

DISTRICT OFFICES:
209 E. Washington, #200-D, Jackson 49201; (517) 783-4486; Fax: (517) 783-3012; District Administrative Assistant: Mary Douglass.

121 S. Cochran Ave., Charlotte 48813; (517) 543-0055; Fax: (517) 543-7116; District Administrative Assistant: Mary Douglass.
118 W. Church St., Adrian 49221; (517) 265-5012; Fax: (517) 265-3375; District Administrative Assistant: Mary Douglass.

COMMITTEE ASSIGNMENTS:
Agriculture
Budget
Science, Space, and Technology

Snowe, Olympia J., R-Maine (2)
CAPITOL HILL OFFICE:
2268 RHOB 20515; 225-6306
Fax: 225-8297
Admin. Assistant   Judith Butler

DISTRICT OFFICES:
2 Great Falls Plaza, #7B, Auburn 04210; (207) 786-2451; Fax: (207) 782-1438; Office Director: John Richter.
1 Cumberland Place, #306, Bangor 04401; (207) 945-0432; Fax: (207) 941-9525; Field Representative: Kevin Raye.
169 Academy St., Presque Isle 04769; (207) 764-5124; Fax: (207) 764-6420; Office Director: Marion Higgins.

COMMITTEE ASSIGNMENTS:
Budget
Foreign Affairs

Solomon, Gerald B. H., R-N.Y. (22)
CAPITOL HILL OFFICE:
2265 RHOB 20515; 225-5614
Fax: 225-6234
Admin. Assistant   Herb Koster

DISTRICT OFFICES:
285 Broadway, Saratoga Springs 12866; (518) 587-9800; Staff Assistant: Mary Ellen Tarantino.
337 Fairview Ave., Hudson 12534; (518) 828-0181; Staff Assistant: Pat Hart.
21 Bay St., Glens Falls 12801; (518) 792-3031, Office Assistant: Dan Orsini.

COMMITTEE ASSIGNMENT:
Rules (Ranking)

Spence, Floyd D., R-S.C. (2)
CAPITOL HILL OFFICE:
2405 RHOB 20515; 225-2452
Fax: 225-2455
Admin. Assistant   Craig Metz

DISTRICT OFFICES:
220 Stoneridge Dr., #202, Columbia 2921((803) 254-5120; Fax: (803) 779-3406; District Admin Mary T. Howard.

1681 Chestnut St. N.E., P.O. Box 1609, Orangeburg 29115; (803) 536-4641; Fax: (803) 536-5754; District Admin.: Chessye B. Powell.

916 Bay St., P.O. Box 1538, Beaufort 29902; (803) 521-2530; Fax: (803) 521-2535; Field Representative: Sara S. Breedlove.

66 E. Railroad Ave., P.O. Box 550, Estill 29918; (803) 625-3177; Field Representative: Mary Eleanor Bowers.

COMMITTEE ASSIGNMENTS:
Armed Services (Ranking)
Veterans' Affairs

Spratt, John M., Jr., D-S.C. (5)
CAPITOL HILL OFFICE:
1536 LHOB 20515; 225-5501
Fax: 225-0464
Admin. Assistant   Ellen Wallace Buchanan

DISTRICT OFFICES:
Federal Bldg., P.O. Box 350, Rock Hill 29731; (803) 327-1114; Fax: (803) 327-4330; District Admin.: Robert H. Hopkins.

39 E. Calhoun St., Sumter 29150; (803) 773-3362; Fax: (803) 773-7662; Congressional Aide: Carolyn McCoy.

88 Public Square, P.O. Box 25, Darlington 29532; (803) 393-3998; Congressional Aide: Joanne Langley.

COMMITTEE ASSIGNMENTS:
Armed Services
Government Operations

Stark, Pete, D-Calif. (13)
CAPITOL HILL OFFICE:
239 CHOB 20515; 225-5065
Fax: 225-0902
Admin. Assistant   Bill Vaughan

DISTRICT OFFICE:
22320 Foothill Blvd., #500, Hayward 94541; (415) 635-1092; Office Director: Annie Zatlin.

COMMITTEE ASSIGNMENTS:
District of Columbia (Chairman)
Joint Economic
Ways and Means

Stearns, Cliff, R-Fla. (6)
CAPITOL HILL OFFICE:
332 CHOB 20515; 225-5744
Fax: 225-3973
Admin. Assistant   Jack Seum

DISTRICT OFFICES:
115 S.E. 25th Ave., Ocala 34471; (904) 351-8777; Fax: (904) 351-8011; District Manager: Sharon Brooks.

111 S. 6th St., Leesburg 34748; (904) 326-8285;

Fax: (904) 326-9430; Caseworker: Catherine Potter.

1726 Kingsley Ave., #8, Orange Park 32073; (904) 269-3203; Fax: (904) 269-3343; Staff Assistant: Todd Schnick.

COMMITTEE ASSIGNMENTS:
Energy and Commerce
Veterans' Affairs

Stenholm, Charles W., D-Texas (17)
CAPITOL HILL OFFICE:
1211 LHOB 20515; 225-6605
Admin. Assistant   Lois Auer

DISTRICT OFFICES:
P.O. Box 1237, Stamford 79553; (915) 773-3623; Office Director: Bill Longley.

P.O. Box 1101, Abilene 79604; (915) 673-7221; Office Director: Elaine Talley.

33 E. Twohig, San Angelo 76903; (915) 655-7994; Office Director: Jayne Schoonmaker.

COMMITTEE ASSIGNMENTS:
Agriculture
Budget

Stokes, Louis, D-Ohio (11)
CAPITOL HILL OFFICE:
2365 RHOB 20515; 225-7032
Admin. Assistant   Leslie Atkinson

DISTRICT OFFICES:
1240 E. 9th St., #2947, Cleveland 44199; (216) 522-4900; Fax: (216) 522-4906; Office Manager: Jewell Gilbert.

2140 Lee Rd., #211, Cleveland Heights 44118; (216) 522-4907; Fax: (216) 397-0445; Staff Assistant: Juanita Philips.

COMMITTEE ASSIGNMENT:
Appropriations

Strickland, Ted, D-Ohio (6)
CAPITOL HILL OFFICE:
1429 LHOB 20515; 225-5705
Admin. Assistant   Frances Strickland

DISTRICT OFFICE:
1236 Gallia St., Portsmouth 45662; (614) 353-5171; Fax: (614) 354-2124; Executive Assistant: Carolyn Andrews.

COMMITTEE ASSIGNMENTS:
Education and Labor
Small Business

Studds, Gerry E., D-Mass. (10)
CAPITOL HILL OFFICE:
237 CHOB 20515; 225-3111
Admin. Assistant   Steven Schwadron

DISTRICT OFFICES:
146 Main St., Hyannis 02601; (508) 771-0666; Fax: (508) 790-1959; Office Director: Mark Forest.
1212 Hancock St., Quincy 02169; (617) 770-3700; Fax: (617) 770-2984; Office Director: Gerard Dhooge.
166 Main St., Brockton 02401; (508) 584-6666; Fax: (508) 580-4692; Office Director: Kate Kelliher.
225 Water St., Plymouth 02360; (508) 747-5500; Fax: (508) 747-6990; Office Director: Kim Arouca.

COMMITTEE ASSIGNMENTS:
Energy and Commerce
Merchant Marine and Fisheries (Chairman)

Stump, Bob, R-Ariz. (3)
CAPITOL HILL OFFICE:
211 CHOB 20515; 225-4576
Fax: 225-6328
Admin. Assistant   Lisa Jackson

DISTRICT OFFICE:
230 N. 1st Ave., #2001, Phoenix 85025; (602) 379-6923; Office Manager: Arlene Lassila.

COMMITTEE ASSIGNMENTS:
Armed Services
Veterans' Affairs (Ranking)

Stupak, Bart, D-Mich. (1)
CAPITOL HILL OFFICE:
317 CHOB 20515; 225-4735
Fax: 225-4744
Admin. Assistant   John Wyma

DISTRICT OFFICES:
1229 W. Washington, Marquette 49855; (906) 228-3700; District Admin.: Scott Schloegel.
111 W. Chisolm, Alpena 49707; (517) 356-0690; Staff Assistant: Karl Opheim.
160 E. State St., Traverse City 49684; (616) 929-4711; District Admin.: Scott Schloegel.
2501 14th Ave. South, Escanaba 49829; (906) 786-4504; Staff Assistant: Cindy Frazer.
616 Sheldon, Houghton 49931; (906) 482-1371.

COMMITTEE ASSIGNMENTS:
Armed Services
Government Operations
Merchant Marine and Fisheries

Sundquist, Don, R-Tenn. (7)
CAPITOL HILL OFFICE:
339 CHOB 20515; 225-2811
Fax: 225-2814
Admin. Assistant   Thomas J. McNamara

DISTRICT OFFICES:
5909 Shelby Oaks Dr., #213, Memphis 38134; (901) 382-5811; Office Director: Gwen Hurd.
117 S. 2nd St., Clarksville 37040; (615) 552-4406; Office Director: Kathy Higginbotham.
149 Cypress St., P.O. Box 68, Selmer 38375; (901) 645-4402; Office Director: Jimmy Daniel.

COMMITTEE ASSIGNMENT:
Ways and Means

Swett, Dick, D-N.H. (2)
CAPITOL HILL OFFICE:
230 CHOB 20515; 225-5206
Admin. Assistant   Kay A. King

DISTRICT OFFICES:
18 N. Main St., Concord 03301; (603) 224-6621; District Director: Shireen Tilley.
5 Coliseum Ave., Nashua 03063; (603) 880-6142; Office Manager: Paul Bagley.
127 Main St., Littleton 03561; (603) 444-1321; Office Manager: Richard Polonsky.

COMMITTEE ASSIGNMENTS:
Public Works and Transportation
Science, Space, and Technology

Swift, Al, D-Wash. (2)
CAPITOL HILL OFFICE:
1502 LHOB 20515; 225-2605
Fax: 225-2608
Admin. Assistant   Janet Thiessen

DISTRICT OFFICES:
104 W. Magnolia, #308, Bellingham 98225; (206) 733-4500; Office Director: Andy Anderson.
3002 Colby Ave., #201, Everett 98201; (206) 252-3188; Office Director: Jill McKinnie.

COMMITTEE ASSIGNMENTS:
Energy and Commerce
House Administration

Synar, Mike, D-Okla. (2)
CAPITOL HILL OFFICE:
2329 RHOB 20515; 225-2701
Fax: 225-2796
Admin. Assistant   Vivek Varma

DISTRICT OFFICE:
125 S. Main St., #2B22, Muskogee 74401; (918) 687-2533; Office Director: Gene Wallace.

COMMITTEE ASSIGNMENTS:
Energy and Commerce
Government Operations
Judiciary

Talent, James M., R-Mo. (2)
CAPITOL HILL OFFICE:
  1022 LHOB 20515; 225-2561
  Fax: 225-2563
    Admin. Assistant   Mark Strand

DISTRICT OFFICES:
  555 N. New Vallas, #315, St. Louis 63141; (314)
872-9561; District Director: Barbara Cooper.
  820 S. Main St., #206, St. Charles 63301; (314)
949-6826; District Manager: Barbara Cooper.

COMMITTEE ASSIGNMENTS:
  Armed Services
  Small Business

Tanner, John, D-Tenn. (8)
CAPITOL HILL OFFICE:
  1427 LHOB 20515; 225-4714
  Fax: 225-1765
    Admin. Assistant   Vickie Walling

DISTRICT OFFICES:
  2836 Coleman Rd., Memphis 38128; (901) 382-
3220; Staff Assistant: Margaret Black.
  Post Office Bldg., #B-7, Jackson 38302; (901)
423-4848; Staff Assistant: Martha Truell.
  203 W. Church St., Union City 38261; (901) 885-
7070, Staff Assistant: Joe Hill.

COMMITTEE ASSIGNMENTS:
  Armed Services
  Science, Space, and Technology

Tauzin, W. J. "Billy," D-La. (3)
CAPITOL HILL OFFICE:
  2330 RHOB 20515; 225-4031
    Admin. Assistant   Emily Young Shaw

DISTRICT OFFICES:
  501 Camp St., #1041, New Orleans 70130; (504)
589-6366; District Representative: Peggy Bourgeois.
  107 Federal Bldg., Houma 70360; (504) 876-
3033; District Representative: Patrick Bell.
  210 E. Main St., New Iberia 70560; (318) 367-
8231; Staff Assistant: Jan Viator.
  828 S. Irma Blvd., Gonzales 70737; (504) 621-
3490; District Director: Martin Cancienne.

COMMITTEE ASSIGNMENTS:
  Energy and Commerce
  Merchant Marine and Fisheries

Taylor, Charles H., R-N.C. (11)
CAPITOL HILL OFFICE:
  516 CHOB 20515; 225-6401
    Admin. Assistant   Roger France

DISTRICT OFFICE:
  22 S. Pack Square, Asheville 28801; (704) 251-
1988; District Representative: Charles Queller.

COMMITTEE ASSIGNMENTS:
  Appropriations
  Merchant Marine and Fisheries

Taylor, Gene, D-Miss. (5)
CAPITOL HILL OFFICE:
  215 CHOB 20515; 225-5772
  Fax: 225-7074
    Admin. Assistant   Wayne Weidie

DISTRICT OFFICES:
  2424 14th St., Gulfport 39501; (601) 864-7670;
Office Director: Margaret Hadden.
  701 Main St., #215, Hattiesburg 39401; (601)
582-3246; District Manager: Jerry Martin.
  706 Watts Ave., Pascagoula 39567; (601) 762-
1770; Office Director: Brian Martin.

COMMITTEE ASSIGNMENTS:
  Armed Services
  Merchant Marine and Fisheries

Tejeda, Frank, D-Texas (28)
CAPITOL HILL OFFICE:
  323 CHOB 20515; 225-1640
  Fax: 225-1641
    Admin. Assistant   Jeff Mendelsohn

DISTRICT OFFICE:
  1313 S.E. Military Dr., #115, San Antonio 78214;
(210) 924-7383; District Director: Frances Lozano.

COMMITTEE ASSIGNMENTS:
  Armed Services
  Veterans' Affairs

Thomas, Bill, R-Calif. (21)
CAPITOL HILL OFFICE:
  2209 RHOB 20515; 225-2915
  Fax: 225-8798
    Admin. Assistant   Cathy Abernathy

DISTRICT OFFICES:
  4100 Truxtun Ave., #220, Bakersfield 93301;
(805) 327-3611; Fax: (805) 631-9535.
  319 W. Murray St., Visalia 93291; (209) 627-6549;
District Representative: Marjorie Lancaster.

COMMITTEE ASSIGNMENTS:
  House Administration (Ranking)
  Ways and Means

Thomas, Craig, R-Wyo. (AL)
CAPITOL HILL OFFICE:
  1019 LHOB 20515; 225-2311

Fax: 225-0726
Admin. Assistant   Elizabeth Brimmer

DISTRICT OFFICES:
Federal Bldg., #4003, Casper 82601; (307) 261-5413; Fax: (307) 265-6706; Office Director: Carol Leffler.
Federal Bldg., #2015, Cheyenne 82001; (307) 772-2451; Fax: (307) 638-3512; Office Director: Ruthann Norris.
2632 Foothill Blvd., #101, Rock Springs 82901; (307) 362-5012; Fax: (307) 362-5129; Office Director: Pati Smith.

COMMITTEE ASSIGNMENTS:
Banking, Finance, and Urban Affairs
Government Operations
Natural Resources

Thompson, Bennie, D-Miss. (2)
CAPITOL HILL OFFICE:
1408 LHOB 20515; 225-5876
Fax: 225-5898
Chief of Staff   Bonnie Walker-Armstrong

DISTRICT OFFICE:
107 W. Madison St., P.O. Box 610, Bolton 39041; (601) 866-9003; District Director: Charles Horhn.

COMMITTEE ASSIGNMENTS:
Agriculture
Merchant Marine and Fisheries
Small Business

Thornton, Ray, D-Ark. (2)
CAPITOL HILL OFFICE:
1214 LHOB 20515; 225-2506
Fax: 225-9273
Staff Director   Ed Fry

DISTRICT OFFICE:
700 W. Capitol Ave., #1527, Little Rock 72201; (501) 324-5941; Fax: (501) 324-6029; District Assistant: Julie Speed.

COMMITTEE ASSIGNMENT:
Appropriations

Thurman, Karen L., D-Fla. (5)
CAPITOL HILL OFFICE:
130 CHOB 20515; 225-1002
Admin. Assistant   Nora Matus

DISTRICT OFFICES:
1 Courthouse Square, #102, Inverness 34450; (904) 344-3044; Fax: (904) 637-1789; District Manager: Anne Morgan.
5700 S.W. 34th St., #425, Gainesville 32608; (904) 336-6614; Fax: (904) 336-6376; Caseworker: Audrey Nuzzo.
5623 U.S. 19 South, #206, New Port Richey

34652; (813) 849-4496; Fax: (813) 845-0462; Caseworker: Linda Tucker.

COMMITTEE ASSIGNMENTS:
Agriculture
Government Operations

Torkildsen, Peter G., R-Mass. (6)
CAPITOL HILL OFFICE:
120 CHOB 20515; 225-8020
Admin. Assistant   Steven Sutton

DISTRICT OFFICES:
70 Washington St., Salem 01970; (508) 741-1600; District Manager: Judy Cypret.
156 Broad St., #106, Lynn 01901; (617) 599-2424; Office Director: Pat Warnock.
160 Main St., Haverhill 01830; (508) 521-0111; Office Manager: Vacant.
61 Center St., Burlington 01803; (617) 273-4400; Office Manager: Vacant.

COMMITTEE ASSIGNMENTS:
Armed Services
Merchant Marine and Fisheries
Small Business

Torres, Esteban E., D-Calif. (34)
CAPITOL HILL OFFICE:
1740 LHOB 20515; 225-5256
Chief of Staff   Albert Jacquez

DISTRICT OFFICE:
8819 Whittier Blvd., #101, Pico Rivera 90660; (310) 695-0702; Chief of Staff: James Casso.

COMMITTEE ASSIGNMENT:
Appropriations

Torricelli, Robert G., D-N.J. (9)
CAPITOL HILL OFFICE:
2159 RHOB 20515; 225-5061
Fax: 225-0843
Admin. Assistant   James P. Fox

DISTRICT OFFICE:
25 Main St., Hackensack 07601; (201) 646-1111; District Admin.: John Dressner.

COMMITTEE ASSIGNMENTS:
Foreign Affairs
Science, Space, and Technology
Select Intelligence

Towns, Edolphus, D-N.Y. (10)
CAPITOL HILL OFFICE:
2232 RHOB 20515; 225-5936
Admin. Assistant   Brenda Pillors

DISTRICT OFFICES:
    545 Broadway, Brooklyn 11206; (718) 387-8696; District Director: Vacant.
    16 Court St., #1505, Brooklyn 11241; (718) 855-8018; District Director: Vacant.

COMMITTEE ASSIGNMENTS:
    Energy and Commerce
    Government Operations

Traficant, James A., Jr., D-Ohio (17)
CAPITOL HILL OFFICE:
    2446 RHOB 20515; 225-5261
    Chief of Staff   Paul Marcone

DISTRICT OFFICES:
    125 Market St., Youngstown 44503; (216) 788-2414; Office Director: Charles P. O'Nesti.
    5555 Youngstown-Warren Rd., #2700, Niles 44446; (216) 652-5649; Staff Assistant: Betty Manente.
    109 W. 3rd St., East Liverpool 43920; (216) 385-5921; Office Director: Carrie Davis.

COMMITTEE ASSIGNMENTS:
    Public Works and Transportation
    Science, Space, and Technology

Tucker, Walter R., III, D-Calif. (37)
CAPITOL HILL OFFICE:
    419 CHOB 20515; 225-7924
    Fax: 225-7926
    Admin. Assistant   Marcus Mason

DISTRICT OFFICE:
    145 E. Compton Blvd., Compton 90220; (310) 884-9989; Fax: (310) 884-9902; District Manager: Audrey Gibson.

COMMITTEE ASSIGNMENTS:
    Public Works and Transportation
    Small Business

Underwood, Robert Anacletus, D-Guam (AL)
CAPITOL HILL OFFICE:
    507 CHOB 20515; 225-1188
    Admin. Assistant   Terri Schroeder

DISTRICT OFFICE:
    190 Hernan Cortez St., #106, Agana 96910; (671) 477-4272; Acting District Manager: Vince Leon-Guererro.

COMMITTEE ASSIGNMENTS:
    Armed Services
    Education and Labor
    Natural Resources

Unsoeld, Jolene, D-Wash. (3)
CAPITOL HILL OFFICE:
    1527 LHOB 20515; 225-3536
    Fax: 226-1048
    Chief of Staff   Jim Hoff

DISTRICT OFFICES:
    601 Main St., #505, Vancouver 98660; (206) 696-7942; District Representative: Donna Levin.
    1110 Capitol Way South, #404, Olympia 98501; (206) 753-9528; District Coordinator: Clover Lockard.

COMMITTEE ASSIGNMENTS:
    Education and Labor
    Merchant Marine and Fisheries

Upton, Fred, R-Mich. (6)
CAPITOL HILL OFFICE:
    2439 RHOB 20515; 225-3761
    Fax: 225-4986
    Admin. Assistant   Joan Hillebrands

DISTRICT OFFICES:
    421 Main St., St. Joseph 49085; (616) 982-1986; Office Director: Jack Baker.
    535 S. Burdick, #225, Kalamazoo 19007, (616) 385-0039; Office Manager: Jeff Breneman.

COMMITTEE ASSIGNMENT:
    Energy and Commerce

Valentine, Tim, D-N.C. (2)
CAPITOL HILL OFFICE:
    2229 RHOB 20515; 225-4531
    Fax: 225-1539
    Admin. Assistant   Ed Nagy

DISTRICT OFFICES:
    3310 Croasdaile Dr., #302, Durham 27705; (919) 383-9404; Fax: (919) 383-9606; Staff Assistant: Sandra Massenburg.
    101 Triangle Court, Nashville 27856; (919) 459-8881; Fax: (919) 459-7674; Admin. Assistant: A.B. Swindell.

COMMITTEE ASSIGNMENTS:
    Public Works and Transportation
    Science, Space, and Technology

Velazquez, Nydia M., D-N.Y. (12)
CAPITOL HILL OFFICE:
    132 CHOB 20515; 225-2361
    Fax: 226-0327
    Admin. Assistant   Karen Ackerman

DISTRICT OFFICES:
815 Broadway, Brooklyn 11206; (718) 599-3658;
Fax: (718) 599-4537; District Administrator: Marta Garcia.
98-100 Avenue C, New York 10009; (212) 673-3997; Fax: (212) 473-5242; District Administrator: Vacant.
50-07 108th St., 2nd Floor, Queens 11368; (718) 699-2602; District Administrator: Vacant.

COMMITTEE ASSIGNMENTS:
Banking, Finance, and Urban Affairs
Small Business

Vento, Bruce F., D-Minn. (4)
CAPITOL HILL OFFICE:
2304 RHOB 20515; 225-6631
Admin. Assistant   Larry Romans

DISTRICT OFFICE:
175 5th St. East, #727, St. Paul 55101; (612) 224-4503; Fax: (612) 224-0575; District Director: Molly Grove.

COMMITTEE ASSIGNMENTS:
Banking, Finance, and Urban Affairs
Natural Resources

Visclosky, Peter J., D-Ind. (1)
CAPITOL HILL OFFICE:
2464 RHOB 20515; 225-2461
Fax: 225-2493
Admin. Assistant   Chuck Brimmer

DISTRICT OFFICES:
215 W. 35th Ave., Gary 46408; (219) 884-1177; District Director: Adam Adams.
6070 Central Ave., Portage 46368; (219) 763-2904; District Director: Adam Adams.
166 Lincolnway, Valparaiso 46383; (219) 464-0315; District Director: Adam Adams.

COMMITTEE ASSIGNMENT:
Appropriations

Volkmer, Harold L., D-Mo. (9)
CAPITOL HILL OFFICE:
2409 RHOB 20515; 225-2956
Admin. Assistant   Jim Spurling

DISTRICT OFFICES:
370 Federal Office Bldg., Hannibal 63401; (314) 221-1200; District Supervisor: Lee Viorel.
122 Bourke St., Macon 63552; (816) 385-5615; Office Director: Carol Phillips.
912 E. Walnut St., Columbia 65201; (314) 449-5111; Office Director: Ewell Lawson.
317 Lafayette, Washington 63090; (314) 239-4001; Office Director: Virginia Brumit.

COMMITTEE ASSIGNMENTS:
Agriculture
Science, Space, and Technology

Vucanovich, Barbara F., R-Nev. (2)
CAPITOL HILL OFFICE:
2202 RHOB 20515; 225-6155
Fax: 225-2319
Admin. Assistant   Michael Pieper

DISTRICT OFFICES:
300 Booth St., #3038, Reno 89509; (702) 784-5003; District Representative: Olive Hill.
368 7th St., Elko 89801; (702) 738-4064; Regional Representative: Frances Thiercof.
6900 Westcliff Dr., #509, Las Vegas 89128; (702) 399-3555; Regional Representative: Joan Dimmitt.

COMMITTEE ASSIGNMENTS:
Appropriations
Natural Resources

Walker, Robert S., R-Pa. (16)
CAPITOL HILL OFFICE:
2369 RHOB 20515; 225-2411
Fax: 225-1116
Admin. Assistant   Connie Thumma

DISTRICT OFFICES:
50 N. Duke St., Lancaster 17604; (717) 393-0666; District Administrator: Marc Phillips.
Exton Commons, #595, Exton 19341; (610) 363-8409; District Administrator: Marc Phillips.

COMMITTEE ASSIGNMENT:
Science, Space, and Technology (Ranking)

Walsh, James T., R-N.Y. (25)
CAPITOL HILL OFFICE:
1330 LHOB 20515; 225-3701
Fax: 225-4042
Admin. Assistant   Art Jutton

DISTRICT OFFICES:
1269 Federal Bldg., P.O. Box 7306, Syracuse 13261; (315) 432-5669; Fax: (315) 423-5669; District Representative: John McGuire.
1 Lincoln St., Auburn 13021; (315) 255-0649; Fax: (315) 255-1369; Staff Assistant: Vivien Norman.

COMMITTEE ASSIGNMENT:
Appropriations

Washington, Craig, D-Texas (18)
CAPITOL HILL OFFICE:
1711 LHOB 20515; 225-3816
Fax: 225-6186
Admin. Assistant   Natalie Warner

DISTRICT OFFICE:
1919 Smith St., #820, Houston 77002; (713) 739-7339; Legal Counsel: Sidney Braquet.

COMMITTEE ASSIGNMENTS:
Energy and Commerce
Government Operations
Judiciary

Waters, Maxine, D-Calif. (35)
CAPITOL HILL OFFICE:
1207 LHOB 20515; 225-2201
Fax: 225-7854
Chief of Staff   Kelly Ganges

DISTRICT OFFICE:
10124 S. Broadway, #1, Los Angeles 90003; (213) 757-8900; Fax: (213) 757-9506; District Director: Roderick Wright.

COMMITTEE ASSIGNMENTS:
Banking, Finance, and Urban Affairs
Small Business
Veterans' Affairs

Watt, Melvin, D-N.C. (12)
CAPITOL HILL OFFICE:
1232 LHOB 20515; 225-1510
Fax: 225-1512
Admin. Assistant   Joan Kennedy

DISTRICT OFFICES:
214 N. Church St., #130, Charlotte 28202; (704) 344-9950; Fax: (704) 344-9971; District Manager: Don Baker.
301 S. Greene St., #210, Greensboro 27401; (910) 379-9403; Fax: (910) 379-9429; District Aide: Pamelyn Stubbs.
315 E. Chapel Hill St., #202, Durham 27702; (919) 688-3004; Fax: (919) 688-0940; District Aide: Tracy Lovett.

COMMITTEE ASSIGNMENTS:
Banking, Finance, and Urban Affairs
Judiciary
Post Office and Civil Service

Waxman, Henry A., D-Calif. (29)
CAPITOL HILL OFFICE:
2408 RHOB 20515; 225-3976
Fax: 225-4099
Admin. Assistant   Philip Schiliro

DISTRICT OFFICE:
8436 W. 3rd St., #600, Los Angeles 90048; (213) 651-1040; Office Director: Howard Elinson.

COMMITTEE ASSIGNMENTS:
Energy and Commerce
Government Operations

Weldon, Curt, R-Pa. (7)
CAPITOL HILL OFFICE:
2452 RHOB 20515; 225-2011
Fax: 225-8137
Admin. Assistant   Doug Ritter

DISTRICT OFFICES:
1554 Garrett Rd., Upper Darby 19082; (610) 259-0700; Office Director: Dennis Lynch.
30 S. Valley Rd., #212, Paoli 19301; (610) 640-9064; Office Director: Vacant.

COMMITTEE ASSIGNMENTS:
Armed Services
Merchant Marine and Fisheries

Wheat, Alan, D-Mo. (5)
CAPITOL HILL OFFICE:
2334 RHOB 20515; 225-4535
Fax: 225-5990
Admin. Assistant   Margaret E. Broadaway

DISTRICT OFFICES:
811 Grand, #935, Kansas City 64106; (816) 842-4545; Office Director: Gerard Grimaldi.
301 W. Lexington, #221, Independence 64050; (816) 833-4545; Caseworker: Shelila Thompson.

COMMITTEE ASSIGNMENTS:
District of Columbia
Rules

Whitten, Jamie L., D-Miss. (1)
CAPITOL HILL OFFICE:
2314 RHOB 20515; 225-4306
Fax: 225-4328
Admin. Assistant   Hal DeCell

DISTRICT OFFICES:
Post Office Bldg., Charleston 38921; (601) 647-2413; Office Director: Isabelle Hayes.
Post Office Bldg., Oxford 38655; (601) 234-9064; Office Director: Debbie Little.
Federal Bldg., Tupelo 38801; (601) 844-5437; Office Director: Billy Ballard.

COMMITTEE ASSIGNMENT:
Appropriations

Williams, Pat, D-Mont. (AL)
CAPITOL HILL OFFICE:
2457 RHOB 20515; 225-3211
Admin. Assistant   Jim Foley

DISTRICT OFFICES:
316 N. Park Ave., Helena 59601; (406) 443-7878; Staff Assistant: Joe Lamsom.
302 W. Broadway, Missoula 59802; (406) 549-5550; District Director: Mike Barton.
Finlen Complex, Broadway and Wyoming, Butte

59701; (406) 723-4404; Office Director: Art Noonan.
325 2nd Ave. North, Great Falls 59401; (406) 771-1242; Staff Assistant: T.J. Gilles.
2806 3rd Ave. North, Billings 59101; (406) 256-1019; Staff Assistant: Kathy McCleary-Wilson.

COMMITTEE ASSIGNMENTS:
Agriculture
Education and Labor
Natural Resources

Wilson, Charles, D-Texas (2)
CAPITOL HILL OFFICE:
2256 RHOB 20515; 225-2401
Admin. Assistant   Peyton Walters

DISTRICT OFFICE:
701 N. 1st St., #201, Lufkin 75901; (409) 637-1770; Fax: (409) 632-8588; District Director: Shaun Davis.

COMMITTEE ASSIGNMENT:
Appropriations

Wise, Bob, D-W.Va. (2)
CAPITOL HILL OFFICE:
2434 RHOB 20515; 225-2711
Admin. Assistant   Lowell Johnson

DISTRICT OFFICES:
107 Pennsylvania Ave., Charleston 25302; (304) 342-7170; Office Director: Sandy Casdorph.
102 E. Martin St., Martinsburg 25401; (304) 264-8810; Office Director: Chip Slaven.

COMMITTEE ASSIGNMENTS:
Budget
Public Works and Transportation

Wolf, Frank R., R-Va. (10)
CAPITOL HILL OFFICE:
104 CHOB 20515; 225-5136
Admin. Assistant   Charles E. White

DISTRICT OFFICES:
13873 Park Center Rd., #130, Herndon 22071; (703) 709-5800; Fax: (703) 709-5802; Office Director: Judy McCary.
110 N. Cameron St., Winchester 22601; (703) 667-0990; Fax: (703) 678-0402; Office Director: Donna Crowley.

COMMITTEE ASSIGNMENT:
Appropriations

Woolsey, Lynn, D-Calif. (6)
CAPITOL HILL OFFICE:
439 CHOB 20515; 225-5161
Admin. Assistant   Mark Isaac

DISTRICT OFFICES:
1301 Redwood Way, #205, Petaluma 94954; (707) 795-1462; Fax: (707) 795-4903; District Director: Danielle Tinman.
1050 Northgate Dr., #140, San Rafael 94903; (415) 507-9554; Fax: (415) 507-9601; Senior District Field Representative: Grant Davis.

COMMITTEE ASSIGNMENTS:
Budget
Education and Labor
Government Operations

Wyden, Ron, D-Ore. (3)
CAPITOL HILL OFFICE:
1111 LHOB 20515; 225-4811
Fax: 225-8941
Admin. Assistant   Josh Kardon

DISTRICT OFFICE:
500 N.E. Multnomah, Portland 97232; (503) 231-2300; Office Director: Lou Savage.

COMMITTEE ASSIGNMENTS:
Energy and Commerce
Joint Economic
Small Business

Wynn, Albert R., D-Md. (4)
CAPITOL HILL OFFICE:
423 CHOB 20515; 225-8699
Admin. Assistant   Luis A. Navarro

DISTRICT OFFICES:
8700 Central Ave., #307, Landover 20785; (301) 350-5055; Fax: (301) 336-6418; District Director: Don Juan Williams.
8601 Georgia Ave., #201, Silver Spring 20901; (301) 588-7328; District Representative: Lou D'Vidio.
6009 Oxon Hill Rd., #208, Oxon Hill 20745; (301) 839-5570; Fax: (301) 567-3853; Chief of Staff: Bill Boston.

COMMITTEE ASSIGNMENTS:
Banking, Finance, and Urban Affairs
Foreign Affairs
Post Office and Civil Service

Yates, Sidney R., D-Ill. (9)
CAPITOL HILL OFFICE:
2109 RHOB 20515; 225-2111
Fax: 225-3493
Admin. Assistant   Mary Bain

DISTRICT OFFICES:
230 S. Dearborn St., Chicago 60604; (312) 353-4596; Executive Assistant: Eddy Engelhard.

2100 Ridge Ave., #2700, Evanston 60201; (708) 328-2610; Executive Assistant: George Van Dusen.

COMMITTEE ASSIGNMENT:
Appropriations

Young, C. W. Bill, R-Fla. (10)
CAPITOL HILL OFFICE:
2407 RHOB 20515; 225-5961
Admin. Assistant   Douglas Gregory

DISTRICT OFFICES:
144 1st Ave. South, #627, St. Petersburg 33701; (813) 893-3191; Admin. Assistant: George Cretekos.
801 W. Bay Dr., #606, Largo 34640; (813) 581-0980; Admin. Assistant: George Cretekos.

COMMITTEE ASSIGNMENTS:
Appropriations
Select Intelligence

Young, Don, R-Alaska (AL)
CAPITOL HILL OFFICE:
2331 RHOB 20515; 225-5765
Admin. Assistant   Lloyd Jones

DISTRICT OFFICES:
222 W. 7th Ave., #3, Anchorage 99513; (907) 271-5978; State Coordinator: Bill Sharrow.
101 12th Ave., P.O. Box 10, Fairbanks 99701; (907) 456-0210; Office Director: Royce Chapman.
401 Federal Bldg., P.O. Box 1247, Juneau 99802; (907) 586-7400; Office Director: Lucy Hudson.
109 Main St., Ketchikan 99902; (907) 225-6880; District Representative: Sherrie Slick.
130 Trading Bay Rd., #350, Kenai 99611; (907) 283-5808; District Representative: Peggy Arness.

COMMITTEE ASSIGNMENTS:
Merchant Marine and Fisheries
Natural Resources (Ranking)
Post Office and Civil Service

Zeliff, Bill, R-N.H. (1)
CAPITOL HILL OFFICE:
224 CHOB 20515; 225-5456
Chief of Staff   Marshall W. Cobleigh

DISTRICT OFFICES:
340 Commercial St., Manchester 03101; (603) 669-6330; Special Assistant: Shirly Higgins.
601 Spaulding Turnpike, #28, Portsmouth 03801; (603) 433-1601; District Director: Pamela Kocher.

COMMITTEE ASSIGNMENTS:
Government Operations
Public Works and Transportation
Small Business

Zimmer, Dick, R-N.J. (12)
CAPITOL HILL OFFICE:
228 CHOB 20515; 225-5801
Fax: 225-9181
Admin. Assistant   David Karvelas

DISTRICT OFFICES:
133 Franklin Corner Rd., Lawrenceville 08648; (609) 895-1559; District Representative: Tom Blakely.
36 W. Main St., #201, Freehold 07728; (908) 303-9020; Office Manager: Vacant.
119 Main St., Flemington 08822; (908) 788-1952; Office Manager: Vacant.

COMMITTEE ASSIGNMENTS:
Government Operations
Science, Space, and Technology

Senators' Offices, Committee Assignments

The list below gives the names of senators in alphabetical order followed by the addresses and telephone numbers for their Washington offices. The address abbreviations used are SD (Dirksen Senate Office Bldg., Constitution Ave. between 1st and 2nd Sts. N.E.), SH (Hart Senate Office Bldg., 2nd St. and Constitution Ave. N.E.), and SR (Russell Senate Office Bldg., Constitution Ave. between Delaware Ave. and 1st St. N.E.). The telephone area code for Washington is 202. The list also gives the name of a top administrative aide for each senator.

The address, telephone number, and director of the senators' state offices are listed. Each senator's committee assignments, except for partisan committees, are given as the final entry. For senators' partisan committee assignments, see p. 1016. As of May 13, 1994, there were 56 Democrats and 44 Republicans in the Senate.

The information for this list was gathered by Congressional Quarterly from Senate offices in Washington, D.C. For the vice president's Capitol and Senate offices, see p. 747.

Akaka, Daniel K., D-Hawaii
CAPITOL HILL OFFICE:
  SH-720 20510; 224-6361
  Fax: 224-2126
  Admin. Assistant James Sakai

STATE OFFICE:
  P.O. Box 50144, Honolulu 96850; (808) 541-2534; Fax: (808) 545-4683; Office Director: Mike Kitamura.

COMMITTEE ASSIGNMENTS:
  Energy and Natural Resources
  Governmental Affairs
  Indian Affairs
  Veterans' Affairs

Baucus, Max, D-Mont.
CAPITOL HILL OFFICE:
  SH-511 20510; 224-2651
  Admin. Assistant Greg Mastel

STATE OFFICES:
  211 N. Higgins Ave., #102, Missoula 59802; (406) 329-3123; State Director: Sharon Peterson.
  23 S. Last Chance Gulch, Helena 59601; (406) 449-5480; State Director: Sharon Peterson.
  125 W. Granate, Butte 59701; (406) 782-8700; State Director: Sharon Peterson.
  107 5th St. North, Great Falls 59401; (406) 761-

1574; State Director: Sharon Peterson.
  2817 2nd Ave. North, #202, Billings 59101; (406) 657-6790; State Director: Sharon Peterson.
  Federal Bldg., P.O. Box 1689, Bozeman 59771; (406) 586-6104; State Director: Sharon Peterson.
  220 1st Ave. East, Kalispell 59901; (406) 756-1150; State Director: Sharon Peterson.

COMMITTEE ASSIGNMENTS:
  Joint Taxation
  Agriculture, Nutrition, and Forestry
  Environment and Public Works (Chairman)
  Finance
  Select Intelligence

Bennett, Robert F., R-Utah
CAPITOL HILL OFFICE:
  SD-241 20510; 224-5444
  Admin. Assistant Greg Hopkins

STATE OFFICE:
  125 South St., #4225, Salt Lake City 84138; (801) 524-5933; State Director: Dixie Minson.

COMMITTEE ASSIGNMENTS:
  Joint Economic
  Banking, Housing, and Urban Affairs
  Energy and Natural Resources
  Governmental Affairs
  Small Business

Biden, Joseph R., Jr., D-Del.
CAPITOL HILL OFFICE:
SR-221 20510; 224-5042
Chief of Staff   Ted Kaufman

STATE OFFICES:
844 King St., #6021, Wilmington 19801; (302) 573-6345; State Director: Bert Di Clemente.
300 S. New St., Dover 19901; (302) 678-9483; Office Director: Arlene La Porte.
600 Dupont Highway, #108, Georgetown 19947; (302) 856-9275; Office Director: Kevin Smith.

COMMITTEE ASSIGNMENTS:
Foreign Relations
Judiciary (Chairman)

Bingaman, Jeff, D-N.M.
CAPITOL HILL OFFICE:
SH-110 20510; 224-5521
Admin. Assistant   Patrick Von Bargen

STATE OFFICES:
119 E. Marcy, #101, Santa Fe 87501; (505) 988-6647; Office Director: Joan Parman.
625 Silver S.W., #130, Albuquerque 87102; (505) 766-3636; Office Director: Liz Gallegos.
505 S. Main, #148, Las Cruces 88001; (505) 523-6561; Office Director: Alice Salcido.
114 E. 4th, #103, Roswell 88201; (505) 622-7113; Office Director: Lynn Ditto.

COMMITTEE ASSIGNMENTS:
Joint Economic
Armed Services
Energy and Natural Resources
Labor and Human Resources

Bond, Christopher S., R-Mo.
CAPITOL HILL OFFICE:
SR-293 20510; 224-5721
Admin. Assistant   Warren Erdman

STATE OFFICES:
339 Broadway, #214, Cape Girardeau 63701; (314) 334-7044; District Manager: Tom Schulte.
312 Monroe St., Jefferson City 65101; (314) 634-2488; Director: Mary Beth Dobbs.
600 Broadway, #420, Kansas City 64105; (816) 471-7141; District Manager: Brad Scott.
8000 Maryland, #1080, St. Louis 63105; (314) 727-7773; District Manager: Catherine Moore.
1736 Sunshine, #705, Springfield 65804; (417) 881-7068; District Manager: Kyle McClure.

COMMITTEE ASSIGNMENTS:
Appropriations
Banking, Housing, and Urban Affairs
Budget
Small Business

Boren, David L., D-Okla.
CAPITOL HILL OFFICE:
SR-453 20510; 224-4721
Admin. Assistant   David Cox

STATE OFFICES:
621 N. Robinson, #370, Oklahoma City 73102; (405) 231-4381; Office Manager: Jim Hopper.
409 S. Boston, Tulsa 74103; (918) 581-7785; Office Manager: Shreese Wilson.
211 E. Oak, Seminole 74868; (405) 382-6480; Office Manager: Anne Dubler.

COMMITTEE ASSIGNMENTS:
Joint Taxation
Agriculture, Nutrition, and Forestry
Finance

Boxer, Barbara, D-Calif.
CAPITOL HILL OFFICE:
SH-112 20510; 224-3553
Admin. Assistant   Karen Olick

STATE OFFICES:
1700 Montgomery St., #240, San Francisco 94111; (415) 403-0100; State Director: Rose Kapolczynski.
2250 E. Imperial Highway, #545, Los Angeles 90245; (310) 414-5700; State Director: Rose Kapolczynski.
525 B St., San Diego 92101; (619) 239-3884; State Director: Rose Kapolczynski.
2300 Tulare St., #130, Fresno 93721; (209) 497-5109; State Director: Rose Kapolczynski.

COMMITTEE ASSIGNMENTS:
Joint Economic
Banking, Housing, and Urban Affairs
Budget
Environment and Public Works

Bradley, Bill, D-N.J.
CAPITOL HILL OFFICE:
SH-731 20510; 224-3224
Fax: 224-8567
Admin. Assistant   Nan Stockholm

STATE OFFICES:
1 Newark Center, 16th Floor, Newark 07102; (201) 639-2860; State Director: Kevin Rigby.
1 Greentree Centre, #303, Route 73, Marlton 08053; (609) 983-4143; Office Manager: Gloria Robertson.

COMMITTEE ASSIGNMENTS:
Energy and Natural Resources
Finance
Special Aging

Breaux, John B., D-La.
CAPITOL HILL OFFICE:
SH-516 20510; 224-4623
Chief of Staff   Vacant

STATE OFFICES:
501 Magazine St., #105, New Orleans 70130; (504) 589-2531; Office Director: Norma Jane Sabiston.
705 Jefferson St., #301, Lafayette 70501; (318) 264-6871; Office Director: Raymond Cordova.
211 N. 3rd St., #102A, Monroe 71201; (318) 325-3320; Office Director: Jean Bates.
1 American Place, #2030, Baton Rouge 70825; (504) 382-2050; Office Director: Ashley Wall.

COMMITTEE ASSIGNMENTS:
Commerce, Science, and Transportation
Finance
Special Aging

Brown, Hank, R-Colo.
CAPITOL HILL OFFICE:
SH-716 20510; 224-5941
Fax: 224-6471
Chief of Staff   Bill Brack

STATE OFFICES:
228 N. Cascade, #106, Colorado Springs 80903, (719) 634-6071; Field Representative: Carley Johnson.
1200 17th St., #2727, Denver 80202; (303) 844-2600; State Director: Gary Hickmon.
400 Rood Ave., #215, Grand Junction 81501; (303) 245-9553; Field Representative: Craig Glogowski.
1100 10th St., #401, Greeley 80631; (303) 352-4112; Field Representative: Diane Hoppe.
411 Thatcher, 5th and Main Sts., Pueblo 81003; (719) 545-9751; Field Representative: David Vickers.

COMMITTEE ASSIGNMENTS:
Budget
Foreign Relations
Judiciary

Bryan, Richard H., D-Nev.
CAPITOL HILL OFFICE:
SR-364 20510; 224-6244
Admin. Assistant   Jean Marie Neal

STATE OFFICES:
300 Booth St., #2014, Reno 89509; (702) 784-5007; State Director: Marlene Joiner.
600 E. William, #304, Carson City 89701; (702) 885-9111; Rural Field Representative: Tom Baker.
300 Las Vegas Blvd. South, #1110, Las Vegas 89101; (702) 388-6605; Office Manager: Sara Besser.

COMMITTEE ASSIGNMENTS:
Armed Services

Banking, Housing, and Urban Affairs
Commerce, Science, and Transportation
Select Ethics (Chairman)
Select Intelligence

Bumpers, Dale, D-Ark.
CAPITOL HILL OFFICE:
SD-229 20510; 224-4843
Admin. Assistant   Mary Hope Davis

STATE OFFICE:
2527 Federal Bldg., Little Rock 72201; (501) 324-6286; Office Manager/Arkansas Representative: Martha Perry.

COMMITTEE ASSIGNMENTS:
Appropriations
Energy and Natural Resources
Small Business (Chairman)

Burns, Conrad, R-Mont.
CAPITOL HILL OFFICE:
SD-183 20510; 224-2644
Admin. Assistant   Tony Payton

STATE OFFICES:
208 N. Montana Ave., #202A, Helena 59601; (406) 449-5401; Field Representative: Worleta Branstetter.
2708 1st Ave. North, Billings 59101; (406) 252-0550; State Director: Dwight MacKay.
415 N. Higgins, Missoula 59802; (406) 728-3606; Field Representative: Julie Altemus.
104 4th St. North, Great Falls 59401; (406) 452-9585; Staff Assistant: Kathy Sparr.
324 W. Towne, Glendive 59330; (406) 365-2391; Field Representative: Pamela Tierney-Crisafully.
10 E. Babcock, #106, Bozeman 59715; (406) 586-4450; Field Representative: Susan Brooke.
125 W. Granite, #211, Butte 59701; (406) 723-3277; Field Representative: Judy Martz.
575 Sunset Blvd., #101, Kalispell 59901; (406) 257-3360; Field Representative: Linda Paulson.

COMMITTEE ASSIGNMENTS:
Appropriations
Commerce, Science, and Transportation
Small Business
Special Aging

Byrd, Robert C., D-W.Va.
CAPITOL HILL OFFICE:
SH-311 20510; 224-3954
Admin. Assistant   Joan Drummond

STATE OFFICE:
1006 Federal Bldg., 500 Quarrier St., Charleston 25305; (304) 342-5855; Office Director: Anne Barth.

COMMITTEE ASSIGNMENTS:
Appropriations (Chairman)
Armed Services
Rules and Administration

Campbell, Ben Nighthorse, D-Colo.
CAPITOL HILL OFFICE:
SR-380 20510; 224-5852
Fax: 224-1933
Admin. Assistant   Ken Lane

STATE OFFICES:
1129 Pennsylvania St., Denver 80203; (303) 866-1900; State Director: Sherrie Wolff.
743 Horizon Ct., #366, Grand Junction 81506; (303) 241-6631; State Aide: Dee Jacobson.
835 2nd Ave., #228, Durango 81301; (303) 247-1609; State Aide: Ann Brown.
720 N. Main St., #210, Pueblo 81003; (719) 542-6987; State Aide: Alberta Vega.
19 Old Town Square, Fort Collins 80524; (303) 224-1909; State Aide: Steve Holdren.
105 E. Vermijo, #600, Colorado Springs 80903; (719) 636-9092; State Aide: Laura DiBiase.

COMMITTEE ASSIGNMENTS:
Banking, Housing, and Urban Affairs
Energy and Natural Resources
Indian Affairs
Veterans' Affairs

Chafee, John H., R-R.I.
CAPITOL HILL OFFICE:
SD-567 20510; 224-2921
Chief of Staff   David A. Griswold

STATE OFFICE:
10 Dorrance St., #221, Providence 02903; (401) 528-5294; Office Director: Mike Ryan.

COMMITTEE ASSIGNMENTS:
Environment and Public Works (Ranking)
Finance
Select Intelligence
Small Business

Coats, Daniel R., R-Ind.
CAPITOL HILL OFFICE:
SR-404 20510; 224-5623
Chief of Staff   Dave Gribbin

STATE OFFICES:
10 W. Market St., #1180, Indianapolis 46204; (317) 226-5555; State Director: Curt Smith.
101 N.W. 7th St., Evansville 47708; (812) 465-6313; Regional Director: Frank Gulledge.
1201 E. 10th St., #103, Jeffersonville 47132; (812) 288-3377; Office Director: Patricia McClain.
5530 Sohl Ave., #103, Hammond 46320; (219) 937-5380; Regional Director: Tim Sanders.
1300 S. Harrison St., #3158, Fort Wayne 46802; (219) 422-1505; Regional Director: Matt Kelty.

COMMITTEE ASSIGNMENTS:
Armed Services
Labor and Human Resources

Cochran, Thad, R-Miss.
CAPITOL HILL OFFICE:
SR-326 20510; 224-5054
Admin. Assistant   Haley Fisackerly

STATE OFFICE:
188 E. Capitol, #614, Jackson 39201; (601) 965-4459; Admin. Assistant: Wiley Carter.

COMMITTEE ASSIGNMENTS:
Agriculture, Nutrition, and Forestry
Appropriations
Governmental Affairs
Indian Affairs
Rules and Administration

Cohen, William S., R-Maine
CAPITOL HILL OFFICE:
SH-322 20510; 224-2523
Fax: 224-2693
Admin. Assistant   Robert Tyrer

STATE OFFICES:
150 Capitol St., P.O. Box 347, Augusta 04332; (207) 622-8414; Office Director: Vacant.
202 Harlow St., #204, P.O. Box 1384, Bangor 04402; (207) 945-0417; Office Director: Judy Cuddy.
109 Alfred St., Biddeford 04005; (207) 283-1101; Office Director: Linda Leeman.
11 Lisbon St., Lewiston 04240; (207) 784-6969; Office Director: Amy Naylor.
10 Moulton St., P.O. Box 1938, Portland 04104; (207) 780-3575; Office Director: Bill Johnson.
169 Academy St., Presque Isle 04769; (207) 764-3266; Office Director: Dayle Ashby.

COMMITTEE ASSIGNMENTS:
Armed Services
Governmental Affairs
Judiciary
Special Aging (Ranking)

Conrad, Kent, D-N.D.
CAPITOL HILL OFFICE:
SH-724 20510; 224-2043
Chief of Staff   Mary Wakefield

STATE OFFICES:
228 Federal Bldg., 3rd and Rosser Sts., Bismarck 58501; (701) 258-4648; State Director: Lynn Clancy.
657 2nd Ave. North, #306, Fargo 58102; (701) 232-8030; Office Director: Lois Schneider.
102 N. 4th St., #104, Grand Forks 58203; (701) 775-9601; Office Director: Jim Hand.
100 1st St. S.W., #105, Minot 58701; (701) 852-0703; Office Director: Mavis Williamson.

COMMITTEE ASSIGNMENTS:
Agriculture, Nutrition, and Forestry
Budget
Finance
Indian Affairs

Coverdell, Paul, R-Ga.
CAPITOL HILL OFFICE:
SR-200 20510; 224-3643
Fax: 228-3783
Chief of Staff   William Earl McClure

STATE OFFICE:
100 Colony Square, #300, 1175 Peachtree St., Atlanta 30361; (404) 347-2202; State Director of Constituent Services: Shirley Puchalski.

COMMITTEE ASSIGNMENTS:
Agriculture, Nutrition, and Forestry
Foreign Relations
Small Business

Craig, Larry E., R-Idaho
CAPITOL HILL OFFICE:
SH-313 20510; 224-2752
Chief of Staff   Greg Casey

STATE OFFICES:
304 N. 8th St., #149, Boise 83702; (208) 342-7985; Regional Director: Missy Guisto.
103 N. 4th St., Coeur d'Alene 83814; (208) 667-6130; Regional Director: Sandy Patano.
633 Main St., Lewiston 83501; (208) 743-0792; Regional Assistant: Susan Fagan.
250 S. 4th Ave., #216, Pocatello 83201; (208) 236-6817; Regional Director: Valorie Watkins.
1292 Addison Ave. East, Twin Falls 83301; (208) 734-6780; Regional Director: Lewie Eilers.
2539 Channing Way, Idaho Falls 83404; (208) 523-5541; Regional Assistant: Jeff Schrade.

COMMITTEE ASSIGNMENTS:
Joint Economic
Agriculture, Nutrition, and Forestry
Energy and Natural Resources
Select Ethics
Special Aging

D'Amato, Alfonse M., R-N.Y.
CAPITOL HILL OFFICE:
SH-520 20510; 224-6542
Fax: 224-5871
Admin. Assistant   Michael T. Kinsella

STATE OFFICES:
7th Ave., 7 Penn Plaza, #600, New York 10001; (212) 947-7390; Fax: (212) 564-5066; Office Director: Miriam Madden.
111 W. Huron St., #620, Buffalo 14202; (716) 846-4111; Fax: (716) 846-4113; Office Director: Jane O'Bannon.

Leo O'Brien Office Bldg., #420, Albany 12207; (518) 472-4343; Fax: (518) 472-4414; Office Director: David Poleto.
100 State St., #304, Rochester 14614; (716) 263-5866; Fax: (716) 263-3173; Office Director: Joan Mueller.
100 S. Clinton St., #1259, Syracuse 13260; (315) 423-5471; Fax: (315) 423-5185; Office Director: Gretchen Ralph.

COMMITTEE ASSIGNMENTS:
Appropriations
Banking, Housing, and Urban Affairs (Ranking)
Select Intelligence

Danforth, John C., R-Mo.
CAPITOL HILL OFFICE:
SR-249 20510; 224-6154
Admin. Assistant   Robert D. McDonald

STATE OFFICES:
8000 Maryland Ave., #440, Clayton 63105; (314) 725-4484; Office Director: Karla Roeber.
811 Grand Ave., #943, Kansas City 64106; (816) 426-6101; Admin. Assistant: Rachael Steele.
1736 E. Sunshine, #705, Springfield 65804; (417) 881-7068; Office Director: Becky Supak.
1233 Jefferson St., Jefferson City 65109; (314) 635-7292; Office Director: Clair Elsberry.

COMMITTEE ASSIGNMENTS:
Commerce,   Science,   and   Transportation (Ranking)
Finance
Select Intelligence

Daschle, Tom, D-S.D.
CAPITOL HILL OFFICE:
SH-317 20510; 224-2321
Admin. Assistant   Peter Rouse

STATE OFFICES:
20 6th Ave., S.E., Suite B, Aberdeen 57401; (605) 225-8823; Office Director: Beth Smith.
816 6th St., Rapid City 57701; (605) 348-7551; West River Director: Jeff Fransen.
810 S. Minnesota Ave., Sioux Falls 57104; (605) 334-9596; State Director: Rick Weiland.

COMMITTEE ASSIGNMENTS:
Agriculture, Nutrition, and Forestry
Finance
Indian Affairs
Select Ethics
Veterans' Affairs

DeConcini, Dennis, D-Ariz.
CAPITOL HILL OFFICE:
SH-328 20510; 224-4521
Fax: 224-2302
Admin. Assistant   Gene Karp

STATE OFFICES:
323 W. Roosevelt, #C100, Phoenix 85003; (602) 379-6756; Office Director: Barry Dill.
2730 E. Broadway, #160, Tucson 85716; (602) 670-6831; Office Director: Bonnie Fricks.
40 N. Center St., Mesa 85201; (602) 379-4998; Office Director: Mary Jane Perry.

COMMITTEE ASSIGNMENTS:
Joint Library
Joint Printing
Appropriations
Indian Affairs
Judiciary
Rules and Administration
Select Intelligence (Chairman)
Veterans' Affairs

Dodd, Christopher J., D-Conn.
CAPITOL HILL OFFICE:
SR-444 20510; 224-2823
Admin. Assistant Vacant

STATE OFFICE:
100 Great Meadow Rd., Wethersfield 06109; (203) 240-3470; State Director: Joan Hogan-Gillman.

COMMITTEE ASSIGNMENTS:
Banking, Housing, and Urban Affairs
Budget
Foreign Relations
Labor and Human Resources
Rules and Administration

Dole, Bob, R-Kan.
CAPITOL HILL OFFICE:
SH-141 20510; 224-6521
Admin. Assistant Dan Stanley
S-230 The Capitol 20510; 224-3135
(Minority Leader's office)

STATE OFFICES:
500 State Ave., #176, Kansas City 66101; (913) 371-6108; Office Director: Gale Grosch.
444 S.E. Quincy, #392, Topeka 66683; (913) 295-2745; Office Director: Judy Brown.
100 N. Broadway, Wichita 67202; (316) 263-4956; State Director: Dave Spears.
Mobile Office: 444 S.E. Quincy, #392, Topeka 66683; (913) 295-2745; Regional Representative: Jill Maycumber.

COMMITTEE ASSIGNMENTS:
Joint Taxation
Agriculture, Nutrition, and Forestry
Finance
Rules and Administration

Domenici, Pete V., R-N.M.
CAPITOL HILL OFFICE:
SD-427 20510; 224-6621
Admin. Assistant R. Charles Gentry

STATE OFFICES:
625 Silver S.W., #120, Albuquerque 87102; (505) 766-3481; Field Representative: Ginny Garland.
120 S. Federal Place, Santa Fe 87501; (505) 988-6511; Office Manager: Maggie Murray.
1065 S. Main St., Bldg. D-13, Suite I, Las Cruces 88005; (505) 526-5475; Southwestern Regional Office Director: Darlene Garcia.
140 Federal Bldg., Roswell 88201; (505) 623-6170; Office Manager: Nancy Smith Corn.

COMMITTEE ASSIGNMENTS:
Appropriations
Banking, Housing, and Urban Affairs
Budget (Ranking)
Energy and Natural Resources
Indian Affairs

Dorgan, Byron L., D-N.D.
CAPITOL HILL OFFICE:
SH-713 20510; 224-2551
Fax: 224-1193
Admin. Assistant Lucy Calautti

STATE OFFICES:
P.O. Box 871, Bismarck 58502; (701) 250-4618; Fax: (701) 250-4484; State Director: Bob Valeu.
110 Roberts St., Fargo 58102; (701) 239-5389; Fax: (701) 239-5112; District Representative: Kevin Carvell.

COMMITTEE ASSIGNMENTS:
Joint Economic
Commerce, Science, and Transportation
Energy and Natural Resources
Governmental Affairs
Indian Affairs

Durenberger, Dave, R-Minn.
CAPITOL HILL OFFICE:
SR-154 20510; 224-3244
Admin. Assistant Rick Evans

STATE OFFICE:
12 S. 6th St., #1020, Minneapolis 55402; (612) 370-3382; Office Director: Jon Schroeder.

COMMITTEE ASSIGNMENTS:
Special Aging
Environment and Public Works
Finance
Labor and Human Resources

Exon, Jim, D-Neb.
CAPITOL HILL OFFICE:
SH-528 20510; 224-4224
Chief of Staff Greg Pallas

STATE OFFICES:
287 Federal Bldg., 100 Centennial Mall North,

Lincoln 68508; (402) 437-5591; State Coordinator: Mark Bowen.

    1623 Farnam St., #700, Omaha 68102; (402) 341-1776; District Director: Catherine Dahlquist.

    300 E. 3rd St. North, #275, Platte 69101; (308) 534-2006; Representative: Claire Nicholas.

    2106 1st Ave., Scottsbluff 69361; (308) 632-3595; Representative: Patty Rapp.

COMMITTEE ASSIGNMENTS:
Armed Services
Budget
Commerce, Science, and Transportation

Faircloth, Lauch, R-N.C.
CAPITOL HILL OFFICE:
SH-702 20510; 224-3154
    Admin. Assistant   Vic Barfield

STATE OFFICES:
    401 W. Trade St., #219, Charlotte 28202; (704) 375-1993; Office Manager: Susan Hays.

    37 Battery Park, #16, Asheville 28801; (704) 251-0165; Office Director: Scotty Morgan.

    310 New Bern Ave., #366, Raleigh 27601; (919) 856-4791; Office Director: Mary Bear.

    251 Main St., #422, Winston-Salem 27101; (919) 631-5313; Office Director: Mary Bagnal.

    109A W. Main St., Clinton 28328; (910) 590-3200; Office Manager: Betty Jo Faircloth.

COMMITTEE ASSIGNMENTS:
Armed Services
Banking, Housing, and Urban Affairs
Environment and Public Works

Feingold, Russell D., D-Wis.
CAPITOL HILL OFFICE:
SH-502 20510; 224-5323
    Admin. Assistant   Ruth LaRocque

STATE OFFICE:
    8383 Greenway Blvd., Middleton 53562; (608) 828-1200; State Director: Moira Harrington.

COMMITTEE ASSIGNMENTS:
Agriculture, Nutrition, and Forestry
Foreign Relations
Special Aging

Feinstein, Dianne, D-Calif.
CAPITOL HILL OFFICE:
SH-331 20510; 224-3841
Fax: 228-3954
    Chief of Staff   Mike McGill

STATE OFFICES:
    1700 Montgomery St., #305, San Francisco 94111; (415) 249-4777; State Director: Hadley Roff.

    11111 Santa Monica Blvd., #915, Los Angeles 90025; (310) 914-7300; State Director: Hadley Roff.

    705 B St., #1030, San Diego 92101; (619) 231-9712; State Director: Hadley Roff.

    1130 O St., #4015, Fresno 93721; (209) 485-7430; State Director: Hadley Roff.

COMMITTEE ASSIGNMENTS:
Appropriations
Judiciary
Rules and Administration

Ford, Wendell H., D-Ky.
CAPITOL HILL OFFICE:
SR-173A 20510; 224-4343
    Admin. Assistant   James T. Fleming

STATE OFFICES:
    600 Dr. Martin Luther King Jr. Place, #1072, Louisville 40202; (502) 582-6251; District Representative: Ann Woods.

    305 Federal Bldg., Frederica St., Owensboro 42301; (502) 685-5158; District Representative: Joanne Hare.

    343 Waller Ave., #204, Lexington 40504; (606) 233-2484; District Representative: Pat Gregory.

    19 U.S. Post Office and Courthouse, Covington 41011; (606) 491-7929; District Representative: Jan Celella.

COMMITTEE ASSIGNMENTS:
Joint Inaugural Ceremonies
Joint Printing (Chairman)
Commerce, Science, and Transportation
Energy and Natural Resources
Rules and Administration (Chairman)

Glenn, John, D-Ohio
CAPITOL HILL OFFICE:
SH-503 20510; 224-3353
Fax: 224-7983
    Admin. Assistant   Mary Jane Veno

STATE OFFICES:
    200 N. High St., #600, Columbus 43215; (614) 469-6697; Fax: (614) 469-7733; Office Director: Jan Denney.

    1240 E. 9th St., #2957, Cleveland 44199; (216) 522-7095; Fax: (216) 522-7097; Office Director: Pat Bluso.

    550 Main St., #10407, Cincinnati 45202; (513) 684-3265; Fax: (513) 684-3269; Office Director: Rosemary Matthews.

    234 N. Summit St., #726, Toledo 43064; (419) 259-7592; Fax: (419) 259-7537; Office Director: Mike Entinghe.

COMMITTEE ASSIGNMENTS:
Armed Services
Governmental Affairs (Chairman)
Select Intelligence
Special Aging

Gorton, Slade, R-Wash.
CAPITOL HILL OFFICE:
SH-730 20510; 224-3441
Fax: 224-9393
    Admin. Assistant   Larry Ehl

STATE OFFICES:
915 2nd Ave., #3206, Seattle 98174; (206) 553-0350; State Director: Veda Jellen.

697 U.S. Courthouse, West 920 Riverside, Spokane 99201; (509) 353-2507; Fax: (509) 353-2547; Eastern Washington Regional Director: Dan Kirschner.

500 W. 12th St., Vancouver 98660; (206) 696-7838; Fax: (206) 696-7844; Southwest Washington Regional Director: Kathy Treadwell.

23 S. Wenatchee Ave., #119, Wenatchee 98801; (509) 663-2118; Fax: (509) 663-1085; Office Director: Don Moos.

402 E. Yakima Ave., Box 4083, Yakima 98901; (509) 248-8084; Fax: (509) 248-8167; Office Director: Sandra Linde.

1530 Grandridge Blvd., #212, Kennewick 99336; (509) 783-0640; Fax: (509) 785-7559; Office Director: Suzanne Heaston.

15600 Redmond Way, #300, Redmond 98052; (206) 883-6072; Fax: (206) 883-6103; Office Director: Candy Horchover.

Transpacific Trade Center, 3700 PCH East, #411, Fife 98424; (206) 926-3984; Fax: (206) 926-3986; Office Director: Lura Lawson.

COMMITTEE ASSIGNMENTS:
Appropriations
Budget
Commerce, Science, and Transportation
Indian Affairs
Select Intelligence

Graham, Bob, D-Fla.
CAPITOL HILL OFFICE:
SH-524 20510; 224-3041
Admin. Assistant Samuel "Buddy" Shorstein

STATE OFFICES:
44 W. Flagler St., #1715, Miami 33130; (305) 536-7293; South Florida Director: Ellen Roth.

325 John Knox Rd., Bldg. 600, Tallahassee 32303; (904) 422-6100; North Florida Director: Mary Chiles.

101 E. Kennedy Blvd., #3270, Tampa 33602; (813) 228-2476; Central Florida Director: Adam Smith.

COMMITTEE ASSIGNMENTS:
Armed Services
Environment and Public Works
Select Intelligence
Special Aging
Veterans' Affairs

Gramm, Phil, R-Texas
CAPITOL HILL OFFICE:
SR-370 20510; 224-2934
Chief of Staff Ruth Cymber

STATE OFFICES:
2323 Bryan, #1500, Dallas 75201; (214) 767-3000; Regional Director: Kevin Brannon.

222 E. Van Buren, #404, Harlingen 78550; (512) 423-6118; Office Manager: Delfina Medina.

712 Main, #2400, Houston 77002; (713) 229-2766; Regional Director: Scott Carter.

1205 Texas Ave., #113, Lubbock 79401; (806) 743-7533; Regional Director: Jennifer Crabtree.

310 N. Mesa St., #318, El Paso 79901; (915) 534-6896; El Paso Representative: Margie Velez.

102 N. College Ave., #201, Tyler 75702; (903) 593-0902; State Director: Steve Moss.

404 E. Ramsey, #200, San Antonio 78216; (210) 366-9494; Regional Director: Scott Keith.

COMMITTEE ASSIGNMENTS:
Appropriations
Banking, Housing, and Urban Affairs
Budget

Grassley, Charles E., R-Iowa
CAPITOL HILL OFFICE:
SH-135 20510; 224-3744
Admin. Assistant Robert J. Ludwiczak

STATE OFFICES:
531 Commercial St., #210, Waterloo 50701; (319) 232-6657; Field Representative: Fred Schuster.

210 Walnut St., #721, Des Moines 50309; (515) 284-4890; Special Representative: Doug Stout.

320 6th St., #103, Sioux City 51101; (712) 233-1860; Field Representative: Marliss DeJong.

101 1st S.E., #206, Cedar Rapids 52401; (319) 363-6832; Field Representative: Jan Swanson.

131 E. 4th St., #116, Davenport 52801; (319) 322-4331; Field Representative: Vada Reed.

COMMITTEE ASSIGNMENTS:
Agriculture, Nutrition, and Forestry
Budget
Finance
Judiciary
Special Aging

Gregg, Judd, R-N.H.
CAPITOL HILL OFFICE:
SR-393 20510; 224-3324
Admin. Assistant Martha Austin

STATE OFFICES:
125 N. Main St., Concord 03301; (603) 225-7115; State Director: Joel Maiola.

28 Webster St., Manchester 03104; (603) 622-7979; State Director: Joel Maiola.

99 Pease Blvd., Portsmouth 03801; (603) 431-2171; State Director: Joel Maiola.

136 Pleasant St., Berlin 03570; (603) 752-2604; State Director: Joel Maiola.

COMMITTEE ASSIGNMENTS:
Budget
Foreign Relations
Labor and Human Resources

Harkin, Tom, D-Iowa
CAPITOL HILL OFFICE:
 SH-531 20510; 224-3254
 Fax: 224-9369
 Admin. Assistant   Dan Smith

STATE OFFICES:
 210 Walnut St., #733, Des Moines 50309; (515) 284-4574; State Admin.: Jack Hatch.
 Lindale Mall, Box 74884, Cedar Rapids 52407; (319) 393-6374; Regional Director: Beth Freeman.
 131 E. 4th St., #314B, Davenport 52801; (319) 322-1338; Regional Director: Beth Freeman.
 307 Federal Bldg., Box H, Council Bluffs 51502; (712) 325-0036; Staff Assistant: Vacant.
 320 6th St., Sioux City 51101; (712) 252-1550; Staff Assistant: Maureen Wilson.
 350 W. 6th St., Dubuque 52001; (319) 582-2130; Case Worker: Linda Lucy.

COMMITTEE ASSIGNMENTS:
 Agriculture, Nutrition, and Forestry
 Appropriations
 Labor and Human Resources
 Small Business

Hatch, Orrin G., R-Utah
CAPITOL HILL OFFICE:
 SR-135 20510; 224-5251
 Fax: 224-6331
 Admin. Assistant   Wendy Higginbotham

STATE OFFICES:
 125 S. State, #8402, Salt Lake City 84138; (801) 524-4380; State Office Director: Ron Madsen.
 51 S. University, #320, Provo 84606; (801) 375-7881; Office Director: Karen Thorn.
 324 25th St., #1006, Ogden 84401; (801) 625-5672; Office Director: Norma Holmgren.
 10 N. Main, P.O. Box 99, Cedar City 84720; (801) 586-8435; Office Director: Jeannine Holt.

COMMITTEE ASSIGNMENTS:
 Finance
 Judiciary (Ranking)
 Labor and Human Resources

Hatfield, Mark O., R-Ore.
CAPITOL HILL OFFICE:
 SH-711 20510; 224-3753
 Fax: 224-0276
 Admin. Assistant   Steve Nousen

STATE OFFICES:
 727 Center St. N.E., #305, Salem 97301; (503) 588-9510; State Director: Ray Naff.
 121 S.W. Salmon St., #1420, Portland 97204; (503) 326-3386; District Office Manager: Mike Salsgiver.

COMMITTEE ASSIGNMENTS:
 Joint Library (Ranking)

 Joint Printing
 Appropriations (Ranking)
 Energy and Natural Resources
 Indian Affairs
 Rules and Administration

Heflin, Howell, D-Ala.
CAPITOL HILL OFFICE:
 SH-728 20510; 224-4124
 Admin. Assistant   Stephen Raby

STATE OFFICES:
 437 Federal Courthouse Bldg., Mobile 36602; (205) 432-7712; Field Representative: Bob Morrisette.
 Federal Courthouse B-29, 15 Lee St., Montgomery 36104; (205) 834-7367; Field Representative: Tim Brown.
 P.O. Box 228, Tuscumbia 35674; (205) 381-7060; Chief of Staff: Bill Gardiner.
 1800 5th Ave. North, #355, Birmingham 35203; (205) 731-1500; Field Representative: Stanley Vines.

COMMITTEE ASSIGNMENTS:
 Agriculture, Nutrition, and Forestry
 Judiciary
 Small Business

Helms, Jesse, R N.C.
CAPITOL HILL OFFICE:
 SD-403 20510; 224-6342
 Fax: 224-7588
 Admin. Assistant   Darryl Nirenberg

STATE OFFICES:
 Century Post Office Bldg., P.O. Box 2888, Raleigh 27602; (919) 856-4630; Office Director: Frances Jones.
 P.O. Box 2944, Hickory 28603; (704) 322-5170; Office Director: Jo Murray.

COMMITTEE ASSIGNMENTS:
 Agriculture, Nutrition, and Forestry
 Foreign Relations (Ranking)
 Rules and Administration

Hollings, Ernest F., D-S.C.
CAPITOL HILL OFFICE:
 SR-125 20510; 224-6121
 Admin. Assistant   David Rudd

STATE OFFICES:
 1835 Assembly St., #1551, Columbia 29201; (803) 765-5731; Fax: (803) 765-5742; Home Secretary: Trip King.
 103 Federal Bldg., Spartanburg 29301; (803) 585-3702; Fax: (803) 585-2559; Office Director: Lynn Cazallis.
 200 E. Bay, #112, Charleston 29401; (803) 727-4525; Fax: (803) 722-4923; Low Country Representative: Joe Maupin.

126 Federal Bldg., Greenville 29603; (803) 233-5366; Fax: (803) 233-2923; Office Director: Ben Alexander.

COMMITTEE ASSIGNMENTS:
Appropriations
Budget
Commerce, Science, and Transportation (Chairman)

Hutchison, Kay Bailey, R-Texas
CAPITOL HILL OFFICE:
SH-703 20510; 224-5922
Admin. Assistant   Cliff Shannon

STATE OFFICES:
300 E. 8th St., #961, Austin 78701; (512) 482-5834; Regional Director: Cynthia Hall.
10440 N. Central Expressway, #1160, Dallas 75231; (214) 361-3500; Regional Director: Gray Rather.
1919 Smith St., #800, Houston 77002; (713) 653-3456; State Director: Dale Laine.

COMMITTEE ASSIGNMENTS:
Armed Services
Commerce, Science, and Transportation
Small Business

Inouye, Daniel K., D-Hawaii
CAPITOL HILL OFFICE:
SH-722 20510; 224-3934
Admin. Assistant   Patrick DeLeon

STATE OFFICE:
300 Ala Moana Blvd., #7325, Honolulu 96850; (808) 541-2542; Executive Director: Alexis Lum.

COMMITTEE ASSIGNMENTS:
Appropriations
Commerce, Science, and Transportation
Indian Affairs (Chairman)
Rules and Administration

Jeffords, James M., R-Vt.
CAPITOL HILL OFFICE:
SH-513 20510; 224-5141
Chief of Staff   Susan Boardman Russ

STATE OFFICES:
95 St. Paul St., #100, Burlington 05401; (802) 658-6001; Office Coordinator: Jessica Comai.
58 State St., Montpelier 05602; (802) 223-5273; State Director: Jolinda LeClair.
2 S. Main St., 2nd Floor, Rutland 05701; (802) 773-3875; Office Coordinator: Mary Sheldon.

COMMITTEE ASSIGNMENTS:
Foreign Relations
Labor and Human Resources
Special Aging
Veterans' Affairs

Johnston, J. Bennett, D-La.
CAPITOL HILL OFFICE:
SH-136 20510; 224-5824
Fax: 224-2952
Chief of Staff   John Lynn

STATE OFFICES:
500 Camp St., #1010, New Orleans 70130; (504) 589-2427; Fax: (504) 589-4023; Louisiana Executive Assistant: Charmaine Caccioppi.
300 Fannin St., Shreveport 71101; (318) 676-3085; Fax: (318) 676-3100; Office Director: Julie Rogers.
1 American Place, #1510, Baton Rouge 70825; (504) 389-0395; Fax: (504) 389-0660; State Director: Jim Oakes.

COMMITTEE ASSIGNMENTS:
Appropriations
Budget
Energy and Natural Resources (Chairman)
Select Intelligence
Special Aging

Kassebaum, Nancy Landon, R-Kan.
CAPITOL HILL OFFICE:
SR-302 20510; 224-4774
Chief of Staff   Dave Bartel

STATE OFFICES:
155 N. Market, #120, Wichita 67202; (316) 263-0416; Regional Representative: Georgia Ptacek.
911 N. Main St., Garden City 67846; (316) 276-3423; Regional Representative: Betty Joe Roberts.
444 S.E. Quincy, P.O. Box 51, Topeka 66683; (913) 295-2888; Regional Representative: Jacque Kimbrough.
4200 Somerset, #152, Prairie Village 66208; (913) 648-3103; State Admin. Assistant: Mike Harper.

COMMITTEE ASSIGNMENTS:
Foreign Relations
Indian Affairs
Labor and Human Resources (Ranking)

Kempthorne, Dirk, R-Idaho
CAPITOL HILL OFFICE:
SD-367 20510; 224-6142
Fax: 224-5893
Chief of Staff   Phil Reberger

STATE OFFICES:
304 North 8th St., #338, Boise 83702; (208) 334-1776; Fax: (208) 334-9044; Idaho Offices Manager: Julie Harwood.
633 Main St., #103, Lewiston 83501; (208) 743-1497; Fax: (208) 743-6484; State Assistant: Carolyn Durant.

250 S. 4th, #207, Pocatello 83201; (208) 236-6775; Fax: (208) 236-6935; State Assistant: Sally Taniguchi.

118 N. 2nd St., Coeur d'Alene 83814; (208) 664-5490; Fax: (208) 664-0889; State Assistant: Steve Judy.

401 2nd St. North, #106, Twin Falls 83301; (208) 734-2515; Fax: (208) 733-0414; State Assistant: Orrie Sinclair.

2539 Channing Way, #240, Idaho Falls 83404; (208) 522-9779; Fax: (208) 529-8367; State Assistant: Dixie Richardson.

COMMITTEE ASSIGNMENTS:
Armed Services
Environment and Public Works
Small Business

Kennedy, Edward M., D-Mass.
CAPITOL HILL OFFICE:
SR-315 20510; 224-4543
Fax: 224-2417
Admin. Assistant   Paul Donovan

STATE OFFICE:
2400 John F. Kennedy Federal Bldg., Boston 02203; (617) 565-3170; Admin. Assistant: Barbara Souliotis.

COMMITTEE ASSIGNMENTS:
Joint Economic
Armed Services
Judiciary
Labor and Human Resources (Chairman)

Kerrey, Bob, D-Neb.
CAPITOL HILL OFFICE:
SH-303 20510; 224-6551
Chief of Staff   Paul Johnson

STATE OFFICES:
7602 Pacific, #205, Omaha 68114; (402) 391-3411; State Director: Lonnie Michael.

294 Federal Bldg., 100 Centennial Mall North, Lincoln 68508; (402) 437-5246; State Director: Lonnie Michael.

2106 1st Ave., Scottsbluff 69361; (308) 632-3595; Office Manager: Patty Redel.

COMMITTEE ASSIGNMENTS:
Agriculture, Nutrition, and Forestry
Appropriations
Select Intelligence

Kerry, John, D-Mass.
CAPITOL HILL OFFICE:
SR-421 20510; 224-2742
Fax: 224-8525
Admin. Assistant   David J. Leiter

STATE OFFICES:
1 Bowdoin Square, 10th Floor, Boston 02114; (617) 565-8519; Office Director: Chris Greeley.

145 State St., #504, Springfield 01103; (413) 785-4610; Office Director: Dusty Houser.

COMMITTEE ASSIGNMENTS:
Banking, Housing, and Urban Affairs
Commerce, Science, and Transportation
Foreign Relations
Select Intelligence
Small Business

Kohl, Herb, D-Wis.
CAPITOL HILL OFFICE:
SH-330 20510; 224-5653
Fax: 224-9787
Chief of Staff   Ted Bornstein

STATE OFFICES:
205 E. Wisconsin Ave., Milwaukee 53202; (414) 297-4451; Fax: (414) 297-4455; State Director: Jeff Gillis.

14 W. Mifflin St., #312, Madison 53703; (608) 264-5338; State Office Director: Eve Galanter.

402 Graham Ave., #206, Eau Claire 54701; (715) 832-8424; Regional Representative: Marjorie Bunce.

4321 W. College Ave., #235, Appleton 54914; (414) 738-1640; Regional Representative: Marlene Mielke.

625 52nd St., #303, Kenosha 53140; (414) 657-7719; Office Director: Rosanne Rogers.

COMMITTEE ASSIGNMENTS:
Appropriations
Judiciary
Small Business
Special Aging

Lautenberg, Frank R., D-N.J.
CAPITOL HILL OFFICE:
SH-506 20510; 224-4744
Fax: 224-9707
Admin. Assistant   Eve Lubalin

STATE OFFICES:
One Gateway Center, #1001, Newark 07102; (201) 645-3030; Director of State Office: Kathryn Forsyth.

208 White Horse Pike, Barrington 08007; (609) 757-5353; Deputy State Director: Karin Elkis.

COMMITTEE ASSIGNMENTS:
Appropriations
Budget
Environment and Public Works
Small Business

Leahy, Patrick J., D-Vt.
CAPITOL HILL OFFICE:
SR-433 20510; 224-4242
Chief of Staff   Luke Albee

STATE OFFICES:
199 Main St., Burlington 05401; (802) 863-2525; Vermont Staff Director: Vacant.
338 Federal Bldg., Montpelier 05602; (802) 229-0569; Vermont Staff Director: Vacant.

COMMITTEE ASSIGNMENTS:
Agriculture, Nutrition, and Forestry (Chairman)
Appropriations
Judiciary

Levin, Carl, D-Mich.
CAPITOL HILL OFFICE:
SR-459 20510; 224-6221
Admin. Assistant Gordon Kerr

STATE OFFICES:
145 Water St., #102, Alpena 49707; (517) 354-5520; Regional Representative: Thad McCollum.
477 Michigan Ave., #1860, Detroit 48226; (313) 226-6020; State Director: Chuck Wilbur.
623 Ludington, #200, Escanaba 49829; (906) 789-0052; Regional Representative: Rosemary Forrester.
110 Michigan Ave. N.W., #134, Grand Rapids 49503; (616) 456-2531; Regional Representative: Rick Tormala.
124 W. Allegan, #1810, Lansing 48933; (517) 377-1508; Regional Representative: Jim Turner.
301 E. Genesee, Saginaw 48607; (517) 754-2494; Regional Representative: Gerald Smith.
24580 Cunningham, #114, Warren 48091; (313) 759-0477; Regional Representative: David Lossing.
15100 Northline Rd., #107, Southgate 48195; (313) 285-8596; Regional Representative: Lisa Tucker.

COMMITTEE ASSIGNMENTS:
Armed Services
Governmental Affairs
Small Business

Lieberman, Joseph I., D-Conn.
CAPITOL HILL OFFICE:
SH-316 20510; 224-4041
Fax: 224-9750
Admin. Assistant William G. Andresen

STATE OFFICE:
1 Commercial Plaza, 21st Floor, Hartford 06103; (203) 240-3566; Fax: (203) 240-3565; State Office Director: Sherry Brown.

COMMITTEE ASSIGNMENTS:
Armed Services
Environment and Public Works
Governmental Affairs
Small Business

Lott, Trent, R-Miss.
CAPITOL HILL OFFICE:
SR-487 20510; 224-6253
Fax: 224-2262
Admin. Assistant John Lundy

STATE OFFICES:
101 S. Lafayette, Starkville 39759; (601) 323-1414; District Representative: Jack Miller.
1 Government Plaza, #428, Gulfport 39501; (601) 863-1988; District Representative: Mercer Miller.
200 E. Washington St., #145, Greenwood 38930; (601) 453-5681; Staff Assistant: Carolyn Overstreet.
245 E. Capitol St., Jackson 39201; (601) 965-4644; State Director: Guy Hovis.
P.O. Box 1474, Oxford 38655; (601) 234-3774; District Representative: Bill Canty.
3100 S. Pascagoula St., Pascagoula 39567; (601) 762-5400; District Representative: Bill Pope.

COMMITTEE ASSIGNMENTS:
Armed Services
Budget
Commerce, Science, and Transportation
Energy and Natural Resources

Lugar, Richard G., R-Ind.
CAPITOL HILL OFFICE:
SH-306 20510; 224-4814
Admin. Assistant Marty Morris

STATE OFFICES:
10 W. Market St., #1180, Indianapolis 46204; (317) 226-5555; State Director: Ellen Whitt.
101 N.W. Martin Luther King Blvd., #122, Evansville 47708; (812) 465-6313; Office Director: Frank Gulledge.
1300 S. Harrison St., #3158, Fort Wayne 46802; (219) 422-1505; Office Director: Matthew Kelty.
5530 Sohl Ave., #103, Hammond 46320; (219) 937-5380; Office Director: Timothy Sanders.
1201 E. 10th St., #103, Jeffersonville 47132; (812) 288-3377; Office Director: David Graham.

COMMITTEE ASSIGNMENTS:
Agriculture, Nutrition, and Forestry (Ranking)
Foreign Relations
Select Intelligence

Mack, Connie, R-Fla.
CAPITOL HILL OFFICE:
SH-517 20510; 224-5274
Fax: 224-8022
Admin. Assistant Mitch Bainwol

STATE OFFICES:
1342 Colonial Blvd., #27, Ft. Myers 33907; (813) 275-6252; Regional Director: Sharon Thierer.
777 Bickell Ave., #704, Miami 33130; (305) 530-7100; Deputy State Director: Javier Vazquez.
600 N. Westshore Blvd., #602, Tampa 33609; (813) 225-7683; Communications Director: Mark Mills.
1211 Governors State Blvd., #404, Tallahassee 32301; (904) 877-6724; Regional Director: Jennifer Cannon.

6706 N. 9th Ave., #C8, Pensacola 32504; (904) 479-9803; Regional Director: Dave Stafford.
1 San Jose Place, #9, Jacksonville 32257; (904) 268-7915; Regional Director: Lisa Sandifer.

COMMITTEE ASSIGNMENTS:
Joint Economic
Appropriations
Banking, Housing, and Urban Affairs
Small Business

Mathews, Harlan, D-Tenn.
CAPITOL HILL OFFICE:
SD-506 20510; 224-4944
Fax: 228-3679
Admin. Assistant   Estie Harris

STATE OFFICES:
3322 West End Ave., #120, Nashville 37203; (615) 736-5129; State Director: Sandy McQuain.
167 N. Main St., #403, Memphis 38103; (901) 544-4224; Caseworker: Terry Owens.
501 Main St., #315, Knoxville 37902; (615) 545-4253; Caseworker: Mary Enkema.
109 S. Highland St., Suite B-9, Jackson 38301; (901) 424-0505; Field Representative: Benny Roberts.
Tri-City Regional Airport, Blountville 37601; (615) 323-6217; Caseworker. Patsy Johnson.
900 Georgia Ave., #256, Chattanooga 37402; (615) 756-1328; Caseworker: Paula Edwards.

COMMITTEE ASSIGNMENTS:
Joint Printing
Commerce, Science, and Transportation
Energy and Natural Resources
Foreign Relations
Rules and Administration

McCain, John, R-Ariz.
CAPITOL HILL OFFICE:
SR-111 20510; 224-2235
Fax: 228-2862
Admin. Assistant   Mark Salter

STATE OFFICES:
1839 S. Alma School Rd., #375, Mesa 85210; (602) 491-4300; Office Manager: Kaye Temple.
2400 E. Arizona, Biltmore Circle, #1150, Phoenix 85016; (602) 952-2410; Office Manager: Babs Donaldson.
450 W. Paseo Redondo, #200, Tucson 85701; (602) 670-6334; Office Manager: Rosemary Alexander.

COMMITTEE ASSIGNMENTS:
Armed Services
Commerce, Science, and Transportation
Governmental Affairs
Indian Affairs (Ranking)
Special Aging

McConnell, Mitch, R-Ky.
CAPITOL HILL OFFICE:
SR-120 20510; 224-2541
Fax: 224-2499
Admin. Assistant   Steven Law

STATE OFFICES:
600 Dr. Martin Luther King Jr. Place, #451, Louisville 40202; (502) 582-6304; Fax: (502) 582-5326; State Director: Larry Cox.
241 E. Main St., #102, Bowling Green 42101; (502) 781-1673; Fax: (502) 782-1884; Field Representative: Robbin Morrison.
700 Scott St., #307, Covington 41011; (606) 261-6304; Fax: (606) 261-9228; Field Representative: Kathy Mueller.
155 E. Main St., #210, Lexington 40508; (606) 252-1781; Fax: (606) 252-1783; Field Representative: Kevin Atkins.
1501-N S. Main St., London 40741; (606) 864-2026; Fax: (606) 864-2035; Field Representative: Janie Catron.
602 Broadway, Paducah 42001; (502) 442-4554; Fax: (502) 443-3102; Field Representative: Gordon Rahn.

COMMITTEE ASSIGNMENTS:
Agriculture, Nutrition, and Forestry
Appropriations
Rules and Administration
Select Ethics (Ranking)

Metzenbaum, Howard M., D-Ohio
CAPITOL HILL OFFICE:
SR-140 20510; 224-2315
Fax: 224-6519
Admin. Assistant   Joel Johnson

STATE OFFICES:
10411 Federal Bldg., Cincinnati 45202; (513) 684-3894; Office Manager: Patricia Phelan.
200 N. High St., #405, Columbus 43215; (614) 469-6774; District Director: John Maynard.
1240 E. 9th St., #2915, Cleveland 44199; (216) 522-7272; Office Manager: Candy Korn.
234 N. Summit St., #722, Toledo 43603; (419) 259-7536; Assistant: Jerry Brown.
City Centre One Ltd., 100 Federal Plaza East, #510, Youngstown 44503; (216) 746-1132; Staff Assistant: Jennifer Cooper.

COMMITTEE ASSIGNMENTS:
Environment and Public Works
Judiciary
Labor and Human Resources
Select Intelligence

Mikulski, Barbara A., D-Md.
CAPITOL HILL OFFICE:
SH-709 20510; 224-4654
Fax: 224-8858
Chief of Staff   Stephenie Foster

STATE OFFICES:
60 West St., #202, Annapolis 21401; (410) 263-1805; Office Director: Denise Nooe.
401 E. Pratt St., #253, Baltimore 21202; (410) 962-4510; Fax: (410) 962-4760; Interim State Admin.: Terry Curtis.
82 W. Washington St., #402, Hagerstown 21740; (301) 797-2826; Fax: (301) 797-2241; Western Maryland Representative: Brien Poffenberger.
9658 Baltimore Ave., #208, College Park 20740; (301) 345-5517; Office Director: Patrice Murray.
213-219 W. Main St., Salisbury 21801; (410) 546-7711; Eastern Shore Representative: Cindy Birge.

COMMITTEE ASSIGNMENTS:
Appropriations
Labor and Human Resources
Select Ethics

Mitchell, George J., D-Maine
CAPITOL HILL OFFICE:
SR-176 20510; 224-5344
Admin. Assistant   Mary McAleney
S-221 The Capitol 20510; 224-5556
(Majority Leader's office)

STATE OFFICES:
202 Harlow St., P.O. Box 1237, Bangor 04402; (207) 945-0451; Office Director: Clyde MacDonald.
231 Main St., Biddeford 04005; (207) 282-4144; Office Director: Judith Cadorette.
157 Main St., Lewiston 04240; (207) 784-0163; Office Director: Jeffrey Porter.
537 Congress St., P.O. Box 8300, Portland 04104; (207) 874-0883; Office Director: Larry Benoit.
541 Main St., Suite B, Presque Isle 04769; (207) 764-5601; Office Director: Mary Leblanc.
Main and Winter Sts., Rockland 04841; (207) 596-0311; Office Director: Tom Bertocci.
33 College Ave., P.O. Box 786, Waterville 04903; (207) 873-3361; Office Director: Janet Dennis.
40 Western Ave., P.O. Box 5248, Augusta 04332; (207) 622-8292; Office Director: Tom Bertocci.

COMMITTEE ASSIGNMENTS:
Environment and Public Works
Finance
Veterans' Affairs

Moseley-Braun, Carol, D-Ill.
CAPITOL HILL OFFICE:
SH-320 20510; 224-2854
Chief of Staff   Olga Corey

STATE OFFICES:
230 S. Dearborn, Chicago 60604; (312) 353-5420; Fax: (312) 353-2560; Office Director: Jill Zwick.

600 E. Monroe St., #117, Springfield 62701; (217) 492-4126; Office Director: Bill Houlihan.
6 Executive Dr., #6, Fairview Heights 62208; (618) 632-7242; Office Director: Kittie Connor.

COMMITTEE ASSIGNMENTS:
Banking, Housing, and Urban Affairs
Judiciary
Small Business

Moynihan, Daniel Patrick, D-N.Y.
CAPITOL HILL OFFICE:
SR-464 20510; 224-4451
Admin. Assistant   Roy Kienitz

STATE OFFICES:
405 Lexington Ave., #4101, New York 10174; (212) 661-5150; Staff Contact: David Warner.
28 Church St., #203, Buffalo 14202; (716) 846-4097; District Director: Jim Kane.
214 Main St., Oneonta 13820; (607) 433-2310; District Director: Barbara Rainville.

COMMITTEE ASSIGNMENTS:
Joint Library
Joint Taxation (Chairman)
Environment and Public Works
Finance (Chairman)
Foreign Relations
Rules and Administration

Murkowski, Frank H., R-Alaska
CAPITOL HILL OFFICE:
SH-706 20510; 224-6665
Chief of Staff   Gregg Renkes

STATE OFFICES:
222 W. 7th Ave., #1, Anchorage 99513; (907) 271-3735; Staff Assistant: Pat Heller.
101 12th Ave., Box 7, Fairbanks 99701; (907) 456-0233; Staff Assistant: Marcia Kozie.
709 W. 9th St., P.O. Box 21647, Juneau 99802; (907) 586-7400; Staff Assistant: Gen Dickey.
130 Trading Bay Rd., #350, Kenai 99611; (907) 283-5808; Staff Assistant: Peggy Arness.
109 Main St., Ketchikan 99901; (907) 225-6880; Staff Assistant: Sherrie Slick.

COMMITTEE ASSIGNMENTS:
Energy and Natural Resources
Foreign Relations
Indian Affairs
Veterans' Affairs (Ranking)

Murray, Patty, D-Wash.
CAPITOL HILL OFFICE:
SH-302 20510; 224-2621
Fax: 224-0238
Admin. Assistant   Michael Timmeny

STATE OFFICES:
915 2nd Ave., #2988, Seattle 98174; (206) 553-

5545; Fax: (206) 553-0891; State Director: Dan Evans.

500 W. 12th St., #140, Vancouver 98660; (206) 696-7797; Office Director: Annette Cleveland.

W. 601 1st Ave., Spokane 99201; (509) 624-9515; Fax: (509) 624-9561; Office Director: Jenny Polek.

COMMITTEE ASSIGNMENTS:
Appropriations
Banking, Housing, and Urban Affairs
Budget

Nickles, Don, R-Okla.
CAPITOL HILL OFFICE:
SH-133 20510; 224-5754
Fax: 224-6008
Admin. Assistant   Les Brorsen

STATE OFFICES:
100 N. Broadway, #1820, Oklahoma City 73102; (405) 231-4941; Office Manager: Mark Nichols.

1916 Lake Rd., Ponca City 74601; (405) 767-1270; State Director: Cheryl Fletcher.

409 S. Boston, #3310, Tulsa 74103; (918) 581-7651; Office Manager: Sharon Keasler.

601 D Ave., #201, Lawton 73501; (405) 357-9878; Office Manager: Billie Penn.

COMMITTEE ASSIGNMENTS:
Appropriations
Budget
Energy and Natural Resources
Indian Affairs

Nunn, Sam, D-Ga.
CAPITOL HILL OFFICE:
SD-303 20510; 224-3521
Fax: 224-0072
Admin. Assistant   Bob Hurt

STATE OFFICES:
75 Spring St. S.W., #1700, Atlanta 30303; (404) 331-4811; Office Manager: Elizabeth Way.

915 Main St., Perry 31069; (912) 987-1458; Field Representative: Jim Peterson.

120 Barnard St., #A307, Savannah 31402; (912) 944-4300; Field Representative: Roy Robinson.

130 Federal Bldg., Gainesville 30501; (404) 532-9976; Field Representative: Mike Giles.

101 Post Office and Courthouse Bldg., Columbus 31902; (706) 327-3270; Field Representative: Olan Faulk.

600 E. 1st St., #361, Rome 30161; (706) 291-5696; Field Representative: Mike Giles.

COMMITTEE ASSIGNMENTS:
Armed Services (Chairman)
Governmental Affairs
Small Business

Packwood, Bob, R-Ore.
CAPITOL HILL OFFICE:
SR-259 20510; 224-5244
Fax: 228-3576
Chief of Staff   Elaine Franklin

STATE OFFICE:
101 S.W. Main St., #240, Portland 97204; (503) 326-3370; State Director: Karen Belding.

COMMITTEE ASSIGNMENTS:
Joint Taxation
Commerce, Science, and Transportation
Finance (Ranking)

Pell, Claiborne, D-R.I.
CAPITOL HILL OFFICE:
SR-335 20510; 224-4642
Chief of Staff   Thomas G. Hughes

STATE OFFICE:
Exchange Terrace, 418 Federal Courthouse, Providence 02903; (401) 528-5456; Staff Director: Jack Cummings.

COMMITTEE ASSIGNMENTS:
Joint Library (Vice Chairman)
Foreign Relations (Chairman)
Labor and Human Resources
Rules and Administration

Pressler, Larry, R-S.D.
CAPITOL HILL OFFICE:
SR-283 20510; 224-5842
Admin. Assistant   Douglas L. Miller

STATE OFFICES:
1923 6th Ave. S.E., Aberdeen 57401; (605) 226-7471; Caseworker: Shannon Garry.

112 Rushmore Mall, Rapid City 57701; (605) 341-1185; State Director: Darrell Sawyer.

309 S. Minnesota Ave., Sioux Falls 57101; (605) 335-1990; Field Representative: Jill Schieffer.

COMMITTEE ASSIGNMENTS:
Special Aging
Commerce, Science, and Transportation
Foreign Relations
Judiciary
Small Business (Ranking)

Pryor, David, D-Ark.
CAPITOL HILL OFFICE:
SR-267 20510; 224-2353
Admin. Assistant   Frank Thomas

STATE OFFICE:
3030 Federal Bldg., Little Rock 72201; (501) 324-6336; Fax: (501) 324-5320; State Director: Kelly Robbins.

COMMITTEE ASSIGNMENTS:
Agriculture, Nutrition, and Forestry
Finance
Governmental Affairs
Special Aging (Chairman)

Reid, Harry, D-Nev.
CAPITOL HILL OFFICE:
SH-324 20510; 224-3542
Chief of Staff Reynaldo Martinez

STATE OFFICES:
600 E. Williams St., #302, Carson City 89701;
(702) 882-7343; Regional Director: Lee Currier.
500 E. Charleston Blvd., Las Vegas 89104; (702)
474-0041; Office Manager: Eric Jordan.
245 E. Liberty St., #102, Reno 89501; (702) 784-
5568; Office Director: Blaine Rose.

COMMITTEE ASSIGNMENTS:
Appropriations
Environment and Public Works
Indian Affairs
Special Aging

Riegle, Donald W., Jr., D-Mich.
CAPITOL HILL OFFICE:
SD-105 20510; 224-4822
Admin. Assistant David Krawitz

STATE OFFICES:
1155 Brewery Park Blvd., Detroit 48207; (313)
226-3188; Regional Representative: Cecilia Walker.
352 S. Saginaw St., #910, Flint 48502; (313) 766-
5115; Regional Representative: Inez Brown.
110 Michigan Ave. N.W., #716, Grand Rapids
49503; (616) 456-2592; Regional Representative:
Brad Miller.
109 W. Michigan St., #705, Lansing 48933;
(517) 377-1713; Regional Representative: Tim
McNeilly.
309 E. Front St., Traverse City 49685; (616) 946-
1300; Regional Representative: Chris Wright.
200 W. Washington, #323, Marquette 49855;
(906) 228-7457; Regional Representative: John
Nelson.
30800 Van Dyke, #31, Warren 48093; (313)
573-9017; Regional Representative: Bill Wenzel.

COMMITTEE ASSIGNMENTS:
Banking, Housing, and Urban Affairs (Chairman)
Budget
Finance
Special Aging

Robb, Charles S., D-Va.
CAPITOL HILL OFFICE:
SR-493 20510; 224-4024
Chief of Staff Thomas Lehner

STATE OFFICES:
530 Main St., Danville 24541; (804) 791-0330;
Regional Representative: Anne Turner.

999 Waterside Drive, #107, Norfolk 23510;
(804) 441-3124; Regional Representative: Barbara
Blount.
8229 Boone Blvd., #888, Vienna 22182; (703)
356-2006; Regional Representative: David Link, III.
310 Church St. S.W., #102, Roanoke 24011;
(703) 985-0103; Regional Representative: Debbie
Lawson.
1 Court Square, #340, Harrisonburg 22801;
(703) 432-1551; Regional Representative: Shelley
Spears.
1001 E. Broad St., #150, Richmond 23219; (804)
771-2221; State Director: Christine Bridge.
P.O. Box 1009, Clintwood 24228; (703) 926-
4104; Regional Representative: Jim O'Quinn.

COMMITTEE ASSIGNMENTS:
Joint Economic
Armed Services
Commerce, Science, and Transportation
Foreign Relations

Rockefeller, John D., IV, D-W.Va.
CAPITOL HILL OFFICE:
SH-109 20510; 224-6472
Admin. Assistant R. Lane Bailey

STATE OFFICES:
405 Capitol, #608, Charleston 25301; (304) 347-
5372; State Director: Lou Ann Martin.
207 Prince St., Beckley 25801; (304) 253-9704;
State Director: Lou Ann Martin.
200 Adams St., Suite A, Fairmont 26554; (304)
367-0122; State Director: Lou Ann Martin.

COMMITTEE ASSIGNMENTS:
Commerce, Science, and Transportation
Finance
Veterans' Affairs (Chairman)

Roth, William V., Jr., R-Del.
CAPITOL HILL OFFICE:
SH-104 20510; 224-2441
Fax: 224-2805
Admin. Assistant John M. Duncan

STATE OFFICES:
844 King St., #3021, Wilmington 19801; (302)
573-6291; Assistant to the Senator: Michae
Fleming.
300 S. New St., #2215, Dover 19901; (302) 674
3308; Assistant to the Senator: Marlene Elliot.
12 The Circle, Georgetown 19947; (302) 856
3566; Assistant to the Senator: Marlene Elliot.

COMMITTEE ASSIGNMENTS:
Joint Economic (Ranking)
Banking, Housing, and Urban Affairs
Finance
Governmental Affairs (Ranking)

Sarbanes, Paul S., D-Md.
CAPITOL HILL OFFICE:
SH-309 20510; 224-4524
Fax: 224-1651
Admin. Assistant   Marvin Moss

STATE OFFICES:
100 S. Charles St., #1010, Baltimore 21201;
(410) 962-4436; Fax: (410) 962-4156; Field Director:
Emily Gibbs.
1110 Bonifant St., #450, Silver Spring 20910;
(301) 589-0797; Fax: (301) 589-0598; Field Representative: Becky Wagner.
15499 Potomac River Dr., Box 331, Cobb Island
20625; (301) 259-2404; Field Representative: Ursula
Culver.
141 Baltimore St., #206, Cumberland 21502;
(301) 724-0695; Fax: (301) 724-4660; Field Representative: Nina Conway.
111 Baptist St., #115, Salisbury 21801; (410)
860-2131; Fax: (410) 860-2134; Field Representative:
Lee Whaley.

COMMITTEE ASSIGNMENTS:
Joint Economic (Vice Chairman)
Banking, Housing, and Urban Affairs
Budget
Foreign Relations

Sasser, Jim, D-Tenn.
CAPITOL HILL OFFICE:
SR-363 20510; 224-3344
Chief of Staff   John Callahan

STATE OFFICES:
569 U.S. Courthouse, Nashville 37203; (615)
736-7353; State Director: Bill Hawks.
167 N. Main, #390, Memphis 38103; (901) 544-
4187; Field Representative: Calvin Anderson.
501 W. Main Ave., #320, Knoxville 37902; (615)
545-4264; Field Representative: Vickie Nance.
109 S. Highland, #B-8, Jackson 38301; (901)
424-6600; West Tennessee Field Representative:
Neal Smith.
Tri-Cities Airport, Blountville 37617; (615) 323-
6207; East Tennessee Field Representative: Paul
Bivens.
239 Federal Bldg., Chattanooga 37402; (615)
756-8836; Field Representative: Beth Jones.

COMMITTEE ASSIGNMENTS:
Appropriations
Banking, Housing, and Urban Affairs
Budget (Chairman)
Governmental Affairs

Shelby, Richard C., D-Ala.
CAPITOL HILL OFFICE:
SH-509 20510; 224-5744
Fax: 224-3416
Chief of Staff   Tom Young

STATE OFFICES:
P.O. Box 2570, Tuscaloosa 35403; (205) 759-

5047; Fax: (205) 759-5067; State Director: Connie
Morton.
1800 5th Ave. North, #321, Birmingham 35203;
(205) 731-1384; Fax: (205) 731-1386; Office Director:
Blair Agricola.
1000 Glenn Hearn Blvd., Box 20127, Huntsville
35824; (205) 772-0460; Fax: (205) 772-8387; Office
Director: LeAnn Hill.
438 U.S. Courthouse, Mobile 36602; (205) 694-
4164; Fax: (205) 694-4166; Office Director: Laura
Breland.
B-28A U.S. Courthouse, Montgomery 36104;
(205) 223-7303; Fax: (205) 223-7317; Office Director:
Carol Estes.

COMMITTEE ASSIGNMENTS:
Armed Services
Banking, Housing, and Urban Affairs
Energy and Natural Resources
Special Aging

Simon, Paul, D-Ill.
CAPITOL HILL OFFICE:
SD-462 20510; 224-2152
Admin. Assistant   Jeremy Karpatkin

STATE OFFICES:
230 S. Dearborn, 38th Floor, Chicago 60604;
(312) 353-4952; Office Director: Nancy Chen.
3 W. Old Capitol Plaza, #1, Springfield 62701;
(217) 492-4960; Executive Assistant: Joe Dunn.
250 W. Cherry, #115-B, Carbondale 62901;
(618) 457-3653; Executive Assistant: Donna
Eastman.

COMMITTEE ASSIGNMENTS:
Budget
Foreign Relations
Indian Affairs
Judiciary
Labor and Human Resources

Simpson, Alan K., R-Wyo.
CAPITOL HILL OFFICE:
SD-261 20510; 224-3424
Chief of Staff   Don Hardy

STATE OFFICES:
1731 Sheridan Ave., #1, P.O. Box 430, Cody
82414; (307) 527-7121; Field Office Director: Karen
McCreery.
2120 Capitol Ave., #2007, Cheyenne 82001;
(307) 772-2477; State Coordinator: Dee Rodekohr.
2020 Grand Ave., #411, P.O. Box 335, Laramie
82070; (307) 745-5303.
2515 Foothill Blvd., #220, Rock Springs 82901;
(307) 382-5079.
Federal Center, #3201, Casper 82601; (307)
261-5172; Field Office Director: Cherie Burd.
2201 S. Douglas Highway, P.O. Box 3155, Gillette 82716; (307) 682-7091; Field Representative:
Robin Bailey.
1120 Maple Way, Suite C, P.O. Box 3634, Jackson 83001; (307) 739-9507; Field Representative:
Lyn Shanaghy.

COMMITTEE ASSIGNMENTS:
Environment and Public Works
Judiciary
Special Aging
Veterans' Affairs

Smith, Robert C., R-N.H.
CAPITOL HILL OFFICE:
SD-332 20510; 224-2841
Admin. Assistant   Patrick Pettey

STATE OFFICES:
46 S. Main St., Concord 03301; (603) 228-0453;
Office Director: Mary Jane Colton.
50 Phillippe Cote St., Manchester 03101; (603)
634-5000; Office Director: Mark Aldrich.
1 Harbor Place, #435, Portsmouth 03801; (603)
433-1667; Office Director: Carol St. Clair.

COMMITTEE ASSIGNMENTS:
Armed Services
Environment and Public Works
Select Ethics

Specter, Arlen, R-Pa.
CAPITOL HILL OFFICE:
SH-530 20510; 224-4254
Admin. Assistant   Barry Caldwell

STATE OFFICES:
600 Arch St., #9400, Philadelphia 19106; (215)
597-7200; Executive Director: Patrick Meehan.
Federal Bldg., #2031, Liberty Ave. and Grant
St., Pittsburgh 15222; (412) 644-3400; Executive Director: Yvonne O'Connor.
6th and State Sts., #118, Erie 16501; (814) 453-
3010; Executive Director: Patsy Root.
P.O. Box 1092, Harrisburg 17108; (717) 782-
3951; Executive Director: Tom Bowman.
102 Post Office Bldg., 5th and Hamilton Sts.,
Allentown 18101; (215) 434-1444; Executive Director: Mary Joe Bierman.
225 N. Washington Ave., Scranton 18503; (717)
346-2006; Executive Director: Andy Wallace.
116 S. Main St., #306, Wilkes-Barre 18701;
(717) 826-6265; Executive Director: Andy Wallace.

COMMITTEE ASSIGNMENTS:
Appropriations
Energy and Natural Resources
Judiciary
Special Aging
Veterans' Affairs

Stevens, Ted, R-Alaska
CAPITOL HILL OFFICE:
SH-522 20510; 224-3004
Chief of Staff   Lisa Sutherland

STATE OFFICES:
222 W. 7th Ave., #2, Anchorage 99513; (907)
271-5915; State Director: Barbara Andrews.

101 12th Ave., #206, Fairbanks 99701; (907)
456-0261; Staff Director: Janet Halvarson.
Federal Bldg., #965, P.O. Box 020149, Juneau
99802; (907) 586-7400; Staff Director: Gen Dickey.
109 Main St., Ketchikan 99901; (907) 225-6880;
Staff Director: Sherrie Slick.
130 Trading Bay Rd., #350, Kenai 99611; (907)
283-5808; Staff Director: Peggy Arness.

COMMITTEE ASSIGNMENTS:
Joint Inaugural Ceremonies
Joint Library
Joint Printing (Ranking)
Appropriations
Commerce, Science, and Transportation
Governmental Affairs
Rules and Administration (Ranking)
Select Intelligence

Thurmond, Strom, R-S.C.
CAPITOL HILL OFFICE:
SR-217 20510; 224-5972
Chief of Staff   R.J. Duke Short

STATE OFFICES:
1835 Assembly St., #1558, Columbia 29201;
(803) 765-5494; State Director: Warren Abernathy.
211 York St. N.E., #29, Aiken 29801; (803) 649-
2591; Office Manager: Elizabeth McFarland.
334 Meeting St., Charleston 29403; (803) 727-
4596; Office Manager: Gerry Dickinson.
401 W. Evans St., Florence 29501; (803) 662-
8873; Office Manager: Raleigh Ward.

COMMITTEE ASSIGNMENTS:
Armed Services (Ranking)
Judiciary
Labor and Human Resources
Veterans' Affairs

Wallop, Malcolm, R-Wyo.
CAPITOL HILL OFFICE:
SR-237 20510; 224-6441
Admin. Assistant   Patricia Ann McDonald

STATE OFFICES:
2009 Federal Center, Cheyenne 82001; (307)
634-0626; State Director: Byra Kite.
2201 Federal Bldg., Casper 82601; (307) 261-
5415; Field Representative: Sue Cole.
Post Office Bldg., P.O. Box 1014, Lander 82520
(307) 332-2293; Field Representative: Pam Buline.
2515 Foothill Blvd., Rock Springs 82901; (307)
382-5127; Field Representative: Rillee Jelouchan.
40 S. Main, Sheridan 82801; (307) 672-6456
Field Representative: Evelyn Ebzery.

COMMITTEE ASSIGNMENTS:
Energy and Natural Resources (Ranking)
Finance
Select Intelligence
Small Business

Warner, John W., R-Va.

CAPITOL HILL OFFICE:
SR-225 20510; 224-2023
Fax: 224-6295
Admin. Assistant   Susan Magill

STATE OFFICES:
600 E. Main St., Richmond 23219; (804) 771-2579; Fax: (804) 782-2131; State Representative: Millie Victor.
4900 World Trade Center, Norfolk 23510; (804) 441-3079; Fax: (804) 441-6250; Office Manager: Loretta Tate.
180 W. Main St., #235, Abingdon 24210; (703) 628-8158; Fax: (703) 628-1036; Office Manager: Cathie Gollehon.
213 S. Jefferson St., #1003, Roanoke 24011; (703) 857-2676; Fax: (703) 857-2800; Caseworker: Camellia Crowder.

COMMITTEE ASSIGNMENTS:
Armed Services
Environment and Public Works
Rules and Administration
Select Intelligence (Ranking)

Wellstone, Paul, D-Minn.

CAPITOL HILL OFFICE:
SH-717 20510; 224-5641
Fax: 224-8438
Admin. Assistant   Kari Moe

STATE OFFICES:
2550 University Ave., #185S, St. Paul 55114; (612) 645-0323; Office Director: Jeff Blodgett.
105 2nd Ave. South, P.O. Box 281, Virginia 55792; (218) 741-1075; District Representative: Jim Shaw.

417 Litchfield Ave. S.W., Willmar 56201; (612) 231-0001; District Representative: Tom Meium.

COMMITTEE ASSIGNMENTS:
Energy and Natural Resources
Indian Affairs
Labor and Human Resources
Small Business

Wofford, Harris, D-Pa.

CAPITOL HILL OFFICE:
SD-521 20510; 224-6324
Fax: 224-4161
Chief of Staff   Steve Schutt

STATE OFFICES:
600 Arch St., #9456, Philadelphia 19106; (215) 597-9914; Fax: (215) 597-4771; Office Director: Todd Bernstein.
1001 Liberty Ave., #1306, Pittsburgh 15222; (412) 562-0533; Fax: (412) 562-0533; Office Director: Mary Esther Van Shura.
Federal Square Station, P.O. Box 55, Harrisburg 17108; (717) 233-5849; Office Director: LaVerna Fountain.
116 N. Washington Ave., #3K, Scranton 18503; (717) 347-2341; Fax: (717) 347-7863; Office Director: Tim McGrath.
617 State St., #107, Erie 16501; (814) 454-7114; Fax: (814) 459-2096; Office Director: Mary Fiolek.

COMMITTEE ASSIGNMENTS:
Environment and Public Works
Foreign Relations
Labor and Human Resources
Small Business

House Committees and Subcommittees

The standing and select committees of the U.S. House of Representatives are listed below in alphabetical order. The listing includes the room number, telephone number, party ratio, and jurisdiction for each full committee. Membership is given in order of seniority on the committees. Subcommittees are listed alphabetically under each committee. Membership is listed in order of seniority on the subcommittees.

Address abbreviations used are as follows: CHOB (Cannon House Office Bldg.), LHOB (Longworth House Office Bldg.), RHOB (Rayburn House Office Bldg.), OHOB (O'Neill House Office Bldg., formerly House Annex #1, at 300 New Jersey Ave. S.E.), FHOB (Ford House Office Bldg., formerly House Annex #2, at 2nd and D Sts. S.W.), and CAP (Capitol). The telephone area code for Washington is 202.

Members of the majority party, Democrats, are shown in roman type; members of the minority party, Republicans, are shown in italic type. The word *vacancy* indicates that a committee or subcommittee seat had not been filled as of May 13, 1994. Subcommittee vacancies do not necessarily indicate vacancies on full committees, or vice versa.

The partisan committees of the House are listed on p. 997. Members of these committees are listed in alphabetical order, not by seniority.

Agriculture

Phone: 225-2171   Room: 1301 LHOB

Majority Staff Director:
Dianne Powell   225-2171   1301 LHOB

Minority Staff Director:
Gary Mitchell   225-0029   1304 LHOB

Agriculture generally; production, marketing, and stabilization of agricultural prices; animal industry and diseases of animals; crop insurance and soil conservation; dairy industry; farm credit and security; forestry in general; human nutrition and home economics; inspection of livestock and meat products; plant industry, soils, and agricultural engineering; rural electrification; commodities exchanges; rural development. Chairman and ranking minority member are members ex officio of all subcommittees of which they are not regular members.

Party Ratio: D 29 - R 19

E. "Kika" de la Garza, Texas, chairman

Pat Roberts, Kan., ranking member

George E. Brown Jr., Calif.
Charlie Rose, N.C.
Dan Glickman, Kan.
Charles W. Stenholm, Texas
Harold L. Volkmer, Mo.
Timothy J. Penny, Minn.
Tim Johnson, S.D.
Bill Sarpalius, Texas
Jill L. Long, Ind.
Gary A. Condit, Calif.
Collin C. Peterson, Minn.
Cal Dooley, Calif.
Eva Clayton, N.C.
David Minge, Minn.
Earl F. Hilliard, Ala.
Jay Inslee, Wash.
Tom Barlow, Ky.
Earl Pomeroy, N.D.
Tim Holden, Pa.
Cynthia A. McKinney, Ga.
Scotty Baesler, Ky.
Karen L. Thurman, Fla.
Bennie Thompson, Miss.
Sanford D. Bishop Jr., Ga.
Sam Farr, Calif.
Pat Williams, Mont.

Bill Emerson, Mo.
Steve Gunderson, Wis.
Tom Lewis, Fla.
Bob Smith, Ore.
Larry Combest, Texas
Wayne Allard, Colo.
Bill Barrett, Neb.
Jim Nussle, Iowa
John A. Boehner, Ohio
Thomas W. Ewing, Ill.
John T. Doolittle, Calif.
Jack Kingston, Ga.
Robert W. Goodlatte, Va.
Jay Dickey, Ark.
Richard W. Pombo, Calif.
Charles T. Canady, Fla.
Nick Smith, Mich.
Terry Everett, Ala.

Blanche Lambert, Ark.
Vacancy

Subcommittees

Department Operations and Nutrition

Phone: 225-1496   Room: 1301A LHOB

Stenholm, chairman   *Smith (Ore.)*
Brown (Calif.)   *Emerson*
Sarpalius   *Gunderson*
Dooley   *Allard*
Inslee   *Barrett (Neb.)*
Glickman   *Ewing*
McKinney   *Kingston*
Bishop   *Canady*
Volkmer   *Boehner*
Clayton
Holden
Rose
Farr
Johnson (S.D.)
Pomeroy
Lambert
Vacancy

Environment, Credit, and Rural Development

Phone: 225-0301   Room: 1430 LHOB

Johnson (S.D.), chairman   *Combest*
Long   *Gunderson*
Clayton   *Allard*
Minge   *Barrett (Neb.)*
Barlow   *Nussle*
Pomeroy   *Ewing*
Holden   *Dickey*
McKinney   *Pombo*
Thurman   *Smith (Mich.)*
Penny
Sarpalius
Peterson (Minn.)
Hilliard
Inslee
Baesler
Thompson
Farr
Vacancy

Foreign Agriculture and Hunger

Phone: 225-1867   Room: 1336 LHOB

Penny, chairman   *Allard*
Rose   *Lewis (Fla.)*
Barlow   *Doolittle*
McKinney   *Canady*
Baesler   *Everett*
Stenholm
Vacancy
Vacancy

General Farm Commodities

Phone: 225-0301   Room: 1430 LHOB

Sarpalius, chairman   *Emerson*
Glickman   *Smith (Ore.)*
Peterson (Minn.)   *Combest*
Volkmer   *Barrett (Neb.)*
Long   *Nussle*
Dooley   *Boehner*
Minge   *Ewing*
Pomeroy   *Doolittle*
Rose   *Dickey*
Stenholm   *Smith (Mich.)*
Condit
Barlow
Bishop
Thompson
Williams
Vacancy
Vacancy

Livestock

Phone: 225-1867   Room: 1336 LHOB

Volkmer, chairman   *Gunderson*
Condit   *Lewis (Fla.)*
Hilliard   *Smith (Ore.)*
Stenholm   *Boehner*
Holden   *Goodlatte*
Long   *Pombo*
Peterson (Minn.)
Rose
Dooley
Sarpalius

Specialty Crops and Natural Resources

Phone: 225-8906   Room: 105 CHOB

Rose, chairman   *Lewis (Fla.)*
Baesler   *Emerson*
Bishop   *Doolittle*
Brown (Calif.)   *Kingston*
Condit   *Goodlatte*
Clayton   *Dickey*
Thurman   *Pombo*
Minge   *Everett*
Inslee
Pomeroy
Stenholm
Peterson (Minn.)
Farr
Volkmer
Vacancy

Appropriations

Phone: 225-2771   Room: H-218 CAP

Majority Staff Director:
Frederick G. Mohrman   225-2771   H-218 CAP

Minority Staff Director:
James W. Kulikowski 225-3481 1016 LHOB

Appropriation of revenue for support of the federal government; rescissions of appropriations; transfers of unexpended balances; new spending authority under the Congressional Budget Act. Chairman and ranking minority member are members ex officio of all subcommittees of which they are not regular members.

Party Ratio: D 37 - R 23

David R. Obey, Wis., chairman	*Joseph M. McDade, Pa., ranking member*
Jamie L. Whitten, Miss.	*John T. Myers, Ind.*
Neal Smith, Iowa	*C. W. Bill Young, Fla.*
Sidney R. Yates, Ill.	*Ralph Regula, Ohio*
Louis Stokes, Ohio	*Robert L. Livingston, La.*
Tom Bevill, Ala.	
John P. Murtha, Pa.	*Jerry Lewis, Calif.*
Charles Wilson, Texas	*John Edward Porter, Ill.*
Norm Dicks, Wash.	
Martin Olav Sabo, Minn.	*Harold Rogers, Ky.*
Julian C. Dixon, Calif.	*Joe Skeen, N.M.*
Vic Fazio, Calif.	*Frank R. Wolf, Va.*
W. G. "Bill" Hefner, N.C.	*Tom DeLay, Texas*
Steny H. Hoyer, Md.	*Jim Kolbe, Ariz.*
Bob Carr, Mich.	*Dean A. Gallo, N.J.*
Richard J. Durbin, Ill.	*Barbara F. Vucanovich, Nev.*
Ronald D. Coleman, Texas	
Alan B. Mollohan, W.Va.	*Jim Ross Lightfoot, Iowa*
Jim Chapman, Texas	
Marcy Kaptur, Ohio	*Ron Packard, Calif.*
David E. Skaggs, Colo.	*Sonny Callahan, Ala.*
David Price, N.C.	*Helen Delich Bentley, Md.*
Nancy Pelosi, Calif.	
Peter J. Visclosky, Ind.	*James T. Walsh, N.Y.*
Thomas M. Foglietta, Pa.	*Charles H. Taylor, N.C.*
Esteban E. Torres, Calif.	*David L. Hobson, Ohio*
George "Buddy" Darden, Ga.	*Ernest Jim Istook Jr., Okla.*
Nita M. Lowey, N.Y.	
Ray Thornton, Ark.	*Henry Bonilla, Texas*
Jose E. Serrano, N.Y.	
Rosa DeLauro, Conn.	
James P. Moran Jr., Va.	
Pete Peterson, Fla.	
John W. Olver, Mass.	
Ed Pastor, Ariz.	
Carrie P. Meek, Fla.	
Vacancy	

Subcommittees

Agriculture, Rural Development, FDA, and Related Agencies

Phone: 225-2638   Room: 2362 RHOB

Durbin, chairman	*Skeen*
Whitten	*Myers*
Kaptur	*Vucanovich*
Thornton	*Walsh*
DeLauro	
Peterson (Fla.)	

Pastor
Smith (Iowa)

Commerce, Justice, State, and Judiciary

Phone: 225-3351   Room: H-309 CAP

Smith (Iowa), chairman	*Rogers*
Carr	*Kolbe*
Mollohan	*Taylor (N.C.)*
Moran	
Skaggs	
Price	

Defense

Phone: 225-2847   Room: H-144 CAP

Murtha, chairman	*McDade*
Dicks	*Young (Fla.)*
Wilson	*Livingston*
Hefner	*Lewis (Calif.)*
Sabo	*Skeen*
Dixon	
Visclosky	
Darden	

District of Columbia

Phone: 225-5338   Room: H-302 CAP

Dixon, chairman	*Walsh*
Stokes	*Istook*
Durbin	*Bonilla*
Kaptur	
Skaggs	
Pelosi	

Energy and Water Development

Phone: 225-3421   Room: 2362 RHOB

Bevill, chairman	*Myers*
Fazio	*Gallo*
Chapman	*Rogers*
Peterson (Fla.)	
Pastor	
Meek	

Foreign Operations, Export Financing, and Related Programs

Phone: 225-2041   Room: H-307 CAP

Obey, chairman	*Livingston*
Yates	*Porter*
Wilson	*Lightfoot*
Olver	*Callahan*
Pelosi	
Torres	
Lowey	
Serrano	

Interior

Phone: 225-3481   Room: 3481 LHOB

Yates, chairman   *Regula*
Murtha   *McDade*
Dicks   *Kolbe*
Bevill   *Packard*
Skaggs
Coleman

Labor, Health and Human Services, and Education

Phone: 225-3508   Room: 2358 RHOB

Smith (Iowa)   *Porter*
Obey   *Young (Fla.)*
Stokes   *Bentley*
Hoyer   *Bonilla*
Pelosi
Lowey
Serrano
DeLauro
Vacancy

Legislative Branch

Phone: 225-5338   Room: H-302 CAP

Fazio, chairman   *Young (Fla.)*
Moran   *Packard*
Obey   *Taylor (N.C.)*
Murtha
Carr
Chapman

Military Construction

Phone: 225-3047   Room: B-300 RHOB

Hefner, chairman   *Vucanovich*
Foglietta   *Callahan*
Meek   *Bentley*
Dicks   *Hobson*
Dixon
Fazio
Hoyer
Coleman

Transportation

Phone: 225-2141   Room: 2358 RHOB

Carr, chairman   *Wolf*
Durbin   *DeLay*
Sabo   *Regula*
Price
Coleman
Foglietta

Treasury, Postal Service, and General Government

Phone: 225-5834   Room: H-164 CAP

Hoyer, chairman   *Lightfoot*
Visclosky   *Wolf*
Darden   *Istook*
Olver
Bevill
Sabo

Veterans Affairs, Housing and Urban Development, and Independent Agencies

Phone: 225-3241   Room: H-143 CAP

Stokes, chairman   *Lewis (Calif.)*
Mollohan   *DeLay*
Chapman   *Gallo*
Kaptur
Torres
Thornton

Armed Services

Phone: 225-4151   Room: 2120 RHOB

Staff Director:
Marilyn A. Elrod   225-4158   2117 RHOB

Professional Staff Member:
Andrew K. Ellis   225-9647   2340 RHOB

Jurisdiction pursuant to House Rule X: Common defense generally; the Defense Dept. generally, including the departments of the Army, Navy, and Air Force generally; ammunition depots; forts; arsenals; Army, Navy, and Air Force reservations and establishments; conservation, development, and use of naval petroleum and oil shale reserves; pay, promotion, retirement, and other benefits and privileges of members of the armed forces; scientific research and development in support of the armed services; selective service; size and composition of the Army, Navy, and Air Force; soldiers' and sailors' homes strategic and critical materials necessary for the common defense; military applications of nuclear energy. In addition, the committee has special oversight with respect to international arms control and disarmament and military dependents education.

Party Ratio: D 34 - R 22

Ronald V. Dellums, Calif., chairman   *Floyd D. Spence, S.C., ranking member*
G. V. "Sonny" Montgomery, Miss.   *Bob Stump, Ariz.*
     Duncan Hunter, Calif.
Patricia Schroeder, Colo.   *John R. Kasich, Ohio*
Earl Hutto, Fla.   *Herbert H. Bateman, Va.*
Ike Skelton, Mo.
Dave McCurdy, Okla.   *James V. Hansen, Utah*
Marilyn Lloyd, Tenn.   *Curt Weldon, Pa.*
Norman Sisisky, Va.   *Jon Kyl, Ariz.*
John M. Spratt Jr., S.C.   *Arthur Ravenel Jr., S.*

Frank McCloskey, Ind.
Solomon P. Ortiz, Texas
George J. Hochbrueckner,
N.Y.
Owen B. Pickett, Va.
H. Martin Lancaster, N.C.
Lane Evans, Ill.
James Bilbray, Nev.
John Tanner, Tenn.
Glen Browder, Ala.
Gene Taylor, Miss.
Neil Abercrombie, Hawaii
Thomas H. Andrews, Maine
Chet Edwards, Texas
Don Johnson, Ga.
Frank Tejeda, Texas
David Mann, Ohio
Bart Stupak, Mich.
Martin T. Meehan, Mass.
Robert Anacletus Underwood,
Guam
Jane Harman, Calif.
Paul McHale, Pa.
Tim Holden, Pa.
Pete Geren, Texas
Elizabeth Furse, Ore.
Sam Farr, Calif.

Robert K. Dornan, Calif.
Joel Hefley, Colo.
Ronald K. Machtley,
R.I.
H. James Saxton, N.J.
Randy "Duke"
Cunningham, Calif.
James M. Inhofe, Okla.
Steve Buyer, Ind.
Peter G. Torkildsen,
Mass.
Tillie Fowler, Fla.
John M. McHugh, N.Y.
James M. Talent, Mo.
Terry Everett, Ala.
Roscoe G. Bartlett, Md.

Farr
Vacancy

Military Installations and Facilities

Phone: 225-7120   Room: 2120 RHOB

McCurdy, chairman	*Hunter*
Montgomery	*Fowler*
McCloskey	*McHugh*
Ortiz	*Everett*
Hochbrueckner	*Stump*
Bilbray	*Machtley*
Browder	*Saxton*
Taylor (Miss.)	*Torkildsen*
Abercrombie	
Edwards (Texas)	
Johnson (Ga.)	
Tejeda	
Underwood	

Oversight and Investigations

Phone: 225-2086   Room: 2540 RHOB

Sisisky, chairman	*Hansen*
Spratt	*Kyl*
Tanner	*Hefley*
Browder	*McHugh*
Edwards (Texas)	*Everett*
Johnson (Ga.)	*Dornan*
Tejeda	
Mann	
Harman	
Holden	

Subcommittees

Military Acquisition

Phone: 225-6703   Room: 2343 RHOB

Dellums, chairman	*Spence*
Lloyd	*Bateman*
Spratt	*Weldon*
McCloskey	*Ravenel*
Evans	*Dornan*
Tanner	*Hefley*
Taylor (Miss.)	*Machtley*
Abercrombie	*Saxton*
Andrews (Maine)	*Cunningham*
Mann	*Inhofe*
Stupak	
McHale	
Holden	
Geren	
Sisisky	

Readiness

Phone: 225-9644   Room: 2339 RHOB

Hutto, chairman	*Kasich*
Ortiz	*Bateman*
Pickett	*Weldon*
Lancaster	*Dornan*
Evans	*Cunningham*
Browder	*Inhofe*
Meehan	
Underwood	
McHale	
McCurdy	

Military Forces and Personnel

Phone: 225-7560   Room: 2343 RHOB

Skelton, chairman	*Kyl*
Montgomery	*Ravenel*
Pickett	*Buyer*
Lancaster	*Fowler*
Bilbray	*Talent*
Stupak	*Bartlett*
Meehan	
Underwood	
Harman	

Research and Technology

Phone: 225-6527   Room: 2120 RHOB

Schroeder, chairman	*Stump*
Hochbrueckner	*Buyer*
Pickett	*Torkildsen*
Lancaster	*Talent*
Bilbray	*Bartlett*
Edwards (Texas)	*Hunter*
Johnson (Ga.)	*Kasich*
Tejeda	*Hansen*
Meehan	

Harman
Furse
Hutto
McCurdy

Banking, Finance, and Urban Affairs

Phone: 225-4247   Room: 2129 RHOB

Majority Clerk and Staff Director:
Kelsay Meek 225-7057 2129 RHOB

Minority Staff Director:
Tony Cole 225-7502 B-301C RHOB

Banks and banking, including deposit insurance and federal monetary policy; money and credit; currency; issuance and redemption of notes; gold and silver; coinage; valuation and revaluation of the dollar; urban development; private and public housing; economic stabilization; defense production; renegotiation; price controls; international finance; financial aid to commerce and industry.

Party Ratio: D 30 - R 20 - I 1

Henry B. Gonzalez, Texas, chairman	*Jim Leach, Iowa, ranking member*
Stephen L. Neal, N.C.	*Bill McCollum, Fla.*
John J. LaFalce, N.Y.	*Marge Roukema, N.J.*
Bruce F. Vento, Minn.	*Doug Bereuter, Neb.*
Charles E. Schumer, N.Y.	*Tom Ridge, Pa.*
Barney Frank, Mass.	*Toby Roth, Wis.*
Paul E. Kanjorski, Pa.	*Al McCandless, Calif.*
Joseph P. Kennedy II, Mass.	*Richard H. Baker, La.*
Floyd H. Flake, N.Y.	*Jim Nussle, Iowa*
Kweisi Mfume, Md.	*Craig Thomas, Wyo.*
Maxine Waters, Calif.	*Sam Johnson, Texas*
Larry LaRocco, Idaho	*Deborah Pryce, Ohio*
Bill Orton, Utah	*John Linder, Ga.*
Jim Bacchus, Fla.	*Joe Knollenberg, Mich.*
Herb Klein, N.J.	*Rick A. Lazio, N.Y.*
Carolyn B. Maloney, N.Y.	*Rod Grams, Minn.*
Peter Deutsch, Fla.	*Spencer Bachus, Ala.*
Luis V. Gutierrez, Ill.	*Michael Huffington, Calif.*
Bobby L. Rush, Ill.	
Lucille Roybal-Allard, Calif.	*Michael N. Castle, Del.*
Thomas M. Barrett, Wis.	*Peter T. King, N.Y.*
Elizabeth Furse, Ore.	
Nydia M. Velazquez, N.Y.	
Albert R. Wynn, Md.	
Cleo Fields, La.	*Bernard Sanders, Vt.*
Melvin Watt, N.C.	
Maurice D. Hinchey, N.Y.	
Cal Dooley, Calif.	
Ron Klink, Pa.	
Eric D. Fingerhut, Ohio	

Subcommittees

Consumer Credit and Insurance

Phone: 225-8872   Room: 604 OHOB

Kennedy, chairman	*McCandless*
Gonzalez	*Castle*
LaRocco	*King*
Gutierrez	*Pryce*
Rush	*Linder*
Roybal-Allard	*Knollenberg*
Barrett (Wis.)	*Bereuter*
Furse	*Thomas (Wyo.)*
Velazquez	*Lazio*
Wynn	*Grams*
Fields (La.)	*Bachus*
Watt	*Baker (La.)*
Hinchey	
Kanjorski	
Flake	*Sanders*
Waters	
Maloney	
Deutsch	

Economic Growth and Credit Formation

Phone: 226-7315   Room: 109 FHOB

Kanjorski, chairman	*Ridge*
Neal (N.C.)	*McCollum*
LaFalce	*Roth*
Orton	*Nussle*
Klein	*Roukema*
Velazquez	*King*
Dooley	
Klink	
Fingerhut	

Financial Institutions Supervision, Regulation, and Deposit Insurance

Phone: 226-3280   Room: 212 OHOB

Neal (N.C.), chairman	*McCollum*
LaFalce	*Leach*
Vento	*Baker (La.)*
Schumer	*Nussle*
Frank	*Thomas (Wyo.)*
Kanjorski	*Johnson*
Kennedy	*Pryce*
Flake	*Linder*
Mfume	*Lazio*
LaRocco	*Grams*
Orton	*Bachus*
Bacchus	*Huffington*
Waters	
Klein	
Maloney	
Deutsch	
Barrett (Wis.)	
Hinchey	

General Oversight, Investigations, and the Resolution of Failed Financial Institutions

Phone: 225-2828   Room: 139 FHOB

Flake, chairman	*Roth*

Neal (N.C.)
Velazquez
Hinchey

Ridge

Housing and Community Development

Phone: 225-7054   Room: B-303 RHOB

Gonzalez, chairman	*Roukema*
Vento	*Bereuter*
Schumer	*Ridge*
Mfume	*Baker (La.)*
LaFalce	*Thomas (Wyo.)*
Waters	*Knollenberg*
Klein	*Lazio*
Maloney	*Grams*
Deutsch	*Bachus*
Gutierrez	*Castle*
Rush	*Pryce*
Roybal-Allard	*Roth*
Barrett (Wis.)	
Furse	
Velazquez	*Sanders*
Wynn	
Fields (La.)	
Watt	

International Development, Finance, Trade, and Monetary Policy

Phone: 226-7515   Room: B-304 RHOB

Frank, chairman	*Bereuter*
Neal (N.C.)	*McCandless*
LaFalce	*McCollum*
Kennedy	*Roukema*
Waters	*Johnson*
LaRocco	*Huffington*
Orton	*King*
Bacchus	*Baker (La.)*
Gonzalez	*Nussle*
Kanjorski	*Castle*
Rush	
Fields (La.)	
Watt	*Sanders*
Fingerhut	
Vacancy	

Budget

Phone: 226-7200   Room: 214 OHOB

Chief of Staff:
Eileen Baumgartner   226-7200   222 OHOB

Minority Staff Director:
Rick May   226-7270   H2-278 FHOB

Federal budget generally; concurrent budget resolutions; Congressional Budget Office. Chairman and ranking minority member are members ex officio of all task forces of which they are not regular members. The majority leader's designate and the minority leader's designate are ex officio members of all task forces.

Party Ratio: D 26 - R 17

Martin Olav Sabo, Minn., chairman	*John R. Kasich, Ohio, ranking member*
Richard A. Gephardt, Mo.	*Alex McMillan, N.C.*
Dale E. Kildee, Mich.	*Jim Kolbe, Ariz.*
Anthony C. Beilenson, Calif.	*Christopher Shays, Conn.*
Howard L. Berman, Calif.	
Bob Wise, W.Va.	*Olympia J. Snowe, Maine*
John Bryant, Texas	
Charles W. Stenholm, Texas	*Wally Herger, Calif.*
Barney Frank, Mass.	*Jim Bunning, Ky.*
Jim Cooper, Tenn.	*Lamar Smith, Texas*
Louise M. Slaughter, N.Y.	*Christopher Cox, Calif.*
Mike Parker, Miss.	*Wayne Allard, Colo.*
William J. Coyne, Pa.	*David L. Hobson, Ohio*
Barbara B. Kennelly, Conn.	*Dan Miller, Fla.*
Michael A. Andrews, Texas	*Rick A. Lazio, N.Y.*
Alan B. Mollohan, W.Va.	*Bob Franks, N.J.*
Bart Gordon, Tenn.	*Nick Smith, Mich.*
David Price, N.C.	*Bob Inglis, S.C.*
Jerry F. Costello, Ill.	*Martin R. Hoke, Ohio*
Harry A. Johnston, Fla.	
Patsy T. Mink, Hawaii	
Bill Orton, Utah	
Lucien E. Blackwell, Pa.	
Earl Pomeroy, N.D.	
Glen Browder, Ala.	
Lynn Woolsey, Calif.	

District of Columbia

Phone: 225-4457   Room: 1310 LHOB

Majority Staff Director:
Broderick D. Johnson   225-4457   1309 LHOB

Minority Staff Director:
Dennis Smith   225-7158   1307 LHOB

Municipal affairs of the District of Columbia.

Party Ratio: D 8 - R 4

Pete Stark, Calif., chairman	*Thomas J. Bliley Jr., Va., ranking member*
Ronald V. Dellums, Calif.	*Dana Rohrabacher, Calif.*
Alan Wheat, Mo.	
Jim McDermott, Wash.	*H. James Saxton, N.J.*
Eleanor Holmes Norton, D.C.	*Cass Ballenger, N.C.*
John Lewis, Ga.	
William J. Jefferson, La.	
Vacancy	

Subcommittees

Fiscal Affairs and Health

Phone: 225-4457   Room: 1309 LHOB

McDermott, chairman	*Ballenger*
Dellums	*Saxton*
Jefferson	
Wheat	
Norton	

Government Operations and Metropolitan Affairs

Phone: 225-4457   Room: 1309 LHOB

Wheat, chairman   *Saxton*
Stark   *Rohrabacher*
Lewis (Ga.)
Jefferson

Judiciary and Education

Phone: 225-4457   Room: 1309 LHOB

Norton, chairman   *Rohrabacher*
Lewis (Ga.)   *Ballenger*
Stark
Dellums
McDermott

Education and Labor

Phone: 225-4527   Room: 2181 RHOB

Majority Staff Director:
Patricia Rissler   225-4527   2181 RHOB

Minority Staff Director:
James Eagen III   225-6910   2174 RHOB

Education and labor generally; child labor; convict labor; labor standards and statistics; mediation and arbitration of labor disputes; regulation of foreign laborers; school food programs; vocational rehabilitation; wages and hours; welfare of miners; work incentive programs; Indian education; juvenile delinquency; human services programs; Howard University; Columbia Institution for the Deaf, Dumb, and Blind; Freedmen's Hospital. Chairman and ranking minority member are members ex officio of all subcommittees of which they are not regular members.

Party Ratio: D 28 - R 15

William D. Ford, Mich.,   *Bill Goodling, Pa.,*
  chairman   *ranking member*
William L. Clay, Mo.   *Tom Petri, Wis.*
George Miller, Calif.   *Marge Roukema, N.J.*
Austin J. Murphy, Pa.   *Steve Gunderson, Wis.*
Dale E. Kildee, Mich.   *Dick Armey, Texas*
Pat Williams, Mont.   *Harris W. Fawell, Ill.*
Matthew G. Martinez, Calif. *Cass Ballenger, N.C.*
Major R. Owens, N.Y.   *Susan Molinari, N.Y.*
Tom Sawyer, Ohio   *Bill Barrett, Neb.*
Donald M. Payne, N.J.   *John A. Boehner, Ohio*
Jolene Unsoeld, Wash.   *Randy "Duke"*
Patsy T. Mink, Hawaii   *Cunningham, Calif.*
Robert E. Andrews, N.J.   *Peter Hoekstra, Mich.*
Jack Reed, R.I.   *Howard P. "Buck"*
Tim Roemer, Ind.   *McKeon, Calif.*
Eliot L. Engel, N.Y.   *Dan Miller, Fla.*
Xavier Becerra, Calif.   *Michael N. Castle, Del.*
Robert C. Scott, Va.
Gene Green, Texas

Lynn Woolsey, Calif.
Carlos Romero-Barcelo, P.R.
Ron Klink, Pa.
Karan English, Ariz.
Ted Strickland, Ohio
Ron de Lugo, Virgin Islands
Eni F.H. Faleomavaega, Am.
  Samoa
Scotty Baesler, Ky.
Robert Anacletus Underwood,
  Guam

Subcommittees

Elementary, Secondary, and Vocational Education

Phone: 225-4368   Room: B-346A RHOB

Kildee, chairman   *Goodling*
Miller (Calif.)   *Gunderson*
Sawyer   *McKeon*
Owens   *Petri*
Unsoeld   *Molinari*
Reed   *Cunningham*
Roemer   *Miller (Fla.)*
Mink   *Roukema*
Engel   *Boehner*
Becerra
Green
Woolsey
English (Ariz.)
Strickland
Payne (N.J.)
Romero-Barcelo

Human Resources

Phone: 225-1850   Room: B-346C RHOB

Martinez, chairman   *Molinari*
Kildee   *Barrett (Neb.)*
Andrews (N.J.)   *Miller (Fla.)*
Scott   *Castle*
Woolsey
Romero-Barcelo
Owens
Baesler

Labor Standards, Occupational Health and Safety

Phone: 225-1927   Room: B-345A RHOB

Murphy, chairman   *Fawell*
Clay   *Ballenger*
Andrews (N.J.)   *Hoekstra*
Miller (Calif.)
Strickland
Faleomavaega
Vacancy

Labor-Management Relations

Phone: 225-5768   Room: 320 CHOB

Williams, chairman	*Roukema*
Clay	*Gunderson*
Kildee	*Armey*
Miller (Calif.)	*Barrett (Neb.)*
Owens	*Boehner*
Martinez	*Fawell*
Payne (N.J.)	*Ballenger*
Unsoeld	*Hoekstra*
Mink	*McKeon*
Klink	
Murphy	
Engel	
Becerra	
Green	
Woolsey	
Romero-Barceló	

Postsecondary Education and Training

Phone: 226-3681   Room: 2451 RHOB

Ford (Mich.), chairman	*Petri*
Williams	*Gunderson*
Sawyer	*Cunningham*
Unsoeld	*Miller (Fla.)*
Mink	*Roukema*
Andrews (N.J.)	*Hoekstra*
Reed	*McKeon*
Roemer	*Armey*
Kildee	*Castle*
Scott	
Klink	
English (Ariz.)	
Strickland	
Becerra	
Green	

Select Education and Civil Rights

Phone: 226-7532   Room: 518 OHOB

Owens, chairman	*Ballenger*
Payne (N.J.)	*Barrett (Neb.)*
Sawyer	*Fawell*
Scott	
Vacancy	
Vacancy	

Energy and Commerce

Phone: 225-2927   Room: 2125 RHOB

Majority Staff Director and Chief Counsel:
Alan J. Roth   225-2927   2125 RHOB

Minority Chief Counsel and Staff Director:
Margaret A. Durbin   225-3641   2322 RHOB

Interstate and foreign commerce generally; national energy policy generally; exploration, production, storage, supply, marketing, pricing, and regulation of energy resources; nuclear energy; solar energy; energy conservation; generation and marketing of power; inland waterways; railroads and railway labor and retirement; communications generally; securities and exchanges; consumer affairs; travel and tourism; public health and quarantine; health care facilities; biomedical research and development; Energy Dept.; Federal Energy Regulatory Commission. Chairman and ranking minority member are members ex officio of all subcommittees of which they are not regular members.

Party Ratio: D 27 - R 17

John D. Dingell, Mich., chairman	*Carlos J. Moorhead, Calif., ranking member*
Henry A. Waxman, Calif.	*Thomas J. Bliley Jr., Va.*
Philip R. Sharp, Ind.	
Edward J. Markey, Mass.	*Jack Fields, Texas*
Al Swift, Wash.	*Michael G. Oxley, Ohio*
Cardiss Collins, Ill.	*Michael Bilirakis, Fla.*
Mike Synar, Okla.	*Dan Schaefer, Colo.*
W. J. "Billy" Tauzin, La.	*Joe L. Barton, Texas*
Ron Wyden, Ore.	*Alex McMillan, N.C.*
Ralph M. Hall, Texas	*Dennis Hastert, Ill.*
Bill Richardson, N.M.	*Fred Upton, Mich.*
Jim Slattery, Kan.	*Cliff Stearns, Fla.*
John Bryant, Texas	*Bill Paxon, N.Y.*
Rick Boucher, Va.	*Paul E. Gillmor, Ohio*
Jim Cooper, Tenn.	*Scott L. Klug, Wis.*
J. Roy Rowland, Ga.	*Gary A. Franks, Conn.*
Thomas J. Manton, N.Y.	*James C. Greenwood, Pa.*
Edolphus Towns, N.Y.	
Gerry E. Studds, Mass.	*Michael D. Crapo, Idaho*
Richard H. Lehman, Calif.	
Frank Pallone Jr., N.J.	
Craig Washington, Texas	
Lynn Schenk, Calif.	
Sherrod Brown, Ohio	
Mike Kreidler, Wash.	
Marjorie Margolies-Mezvinsky, Pa.	
Blanche Lambert, Ark.	

Subcommittees

Commerce, Consumer Protection, and Competitiveness

Phone: 226-3160   Room: 151 FHOB

Collins (Ill.), chairman	*Stearns*
Towns	*McMillan*
Slattery	*Paxon*
Rowland	*Greenwood*
Manton	
Lehman	
Pallone	

Energy and Power

Phone: 226-2500   Room: 331 FHOB

Sharp, chairman	*Bilirakis*

Markey
Lehman
Washington
Kreidler
Lambert
Swift
Synar
Tauzin
Hall (Texas)
Boucher
Cooper

Hastert
Stearns
Gillmor
Klug
Franks (Conn.)
Crapo
Moorhead

Health and the Environment

Phone: 225-4952   Room: 2415 RHOB

Waxman, chairman
Synar
Wyden
Hall (Texas)
Richardson
Bryant
Rowland
Towns
Studds
Slattery
Cooper
Pallone
Washington
Brown (Ohio)
Kreidler

Bliley
Bilirakis
McMillan
Hastert
Upton
Paxon
Klug
Franks (Conn.)
Greenwood

Oversight and Investigations

Phone: 225-4441   Room: 2323 RHOB

Dingell, chairman
Brown (Ohio)
Margolies-Mezvinsky
Waxman
Collins (Ill.)
Wyden
Bryant

Schaefer
Moorhead
Barton
Upton

Telecommunications and Finance

Phone: 226-2424   Room: 316 FHOB

Markey, chairman
Tauzin
Boucher
Manton
Lehman
Schenk
Margolies-Mezvinsky
Synar
Wyden
Hall (Texas)
Richardson
Slattery
Bryant
Cooper

Fields (Texas)
Bliley
Oxley
Schaefer
Barton
McMillan
Hastert
Gillmor

Transportation and Hazardous Materials

Phone: 225-9304   Room: 324 FHOB

Swift, chairman
Lambert
Tauzin
Boucher
Rowland
Manton
Studds
Pallone
Schenk
Sharp
Markey
Richardson

Oxley
Fields (Texas)
Schaefer
Upton
Paxon
Gillmor
Crapo

Foreign Affairs

Phone: 225-5021   Room: 2170 RHOB

Majority Chief of Staff:
Michael H. Van Dusen   225-5021   2170 RHOB

Minority Chief of Staff:
Richard J. Garon Jr.   225-6735   B360 RHOB

Relations of the United States with foreign nations generally; foreign loans; international conferences and congresses; intervention abroad and declarations of war; diplomatic service; foreign trade; neutrality; protection of Americans abroad; Red Cross; United Nations; international economic policy; export controls including non-proliferation of nuclear technology and hardware; international commodity agreements; trading with the enemy; international financial and monetary organizations; international education.

Party Ratio: D 27 - R 18

Lee H. Hamilton, Ind., chairman
Sam Gejdenson, Conn.
Tom Lantos, Calif.
Robert G. Torricelli, N.J.
Howard L. Berman, Calif.
Gary L. Ackerman, N.Y.
Harry A. Johnston, Fla.
Eliot L. Engel, N.Y.
Eni F.H. Faleomavaega, Am. Samoa
James L. Oberstar, Minn.
Charles E. Schumer, N.Y.
Matthew G. Martinez, Calif.
Robert A. Borski, Pa.
Donald M. Payne, N.J.
Robert E. Andrews, N.J.
Robert Menendez, N.J.
Sherrod Brown, Ohio
Cynthia A. McKinney, Ga.
Maria Cantwell, Wash.
Alcee L. Hastings, Fla.
Eric D. Fingerhut, Ohio
Peter Deutsch, Fla.
Albert R. Wynn, Md.

Benjamin A. Gilman, N.Y., ranking member
Bill Goodling, Pa.
Jim Leach, Iowa
Toby Roth, Wis.
Olympia J. Snowe, Maine
Henry J. Hyde, Ill.
Doug Bereuter, Neb.
Christopher H. Smith, N.J.
Dan Burton, Ind.
Jan Meyers, Kan.
Elton Gallegly, Calif.
Ileana Ros-Lehtinen, Fla.
Cass Ballenger, N.C.
Dana Rohrabacher, Calif.
David A. Levy, N.Y.
Donald Manzullo, Ill.
Lincoln Diaz-Balart, Fla.
Ed Royce, Calif.

Don Edwards, Calif.
Frank McCloskey, Ind.
Tom Sawyer, Ohio
Luis V. Gutierrez, Ill.

Subcommittees

Africa

Phone: 226-7807 Room: 709 OHOB

Johnston, chairman	*Burton*
Payne (N.J.)	*Diaz-Balart*
Hastings	*Royce*
Torricelli	*Vacancy*
Edwards (Calif.)	
Engel	

Asia and the Pacific

Phone: 226-7801 Room: 707 OHOB

Ackerman, chairman	*Leach*
Faleomavaega	*Rohrabacher*
Martinez	*Royce*
Torricelli	*Roth*
Brown (Ohio)	
Fingerhut	
Gutierrez	

Economic Policy, Trade, and the Environment

Phone: 226-7820 Room: 702 OHOB

Gejdenson, chairman	*Roth*
Oberstar	*Manzullo*
McKinney	*Bereuter*
Cantwell	*Meyers*
Fingerhut	*Ballenger*
Wynn	*Rohrabacher*
Johnston	
Engel	
Schumer	

Europe and the Middle East

Phone: 225-3345 Room: B-359 RHOB

Hamilton, chairman	*Gilman*
Engel	*Goodling*
Schumer	*Meyers*
Borski	*Gallegly*
Andrews (N.J.)	*Levy*
Brown (Ohio)	*Leach*
Hastings	
Deutsch	
Lantos	

International Operations

Phone: 225-3424 Room: 2103 RHOB

Berman, chairman	*Snowe*

Faleomavaega	*Hyde*
Martinez	*Diaz-Balart*
Andrews (N.J.)	*Levy*
Menendez	*Manzullo*
Lantos	
Johnston	
Edwards (Calif.)	

International Security, International Organizations, and Human Rights

Phone: 226-7825 Room: B-358 RHOB

Lantos, chairman	*Bereuter*
Berman	*Snowe*
Ackerman	*Smith (N.J.)*
Martinez	*Burton*
McCloskey	
Sawyer	

Western Hemisphere Affairs

Phone: 226-7812 Room: 705 OHOB

Torricelli, chairman	*Smith (N.J.)*
Menendez	*Ros-Lehtinen*
Oberstar	*Ballenger*
McKinney	*Gallegly*
Deutsch	
Wynn	

Government Operations

Phone: 225-5051 Room: 2157 RHOB

Majority Staff Director:
Julian Epstein 225-5051 2157 RHOB

Minority Staff Director:
Matthew Fletcher 225-5074 2153 RHOB

Budget and accounting measures; overall economy and efficiency in government, including federal procurement; executive branch reorganization; general revenue sharing; intergovernmental relations; National Archives; off-budget treatment of federal agencies or programs. Chairman and ranking minority member are members ex officio of all subcommittees of which they are not regular members.

Party Ratio: D 26 - R 17 - I 1

John Conyers Jr., Mich., chairman	*William F. Clinger, Pa., ranking member*
Cardiss Collins, Ill.	*Al McCandless, Calif.*
Henry A. Waxman, Calif.	*Dennis Hastert, Ill.*
Mike Synar, Okla.	*Jon Kyl, Ariz.*
Stephen L. Neal, N.C.	*Christopher Shays, Conn.*
Tom Lantos, Calif.	
Major R. Owens, N.Y.	*Steven H. Schiff, N.M.*
Edolphus Towns, N.Y.	*Christopher Cox, Calif.*
John M. Spratt Jr., S.C.	*Craig Thomas, Wyo.*
Gary A. Condit, Calif.	*Ileana Ros-Lehtinen, Fla.*
Collin C. Peterson, Minn.	

Karen L. Thurman, Fla.
Bobby L. Rush, Ill.
Carolyn B. Maloney, N.Y.
Thomas M. Barrett, Wis.
Donald M. Payne, N.J.
Floyd H. Flake, N.Y.
Jimmy Hayes, La.
Craig Washington, Texas
Barbara-Rose Collins, Mich.
Corrine Brown, Fla.
Marjorie Margolies-
Mezvinsky, Pa.
Lynn Woolsey, Calif.
Gene Green, Texas
Bart Stupak, Mich.
Vacancy

Dick Zimmer, N.J.
Bill Zeliff, N.H.
John M. McHugh, N.Y.
Steve Horn, Calif.
Deborah Pryce, Ohio
John L. Mica, Fla.
Rob Portman, Ohio
Vacancy

Bernard Sanders, Vt.

Subcommittees

Commerce, Consumer, and Monetary Affairs

Phone: 225-4407   Room: B-377 RHOB

Spratt, chairman   *Cox*
Rush   *Shays*
Margolies-Mezvinsky   *Horn*
Collins (Mich.)
Green

Employment, Housing, and Aviation

Phone: 225-6751   Room: B-349A RHOB

Peterson (Minn.), chairman   *Zeliff*
Lantos   *Shays*
Rush   *McHugh*
Flake
Thurman
Collins (Mich.)

Environment, Energy, and Natural Resources

Phone: 225-6427   Room: B-371C RHOB

Synar, chairman   *Hastert*
Thurman   *McHugh*
Maloney   *Pryce*
Hayes   *Mica*
Washington
Towns   *Sanders*

Human Resources and Intergovernmental Relations

Phone: 225-2548   Room: B-372 RHOB

Towns, chairman   *Schiff*
Waxman   *Mica*
Barrett (Wis.)   *Portman*
Payne (N.J.)
Washington   *Sanders*

Information, Justice, Transportation, and Agriculture

Phone: 225-3741   Room: B-349C RHOB

Condit, chairman   *Thomas (Wyo.)*
Owens   *Ros-Lehtinen*
Thurman   *Horn*
Woolsey
Stupak

Legislation and National Security

Phone: 225-5147   Room: B-373 RHOB

Conyers, chairman   *McCandless*
Collins (Ill.)   *Clinger*
Neal (N.C.)   *Kyl*
Maloney   *Zimmer*
Lantos
Brown (Fla.)
Vacancy

House Administration

Phone: 225-2061   Room: H-326 CAP

Majority Staff Director:
Robert E. Shea   225-2061   H-326 CAP
Minority Staff Director:
Stacy Carlson   225-8281   H-330 CAP

House administration generally; contested elections; federal elections generally; corrupt practices; qualifications of members of the House; Congressional Record; the House wing of the Capitol; Library of Congress; Smithsonian Institution; Botanic Garden. Chairman and ranking minority member are nonvoting members ex officio of all subcommittees of which they are not regular members.

Party Ratio: D 12 - R 7

Charlie Rose, N.C.,
 chairman
Al Swift, Wash.
William L. Clay, Mo.
Sam Gejdenson, Conn.
Martin Frost, Texas
Thomas J. Manton, N.Y.
Steny H. Hoyer, Md.
Gerald D. Kleczka, Wis.
Dale E. Kildee, Mich.
Butler Derrick, S.C.
Barbara B. Kennelly, Conn.
Benjamin L. Cardin, Md.

Bill Thomas, Calif.,
 ranking member
Newt Gingrich, Ga.
Pat Roberts, Kan.
Robert L. Livingston,
 La.
Bill Barrett, Neb.
John A. Boehner, Ohio
Jennifer Dunn, Wash.

Subcommittees

Accounts

Phone: 226-7540   Room: 611 OHOB

Frost, chairman
Swift
Gejdenson
Hoyer
Kildee
Kennelly
Cardin

Roberts
Gingrich
Boehner
Dunn

Administrative Oversight

Phone: 225-2061   Room: H-326 CAP

Rose, chairman
Clay

Thomas (Calif.)
Barrett (Neb.)

Elections

Phone: 226-7616   Room: 717 OHOB

Swift, chairman
Frost
Hoyer
Kleczka
Cardin

Livingston
Roberts
Dunn

Libraries and Memorials

Phone: 226-2307   Room: 612 OHOB

Clay, chairman
Frost
Derrick
Kennelly

Barrett (Neb.)
Roberts

Office Systems

Phone: 225-1608   Room: 720 OHOB

Gejdenson, chairman
Frost
Kleczka
Kennelly

Boehner
Barrett (Neb.)

Personnel and Police

Phone: 226-7641   Room: 722 OHOB

Manton, chairman
Clay
Kleczka
Derrick

Dunn
Livingston

Judiciary

Phone: 225-3951   Room: 2138 RHOB

General Counsel:
Jon Yarowsky   225-3951   2138 RHOB

Minority Chief Counsel:
Alan F. Coffey Jr.   225-6906   B-351C RHOB

Civil and criminal judicial proceedings generally; federal courts and judges; bankruptcy, mutiny, espionage, and counterfeiting; civil liberties; constitutional amendments; immigration and naturalization; interstate compacts; claims against the United States; apportionment of representatives; meetings of Congress and attendance of members; penitentiaries; patent office; patents, copyrights, and trademarks; presidential succession; monopolies and unlawful restraints of trade; internal security; revision and codification of U.S. statutes; state and territorial boundary lines. Chairman and ranking member are nonvoting members ex officio of all subcommittees of which they are not regular members.

Party Ratio: D 21 - R 14

Jack Brooks, Texas, chairman
Don Edwards, Calif.
John Conyers Jr., Mich.
Romano L. Mazzoli, Ky.
William J. Hughes, N.J.
Mike Synar, Okla.
Patricia Schroeder, Colo.
Dan Glickman, Kan.
Barney Frank, Mass.
Charles E. Schumer, N.Y.
Howard L. Berman, Calif.
Rick Boucher, Va.
John Bryant, Texas
George E. Sangmeister, Ill.
Craig Washington, Texas
Jack Reed, R.I.
Jerrold Nadler, N.Y.
Robert C. Scott, Va.
David Mann, Ohio
Melvin Watt, N.C.
Xavier Becerra, Calif.

Hamilton Fish Jr., N.Y., ranking member
Carlos J. Moorhead, Calif.
Henry J. Hyde, Ill.
F. James Sensenbrenner Jr., Wis.
Bill McCollum, Fla.
George W. Gekas, Pa.
Howard Coble, N.C.
Lamar Smith, Texas
Steven H. Schiff, N.M.
Jim Ramstad, Minn.
Elton Gallegly, Calif.
Charles T. Canady, Fla.
Bob Inglis, S.C.
Robert W. Goodlatte, Va.

Subcommittees

Administrative Law and Governmental Relations

Phone: 225-5741   Room: B-351A RHOB

Bryant, chairman
Glickman
Frank
Berman
Mann
Watt

Gekas
Ramstad
Inglis
Goodlatte

Civil and Constitutional Rights

Phone: 226-7680   Room: 806 OHOB

Edwards (Calif.), chairman
Schroeder
Frank
Washington
Nadler

Hyde
Coble
Canady

Crime and Criminal Justice

Phone: 226-2406   Room: 362 FHOB

Schumer, chairman   *Sensenbrenner*
Edwards (Calif.)   *Smith (Texas)*
Conyers   *Schiff*
Mazzoli   *Ramstad*
Glickman   *Gekas*
Sangmeister
Washington
Mann

Economic and Commercial Law

Phone: 225-2825   Room: B-353 RHOB

Brooks, chairman   *Fish*
Conyers   *Gallegly*
Synar   *Canady*
Schroeder   *Inglis*
Glickman   *Goodlatte*
Berman   *Moorhead*
Boucher
Scott
Mann
Watt

Intellectual Property and Judicial Administration

Phone: 225-3926   Room: 207 CHOB

Hughes, chairman   *Moorhead*
Edwards (Calif.)   *Coble*
Conyers   *Fish*
Mazzoli   *Sensenbrenner*
Synar   *McCollum*
Frank   *Schiff*
Berman
Reed
Becerra

International Law, Immigration, and Refugees

Phone: 225-5727   Room: B-370B RHOB

Mazzoli, chairman   *McCollum*
Schumer   *Smith (Texas)*
Bryant   *Gallegly*
Sangmeister   *Canady*
Nadler
Becerra

Merchant Marine and Fisheries

Phone: 225-4047   Room: 1334 LHOB

Majority Staff Director:
Jeffrey R. Pike   225-8183   1334 LHOB
Minority Staff Director:
Harry F. Burroughs 225-2650 1337 LHOB

Merchant marine generally; oceanography and marine affairs including coastal zone management; Coast Guard; fisheries and wildlife; regulation of common carriers by water and inspection of merchant marine vessels, lights and signals, lifesaving equipment, and fire protection; navigation; Panama Canal, Canal Zone and interoceanic canals generally; registration and licensing of vessels and small boats; rules and international arrangements to prevent collisions at sea; international fishing agreements; Coast Guard and Merchant Marine academies and state maritime academies. Chairman and ranking minority member are members ex officio of all subcommittees of which they are not regular members.

Party Ratio: D 29 - R 19

Gerry E. Studds, Mass.,   *Jack Fields, Texas,*
  chairman   *ranking member*
William J. Hughes, N.J.   *Don Young, Alaska*
Earl Hutto, Fla.   *Herbert H. Bateman,*
W. J. "Billy" Tauzin, La.   *Va.*
William O. Lipinski, Ill.   *H. James Saxton, N.J.*
Solomon P. Ortiz, Texas   *Howard Coble, N.C.*
Thomas J. Manton, N.Y.   *Curt Weldon, Pa.*
Owen B. Pickett, Va.   *James M. Inhofe, Okla.*
George J. Hochbrueckner,   *Arthur Ravenel Jr., S.C.*
  N.Y.   *Wayne T. Gilchrest,*
Frank Pallone Jr., N.J.   *Md.*
Greg Laughlin, Texas   *Randy "Duke"*
Jolene Unsoeld, Wash.   *Cunningham, Calif.*
Gene Taylor, Miss.   *Jack Kingston, Ga.*
Jack Reed, R.I.   *Tillie Fowler, Fla.*
H. Martin Lancaster, N.C.   *Michael N. Castle, Del.*
Thomas H. Andrews, Maine   *Peter T. King, N.Y.*
Elizabeth Furse, Ore.   *Lincoln Diaz-Balart,*
Lynn Schenk, Calif.   *Fla.*
Gene Green, Texas   *Richard W. Pombo,*
Alcee L. Hastings, Fla.   *Calif.*
Dan Hamburg, Calif.   *Helen Delich Bentley,*
Blanche Lambert, Ark.   *Md.*
Anna G. Eshoo, Calif.   *Charles H. Taylor, N.C.*
Tom Barlow, Ky.   *Peter G. Torkildsen,*
Bart Stupak, Mich.   *Mass.*
Bennie Thompson, Miss.
Maria Cantwell, Wash.
Peter Deutsch, Fla.
Gary L. Ackerman, N.Y.

Subcommittees

Coast Guard and Navigation

Phone: 226-3587   Room: 541 FHOB

Tauzin, chairman   *Coble*
Hughes   *Bateman*
Hutto   *Gilchrest*
Lancaster   *Fowler*
Barlow   *Castle*
Stupak   *King*
Lipinski   *Diaz-Balart*
Pickett   *Inhofe*
Hochbrueckner   *Pombo*
Pallone

Laughlin
Schenk
Hastings
Lambert
Taylor (Miss.)

Environment and Natural Resources

Phone: 226-3547   Room: 545 FHOB

Studds, chairman	*Saxton*
Hochbrueckner	*Young (Alaska)*
Pallone	*Weldon*
Laughlin	*Ravenel*
Unsoeld	*Gilchrest*
Reed	*Cunningham*
Furse	*Castle*
Hamburg	*Taylor (N.C.)*
Lambert	
Eshoo	
Hutto	
Tauzin	
Ortiz	
Thompson	

Fisheries Management

Phone: 226-3514   Room: 534 FHOB

Manton, chairman	*Young (Alaska)*
Hughes	*Coble*
Unsoeld	*Ravenel*
Taylor (Miss.)	*Kingston*
Lancaster	*Torkildsen*
Hamburg	
Cantwell	
Hutto	

Merchant Marine

Phone: 226-3533   Room: 543 FHOB

Lipinski, chairman	*Bateman*
Pickett	*Inhofe*
Taylor (Miss.)	*Cunningham*
Andrews (Maine)	*Kingston*
Schenk	*Fowler*
Green	*King*
Hastings	*Diaz-Balart*
Reed	*Bentley*
Furse	
Stupak	
Manton	
Ackerman	
Thompson	

Oceanography, Gulf of Mexico, and the Outer Continental Shelf

Phone: 226-2460   Room: 575 FHOB

Ortiz, chairman	*Weldon*
Green	*Saxton*
Eshoo	*Bentley*

Laughlin
Schenk
Hughes

Natural Resources

Phone: 225-2761   Room: 1324 LHOB

Majority Staff Director:
John Lawrence   225-2761   1324 LHOB
Minority Staff Director:
Daniel V. Kish   225-6065   1329 LHOB

Public lands, parks, and natural resources generally; Geological Survey; interstate water compacts; irrigation and reclamation; Indian affairs; minerals, mines, and mining; petroleum conservation on public lands; regulation of domestic nuclear energy industry, including waste disposal; territorial affairs of the United States. Chairman and ranking minority member are nonvoting members ex officio of all subcommittees of which they are not regular members.

Party Ratio: D 28 - R 15

George Miller, Calif., chairman	*Don Young, Alaska, ranking member*
Philip R. Sharp, Ind.	*James V. Hansen, Utah*
Edward J. Markey, Mass.	*Barbara F. Vucanovich, Nev.*
Austin J. Murphy, Pa.	
Nick J. Rahall II, W.Va.	*Elton Gallegly, Calif.*
Bruce F. Vento, Minn.	*Bob Smith, Ore.*
Pat Williams, Mont.	*Craig Thomas, Wyo.*
Ron de Lugo, Virgin Islands	*John J. "Jimmy" Duncan Jr., Tenn.*
Sam Gejdenson, Conn.	
Richard H. Lehman, Calif.	*Joel Hefley, Colo.*
Bill Richardson, N.M.	*John T. Doolittle, Calif.*
Peter A. DeFazio, Ore.	*Wayne Allard, Colo.*
Eni F.H. Faleomavaega, Am. Samoa	*Richard H. Baker, La.*
Tim Johnson, S.D.	*Ken Calvert, Calif.*
Larry LaRocco, Idaho	*Scott McInnis, Colo.*
Neil Abercrombie, Hawaii	*Richard W. Pombo, Calif.*
Cal Dooley, Calif.	*Jay Dickey, Ark.*
Carlos Romero-Barcelo, P.R.	
Karan English, Ariz.	
Karen Shepherd, Utah	
Nathan Deal, Ga.	
Maurice D. Hinchey, N.Y.	
Robert Anacletus Underwood, Guam	
Sam Farr, Calif.	
Lane Evans, Ill.	
Patsy T. Mink, Hawaii	
Tom Barlow, Ky.	
Thomas M. Barrett, Wis.	

Subcommittees

Energy and Mineral Resources

Phone: 225-8331   Room: 818 OHOB

Lehman, chairman
Sharp
Murphy
Markey
Rahall
LaRocco
Deal
DeFazio
Barlow
Farr

Vucanovich
Thomas (Wyo.)
Doolittle
Allard
McInnis
Pombo

Insular and International Affairs

Phone: 225-9297   Room: 1626 LHOB

de Lugo, chairman
Faleomavaega
Romero-Barcelo
Underwood
Murphy
Miller (Calif.)
Vacancy

Gallegly
Vucanovich

National Parks, Forests, and Public Lands

Phone: 226-7736   Room: 812 OHOB

Vento, chairman
Markey
Murphy
Rahall
Williams
Richardson
DeFazio
Johnson (S.D.)
LaRocco
Abercrombie
Romero-Barcelo
English (Ariz.)
Shepherd
Hinchey
Underwood
Mink
de Lugo

Hansen
Smith (Ore.)
Thomas (Wyo.)
Duncan
Hefley
Doolittle
Baker (La.)
Calvert
Dickey

Native American Affairs

Phone: 226-7393   Room: 1522 LHOB

Richardson, chairman
Williams
Gejdenson
Faleomavaega
Johnson (S.D.)
Abercrombie
English (Ariz.)

Thomas (Wyo.)
Young (Alaska)
Baker (La.)
Calvert

Oversight and Investigations

Phone: 225-2761   Room: 1324 LHOB

Miller (Calif.), chairman
Gejdenson
Dooley

Smith (Ore.)
Hansen
Vucanovich

Deal
Sharp
Vento
Lehman
DeFazio
English (Ariz.)
Shepherd
Hinchey
Abercrombie
Evans
Barrett (Wis.)

Duncan
Doolittle
Allard
Calvert
Pombo
Dickey

Post Office and Civil Service

Phone: 225-4054   Room: 309 CHOB

Majority Staff Director:
Gail E. Weiss   225-4054   309 CHOB
Minority Staff Director:
Joseph A. Fisher   225-8036   300 CHOB

Postal and federal civil service; census and the collection of statistics generally; Hatch Act; holidays and celebrations; commemorative bills and resolutions.

Party Ratio: D 15 - R 9

William L. Clay, Mo.,
  chairman
Patricia Schroeder, Colo.
Frank McCloskey, Ind.
Gary L. Ackerman, N.Y.
Tom Sawyer, Ohio
Paul E. Kanjorski, Pa.
Eleanor Holmes Norton, D.C.
Barbara-Rose Collins, Mich.
Leslie L. Byrne, Va.
Melvin Watt, N.C.
Albert R. Wynn, Md.
Greg Laughlin, Texas
Sanford D. Bishop Jr., Ga.
Sherrod Brown, Ohio
Alcee L. Hastings, Fla.

John T. Myers, Ind.,
  ranking member
Benjamin A. Gilman,
  N.Y.
Don Young, Alaska
Dan Burton, Ind.
Constance A. Morella,
  Md.
Tom Ridge, Pa.
Tom Petri, Wis.
Sherwood Boehlert,
  N.Y.
Vacancy

Subcommittees

Census, Statistics, and Postal Personnel

Phone: 226-7523   Room: 515 OHOB

Sawyer, chairman
McCloskey
Wynn

Petri
Ridge

Civil Service

Phone: 225-4025   Room: 122 CHOB

McCloskey, chairman
Schroeder
Kanjorski

Burton
Morella

Compensation and Employee Benefits

Phone: 226-7546   Room: 209 CHOB

Norton, chairman   *Morella*
Ackerman   *Young (Alaska)*
Byrne

Oversight and Investigations

Phone: 225-6295   Room: 219 CHOB

Clay, chairman   *Boehlert*
Hastings   *Vacancy*
Laughlin

Postal Operations and Services

Phone: 225-9124   Room: 406 CHOB

Collins (Mich.), chairman   *Young (Alaska)*
Watt   *Gilman*
Bishop

Public Works and Transportation

Phone: 225-4472   Room: 2165 RHOB

Chief of Staff:
Paul Schoellhamer   225-4472   2165 RHOB
Minority Chief Counsel and Staff Director:
Jack Schenendorf   225-9446   2163 RHOB

Flood control and improvement of rivers and harbors; construction and maintenance of roads; oil and other pollution of navigable waters; public buildings and grounds; public works for the benefit of navigation, including bridges and dams; water power; transportation, except railroads; Botanic Garden; Library of Congress; Smithsonian Institution. Chairman and ranking minority member are members ex officio of all subcommittees of which they are not regular members.

Party Ratio: D 40 - R 25

Norman Y. Mineta, Calif.,   *Bud Shuster, Pa.,*
   chairman   *ranking member*
James L. Oberstar, Minn.   *William F. Clinger, Pa.*
Nick J. Rahall II, W.Va.   *Tom Petri, Wis.*
Douglas Applegate, Ohio   *Sherwood Boehlert,*
Ron de Lugo, Virgin Islands   *N.Y.*
Robert A. Borski, Pa.   *James M. Inhofe, Okla.*
Tim Valentine, N.C.   *Bill Emerson, Mo.*
William O. Lipinski, Ill.   *John J. "Jimmy"*
Bob Wise, W.Va.   *Duncan Jr., Tenn.*
James A. Traficant Jr., Ohio   *Susan Molinari, N.Y.*
Peter A. DeFazio, Ore.   *Bill Zeliff, N.H.*
Jimmy Hayes, La.   *Thomas W. Ewing, Ill.*
Bob Clement, Tenn.   *Wayne T. Gilchrest,*
Jerry F. Costello, Ill.   *Md.*
Mike Parker, Miss.   *Jennifer Dunn, Wash.*
Greg Laughlin, Texas   *Tim Hutchinson, Ark.*
Pete Geren, Texas   *Bill Baker, Calif.*

George E. Sangmeister, Ill.   *Mac Collins, Ga.*
Glenn Poshard, Ill.   *Jay C. Kim, Calif.*
Dick Swett, N.H.   *David A. Levy, N.Y.*
Robert E. "Bud" Cramer, Ala.   *Steve Horn, Calif.*
Barbara-Rose Collins, Mich.   *Bob Franks, N.J.*
Eleanor Holmes Norton, D.C.   *Peter I. Blute, Mass.*
Lucien E. Blackwell, Pa.   *Howard P. "Buck"*
Jerrold Nadler, N.Y.   *McKeon, Calif.*
Sam Coppersmith, Ariz.   *John L. Mica, Fla.*
Leslie L. Byrne, Va.   *Peter Hoekstra, Mich.*
Maria Cantwell, Wash.   *Jack Quinn, N.Y.*
Pat Danner, Mo.   *Vernon J. Ehlers, Mich.*
Karen Shepherd, Utah
Robert Menendez, N.J.
James E. Clyburn, S.C.
Corrine Brown, Fla.
Nathan Deal, Ga.
James A. Barcia, Mich.
Dan Hamburg, Calif.
Bob Filner, Calif.
Walter R. Tucker III, Calif.
Eddie Bernice Johnson, Texas
Peter W. Barca, Wis.

Subcommittees

Aviation

Phone: 225-9161   Room: 2251 RHOB

Oberstar, chairman   *Clinger*
de Lugo, vice chairman   *Boehlert*
Lipinski   *Inhofe*
Geren   *Duncan*
Sangmeister   *Ewing*
Collins (Mich.)   *Gilchrest*
Coppersmith   *Dunn*
Borski   *Collins (Ga.)*
Valentine   *Kim*
DeFazio   *Levy*
Hayes   *Horn*
Clement   *McKeon*
Costello   *Mica*
Parker
Laughlin
Swett
Cramer
Blackwell
Cantwell
Danner
Shepherd
Brown (Fla.)
Rahall

Economic Development

Phone: 225-6151   Room: B-376 RHOB

Wise, chairman   *Molinari*
Blackwell, vice chairman   *Boehlert*
Coppersmith   *Ewing*
Clyburn   *Dunn*
Deal   *Hutchinson*
Barcia   *Baker (Calif.)*

Filner
Oberstar
Traficant
Clement
Costello
Parker
Swett
Nadler
Danner
Shepherd
Menendez
Brown (Fla.)
Hamburg
Norton
Johnson
Barca

Collins (Ga.)
Kim
Franks (N.J.)
Blute
Mica
Hoekstra
Quinn

de Lugo
Lipinski
Traficant
Barca

Investigations and Oversight

Phone: 225-3274   Room: 586 FHOB

Borski, chairman
Collins (Mich.), vice chairman
Wise
Blackwell
Byrne
Barcia
Filner
Barca
Poshard

Inhofe
Duncan
Molinari
Zeliff
Gilchrest
Baker (Calif.)

Public Buildings and Grounds

Phone: 225-9961   Room: B-376 RHOB

Traficant, chairman
Norton, vice chairman
Johnson
Applegate
Clyburn
Tucker

Duncan
Petri
Emerson

Surface Transportation

Phone: 225-9989   Room: B-376 RHOB

Rahall, chairman
Valentine, vice chairman
Clement
Costello
Laughlin
Poshard
Swett
Cramer
DeFazio
Nadler
Byrne
Cantwell
Danner
Menendez
Clyburn
Tucker
Hamburg
Johnson
Applegate

Petri
Clinger
Emerson
Zeliff
Dunn
Hutchinson
Baker (Calif.)
Collins (Ga.)
Kim
Levy
Franks (N.J.)
Blute
McKeon

Water Resources and Environment

Phone: 225-0060   Room: B-370A RHOB

Applegate, chairman
Hayes, vice chairman
Parker
Shepherd
Brown (Fla.)
Deal
Barcia
Filner
Oberstar
Rahall
Wise
Geren
Sangmeister
Poshard
Norton
Nadler
Byrne
Menendez
Hamburg
Tucker
Borski
Valentine
Lipinski

Boehlert
Clinger
Petri
Inhofe
Emerson
Molinari
Zeliff
Ewing
Gilchrest
Hutchinson
Horn
Hoekstra
Quinn

Rules

Phone: 225-9486   Room: H-312 CAP

Majority Staff Director:
George C. Crawford   225-9486   H-312 CAP

Minority Chief of Staff:
Don Wolfensberger   225-9191   H-305 CAP

Rules and joint rules order of business of the House; recesses and final adjournments of Congress; authorized to sit and act whether or not the House is in session.

Party Ratio: D 9 - R 4

Joe Moakley, Mass.,
  chairman
Butler Derrick, S.C.
Anthony C. Beilenson, Calif.
Martin Frost, Texas
David E. Bonior, Mich.
Tony P. Hall, Ohio
Alan Wheat, Mo.
Bart Gordon, Tenn.
Louise M. Slaughter, N.Y.

Gerald B. H. Solomon,
N.Y., ranking member
James H. Quillen, Tenn.
David Dreier, Calif.
Porter J. Goss, Fla.

Subcommittees

Legislative Process

Phone: 225-2430   Room: 1629 LHOB

Derrick, chairman   *Quillen*
Frost   *Goss*
Wheat
Gordon
Moakley

Rules of the House

Phone: 225-9588   Room: 1628 LHOB

Beilenson, chairman   *Dreier*
Bonior   *Solomon*
Hall (Ohio)
Slaughter
Moakley

Science, Space, and Technology

Phone: 225-6371   Room: 2320 RHOB

Chief of Staff:
Robert E. Palmer   225-6375   2320 RHOB
Minority Staff Director:
Dave Clement   225-8772   2320 RHOB

Astronautical research and development, including resources, personnel, equipment, and facilities; National Institute of Standards and Technology, standardization of weights and measures, and the metric system; National Aeronautics and Space Administration; National Aeronautics and Space Council; National Science Foundation; outer space, including exploration and control; science scholarships; scientific research, development, and demonstration; federally owned or operated nonmilitary energy laboratories; civil aviation research and development; environmental research and development; energy research, development, and demonstration; National Weather Service. Chairman and ranking minority member are members ex officio of all subcommittees of which they are not regular members.

Party Ratio: D 33 - R 22

George E. Brown Jr., Calif.,   *Robert S. Walker, Pa.,*
  chairman   *ranking member*
Marilyn Lloyd, Tenn.   *F. James Sensenbren-*
Dan Glickman, Kan.   *ner Jr., Wis.*
Harold L. Volkmer, Mo.   *Sherwood Boehlert,*
Ralph M. Hall, Texas   *N.Y.*
Dave McCurdy, Okla.   *Tom Lewis, Fla.*
Tim Valentine, N.C.   *Harris W. Fawell, Ill.*
Robert G. Torricelli, N.J.   *Constance A. Morella,*
Rick Boucher, Va.   *Md.*
James A. Traficant Jr., Ohio   *Dana Rohrabacher,*
Jimmy Hayes, La.   *Calif.*
John Tanner, Tenn.   *Steven H. Schiff, N.M.*
Pete Geren, Texas   *Joe L. Barton, Texas*

Jim Bacchus, Fla.   *Dick Zimmer, N.J.*
Tim Roemer, Ind.   *Sam Johnson, Texas*
Robert E. "Bud" Cramer, Ala. *Ken Calvert, Calif.*
Dick Swett, N.H.   *Martin R. Hoke, Ohio*
James A. Barcia, Mich.   *Nick Smith, Mich.*
Herb Klein, N.J.   *Ed Royce, Calif.*
Eric D. Fingerhut, Ohio   *Rod Grams, Minn.*
Paul McHale, Pa.   *John Linder, Ga.*
Jane Harman, Calif.   *Peter I. Blute, Mass.*
Don Johnson, Ga.   *Jennifer Dunn, Wash.*
Sam Coppersmith, Ariz.   *Bill Baker, Calif.*
Anna G. Eshoo, Calif.   *Roscoe G. Bartlett, Md.*
Jay Inslee, Wash.   *Vernon J. Ehlers, Mich.*
Eddie Bernice Johnson, Texas
David Minge, Minn.
Nathan Deal, Ga.
Robert C. Scott, Va.
Xavier Becerra, Calif.
Peter W. Barca, Wis.
Bobby L. Rush, Ill.

Subcommittees

Energy

Phone: 225-8056   Room: H2-390 FHOB

Lloyd, chairman   *Fawell*
Scott   *Schiff*
Cramer   *Baker (Calif.)*
Swett   *Grams*
Klein   *Bartlett*
McHale   *Ehlers*
Coppersmith
Inslee
Roemer
McCurdy

Investigations and Oversight

Phone: 225-4494   Room: 822 OHOB

Hayes, chairman   *Morella*
Tanner   *Barton*
Lloyd   *Ehlers*
Johnson (Ga.)
Coppersmith
Vacancy

Science

Phone: 225-8844   Room: 2319 RHOB

Boucher, chairman   *Boehlert*
Hall (Texas)   *Barton*
Valentine   *Johnson*
Barcia   *Smith (Mich.)*
Johnson (Ga.)   *Blute*
Eshoo
Johnson
Minge
Barca

Space

Phone: 225-7858 Room: 2320 RHOB

Hall (Texas), chairman | *Sensenbrenner*
Volkmer | *Rohrabacher*
Torricelli | *Zimmer*
Traficant | *Johnson*
Bacchus | *Hoke*
Cramer | *Royce*
Barcia | *Dunn*
Fingerhut | *Schiff*
Hayes | *Calvert*
Tanner | *Bartlett*
Geren
Roemer
Harman
Eshoo
McCurdy
Vacancy
Vacancy

Technology, Environment, and Aviation

Phone: 225-9662 Room: B-374 RHOB

Valentine, chairman | *Lewis (Fla.)*
Glickman | *Morella*
Geren | *Calvert*
Roemer | *Smith (Mich.)*
Swett | *Grams*
Klein | *Linder*
McHale | *Blute*
Harman | *Bartlett*
Johnson (Ga.) | *Rohrabacher*
Coppersmith | *Zimmer*
Eshoo | *Hoke*
Inslee | *Royce*
Johnson
Minge
Deal
Becerra
Torricelli
Bacchus
Barca

Select Intelligence

Phone: 225-4121 Room: H-405 CAP

Chief Counsel:
Michael Sheehy   225-4121   H-405 CAP

Minority Counsel:
Stephen D. Nelson   225-8246   H-405 CAP

Legislative and budgetary authority over the Central Intelligence Agency and the director of central intelligence, the Defense Intelligence Agency, the National Security Agency, intelligence activities of the Federal Bureau of Investigation, and other components of the federal intelligence community. House majority leader and minority leader are nonvoting members ex officio of the full committee.

Party Ratio: D 12 - R 7

Dan Glickman, Kan., chairman | *Larry Combest, Texas, ranking member*
Bill Richardson, N.M. | *Doug Bereuter, Neb.*
Norm Dicks, Wash. | *Robert K. Dornan, Calif.*
Julian C. Dixon, Calif. | *C. W. Bill Young, Fla.*
Robert G. Torricelli, N.J. | *George W. Gekas, Pa.*
Ronald D. Coleman, Texas | *James V. Hansen, Utah*
David E. Skaggs, Colo. | *Jerry Lewis, Calif.*
James Bilbray, Nev.
Nancy Pelosi, Calif.
Greg Laughlin, Texas
Robert E. "Bud" Cramer, Ala.
Jack Reed, R.I.

Subcommittees

Legislation

Phone: 225-7311 Room: H-405 CAP

Coleman, chairman | *Gekas*
Dicks | *Hansen*
Bilbray | *Lewis (Calif.)*
Pelosi
Laughlin
Cramer

Oversight and Evaluation

Phone: 225-5658 Room: H-405 CAP

Dicks, chairman | *Young (Fla.)*
Pelosi | *Hansen*
Reed | *Bereuter*
Torricelli
Coleman
Skaggs

Program and Budget Authorization

Phone: 225-7690 Room: H-405 CAP

Glickman, chairman | *Combest*
Richardson | *Bereuter*
Dixon | *Dornan*
Torricelli | *Lewis (Calif.)*
Skaggs
Bilbray
Laughlin
Cramer

Small Business

Phone: 225-5821 Room: 2361 RHOB

Majority Staff Director:
Jeane Roslanowick   225-5821   2361 RHOB

Minority Staff Director:
Steve Lynch   225-4038   B-343C RHOB

Assistance to and protection of small business including

financial aid; participation of small business enterprises in federal procurement and government contracts. Chairman and ranking minority member are members ex officio of all subcommittees of which they are not regular members.

Party Ratio: D 27 - R 18

John J. LaFalce, N.Y., chairman	*Jan Meyers, Kan., ranking member*
Neal Smith, Iowa	*Larry Combest, Texas*
Ike Skelton, Mo.	*Richard H. Baker, La.*
Romano L. Mazzoli, Ky.	*Joel Hefley, Colo.*
Ron Wyden, Ore.	*Ronald K. Machtley, R.I.*
Norman Sisisky, Va.	
John Conyers Jr., Mich.	*Jim Ramstad, Minn.*
James Bilbray, Nev.	*Sam Johnson, Texas*
Kweisi Mfume, Md.	*Bill Zeliff, N.H.*
Floyd H. Flake, N.Y.	*Mac Collins, Ga.*
Bill Sarpalius, Texas	*Scott McInnis, Colo.*
Glenn Poshard, Ill.	*Michael Huffington, Calif.*
Eva Clayton, N.C.	
Martin T. Meehan, Mass.	*James M. Talent, Mo.*
Pat Danner, Mo.	*Joe Knollenberg, Mich.*
Ted Strickland, Ohio	*Jay Dickey, Ark.*
Nydia M. Velazquez, N.Y.	*Jay C. Kim, Calif.*
Cleo Fields, La.	*Donald Manzullo, Ill.*
Marjorie Margolies-Mezvinsky, Pa.	*Peter G. Torkildsen, Mass.*
Walter R. Tucker III, Calif.	*Rob Portman, Ohio*
Ron Klink, Pa.	
Lucille Roybal-Allard, Calif.	
Earl F. Hilliard, Ala.	
H. Martin Lancaster, N.C.	
Thomas H. Andrews, Maine	
Maxine Waters, Calif.	
Bennie Thompson, Miss.	

Subcommittees

Minority Enterprise, Finance, and Urban Development

Phone: 225-7673   Room: 557 FHOB

Mfume, chairman	*Machtley*
Conyers	*Talent*
Flake	*Knollenberg*
Velazquez	*Dickey*
Tucker	*Vacancy*
Fields (La.)	
Roybal-Allard	
Hilliard	

Procurement, Taxation, and Tourism

Phone: 225-9368   Room: B-363 RHOB

Bilbray, chairman	*Baker (La.)*
Sisisky	*Knollenberg*
Hilliard	*Portman*
Mfume	*Vacancy*
Clayton	
Klink	

Regulation, Business Opportunities, and Technology

Phone: 225-7797   Room: B-363 RHOB

Wyden, chairman	*Combest*
Skelton	*Johnson*
Strickland	*Dickey*
Andrews (Maine)	*Kim*
Sisisky	*Torkildsen*
Bilbray	*Huffington*
Meehan	
Tucker	
Vacancy	

Rural Enterprises, Exports, and the Environment

Phone: 225-8944   Room: 1F CHOB

Sarpalius, chairman	*Hefley*
Clayton	*Ramstad*
Danner	*Manzullo*
Poshard	*Collins (Ga.)*
Strickland	
Thompson	

SBA Legislation and the General Economy

Phone: 225-5821   Room: 2361 RHOB

LaFalce, chairman	*Meyers*
Smith (Iowa)	*Zeliff*
Mazzoli	*Collins (Ga.)*
Poshard	*Huffington*
Meehan	*Talent*
Fields (La.)	*Ramstad*
Margolies-Mezvinsky	
Klink	
Roybal-Allard	

Standards of Official Conduct

Phone: 225-7103   Room: HT-2 CAP

Chief Counsel:
Bernard Raimo Jr.   225-7103   HT-2M CAP

Measures relating to the Code of Official Conduct; conduct of House members and employees; functions designated in the Ethics in Government Act and the U.S. Code.

Party Ratio: D 7 - R 7

Jim McDermott, Wash., chairman	*Fred Grandy, Iowa, ranking member*
George "Buddy" Darden, Ga.	*Nancy L. Johnson, Conn.*
Benjamin L. Cardin, Md.	*Jim Bunning, Ky.*
Nancy Pelosi, Calif.	*Jon Kyl, Ariz.*
Kweisi Mfume, Md.	*Porter J. Goss, Fla.*
Robert A. Borski, Pa.	*David L. Hobson, Ohio*
Tom Sawyer, Ohio	*Steven H. Schiff, N.M.*

Veterans' Affairs

Phone: 225-3527   Room: 335 CHOB

Majority Counsel and Staff Director:
Mack G. Fleming   225-3527   335 CHOB

Minority Counsel and Staff Director:
Carl Commenator   225-9756   333 CHOB

Veterans' measures generally; compensation, vocational rehabilitation, and education of veterans; armed forces life insurance; pensions; readjustment benefits; veterans' hospitals, medical care, and treatment. Chairman and ranking minority member are members ex officio of all subcommittees of which they are not regular members.

Party Ratio: D 21 - R 14

G. V. "Sonny" Montgomery, Miss., chairman	Bob Stump, Ariz., ranking member
Don Edwards, Calif.	Christopher H. Smith, N.J.
Douglas Applegate, Ohio	
Lane Evans, Ill.	Dan Burton, Ind.
Timothy J. Penny, Minn.	Michael Bilirakis, Fla.
J. Roy Rowland, Ga.	Tom Ridge, Pa.
Jim Slattery, Kan.	Floyd D. Spence, S.C.
Joseph P. Kennedy II, Mass.	Tim Hutchinson, Ark.
George E. Sangmeister, Ill.	Terry Everett, Ala.
Jill L. Long, Ind.	Steve Buyer, Ind.
Chet Edwards, Texas	Jack Quinn, N.Y.
Maxine Waters, Calif.	Spencer Bachus, Ala.
Bob Clement, Tenn.	John Linder, Ga.
Bob Filner, Calif.	Cliff Stearns, Fla.
Frank Tejeda, Texas	Peter T. King, N.Y.
Luis V. Gutierrez, Ill.	
Scotty Baesler, Ky.	
Sanford D. Bishop Jr., Ga.	
James E. Clyburn, S.C.	
Mike Kreidler, Wash.	
Corrine Brown, Fla.	

Subcommittees

Compensation, Pension, and Insurance

Phone: 225-3569   Room: 335 CHOB

Slattery, chairman	Bilirakis
Applegate	Everett
Evans	Stearns
Sangmeister	King
Edwards (Texas)	
Tejeda	

Education, Training, and Employment

Phone: 225-9166   Room: 337A CHOB

Montgomery, chairman	Hutchinson
Penny	Stump
Clyburn	Ridge
Rowland	Quinn
Slattery	
Clement	

Hospitals and Health Care

Phone: 225-9154   Room: 338 CHOB

Rowland, chairman	Smith (N.J.)
Applegate	Stump
Kennedy	Burton
Long	Bilirakis
Edwards (Texas)	Hutchinson
Clement	Everett
Filner	Buyer
Tejeda	Linder
Gutierrez	
Baesler	
Bishop	
Kreidler	
Brown (Fla.)	

Housing and Memorial Affairs

Phone: 225-9164   Room: 337 CHOB

Sangmeister, chairman	Burton
Bishop	Spence
Brown (Fla.)	Buyer
Kreidler	

Oversight and Investigations

Phone: 225-9044   Room: 335 CHOB

Evans, chairman	Ridge
Waters	Bachus
Filner	Everett
Gutierrez	Quinn
Clyburn	
Kreidler	
Long	

Ways and Means

Phone: 225-3625   Room: 1102 LHOB

Majority Chief Counsel:
Janice A. Mays   225-3625   1102 LHOB

Minority Chief of Staff:
Phillip D. Moseley   225-4021   1106 LHOB

Revenue measures generally; reciprocal trade agreements; customs, collection districts, and ports of entry and delivery; bonded debt of the United States; deposit of public moneys; transportation of dutiable goods; tax exempt foundations and charitable trusts; Social Security. Chairman and ranking minority member are members ex officio of all subcommittees of which they are not regular members.

Party Ratio: D 24 - R 14

Sam M. Gibbons, Fla., acting chairman	Bill Archer, Texas, ranking member

Dan Rostenkowski, Ill.
J. J. Pickle, Texas
Charles B. Rangel, N.Y.
Pete Stark, Calif.
Andrew Jacobs Jr., Ind.
Harold E. Ford, Tenn.
Robert T. Matsui, Calif.
Barbara B. Kennelly, Conn.
William J. Coyne, Pa.
Michael A. Andrews, Texas
Sander M. Levin, Mich.
Benjamin L. Cardin, Md.
Jim McDermott, Wash.
Gerald D. Kleczka, Wis.
John Lewis, Ga.
L. F. Payne Jr., Va.
Richard E. Neal, Mass.
Peter Hoagland, Neb.
Michael R. McNulty, N.Y.
Mike Kopetski, Ore.
William J. Jefferson, La.
Bill Brewster, Okla.
Mel Reynolds, Ill.

Philip M. Crane, Ill.
Bill Thomas, Calif.
E. Clay Shaw Jr., Fla.
Don Sundquist, Tenn.
Nancy L. Johnson,
  Conn.
Jim Bunning, Ky.
Fred Grandy, Iowa
Amo Houghton, N.Y.
Wally Herger, Calif.
Jim McCrery, La.
Mel Hancock, Mo.
Rick Santorum, Pa.
Dave Camp, Mich.

Select Revenue Measures

Phone: 225-9710   Room: 1105 LHOB

Rangel, chairman   *Hancock*
Payne (Va.)   *Sundquist*
Neal (Mass.)   *McCrery*
Hoagland   *Camp*
McNulty
Kopetski
Jacobs

Social Security

Phone: 225-9263   Room: B-316 RHOB

Jacobs, chairman   *Bunning*
Pickle   *Crane*
Jefferson   *Houghton*
Brewster
Reynolds

Subcommittees

Health

Phone: 225-7785   Room: 1114 LHOB

Stark, chairman   *Thomas (Calif.)*
Levin   *Johnson (Conn.)*
Cardin   *Grandy*
Andrews (Texas)   *McCrery*
McDermott
Kleczka
Lewis (Ga.)

Human Resources

Phone: 225-1025   Room: B-317 RHOB

Ford (Tenn.), chairman   *Santorum*
Matsui   *Shaw*
McDermott   *Grandy*
Levin   *Camp*
Kopetski
Reynolds
Cardin

Oversight

Phone: 225-5522   Room: 1135 LHOB

Pickle, chairman   *Houghton*
Ford (Tenn.)   *Herger*
Rangel   *Hancock*
Jefferson   *Santorum*
Brewster
Kleczka
Lewis (Ga.)

Trade

Phone: 225-3943   Room: 1136 LHOB

Matsui, acting chairman   *Crane*
Gibbons   *Thomas (Calif.)*
Rostenkowski   *Shaw*
Kennelly   *Sundquist*
Coyne   *Johnson (Conn.)*
Payne (Va.)
Neal (Mass.)
Hoagland
McNulty

Partisan Committees

Democratic Congressional Campaign Committee

430 S. Capitol St. S.E. 20003; 863-1500

Campaign support committee for Democratic House candidates.

Vic Fazio, Calif., chairman
Dan Rostenkowski, Ill., vice chairman
Thomas S. Foley, Wash., ex officio
Richard A. Gephardt, Mo., ex officio
David E. Bonior, Mich., ex officio
Steny H. Hoyer, Md., ex officio
Butler Derrick, S.C., ex officio

Barbara B. Kennelly, Conn., ex officio
John Lewis, Ga., ex officio
Bill Richardson, N.M., ex officio
Benjamin L. Cardin, Md., co-chairman
Robert E. "Bud" Cramer, Ala., co-chairman
Barney Frank, Mass., co-chairman
Bart Gordon, Tenn., co-chairman
Greg Laughlin, Texas, co-chairman
Thomas J. Manton, N.Y., co-chairman
John P. Murtha, Pa., co-chairman
Nancy Pelosi, Calif., co-chairman
Jim Slattery, Kan., co-chairman
Rosa DeLauro, Conn., speaker's appointment
Lee H. Hamilton, Ind., speaker's appointment
David R. Obey, Wis., speaker's appointment
Lynn Schenk, Calif., speaker's appointment
Charles W. Stenholm, Texas, speaker's appointment
W. J. "Billy" Tauzin, La., speaker's appointment
Maxine Waters, Calif., speaker's appointment
Ron Wyden, Ore., speaker's appointment

Neil Abercrombie, Hawaii	John P. Murtha, Pa.
Gary L. Ackerman, N.Y.	Richard E. Neal, Mass.
Thomas H. Andrews, Maine	Eleanor Holmes Norton,
Tom Barlow, Ky.	D.C.
Thomas M. Barrett, Wis.	James L. Oberstar, Minn.
Tom Bevill, Ala.	Bill Orton, Utah
James Bilbray, Nev.	Frank Pallone Jr., N.J.
Rick Boucher, Va.	Mike Parker, Miss.
Bill Brewster, Okla.	Pete Peterson, Fla.
George "Buddy" Darden, Ga.	Earl Pomeroy, N.D.
Ron de Lugo, Virgin Islands	Jack Reed, R.I.
Norm Dicks, Wash.	Bill Richardson, N.M.
John D. Dingell, Mich.	Carlos Romero-Barcelo,
Cal Dooley, Calif.	P.R.
Richard J. Durbin, Ill.	Patricia Schroeder,
Karan English, Ariz.	Colo.
Eni F.H. Faleomavaega, Am.	Neal Smith, Iowa
Samoa	John M. Spratt Jr., S.C.
Eric D. Fingerhut, Ohio	Dick Swett, N.H.
Dan Glickman, Kan.	John Tanner, Tenn.
W. G. "Bill" Hefner, N.C.	Ray Thornton, Ark.
Peter Hoagland, Neb.	Robert Anacletus
William J. Jefferson, La.	Underwood, Guam
Tim Johnson, S.D.	Harold L. Volkmer, Mo.
Barbara B. Kennelly, Conn.	Craig Washington,
Mike Kopetski, Ore.	Texas
Larry LaRocco, Idaho	Pat Williams, Mont.
Frank McCloskey, Ind.	
Kweisi Mfume, Md.	
Alan B. Mollohan,	
W.Va.	

Personnel Committee

B343 RHOB; 225-4068

Selects, appoints, and supervises Democratic patronage positions.

Jack Brooks, Texas, chairman

Democratic Steering and Policy Committee

H-324 CAP; 225-8550

Scheduling of legislation and Democratic committee assignments.

Thomas S. Foley, Wash., chairman
Richard A. Gephardt, Mo., vice chairman
Steny H. Hoyer, Md., second vice chairman

David E. Bonior, Mich.	Thomas J. Manton,
Jack Brooks, Texas	N.Y.
Maria Cantwell, Wash.	Patsy T. Mink, Hawaii
Benjamin L. Cardin, Md.	Joe Moakley, Mass.
E. "Kika" de la Garza, Texas	John P. Murtha, Pa.
Butler Derrick, S.C.	David R. Obey, Wis.
John D. Dingell, Mich.	Ed Pastor, Ariz.
Julian C. Dixon, Calif.	Bill Richardson, N.M.
Richard J. Durbin, Ill.	Dan Rostenkowski, Ill.
Vic Fazio, Calif.	J. Roy Rowland, Ga.
Sam Gejdenson, Conn.	Al Swift, Wash.
Dan Glickman, Kan.	Mike Synar, Okla.
Barbara B. Kennelly, Conn.	W. J. "Billy" Tauzin,
Gerald D. Kleczka, Wis.	La.
Ron Klink, Pa.	Melvin Watt, N.C.
John Lewis, Ga.	Alan Wheat, Mo.

National Republican Congressional Committee

320 1st St. S.E. 20003; 479-7000

Campaign support committee for Republican House candidates.

Bill Paxon, N.Y., chairman
Susan Molinari, N.Y., chief vice chair
Rick Santorum, Pa., chief vice chair
H. James Saxton, N.J., chief vice chair
John A. Boehner, Ohio, vice chair
John T. Doolittle, Calif., vice chair
Nancy L. Johnson, Conn., vice chair
Robert L. Livingston, La., vice chair
Jim Nussle, Iowa, vice chair
Deborah Pryce, Ohio, vice chair
Dick Armey, Texas, ex officio
Tom DeLay, Texas, ex officio
Newt Gingrich, Ga., ex officio
Duncan Hunter, Calif., ex officio
Henry J. Hyde, Ill., ex officio
Bill McCollum, Fla., ex officio
Robert H. Michel, Ill., ex officio

Spencer Bachus, Ala.
Bill Barrett, Neb.
Michael Bilirakis, Fla.
Sherwood Boehlert, N.Y.
Dan Burton, Ind.
Sonny Callahan, Ala.
Dave Camp, Mich.
Michael N. Castle, Del.
Howard Coble, N.C.
Mac Collins, Ga.
Christopher Cox, Calif.
Michael D. Crapo, Idaho
Helen Delich Bentley, Md.
Jennifer Dunn, Wash.
Harris W. Fawell, Ill.
Jack Fields, Texas
Bob Franks, N.J.
Gary A. Franks, Conn.
James V. Hansen, Utah
Dennis Hastert, Ill.
Tim Hutchinson, Ark.
Bob Inglis, S.C.
James M. Inhofe, Okla.
Scott L. Klug, Wis.
Joe Knollenberg, Mich.
Jim Kolbe, Ariz.
Jon Kyl, Ariz.
John Linder, Ga.
Ronald K. Machtley, R.I.
Constance A. Morella, Md.
Jim Ramstad, Minn.

Pat Roberts, Kan.
Ileana Ros-Lehtinen, Fla.
Ed Royce, Calif.
Dan Schaefer, Colo.
Steven H. Schiff, N.M.
F. James Sensenbrenner Jr., Wis.
Bud Shuster, Pa.
Joe Skeen, N.M.
Bob Smith, Ore.
Christopher H. Smith, N.J.
Olympia J. Snowe, Maine
Gerald B. H. Solomon, N.Y.
Don Sundquist, Tenn.
James M. Talent, Mo.
Craig Thomas, Wyo.
Peter G. Torkildsen, Mass.
Barbara F. Vucanovich, Nev.
Robert S. Walker, Pa.
Frank R. Wolf, Va.
Don Young, Alaska
Bill Zeliff, N.H.
Vacancy

Republican Committee
on Committees

H-230 CAP; 225-0600

Makes Republican committee assignments.

Robert H. Michel, Ill., chairman

Wayne Allard, Colo.
Bill Archer, Texas
Bill Baker, Calif.
Cass Ballenger, N.C.
Thomas J. Bliley Jr., Va.
Jim Bunning, Ky.
Jennifer Dunn, Wash.
Dean A. Gallo, N.J.
Newt Gingrich, Ga.
Dennis Hastert, Ill.
James M. Inhofe, Okla.
Scott L. Klug, Wis.

John Linder, Ga.
Joseph M. McDade, Pa.
Ron Packard, Calif.
Ralph Regula, Ohio
Gerald B. H. Solomon, N.Y.
Floyd D. Spence, S.C.
Bob Stump, Ariz.
Fred Upton, Mich.
C. W. Bill Young, Fla.
Don Young, Alaska

Republican Policy Committee

1616 LHOB; 225-6168

Advises on party action and policy.

Henry J. Hyde, Ill., chairman

Bill Archer, Texas
Dick Armey, Texas
Doug Bereuter, Neb.
John A. Boehner, Ohio
Steve Buyer, Ind.
Michael D. Crapo, Idaho
Tom DeLay, Texas
Tillie Fowler, Fla.
Gary A. Franks, Conn.
Dean A. Gallo, N.J.
Newt Gingrich, Ga.
Bill Goodling, Pa.
Steve Gunderson, Wis.
Mel Hancock, Mo.
Dennis Hastert, Ill.
Peter Hoekstra, Mich.
Duncan Hunter, Calif.
Ernest Jim Istook Jr., Okla.

Nancy L. Johnson, Conn.
John R. Kasich, Ohio
Tom Lewis, Fla.
Bill McCollum, Fla.
Joseph M. McDade, Pa.
Jan Meyers, Kan.
Robert H. Michel, Ill.
Michael G. Oxley, Ohio
Bill Paxon, N.Y.
Ileana Ros-Lehtinen, Fla.
Ed Royce, Calif.
Lamar Smith, Texas
Gerald B. H. Solomon, N.Y.
Floyd D. Spence, S.C.
Craig Thomas, Wyo.
Barbara F. Vucanovich, Nev.

Republican Research Committee

1622 LHOB; 225-0871

Serves as an advisory body to Republican members of Congress. The committee and its task forces work to develop various policy options for the Republican Conference.

Duncan Hunter, Calif., chairman

Dick Armey, Texas
Doug Bereuter, Neb.
John A. Boehner, Ohio
Dan Burton, Ind.
Charles T. Canady, Fla.
Michael D. Crapo, Idaho
Tom DeLay, Texas
Newt Gingrich, Ga.
Mel Hancock, Mo.
Duncan Hunter, Calif.
Henry J. Hyde, Ill.
Jim Ross Lightfoot, Iowa

Bill McCollum, Fla.
Robert H. Michel, Ill.
Susan Molinari, N.Y.
Jack Quinn, N.Y.
H. James Saxton, N.J.
Steven H. Schiff, N.M.
Olympia J. Snowe, Maine
Cliff Stearns, Fla.
Barbara F. Vucanovich, Nev.
Vacancy

Joint Committees of Congress

The joint committees of Congress are listed below in alphabetical order. The listing includes the room number, telephone number, and jurisdiction for each full committee. Address abbreviations used are as follows: SD (Dirksen Senate Office Bldg.), SH (Hart Senate Office Bldg.), SR (Russell Senate Office Bldg.), LHOB (Longworth House Office Bldg.), and OHOB (O'Neill House Office Bldg., formerly House Annex #1, at 300 New Jersey Ave. S.E.). The telephone area code for Washington is 202. Membership is drawn from both the Senate and House and from both parties. Membership is given in order of seniority on the committees.

Democrats are shown on the left in roman type; Republicans are on the right in italic type. When a senator serves as chairman, the vice chairman usually is a representative, and vice versa. The chairmanship usually rotates from one chamber to the other at the beginning of each Congress.

Economic

Phone: 224-5171   Room: SD-G01

Executive Director:
Richard McGahey   224-5171   SD-G01
Minority Staff Director:
Larry Hunter   224-0374   SH-802

Studies and investigates all recommendations in the president's annual economic report to Congress. Reports findings and recommendations to the House and Senate.

Senate Members

Paul S. Sarbanes, Md., vice chairman	*William V. Roth Jr., Del., ranking member*
Edward M. Kennedy, Mass.	*Connie Mack, Fla.*
Jeff Bingaman, N.M.	*Larry E. Craig, Idaho*
Charles S. Robb, Va.	*Robert F. Bennett, Utah*
Byron L. Dorgan, N.D.	
Barbara Boxer, Calif.	

House Members

David R. Obey, Wis., chairman	*Dick Armey, Texas*
Lee H. Hamilton, Ind.	*H. James Saxton, N.J.*
Pete Stark, Calif.	*Christopher Cox, Calif.*
Kweisi Mfume, Md.	*Jim Ramstad, Minn.*
Ron Wyden, Ore.	
Michael A. Andrews, Texas	

Library

Phone: 226-7633   Room: SR-305

Staff Director:
William M. Cochrane   224-6352   SR-305
Vice Staff Director:
Hilary Lieber   226-7633   103 OHOB

Management and expansion of the Library of Congress; receipt of gifts for the benefit of the library; development and maintenance of the Botanic Garden; placement of statues and other works of art in the Capitol.

Senate Members

Claiborne Pell, R.I., vice chairman	*Mark O. Hatfield, Ore.*
Dennis DeConcini, Ariz.	*Ted Stevens, Alaska*
Daniel Patrick Moynihan, N.Y.	

House Members

Charlie Rose, N.C., chairman	*Vacancy*
Vacancy	*Vacancy*
Vacancy	

Printing

Phone: 224-5241   Room: SH-818

Staff Director:
John Merritt   224-5241   SH-818

Professional Staff Member:
Linda Kemp   224-5241   SH-818

Probes inefficiency and waste in the printing, binding, and distribution of federal government publications. Oversees arrangement and style of the Congressional Record.

Senate Members

Wendell H. Ford, Ky.,   *Ted Stevens, Alaska*
chairman   *Mark O. Hatfield, Ore.*
Dennis DeConcini, Ariz.
Harlan Mathews, Tenn.

House Members

Charlie Rose, N.C.,   *Pat Roberts, Kan.,*
vice chairman   *ranking member*
Sam Gejdenson, Conn.   *Newt Gingrich, Ga.*
Gerald D. Kleczka, Wis.

Taxation

Phone: 225-3621   Room: 1015 LHOB

Chief of Staff:
Harry Gutman   225-3621   1015 LHOB

Operation, effects, and administration of the federal system of internal revenue taxes; measures and methods for simplification of taxes.

Senate Members

Daniel Patrick Moynihan,   *Bob Packwood, Ore.*
N.Y., chairman   *Bob Dole, Kan.*
Max Baucus, Mont.
David L. Boren, Okla.

House Members

Dan Rostenkowski, Ill.,   *Bill Archer, Texas*
vice chairman   *Philip M. Crane, Ill.*
Sam M. Gibbons, Fla.
J. J. Pickle, Texas

Senate Committees and Subcommittees

The standing and select committees of the U.S. Senate are listed below in alphabetical order. The listing includes the room number, telephone number, party ratio, and jurisdiction for each full committee. Membership is given in order of seniority on the committee. Subcommittees are listed alphabetically under each committee. Membership is listed in order of seniority on the subcommittee.

Address abbreviations used are as follows: SD (Dirksen Senate Office Bldg.), SH (Hart Senate Office Bldg.), SR (Russell Senate Office Bldg.), and CAP (Capitol) The telephone area code for Washington is 202.

Members of the majority party, Democrats, are shown in roman type; members of the minority party, Republicans, are shown in italic type.

The word *vacancy* indicates that a committee or subcommittee seat had not been filled as of May 13, 1994. Subcommittee vacancies do not necessarily indicate vacancies on full committees, or vice versa.

The partisan committees of the Senate are listed on p. 1016. Members of these committees are listed in alphabetical order, not by seniority.

Agriculture, Nutrition, and Forestry

Phone: 224-2035   Room: SR-328A

Majority Chief of Staff:
Charles Riemenschneider   224-2035   SR-328A
Minority Staff Director:
Chuck Conner   224-6901   SR-328A

Agriculture in general; animal industry and diseases; crop insurance and soil conservation; farm credit and farm security; food from fresh waters; food stamp programs; forestry in general; home economics; human nutrition; inspection of livestock, meat, and agricultural products; pests and pesticides; plant industry, soils and agricultural engineering; rural development, rural electrification, and watersheds; school nutrition programs. Chairman and ranking minority member are members ex officio of all subcommittees of which they are not regular members.

Party Ratio: D 10 - R 8

Patrick J. Leahy, Vt., chairman
David Pryor, Ark.
David L. Boren, Okla.

Richard G. Lugar, Ind., ranking member
Bob Dole, Kan.
Jesse Helms, N.C.

Howell Heflin, Ala.
Tom Harkin, Iowa
Kent Conrad, N.D.
Tom Daschle, S.D.
Max Baucus, Mont.
Bob Kerrey, Neb.
Russell D. Feingold, Wis.

Thad Cochran, Miss.
Mitch McConnell, Ky.
Larry E. Craig, Idaho
Paul Coverdell, Ga.
Charles E. Grassley, Iowa

Subcommittees

Agricultural Credit

Phone: 224-2035   Room: SR-328A

Conrad, chairman
Daschle
Boren
Baucus

Grassley
Craig
Coverdell

Agricultural Production and Stabilization of Prices

Phone: 224-2035   Room: SR-328A

Pryor, chairman
Baucus
Kerrey
Feingold
Boren

Helms
Dole
Cochran
McConnell
Craig

Heflin   *Grassley*
Harkin

Agricultural Research, Conservation, Forestry, and General Legislation

Phone: 224-2035   Room: SR-328A

Daschle, chairman   *Craig*
Kerrey   *Cochran*
Harkin

Domestic and Foreign Marketing and Product Promotion

Phone: 224-2035   Room: SR-328A

Boren, chairman   *Cochran*
Pryor   *Helms*
Conrad   *Coverdell*
Baucus   *McConnell*
Feingold   *Grassley*
Heflin

Nutrition and Investigations

Phone: 224-2035   Room: SR-328A

Harkin, chairman   *McConnell*
Pryor   *Dole*
Kerrey   *Helms*
Feingold

Rural Development and Rural Electrification

Phone: 224-2035   Room: SR-328A

Heflin, chairman   *Coverdell*
Conrad   *Dole*
Daschle

Appropriations

Phone: 224-3471   Room: S-128 CAP

Majority Staff Director:
James H. English   224-7200   S-128 CAP

Minority Staff Director:
J. Keith Kennedy   224-7251   SD-135

Appropriation of revenue; rescission of appropriations; new spending authority under the Budget Act. Chairman and ranking minority member are members ex officio of all subcommittees.

Party Ratio: D 16 - R 13

Robert C. Byrd, W.Va.,   *Mark O. Hatfield, Ore.,*
  chairman   *ranking member*
Daniel K. Inouye, Hawaii   *Ted Stevens, Alaska*
Ernest F. Hollings, S.C.   *Thad Cochran, Miss.*

J. Bennett Johnston, La.   *Alfonse M. D'Amato,*
Patrick J. Leahy, Vt.   *N.Y.*
Jim Sasser, Tenn.   *Arlen Specter, Pa.*
Dennis DeConcini, Ariz.   *Pete V. Domenici, N.M.*
Dale Bumpers, Ark.   *Don Nickles, Okla.*
Frank R. Lautenberg, N.J.   *Phil Gramm, Texas*
Tom Harkin, Iowa   *Christopher S. Bond,*
Barbara A. Mikulski, Md.   *Mo.*
Harry Reid, Nev.   *Slade Gorton, Wash.*
Bob Kerrey, Neb.   *Mitch McConnell, Ky.*
Herb Kohl, Wis.   *Connie Mack, Fla.*
Patty Murray, Wash.   *Conrad Burns, Mont.*
Dianne Feinstein, Calif.

Subcommittees

Agriculture, Rural Development, and Related Agencies

Phone: 224-7240   Room: SD-140

Bumpers, chairman   *Cochran*
Harkin   *Specter*
Kerrey   *Bond*
Johnston   *Gramm*
Kohl   *Gorton*
Feinstein

Commerce, Justice, State, and Judiciary

Phone: 224-7277   Room: S-146A CAP

Hollings, chairman   *Domenici*
Inouye   *Stevens*
Bumpers   *Hatfield*
Lautenberg   *Gramm*
Sasser   *McConnell*
Kerrey

Defense

Phone: 224-7255   Room: SD-119

Inouye, chairman   *Stevens*
Hollings   *D'Amato*
Johnston   *Cochran*
Byrd   *Specter*
Leahy   *Domenici*
Sasser   *Nickles*
DeConcini   *Gramm*
Bumpers   *Bond*
Lautenberg
Harkin

District of Columbia

Phone: 224-2731   Room: S-205 CAP

Kohl, chairman   *Burns*
Murray   *Mack*
Feinstein

Energy and Water Development

Phone: 224-7260   Room: SD-132

Johnston, chairman
Byrd
Hollings
Sasser
DeConcini
Reid
Kerrey

Hatfield
Cochran
Domenici
Nickles
Gorton
McConnell

Foreign Operations

Phone: 224-7209   Room: SD-136

Leahy, chairman
Inouye
DeConcini
Lautenberg
Harkin
Mikulski
Feinstein

McConnell
D'Amato
Specter
Nickles
Mack
Gramm

Interior

Phone: 224-7233   Room: SD-127

Byrd, chairman
Johnston
Leahy
DeConcini
Bumpers
Hollings
Reid
Murray

Nickles
Stevens
Cochran
Domenici
Gorton
Hatfield
Burns

Labor, Health and Human Services, and Education

Phone: 224-7283   Room: SD-186

Harkin, chairman
Byrd
Hollings
Inouye
Bumpers
Reid
Kohl
Murray

Specter
Hatfield
Stevens
Cochran
Gorton
Mack
Bond

Legislative Branch

Phone: 224-7338   Room: SD-126

Reid, chairman
Mikulski
Murray

Mack
Burns

Military Construction

Phone: 224-7276   Room: SD-131

Sasser, chairman
Inouye
Reid
Kohl

Gorton
Stevens
McConnell

Transportation

Phone: 224-7281   Room: SD-156

Lautenberg, chairman
Byrd
Harkin
Sasser
Mikulski

D'Amato
Domenici
Hatfield
Specter

Treasury, Postal Service, and General Government

Phone: 224-8271   Room: SD-190

DeConcini, chairman
Mikulski
Kerrey

Bond
D'Amato

VA, HUD, and Independent Agencies

Phone: 224-7211   Room: SD-142

Mikulski, chairwoman
Leahy
Johnston
Lautenberg
Kerrey
Feinstein

Gramm
D'Amato
Nickles
Bond
Burns

Armed Services

Phone: 224-3871   Room: SR-228

Majority Staff Director:
Arnold Punaro   224-3871   SR-228
Minority Staff Director:
Richard L. Reynard   224-9348   SR-228

Defense and defense policy generally; aeronautical and space activities peculiar to or primarily associated with the development of weapons systems or military operations; maintenance and operation of the Panama Canal, including the Canal Zone; military research and development; national security aspects of nuclear energy; naval petroleum reserves (except Alaska); armed forces generally; Selective Service System; strategic and critical materials. Chairman and ranking minority member are nonvoting members ex officio of all subcommittees of which they are not regular members.

Party Ratio: D 12 - R 10

Sam Nunn, Ga., chairman
Jim Exon, Neb.
Carl Levin, Mich.
Edward M. Kennedy, Mass.
Jeff Bingaman, N.M.
John Glenn, Ohio
Richard C. Shelby, Ala.
Robert C. Byrd, W.Va.

Strom Thurmond, S.C., ranking member
John W. Warner, Va.
William S. Cohen, Maine
John McCain, Ariz.
Trent Lott, Miss.
Daniel R. Coats, Ind.
Robert C. Smith, N.H.

Bob Graham, Fla.
Charles S. Robb, Va.
Joseph I. Lieberman, Conn.
Richard H. Bryan, Nev.

Dirk Kempthorne,
Idaho
Lauch Faircloth, N.C.
Kay Bailey Hutchison,
Texas

Subcommittees

Coalition Defense and Reinforcing Forces

Phone: 224-3871   Room: SR-228

Levin, chairman	*Warner*
Exon	*Cohen*
Glenn	*Coats*
Shelby	*Smith*
Byrd	*Kempthorne*
Graham	*Hutchison*
Lieberman	

Defense Technology, Acquisition, and Industrial Base

Phone: 224-3871   Room: SR-228

Bingaman, chairman	*Smith*
Levin	*Cohen*
Kennedy	*Lott*
Byrd	*Coats*
Graham	*Kempthorne*
Robb	*Faircloth*
Lieberman	

Force Requirements and Personnel

Phone: 224-3871   Room: SR-228

Shelby, chairman	*Coats*
Kennedy	*McCain*
Byrd	*Faircloth*
Bryan	

Military Readiness and Defense Infrastructure

Phone: 224-3871   Room: SR-228

Glenn, chairman	*McCain*
Bingaman	*Smith*
Shelby	*Faircloth*
Robb	*Hutchison*
Bryan	

Nuclear Deterrence, Arms Control, and Defense Intelligence

Phone: 224-3871   Room: SR-228

Exon, chairman	*Lott*
Levin	*Warner*
Bingaman	*Kempthorne*
Glenn	*Hutchison*
Bryan	

Regional Defense and Contingency Forces

Phone: 224-3871   Room: SR-228

Kennedy, chairman	*Cohen*
Exon	*Warner*
Graham	*McCain*
Robb	*Lott*
Lieberman	

Banking, Housing, and Urban Affairs

Phone: 224-7391   Room: SD-534

Majority Staff Director:
Steven Harris   224-7391   SD-534

Professional Staff Member:
Howard A. Menell   224-1572   SD-548

Banks, banking, and financial institutions; price controls; deposit insurance; economic stabilization and growth; defense production; export and foreign trade promotion; export controls; federal monetary policy, including Federal Reserve System; financial aid to commerce and industry; issuance and redemption of notes; money and credit, including currency and coinage; nursing home construction; public and private housing, including veterans' housing; renegotiation of government contracts; urban development and mass transit; international economic policy. Chairman and ranking minority member are members ex officio of all subcommittees of which they are not regular members.

Party Ratio: D 11 - R 8

Donald W. Riegle Jr., Mich.,
chairman
Paul S. Sarbanes, Md.
Christopher J. Dodd, Conn.
Jim Sasser, Tenn.
Richard C. Shelby, Ala.
John Kerry, Mass.
Richard H. Bryan, Nev.
Barbara Boxer, Calif.
Ben Nighthorse Campbell,
Colo.
Carol Moseley-Braun, Ill.
Patty Murray, Wash.

Alfonse M. D'Amato,
N.Y., ranking member
Phil Gramm, Texas
Christopher S. Bond,
Mo.
Connie Mack, Fla.
Lauch Faircloth, N.C.
Robert F. Bennett, Utah
William V. Roth Jr.,
Del.
Pete V. Domenici, N.M.

Subcommittees

Economic Stabilization and Rural Development

Phone: 224-7391   Room: SD-534

Shelby, chairman	*Faircloth*
Campbell	*Bennett*
Dodd	*Gramm*
Kerry	*Mack*
Bryan	

Housing and Urban Affairs

Phone: 224-6348 Room: SD-535

Sarbanes, chairman	*Bond*
Kerry	*Domenici*
Bryan	*Mack*
Boxer	*Faircloth*
Moseley-Braun	*Roth*
Dodd	

International Finance and Monetary Policy

Phone: 224-1564 Room: SD-534

Sasser, chairman	*Mack*
Murray	*Gramm*
Sarbanes	*Bennett*
Kerry	*Roth*
Boxer	*Bond*
Campbell	

Securities

Phone: 224-9213 Room: SD-534

Dodd, chairman	*Gramm*
Sasser	*Roth*
Shelby	*Bond*
Bryan	*Faircloth*
Moseley-Braun	*Domenici*
Murray	

Budget

Phone: 224-0642 Room: SD-621

Majority Staff Director:
Larry Stein 224-0553 SD-621

Minority Staff Director:
William G. Hoagland 224-0769 SD-634A

Federal budget generally; concurrent budget resolutions; Congressional Budget Office.

Party Ratio: D 12 - R 9

Jim Sasser, Tenn., chairman	*Pete V. Domenici, N.M., ranking member*
Ernest F. Hollings, S.C.	*Charles E. Grassley, Iowa*
J. Bennett Johnston, La.	
Donald W. Riegle Jr., Mich.	*Don Nickles, Okla.*
Jim Exon, Neb.	*Phil Gramm, Texas*
Frank R. Lautenberg, N.J.	*Christopher S. Bond, Mo.*
Paul Simon, Ill.	
Kent Conrad, N.D.	*Trent Lott, Miss.*
Christopher J. Dodd, Conn.	*Hank Brown, Colo.*
Paul S. Sarbanes, Md.	*Slade Gorton, Wash.*
Barbara Boxer, Calif.	*Judd Gregg, N.H.*
Patty Murray, Wash.	

Commerce, Science, and Transportation

Phone: 224-5115 Room: SD-508

Majority Chief Counsel and Staff Director:
Kevin Curtin 224-0427 SR-254
Republican Staff Director:
Jonathan Chambers 224-5183 SD-554

Interstate commerce and transportation generally; Coast Guard; coastal zone management; communications; highway safety; inland waterways, except construction; marine fisheries; Merchant Marine and navigation; nonmilitary aeronautical and space sciences; oceans, weather, and atmospheric activities; interoceanic canals generally; regulation of consumer products and services; science, engineering, and technology research, development, and policy; sports; standards and measurement; transportation and commerce aspects of Outer Continental Shelf lands. Chairman and ranking minority member are nonvoting members ex officio of all subcommittees of which they are not regular members.

Party Ratio: D 11 - R 9

Ernest F. Hollings, S.C., chairman	*John C. Danforth, Mo., ranking member*
Daniel K. Inouye, Hawaii	*Bob Packwood, Ore.*
Wendell H. Ford, Ky.	*Larry Pressler, S.D.*
Jim Exon, Neb.	*Ted Stevens, Alaska*
John D. Rockefeller IV, W.Va.	*John McCain, Ariz.*
John Kerry, Mass.	*Conrad Burns, Mont.*
John B. Breaux, La.	*Slade Gorton, Wash.*
Richard H. Bryan, Nev.	*Trent Lott, Miss.*
Charles S. Robb, Va.	*Kay Bailey Hutchison, Texas*
Byron L. Dorgan, N.D.	
Harlan Mathews, Tenn.	

Subcommittees

Aviation

Phone: 224-9350 Room: SH-428

Ford, chairman	*Pressler*
Exon	*McCain*
Inouye	*Stevens*
Kerry	*Gorton*
Bryan	

Communications

Phone: 224-9340 Room: SH-227

Inouye, chairman	*Packwood*
Hollings	*Pressler*
Ford	*Stevens*
Exon	*McCain*
Kerry	*Burns*
Breaux	*Gorton*
Rockefeller	
Robb	

Consumer

Phone: 224-0415   Room: SH-227

Bryan, chairman	*Gorton*
Ford	*McCain*
Dorgan	*Burns*
Mathews	

Foreign Commerce and Tourism

Phone: 224-9325   Room: SH-428

Kerry, chairman	*McCain*
Hollings	*Packwood*
Rockefeller	*Pressler*
Bryan	
Dorgan	
Mathews	

Merchant Marine

Phone: 224-4914   Room: SH-425

Breaux, chairman	*Lott*
Inouye	*Stevens*
Mathews	

National Ocean Policy Study

Phone: 224-4912   Room: SH-425

Hollings, chairman	*Stevens*
Kerry, vice chairman	*Danforth*
Inouye	*Packwood*
Ford	*Pressler*
Breaux	*Gorton*
Robb	*Lott*
Vacancy	*Hutchison*

Science, Technology, and Space

Phone: 224-9360   Room: SH-427

Rockefeller, chairman	*Burns*
Hollings	*Pressler*
Kerry	*Lott*
Bryan	*Hutchison*
Robb	

Surface Transportation

Phone: 224-9350   Room: SH-428

Exon, chairman	*Hutchison*
Rockefeller	*Packwood*
Inouye	*Burns*
Breaux	*Lott*
Robb	*McCain*
Dorgan	
Mathews	

Energy and Natural Resources

Phone: 224-4971   Room: SD-304

Majority Staff Director:
Benjamin Cooper   224-5360   SD-358
Minority Staff Director:
G. Robert Wallace   224-1017   SD-312

Energy policy, regulation, conservation, research, and development; coal; energy-related aspects of deep-water ports; hydroelectric power, irrigation, and reclamation; mines, mining, and minerals generally; national parks, recreation areas, wilderness areas, wild and scenic rivers, historic sites, military parks, and battlefields; naval petroleum reserves in Alaska; nonmilitary development of nuclear energy; oil and gas production and distribution; public lands and forests; solar energy systems; territorial possessions of the United States. Chairman and ranking minority member are members ex officio of all subcommittees of which they are not regular members.

Party Ratio: D 11 - R 9

J. Bennett Johnston, La., chairman	*Malcolm Wallop, Wyo., ranking member*
Dale Bumpers, Ark.	*Mark O. Hatfield, Ore.*
Wendell H. Ford, Ky.	*Pete V. Domenici, N.M.*
Bill Bradley, N.J.	*Frank H. Murkowski, Alaska*
Jeff Bingaman, N.M.	
Daniel K. Akaka, Hawaii	*Don Nickles, Okla.*
Richard C. Shelby, Ala.	*Larry E. Craig, Idaho*
Paul Wellstone, Minn.	*Robert F. Bennett, Utah*
Ben Nighthorse Campbell, Colo.	*Arlen Specter, Pa.*
Harlan Mathews, Tenn.	*Trent Lott, Miss.*
Byron L. Dorgan, N.D.	

Subcommittees

Energy Research and Development

Phone: 224-7569   Room: SH-312

Ford, chairman	*Domenici*
Shelby, vice chairman	*Specter*
Bumpers	*Nickles*
Bingaman	*Craig*
Wellstone	*Lott*
Mathews	
Dorgan	

Mineral Resources Development and Production

Phone: 224-7568   Room: SD-362

Akaka, chairman	*Craig*
Mathews, vice chairman	*Murkowski*
Bumpers	*Nickles*
Ford	*Bennett*
Campbell	

Public Lands, National Parks, and Forests

Phone: 224-8115   Room: SD-308

Bumpers, chairman   *Murkowski*
Campbell, vice chairman   *Hatfield*
Bradley   *Lott*
Bingaman   *Domenici*
Akaka   *Bennett*
Shelby   *Craig*
Wellstone   *Specter*
Dorgan

Renewable Energy, Energy Efficiency, and Competitiveness

Phone: 224-4756   Room: SH-212

Bingaman, chairman   *Nickles*
Wellstone, vice chairman   *Specter*
Bradley   *Lott*
Akaka   *Hatfield*
Shelby   *Domenici*
Mathews

Water and Power

Phone: 224-6830   Room: SD-306

Bradley, chairman   *Bennett*
Ford   *Hatfield*
Campbell   *Murkowski*
Dorgan

Environment and Public Works

Phone: 224-6176   Room: SD-456

Majority Staff Director:
Peter L. Scher   224-7845   SD-456
Minority Staff Director and Chief Counsel:
Steven J. Shimberg   224-7854   SD-410

Environmental policy, research, and development; air, water, and noise pollution; construction and maintenance of highways; environmental aspects of Outer Continental Shelf lands; environmental effects of toxic substances other than pesticides; fisheries and wildlife; flood control and improvements of rivers and harbors; nonmilitary environmental regulation and control of nuclear energy; ocean dumping; public buildings and grounds; public works, bridges, and dams; regional economic development; solid waste disposal and recycling; water resources.

Party Ratio: D 10 - R 7

Max Baucus, Mont.,   *John H. Chafee, R.I.,*
  chairman   *ranking member*
Daniel Patrick Moynihan,   *Alan K. Simpson, Wyo.*
  N.Y.   *Dave Durenberger,*
George J. Mitchell, Maine   *Minn.*
Frank R. Lautenberg, N.J.   *John W. Warner, Va.*
Harry Reid, Nev.   *Robert C. Smith, N.H.*

Bob Graham, Fla.   *Lauch Faircloth, N.C.*
Joseph I. Lieberman, Conn. *Dirk Kempthorne,*
Howard M. Metzenbaum,   *Idaho*
  Ohio
Harris Wofford, Pa.
Barbara Boxer, Calif.

Subcommittees

Clean Air and Nuclear Regulation

Phone: 224-3597   Room: SH-505

Lieberman, chairman   *Simpson*
Moynihan   *Faircloth*
Graham   *Kempthorne*
Metzenbaum

Clean Water, Fisheries, and Wildlife

Phone: 224-3597   Room: SH-505

Graham, chairman   *Chafee*
Mitchell   *Durenberger*
Lautenberg   *Faircloth*
Reid   *Kempthorne*
Lieberman
Wofford

Superfund, Recycling, and Solid Waste Management

Phone: 224-3597   Room: SH-505

Lautenberg, chairman   *Durenberger*
Moynihan   *Simpson*
Graham   *Smith*
Metzenbaum   *Warner*
Wofford
Boxer

Toxic Substances, Research, and Development

Phone: 224-3597   Room: SH-505

Reid, chairman   *Smith*
Lautenberg   *Warner*
Lieberman   *Simpson*
Wofford   *Faircloth*
Boxer

Water Resources, Transportation, Public Buildings, and Economic Development

Phone: 224-5031   Room: SH-415

Moynihan, chairman   *Warner*
Mitchell   *Durenberger*
Reid   *Smith*
Metzenbaum   *Kempthorne*
Boxer

Finance

Phone: 224-4515   Room: SD-205

Majority Staff Director:
Lawrence O'Donnell Jr.   224-4515   SD-205

Minority Staff Director:
Lindy Paull   224-5315   SH-203

Revenue measures generally; taxes; tariffs and import quotas; reciprocal trade agreements; customs; revenue sharing; federal debt limit; Social Security; health programs financed by taxes or trust funds. Chairman and ranking minority member are members ex officio of all subcommittees of which they are not regular members.

Party Ratio: D 11 - R 9

Daniel Patrick Moynihan, N.Y., chairman	*Bob Packwood, Ore., ranking member*
Max Baucus, Mont.	*Bob Dole, Kan.*
David L. Boren, Okla.	*William V. Roth Jr.,*
Bill Bradley, N.J.	*Del.*
George J. Mitchell, Maine	*John C. Danforth, Mo.*
David Pryor, Ark.	*John H. Chafee, R.I.*
Donald W. Riegle Jr., Mich.	*Dave Durenberger,*
John D. Rockefeller IV, W.Va.	*Minn.*
Tom Daschle, S.D.	*Charles E. Grassley,*
John B. Breaux, La.	*Iowa*
Kent Conrad, N.D.	*Orrin G. Hatch, Utah*
	Malcolm Wallop, Wyo.

Subcommittees

Deficits, Debt Management, and Long-Term Economic Growth

Phone: 224-4515   Room: SD-205

Bradley, chairman	*Wallop*
Riegle	

Energy and Agricultural Taxation

Phone: 224-4515   Room: SD-205

Daschle, chairman	*Hatch*
Boren	*Dole*
Breaux	*Wallop*

Health for Families and the Uninsured

Phone: 224-4515   Room: SD-205

Riegle, chairman	*Chafee*
Bradley	*Roth*
Mitchell	*Durenberger*
Rockefeller	*Danforth*

International Trade

Phone: 224-4515   Room: SD-205

Baucus, chairman	*Danforth*
Moynihan	*Packwood*
Boren	*Roth*
Bradley	*Chafee*
Mitchell	*Grassley*
Riegle	*Hatch*
Rockefeller	*Wallop*
Daschle	
Breaux	
Conrad	

Medicare and Long Term Care

Phone: 224-4515   Room: SD-205

Rockefeller, chairman	*Durenberger*
Baucus	*Packwood*
Mitchell	*Dole*
Pryor	*Chafee*
Daschle	*Grassley*
Conrad	*Hatch*

Private Retirement Plans and Oversight of the Internal Revenue Service

Phone: 224-4515   Room: SD-205

Pryor, chairman	*Grassley*
Moynihan	

Social Security and Family Policy

Phone: 224-4515   Room: SD-205

Breaux, chairman	*Dole*
Moynihan	*Durenberger*

Taxation

Phone: 224-4515   Room: SD-205

Boren, chairman	*Roth*
Baucus	*Packwood*
Pryor	*Danforth*
Conrad	

Foreign Relations

Phone: 224-4651   Room: SD-446

Majority Staff Director:
Geryld B. Christianson   224-4651   SD-446

Minority Staff Director:
James W. Nance   224-3941   SD-452

Relations of the United States with foreign nations generally; treaties; foreign economic, military, technical and humanitarian assistance; foreign loans; diplomatic service; International Red Cross; international aspects of nuclear energy; International Monetary Fund; intervention abroad and declarations of war; foreign trade; national security; oceans and international environmental and scientific affairs; protection of U.S. citizens abroad

United Nations; World Bank and other development assistance organizations. Chairman and ranking minority member are members ex officio of all subcommittees of which they are not regular members.

Party Ratio: D 11 - R 9

Claiborne Pell, R.I., chairman	*Jesse Helms, N.C., ranking member*
Joseph R. Biden Jr., Del.	*Richard G. Lugar, Ind.*
Paul S. Sarbanes, Md.	*Nancy Landon*
Christopher J. Dodd, Conn.	*Kassebaum, Kan.*
John Kerry, Mass.	*Larry Pressler, S.D.*
Paul Simon, Ill.	*Frank H. Murkowski,*
Daniel Patrick Moynihan, N.Y.	*Alaska*
	Hank Brown, Colo.
Charles S. Robb, Va.	*James M. Jeffords, Vt.*
Harris Wofford, Pa.	*Paul Coverdell, Ga.*
Russell D. Feingold, Wis.	*Judd Gregg, N.H.*
Harlan Mathews, Tenn.	

Subcommittees

African Affairs

Phone: 224-4651   Room: SD-446

Simon, chairman	*Jeffords*
Moynihan	*Kassebaum*
Feingold	

East Asian and Pacific Affairs

Phone: 224-4651   Room: SD-446

Robb, chairman	*Murkowski*
Biden	*Lugar*
Kerry	*Pressler*
Mathews	

European Affairs

Phone: 224-4651   Room: SD-446

Biden, chairman	*Lugar*
Pell,	*Kassebaum*
Sarbanes	*Brown*
Simon	*Gregg*
Feingold	

International Economic Policy, Trade, Oceans, and Environment

Phone: 224-4651   Room: SD-446

Sarbanes, chairman	*Kassebaum*
Biden	*Helms*
Dodd	*Murkowski*
Kerry	*Brown*
Wofford	*Jeffords*
Feingold	

Near Eastern and South Asian Affairs

Phone: 224-4651   Room: SD-446

Moynihan, chairman	*Brown*
Pell,	*Pressler*
Sarbanes	*Jeffords*
Robb	*Coverdell*
Wofford	*Gregg*
Mathews	

Terrorism, Narcotics, and International Operations

Phone: 224-4651   Room: SD-446

Kerry, chairman	*Pressler*
Pell	*Helms*
Dodd	*Murkowski*
Simon	*Coverdell*
Moynihan	

Western Hemisphere and Peace Corps Affairs

Phone: 224-4651   Room: SD-446

Dodd, chairman	*Coverdell*
Robb	*Helms*
Wofford	*Lugar*
Mathews	

Governmental Affairs

Phone: 224-4751   Room: SD-340

Majority Staff Director:
Leonard Weiss   224-4751   SD-340

Minority Staff Director:
Franklin G. Polk   224-2627   SD-350

Archives of the United States; budget and accounting measures; census and statistics; federal civil service; congressional organization; intergovernmental relations; government information; District of Columbia; organization and management of nuclear export policy; executive branch organization and reorganization; Postal Service; efficiency, economy, and effectiveness of government. Chairman and ranking minority member are nonvoting members ex officio of all subcommittees of which they are not regular members.

Party Ratio: D 8 - R 6

John Glenn, Ohio, chairman	*William V. Roth Jr., Del., ranking member*
Sam Nunn, Ga.	*Ted Stevens, Alaska*
Carl Levin, Mich.	*William S. Cohen,*
Jim Sasser, Tenn.	*Maine*
David Pryor, Ark.	*Thad Cochran, Miss.*
Joseph I. Lieberman, Conn.	*John McCain, Ariz.*
Daniel K. Akaka, Hawaii	*Robert F. Bennett, Utah*
Byron L. Dorgan, N.D.	

Subcommittees

Federal Services, Post Office, and Civil Service

Phone: 224-2254   Room: SH-601

Pryor, chairman   *Stevens*
Sasser   *Cochran*
Akaka

General Services, Federalism, and the District of Columbia

Phone: 224-4718   Room: SH-432

Sasser, chairman   *McCain*
Lieberman   *Stevens*
Akaka

Oversight of Government Management

Phone: 224-3682   Room: SH-442

Levin, chairman   *Cohen*
Pryor   *Stevens*
Lieberman   *Cochran*
Akaka   *McCain*
Nunn   *Bennett*
Dorgan

Permanent Subcommittee on Investigations

Phone: 224-3721   Room: SR-100

Nunn, chairman   *Roth*
Glenn, vice chairman   *Stevens*
Levin   *Cohen*
Sasser   *Cochran*
Pryor   *McCain*
Lieberman   *Bennett*
Dorgan

Regulation and Government Information

Phone: 224-9000   Room: SH-605

Lieberman, chairman   *Cochran*
Nunn   *Cohen*
Levin   *McCain*
Dorgan

Indian Affairs

Phone: 224-2251   Room: SH-838

Majority Staff Director:
Patricia Zell   224-2251   SH-838
Minority Staff Director:
Daniel N. Lewis   224-2251   SH-838

Problems and opportunities of Indians, including Indian land management and trust responsibilities, education, health, special services, loan programs and claims against the United States.

Party Ratio: D 10 - R 8

Daniel K. Inouye, Hawaii, chairman   *John McCain, Ariz., ranking member*
Dennis DeConcini, Ariz.   *Frank H. Murkowski, Alaska*
Tom Daschle, S.D.
Kent Conrad, N.D.   *Thad Cochran, Miss.*
Harry Reid, Nev.   *Slade Gorton, Wash.*
Paul Simon, Ill.   *Pete V. Domenici, N.M.*
Daniel K. Akaka, Hawaii   *Nancy Landon Kassebaum, Kan.*
Paul Wellstone, Minn.
Byron L. Dorgan, N.D.   *Don Nickles, Okla.*
Ben Nighthorse Campbell, Colo.   *Mark O. Hatfield, Ore.*

Judiciary

Phone: 224-5225   Room: SD-224

Majority Chief Counsel:
Cynthia Hogan   224-5225   SD-224
Minority Chief Counsel:
Sharon Prost   224-7703   SD-147

Civil and criminal judicial proceedings in general; penitentiaries; bankruptcy, mutiny, espionage, and counterfeiting; civil liberties; constitutional amendments; apportionment of representatives; government information; immigration and naturalization; interstate compacts in general; claims against the United States; patents, copyrights, and trademarks; monopolies and unlawful restraints of trade; holidays and celebrations. Chairman and ranking minority member are members ex officio of all subcommittees of which they are not regular members.

Party Ratio: D 10 - R 8

Joseph R. Biden Jr., Del., chairman   *Orrin G. Hatch, Utah, ranking member*
Edward M. Kennedy, Mass.   *Strom Thurmond, S.C.*
Howard M. Metzenbaum, Ohio   *Alan K. Simpson, Wyo.*
Dennis DeConcini, Ariz.   *Charles E. Grassley, Iowa*
Patrick J. Leahy, Vt.   *Arlen Specter, Pa.*
Howell Heflin, Ala.   *Hank Brown, Colo.*
Paul Simon, Ill.   *William S. Cohen, Maine*
Herb Kohl, Wis.
Dianne Feinstein, Calif.   *Larry Pressler, S.D.*
Carol Moseley-Braun, Ill.

Subcommittees

Antitrust, Monopolies, and Business Rights

Phone: 224-5701   Room: SH-308

Metzenbaum, chairman   *Thurmond*
DeConcini   *Specter*

Heflin   *Hatch*
Simon

Constitution

Phone: 224-5573   Room: SD-524

Simon, chairman   *Brown*
Metzenbaum   *Hatch*
DeConcini
Kennedy

Courts and Administrative Practice

Phone: 224-4022   Room: SH-223

Heflin, chairman   *Grassley*
Metzenbaum   *Thurmond*
Kohl   *Cohen*
Moseley-Braun

Immigration and Refugee Affairs

Phone: 224-7878   Room: SD-520

Kennedy, chairman   *Simpson*
Simon

Juvenile Justice

Phone: 224-4933   Room: SH-305

Kohl, chairman   *Cohen*
Biden   *Pressler*
Moseley-Braun

Patents, Copyrights, and Trademarks

Phone: 224-8178   Room: SH-327

DeConcini, chairman   *Hatch*
Kennedy   *Simpson*
Leahy   *Grassley*
Heflin   *Brown*
Feinstein

Technology and the Law

Phone: 224-3406   Room: SH-815

Leahy, chairman   *Specter*
Kohl   *Pressler*
Feinstein

Labor and Human Resources

Phone: 224-5375   Room: SD-428

Majority Staff Director and Chief Counsel:
  Nick Littlefield   224-5465   SD-428
Minority Staff Director:
  Susan K. Hatten   224-6770   SH-835

Education, labor, health, and public welfare in general; aging; arts and humanities; biomedical research and development; child labor; convict labor; domestic activities of the Red Cross; equal employment opportunity; handicapped and statistics; mediation and arbitration of labor disputes; occupational safety and health; private pensions; public health; railway labor and retirement; regulation of foreign laborers; student loans; wages and hours; agricultural colleges; Gallaudet University; Howard University; St. Elizabeths Hospital in Washington, D.C. Chairman and ranking minority member are members ex officio of all subcommittees of which they are not regular members.

Party Ratio: D 10 - R 7

Edward M. Kennedy, Mass.,   *Nancy Landon*
  chairman   *Kassebaum, Kan.,*
Claiborne Pell, R.I.   *ranking member*
Howard M. Metzenbaum,   *James M. Jeffords, Vt.*
  Ohio   *Daniel R. Coats, Ind.*
Christopher J. Dodd, Conn.   *Judd Gregg, N.H.*
Paul Simon, Ill.   *Strom Thurmond, S.C.*
Tom Harkin, Iowa   *Orrin G. Hatch, Utah*
Barbara A. Mikulski, Md.   *Dave Durenberger,*
Jeff Bingaman, N.M.   *Minn.*
Paul Wellstone, Minn.
Harris Wofford, Pa.

Subcommittees

Aging

Phone: 224-3239   Room: SH-615

Mikulski, chairman   *Gregg*
Pell   *Coats*
Metzenbaum   *Durenberger*
Dodd
Wofford

Children, Families, Drugs, and Alcoholism

Phone: 224-5630   Room: SH-639

Dodd, chairman   *Coats*
Pell   *Kassebaum*
Mikulski   *Jeffords*
Bingaman   *Gregg*
Kennedy   *Thurmond*
Wellstone   *Durenberger*
Wofford

Disability Policy

Phone: 224-6265   Room: SH-113

Harkin, chairman   *Durenberger*
Metzenbaum   *Jeffords*
Simon   *Hatch*
Bingaman

Education, Arts, and Humanities

Phone: 224-7666   Room: SD-648

Pell, chairman
Metzenbaum
Dodd
Simon
Mikulski
Bingaman
Kennedy
Wellstone
Wofford
Harkin

Jeffords
Kassebaum
Coats
Gregg
Thurmond
Hatch
Durenberger

Employment and Productivity

Phone: 224-5575   Room: SD-644

Simon, chairman
Harkin
Mikulski
Bingaman
Wofford

Thurmond
Coats
Gregg
Hatch

Labor

Phone: 224-5546   Room: SH-608

Metzenbaum, chairman
Harkin
Dodd
Kennedy
Wellstone

Hatch
Kassebaum
Jeffords
Thurmond

Rules and Administration

Phone: 224-6352   Room: SR-305

Majority Staff Director:
James O. King   224-6351   SR-305
Minority Staff Director:
Al McDermott   224-5647   SR-479

Senate administration in general; corrupt practices; qualifications of senators; contested elections; federal elections in general; Government Printing Office; Congressional Record; meetings of Congress and attendance of members; presidential succession; the Capitol, congressional office buildings, the Library of Congress, the Smithsonian Institution, and the Botanic Garden.

Party Ratio: D 9 - R 7

Wendell H. Ford, Ky.,
chairman
Claiborne Pell, R.I.
Robert C. Byrd, W.Va.
Daniel K. Inouye, Hawaii
Dennis DeConcini, Ariz.
Daniel Patrick Moynihan,
N.Y.
Christopher J. Dodd, Conn.
Dianne Feinstein, Calif.
Harlan Mathews, Tenn.

Ted Stevens, Alaska,
ranking member
Mark O. Hatfield, Ore.
Jesse Helms, N.C.
John W. Warner, Va.
Bob Dole, Kan.
Mitch McConnell, Ky.
Thad Cochran, Miss.

Select Ethics

Phone: 224-2981   Room: SH-220

Staff Director and Chief Counsel:
Victor M. Baird   224-2981   SH-220

Studies and investigates standards and conduct of Senate members and employees and may recommend remedial action.

Party Ratio: D 3 - R 3

Richard H. Bryan, Nev.,
chairman
Barbara A. Mikulski, Md.
Tom Daschle, S.D.

Mitch McConnell, Ky.,
vice chairman
Robert C. Smith, N.H.
Larry E. Craig, Idaho

Select Intelligence

Phone: 224-1700   Room: SH-211

Majority Staff Director:
Norm Bradley   224-1700   SH-211
Minority Staff Director:
David Addington   224-1700   SH-211

Legislative and budgetary authority over the Central Intelligence Agency, the Defense Intelligence Agency, the National Security Agency, and intelligence activities of the Federal Bureau of Investigation and other components of the federal intelligence community. The majority leader and minority leader are members ex officio of the committee.

Party Ratio: D 9 - R 8

Dennis DeConcini, Ariz.,
chairman
Howard M. Metzenbaum,
Ohio
John Glenn, Ohio
Bob Kerrey, Neb.
Richard H. Bryan, Nev.
Bob Graham, Fla.
John Kerry, Mass.
Max Baucus, Mont.
J. Bennett Johnston, La.

John W. Warner, Va.,
vice chairman
Alfonse M. D'Amato,
N.Y.
John C. Danforth, Mo.
Slade Gorton, Wash.
John H. Chafee, R.I.
Ted Stevens, Alaska
Richard G. Lugar, Ind.
Malcolm Wallop, Wyo.

Small Business

Phone: 224-5175   Room: SR-428A

Majority Staff Director:
John W. Ball III   224-5175   SR-428A
Minority Staff Director:
Thomas G. Hohenthaner   224-8494   SR-428A

Problems of small business; Small Business Administration.

Party Ratio: D 12 - R 10

Dale Bumpers, Ark., chairman	*Larry Pressler, S.D., ranking member*
Sam Nunn, Ga.	*Malcolm Wallop, Wyo.*
Carl Levin, Mich.	*Christopher S. Bond, Mo.*
Tom Harkin, Iowa	
John Kerry, Mass.	*Conrad Burns, Mont.*
Joseph I. Lieberman, Conn.	*Connie Mack, Fla.*
Paul Wellstone, Minn.	*Paul Coverdell, Ga.*
Harris Wofford, Pa.	*Dirk Kempthorne, Idaho*
Howell Heflin, Ala.	
Frank R. Lautenberg, N.J.	*Robert F. Bennett, Utah*
Herb Kohl, Wis.	*John H. Chafee, R.I.*
Carol Moseley-Braun, Ill.	*Kay Bailey Hutchison, Texas*

Subcommittees

Competitiveness, Capital Formation, and Economic Opportunity

Phone: 224-5175   Room: SR-428A

Lieberman, chairman	*Mack*
Harkin	*Bond*
Lautenberg	

Export Expansion and Agricultural Development

Phone: 224-5175   Room: SR-428A

Wofford, chairman	*Coverdell*
Harkin	*Bennett*
Bumpers	*Chafee*
Lautenberg	*Hutchison*
Moseley-Braun	

Government Contracting and Paperwork Reduction

Phone: 224-5175   Room: SR-428A

Nunn, chairman	*Bond*
Lieberman	*Wallop*
Harkin	*Hutchison*
Kohl	

Innovation, Manufacturing, and Technology

Phone: 224-5175   Room: SR-428A

Levin, chairman	*Burns*
Kerry	*Kempthorne*
Bumpers	*Bennett*
Heflin	

Rural Economy and Family Farming

Phone: 224-5175   Room: SR-428A

Wellstone, chairman	*Pressler*
Nunn	*Wallop*
Levin	*Burns*
Bumpers	*Coverdell*
Heflin	*Kempthorne*
Kohl	

Urban and Minority-Owned Business Development

Phone: 224-5175   Room: SR-428A

Kerry, chairman	*Chafee*
Nunn	*Mack*
Wellstone	*Pressler*
Wofford	
Moseley-Braun	

Special Aging

Phone: 224-5364   Room: SD-G31

Majority Staff Director:
Theresa M. Forster   224-5364   SD-G31
Minority Staff Director:
Mary Gerwin   224-1467   SH-628

Problems and opportunities of older people, including health, income, employment, housing, and care and assistance. Reports findings and makes recommendations to the Senate, but cannot report legislation.

Party Ratio: D 11 - R 10

David Pryor, Ark., chairman	*William S. Cohen, Maine, ranking member*
John Glenn, Ohio	
Bill Bradley, N.J.	*Larry Pressler, S.D.*
J. Bennett Johnston, La.	*Charles E. Grassley, Iowa*
John B. Breaux, La.	
Richard C. Shelby, Ala.	*Alan K. Simpson, Wyo.*
Harry Reid, Nev.	*James M. Jeffords, Vt.*
Bob Graham, Fla.	*John McCain, Ariz.*
Herb Kohl, Wis.	*Dave Durenberger, Minn.*
Russell D. Feingold, Wis.	
Donald W. Riegle Jr., Mich.	*Larry E. Craig, Idaho*
	Conrad Burns, Mont.
	Arlen Specter, Pa.

Veterans' Affairs

Phone: 224-9126   Room: SR-414

Majority Staff Director:
Jim Gottlieb   224-9126   SR-414
Minority Staff Director:
John H. Moseman   224-2074   SH-202

Veterans' measures in general; compensation; life insurance issued by the government on account of service in the armed forces; national cemeteries; pensions; readjustment benefits; veterans' hospitals, medical care, and treatment; vocational rehabilitation and education.

Party Ratio: D 7 - R 5

John D. Rockefeller IV, W.Va., chairman
Dennis DeConcini, Ariz.
George J. Mitchell, Maine
Bob Graham, Fla.
Daniel K. Akaka, Hawaii
Tom Daschle, S.D.
Ben Nighthorse Campbell, Colo.

Frank H. Murkowski, Alaska, ranking member
Strom Thurmond, S.C.
Alan K. Simpson, Wyo.
Arlen Specter, Pa.
James M. Jeffords, Vt.

Partisan Committees

Democratic Policy Committee

S-118 CAP; 224-5551

An arm of the Democratic Caucus that advises on legislative priorities.

George J. Mitchell, Maine, chairman
Tom Daschle, S.D., co-chairman
Jeff Bingaman, N.M., vice chairman
John Glenn, Ohio, vice chairman
Paul S. Sarbanes, Md., vice chairman

Daniel K. Akaka, Hawaii
Dale Bumpers, Ark.
Ben Nighthorse Campbell, Colo.
Byron L. Dorgan, N.D.
Russell D. Feingold, Wis.
Wendell H. Ford, Ky.
Howell Heflin, Ala.
Ernest F. Hollings, S.C.
Herb Kohl, Wis.
Frank R. Lautenberg, N.J.

Carol Moseley-Braun, Ill.
Daniel Patrick Claiborne Pell, R.I. Moynihan, N.Y.
David Pryor, Ark.
Donald W. Riegle Jr., Mich.
Charles S. Robb, Va.
John D. Rockefeller IV, W.Va.

Democratic Senatorial Campaign Committee

430 S. Capitol St. S.E. 20003; 224-2447

Campaign support committee for senatorial candidates.

Bob Graham, Fla., chairman

Max Baucus, Mont.
Barbara Boxer, Calif.
John B. Breaux, La.

Barbara A. Mikulski, Md.
George J. Mitchell, Me.

Ben Nighthorse Campbell, Colo.
Christopher J. Dodd, Conn.
Tom Harkin, Iowa
John Kerry, Mass.

Patty Murray, Wash.
David Pryor, Ark.
Charles S. Robb, Va.
John D. Rockefeller IV, W.Va.
Richard C. Shelby, Ala.

Democratic Steering Committee

S-309 CAP; 224-3735

Makes Democratic committee assignments.

Daniel K. Inouye, Hawaii, chairman

Max Baucus, Mont.
Joseph R. Biden Jr., Del.
David L. Boren, Okla.
Barbara Boxer, Calif.
John B. Breaux, La.
Richard H. Bryan, Nev.
Robert C. Byrd, W.Va.
Kent Conrad, N.D.
Dennis DeConcini, Ariz.
Christopher J. Dodd, Conn.
Jim Exon, Neb.
Wendell H. Ford, Ky.
Bob Graham, Fla.
Tom Harkin, Iowa

Edward M. Kennedy, Mass.
John Kerry, Mass.
Herb Kohl, Wis.
Patrick J. Leahy, Vt.
Carl Levin, Mich.
Howard M. Metzenbaum, Ohio
George J. Mitchell, Maine
Sam Nunn, Ga.
David Pryor, Ark.
Jim Sasser, Tenn.

National Republican Senatorial Committee

425 2nd St. N.E. 20002; 675-6000

Campaign support committee for Republican senatorial candidates.

Phil Gramm, Texas, chairman

Robert F. Bennett, Utah
Hank Brown, Colo.
Conrad Burns, Mont.
Daniel R. Coats, Ind.
Paul Coverdell, Ga.
Alfonse M. D'Amato, N.Y.
Lauch Faircloth, N.C.
Slade Gorton, Wash.

Dirk Kempthorne, Idaho
Richard G. Lugar, Ind.
Connie Mack, Fla.
John McCain, Ariz.
Bob Packwood, Ore.
Ted Stevens, Alaska
John W. Warner, Va.

Republican Committee on Committees

SR-487; 224-6253

Makes Republican committee assignments.

Conrad Burns, Mont., chairman

Robert F. Bennett, Utah
Paul Coverdell, Ga.
Lauch Faircloth, N.C.
Judd Gregg, N.H.

Dirk Kempthorne,
  Idaho
Frank H. Murkowski,
  Alaska

Republican Policy Committee

SR-347; 224-2946

Advises on party action and policy.

Don Nickles, Okla., chairman

John H. Chafee, R.I.
Thad Cochran, Miss.
Alfonse M. D'Amato, N.Y.
John C. Danforth, Mo.
Bob Dole, Kan.
Pete V. Domenici, N.M.
Phil Gramm, Texas
Orrin G. Hatch, Utah
Mark O. Hatfield, Ore.
Jesse Helms, N.C.
Nancy Landon Kassebaum,
  Kan.
Trent Lott, Miss.

Richard G. Lugar, Ind.
Frank H. Murkowski,
  Alaska
Bob Packwood, Ore.
Larry Pressler, S.D.
William V. Roth Jr.,
  Del.
Alan K. Simpson, Wyo.
Ted Stevens, Alaska
Strom Thurmond, S.C.
Malcolm Wallop, Wyo.
John W. Warner, Va.

Freedom of Information Act

Public access to government information remains a key issue in Washington. In 1966 Congress passed legislation to broaden access: the Freedom of Information Act (PL 89-487; codified in 1967 by PL 90-23). Amendments to expand access even further were passed into law over President Ford's veto in 1974 (PL 93-502).

Several organizations in Washington specialize in access to government information. See "Freedom of Information Act" section in the Communications and the Media chapter for details *(p. 23)*.

1966 Act

The 1966 act requires executive branch agencies and independent commissions of the federal government to make records, reports, policy statements, and staff manuals available to citizens who request them, unless the materials fall into one of nine exempted categories:
- secret national security or foreign policy information
- internal personnel practices
- information exempted by law (e.g., income tax returns)
- trade secrets, other confidential commercial or financial information
- inter-agency or intra-agency memos
- personal information, personnel, or medical files
- law enforcement investigatory information
- information related to reports on financial institutions
- geological and geophysical information

1974 Amendments

Further clarification of the rights of citizens to gain access to government information came in late 1974, when Congress enacted legislation to remove some of the obstacles that the bureaucracy had erected since 1966. Included in the amendments are provisions that:
- Require federal agencies to publish their indexes of final opinions on settlements of internal cases, policy statements, and administrative staff manuals. If, under special circumstances, the indexes are not published, they are to be furnished to any person requesting them for the cost of duplication. The 1966 law simply required agencies to make such indexes available for public inspection and copying.
- Require agencies to release unlisted documents to someone requesting them with a reasonable description (a change designed to ensure that an agency could

not refuse to provide material simply because the applicant could not give its precise title).

• Direct each agency to publish a uniform set of fees for providing documents at the cost of finding and copying them. The amendment allows waiver or reduction of those fees when in the public interest.

• Set time limits for agency responses to requests: 10 working days for an initial request; 20 working days for an appeal from an initial refusal to produce documents; a possible 10-working-day extension which can be granted only once in a single case.

• Set a 30-day time limit for an agency response to a complaint filed in court under the act; provides that such cases should be given priority attention by the courts at the appeal, as well as the trial, level.

• Empower federal district courts to order agencies to produce withheld documents and to examine the contested materials privately *(in camera)* to determine if they are properly exempted.

• Require annual agency reports to Congress, including a list of all agency decisions to withhold information requested under the act; the reasons; the appeals; the results; all relevant rules; the fee schedule; and the names of officials responsible for each denial of information.

• Allow courts to order the government to pay attorneys' fees and court costs for persons winning suits against them under the act.

• Authorize a court to find that an agency employee has acted capriciously or arbitrarily in withholding information; disciplinary action is determined by Civil Service Commission proceedings.

• Amend and clarify the wording of the national defense and national security exemption to make clear that it applies only to *properly* classified information.

• Amend the wording of the law enforcement exemption to allow withholding of information which, if disclosed, would interfere with enforcement proceedings, deprive someone of a fair trial or hearing, invade personal privacy in an unwarranted way, disclose the identity of a confidential source, disclose investigative techniques, or endanger law enforcement personnel; protect from disclosure all information from a confidential source obtained by a criminal law enforcement agency or a lawful national security investigation.

• Provide that separable non-exempt portions of requested material be released after deletion of the exempt portions.

• Require an annual report from the attorney general to Congress.

1984 Amendments

In 1984 Congress enacted legislation that clarified the requirements of the Central Intelligence Agency to respond to citizen requests for information. Included in the amendments are provisions that:

• Authorize the CIA to close from FOIA review certain operational files that contain information on the identities of sources and methods. The measure removed the requirement that officials search the files for material that might be subject to disclosure.

• Reverse a ruling by the Justice Dept. and the Office of Management and Budget that invoked the Privacy Act to deny individuals FOIA access to information about themselves in CIA records. HR 5164 required the CIA to search

files in response to FOIA requests by individuals for information about themselves.
  • Require the CIA to respond to FOIA requests for information regarding covert actions or suspected CIA improprieties.
  All agencies of the executive branch have issued regulations to implement the Freedom of Information Act. To locate a specific agency's regulations, consult the general index of the *Code of Federal Regulations* under "Information availability."

Privacy Act

To protect citizens from invasions of privacy by the federal government, Congress passed the Privacy Act of 1974 (PL 93-579). The act permitted individuals for the first time to inspect information about themselves contained in federal agency files and to challenge, correct, or amend the material. The major provisions of the act:
  • Permit an individual to have access to personal information in federal agency files and to correct or amend that information.
  • Prevent an agency maintaining a file on an individual from making it available to another agency without the individual's consent.
  • Require federal agencies to keep records that are necessary, lawful, accurate, and current, and to disclose the existence of all data banks and files containing information on individuals.
  • Bar the transfer of personal information to other federal agencies for non-routine use without the individual's prior consent or written request.
  • Require agencies to keep accurate accountings of transfers of records and make them available to the individual.
  • Prohibit agencies from keeping records on an individual's exercise of First Amendment rights unless the records are authorized by statute, approved by the individual, or within the scope of an official law enforcement activity.
  • Permit an individual to seek injunctive relief to correct or amend a record maintained by an agency and permit the individual to recover actual damages when an agency acts in a negligent manner that is "willful or intentional."
  • Exempt from disclosure: records maintained by the Central Intelligence Agency; records maintained by law enforcement agencies; Secret Service records; statistical information; names of persons providing material used for determining the qualification of an individual for federal government service; federal testing material; and National Archives historical records.
  • Provide that an officer or employee of an agency who violates provisions of the act be fined no more than $5,000.
  • Prohibit an agency from selling or renting an individual's name or address for mailing list use.
  • Require agencies to submit to Congress and to the Office of Management and Budget any plan to establish or alter records.
  Virtually all agencies of the executive branch have issued regulations to implement the Privacy Act. To locate a specific agency's regulations, consult the general index of the *Code of Federal Regulations* under "Privacy Act."

Name Index

In the name index, page numbers in **boldface** indicate the main entries of senators and representatives.

Aaron, Henry J., 51
Abbey, Joseph L. S., 785
Abbott, Rebecca Phillips, 118
Abdal-Haqq, Irshad, 523
Abdo, Judy, 876
Abdul Majid, Dato, 790
Abercrombie, Neil, D-Hawaii, 886, **891**, 979, 000, 000, 000
Abernathy, Cathy, 947
Abernathy, Warren, 972
Abernethy, David, 322, 341, 348, 355
Abernethy, Durant, 256
Able, Edward H., Jr., 117
Abler, Ronald F., 693
Aborn, Richard M., 512
Abraham, Cathy, 930
Abraham, Herbert, 609
Abraham, Katharine G., 11, 94, 166, 196
Abramowitz, Morton I., 447
Abrams, Robert, 871
Abramson, Jerry, 878
Abrecht, Gary L., 743
Abshire, David M., 447
Accardi, Thomas C., 712
Acevedo, Hector Luis, 881
Acheson, David C., 78, 447, 533
Acheson, Eleanor Dean, 490, 499
Achtenberg, Roberta, 9, 376, 400, 401
Ackerman, Gary L., D-N.Y., 443, 757, 887, **891**, 984, 985, 988, 989, 990, 991, 998
Ackerman, Karen, 949
Ackerman, Kenneth D., 604
Acosta, Renee, 454
Ada, Joseph, 867
Adair, John J., 299
Adair, Marshall P., 461
Adams, Adam, 950
Adams, Alvin, Jr., 793
Adams, Dave, 520

Adams, Eben, 761
Adams, John, 625
Adams, John M., 579
Adams, Robert McCormick, 19, 117
Adams, Wayne, 904
Adams, William T., 719
Adcock, Mike, 902
Addington, David, 1014
Addlestone, David, 434, 436
Adkins, Charles E., 193
Adkins, Roger, 702
Adler, Wendy, 179, 186, 266, 273, 287, 387
Aesch, Mark, 934
Afande, Denis D., 788
Afes, Diane, 375, 424
Agricola, Blair, 971
Agrimonti, Madolyn L., 876
Aguirre, Juan Esteban, 793
Ahlberg, Brian, 612
Ahouansou, Candide Pierre, 781
Ahumada, Pat, 881
Aiken-O'Neill, Patricia, 359
Ainina, Mohamed Fall, 791
Aiston, Kevin, 782, 794
Aitken, Gwen R., 24
Akaka, Daniel K., D-Hawaii, 211, 215, 230, 237, 644, 646, 648, 665, 681, 715, 886, **955**, 1008, 1009, 1011, 1012, 1016
Alaini, Mohsin A., 799
Albee, Luke, 965
Alberts, Bruce, 666
Albright, David, 337
Alder, Thomas, 555, 584
Aldrich, Arnold D., 699
Aldrich, Mark, 972
Aldridge, Bill G., 129, 675
Alejandro, Aaron, 940
Alepa, John, 308
Alexander, Arthur J., 460
Alexander, Ben, 964

Alexander, Duane F., 334
Alexander, Jane, 17, 98, 101, 158
Alexander, Leslie, 791
Alexander, Robert, 139, 428
Alexander, Robert M., 566
Alexander, Rosemary, 967
Alford, Beverly, 35
Allard, Dean C., 558
Allard, Wayne, R-Colo., 885, **891**, 975, 976, 981, 989, 990, 999
Allbritten, Drew, 144
Allegretti, Thomas, 716
Allen, Carolyn, 880
Allen, Ernest, 418
Allen, Gary W., 707, 713
Allen, George F., 873
Allen, James, 383
Allen, Janet, 311
Allen, Kenneth B., 165
Allen, Larry, 60
Allen, Marc S., 698, 699
Allen, Martha Leslie, 37
Allen, Mike, 914
Allen, Peggy, 902
Allen, William, 931
Alley, Sandra, 122
Allison, Richard G., 259
Allsup, Jerry, 236
Alonso, Julio, 927
Alpern, Robert Z., 280
Alpern, Stephen E., 290
Alsace, Juan, 789
Alston, Frank, 180
Alt, Konrad S., 255
Altemus, Julie, 957
Altenstadter, Shelley G., 471, 475, 506
Alter, Rosilyn, 121
Alterman, Stephen A., 709
Altier, Michael, 256
Altman, Roger C., 19, 42, 62
Alvarez, Emmett, 923
Alvarez, Jose, 929

Explanatory Note

If the name of an agency or organization begins with one or more of the words listed below, it is not listed under those words; rather, it is indexed under the next word in the name. For example, the National Gallery of Art is listed alphabetically not under *National* but under *Gallery of Art, National.*

Academy	Department
Advisory	Federal
Agency	Federation
American	Foundation
Association	Fund
Bureau	Institute
Center	International
Coalition	League
College associations	National
College of	Office
Commission	Society
Committee	United
Conference of/on	U.S.
Council	United States

Subject Index

In the subject index, page numbers in **boldface** indicate the main entries for congresional committees and subcommittees.

Federal and Private Toll-Free Numbers...

Departments

Agriculture
Meat and poultry safety inquiries .... (800) 535-4555; 720-3333 in Washington, D.C.

Commerce
Export counseling .... (800) 872-8723; (410) 962-3560 in Maryland and Washington, D.C.

Defense
Army espionage hotline .... (800) 225-5779

Education
Student financial aid info. .... (800) 433-3243

Energy
Renewable energy conservation info. ...... (800) 523-2929

Health and Human Services
AIDS info. .... (800) 342-2437; 332-2437 in Washington, D.C. Spanish speaking, (800) 344-7432; 328-0697 in Washington, D.C.; TDD, (800) 243-7889
Cancer info. .... (800) 422-6237
Civil rights info. .... (800) 368-1019; 863-0100 in Washington, D.C.
General health info. .... (800) 336-4797
Medicare hotline .... (800) 638-6833
National Runaway Switchboard .... (800) 621-4000
Social Security benefits info. .... (800) 772-1213

Housing and Urban Development
Housing discrimination hotline .... (800) 669-9777; TDD, (800) 927-9275

Justice
Juvenile justice info. .... (800) 638-8736; (301) 251-5500 in Maryland
Racial, religious, and sexual preference
  disputes hotline .... (800) 347-4283

Transportation
Airline safety hotline .... (800) 322-7873; 267-8592 in Washington, D.C.
Auto safety hotline .... (800) 424-9393; 366-0123 in Washington, D.C.
Hazardous material, chemical, and oil spills (800) 424-8802[a]; 426-2675 in Washington, D.C.

Treasury
Drug smuggling reports .... (800) 232-5378
Explosive materials discovery,
  theft, loss reports .... (800) 800-3855; 927-7777 in Washington, D.C.
Tax form requests .... (800) 829-3676
Tax refund info. .... (800) 829-4477
Taxpayer assistance .... (800) 829-1040; (410) 962-2590 in Baltimore, Md.

Agencies

Consumer Product Safety Commission
Product safety info. .... (800) 638-2772

Environmental Protection Agency
Safe drinking water hotline .... (800) 426-4791
Hazardous waste and cleanup info. .... (800) 424-9346; (703) 412-9810 in Washington, D.C., area
Pesticides and related medical info. ...... (800) 858-7378

Export-Import Bank
Export finance hotline .... (800) 424-5201; 566-8860 in Washington, D.C.